Comprehensive
Textbook of
Psychiatry

VOLUME 1

THIRD EDITION

Dedicated to Nancy,
Marcia, and Virginia

Comprehensive Textbook of Psychiatry/III

VOLUME 1   **THIRD EDITION**

Harold I. Kaplan, M.D.
Professor of Psychiatry, New York University School of Medicine;
Attending Psychiatrist, University Hospital of the New York University Medical Center;
Attending Psychiatrist, Bellevue Hospital, New York, New York

Alfred M. Freedman, M.D.
Professor of Psychiatry and Chairman,
Department of Psychiatry, New York Medical College;
Chairman, Department of Psychiatry, Psychiatric Institute,
Westchester Medical Center, Valhalla, New York;
Chairman, Department of Psychiatry, Metropolitan Hospital and
Bird S. Coler Memorial Hospital and Home, New York, New York

Benjamin J. Sadock, M.D.
Professor of Psychiatry, New York University School of Medicine;
Attending Psychiatrist, University Hospital of the New York University Medical Center;
Attending Psychiatrist, Bellevue Hospital, New York, New York

WILLIAMS & WILKINS
Baltimore/London

NOTICE

The Editors and the Publisher of this work have made every effort to ensure that the drug dosage schedules herein are accurate and in accord with the standards accepted at the time of publication. The reader is strongly advised, however, to check the product information sheet included in the package of each drug he or she plans to administer to be certain that changes have not been made in the recommended dose or in the contraindications for administration.

Library of Congress Cataloging in Publication Data.

  Kaplan, Harold I.
  Comprehensive Textbook of Psychiatry.
  Includes bibliographies.
  1. Psychiatry. I. Freedman, Alfred M., joint author. II. Sadock, Benjamin J., joint author. III. Title [DNLM: 1. Mental disorders. 2. Psychiatry. 3. Psychiatry—History. WM100 F855c]
  RC454.F74   1975   616.8′9   74-20808
  ISBN 0-683-03357-3

Composed and Printed at the Waverly Press, Inc.
Mount Royal and Guilford Avenues
Baltimore, Maryland, 21202, USA.

Preface to the Third Edition

The organization and the orientation of this book were determined in large measure by the editors' assessment of the distinctive characteristics of modern American psychiatry and philosophy. In addition, our efforts were guided by certain practical considerations. As a manual of instruction, this textbook has the prescribed aim of fostering professional competence. Accordingly, the content follows the psychiatric curriculum recommendations of the National Board of Medical Examiners and the American Board of Psychiatry and Neurology. On the other hand, the presentation of the material we consider essential to competence in this field was subject to certain restrictions imposed by limitations of time and space.

BASIC DECISIONS

To translate our ideals into the reality of a textbook, we had to resolve many practical problems and make some basic decisions. Specifically, we decided (1) that the approach would be eclectic and multidisciplinary; (2) that the book would be comprehensive in scope—that is, it would include contributions on topics fundamental to psychiatry in addition to the traditional clinical material; and (3) that the textbook would continue to present contributions written by many experts.

Eclectic orientation. Since psychiatry is currently in a state of rapid development and change, commitment to any one approach would be unwise at this time and in our opinion would constitute a disservice to the discipline and to the young student, who bears the responsibility for its progress. To avoid premature closure, we have included different theoretical models or schools of thought and contributions from various related disciplines, such as neurophysiology, psychology, and sociology.

We have tried to pursue this eclectic orientation throughout the textbook, although our approach has varied, depending on the material under consideration. For example, in the part of the book that deals with the basic behavioral and psychological sciences, the various theoretical models and disciplines stand side by side, and their very juxtaposition transmits the message of eclecticism. In the sections covering clinical material, the dynamics and the treatment of a given disorder are presented with emphasis on the particular theoretical orientation that is most widely accepted at the present time. However, in each instance alternate approaches and assumptions are also delineated.

Comprehensive scope. The editors believe that psychiatry can no longer be taught as a technical trade. Obviously, clinical competence is an essential goal of training, but it is not the only goal. A knowledge of the behavioral sciences and of underlying theoretical models is fundamental to true understanding and clinical skill in psychiatry. Moreover, psychiatry is currently faced with the challenge of distributing its services to previously unreached populations. Therefore, in addition to clinical material on the description and treatment of the various disorders that constitute the content of the traditional psychiatric text, this book includes germane biological, psychological, and sociological information; presentations of current concepts and theoretical models; and discussions of various aspects of community psychiatry and of the delivery of mental health services.

Multiauthorship. As stated in the second edition, the editors believe that the scope of psychiatry has grown to such an extent that no one person or small group of people can properly present the entire field to the student or practitioner. It is true that multiauthorship may produce duplication of material and certain inconsistencies in writing style. But we believe that careful editorial attention has minimized that risk. In addition, that risk is more than compensated for by the fact that we have brought together the leaders of modern psychiatry, each describing his work in his own words.

Every contribution to the third edition of *Comprehensive Textbook of Psychiatry* is original; none is a reprint of an article published elsewhere. And every contribution in the third edition that was written by the same contributor as in the second edition was rewritten; most of those contributions were rewritten completely. Each section represents the most up-to-date exposition on the subject to be found anywhere in the world literature.

MAJOR MODIFICATIONS IN THE THIRD EDITION

DSM-III. All major psychiatric disorders discussed in this textbook are in accord with the nosology of the third edition of the American Psychiatric Association's *Diagnostic and Statistical Manual of Mental Disorders* (DSM-III), which was prepared during the same time that this textbook was written. As a result, our contributors had to do a great deal of rewriting as the committees that were writing DSM-III revised the various parts of that nosological manual.

There was much disagreement within the profession about DSM-III and its contents up to the last minute before its approval by the various bodies of the American Psychiatric Association. The controversy about whether to include the term "neurosis" stands out as one notable example. Many of our contributors had and still do have distinct reservations about some of the modifications introduced in DSM-III. In some of the descriptions of the organic mental disorders, many of the DSM-II terms were used by some of our contributors because they believed that those terms followed the medical model more closely than did the DSM-III terms. However, in the introduction to the chapter on organic mental disorders, a comprehensive table comparing the terminology used in DSM-II and that used in DSM-III is included for the student's benefit. We believe that the nosological issues regarding organic mental disorders and organic brain syndromes remain confused at this time.

In several sections of this book, contributors wished to express their objections to the changes made by DSM-III, and the editors encouraged them to do so as they chose. In fact, most of our contributors did not agree with DSM-III's limitation on the use of the terms "neurotic," "psychoneurotic," "psychosomatic," and "psychophysiological," and the reader will find these words used throughout this book.

As future editions of the *Diagnostic and Statistical Manual of Mental Disorders* appear—and we believe that such modifications are in the offing, appearing perhaps every 5 years—there must be more room for dissent, *before and especially after* every new edition of the manual appears. We firmly believe that a major textbook such as *Comprehensive Textbook of Psychiatry* must provide a forum for free discussion and disagreement, while giving due acknowledgment to the official nomenclature. A manual on nomenclature is just that; it is *not* a textbook.

Added material. Although we have retained the basic organization of the second edition of *Comprehensive Textbook of Psychiatry*, many changes and modifications have been added. For example, in the area of the behavioral sciences, major new contributions have been added, including sections on the life cycle, sociobiology, and Jean Piaget. Almost all the clinical sections have been rewritten to make them consistent with DSM-III. Fresh new case material and recent treatment trends have been added, as well as a section on the overview of treatment methods of schizophrenia. And other new overview sections have been introduced, covering schizophrenia, affective disorders, and psychiatric hospitalization.

A major new chapter has been introduced on psychiatric education. It includes sections on the psychiatrist, his training, the American Board of Psychiatry and Neurology, and objective examinations in psychiatry. And we have included a special chapter on psychiatric research.

In the chapter on contemporary issues in psychiatry, new sections have been written on confidentiality, sports, gambling, peer review, and foreign affairs.

The psychiatric glossary has been significantly expanded and correlated with the terminology of DSM-III.

Innovations in the last edition, such as the asterisk (*) next to the outstanding references listed after each article and the increased use of illustrations and tables, have been retained.

Three volumes. Although paper stock, type size, and margin size are identical to those used in the second edition, the number of pages in this edition has escalated from 2,800 pages to nearly 4,000 pages, necessitating a third volume. The increase in the number of pages was itself necessitated by a number of factors: There has been a marked increase in knowledge in our field; with the introduction of DSM-III, sections on almost all the clinical syndromes had to be heavily rewritten and expanded; new subjects were introduced; and the contributions from the second edition were heavily revised and expanded.

ACKNOWLEDGMENTS

Completing a task of this magnitude required 5 years of prodigious effort and an accomplished and dedicated staff. Norman Sussman, M.D., Robert Gelfand, M.D., and Nancy Barrett provided important aid and assistance throughout the project.

This was in many ways our most difficult edition to produce because it was written at the same time that DSM-III was being written. We are deeply appreciative of the outstanding cooperation received from Robert L. Spitzer, M.D., chairman of the American Psychiatric Association's Task Force on Nomenclature and Statistics, and Janet B. W. Williams, M.S.W., DSM-III Project Coordinator, in keeping the editors and the contributors informed, almost on a day-to-day basis, of changes being made in DSM-III, so that changes could be made in the manuscripts and galley proofs of CTP-III. They afforded us magnificent cooperation in this effort. We appreciate the warm friendship that developed as a result of this collaboration.

Lois Baken was in charge of our secretarial and office staff and served with distinction. Proofreading was directed by Batya Bauman. We wish to offer special thanks to Joan Welsh, head of editorial supervision, for her excellent skills and superb performance in the editing of this book. Both her talents and her friendship are deeply valued.

Virginia A. Sadock, M.D., in addition to writing a number of sections for this book, served admirably as assistant to the editors, and she deserves particular mention for her outstanding help in the many editorial discussions and decisions in which she participated.

Others who helped in the production of this book and who deserve mention are Gail Brenner, M.D., Peter Kaplan, Robin Segal, and Robert Simon. At Williams & Wilkins, Nan Tyler, the editor in charge of this edition, was an outstanding new addition to our team and was of inestimable help. Robert Grose, Book Division President of Williams & Wilkins, and G. James Gallagher, Journal Division President, were also most helpful.

Finally, we wish to express appreciation to our 236 contributors, who worked with enthusiasm and were cooperative in every aspect of this book.

HAROLD I. KAPLAN, M.D.
ALFRED M. FREEDMAN, M.D.
BENJAMIN J. SADOCK, M.D.

New York

From the Preface to the Second Edition

PHILOSOPHY

The second edition of *Comprehensive Textbook of Psychiatry* has evolved from the editors' experience in establishing undergraduate, graduate, and postgraduate continuing education programs in psychiatry. The responsibility for preparing a teaching program for students of psychiatry at every level has made us acutely conscious of the expansion of the field and of the many important additions to the traditional body of the discipline.

The superstructure of clinical psychiatry has expanded and strengthened; thus, the practitioner now has at his disposal a great deal of new information in various major areas of behavioral science, information that he must incorporate into the existing theoretical and therapeutic knowledge in psychiatry. Among these areas are the basic sciences, such as neurophysiology and neuropharmacology; the social sciences that pertain to individual persons; and those that concern the behavior of groups and of systems. Knowledge in these areas is important not merely as an intellectual exercise but because it is a vital part of the practice of psychiatry. It is, in fact, a prerequisite for clinical competence. The perplexing array of therapeutic drugs, for example, demands that the practitioner have a full understanding of their properties—in particular, their effects on the central nervous system—so that he may dispense them in the most sophisticated manner possible. Similarly, increasing awareness of the contribution of social factors to the development and the continuance of mental illness requires that the student be systematically trained in pertinent aspects of the social sciences. The interplay between the individual person and the social structure is especially important in such disorders as drug addiction, alcoholism, delinquency, and educational disabilities—problem areas that psychiatry can no longer avoid.

Modern psychiatric practice should evolve in a manner complex enough to allow for new inputs and yet sufficiently flexible to adapt to a rapidly changing social scene. Such a structure permits taking into account certain features of American life that distinguish it from life in other highly developed countries.

Pluralism. This textbook is organized according to principles derived from certain distinctive characteristics of American life that are rooted in our history and that form the guidelines for the development of our social institutions. The first of these characteristics is pluralism. American communities are composed of a multitude of governmental structures and private groups, each with a measure of power and strength. Sometimes these structures and groups cooperate, but often they act in competition with one another. Each has its own responsibilities, and the fulfillment of these responsibilities gives rise to diffuse goals. The operation of such groups is seldom conducive to the formation of unified conceptual systems, and the history of American psychiatric schools is no exception to this rule. This diversity is caused not only by the steady growth of knowledge within the United States but also by the constant enrichment of American intellectual life through immigration. New ideas brought here by our colleagues from abroad have taken root and flourished. Much of this new knowledge is now incorporated into the body of American psychiatry and has enhanced it immeasurably. To present this diversity in all its richness and contradiction, one must be truly eclectic. It has been our aim in this textbook to include all the major contributions and trends that are now influencing the direction of the discipline.

Pragmatism. If pluralism is a feature of American life that demands recognition, then pragmatism is one that requires compensation. Although truth needs testing by the practical consequences of belief, commonplace American pragmatism often goes beyond empiricism to a disregard for theory. Thus, American psychiatry has shown strength in the development and application of treatment methods while neglecting nosology and clinical description. Nosology is of relatively minor interest when psychiatric therapies are nonspecific; indeed, classification is not a practical use for those who are wedded to single general-purpose therapies. To compensate for these weaknesses, we have stressed the development of theoretical models, the presentation of adequate clinical description, and the importance of classification schemes. To the same end, we have emphasized the behavioral science materials, the full comprehension of which is required not only for practice but for the expansion of theoretical understanding.

Traditional societies have revered what is old, but Americans are typically engaged mainly by what is new. A veneration for change gives rise to a galloping faddism in intellectual life. We have attempted to deal with this problem conservatively by preserving significant knowledge developed over a period of time while presenting new approaches. We have applied this principle not only to treatment methods but also to theoretical issues that are not immediately translated into therapeutic technique.

As a result of the fascination with change, new ideas become superimposed on older ones that are still viable. Thus, one sees change by accretion. New hypotheses and treatment methods are promulgated before older ones have been either validated or discarded. Because both old and new exist at the same time, they must both be presented in a comprehensive psychiatric text, even at the risk of overinforming the reader. American psychiatry cannot be presented adequately in a simple fashion. To oversimplify what is complex would be a disservice to the student and a backward step in the field. It is hoped that this textbook will be an organizing statement for the multitude of relevant variables and an initial approach to a complex model. More parsimonious statements must await further research and developments in the field. In the meantime, it is important not to exclude any aspect of psychiatry and to encourage constant evaluation methods.

Contributors

Gerald Adler, M.D.
Director of Medical Student Education in Psychiatry, Massachusetts General Hospital; Lecturer in Psychiatry, Harvard Medical School; Supervising and Training Analyst, Boston Psychoanalytic Society and Institute, Boston, Massachusetts.

Nancy C. Andreasen, Ph.D., M.D.
Associate Professor of Psychiatry, University of Iowa College of Medicine, Iowa City, Iowa.

Heinz L. Ansbacher, Ph.D.
Professor of Psychology (Emeritus), University of Vermont, Burlington, Vermont.

Haroutun M. Babigian, M.D.
Professor and Chairman, Department of Psychiatry, University of Rochester School of Medicine and Dentistry, Rochester, New York.

Arthur J. Bachrach, Ph.D.
Director, Environmental Stress Program Center, Naval Medical Research Institute, National Naval Medical Center; Adjunct Professor of Medical Psychology, Uniformed Services University for the Health Sciences, School of Medicine, Bethesda, Maryland.

Anita K. Bahn, M.D., Sc.D.
Professor of Epidemiology, Director of Program for Epidemiology Research and Training, Chairperson of Graduate Group in Epidemiology, Department of Research Medicine, University of Pennsylvania School of Medicine, Philadelphia, Pennsylvania.

James B. Bakalar, J.D.
Lecturer in Law, Department of Psychiatry, Harvard Medical School, Boston, Massachusetts.

Lorian Baker, Ph.D.
Research Associate, Department of Psychiatry, Division of Mental Retardation and Child Psychiatry, Neuropsychiatric Institute, University of California at Los Angeles, Los Angeles, California.

Stewart L. Baker, Jr., M.D.
Associate Director, Mental Health and Behavioral Sciences Service, Veterans Administration Central Office; Clinical Professor of Psychiatry and Behavioral Sciences and of Child Health and Development, George Washington University Medical School, Washington, D.C.; Consultant in Psychiatry, Office of the Surgeon General, United States Army, Department of Defense, McLean, Virginia.

Annette Baran, M.S.W.
Co-founder, Adoption Research Project, Los Angeles, California.

David P. Barash, Ph.D.
Associate Professor of Psychology and Zoology, University of Washington, Seattle, Washington.

Robert A. Baron, Ph.D.
Program Director, Social and Developmental Psychology, National Science Foundation, Washington, D.C.; Professor of Psychology, Department of Psychological Sciences, Purdue University, West Lafayette, Indiana.

John Elderkin Bell, Ed.D.
Clinical Associate Professor (Emeritus) of Psychiatry and Behavioral Sciences, Stanford University, Stanford, California; Lecturer (Clinical), Department of Psychiatry, University of California, San Francisco, California; Adjunct Professor and Reader, San Francisco Theological Seminary, San Anselmo, California.

Arthur L. Benton, Ph.D., D.Sc.
Professor Emeritus of Neurology and Psychology, University of Iowa College of Medicine, Iowa City, Iowa.

Irving N. Berlin, M.D.
Professor of Psychiatry and Pediatrics, Director, Division of Child and Adolescent Psychiatry, University of New Mexico School of Medicine, Department of Psychiatry; Director, New Mexico Children's Psychiatric Center, Albuquerque, New Mexico.

Victor Bernal y del Rio, M.D.
Executive Director, Puerto Rico Institute of Psychiatry; Lecturer, Inter-American University School of Law; Professor of Psychiatry, Universidad del Caribe, School of Medicine, San Juan, Puerto Rico.

Grady L. Blackwood, Jr., Ph.D.
Staff Psychologist, Alcohol Treatment Unit, Veterans Administration Medical Center; Assistant Professor, Department of Psychiatry and Behavioral Sciences, University of Oklahoma Medical Center, Oklahoma City, Oklahoma.

Paul Bohannan, D. Phil. (Oxon.)
Professor of Anthropology, University of California, Santa Barbara, California.

James A. Boydstun, M.D.
Colonel, United States Air Force; Military Consultant in Psychiatry to the Surgeon General of the United States Air Force; Commander, United States Air Force Hospital Fairchild (Strategic Air Command), Fairchild Air Force Base, Washington.

John Paul Brady, M.D.
Kenneth E. Appel Professor of Psychiatry and Professor of Psychology, University of Pennsylvania, Philadelphia, Pennsylvania.

H. Keith H. Brodie, M.D.
Professor and Chairman, Department of Psychiatry, Duke University School of Medicine; Chief, Psychiatry Service, Duke University Hospital, Durham, North Carolina.

Bertram S. Brown, M.D.
Assistant Surgeon General, United States Public Health Ser-

vice; Former Director, National Institute of Mental Health; Clinical Professor of Psychiatry and Behavioral Sciences, George Washington University Medical School, Washington, D.C.

Robert N. Butler, M.D.
Director, National Institute on Aging, National Institutes of Health, Bethesda, Maryland.

Justin D. Call, M.D.
Professor and Chief of Child and Adolescent Psychiatry Division, Department of Psychiatry and Human Behavior, University of California at Irvine, Irvine, California; Supervising and Training Analyst, Los Angeles Psychoanalytic Society and Institute, Los Angeles, California.

Robert Cancro, M.D., Med. D.Sc.
Professor and Chairman, New York University School of Medicine; Director, Department of Psychiatry, Bellevue Hospital Center, New York, New York.

Dennis P. Cantwell, M.D.
Professor of Child Psychiatry; Director, Residency Training, Child Psychiatry, Department of Psychiatry, Division of Mental Retardation and Child Psychiatry, Neuropsychiatric Institute, University of California at Los Angeles, Los Angeles, California.

Arthur C. Carr, Ph.D.
Professor of Clinical Psychology in Psychiatry, Cornell University Medical College, New York, New York; Attending Psychologist, Westchester Division of New York Hospital, White Plains, New York.

Raymond Bernard Cattell, Ph.D., D.Sc.
Distinguished Research Professor Emeritus in Psychology, University of Illinois, Urbana, Illinois.

Stanley Cheren, M.D.
Associate Professor of Psychiatry; Head, Department of Psychosomatic Medicine, Boston University School of Medicine; Associate in Psychiatry, Head of Consultation-Liaison Service, University Hospital, Boston, Massachusetts.

John A. Clausen, Ph.D.
Professor of Sociology and Research Sociologist, Institute of Human Development, University of California, Berkeley, California.

Ralph Colp, Jr., M.D.
Psychiatrist in Charge, Columbia University Health Service; Assistant Clinical Professor of Psychiatry, Columbia University College of Physicians and Surgeons; Attending Psychiatrist, St. Luke's Hospital, New York, New York.

Joseph B. Cramer, M.D.
Professor of Psychiatry and Pediatrics, Albert Einstein College of Medicine, New York, New York.

Leon Cytryn, M.D.
Clinical Professor of Psychiatry and Behavioral Sciences, Clinical Professor of Child Health and Development, George Washington University School of Medicine; Senior Attending Physician, Children's Hospital, Washington, D.C., Staff Psychiatrist, Unit on Childhood Mental Illness, Biological Psychiatry Branch, National Institute of Mental Health, Bethesda, Maryland.

Allan J. D. Dale, M.D.
Associate Professor in Neurology, Mayo Medical School; Consultant, Department of Neurology, Mayo Clinic-Mayo Foundation, Rochester, Minnesota.

John M. Davis, M.D.
Director of Research, Illinois State Psychiatric Institute; Pro-

fessor of Psychiatry, University of Chicago Pritzker School of Medicine, Chicago, Illinois.

Robert Dickes, M.D.
Professor of Psychiatry, Downstate Medical Center, State University of New York; Director of the Center for Human Sexuality, Downstate Medical Center, Brooklyn, New York.

John Donnelly, M.D., Sc.D.
Psychiatrist-in-Chief, Institute of Living, Hartford, Connecticut; Professor of Psychiatry, University of Connecticut School of Medicine, Farmington, Connecticut.

John M. Dusay, M.D.
Assistant Clinical Professor of Psychiatry, University of California School of Medicine; President, International Transactional Analysis Association; Attending Psychiatrist, Langley Porter Institute, San Francisco, California.

James S. Eaton, Jr., M.D.
Chief, Psychiatry Education Branch, National Institute of Mental Health, Bethesda, Maryland; Clinical Professor of Psychiatry, Georgetown University School of Medicine, Washington, D.C.; Lecturer in Medicine and Psychiatry, Tulane University School of Medicine, New Orleans, Louisiana.

Lloyd O. Eckhardt, M.D.
Assistant Professor of Psychiatry and Pediatrics, University of Colorado School of Medicine, Denver, Colorado.

Leon Eisenberg, M.D.
Maude and Lillian Presley Professor of Psychiatry, Harvard Medical School; Senior Associate in Psychiatry, Children's Hospital Medical Center, Boston, Massachusetts.

David Elkind, Ph.D.
Professor and Chairman, Eliot-Pearson Department of Child Study, Tufts University, Medford, Massachusetts.

Jean Endicott, Ph.D.
Associate Professor of Clinical Psychology, Department of Psychiatry, Columbia University, College of Physicians and Surgeons, New York, New York.

Allen J. Enelow, M.D.
Chairman, Department of Psychological and Social Medicine, Pacific Medical Center; Clinical Professor of Psychiatry, University of California, San Francisco, California.

Dennis W. Engels, M.D.
Associate Professor, McGill University School of Medicine; Clinical Director, Allan Memorial Institute of Psychiatry (Royal Victoria Hospital), Montreal, Quebec, Canada.

Dana L. Farnsworth, M.D.
Henry K. Oliver Professor of Hygiene, Emeritus, Harvard University, Cambridge, Massachusetts.

Armando R. Favazza, M.D., M.P.H.
Associate Professor and Chief, Section of Adult Psychiatry, University of Missouri-Columbia School of Medicine, Columbia, Missouri.

Eugene B. Feigelson, M.D.
Professor and Chairman, Department of Psychiatry, State University of New York, Downstate Medical Center, Brooklyn, New York.

Sherman C. Feinstein, M.D.
Director, Child Psychiatry Research, Michael Reese Hospital and Medical Center; Clinical Professor of Child Psychiatry, University of Chicago Pritzker School of Medicine, Chicago, Illinois.

Ronald R. Fieve, M.D.
Professor of Clinical Psychiatry, Columbia University College of Physicians and Surgeons; Chief of Psychiatric Research,

Lithium Clinic and Department of Lithium Studies in Manic Depressive Disorders, New York State Psychiatric Institute; Attending Psychiatrist, Presbyterian Hospital; Medical Director, Foundation for Depression and Manic Depression, New York, New York.

Stuart M. Finch, M.D.
Lecturer, Department of Psychiatry, Arizona College of Medicine, Tucson, Arizona.

Paul Jay Fink, M.D.
Professor and Chairman, Department of Psychiatry and Human Behavior, Thomas Jefferson University, Philadelphia, Pennsylvania.

Stephen Fleck, M.D.
Professor of Psychiatry and Public Health, Yale University School of Medicine; Psychiatrist-in-Chief, Yale Psychiatric Institute; Psychiatrist-in-Chief, Connecticut Mental Health Center, New Haven, Connecticut.

Vincent J. Fontana, M.D.
Medical Director and Pediatrician-in-Chief, New York Foundling Hospital Center for Parent and Child Development; Professor of Clinical Pediatrics, New York University College of Medicine; Chairman, Mayor's Task Force on Child Abuse and Neglect, New York, New York.

Shervert H. Frazier, M.D.
Professor of Psychiatry, Harvard Medical School, Boston, Massachusetts; Psychiatrist-in-Chief, McLean Hospital, Belmont, Massachusetts.

Alfred M. Freedman, M.D.
Professor of Psychiatry and Chairman, Department of Psychiatry, New York Medical College; Chairman, Department of Psychiatry, Psychiatric Institute, Westchester Medical Center, Valhalla, New York; Chairman, Department of Psychiatry, Metropolitan Hospital and Bird S. Coler Memorial Hospital and Home, New York, New York.

Alfred P. French, M.D.
Assistant Visiting Professor of Child Psychiatry, University of California at Davis, Davis, California.

John R. Fulton, M.S.W.
Chief, Social Work Service, Brentwood Veterans Administration Medical Center, Los Angeles, California.

Robert Gelfand, M.D.
Teaching Assistant, Department of Medicine, New York University School of Medicine, New York, New York.

Mark A. Geyer, Ph.D.
Assistant Professor of Psychiatry, University of California (San Diego) School of Medicine, La Jolla, California.

Peter L. Giovacchini, M.D.
Clinical Professor of Psychiatry, University of Illinois College of Medicine, Chicago, Illinois.

Bernard C. Glueck, M.D.
Senior Associate in Research, Institute of Living, Hartford, Connecticut; Professor of Psychiatry, University of Connecticut Medical School and Health Center, Farmington, Connecticut; Lecturer, Department of Psychiatry, Yale University School of Medicine, New Haven, Connecticut.

William Goldfarb, M.D., Ph.D.
Director, Henry Ittleson Center for Child Research; Clinical Professor of Psychiatry, Columbia University College of Physicians and Surgeons, New York, New York.

John F. Greden, M.D.
Associate Professor of Psychiatry; Medical Director, Clinical Studies Unit, Inpatient Program; Director, Neural and Behavioral Sciences, University of Michigan Medical Center, Ann Arbor, Michigan.

Richard Green, M.D.
Professor, Department of Psychiatry and Behavioral Science, and Psychology, State University of New York at Stony Brook, Stony Brook, New York.

Harvey R. Greenberg, M.D.
Associate Clinical Professor of Child Psychiatry, Albert Einstein Medical College; Lecturer in Adolescent Psychiatry, Bronx Children's Psychiatric Center, New York, New York.

Milton Greenblatt, M.D.
Director, Neuropsychiatric Institute Hospital and Clinics; Professor and Executive Vice-Chairman, Department of Psychiatry and Biobehavioral Sciences; University of California at Los Angeles School of Medicine, Los Angeles, California.

Lester Grinspoon, M.D.
Associate Professor of Psychiatry, Harvard Medical School, Boston, Massachusetts.

Ernest M. Gruenberg, M.D., D.P.H.
Professor and Chairman, Department of Mental Hygiene, School of Hygiene and Public Health; Professor of Psychiatry, School of Medicine, Johns Hopkins University, Baltimore, Maryland.

Samuel B. Guze, M.D.
Spencer T. Olin Professor of Psychiatry; Head, Department of Psychiatry; Vice Chancellor for Medical Affairs, Washington University School of Medicine; Psychiatrist-in-Chief, Barnes and Renard Hospitals, St. Louis, Missouri.

Seymour Halleck, M.D.
Professor of Psychiatry, University of North Carolina, Chapel Hill, North Carolina.

Katherine A. Halmi, M.D.
Associate Professor of Psychiatry, Cornell University Medical College, New York Hospital-Cornell Medical Center, Westchester Division, White Plains, New York.

Harry F. Harlow, Ph.D.
G. C. Comstock Research Professor in Psychology, University of Wisconsin, Madison, Wisconsin; Visiting Scientist, University of Arizona, Tucson, Arizona.

Robert J. Harmon, M.D.
Assistant Professor of Psychiatry (Child), University of Colorado School of Medicine, Denver, Colorado.

Saul I. Harrison, M.D.
Professor of Psychiatry and Director of Child and Adolescent Psychiatry Education, University of Michigan Medical Center, Ann Arbor, Michigan.

Ernest L. Hartmann, M.D.
Professor of Psychiatry, Tufts University School of Medicine; Director, Sleep Laboratory; Director, Schizophrenia Research Laboratory, Boston State Hospital; Senior Psychiatrist, West-Ros-Park Mental Health Center; CoDirector, Sleep Disorder Clinic, Peter Bent Brigham Hospital and Boston State Hospital, Boston, Massachusetts.

Marvin I. Herz, M.D.
Professor and Chairman, Department of Psychiatry, State University of New York at Buffalo School of Medicine; Director of Psychiatry, Erie County Medical Center; Director of Psychiatry, Buffalo General Hospital, Buffalo, New York.

J. Cotter Hirschberg, M.D.
Chief of Professional Services and William C. Menninger Distinguished Professor of Psychiatry, Menninger Foundation; Training and Supervising Analyst, Topeka Institute for Psy-

choanalysis, Topeka, Kansas; Clinical Professor of Psychiatry, University of Kansas Medical Center College of Health Sciences and Hospital, Kansas City, Kansas.

Marc H. Hollender, M.D.
Professor and Chairman, Department of Psychiatry, Vanderbilt University School of Medicine, Nashville, Tennessee.

Richard R. Hurtig, Ph.D.
Assistant Professor of Psychology, and Speech Pathology and Audiology, University of Iowa, Iowa City, Iowa.

Steven E. Hyler, M.D.
Assistant Clinical Professor of Psychiatry, College of Physicians and Surgeons, Columbia University, New York, New York.

Eric Jackson, B.D.S., Ph.D.
Associate Professor of Behavioral Sciences, Department of Community Dentistry, Temple University School of Dentistry, Philadelphia, Pennsylvania.

Elizabeth Janeway, D. Litt.
Author, *Man's World, Woman's Place*; *Between Myth and Morning: Women Awakening*; Trustee, Barnard College, New York, New York; Associate Fellow, Berkely College, Yale University, New Haven, Connecticut.

Jeannette Jefferson Jansky, Ph.D.
Assistant Clinical Professor of Pediatrics, Columbia University; Educational Director, Robinson Reading Clinic, Columbia-Presbyterian Medical Center, New York, New York.

Gordon D. Jensen, M.D.
Professor of Psychiatry and Pediatrics, University of California (Davis) School of Medicine, Davis, California.

Edward D. Joseph, M.D.
Professor of Psychiatry, Mount Sinai Medical School, City University of New York; President, International Psychoanalytic Association, Attending Psychiatrist, Mount Sinai Hospital, New York, New York.

Lothar B. Kalinowsky, M.D.
Clinical Professor of Psychiatry, New York Medical College, Valhalla, New York.

Francis J. Kane, Jr., M.D.
Professor of Psychiatry, Baylor College of Medicine, Texas Medical Center; Deputy Chief of Psychiatry, Methodist Hospital, Houston, Texas.

Harold I. Kaplan, M.D.
Professor of Psychiatry, New York University School of Medicine; Attending Psychiatrist, University Hospital of the New York University Medical Center; Attending Psychiatrist, Bellevue Hospital, New York, New York.

Steven Keller, Ph.D.
Assistant Professor of Psychiatry, Mount Sinai School of Medicine, New York, New York.

Otto F. Kernberg, M.D.
Medical Director, New York Hospital-Cornell Medical Center, Westchester Division; Professor of Psychiatry, Cornell University Medical College; Training and Supervising Analyst, Columbia University Center for Psychoanalytic Training and Research, New York, New York.

Mitchell L. Kietzman, Ph.D.
Professor of Psychology, Queens College, City University of New York; Associate Research Scientist, Department of Psychophysiology, New York State Psychiatric Institute; Research Associate, Department of Psychiatry, Columbia University College of Physicians and Surgeons, New York, New York.

Susan T. Kleeman, M.D.
Assistant Clinical Professor of Psychiatry, University of California (San Diego) Medical School, La Jolla, California.

Gerald L. Klerman, M.D.
Administrator, Alcohol, Drug Abuse, and Mental Health Administration, Public Health Service, Department of Health and Welfare, Rockville, Maryland; Professor of Psychiatry, Harvard Medical School, Massachusetts General Hospital, Boston, Massachusetts.

Peter H. Knapp, M.D.
Professor and Associate Chairman, Division of Psychiatry, Boston University School of Medicine, Boston, Massachusetts.

Donald S. Kornfeld, M.D.
Professor of Clinical Psychiatry, Columbia University College of Physicians and Surgeons; Chief, Psychiatric Consultation and Liaison Service, Presbyterian Hospital, New York, New York.

Irvin A. Kraft, M.D.
Clinical Professor of Mental Health, University of Texas School of Public Health; Clinical Professor of Psychiatry, Baylor College of Medicine; Staff, Texas Children's Hospital, Methodist Hospital, and Bellaire General Hospital, Houston, Texas.

Donald G. Langsley, M.D.
Professor and Chairman, Department of Psychiatry, University of Cincinnati College of Medicine, Cincinnati, Ohio.

Maurice W. Laufer, M.D. (deceased)
Professor of Psychiatry and Human Behavior, Brown University, Providence, Rhode Island; President and Physician-in-Chief, Emma Pendleton Bradley Hospital, Riverside, Rhode Island.

Ruth L. LaVietes, M.D.
Professor of Clinical Psychiatry, Director of Child and Adolescent Psychiatry, New York Medical College, Valhalla, New York.

Heinz E. Lehmann, M.D.
Professor of Psychiatry, McGill University, Montreal, Quebec, Canada.

Melvin Lewis, M.B., B.S. (London) F.R.C. Psych., D.C.H.
Professor of Pediatrics and Psychiatry, Director of Medical Studies, Child Study Center, Yale University; Attending Physician in Pediatrics and Psychiatry, Yale-New Haven Hospital; Editor, *Journal of the American Academy of Child Psychiatry*, New Haven, Connecticut.

Theodore Lidz, M.D.
Sterling Professor of Psychiatry, Emeritus, Yale University School of Medicine, New Haven, Connecticut.

Robert Jay Lifton, M.D.
Foundations Fund Research Professor of Psychiatry, Yale University School of Medicine, New Haven, Connecticut.

Louis Linn, M.D.
Clinical Professor of Psychiatry, Mount Sinai School of Medicine, City University of New York; Attending Psychiatrist, Mount Sinai Hospital, New York, New York.

Zbigniew J. Lipowski, M.D.
Professor of Psychiatry, Dartmouth Medical School; Director, Psychiatric Consultation Service, Dartmouth-Hitchcock Medical Center, Hanover, New Hampshire.

Judith E. Lipton, M.D.
Clinical Instructor, Department of Psychiatry and Behavioral Sciences, University of Washington, Seattle, Washington.

Samuel Livingston, M.D.
Director, Samuel Livingston Epilepsy Diagnostic and Treatment Center; Associate Professor Emeritus of Pediatrics, Johns Hopkins University School of Medicine; Director Emeritus, Johns Hopkins Hospital Epilepsy Clinic; Honorary Consultant

in Pediatrics and Consultant in Internal Medicine, Sinai Hospital, Baltimore, Maryland.

Reginald S. Lourie, M.D., Med. Sc.D.
Professor Emeritus of Child Health and Development Psychiatry and Behavioral Sciences, George Washington University School of Medicine; Senior Consultant, Psychiatric Institute of Washington, Washington, D.C.; Senior Research Scientist, National Institute of Mental Health; Clinical Professor of Psychiatry, Uniformed Services University for the Health Sciences, School of Medicine, Bethesda, Maryland.

Arnold M. Ludwig, M.D.
Evalyn A. Edwards Professor, Department of Psychiatry, University of Kentucky College of Medicine, Lexington, Kentucky.

Roger A. MacKinnon, M.D.
Clinical Professor of Psychiatry, Columbia University College of Physicians and Surgeons; Training and Supervising Analyst, Columbia University Center for Psychoanalytic Training and Research; Attending Psychiatrist, Presbyterian Hospital and New York State Psychiatric Institute, New York, New York.

Robert B. Malmo, Ph.D., LL.D.
Professor of Psychology and Director, Neuropsychology Laboratory, Department of Psychiatry, McGill University; Associated Scientist, Royal Victoria Hospital, Montreal, Quebec, Canada.

Arnold J. Mandell, M.D.
Professor of Psychiatry, University of California (San Diego) School of Medicine, La Jolla, California.

Maurice J. Martin, M.D.
Professor and Chairman, Department of Psychiatry and Psychology, Mayo Clinic and Mayo Medical School, Rochester, Minnesota.

Peter A. Martin, M.D.
Clinical Professor of Psychiatry, University of Michigan Medical Center, Ann Arbor, Michigan; Clinical Professor of Psychiatry, Wayne State University Medical School, Detroit, Michigan; Lecturer, Michigan Psychoanalytic Institute, Southfield, Michigan.

Jules H. Masserman, M.D.
Professor of Psychiatry and Co-Chairman Emeritus, Northwestern University Medical School; President, American Psychiatric Association (1978–1979); Honorary Life President, International Association for Social Psychiatry, Chicago, Illinois.

Joseph D. Matarazzo, Ph.D.
Professor and Chairman, Department of Medical Psychology, School of Medicine, University of Oregon Health Sciences Center, Portland, Oregon.

Philip R. A. May, M.D.
Director, Health Services Research and Development Laboratory, Veterans Administration Medical Center, Brentwood, California; Professor of Psychiatry, Neuropsychiatric Institute, University of California at Los Angeles Center for the Health Sciences, Los Angeles, California.

John F. McDermott, Jr., M.D.
Professor and Chairman, Department of Psychiatry, University of Hawaii School of Medicine, Honolulu, Hawaii.

F. Patrick McKegney, M.D.
Professor of Psychiatry and Medicine, University of Vermont College of Medicine; Chief, Consultation-Liaison Service, Medical Center Hospital of Vermont, Burlington, Vermont.

Donald H. McKnew, Jr., M.D.
Associate Clinical Professor of Child Health and Development and of Psychiatry and Behavioral Sciences, George Washington University School of Medicine, Washington, D.C., Staff Psychiatrist, Unit on Childhood Mental Illness, Biological Psychiatry Branch, National Institute of Mental Health, Bethesda, Maryland.

Alan A. McLean, M.D.
Clinical Associate Professor of Psychiatry, Cornell University Medical College, New York, New York; Associate Attending Psychiatrist, New York Hospital, Westchester Division, White Plains, New York; Eastern Area Medical Director, IBM Corporation, New York, New York.

John E. Meeks, M.D.
Director, Child and Adolescent Services, Psychiatric Institute of Washington; Associate Clinical Professor of Psychiatry, George Washington University Medical Center, Washington, D.C.

William W. Meissner, S.J., M.D.
Associate Clinical Professor of Psychiatry, Harvard Medical School; Faculty Member, Boston Psychoanalytic Institute; Staff Psychiatrist, Massachusetts Mental Health Center, Boston, Massachusetts.

Alvin M. Mesnikoff, M.D.
Professor of Psychiatry, State University of New York, Downstate Medical Center, Brooklyn, New York; Lecturer in Psychiatry, Columbia University College of Physicians and Surgeons; Deputy Commissioner for Research, New York State Office of Mental Health, New York, New York.

Carol H. Meyer, D.S.W.
Professor of Social Work, Columbia University School of Social Work, New York, New York.

Jon K. Meyer, M.D.
Associate Professor of Psychiatry, Johns Hopkins University School of Medicine; Director, Sexual Behaviors Consultation Unit, Johns Hopkins Medical Institutions, Baltimore, Maryland.

Juan E. Mezzich, M.D., Ph.D.
Associate Professor of Psychiatry and Director, Clinical Information Systems, Western Psychiatric Institute and Clinic, University of Pittsburgh School of Medicine, Pittsburgh, Pennsylvania.

Michael R. Milano, M.D.
Associate Clinical Professor of Psychiatry, Columbia University College of Physicians and Surgeons, New York, New York.

James Grier Miller, M.D., Ph.D.
President, University of Louisville; Professor of Psychiatry and Behavioral Science and Professor of Psychology, University of Louisville, Louisville, Kentucky.

Neal E. Miller, Ph.D.
Professor and Head, Laboratory of Physiological Psychology, The Rockefeller University, New York, New York.

Herbert C. Modlin, M.D.
Professor of Community Psychiatry, Menninger Foundation, Topeka, Kansas.

George Mora, M.D.
Assistant Clinical Professor of Psychiatry, New York Medical College, Valhalla, New York; Lecturer, Department of Psychiatry, Columbia University College of Physicians and Surgeons, New York, New York; Clinical Associate Professor of Psychiatry, Albany Medical College, Albany, New York; Research Associate, Department of History of Science and Medicine, Yale University School of Medicine, New Haven, Connecticut; Medical Director, Astor Home for Children, Rhinebeck, New York.

Loren R. Mosher, M.D.
Chief, Center for Studies of Schizophrenia, Clinical Research

Branch, Division of Extramural Research Programs, National Institute of Mental Health, Bethesda, Maryland; Clinical Professor of Psychiatry, Georgetown Medical School, Washington, D.C.

Donald W. Mulder, M.D.
Professor of Neurology, Mayo Medical School; Senior Consultant in Neurology, Mayo Clinic, Rochester, Minnesota.

Patrick F. Mullahy, M.A.
Associate Professor of Psychology (Retired), Manhattan College, New York, New York.

Evelyn S. Myers, M.A.
Coordinator, Psychiatric Care Insurance Coverage, American Psychiatric Association; Managing Editor, *American Journal of Psychiatry*, Washington, D.C.

John C. Nemiah, M.D.
Professor of Psychiatry, Harvard Medical School; Psychiatrist-in-Chief, Beth Israel Hospital, Boston, Massachusetts.

Daniel Offer, M.D.
Chairman, Department of Psychiatry and Director, Institute for Psychosomatic and Psychiatric Research and Training, Michael Reese Hospital and Medical Center; Professor of Psychiatry, Pritzker School of Medicine, University of Chicago, Chicago, Illinois.

William V. Ofman, Ph.D.
Associate Professor of Counseling, University of Southern California, Los Angeles, California; Director, Psychological Affiliates, Beverly Hills, California.

Mary Oman, M.A.
Research Assistant (Anthropology), Department of Psychiatry, University of Missouri-Columbia School of Medicine, Columbia, Missouri.

Mortimer Ostow, M.D., Med. Sc.D.
Edward T. Sandrow Visiting Professor, Department of Pastoral Psychiatry, Jewish Theological Seminary of America, New York, New York.

Anita Werner O'Toole, R.N., Ph.D.
Professor of Nursing and Director, Graduate Program in Psychiatric Mental Health Nursing, Kent State University, Kent, Ohio.

Reuben Pannor, M.S.W.
Director of Community Services, Vista del Mar Child-Care Service; Co-Director, Adoption Research Project, Los Angeles, California.

Lydia L. Pauli, M.D.
Assistant Professor of Pediatrics, Johns Hopkins University School of Medicine; Associate Director, Samuel Livingston Epilepsy Diagnostic and Treatment Center, Baltimore, Maryland.

Ira B. Pauly, M.D.
Professor and Chairman, Department of Psychiatry and Behavioral Sciences, University of Nevada School of Medical Sciences, Reno, Nevada.

Carlos J. G. Perry, M.D.
Chairman, Department of Psychiatry, Wilford Hall United States Air Force Medical Center; Military Consultant in Psychiatry, United States Air Force Surgeon General; Clinical Professor of Psychiatry, University of Texas Health Sciences Center, San Antonio, Texas.

J. Christopher Perry, M.D.
Instructor in Psychiatry, Harvard Medical School, Boston, Massachusetts; Assistant Director, Psychiatric Emergency Service, Cambridge Hospital, Cambridge, Massachusetts.

Gerald C. Peterson, M.D.
Assistant Professor of Psychiatry and Director of Undergraduate Education in Psychiatry, Mayo Medical School; Consultant in Psychiatry; Mayo Clinic, Rochester, Minnesota.

Steve R. Pieczenik, M.D.
Deputy Assistant Secretary of State for Management, Department of State; Assistant Clinical Professor of Psychiatry, George Washington University, Washington, D.C.

Chester M. Pierce, M.D.
Professor of Education and Psychiatry, Faculty of Medicine, Graduate School of Education, Harvard University, Cambridge, Massachusetts; Professor of Education and Psychiatry, Harvard Medical School; Visiting Psychiatrist, Massachusetts General Hospital, Boston, Massachusetts.

Jonathan H. Pincus, M.D.
Professor of Neurology, Yale University School of Medicine, New Haven, Connecticut.

George H. Pollock, M.D., Ph.D.
Director, Chicago Institute for Psychoanalysis; Professor of Psychiatry, Northwestern University School of Medicine; President, Center for Psychosocial Studies, Chicago, Illinois.

Alvin F. Poussaint, M.D.
Associate Professor of Psychiatry and Senior Associate Psychiatrist, Children's Hospital Medical Center and the Judge Baker Guidance Center; Associate Dean of Student Affairs, Harvard Medical School, Boston, Massachusetts.

Sally Provence, M.D.
Professor of Pediatrics, Child Study Center, Yale University School of Medicine; Attending Physician in Pediatrics, Yale-New Haven Hospital; Faculty, Western New England Institute for Psychoanalysis, New Haven, Connecticut.

Irving Pruce, B.S.
Director of Research, Samuel Livingston Epilepsy Diagnostic and Treatment Center, Baltimore, Maryland.

Dane G. Prugh, M.D.
Professor of Psychiatry and Pediatrics, University of Colorado School of Medicine; Director of Training in Child Psychiatry, Department of Psychiatry, University of Colorado Medical Center, Denver, Colorado.

John D. Rainer, M.D.
Professor of Clinical Psychiatry, Columbia University College of Physicians and Surgeons; Chief of Psychiatric Research (Medical Genetics), New York State Psychiatric Institute, New York, New York.

Morton F. Reiser, M.D.
Charles B. G. Murphy Professor of Psychiatry and Chairman, Department of Psychiatry, Yale University School of Medicine, New Haven, Connecticut.

H. L. P. Resnik, M.D.
Clinical Professor of Psychiatry, George Washington University School of Medicine, Washington, D.C.; Clinical Professor of Psychiatry, Uniformed Services University for the Health Sciences, School of Medicine, Bethesda, Maryland; Lecturer in Psychiatry, Johns Hopkins University School of Medicine, Baltimore, Maryland.

Lewis L. Robbins, M.D.
Psychiatrist-in-Chief, Emeritus, Long Island Jewish-Hillside Medical Center, New Hyde Park, New York; Professor of Psychiatry, State University of New York at Stony Brook, Stony Brook, New York.

Carl R. Rogers, Ph.D.
Resident Fellow, Center for Studies of the Person, La Jolla, California.

Lester H. Rudy, M.D.
Professor and Head, Department of Psychiatry, Abraham Lincoln School of Medicine, University of Illinois; Psychiatrist-in-Chief, University of Illinois Hospital; Executive Director, American Board of Psychiatry and Neurology, Chicago, Illinois.

Jurgen Ruesch, M.D.
Professor of Psychiatry, The Langley Porter Institute, University of California School of Medicine, San Francisco, California.

Melvin Sabshin, M.D.
Medical Director, American Psychiatric Association, Washington, D.C.; Clinical Professor Emeritus, Department of Psychiatry, Abraham Lincoln School of Medicine, University of Illinois College of Medicine, Chicago, Illinois.

Benjamin J. Sadock, M.D.
Professor of Psychiatry, New York University School of Medicine; Attending Psychiatrist, University Hospital of the New York University Medical Center; Attending Psychiatrist, Bellevue Hospital, New York, New York.

Virginia A. Sadock, M.D.
Assistant Professor of Psychiatry and Director, Human Sexuality Program, New York Medical College, Valhalla, New York; Assistant Visiting Psychiatrist, Metropolitan Hospital, New York, New York.

Eugene C. Sandberg, M.D.
Associate Professor of Gynecology and Obstetrics, Stanford University School of Medicine, Stanford, California.

Burton A. Sandok, M.D.
Associate Professor of Neurology, Mayo Medical School; Consultant and Head of Section, Department of Neurology, Mayo Clinic, Rochester, Minnesota.

Steven Schleifer, M.D.
Instructor in Psychiatry, Mount Sinai School of Medicine, City University of New York, New York, New York.

Abraham Schmitt, D.S.W.
Author, *Dialogue with Death* and *The Art of Listening with Love*, Souderton, Pennsylvania.

Bernard Schoenberg, M.D. (deceased)
Professor of Clinical Psychiatry and Associate Dean for Academic Programs, Columbia University College of Physicians and Surgeons.

Helen Schucman, Ph.D.
Associate Professor of Medical Psychology (Retired), Columbia University College of Physicians and Surgeons, New York, New York.

Arthur H. Schwartz, M.D.
Associate Professor of Psychiatry and Director, Ambulatory Services, Department of Psychiatry, Mount Sinai School of Medicine, City University of New York, New York, New York.

Anne M. Seiden, M.D.
Chairperson, Department of Psychiatry, Cook County Hospital; Associate Professor of Psychiatry, Abraham Lincoln School of Medicine; Associate Professor of Health Services, School of Public Health, University of Illinois; Attending Psychiatrist, Michael Reese Hospital, Chicago, Illinois.

Melvin L. Selzer, M.D.
Clinical Associate Professor of Psychiatry, University of California, San Diego, California.

Robert A. Senescu, M.D.
Adjunct Professor of Psychiatry, University of New Mexico School of Medicine; Professor of Law, University of New Mexico School of Law, Albuquerque, New Mexico.

Charles Shagass, M.D.
Professor of Psychiatry, Temple University School of Medicine; Chief, Temple University Clinical Services, Eastern Pennsylvania Psychiatric Institute, Philadelphia, Pennsylvania.

David Shakow, Ph.D.
Senior Research Psychologist, National Institute of Mental Health, Bethesda, Maryland.

Johanna Shaw, M.D.
Assistant Clinical Professor of Psychiatry, University of Vermont School of Medicine; Attending Psychiatrist, Medical Center Hospital of Vermont, Burlington, Vermont; Attending Psychiatrist, Hartford Hospital, Hartford, Connecticut.

Taranath Shetty, M.D.
Clinical Assistant Professor of Pediatrics and Neurology, Brown University Program in Medicine; Director, Pediatric Neurology, Rhode Island Hospital, Providence, Rhode Island.

Peter E. Sifneos, M.D.
Professor of Psychiatry, Harvard Medical School; Associate Director, Department of Psychiatry, Beth Israel Hospital, Boston, Massachusetts.

Larry B. Silver, M.D.
Special Assistant to the Director, National Institute of Mental Health, Bethesda, Maryland.

Albert J. Silverman, M.D.
Professor and Chairman, Department of Psychiatry, University of Michigan Medical Center, Ann Arbor, Michigan.

George M. Simpson, M.B., Ch.B. (Liverpool)
Professor of Psychiatry, University of Southern California School of Medicine, Los Angeles, California; Director, University of Southern California—Metropolitan State Hospital Psychopharmacology Service, Metropolitan State Hospital, Norwalk, California.

Margaret Thaler Singer, Ph.D.
Professor of Psychology, Department of Psychiatry (Psychology), University of California Langley Porter Institute, San Francisco, California; Research Scientist, National Institute of Mental Health, Bethesda, Maryland.

William H. Sledge, M.D.
Assistant Professor of Psychiatry, Associate Director of Graduate Education, Yale University School of Medicine, New Haven, Connecticut.

Ralph Slovenko, LL.B., Ph.D.
Professor of Law and Psychiatry, Wayne State University School of Law, Detroit, Michigan; Author, *Psychiatry and Law*; Editor, American Lecture Series in Behavioral Science and Law.

Iver F. Small, M.D.
Professor of Psychiatry, Indiana University School of Medicine, Assistant Medical Director, Larue D. Carter Memorial Hospital, Indianapolis, Indiana.

Joyce G. Small, M.D.
Professor of Psychiatry, Indiana University School of Medicine; Director of Research, Larue D. Carter Memorial Hospital, Indianapolis, Indiana.

S. Mouchly Small, M.D.
Professor of Psychiatry, State University of New York at Buffalo School of Medicine, Buffalo, New York; Director, American Board of Psychiatry and Neurology.

Solomon H. Snyder, M.D.
Distinguished Service Professor of Psychiatry and Pharmacol-

ogy, Johns Hopkins University School of Medicine, Baltimore, Maryland.

Albert J. Solnit, M.D.
Sterling Professor of Pediatrics and Psychiatry, Yale University School of Medicine and Director, Child Study Center, Yale University; Attending Physician in Pediatrics and Psychiatry, Yale-New Haven Hospital, New Haven, Connecticut.

Philip Solomon, M.D.
Clinical Professor of Psychiatry, University of California (San Diego) Medical School, La Jolla, California.

Seymour Solomon, M.D.
Professor of Neurology, Albert Einstein College of Medicine, Yeshiva University; Attending Neurologist, Montefiore Hospital and Medical Center, Bronx Lebanon Hospital Center, New York, New York.

Arthur D. Sorosky, M.D.
Associate Clinical Professor of Psychiatry, Division of Child Psychiatry, University of California at Los Angeles School of Medicine; Co-Director, Adoption Research Project, Los Angeles, California.

David Spiegel, M.D.
Assistant Professor of Psychiatry and Behavioral Sciences, Stanford University School of Medicine, Stanford, California; Director, Social Psychiatry and Community Services, Palo Alto Veterans Administration Medical Center, Palo Alto, California.

Herbert Spiegel, M.D.
Clinical Professor of Psychiatry, Columbia University College of Physicians and Surgeons; Attending Psychiatrist, Columbia Presbyterian Medical Center, New York, New York.

Herzl R. Spiro, M.D., Ph.D.
Professor and Chairman, Department of Psychiatry and Mental Health Sciences, Medical College of Wisconsin; Director of Psychiatry, Milwaukee County Mental Health Institute; Director of Psychiatry, Milwaukee County Medical Complex; Milwaukee, Wisconsin.

Robert L. Spitzer, M.D.
Professor of Psychiatry, Columbia University College of Physicians and Surgeons; Chief, Psychiatric Research, Biometric Research Department, New York State Psychiatric Institute, New York, New York.

Bonnie Spring, Ph.D.
Assistant Professor of Psychology, Harvard University; Assistant Psychologist, McLean Hospital; Clinical Assistant in Psychology, Department of Psychiatry, Massachusetts General Hospital, Boston, Massachusetts; Lecturer, Department of Psychiatry, Columbia University College of Physicians and Surgeons, New York, New York.

Marvin Stein, M.D.
Esther and Joseph Klingenstein Professor and Chairman, Department of Psychiatry, Mount Sinai School of Medicine, City University of New York, New York, New York.

Robert L. Stewart, M.D.
Training and Supervising Analyst, Cincinnati Psychoanalytic Institute, Cincinnati, Ohio; Professor of Psychiatry, University of Cincinnati College of Medicine, Cincinnati, Ohio.

Robert J. Stoller, M.D.
Professor of Psychiatry, University of California at Los Angeles School of Medicine, Los Angeles, California.

Charles F. Stroebel, Ph.D., M.D.
Director of Research and Director of Psychophysiology Clinic and Laboratories, Institute of Living, Hartford, Connecticut; Professor of Psychiatry, University of Connecticut Medical School and Health Center, Farmington, Connecticut; Lecturer

in Psychiatry, Yale University School of Medicine, New Haven, Connecticut.

Hans H. Strupp, Ph.D.
Distinguished Professor of Psychology, Vanderbilt University, Nashville, Tennessee.

Albert J. Stunkard, M.D.
Professor of Psychiatry, University of Pennsylvania, Philadelphia, Pennsylvania.

Frida G. Surawicz, M.D.
Professor of Psychiatry, University of Kentucky Medical College; Chief of Psychiatry, Veterans Administration Medical Center, Lexington, Kentucky.

Norman Sussman, M.D.
Instructor, Department of Psychiatry and Lecturer, Division of Continuing Education in Psychiatry, New York Medical College, Valhalla, New York.

Alexandra Symonds, M.D.
Clinical Associate Professor of Psychiatry, Department of Psychiatry, New York University School of Medicine, New York, New York; Training and Supervising Analyst, American Institute of Psychoanalysis; Karen Horney Center, New York, New York.

Martin Symonds, M.D.
Clinical Associate Professor of Psychiatry, New York University School of Medicine; Assistant Dean, American Institute for Psychoanalysis; Assistant Attending Psychiatrist, University Hospital and Bellevue Hospital, New York, New York.

Bryce Templeton, M.D.
Principal Investigator, Comprehensive Qualifying Evaluation Program, National Board of Medical Examiners; Clinical Assistant Professor of Psychiatry, University of Pennsylvania School of Medicine, Philadelphia, Pennsylvania.

William N. Thetford, Ph.D.
Professor of Medical Psychology, Department of Psychiatry, Columbia University College of Physicians and Surgeons, New York, New York.

Pamela J. Trent, Ph.D.
Assistant Medical Research Professor, Department of Psychiatry, Duke University Medical Center, Durham, North Carolina.

Gary J. Tucker, M.D.
Professor and Chairman, Department of Psychiatry, Dartmouth Medical School, Hanover, New Hampshire.

Montague Ullman, M.D.
President, American Society for Psychical Research; Faculty, Westchester Center for the Study of Psychoanalysis and Psychotherapy, White Plains, New York; Professor of Psychiatry, Albert Einstein College of Medicine, Yeshiva University, New York, New York.

George E. Vaillant, M.D.
Professor of Psychiatry, Harvard Medical School, Boston, Massachusetts; Director of Training, Cambridge Hospital, Cambridge, Massachusetts.

J. Ingram Walker, M.D.
Assistant Professor of Psychiatry, Duke University Medical Center; Staff Psychiatrist, Veterans Administration Hospital, Durham, North Carolina.

Roger Walsh, M.D., Ph.D. MRANZCP
Assistant Professor of Psychiatry and Human Behavior, University of California at Irvine School of Medicine; Assistant Professor, School of Social Sciences, University of California at Irvine, Irvine, California; Director of Residency Education, Metropolitan State Hospital, Norwalk, California.

Jack Weinberg, M.D.
Director, Illinois Mental Health Institute; Professor of Psychiatry, Abraham Lincoln School of Medicine, University of Illi-

nois; Professor of Psychiatry, Rush Medical College, Rush-Presbyterian-St. Luke's Medical Center, Chicago, Illinois; Distinguished Senior Scholar, Center for the Study of the Mental Health of the Aging, National Institute of Mental Health, Bethesda, Maryland.

Herbert Weiner, M.D.
Professor of Psychiatry and Neuroscience, Albert Einstein College of Medicine; Chairman, Department of Psychiatry, Montefiore Hospital and Medical Center, Albert Einstein College of Medicine, New York, New York.

Avery D. Weisman, M.D.
Professor of Psychiatry, Massachusetts General Hospital; Professor of Psychiatry, Harvard Medical School; Training and Supervisory Analyst, Boston Psychoanalytic Society and Institute, Boston, Massachusetts.

Charles E. Wells, M.D.
Professor of Psychiatry and Neurology; Vice-Chairman, Department of Psychiatry, Vanderbilt University School of Medicine, Nashville, Tennessee.

Sidney Werkman, M.D.
Professor of Psychiatry, University of Colorado School of Medicine, Denver, Colorado.

Louis J. West, M.D.
Professor and Chairman, Department of Psychiatry, University of California at Los Angeles School of Medicine; Psychiatrist-in-Chief, University of California Hospitals and Clinics; Director, Neuropsychiatric Institute, University of California Center for the Health Sciences, Los Angeles, California; Consultant in Psychiatry, Veterans Administration Center for Psychosocial Medicine, Brentwood, California; Consultant in Psychiatry, Veterans Administration Hospital, Sepulveda, California.

Barbara F. Westmoreland, M.D.
Associate Professor of Neurology, Mayo Medical School; Consultant in Electroencephalography, Mayo Clinic, Rochester, Minnesota.

Lynn Whisnant, M.D.
Assistant Clinical Professor of Psychiatry and Associate Director of Undergraduate Education, Department of Psychiatry, Yale University School of Medicine, New Haven, Connecticut.

Jerry M. Wiener, M.D.
Professor and Chairman, Department of Psychiatry and Behavioral Sciences; Professor of Child Health and Development, George Washington University School of Health Sciences; Attending Psychiatrist, Children's Hospital National Medical Center, Washington, D.C.

Otto Allen Will, Jr., M.D.
Formerly Clinical Professor of Psychiatry, University of Massachusetts School of Medicine, Boston, Massachusetts; Visiting Professor of Psychiatry, University of Cincinnati College of Medicine, Cincinnati, Ohio; Formerly Medical Director, Austen Riggs Center, Stockbridge, Massachusetts.

Janet B. W. Williams, M.S.W.
Instructor in Clinical Psychiatric Social Work, Department of Psychiatry, Columbia University College of Physicians and Surgeons; Research Scientist, Biometric Research Department, New York State Psychiatric Institute, New York, New York; DSM-III Project Coordinator.

Jerome A. Winer, M.D.
Associate Professor of Psychiatry and Director, Residency Training Program, Department of Psychiatry, Abraham Lincoln School of Medicine, University of Illinois, Chicago, Illinois.

E. D. Wittkower, M.D.
Emeritus Professor of Psychiatry, McGill University School of Medicine; Honorary Consulting Psychiatrist, Queen Elizabeth Hospital, Montreal General Hospital, Royal Victoria Hospital, and Reddy Memorial Hospital, Montreal, Quebec, Canada.

Jack A. Wolford, M.D.
Professor of Psychiatry, Department of Psychiatry, University of Pittsburgh School of Medicine, Western Psychiatric Institute and Clinic, Pittsburgh, Pennsylvania.

Edward A. Wolpert, M.D., Ph.D.
Director of the Hospital, Institute for Psychosomatic and Psychiatric Research and Training, Michael Reese Hospital and Medical Center; Clinical Professor of Psychiatry, University of Chicago, Pritzker School of Medicine; Consultant, Sonia Shankman Orthogenic School, University of Chicago, Chicago, Illinois.

Leon J. Yarrow, Ph.D.
Chief, Social and Behavioral Sciences Branch, National Institute of Child Health and Human Development, National Institutes of Health, Bethesda, Maryland.

Joseph Zubin, Ph.D.
Distinguished Research Professor of Psychiatry, University of Pittsburgh Medical School; Research Career Scientist, Veterans Administration Medical Center, Pittsburgh, Pennsylvania; Professor Emeritus of Psychology and Special Lecturer in Psychiatry, Columbia University; Attending Biometrician, New York State Psychiatric Institute; Adjunct Professor of Psychology, Queens College, City University of New York, New York, New York.

Contents

VOLUME ONE

VOLUME TWO

VOLUME THREE

Introduction

Psychiatry: The Inexhaustible Science

JOHN C. NEMIAH, M.D.

I have often amused myself with thinking how different a place London is to different people. They, whose narrow minds are contracted to the consideration of some one particular pursuit, view it only through that medium. A politician thinks of it merely as the seat of government in its different departments; a grazier, as a vast market for cattle; a mercantile man, as a place where a prodigious deal of business is done upon 'Change; a dramatick enthusiast, as the grand scene of theatrical entertainments; a man of pleasure as an assemblage of taverns, and the great emporium for ladies of easy virtue. But the intellectual man is struck with it, as comprehending the whole of human life in all its variety, the contemplation of which is inexhaustible.

— James Boswell, *The Life of Samuel Johnson*

Modern psychiatry is a great, brawling metropolis which has engulfed in its urban sprawl a host of arts and sciences. The courageous traveler who sets out to explore its labyrinthine ways, skillfully mapped in the pages of these volumes, will find the thoroughfares thronged with scholars from a multitude of disciplines and crowded with artisans displaying a bewildering array of clinical skills. He will rub shoulders with a myriad of pilgrims come to seek help for an astonishing diversity of human infirmities. And he will learn at first hand the immense, inexhaustible complexity that is at once psychiatry's glory and its curse.

The confusion is reminiscent of an earlier period in the erratic history of psychiatric theory and practice. In the Great Confinement of the 17th and 18th centuries (Foucault, 1965), the mentally ill were indiscriminately locked away with a mass of other unfortunates of every description. Prisons, workhouses, bridewells, and those vast warehouses of human misery, the *hôpitals generaux*, detained behind their grim walls a farrago of the destitute, the crippled, the aged and senile, of orphans, beggars, vagabonds, criminals, and the insane. The single thread that stitched these markedly dissimilar outcasts together was their idleness and unproductivity in an increasingly mercantile society. They were segregated by the authorities more out of vengeance and fear than from a wish to help or reform. Their banishment was a quarantine to protect the rest of society from a loathsome infection—a quarantine that initially failed to take cognizance of individual conditions and needs among those so summarily sequestered.

Before long, however, it became clear even to the most obtuse and unfeeling of governments that many of those they had sentenced to exile were not willfully lazy or miscreant but victims of circumstances beyond their control. The insane, in particular, were marked as a group apart by their bizarreness, their social ineptitude, their disordered perceptions and thinking, and their often wildly irrational or self-destructive behavior. It was increasingly evident that they were not vicious but deranged, that they were in need of rehabilitation, not punishment. The madhouses that sprang up to dot the 18th-century landscape in England and on the continent were testimony to that change in perception (Parry-Jones, 1972).

The change was not, of course, evidence of a complete break with the attitudes of the immediate past. Madhouses were, after all, still places in which the insane were confined against their will, and that confinement was still often motivated by fear and loathing. At the same time, the very fact that facilities were specifically created for the reception and care of the mentally disordered reflected a growing recognition that their inmates were ill, that they needed retreats to buffer them from the stresses of the workaday world, and that special kinds of treatment were required to bring them back to reason and sanity. If madhouse keepers were often opportunists who exploited their charges to satisfy financial greed and treated them with neglect, even outright cruelty, there were a growing number of Pinels and Tukes whose compassion and concern for their patients foreshadowed the sweeping humanitarian reforms that came a generation later.

Reforms, although they are often set in motion by the initiative of private citizens, require, if they are to be lasting, governmental intervention in the form of laws and regulations that create formal institutions. The care of the insane was no exception, and that fact is perhaps nowhere more clearly seen than in the social history of England in the early decades of the 19th century. Widespread clamor over the shocking abuses found in the many private madhouses and public hospitals, like Bethlem and St. Luke's, led to parliamentary investigations, legislative acts, regulatory commissions, and, by mid-century, the creation of a network of tax-supported county asylums specifically erected for the care and treatment of the mentally ill (Jones, 1955).

The social concern for the insane was, furthermore, accompanied by a rising professionalism among those who cared for them. The administration of the 18th-century madhouses had been a haphazard and individual affair, and as often as not, they were run by laymen whose interests were more monetary than clinical. With reform and governmental intervention there came a demand for medical attention for the swelling populations of the recently built asylums. The demand created supply, and the specialty of psychiatry was born as physicians increasingly directed and staffed the new mental institutions and, with a newfound sense of cohesion, created professional societies and journals to promote their scientific and practical activities (Scull, 1979). Although the word "psychiatry" first appeared in print in 1847 (Murray et al., 1970), it did not come into general usage for several decades, and physicians who focused their professional attention on the insane were known as "alienists" throughout much of the 19th century.

The organization of professional groups can, of course, lead to self-interested conservatism and stultifying intellectual parochialism. No doubt, that was a feature of psychiatry as it developed through the 19th century. But at the same time it provided a forum for the exchange of ideas among physicians of similar interests. Of perhaps even greater importance, it acted as a lens to focus scientific attention on the phenomena of mental illness. Viewed through the rich, often dismaying diversity of the modern study of mental disorders, 19th-century psychiatry is invitingly simple. A hundred years ago the alienist concentrated on the study and the treatment of persons with major mental disorders, and the locus of his work was in the huge asylums that housed his patients. His clinical scientific interests were mainly centered on the accurate description of psychiatric symptoms and their classification into empirically defined diagnostic categories. When he entered the laboratory, it was to search for the lesions in the brain that determined the pathological behavior of the living psychotic patient.

If the alienist entertained psychological notions in his clinical practice, his concepts were rudimentary at best. Since the time of Pinel, clinicians had known that his human environment could affect the course of a patient's mental disorder. Moral treatment surrounded the sick person with a kindly, if author-itarian, social structure designed to encourage his return to health. Based on empirical observation and traditional faculty psychology, moral treatment aimed to quiet the passions and to restore reason to its rightful place of supremacy in the human psyche. The fact that it often worked was a tribute to the skill and the sensitivity of those who practiced it. The loss of faith in its efficacy as the 19th century wore on meant the loss to psychiatry of the beginnings of a humanistic approach to mental illness that had to be rediscovered several generations later. Late 19th-century psychiatry became largely a medical discipline, rooted in the same biologically oriented science that ⌐urished all contemporary medicine. Increasingly restricted in its outlook, psychiatry became temporarily sterile until an infusion of new ideas at the close of the century set the stage for a renascence of its creativity.

The breath of fresh air that Freud brought to psychiatry eventually became a gale that has threatened to blast the discipline from its medical moorings. Raised in the biological medicine of his day, Freud was basically a psychologist (Levin, 1968), and the source of his ideas is to be found outside the medical tradition. Sired by the romantic reaction to rational-ism, the concept of an unconscious mind was, throughout much of the 19th century, the plaything of poets, artists, and philos-ophers. The concept found support in the findings of magnet-ism or mesmerism—as it was sometimes called, after its pro-genitor, Mesmer. Magnetism led an early life that was check-ered if not disreputable. Scorned, with a few notable exceptions, by the medical fraternity, its phenomena were largely explored by French noblemen, Church of England vicars, mountebanks, and assorted curious laymen. Central to the phenomena was the discovery of areas of mental functioning inaccessible to ordinary conscious awareness or control—what later were called "dissociated" or "subconscious" mental states that could be produced or uncovered by the procedures of magnetic operators. Magnetism first became partially legitimized for the medical profession in the work of the Manchester surgeon James Braid, who renamed it "hypnotism" and convincingly demonstrated its psychological nature.

Hypnotism initially made little headway in England, but Braid's ideas profoundly influenced an important group of French clinicians, foremost of whom was Jean-Martin Char-cot, the founder of the seminal school of neurology at the Salpêtrière in Paris. It was during his period of study with Charcot that Freud became conversant at first hand with the phenomena of hypnosis and of the closely related, naturally occurring clinical features of hysteria; it was there that he first learned that unconscious memories, ideas, and emotions can produce the symptoms of illness, as well as determine their form. To the explanatory concept of dissociation proposed by Charcot and his colleagues, Freud added the revolutionary theoretical notion of psychological conflict. The idea that man's dark underworld of forbidden desires and fantasies could come into conflict with his rational controlling ego and that the symptoms of his illnesses could be explained as the compromise reached in the resolution of that conflict revitalized psychia-trists' interest in the causes and treatment of emotional disor-ders. The influence of Freud's ideas has been profound, and the importance of psychoanalysis for the development of psy-chiatry in America cannot be underestimated. But, along with its vital contributions to clinical theory and practice, its wide-spread adoption by the psychiatric profession has created significant difficulties.

Perhaps more than any other factor, psychoanalysis has led to the confusing complexity that besets psychiatry today. Psy-choanalysis began as a clinical science and shed new light on the cause of psychiatric symptoms. But its explanatory power went beyond the confines of the clinic; the concept of psycho-logical conflict between opposing forces in a structured psyche formed the basis of a general psychology that pertained not just to symptoms and illness but to the formation of personality and the origins of behavior as well. In its general applications, it seemed that there was no aspect of human activity that could not be illuminated and understood in terms of unconscious motivations. Psychoanalytic clinicians and theorists alike turned their attention to an ever-widening circle of human concerns. Crime, delinquency, creativity, religion, physical ill-ness, child development, education, sexual deviancy, and the manifold aberrations of personality, behavior, and human relationships—all came under analytic scrutiny. It appeared as if history had come full circle; once again, as in the age of the Great Confinement, an almost infinite diversity of seemingly disparate human phenomena were lumped together, intermin-gled now not within the walls of an all-encompassing prison but on the analyst's couch. The stark, beautiful simplicity of 19th-century psychiatry had vanished.

In the eventual development of analytic observation and theory to include the mosaic of ego theory, yet further com-plexities ensued. As human beings came to be viewed not simply as the resultants of intrapsychic conflicts but also as beings required to adapt to the stresses of their human and physical environments, the scope of psychiatric inquiry and practice was extended. It was now necessary to look beyond the individual person to the nature of his transactions in human relationships, ranging from the simplest to the most complex. It was important to define the characteristics of the stresses to which he was subject—the losses, the bereavements, and the significant changes in social status that could lead to emotional strain and distress. And it was essential to understand the influence on a person's life and health of the deprivations inherent in adverse social circumstances, such as poverty, bro-ken homes, and belonging to an underprivileged minority. As psychiatry moved out from its restricted clinical center, it rubbed shoulders with professionals from other disciplines who brought different and often perplexingly strange techniques to bear on the phenomena under study. In its exodus into the suburbs, psychiatry had to learn the ways of sociologists and anthropologists, of epidemiologists and demographers, of ur-ban planners and others concerned with social change. In those unaccustomed regions it was always in jeopardy of losing its orientation. What was perhaps of even greater potential danger was the fact that, in its enthusiasm for new avenues of approach and in its hope of preventing human misery through effecting changes in the structure of society, psychiatry pledged more than it could pay. Psychiatrists have already reaped some of the disillusionment that has resulted from their shortcomings in community activities and are making a cautious but healthy withdrawal to more realistic goals.

Although psychiatry focused on the understanding of the human being as a psychological and social being, it lost sight of its biological underpinnings. That is not surprising, since for several decades the development of knowledge of human psychological functioning outstripped the understanding of neurophysiology and neurochemistry. For a considerable period of time, the exciting observations and concepts concerning behavior came from psychoanalysis, which, as the basis for psychodynamic psychiatry, was and remains the most useful model for the understanding of many clinical disorders. At the same time, this casting loose from its biological mooring has had unfortunate consequences. It has led to a loosening of psychiatry's ties with the rest of medicine, has created confusion and differences of opinion about the prerequisites for training in psychiatry, and has caused psychiatrists to lose stature as physicians in the eyes of the public, if not of their patients. Psychiatrists have quite rightly, if ingenuously, pointed out that one does not necessarily need a medical background to be a skilled psychotherapist. That statement has been taken at face value by colleagues in the ancillary professions; indeed, they have gone one better in their claims that they are as competent as psychiatrists to perform almost all the functions traditionally considered those of the psychiatrist. One needs only to observe the dismay of first-year psychiatric residents as they strive to find a professional identity to be convinced of the confusion that arises from this blurring of customary roles. And on a larger stage, the battle is joined in legislatures and courts as the various professional groups seek autonomy in the care of psychiatric patients—a battle whose issue is by no means certain.

In the face of these forays, psychiatry has been reassessing its position. It is fortunate that the current self-reflection coincides with recent major advances in knowledge of the biological side of psychiatric illness and human behavior. The understanding of brain function is beginning to approximate the sophistication of psychological observations and theories, inspiring the hope that psychiatrists are coming closer to substantial correlations between those two complementary approaches. Already, the contributions of psychopharmacology have made it possible for psychiatrists to alleviate the symptoms of the major psychoses that were formerly generally beyond the reach of their skills.

Biological knowledge, in other words, is beginning to restore the balance that has been long tipped steeply toward psychology. There is a danger in this, too—a danger that the balance will dip too far in the opposite direction and that psychiatrists will forget the important gains that have been made in the psychological and social understanding of human behavior. There are even now straws in the wind—the disappearance of the psychodynamic approach from some training programs, the strongly syndromatic view of emotional disorders in the 1980 edition of the American Psychiatric Association's classification manual, to the exclusion of the psychological knowledge gained over the past half-century, the tendency on the part of some to think too narrowly, to contract their minds "to

the consideration of some one particular pursuit" and to view psychiatric phenomena "only through that medium." It would be sad if psychiatry, through internal faction and dissent, lost sight of the message it has preached for so many years—that man is at once a biological, a psychological, and a social creature and that his ailments can be understood fully only as the product of factors derived from all three dimensions of his being.

Psychiatry is clearly in a period of transition as it approaches the end of the century. It would be the height of folly to predict where psychiatry will be by the year 2000, but perhaps one can erect a signpost or two to point the way. Human illness has its roots in the biological, psychological, and social elements of human nature, and those conditions designated "psychiatric disorders" are no exception. In the treatment of a patient with a psychiatric illness, one may, with profit to the patient, enlist the help of therapists from a variety of professional disciplines, but the responsibility for the patient's diagnosis, for the determination of the nature of his treatment, and for his over-all care must rest with the psychiatric physician, for only he, with his biological medical education joined to his postgraduate psychiatric training, has the background to understand and to assess the contributions made by these three spheres of his being to the patient's illness. At the same time, when it comes to the scientific investigation of psychiatric disorders, the psychiatrist has no claim to preeminence. On the contrary, knowledge must be sought wherever it lies and from every discipline that has a contribution to make. Research is a partnership of equals, working side by side with mutual appreciation and respect. Factionalism and interdisciplinary strife can only delay the attainment of the solutions that all seek.

Stanley Cobb once said to an aspiring young colleague:

> Psychiatry is an immense field, and you cannot possibly learn it all. The best you can do is to pick an area that interests you and make yourself the master of that. But above all, keep an open mind about what others are thinking and doing.

The reader of these volumes will rapidly discover that their editors have been deeply imbued with the spirit of that message. They have accurately delineated each highway and byway of every borough in the great metropolis of Psychiatry. And they have done so with an admirable evenhandedness, with a profound respect for all points of view, and with an open willingness to allow every author to develop his subject according to his own lights. In the process they have created a textbook unique in the annals of psychiatric publications. Here, then, is a truly comprehensive Baedeker, skillfully compiled so as to reveal psychiatry to each intellectual man and woman "as comprehending the whole of human life in all its variety, the contemplation of which is inexhaustible."

REFERENCES

Boswell, J. *The Life of Samuel Johnson.* Oxford University Press, New York, 1933.
Foucault, M. *Madness and Civilization.* Pantheon Books, New York, 1965.
Jones, K. *Lunacy, Law, and Conscience.* Routledge & Kegan Paul, London, 1955.
Levin, K. *Freud's Early Psychology of the Neuroses.* University of Pittsburgh Press, Pittsburgh, 1968.
Murray, J. A. H., Bradley, H., Craigie, W. A., and Onions, C. T., editors. *The Oxford English Dictionary.* Clarendon Press, Oxford, 1970.
Parry-Jones, W. *The Trade in Lunacy.* Routledge & Kegan Paul, London, 1972.
Scull, A. *Museums of Madness.* St. Martin's Press, New York, 1979.

chapter

1

Historical and Theoretical Trends in Psychiatry

1.1 ● ● ●

GEORGE MORA, M.D.

Introduction

In recent years a distinct increase of interest in the history of psychiatry has become noticeable in this country, as well as elsewhere. In addition to books, articles on the development of psychiatric theories and practices frequently appear in psychiatric and medicohistorical periodicals. References to analogies, derivations, and relations between current and past psychiatric methods are frequently brought up in the literature. In particular, a number of studies on the history of attitudes toward the mentally ill throughout the centuries have been published by scholars from the fields of history, philosophy, sociology, and the like. The practicing psychiatrist and, especially, the trainee in psychiatry may feel somewhat disoriented toward this situation. This section tries to clarify the issues, methodological procedures, and relevance of the history of psychiatry for the psychiatrist. Such clarification will, it is hoped, enhance the comprehension of the historical development of psychiatry that follows.

Methodological Aspects

Psychiatry, a vast body of doctrine and practice regarding a large number of patients, was the last specialty to be incorporated into the over-all field of medicine, about a century and a half ago. Before that time, mental diseases were considered the province of philosophy; further back, from early times to the Middle Ages, the mentally ill, when not ignored, were usually taken care of—that is sheltered, punished, or exorcized—by medicine men and clergymen. That history is easily understandable, since diseases of the mind—regardless of whether one adheres to a theory of the mind as distinct from the body or a theory of the mind united to the body—have always appeared in the past as very puzzling and difficult to treat.

In *The Structure of Scientific Revolutions*, Kuhn (1970) convincingly showed that scientific principles are meaningful and understandable in the context of a paradigm—that is, of a disciplinary world view that is culturally transmitted and sustained by a set of social institutions. Scientific revolutions occur when the introduction of new notions provokes a crisis that necessitates the creation of a new paradigm.

The behavioral sciences, in particular psychiatry, are still at a preparadigmatic level because of the uncertainties regarding the body-mind relationship—uncertainties that reflect the difficulty of defining their focus, their methodology, their boundaries, and their reciprocal relations. In discussing the development of psychology, Watson (1967) called the field a prescriptional science; prescriptions, which are part of the intellectual equipment of the scientist, more than classifications, are oppositional trends (either dominant or counterdominant), represented by such dichotomies as rationalism versus empiricism and monism versus dualism and identified at various times as operationalism, phenomenalism, or, more concretely, behaviorism, Gestalt theory, psychoanalysis, and structuralism (see Tables I–V). That characteristic goes for psychiatry even more than for psychology, since a great variety of contrasting trends and assumptions are at the base of psychiatry's theoretical and practical foundations. The current proliferation of psychiatric concepts and methods of treatment certainly bears witness to that fact.

Those trends tend to persist and never die; in fact, they are subsumed under different names into broader intellectual and social contexts at various historical periods according to national and cultural characteristics.

Boring (1963), a historian of psychology, particularly emphasized the importance of the cultural configurations, for which he used the term *zeitgeist* (coined by Goethe) to indicate the climate of opinion, the "current of credence,"

the total body of knowledge and opinion available at any time to a person living within a given culture.

The issue of the *zeitgeist* has become increasingly important in the history of science; the creative moment that brings a new discovery appears to be the result of the interplay between the cultural substratum and the individual genius. Boring (1963) wrote:

It may be true that it is the great man who perceives significance, but it is also true that the significance shows the problem to the "great" man. This is why great discoveries do not occur until times are ready for them or, when they occur too early, are not great. In other words, the state of the times works both before and after discovery.

That is a radical departure from the old-fashioned view of history as the unfolding of the great-man theory—that is, as a succession of unrelated creative flashes by individual men, quite often in the assumption of unproved teleological postulates.

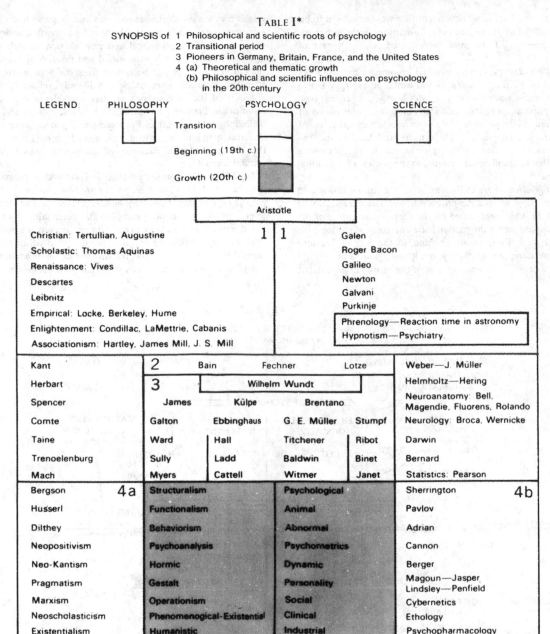

TABLE I*

SYNOPSIS of 1 Philosophical and scientific roots of psychology
2 Transitional period
3 Pioneers in Germany, Britain, France, and the United States
4 (a) Theoretical and thematic growth
(b) Philosophical and scientific influences on psychology
in the 20th century

LEGEND: PHILOSOPHY   PSYCHOLOGY   SCIENCE

Transition

Beginning (19th c.)

Growth (20th c.)

Aristotle

1	1	
Christian: Tertullian, Augustine		Galen
Scholastic: Thomas Aquinas		Roger Bacon
Renaissance: Vives		Galileo
Descartes		Newton
Leibnitz		Galvani
Empirical: Locke, Berkeley, Hume		Purkinje
Enlightenment: Condillac, LaMettrie, Cabanis		Phrenology—Reaction time in astronomy
Associationism: Hartley, James Mill, J. S. Mill		Hypnotism—Psychiatry.

Kant	2	Bain	Fechner	Lotze		Weber—J. Müller
Herbart	3	Wilhelm Wundt				Helmholtz—Hering
Spencer		James	Külpe	Brentano		Neuroanatomy: Bell, Magendie, Fluorens, Rolando
Comte		Galton	Ebbinghaus	G. E. Müller	Stumpf	Neurology: Broca, Wernicke
Taine		Ward	Hall	Titchener	Ribot	Darwin
Trenoelenburg		Sully	Ladd	Baldwin	Binet	Bernard
Mach		Myers	Cattell	Witmer	Janet	Statistics: Pearson

Bergson	4a	Structuralism	Psychological	Sherrington	4b
Husserl		Functionalism	Animal	Pavlov	
Dilthey		Behaviorism	Abnormal	Adrian	
Neopositivism		Psychoanalysis	Psychometrics	Cannon	
Neo-Kantism		Hormic	Dynamic	Berger	
Pragmatism		Gestalt	Personality	Magoun—Jasper Lindsley—Penfield	
Marxism		Operationism	Social	Cybernetics	
Neoscholasticism		Phenomenogical-Existential	Clinical	Ethology	
Existentialism		Humanistic	Industrial	Psychopharmacology	

* From Misiak, H., and Sexton, V., *History of Psychology, An Overview.* Grune & Stratton, New York, 1966.

In an essay on the historiography of science, Agassi (1963) discussed the problem of whether history should be written from the viewpoint of the inductionist or of the conventionalist method—that is, whether the history of science should be represented as a succession of men and discoveries in black and white terms or, rather, as a simple sequence of events that assume different heuristic values at different times. His conclusion was that history should be viewed from the perspective of a continuity—that is, as a slow development of events, each occurring in the context of a given historical background, characterized by the prevalence or, conversely, inhibitions of particular themes or clusters of prescriptions, according to Watson.

Historiography of Psychiatry

Far from being pure speculations, the above points are important for the proper understanding of the significance of the history of psychiatry for the psychiatrist. Psychiatry as a field of medicine and the history of psychiatry developed at the same time, at the end of the 18th century, in the intellectual climate of the Enlightenment, in which humans for the first time discovered their own history. Of the three men who most contributed to the rise of a new attitude toward the mentally ill—Chiarugi in Florence, Tuke in England, and Pinel in Paris—only Pinel (1962) was aware of the historical meaning of his work. He wrote a historical introduction to his *Treatise on Insanity* and was able to provide historical continuity to his ideas by founding a school of clinical psychiatry in Paris, then the center of intellectual life and shortly thereafter, during the Napoleonic era, of political life. Although he held a staunch belief in the scientific approach to psychiatry as a branch of medicine, he was still imbued with a strong humanistic tradition, based on familiarity with the classics.

The same can be said of all other physicians of the psyche—that is, psychiatric pioneers—who came to the fore during the succeeding decades in the countries of Western culture. A number of articles in the early volumes of the first psychiatric journals in France, England, Germany, and the United States bear evidence of that strong interest in historical concerns. No matter how scientific psychiatry ought to be, in reality it was still solidly anchored in the humanities; and psychology, on which the theories of the mind were based, was still part of philosophy.

By the mid-19th century, nationalism had become a pervasive force in continental Europe on the wave of the romantic aspiration of a return to the glorious traditions of the Middle Ages, when national languages and popular lores first came into being. The universality of Latin, which had made possible the rise of academics—that is, of societies of learned men—in the 17th century and later in the Enlightenment, was superseded by the nationalistic trend of viewing history and the background of each culture in the context of individual political entities.

Psychiatry was affected by that trend, too, and broke down into French, German, English, and American schools. The universality of the so-called moral treatment, based on the therapeutic milieu of the small mental hospital under the paternalistic approach of the superintendent, spread from France and England to the rest of Western Europe and, especially, to this country, but it had a short life.

By the middle of the 19th century, most of the historical psychiatric

studies focused on illustrious pioneers and, in general, on the antecedents of each national group. In the decades thereafter, under the impact of the prevailing biochemical and physiological models of the mind then taught in the newly established and flourishing German universities, psychiatry came to be viewed from the organicistic perspective. If mental diseases were to be considered exclusively in terms of disorders of the nervous system, then the relevance of cultural and historical influences on their clinical manifestations and therapeutic philosophy was negligible. For example, if general paresis was due to bacterial infection—as, indeed, was shown by some French clinicians—then the pathological ideation of the patient was independent of cultural factors.

In 1845 two important psychiatric textbooks appeared, von Feuchtersleben's (1847) *The Principles of Medical Psychology* and Griesinger's (1965) *Mental Pathology and Therapeutics*. The first, presented from a psychological perspective of the personality, had a historical introduction that went back to early times; Griesinger's book, presented from an organicistic perspective of the mind, dismissed historical antecedents entirely and soon became the standard handbook in medical schools. As mental illness was then seen exclusively in terms of

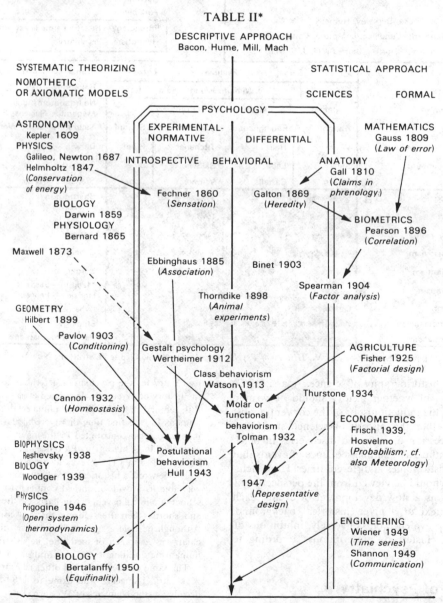

TABLE II*

* From Sexton, V., and Misiak, H., editors, *Historical Perspectives in Psychology: Readings.* Brooks/Cole, Belmont, Calif., A Division of Wadsworth Publishing Company, Inc., 1971.

TABLE III
*The Schools of Psychology and What They Stood For**

School (and representative adherents)	Structuralism (Wundt, Titchener)	Functionalism (Angell, Carr, Thorndike, Woodworth)	Behaviorism (Watson, Hunter, Hull)	Gestalt Psychology (Wertheimer, Koffka, Köhler)	Psychoanalysis (Freud, Jung, Adler)
Unit of study	Mental elements	Mental elements and adaptive processes	S–R elements	Antielements (natural wholes or gestalten)	Elements and processes
Subjective or objective?	Mentalism (subjective)	Mostly mentalism (subjective)	Antimentalism (objective)	Both subjective and objective	Mentalism (subjective)
What should psychology study?	Content	Mostly function but also content	Content and function	Content and function	Content and function
Preferred method	Introspection	Introspection; later, behavior observation, too	Behavior observation	Phenomenology and behavior observation	Free association
Purpose: pure or applied?	Pure	Pure and applied	Pure and applied	Mostly pure	More applied than pure
Nomothetic or idiographic?	Global laws (nomothetic)	Some individual differences (idiographic) but mostly global laws	Both	Both	More individual differences than global laws
Physiological explanation	Physiological hookups	Physiological why or what for	Physiological hookups	Physiological fields	Biological drives?

* From Wertheimer, M., *A Brief History of Psychology*. Holt, Rinehart and Winston, New York, 1970.

TABLE IV
*How the Schools of Psychology Exemplified the Eight Trends**

	Structuralism	Functionalism	Behaviorism	Gestalt Psychology	Psychoanalysis
Physiology	A bit, for explanation	Yes: adaptive processes	Yes: neural hookups	Yes: brain model	Not really
Biology	Not really	Yes: strongly evolutionary	Yes: behavior and evolution	A little: living systems are gestalten	Somewhat: the id drives
Atomism	Yes: mental elements	Yes: mental elements	Yes: S–R bonds	No: antielementism	Maybe: traumatic experiences
Quantification	Yes, some	Yes, some	Yes	Yes	No
Laboratories	Yes	Yes	Yes	Yes	No
Critical empiricism	Yes	Yes	Yes	Yes	Yes, loosely
Associationism	Yes	Yes	Yes	No: antiassociationistic	Maybe: free association
Scientific materialism	Some	Yes: study of the organism	Strongly: objectivism	Yes: brain model	Not really

* From Wertheimer, M., *A Brief History of Psychology*. Holt, Rinehart and Winston, New York, 1970.

psychotic pictures in hospitalized patients, it is no wonder that the only psychiatric history written at that time consisted of histories or, rather, chronicles of the development of mental hospitals, increasingly seen (in this country, under the influence of the crusader Dorothea Dix) as repositories for all kinds of mentally ill. As late as 1906, the Austrian Kornfeld (1905), in his history of psychiatry, included in a comprehensive handbook of the history of medicine, began his presentation with the Renaissance, the time of the advent of experimental science, on the assumption that no psychiatric event worth recording had occurred before that period.

The organicistic trend culminated in the so-called theory of degeneration by the Frenchmen Morel and Magnan. According to that theory, mental diseases were stages of a malignant pathological process, slowly progressing from neurosis to psychosis to mental deficiency and, finally, to extinction of the line. Far from being only an expression of organicistic philosophy, the trend also embodied views of nationalistic

psychiatry, inasmuch as certain nations were supposed to be more degenerated than others. The trend led to Lombroso's theory of atavistic signs in the assessment of the delinquent and, through him, to the biographical study of the delinquent personality. Others—in particular, the German psychiatrist Möbius—published a number of pathographies—that is, psychiatric studies of geniuses—on the assumption of a correlation between genius and insanity.

That trend was a step in the slow transition of emphasis from the hospitalized psychotic to the neurotic patient. Neurotics were still not the province of the psychiatrists. Throughout the 17th and 18th centuries, neurotic symptoms had occasionally been described by general practitioners; toward the end of the 19th century, they were becoming the domain of the neurologist. Weir Mitchell's rest cure—consisting of a period of isolation, overfeeding, and suggestion for wealthy neurotic women—was perhaps the best-known example of interest in neurosis.

Recent studies have pointed to the many currents that slowly contributed to the rise of dynamic psychology at the beginning of the 20th century. Social Darwinism, naturalism and decadentism in literature, the cult of the hero (Nietzsche), and interest in hypnotic and other obscure phenomena in psychiatry proper led to the Freudian revolution. Freud very early became aware of the importance of his new approach to the study of the unconscious, mainly through the interpretation of dreams and free associations, and, in general, to the treatment of neurotic patients. Therefore, he took an attitude of unconcern for psychiatric events of the past and, particularly, for the antecedents of his concepts.

Seen in retrospect, such an attitude was understandable and historically fortunate, since considerations for the past might have interfered with the free expression of his creativity. His pupils followed his steps and remained essentially involved with clinical matters. But, since they were all imbued with a humanistic education, they eventually became attracted to themes of historical interest. So Freud himself published monographs on some unusual personalities, such as Leonardo and Moses, and others—mainly Rank and, above all, Jung—wrote extensively on mythology, archeology, and literature. The common focus of that production was the study of these various subjects from the strict psychoanalytic viewpoint of the unconscious.

During the same period, the early decades of this century, the few psychiatric historical studies continued to deal mainly with themes related to hospitalized psychotic patients. Typical expressions of the trend were several monographs on the development of mental hospitals, on the changes in the methods of treatment, and on current clinical issues, such as degeneration, body-mind relationship, suicide, and hallucinations. Still important today are the collaborative collections

TABLE V
Schools of Academic Psychology (1870–1930)

School of Psychological Thought	Workers	Specific Emphasis
Structuralism	Wundt, Titchener	The study of conscious experience through introspective experimentation. Elementary psychological states—such as sensations, images, and feelings—that make up consciousness are observed and analyzed.
Functionalism	Titchener, Dewey, Angell	Like structuralism, functionalism emphasizes the study of consciousness but in relation to environmental adaptation through application to education (educational psychology) and people (clinical psychology).
Associationism	During the 17th century, philosophers like Hobbes, Berkeley, Locke, Brown, Hartley, Mills, and Bain. In the early 19th century, Herbart. From 1885 on, psychologists like Ebbinghaus, Pavlov, Thorndike, Skinner	The study of learning and memory, as exemplified by Thorndike's law of effect, Pavlov's law of reinforcement, and Skinner's study of learning in animals and human beings, through application of the "Skinner box."
Behaviorism	Watson, Meyer, Weiss, Hunter, Lashley, Tolman, Hull, Skinner	The objective study of human and animal behavior. "Mental" concepts, such as sensation and emotion, are replaced by concepts of stimulus, response, learning, habit, and receptor and effector function. Even the study of consciousness is avoided.
Gestalt psychology	Wertheimer, Koffka, Köhler, Lewin	The total perceptual configuration and the interrelation of its parts are studied. Total experience or behavior is considered to represent more than the sum of its parts. Perception and memory are studied through introspection and observation.
Purposive or hormic psychology	McDougall	The study of goal-seeking behavior. Emphasizes striving and foresight. Human propensities (instincts) constitute the ultimate, primary motivation for behavior. Observations on social behavior stimulated the field of social psychology.
Organismic psychology	Coghill, Kurt Goldstein, Kantor	The holistic, biological study of the individual.
Personalistic psychology	Calkins, Stern	The holistic, social study of the individual.

of biographies of German and French psychiatrists, as well as single biographical studies, such as the ones on Benjamin Rush and Dorothea Dix in this country and on Mesmer in Europe. Other important studies on the Greek and Roman antecedents of modern psychiatry passed almost entirely unnoticed, not unlike the few valuable 19th-century monographs on antiquity, on psychological interpretations of historical personages, and on psychiatric development in a national entity. Comprehensive presentations of the development of psychiatry continued to be viewed as introductions to psychiatric textbooks or to a particular psychological system.

The end of the third decade of this century marks a definite turning point in psychiatry. Psychoanalysis and, in general, dynamic psychology came to be increasingly ostracized and eventually forbidden in Central European countries and later under Nazism, leading to a massive immigration of psychiatrists to this country. At the same time, a decline occurred in the trend of studying writers and artists of the past, of a past culture, and of unconscious productions, such as dreams and collective phenomena, from the psychoanalytic perspective, as well as of investigating the historical antecedents of psychoanalysis.

From then on, for more than a decade, most of the historical psychiatric studies appeared in this country. To be sure, the tendency of the early generation of psychoanalysts was to view the development of psychiatry only in the role of anticipations of dynamic psychology. That tendency is the main criticism that is today expressed of Zilboorg's (1941) *A History of Medical Psychology*, which is otherwise still valuable in many respects. It had been preceded in 1937 by *The Mentally Ill in America*, the work of the layman Deutsch (1948), based on a thorough study of primary sources.

Both these volumes can be considered as the beginning of a new period in psychiatric historiography. The experience of World War II had helped broaden the horizons of many—in regard to psychiatry, by pointing to the great incidence of emotional disorders in the general population, and in regard to history, by showing cultural continuities, derivations, and transitions through the first-hand experiences of many servicemen in foreign lands. The developments in the history of psychiatry, as in the field of history in general, have been so many and so complex that their critical presentation is a difficult one.

Psychiatrists have become interested in historical matters in increasing numbers, especially since the occurrence of the centenary of the American Psychiatric Association in 1944, which greatly contributed to focusing on the significance of the development of psychiatry. It is likely that at the base of this interest is the need for recapturing the spirit of the humanities, which is now lost in the strict biological philosophy of medical schools and which is, indeed, pertinent to psychiatry, which is both a scientific field and a humanistic field. Yet psychiatrists have been thus far ill equipped to deal with historical matters because of their amateurish historical perspective, a tendency to focus on the great men and to disregard the *zeitgeist*, and, even more important, an inclination to view history, as in the case of Zilboorg, from the biased adherence to a particular school of thought.

Since its inception in 1942, the Committee on History of the American Psychiatric Association (APA) has been involved in preparing exhibits of great psychiatrists, in collecting archives, in establishing a museum at the APA headquarters in Washington, in republication of classic psychiatric texts and other material (such as the presidential addresses of the APA from 1944 to 1969), in gathering oral data, and in sponsoring the annual Benjamin Rush Lecture on Psychiatric History.

Individual psychiatrists and clinicians in general, here as in Europe, have been active in publishing comprehensive histories of psychiatry and histories of psychotherapy or histories of their own particular field, of their own particular country, of a particular period, or of a particular institution. Others have focused on the study of nosology, of a clinical entity, of psychiatrists of the past, of psychoanalytic pioneers, and of leaders of psychoanalytic movements—in particular, Adler and Jung. Autobiographies by some well-known psychiatrists have appeared throughout the years, although their historical value remains limited.

The same can be said of some of the studies mentioned above and of others that focused on broad topics requiring special training in historical research. More valuable, however, have been the many psychiatric and psychoanalytic studies of great men of the past written by clinicians, as shown in the bibliographies published by Kiell (1963).

Throughout the years, the methodology of clinicians writing on historical matters has become more sophisticated. Particular events, such as the centenary of Freud's birth in 1956, drew attention to the importance of history. By that time Jones's (1953–1957) biography of Freud—a thorough but not unbiased endeavor, as is typical of a pupil writing about his master—was almost completely published. Since then, Freud's life and work, presented earlier in some monographs, have continued to be the subject of comprehensive studies based on traditional sources.

During the same period, some medical historians published valuable studies based on knowledge of primary sources and other documents—notably Temkin's (1971) historical study of epilepsy. They were followed shortly thereafter by two general histories of psychiatry written by two German-born medical historians, Leibbrand (Leibbrand and Wettley, 1959) and Ackerknecht (1968), the first one mostly dealing with theoretical concepts, the second with clinical matters. Still later, medical historians produced important studies of clinical pictures, such as hysteria and hypochondria, or of psychiatrists of the past. Under the impact of that new approach, a number of psychiatric themes have been investigated in the Institute for the History of Medicine of the University of Zurich, under the leadership of Ackerknecht, which resulted in many publications on broad psychiatric topics.

The differences in methodology between the old approach and the new approach can be clearly seen in the historical study of dreams, on which an extensive literature has been available for a long time. In the past, dreams were reported as a matter of curiosity, but now dreams are investigated in their own historical context, with the help of anthropological, ethnological, and religious notions.

Naturally, since clinicians are by nature and training inclined to the study of the individual personality, it is understandable that they have applied that more sophisticated methodology especially to research on psychiatrists of the past, such as Pinel. No one, however, has been studied as intensively as Freud, on the basis of new data. In particular, several volumes of correspondence between him and his pupils and others have been published.

All that interest has led to a critical evaluation of some new aspects of Freud's thinking—that is, his political, literary, and aesthetic views. Also, unknown sides of his relationship to his early adherents have been investigated, leading at times to acrimonious disputes. On the basis of new documents, including his school records, even his academic career and the issue of the negative influence of his Jewish background on it have become controversial. Freud's study on Leonardo has also become the target of criticism by some art connoisseurs and of passionate defense by others. In psychiatric history, perhaps the only other controversy of the same intensity has been the one concerning the traditionally accepted emotional cause of the mental disease that affected George III, the last king of America, which is now being challenged by some.

Regardless of those controversial aspects, in the past 3 decades several important volumes concerning the pre-Freudian origins of psychiatric concepts and the background of Freud's original ideas have appeared. Also matter for investigation have been the lives of some famous patients—in particular, the so-called Anna O., who, like some other intelligent and attractive young women, influenced the early psychotherapists. A remarkable event in psychiatric history was the publication of Ellenberger's (1970) *The Discovery of the Unconscious*, based on thorough and original research on the development of the early psychoanalytic schools. Other monographs dealing with the history of the psychoanalytic development in this country can serve as evidence of the development in the level of methodological approach. In the past, such a history was seen as a chronicle of events, but in recent years it has been studied in depth from the perspective of American psychology or of the over-all culture in general.

Increasingly, studies on psychiatric matters by historians tend to be based on cultural factors. The range of those cultural factors has rapidly grown in the last few years to include areas belonging to humanities, anthropology, and sociology.

About 3 decades ago, with the advent of ego psychology, similarities had been found between psychoanalysis and history, and consideration had been given to the study of history on the basis of the interplay in men of defense mechanisms with the unconscious, either of a microscopic (biographical) or of a macroscopic (social) type. Those discussions remained at somewhat of a theoretical level until Erikson's book *Young Man Luther* appeared in 1958. In an original way, the beginning of the revolt against the power of Rome, eventually leading to the Reformation, was linked to Luther's personal conflicts and identity crisis. Regardless of the reasons professional historians had for ignoring or criticizing the book, it undoubtedly opened the new field of psychohistory, to which Erikson (1969), with his important study on Gandhi, and others have continued to contribute.

In the same year, 1958, the historian Langer, in his presidential address to the American Historical Association, proposed that the next assignment be the application of psychological and, in particular, psychoanalytic concepts to historical interpretations. Other historians presented similar views, and slowly the field of psychological interpretation of history has come into existence, as evidenced by some monographs and collaborative publications. Other contributions to the field of psychohistory, in regard to political figures particularly, have appeared since then.

In the past few years, a number of studies conducted with a fresh methodological approach—such as the evaluation of hospital reports, records of patients, newspaper accounts, and legislative decisions—have been published. Those studies have dealt with a variety of topics, apparently unconnected but essentially centered on the attitudes of cultural groups toward the mentally ill at different historical periods, as reflected in concepts of mental illness, systems of institutionalization, and methods of treatment.

Pioneering efforts have been represented in the monographs by the German philologist Snell (1953) and by the British scholar Dodds (1951) on the characteristics of the Greek mind and by the Spanish medical historian Lain Entralgo (1970) on verbal therapeutic techniques in the Greek culture anticipated by the study of Greek beliefs about the soul by the German philologist Rhode (1925); by the French philosopher Foucault (1965), by the American medical historian Rosen (1968), and by the German clinician Dörner (1969) on the attitude toward the mentally ill from the Renaissance to the 19th century in Western countries; and by scholars with various backgrounds on the significance of broad concepts—such as melancholia, hysteria, insanity, and institutional treatment—as well as psychiatric developments in general. Others have limited themselves to a more restricted theme of either clinical or social interest. New topics, such as the development of the concept of childhood, have become prominent since the study by the Frenchman Ariès (1963); other topics, such as the history of mind-altering drugs, have been investigated from a complex ethnological, anthropological, and religious perspective.

The feeling is prevalent in many from the fields of the humanities and psychiatry that today's situation represents a transitional stage in psychiatric historiography, halfway between the amateur and the scholarly perspective. Increasingly, research projects in the history of the behavioral sciences are carried on by many; seminars and symposiums on historical matters are held involving scientists and clinicians; since 1965 the multidisciplinary *Journal of the History of the Behavioral Sciences* has been published; an international society for the history of the behavioral and social sciences (Cheiron) was founded in 1968.

Methodological issues concerning the history of individual fields of behavioral sciences have begun to come to the fore. With regard to psychiatry, methodological principles for the study of its history were discussed at a special meeting held at Yale University some years ago. At least one of the main suggestions brought forward at that meeting— the importance of relying on primary sources—seems to receive increasing consideration. In the past few decades, a number of psychiatric classics have been either reprinted or translated, thus making available the basic literature of ancient times, of the Renaissance, of the 18th century, of the period of moral treatment, of the period of German romanticism, of 19th-century clinical psychiatry, and of the beginning of dynamic psychiatry. Autobiographical memoirs of mentally ill persons have also been reprinted, and useful psychiatric historical anthologies of certain periods have appeared.

All that activity represents a good beginning, but much more remains to be done. There is a need of a better clarification of basic psychiatric concepts in historical perspective—for example, anxiety—of studies in depth of well-defined topics and periods, and especially of a fresh approach to the investigation of attitudes toward the mentally ill and systems of treatment based on solid historical methodology, with the help of specialists in collateral fields, such as anthropology and sociology.

Many clinicians recognize by now the relevance of the history of psychiatry for the comprehension of many psychiatric matters. Far from being a futile intellectual exercise, the study of the development of attitudes toward mental disorders and the methods of treating mental patients is essential to the development of the psychiatrist for four main reasons: (1) the analogies between the genetic—that is, the historical—approach to the study of the individual personality and collective attitudes and therapeutic modalities; (2) the apparently cyclic recurrence throughout history in different countries of such group attitudes and therapeutic systems as an enlightened approach toward the mentally ill or, conversely, mistreatment or neglect of the mentally ill; (3) the inclination of many clinicians to go back to the origins and study the development of contemporary concepts and therapeutic modalities in an attempt to place their scientific training on a broader humanistic tradition; (4) the help offered by historical insight in overcoming the increasingly skeptical feeling related to the current fragmentation of psychiatric schools.

No longer a matter to be leisurely left for retirement years, the study of the history of psychiatry is an intrinsic part of psychiatry and, thus, rightly represents the introduction of a comprehensive psychiatric textbook, such as this one. In this section, an effort is made to present the development of psychiatric concepts and practices on the basis of today's historiography. But since this is a general textbook of psychiatry and not a textbook on psychodynamics, events that anticipated modern methods of physical psychiatric therapy, psychopharmacology, and hospital care, as well as those that led to the focus on psychodynamics, have been given due recognition. It is hoped that each reader will be able to identify the historical antecedents of his own philosophy of psychiatry and, thus, to acquire a deeper and broader understanding of it.

Psychological Aspects of Prehistoric Humans

The psychology of prehistoric humans is still largely unknown. What is known is that a slow process of evolution took place through the millennia and that the Hominids appeared sometime between the Pliocene and the Pleistocene (the date of the Pleistocene spans between 70,000 and 8,000 B.C.). Such an evolution, favored by huge migrations of animals and humans related to wide variations in temperature, was characterized by the incidence of mutations of genes and critical stages of the environment leading to a biosocial maturation.

Slowly, a marked difference between primates and *Homo sapiens* emerged, especially in terms of the amount of cerebral matter and of the relation among the various lobes. It was found that the analogies between primates and human beings are mostly marked in the earliest stages of development of both; from the viewpoint of his ability to learn, the human is always a newborn, in the sense of having endless potential for improvement. How much such potential is due to genetic or environmental factors remains an open question.

It is unquestionable, however, that human evolution is strictly dependent on the evolution of the psyche, which is related to the development of the process of cerebration. During the process from the Sinanthropus and the Pithecanthropus to the Neanderthal, the amount of the cerebral mass steadily increased to almost double, the shape of the brain changed, the circumvolutions became more differentiated, and the skull modified itself under the influence of the brain; then the erect posture and the use of the hands developed, which slowly led to the appearance of thought and intelligence—indeed, a prototype of the close body-mind unit.

Regardless of the preeminence assigned to the genetic role of the DNA or, conversely, to the environmental use of tools, the important point is that the structural and functional evolution of the central nervous system slowly led to a biocultural unity that presented different characteristics in various areas in which remnants of the representatives of such a unity have been found—on the island of Java, in China, in Rhodesia, in the Middle East, and in Neanderthal (West Germany). Common to all those types of humans were affective sensibility, awareness of the emotional realm, the use of instruments for hunting and defense and offense, and the presence of a sort of magicoreligious thinking, as evidenced by the tendency to bury the dead and to open the skull for propitiatory reasons.

The Neanderthal man disappeared about 50,000 years ago and, after a mysterious gap, the earliest evidence of *Homo sapiens* is the discovery of the so-called Cro-Magnon in southern France about 35,000 BC. Endowed with a large cerebral mass, the Cro-Magnons left paintings in caverns that attest to their intelligence, their creative ability, their vivid imagination, their skill and shrewdness in hunting and fishing and fighting, and, even more important, their degree of self-awareness. Their tendency toward nomadic life and hunting probably favored their belief in a fantastic world full of magical beings.

That tendency slowly subsided and was replaced by a movement toward the cultivation of land and the breeding of cattle and, in general, by a more sedentary life in the succeeding Mesolithic period, characterized by the appearance of the bow and cutting tools, and later in the Neolithic period (beginning about 10,000 years ago), characterized by the development of farming and the making of technically advanced stone implements. (Areas of Neolithic cultures still survive today in some Pacific islands.) The new freedom and potentiality of humans, favored by an adequate supply of food, led to novel expressions of thought and exchanges of ideas, bringing about involvement in the worship of the dead and strong religious beliefs. Experimentation resulted in the creation of new forms and ways of doing things—vases, carriages on wheels, the use of animals for transportation, the preparation of bronze.

From the evolutionary perspective, the acquisition of language assumes paramount importance. Whether language developed according to the interjectional theory—that is, essentially from exclamations and shouts—or to the onomatopoeic theory—that is, from imitations of the sounds of animals—the notion of symbolization is central to language, which is the basis of the development of civilization.

The advances achieved by archeology in the 19th century through various expeditions carried on by many scientists led to the uncovering of many remnants of prehistoric cultures. In view of the similarities found among those remnants—such as burial places, vases, tools, and weapons—it is now postulated that civilization began independently in various sites in the Middle East in the Mesolithic era and then spread during the succeeding Neolithic era along the valleys of the Tigris, Euphrates, and Nile rivers; then into Cyprus and Crete; later into the Indus river valley and Central Asia up to the Yangtze; then independently to Mesoamerica; and, finally, to the Andean areas.

In spite of the wide geographical and chronological spans, the common characteristics of those various cultures are impressive: life in the clans composed of many families, probably a necessity for protec-

tion and a result of newly established ecological principles of population growth; the rituals and magical practices related to an array of beliefs concerning the sources of life, the dead, and many mysterious phenomena of the world; the artistic productions, ranging from paintings to statues for propitiatory purposes.

Regardless of the dichotomy—now largely bypassed by Lévi-Strauss's structuralism—between the prelogical mind of the primitive and the logical mind of modern humans, the consensus among students has focused on the propensity of the primitive to think by images—that is, in a way strictly bound to sensorial stimuli. More recently, following Piaget's studies, important characteristics of the primitive mind have been stressed: egocentrism (the tendency to subsume any personal experiences as objective and real, regardless of the influence of the personal perspective); realism (the tendency to accept things at face value independently of a critical and objective evaluation); animism (the tendency to consider as alive the entire world of material things). All that justifies the sincretistic attitude of the primitive mind to consider the world as penetrated by spirits and its inability to distinguish the self from the nonself and, consequently, the inclination toward a mystical anthropomorphic cosmogony.

At variance with that widely accepted interpretation of the primitive mind stands Jaynes's (1976) postulate of the bicameral mind. That bold and challenging interpretation of the entire primitive and archaic world is based on the contention that in early times the two hemispheres of the brain were not integrated; consequently, the silent areas of the right hemisphere corresponding to the speech areas of the left hemisphere of today's humans generated stimuli that were perceived as outside voices and attributed to gods, either represented in or personified by kings. That theory would explain much of the thus-far hidden meaning of many remnants of past civilizations—statues, hieroglyphics, cuneiform tablets, religious ceremonies, and, especially, burial practices, in which the burial of one king over another in the royal tomb signifies the transmission of the power of the hallucinatory voices perceived by people as gods' voices from one king to another. It was Jaynes's thesis that the bicameral mind, by fostering an attitude of obedience to the divine authority as exercised by the king, served as a system of social control and that the cultural upheavals resulting from a series of atmospheric calamities in the 13th to 11th centuries B.C. led to the slow disappearance of the bicameral mind and to the emergence of individual consciousness.

Psychiatry in Preliterate Cultures

In the past few decades, the study of psychiatry in preliterate cultures (a term preferable to primitive cultures)—the field of the so-called folk psychiatry or ethnopsychiatry or transcultural psychiatry—has become increasingly relevant to psychiatry in general. On the anthropological side, the advent of the schools of functionalism and cultural relativism brought to the fore the need for a more sophisticated approach to the study of normal and abnormal conditions, far above the dichotomy of primitive versus Western ways of feeling, thinking, and living found in the school of cultural evolution. On the psychiatric side, the acceptance of psychoanalytic principles led to a progressive disregard for the Kraepelinian psychiatric classification, which was based on the existence of clinical pictures clearly distinct from each other, and, instead, led to the emphasis on universal occurrences of personality stages and mechanisms underlying psychopathological symptoms. On the sociological side, increasing attention has been given recently to the common factors found in the so-called culture of poverty (Lewis 1959), a culture that includes most of the preliterate groups, regardless of ethnic, religious, or national entities.

Studies in the field of ethnopsychiatry have presented considerable variations, depending on the researcher's basic working hypotheses and adherence to a particular school of thought, the methodological approach used, and other dimensions. Most of those studies appear to fall into the following groups: (1) studies pointing to a different incidence, prevalence, and type of psychopathology in primitive versus advanced cultures (for example, Goldhamer and Marshall's (1953) *Psychosis and Civilization*); (2) studies usually identified as culture and personality and designed to investigate the correlation between personality development and psychopathology (for example, Malinowski's (1927) *Sex and Repression in Savage Society* in regard to the supposed universality of the oedipal conflict); (3) epidemiological studies in Western cities (for example, the Faris and Dunham (1939) study in Chicago, the Hollingshead and Redlich (1958) work in New Haven, and the Srole et al. (1962) Midtown study in Manhattan) and in non-Western cities, pointing to the importance of sociological and economic factors in the occurrence of mental diseases and in their treatment. An even more recent school of thought is represented by Lévi-Strauss's (1966) structuralism, which postulates a reduction of all sorts of cultural forms and symbols to the structure of the human mind.

Those various contributions to the field of ethnopsychiatry have helped to focus on some basic points. First, regardless of the allegiance of the individual researcher to a particular school, it is impossible for any Western scientist to entirely disregard his *forma mentis*; consequently, he is influenced by naiveté and ethnocentrism in investigating other cultures.

Second, the differentiation introduced by the historian Ackerknecht (1942) almost 40 years ago still remains valid. Probably under the impact of cultural relativism, he differentiated between autonormal or autopathological, as applied to persons regarded as normal or pathological by their own society, and heteronormal or heteropathological, as applied to persons regarded as normal or pathological by members of another society observing them. The validity of that differentiation is borne out by the facts that certain special experiences, such as glossolalia and extrasensory powers, are accepted as nonpathological, even in groups of the Western culture; that certain phenomena, such as homosexuality and the use of mind-altering drugs, are viewed differently in different cultures; and that certain well-established clinical entities are more frequent in some areas than in others—for example, in the African countries, depression is rare, and entities resembling acute and temporary schizophrenia are frequent. On the other hand, it is commonly accepted that the incidence of mental illness does not differ substantially in various cultures and, as Kiev (1964) wrote, that

> the emphasis must be placed less on the strangeness of the ideas than on the relationship they bear to the inner insecurities and morbid experiences of the patient.

A third point is that most of the research in the area has been conducted from the cross-cultural perspective—that is, using a comparative approach among various groups.

The cross-cultural method has focused on comparable units of sociocultural environment, but not enough attention has been paid to the kinds of units studied. Some have studied the tribe, as in Kardiner's (1945) and Linton's (1956) studies on the basic personality in preliterate and Western groups; others have studied the community, as in Eaton and Weil's (1955) study of the Hutterite community and Leighton's (1961) Stirling County study; others have studied the city, especially in recent years on the wave of the emphasis on urban problems—overpopulation, ecology, public health, preventive medicine, epidemiology, environmental engineering—on the assumption of a rural-urban dichotomy; others have studied the nation, as in Lerner's (1957) *America as a Civilization* for this country and Benedict's (1940) *The Chrysanthemum and the Sword* for the Japanese culture; others have compared Western nations with non-Western nations; still others have used the concepts of discontinuous and continuous cultures (Benedict, 1940) in terms of stressful and nonstressful culture and personality, modes of child rearing, tough and easy cultures, shame and guilt cultures, and simple and complex cultures.

In the past few years the limitations of the cross-cultural approach have become evident in the light of international developments. Cultures can no longer be considered as static or even as slowly moving but, rather, as changing rapidly, at least in many parts of the world. Since the end of World War II, the world has been witnessing the rapid Americanization of a number of European countries and of Japan, the amazing growth of the Western-like nation of Israel because of the immigration of large groups tied by a common religious tradition, the migration of populations and other cultural upheavals because of a succession of wars in the Middle East and in the Far East, and the superimposition of elements of Western culture on autochthonous cultures in many African and Asian nations of the so-called third world.

All those events have been accompanied by a good deal of stress, mainly related to conflicts of values, and have resulted in an increase in personal and interpersonal problems. It remains controversial whether mental diseases are also increasing, in view of the difficulty in conducting sound epidemiological studies, the tendency being to identify more mentally ill persons as each culture becomes increasingly Western oriented.

Clearly, the tempo has accelerated, and many cultures today find themselves at different levels of acculturation—that is, made up of poorly integrated and even contrasting elements. That fact calls for consideration of the historical dimension in research on preliterate cultures, aside from the common cross-cultural approach.

CONCEPTS OF DISEASES

The difficulties in doing research on ethnopsychiatry are many. A guide recently compiled includes the following categories: normal and abnormal person, magic, practitioners of magic or ritual experts, social hierarchy, religion, birth and child rearing, genital customs, education, death and burial customs, dreams and other symbolism, demonology and possession, secret societies, politics, suicide, murder and cannibalism, justice, alcohol and drugs, sex habits, stories and myths, dances and music, art and artifacts. The methods used to acquire such a knowledge extend from observation, interviews, and language to tales and myths, art, the study of artifacts, photography, sound recording, and laboratory aids. In view of the methodological complexity, it is no wonder that relatively few solid data have been accumulated and that, increasingly, field work is done by teams of experts, rather than by individual researchers.

The situation is even more difficult in cultures of the past, in which only scattered art and literary remnants are available—notably ruins of buildings erected for religious and healing purposes, religious and votive statues, paintings (such as the representations of the witch doctor on the walls of the prehistoric cave of the three brothers in France, in the Ariège department), amulets and talismans, and literary fragments, recorded in the form of cuneiform tablets and papyri.

Yet, on the basis of the research thus far done in the field, there is general concensus on some universal concepts. As a matter of fact, this research has been used as evidence that cultures migrated from Central Asia to the Near East on the one side and to America, by way of Alaska, on the other side. Common to many cultures of the eastern Mediterranean, pre-Columbian America, and African areas is the belief that mental diseases, like other diseases, were sent by a god or by gods, thus justifying all sorts of propitiatory and expiatory rituals. In addition, all kinds of misfortunes were attributed to the actions of devils; to control them, practices of so-called white magic—that is, permissible magic—and of black magic—that is, forbidden magic—such as the evil eye and spells, were used. Prognosis was based on the study of numbers, of astrology, of the configuration of the interiors of animals (especially hepatoscopy), of divination by some persons endowed with extrasensory powers, and on the interpretation of dreams.

A few basic postulates seem to be common to the beliefs of preliterate cultures: the liberation of immaterial forces by divine power or magical arts; the principle of solidarity or contagion (Frazer, 1922), implying a continuity between the human being and his surroundings; the belief in sympathetic, imitative forms of magic occurring by telepathy (Frazer, 1922) and in the synergic or antagonistic interactions between similar elements, such as homeopathic medicine's method of treatment by similars; the symbolism of certain elements, such as the purifying role of water; and, especially, the power attributed to the utterance of certain words. As a matter of fact, one thing that appears central to almost all the religions of the world is the action of words, whether in the form of spells and incantations, orders to spirits to leave the patient, exorcisms and prayers, or penitential formulas asking the forgiveness of the offended deity. Words are often accompanied by movements, such as the imposition of hands, mimicry, and ritual dances.

Other therapeutic practices consist of the prescription of drugs, obtained either from vegetables or from animals, quite often combined in a complex and secret way, and prepared according to certain rituals. The medicines are believed to act according to some basic principles: by expulsion or evacuation of the harmful spirit through emetics, cathartics, and bloodletting; less often, by skull trepanning and mouth suction; by interaction between similars (for example, the extract of animal testes for impotency); by repulsion—that is, by forcing the spirit to vacate the person through the use of antagonistic substances, such as revolting drugs.

Some procedures are based on substitute methods—that is, on transferring a disease to a scapegoat, usually an animal, as in cases of expiatory sacrifice. The prevention of diseases is assured by the use of magic objects, mainly amulets that protect the person, talismans that symbolize power, and fetishes that represent the protecting deity. Mental diseases or, rather, diseases considered to be mental by Western observers are mainly attributed to the violation of taboos, the neglect of ritual obligations, the loss of a vital substance from the body (mainly the soul), the introduction of a foreign and harmful substance into the body (possession by spirits), and witchcraft.

Simply to mention those tenets of medical concepts in preliterate cultures brings up three main points: (1) their relevance to psychiatry, based on a unitary concept of the person, at variance with the body-mind dichotomy of the Western tradition; (2) their occurrence in historical periods, not only in the Eastern Mediterranean and later the Judaic and Arabian cultures, the pre-Columbian civilizations, and the Greco-Latin world but, even later, during the period of German mystic romantism of the early 19th century and up to the current wave of superstitious beliefs; (3) their attempt to introduce rationality and stability in the culture when viewed in the context of a solid structured system of beliefs and rituals underlying apparent disconnected cultural expressions, as is shown by Lévi-Strauss's (1966) work.

TREPANATION OF THE SKULL

Trepanation (or trephination, from the French) of skulls performed during the Neolithic period first came to the attention of investigators in France a century ago. The French anthropologist and neurologist Paul Broca (1877), who first described aphasia, wrote a book on the subject. Since then, evidence of the surgical procedure has been accumulated in many parts of the world, prompting William Osler (1922) to refer to it as "the oldest existing evidence of a very extraordinary practice."

It is believed that the practice was carried on in Eastern Mediterranean and North African countries in the Neolithic age as early as 4,000 to 5,000 years ago, that it was widespread—not, however, in China, Japan, or Egypt—and that it reached its highest development in Stone Age Peru of 1,000 to 2,000 years ago, especially in connection with surgical traumas during wars. The surgical procedure consisted of boring a hole (perforation) or of removing a portion of the bone with the help of sharpened and saw-like instruments (trepanation). The average diameter of the opening was about 2 cm., and holes have been found in all areas of the skull, with distinct predominance, however, in the left parietal region. The lack of signs of osteomyelitis and the finding in some skulls of more than one hole support the opinion that the operation was not fatal. Indeed, some reports indicate that the mortality may have been as low as 10 per cent, an astonishing fact in view of the difficult surgical procedure.

The relevance of the procedure for psychiatry lies in the opinion—strongly voiced by the two American researchers Muniz and McGee (1897), who exhibited a number of trephined skulls at the World's Congress of Anthropology held in connection with the Columbian Exposition in Chicago in 1894—that the operation was done to liberate the evil spirits supposedly causing the symptoms. That opinion, anticipated by Broca in 1876, was subsequently enlarged to include, as other reasons for the procedure, combat of sorcery, a way of permitting something to enter the body of the person, and interest in obtaining a piece of bone (rondelle) for magic-religious purposes. That view was upheld by other researchers involved in extensive studies of the large number of skulls found in Peru as remnants of pre-Columbian civilizations. The opposite view—that the operation was mainly performed for therapeutic reasons, based on the frequency of the procedures on the left side of the skull, which is more vulnerable to attack by right-handed enemies during wars—has not been generally accepted. As a matter of fact, the finding that mutilating cranial procedures have continued to be performed from early historical times up to the present to treat epilepsy, idiocy, and mental diseases has further corroborated the thesis of their magic-religious meaning.

SHAMANISM

In contrast to the trepanation of skulls, shamanism is still widely practiced in many cultures of the world; as a matter of fact, it has gained impetus in some areas in the past few years in connection with conflicts related to acculturation. Concurrently, the literature on shamanism has continued to grow; the 650-item bibliography published by the Russian scholar Popov in 1932 can now be extended to several thousand items. The Russians are interested in the topic because of the widespread occurrence of shamanism in North Eurasian countries. The very word "shaman," comparable to the term "medicine man," derives from the Tungus language of northern Siberia.

The most commonly held picture of the shaman is that of an inspiration-type medicine man who is quite vulnerable to possession by spirits and through whom the spirits communicate with human beings (see Figure 1). Typically, the shamanistic séance takes place in the presence of a selected group of participants. It involves a progressively increasing state of excitement on the part of the shaman; the state of excitement is induced by heavy smoking, drinking, and the use of drugs,

FIGURE 1. Wooden statue of shaman. North Pacific coast.

accompanied by rhythmic music, especially drums, to the point of paroxysm, characterized by partial loss of consciousness and unusual movements. The shaman reveals the presence of the spirits through utterances and violent actions. Mentally disturbed patients, in the course of active participation in the ceremony, may confess their sins or ask for the removal of certain disturbances specifically attributed to an evil spirit. The excursion of the shaman into the realm of the spirits is symbolic of the restoration of the patient's peace of mind through sacrifices and other symbolic means. Frequently, the patient's liberation from the evil spirit is expressed concretely through the actual expulsion of an object—such as a stone, insect, or hair—from the mouth of the shaman.

The personalities of both the shaman and the mental patient treated by him have been the focus of much controversy. The opinion most commonly held is that the shaman is not psychotic or epileptic, as originally believed, but is essentially neurotic. As such, he may find an outlet for his own emotional instability through the séance, which represents almost an unconscious attempt at self-healing. Eligibility for the role of shaman requires a particular state of receptivity to dreams and other psychological phenomena, elicited with the help of drugs and medicinal plants; a novitiate period is passed in isolation from the community. With regard to the patients who ask for

the shaman's help, their symptoms, although difficult to translate into current psychiatric terminology, seem to range widely from depression to withdrawal; for the most part, their symptoms seem to be acute.

Early anthropological reports emphasized the dramatic aspects of the shaman's performance—that is, the actual appearance of the spirits in the course of the highly emotionally charged séance. Recent literature, however, has focused on the anthropological, sociological, and psychological dimensions.

From the anthropological perspective, the main issues deal with the characterization of shamanism as a universal phenomenon that acquires particular forms according to the culture or as a singular phenomenon that has emerged independently in various cultures; the essence of the shamanistic phenomenon— that is, the ecstasy—is viewed as a sort of possession and illness, a lower form of mysticism, or, conversely, as a technique for passing unhindered through different layers of the world, not unlike other psychological techniques, such as hypnosis. Depending on their orientation, some limit shamanism to the Arctic, from which it eventually spread to other areas and became complex; others believe it occurs in any part of the world; then there are those, especially Russian authors, who emphasize the development of shamanism from a stage of pure natural healing to a more elaborate stage of ecstasy.

From the sociological perspective, recent studies consistently stress the leading role of the shaman in his community. The role of the shaman becomes meaningful only in the context of a community that expects him to acquire supernatural powers according to a traditional way and to make use of them for healing purposes according to a well-established ritual. The shaman is, thus, an essential element in preserving traditional forms of culture and in guarding them from inner disintegrating forces, especially in societies that feel threatened by the advancing Western civilization. Moreover, he can be of help in exploiting and channeling existing neurotic leanings in the community and in relieving mutual stress.

From the psychological perspective, a comparison between shamanistic and modern psychotherapeutic procedures can be made. In both cases, the candidates for the role of healer have to undergo a period of relative seclusion from the community. That seclusion carries a literal interpretation with regard to the shaman, but it is comparable to the period of intensive study implied in all psychotherapeutic training, particularly in psychoanalysis. Similarly, in both cases the acquisition of healing powers is facilitated by the interpretation of the potential healer's dreams and other unconscious life events in the highly ambivalent context of the candidate-teacher relationship. Furthermore, similarities can be found between the shamanistic séance and the many forms of psychotherapeutic group approaches that have mushroomed in this country in the past few years in terms of the personality of the leader, group interaction, the cathartic effect of verbal expressions (including confessions), and other dimensions.

It has been pointed out that magical beliefs are accepted for their compatibility with personality variables, such as childrearing practices, rather than for their physiological usefulness (Whiting and Child, 1953); that, spontaneously, the emphasis is on catharsis in highly organized sociocultural systems and on control in poorly organized systems; and that shamanism provides not a cure or improved functioning but a social remission without insight (Devereux, 1940) or simply symptom relief (Frank, 1973).

Regardless of all that, the literature increasingly points to many similarities between ethnopsychiatry and modern psychiatry—mainly, the difficulty in assessing, measuring, and controlling the many variables entering the psychotherapeutic process and the common elements of suggestion, reassurance, and direct influences present in all forms of psychotherapy. In *Persuasion and Healing*, Frank (1973) convincingly showed the universality of certain elements of the psychotherapeutic approach and the relevance of some cultural factors, especially societal expectation, both to the content and to the technique of psychotherapy. Even more striking is the book by Torrey (1972), *The Mind Game: Witch Doctors and Psychiatrists*, in which many common points between the two kinds of healers were suggested in the light of four basic components of psychotherapy: (1) a shared world view that makes possible the naming of the pathological factor; (2) certain personal qualities of the therapist that seem to produce favorable results; (3) the patient's expectation of getting well, which is increased by societal mores, such as the aura of the therapeutic setting and of the therapist's reputation; (4) techniques of therapy based on similar principles. Others, in discussing psychotherapy, have stressed the importance of cultural factors (Horney, 1937; Fromm, 1941; Opler, 1956), the cathartic values of confession (Hallowell, 1934), the role of group support and of traditional values (Leighton and Hughes, 1961), the similarities between psychoanalytic and primitive forms of therapy (Pfister, 1932, in the case of Navaho rituals), and the importance of cultural factors in the selection of psychotherapeutic techniques (Devereux, 1940).

The historical study of ethnopsychiatry is of considerable relevance to today's psychiatry. As psychiatry is increasingly viewed no longer as a dyadic interaction between the patient and the doctor but as a triadic interaction between the patient, the doctor, and the community, the study of ethnopsychiatry can broaden and deepen the perspective for today's psychiatrist. In particular, methods of psychological healing successfully carried on in preliterate cultures and in areas in process of acculturation may have considerable relevance for the development of a proper philosophy of psychiatry, especially of effective treatment systems for large low-income segments of the population.

Psychiatry at the Dawn of Civilization

Western civilization had its beginnings in various areas of the Middle East at different times during the first 2,000 years B.C. Increasingly, however, evidence has pointed to connections and interrelations between cultures that flourished in those areas and cultures that flourished in the Far East. The remnants of those early civilizations have made it possible for researchers to reconstruct the high level of knowledge that was achieved in many fields of science; however, there is much less certainty about concepts of mental health and disease during that period because psychological concepts are closely interwoven with religious concepts, making their study and differentiation difficult. In spite of that, there is evidence of early attempts to describe mental phenomena, albeit in less concrete terms than those used in preliterate cultures.

CONCEPTS OF THE MIND IN FAR EASTERN CULTURES

Of the three major Far Eastern cultures—Indian, Chinese, and Japanese—the Indian is by far the most important for various reasons: (1) It was the first to be discovered and studied by British scholars during the 19th century (the *Yoga Sutras* were translated in 1852; the *Bhagavad-Gita* was translated in 1875). (2) It is the oldest of the three cultures and has exten-

sively influenced the other two cultures for centuries. (3) More markedly than those cultures, it represents an unbroken and elaborate tradition at variance with the discontinuities of Western cultures. (4) Many of its tenets have close similarities to modern psychology concepts, from psychoanalysis to conditioning. (5) On the wave of criticism of ethnocentrism and of the spread of structuralism, its concepts have increasingly gained recognition; as a matter of fact, some of its practices, notably Yoga and Zen, have been adapted by many as a means of escape from the strictures of the Western cultures. (6) The trend toward a rapprochement between Eastern and Western cultures is progressively becoming acknowledged by many.

True, epistemological difficulties of all kinds have hampered the reciprocal understanding between Eastern and Western concepts. Semantic difficulties have to be taken into consideration, too, as it has been claimed that for every psychological term in English there are four in Greek and 40 in Sanskrit. Yet there is no equivalent for the "unconscious" in Indian or Chinese terms. In Chinese, the ideographs used to denote the prefix "psycho," as in psychoanalysis and psychology, can be translated approximately as "the reason or principles of the heart." Furthermore, language has contributed to the split between the organism-environment relationship because language is unable to express the unity of differences. At a deeper level, the Western approach to philosophy has been considered primarily analytic and objective, the Eastern approach primarily intuitive and existential; moreover, it has been said that the Western philosopher is primarily a natural philosopher, the Chinese philosopher a social philosopher, and the Indian philosopher a psychological philosopher. The attitude of the Westerner toward the Eastern culture has been, by and large, characterized by a great deal of ambivalence—resentment of the Eastern attitude of contempt for industrial progress and, in general, for the capitalistic world view but envy of the Easterner's ability to overcome the temptations of the world and of the body in search of an all-embracing supernatural reality.

Moreover, several important points have to be taken into consideration to explain the difficulty for Westerners in understanding the Eastern way of life: (1) the inability to transcend the dualism residing in the very nature of the person, as long as they cling to their historical-theological tradition of God-man or man-God; (2) for today's scientist, the difficulty in having to approach psychological concepts that cannot be considered independently from a philosophical view of man; (3) the pervasive influence of 19th-century anthropological theories of a human as an angel riding a wild animal, based on Darwin's doctrine of evolution and leading to the belief that nonrational behavior is due to regression; (4) the narrow view that repression is due to a psychological organ, such as the ego, rather than to social and cultural pressures.

That being the case, a presentation of the Far Eastern psychological concepts also has to deal with their philosophical postulates. Among them, three are particularly antithetic to Western concepts: (1) cyclical time, rather than Western objective time, considered as a psychological measurement; (2) rhythm of death-life-death displacing Western progress; (3) the Western tendency toward polarity of contrasting opposites (man-world, conscious-unconscious, existential being-God) being substituted by juxtaposition and identity of polarities.

Indian. It is generally agreed that around 3000 to 1600 B.C. light-skinned Aryans took over the area occupied by dark-skinned Indians, resulting in the hereditary division into six casts. The oldest literary remnants of that period and of world literature are the Vedas (knowledge), written in Sanskrit (=pure, perfect, sacred). Of the four Vedas that have survived, the most important is the Rig-Veda (or knowledge of the hymns of praise), which are hymns of worship to the various forces of sun, sky, fire, light, winds, water, and sex. Each of the four Vedas is divided into four sections, of which the most important for psychology are the Upanishads (from "sitting near," as a student listening to a teacher's secret teaching, about 800 B.C.)—that is, discussions of philosophers presenting many opinions, at times even contradictory.

Throughout the centuries many philosophical schools have developed in India—sometimes with overlapping concepts, other times bringing forward new concepts. Common to all the schools is the principle that there is no essential distinction between the inorganic and the organic, between the vegetable and the animal, and between the animal and the human; that is, the animating principle of plants, animals, and humans is the same. Central to the school of Samkhya, the most important of the post-Veda Indian schools of philosophy, is the notion of nature (Prakrti), dynamic and creative, in contrast to the spirit (Purusha), which is passive. Prakrti manifests itself in three different fashions, called Gunas: Sattva (light, intelligence), Rajas (motor energy, mental activity), and Tamas (static inertia, psychic obscurity). Prakrti proceeds spontaneously toward a state of obscure consciousness of being an ego and acquires different characteristics according to the predominance of each one of the Gunas: with Sattva, the five senses and the inner sense; with Rajas, the conative senses; with Tamas, the five elements, out of which come the atoms, the molecules, and eventually the human body.

All Indian philosophies accept the spirit as a transcendent and autonomous principle. However, for the Vedanta, Atman—that is, the true self, the Supreme existence of being is defined as Saccinanda (*sat*, "being"; *cit*, "consciousness"; *ananda*, "blessedness")—is entangled in the temporal illusion of the creation (Maya); for Samkhya the spirit has no attribute.

The important point for the psychological perspective is that the immortal soul can never be a personality in the ordinary sense, and the individual person is not really a permanent, unchangeable unity; he is a link in the endless chain of life. The souls or, rather, the multitude of physical and social relations embodied in humans and animals pass from humans into animals and back again. All beings are woven into an infinite web of Karma—that is, the power of the deeds done in past existences to condition or even to create further existences—and reincarnation as a way matter is purified from iniquities and its own potentialities released. The doctrine of reincarnation may seem quite unpalatable to the Western mind, although in the Greek culture metempsychosis was intrinsic to Pythagoras's school and to the Orphic mysteries. It may make it possible to overcome the difficulty that the short span of life in this world determines forever the fate of a soul that is immortal.

The illusion of the creation is due to the confusion between the real self and the psychoneutral states. Such a confusion is the result of primal ignorance (Avidya), not of divine punishment or of sin. Hence, the endless perpetuation through Karma of the five matrices that produce psychomental states: (1) ignorance, (2) individuality, (3) passion, (4) disgust, and (5) love of life. The only way to interrupt the meaningless cycle of earthly life and to eliminate suffering is through knowledge achieved not in an intellectual way but in an experiential way. That leads to the obliteration of the dichotomy of subject and object and to the final dissolution into Brahman, the supreme reality.

In order to do that, a person must make a long journey involving all his forces. Of the various systems, that of Yoga ("to bind closely," "to link together," "to bring under the yoke"), described by Patanjali (1927) in the 4th century, is by far the best known. Defined by him as the abolition of the states of consciousness, at the beginning of his famous treatise *Yoga Sutras*, such a system is so sophisticated as to justify the claim that the Oriental psychologist carries his laboratory within him. Essentially, its aim is to gradually move from states of waking to dream to deep sleep and, eventually, to self-realization through a progression from errors and illusions—dreams, hallucina-tions—to the totality of normal psychological experiences—usual aspects of the well-integrated personality—and, finally, to parapsychological experiences achievable only by the initiators.

For the practice of Yoga (Sadhana), the pupil (sisya or chela) must put himself under the spiritual guidance of a teacher (guru). The initial step of the practice, the concentration on a single object, enables the pupil to control the two sources of mental fluidity: sensory activity and subconscious activity. Of the two, the specific subconscious sensations—that is, the latencies embodied in the subconscious (Vasana)—are the most important, as they constitute the matrix for the psychomental states that interefere with the attainment of the self.

Once the proper concentration is reached, the spiritual itinerary of Yoga goes through eight different stages: (1) restraints (Yama), (2) disciplines (Niyama), (3) attitudes and positions of the body (Asana), (4) respiratory rhythm (Pranayama), (5) emancipation of sensory activity from the mastery of external objects (Pratyahara), (6) concentration (Dharana), (7) yogic meditation (Dhyana), and (8) an invulnerable state completely impervious to stimuli (Samadhi). At that point the circuit of psychic matter is closed; the unconscious that emerged into consciousness returns into the unconscious. Deliverance is then reached, a kind of Nirvana unknown to mortals because it is absolute.

In addition to the above, other practices focus on the use of mantras—that is, a sacred saying—usually uttered silently (mentally), representing the Supreme Being in the guise of sounds. Progressively, the sound vibrations and the thought vibrations melt into one until the perfect silence of the absolute is attained. Mantras have their graphic counterpart in the yantras, as a field of energy, most typically represented by the human body. Some yantras are of circular form, referred to as mandalas, on which Jung (1931) elaborated.

The method of Yoga and its main philosophical assumptions have been described here because of their importance in understanding Eastern thinking in relation to the Western culture. But the fact is that the tradition of Indian philosophy is maintained in only small and widely scattered circles today. A number of other philosophical systems have flourished throughout the centuries, some in direct opposition to the above, emphasizing materialism and hedonism (the latter typified in the Kama-Sutri). Some of those systems also include concepts that are relevant to psychological medicine.

According to the Aharva-Veda, a collection of charms and magic formulas, the mind (Manas) is located in the heart and comprises four functions: coordination of the senses, control of itself, reasoning, and judgment. The fundamental principle of health is the proper balance between the five elements (Buthas) and the three humors (Dosas) that occur at different levels: physical, physiological, psychological and, finally, spiritual—the state of bliss in which the ultimate goal is tranquility. When the humors in the brain affect the mind and then involve the heart, the understanding is impaired, and that leads to madness.

In the Ayurveda (from *ayur*, "life," and *veda*, "knowledge"), which is the ancient Indian system of medicine that flourished between the 6th century B.C. and the 2nd century A.D., the major cause of mental disorder is the imbalance of the humors—that is, it has a somatic origin, rather than a psychic origin. According to the famous physicians Araka, Susrutha, and Bhela in the 1st and 2nd centuries, some of the premonitory symptoms of unmada (madness) are fits of unconsciousness, an agitated state of mind, a ringing in the ears, emaciation of the body, excessive energy of action, and aversion to food. When the disease develops, the symptoms vary, depending on the prevailing influence of mind, bile, or phlegm or a combination of those humors.

Therapy was aimed at the restoration of the balance of the humors and was carried on through the decoction of many herbs, whose substances counteracted the humors, and through nasal packs and nasal draining, used in an attempt to loosen the dried phlegm and expel it from the head through the nasal passage. A popular drug for insanity was *Rauwolfia serpentina*, called Sarpagandha in Sanskrit, which, according to an ancient text (Rao, 1964),

> is effective in giving sound sleep and peace of mind. It eradicates . . . sleeplessness, lunacy, passion, misapprehensions, or delusions.

Other therapeutic measures included purification procedures by emetics, venesection, words of sympathy and comfort, and terrorizing by means of snakes; worship sacrifices, incantations, propitiatory rites, and pilgrimages to sacred places were also used.

Three main personality types described in detail in the Bhagavad-Gita—the most popular mystical-philosophical poem of India, in which the various above-mentioned doctrines are blended together for the purpose of edification—are: contemplative (Sattvic), passionate (Rajas), and dull (Tamas), reflecting the Indian trinity of the gods Vishnu, Brahma, and Siva. In the same Gita a process of disintegration of reasoning leading to dementia is mentioned:

> A man thinking of objects of senses becomes attached to them; attachment causes longing; from longing grows anger; from anger arises delusions; from delusions arises a loss of memory; from the loss of memory rises a ruin of discrimination and from this loss of discrimination, he ultimately perishes.

Chinese. The development of the Chinese culture has been heavily influenced by three main religious philosophies: Taoism, Buddhism, and Confucianism.

Taoism is based on the teaching of Lao-Tzu (604–531 B.C.), also spelled Lao-Tze, a legendary figure whose historicity is questioned. Tao is considered as metaphysical, eternal, all pervading, the source of all things and cannot be defined. Taoism is a counterculture without schools, hierarchy, or disciples. According to the sage Chuang-tzu (4th century B.C.), the Tao man has acquired special powers through the use of yoga. Central to the understanding of Taoistic doctrine is a small controversial book called *Tao Te Ching* (Ross, 1966), usually translated as *The Way and Its Power*, in which a contradictory, seemingly illogical style is used in order to shake up the reader's familiar beliefs.

Siddhartha Gautama or Buddha (the Enlightened or Awakened) is a historical personage who lived in the 6th century B.C. Born in the foothills of the Himalayas, on the Nepalese-Indian border, supposedly as the final incarnation of previous Indian sages, his life was marked by legendary events. It is known, however, that he left his family, went through a period of severe asceticism, and then began his teaching by advocating the Middle Path, warning against the two extremes of devotion to passion and devotion to self-mortification, and finally preached his doctrine of the Aryan (noble) Eightfold Path—that is, right views, right aspirations, right speech, right conduct, right mode of livelihood, right effort, right mindfulness, and right rapture—until his death at the age of 80. Buddhism does not recognize the supernatural or the existence of the soul; instead, it emphasizes a disgust for the body, for sensations, and for consciousness. Nirvana—that is, the immediate experience of the egoless self with the Supreme—can be achieved in different ways according to various schools. After a period of great popularity in the 3rd century B.C., Buddhism declined in India but many of its concepts continued to find their way in folklore, superstition, and magic. In the Western perspective, Nirvana has been characterized by pessimism and passivity and has greatly influenced some thinkers, notably Schopenhauer.

Confucius (551–479 B.C.), the most famous of the ancient Chinese sages, spent most of his life in government service under a variety of rulers. Surrounded by an increasing number of pupils, in later years he assembled the essentials of his wisdom in six works, of which some are basic compilations from previous works. Of them, the most important is the *I Ching* or *Yü King* (*The Book of Changes*), consisting of 64 hexagrams, made up of full or broken lines, each hexagram being composed of two trigrams. The hexagrams, selected through the procedure of tossing sticks, are read and commented on. Crucial to Chinese thought is the concept of change, for which one must always be ready, although at times one must wait patiently for the right moment. A distinction is made among three kinds of changes: nonchange, cyclic change, and sequent change. Nonchange is the background against which change is made possible, presented as an interplay of heaven (the creative) and earth (the receptive), which do not oppose but complement each other. Cyclic change is explained as a rotation of phenomena, each succeeding the other until the starting point is reached again, as is typical of the life cycle. Sequent change is typical of many natural events. Also well known are Confucius's *Analects*, a collection of his sayings based on humanitarianism and a love for the world, spreading to the family and to all mankind. Confucianism, not a religion but an ethical code for right living, is based on the use of simple virtues and on the search for harmony among the various forces of the universe. The most illustrious representative of Confucianism was the 4th-century B.C. scholar Mencius, who elaborated on the Fourfold Rule of Conduct, also called the Four Limits of Man—that is, the feeling of compassion, the feeling of shame, the feeling of consideration for others, and the feeling of right and wrong. Although hindered by the influence of Taoism and Buddhism, Confucianism went through a period of revival in the 6th century and was adopted by the state as its formal cult in the 12th century. It maintained that role until the beginning of the 20th century.

Regardless of particular schools of thought and emphases, the old Chinese concepts of humans and the universe center on three main tenets: (1) The world was not created by a divine or supernatural being but by Tao, an abstract principle that turned into an active moral guide after creation was accomplished. (2) Humans are composed of the same elements of the universe and reflect in themselves the principles of the macrocosm. (3) Mental functions are not conceived distinct from physical functions and are not localized in any part of the organism, although the heart is given particular importance as a guide for the mind. The cosmic forces are the tao (the way); the yin and the yang (opposite forces of the female and of the male, in a perennial state of opposition and attraction); and the five elements (water, fire, wood, metal, and earth), brought forth during the creation by yin and yang. Yin represents the shady, cloudy element (moon, earth, night, water, cold, dampness, darkness, female); yang stands for the sunny, clear element (sun, heaven, day, fire, heat, dryness, light, male). However, both male and female are products of yang and yin, so those qualities are contained in both sexes.

The cyclic occurrence of events in nature, such as the rising and the setting of the sun and seasonal sequences, depends on the correct proportion of those elements. Traditionally, proper behavior was guided by Tao, the principle of all human conduct. Basic to such conduct was reverence for the elders and the ancestors, as typically expressed in the hsiao king or classic of filial piety, and the social image of the person, as revealed through lien (face)—that is, the confidence of society in the moral character of the ego.

Both deviation from filial piety and loss of face were believed to be important contributing factors in acute psychosis, leading even to suicide. Evidence of knowledge of other mental diseases is substantiated by the number of ideographs describing them. And in the medical textbook *The Yellow Emperor's Classic of Internal Medicine* (about 1000 B.C.) (Huarg Ti Nei Ching Su Wen, 1966), the most important Chinese medical book, reference is made to insanity, dementia, violent behavior, and convulsions.

It was there stated that the treatment of the spirit consists in guiding toward Tao those persons who by infringement

of the basic rules of the universe severed their own roots and ruined their true selves [for] those who disobey the laws of Heaven and Earth have a lifetime of calamities, while those who follow the laws remain free from dangerous illness.

The principle of prevention achieved through proper education was also stressed:

The ancient sages did not treat those who were already ill; they instructed those who were not ill.

The importance of dreams was also recognized:

When Yin is flourishing then there occur dreams, as if one had to wade through great waters, which cause bad fears; when Yang is flourishing, there occur dreams of great fires which burn and cauterize. When Yin and Yang both are flourishing there occur dreams in which both forces destroy and kill each other or wound each other. . . . When one is replete with food then one dreams that one gave up one's inner surplus; when one is hungry or starved, then one dreams that one obtained enough to satisfy one's interior.

As for practical treatment, it is likely that mentally ill persons, when not violent, were left wandering in the country. The belief that yin and yang, the carriers of psychic balance, were equally distributed throughout the body offered the rationale for the practices of acupuncture and moxibustion (from the Japanese *Moe Kusa* or burning herbs)—that is, the application of needles and ignited substances on certain areas of the body—since they both attempted to facilitate the proper flow of yin and yang along the channels of the body (see Figure 2).

Japanese. Buddhism reached China as early as the 1st century after Christ and from there, through Korea, it passed into Japan in succeeding centuries. Zen (from the Chinese *Ch'an*, a transliteration of the Sanskrit *Dhyana*, meaning meditation or contemplation leading to a union with reality) is a blending of Indian metaphysical abstraction, Taoistic paradox, and Confucian pragmatism. According to tradition, Zen was brought to China from India in 520 A.D. by a monk called Budhidharma, The First Patriarch. Fundamental to Zen is the concept of nonresistance—of letting things happen, rather than being taken by ideas. The point is that the idea of human life as a problem is a wrong issue, though unfamiliar to most people. In particular, the opposition between a human being existing in this world as subject and object is a wrong problem based on ignorance—that is, on the exclusive focus of consciousness and attention, which tend to separate things from their context. Zen is seeing into one's own nature from one's own life experiences. Through correct use or posture of the body, contemplation leads to the attainment of self-realization. Indeed, the emphasis is to find in the self, rather than in ceremony or doctrine, the path to wisdom: the less done, the clearer is reality; the less said, the more direct is the comprehension. That emphasis is also related to Buddha's noble silence, which he maintained when questioned about issues such as the meaning of life, the reality of self, the origin of the universe, and the nature of Nirvana. The lengthy process leading to the discovery of the true self and to Nirvana can be accomplished only with the help of a master or guru.

There are two chief schools of Zen teaching in Japan today, both of which were imported from China around the 13th century: the Rinzai school, known as the Sudden school, and the Soto school, known as the Gradual school. Individual and group meditation is common to both. However, Rinzai emphasizes a formal personal interview (*Zanzen* or *Zazen*) between master and individual pupil, during which the pupil is asked to answer the *Koan*—an enigma or puzzle that forces the student's mind outside normal thought processes in order to gain instant enlightenment (Satori). The *Koans*, which have been called spiritual dynamite, defy logic, analysis, and reasoning and create a mental impasse and a state of tension, out of which, with proper instruction and perseverance, an illumination sudden as a flash of lightning takes place. The guru initiates a countergame aimed at contradicting the game of social life (of play being the main concern of human beings, who, however, pretend that most of such play is work) which the pupil tends to repress.

In the Soto method, the pupil, under the guidance of the guru, undergoes a process of transcending the antithetic experience of subject and object, good and bad, mine and yours, through a progressive discovery of the true self and by overcoming the limiting and excessive dominant ego, which manifests itself under the form of escape mechanism in much of ordinary daily activity. That is accomplished through an inner journey, whose stages can be defined as follows: (1) nonreligious consciousness, (2) secular morality, (3) religious morality, (4) denial of God or humans as entities, (5) interdependence of all beings, (6) mercy, (7) mind regarded as void, (8) negation of negation, affirmation of the absolute reality, (9) denial of the reality of the absolute reality, and (10) communication and identification with Buddha. At that point there is no knowledge except knowledge of the present; for the Easterner, eternity is now, and the physical organism and the physical world turn out to be the divine world. Zen had a vast influence on Japanese culture and life, notably on kendo (the art of the sword), judo (the art of aggressive self-defense), art, literature, drama, and the art of flower arranging and gardening.

As for mental illness proper, descriptions of mental diseases can be found in the old Japanese medical literature which was influenced by Chinese concepts imported through Korea, especially in the period of great cultural advances between 700 and 1000 A.D. In regard to treatment, emetics, a variety of vegetable substances, heat, water, massage, and other methods were applied. For several centuries many mentally ill people were brought to a small temple in Iwakura near Kyoto in the belief that those sick human beings could be healed by the local divinity after they had undergone a proper ritual of purification with water. A number of them found shelter in the homes of neighboring peasants; they lived there and worked in the homes and the fields, constituting a colony based on family care.

FAR EASTERN AND WESTERN PSYCHOLOGICAL CONCEPTS AND PRACTICAL INFLUENCES

The concepts and practices described above are basic aspects of Indian, Chinese, and Japanese cultures. After a long period of neglect and condemnation by the Judeo-Christian tradition of the Western world, they have gained popularity in recent years, especially in the United States and more progressive countries of Europe.

Yet, from the historical perspective, two points have to be taken into consideration. In the first place, parallel to philosophical and medical thinking, folk beliefs and practices have continued uninterrupted from the early times to the present in all the cultures of the Far East, as well as in the West. As mentioned previously, central to such beliefs and practices is the notion of superstitious causation of disease as related to the invasion of the mind by noxious spirits, a notion that presupposes a consideration of body and soul as separate entities. In China special priests, designated by the symbol *Wu*, acted as exorcists and performed ceremonies especially geared to propitiating the ancestors. Of the animate and inanimate sub-

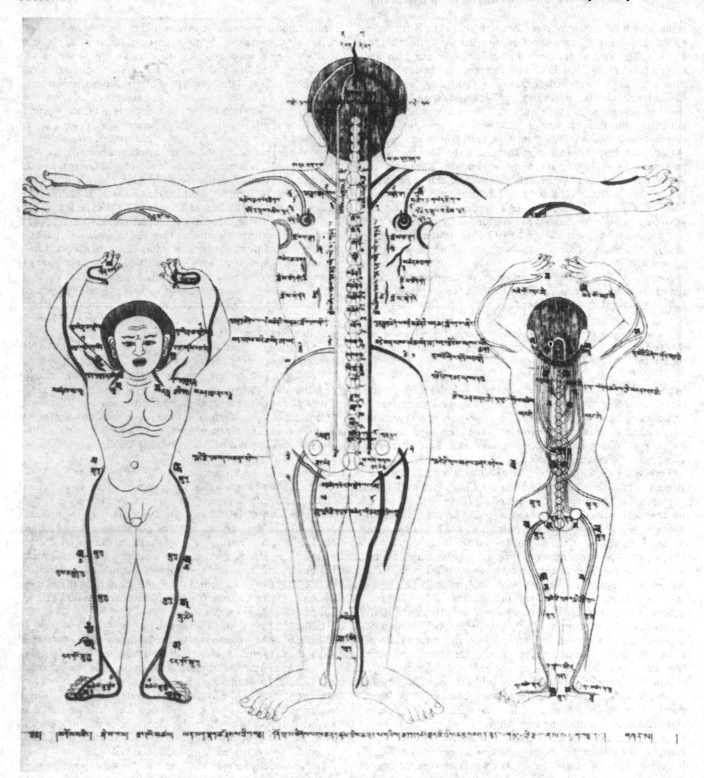

FIGURE 2. Diagram showing the many channels that convey the soul throughout the body. Yoga exercises are intended to affect that aspect of the soul that is related to the channels involved. From the Tibetan medical scrolls on the walls of the temple dedicated to Bhaishaajaguru (or Yao-shih-fo), the Buddha of the healing art (5th century B.C.?).

stances endowed with harmful power, no single figure has had as important a role in Chinese and Japanese fantasy as that played by the fox, somewhat corresponding to the witch in Western culture. The folklore related to the role of the fox in the causation of all forms of mental aberrations, including such sexual disturbances as impotence and frigidity, is extensive and has continued to this day.

In the second place, many of the beliefs and practices as they exist today are no longer an autochthonous expression of India, China, and Japan, inasmuch as those countries have been influenced by Western concepts for a long time. The Portuguese established trade centers in all of them in the 16th century. Later, India came under the influence of the British from the early 17th century until 1947, first through commerical enterprises (mainly the British East India Company) and then through political administration. In China and Japan Christian missionaries, especially Jesuit priests, exercised a strong influence from the 16th century on; however, in Japan they were expelled in the early 17th century. In both China and Japan, Western influence became more marked in the 19th century—in China, especially in the Canton area, by a number of Western nations (in 1898 the Refuge for the Insane was opened in that city by John G. Kerr) and later at the Peking Union Medical College (founded in 1906 under British-American auspices); in Japan through the Europeanization of the country that took place from the second half of the 19th century and through the heavy influence of German and later of American science and medicine.

A comparison between contemporary psychodynamic theories and Far Eastern concepts is difficult because of the historical and cultural differences. As Jung (1931) put it:

> The West emphasizes the human incarnation, and even the personality and historicity of Christ, while the East says: "Without beginning, without end, without past, without future."

Moreover, in all the Western ideologies—Judaic, Christian, capitalist, and communistic—morality is based on renunciation or postponement; for the Easterner, liberation is achieved in the immediate present. Nevertheless, since the advent of dynamic psychology, many analogies have been found between Eastern and Western concepts and practices.

To begin with, Zen has been equated with the unconscious. In particular, Jung (1931) considered *I Ching* as a method of exploring the unconscious because of the focus on the element of chance involved. Many aspects point to the similarities between psychotherapy and the Eastern way to liberation—for instance, the Freudian tenets that knowledge leads to transformation and that apparently nonlogical free associations are essential to the therapeutic process. True, Westerners have tended to identify the Eastern notion of liberation with regression, with a state of advanced autism, or with an extreme experience of autosuggestion, unaware of the differences Easterners draw between primal narcissism in children and cosmic consciousness in adults and unaware of the importance of higher states of consciousness, revealed in the abundant mystic literature, a natural link between the East and the West.

Also common to psychotherapy and the Eastern way of liberation are the transformation of consciousness, of the inner feeling of one's own existence, and the release of the person from forms of conditioning imposed on him by social institutions, so that the liberated—like the well-analyzed person—can play his role in the social game of society without taking it too seriously. Of course, the similarity becomes even stronger when the process of liberation and psychotherapy takes place in the context of a pupil-master (novice-guru, patient-therapist) relationship, as the master stands for the authority of nature, rather than the authority of men. On the other hand, interpretation of dreams has not been practiced in Eastern cultures for the simple reason that interpretation of dreams presupposes a subjective and individual unconscious at variance with the cosmic unconscious resulting from the unassimilated residues of many former lives.

It is natural to expect that many parallels can be drawn between yoga and psychotheraeutic techniques, especially in terms of the importance yoga assigned to the unconscious long before psychoanalysis. Some even consider yoga superior to psychoanalysis, inasmuch as it does not see the libido only in the unconscious but, rather, considers the unconscious as one with the matrix and the recipient of all the actions, movements, and intentions of the ego. From the unconscious everything emerges that seeks to manifest itself, and it is to the unconscious that it returns. The over-all consensus is that yoga is not hypnosis; on the contrary, it is a higher state of consciousness. However, hypnotic suggestion or temple sleep may have originated in India before appearing in Egypt and Greece, and the three Englishmen who introduced hypnotherapy into England in the mid-19th century—Braid, Esdaile, and Ellioston—undoubtedly got their ideas and some of their experience from contact with India. Moreover, similarities have been found between the experiential, rather than the intellectual, approach of Zen and of psychoanalytic training, inasmuch as both rely on the use of free association—verbalized in Western therapy, unexpressed in the Eastern approach. In recent years, comparisons have been made between the various psychophysiological stages leading to Zen and deconditioning, as well as states of mind reached under the influence of drugs, such as lysergic acid diethylamide (LSD).

Erikson's (1959) concept of stages of development of the personality certainly represents a major advance in modern psychology. The notion was anticipated by ancient Hindus with the four stages (*Ashramas*) in the pilgrimage of the life of a person: (1) initial stage devoted to the training of the body, (2) matrimony as an important avenue to spiritual growth, (3) abandonment of domestic responsibilities to retire to a forest life, (4) final stage of renunciation and asceticism.

That final stage was emphasized by Jung (1931) in his description of the process leading to individuation. It is also relevant to the focus on death in recent Western psychological literature; the difference is that, for the Westerner, anxiety is the expression of death, but, for the Easterner, death means denial not of the person or of the person-environment unity but of the ego. Yet Jung, a long-standing student of Eastern philosophies, strongly warned the Westerner against the use of Eastern techniques, such as yoga, arguing that beyond the egoless state of consciousness of the Easterner there is an undifferentiated awareness based on ancestral maturity that is unknown to the Westerner.

In his comment on *The Secret of the Golden Flower*—a Chinese book transmitted orally for centuries, finally published some decades ago, and now translated into English—Jung (1931) emphasized the core of Tao as unity of the two opposites of life and consciousness, stating that the Chinese way of keeping the opposites in a state of balance is a sign of high maturity. He found analogies between that trend and some of his main concepts, such as the dichotomies of introvert and extrovert and of animus and anima. Buddha himself preached the middle way between asceticism and hedonism.

It has been pointed out that the Western equivalent of reincarnation is an obsession with history, a forward-moving *recherche du temps perdu*, directly opposite to the Eastern ahistorical approach. Yet historical dimensions of such an approach have also been noticed: Karma may be viewed as an excellent way for dissuading the human beast from murder, theft, and other antisocial acts and for extending the moral unity and obligations to all life, as in the precept of *Ahimsa* of not injuring living things. The opposition of Taoists to artificiality and technology may have been the way of opposing a feudal system in which the laws were a protection of exploitation, and technology was the manufacture of weapons. Gandhi's crusade for nonviolence had, indeed, historical significance, as it led to the independence of India. And the current reevaluation of Confucianism in today's China has definite historical implications.

Many of the centuries-old tenets of the Eastern concepts of mental functions and the practices based on them can become quite relevant to Western psychology, once it liberates itself from ethnocentric bias. True, major differences between the two cannot be denied—in particular, the secular orientation of the Westerner, as opposed to the spiritual orientation of the Easterner, and the Western emphasis in mental health on heredity and environment—that is, essentially on the past—as opposed to the Eastern emphasis on self-management—that is, essentially on the present. Yet, it is felt that the time is ripe for a synthesis of the timeless wisdom of Asia and the Western bent for practical accomplishments.

CONCEPTS OF THE MIND IN MIDDLE EASTERN CULTURES

Egyptian. Two main methodological difficulties have prevented scholars from achieving consensus on the concepts of the mind in the Egyptian culture—the accidental and biased sample of the culture, mainly temples and tombs of the mortuary cult, which was obviously only a minute fraction of the whole culture, and the many uncertainties related to the hieroglyphics (half pictures and half symbols) that preceded hieratic and cuneiform writings.

In that culture, kings were viewed as gods, to be worshiped as such even after their death, as evidenced by their sumptuous burials in the pyramids. Whether or not one accepts Jaynes's (1976) notion of the bicameral mind—according to which the hallucinated voice of the dead king was perceived by people as the voice of God—the fact is that such a divine concept of the king served as a means of social control. Life was viewed as a balance between a person's static experience and his relationship to the universe—that is, as an interaction between internal and external forces. That balance gave rise to rhythmic and cyclic happenings from birth to death, probably related to the cyclic harvests caused by the flooding of the Nile. The total personality was the result of seven forces, which included emotional, intellectual, and creative components.

Data from various sources point to the firm belief in the heart as the source of all psychological activities—a notion that would continue to persist in Aristotle and others—and the brain was not given any importance whatsoever. In fact, in the process of mummification of the dead rulers before 2700 B.C., the brain was extracted with a metal hook, bit by bit through the nostril, then discarded as waste. Moreover, much of what was found written on papyrus rolls in the popularly called *Books of the Dead* deals with the preservation of the heart. In the Edwin Smith medical papyrus, in the Papyrus Ebers, and elsewhere, the heart was considered to be at the center of a system of vessels that carried body products. In a passage in another text it is recorded:

The sight of the eyes, the hearing of the ears, and the smelling the air by the nose, they report to the heart. It is this which causes every completed concept to come forth, and it is the tongue which announces what the heart thinks.

Among the other psychological forces were the name (Ren) of a person or of a thing, which stands for the person himself or the thing itself and whose pronunciation is essential for the effectiveness of a prayer or exorcism (hence, the importance of keeping the name of rulers or of a god secret or known only to the initiates, as also occurred later in the Jewish culture); the Ba or a man-headed bird, representing the physical and spiritual might of the dead person and charged after death with responsibility for maintaining contact between the dead person as a supernatural being and his corpse, tomb, and survivors in this world; the Ka, a very controversial term generally indicating a generative or vital force or, perhaps, will power based on introjected parental authority, not unlike the source of motion called *thymos* in the *Iliad* and the *Odyssey*.

Emphasis on the supernatural—especially communication with the dead, such as the spirits of the Pharaohs—was possible through a healing sleep induced by incubation techniques—a method that may have had therapeutic implications for the mentally ill. Interpretation of dreams was extensively used in the Egyptian culture. Of particular historical significance is Joseph's interpretation of the Pharaoh's dream of the seven fat and seven lean cows, reported in detail in Genesis. It is likely that the treatment of mental disorders involved the integration of physical, psychic, and spiritual factors, accomplished through identification with positive constructive forces.

Judaic. Evidence of the recognition of mental illness, as differentiated from mental deficiency and from physical diseases that show such psychiatric symptoms as delirium is presented by the Old and New Testaments and by the Babylonian and Jerusalem Talmud. Of the various words expressing mental conditions, *shiggayon* means madness and is etymologically related to *meshuggai*, which stands for madman.

In one of the oldest books of the Bible, Deuteronomy, it is said that God will punish those who violate his commands with "madness, and blindness, and astonishment of heart"—that is to say, with mania, dementia, and stupor.

Perhaps the most famous episode of insanity in the Bible refers to the case of Saul, who, after some disturbed behavior early in life, developed abnormal irritability, great suspiciousness (especially toward David), and uncontrollable impulses that ended in suicide; apparently, he was affected by manic-depressive psychosis. It was said that

the spirit of the Lord departed from Saul and an evil spirit from the Lord suddenly terrified him.

His servants, however, did not consider him possessed, perhaps because he had already given some evidence of poor judgment and impulsive behavior; at one time he had forbidden his people to eat any food during the course of a long and strenuous fight; another time he had been considered to be suffering from witchcraft for his rebellious attitude toward the high priest. Thus, he followed his servants' therapeutic advice, in line with a centuries-old tradition that music alleviates emotional conditions, that a man who is a skillful player on the harp should be sought out,

and it shall be, when the evil spirit from the Lord cometh upon thee, that he shall play with his hand, and thou shall be well.

In spite of his good will and submissive attitude, David, who was well liked by the people for having killed the giant Philistine, Goliath, elicited a paranoid reaction in Saul. This latter became very aggressive—

an evil spirit from the Lord came mightly upon Saul, and he raved in the midst of the house—

and eventually turned the aggression on himself by committing suicide.

Also worth remembering is the case of Nebuchadnezzar,

king of Babylon, who became very depressed, irritable, and uncontrollable and finally fell into a conditon called lycanthropy—a form of mental disorder in which the patient imagines himself to be a wolf or other wild beast and that was reported in the literature until the 17th century—which is probably a form of melancholia.

Attempts have been made, even recently, to delineate the personality characteristics of the most important personages in the Bible. Abraham has been viewed as constantly struggling to grow in emotional and spiritual maturity; Jacob as wrestling with his own projected image of himself; Joseph, who achieved stature through interpreting the famous dream of the Pharaoh, as influenced by the problem of sibling rivalry. In general, the psychological core of the Old Testament has been described as the oedipal struggle, the struggle between human instinctual impulses and the wish and need for socialization; and the love for the mother has been viewed as sublimated in the love for the land "flowing with milk and honey."

In the realm of psychopathology proper, a renowned simulation of mental illness was described by the Chronicles of David when he was with the King of Gath:

and he changed his behavior before them, and feigned himself mad in their hands; he scratched on the doors of the gate and let his spittle fall down upon his beard.

An example of auditory hallucinations, related to mass suggestion, was reported in the Book of Kings:

for the Lord had made the host of the Arameans to hear a noise of chariots, and a noise of horses, and even the noise of a great host.

The question was raised, and it was generally answered negatively, of whether Saul manifested a behavior similar to those of the prophets. Prophecy has a long history in the Judaic culture, and prophecy eventually became formalized in the period from the 8th century to the 4th century B.C., at the time of Samuel and the establishment of the monarchy under Saul. Probably derived from divination and linked to rites of an imitative or sympathetic character, prophecy was a form of ecstasy that belonged to borderline psychological states. The important point is that the prophet's personal experience of God was not merely a private matter; rather, it increasingly became a political-religious function that, by keeping the rulers in contact with supernatural forces, contributed to the stability of the nation. In line with the over-all biblical tradition, prophecy was an expression of the power of words, as illustrated by blessings and curses.

In the New Testament many passages are of relevance to psychopathology. On the personality of Jesus himself, there is extensive literature, including the two monographs by Stanley Hall (1917), one of the earliest American psychologists, and by Albert Schweitzer (1910). The Evangelists portray the possessed as the one who wears no clothes and resides in no one's house; rather, he spends his days and nights on the mountain and in the tombs, and he cries and hits himself with stones; moreover, no one can bind him, not even with chains. In the most striking miracle of mental healing in the Gospels, Christ liberated the insane man from a legion of demons, an excellent example of personality split, and the expelled devil was forced to enter into a sow, which then plunged into the ocean during a storm and drowned.

Aside from evil spirits, the causes of mental illness included inheritance, physiological processes, lewdness and improper sexual relations, dirt, and idleness. Essentially, those various causes can be divided into two main groups—fatalistic occur-

rences of madness by divine decree and punishment for something done by the person.

It is likely that the margin of tolerance for mental abnormalities was rather wide. Well-to-do patients were probably kept confined at home; others were left wandering on their own. In the book of Jeremiah, Zephaniah had every madman (*meshuggai*) and every prophetizer (*mithnabe*) placed in prison or in the stocks. In the *Mishnah*, the collection of oral laws made in the 2nd century that forms the basis of the *Talmud*, a large number of individual regulations were given concerning the legal status of the absent-minded and of the imbecile (*shoteh*): He was not entrusted with official functions; he was legally equated with a child; his marriage could be invalidated; he could not be used as a witness in court; he was assigned a guardian when judged incompetent; he was considered healthy during lucid intervals. It is likely that by that time some of those concepts may have resulted from the interface with the Greek and Roman cultures.

Psychiatry in Greek and Roman Cultures

During the second part of the 19th century, as a concomitant of the philological and archaeological investigations of the Greek world, several studies, among which Rhode's (1925) is particularly prominent, touched on psychological and psychiatric concepts. The initial interest engendered by those studies gradually declined. Recently, however, it has been revived by modern psychodynamic theories that follow Jung's and Rank's early applications of mythological concepts to human behavior. The studies of Snell (1953), Onians (1951), and, more recently, the work of Dodds (1951), Adkins (1970), and Simon (1978) are particularly significant in that connection.

GREEK CONCEPTS OF MADNESS

Essentially, the description of madness in Greek culture derives from four main sources: popular concept, poetic tradition, medical concepts, and philosophical concepts. Each of those viewpoints prevailed at certain times, and, inevitably, they influenced each other. Consequently, a systematic presentation is almost impossible.

Popular concept. The popular concept of madness that was evident in primitive times, as represented in the vase paintings of that period, persisted throughout the development of the Greek culture and, in fact acquired further impetus during the Hellenistic era. Characteristic of the popular view was the belief in the supernatural causation of mental disorders. A typical case was the mental illness of the Persian king Cambyses and of Cleomenes I, king of Sparta, as reported by Herodotus (1899) in his *Histories*. Persons who were so afflicted were believed to be possessed by evil spirits, personified by the dread goddesses Mania and Lyssa, that had been sent by the gods in a state of anger. The habit of wandering around and the proneness to violence were especially considered signs of mental disorder. At the same time, however, there is some indication that those persons who manifested behavioral aberrations and who were, therefore, believed to be possessed by evil spirits may also have been regarded as sacred, as was the case in primitive cultures. Presumably, that belief was based on an unconscious fear of death, for the spirits represented the cult of the dead—the malign spirits keres were, in fact, the ghosts of the dead—and their persisting influence on the living.

As might be expected, that popular view provided no facilities for the treatment of the mentally ill. Mild cases were simply left to fare for themselves as objects of contempt, ridicule, and abuse. Those who were considered violent were kept at home, often in chains, on the assumption that the same gods who made people mad could cure them of it, in line with the homeopathic trend of Greek medical thinking.

Poetic tradition. In the time of Homer (10th to 9th century B.C.), no definition of personality was advanced that might be equated with current concepts of personality in terms of a psychic structure, of inner mental states, and of a self in an abstract sense. The three somewhat differentiated components of the soul—*psyche, noos,* and *thymos*—corresponded to the organs of life, rather than to psychological functions, for action—that is, thinking—had not yet been separated from its physical substrata, the brain. Thus, psyche (Greek *psyche,* to breathe) was conceptualized as the breath of life, the force that kept the human being alive. Moreover, it persisted after life as the spirit of the dead, so that it might continue to influence one's living descendants.

In the *Iliad*, human beings lacked personal motivation; instead, they were possessed by sudden feelings of power, almost comparable to states of temporary insanity. Typically, the ate—that is, infatuation—sent by a god was used to explain the aberrant behavior and thoughts of the heroes. Those unusual feelings were believed to originate in the *thymos* or *phrenes* and were attributed to the gods, to *moira* (destiny), or to the Erinyes, the goddesses of vengeance. In general, mental activity was regarded not as something intrinsically private and inaccessible to others but, rather, as something resulting from the interchange among several characters, either human or divine; and gods were often portrayed as initiating human action by putting into a man a drive or an idea, so that the Homeric man experienced himself as a plurality, rather than a unity, with uncertain boundaries. It has been claimed that the Homeric model of mental activity of the heroes is a reflection of the collective mental attitudes transmitted in dramatic form by oral epic poetry from generation to generation.

Moreover, it has been claimed that a process of identification took place between the bard and his audience and that the bard exercised some sort of therapeutic function. There is no description of insanity in Homer; even Achilles' wrath is not called a disease. Rather, insanity seemed to represent the hero's falling out with the social order. That belief was in him with the characteristics of the Mediterranean shame culture, as opposed to the characteristics of the Northern guilt culture.

In the *Odyssey*, however, there were implications of moral criticism; and in time the concept of *hybris* (arrogance) became prominent in terms of its link with success, complacency, sin, and guilt. In other words, the poetic works of the period began to evidence an awareness of the fact that moral principles—that is, conscience—were internalized. They further stressed the relationship between the violation of those principles and consequent punishment by the gods as an inevitable part of human destiny (*moira*). Such punishment might be inflicted in this life, in the other life—that is, after death—or even on one's descendants.

Important for cathartic liberation from disturbing emotions was the function of the theater, which in the Greek culture was attended by the entire community at intervals. The actions performed in the theater portrayed the conflict between various contrasting and instinctual tendencies, and the chorus represented the instances of a collective superego, although often identifying with the protagonist. Murders, suicide, and madness were themes quite often represented in the tragedies for the purpose of arising terror and pity. The personages affected by madness seemed to be in a state of imbalance between opposite tendencies, such as to yield too much to impulses or to deny

them. At the root of that imbalance, conflicts of various nature and ambivalence seemed to be paramount. In the *Bacchae*, though, the main issue of the drama was confusion of identity—probably a reflection of the great changes occurring then in Greek life. Thus, the aim of the dramatist was to find the right balance between passion and reason—that is *soprhosyne* (moderation or temperance).

In some of the most important dramatic productions, the key figures were afflicted with madness vividly pictured on the stage: in the *Eumenides* by Aeschylus (525–456 B.C.) Orestes's violent and erratic behavior subsequent to his matricide, a theme later repeated in Euripides's *Iphigenia in Tauris*; in *Ajax* by Sophocles (ca. 496–406 B.C.) the hero's violent behavior leading to suicide related to pride (*hybris*); in *Heracles* by Euripides (ca. 484–407 B.C.) the progressive state of insanity caused by Lyssa, the goddess of madness, resulting in the hero's murdering his own children; in the *Bacchae* by Euripides the murder of Pentheus by the hand of his own mother, who, as a Maenad, was involved in ritual orgies. In Sophocles, the madman lived in an unreal, rather than a supernatural, world. But in Euripides, behavioral expressions of madness, such as hallucinations, were purposely exaggerated for dramatic effect. Of course, no Greek play has enjoyed as much recognition in psychiatry as Sophocles's *Oedipus Rex*, from which Freud derived his famous notion of the oedipal conflict.

Medical concepts (hysteria and collective psychopathology). The medical concept of madness, as elaborated in the Hippocratic writings (4th century B.C.), centered on the interactions of the four bodily humors—blood, black bile, yellow bile, and phlegm—which resulted from the combination of the four basic qualities in nature—heat, cold, moisture, and dryness. Persons were classified according to four corresponding temperaments—sanguine, choleric, melancholic, and phlegmatic—which classification was considered to indicate their prevailing emotional orientation. That notion had been anticipated by Alcmaeon of Croton in the 5th century B.C. He was the first to consider the brain as the seat of the senses and of intellectual life, and he did experimental research on animals. Personality functioning reached an optimal level when crasis—that is, the appropriate interaction of internal and external forces—had been achieved. Conversely, conflict between those forces, termed dyscrasia, indicated the presence of excessive bodily humor, which had to be removed by purging.

Of greater significance, however, were the initial indications of a radical change in the concept of madness, in the sense of diseases of the nervous system, which began to emerge at that time. The change was first expressed by Hippocrates (460–355 B.C.) in the introduction to his treatise on epilepsy, *The Sacred Disease* (Hippocrates, 1950). Even after many centuries, the viewpoint elaborated therein has not lost its philosophical value:

> I do not believe that the "sacred disease" is any more divine or sacred than any other disease but, on the contrary, has specific characteristics and a definite cause. Nevertheless, because it is completely different from other diseases, it has been regarded as a divine visitation by those who, being only human, view it with ignorance and astonishment.

And, from a more general perspective, he stated:

> Men ought to know that from nothing else but thence [from the brain] come joys, delights, laughter, and sports; and sorrows, griefs, despondency, and lamentations. And by this in an especial manner, we acquire vision and knowledge, and we see and hear. And by the same organ we become mad and delirious, and fears and terrors assail us,

some by night and some by day.... All these things we endure from the brain, when it is not healthy.

In Hippocrates's classic work other clinical entities, apart from epilepsy, are today recognizable—namely, cases of psychoses (delusions due to distortions in sensory perceptions); impulse behavior disorders; melancholia; and, possibly, phobias. However, in the light of modern diagnostic criteria, those distinctions seem superficial and uncritical. All too frequently, case histories were restricted to the patient's own account of the onset of his illness and referred to causative factors relating to malfunctioning of the brain or heart. Notably, madness was commonly attributed to disturbances in the interaction of the four bodily humors, and an excess of black bile was mentioned with particular frequency as the cause of mental illness. Typically, the treatment in such cases involved the administration of a purgative—specifically, black hellebore. Thus, the line "Go to Anticyra," which appears in Aristophanes's (448–385 B.C.) *Vespae,* can be interpreted as a colloquialism that meant, "You're crazy," for Anticyra was famous as a source of hellebore. The treatment prescribed in such cases also included vapors, baths, and appropriate diet.

In spite of the medical emphasis, no clear legal status was outlined for the mentally ill person. Since his antisocial behavior was viewed as punishment by the gods, administered either directly or by their emissaries, the mentally ill criminal was relieved of any legal responsibility for his actions. Rather, the person convicted of a crime by reason of insanity was, as suggested by Plato, exiled from his city voluntarily or was forced to flee and to undergo purification rites. There was no psychiatric examination, except in cases involving slaves; in controversial cases—such as those involving marriage, divorce, and adoption—appeal on psychiatric grounds was made to the guardians of the law, rather than to physicians.

Yet at least one definite emotional condition, hysteria, fell under the medical realm in Greek times. Hysteria (from *hystera,* uterus) was a complex disease characterized by a variety of symptoms that were related to alleged movements of the uterus. Typically, the globus hystericus—that is, inability to swallow—was attributed to the pressure of the uterus on the throat. Likewise, convulsions, disorders of menstruation, vomit, headaches, and many other types of malaise were explained as movements of the uterus. In the *Epidemics,* one of the Hippocratic books, one of the earliest known case histories of hysterical disorder is given (Hippocrates, 1950).

The wife of Polemarchus felt a sudden pain in her groin; her menses having failed to set in ... she was without voice through the entire night until the middle of the next day ... [and only able] to indicate with her hand that the pain was in her groin.

Quite often, hysteria occurred in virgins. Consequently, treatment consisted of physical methods, mainly of fetid fumigations to the nose to repel the ascended uterus and of aromatic fumigations to attract the wandering uterus back to its proper place. Marriage, intercourse, and procreation were frequently prescribed.

Unquestionably, as lately described by Freud, such hysteric phenomena found their origin in the emotional condition of the woman in Greek society. Women were considered inferior to men, even legally, and female sexuality as a pejorative of male sexuality—hence, the praise of homosexuality, especially between a master and a pupil. Underneath the contempt of men for women was their fear of women, probably because of castration anxiety, as evidenced by the large number of female

figures who could bring calamities and even death to men— the Erinyes, the Harpies, the Sirens, the Sphinxes, and the snake-haired Furies. It seems that the woman expressed her deep resentment toward the man by displacing her feeling to her sons, who would grow up hostile toward females, narcissistic, and very competitive toward each other. Moreover, because in the Greek culture the image of the woman was split in two— that of a wife and mother and that of an object of pleasure—it is likely that the hysteric symptoms represented the woman's inability to integrate those two conflicting images.

Yet the culture itself offered opportunities to overcome the imbalance between the sexes and to provide women with a cathartic outlet for the public expression of repressed feelings of sexuality and aggression. Various kinds of rituals largely attended by women—such as the Dionysiac, the Corybantic, and the Bacchic—in which orgiastic dances and ceremonies accompanied by stimulating music in the Phrygian mode up to the point of paroxysm took place, represented the most socially acceptable and desirable mode for such an outlet. In the *Laws,* Plato (1961) subsumed the same therapeutic principle for the Corybantic rites and for the practice of rocking babies (today looked on as a sign of psychological regression):

They restore the sufferers to a state of inner calm and repose and bring them back to their sober senses. Thus, the inner tumult is cured by outer activity; unwholesome mania is driven out by beneficient mania, and in the end both kinds of mania are gone.

The alleged supernatural phenomena of divination and precognition, to which Dodds (1951) called attention, occurred only through women, notably through the priestesses of the shrine of Delphi called Pythia or sometimes Pythonesses.

Philosophical concepts. It is difficult to translate the psychological vocabulary of the philosophical writings of 5th century B.C. Greece into modern terms. What is certain is that the pre-Socratic philosophers were the first to attempt to define abstract, as opposed to concrete. As a matter of fact, the concept of the soul divorced from the qualities of the body and its physical organs was expressed for the first time by Heraclitus (540–475 B.C.) (Kirk and Raven, 1960):

You could not find the ends of the soul though you traveled everywhere, so deep is its "logos."

In general, the over-all tendency was to consider *physis,* the qualities with which a person is endowed by birth, as responsible for the achievement of *arete* (goodness) by the *agatoi* (the outstanding people). In time, a distinction between *soma* (body) and *psyche* comes to the fore; in Plato's dialogues the psyche appears to be longing for the world of ideas. But the 5th century was characterized by an agglomeration of contrasting beliefs. Passion and immorality were conceived of, on the one hand, as an expression of natural law (*physis*) and, on the other hand, as a conglomeration of irrational customs (*nomos*). Protagoras (481–411 B.C.) believed that virtue must be acquired, like a habit, but Socrates (470–399 B.C.) maintained that it had to be taught intellectually.

It is likely that the structure of the *polis,* the Greek society in the small city, may, by favoring the role of external forces in human actions and by minimizing the importance of personal intentions, have delayed the development of the ego in the individual personality that is paramount to modern psychological theories. Moreover, it may have caused considerable stress in some—especially in outstanding citizens—to the point of eliciting emotional instability and even madness.

True, certain aspects of the Greek culture point to a view of the psyche as independent from the body. For example, dreams came to be considered as liberating the person from adverse external forces and, later on, from the impediment of his own body—the orphic tradition—and, thus, to have a therapeutic function. Furthermore, the highly emotional group rites in praise of Dionysius—the Greek god of fruitfulness and vegetation, especially wine—came to be replaced by mystic individualistic expressions, as typified by the puritanic community established by Pythagoras (6th century B.C.), which emphasized vegetarianism and purification by ritual means. Typically, such rituals included recollection, to the degree that, in time, catharsis was considered the only means of salvation. Clearly, these practices might serve as a substitute for religious ritual.

Plato's concepts. From the 19th century on, students of the dialogues of Plato (428–348 B.C.) divided on the issue of considering them as the expression of separate periods of mysticism and rationalism or, on the other hand, of a progressive evolution. Western philosophy has been imbued with Platonic concepts, to the extent that there is no theory of the mind that has not been affected by them.

Central to Plato's philosophy are the notions that the psyche is active and immortal and that sickness of the psyche is due either to discord among one's various personal traits or to ignorance—the worse kind of ignorance being, in a Socratic vein, ignorance of oneself, self-deception.

Also well known is the concept of health as harmony between body and mind, which has led to the conception that mental health was Plato's invention. Conversely, it is said in *Timaeus* that disharmony between body and mind causes mental aberrations based on either mania or gross ignorance. In *Phaedrus* Plato described four kinds of madness: prophetic, telestic or ritual, poetic, and erotic. Prophetic madness was defined as a unique form of temporary insanity that was reserved for the few persons who were able to reach the paroxysm of enthusiasm characteristic of the shamanistic trance, as typified by the ecstatic prophecy of Apollo's oracle at Delphi and as immortalized in Aeschylus's (525–456 B.C.) *Cassandra.* Telestic or ritual madness typically signified freedom from instinctual needs, and it was achieved collectively during the Corybantic religious rites. Poetic madness, due to possession by the muses, was described as a state of particular inspiration that was bestowed by the gods on the artist in order to facilitate the process of creation. Erotic madness was associated with human love, which in the Greek culture included homosexual, as well as heterosexual, relationships (Dover, 1978).

In the *Laws* psychiatric issues are openly discussed. Mentally ill persons presenting psychopathic behavior were to be sentenced by the judge to a house of correction for a term of not less than 5 years, during which time their contact with the community was to be kept to a minimum. After the term of confinement expired, the prisoner was to be freed if he had improved, or, if not, he was to be put to death. Lunatics were to be kept in safe custody at home, and stiff penalties were to be given to relatives who did not take care of them. Definite rules were also to be followed in matters of competency in relation to marrying and leaving a will and in other legal issues. It has been said that in *The Republic* Plato applied a medical model to social life, inasmuch as he portrayed both the state and the soul as an organism that can be in a state of health or not; in the latter case, the judge functions as a doctor. That model is not far from today's discussions about the medical versus the moral notion of mental health.

Several attempts have been made to gain insight into Plato's concepts by exploring his own personality. Brès (1968) submitted that the dialogues of the mature period—especially *Symposium, Phaedon,* and *Phaedrus*—give evidence of the insufficiency of Plato's return to his personal past, through dreams and reminiscences, possibly related to a love experience and his contact with the Pythagoric school while in Sicily. Such an insufficiency could have caused the projection of his personal motives in his famous theses of the immortality of the soul, the contemplation of divine ideas, and the supremacy of Good. It was Brès's contention that the dialogues of maturity portray a dynamic psychology, in contrast to the static psychology of the later dialogues—that is, love is replaced by reason (*logos*) and by law (*nomos*). That contention is, of course, debatable.

Analogies have been drawn between Plato's concepts and Freud's concepts. The tripartite subdivision of the soul, which parallels the structure of the state, in *The Republic* into appetite, reason, and temper has been compared by many to the psychoanalytic subdivision of the psyche into id, ego, and superego, the main differences being that the appetite, in contrast to the id, is largely conscious and that the superego, although largely irrational and punitive, is not limited to the emotions. A similar concept is expressed by the analogy between the tripartite soul and the charioteer with a pair of winged steeds, which occurs in *Phaedrus,* as well as in Freud's writings. Most of the similarities between the two center on several main points—the dichotomy between conscious and unconscious, the model of the mind as a conflict among various drives eventually leading to control by one over the others, the similarities between Plato's eros and Freud's libido, the attempt to find an outlet for instinctual impulses into socially acceptable activities, the attribution of the sickness of the psyche to a form of ignorance to be overcome in Plato's philosophical dialogue and in Freud's analytic dialogue. The *locus classicus,* anticipating the oedipal conflict of the Freudian school, occurs in *The Republic* (Plato, 1961):

> In sleep the wild beast in us, full-fed with meat or drink, becomes rampant and shakes off sleep to go in quest of what will gratify its own instincts . . . . In phantasy it will not shrink from intercourse with a mother or anyone else, man, god, or brute, or from forbidden food or any deed of blood.

Recently, Simon (1978) submitted that the basis of the unconscious meaning of madness in the Platonic dialogues is the wild, confused, and combative scene of parental intercourse as perceived by the child, which Freud called the primal scene. Support for that thesis has been found in the famous image of the cave in *The Republic*—that is the confused picture of the reality obtained by prisoners condemned to see only the shades or shadows on the wall of a cave of people acting in front of a fire. That, in itself, can be viewed as a representation of the primal scenes and fits into Plato's continuous emphasis of opposing light to darkness and of condemning drama as leading to extravagant expressions of emotion and immorality through its contagious effect on the audience. Simon (1978) also proposed that the similarities in Plato's and Freud's oedipal orientation and primal scene conflicts may be related to similarities in their family dynamics, a view that is certainly open to debate.

Aristotle's empirical psychology. Plato made an impressive effort to explain irrational events and behavior as an inevitable part of human life, rather than as the result of noxious influences. Concurrently, he attempted to subject them to the rational control of the mind. In contrast, Aristotle (384–322

B.C.) approached the various expressions of human behavior from an empirical viewpoint, which is more in keeping with today's psychology.

Like others, Aristotle supported the view that the black bile (Greek *melaina chole,* from which the word "melancholia" derives) caused disturbed sensory perception and hallucinations, a notion that persisted through the Middle Ages right up to the Renaissance (Klibansky et al., 1964). In Aristotle, the mediating aspect of the bile between the body and the mind offered one more argument in support of his organicistic philosophy of body-mind unity, which has influenced Western thought to the present day.

In a famous passage of a treatise called *Problems,* he said (Aristotle, 1927):

Why is it that all those who have become outstanding in philosophy, in statesmanship, poetry, or other arts are melancholic, and some to such an extent that they are affected by diseases arising from black bile? . . . Even many [of our earlier] heroes seem to have suffered in the same way. In later times there have been such men as Empedocles, Plato, Socrates, and many other well-known men. The same is true of most of those who have handled poetry.

In a similar vein, Socrates had spoken of the demon as an inspiring and divine force that gives supernatural attributes to thought. All that is an anticipation of the thesis of a relationship between genius and insanity that was brought forward by Lombroso and his pupils at the end of the 19th century.

Croissant's (1932) presentation of Aristotle's explanation of the mysteries clearly establishes that he conceived of them as ritual happenings in the course of which mental disorder could be healed. Essentially, in accordance with the basic orphic theme, which Plato ascribed to as well, Aristotle believed that the disordered movement of the mysteries was ultimately conducive to order. Nor did he deviate substantially from general belief in his identification of the three irrational elements presented in those rituals—enthusiasm, a state of temporary madness, related to sexuality; divination through dreams; and divination through chance. However, whereas according to the classical Pythagorical tradition the music that accompanied such rituals was considered to evoke harmony, Aristotle postulated that its therapeutic function was to arouse passions. That was the first clear statement that the release of repressed emotions or passions—that is, abreaction—was an essential prerequisite for the effective treatment of mental illness, a viewpoint that was to serve as the basis for the moral treatment of the early 19th century.

Aristotle further advocated the use of catharsis, wine, aphrodisiacs, and music, since, in the final analysis, they were all found to produce similar effects, especially in people with melancholic constitutions. In summary, Aristotle discussed catharsis from a naturalistic viewpoint. In contrast to Plato, he did not emphasize the occult and supernatural character of catharsis; rather, he conceived of it as a natural outlet for disturbing passions. In fact, passions must be purged consistently to avoid violence. The use of the theater as a civic and collective cathartic device in Greek culture may be attributed largely to the wide acceptance of that belief.

Triumph of rationalism. Aristotle's empirical psychology did not undergo further development by his disciples. Instead, *ataraxia,* a mental state of imperturbability, became the ideal of the Epicureans and Stoics during the 3rd century B.C., and the foundation of psychology became much more rationalistic. Leibbrand and Wettley (1959) pointed out that the basic Stoic concept of *apatheia,* which emphasized the moderation of passions in every human act, played an eminent role throughout the development of psychopathology up to the present. In the 4th century B.C., the conglomerate, the term used by Dodds (1951) to express the combination of rational and irrational motives in Platonic philosophy, broke down. With the rise of Hellenism, religion became more rationalistic. At the same time, astrology, neo-Pythagorism, and other irrational beliefs gained momentum. In general, there was a preoccupation with those beliefs that applied to individual salvation, and that preoccupation anticipated some of the major tenets of Christianity.

This description of the development of psychiatry in Greek culture might be appropriately concluded by a brief description of concurrent developments in other medical disciplines. Various schools of medical thought had begun to emerge and to acquire the distinct characteristics that were later to become well known in medical history: dogmatic, empirical, methodical, pneumatic, and eclectic. Alexandria became the new center of learning, and it was there, in the 3rd century B.C., that Erasistratus and Herophilus first correctly described parts of the nervous system, such as the ventricles, the sensory and motor nerves, the circumvolutions, the vessels at the base of the brain, the arachnoid, and the dura mater.

ROMAN CONCEPTS OF MADNESS

In the succeeding two centuries. Rome acquired increasing political importance, but Greek culture continued to dominate those aspects of Roman life that related to philosophy and art. On the other hand, the Romans were particularly concerned with the practical aspects of existence, such as architecture, economics, and jurisprudence. With specific reference to psychiatry, the popular and medical concepts of madness, as well as literary and philosophical writings, repeated the Greek themes for the most part, with minor variations.

Popular concepts. Superstitious practices, influenced by autochthonous Etruscan beliefs, continued to determine the popular attitude toward the mentally ill, who were neglected, banned, or persecuted. Thus, according to the *Twelve Tables* (451–450 B.C.) (Semélaigne, 1869) the mentally ill were deprived of freedom of action and were judged incompetent to control their own personal and business affairs. The *furiosi* were to be placed under the care of their *agnati* (relatives through the male line) or, those failing, of their *gentiles* (name-related family). It is likely that the original purpose of the law was to keep property in the family.

On the stage, the Romans portrayed madness in the form of bacchantes, in which women carried snakes, wore bizarre costumes, and performed in frenzied ecstasy. In the *Aeneid,* Vergil (70–19 B.C.) conceived of madness as representing the same bacchic frenzy. Later, the Fury was used to imply an even more dramatic picture of madness, and in *Metamorphoses* Ovid (43 B.C.–17 A.D.) (Wedeck, 1963) used not only the Fury but hell broth, magic philters, and love potions, thus anticipating the paraphernalia typical of the medieval traditions and folk beliefs. Incubation practices became more frequent in Rome at the beginning of the 3rd century, when an Asclepean temple was built on the Tiberine Island, where the Fatebenefratelli Hospital now stands.

Medical concepts. Roman physicians continued to believe in the premonitory value of dreams and, in general, continued to be influenced by Greek concepts. That influence became particularly evident after Julius Caesar issued an edict permitting foreign physicians to practice and to teach in Rome.

In the 1st century B.C., Asclepiades, originally from Asia Minor and a founder of the methodical school, rejected the doctrine of vital fluids and built his theories on the atomic hypotheses of Democritus. He described phrenitis as a fever accompanied by mental excitement and mania as continuous excitement without fever. Anticipating Esquirol, Asclepiades further differentiated illusions from hallucinations and prescribed treatment in light rooms for patients afflicted with hallucinations because of their characteristic fear of the dark. Treatment also emphasized the proper use of food and wine, physiotherapy, and other activities that imposed minimal physical restrictions, and it included such psychotherapeutic techniques as music and intellectual stimulation; patients were encouraged to form emotional relationships with others.

In the 1st century after Christ, Celsus, the author of the classic eight-volume *De Re Medica,* dealt at length with mental diseases in volume 3 of that work. Essentially, the originality of Celsus's approach lay in the emphasis he placed on the value of the individual doctor-patient relationship. Celsus anticipated modern psychotherapy in that he proposed that such a relationship might evolve from the use of specific techniques to cheer depressed patients and to quiet those who are manic; furthermore, he advocated the proper use of language and music and, possibly, some group activities, such as reading groups. Once again, passions were recognized as constituting the essential ingredient for the treatment of the mental patient.

Literary-philosophical concepts. Cicero (106–43 B.C.) must be credited with the first detailed description of passions, which is included in his *Tisculanae Disputationes,* as part of his attempt to clarify psychological terminology. Having defined *animus* as corresponding to the Greek *psyche* and *anima* as corresponding to the Greek *pneuma,* Cicero proceeded to describe four main groups of *pate* (same root as "passions"), which can be translated literally as perturbations. Those four groups comprised *aegritudo* (discomfort), *metus* (fear), *voluptas* or *laetitia* (pleasure, joy), and, the strongest of all, *libido* (violent desire). It was Cicero, then, who used the word "libido" in a psychological sense for the first time. Cicero further stated that excessive perturbation might give rise to *morbi,* actual diseases of the soul, and that, basically, they were caused by a contempt or abuse of *ratio*—that is, by errors in judgment. In essence, the concepts elaborated by Cicero were based on the philosophical doctrine of Stoicism.

Belonging to the same school was the Spanish-born Seneca (4–65 A.D.), one of the greatest moralists of all times. He considered reason as basic for proper human behavior and passions as perturbations of the soul, to be differentiated from mental diseases. He advocated, as medicine of the soul, the rationalization of morbid processes—that is, philosophical examination of the realities of death, pain, and infirmity—and the cultivation of wisdom and of friendship. It has been claimed that Seneca's constant moralistic struggle constituted an attempt to overcome the feelings of overprotection by his mother that accompanied him throughout his life.

In contrast, Lucretius's (ca. 99–55 B.C.) *De Rerum Natura,* which exerted wide influence during the Middle Ages, followed the Epicurean doctrine. Lucretius conceived of both the mind (*animus*) and the soul (*anima*) as corporal and mortal, being made of atoms. The mind was located in the breast—the seat of feelings and intelligence—but the soul was dispersed throughout the body.

GALEN

A complex and prolific writer on philosophy and on medicine, Galen (ca. 130–200) was undoubtedly the greatest physician of Roman times. For centuries, the impact of his ideas on medical theory and practice continued under the name of Galenism. Born in Pergamon in Asia Minor, then the seat of the famous temple of Asclepius, he was mainly influenced by the Hippocratic writings, by the anatomical school of Alexandria, and by the Stoic philosophy. Eventually, he settled in Rome, where he taught extensively and carried on a large practice.

Eclectic in medical theory, Galen (1963) was especially influenced by the doctrine of the four humors. Health was due to the proper proportions of blood, phlegm, yellow bile, and black bile; dyscrasia, leading to disease, was due to an improper mixture. Thus, apoplexy was caused by a dyscrasia of the brain, headache by vapors rising from the stomach or by fever, melancholia by an excess of black bile. In the last case, he described many types of melancholic aberrations (*paranoia*) arising partly from false sense impressions (*phantasis*); common to all of them, however, were fear and despair (*dysthymia*). As far as treatment was concerned, the excess of bile had to be eliminated through phlebotomy or by cathartics.

Galen pointed out that the retention of male sperm or the delay of uterine discharges also contributed to psychic imbalance and to manifestations of anxiety. He was aware of the correlation between hysterical symptoms and the absence of sexual relations and noted the curative effect of sexual relations and the release of tension provided by masturbation. That modern concept of sexuality may be viewed as an example of the interaction between psychic components and somatic illnesses; Galen gave many clinical descriptions of that interaction.

It has been claimed that the close association between the aberration of the soul and the dyscrasia of the body tended to remove any stigma attached to mental disease. Be that as it may, Galen has essentially remained best known for his theory of the spirits, which stated that the natural or physical spirits carried by the blood as a result of the digestive and reproductive functions become transformed into vital spirits in the veins and heart under the influence of the circulatory and respiratory functions and are finally transformed into animal or psychic spirits through a process of distillation occurring in the brain and the nerves. That triadic subdivision of the soul is similar to that earlier proposed by Plato: the concupiscible, irascible, and rational powers were located in the liver, in the heart, and in the brain, respectively. Those concepts exerted a strong influence on medical thought and on Western thought in general up until the time of the scientific revolution of the 17th century.

With specific reference to psychology, Galen attempted to disprove the Stoic dogma that psychological deviations (*pate* or perturbations) were due to defects of reason, the dogma Cicero had ascribed to. Instead, he maintained that the health of the soul depended on the proper harmony of the rational, irrational, and lustful parts of the soul. When errors in judgment were made unconsciously, they might be corrected by proper education. However, when such erroneous acts of judgment were reached consciously, for personal gain, they might prove more difficult if not impossible to correct. From his treatise *On Passions,* it would appear that the insight Galen acquired later in life into his own personal difficulties helped him to master his own passions. That accomplishment was due in no small measure to his relationship with a loved and respected mentor, a carryover from his warm relationship with his father, in contrast to his difficult relationship with his mother. Thus, his personal experience, in combination with his clinical experience, fostered his understanding of the human mind.

CONTRIBUTION TO FORENSIC PSYCHIATRY

It is in relation to the legal aspects of mental illness that the Romans made their most important contribution to psychiatry. Previously, the various terms that defined the mentally ill—*furiosi, mente capti, dementes,* and *fatui*—had been used interchangeably. In contrast, the classic legal text of the late Roman times, *Corpus Juris Civilis* (Lee, 1922), detailed the various conditions—insanity, drunkenness, and so on—that, if present at the time the criminal act was committed, might decrease the criminal's responsibility for his actions. Apparently, however, the defendant's state of mind was determined by a judge; physicians were not consulted in such matters. And, for the most part, those persons who were considered to be mentally ill, including those who might be diagnosed as criminal psychopaths today, were placed under the custody of relatives or guardians appointed by legal authorities. In addition, laws were passed that defined the ability of the mentally ill to contract marriage, to be divorced by a spouse, to dispose of their possessions, to leave a will, and to testify. During the rule of the emperor Justinian (483–565), a number of mentally ill patients, for whom facilities had not been provided earlier, were admitted to institutions for the poor and infirmed, perhaps as a result of the influence of Christianity.

TREATMENT OF MENTAL ILLNESS

That more humane attitude toward mental patients, as evidenced in the philosophy of two great physicians of the time, is described by Caelius Aurelianus, (1950) in his treatise *On Acute Diseases and on Chronic Diseases.* The first of these great physicians, Aretaeus of Cappadocia (1st century), who belonged to the pneumatic school of thought, described forms of melancholia that terminated in mania, thus anticipating the manic-depressive syndrome. Of particular interest is the psychological insight Aretaeus demonstrated in defining the influence of the emotions on mental functioning—for example, the influence of love on melancholia. A hundred years later, Soranus of the methodical school described the ideational content of mental disturbances and of various forms of stupor. However, Soranus (1st to 2nd centuries) is known in particular for the truly humanitarian principles he applied in the treatment and management of the mentally ill. Rooms were to be kept free from disturbing stimuli; visiting by relatives was restricted; the personnel responsible for the care of the patients were instructed to be sympathetic; during lucid intervals mental patients were encouraged to read and then to discuss what they had read, to participate in dramatic performances—tragedy was prescribed to counteract mania, comedy to counteract depression—and to speak at group meetings. And, of course, those procedures are basic to the therapeutic regimen in the modern mental hospital. Historically, those enlightened practices, which prevailed in the Roman culture at the time of the emperor Trajan, appeared to reflect a tolerant political attitude, along with a pessimistic view of the value of reason in the pursuit of absolute knowledge. Also, it is likely that relatively few people could afford the treatment advocated by Soranus. For the others, therapeutic means may have been limited to drugs, spells, or visits to religious shrines.

Other writers representative of the period of late Roman civilization repeated the themes of classic antiquity in describing the treatment of mental disorders. In addition, three forms of melancholia—due to general physiological, nervous, and intestinal factors—were described. The brain was considered of central importance in the causation of mental disorders: the forebrain was the site of disturbances of imagination; the midbrain gave rise to disturbances of reason; and the middle and the posterior parts of the brain together were the locus for disturbances of thought affecting imagination and reason.

ANCIENT THERAPEUTIC METHODS

Among the various psychotherapeutic interventions for emotional disorders in antiquity, three stand out because of their widespread use for many centuries in various cultures in the Near East and the Mediterranean areas—the interpretation of dreams, incubation techniques, and therapy with words. They are discussed here separately, but in many ways they are interrelated. In general, those various methods, officially disregarded by psychiatry in the 18th and 19th centuries as expressions of magic and superstition, have become quite relevant since the advent of dynamic psychiatry in the 20th century. Increasingly, attention has been given to them by the psychoanalytic literature, which, until recently, had focused almost exclusively on psychotherapeutic methods in preliterate cultures.

Interpretation of dreams. With the help of studies by Oppenheim (1956) and others, it has been possible to gather considerable information on this subject. Divination through dreams flourished especially in ancient Mesopotamia from the middle of the second millenium B.C. on, as evidenced by the Assyrian dream books and other documents preserved in cuneiform tablets. Three types of dreams can be differentiated: dreams that served as a vehicle for the revelation of a deity and that might or might not require interpretation, dreams that foretold future events, and dreams reflecting the state of mind of the dreamer, which was implied but never recorded.

Message or theological dreams. The message dream appeared within a conventional frame. Characteristically, the circumstances of the dream were reported with emphasis on the shocking experience undergone by the dreamer in the presence of the deity or of the hero, who was usually represented as standing near his head and giving him a message. The reports then emphasized his surprise at awakening, and mention was made of the fulfillment of the prediction or promise revealed in the dream. The message was expressed clearly or presented symbolically, as in two dreams of Joseph in the Old Testament, where symbolic dreams are reported solely by gentiles. In the case of a symbolic dream, the dreamer required the services of an interpreter capable of decoding it. The decoding had to be accomplished as quickly as possible, so that the dreamer might not suffer unnecessarily from the enigma of the dream and, if necessary, might undergo purifying—that is, cathartic rituals. Thus, the decoding of dreams served much the same purpose as the analysis of dreams does today. The difference lies in the fact that during that period dreams were always believed to refer to the future. In contrast, psychoanalysis has clearly established that dreams refer to the patient's past experiences.

Prophetic or mantic dreams. These dreams occurred in the context of a divination lore codified in extensive collections of highly formalized one-sentence units, called omens by the Assyriologists. Each omen consists of a protasis, in which the ominous feature or event is described, and an apodosis, which makes a prediction. Both observation and description are strikingly devoid of irrational attitudes, of a priori explanations, or of direct references to divine agents. It has been claimed that this characteristic represents a scientific attitude toward the divinatory aspect of dreams, in contrast to the folkloristic attitude, in which the focus is not on the predictions of dreams but on their acceptance as a psychological phenomenon. Basic to either attitude is the cultural context in which each occurs. In the Mesopotamian culture the essential reality of the dream was a communication for divine expressions; in the Old Testament culture this reality consisted of the acts of the deity and of the mediating role of the wise and pious man.

In the larger majority of omens, however, it is impossible to discover a rational relationship between omen content and prediction.

Subjective or evil dreams. Several coexisting causes of the dream can be found in each of the ancient cultures. Frequently appearing is the belief that the soul moves out of the body of the sleeping person and actually visits, in some mysterious way, the places and persons the dreamer sees in his sleep. At times, because of their disturbing contents, dreams are thought of as evil and as demonic phenomena. In this case the dreamer may have to undergo cathartic rites to rid himself of their influence. The subjective state of mind of the dreamer, as reflected by the impact of physiological functions—such as sex, thirst, hunger, and indigestion—on the dream experience, is seldom mentioned, for fear that a description of the content of unpleasant dreams would make the evil things they portray come true.

In the Greek culture the evaluation of the concept of dreams can be followed rather closely through literary, philosophical, and medical writings. Initially, dreams were thought of as real events. Subsequently, the dream was thought to be the creation of the gods, who used it as a mode of communicating with the dreamer. Still later, the dream was recognized as the product of the dreamer, and it was further recognized that the events portrayed therein might be interpreted in the light of their symbolic meaning, in the manner outlined by Hippocrates in *On Regimen*. In the Homeric poems, only men's dreams are described in the *Illiad* and only women's dreams in the *Odyssey*. Dreams were looked on as messages from the gods appearing in sleep when the soul is freed from its tomb (body) in accordance with the Orphic tradition. For Plato, the content of the dream was determined by the particular part of the psyche that was active—the instinctual, the rational, or the emotional. For Aristotle, the dream was the result of residual movements during sleep left over from the waking activities of the senses. Thus, the mental pictures were close to reality, like reflections in water. The Stoics thought that dreams offered an opportunity to become aware of the interrelation of all things—in particular, of the concatenation of causes and effects in the universe. In the Hippocratic writings the health of the dreamer was thought to be reflected in his dreams, as the soul could perceive the causes of illness in images—that is, by analogies—during sleep; bodily disorder was portrayed by wars, conflicts, and the like.

In the few surviving books on dreams written in the Hellenistic period, dreams were considered exclusively for their prophetic character. The most important surviving book is the one by the Roman Artemidorus Daldianus (1975) in the 2nd century. His book *Oneirocritica*, a scientific study of divination by dreams, enjoyed high popularity again in the 17th and 18th centuries. It was based on a thorough familiarity with the literature and on the personal knowledge of 3,000 dreams. For Artemidorus, there was always some point of similarity between the object or act of the dream and the event it foretold; moreover, all dreams were judged mainly in terms of future actual events and according to whether they turned out favorably or unfavorably. It was important to know the character and disposition or animal in a dream; the location in which the dream took place; and the proverbial expressions, common metaphors, references to mythical or historical stories, verbal quibbles, and the dual meanings of some words, literal and figurative, brought forth in the dream. Much less emphasis was put on the personality and circumstances of the dreamer, although it was accepted that the same dream could have entirely different meanings in two different persons. Typically, dream presages were good when they were fitting and appropriate to the dreamer, bad when they were not.

Today, on the basis of the psychoanalytic interpretation of dreams, the focus is put on Artemidorus's philosophy of the interpretation of dreams—mainly, the dream representing the presage of a happening about to become a reality or, the reverse, of a happening of a seemingly opposite realization. From the perspective of the cosmological philosophy of the Greeks, antithetic dreams, as in the twenty-fourth song of the *Odyssey*, were thought to inhabit a region outside the real cosmos—that is, the infernal regions of the dead, where the primordial powers of darkness prevail. That explanation can be translated easily into the contemporary notion of the content of the dream being related to unconscious factors and to the ambivalent attitude of the dreamer toward people and things in his environment.

Incubation techniques. Similarities have been found between the techniques of incubation (from the Latin *incubare*, to sleep in the holy room) used by the Greeks and those used in other cultures or, in later times, in the Western culture in shrines and other communal places of worship. Actually, most of the cults practiced by adherents of official Western religions fall into the category of Apollonian—that is, rational and harmonious—rather than of Dionysian—that is, ecstatic, orgiastic, and irrational—manifestations. That dichotomy was introduced by Nietzsche (1956) in *The Birth of Tragedy* in 1872. From today's perspective, Apollonian manifestations can be attributed to the realm of the conscious, Dionysian to the realm of the unconscious. In the Greek culture the cult of Apollo, the god of beauty and harmony, took place at the shrine of Delphi, where the priestess Pythia went into ecstasy and prophesied. According to Rollo May (1968), the function of the shrine was to bring to light unconsciously disturbing contents (often related to collective experiences) in the participants and to integrate them with individual processes of consciousness.

In essence, this phenomenon derives from the chthonic belief in the omnipotence of the souls of one's ancestors and from the concomitant homeopathic postulate that the gods who inflicted diseases could also cure them. The god Asclepias played a central role in this phenomenon. Originally a demon of Thessalian origin, Asclepias had undergone an interesting metamorphosis, from a mortal god in Homer to an underworld oracle-demon and then to an Apollonian god, whose healing role was similar in certain respects to that of Christ. Of the many Greek temples—probably about 420, all located in a natural environment of exquisite beauty—dedicated to Asclepias as setting for his divine manifestation (*epiphanias*), perhaps the most famous today is situated in Epidaurus, in the Peloponnesus (see Figure 3).

Typically, the phenomenon of incubation, as described by Pausanias (1913) in the 2nd century, consisted of several stages: Postulants, who were afflicted with a variety of physical and psychic diseases, were first subjected to ritual purification, special diet, and fumigations with various sleep-inducing drugs. They then went to sleep in the abaton of the temple—namely, in underground corridors constructed to form a maze in which music was played. While the patient slept, Asclepias appeared in his dreams as a man or a child or as a snake or a dog; he then touched the sick part of each patient's body, after which he disappeared. The patient awoke healed and had his dream decoded by an interpreter. The patient's dream and his subsequent recovery were regarded as a reward for his devotion to the god Asclepias, to whom he would then make further votive offerings, as in Plato's *Phaedo*.

Important clues to the rituals practiced in the healing temples of ancient Greece are offered by the inscribed tablets or steles, a group of which were found in 1883 in the remains of the

FIGURE 3. Asclepian of Epidaurus in its present status. The labyrinthine structure of the *tholos*, where mental patients had to walk and to sleep in order to be able to reach the center. In the course of that highly symbolic process, they were "healed" by the god while dreaming. (From Kereny, C. *Asklepios: Archetypal Image of the Physician's Existence,* p. 44. Pantheon Books, New York, 1959.) (With permission, Bildarchio Foto Marburg, Marburg, West Germany.)

FIGURE 4. Asclepias healing. Bas-relief in the Athens Museum.

Asclepian temple at Epidaurus (see Figure 4). The following is an example of the healing procedure.

A man whose fingers, with the exception of one, were paralyzed came as a suppliant to the god. While looking at the tablets in the temple, he expressed incredulity regarding the cures and scoffed at the incriptions. But in his sleep he saw a vision. It seemed to him that he was playing at dice below the temple and was about to cast the dice [when] the god appeared, sprang upon his hand, and stretched out his [the patient's] fingers. When the god had stepped aside, it seemed to the patient that he could bend his hand, and [he] stretched out all his fingers one by one. When he had straightened them all, the god asked him if he could still be incredulous of the inscriptions on the tablets in the temple. He answered that he would not, [and the god said to him:] "Since, then, formerly you did not believe in the cures, though

they were not incredible, for the future your name shall be 'Incredulous.'" When day dawned, he walked out sound.

It is likely that the above was a case of hysterical paralysis and that the suggestive power of the dream and of the environment had a healing effect. Other cases, however, were not so simple. It is known, for instance, that the rhetorician Aelius Aristides (Philostratus, 1952)—author of the *Sacred Discourses,* the only known pre-Christian religious autobiography—afflicted with a severe form of asthma and other psychosomatic disorders, remained at the shrine of Asclepias in Pergamum for more than 10 years in the 2nd century, taking part in group discussions and other activities with the participants, until he regained complete health.

Jungian psychiatrist Meier (1967) elaborated an interpretation of the phenomenon of incubation in the light of modern dynamic psychiatry, emphasizing the symbolism of various aspects of the ritual. The spring connected with the place of altar or of sacrifice (*tholos*) was seen to have a therapeutic significance. The purifying process undergone by the postulant and his unusual experience underground were equated with disintegration and reintegration. The fact that the experience, the dream, occurred during an altered state of consciousness under the effect of music in the darkness of the night might be compared to the ego regression that is a prerequisite for free association. And just as psychoanalytic theory postulates that the goal of treatment is to make the patient conscious of the unconscious, the phenomenon of incubation equated cure with the patient's acceptance and understanding of the unconscious meaning of his disease.

Today, with the emphasis on community mental health, many analogies can be drawn between those ancient therapeutic techniques and modern group psychotherapeutic approaches based on charismatic leadership, group interaction, collective suggestion, and societal expectations.

Therapy with words. From what has been said thus far in regard to therapy for mental illness in antiquity, it is clear that, in all cultures, verbal expressions in various forms accompanied practically all kinds of therapeutic interventions.

Etymologically, the word *psyche* meant to breathe, and breathing was the expression of life. But in human beings, breathing also makes it possible to pronounce words; thus, the concept of human life is intrinsically united to that of the word, a notion that would later be carried to the extreme in the Christian *logos*. That connection between life and words helps one understand the pervasiveness of the power of words in all forms of therapy. Of course, the role played by verbal expressions and the value of that role varied according to different historical periods, concepts of humans, and philosophies of health and disease in the Greek culture.

In the Homeric poems one finds three forms of utterances used for the occurrence of illness: the prayer (*euche*), the magic charm (*epaoidé*), and the suggestive or cheering speech (*terpnos logos*). Only in post-Homeric times, however, did many become aware of the power of the word. That awareness coincided with the belief that life is governed by rational and logical principles that can be discovered and followed. The famous motto "Know yourself" (*Gnoti sauton*) inscribed on the door of the Delphic temple was echoed by Heraclitus, who said, "I have explored myself."

Plato's emphasis on the need for harmony between body, psyche, and soul is reflected in the Socratic dialogues, which can be viewed as a long journey toward the achievement of *sophrosine*—that is, moderation and self-control necessary for good behavior. Typically, Charmides agreed to continue to investigate with Socrates the way to attain *sophrosine* and to be "questioned every day until you [Socrates] say, it was enough." Plato was quite impressed by the power of the suggestive word (*epode*) expressed through "beautiful speech" (*logos kalós*) and leading to a harmonious and rightful ordering of all the ingredients of the psychic life: beliefs, feelings, impulses, knowledge, thoughts, and value judgments. Therefore, it was not the words alone that had a therapeutic effect; rather, they represented an a priori condition for the best and greatest efficacy of medicaments. When Charmides asked for a reliable drug for his headache, Socrates knew that the drug itself would not be effective without an accompanying *epode*— kind words.

Less impressed with the power of words were the Hippocratic physicians, who unwisely preferred not to take up the legacy from Plato. They believed only in a restricted use of words to win the confidence of the patient while using drugs and physical means of treating him.

Aristotle devoted his treatise *Rhetoric* entirely to the role of the persuasive word and to the techniques for its use, thus offering the first characterological thesis for the study of emotions, moral qualities, virtues, and vices, a trend that continued in rhetorical literature up to modern times. Anticipating a basic tenet of today's psychotherapy, Aristotle (1926) stated in the same treatise,

> the most effective means of persuasion is the speaker's character itself.

Moreover, words are most efficacious when they are pronounced by a man of prestige; and the prestige of the speaker is based on his internal qualities (talent for pathetic eloquence), his moral qualities (integrity, prudence), and his skills (mastery of the matter in question and of the art of speaking). In *Poetics* Aristotle called catharsis the purgation that certain words, especially those of the tragic poems, can produce in the whole reality of the human being. He described three distinct types of logos: dialectical or convincing; rhetorical or persuasive, related to verbal psychotherapy; and purgative or cathartic, related to medicine.

Among Aristotle's followers, some continued the trend initiated by him. For instance, the physician Diocles (Jaeger, 1938) of Carystus, as reported in Fragment 92:

> considered friendly solace as a charm [*epaoide*]. For it stops the flow of blood when the "pneuma" of the wounded man is attentive [that is, when the attention of the mind of the wounded man is great] and remains as if bound to the one who is speaking to him,

a beautiful example, indeed, of the psychotherapeutic relationship. Theophrastos (1970) (372–287 B.C.), physician and head of the peripatetic school, is most often remembered for his work *The Character Sketches,* in which he described, in 30 sketches, personality traits and moral types in a lively style. Translated into French by Jean de la Bruyére in 1687, the book enjoyed considerable renown in the moralistic literature that preceded the advent of modern psychology.

At the time of the Sophists, the power of words was recognized as a technique. As Socrates put it in *Theatetus,*

> The physician obtains changes he wishes through drugs, the Sophists, instead, through the word.

According to Plutarch, the Sophist Antiphon had a doorplate on his house in Corinth indicating that he was qualified to heal by words those who suffered from grief and melancholy— possibly the first direct antecedent of today's psychotherapist in the Western culture. In the post-Socratic period, scepticism and hedonism came to prevail in the schools of Epicureans, Sceptics, and Stoics. Regardless of their different orientation toward human behavior and ethics, they were all united in their claim that without philosophy there could be no goodness. The persuasive and suggestive power of the word previously used by wise and enlightened men degenerated into easily dispensed wisdom by "obscure coiners of phrases," as Cicero (1950) put it in *Tusculanae*. As a matter of fact, Cicero himself anticipated modern psychotherapeutic notions by stating that the patient has to be ready to suffer to be cured—that is, anxiety is a necessary condition for the success of psychotherapy.

Lain Entralgo (1970) concluded his book on the therapeutic influence of the word in the classical world with the following statement:

> The bond that the Greeks saw between the action of the word and the curing of illness was threefold. The good order of the soul always has beneficial physical consequences, both in the state of health as well as in the state of illness. Moreover, that good psychic order would be a necessary condition to make best and most effective the curative action of drugs, diet, and surgery. And in the case of Aristotelian verbal catharsis the action of the word is so intense that it operates as though the speech itself were an actual medicament.

Psychiatry in the Middle Ages

The era spoken of as the Middle Ages seems to present many uncertainties. There is no agreement even on the dates of that historical period. Many medical historians say that it begins with the death of Galen (ca. 200 A.D.) and terminates with the date of publication of the work of Vesalius (*De Corporis Humani Fabrica*, 1543). Traditionally, the Middle Ages has been looked on as a period of stagnation or even retrogression, during which medicine was almost entirely under the sway of humoral pathology, demonology, astrology, witchcraft, and sorcery. Today, with the increased knowledge of that period and the decline of some unrealistic expectations of science, many expressions of the Middle Ages are seen in a more positive way. Writing more than 5 decades ago, the historian of science George Sarton (1927) stated that charity was the main focus of that period, at the expense of science, and he criticized the antithetical attitude taken by medieval persons. Crombie (1959), another historian of science, indicated, instead, that an activist attitude toward technical progress and the confluence of the empiricism of technique with the rationalism of philosophy and mathematics and with the Aristotelian tradition resulted in

> a new conscious empirical science seeking to discover the rational structure of nature.

Likewise, the situation is neither clear nor unanimous in regard to psychiatry. Two points, however, are generally accepted: the remarkable stability of views in clinical psychiatry, which presented only minor changes from the times of later Hellenism on, and the persistence of neglect and the use of cruel methods in handling the mentally ill.

ST. AUGUSTINE

One gigantic figure, St. Augustine (354–430), stands out in the time between classical antiquity and the Middle Ages; since his influence spans a number of centuries, he is rightly considered as belonging to the Middle Ages. A philosopher and a theologian, St. Augustine was not interested in psychology proper and even less in mental disorders. Yet it has been pointed out that some of his observations represent the anticipation of many current concepts. From the psychodynamic perspective, it is understandable that he may have gained a good deal of insight into his own psychology through his painstaking self-analysis, as revealed in his *Confessions* (1953), a highly moving and appealing document. Possibly his own emotional difficulties—mainly his strong attachment to his mother, Monica, his unconscious admiration for his father, and the struggle to curb his strong sexual urge—may have contributed to his passion for introspection.

The theme of his religious conversion has been the object of

psychological investigation by many. Also relevant to psychology has been his analysis of time; since neither the past nor the future exist experientially, only the present exists as inner experience—that is, in a psychological sense. Likewise, in regard to memory, he pointed to the evidence of unconscious, preconscious, and associative processes. Strongly influenced by the Platonic dichotomy of body and soul, he subscribed to the widely accepted division of the mind into the three faculties of reason, memory, and will. He accepted Cicero's description of four main passions or perturbations—namely, desire (libido), fear, joy, and sorrow—which could be moderated by reason. However, he pointed out that, if the soul is not intent—that is, if there is insufficient motivation—the effect of external agents, however powerful, remain unnoticed. That statement, which gives preeminence to the will, represents the essence of the voluntaristic Augustinian philosophy.

Recently, it has been noted (Block, 1966) that his observations in many areas—on educational methods, on the nature of children, on the joy of being with friends, on the sense of power one derives from doing what is forbidden—reveal great psychological insight. Even more cogent for psychiatry are his notions of child psychology.

The following is a pertinent passage, as it occurs in the first book of St. Augustine's (1953) *Confessions*.

> At that time, I knew only to suckle and to be satisfied with enjoyable things and to cry at injuries to my flesh—nothing more. Later, I began to smile: first, while sleeping; then, while waking .... Then, gradually, I became aware of where I was and began to desire to make known my wishes to those who might take care of them. But I could not, because these wishes were inside and those people outside. These latter were not endowed with any sense whereby they may enter into my soul. So I began to toss about my limbs and my cries, as signs indicating my wishes, doing the few things that I could, as well as I could, for they were not like the truth. When I was not heeded, either because not understood or because of a harmful request, I became indignant at the fact that my elders did not obey and, independent, would not serve me. So, I got even with them by crying.

Here, in a few lines, are anticipated the notions that the neonate cannot differentiate between the self and the nonself; that the smiling response is the earliest expression of the stage of object recognition, later followed by the expression of omnipotent fantasies; and that aggression has to be accepted as a basic ingredient of the human condition. In another passage of Freudian flavor, the myth of the innocence of babies is openly dispelled:

> The weakness of infant limbs is innocent, but not the minds of infants. I myself have seen and have had experience with a jealous child: he could not speak, but, growing pale, would stare with a bitter look at his foster brother. Who does not know this?

A similarity has also been found between Augustine's self-observation of his grief reaction after his mother's death and Freud's classical description of mourning and melancholia in 1917. Unfortunately, in the light of his religious orientation, the psychological implications of his introspective findings were not recognized by him or by his followers. When St. Augustine died, the Vandals were at the doors of his city of Hippo.

PSYCHOPATHOLOGICAL CONCEPTS

In regard to the causes of mental disorders and the humoral doctrine of the black bile, increasing attention was given to the notion of localizing imagination in the forebrain, understanding in the midventricles of the brain, and memory in the back part of the brain (see Figure 5); in a way, that triadic function of the brain can be viewed as an anatomical version of Plato's triadic division of the soul. Initially advanced by the physician Posidonius (Edelstein, 1936) in the 4th century and supported by the anatomical research of Herophilus and Erasistratus (Souques, 1936), that notion had considerable appeal throughout the Middle Ages, probably because it was consonant with Platonic and Christian views regarding the subdivision of the soul. Melancholia was then attributed not to noxious humors but to damaged faculties of the mind.

Morcover, considerable difficulty surrounded the traditional pathogenic view of the black bile. In the famous passage in *Problems*, Aristotle (1927) praised the highly gifted melancholic. Was the melancholic humor, then, a positive or a negative factor in the psychic economy of the person? Klibansky et al. (1964), who dealt with the issue extensively, stated that Aristotle's point was forgotten during the first 12 centuries of Christianity and that it was only picked up again in the 13th century by Albert the Great.

Regardless of that question, throughout the early Middle Ages many attempts were made to view the humoral doctrine from a Christian perspective. In the 4th century the religious

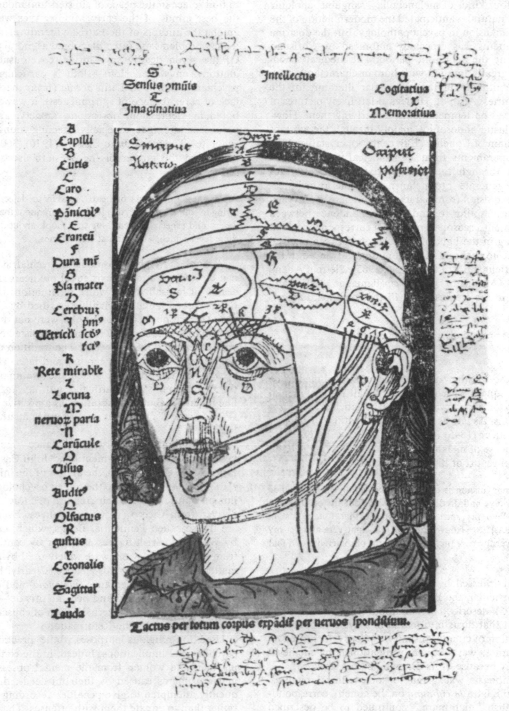

FIGURE 5. The functions of the brain. (From Magnus Hundt the Elder. *Anthropologium de Hominis Dignitate Natura et Proprietatibus.* Manacensis, Leipzig, 1501.)

preacher John Chrysostom considered melancholia as a trial that could be made tolerable by reason. Later on, the physician and abbess St. Hildegard of Bingen (ca. 1098–1179), by attributing the origin of black bile to the fall of Adam, transformed an individual disorder into a calamity of all mankind. Still later, the theologian William of Auvergne (ca. 1180–1249) praised the melancholic disposition as leading to withdrawal from pleasure and, thus, to asceticism.

Another concept relevant to psychopathology that came to the fore during the Middle Ages was the doctrine of temperaments. Even non-Christians followed that doctrine. For instance, the Persian-born physician Avicenna (1930) (980–1037), by considering four kinds of melancholia—sanguine, choleric, phlegmatic, and natural—anticipated the modern notion of the constitutional dimension in psychopathology. But the doctrine of the temperaments was especially embraced by Christian philosophy during the Scholastic period. The medical school of Salerno was greatly imbued with human characterology, a tradition that continued in the vernacular literature of the succeeding centuries. Also, St. Hildegard left lively pictures of sexual types based on temperaments, underlying them. However, only Scholastic philosophy, mainly through the work of the scholar William of Conches (12th century), crystallized the doctrine of temperaments from a theological perspective: A person, created through the proper mixture—that is, sanguine—could degenerate into melancholic, choleric, or phlegmatic after his expulsion from paradise. From here, it was only a step toward attempting to find a correspondence between humors and elements, seasons, and ages, a correspondence that acquires meaning in the light of the relation between medical thought and astrological and magical notions advanced in the Middle Ages (Michael Scot (Thorndike, 1965), Pietro d'Abano (Tanfani, 1934), Arnold of Villanova (Paniague, 1963)) and greatly stressed in the Renaissance (Ficino, Agrippa, Paracelsus).

CLINICAL CONCEPTS AND THERAPEUTIC PRACTICES

Throughout the Middle Ages, melancholia continued to be the term most frequently used in describing all kinds of mental disorders, many of which would today be labeled as schizophrenic symptoms. As late as the mid-14th century, in *Book of the Duchess* Chaucer (1845) (ca. 1340–1400) gave an excellent description of a case of melancholia, considered by some as an autobiographical report of his own depression:

For sorwful ymagynacion is always hoolly [wholly] in my mynde . . . . This melancholye and drede I have for dye, defaute of slepe and hevynesse hath sleyn my spirit of quycknesse that I have lost al lustihede [happiness] . . . . I have suffered this eight yere and yet my boote [cure] is never the nere [nearer]: for ther is phisicien but oon that may me hele.

Others were impressed by the cyclic occurrence of mental disorders. In particular, the Byzantine physician Alexander of Tralles (525–605) described a condition that is not simply melancholia but that turns into mania in a cycle—apparently the first description of circular insanity. Epilepsy, identified by a variety of names, was frequently mentioned by medieval writers, probably because of its dramatic manifestations.

Particular emphasis was given to some clinical pictures. Incubus (from the latin *in cubitum*, on the couch), corresponding to the English "nightmare," continued to be described through the Renaissance. It was attributed to various causes but most often to a male demon attacking chaste girls, as opposed to the succubus—that is, a female demon molesting men. Also related to sexuality was the picture of effeminacy or pathic disorder in a man, attributed by Avicenna to a degraded mind, a vicious nature, and bad habits. Lycanthropy, a species of melancholy in which the patient wanders about at night—in sepulchers, woods, and elsewhere—imitating wolves and wild animals, was also mentioned by some.

As with etiological concepts of the humors, clinical concepts became overshadowed by moral and religious considerations, to the extent that it is difficult today to obtain a clear picture of them. That is particularly the case with many who, disillusioned by the social and cultural conditions of the time, tried to find solace in the peace of cloisters and monasteries. Indeed, the best minds of the early Middle Ages were to be found among the authors of the Patristic literature, in which psychological problems are often diagnosed as moral and theological. Of the seven deadly sins—pride, covetousness, lust, anger, gluttony, envy, and sloth—sloth is particularly relevant for psychiatry. Called in Latin *acedia* (from the Greek *akedia*—lack of care, absence of spiritual zest), it was characterized by boredom, depression, obsessions, anxiety, and a variety of psychosomatic signs, especially affecting young anchorites and cenobites. The monk John Cassian (1936) (360–435), generally considered the master of the Western ascetic tradition, described it as

weariness or distress of heart . . . akin to dejection . . . especially trying to solitaries, and a dangerous and frequent foe to dwellers in the desert; and especially disturbing to a monk about the sixth hour, like some fever which seizes him at stated times.

Perhaps more than to modern psychiatric diseases, *acedia* can be compared to the existential predicament of a person in search of himself, made worse in situations of isolation from others. Erotic fantasies, vividly described by Cassian in regard to the sexual obsessions of monks, were not thought by him to be important for *acedia*. Treatment consisted of prayer, mixing with others, and manual work. The tradition of *acedia* continued throughout the 13th century and later. Dante placed the *accidiosi* in the fifth circle of hell, the swamp of Styx. Petrarch, the first humanist, was afflicted with *acedia*. He regarded it, like the melancholic constitution, as a positive condition—that is, as a state of mind that was essential for the contemplative life.

A rich literature on pastoral guidance—mainly by St. Ambrose, St. Jerome, above-mentioned John Cassian (1936), and Gregory the Great (1955), the author of the influential *Book of Pastoral Rule*—pointed to their keen psychological insight into human nature and to their free use of Stoic concepts, mainly derived from Cicero (1950) and Seneca. Even more relevant are the so-called Penitential Books, which, originally written by Welsh and Irish monks and later by continental imitators from the 6th century on, were widely used by parish priests on matters of confession and penance. Clearly, by that time the practice of public repentance (*metanoia*) and confession (*exomologesis*) had changed and become private—almost a beginning of that process of internalization of conscience that would be accomplished by the Reformation.

Used for religious purposes, those practices had definite psychological implications. Indeed, in the concern for delivering men and women from the mental obsessions and social maladjustments caused by their misdeeds, the confessor frequently attempted to give penalties according to personalities, rather than to equate them with offenses. The physician of the soul, like the modern psychiatrist, was inclined to identify himself with the penitent; and the penitentials offered to the sinners the means of rehabilitation and of character reconstruction in a climate free from social censure.

Thus, the personalistic aspect ultimately concerned with salvation and the social aspect aimed at community action may be viewed as the two opposed yet complementary poles of Christianity, alternately emphasized at various historical times. The development of the early Church in the Eastern Mediterranean area offers an interesting example of that interplay.

It was there, in fact, that monachism had its beginning, approximately in the 4th century, by a few men eager to abandon civilization and, perhaps, disillusioned by the decline of values. In pursuing the ideals of ascetic life, based on a devaluation of earthly needs for the attainment of spiritual goals, they underwent a ritual that has been related to the incubation process and to the Far Eastern techniques of meditation. They experienced all kinds of subjective phenomena, such as hallucinations, that, when stripped of their religious and highly symbolic meaning, have definite relevance for psychopathology, especially in the light of sensory deprivation.

Regardless of all that, it is the social and cultural aspects of monastic life that are of main interest here. Although monachism flourished especially in the Oriental empire of Byzantium until the 15th century, even in the West it managed to create a vast network of services for the poor, sick, neglected, crippled, and elderly. Patients ailing from all sorts of diseases, including mental diseases, were often cared for in charitable centers supported by various religious orders, such as Cluny in France, St. Gallen in Switzerland, Fulda in Germany, Bobbio and Montecassino in Italy, and Montserrat in Spain.

In regard to treatment, bloodletting and purgatives continued to prevail throughout the Middle Ages. Skull trepanation was apparently practiced in cases of epilepsy and dementia (see Figure 6). According to Roger of Salerno (12th century), the skull should be perforated so that the noxious matter might escape to the exterior. For the Catalan Arnaldus de Villanova (ca. 1235–1315) (Paniagua, 1963), the skin should be incised in the fashion of a cross, perhaps another example of combining medical and theological ideas.

Not all the treatment was so cruel, however. Anticipating a method used in the 18th century, the Byzantine physician Paulus of Aegina (7th century) advised that the mentally ill be swung in a wicker basket bed suspended from the ceiling. Bartholomeus Salernitanus (12th century) prescribed silence and solitary confinement for the mentally ill; quite to the contrary, Bernard of Gordon (13th century) recommended a bright and light facility filled with fragrant odors and located in a pleasant and cheerful surroundings (Whitwell, 1936). The Arabian Rhazes was in favor of frequent sexual intercourse and the moderate use of alcohol.

ARAB CONTRIBUTIONS TO PSYCHIATRY

For many centuries, under the influence of the Judeo-Christian tradition, the contribution of the Arabs to civilization has been overlooked. Such a disregard may have been particularly evident in the field of psychology because the domain of the mind is indissolubly linked to religion. The Moslem religion was, until recently, taboo in Western nations, perhaps also as a reaction against the impetuous stance of its founder, the Prophet Mohammed, in the early 7th century.

The Mohammedan era, which began in 622, was strongly influenced by the Koran (Schipperges, 1961 a, b), the holy book that was to serve as a guide for the conduct of life. A number of its topics, drawn from past events and experiences, deal with psychological matters related to individual, family,

and social occurrences. Even after the victory by Charles Martel (Charlemagne's grandfather) at Tours near Poitiers in 732, the Arab domain, ranging from Spain to Persia, continued to grow in cultural and religious unity.

The Arabs created a splendid civilization in Spain, with many learning centers, where Greek, Latin, and Judaic literature could be translated and thus become available to Western civilization. Of the four most important Arab medical writers, Rhazes (865–925) and Avicenna (980–1037) came from Persia, and Avenzoar (ca. 1090–1162) and Averroes (1126–1198) came from Spain. Rhazes (Schipperges, 1961b), from Baghdad, considered the Arabian Galen, wrote many books, including a comprehensive guide to physiognomy and a treatise on dreams (Hoffmeister, 1969). Avicenna (1930) became universally known as the author of the *Canon of Medicine*, an attempt to coordinate systematically the medical doctrines of Hippocrates and Galen with the biological concepts of Aristotle. In it, mention was made of balanced emotions between excess and deficiency as proof of normal temperament, and an effort to be pleasant to patients and to avoid anything that is harmful to them was advocated.

Traditionally, it was believed that the Arabs lacked originality because their approach to mental diseases was largely influenced by Greek medical science, by the tenets of Christianity, and by the enlightened Byzantine administration. After they came in contact, in the 6th and 7th centuries, with the scientists in Alexandria and with the medical schools established by heterodox Nestorians and pagan philosophers in Syria and Persia, Arabs translated into Arabic many Greek classic texts and, in turn, established flourishing medical schools. Furthermore, a number of asylums were founded in Baghdad in the 8th century, in Damascus in the 9th century, and in Aleppo, Kalaoma, Cairo, and Fez in the 13th century. As early as the 12th century, travelers returning to Europe reported on the enlightened treatment mental patients received in those institutions. In his description of the psychiatric hospital built by the sultan Bajazet II in Adrianopolis in approximately 1500 A.D., the historian Evilija (Staehelin, 1957) described in detail the relaxed atmosphere of that establishment, surrounded by charming fountains and gardens, and the therapeutic regimen, which included special diets, baths, drugs, perfumes, and concerts at which the instruments were tuned in a special way, so they would not jar the patients' nerves. An outpatient clinic and a medical school, where teaching was conducted in the Greek tradition, were attached to each hospital. The same treatment facilities were available to rich and poor patients alike, the majority of whom appear to have been manic-depressive psychotics.

At the root of that humanitarian attitude was the Moslem belief, stated by the Prophet, that the insane person is loved by God and is particularly chosen by Him to tell the truth. Therefore, the difference between insanity and possession was thought to be minimal, and the mentally ill were frequently worshiped as saints. From a modern viewpoint, it seems that the attitude might facilitate the patient's recovery, since it permitted the free expression of his sexual and aggressive instincts. In any event, although the Arab approach to mental illness was influenced by Greek and Christian tenets and, in fact, was based on the mystical and superstitious tendencies of the Eastern Mediterranean countries, its application of those concepts was original and unique.

SCHOOL OF SALERNO

It is not surprising that, in such a climate of liberal inter-

FIGURE 6. Cutting for stone in head. By Hieronymus (Jerome) Bosch (1450–1516). Prado Museum, Madrid.

change of ideas, many scholars found it easier to accept an eclectic viewpoint. Among those scholars was Constantinus Africanus (ca. 1020–1087), who is recognized as the founder of the medical school of Salerno, near Naples, which enjoyed great renown in the late Middle Ages.

Like the treatises by his contemporaries and disciples, Africanus's *De Melancholia* (Constantino Africano, 1959) was based on the amalgamation of classic and Arab influences. Typically, an excess of bile, which was attributed to an imbalance of the systems of the body, could cause melancholia. And, as was true in the past, the recommended treatment included proper diet, kind and sensible words, music, baths, cathartics, rest, physical exercise, and sexual gratification. However, Africanus's concept of two forms of melancholia was more indicative of his originality. According to that hypothesis, which became a basic formulation in 18th- and 19th-century literature, the site of the first form of melancholia was the brain; the site of the second was the stomach (hypochondriasis). He then proceeded to describe for the first time the symptoms that characterized this syndrome—sadness (due to loss of the loved object), fear (of the unknown), withdrawal (staring into space), delusions surrounding siblings and parents (which today would be attributed to ambivalence), and intense fear and guilt in religious people. Africanus also advanced certain hypotheses regarding prognosis that are generally accepted today—for example, the prognosis was more favorable in acute reactive conditions and when the patient had not reached an extreme state of withdrawal.

EARLY RENAISSANCE OF THE 13TH CENTURY

The 13th century has been considered an early Renaissance, primarily because it brought about a more proper and realistic understanding of human nature, as typified by the poetry of Dante and the art of Giotto, and because of concepts formulated during that period that preannounced the foundation of modern science. All the psychological theories of that period were greatly influenced by the Arab-imported Aristotelian writings, which stressed the body-mind unity and, thus, the biological foundation of psychology. In the preceding century, the famous Spanish-born Jewish physician Moses Maimonides (1135–1204), who was influenced by biblical and Talmudic teaching in Egypt, had outlined a way of rational religion based on sound psychological principles in *The Guide for the Perplexed*. Petrus Hispanus (1200–1277) (Schipperges, 1961a), who in 1276 became Pope John XXI and who was the only "psychologist" to achieve that honor, viewed psychology as the *pars nobilissima* of nature and maintained that the study of such phenomena belonged to the realm of the natural sciences, rather than to philosophy. Concomitantly, the *physicus*, whose efforts centered on the functioning of the psyche, was defined as a specialist in the fields of psychology and psychiatry. Passions, which Hispanus classified in accordance with Cicero's scheme, must be considered in a relation to both psyche and soma. And within that framework, psychic disturbance was the result of multiple causative factors. Thus, Hispanus foresaw, with remarkable accuracy, modern views of psychosomatic medicine.

Pietro d'Abano (Tanfani, 1934) (ca. 1250–1316)—the Averroistic philosopher who taught medicine, physiology, and astrology in Padua—anticipated some concepts of modern psychotherapy in *Conciliator Differentiarum*, which was published posthumously in 1476. For example, in discussing enchantment (*praecantatio*), he maintained that suggestion played a crucial role in the treatment of diseases. That technique might be particularly effective for those patients who were vulnerable to the physician's influence, provided he had the proper personality—kind yet authoritative. In addition, in the tradition of Albert the Great and other thinkers of medieval times, Pietro d'Abano attempted to evolve a scientific explanation of dreams by relating dream content to the personality of individual patients and to their moral characteristics.

Outstanding among the thinkers of the 13th century were Albert the Great (1193–1280) and Thomas Aquinas (1225–1274), who have had considerable impact up to the present day through the teaching of scholastic philosophy. Thomas, of course, is the universally known author of the *Summa against the Pagans* and of the *Summa Theologica* and many other works, among which is his commentary on Aristotle's *De Anima* (on Soul). Aside from Aristotle's teaching, both were influenced by the views of Hippocrates, Galen, and the Arabs, according to whom the body, conceived of in terms of the four classic elements, influenced all psychic phenomena, and the soul was the form of the body.

Psychic apparatus. The structure of the psyche was conceived of as comprising three levels—anima vegetativa, anima sensitiva, and anima intellectiva—a concept that anticipated Jackson's theory of integration.

The anima vegetativa referred to physiological functions.

The anima sensitiva was concerned with (1) the external and the internal senses, including common sense (the inner center of the external senses), imagination or fantasy, memory, and the cognitive aspect of instinct, all of which originated in the brain; and (2) the appetitus sensitivus, which represented movement—that is, the dynamic forces of the psyche, which lay somewhere between somatic and spiritual forces, which included lustful and irascible tendencies, and which, in a broad sense, corresponded to the sexual and aggressive instincts of today's psychology. Those tendencies, which were located in the heart, were the source of all passions.

The anima intellectiva alluded to those qualities in the senses that made possible the cognitive functions of ratio—that is, judgment and intelligence—which derived their impetus from the appetitus intellectivus or will.

Theory of psychopathology. Central to the theory of psychopathology postulated by Albert the Great and Thomas Aquinas was the notion that the soul could not become sick. Therefore, insanity was primarily a somatic disturbance. Ultimately, mental disturbance was attributed to the deficient use of reason, which was due to one of two factors: Either passions were so intense that they interfered with proper reasoning, or reason could not prevail because of the peculiar functioning of the physical apparatus—in dream states or states of intoxication, for example. Even the pathological character traits described by Albert—such traits as timidity, arrogance, resentment, and impulsiveness—were attributed to somatic factors.

That theory has prompted some psychiatric historians to consider Thomas Aquinas the precursor of the so-called organicistic school of psychiatry that became prevalent during the second part of the 19th century in Germany. The Thomistic influence on cultural life, including medicine, in countries of the Latin tradition may explain the adherence of the psychiatric schools there to an organicistic frame of reference until recently.

Both Albert and Thomas Aquinas described various psychotic symptoms, such as hallucinations, and different types of mental patients; those descriptions, although highly intuitive, show a lack of clinical experience. In addition to melancholia, which he attributed to altered body humors, Thomas Aquinas described mania (pathological anger), organic psychosis (loss of memory), and epilepsy, which he attributed to an increased formation of vapors in the brain. His further elaboration of *stultitia, hebetudo,* and *ignorantia* correspond, respectively, to current concepts of the psychopathic personality, mental deficiency, and social retardation.

Although mental patients (*amentes*) might have lucid intervals, they were, from a legal viewpoint, incapable of distinguishing right from wrong; therefore, they could not be held responsible for any crimes they committed. Sleep and baths were recommended treatment procedures. However, neither Albert the Great nor Thomas Aquinas was immune to the beliefs held by other thinkers of medieval times, according to which both the cause and the treatment of mental illness depended largely on astrological influences on the psyche and on the evil power of demons.

POPULAR ATTITUDES TOWARD MENTAL DISORDER

That even the greatest men of the time were not immune from superstitious beliefs should not be a surprise. The medieval psychopathological concept and therapeutic methods were relevant to only a small group of the intellectual elite of the time, who were active mainly in cloisters and monasteries, where much of the classical heritage continued to be cherished and preserved.

The ignorant population, which represented the great majority, were influenced by all sorts of mystic and occult beliefs, mainly of Eastern origin. In fact, there is evidence that, even after the Christianization of the Northern countries, magical practices, which were carried over from the earliest Indo-European cultures to the Anglo-Saxon cultures, continued unin-

terrupted. There are written records by Bede and other historians of charms and of ceremonies involving idolatry, the worship of demons, the cult of the dead, the worship of trees and stones and fire, augury, and divination. "Devil" often meant pagan deity, rather than spirit of evil. Contests between saints and pagan magicians were reported; in many instances, Christian and pagan festivals coincided, and the cult of the pagan god was often replaced by that of the local saint.

Possession of the mind of the mentally ill by an evil spirit, with or without the will of the subject, resulting in all sorts of verbal manifestations and abnormal behavior, came to be accepted as a common cause of mental disorders. Following the example of Christ, who in several passages of the New Testament is reported to have ordered the evil spirits to leave the possessed, the exorcising of persons allegedly possessed by harmful intruders became a frequent practice in the Middle Ages. The rich iconography on the subject is further evidence of the wide belief in that form of treatment for the mentally ill (see Figure 7).

At the base of those superstitious concepts was a static and theocentric notion of the architecture of the world, quite alien to today's preoccupation with scientific improvement and progress. Feudalism itself, with its fundamental antithesis of empire

FIGURE 7. St. Catherine exorcising a possessed woman. By Girolamo di Benvenuto (1470–1524) of Siena. Denver Art Museum. Samuel H. Kres Collection.

versus papacy, was a concrete representation of the order that reigned supreme in the world, an order that was reflected in all sorts of monastic, religious, penitential, and knighthood orders.

From that perspective, insanity was alienation. But alienation had two opposite meanings—on the one side, failure to love God and refusal to adhere to the order he had given; on the other side, lack of involvement in the world for the purpose of being rewarded in the other world. In either case—estrangement from God or estrangement from the world—the image of a human was that of a wayfarer. Madmen, left wandering on their own, were a testimony of the greatness of God and of the frailty of humans. Probably they were not mistreated or neglected but simply viewed as a necessary, although at times annoying, part of the community.

There is plenty of evidence that, regardless of the beautiful order of the theological systems of Dante and St. Thomas—in which a place was given to alienation, too—the medieval culture allowed for expressions of disorder, as in the case of insanity. Many may have found relief from their overwhelming aggressive and sexual impulses through participation in religious wars and crusades and in long pilgrimages; others preferred to embrace emotionally charged heretic movements. Typical manifestations of disorder available to large portions of the population were religious dances, up to the famous dance epidemics of the 14th century (see Figure 8); seasonal festivals, such as carnival and the so-called feast of fools; and other rituals in which release was given to pent-up impulses and to fear of insanity. In a few instances the record of the emotional disorder of some heroes—notably Lancelot and Tristan—has been reported in the context of the ideals of chivalry in the French medieval literature.

Psychiatry in the Renaissance

IMAGE OF THE FOOL

The strict order of the late Middle Ages contained in itself the germs of disintegration. In literature, philosophy, and the visual arts, people were slowly becoming conscious of themselves and were developing a different view of the world—as a setting for existence, rather than for a return to God. Although the rise of humanism in Italy in the 15th century and later throughout the rest of Europe is no longer considered an antireligious expression, which was the interpretation attached to those events in historical accounts of the 19th century, the fact remains that a person's awareness of himself as an individ-

FIGURE 8. Dance epidemics of 1564. Pen drawing by Pieter Brueghel the Elder (ca. 1525–1569). Albertina Collection of Vienna.

ual being whose creation enhanced God coincided with the diminishing influence of the Church and with the process of secularization of institutions that has continued to the present day. Throughout the 15th and the 16th centuries, however, old-style systems tended to prevail in civic and political life, resulting in a deep conflict with the upsurging creative forces stemming from many great personalities. Alienation came to be viewed no longer from the theocentric order but from the lower key of the human perspective. In that era of contrast between the new humanism and the medieval social structures—which led to all sorts of wars, migrations, and other upheavals, notably witchcraft—insanity came to the fore in a patent, almost paroxistic, way.

The preeminent role occupied by the pilgrim and the wayfarer during the Middle Ages was now taken over by the fool. The court buffoon, by embodying the roles of a flattering and laughter-making official parasite, helped break down the distinction between folly and wisdom, life and art. The monstrosity of the fool, quite often an odd-looking dwarf, had appeal because of its mysterious character. In line with an old tradition, especially in the Arab culture, the fool was considered a clairvoyant. Aside from its obvious apotropaic meaning—that is, of averting calamity—folly was thought of as a deep and innocent state of knowledge—and, thus, was often represented by animals—and as a satire of the seductive and diabolic search for knowledge by people attempting to emulate God.

In literature, the great humanist Erasmus presented a satirical view of wise folly in *The Praise of Folly* (1509). Other representations of the fool were given in *Orlando Furioso* (1532) by Ariosto, in Panurge by Rabelais in *Tiers Livre* of *Gargantua and Pantagruel* (1546) and, later on, in Falstaff by Shakespeare in *Henry IV* (1598) and in *Don Quixote* (1605) by Cervantes. In them, a progression is evident from a philosophical theme to a literary genre.

In the Renaissance, however, the literary figure of the fool had considerable pathos. Sebastian Brant's *Das Narrenschiff (Ship of Fools)*, published in 1494, was meant to be satirical, but it provided an accurate picture of the prevailing attitude toward the mentally ill. Indeed, many of them were left wandering in the country or drifting on the sea (see Figure 9). The ship of fools can be viewed as a symbolism of the madman's voyage, as the journey for excellence between two countries—that from which he was rejected and that for which he longs but to which he does not belong. A few years later, in 1499, Hieronymus Bosch painted "The Ship of Fools," in which the figures, in their isolation and animal appearance, are a symbol of alienation, of the nothingness of sin, of the demonic. The contrast between the comedy of the details and the tragedy of the whole dramatically elicits nostalgia for the state of innocence that was lost in the original fall. Satanism has contributed to erasing the memory of it; only folly can return humans to that state of innocence.

In recent years a considerable effort has been made by students from different disciplines—philosophy, intellectual history, history of art, religion—to explain the meaning of a number of paintings by the Flemish School—Hieronymus Bosch, Peter Bruegel the Elder, and others—relevant to the theme of folly. In spite of a considerable difference of opinion by scholars such as E. H. Gombrich, E. Panofsky, C. De Tolnay, and W. Fraenger, there is some agreement on the meaning of the most famous of those paintings: "The Haywain," "The Temptations of St. Anthony," "The Garden of Earthly Delights," and the "Last Judgment" by Bosch. It seems that the gross distortion of form and body images, the condensation of part-objects and ideas, the mutilation and dismem-

FIGURE 9. Xylograph on the title page of Sebastian Brant's *La Nef des Fols du Monde* (Paris, Jean Lambert, 1497).

FIGURE 10. Melancholia. Engraving by Albrecht Dürer (1514). Gabinetto Nazionale delle Stampe, Rome. Anticipating contemporary existential themes, the main figure, representing human self-assurance, cannot take flight, being tied to transient matter (the passing-bell and the magic square, symbol of the vain human attempt to discover the hidden meaning of phenomena). Human knowledge (tools) and the subjugation of nature (the dog) represent the impotence of humans in reaching the distant horizon of the eternity. The angel recording human actions signifies the guilt that is intrinsic to human life.

berment of the human body, the distortion of space, and the blending of the animate with the inanimate are attempts at presenting madness.

The fantasmagoric figures of those paintings are symbols of alienation, in the sense of each one being isolated, without time, space, or relationship to each other; and the naked figures are not tempting or sensuous but are symbols representing the nothingness of sin. The fool's irrational journey through the seductive aspects of the nonnatural, in contrast to nature that comes from God, promises an inverse wisdom and points to the failure of achieving a purely rational view of humans (see Figure 10).

WITCHCRAFT MANIA

Historical interpretation. The phenomenon of witchcraft is particularly interesting for the history of psychiatry on various grounds: (1) It unequivocally points to the close connection between psychiatric pictures and the cultural scene and, in general, to the relativity of the concepts of mental health and psychiatric diagnosis. (2) It corroborates the element of magic commonly shared by all religions of the world. (3) It can be followed from early times to the present, as it has been argued with some justification, particularly by the psychiatrist Szasz (1973) in recent years in this country, that the nonconformist— either the medieval witch or today's mentally ill person—tends to be placed in the role of a scapegoat by society. If one also takes into consideration the opinion, commonly held by

scholars, that witchcraft and beliefs in occult and supernatural powers tend to prevail in times of social stress and the decline of traditional institutions—as, indeed, the present time seems to be—then the relevance of witchcraft for the present situation of psychiatry is beyond dispute.

In the late 19th century, at the time of the antireligious belief in rationalism and in science, medieval witchcraft was viewed as an expression of superstition by such American scholars as the historian Lea, by White—the president of Cornell University who gathered there the world's finest collection of printed material relating to witchcraft—and by his pupil Burr. Later on, at the end of the century, remarkable collections on the source of witchcraft were published in Germany by Hansen and by Soldan, with his revisors, Heppe and Bauer. Early in the 20th century, with the rise of anthropology, witchcraft was studied from the perspective of a folkloristic phenomenon in many cultures, notably by Frazer and Evans-Pritchard. That trend culminated in Murray's book *The Witch-Cult in Western Europe* (1921), in which the phenomenon—through its link to Greco-Roman, Teutonic, and Celtic traditions—was viewed as a typical example of continuity in cultic beliefs and rites. A little later, with the advent of the psychoanalytic application to anthropology—as in Freud's *Totem and Taboo*, published in

1913—the psychopathological aspects of witchcraft became the object of much interest. Was the ritual of witchcraft a form of escape from or of rebellion against society? Were the fantasies of the alleged witches a projection of wishful thinking related to their frustrated lives? Was the attitude of the inquisitors dominated by an unconscious fear of women and lustful gratification of their repressed sexual desires? Freud (1949) in his monograph *A Neurosis of Demoniacal Possession in the Seventeenth Century* (1949), attributed the pact with the devil made by the painter Christian Haitzmann to his ambivalent feelings toward his dead father, endowed by him with good and bad attributes. In the 1950's, with the progress made in psychopharmacology, some came out strongly in support of a purely chemical cause of witchcraft, based on the evidence that quite often alleged witches used ointments, philters, drugs, and fumigations that may have contained such active principles as belladonna, mescaline, and Solanaceae.

This point brings up the vexatious question of the state of mind of the alleged witches, a question that is of particular relevance for psychiatry. Scholars admit that there is a lack of psychological description and of personal and family history in all cases of accused witches; in fact, all the available reports are by opposers of witchcraft. That fact may throw some light on the antithetical position found in the literature between those who stated that all witches were mentally ill and those who, in equally strong terms, asserted that no one was. Obviously, it is largely a matter of guessing. In the first group, some, rather conservative, attributed the impaired state of mind of the alleged witches mainly to senility. That old theory can be traced back to the 16th century. In *De Subtilitate* (1550) Jerome Cardan (Rivari, 1906) described them as

miserable old women, beggars, existing in the valley on chestnuts and field herbs ... emaciated, deformed, with prying eyes, pallid, showing in their face black bile and melancholy ... taciturn, stupid ... fixed in their opinions and stubborn.

That description is closely matched by that of the country squire Reginald Scot (1584), who, in *Discovery of Witchcraft*, calls them

Old, lame, bleare-eyed, pale, fowle and full of wrinkles ... in whose drowsie minds the divell hath gotten a fine seat ... leane and deformed, showing melancholie in thier faces ... doting, scolds, mad, divellish

and indicates

their humor melancholicale to be full of imaginations, from whence cheefely proceedeth the varieties of their confessions.

To the second group belonged Zilboorg (1935), who hinted that people put to death at the stake may have been cases of dementia precox, senile psychoses, general paralysis, and involutional melancholia. Others were even more liberal in their criteria and included cases of mania, delirium, alcoholism, brain damage, avitaminosis, hysteria, epilepsy, and psychosomatic disorder—in sum, the entire spectrum of psychopathology.

Some years ago, in a detailed review of the literature on witchcraft from the psychiatric perspective, Hoffmann (1935) stressed the regressive aspect of the psychopathology of the alleged witches, related to the prevalence of collective autosuggestion and mass hysteria during the period of social upheaval in the15th and 16th centuries. In a similar vein, Russell (1972) stated:

the concept of madness is of only limited use in explaining the medieval witch phenomenon, for not all witches were psychologically disturbed or psychotic individuals.

Rather than from the perspective of today's clinical psychiatry, witchcraft can best be understood by the contemporary scientist in the light of psychological phenomena, the role of which, however, can become clear only from a discussion of the phenomenon of witchcraft in its totality.

Meaning of witchcraft. Witchcraft was defined by Russell (1972) as

a composite phenomenon drawing from folklore, sorcery, demonology, heresy and Christian theology.

Immediately, two points stand out; on the one side, the similarity of notions between witchcraft in Europe and other cultures—supernatural powers, change into animals, intercourse with evil spirits, ability of leaving the body temporarily, involvement with all sorts of black practices, such as the evil eye and the use of initiation rites—and, on the other side, the intrinsic resistance to apply attitudes and categories of cultural anthropology to a phenomenon that, initiated in the Middle Ages, achieved its apex during the Renaissance and the Reformation—at the time of Leonardo, Michelangelo, Vesalius, Copernicus, and many other great men—so as to be considered

quantitatively and qualitatively the single greatest threat to Christian European civilization.

References to Satan and the devil can be found in the Old and New Testaments, in apocryphal writings, in St. Paul, and in St. Augustine. In St. Augustine the antithesis between God and the devil acquires a particularly dramatic character. In the early Middle Ages some ceremonies were held at night in solitary places and attended by women for the worship of Diana—the goddess who looked after maidens and women in childbirth and perhaps confused then with Hecate, a goddess of sorcerers, witches, and ghosts—probably for rather innocuous purposes. The Canon Episcopi, composed about 906, stated that the acts of alleged witches, such as transvestism and intercourse with animals, were all illusions or fantasies originating in dreams, for which, at the most, religious sanctions should be applied. In the 12th century groups of heretics, notably the Albigensians aiming at a return to the early evangelic ideals and at opposition to the growing power of the papacy, grew rapidly in southern France, in the Low Countries, in the Rhineland, and in northern Italy—that is, in rather healthy areas that were undergoing rapid social changes. The Roman Inquisition was established by Pope Innocent III in 1199 for the purpose of exterminating the heretics; shortly thereafter, heresy, a crime punishable by death, was transferred from canon law to civil law throughout the Holy Roman Empire.

Around that time a transition occurred from accusations of a crime of doing to accusations of a crime of imagining. The heretics were accused of all kinds of wrongdoing, as were two other groups of outcasts, the Jews and the lepers. It remains controversial whether the custom of confiscating the property of the convicted resulted in a substantial increase in the number of accusations of witchcraft and of subsequent trials, but there was a rapid decline in the incidence of witchcraft when confiscation was officially forbidden in the early 17th century. The main point remains the peculiar distortion of logic that affected not only the ignorant populace but also the cultivated—popes of the Renaissance, great Protestant reformers, saints of the Counterreformation, and scholars of the caliber of Bacon, Grotius, and Pascal.

Early in the 14th century in southern France, the inquisitory probing trials began to show the crystallization of the image of the witch and of the ritual of witchcraft as it appears now. An accusation based on suspicion or rumor would be brought to the Inquisition; then secular power would apprehend the alleged witch; particular marks supposedly made by the devil, such as birthmarks and patches of anesthesia, would be found; under tortures of various kinds (see Figure 11), the accused would confess the pact with the devil, based on infamous practices, or the selling of her soul to the devil and, consequently, the participation in all sorts of revolting practices—the orgiastic sabbats, intercourse with the devil, eating babies—and to all sorts of misfortunes—from impotence in men to drought, famine, plague, and death of animals—she would reveal the names of other witches; quite often she would be found guilty and sentenced to death in a cruel way. Events corroborating the innocence of the alleged witch were discarded as deceptions by the devil, since the judges themselves were afraid of being accused of excessive leniency based on connivance with the devil. With that kind of logic, it is no wonder that conservative estimates put the figure of executed men, women, and children at more than 100,000 in Germany and a similar number in France. Only in England, where the pagan Anglo-Saxon law persisted, according to which a person was

innocent unless proved guilty, very few people were killed; paradoxically, in Spain, too, the attack on witchcraft was restricted because of the nationalistic and independent attitude of the Spanish Inquisition.

Several treatises on witchcraft began to appear in the early 15th century, and they contributed to the spread of the belief, with the help of the newly discovered system of printing. The most influential treatise was *Formicarius* (*Ant Heap*) published in 1437 by the Dominican Johann Nider. In that treatise the supposed sexual activities between women and the devil were discussed in detail. The highest peak in the adherence to the tenets of witchcraft was reached in 1484, when Pope Innocent VIII issued the bull *Summis Desiderantes Affectibus*, which aimed to remove any possible hesitation in persecuting those accused of the calamity. It was followed shortly thereafter by the unfortunately famous *Malleus Maleficarum* (*The Witches' Hammer*) by the two Dominicans Jakob Sprenger and Heinrich Kramer (1928), published in Cologne in 1486 (see Figure 12). Zilboorg (1935) pointed out that the book was

so replete with sexual details that at times it may well be considered a handbook of sexual psychopathies.

In addition, it was a document of gross misogyny. According to its two authors, a person who became delusional or hallucinated was considered to be possessed of the devil and to be a witch. *Malleus Maleficarum*, which has been described as "the most horrible document of that age" (Zilboorg, 1935), became the standard reference for Church and state alike in

FIGURE 11. Instruments of torture for witches, some of whom may have been mentally ill. (From a German engraving of 1527 at the Cornell University Library. From Robbins, R. H. *The Encyclopedia of Witchcraft and Demonology*, p. 507. Crown, New York, 1959.)

FIGURE 12. Title page of the *Malleus Maleficarum* (1486) by the two Dominicans Jacob Sprenger and Heinrich Kramer.

regard to matters concerning the indictment, trial, judgment, and punishment of alleged witches. It went through 29 editions up to 1669.

It was as late as 1682, in fact, that Colbert, Louis XIV's minister, decried the abolition of capital punishment for sorcerers and witches. That abolition, however, did not eradicate superstitions and fanaticisms, as evidenced by the fact that, 10 years later, there was a revival of the witchcraft mania in Salem, Massachusetts. There, within a single year, 25 alleged witches were placed on trial, and 19 were executed. Witch trials even continued throughout the 18th century in some areas. As late as 1768 John Wesley wrote that

> the giving up of witchcraft is, in effect, giving up the Bible.

The important point here is that the Western civilization belief in witchcraft, based on elements of religion and magic common to all cultures, underwent a transformation from a probable fertility cult, the so-called society of Diana of women in the early Middle Ages, to a definite ritual sanctioned by ecclesiastic authorities. That transition, which historically is characterized by a switch of emphasis from anthropology to theology, occurred at a particular period of great social upheavals. In such circumstances, no different from the persecution of the Jews by the Nazis during World War II, men subjected to all kinds of frustrations tend to discharge their pent-up aggression on a scapegoat. The crystallization of the belief in witchcraft made possible the establishment of a system of counterwitchcraft—that is, of an attempt to apply a system of putative knowledge to maintain order in the world—a fact that explains why all the rulers of that period, feeling their status threatened, actively contributed to the belief in witchcraft.

The above considerations belong to the field of social psychology proper and, therefore, transcend the historical period under consideration and are of relevance even in the present day. As a matter of fact, magic, including witchcraft, is on the increase in many marginal groups of Western civilization and in many cultures undergoing a stressful period of acculturation. Certain dimensions seem to be common to all cultures—notably, the archetypal image of the witch as frightening, numinous, and threatening, associated with awe, wildness, and evil; the social expectation that witches would behave just as they did; and the sense of superiority related to the awesome dread of being in contact with the demonic.

Other dimensions, however, seem to be particularly fitting to the medieval and Renaissance witch craze. In the compact and socially rigid society of the time, witchcraft acquired the characteristic of alienation—that is, of repudiation of the existing order. In view of the theocentric view of the world, such a repudiation was expressed essentially through religious means. That fact explains why much of the witchcraft rituals represented a parody of the Christian sacraments—for instance, the kiss on the devil's fundament, as opposed to the Christian kiss of peace or the kiss on the altar.

Even more important is the fact that, in most instances, women were involved in the witchcraft rituals. At the base of their phenomenon is the overwhelmingly antifeminine trend of the Christian tradition. From the very beginning, sin entered the world through Eve, and the demons originally fell because they lusted after the daughters of men; later on, from St. Augustine and St. Jerome to all the other Christian fathers, sexuality was viewed as degrading for men, even in the context of marriage. In the Middle Ages, the traditional image of the woman as a passive being bearing children and tending to the house split into contrasting images—on the one side, the courtly lady of the troubadours and of the heroes, almost a mundane version of the Virgin Mary; on the other side, a dangerous creature ready to use and misuse sex to control men or to lead them into perdition. The fact that many more women than men were involved in heretical movements and in witchcraft rituals may then be viewed, as proposed by Marxist writers, as a form of rebellion against the male establishment—an issue that is relevant to the contemporary scene.

EMERGENCE OF HUMANISM

The confluence of witchcraft and the position of women in the Middle Ages and the Renaissance is also reflected in the work of some great humanists of the time—notably Vives, Agrippa, and Weyer. It is significant that, in direct opposition to the belief in witchcraft, those three men held enlightened views about the roles of women and about the mentally ill.

Juan Luis Vives was born in Valencia, then the prosperous metropolis of the Crown of Aragon, an area in which the successful blending of Christians, Jews, and Moriscos (Arabs) had resulted in enlightened forms of civic life. The year of his birth, 1492, *annus mirabilis*, marked the date of the discovery of America and of the unification of Spain under the Catholic kings. Traditionally held as a champion of Catholic faith for his many religious works and his friendship with Erasmus, he was, it has recently been demonstrated beyond dispute, born of Jewish parents, who, though converted, suffered persecution. Probably because of that fact, he left Spain at the age of 16 and never returned, living the rest of his life mainly in Flanders and England, until his death in 1540.

In 1524 Vives wrote a treatise on the education of women, a pioneering concept at that time, and dedicated it to the daughter of Catherine of Aragon, wife of Henry VIII, to whom, like Thomas More and Linacre, he was quite close. The next year he published *On Poor Relief* (Vives, 1917) in which he advanced modern views on welfare, stating that particular attention should be given to those who are sick in the mind, for whom the authorities should build special hospitals.

> When a man of unsettled mind is brought to a hospital, it must be determined, first of all, whether his illness is congenital or has resulted from some misfortune, whether there is hope for recovery or not. One ought to feel compassion for so great a disaster to the health of the human mind, and it is of utmost importance that the treatment be such that the insanity be not nourished and increased, as may result from mocking, exciting or irritating madmen, approving or applauding the foolish things that they say or do, inciting them to act more ridiculously, applying fomentations as if it were to their stupidity and silliness. What could be more inhuman than to drive a man insane just for the sake of laughing at him and amusing one's self at such a misfortune.

And later on he wrote:

> Remedies suited to the individual patients should be used. Some need medical care and attention to their mode of life; others need gentle and friendly treatment, so that like wild animals they may gradually grow gentle; still others need instruction. There will be some who will require force and chains, but these must be used so that the patients are not made more violent. Above all, as far as possible, tranquility must be introduced in their minds, for it is through this that reason and sanity return.

In 1538, while in Bruges, Vives published *De Anima et Vita* (1948), in which, probably on the basis of a careful exploration of his own inner life, he dealt with the mind from an empirical viewpoint.

What the soul is, is of no concern to us; what it is like, what its manifestations are, is of very great importance.

Among the many interesting points in the book are the awareness of psychological associations and the recognition of their emotional origin, the emphasis given to the role of instinct in human behavior, and the belief in the ambivalent aspect of certain emotions. Called the father of modern, empirical psychology, Vives should also be recognized as the forerunner of dynamic psychology.

The wandering scholar Cornelius Agrippa (ca. 1486–1535) was even more outspoken in his opposition to misogyny. *On the Nobility and Pre-eminence of the Feminine Sex* was written in 1509 as a general defense of women. Furthermore, in 1519 he underscored his beliefs by risking his life in Metz to liberate a woman who had been accused of witchcraft.

In combination, those events clearly indicate the emergence of a new trend. There was an increasing tendency to take a fresh look at humans, from the viewpoint of classic wisdom, grounded in the Christian tradition. The many treatises on family life and the education of children that were published in Italy during the 15th century may be regarded as a further expression of the gathering momentum of this humanistic—and human—outlook.

JOHANN WEYER: A PIONEER OF MODERN PSYCHIATRY

Because of his books on the occult sciences, Agrippa was generally regarded as a rather controversial figure. Nevertheless, the benefits that were to derive from the influence he exerted on Johann Weyer (see Figure 13) during his adolescence are universally acknowledged.

Weyer was born in 1515 in Graves, a town on the border between Holland and Germany, and later studied medicine in Paris, where he became acquainted with a number of scholars. After he had completed his medical studies, which were in the medieval tradition, and until his death 38 years later, in 1588, Weyer served as personal physician to Duke William of Jülich, Cleves, and Berg. Although the duke would undoubtedly be

FIGURE 13. Johann Weyer (or Wier), 1515–1588, author of the *De Praestigiis Daemonum* (1563). (From Ioannis Wieri, *Opera Omnia*, 1660.)

considered an enlightened man by any standards, in later life he became mentally ill, and that fact may explain his particular sensitivity to psychological issues and his interest in Weyer's investigation in that area. One can only speculate as to the extent to which Weyer's efforts were influenced by Duke William. The fact remains, however, that Weyer gradually turned his interest from general medicine to the study of individual human behavior, in particular to the study of women who had been accused of witchcraft. The conclusions he reached in the course of his investigations were ultimately incorporated into *De Praestigiis Daemonum* (Weyer, 1967) which was published in Basel in 1563. It is today universally recognized that this book represents a landmark in the history of psychiatry.

Weyer began with an adamant rejection of the belief in witchcraft and a strong condemnation of the clergy who supported it. He then proceeded patiently to explain a variety of the so-called supernatural signs with which witches were usually identified, on the basis of pure medical knowledge, and when such knowledge proved inadequate, as in the case of hallucinations, to attribute such phenomena to a combination of natural and supernatural factors. Since Weyer was a 16th-century man, it is likely that he genuinely believed that the devil participated, to some extent and in some special way, in human behaviors. His determination to "make clinical situations as clear as daylight" and to proceed to a careful psychological examination of mental patients is all the more remarkable in the light of his personal convictions. Weyer had acquired extensive clinical experience, which enabled him to describe a wide range of diagnostic entities and associated symptoms, including toxic psychoses, epilepsy, senile psychoses, nightmares, hysteria, delusions, paranoia, *folie a deux*, and depression.

Two examples reported in his book may be sufficient to show Weyer's (1967) clinical acuity:

I knew once a melancholic Italian who thought that he was the King and Emperor of the whole world, and who insisted that these titles were only for him. He was quite articulate, relaxed, and showed no other symptoms. However, he kept repeating some Italian verses of his own in which he discussed the condition of the Christian world, especially as far as the different religions were concerned, and the methods of handling the trouble of France and Flanders; he referred to all these problems as if they had been revealed to him from God. In every occasion he would announce his titles with the letters R.R.D.D.M.M., namely, Rex Regum, Dominus Dominatium, Monarcha Mundi.

And elsewhere he wrote:

There was a woman in Buderic who was affected by a form of melancholia, or rather, mania, each year. For several weeks she could not depart from the graves of the cemetery, then she would break the door of someone's house and the windows of someone else's house, and she would at times run away to solitary places in the country. As her trouble occurred each year usually around Easter, when the bodily humors frequently are agitated, people thought that she was possessed by an evil spirit.

However, it is in the realm of psychotherapy that Weyer's contribution to psychiatry is truly outstanding and unique. For example, he recommended that nuns in convents, who manifested psychological symptoms, frequently of an erotic nature, be isolated first and then permitted to return to their own families. But, above all, he insisted that the needs of the individual, rather than the rules of the institution, must be given primary consideration.

That attitude was further exemplified in an account of his treatment of Barbara Kremers, a 10-year-old girl who, supposedly, had existed for over a year without food or drink. Weyer moved the patient and her older sister to his own house, where they lived among his family. After a period of observation, he concluded that the patient's behavior represented an unconscious desire to malinger. The important point is that there and elsewhere he tried to initiate a new approach to treatment that was to provide the framework for modern psychotherapy. Weyer recognized the importance of the therapeutic relationship and of the kindness and understanding the therapist must extend toward his patient. However, he further postulated that, to be truly effective, the benevolent attitude must be based on scientific principles—that is, careful psychiatric examination and observation.

Weyer's book also included a discussion of matters relating to the trial and punishment of alleged witches; that discussion represents an important contribution to legal psychiatry. The book also presented his pioneer views on possible areas for collaboration between physicians and clergymen and the benefits to be derived from such collaboration.

Weyer's radical approach was, of course, completely alien to the thinking of his times. As a result, his work evoked hostility at first and then was simply ignored by theologians, philosophers, physicians, and lawyers alike—the very audience to whom his book had been directed. In fact, among the leading demonologists of the 16th and 17th centuries—Bodin, Delrio, Guaccius, Remy, King James I, Cotton Mather—only Reginald Scot, in *Discovery of Witchcraft*, published in 1584, came to Weyer's defense. Weyer himself had expected that his book would encounter some opposition. However, he could not have anticipated that it would be listed in the *Index Librorum Prohibitorum* until the beginning of the 20th century. Nor could Weyer have predicted that his observations would be disregarded by physicians who were mainly interested in mental disorders, specifically in problems involving nosology, during the 17th and 18th centuries and by those interested in organic pathology in the 19th century. Only recently, with the advent of dynamic psychiatry, was the historical significance of Weyer's contributions evaluated in proper perspective, thanks to the efforts of Binz (1969) and Cobben (1976).

HUMANISM OF PARACELSUS AND CARDAN

As might be expected, Weyer remained without peer during the 16th century in terms of the originality and imagination evident throughout his writings. Nevertheless, it seems appropriate in this context to refer briefly to the views advanced by two other enlightened scholars of this period, Paracelsus and Cardan.

The Swiss-born physician Paracelsus (ca. 1493–1541) advocated a more humane approach to all patients, including those who were afflicted with mental illness. Throughout his active life, he was dominated by an inner restlessness that prevented him from settling down in any of the places where he lived—Basel, Würzburg, Paris, Montpelier, Ferrara, Alsace, Augsburg, Carinthia, and many others—and from presenting his thinking in a systematic way. Influenced by gnostic (Manichean opposition of good and evil), cabalistic, astrological, pantheistic, and alchemical trends, he substituted the three principles—sulfur, salt, and mercury—for the four humors of classical medicine and based his system, which has been called a cosmological

anthropology, on a symbolic and intuitive correspondence between humans and the universe.

In regard to psychiatry proper, the introduction to his book *The Diseases Which Deprive Man of His Reason* (Paracelsus, 1941), written in 1526 but published posthumously in 1567, clearly represents his philosophical position:

In nature there are not only diseases which afflict our body and our health, but many others which deprive us of sound reason, and these are the most serious. While speaking about the natural diseases and observing to what extent and how seriously they afflict various parts of our body, we must not forget to explain the origin of the diseases which deprive man of reason, as we know from experience that they develop out of man's disposition. The present-day clergy of Europe attribute such diseases to ghostly beings and three-fold spirits; we are not inclined to believe them. For nature proves that such statements by earthly Gods are quite incorrect and, as we shall explain in these chapters, that nature is the sole origin of diseases.

From that book, as well as from other passages in his writings, it is evident that many of Paracelsus's concepts, simply dismissed in the past as too obscure or nonscientific, may be considered in a more favorable light from the perspective of today's psychology. In particular, he presented a dynamic view of the personality and emphasized its total involvement in each mental illness; he attempted to clarify definite clinical pictures of mental diseases—especially manic-depressive psychoses, psychopathic personality, and mass psychic contagion; he posited that mental illness is a deviation from normality, with a consequent search for causative factors and for therapeutic methods to reintegrate the patient to his original state of health; and he held the basic tenet that the mental patient is neither a criminal nor a sinner but a sick person in need of medical help.

From the perspective of psychodynamics, Paracelsus anticipated the concepts of projection, ambivalence, unconscious self-destructive trends, and the economy of the libido. According to Zilboorg (1941), the first reference to the unconscious motivation of neuroses in the history of medical psychology occurred in a passage of Paracelsus's (1941) book concerning St. Vitus' dance:

The cause of the disease "chorea lasciva" is a mere opinion and idea, assumed by imagination, affecting those who believe in such a thing. This opinion and idea are the origin of the disease both in children and adults. In children, the cause is also imagination, based not on thinking but on perceiving, because they have heard or seen something. The reason is this: their sight and hearing are so strong that *unconsciously* [italics added] they have fantasies about what they have seen or heard.

Paracelsus strictly adhered to the notion that psychic conditions should be treated with psychic methods. Consequently, he practiced a method of psychotherapy based on counseling, suggestion, reasoning, and encouraging the patient. From the developmental perspective, as the psychiatric historian Galdston (1967) put it:

The magnet, magnetism, hypnotism, suggestion, psychocatharsis, and psychoanalysis represent a series of stages in the progressive development of modern psychiatric thought and knowledge. The initial impulse to this development came from Paracelsus.

Jerome Cardan (Rivari, 1906) (1501–1576)—a mathematician, philosopher, and physician—was among the first to use his personal experiences as the basis for his efforts to understand psychological phenomena. In his *Autobiography*, which he completed in 1570, Cardan described in detail the emotional disorders he underwent during his childhood (nightmares and stuttering, which he ascribed to his father's pathological influence) and as an adolescent (sexual impotence, hallucinations, and grandiose ideas). Cardan's son—who, in turn, was adversely influenced by his father's neurotic tendencies—became so disturbed in later life that he killed his wife. Cardan's awareness of the psychological factors he believed had precipitated his son's behavior led him to postulate, albeit not for the first time, that the mentally ill should not be considered responsible for their criminal acts, a view that is similar to the later concept of moral insanity. Apart from his *Autobiography*, Cardan wrote a number of other works. At various times in his numerous publications, he opposed persecution of people for so-called witchcraft, detailed the prerequisites for mental health, and described various character types and their somatic correlations.

PHYSIOGNOMY AND MORPHOLOGY

An attempt to correlate character type with somatic variables properly includes physiognomy, a field of study that became popular during the Renaissance at the time of the "discovery" of anatomy by Vesalius (1514–1564) and the concomitant emphasis on humans as a microcosm that reflected the macrocosm. In fact, however, physiognomy has a long history in human development and can be traced back to the Arabs; to Pietro d'Abano; to Michael Scot, the 13th-century astrologist of Frederick II; and to Michael Savonarola, grandfather of the proponent of Florentine religious reforms.

Many volumes on physiognomy were published in the late 15th century, but none acquired such wide popularity as *De Humana Physiognomia* by Giambattista della Porta (1538–1615), the Neapolitan writer of scientific or pseudoscientific subjects. The main thesis of his book, which is presently termed "teriological physiognomy," was that the physical resemblance of humans to animals may be extended to apply to behavioral characteristics as well—for instance, sharpness of sight, cautiousness, and aggressiveness. della Porta also attempted to support the validity of that concept by inserting throughout his book numerous illustrations, which have become justly famous. In a broader sense, however, physiognomy represented the culmination of a series of means of divination used by humans. In early religions, magic traits were assigned to anthropomorphic gods, then in astrology to the planets and stars, and in physiognomy to the parts of the human body, such as the hand and the head. Thus, physiognomy represents the final stage of a cycle that starts and ends with humans. That final concept of humans as the focus of the entire universe is crucial to Renaissance thinking and led to various currents of thought that ultimately produced certain current theoretical trends, including the modern concept of the biological constitution in relation to psychological functioning.

As a result of his studies of the morphological constitution, the Spaniard Juan Huarte (1594) (ca. 1530–1592), in his book *The Examination of Men's Wits*, published in 1574, advanced the thesis that variations in the intellectual capacity of people may be attributed to differences in temperament. Thus, Huarte came even closer to modern character analysis and the concepts of vocational orientation.

SCIENTIFIC CONTRIBUTIONS TO PSYCHOLOGY

The contributions to psychology and psychopathology by Cardan and della Porta and other physicians must be considered a reflection of their ability as scientists, rather than clinicians. With the notable exception of Weyer, Renaissance clinicians, although renowned for their anatomical and physiological discoveries, added very little to the knowledge of human psychopathology.

To mention only some of the more outstanding among them, Girolamo Fracastoro (1483–1553), mainly known for his poem on syphilis, accurately described the anxious state of mind of melancholics and suggested methods for the prevention of suicide; Girolamo Mercuriale (1530–1606) related melancholia to a disturbance in the heart, rather than in the brain; Jean Schenck (1530–1598) described various psychiatric signs, such as incubus, and manifestations of collective psychopathology (St. Vitus' dance, demonopathies); Konrad von Gesner (1516–1565), a scientist from Zürich, described several kinds of epilepsy and mental disorders, among which he included *amoris morbus* (the disease of love), and emphasized psychological aspects of dreams and the fact that they reflected the past, as well as present and future events.

The concepts advanced by each of those clinicians are lacking in originality. Nevertheless, that quality did exist in Renaissance thought. To find it, one must go back to Leonardo da Vinci (1452–1519), who, even before Galileo and Bacon, attempted to establish some kind of scientific methodology by means of various experiments involving humans and their functions. His efforts included the careful study of the cerebral ventricles through injection of cadavers. In addition, he anticipated modern concepts of the functioning of the nervous system (Jackson's motor automatisms) and the Rorschach Test by pointing to the individual reaction to the configuration of spots and clouds. He investigated the psychophysiology of perception (stereoscopic vision, binomial character of colors, persistence of images), the expression of emotions in physiognomy, and the emotional selectivity of memory. He hinted at the importance of self-suggestion (hypnotic fascination, especially in women) and of dreams. And, in general, he emphasized the instinctual component of the mind.

PIONEER HOSPITAL TREATMENT

Despite advances in psychology and psychiatry, the fact remains that in the 16th century—at which point the Renaissance had reached its peak—the attitude of the general public toward mental illness remained essentially the same as the attitude that had prevailed in ancient and medieval times. It has frequently been pointed out that this phenomenon, which ultimately led to the psychiatric revolution of the 19th century, was due to the lag between persisting medieval social institutions, on the one hand, and individual creativity, on the other. That basic discrepancy accounted for the lack of community responsibility and humanitarian attitudes that characterized the period. Reports of mentally ill patients kept in institutions can be traced back to the late Middle Ages in the Christian world. *The Book of Foundation of St. Bartholomew's Church*, which dealt with patients treated at the nearby St. Bartholomew's Hospital in London, showed the survival of pagan practices under a Christian version. The general belief was that mental patients were cured by supernatural forces—that is, the intercession of saints. In fact, there was a similarity with the ancient practice of incubation, for such intercession was held to occur for the most part while the patient was asleep. When the saints failed to intervene, physical treatment methods—such as cathartics, emetics, and bloodletting—were used.

By the 14th century, several institutions had been established for the care or, more accurately, the custody of mental patients in Metz (1100), Uppsala (1305), Bergamo (1325), and Florence (1385). Furthermore, the town of Gheel in Belgium had become a center for the care of mental patients during the Middle Ages as a result of the miraculous renown that the Church of St. Dyphna—named after an Irish princess persecuted and killed there by her incest-ridden father—had acquired for the healing of many patients.

Traditionally, however, the founding of the first mental hospital in Valencia in 1409 is attributed to Father Gilabert Jofré (1350–1417), a Spanish priest (Bassoe, 1945; Chamberlain, 1966; Dominguez, 1967). Legend has it that Father Jofré decided to enlist the help of his parishioners to build a hospital for the insane after he had witnessed a street scene of mockery and sadism toward the mentally ill that was typical of the customs of the time. Apparently, Father Jofré was sufficiently impressed by his experience to press toward his goal; his hospital was completed within the year. Moreover, in the period from 1412 to 1489, five similar institutions were established in various cities in Spain, and in 1567, under Spanish influence, the first mental hospital was established in Mexico City (Rumbaut, 1972). Without question, then, the role of Spain in regard to the hospital care of mental patients, in both the Old World and the New World, remains of primary significance.

It is equally certain that the Arabs exerted a major influence in shaping the new attitude of the Spaniards toward mental patients. That fact is borne out by the many similarities between those early mental hospitals and some of the Arab institutions that were apparently devoted to mental patients, such as the one built by Mohammed V in Granada in 1365.

Whether mentally ill patients showed evidence of improvement in those facilities cannot be ascertained today, in the absence of reliable reports and data concerning staff and institutional practices. When those patients were kept at home, their families frequently resorted to the use of chains. And, with few exceptions, the conditions to which the hospitalized mental patient was exposed were equally deplorable. Apparently, hospital administrators shared the popular view of mental illness, for, until the 19th century, mental patients were regularly placed on exhibition at Bethlehem Hospital in London (see Figure 14), where they could be viewed by the public for a few pennies; nor is there any indication that the Hospital of St. Maria della Pietà in Rome was an exception to the general rule, despite the fact that it was administered by a religious order established by the Portuguese Juan Ciudad (1495–1550), called John of God, and was dedicated to the care of all sick people, including those who were mentally sick.

LAY VIEW OF MENTAL ILLNESS

The lay attitude toward the contemporary mental hospital was vividly described by the learned monk Tomaso Garzoni (1549–1589) in *The Hospital of Incurable Fools*, (Garzoni, 1967), originally published in Italian in 1586 and translated into English (Padovani, 1949) in 1600 (see Figure 15). Garzoni presented a broad spectrum of psychiatric entities, ranging from alcoholism to melancholia, paranoia, and malingering. But apart from the stereotyped descriptions of the typical behavior of patients in each of those diagnostic entities, there is an occasional hint of Garzoni's awareness of their inner psychological condition—for instance, the longing for life and death of the "insane for love."

Evidence of an awareness of inner struggle, reaching the highest level of existential pathos, is present to a much greater degree in many of Shakespeare's characters. Long before the advent of modern psychiatry, Pope, Johnson, Coleridge, Goethe, Lessing, the Schlegels, and many others stressed Shakespeare's ability to depict human psychology. More than a century ago the English psychiatrist Bucknill (1859) devoted a monograph to Shakespeare's personages who particularly seemed to present mental abnormalities, such as Macbeth, Hamlet, and King Lear. The interest by psychiatrists in Shakespeare received impetus from Freud's interpretation of Hamlet at the time of his own self-analysis at the dawn of the 20th century. Since then, the extensive psychological literature on Shakespeare's work (Holland, 1964; Edgar, 1970; Faber, 1970; Eissler, 1971b) has focused on some critical points—mainly the conflict with the father figure, the aggressive struggle between men for power and sex, and passive and submissive attitude of the sons vis-à-vis the fathers up to Erikson's recent view of Hamlet (1964) as an expression of identity crisis—for which conflicts explanations have been sought in Shakespeare's own personality.

Contrasting and at times opposing etiological factors in mental diseases based on the humoral theory, on a mysterious correspondence between human behavior and the planets, and on other unproved notions are typical of the so-called Eliza-

THE
HOSPITALL
OF INCVRABLE
FOOLES:

Erected in Englifh, as neer the firft
Jtalian modell and platforme, as
the vnskilfull hand of an ignorant *Architect could*
deuife.

I pazzi, é li prudenti, fanno
giuftiſsima bilancia.

Printed by Edm. Bollifant,
for Edward Blount.

1 6 0 0

FIGURE 15. Title page of *The Hospital of Incurable Fools* by the learned Italian monk Tomaso Garzoni (1549–1589). It appeared in English translation in 1600.

FIGURE 14. Bethlehem Hospital in 1676.

bethan malady, described with unwarranted frequency in the English literature from the late 16th century to the middle 17th century. As Babb (1951) put it:

The physiological psychology of the Renaissance is a body of theories containing so many contradictions, semicontradictions, and disharmonies that any exposition of it is likely to misrepresent by introducing into it an orderliness which it does not really have.

However, recognition of the importance of passions as an internal force that, when it was not regulated by reason, could produce melancholia through the mediating action of the body suggests that the foundation had been laid for a more modern view of a human psychological functioning as representing a continuum that ranged from normality to disease. The Renaissance picture of the fool slowly faded, and in its place modern conscience slowly advanced as a concomitant of the Reformation, of pietism and other religious trends, of philosophical criticism, and of early liberal tendencies in the new atmosphere of growing national entities.

Psychiatry in the 17th and Early 18th Centuries

ORIGINS OF MODERN MEDICINE AND SCIENCE

The 17th century represents a period of transition from uncritical dependence on the ancients' belief in the gods, which in the Renaissance had found expression in the witchcraft mania, to the specification and application of methodological criteria in science. Galileo and Bacon must be credited with the formulation of the basic criteria for scientific experimentation. The widespread application of their concepts may be attributed to the fact that they were elaborated in Latin, then the universal language of science. In addition, the promulgation of those new theories may be ascribed to the establishment, in the years from 1657 to 1700, of the first four scientific societies—the Academia del Cimento, the Royal Society, the Academie des Savants, and the Berlin Akademie—and the first professional journals, *The Philosophical Transactions of the Royal Society* and the *Journal des Savants*.

The Copernican revolution, by demoting earth from a central role in the universe, had paved the way for a more critical and objective view of the world and, subsequently, of humans themselves. Obviously, the old beliefs in astrology and alchemy could not be expected to disappear overnight. However, those tenets now contributed to the foundation of the new sciences of astronomy and chemistry, which were further implemented by the many technological advances during the period. That new dynamic concept of the world was soon expanded to include humans, and Harvey's description of the circulation of the blood in 1628 fostered that view. Subsequently, Santorio did pioneer work on metabolism; Malpighi, on capillary circulation; Redi, on the generation of life; and Bonet, on pathological anatomy; later, in the 18th century, Galvani developed his theories in physiology. Whatever their specific area of investigation, all those men shared certain interests in common: the forces that generate life, the nature of death, the study of microorganisms and of cells and chemical compounds as basic constituents of the human body. After the Greek word *jatros* for physician, these scientists were called jatrophysicists, jatrochemists, or jatromechanics, depending on their particular focus.

NEW ANATOMICAL AND PHYSIOLOGICAL CONCEPTS OF THE MIND

In psychology, a word coined in 1590 by the German philosopher Göckel (1547–1628), the emphasis was placed on the organs that mediated between passions and body humors—namely, on the body-mind relationship. The *sensorium commune* that was considered central to that relationship was variously located in the pineal gland (Descartes), in the corpora striata (Vieussens), in the centrum ovale (Boerhaave), in the corpus callosum (Lancisi), and in the medulla oblongata (Malpighi, Willis).

Of all those men, René Descartes (1596–1650) was undoubtedly the most important. Indeed, his philosophical postulate concerning the essential distinction between body and mind continued to influence psychology until the beginning of the 20th century and was responsible for the split between morphology and psychology. Descartes's theories were subsequently rejected because of their strict materialism. However, today an increasing number of scientists no longer subscribe to that viewpoint. Thus, his attempt to locate the mind in the pineal gland is seen as a dynamic concept, rather than a static concept. Descartes defined the seat of the soul as the site of its activity, rather than its locale, which implies that he conceived of the soul as a physical force, *vertu*. He continued to subscribe to the Galenic concept of spirits; however, he related differences of temperament or natural propensities to differences in the number, size, shape, and movements of the spirits. And he concluded that each reflex action reflected the *total* functioning of the nervous system. Furthermore, he maintained that movements—that is, mental phenomena—could occur only after a rational soul had been joined to the body machine, a view clearly opposed to the concept of the homme-machine, which many workers have incorrectly attributed to Descartes.

Traditionally, Descartes is considered the most outstanding representative of 17th-century rationalism. Nevertheless, he attached great significance to emotional factors. That fact has been substantiated by evidence from still another source; obviously, one's life experience is inevitably reflected in one's work. The fact that, in his own life, Descartes was guided by strong emotions, as well as reason, is illustrated by his performance in two life crises. The first occurred when, at 17, he rejected Jesuit teachings. The second occurred at the age of 23, when he had his three famous dreams, which several of his biographers have explained as mystical crises. It is likely that those dreams, by bringing forth an emotional conflict based on sexual confusion, led Descartes to lay the foundation of his philosophical system, based on mathematical principles devoid of feelings. That system dominated philosophy for the next three centuries. A personal crisis thereby developed into a major influence in Western civilization, not unlike Luther's conflict with the father image, which, according to Erikson (1958), resulted in the Reformation. In any event, by the time he was in his fifties, his major conflicts were apparently resolved for the most part, for in 1649 he was able to write *Traité des passions de l'âme* which consists primarily of his correspondence with his pupil Princess Elizabeth of Bohemia.

CLASSIFICATION OF MENTAL DISEASES

In line with the contemporary taxonomic trend in many fields of science, a preoccupation with the classification of mental disorders also emerged. The first medical textbook published in the 17th century to deal with psychiatry, *Praxix Medica*, written in 1602 by the Swiss physician Felix Platter

(1536–1614), begins with a 75 quarto-page introduction on the classification of mental diseases (Diethelm and Hoffernan, 1965). Like his contemporaries, Platter subscribed to a theory of organic humoral causation; however, that view did not necessarily outrule the devil as a causative factor, at least in some cases of possessed female patients. Platter's contribution is historically significant. Undoubtedly, however, the two physicians who were most important for the history of psychiatry in the 17th century were Zacchia and Sydenham, who differed radically in orientation.

LEGAL PSYCHIATRY (ZACCHIA)

Paolo Zacchia (1584–1659), who is generally regarded as the father of legal medicine, served as the Pope's personal physician for many years. In that capacity he was called on frequently to give *consilia* to the Court of the Sacra Rota, the highest judicial body of the Catholic Church. In his lengthy volume *Quâestiones Medico-Legales* (1621–1635), he presented many case reports and then made many recommendations that would be considered valid even today. Zacchia's discussion of those cases began with a statement that, in his opinion, only a physician was competent to judge the mental condition of a person. He then suggested that such an examination should be based on observation of the person's behavior, language, actions, ability to exercise sound judgment, and emotional state. Mental disorders were classified as (1) *fatuitas*, which denoted the symptom complex generally associated with immature and psychopathic persons; (2) *insania*, comprising mania, melancholia, and disorders of passion; and (3) *phrenitis*, which, for the most part, was thought to be organic conditions, in the Hippocratic tradition. For persons in each of those categories, Zacchia outlined certain rules regarding imputability and ability to testify, to marry, to enter a religious order, to leave a will, and so on. Above all, Zacchia's importance lies in the liberal attitude reflected in those concepts, which stressed that the person, rather than the law, was to be given primary consideration. Thus, manic patients who had lucid intervals could be held only partly responsible for their criminal acts; marriage might be beneficial for some melancholics, who could also hold positions with limited responsibilities. Persons who committed crimes of passion should be acquitted; alcoholics should be studied carefully; epileptics should be made to undergo a period of intensive study and observation before they were accepted into religious orders. In cases of malingering, one should keep in mind that not all symptoms are known to the patients and can be reproduced by them. And melancholia led possessed persons to believe they were persecuted by the devil. That brief summary of Zacchia's concepts underscores his progressive viewpoint. Certainly, on the basis of his contribution, his name should, at long last, be removed from oblivion, so that he may assume his proper role in the history of psychiatry.

ADVANCES IN CLINICAL OBSERVATION (SYDENHAM)

The second 17th-century physician whose work was of particular significance in the history of psychiatry was Thomas Sydenham (1624–1689), who is generally thought to have initiated the clinical approach in modern medicine. Although Sydenham was not specifically interested in diseases of the mind, he had, in the course of his clinical experience, become aware of the importance of neurotic and hysteric symptoms and the frequency with which they occurred among his pa-

tients. He described those symptoms in detail. He pointed out that, contrary to popular belief, hysteric manifestations were not restricted to women but might be observed in men and children as well. Moreover, hysterical illness might include a wide range of symptoms, such as vomiting, convulsive coughing, spasm of the colon, pain in the bladder and back, and retention of urine. Sydenham's therapeutic armamentarium in such cases did not extend beyond the usual methods of bloodletting and the use of cathartics and emetics. Rather, his great importance derives from the fact that, whereas psychiatry had focused exclusively on psychotic phenomena, now, for the first time, attention was drawn to the symptoms of neurosis. That new era of emphasis was not fully explored, however, until the beginning of the 20th century, largely as a result of the work of Sigmund Freud.

DESCRIPTIONS OF PSYCHIATRIC SYNDROMES

Throughout the 17th and 18th centuries, other workers adopted the clinical approach initiated by Sydenham for the observation and description of emotional disturbances. As a matter of fact, despite its initial significance, the classification of mental disorders had, in much the same way as Linnaeus's major opus in botany (1758), degenerated into a taxonomic compulsion. The advances in psychiatric knowledge achieved during those two centuries consisted of isolated descriptions of symptoms and clinical pictures, which were often ignored or forgotten. In Zilboorg's (1941) words,

The original and refreshing parts of the literary contribution to medical psychology [of this period] are to be found in the ever increasing number of case reports, in the observations of certain psychological details which, even though not a little desultory, represent an important contribution and a remarkable step forward.

That orientation was evident in the description by Charles Lepois (1611–1675) of postpartum psychosis and in the descriptions by Herman Boerhaave (1668–1738) and, particularly, his successor Jerome Gaub (1705–1780) (Rather, 1965) of psychosomatic conditions. It was from that viewpoint that Tissot (1728–1797) explored the problem of nervous diseases (epilepsy). It is reflected in a report by Kenelm Digby (1603–1665) of a case of *folie à deux* (Digby, 1658) and in the lengthy dissertation by Giorgio Baglivi (1668–1707) on tarantism (Baglivi, 1841). That attention to psychological detail led de Bienville (1726–1813) to introduce the term "nymphomania" in 1771 to describe uterine furor. Furthermore, the *maladie des vapours*, a favorite symptom of many fashionable ladies, came to signify hysteric symptoms caused by the spreading to the upper part of the body and the brain of noxious substances that supposedly emanated from the uterus; spleen was attributed to the particular disposition of the English people. In addition to appearing in the professional literature—John Purcell's *A Treatise of Vapours, or Hysterical Fits* published in 1702; Richard Blackmore's *A Treatise of the Spleen and Vapours*, which appeared in 1725—those terms were used widely in colloquial expressions.

The concept of hypochondria underwent a significant transformation, as described by Fischer-Homberger (1970). Originally equated with the melancholia of the Greeks, hypochondria slowly took over the humoral and nervous symptoms of melancholia. By the early 18th century it had become a disease à la mode, called "English malady" by George Cheyne (1733) (1671–1743) and attributed to the social and economic progress at which England then excelled. The causative emphasis came to be put on emotions, such as nostalgia—that is, French *ennui* and German *Heimweh*—eventually resulting in the narrower but clearer concept of hypochondria as fear of diseases.

LAY CONCEPTS OF MENTAL DISORDERS

The attempts by a few enlightened physicians to identify some psychiatric syndromes did not substantially modify the traditional view of mental illness as related to melancholia. That persistence accounts for the success for more than a century and a half of *The Anatomy of Melancholy* (1621) by Robert Burton (1577–1640), a divine at St. Thomas, near Oxford. Burton (1960) defined melancholia as

a kind of dotage without a fever, having for his ordinary companions fear and sadness without any apparent occasion.

By such a broad definition, melancholia could denote any kind of human folly, irrationality, or malaise; indeed, Burton's book easily became a treatise on the condition of humans. Heavily based on quotations from ancient literature, quite often self-contradictory, rather than on direct experience, although not void of autobiographical references, and written in a prolix and discursive style, the book had success because of the moralistic tone, consonant to the puritanical view of the world.

To those who wish good health of body and mind, give not way to solitude and idleness. Be not solitary: be not idle

was Burton's parting advice at the end of his voluminous work, which strikes an appealing note in light of today's concern with alienation. Nevertheless, his elucidation of the psychological and social causes of insanity—for example, jealousy, solitude, fear, poverty, unrequited love, excessive religiosity—justifiably appealed to his contemporaries and their descendants. That emphasis on emotional factors in the causation of mental illness, combined with the rejection of supernatural factors and occult practices, marked a new stage in the development of a more humane and understanding concept of people that anticipated the English liberal philosophy. That trend was similarly reflected in the spiritual and moral Christian guidance movement that developed during the 17th century as an expression of Protestant piety and of the Catholic counterreformation and the religious orders that evolved from it. In brief, concern for the moral and spiritual welfare of the soul could not be divorced from consideration of psychological factors, as typified by the casuistry of the Jesuits, which was based on counseling and on establishing a relationship with the person. On the philosophical level, the Jewish philosopher Baruch Spinoza (1632–1677) provided the foundation for an integrated approach to physical and psychological phenomena by considering them as two aspects of the same living organism; in so doing, he anticipated some concepts of the dynamic unconscious.

CONTRADICTIONS IN ATTITUDES TOWARD THE MENTALLY ILL

With the rise of liberalism in economy and Puritanism in religion, labor became equated with morality and idleness with sin. That marked the beginning of the Protestant ethic, which has exercised the greatest influence on Western culture to the present day. During the period of so-called enlightened absolutism, the king of each European nation, as typified by Louis XIV, was idealized as a benign father figure who was responsible not only for the safety of his subjects but for their health, mental and physical. Accordingly, general hospitals for the care of elderly people, people with venereal diseases, epileptics, and the mentally ill were built in several cities in France (in Paris, the Hôtel-Dieu in 1656) and in Germany (the Zuchthaus in Hamburg in 1620). According to descriptions that have appeared recently in the literature, those installations, each one containing several thousand inmates, combined the characteristics of a penal institution, an insane asylum, a sheltered workshop, and a hospital. An elaborate system for the commitment of that patient category was instituted. The family brought charges against the "correctionnaires" to the police, who verified the facts and obtained an order for their institutionalization (*lettre de cachet*) from the king. The king's responsibility was extended to include not only the general health of each family in his domain but supervision of their moral standards as well.

Madness was confined to the realm of the absurd and irrational, as portrayed in Molière's comedies. The glorification of reason and the concomitant lack of tolerance for the irrational, by condemning and denying irrationality, culminated in a complete rejection of the mentally ill from a philosophical viewpoint. Although passions were discussed to an increasing extent in the literary salons and in the lucid prose of the French moralists, such as La Bruyère and La Rochefoucault, they were also considered a great potential evil when they were not controlled by reason. Reason took the place of the medieval god; but in the eyes of God, madness had to be exposed; in the eyes of reason, madness had to be hidden.

In his volume on the history of insanity in the age of reason, the French philosopher Foucault (1965) advanced several new ideas on the matter. According to him, the asylums were viewed as cages in which the insane, like animals, were to be kept for the protection of society. The animality was thought to afford them a sort of invulnerability; for instance, it was thought that it protected them from sickness, a belief that persisted for a long time. That theory justified all sorts of discipline methods, including brutalization. Before psychology acquired autonomy and before the separation of physical and moral treatment, the contemporary therapeutic methods were aimed at correcting the distorted movements of the spirits, which, in the light of the new dynamic concept of life, had then come to be accepted in medicine. Accordingly, consolidation—that is, reinforcement of the spirits and the nervous fibers—was obtained through the use of vapors and the ingestion of iron; purification was obtained through blood transfusion, the creation of local infections to expunge noxious agents, and the use of soap and vinegar; immersion was obtained through purification with water, almost a symbolic return to nature, and through the use of hot and cold water in baths, which later led to surprise baths and showers; and regulation of movements—that is, renormalization of mind and body through the use of movements, from walking to running—later resulted in all sorts of rotatory and swinging devices

By the second half of the 18th century, the fear of madness, perhaps influenced by the idea of contagion then brought forward by the new field of public health, grew out of proportion. Madness became linked to liberty—that is, to the incipient democratic progress, to religion, and, in general, to the movement of civilization and, ultimately, to poverty—a dim view in the light of the rapidly increasing concern with economic factors and the rise of industrialization.

There was a basic contradiction in the attitude toward mental illness. On the one hand, the mentally ill were rejected by medical and other professional societies. On the other hand, the impressive scientific and social accomplishments during the period led to the establishment of modern science and initial acceptance of the liberal ideas of Locke and Montesquieu, which ultimately laid the foundation for modern democracy in the 19th century. Thus, even as cultivated persons all over Europe were engaged in philosophical discussion of the human mind and its functions and of social and economic theories, mental patients continued to be objects of ridicule and neglect. Hogarth's painting of Bethlehem's wards in the eighth scene of *A Rake's Progress* (1733) was a representation of the customs of the time (see Figure 16). Obviously, the custom of exhibiting lunatics for a penny every Sunday was quite popular if, on the basis of 400 pounds of annual revenue, the number of visitors can be calculated as close to 100,000. Essentially, that custom represented a revenge that irrationality played on reason for the kind of forbidden pleasure that the sight of the inmates offered to the excited senses. Such dramatic forms of sadomasochism are typically represented in the episode of the flagellants of Urban Grandier of 1634 and in the expression of mass psychopathology of the French Revolution in the next century, reflected in the works of the Marquis de Sade.

TRENDS IN THE STUDY OF THE MIND AND OF MENTAL ILLNESS IN THE 18TH CENTURY

The contradictions mentioned above largely reflected the thorough transformations of society that were taking place in the 18th century, mainly in England and France and to a smaller extent in other Western countries. At the same time, an entirely new reelaboration of psychological concepts was put forward by some representatives of the Enlightenment. Although such a reelaboration tended to remain at the theoretical level, it still portrayed a new image of humans in transition from the constrictions of the political and religious absolutism of the past to a longing for freedom and experimentation in all domains. Thus, even if the movement resulted in few changes in the care of the mentally ill, it was the basis of the new orientation that resulted in an entirely new approach to mental illness at the end of the century.

Regardless of many common aspects in the Western countries, trends in the study of the mind and of mental disorders present substantial differences in Germany, England, and France. It is, therefore, necessary to deal with the trends in those three countries separately.

FIGURE 16. Sketch of Bedlam (Bethlehem Hospital) by William Hogarth (1697–1764). (From *A Rake's Progress*. Plate VIII.)

Germany. In Germany, the emphasis remained on a search for the metaphysical aspect of reality and for the ontological nature of humans, influenced by mystic, pantheistic, and occult notions. Medicine, too, was affected by such an emphasis.

G. E. Stahl (1660–1734), the German physician who was well known for his phlogiston theory, attempted to superimpose the chemical orientation of 18th-century medicine on the Aristotelian tradition. It was Stahl's contention that the soul was not a spirit but a special force, a drive characteristic of every living organism—a viewpoint that some workers regard as a direct antecedent of the psychodynamic theory of behavior. Similary, C. F. Wolff (1733–1794), in his doctrine of epigenesis, stated that the living forces of the primary substance (protoplasm) shape each body organ. Both theories are representative of vitalism, a trend that was to become particularly popular among the German romanticists.

An all-encompassing approach to the study of humans is evident in Kant's (1974) *Anthropology from a Pragmatic Point of View* (1798) in which "pragmatic" means a view of humans as free beings full of potentialities. At the basis of Kant's volume is the principle of traditional psychology of the innate faculties conceived of in relation to the unity of consciousness. For him, all the deficiencies and diseases of the soul depended on the intellective faculty, hypochondria was a disease of the imagination, and real insanity was represented by delirium. Only delirium accompanied by fever was within the competence of the physician; insanity proper was to be treated by the philosopher. The causative aspects of insanity were hereditary disturbances and the loss of the *sensus communis*; the former was incurable, and the latter was responsive to treatment. Passions were for him diseases of the soul—a stance that, in view of Kant's influence on German thought, led to rigid, if not cruel, forms of treatment.

Physiognomy—that is, the belief in the correspondence between psychic and facial features—represented another attempt to view a human as a unity from the ontological perspective (see Figure 17). In his *Essays on Physiognomy, Designed to Promote the Knowledge and the Love of Mankind* (1789) the Swiss pastor, Johann Kasper Lavater (1741–1801), presented a human being as a microcosm, created according to a unitary plan that, through the identity of interior and exterior, determines the infinite diversity among people and, thus, the uniqueness of individuality.

An expression of that movement was the journal *Gnotzi Sauton oder Magazin zur Erfahrungsselenkunde* (*Know Yourself or Journal of the Psychology of Experience*), published in Berlin between 1783 and 1793 by the writer Carl Philipp Moritz, in which descriptions of journeys into human interiority, unusual psychological situations, and therapeutic recommendations were presented in a nonscientific way. Moritz (1785) was the author of *Anton Reiser, a Psychological Novel* (1785–1790), which, together with the Jewish philosopher Salomon Maimon's *Autobiography* (1792), represent a new search into the inner meaning of humans. Common to those various expressions of the German Enlightenment was the rejection of atheistic and materialistic themes, obviously under the influence of the deep-rooted Pietistic movement that prevailed in the many small German states.

For the later developments of psychiatry, however, no one was as important as the philosopher Schelling, who, like Spinoza, advocated a unity of spirit and matter and the identity between the absolute Being and the one and unchangeable I, the absolute I, at the base of a person. In a person the breaking and separation of the conscious from the unconscious awakens a desire for union and reconciliation of separated elements,

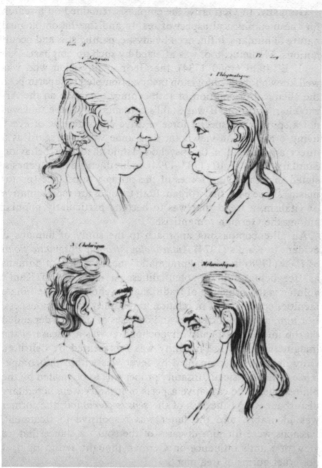

FIGURE 17. Eighteenth-century engraving representing the four main temperaments according to Johann Kasper Lavater (1741–1801): sanguine (*upper left*), phlegmatic (*upper right*), choleric (*lower left*), and melancholic (*lower right*).

almost as a progressive transformation of primordial chaos into conscious chaos. That unconscious, however, was seen from the metaphysical viewpoint, rather than from the psychological viewpoint. Regardless of the romantic emphasis on processes of flux and growth of all kinds of phenomena and of the special place assigned to humans at the highest level of the animal kingdom, the romantic evolutionism of the Naturphilosophie was static, immobile, as typified by Herder's so-called organic anthropocentrism.

Clearly, those highly speculative views, no matter how engaging, reflected a traditional view of society still tied to the slow pace of life in the various courts and bureaucratic administrations. After the closing of many convents and religious institutions that had until then taken care of many paupers, including the insane, the mentally ill became a charge of the state, and their situation of neglect worsened. The use of cages of the insane (*Dollkästen*) to transport the mentally ill was a typical example of such a situation.

True, some absolutistic and enlightened states initiated reform movements in the economic area but had difficulty in bringing them to completion because of their bureaucratic organizations. Notably, the attempt made by the Austrian Emperor Joseph II to separate the insane from other inmates by placing them in the Narrenturm (the tower of the insane) in 1784 had little success. Johann Peter Frank (1788), who attempted to set up rules for the entire society in his encyclopedic *A System of Complete Medical Police* (1976), still considered

the insane from the viewpoint of their social danger.

Ambulatorial psychiatry had little influence in Germany, mainly because of the lack of a proper public milieu of bourgeois consciousness. No physician had submitted the insane to prolonged observation in the 18th century. Rather, philosophers, educators, anthropologists, and poets turned their interest into their interiority and nonreason. That fascination with the abnormal and the nightside of human life—dreams, the unconscious, nostalgia, childhood, medieval poems—prompted Goethe to call the trend *Lazarett-poesie*. Some literary persons had even long-time contact with the mentally ill and tried to treat them in a variety of ways.

England. In England at the beginning of the 17th century, the Elizabethan Poor Law Act (1601), which placed the responsibility for the care of the poor and frequently the insane on local authorities, led to their exile from one community to another. During the era of confinement that followed, the mentally ill became the object of contempt and ridicule. But, slowly, various trends led to a more pragmatic approach to the study of the mind—Locke's sensism, Berkeley's idealism, Hume's skepticism, the Scottish philosophy of common sense alien both to sensism and to metaphysics and, no less important, the rise of liberalism in politics.

In 1714 an act of Parliament focused for the first time on pauper lunatics and on the need to distinguish them from other kinds of inmates for the purpose of treatment. It was followed in 1736 by another act of abrogation of all the laws against conjuration, enchantments, and witchcrafts and, in 1744, by a decree directing local administrations to provide for the placement and treatment of their pauper lunatics. Six years later, in 1750, St. Luke's Hospital was opened at Moorsfield. In 1774, the first Act of Parliament for Regulating Madhouses was passed; it was essentially geared to ensure the rights and the care of well-to-do patients to the exclusion of the pauper lunatics. By that time, however, a few asylums for the pauper lunatics had been opened—in Manchester in 1766, in Newcastle upon Tyne in 1767, in York in 1777, and in Liverpool in 1790.

The person behind that movement was William Battie (1704–1776), a physician who, after several years of study of the insane at Bethlehem Hospital as governor, devoted himself to the treatment, rather than to the care only, of the mentally ill. Although his contribution has passed largely unknown, Battie's (1962) *A Treatise on Madness* (1758) was the first psychiatric text based on a large personal experience. In it, madness was attributed to a disorder of sensations, either overexcitement of sensation or insensibility, and was divided into original madness, caused by an internal disorder of the nervous matter, and consequential madness, caused by an external disorder. The essential characteristics of the moral management of the mentally ill were complete separation from family and environment, elimination of exciting stimuli, distraction from fixed ideas, acquisition of a proper daily routine, and involvement in a proper occupation. John Monro (1715–1791), who was physician at Bethlehem Hospital for almost 40 years, took issue with that novel view of the treatment of the mentally ill in his *Remarks on Dr. Battie's Treatise on Madness* (1758), considering it absurd that madness caused by vitiated judgment be made the object of medical discussion.

A little later appeared the work of the Scot William Cullen (1710–1790), who founded almost the entire medicine on neurophysiology and neuropathology by conceiving muscles and nerves as a unitary nervous force and by considering all diseases as movements against the nature of that nervous force—that is, neuroses, a term he coined in 1777. Diseases were due to the various alternations of excitement and atony in the nervous system. In contrast to the existing, more complicated classifications of mental disorders, his classification defined mania as a state of excitement of the intellectual functions that was to be treated with sedative measures, including opium, which began to be used extensively for that purpose during that time. The concept of states of excitement and of atony of the nervous system was further elaborated by Cullen's pupil, John Brown (1735–1788), in his *Elementa Medicinae* (1780): sthenic diseases, such as mania, were due to excessive excitement, as opposed to asthenic diseases, such as melancholia, which were due to deficient excitement. Those views of the polarity of the nervous system had considerable influence on Schelling and, in general, on all the romantics, for whom the asthenic personality was equated with the romantic sensibility.

On a more clinical level, another dichotomy was introduced by another Scottish physician, Robert Whytt (1714–1766), between two nervous disorders: hysteria, considered by him to be more frequent in women, and hypochondria, more frequent in men. In such a way, the emphasis was now put on less severe mental conditions and on disorders that mainly affected the newly rising bourgeois class. That meant a shift from nonreason as object of external confinement to nonreason stemming from the interiority of a person. Many personages of the literature of the time, such as *Rasselas* of Samuel Johnson, were endowed with a deep personal problem. Moderation in expressing passion and renunciation of earthly pleasures, which are the tenets of the Scottish philosophy of common sense and of Puritanism in religion, slowly passed from the field of ethics into the field of the mind, pointing to a connection between mental disease and sin. In the climate of Rousseau's *Emile* (1762), the answer to that danger was to be found in escaping society either through long trips or through a return to nature. Thomas Arnold (1742–1816), founder of the Leicester Lunatic Asylum, in his *Observations on the Nature, Kinds, Causes, and Prevention of Insanity* (1782) identified as a cause of insanity the spread of power, of wealth, and of luxe. Paradoxically, it seemed that the economic success of 18th-century England carried in itself the seeds of its collapse.

Even more important from the social perspective, the rapid process of industrialization led to the oppression and poverty of many workers. The pauper lunatics represented an expression of the malaise and of the crisis that was rising in the second half of the 18th century. The physician J. Aikin, in his book *Thoughts on Hospitals* (1771), was the first to focus on the problem of the pauper lunatics, stating that in the long run their institutionalization was economical—obviously, a statement related to the passage from the extended family of the country to the small family of the city.

That opinion found support in the well-known report by John Howard, the prison reformer, *An Account of the Principal Lazarettos in Europe* (1789)—that is, on jails, hospitals, and asylums. Two years later, Jeremy Bentham (1748–1832), another great reformer, presented his proposal of building institutions as wings departing from a central office, which he called Panopticon or the Inspection House, to facilitate the supervision of the inmates. Such an idea was, indeed, followed in the construction of many institutions in England. Bentham should be remembered for having introduced two basic psychiatric concepts: psychological dynamics—that is, psychodynamics—and psychological pathologie—that is, psychopathology. That was his way of expressing not clinical concepts but the relation between pleasure and nonpleasure as the basis of human actions.

As could be anticipated, further impetus toward the consideration of mental illness came from the mental disorder attacks of King George III in 1788 to 1789 and the remarkable therapeutic success achieved by his therapist, the Reverend Dr. Francis Willis. Willis applied literally his principles of moral management to the king. Not only did he separate the king from his family, but he submitted the king to his power through fear and, especially, through fixing him in the eyes, a method that was to be followed later on by Pinel and others (Guttmacher, 1941; Macalpine and Hunter, 1969).

A similar system was used by another physician, William Perfect, owner of a private "madhouse" and author of the successful book *Methods of Cure in Some Particular Cases of Insanity and Nervous Disorders* (1778). But methods of containing the mentally ill continued to be used extensively, as evident in the success obtained by the rotatory machine described by the physician J. M. Cox as late as 1804.

France. In France, aside from the confinement of many mentally ill in the various types of *hôpital général* mentioned above, a number of them were still taken care of by religious orders in the realm of the Catholic Church. Research (Vié, 1930; Bonnafous-Sérieux, 1936) on those charitable institutions has disclosed that both open and closed wards were provided for the patients, depending on their condition. In addition, there is evidence that they received both physical and psychological treatment, consisting of isolation, reading, personal interviews with the religious staff, spiritual exercises, and controlled contact with their families. A similar program, which seems to have been held in high esteem by such leading figures of the period as Voltaire, was instituted in some small institutions, the most famous of those, at the end of the 18th century, being the Maison Belhomme in Paris.

The religious order of St. Vincent de Paul founded Saint Lazare in 1632, and the Brothers of Charity founded the Charité de Senlis in 1668 for the care of the insane and of correctionnaires—namely, patients who today would be called juvenile delinquents or psychopaths, primarily in need of supervision and rehabilitation.

In the meantime, attempts at finding the causes of pathological processes, including mental pathology, were taking place. The school of Montpelier, mainly represented by Théophile Bordeu, acquired renown around the middle of the 18th century. It had been influenced by the views of the Swiss scientist Albrecht von Haller (1708–1777), according to whom in humans there are two fundamental forces or qualities—the irritability, located in the muscular fibers and capable of effecting movements, and the sensibility, located in the nervous fibers related to the cerebral-conscious center. Haller, in turn, was especially influenced by the German physician Georg Ernst Stahl (1660–1734), who strongly asserted that the anima was the principle of life, responsible for the movements in the organism. For the adherents to the school of Montpellier, the vital principle resided in every part of the body and regulated functions by means of sensibility and motility.

From that perspective, much of the ambulatorial psychiatry related to nervous disturbances, hypochondrias, vapors, and melancholy, was based on that new model of the nervous system—that is, on the vital quality of sensibility or on the notion of nerves that are in a state of tension or relaxation and that transmit vibrations. For Anne-Charles Lorry (1726–1783), well-being was the result of the proper state of tension of the nervous fibers, and melancholia nervosa was due to a disturbance of the solid part of the nervous system. For Simon-André Tissot (1728–1787), nervous disorders were due to a sensibility that may be altered under the influence of unnatural stimuli of the social life.

As is well known, the theme of the return to nature is central to Jean-Jacques Rousseau (1712–1778), the famous author of *Emile* (1762) and of *Le contrat social* (1762). His books convinced an entire generation that the means of the Enlightenment were inadequate to fight absolutism and aristocratic rationalism. It is likely that his pervasive interest in self-observation, as revealed in the bold autobiographical details of his *Confessions* (1782–1789), and his own emotional difficulties, revealed in his wandering existence, may have given him insight into human psychology.

However, the movement that most influenced French thought in the late 18th century was that of the so-called Ideologues, considered the final stage in the process of secularization that eventually led to the French Revolution. The main representatives of that movement—Diderot, d'Holbach, La Mettrie, Condillac, Helvétius—produced their main works during that period. The most important of them, Condillac, built his entire system of philosophy, especially in *Traité des sensations* (1754), on the concept that the human psyche is formed initially by sensations, from which eventually feelings and reason develop; consequently, the study of humans should begin with the analysis of sensations. Ideology was thus a method for investigating the instruments and results of human knowledge and for placing on a concrete basis the fields of morality, economics, and education, at variance with the traditional emphasis on reason and authority. The ideologists occupied themselves with concrete services and positive facts related to psychophysiology, the education of the deaf and dumb, the reform of the school, the study of primitive societies, and, last but not least, the theoretical and practical reform of psychiatry.

Pierre-Jean Georges Cabanis (1757–1808) is especially important for the field of psychiatry. Influenced by the Ideologists, especially through the contacts established at the salon of Mme. Helvétius, where the elite of the Parisian minds congregated, from 1796 to 1802 he wrote his famous *Mémoirs* on the relationship between the physical and moral aspects of humans, which were eventually published in 1802 as *Rapports du physique et du moral de l'homme* (Cabanis, 1956). In it, in addition to pointing to sensibility based on the perception of the external reality through the various senses, as advocated by Condillac, he claimed that there were two other sources of sensibility— one resulting from the nervous system itself and the other resulting from the functioning of the internal organs, both unconscious and both apt to become conscious only when they were increased in pathological conditions, both already present at birth and acquiring importance at different chronological ages in relation to the development of particular organs, especially the sexual organs. For him, insanity had four causes: (1) sensations proper, related to the contact of the nervous system with the external world; (2) sensations received by the inner nervous extremities, particularly those innervating the digestive system and the sexual organs; (3) impressions occurring in the matter of the nervous system itself; and (4) instinctual desires and urges caused by actions of sympathies—that is, of unconscious affinities—among different organs.

It is clear that Cabanis anticipated current notions of the unconscious, of cenesthesis, of instinctual urges, of psychosomatic medicine, and, in general, of the unity of the personality. At least equally important was his action on behalf of the mentally ill. In 1791 he was named a member of a five-man Commission des Hôpitaux, charged with the reorganization of the hospitals, especially in Paris. Before that, the physician Jean Colombier had published a report in 1785 on the condition of the mentally ill, exposing the neglect of the communities toward them and cruelties that took place in the institutions that housed them. It was followed 3 years later by a report by Jacques-René Tenon, then surgeon at the Salpétrière, in which he disclosed the horrible conditions of the inmates of the Hôtel-dieu.

In 1792 Cabanis himself published a report in which he advocated that, as much as possible, the mentally ill person should remain in the care of his family and that commitment to an institution should take place solely in cases of dangerous behavior. Only the truly mentally ill pauper should be accepted in public institutions to avoid unnecessary crowding; and the single method of restraint should be the straitjacket. Influenced by revolutionary ideals, he hoped that the improvement of society would result in a decrease of mental illness. Although such a goal was not reached, at least Cabanis accomplished a very important thing: He managed to have Pinel named to the position of physician at Bicêtre.

Psychiatry in the Late 18th and Early 19th Centuries

Traditionally, the credit for the elimination of the objectionable methods of restraint has been ascribed to the French physician Pinel. His dramatic efforts to free the mentally ill from their chains at Bicêtre in 1793 have been described at length in the literature. More properly, Pinel should share the credit for that achievement with an Italian, Vincenzo Chiarugi, and an Englishman, William Tuke. Thus, here one has a striking example of *zeitgeist* in the history of psychiatry. Actually, the existing facilities for the care of mental patients had been criticized strongly in France in earlier reports by Colombier (1785), Tenon (1788), and La Rochefoucault-Liancourt (1791). Furthermore, proper treatment methods had been proposed by the physician and philosopher Cabanis. The French revolution outruled any attempt to initiate improvements in the existing institutions, but other equally important events occurred in Florence, Italy, in York, England, and even in France, in Chambéry and Paris.

VINCENZO CHIARUGI

The rulers of Florence during the 17th and 18th centuries, the Medicis and the Lorenas, had continued to encourage the scientific research initiated by Galileo and carried on by others, especially in biology and medicine. Italian enlightenment, in contrast to that of the French and the English, acquired a practical character, which crystallized under the rule of the Grand Duke Peter Leopold (1747–1792) in a number of economic, financial, judiciary, educational, and religious reforms, culminating in the project for a constitution of 1778, a unique instance in which peaceful revolution almost led to modern democracy. Although many of those proposed economic and social reforms could not be put into effect by the Grand Duke and his ministers because the general population was simply not ready for them, several programs of importance to the future development of psychiatry were implemented.

The law on the insane—which established the specific rules, including a mental examination, to be followed in cases of proposed commitment—was passed in 1774. In 1785 the Grand Duke began the construction of the Hospital Bonifacio, which was opened 3 years later under the medical direction of a young physician, Vincenzo Chiarugi (1759–1820). The 1789 regulations of the hospital (see Figure 18), which were obviously prepared under Chiarugi's (1793) supervision, specifically stated:

It is a supreme moral duty and medical obligation to respect the insane individual as a person.

Accordingly, neither physical force nor cruel methods of restraint were to be applied to patients, except for the occasional use of a straitjacket, designed so that it would not cause the patient undue discomfort. Hygienic and safety measures were also described in the regulations, and, despite their unpretentious character, they represented a radical change in treatment of the mentally ill. Chiarugi's three-volume work *Medical Treatise on Insanity* (1793–1794) is somewhat obscure in the passages that describe the psychological foundations of personality, which represent an amalgamation of Aristotelian-Thomistic and modern concepts. Nevertheless, it is important for its pathological and clinical views. Those volumes included descriptions of 100 clinical cases, accompanied in many instances by descriptions of the condition of the patient's brain at autopsy. With regard to diagnosis, evaluation procedures were outlined, and mental illnesses were divided into three general categories: melancholia (partial insanity), mania (general insanity), and amentia (abnormal functioning of intellect and will), which might be either congenital or acquired. The causes of mental disease were discussed, and possible congenital and environmental causes were listed. Most important, the prescribed principles of treatment emphasized the importance of handling patients with tact and understanding and of using an authoritative and impressive but, at the same time, pleasant and individualized approach. Apparently, that therapeutic program, which was similar to what was later known as moral treatment, was carried out by nurses and attendants under medical supervision. Unfortunately, Chiarugi's reform program fell into complete oblivion, first because of the peripheral role played by Florence on the European scene and, especially, because of the preoccupation with the succession of wars and revolutions that took place throughout Italy shortly thereafter.

THE TUKES AND THE YORK RETREAT

In England, among the religious movements aimed at returning to the basic principles preached in the Gospels was that of the Quakers, founded by George Fox (1624–1691) and later continued by William Penn (1644–1718). After a period of persecution, the movement progressively spread, even to the United States, after the Toleration Act of 1689. Opposed to any form of religious dogmatism and power, the Friends, as the adherents to the movement called themselves, in their yearly meetings became involved in all kinds of charitable and social endeavors—relief of the poor, sound education, prison reform, the battle against alcoholism, and the abolition of slavery. The care of the insane was also among their goals.

As early as 1671, at one of their meetings, it was suggested (Tuke, 1964):

REGOLAMENTO

DEI REGI SPEDALI

DI SANTA MARIA NUOVA

e

DI BONIFAZIO

FIRENZE MDCCLXXXIX.
Per Gaetano Cambiagi Stampator Granducale.

CON APPROVAZIONE.

FIGURE 18. Title page of the *Regolamento Leopoldino* of 1789, in which were established the principles of the reform in the treatment of mental patients by Vincenzo Chiarugi (1759–1820).

FIGURE 19. William Tuke (1732–1819), founder of the Retreat near York, England.

That frends doe seeke some place convenient In or about ye Citty wherein they may put any person that may be distracted or troubled in minde, that soe they may not be put amongst ye world's people or Run about ye Streets.

Nothing came of that proposal. In 1791, however, a woman belonging to the Society of Friends was placed in St. Luke's Asylum; her family was denied access to her, and in a few weeks she died. That event gave the final impetus for the Society of Friends to found their own institution for the care and treatment of their insane members—their concern being that the indiscriminate mixture of persons of different religious sentiments and practices, as occurs in large public institutions, would enhance melancholic ideas and make their condition worse.

William Tuke (1732–1822) (see Figure 19), a successful wholesale tea and coffee merchant, although already 60, at the quarterly meeting of 1792 took the initiative with others to found a facility for insane Quakers. The money necessary for the building and the maintenance of the asylum was to come from paid-up capital sums, in exchange for which annuities were to be issued, paid from gifts and annual contributions. The charge for the complete maintenance of the patient—the cost of clothing alone being excluded—was first set at 14 or 15 shillings a week.

The institution was formally opened in May 1796 as the Retreat near York (see Figure 20). Its history and philosophy of treatment were later presented in detail in Samuel Tuke's (1964) *Description of the Retreat* (1813). Samuel Tuke (1784–1857), like his grandfather William Tuke and his father Henry Tuke (1755–1814), devoted his life to the endeavor. The inmates were divided into two sections, one for men under the supervision of a superintendent and one for women under the supervision of a matron. Their number continued to increase, up to 66 in 1812, of whom 26 were men and 40 were women.

Although a physician was soon hired, the treatment was essentially nonmedical, and no consideration whatsoever was given to the possible organic causes of mental illness. As a matter of fact, all traditional means of medical treatment were disregarded, with the exception of hot baths. Instead, the therapeutic philosophy followed at the Retreat was exclusively based on the so-called moral treatment. The spacious and

cheerful building was located in a nice area in the country; there were no bars on the windows, and a thick edge of shrubs replaced iron gates around the property; the only means of restraint were strait-waistcoats and a room for temporary confinement; ample courts and space for activities and recreation were available.

As Samuel Tuke (1964) put it:

The moral treatment of the insane seems to divide itself into three parts ... 1. By what means the power of the patient to control the disorder is strengthened and assisted. 2. What modes of coertion are employed when restraint is absolutely necessary, and 3. By what means the general comfort of the insane is promoted.... The principle of fear, which is rarely decreased by insanity, is considered as of great importance in the management of the patients. But it is not allowed to be existed, beyond that degree which naturally arises from the necessary regulations of the family..... The patients are arranged into classes, as much as may be, according to the degree in which they approach rational or orderly conduct.... To the mild system of treatment adopted at the Retreat, I have no doubt we may partly attribute, the happy recovery of so large a proportion of melancholy patients.

Later on Tuke (1964) said:

In an early part of this chapter, it is stated, that the patients are considered capable of rational and honourable inducement; and though we allowed *fear* a considerable place in the production of that restraint, which the patient generally exerts on his entrance in a new situation; yet, the *desire of esteem* is considered, at the Retreat, as operating, in general, still more powerfully. This principle ... is found to have great influence, even over the conduct of the insane ... when properly cultivated, it leads many to struggle to conceal and overcome their morbid propensities.... This struggle is highly beneficial to the patient, by strengthening his mind, and conducing to a salutary habit of self-restraint.... That fear is not the only motive, which operates in producing *self-restraint* in the minds of maniacs, is evident from its being often exercised in the presence of strangers, who are merely passing through the house; and which, I presume, can only be accounted for, from that desire of esteem, which has been stated to be a powerful motive to conduct.

And still later Tuke (1964) said:

It is probably from encouraging the action of this principle, that so much advantage has been found in this Institution, from treating the patient as much in the manner of a rational being, as the state of his mind will possibly allow. The superintendent is particularly attentive to this point, in his conversation with the patients.... Indeed, [the

The "Retreat" at York, England.

FIGURE 20. The Retreat near York, England, in the late 18th century.

insane] perceive, or if not, they are informed on the first occasion that their treatment depends, in great measure, upon their conduct.

As a matter of fact:

there is much analogy between the judicious treatment of children, and that of insane persons.

In the effort to individualize the treatment for each patient:

considerable advantage may certainly be derived, in this part of moral management, from an acquaintance with the previous habits, manners, and prejudices of the individual. Nor must we forget to call to our aid, in endeavoring to promote self-restraint, the mild but powerful influence of our holy religion.

Elsewhere it is said that the superintendent

introduces such topics as he knows will most interest them [the patients]; and which, at the same time, allows them to display their knowledge to the greatest advantage; . . . every means is taken to reduce the mind from its favourite but unhappy musings, by bodily exercise, walks, conversation, reading, and other innocent recreations. . . . Those who are not engaged in any useful occupation are allowed to read, write, draw, play at ball, chess, crafts, etc. . . . [T]he female superintendent, who possesses an uncommon share of benevolent activity, and who has the chief management of the female patients, as well as of the domestic department, occasionally gives a general invitation to the patients to a tea-party . . . the patients control, in a wonderful degree, their different propensities; and the scene is at once curious, and affectingly gratifying. Some of the patients occasionally pay visits to the friends in the city; and female visitors are appointed every month to pay visits to those of their own sex.

The moral treatment developed at the Retreat near York served as a model for several institutions that were opened in England, as well as in the United States, in the early 19th century.

PINEL'S MORAL TREATMENT

In the meantime, in 1791, Joseph Daquin (1733–1815), an obscure physician in charge of an institution at Chambéry, a village in the then French duchy of Savoy, published *La philosophie de la folie*, in which he advocated a more humane approach to the care of the mentally ill. However, that contribution—like the work of Chiarugi and, to a smaller extent, William Tuke—was soon overshadowed by the renown that Pinel acquired throughout Europe.

Philippe Pinel (1745–1826) was born in southern France and was influenced by the vitalism of the medical school at Montpelier. Later, when he moved to Paris, Pinel became part of the intellectual group of ideologists (Cabanis, d'Holbach). In 1793, after he had been associated with the Maison Belhomme for 5 years, Pinel became superintendent of the Bicêtre (for male patients) and later of the Salpêtrière (for female patients), where criminals and mentally retarded patients, as well as the mentally ill, were housed. One of Pinel's first accomplishments at the Bicêtre was to free the mentally ill from their chains (see Figure 21). On the one hand, since he took that radical action during the Reign of Terror, the step was widely acclaimed as an act of personal courage. On the other hand, its significance lies in its far-reaching implications for the development of psychiatry. Pinel is remembered for two other major contributions to psychiatry: his attempt to analyze and categorize symptoms and his application of moral treatment.

Under the influence of the Ideologists, Pinel considered basic to his system the psychological analysis of ideas, to be integrated with that of the emotional drives. Only if patients were free to move around at their ease and if developmental data related to the patient's biography were available was it possible to arrive at the understanding of the symptoms and of the succeeding stages of the disease. He conceived of insanity as a disturbance of self-control and identity, for which he preferred the denomination of "alienation"; hence, the term "reasoning

FIGURE 21. Philippe Pinel (1745–1826), the founder of modern psychiatry, liberating mental patients at the Salpêtrière in 1795. (From the painting by Robert Fleury.)

T R A I T É

MÉDICO–PHILOSOPHIQUE

S U R

L'ALIÉNATION MENTALE,

O U

L A M A N I E,

PAR PH. PINEL,

Professeur de l'École de Médecine de Paris,
Médecin en chef de l'Hospice National des
femmes, ci-devant la Salpêtrière, et Membre
de plusieurs Sociétés savantes.

Avec Figures représentant des formes de crâne ou des
portraits d'Aliénés.

A P A R I S,

CHEZ RICHARD, CAILLE ET RAVIER,
Libraires, rue Haute-Feuille, N°. ii.

A N I X.

FIGURE 22. Title page of *A Treatise on Insanity* (1801) by Philippe
Pinel (1745–1826).

mania" (*manie raisonnante*) to describe the nonreason due to
the uncontrolled discharge of instinctual energies.

Pinel (1962) described clinical symptoms in a very simple
manner but with great clarity in the best medical tradition in
his *Traité médico-philosophique sur la manie* (1801) (see Figure
22). In it five forms of insanity were presented: (1) melancholia—that is, the predominance of an exclusive delirious idea
while the other intellectual faculties remain intact; (2) mania
without delirium (*manie sans délire*)—that is, a pure disturbance of will in the absence of intellectual disturbances; (3)
mania with delirium, the most typical form of mental illness;
(4) dementia—that is, a disturbance in thought processes; and
(5) idiocy—that is, the obliteration of intellectual faculties and
affects. Detailed data were accumulated for each patient. Most
of the data were gathered by Pinel himself, a fact that accounts
for the abundance of clinical examples throughout the book.
Written in a clear and simple style, his presentations on the
course of the diseases as they affected the patients soon acquired renown and greatly helped the cause of psychiatry.

The following is an example of a case report:

A 20-year-old girl, thrown into confusion by an unhappy love, still
had her eyes full of life. She passed from one subject to another entirely
different one with the rapidity of the flashing of lightning. At times her
utterances were soft and full of decency, but at times obscene, conveying an unveiled invitation to love. The next moment she indulged in
vanity, using conceited and commanding language. Then she believed
she was a queen, her gait was proud and majestic, and she looked

disdainfully at the companions of her misfortune. Advice and admonition were of no use, she did not seem to listen. Yielding to sudden
impulses, she was running or singing, screaming, dancing, laughing, or
beating the nearby persons, though aimlessly and with no malice, not
unlike a child.

More important than environmental factors were those factors that were thought to indicate a predisposition to the later
development of insanity; among them, passions were considered of particular importance. Accordingly, moral treatment
was based on Aristotle's concept of mental health as dependent
on the balance of passions, a word that in 18th-century literature corresponded to the present use of the word "emotions."
Moreover, in anticipation of later theories of psychosomatic
functioning, passions (emotions) were considered the link between mind and body. With regard to specific therapeutic
techniques, the doctor initially had to exert the greatest firmness in his approach to the patient and hold his attention and
control his will with his eyes. Once the patient was subdued
and had been completely dominated by the doctor, treatment
consisted of a combination of kindness, firmness, and coercion.
Although his book emphasized that phase of treatment, which
Pinel conducted with the assistance of his remarkable male
nurse Poussin, there is evidence that the patient's participation
in various activities within a structured environment greatly
contributed to the success of Pinel's moral treatment.

OVERVIEW OF EARLY CONTRIBUTIONS
TO PSYCHIATRIC REFORM

A comparison of the therapeutic orientations of Chiarugi,
Tuke, and Pinel reveals that each of those pioneers in psychiatric reform emphasized the healthy part of the patient's personality—that is, to use modern terminology, the conflict-free
sphere of ego functioning. In addition, they shared the belief
than any meaningful therapeutic approach had to be geared to
the healthy part of the personality and that, consequently, the
right treatment consisted of a combination of support and
dependency. The course of treatment might be affected by the
nature of the doctor-patient relationship—that is, the transference—but, without exception, the treatment success required
that the patient be separated from his family so that he might
receive therapy in the structured environment of the hospital,
where the patient was treated as a child in a sort of artificial
family.

Apart from those basic similarities in viewpoint, Chiarugi's
innovations were made possible by the various reform measures
introduced by the Grand Duke Peter Leopold, a fact that
implies a close connection between politics and psychiatry.
Today, the desirability of such a connection would be debated
at length. In fact, however, Chiarugi was practically unaware
of the importance of the therapeutic reforms he initiated.
Rather, he felt that the value of his work lay in his emphasis
on the study of the anatomical changes in the brain of mental
patients.

At the York Retreat, the external constrictions were replaced
by internal constrictions, and the philosophy underlying that
change was based on the puritanical and bourgeois ideals of
the time. The Retreat was conceived of as a large family under
the attentive and mildly disciplinarian father figure of the
superintendent, and the patients were treated like children. The
methods used were close to today's behavior modification.
Underneath all that was the belief in the spontaneous improvement in the patient when he was separated from his family and

influenced by moral and religious constraints in an idyllic place in the country. No medical consideration was given to the course of the mental illness; nor was any thought given to the teaching of students.

As for Pinel, the French Revolution, through its emphasis on freedom and equality, led to a reorganization in the structuring of the asylum and to the achievement of the principles of moral treatment through reasoning; at the same time, it uncovered the influence of instincts, passions, and social needs on the economy of the person. Pinel was quite aware of the fact that the revolutionary impetus—by liberating the perverse instincts of the populace, notably the poor—might lead to insanity; on the other side, he noticed that aristocrats who were not involved in regular work were also prone to insanity. Although, in the spirit of the Ideologists and of the Revolution, Pinel was anticlerical, he recognized the importance of religion as a value, together with the other values of the bourgeois system, such as the importance of cultivating the land, of dividing labor according to skills, of competing in achieving goals and in perpetuating the system.

At variance with the philosophy of the York Retreat, however, Pinel combined scientific observation with moral treatment; a distinguished physician himself, he advocated the importance of confronting the patient with his own disease, even by facing the patient with a caricature of his condition or by using pedagogical lies—such as, by administering an emetic to a patient who believed he had a snake in his stomach and by hiding a snake in his vomit. In spite of those differences, it has been argued in recent years, especially by Foucault (1965), that the internal restraints provided to the patients through confinement in the asylum were as objectionable as the external restraints; in line with Marxist views, Dörner (1969) stressed that the basis of the confinement of the mentally ill in the asylum was the bourgeois attempt to isolate the poor and to increase their labor capacity in the context of the institution. Both arguments have remained highly controversial and have generated much discussion.

Two other independent movements, somewhat opposed but equally appealing to many laymen—namely, phrenology and mesmerism—reached the peak of their popularity in the early part of the 19th century.

PHRENOLOGY

Franz Josef Gall (1758–1828), the founder of phrenology, was a distinguished physician from Vienna who taught brain physiology there for several years. On the basis of physiognomic concepts—especially those developed by the Swiss pastor Johann Kasper Lavater (1741–1801), who was a close friend of Goethe—Gall postulated that mental faculties were innate and that they depended on the topical structures of the brain, to which corresponded particular protuberances of the external cranial surface. Eventually, he identified 27 organs in the human brain—19 of which were found in animals as well. Those organs corresponded to an equal number of faculties that, being fixed from birth, could not be modified by education. Although Gall tried to avoid criticism by theologians by including among the faculties he listed such factors as goodness and religious sentiment, he was accused of materialism and was ultimately forced to leave Vienna for Paris, where he was influenced by the Ideologists. In Paris he continued his neurological studies, in the course of which he anticipated the concept of cerebral localizations that was to prove fruitful for future investigators. His phrenological teaching was carried on

by his pupil Johann Casper Spurzheim (1776–1832), who lectured extensively on phrenology in the United States, where the new doctrine had already been introduced by two Scottish laymen, George and Andrew Combe. Eventually, phrenological societies and journals were founded in several American cities, and the movement became increasingly popular, owing to the efforts of its two principal proponents, the Fowler brothers. It did not decline in popularity until the latter half of the century.

MESMERISM

The second movement, mesmerism, was initiated by Franz Anton Mesmer (1734–1815), who in 1766, in his doctoral dissertation at the University of Vienna Medical School, subscribed to the concept that planets influence physiological and psychological phenomena, a concept that derived from the writings of some Paracelsists, such as Robert Fludd, and from the writings of William Maxwell and Richard Mead. In a later publication, entitled *Memory on the Discovery of Animal Magnetism* (1779), Mesmer (1948) hypothesized that humans are endowed with a special magnetic fluid, a kind of sixth sense, that, when liberated, can produce amazing healing effects. Mesmer himself claimed to have magnetized and cured many patients, but the controversy that arose over his treatment of Miss Paradis—a gifted musician who, quite possibly, had been afflicted by hysterical blindness—forced him to leave Vienna and to move to Paris in 1778. There, his miraculous cure achieved great success (see Figure 23), and, as a result, he elicited the support of many distinguished and wealthy people—and an equal amount of opposition from the medical profession. A royal commission that was appointed in 1784 and that included Benjamin Franklin investigated mesmerism and handed down an unfavorable report. After that defeat, Mesmer retired to Switzerland, where he died in poverty and oblivion (Buranelli, 1975; Rausky, 1977). However, his pupils continued to practice mesmerism, and eventually the Marquis du Puységur (1751–1825) came to the conclusion that mesmerized patients were actually in a trance state. That observation was subsequently confirmed by James Braid (1795–1860) (1960), who coined the word "hypnosis." Even as the teaching of mesmerism flourished in Germany, the physicians James Esdaile (1808–1859) (1957) and John Ellioston (1791–1868) made good use of mesmerism as a method of anesthetizing surgical patients in India and in England, respectively. The importance of mesmerism for psychiatry lies in the fact that it

FIGURE 23. A mesmeric seance held around the banquet in Mesmer's clinic in Paris around 1780.

represented the most notable attempt to focus on neurotic phenomena, as opposed to psychoses.

MENTAL HOSPITALS AND THE APPLICATION OF MORAL TREATMENT IN THE UNITED STATES

Colonial period. The United States presented an ideal testing ground for some of the new ideas advanced by Pinel and William Tuke. During the Colonial period, insanity was linked to superstitious beliefs of all kinds, including witchcraft. In 1647, in Connecticut, the first alleged witch was hanged. A few decades later, as related by Cotton Mather (Wendell, 1963) in his *Memorable Providences* (1689), many citizens began to be impressed by a series of strange events apparently caused by wild women. Under the influence of narrow Puritanism and obviously misogynic views, the community of Salem, Massachusetts, was filled with terror of the invisible world—that is, unexplainable phenomena. The accusations of some suggestible young girls resulted in the Salem witchcraft trials in 1692, when 250 persons were arrested and tried; 50 were condemned, 19 were executed, two died in prison, and one died of torture. The next year Governor Phips released from custody all persons accused of witchcraft, but superstitious beliefs persisted.

The Elizabethan Poor Law Act of 1601 also affected the American colonies. By 1676 Massachusetts had enacted a statute (Deutsch, 1948):

> Whereas, there are distracted persons in some tounes, that are unruly, whereby not only the familyes wherein they are, but others suffer undue damages by them, it is ordered by this Court and the authoritye thereof, that the selectmen in all tounes where such persons are hereby impowered & injoyned to take care of all such persons, that they doe not damnify others.

In practice, it seems that a few mentally ill were left at home or boarded for a lump sum in private homes, where they were likely exploited. Violent and dangerously sick persons were put in jails, such as the Poor House, Work-House, and House of Correction of New York City, founded in 1736. Other mentally ill persons, less fortunate, were either sold on the auction block or simply brought to the town line and left to wander on their own. Except for a few champions of the right of the individual, such as Roger Williams, the basic attitude of the general population toward the mentally ill was uncharitable and punitive.

In the late 18th century, however, under the influence of the Enlightenment, a more optimistic view of humans as innately good and as possessing perfectibility slowly came to prevail. The Quakers, especially, like their counterparts in Europe, played a paramount role in fostering a humanitarian approach to the mentally ill. Under the influence of some of the prominent people, beginning with Benjamin Franklin, who founded the Pennsylvania Hospital, the first general hospital in America, in 1756, the provincial Assembly passed an act on January 3, 1751,

> to encourage the establishment of a Hospital for the Relief of the Sic Poor of this Province, and for the Reception and Cure of Lunaticks.

Thus, in 1756, the first group of mentally ill patients were admitted in the cellar of the new Pennsylvania Hospital. The methods of treatment were rudimental, and great faith was placed on work as a way to restore health. Patients were cared for by cell-keepers—that is, attendants. When violent, the patients were restrained by handcuffs, ankle-irons, or the

maddshirt, a strait-waistcoat. As in England, the patients could be exhibited on Sunday to curious sightseers for a set admission fee. Eventually, in 1796, a new wing was erected especially for the mental patients (see Figure 24). Meanwhile, in 1773 the first American asylum exclusively for the mentally ill had been opened under government auspices and with the support of the state, in Williamsburg, then the flourishing capital of Virginia. Under the leadership of the Galt family, who were connected with that institution for nearly a century, the therapeutic approach used there was benign and humanitarian and considerable use was made of agricultural work and recreational programs, mainly music and reading. However, because of the geographical isolation of the hospital from the rapidly growing Northern states, where moral treatment was soon to develop; because of the prevailing lay, rather than medical, operation; and because of the unconcern for publishing annual reports, which were a viable source of information and public support in the Northern hospitals, the Williamsburg asylum went through a period of decline in the succeeding decades, even before the social deterioration of the South related to the Civil War.

Benjamin Rush. The early treatment of the mentally ill at Pennsylvania Hospital is closely connected with the work of Benjamin Rush, who is called the father of American psychiatry and whose picture is reproduced in the seal of the American Psychiatric Association. Born in Philadelphia in 1745 of Quaker parents, he graduated from Princeton, then New Jersey College, at the age of 15 and then attended the prestigious medical school of Edinburgh, where he was especially influenced by the teachings of Cullen and Sydenham. After his graduation in 1767, Rush spent some time in London and Paris. Endowed with an appealing and warm personality not immune to some vanity, he came in contact with several outstanding men there. Back home, he was appointed professor of chemistry in the College of Philadelphia—the country's first medical school, founded in 1765—and had his *Course of Lectures on Chemistry* published in 1770.

In the meantime, he became involved in many other activities, in which he proved to be a skillful propagandist: the movement for the abolition of slavery; the recognition of the need to overcome attitudes of discrimination against members from minority groups, such as Indians; temperance and treatment for alcoholics; and, later, the alleviation of hardship for prisoners and the fight against the use of tobacco. More important, however, was his involvement in political action, which led to his appointment to the Pennsylvania delegation in the Continental Congress and, eventually, to his signing of the Declaration of Independence in 1776. Except during his service

FIGURE 24. The Pennsylvania Hospital for the Insane in the late 18th century.

in the Revolutionary Army and his involvement in teaching and social action, Rush carried on an extensive medical practice in Philadelphia; he mainly followed the theories of the Dutchman Boerhaave and his former teacher Cullen. His medical career was clouded by his controversial and extensive use of purging and bloodletting during the epidemics of yellow fever in 1793.

Throughout his professional career Rush maintained a constant interest in the problem of mental illness. In 1786, he was invited to address the Philosophical Society; in "An Inquiry into the Influence of Physical Causes upon the Moral Faculty," he advocated a distinction between moral rules based on law and customs and ethical rules based on the individual tendency toward perfection and self-realization. Since those ethical rules are conditioned by constitutional and environmental factors, it follows that not only madness but also hysteria and hypochondria, regardless of moral implications, fall into the realm of medicine.

A few years before, in 1783, he had become a regular member of the staff of the Pennsylvania Hospital, and for many years he was in charge of the mental patients housed there. Slowly, through his own observation and under the influence of Pinel and others, Rush (1962) developed his psychiatric concepts and finally presented them in 1812, the year before his death, in *Medical Inquiries and Observations upon the Diseases of the Mind*, which remained for 70 years the only American textbook of psychiatry (see Figure 25). Rush regarded insanity as a disease of the brain:

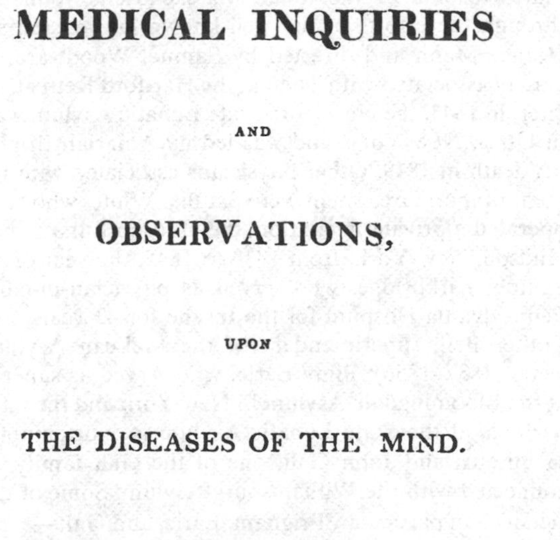

MEDICAL INQUIRIES

AND

OBSERVATIONS,

UPON

THE DISEASES OF THE MIND.

BY BENJAMIN RUSH, M. D.

Professor of the Institutes and Practice of Medicine, and of Clinical Practice, in the University of Pennsylvania.

PHILADELPHIA:

PUBLISHED BY KIMBER & RICHARDSON,

NO. 237, MARKET STREET.

Merritt, Printer, No. 9, Watkin's Alley.

1812.

FIGURE 25. Title page of the textbook on mental diseases by Benjamin Rush (1745–1813).

The cause of madness is seated primarily in the blood vessels of the brain ... madness is a chronic form, affecting that part of the brain which is the seat of the mind.

Probably under the influence of Brown's doctrine of stimulus and counterstimulus, Rush classified the remote and exciting causes of mental disorders in two groups, those acting directly on the body or the brain—congenital malformations, cerebral diseases, systemic diseases affecting the central nervous system—and those acting on the body or the brain through the medium of the mind—intensive study, strong emotional impressions, moral preoccupations, such as guilt feelings.

Rush listed as predisposing factors to mental diseases: heredity, young age, female sex, single status, intellectual occupations, excesses of climate, certain forms of government, revolutions, and particular religious tenets. Under the impact of the Scottish philosophers and of the phrenologists, he stated that the morbid action of the blood vessels affects the functions of the mind that are located there—that is, the internal senses or faculties. He distinguished nine faculties of the mind—three intellectual, three moral, and three miscellaneous—and he left a description of each one of them, which is today obsolete. Rather appealing, however, is his definition of mental diseases:

By derangement of the understanding I mean every departure of the mind in its perceptions, judgments, and reasonings from its natural and habitual order, accompanied with corresponding actions.

In retrospect, Rush's importance lies not in his elaborate classification but in the role he attributed to the derangement of passions—love, grief, fear, anger, joy, envy, malice, and hatred—and of the sexual appetite, in his lengthy discussion about dreams and sleep, and in his description of certain clinical pictures, such as hysteria. Regardless of his conviction of the organic nature of insanity, in actuality he believed in the psychogenic origin of many forms of mental disorders, including some attributed to moral derangement, which today is no longer considered as belonging to psychiatry.

Rush advocated two types of treatment—one intended to act directly on the body and another intended to act indirectly on the body through the medium of the mind. To the first type belonged bloodletting (of which he made great use), purges, emetics, reduced diet, drugs, and, in particular cases, the use of two curious mechanical devices: the tranquilizer, a chair to which the patient was strapped hand and foot, and the gyrator, a modification of a circulating swing, introduced in England by Cox and consisting of a rotating board to which the patient was strapped with the head farthest from the center in an attempt to cause the blood to rush to the head. To the second and more enlightened type of treatment belonged the attempt to eliminate all old associations and ideas through removal of the patient from his family and from all remote and exciting causes, the writing of a personal account of the symptoms, a complete change of activities, the encouragement to memorize passages of verse and prose, and the use of work, amusements of various types, and travel.

In the hospital the physician was urged to listen sympathetically to patients and thus give them the opportunity to relieve their minds and their consciences while he exercised control over them through his eye, his voice, and his countenance, so as to secure their obedience; very noisy and disturbing patients were to be housed in separate buildings; patients were to be divided by sexes; intelligent men and women were to be hired as attendants; and visitors were to be rigidly excluded. With slight modifications, such a program is still basic to today's philosophy of institutional treatment.

Rush's book passed largely unnoticed, perhaps because of the rather controversial nature of his personality, his intolerance of criticism, and his inclination to uncritically follow all sorts of ideas and to espouse unpopular causes. However, evidence of his prestige is seen in his appointment as dean of the medical school and his close association, to the very end, with Thomas Jefferson and John Adams.

Pioneers of moral treatment. The year of Rush's death, 1813, saw the appearance in London of *Description of the Retreat near York* by Samuel Tuke (see Figure 26), the grandson of William Tuke. In it Tuke (1964) described the general atmosphere of kindness and sympathy and the optimistic view of mental illness that prevailed among the Quakers involved in the operation of the York Retreat, an atmosphere and view generally subsumed under the term "moral treatment." The word "moral," then used in the sense of emotional or psychological, carried the connotations of hope and confidence, as well as of moral responsibility. Interestingly enough, moral treatment as a therapeutic philosophy was never defined by Tuke's adherents or opponents; as a matter of fact, it was completely forgotten until recently, when it was revived by some psychiatric historians.

In this country moral treatment essentially came to signify the philosophy of treatment applied at the York Retreat, a fact certainly understandable in view of the close intellectual and social dependence of this country on England, even after the Revolution. However, Pinel's ideas also came to be known soon for at least two reasons: the paramount role in all aspects of literary, scientific, and political life then played by Paris and, specifically, the availability of Pinel's treatise in an English translation in 1806.

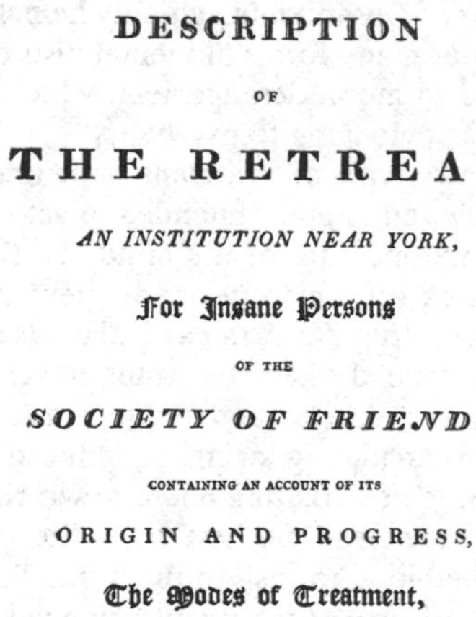

DESCRIPTION

OF

THE RETREAT,

AN INSTITUTION NEAR YORK,

For Insane Persons

OF THE

SOCIETY OF FRIENDS.

CONTAINING AN ACCOUNT OF ITS

ORIGIN AND PROGRESS,

The Modes of Treatment,

AND

A STATEMENT OF CASES.

By SAMUEL TUKE.

With an Elevation and Plans of the Building.

YORK:

PRINTED FOR W. ALEXANDER, AND SOLD BY HIM;
SOLD ALSO BY M. M. AND E. WEBB, BRISTOL;
AND BY DARTON, HARVEY, AND CO.; WILLIAM PHILLIPS; AND
W. DARTON, LONDON.

1813.

FIGURE 26. Title page of *Description of the Retreat near York* by Samuel Tuke (1784–1857), son of William Tuke.

Strongly influenced by optimistic and humanitarian trends about human nature, some community leaders—educators, businessmen, clergymen, and physicians—took the initiative of opening a few mental hospitals early in the 19th century. Under private auspices, the Friends Asylum at Frankford, Pennsylvania, was opened in 1817 by some Quakers; the Bloomingdale Asylum in New York was opened in 1821 (under the auspices of the New York Hospital, founded in 1771) by the layman Thomas Eddy, a Quaker merchant; the McLean Asylum in Massachusetts was opened in 1818 under the leadership of Rufus Wyman, the first physician appointed to this post in America; the Hartford Retreat in Connecticut was opened in 1824, first under the superintendency of Eli Todd and later, from 1843 to 1872, of John Butler; the Brattleboro Retreat in Brattleboro, Vermont, was opened in 1836 under William Rockwell; and the Butler Hospital in Providence, Rhode Island, was opened in 1847 under Isaac Ray. Among the earliest state-supported institutions were the Eastern State Hospital at Lexington, Kentucky, opened in 1824; the Manhattan State Hospital in New York City, opened in 1825; the Western State Hospital in Staunton, Virginia, opened in 1828; and the South Carolina State Hospital in Columbia, South Carolina, opened in 1828. In contrast with the private or corporate hospitals, in which moral treatment was applied, those state institutions remained largely custodial.

Within 30 years, 18 hospitals were built; from 1825 to 1865 the number of asylums grew from nine to 62. The first state institution that relied on moral treatment and one that carried a brilliant tradition in American psychiatry was the Worcester State Hospital in Worcester, Massachusetts, founded largely through the efforts of the well-known lawyer and statesman Horace Mann and directed by Samuel Woodward, who was closely associated with Todd at the Hartford Retreat. Ten years later, in 1843, the New York State Lunatic Asylum was opened in Utica, New York, and was led by Amariah Brigham until his death in 1849. Other physicians associated with the movement of moral treatment were Samuel White, who successfully operated a private institution, the Hudson Lunatic Asylum, in Hudson, New York, from 1830 to 1845, the year of his death; Samuel Kirkbridge, who served as physician-in-chief of the Pennsylvania Hospital for the Insane for 43 years, until 1883; Luther Bell, superintendent of the McLean Asylum for 20 years (1837–1856); Pliny Earle, who served as superintendent at the Bloomingdale Asylum in New York and then, from 1864 to 1885, at the State Lunatic Asylum in Northampton, Massachusetts; and John Galt, one of the Galt family, who was connected with the Williamsburg Asylum. Some of these physicians—in particular, Brigham, Earle, and Galt—exhaustively visited mental institutions in Europe early in their careers; all were familiar with the movement of moral treatment carried on in England and France.

Philosophy of moral treatment. Since moral treatment came into existence before the development of modern psychology in the latter part of the 19th century, the pioneers could not be expected to formulate it in psychological terms. Moreover, they were not aware that the various attitudes and methods in dealing with the mentally ill and in protecting the community from them could be harmoniously and logically organized into a comprehensive system. Rather, they initiated various aspects of the moral treatment according to the circumstances of the moment. That lack of systematization made moral treatment's conceptual transmission to others impossible and hampered the recognition of its importance, a fact that undoubtedly contributed to its decline in the space of a few decades.

That is not to say that the main characteristics of the moral treatment were not a rational expression of the same general philosophy; indeed, a unity of intent strongly bound all those involved in it. As Horace Mann (M. Mann, 1888) broadly put it in 1833:

The whole scheme of moral treatment is embraced in a single idea—humanity—the law of love that sympathy which appropriates another's consciousness of pain and makes it a personal relief from suffering whenever another's sufferings are relieved.

The foundations of the Protestant ethic were at the base of the pioneers' philosophy of moral treatment: a humanistic background, an enlightened and humanitarian approach toward other fellow men, middle-class values, and a community-oriented way of operating. In addition to the moral treatment for the mentally ill, those same men shared similar interests in many other reforms, such as the fight against alcoholism and the improvement of the prison system.

The theoretical foundation underlying that reform program was far from clear and consistent. It was a mixture of Locke's sensationism and associationism, of Scottish common sense, of phrenology's "scientific" localization of faculties, and of the Quakers' belief in the perfectibility of man. Regardless of the emphasis on the psychological, on the somatic, or on the mixed causes of mental diseases, there was a widespread conviction that mental aberrations did not affect the immortal soul, a theory in line with the Christian tradition. Necessarily, mental diseases had to be diseases of the brain, which could be caused by physical factors or—and this is most important—by psychological factors. As Brigham put it in 1844:

Insanity is a chronic disease of the brain, producing either derangement of the intellectual faculties, or, prolonged change of the feelings, affections, and habits of our individual.

From that perspective, it was logical to assume that psychological therapy, by affecting those psychopathogenic factors, may restore health. Functional disorders, as described by Pinel and Esquirol, who both believed that in the majority of instances there is no organic lesion of the brain, could then be attributed to not yet visible changes in the structure of the brain. The developments of histopathology, chemistry, and neurophysiology from the latter 19th century to the present have not basically changed that philosophical position.

The main causes leading to mental disorders were considered to be psychological and environmental and were divided into predisposing and precipitating, then called "exciting." Among the causes were heredity, passions, unhappy childhood, faulty education based on too much strictness or leniency, excessive masturbation (on which much was written at that time), sudden shocks, frightening and lustful novels, lack of sleep, rapid changes of habits (related to wars, revolutions, economic recessions), religious overemphasis (enhanced by terrifying sermons, fastings, penances, revival meetings, and millenarian expectations brought forward by apocalyptic groups), and, in general, the many dangers of civilization, ranging from political freedom to the appearance of industry, the growth of cities, and economic uncertainties.

Moral treatment attempted to prevent, treat, and correct those various causes of mental disorders. Among the preventive measures were compliance with phrenological and eugenic principles, as by discouraging intermarriage; developing proper habits of life, possibly in rural communities and based on a balanced regimen of work and recreation and on the cultivation of self-control and self-discipline by enlightened parents; avoid-

ance of intensive study in childhood, stressed by Brigham in *Remarks on the Influence of Mental Cultivation and Mental Excitement upon Health* in 1832; and caution in overinvolvement in religious matters, also brought forward by Brigham in his controversial *The Observations on the Influence of Religion upon Health and Physical Welfare of Mankind* in 1835.

The therapeutic and corrective measures fell more directly into the realm of psychiatry proper, constituted the bulk of moral treatment, and were applied to institutionalized patients. Essentially, they consisted of a therapeutic milieu in which the emphasis was on building up the personal self-esteem and self-control of the patient through the rational use of rewards and punishments in the context of a strong emotional relationship with a doctor. The doctor, viewed by the patients as a father figure, was expected to be intelligent, courageous, firm but kind, understanding, hopeful and cheerful, and able to achieve dominance over the patient tactfully. As Isaac Ray put it in his paper "Ideal Characters of the Officers of a Hospital for the Insane" in 1873:

[The superintendent] never grudgeth the moments spent in quiet, familiar intercourse with them [the patients], for thereby he gaineth many glimpses of their inner life, that may help him in their treatment .... He maketh himself the center of their system around which they all revolve, being held in their places by the attraction of respect and confidence ... he considereth that their hearts are sore and distracted with apprehension, and therefore he pardoneth their impatience and returneth a gentle answer to their unreasonable complaints ... he giveth them all the encouragement he fairly can, and by dwelling on every favorable circumstance, he breaks the force of the final shock.

In summary, it may be said that moral treatment was a method of reeducating the patient in a proper environment.

It is not clear today how other facets of such programs were carried on—for instance, the roles and functions of other staff physicians, nurses, and attendants vis-à-vis the patients and the superintendent. But it is clear that moral treatment was a movement well supported by the community; that it was applied to relatively small numbers of patients in each hospital, then housing a maximum of 200 patients; that almost all patients were from homogeneous New England middle-class or upper-class backgrounds (paupers, especially if from other communities, and blacks were not admitted and tended to be sent to workhouses and jails); and that there were some differences in the treatment of the patients, depending on their symptoms (violent patients were confined in separate wards and were not expected to do manual work).

That philosophy of treatment was carried on mainly in the private or corporate hospitals and in the two outstanding state hospitals at Williamsburg and at Worcester from the time of their beginning to about the mid-1840's. Typically, patients were divided into groups according to their behavior and degree of illness, they were expected to work 3 or more hours a day, various amusements and activities were provided—parties and trips, during which male and female inmates frequently met—social gatherings and mental occupations were encouraged—the use of a library, listening to lectures and music and increasing freedom was given to convalescent patients. The attitudes of physicians and of the well-informed segment of the population varied but were, in general, well disposed toward moral treatment. Clergymen also tended to support moral treatment, although they were eager to dismiss the charges that religion, notably as represented by evangelism, could lead to insanity. Evidence of the beneficial atmosphere of moral treatment is confirmed by the reports of a number of mental hospital visitors from this country and abroad. In particular, Charles Dickens, who was not well disposed toward the United States, left a positive description of his visit to the Boston Lunatic Asylum in *American Notes* in 1842. He was especially impressed by the wide variety of activities available to the patients, including carriage rides in the open air and work with sharp-edged tools, by the fact that meals were served with knives and forks, by the self-respect inculcated in the patients, and by the close association between the superintendent and the patient.

Controversial issues. Two main issues became controversial during the period of moral treatment. The first concerned the prognosis of mental diseases. Clearly, such an individualized, promising, and stimulating therapeutic approach could not fail to achieve results. However, the recovery rates published in the asylums' annual reports, valuable sources of information, were open to criticism in the light of several factors: the criteria used in dividing curable from incurable cases; the selection applied in admitting patients; the tendency to compute percentages of cures from the number of patients discharged from the institution, rather than from the number of patients admitted, thus counting as a separate cure each discharge of a patient who had multiple commitments; and the principles used in determining the level of recovery. At the Friends Asylum in Frankford, Pennsylvania, the percentage of cured patients was reported as 50 per cent annually, excluding those who relapsed; at the Worcester State Hospital the figure was about 40 per cent during the years 1833 to 1847. In some hospitals the figure was reported as higher than 80 per cent. Basil Hall, an English captain, in a widely publicized report published in 1829, stated that the recovery rate was as high as 90 per cent. Not everyone was convinced of such extraordinary success in mental institutions, and that point was debated in the next decades.

The second controversial issue concerned the definition of moral insanity offered by the Englishman James Prichard in *Treatise on Insanity and Other Diseases Affecting the Mind* in 1835. He defined moral insanity as a disorder of emotions and habits, with no injury to the intellectual faculties, corresponding to Pinel's *manie sans délire*. Such a concept—accepted by Isaac Ray (1962) in his classic *A Treatise on the Medical Jurisprudence of Insanity* of 1838, which has remained important to the present day—opened the door to the frequent plea of insanity in courts. As long as phrenology was in vogue, it provided a link between somatic and psychological factors and an escape from strict materialism by postulating the possibility of moral faculties in specific areas of the brain. With the decline of phrenology in the early 1840's, the question of the acceptance or rejection of moral insanity became the frequent subject of debate.

NATIONAL TRENDS IN PSYCHIATRY

As the various national entities began to take shape in Europe at the end of the Napoleonic era, medicine in general, including psychiatry, began to acquire definite characteristics in each country. Thus, at that point in its history, developments in psychiatry can best be understood within the context of specific cultural and medical trends that influenced scientific developments in particular nations. In general, during that period psychiatry gradually achieved recognition as a separate medical discipline. The term "psychiatry" was first used in specific journals devoted to that area of study that were founded in Germany at the beginning of the 19th century but that, unfortunately, were short lived.

German school. Germany remained essentially excluded from the rising movement of social and political consciousness coupled with the spread of industrialization that characterized England and France in the late 18th and early 19th centuries. The princes of the various small German states continued to rule in a paternalistic way, with the help of a heavy bureaucratic administration that maintained a great deal of ambivalence toward the Napoleonic reforms in the fields of health, welfare, and education. Rather, German intellectuals interested in mental illness—philosophers, theologians, and physicians—tended to be influenced by the romantic movement and by the personal piety stemming from the Reformation.

The philosopher Novalis, who had many intuitive insights into the realm of the unconscious, under the impact of Brown's polarity of sthenia versus asthenia, considered insanity due to asthenia—not to the lack of but to excess of stimulation, like being dazzled by too much light. Likewise, the work of the physician Johann Christian Reil (1759–1813), who coined the word "psychiatry," remained alien from practical application. A professor of medicine at Halle and then Berlin, he was attracted by the problem of the relation between mind and body, which he attempted to solve with a kind of dynamic materialism (see Figure 27). In his well-known book *Rhapsodies on the Application of Psychic Methods in the Treatment of Mental Disturbances* (1803), Reil, like Pinel, gave a vivid description of the miserable conditions to which the mentally ill were exposed. However, in contrast to Pinel, Reil did not offer a classification of mental disorders, limiting himself to describing disturbances of common sense—that is, of the connection between the nervous system and the body (hysteria, hypochondria, delusions), of the sensorial organs (illusions), and of the brain itself (loss of reasoning). Thus, for him mental disorders were essentially due to somatic causes; however, the methods of treatment had to be psychological, inasmuch as they all acted through the body. The array of methods to be prescribed

FIGURE 27. Title page of the first psychiatric journal edited by Johann Christian Reil and Anton August Adalbert Kayssler.

by the "psychologist"—a mixture of physician, philosopher, and theologian—was truly fantasmagoric—from cruel actions (including corporal punishment) to terrifying scenes (threats with sounds, lights, animals, a sudden fall in water) to theatrical performances.

Although Reil's work led many to mental excitement more than to action, some progress was being made in the care of the mentally ill. The progress was slow, however, as it was achieved not with the help of a progressive social consciousness, as in England and France, but through bureaucratic action, quite often under the influence of the French occupation of the left bank of the Rhine. In fact, after the introduction of the Napoleonic code and the decentralization of the administration, several general hospitals were founded in Cologne, Mainz, Trier, and Coblenz, and the principle that all kinds of sick people, including the mentally sick, were entitled to care was progressively being accepted.

To the physician Johann Gottfried Langermann (1768–1832) goes the credit for having introduced in 1804, at the suggestion of the Prussian statesman Hardenberg, a project concerning changes in the asylum of Bayreuth. Such changes included the acceptance in the same facility of all insane paupers who were curable and, among the incurable, of all dangerous persons; the use of a rigid system of care based on rewards and punishment, not unlike the education of children, under the physician's prescription; and, even more important, the underlying assumption that the state sanctioned the curability of insanity.

The trend toward the rigid treatment of the mentally ill reached the extreme point in the work of the professor of medicine Ernst Horn (1774–1848), who introduced a detailed routine of comprehensive care, education, order, religious training, and corporal punishment for the mentally ill at the famous hospital Charité in Berlin. Eventually, after the death of a patient who had been restrained in a sack of his own invention, Horn was found guilty of homicide and dismissed.

Clearly, the discrepancy between the idealistic notions of the mind and the repressive, if not brutal, approach to the practical care of the mentally ill was not conducive to much-needed reforms. What led to those reforms was the exposure of some young German physicians to the new methods of treatment for the mentally ill in England and France, obtained through long travels and visits to institutions in those countries. C. A. F. Hayner and E. Pienitz, who had studied under Pinel and Esquirol in Paris, fought against physical abuses, eliminated cruel methods of restraint for the mentally ill, and introduced the French *traitement moral* at the asylums of Sonnenstein Pirna and of Waldheim in Saxony in 1811.

At the same time that those reforms were slowly being introduced, the theoretical approach to the study of the mind remained heavily influenced in Germany by philosophical and theological concepts. In line with Brown's bipolarity, the philosopher Schelling, who had a particularly large following, considered receptivity and activity as a state of bipolar tension between the person and the totality of nature; he further divided receptivity into sensibility and irritability, and he regarded diseases as the result of the varied interplay of those two factors. Moreover, he attributed diseases to the original fall of man, as a sort of false unity between virtue and evil, not unlike poverty, vice, error, and many other expressions of human frailty. For him, there were three aspects in a person: the psyche (*Gemüt*)—that is, the unconscious principle of the spirit; the mind (*Geist*), the personal, conscious principle; and the soul (*Seele*), the divine principle in humans. Mental diseases occurred along an uninterrupted line intersecting those three principles. Insanity represented both the divine and the corrupted element in humans that manifests itself in the demonic aspect as clairvoyance or, conversely, as mental illness.

That idea of illness as due to the fall of man—that is, to sin—had a considerable impact on the early generation of physicians and philosophers involved with the mentally ill. Among that group of intellectuals interested in the diseases of the mind, which was later called the Christian German school, were a number of well-known university professors—J. N. Ringeis; C. G. Carus (1970), who anticipated notions of the unconscious in his book *Psyche* (1846); D. G. Kieser, a student of sleep and somnambulism; G. H. von Schubert, the author of *Symbolism of Dreams* (1814); J. Kerner, whose book *The Seeress of Prevost* (1829) became a best seller. To that period also belongs Alexander Haindorf (1782–1862), the first Jewish psychiatrist in Germany and the author of *Attempt at a Pathology and Therapy of Emotional and Mental Disorders* (1811). In it a distinction was made between diseases of the mind—that is, free activity aimed at the world—and diseases that are an expression of the unfree life—that is, a distortion of the normal self-feeling; the various pathological pictures were related to stages in the mental and emotional life; and therapy consisted of psychic, chemical, and dynamic means, including the use of electricity and animal magnetism.

Undoubtedly, the most important psychiatrist of that period was Johann Christian Heinroth (1773–1843), who for many years worked at the St. George Home, an asylum in Saxony, and taught at the University of Leipzig. An exceptionally well-read man, as shown by his numerous translations of French and English psychiatric works, he published several books, of which the most important (Heinroth, 1975) was *Textbook of Disturbances of Mental Life or Disturbances of the Soul and Their Treatment* (1818). In it he accepted a developmental view of humans, passing through the stages of world-consciousness (sensory-perception level), self-consciousness (ego level), and reason-consciousness (ego-ideal level).

For Heinroth (1975), the complete concept of mental disturbances includes permanent loss of freedom or loss of reason, independent and of itself, even when bodily health is apparently unimpaired, which manifests itself as a disease or a diseased condition, and which comprises the domains of disease of temperament, spirit and will.

Although "madness is a disease of the reason and not of the soul," there cannot be mental disturbance without a total fall from grace. In spite of that theological influence and his apparently limited direct experience with patients, he showed some notable insights: Mental disturbances were the result of the combination of constitutional and environmental factors, and, as a result of the pathological process, a person developed a secondary organization at a lower level, of which he gave an example in the melancholia attonita, which corresponded to the later catatonia. Heinroth (1975) first defined the role of the psychiatrist, stating that

a doctor of the psyche must be especially schooled by the psychologist, by the cleric, and by the educator, or rather, he must develop in himself the gift for psychological observation.

In fact, the physician of the psyche was expected to observe the behavior and the state of mind of the patient so as to be able to formulate a diagnosis. Treatment consisted of a mixture of firmness and kindness, to be administered by the physician and his assistants in a peaceful milieu away from the patient's relatives and from obnoxious stimuli. The curable patients were to be treated in the hospital; the incurable were to be treated in the asylum.

In conjunction with the industrial revolution of the 1830's, the physicians working in the asylums acquired more power than the university professors involved in theoretical discussions of the mind. Beginning with the mental hospital of

Sachsenberg near Schwerin in 1830, several institutions were built purposely for the care and treatment of the mentally ill. Although still built on the model of prisons to protect society from the alleged dangerousness of the inmates and although rigidly run by the state, they represented progress.

It was around that time, roughly during the first 4 decades of the 19th century, that a schism occurred in German psychiatry between the so-called *Psychiker* and the *Somatiker*—that is, between those advocating a psychological and moral cause and those advocating a material cause of mental illness, a conflict that is far from being solved to this day.

The first of the *Psychiker* was C. W. Ideler (1795–1860), who for many years was in charge of the psychiatric ward of the Charité in Berlin. A very learned man, the author of many works on the history of psychiatry, including one on the Bible, he did not introduce any change in the practical approach to the mentally ill, in the belief that they, too, had to comply with the absolutism of ethics, rather than be controlled by passions. Ideler's psychological views are thus consonant with his conservative views on the repressive and educational functions of the state.

Among the other *Psychiker* worth mentioning are F. Groos, from Heidelberg, who viewed mental disease as an obstacle either psychological or somatic; F. E. Beneke, who believed in a symbolic relationship between psychological states and bodily processes; and, the most important of the group, the Baron Ernst von Feuchtersleben (1806–1849), dean of the faculty of medicine at Vienna and author of *The Principles of Medical Psychology* (1845), which was soon translated into English. In it von Feuchtersleben (1847) considered the mind as the union between the body and the spirit; he outlined degrees in the relationship between physiological and psychological phenomena not unlike today's psychosomatic approach; he called mental disturbances "diseases of the personality"; and he advocated physical and psychic forms of treatment to be administered by the physician. On the whole, in spite of Zilboorg's (1941) statement that the *Psychiker* approached medicopsychological problems from a broader and more inclusive point of view than did their successors in the second half of the century and that, therefore, they anticipated notions of modern psychodynamic theories, their importance remained quite limited, partly because of their lack of clinical experience.

In contrast to them, the psychiatrists belonging to the school of *Somatiker*, almost all of them superintendents of hospitals, relied on empirical observations of patients. They were affected by the advances made in French and English institutions and believed in a lenient approach to the mentally ill. Outstanding among them was Maximilian Jacobi (1775–1858), who studied also in England and then worked for many years in the mental hospital of Sieburg in the Rhine valley. In Jacobi's most important work, *Observations on the Pathology and Therapy of the Diseases Related to Insanity* (1830), he forcefully stated that insanity is only a symptom of a somatic disease, that psychopathology cannot be understood on the basis of normal psychology, that the seat of the psyche (*Seele*) is the entire organism of a person, and that the predominance of organic or psychological symptoms in a disease depends only on constitutional differences. Among the other *Somatiker* were Johannes Friedreich (1796–1862), a professor in Würzburg, and Fridrich Nasse (1778–1851), a professor in Bonn, who attempted to systematize medical methods on the basis of clinical observations. Common to all was their activity in areas formerly occupied by the French and their interest in legal medicine, which also contributed to their practical orientation, as well as their belief that insanity had to be a somatic disease because the soul, being the divine element in a person, cannot become sick.

In 1844 the *Allgemeine Zeitschrift für Psychiatrie* was founded; it was a journal intended by its editor, H. Damerow, to serve as a point of convergence of the various trends of psychiatry in the attempt to lead to a German psychiatry. Basically, however, the journal remained anchored to the anthropological and religious positions of the past, tied to the bureaucracy of the government, and insensitive to the new concern for the increasing number of insane paupers relegated to the fringe of society by the rising bourgeois and by rapid industrialization. Consequently, many psychiatrists found themselves opposed to their government, ostracized by the official authorities, and involved in the revolution of 1848.

The movement of the *Somatiker* found its final expression in the work of Wilhelm Griesinger (1817–1868), who paved the way for the development of a more strictly scientific psychiatry in the latter part of the century. In 1845, at the age of 28, Griesinger (1965) published *Mental Pathology and Therapeutics*, which was to remain the most influential textbook in the field for many years. His methods were based on physiology in the amplest sense of the term, on anatomopathology, and on the developmental dimension. For him there was a gradual, imperceptible passage from the reflex action to the voluntary action, and the psychic disturbance was conceived of as a purely quantitative variation of the physiological states. Mental diseases were diseases of the brain that could occur either because of sympathic irritation or because of the most various external experiences. Conflicts that developed in the person—especially at certain stages, such as puberty—could be overcome by the integrating function of the ego. As a matter of fact, he advanced views that anticipated recent developments in ego psychology—views that, unfortunately, have been forgotten. As Griesinger (1965) put it:

> The mind appears as a higher and conscious unity, forming out of changing mental states, one of which remains constant, *das Ich*.... The emotions are more active when, through a sudden change occurring within the consciousness, the masses of ideas belonging to *das Ich* are violently shaken and reshaken, and *das Ich* thereby suffers an abrupt disturbing enhancement or inhibition.... [the patient can improve when], through strengthening of the former normal direction of the thoughts, the false judgments which were bound to *das Ich* gradually loosen themselves and eventually can be entirely repressed. When, however, the old *Ich* is vitiated, corrupted, and distorted on all sides by the morbid false ideas, when finally the complexes of thought of the former *Ich* are so completely repressed that, without any trace of emotion, the patient has exchanged his whole personality for a new one and has scarcely any remembrance of the old one, then recovery is almost impossible.

Predisposing factors for him were malnutrition, poverty, alcohol, the lack of education, and heredity. The pathological process progressed according to definite stages, and the symptoms, such as hallucinations and delusions, were the result of the reaction of the person to such a process. As for his practical action on behalf of the mentally ill, Griesinger, while a professor in Zurich in 1860, transformed the old asylum into a university clinic and practiced the principle of nonrestraint. Appointed a professor in Berlin in 1864, he combined the psychiatric and the neurological clinic, a model that remained for the next century, and 3 years later, in 1867, founded the *Archiv für Psychiatrie und Nervenkrankheiten*. However, some of his ideas were so advanced that they are still to be implemented today: In each city there should be a psychiatric facility free of cost not only to the poor but to the middle-income class; such a facility, built like a general hospital, should be open day and night and should also serve for teaching; the physician on the staff there should visit each patient's home to become aware of the conditions in which he has lived; patients should be given as much freedom as possible; many of them should be placed in families and in agricultural colonies; chronic patients, especially if mentally defective, should be placed in large institutions run by religious orders.

British school. The success of the Retreat near York, especially after the publication of Samuel Tuke's (1964) *Description of the Retreat,* contributed toward mobilizing public opinion on the need of the state to take care of the insane, since insanity was viewed as one of the consequences of social maladjustment. In fact, a parliamentary inquiry into the madhouses, which took place between 1815 and 1816, resulted in a plea for the increased involvement of physicians in the matter of insanity; for the protection of the rights of the insane, rather than of society from the insane; and for a delay in the cure caused by physical abuses.

In 1816 there was a shake-up in the organization of Bethlehem Hospital that resulted in the dismissal of Dr. Monro and of the apothecary John Haslam (1764–1844). Haslam, nominated to his position in 1795, had published *Observations on Insanity* in 1798, in which he had first presented statistical data. It was followed by *Illustrations of Madness* (1810), which dealt with the detailed account of a paranoid schizophrenic, and by *Medical Jurisprudence, as It Relates to Insanity According to the Law of England* (1817), the first work on forensic psychiatry in that country. In spite of those contributions, criticism of the methods used by Haslam continued even after his departure, as evidenced by the anonymous *Sketches in Bedlam,* which appeared in 1823.

Shortly thereafter, the name of George M. Burrows, a physician-owner of a private asylum, became known for his book *Commentaries on the Causes, Forms, Symptoms, and Treatment, Moral and Medical, of Insanity* (1828). For him, insanity was essentially due to environmental factors, such as economic, political, and religious crises that affected the physical constitution of a person; therefore, therapy should be a combination of medical and environmental means. Although well-to-do patients were to be treated in private madhouses, the insane paupers were to be charges of the state. In the meantime, some progress was made in the understanding of the causes of some mental disorders. In particular, Burrows made known the discovery by French students of the connection between general paralysis and insanity. Most of that generation of psychiatrists were greatly influenced by phrenology, introduced in England by Andrew Combe in 1831.

Among his contemporaries who acquired stature was James Cowles Prichard (1786–1848), a distinguished psychiatrist and anthropologist. In Prichard's book *A Treatise on Insanity and Other Disorders Affecting the Mind* (1835), he was greatly influenced by French authors, especially Pinel and Esquirol. His originality consisted in the concept of moral insanity, in which the term "moral" was used both in the sense of ethical and of emotional. That concept corresponded to Pinel's *manie sans délire* and was defined as a disorder that affects the feelings and emotions or what were termed the moral powers, in contradistinction to those of the understanding and intellect. Prichard's views gained considerable attention for many years through his position as a member of the Commission on Lunacy.

However, no other issue achieved such momentum in British psychiatry as that of the nonrestraint system—that is, the abrogation of all systems of restraint. Although moral treatment was especially used in institutions for middle-class and well-to-do patients, the nonrestraint system was developed in large public institutions. It was initiated in 1835 by the surgeon Robert Gardiner Hill (1811–1878) while he was working at the public asylum of Lincoln. Soon it became clear that, in conjunction with the decrease of the system of restraint, the percentage of cures increased, suicides disappeared, and the number of incidents of violent behavior, especially toward attendants, became much rarer than in the past. Hill published his results in 1839. However because of the campaign against him by the public, who were afraid of possible acts of violence by the mentally ill, he was forced to resign in 1840.

The year before, John Conolly (1794–1866) had learned of Hill's nonrestraint system and had introduced it at the provincial asylum at Hanwell. Conolly, who lived in France for a while, studied medicine in England and soon became involved in several causes tied to liberal progress and to the improvement of the working class. A founder of the British Medical Association (1832) and of the Medico-Psychological Association (1841), he began to teach clinical psychiatry in 1842 and to train psychiatric attendants. In Conolly's main work, *The Treatment of the Insane without Mechanical Restraints* (1856), he considered insanity as a cerebral disorder related to external physical and social factors, such as malnutrition, poor health, and faulty education. Means of physical restraint were replaced by a well-structured environment. Essential to the treatment was the work of sensitive and well-trained attendants who assisted the superintendent—all benign father figures who were always available to their "crazy children." Work therapy was maintained in reasonable limits and was often replaced by social activities, which included entertainment on the grounds, such as concerts and dances, to which even the public was invited. In such a way, Conolly attempted to make psychiatry relevant to the social problems of the time, especially the needs of the insane paupers, while trying to establish psychiatry on a scientific basis. Much of the literature on psychiatry was then appearing in *The Journal of Psychological Medicine and Mental Pathology,* which was founded in 1848.

French school. In France, where the most important developments occurred, psychiatrists stressed the clinical study of the patient—that is, the clarification of symptoms and their detailed description, the close relationship between psychiatry and neurology, and the medicolegal aspects of psychiatry. Concomitantly, a continuous effort was made to improve institutions and hospitals for the mentally ill.

Among the contributions from the members of that school were those of Jean Etienne Esquirol (1772–1840). Like Pinel, he was born in southern France and studied medicine at Montpellier. In 1805 he presented his thesis entitled, "Passions Considered as Causes, Symptoms, and Therapeutic Means of Mental Disease." While in Paris, Esquirol became a faithful pupil of Pinel. In 1811 he was named regular physician at the Salpétrière; in 1817 he inaugurated the first official course on mental diseases; among his pupils were most of the French psychiatrists of the mid-19th century. Charged with surveying many French asylums by the Minister of the Interior, he submitted a report in which, after an exposé of the miserable conditions in which the mentally ill were kept, he recommended the creation of regional asylums to be supported by the local administrations, each asylum to house no more than 150 patients; those patients who did not improve after 2 years were to be placed in institutions for the incurable. Although nothing came of that recommendation, Esquirol continued his work on behalf of the mentally ill for the rest of his life at the Charenton, the institution that became famous for having housed the Marquis de Sade, where he was appointed superintendent in 1825.

In 1838 appeared Esquirol's (1965) textbook, *Des maladies mentales* (see Figure 28), which was recognized as outstanding and was eventually translated into several languages. In it, insanity was attributed to a disturbance of passions, which, in turn, were linked to the conditions of society; hence, it was a pessimistic diagnosis of the contemporary scene of the anarchy

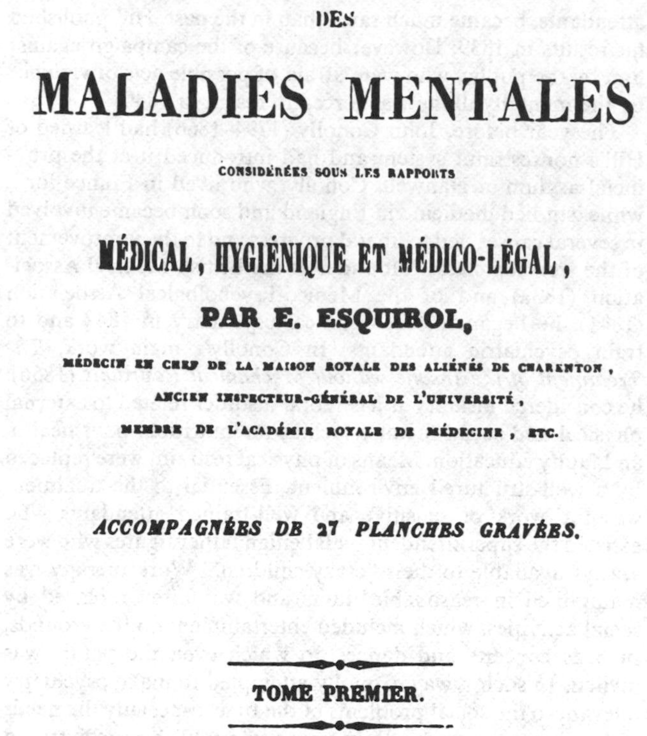

DES

MALADIES MENTALES

CONSIDÉRÉES SOUS LES RAPPORTS

MÉDICAL, HYGIÉNIQUE ET MÉDICO-LÉGAL,

PAR E. ESQUIROL,

MÉDECIN EN CHEF DE LA MAISON ROYALE DES ALIÉNÉS DE CHARENTON,

ANCIEN INSPECTEUR-GÉNÉRAL DE L'UNIVERSITÉ,

MEMBRE DE L'ACADÉMIE ROYALE DE MÉDECINE, ETC.

ACCOMPAGNÉES DE 27 PLANCHES GRAVÉES.

TOME PREMIER.

FIGURE 28. Title page of Esquirol's classic textbook, *Des maladies mentales,* published in 1837.

created by the French Revolution and of the changing mores, leading to a linkage between poverty and insanity. Esquirol was the first psychiatrist who attempted to substantiate his statements with the use of statistics. Probably under the influence of Comte's positivistic method, he conceived of insanity as a disease process that went through stages caused by heredity, constitution, and experiences in early childhood. He classified mental diseases into five groups: (1) lipemania (immobility of the body, fixation of the eyes, expression of pain); (2) mania (excitement of all the mental faculties, including monomania, a word coined by him, indicating the prevalence of a delusion centered on a particular theme); (3) melancholy (reduction of movement, restriction of emotional life, and a self-deprecatory attitude); (4) dementia (weakening of all the mental faculties); and (5) idiocy (congenital deficiency of all the mental faculties). Esquirol's originality consisted mainly of two points: (1) the distinction between hallucinations (true perceptions, like awakened dreams, without due intervention of the senses) and illusions (due to heightened, weakened, or perverted sensitivity of the nerve ends) and (2) the description of monomania, divided into intellectual (wrong conviction based on one faulty principle), affective (disturbance of emotions with inappropriate behavior and apparently intact intellectual functions), and instinctive (disturbance of the will, resulting in impulsive and irrational actions). In line with Esquirol's critical view of society, in monomania he gave a concrete description of the excess of normal impulses—hence, the specific terms "megalomania," "kleptomania," "dipsomania" (tendency to drink), "pyromania" (tendency to arson), and so forth. Eventually, monomania was found to be close to Prichard's moral insanity, and it became important mainly in relation to legal psychiatry.

Esquirol's therapeutic principles followed those introduced by Pinel—initial subjugation of the patient's will by fixing him

in the eye, individualized treatment for each patient under the guidance of the physician, encouraging healthy emotions, providing a serene and varied milieu in the institution, and resorting to isolation and the straitjacket only when necessary. Esquirol's effort in ensuring the passing of legislation concerning the mentally ill in 1838 was highly original. It established a definite procedure for the commitment of mentally ill persons throughout France; special forms were to be filled out and signed by competent physicians and then made official through court action; voluntary admissions were encouraged; and for each new patient there was to be a period of observation until a definite plan could be made for his treatment. Similar legislation was passed in Switzerland (1838), England (1842), and elsewhere.

A number of other psychiatrists who were disciples of Pinel and Esquirol achieved prominence during that period. In his thesis for a medical degree in 1822, A. L. J. Bayle first described dementia paralytica as a disease that passes through various stages, leading to the complete deterioration of the mental faculties, and that was attributed to a chronic inflammation of the arachnoid membrane of the brain. In 1826 J. L. Calmeil in his book *De la paralysie considérée chez les aliénés* described dementia paralytica as a specific disease, always accompanied by mental disorder, due to definite causes with particular symptoms, course, and outcome. Etienne Georget, who died at age 33, attempted in his work *About Insanity* (1820) to prove that those suffering from monomanias should be considered in courts as not responsible for their actions, which often represented repressed thoughts. Pinel's oldest son, Scipion Pinel, under the influence of Comte's positivism, in various writings conceived of mental diseases as belonging to stages on a scale ranging from normality to complete deterioration. Guillaume Ferrus asked for the creation of special departments for the criminally insane and initiated psychiatric teaching at Bicêtre in 1833. Felix Voisin organized a department for idiots that was later transferred to Bicêtre (1836), and in 1843 he published a work on idiocy that soon became a classic. The study of mental deficiency was especially enhanced by Edward Seguin (1866), who, in his treatise *Idiocy and Its Treatment by the Physiological Method* (1846), advocated a method of teaching based on fostering perceptual faculties before conceptual functions; in 1848 he emigrated to the United States and was instrumental in developing programs for the mentally defective in this country. François Leuret attempted to differentiate between a criminal and a homicidal monomaniac, and he anticipated some of the concepts that were later described as split personality. Much of the literature of the period appeared in *Annales médico-psychologiques,* which was founded in 1843 and followed 4 years later by the establishment of the Société Médico-psychologique.

Other developments in European psychiatry. Elsewhere in Europe during that period, the contributions of two men were particularly outstanding. First, the Italian layman Pietro Pisani (1760–1837), who was superintendent of the mental hospital in Palermo, applied advanced methods of treatment that anticipated current concepts of milieu therapy. Second, the Belgian Joseph Guislain (1797–1860) became well known for his textbooks and for his many activities on behalf of mental patients in his own country.

In summary, developments in psychiatry during the first half of the 19th century, although often idealistic and prescientific, played a significant role in building the foundation of modern psychiatry. It is difficult to delineate the many trends that influenced psychiatrists of that period. Nevertheless, many current psychiatric concepts may be traced back to the concerns that dominated psychiatric thinking at that phase of its historical development.

Psychiatry in the Late 19th Century

During the second half of the 19th century, psychiatry underwent considerable development, with marked differences in the European nations, according to varying traditions and cultural characteristics. The process of industrialization, with urbanization and the formation of areas of poverty, spread from England and France to the rest of the continent. As the people of such nations as Germany and Italy rebelled against their ruling dynasties and acquired political independence, a zeal for social reform replaced the former preoccupation with religion. Concurrently, positivism and materialism became the prevailing trends in philosophy. Medicine became increasingly scientific and materialistic, and, as might be expected in that context, psychological phenomena came to be attributed to physiological factors.

Regardless of the over-all direction of these trends, the empirical orientation persisted in England and the clinical orientation persisted in France. In Germany, under the influence of Griesinger, the orientation became strictly scientific and academic.

ENGLAND

In England, psychiatry depended largely on the development of mental hospitals, as there were no university psychiatric clinics. The split between neurology and psychiatry, initiated by the foundation of the National Hospital for Nervous Diseases in 1860, has continued to the present day. Although the somatic origin of mental illness progressively gained acceptance there, the concern with the improvement of the conditions of the mentally ill in psychiatric hospitals contributed to maintaining a view of the global personality, in contrast to the fragmentary attitude of other schools. Among the psychiatrists who acquired renown were John Charles Bucknill (1817–1897), for many years the superintendent of the Devon Asylum and the first editor of *Asylum Journal* (subsequently *Journal of Mental Science* and *British Journal of Psychiatry*); Daniel Hack Tuke (1827–1895), who continued the tradition of his family as the superintendent of the Retreat near York; and Henry Maudsley (1835–1918), the son-in-law of Conolly, who taught medical jurisprudence at University College in London for many years. Bucknill and Tuke (1968) published together in 1858 *A Manual of Psychological Medicine*, which presented a new classification of mental diseases. After writing two volumes on the history of psychiatry in England and the United States, Tuke edited the important *A Dictionary of Psychological Medicine* (1892), to which 67 specialists contributed. Maudsley's first important publication was *The Physiology of the Mind* and *The Pathology of the Mind* (1867), wherein he recognized the role of the unconscious in mental activity and devoted a pioneering chapter to mental disturbances in children; it was followed by *Body and Mind* (1870), in which emphasis was placed on the emotions as affecting every part of the body and on the value of taking a full history and of individualizing the treatment for every patient.

Undoubtedly, Charles Darwin's main works—*The Origin of Species* (1859), *The Descent of Man* (1871), and, of particular interest for psychology, *The Expression of Emotions in Man and Animals* (1872)—influenced many toward an evolutionary concept of humans. That influence is especially noticeable in Hughlings Jackson's formulation of the nervous system as composed of three evolutionary levels—the lowest in the spine, the middle in the basal ganglia, and the highest in the cortex—normality representing an evolution from automatic to purposive movements, and pathology representing a dissolution from the purposive to the automatic.

FRANCE

In France, the clinical orientation remained paramount, as evidenced in the description of a number of syndromes found in patients hospitalized in the few large psychiatric centers in Paris. Jean Pierre Falret in 1854 described cyclic insanity (*folie circulaire*)—that is, a disease characterized by consecutive and regular alternation of a manic state, a melancholic state, and lucid intervals. Jules Baillarger called that same syndrome *folie à double forme*. Ulysse Trélat in 1861 published a monograph on the *folie lucide*—that is, on the borderline state leading to paranoia. In 1877 Charles Lasègue and Jules Falret described *folie à deux* in terms still relevant to modern psychodynamic concepts. Before then, in 1852, Lasègue had already described the *délire de persecution*. In 1845 appeared the book *Du hascisch et de l'aliénation mentale* by J. Moreau de Tours (1973). In it an attempt was made to understand the basic mental disturbance or primary fact (*fait primordial*) from the point of view of subjective introspection, rather than of objective observation by an outsider. Moreover, having postulated two entirely different modes of existence, one determined by relations to the outer world and the other to the world of dreams, he submitted that in insanity there is a fusion between the two modes of existence, the mentally ill person finally emerging as an awakened dreamer. In order to gain first-hand experience of subjective sensations, Moreau went so far as to take hashish. In retrospect, Moreau's work represents an anticipation of psychodynamic and phenomenological concepts.

No other trend, however, gained more importance in the mid-19th century in France than the theory of degeneration. The concept of degeneration was the result of the confluence of various trends—the disillusion with the traditional causative theories, with the exception of senile psychoses and general paralysis; the new interest in hereditary studies; and the pessimistic climate of the time, coinciding with the political and scientific decline of France and the corresponding ascendance of Germany. From the historical perspective, it is clear that the theory of degeneration received its greatest impetus with the publication of Darwin's *The Origin of Species* in 1859, notwithstanding the almost opposite position between the theories of evolution and degeneration.

In 1857 appeared the *Traité des dégénérescences physiques, intellectuelles et morales de l'espèce humaine* by Benedict Augustin Morel, who combined a staunch adherence to Catholicism with an interest in prophylactic and social measures. For him, degeneration could be caused by intoxication, environmental factors, a pathological constitution, moral sickness, inborn or acquired damage, and heredity. In any case, in the first generation there was a certain predominance of a nervous temperament, followed in the second generation by an increase in all those morbid characteristics, leading in the third generation to a full-fledged occurrence of mental illness, and, finally, leading in the fourth generation to a complete deterioration in the intellectual and emotional spheres, such as deafness, inborn weakness of the psyche, and early dementia (*démence précoce*).

Morel's views, although unilateral, represented a pioneering effort in at least three areas: (1) extension of the factors of degeneration to an unusually broad base, which included alcoholism, infectious diseases, poverty, and too-strenuous labor under unhygienic conditions; (2) emphasis on the affective tone in the origin of mental diseases, which was especially important in a period of ascendancy of a purely intellectual psychology; and (3) attempt to unite under one generalization the scattered pictures that were regarded as independent diseases. Certainly related to Morel's ideas were the establishment of temperance societies in many nations and the founding of hospitals for alcoholics in Germany, Switzerland, and the United States.

The other well-known adherent to the theory of degeneration was Valentin Magnan, who worked for 45 years at the Asylum of St. Anne in Paris. His early work dealt with alcoholism, on which subject he acquired a great deal of knowledge, especially since the condition spread in France in the years after the defeat of France by Germany in 1870. Later Magnan applied the concept of degeneration not only to psychotics but also to neurotics and not only to persons but to nations as well, getting involved in an acrimonious controversy regarding the degenerative aspects of the French and the Germans. The influence of the theory of degeneration was reflected in much of the literature of the Western nations until the beginning of the 20th century.

GERMANY

In Germany, Griesinger's work acquired wide recognition in a short time. He was the first psychiatrist to occupy a professional position on a full-time basis, and under his influence psychiatry became unified with neurology and was tied to academic life. That fact contributed to placing psychiatry in Germany in a position of leadership vis-à-vis all the other countries. As for his treatise on mental illness, very little notice was given to the part devoted to ego psychology, although his concept that mental diseases are brain diseases became universally accepted.

That concept fitted well with the spread of the physicochemical reductionism in the development of physiological theories in that period. According to those theories, vital phenomena, stripped of their uniqueness and finality, could be entirely explained according to physical and chemical laws. Johannes Müller, Theodor Schwann, Emil du Bois-Reymond, Carl Ludwig, Hermann von Helmholtz, Ernst Brücke—all well known in the history of physiology—were among the main exponents of that movement. As a result, considerable progress was made in the acquisition of knowledge of the functions of the brain, especially after the introduction of histological techniques. On the other side, such a materialistic approach, by focusing on the common physicochemical aspects of the person, lost sight of the global aspect of the personality.

In less than 20 years, from 1864 to 1882, professorial chairs were established in Berlin, Göttingen, Zurich, Vienna, Heidelberg, Leipzig, and Bonn. In spite of their theoretical orientation, some of the representatives of university psychiatry contributed to advances in the clinical field. At variance with the contemporary interest in the classification of mental disorders, Heinrich Neumann stressed that there is but one type of mental disturbance, called insanity, and that the human personality should be viewed as a functional whole. Karl Westphal, Griesinger's successor in Berlin and known for the exceptional clarity of his thinking, in 1877 described obsessional ideas as appearing in one's consciousness against and regardless of one's desire. Karl Kahlbaum named as a symptom complex a particular constellation of symptoms that tended to present themselves in a cluster without constituting a disease. In particular, in his monograph (Kahlbaum, 1973) on catatonia (1874) he described the main features of that condition—fixed

position, negativism, stereotyped movements, and *flexibilitas cerea*. His pupil Ewald Hecker in 1871 described hebephrenia as a special form of psychosis observed during adolescence. Theodore Meynert (1968), who eventually became Freud's teacher while a professor in Vienna, in 1884 published a textbook with the significant title of *Psychiatry, A Clinical Treatise on the Diseases of the Fore-brain, Based on Its Structure, Functions, and Nutrition*. In it, he first regarded the brain as a projection surface, on which is reflected the whole periphery of the body; moreover, he conceived of the functions of the brain as being in a state of balance between the excitation of the subcortical ganglia and the inhibition of the forebrain; consequently, mental diseases could be due to the alteration of such a balance.

By that time—after the discovery by the French Paul Broca in 1863 that aphasia was due to a lesion of the third frontal convolution, on which depended the function of speech—the path was opened for many discoveries of the localization of functions of the brain by such men as Wernicke, Fritsch, Hitzig, Ferrier, and Flechsig. Of particular importance in that group was Karl Wernicke, who in his monograph on aphasia (1874) attempted to interpret the various aphasic symptom complexes as consequences of the impairment of specific elementary psychic processes, localized in different parts of the cerebral cortex and their subcortical connections. Among the other psychiatrists of that period, also worth remembering were Richard Krafft-Ebing (1894), a specialist in forensic psychiatry who succeeded Meynert in Vienna and who became especially known for his book *Psychopathia Sexualis* (1886), which was translated into many languages and became a best seller everywhere among both physicians and laymen; and Paul Möbius, especially known as the author of pathographies—that is, biographies of prominent men from the viewpoint of psychopathology—on Rousseau, Goethe, Schopenhauer, and others.

Thus, unquestionably, in the second part of the 19th century, German psychiatry, which had previously lagged far behind British and French psychiatry, took a leading position in Europe. German medical schools came to play a dominant role for their excellent system of teaching and their outstanding laboratories. With few exceptions, most of the discoveries in the field of the nervous system in its relation to psychiatry were attributed to scientists from German-speaking countries. In retrospect, although much of that trend toward the classification of mental diseases based on the theory of localization was called brain mythology and speculative anatomy, the importance of that period of German psychiatry cannot be underestimated.

OTHER EUROPEAN COUNTRIES

Of the other European countries, Russia and Italy should be mentioned briefly.

Russia. In Russia the system of care of the mentally ill lagged behind that of the more progressive Western countries. Slowly, more human methods of treatment, including nonrestraint, were introduced in some hospitals. University psychiatry began in the military medical academy of Petersburg under the leadership of Ivan Balinsky, who opened a clinic and introduced psychiatric teaching in 1867. By that time Ivan Sechenov (1935) had published his major work, *The Reflexes of the Brain* (1863), in which he submitted that the nature of the muscular response is elicited in the peripheral sense organs and mediated by the nervous system, especially the centers of the midbrain that serve in an inhibitory capacity. His assertion that the initial cause of any human action lies outside the person ran counter to the political point of view of the Czarist government, then greatly influenced by the Church, and he encountered much opposition in many quarters. However, his work was considered pioneering by physiologists and was a source of inspiration to Pavlov. In 1877 the first Russian psychiatric journal was published, *Archives of Psychiatry, Neurology, and Forensic Psychopathology*.

In 1887 Sergei Korsakoff published his dissertation "About Alcoholic Paralysis"; 3 years later he presented a paper entitled, "About One Form of Mental Disease, Combined with Degenerative Polyneuritis" at the International Medical Congress in Paris (Korsakoff, 1890). As alcoholism was quite common in Russia, such studies gained a great deal of attention, to the point that at the twelfth International Medical Congress in Moscow in 1897 a proposal was passed to call polyneuritis psychosis "Korsakoff's syndrome," an eponym that has remained in psychiatry. Later, Vladimir Bekhterev, who founded the Psychoneurological Institute in Leningrad in 1907, acquired renown for his doctrine of psychoreflexology, based on the notion of associative reflexes, which, having originated from physiology, became relevant to clinical methods and anticipated today's behavior school. Bekhterev's name was later overshadowed by that of Ivan Pavlov, the discoverer of the conditioned reflex and a Nobel Prize winner in 1904.

Italy. Many of the pioneering ideas and endeavors of relevance to psychiatry that developed in Italy in the 17th and 18th centuries—notably, Chiarugi's progressive attitude in the care of the mentally ill—could not be continued because of the political unrest and the wars among the rulers of that country that finally resulted in the unification of the peninsula. Conceptually, Italian psychiatry was heavily influenced first by the French school, including the phrenological movement, and then, after the middle of the century, by the German school. The teaching of psychiatry was begun in Turin in 1850; in 1874 the *Rivista Sperimentale di Freniatria e di Medicina Legale* started publication. In the same year, Camillo Golgi, a professor in Pavia, developed the method of silver-staining nervous tissue that carries his name and for which he was later awarded the Nobel Prize.

Undoubtedly, however, the best-known Italian psychiatrist was Cesare Lombroso, a versatile and prolific writer who was greatly influenced by positivism and evolutionism. In Lombroso's (1889) *The Man of Genius* (1864), under the influence of Morel's idea of degeneration, he postulated a connection between psychic degeneration, criminality, epilepsy, and the characteristics of the genius. In *The Delinquent Man* (1876) Lombroso emphasized the atavistic traits of delinquents and advocated the substitution of social responsibility for moral responsibility and of prevention and rehabilitation for punishment. In spite of some opposition to his ideas, Lombroso was able to found the movement of criminal anthropology. His writings were translated into many languages, and his journal, *Archivio di Psichiatria, Antropologia Criminale e Scienze Penali*, soon imitated in other countries, influenced the coming together of a group of outstanding psychiatrists and lawyers who became known as the positive school of criminology (*scuola positiva*). That group focused on the biological and anthropological study of the individual delinquent and played an important role in prevention, education, and rehabilitation, thus anticipating the study of the individual personality undertaken later by the psychodynamic school.

EUROPEAN MENTAL HOSPITALS

Several issues are important in dealing with the concrete treatment and care of the mentally ill during the second half of the 19th century: (1) The rise of a democratic consciousness in many countries at the time of the disappearance of some of the old dynasties and the establishment of independent governments contributed to the rejection of cruel methods of restraint and treatment and to the gradual acceptance of nonrestraint and moral treatment. (2) Legislation concerning the commitment of dangerous mentally ill persons and regulations concerning the standards of public and private mental institutions were passed in many countries. (3) In contrast to the efforts made by reformers because of overcrowding in the few mental hospitals, in many countries mentally ill paupers continued to be kept in large institutions or in workhouses, together with all sorts of social outcasts. (4) A large proportion of the inmates in mental hospitals, perhaps up to 30 per cent, consisted of patients affected by general paralysis or other organic conditions, thus contributing to a rather pessimistic view of mental illness on the part of both professionals and lay people.

In that situation, it is no wonder that, in spite of the many reports left by visitors, quite often psychiatrists from other countries, to many institutions, it is quite difficult to obtain a reliable picture of the methods of care and treatment practiced in them. On the one side, regardless of all the reform efforts, brutal systems of restraint, punishment, and confinement continued to be used with or without the knowledge of the authorities well into the 20th century. On the other side, those cruel systems, notably the mechanical gadgets of restraint described in some books, were used rather seldom, pointing to a discrepancy between theory and practice.

As mentioned above, in the first half of the century a few enlightened people had introduced humane and rational methods of care and treatment in a few institutions in England and France. In the second part of the century, the leadership for introducing new reforms passed to Germany for various reasons: the healthy competition among the various states into which Germany was then divided; the need for building new institutions, in contrast to the trend of converting old monasteries into mental hospitals, as so often happened in Catholic countries; the tendency, following Griesinger's example, to affiliate mental hospitals with medical schools, resulting in a rise of standards and interest in providing training and research, along with regular service.

In an attempt to solve the problem of overcrowded institutions, a division was made between curable and incurable patients; the curable patients were admitted to mental hospitals (*Heilanstalten*), and the incurable patients were admitted to custodial institutions (*Pflegeanstalten*), a quite arbitrary system that lasted only a few decades. Considerable emphasis was put on the best type of architecture for mental hospitals, a topic on which monographs were written by several psychiatrists, notably the French A. Brierre de Boismont (1847) and J. B. M. Parchappe (1853) and the German M. Jacobi (1834) and H. Damerow (1840).

Regardless of the physical plant, some institutions achieved renown and became the favored place of training by many young psychiatrists. In France that role was taken for decades by the Salpétrière, Saint Anne, and the Maison de Charenton. In Germany the mental hospitals of Illenau in Baden and Alt-Scherbitz in Saxony were particularly important. Alt-Scherbitz, aside from the hospital, included a colony composed of various cottages for convalescent patients, as suggested by Griesinger (1965) in his textbook. While a professor of medicine at the University of Zurich, Griesinger had made plans for a mental hospital; it was opened in 1870 under the name of Burgölzli and probably became the most famous mental hospital in the world. Griesinger's other suggestion for an urban hospital of no more than 100 patients was carried out in connection with university clinics, of which there were 20 at the end of the century. In addition, a number of so-called sanatoriums for the treatment of nonpsychotic patients were in operation in Germany, and institutions for epileptics, idiots, and alcoholics were opened in various countries during that period. Finally, institutions for the criminally insane were established in England (Broadmoor), France (Maison Centrale de Gaillon), Germany (Bruchsal and Waldheim), and Italy (Aversa and Reggio Emilia).

In most instances, the head of an institution was a physician who also had administrative responsibilities. The ratio of physicians to patients varied from program to program; for instance, in Baden in 1865 there were 9 physicians for 800 patients. The role of the nurses was also very important; the ratio of nurses to patients was about 1 to 10. In England and then elsewhere, female nurses were found to be very helpful, even in male wards. The training of nurses was initiated in Germany and was generally provided in the context of each institution.

As for the treatment itself, in most places it was eclectic and consisted of a variety of means. Separation of the patients from their families was practically a canon accepted everywhere. In a few institutions there was an admission cottage. Although a description of treatment was not given anywhere, the use of a system of rewards and punishments to control patients was widespread. The individual positive relationship between patients and attendants was important. Conversely, as the object of paranoid feelings, a number of physicians were murdered by patients. The most notable case was that of the distinguished psychiatrist Bernhard von Gudden, who died under mysterious circumstances near Münich while in the company of the insane King Ludwig II of Bavaria.

A number of medications—such as belladonna, aconite, and opium—were used for various purposes. The relaxing and sleep-inducing effect of prolonged hot baths was emphasized by many. Electricity in various forms—such as electrical shocks and galvanization— was also used. Various methods to produce a state of shock in the patient were also mentioned. Considered particularly beneficial by many was the rest treatment, which entailed keeping the patients in bed for a long time. On the opposite side, others recommended keeping the patients involved in work, such as farming and gardening; in some institutions up to 80 per cent of the patients were engaged in different kinds of work. Concerts, plays, and intellectual activities were also advocated. How effective those various methods of treatment were is far from clear. Contemporary reports, however, were rather optimistic; cures were described in about 60 per cent of the cases of acute psychosis and up to 70 per cent in institutions with a high percentage and quality of staff. Finally, the aftercare movement at the end of the century resulted in the establishment of associations on behalf of patients and former patients in various countries.

AMERICAN PSYCHIATRY

Trend toward institutionalization. By the mid-1840's American psychiatry was definitely going through a transitional stage of ambivalence toward commitment to the ideals of moral treatment and to new emerging needs, whose meaning has become clear only recently. In a few years a number of events brought about a new situation: the rapid process of urbanization and industrialization, the increase in the population, the massive arrival of immigrant Irish, and the appearance of the vicious cycle of poverty, disease, and delinquency.

Correspondingly, the scene of psychiatry changed quickly. In private hospitals and in a few state hospitals, the philosophy of moral treatment continued to prevail for some time. But most of the state hospitals rapidly became overcrowded with state paupers, criminals, alcoholics, and vagrants. All those persons constituted a burden on the taxpayers, leading to a negative reaction against the use of moral treatment and to a justification for excluding them from the mental hospitals. The 1840 census had established that free northern Negros had a higher frequency of insanity than did either the white population of the nation or the Negro slaves of the South, a finding that was soon to be challenged as incorrect. More important was the survey of a sample of mentally ill patients by the physician and statistician Edward Jarvis (1971). *Insanity and Idiocy in Massachusetts: Report of the Commission on Lunacy, 1855*, concluded that there was a definite correlation between poverty and insanity; that most of the mentally ill were incurable, probably because of hereditary factors; and that the Irish were prone to mental diseases because they were ill adapted to American life. Jarvis recommended that the state take over the responsibility for treating, rather than just sheltering, all the mentally ill—in the long run treating was a more economic system—and that several new small hospitals for no more than 250 patients be built in various communities, in anticipation of today's concept of catchment areas. In contrast with those enlightened views, however, he added that curable and incurable native-born patients should be mixed together but that mentally ill aliens should be transferred to poorhouses and jails.

Regardless of some criticism expressed toward the report, mainly by Isaac Ray on statistical grounds, the trend toward hospitalizing patients in large mental institutions to keep expenditures low could not be stopped. Historically, the trend was similar to one that had become evident in Europe in the late 17th century; as in Europe, the aim was to remove and isolate not only the mentally ill but all outcasts of society, such as paupers, criminals, and vagrants. To a significant degree, the almshouse, the penitentiary, and the asylum all grew from the same sources. The movement toward institutionalizing the mentally ill was enhanced by several lay crusaders motivated by humanitarian reasons, notably Dorothea L. Dix (1802–1887) (see Figure 29). Endowed with an emotional personality and influenced by the Unitarian movement after a call to help the insane in 1841, she devoted the next 30 years of her life to founding mental hospitals in this country and abroad, mainly by appealing to the legislatures of the various states. By 1861 there were 48 asylums in the United States—one federally run in the District of Columbia, 27 state supported, five maintained by cities and counties, 10 corporate institutions, and five privately owned. The total number of hospitalized patients was about 8,500 in a United States population of more than 27 million.

In this country, in contrast to Europe, there were no big buildings, such as monasteries and manor houses, that could possibly be converted into hospitals, and an attempt by Dorothea Dix to convince the federal government to reserve

FIGURE 29. Dorothea Lynde Dix (1802–1887).

12,225,000 acres of wild land for the support of the insane was vetoed by President Franklin Pierce in 1854. Therefore, the problem of overcrowding became quickly endemic in mental institutions. In the meantime, the superintendents of asylums had recognized the need to form an official association for the purposes of sharing views, establishing a common platform on important issues, and, especially, providing better care for the mentally ill through joint action. On October 16, 1844, in Philadelphia, 13 superintendents of mental hospitals (The Original Thirteen) founded the Association of Medical Superintendents of American Institutions for the Insane, later called the American Medico-Psychological Association and now called the American Psychiatric Association, the oldest national medical association in this country (see Figure 30). The same year the *American Journal of Insanity*, now entitled the *American Journal of Psychiatry*, was founded by Brigham and published for many years at the New York State Lunatic Asylum in Utica.

Because of the ambivalence toward continuing the philosophy of moral treatment and the need to provide for large numbers of mentally ill patients, the psychiatric events of the decades from about the 1840's to the 1870's appear, in retrospect, complex and hard to define. Clearly, moral treatment was in decline, as evidenced by a number of signs—the etiological emphasis on heredity at the expense of environmental factors, thus leading to a pessimistic concept of prognosis; the increasing use of drugs for disturbed patients; the virtual rejection of the method of nonrestraint introduced in England by Hill and Conolly in the 1840's; the prevailing opposition to the notion of moral insanity as grounds for acquittal in courts, as shown by the uncertain position of the psychiatric profession toward the assassin of President Garfield, Charles Guiteau, a man who had a long history of irrationality; and the constant decrease of cost per patient and of patient-physician interaction, paralleled by the increase in the ratio between the physician and nurses, attendants, and aides.

The pioneers in the philosophy of moral treatment were disappearing from the scene. After the deaths of Brigham in 1849 and of Woodward the next year, Bell resigned from the medical superintendents association in 1856, John Galt died in 1862, Isaac Ray resigned in 1867, and 5 years later Butler resigned from the Hartford Retreat. Of the original 13 fathers of American psychiatry, only two were still active in the 1870's, Kirkbride, author of the standard *On the Construction, Organization, and General Arrangements of Hospitals for the Insane* (1854), at the Pennsylvania Hospital and Earle at the Northampton (Massachusetts) State Hospital. Even with them, however, the focus was shifting away from moral treatment and toward the categorization and assignment of mental patients to different wards, the protection of society from the insane, the division of the curable from the incurable patients, and the decrease of work programs.

By the mid-1850's—under the influence of the new research on brain pathology then flourishing in German universities and of the success of Griesinger's (1965) textbook on mental diseases, available in English translation in 1867, strictly linking behavior to organic factors—almost all American psychiatrists came to believe in the physiopathological cause of mental disorders. Postmortem examinations became more important than individual contacts with patients, physicians progressively lost contact with the families of their patients and with the community, and the psychiatric guild found itself more and more isolated from the stream of medicine and the public. An aura of pessimism seemed to pervade psychiatry. The high recovery rates that in the 1830's had constituted tangible proof of the validity of moral treatment were challenged on various grounds by Earle in *The Curability of Insanity* (1887), leading to the controversies surrounding the so-called myth of curability. Further pessimism was conveyed by the acceptance by many of Morel's causative concept of the degeneration of

FIGURE 30. Signatures of the original 13 founders of the American Psychiatric Association, 1844.

philosophy of society that was based on the survival of the fittest and that justified the neglect of its weakest members. Such a pessimistic outlook was also shared by official bodies, such as the commissions of lunacy established in some states. The *American Journal of Insanity*, edited by John Gray from 1854 to 1886, unilaterally reflected the adherence to the organogenesis of mental diseases. The gap between the empirical field of psychiatry and the other more scientifically based fields of medicine was increasing. Moreover, American psychiatry was clearly lagging behind the various schools of psychiatry then prospering in some European centers.

By the late 1870's and 1880's, criticism of asylums—especially in relation to the wide use of methods of restraint, dubious practices of patient commitment, the qualifications of the staff, and patent political appointments of superintendents—had crystallized. The National Organization for the Protection of the Insane and the Prevention of Insanity was founded in 1880. *The Journal of Nervous and Mental Disease* appeared in 1874 under the sponsorship of some neurologists who were also involved in private practices with disturbed patients. The movement of reforms became particularly evident in some states, notably New York, where the attempt to place the responsibility for the care of the mentally ill on counties and to commit all the chronic insane to a single asylum, the Willard Asylum, in 1865 had failed. The newly formed State Commission of Lunacy in 1893 included mental hospital positions under the civil service laws, established that the insane were wards of the state, and attempted to eliminate most of the abuses in institutions through the State Care Bill of 1890. In 1896 New York passed the Insanity Law, which aimed at dealing with the problem of mental illness in a comprehensive way by delegating to the Commission of Lunacy, composed of three men appointed for 6 years, the responsibility of supervising mental institutions through boards of managers; executing all laws pertinent to the custody, care, and treatment of the insane; and centralizing and unifying the systems of civil service examinations, transferrals of patients, and fee problems.

Contribution of neurology to psychiatry. One effect of the large number of medical casualties during the Civil War was to focus attention on the importance of neurology. Apart from their contributions to that discipline, William Hammond, E. C. Spitzka, and S. Weir Mitchell (1829–1914) were the neurologists whose names are most frequently associated with progress in psychiatry during that period: Hammond and Spitzka for their textbooks on psychiatry (respectively, *A Treatise on Insanity in Its Medical Relations* (Hammond, 1883) and *Insanity: Its Classification, Diagnosis, and Treatment* (Spitzka, 1883)); Mitchell for his outspoken criticism of the isolation of psychiatry from medicine and for the disinterest in research and training (in a famous address before the American Medical Psychological Association in 1894) and for his rest cure method, which he considered particularly beneficial in the treatment of neurotic women and which was a logical outgrowth of the concept of neurasthenia, developed by George Beard in 1880. Toward the end of the century, refreshing signs of a more positive and individualized approach to the mentally ill were becoming evident. Functional insanity was linked to faulty habits of life; separate facilities for acute cases were advocated; new forms of physical therapy—diet, massage, hydrotherapy, electrotherapy—were introduced; family care and the cottage system were initiated; and training courses for nurses and attendants were established. As a reaction to Mitchell's criticism, a few psychiatrists became interested in research, and that interest led to the founding in 1895 of the Pathological

Institute of New York Hospital, which later became the New York State Psychiatric Institute. A few years later, in 1902, the young Swiss psychiatrist Adolf Meyer (1866–1950) was appointed to the staff of the Institute, where he remained until 1913, when he became director of the newly built Henry Phipps Psychiatric Clinic at The Johns Hopkins University. By that time, important psychopathic hospitals for training and the active treatment of patients had been established in Michigan (1907) and in Boston (1912), the latter under the supervision of Southard, who is noted for his pioneer views on the importance of social work for psychiatry.

Mental hygiene movement. One other event during that period was of particular importance for the development of psychiatry: Clifford Beers, a distinguished businessman, published *A Mind That Found Itself* in 1908, after his recovery from a mental breakdown. In so doing, he launched the mental hygiene movement. Despite the implications for organic psychiatry of Noguchi's and Moore's discovery of *Treponema palidum* in 1913, a social orientation was soon to prevail, and that orientation was followed by dynamic psychiatry, with its emphasis on the psychological functioning of the patient.

KRAEPELIN

Although he was Freud's contemporary, Emil Kraepelin (1855–1926) can be considered the last representative of the predynamic school of psychiatry. After many years of training in some of the best neuropathological schools, Kraepelin turned to clinical psychiatry and taught that subject at the University of Munich for nearly 2 decades (1903–1921). Then he became head of the Research Institute of Psychiatry there, the so-called Kraepelin Institute, rapidly recognized as the leading place for psychiatric training. The development of his clinical concepts can be followed in his handbook of psychiatry, which, modestly initiated as a compendium in 1883, went through nine editions and, in 1927, became a 2,500-page textbook. In line with Virchow's idea of the disease concept, Kraepelin attempted to identify definite clinical syndromes by following and statistically recording their signs, their course, and their outcome. That method was, thus, objective and limited to the patient— that is, it took no consideration of his family and environment. On the basis of the voluminous data gathered, Kraepelin clearly differentiated manic-depressive psychosis from dementia precox, which was characterized by a weakening of emotional activities and a loss of inner unity. Unfortunately, that differentiation was carried one step further than necessary, and dementia precox patients came to be considered incurable. Because of its appealing structure, Kraepelin's classification was accepted all over the world; consequently, schizophrenia acquired a fatalistic connotation.

Only after the introduction of various organic therapies— such as malaria therapy by the Nobel Prize winner Julius von Wagner-Jauregg (1857–1940) in 1917 and, between 1935 and 1937, insulin coma treatments by Manfred Sakel (1900–1957), cardiazol shock treatments by Ladislau J. von Meduna (1896–1964), electric shock treatments by Ugo Cerletti (1877–1963) and Lucio Bini, and psychosurgery by Egas Moniz (1874–1955)—was the prognosis for psychosis viewed with greater optimism. Less well known but also significant is the method of psychological and social reintegration used extensively in Russia, based on the studies of conditioned reflexes by Ivan Petrovitch Pavlov (1849–1936) (see Figure 31).

RELATIONSHIP BETWEEN CONSTITUTION AND PERSONALITY

From earliest times, humans have attempted to correlate constitution—that is, the intrinsic physical endowment—with personality type, temperament, and emotional disorder. Kallmann's (1953) summary of the various schools of constitutional

FIGURE 31. Ivan P. Pavlov (1849–1936). (Courtesy of the National Library of Medicine.)

typology is reproduced in Table VI. In psychiatry, the classifications of Kretschmer and Sheldon in that regard are considered most noteworthy. Kretschmer correlated the short, stocky, round pyknic habitus with extroversion, cyclothymic (cycloid), and manic-depressive psychosis; the thin asthenic leptosomic constitution with introversion, schizoid tendencies, and schizophrenia; and the abnormally proportioned dysplastic habitus with endocrine and pituitary disorders. Many workers consider his muscular, well-proportioned, athletic habitus a variation of the asthenic constitution. According to Sheldon, who applied the methods of anthropometrics, the endomorph was temperamentally viscerotonic (sociable, relaxed, enjoys eating), the ectomorph was temperamentally cerebrotonic (antisocial, hypersensitive, secretive), and the mesomorph was somatic (energetic, competitive, action oriented).

Psychoanalysis and Recent Trends in Psychiatry

The psychiatric events described above refer, for the most part, to psychotic or, at least, grossly disturbed patients. In fact, even those workers, such as Mesmer and his followers, who did attempt to describe and treat neurotic symptoms were largely unaware of the true origins of those symptoms in the unconscious.

19th-CENTURY CONCEPTS OF THE UNCONSCIOUS

Interest in the unconscious, which may be attributed primarily to the romantic movement, was evident throughout the 19th century and found expression in the five main currents of thought preeminent during that period.

Metaphysical concepts. The unconscious was equated with will by the philosophers Schelling, Schopenhauer, and von Hartmann. Carus (1970) in *Psyche* (1846) described an "absolute unconscious" and stated:

the key to the knowledge of the nature of the conscious life of the soul lies in the realm of the unconscious.

Biological concepts. These concepts included the "physiological unconscious" of von Hartmann, which was followed later by the "mnene" of Semon and the "psychoid" of Dreisch and Bleuler.

TABLE VI
*Schools of Constitutional Typology**

Nationality of School	Name of Main Investigator	Name of Constitutional Types			
		Type I	Type II	Type III	Type IV
Greek	Hippocrates	Apoplecticus	Phthisicus		
Roman	Galen	Sanguine	Melancholic	Phlegmatic	Choleric
French	Rostan	Digestive	Respiratory cerebral	Muscular	
Italian	De Giovanni	Megalosplanchnic	Microsplanchnic	Normosplanchnic	
	Viola	Brachymorphic	Dolichomorphic	Eumorphic	
German	Gall-Beneke	Hyperplastic	Hypoplastic		
	Kretschmer	Pyknic	Asthenic	Athletic	Dysplastic
Anglo-American	Stockard	Lateral	Linear		
	Rees-Eysenck	Eurymorphic	Leptomorphic	Mesomorphic	
	Sheldon	Endomorphic (viscerotonic)	Ectomorphic (cerebrotonic)	Mesomorphic (somatotonic)	Dysplastic

* Adapted from Kallmann, F. J., *Heredity in Health and Mental Disorder*, p. 56. W. W. Norton, New York, 1953.

TABLE VII

The Successive Discovery of the Cognitive, Vital, and Pathological Aspects of the Unconscious Mind in Post-Cartesian Europe
Four aspects have been so widely recognized or are so subtly connected that they fall outside this historical analysis: (1) the *mystical* (from earliest times to Kierkegaard), (2) *memory*, (3) *dreams*, and (4) the *collective* (from Vico to Jung). What is here called the Vital Unconscious, properly understood, should include the others as its varied expressions.

COGNITIVE (Apperceptions, perceptions, images, ideas)	VITAL (Instinct, will, motives, emotions, imagination)	PATHOLOGICAL
1650	Paracelsus (1493–1541) Montaigne (1544–1592) Shakespeare (1546–1616) Pascal (1623–1662) and Spinoza (1632–1677), all show a background awareness	
From about 1680 Cudworth Norris		
1700 Malebranche Leibniz Vico v. Wolff Kames	(Shaftesbury)	
1750 Crusius Condillac Tucker Kant	(Rousseau)	from about 1780
	Herder Lichtenberg Fichte, Goethe	Herder Mesmer Moritz
1800 Fichte	Schelling The Romantics Troxler	Reill Langermann Bertrand
Herbart Maine de Biran	Herbart Maine de Biran Schopenhauer	Herbart Schopenhauer Benecke
1850 Hamilton Marx-Engels Carpenter	Hamilton Carus Fortlage Dostoevski Amiel von Hartmann	Morell, Griesinger Laycock, Maudsley Charcot, Brentano Bernheim, Janet Breuer, Lipps
Galton		
1900	Freud	Freud
Jung	Jung	Jung

Concepts based on depth psychology. These concepts of the unconscious were expressed by the mystics, the mesmerists, and the parapsychologists, such as von Schubert (1814), who, in his work on dreams (1837), focused on the creative activity and symbolism of the unconscious, anticipating Freudian and, to an even greater extent, Jungian views.

Prescientific concepts. Within this category of concepts of the unconscious are the forgotten memories and the subliminal perceptions of Leibnitz, Herbart, and Fechner. Herbart is particularly important for his emphasis on unconscious representations as the background for the conscious, which strongly influenced German psychology; Fechner was significant for his attempt to express the relationship between mind and body in mathematical form.

Concept of the dynamic unconscious. The concept of the dynamic unconscious was developed as a concomitant of hypnosis by a number of physicians of the French school. For purposes of this presentation, only this last concept of the unconscious is of interest (see Table VII).

SCIENTIFIC STUDY OF HYPNOSIS

Jean Martin Charcot (1825–1893), a neurologist and literary man, early in his career at the Salpétriére described several neurological syndromes in *Leçons sur les maladies du système nerveux* (1872–1873) (Charcot, 1877–1889). Later on, he was attracted by the puzzling symptoms of hysteria and investigated it thoroughly from the psychological perspective. He described hysterical stigmata, hysterogenous zones, the attacks, and the labile affect of the patients, characterized by emotional indifference (*la belle indifférence*). Eventually, Charcot came to recognize that a trauma, mainly of a sexual nature, quite often touched off ideas and feelings that become unconscious (*condition seconde*). Symptoms similar to hysteria, such as the idea of a paralysis, could be reproduced experimentally through hypnosis. Because of Charcot's prestige at the Salpétriére, where his Tuesday and Friday morning lectures were attended by the Parisian elite, hypnosis soon acquired wide popularity and an equal amount of opposition from the medical profession. Charcot believed that hysteria could be cured by hypnosis, which he divided into three successive stages—lethargy, catalepsy, and somnambulism.

Opposed to Charcot's thesis that only hysterical persons could be hypnotized were two physicians, A. A. Liébeault (1823–1904) and Hippolyte Bernheim (1837–1919), of the school of Nancy. They stressed that anybody who could be influenced by suggestion could be hypnotized. After a bitter controversy and in spite of the prestige carried by Charcot, the school of Nancy eventually proved to be right. Regardless of that setback and of the criticism that some patients unconsciously performed for the public to please their doctor, Charcot's distinction for having directed the attention of many students from all over Europe, including the young Freud, to the problem of hysteria remains beyond dispute. Even more important is the fact that the emphasis in psychiatry shifted from the study of psychoses to the study of neuroses.

PIERRE JANET

Relatively little is known outside of France of the work of Pierre Janet (1859–1947), although many of his concepts paralleled some tenets of the psychodynamic school. Originally a teacher of philosophy, Janet worked at the Salpétrière for several years and eventually obtained the chair of experimental psychology at the Collège de France. He lectured in the United States on psychopathology in 1904 in St. Louis, Missouri, and on hysteria in 1906 at Harvard University and again at Harvard in 1936 on the occasion of the tercentenary of its foundation. Like Myers in England and Prince in the United States, Janet was attracted to psychiatry by the interest early in this century in exotic psychopathology, such as hysteria and somnambulism, recently called Victorian melodrama. He then developed the notion of psychological automatism—that is, the appearance of lower psychological functions when the higher functions are impaired. He excelled in the clinical descriptions of hysteria (Janet, 1965), amnesia, fugues, anorexia, tics, and other syndromes. Common to most of those syndromes was the emergence of subconscious contents related to forgotten dimensions of the psyche, with which contact could be established in particular situations of suggestibility. Central to his theory of psychopathology was the concept of psychoasthenia, which he described as loss of "the function of the real," partial dissociation and inability to keep ideas in full consciousness due to weakness of the highest integrative activities. The fact that Janet was influenced by the concepts related to hysteria and hypnosis developed by Charcot undoubtedly explains the many similarities between his own publications in clinical psychiatry and those of Freud at the end of the 19th century. Hailed as a true pioneer of the psychodynamic school by the leading French psychiatrists—such as Baruk, Ey, and Delay—Janet's name is practically forgotten today. Several factors may account for that lack of fame—namely, his reserved personality, his unrelenting independence of thought and the lack of an organized school of disciples, the bitter opposition by the psychoanalytic school, and the philosophical style of his writing, most of which appeared in the 1920's, when psychoanalysis was already well established.

ROLE OF SWITZERLAND

In addition to the great influence exercised on the development of modern psychiatry by the French clinicians at the turn of the century, brief mention should be made of the Swiss school, notably represented by the mental hospital Burghölzli

in Zurich. In spite of its small size, Switzerland has played a major role in psychiatry, probably because of its geographical location, its variety of ethnic and linguistic influences, and its traditional political neutrality.

The Burghölzli Hospital, founded in the mid-19th century, achieved great renown under the leadership of August Forel (1879–1898), who studied hypnosis extensively, vigorously fought against alcoholism, and presented enlightened views on sex in *The Sexual Question* (1905). He was succeeded as director of Burghölzli by Eugen Bleuler (1857–1939), who, during his tenure there (1898–1927), coined the word "schizophrenia" (from the Greek words for split mind—that is, dissociation between thoughts and affects); classified the disorder into hebephrenic, catatonic, and paranoid; differentiated the primary disturbances, essentially loose associations, from the secondary disturbances, such as autism and hallucinations; under the influence of psychoanalysis focused on the content of the syndrome, such as displacement and condensation; and presented a much more optimistic view of its outcome than the one held by Kraepelin. Although Bleuler's (1950) monograph *Dementia Praecox or the Group of Schizophrenias* (1911) was not translated into English until 4 decades later, his *Textbook of Psychiatry* (1916) (Bleuler, 1924) soon became well known and helped to disseminate his ideas.

The physician Hermann Rorschach (1884–1922) also worked at Burghölzli. Under the influence of Jung's studies on associations and the complex, Rorschach published *Psychodiagnostik* in 1921, a fusion of clinical psychiatry, psychoanalysis, and applied psychology. By that time, three other Swiss physicians trained at Burghölzli had left Switzerland and established themselves permanently in the United States: August Hoch, who became active in the New York State psychiatric system; Emil Oberholzer, who introduced the Rorschach Test in this country; and Adolf Meyer, who greatly influenced the entire American psychiatric field. The psychiatric tradition of Burghölzli has continued to this day under the leadership of Eugen Bleuler's son Manfred, the author of a number of studies on hereditary and endocrinological aspects of mental diseases.

Burghölzli was also the first mental hospital to accept psychoanalysis as a modality of treatment on the part of Eugen Bleuler, Carl Jung, and Ludwig Binswanger, who eventually became an exponent of the existentialist movement. As a number of physicians from many countries, including the United States, trained at Burghölzli early in the 20th century, the therapeutic methods used there were soon practiced elsewhere. Among those methods were emphasis on work therapy and the placement of patients in colonies and halfway houses. Not far from Zurich, in Bern, Jacob Klaesi introduced the therapy of prolonged sleep for psychotic disorders in 1922; since then, sleep therapy has been extensively used in Russia and other countries. In Zurich, important neurological studies were carried on by von Monakow, Minkowski, and the Nobel Prize winner Hess.

Furthermore, Switzerland is known for its long-standing interest in education, which can be traced back to Rousseau (1712–1778) and Pestalozzi (1746–1827). It is, therefore, not surprising that Switzerland played a preeminent role in the study and treatment of children. Child psychology has been especially cultivated in Geneva. There, the first chair of psychology was occupied by Flournoy (1854–1920), a pioneer in the study of parapsychology and a friend of William James. His successor, Claparède (1873–1940), founded the Institut J. J. Rousseau, which later acquired international renown for the studies on genetic psychology made there by Jean Piaget. The first residential treatment center in the field of child psychiatry was established by Burghölzli near Zurich in 1920; since the 1930's, the child guidance movement has flourished in many regions of Switzerland.

During World War II many people from various countries found refuge in Switzerland and carried on some important psychiatric studies, especially of children separated from their families. Since then, the international role played by Switzerland has been continued there with the publication of several psychiatric journals and, in the 1950's, with the great impetus given to psychopharmacology by important chemical industries in Basel.

PSYCHOANALYTIC MOVEMENT

It is likely that the concepts and therapeutic techniques developed by Charcot and Janet would never have passed the limits of their respective schools, in spite of their position of prestige in academic circles, were it not for their importance in relation to the psychoanalytic movement. Such a movement in its early stage is so closely connected with the life and work of its founder, Sigmund Freud (1856–1939), that it is necessary to focus on that great personality, who opened many new paths in the comprehension of human psychology.

Significantly, the 20th century opened with Freud's *The Interpretation of Dreams* (1900), a milestone in the history of psychology by any standard. Although the book at that time passed almost unnoticed, it represented a major breakthrough in the understanding of the human mind on three different grounds: (1) It introduced a strict methodological technique in the study of dreams, a field that has puzzled people for centuries and that has been greatly influenced by all sorts of absurd beliefs and superstitions. (2) It relied on the introspective study of the self, in contrast to the objective psychology of the times, which made use only of other subjects, disregarding the importance of the subjective state of mind of the researcher. (3) It posed the basis for a foundation of psychology in which normality and pathology were conceived of as an uninterrupted continuum, thus opening the way for a more comprehensive attitude toward anyone affected by emotional disorders.

As one would expect, all that was not recognized at the time. In the academic circles of Vienna, Freud was known as a neurologist who had progressively turned his attention to the study of mental phenomena. Today, after the biography by Ernest Jones (1953–1957) and the publication of selected letters (Freud, 1960), it is possible to reconstruct Freud's personality rather accurately.

Born in the small industrial town of Freiberg, Moravia— then belonging to Austria, now part of Czechoslovakia—in 1856 to a Jewish family of limited means, Freud distinguished himself early for his brilliant mind, for his tenacity in pursuing his studies, and for an innate desire to excel. His scientific curiosity, accompanied by the boldest inclination to maintain intellectual independence at any cost, developed early and accompanied him throughout his life, giving him a certain feeling of loneliness, which he seemed to cherish and to resent at the same time.

As a medical student, he held an apprenticeship in the scientific investigation of physiology under Ernest Brücke, who belonged to the circle of researchers influenced by Johann Müller. However, Freud's interests ranged well beyond medicine, and he followed the courses in philosophy given by Franz Brentano, a scholar of Aristotle and a staunch defender of intentionality in human motivation. The translation of a book by the English philosopher John Stuart Mill provided another philosophical influence. After having obtained a medical de-

gree in 1881, Freud, beset by financial difficulties, turned to neurology, did research in Meynert's psychiatric institute, and became *Privatdozent* in 1885. In the next 2 years he published two books, one on infantile cerebral paralysis and one on aphasia. In 1886 he studied in Paris under Charcot and, on his return to Vienna, became a vigorous defender of the value of hypnosis. He was influenced by the Viennese internist Josef Breuer (1842–1925), who in 1880 had successfully treated a young woman affected by hysterical symptoms with a new talking cure, catharsis. After a second period of study in Nancy, France, in 1889, under Hippolyte-Marie Bernheim, Freud became convinced that suggestion was the psychological foundation of hypnosis. In *Studies on Hysteria* (1895) Breuer and Freud related the cure of hysteric symptoms to the release of blocked emotions. The same year Freud discovered the method of free association and gave up hypnosis completely. He called his method "psychoanalysis" for the first time in 1896.

Around that time Freud shared his most intimate thoughts related to his work with the German otorhinolaryngologist Wilhelm Fliess. In retrospect, it is clear that through that relationship Freud underwent a sort of personal analysis, which eventually resulted in *The Interpretation of Dreams*.

For the next 2 decades Freud dedicated himself entirely to clinical matters, which he presented with great care in a number of books and articles. Having discovered the importance of the dynamic unconscious, he proceeded to investigate the laws and mechanisms that regulate it. In *Psychopathology of Everyday Life* (1901), he described, in succession, primary process, condensation, displacement, and such other phenomena as slips of the tongue and parapraxias. Impressed by the importance of sexual disturbances in neuroses and by a hint at the Oedipus complex through his own analysis, Freud posed the foundations of the libido theory in *Three Essays on the Theory of Sexuality* (1905). In line with evolutionary concepts, he described an oral, an anal, and a phallic phase, all preceding the genital phase of maturity. He also described the fixation and regression that are typical of neurotic and psychotic symptoms.

Those concepts were so much at variance with the standards of Victorian morality that, no matter how much they were supported by clinical evidence, they drew considerable criticism and aroused animosity against their proponent. Freud, having lost Breuer's support some years previously, worked in isolation for several years. However, some young physicians were attracted by Freud's ideas, and in 1907 the first formal psychoanalytic society was formed in Vienna. Its original members were Alfred Adler, Wilhelm Steckel, Sandor Ferenczi, Otto Rank, Carl Jung, Karl Abraham, and Max Eitington. The last three were on the staff of the Burghölzli Psychiatric Hospital of Zurich, whose director, Bleuler, was originally well disposed toward psychoanalysis. In 1908 the first international meeting of psychoanalysts was organized by Jung in Salzburg.

In 1909 both Freud and Jung were invited by Stanley Hall and James Putnam to lecture at Clark University in Worcester, Massachusetts. As a reaction against the social Darwinism and the civilized morality of the late 19th century, the United States was then ready to try many new social and educational reforms, such as settlement houses and juvenile courts, in that climate of optimistic moralism that characterized the progressive movement. In psychiatry itself, Adolf Meyer was then introducing the clinical and developmental study of the patient in hospital settings. This country seemed ready to try Freud's clinical formulations, but at home Freud experienced many difficulties, mainly related to the lack of academic support, made worse by Bleuler's resignation from the international psychoanalytic association in 1910. Together with the influence of Freud's domineering personality, that lack of support had the effect of perpetuating the isolation of the various psychoanalytic societies in Vienna, Zurich, Berlin (organized in 1908), Munich (1910), and New York (1911), in spite of the founding of some specialized journals—*Zentralblatt für Psychoanalyse* in 1911 and *Internationale Zeitschrift für Psychoanalyse* and *Imago*, both in 1913. The tendency toward isolation reached an extreme point in the creation of the inner circle of Freud's most faithful pupils—originally Abraham, Jones, Ferenczi, Sachs, and Otto Rank and, later, Max Eitington.

By that time, Jung and Adler were no longer associated with Freud. Jung was already well known in psychiatry for his studies on word associations and on dementia precox. His work on the psychology of the unconscious (1911–1912), in which he denied the sexual role of the libido, brought the final break with Freud. Adler, too, broke with Freud when he substituted the aggressive drive for the sexual drive in the economy of the libido. Later on, around 1923, Rank departed from Freud's philosophy with his repudiation of the Oedipus complex and preference for unorthodox theoretical and practical views.

As could be expected, World War I resulted in the isolation of the few psychoanalysts and in a decrease in activities. Freud, however, continued his work and in 1916–1917 published *Introductory Lectures to Psychoanalysis*, in which he dealt extensively with defense mechanisms, such as overcompensation, reaction formation, rationalization, projection, and displacement. Neurotic symptoms were considered unsuccessful attempts to achieve self-healing—unsuccessful because of the handicap posed by the defense mechanisms themselves.

The second decade of the 20th century marked the publication of Freud's metapsychological—that is, theoretical—writings. In *Beyond the Pleasure Principle* (1920), he differentiated between ego drives and sexual libido, proposing a new theory of two primary instincts, the life instinct (Eros) and the death instinct (Thanatos); the life instinct deals with the preservation of the individual, and the death instinct deals with the preservation of the race. Three years later, in *The Ego and the Id*, Freud continued to elaborate on a general theory of personality: The id is the common matrix of the unconscious from which each person, from birth on, gradually develops his own ego, progressively substituting the reality principle for the pleasure principle. That substitution takes place under the influence of the superego, which consists of largely unconscious parental and social mores and rules; ultimately, the function of the ego is to harmonize the needs of the instincts with external expectations. In *Inhibitions, Symptoms, and Anxiety* (1925), his last great clinical contribution, Freud replaced the earlier notion of anxiety as a product of frustrated sexual libido with a new concept of anxiety as a signal of approaching internal danger; in contrast to anxiety, fear is a signal of approaching external danger. Anxiety, rather than sexuality, became paramount in the pathogenesis of neurosis, and the importance of the ego slowly began to overshadow the earlier emphasis on the unconscious.

The last group of Freud's writings deals with cultural phenomena and represents the beginning of the trend of applying psychoanalysis to social sciences. In *Totem and Taboo* (1913), under the influence of James Frazer's emphasis on the universality of taboos toward incest and toward the killing of the totem animal, Freud explained the origin of society as related to the ancestral killing of the father by the jealous sons, with the consequent rise of fraternal guilt and of worship of the totem, which represents the killed father.

In *Group Psychology and the Analysis of the Ego* (1920), Freud, under the influence of the studies of the French soci-

ologist Gustave Le Bon, attributed the cohesion and dynamics of any group to the libidinous relationship of each individual member to the leader, who can exercise a positive or a negative influence. Under stress, the group tends to regress to the extreme level of disorganization in conditions of panic—indeed, an anticipation of the fate of Fascism and Nazism 2 decades later. Less convincing, however, was his attempt to apply the same dynamics to two organized groups, the church and the army.

Progressively, Freud's interest in social factors broadened to include the whole society. A few years later, Freud published *The Future of an Illusion* (1927), in which he related the universal need for a religion to dependency needs. As could be anticipated, that book caused a great deal of controversy and led to the impression in many circles in Austria and in other Catholic countries that psychoanalysis was immoral, a notion that has been dispelled in recent years. In *Civilization and Its Discontents* (1929), Freud attributed the dynamics of society to a balance between aggressive impulses and the need of its individual members for security. Necessarily, freedom has to be limited in order to obtain security, and that limitation arouses guilt feelings that are unavoidable in any society.

Freud's interest in social factors was greatly enhanced by the 1920's political situation in Central Europe that followed the catastrophe of World War I and that progressively led to the rise of Nazism. Since his childhood, however, Freud was intrigued by the individual dynamics of great personages of the past. Throughout the years, he applied the psychoanalytic method to Jensen's *Gradiva* (1907); to Shakespeare's Lady Macbeth, Hamlet, and Richard III; to Dostoevski's *The Brothers Karamazov;* to Leonardo da Vinci; and to Michelangelo's Moses—all in such a lucid prose as to earn him the Goethe Prize in 1930, the only outstanding award granted to him during his life.

The theme of Moses fascinated Freud for years and culminated in the publication of his final book, *Moses and Monotheism* (1939), which combined his two interests, the study of the individual personality and the study of society. Unquestionably, his interest in the origin of his own ancestors, the Jewish people, was greatly enhanced by the mass persecutions of Jews carried on by the Nazis. Freud's theory was that Moses was originally an Egyptian who embraced monotheism while in Egypt and then converted the Jews to that belief. Later on, however, Moses was murdered by his followers, and that murder is the origin of the unconscious feeling of guilt that is a pervasive characteristic of the Jews and that is cyclically reenacted—typically, in the death of Christ.

By the time the book appeared, Freud was safe in London. Although, being a Jew, he always felt somewhat discriminated against academically by the strictly Catholic Austrian society, a matter that has given rise to controversies in recent years, he felt quite attached to Vienna and appeared to enjoy a position of isolation. But, after the *Anschluss* in 1938, the situation in Austria became quite dangerous for the Jews, and there was fear for his life. Thanks to the intervention of many friends—in particular, Princess Marie Bonaparte—he was allowed to leave, and he settled with his daughter Anna in London, where he died in 1939.

From a historical perspective, undoubtedly Freud's work has the characteristics and originality of genius. Nevertheless, it should be recognized that some of his basic concepts can be followed throughout the development of medical and cultural history. The value of catharsis was recognized in ancient Greek culture. Symptoms were believed to represent a compromise between opposing forces—unconscious, sexual, life, and death—during the romantic movement and in early 19th century medicine. The unconscious was thought to play an essential role as conducive to self-knowledge by the French moralists of the 18th century and the philosophers and biologists of the 19th century. The interpretation of dreams was part of ancient tradition and was essential to the technique of incubation. Descriptions of the gradual unfolding of the sexual instinct and the developmental nature of neuroses may be found in the evolutionary concepts of Goethe, Darwin, and others. The teleological, sexual, and self-preservation aims of the instincts were fundamental to Plato's basic concept of the immutability of things and their mythical return to an earlier state. Freud's concept of regression was stated earlier by Hughlings Jackson as part of his neurological concept of dissolution. The scientific character of psychoanalytic technique and its concept of behavior as predetermined are evident in the deterministic and experimental frame of reference of 19th-century medicine. And Freud's belief that the cure depended on the insight gained by the patient was in the Platonic and orphic tradition—that is, once a person is purged of his prejudices, knowledge replaces ignorance, and *logos*, thought, prevails.

Adler, Jung, and Rank. Among those who were particularly influenced by Freud at the beginning of the 20th century, three stand out for their initial adherence to his doctrines and their later dissension and elaboration of independent schools of thought: Adler, Jung, and Rank.

Adler. Alfred Adler was born in a suburb of Vienna in 1870 to a Jewish family of merchants well integrated in the prevailing Catholic community. The second in a family of six children, he appeared to have headstrong feelings of sibling rivalry toward his older brother, Sigmund. Early in his life he was influenced by rationalistic trends in philosophy and by the writings of Marx and Nietzsche. Shortly after he graduated from the medical school of Vienna in 1895, he became an outspoken proponent of ideas of social medicine and advanced enlightened views on the education of children and on sexual matters.

He was converted to the Protestant faith in 1904. From 1902 to 1911 he belonged to Freud's small psychoanalytic circle and was elected president of the International Psychoanalytic Society. By that time, he had already published *Studies of Organ Inferiority* (1907), in which he submitted that, as a reaction to an organ inferiority due to organic or functional causes, the patient develops a compensation that often takes neurotic form—typically, masculine protest in women.

Because of his many conflicts with Freud, which were related mainly to Adler's denial of the sexual element in neuroses, he departed from Freud in 1911 and founded the Society for Individual Psychology. The next year he published *The Nervous Character*, rich in ideas and clinical data, in which he stated that neurosis stems from feelings of inferiority brought forth by social factors and that the emphasis should be on the individuality of the person viewed in the temporal dimension.

In the decade after Austria's defeat of 1918, during the period of great development of social institutions supported by the Social-Democrats, Adler founded a variety of programs in Vienna: consultations for teachers, medicopedagogical consultations—that is, pioneering child guidance clinics—kindergartens, and experimental schools. In 1924 he was appointed a professor at the Pedagogical Institute of the City of Vienna. He further elaborated on his concepts in *Understanding Human Nature* (1927), which was based on *Menschenkenntnis*—that is, concrete psychology. In it he stressed various principles: the indivisibility of the human being, the dynamism of the psyche, and the style of life (*Lebensstil*) of each person. He paid special attention to the dynamics of interpersonal relations—typically, the position of a person vis-à-vis his siblings—out of which inferiority feelings, educational errors, and, eventually, social disorders may develop.

Progressively, Adler became involved in teaching in the United States—first at Columbia University and then, from 1932 on, at the Long Island Medical College. By that time, the tenets of his psychotherapeutic methods had reached full expression. The emphasis was on the patient's gradually becoming aware of his fictitious life goal and life style and being motivated to change them in the context of a cooperative patient-doctor relationship. Adler settled permanently in this country in 1934. He died while on a lecture tour in England in 1937.

From the historical viewpoint, it has become clear that Adler's work represents a pioneering effort in some fields, notably in psychosomatic medicine (organ inferiority), in group therapy and community psychiatry (social factors in psychopathology), and in existential psychiatry (life style). Moreover, the primacy he attributed to the aggressive drive over the libido has been considered favorably by many. Therefore, it remains puzzling why Adler's work has not received more attention, considering the fact that many of his original ideas have found their way into psychiatry. In attempting to answer this question, Ellenberger brought forward several points: Adler's unassuming and down-to-earth personality, which was at variance with Freud's intellectual stature; his rejection of his Jewish background, coupled with his inability to organize a strong society of followers, as had been done by the psychoanalytic group; the poor form of his writings; and his lack of a stable academic position.

Jung. Carl Gustav Jung was born in the little Swiss village of Kesswil, near Lake Constance, in 1875. His paternal grandfather, considered by some to be an illegitimate son of Goethe, was influenced early by the German romantic movement and then became a prominent physician in Basel, where he was elected rector of the university. His father was a Protestant pastor well versed in the Scriptures. In his autobiography Jung elaborated on his childhood fantasies, dreams, and anxieties. While studying medicine at Basel University, he was particularly influenced by Goethe, Schopenhauer, Nietzsche, and authors who had studied parapsychological phenomena—such as Swendenborg, Mesmer, Kerner, and Lombroso. In a talk to a student society in 1897, Jung stated that the existence of the soul was based on transcedent hopes after death and that somnambulism, hypnosis, and spiritistic phenomena were means of investigating the soul. His direct experiences while participating in spiritual seances with a young woman, a cousin of his, convinced him that split-off contents of the unconscious can take the appearance of a human personality. His dissertation, based on that experience of multiple personality, was entitled "Psychology and Pathology of the So-called Occult Phenomena." The origins of his many ideas, later elaborated in his books, can be found in his writings of that period.

From 1900 to 1909, except for a short period of study with Janet in Paris, Jung was assistant to Bleuler at the Burghölzli Hospital in Zurich. At the suggestion of Bleuler, Jung did extensive research on word association and published a book on it in 1906, *Studies in Word Association,* wherein for the first time he discussed the notion of complex—that is, an emotionally charged complex of representations. In the next year *The Psychology of Dementia Praecox* appeared, the first monograph in which the new dynamic psychology was applied to a psychotic patient. He advanced the hypothesis that the cause of the disease was a toxin produced by the complexes.

During that period Jung was greatly influenced by Freud's principles, which, with Bleuler's encouragement, were then applied at Burghölzli. As a matter of fact, Freud soon recognized in Jung a superior mind and, in the attempt to counteract the impression that psychoanalysis was purely a Jewish matter, considered him as his favorite disciple. In 1909, the year he left Burghölzli, Jung joined Freud in lecturing at Clark University in Worcester, Massachusetts, and shortly thereafter Jung became the first president of the International Psychoanalytic Association.

Soon, however, the discrepancies between Freud and Jung, characterized by mutual ambivalence, came to the fore. Freud expected that Jung would remain his faithful disciple; instead, Jung revealed independence of thinking in rejecting the Oedipus complex and the exclusively sexual origin of the libido. In Jung's *Metamorphosis and Symbols of the Libido* (1911–1912), translated into English as *The Psychology of the Unconscious*, which was based on a comprehensive study of myths from early times up to the present, he considered the libido as psychic energy, manifesting itself in three stages in the development of the child up to sexual maturity. Psychotherapy was to be based largely on the analysis of dreams, and the psychoanalyst was to undergo analysis himself—apparently, the first statement to that effect. That same year, 1912, Jung gave some lectures on psychoanalysis in New York, and the next year he resigned from the International Psychoanalytic Association.

In the period from 1913 to 1919, Jung apparently went through a personal crisis, during which he forced unconscious material to the fore of his personality through dreams, fantasies, and other forms. At the end of that period of what Ellenberger called "creative illness," Jung emerged as head of the new school of analytic psychology and a famous therapist. In 1921 he published *Psychological Types,* in which, on the basis of a contrast between the psychological syndromes of hysteria and of schizophrenia, he presented an entirely new system of dynamic psychiatry, centered on the two opposite concepts of extroversion and introversion, for which he found confirmation in philosophy, theology, and literature.

From then on, Jung developed the various original concepts with which analytic psychology has been especially identified: psychic energy stemming from the instincts; the collective unconscious from which universal archetypes emerge, regardless of cultures and historical periods; the structure of the human psyche as a composite of persona (social mask), shadow (hidden personal characteristics), anima (feminine identification in a man), animus (masculine identification in a woman), and self (the innermost center of the personality); the individuation, the slow process of achieving wisdom in the second half of life through the emergence of an archetypal image of the self; and, at variance with Freud's analytic-reductive therapy, Jung's synthetic-hermeneutic therapy of helping the patient achieve individuation.

Progressively, Jung came to be influenced by the writings of Paracelsus, of mystics, of gnostics, and of alchemists and by Indian and Chinese religious traditions. Many of his late concepts, as well as those of his sympathizers, in the fields of religion, mythology, archeology, literature, and philosophy were presented at the Eranos yearly conferences held in Ascona, Switzerland, and were published in the *Eranos Yearbooks*. As the last part of his production, typified by his books on religious and cultural matters—*Psychology and Religion,* 1940; *Psychology and Alchemy,* 1944; *Aion,* 1951; *Answers to Job,* 1952; *Mysterium Coniunctionis,* 1955—is outside of the field of psychiatry proper, a simple mention of this period is sufficient here. Only his study on syncronicity (1952), postulating the connection between apparently unrelated phenomena, falls on the borderline of psychology. By the time of his death, in 1961, Jung's rich heritage had been taken over by the C. G. Jung Institute, which opened in Zurich in 1948. In the United States Jung's concepts have had only limited success, mainly because of their esoteric formulation, which is alien to the American pragmatic mentality; moreover, few of Jung's pupils had to emigrate to this country because of racial persecution.

Rank. Otto Rank was born in Vienna in 1884 to a Jewish family in which relationships were strained because of the father's alcoholism. Influenced toward pessimism by Schopenhauer and Nietzsche, he soon became interested in great men of the past and in the psychology of creativity, on which he wrote his first book, *The Artist* (1907), in which he considered creativity as a constructive outlet for neurotic conflicts.

In his early twenties, he developed a filial sort of relationship toward Freud; the relationship was probably based on Rank's craving for a good father image. Conversely, Freud was very impressed by his exceptional knowledge of literature and mythology and by his good disposition. From 1906 to 1915 Rank was the secretary of the Vienna Psychoanalytic Society and kept records of the meetings. In *The Myth of the Birth of the Hero* (1909), a common myth in many cultures, he submitted that the son's rebellion against the father is provoked by the hostile behavior of the father. In 1912, the same year in which he received a doctoral degree from the University of Vienna, he published *The Incest Motive in Poetry and Saga,* a thorough study of the Oedipus conflict in literature, pointing to the unconscious gratification derived by the artist through his creation. Also in that year, he and Sachs started to edit the journal *Imago,* devoted to the application of psychoanalysis to literature and art. Shortly thereafter, Rank began to act as private secretary to Freud on many occasions.

In 1913 Rank coauthored with Sachs *The Significance of Psychoanalysis for the Mental Sciences;* the next year, he published *Doppelgänger (The Double),* in which he discussed the mirror reflection of the person described by many authors and considered by him a narcissistic protection against the destruction of the ego. It was followed by *Don Juan* (1922), in which the theme of the gallant man is related to his search for an ideal woman. Shortly thereafter, in spite of the antagonism that developed between him and Abraham and Jones, Rank published with Ferenczi *The Development of Psychoanalysis* (1924), in which the notion of acting out is mentioned for the first time in psychiatric literature.

The same year, 1924, marked the publication of *The Trauma of the Birth* and the beginning of Rank's separation from the psychoanalytic movement. In that book Rank minimized the importance of the Oedipus conflict and considered the separation anxiety connected with birth (primary anxiety) as the most important element in the future development of the person and also as the source of neurosis. Freud was initially inclined to absorb that new notion into the psychoanalytic doctrine but, in the face of the strong rejection by all his colleagues, eventually repudiated it in 1926. In retrospect, such a notion anticipated a number of current concepts, such as primal fixation, primal anxiety, good and bad mother, and return-to-womb fantasies. The same can be said of the active therapy of a limited number of sessions, postulated by Rank and Ferenczi, which presaged today's brief therapy.

Between 1926 and 1935 Rank lived in Paris, except for several trips to the United States; he lectured in psychoanalytic quarters, eliciting a rather cold response. In 1935 he moved to

New York, where he worked on his later books—*Art and Artist* (1932), *Modern Education* (1932), *Will Therapy* (1936), *Truth and Reality* (1936), and his posthumously published *Beyond Psychology* (1941). In them, therapy was viewed as an emotional, rather than an intellectual, change, taking place only in the present situation; the personality was conceived of as a total unit—a will, to use Schopenhauer's term. The emphasis on the present, rather than on the past, was carried on by a few of Rank's pupils in the so-called functional school of social work at the University of Pennsylvania. As with Adler, many of Rank's ideas have been incorporated into psychiatry without proper recognition being given him. The main reason for that lack of recognition is that all his life Rank remained a tremendous creator, an artist in the global sense of the term, and that artistic orientation of his personality, as revealed by his unsystematic and one-sided writings, hindered his acceptance by official psychoanalysis and, thus, by psychiatry.

Other exponents of psychoanalysis

Sachs. Hanns Sachs (1881–1947), a lawyer by training, joined Freud's group in 1909 and was soon included among his closest collaborators. In 1912, with Rank, he became coeditor of *Imago*, in which post he continued for 20 years. From 1923 to 1929 he was active at the Berlin Psychoanalytic Institute and from 1932 to his death at the Boston Psychoanalytic Institute. In 1913 he coauthored with Rank *The Significance of Psychoanalysis for the Mental Sciences*. From his longstanding interest in literary works came his volume *Creative Unconscious* (1942). In 1944 he published *Freud, Master and Friend*, a biography for which he is mostly remembered today.

Jones. Ernest Jones (1879–1958), a Welshman, is considered the most faithful of the pupils of Freud, whom he defended in any circumstance, with the result that he attracted a great deal of hostility from other analysts. Interested in the problems of art and creativity, he published many studies, among which are *On the Nightmare* (1909) and *Hamlet and the Oedipus* (1910). After a brief period in Toronto, Canada (1908–1912), he became acquainted with some American psychiatrists and—together with William A. White, Smith E. Jelliffe, James Putnam, and A. A. Brill—he founded the American Psychoanalytic Association in 1911. Back in London in 1914, he was responsible for founding the British Psychoanalytic Association, for editing the *International Journal of Psychoanalysis*, and, in general, for the spread of psychoanalytic ideas in English-speaking countries. Today, Jones is best remembered for his three-volume biography of Freud (1953–1957), which is based on much unpublished material and praised for its thoroughness but is criticized for the uncritical idealization of his hero.

Hitschmann. Edward Hitschmann (1871–1957), an internist from Vienna, wrote *Freud's Theories of the Neuroses*, a well-organized presentation of psychoanalytic concepts, in 1909. In 1922 he founded the Vienna Psychoanalytic Clinic and directed it until 1938, when he joined the Boston Psychoanalytic Institute. His name is connected especially with the psychoanalytic studies that he wrote on literary figures of the past.

Federn. Paul Federn (1871–1950), another internist from Vienna, became Freud's personal deputy in 1924, after a decade of didactic analyses. In 1926, together with Meng, he published *Psychoanalytische Volksbuch* (*The People's Book of Psychoanalysis*). His most original contribution lies in his emphasis on ego psychology and in his belief that the psychoses are due to a deficient ego, an idea that he further elaborated after he moved to New York in 1939.

Ferenczi. Sandor Ferenczi (1873–1933), born near Budapest, studied medicine in Vienna and became closely associated with Freud, whom he accompanied on his trip to Worcester, Massachusetts, in 1909. Soon recognized as an outstanding therapist, Ferenczi was among the first to link homosexuality to the pathogenesis of paranoia. In his classical essay "Stages in the Development of the Sense of Reality" (1913), he anticipated the later emphasis on ego psychology and attempted to

define the succession of stages progressively leading from magic-hallucinatory omnipotence to magic thoughts and words and finally to acceptance of reality. In his 1924 book *Thalassa: A Theory of Genitality* (*thalassa* means sea in Greek), he maintained that all beings have an innate craving to reestablish their previous state of existence in the ocean—namely, the amniotic fluid of the uterus. Less speculative was his concept of sphincter morale, a physiological forerunner of the superego. Even more practical, although controversial, was his active therapy—described in the book he coauthored with Rank, *The Development of Psychoanalysis* (1923). In active therapy the patient was encouraged to act and behave in a way to mobilize unconscious material. Named professor of psychoanalysis at the University of Budapest in 1919, the first professorship of that kind, Ferenczi taught at the New York School for Research in New York City in 1926.

Abraham. Karl Abraham (1877–1925), born in Bremen, graduated from the medical school of Berlin and became acquainted with Freud while studying under Bleuler at Burghölzli in Zurich. A linguist and a widely read man of high integrity, Abraham was the first German physician to initiate a psychoanalytic practice in 1907. A close friend of Freud, in 1910 he founded the Berlin Psychoanalytic Society and Institute, which was soon to become the model for similar settings in several places. He himself was instrumental in analyzing many colleagues who eventually joined the staff of the institute. His main contribution lies in the study of character formation. On the basis that the character is formed in the pregenital stage of the development of the personality, he opposed the expansive oral character to the constricted anal character and assumed an anal-sadistic fixation for the obsessional neuroses and an oral fixation for melancholia. That concept, which greatly influenced Melanie Klein, found later confirmation in René Spitz's research on hospitalism and motherless orphans.

Pfister. Oscar Pfister (1873–1956), the first educator to apply psychoanalytic concepts to education, was born in Zurich. After obtaining degrees in theology and philosophy, he was elected pastor of the Prediger Church in Zurich in 1902 and remained there for 37 years. In 1909 he founded, with Bleuler, a psychoanalytic group that was dissolved in 1914 and eventually reorganized in 1919 as the Swiss Society for Psychoanalysis. By the time Pfister published *The Psychoanalytic Method* in 1917, he had developed a deep friendship with Freud that, regardless of Freud's disregard for religion, lasted to the latter's death. In the 1920's, during a stay in the United States, Pfister proposed a psychoanalytic interpretation of the healing ceremonies performed by the Navaho Indians. His work greatly contributed to the dissemination of psychoanalytic ideas among educators and clergymen. After his retirement, he published the important book *Christianity and Fear* (1944).

Tausk. Victor Tausk (1877–1919), born in Croatia, graduated in medicine from the University of Vienna. Regardless of the recent controversies about Freud's supposed envy of him and the vicissitudes of his personal analysis, which allegedly drove him to suicide at the age of 42, Tausk is remembered most for his paper "On the Origin of the 'Influencing Machine' in Schizophrenia." By linking the symbol of the machine to the patient's unconscious sexual fantasies, he opened the way to the psychoanalytic study of psychosis.

Róheim. Geza Róheim (1891–1953), originally from Budapest, was early influenced by psychoanalysis through Ferenczi while studying anthropology in Leipzig and Berlin. Appointed professor of anthropology in Budapest, he pioneered the introduction of psychoanalysis into anthropological thinking. Thanks to the generosity of Marie Bonaparte, from 1928 to 1931 he conducted field trips in Africa, Asia, and the United States, where eventually he settled permanently. His anthropological works from "Australian Totemism," which was highly praised by Freud, to *The Riddle of the Sphinx* (1935) and *The Origin and Function of Culture* (1945) were criticized in anthropological quarters because of his tendency to consider social phenomena from the perspective of the individual personality, rather than from the perspective of the culture. Likewise, *Magic and Schizophrenia* (1952)—which posited a relation between the state of magic and symbolic thinking of early cultures on the one hand and schizophrenia, dreams, and creativity on the other hand—has been rejected by anthropologists. A vehement and expansive personality and essentially an autodidact, Róheim is important because of his introduction of psychoanalytic thinking into anthropology.

Groddeck. Georg Groddeck (1866–1934)—born in Baden-Baden, Germany—was a colorful personality. After graduation from medical school, he became director of a small sanitarium in his home town, where he practiced a variety of treatments. Early in his career, he conceived of illness as a physical reaction of the body to trauma and also as a symbolic creation, expressing the inner needs of the "it"— that is, the unknown forces influencing human beings. The term "it" was eventually accepted by Freud in the modified form of "id." Groddeck further elaborated on this theme in *The Book of the It* (1921), in which he postulated that a person is born with a knowledge of it that he later loses; he is constantly lived by his "it" whose expressions are to be found in dreams, symbols, and illnesses. Because of those rather startling statements, Groddeck was soon identified as a wild analyst. In retrospect, he seems to have anticipated the theory and practice of natural childbirth and some contemporary methods of psychotherapy of the psychoses.

Brill. Abraham Brill (1874–1948) was born in Austria and graduated from the Columbia University College of Physicians and Surgeons in 1903. While working at Burghölzli in Zurich under Bleuler, he came in contact with Freud, toward whom he developed strong feelings of veneration. After Brill returned to this country, he was, between 1908 and 1910, the only analyst in New York City. In 1911 he founded the New York Psychoanalytic Society and was instrumental in the formation of the American Psychoanalytic Association several months later. By 1924 he had completed the translation of 10 of Freud's works, translations that were later considered not very accurate, and in 1938 he published *The Basic Writings of Sigmund Freud.* His most original contribution consists of the book *Lectures on Psychoanalytic Psychiatry* (1946), which was based on his long teaching experience, first at Columbia University and then at New York University.

Jelliffe. Smith Ely Jelliffe (1866–1945) was born in New York City and graduated from Columbia University's College of Physicians and Surgeons. By 1899 he was already associate editor of *The Journal of Nervous and Mental Disease.* With William Alanson White (1870–1937), superintendent of the St. Elizabeth's Hospital in Washington, D.C., he initiated the Nervous and Mental Disease Monograph Service, in which important psychiatric publications were presented. Also with White, he launched in 1913 the first psychoanalytic journal in English, *The Psychoanalytic Review,* which has continued to this day. A distinguished neurologist and a pioneer in psychosomatic medicine, Jelliffe also wrote several papers on the history of psychiatry in antiquity.

Rado. Sandor Rado (1890–1971), born in Hungary, first obtained a degree in political science (1911) and then a degree in medicine (1915). Under the influence of Ferenczi, he became secretary of the Hungarian Psychoanalytic Society in 1913. In 1922 he joined the faculty of the Berlin Psychoanalytic Institute and taught there until 1931, the year in which he moved to New York. By that time he had been appointed managing editor of *Internationale Zeitschrift für Psychoanalyse* (1924) and of *Imago* (1927). In 1944 he became the head of the Psychoanalytic Institute of Columbia University, the first psychoanalytic institute within a university. On his retirement in 1957, he organized the New York School of Psychiatry. The most original aspect of his contribution concerns adaptational psychodynamics, which has many similarities to psychoanalytic ego psychology. Adaptational psychodynamics is an attempt, based on evolutionary biological concepts, to stress the integrative act of instinctual urge and reality testing leading to purposeful adaptive behavior.

Reik. Theodor Reik (1888–1969) was born in Vienna and received his Ph.D. in psychology in 1912. After a year of training analysis in Berlin with Karl Abraham, he worked for 10 years, from 1918 to 1928, in Vienna, where he also functioned as secretary of the Vienna Psychoanalytic Society. From 1928 to 1934 he taught in the Berlin Psychoanalytic Institute and then, after a short stay in The Hague, emigrated to the United States in 1938. His arrival in this country was marked by bitterness because of the refusal of the New York Psychoanalytic Society to grant him full membership, which was given only to physicians. Eventually, in 1948, he founded the National Psychological Association for Psychoanalysis. A gifted and widely read man who was highly praised by Freud, Reik wrote extensively, and his books were directed largely to the intelligent public, rather than to the restricted field of specialists. Among his most important publications are his psychoanalytic studies of the couvade, an old practice in which the husband of a woman in labor takes to his bed, as if he were bearing the child; of the puberty rites of savages, such as circumcision and death rites; and of criminals—in particular, the criminal's unconscious need to confess. Among the many books of his last 2 decades are *Listening with the Third Ear* (1948), *Masochism in Modern Man* (1949), *Fragment of a Great Confession* (1949), *The Search Within* (1956), *Of Love and Lust* (1959), and *Jewish Wit* (1962).

Helene Deutsch. Helene Deutsch, born in 1884, was originally from Galicia, a Polish area under Austria. She grew up in a highly intellectual environment marked by the figure of her father, a well-known scholar of international law. A very independent personality from the beginning, she graduated from the medical school of Vienna in 1912, the same year in which she married Felix Deutsch. After several years of training at the neuropsychiatric clinic of Vienna under Wagner-Jauregg, she became an ardent follower of Freud and, in 1918, a full member of the Vienna Psychoanalytic Society; she was the second woman member, the first being Hermine von Hug-Hellmuth, a pioneer in the psychoanalytic treatment of children. For 10 years she served as director of the Vienna Psychoanalytic Institute, founded in 1925. There she introduced the system of the continuous case seminar. In 1935 she accepted an invitation to move to Boston with her husband; from then on, her activity was closely identified with the Boston Psychoanalytic Institute. Her original contributions to clinical psychoanalysis were gathered in her book *Psychoanalysis of the Neuroses* (1930). Her name, however, is mainly associated with her two-volume *The Psychology of Women* (1944–1945), which has remained a classic to this day. Challenging Freud's statement that the enigma of the woman could be fully understood neither by men nor by women—a chauvinistic statement in line with the over-all masculine orientation of the psychoanalytic movement—her work represented the culmination of 2 decades of intensive research on the subject. The entire life cycle of women, from prepuberty to climacterium, was thoroughly presented from a comprehensive physiological, psychological, and sociohistorical perspective: the essential passive-masochistic disposition of women, the early identification of the girl with the mother and then the libidinal relationship to the father, the slow transition at puberty from a clitoral to a vaginal orientation, the meaning of the sexual act, the orientation of libidinal forces during pregnancy and after delivery, and the maternal role. From the historical perspective, Helene Deutsch's work is currently being reassessed in the light of the present sexual revolution and of the new alignment of the woman's role. Recently, her autobiography, *Confrontations with Myself: An Epilogue,* appeared in 1973.

Felix Deutsch. Felix Deutsch (1884–1964) was born in Vienna. After graduating from medical school in 1912, he embarked on a distinguished career of internal medicine and wrote a standard book on sports medicine. Influenced by Freud's ideas, he established in 1919 the first clinic on organ neurosis and presented the first seminar on that subject at the Vienna Psychoanalytic Institute. After coming to the United States in 1935, he was active in the Boston Psychoanalytic Institute and in other academic settings during the last 3 decades of his life. In his many publications he continuously stressed the principle of the homeostatic balance and reciprocal interaction between organic functions and psychic processes. Specific methods advocated by him in *Applied Psychoanalysis* (1949) include the activation of the autonomic nervous system to release emotional conflict, and the use of associative anamnesis, to which he later added sector psychotherapy—that is, the aim of keeping the material brought forth by the patient centered on certain symptoms or certain conscious and unconscious conflicts to avoid an unnecessary spread of energy. His last works included *The Clinical Interview* (1955) with William Murphy and *On the Mysterious*

Leap from the Mind to the Body (1959), in which he studied the unconscious motivations of postural behavior.

Simmel. Ernst Simmel (1882–1947) was born in Breslau, Germany. After receiving a medical degree from the University of Vienna in 1908, he practiced general medicine and then got involved in the treatment of war neuroses, for which he used hypnosis and psychoanalytic techniques. In his book *On the Psychoanalysis of War Neuroses* (1918), he discussed the military ego—that is, the substitution of the parental superego by the military unit—the value of group identity for the support of the ego and other phenomena, and advocated a therapeutic method based on cathartic abreactions under the influence of hypnosis, which was later used again during World War II. A founder of the Berlin Psychoanalytic Institute, Simmel became president of the Berlin Psychoanalytic Society in 1925. The next year he established his psychiatric sanitarium on the grounds of a large and beautiful castle on the outskirts of Berlin, where he pioneered in the application of psychoanalytic principles to hospitalized patients. He particularly emphasized the removal of the patient from his neurotic constellation and the infantile gratification provided by the analyst in the hospital setting. Simmel joined a group of analysts in Los Angeles in 1934 and later on became president of the newly formed San Francisco Psychoanalytic Society. In his late years he became interested in the problem of addiction, which he attributed to a protection against the depression resulting from the introjection of a disappointing love object, and of anti-Semitism, a prejudice that he related to a defense against latent homosexuality.

Bernfeld. Siegfried Bernfeld (1892–1953) was born in Lemberg, then Austria, and received his Ph.D. from the University of Vienna, where he was closely identified with the Zionist cause. He became involved in psychoanalysis while working in a children's home for Polish Jewish refugee children. Among his early works are *Concerning the Poetic Creativeness of Youth* (1924), *Sisyphus or the Boundaries of Education* (1925), in which he emphasized the sociological and psychological dimensions of education, and *The Psychology of the Infant* (1925), which was presented exclusively from the viewpoint of the unconscious, with no regard for ego psychology, and thus it is outdated today. While in Berlin, from 1926 to 1932, he taught at the Berlin Institute for Psychoanalysis and was occupied with political issues. After he relocated himself in San Francisco in 1937, he wrote a number of scholarly papers on Freud's early life and scientific beginnings.

Reich. Wilhelm Reich (1897–1957), born in Austria, received a medical degree from the University of Vienna and then worked at the Vienna Neuropsychiatric Institute. Soon accepted as a member of the Vienna Psychoanalytic Society, he functioned as director of the prestigious Seminar for Psychoanalytic Therapy from 1924 to 1930. During that time he analyzed many candidates who were there for training, including several candidates from the United States. In some studies published during that period—*The Impulsive Character* (1925), *The Function of the Orgasm* (1927), and others—he advanced views at variance with his more orthodox colleagues; for instance, he did not hesitate to encourage genital masturbation as a step toward genital maturity. His most important contribution to psychiatry during that period is undoubtedly *Character Analysis* (1928), essentially a phenomenological description of character formation as an outgrowth and development of oral, anal, and genital ego types. In that book Reich convincingly proved that the characterological substructure of the personality, based on the repression of instinctual demands, serves as a compact defense mechanism and as a resistance against therapeutic efforts; that fact justifies the therapist's eliciting of a negative transference in the patient as a way to overcome such a resistance.

At that time, 1927, in line with with his official adherence to Marxism, Reich had already expressed his dissatisfaction with Freud's neglect of social factors in the causes of neuroses. Reich's voluminous production during those years—"Dialectic Materialism and Psychoanalysis" (1929), *The Mass Psychology of Fascism,* (1933), *The Sexual Revolution* (1936), and other popular publications—aimed at integrating basic psychoanalytic findings with Marxist theory. To that end, Reich in 1929 organized the Socialist Society for Sexual Advice and

Sexual Research and, moving to Berlin in 1930, joined the Communist Party. It was his contention that Marx's concept of alienation should be broadened to include the sexual realm, as reflected in the inability of people to come to grips with their life situation because of sexual repression. To Freud's main tenets of sexuality—that is, of being controlled by the unconscious, of being present in small children, of remaining active when repressed, and of being repressed by society—Reich added the concepts of orgastic potency—that is, the capacity for complete and uninhibited sexual gratification over and above the sexual act—and of orgastic impotence—that is, the burdening of the character structure to avoid instinctual gratification. Moreover, he linked sexual blockage to the performance of boring, mechanical work by most people in a capitalistic society in the interest of the society's maintaining its existing class structure by perpetuating sexual repression with the help of education, the family, and, in general, the prevailing ideology.

Reich's philosophy was not, as many erroneously believed, to advocate free sexual intercourse but to make possible a satisfactory love life in the belief that the sexual need had been neglected in Marx's writings, in which the economic factor was limited to the need for nourishment. Perhaps the reason for the difference between those two authors is that Marx was limiting his analysis of society to the past few centuries, but Reich was basing his analysis on a much broader spectrum. At any rate, Reich's bold views represented such a threat to the existing institutions that he was expelled from the Communist Party in 1932 and from the International Psychoanalytic Association the next year. First in Denmark and then in Sweden and Norway, he continued his work with few followers and, under the name of Sexpol, issued the *Journal of Political Psychology and Sexual Economy* from 1934 to 1938. He emigrated to the United States in 1939 and, in spite of his belief and his continuous adherence to psychoanalytic principles, rapidly drifted away from both psychoanalysis and Marxism and was ostracized by both. He increasingly got involved in highly speculative problems of biology and insisted that he had discovered the physical basis of sexual energy (libido) and a new therapeutic method based on cosmic radiation, his theory of biones. When he tried to ship material related to those biones from his large estate in Maine, where he had settled, he was prosecuted by the United States Food and Drug Administration and was sentenced to a 2-year term. He died in prison during that term. Almost completely forgotten in the 1950's, even by such enlightened authors as Herbert Marcuse and Norman Brown, Reich has recently been heralded as a champion of liberation from sexual and political constrictions by the radicals of the New Left in this country, as well as elsewhere, and his writings are now enjoying considerable popularity.

Horney. Karen Horney (1885–1952) was born in Hamburg. After her graduation in medicine from the University of Berlin in 1913, she became a member of the Berlin Psychoanalytic Institute. At that time, under the influence of Adler, she was already dissatisfied with some of the rather deterministic psychoanalytic theories, and she advocated that a greater role be assigned to cultural factors in the development of neuroses. For instance, she reversed Freud's view that penis envy is of basic importance in the psychological development of the girl; she favored a view that the widespread male dread of women comes from a basic dread of the vagina. Later on, she challenged the universality of the Oedipus complex, again on cultural grounds. Always an independent thinker, she was at the Chicago Institute for Psychoanalysis from 1932 to 1934 and then continued her work in New York, where she eventually broke with the New York Psychoanalytic Institute and founded, with Clara Thompson and others, the American Institute for Psychoanalysis in 1941. In her later books, written especially for the general public, she elaborated the concepts of the neurotic process as moving toward, moving away, and moving against; of the major solutions of self-effacement, expansiveness, and resignation, and of the clinical pictures of masochistic, perfectionistic, and narcissistic characters. Moreover, she anticipated today's notion of alienation. Her contention that feminine psychology is not understood because of the prevailing masculine bias in psychoanalysis credits her with a definite pioneering role in the light of today's women's movement.

Schilder. Paul Ferdinand Schilder (1886–1940) was an independent man who opened many new paths. Born in Vienna, he graduated there in medicine and philosophy. By 1913 he published his classic description of encephalitis periaxilis diffusa, which bears his name. A true scholar and a man of universal interests, he worked for many years at the psychiatric clinic of the University of Vienna and eventually became a member of the Vienna Psychoanalytic Society. Under the influence of the philosopher Edmund Husserl, the founder of phenomenology—that is, of the philosophical movement based on the study of phenomena as they are experienced or present themselves in consciousness—Schilder carried on many studies of the body image in a person's relation to himself, to his fellow human beings, and to the world around him, culminating in his classic *The Image and Appearance of the Human Body* (1935). By that time he had already published *Plan for a Psychiatry on a Psychoanalytic Basis* (1925) and *Brain and Personality* (1931), a book of lectures intended to fill the gap between the organic and the functional. In 1930 he moved to this country and became clinical director of the psychiatric division of Bellevue Hospital and research professor of psychiatry at New York University College of Medicine. At variance with Freud's tendency to think in terms of opposites and dichotomies, such as Eros versus Thanatos, as well as with the static approach of the Gestalt theory, Schilder constantly pointed to the simultaneous and integrated aspects of the psychological and the somatic viewpoints and to the constructive and world-oriented fundamental attitude of human beings, above the narrow interest of self-preservation. Typically, perception, rather than being passive, had to be viewed as a continuous process of construction and reconstruction, and the body image had to be viewed as a dynamic process of interrelationship between a person's libidinous drives and his social experiences. During his years in the United States, Schilder did pioneering work on psychoanalytically oriented group psychotherapy and child psychopathology, a trend that was followed by his wife, Lauretta Bender. In retrospect, it may be said that Schilder anticipated some contemporary concepts of ego psychology—in particular, ego identity.

Alexander. Franz Alexander (1891–1964) shares with Schilder a universality of intellectual grasp and a definite independence from the psychoanalytic school proper. Born in Budapest to a distinguished family, Alexander graduated in medicine in 1912 and moved to Berlin, where he became the first student of the Berlin Institute for Psychoanalysis and eventually a member of its teaching staff. His creative and synthetic skill was manifested in his first book, *Psychoanalysis of the Total Personality* (1929), in which he proposed that conversion hysteria, obsessive-compulsive neurosis, and manic-depressive disease are different forms of disturbances in the interplay between the repressive functions of the ego and the repressed tendencies. In 1929 he published *The Criminal, the Judge, and the Public* with Hugo Staub; there he presented a psychoanalytic study of criminology, emphasizing the unconscious motivations prevailing in the criminal's sense of justice, in the judge's attitude, and in the public's expectation. Shortly thereafter, Alexander visited the United States and was appointed visiting professor of psychoanalysis, the first chair of that kind, at the University of Chicago. In 1932 he founded the Chicago Institute for Psychoanalysis, modeled after the Berlin Institute, and remained its director for 25 years. In 1938 he became professor of psychiatry at the University of Illinois.

In his many contributions to psychoanalytic therapy, such as *Psychoanalytic Therapy* (1946) and *Fundamentals of Psychoanalysis* (1948), Alexander stressed the role of countertransference and advocated a flexible technique, including short-term therapy, leading to a reexperiencing of past reactions in the new and different setting of the patient-physician relationship, a process he called "corrective emotional experience." At the Chicago Institute for Psychoanalysis, surrounded by a number of active and brilliant collaborators, he developed an extensive program of research in psychosomatic medicine, undoubtedly the best scientific endeavor thus far attempted in the field of psychoanalysis. He introduced the concept of vector analysis—that is, the wish of

the organs of the body either to receive, to retain, or to eliminate in the context of loving or, conversely, aggressive and hateful connotations. Moreover, he introduced the notion of specificity—that is, of a specific correlation between a particular conflict and a psychosomatic disorder—for instance, chronic, inhibited rage in cases of patients with blood hypertension. Also important is his concept of surplus energy discharged through sexuality, generativity, and creativity after physical growth has reached its peak in late adolescence.

In 1956 Alexander accepted an invitation to become the director of the new psychiatric research department at Mount Sinai Hospital in Los Angeles. There he initiated a vast program of research aiming at investigating as scientifically as possible the various dimensions of the psychotherapeutic process. He also attempted to integrate psychoanalysis slowly into academic psychiatry, with the goal of preserving the future of psychoanalysis as a science. Finally, in his books directed to the general public—mainly, *Our Age of Unreason* (1942) and *The Western Mind in Transition* (1960)—he discussed many of his views related to broad historical and philosophical topics—especially, the cultural lag concept—that is, the tendency of old-fashioned attitudes to outlive the sociological structure that created them and the dangers involved in the emergence of the mass man. Alexander's role in the development of American psychoanalysis and of psychiatry in general has been remarkable, and many of his ideas continue to be relevant today.

Anna Freud. Anna Freud, the daughter of Sigmund Freud, was born in 1895. Originally a teacher, she devoted herself to the psychoanalytic study of children, in which area she opened many new paths. From the historical perspective, her major contribution is *The Ego and the Mechanisms of Defense* (1937), a combination and refinement of Sigmund Freud's 1926 work *Inhibition, Symptoms, and Anxiety*, in which the concept of the signal function of anxiety implied the concept of the adaption of reality. Her book is essentially an attempt to investigate the ego processes as revealed by the defense mechanisms that the ego uses against drive impulses. She discussed several mechanisms—such as regression, repression, projection, introjection, and reaction formation—but, essentially, repression continued to be the chief factor at work in the genesis of neuroses. That book marks, historically, the definite switch of emphasis from the unconscious to the ego in psychoanalytic theory and practice. When Anna Freud emigrated to England in 1938 with her father, she continued her clinical work with children and their parents and stressed the educational component of child analysis and the substantial differences between adult analysis and child analysis, especially the inability of children to develop a full-fledged transference neurosis. During World War II the circumstances of many children separated from their families offered her the opportunity to study the emotional impact of the mother-child separation, which she and Dorothy Burlingham presented in *War and Children* (1943) and *Infants without Families* (1943). Anna Freud's contributions to psychoanalytic study have continued to this day.

Other analysts in the United States. Brief mention should be made here of the work of some analysts belonging to the first psychoanalytic generation who either emigrated to the United States from Europe or were born in this country. Otto Fenichel (1898–1946) is remembered mainly for his encyclopedic book *The Psychoanalytic Theory of Neurosis* (1945). In the area of psychosomatic medicine, some outstanding workers, in addition to Franz Alexander, were Therese Benedek (for the psychoanalytic investigation of the sexual cycle of women), Carl Binger, Leon Saul, Flanders Dunbar (*Emotions and Bodily Changes*, 1938), George Daniels, Thomas French (for the study of asthma), and Roy Grinker (for studies on anxiety and stress, especially during World War II). The field of child psychiatry has been represented by the work of Berta Bornstein, Beata Rank, Marion Putnam, Frederick Allen, Margaret Gerard, David Levy, O. Spurgeon English, Gerald Pearson, and Emmy Sylvester. Innovating concepts and practices were introduced in the 1930's and early 1940's by Jules Masserman (experimental neuroses created in animals, described in *Behavior and Neuroses*, 1943), by Abraham Kardiner (concept of basic personality, resulting from the interplay of constitutional endowment and social institutions, described in *The Individual and His Society,* 1939; traumatic neuroses as unsuccessful results of the ego's adaptive efforts, described in *The Traumatic Neuroses of War,* 1941); by William Healy (psychoanalytic contributions to the field of juvenile delinquency and to the prevention of behavior disorders in children, described in *New Light on Delinquency and Its Treatment,* 1936, and *Personality in Formation and Action,* 1938); by Benjamin Karpman (psychoanalytic treatment of criminals, described in *The Individual Criminal,* 1941); and by Samuel R. Slavson (*An Introduction to Group Therapy,* 1943). In the same period broad presentations of psychoanalytic concepts were published by William Healy (*Structure and Meaning of Psychoanalysis,* 1930), Sandor Lorand (*Psychoanalysis Today: Its Scope and Function,* 1933), Lawrence Kubie (*Practical Aspects of Psychoanalysis,* 1936), Karl Menninger (*The Human Mind,* 1937, and *Man against Himself,* 1938), Ives Hendrick (*Facts and Theories of Psychoanalysis,* 1939), and Maurice Levine (*Psychotherapy in Medical Practice,* 1942). Historical presentations were devoted either to the founder of psychoanalysis (Fritz Wittels's *Freud and His Time,* translated into English in 1931) or to psychiatry in general (Gregory Zilboorg's *A History of Medical Psychology,* 1941). Early American contributions to psychoanalysis were presented by many, among whom the following names are worth mentioning: Kenneth Appel, Leo Bartemeier, Edmund Bergler, Grete and Edward Bibring, Ludwig Eidelberg, Kurt Eissler, Phyllis Greenacre, Martin Grotjahn, Ludwig Jekels, M. Ralph Kaufmann, Robert Knight, Bertrand Lewin, Robert Lindner, Bela Mittelman, Herman Nunberg, Clarence Oberndorf, Norman Reider, Editha and Richard Sterba, and Edith Weigert.

Most of the above analysts belonged to the American Psychoanalytic Association, which was founded by Ernest Jones and a few others in 1911, 3 months after the founding of the New York Psychoanalytic Society by Abraham Brill. Clarence Oberndorf's *A History of Psychoanalysis in America* (1953) traced the highlights of that movement, which was characterized by success in spreading psychoanalytic concepts in many quarters, especially medical schools; efforts at the centralization and standardization of training; and conflicts, which eventually resulted in secessions by some and the formation of independent groups. The main differences of opinion concerned the questions of lay analysis, favored by Freud and some European analysts but opposed by most American analysts; of Freud's ambivalent attitude toward the United States, based on his fear that the great acceptance of psychoanalysis in this country would lead to the loss of the movement's identity; and, later on, of the autonomy of psychoanalysis or, conversely, the integration of psychoanalysis in medical schools. Freud and the American analysts reached a compromise in the early 1930's in regard to lay analysis, thereby averting the split that had occurred between the American association and the international association a decade earlier.

The earliest psychoanalytic institutes were established in Boston (1930), New York (1931), Chicago (1932), Philadelphia (1937), and Topeka (1938). By 1939 the American Psychoanalytic Association was strong enough to declare its independence from the International Psychoanalytic Association. On the grounds of lack of academic freedom in the American Psychoanalytic Association, Karen Horney established the Association for the Advancement of Psychoanalysis in 1941 in New York City. In 1943 the William Alanson White Institute was founded by Clara Thompson, Erich Fromm, and Harry Stack Sullivan. The first medical school-affiliated psychoanalytic training institute was started at the New York Medical College-Flower-Fifth Avenue Center in 1944. The next year a new psychoanalytic clinic in the Department of Columbia University's College of Physicians and Surgeons was established by Sandor Rado and a few others. In New York the main psychoanalytic group split into the New York Psychoanalytic Society and the Psychoanalytic Association of New York, both adherent to rather orthodox techniques of training. In the 1950's a number of new psychoanalytic societies and associations were established in cities, most of them in the Midwest and on the Pacific coast. In 1956 the Academy of Psychoanalysis was founded in Chicago by a group of analysts eager to overcome the conformism of the American Psychoanalytic Association and to establish a free forum for scientific discussion and the exchange of views with scientists from allied disciplines.

Other European analysts. Switzerland, already known for the school of Burghölzli and the work of Jung and Pfister, has been the motherland of a number of analysts: Alphonse Maeder, Hans Christoffel (the author of a historical monograph on enuresis), Charles Baudouin (who published several books on psychoanalysis for the general public), Gustav Graber, Raymond De Saussure (who wrote scholarly studies on the history of French psychiatry), Charles Odier (who attempted to combine Freud's and Piaget's concepts), Rudolph Brun (the author of *General Theory of Neuroses,* translated into English in 1951), Ernst Schneider, Gustav Bally, and especially Hans Zulliger (an elementary school teacher and poet who successfully applied psychoanalytic principles to education and developed the Z-test, a collective Rorschach test). Among the foreign born who settled in Switzerland was Heinrich Meng (1887–1961), who was originally from Germany, where he edited with Paul Federn *The Popular Book on Psychoanalysis* (1924) and where he founded the Institute for Psychoanalysis at the University of Frankfurt, which was connected with the famous Frankfurt School of Sociology of Max Horkheimer, Theodore W. Adorno, and Herbert Marcuse. When the institute closed, he settled in Basel as a professor of mental hygiene.

In Austria psychoanalysis was virtually wiped out as a result of the *Anschluss* of 1938 and the racial persecutions. Only August Aichorn (1878–1949), who came from a Catholic background, was able to continue his work. Early in his career as a schoolmaster in Vienna, he postulated that antisocial behavior was due to an inadequate superego and that the treatment consisted of providing a positive relationship to a parental representative. He successfully applied those principles in the reformatory schools at Ober-Hollabrunn and then at St. Andra, and he illustrated them in his book *Wayward Youth* (1925) and in other works up to the time of his death.

In France the early stage of the psychoanalytic movement was dominated by the rather complex figure of Princess Marie Bonaparte (1882–1962). A descendant of Napoleon, she soon developed a filial relationship toward Freud. A founder-member of the Société Psychanalytique de Paris in 1926, she founded and supported the *Revue Française de Psychanalyse* the next year and the Institut de Psychanalyse in 1934. In 1938 she played a vital role in arranging for Freud's departure from Vienna and emigration to England. Aside from her book *Female Sexuality,* she is especially remembered for her psychoanalytic study of Edgar Allen Poe (1949). Among the early French psychoanalysts were A. Hesnard, Réné Allendy, Sacha Nacht, and Réné Laforgue. In 1955 a group of dissidents, led by Daniel Lagache and Jacques Lacan, established the French Psychoanalytic Society, which is interested in the social and cultural aspects of psychoanalysis.

In England, the early history of the psychoanalytic movement is closely identified with the work of Ernest Jones, who in 1913 established the London Psychoanalytic Society and, in 1919, the British Psychoanalytic Society, which was later affiliated with the International Psychoanalytic Association. That early group included J. C. Flugel (the author of *The Psychology of Clothes,* 1930; *Psychoanalytic Study of the Family,* 1931; *A Hundred Years of Psychology,* 1934; and other books), Cyril Burt (the author of *The Young Delinquent,* 1925; *The Subnormal Mind,* 1935; and many other studies), W. H. Rivers (the author of *The Development of the Psychoanalytic Theory of the Psychoses,* 1928), James and Edward Glover, Ella Sharpe (the author of *Dream Analysis,* 1937), James and Alix Strachey, and Susan Isaacs (who, on the basis of her long experience at the experimental Malting House School, wrote many books, notably *Childhood and After,* 1948). In 1926 Melanie Klein emigrated to London; that event marked the beginning of a new stage in the British psychoanalytic movement.

Melanie Klein (1882–1960), born in Vienna, moved early in life with her family to Budapest and became a member of the Budapest Psychoanalytic Society in 1919. From 1920 to 1925 she worked at the Berlin Psychoanalytic Institute, where she was greatly influenced by Karl Abraham. Her ideas about the fantasies and anxieties expressed by children in play and about the feasibility of analyzing children outside of the educational context gained much more acceptance in England, where she moved in 1926, than on the continent. Convinced that the unconscious is much less close to the surface in children than in adults because of the weak power of repression in children, she developed her main tenets in *The Psychoanalysis of Children* (1932) and in later publications. She postulated that projective and introjective mechanisms, based on the internalization by the child of parts of the mother (breast, face, hands) and of the splitting of impulses and objects into good and bad aspects, are essential for the building of the child's internal world and of an embryonic superego; a depressive position, related to the infant's awareness of his mother as a separate person, is normal; a paranoid-schizoid position can inhibit the capacity to form and use symbols and can lead to a fixation in psychotic illness. Those concepts, by stressing the preoedipal cause of psychopathology, were in direct contrast with Freudian psychoanalysis. Also unorthodox were her beliefs that children can be helped by being given direct interpretations of unconscious motivations and that a transference neurosis can develop between the therapist and the child.

Those views had a considerable following among many members of the British Psychoanalytic Society for various reasons: They were supported by Ernest Jones, they represented challenging suggestions, and they may have helped alleviate the British psychoanalysts' feeling of inferiority toward their European colleagues. The development of psychoanalysis in Britain in the past few decades has been characterized by marked dissensions between the Freudians, mainly those close to Anna Freud, and the Kleinians and by the formation of in-between groups. Nevertheless, the work carried on at the Tavistock Clinic and at the Institute of Human Relations, both strongly influenced by psychoanalysis, has maintained high standards. The same can be said of the Hampstead Child Therapy Clinic and Training Center, founded in 1947 at the suggestion of Kate Friedländer, the author of *The Psychoanalytical Approach to Juvenile Delinquence* (1947), and directed since then by Anna Freud. There—with the help of an index project, aimed at categorizing and classifying all sorts of clinical items—solid research has been carried on up to the present on the diagnostic evaluation of children and on the assessment of pathology and normality along developmental lines, resulting in important publications, such as *Normality and Pathology in Childhood* (1962).

Of the other British psychoanalysts, Edward Glover, a critic of Klein's theories, is remembered mostly for *The Technique of Psychoanalysis* (1955); W. Ronald Fairbairn, a follower of Klein, advocated in *An Object-Relations Theory of Personality* (1954) a personality theory based on the interplay of introjected good and bad objects and a psychopathological etiology based on a split within the ego occurring before the inception of the Oedipus complex; and Donald Winnicott introduced in 1953 the concept of transitional objects in the early development of the child. In general, Klein's ideas, although very influential in England, have had little following in the United States, but much of her technique has been incorporated in the present practice of child analysis.

PSYCHIATRY IN THE PAST 4 DECADES

The great number of psychiatric casualties during World War II had the effect of bringing the attention of many—including legislators—to the problem of mental illness and emotional disorders in general. In the United States the need for a treatment and rehabilitation program for many service people and veterans led to the establishment of vast psychiatric services by the Veterans' Administration, out of which eventually emerged a pioneering effort toward the systematic training of psychiatrists. After the Vocational Rehabilitation Act of 1942, the National Mental Health Act was passed in 1946, resulting in the opening of the National Institute of Mental Health in Bethesda, Maryland, in 1949 for the purposes of research, training, and assistance to the states in providing preventive, therapeutic, and rehabilitative services.

From the mid-1940's to the mid-1950's. From the mid-1940's to the mid-1950's the development of psychiatry, especially in the United States, was characterized by a rather strong dichotomy between the biological orientation and the dynamic orientation.

The biological school had a brilliant tradition, especially in European countries. Histopathological, biochemical, and genetic studies had opened the path for the scientific understanding and treatment of a number of psychiatric conditions. Constitutional theories linking the leptosome or asthenic type to schizophrenia and the rotund, pyknic type to manic-depressive psychosis had acquired ample renown in the 1920's, mainly through the work of the German Ernst Kretschmer (1888–1964), the author of *Physique and Character*, which was translated into English in 1925. Those theories were followed in this country by the studies of William Sheldon, who described the mesomorph, the ectomorph, and the endomorph types. Important research on the heredity of mental disease was carried on for many years at the New York Psychiatric Institute by Franz Kallmann (*Heredity in Health and Mental Disorders,* 1953), who studied schizophrenic identical twins. The introduction of shock treatment and psychosurgery in the late 1930's and the 1940's had had the effect of offering a more optimistic outlook for the treatment of severe mental disorders; however, after the initial period of unrealistic expectations, the indications for shock treatment and, even more, psychosurgery were limited to specific clinical conditions.

Historically, that biological orientation represented a return to the emphasis on the study and treatment of psychoses, which had been replaced by the emphasis on neuroses with the advent of the psychodynamic schools. Regardless of the limited and uncertain results achieved by studies of the physiological and psychological aspects of shock treatment and psychosurgery, the biological orientation led to progress in research methods and in the formulation of some important notions. Still under the over-all influence of Watson's behaviorism and of Cannon's main ideas—the concept of homeostasis and the study of the autonomic reactions (fight or flight) of the organism under stress—new concepts were brought forward: James Papez's theory of emotions, Paul MacLean's visceral brain, Giuseppe Moruzzi's and Horace Magoun's reticular system, Donald Hebb's sensory deprivation, Wilder Penfield's stimulation of the cerebral cortex, John Fulton's effects of the ablation of the frontal lobes, and, from a comprehensive perspective, Hans Selye's stress syndrome and general adaptational syndrome. Other studies dealt with the biological dimensions of anxiety—for example, Stewart Wolf's and Harold Wolff's studies of the effects of anxiety on gastric secretion and Daniel Funkenstein's distinction between fear and anger through the assessment of the level of epinephrine and norepinephrine.

Research in psychosomatic medicine, viewed as the most natural expression of the body-mind interaction, received great impetus in the 1940's and 1950's. At the Chicago Psychoanalytic Institute, under the influence of Alexander's vector theory, a specificity was found in the psychodynamic constellation of six chronic diseases: ulcerative colitis, asthma, hypertension, rheumatoid arthritis, neurodermatitis, and hyperthyroidism. Other researchers established a correlation between phases of the ovarian cycle and emotional attitudes, particularly the content of dreams, in a group of women (Therese Benedek); still others identified the somatic factor in duodenal ulcer as a constitutional tendency to gastric hypersecretion (I. Arthur Mirsky).

In the psychoanalytic field proper, Jules Masserman's pioneering studies on experimentally induced neuroses in the

1930's were followed by research in the area of the mother-child relationship. Early in the 1940's Leo Kanner attributed the syndrome of autism in children to a lack of maternal emotional involvement; David Levy studied the detrimental consequences of maternal overprotection for personality development; René Spitz described hospitalism in children raised in an environment void of proper maternal stimulation and anaclitic depression in children who, as infants, were denied proper maternal care. Along similar lines in England, John Bowlby identified three phases—protest, despair, and detachment—in children separated from their mothers, and he related those phases to mourning and to later psychopathology. New theoretical notions in the field of psychoanalysis were advanced by Thomas French, who considered psychoanalysis as a process of progressive adaptation on the part of the personality moved by a chain of motivation to achieve a complex process of integration, and by Sandor Rado, who described his adaptational psychodynamics as a study of behavior focused on the motivational context and on the interplay of emotions and leading to flexible therapeutic techniques.

However, it was in the area of ego psychology that a significant development took place in the 1940's and 1950's. The shift of emphasis from the unconscious to the ego in psychoanalysis can be traced back to the basic study *Ego Psychology and the Problem of Adaptation* (1939) by Heinz Hartmann (1894–1972), a physician born and trained in Vienna who was active in the New York Psychoanalytic Institute during the last 3 decades of his life. In his monograph he distinguished two groups of ego functions, those specifically involved in conflict and those that develop outside of conflict and that constitute the conflict-free ego sphere. Those functions of the ego, independent of instinctual drives and outside reality, are of fundamental importance in a person's adaptation to his environment and have a survival value and a biological purposefulness in terms of the average expectable environment. In the early 1950's those concepts were further defined by Hartmann in association with two other distinguished psychoanalysts: Ernst Kris (1900–1957), a brilliant art historian who in 1933 became editor of the journal *Imago* and who in 1940 settled permanently in New York, where he published a number of important essays, gathered together in *Psychoanalytic Explorations in Art* (1952), and later organized a longitudinal study of child development with Milton Senn at the Yale Child Study Center; and Rudolf M. Loewenstein, a physician born in Poland in 1898 and trained in Germany who spent several years in France and then settled in New York during World War II. Together, those men, who were three of the coeditors of the series *Psychoanalytic Study of the Child,* further developed the concepts of primary autonomous ego functions, secondary autonomous ego functions, and neutralized energy as desexualized and aggression-free energy.

Further contributions to the study of ego psychology came from the research carried on by David Rapaport (1911–1960), a Hungarian-born psychologist who in 1938 emigrated to this country and worked for many years at the Menninger Clinic and then at the Austen Riggs Center in Stockbridge, Massachusetts. A scholarly and well-read man—as evidenced by his *Organization and Pathology of Thought* (1951), an important selection of sources—he postulated for the optimal functioning of the organism a constant balance of mutually controlling factors, ego autonomy from the id and ego autonomy from the environment.

Historically, ego psychology signifies a trend toward rapprochement with genetic psychology, as represented by the work of the German-born Heinz Werner (1890–1964), who taught for many years at Clark University and who published in 1940 *Comparative Psychology of Mental Development,* and of the Swiss Jean Piaget (born in 1896), the author of many books on child development and a pioneer in the field of genetic epistemology.

Thus, the trend of ego psychology emerged as a further elaboration of psychoanalytic tenets related to the development of the individual personality and of neuroses on the part of some European-born researchers. It was only natural that in this country, where behaviorism had flourished in the 1920's and the social sciences in the 1930's, trends more consonant with the social dimensions in life should emerge. Several psychiatric schools of thought, apparently unrelated, have in common that emphasis on the social component. Karen Horney's concern with environmental influences in the causation of neuroses is an example.

Even more original and fruitful are the concepts developed by Harry Stack Sullivan (1892–1949), the only American-born psychiatrist founder of an independent school during that period. He was active mainly at the Sheppard Pratt Hospital in Towson, Maryland, and at St. Elizabeths Hospital in Washington, D.C. Trained in Meyer's psychobiology and in classical psychoanalysis—he was, in fact, a charter member of the Washington Psychoanalytic Society—he was influenced by such social scientists as Ruth Benedict, Margaret Mead, Edward Sapir, L. Cattrell, and Harold Lasswell. Central to his thinking was the emphasis on a behavioristic approach in psychopathology, based on the interpersonal theory, which was at variance with the strictly individual emphasis in psychoanalysis. His denomination of prototaxic, parataxic, and syntactic modes of experiencing reality is today forgotten; but still appealing are his concepts of anxiety as related to feelings of disapproval by others, of stages of personality development as an outgrowth of interpersonal experiences, and of psychopathological phenomena as substitutive (neurotic) or disintegrative (psychotic) processes in the distressing effects of anxiety. His main contribution, however, consisted of his pioneering method of psychotherapy of the psychoses. He aimed at the understanding and correction of the patient's distorted communication process in the context of a patient-therapist relationship based on a reciprocal learning situation. After his first book, *Conception of Modern Psychiatry* (1947), several other books appeared posthumously under his name.

Eventually, the psychotherapy of the psychoses received great impetus from the work at Chestnut Lodge Hospital, in Rockville, Maryland, by Frieda Fromm-Reichmann (1899–1957), a friend of Groddeck, a member of the Frankfurt Institute for Psychoanalysis, and the author of *The Principles of Intensive Psychotherapy* (1950). That work was followed shortly thereafter by John Rosen's method of direct analysis for schizophrenic patients (*Direct Analysis,* 1953), a method that has remained controversial.

Even more influenced by social and anthropological ideas are the concepts expressed by the exponents of the culturalistic and neo-Freudian schools. Ruth Benedict (1887–1948), who wrote *Patterns of Culture* (1934), studied the influence of the culture, defined as a consistent cohesive ideological pattern, on child rearing and mental development. Margaret Mead (1901–1978) showed in many of her publications, such as *The Balinese Character* (1942) and *Male and Female* (1949), how individual and family traits are culturally determined.

Also typically American and again related to the social dimension has been the field of group psychotherapy. Anticipated in Vienna in the 1920's by Jacob Moreno's use of dramatic classes with disturbed children and in this country by the lecture classes for mental patients organized by Edward Lazell at St. Elizabeths Hospital in Washington in 1919 and, later on, by L. Cody Marsh in New York, group psychotherapy acquired momentum in the 1940's and 1950's. Moreno (1892–1974) developed a method he called "psychodrama" (presented in his book *Sociometry*, 1951, and others), which allows the patient to act out his conflicts on the stage through the use of particular techniques (auxiliary ego, mirror, double, and role reversal). Samuel R. Slavson (*An Introduction to Group Therapy*, 1943, and other volumes) used play therapy in his group work with children at the Jewish Board of Guardians in New York.

Dissatisfied with the empirical and intuitive approach to psychotherapy, a few researchers attempted to introduce a more objective method in the therapeutic process. Outstanding in that area was the work of the psychologist Carl Rogers, first at Ohio State University and then at the Counseling Center of the University of Chicago. His name is mainly associated with his client-centered therapy, which is characterized by genuineness, unconditioned positive regard for the patient, and accurate empathic understanding. However, his painstaking search for ways of measuring the dimensions and the results of the psychotherapeutic process, as presented in *Client-centered Therapy* (1951), is probably more important than his theories.

Even old forms of therapy were revitalized and made the subject of fresh investigation. Hypnosis, for instance, after the pioneering study by Clark Hull (*Hypnosis and Suggestibility: An Experimental Approach,* 1933), was critically presented by Lewis Wolberg and later by Milton Erickson, Jerome Schneck, and others. Under the influence of the learning theories and cognitive theories, others attempted to subject the psychoanalytic tenets to an experimental approach. Notably, John Dollard and Neal E. Miller at Yale, after their original study *Frustration and Aggression* (1939), showing that hostility in animals results from frustration, attempted to correlate learning theories and psychoanalysis (*Personality and Psychotherapy*, 1950). Still others tried to introduce a mathematical terminology in human behavior by making use of the field-theory system developed by the German-born and German-trained Kurt Lewin (1890–1947). His work has been continued at the Department of Social Relations at Harvard University and at the Center for Group Dynamics at the University of Michigan. Lewin developed a topological system, according to which the life-space of a person is the result of the interplay of positive (reward-giving) and negative (punishment-giving) values (*A Dynamic Theory of Personality*, 1935; and *Principles of Topological Psychology*, 1938).

Quite apart from those attempts to objectify psychiatry, some new concepts slowly started to emerge in the early 1950's, perhaps as forerunners of the great social upheavals and debates over basic values that would become prominent in the 1960's. Mainly influenced by the works of two exponents of existentialism—the German Martin Heidegger, born in 1889, and the Swiss Ludwig Binswanger (1881–1966)—the American psychologist Rollo May, born in 1909, who was a training and supervisor analyst at the William Alanson White Institute of Psychiatry in New York, published *The Meaning of Anxiety* in 1950. In it he considered anxiety as a threat to the very foundation of existence—that is, the experiencing of the dissolution of the existence of the person as a self—a stance that, according to its author, was of considerable relevance for psychopathology and for psychotherapy. Shortly thereafter appeared *The Courage to Be* (1953) by the German-born Paul Tillich (1886–1965), for many years professor of philosophical theology at the Union Theological Seminary in New York and

then at the Harvard Divinity School. The courage to be is authenticity as a search for the ultimate individual potentialities, despite the threat it presents of not being. By that time some works of Erich Fromm—a social philosopher born in Germany in 1900 and trained at the Universities of Heidelberg and Frankfurt and at the Berlin Psychoanalytic Institute and later a founder of the William Alanson White Institute of Psychiatry—had become known. *Escape from Freedom* (1941) and *Man for Himself* (1947) were followed by *The Sane Society* (1955) and *The Art of Loving* (1956). In those books Fromm presented with dramatic pathos the situation of malaise of the person aspiring to freedom but having to comply with the overwhelming collective systems. Taking issue with some of the basic Freudian postulates, he delineated several personality types—the receptive, exploitive, hoarding, marketing, and productive.

Those various authors, however, have remained somewhat peripheral to the central core of psychiatry. Much more relevant for psychiatry has been the work of the German-born Erik H. Erikson, born in 1902. Trained as a psychoanalyst in Europe, he emigrated to this country in 1933. After a decade at the Austen Riggs Center in Stockbridge, Massachusetts, he conducted research at Harvard, Yale, and other settings and is now professor of human development at Harvard. As a result of his thorough studies on the psychological development of the person in the 1930's and 1940's, including anthropological work with the Sioux and Yurok Indians, he published *Childhood and Society* in 1950. In that book he presented a psychosocial theory of development based on the interplay of the biological epigenesis with societal dimensions and encompassing a total life cycle from birth to senescence through the progressive unfolding of eight polarities. As is usual in the case of pioneers, it was some time before Erikson's innovating formulations had a significant impact on psychiatry. During the 1940's and 1950's the prevailing theoretical frame remained the psychoanalytic one, progressively influenced by the trend of ego psychology.

Teaching in psychiatry—first enhanced by the Veterans' Administration and supported by such private foundations as the Rockefeller Foundation, the Commonwealth Fund, and the Menninger Foundation—progressively became more formal and homogeneously organized because of the requirements of the American Board of Psychiatry, established in 1934. After some conferences on psychiatric education held at Cornell University in the early 1950's and proposals advanced by the Committee on Medical Education of the Group for the Advancement of Psychiatry, an active group of research-oriented and teaching-oriented psychiatrists established in 1946, psychiatry came to play an increasing role in medical schools, both at the undergraduate level and at the graduate level. The National Institute of Mental Health, founded in 1949, has since its inception given priority to training, as well as research, in psychiatry by establishing a program of fellowship that in time extended to many centers in the country. The philosophy of teaching was based mainly on the understanding of psychodynamics and the acquisition of psychotherapeutic skills with the help of individual supervision. A personal analysis was strongly recommended in many training centers as a way of achieving better insight and self-knowledge.

From the mid-1950's to the mid-1960's. By the mid-1950's some early signs indicated that psychiatry was entering a new stage. At that time, those signs passed almost unnoticed, but their significance for the historical perspective cannot be questioned today. To be sure, such a new orientation did not take place to a meaningful degree in a short time. The psychoanalytic ideology, increasingly tinged with ego psychology, remained prevalent. Even some innovating concepts had appeared in the literature—for instance, Thomas French's description of goal-directed behavior from the viewpoint of biological adaptation (*The Integration of Behavior,* 1952–1958); Ernst Kris's and Lawrence Kubie's views linking creativity to the preconscious as a regression in the service of the ego (as seen in Kubie's *Neurotic Distortion of the Creative Process,* 1958); Adelaide Johnson's and Stanislaus Szurek's attribution of much of children's delinquent behavior to superego lacunae, a defect in the superego structure of one or both of the parents; and new and enlightening vistas in the understanding of alcoholics, sexual psychopaths, and criminals.

Particularly significant was the interest in the psychodynamics and psychotherapy of schizophrenia. In 1955 Silvano Arieti's *Interpretation of Schizophrenia,* a comprehensive presentation of the condition, appeared. In that study, the emphasis was put for the first time on the formal mechanisms—that is, on how rather than on what the patients think—in line with previous studies by Jacob S. Kasanin (*Language and Thought in Schizophrenia,* 1946) and Ellhard von Domarus. Arieti's book was followed by a flow of many other publications on that most puzzling psychiatric condition, a flow that has continued uninterrupted to this day.

Shortly thereafter in 1956, Erikson introduced the concepts of ego identity, ego diffusion, and identity crisis to explain the complex development of the personality in passing from childhood to adulthood. Those concepts, then considered rather theoretical, became very meaningful in the mid-1960's, during the conflict of values.

Existentialism and other related currents—in spite of some fresh presentations (as in Rollo May's *Existence: A New Dimension in Psychiatry and Psychology,* 1958), translations of important volumes (by Ludwig Binswanger, Karl Jaspers, Maurice Merleau-Ponty, Jean Paul Sartre, Erwin Strauss, Igor Caruso, Viktor Frankl), and support by some psychologists (notably Robert MacLeod and Abraham Maslow, the author of *Toward a Psychology of Being,* 1962)—never developed into a significant force, probably because of the innate tendency of the American culture to find solutions for deep-seated issues in collective, rather than individual, forms of expressions, as has been the case in Europe. Likewise stimulating but essentially limited to the intellectual elite were the reinterpretations of psychoanalytic concepts by Norman Brown (*Life against Death,* 1959), Paul Rieff (*Freud: The Mind of a Moralist,* 1959), and a few others.

Historically rather significant were some early signs of dissatisfaction with prevailing theories and methods that came to the fore from psychoanalytic quarters themselves. The issue of incorporating psychoanalytic didactic training into the over-all psychiatric training was amply discussed by many, especially by Franz Alexander in *Psychoanalysis and Psychotherapy* (1956). Research on the various dimensions of psychoanalytic therapy was initiated in some quarters, such as the Menninger psychotherapy research project and the ad hoc committee on central fact gathering of the American Psychoanalytic Association. Considerable interest, mixed with accusations of secession by some orthodox analysts, accompanied the introduction of brief psychotherapy by Alexander and a few others.

Much more important, however, were two developments that took place in the mid-1950's and that pointed to an interesting example of *zeitgeist*—the introduction of psychopharmacology and the revolution that took place in mental hospitals.

Organic therapies have had an illustrious tradition in psychiatry. As a matter of fact, drugs of the mind have been used incessantly in preliterate cultures and up to the present day, psychosurgery was preceded by skull trepanation, and methods of shock have been used at various times, especially in the early 19th century. In the context of modern psychiatry, shock treatment, mainly electric shock and insulin shock, enjoyed great popularity in the 1940's and contributed to the focusing of interest on many severely psychotic patients and raised hopes for a more favorable prognosis. In spite of extensive experimental and clinical research, the mechanism of action of shock treatment remained obscure and was further clouded by the ambivalence between the physiological interpretation and the psychological interpretation of the phenomenon. Clearly negative was the reaction of many, from the Catholic Church to Soviet Russia, to psychosurgical procedures.

That apparently stagnant situation was rather suddenly overturned by the introduction of chemotherapy—tranquilizers and psychic energizers—in the early 1950's. What had been for many years a specialized field of experimental and clinical research—as represented in the pioneering book by L. Lewin (1931) and by C. Bradley's 1937 introduction of amphetamines for the treatment of hyperkinetic children—became in a few years one of the most active and promising areas of psychiatry. After the discovery of the beneficial effect of chlorpromazine in psychotic and agitated mental patients by the Frenchmen Pierre Deniker, Henri Leborit, and Jean Delay in 1953, meprobamates, synthetized by Frank Berger and B. Ludwig in 1950, were introduced in clinical practice in 1954; lysergic acid, first accidentally discovered by Albert Hoffman, was made the subject of clinical investigation by Joel Elkes and others; reserpine, empirically used in India for centuries, was synthetized by Hugo Bein and R. Kuhn in 1956; chlordiazepoxide was first used by I. Cohen at the University of Texas in 1960; and lithium was successfully used by J. Cade in the 1960's. *Discoveries in Biological Psychiatry* (1970), edited by Frank Ayd and Barry Blackwell, offered a valuable historical perspective on psychopharmacology.

Those developments in psychopharmacology meant that, beginning in the early 1950's, many mental patients were able to function in a more integrated and acceptable way in institutional settings, and, even more important, many of them could avoid hospitalization or could be returned earlier to their families and communities. Around that same time a new atmosphere of innovation and hopefulness became noticeable in some mental institutions. Social psychiatry, a term coined by Thomas Rennie in 1956, acquired quick prominence in its various environmental, sociocultural, ecological, interdisciplinary, and cross-cultural dimensions. To be sure, social factors in relation to psychopathology and treatment had been anticipated by some pioneering educational and sociological influences—such as settlement houses, visiting nurses, and juvenile courts—early in the century under the influence of the progressive movement and with the support of private organizations. Even the initial child guidance movement in the 1920's had been affected by those trends. The main field of psychiatry, however, still consisted of institutionalized patients in mental hospitals that had remained largely isolated from their communities and from the mainstream of medicine. The mental hygiene movement, launched by Clifford Beers, had acquired a more scientific aspect through the leadership of Thomas Salmon, and the First International Congress on Mental Hygiene was held in Washington in 1930, but the movement was still largely limited to lay participation. The application of the social sciences to psychology in the 1930's, mainly at the University of Chicago, had not gone beyond theoretical studies. The wide acceptance of long-term individual treatment, based on psychoanalytic ideas and administered mainly to neurotic middle-class and upper-class patients from urban areas, had further contributed to the isolation of psychiatry from mental hospitals.

Not until the mid-1950's, at the time of the initial surge in the use of chemotherapy, did some innovating concepts and procedures, introduced in England a few years before, become known in this country: the open-door policy, successfully used by some; the tenets of the therapeutic community, based on a better staff-patient relationship and increased patient participation in the therapeutic program, as spelled out by Maxwell Jones and others in *The Therapeutic Community* (1953); and the beginning attempts to try new methods, such as halfway houses, family care, aftercare services, and the involvement of volunteers in mental institutions. All those developments generated considerable hope and helped to open new vistas in this country, too. In 1954 appeared the monograph by Alfred Stanton and Morris Schwartz, *The Mental Hospital,* a study of the social structure of the Chestnut Lodge Hospital in Rockville, Maryland. That monograph was followed shortly thereafter by the collaborative books edited by Milton Greenblatt and others, *From Custodial to Therapeutic Patient Care in Mental Hospitals* (1955) and *The Patient and the Mental Hospital* (1957). In 1958 August Hollingshead and Frederick Redlich published *Social Class and Mental Illness,* a report of a sociological investigation carried on in New Haven that unequivocally showed that middle-class and upper-class people tended to make use of outpatient clinics and of private practitioners and that lower-class patients tended to use hospitals.

By that time, with typical American enthusiasm and urge for action, the issue of mental illness was becoming national. With the strong support of the National Institute of Mental Health (headed for a decade and a half by Robert Felix), of the Governors Conference on Mental Health, and of many private organizations and professional associations, the Mental Health Study Act was passed in 1955. It established the Joint Commission on Mental Illness and Health, under the presidency of Kenneth Appel and Leo Bartemeier, for the purposes of establishing priorities and viable methods of services for the mentally ill throughout the country. After 5 years of intensive work under the leadership of Jack Ewalt and his associates, the commission came to the conclusion that the present psychiatric personnel and the network of mental hospitals were totally inadequate to serve the country. The final report of the commission, *Action for Mental Health* (1961), was essentially a proposal for a concerted attack on mental illness through a better redistribution and a community-oriented philosophical reorientation of psychiatrists; increasing participation of many lay people at various levels in a massive program of prevention, treatment, and rehabilitation of the mentally ill; a progressive shift of emphasis from institutional to community services; and plans for shared federal, state, and local funding of community mental health centers.

In the next 2 years, with the help of many professionals and lay people, including some prominent legislators, the community mental health movement was launched. On February 5, 1963, President John F. Kennedy, in a message to the Eighty-eighth Congress, clearly identified the national aspect of the problem of mental illness and the need for returning mental illness to the mainstream of American medicine and for upgrading mental health services. On October 31, 1963, the Community Mental Health Act was passed, mandating the National Institute of Mental Health to establish and fund community mental health centers, each one located in a homogeneous catchment area of about 75,000 to 200,000 people and encompassing several essential services in addition to other

optional ones. Historically, that event represented the culmination of the effort to view mental health and mental illness as a national responsibility, a view that had been initiated in the mid-19th century and that had been anticipated by Adolf Meyer early in this century. After the appropriation of funds for the construction of many community mental health centers, other funds became available in 1965, under President Johnson's leadership, for staffing a number of such centers.

So, in the space of a decade, a national program of community mental health had become a reality. That does not mean, however, that the goals concerning the reorientation of priorities, professional ideals, and methods of treatment were accomplished in that short time. Such a reorientation has continued to the present time—punctuated by unrealistic expectations, conflicts of values, and fluctuations between hopefulness and disillusion in many.

The over-all trend during the decade was characterized by an enlightened and optimistic view of the problem of mental illness not only on the part of professionals and well-informed lay people but also on the part of the general public. In the field of psychiatry proper, several currents slowly emerged. Research received great impetus, mainly with the support of the National Institute of Mental Health—a commendable endeavor that may, however, lead to a certain degree of monopolization. Research—mainly interdisciplinary and led by behavioral scientists, rather than by psychiatrists, who tend to lack a proper foundation in research methods—has centered on biological dimensions (chemotherapy, sensory deprivation, electroencephalography, biochemistry of schizophrenia and depression, neurophysiology of dreams, genetic aspects of the deoxyribonucleic acid molecule and of the ribonucleic acid, and identification of inborn errors of metabolism, enzymatic defects, and chromosexual abnormalities), on epidemiological dimensions (large epidemiological surveys with the help of up-to-date statistical techniques, such as the Midtown Manhattan survey in 1962; the definition of the concept of normality; the application of computing techniques to psychiatry), on psychosomatic aspects, and on child development, such as Harry Harlow's studies on the mother-child relationship in monkeys.

Some virtually new fields acquired prominence during the decade. Through the long-term efforts of Nathan Ackerman (1908–1971), the author of *The Psychodynamics of Family Life* (1958), and of a few others, such as John Spiegel and Norman Bell, family therapy came to be viewed as a treatment of choice in many cases. A few years later the Palo Alto group (Gregory Bateson, Don Jackson, Virginia Satir), the Yale group (Theodore Lidz, Alice Cornelison), and others involved in research on communication attempted to introduce a more objective methodological technique in the study of family dynamics, which led to the identification of the double-bind message in the causes of schizophrenia. In the broad context of communication theory, transactional analysis—essentially an abridged combination of psychoanalysis, Adler's life style, and Reich's character analysis—was developed and popularized by Eric Berne in *Games People Play* (1964). Group psychotherapy of various kinds, including psychodrama, became increasingly popular, partly because of its relatively low cost. Anticipated in the studies by Elaine and John Cumming (*Ego and Milieu,* 1962), milieu therapy, which focused on the strengthening of the ego in a suitable therapeutic setting, became the center, rather than the context, of the psychotherapeutic process. And brief psychotherapy, in the past considered as a modality of psychoanalysis, became an independent technique that was especially useful for many reactive and acute conditions and for crisis intervention.

Even bolder were two trends that emerged in the 1960's and that have since been continuously expanded. On the theoretical side, the general system theory initiated by Ludwig von Bertalanffy, who was for many years active in Vienna and then in Canada, made its appearance. It postulated a reciprocally influencing system of homeostasis, transaction, and communication among all aspects of life, leading to optimal function or, conversely, dysfunction in particular circumstances. Representatives of that trend are James Miller, Roy Grinker (*Toward a Unified Theory of Human Behavior*, 1956), and, to a certain extent, Karl Menninger (*The Vital Balance*, 1963). On the practical side, rapid growth marked the introduction of behavior therapy, essentially a combination of Pavlov's Russian reflexology and Thorndike's and Hull's American instrumentalism, popularized mainly by the psychiatrist Joseph Wolpe (author of *Psychotherapy by Reciprocal Inhibition*, 1958, and, with Arnold Lazarus, *Behavior Therapy Techniques*, 1966), first in South Africa and then at Temple University, and by a number of other scientists.

From the mid-1960's to the present and into the future. By the mid-1960's it appeared that psychiatry was going to enjoy an increasingly favorable condition in this country, with the massive support of the federal government and the growing acceptance by the general population. The number of psychiatrists was rapidly rising with the help of training grants from the National Institute of Mental Health, the number of hospitalized mental patients was constantly decreasing, and plans for the construction of 2,000 mental health centers were on their way.

However, a number of stressful and interrelated events challenged that optimistic view—the Vietnam War, the outbreak of violence in urban and academic settings, the racial confrontations that were characterized by the broad issues of school integration and black militancy, the women's movement, the endemic spread of all sorts of drugs of the mind, the less inhibited attitudes toward sex and marriage, the concern with environmental problems of ecology and survival, and the rise of the third world among Afro-Asian nations.

Those trends and others were met with varying reactions by psychiatrists. Initially, the reaction of most psychiatrists was rather defensive, on the assumption that those trends were outside the realm of psychiatry proper. Increasingly, however, many psychiatrists have become involved in a number of social issues in different ways. The success of the historical overtures to psychoanalysis offered by Erikson in *Young Man Luther* (1958) and *Gandhi's Truth* (1969) was an expression of that new attitude by many. Since then, there has been a noticeable change in the self-image of psychiatrists and in the perception of psychiatry by the general population—more involvement in community affairs, less emphasis on didactic analysis and psychoanalysis, more inclination toward an eclectic approach to theory and practice, and a closer relationship with other professionals and lay people concerned with mental health.

The field of psychiatry is now in a state of uncertainty and restlessness, unable to abandon the traditional theoretical models and unprepared to face the challenge of the great social issues at stake. Yet some progress is being made, at least in psychiatrists' increased flexibility of approach toward new ideas. B. F. Skinner's operant conditioning, Herbert Marcuse's one-dimensional man, Kenneth Keniston's uncommitted youth, Thomas Szasz's myth of mental illness, Abraham Maslow's third-force psychology, Claude Lévi-Strauss's structuralism, the new integration of Piaget's work in psychology, Konrad Lorenz's ethology, R. D. Laing's bold views on schizophrenia, William Masters's and Virginia Johnson's new approach

to the treatment of sexual disorders, more enlightening views on parapsychology and legal matters and even on clinical matters (typically, homosexuality), an entire new range of psychotherapeutic techniques from sensitivity training to encounter and marathon groups, and self-hypnotic ascetic practices derived mainly from Yoga and Zen Buddhism—those are some of the most remarkable developments that have taken place in psychiatry. In the past few years, there has been an upsurge of interest in psychopharmacology in the treatment of mental disorders.

All those developments point to a growing sense of social responsibility on the part of the psychiatrist, perhaps as a result of the apparent decline of traditional institutions, the change of mores, and the search for new values. That sense of responsibility is being enhanced by the decrease of governmental financial support in the past few years. On a broader scale, the rapidly spreading concern that many issues—wars, poverty, famine, endemic diseases, environmental contamination, and now the depletion of sources of energy—can be coped with only through international effort, points to the need for an entire reevaluation of the ideology of psychiatry. Far from being molded by the prevailing social forces of a few affluent nations, such an ideology may be increasingly influenced by many other cultures and nations of the world. History, however—by pointing to the similarities between now and the past, to the apparent cyclic occurrence of attitudes and customs, and to the basic constancy of human needs and ways of solving problems—may offer much-needed guidelines for the future.

Suggested Cross References

Many sections in this textbook contain historical information related to their specific subjects. Of particular interest may be the sections on psychiatric theories of the 20th century (Chapters 8 through 11), the history of schizophrenia (Section 15.2), the history of psychosomatic medicine (Section 26.1), the history of child psychiatry (Section 34.1), the development of community psychiatry concepts (Section 45.1), and contemporary issues in psychiatry (Chapter 56).

REFERENCES

Ackerknecht, E. H. Psychopathology, primitive medicine, and primitive culture. Bull. Hist. Med., *14:* 30, 1942.
* Ackerknecht, E. H. *Short History of Psychiatry*, ed. 2. Hafner Press, New York, 1968.
Ackerknecht, E. H., Galdston, I., and Rosen, G. Mesmerism. Ciba Found. Symp., *9:* 326, 1948.
Adkins, A. W. H. *From the Many to the One: A Study of Personality and Views of Human Nature in the Context of Ancient Greek Society, Values, and Beliefs.* T. & A. Constable, London, 1970.
Agassi, J. *Towards a Historiography of Science.* Mouton, The Hague, 1963.
Agrippa von Nettesheim. *Opera.* Beringos, Lyon, 1550.
Aikin, J. *Thoughts on Hospitals.* London, 1771.
Alexander, F., Eisenstein, S., and Grotjahn, M., editors. *Psychoanalytic Pioneers.* Basic Books, New York, 1966.
* Alexander, F., and Selesnick, S. T. *The History of Psychiatry.* Harper & Row, New York, 1966.
Alphandéry, P. De quelques documents médiévaux relatifs à des états psychasthéniques. J. Psychol. Norm. Pathol., *26:* 763, 1929.
Altschule, M. D. *Roots of Modern Psychiatry: Essays on the History of Psychiatry,* ed. 2. Grune & Stratton, New York, 1965.
Altschule, M. D. *The Development of Traditional Psychopathology: A Sourcebook.* John Wiley & Sons, New York, 1976.
Alvarez, W. *Minds That Came Back.* J. B. Lippincott, Philadelphia, 1961.
Amdur, M. K. The dawn of psychiatric journalism. Am. J. Psychiatry, *100:* 205, 1943.
Andersson, O. *Studies in the Prehistory of Psychoanalysis.* Svenska Borkforlaget, Norstedts, Sweden, 1962.
Andreas-Salome, I. *The Freud Journal of Lou Andreas Salomé.* Basic Books, New York, 1964.
Andrew, G., and Vinkenoog, S., editors. *The Book of Grass: An Anthology of Indian Hemp.* Grove Press, New York, 1967.
Ariès, P. *Centuries of Childhood.* Alfred A. Knopf, New York, 1963.

Artemidorus. *The Interpretation of Dreams*. Noyes Press, Park Ridge, N. J., 1975.

Aristotle. *Works*. Vol. VII: *Problemata*. Oxford University Press, Oxford, 1927.

Aristole. *Poetics*. Clarendon Press, Oxford, 1968.

Aristole. *Rhetorica*. G. P. Putnam's Sons, New York, 1926.

Arnold, T. *Observations on the Nature, Kinds, Causes, and Prevention of Insanity*. Robinson, Leicester, 1782.

Avicenna. *A Treatise on the Canon of Medicine*. Luzac, London, 1930.

Ayd, F. J., and Blackwell, B., editors. *Discoveries in Biological Psychiatry*. J. B. Lippincott, Philadelphia, 1970.

Ayers, G. M. *England's First State Hospitals, 1867–1930*. University of California Press, Berkeley, 1971.

Babb, L. *The Elizabethan Malady: A Study of Melancholia in English Literature from 1580 to 1642*. Michigan State University Press, East Lansing, 1951.

Babkin, B. P. *Pavlov: A Biography*. University of Chicago Press, Chicago, 1949.

Back, K. W. *Beyond Words: The Story of Sensitivity Training and the Encounter Movement*. Russell Sage Foundation, New York, 1973.

Baglivi, G. Intorno all'anatomia, morso ed effetti della tarantella. In *Opere Complete*. Coen, Firenze, 1841.

Baillarger, J. G. F. De la folie à double forme. Ann. Méd.-Psychol., *6:* 369, 1854.

Bamborough, J. B. *The Little World of Man*. Longman's, Green, New York, 1952.

Barbu, Z. *Problems of Historical Psychology*. Grove Press, New York, 1960.

Barnett, B. Witchcraft, psychopathology, and hallucinations. Br. J. Psychiatry, *111:* 439, 1965.

Barrucand, D. *Histoire de l'hypnose en France*. Presses Universitaires de France, Paris, 1967.

Baruk, H. *La psychiatrie française de Pinel à nos jours*. Presses Universitaires de France, Paris, 1967.

Bassoe, P. Spain as the cradle of psychiatry. Am. J. Psychiatry, *101:* 731, 1945.

Bateson, G., editor. *Perceval's Narrative: A Patient's Account of His Own Psychosis, 1830–1832*. Stanford University Press, Palo Alto, Calif., 1961.

Battie, W. *A Treatise on Madness*. Brunner/Mazel, New York, 1969.

Bayle, A. L. J. *Recherches sur les maladies mentales*. These, Paris, 1822.

Beers, C. W. *A Mind That Found Itself*. Longman's, Green, New York, 1908.

Bellak, L., editor. *Contemporary European Psychiatry*. Grove Press, New York, 1961.

Benedict, R. *The Chrysanthemum and the Sword*. Houghton Mifflin, Boston, 1940.

Bernheim, H. *Suggestive Therapeutics: A Treatise on the Nature and Uses of Hypnotism*. London Book, New York, 1947.

Binger, C. *Revolutionary Doctor: Benjamin Rush, 1746–1813*. W. W. Norton, New York, 1966.

Binion, R. *Frau Lou: Nietzsche's Wayward Pupil*. Princeton University Press, Princeton, 1968.

Binswanger, L. *Sigmund Freud: Reminiscences of a Friendship*. Grune & Stratton, New York, 1957.

Binz, C. *Doctor Johann Weyer*, ed. 2. Sändig, Wiesbaden, 1969.

Blackmore, R. *A Treatise of the Spleen and Vapours*. London, 1725.

Blaine, D. and Barton, D. *The History of American Psychiatry: A Teaching and Research Guide*. American Psychiatric Association, Washington, D.C., 1979.

Bleuler, E. *Textbook of Psychiatry*. Macmillan, New York, 1924.

Bleuler, E. *Dementia Praecox or the Group of Schizophrenias*. International Universities Press, New York, 1950.

Bleuler, E. *Autistic Undisciplined Thinking in Medicine and How to Overcome It*. Hafner, Darien, Conn., 1970.

Block, S. L. St. Augustine: On grief and other psychological matters. Am. J. Psychiatry, *122:* 943, 1966.

Blum, R. H. *Society and Drugs*, vol. I. Jossey-Bass, San Francisco, 1970.

Bockoven, J. S. *Moral Treatment in Community Mental Health*. Springer, New York, 1972.

Bond, E. D. *Dr. Kirkbride and His Mental Hospital*. J. B. Lippincott, Philadelphia, 1947.

Bonnafous-Sérieux, H. *Une maison d'aliénés et de correctionnaires au XVIIIe siècle: La Charité de Senlis*. Presses Universitaires de France, Paris, 1936.

Boring, E. *History, Psychology, and Science: Selected Papers*. John Wiley & Sons, New York, 1963.

Bottome, P. *Alfred Adler*. Vanguard, New York, 1957.

Braceland, F. J. *The Institute of Living: The Hartford Retreat, 1822–1972*. Hartford, Conn., 1972.

Braid, J. *Braid on Hypnotism: The Beginnings of Modern Hypnotism*. Julian Press, New York, 1960.

Brand, J. L. The United States: A historical perspective. In *Community Mental Health: An International Perspective*, R. H. Williams and L. D. Ozarin, editors, p. 180. Jossey-Bass, San Francisco, 1968.

Brès, Y. *La psychologie de Platon*. Presses Universitaires de France, Paris, 1968.

Brierre de Boismont, A. J. F. Remarques sur quelques établissements d'aliénés de la Belgique, de la Hollande et de l'Angleterre. Ann. Hyg. Med. Légale, *37:* 44, 1847.

Brigham, A. *Remarks on the Influence of Mental Excitement upon Health*. Marsh, Capen and Lyon, Boston, 1832.

Brigham, A. *Observations on the Influence of Religion upon the Health and Physical Welfare of Mankind*. Marsh, Capen and Lyon, Boston, 1835.

Brigham, A. Definition of insanity. Am. J. Insanity, *1:* 97, 1844.

Broca, P. *Sur la trépanation du crâne et les amulettes crâniennes à l'époque néolithique*. Leroux, Paris, 1877.

Bromberg, W. *Man above Humanity: A History of Psychotherapy*. J. B. Lippincott, Philadelphia, 1954.

Bromo, V. *Freud and His Early Circle*. Morrow, New York, 1968.

Brown, J. *Elementa Medicinae*. London, 1780.

Brozek, J. History of psychology: Diversity of approaches and uses. Trans. N. Y. Acad. Sci., *31:* 115, 1969.

Brozek, J., and Slobin, D. I., editors. *Psychology in the U.S.S.R.: An Historical Perspective*. International Arts and Sciences Press, White Plains, N. Y., 1972.

Bry, I. Freud and the history of ideas. In *Science and Psychoanalysis*, J. Masserman, editor, vol. 5, p. 6. Grune & Stratton, New York, 1962.

Bucknill, J. C. *The Psychology of Shakespeare*. Longman, London, 1859.

Bucknill, J. C., and Tuke, D. H. *A Manual of Psychological Medicine*. Hafner Press, New York, 1968.

Bulferetti, L. *Cesare Lombroso*. Union Tipographica Editria Torinese, Torino, 1975.

Bullough, V. L. *Sexual Variance in Society and History*. John Wiley & Sons, New York, 1976.

Buranelli, V. *The Wizard from Vienna: Franz Anton Mesmer*. Coward, McCann & Geoghegan, New York, 1975.

Burnham, J. C. *Psychoanalysis and American Medicine, 1894–1918: Medicine, Science, and Culture*. International Universities Press, New York, 1967.

Burr, G. L., editor. *Narratives of the Witchcraft Cases, 1648–1706*. Charles Scribner's Sons, New York, 1914.

Burrows, G. M. *Commentaries on the Causes, Forms, Symptoms, and Treatment, Moral and Medical, of Insanity*. Underwood, London, 1828.

Burstein, S. R. Aspects of the psychopathology of old age revealed in witchcraft cases of the sixteenth and seventeenth centuries. Br. Med. J., *6:* 63, 1949.

Burton, R. *The Anatomy of Melancholy*. Tudor, New York, 1960.

Byrd, M. *Visits to Bedlam: Madness and Literature in the Eighteenth Century*. University of South Carolina Press, Columbia, 1974.

Cabanis, P. J. G. Rapports du physique et du moral de l'homme. In *Oeuvres Philosophiques*, vol. 1. Presses Universitaires de France, Paris, 1956.

Caelius Aurelianus. *On Acute Diseases and on Chronic Diseases*. University of Chicago Press, Chicago, 1950.

Calmeil, L. F. *De la paralysie considérée chez les aliénés*. Paris, 1826.

Caplan, R. B. *Psychiatry and the Community in Nineteenth-century America*. Basic Books, New York, 1969.

Carlson, E. T., and Simpson, M. M. Benjamin Rush's medical use of the moral faculty. Bull. Hist. Med., *39:* 22, 1965.

Carus, C. G. *Psyche*. Springer, New York, 1970.

Cassian, J. On Accidie. In *The Desert Fathers*. Constable, London, 1936.

Castelli, E., editor. *L'Umanesimo e "la Follia."* Abete, Rome, 1971.

Centenary issue. Am. J. Psychiatry, *100:* 1, 1944.

Chamberlain, A. S. Early mental hospitals in Spain. Am. J. Psychiatry, *123:* 143, 1966.

Charcot, J. M. *Lectures on the Diseases of the Nervous System*. New Sydenham Society, London, 1877–1889.

Charcot, J. M. *Clinical Lectures on Certain Diseases of the Nervous System*. Davis, Detroit, 1888.

Chaucer, G. Booke of the Dutchesse. In *Poetical Works*. W. Pickering, London, 1845.

Chertok, L., and De Saussure, R. *Naissance du psychanalyste: de Mesmer à Freud*. Payot, Paris, 1973.

Chesney, E. The theme of folly in Rabelais and Ariosto. J. Med. Renaiss. Stud., *7:* 67, 1977.

Cheyne, G. *The English Malady*. London, 1733.

Chiarugi, V. *Della Pazzia in genere e in specie*. Carlieri, Firenze, 1793–1794.

Cicero. *Tusculan Disputations*. Harvard University Press, Cambridge, Mass., 1950.

Clark, S. R. L. *Aristotle's Man: Speculations upon Aristotelian Anthropology*. Clarendon Press, Oxford, 1975.

Clarke, E., and Dewhurst, K. *An Illustrated History of Brain Function*. University of California Press, Berkeley, 1972.

Clarke, E., and O'Malley, C. D. *The Human Brain and Spinal Cord: A Historical Study with Writings from Antiquity to the Twentieth Century*. University of California Press, Berkeley, 1968.

Coles, R. *Erik H. Erikson: The Growth of His Work*. Little, Brown, and Co., Boston, 1970.

Cobben, J. J. *Jan Wier, Devils, Witches and Magic*. Dorrance, Philadelphia, 1976.

Colombo, G. *La scienza infelice. Il Museo di Antropologia Criminale di Cesare Lombroso*. Boringhieri, Torino, 1975.

Combe, A. *Observations on Mental Derangement*. Scholars' Facsimiles & Reprints, Delmar, N. Y., 1972.

Conolly, J. *The Treatment of the Insane without Mechanical Restraints*. Smith, Elder & Co., London, 1856.

Conolly, J. *The Indications of Insanity*. Dawson, London, 1964a.

Conolly, J. *An Inquiry Concerning the Indications of Insanity*. Dawson, London, 1964b.

Constantino Africano. *Della Melancolia*. Instituto di Storia della Medicina, Rome, 1959.

Coury, C. The basic principles of medicine in the primitive mind. Med. Hist., *11:* 111, 1967.

Croissant, Jr. *Aristotle et les mystères*. Faculté de Philosophie et Lettres, Liège, 1932.

Crombie, A. C. *Medieval and Early Modern Science*, vol. 1. Doubleday, Garden City, N. Y., 1959.

Cuny, H. *Ivan Pavlov: The Man and His Theories.* Erikkson, New York, 1965.

Dain, N. *Concepts of Insanity in the United States, 1789–1865.* Rutgers University Press, New Brunswick, N. J., 1964.

Dain, N. *Disordered Minds: The First Century of Eastern State Hospital in Williamsburg, Virginia, 1766–1866.* University Press of Virginia, Charlottesville, 1971.

Dalma, G. Leonardo precursore della psicofisiologia e psicologia dinamica moderna. Nevrasse, *6:* 231, 1956.

Damerow, H. *Ueber die relative Verbindung der Irren- Heil- und Pflege-Anstalten.* Wigand, Leipzig, 1840.

Daquin J. *La Philosophie de la folie.* Chambéry, 1791.

Davies, J. P. *Phrenology: Fad and Science.* Yale University Press, New Haven, Conn., 1955.

De Becker, R. *The Understanding of Dreams and Their Influence on the History of Man.* Hawthorn Books, New York, 1968.

de Bienville, D. T. *La nymphomanie ou traité de la fureur utérine.* London, 1771.

Decker, H. S. *Freud in Germany: Revolution and Reaction in Science, 1893–1907.* International Universities Press, New York, 1977.

della Porta, G. B. *Della Fisionomia dell'uomo.* Carlino, Napoli, 1610.

De Saussure, R. French psychiatry in the eighteenth century. Ciba Found. Symp., *11:* 1222, 1950a.

De Saussure, R. Psychoanalysis and history. In *Psychoanalysis and Social Sciences,* G. Roheim, editor, vol. 2, p. 7. International Universities Press, New York, 1950b.

Desruelles, M., and Bersot, H. L'assistance aux aliénés chez les Arabes du VIII au XII siècle. Ann. Med. Psychol., *96:* 689, 1938.

* Deutsch, A. *The Mentally Ill in America,* ed. 2. Columbia University Press, New York, 1948.

Deutsch, H. *Confrontations with Myself: An Epilogue.* W. W. Norton, New York, 1973.

Devereux, G. Primitive psychiatry. Bull. Hist. Med., *8:* 1194, 1940.

Dickens, C. *American Notes and Pictures from Italy.* Oxford University Press, London, 1957.

Diethelm, O. *Medical Dissertations of Psychiatric Interest Printed before 1750.* S. Karger, New York, 1971.

Diethelm, O., and Hoffernan, T. F. Felix Platter and psychiatry. J. Hist. Behav. Sci., *1:* 10, 1965.

Digby, K. *A Late Discourse: Touching the Cure of Wounds by the Power of Sympathy.* London, 1658.

Dodds, E. R. *The Greeks and the Irrational.* University of California Press, Berkeley, 1951.

Dodds, E. R. Supernatural phenomena in classical antiquity. Proc. Soc. Psychical Res., *55:* 189, 1971.

Dominguez, E. J. The Hospital of Innocents: Humane treatment of the mentally ill in Spain: 1409–1512. Bull. Menninger Clin., *31:* 285, 1967.

Dörner, K. *Bürger and Irre: Zur Sozialgeschichte und Wissenschaftsoziologie der Psychiatrie.* Europäische Verlagsanstalt, Frankfurt, 1969.

Dover, K. F. *Greek Homosexuality.* Harvard University Press, Cambridge, Mass., 1978.

Drabkin, I. E. Remarks on ancient psychopathology. Isis, *46:* 223, 1955.

Earle, P. *The Curability of Insanity.* J. B. Lippincott, Philadelphia, 1887.

Earle, P. *Memoirs of Pliny Earle, M. D.* Damrell & Upham, Boston, 1898.

Eaton, J. W., and Weil, R. *Culture and Mental Disorder.* Free Press of Glencoe, New York, 1955.

Ebin, D. *The Drug Experience.* Orion, New York, 1961.

Edelstein, L. The philosophical system of Posidonius. Am. J Philol., *15:* 286, 1936.

Edgar, I. I. *Shakespeare, Medicine and Psychiatry.* Philosophical Library, New York, 1970.

The Egyptian Book of the Dead. British Museum, London, 1895.

Eissler, K. R. *Sigmund Freud und die Universität.* H. Huber, Bern, 1966.

Eissler, K. R. *Talent and Genius: The Fictitious Case of Tausk Contra Freud.* Quadrangle, New York, 1971a.

Eissler, K. R. *Discourse on Hamlet and Hamlet: A Psychoanalytic Inquiry.* International Universities Press, New York, 1971b.

Eliot, T. D. Interactions of psychiatric and social theory prior to 1940. In *Mental Health and Mental Disorder,* A. Rose, editor, p. 18. W. W. Norton, New York, 1955.

Ellenberger, H. La psychiatrie suisse. Evol. Psychiatr. (Paris), *16:* 321, 619, 1951; *17:* 139, 369, 593, 1952; *18:* 299, 1953.

Ellenberger, H. Hermann Rorschach, M.D., 1884–1922. Bull. Menninger Clin., *18:* 173, 1954.

* Ellenberger, R. *The Discovery of the Unconscious: The History and Evolution of Dynamic Psychiatry.* Basic Books, New York, 1970.

Engelman, E., editor. *Berggasse 19: Sigmund Freud's Home and Offices, Vienna 1938.* Basic Books, New York, 1976.

Erikson, E. H. *Young Man Luther: A Study in Psychoanalysis and History.* W. W. Norton, New York, 1958.

Erikson, E. H. *Identity and the Life Cycle.* International Universities Press, New York, 1959.

Erikson, E. H. *Insight and Responsibility.* W. W. Norton, New York, 1964.

Erikson, E. H. *Ghandi's Truth: On the Origin of Militant Non-Violence.* W. W. Norton, New York, 1969.

Esdaile, J. *Hypnosis in Medicine and Surgery.* Julian Press, New York, 1957.

Esquirol, J. E. D. *Mental Maladies.* Hafner Press, New York, 1965.

Ewalt, J. R., and Ewalt, P. L. History of the community psychiatric movement. Am. J. Psychiatry, *126:* 43, 1969.

Ey, H. Pierre Janet: The man and the work. In *Historical Roots of Contemporary Psychology,* B. B. Wolman, editor, p. 177. Harper & Row, New York, 1968.

Faber, M. D. *The Design Within: Psychoanalytic Approach to Shakespeare.* Science House, New York, 1970.

Falret, J. P. De la folie circulaire. Bull. Acad. Med., *19:* 382, 1854.

Faris, R. E. L., and Dunham, H. W. *Mental Disorders in Urban Areas.* University of Chicago Press, Chicago, 1939.

Fearing, F. *Reflex Action: A Study in the History of Physiological Psychology.* Williams & Wilkins, Baltimore, 1930.

Ferrus, G. M. A. *Des aliénés.* Paris, 1834.

Fine R. *A History of Psychoanalysis.* Columbia University Press, New York, 1979.

Fischer, H. *Die Heilige Hildegard von Bingen.* (Münchener Beiträge zur Geschichte und Literatur der Naturwissenschaften und Medizin, Heft 7/8.) Verlag der Münchner Drucke, Munchen, 1927.

Fischer-Homberger, E. *Hypochondrie, Melancholie bis Neurose: Krankheiten und Zustandsbilder.* H. Huber, Bern, 1970.

Fish, F. The historical development of modern psychiatry in Britain and Germany. Anglo-Ger. Med. Rev., *2:* 296, 1964.

Folie et Déraison à la Rénaissance. (Travaux de l'Institut pour l'Etude de la Rénaissance et de l'Humanisme.) Editions de l'Université de Bruxelles, Bruxelles, 1976.

Forel, A. *The Sexual Question.* Heinemann, London, 1906.

Forel, O. *Out of My Life and Work.* Allen, London, 1937.

Fortenbaugh, W. W. *Aristotle on Emotion.* Barnes & Noble, New York, 1975.

Foucault, M. *Madness and Civilization: A History of Insanity in the Age of Reason.* Pantheon Books, New York, 1965.

Frank, J. D. *Persuasion and Healing: A Comparative Study of Psychotherapy,* ed. 2. Johns Hopkins University Press, Baltimore, 1973.

Frank, J. P. *A System of Complete Medical Police: Selections from J. P. Frank.* Johns Hopkins University Press, Baltimore, 1976.

Frazer, J. G. *The Golden Bough: A Study in Magic and Religion.* Macmillan, New York, 1922.

Freedman, A. M. Historical and political roots of the Community Mental Health Centers Act. Am. J. Orthopsychiatry, *37:* 487, 1967.

Freeman, W. *The Psychiatrist: Personalities and Patterns.* Grune & Stratton, New York, 1968.

Freud, S. A neurosis of demoniacal possession in the seventeenth century. In *Collected Papers,* vol. 4, p. 436. Hogarth Press, London, 1949.

Freud, S. *Standard Edition of the Complete Psychological Works of Sigmund Freud.* Hogarth Press, London, 1953–1966.

Freud, S. *The Origins of Psychoanalysis: Letters of Wilhelm Fliess, 1887–1902.* Basic Books, New York, 1954.

Freud, S. *Letters of Sigmund Freud.* Basic Books, New York, 1960.

Freud, S. *The Letters of Sigmund Freud and Karl Abraham, 1907–1926.* Basic Books, New York, 1965.

Freud, S. *The Letters of Sigmund Freud and Arnold Zweig.* Harcourt, Brace, New York, 1970.

Freud, S. *Sigmund Freud and Lou Andreas-Salomé: Letters.* Harcourt, Brace, Jovanovich, New York, 1972.

Freud, S., and Pfister, O. *Letters, Psychoanalysis, and Faith.* Basic Books, New York, 1963.

Fromm, E. *Escape from Freedom.* Holt, Rinehart and Winston, New York, 1941.

Galdston, I. Descartes and modern psychiatric thought. Isis, *35:* 118, 1944.

Galdston, I. Community psychiatry, its social and historic derivations. J. Can Psychiatr. Assoc., *10:* 461, 1965.

Galdston, I., editor. *Historic Derivations of Modern Psychiatry.* McGraw-Hill, New York, 1967.

Galen. *On the Passions and Errors of the Soul.* Ohio State University Press, Columbus, 1963.

Garzoni, T. *L'hospidale de' pazzi incurabili.* Ferro, Milan, 1967.

Gay, F. *Elmer Ernest Southard (1876–1920).* Normandie House, Chicago, 1938.

Gedo, J. E., and Pollock, G. H., editors. *The Fusion of Science and Humanism: The Intellectual History of Psychoanalysis.* International Universities Press, New York, 1976.

Genil-Perrin, G. *L'idée de dégénerescence en médecine mentale.* Lecler, Paris, 1913.

Georget, E. J. *De la folie.* Paris, 1820.

Gifford, E. J. J. *Psychoanalysis, Psychotherapy and the New England Scene.* Science History Publications, New York, 1978.

Glickhorn, J., and Glickhorn, R. *Sigmund Freud's Akademische Laufbahn im Lichte der Dokumente.* Urban & Schwarzenburg, Wien, 1960.

Gode von Aesch, A. *Natural Science in German Romanticism.* Columbia University Press, New York, 1941.

Goldhamer, H., and Marshall, A. W. *Psychosis and Civilization: Two Studies in the Frequency of Mental Disease.* Free Press of Glencoe, New York, 1953.

Goodman, N. G. *Benjamin Rush: Physician and Citizen, 1746–1813.* University of Pennsylvania Press, Philadelphia, 1934.

Gregory the Great. *Pastoral Care.* Newman Press, Westminster, Md., 1955.

Griesinger, W. *Mental Pathology and Therapeutics.* Hafner Press, New York, 1965.

Grob, G. N. *The State and the Mentally Ill: A History of the Worcester State Hospital in Massachusetts, 1830–1920.* University of North Carolina Press,

Chapel Hill, 1966.

Grob, G. N. *Mental Institutions in America: Social Policy to 1875.* Free Press of Glencoe, New York, 1973.

Grossman, C. M., and Grossman, S. *The Wild Analyst: The Life and Work of Georg Groddeck.* Braziller, New York, 1965.

Gruhle, H. *Geschichtsschreibung und Psychologie.* Bouvier, Bonn, 1953.

Guerra, F. *The Pre-Columbian Mind.* Seminar Press, New York, 1971.

Guillain, G. *J. M. Charcot. 1825-1893: His Life, His Work.* Harper & Row, New York, 1959.

Guttmacher, M. S. *America's Last King: An Interpretation of the Madness of George III.* Charles Scribner's Sons, New York, 1941.

Guttmacher, M. S. An historical outline of the criminal law's attitude toward mental disorders. Arch. Crim. Psychodynamics, *4:* 647, 1961.

Hadfield, J. A. *Introduction to Psychotherapy: Its History and Modern Schools.* George Allen & Unwin, London, 1967.

Haindorf, A. *Versuch einer Pathologie und Therapies der Geistes- und Gemütskrankheiten.* Heidelberg, 1811.

Hale, N. G. *Freud and the Americans: The Beginnings of Psychoanalysis in the United States, 1876-1917.* Oxford University Press, New York, 1971.

Hall, J. K., editor. *One Hundred Years of American Psychiatry.* Columbia University Press, New York, 1944.

Hall, S. *Jesus the Christ in the Light of Psychology.* Doubleday, New York, 1917.

Halleck, S. American psychiatry and the criminal: An historical review. Am. J. Psychiatry, *121:* 939, 1965.

Haller, J. S. Neurasthenia: Medical profession and the urban "blahs." N. Y. State J. Med., *70:* 2489, 1970.

Hallowell, A. I. Culture and mental disorder. J. Abnorm. Psychol., *29:* 1, 1934.

Hammond, W. A. *A Treatise on Insanity in Its Medical Relations.* Appleton, New York, 1883.

Hansen, J. *Zauberwahn, Inquisition und Hexenprozess im Mittelalter.* Oldenbourg, Munchen, 1900.

Hare, E. H. Masturbatory insanity: The history of an idea. J. Ment. Sci., *108:* 1, 1962.

Harms, E. *Origins of Modern Psychiatry.* Charles C Thomas, Springfield, Ill., 1967.

Harvey, E. R. *The Inward Wits: Psychological Theory in the Middle Ages and the Renaissance.* The Warburg Institute, University of London, London, 1975.

Haslam, J. *Observations on Insanity.* Rivington, London, 1798.

Haslam, J. *Illustrations of Madness.* Hayden, London, 1810.

Haslam, J. *Medical Jurisprudence, as It Relates to Insanity According to the Law of England.* Hunter, London, 1817.

Havens, L. H. *Approaches to the Mind: Movement of the Psychiatric Schools from Sects toward Science.* Little, Brown, and Co., Boston, 1973.

Hawke, D. F. *Benjamin Rush: Revolutionary Gadfly.* Bobbs-Merrill, Indianapolis, 1971.

Hecker, E. Die Hebephrenie. Arch. Pathol. Anat. Physiol. *52:* 76, 1871.

Hecker, J. F. C. The dancing mania. In *The Epidemics of the Middle Ages.* Sydenham Society, London, 1846.

Heinroth, J. C. *Textbook of Disturbances of Mental Life.* Johns Hopkins University Press, Baltimore, 1975.

Hemphill, R. E. Historical witchcraft and psychiatric illness in Western Europe. Proc. Soc. Med., *59:* 891, 1966.

Herodotus. *Histories.* Appleton, New York, 1899.

Hes, J. P., and Wollstein, S. The attitude of the ancient Jewish sources to mental patients. Israel Ann. Psychiatry, *2:* 103, 1964.

Hill, R. G. *A Lecture on the Management of Lunatic Asylums.* Simpkin, Marshall & Co., London, 1839.

Hippocrates. *The Medical Works of Hippocrates.* Blackwell, Oxford, 1950.

The History and Philosophy of Knowledge of the Brain and Its Functions. Blackwell, Oxford, 1958.

Hodgkinson, R. G. Provision for pauper lunatics, 1834-1871. Med. Hist., *10:* 138, 1966.

Hoffmeister, G. Rasis' Traumlehre. Traumbücher des Spätmittelalters. Arch. Kulturgeschichte, *51:* 138, 1969.

Hoffmann, H. *Der Hexen- und Besessenenglaube des 15 und 16: Jahrhunderts im Spiegel des Psychiaters.* Universitätsverlag Ratsbuchhandlung Balberg, Greisfald, 1935.

Holland, N. N. *Psychoanalysis and Shakespeare.* McGraw-Hill, New York, 1964.

Hollingshead, A. B., and Redlich, F. C. *Social Class and Mental Illness: A Community Study.* John Wiley & Sons, New York, 1958.

Holmstedt, B. Historical survey. In *Psychoactive Drugs.* D. Efron, editor, p. 3. United States Government Printing Office, Washington, D.C., 1967.

Horney, K. *The Neurotic Personality of Our Time.* W. W. Norton, New York, 1937.

Howard, J. *An Account of the Principal Lazarettos in Europe.* Warrington, London, 1789.

Howells, J. G., editor. *World History of Psychiatry.* Brunner/Mazel, New York, 1975.

Huang Ti Nei Ching Su Wen. *The Yellow Emperor's Classic of Internal Medicine,* ed. 2. University of California Press, Berkeley, 1966.

Huarte, J. *The Examination of Men's Wits.* Islip, London, 1594.

Hunter, R., and Macalpine, I. *Three Hundred Years of Psychiatry, 1535-1860.* Oxford University Press, London, 1963.

Hurd, H., editor. *The Institutional Care of the Insane in the United States and Canada.* Johns Hopkins University Press, Baltimore, 1914-1917.

Jackson, S. W. Unusual mental states in medieval Europe. I. Medical syndromes of mental disorders: 400-1100 A.D. J. Hist. Med. *27:* 262, 1972.

Jacobi, M. *Beobachtungen über die Pathologie und Therapie der mit Irreseyn verbundenen Krankheiten.* Elberfeld, 1830.

Jacobi, M. *Ueber die Anlegung und Einrichtung von Irren-Heilanstalten.* Berlin, 1834.

Jacobs, H. *Western Psychotherapy and Hindu-Sadhana.* International Universities Press, New York, 1961.

Jaeger, W. *Diokles von Karystos: Die griechische Medizin und die Schule des Aristoteles.* de Druyter, Berlin, 1938.

Janet, P. *Principles of Psychotherapy.* Macmillan, New York, 1924.

Janet, P. *Psychological Healing: A Historical and Clinical Study.* Macmillan, New York, 1925.

Janet, P. *The Major Symptoms of Hysteria.* Hafner Press, New York, 1965.

Jarvis, E. *Insanity and Idiocy in Massachusetts: Report of the Commission on Lunacy, 1855.* Harvard University Press, Cambridge, Mass., 1971.

Jaynes, J. *The Origin of Consciousness in the Breakdown of the Bicameral Mind.* Houghton Mifflin, Boston, 1976.

* Jones, E. *The Life and Work of Sigmund Freud.* Basic Books, New York, 1953-1957.

Jones, K. *A History of Mental Health Services.* Routledge & Kegan Paul, London, 1972.

Jung, C. G. *Commentary to The Secret of the Golden Flower. A Chinese Book of Life.* Harcourt, Brace & World, New York, 1931.

Jung, C. G. *Psychology and Religion.* Yale University Press, New Haven, Conn., 1938.

Jung, C. G. *Memories, Dreams, Reflections.* Pantheon Books, New York, 1961.

Jung, C. G. *C. G. Jung's Letters,* vol. 1. Princeton University Press, Princeton, 1973.

Kahlbaum, K. L. *Catatonia.* Johns Hopkins University Press, Baltimore, 1973.

Kahn, E. The Emil Kraepelin Memorial Lecture. In *Epidemiology of Mental Disorders.* American Association for the Advancement of Science, Washington, D.C., 1959.

Kaiser, W. *Praisers of Folly: Erasmus, Rabelais, Shakespeare.* Harvard University Press, Cambridge, Mass., 1963.

Kalant, O. J. Moreau, hashish, and hallucinations. Int. J. Addict., *6:* 553, 1971.

Kallman, F. J. *Heredity in Health and Mental Disorders.* W. W. Norton, New York, 1953.

Kant, I. *Anthropology from a Pragmatic Point of View.* Martinus Nijhoff, The Hague, 1974.

Kardiner, A., Linton, R., DuBois, C. and West, J., editors. *The Psychological Frontiers of Society.* Columbia University Press, New York, 1945.

Kenny, A. J. P. Mental health in Plato's Republic. Proc. Br. Acad., *55:* 230, 1969.

Kereny, C. *Asklepios: Archetipal Image of the Physician's Existence.* Pantheon Books, New York, 1959.

Kerner, J. *Die Seherin von Prevost.* Cotta, Stuttgart, 1829.

Kiell, N. *Psychoanalysis, Psychology, and Literature: A Bibliography.* University of Wisconsin Press, Madison, 1963.

Klev, A. The study of folk psychiatry. In *Magic, Faith, and Healing.* A, Kiev, editor, p. 3. Free Press of Glencoe, New York, 1964.

Kirchhoff, T. *Deutsche Irrenärzte.* Springer Verlag, Berlin, 1921-1924.

Kirk, G. S., and Raven, J. E. *The Presocratic Philosophers.* Cambridge University Press, Cambridge, 1960.

Kirkbride, T. S. *On the Construction, Organization, and General Arrangements of Hospitals for the Insane.* Lindsay & Blakiston, Philadelphia, 1854.

Klibansky, R., Panofsky, E., and Saxl, F. *Saturn and Melancholy.* Basic Books, New York, 1964.

Kolle, K., editor. *Grosse Nervenarzte.* Thieme, Stuttgart, 1956-1963.

Kornfeld, S. Geschichte der Psychiatric. In *Handbuch der Geschichte der Medizin,* T. Puschmann, editor, p. 601. Fischer, Jena, 1905.

Kors, A. C., and Peters. E. *Witchcraft in Europe, 1100-1700: A Documentary History.* University of Pennsylvania Press, Philadelphia, 1972.

Korsakoff, S. S. Eine psychische Störung combiniert mit multipler Neuritis. Allgemeine Z. Psychiatrie, *46:* 475, 1890.

Kraepelin, E. *Manic-Depressive Insanity and Paranoia.* E. and S. Livingstone, Edinburgh, 1921.

Kraepelin, E. *One Hundred Years of Psychiatry.* Citadel Press, New York, 1962.

Kraepelin, E. *Lectures on Clinical Psychiatry.* Hafner Press, New York, 1968.

Krafft-Ebing, R. *Psychopathia Sexualis.* F. A. Davis, Philadelphia, 1894.

Krapf, E. *Thomas de Aquino y la Psicopatologia.* Index, Buenos Aires, 1943.

Kuhn, T. S. *The Structure of Scientific Revolutions,* ed. 2. University of Chicago Press, Chicago, 1970.

Ladner, G. B. Homo viator: Medieval ideas on alienation and order. Speculum, *42:* 233, 1967.

Lain Entralgo, P. *The Therapy of the Word in Classical Antiquity.* Yale University Press, New Haven, Conn., 1970.

Landis, C., and Mettler, F. A. *Varieties of Psychopathological Experience.* Holt, Rinehart and Winston, New York, 1964.

Langer, W. The next assignment. Am. Hist. Rev., *63:* 283, 1958.

Lassek, A. M. *The Unique Legacy of Doctor Hughlings Jackson.* Charles C Thomas, Springfield, Ill., 1970.

Lavater, J. K. *Essays on Physiognomy, Destined to Promote the Knowledge and Love of Mankind.* Holloway, London, 1789-1798.

Laver, A. B. Precursors of psychology in ancient Egypt. J. Hist. Behav. Sci., *8:* 181, 1972.

Lea, H. C. *Materials toward a History of Witchcraft.* University of Pennsylvania Press, Philadelphia, 1939.

Lee, G. C. *Historical Jurisprudence.* Macmillan, New York, 1922.

Leibbrand, W. Stoiche Reliquien im geschichtlichen Gang der Psychopathologie. Conf. Psychiatrica, *2:* 1, 1959.

Leibbrand, W., and Wettley, A. *Der Wahnsinn: Geschichte der Abandländischen Psychopathologie.* Alber, Freiburg-München, 1961.

Leibbrand, W., and Wettley, A. Die Stellung des Geisteskranken in der Gesellschaft des 19: Jahrhunderts. In *Der Arzt und der Kranke in der Gesellschaft des 19. Jahrhunderts,* W. Artelt and Rüegg, editors. Enke, Stuttgart, 1967.

Leigh, D. *The Historical Development of British Psychiatry,* vol. 1. Pergamon Press, New York, 1961.

Leighton, A. H., and Hughes, J. H. Cultures as causative of mental disorder. In *Causes of Mental Disorders: A Review of Epidemiological Knowledge,* p. 341. Millbank Memorial Fund, New York, 1961.

Lerner, M. *America as a Civilization.* Simon & Schuster, New York, 1957.

Lessa, W. A. Somatomancy: Precursor of the science of human constitution. Sci. Monthly, *75:* 355, 1952.

Levine, M., and Levine, A. *A Social History of Helping Services: Clinic, Court, School, Community.* Appleton-Century-Crofts, New York, 1970.

Lévi-Strauss, C. *The Savage Mind.* University of Chicago Press, Chicago, 1966.

Lewin, L. *Phantastica, Narcotic, and Stimulant Drugs.* Kegan Paul, Trench, and Trubner, London, 1931.

Lewis, O. *Five Families: Mexican Case Studies in the Culture of Poverty.* Basic Books, New York, 1959.

Linton, R. *Culture and Mental Disorders.* Charles C Thomas, Springfield, Ill., 1956.

Lisowski, F. P. Prehistory and early historic trepanation. In *Diseases of Antiquity,* D. Brothwell and A. T. Sandison editors, p. 651. Charles C Thomas, Springfield, Ill., 1967.

Lombroso, C. *L'uomo delinquente.* Bocca, Torino, 1876.

Lombroso, C. *The Man of Genius.* Charles Scribner's Sons, New York, 1889.

Lyons, B. G. *Voices of Melancholy: Studies in Literary Treatments of Melancholy in Renaissance England.* Routledge & Kegan Paul, London, 1971.

Macalpine, I., and Hunter, R. A. *Schizophrenia 1677: A Psychiatric Study of an Illustrated Autobiographical Record of Demoniacal Possession.* Dawson, London, 1956.

Macalpine, I., and Hunter, R. A. *George III and the Mad-Business.* Pantheon Books, New York, 1969.

Mack, J. E. Psychoanalysis and historical biography. J. Am. Psychoanal. Assoc., *19:* 143, 1971.

MacKenzie, N. *Dreams and Dreaming.* Vanguard, New York, 1965.

Magnus Hundt the Elder. *Anthropologium de Hominis Dignitate Natura et Propietatibus.* Manacensis, Leipzig, 1501.

Maimon, S. *Salomon Maimon, with an Essay on Maimon's Philosophy,* Hugo Bergman. East and West Library, London, 1954.

Maimonides, M. *The Guide for the Perplexed.* University of Chicago Press, Chicago, 1963.

Malinowski, B. *Sex and Repression in Savage Society.* Humanities Press, New York, 1927.

Mann, H. *The Life of Horace Mann.* Lee and Shepard, Boston, 1888.

Margetts, E. L. Historical notes on psychosomatic medicine. In *Recent Developments in Psychosomatic Medicine,* E. D. Wittkower and R. A. Cleghorn, editors, p. 41. J. B. Lippincott, Philadelphia, 1954.

Margetts, E. L. Trepanation of the skull by the medicine-men of primitive cultures. In *Diseases in Antiquity,* D. Brothwell and A. T. Sandison, editors. Charles C Thomas, Springfield, Ill. 1967.

Margetts, E. L. African ethnopsychiatry in the field. Can. Psychiatr. Assoc. J., *13:* 521, 1968.

Marshall, H. E. *Dorothea Dix: Forgotten Samaritan.* University of North Carolina Press, Chapel Hill, 1937.

Marwick, M. *Witchcraft and Sorcery: Selected Readings.* Penguin Books, Baltimore, 1970.

Marx, O. Nineteenth-century medical psychology: Theoretical problems in the work of Griesinger, Meynert, and Wernicke. Isis, *61:* 355, 1970.

Maudsley, H. *The Physiology of the Mind.* Macmillan, London, 1867a.

Maudsley, H. *The Pathology of the Mind.* Macmillan, London, 1867b.

Maudsley, H. *Body and Mind.* Macmillan, London, 1870.

May R. The Delphic oracle as therapist. In *The Reach of Mind: Essays in Memory of Kurt Goldstein,* M. L. Simmel, editor, p. 211. Springer, New York, 1968.

Mazlich, B., editor. *Psychoanalysis and History.* Prentice-Hall, Englewood Cliffs, N. J., 1963.

McHenry, L. C., editor. *Garrison's History of Neurology.* Charles C Thomas, Springfield, Ill., 1969.

McReynolds, P. Historical antecedents of personality assessment. In *Advances in Psychological Assessment,* vol. 3. Jossey-Bass, San Francisco, 1975.

Meier, C. A. *Ancient Incubation and Modern Psychotherapy.* Northwestern University Press, Evanston, Ill., 1967.

Mendelsohn, E. Physical models and physiological concepts: Explanations in nineteenth century biology. In *Boston Studies in the Philosophy of Science,* R. S. Cohen and M. W. Wartofsky, editors. Humanities Press, New York, 1965.

Menninger, K., Ellenberger, H., and Pruyser. P. The unitary concept of mental illness. Bull. Menninger Clin., *22:* 4, 1958.

Mesmer F. A. *Mesmerism.* MacDonald, London, 1948.

Meynert, T. *Psychiatry. A Clinical Treatise on Diseases of the Fore-Brain Based upon a Study of Its Structure, Functions, and Nutrition.* Hafner Press, New York, 1968.

Middleton, J., editor. *Magic, Witchcraft, and Curing.* Natural History Press, Garden City, N. Y., 1967.

Miller, J., editor. *Freud: The Man, His World, His Influence.* Little, Brown, and Co., Boston, 1972.

Mishra, R. S. *The Textbook of Yoga Psychology.* Julian Press, New York, 1963.

Misiak, H., and Sexton, V. S. *History of Psychology.* Grune & Stratton, New York, 1966.

Misiak, H., and Saxton, V. S. *Phenomenology, Existentialism, and Humanistic Psychologies: A Historical Survey.* Grune & Stratton, New York, 1973.

Mitchell, S. W. Address before the 50th annual meeting. J. Nerv. Ment. Dis., *21:* 413, 1894.

Monro, J. *Remarks on Dr. Battie's Treatise on Madness.* Dawson, London, 1962.

Mora, G. Vincenzo Chiarugi (1759–1820) and his psychiatric reforms in the late 18th century. J. Hist. Med., *14:* 424, 1959a.

Mora, G. Pietro Pisani and the mental hospital of Palermo in the early 19th century. Bull. Hist. Med., *33:* 230, 1959b.

Mora, G. On the 400th anniversary of Johann Weyer's "De Praestigiis Daemonum." Am. J. Psychiatry, *120:* 417, 1963.

Mora, G. One hundred years from Lombroso's first essay "Genius and Insanity." Am. J. Psychiatry, *121:* 562, 1964.

Mora, G. Paracelsus' psychiatry: On the occasion of the 400th anniversary of his book *Diseases That Deprive Man of His Reason* (1567). Am. J. Psychiatry, *124:* 803, 1967.

Mora, G. Introduction. In *New Directions of American Psychiatry, 1944–1968,* p. vii. American Psychiatric Association, Washington, D.C., 1969.

Mora, G. The history of psychiatry: Its relevance for the psychiatrist. Am. J. Psychiatry, *126:* 957, 1970.

Mora, G. On the bicentenary of the birth of Esquirol (1772–1840), the first complete psychiatrist. Am. J. Psychiatry, *129:* 562, 1972.

Mora, G. Introduction. In *Catatonia,* K. L. Kahlbaum. Johns Hopkins University Press, Baltimore, 1973.

Mora, G. Introduction. In *Textbook of Disturbances of Mental Life,* J. C. Heinroth. Johns Hopkins University Press, Baltimore, 1975.

Mora, G. Dynamic psychiatry: Historical review. In *International Encyclopedia of Psychiatry, Psychology, Psychoanalysis, and Neurology,* B. B. Wolman, editor. D. Van Nostrand, New York, 1977a.

Mora, G. Juan Huarte: The examination of men's wits (1575). J. Hist. Behav. Sci., *13:* 67, 1977b.

Mora, G. Thomas Aquinas and modern psychology: A reassessment. Psychoanal. Rev., *64:* 495, 1977c.

Mora, G. French ideology at the dawn of the American nation: Cabanis and Jefferson on psychology and mental health. In *Historical Explorations in Medicine and Psychiatry,* H. Riese, editor. Springer, New York, 1978.

Mora, G. Mind-body concepts in the Middle Ages. I. The classical background and its merging with the Judeo-Christian tradition in the early Middle Ages. J. Hist. Behav. Sci., *14:* 344, 1978b.

Mora, G., and Brand, J., editors. *Psychiatry and Its History.* Charles C Thomas, Springfield, Ill., 1970.

Moreau, J. J. *Hashish and Mental Illness.* Raven Press, New York, 1973.

Morel, B. A. *Traité des dégénéréscences physiques, intellectuelles et morales de l'espèce humaine.* Baillière, Paris, 1857.

Moritz, K. P. *Anton Reiser.* Berlin, 1785–1790.

Muniz, M. A., and McGee, W. J. Primitive trephining in Peru. In *16th Annual Report of the Bureau of American Ethnology for 1894–95,* p. 3. Washington, D.C., 1897.

Murphy, G., and Murphy, L. B. *Asian Psychology.* Basic Books, New York, 1968.

Murray, M., and Wax, R. The notion of magic. Curr. Anthropol., *4:* 495, 1963.

Murray, M. A. *The Witch-Cult in Western Europe: A Study in Anthropology.* Clarendon Press, Oxford, 1921.

Nardi, M. G. Marsino Ficino, medico. Minerva Med., *43:* 898, 1952.

Nelson, B., editor. *Freud and the 20th Century.* Meridian Books, New York, 1957.

Nelson, B. Self-images and systems of spiritual directions in the history of European civilization. In *The Quest for Self-control: Classical Philosophies and Scientific Research,* S. Z. Klausner, editor, p. 49. Free Press of Glencoe, New York, 1965.

Neuburger, M. British and German psychiatry in the second half of the eighteenth and the early nineteenth century. Bull. Hist. Med., *18:* 121, 1945.

Nietzsche, F. W. *The Birth of Tragedy.* Doubleday, Garden City, N. Y., 1956.

North, E. *Sophrosyne: Self-knowledge and Self-restraint in Greek Literature.* Cornell University Press, Ithaca, N. Y., 1966.

Nunberg, H., and Federn, E., editors. *Minutes of the Vienna Psychoanalytic Society.* International Universities Press, New York, 1962–1974.

Oberndorf, C. P. *A History of Psychoanalysis in America.* Grune & Stratton, New York, 1953.

Obeyesekere, G. Ayurveda and mental illness. Comp. Stud. Soc. Hist., *12:* 292, 1970.

Obeyesekere, G. The theory and practice of psychological medicine in the Ayurvedic tradition. Culture, Med. Psychiatry, *1:* 155, 1977.

O'Donoghue, E. G. *The Story of Bethlehem Hospital.* Fisher Unwin, London, 1914.

Onians, R. B. *The Origins of European Thought about the Body, the Mind, the Soul, the World, Time, and Faith.* Cambridge University Press, Cambridge, England, 1951.

Opler, M. *Culture, Psychiatry and Human Values.* Charles C Thomas, Springfield, Ill., 1956.

Oppenheim, A. L. The interpretation of dreams in the ancient Near East. Trans. Am. Philos. Soc., *46:* 179, 1956.

Orgler, H. *Alfred Adler: The Man and His Work.* Liveright, New York, 1963.

Osler, W. *The Evolution of Modern Medicine.* Yale University Press, New Haven, Conn., 1922.

Padovani, G. "L'hospidale de' pazzi incurabili" di Tommaso Garzoni. Rass. Studi Psichiatrici, *38:* 217, 1949.

Palmai, G., and Blackwell, B. The Burghölzli centenary. Med. Hist., *10:* 257, 1966.

Paniague, J. A. La psicoterapia en las obras médicas de Arnau de Vilanova. Arch. Iberoam. Hist. Med., *15:* 3, 1963.

Paracelsus. The diseases that deprive man of his reason. In *Four Treatises of Theophrastus von Hohenheim Called Paracelsus,* p. 127. Johns Hopkins University Press, 1941.

Parchappe, J. B. M. *Des principes à suivre dans la fondation et la contruction des asiles d'aliénés.* Baillière, Paris, 1853.

Parry-Jones, W. L. *The Trade Lunacy: A Study of Private Madhouses in England in the Eighteenth and Nineteenth Centuries.* Routledge & Kegan Paul, London, 1972.

Patanjali. *The Yoga System of Patanjali.* Harvard University Press, Cambridge, Mass., 1927.

Pausanias. *Pausanias' Description of Greece.* Macmillan, London, 1913.

Perfect, W. *Methods of Cure in Some Particular Cases of Insanity and Nervous Disorders.* London, 1778.

Pfister, O. Instructive psychoanalysis among the Navahos. J. Nerv. Ment. Dis., *76:* 251, 1932.

Philostratus. Lives of the Sophists. In *Philostratus and Eunapias,* p. 214. Harvard University Press, Cambridge, Mass., 1952.

Pinel, P. *A Treatise on Insanity.* Hafner Press, New York, 1962.

Pinel, S. *Physiologie de l'homme aliéné.* Paris, 1833.

Pinero, J. M. L., and Meseguer, J. M. M. *Neurosis y Psicoterapia: Un Estudio Historico.* Espasa-Calpe, Madrid, 1970.

Plato. *The Collected Dialogues.* Pantheon Books, New York, 1961.

Podolsky, S. Skull surgery by prehistoric man. Med. Ann. D. C., *31:* 268, 409, 1962.

Policier, Y. *Histoire de la psychiatrie.* Presses Universitaires de France, Paris, 1971.

Popov, A. *Materialy dlja Bibliografi Russkoj Literatury po Izuceniju Samanstva.* Leningrad, 1932.

Poynter, F. N. L. *The History and Philosophy of Knowledge of the Brain and Its Functions.* Blackwell, Oxford, 1958.

Prévost, C. M. *La psycho-philosophie de Pierre Janet.* Payot, Paris, 1973.

Pribram, K. H., and Gill, M. M. *Freud's "Project" Re-assessed.* Basic Books, New York, 1976.

Prichard, J. C. *A Treatise on Insanity and Other Disorders Affecting the Mind.* Sherwood, Gilber & Piper, London, 1835.

Pruyser, P. Appendix. In *The Vital Balance,* K. Menninger, p 419. Viking Press, New York, 1963.

Purcell, J. *A Treatise of Vapours, or Hysterick Fits.* London, 1702.

Quen, J. M., and Carlson, E. T., editors. *American Psychoanalysis: Origins and Development.* Brunner/Mazel, New York, 1978.

Rank, G. Shamanism as a research subject. In *Studies in Shamanism,* C. M. Edsman, editor, p. 15. Amquist & Wiksell, Stockholm, 1967.

Rao, A. V. Some ancient Indian concepts of mind, insanity and mental hygiene. Ind. J. Hist. Medi., *9:* 13, 1964.

Rather, L. J. *Mind and Body in the Eighteenth Century Medicine: A Study Based on Jerome Gaub's "De Regimine Mentis."* University of California Press, Berkeley, 1965.

Rausky, F. *Mesmer ou la révolution thérapeutique.* Payot, Paris, 1977.

Ray, I. Ideal characters of the officers of a hospital for the insane. Am. J. Insanity, *30:* 64, 1873.

Ray, I. *A Treatise on the Medical Jurisprudence of Insanity.* Harvard University Press, Cambridge, Mass., 1962.

Ray, I. *Mental Hygiene.* Hafner Press, New York, 1968.

Regolamento dei Regi Spedali di Santa Maria Nuova e di Bonifazio. Cambiagi, Firenze, 1789.

Reich, O. *Wilhelm Reich: A Personal Biography.* St. Martin's Press, New York, 1969.

Reil, J. C. *Rhapsodien über die Anwendung der Psychischen Curmethode auf Geisterzerrüttungen.* Halle, 1803.

Rhode, E. *Psyche: The Cult of Souls and Belief in Immortality among the Greeks.* Kegan Paul, Trench and Trubner, London, 1925.

Ridenour, N. *Mental Health in the United States: A Fifty-Year History.* Harvard University Press, Cambridge, Mass., 1961.

Riese, W. *A History of Neurology.* MD Publications, New York, 1959.

Riese, W. The pre-Freudian origins of psychoanalysis. In *Science and Psychoanalysis,* J. Masserman, editor, vol. 1, p. 29. Grune & Stratton, New York, 1962.

Riese, W. *La théorie des passions à la lumière de la pensée médicale du XVII Siecle.* S. Karger, New York, 1965.

Riese, W. *The Legacy of Philippe Pinel.* Springer, New York, 1969.

Rivari, E. *La mente di Girolamo Cardano.* Zanichelli, Bologna, 1906.

Roazen, P. *Brother Animal: The Story of Freud and Tausk.* Alfred A. Knopf, New York, 1969.

Roazen, P. *Freud and His Followers.* Alfred A. Knopf, New York, 1971.

Roback, A. A., and Kiernan, T. *Pictorial History of Psychology and Psychiatry.* Philosophical Library, New York, 1969.

Robbins, R. H. *Encyclopedia of Witchcraft and Demonology.* Crown, New York, 1959.

Robert, M. *The Psychoanalytic Revolution: Sigmund Freud's Life and Achievement.* Harcourt, Brace and World, New York, 1966.

Robinson, P. A. *The Freudian Left: Wilhelm Reich, Geza Róheim, Herbert Marcuse.* Harper & Row, New York, 1969.

Robinson, T. M. *Plato's Psychology.* University of Toronto Press, Toronto, 1970.

Rorschach, E. *Psychodiagnostik.* Bircher, Bern, 1921.

Rosen, G. The philosophy of ideology and the emergence of modern medicine in France. Bull. Hist. Med., *20:* 328, 1946.

Rosen, G. *Madness in Society: Chapters in the Historical Sociology of Mental Illness.* University of Chicago Press, Chicago, 1968.

Rosenberg, C. The place of George M. Beard in nineteenth century psychiatry. Bull. Hist. Med., *36:* 245, 1962.

Ross, N. W. *Three Ways of Asian Wisdom.* Simon and Schuster, New York, 1966.

Rossi, A. M. Some pre-World War II antecedents of community mental health theory and practice. Ment. Hyg., *46:* 78, 1962.

Rothman, D. J. *The Discovery of the Asylum: Social Order and Disorder in the New Republic.* Little, Brown, and Co., Boston, 1971.

Ruitenbeek, H. M., editor. *Freud as We Knew Him.* Wayne State University Press, Detroit, 1973.

Rumbaut, R. D. The first psychiatric hospital of the Western world. Am. J. Psychiatry, *128:* 1305, 1972.

Rush, B. *The Selected Writings of Benjamin Rush,* D. D. Runes, editor. Philosophical Library, New York, 1947.

Rush, B. *The Autobiography of Benjamin Rush,* G. W. Corner, editor. Princeton University Press, Princeton, 1948.

Rush, B. *Medical Inquiries and Observations upon the Diseases of the Mind.* Hafner Press, New York, 1962.

Rush, B. *Two Essays on the Mind.* Brunner/Mazel, New York, 1972.

Russell, J. B. *Witchcraft in the Middle Ages.* Cornell University Press, Ithaca, N. Y., 1972.

Sackler, A. M. *The Great Physiodynamic Therapies in Psychiatry.* Harper, New York, 1956.

Sarton, G. *Introduction to the History of Science,* vol. 1. Williams & Wilkins, Baltimore, 1927.

Sauri, J. J. *Historia de la ideas psiquiatricas.* Lohle, Buenos Aires, 1969.

Schipperges, H. Zur Psychologie und Psychiatrie des Petrus Hispanus. Confin. Psychiatr., *4:* 137, 1961a.

Schipperges, H. Der Narr und sein Humanum im islamischen Mittelalter. Gesnerus, *18:* 1, 1961b.

Schmidbauer, W. *Psychotherapie: Ihr Weg von der Magie zur Wissenschaft.* Nymphenburger, München, 1971.

Schneck, J. M. *A History of Psychiatry.* Charles C Thomas, Springfield, Ill., 1960.

Schreber, D. P. *Memories of My Nervous Illness.* Dawson, London, 1955.

Schur, M. *Freud: Living and Dying.* International Universities Press, New York, 1972.

Schweitzer, A. *The Quest of the Historical Jesus.* A. & C. Black, London, 1910.

Scot, R. *Discovery of Witchcraft.* London, 1584.

Sechehaye, M. *Autobiography of a Schizophrenic Girl.* Grune & Stratton, New York, 1968.

Sechenov, I. *Selected Works of Sechenov.* State Publishing House of Biological Medical Literature, Moscow, 1935.

The Secret of the Golden Flower: A Chinese Book of Life. Harcourt, Brace and World, New York, 1931.

Seguin, E. O. *Idiocy and Its Treatment by the Physiological Method.* Wood, New York, 1866.

Semélaigne, A. *Etudes historiques sur l'aliénation mentale dans l'antiquité.* Asselin, Paris, 1869.

Semelaigne, R. *Alienistes et philantropes: Les Pinel et les Tuke.* Steinheil, Paris, 1912.

Semelaigne, R. *Les Pionners de la psychiatrie française avant et après Pinel.* Baillière, Paris, 1930–1932.

Sexton, V. S., and Misiak, H., editors. *Historical Perspectives in Psychology: Readings.* Brooks/Cole, Belmont, Calif., 1971.

Shakow, D., and Rapaport, D. *The Influence of Freud on American Psychology.* International Universities Press, New York, 1964.

Siegel, R. E. *Galen on Psychology, Psychopathology, and Function and Diseases of the Nervous System.* S. Karger, New York, 1973.

Simon, B. *Mind and Madness in Ancient Greece: The Classical Roots of Modern Psychiatry.* Cornell University Press, Ithaca, N. Y., 1978.

Simon, B., and Weiner, H. Models of mind and mental illness in ancient Greece. J. Hist. Behav. Sci., *2:* 303, 1966; *8:* 389, 1972; *9:* 3, 1973.

Snell, B. *The Discovery of the Mind.* Harvard University Press, Cambridge, Mass., 1953.

Soldan-Heppe. *Geschichte der Hexenprozesse.* Müller, München, 1912.

Souques, A. *Etapes de la neurologie dans l'antiquité grècque.* Masson, Paris, 1936.

Spehlmann, R. *Sigmund Freud's Neurologischen Schriften: Eine Untersuchung zur Vorgeschichte der Psychoanalyse.* Springer Verlag, Berlin, 1953.

Spitzka, E. C. *Insanity: Its Classification, Diagnosis, and Treatment.* Bermingham, New York, 1883.

Sprenger, J., and Kramer, H. *Malleus Maleficarum*. Rodker, London, 1928.

Srole, L., Langner, T. S., Opler, M. K., and Rennie, T. A. C. *Mental Health in the Metropolis*. McGraw Hill, New York, 1962.

St. Augustine. *Confessions*, p. 9. Fathers of the Church, New York, 1953.

Staehelin, J. E. Zur Geschichte der Psychiatrie des Islams. Schweiz. Med. Wochenschr., *87:* 1151, 1957.

Stainbrook, E. The use of electricity in psychiatric treatment during the nineteenth century. Bull. Hist. Med., *22:* 156, 1948.

Stainbrook, E. Psychosomatic medicine in the nineteenth century. Psychosom. Med., *14:* 211, 1952.

Stern, M. B. *Heads and Headlines: The Phrenological Fowlers*. University of Oklahoma Press, Norman, 1971.

Sterns, E. Isaac Ray: Psychiatrist and pioneer in forensic psychiatry. Am. J. Psychiatry, *101:* 573, 1945.

Stewart, W. A. *Psychoanalysis: The First Ten Years, 1888–1898*. Macmillan, New York, 1967.

Stocking, G. W. On the limits of "presentism" and "historicism" in the historiography of the behavioral sciences. J. Hist. Behav. Sci., *1:* 211, 1965.

Swain, B. *Fools and Folly during the Middle Ages and Renaissance*. Columbia University Press, New York, 1932.

Szasz, T. S. *The Age of Madness: The History of Involuntary Mental Hospitalization Presented in Selected Texts*. Doubleday, Garden City, N. Y., 1973.

Taft, J. *Otto Rank*. Julian Press, New York, 1958.

Tanfani, G. Le conoscenze neurologiche al tempo di Pietro d'Abano. G. Psichiatr. Neuropatol., *62:* 180, 1934.

Temkin, O. Gall and the phrenological movement. Bull. Hist. Med., *21:* 275, 1947.

Temkin, O. Basic science, medicine, and the romantic era. Bull. Hist. Med., *37:* 97, 1963.

Temkin, O. The history of classification in the medical sciences. In *The Role and Methodology of Classification in Psychiatry and Psychopathology*, M. J. Katz, J. O. Cole, and W. E. Barton, editors, p. 11. Department of Health, Education, and Welfare, Washington, D.C., 1968.

Temkin, O. *The Falling Sickness: A History of Epilepsy from the Greeks to the Beginnings of Modern Neurology*, ed. 2. Johns Hopkins University Press, Baltimore, 1971.

Theophrastus, *The Character Sketches*. Kent State University Press, Kent, Ohio, 1970.

Thorndike, L. *Michael Scot*. Nelson, London, 1965.

Tiffany, F. *Life of Dorothea Lynde Dix*. Houghton Mifflin, Boston, 1890.

Tinterow, M. M. *Foundations of Hypnosis, from Mesmer to Freud*. Charles C Thomas, Springfield, Ill., 1970.

Tissot, S. A. A. D. *Traité des nerfs et de leurs maladies*. Lausanne, Paris, 1778–1780.

Torrey, E. F. *The Mind Game: Witch Doctors and Psychiatrists*. Emerson Hall, New York, 1972.

Tourney, G. A history of therapeutic fashions in psychiatry, 1800–1966. Am. J. Psychiatry, *124:* 784, 1967.

Tourney, G. History of biological psychiatry in America. Am. J. Psychiatry, *126:* 29, 1969.

Tourney, G. Psychiatric therapies: 1880–1968. In *Changing Patterns in Psychiatric Care*, T. Rothman, editor, p. 3. Crown, New York, 1970.

Trélat, L. A. *La folie lucide etudiée et considérée au point de vue de la famille et de la société*. Paris, 1861.

Tseng, W. The concept of personality in Confucian thought. Psychiatry, *36:* 191, 1973.

Tuke, H., editor. *A Dictionary of Psychological Medicine*. J. & A. Churchill, London, 1892.

Tuke, S. *Description of the Retreat*. Dawson, London, 1964.

Veith, I. Psychiatric thought in Chinese medicine. J. Hist. Med., *10:* 261, 1955.

Veith, I. Psychiatric nosology: From Hippocrates to Freud. Am. J. Psychiatry, *114:* 385, 1957.

Veith, I. The supernatural in Far Eastern concepts of mental disease. Bull. Hist. Med., *37:* 139, 1963.

Veith, I. *Hysteria: The History of a Disease*. University of Chicago Press, Chicago, 1965.

Venkoba Rao, A. Some ancient Indian concepts of mind, insanity, and mental hygiene. Indian J. Hist. Med. *2:* 13, 1964.

Vié, J. *Les aliénés et les correctionnaires à Saint-Lazare au XVIIe et au XVIIIe siècles*. Alcan, Paris, 1930.

Vives, J. L. *On Poor Relief*. New York School of Philanthropy, New York, 1917.

Vives, J. L. Tratado del alma. In *Obras Completas*. Aguilar, Madrid, 1948.

Voisin, F. *De l'Idiotie chez les enfants*. Paris, 1843.

von Feuchtersleben, E. *The Principles of Medical Psychology*. Sydenham Society, London, 1847.

von Grunebaum, G. E., and Caillois, R., editors. *The Dream in Human Societies*. University of California Press, Berkeley, 1966.

von Schubert, G. H. *Die Symbolik des Traumes*. Brockhaus, Leipzig, 1814.

Walker, N. *A Short History of Psychotherapy*. Routledge & Kegan Paul, London, 1957.

Walmsley, D. M. *Anton Mesmer*. Hale, London, 1967.

Walter, R. D. S. *Weir Mitchell, M. D., Neurologist: A Medical Biography*. Charles C Thomas, Springfield, Ill., 1970.

Watson, R. I. Psychology: A prescriptive science. Am. Psychol., *22:* 435, 1967.

Watson, R. I. *Eminent Contributors to Psychology: A Bibliography of Primary References*. Springer, New York, 1974, 1976.

Watson, R. I. *The History of Psychology and the Behavioral Sciences: A Bibliographical Guide*. Springer, New York, 1978.

Watts, A. W. *Psychotherapy East and West*. Pantheon Books, New York, 1961.

Wedeck, H. E. *Love Potions through the Ages*. Citadel Press, New York, 1963.

Wehr, G. *Portrait of Jung: An Illustrated Biography*. Herder & Herder, New York, 1971.

Wendell, B. *Cotton Mather: The Puritan Priest*. Harcourt, Brace and World, New York, 1963.

Wenzel, S. *The Sin of Sloth: Acedia in Medieval Thought and Literature*. University of North Carolina Press, Chapel Hill, 1960.

Wernicke, C. *Der aphasische Symptomkomplex*. Weigert, Breslau, 1874.

Westphal, C. Ueber Zwangsvorstellungen. Berl. Klin. Wochenschr., *14:* 346, 1877.

Wertheimer, M. *A Brief History of Psychology*. Holt, Rinehart and Winston, New York, 1970.

Weyer, J. *Histories, Disputes, et Discours*. Delahayet et Lecrosnier, Paris, 1885.

Weyer, J. *De Praestigiis Daemonum*. Bonset, Amsterdam, 1967.

White, W. *The Autobiography of a Purpose*. Doubleday, Garden City, N. Y., 1938.

Whiting, J. W. M., and Child, I. L. *Child Training and Personality: A Cross-cultural Study*. Yale University Press, New Haven, Conn., 1953.

Whitwell, J. R. *Historical Notes on Psychiatry*. Lewis, London, 1936.

Whyte, L. *The Unconscious before Freud*. Basic Books, New York, 1960.

Whytt, R. *Observations on the Nature, Causes, and Cure of Those Disorders Which Have Been Commonly Called Hypochondriac, or Hysteric*. Edinburgh, 1765.

Wilson, J. V. K. Mental diseases of ancient Mesopotamia. In *Diseases of Antiquity*. D. Brothwell and A. T. Sandison, editors, p. 723. Charles C Thomas, Springfield, Ill., 1967.

Wolman, B., editor. *The Psychoanalytic Interpretation of History*. Basic Books, New York, 1971.

Woods, R. L., and Greenhouse, H. B., editors. *The World of Dreams*. Macmillan, New York, 1974.

Wyckhoff, J. *Wilhelm Reich: Life Force Explorer*. Fawcett, Greenwich, Conn., 1973.

Wyss, D. *Depth Psychology: A Critical History*. W. W. Norton, New York, 1966.

The Yi King (Book of Changes), Sacred Book of the East. vol. XVI. Oxford, 1899.

Young, R. M. *Mind, Brain, and Adaptation in the Nineteenth Century: Cerebral Localization and Its Biological Context from Gall to Ferrier*. Clarendon Press, Oxford, 1970.

Zacchia P. *Quaestiones Medico-Legales*. Roma, 1621–1635.

Zakopoulos, A. N. *Plato on Man*. Philosophical Library, New York, 1975.

Zilboorg, G. *The Medical Man and the Witch during the Renaissance*. Johns Hopkins University Press, Baltimore, 1935.

* Zilboorg, G. *A History of Medical Psychology*. W. W. Norton, New York, 1941.

1.2   General Living Systems Theory

JAMES GRIER MILLER, M.D., Ph.D.

Introduction

General systems theory asserts that the universe is composed of a hierarchy of concrete systems, defined as accumulations of matter and energy organized into coacting, interrelated subsystems or components and existing in a common space-time continuum. General living systems theory is concerned with a subset of all such systems, the living systems (Miller, 1965 a, b, c; 1971 a, b, c; 1972, 1973; 1975; 1976; 1978). It provides a conceptual framework within which the content of biological and social sciences can be logically integrated with that of the physical sciences. It seeks to eliminate the firm disciplinary boundaries that obscure the orderly relationships among parts of the real world and lead many to overlook their shared characteristics. In the field of psychiatry, it provides a new resolution of the mind-matter dilemma, a new integration of biological and social approaches to the nature of human beings, and a new approach to psychopathology, diagnosis, and therapy.

Basic Concepts

SYSTEM

The term "system" has a number of meanings that are often confused. The most general definition is: A system is a set of units with relationships among them. The state of each unit is constrained by the state of other units. A conceptual system has, as units, terms such as words, numbers, and other symbols, including those in computer programs. The relationships of the units in a conceptual system are expressed by words or by logical or mathematical symbols. A concrete system, except the least complex ones, is composed of multiple constituent units that are themselves systems at a lower level. Such systems are studied by physical and biological scientists, engineers, and some social scientists and psychiatrists. Abstracted systems are often topics of study by psychoanalysts, personologists, and social scientists. The units of such systems are relationships abstracted or selected by an observer in the light of his interests. Human beings are viewed as having such relationships. Statements about abstracted systems can be transformed into statements about concrete systems.

LEVEL

The universe contains a hierarchy of systems, each more advanced or higher level made of systems of lower levels. Atoms are composed of particles, molecules of atoms, crystals and organelles of molecules. Above the level of crystallizing viruses, like the tobacco mosaic virus, the subset of living systems begins. Viruses are necessarily parasitic on cells, so cells are the lowest level of living systems. Cells are composed of atoms, molecules, and multimolecular organelles; organs are composed of cells aggregated into tissues; organisms of organs; groups—for example, herds, flocks, families, teams, and tribes—of organisms; organizations of groups and sometimes single individual organisms; societies of organizations, groups, and individuals; and supranational systems of societies and organizations. Higher levels of systems may be of mixed composition, living and nonliving. They include ecological systems, planets, solar systems, galaxies, and so forth (Watt, 1973; Emlen, 1973).

This section, in presenting general living systems theory, is limited to the subset of concrete living systems—cells, organs, organisms, groups, organizations, societies, and supranational systems.

TYPE

If a number of individual living systems have similar characteristics, they are often classed together as a type. Types are abstractions made by an observer. Agricultural societies, for example, may be contrasted with industrial societies or primitive societies contrasted with advanced societies. Free-living cells may be considered a type, as opposed to those that are aggregated into the tissues of organisms. Species is also an abstraction. It is similar in meaning to type but is usually restricted to living systems at cell and organism levels so closely related genetically that individuals can interbreed.

SUPRASYSTEM

Any living system's suprasystem is the next higher system in which it is a component or subsystem. For example, the suprasystem of a cell or tissue is the organ it is in; the suprasystem of an organism is the group it is in at the time. The suprasystem is differentiated from the environment. The immediate environment is the suprasystem minus the system itself. The entire environment includes the systems at all higher levels that contain the suprasystem.

COMPONENT OR SUBSYSTEM

Components, sometimes called members or parts, of a system are the structures of which it is composed. Its subsystems are defined by the processes they carry out. The totality of all the parts in a system that carry out a particular process is a subsystem.

MATTER-ENERGY, INFORMATION, AND MEANING

Besides the concepts of matter and energy, which are used in the same senses as they are in the physical sciences, the term "information" is basic to general systems theory. Matter and energy are referred to here as "matter-energy" except when one or the other is specifically intended. The term "information" is used as it appears in communications theory, in which it refers to the amount of complexity, patterning, or organization in a signal or message. The statistical measure of information can also be used to measure the complexity of a system. Information is not equivalent to meaning, although the concepts are closely related. The meaning of an information transmission is the change it brings about in a receiver, either overtly or in his or her internal processes.

OPEN AND CLOSED SYSTEMS

Both living and nonliving systems are more or less open systems. They exchange certain sorts of inputs and outputs of matter-energy and information across their boundaries. Closed systems, with completely impermeable boundaries, do not occur, although some boundaries, like the outer coverings of encysted spores and the lead shielding of an atomic reactor, are highly impermeable.

Living systems are much more open than are nonliving systems. Unlike nonliving systems, living systems are able to maintain their steady states and repair themselves by taking in inputs of matter-energy higher in complexity or organization or lower in entropy than their outputs. Thus, they are able to combat for varying periods of time the entropy to which all systems are subject.

CROSS-LEVEL IDENTITIES

That important uniformities can be generalized about across all levels of living systems is not surprising. All are composed of comparable compounds of carbon—organic molecules. Most important, they all contain a score of amino acids organized into proteins, which are produced in nature only in living systems. All are equipped to live in a water-oxygen world, rather than, for example, on the methane and ammonia planets so dear to science fiction. Also, they are all adapted only to environments in which the physical variables—like temperature, hydration, pressure, and radiation—remain within relatively narrow ranges. Moreover, they all presumably have arisen from the same primordial genes or DNA template, diversified by evolutionary change.

Perhaps the most convincing argument for the plausibility of cross-level generalization derives from analysis of the evolutionary development of living systems. Although increasingly complex types of living systems have evolved at a given level, followed by higher levels with even greater complexity, certain basic necessities did not change. All those systems, if they were to survive in their environment, had to carry out, by some means or other, the same vital subsystem processes. Free-living cells like protozoans carry out those processes with relative simplicity, but the corresponding processes are more complex in multicellular organisms like mammals and even more complex at higher levels.

SHRED-OUT

The increase in complexity came about by a process of shred-out. It is as if each strand of a many-stranded rope had unraveled progressively into more and more pieces. Shred-out is a process of progressive division of labor, differentiation, or specialization of function of each subsystem from the least to the most advanced level of a living system. Every one of the 19 critical subsystem processes that must be performed by all living systems, or that must be performed for them by some other system, was essential for the continuation of life at every point in that evolution. If any one of those subsystems had failed to appear in a generation of any type of system, such systems would have been eliminated.

Shred-out is illustrated in Figure 1, which shows generalized living systems at each level, from cell to supranational system, and which indicates that the 19 subsystems appear at each level with increasing complexity. The approximate number of years since each level evolved and the approximate size of typical systems at each level are also shown.

EMERGENTS

The more complex systems at higher levels have characteristics that cannot be described only in terms used for their lower level subsystems and components without neglecting significant aspects of those systems. Such characteristics are emergents. Life itself, for instance, emerged at the level of the cell. The ability to adjust to more and severer stresses by pooling resources among the cells of a multicellular organ emerged at the organ level. At the organism level, with the evolution of human beings, the capacity to use symbolic language emerged. Groups developed the ability to perform motor activities and to make artifacts beyond the capacity of a single organism. Above that level, emergents include new forms of social organization.

STRUCTURE AND PROCESS

Each living system, as well as each of its subsystems, has two aspects: structure and process. "Structure" is used straightforwardly in the biological sciences to refer to the arrangement of a system's subsystems and components in three-dimensional space at a given moment of time. That is its meaning in general systems theory. In the social sciences, however, there is confusion as to what structure means. It is well to keep in mind that structure, even in a relatively stable system like an organism,

can change rapidly, so it must always be studied as of a given moment, as if time stood still and process were arrested.

DISPERSAL

Subsystem processes are not necessarily limited to a single component but may be dispersed into a number of components. At the level of the organism, for example, an organ that is a subsystem of a complex animal may include several spatially separate components. Conversely, a single structure, like the pancreas, may have components that perform parts of more than one subsystem process. Processes can, on occasion, be dispersed to other systems, living or nonliving, at the same, a higher, or a lower level. Nonliving systems that carry out such processes are manufactured artifacts, called prostheses, machines, or technology.

Table I lists the critical subsystems whose processes every living system must have if it is to survive. The subsystems can be classified into those involved in the metabolism of matter-energy (the left column), those involved in the metabolism of information (the right column), and those involved in both metabolisms (crossing both columns). The order in which the subsystems are listed is meaningful, indicating the commonest sequence followed by the processes that make up the metabolism of matter-energy or of information. In the table, a given subsystem in one column carries out processes analogous to those of any subsystem that appears opposite to it on the same line in the other column.

SUBSYSTEMS THAT PROCESS BOTH MATTER-ENERGY AND INFORMATION

Reproducer. This subsystem is capable of giving rise to other systems similar to the one in which it is found. The reproducing process at all levels involves the transmission of information—the blueprint, template, or charter of the new system—and the organization of matter-energy to compose the new system. At the level of the organism, the fundamental process is the combining of the genetic information of the parents, in sexual species, into the zygote. Other processes aid in achieving that union and support the new system until it becomes independent. Those processes include courtship, nesting, and care of the young.

Among animals, the following components all together constitute the structure of the reproducer: the male and/or female genitalia and sex glands, with the eggs and the sperm that they contain and their accessory structures, as well as the endocrine, neural, and motor components associated with them; a variety of other structures—which may or may not be present, depending on the species and the sex of the organism—such as lacteal glands, breasts, nipples, marsupial pouches, and other sex-specific structures, like antlers, colored feathers, and wattles.

The family, a genetically based group, has as its reproducer a mating dyad that, by reproducing new organisms and caring for them over a period of time, founds a new family. Other sorts of groups and systems at levels above the group have as their fundamental reproductive event the transmission of information that provides an implicit or explicit charter for a newly forming system.

A line separates the reproducer subsystem from the other subsystems in Table I to signify that, among the critical subsystems, the reproducer is the only one not necessary for the

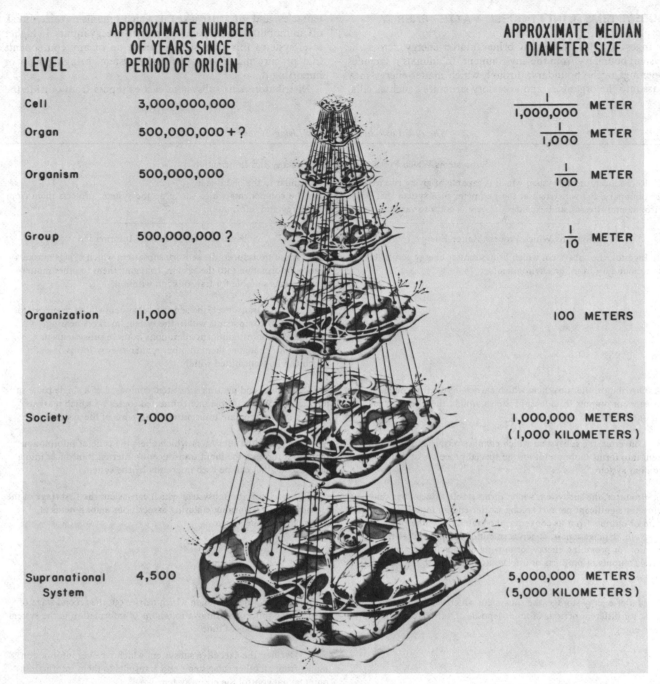

LEVEL	APPROXIMATE NUMBER OF YEARS SINCE PERIOD OF ORIGIN	APPROXIMATE MEDIAN DIAMETER SIZE
Cell	3,000,000,000	$\frac{1}{1,000,000}$ METER
Organ	500,000,000 + ?	$\frac{1}{1,000}$ METER
Organism	500,000,000	$\frac{1}{100}$ METER
Group	500,000,000 ?	$\frac{1}{10}$ METER
Organization	11,000	100 METERS
Society	7,000	1,000,000 METERS (1,000 KILOMETERS)
Supranational System	4,500	5,000,000 METERS (5,000 KILOMETERS)

FIGURE 1. Shred-out. (Modified from Miller, J. G. *Living Systems*, p. 1034. McGraw-Hill, New York, 1978. © McGraw-Hill Book Company, 1978. Reprinted by permission.)

continuance of the individual system. It is critical, however, for the continuance of the species or type of system.

Boundary. This subsystem, at the perimeter of a system, holds together the components that make up the system, protects them from environmental stresses, and excludes or permits entry to various sorts of matter-energy and information. Components that carry out boundary processes for information may be different from those that process matter-energy. The skin or other outer covering of an organism is the boundary to both matter-energy and information, but the points at which boundary processes are carried out are different for the two sorts of transmissions. The skin provides protection by its relative impermeability, preventing excessive inputs and outputs of matter-energy such as moisture, heat, and radiant energy. Visual information may be excluded by closing the eyes.

Boundaries of systems above the level of the organism do not necessarily have immediate physical continuity. They may have very complex shapes as the components of the system move about in space. Matter-energy boundary processes are carried out in groups by individual organisms or by subgroups, such as doorkeepers and a membership chairman. In organizations and larger systems, groups or organizations perform boundary functions. Similar groups or organizations filter information at the boundary. Artifacts such as clothing, buildings, and weapons may be used in carrying out boundary processes.

SUBSYSTEMS THAT PROCESS MATTER-ENERGY

Ingestor. This subsystem brings matter-energy across the system boundary from the environment. In animals it includes openings in the boundary, through which matter-energy may pass into the organism, and accessory structures, such as cilia, tentacles, and muscular jaws by which organisms seize, break off, immobilize, or kill potential matter-energy inputs. In higher level systems this subsystem is made up of any components that procure matter-energy for the system, bringing it in or importing it.

Distributor. This subsystem carries inputs from outside the

TABLE I

The 19 Critical Subsystems of a Living System*

Subsystems Which Process Both Matter-Energy and Information

1. Reproducer, the subsystem which is capable of giving rise to other systems similar to the one it is in
2. Boundary, the subsystem at the perimeter of a system that holds together the components which make up the system, protects them from environmental stresses, and excludes or permits entry to various sorts of matter-energy and information

Subsystems Which Process Matter-Energy	Subsystems Which Process Information
3. Ingestor, the subsystem which brings matter-energy across the system boundary from the environment	11. Input transducer, the sensory subsystem which brings markers bearing information into the system, changing them to other matter-energy forms suitable for transmission within it
	12. Internal transducer, the sensory subsystem which receives, from subsystems or components within the system, markers bearing information about significant alterations in those subsystems or components, changing them to other matter-energy forms of a sort which can be transmitted within it
4. Distributor, the subsystem which carries inputs from outside the system or outputs from its subsystems around the system to each component	13. Channel and net, the subsystem composed of a single route in physical space or multiple interconnected routes by which markers bearing information are transmitted to all parts of the system
5. Converter, the subsystem which changes certain inputs to the system into forms more useful for the special processes of that particular system	14. Decoder, the subsystem which alters the code of information input to it through the input transducer or internal transducer into a private code that can be used internally by the system
6. Producer, the subsystem which forms stable associations that endure for significant periods among matter-energy inputs to the system or outputs from its converter, the materials synthesized being for growth, damage repair, or replacement of components of the system or for providing energy for moving or constituting the system's outputs of products or information markers to its suprasystem	15. Associator, the subsystem which carries out the first stage of the learning process, forming enduring associations among items of information in the system
7. Matter-energy storage, the subsystem which retains in the system, for different periods of time, deposits of various sorts of matter-energy	16. Memory, the subsystem which carries out the second stage of the learning process, storing various sorts of information in the system for different periods of time
	17. Decider, the executive subsystem which receives information inputs from all other subsystems and transmits to them information outputs that control the entire system
	18. Encoder, the subsystem which alters the code of information input to it from other information processing subsystems from a private code used internally by the system into a public code which can be interpreted by other systems in its environment
8. Extruder, the subsystem which transmits matter-energy out of the system in the forms of products or wastes	19. Output transducer, the subsystem which puts out markers bearing information from the system, changing markers within the system into other matter-energy forms which can be transmitted over channels in the system's environment
9. Motor, the subsystem which moves the system or parts of it in relation to part or all of its environment or moves components of its environment in relation to each other	
10. Supporter, the subsystem which maintains the proper spatial relationships among components of the system, so that they can interact without weighting each other down or crowding each other	

* From Miller, J. G. *Living Systems*, p. 3. McGraw-Hill, New York, 1978. © McGraw-Hill Book Company, 1978. Reprinted by permission.

system or outputs from its subsystems around the system to each component. Vascular components of organs and organisms are parts of their distributors. Transportation systems are parts of the distributors at higher levels.

Converter. This subsystem changes certain inputs to the system into forms more useful for the special processes of that particular system. Conversion is carried out in cells and organs by chemical processes and in animal organisms by the mouth, teeth, tongue, associated musculature, salivary glands, stomach, liver, gallbladder, pancreas, and small intestine. In groups, a member may be assigned the task of cutting, grinding, or otherwise breaking down food as a part of its preparation or of cutting wood or cloth for use in clothing. Factories that change raw materials to other forms of matter or energy do converting at higher levels.

Producer. This subsystem forms stable associations that endure for significant periods among matter-energy inputs to the system or outputs from its converter, the materials synthesized being for growth, damage repair, or replacement of components of the system, or for providing energy for moving or constituting the system's outputs of products or information markers to its suprasystem. Cells carry out the process for organisms, so in organisms the subsystem is downwardly dispersed. Factories of a society that make finished materials are components of its producer. Subsidiary organizations and groups of production workers in factories are producers at the level of the organization, such as cooks and bakers in a hospital's dining facilities.

Matter-energy storage. This subsystem retains in the system, for different periods of time, deposits of various sorts of matter-energy. All organisms also store supplies of matter-energy for the frequent situations when outputs temporarily occur faster than inputs or when outputs must be delayed. In cells and organs, matter-energy is stored as adenosine triphosphate, glucose, fat, glycogen, or other forms. In complex animals the subsystem has many components throughout the body, including fatty tissue, liver, gallbladder, bone marrow, muscles, bladder, and lower bowel. Organizations have groups or subsidiary organizations charged with having on hand supplies of necessary matter-energy. Societies similarly hold matter-energy in storage facilities managed by organizations of many kinds, among which are warehouses, grain elevators, and reservoirs. The supplies of ores and petroleum beneath the earth's surface and the forests within the society's boundaries can also be regarded as storage for future use. At the levels of the organization and the society, storage can be divided according to the holding time into long-term, short-term, and buffer storage, the last being storage of people or other matter-energy in queues. The storage process at all levels includes storing and maintaining in storage, loss from storage, and retrieval from storage.

Extruder. This subsystem transmits matter-energy out of the system in the form of either products or wastes. Excretory vacuoles of cells, output arteries and ducts of organs, and excretory organs of animal organisms, together with the structures involved in giving birth and in suckling young, are included in the subsystem. Maids, housewives, and workmen rid buildings of unwanted wastes. Cities and other organizations have street cleaners and garbage and trash-removal teams among their extruder components. Large societies have special problems with the subsystem process because it is often difficult to remove the wastes of their components from the parts of the environment included within the system boundaries. Such large systems are in continual danger of being poisoned by their own wastes. They generally have few components of the subsystem

but disperse its processes downward to components at lower levels and subcomponents that discharge wastes into the system's environment. Other components are those associated with shipping or exporting products over organizational or societal boundaries.

Motor. This subsystem moves the system or parts of it in relation to all or part of its environment, or it moves components of its environment in relation to each other. Striated skeletal muscles are the principal components of the motors of vertebrates. Smooth muscles form the motors of organs that contract or move in other ways. Cardiac muscle is the motor of the blood vascular system. The motors of organizations are usually human beings or human-machine systems, the human components of which are such groups and subsidiary organizations as crews, pilots, drivers, operators, and maintenance personnel. The transportation industry forms the motors of modern industrialized societies.

Supporter. This subsystem maintains the proper spatial relationships among components of the system, so that they can interact without weighting each other down or crowding each other. A cell has ground substance, a cytoskeleton, and a cell wall or membrane. An organ has a stroma. Bones and other connective tissues form the supporters of vertebrate animals. Groups, organizations, and societies use land, buildings, and other artifacts as supporters of their components.

SUBSYSTEMS THAT PROCESS INFORMATION

Input transducer. This sensory subsystem brings markers bearing information into the system, changing them to other matter-energy forms suitable for transmission within it. The input transducers of cells are specialized receptor regions that react to chemical or electrical markers. A chemical change or a patterned excitatory state causes a bioelectric pulse to be propagated. The propagation of such a pulse is followed by the rapid disappearance of the excitation at the receptor site and the restoration of the conditions of sensitivity that existed before the input occurred. The transduction is from the energy of the marker carrying the information to the chemical state or pulse. The totality of an organism's apparatus for receiving signals from the environment is the structure of the subsystem. Groups, organizations, and societies use the input transducers of human components or subcomponents in such groups or organizations as guards, lookouts, intelligence agencies, and research departments. Such components are often supplemented by electronic transducers, like television or radar systems, and meteorological or astronomical instruments.

Internal transducer. This sensory subsystem receives, from subsystems or components within the system, markers bearing information about significant alterations in those subsystems or components, changing them to other matter-energy forms of a sort that can be transmitted within it. Enzymes, repressor molecules controlled by regulatory genes, and postsynaptic regions of neurons are cellular internal transducer components. The postsynaptic regions of neurons that synapse with neurons carrying sensory signals of pain, pressure, stretch, and temperature are internal transducers of organisms, and so are receptor cells in the central nervous system and receptor cells in target tissues that react to hormones or to other components. The totality of all the endocrine or neural receivers that react to bodily states is an organism's internal transducer. All persons who report on states of the group they are in are members of the subsystem at the group level. All departments or divisions responsible for making internal reports of various sorts within organizations and at higher levels belong to the subsystem.

Channel and net. This subsystem is composed of a single route in physical space or multiple interconnected routes by which markers bearing information are transmitted to all parts of the system. In cells, substances that convey chemical or electrical signals constitute the subsystem. In organs, hormonal and neural pathways are the channel and net. In animal organisms, the distributor components conveying endocrine secretions also act as components of information channels. The neural network that carries information throughout the organism is a second component. The two components are interconnected in various ways. The basic components of the channel and net in systems above the organism level are person-to-person communication structures that include all persons in the system. Their communication may be supplemented by mechanical or electronic artifacts and may make use of markers such as ink on paper, radio or television signals transmitted through the air, and pulses along a wire or cable.

Decoder. This subsystem alters the code of information input to it through the input transducer or the internal transducer into a private code that can be used internally by the system. In cells, its components are various molecular binding sites or membrane areas where chemical or bioelectric codes are changed. In organs, they are receptor or second-echelon sensory cells, other neurons, and hormonal receptor sites. In animal organisms with complex nervous systems, the components of the subsystem are widely dispersed. Sensory information is subjected to repeated decodings between the peripheral sense organs and the highest sensory association areas of the central nervous system. Those recordings may emphasize specific aspects of the input signal to which the particular species reacts selectively. Decoding also occurs at many points on motor and other information channels of organisms. Above the level of the organism, decoding may involve translation into technical language or into a language different from that in which the message was received. Appropriate persons, groups, or organizations carry out the process for the system, or it may be downwardly dispersed to all persons in it.

Associator. This subsystem carries out the first stage of the learning process, forming enduring associations among items of information in the system. The structure of the subsystem is unknown in cells, but much research suggests that macromolecules like ribonucleic acid or proteins may be involved. The structure in organs is also unknown. Areas of the cerebral cortex, subcortical regions, and spinal centers are involved in the processes of the subsystem in higher animals. Removal of no single center in a human being however, eliminates the process, so it must be dispersed. Systems at levels above the organism depend fundamentally on the associative capacities of the organisms that compose them, although special research or brainstorming teams that work together may make associations jointly. Computers may be used in the subsystem.

Memory. This subsystem carries out the second stage of the learning process—storing various sorts of information in the system for different periods of time. The memory process at all levels includes reading into storage; the maintenance of storage, including some loss from storage; and the retrieval of information from storage. Memory cells are known to include DNA molecules and probably other molecules yet unidentified. No memory has been discovered in organs. The structural basis for the memory of animal organisms is being investigated

vigorously, and many interesting hypotheses have been tested, with, as yet, no definitive answers. The storage may be in cells or in the connections of the neural channels and nets. The hippocampus, the fornix, the mammillary bodies, some thalamic nuclei, the floor and sides of the third ventricle, and the temporal lobes of the cerebral cortex seem to be related to memory in human beings, but none by itself is the storehouse. Specialized memory for language is related to the temporal lobe of the dominant hemisphere. Groups, organizations, and societies may rely entirely on the memories of their human components and subcomponents or may store written or otherwise recorded material in libraries, files, computers, or other places.

Decider. This executive subsystem receives information inputs from all other subsystems and transmits to them information outputs that control the entire system. The deciding process at all levels has four distinguishable stages: discovering purposes or goals, analysis, synthesis, and implementing. Many complex living systems at various levels are organized into two or more echelons, from lowest to highest, one type of decision being made by decider components at one echelon and another type at another echelon. The decider subsystem of cells includes a higher echelon of genes in the nucleus and a lower echelon of effectors and regulator enzymes in the cytoplasm. It also includes the axon hillock in neurons. Many organs may not have autonomous deciders, but the heart has regulatory nodes and fibers, and some other organs seem to have plexuses that act as deciders. In human organisms, processes are controlled and regulated by structures from local axons in all parts of the body to the spinal cord to the medulla to the cortex. Lower echelon structures regulate reflexive activities, and the highest echelon, the cerebral cortex, controls actions and cognitions that human beings report they are aware of and are carrying out voluntarily. Echelons are clearly identifiable in organizations, and tables of organization place some decider components in each one. Lower echelon decider components are more limited in scope and tend to control more specific processes than do higher echelon deciders.

Encoder. This subsystem alters the code of information input to it from other information-processing subsystems from a private code used internally by the system into a public code that can be interpreted by other systems in its environment. The parts of free-living cells and cells in organisms that synthesize molecules that they put out and that carry signals and the parts of neurons and other cells that produce bioelectric pulses are components of the cellular encoder. Presynaptic regions and perhaps some parts of cell bodies of neurons, as well as cells that secrete hormones, are organ encoder subsystem components. At the level of organisms, the encoding process selects from the organism's repertoire of signals those that are appropriate for communication over a particular channel to a particular sort of receiver and that will convey the intended message. In a human being it can involve a choice among a number of languages to be spoken or written or some other system of signals, such as the hand alphabet of the deaf or a semaphore code. Neural components responsible for the subsystem process are not known, although the dominant hemisphere of the cerebral cortex is essential for any linguistic activity. Encoding at higher levels of living systems may be carried out by single persons or by groups—translators, speechwriters, and advertising copywriters, among others.

Output transducer. This subsystem puts out markers bearing information from the system, changing markers within the system into other matter-energy forms that can be transmitted over channels in the system's environment. Output transducing in cells may be done by components that are also part of the extruder or that put out markers bearing chemical signals or by parts of the cell membrane, particularly specialized presynaptic regions in neurons. In organs, output transducing is done by presynaptic regions of output neurons from organs and by cells that output hormones from glands, as well as vessels that convey them out of organs. An organism's output transducing may be done by laryngeal muscles that control vocal cords, by various muscles of expression, or by glands that put out pheromones carrying chemical signals. Any organ component that is used in signaling—like the hand of a man, the tail of a dog, or the minute muscles that raise the hairs of a cat—is an output transducer component. Output transducers at higher levels are spokespersons who speak for groups, organizations, or societies or who send messages over electronic or other communications media.

VARIABLES

The processes of each of those subsystems can vary, within limits, in a number of respects. Some of the variables, measurable for each subsystem, are the rates at which they can process matter-energy or information, the amount of information or matter-energy that can be processed per unit time, the number of omissions or errors made in the processing, the meaning of the information processed, and the costs to the system of carrying out the processes. They may all vary with changed circumstances and over time, much as do the many variables that indicate the states of different organs that a physician measures by physical, neurological, and laboratory examinations.

STEADY STATES

When opposing variables in a system are in balance, that system is in equilibrium with regard to them. The equilibrium may be static and unchanging, or it may be maintained in the midst of dynamic change. Since living systems are open systems, with continually altering input-output fluxes of matter-energy and of information, many of their equilibria are dynamic and are often referred to as flux equilibria or steady states.

All living systems tend to maintain steady states or homeostasis of many variables, keeping an orderly balance among subsystems that process matter-energy or information. Not only are subsystems usually kept in such equilibria, but also systems ordinarily maintain steady states with their environments and suprasystems, which have outputs to the systems and inputs from them. That prevents variations in the environment from destroying systems. The variables of living systems are constantly fluctuating. A moderate change in one variable may produce greater or smaller alterations, reversible or irreversible, in other related variables.

There is a range of stability for each of numerous variables in all living systems. Within that range the rate of correction of deviations is minimal or zero, and beyond that range correction occurs. An input or output of either matter-energy or information, which by lack or excess of some characteristic forces one or more variables beyond the range of stability, constitutes a stress and produces a strain or strains. Stress may be anticipated. An input signal, which an organism has learned indicates that a stress is imminent, constitutes a threat to the system and creates a strain.

ADJUSTMENT PROCESSES

Living systems seek to maintain their steady states by adjustment processes among subsystems or components. The phrase "adjustment process" is preferable to "coping mechanism" or "defense mechanism" for two reasons: (1) The word "mechanism" ordinarily refers to a structure, but this is a process. It is important to distinguish structure and process clearly. (2) "Defense" refers to the psychoanalytic concept of defensiveness, which in Freudian theory carries the connotation of pathological adaptation, when actually most adjustment processes are healthy and normal. Furthermore, "defense mechanism," being a psychoanalytic term, has overwhelmingly been applied to psychological or informational processes, but "adjustment process" is equally applicable to matter-energy and information processing, as is essential in this conceptual system because of the many parallels between the two sorts of processes.

Adjustment processes change the rates or other aspects of the system variables in such a way that the matter-energy or information processing of the system or significant parts of it is adjusted to the changed conditions within the system or in its environment. An example of such a process is the negative feedback process that elicits an adjustment to depletion of water within the tissues of an organism. When electrolyte concentration in tissue fluids increases as a result of a lack stress of water, information flows through the blood stream, in its role as an information channel, to hypothalamic receptors. Signals pass from them to the pituitary, which secretes vasopressin. That hormone adjusts the extruder process so that more water is resorbed from the kidney tubules, and the volume of urine is decreased. At the same time, hypothalamic centers receiving signals from the nearby receptors initiate thirst signals, and the rate of ingestion of water increases. In that example, both matter-energy and information-processing components participated in the restoration of the system's steady state with respect to the amount of water in its tissues.

Systems at five levels—cell, organ, organism, group, organization—have been shown (Miller, 1960, 1964, 1978) to use similar adjustment processes to information input overload, although more complex systems at higher levels use more such processes. As the rate of information input increases, the system is at first able to cope with it by increasing the rates at which it is processed by its information-processing subsystems. However, increase beyond a certain rate, different for each type of system, constitutes a stress and produces a strain. The system may adjust to such strain at first by randomly omitting the processing of some signals in the input information. For example, a neuron may respond with an action current to every third stimulation, the others being lost because of its refractory period. As rates continue to increase, errors in processing occur. Other adjustment processes to that stress are: queuing, filtering, abstracting, multiple channels, and escape. The use of a similar adjustment process by systems at different levels constitutes a cross-level formal identity, a system characteristic that is of major significance to general living systems theory.

Adjustment processes may be classified, according to the sort of strains to which they adjust, as matter-energy input, information input, matter-energy internal, information internal, matter-energy output, and information output adjustments.

FEEDBACKS

Many adjustment processes of all classes are feedback processes. The term "feedback" refers to a situation in which there are two channels carrying information, such that channel B loops back from the output of channel A to its input, transmitting some portion of the signals emitted by channel A (Rosenblueth et al., 1943). Those feedback signals on channel B are telltales or monitors of the outputs of channel A. The transmitter on channel A is a device with two inputs, one the signal to be transmitted over channel A and the other a resultant of a previously transmitted signal on channel A, fed back on channel B. If the new signal transmitted on channel A is selected to decrease the strain resulting from any error or deviation of the feedback signal from a criterion, comparison, or reference signal indicating the state of the output of channel A that the system maintains steady, a negative feedback exists. That controls the output of channel A on the basis of actual immediate past performance, rather than on the basis of expected performance. Steering devices and thermostats are negative feedback devices. Living systems that guide their behavior partly as a result of observing the effect of their past behavior are using negative feedback. Most steady states in living systems are maintained by negative feedbacks.

COSTS

All adjustment processes are carried out at some cost to the system. That cost may be in matter-energy or information available to satisfy needs, in the special sort of information called money, in time, in lost opportunities, or in the worsening of competitive position.

Most adjustment processes of systems are normal, healthy interactions among subsystems and components that keep the system functioning as well as it can. Some, however, are carried out at such high cost that they must be classed as pathological because less expensive adjustments could achieve the same results.

Applications of General Living Systems Theory to Psychiatry

The value of general living systems theory to psychiatry is becoming clear to many in the field. A theory that embraces both biological and social approaches to the study of living systems is necessarily concerned with conceptual issues basic to psychiatry. A beginning has been made in applications to diagnosis, therapy, and pathology, but the detailed conceptual system presented here has much more potential usefulness than has yet been realized. In addition, general systems theory is already making a significant contribution to the delivery of services in community and hospital settings (Kilburg, 1977).

Grinker (1975) listed psychotherapy and psychoanalysis, health, illness, education, community and social psychiatry, affect, stress and coping, and schizophrenia as presenting problems that systems theory could assist in answering. He predicted that in the future there will be more and more use of systems theory in research and that such use will enhance the knowledge of the causes, courses, and treatments of psychological disturbances.

An advantage of general living systems theory is that an interdisciplinary approach to problems is inherent in it. As Cooper and Marshall (1976) pointed out in their review of research on the relationship of occupational stress to coronary heart disease and mental ill health, much research is carried out within and not between such disciplines as psychology, management, sociology, and medicine. They concluded that gaps in the research result from researchers' inability to see the field as essentially interdisciplinary. The interdisciplinary aspects of general living systems theory derive naturally from its emphasis on the related flows of matter-energy and information and the insistence on the interrelatedness of subsystem processes throughout living systems.

A general living systems approach in psychiatry requires that the system of reference—the patient or group—be viewed in the context of the higher level systems—including the dyad of patient and therapist—of which it is a component and of the environment that surrounds it. The flows of matter-energy and information over its boundaries in both directions and the adjustment processes they elicit are explicitly considered. At the same time, the matter-energy and information flows through its subsystems and components and the internal adjustment processes among them are not neglected.

CONCEPTUAL ISSUES

Mind-matter dilemma. The view of organisms as living systems with inputs, internal processing, and outputs of matter-energy is not new to medically trained scientists. The comparability of the metabolism of information to the metabolism of matter-energy and the emphasis in the theory on the necessary interrelatedness of the two sorts of flows complete the conceptualization of the organism as a system and contribute to the clarification of the ancient mind-matter dilemma.

Psychiatry has long been segregated from the other medical specialties because the classical distinction between mind and matter, going back to ancient times and enduring to the present, has separated mental disease from physical disease. That conceptual dichotomy is also manifested in the gap that exists between the usually objective, biological study of human beings and the frequently subjective, psychosocial study of human beings. The literature of the biotropic sciences of human beings rarely refers to the literature of the sociotropic sciences of human beings and vice versa. A cursory survey of the references in scientific articles on psychiatry and the other behavioral sciences clearly reveals that conceptual segregation.

General systems theory provides a resolution for that unhealthy situation. The proper dichotomy is not between mind and matter but between information processing and matter-energy processing. There is no mind-matter dichotomy in computer science. The computer is made of matter. It has inputs of electrical energy and outputs of electrical energy or mechanical energy conveying markers bearing information. Also, information is input by typewriter, keypunched cards, or other means and output as characters on cathode ray tubes, computer printouts, or other markers. The energy flows through the computer to activate its many parts. The information flows through it and is transformed in the process by various computations controlled by stored, programed information. All that is clear to persons who use computers; there is no mind-matter dichotomy.

Often the behavior of a computer is pathological—its output is incorrect. Then computer operators diagnose the reasons for the maladaptive performance and try to cure or correct it, just as psychiatrists do. There are various possible explanations, and the similarities between the classes of causes for computer malfunctioning and pathological behavior are striking:

The computer may not operate correctly because it has inadequate energy inputs. Similarly, there are psychiatric diseases caused by nutritional deficiencies.

The computer may receive too much energy input, destroying memory or creating abnormal energy processing. Electro-shocks, epilepsy, and strychnine can do that to the human brain.

The computer may—rarely—break down because it received the wrong sort of matter or energy input—the wrong shape of punches or cards or electricity of the wrong voltage. The wrong inputs to the human being—poisons such as overdoses of barbiturates or carbon monoxide—can alter behavior.

The computer may not be programed or may not receive data inputs, so it cannot produce information outputs. Inadequate information inputs—sensory deprivation—can cause pathological human behavior.

Computer processing breaks down if information is fed into the computer at rates it cannot handle. So do some sorts of human behavior.

The computer does not function properly if all its parts are not constructed correctly. Human behavior is pathological if there are genetic faults.

If a computer is wired wrong internally, it does not process electrical energy correctly, and so its information outputs are incorrect. In human beings many sorts of internal matter-energy pathology—metabolic disease or cancer, for example—can produce psychiatric disease.

If information is processed incorrectly within a computer—say, because of incorrect programing—the output is wrong. Similarly, incorrect internal information processing, as in brain disease and many neuroses and psychoses, produces abnormal behavior.

Of course, those analogies are not exact. A computer does not seem to have subjective experience like a person. Nevertheless, the above parallels make it clear that the mind-matter dichotomy need not cleave psychiatry from medicine and biopsychiatry from social psychiatry if the concepts of general systems theory as to how matter-energy and information transmissions interact are accepted.

Decoding and encoding. In the conceptual scheme outlined above, the decoder and the encoder are two of the information-processing subsystems considered essential to living systems. The understanding of cognitive and affective human communication, normal and abnormal, can be facilitated by that theoretical approach. One may consider, for example, aphasia and emotional expression.

Like perception of the environment, the comprehension of language is a complex information-processing function in which certain patterns of input signals are decoded to other patterns that represent them in the ensemble of an internal code of the nervous system. Studies of patients suffering from aphasia indicate that damage to the temporoparietal lobe of the dominant side of the brain can render the patient unable to comprehend symbolic inputs (damage to the decoder) or to produce normal linguistic outputs (damage to the encoder or, perhaps, to the output transducer) or both. Understanding which of the multiple information-processing subsystems are involved clarifies the findings in aphasia.

Human beings and higher animals can receive and decode information that comes to them, often simultaneously, over different bands (Osgood and Sebeok, 1954). On each band, information is coded in a way suitable for transmission over that particular sort of channel and for reception by that particular sort of transducer. Each band has its characteristic variables. Since multiple bands may be used simultaneously, supplementary and even contradictory messages can be received from the same source. When a watchdog growls and wags its tail at the same time, the interpretation is difficult.

The auditory band carries verbally coded messages and expressive tones and sounds, such as cries and whimpers and the sound communications of animals. Human speech also carries messages encoded in other ways than in words. When a contentless flow of recorded low frequency (100 to 550 cycles a second) vowel tones is played, produced by filtering out the high-frequency sounds of consonants that carry most of the semantic information in speech, there is reasonably good agreement among judges on the speaker's emotional state (Soskin and Kauffman, 1961). With the verbally coded meaning included or with it filtered out, voice samples can be reliably judged to convey either aggressive or pleasant feelings (Starkweather, 1956, 1961). Singing, with or without words, also carries emotional content. The understanding that human beings process information to others simultaneously on several distinct bands or channels clarifies the nature of cognitive and emotional communication.

A general systems theory of personality. A personality theory proposed by Karl Menninger (1963) described normal personality function and psychopathology in systems theory terms. He related classical psychoanalytic concepts to present-day systems theory. A central feature of his approach is a detailed analysis of internal information-adjustment processes that he calls coping devices, which are much like Freudian defense mechanisms or the adjustment processes of general systems theory. His theory deals with four major issues: adjustment or individual-environmental interaction; the organization of living systems; psychological regulation and control, known as ego theory in psychoanalysis; and motivation, which in psychoanalysis is often called instinct theory. Like other systems theorists, Menninger made a salient point of the principle of homeostasis. He considered the maintenance of steady states to be basic to both psychological and physical processes. Also, he contended that certain forces cause living systems to search for new and unsettled states. Menninger (1963) agreed with Ali Ibn Hazm, who lived from 994 to 1064, that all human beings are constantly attempting to escape anxiety, the primary principle of human motivation being that

no one is moved to act, or resolves to speak a single word, who does not hope by means of this action or word to release anxiety from his spirit.

Also, Menninger believed that negative feedbacks maintain the steady states in living systems, which he called their vital balance. He recognized that all living systems are open systems and that they are hierarchies composed of subsystems and subsubsystems. He interpreted Freudian personality theory in terms of that systems approach. The ego, he said, is the central executive (in the author's terms, the decider, concerned with the governance of the organism). The instincts of the id are dual drives that alter adjustments in either of two opposite directions. The one drive, sex, tends toward positive relationships with other organisms, human and nonhuman. The other drive, aggression, tends toward disruption of such relationships. (Those drives, in the author's terms, are concerned with the governance of the organism's subsystems. The introjected superego is concerned with the governance of the organism's suprasystem.)

Pointing out that all coping devices have costs in the energy expenditures they entail, Menninger listed the following normal adjustment processes commonly used to cope with the emergencies of everyday life: reassurances by touch, rhythm, sound, and speech; food and food substitutes—smoking, chewing gum; alcoholic beverages and other self-medications; self-discipline; laughing; crying and cursing; boasting; sleep; talking issues and feelings out; thinking through stressful problems; rationalization; working off aggression by physical exercise; acting to alter situations to reduce strains; pointless overactivity to reduce strains, such as finger tapping and floor walking; fantasy formation and daydreaming; dreaming; slips of the pen and the tongue and other minor errors; symbolic acts; reaction formation; seeking out dangerous situations to relieve anxiety that one is cowardly; and physical and physiological processes such as sneezing, coughing, itching, scratching, yawning, and blushing.

Noting that stresses on organisms and strains within them are of different orders of magnitude, Menninger asserted the validity for the human organism of the general systems principle that the greater a threat or stress on a system is, the more of the system's components are involved in adjusting to it. When no further components with new adjustment processes are available, the function of the system collapses.

DIAGNOSIS

A number of aspects of general living systems theory can contribute to psychiatric diagnosis. One principle is that every process should, when possible, be identified with the structure that carries it out. If, as is currently true, not all neural structures that mediate behavior can be identified, then a reasonable hypothesis can be proposed until research identifies the structure. Basic research can then confirm or refute such hypotheses.

A second principle is to include, as part of diagnosis, a tracing of the routes of all separate sorts of matter-energy and information transmissions, including feedbacks, from inputs to outputs of systems and subsystems. The principle requires greater precision than is possible when one uses the common terms "stimulus" and "response." Stimuli should be separated into matter-energy inputs and information inputs, and responses should be separated into matter-energy outputs and information outputs. Then each sort of transmission can be traced through the system to determine whether the relevant variables are within normal ranges or to locate the places where they are not—the loci of pathology. Also, research can reveal the quantitative relationships of the variables.

A third principle, the existence of 19 critical subsystems in all living systems, gives a basis for agreement among diagnosticians as to what are the basic parts and processes of the system. The variables of each subsystem can be tested to determine whether they are within normal steady-state ranges. If they are not, the controlling feedbacks can be tested to determine why the relevant adjustment processes are not working properly.

THERAPY

General systems theory has appealed to group therapists as a means of conceptualizing the role of the therapist in the group and describing group processes. The concept of levels has been found to be useful in the field, although it is not always used exactly as it is defined in the presentation. Thus, Gray (1974) pointed out that a group, such as a family, may have somewhat different laws than an individual and that laws also differ at the oedipal and anal intrapsychic "levels." Those two levels are abstractions, rather than concrete levels of living systems, as they are defined above. He described group therapy

as proceeding from an equilibrium that becomes unstable and experiences a perturbation to a new position of metastability, a cycle that can be repeated many times. As an example, in group therapy he used a defensive posture of seductiveness as an initial equilibrium, rejection by the group as a perturbation, proceeding to a new equilibrium of hostility covering love or pain.

Gray (1974) also discussed stabilizing activity on the part of the therapist to prevent a continually escalating series of positive feedbacks. He also discussed the concept of boundaries. He pointed out that rate changes, which take place at boundaries, are crucial to change. Gray (1974) wrote:

My own view of the importance of boundary functions in a general systems view of personality is the realization that, without them, life is impossible; that without an ability to shift permeability, life is also impossible, and that rate changes, upon which rests the whole concept of how change occurs, take place at boundaries. Thus a formation of a dyad in a group, a pulling away of a patient in a therapy session, or the occurrence of manifestations of positive or negative transference are all very important because they signify boundary changes.... So, the general systems principle here is that boundaries are to be recognized, their function understood, and ways of changing them conceptualized, with the rather glorious understanding that boundary changes mean system changes, thus giving a sort of short cut to our understanding of how patients change.

Gray (1974) also described the function of a group in terms of competing information programs being processed and of the development of codes and group norms.

Barcai (1977) used case examples to describe how change in a single member can elicit reactions from a family group. He preferred to describe individuals in terms of a psychodynamic model, confining his systems analysis to the group. He emphasized the importance to a psychotherapist of taking into account a patient's total social climate. He pointed out that the therapist should anticipate the effect of change in the patient, prepare the family system for the change, and offer support to both the patient and the members of the family to protect against the shock produced by change. Barcai (1977) wrote:

The family is seen as a system with interlocking parts. Each individual is a part of that system and has a certain amount of private and individual, however limited, degree of freedom, until his action begins to affect the totality of the system. A drastic change, be it planned and external, or developmental and normative in one member requires accommodation and response in the other family members.

Linton and Estock (1977) discussed the therapy for anxiety phobic depersonalization, making use of some general systems theory ideas. A patient with this syndrome experiences, as an initial episode, an acute attack of anxiety or panic. A second phase is marked by a fear of losing control and of doing or saying something embarrassing or humiliating. Such a patient may fear insanity. As a result, he withdraws and avoids new experiences or unfamiliar surroundings. That withdrawal creates sensory isolation and is followed by depersonalization, defined as a state of awareness in which feelings, thoughts, memories, and bodily sensations are no longer experienced as being his own. The world appears strange or dream-like. He may report a feeling of being outside his body, watching himself. That syndrome is said to occur in extroverted persons who are dependent on external reality for optimum functioning. Treatment of such a patient is usually aimed at reducing the anxiety, but the drugs used for that purpose reduce stimulus intensity and increase the stress response. The authors suggested that an antidepressant be used during the day and a mild hypnotic at night. Tranquilization should be avoided during the day. After the initial crisis has been resolved, psychotherapy is ordinarily helpful. The authors related that analysis to the general systems theory concept that organisms need an optimal amount of stimulation. That notion is related to the concepts of information input underload and information input overload discussed below. Variation from a patient's own preferred amount of input produces stress that manifests itself as anxiety phobic depersonalization syndrome.

A major contribution of general living systems theory to psychotherapy is its emphasis on analysis of the subsystem processes of the patient and of his or her relationship to higher level systems—such as family, work group, organization, and society—to discover what variable has been forced out of normal range or what specific feedback or adjustment process is not operating correctly. Choice of a type of intervention— such as drugs, psychotherapy, alteration in the patient's suprasystem or environment, or a combination of those therapies— is then facilitated. Cooper and Marshall (1976) in their discussion of the contribution of occupational stress to coronary heart disease and mental health, suggested changes that can be made in industrial life—that is, at the organization level—to reduce the strains that contribute to the development of those conditions. They included fundamental changes in organizations, bridging the gap between the organization and the family to increase the family's understanding of the job and permit the spouse to express his or her feelings about the effect of the work on family life, and the use of social and interactive skill-training programs to help clarify role difficulties and interpersonal difficulties in organizations.

PATHOLOGY

Of interest to psychiatrists are all levels of living systems, including cells and organs—the structures that mediate a person's behavior—and organizations, societies, and supranational systems—the concerns of community and social psychiatry. The systems that are usually of most importance to them, however, are human organisms and human groups, usually families and therapy groups. Just as the various levels of living systems have comparable adjustment processes, so they have comparable pathologies, caused by lacks of matter-energy inputs, excesses of matter-energy inputs, inputs of inappropriate forms of matter-energy, lacks of information inputs, excesses of information inputs, inputs of maladaptive genetic information in the template, abnormalities in internal matter-energy processes, and abnormalities in internal information processes. Since people usually live in families or other groups and participate in numerous organizations that are parts of total societies, the pathology must be identified according to the level at which it occurs. That need is recognized by many psychiatrists, who find that they cannot treat one member of a family in isolation from the others because the pathology is in the family interrelationships. With the aid of the above classification of pathologies, a few examples are given here of general living systems approaches to pathology at five levels, situations in which stresses and threats produce strains that alter steady states because adjustment processes do not cope adequately with them.

Cell level. Addictive drugs like heroin apparently create abnormalities in internal cellular information processes by altering enzymatic controls (decider processes). At least some behavioral changes follow from those cellular alterations. Also, inputs to vertebrate cells of hormonal molecules, such as thyroxine, bearing chemically coded information, at ordinary rates convey signals that promote the normal functions of those cells by regulating the rates of certain enzymatic processes. Abnormally high rates of hormonal inputs—excesses of information inputs—can produce thyrotoxicosis; when they affect neural cells, such excess inputs can produce toxic psychoses. Furthermore, various neuropsychiatric disease syndromes result from inputs of maladaptive genetic information, as in the DNA of the human chromosomes, whose code is now known as a result of many research efforts of recent years. One of those maladaptive inputs is mongolism or Down's syndrome—mental retardation, eyes somewhat like those of Mongolians, multiple physical deformities, and reduced vitality, usually leading to early death.

Certain psychoses may be determined by aberrations in the genetic signal. Some studies of schizophrenic patients and their relatives have been interpreted as showing such inheritance, but the exact nature of the genetic defect, the gene or genes involved, and the probability that the disease will appear in a relative of a schizophrenic patient are not clear (McClearn and Meredith, 1966).

Organ level. A blood clot or tumor can produce a lack of matter inputs, such as oxygen from the blood stream, into a component of the brain and cause a stroke. Shrapnel (excess matter inputs) in the temporoparietal area of the cortex can cause aphasia. In addition, endocrine and neural information-processing components are subject to the effects of trauma, infection, tumors, and other types of abnormalities in internal matter-energy processes. They may or may not cause illnesses. A few examples of diseases with neuropsychiatric implications that affect those components are diabetes insipidus, in which damage to the posterior pituitary prevents it from secreting vasopressin, so that it cannot signal the kidney tubules to resorb water, and, consequently, abnormally large amounts of urine are extruded; the neuritis and psychotic manifestations of severe pellagra, a disease produced by nicotinic acid (vitamin B_6) deficiency; the distinctive electroencephalographic patterns, convulsions, and other abnormal behavior seen in epilepsy, which arises after brain trauma or from brain tumor or other causes; stuttering and related speech defects; the motor weakness of myasthenia gravis, which arises from abnormalities in acetylcholine metabolism.

Organism level. A systems theory explanation of some of the motor behavior in schizophrenia was presented by Glassman (1976).

As a result of the drugs used in the treatment of psychoses, patients develop tardive dyskinesia, a condition in which the patient displays uncontrolled active movement similar to the motor behavior of Huntington's chorea. The condition is mediated through the extrapyramidal system. Glassman (1976) explained it as a result of the development of semiautonomy of behavioral fragments. He postulated three echelons of behavioral control. The lowest echelon includes small fragments of coordinated movements. Those fragments run free in dyskinesias. Neural structure for that echelon is in the nuclei of the extrapyramidal system below the diencephalon. The second echelon is contained largely in the basal ganglia in the forebrain; it exerts tonic inhibition on the third echelon and produces coordinated sequences of movement by selective disinhibition. The first echelon lies largely in the frontal cortex; it helps to integrate movement sequences into the life of the organism, making use of memory, and, through its connections with the limbic system, makes use of planning and evaluation. Glassman believed that, in schizophrenia, the problem is a deficiency in the ability of the first echelon to exert sufficient tonic inhibition on the second echelon. Patterns of the second echelon then organize the whole system around themselves. This leads to fragmentary sequences of thought or action or, in less deteriorated cases, to a delusion which is not adequately tested against reality.

Neuroleptic agents allow the control of the first echelon to continue, but they do it by disrupting the second echelon, rather than by enhancing the inhibitory capability of the first echelon. That disruption results in the dyskinesias.

Pathological adjustment processes. According to Menninger (1963), normal adjustments to ordinary matter-energy and information lack and excess stresses and the resultant strains include such information processes as general irritability, feelings of tension, overtalkativeness, repeated laughter, frequent losses of temper, restlessness, sleepless worrying at night, and fantasies about solutions to real problems. Beyond those adjustments, more costly and more pathological adjustments are resorted to in response to stresses of greater magnitude. They are pathological if more expensive adjustment processes are used when less costly ones would suffice. Menninger (1963) identified the following five degrees of internal information-processing pathology: (1) nervousness, a slight impairment of smooth adaptive control; (2) neurotic hysterical, obsessional, or anxiety symptoms, including character disorders; (3) directed aggression and violence, including some forms of self-defense or warfare that are condoned in many social contexts, as well as chronic repetitions of mild aggressions and explosive outbursts of serious violent and socially unacceptable aggressions, such as murder, associated with pathological lack of self-control; (4) psychotic states of extreme disorganization, regression, and repudiation of the reality of inputs from the environment; (5) extreme disorganization of control with malignant anxiety and depression, often resulting in death, frequently by suicide. The diagnosis, treatment, and cure of cognitive and affective disorders and pathologies of social adjustment were analyzed by Menninger, using this general systems approach.

The effects of abnormalities in a human organism's internal information flows in altering normal matter-energy processing are recognized in psychiatry. A great variety of symptoms—including pain, paralyses, and anesthesias of parts of the body—are seen in patients with neurotic conflicts. The symptoms often have only a superficial resemblance to symptoms resulting from damage to neural or muscular components.

The importance of lacks or excesses of matter-energy or information stresses in producing diverse clinical symptoms is accepted in clinical medicine. Some kinds of hypertension, rheumatic diseases, arthritis, kidney diseases, vascular diseases (including possibly atherosclerosis), and a number of other illnesses have been classified by Selye (1956) as diseases of adaptation, brought about by the excess of anterior-pituitary and adrenocortical hormones that characterizes bodily responses to stresses. Overdosages with such hormones can cause the formation and eventual perforation of a peptic ulcer. Those hormones are assumed to accelerate the flow of the gastric juices as a result of the more rapid secretion of acetylcholine and consequent increased vagal activity. Experimental results support some of those conclusions.

For example, rats placed in a dark box and shocked on a random schedule developed more peptic ulcers than did similar rats that were shocked at regular intervals (Sawrey, 1961). Presumably, the rats on the random schedule experienced more strain because of the threat of shock every moment without letup. In another study, the predictability of a painful input also affected monkeys during conditioned emotional

disturbances (Mason et al., 1961). Norepinephrine and 17-hydroxycorticosteroid concentrations in the blood plasma rose in a number of experimental situations involving such disturbances. If the situations involved uncertainty about when a painful input would occur, the concentration of epinephrine also rose.

Anxiety. This unpleasant emotional experience, like pain, may be viewed as information, a signal that a steady state has been or threatens to be seriously disturbed. In the presence of a lack or excess stress or threat, the intensity of the anxiety probably signals the relative strength of the stress or threat, on the one hand, and the adjustment processes available to counter it, on the other hand. Either an increase in the stress or threat or a decrease in the adjustment processes as perceived by the organism can produce the signal. Anxiety can be pathological in some patients, but it is often like pain—a useful signal in normal people that a steady state does not exist because available adjustment processes seem to be inadequate to cope with a potential or actual stress (Freud, 1959).

When a person experiences anxiety, physiological measures often indicate that he is under stress. The anxiety signal is transmitted up to and through the frontal lobes of the brain. It can be blocked by tranquilizers, sedatives, and other psychoactive drugs. It can also be blocked by operative techniques that separate the prefrontal areas from their related thalamic nuclei. Although the destructive procedure is followed by profound personality changes, it has sometimes been carried out in the hope of ending the anxiety signal of patients suffering intractable pain from terminal cancer (Crosby et al., 1962; Grinker and Sahs, 1966).

Adjustment processes to lacks of information inputs. Information input underload is a lack stress. Under normal conditions most people are able to adjust information flows to comfortable levels by seeking or avoiding other people, shifting attention, increasing physical activity, or making adjustments in the environment, such as lowering window shades or turning on lights. Sensory deprivation has been investigated extensively in recent years. A minimum rate of information inputs to a system must be maintained for it to function normally, and organisms strive to get such inputs.

For instance, after light deprivation of several hours, monkeys press a bar almost insatiably to obtain a brief moment of light for each bar press (Fox, 1962; Wendt et al., 1963). In one experiment the rate of bar presses, which provided 0.5 second of light each, increased from about 800 an hour after no period of deprivation to about 3,800 an hour after 8 hours of deprivation. The adjustment process of bar pressing was available to those monkeys as a way to maintain a minimum rate of visual information inputs. They put out a significant amount of energy to keep up the input rate—the longer the deprivation, the greater their energy expenditure. Human subjects, given the opportunity to relieve the underload conditions by pressing buttons for flashes of light, pressed more frequently for light presentations that provided more information than for those that provided less information (Jones et al., 1966).

The effects of social isolation and lack of variability in information inputs on people—like truck drivers who must spend long hours driving alone, prisoners in solitary confinement, patients in respirators, and explorers alone on the sea or in the wilderness—have been described as an isolation syndrome (Wheaton, 1959). Rather extreme subjective experiences, like hallucinations, have been reported with even relatively mild sensory deprivation, such as is experienced in a long drive alone at night (Wheaton, 1959). Experimental subjects have experienced similar symptoms.

The isolation syndrome has a number of stages, commonly including the following: At first, the person is able to pass time thinking, but he finally becomes sleepy and may fall asleep. As time goes on, he is unable to direct his thoughts or to think clearly. He becomes irritable, restless, and hostile. Then he may make an explicit attempt to use fantasy material as an adjustment process to substitute for needed information inputs. Later, he becomes child-like in his emotional variability and behavior. A stage of vivid visual, auditory, or kinesthetic hallucinations follows, succeeded by a final stage in which there is a sensation of otherness. He may "see" his subjective experience as a bright area in darkness. Termination of the information input lack stress does not immediately return the person to normal. He slowly readjusts to society. Hallucinations and blank periods may continue to bother him. He often finds it difficult to concentrate attention, and he must take care to keep his fantasies out of his speech.

In a variety of experiments, the first carried out at McGill University in the early 1950's, information inputs to subjects have been severely limited. Probably the most extreme experimental form of sensory deprivation or information input underload was experienced by only two subjects, one of whom was the experimenter himself (Lilly, 1956; Solomon et al., 1957). Each subject was suspended in a tank of slowly flowing water kept at about body temperature. He wore only a blacked-out head mask, through which he breathed, that eliminated visual inputs. Auditory inputs were limited to faint noises from the water pipes and the subject's own breathing sounds. Pressures from the harness and the mask were kept constant. Both subjects developed vivid fantasies, illusions, delusions, hallucinations, and anxiety in from 2½ to 3 hours. In less severe sensory deprivation situations, symptoms have been less extreme and have appeared after longer periods of time, although subjects differ markedly in their responses (Heron et al., 1956; Solomon et al., 1957; Mendelson et al., 1961).

An organism experiencing information input lack stresses can increase its activity in the environment in order to speed the rate of information inputs to it. Blind rats moved more than seeing rats when put in an activity wheel that turned whenever they walked (Rhodes and Wyers, 1956). Blind rats also consumed more saccharin than did seeing rats when they were free to do so. That consumption increased their matter-energy and also their information inputs. Furthermore, blind rats were more active than seeing rats in operating a clicker device that provided information inputs. However, most of the adjustments that subjects in such experiments can use concern internal information processing. A person or animal can move his joints and so send signals from his internal transducer through his nervous system. The subjects in the tank did that and reported that the resultant information flow was so pleasant that it was almost erotic. One can also sleep. In sleep, time passes quickly while the sleeper dreams and is unaware of the lack of information inputs. Organized thought, possible during early deprivation, also maintains a flow of information that is fairly comfortable for the subject. A prisoner in solitary confinement in a prison in China made up for his information input underload by spending hours every day searching through the information stored in his memory—recycling poems, historical facts, and mathematical principles he had once learned (Byrd, 1938). When such organized thought breaks down, fantasies and hallucinations, sometimes frightening and sometimes not, take over.

The bulk of the research evidence is that the drastic curtailment of information inputs has an important influence on behavior. There are individual differences in the optimal rate of information input for a person to maintain arousal, think well, act effectively, and feel good. In an overview of the present knowledge about sensory deprivation, Goldberger (1970) wrote:

> one would no longer claim "hallucinations" (or its current operational variant, "reported visual sensations") as effects due directly to sensory reduction; the current view would require more qualification and would speak of them as being facilitated by or occurring with greater frequency in sensory reduction as compared with a number of other conditions, depending on arousal level, set, personality, and so on. Certainly today's researcher would be most cautious about linking these phenomena to psychosis. Similarly, the current position on cognitive impairment would specify that it is more likely to occur on tasks requiring complex, self-directed efforts; and so on down the line with each behavioral index. Nevertheless, the overall conclusion of the early McGill studies remains: namely, that sensory stimulation is an important ingredient in the maintenance of effective functioning. In fact Zuckerman ... offers the reader a stronger version of the old aphorism when he suggests that variety (in stimulation) is the *bread*, not simply the spice, of life.

Adjustment processes to excesses of information inputs. Information input overload can produce major pathology in organisms. That effect has been demonstrated in rats (Sebeok, 1962).

Over several years Calhoun (1961) conducted controlled observations of rat communities in enclosures. In communities in which the rats were crowded together and encountered other rats frequently, overpopulation produced various sorts of pathology, different from one animal to another. Although the pregnancy rates of the females were not abnormal, their pregnancies produced a lower percentage of live births than did the pregnancies of female rats in less crowded communities. Of the infants born in crowded communities, 80 per cent or more died before they were weaned. Their mothers often failed to feed them, did not build them nests, and frequently would forget to care for them when they were in danger. The adult males in the overcrowded pens also showed a variety of pathological behaviors. Some indulged frequently in homosexual or pansexual contacts; some withdrew passively from the other rats, ignoring even females in estrus; others—called "probers" by Calhoun—were hyperactive, hypersexual, and homosexual, insistently and abnormally pursuing females in estrus and sometimes indulging in cannibalism of the young.

Those various sorts of pathology in rats in the crowded pens apparently were not caused by matter-energy stresses of any sort. Rather, As Spitz (1964) concluded from Calhoun's work, they arose from the fact that each animal was subjected to an excessive rate of information inputs. Those rapid inputs elicited various abnormal internal cognitive and affective processes and overt behaviors, particularly frenetic activity and pathological withdrawal. According to Spitz, repeated interruptions before completion of normal input-output sequences by new inputs produce the pathology. In his view, human infants are particularly susceptible to such pathogenic processes.

Such states of information input overload are like those that Toffler (1970) called "future shock." In severe or irreversible form, the condition has been explicitly identified by Lipowski (1970, 1971) as a form of pathology. He explained its origins as follows: Today's affluent, technical society is characterized by an excess of attractive information inputs. The many communication media increase the surfeit, as do the increasing density of population and the ease of the spread of information in a society that advocates free and often discordant expression. Social influences pressure the individual person to choose among those attractive inputs, creating in him conflicts as to which of several desirable behaviors he should carry out.

Anxiety is associated with those conflicts. The person attempts to cope with them by such adjustment processes as filtering, escape, repeated approaches to many different goals or sources of information inputs, aggressive or violent behavior, and passive surrender. The young seem to be more vulnerable to excesses of information inputs because they have not learned how to choose among attractive alternatives and to strive in a sustained manner for selected goals.

Various practitioners have called attention to case histories that suggest that information input overload can give rise to psychopathology in individual human beings.

For example, C. A. Ullman in a personal communication reported the case of a supervisor in a government agency who voluntarily withdrew from a Civil Service internship training program intended to prepare him for a position with a higher rating, which would have given him more status and salary, because he believed that the training program was jeopardizing his health. He complained of nervousness, insomnia, and elevated blood pressure, which persisted in spite of medical care. He had received counseling and guidance concerning his worries that his progress in the training program was steadily deteriorating. His training and writing skills were more limited than those of other interns in the training program, and he felt that he was doing poorly on a required project. His educational background was well below the average of the group, and his general intelligence and information were also low for the group. He was poor in self-insight, as measured by tests. He was unwilling to accept help in his work, even though others in the program were willing to give him help. Moreover, he seemed unable to escape from the confines imposed by the necessity he felt to process information in minute detail. He had a reasonably strong need to achieve but also marked inferiority feelings and a strong need to defer to the opinions of others. He contended that his performance was poor because his preparation was inadequate and that he overworked in order to compensate for that lack. When he felt that he was not meeting his own high goals of performance and that he would be unable to do so, he withdrew from the program, a victim of information overload.

It is common for executives in industry, government, and elsewhere to feel strains from a sort of stress that French and Kahn (1962) called "role overload." They explicitly regarded it as a sort of information input overload. They found that, in general, the more important the executive position, the greater the stress. Increasing demands are pressed on the executive by his various colleagues and by the total mission of the organization. He does not find time in his busy life to cope adequately with those demands. He uses various adjustment processes to the overload in order to handle them as well as possible, but he still has a constant feeling of guilt that he is not meeting expectations. Many nights he may carry home a briefcase of work but be too exhausted to complete it.

Information overloads on airplane pilots seem to be capable of causing potentially dangerous panic.

In one case, an experienced, mature, and stable B-47 pilot was flying a plane whose landing wheels had just malfunctioned (Flinn, 1965). He had also received an erroneous message from a ground controller and had been concentrating intensely on his instrument panel, on which red collision lights were flashing. He froze at the plane's controls and almost crashed it into some mountains. A later review of the situation indicated that, when the pilot froze at the controls, he was apparently overwhelmed by sensory overload.

Clinical and experimental evidence suggests that overloads of information may have some relation to schizophrenic behavior. In schizophrenia a genetically determined metabolic fault or some other source of increased neural noise may lower the capacities of certain as yet unidentified channels involved in cognitive information processing. Various studies suggest that input channels are particularly affected.

On the basis of work on information overload, Luby et al. (1962) suggested that schizophrenic withdrawal, manifested in its most extreme form as schizophrenia, may be an attempt by the patient to use escape as an adjustment process to reduce the rate at which information impinges on him in order to prevent overload and keep the rate within a range he can handle. That may be why a psychotic beachcomber or vagrant or hippie shuns much human contact. Also, a catatonic schizophrenic may be unable to respond to information inputs because they overload him and create confusion.

Various case histories of schizophrenic patients (Jaffe, 1958), together with a large mass of other observations and experiments on schizophrenics, make it apparent that they have difficulty in ordering and organizing the large fluxes of information inputs that impinge on their input channels (Yates, 1966). Among the many formulations of the basic pathology in schizophrenia are the following: a defect in central nervous system organization, an abnormality of a cortical regulatory system, a defect in the reticular activating or limbic system, a biochemical fault, and a metabolic disorder of nervous tissue (Snyder et al., 1961; Robertson, 1962; Venables, 1963 a, b; Belmont et al., 1964; Weckowicz, 1964). Regardless of whether one or more of those pathologies or some other one is the normal basis of schizophrenia, the fundamental defect, according to Chapman and McGhie (1962) is an inability to process input information accurately. They showed that schizophrenics did as well as normal subjects on tasks involving distraction but were worse when selective attention was involved, particularly when information was put in simultaneously on competing sensory channels. Schizophrenics, they contended, are unable to use the adjustment process called "filtering" to shut out irrelevant information inputs (Chapman and McGhie, 1964). Consequently, their short-term memory is overloaded. One indication of that overload is that schizophrenics are as good as normal subjects in repeating sentences of low redundancy, but they do not improve as much as normal subjects when repeating sentences of higher redundancy. In normal speech, redundant words are distractors for a schizophrenic (Lawson et al., 1964; Nidorf, 1964). His channel capacity is lowered, according to Pishkin et al. (1962). He takes longer than a normal person to perceive single and multiple units of inputs, according to Harwood and Naylor (1963). And his use of the filtering adjustment process is abnormal, according to Payne et al. (1963).

Lipowski (1975) also used the concept of information input overload in explaining the observed pathological responses of schizophrenics, using Broadbent's (1971) concept of a filter protecting a nervous system with a limited capacity to process information. Schizophrenic patients have defective filtering processes, with the result that they suffer information input overload with a level of input that is quite comfortable for healthy people.

The responses of normal subjects reacting at their own rates and of normal subjects reacting under forced pace on a word-association test were compared by Flavell et al. (1958) with the responses of schizophrenics. Normal subjects under time pressure made responses more like those of schizophrenics than did normal subjects under no time pressure. A related study by Usdansky and Chapman (1960) seems to lend support to the general viewpoint presented here. They found that increased rates of information input evoked schizophrenic-like associative errors in normal subjects.

Those research findings and other data suggest that the differences in speech between schizophrenics and normal subjects arise from overloading some information-processing component or components that in schizophrenia have abnormally low channel capacity (Miller, 1964, 1978). Consequently, schizophrenics cannot process signals as quickly or as correctly as normal persons can. All the evidence cited above suggests that schizophrenia, by some as yet unknown process that increases neural noise or distortion, lowers channel capacity. Infections, trauma, or other events that, as Menninger (1930) indicated, can precipitate schizophrenia may perhaps further lower channel capacity biochemically, exacerbating abnormal states that were themselves caused by some prior lowering of channel capacity of uncertain origin (Yates, 1966).

Hemsley (1977) related the clinical phenomena of schizophrenia to the adjustment processes to input overload discussed above (see p. 105). For each adjustment process he listed a set of schizophrenic symptoms:

Errors are related to inappropriate responding and to incoherence of speech.

Omission includes underresponsiveness, poverty of speech, and flatness of affect.

Abstracting includes undifferentiated responding and delusions.

Escape is shown by social withdrawal and catatonic symptoms.

Queuing is manifested in retardation.

Filtering results in narrowed attention.

Hemsley (1977) wrote:

Several factors might be expected to influence the choice of preferred mode of adaptation if information overload is viewed as the primary disturbance in schizophrenia. Firstly, it would be dependent on the severity of such overload. It will be recalled that in Miller's [1960, 1978] experiment, "omission" was the most prominent mechanism of adaptation for normal subjects at high levels of overload. The "omission" and the "escape" adaptations may be the only viable methods at high levels of overload. Both are more prominent in chronic patients; it is likely that those patients who eventually become chronic are those with the greatest cognitive disturbance. At more moderate levels of disorganization, all methods of adaptation might be attempted. The conventional criteria for a diagnosis of paranoid schizophrenia require only moderate intellectual disorganization; in such patients the limited degree of overload may allow the "approximation" [abstracting] adaptation. Unlike under-responsiveness and social withdrawal, paranoid delusions are not more prominent in chronic patients ... there may indeed be a disappearance of paranoid symptoms with chronicity.

Group level. Conflict may arise in a group like a family if there is a lack of matter-energy inputs, such as a shortage of food, water, or clothing. Excess or unwanted matter-energy inputs, like the destruction of a house or the arrival of a chronic invalid in a home, can also subject a family to severe strains. Lacks of information inputs, like sensory deprivation to a team of astronauts during a long space journey or inadequate income to feed a family, can produce pathological behavior (Cramer and Flinn, 1963). Also, when certain arrangements of the channel and net subsystems of groups centralize communications in one or a few members and they consequently tend to suffer from excesses of information inputs, frequently one member of a group—like the chairman of a committee, the quarterback of a football team, or the ranking officer of a command post—takes on an undue proportion of the total information processing being carried out by his group. Under such circumstances, pathological group processes can easily arise. Undue physical aggressiveness and unfair acquisitiveness, resulting in inputs of inappropriate forms of matter-energy and abnormalities in internal information processes, can also produce group pathology. All such situations are psychiatrically important.

Organization level. Many problems of community, military, and industrial psychiatry and of hospital organization and management fall under this rubric. Inadequate food in a community and insufficient food, drugs, and other supplies in a hospital are lacks of matter-energy inputs that can result in pathological functioning of the system. Excesses of matter-energy inputs, like overpopulation in a city and overcrowding in hospitals and prisons, cause organizational pathology, such as delays in providing essential services. Pollution and accumulated wastes in cities are inputs of inappropriate forms of matter-energy that cause them to function unsatisfactorily.

Lacks of information inputs about the suprasystem in which it exists can result in the inadequate performance of an organization. A psychiatric hospital can serve the needs of the community best only if it carefully and continuously assesses those needs by direct study of the community. Persons in the primary communication nodes of large organizations, particularly the executives, are often overloaded by excesses of information inputs. Such overloads fatigue those who suffer from them. The overloads also delay communications and decisions, make the decisions erratic or wrong, and may result in the decisions' not being made or being made by persons not properly equipped to do so. All those causes can produce pathological effects in cities, hospitals, corporations, armies, and other types of organizations.

Abnormalities in internal matter-energy processes include requiring laborers to work in unattractive surroundings, prisoners to live under inhumane conditions, and outpatients to wait idly for hours to be treated. Abnormalities in internal information processes include the management styles of administrators that neglect worker needs and produce poor organizational morale. Breakdowns in communications between component units are common causes of inadequate performance in all types of organizations. Similar breakdowns in information flows among ethnic groups destroy the relationships among citizens in a city. Such forms of pathology must be dealt with by psychiatrists who care for patients who live or work in organizations.

Suggested Cross References

Many of the psychotic disorders and therapies discussed in this book are relevant to general living systems theory, and the reader is directed to them, particularly the discussions of schizophrenia (Chapter 15), organic mental disorders (Chapter 20), mental retardation (Chapter 36), psychosomatic disorders (Chapter 26), psychotherapies (Chapter 30), and organic therapies (Chapter 31). Also of interest are the discussions of computers (Section 6.2), experimental disorders (Section 6.3), and sensory deprivation (Section 6.5).

REFERENCES

Barcai, A. The reaction of the family system to rapid therapeutic change in one of its members. Am. J. Psychother., *31:* 105, 1977.
Belmont, I., Birch, H. G., Klein, D. F., and Pollack, M. Perceptual evidence of CNS dysfunction in schizophrenia. Arch. Gen. Psychiatry, *10:* 395, 1964.
Broadbent, D. E. *Decision and Stress.* Academic Press, London, 1971.
Byrd, R. E. *Alone.* G. P. Putnam's Sons, New York, 1938.

Calhoun, J. B. Determinants of social organization exemplified in a single population of domesticated rats. N. Y. Acad. Sci. Trans., *25:* 437, 1961.

Chapman, J., and McGhie, A. A comparative study of disordered attention in schizophrenia. J. Ment. Sci., *108:* 487, 1962.

Chapman, J., and McGhie, A. Echopraxia in schizophrenia. Br. J. Psychiatry, *110:* 365, 1964.

Cooper, C. L., and Marshall, J. Occupational sources of stress: A review of the literature relating to coronary heart disease and mental ill health. J. Occup. Psychol., *49:* 11, 1976.

* Cramer, E. H., and Flinn, D. E. *Psychiatric Aspects of the SAM Two-Man Space Cabin Simulator.* United States Air Force School of Aerospace Medicine, Brooks Air Force Base, San Antonio, Tex., 1963.

Crosby, E. C., Humphrey, T., and Lauer, E. C. *Correlative Anatomy of the Nervous System.* Macmillan, New York, 1962.

Emlen, J. M. *Ecology: An Evolutionary Approach.* Addison-Wesley, Reading, Mass., 1973.

Flavell, J. H., Draguns, J., Feinberg, L. D., and Budin, W. A microgenetic approach to word association. J. Abnorm. Soc. Psychol., *57:* 1, 1958.

Flinn, D. E. Functional states of altered awareness during flight. Aerosp. Med., *36:* 540, 1965.

Fox, S. S. Self-maintained sensory input and sensory deprivation in monkeys: A behavioral and neuropharmacological study. J. Comp. Physiol. Psychol., *55:* 438, 1962.

French, J. R. P., and Kahn, R. L. A programmatic approach to studying the industrial environment and mental health. J. Soc. Issues, *18:* 3, 1962.

* Freud, S. Inhibitions, symptoms, and anxiety. In *Standard Edition of the Complete Psychological Works of Sigmund Freud*, vol. 20, p. 87. Hogarth Press, London, 1959.

Glassman, R. B. A neural systems theory of schizophrenia and tardive dyskinesia. Behav. Sci., *21:* 274, 1976.

Goldberger, L. In the absence of stimuli. Science, *168:* 709, 1970.

Gray, W. Current issues in general systems theory and psychiatry. Gen. Systems, *19:* 97, 1974.

Grinker, R. R. The relevance of general systems theory to psychiatry. In *American Handbook of Psychiatry*, S. Arieti, editor, ed. 2, vol. 6, p. 251. Basic Books, New York, 1975.

Grinker, R. R., and Sahs, A. L. *Neurology*, ed. 6. Charles C Thomas, Springfield, Ill., 1966.

Harwood, E., and Naylor, G. F. K. Nature and extent of basic cognitive deterioration in a sample of institutionalized mental patients. Aust. J. Psychol., *15:* 29, 1963.

Hemsley, D. R. What have cognitive deficits to do with schizophrenic symptoms? Br. J. Psychiatry, *130:* 167, 1977.

Heron, W., Doane, B. K., and Scott, T. H. Visual disturbances after prolonged perceptual isolation. Can. J. Psychol., *10:* 13, 1956.

Jaffe, J. Language of the dyad, a method of interaction analysis in psychiatric interviews. Psychiatry, *21:* 249, 1958.

Jones, A., Wilkinson, H. J., and Braden, I. Information deprivation as a motivational variable. J. Exp. Psychol., *62:* 126, 1966.

Kilburg, R. General systems theory and community mental health: A view from the boiler room. Int. J. Ment. Health, *5:* 73, 1977.

Lawson, J. S., McGhie, A., and Chapman, J. Perception of speech in schizophrenia. Br. J. Psychiatry, *110:* 375, 1964.

Lilly, J. In *Illustrative Strategies for Research on Psychopathology in Mental Health*, J. G. Miller, editor. Group for the Advancement of Psychiatry, New York, 1956.

Linton, P. H., and Estock, R. E. The anxiety phobic depersonalization syndrome: Role of the cognitive-perceptual style. Dis. Nerv. Syst., *38:* 138, 1977.

Lipowski, Z. J. The conflict of Buridan's ass or some dilemmas of affluence: The theory of attractive stimulus overload. Am. J. Psychiatry, *127:* 273, 1970.

Lipowski, Z. J. Surfeit of attractive information inputs: A hallmark of our environment. Behav. Sci., *16:* 467, 1971.

Lipowski, Z. J. Sensory and information inputs overload: Behavioral effects. Compr. Psychiatry, *16:* 199, 1975.

Luby, E. D., Gottlieb, J. S., Cohen, B. D., Rosenbaum, G., and Domino, E. F. Model psychoses and schizophrenia. Am. J. Psychiatry, *119:* 61, 1962.

Mason, J. W., Mangan, J. G., Brady, J. V., Conrad, D., and Rioch, D. M. Concurrent plasma epinephrine, norepinephrine and 17-hydroxycorticosteroid levels during conditioned emotional disturbances in monkeys. Psychosom. Med., *23:* 344, 1961.

McClearn, G. E., and Meredith, W. Behavioral genetics. Annu. Rev. Psychol., *17:* 515, 1966.

McGhie, A., Chapman, J., and Lawson, J. S. Disturbances in selective attention in schizophrenia. Proc. R. Soc. Med., *57:* 419, 1964.

Mendelson, J. H., Kubzansky, P. E., Leiderman, P. H., Wexler, D., and Solomon, P. Physiological and psychological aspects of sensory deprivation: A case analysis. In *Sensory Deprivation*, P. Solomon, P. E. Kubzansky, P. H. Leiderman, J. H. Mendelson, R. Trumbull, and D. Wexler, editors, p. 91. Harvard University Press, Cambridge, Mass., 1961.

Menninger, K. The amelioration of mental disease by influenza. J. A. M. A., *94:* 631, 1930.

Menninger, K. A. *The Vital Balance.* Viking Press, New York, 1963.

* Miller, J. G. Information input overload and psychopathology. Am. J. Psychiatry, *116:* 695, 1960.

Miller, J. G. Psychological aspects of communication overloads. In *International Psychiatry Clinics: Communication in Clinical Practice*, R. W. Waggoner and D. J. Carek, editors, p. 201. Little, Brown, and Co., Boston, 1964.

Miller, J. G. Living systems: Basic concepts. Behav. Sci., *10:* 193, 1965a.

Miller, J. G. Living systems: Cross-level hypotheses. Behav. Sci., *10:* 380, 1965b.

Miller, J. G. Living systems: Structure and process. Behav. Sci., *10:* 337, 1965c.

Miller, J. G. Living systems: The cell. Curr. Mod. Biol., *4:* 78, 1971a.

Miller, J. G. Living systems: The group. Behav. Sci., *16:* 302, 1971b.

Miller, J. G. Living systems: The organ. Curr. Mod. Biol., *4:* 207, 1971c.

Miller, J. G. Living systems: The organization. Behav. Sci., *17:* 1, 1972.

Miller, J. G. Living systems: The organism. Q. Rev. Biol., *48:* 92, 1973.

Miller, J. G. Living systems: The society. Behav. Sci., *20:* 366, 1975.

Miller, J. G. Living systems: The supranational system. Behav. Sci., *21:* 320, 1976.

* Miller, J. G. *Living Systems.* McGraw-Hill, New York, 1978.

Nidorf, L. J. The role of meaningfulness in the serial learning of schizophrenics. J. Clin. Psychol., *20:* 92, 1964.

Osgood, C. E., and Sebeok, T. A., editors. Psycholinguistics: A survey of theory and research problems. J. Abnorm. Soc. Psychol., *49* (Suppl.): 1, 1954.

Payne, R. W., Ancevich, S. S., and Laverty, S. G. Overinclusive thinking in symptom-free schizophrenics. Can. Psychiatr. Assoc. J., *8:* 225, 1963.

Pishkin, V., Smith, T. E., and Liebowitz, H. W. The influence of symbolic stimulus value on perceived size in chronic schizophrenia. J. Consult. Psychol., *26:* 323, 1962.

Rhodes, J. M., and Wyers, E. J. Effect of blindness on saccharine intake and manipulatory activity in rats. Am. Psychol., *11:* 445, 1956.

Robertson, J. P. S. Perceptual-motor disorders in chronic schizophrenia. Br. J. Soc. Clin. Psychol., *1:* 1, 1962.

Rosenblueth, A., Wiener, N., and Bigelow, J. Behavior, purpose, and teleology. Philos. Sci., *10:* 18, 1943.

Sawrey, W. L. Conditioned responses of fear in relationship to ulceration. J. Comp. Physiol. Psychol., *54:* 347, 1961.

Sebeok, T. A. Coding in the evolution of signalling behavior. Behav. Sci., *7:* 430, 1962.

Selye, H. *The Stress of Life.* McGraw-Hill, New York, 1956.

Snyder, S., Rosenthal, D., and Taylor, I. A. Perceptual closure in schizophrenia. J. Abnorm. Soc. Psychol., *63:* 131, 1961.

Solomon, P., Leiderman, P. H., Mendelson, J., and Wexler, D. Sensory deprivation: A review. Am. J. Psychiatry, *114:* 357, 1957.

Soskin, W. F., and Kauffman, P. E. Judgment of emotion in word-free voice samples. J. Commun., *11:* 73, 1961.

* Spitz, R. A. The derailment of dialogue: Stimulus overload, action cycles, and the completion gradient. J. Am. Psychoanal. Assoc., *12:* 752, 1964.

Starkweather, J. A. Content-free speech as a source of information about the speakers. J. Abnorm. Soc. Psychol., *52:* 394, 1956.

Starkweather, J. A. Vocal communication of personality and human feelings. J. Commun., *11:* 63, 1961.

* Toffler, A. *Future Shock.* Random House, New York, 1970.

Usdansky, G., and Chapman, L. J. Schizophrenic-like responses in normal subjects under time pressure. J. Abnorm. Soc. Psychol., *60:* 143, 1960.

Venables, P. H. Changes due to noise in the threshold of fusion of paired light flashes in schizophrenics and normals. Br. J. Soc. Clin. Psychol., *2:* 94, 1963a.

Venables, P. H. The relation between level of skin potential and fusion of paired light flashes in schizophrenic and normal subjects. J. Psychiatr. Res., *1:* 279, 1963b.

Watt, K. E. *Principles of Environmental Science.* McGraw-Hill, New York, 1973.

Weckowicz, T. E. Shape constancy in schizophrenic patients. J. Abnorm. Soc. Psychol., *68:* 177, 1964.

Wendt, R. H., Lindsley, D. F., Adey, W. R., and Fox, S. S. Self-maintained visual stimulation in monkeys after long-term visual deprivation. Science, *139:* 336, 1963.

Wheaton, J. L. Fact and fancy in sensory deprivation studies. Aeromed. Rev., *5:* 59, 1959.

Yates, A. J. Psychological deficit. Annu. Rev. Psychol., *17:* 111, 1966.

1.3 The Life Cycle

THEODORE LIDZ, M.D.

Introduction

An understanding of the life cycle and its vicissitudes is fundamental to dynamic psychiatry and psychotherapy. Like all higher organisms, humans go through a cycle of gestation, birth, immaturity, maturation, decline, and death largely determined by their biological make-up, but the unique means of adaptation of *Homo sapiens* greatly complicates the process, allowing people to live in greatly divergent ways but almost inevitably leading to interpersonal and intrapsychic impasses and conflicts.

The human species evolved largely through the selecting out of those mutations that favored the extension of inborn physical capacities by the use of tools, including that most valuable and intangible of all tools, language. Through the ability to communicate verbally, proto-humans gradually developed languages and, by transmitting the fruits of experience across generations, evolved cultures, different bodies of techniques for coping with the environment and for living with one another. As in all other animals, the biological make-up of humans was suited to maintain its essential physiological homeostasis only within rather limited physical environments, but people developed techniques of modifying environments to suit those limits. Through the ability to communicate with themselves—to think—humans could fragment past experiences, recall selectively, and use the past to project a future and to plan ahead. Thus, they were freed from learning primarily through conditioning and from being motivated mainly by physiological needs and basic drives. They also became aware at an early age of their ultimate death.

As an essential concomitant of their dependence on learned, rather than built-in, techniques, human beings mature so slowly that they are not fully grown until almost a third of the usual life-span has passed. Each person begins life totally dependent on parental figures and remains dependent on them for many years. During those years individuals assimilate the culture's techniques from those who raise them and take on not only their ways of doing things but also their ways of thinking and reacting emotionally; many of the cultural and parental directives become self-directives. Each person's patterns of reacting to family members deeply influence the ways of interacting with all subsequent significant individuals. The emotional ties to parents and the family become intense, but children must be so raised that they can eventually form intimate relationships with others and form families of their own. Although the family is a social system, it is an essential concomitant of the human biological make-up because the infant's development into a reasonably independent person requires care by persons to whom the child's survival is of paramount importance and who provide a shelter within the larger society, furnish models for identification, and knowingly or unknowingly enculture the child by conveying the society's techniques while providing for the child's biological needs. The development of an individual cannot be studied in isolation or, even as has often been done, in relation to the mothering figure alone, for the transactions within the family not only are an essential shaping force but enter into and become part of the developing person. Any attempt to study the child's development without considering the family in which it transpires is bound to err, as it leaves out an essential aspect of the process.

The study of personality development and maldevelopment and, concomitantly, the study of psychiatry would be relatively simple if the person just unfolded like an embryo from a fertilized germ cell and became an integrated, well-functioning person unless he was seriously deprived of emotional nutriment in early childhood or some emotional trauma disrupted the developmental process. Many students of personality dysfunction would like to believe it is so and, in seeking the reasons for personality disorders, focus on the search for physiological dysfunctions, currently primarily on defects in neurochemical transmitters. However, the journey from the womb to adulthood and then through maturity into old age is lengthy, circuitous, and beset by countless contingencies. Newborn infants are extremely malleable; the sort of persons they will become and how emotionally stable they will be depends greatly on where they are born, how their parents relate to each other as well as to them, the culture they assimilate, and the language they learn. The less the developmental process is genetically predirected and physiologically governed, the greater the chances that it will go awry.

The complexity of the topic is inordinate, probably the most complex matter that people have sought to study. In some respects, novelists and playwrights have been more successful than scientists in providing an understanding of how persons develop and in lending insights into the human condition. Those who study developmental psychology know that their subject will never be comprehended fully for it is limitless. Here, one can only offer an orientation and provide an outline that those who study human functioning can fill in by research and study and by gaining experience through the study of patients and perhaps even more pertinent, through the scrutiny of their own lives.

Phasic Development

The first 12 to 25 years of the life cycle involve the slow separation of the person from the mother and then from the family with the development of boundaries between the self and others and through individuation—the attainment of personality structure and the capacities for self-guidance to replace the care and guidance provided by parents and the structure and shelter of the family. The development of the personality, however, does not proceed at a steady pace but phasically. Children go through periods in which there is simply an expansion of skills attained and when progress may seem slight, and then they enter a new developmental phase and undergo a marked shift in the tasks with which they are coping.

During the period of physical maturation when children are acquiring the intrapsychic structure, security, knowledge, and skills necessary for life as adults, the epigenetic principle is extremely important. The principle holds that the critical tasks of each phase of development must be met and mastered at the proper time and sequence to enable the child to cope with the tasks of the next phase. If something happens to disturb the satisfactory passage through one phase, a series of maldevelopments follow in chain. The principle was adopted by psychoanalysis from embryology, for fetal development depends on each organ's arising from its anlage in the proper sequence. Although personality development is not as rigidly set as embryonic development, a child who does not acquire adequate autonomy from the mother has difficulty in going to school and relating to teachers and classmates. Moreover, compensations are possible, and deficiencies can sometimes be turned into assets, which is not the case with embryonic development.

The epigenetic principle does not apply to adult life as strictly as it does to childhood, but just how successfully persons manage any period in life rests to a considerable degree on how they lived through earlier stages.

The phasic nature of the life cycle results from several interrelated factors.

1. The acquisition of many abilities must wait on the physical maturation of the organism. For example, the infant cannot become a toddler until the pyramidal nerve tracts that permit voluntary discrete movements of the lower limbs become functional. Then, after such maturation occurs, it takes considerable practice to gain the skills needed to master a function, but the function becomes amenable to training and education. Adequate mastery of simple skills must precede their incorporation into more complex activities.

In a somewhat different way, shifts in the physiological equilibrium can initiate a new phase in the life cycle, as when the new inner forces that come with puberty require changes in personality functioning, whatever the preparation in prior phases of childhood.

2. Cognitive development plays a significant role in creating phasic shifts. The ability to communicate needs and desires verbally and to understand what parents say is a major factor

in ending the period of infancy, and the child's ability to attend school depends to a great extent on gaining the ability to form concrete categories at the age of 5 or 6. Cognitive development does not progress at an even pace, for qualitatively different capacities emerge in rather discrete stages.

3. Society establishes roles and sets of expectations for persons of different ages and statuses. At 5 or 6, a child becomes a schoolchild with new demands, opportunities, and interpersonal relationships. Marriage includes the expectation that areas of independence will be rescinded and the needs of the spouse will become major directives.

4. Children attain many attributes and capacities for directing the self and controlling impulses by internalizing parental characteristics in order to overcome gradually the need for surrogate egos to direct their lives and provide security. Such internalizations take place in stages in relation to the child's physical, intellectual, and emotional development.

5. Time itself is a determinant of phasic changes not only because of the need to move into age-appropriate roles but because changes in physical make-up—as at puberty and old age—require changes in self-concepts and attitudes. Awareness of the passage of time also fosters entry into new stages of life, as when persons realize that more time lies behind than ahead of them as they enter middle age.

Each phase of the life cycle presents critical tasks to be surmounted to enable the person to cope with the tasks of the next phase. Through mastering those crises, the person gains greater confidence, self-sufficiency, and integration. Many of the so-called traumas that initiate neuroses are simply the person's inability or difficulty in coping with those critical events that are an inevitable aspect of the developmental process. Although each person meets each developmental crisis somewhat differently, there are similarities in the ways people meet and seek to cope with similar developmental problems. The similarities in the developmental tasks, common problems in coping with them, and knowledge of the likely consequences of failures in mastering them provide major guidelines for psychotherapists.

A child or an adolescent often pauses before gaining the confidence to venture into the uncertainties of a new phase of life, much as many young adults pause before marrying. The pace of development is limited by the need for emotional security. The child is caught up in opposing motivations. There is an impulsion to expand, to achieve new skills, enter new situations, gain greater independence, and become more grown up, but the insecurity of acquiring new ways and rescinding some degree of dependency creates insecurity. The ensuing anxiety tends to impel the child to retain or regain the security possessed and to renounce, at least temporarily, forward movement or even to fall back to more childish ways of gaining security.

The tendency to stay put or to regress is more pronounced in those who have not yet mastered critical tasks of an earlier period. However, children need support and guidance to progress properly. At times they may need to be restrained from premature and unbridled use of new capacities, as when they begin to ambulate, and at other times they may need help and even urging to move into the next phase. Too much support can lead a child to become overly dependent; too little can leave the child struggling to keep afloat, creating anxieties that deter progression. The child may give up; more often the child moves ahead in some areas but squanders energies in repetitive efforts to cope with old, unresolved problems. A boy who has never felt secure away from his mother may remain at home,

seeking maternal affection or protection, while his peers are happy at the playground, secure with one another.

Such developmental arrests are termed fixation, and movement back to an earlier phase of development to gain security is termed regression. Paradoxically, both fixation and regression are part of normal development, for all children, at times, fall back to regain security after a forward thrust or when one of the inevitable exigencies of life upsets their equilbrium. Children generally progress with security when they feel they can find parental protection and understanding at the center of their expanding worlds. Although fixations and regressions are anticipated aspects of development, they create insecurities in turn if they are more than temporary expedients. The child remains unprepared for the next stage, which can lead to cumulative failures; or, if the tasks of later stages are managed, an underlying insecurity remains that limits and serves as a locus to which the person regresses when seriously frustrated in subsequent years.

Although the epigenetic principle, including the concepts of fixation and regression, is extremely important in understanding personality development and maldevelopment, as well as psychopathology in general, important panphasic influences must also be taken into account. The same parents, socioeconomic conditions, and cultural influences usually affect children throughout their formative years and often influence a child's transition through different phases in similar ways. Then, too, the intrafamilial transactions, including the manner in which parents relate to each other and the family ways of communicating, are major influences on the emerging personality.

Approaches to the Life Cycle

The outline of the stages of the life cycle and the critical developmental tasks of each stage that follows rests on four different approaches to understanding the phasic emergence of personality attributes as presented by Freud, Sullivan, Erikson, and Piaget, but it is more comprehensive and integrated than any of those models. As familiarity with each of those orientations is essential to the understanding of the literature and the language used in discussing personality development and psychopathology, the basic contributions of each are included in the presentation of the various stages when they apply, even when they differ from or run counter to the concepts of the writer. It is necessary, however, to understand the differing purposes of those several theories, as well as their sequential positions in the conceptualization of the developmental process.

FREUD

As an outgrowth of his epoch-making studies of childhood sexuality, based on his analysis of adult patients, Freud (1954) conceptualized five phases of psychosexual development between birth and maturity: the oral, anal, phallic or oedipal, latency, and genital phases. He was not actually proposing stages in personality development but tracing the vicissitudes of the sexual energy which he posited and termed libido and deemed the prime motivating force in human development and behavior. He believed that the libido becomes invested (cathected) in the oral, anal, and phallic zones in turn and then, after a lengthy period free of libidinal pressures, invests the maturing genitals at the onset of puberty. Whatever the merit of those concepts, they continue to exert a profound influence on psychoanalytic theory and therapy, and they served to draw attention to the phasic nature of child development, the importance of parent-child interaction to personality development, and the influence of the various phases of childhood development on subsequent character formation. Freud did not consider developmental tasks beyond the achievement of "genital sexuality" in early adolescence, and he tended to attribute all subsequent development problems to fixations at one of the childhood phases of psychosexual development.

SULLIVAN

Harry Stack Sullivan (1971) greatly modified psychoanalytic developmental theory by emphasizing its interpersonal aspects, particularly the importance of the interactions between mother and child to personality development and its pathology. Further, by considering the child's development within a social system, Sullivan sought to bring psychoanalytic theory into conjunction with the behavioral sciences. He was considering not only libidinal or psychosexual development but the interpersonal, social, and biological influences on personality development. Rather than considering the juvenile period as a time of latency, he emphasized the importance of the close friendships that developed as the child moved away from home and how a close friendship, as well as relations with other adults, could offset the damage from noxious family environments. He anteceded Erikson in considering the critical moment of adolescence in the developmental process.

ERIKSON

Erikson (1968), although tending to adhere to Freud's psychosexual phases, opened new approaches by superimposing an epigenesis of psychosocial development on them, and he went beyond the traditional psychosexual phases to consider the entire life cycle through old age. He emphasized the importance of late adolescence and early adult life, when the personality must jell and the person must achieve an ego identity and then the capacity for intimacy in order to become a reasonably stable adult. He formulated eight major stages in the life cycle and designated for each stage a crucial psychosocial task that the person has to surmount or suffer a setback that more or less permanently affects further development. The specific dichotomies used to characterize the crucial issues of each phase—such as the young adult period's requiring the achievement of true intimacy, with failure leading to self-absorption—sharpen the appreciation of the need to cope with tasks, rather than simply pass through the phase without succumbing to traumatic influences. However, the focus on a single critical issue for each phase of life has led to a gross oversimplification of the developmental process and a neglect of other tasks that are just as vital and some that may well be more important.

PIAGET

The theoretical approaches already mentioned virtually neglect linguistic and cognitive development, even though they are essential to understanding much of what is unique to human development. Although a number of investigators have studied cognitive development, Jean Piaget's (Piaget and Inhelder, 1969) studies of the epigenesis of cognition seem best suited to the study of personality development. Piaget's primary interest has been epistemology, but, in seeking the psychological foundations of knowing, Piaget and his co-workers examined the development of intellect—including language, reasoning, conceptualizing, and understanding time and space—and, concomitantly, the child's ethical development. They traced the ever-widening scope of the child's cognitive abilities by the constant process of adaptation of the existing organization of the organism to new experiences.

Children cannot properly use experiences that their cognitive capacities are not yet prepared to assimilate. The existing capacities undergo a process of adaptation—that is, they expand and reorganize—through accommodating to what has been assimilated and thereby become prepared to react to and assimilate new and more complex experiences. The organism is, so to speak, ever reaching out to incorporate new experiences within the limits permitted by its capacities and organization at that moment in its development.

Piaget's theory is more dynamic than associational psychology, learning theory, and operant conditioning as it posits a constant reorganization of the cognitive capacities. His theory and observations are of considerable moment to a conceptualization of the life cycle because they provide guides to how the child and the adolescent can understand their worlds at each stage of development, as well as because of the fundamental relationship between increasing autonomy and cognitive capacities.

Piaget divided cognitive development into four major periods with various subdivisions. The sensorimotor period is essentially concerned with preverbal cognition. The preoperational state covers the period when the child is learning to use symbols and language but does not yet think logically or conceptually. The period of concrete operations concerns the prepubertal school-age period, when the child gains a coherent cognitive system into which experiences can be fitted but is not yet capable of abstract conceptualization. In early adolescence the child first becomes capable of formal operations, thinking in propositions, reasoning on the basis of hypotheses, and using abstract concepts, but only a minority of people achieve more than the rudiments of such capacities.

AN ORIENTATION TO THE PHASES OF LIFE CYCLE

The division of the life cycle presented here follows fairly clear lines of demarcation. Infancy covers approximately the first 15 months, when children, unable to talk or walk properly, are completely dependent on others for their essential needs. In the toddler stage, crucial problems arise because of the imbalance between newfound motor skills and the baby's meager mental abilities, knowledge, and capacities for self-direction and control. At about 2½ or 3 years of age, the baby becomes a preschool or so-called oedipal child and moves away from a primary, erotized attachment to the mother to find a place as a boy or a girl member of the family. The child completes the process of basic socialization within the family to become a juvenile capable of attending school and moving into peer groups. Adolescence, which involves the discrepancy between sexual maturation and incomplete physical maturity and the unpreparedness for marriage and parenthood, is divided into three substages: early adolescence, including the prepubertal stage, when changes in bodily configuration herald the upsurge in sexual drives; midadolescence, with its expansive strivings and movement away from parental controls and standards; and late adolescence, when delimitation and the attainment of an ego identity are central issues. The young adult period is a time for commitments—to a career, marriage, and parenthood. The middle adult years concern the attainment of maturity and the passage over the crest, when a period of stocktaking occurs. As those years are not demarcated by any clear boundaries, the movement into the middle adult years or into middle age is a rather arbitrary matter. In old age physical abilities and usually mental capacities become limited, and sooner or later the aged become more or less dependent on others. Death, the end of the life cycle, profoundly influences how people live their lives.

It is not always feasible to sum up the tasks of a developmental stage under a common rubric, as Erikson does, nor is it always wise, because the rubric tends to oversimplify a very complex process. As Anna Freud (1965) emphasized, various aspects of the personality develop at different tempos, and the interrelationships between the development of such essentials as separation from the mother and the family, individuation, cognition, object constancy, interpersonal relations, gender identity, and ethical concepts require continuing study. Nevertheless, dividing the life cycle into phases enables one to compare various developmental lines and to study how a person's development may be globally or partially impeded, fixated, or regressed at any stage of life.

The presentation of the stages of the life cycle that follows can be only a sketch of the major aspects and critical tasks of each stage. For a more comprehensive presentation, the writer must immodestly refer the reader to his book *The Person* (Lidz, 1976)—which, as far as he knows, is the only effort to offer an integrated and reasonably comprehensive account of the entire life cycle—and to the excellent collection of relevant papers in *The Human Life Cycle* (Sze, 1975).

Infancy

Infancy consists of the first 15 months of life, lengthy months during which the helpless and totally dependent neonates become transformed into alert toddlers who actively seek to gain some mastery over their surrounding, limited world by constant exploration and experimentation. During the period the infant's weight triples to about 22 pounds, and the bodily proportions change markedly as the trunk and the extremities grow more rapidly than the head that seems so large at birth. The acquisition of six teeth permits some biting and chewing, and the myelinization of the pyramidal tracts of the spinal cord makes them functional and permits motor control of the lower extremities, enabling the child to stand, learn to walk, and begin to gain sphincter control.

An infant's capacities and needs change so markedly that it is difficult to discuss infancy as a unit. The period is unified by the baby's inability to walk or talk, except haltingly during the latter part of the period and by the extent of the baby's dependency. A mothering person is needed to surmise the baby's needs with relatively little direction from the child. The infant is completely dependent on others not only for sustenance and bodily care but also for the stimulation needed for proper cognitive development and the affection that fosters emotional stability.

A central theme and critical task of infancy concerns the establishment of feelings of confidence in the world (Benedek, 1959). If children's essential needs are met and untoward tensions do not repeatedly arise within them when unable to provide for themselves, they will, in Erikson's (1950) terms, attain a basic trust in others which forms the nucleus for achieving trust in the self. If needs are not met, the child is left with an enduring sense of distrust.

Psychoanalytic psychology has termed infancy the oral phase of psychosexual development, emphasizing that the infant's life centers on taking in nutriment through sucking, that the oral area is erotized to promote the enjoyment of feeding, and,

moreover, that the first critical relationships with others form while completely dependent on mothering persons and receiving vital nourishment from them. An enduring relationship is thereby established between affection and feeding, between a need for others and oral activity, and the basis is laid to regress or wish to regress to such oral dependency on others when overwhelmed by life's difficulties. Other later types of sensuous or erotic activity are related to those first oral sensuous gratifications and thereby connect orality to sexuality.

The concept of orality should not be taken literally to imply that how well the infant is fed is the only matter of primary importance. The oral relatedness properly includes the relationship through feel, odor, voice, body position and warmth, and the visual connections to the mother's eyes and face that are important aspects of nursing. And the sense of confidence and trust engendered in the infant relates to the tenderness, security, and conviction with which the mother carries out her many maternal tasks.

Salubrious development during infancy depends greatly on the establishment of a mutuality between a mothering person and the baby—the mother becoming able to interpret the infant's many nonverbal signals, the infant being able to feel at ease with the mother, gain a sense of predictability from her behavior, and find comfort and pleasure from interactions with her. Some mothers, because of their own experiences, have difficulty in empathizing; and some infants are cuddly and receptive, and others are rigid or loose and less responsive. In any case, the infant cannot purposefully change the nature of the relationship, but the mothering person may be able to find ways of doing so. Nevertheless, babies seem to have innate ways of helping assure their mothers' attachments to them (Bowlby, 1969). The infant's lips and the mother's nipples are both erogenous zones, and the baby's sucking provides the mother with sensuous pleasure, including genital stimulation; the mother's odor may, as in many animals, form a basic linkage between babies and their own mothers; the infant's cry may arouse a need in adults to alleviate the infant's discomfort. When the baby engages in eye-to-eye contact at about 4 weeks of age, the parents are apt to experience a deeper sense of attachment; and the baby's babbling that starts soon thereafter usually evokes a vocal response from an adult. The smile that at first is elicited by a soft, high-pitched voice and then by a nodding human face when the baby is 4 to 6 weeks old tends to arouse warmth and responsiveness in parents. The very young infant, however, is not yet smiling at the parents, for the smile is a built-in bit of attachment behavior that can be induced by a mask depicting a forehead, eyes, and a nose (Spitz, 1965).

During the first month of life, the infant is considered a neonate or newborn. The neonate is totally dependent on a mothering person. The primary needs seem to be for milk and sleep to foster growth and maturation. However, within a day or two of birth, the infant begins to follow objects within its field of vision and turns its head to the side on which a loud, sharp noise is made (Wolff, 1966) when in a state of alert inactivity but not when active, although, after 10 days or so, activity may stop if the infant begins to pursue an object visually. It appears that, aside from the purely reflex activity usually attributed to the neonate, the newborn's assimilation of some sensations begins soon after birth. Several types of crying can be differentiated that serve as guides to some parents; a rhythmic cry when hungry, an angry cry, and a pain cry can be differentiated (Wolff, 1966). Then, at about 3 weeks of age, a low-pitched moaning cry sets off a circular reaction, which the baby practices, thereby acquiring a way of obtaining attention. By the end of the first month, the baby laughs to proper physical stimulation and smiles to a nodding face or to cooing when in a proper state of arousal. Neonates, in their helplessness, paradoxically possess an omnipotence they will never again have—an omnipotence of helplessness when, with proper parenting, all their needs are served.

Although the importance of proper adequate nourishment for growth, the alleviation of discomfort, and the provision of affectionate care to foster basic trust have been emphasized, adequate stimulation to promote cognitive development is also vital to proper development. A fine balance holds between what attracts infants' attention and what they ignore on the one hand and what causes discomfort or even disorganizing fear on the other. Starting with innate reflex responses, sensorimotor schema (Piaget, 1963) or patterns are built up by the modification of the reflex responses by experiences. Then, unless a schema exists to which a new experience can be assimilated, babies pay no attention unless it intrudes on them when it may cause distress. If a new sensation or action is assimilated to a schema, the child tries to repeat the experience (termed a circular reaction by Piaget) until it has been accommodated into the schema or, in other terms, the child has become habituated to it. Infants of all ages can be active in fostering such assimilation until accommodation has taken place and the act or sensation no longer stimulates, and the infant is then ready to expand by assimilating new pertinent experiences. Thus, a cumulative change in the infant's behavior goes on through the repetition of circular reactions, each repetition altering behavior almost imperceptibly. The stimulation provided by an object changes with experience; a thumb is, at first, simply something to suck (as part of a sucking schema), later to be looked at (as part of a visual schema), still later something to play with, and so on.

During the first 4 months, the baby's physical maturation is of prime importance, and the care of his physical needs takes precedence over socialization. The mother is not yet an individual person to the baby. There is no proper distinction between what is internal and what is external, between self and environment, or between objects and the sensorimotor patterns through which the infant interacts with objects. Yet the mother is distinguished from others if she habitually cares for the baby. A child may cry if picked up by a stranger, and the mother's face is likely to produce a more pronounced smile than does another face. Innate reflexes are being modified by the repetition and expansion of circular reactions. The thumb no longer goes to the mouth simply by accident; sucking has been altered by experience. The infant can now control some hand movements, differentiate some sounds, respond to faces with a smile accompanied by babbling and kicking and arm waving, and anticipate sufficiently to stop crying at the sight of the mother or the sound of her voice. Parents' efforts to keep their infant satisfied are not always successful; and it is difficult to tell if the problem lies in a sensitive or irritable baby or in the parental handling. Most disturbances are short lived, but colic at around 3 months can present a major problem. It is a time when disturbances in the parent-child relationship are likely to give rise to physiological dysfunction, particularly in feeding and gastrointestinal functioning.

The middle third of the first year brings notable changes as the infant increasingly becomes a separate person and is very responsive to the parents. The infant becomes a lively character with a distinctive personality whose behavior can elicit warm responsiveness from parents. Mahler et al. (1975) considered that the first subphase of the separation-individuation process takes place at about the fourth month. Separation concerns the child's disengagement and differentiation from the mother; individuation involves gaining a stable inner representation of the mother, a capacity for testing reality, and the realization that others have an existence discrete from the child's. In a larger sense, individuation concerns the slow development of a self-structure that can replace the care and directives provided by parental figures. At 4 months of age, the infant moves from an autistic, self-contained state that Freud termed primary narcissism into a state of symbiosis with the mother.

By 7 months of age, a critical change takes place; parents clearly become specific persons to the child, who has become much more of a social being. Now babies can sit without effort and usually begin to make crawling movements when prone, and they babble incessantly, stimulated by their own voices and the voices of others. At about midyear, the infant seeks to repeat actions that accidentally produced a new experience. Through repetition, increasing control is attained, as when the baby learns to control the amplitude of the swing of a hanging toy by hitting it with different degrees of force. Now some movements that had been used to start a circular reaction are modified into slight movements as a token of recognition, rather than as an attempt to promote a repetition, and thus have taken on something of a symbolic connotation. Infants also now make movements that seem to be efforts to control distant objects as if by magic, but they are simply repeating what they did before some happening to bring about a repetition of the happening, such as shaking the crib to make the door open—actions that have something of an intentional character.

By the sixth or seventh month, the infant, as Piaget demonstrated, gains a new organizing principle by relating to the mother as a specific person (Spitz, 1965). The infant now needs specific parenting persons to feel secure. Stranger anxiety occurs, for now, instead of responding favorably to a stranger's smile, the baby shows evidence of apprehension and may start to cry. During the second half of infancy, lengthy separation from the mother produces a reaction similar to grief or an anaclitic depression that can go on to serious apathy and retardation, depending on the duration of the separation and the quality of the substitute. Now, too, prolonged deprivation of stimulation, as well as of affectionate nurturance, leads to serious impairments of cognitive and emotional development.

At around the seventh or eighth month, the infant gains an idea of an object, in contrast to the earlier inclusion of the object as part of a sensorimotor schema. If a pillow is placed between the child and a ball, the child pushes away the pillow and then grasps the ball. Actions are moving away from modifications of reflex acts to the pursuit of ends in view. Concomitantly, the infant enters what Mahler et al. (1975) called the practicing period of the separation-individuation process, which lasts until the end of infancy. Now, when children can crawl easily and then begin to walk, they make tentative trials at moving away from the mother but still require her presence to feel secure.

At about 10 months of age, the child not only begins to crawl but, if held by both hands, may walk in a tottering fashion. Babbling has moved toward the sounds of the language spoken to the child, and the parents are pleased with "da-da" and "ma-ma," even though those incipient words do not yet designate a parent. However, toward the end of the first year, a major landmark occurs—a step away from the unblemished innocence of infancy—when the baby begins to respond to "no." Although limited, the word is a control that can be exerted from a distance and marks a beginning of internalization of parental directives. Another half year passes before the children use "no" themselves.

By the time the child is a year old, a favorite blanket, sweater, or stuffed animal may have been adopted as a transitional object (Winnicott, 1953) that provides a sense of security in the mother's absence, particularly when going to sleep. As the child grows older, it often becomes difficult to take the object away or even provide a substitute for it without provoking serious upsets. The use of such transitional objects is a common aspect of the separation-individuation process.

In the beginning of the second year, the child clearly differentiates the self from the object and the object from the act; an exploration of objects turns into an experimentation with how objects can be manipulated. The child is experimenting to see what happens, rather than simply repeating experiences. What is learned in manipulating one object can be transferred to another object. Now, if a ball is rolled under a chair where the child finds it and is then rolled under another chair, rather than repeat the former successful search under the first chair, as a younger child would do, the child looks directly under the second chair. However, the limitations of the child's cognitive abilities are noteworthy, for, should the ball not be found under the second chair, the child will look under the first chair, where he had previously found it.

As children approach 15 months, they are usually filled with vitality and curiosity and are exploring their expanding surroundings and finding ways of mastering them. However, not all children flourish so; some may become apathetic and lack a glow, and others do not reach anticipated levels of intellectual capabilities. The studies of Spitz (1945) of institutionalized children indicated how seriously and irretrievably impaired children who receive little affection and stimulation can become; and Provence and Lipton (1962) documented institutionalized children's severe retardation, which cannot be fully overcome by later measures. The serious impairments of children raised in disorganized families has also been systematically studied, but much remains to be learned about the lasting effects of various types of emotional deprivation and deficient stimulation (Pavenstedt, 1967).

In psychoanalytic theory, developmental difficulties during infancy lead to oral fixations and to oral character traits of two types. Oral-incorporative characters, supposedly due to problems in the first 6 months, consistently seek to get from others and passively seek to be dependent on others, with little confidence in their abilities to survive unless someone feeds and takes care of them. Oral-aggressive characters seek to satisfy their needs for care aggressively, by grasping after what they need, hurting or exploiting others in the process. Those concepts are simplifications of a complicated matter, but oral traits need not be an epithet, simply a useful descriptive term for character traits, including traits that may be highly useful, such as the orality of an author who boundlessly takes in and then pours forth words or a financier who aggressively seeks money, as he feels insecure without endless supplies of funds to acquire food and insurance against want.

The Toddler Years

When babies start to walk and talk, they enter a phase that lasts for about a year and a half, during which many of the developmental problems derive from the imbalance between their newfound motor skills and their meager mental capacities. Their verbal and intellectual abilities lag far behind their impulses to use their new abilities to explore their surroundings. Limits must be placed on them for their own safety and for the preservation of the family possessions. With little ego of their own, parents must function as surrogate egos for them more than at any other time. Children find themselves in a relationship with their parents very different from the one they had before. The person who had nurtured them and encouraged expansiveness must now delimit, but the toddler does not understand, so the parents cannot properly explain reasons for the limitations. Parents expect children to respect limits and renounce immediate gratification, but toddlers are only beginning to be able to brook delay and frustration. They are also caught between their need for their mother and their wish to have greater autonomy. It is a difficult transition for an unreasoning and unreasonable baby.

Toddlers are moving away from the need for complete care and a symbiotic existence with a mothering person. In moving toward greater independence, they display several types of behavior that may seem paradoxical. They seem rather independent, comfortable, and active when the mother or some familiar nurturant person is about; but, when left with a stranger, they take less interest in their surroundings and appear preoccupied, and their activity slows; if upset, an unfamiliar person may be unable to comfort them. The condition disappears when the mother returns but, strangely, sometimes only after a brief crying spell—which may mark a release of pent-up tension. Then, during what Mahler et al. (1975) termed the rapprochement phase, some time after 18 months of age,

children may seem to regress and seek more attention from and closeness to their mothers. They are apt to follow their mother about and want the mother to interact with them more than previously. Parents may be annoyed by what seems an increased babyishness, but the toddler has not really regressed; he is forming a more real relationship than simply requiring the mother's presence. The mother's absence may now lead to greater activity, rather than a dampening effect, as it did earlier, as activity is used to help master the separation anxiety. However, when the child is away from home, as at nursery school, it may not help to know the mother is near or will soon return. A child may be too miserable to play and simply cling to a teacher. The child may reject everything the teacher does to comfort or distract, fall asleep to withdraw from the situation, or perhaps eat large amounts of cookies to replace the feeder with food.

The toddler phase is critical to the establishment of a basic trust in the self and a sense of initiative; when initiative is thwarted, the child develops a basic inhibition of expression and a tendency toward negativism. Toddlers are in the process of establishing boundaries between themselves and their mothers, physical and psychic boundaries, and gaining a sense that they can do things as separate individuals. They increasingly realize that parents are separate from them, and, as they cannot yet take care of themselves, the realization inevitably evokes anxieties.

The dangers lie on both sides. Driven by an inner impulse to activity and pulled by the attractions they wish to explore, they can readily injure themselves. Their venturesomeness depends, however, on having a shelter of a parent's arms nearby to which they can retreat when they overreach themselves. Mothers who become too anxious about activities that lead into a world containing real dangers may overly restrict with gates, playpens, and a barrier of no's that stifle both initiative and self-confidence. Parents who cannot tolerate disorder or messiness or who overestimate the toddler's abilities to conform can convey a sense of being bad or being dirty that inculcates a lasting sense of guilt or shame. The child may be forced into an overconformity that placates the parents but covers a hostile negativism and stubbornness.

Erikson (1950) considered the critical task of this phase of life to be the development of autonomy, with initiative the essential task of the next developmental phase. The difference is, in part, how the words are used and, in part, a matter of emphasis. Here, the development of autonomy is considered a primary task in the next phase, during the oedipal transition.

In psychoanalytic theory, the toddler period is the anal phase of psychosexual development, the period when, theoretically, the child's libido shifts its investment (cathexis) from the oral zone to the anal zone. The child now gains erogenous pleasure from passing or withholding bowel movements and from the stimulation experienced when the mother cleans the anal region. Giving or withholding, compliance or stubbornness, and related behaviors become important and influence character formation. It is clear that strict bowel training, as often practiced in Western societies, can epitomize all other requirements of primary socialization, but when early bowel training is not imposed on the child, very similar problems can arise simply from the need to accept delimitations and to begin to achieve some degree of self-control. The child can become engaged in a struggle for mastery, and a clash of wills with parents often ensues. Bowel training forms a good area for the conflict because parents cannot make the child perform when and as they wish; however, currently, the struggle almost as often focuses on eating.

Learning language is also a crucial task of the toddler period; indeed, the period terminates at the end of the third year, when children have gained sufficient vocabulary and syntax to comprehend much of what they are told and can convey most needs and desires verbally. They have internalized enough of their world to begin to reason and to listen to patient explanations that help them tolerate delay. When a reasonable equilibrium is established between their motor abilities and the more slowly acquired language, the problems concerning control that frequently make the toddler period trying for parents diminish markedly.

In learning language, children are beginning to acquire the adaptive technique that is uniquely human and on which much of their future learning rests. In the process, they are not only learning to communicate verbally but assimilating the culture's system of meanings and its ways of thinking and reasoning. Each society divides its ways of experiencing into somewhat different categories, and its vocabulary forms a catalogue of the categories it uses. The acquisition of language rests on the prior elaboration of sensorimotor schema during the first 15 to 18 months of life, but it is not a direct continuation of that form of cognitive development. It requires the assimilation of a system developed by others, rather than the further elaboration of the child's own schema; therefore, the development of language requires a new start, so that verbal communication at first plays a relatively small part in directing the baby's behavior.

The capacity to learn language is part of every intact person's innate endowment, but which language they learn and how effectively and rapidly they learn it depends on where they live and how effective their tutors, usually the members of their families, are. At the toddler stage, to gain proper language facility, they need a mothering person who is thoroughly familiar with them, and who can interpret their needs, gestures, and primitive use of words with reasonable accuracy and can teach them how things can be conveyed verbally. The consistency of the tutors' interactions with the child and the tutors' ability to suit the teaching to the child's capacities are extremely important.

All normal children start to babble early in life, the sounds they make stimulate them to repeat the sounds as a circular reaction and then to vary them. Vocalizations of others also stimulate babbling and, later, efforts to mimic and repeat the sounds heard. Certain repetitive sounds, such as "dadada," are selected out and repeated and thus reinforced. However, the young infant's use of "mama" is far from a designation of his mother. It first serves the simple instrumental function of calling attention to a wish or a need and only becomes limited to designate the mother between the ages of 10 and 15 months. Basic baby language is built on the same archetypical sounds made by infants everywhere that are reinforced and expanded into transitional words, such as "nana" for nurse or grandmother—a baby still being unable to vocalize "nurse" or "grandma." The parents, in accord with the child's expanding abilities, gradually use and teach sounds that more closely approximate the proper word.

Meanings expand before they narrow down to usage that is approximately correct. "Wawa," first used to ask for a drink, may expand to the glass and anything shiny like the glass but also to any fluid and only gradually narrows down to mean water to drink. It may then go through other false expansions when applied to running water or to rain. A word gradually takes on a discrete meaning and becomes a symbol for an object perceived in different perspectives and at different times and, with greater difficulty, for different objects with the same critical attributes that are categorized together by the same noun. "Doggie" may well be used correctly for the family dog, but for a time it may indicate any four-legged animal.

The development of syntax is gradual. Usually, the mothering person unknowingly turns a single word toddlers use at 18 or 20 months into a short phrase or sentence she believes the baby will understand. "Eat" is expanded into "Jimmy eat" or "doggy eat," depending on the situation. When children at about the age of 2 years begin to use two- to four-word expressions, the specificity of their communications increases markedly, despite their simplicity. "Mommy eat" is much more specific than a plaintive "mommy." Parents continue to expand the child's phrases in a way that only a person very familiar with the child can do and in the process teach the rudiments of syntax. In the third year, children begin to ask questions, often playing the naming game, and, if they have proper respondents, their language and comprehension increase rapidly.

There are indications that failures to learn language during this period may lead to permanent cognitive limitations, but intensive tutoring at a later date may be able to make up for the deficit, as in the case of Helen Keller. Children's dependence on their mothering persons for understanding is great, for no other persons are likely to be able to communicate as effectively with the toddler. It is one of the reasons why separation from the mother at the age of 2 or 3 years is traumatic for a child.

There is also considerable evidence that the child's basic gender identity is established by the age of 2½ or 3 years. Whether a child is a boy or a girl has always been and almost surely will continue to be one of the most important determinants of personality characteristics. It is difficult to determine how much of the gender-linked traits are innate and how much is due to environment, but studies by Hampson and Hampson (1961) and Money (1965) of various types of pseudohermaphrodites indicate that a major factor in determining gender identity is gender assignment, including the ways in which parents relate to a child they consider a boy or a girl and the child's identification with the parent of the same sex. It has been found that efforts to change the child's gender identity after the age of 3 years encounter serious difficulties and are not likely to be fully successful. However, the security of the child's gender identity can be affected by later events, particularly by the oedipal transition.

Although the emphasis here has been on the attainment of trust in the self and a sense of initiative as the major developmental tasks for the child between 18 and 36 months, it is apparent that other matters, including language development and the achievement of an identity as a boy or a girl, are also critical.

The Preschool or Oedipal Years

Around the age of 3 years, children enter a particularly important phase of the life cycle that has been termed the oedipal transition. The basic task lies in rescinding the close and erotized relationship with the mothering person that they needed as babies to become sufficiently autonomous as a boy or girl member of the family. The transition helps provide structure and integration to their emerging personalities and requires greater attention to the reality of their position in life and thus helps in the development of the cognitive capacities they need to manage with less parental guidance when they move beyond the family into school and the company of playmates.

By the time the phase ends at the age of 5 or 6, children are ready to enter school. They have mastered the tasks of primary socialization—to control their bowels and urine, dress and feed themselves, and control their tears and temper outbursts, at least most of the time. Even though they may spend part of the day in the tolerant and understanding environment of a nursery school, the preschool children's lives still center in the home. It is within the shelter of the family that coming to terms with reality as a boy or a girl, attaining the requisites of basic socialization, and establishing workable patterns of relating to others properly take place.

The process of attaining autonomy as a person distinct from the mother depends to some degree on the mother's ability gradually to frustrate the child's attachment to her, as well as the child's increasing desire for self-direction. The child, however, can now recognize that the mother's life does not center entirely on the child, and that the father and siblings have prerogatives. Children, therefore, experience frustrations and jealousies that arouse their anger, and become anxious lest their aggressive actions and feelings are reciprocated, but anxiety also arises almost inevitably because of the insecurities inherent in losing the close bond to the mother. The anxieties create regressive pulls toward regaining security by remaining dependent, and fixations at this oedipal phase are common.

It is necessary to comprehend the general nature of children's cognitive capacities and their understanding of their experiences to grasp the nature of the oedipal transition properly. Although 3-year-olds have acquired sizable vocabularies and have mastered the essentials of syntax, their cognitive capacities and their understanding of their surroundings and experiences are very limited. Their newly gained abilities to manipulate symbols imaginatively will ultimately permit reflective intelligent decisions, but for a time they interfere with problem-solving behavior. It is obviously simpler to solve problems in fantasy than to solve them in reality, and children do not yet have the experience to know what is reality and what is imagined. They are not at all certain that they cannot change the world to suit their needs or even to change themselves.

The nouns the child has learned are labels for categories, but, when they are first learned, they are virtually empty folders into which experiences that belong to the given category will be placed. Thinking is precategorical or, in Piaget's term, preoperational. The preschool child still focuses on the specific experience, rather than on the categorical meaning. Further, they still lack the organized frames of reference into which they can fit what they learn or the various systems developed by the culture—its measures of time and space, its value systems, and its ways of categorizing—to provide bases for comparison and evaluation.

During the preoperational period (Piaget and Inhelder, 1969) children are animistic and believe that inanimate objects have feelings, ideas, and wills of their own. Aspects of nature are explained by artificialism; as Piaget (1962) noted, the child believes that

the sky is a man who goes up in a balloon and makes the clouds and everything.

Everything in nature was made by man or for man; and parents are more or less omnipotent. Names are an inherent part of a thing or place. The rules of games, like their names, are something inherent to it or something that God or ancestors made up. Fantasy and reality are intermingled, and stories they tell may be considered as outright lies by adults who do not understand the limitations of the child's cognition. Further, children are profoundly egocentric, not only because the world centers on them, but also because of their lack of realization of the limits of fantasy.

As noted earlier, the little child's attachment to the mother includes strong erotic components; the baby requires erotically toned nurturance that stimulates sensuous oral, anal, genital, and tactile feelings that generalize to the child's entire relationship to his mother. The boundaries between self and mother that are at first nebulous gradually become more definite. The father becomes an increasingly important figure to a degree that depends on the family style. The initial symbiosis with the mother divides into an identification, with the child seeking to be like the mother, and into an object relationship, in which the child seeks to maintain a tender and erotized relationship with her. In the young girl, many factors lead to an increase in the identification, whereas the boy's identification with his mother diminishes, but he seeks to retain her as a primary love object.

The preschool child is egocentric and nowhere are little children more egocentric than in their relationship with their mothers. They consider themselves central to their mothers' lives, just as the mother is central to their lives. They resist accepting the changes in the relationship that are part of growing up and of individuation, but reality inevitably forces the child to come to terms. The renunciation of priority with the mother and the resolution or repression of the erotic components of the attachment to her—the resolution of the oedipal attachment—seem to be the pivot about which many changes in the organization of the child's personality consolidate. Just how the process transpires greatly influences all future relationships to significant persons, as well as the security of the child's gender identity.

Freud's discovery of the Oedipus complex was one of the great advances in human beings' understanding of themselves, and, as it forms a cornerstone of analytic theory, Freud's version of the transition is presented here briefly, and then its modification in the light of contemporary understanding of children is considered.

Freud recognized the little boy's intense attachment to his mother. He understood the upsurge in the boy's sensuous love for his mother in terms of the vicissitudes of the child's libido. After the anal phase, the libido becomes invested in the boy's phallus and in the girl's clitoris. The shift causes an upsurge of sexual feelings that leads to a boy's sexual desires for and fantasies about his mother and a girl's desire for her father. The child has fantasies of sexually possessing the parent of the opposite sex and resents the parent of the same sex as an intruder and rival. Wishing to be rid of the rival parent, hoping for his death, or having fantasies of killing that parent, the child projects his or her hostile feelings onto the same-sex parent and fears harm from that parent. Typically, the boy, experiencing genital sensations that accompany his erotic fantasies, fears that his father will cut off his penis, which Freud called castration anxiety. At times, Freud believed that castration anxiety was the cause of virtually all anxiety, including the fear of death. Unable to stand the anxiety, the boy represses his erotic desires for his mother and, instead, decides to become a person like his father who can gain the love of a woman like his mother. In the process, the boy gains a superego (Freud believed that the libidinal energy now went into repressive, socializing forces) by taking over the father's restrictions and prohibitions to enable him to maintain the repression of the oedipal desires. The boy is also strengthened in his masculinity by his identification with his father.

Freud's explanation of the girl's oedipal transition as a mirror image of the boy's, impelled by fears that her mother will reject or kill her, was never satisfactory. He believed that the girl turns from her attachment to her mother because the mother does not have a penis or because the girl blames her mother for depriving her of a penis. She comes to desire her father because he can provide her with a baby to compensate for the absence of a penis. However, the fear of the mother's jealousy leads her to abandon her desire for the father and to identify with her mother. Late in his career, Freud (1962) recognized that, when the girl gives up her libidinal attachment to her mother, she finds a new love object within the family in her father and that she does not usually repress that erotized attachment to her father until pubescence. Thus, the girl's oedipal transition occurs in two stages, widely separated in time.

There is, however, no evidence that a preschool-age child experiences an upsurge of libido caused by increased sexual drive, such as occurs at puberty. Children masturbate earlier than the oedipal years, and biochemical assays show that gonadotrophic hormones are not detectable in preschool-age children and that the androgen and estrogen contents of the blood are negligible at that phase of life.

Nevertheless, the oedipal transition is critical because, at that time of childhood, children of both sexes must overcome their intense bonds to their mothers. Now that children are becoming capable of getting along without constant care and can look after themselves in many ways, the mother turns her energies elsewhere and frustrates the child. Children suffer a narcissistic blow when they learn that they are not central to their mothers' lives, and that her affections are divided between her husband and her other children as well. It becomes apparent that the father has prerogatives denied the child. The blow to the child's self-esteem and security may be severe. Wertham (1941) noted that the resentment toward the mother can reach matricidal proportions and can form the basis for lasting misogynistic tendencies. Most children, however, develop defenses against that blow to their narcissism. The boy decides to marry his mother and retain her care and love. The girl turns to her father, who admires her mother. Whether such wishes are expressions of infantile sexuality, as Freud believed, or natural security operations remains debatable. However, when and if the child recognizes the parents' priority with one another and other reality factors—augmented, at times, by fears of the jealousy of the other parent—the child develops a new and more lasting defensive pattern.

The boy may, as Freud found, give up his mother because of fear of his father and gain strength by identifying with his father. However, when the relationship between the parents is good and the father has an affectionate relationship with the son, a more salubrious outcome often occurs. The boy simply identifies with his father, whom his mother loves, in order to retain his mother's love and to become a person who will eventually be able to gain a wife like his mother, and thus he gains a model to follow into adulthood, as well as his father's approval and protection.

Obviously, there are other ways to defend against anxiety and depressive feelings that come when a boy loses his primacy with his mother. The various patterns that develop lead into different types of personality development. As noted, lasting resentment against the mother can lead to misogynistic tendencies; on the other hand, a clinging to the mother and a continuing identification with her promotes gender confusions. Much depends on how the parents relate to each other as well as to the child.

Freud considered female development more complicated than male development because the girl has to shift from her primary erotized attachment to her mother to find a basic love object in her father. However, as the girl can continue her primary identification with her mother, in contrast to the boy, and can then find a new love object within the family in her father, her developmental task is in many ways simpler. The difference may account both for the tendency for the school-age or latency girl to remain centered within the home more than the boy and for the greater frequency of developmental disturbances in school-age boys than in girls. In a sense, the girl first forms an intense oedipal attachment to her father at the age when the boy is overcoming his oedipal attachment to his mother. Then, at about the time of puberty, the girl becomes anxious about her erotized fantasies about her father and begins to take distance from him, a move usually abetted by the father's need to move away from his sexually attractive daughter. The girl's oedipal transition then usually occurs in two stages—giving up of the intense attachment to the mother as a pre-school child and repressing the libidinal attachment to the father just before or during pubescence.

The outcome of the oedipal situation depends on many factors. A properly structured family, particularly when there is a firm coalition between the parents and clear boundaries between the generations, keeps the child from seeking to insert himself or herself between the parents and directs the child into finding a relatively conflict-free place as a boy or a girl member of the family. The need to rescind the wish to preempt a parent brings about a reevaluation of the child's world. The child will never again view life so egocentrically, and fantasy now yields to reality. A giant step has been taken toward becoming autonomous individuals, even though children recognize that it will still be a long time before they can become independent and gain adult prerogatives. The manner in which the oedipal situation or family romance has been lived through is likely to set a pattern that will be relived in different variations in later life.

The Juvenile Years

The half dozen years from the time children enter school to the spurt of growth that precedes puberty constitute the juvenile period, during which the personality integration achieved with the completion of the oedipal transition has time to consolidate before the emotional upsurge of puberty initiates the need for a reintegration. However, consolidation is not the major issue, for children enter a new phase of the separation-individuation process as they emerge from the home to venture into school and into play groups consisting of peers. Although the family remains central to their lives, they are now not only practicing being on their own but also gaining a sense of how they will fit into the broader society.

Classical psychoanalytic theory considers the juvenile period as the latency phase, a transition between the oedipal period and the onset of puberty; it is a time when a biological subsidence of sexual drives ushers in a period of relative calm. However, as there has not been any evidence of an increased sexual drive during the oedipal period, there is no reason to believe that a diminution of drive accounts for the critical aspects of the period. Still, having come to terms with their positions in their families and having repressed or resolved much of their sensuous attachments to the mother, energies are liberated for learning and for freer involvement with peers. Children now require less immediate care and less physical care from their parents; with activities and interests centering more on school, friends, and learning, there is usually less turmoil at home.

Many of the crucial tasks of the juvenile period arise because of the shift from ascribed to achieved status and acceptance. Young children's positions in their families are determined largely by biological factors—sex, age, and ordinal position—and they receive love or acceptance simply because they are their parents' children. In contrast, in school and with peers at play, children are judged by their own capabilities and personality traits. As a member of a group, each is often treated as a part of a collectivity, rather than with individualized attention. Further, teachers evaluate children differently from the way their parents do, peers differently from teachers, and often playmates differently from schoolmates. Indeed, the teacher has the obligation increasingly to evaluate on the basis of achievement, rather than by ascription (Parsons, 1964). In the process children overcome much of their family-centered orientation to the world and themselves and gain more of a sense of self by how others relate to them and value them.

Harry Stack Sullivan (1971) was among the first to emphasize the importance of the juvenile period and the child's finding a place in the peer group, particularly the significance of a chum relationship as the first major emotional investment in a peer other than a family member. He also noted how the relationship with a chum or a significant adult can rescue a child from destructive family relationships. Erikson (1959) considered the development of a sense of industry crucial to the juvenile period; the negative outcome of the period, the development of pervasive feelings of inferiority and inadequacy. The trait of industriousness is encompassed, on one side, by the danger of compulsive striving to excel competitively—a trait so highly valued in American society that its pathological aspects often remain unrecognized—and, on the other side, by the danger of defeatism and unwillingness to face meaningful challenges.

In accord with the transition to achieved status, other important characteristics develop. A sense of belonging to the group, as against feeling like an outsider; the sense of belonging may involve commitment to the values, beliefs, and ethics of the society, as against alienation. It is also the time when a sense of responsibility develops—a willingness and a capacity to live up to expectations and to consider the rights and needs of others. Children now begin to assume their position in society as leaders, helpers, followers, dissidents, outsiders.

In moving into the world beyond the family, children take on new values, view their social worlds from different perspectives, and thus move beyond the egocentric and family-centered orientation of early childhood—a change that plays a major role in the child's further cognitive and ethical development.

The maturing child gradually moves into a new stage of cognitive development under the influence of formal education, as well as through the new perspective and experiences gained outside the family. At the age of 6 or 7, children are often still unconcerned by obvious contradictions and may continue to confuse their fabulations with reality, sometimes making assertions with the conviction that something is so simply because they believe it to be so. Piaget (1963) emphasized the child's inability to carry out the mental operations of conservation and reversibility. When, for example, water from a container is poured into a narrower container, the child states that the narrower container has more water because the water rises higher in it. They do not realize that, if the operation were reversed, the water would be at the previous level in the original container. They do not retain the original image or mentally reverse the procedure. They are also unable to use two factors at the same time and consider either only the width or only the height of the column of water. Children begin to master such problems at about the age of 7 and so enter the stage of concrete operations. They become capable of classifying objects according to increasing size, weight, color, and so on, and then begin to classify them by using two attributes, such as color and shape, simultaneously. At least some of the ability to form concrete categories comes from learning an integrated cognitive system into which they can fit their experiences and ways of solving problems. Not until adolescence will they become able to think reflectively and develop the capacity to form abstract concepts.

A number of factors are leading to profound changes in moral development. The chum relationship leads the child to think in terms of "we," instead of "I," and to achieve an incipient altruism. Kohlberg (1964) showed that ethical development more or less parallels cognitive development. Whereas preschool-age children only imitate the using of rules and bend the rules to their wishes, juveniles are likely to consider the rules of a game immutable, something inherent in the game that cannot be changed by agreement. A young juvenile does not properly know the difference between a lie and a mistake. Whereas a preschool-age child decides what is right or wrong by what elicits punishment, the juvenile may recognize that a child has been punished erroneously. By and large, however, the juvenile exhibits what Piaget (1948) termed the morality of constraint, believing that the same punishment should be meted out for the same offense, regardless of the circumstances. They do so because they largely accept the adults' value system, which they do not understand and cannot yet analyze.

The society of playmates has a socializing influence as a subculture of its own in which mores and skills are transmitted

relatively independently of the family or the school; the mores and skills are passed on from one age group to the next entering the age group in constant succession and with a much more rapid turnover than the generational cycle. The age roles have been established over countless generations and afford children the opportunity to use their expanding abilities and gain acceptance according to their worth to the peer group.

By and large, the two sexes are more completely separated in the juvenile years than at any other time of life—at least, they have been in the past. The division into different gender groups may be instigated by boys more than by girls. The boy is overcoming his initial identification with his mother and his dependence on her. He may also be countering an envy of a girl's prerogative to remain more dependent. The boy convinces himself that there is nothing he would less want to be than a girl, and repressing any such desire is one of the important tasks of the juvenile period. How much of the differences in a boy's behavior and a girl's behavior is innate and how much is socially fostered remains problematical. The contemporary trend to insist that girls be permitted to join boys' games is also problematical, for it may interfere with the process by which the boy gains a firm gender identity, particularly in view of a girl's earlier physical maturation, which can impart a temporary superior physical prowess. Toward the end of the juvenile period, when the boy feels more secure of his masculinity, the two sexes may mingle more freely and have the opportunity to gain some familiarity with the ways of the opposite sex before the shyness and tensions that often accompany adolescence interfere with boy-girl relationships.

Adolescence

Adolescence can be defined as the period between the onset of sexual maturation and the completion of physical growth. However, in considering the life cycle, one starts with the preadolescent spurt of growth that initiates the transition from childhood. The adolescent period involves the discrepancy between sexual maturation, when the child undergoes a physical metamorphosis that initiates a drive toward procreation, and the physical, emotional, and social unpreparedness for marriage and parenthood. Adolescence ends when the person is ready to make the commitments concerning career and marriage that greatly determine the further course of his life.

During the passage through adolescence, the dependent children with still unshaped futures become persons responsible for themselves with definite ego identities and the capacities to share one's life with a person of the opposite sex. A successful passage through adolescence depends not only on an earlier satisfactory resolution of the oedipal transition and the other earlier developmental phases but, as Erikson (1956) emphasized, also on surmounting some developmental hurdles specific to adolescence that lead to a reorganization and reintegration of the personality to permit the person to function as an adult. The adolescent is moving toward the closure of dependence on parents and to an identity as a person in his or her own right and not simply as someone's son or daughter. Erikson (1956) considered achieving an ego identity as the basic task of adolescence, with ego diffusion as the negative outcome. There are, however, other negative outcomes, such as identity foreclosure (Hauser, 1971), which occurs when a person fails to develop beyond the juvenile stage or early adolescence and which sometimes includes the assumption of a negative identity, the identification with persons who are feared, hated, despised, or shunned—developments usually related to deprivation and the aberrant role models provided in the inner-city slum. Continued dependence and inability to assume responsibility for the self is another potential negative outcome. For many, however, gaining an ego identity involves also achieving a capacity for intimacy, the ability to form a significant relationship with commitment to another person without fear of loss of the self. Adolescence, however, is a lengthy developmental period, during which other important developmental tasks must be surmounted before an ego identity and a capacity for intimacy can be attained.

Although the years of adolescence can be subdivided in various ways, here they are somewhat arbitrarily divided into early, middle, and late subphases, each with different basic developmental tasks.

EARLY ADOLESCENCE

The gradual growth and maturation of the child and the gradual development toward increasing independence is disrupted by the metamorphosis of puberty that impels the child toward a more adult perspective simply by the change in size and contours. New sexual impulses create strange feelings and longings that add an irrational force with which the child has not had prior experience. The metamorphosis brings about a new and clear differentiation between the sexes but also increases the attraction between them. The need for readjustment starts about 2 years before pubescence with a marked increase in the rate of growth and weight gain.

Two aspects of the changes in size, contours, and drives are important in changing the child's social milieu and the relations between the sexes: the maturation of girls about 2 years earlier than boys, with puberty occurring at a median age of 12½ in girls and about 14½ in boys, and the notable variation in onset in different children. The relationships between boys and girls are often disrupted by the greater height of girls and then by the girls' earlier sexual maturation, which changes their interests, as well as their physiques. Relationships between friends of the same sex may be affected by the relatively early or late start of the changes in physique. A very early onset may cause embarrassment, particularly to a girl, and difficulties in coping with internal drives and the changes in the way others relate to her.

With menarche, the girl not only begins to experience an increase in sexual impulses but also comes under the influence of the cyclic changes in hormonal balance that directly or indirectly affect mood and behavior. She must also now definitively come to terms with being female, a fact that she may have managed to avoid. Although the onset of menstruation is traumatic to some girls, the vast majority of adolescent girls have been looking forward—although usually with some trepidation—to the signal event that marks a major turning point in their lives. The girl now feels confirmed in her femininity. Unfortunately, she is often told that she has now become a woman, whereas in contemporary society, at least, she is still far from being a woman or being ready to cope with the responsibilities of womanhood. She also becomes aware that men now regard her differently, perhaps lustfully, which she may simultaneously resent and desire.

Although the changes in the boy are also marked—his body mass and strength double between the ages of 12 and 17, his genitals develop, and his voice changes—there is no definitive marker of the onset of puberty, as in the girl. In most societies, the change is marked by a ritual, often a confirmation of the boy as a man and the girl as a woman. The ritual may be more important for the boy, who lacks the natural marker of menarche, but for both sexes the ritual often seeks to deepen the sense of responsibility for the self and for one's sexual behavior. At that time of life, both boys and girls need confirmation of their status and worth, and confirmation by the trust and admiration of parents may be more important than the societal ritual.

Young adolescents are particularly prone to feelings of embarrassment, shame, and guilt. They fear that others detect their crushes or sexual feelings. A girl fears that boys know she is menstruating, or she feels that her growing breasts are ungainly. The boy is embarrassed by an unexpected erection he must seek to conceal. Acne becomes a source of concern and shame. Guilt over masturbation and sexual dreams may preoccupy and frighten; a boy's inability to control masturbatory urges may lead to fears that he is promoting eventual insanity or impotence. Self-consciousness concerning one's physique is an almost inevitable concomitant of puberty.

The young adolescent's life continues to be family centered. Sexual drives are usually sublimated into fantasy and channeled into other activities, rather than acted upon. A reawakening of oedipal feelings frequently takes place, particularly in the boy, who idealizes his mother; but the girl, whose erotized attachment to her father had often just been renounced, may be left feeling lonely and deserted. The renewed attraction to a parent, accompanied by unconscious or not so unconscious sexual feelings and fantasies, may arouse intense guilt or may be countered by an irritability that threatens to disrupt family relationships. A father's withdrawal of attention and affection in response to his daughter's sexual attractiveness is, unfortunately, frequently interpreted by the daughter to mean that she has become unattractive to him now that she has developed physically. As sexual drives can now be repressed only with difficulty, fantasies turn toward members of the opposite sex, often toward older idealized figures before turning toward age-mates. When parents fail to maintain the boundaries between the generations, incestuous thoughts are apt to become conscious and require pathological defenses that distort the adolescent's development and may impel him or her to premature sexual activity.

Just when children are beset by the awakening of sexual drives that can lead to impulsive activities with lasting consequences, they enter a new phase of cognitive development and acquire new intellectual abilities that can help them cope with their drives and feelings more effectively. It is not merely a quantitative increase in cognitive abilities but a qualitative change. Adolescents enter Piaget's period of formal operations (Inhelder and Piaget, 1958) and become capable of understanding and constructing abstract concepts, of thinking about thinking, of reasoning on the basis of hypotheses, of trying out mentally what the various consequences of a potential act may be for their ultimate goals. The capacity to think conceptually develops gradually throughout adolescence, and a large proportion of people never develop such abilities except in rudimentary form (Dulit, 1972). As a concomitant of the change in cognitive abilities, the adolescent characteristically overvalues cognitive solutions of problems, not yet recognizing the extent of the difficulties in changing fantasied solutions or achievements into actuality. There is also an increased ability to think about the future they tentatively conceptualize, and to become involved with ideals and ideologies into which they can sublimate their increasing sexual drives. The need to contain the body's demands for sexual release and fulfillment increases the role of unconscious processes in directing behavior and augments the role of the irrational just at the time when cognitive development has opened new ways of achieving rational solutions.

MIDADOLESCENCE

A year or two after pubescence, the increase in sexual drives creates a need to gain emotional and sometimes physical distance from the parents. Adolescents now enter a pivotal time, when they turn away from the family, which has formed the center of their existence. They now seek to feel competent to direct their own lives and no longer act as dependent children. The adolescent's inner equilibrium is upset by the intense libidinal drives with which the child has had little experience. The interdict on the expression of sexuality needs to be lifted, but the repression on linking sex with affection for family members must be maintained and even strengthened. Conflicts are increased by the upsurge of oedipal attachments that confuse and can threaten the integrity of the adolescent and the family. There is a longing for intimacy and sexual release, but most midadolescents are not yet ready for real sexual intimacy. It is often a time of considerable turmoil, as the shift in relationships with parents and the need for ways to cope with libidinal desires require a profound inner reorientation. Most adolescents are helped in finding their way through by the ways and mores of the peer group, as well as by firm but understanding guidance by parental figures.

Midadolescence is, by and large, a time of revolt and conformity. The revolt is against parents and their standards, which must be denied to enable adolescents to try things out on their own. They must prove to themselves that they no longer need to rely on parental judgment and directives. However, much of their own inner directives derive from their parents. The parental restrictions suited to childhood must be loosened to permit more adult behavior but more firmly internalized to enable the adolescent to direct the self with less parental supervision.

Although modification of the superego is an intrapsychic matter, at this time of life it usually involves changing perceptions and evaluations of the parents, whose values have been internalized. Adolescents seek to convince themselves that their parents do not always know what is correct and that their parents are far from perfect themselves. They may begin to act and talk as if nothing the parents do and say is acceptable. They are caught up in their own ambivalences—wanting and needing the parents and their guidance and wanting to be free of them. Arguments can become blindly irrational to help overcome their contradictory needs. Midadolescence is the proper time to want to be and to need to be both dependent and independent. Adolescents at this stage are not yet ready to be on their own but, rather, have entered a third and final practicing period in the lengthy process of separation and individuation; as it is still a practicing period, they still need support, guidance, and a haven from which they can venture and to which they can return and still receive acceptance and affection.

The process of gaining independence from the parents is complicated and aggravated by the resurgence of oedipal feelings that generally accompanies the upsurge of sexual impulses—feelings that contribute to the need for separation. Many of the expressed causes of conflicts between adolescents and parents are but surface manifestations, displacements and rationalizations of the sexual struggle that both attracts and repels the adolescent from the parents. The adolescent often engages in fantasies that are thinly disguised daydreams of gaining the parent of the opposite sex and being rid of the parent of the same sex. Occasionally, awareness of the sexual attraction breaks through or an incestuous dream frightens, but the unconscious fantasies exert an influence. Displays of affection may be suddenly replaced by irritability with everything a parent does or by avoidance of being close to the parent. It requires unusual empathy and understanding for a parent not to be perplexed and troubled by the child's inconsistency and criticisms. Temporarily, guilt over sexuality causes renewed sexual repression, but, ultimately, it is the attraction to the parent that is repressed. Serious problems arise when parents cannot contain their own seductiveness, when a parent conveys that the child is preferred to the spouse, and when the child is parentified to meet the emotional and sensual needs of a parent.

The conformity is to the youth group. As adolescents seek to move away from their parents, the adolescent peer group gains in importance. The youth group tends to have something of an antiadult orientation, but, as it tends to be composed of adolescents with similar backgrounds and interests, it is not usually a counterculture. The youths band together for support and guidance, as well as companionship. In the group they feel free of parental guidance; but, uncertain of themselves they often conform rigidly to the ways of the group. Here they try out more adult behavior, which may mean daring to do things that had been forbidden in childhood. In the group they find others who admire them and others who serve as models, and thus they have replacements for the losses suffered in withdrawing from the family. With the support of the group and of particular close friends within the group, they learn to manage without parental supervision. The group serves an important function both in modifying the superego and in fostering a sense of identity. By observing and identifying with others in the group and noting the group's reaction to the self, by taking on the group mores, and by constant discussions, the adolescents alter their guiding principles and gain a sense of how they fit into social groups.

The adolescent group is usually monosexual at first, for throughout midadolescence friendships with members of the same sex take prece-

dence, particularly for boys. There is still considerable narcissism in the admiration of others, and teenagers are apt to be close to others with whom they can identify and thus gain guidance and a clearer sense of self.

Although adolescent groups are sometimes thought of as gangs that raise parents' concerns, the composition of a group of teenagers from similar backgrounds means that the group usually exerts a modifying and restraining influence on its members, even though it fosters activities toward the limit of what is acceptable to parents. A member is not likely to risk ostracism by going beyond what is acceptable to the group. When youths from good neighborhoods join groups with delinquent mores, they almost always come from homes that somehow foster antisocial tendencies or are so restrictive that they permit no latitude for the expansion necessary for the adolescent.

Movement toward the opposite sex usually starts slowly. The adolescent must first become more secure of his or her sexual identity before daring to engage with the other sex. The need for narcissistic supplies that are more likely to come from the opposite sex may motivate as much as sexual drive. Crushes antedate going together, and achieving real sexual intimacy usually awaits late adolescence, even though many younger adolescents engage in sexual relations. Sexual activity starts tentatively and may involve trying out feelings, gaining experience and courage, and testing one's limits; if sexual intercourse occurs, it is not likely to be satisfactory. Adolescents of both sexes must not only overcome deeply entrenched repressions of sexuality but also disengage their sexual feelings from their intrafamilial love objects. The boy may need to overcome castration fears involving his own or the girl's father and feelings that females in the image of his mother are powerful and enveloping. The girl may have to overcome fears of penetration and the fears of annihilation that come with impending orgasm. The girl may pause before losing her virginity and all it symbolizes, although she may also be anxious to have the experience behind her and to feel herself a knowledgeable woman. Whether or not to engage in sexual intercourse is often considered in terms of morals, but successful sexual relations require maturity, and the immaturity of the midadolescent provides proper and sufficient reason for delay.

Midadolescence is properly a time for expansion, a time to explore one's own feelings and capacities, as well as the ways of the opposite sex. It is also a time when fantasy formation helps provide solace for the lack of romantic involvements and worldly achievements. It is a time when ideals and ideologies may replace parental teachings and provide guidance; a youth may practice ascetic denial for ideological purposes, unaware that it also serves to control sexual and aggressive drives. The adolescent is filled with potentiality, and the intensity of feeling about beauty and desire may be almost too much to bear; it is a time for dreams of future greatness and fulfillment.

LATE ADOLESCENCE

The expansiveness of midadolescence tends to give way to a need to consolidate and imaginatively and realistically try out ways of life, including trials at relating meaningfully to persons of the opposite sex. Achieving an ego identity and achieving the capacity for intimacy are the interrelated major tasks of late adolescence. The question "Who am I?" is repeated consciously and unconsciously as the young person tries to decide what to do with his or her life. They realize that time is running out, and they will soon be expected to assume adult roles; if they do not make decisions, the passage of time will make them instead. Yet they cannot make decisions concerning careers and marriage without knowing who they are.

The individual has passed through a series of developmental phases and at each stage has had an identity, but those identities each had a tentative quality, for they were each part of the process of becoming. Now it has become time to be. The transition to adulthood involves becoming someone in one's own right and not simply someone's son or daughter. It involves the crystallization of a person from the developmental process that has been going on since birth.

The concept of ego identity was formulated by Erikson (1956) to signify that the various developmental stages are not ends in themselves but are part of the process of developing into an integrated and reasonably self-sufficient person who fits into the social system in which the individual lives. Although the concept of ego identity cannot be defined precisely, it concerns the constancy that characterizes individuals as they move into the various roles they fill at any one period in their lives and the consistency that will exist throughout their lives. It permits others, as well as the person, to have some idea of how he or she will behave, react, relate, and feel in various situations. Identity formation emerges out of a person's past identifications and the lost love objects that have been internalized and their fusion into a new integrate. It involves identifications with groups, as well as individuals, not only parents but also the family as a unit; with one's social class, religion, nation, and the particular time in history in which one lives; and, of course, with one's gender, which forms the keystone of a person's ego identity.

For many, achieving an ego identity presents little difficulty. They follow the expectations of parents, teachers, or other significant figures; but some pass through an identity crisis, seeking inward to find what they are about, where they wish to go, how to find a sense of completeness and ultimate completion.

Adolescents have been seeking a way and sampling. Some find it difficult to renounce one potentiality in favor of another, and yet they know that each person has only one life to lead. They must delimit to gain organization. They may feel that everything hangs in the balance and that a single decision can determine an entire life. The late adolescent or young adult may become paralyzed into indecision. The danger lies in suffering ego diffusion when unable to decide on a way; one drifts, and the personality and the person's life fail to jell. At that time in life, with numerous potential futures ahead, the adolescent may find it difficult to realize that the question is not so much "Who am I?" but "What do I wish to become that I have the potential to become?"

Currently, an adolescent girl may have particular difficulty in achieving a firm identity because she is caught up in a historical crisis in which women's traditional roles provide less satisfaction than in the past and when opportunities to pursue virtually any career are opening; but there are a paucity of female role models to follow into some careers. The adolescent girl whose primary objectives are to become a wife and mother—and she is one of the large majority—realizes that motherhood will occupy her for only 10 to 15 years, that being married is not as permanent a status as it formerly was, and that combining motherhood with a career presents real difficulties. Most girls expect to marry and have at least one child, but combining a real career with marriage requires finding a man who will consider his wife's career on a par with his own.

Although late adolescents have almost always had some sexual experiences and have probably fallen in and out of love, they have a less self-centered and narcissistic orientation to their sexual and affectional needs as they begin to gain fairly definite ego identities. They feel incomplete alone and seek someone whose ways of relating and loving are complementary to their own, someone who will gain satisfaction from what they do, someone who needs them and will be a partner, not a rival.

Couples are drawn together in such ways that the life of each encompasses the other, and "we" becomes an important part of their thoughts and talk. Separation can be painful, and thoughts of losing the lover engender real suffering. The experience of being drawn beyond one's own confines into such intimate involvement leads to a loosening of self-boundaries, and an attachment is achieved in which the affectional and the erotic can be combined to replace the attachment to a parent that had to be renounced and repressed many years earlier. The relationship may not endure, but the ability to have achieved it gives the person a new sureness and sense of self-esteem. After all, much of the question of "Who am I?" is answered by knowing that one can love and be loved by whom one loves and from whom one desires love. The sense of an ego identity is furthered by having moved beyond concerns with the self alone and by feeling needed by another and being able to share the self and one's experiences with another. For many, striving after fame or fortune or even the furtherance of an ideal becomes less important than becoming meaningful and necessary to some specific person. The problems of achieving an ego identity and gaining fulfillment through intimacy become united.

Adolescence sooner or later comes to an end—in general after the person feels independent enough and has explored what various ways of life have to offer and when the need to join forces with another in a permanent relationship becomes a dominant desire. Persons feel that the world is too large, and they feel lost in it. They recognize that success in a chosen career requires determined and single-minded effort. They may develop an obsessiveness in their efforts to overcome their anxieties about success, for they cannot afford to fail, now that they have decided about their futures. They may now miss their ties to a family, rather than be pleased by the breaking of those ties, and they seek to establish a new family.

Now, at the end of adolescence, the youth may develop beyond the egocentricity of formal operations. They realize that to change the course of the world or even their own university or city will take years of effort, and they may either doubt their own capacities to bring about such changes or doubt that it is worth devoting one's life to it. They begin to see themselves as single individuals moving through a complex world filled by masses of people, rather than as the center of a world that others pass through. They begin to hope that they will find meaning in existence and not get lost in their insignificance. Their perspectives change, and they now see their parents as persons with lives of their own, not simply as parents; and if they are fortunate, they begin to understand their parents' limitations, foibles, and inadequacies and may even hope that they, in their time that is about to start, will do as well.

The Adult Years

The passage through the various stages of adult life rests on the manner in which the person mastered the phases of childhood and adolescence. Many of the serious emotional problems from which adults suffer arise from fixations in childhood and adolescence and the distorted transactions of the intrafamilial environment in which the person grew up; but adults continue to be faced with new developmental challenges throughout their life-span, and with new critical tasks that must be surmounted as they move from one phase to the next; they may undergo a profound reorientation in their attitudes toward life and toward themselves as they enter a new phase of adult life. The stages and substages are not as set as those of childhood and adolescence; their start and end may vary with the culture, socioeconomic factors, and the person's life patterns and objectives. The developmental tasks of a man and a woman often differ markedly because of the central role of childbearing and child rearing in most women's lives. The epigenetic principle is not as pertinent as earlier in life, as phases may be delayed or deleted without leaving permanent vulnerabilities.

Students of adult life may divide adulthood somewhat differently, but there is reasonable agreement concerning the nature of the crucial tasks that confront a person and the critical transitions in their outlook that are apt to occur as they move through the adult years.

THE YOUNG ADULT YEARS

The age when adult life begins varies. Some persons have chosen their careers and their spouses in their teens and are more adult than adolescent. Some, particularly those who are gaining a higher education and who remain more or less dependent on their parents, may be considered by some to be adolescents into their midtwenties. Keniston (1974) inserted a stage of youth for the small proportion of persons who, having gained an ego identity, become caught up in tensions between the self and society and who struggle through their twenties to overcome the disparity between their emergent selves and the social order; the youth stage may also apply for those young persons who have trouble finding their way in a relativistic world.

A critical task of personality development during youth lies in achieving individuation (Jung, 1961)—the ability to acknowledge reality and cope with it through acceptance or revolutionary opposition while preserving an intactness of self distinct from society. Failure to individuate properly leads to uncritical acceptance of the societal norms of one's immediate group, which, although the lot of most persons, can be scorned by youth as a selling out to the Establishment and can lead to a denial of the self when it becomes overconformity. The opposite danger lies in alienation, in which efforts to preserve autonomy lead to withdrawal from the societal matrix, including dropping out, and to seeking to find oneself through mystical experiences and drugs, rather than continuing to develop. Others, who are highly developed intellectually and ethically, become caught up in problems of relativism. Gaining perspective from the study of other cultures and other times and recognizing the validity of the ways and beliefs of other peoples, they appreciate that the standards of their own society are more or less arbitrary. They wonder about their obligations to adhere to societal norms; recognizing the relativity of values and meanings, they find it difficult to find purpose and direction. Further, the increased awareness that what they or anyone becomes depends on how and where one is brought up leads some to become caught up in the omnipotentiality of their capabilities to change themselves and the direction of their lives. The apparent freedom to choose can almost paralyze.

Many of the contemporary problems of female youths derive, in a sense, from the recently gained potentiality and awareness of their omnipotentiality. New potential futures have been opened for women by the more secure modes of separating sex and procreation, which permit a woman to lead an active sexual life and still have the choice of when and if she will have children, and by the high level of education that enables her to choose among many careers that had formerly been closed to women. In some respects she has greater freedom than her male age-mates in the choice of future roles. She can move beyond stereotypic female roles and occupations and consider herself capable of doing almost anything a man can do, and she is also free to become a housewife and mother and gain gratification from the choice; but being a husband and father has not yet become a career for a man. The ability to choose here, as elsewhere, opens the way for inner conflict and is accentuated by the paucity of role models to follow if she decides to pursue a career traditionally closed to women. The desire for a career and also to be a mother further complicates her life.

Young adults, sooner or later and usually early in their twenties, come to recognize that the time has come to make commitments and that those commitments will determine to a very great extent how their future lives will go. They can delay and delay and linger in the shelter of their home or in the arms of their alma mater, but they cannot tarry too long without commitments and obtain the direction and motivation they provide. Some, who are caught up in the indecision that can come with awareness of their own malleability, require a moratorium (Erikson, 1956) before committing themselves, but all are apt to feel, perhaps in an exaggerated form, that all has been preparation, and now the time has come to start life in earnest. The choice of an occupation and the choice of a mate are apt to start young adults on their way, usually sometime

between the ages of 18 and 30. Both of those major decisions greatly influence the further development of the personality and the chances for future happiness.

Occupational choice. Occupational choice is usually of two general types. In one, an occupation is chosen primarily to make a living—to enable the person to support a family and attain security, whereas the major sources of contentment, satisfaction, and enjoyment are sought elsewhere—from a family, sports, affairs, or some avocation, rather than one's vocation. In the other type, the occupation is an expansion of the self, as in the professions and the arts.

The choice of an occupation depends greatly on personality characteristics, as well as on many other conscious and unconscious factors, but the occupation chosen greatly influences the further development of the personality. An occupation concerns more than a set of skills and functions, for it does much to determine a way of life. To a considerable degree an occupation establishes the social and physical environment in which the person lives. By determining the type of persons with whom one spends much of one's life, a vocation influences value judgments, goals, and ethical standards. It selects out traits to be strengthened and provides social roles and patterns for living. Physicians are supposed to be idealistic; politicians need to be wily; scientists devote themselves to increasing human knowledge; industrialists keep their eyes on profits. A person may be capable of becoming an artist, a physician, an architect, or a teacher, but the future personality will differ greatly, according to which career one decides to pursue (Lidz, 1976).

As has been noted, the problem of occupational choice for a woman poses particular difficulties today. For the majority of women, occupational choice is still a relatively secondary matter, as marriage and motherhood are dominant goals. Many young women find and keep jobs until they have children and are not concerned about a career outside the family. However, serious conflict can ensue when a young woman attempts to decide whether to pursue a career or profession or to marry and have children. If she decides on both a career and motherhood, she may find the rewards of choosing both to be eminently fulfilling and gratifying, but she must also be aware that, unless she is extremely fortunate, serious difficulties and frustrations will be encountered. The potentiality depends not on the liberation of the specific woman alone but on the choice of a husband who will share parental responsibilities and foster his wife's career. Dual-career marriages can be highly stimulating to both spouses, but they permit little time for relaxation after working hours. Many women decide to delay having children until they are well enough along in a career to take some years of leave or until they can afford domestic help; others set their career ambitions aside until their children are in school. Increasingly, the problems of occupational and marital choice intertwine.

Marital choice. Marital choice is not a necessary step in the life cycle, and a person can lead a happy and satisfactory life without marrying, but about 97 per cent of the people in the United States do marry. When the number of mentally retarded, mentally ill, and physically incapacitated are excluded, that means that very few mentally and physically competent persons never marry.

There are many reasons, both good and bad, why people marry. The impulsion to marry rests on the biological nature of humans and the prolonged period of nurturance in the family of origin. Growing up in a family, children can feel secure because their well-being is of paramount importance to their parents and because they are accepted for affectional reasons, rather than because of achievements. The movement toward separation and individuation has always had a conscious or unconscious counterweight in a pull toward dependence and a total relatedness to another. Having achieved freedom from parents, the person comes to feel insecure and alone and seeks a new relationship in which one's welfare is as essential to the spouse as the spouse's own well-being because the two lives are, at least theoretically or ideally, irretrievably interrelated; one seeks a relationship in which acceptance depends primarily not on achievement, as in the working world, but on affection. The two sexes differ in anatomy and biological functions and are suited to each other for the satisfactory release of sexual tensions, but the developmental process everywhere has also, at least until the present, prepared males and females to fill different but complementary roles. In all societies children are reared in a way that leads to a need for interdependence with a member of the opposite sex to provide a sense of completion, particularly to carry out the critical task of child rearing. The desire to propogate also fosters a more permanent relationship, as children require protective nurturance for many years. However, a major impetus to marry comes from the unconscious desire to complete the oedipal strivings that had to be frustrated in the family of origin and, finally, to be able to unite love and sex and to become the wife or the husband, rather than be relegated to a place in the childhood generation of a family.

The choice of a marital partner is probably the major decision of a voluntary nature that can complement and alter the personality and afford opportunities for self-completion before the production of a new generation. Individuals making the decision are aware that much of their future happiness and the well-being of their children depends on this choice. In most societies, the decision is considered too important to leave to a relatively inexperienced person, who may be swayed by passion. In American society, however, love is expected to be a major motivation, and it often is, although many other considerations—such as pregnancy, security, and anger at a third party—may enter into the decision. Indeed, the choice of a spouse is a highly overdetermined matter and, in a sense, the resultant of the person's total experience. It is significant that much of the process of falling in love depends on unconscious determinants that trail back into infancy, but the unconscious processes may be more suited than is conscious deliberation for drawing together and weighing the diffuse needs that enter into the matter—the feeling-tone remembrances; the resemblances and differences from parents; the feel, odor, and responsiveness of the other; and many other variables with which intellect could scarce cope, even if they were consciously available. Although the unconscious processes can designate whom one loves, they are not as capable of judging correctly with whom one can live. Logical appraisals usually check the chances for success and failure. Currently, increasing numbers of young adults go through a trial of living together before making the decisive step.

Marital adjustment. Marriage leads to the critical task of marital adjustment. The topic encompasses far more than sexual adjustment, even though the sexual adjustment of the couple is extremely important, for a good sexual relationship serves as a lubricant to reduce frictions arising elsewhere and the lack of sexual fulfillment is likely to aggravate other sources of conflict. Marital problems not only shortly after marriage but throughout life are apt to be major factors in emotional disorders, even though much of the difficulty stems from earlier problems or is an almost inevitable outcome of the choice of a spouse.

Although the topic is extremely involved, the essence of the process of marital adjustment can be stated in terms of the psychoanalytic structural hypothesis. The ego functions of each partner must now take into account and encompass the id impulses and superego standards of the other. Optimally, the spouse becomes an alter ego whose well-being is considered on a par with one's own and whose needs, wishes, and opinions are taken into account in reaching decisions in areas of common interest. Easily stated, the process almost always requires a marked shift in thinking and behavior. Satisfying another and being needed by another and not just being satisfied and being taken care of must provide gratification. Various developmental problems and fixations impair the marital adjustment—oral or anaclitic dependency needs, gender identity problems, unresolved oedipal attachments, undue needs for narcissistic gratification—indeed, the capacity to make a good marital adjustment is, in many respects, a measure of the success of the developmental process. However, many marriages succeed because the personality weaknesses of one or both spouses gain support from the strength of the other spouse or simply from the support each partner affords the other.

A new marriage is in many respects a fusion of the two families in which the partners grew up into a new pattern congenial to both members. The expectations of the marital partner, the roles assumed, the tacit understandings, the unconscious communications, and many other matters that are simply taken for granted in a family are often very disparate in the two families from which the spouses have emerged. The center of gravity of the life of each spouse properly shifts from the family of origin and peer groups to the new family, although in some socioeconomic groups male and female roles and activities tend to remain quite discrete (Bott, 1955).

Parenthood. With the birth of the first child, the marital partners enter a different phase of their development (Benedek, 1959). They have become members of the parental generation, and the future well-being of their child depends greatly on their abilities to give of themselves so that the child can grow, learn, and develop. Their orientation toward the future, the roles they occupy, and the tasks with which they cope change markedly. Some young couples are surprised to find that the arrival of the child changes their lives even more than did their marriage.

The birth of the child transforms a marriage into a family, and there is a need to make emotional room for a third person. The family unit is not as malleable as a marriage. A childless couple can relate in an endless variety of ways as long as those ways are acceptable to the spouses, but the maintenance of a family, particularly of a family suited for the salubrious rearing of children, requires a dynamic structuring of the family in which each spouse fills certain roles and carries out definite responsibilities.

The infant is not just a physical fusion of the parents; their personalities also unite within the child they raise. The parents are united in the child and by the child, whose experiences they share and with whom they both identify. But the child is also a potential source of friction—by preempting the attention of a parent, by bringing differences in family patterns to the fore, by arousing insecurities in one or both parents. However, as is the case with many responsibilities, the child fosters growth in the parents as they rise to the challenges placed on them.

For many, probably most, married women a deep sense of fulfillment comes with the creation of a child. A woman's sexuality is more complex than a man's. A woman is consciously and unconsciously kept in close feeling touch with procreation through the menstrual cycle, and her sexuality encompasses conception, the fetus within, childbirth, and nursing, as well as the sexual act. Many feel that their lives are incomplete unless they produce and nurture a child. The child specifically affords the profound gratification that comes from being necessary to another, giving of oneself to another, and being loved for having given of oneself. The mother now finds compensation for many deprivations she may have felt by not having been born a boy, although some mothers with little esteem for themselves as women can gain such recompense only from having a son.

The father, too, usually grows through having a child and may be transformed by the event. To some, having a child provides an important sign of virility, and among some ethnic groups the ability to father a child is an essential indication of masculinity. However, while heightening a man's sense of masculine self-esteem, having a child also affords an opportunity for him to express the nurturant qualities gained from his early childhood identification with his mother that have often had few acceptable outlets and that required repression. Then, too, as the child grows older, the child's admiration of the father provides narcissistic supplies, and the man gains the status of father that he had envied since early childhood. Nevertheless, deep rivalries with the child for the wife's attention may unleash old oedipal and sibling rivalries that interfere with paternal feelings and even arouse fears of the child's oedipal hostility toward him.

The impact of children on parents changes as the children and the parents move into different stages of life. As children change, they offer new problems and concerns to the parents but also a constant opportunity for the parents' growth, as they are forced to relate differently than before. Such changes provide a source of renewal for the parents and their marriage.

THE MIDDLE ADULT YEARS

As young adults move into their thirties, they usually undergo a reorientation in their attitudes toward life. One can consider the start of the thirties as a transition to the middle adult years, when—having achieved maturity and possessing the skills, knowledge, and assurance needed to settle into their careers and family lives—they become caught up in making the most of their abilities and opportunities. They are in their prime, moving toward the onset of middle age around the age of 40, which is often ushered in by a period of stocktaking. In a fair proportion of persons, the turn from the twenties into the thirties is marked by something of a crisis. They feel that their youth has ended and that more definitive commitments must be made. Or, unhappy about the choice of a career, they may decide that the time has come for a change. Marriages are disturbed by what has been termed the 7-year itch as one or both members of a couple decide that the marriage has not brought happiness and seek new sources of sexual satisfaction outside the marriage or decide to find a new marital partner. In general, however, persons are likely to feel the pleasure of mastery. Established in their own families, they feel that they are finally free from parental control. Indeed, they often begin to see their parents from a different perspective, now that they are experiencing problems of parenthood themselves, and gain a new regard for what their parents accomplished. Having gained the necessary knowledge and skills, they settle in at their occupations and become concerned with making it (Levinson, 1977; Levinson et al., 1978). They realize that just how far they get in their thirties will determine to a great extent their ultimate success. They assume increasing responsibility, even though they are usually still considered junior members in their business or profession. Some will move to the fore and be granted major responsibilities, for this is the time when truly creative persons show their capacities.

A woman who has been busy with her career realizes that the time has come to have children if she is going to have any, and she plans to change her way of life. If she has children now, she has the skills needed to bring a second or third child through infancy and early childhood without feeling overwhelmed. Currently, with the limited number of children in most families, a woman may undergo major changes in her life pattern when her children become adolescent or, at least, when they are all in school. She may return to pursue the career she had deferred to become a mother; or she may begin to prepare for a new career, a shift that is very different from what is going on in the lives of men at this stage of life. The patterns of middle life in women are so variant that it is difficult to make generalizations.

As ambitious persons, particularly men with careers, move past the age of 35, they become impatient at being subordinates or juniors, and they are apt to enter a phase in which they are impatient to become one's own man (Levinson el al., 1974, 1978). They may enter a period of intense striving to gain a promotion. Some may grow resentful and perhaps depressed because they are not appreciated and then face the decision of whether to move to another firm or risk the insecurity of striking out on their own. Which decision is made may depend on basic traits that derive from childhood experiences; an orally dependent person may chafe and become resentful over a lack of promotion but stay put, needing the security; old oedipal rivalries may push another to surpass his elders by establishing his own firm; still another may be highly competitive, as he was with siblings.

The start of middle age is usually placed around the age of 40. It is properly a time when years of effort reach fruition. However, for many it is ushered in by several difficult years that have been termed the midlife crisis or midlife transition. It is a time of stocktaking that comes with the realization that one's life is reaching its climax and has even begun to move toward its inevitable conclusion. Middle-aged adults usually gain insight into the way their lives are going to turn out and try to assess whether goals can be achieved, dreams fulfilled, satisfaction attained. Do one's most significant relationships provide fulfillment and happiness? Must one come to terms with just getting by or accept disappointment, disillusionment, and relative failure? They realize that they have now become members of the older, responsible generation. Will they be in a responsible position themselves? At the start of middle age, there is still time to revise, time to start afresh or, at least, to salvage the years that are left, but there can be no further delay. The crisis is set off not by any significant event but, rather, by the realization that more time stretches behind one than stretches before one. The balance of life is upset by an awareness of the limits of life's span, and there is apt to be a recrudescence of existential anxiety concerning the insignificance of the individual life in an infinity of time and space. Two of the world's literary masterpieces start on that note. Dante's *The Divine Comedy* opens with the lines

Midway in the journey through life, I found myself lost in a dark wood, having strayed from the true path.

And Goethe's *Faust* finds that—although he has studied philosophy, medicine, and law thoroughly—he is fundamentally no wiser than the poorest fool, and he makes a pact with Mephistopheles in an attempt to salvage something in life. For some, middle age brings neither fruition nor disappointment so much as angry bewilderment at finding that their neglect of meaningful relationships in the frenetic striving for success now makes life seem empty.

The competitive striving for success is far from a universal phenomenon; it is, rather, a manifestation of industrial or postindustrial society, to some degree an aberration that is looked on in the United States as a high virtue, as it is simply an exaggeration of individualistic ways. The Hopi, who cherish an inner calm above all, and the Fijians, who have a taboo against individual ambition, find it very strange, indeed. However, stocktaking concerns more than external success. It has to do with inner satisfactions, with whether achievements are compatible with one's earlier dreams and ideals and with disparities between one's way of life and what really provides a sense of self-esteem.

Although life for most continues along the well-trodden path, with satisfactions found along the way and with ambitions tempered by experience and concerns countered by religion or philosophy, stocktaking and reassessment are characteristics of the first years of middle age.

There are other potential problems as a person crosses the crest. The burning narcissistic need for reassurance concerning potency or attractiveness or the longing for affection when marital love has been devoured by resentments may impel a person to seek a final fling before the closing of the gates. It is a fling that can sabotage a career or disrupt a marriage that has been reasonably satisfactory. Or a person may decide to terminate a marital relationship that he or she has put up with for the sake of the children, now that the children are adolescents or young adults. Such shifts in midlife can work out well for many who have matured sufficiently to use better judgment in choosing a spouse than they did in the impetuousness of youth. However, a striking number select a second spouse much like the first spouse.

Traditionally, the late forties have been a time of trial for a menopausal woman because of the physical discomforts or because of her expectation that the menopause entails the end of active sexuality or even a depressive episode. Endocrine therapy can alleviate or even abolish her discomforts, and the expectation of serious emotional instability is unwarranted, but the menopause often brings with it a transitory period of depression as the woman loses her badge of womanhood, the indicator of her capacity to reproduce that has provided feelings of worth. Actually, there may be an upsurge in sexual interest and enjoyment when concerns over pregnancy disappear, and the continuing sexual capacities of the wife may create difficulties for the husband, whose potency is now diminishing.

A woman whose life has centered on her children, particularly if she is widowed or divorced, may suffer from the empty-nest syndrome, no longer feeling wanted or needed. But many mothers today look forward to new vocations or avocations and welcome their greater freedom when their children have all left home. The end of active parenthood can bring great changes in the lives of both spouses with a new sense of freedom and opportunity to use their income on themselves. In recent years, more and more women have moved into new careers and, having already gained a sense of worth and accomplishment through raising a family, do so without the pressure to prove themselves that can plague men.

Although the middle-aged may be in the prime of life, their bodies no longer respond to demands without aches and stiffness. Men are aware that, between 40 and 50, heart attacks are particularly dangerous. Diet and exercise become important to maintain a trim figure, and more time is required to cover signs of aging. Women are advised to check their breasts regularly for masses and to have semiannual gynecological examinations. Obituary columns are scanned for names of friends and acquaintances. The middle-aged become aware that ill health and death are potentialities that hover over them and consciously and unconsciously influence the patterns of their lives.

Although middle age has its gloomy aspects, it is properly a time of fruition, when the strivings and efforts of earlier years are producing tangible rewards. In many respects, life seems just to be getting under way, as the person feels complete and free to use his capacities to realize ambitions. Most persons are now at the height of their potential. Even though they may be somewhat past their physical prime, they can use their heads effectively and have learned to conserve their energies. They know what will work and what will be a waste of time and effort. They know their areas of competence and have the satisfaction of feeling in control of them. They have moved to the center of the stage of life and are among those who innovate, manage, and assume responsibility. Some enjoy the prestige and power, and they are impelled to seek more power over others, but the sense of mastery in itself provides pleasure to less driven individuals. A truly sucessful person has acquired not only power, knowledge, and skills but also wisdom in making decisions, approaching tasks, and working with others.

Persons are now established in their work. In executive circles, the years between 40 and 55 may involve intense striving to capture a top position or to climax a career by gaining the prestige or wealth that has come within their grasp. However, many persons with their parental functions virtually completed are now likely to find gratification in a different type of generativity. They can now become mentors, seeking to develop heirs in their fields of endeavor who will carry on their teachings and interests. They become involved in the future of the firms, universities, or towns—the institutions in which they have invested their interests and energies. They seek to sponsor the younger person or persons who, they believe, have the abilities to assume major responsibilities. Erikson (1959) considered such generativity a crucial aspect of middle age, with stagnation the negative outcome. The stagnation comes with falling into an uninteresting routine or a rut, no longer seeking to learn, or from embittered disillusionment that one's worth has not been appreciated or, perhaps more often, from lack of interest in anyone or any purpose beyond self-interest.

One of the critical aspects of middle age concerns coming to terms with one's accomplishments and future potential—not only to accept the limits of achievement and not become resentful and depressed over inadequate recognition but also to be able to enjoy the prestige attained and to accept the responsibilities that accompany it. Many find it difficult to gain satisfaction from what they have accomplished if the accomplishments are not recognized and rewarded or to find pleasure in what they have made of themselves unless others appreciate who they have become. Even the reward of promotion can bring trouble at this time of life. After a much desired promotion or some specific award in recognition of one's abilities, a person may become depressed—the so-called promotion depression. A man feels vulnerable because he feels he has surpassed his father—an adult version of the childhood fantasy of displacing the father and the old haunting fears that the father will gain vengeance—and a man punishes himself for his hubris. Or, as much as he wished for the promotion, he may resent being burdened with new expectations and responsibilities at a time when he wishes to work less arduously or no longer feels up to the continuing pressure.

The realization that one has rounded the turn toward the end of life allows a sense of satisfaction and accomplishment or provokes anxiety and despair in proportion to feelings that one has really lived and loved. As old age approaches, one may have regrets, but it serves little to become caught up in them. Most can enjoy the benefits that come with maturity and the opportunities it presents.

OLD AGE

The onset of old age is a rather indefinite and arbitrary matter that clearly varies from person to person, but currently in the United States a rite of passage marks the moment. Shortly before the sixty-fifth birthday, each person makes a brief visit to the Social Security office and presents a few documents to establish qualifications for future Social Security benefits. Although the visit is brief, polite, and painless, those who make it are likely to experience a slight inner chill, for they have now become senior citizens. They now begin to measure time in terms of years left, rather than in terms of years lived. Aware of the precariousness of their future health and earning capacities, they become concerned with income and the ability to receive adequate health care.

Almost 40 per cent of the women reaching the age of 65 have already become widows, but only 10 per cent of the men have lost their wives. However, having reached the age of 65, a man has a life expectancy of another 13 years, and a woman has a life expectancy of another 16 years. But they know that they will be fortunate if the remaining years are relatively healthy and untroubled and if they can escape becoming unduly dependent before they die. For many persons little has changed significantly, and the critical transition comes at the time of retirement or for the housewife, at the time of her husband's retirement.

Erikson (1959) designated the achievement of integrity as the critical task of old age—the acceptance of one's one and only life and of the people who have become significant to it as something that had to be and that, by necessity, permitted no substitutions. Integrity requires the wisdom to realize that there are no "ifs" in life—that one was born with certain capacities, of a set of parents, into specific life circumstances, and in a particular time in history and that one encountered various conditions and made numerous decisions. Whether any of those circumstances could have been changed is questionable, but the past cannot be altered, although one's attitudes toward the past can be. The negative outcome of this stage of life is despair—despair that the one and only lifetime has been wasted, leading to bitterness toward others or self-hatred that precludes the constructive uses of the experiences of a lifetime. Now persons are moving toward the completion of the life cycle, some may feel that they are left standing at the outskirts of life, at the end of the line, with only a void before them; or they may seek to bring a sense of closure to their lives and make efforts to round out what they have accomplished. In so doing many elderly persons may review where they have been, a process that may keep them rather fully occupied. Others may still be achieving or helping others on their way.

In a sense, the aged person goes through a reversal of some critical aspects of adolescence (Lidz, 1976). The force of the sexual drive diminishes, and much of the elderly person's sexual strivings come from desires for affectionate and sensuous sharing, much as in childhood. Then, as the woman loses the subcutaneous padding that rounded her contours and her secondary sexual characteristics and as the man's masculinity diminishes, physical differences between the sexes lessen. Instead of being future oriented, aging persons increasingly turn to the past and what they have accomplished and experienced, rather than to what is still to come. They become increasingly dependent on their children or on others of the succeeding generation; sometimes they must again become virtually obedient to caretaking persons, as in childhood, lest they be rejected. Whereas adolescents move toward sharing their lives intimately with another, aged persons must sooner or later absorb the loss of the persons with whom they shared their lives. Nevertheless, early old age is autumn, not winter, and it is properly a time of contentment and a gathering of the harvest.

The potential pleasures and contentment of old age are somewhat less in contemporary United States than in former times. Knowledge of the uses of the past is valued less in a rapidly changing technical society, and television, films, and sports afford the young little time to listen to the tales of the elderly or to learn to value their sagacity. Then, too, the isolated nuclear family often contains little place or space for the elderly. Nevertheless, the wisdom that comes with aging and having lived through repetitive cycles of events is still appreciated by many.

On the other hand, advances in medicine, improved living conditions, and various modern inventions have made life more satisfactory for many elderly persons. The removal of cataracts can restore vision; the electronic hearing aid has greatly diminished the number of aged persons who are cut off from social contact by deafness; dentures not only permit the enjoyment of food but lessen the occurrence of nutritional deficits. The automobile makes continued mobility possible, and television keeps those who are physically limited in touch with the world and provides entertainment that is satisfactory to most.

The elderly person remains essentially unchanged from the middle years except for the differences in the way of life that may be created by retirement. Being retired may be resented, whereas retiring may be welcomed. However, much of the resentment and distress of retirement comes from the accompanying relative or real poverty. If the elderly persons have good financial provisions for retirement they are likely to welcome it, happy to be free of the cares and monotony of work and to have time to enjoy the many things they have put off and would still like to experience. Of course, a housewife does not retire, but her life is changed for better or worse by having her husband at home much of the day. Increasingly, retired couples in the United States move to the sun belt and find a different way of life in a new community.

By and large, old age goes best if there is still not enough time to do all the things one would like, if one is still caught up in a profession or the pursuit of an avocation. A number of gifted persons have reached the heights of accomplishment long after they entered old age. Churchill guided the British empire through the tribulations of World War II, Golda Meir became Prime Minister of Israel, Picasso poured out endless innovations in his painting and sculpture—all after they reached the age of 65.

When persons are fortunate and both members of the marital couple are still alive at 65, their relationship tends to become increasingly important as they grow older. A couple not only care for one another but take care of one another and can accept each other's help and hope that they will never need the help of any other. An upsurge of deeply felt and rather romantic love may occur. Contrary to the beliefs of the young, the elderly can and often do remain sexually active into advanced old age, although the comfort of sensual closeness may become more important than orgasmic pleasure. However, sooner or later the invalidism of one partner usually brings the need for major readjustments.

Life as a single person can be particularly lonesome for the elderly because of limitations and the loss of friends. Remarriage has become more common of late, and sometimes it brings the first real marital happiness a person has known. Mores have changed for the old, as well as for the young, and increasingly elderly couples live together without marrying, eschewing marriage for sentimental reasons, to avoid the commitment, or for tax and inheritance purposes. Because of the gender imbalance among the elderly, a man has a greater opportunity to find a new partner than does a woman.

Social relationships can become increasingly difficult to maintain as friends and relatives die or move away and as infirmities restrict mobility. Relatives, even those who have rarely been seen since childhood, become important because of old ties and common memories. Retirement villages, southern resorts, and golden age clubs help people find new acquaintances.

Advanced old age may be said to start at about the age of 75. Hopes for the years ahead have usually become modest, as persons hope to find ways in which they can still be useful if not essential, but they are most concerned that they not become a burden to anyone. Completing life in an old-age home or a nursing home, separated from family and friends, is a dreaded possibility but often seems preferable to burdening those one loves.

Those who enter advanced old age are a rather select group, for those who survive to 80 still have a life expectancy of another 10 years. It is often difficult to convince a person of 80 that he or she has a good chance of living another 15 or 20 years and must plan accordingly. Some remain very vital, despite some infirmities, and continue to live full lives, using their inner resources and making the most of what life offers until the end; or they may accept what comes and try to make the most of it, despite the loss of capacities. However, most persons who reach advanced old age are or will soon become dependent on others, and the status is difficult for many to assimilate. Self-esteem based on self-sufficiency is undermined. Even if children are willing or glad to be attentive, dependency can provoke frictions. The old person may react to needing help by becoming irritable or assertive, or may become burdensome by insisting on his independence and capabilities. Not all children feel devoted to their parents, and some gain satisfaction from dominating the parent who once dominated them. Some grown children do not wish a parent to rejoin them, and they refuse to accept any responsibility. Social Security payments have at least freed old people from being completely dependent financially, and improved pension plans are increasingly providing financial independence for the elderly. Old people are rightly concerned about losing their autonomy, for, when independence goes, individuality often follows.

All aged persons suffer some decrement in cognitive capacities, but the loss is offset by the knowledge and skills acquired throughout life. Finding proper names becomes a common problem. Most aged persons retain their intellectual capacities reasonably intact into advanced age, but a small proportion become senile and can no longer care for themselves. Sufficient numbers of cortical cells disappear because of senile changes or more precipitously because of a stroke affecting an area essential for symbolic functioning. With senile changes, the most notable decrement is the loss of memory for recent events. It is as if a shade had rolled down over the recent past until only memories of childhood remain. Without memory of recent events, the aged persons cannot guide themselves into the future, and eventually even routines become disrupted by faulty placement of the present into the remote past, and then a person requires supervisory care. Some aged persons become mentally incompetent after a stroke. Those who remain reasonably intact mentally as they become very old usually await their end with equanimity and may regard death as a haven from loneliness and from the efforts needed to continue living.

Very old persons have passed the stage of being procreative or even creative, but the type of life they lead and the life afforded them by others still profoundly influence those who come after them.

Death

Death brings the end of the life cycle, the inevitable outcome of the life story. Because humans from early childhood are aware of their ultimate fate, death influences their development and their way of life profoundly. Religions provide ways of denying that death is the final outcome and use beliefs of what transpires after death as a means of controlling behavior. The vast majority of persons in Western societies believe in life after death, and some in old age attain a clear idea of what they will find on the other side, whereas others are content with nebulous concepts. Some among the elderly cling to life tenaciously as long as any glimmer of hope remains. Paradoxically, those who have never been able to live because others have restricted them or because of their own neurotic limitations may fear death most. Some not only suffer anxiety but become agitated when they know they are going to die, and they cause others to suffer with them. Still, persons almost always are able to accept the inevitable. Those who do not wish to know that they will soon die usually have strong defense mechanisms against perceiving what may seem obvious.

All too often, efforts made to protect persons from knowing that they will soon die have unfortunate consequences. A wall of deception separates the dying person from his family and friends at a time when they wish to be particularly close. The dying often wish to discuss various matters that will concern the living. Some do not wish to be deprived of experiencing their final experience. At times, the insistence to persons with terminal illnesses that they are doing well and will recover can confuse the patients, provoke mistrust in those caring for them, and even lead to disorganization and delusions. They are not permitted to believe what they know to be a fact. If they have gained wisdom in old age, they have usually ceased fearing death and may even welcome it as a relief from the tribulations of life, particularly if those who have made life meaningful for them have already preceded them through the gates of death. They are consciously or unconsciously aware that life is na-

ture's greatest invention and that death is her means of making much life possible.

Suggested Cross References

Freud's theories are discussed in Chapter 8, Sullivan's theories in Section 9.3, Erikson's theories in Section 10.1, and Piaget's theories in Section 4.2. Normal child development is discussed in Section 34.2 and normal adolescent development in Section 34.3. Maternal deprivation is discussed in Section 43.1, parenthood in Section 43.7, and the family in Section 5.3. Gender identity is discussed in Section 24.4. Marriage is discussed in Section 56.17. Sex and the life cycle are discussed in Section 24.5. Psychiatry and psychology of the middle-aged are discussed in Chapter 52 and geriatric psychiatry in Chapter 53. Thanatology is discussed in Section 28.2.

REFERENCES

Benedek, T. Parenthood as a developmental phase: A contribution to libido theory. J. Am. Psychoanal. Assoc. 7: 389, 1959.

Bott, E. Urban families: Conjugal roles and social networks. Hum. Relat., 8: 345, 1955.

Bowlby, J. Attachment and Loss. Vol. 1: Attachment. Basic Books, New York, 1969.

Dulit, E. Adolescent thinking à la Piaget: The formal stage. J. Youth Adol., 1: 281, 1972.

* Erikson, E. Childhood and Society. W. W. Norton, New York, 1950.

Erikson, E. The problem of ego identity. J. Am. Psychoanal. Assoc., 4: 56, 1956.

Erikson, E. Growth and crises of the "healthy" personality. Psychol. Issues, 1: No 1, 1959.

Erikson, E. Identity: Youth and Crises. W. W. Norton, New York, 1968.

Freud, A. Normality and pathology in childhood: Assessments of development. In The Writings of Anna Freud, vol. 6. International Universities Press, New York, 1965.

Freud, S. Introductory lectures on psychoanalysis. In Standard Edition of the Complete Psychological Works of Sigmund Freud, vol. 16, p. 243. Hogarth Press, London, 1954.

Freud, S. New introductory lectures. In Standard Edition of the Complete Psychological Works of Sigmund Freud, vol. 22, p. 7. Hogarth Press, London, 1962.

Hampson, J. L., and Hampson, J. G. The ontogenesis of sexual behavior in man. In Sex and Internal Secretions, W. C. Young, editor, vol. 2, p. 1401. Williams & Wilkins, Baltimore, 1961.

Hauser, S. Black and White Identity Formation: Explorations in the Psychosocial Development of White and Negro Male Adolescents. Wiley-Interscience, New York, 1971.

* Inhelder, B., and Piaget, J. The Growth of Logical Thinking from Childhood to Adolescence. Basic Books, New York, 1958.

Jung, C. Psychological Types: The Psychology of Individuation. Harcourt, Brace, New York, 1961.

Keniston, K. The Uncommitted: Alienated Youth in American Society. Harcourt, Brace and World, New York, 1974.

Kohlberg, L. Development of moral character and moral ideology. In Review of Child Development Research, M. L. Hoffman and L. W. Hoffman, editors, p. 6. Russell Sage Foundation, New York, 1964.

Levinson, D. The mid-life transition: A period in adult psycho-social development. Psychiatry, 40: 99, 1977.

Levinson, D., Darrow, C., Klein, E., Levinson, M., and McKee, J. B. The psychosocial development of men in early adulthood and the mid-life transition. In Life History Research in Psychopathology, D. F. Ricks, A. Thomas, and M. Roff, editors, vol. 3. University of Minnesota Press, Minneapolis, 1974.

Levinson, D., Darrow, C., Klein, E., Levinson, M., and McKee, J. B. The Seasons of a Man's Life. Alfred A. Knopf, New York, 1978.

* Lidz, T. The Person, revised ed. Basic Books, New York, 1976.

Mahler, M., Pine, F., and Bergman, A. The Psychological Birth of the Infant. Basic Books, New York, 1975.

Money, J. Psychosexual Differentiation in Sex Research: New Developments. Holt, Rinehart and Winston, New York, 1965.

Parsons, T. The school class as a social system: Some of its functions in American society. In Social Structure and Personality, T. Parsons, editor, p. 129. Free Press of Glencoe, New York, 1964.

Pavenstedt, E., editor. The Drifters: Children of Disorganized Lower-class Families. Little, Brown and Co., Boston, 1967.

Piaget, J. The Moral Judgment of the Child. Free Press, Glencoe, Ill., 1948.

Piaget, J. Play, Dreams, and Imitation in Childhood. W. W. Norton, New York, 1962.

Piaget, J. The Origins of Intelligence in Children. W. W. Norton, New York, 1963.

Piaget, J., and Inhelder, B. The Psychology of the Child. Basic Books, New York, 1969.

Provence, S., and Lipton, R. *Infants in Institutions: A Comparison of the Development with Family-reared Infants during the First Year of Life.* International Universities Press, New York, 1962.

Spitz, R. Hospitalism: An inquiry into the genesis of psychiatric conditions in early childhood. Psychoanal. Study Child, *1:* 53, 1945.

Spitz, R. *The First Year of Life: A Psychoanalytic Study of Normal and Deviant Development of Object Relations.* International Universities Press, New York, 1965.

Sullivan, H. S. *Personal Psychopathology.* W. W. Norton, New York, 1971.

Sze, W., editor. *The Human Life Cycle.* Jason Aaronson, New York, 1975.

Wertham, F. The matricidal impulse: Critique of Freud's interpretation of Hamlet. J. Crim. Psychopathol., *2:* 455, 1941.

Winnicott, D. W. Transitional objects and transitional phenomena: A study of the first not-me possession. Int. J. Psychoanal., *34:* 89, 1953.

Wolff, P. H. The causes, controls, and organization of behavior in the neonate. Psychol. Issues, *5:* 1, 1966.

chapter

2

Science of Human Behavior: Contributions of the Biological Sciences

2.1 Genetics and Psychiatry

JOHN D. RAINER, M.D.

Introduction and History

Genetics plays a key role in modern psychiatric research and practice. Rooted in the evolutionary process and incorporating scientific advances in such fields as molecular biology, biochemistry, cytology, and population dynamics, genetics has paced the development of psychiatry as a biological discipline and a responsible medical specialty. That this has come about is due to rapidly increasing sophistication in the techniques and formulations of human genetics, including the principles of dynamic interaction with the environment, and to the growing interdisciplinary framework of psychiatric thought.

Until the early 1930's in this country, development in the fields of genetics and psychiatry followed separate paths. In the behavioral sciences, heredity and environmental factors were considered as separate—indeed, as competing—agents. Many psychiatrists were caught up in the ancient dichotomies between nature and nurture and between mind and matter. As a result, they tended to distinguish and choose between biological and psychological approaches.

For many years the behavioral sciences were dominated by oversimplified views on one side or the other. In the United States, psychogenic or environmental forces were assigned exclusive roles; in psychology the behaviorism of J. B. Watson and in psychiatry the psychobiology of Adolf Meyer emphasized the role of external forces in the development of psychopathology in the individual. A number of genetic family studies of the major psychoses were reported by Rosanoff, Pollock, Malzberg, and others, and biologists such as Raymond Pearl worked in the tradition of Galton and Pearson. But in the transplantation of psychoanalysis from Europe to the United States in the middle 1930's and its flourishing during and immediately after World War II, the attention that Freud and Ernest Jones had given to inborn differences was largely forgotten. The unifying concepts that could define the interaction between organism and environment had not yet clearly emerged, and therapeutic aims seemed to demand exclusive attention to psychogenesis.

A few of that generation of psychoanalysts showed exceptions to this trend. Among these were Rado—who conceived of a unitary scheme of psychology, with psychodynamics resting on the solid bases of genetics and physiology—and Hartmann, who studied inborn characteristics of the ego. The publication of Kallmann's Berlin family study and later of his New York twin investigation in schizophrenia changed American psychiatry profoundly by calling attention to the interacting role of genetics in many psychiatric conditions. The area of Kallmann's work included schizophrenia, manic-depressive psychoses, homosexuality, mental deficiency, aging and longevity, tuberculosis, early deafness, and genetic counseling.

For a time, political events and pseudoeugenic horror put the scientific evaluation of human genetics into disrepute. But in the past 2 or 3 decades a general shift in American psychiatry could be seen. Major advances in cytological, biochemical, and population genetics not only captured the imagination of many psychiatrists but pointed to an understanding of the possible mechanisms of genetic influence that were fully compatible with human rights, values, and individuality. Experimental psychology was studying individual differences in various species from Drosophila to dogs. The theory of interaction of genetic and ecological forces in human development became predominant, and problems of population growth began to draw attention to important aspects of ecology and evolution. At the same time, on the basis of clinical observations, psychiatrists were beginning to be aware of the importance of family patterns, individual differences, and metabolic and pharmacological distinctions. Investigations of families and twins were combined with analysis of enzymes and studies of gene localization and linkage to chromosomal markers and were supplemented by studies of adoptees and high-risk persons to tease out the role of the environment.

In considering the relation of genetics to psychiatry throughout the material that follows, one can conceive a series of organization levels: the molecular and cellular, the biochemical and neurophysiological, the psychodynamic, the demographic, and the social. In each of these areas, the continuous interaction of the organism with its surrounding forces determines its status at any given time; that is, there is an interplay of all the factors affecting human development, whether genetic, chromosomal, biochemical, embryological, metabolic, experiential, or social. The goal of psychiatric genetics as a science may be considered, in the broadest sense, to be the clarification of the mechanisms of human variation and development not only in psychiatric disorders but also in normal behavior.

Human Genetics in the Framework of Evolution

The theory of biological evolution provides the framework in which to understand both the success of humans as a species and the individual failures and problems seen by the physician and psychiatrist. On the scale of evolutionary time, the structures and functions of all living organisms, including humans, are adapted to survival and reproduction in the environment; in the case of humans, a built-in plasticity has evolved over eons that greatly extends the range of livable environments. An essential part of this evolutionary process, as foreseen by

Darwin, is the existence of a storehouse of variation that acts as raw material for the action of selective processes. On the much smaller time scale represented by the lifetime of a person and his or her family, these variations may include some that are poorly adaptive or relatively maladaptive.

Interacting with a wide range of physical and affective environments over the course of a life from conception to death, these genetic components of health and disease, of feeling and behavior are the true subject of this section.

To better understand the methods, results, and application of genetics in psychiatry, one may usefully survey the basic genetic principles. This survey includes the classical rules of Mendelian genetics, which are given richer meaning and cogency by modern biochemical and cytological science.

CLASSICAL GENETICS

Gregor Mendel's report on his garden pea experiments in 1865 paved the way for the modern theory of genetics. His observations led to the postulation that a genetic substance—which was not blended but rather remained intact during an individual's life—was transmitted in the form of stable units to its offspring. His idea led to the description of population in mathematical terms, and the development of genetics later merged with that of the theory of evolution. Originally, Mendel's conclusions were statistical in nature. Counting the variations that he found in the progeny of certain matings, he inferred that each trait existed as if determined by paired particles (later called genes) in the germ plasm. From this inference, a number of general principles of inheritance were derived.

In classical genetics, it is assumed that single genetic traits in sexually reproducing species are determined by paired genes, one of which is derived from the male germ cell and the other from the female germ cell. In human genetics, for example, one may speak of the total genetic constitution of a person as his genotype and of his appearance at any given time as his phenotype. A person receiving a given gene from both parents is called a homozygote for that particular gene, and, under proper environmental conditions, he will be certain to show the characteristics. If a person receives the given gene from one parent and a different gene at the corresponding locus from the other parent, he is known as a heterozygote. In some cases the heterozygote displays traits intermediate between those represented by homozygotes; in other cases he displays the traits as a homozygote does. In the latter instance, the trait is known as dominant. In still other cases he does not display the trait; in this instance the trait is known as recessive—that is, it is expressed only if both genes are present.

Single-gene inheritance. At any locus a mutation can occur at the molecular level that may alter the phenotypic manifestation of the given gene. Once in a while such a mutation, random in nature, becomes the building block that leads by selection to evolutionary change. For the most part, however, if a single mutant gene can express itself against the genetic background of many other factors, its phenotype effect tends to be pathological.

One of the classic writings on genetics early in this century was the series of papers by Garrod (1909), which deal with such inborn errors of metabolism. Garrod foresaw the concept of genes determining enzyme production and conceived of the idea of metabolic blocks in which the absence of a necessary enzyme causes the intermediary metabolism of a certain substance to proceed in a faulty direction. His theory also foreshadowed the one gene-one enzyme hypothesis of Beadle and Tatum. Among the genetic defects of this nature may be listed phenylketonuria, alcaptonuria, albinism, tyrosinosis, galactosemia, some of the aminoacidurias, and Wilson's disease.

Simple dominant traits tend to be rare and incompletely expressed. When they appear, they are transmitted in the direct line of descent by inheritance from one parent. They may easily be studied in pedigrees, and they appear in about 50 per cent of the offspring of one affected parent (see Figure 1). Matings between two affected persons are rare, and a negligible role is played by consanguineous marriages.

In simple recessive traits, inheritance from both parents is necessary. The parents themselves are frequently unaffected, since they are usually heterozygotes. If two heterozygotes mate, each child has a 25 per cent chance of being a homozygote and, therefore, an affected offspring (see Figure 2). In relatively rare disorders, consanguineous marriages are apt to increase the chances of such affected offspring. Transmission of a simple recessive trait is usually along collateral, rather than direct, lines of descent.

A modification of these modes of inheritance is X-linkage, in which the given gene is on the X chromosome. The inheritance is unequally distributed between the sexes, since a male transmits his X chromosome to none of his sons and to each of his daughters. In X-linked recessive inheritance, with an affected father, all sons are unaffected, and all daughters are carriers; with an affected mother, the sons have a 50 per cent risk of being affected, and the daughters have a 50 per cent risk of being carriers. In X-linked dominant inheritance, the affected female transmits the trait to half her sons and to half her daughters; the affected male transmits the trait to none of his sons and to all of his daughters.

Not all mutant genes in humans conform to a simple mode of inheritance. A gene does not produce a given trait directly. It merely begins a long series of reactions that may be modified by environmental factors, both prenatal and postnatal, and by the action of other genes. Gene effects, therefore, may vary from complete expression to no apparent expression at all. There are genes that are neither completely dominant nor completely recessive but somewhere in between. Since

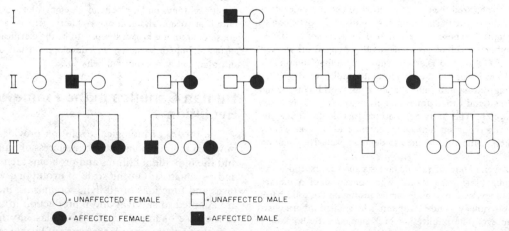

FIGURE 1. A pedigree of Huntington's chorea, illustrating dominant inheritance. (From the Department of Medical Genetics, New York State Psychiatric Institute.)

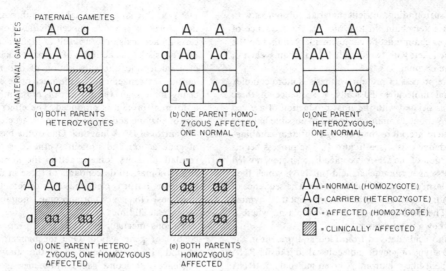

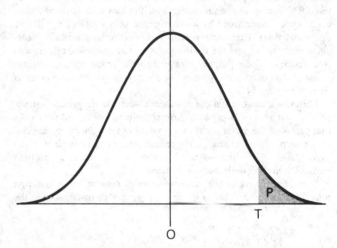

FIGURE 2. Diagram of theoretical expectations in simple recessive inheritance, e.g., phenylketonuria. (From the Department of Medical Genetics, New York State Psychiatric Institute.)

recessive genes may express themselves mildly in heterozygotes, methods for their detection are of great importance in the practical application of genetic counseling.

Multiple-gene inheritance. In addition to single-factor types of inheritance, certain traits are determined by the action of several or many genes. This type of inheritance is called polygenic, with contributions made in a cumulative manner by a number of genes that by themselves produce only minor effects. Such genes may be dominant, recessive, or additive in their effect. Some genes may modify the expression of a major gene, and others may suppress its effect entirely. For many traits such as height, weight, intelligence, and perhaps personality variations that show small gradations within the range of normality, polygenic inheritance may be at work.

If a trait is determined by the additive effect of many genes in a randomly mating population and the trait is continuously measurable—for example, height, intelligence, blood pressure—it is distributed in a normal bell-shaped fashion. When the multiple factors contributing to the trait are nongenetic as well as genetic, the trait is called multifactorial, and the same type of distribution is found. Multifactorial inheritance may also apply to a discontinuous (affected or unaffected) trait—for example, diabetes, schizophrenia, spina bifida—if one assumes that there is an underlying graded attribute called liability, which is related to the disorder and is made up of genetic and environmental factors. This liability is considered to have a normal distribution, but there is a threshold below which individuals are unaffected and above which all individuals are affected (see Figure 3).

Other forms of transmission. There are instances of vertical transmission in families formerly thought to have a hereditary basis that are probably due to a transmissible viral agent, such as kuru or hepatitis B (Australia antigen). The importance of genetic factors in susceptibility remains unclear in kuru, but they are probably important in hepatitis B.

BIOCHEMISTRY OF GENETIC SUBSTANCE

Structure of DNA. In recent decades there have been outstanding advances in elucidating the nature of the genetic substance itself. By 1952 chemists had determined that the genetic material transferred from generation to generation and carrying genetic information is not protein, as had long been thought, but deoxyribonucleic acid (DNA). It was found possible to transform a bacterium of one type to another by injecting it into an animal together with pure DNA of the second type. It was also found that, in certain viruses, the effective part was DNA. Chromosomes are composed of DNA and protein, but DNA appeared to be the primary genetic material.

FIGURE 3. Threshold model, multifactorial inheritance. *Horizontal axis* represents liability; *vertical axis* represents frequency. Individuals whose liability exceeds a value T are affected. The area under the *curve* beyond *T* represents the proportion (*P*) of affected individuals in the given population.

In 1953 the structure of this molecule was proposed by Watson and Crick. It had been known that DNA contains deoxyribose (a five-carbon sugar), phosphate, and four nitrogenous bases—two purines (adenine and guanine) and two pyrimidines (cytosine and thymine)—and that the number of adenine molecules equals that of thymine and the number of guanine molecules equals that of cytosine. Watson and Crick suggested that DNA consists of two sugar-phosphate chains and that the chains are twisted around each other in the form of a double helix. From a sugar on one chain to a corresponding sugar on the other, there is a hydrogen bond linkage through either adenine on one chain and thymine on the other or guanine on one chain and cytosine on the other. A DNA molecule may consist of thousands of such nucleotide linkages.

Functions of DNA. On the basis of this DNA structure, it is possible to explain the two main functions of the genetic material (1) its ability to duplicate itself exactly in cell division and (2) its ability to transmit information to the cytoplasm of the cell and bring about the synthesis of unique enzymes or other proteins.

Replication. If the two chains forming the double helix untwist and separate, breaking the linkages between the nucleotides, each half can then extract, from the surrounding nutrient material, substances with which to reconstruct a sister chain. In this process, the sequence of nucleotides on each sister chain must be complementary to that on the original half chain. One is left with two double helical chains, each of which is identical to the original.

Protein synthesis. The process of protein synthesis is more complex and involves additional molecules. Basically, a sequence of three nucleotide linkages is associated with the final production of a given amino acid. As there are about 20 amino acids and 64 possible linkages of three nucleotides, there are more than enough different combinations, and some redundancy exists (see Figure 4). The process begins as the message on a portion of the DNA is copied by a single-stranded molecule known as messenger ribonucleic acid (mRNA), which then migrates into the cytoplasm of the cell (transcription). The sequence of nucleotides in the RNA is the same as in the DNA, except that thymine is replaced by uracil. The mRNA travels to the cytoplasm, where it attaches to structures known as ribosomes.

Meanwhile, the amino acids derived from food and present in the cytoplasm are joined to a type of genetic molecule called transfer RNA (tRNA), a long chain bent like a hairpin. A given molecule of tRNA is able to be joined at its free end to one and only one of the amino acids. At one bend of the hairpin, a sequence of three nucleotides is ready to attach itself to its unique complementary sequence on the mRNA as that sequence moves across the ribosome. In this manner the mRNA serves as a template that specifies how a sequence of amino acids, each accompanied by its appropriate tRNA molecule, will line up (translation). These amino acids join together as the tRNA molecules separate off, and the resulting chain of amino acids, or polypeptide, remains. These polypeptides assume the proper spatial configuration and form proteins, which may be enzymes or structural proteins such as hemoglobin.

Mutations. Gene mutations represent changes in the genetic instruction so that new cells produce different substances than do the cells that preceded the mutation. If these mutations take place in germ cells, they may produce a change in the genetic information contained in the zygote and, depending on the locus of the mutation, a resultant particular enzyme deficiency or disease.

In the framework of the modern theory of gene action, a mutation may be considered as a change in the sequence of nucleotides in the DNA. Such changes may take place through a mistake in the replication process at the time the cell divides, possibly through the action of certain chemicals or as a result of high energy radiation. The changes may consist of the addition of an extra nucleotide pair, the subtraction of a nucleotide, the substitution of one nucleotide for another, or various rearrangements of the nucleotide sequence. From then on, a changed message is sent by means of the mRNA to the cytoplasm, and a different protein is produced. The effect may be a modification or loss of enzyme activity or an altered structure, as in hemoglobin.

Control of DNA function. One of the basic questions in this picture of gene action and protein synthesis is the problem of control or regulation. Every somatic cell in the human being has the same 46 chromosomes, all descendants of those in the original fertilized ovum or zygote, but it is clear that cells differentiate and perform different functions. Not every chromosome, therefore, is transferring its total message at all times.

Various mechanisms have been propounded to account for the control of gene action. One mechanism discovered by Jacob and Monod (1961) on the basis of the study of bacteria involves the existence of structural genes, whose message determines the production of enzymes or structural materials produced by the cell, and regulatory genes. The regulatory genes are controlled by external molecules (inducers and repressors) and, in turn, control the synthesis of mRNA—in effect, switching the structural genes on and off, depending on the presence and quantity of the substrate on which the genes act or of the product that the genes produce. Thus, a type of feedback mechanism ensures a regulation of the genes by their surroundings. More complex mechanisms, including the action of hormones, may play a role in higher organisms, representing the basic prototypes of gene-environment interaction, a concept of primary importance in psychiatric genetics.

Population Genetics and Human Variation

Genetic factors determine important short-range and long-range effects in human populations. A population may be defined as a group of individuals tending to mate among each other. Such a reproductive community shares a common gene pool, within which the relative frequencies of various genes

2nd base

1st base		U	C	A	G	3rd base
U		Phenylalanine	Serine	Tyrosine	Cysteine	U
		Phenylalanine	Serine	Tyrosine	Cysteine	C
		Leucine	Serine	(Term)*	(Term)	A
		Leucine	Serine	(Term)	Tryptophan	G
C		Leucine	Proline	Histidine	Arginine	U
		Leucine	Proline	Histidine	Arginine	C
		Leucine	Proline	Glutamine	Arginine	A
		Leucine	Proline	Glutamine	Arginine	G
A		Isoleucine	Threonine	Asparagine	Serine	U
		Isoleucine	Threonine	Asparagine	Serine	C
		Isoleucine	Threonine	Lysine	Arginine	A
		Methionine	Threonine	Lysine	Arginine	G
G		Valine	Alanine	Aspartic acid	Glycine	U
		Valine	Alanine	Aspartic acid	Glycine	C
		Valine	Alanine	Glutamic acid	Glycine	A
		Valine	Alanine	Glutamic acid	Glycine	G

FIGURE 4. The genetic code. Associations between amino acids and combinations of three nucleotide bases in RNA molecule. * Chain terminating.

may be specified. In a human population other distinguishing features may be of a geographic, cultural, socioeconomic, ethnic, or psychological nature. These considerations may tend to isolate certain subpopulations within the main population. The changing stratification of such subpopulations exerts a definite effect on the genetic composition of the given population groups.

HARDY-WEINBERG EQUILIBRIUM

The basis for a systematic approach to population genetics is a simple formula called the Hardy-Weinberg principle. This principle describes an equilibrium state in an ideal population that will exist from generation to generation. Dealing with the variation in a population of genotypes at a particular locus (polymorphism), it expresses, in terms of the gene frequencies, the expected equilibrium values of the various genotypes if the following conditions are met: random mating, with every individual having the same chance to mate with any other individual of the opposite sex; no selective advantage or disadvantage of any one gene over the others at the same locus; and absence of mutations. In addition, the ideal Hardy-Weinberg equilibrium assumes a very large and geographically stable population.

The main importance of the principle lies in the fact that it demonstrates a continuation of population variations from generation to generation, rather than a trend toward increasing uniformity. If any of its conditions are not fulfilled, there is interference with the population equilibrium.

CAUSES OF DISEQUILIBRIUM

Interference with random mating. A change in the relative proportion of homozygotes and heterozygotes is brought about by any interference with random mating, such as consanguineous marriage, assortative mating, and the persistence or development of population isolates. Such practices result in an increase of recessive phenotypes, particularly in the case of relatively rare conditions, since there is an increased trend for two heterozygous carriers of recessive genes to mate and produce homozygous offspring.

Genetic drift. In small populations, even with random mating, there are chance variations in the relative frequency of genes from generation to generation. This phenomenon, known as genetic drift, leads to fluctuations of gene frequencies, even in the absence of mutation, selection, and assortative mating.

Mutation and selection. Mutations, now understood in biochemical terms as changes in the DNA molecule, may be described in terms of calculable frequencies with definite effect on the gene pool for future generations. Mutations tend to cause changes not only in gene frequencies but also in the adaptiveness of individuals. In this process these individuals become subject to the action of selection, which may be defined as genetic advantage or disadvantage measured in terms of mean family size. If individuals of a certain genetic constitution produce an increased number of offspring, this is known as positive selection. A trend toward elimination of a trait due to a disadvantage is known as negative selection. In some instances a trait in heterozygous form is advantageous, whereas in the homozygous state it is detrimental. For example, individuals with the sickle-cell trait (heterozygotes) are relatively resistant to falciparum malaria, a phenomenon that tends to stabilize the frequency of the given gene in populations living in malarial regions, even though the rarer homozygote with sickle-cell anemia is at a severe disadvantage.

To be sure, advantage is determined not only by the effect of individual genes determining unit characters but by general genetic aspects of fitness and adaptiveness to the environment, which may be determined by the action of many genes, in both homozygous and heterozygous form. Selection may be mediated by differences in mating, fertility, migration, and early mortality.

Human Cytogenetics

During the 3 decades in which Mendel's findings remained unnoticed, the discovery of the chromosomes in the cell nucleus took place. These specially staining thread-like bodies were observed to divide in the process of cell division and to be distributed as exact duplicates. But in the formation of germ cells, each cell received only half of the chromosomes in the parental cells. These facts turned out to be consistent with the statistical findings of Mendel, and thus it became possible to combine data derived from breeding experiments with the microscopic study of cells and chromosomes.

Nevertheless, the study of chromosomes in humans was long neglected. There was no agreement on such simple matters as the number of chromosomes and the mechanism by which sex was determined chromosomally. Most textbooks stated that the total number of chromosomes in each normal human cell was 48, a figure later found to be incorrect; the number is now established as being 46. Although it was known that females had two X chromosomes and males one X and one Y, it had erroneously been thought that the Y chromosome was inactive, sex being determined by the number of X chromosomes. Actually, it is a locus on the Y chromosome that determines the development of male characteristics in a human being. And until recently, methodology was not advanced to the point where clinical abnormalities could be correlated with chromosomal aberrations.

SEX CHROMATIN

In 1949, the first recent major discovery in human cytogenetics was made by two Canadians, Barr and Bertram, who uncovered an important difference between male and female cells while studying neurons of the cat. The investigators found a dark-staining mass of chromatin in the nuclei of many cells. They soon made the crucial observation that it was the female that had this chromatin substance. Before long, this difference was shown to exist in other somatic cells and in other mammals, including humans.

The determination of sex chromatin in humans is not a difficult procedure. It is done most easily by examining a smear of buccal mucosal cells. The cells are scraped from the inside of the mouth, put on specially prepared slides, fixed, and stained, and 100 to 200 cells are counted. The mass is seen as a lens-shaped body adjacent to the nuclear membrane. From 30 to 60 per cent of the cells of the normal woman show this dark-staining mass, which is now referred to as sex chromatin or, after its discoverer, a Barr body (see Figure 5). Originally, it was believed that the sex chromatin body consisted of parts of both X chromosomes. This theory was discarded in favor of one derived from the so-called Lyon hypothesis, which states that, in the early embryonic development of the female, one X chromosome in each cell is inactivated. Accordingly, the Barr body is thought to represent all or part of this inactivated chromosome.

DEVELOPMENT OF CHROMOSOME TECHNIQUE

In 1956 improved methods of visualizing and counting human chromosomes led to the clarification of many cytogenetic problems. Since chromosomes become visible and distinguishable only at the metaphase stage of a dividing nucleus, it was necessary to obtain cells in the process of division. Early investigations had been done with testicular tissue, and individual cells with visible and distinguishable chromosomes had been observed. However, these chromosomes clumped together and overlapped, rendering attempted counts inaccurate.

The problem of obtaining many cells in a dividing stage was dealt with by the use of tissue culture methods whereby cells from skin biopsy or from blood could grow and divide in vitro in tissue culture media. To arrest the cells at the metaphase stage, where the chromosomes may be distinguished, researchers added colchicine or other mitotic poisons to the culture medium shortly before the cells were harvested. To avoid clumping and overlapping of the chromosomes, researchers suspended the cells in a hypotonic solution in the stage before staining. This hypotonic solution swelled the nucleus and spread the chromosomes over a larger area to make them discretely visible.

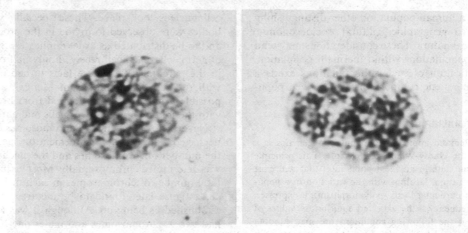

FIGURE 5. Sex chromatin in buccal epithelial cells (thionin stain). *Left,* chromatin positive. *Right,* chromatin negative.

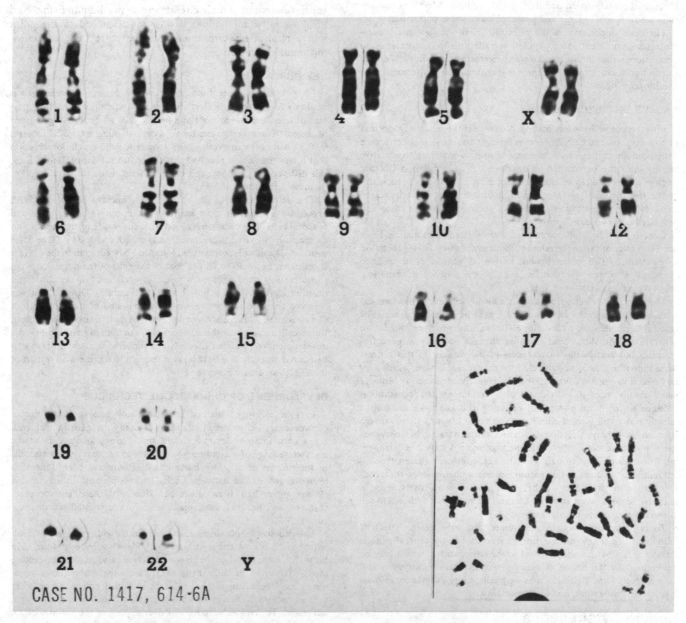

FIGURE 6. Banding patterns in human chromosomes. Karyotype of normal female, Giemsa (G-) banding.

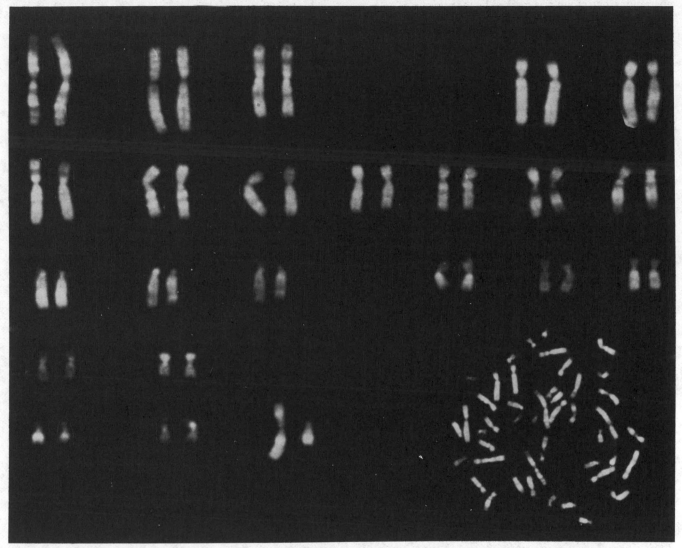

FIGURE 7. Banding patterns in human chromosomes. Karyotype of normal male fluorescent quinacrine (Q-) banding.

Finally, the cells were centrifuged, spread on slides, dried, and stained. In the case of leukocyte cultures from peripheral blood, the addition of an extract of kidney bean, phytohemagglutinin, was found not only to agglutinate the red blood cells but also to initiate cell division (mitosis) in leukocytes. This action is probably on an immunological basis. Harvesting of cells is done after 72 hours.

NORMAL HUMAN KARYOTYPE

In 1956 Tjio and Levan found, by tissue culture methods, that the number of chromosomes in humans is 46. It was possible, by enlarging the photograph of the microscopic field and cutting each chromosome out, to arrange the chromosomes in descending order of size, thus producing a visual representation of the chromosome complement or karyotype. Since the chromosomes are photographed after replication, they appear as two chromatids attached at one point called the centromere. The chromosomes are distinguishable within size groups by the position of this centromere, which may be median, submedian, or toward one end; the corresponding chromosomes are known as metacentric, submetacentric, and acrocentric.

In 1960 the numbering system was standardized at a conference in Denver, the first 22 pairs of autosomes being divided into seven groups labeled A to G and numbered 1 to 22. The twenty-third pair represents the sex chromosomes—namely, XX in women, XY in men. In later conferences further standardization of nomenclature was achieved,

with more detailed methods of symbolizing chromosome abnormalities. At the same time, new techniques were developed and described to differentiate among chromosomes that were not precisely distinguishable by morphology under the usual stains used.

Autoradiography, a technique in which cells are grown in a labeled medium and the uptake of radioactive thymidine at various stages in chromosome replication is measured and visualized, has been superseded by newer staining methods of chromosome characterization. These are based on the banding patterns that appear as fluorescent segments after staining by quinacrine mustard or quinacrine hydrochloride or by dark and light segments when the Giemsa dye mixture is used as the staining agent. These developments have made possible the identification of each of the human chromosomes (see Figures 6 and 7).

CHROMOSOMAL ABERRATIONS

Nondisjunction leading to trisomy. The 3 years after the correct description of the human karyotype were fruitful ones in cytogenetics, and a number of aberrations were described. Since then, many clinical syndromes involving chromosomal aberrations (changes in number or structure) have been reported; most of these syndromes are rare (de Grouchy and Turleau, 1977). Among the more common or prototypical aberrations, one group was marked by the presence of an extra chromosome, so that there were 47, rather than 46, chromosomes in the karyotype. The extra chromosome represented the presence of three, rather than two, of a given chromosome. Such an anomaly arises through a process of nondisjunction, usually in the formation of the sperm or the egg cell. In the splitting of the cell, one chromosome of each pair ordinarily goes to each of the daughter cells. If the two chromosomes of a given pair remain joined and enter one of the daughter cells together, that cell has an extra chromosome. When that daughter cell combines in fertilization with a normal gamete, a zygote or single-cell-stage individual is formed with the extra chromosome, a condition known as trisomy.

Three classical instances of nondisjunction causing trisomic conditions have been described in which the autosomes, as distinguished from the X and Y or sex chromosomes, are involved. The first of these instances was the trisomy of chromosome 21 in mongolism, better termed Down's syndrome, after the man who first described it in 1866 (see Figure 8). It had been known for a long time that most cases of this syndrome occurred in children born to older mothers. At the same time, however, the concordance rate in one-egg twins was close to 100 per cent. These findings foreshadowed an early germinal, possibly chromosomal, defect as the responsible agent. In 1959 Lejeune and others demonstrated by tissue culture methods the presence of an extra small acrocentric chromosome in patients with Down's syndrome. It is very likely that this condition arises by nondisjunction in the formation of the maternal ovum, related somehow to the age of the mother. A second autosomal trisomy is the trisomy 18 (Edwards's) syndrome, and a third trisomy found in living infants involves chromosome 13 (Patau). Both of these are rare (one in several thousand births), and infants do not survive beyond 1 year.

Mosaicism. In a trisomic condition, if the extra chromosome is lost through disjunction in the early cell divisions of the zygote, two cell lines may persist, one with 46 and one with 47 chromosomes. Such a person, an example of mosaicism, may have an intermediate degree of symptomatology.

Translocation. Another mechanism in Down's syndrome was first postulated by Polani on the basis of the investigation of the chromosome complement in an affected child born to a young mother. Chromosome count revealed the normal number of 46, but one of the chromosomes in group D turned out

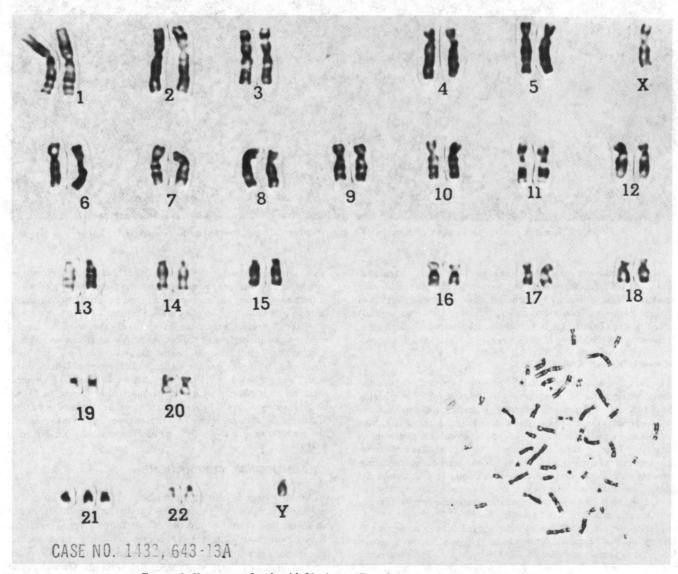

CASE NO. 1432, 643-13A

FIGURE 8. Karyotype of male with 21 trisomy (Down's syndrome), Giemsa (G-) banding.

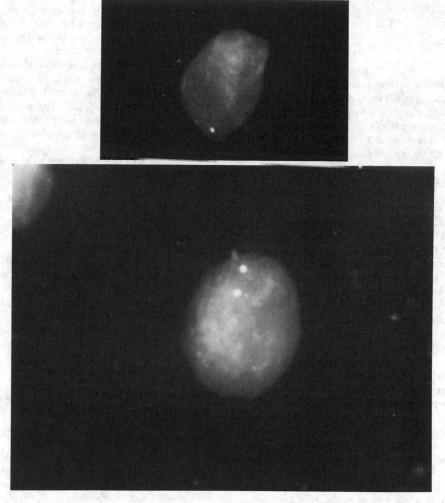

FIGURE 9. Fluorescent Y chromosome in buccal mucosal cells. *Above,* normal male; *below,* male with XYY karyotype.

to be longer than normal. It was suggested that this oversized chromosome consisted of the long arm of the D chromosome plus that of an extra chromosome 21; in such cases it appears that the mother or the father also has such a long D chromosome, but the added unit is balanced by the absence of one of the unattached chromosomes 21, leaving the person with a total number of only 45 chromosomes.

The population risk for Down's syndrome over all is 1 in 700, but it increases exponentially with maternal age; at age 20 it may be as low as 1 in 2,000, but it is about 1 in 50 for mothers over 45. If either parent has a balanced translocation, however, his or her children can be expected theoretically to have 1 chance in 3 of being affected, although empirically the risk is actually about 15 per cent if the mother is a carrier and 2 to 3 per cent if the father has the aberration.

This interchange of chromosomal material is known as translocation. In Down's syndrome it may also occur between two chromosomes 21, in which case the risk for a trisomic child is 100 per cent. The difference between trisomy and translocation is very important from a practical point of view. If a child with Down's syndrome is a trisomy or if the child is a translocation but both parents are normal, the risk of recurrence is only slightly increased, taking maternal age into account.

Deletion. In addition to nondisjunction and translocation, a third mechanism causing chromosomal anomalies is that of deletion. In this condition part of a chromosome breaks off

during cell replication and is lost, so that future cells have a smaller sized chromosome than usual. The cri-du-chat syndrome described by Lejeune is associated with a deletion of part of the short arm of chromosome 5.

Abnormalities involving sex chromosomes. Contrary to the normal patterns, certain males show the sex chromatin mass and certain females do not. Chromatin–positive male patients with Klinefelter's syndrome generally have 47 chromosomes. They do, indeed, have two X chromosomes, but they also possess a Y chromosome. The two X chromosomes are sufficient to cause the appearance of the Barr body, but the Y chromosome causes them to have male gonads and essentially male genitals. In each case, the abnormal gamete is the result of nondisjunction. Similarly, most girls with Turner's syndrome and no Barr body are found to have a karyotype containing only 45 chromosomes; they have only one X chromosome, the other sex chromosome being missing.

Other abnormalities involving the sex chromosomes are seen in females having 47 chromosomes with three X chromosomes and two Barr bodies and in males with an extra Y chromosome (XYY). These men have given rise to much discussion, since they were originally described as tall, criminal, or psychopathic males with mental subnormality. Screening of newborns with the use of fluorescent staining techniques in buccal epithelial cells (see Figure 9—the Y chromosome shines brightly, even in interphase) may provide better data on both the incidence of the karyotype abnormality and its possible consequences in the course of development, but longitudinal studies have been few because of some real ethical and methodological concerns.

Biological and Clinical Models for Interaction

To set the framework in which to describe in more detail basic genetics or clinical applications, one may usefully consider first some ways of conceptualizing, describing, and illustrating the interaction of genetic and environmental forces. The genetic forces are transmitted by cells and are expressed by a complex transcription and translation machinery. The environmental forces are either natural or man-made and modify, at all levels, both the transmission and the expression of genetic information. This modification may be in the form of activation or repression; both are needed if there is to be cell differentiation and specialization of function and if cell and tissue functions are to be smoothly regulated, in cybernetic fashion, to the needs of the organism. In bacteria the model for such orderly regulation provided by Jacob and Monod (1961) has been referred to above. The production of a specific antibody in response to antigenic stimulation is another example of the interlocking of genetic and environmental information. These mechanisms are usually adaptive to the organism. On the other hand, the disruption of genes or chromosomes by chemical or other environmental mutagens or the intrusion of foreign genetic information by viruses may lead, at least in the individual, to disease or death.

If environmental and genetic factors are inseparably related at the cellular level, they work together no less closely at the other extreme on the scales of number and time in large populations and over many generations. The genetic constitution of populations undergoes changes over the short run or the long run, and evolution proceeds in response to positive or negative forces in the environment, together with the workings of chance, geography, and human ingenuity.

Although these basic mechanisms of interaction are not yet completely understood, they may help the psychiatrist to conceptualize and accept the dynamic functioning of genetics in individual development and psychopathology without subordinating the complementary role of the environmental factors he has studied. More than a static combination of two factors added together, the interaction is a continuous process with mutual feedback and spiral development through a series of critical stages. A few examples of clinical efforts to describe the interworking of genetic and nongenetic factors may illustrate these points.

GENETICS AND PSYCHODYNAMICS

The science of psychodynamics was always postulated by some psychoanalysts to be part of a unitary conceptual scheme in human biology. These psychoanalysts, such as Rado, analyzed behavioral variations in the gene-specific physiological (that is, biochemical) context of the organism. In such a scheme, the psychodynamic approach, focused on an understanding of motivation and emotional control, may uncover and delineate behavior problems that require for their complete explanation the clarification of the role of genetic transmission. Indeed, this approach was formulated in the writings of Freud. He always took into consideration both the constitutional and the accidental causes of neurotic disease, and he spoke of primary congenital variations in the ego and in the defense mechanisms a person selects. And in an early essay on the study of twins, Hartmann (1964) wrote of personality structure as the result of interaction between heredity and environment. He considered

the possibility of character *anlagen* that, in the course of development, differentiate into character traits. He thought that studies of twins may throw light on the possible substitution of one trait for another.

Such an integrated approach may assume a central role in future psychodynamic work. In essence, this approach affords an opportunity to recognize fundamental genetic differences among persons and to correlate these differences with various forms of developmental interaction both before and after birth. Although the role of genetics is not always made explicit in these studies, there are many advantages and potentialities within the scope of workers who combine the methods of both disciplines.

INNATE DIFFERENCES AND PERSONALITY DEVELOPMENT

In the field of infant and child psychiatry, Levy was one of the first to call attention to intrinsic differences among children as equipotent with maternal attitudes in determining final behavior patterns. These differences have been measured along various dimensions—sleep, feeding, sensory responses, activity and passivity, and motor behavior. Thomas and Chess (1977) have identified a group of temperamental qualities in young infants that tend to persist into early childhood and become associated in some cases with behavior. These traits include activity level, rhythmicity, approach-withdrawal, adaptability, intensity of reaction, threshold of response to stimulation, quality of mood, distractibility, and attention span and persistence. Another approach to early differences has been through psychophysiological studies of neonates.

The concept of average expectable environment has been matched by that of significant congenital deficit. The study of deaf children and blind children has begun to serve as a prototype for the investigation of innate somatic deficits upon character development.

Not all constitutional variations are hereditary, since prenatal and perinatal factors must be taken into account, but refined techniques of observation and of genetic analysis can be expected to help in this difficult matter.

PSYCHOSOMATIC DISORDERS AS MODELS OF GENETIC INTERACTION

The cumulative effect of genetic predisposition, early parent-child relationship, and social pressure on psychopathology is exemplified in studies of the causes of peptic ulcer (Mirsky, 1958) and of infantile eczema (Spitz, 1965). Variability among healthy persons, newborn and older, in the level of pepsinogen secretion, as measured in urine and blood, appears to be genetically determined. Dividing a group of army inductees into high-secretion and low-secretion groups, Mirsky found that, under the stress of army training, a large number of persons in the high-secretion group developed signs and symptoms of duodenal ulcer. His hypothesis was that infants who secrete large amounts of pepsinogen have difficulty in satisfying their oral needs, even with a normally good mother; the ensuing anxiety is revived in later life under conditions of deprivation, and this anxiety may lead to ulcer formation. The somatic pathways may be chemical or neurological and may involve hypothalamus, autonomic nervous system, hyperchlorhydria, hyperexcretion of pepsinogen, or hypermotility.

In the study of infantile eczema, Spitz focused on a group of neonates living in an institution along with their unwed mothers. The children were dichotomized into those with and without hypersensitive cutaneous reflexes. It was the hypersensitive group that tended to develop eczema in the second half year of life, when to their congenital predisposition were added manifest anxiety and repressed hostility on the part of their mothers. Deprived of normal touch, care, or skin contact, the very cutaneous need that had been found to be increased, this group of infants developed the somatic lesion, which usually lasted until their motility increased. Although the pathways are not clear, the interaction of innate and nurturing factors provides the kind of model in which genetics may play a dynamic, rather than a mechanical, role in etiology.

Methods of Genetic Investigation in Psychiatry

The aims of genetic investigation in psychiatry are (1) to demonstrate the existence and relative contribution of gene-borne influences, (2) to determine their modes of inheritance, and (3) to elucidate their mechanisms by discovering the chain connecting primary gene products with symptoms or syndromes. The first of these aims has been achieved to the general satisfaction by family, twin, and adoption studies; the second aim is currently being investigated by fitting segregation analysis models to pedigrees or liability threshold models to population family risk data. The study of genetic markers (association of vulnerability with heritable biochemical variables) and longitudinal studies of high-risk persons are among the newer techniques that may further the third aim and eventually unravel mechanisms in a developmental framework. Complicating the design of all these investigational methods are the problems of diagnosis and classification and of interaction with environmental factors.

FAMILY RISK STUDIES

A classical method of genetic investigation has been termed the contingency method of statistical prediction. The aim of this method is to compare the expectancy of a given medical condition developing among relatives of affected persons with the expectancy in the general population. The condition in question must be well defined, so that a number of independent observers may reliably diagnose persons coming into the study. And the original group of patients whose relatives are to be investigated must be either a consecutively reported series representing a complete ascertainment or a random sample thereof. If this criterion is met, members of the group may be called *index cases* or *probands*. They generally represent all admissions to a given hospital system or clinic over a given period of time or, at least, a properly selected sample of such a list.

Not all relatives who are free of symptoms necessarily remain so if they live to an older age. For relatives, therefore, one cannot simply consider the prevalence of the condition; one must also obtain a corrected figure known as the expectancy rate. A simple means of calculating this rate is Weinberg's abridged method. The number of observed cases among relatives (the numerator) is related not to the total number of relatives but to all those who have survived the period in which the disease may be certain to be manifested plus half the number who are still within the age limits during which the disease may be manifested (the denominator). Persons who died before the earliest manifestation age of the given disease or who are still under that age are not counted as part of the denominator. This method yields morbidity risks that approach the average expectancy of developing the given condition in persons who remain alive through its manifestation period.

These expectancy rates for various groups of relatives may be compared with one another and with the expectancy rates for the general population. General population rates have been obtained in many medical conditions through careful demographical studies of whole populations of small areas or of samples of populations of larger districts.

Family risk studies are able to provide empirical risks of developing given conditions in relatives of patients, and these data are useful in genetic counseling. Such studies may suggest the relative action of genetic and environmental factors or the mode of inheritance but are inconclusive in this regard without the further sophistication provided by segregation and threshold models.

In segregation models, genetic hypotheses are tested by pooling data from different pedigrees to compare the observed proportion of affected relatives with that expected according to the given hypothesis. Biases arise due to methods of ascertainment, size of family, and variable age of onset, and various statistical methods have been developed to eliminate or minimize these biases (Emery, 1976).

In the threshold models, a graded attribute termed "liability" is shared by all persons in a given population, this liability being the sum of all genetic and environmental factors determining one's likelihood to develop a given disease. This liability is assumed to be distributed normally in the general population and, with a higher mean value, in the relatives of affected persons. A threshold is defined above which the disorder is manifest, the position of the threshold being a function of the prevalence of the disorder in each group (Falconer, 1965). A more refined version of this method assumes two or more thresholds corresponding, for example, to more or less severity (Reich et al., 1972). A set of best-fit parameters can then be found for the liability distribution of the general population and of relatives of affected persons; these parameters can be tested for goodness of fit of expected to observed prevalences. It may thereby be possible to specify uniquely the existence and mode of inheritance—distinguishing, for example, between single-gene transmission and polygenic transmission.

TWIN AND TWIN-FAMILY METHODS

Twin studies are useful to separate and hence evaluate genetic and environmental influences and to seek for protective and precipitating factors. The use of twins in genetic research was initiated by Galton and is based on the occurrence of two genetically different types of twins: those derived from one fertilized ovum and those derived from two fertilized ova. The one-egg twins are always of the same sex (barring a rare chromosomal loss before the first cell division, which may result in a pair of identical twins comprising a normal male and a Turner's syndrome female); two-egg twins may be either of the same sex or of opposite sexes.

In the twin-family method, data are obtained on complete sibships of twin index cases and their parents. These data may be concordance rates in all-or-nothing traits or correlations in continuous characters. Comparisons are made between one-egg twins, two-egg twins of the same sex, two-egg twins of opposite sexes, full siblings, half siblings, and stepsiblings. This procedure provides a unique opportunity to investigate intrafamily variations with a minimum of uncontrolled variables. Comparisons can be made between one-egg twins brought up and living together, two-egg twins under the same conditions, and other siblings. It is more difficult to find one-egg twins who have been raised apart and who present a particular syndrome—at least in sufficient numbers to warrant drawing conclusions from concordance rates.

Certain significant misunderstandings concerning twin studies should be noted. Carefully stated hypotheses should not be questioned simply because pairs of dissimilar one-egg twins have been found. Genes actually determine a norm of reaction, the exact expression of which depends on many interactions taking place before, at, and after birth. Indeed, one-egg twins, especially those with a common chorion, are subject to more disparate influence before birth than are two-egg pairs, as a result of circulatory variations. Parents are often unsure of which type of twins they have, and similar patterns of family dynamics occur in both types.

It is important to be certain that a condition to be studied by twin concordance methods be no more prevalent in twins than in singletons. A complete sample of monozygotic and dizygotic twins has to be obtained, and diagnosis of illness and zygosity must be made independently.

There are many pathways from identical genetic structures to later expression of behavioral traits, and minor shifts in the process of interaction at crucial points may lead to wide divergence in phenotypes. Preconceived ideas on the locus of such crucial points often prove to be invalid. A spiral-like development toward marked dissimilarity in behavior may arise as a result of influences at all stages from the chromosomal to the postnatal ones. Conversely, similar development is often found to exist in two-egg twins.

The statistical value of investigating twins, with primary genetic factors maintained constant, does not preclude more intensive studies in the fields of biochemical and clinical investigation. One of these studies is represented by the co-twin control method in which longitudinal data are obtained from a few selected pairs of one-egg twins. Their reactions and patterns are compared under different life conditions or in response to planned differences in management. In general, the careful study of discordant or dissimilar identical twin pairs may furnish important findings. Often the discordance turns out to be only a partial one, and much is learned about expressivity. In other cases the divergent development may be associated with certain key life factors.

ADOPTION STUDIES

Another useful method of separating biological from rearing influences is the study of children cared for since early infancy by nonrelated foster or adoptive parents. It is possible to compare psychopathology in adopted children whose biological parents were ill with children with unaffected biological parents, or to compare psychopathology in the biological parents and the adoptive parents of affected children. It is also possible to compare parents, biological and adoptive, of affected adopted children with parents of control adoptees without psychopathology or of control children with nongenetic disorders. All these methods have been variously used in recent studies in schizophrenia, psychopathy, alcoholism, and manic-depressive disorder.

Biasing factors to be considered in this method are possible genetic bases for the decision to give a child for adoption or to accept a given child, nonrandom assignment of adoptees according to the socioeconomic status of both families, and the effect on adoptive parents of raising a difficult child.

LONGITUDINAL STUDIES

To learn about the expression of genetic factors and perhaps about means of early detection and intervention, researchers often use longitudinal studies, perhaps the most valuable approach to the understanding of the vicissitudes of genetic interaction in psychiatry. Although these studies can be retrospective, there is much chance for bias in sampling and in the data remembered or recorded; prospective observation of high-risk groups, particularly the children of one or two affected parents, can best provide data on early signs—behavioral, neurological, psychophysiological, and biochemical—and provide leads for prevention. In schizophrenia, such studies have been conducted by Mednick, by Anthony, and by Erlenmeyer-Kimling and are currently being coordinated nationally through a research consortium. This approach avoids confusing precursor signs with the effects of illness and makes for economy and precision.

GENETIC MARKERS, ASSOCIATION, AND LINKAGE

More than 200 genes have been localized on human chromosomes since the color blindness gene was first assigned to a specific chromosome, the X, in 1911. These genes include about 110 assigned to specific autosomes and 100 to the X chromosome. For example, ABO, Rh, and HLA loci have been localized on chromosomes 9, 1, and 6, respectively; in addition to color blindness, the X chromosome map includes genes for forms of muscular dystrophy, hemophilia, and the Xg blood group (McKusick, 1975; McKusick and Ruddle, 1977). Although accounting for only a small number of the 50,000 postulated structural genes or even the 1,200 or so genes whose phenotypes are known, the genes that have been mapped may serve as markers. Specificity of a genetic syndrome may be surmised if it can be shown to be associated with a gene whose locus is linked to that of a known gene—that is, with the two loci on the same chromosome and only a short distance apart. In practice, it is possible to study individual family pedigrees and determine one of two possible types for each offspring—one type in which the given syndrome appears together with a known trait and one in which they appear separately. If the genes are not linked, these two types should be equally likely; if they are linked, most of the offspring will be of one type, depending on the arrangement in the parent. Mathematical methods exist for describing the closeness and the likelihood of linkage.

Other methods of localizing genes depend on hybridization of human somatic cells with cells of other species in vitro, where progressive loss of human chromosomes can map the markers for particular enzymes under conditions of selection. Association of a trait with a given marker, in which the two are mainly found together, implies a causal connection; for example, ankylosing spondylitis is strongly associated with HLA-w27 on chromosome 6, implying that there is a causal connection, not merely a geographical closeness. Both linkage and association studies should turn out to be valuable in psychiatric genetics.

Genetics and Nosology

The ultimate contribution of genetics to nosological distinction in psychiatry would be the identification of genetic mutations directly in the DNA code or, more likely, through their production of abnormal or deficient enzymes in brain or nervous tissue. Quantitative differences, such as in heterozygotes, may be detected by loading techniques, akin to tolerance tests. The study of genetic linkage and association can provide another method for establishing homogeneous diagnostic groups.

Family studies themselves may help to refine psychiatric nosology; a wide catch of symptom complexes may be narrowed if certain forms of illness seem to preponderate in particular family groups. In addition, similarity of symptoms and prevalence across widely varied cultural or geographical groups tends to specify an essential genetic basis. In such a case, differences in frequency may, indeed, be caused by population-genetic variables, such as mating customs, migration patterns, and specific environmental selective factors, or they may be an artifact of differences in diagnostic criteria, but they will not vary greatly with changes in cultural practices over a short time span.

Pharmacogenetics

There is evidence that there may be inherited differences in responses to drugs (Vesell, 1976). In the first place, the therapeutic value of certain drugs may vary with the genetic form of a given syndrome; for example, there are current indications that response to lithium may be correlated with genetically distinct forms of cyclic mood disorder. Second, side effects of drugs may depend quantitatively or qualitatively on genetic differences. Persons with atypical forms of the enzyme pseudocholinesterase may show a prolonged reaction to the administration of succinylcholine. Used before electroconvulsive treatment, this muscle relaxant may cause prolonged apnea in a patient with this rare (1 in about 3,000) gene-controlled metabolic disorder. Hereditary predisposition to phenothiazine-induced parkinsonism has been described, and the acute paralytic effect of barbiturates in persons with porphyria is of essential clinical importance. The therapeutic and side effects of phenelzine, isoniazide, phenytoin sodium, and nortriptyline have also been related to gene-controlled pathways of metabolic excretion or inactivation.

At the level of the gene and the chromosome, the mutagenic effects of ionizing radiation and various chemicals in the natural or the man-created environment may lead to somatic changes or hereditary damage. In addition, certain substances have been implicated in causing chromosome damage in vivo and in vitro. Lysergic acid diethylamide has been found by some investigators to increase the number of chromosome breaks when added to lymphocyte cultures in low concentration; its effect on the cultured cells of subjects who have ingested it seems to vary with the individual. Other more commonly used agents—such as aspirin, caffeine, and ergonovine maleate—have also been shown to cause chromosome breaks when added to cultures; the mechanism, duration, and clinical significance of the damage have yet to be elucidated.

More sensitive than measuring chromosome fragments is the sister chromatid exchange technique, whereby exchanges of material between chromosomes and their replicas formed in vitro during mitosis may be detected by fluorescent staining methods.

Psychiatric Genetics

SCHIZOPHRENIC DISORDERS

In the early literature of psychiatric genetics, there are a number of case reports tending to confirm the common notion that psychoses run in families. However, such studies are of limited value. At the time of their origin, the science of genetics itself had not developed, and the reports themselves were usually restricted to families having many cases, of doubtful diagnosis, and in which intrafamilial causes other than those of a genetic nature were in no way ruled out.

Early studies of expectancy rates. In 1916 Rüdin studied the genetics of schizophrenia in representative and clinically homogeneous samples, obtaining statistically corrected expectancy rates for schizophrenia in relatives of schizophrenic patients as compared with the general population. Based on the families of a series of almost 1,000 patients, the rate for sibs ranged from about 4½ per cent to almost 23 per cent, depending on the psychiatric diagnoses of the parents. In 1932 Schulz reexamined these data and found higher sib expectancies for patients whose illness had an insidious onset and lower sib expectancies for those with an acute onset, precipitating cause, and benign course. In his large family study conducted in Berlin, Kallmann (1938) investigated the families of 1,087 patients; the over-all expectancy rate for sibs was 11 per cent, but it was higher for the sibs of nuclear (catatonic, hebephrenic) patients than of peripheral (paranoid, simple) ones. In reviewing a series of 25 investigations and combining their findings, Zerbin-Rüdin presented 8.7 per cent as the minimal expectancy in sibs. For children of index cases in which one parent was schizophrenic, the expectancy rate in the combined findings was 12 per cent; in Kallmann's it was 16.4 per cent, with about 20 per cent for the nuclear group and 10 per cent for the peripheral. With both parents schizophrenic, the range of expectancy in children was between 35 and 68 per cent in the various studies. All these figures, compared with the 1 to 2 per cent expectancy consistently found in the general population, give strong evidence that genetic factors are necessary, although not sufficient, in the pathogenesis of schizophrenia.

Regarding the mode of inheritance, Kallmann assumed that a single unit factor was responsible for schizophrenia and that this factor was autosomal recessive in nature and subject to modification by other genes conferring a greater or lesser degree of resistance. Other hypotheses that have been advanced include a dominant mode of inheritance with incomplete penetrance in heterozygotes, a polygenic form of inheritance with a threshold, and a heterogenetic model specifying a variety of separate genes, dominant or recessive, any one of which may be involved in the etiology of schizophrenia. Environmental stress as an interacting factor is presumed in all these hypotheses. The diversity of the various theories seems to indicate that theories as to the exact mode of inheritance will remain inconclusive until the biochemical and physiological nature of the inherited vulnerability factor is identified.

Twin studies. In the now classic early twin studies—that is, those reported in Europe, Japan, and the United States between 1928 and 1961—there was noteworthy agreement among many investigators. It has been calculated over all that in these studies the concordance for monozygotic twins of schizophrenic patients without age correction is 65 per cent and for dizygotic twins about 12 per cent, close to the figure for all sibs. Kallmann's (1946) figures, based on the largest series of index cases, were 69 per cent and 10 per cent, respectively; with age correction these yielded the well-known expectancies of 86 per cent and 15 per cent. Although twin studies cannot establish the mode of inheritance, one aim of these studies was to explore the nature of the protective factors at work in discordant pairs. Foreshadowing later findings were the differences in concordance rates even in Kallmann's series, in which the over-all expectancies given above masked the wide range depending on the severity of illness in the index case. With little or no deterioration in the index case, the monozygotic twin expectancy rate was as low as 26 per cent and the dizygotic 2 per cent, whereas, for those with extreme deterioration, the rates were as high as 100 and 17 per cent, respectively.

These findings related to severity anticipated some of the

methodological refinements that typify the group of more recent twin studies in Scandinavia, England, and the United States. In the main, these studies tried to use as a source of index cases either all twins in the population, looking afterward for those with schizophrenia, or at least a group that included clinic and day hospital patients, as well as more chronic patients on the wards. In either case, less severe or more acute patients could now enter the study as index cases, along with the more typical chronic ones. The more recent studies also used newer methods of zygosity analysis, particularly blood groups, thus reducing possible sources of error, although it had been shown that such errors must have been rare and could not have been crucial even in the older reports.

The largest of the newer studies in which personal survey was made of the twin partners was reported by Kringlen in 1967. This study was based on all 25,000 pairs of twins born in Norway between 1901 and 1930, a list made possible by the existence of a Central Birth Registry. Concordance rates for pairs with schizophrenia in one twin ranged from 25 to 38 per cent for monozygotic pairs and 4 to 10 per cent for dizygotic, variations depending on whether only hospitalized co-twins were counted or others based on personal investigation and on the strictness of the diagnostic criteria used. Similarly, Gottesman and Shields (1972), studying all twins treated as outpatients or short-stay inpatients at the Maudsley Hospital in London between 1948 and 1964, found over-all concordance expectancy rates of 50 per cent for monozygotic twins and 10 per cent for dizygotic. The Maudsley rates also varied with severity, so that, if, for example, length of hospitalization of the index case was taken as the criterion, the monozygotic rates were 70 per cent with more than 1 year in a hospital and 33 per cent with less than 1 year in a hospital. Using broad criteria for inclusion of co-twins, Fischer (Fischer et al., 1969) found 56 per cent concordance in monozygotic and 26 per cent in dizygotic co-twins of chronic schizophrenic probands in a Danish sample extracted from a general twin register. With stricter criteria, the rates were 36 per cent and 18 per cent, respectively.

Many of these studies provided ample case material to explore some of the nongenetic factors associated with pathogenesis. This problem is central to the National Institute of Mental Health study by Pollin and Stabenau (1968), in which discordant pairs were carefully examined. In general, it seemed to be the smaller and physiologically less competent twin at birth who later developed schizophrenia in these vulnerable pairs; whether the divergence is mediated through neurological pathways or by way of intrafamilial role assignment has remained an unanswered question.

Finally, a survey of 274 pairs in which one or both twins had a diagnosis of schizophrenia taken from a register of 15,909 male veterans of the armed forces yielded concordance rates of 27.4 per cent for monozygotic and 4.8 per cent for dizygotic twins (Allen et al., 1972). Limited to a group already screened for relative health, these figures continue the trend for lower concordance rates in less chronic schizophrenia, but the ratio of monozygotic versus dizygotic concordance rates is maintained even in this group. Many formulations have been made in the attempt to assess the meaning of the various twin studies in conceptualizing the role of heredity in schizophrenia. The same results have been interpreted as evidence for or against a strong genetic component. What are yet needed are ways to define more precisely the important environmental and genetic factors, to describe in mathematically meaningful terms their interaction, and to observe this process developmentally in well designed longitudinal studies. Whether genetic determination varies with severity of illness and is related to clinical types is a question that may only be answered when a definitive biochemical or psychological trait is found that characterizes all schizophrenic genotypes, whether expressed clinically or not.

Adoption studies. Coming at a time when twin and family studies were being criticized for not fully disentangling genetic and experiential influences, the publication of Heston's Oregon adoption study in 1966 came as a welcome event. The ideal experimental situation—identical twin pairs randomly selected for separation at birth and for rearing by families bearing only a random resemblance to the biological ones—did not, of course, exist except anecdotally, and the converse paradigm—monozygotic twins, dizygotic twins, sibs, half sibs, and stepsibs variously reared in the same families—did not satisfy those who felt that there were postnatal or even prenatal experiential influences that differed among these groups. Heston's study found the rate for schizophrenia to be 16.6 per cent in 47 children of a series of schizophrenic mothers, with no schizophrenia among children of a matched group of control mothers. Other significant differences between the index and the control adoptees were in sociopathic personality, spending more than 1 year in a penal or psychiatric institution, and discharge from the armed forces on psychiatric or behavioral grounds. The study showed no evidence that adult adjustment of the adoptees was affected by the social class of the childhood home, by whether the child was reared in a foster or a foundling home, or by the length of time in a foundling home before being adopted.

Heston's study was followed by the well-known series of reports by Kety, Rosenthal, Wender, Schulsinger, and colleagues, conducted mostly in Denmark (all described by Rosenthal and Kety, 1968). These were of two basic designs, one like Heston's, in which the children of schizophrenic biological parents were reared by adoptive parents and compared with a group of matched control adoptees, and the other in which the biological families of schizophrenic adoptees were compared with the biological families of matched nonschizophrenic control adoptees.

In the first design, the prevalence of schizophrenia and schizophrenia-like disorders was found to be greater among the adopted-away offspring of schizophrenics than among the adopted-away offspring of nonschizophrenics. An extension of this study by Wender et al. (1974) introduced a cross-fostering design by adding a group of adopted-away offspring of normal biological parents reared by schizophrenic parents. The latter group showed no increase in psychopathology; the only increase remained in the adopted-away offspring of schizophrenic parents.

In the opposite design, diagnoses in the schizophrenia spectrum were concentrated in the biological relatives of adoptees who became schizophrenic; the biological relatives of controls, adoptive relatives of schizophrenics, and adoptive relatives of controls had significantly lower schizophrenic psychopathology. Most important, there was a significant concentration of schizophrenia diagnoses in the biological paternal half siblings of schizophrenic adoptees as compared with paternal half siblings of controls, thus excluding intrauterine influences and early mothering experiences as common environmental factors.

In a New York State study by Wender et al. (1977), adoptive parents of schizophrenic adoptees were compared with biological parents of a matched group of schizophrenic patients and with biological parents of nonschizophrenic retardates, the latter group to control for the possible effect on parents of rearing a difficult child. The biological parents of schizophrenics showed more psychopathology in structured clinical evaluation and Rorschach Tests than did the other two groups.

High-risk longitudinal studies. Studies of persons deemed particularly vulnerable to schizophrenia before the manifestation of illness are designed to distinguish between characteristics that are a cause and those that are a consequence of illness. They are also designed to foster preventive intervention based on a better understanding of early precursors of the disorder. On the basis of expectancy rates in genetic family studies, the children of one schizophrenic parent (with a 10 to 15 per cent risk) and of two schizophrenic parents (with a 40 per cent risk) represent strategic populations for study. By following these children from early years through the period of risk, researchers hope to identify preexisting biochemical, psychophysiological, neurological, behavioral, and environmental characteristics that differentiate those who ultimately become schizophrenic. One ongoing study by Erlenmeyer-Kimling and colleagues is focused on hypotheses concerned with distractibility and attentional dysfunction.

Biochemical genetic markers. Various enzymes have been studied that may be controlled quantitatively or qualitatively by genetic mechanisms and that may show differences in schizophrenics. Monoamine oxidase (MAO) activity as measured in blood platelets has been shown to be heritable. Although the results are still inconclusive, a decrease in enzyme activity has been found in some chronic schizophrenics as compared with controls, and a significant correlation has been reported between members of discordant twin pairs.

Association with HLA genes has not yet been established; such association would bolster theories relating to immune mechanisms in schizophrenia. Establishing linkage of clinical symptoms or a biochemical correlate of schizophrenia with a known genetic locus would be another powerful method of pinpointing a major gene for the disease on the genetic map.

Deafness and schizophrenia. A unique study by Altshuler and Sarlin (1969) explored the effect of early total deafness, a severe sensory deprivation, on the vulnerability to schizophrenia. Families of patients with both schizophrenia and deafness were studied. Although the schizophrenia rate among the general deaf population was no more than 2 per cent (Rainer et al., 1969), the rate among the siblings of deaf schizophrenics was 12 to 14 per cent. This figure was significantly higher than that for the general population and was similar to that observed for siblings of hearing schizophrenics. Of major importance was the fact that the schizophrenia rates between deaf siblings and hearing siblings did not differ significantly. These findings confirmed the genetic transmission of schizophrenia without significant interaction with a severe communicative defect.

Genetics and adaptational psychodynamics. The work of Sandor Rado and his school based on the genetic theory of schizophrenia was directed at exploring the basic psychological organization of the genetically defined schizotype. The two most consistent factors Rado found were a deficiency of the motivating power of pleasure and proneness to a distorted awareness of bodily self (an integrative pleasure deficiency and a proprioceptive diathesis). He foresaw the time when discovery of the presumably inherited biochemical traits of schizotypal organization will place its psychodynamics on a firm physiological basis and open up truly radical ways of treatment.

AFFECTIVE DISORDERS

Manic-depressive psychosis. Genetic studies in the affective disorders have been very much tied with problems of diagnosis, as well as with patterns of inheritance. Early studies of psy-

chosis dealt with the Kraepelinian category of manic-depressive psychosis and its distinction from schizophrenia. Kraepelin himself found large numbers of relatives of manic-depressives to have the same illness, but he did not find an increase in dementia precox among these relatives. In family studies of manic-depressive index cases, investigators reported a rate of manic-depressive psychosis of 10 to 15 per cent in parents and a similar range in siblings and children. Stenstedt (1952), in Sweden, conducted a careful population study from 1949 to 1952 and found morbidity risks of 12.3 per cent for siblings, 7.4 per cent for parents, and 9.4 per cent for children.

The largest twin family study, reported in 1953 by Kallmann in New York, involved 27 one-egg and 58 two-egg pairs. In this series the expectancy of manic-depressive psychosis varied from 16.7 per cent for half siblings to 22.7 and 25.5 per cent for siblings and two-egg co-twins, respectively, and 100 per cent for one-egg co-twins. Parents of index cases showed a rate of 23.4 per cent. The apparently perfect concordance rate of 100 per cent for one-egg twins was considered an artificial maximum value, since only patients admitted to a mental hospital, and hence the most severe cases, were included as index cases.

It was concluded by both Stenstedt and Kallmann that manic-depressive psychosis followed a dominant type of inheritance with incomplete penetrance and variable expressivity of a single autosomal gene. Although there were more females than males among the index cases in both studies, the sex ratio among siblings, parents, and children was no different from that of the normal population.

An important offshoot of Kallmann's study of manic-depressive illness in families was the differentiation of depressive illness from schizophrenia. In no case was a pair of twins found with a schizophrenic psychosis in one partner and a cyclic psychosis in the other, and the morbidity risk for schizophrenia among families of manic-depressive index cases was not statistically different from that in the general population.

Bipolar disorder. In 1959 Leonhard made a clinical distinction in affective disorders of a psychotic nature between bipolar illness, with periods of mania, and unipolar illness, with recurring depressions only. In reviewing twin studies, Zerbin-Rüdin (1969) found, indeed, that most pairs were either both unipolar or both bipolar. This suggests that some of the unipolar relatives of bipolar patients have the bipolar genotype. Leonhard and others found higher incidences of affective psychoses in the relatives of bipolar than in relatives of unipolar patients. Angst and Perris (1972) noted that the affected relatives of bipolar patients were both unipolar and bipolar in type, whereas affected relatives of unipolar patients were only of the recurrent depression variety.

Although unipolar illness is the more common form, most progress has been made to date in the genetics of bipolar (manic-depressive) illness. This form has the earlier age of onset and greater genetic loading and is more often responsive to lithium treatment.

Bipolar illness has been variously subdivided clinically into rapid-cycling and slow-cycling forms, into forms with severe manic episodes (bipolar I) and those with hypomanic episodes (bipolar II), into those with early versus late onset, and from the point of view of family history. A study of bipolar patients with and without affected first-degree relatives (Mendlewicz et al., 1972) showed that those with affected relatives have an earlier onset age, more psychotic episodes in the manic phase, and the likelihood of single-gene, rather than polygenic, inheritance. Alcoholism in the positive family history group, if present, was of the episodic type, rather than the chronic type. Finally, those with other bipolar cases in the family have been reported to respond more favorably to lithium prophylaxis than do those with a negative family history (Mendlewicz et al., 1973).

Family studies by Winokur and Clayton (1969) revealed a 34 per cent risk in parents and 35 per cent in sibs through family histories or, if relatives were actually interviewed, 41 per cent in parents, 42 per cent in sibs, and 50 per cent in children. Both bipolar and unipolar disease were found in first-degree relatives. The risk for female first-degree relatives was considerably higher than for males. Mendlewicz and Rainer (1974) found morbidity risks for all affective illness of 33.7 per cent for parents, 39.2 per cent for sibs, and 59.9 per cent for children. The risk was significantly higher for female relatives (48.2 per cent) than for male relatives (30.7 per cent).

Mendlewicz and Rainer (1977) also reported a study of manic-depressive adoptees in which a greater degree of psychopathology, particularly of affective illness, was found in parents genetically related to these manic-depressive probands than in parents who adopted and raised these same patients.

Linkage studies. In many family studies the rates of affective illness among fathers and sons of male probands were lower than those found among mothers and daughters. The rates and sex distribution are consistent with an X-linked dominant pattern of inheritance with diminished penetrance. Linkage studies have been carried out with X chromosome markers in informative families of bipolar (manic-depressive) and unipolar (depressive) probands (Winokur and Tanna, 1969; Mendlewicz and Fleiss, 1974). Close linkage was demonstrated between bipolar illness and both deutan and protan color blindness; linkage between bipolar illness and the Xg blood group, although measurable, was found to be less close. In contrast, there was no measurable linkage between unipolar illness and either protanopia or the Xg blood group. These results, if confirmed, indicate that, within the families described in the study, a dominant X-linked gene is involved in the transmission of bipolar illness. They have been criticized, however, from the point of view of diagnosis of young family members, and clearly families with bona fide father-to-son transmission exemplify a mode of transmission that is not X-linked.

An over-all heterogeneity in the heredity of this illness seems to be indicated, though it remains to be seen whether family data fit multiple threshold models that are consistent with a shared genetic diathesis for unipolar and bipolar disorders. Such a model would assume that a greater genetic or environmental loading—or both—would produce bipolarity (Gershon et al., 1975).

Unipolar disorder. In unipolar illness Winokur distinguished between depressive spectrum disease—with early onset and a family history of depression, alcoholism, and sociopathy—and pure depressive illness—with late onset and only depression in the family.

Schizoaffective and involutional disorders. The status of schizoaffective illness is changing; formerly considered a subtype of schizophrenia, it seems to be genetically related in many families to bipolar affective disorder by morbidity risk and linkage criteria.

Involutional psychosis as formerly defined was also variously associated genetically with schizophrenia on the one hand and affective disorder on the other. In one study Kallmann (1953) found no increase in involutional psychosis among the families of manic-depressives. In the families of 96 involutional twin index cases, the risk of involutional psychosis was increased (6.4 per cent for parents, 6 per cent for full siblings, 6 per cent for dizygotic co-twins, and 60.9 per cent for monozygotic co-twins). The risk for schizophrenia was somewhat elevated (5.5 per cent in parents and 4.2 per cent in siblings), but the risk for manic-depressive psychosis was hardly raised at all. Finally, the expectancy of involutional psychosis among the parents and siblings of schizophrenic twin index cases was increased to 6.6 per cent. From these data it was concluded that the diagnostic category of involutional psychosis was more complex pathogenetically than schizophrenia and manic-depressive psychosis, but that it was more closely associated with the group of schizoid personality traits than with manic-depressive psychosis.

In other studies, an increased risk for manic-depressive illness was found in the relatives of persons with involutional disease. Differences in diagnostic criteria may be responsible for these discrepancies, or, equally likely, these categories (schizoaffective illness, involutional psychosis) may be genetically and causatively heterogeneous.

SOCIOPATHIC BEHAVIOR AND CRIMINALITY

Antisocial personality disorder is marked by a history of continuous and chronic antisocial behavior of a defined nature with onset before the age of 15 and in the absence of symptoms of severe mental retardation or schizophrenic, schizoaffective, or manic disorder. In this syndrome it is especially difficult to separate the effect of family and social environment from genetic predisposing factors. Early studies, particularly in Germany, revealed a high degree of concordance among groups of monozygotic twins for having a criminal record, but the rate for same-sexed dizygotic twins was not much lower. In general, the distribution of concordance rates in sibs, opposite- and same-sexed dizygotic twins, and monozygotic twins has consistently led genetic investigators to suspect a large environmental role in the pathogenesis of criminal behavior. Kallmann (1959), for instance, said that the distribution

indicates that both family milieu and basic personality traits play important parts in shaping the habitual criminal [and] the trend toward similar criminal behavior in two-egg pairs may stem largely from the effect of unfavorable environmental influences.

Slater and Cowie (1971) pointed out also that concordance rates among male dizygotic pairs were relatively high, something that can only be accounted for if family tradition and parental example play a part in determining criminality.

In the Danish adoption study reported by Schulsinger (1972) on the biological and adoptive relatives of 57 psychopathic adoptees and 57 matched controls, the frequency of all mental disorders was found to be higher in the biological relatives of the psychopathic probands than among their adoptive relatives or either group of relatives of the controls. The difference was even greater when only psychopathic spectrum disorders were considered and was highest of all among biological fathers. Psychopathy actually occurred more than 5 times as frequently among the biological fathers of the psychopathic adoptees than among their adoptive fathers or the biological fathers of the controls.

The converse study of a group of 37 children born to female offenders and subsequently raised in adoptive homes showed a significant increase over a control group in arrests and incarcerations and in psychiatric hospitalizations (Crowe, 1975). Because of assortative mating, many of the fathers must also have shown antisocial personality traits. The various adoption studies did show an effect of criminality of adoptive parents on their children, though it was not as strong as with biological parents.

The pathogenic pathways by which genes may influence impulsive or sociopathic behavior are certainly not clear, though brain electrical activity has been implicated in some cases. The relation to chromosomal defects, particularly in the XYY male, is discussed below.

ORGANIC MENTAL DISORDERS

Senile and presenile dementias have similar neuropathological findings, and, under the heading of Alzheimer's disease, a dominant form of genetic transmission has been suggested (Sjögren et al., 1952).

In senile disease, alternatively, a higher frequency of chromosome loss has been noted in peripheral leukocyte cultures taken from women with organic mental disorder without evidence of cerebral arteriosclerosis than in women without organic mental disorder (Jarvik et al., 1971). The same findings were not evident in men. These results suggest that the aneuploidy found in the blood cells also exists in glial cells, but this theory has not been studied directly. The senile plaques found in these conditions are similar to those found in patients with Down's syndrome who have died at a younger age.

Huntington's chorea is a classical example of a dominantly inherited genetic disease with neurological and psychiatric symptoms and variable age of onset. Until a reliable biochemical or neurological test for early signs of the disease is found, the son or daughter of an affected parent remains under the threat of a 50 per cent risk of disease, often into adulthood, making counseling and family decisions difficult.

Lesch-Nyhan syndrome is an example of a behavioral disorder, inherited as an X-linked recessive trait, whose biochemistry is known. A deficiency of hypoxanthine guanine phosphoribosyl transferase results in hyperuricemia with mental retardation, spastic cerebral palsy, choreoathetosis, and self-destructive biting of fingers and lips. The bizarre behavior also includes aggression against others. Children with this syndrome feel pain, do not want to bite themselves, and welcome restraint. The illness is a classical instance in which a stereotyped pattern of behavior is associated with a distinct genetically controlled enzymatic defect. Aside from restraint, certain pharmacological and behavioral modification approaches have been used for treatment with limited success. In the future, prenatal detection and gene replacement may represent a form of genetic engineering useful in disorders of this type.

Alcoholism, a substance-induced organic disorder, has consistently shown increased rates in families. In the Danish adoption data (Goodwin et al., 1977), sons of alcoholics were about 4 times more likely to be alcoholic than were sons of nonalcoholics, whether they were raised by foster parents or by their own alcoholic parents. The rate for both adopted and nonadopted daughters of alcoholics was much lower, though still above the population norm. Depression and alcoholism seemed to overlap in daughters if they were raised by their own alcoholic parents, so that genetic and environmental contributants to this combination remained confounded.

NONPSYCHOTIC DISORDERS

In the anxiety and personality disorders, genetic studies have been hampered by problems of diagnosis and the need to develop quantitative methods. Reviewing the literature, Slater and Cowie (1971) found an increase in neurotic illnesses and neurotic personality traits of a like kind among relatives of obsessional neurotics, anxiety neurotics, and persons diagnosed as hysterics, with the evidence much stronger in the first of these than in the last. The evidence supported a multifactor type of inheritance with continuous and probably multidimensional variation in traits.

Studies based on psychological tests have involved general neurotic traits, as well as factors within the normal range of personality variation. For example, applying factor analysis to personality characteristics as measured by a wide variety of psychological techniques, Eysenck observed that many differently formulated theories of neurosis were on the same descriptive level and concerned with the same fundamental dimension of personality. On the basis of data obtained from 25 one-egg and 25 two-egg pairs, Eysenck and Prell (1951) classified the neurotic personality factor as a biological and largely gene-specific entity, estimating the genetic contribution to this neurotic unit predisposition at 80 per cent.

In another twin study by Claridge et al. (1973), a sample of 95 pairs was used to test some of Claridge's hypotheses concerning the psychophysiological classification of personality. Two principal factors were isolated, one termed "tonic arousal," referring to autonomic reactivity, the other factor termed "arousal modulation," concerned with the monitoring of sensory input and with such processes as narrowing and broadening of attention. Arousal modulation is mainly associated with electroencephalogram parameters and is the one that seems to be more influenced by heredity. Both factors form the parameters of Claridge's elaborate descriptive model of personality, which has two major dimensions, neuroticism and psychoticism. In neuroticism, tonic arousal and arousal modulation are positively associated, the hysteroid being low in both and the obsessoid high in both; in psychoticism, low tonic arousal and high modulation are found in the schizoid and the opposite in the cycloid.

Using the Minnesota Multiphasic Personality Inventory, Gottesman (1963) studied twins to investigate heritability on the various scales. Depression, social introversion, and psychopathic deviation showed the highest heritability; hypochondriasis, hysteria, paranoia, and pathological sexuality showed the lowest heritability. From these trait findings, he postulated that neuroses with anxiety and schizoid reaction have a high genetic component, under environmental conditions similar to those of his subjects; that those with depressive, phobic, and obsessive-compulsive symptoms have a lower genetic component; and that those with hypochondriacal and hysterical elements have little or no genetic component.

MALE HOMOSEXUALITY

Early hypotheses regarding genetic factors in male homosexuality centered on the conception that male homosexuals may have a female chromosome structure. Certain investigators found a greater proportion of males among the siblings of male homosexuals than would normally be expected. However, with the onset of sex chromatin studies and karyotype analysis, no abnormalities in sex chromatin or sex chromosomes were discovered in male homosexuals. Nevertheless, Slater (1962) reported a later birth order and a high maternal age in a group of 401 consecutive admissions of male homosexuals. These findings were thought to suggest a chromosomal anomaly in some male homosexuals. Klinefelter's syndrome has been associated with a number of cases of homosexuality, transvestism, and pedophilia, but these symptoms are not generally characteristic of the syndrome. There are reports of abnormal hormone excretion in homosexuals and sexual identity problems connected with prenatal hormone administration. Even if confirmed, there will be many questions to answer regarding causative pathways and hormonal imbalance.

Some of the highest monozygotic twin concordance rates have been those of homosexual behavior in the adult male. In Kallmann's (1952) series of 40 male homosexuals with identical twins, almost perfect concordance was found, whereas in 45 dizygotic male homosexual twins, the degree of concordance in the co-twin was no higher than what might be anticipated on the basis of Kinsey's statistics for the general population.

These findings were interpreted as suggesting a gene-controlled disarrangement between male and female psychosexual maturation patterns. In this formulation, homosexuality appears to be a part of the personality structure, rather than directly determined by the gonadal apparatus. If this is so, the processes whereby this orientation develops may be studied within the interactional framework of psychiatric genetics. A normal rate of maturation of personality development and an ability to perceive and respond to sexual stimuli, to recognize satisfaction and success, and to use these experiences as integrating forces may be crucial to normal sexual role development. Vulnerability factors in these areas may render a person susceptible to deviant behavior, which is then reinforced accidentally or by family or social surroundings.

A few one-egg twin pairs discordant for homosexual behavior have been discovered who also showed important similarities, principally in psychological test findings that indicated sexual confusion and body image distortion (Rainer et al., 1960). Divergent patterns of experience may be influenced by such factors as differences in the twins' relationships with their parents, frustration in heterosexual contacts, and poor masculine identification in the case of the homosexual twin.

INTELLIGENCE AND MENTAL DEFECT

A great deal of heated discussion is still current regarding the role of heredity in intelligence. The issue has encompassed the value of compensatory education in early childhood, the nature of learning, and the problem of underprivileged groups. Decisions on Head Start programs have been based on one's stand in assigning priorities in intelligence to nature or nurture. Underlying much of the divergence of opinion is the basic difficulty of measuring intelligence apart from environmental influence. Although intelligence scores, largely consisting of intelligence quotients (I.Q.'s), show remarkable correlation with genetic closeness, there has been much debate over the question of whether a difference in performance on intelligence tests between two groups in different environments is, therefore, also in some degree due to heredity. It is also not clear what factors are measured by the various tests or how their results are affected by such environmental factors as maternal health and nutrition, communication, and educational patterns at home and in school.

Mental defect, as distinguished from below-normal intelligence, may be due to trauma or to specific gene mutations and chromosomal aberrations. Specific genetic factors and obvious infectious or birth-traumatic incidents, however, account for barely half of all persons with I.Q.'s below 70. Polygenic inheritance is probably responsible for most of the others, with social deprivation usually playing a secondary or modifying role. In a large study by Reed and Reed (1965), it is concluded that more than 80 per cent in the low I.Q. range have had at least one parent or an aunt or an uncle similarly retarded.

Chromosomes and Behavior

Aside from Down's syndrome (marked by mental deficiency but no specific behavior disturbance), most major chromosomal aberrations in persons surviving past infancy involve the sex chromosomes. Conclusions regarding behavior in these groups will be tentative and perhaps biased until more widely applicable screening methods are perfected. Until the incidence at birth and the subsequent fate of persons with the various chromosomal anomalies in the general population is better known, the role of the karyotype in determining behavior will not be clearly evaluated. Interaction with biological, social, and educational forces will undoubtedly account for differences within the various groups.

Klinefelter's syndrome includes, more often than expected by chance, weak libido, mental subnormality, and nonspecific personality disorders ranging from inadequate personality and delinquency to schizophrenia-like behavior. Since the XXY karyotype occurs as frequently as 2 to 3 per 1,000 male newborns, it is not at all certain whether behavior disorder, when it occurs, results from the chromosome imbalance or whether the chromosomal syndrome precipitates an otherwise determined psychosis by adding an additional biological or social burden, perhaps connected with body frame or eunuchoid habitus. Similarly, among females with an extra X chromosome, some persons have been found in clinics and hospitals who are mildly retarded and socially withdrawn; they usually suffer from menstrual disturbances. Again, no specific behavior correlate can safely be postulated, though Vartanyan and Gindilis (1972) have reported XXX mosaicism in some schizophrenic women.

In Turner's syndrome, the typical patient is a short and sexually undeveloped female. This syndrome is usually marked by the absence of the second sex chromosome, leaving 45 chromosomes with a single X. Sexual immaturity and body defects do not seem to result in any emotional disturbance in this group; in fact, these girls and women have been described as resilient to adversity, stable in personality, and maternal in temperament. They are not mentally retarded, but they have been reported to show a specific defect in space-form appreciation and constructional skills, one of the few examples of a specific intellectual correlate of a karyotypic defect. Turner's syndrome is comparatively rare in living infants (less than 1 in 1,000).

Medical-legal interest has centered on the 47-chromosome XYY genotype, which seems to occur to excess among aggressive, impulsive, and criminally inclined persons, who also tend to be tall and of low intelligence. Persons who have been studied intensively appear to show episodic violence, often with signs and symptoms of a convulsive diathesis, and are often the only delinquent members of their families. They have been described as loners, generally mild, passive, docile, and inadequate, with occasional episodes of impulsive behavior triggered by sexual stimuli or authority figures in the environment. A relation of this episodic behavior to possible seizure-like electrical activity in the brain has been suggested.

In considering the effect of the XYY chromosome anomaly, one must note that its incidence among newborns has been estimated from as frequent as 1 in 250 to 1 in 2,000, with the most likely figure using present techniques of ascertainment being about 1 in 1,000. Also, there have been reports of adults with the anomaly who have no history of violent behavior. Both legal and preventive considerations require more knowledge about the interaction of genetic and environmental factors in the development of children with an extra Y chromosome.

Social and Ethical Problems

Many social problems are raised by medical genetics, population growth, and evolutionary change. The psychiatrist who is concerned with individual and community mental health, as well as some of the broader questions of social planning, cannot avoid taking part in the discussion and implementation of pertinent issues. Dysgenic trends in human populations include wars, certain differential reproductive patterns, improvement in the efficiency of therapeutic procedures not accompanied by attention to reproductive trends, and such mutagenic procedures as exposure to radiation. At the same time, diversity in the human genotype may increase human adaptability to present and future environments.

In the narrower area of psychiatric genetics, the scientific, as well as the ethical and legal, issues involved in genetic screening, genetic counseling, and the handling of genetic information are being widely discussed by geneticists, psychiatrists, philosophers, clergymen, and lawyers.

Genetic engineering—the transfer of DNA fragments into the gene structure of another organism—has great potential for definitive treatment of much genetic disease but also, in the minds of many, much potential for severe environmental danger. Cloning of humans, if it ever becomes technically possible, poses problems not only of control but also of the ethical basis for creating a human identical to another, with all its psychological implications.

Genetic Counseling

In clinical practice, the final common pathway of increased knowledge in the areas of genetics and family guidance is the responsible practice of marriage and parenthood counseling when there is a gene-borne condition present in one of the families concerned. When doubt exists regarding important and emotion-laden decisions as to marriage and parenthood, people must have access to trained professional advisers who are able not only to elicit the facts and evaluate them scientifically but also to resolve fears and misunderstandings and to be aware of the impact of their procedures on their patients.

Genetic counseling may represent a short-term course of psychotherapy based on psychological understanding and conducted according to established techniques of psychiatric interviewing. The psychiatrist is best equipped to diagnose emotional illness, to be aware of nosological distinctions and alternate forms of the same syndrome, and to understand the impact of knowledge and discovery on the individual or couple, depending on level of maturity, guilt and conflicts, defense mechanisms, and ego strengths and weaknesses. The counselor must be equally well versed in the medical, legal, and psychological implications of such procedures as amniocentesis, contraception, sterilization, abortion, artificial insemination, and adoption.

Counseling ought to be done in person, not by telephone or mail, since there needs to be interaction with the client. The emotional reactions of the counselor, as in all psychotherapy, have to be considered, as well as his or her prejudices or blind spots. Other family members may be involved. Counseling varies in its techniques and its impact with the time it is given relative to marriage, parenthood, or the birth of an affected child. The counselor has to be ready to deal with depression, while not preventing the person counseled from expressing his wishes, fears, and emotions.

From the clinical point of view, responsible genetic counseling provides the most direct application of medical knowledge in the field of genetics to the patient and his family.

Suggested Cross References

For more detailed descriptions of the various clinical syndromes discussed in this section, see Chapter 15, on schizophrenic disorders, Chapter 16, on paranoid disorders, Chapter 17, on schizoaffective disorders, Chapters 18 and 19, on affective disorders, Chapter 36, on mental retardation, and Section 24.4, on gender identity disorders.

REFERENCES

Allen, M. G., Cohen, S., and Pollin, W. Schizophrenia in veteran twins: A diagnostic review. Am. J. Psychiatry, *128:* 939, 1972.

Altshuler, K. Z., and Sarlin, M. B. Deafness and schizophrenia: A family study. In *Family and Mental Health Problems in a Deaf Population*, J. D. Rainer, K. Z. Altshuler, F. J. Kallmann, and W. E. Deming, editors, ed 2., p. 204. Charles C Thomas, Springfield, Ill., 1969.

Angst, J., and Perris, C. The nosology of endogenous depression. Int. J. Ment. Health, *1:* 145, 1972.

Claridge, G., Canter, S., and Hume, W. I. *Personality Differences and Biological Variations: A Study of Twins*. Pergamon Press, Oxford, 1973.

Crowe, R. R. An adoptive study of psychopathy. In *Genetic Research in Psychiatry*, R. R. Fieve, D. Rosenthal, and H. Brill, editors, p. 95. Johns Hopkins University Press, Baltimore, 1975.

*de Grouchy, J., and Turleau, C. *Clinical Atlas of Human Chromosomes*. John Wiley & Sons, New York, 1977.

Ehrman, L., Omenn, G., and Caspari, E., editors. *Genetics, Environment, and Behavior*. Academic Press, New York, 1972.

Ehrman, L., and Parsons, P. A. *The Genetics of Behavior*. Sinauer Associates, Sunderland, Mass., 1976.

Emery, A. E. H. *Methodology in Medical Genetics*. Churchill Livingstone, Edinburgh, 1976.

Eysenck, H. J., and Prell, D. B. The inheritance of neuroticism: An experimental study. J. Ment. Sci., *97:* 441, 1951.

Falconer, D. S. The inheritance of liability to certain diseases, estimated from the incidence among relatives. Ann. Hum. Genet., *29:* 51, 1965.

*Fieve, R. R., Rosenthal, D., and Brill, H., editors. *Genetic Research in Psychiatry*. Johns Hopkins University Press, Baltimore, 1975.

Fischer, M., Harvald, B., and Hauge, M. A Danish twin study of schizophrenia. Br. J. Psychiatry, *115:* 981, 1969.

Garrod, A. E. *Inborn Errors of Metabolism*. Frowde, London, 1909.

Gershon, E. S., Baron, M., and Leckman, J. F. Genetic models of the transmission of affective disorders. J. Psychiatr. Res., *12:* 301, 1975.

Goodwin, D. W., Schulsinger, F., Knop, J., Mednick, S., and Guze, S. R. Psychopathology in adopted and nonadopted daughters of alcoholics. Arch. Gen. Psychiatry, *34:* 1005, 1977.

Gottesman, I. I. Heritability of personality: A demonstration. Psychol. Monogr., *77:* 1, 1963.

*Gottesman, I. I., and Shields, J. *Schizophrenia and Genetics: A Twin Study Vantage Point*. Academic Press, New York, 1972.

Hartmann, H. Psychiatric studies of twins. In *Essays in Ego Psychology*, p. 419. International Universities Press, New York, 1964.

Heston, L. Psychiatric disorders in foster home reared children of schizophrenic mothers. Br. J. Psychiatry, *112:* 819, 1966.

Jacob, F., and Monod, J. On the regulation of gene activity. Cold Spring Harbor Symp. Quant. Biol., *26:* 193, 1961.

Jarvik, L. F., Altshuler, K. Z., Kato, T., and Blumner, B. Organic brain syndrome and chromosome loss in aged twins. Dis. Nerv. Syst., *32:* 159, 1971.

Kallmann, F. J. *The Genetics of Schizophrenia*. Augustin, New York, 1938.

Kallmann, F. J. The genetic theory of schizophrenia. Am. J. Psychiatry, *103:* 309, 1946.

Kallmann, F. J. Comparative twin study on the genetic aspects of male homosexuality. J. Nerv. Ment. Dis., *115:* 283, 1952.

Kallmann, F. J. *Heredity in Health and Mental Disorder*. W. W. Norton, New York, 1953.

Kallmann, F. J. Psychogenetic studies of twins. In *Psychology: A Study of a Science*, S. Koch, editor, vol. III, p. 328. McGraw-Hill, New York, 1959.

Kringlen, E. *Heredity and Environment in the Functional Psychoses*. Universitetsforlaget, Oslo, 1967.

Leonhard, K. *Aufteilung der endogenen Psychosen*. Akademie-Verlag, Berlin, 1959.

McKusick, V. A. *Mendelian Inheritance in Man*, ed. 4. Johns Hopkins University Press, Baltimore, 1975.

McKusick, V. A., and Ruddle, F. H. The status of the gene map of the human chromosomes. Science, *196:* 390, 1977.

Mendlewicz, J., Fieve, R. R., Rainer, J. D., and Fleiss, J. L. Manic-depressive illness: A comparative study of patients with and without a family history. Br. J. Psychiatry, *120:* 525, 1972.

Mendlewicz, J., Fieve, R. R., and Stallone, F. Relationship between the effectiveness of lithium therapy and family history. Am. J. Psychiatry, *130:* 1011, 1973.

Mendlewicz, J., and Fleiss, J. L. Linkage studies with X chromosome markers in bipolar (manic-depressive) and unipolar (depressive) illness. Biol. Psychiatry, *9:* 261, 1974.

Mendlewicz, J., and Rainer, J. D. Morbidity risk and genetic transmission in manic-depressive illness. Am. J. Hum. Genet., *26:* 692, 1974.

Mendlewicz, J., and Rainer, J. D. Adoption study supporting genetic transmission in manic-depressive illness. Nature, *268:* 327, 1977.

Mirsky, I. A. Physiologic, psychologic, and social determinants in the etiology of duodenal ulcer. Am. J. Dig. Dis., *3:* 285, 1958.

Pollin, W., and Stabenau, J. R. Biological, psychological, and historical differences in a series of monozygotic twins discordant for schizophrenia. In *The Transmission of Schizophrenia*, D. Rosenthal and S. Kety, editors, p. 317. Pergamon Press, Oxford, 1968.

Rainer, J. D. Genetic knowledge and heredity counseling: New responsibilities for psychiatry. In *Genetic Research in Psychiatry*, R. R. Fieve, D. Rosenthal, and H. Brill, editors, p. 289. Johns Hopkins University Press, Baltimore, 1975.

Rainer, J. D. Genetics of intelligence: Current issues and unsolved questions. Res. Communications Psychiatry, Psychol., and Behav., *1:* 607, 1976.

Rainer, J. D., Altshuler, K. Z., Kallmann, F. J., and Deming, W. E., editors. *Family and Mental Health Problems in a Deaf Population*, ed. 2. Charles C Thomas, Springfield, Ill., 1969.

Rainer, J. D., Mesnikoff, A., Kolb, L. C., and Carr, A. Homosexuality and heterosexuality in identical twins. Psychosom. Med., *22:* 251, 1960.

Reed, E. W., and Reed, S. C. *Mental Retardation: A Family Study*. W. B. Saunders, Philadelphia, 1965.

Reich, T., James, J. W., and Morris, C. A. The use of multiple thresholds in determining the mode of transmission of semi-continuous traits. Ann. Hum. Genet., *36:* 163, 1972.

Rosenthal, D. *Genetic Theory and Abnormal Behavior*. McGraw-Hill, New York, 1970.

*Rosenthal, D., and Kety, S., editors. *The Transmission of Schizophrenia*. Pergamon Press, Oxford, 1968.

Schulsinger, F. Psychopathy, heredity, and environment. Int. J. Ment. Health, *1:* 190, 1972.

Seixas, F. A., Omenn, G. S., Burk, E. D., and Eggleston, S., editors. *Nature and Nurture in Alcoholism*. Ann. N. Y. Acad. Sci., *197:* 1972.

Sjögren, T., Sjögren, H., and Lindgren, A. *Morbus Alzheimer and Morbus Pick*. Munksgaard, Copenhagen, 1952.

Slater, E. *Psychotic and Neurotic Illnesses in Twins*. Her Majesty's Stationery Office, London, 1953.

Slater, E. Birth order and maternal age of homosexuals. Lancet *1:* 69, 1962.

*Slater, E., and Cowie, V. *The Genetics of Mental Disorders*. Oxford University Press, London, 1971.

Spitz, R. A. *The First Year of Life*. International Universities Press, New York, 1965.

Stenstedt, A. A study in manic-depressive psychosis: Clinical, social, and genetic investigations. Acta Psychiatr. Neurol. Scand., *79* (Suppl.): 1952.

Thomas, A., and Chess, S. *Temperament and Development*. Brunner/Mazel, New York, 1977.

Tjio, J. H., and Levan, A. The chromosome number in man. Hereditas, *42:* 1, 1956.

Vartanyan, M. E., and Gindilis, V. M. The role of chromosomal aberrations in the clinical polymorphism of schizophrenia. Int. J. Ment. Health, *1:* 93, 1972.

Vesell, G. S. Pharmacogenetics. In *Psychotherapeutic Drugs*, E. Usdin and I. S. Forrest, editors, p. 139. Marcel Dekker, New York, 1976.

*Watson, J. D. *Molecular Biology of the Gene*, ed. 3. W. A. Benjamin, New York, 1976.

Wender, P. H., Rosenthal, D., Kety, S. S., Schulsinger, F., and Welner, J. Crossfostering. Arch. Gen. Psychiatry, *30:* 121, 1974.

Wender, P. H., Rosenthal, D., Rainer, J. D., Greenhill, L., and Sarlin, M. B. Schizophrenics adopting parents. Arch. Gen. Psychiatry, *34:* 777, 1977.

Winokur, G., and Clayton, P. *Manic-Depressive Illness*. C. V. Mosby, St. Louis, 1969.

Winokur, G., and Tanna, V. L. Possible role of X-linked dominant factors in manic-depressive disease. Dis. Nerv. Syst., *30:* 89, 1969.

Zerbin-Rüdin, E. Zur Genetik der depressiven Erkrankungen. In *Das Depressive Syndrom*. H. Hippius and H. Selbach, editors, p. 35. Urban & Schwarzenberg, Munich, 1969.

2.2 Basic Science of Psychopharmacology

SOLOMON H. SNYDER, M.D.

Introduction

What are the basic sciences of psychopharmacology? A large number of disciplines have been involved in the study of the action of psychotropic drugs, including biochemistry, physiology, neuroanatomy, and clinical psychiatry. All these disci-

plines aid in understanding how drugs act on the mind. In the 30 years since the initiation of vigorous research with psychotropic drugs, it has become evident that the effects of greatest relevance to understanding the clinical actions of the drugs are exerted on neurotransmitter disposition. Accordingly, a fundamental understanding of psychopharmacology demands a familiarity with central nervous system neurotransmitters. A detailed elucidation of central neurotransmission is quite recent and has paralleled the development of psychotropic drugs. Indeed, those drugs are as valuable as tools in elucidating synaptic transmission in the brain as they are in the treatment of psychiatric patients.

Neurotransmitters

Acetylcholine has the longest history of investigation as a neurotransmitter, followed in close historical sequence by norepinephrine (see Figure 1). Interactions of psychotropic drugs with the catecholamines, norepinephrine and dihydroxyphenylethylamine (dopamine), have been discovered by numerous investigators and seem to account for the actions of numerous drugs. Accordingly, some people have gained the impression that the catecholamines and acetylcholine, along with the indoleamine serotonin, account for the bulk of synaptic transmission in the brain. Quantitatively, those compounds are all only minor transmitters in the brain, although they may have particular importance in the areas of the brain concerned with emotional behavior. Even in the corpus striatum, the area of the brain with the highest concentration of dopamine, only about 15 per cent of the nerve terminals use dopamine as their transmitter. In the hypothalamus, the brain region richest in norepinephrine, only about 5 per cent of the nerve terminals are noradrenergic. In the brain as a whole, the two catecholamines probably account for synaptic transmission at no more than about 1 to 2 per cent of synapses. Serotonin is the transmitter at considerably fewer synapses than the catecholamines. Although such estimates are more difficult to obtain for acetylcholine, it is likely that no more than 5 to 10 per cent of the synapses in the brain are cholinergic. There is now considerable evidence that histamine is a neurotransmitter in "emotional" areas of the brain, such as the hypothalamus. However, its levels in the brain are substantially lower than those of serotonin and the catecholamines, and it probably accounts for fewer synapses than the other biogenic amines.

What, then, are the major neurotransmitters in the central nervous system? It is likely that a variety of amino acids are transmitters at the major excitatory and inhibitory synapses. In various brain regions γ-aminobutyric acid (GABA) probably accounts for transmission at between 25 and 40 per cent of synapses. GABA inhibits the firing of neurons and is, therefore, a major inhibitory transmitter. In the spinal cord and brain stem, the amino acid glycine, in addition to its other metabolic functions, seems to be a prominent inhibitory transmitter at about the same percentage of synapses as GABA. It should be borne in mind at all times that a given neuron presumably uses only a single neurotransmitter. Thus, GABA and glycine are transmitters at distinct synapses. The identity of the major excitatory neurotransmitters is somewhat less certain. However, glutamic and aspartic acids, which uniformly excite neurons, satisfy many characteristics demanded of the prominent excitatory neurotransmitters.

A major recent development has been the awareness that numerous peptides may also be neurotransmitters (see Table I). The most studied peptide transmitters are the opiate-like peptides, the enkephalins. Their discovery derives from fun-

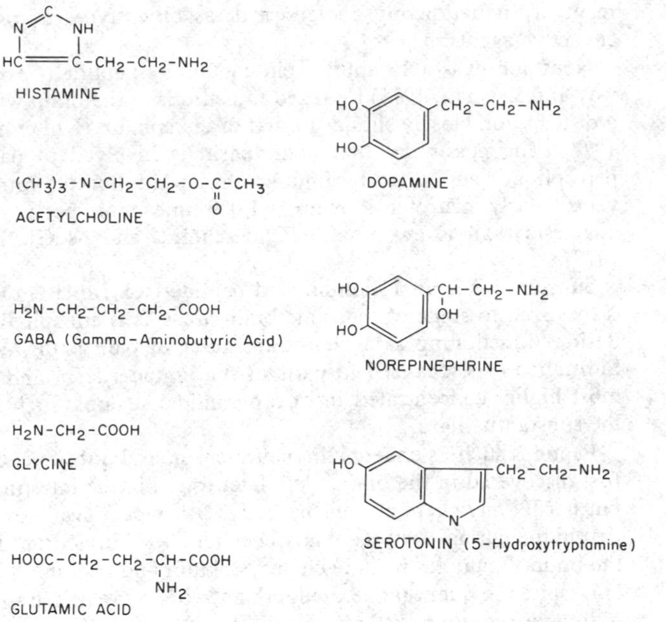

FIGURE 1. Structures of neurotransmitter candidates in the brain.

TABLE I
Peptide Structures

Substance P	Arg-Pro-Lys-Pro-Gln-Gln-Phe-Phe-Gly-Leu-Met-NH$_2$
Bradykinin	Arg-Pro-Pro-Gly-Phe-Ser-Pro-Phe-Arg-COOH
CCK-33	Lys-Ala-Pro-Ser-Gly-Arg-Val-Ser-Met-Ile-Lys-Aln-Leu-Gln-Ser-Leu-Asp-Pro-Ser-His-Arg-Ile-Ser-Asp-Arg-Asp-Tyr(SO3)-Met-Gly-Trp-Met-Asp-Phe-NH$_2$
CCK-8	Asp-Tyr$^{(SO3)}$-Met-Gly-Trp-Met-Asp-Phe-NH$_2$
Neurotensin	pyroGlu-Leu-Tyr-Glu-Asn-Lys-Pro-Arg-Arg-Pro-Tyr-Ile-Leu-OH
VIP	His-Ser-Asp-Ala-Val-Phe-Thr-Asp-Asn-Tyr-Thr-Arg-Leu-Arg-Lys-Gln-Met-Ala-Val-Lys-Lys-Tyr-Leu-Asn-Ser-Ile-Leu-Asn-NH$_2$
Angiotensin II	Asp-Arg-Val-Tyr-Val-His-Pro-Phe
TRH	pyroGlu-His-Pro-NH$_2$
Somatostatin	Ala-Gly-Cys-Lys-Asn-Phe-Phe-Trp-Lys-Thr-Phe-Thr-Ser-Cys-OH

TABLE II
Localization and Possible Function of Opiate Receptors

Location	Functions Influenced by Opiates
Spinal cord	
Laminae I and II	Pain perception in body
Brain stem	
Substantia gelatinosa of spinal tract of caudal trigeminal	Pain perception in head
Nucleus of solitary tract, nucleus commissuralis, nucleus ambiguus	Vagal reflexes, respiratory depression, cough suppression, orthostatic hypotension, inhibition of gastric secretion
Area postrema	Nausea and vomiting
Locus coeruleus	Euphoria
Habenula-interpeduncular nucleus-fasciculus retroflexus	Limbic, emotional effects, euphoria
Pretectal area (medial and lateral optic nuclei)	Miosis
Superior colliculus	Miosis
Ventral nucleus of lateral geniculate	Miosis
Dorsal, lateral, medial terminal nuclei of accessory optic pathway	Endocrine effects through light modulation
Dorsal cochlear nucleus	Unknown
Parabrachial nucleus	Euphoria in a link to locus coeruleus
Diencephalon	
Infundibulum	Antidiuretic hormone secretion
Lateral part of medial thalamic nucleus, internal and external thalamic laminae, intralaminar (centromedian) nucleus, periventricular nucleus of thalamus	Pain perception
Telencephalon	
Amygdala	Emotional effects
Caudate, putamen, globus pallidus, nucleus accumbens	Motor rigidity
Subfornical organ	Hormonal effects
Interstitial nucleus of stria terminalis	Emotional effects

damental investigations of opiate receptors. By monitoring the binding of radioactive opiates to brain membranes, investigators were able to identify specific binding sites that represent the loci at which pharmacological effects of opiates are mediated (Snyder, 1978). Opiate receptors are highly localized to parts of the central nervous system mediating pain perception and emotional regulation, as well as a limited number of other areas not classically associated with opiate actions. In general, the precise microscopic localizations of opiate receptors can explain all the major pharmacological effects of opiates (see Table II). The pharmacological properties of opiates as agonists, antagonists, or mixed agonist-antagonists with potential as relatively nonaddicting analgesics can be predicted from their interactions with receptors. Sodium ion greatly decreases the affinity of pure agonists such as morphine for the receptor, has no effect on the affinity of pure antagonists such as naloxone, and affects mixed agonist-antagonists such as pentazocine (Talwin) in an intermediate fashion. The potent and selective effects of sodium on opiate-receptor binding suggest that sodium may be the ion whose permeability is affected in converting the recognition of opiates at receptor sites into alterations in neuronal function.

The dramatic properties of the opiate receptor suggest that it is not an evolutionary vestige but may serve to interact with a normally occurring morphine-like substance. By monitoring the effects of brain extracts on smooth muscle or by measuring the competition of brain extracts for opiate-receptor binding, one can measure the amount of opiate-like substance, purify and finally isolate it, and determine its structure, a task accomplished by Hughes et al. (1975) and confirmed soon thereafter (Simantov and Snyder, 1976). The opiate-like substance is a mixture of two peptides, five amino acids in length and differ-

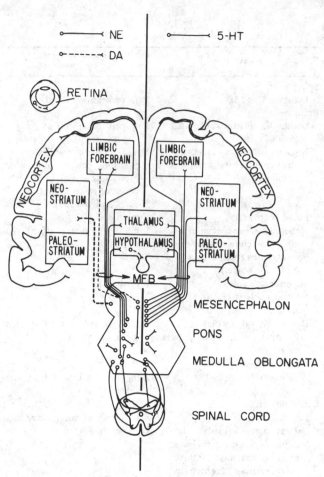

FIGURE 2. Pathways of serotonin (*5-HT*), norepinephrine (*NE*), and dopamine (*DA*) neuronal systems in the central nervous system. (Adapted from Anden, N. E., Dahlström, A., Fuxe, K., Larsson, K., Olson, K., and Ungerstedt, U. Ascending monoamine neurons to the telencephalon and diencephalon. Acta Physiol. Scand., *67:* 3131, 1966.)

ing only in one amino acid. They are referred to as methionine-enkephalin (met-enkephalin) and leucine-enkephalin (leu-en-kephalin), respectively.

The pituitary gland also contains large concentrations of an opioid peptide, β-endorphin, consisting of 31 amino acids that include the five amino acids of met-enkephalin. The biological significance of an opioid peptide in the pituitary is unclear, because β-endorphin does not enter the brain to a major extent. However, the brain does contain low levels of β-endorphin that are synthesized in specific neuronal systems.

By using immunohistochemical techniques in which fluorescent probes label antisera to peptides, one can visualize peptides such as enkephalin at a microscopic level and map their localizations. Enkephalins are highly concentrated in the same brain regions as those enriched in opiate receptors. In the dorsal part of the spinal cord, enkephalin seems to act on opiate receptors contained on the surface of sensory nerve terminals conveying information about pain perception. Enkephalin inhibits the release of the sensory neurotransmitter Substance P, which normally conveys pain sensation. In the limbic system, enkephalins and opiate receptors are highly concentrated in certain parts of the amygdala.

A great deal of effort has been devoted to the development of stable analogues of enkephalins that may offer promise as relatively nonaddicting analgesics or as other types of psychoactive agents.

Neurotensin is a 13 amino acid-containing peptide (Carraway and Leeman, 1975) localized to neurons in the brain with a distribution closely similar to that of enkephalin (Uhl et al., 1977). The possibility that neurotensin is involved in pain perception is supported by findings that, when injected intraventricularly, neurotensin is up to 1,000 times more potent an analgesic than is enkephalin (Clineschmidt and McGuffin, 1977).

Substance P is an 11-amino-acid peptide (see Table I) that is localized to some of the same brain areas as is enkephalin. Besides functioning as a neurotransmitter of pain pathways, Substance P is localized to parts of the limbic system and is most highly concentrated in extrapyramidal regions, such as the substantia nigra.

Peptides such as enkephalin, neurotensin, and Substance P, first discovered in the brain, were later found in the intestines but hardly anywhere else in the body. Other peptides known first in the gut have subsequently been identified in neurons in the brain. Examples include cholecystokinin and insulin.

Despite the quantitative predominance of amino acid transmitters in the brain, little is currently known of their interactions with psychotropic drugs. The most detailed information is available for the biogenic amines norepinephrine, dopamine, and serotonin and for the opioid peptide enkephalins.

AMINE TRACTS

A major advance in understanding the functions of the amines in the brain occurred when histochemical techniques were developed to localize neurons containing norepinephrine, dopamine, and serotonin. In the histochemical fluorescence method, serotonin can be distinguished from the catecholamines by the wave length of fluorescence, which varies in such a way that serotonin appears bright yellow and the catecholamines appear bright green. Although both dopamine and norepinephrine fluoresce green, they can be differentiated by their response to drugs. What are the pathways of the monoamine neuronal systems? The cell bodies of all the systems are within the brain stem. Axons ascend and descend throughout the brain and into the spinal cord. For each of the amines, there are several separate and distinct tracts (see Figure 2).

Norepinephrine. There are two major norepinephrine tracts. The ventral pathway has cell bodies in several locations in the brain stem and axons that ascend in the medial forebrain bundle to give off terminals predominantly in the hypothalamus and limbic system. The cell bodies of the dorsal norepinephrine pathway are discretely localized in a single nucleus of the brain stem, the locus coeruleus. Its axons also ascend in the medial forebrain bundle but more dorsally than do those of the ventral pathway. Terminals of the dorsal pathway are located predominantly in the cerebral cortex and hippocampus. Some axons from the locus coeruleus descend to give off nerve terminals synapsing on the Purkinje cells of the cerebellum. Certain cells from the locus coeruleus give off axons that bifurcate, sending one branch to the cerebral cortex and another to the cerebellum. In this way a single neuron can influence widely separated parts of the brain.

By knowing the course of these neurons, one can readily speculate as to their function. It is is likely that the ventral norepinephrine pathway, with terminals in the pleasure centers in the lateral hypothalamus, subserves such affective behaviors as euphoria and depression. One may speculate that the dorsal norepinephrine pathway to the cerebral cortex is associated with alerting actions of these neurons.

Other norepinephrine pathways with cell bodies in the brain stem send axons down in the lateral sympathetic columns of the spinal cord, terminating at various levels. These neurons influence a variety of spinal cord reflexes. It is conceivable that in this way norepinephrine pathways mediate apparent emotional influences on muscle tone in conditions such as anxiety and tension.

Dopamine. There are several discrete dopamine pathways. The most prominent pathway has cell bodies in the substantia nigra and gives rise to axons that terminate in the caudate nucleus and putamen of the corpus striatum. This pathway is degenerated in Parkinson's disease, accounting for major symptoms of the condition. Restoration of the depleted dopamine by treatment with its amino acid precursor dihydroxy-L-phenylalanine (L-dopa) greatly alleviates the symptoms of Parkinson's disease. Other dopamine pathways in the brain have cell bodies close to the substantia nigra, just dorsal to the interpeduncular nucleus, with terminals in the nucleus accumbens and olfactory tubercle, both parts of the limbic emotional areas of the brain. There are also dopamine neurons in the cerebral cortex. The functions of these dopamine pathways are poorly understood, but they may relate to emotional behavior. Dopamine cells in the arcuate nucleus of the hypothalamus with terminals in the median eminence probably regulate release of hypothalamic tropic hormones, which then act on the pituitary gland. Dopamine seems to be a physiological inhibitor of prolactin release. Neuroleptic drugs, by blocking dopamine receptors, elevate plasma prolactin. There are also dopamine neurons in the retina whose function is obscure but tantalizing, inasmuch as the retina contains no norepinephrine or serotonin fibers.

Serotonin. All cell bodies of the serotonin-containing neurons are localized in a series of nuclei in the lower midbrain and upper pons that are called the raphe nuclei. Serotonin is so highly concentrated in raphe nuclei that almost all their cells are probably serotonergic. Axons of those cells ascend primarily in the medial forebrain bundle and give off terminals in all brain regions but with the majority in the hypothalamus and the fewest in the cerebral cortex and cerebellum. Selective destruction of the raphe nuclei in animals results in insomnia. Restoring the depleted serotonin with tryptophan or 5-hydroxytryptophan, the amino acid precursors of serotonin, puts such insomniac animals to sleep. Similarly, stimulation of the raphe nuclei at physiological frequencies makes animals somnolent. Thus, the serotonin neurons play some role in regulating sleep-wakefulness cycles.

AMINE METABOLISM

Understanding the metabolic pathways of the biogenic amines greatly enhances one's ability to appreciate their interactions with psychotropic drugs. The amino acid tyrosine is the dietary precursor of the catecholamines (see Figure 3). The first enzyme in the biosynthetic pathway of the catecholamines is tyrosine hydroxylase, which converts tyrosine into dihydroxyphenylalanine. Tyrosine hydroxylase is believed to be the major rate-limiting enzyme in catecholamine biosynthesis, because increasing or decreasing its activity produces corresponding changes in the levels of the catecholamines. Dopa is then decarboxylated by the enzyme dopa-decarboxylase to dopamine. Dopa-decarboxylase is often referred to as aromatic amino acid decarboxylase, as it acts on any aromatic amino acid, with important consequences when certain amino acids are used as drugs. For instance, if one treats a patient with 5-hydroxytryptophan, which is an aromatic amino acid that is decarboxylated into serotonin, the catecholamine neurons form serotonin from 5-hydroxytryptophan just as efficiently as do the serotonin neurons, so that after such treatment serotonin accumulates as a false transmitter in catecholamine neurons.

In norepinephrine neurons, dopamine is then converted to norepinephrine by the addition of a hydroxyl group by the enzyme dopamine-β-hydroxylase. Dopamine neurons do not contain any dopamine-β-hydroxylase, so dopamine is the major catecholamine in those neurons.

A detailed appreciation of catecholamine metabolism enables one to monitor biochemically the firing rate of catecholamine neurons. Under normal conditions, when a neuron fires and releases a molecule of a catecholamine, the neuron must synthesize a new catecholamine molecule to replace the one just released. Accordingly, when the firing rate of catecholamine neurons is accelerated, there is a parallel increase in the conversion of tyrosine to new catecholamines. Pharmacologists have applied this principle with great success to an analysis of the influence of psychotropic drugs on the firing rates of catecholamine neurons.

Catecholamines can be metabolically degraded primarily by two enzymes, monoamine oxidase and catechol-*O*-methyl-

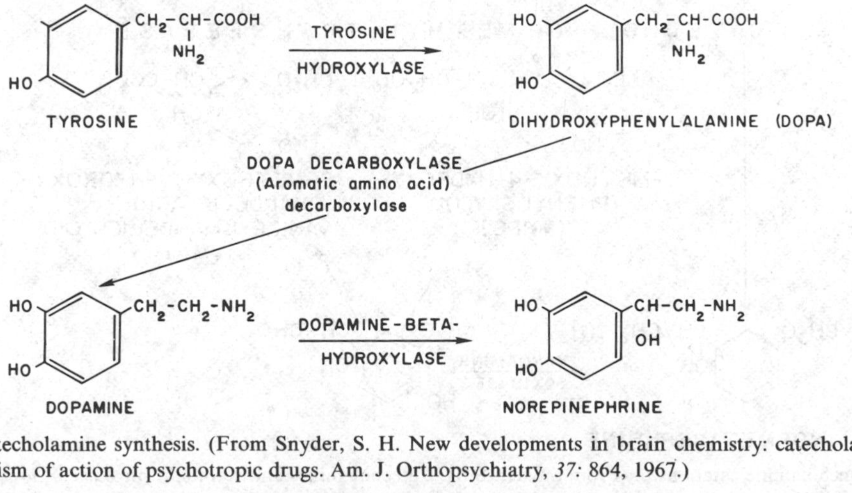

FIGURE 3. Pathways of catecholamine synthesis. (From Snyder, S. H. New developments in brain chemistry: catecholamine metabolism and its relationship to the mechanism of action of psychotropic drugs. Am. J. Orthopsychiatry, *37*: 864, 1967.)

transferase (COMT) (see Figure 4). Monoamine oxidase oxidatively deaminates dopamine or norepinephrine to the corresponding aldehydes. Those in turn can be converted by aldehyde dehydrogenase to corresponding acids. The aldehydes may also be reduced to form alcohols. Dietary factors, such as the ingestion of ethanol, can determine the relative amounts of catechol acids or alcohols formed from the catecholamines because ethanol also competes for aldehyde dehydrogenase.

Catecholamines can be methylated by COMT, which transfers the methyl group of *S*-adenosylmethionine to the meta (3 position) hydroxyl of the catecholamines. COMT acts on any catechol compound, including the aldehydes and acids formed from the action of monoamine oxidase on the catecholamines. When norepinephrine is methylated by the enzyme, the product is called normetanephrine. There is no corresponding name for the methylated derivative of dopamine, which is simply referred to as 3-*O*-methyldopamine.

Like COMT, monoamine oxidase is relatively nonspecific and acts on any monoamine—including serotonin, normetanephrine, and 3-*O*-methyldopamine—converting them first into their respective aldehydes and then into acids or alcohols. Thus, an *O*-methylated alcohol or acid results from the combined actions of monoamine oxidase and COMT. In the peripheral sympathetic nervous system, the *O*-methylated acid product of norepinephrine degradation is called vanillylmandelic acid. Its levels are measured in clinical laboratories as an index of sympathetic nervous function and to diagnose tumors that produce norepinephrine or epinephrine, such as pheochromocytomas and neuroblastomas. Dopamine *O*-methylation and deamination gives rise to homovanillic acid.

In the brain, reduction of the aldehyde formed from the action of monoamine oxidase on norepinephrine or normetanephrine predominates, so that the major metabolite in the brain is an alcohol derivative called 3-methoxy-4-hydroxylphenylglycol (MHPG). The MHPG formed in the brain is conjugated to sulfate. Because MHPG can diffuse from the brain to the general circulation, estimates of its levels in the urine might be thought to reflect directly the activity of norepinephrine neurons in the brain. However, although MHPG is proportionately only a minor breakdown product of norepinephrine in the periphery, quantitatively it seems that a significant portion of urinary MHPG still derives from the periphery, with a variable amount coming from the brain. Nonetheless, measuring urinary MHPG seems to be a valuable tool in estimating the function of brain norepinephrine neurons and has value in predicting the response of depressed patients to antidepressant drugs.

Serotonin. Tryptophan, the dietary amino acid precursor of serotonin, is hydroxylated by the enzyme tryptophan hydroxylase to form 5-hydroxytryptophan (see Figure 5). 5-Hydroxytryptophan is decarboxylated to serotonin by 5-hydroxytryptophan decarboxylase, which is also referred to as aromatic amino acid decarboxylase, because its range of substrate preference is the same as that of dopa-decarboxylase. Thus, when parkinsonian patients are treated with L-dopa, dopamine is formed not only in dopamine neurons but also in serotonin neurons and has been demonstrated to displace serotonin so that dopamine becomes a false transmitter in brain serotonin neurons of those patients, with unknown consequences. Serotonin is destroyed by monoamine oxidase, which oxidatively deaminates it to the aldehyde, just as the enzyme does with the

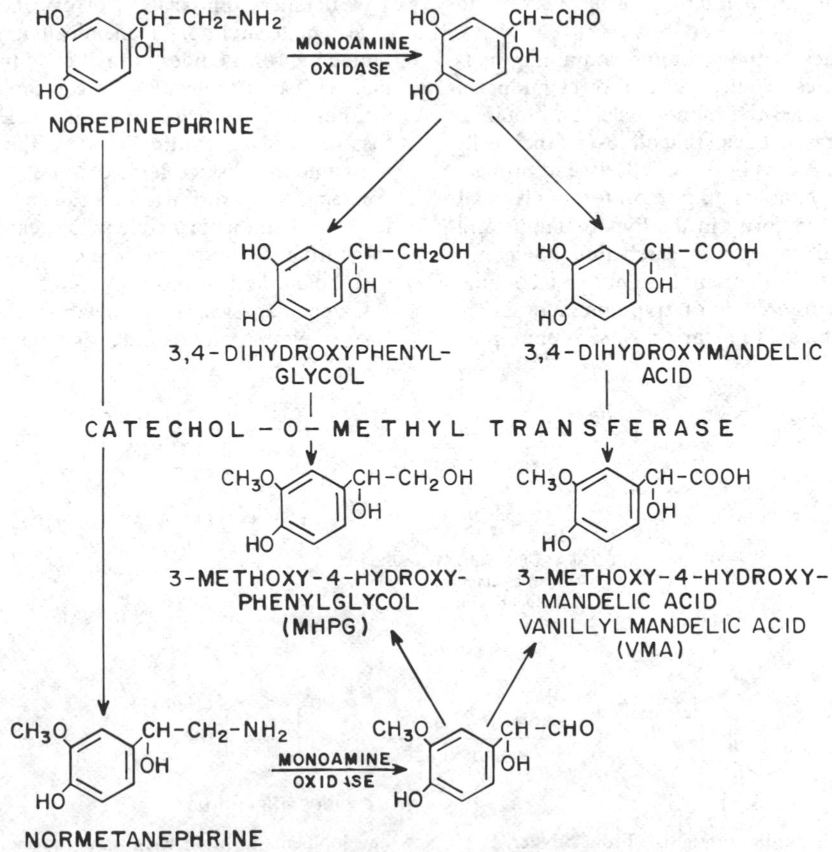

FIGURE 4. Pathways of catecholamine catabolism. (From Snyder, S. H. Catecholamines and serotonin. In *Basic Neurochemistry*, R. W. Albers, G. I. Siegal, R. Katzman, and B. W. Agranoff, editors, p. 89. Little, Brown, and Co., Boston, 1972.)

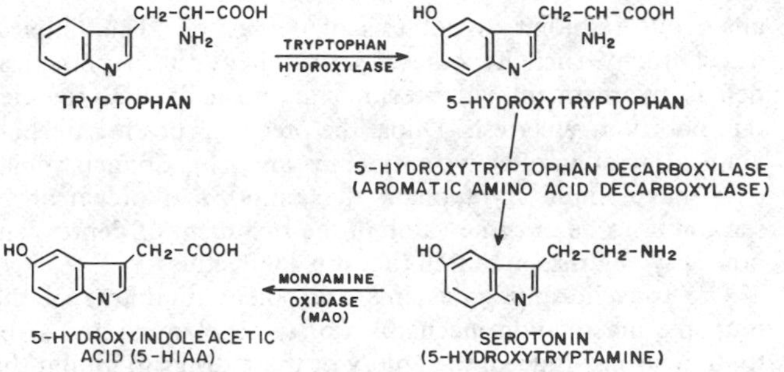

FIGURE 5. Pathways of serotonin synthesis and degradation. (From Snyder, S. H. Catecholamines and serotonin. In *Basic Neurochemistry*, R. W. Albers, G. I. Siegal, R. Katzman, and B. W. Agranoff, editors, p. 89. Little, Brown, and Co., Boston, 1972.)

catecholamines. The aldehyde formed from serotonin is predominately oxidized to 5-hydroxyindoleacetic acid, although a limited amount is reduced to the alcohol, 5-hydroxytryptophol.

Reuptake inactivation. After discharge at synapses, acetylcholine is inactivated through hydrolysis by the enzyme acetylcholinesterase. None of the enzymes that degrade serotonin or the catecholamines seems to be responsible for their synaptic inactivation. Instead, these amines are predominantly inactivated by reuptake into the nerve terminals that released them. The process was first discovered and shown to be responsible for synaptic inactivation of norepinephrine in the peripheral sympathetic nervous system by Axelrod (1965). Subsequently, highly efficient and specific uptake systems have been demonstrated for all the neurotransmitter candidates in the central nervous system—for norepinephrine, dopamine, serotonin, GABA, glutamic and aspartic acids, and glycine but not for histamine and acetylcholine. It seems likely that reuptake inactivation is the universal mechanism for neurotransmitter inactivation and that enzymatic degradation in the case of acetylcholine is an exception to the rule. Interference with reuptake inactivation is a major mechanism of action of several psychotropic drugs.

Psychotropic Drug Action

STIMULANTS

Amphetamines and related stimulants bear striking structural resemblances to the catecholamines (see Figure 6). Pharmacologists have generally assumed that amphetamines act through one of the two catecholamines in the brain. Amphetamine can act in two ways. It causes a direct release of catecholamines into the synaptic cleft and, hence, onto postsynaptic receptor sites. Amphetamine can also efficiently block the reuptake inactivation mechanism of catecholamines, thus prolonging the effects of synaptically released norepinephrine and dopamine. These two actions, release and reuptake blockade, are closely related, and it is not clear to what extent each accounts for amphetamine effects, although release seems to be more important.

By either means, amphetamine facilitates synaptically released catecholamines. One can well imagine how the alerting action of amphetamine may be mediated by effects on the dorsal norepinephrine pathway to the cerebral cortex. Similarly, it is reasonable to suppose that facilitation of the ventral norepinephrine neuronal activity in the pleasure centers of the hypothalamus could account for the euphoria-producing ac-

tions of amphetamine. The ability of amphetamine to decrease appetite poses a more complex problem. Some researchers think that norepinephrine neurons in the hypothalamus in so-called eating centers are responsible for amphetamine-induced anorexia, but there is other evidence that dopamine neurons play a major role in this action.

Various amphetamine analogues were developed in an effort to produce agents that are selective central stimulants with little anorexic activity or that selectively decrease appetite without causing central stimulation. One may anticipate that appetite suppressants with no central stimulant actions would not be as liable to abuse as amphetamine itself. Drugs such as phenmetrazine (Preludin) and diethylpropion (Tenuate) were developed to decrease appetite selectively. However, when amphetamine was proscribed in Sweden to combat a widespread epidemic of amphetamine abuse, addicts turned to phenmetrazine, which was then abused even more widely than amphetamine itself. Of the two optical isomers of amphetamine, *d*-amphetamine (Dexedrine) is about 5 times as potent a central stimulant as *l*-amphetamine. Fenfluramine (Pondamin), an amphetamine analogue, effectively decreases appetite and is not a central stimulant. In fact, fenfluramine gives rise to somnolence in human beings and, accordingly, may be thought of as an ideal appetite-suppressing drug. Methylphenidate (Ritalin) is an amphetamine analogue that is a powerful central stimulant but is essentially devoid of appetite-suppressing activity. It is the amphetamine analogue of choice in the treatment of hyperactive children in whom loss of appetite would be a serious side effect. The mechanism of this paradoxical action of amphetamines in hyperactive children is unclear. Some investigators think that the drug is not paradoxical at all. Instead, by its alerting effect, amphetamine enables the child to focus his attention on his work and hence be less distractible and hyperactive.

Because antidepressant drugs are thought to act by facilitating the synaptic effects of catecholamine, one might anticipate amphetamine to be a useful antidepressant. Surprisingly, amphetamine generally tends to worsen the symptoms of endogenous depression. However, there is evidence that single doses of amphetamine do selectively produce euphoria in those patients who subsequently display a favorable therapeutic re-

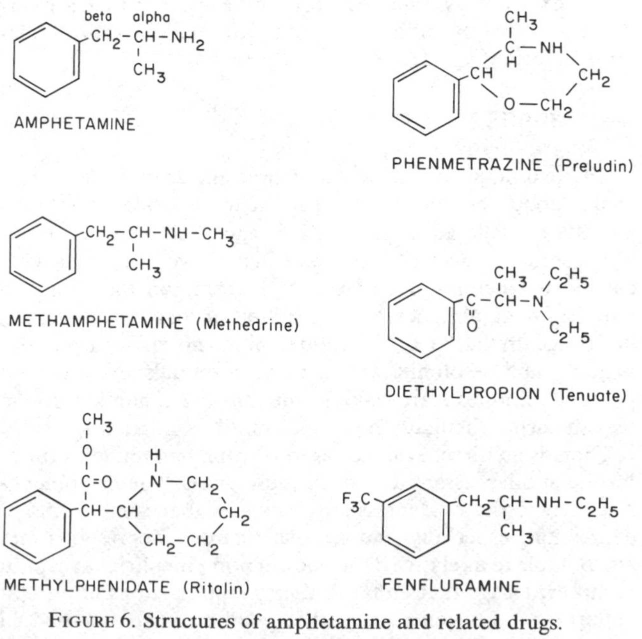

FIGURE 6. Structures of amphetamine and related drugs.

sponse to tricyclic antidepressants. In this way, amphetamine affords a test substance to determine therapeutic response to antidepressant drugs. The patients who respond to amphetamine with euphoria and whose depression is alleviated by imipramine (Tofranil) have lower urinary MHPG levels before drug treatment than do patients who respond less well (Maas et al., 1973). Patients with higher MHPG levels respond better to amitriptyline (Elavil) (Schildkraut, 1974; Beckman and Goodwin, 1975). Conceivably, amphetamine has a certain potential for alleviating certain factors in depression, but, perhaps because of its dynamics of action—directly releasing catecholamines into the synaptic cleft, besides blocking their reuptake—it produces adverse psychic effects that counteract its therapeutic actions.

Amphetamine addicts—speed freaks—self-administer huge amounts of amphetamine intravenously. Such persons frequently develop an acute paranoid psychosis, which may be clinically indistinguishable from acute paranoid schizophrenia and which provides the best drug model of schizophrenia. Accordingly, it is conceivable that understanding brain mechanisms in the mediation of amphetamine psychosis may shed light on the pathophysiology of schizophrenia. Several indirect lines of evidence suggest that brain dopamine mediates the symptoms of amphetamine psychosis. Besides producing a model schizophrenia, small doses of amphetamine administered intravenously to schizophrenic patients produce a florid exacerbation of their schizophrenic symptoms (Davis and Janowsky, 1973). Methylphenidate is more effective in this regard than is amphetamine itself.

Amphetamine can be metabolized by a variety of routes. The most prominent ones involve the introduction of a hydroxyl group on the ring opposite (para) to the side chain and the deamination of the side chain nitrogen by a drug-metabolizing system in the liver that is different from monoamine oxidase. However, those metabolic pathways are not especially prominent in humans, and a major amount of amphetamine is excreted in the urine unchanged. In treating toxic reactions to amphetamine, one should attempt to hasten amphetamine excretion. Because amphetamine is an amine, it is un-ionized at alkaline pH values and, accordingly, predominantly reabsorbed into the circulation from the kidney tubules and poorly excreted. To facilitate amphetamine excretion, one wants to increase the positive charge on the amine nitrogen by acidifying the urine—for example, by treating the patient with ammonium chloride.

ANTIDEPRESSANT DRUGS

The two major classes of antidepressant drugs were discovered at about the same time: the monoamine oxidase inhibitors and the tricyclic antidepressants. Monoamine oxidase inhibitors comprise a group of agents that have widely varying chemical structures but that have in common the ability to inhibit monoamine oxidase. Inhibition of that enzyme results in an accumulation of the monoamines norepinephrine, dopamine, and serotonin within nerve terminals. At a certain point the amines start leaking out into the synaptic cleft, so that the drugs facilitate the actions of all monoamines.

There is no direct evidence as to which monoamine is crucial for the antidepressant actions of those drugs. The norepinephrine hypothesis of depression postulates that some forms of depression, especially endogenous retarded depressions, are attributable to a relative deficiency of norepinephrine at central synapses. Drugs that enhance the synaptic actions of norepinephrine tend to relieve depression. Others have proposed an analogous serotonin hypothesis of depression. The simplest direct test of such hypotheses is to relieve the hypothetical deficits by treatment with precursor amino acids. Both theories fare poorly in such tests. Dopa, the precursor of the catecholamines, is not an effective antidepressant drug. Some psychiatrists have found tryptophan, the amino acid precursor of serotonin, to be of some value in the treatment of depression; other psychiatrists maintain that it is ineffective.

The tricyclic antidepressants are potent inhibitors of the reuptake inactivation mechanism of catecholamine and serotonin neurons. Indeed, the ability of those drugs to inhibit the reuptake process is a powerful predictor of their antidepressant efficacy. The chemical structures of the tricyclic antidepressants closely resemble those of the phenothiazines (see Figure 7). Those antidepressants were initially developed as antischizophrenic drugs, although they were relatively ineffective in treating schizophrenic patients. Like certain phenothiazines, the tricyclic antidepressants, such as imipramine (Tofranil) and amitriptyline (Elavil), tend to sedate normal people and yet, paradoxically, relieve depression. In the treatment of depression, these drugs, as well as the monoamine oxidase inhibitors, require a latency period of 1 to 3 weeks before they are fully effective. Whether this latency period is related simply to the

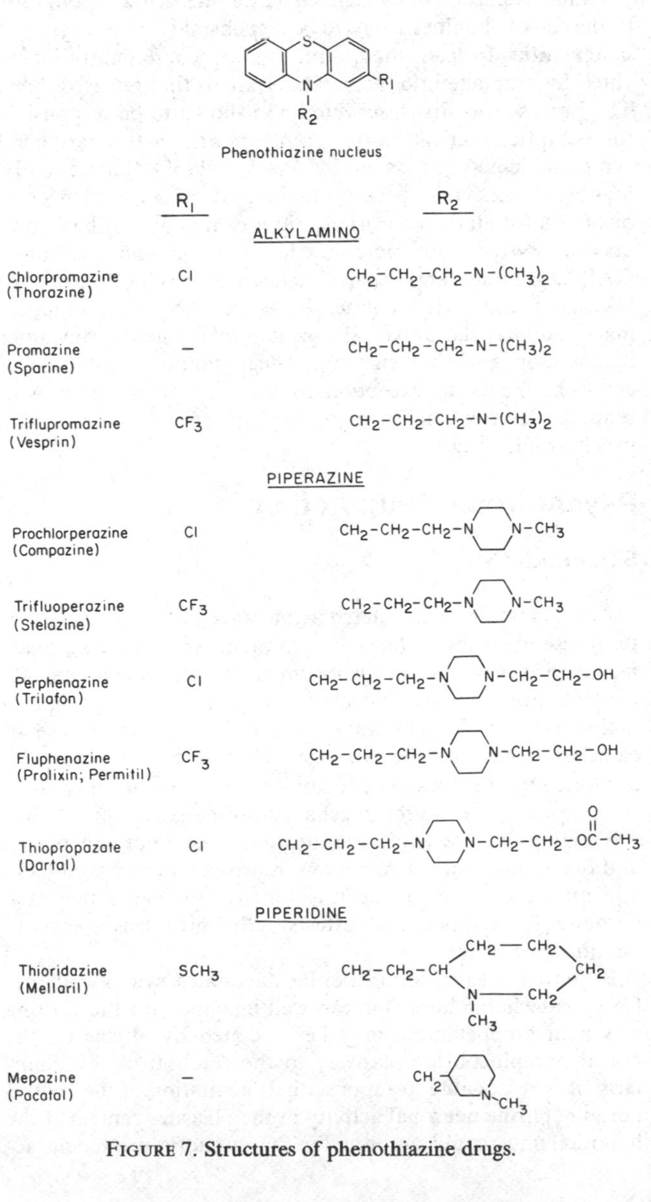

FIGURE 7. Structures of phenothiazine drugs.

duration required to obtain consistently high brain levels of the drugs or to other factors is unclear.

Some recently developed effective antidepressant drugs, such as iprindole and mianserin, inhibit neither the amine reuptake process nor monoamine oxidase. That fact has prompted investigators to seek other effects. Tricyclic antidepressants block histamine H_2 receptors in the brain more potently than they inhibit amine uptake (Green and Maayani, 1977; Kanof and Greengard, 1978), and they are even more potent at blocking cerebral histamine H_1 than H_2 receptors (Tran et al., 1978). All tricyclic antidepressants, as well as iprindole and mianserin, exert these antihistamine actions.

In the periphery, histamine H_1 receptors mediate the classical effects of histamine on smooth muscle, and the H_1 antihistamines comprise the traditional antiallergic antihistamines. H_2 receptors are best characterized in the stomach, where they mediate acid secretion. The H_2 antihistamine cimetidine (Tagamet) is a potent blocker of acid secretion, with major therapeutic benefits in duodenal ulcer treatment. The function of either type of histamine receptor in the brain is unclear.

Both the tricyclic antidepressants and the monoamine oxidase inhibitors presumably owe their clinical actions to the facilitation of the synaptic actions of norepinephrine or serotonin in the brain. These drugs also facilitate the effects of norepinephrine released at sympathetic synapses in the peripheral nervous system. This action can give rise to major side effects associated with enhanced sympathetic function. In some patients these drugs produce marked hypertension. Because the two classes of drugs facilitate norepinephrine effects in different ways, they enhance the activities of each other in a synergistic fashion. Extremely severe, even fatal, hypertensive crises have occurred in certain patients treated simultaneously with monoamine oxidase inhibitors and tricyclic antidepressant drugs. American practice warns against treating patients simultaneously with the two drugs. Authorities generally recommend at least a 10-day interval between treatment with drugs of the two classes. However, those hypertensive crises are rare, and many European psychopharmacologists believe that the combination of those two classes of drugs is relatively safe.

The metabolism of the monoamine oxidase inhibitors is as varied as their structures. No well-defined clinical features depend on differential metabolism of those drugs. By contrast, the metabolism of the tricyclic antidepressants has some clinically relevant aspects. The liver microsomal drug-metabolizing enzymes demethylate the dimethylated tricyclic antidepressants into monomethylated forms. Thus, imipramine is converted to desmethylimipramine (Pertofran, Norpramin). Similarly, amitriptyline is converted to nortriptyline (Aventyl). In rats, desmethylimipramine is more potent than imipramine, and some authors have proposed that demethylation activates the tricyclic antidepressants. Although both dimethylated and monomethylated forms of the drugs are clinically useful in depression, demethylation does not appear to be crucial for antidepressant action.

Tricyclic antidepressants block the metabolism of amphetamine and slow its disappearance from the brain. Accordingly, those drugs potentiate the central stimulant effects of amphetamine. Some limited evidence indicates that amphetamines retard metabolism of the tricyclic antidepressants and in that way facilitate their therapeutic actions.

ANTISCHIZOPHRENIC DRUGS

The most important drugs in psychiatry are probably the antischizophrenic phenothiazines and butyrophenones, which are generally referred to as neuroleptics. Abundant evidence supports the contention that these drugs exert a selective antischizophrenic action, so that neuroleptics have been used as tools to discern abnormal brain mechanisms in schizophrenia. The phenothiazines are complex three-ringed structures with side chains, quite similar in structure to the tricyclic antidepressants (see Figure 7). The butyrophenones, such as haloperidol (Haldol), differ markedly from the phenothiazines in chemical structure but have extremely similar pharmacological activities.

Because of the extreme chemical reactivity of the aromatic portions of the phenothiazines, those drugs exert multiple neurophysiological and biochemical effects. Actions on a wide variety of metabolic systems have been proposed as the antischizophrenic action of the phenothiazines. It is the task of the pharmacologist to determine which of those effects represents the mechanism of therapeutic action and which are secondary or irrelevant to therapeutic efficacy. When one has a class of drugs with many members, as is the case with the phenothiazines, a valuable approach is to ascertain whether a given biochemical effect correlates with the therapeutic efficacy of the various drugs. Some phenothiazine drugs, such as the antihistamine promethazine (Phenergan), differ very little from the parent phenothiazine chlorpromazine (Thorazine), yet lack antischizophrenic actions. The vast majority of the biochemical effects of phenothiazines do not correlate at all with the antischizophrenic actions of those drugs. One neurochemical effect does correlate: the ability to block dopamine receptors.

In 1963 the Swedish pharmacologist Arvid Carlsson (Carlsson and Lindquist, 1963) observed that phenothiazines that are effective antischizophrenic agents tend to elevate brain levels of methoxydopamine, but clinically ineffective phenothiazines do not. That observation suggested that effective antischizophrenic drugs cause an increased release of dopamine and, to a smaller extent, of norepinephrine. Later, it was found that phenothiazines and butyrophenones accelerate the formation of dopamine from tyrosine in proportion to their clinical efficacy. Haloperidol, which is about 10 times as potent as chlorpromazine, is also about 100 times as potent in accelerating dopamine formation, but promethazine, which is ineffective in the treatment of schizophrenia, does not accelerate dopamine formation. An acceleration of norepinephrine synthesis occurs with those drugs but correlates much less with their antischizophrenic activity. Indeed, some potent butyrophenones are highly effective in accelerating dopamine synthesis with no actions on norepinephrine synthesis. As described above, an enhancement of new catecholamine synthesis may reflect the activity of the neurons to replace catecholamines lost because of an increased firing rate of the neurons. That suggests that those drugs accelerate the firing rate of dopamine neurons in proportion to their antischizophrenic activity. Aghajanian and Bunney (1973) obtained direct evidence that phenothiazines do, indeed, accelerate the firing of dopamine neurons.

However, none of those approaches directly measures the effects at dopamine receptors. The first biochemical means of examining dopamine receptors derives from the observation that dopamine selectively increases cyclic adenosine monophosphate formation by stimulating its biosynthetic enzyme adenylate cyclase in dopamine-rich parts of the brain (Kebabian et al., 1972). The dopamine-sensitive adenylate cyclase is blocked by phenothiazines in rough proportion to their clinical potencies but is affected only weakly by butyrophenones such as haloperidol (Haldol). Because butyrophenones exert the same pharmacological actions as phenothiazines and are even more potent than phenothiazines, those findings suggest that neuroleptics do not act through dopamine receptors. However, recent findings indicate that the dopamine-sensitive adenylate cyclase reflects only one of at least two distinct populations of dopamine receptors. Using binding techniques that had proved effective in labeling the opiate receptor, investigators have been able to monitor, by binding of ^{3}H-haloperidol, a population of dopamine receptors that are, for the most part, physically distinct from the dopamine receptors associated with the cyclase (Schwarcz et al., 1978). The relative potencies of neuroleptics in competing for dopamine receptors labeled by ^{3}H-haloperidol parallels quite closely their clinical potencies, demonstrating clearly that neuroleptics act by blocking those dopamine receptors (Creese et al., 1976; Seeman et al., 1976).

The phenothiazines and butyrophenones all share an antischizophrenic action. In addition, they possess several other clinically useful actions, which vary among the drugs. Phenothiazines elicit postural hypotension, and some of those drugs are quite sedating. Most phenothiazines exert an antiemetic effect by acting directly on the chemoreceptor trigger zone in the brain stem. Some phenothiazine derivatives are marketed primarily for their antiemetic actions. The alkylamino and piperidine side chain phenothiazines produce more hypotensive and sedating effects than do the piperazine side chain phenothiazines. By contrast, the piperazine phenothiazines are more potent antiemetics and provoke more extrapyramidal side effects than do the alkylamino and piperidine phenothiazines. The butyrophenones tend most to resemble the piperazine phenothiazines in their side effects.

The extrapyramidal side effects of the phenothiazines frequently resemble the symptoms of Parkinson's disease, with akinesia, rigidity, and tremor. In addition, there are other extrapyramidal effects, such as akathisia, which refers to a peculiar sort of restlessness, almost a muscular itchiness, in which patients cannot sit still and so pace up and down the floors of the hospital. Other extrapyramidal symptoms include abnormal muscular movements, such as torticollis. The symptoms of idiopathic Parkinson's disease are presumed to result from a deficiency of dopamine because of the degeneration of the dopamine neurons in the corpus striatum. The extrapyramidal side effects of phenothiazine drugs seem to result from dopamine receptor blockade. By blocking dopamine receptors in the corpus striatum, phenothiazines can produce a pharmacological model of Parkinson's disease. Because the therapeutic action of the phenothiazines also seems to be related to a blockade of dopamine receptors, one wonders which dopamine tracts are involved in the antischizophrenic activity. Because there are no satisfactory animal models of schizophrenia, it is difficult to study this problem. Potential candidates include the dopamine tracts to the nucleus accumbens and olfactory tubercle, parts of the limbic system of the brain thought by many investigators to be prominent in mediating emotional behavior, and the dopamine neurons in the cerebral cortex.

Studies of neurotransmitter receptors have also clarified the side effects of neuroleptics. The incidence of extrapyramidal side effects of neuroleptics is related inversely to their affinities for muscarinic cholinergic receptors (Snyder et al., 1974). Atropine-like muscarinic anticholinergic drugs such as benztropine (Cogentin) and trihexiphenidyl (Artane) are effective antiparkinsonian agents and block the extrapyramidal effects of neuroleptics. Neuroleptics all have some muscarinic anticholinergic properties. Those with greater anticholinergic potency, such as thioridazine (Mellaril) produce fewer extrapyramidal effects than do the weaker anticholinergics, such as fluphenazine (Prolixin) and haloperidol.

The sedative-hypotensive effects of the neuroleptics seem to be due to the blockade of α-noradrenergic receptors (Peroutka et al., 1977). Neuroleptics that, at therapeutic doses, block a greater proportion of central α-receptors, such as promazine and chlorpromazine, are more sedative-hypotensive than are those occupying fewer α-receptors, such as haloperidol and fluphenazine.

Patients treated for a long period of time with phenothiazines develop a side effect that seems to be the opposite of the parkinsonian-like side effects of the drugs, namely tardive dyskinesia. The side effect consists of a hypermotility of facial muscles and the extremities. Even though tardive dyskinesia follows prolonged phenothiazine treatment, phenothiazines and butyrophenones relieve the symptoms of tardive dyskinesia. That effect suggests that the mechanism responsible for tardive dyskinesia is an overcompensation of the dopamine system for the dopamine receptor blockade. For instance, after prolonged treatment with phenothiazines, the dopamine receptors may become supersensitive to the effects of dopamine. Such a mechanism has been directly demonstrated in animals. The number of dopamine receptor binding sites in rats treated chronically with neuroleptics increases significantly, which may account for behavioral supersensitivity (Burt et al., 1977).

Phenothiazines can be metabolized by a large number of pathways. More than 100 metabolites of chlorpromazine have been reported in the urine. There are wide individual variations in blood levels of chlorpromazine after fixed doses, suggesting that there are wide variations in phenothiazine metabolism. It is quite possible that those variations are responsible in part for the striking differences among patients in dose requirements. Conceivably, when sensitive and simple assay measures for blood phenothiazines are developed, it may be possible to adjust the dosage according to blood level, rather than attempting to gauge subjectively when a patient has reached maximum therapeutic benefit. A variety of chemical techniques have been used to measure neuroleptic levels; most of them are selective for given drugs but are often tedious and too complex for hospital laboratories. Recently, a radioreceptor assay was developed that is based on the ability of neuroleptics in a patient's blood to compete with ^{3}H-neuroleptics for binding to dopamine receptors (Creese and Snyder, 1977). That assay detects all clinically used neuroleptics, as well as any pharmacologically active metabolites. Because it is simple, sensitive, and specific, it can be readily used in routine clinical laboratories.

PSYCHEDELIC DRUGS

The psychedelic drugs comprise a wide range of chemical structures that, despite their marked chemical differences, produce a strikingly similar set of profound subjective effects. Although the psychological effects of lysergic acid diethylamide (LSD) were initially likened to a model schizophrenia, most authors do not now think that the symptoms elicited by LSD mimic schizophrenia nearly so well as do the symptoms of amphetamine psychosis. For instance, psychedelic drugs produce primarily perceptual alterations in the visual sphere, but schizophrenic hallucinations are auditory. Psychedelic drugs rarely produce hallucinations but usually just elicit distortions of perception.

After the interest of psychiatric researchers in LSD psychosis as a model of schizophrenia subsided, a new interest in these agents as psychedelic tools emerged. Humphrey Osmond coined the word "psychedelic"—which is derived from the Greek, meaning mind manifesting—to emphasize the extraordinary changes in state of consciousness brought about by those agents. By "mind manifesting," he really meant mind expanding. Under the influence of LSD, persons do feel as if their vision were much more acute than normal, so much so that they feel able to see the pores in another person's skin. Changes in the sense of time are so profound that a minute may seem like a month, and 30 minutes is like all eternity. Space changes, so that wandering from one room to the next is tantamount to traversing the farthest reaches of the universe. Even if those psychological effects of LSD do not teach anything about schizophrenia, they may aid in explaining ways in which the brain normally mediates perception and self-awareness.

The chemical structure of LSD possesses certain similarities to that of serotonin. It seems reasonable to seek the mechanism of action of LSD through brain serotonin.

In 1953 the British pharmacologist John Gaddum found that LSD is a potent antagonist of the effects of serotonin on smooth muscle, especially of the uterus. The ability of serotonin to contract the uterus was exerted at low doses, and LSD in extremely small concentrations was able to antagonize the effects of serotonin. That finding led to the speculation that LSD acts in the brain as a serotonin antagonist. But the behavior of chemicals in the brain is often very different from their actions in the periphery. Thus, it was not surprising when it was observed that brom-LSD, which is essentially devoid of psychedelic action, was just as potent as LSD in antagonizing the effects of serotonin on the uterus, casting doubt on whether LSD exerts its clinical effects through serotonin antagonism. Again, as discussed above with the phenothiazines, the test of whether a given pharmacological effect correlates with clinical actions proved useful in evaluating the relationship of serotonin antagonism to LSD action.

Of the many biochemical and neurophysiological effects of LSD, most have not been able to adequately pass the test of correlation with clinical potency. One dramatic effect of LSD closely parallels its clinical actions: reduced firing of serotonin neurons. Aghajanian et al. (1970) made the observation that LSD, in miniscule doses, slows or stops the firing of the serotonin cells in the raphe nuclei of the brain stem. When the microelectrode was moved a small distance from the raphe nuclei, LSD no longer exerted that effect. The only cells in the brain affected in so potent a fashion by LSD were the raphe nuclei. The effect of LSD on raphe cells was shared by all other psychedelic drugs and by no other drugs. That effect represents a direct action on the raphe cells because direct application of LSD in very small amounts to the raphe cells produced the same effects as did intravenous injections. By contrast, LSD had no effect on serotonin receptors of neurons that received serotonin nerve terminals and that were hyperpolarized by serotonin. At postsynaptic serotonin receptor sites, LSD neither mimicked nor antagonized serotonin. The extraordinary specificity of LSD and other psychedelic drugs for raphe cells strongly suggests that serotonin neurons are intimately associated with psychedelic drug effects.

Very early research with LSD showed that the drug is rapidly metabolized and excreted from the body, even though its psychological effects last for 8 hours or more. Several researchers concluded that LSD does not act by itself but triggers some effect that produces psychedelic actions several steps removed or that a metabolite of LSD is the active drug. Later, however, it was shown that, although LSD is rapidly metabolized, substantial amounts remain in the plasma long enough to account for the psychological effects of the drug.

The various psychedelic drugs differ from each other in certain nuances of their subjective effects and in their duration of action. However, their effects are far more similar than they are dissimilar. Most work by mouth, although dimethyltryptamine (DMT) is not active by mouth and is usually injected or inhaled. LSD effects persist about 8 hours; mescaline is a little longer lasting. DMT is the shortest-acting psychedelic drug; its effects persist for only about 1 hour. Certain methoxyamphetamines, such as 2,5-dimethoxy-4-methylamphetamine, or DOM (STP), are less susceptible to metabolism than is mescaline, from which they are derived. They are active in much smaller doses, and their effects continue for long periods, sometimes as long as 24 hours.

ANTIANXIETY AGENTS

The term "antianxiety drug" is somewhat controversial. The notion of prescribing a sedative drug to reduce emotional tension and produce mild skeletal muscle relaxation is a long-standing one in clinical medicine. Phenobarbital has been a favorite drug for this use since its introduction in the early part of the 20th century. Of the many available barbiturates, phenobarbital seems to be the most valuable drug in this regard, primarily because of its slow onset and long duration of action. Barbiturates with steep dose-response curves, such as secobarbital, are better sleeping medications but less satisfactory as tranquilizers. They produce sleep in doses not much greater than those necessary to minimally sedate. By contrast, drugs such as phenobarbital, with relatively shallow dose-response curves, produce calming without drowsiness, sleep, ataxia, or slurred speech over a wide range of doses. Phenobarbital has a shallower dose-response curve than do the other barbiturates because it is more slowly metabolized, excreted, and absorbed into the brain.

The controversy in the area of daytime sedation has to do with newer drugs. In the early 1950's meprobamate (Miltown, Equanil) was introduced as a totally novel agent specifically designated to alleviate anxiety without causing sedation (see Figure 8). In particular, it was emphasized that meprobamate, in contrast to the barbiturates, was not addicting and was not lethal, even in large doses. Unfortunately, neither of those contentions is altogether valid. Meprobamate can be addicting, although it may not be as addictive as barbiturates, and there have been numerous suicides with meprobamate. However, it is true that the lethal dose of the drug is proportionately greater than the barbiturates' lethal dose.

As the medical public became disenchanted with meprobamate, two new antianxiety agents became widely available: chlordiazepoxide (Librium) and diazepam (Valium). Although differing in their chemical structure from meprobamate and the barbiturates, chlordiazepoxide and diazepam share many

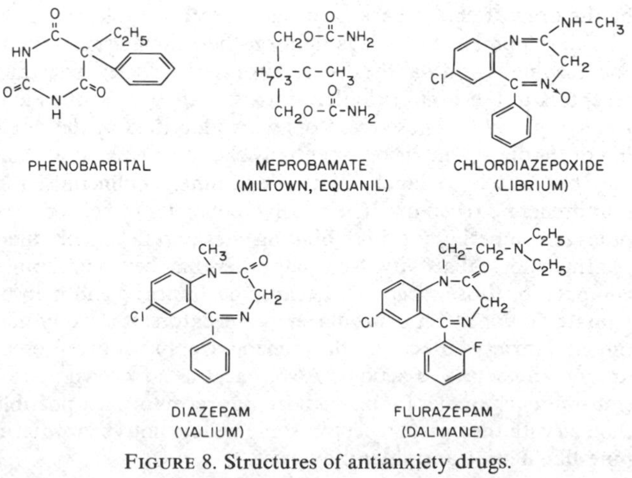

PHENOBARBITAL   MEPROBAMATE (MILTOWN, EQUANIL)   CHLORDIAZEPOXIDE (LIBRIUM)   DIAZEPAM (VALIUM)   FLURAZEPAM (DALMANE)

FIGURE 8. Structures of antianxiety drugs.

pharmacological actions with those drugs. Like meprobamate, chlordiazepoxide and diazepam are effective muscle relaxants. Diazepam seems to be the most clinically useful of all available muscle relaxants and is the drug of choice for most conditions involving muscle spasm.

Diazepam and chlordiazepoxide are both less subject to addictive abuse and less lethal than is meprobamate. In this way they represent the safest available antianxiety agents. Although it is possible to become tolerant to the actions of those two drugs and there are some withdrawal-like symptoms on termination of use, the reactions are mild. Apparently, the only difficulty encountered with those agents occurs when they are prescribed for a prolonged, indefinite period, during which considerable tolerance can develop. When used for a self-limited time to treat a specific anxiety episode, they present very little addictive danger. In this way they constitute drugs the physician can justly prescribe to be taken as needed, leaving some of the decision making up to the patient. Still, to prevent chronic use of increasing doses, the physician should prescribe the drugs in limited quantities.

Do those drugs exert a selective antianxiety effect that can be reliably discriminated from their sedative actions? Many studies have been performed with anxious outpatients in which phenobarbital has been compared with meprobamate, chlordiazepoxide, and diazepam. The powerful placebo effect associated with treating anxious patients complicates the studies. Some researchers have shown that anxious patients respond to a placebo even when told that the pill contains only sugar. As methods have become more sophisticated, true antianxiety actions have been demonstrated for phenobarbital, meprobamate, chlordiazepoxide, and diazepam. In the relief of acute anxiety, meprobamate, diazepam, and chlordiazepoxide are no better than barbiturates. However, in the treatment of chronic anxiety, there is evidence that the antianxiety agents, especially chlordiazepoxide and diazepam, are more efficacious than meprobamate, but the converse has rarely, if ever, been demonstrated. Of the antianxiety agents, chlordiazepoxide and diazepam seem to be the most effective. Moreover, they are safer than meprobamate and barbiturates and, therefore, seem to be the drugs of choice in treating anxious outpatients.

Pharmacologically, there is considerable overlap of alcohol, barbiturates, meprobamate, chlordiazepoxide, and diazepam. The symptoms of withdrawal from all those drugs are almost the same, with insomnia, tremulousness, great anxiety, convulsions, and a confusional psychosis resembling delirium tremens. For that reason, one can relieve withdrawal symptoms from one drug by the administration of any of the others. Diazepam is highly effective in treating the symptoms of delirium tremens or of barbiturate withdrawal and may well be the drug of choice because of its general over-all safety.

A development that sheds light on the mechanisms of benzodiazepine action was the discovery of specific benzodiazepine receptors in the brain (Mohler and Okada, 1977; Squires and Braestrup, 1977). Those receptors were identified by the binding of ^{3}H-diazepam, using essentially the same techniques that had been used to label opiate, dopamine, cholinergic, and noradrenergic receptors. The relative potencies of benzodiazepines in competing for those binding sites parallel closely their pharmacological activity. No drugs other than benzodiazepines compete for those receptors. Because barbiturates and meprobamate do not affect benzodiazepine receptors, it is likely that the antianxiety effects of the benzodiazepines do represent unique and selective actions. Also, because no known neurotransmitter competes for benzodiazepine receptors, it is possible that, as with the opiate receptor, some endogenous benzodiazepine-like neurotransmitter may exist.

The barbiturates stimulate liver drug-metabolizing enzyme systems, including those that metabolize barbiturates. That effect explains, in part, tolerance to barbiturates. There must, in addition, be a tolerance at receptor sites in the brain because, even at identical brain levels of barbiturates, an animal that has received the drugs chronically displays less of a pharmacological response than does a naive animal. Because meprobamate and barbiturates induce a wide variety of drug-metabolizing enzymes, metabolic tolerance to them is associated with metabolic tolerance to other drugs.

Suggested Cross References

Neurology is described at great length in Chapter 3. The neurochemistry of behavior is discussed in Section 2.4, and the neurophysiology of behavior in Section 2.5. The hallucinogens are discussed in Section 6.4. The various psychiatric disorders are discussed in other parts of this book: schizophrenic disorders in Chapter 15, paranoid disorders in Chapter 16, schizoaffective disorders in Chapter 17, affective disorders in Chapters 18 and 19, neurotic disorders in Chapter 21, and drug dependence in Chapter 23. The clinical use of antipsychotic drugs is discussed in Section 31.1, antidepressant drugs in Section 31.2, and minor tranquilizers, sedatives, and hypnotics in Section 31.3. The use of drugs in child psychiatry is discussed in Section 42.3.

REFERENCES

*Aghajanian, G. K., and Bunney, B. S. Central dopamine neurons: Neurophysiological identification and responses to drugs. In *Frontiers in Catecholamine Research*, E. Usdin and S. H. Snyder, editors, p. 643, Pergamon Press, Oxford, 1973.

*Aghajanian, G. K., Foote, W. E., and Sheard, M. H. Action of psychotogenic drugs on single midbrain raphe neurons. J. Pharmacol. Exp. Ther., *171*: 178, 1970.

*Anden, N. E., Dahlstrom, A., Fuxe, K., Larsson, K., Olson, K., and Ungerstedt, U. Ascending monoamine neurons to the telencephalon and diencephalon. Acta Physiol. Scand., *67*: 3131, 1966.

Axelrod, J. The metabolism, storage and release of catecholamines. Rec. Progr. Horm. Res., *21*: 597, 1965.

Beckman, H., and Goodwin, F. K. Antidepressant response to tricyclics and urinary MHPG in unipolar patients. Arch. Gen. Psychiatry, *32*: 17, 1975.

Burt, D. R., Creese, I., and Snyder, S. H. Antischizophrenic drugs: Chronic treatment elevates dopamine receptor binding in brain. Science, *196*: 326, 1977.

Carlsson, A., and Lindquist, M. Effect of chlorpromazine and haloperidol on formation of 3-methoxytyramine and normetanephrine in mouse brain. Acta Pharmacol. Toxicol., *20*: 140, 1963.

Carraway, R., and Leeman, S. The amino acid sequence of a hypothalamic peptide, neurotensin. J. Biol. Chem., *250*: 1907, 1975.

Clineschmidt, B. V., and McGuffin, J. Neurotensin administered intracisternally inhibits responsiveness of mice to noxious stimuli. Eur. J. Pharmacol., *46*: 395, 1977.

Creese, I., Burt, D. R., and Snyder, S. H. Dopamine receptor binding predicts clinical and pharmacological potencies of antischizophrenic drugs. Science, *192*: 481, 1976.

Creese, I., and Snyder, S. H. A simple and sensitive radioreceptor assay for antischizophrenic drugs in blood. Nature, *270*: 180, 1977.

Davis, J. M., and Janowsky, D. Amphetamine psychosis. In *Frontiers in Catecholamine Research*, E. Usdin and S. H. Snyder, editors, p. 977, Pergamon Press, Oxford, 1973.

Gaddum, J. H. Antagonism between LSD and 5-hydroxytryptamine. J. Physiol. Lond., *121*: 15, 1953.

Green, J. P., and Maayani, S. Tricyclic antidepressants block histamine H$_2$ receptors in brain. Nature, *269*: 163, 1977.

Hughes, J. T., Smith, T. W., Kosterlitz, H. W., Fothergill, L., Morgan, B. A., and Morris, H. R. Identification of two related pentapeptides from the brain with potent opiate agonist activity. Nature, *258*: 577, 1975.

Kanof, P. D., and Greengard, P. Brain histamine receptors as targets for antidepressant drugs. Nature, *272*: 329, 1978.

Kebabian, J. W., Petzold, G. L., and Greengard, P. Dopamine-sensitive adenylate cyclase in caudate nucleus of rat brain and its similarity to the "dopamine receptor." Proc. Natl. Acad. Sci. U.S.A., *69*: 2145, 1972.

*Klein, D. F., and Davis, J. M. *Diagnosis and Drug Treatment of Psychiatric Disorders.* Williams & Wilkins, Baltimore, 1969.

*Maas, J., Dekirmajian, H., and Jones, F. The identification of depressed patients who have a disorder of norepinephrine metabolism and/or disposition. In *Frontiers in Catecholamine Research*, E. Usdin and S. H. Snyder, editors, p. 1081. Pergamon Press, Oxford, 1973.

Mohler, H., and Okada, T. Benzodiazepine receptors in the central nervous system. Science, *198*: 849, 1977.

Peroutka, S. J., U'Prichard, D. C., Greenberg, D. A., and Snyder, S. H. Neuroleptic drug interactions with norepinephrine α-receptor binding sites in rat brain. Neuropharmacology, *16*: 549, 1977.

Schildkraut, J. J. Biochemical criteria for classifying depressive disorders and predicting responses to pharmacotherapy: Preliminary findings from studies of norepinephrine metabolism. Pharmacopsychiatry, *7*: 98, 1974.

Schwarcz, R., Creese, I., Coyle, J. T., and Snyder, S. H. Dopamine receptors localized on cerebral cortical afferents to rat corpus striatum. Nature, *271*: 766, 1978.

Seeman, P., Lee, T., Chau-Wong, M., and Wong, K. Antipsychotic drug doses and neuroleptic/dopamine receptors. Nature, *261*: 717, 1976.

Simantov, R., and Snyder, S. H. Morphine-like factors in mammalian brain: Structure elucidation and interactions with the opiate receptor. Proc. Natl. Acad. Sci. U.S.A., *73*: 2515, 1976.

Snyder, S. H. New developments in brain chemistry: Catecholamine metabolism and its relationship to the mechanism of action of psychotropic drugs. Am. J. Orthopsychiatry, *37*: 864, 1967.

*Snyder, S. H. Catecholamines and serotonin. In *Basic Neurochemistry*, ed. 2, R. W. Albers, G. I. Siegal, R. Katzman, and B. W. Agranoff, editors, p. 203. Little, Brown, and Co., Boston, 1976.

Snyder, S. H. The opiate receptor and morphine-like peptides in the brain. Am. J. Psychiatry, *135*: 645, 1978.

Snyder, S. H., Greenberg, D., and Yamamura, H. I. Antischizophrenic drugs and brain cholinergic receptors. Arch. Gen. Psychiatry, *31*: 58, 1974.

Squires, R. F., and Braestrup, C. Benzodiazepine receptors in rat brain. Nature, *266*: 732, 1977.

Tran, V. T., Chang, R. S. L., and Snyder, S. H. Histamine H_1 receptors identified in mammalian brain membranes with ^{3}H-mepyramine. Proc. Natl. Acad. Sci. U.S.A., *75*: 6290, 1978.

Uhl, G. R., Kuhar, M. J., and Snyder, S. H. Neurotensin: Immunohistochemical localization in rat central nervous system. Proc. Natl. Acad. Sci. U.S.A., *74*: 4059, 1977.

2.3 Sleep

ERNEST L. HARTMANN, M.D.

Definition

Sleep is a regular, recurrent, easily reversible state of the organism that is characterized by relative quiescence and by a great increase in the threshold of response to external stimuli relative to the waking state.

Thus, sleep is basically a behavioral state. However, certain electroencephalographic (EEG) and polygraphic characteristics can now be accepted as part of a definition of sleep because of their regular and constant association with the behavior of sleep. The individual EEG changes often considered characteristic of sleep may be deceptive. The deep, slow waves usually associated with sleep, for instance, can be found in the waking state under certain pharmacological conditions and are also seen during certain phases of anesthesia and coma. Thus, when an EEG tracing is used to make the diagnosis of sleep, it is the regular cyclic pattern, rather than any single characteristic wave form, that is most important.

Study Methods

Physicians and psychiatrists are and should be interested in sleep for a number of reasons. First of all, complaints of sleep disturbance are among the most common of all symptoms; it is important to know when they signal a specific serious and treatable illness and when they are nonspecific and part of a general malaise or anxiety. For instance, sleep disturbance is one of the earliest symptoms of impending psychosis and of an impending suicide attempt (Detre, 1966). Specific sleep patterns can help differentiate different kinds of depression (Kup-

fer et al., 1976) and may be of use in other conditions as well. Recently, several distinct sleep disorders have been identified, and it is important to differentiate them from the better-known psychiatric disorders.

Finally, there are theoretical relationships between sleep and dream research and research into mental illness. It has repeatedly been pointed out that we are all psychotic in our dreams. Many researchers, including the author, believe, despite some initial disappointments, that, in studying the biology of sleep—especially the biology of dreaming—they are studying aspects of the biology of psychosis or of the biology underlying primary-process mental functioning (Hartmann, 1967a, 1976a).

There have been sporadic attempts for many years to study the amount, depth, and quality of sleep. One classic method of sleep study is the simple subjective report. The doctor asks the patient whether he or she has been sleeping better or worse than usual. That is a simple and inexpensive way of evaluating sleep. It can be refined to a certain extent by the use of questionnaires that ask specific questions of interest to the clinician or researcher. Although the information obtained from subjective reports may be somewhat biased and not very precise, such reports do supply information not obtainable by any other means. For instance, a sleeping medication that looks perfect from the point of view of various objective laboratory studies but that leaves the patient feeling miserable in the morning is clearly a poor medication.

The report of an objective observer who checks the sleeper every 15 or 30 minutes during the night can be used in some settings to supplement the sometimes biased subjective report. That method can be applied to a large number of sleeping persons at the same time at relatively low cost, and such observations have been found to correlate fairly closely with EEG measures of sleep. Of course, only limited information is obtained at each check time—namely, whether the patient was judged to be asleep or awake.

For a time, a popular technique for measuring the length and depth of sleep was to attach a movement-sensitive device to the bedsprings and record the amount of bed movement during the night. That method was based on the oversimplified notion that sleep can be gauged by a diminution of movement and that the deepest sleep is the sleep with the least movement. Still, those studies did lead to rough estimates of changes in the length of sleep and to a general notion that the early hours of sleep are the deepest, at least in the sense of containing the least movement. Those observations, insofar as they go, are still valid.

More recently, EEG and polygraphic studies of sleep have become commonplace. They usually involve the continuous measurement of the occipital and parietal EEG, eye movements, muscle potential, and, in certain cases, the electrocardiogram, measures of respiration, and other measures of interest. That method has the obvious advantage of providing a continuous minute-by-minute record of the entire night's sleep, and it provides a great deal of precise information on whatever measures are being recorded. Among the disadvantages of the technique are the expense and the fact that the application of the necessary electrodes for recording may be somewhat disturbing to sleep, necessitating one, two, or even more nights of adaptation to the sleep laboratory before a proper evaluation of a person's sleep can be made.

Phenomenology

Information about the phenomenology of sleep—what occurs during a typical night of sleep in a healthy young human adult—is derived chiefly from polygraphic studies (Aserinsky and Kleitman, 1953; Dement and Kleitman, 1957; Williams et al., 1974), but many of the findings mentioned here are amenable to study by other techniques, including visual observation.

As a person falls asleep, his brain waves go through certain characteristic changes, classified as stages 1, 2, 3, and 4 (see Figure 1). The waking EEG is characterized by α-waves of 8 to 12 cycles a second and low-voltage activity of mixed frequency. As the person falls asleep, he begins to show a disappearance of α-activity. Stage 1, considered the lightest stage of sleep, is characterized by low-voltage desynchronized activity and sometimes by low-voltage, regular activity at 4 to 6 cycles a second. After a few seconds or minutes, this stage gives way to stage 2, a pattern showing frequent spindle-shaped tracings at 13 to 15 cycles a second (sleep spindles) and certain high-voltage spikes known as K-complexes. Soon thereafter, δ-waves—high-voltage activity at 0.5 to 2.5 cycles a second—make their appearance (stage 3). Eventually, in stage 4, those δ-waves occupy the major part of the record (Rechtschaffen and Kales, 1968; Williams et al., 1974). The division of sleep into stages 1 through 4 is a somewhat arbitrary division of a continuous process.

Sleep is cyclical, with four or five periods of emergence from stages 2, 3, and 4 to a stage similar to stage 1 (see Figure 2). Persons awakened during those periods of emergence frequently—60 to 90 per cent of the time—report that they have been dreaming. Such periods are characterized not only by stage 1 EEG patterns and by rapid conjugate eye movements but by a host of other distinguishing factors, including irregu-

larity in pulse rate, respiratory rate, and blood pressure; the presence of full or partial penile erections; and generalized muscular atony interrupted by sporadic movements in small muscle groups. Those periods differ markedly from typical stage 1 sleep, as well as from the other three stages. Because of their distinguishing characteristics and specific neurophysiological and chemical character, those periods are now almost universally seen as constituting a separate state of sleep. That view is reinforced by the fact that similar periods differing from the remainder of sleep are found in nearly all mammals and birds studied (Allison and Van Twyver, 1970; Allison et al., 1970). This distinct state of sleep is referred to as D-sleep (desynchronized or dreaming sleep) and the remainder of sleep as S-sleep (synchronized sleep). These two states of sleep are also known as REM sleep (rapid eye movement sleep) and NREM sleep (nonrapid eye movement sleep), as paradoxical sleep and orthodox sleep, and as active sleep and quiet sleep.

Several important characteristics of the typical night's sleep should be noted (see Figure 2). First of all, there are four or five D-periods during the night, and the total time taken up by the periods (D-time) is about 1½ hours, a little more than 20 per cent of the total sleep time. There is some variation, of course, but all the many hundreds of humans studied have such D-periods, and in young adults those periods almost always take up 20 to 25 per cent of the total night's sleep. The first D-period occurs about 70 to 120 minutes after the onset of sleep; the interval may be longer in some normal persons, but it is significantly shorter only in a few abnormal clinical and experimental conditions, such as D-deprivation and narcolepsy.

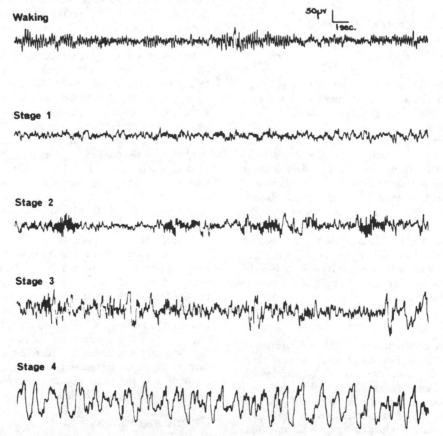

FIGURE 1. The electroencephalogram of sleep in a human adult. A single channel of recording—a monopolar recording from the left parietal area, referred to the ears as a neutral reference point—is shown for each stage.

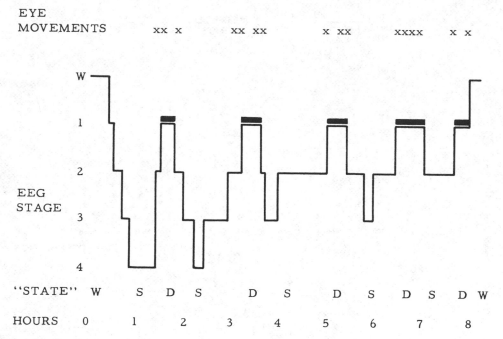

EYE
MOVEMENTS   xx x   xx xx   x xx   xxxx   x x

"STATE"   W   S   D   S   D   S   D   S   D   W

HOURS   0   1   2   3   4   5   6   7   8

FIGURE 2. A typical night's sleep in a young adult. *W*, waking state; *S*, synchronized or nondreaming sleep; *D*, desynchronized or dreaming sleep.

The cyclical nature of sleep is quite regular and reliable; a D-period occurs about every 90 to 100 minutes during the night. The first D-period tends to be the shortest, usually lasting less than 10 minutes; the later D-periods may last 15 to 40 minutes each. Most D-time occurs in the last third of the night, whereas most stage 4 sleep occurs in the first third of the night.

S-sleep (synchronized or nondreaming sleep) can be neatly organized according to depth: Stage 1 is the lightest stage, and stage 4 is the deepest stage, as measured by arousal threshold and by the appearance of the EEG. D-sleep (dreaming sleep), however, does not fit into that continuum. Human EEG data alone might indicate that D-sleep is a light sleep. But the arousal threshold in animals is higher in D-sleep than in S-sleep, and resting muscle potential is lowest during D-sleep. Thus, D-sleep is neither truly light sleep nor deep sleep but a qualitatively different kind of sleep (Jouvet, 1962; Snyder, 1963; Hartmann, 1967a).

The constant and regular characteristics of a night of normal sleep are sensitive indicators of disturbance. They can be used to study alterations associated with various forms of pathology or produced by various drugs.

Much of the basic work on sleep derives from studies by Aserinsky, Kleitman, and Dement in the 1950's (Aserinsky and Kleitman, 1953; Dement and Kleitman, 1957; Kleitman, 1963). A number of recent reviews are also available (Hartmann, 1973; Williams et al., 1974; Mendelson et al., 1977).

Phylogeny

According to the behavioral definition of sleep, most vertebrates may be said to display some form of sleep. Fish and amphibians have periods of quiescence accompanied by increased response threshold. However, concomitant EEG or other recordings have not demonstrated clear-cut differences between sleep and waking. Reptiles show behavioral sleep and recordings somewhat similar to mammalian S-sleep; in a few instances, brief episodes of a state resembling D-sleep have also been recorded. Birds have definite periods of both S-sleep and D-sleep,

although the D-periods are generally very short and account for only a small percentage of total sleep time (Allison et al., 1970).

Among mammals, the two states of sleep have been studied in a wide variety of species. Almost all mammals have S-sleep and D-sleep. D-sleep seems to be absent in a single very primitive mammal, the spiny anteater (Allison et al., 1970). That fact could have important implications in helping to determine when the differentiation of the two states of sleep arose phylogenetically. Also, the spiny anteater has surprisingly complicated-looking cerebral hemispheres for an otherwise primitive species. D-sleep may be an innovation, one that allows later mammals to do more efficiently whatever tasks the anteater's elaborate hemispheres perform. The exact tasks are not yet certain.

No obvious relationships have yet emerged among mammalian species in terms of amounts of S-sleep and D-sleep (Allison and Van Twyver, 1970; Zepelin and Rechtschaffen, 1974), but there are some differences, and many explanations have been proposed. The so-called higher mammals, such as humans and apes, show neither more or less sleep nor more or less D-time than the lower forms. Within closely related species like the rodents, the animals that are usually preyed on—rabbits, for example—have less D-time than do the predators, such as rats. To some extent that distinction holds true across many groups of mammals—carnivores tend to have more D-time than do herbivores, and the amount of D-time recorded in omnivores falls between the two—and makes sense from the point of view of adaptation and selection, since the muscular relaxation of the D-state makes an animal especially vulnerable, and long D-periods are especially disadvantageous to the herbivores and other preyed-on animals.

Even though the relationship of D-sleep and S-sleep among species is not entirely clear, a definite relationship can be seen between the basal metabolic rate of a species and the length of its sleep-dream cycle, usually defined as the time from the end of one D-period to the end of the next. Small mammals with high metabolic rates have shorter sleep-dream cycles than do larger mammals with lower metabolic rates. There is an inverse relationship between the metabolic rate of a species and its sleep-dream cycle length (Hartmann, 1967a, 1968b) (see Figure 3). Indeed, the same relationship can be found between the metabolic rate and the length of the pulse cycle, the respiratory cycle, the gestation period, and the life-span. That similarity helps establish the fact that the sleep-dream cycle is one of the basic bodily cycles in mammals.

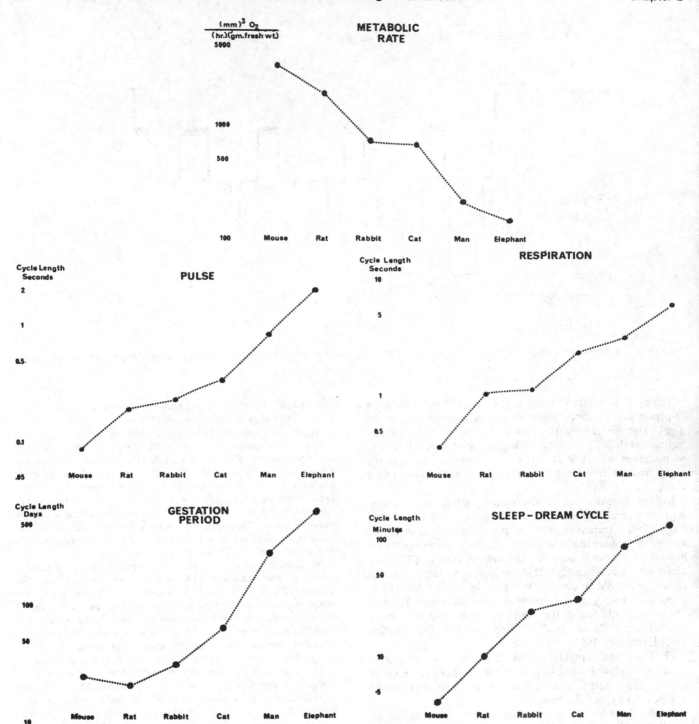

FIGURE 3. Cycle length of four cycles and basal metabolic rate in six mammalian species. (From Hartmann, E. *The Biology of Dreaming*. Charles C Thomas, Springfield, Ill., 1967a.)

Ontogenetic Development

One of the consistent findings in sleep research is that the young of any species always have more sleep time and considerably more D-time than do the adults. The young adult human spends 16 to 17 hours awake every day and 7 to 8 hours asleep, and perhaps 6 of the sleeping hours are spent in S-sleep and 1½ hours in D-sleep. Both S-sleep and D-sleep, on the average, decrease slightly with increasing age (Roffwarg et al.,

1966) (see Figure 4). The newborn child sleeps 16 to 18 hours a day, at least half of it in D-sleep. Although exact definitions and scorings of S-sleep and D-sleep are somewhat problematic in young children, that finding has been repeatedly confirmed and suggests that D-sleep is, developmentally, a very primitive state.

The same ontogenetic relationship seems to hold for other mammalian species. The young mammal always sleeps more than the adult and has an especially high percentage of D-time.

In addition, the sleep-dream cycle is clearly present at birth and is generally shorter in the newborn of any species than in the adult of that species.

Peripheral Physiology

One of the most intriguing aspects of recent sleep research was the finding of the differences in physiological functioning and control mechanisms in sleep and waking—or, more accurately, differences between the states of waking, S-sleep, and D-sleep. The control of physiological functions during sleep is not only of theoretical interest but proving important in terms of the understanding of the recently discovered sleep disorders.

Simple recordings of various physiological measures—pulse, blood pressure, respiration, muscle potential, galvanic skin response, penile erections—reveal some fairly clear-cut patterns. In normal persons, S-sleep is a peaceful state relative to waking (Dement and Kleitman, 1957; Snyder et al., 1964; Hartmann, 1967a). Pulse rate is typically slowed, 5 or 10 beats a minute below the level of restful waking, and the pulse during S-sleep is very regular. Respiration behaves in the same way, and blood pressure also tends to be low, with few minute-to-minute variations (Snyder et al., 1964). Resting muscle potential of body musculature is lower in S-sleep than in waking. There are no or few rapid eye movements and seldom any penile erections. Blood flow through most tissues, including cerebral blood flow, is also slightly reduced.

Thus, in most ways S-sleep is a quiet and peaceful sleep. However, the deepest portions of S-sleep—stages 3 and 4—are sometimes associated with unusual arousal characteristics. When someone is aroused ½ to 1 hour after sleep onset—usually in stage 3 or stage 4—he finds himself disoriented and would probably do poorly on a formal mental status examination at such a time. In certain persons the disorganization during arousal from stage 3 or stage 4 results in specific problems, including enuresis, somnambulism, and stage 4 nightmares or night-terrors (Gastaut and Broughton, 1965). Also, the galvanic skin response (GSR), which shows little activity during most of S-sleep, sometimes suddenly demonstrates greatly heightened activity (GSR storms) during stage 4 sleep (Shapiro, 1962). That phenomenon may also represent an unusual partial arousal during what is normally the deepest and most peaceful sleep.

D-sleep is considerably different. Many polygraphic measures show irregular patterns sometimes close to aroused waking patterns. Indeed, if one were not aware of the behavioral state of the person or animal and one happened to be recording a variety of physiological measures (but not muscle potential) during D-periods, one would undoubtedly conclude that the person or animal was in an active waking state. Pulse, respiration, and blood pressure in humans are all high during D-sleep—much higher than during S-sleep and quite often higher than during waking. Even more striking than the level or rate is the variability from minute to minute. The highest and the lowest pulse and respiratory rates of the night usually occur during D-sleep (Snyder et al., 1964). D-sleep is also associated with rapid conjugate movements of the eyes and, in the very young human or animal, rapid phasic movements of other small muscles (Parmelee et al., 1962; Roffwarg et al., 1966). Almost every D-period is accompanied, in the human male, as well as in other species, by a partial or full penile erection; this has been demonstrated in the monkey, as well as in man (Ohlmeyer and Brilmayer, 1947; Fisher et al., 1965; Karacan et al., 1972). All that aroused-appearing activity is superimposed on a very relaxed muscular state: muscular potential recorded from the major skeletal muscles, especially the antigravity muscles, shows the least activity during D-sleep; the muscles are even more relaxed during D-sleep than during S-sleep (Jouvet, 1962; Jacobson et al., 1964). That "arousal," combined with a relaxed musculature and a relatively high arousal threshold, is the reason D-sleep or REM sleep has also been called paradoxical sleep.

As far as the body's physiology is concerned, D-sleep could be called an active and aroused state—but with muscular immobility. That description could also be applied to the psychological state during dreaming; most typical dreams are reported from D-sleep. In a dream, one is conscious and apparently aware—watching things, experiencing emotions, getting involved—and yet all without being able to move a muscle.

Control Mechanisms

The above has referred simply to what can be learned from straightforward recordings across time of a given physiological variable. Recent investigations have begun to attack questions about control mechanisms. For instance: How does the body's respiratory apparatus respond to hypoxia and to hypercapnia? How does the body's temperature-regulating system respond to cold and to heat? Each control system, controlling a physiological function, has its own peculiarities. However, an important over-all statement is that control systems cannot be expected to act in the same way during the sleep states as they do during waking. There are numerous instances of different control mechanisms in sleep, especially during D-sleep. For instance, Chase (1974, 1975) demonstrated that a given stimulus that produces contraction of a jaw muscle group (the digastric reflex) produces one effect during waking and S-sleep but the opposite effect during D-sleep. In other words, some of the brain's control mechanisms are state dependent; they are heavily dependent on whether the organism is awake, in S-sleep, or in D-sleep.

Aside from that general change in control mechanisms, one striking over-all finding recurs over and over in different control systems. Parmeggiani and Sabattini (1972) did a series of studies of temperature control and concluded that, whereas homeothermic temperature control is present during S-sleep and not too different from that during waking, during D-sleep the mammal becomes cold-blooded—that is, there is no proper homeothermic control of temperature. Papousek (1975) demonstrated that during D-sleep there is no longer the normal adaptation in certain reflex responses involving facial muscles in children. There is also a major disturbance in the control of respiration during D-sleep (Parmeggiani et al., 1976; Phillipson

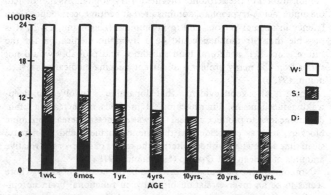

FIGURE 4. Time spent in waking (*W*) and the two sleep stages.

et al., 1976). Putting all those findings together with the information about the extreme irregularity of most measures during D-sleep, one could conclude that D-sleep is characterized by poorly controlled feedback characteristics. In 1967, the author pointed out that D-sleep is a state with a high activity level but poorly regulated feedback control (Hartmann, 1967a). The organism seems to have lost its normal subtle capacities for monitoring the environment and adjusting its own parameters necessary to maintain a homeostasis. This may be of importance, because the lack of feedback monitoring of the environment and lack of normal homeostasis may also be characteristic of schizophrenia (Hartmann, 1976b). That is one of the ways in which the biology of dreaming may be related to the biology of schizophrenia.

Neurophysiology

Maintenance of the waking state depends on the activity of the ascending reticular activating system (ARAS), which sends impulses to the forebrain. For some time after the discovery of the ARAS, it was assumed that sleep supervenes whenever ARAS activity falls below a certain level—the passive theory of sleep. It now appears that several active processes subserve sleep. Synchronized sleep in animals probably depends on the activity of certain centers in the brain stem (Jouvet, 1962; Moruzzi, 1962), especially the raphe nuclei (Jouvet and Renault, 1966), and certain areas in the medial forebrain; other areas in the hypothalamus and the thalamus, among others, cannot be entirely excluded. It is possible but not certain that all those regions eventually exert an influence on ARAS activity. In addition, a brain stem system is necessary for the initiating and the maintenance of D-sleep; several pontine areas may be involved (Jouvet, 1962, Hobson et al., 1975). A great many studies have delineated the specific neurophysiological characteristics of the two states of sleep (Jouvet, 1962; Moruzzi, 1962; Koella, 1963). There has been great interest in certain brain waves occurring phasically during D-sleep—the pontogeniculooccipital (PGO) waves and other neural patterns characteristic of D-sleep (Brooks and Bizzi, 1963)—since those patterns show a rebound after deprivation and may be related to eye movements and to dreaming (Dement et al., 1969).

The question of whether there are one or more true sleep centers has intrigued investigators for many years. The weight of the evidence indicates that a number of important sleep centers or systems are located in the brain stem or, at least, originate in the brain stem. Concentrating on them by no means implies that the remainder of the brain is unnecessary or unimportant for normal sleep; rather, the initiation of various states probably involves those brain stem areas.

First, the broad central gray matter of the brain stem—called the ascending reticular activating system (ARAS)—is definitely involved in maintaining wakefulness (Moruzzi and Magoun, 1949). Within that broad area, specific monoamine-containing pathways—especially the dopamine pathways, with cell bodies in the mesencephalon and widespread endings in the forebrain—seem to be implicated in arousal or waking. Some evidence also implicates norepinephrine.

Second, the serotonin in the raphe nuclei of the brain stem, containing almost all the brain's serotonergic cell bodies, definitely plays a role in sleep. The destruction of that area (Jouvet and Renault, 1966) or the prevention of serotonin synthesis (Koella et al., 1968; Dement et al., 1972) reduces sleep for a considerable time. The raphe system has sometimes been said to influence only S-sleep, but the data suggest, rather, that the serotonin-containing raphe system is definitely necessary, although not sufficient, for normal sleep of both kinds to occur. Brain noradrenergic systems, with cell bodies in the brain stem, are clearly involved in regulating the states of sleep. The best evidence from many investigations, including the studies in the author's own laboratory, is that the ascending noradrenergic systems originating from the locus coeruleus and other brain stem norepinephrine regions play an inhibitory role in D-sleep (Hartmann, 1970, 1973).

A region in the lower brain stem containing giant cells—the frontal gigantocellular fields (FTG)—may play a direct role in initiating D-periods. Those cells were first reported to fire almost exclusively just before and at the end of D-periods (Hobson et al., 1974). McCarley and Hobson proposed a hypothesis that the states of sleep are regulated by a process of reciprocal inhibition between those FTG cells and the locus coeruleus (Hobson et al., 1975; McCarley and Hobson, 1975). However, it has recently been shown that those neurons fire quite actively during certain waking movements (Siegel et al., 1977; Vertes, 1977) and are thus not as specific to D-sleep as was first postulated. Nonetheless, the concept of reciprocal inhibition or something similar may be useful in explaining such phenomena as the oscillation between the two states of sleep; such regulation is somewhat similar to the reciprocal inhibition that regulates the inspiratory and expiratory phases of the respiratory cycle. It seems likely that a reciprocal relationship involves the raphe nuclei and perhaps other areas in addition to the relation between the FTG cells and the locus coeruleus.

The most probable conclusion at present is that there is not one sleep center but a small number of systems or centers, probably located chiefly in the brain stem, which mutually activate and inhibit one another—while accepting various inputs from other systems—and among them regulate the states of sleep and waking.

Chemistry

A great deal of work has helped to elucidate the basic neurochemistry of sleep. The best evidence involves the monoamines, with cell bodies in the brain stem. The neurohumor most clearly involved is brain serotonin. The author suggested in the mid-1960's that serotonin is involved in the mechanisms underlying sleep, especially D-sleep (Hartmann, 1966, 1967c). Studies demonstrated that the administration of the serotonin precursor *l*-tryptophan induces sleep (reduces sleep latency) and tends to increase total sleep and to increase D-sleep time in humans, as well as in animals, without altering the states and stages of sleep (Hartmann, 1967c, 1977; Hartmann et al., 1971b).

In 1966 anatomical studies in Sweden demonstrated by fluorometric methods that most or all brain serotonin derives from neurons in a small brain stem area—the raphe system (Dahlstrom and Fuxe, 1965; Hillarp et al., 1966). Jouvet's group then performed studies investigating lesions of those systems (Jouvet and Renault, 1966). In the cat, the greater the amount of raphe nuclei destroyed, the lower was the total brain serotonin level, and the lower were the animal's total sleep levels. At the same time, Koella and others demonstrated that inhibition of tryptophan hydroxylase, which reduces serotonin levels, also reduced total sleep levels greatly (Koella et al., 1968; Dement et al., 1972).

A large number of studies support the role of serotonin in sleep. The best evidence supports a role for serotonin underlying both states of sleep. In cats serotonin seems more closely related to S-sleep, but in humans some evidence links it more closely to D-sleep (Hartmann, 1967c, 1970; Mendelson et al., 1977; Gillin et al., 1978). These findings have important practical implications. One of the best ways to raise brain serotonin levels at its normal sites of occurrence is by the administration of the serotonin precursor *l*-tryptophan. As mentioned, the amino acid *l*-tryptophan, administered at bedtime, can reduce sleep latency in normal persons and in insomniacs (Hartmann, 1977). It is possible that *l*-tryptophan could be a hypnotic medication for the future, since it is a natural food substance and probably would not suffer from the many problems of current sleeping medications (Hartmann, 1978b).

There is also good evidence that dopamine is involved in sleep-waking mechanisms. Pharmacological methods of increasing brain dopamine tend to produce arousal and wakefulness, whereas dopamine blockers, such as pimozide and the phenothiazines, tend to increase sleep time somewhat, without altering the cycles of sleep or the relative amounts of S-sleep and D-sleep (Hartmann, 1978a).

Norepinephrine may also be involved in the control of sleep. There seems to be an inverse relationship between functional brain norepinephrine and D-sleep. Drugs and manipulations that increase the available brain norepinephrine produce a marked decrease in D-sleep, whereas reducing brain norepinephrine levels increases D-sleep (Hartmann, 1970, 1973, 1978a). That action of norepinephrine almost certainly involves α-adrenergic receptors, since an α-blocker, such as phenoxybenzamine, increases D-time, but a β-blocker, such as propranolol, has no effect (Hartmann and Zwilling, 1976; Hartmann, 1978a).

There is little question that acetylcholine is also involved in sleep, and at one point Hernandez-Peon and Ibarra-Chavez (1963) outlined a series of cholinergic systems that possibly underlie sleep. Recently, it has been demonstrated that physostigmine and similar cholinergic agents can trigger D-sleep in humans (Gillin et al., 1978). Acetylcholine does not occur in well-delineated systems, as do the monoamines, but is extremely widespread in the brain. Thus, it is difficult to relate chemical to neurophysiological findings. However, one aspect of importance may be that the FTG cells—which, as noted above, may play a role in initiating D-periods—appear to be cholinergic. Cholinergic FTG neurons, with synapses at the locus coeruleus, and noradrenergic locus coeruleus neurons, with synapses on FTG cells, could be part of the reciprocal inhibition discussed above.

In addition to the fairly well-established neurochemistry involving amines in the brain stem, substances found by some workers in the cerebrospinal fluid and the blood of sleep-deprived animals may have something to do with initiating sleep. Monnier and Hösli (1964) repeatedly found a sleep-inducing substance in the blood of sleep-deprived rabbits. Similarly, Pappenheimer et al. (1975) found a sleep-inducing substance in the spinal fluid of sleep-deprived goats. Monnier's substance is a nine-amino-acid peptide; Pappenheimer's substance may be an even shorter peptide containing only two to five amino acids. Those findings are intriguing, especially in view of recent work demonstrating the presence of many endogenous peptides in the human brain; however, it is not yet established that those peptides play any role in normal sleep.

Functions

The largest, perhaps most important, and perhaps impossible question in sleep research is: Why sleep? What are the functions of sleep? It is safe to say that the functions of sleep are not yet fully understood. Some researchers have even implied that sleep is a sort of vermiform appendix that may have once served the function of keeping ancestors out of harm's way for a portion of the day but has no remaining function now. Most researchers, however, believe that sleep does serve some restorative function. The problem of function has been approached in a number of ways (Hartmann, 1973). One of the classical techniques in medicine for discovering the function of an organ or system is to attempt to remove it and observe what deficits follow. The technique of sleep deprivation follows that logic.

SLEEP DEPRIVATION

Literally hundreds of investigators have studied sleep deprivation (Williams et al., 1959; Kleitman, 1963; Wilkinson, 1965; Hartmann, 1973). Physiologically, a sleep-deprived subject shows a central (brain) hypoarousal that is combined, at least in certain stages, with an autonomic hyperarousal. After several days of sleep deprivation, the waking EEG shifts away from α and in the direction of lower frequencies; pulse and respiratory rates are frequently increased. Recovery sleep after a period of sleep deprivation involves a great deal of slow-wave sleep (stage 3 sleep and stage 4 sleep) in the first hours and an increase in D-time in subsequent hours or days.

The psychological effects of sleep deprivation have not always been easy to determine and obviously depend a great deal on social and environmental factors. For example, a period of sleep deprivation undergone in an army group in which sleep deprivation is seen as a challenge to be overcome has very different effects from sleep deprivation in a 24-hour marathon group, in which the emphasis is on increasing self-awareness. Many studies have investigated what tasks are especially sensitive to sleep deprivation; over-all, the conclusion has been that the length and the dullness of a task, far more than its difficulty, make it susceptible to disruption by sleep deprivation. The only tasks that have reliably picked up differences between rested persons and persons who have experienced half a night's sleep loss involve hours of monitoring a television display, with responses required when certain symbols are seen. Unfortunately, such results can be interpreted as showing merely that a sleep-deprived person is more likely to fall asleep, since the tasks sensitive to sleep deprivation are exactly those during which one might be expected to doze off at least briefly. Although it has been hard to establish sleep-deprivation effects with objective psychological tests, there are undoubted subjective effects; a person tends to feel bad when he has not slept, and results can be measured on mood-rating forms. Various studies involving adjective checklists have, not surprisingly, found decreases in such scales as alertness and vigor and increases in such scales as confusion and fatigue.

Prolonged periods of sleep deprivation sometimes lead to increasing ego disorganization, hallucinations, and delusions. It has been widely assumed that a long enough period of sleep deprivation produces a psychosis in normal persons, but that assumption cannot be proved with certainty, both because of obvious ethical considerations in conducting research and because the occasional persons who either deprive themselves of sleep for long periods or who volunteer for long-term sleep-deprivation studies must be considered somewhat atypical.

Since the advent of EEG techniques, it has become possible to deprive persons selectively of D-sleep or of the deeper portions of S-sleep; it is not possible to deprive someone completely of synchronized sleep without producing total sleep deprivation. Selective D-sleep deprivation produces two unquestioned effects. First, during the night when the person is awakened at the beginning of each D-period, he makes an increasing number of beginnings or attempts to have a D-period; although four or five awakenings are sufficient for total D-sleep deprivation on the first night, 20 to 30 awakenings are often required by the fifth night, and it is often impossible to continue the study much longer than that. Second, the recovery sleep is usually characterized by greatly increased D-sleep (rebound increase) (Dement, 1960). Psychological effects are less certain. Although it was first reported that D-sleep deprivation produced disorganization and would eventually produce psychosis, in line with suggestions by Freud and others, recent results have not been conclusive (Vogel, 1968). It has been possible to differentiate only to a limited extent psychological changes produced by D-sleep deprivation from those produced by stage 4 sleep deprivation. A study by Agnew et al. (1967) did describe some differences: greater physical lethargy in persons deprived of stage 4 sleep and more irritability and social difficulties in the D-sleep-deprived group.

Thus, the studies on sleep deprivation give hints as to the functions of sleep but not much hard data. People are able to get along without sleep for several days without gross disturbances. The hints suggest that S-sleep has some restorative role relating to lethargy or physical fatigue and that D-sleep has some function in restoring more subtle mental and social functioning. But nothing can be considered established on the basis of sleep-deprivation studies alone.

SLEEP REQUIREMENT

Another possible approach to the functions of sleep involves examining the question of sleep requirement. There are considerable differences in sleep requirements. If one can find persons who require much less sleep than most, one can inquire as to what characterizes those persons physiologically or psychologically. The author and his colleagues have completed two studies of long sleepers and short sleepers. Short sleepers are defined as persons who, according to their own reports and supported by a 2-week sleep log, always sleep less than 6 hours a night and are functioning adequately. Long sleepers are persons who always sleep more than 9 hours a night and are functioning adequately. Persons who complained about their sleep (insomniacs) were not included. The more complete of the two studies used only men (Hartmann et al., 1971a, 1972), so the following results are more definitely true of men than of women, although the results in women, at least in female short sleepers, in a smaller study were quite compatible with the results in men (Spinweber and Hartmann, 1977).

First of all, there were no obvious physical differences between the long sleepers, the normal sleepers, and the short sleepers, nor were there differences in the results of standard laboratory tests, tests of thyroid function, and so on. However, studies in the sleep laboratory demonstrated some clear differences. Figure 5 presents the most defi-

nite result. In a comparison of 10 long sleepers, 10 normal sleepers, and 10 short sleepers (comparing nights 3, 4, and 5 of sleep in the laboratory), the length of time spent in slow-wave sleep (stage 3 sleep and stage 4 sleep) was almost exactly equal in the three groups. The amount of D-sleep showed the greatest differences between the two groups: The short sleepers averaged 65 minutes a night, and the long sleepers averaged 121 minutes a night. The researchers went further and looked at numbers of eye movements within D-periods, since those movements are sometimes considered a measure of the intensity of D-sleep and are related to the intensity or the vividness of dreaming. They found that the long sleepers were by no means having long and empty D-periods; rather, they had still more eye movements per time (REM density) than the short sleepers. Over the course of a night, the long sleepers had 1½ times as much sleep as the short sleepers, twice as much D-time, and 3 times as many rapid eye movements during D-periods.

Those sleep laboratory results suggest that there is a relatively constant need for a certain amount of slow-wave sleep; those three different groups of persons all obtained 70 to 80 minutes of slow-wave sleep a night. The data suggest that, insofar as there is a need for D-sleep—which, admittedly, has not been firmly established—the need may be quite different in different groups, and it is worth exploring further in what ways the groups may differ.

The researchers found some interesting psychological results. In quantitative psychological tests, the long sleepers scored significantly higher than did the short sleepers on two subscales of the Cornell Index (nervousness-anxiety, and pathological mood). On the Minnesota Multiphasic Personality Inventory, the long sleepers scored significantly higher on the social introversion scale and significantly lower on the lie scale. The long sleepers also scored significantly lower than the short sleepers on the California Personality Index scales of social presence, tolerance, and flexibility. On the basis of those results and long psychiatric interviews, the researchers felt that the short sleepers could be characterized as a group of persons who were generally efficient, energetic, ambitious, socially adept, and satisfied with themselves and their lives. They were relatively free of psychopathology; insofar as there was any psychopathology, it was in the direction of denial and avoidance problems. In some cases it approached hypomania. The long sleepers were a group who had various types of minor psychopathology—usually mild depression, anxiety, or simply shyness; they were also a group of nonconformist thinkers and worriers. In fact, the simplest one-word differentiation of the groups involves the word "worry." The long sleepers were definitely worriers; they worried about their own lives, about the state of the world, about the research study. The short sleepers were striking nonworriers who tended to take the attitude "Nothing I can do about it; so why worry?" and "I might as well keep busy." In computer terms the long sleepers could be seen as reprograming themselves every day and changing their ways of functioning, whereas the short sleepers appeared to be preprogramed; they had found a way of doing things that they liked, and they kept doing them that way.

Those clear-cut differences quite possibly apply only to extreme groups of constant long sleepers and short sleepers. The persons studied had maintained their pattern of long sleep or short sleep for a period of years. Another group studying long sleepers and short sleepers among college freshmen on the basis of their answers on a questionnaire could find no clear-cut psychological differences between the groups (Webb and Agnew, 1970).

The results provided possible hints about the functions of sleep. They suggest, at least, that more sleep, especially more D-sleep, is required by persons with life styles characterized by worry, mild depression, or anxiety. They suggest that sleep, especially D-sleep, may have some function in dealing with or restoring the brain and the mind after days of such worry and disturbance (Hartmann, 1973).

Aside from the relationship to the functions of sleep, those results confirm that some persons who function normally in

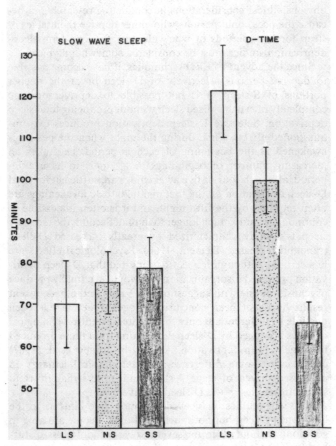

FIGURE 5. Slow-wave sleep (stages 3 and 4) and dreaming sleep (D-time) in long sleepers (*LS*), normal sleepers (*NS*), and short sleepers (*SS*). *Bars* indicate standard deviations. (From Hartmann, E., Baekeland, F., and Zwilling, G. Psychological differences between long and short sleepers. Arch. Gen. Psychiatry, *26*: 463, 1972.)

society always sleep more than 9 hours and others always sleep less than 6 hours. However, after many months of newspaper ads by Hartmann's group in Boston and Baekland's group in New York, they never found a person who regularly slept less than 4½ hours. The over-all conclusion with regard to sleep requirement is that, with perhaps extremely rare exceptions, there is a minimum requirement for at least 4 or 5 hours of sleep in normal humans.

Are there persons who require more sleep at certain times of their lives than at other times in their lives? If so, what characterizes the times of high sleep need and the times of low sleep need? The author and his colleagues asked people about periods lasting at least weeks or months; they were not interested in changes in sleep requirements for a day or a few days. They were definitely not studying insomniacs—persons who complain about their sleep or who were obtaining insufficient sleep. They were studying persons who reported that they required more sleep or less sleep at certain times. It was not a laboratory study, since periods of increased or decreased sleep need could not be predicted and studied in the laboratory. Two studies involved a series of questionnaires and interviews and included a total of 501 persons who gave usable responses (Hartmann, 1973).

The over-all results are tabulated in Table I. The only time when persons routinely reported requiring less sleep were times that could be summarized as "everything is going well." Those times often involved intense involvement in enjoyable work or something of the kind. Increased need for sleep was reported under a number of circumstances. A series of factor analyses separated those circumstances into two groups: One involved increased sleep at times of physical work and exercise, included in Table I, and also times of pregnancy and illness, not included in the table. The other factor involves the four other columns in Table I; more sleep was required at times of change in occupation, increased mental activity, depressed or upset mood, and stressful periods.

More data were obtained as well; over-all increased sleep need was associated with times of worry or concern. For instance, five persons who had been fairly long sleepers reported, somewhat to their surprise, a considerable decrease in sleep requirement over the course of a successful psychoanalysis. They could not associate the change with any specific events in the analysis, and it was not a sudden change, but it seemed to be related to an over-all decrease in psychic conflict—less anxiety and worry—after treatment.

Many persons described definite changes in sleep requirement associated with changes in occupation and life style. One especially striking case involved a student who had a marked change in his life about 2 years before the interview. He was a man in his thirties who had spent much of his life as a laborer. His typical day at that time involved moderately heavy physical work and very little thinking or worry. Two years before the interview, he had entered a distinguished university in a special program for intelligent persons who had not had the opportunity to attend college. His life changed greatly in that for the next 2 years he did chiefly intellectual work, rather than physical work; because of his limited previous schooling and slow reading speed, it was a stressful and emotionally difficult time. He reported that his average sleep time had been 1 or 2 hours more in those last 2 years than previously and that he definitely could not get along without the extra sleep. Again, increased sleep need is associated with intellectual and emotional work. That case is important because the sleep change was clearly in the direction opposite to what would have been convenient—that is, he would have loved to have slept less and to have had more time, rather than less time, available for studying.

Several professional men, reliable and trained observers, reported that, when they retired and stopped the considerable intellectual work and emotional stress that had characterized their working lives, their sleep requirement definitely decreased. Again, more sleep is associated with intellectual and emotional effort, and the change is opposite to what one would expect and what they themselves had expected—that retirement would be associated with more sleep.

Over-all, those results on variable sleepers support the same conclusions as the results on long sleepers and short sleepers. Short sleep times are associated with relatively happy, effortless, preprogramed functioning and with a life style involved in keeping busy and not worrying; long sleep times are associated with worry, conflict, changes in one's life, and reprograming. Sleep, especially D-sleep, may have a role in the restoration of the brain and the mental apparatus after such a change or stress.

OTHER APPROACHES

Many other bits of evidence help in organizing a theory of the functions of sleep. Not only is sleep time greater in the very young organism, but both D-sleep and slow-wave sleep—stage 3 and stage 4—are especially high in young children and young animals, as discussed above. That fact certainly suggests a role for sleep in the development of the body or the brain. Sleep studies in groups of mentally retarded persons and in the aged

TABLE I
*Periods Associated with Increased or Decreased Sleep Need**

	Increased Physical Work or Exercise	A Change in Occupation	Increased Mental Activity	Depressed or Upset Mood	Stressful Period	Times When Everything Goes Well
Study 1						
Reports of:						
Increased sleep need	81	42	57	71	60	9
Decreased sleep need	23	11	31	21	41	46
No definite change (or no such period)	139	190	155	151	142	188
Study 2						
Reports of:						
Increased sleep need	83	29	67	81	69	4
Decreased sleep need	14	3	13	9	16	46
No definite change (or no such period)	161	226	178	168	173	208

* From Hartmann, H., and Brewer, V. When is more or less sleep required: A study of variable sleepers. Compr. Psychiatry, *17*: 215, 1976.

with and without cognitive deficits (Feinberg and Carlson, 1968; Feinberg, 1968) suggest a role for D-sleep in learning processes.

Also important is the fact that D-sleep is increased after certain psychological stimuli, including many different learning situations in animals (Block, 1970), after direct brain stimulation of the reticular activating system (Frederickson and Hobson, 1970), and after many chemical or pharmacological manipulations that result in a reduction of functional brain catecholamines (Hartmann, 1970, 1978a).

Sleep does have a restorative function—in fact, two closely linked restorative functions. The function of S-sleep, which always precedes D-sleep, probably involves the anabolism and synthesis of macromolecules (protein or RNA), some of which may be used during subsequent D-sleep. The functions of D-sleep seem to involve repair, reorganization, the formation of new connections in the cortex and in the norepinephrine systems ascending to the cortex—systems required for optimal attention mechanisms—and secondary-process functions during waking (see Figure 6) (Hartmann, 1973). Obviously, there is not yet total agreement about the functions of sleep, and some workers maintain that sleep may be an unnecessary habit with no real function.

Sleep and Mental Illness

On the whole, laboratory-recorded sleep patterns show a surprising consistency across subjects, and the basic patterns are not easily altered by physical or mental illness. Definite alterations are found in some of the specific sleep disorders—for instance, in narcolepsy—but are not routinely found in mental illness.

Despite expectations based on associations with dreaming, the laboratory sleep of most schizophrenic patients turns out to be relatively normal in its basic structure. There are some differences: During acute episodes, sleep is often disturbed and D-time is low (Mendelson et al., 1977), but it is not likely that the change is intrinsic to the schizophrenic process; it is more probably an effect of extreme anxiety. Some chronic schizophrenic patients show normal sleep patterns. In others, slow-wave sleep (stage 3 and stage 4) is markedly decreased; that decrease may be related to the postulated central hyperarousal of certain schizophrenic patients (Mendelson et al., 1977).

Mania and depression are more regularly associated with unusual sleep patterns. EEG studies have confirmed the short sleep time usually found in manic patients; all stages of sleep seem to be reduced to a certain extent, although there is some disagreement among studies. In the author's investigations, D-sleep especially was reduced, but stage 4 sleep remained close to normal levels (Hartmann, 1968a). The sleep in manic patients can be considered an extreme form of the sleep found in short sleepers; psychologically, manic patients show in extreme form the defenses of keeping busy and denial that are prominent in short sleepers.

Sleep is usually also abnormal in depression, and several distinct patterns can be described. The most frequent sleep pattern in severe depression involves insomnia—especially difficulty in remaining asleep, rather than difficulty in falling asleep. Laboratory sleep studies have confirmed that many severely depressed patients have frequent awakenings during the night, as well as early morning awakenings; in addition, the records show increased shifts between stages, reduced slow-wave sleep time, reduced D-latency, and sometimes reduced D-sleep (Mendelson et al., 1977).

Other depressed patients have hypersomnia—increased total sleep time—without dramatic alterations in sleep stages and usually with increased D-time. That pattern has been seen in neurotic depressions in young patients; the physiology and the

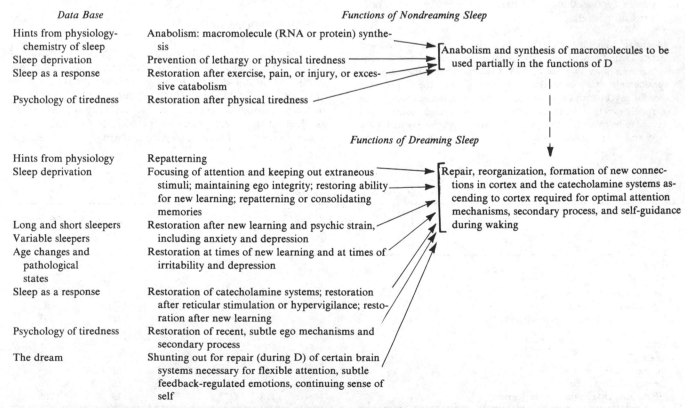

FIGURE 6. The functions of sleep. (From Hartmann, E. *The Functions of Sleep.* Yale University Press, New Haven, Conn., 1973.)

psychology are comparable to those seen in long sleepers. Hypersomnia and increased D-time have also been recorded in more severe depressions, especially in the depressed phase of manic-depressive illness (Hartmann, 1968a).

One could say that most depressed patients demonstrate an increased tendency to have D-sleep. Some actually have increased D-time; others, with severely disturbed sleep patterns, have normal or low D-time. But almost all manifest a decreased D-latency, a lengthened initial D-period, and increased eye movements during D-periods.

There is no general agreement about the theoretical relationship between sleep and depression. The empirical findings could be explained by postulating two factors: (1) an increased requirement or tendency for D-sleep, present in most or all depression; this factor could be related to decreased functional norepinephrine in the brain; (2) an inability to remain asleep, which is present in some severely depressed patients; this factor could be related to decreased functional serotonin and, therefore, a deficient functioning of the serotonin-dependent sleep systems.

At times, sleep patterns, as determined in the laboratory or simply by careful clinical history, can help in diagnosis and prognosis. Sleep disturbance is an important if nonspecific indicator that something is wrong. An acute or subacute onset of insomnia is always worth investigating. It may be related to organic causes, but it has also been shown to be one of the earliest symptoms to precede suicide attempts and psychotic episodes (Detre, 1966).

Some patterns recorded in the sleep laboratory suggest certain psychiatric diagnoses. As mentioned, a pattern involving no problem in sleep onset but frequent awakenings during the second half of the night and early morning awakening, with short D-latency and reduced stage 3 and stage 4 sleep, is characteristic of depression. Such a pattern may lead one to investigate further for occult signs of depression, even in someone who does not present primarily as a depressed patient. Within groups of depressed patients, an inverse relationship has been reported between D-latency and severity of depression (Kupfer and Foster, 1972). D-latency always tends to be short in depressed patients, especially in primary depression, but its length may be a measure of severity. In schizophrenic patients, a short D-latency may characterize those patients with an affective component—schizoaffective patients (Reich et al., 1975).

Certain sleep patterns have also been shown to be characteristic for certain patients with mental deficiencies, but so far sleep study does not seem to be of much use in diagnosis in those areas.

Sleep studies are often useful in the diagnosis of patients who present with specific symptoms of sleep disorder—insomnia (difficulty in sleeping or too little sleep), hypersomnia (too much sleep), excessive daytime sleepiness or sleep attacks, episodic events during the night. Each of these symptoms can have a number of specific courses which are discussed under sleep disorders.

Sleeping Pills

The availability of sleep laboratory recordings and renewed interest in sleep over the past 20 years has brought about greater interest in one of the oldest types of medications: the sleeping pill. Sleeping pills are used in huge quantities by psychiatrists and by other physicians. About 3 billion doses a year are used in the United States. Much of that is unnecessary use and provides a serious cause for concern.

A number of problems are associated with the use of sleeping pills. The effects of sleeping pills and other drugs on laboratory-recorded sleep have been investigated in hundreds of studies, many of them concentrating on sleeping pills (Williams and Karacan, 1976; Hartmann, 1978b). One over-all finding from those sleep laboratory studies is that almost all sleeping pills greatly distort the normal patterns of recorded sleep. The most usual change is a great reduction in D-time, but some of the most widely used sleeping pills, the benzodiazepines, reduce stage 4 sleep as well. Thus, what is recorded after a sleeping pill is taken is not normal sleep by polygraphic criteria but could well be called mild anesthesia or mild coma. It is not yet certain whether those distortions of sleep patterns are in themselves dangerous, but any long-term distortion of brain-wave activity bears at least a potential for danger. Some studies describe problems in psychomotor functioning the morning after a sleeping pill is used (Bixler et al., 1975) and even the possibility of increased death rates in persons taking sleeping medications (Kripke and Simons, 1976), although the relationship has not been proved to be a causal one.

A historical survey makes it clear that, with very few exceptions, sleeping pills have been dangerous drugs. Most of them have a low therapeutic index and frequently cause accidental or intentional death. Sleeping pills have almost invariably become drugs of abuse. Addiction to them is extremely common. In addition, withdrawal from those drugs is often quite unpleasant and may last for a period of weeks. Withdrawal from certain hypnotic medications, such as barbiturates, can also be associated with convulsions.

The body rapidly develops a tolerance to sleeping pills. Therefore, unless the dose is increased, the drugs are usually no longer effective in producing beneficial effects on sleep after a few weeks. That phenomenon has been shown in the sleep laboratory. It is true that most persons taking hypnotic medications for long periods continue to take a low dose, but their sleep on the low dose is in most cases no better than was their sleep without the medication; in other words, they are taking sleeping medication to avoid withdrawal effects, rather than for any direct beneficial effect. Also, sleeping medications are not rapidly cleared by the body; increased enzyme activity must be induced, and the drug itself or one of its active metabolites often has a very long half-life. That fact may account for the frequent complaints of hangover effects after sleeping pills are taken. Finally, there are problems of allergy, hypersensitivity, and interactions with other medications. Some of the hypnotic drugs are well known to be especially problematic in terms of drug interactions.

The author believes that many problems stem from the fact that sleeping pills have simply been nonspecific central nervous system depressants; they have nothing to do with the normal physiology or chemistry of sleep (Hartmann, 1978b). It is possible that in the future a sleeping pill such as l-tryptophan, which is related to the body's normal sleep mechanisms, may avoid most of those problems (Hartmann, 1977).

Insomnia is not an illness for which a sleeping pill is the remedy. Insomnia is a symptom, and it can be a symptom of many different medical and psychiatric conditions, each of which has its own treatment.

Suggested Cross References

The neurochemistry and the neurophysiology of behavior are discussed in Section 2.4 and Section 2.5, respectively. Biological rhythms in psychiatry are discussed in Section 2.6. Neurology is discussed in Chapter 3. Experimental disorders are discussed in Section 6.3. Schizophrenic disorders are discussed in Chapter 15, schizoaffective disorders in Chapter 17, and affective disorders in Chapters 18 and 19. Sleep disorders, including insomnia, are discussed in Section 27.3. Suicide is discussed in Section 29.1. Enuresis is discussed in Section 43.10.

REFERENCES

Agnew, H. W., Jr., Webb, W. B., and Williams, R. L. Comparison of stage four and l-REM sleep deprivation. Percept. Mot. Skills, *24:* 851, 1967.

Allison, T., and Van Twyver, H. The evolution of sleep. Natural History, *79:* 56, 1970.

Allison, T., Van Twyver, G., and Goff, W. F. Electrophysiological studies of the echidna. Tachyglossus aculeatus. Waking and sleep. Arch. Ital. Biol., *110:* 145, 1970.

Aserinsky, E., and Kleitman, N. Regularly occurring periods of eye motility and concomitant phenomena during sleep. Science, *118:* 273, 1953.

Bixler, E. O., Ccharf, M. B., Leo, L. A., and Kales, A. Hypnotic drugs and performance: A review of theoretical and methodical considerations. In *Hypnotics: Methods of Development and Evaluation*, F. Kagan, T. Harwood, K. Rickels, A. D. Rudzik, and H. Sarer, editors, p. 175. Spectrum, New York, 1975.

Block, V. Facts and hypotheses concerning memory consolidation processes. Brain Res., *24:* 561, 1970.

Brooks, D., and Bizzi, E. Brain stem electrical activity during sleep. Arch. Ital. Biol., *101:* 648, 1963.

Chase, M. H. Central neural control of brainstem somatic reflexes during sleeping and waking. Adv. Sleep Res., *1:* 251, 1974.

Chase, M. H. A model of reticular control of motor activity during wakefulness and active sleep. Sleep Res., *4:* 25, 1975.

Dahlstrom, A., and Fuxe, K. Evidence for the existence of monoamine-containing neurons in the central nervous system. 1. Demonstration of monoamines in the cell bodies of brain stem neurons. Acta Physiol. Scand., *62* (Suppl.): 1, 1965.

Dement, W. C. The effect of dream deprivation. Science, *131:* 1705, 1960.

Dement, W. C., and Kleitman, N. Cyclic variations in EEG during sleep and their relation to eye movements, body mobility, and dreaming. Electroencephalogr. Clin. Neurophysiol., *9:* 673, 1957.

Dement, W. C., Mitler, M. M., and Henriksen, S. J. Sleep changes during chronic administration of parachlorophenylalanine. Rev. Can. Biol., *31* (Suppl.): 239, 1972.

Dement, W. C., Zarcone, V., Ferguson, J., Cohen, H., Pivik, T., and Barchas, J. Some parallel findings in schizophrenic patients and serotonin-depleted cats. In *Schizophrenia: Current Concepts and Research*, D. B. Siva Sankar, editor, p. 775. PJD Publications, Hicksville, N. Y., 1969.

Detre, T. Sleep disorder and psychosis. Can. Psychiatr. Assoc. J., *11:* S169, 1966.

Feinberg, I. Eye movement activity during sleep and intellectual function in mental retardation. Science, *159:* 1256, 1968.

Feinberg, I., and Carlson, V. R. Sleep variables as a function of age in man. Arch. Gen. Psychiatry, *18:* 239, 1968.

Fisher, C., Gross, J., and Zuch, J. Cycle of penile erection synchronous with dreaming (REM) sleep. Arch. Gen. Psychiatry, *12:* 29, 1965.

Foulkes, D. *The Psychology of Sleep.* Charles Scribner's Sons, New York, 1966.

Frederickson, C. J., and Hobson, J. A. Electrical stimulation of the brain stem and subsequent sleep. Arch. Ital. Biol., *108:* 564, 1970.

Gastaut, H., and Broughton, R. A clinical and polygraphic study of episodic phenomena during sleep. Recent Adv. Biol. Psychiatry, *7:* 197, 1965.

Gillin, J. C., Mendelson, W. B., Sitaram, N., and Wyatt, R. J. The neuropharmacology of sleep and wakefulness. Annu. Rev. Pharmacol. Toxicol., *18:* 563, 1978.

Hartmann, E. Some studies on the biochemistry of dreaming sleep. Excerpta Med. Int., *150:* 3100, 1966.

Hartmann, E. *The Biology of Dreaming.* Charles C Thomas, Springfield, Ill., 1967a.

Hartmann, E. The effect of tryptophan on the sleep dream cycle in man. Psychonom. Sci., *8:* 479, 1967b.

Hartmann, E. The sleep-dream cycle and brain serotonin. Psychonom. Sci., *8:* 295, 1967.

Hartmann, E. Longitudinal studies of sleep and dream patterns in manic-depressive patients. Arch. Gen. Psychiatry, *19:* 312, 1968a.

Hartmann, E. The 90-minute sleep-dream cycle. Arch. Gen. Psychiatry, *18:* 280, 1968b.

Hartmann, E. The D-state and norepinephrine-dependent system. In *Sleep and Dreaming*, E. Hartmann, editor, p. 308. Little, Brown, and Co., Boston, 1970.

* Hartmann, E. *The Functions of Sleep.* Yale University Press, New Haven, Conn., 1973.

Hartmann, E. The dream as a "royal road" to the biology of the mental apparatus. Int. J. Psychoanal., *57:* 331, 1976a.

Hartmann, E. Schizophrenia: A theory. Psychopharmacology, *49:* 1, 1976b.

Hartmann, E. l-Tryptophan: A rational hypnotic with clinical potential. Am. J. Psychiatry, *134:* 366, 1977.

Hartmann, E. Effects of psychotropic drugs on sleep: The catecholamines and sleep. In *Psychopharmacology: A Generation of Progress.* M. A. Lipton, A. DiMascio, and K. F. Killam, editors, Raven Press, New York, 1978a.

* Hartmann, E. *The Sleeping Pill.* Yale University Press, New Haven, Conn., 1978b.

Hartmann, E., Baekeland, F., and Zwilling, G. Psychological differences between long and short sleepers. Arch. Gen. Psychiatry, *26:* 463, 1972.

Hartmann, E., Baekeland, F., Zwilling, G., and Hoy, P. Sleep need: How much sleep and what kind? Am. J. Psychiatry, *127:* 1001, 1971a.

Hartmann, E., and Brewer, V. When is more or less sleep required: A study of variable sleepers. Compr. Psychiatry, *17:* 275, 1976.

Hartmann, E., Chung, R., and Chien, C. l-Tryptophan and sleep. Psychopharmacologia, *19:* 114, 1971b.

Hartmann, E., and Zwilling, G. The effect of alpha and beta adrenergic receptor blockers on sleep in the rat. Pharm. Biochem. Behav., *5:* 1, 1976.

Hernandez-Peon, R., and Ibarra-Chavez, G. Sleep induced by electrical or chemical stimulation of the forebrain. Electroencephalogr. Clin. Neurophysiol., *24:* 189, 1963.

Hillarp, N. A., Fuxe, K., and Dahlstrom, A. Demonstration and mapping of central neurons containing dopamine, noradrenaline, and 5-hydroxytryptamine and their reactions to psychopharmaca. Pharmacol. Rev., *18:* 727, 1966.

Hobson, J. A., McCarley, R. W., Pivik, R. T., and Freedman, R. Selective firing by cat pontine brainstem neurons in desynchronized sleep. J. Neurophysiol., *37:* 497, 1974.

Hobson, J. A., McCarley, R., and Wyzinski, P. Sleep cycle oscillation: Reciprocal discharge by two brainstem neuronal groups. Science, *189:* 55, 1975.

Jacobson, A., Kales, A., Lehman, D., and Hoedemacher, F. Muscle tonus in human subjects during sleep and dreaming. Exp. Neurol., *10:* 418, 1964.

* Jouvet, M. Recherches sur les structures nerveuses et les mecanisms responsables des differentes phases du sommeil physiologique. Arch. Ital. Biol., *100:* 125, 1962.

Jouvet, M., and Renault, J. Insomnie persistante apres lesions des noyaux du raphe chez le chat. C. R. Soc. Biol., *160:* 1461, 1966.

Karacan, I., Hursch, C. J., Williams, R. L., and Thornby, J. I. Some characteristics of nocturnal penile tumescence in young adults. Arch. Gen. Psychiatry, *26:* 351, 1972.

* Kleitman, N. *Sleep and Wakefulness.* University of Chicago Press, Chicago, 1963.

Koella, W. P. *Sleep.* Charles C Thomas, Springfield, Ill., 1963.

Koella, W. P., Feldstein, A., and Czicman, J. The effect of parachlorophenylalanine on the sleep of cats. Electroencephalogr. Clin. Neurophysiol., *25:* 481, 1968.

Kripke, D. F., and Simons, R. N. Average sleep, insomnia, and sleeping pill use. Sleep Res., *5:* 110, 1976.

Kupfer, D. J., and Foster, F. G. Interval between onset of sleep and rapid eye movement sleep as an indicator of depression. Lancet *2:* 684, 1972.

Kupfer, D. J., Foster, F. G., Reich, L., Thompson, K. S., and Weiss, B. EEG sleep changes as predictors in depression. Am. J. Psychiatry, *133:* 622, 1976.

McCarley, R. W., and Hobson, J. A. Neuronal excitability modulation over the sleep cycle: A structural and mathematical model. Science, *189:* 58, 1975.

Mendelson, W. B., Gillin, J. C., and Wyatt, R. J. *Human Sleep and Its Disorders.* Plenum Publishing Corp., New York, 1977.

Monnier, M., and Hösli, L. Dialysis of sleep and waking factors in blood of the rabbit. Science, *146:* 796, 1964.

Moruzzi, G. Active processes in the brainstem during sleep. Harvey Lect., *58:* 233, 1962.

Moruzzi, G., and Magoun, H. Brainstem reticular formation and activation of the EEG. Electroencephalogr. Clin. Neurophysiol., *1:* 455, 1949.

Ohlmeyer, P., and Brilmayer, H. Periodische Vorgaenge in Schlaf. Pfluegers Arch. Ges. Physiol., *249:* 50, 1947.

Papousek, H. Early human ontogeny of the regulation of behavioral states in relation to information processing and adaptation organizing. In *Sleep*, P. Levin and W. Koelle, editors, p. 384. S. Karger, Basel, 1975.

Pappenheimer, J. R., Koski, G., Fencl, V., Karnovsky, M. L., and Krueger, J. Extraction of sleep-promoting factor S from cerebrospinal fluid and from brains of sleep-deprived animals. J. Neurophysiol., *38:* 1299, 1975.

Parmeggiani, P. L., Franzini, C., and Lenzi, P. L. Respiratory frequency as a function of preoptic temperature during sleep. Brain Res., *111:* 253, 1976.

Parmeggiani, P. L., and Sabattini, L. Electromyographic aspects of postural, respiratory, and thermoregulatory mechanisms in sleeping cats. Electroencephalogr. Clin. Neurophysiol., *33:* 1, 1972.

Parmelee, A., Akiyama, Y., Monod, N., and Flescher, J. EEG patterns in sleep of full-term and premature infants exposed to neutral temperatures. Biol. Neonate, *4:* 317, 1962.

Phillipson, E. A., Murphy, E., and Kozar, L. F. Regulation of respiration in sleeping dogs. J. Appl. Physiol., *40:* 688, 1976.

Rechtschaffen, A., and Kales, A., editors. *A Manual of Standardized Terminology, Techniques, and Scoring System for Sleep Stages of Human Subjects.* United States Government Printing Office, Washington, D.C., 1968.

Reich, L., Weiss, B. L., Coble, P., McPartland, R., and Kupfer, D. J. Sleep disturbance in schizophrenia: A revisit. Arch. Gen. Psychiatry, *32:* 51, 1975.

Roffwarg, H., Muzio, J., and Dement, W. Ontogenetic development of human sleep-dream cycle. Science, *152:* 604, 1966.

Shapiro, A. Observations on some periodic and non-periodic phenomena in normal human sleep. Ann. N. Y. Acad. Sci., *98:* 1139, 1962.

Siegel, J. M., McGinty, D. G., and Breedlove, S. M. Sleep and waking activity of pontine gigantocellular field neurons. Exp. Neurol., *56:* 553, 1977.

Snyder, F. New biology of dreaming. Arch. Gen. Psychiatry, *8:* 381, 1963.

Snyder, F., Hobson, J., Morrison, D., and Goldfrank, F. Changes in respiration, heart rate, and systolic blood pressure in relation to electroencephalographic patterns of human sleep. J. Appl. Physiol., *19:* 417, 1964.

Spinweber, C., and Hartmann, E. Long and short sleepers: MHPG and 17-hydroxycorticosteroid excretion. Sleep Res., *6:* 65, 1977.

Vertes, R. P. Selective firing of rat pontine gigantocellular neurons during movement and REM sleep. Brain Res., *128:* 146, 1977.

Vogel, G. W. REM deprivation. Arch. Gen. Psychiatry, *18:* 312, 1968.

Webb, W. B., and Agnew, H. W., Jr. Sleep stage characteristics of long and short sleepers. Science, *168:* 146, 1970.

Wilkinson, R. T. Sleep deprivation. In *The Physiology of Human Survival*, O. G. Edholm and A. L. Bacharach, editors, p. 399. New York Academy Press, New York, 1965.

Williams, H. L., Lubin, A., and Goodnow, J. J. Impaired performance with acute sleep loss. Psychol. Mongr., *73:* 1, 1959.

Williams, R. L., and Karacan, I., editors. *Pharmacology of Sleep*. John Wiley & Sons, New York, 1976.

Williams, R. L., Karacan, I., and Hursch, C. J. *Electroencephalography (EEG) of Human Sleep: Clinical Applications*. John Wiley & Sons, New York, 1974.

Zepelin, H., and Rechtschaffen, A. Mammalian sleep, longevity, and energy metabolism. Brain Behav. Evol., *10:* 425, 1974.

2.4 Neurochemistry of Behavior

HAROLD I. KAPLAN, M.D.
BENJAMIN J. SADOCK, M.D.

Introduction

The aim in neurochemistry is to identify the chemical accompaniments to nervous system function. Prominent concerns are the characterization of the molecular structure of neural constituents, the process and the regulation of enzymatic activity, the interactions between functional and anatomical parts of the nervous system, and the effects of exogenous substances in neural activity. An ultimate objective of neurochemical research is to elucidate the interrelationships of psychological and biological variables that result in normal and abnormal behavior.

Neurochemistry has become an important adjunct to the psychiatric armamentarium. Biochemical investigation of the brain has enhanced the understanding of human behavior and has aided in the development of new therapeutic agents that palliate disorders of mental function. Familiarity with basic neurochemistry has immediate relevance to the clinician; it facilitates comprehension of the current literature, encourages more appropriate use of psychoactive drugs, and serves as a reminder that the brain is an organ as unique in its chemistry and dynamics as it is in the functions it performs.

History

The search for a cause of madness has long focused on suspected toxins or imbalances of normal body constituents. The ancient Greeks, for example, related dyscrasias of the brain to an excess of primary body fluids. Known as the four humors—black bile, yellow bile, phlegm, and blood—those fluids were held to mediate a wide range of physiological and behavioral processes, including emotion and temperament. The doctrine of humoralism influenced scientific thinking well into the 19th century, when objective experimental evidence revealed the view to be oversimplistic. Thudichum, credited with being the founder of modern neurochemistry, expressed the outlook and the issues confronting 19th-century investigators. In his book *A Treatise on the Chemical Constitution of the Brain*, Thudichum (1884) wrote:

Many forms of insanity are unquestionably the external manifestations of the effects on the brain substance of poisons fermented within the body. These poisons we shall, I have no doubt, be able to isolate after we know the normal chemistry to its uttermost detail. And then will come in their turn the crowning discoveries to which our efforts must ultimately be directed, namely, the discoveries of the antidotes to the poisons of the fermenting causes and processes which produce them.

Thudichum's emphasis on normal biochemical functions foreshadowed the course of scientific investigation, as workers over the past century in a number of disciplines slowly characterized the basic physiochemical organization of the nervous system. Sherrington (1898) outlined a concept of chemical neurotransmission in which messenger molecules act as agents at the synapse. The existence and physiological effects of unseen chemical messengers were later demonstrated by Loewi (1921). He showed that vagal stimulation produces its effect on the heart through a blood-borne chemical agent. That chemical, which he termed *vagusstoff*, was subsequently identified as the neurotransmitter acetylcholine. Dale (1933) later clarified the chemical events at the synapse, providing a general framework for current conceptualization of neurotransmission. Kety (Kety and Schmidt, 1948) provided major breakthroughs in the measurement of cerebral metabolism with Kety later providing evidence of the genetic determinants of mental disorders.

Despite the long-standing interest in the chemical aspects of neural function, the further elucidation of factors related to psychiatric symptoms was inhibited by the state of the existing technology. The brain, physically inaccessible and apparently modulated by infinitely small amounts of substances, required more precise and sensitive research tools than were then available. Only after World War II, as part of the over-all advances in pharmacology and scientific technology, was the modern era of behavioral chemistry able to begin. Between 1950 and 1975, a body of knowledge concerning neurochemistry and behavior gradually evolved, allowing researchers to formulate hypotheses about the chemical accompaniments to behavior based on well-established facts.

Metabolism

All tissue requires constant supplies of oxygen and of oxidizable substrates. Under normal conditions, brain metabolism is characterized by an exceedingly high consumption of oxygen and an almost exclusive dependence on glucose as a source of energy.

NORMAL METABOLISM

As blood traverses brain tissue, compounds that participate in metabolic processes are extracted from the arterial system. The end products of metabolism, in turn, are discharged into the venous circulation. The measurement of that process serves as the primary source of information about cerebral metabolism.

Direct quantitative determination of the average cerebral blood flow in humans was first accomplished by Kety (1948), working in the laboratory of Schmidt. Kety was able to measure arteriovenous differences in oxygen and to calculate the average cerebral metabolic rate for oxygen. That rate is about 3.5 ml. of oxygen per 100 gm. of tissue per minute. Kety also determined another hemodynamic fact—that the average blood flow through brain tissue is about 50 ml. of blood per 100 gm. of brain tissue per minute. His findings demonstrated that the fall in oxygen concentration and the amount of blood flow in the brain are significantly greater than in other organs, and they underscored the unique dependence of the brain on oxygen during normal functions.

Glucose is the primary oxidizable substrate in the central nervous system. Rates of glucose metabolism are highest in the cerebral hemisphere and parts of the cerebellum. The medulla oblongata exhibits the lowest metabolic rate. Carbon dioxide, pyruvic acid, and lactic acid represent the major end products of glucose metabolism under normal conditions.

The brain represents about 2 per cent of adult body mass but consumes nearly 25 per cent of the total oxygen needed by the whole body, receiving about 15 per cent of the resting cardiac output. Those figures are remarkable for an organ with no important mechanical function. In young children, cerebral respiration may represent about 50 per cent of total body oxygen consumption.

In vivo studies of cerebral blood flow and volume show significant regional differences that are related to the functional role of a given area. For example, the rate of glucose uptake in the visual cortex is increased when the eyes are illuminated. When just one eye is illuminated, the area of neuronal activity is decreased accordingly. Grubb and his co-workers (1978) measured the hemodynamics of right-handed people and found the cerebral blood volume to be significantly higher in the left cerebral hemisphere—the dominant hemisphere.

ALTERED BRAIN METABOLISM

A variety of changes, both inside and outside the central nervous system, result in secondary alterations of brain metabolism.

Hypoglycemia. The brain does not store glucose, a carbohydrate that is the major source of energy in the body. Glucose is constantly used in the manufacture of compounds that power the nervous system.

Blood glucose concentrations can be artificially lowered by the administration of exogenous insulin. Resection of the liver, which stores glycogen for synthesis to glucose when needed, also reduces glucose levels. The most common organic cause of hypoglycemia is islet-cell adenoma.

In most people, blood glucose levels normally range between 80 and 100 mg. per 100 ml. A drop below 70 mg. per 100 ml. often induces changes in sensation and behavior, with some people experiencing alterations of mood or consciousness at that concentration. Psychosis, excitement, and abnormal electroencephalographic activity may appear. Nearly 25 per cent of the general population, however, routinely have blood glucose levels below 50 mg. per 100 ml. without concurrent symptoms of hypoglycemia. Some people tolerate even lower transient levels without associated symptoms.

Hypoxia and anoxia. Brain tissue can tolerate a 10 to 20 per cent decrease in the content of ambient air without cerebral respiratory change. That tolerance is due in part to a compensatory increase in cranial blood flow.

Different parts of the brain vary in their sensitivity to oxygen deprivation. Neurons of the globus pallidus, cerebellum, and cerebral white matter are the most readily affected by anoxia. Experiments with mice have demonstrated the high oxidative rate of neurons. In those studies, all brain oxygen was consumed within 1 second of decapitation.

Changes that accompany even mild cerebral hypoxia include a rapid drop, within seconds, of adenosine triphosphate (ATP) and creatinine phosphokinase (CPK) and a precipitous rise in lactate and ammonia. Those products of metabolism seem to be toxic to brain tissue. Associated decreases of neurotransmitters and cyclic nucleotides also take place. If hypoxia is prolonged, cell death results. Extensive destruction of neurons results in brain death.

Brain death. Traditionally, death has been equated with the cessation of the heart beat or the cessation of respiration. The ability of modern medical techniques to restore and artificially maintain those functions has diminished the significance of those findings; they are no longer deemed to be equivalent to death. Increasingly, identification of brain death is used to determine whether a patient is dead. As noted by the Conference of Medical Royal Colleges and their faculties in the United Kingdom, that is true

whether or not the function of some organs, such as a heart beat, is still maintained by artificial means.

Much effort and controversy have been involved in developing a diagnostic routine that can identify with certainty the presence of brain death.

Most criteria for brain death rely heavily on clinical observations. For example, the absence of cerebral function, the absence of cephalic reflexes (which require integrity of the brain stem), and an isoelectric electroencephalogram all suggest a diagnosis of brain death. Deep hypothermia and barbiturate anesthesia must be excluded in forming the diagnosis (see Table I).

Among the currently advocated procedures in determining brain function are angiographic scanning of the brain after intracarotid injection of radioactive isotopes and filling arteriograms.

Aging. Aging may be defined (Diamond, 1978) as "a progressive decline in cellular efficiency that occurs after maturation." The process of aging and its associated changes in neural function have recently been examined from the perspective of altered neurochemical activity.

Landfield and his co-workers (1978) examined the brain endocrine interactive hypothesis of aging. According to that model, neural and endocrine changes are somehow related during aging as either cause or effect. Those studies suggested a possible involvement of adrenocorticoid activity and structural changes in the central nervous system. Specifically, they observed decreased hypocampal astrocyte reactivity when adrenocortical secretory function increased.

Impaired mental functions associated with aging may be a consequence of circulatory changes, which diminish cerebral blood and oxygen supplies. Neurochemical changes include the accumulation of lipfuscin or age pigment. The origin and the pathological effects of that substance remain unclear.

TABLE I
Harvard Criteria of Brain Death*

1. Unresponsive coma
2. Apnea
3. Absence of cephalic reflexes (pupillary, corneal oculocephalic, vestibular, audioocular, snout, pharyngeal, swallow, cough, jaw)
4. Absence of spinal reflexes (biceps, triceps, radial, knee, ankle)
5. Isoelectric electroencephalogram
6. Persistence of conditions for at least 24 hours
7. Absence of drug intoxication or hypothermia

* From Ad Hoc Committee of the Harvard Medical School to Examine the Definition of Brain Death. A definition of brain death. J. A. M. A., *205:* 337, 1968.

Low brain weight. Dekaban and Sadowsky (1978) noted relationships between brain weight, gender, body height, and body weight. They found that the brain weights in males are greater than those in females by 9.8 per cent; the largest increases in brain weight in both sexes occur during the first 3 years of life, when the value quadruples over that at birth; during the subsequent 15 years the brain weight barely quintuples over that at birth. A progressive decline in brain weight begins at about 56 years of age and reaches its lowest value after age 86, by which time the mean brain weight has decreased by about 11 per cent relative to the maximum brain weight attained by young adults at about 19 years of age.

Hepatic disease. Severe damage to the liver, with disruption of its physiological role, results in the accumulation of numerous substances that have a toxic effect on the nervous system. In severe cases, hepatic encephalopathy and coma result. Neurotoxic compounds suspected of producing those disorders currently include several amino acids, ammonia, and progenic amines. Substantial cerebrospinal fluid elevations of the amino acid glutamine are found during hepatic coma, with decreases in levels corresponding to regained consciousness.

Composition

Disturbances in systemic chemistry produce secondary disorders of mental and neurological function. The brain, however, has a constitution quite different from extracerebral organs, and many diseases of mood, behavior, and intellect reflect primary abnormalities of central neural chemistry.

AMINO ACIDS, PEPTIDES, AND PROTEINS

Amino acids, peptides, and proteins are nitrogen-containing compounds that participate in many aspects of neural function. They participate in the maintenance of structural integrity, serve as nutrients, and mediate neuronal communications. Prominent examples of proteins in the nervous system include enzymes, hormones, neurotransmitters, and membrane receptor molecules. Recent findings show those compounds to be extensively involved in the regulation of behavioral and cognitive processes.

Amino acids are a heterogeneous group of substances. They have biological activities of their own but also serve as building blocks of proteins. Each amino acid contains a carboxyl group and an amino group. Proteins are formed when two or more amino acids are linked together. The bond between the carboxyl group of one acid and the amino group of the other is termed a peptide bond. Proteins that contain between two and 40 amino acids are commonly called peptides. Thus, peptides are merely small proteins.

More than two-thirds of the free amino nitrogen in the brain is represented by glutamic acid (glutamate), glutamine, *N*-acetylaspartic acid, and γ-aminobutyric acid (GABA). Amino acids, free or as proteins, account for nearly half the dry weight of the brain. GABA and *N*-acetylaspartic acid are derivatives of dietary amino acids formed by enzymatic action within the central nervous system. Because of their high concentration within the brain, they are considered characteristic of the organ. Other amino acids and related compounds are present in only trace amounts.

Peptides are known to serve a number of important physiological functions, mostly involving the regulation of growth and homeostasis. Interest in the psychiatric and neurological aspects of peptides has been prompted by the rapidly growing body of evidence that suggests that many of those compounds—newly isolated and identified—exert specific behavioral effects.

No adequate organizing scheme has yet been devised for the classification of the expanding list of neuropeptides, but Nemeroff and Prange (1978) presented a scheme based on site of origin (see Table II). According to that system, four anatomical sites of peptide synthesis can be described: the brain, the anterior pituitary gland (adenohypophysis), the posterior pituitary gland (neurohypophysis), and the periphery.

Brain peptides include a number of substances long known to have hormonal effects but now suspected of acting as neurotransmitters, as well as agents only recently discovered but suspected of acting primarily as neurotransmitters. At least five peptides—substance P, neurotensin, somatostatin, endorphin, and the enkephalins—seem to be involved in the regulation of pain.

Many peptides act as hormones for other hormones, serving to influence or regulate the synthesis and release of hormones. For example, luteinizing hormone-releasing hormone (LHRH), thyrotropin-releasing hormone (TRH), somatotropin release-inhibiting hormone (SRIH) (also called somatostatin), and melanocyte-stimulating hormone-release-inhibiting hormone (MIF) regulate the activity of anterior pituitary hormones. Accordingly, they are called hypothalamic hypophysiotropic hormones (HHH). TRH and somatostatin are suspected of having neurotransmitter properties. A number of studies have shown that there is impaired release of thyrotropin after stimulation with TRH in certain depressed patients.

The discovery of endogenous peptides that bind to opiate receptors (Hughes et al., 1975) opened an entirely new area of neurochemical exploration. The initial reports of two related pentapeptides that possess potent opiate-antagonist activity were followed by accounts of possible involvement of schizophrenic behavior. Although it has been implied that those peptides and related substances not only modulate pain perception but also affect behavior, conclusive evidence is lacking. There is, however, no doubt that the endorphins are anatomically associated with areas of the brain and the pituitary that are involved with neuroendocrine regulation.

Enkephalin analogues, such as DAMME (D-Ala^2, MePhe^4, Met(O)-ol enkephalin), have been synthesized and are being used experimentally.

Substance P exhibits many characteristics of a neurotransmitter. In addition to being highly concentrated in the primary afferent neurons of the spinal cord—pathways that mediate pain—the distribution of substance P parallels the anatomical sites that are associated with the regulation of emotion and behavior. Those areas are the amygdala, the septum, the preoptic area, and the hypothalamus.

Nervous system-specific proteins. Extensive biochemical investigation has resulted in the isolation and identification of proteins that seem to be nervous system specific.

One compound, present in the brain of numerous species, has been termed S-100 on the basis of its solubility characteristic; it is soluble in 100 per cent ammonium sulfate at neutral pH. In the human brain, S-100 is found primarily in white matter and is highly concentrated within the glial cells. Chemically, it is a soluble acidic protein with a molecular weight of between 19,500 and 24,000. S-100 has a characteristic amino acid composition that is high in residues of glutamic acid and aspartic acid. Moore (1972) commented on the significance of S-100:

TABLE II
Anatomical Classification of Peptides of Psychoneuroendocrinological Interest*

	Abbreviation	Other Names	Origin	Function
Brain Peptides				
Thyrotropin-releasing hormone	TRH, TRF	Thyroliberin	Brain, spinal cord	Releasing hormone Neurotransmitter?
Luteinizing hormone-releasing hormone	LHRH, LRF, FSH-RH, GnRH	Luliberin	Brain	Releasing hormone
Somatostatin	SRIF, GHIH, GRIF	Growth hormone releasing inhibiting hormone	Brain, pancreas, gut	Release-inhibiting hormone Neurotransmitter?
Melanocyte-stimulating hormone-release-inhibiting hormone	MIF		Brain	Release-inhibiting hormone
Neurotensin			Brain, gut	?
Substance P			Brain, spinal cord, gut	Neurotransmitter?
Enkephalins			Brain, pituitary	?
Bradykinin		Kinin-9	Brain?	?
Learning-related peptides: scotophobin, ameletin, catabathmophobin, chromodiapsins			Brain	Memory?
Carnosine			Muscle, brain	Neurotransmitter?
Anterior-Pituitary (Adenohypophysial) Peptides				
Corticotropin-related peptides Corticotropin	ACTH		Anterior pituitary	Releases adrenal glucocorticoids and (aldosterone); modulates learning and memory processes
Melanocyte-stimulating hormone	MSH		Intermediate lobe	Releases pigment granules from melanocytes in fish and amphibia; function unclear in mammals; modulates behavioral processes
Lipotropins	β-LPH		Posterior and intermediate lobes Brain	Contains sequences of opiate-like peptides (endorphins)
Somatomammotropins Prolactin	PRL	Mammotropin	Anterior pituitary	Initiates and maintains lactation, maternal behavioral homeostasis, osmoregulation, growth promotion, progesterone secretion, synergism with steroids
Growth hormone	GH	Somatotropin	Anterior pituitary	Stimulates tissue growth and protein synthesis
Chorionic somatomammotropin	CS		Placenta	
Glycoprotein hormones Thyroid-stimulating hormone	TSH		Anterior pituitary	Stimulates thyroid hormone release and synthesis; promotes lipolysis in adipose tissue
Luteinizing hormone	LH, ICSH	Interstitial cell-stimulating hormone	Anterior pituitary	Promotes luteinization of the ovary; stimulates Leydig cell function of the testes
Follicle-stimulating hormone	FSH		Anterior pituitary	Stimulates follicular development in the ovary; stimulates gametogenesis in the testes
Chorionic gonadotrophin	CG		Placenta	Stimulates persistence of the corpus luteum
Posterior-Pituitary (Neurohypophysial) Peptides				
Vasopressin	VP, ADH	Antidiuretic hormone	Supraoptic and paraventricular nuclei	Conserves body water (antidiuretic); modulates learning and memory processes
Oxytocin	OXT		Paraventricular and supraoptic nuclei	Affects lactation and uterine muscle contraction
Peripheral Peptides				
Angiotensin II			Plasma Brain?	Regulates circulatory pressure and volume; releases vasopressin from posterior pituitary; modulates aldosterone release; induces drinking behavior
Cholecystokinin	CCK		Intestine	Induces behavioral satiety; stimulates pancreatic secretion

* From Nemeroff, C. B., and Prange, A. J. Peptides and psychoneuroendocrinology. Arch. Gen. Psychiatry, *35:* 999, 1978.

That S-100 is found in a relatively invariant form in the brains of such a wide range of species and that it is present only in the nervous system and that it is present there in fairly large amounts suggest that S-100 is related to some general important, specific nervous system function.

The most probable function of S-100 seems to be related to learning. Hyden and Ronnback (1978) reported

greater amounts of production during the first part of learning, when animals were striving to cope with a new problem.

When the animals were overtrained, further increases in brain concentration of the protein were not observed. A dramatic finding, however, was the impairment of learning rate among animals injected with antibodies against S-100, a procedure that blocks the activity of the protein. Levels of S-100 are lowest at birth. They increase during childhood and adolescence, then stabilize during adulthood. The inhibition of ribonucleic acid synthesis by S-100 has been reported (Bondy and Roberts, 1969). The precise physiological function of S-100 is unknown.

A soluble acidic protein, concentrated in gray matter and thus associated with neurons, also seems to be a brain-specific protein. It is called 14-3-2 because of its column chromatography characteristics, and it is larger than S-100, with a molecular weight of about 50,000. Reports indicate that 14-3-2 is also associated with learning.

Several applications of brain-specific proteins in neuroscientific research have been described. In neuropathology, for example, they are being used as cell markers to establish the origin of tumor cells. That approach has been successfully used in cases of human acoustic neurinomas.

A number of additional nervous system-specific proteins have been identified, including glial pituitary acidic protein and olfactory marker protein.

Inherited metabolic disorders. More than 30 inherited disorders of amino acid metabolism have been found to produce abnormal formation or functioning of the nervous system. Mental retardation is a common feature. Convulsions, ataxia, and disorders of speech are also frequently observed. The primary abnormality in those disorders may involve systemic changes in enzyme activity, the complete absence of an enzyme, changes in enzymatic kinetic properties, or disturbances in the absorption of dietary amino acids. Abnormalities of absorption reflect the involvement of membranes in the inherited amino acid disorders. In contrast with other metabolic genetic diseases, the severe disabilities in mental and neurological function caused by those diseases are often prevented by the dietary restriction of protein or of the specific amino acid whose catabolism is blocked.

LIPIDS

The lipids are a class of compounds that are rich in carbon and hydrogen, with some oxygen, and that frequently contain nitrogen and phosphorus (Davidsohn and Henry, 1969). More than 50 per cent of the dry weight of the brain is represented by lipids, and lipids, more than any other compound, characterize the brain. That is true not only in quantitative terms but in the fact that several lipid compounds are exclusive to the central nervous system. Brain lipids are generally classified according to their structural features.

Cholesterol. Diverse as they are, all lipids except cholesterol contain long-chain aliphatic acids and in some cases, together with sphingomyelin, constitute half the weight of a normal brain.

Cerebrosides. The cerebrosides are a series of myelin lipids that are abundant in white matter but sparsely represented in gray matter. Because they contain a sugar, they are classified as glycolipids, as well as sphingolipids. If the sugar is galactose, the compound is termed galactocerebroside or ceramide-galactose. If the sugar is glucose, the compound is known as glucocerebroside or ceramide-glucose. Glucocerebrosides are present only in pathological conditions.

Sulfatides. The addition of a sulfate group to galactocerebroside results in the formation of a sulfatide or ceramide-galactose-sulfate.

Gangliosides. The concentration of sphingolipids containing sialic acid (N-acylneuraminic acid) in central ganglia serves as the source of their name, the gangliosides. The gangliosides are the richest of all the sphingolipids in carbohydrates.

Ceramide oligohexosides. Present in trace amounts in the normal adult brain are a group of sphingolipids that are also rich in sugar, the oligohexosides. The concentrations of those compounds are elevated during development and in certain disorders.

Lipidoses. The terms "lipidoses" and "lipodystrophies" describe a group of inherited neurometabolic disturbances that result in the accumulation of normal and abnormal lipids in the brain and in various other organs of the body. The deficiency of a hydrolase enzyme results in a disorder. Different clinical syndromes arise, the specific syndrome depending on the enzyme involved and the lipid accumulated. Although systemic involvement is frequent, the outstanding feature of the disorders is neural degeneration as an early presenting sign, followed by death before the age of 5 years.

Prostaglandins. As their name suggests, a series of compounds called prostaglandins is found in high concentrations in seminal plasma. They have also been identified in the human brain in association with microsomes and nerve-ending particles. Because of their presence in the brain, these acidic lipids are being investigated as possible neurotransmitters. The injection of prostaglandins into the cerebral ventricles produces a fever that resists the effects of antipyretics (Goth, 1972).

ELECTROLYTES

Electrolytes play an important role in forming the internal environment by which the human nervous system responds to external events. Ionic compounds participate in the synapse and in the changes associated with the neuronal conduction of impulses. The metabolism of the neurotransmitters depends on electrolytes, and it should be recalled that lithium is an inorganic ion.

Copper. The familial disorder Wilson's disease, hepatolenticular degeneration, is the most widely discussed disturbance of copper metabolism. The disease is characterized by a positive family history of the disorder, early onset, progressive dementia, and the pathognomonic Kayser-Fleischer ring.

Laboratory findings of aminoaciduria, abnormal findings in liver function tests, and a high urinary excretion of copper confirm the diagnosis. Although copper deficiency is rare in humans, being limited mainly to persons with malabsorption syndromes, the lack of copper affects important enzymes involved in the function of the brain. Monoamine oxidase (MAO) and dopamine β-hydroxylase, for example, are copper dependent. The white matter of the central nervous system undergoes severe degeneration in states of copper deficiency.

Manganese. A deficiency of manganese "elicits some interesting and bizarre behavioral aberrations" (Oberleas et al., 1972), primarily due to faulty mucopolysaccharide production. Hyperirritability is a prominent feature.

Iron. Behavioral changes develop in iron-deficient persons, but those changes seem to be the result of impaired hemoglobin function with secondary hypoxia or anoxia in the brain.

Magnesium. Catecholamine uptake by the neuron seems to require magnesium and adenosine triphosphate (ATP). The maintenance of sodium and potassium balance also depends on the presence of magnesium. There are conflicting reports of altered plasma magnesium concentrations in depression, mania, and schizophrenia (Cade, 1964; Frizel et al., 1969).

Zinc. Anorexia, apathy, decreased sexual activity, and lethargy are associated with low body zinc levels. Task performance and emotionality are also decreased (Oberleas et al., 1972).

Calcium. The release of most neurotransmitters depends on the presence of calcium, but the significance of alterations of serum calcium levels in neural activity is poorly understood. Carman and Wyatt (1979) reported transient increases in serum total calcium and inorganic phosphorus levels during certain agitated and manic states. Moreover, they noted that calcitonin, which reduces calcium levels, has a tranquilizing or depressant effect in such patients. Alexander et al. (1978) reported alterations of serum calcium in two subgroups of schizophrenic patients who remitted after neuroleptic withdrawal and in catatonic schizophrenic patients at the onset of catatonic stupor. The first group exhibited lower calcium levels; the second group had increased levels.

Sodium. There is an increase in sodium during depression, and nonpsychiatric patients have been reported to experience psychotic episodes because of low sodium levels, a group of symptoms described as the low-sodium syndrome (Burnell and Foster, 1972). The effects of hypernatremia are most pronounced on central nervous system functioning. Confusion, stupor, and coma are observed. Those symptoms seem to reflect dehydration of brain neurons.

Potassium. There is no direct link between disturbances of potassium levels and psychiatric syndromes, and even an extreme variation from normal concentrations produces no emotional or behavioral changes.

ENZYMES

Enzymes are a class of proteins whose function is the catalysis of chemical reactions. Disorders of amino acid, carbohydrate, lipid, and neurotransmitter metabolism may be ascribed to enzyme defects.

Few enzymes may be called unique to the central nervous system, but many are typical of brain tissue. Most enzymes that characterize the brain are involved in the synthesis and degradation of neurotransmitters. Enzymes mediating γ-aminobutyric acid (GABA), acetylcholine, norepinephrine, and serotonin biosynthesis are the focus of intensive investigation.

Adenosine triphosphatase (ATPase). In addition to membrane receptors and adenylate cyclase, another important enzyme system seems to regulate neuronal activity. This enzyme—a special form of adenosine triphosphatase (ATPase)—serves a transport-facilitating function, catalyzing the transport of substances through the cell membrane.

The best-understood form of ATPase is activated by sodium (Na^+) and potassium (K^+). Because it is activated by Na^+ and K^+ and because it is responsible for the coupled active transport of those cations, the enzyme has been conceptualized as a system—the $(Na^+ + K^+)$-ATPase system. ATPase is highly concentrated in the cerebral cortex.

$(Na^+ + K^+)$-ATPase is best understood if considered in terms of its known biological function—to maintain low cytoplasmic Na^+ concentrations while keeping K^+ levels high. It acts as a pump. Energy for that process is provided by the addition to and the removal of a phosphate group (phosphorylation and dephosphorylation) from ATP. Current evidence suggests that the interaction of intracellular Na^+ with the pump receptor causes the phosphate group to be added to the receptor system, whereas K^+ uptake is associated with the energy-consuming removal of phosphate from the enzyme. Facilitating the task of transporting Na^+ outward while moving K^+ inward is the apparent affinity of receptors on the inner cell membrane for Na^+ and the affinity of receptors on the external membrane for K^+. In that fashion, ionic concentrations between the external medium and the cell are maintained.

Alterations of ionic balance across nerve cell membranes, whether present for a fraction of a second or for extended periods, account for the physiological activity of the neuron. Thus, normal neurophysiological activity, as well as pathological states, can be understood in terms of $(Na^+ + K^+)$-ATPase function. A number of drugs seem to have their therapeutic effects through interaction with the $(Na^+ + K^+)$-ATPase pump.

Lithium carbonate, like Na^+ and K^+, is a monovalent cation. It has been extensively investigated from the perspective of its relationship to the ATPase system. Some current theories state that the lithium in (Li^+) may replace Na^+ in the activation of the internal receptors of the pump system or may stimulate the inner receptors by mimicking Na^+, while also having a K^+-like effect on the external membrane sides. Thus, the biological effects of the lithium ion—that is, the alteration of moods during affective disorders, may result from a correction of biological overswings in the distribution of Na^+ and K^+ (Glen and Reading, 1973).

Cyclases and cyclic nucleotides. It is currently believed that many—if not most—important synaptic reactions involve an interaction between a hormone or neurotransmitter and a cyclase—a membrane enzyme. That interaction, in turn, causes a change in basal levels of cyclic nucleotides, which act as second messengers, triggering the genetically determined biochemical responses.

The two cyclic nucleotides known to mediate neuronal responses to stimuli are cyclic adenosine monophosphate (cAMP) and cyclic guanylate cyclase. Dopamine, prostaglandins, norepinephrine (acting at the β-adrenergic receptor), histamine (acting at the H_2 receptor), and many of the peptides stimulate cAMP synthesis. cGMP synthesis is stimulated by acetylcholine (acting at the muscarinic receptors), histamine (acting at the H_1 receptors), and norepinephrine (acting at the α-adrenergic receptors).

Receptors not associated with adenylate cyclase activity do exist and play an important role in neurotransmission. The dopaminergic autoreceptors on nigrostriatal neurons are a good example.

Some compounds reduce endogenous levels of cAMP in selected neurons. Opiates, for example, inhibit adenylate cyclase and reduce cyclic AMP levels in neuroblastoma-glioma cell cultures, cellular clones that are rich in opiate-receptor kindling sites. That observation has been used to explain the mechanism for opiate addiction at the level of the cell membrane (Snyder, 1979).

Adenylate cyclase, in effect, conveys the message to the cell that a transmitter or hormone has become bound to a membrane receptor. Adenylate cyclase is permanently bound to the membrane, hypothetically facing both the receptor molecule and the interior of the cell. It is theorized that, once a neurotransmitter receptor becomes occupied, it couples with adenylate cyclase within the membrane, thus altering the configuration of the cyclase. Neurotransmitter-sensitive adenylate cyclases are so called because their activation requires the presence of a specific neurotransmitter. Among the changes that accompany activation of the cyclase is an alteration of postsynaptic membrane permeability to ions.

It is not clear how cAMP produces its effects within the cell. It is speculated, however, that the process involves alterations in protein phosphorylation. That requires activation of cell-specific protein kinases, enzymes that catalyze the transfer of inorganic phosphate from ATP to various proteins, thus causing a change in their charge state. Phosphorylation may be a two-step process, starting first with phosphorylation of the protein kinase, which then transfers the inorganic phosphate to phosphorylase b. However, it should be noted that neurotransmitters and hormones activate the biochemical machinery of the cell in a process that involves adenylate cyclase, a cyclic nucleotide, and protein kinase.

Cyclic nucleotides, such as cAMP and cGMP, are considered second messengers in that they seem to be necessary for the translation of messages carried by a transmitter so that biological responses by the receptor cells are possible. Recent experimental work has demonstrated that, after its generation, cyclic AMP persists for several minutes, moving from one site within the neuron to another. As expected, there is a time-related and dose-related increase in the nucleotide content of a neuronal population in response to contact with a neurotransmitter. The application of dopamine to the basal ganglia, where dopaminergic receptors are concentrated, causes an increase in cAMP levels. The administration of exogenous cyclic nucleotides causes physiological responses identical to those induced by a neurotransmitter. The application of cAMP to a dopaminergic neural population mimics the action of dopamine.

All cyclic nucleotides appear to be identical. Thus, all cAMP's are the same, and all cGMP's are the same. It is in the formation within a given neuron that a cyclic nucleotide is dependent on the activation of adenylate cyclase. The adenylate cyclase is specific, responding only to a certain transmitter or its analogue.

The enzyme $3',5'$-cyclic nucleotide phosphodiesterase degrades both cAMP and cGMP to an inactive monophosphate form.

Lithium carbonate seems to inhibit adenylate cyclase, causing a decrease in cAMP formation. Since adenylate cyclase is involved in the regulation of diverse hormone receptors, the numerous signs of endocrine dysfunction associated with lithium—such as weight gain, goiter, diabetes insipidus, and insulin inhibition—may have as their mechanism of action the inhibition of adenylate cyclase.

One hypothesis of schizophrenia holds that patients with high cAMP levels in the cerebrospinal fluid—interpreted tentatively as a reflection of catecholamine activity in the brain—represent a subgroup of patients associated with poor-prognosis process schizophrenia.

VITAMINS

The vitamins are a diverse group of compounds that are required for metabolic processes. Numerous enzyme systems depend on vitamins as co-factors. Vitamin deficiences have long been known to produce defects in neurological and mental functions. Thiamine deficiency, for example, results in Wernicke-Korsakoff's syndrome and beriberi, diseases of the central and peripheral nervous system, respectively. A lack of vitamin B_{12} can cause subacute degeneration of the spinal cord. A deficiency of niacin (nicotinic acid) produces pellagra, a disorder with pronounced psychological manifestations.

The role of vitamins in the causation and treatment of behavioral disturbances has received considerable attention since 1953, when Osmond and Hoffer (Lipton, 1973) introduced the megavitamin hypothesis for the treatment of schizophrenia. The administration of huge vitamin doses to psychotic patients has more recently been the domain of orthomolecular psychiatry (Hawkins and Pauling, 1973). The fundamental theories and methods proposed by advocates of vitamin therapy have been disproved by several distinguished research teams. Nevertheless, reputable workers, such as Smythies (1973), report the successful use of vitamins in the treatment of schizophrenia.

Folic acid deficiency is associated with a number of neurological and psychiatric symptoms. Among the most frequent symptoms are polyneuropathies, fatigue, mild depression, and abnormal intellectual functions. An excess of folate alters sleep patterns and causes malaise, irritability, and overactivity. Work by Botez and his associates (1979) suggested that folate deficiency and folate excess cause similar behavioral and biochemical changes—specifically, irritability, altered sleep patterns, and decreases in brain 5-hydroxytryptamine synthesis. Although the mechanisms of those effects are uncertain, the study revealed that a vitamin deficiency can decrease the synthesis of a neurotransmitter and can influence behavior.

Neurotransmitters

The processes involved in neurotransmission are among the most intensively studied areas in neurobiology. There is little doubt at present that chemicals are the primary mediators of those processes.

A basic principle of neurotransmission—known as Dale's law—is that each neuron produces and releases only one transmitter. Although recent evidence suggests that experimental manipulation can induce a cell to release a mixture of transmitters, Dale's principle seems to be valid for the intact nervous system under normal circumstances.

The list of suspected transmitter substances has been dramatically expanded. In the second edition of this textbook, only a handful of chemicals were listed with any degree of confidence as putative neurotransmitters. They included acetylcholine, norepinephrine, epinephrine, dopamine, serotonin, γ-aminobutyric acid, and several amino acids, most notably glycine, glutamine, and aspartate. At present, the list has grown to include a number of hormones and the endogenous opiate substances and other peptides.

CATECHOLAMINES

Dopamine and norepinephrine are the two major central nervous system catecholamines. Epinephrine is an important peripheral catecholamine but, in terms of current knowledge, is of little consequence in discussions of brain function.

Each of the catecholamines is produced from the same amino acid, tyrosine. The enzymatic machinery of the involved neurons determines which neurotransmitter is synthesized. Thus, tyrosine crosses the blood-brain barrier, then enters dopaminergic and noradrenergic neurons, the distinction between those two neuron populations being the absence of the enzyme dopamine β-hydroxylase in dopaminergic cells. In noradrenergic cells, that enzyme catalyzes the conversion of dopamine to norepinephrine. The entry of tyrosine into the central nervous system is related to the amount of that amino acid in the blood. High blood concentrations cause large amounts to penetrate the blood-brain barrier. Central nervous system uptake may be reduced if other aromatic amino acid levels in the blood are increased, since they compete at the blood-brain barrier.

Tyrosine is converted to dopa in a reaction catalyzed by the enzyme tyrosine hydroxylase. That is the rate-limiting step in the synthesis of dopamine and norepinephrine. The tyrosine analogue *d*-methyl-para-tyrosine (metyrosine) inhibits the enzyme (see Figure 1). It is used in the treatment of pheochromocytoma to lower epinephrine production but does not have a clinical application in psychiatric disorders. It has, however, been used in research. In some instances, for example, the concurrent administration of metyrosine and neuroleptics potentiates the antipsychotic action of the neuroleptics, reducing the amount of medication needed to reduce schizophrenic symptoms (Carlsson et al., 1972; Wålinder et al., 1976). Those findings support the dopamine hypothesis of schizophrenia, which states that schizophrenia is associated with excessive dopaminergic activity. Although metyrosine has been found to potentiate the antipsychotic effect of neuroleptic drugs, metyrosine has not been shown to produce antipsychotic effects when given alone. It is possible that metyrosine needs to be given in large doses in order to act as an antipsychotic agent; however, it is nephrotoxic when used in high doses.

Studies have also shown that the manic symptoms of some patients are reduced after metyrosine administration (Brodie et al., 1971). That finding lends support to the notion that catecholamine activity is increased in mania. Metyrosine reduces cerebrospinal fluid levels of homovanillic acid (HVA), the principal dopamine metabolite.

The enzyme dopamine β-hydroxylase permits the conversion of dopamine to norepinephrine. The drug disulfiram (Antabuse) inhibits the enzyme and has been used experimentally to decrease brain norepinephrine synthesis. As a result of dopamine β-hydroxylase inactivation, the neurotransmitter dopamine accumulates. The increase in dopamine activity may explain why disulfiram induces psychosis in some patients. Wise and Stein (1973) reported reduced dopamine β-hydroxylase activity in some schizophrenic brains.

Two enzymes mediate the breakdown of catecholamines—monoamine oxidase (MAO) and catechol-*O*-methyltransferase (COMT). Two forms of MAO have been identified—MAO-A, which catalyzes the degradation of norepinephrine and serotonin; and MAO-B, which degrades dopamine and, to a smaller degree, norepinephrine and serotonin. Brain norepinephrine is metabolized to 3-methoxy-4-hydroxyphenylglycol (MHPG).

Urinary MHPG is the most frequently used biochemical measure of depression, and it has been applied to the issues of diagnosis and treatment. Preliminary reports from several laboratories suggest that the rate of MHPG excretion is useful in characterizing depressions biochemically and thus helpful in predicting response to pharmacotherapy.

Distinctions have been reported between low excreters and normal or high excreters. When urinary MHPG excretion is low, it is theorized that the altered mood state is associated with decreased central norepinephrine activity. When excretion is normal or high, a central deficiency of serotonin activity is presumed. It has been asserted that low pretreatment urinary MHPG values indicate a favorable response to imipramine but not to amitriptyline. High pretreatment MHPG or normal MHPG values are said to be associated with failure of response to imipramine but positive therapeutic response to amitriptyline (Taube et al., 1978).

Schildkraut et al. (1978) presented evidence of biological differences among different forms of depression. They reported that patients with bipolar manic-depressive illness and a small group of schizoaffective patients with depression had relatively low MHPG urinary levels. Patients with unipolar nonendogenous depressions had relatively high MHPG levels. Patients with schizophrenia-related depressions—that is, with histories of chronic asocial behavior—exhibited low MHPG levels and had low epinephrine and metanephrine levels and high platelet MAO activity. Thus, using two basic measures—urinary excretion of the catecholamines and their metabolites and platelet MAO—Schildkraut and his associates described three biochemically discrete groups of depressive disorders (see Table III). The investigators were unable to characterize unipolar endogenous depressions, since patients in that group were quite heterogeneous with respect to MHPG excretion. Some patients exhibited MHPG levels that were low, and others had MHPG levels that were high.

Although the evidence presented regarding the biochemical markers of depression is persuasive, it is not yet conclusive. Hollister et al. (1978) measured MHPG excretion in normal persons. They found a range of excretion—900 mg. to 3,500 mg. per 24 hours—that would include most of the people who were reported in other studies to be suffering from depression.

An incidental finding in the research on depressive illness was the discovery of an association between catecholamines and anxiety. Sweeney and his associates (1978) noted that low baseline MHPG levels—and, by inference, decreased central nervous system norepinephrine activity—are linked to a tendency to experience anxiety under environmentally activating circumstances. The possible role of norepinephrine in mediat-

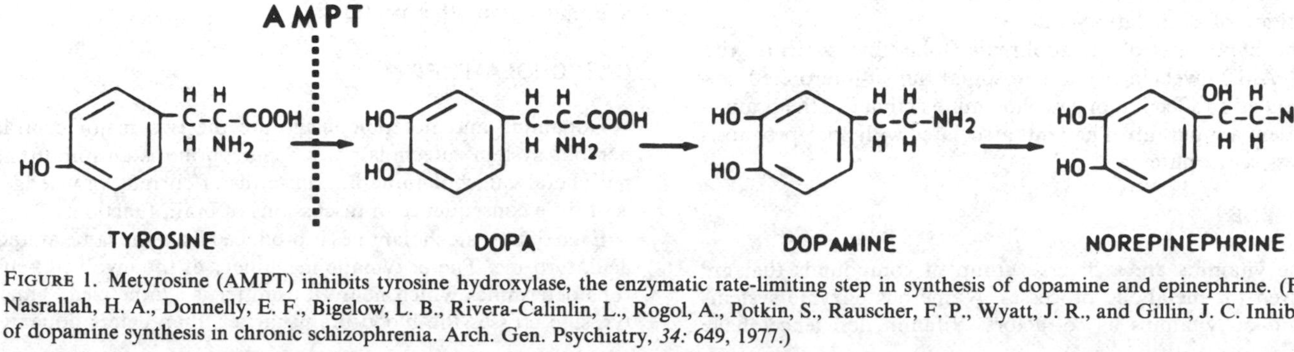

FIGURE 1. Metyrosine (AMPT) inhibits tyrosine hydroxylase, the enzymatic rate-limiting step in synthesis of dopamine and epinephrine. (From Nasrallah, H. A., Donnelly, E. F., Bigelow, L. B., Rivera-Calinlin, L., Rogol, A., Potkin, S., Rauscher, F. P., Wyatt, J. R., and Gillin, J. C. Inhibition of dopamine synthesis in chronic schizophrenia. *Arch. Gen. Psychiatry, 34:* 649, 1977.)

TABLE III

Biochemically Discrete Groups of Depressive Illness

Type of Depression	Biochemical Features
1. Bipolar manic-depressive illness and schizoaffective depressions (without histories of chronic asocial behavior)	Low MHPG excretion
2. Unipolar nonendogenous depressions	High MHPG excretion
3. Schizophrenia-related depressions	Low MHPG excretion Low epinephrine Low metanephrine High platelet MAO activity

* From Schildkraut, J. J., Orsulak, P. J., Schatzberg, A. F., Gudeman, J. E., Cole, J. O., Rohde, W. A., and La Brie, R. A. Toward a biochemical classification of depressive disorders. Arch. Gen. Psychiatry, *35:* 1427, 1978.

ing anxiety suggests a biochemical connection between anxiety and depression, emotional phenomena that are often closely related clinically. It may also explain why tricyclic antidepressants are effective in the treatment of phobic anxiety symptoms.

Pharmacological studies of tricyclic antidepressant activity are consistent with those hypotheses. For instance, different classes of drugs exhibit selective and distinct effects on norepinephrine and serotonin activity.

The presumed mechanism through which tricyclic antidepressants exert their therapeutic effect is the inhibition of neurotransmitter reuptake into the presynaptic neuron. Secondary amine agents—such as desipramine, protriptyline, and nortriptyline—seem to block the reuptake of serotonin and of norepinephrine equally. Tertiary amines, such as imipramine and amitriptyline, selectively inhibit serotonin reuptake, as compared with the reuptake of norepinephrine.

Although the inhibition of amine reuptake seems to be the primary effect of the tricyclic agents, other mechanisms seem to be involved. One of those mechanisms is the actual reduction of neurotransmitter synthesis by the presynaptic neuron. According to Carlsson and Lindqvist (1978), that reduction seems to involve a feedback adjustment involving autoreceptors on the presynaptic cell bodies or dendrites. The mechanism of action for the tricyclic agents may be more complex than had previously been suspected. The standard explanation—namely, that the tricyclic agents act through the inhibition of serotonin and norepinephrine reuptake—may describe only part of the process. Carlsson and Lindqvist (1978), for example, reported that there is a decrease in dopamine synthesis during nortriptyline and protriptyline therapy and that there is an enhancement of dopamine synthesis after large doses of amitriptyline are administered. Thus, Carlsson and Lindqvist observed, the secondary amine tricyclics seem to influence dopamine reuptake, and the tertiary amines may have dopamine receptor-blockade properties.

Halaris (1978) determined plasma MHPG levels through the use of gas chromatography. In his report of a patient with manic psychosis, Halaris provided support for the theory that an excess of norepinephrine activity is associated with manic-depressive illness. It was noted that MHPG levels in the plasma were extremely high at the peak of the patient's manic stage and that the levels returned to normal after treatment with lithium.

Van Kammen and Murphy (1978) provided evidence that response to a 1-day trial of *d*-amphetamine can be used to predict the fourth-week clinical response to imipramine. According to their study, significant correlations are found between *d*-amphetamine-induced changes in the activation of euphoria and of depression and the antidepressant effects of imipramine.

Two biological approaches have been enlisted to determine appropriate antidepressant dosage. One method involves the measurement of plasma drug levels. At present, those procedures are being used primarily with the tricyclic agents. Studies indicate that some, if not all, antidepressant drugs are most effective within a therapeutic window (Åsberg et al., 1971). In simple terms, that window defines the upper and lower limits of drug efficacy. Patients with plasma levels either below or above the limits of that window do not improve. The phenomenon is most evident in research on nortriptyline.

A second approach involves the assay of platelet MAO activity. The determination of platelet enzyme activity has been said to correlate with observed benefits from MAO inhibitor drugs. As described by Davidson and his associates (1978), a minimum of 60 per cent MAO inhibition is needed if a drug is to be consistently beneficial. Measuring MAO type B and the drug phenelzine, their studies suggested that the degree of enzyme inhibition is directly related to the antidepressant effect.

ACETYLCHOLINE

The role of acetylcholine in the regulation of emotional and behavioral phenomena is still unclear. Current interest in the neurotransmitter has been prompted in part by evidence that acetylcholine activity is altered in tardive dyskinesia and some affective disorders.

Acetylcholine is synthesized from choline and acetylcoenzyme in a reaction catalyzed by the enzyme choline acetyltransferase. The brain, unable to manufacture choline, depends on the passage of choline from the periphery through the blood-brain barrier into the central nervous system. The enzyme acetylcholinesterase (AChE) mediates the breakdown of acetylcholine to choline and acetate.

Two classes of cholinergic receptors are found in mammals—the nicotinic postsynaptic receptor and the muscarinic postsynaptic receptor. Nicotinic receptors are stimulated by nicotine and carbachol and are inhibited by curare. Muscarinic receptors are stimulated by muscarine, carbachal, and bethanechol and are inhibited by atropine and scopolamine. Cholinergic receptors in the brain are almost exclusively represented by muscarinic neurons. Nicotinic synapses occur in neuromuscular junctions and in ganglia.

Snyder et al. (1974) conducted extensive studies of the binding affinities of neuroleptic and antidepressant drugs for the muscarinic acetylcholine receptor. They determined that the affinity of neuroleptics for the receptor-binding site is inversely related to both their anticholinergic potency and their ability to cause extrapyramidal side effects. Accordingly, drugs that exhibit the lowest tendency to induce extrapyramidal reactions are the most potent in causing atropine-like side effects. Tricyclic agents can be classified in terms of their strength as muscarinic cholinergic antagonists (Snyder and Yammamura, 1977).

The brain cholinergic system is extremely sensitive to hypoxia. Even mild decreases of oxygen flow to the brain, as evident during cardiopulmonary failure, induce a drop in acetylcholine synthesis.

The rate of acetylcholine synthesis is related to the availability of precursor substances in the blood. Work done by Wurtman (1976) demonstrated that the rate of synthesis for acetylcholine and other transmitters can be significantly altered by either the injection or the dietary intake of amino acids needed for synthesis of the substance. He reported that a dose-related and time-related variation in brain acetylcholine levels existed with respect to the ingestion of dietary sources of choline, such as soybeans, liver, and eggs. In addition, the emulsifying agent lecithin (phosphatidylcholine), which is transformed into choline by the liver and the intestines, was noted to raise central acetylcholine concentrations. The discovery that central cholinergic neurons can be exogenously manipulated through diet was surprising. It prompted a revision of a long-standing belief that the ability to synthesize neurotransmitters is unaffected by the composition of the plasma. It was assumed that the blood-brain barrier protected the central nervous system against fluctuations of substances in the blood and that purely neural requirements determined the flow of information across the synapse (Wurtman, 1976).

Awareness of the positive relationship between choline availability and central cholinergic concentrations has been applied to the treatment of tardive dyskinesia. Although the biochemical nature of that disorder is still poorly understood, current evidence suggests that tardive dyskinesia reflects hypocholinergic function in the brain. Two observations argue for that fact: Scopolamine, which is known to block the muscarinic receptor, tends to exacerbate the symptoms of tardive dyskinesia. And physostigmine, which inhibits AChE and thus prevents the breakdown of acetylcholine, often reduces abnormal movements in tardive dyskinesia patients. A number of studies have reported on the efficacy of dietary choline in the treatment of tardive dyskinesia.

Lecithin may be more desirable than choline, since it produces higher serum concentrations of choline over a more extended period and does not cause offensive gastrointestinal symptoms.

Organophosphates interfere with the activity of AChE. Those compounds are used as nerve gas in combat. Organophosphate insecticides cause psychiatric symptoms. Intoxication produces confusion, impairment of concentration, depression, irritability, nervousness, and psychotic reactions, both affective and schizophrenic.

Deanol was at one time considered a good candidate as a therapeutic agent in the treatment of tardive dyskinesia. The rationale for the use of that drug was the belief that it served as a precursor for brain acetylcholine. But clinical reports failed to demonstrate consistent improvement with deanol. Moreover, it has been shown (Millington et al., 1978) that deanol competes with choline for uptake at the blood-brain barrier, thus antagonizing its intended pharmacological effect.

Changes in central cholinergic activity are noted in Huntington's chorea. Specifically, muscarinic cholinergic activity in the corpus striatum is reduced. Aberrant cholinergic mechanisms have also been implicated in other disorders. Davis and his associates (1978) reported dramatic mood changes in manic patients after the administration of physostigmine. In a number of cases, mood and thought content changed from mania toward depression.

INDOLAMINES

Two neurotransmitters with an indole nucleus, serotonin and melatonin, represent the important central indolamines.

Serotonin is formed through the hydroxylation and decarboxylation of the amino acid tryptophan. The rate of brain serotonin synthesis is, in part, tryptophan dependent, since under normal circumstances the enzyme tryptophan hydroxylase is not saturated. The major end product of serotonin metabolism, 5-hydroxyindolacetic acid (5-HIAA), is excreted in the urine.

The pineal gland contains the enzymes N-acetyltransferase and hydroxyindole-O-methyltransferase, which catalyze the synthesis of melatonin from serotonin. Melatonin, highly concentrated in the pineal gland, is an important agent in chemical processes related to circadian rhythm.

Binkley et al. (1978) produced experimental data that indicate that pineal gland N-acetyltransferase serves as a biological clock—that is, a device that measures time. Levels of melatonin and N-acetyltransferase activity are highest at night.

The circadian rhythm of pineal N-acetyltransferase may also be related to the periodic release of norepinephrine from sympathetic fibers in the superior cervical ganglia. The ganglia, in turn, may be controlled by the hypothalamus (Kasal and Menaker, 1979). There is circadian rhythm to the melatonin content of human urine and plasma that parallels the content observed directly in the pineal gland itself.

Like acetylcholine, brain levels of serotonin can be altered. Wurtman and Growdon (1978) demonstrated that the ability of serotonin-containing neurons to synthesize serotonin depends on the level of tryptophan in the brain, and the brain tryptophan level, in turn, depends on the level of tryptophan and other amino acids in the plasma. Thus, an important factor controlling the rate of serotonin synthesis in the brain is the relative concentration of plasma-free tryptophan and other amino acids with which it competes for uptake into the brain.

One theory of schizophrenia—the indolamine hypothesis—asserts that the aberrant methylation of indolamines plays a causal role in the disorder. The biosynthetic pathway for the methylated indolamine dimethyltryptamine (DMT), a potent hallucinogen, has been elucidated. In addition, trace amounts of DMT have been reported in the blood or the urine of some schizophrenics and controls.

γ-AMINOBUTYRIC ACID

The neurotransmitter γ-aminobutyric acid (GABA) is synthesized from the amino acid glutamine through the removal of a carboxyl group. GABA is distributed throughout the central nervous system but is especially concentrated in the substantia nigra, globus pallidus, and hypothalamus. The major afferent system of the substantia nigra is formed by GABA-releasing neurons that originate in the corpus striatum. GABA is a major inhibitory transmitter. The transmitter does not cross the blood-brain barrier when administered systemically.

Several disorders have been postulated to reflect disorders of GABA function. Huntington's chorea has been reported to be associated with reduced GABA levels in the basal ganglia. Structural changes in the caudate nucleus are pronounced. Bird and his associates (1973) suggested that the hypogabergic state is related to a deficiency of glutamic acid decarboxylase, the enzyme that mediates the conversion of glutamic acid to GABA. GABA dysfunction has also been implicated in parkinsonism, epilepsy, schizophrenia, and senile dementia.

Myelin

The membrane that has long been foremost in neural research is the myelin sheath. Myelin is the white matter of the brain and the spinal cord. Proteins constitute 25 per cent of the total dry weight of myelin. Cholesterol is the largest single component, representing 34 per cent of the dry weight. Phospholipids—such as ethanolamine phospholipids, lecithins, and sphingomyelin—make up another 25 per cent. Cerebrosides, cerebroside sulfates, and gangliosides—collectively termed the glycolipids—make up the remaining 16 per cent of myelin. Myelin represents as much as one-third of the dry weight of the mature brain. The lack of observed ionic movement through the myelin sheath reflects its role as an electrical insulator. Some movement of ions does take place at interruptions in the covering, termed nodes of Ranvier. Those clefts permit the rapid propagation of impulses, known as saltatory conduction. Myelin itself enhances the speed of neural impulses.

Loss of myelin sheaths occurs in many disorders of the central and peripheral nervous systems, but there is a particular category, with certain clinical and pathological features in common, in which loss of myelin is considered to be the primary change, and the axis cylinders may be spared or, if affected, are damaged secondarily. Such disorders are called demyelinating diseases. Thus, a disorder such as metachromatic leukodystrophy, which produces degeneration of myelin secondary to the accumulation of granules in the myelin-forming Schwann cells (see Figure 2), is not considered a demyelinating disease. Multiple sclerosis (disseminated sclerosis) is such a disorder and is the most common nervous system disease in

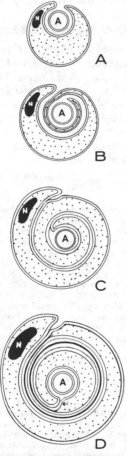

FIGURE 2. Diagram of stages in the development of the myelin sheath about an axon (*A*). Cytoplasm of the Schwann cell is stippled, and its nucleus is indicated (*N*). As additional layers of cell cytoplasm become wrapped around the axon (*B* and *C*), the cytoplasm is reduced in amount, and the double-layered plasma membranes come into apposition (*D*). The outer membrane unit of the Schwann cell will become the *intraperiod line* of myelin. The dark line (*major dense line*) represents the apposition of the inner (cytoplasmic) surface of the unit membrane as shown in *D*. The internal mesaxon is also indicated (*arrow in D.*) (From Truex, R. C., and Carpenter, M. B. *Human Neuroanatomy*, ed. 6. Williams & Wilkins, Baltimore, 1969.)

the northern hemisphere and the most common disease of the myelin system. Another disease characterized by demyelination is the Guillain-Barré syndrome. Both disorders are suspected of being caused by a virus. Hexachlorophene may induce demyelination, and demyelination is sometimes seen in phenylketonuria.

Blood-Brain Barrier

The unique characteristics of brain chemistry depend on the functional integrity of the blood-brain barrier—a series of biologically active membranes that regulate the passage of substances into and out of the central nervous system. That barrier maintains a chemical homeostasis between the cerebrospinal fluid and the other fluid compartments—namely, the venous and the arterial systems.

The concept of the blood-brain barrier evolved from observations made during the 19th century that certain dyes, although present in the blood and able to stain other body organs, consistently failed to discolor tissue in the brain or the spinal cord. It was correctly postulated that an unseen partition somehow excluded those dyes from the central nervous system. It was furthermore noted that the barrier was highly selective in its function. Acidic analine dyes failed to penetrate the barrier, but basic analine dyes readily crossed into the central nervous system.

The anatomy of the blood-brain barrier remains unclear. Sites where the membrane seems to exert its regulatory functions include the choroid plexus, the blood vessels of the brain and the subarachnoid space, and the arachnoid membrane overlying the subarachnoid space. Electron microscopy has shown that those areas are characterized by tight junctions, a type of intercellular connection that is known to restrict the passive exchange of solutes. The presence of numerous energy-forming mitochondria suggests the presence of energy-requiring transport mechanisms. Indeed, a complex system of fluid exchange, involving both active and passive transport mechanisms, occurs at the barrier.

Because of its selective permeability, the barrier presents clinicians and researchers with special problems and, at times, unique opportunities. The existence of the barrier interferes with what might otherwise be rather simple drug therapy. Many antibiotics and dietary substances, for example, cannot pass from the blood into the cerebrospinal fluid. Parkinson's disease is known to be a dopamine-deficiency disease, and rational therapy would include exogenous replacement of dopamine. Dopamine, however, does not penetrate the barrier. That fact necessitates the use of levodopa, a dopamine precursor that freely penetrates the barrier. Once in the brain, levodopa is converted to dopamine, and a biochemical correction is achieved. Ironically, the blood-brain barrier, while necessitating that indirect form of therapy, makes it possible to effectively mitigate some adverse side effects that result from the use of levodopa. Both inside and outside of the central nervous system, levodopa is converted to dopa by the enzyme dopa decarboxylase. Dopa, in turn, may be converted to dopamine, norepinephrine, and epinephrine, which are collectively called the catecholamines. The intended effect of levodopa therapy is to enhance the formation of the catecholamine dopamine in the central nervous system. Peripheral catecholamines, however, induce such symptoms as anorexia, nausea, and vomiting and for years represented an unpleasant component of levadopa treatment. Those side effects have more recently been circumvented through the concurrent administration of carbidopa, an inhibitor of the enzyme dopa decarboxylase. Carbidopa does not enter the brain and thus inhibits only the extracerebral dopa decarboxylase, decreasing the decarboxylation of levodopa in the periphery.

The blood-brain barrier has paradoxical roles. It protects against infection by shielding against infiltration by microorganisms—for example, breakdown of a portion of the blood-brain barrier may permit the spread of blood-borne infection, with subsequent abscess formation—and it also excludes those molecules that normally mediate the immune response, the immunoglobins and the lymphocytes. Under normal conditions, those carriers of systemic immunity do not freely permeate the blood-brain barrier.

The blood-brain barrier, under normal conditions, excludes substances that are directly toxic to the central nervous system. Bilirubin is generally unable to cross the blood-brain barrier. However, in newborns with hemolytic disorders, with a large amount of circulating unconjugated (indirect-reacting) bilirubin, there is high risk of central nervous system toxicity and permanent brain damage.

Investigators seeking biochemical indices of central nervous system function often try to enhance the natural partition provided by the blood-brain barrier. Typically, they measure accumulations of neurotransmitters and their metabolites in the cerebrospinal fluid. A popular technique involves the use of probenecid, a drug that blocks the removal of acidic metabolites of monoamine transmitters from the central nervous system. The degree of accumulation of those metabolites is then used as an indirect measure of central neurotransmitter turnover.

Cimetidine (Tagamet), a histamine H_2-receptor antagonist used for the treatment of upper gastrointestinal bleeding and the prevention of ulcers, is reported to cause mental confusion as a side effect in critically ill patients (Mogelnicki et al., 1979). Since physostigmine has been able to effectively antagonize the stupor, it seems that cimetidine has central anticholinergic activity. According to pharmacological studies, cimetidine does not normally cross the blood-brain barrier. However, concurrent problems with gastrointestinal bleeding, such as uremia, seem to increase the permeability of the blood-brain barrier to cimetidine and other substances.

Cerebrospinal Fluid

The intracellular compartment of the central nervous system is represented by the neurons and the glia. The extracellular compartment is composed of spaces filled with blood, cerebrospinal fluid, or extracellular fluid. The extracellular fluid, also called the interstitial fluid, immediately surrounds the cells of the brain and constitutes 25 per cent of the cerebral volume. Because of its direct contact with the neural cells, the interstitial fluid is the most important medium in contact with the brain. It is the cerebrospinal fluid, however, that generates the most interest of any brain fluid.

The cerebrospinal fluid serves as a protective cushion against trauma and acts as a pathway by which substances are transported to and removed from the central neural tissue. The normal cerebrospinal fluid volume in adults is 130 ml. to 140 ml. The fluid is constantly being secreted into the ventricular system, primarily at the choroid plexuses, and being removed, mainly through the arachnoid granulation of the superior sagittal sinus. The normal rate of cerebrospinal fluid secretion is 0.35 ml. a minute. In the normal state, the fluid is clear and colorless and has a specific gravity of 1.004 to 1.007. When a person is in a horizontal position, cerebrospinal fluid pressure in the lumbar region may be between 100 mm. and 150 mm. H_2O. In the sitting position, the pressure may rise to 200 mm. or 300 mm. H_2O. The important constituents of the fluid are protein, glucose, chloride, and cells. Proteins are present in small amounts, with the normal value of 15 mg. to 50 mg. per 100 ml. Chlorine, mostly as sodium chloride, is present in 118 mEq. to 132 mEq. per 100 ml. The fluid is remarkably free of cells, with zero to five lymphocytes per millimeter representing the normal concentration of mononuclear cells. Potassium, sulfate, phosphate, calcium, and uric acid are present in small amounts.

Conclusion

The application of biochemical techniques to the investigation of psychiatric disorders represents a fruitful and challenging sector of behavioral research. The importance of those efforts is underscored by the recent advances in the pharmacological treatment of mental illness. Nevertheless, the neurochemical assessment of emotional disorders remains an imprecise task, and biochemical measures do not yet provide definitive answers about the causes of most psychiatric diseases. The brain itself remains largely inaccessible to most forms of direct physical examination; as a result, the majority of information about central neural function is derived from studies of peripheral activity. Yet neurochemistry has become a basic medical science, with important clinical implications.

Suggested Cross References

Neurology is discussed at length in Chapter 3. The basic science of psychopharmacology is discussed in Section 2.2, and organic therapies are discussed in Chapter 31. The neurophysiology of behavior is discussed in Section 2.5. Organic mental disorders are described in Chapter 20, schizophrenic disorders in Chapter 15, and affective disorders in Chapters 18 and 19.

The authors wish to thank Norman Sussman, M.D., who collaborated in the preparation of this section.

REFERENCES

Ad Hoc Committee of the Harvard Medical School to Examine the Definition of Brain Death. A definition of brain death. J. A. M. A., *205*: 337, 1968.

Alexander, P. E., Van Kammen, D. P., and Bunney, W. E. Serum calcium and magnesium in schizophrenia: Relationship to clinical phenomena and neuroleptic treatment. Br. J. Psychiatry, *133*: 143, 1978.

Åsberg, M., Cronholm, B., and Sjoqvist, F. Relationship between plasma level and therapeutic effect of nortriptyline. Br. Med. J., *3*: 331, 1971.

Banik, N. L., and Davison, A. N. Isolation of purified basic protein from human brain. J. Neurochem., *21*: 489, 1973.

Barbeau, A. G.A.B.A. and Huntington's chorea. Lancet, *2*: 1499, 1973.

Bell, G. H., Davidson, J. N., and Emslie-Smith, D. *Textbook of Physiology and Biochemistry.* Williams & Wilkins, Baltimore, 1972.

Bickerstaff, E. R. *Neurological Examination in Clinical Practice.* Blackwell, Oxford, 1973.

Binkley, S. A., Riebman, J. B., and Reilly, K. B. The pineal gland: A biological clock in vitro. Science, *202*: 1198, 1978.

Bird, E. D., Mackay, A. V. P., Rainer, C. N., and Iversen, L. L. Reduced glutamic-acid decarboxylase activity of postmortem brain in Huntington's chorea. Lancet, *1*: 1090, 1973.

Bogoch, S. *The Biochemistry of Memory.* Oxford University Press, London, 1968.

Bondy, S. C., and Roberts, S. Developmental and regional variations in ribonucleic acid synthesis on cerebral chromatin. Biochem. J., *115*: 341, 1969.

Botez, M. I., Young, S. N., Bachevalier, J., and Gauthier, S. Folate deficiency and decreased brain S. hydroxytryptamine synthesis in man and rat. Nature (Lond.), *278*: 182, 1979.

Brodie, H. K. H., Murphy, D. C., and Goodwin, F. K. Catecholamines and mania: The effect of alpha-methyl-para-tyrosine on manic behavior and catecholamine metabolism. Clin. Pharmacol. Ther., *12*: 218, 1971.

Burnell, G. M., and Foster, T. A. Psychosis with low sodium syndrome. Am. J. Psychiatry, *128*: 1313, 1972.

Cade, J. F. J. A significant elevation of plasma magnesium levels in schizophrenia and depressive states. Med. J. Aust., *1*: 195, 1964.

* Carlsson, A., and Lindqvist, M. Antidepressants and brain monoamine synthesis. J. Neural Transm., *43*: 73, 1978.

Carlsson, A., Persson, T., and Roos, B. E. Potentiation of phenothiazines by alpha-methyl-tyrosine in treatment of chronic schizophrenia. J. Neural Transm., *33*: 83, 1972.

Carman, J. S., and Wyatt, R. J. Use of calcitonin in psychotic agitation on mania. Arch. Gen. Psychiatry, *36*: 72, 1979.

* Carpenter, M. B. *Human Neuroanatomy,* ed. 7. Williams & Wilkins, Baltimore, 1976.

Dale, H. H. Nomenclature of fibres in the autonomic nervous system and their effects. J. Physiol. (Lond.), *80*: 10P, 1933.

Davidsohn, I., and Henry, J. B. *Clinical Diagnosis by Laboratory Methods.* W. B. Saunders, Philadelphia, 1969.

Davidson, S., McLeod, M. N., and White, H. L. Inhibition of platelet monoamine oxidase in depressed patients treated with phenezine. Am. J. Psychiatry, *135*: 470, 1978.

Davis, K. L., Berger, P. A., Hollister, L. E., and Defraites, E. Physostigmine in mania. Arch. Gen. Psychiatry, *35*: 119, 1978.

Dekaban, A. S., and Herman, M. M. Childhood, juvenile, and adult cerebral lipidoses. Arch. Pathol., *97*: 65, 1974.

Dekaban, A. S., and Sadowsky, D. Changes in brain weights during the span of human life. Ann. Neurol., *4*: 345, 1978.

Diamond, M. C. The aging brain: Some enlightening and optimistic results. Am. Sci., *66*: 66, 1978.

Frizel, D., Coppen, A., and Marks, V. Plasma magnesium and calcium in depression. Br. J. Psychiatry, *115*: 1375, 1969.

Garfinkel, P. E., Warsk, J. J., and Stancer, H. C. Depression: New evidence in support of biological differentiation. Am. J. Psychiatry, *136*: 535, 1979.

Glen, A. I. M., and Reading, H. W. Regulatory action of lithium in manic-depressive illness. Lancet, *2*: 1239, 1973.

Goth, A. *Medical Pharmacology.* C. V. Mosby, St. Louis, 1972.

Greep, R. O., and Weiss, L. *Histology,* ed. 3. McGraw-Hill, New York, 1973.

Grubb, R. L., Raichle, M. E., Higgins, C. S., and Eichling, J. O. Measurement of regional cerebral blood volume by emission tomography. Ann. Neurol., *4*: 322, 1978.

Haglid, K. G., and Starrou, D. Water-soluble and pentanol-extractable proteins in human brain normal tissue and brain tumours, with special reference to S-100 protein. J. Neurochem., *20*: 1523, 1973.

Halaris, A. E. Plasma 3-methoxy-4-hydroxyphenylglycol in manic psychosis. Am. J. Psychiatry, *135*: 493, 1978.

Hawkins, D., and Pauling, L., editors. *Orthomolecular Psychiatry.* W. H. Freeman, San Francisco, 1973.

Hollister, L. E., Davis, K. L., Overall, J. E., and Anderson, T. Excretion of MMPG in normal subjects. Arch. Gen. Psychiatry, *35*: 1410, 1978.

Hughes, J., Smith, T., Kosterlits, H., Fothergill, L., Morgan, B., and Morris, H. Identification of two related pentapeptides from the brain with potent opiate agonist activity. Nature (Lond.), *259*: 577, 1975.

Hyden, H., and Ronnback, L. The brain-specific S-100 protein on neuronal cell membranes. J. Neurobiol., *9*: 489, 1978.

Kasal, C. A., and Menaker, M. Circadian clock in culture: *N*-acetyltransferase activity of chick pineal glands oscillates in vitro. Science, *203*: 656, 1979.

Kety, S. S., and Schmidt, C. F. The nitrous oxide method for the quantitative determination of cerebral blood flow in man: Theory, procedure, and normal values. J. Clin. Invest., *27*: 476, 1948.

Landfield, P. W., Waymire, J. C., and Lynch, G. Hippocampal aging and adrenocorticoids: Quantitative correlations. Science, *202*: 1098, 1978.

Lassen, N. A., Feinberg, I., and Lane, M. H. Bilateral studies of cerebral oxygen uptake in young and aged normal subjects and in patients with organic dementia. J. Clin. Invest., *39*: 491, 1960.

Lassen, N. A., Ingvar, D. H., and Skinhoj, A. Brain function and blood flow. Sci. Am., *239*: 62, 1978.

Lipton, M. A. Schizophrenia: A dubious approach. Med. World News, *23*: 41, 1973.

Loewi, O. Uber humorale Ubertragbarkeit der Herznervenwirkung. Pfluegers Arch., *189*: 239, 1921.

Millington, W. R., McCall, A. L., and Wurtman, R. J. Deanol acetamidobenzoate inhibits the blood-brain transport of choline. Ann. Neurol., *4*: 302, 1978.

Mogelnicki, S. R., Waller, J. L., and Finlayson, D. C. Physostigmine reversal of cimetidine-induced mental confusion. J. A. M. A., *241*: 826, 1979.

Moore, B. W. Chemistry and biology of two proteins, S-100 and 14-3-2, specific to the nervous system. In *International Review of Neurobiology,* C. C. Pfeiffer and J. R. Smythies, editors, p. 215. Academic Press, New York, 1972.

* Murphy, D. L., and Wyatt, R. J. Reduced monoamine oxidase activity in blood platelets from schizophrenic patients. Nature (Lond.), *238*: 225, 1972.

Nasrallah, H. A., Donnelly, E. F., Bigelow, L. B., Rivera-Calimlim, L., Rogol, A., Potkin, S., Rauscher, F. P., Wyatt, J. R., and Gillin, J. C. Inhibition of dopamine synthesis in chronic schizophrenia. Arch. Gen. Psychiatry, *34*: 649, 1977.

* Nemeroff, C. B., and Prange, A. J. Peptides and psychoneuroendocrinology. Arch. Gen. Psychiatry, *35*: 999, 1978.

Oberleas, D., Caldwell, D. F., and Prasad, A. S. Trace elements and behavior. In *Neurobiology of the Trace Metals Zinc and Copper,* C. C. Pfeiffer, editor, p. 83. Academic Press, New York, 1972.

Ouaknine, G., Kosary, I. Z., Braham, J., Czerniak, P., and Nathan, H. Laboratory criteria of brain death. J. Neurosurg., *39*: 429, 1973.

Palmer, G. C., Robison, G. A., Manian, A. A., and Sulser, F. Modification by psychotropic drugs of the cyclic AMP response to norepinephrine in the rat brain in vitro. Psychopharmacologia, *23*: 201, 1972.

Pampiglione, G., and Harden, A. Neurophysiological identification of a late infantile form of "neuronal lipidosis." J. Neurol. Neurosurg. Psychiatry, *36*: 68, 1973.

Prockop, L. D. Disorders of cerebrospinal fluid and brain extracellular fluid. In *Biology of Brain Dysfunction,* G. E. Gaull, editor, vol. 1, p. 229. Plenum Publishing Corp., New York, 1973.

Satake, M. Some aspects of protein metabolism of the neuron. In *International Review of Neurobiology,* C. C. Pfeiffer and J. R. Smythies, p. 189. Academic Press, New York, 1972.

* Schildkraut, J. J., Orsulak, P. J., Schatzberg, A. F., Gudeman, J. E., Cole, J. O., Rohde, W. A., and LaBrie, R. A. Toward a biochemical classification of depressive disorders. Arch. Gen. Psychiatry, *35*: 1427, 1978.

Schultz, J., and Daly, J. W. Adenosine 3'-5'-monophosphate in guinea pig cerebral cortical slices: Effects of α- and β-adrenergic agents, histamine, serotonin, and adenosine. Science, *21*: 573, 1973.

Seiler, N. Enzymes. In *Handbook of Neurochemistry,* A. Lathja, editor, vol. 1, p. 325. Plenum Publishing Corp., New York, 1969.

Sherrington, C. S. *Integrative Action of the Nervous System.* Constable, London, 1898.

Singer, I., and Rotenberg, D. Mechanism of lithium action. N. Engl. J. Med., *289*: 254, 1973.

Smythies, J. R. Nicotinamide treatment of schizophrenia. Lancet, *2*: 1450, 1973.

Snyder, S. H. Receptors, neurotransmitters, and drug responses. N. Engl. J. Med., *300*: 465, 1979.

Snyder, S. H., Greenberg, D., and Yammamura, H. I. Antischizophrenic drugs and brain cholinergic receptors: Affinity for muscarinic sites predicts extrapyramidal effects. Arch. Gen. Psychiatry, *31*: 58, 1974.

Snyder, S. H., and Yammamura, H. I. Antidepressants and the muscarinic acetylcholine receptor. Arch. Gen. Psychiatry, *34*: 236, 1977.

Sweeney, D. R., Maas, J. W., and Heninger, G. R. State anxiety, physical activity, and urinary 3-methoxy-4-hydroxyphenethylene glycol excretion. Arch. Gen. Psychiatry, *35*: 1418, 1978.

Taube, S. L., Kirstein, L. S., Sweeney, D. R., Heninger, G. R., and Maas, J. W. Urinary 3-methoxy-4-hydroxyphenylglycol and psychiatric diagnosis. Am. J. Psychiatry, *135*: 78, 1978.

Thudichum, J. W. L. *A Treatise on the Chemical Constitution of the Brain.* Balliere, Tindall & Cox, London, 1884.

Truex, R. C., and Carpenter, M. B. *Human Neuroanatomy,* ed. 6. Williams & Wilkins, Baltimore, 1969.

Ungar, G., Desiderio, D. M., and Parr, W. Isolation, identification, and synthesis of a specific-behavior-inducing brain peptide. Nature (Lond.), *238*: 198, 1972.

Van Kammen, D. P., and Murphy, D. L. Prediction of imipramine antidepressant response by one-day *d*-ampetamine trial. Am. J. Psychiatry, *135*: 1179, 1978.

Wålinder, J., Skott, A., Carlsson, A., and Roos, B-E. Potentiation by metyrosine of thioridazine effects in chronic schizophrenics. Arch. Gen. Psychiatry, *33*: 501, 1976.

White, A., Handler, P., and Smith, E. S. *Principles of Biochemistry.* McGraw-Hill, New York, 1973.

Wise, C. D., and Stein, L. Dopamine-beta-hydroxylase deficits in the brains of schizophrenic patients. Science, *181*: 344, 1973.

Wurtman, R. J. Control of neurotransmitter synthesis by precursor availability and food consumption. In *Subcellular Mechanisms in Reproductive Neuroendocrinology,* F. Naftolin, editor, p. 149. Elsevier, Amsterdam, 1976.

Wurtman, R. J., and Growdon, J. H. Dietary enhancement of CNS neurotransmitters. Hosp. Pract., *13*: 71, 1978.

Wyatt, R. J., and Murphy, D. L. Low platelet monoamine oxidase activity and schizophrenia. Schizo. Bull., *2*: 77, 1976.

2.5 Neurophysiology of Behavior

HAROLD I. KAPLAN, M.D.

BENJAMIN J. SADOCK, M.D.

Introduction

The brain, by definition, consists of the mass of nervous tissue contained within the cranium; it includes the cerebrum, the cerebellum, the midbrain, the pons, and the medulla oblongata. The field of psychiatry—seeking to understand feelings, perception, intellect, memory, and affect—has often avoided such anatomical designations, making reference, instead, to that faculty of the brain by which those functions are mediated—the mind or psyche. Indeed, during the psychoanalytic era, interest in psychosocial models of behavior overshadowed theories based on faults or lesions in the structure of the nervous system as causes of mental illness. In recent years, however, there has been a revival of interest in theories that propose neurobiological disorders as the basis of emotional and behavioral dysfunction. Increasingly sophisticated and precise research techniques are enabling investigators to probe the deepest aspects of the brain and to observe events that correlate with observed behavior. The rapidly expanding body of information provided by such efforts is obscuring the boundaries of interest between psychiatry and other disciplines. No longer can it be said (Eckstein, 1970) that "no modern surgeon enters the skull to find mind." Similarly, no modern psychiatrist is well prepared to examine the mind unless he is familiar with underlying neuroanatomical and neurochemical mechanisms of the brain.

History

The search for a physical mechanism subserving mental phenomena has a long history. Aristotle spoke of the heart's supremacy as both the source of the nerves and the seat of the soul. In the 2nd century, Galen postulated the circulation of thoughts in the ventricles of the brain and the traveling of emotions in the vascular system. During the 19th century, the phrenologists attempted to localize specific moral qualities to circumscribed areas of the brain. Less fanciful 19th-century views included those of Cannon and Bard, who theorized that the dorsal thalamus is the mediator of emotional feeling and that the hypothalamus is the mediator of emotional expression. Freud, attempting to localize the anatomical basis of emotion, speculated about the existence of toxic compounds in psychiatric disorders. Papez (1937) presented a complex formulation of a neural circuit regulating behavior. He suggested the presence of a harmonious mechanism made up of the anterior thalamic nuclei, the cingulate gyrus, the hippocampus, and their interconnections, which collectively elaborate the functions of emotion and participate in emotional expression. Other workers, such as MacLean (1952) and Heath (1966), later confirmed the soundness of this scheme and expanded on it, leading to what has become conceptualized as the limbic system. In 1949, Moruzzi and Magoun published the results of experiments involving the reticular activating system, a unit of the brain shown to be concerned with electrical activity in the cerebral cortex and with the modulation of sleep and arousal. Another structure, the hypothalamus, is involved with the performance of both the reticular activating system and the limbic system and has been extensively investigated for its influences on behavior. Neuroendocrine research has established that hypothalamic factors or hormones control the release of pituitary hormones. The discovery of hypothalamic peptides that seem to act as neurotransmitters and that profoundly affect emotional states has directed attention to that area of the brain. Pharmacological investigation of psychiatric drugs has become a major source of insight into the mechanisms of neural activity. For example, the finding that antipsychotic drugs produce movement disorders and that drugs used in the treatment of movement disorders induce psychotic symptoms has shed light on the functions of the dopamine systems. The identification of the anatomical and biochemical basis of psychiatric phenomena thus represents a major focus of scientific efforts.

Neuroanatomy

Interest in the anatomy of the brain predates the development of purely psychological models, and familiarity with structure remains fundamental to the practice of psychiatry. Much of the contemporary literature uses anatomical designations for the purposes of description and as part of the standard nomenclature.

EMBRYOLOGY

An adult brain, with its complex anatomical relationships and tortuous connections, develops from a simple embryonic structure, progressing from primitive germinal cells to a mature nervous system.

Bilaminar disc. As the embryo enters its third week of development, it resembles a sphere firmly embedded in the maternal endometrium. When sectioned, the embryo is seen to consist of two cavities separated from one another by a double layer of cells (see Figure 1). One cavity is termed the yolk sac and has as its roof a layer of flattened cells called entoderm. The other space is known as the amniotic cavity and has as its floor tall columnar cells called ectoderm. Both the ectoderm and the entoderm cells lie in direct apposition to one another, forming a bilaminar membrane.

Trilaminar disc. Between the fifteenth and the sixteenth days of development, a narrow groove appears on the ectoderm, facing the amniotic cavity. The indentation proceeds midway across the surface, ending in a pit. Both the groove and the pit are surrounded by bulging areas on their sides. The groove is called the primitive streak, and the pit and its surrounding ridge are termed the node of Hensen (see Figure 2). Evidence suggests that ectodermal cells from the ridges along the primitive streak invaginate downward, then migrate laterally and caudally between the ectoderm and the entoderm, forming an intermediate cell layer, the mesoderm (see Figure 3). There is now a trilaminar membrane, composed of three germinal cell types—ectoderm, mesoderm, and entoderm. Each layer gives rise to specific tissues and organs. The brain and other nervous tissues derive from the ectoderm.

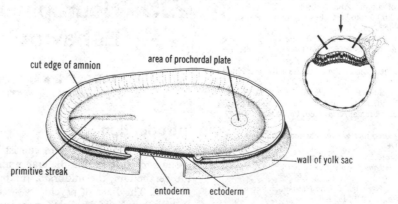

FIGURE 1. Schematic view of the embryo at the end of the second week of development. The amniotic cavity has been opened to permit a dorsal view of the ectodermal germ layer (see *inset*). In one area the amnion and the wall of the yolk sac have been removed to show the entodermal and ectodermal layers in contact with each other. Note that the primitive streak is being formed. (From Langman, J. *Medical Embryology*, ed. 3. Williams & Wilkins, Baltimore, 1975.)

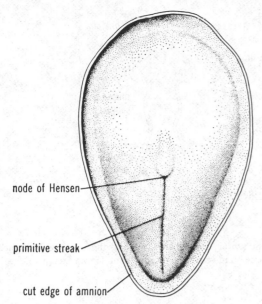

FIGURE 2. Schematic drawing of an 18-day-old embryo. View is from above, with the amnion having been removed. The embryo has a pear-shaped appearance and shows at its caudal end the primitive streak and node of Hensen. (From Langman, J. *Medical Embryology*, ed. 2. Williams & Wilkins, Baltimore, 1969.)

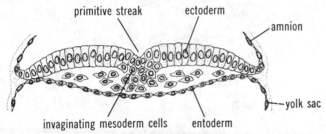

FIGURE 3. Transverse section through the region of the primitive streak, showing the invagination of cells from the ectoderm to form the mesoderm. (From Langman, J. *Medical Embryology*, ed. 2. Williams & Wilkins, Baltimore, 1969.)

Appearance of the nervous system. An oval thickening in the cephalic area of the ectoderm is the first evidence of the future nervous system. The thickening gradually enlongates to form the neural plate, which itself continues to expand toward the caudal end of the embryo. With further development, the edges of the neural plate elevate, forming the neural folds. The depressed midregion is called the neural groove. As the neural folds approach each other in the midline and fuse, the neural tube is formed (see Figure 4). Openings remain temporarily at both ends of the tube, but those neuropores, as they are called, eventually close, creating a sealed tubular structure with a fluid-filled lumen. The narrow caudal portion of the tube becomes the spinal cord, and the broad cephalic portion, with its several dilations, becomes the brain.

Primary brain vesicles. Three distinct bulges in the anterior part of the embryo are the primary brain vesicles. From front to back, those bulges are the prosencephalon or forebrain, the mesencephalon or midbrain, and the rhombencephalon or hindbrain. At the same time that those vesicles appear, the neural tube develops two flexures—a cervical flexure at the rhombencephalon-spinal cord junction and a cephalic flexure in the mesencephalon region (see Figure 5).

Secondary brain vesicles. With further development, the prosencephalon differentiates into two parts. The anterior portion is termed the telencephalon or endbrain. That area is characterized by two lateral outpocketings, the primitive cerebral hemispheres (see Figure 6). Similarly, the posterior part of the prosencephalon, the diencephalon, is discerned by the bulging of the primitive optic vesicles. The mesencephalon undergoes little change. The rhombencephalon, however, divides into two parts. The anterior segment becomes the metencephalon; the posterior segment becomes the myelencephalon.

Late development. The adult structure evolves from the five secondary brain vesicles. During the genesis two major changes occur. First, the nervous tissue derived from the ectoderm experiences a massive increase in size and a transformation in morphology. Second, the neural tube lumen is twisted and compressed as the tissue around it assumes its final shape. By the end of development, that cavity has a definite shape. It constitutes the ventricles through which cerebrospinal fluid flows to provide nourishment and protection to the brain.

Myelencephalon. This, the lowest part of the brain stem, is continuous with the spinal cord. Changes that characterize the region result from the lateral movement of the myelencephalon walls. That movement causes a stretching of the roof plate and widens the lumen of the central cavity, forming the fourth ventricle. Later in development, the thin membrane created by the stretching of the roof becomes a choroid

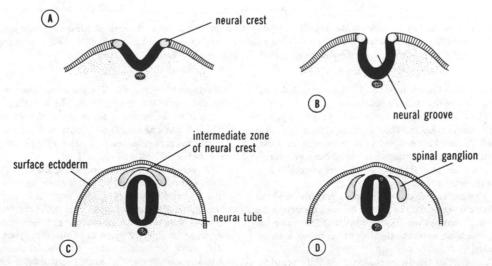

FIGURE 4. Schematic drawing of a number of transverse sections through successively older embryos, showing the formation of the neural folds, neural groove, and neural tube. Cells on the neural crest develop into the spinal and sensory ganglia. (From Langman, J. *Medical Embryology*, ed. 3. Williams & Wilkins, Baltimore, 1975.)

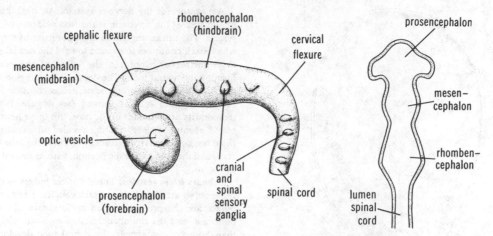

FIGURE 5. Lateral view of a 4-week-old embryo. The cephalic and cervical flexures and sensory ganglia are formed by the neural crest on each side of the rhombencephalon and spinal cord. Diagram at right shows the lumina of the three brain vesicles and spinal cord. (From Langman, J. *Medical Embryology*, ed. 3. Williams & Wilkins, Baltimore, 1975.)

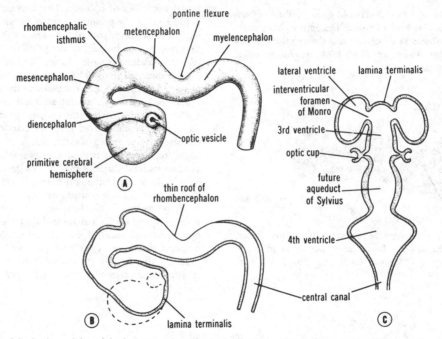

FIGURE 6. *A*. Lateral view of the brain vesicles of the human embryo in the beginning of the sixth week. *B*. Midline section through the brain vesicles and spinal cord of an embryo of the same age as shown in *A*. Note the thin roof of the rhombencephalon. *C*. Diagram of the lumina of the spinal cord and brain vesicles. (From Langman, J. *Medical Embryology*, ed. 3. Williams & Wilkins, Baltimore, 1975.)

plexus, where cerebrospinal fluid is formed. All those morphological features are characteristic of the medulla oblongata.

Metencephalon. The fourth ventrical continues into the next part of the brain stem, the metencephalon. That segment gives rise to two important structures. The cerebellum develops from tissue in the dorsal region, and fiber tracts that act as a bridge between the cerebral cortex and the cerebellar cortex develop from the basal layer of cells. Those bridging tracts give the section its name, the pons.

Mesencephalon. The mesencephalon is the most primitive and the shortest of the brain stem segments. The central lumen, enlarged in the medulla and the pons, becomes remarkably constricted, forming the cerebral aqueduct, which connects the third ventrical below with the fourth ventricle above.

Diencephalon. The cavity of the diencephalon is the third ventricle. At first, it is an oval lumen, but the ventricle becomes compressed and altered in shape as thalamic, hypothalamic, and epithalamic nuclei develop within its walls. The thalamus appears as a thickening in the caudal area of the diencephalon. The hypothalamus develops lower in the wall of the ventricle, above the pituitary gland (hypophysis), with which it has anatomical and functional connections. Eventually, the hemispheres envelop the region, fusing a segment of cerebral cortex to the diencephalon (see Figure 7).

Telencephalon. The telencephalon sits atop the anterior end of the third ventricle (see Figure 8). It is made up of two parts: a midportion and bilateral outpocketings, the cerebral hemispheres. After they appear in the fifth week of development, the cerebral hemispheres expand in an upward direction, compressing the intraventricular foramen, thus reducing its size. The growth of the hemispheres is uneven. At first, they grow forward, creating the frontal lobes. Then they expand laterally and upward to form the parietal lobes. The occipital and temporal lobes are formed last, as the hemispheres grow posteriorly and inferiorly. The result of that tremendous expansion is the burial of

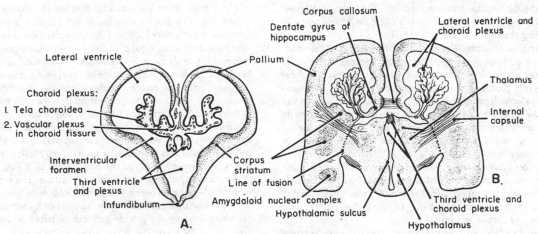

FIGURE 7. Diagrams of frontal sections through the diencephalon, ventricular system, and choroid plexuses of the developing brain. *A.* Growth of choroid plexuses and the corpus striatum into the lateral and third ventricles. *B.* Fusion of the telencephalon with the diencephalon. (From Carpenter, M. B. *Human Neuroanatomy*, ed. 7. Williams & Wilkins, Baltimore, 1976.)

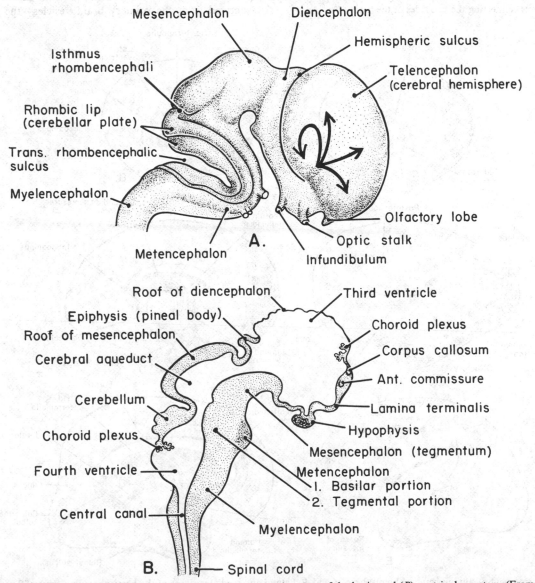

FIGURE 8. Schematic drawings showing simultaneous changes in (*A*) external surface of the brain and (*B*) ventricular system. (From Carpenter, M. B. *Human Neuroanatomy*, ed. 7. Williams & Wilkins, Baltimore, 1976.)

the brain stem by the hemispheres (see Figure 9). The process is likened to rising bread dough, which may completely overflow, enveloping and eventually hiding the pan in which it was mixed.

With further differentiation, the most anterior segment of the telencephalon, the neopallium or suprastriatal region, becomes the cerebral hemispheres; the midportion of the telencephalon, the basal or striatal area, develops into the basal ganglia; the lowest portion of the telencephalon, the paleopallium or rhinencephalon, evolves to contain the structures of the limbic system. The limbic system, in fact, derives its name from its developmental origins, since the limbic lobe is the border between structures of the diencephalon and telencephalon. *Limbus* in Latin means border.

A major process during the growth of the cerebral cortex is the concurrent formation between the cortex and the subcortical structures of a major tract—the internal capsule. The capsule, which has a striated appearance, courses through the basal ganglia, giving part of that region its name, the corpus striatum.

Commissures. Bundles of nerve fibers that cross from one cerebral hemisphere to the other are called commissures. The lamina terminalis—the tissue between the diencephalon roof plate and the optic chiasma—demarcates the cephalic end of the ventricular lumen. It forms a bridge for commissural fibers, acting as the principal path for important tracts connecting the two sides of the brain.

Three major fiber bundles arise that use the lamina terminalis (see Figure 10). The first to develop is the anterior commissure, which connects the olfactory bulb and the temporal lobe of the cortex on one side with their counterparts in the opposite hemisphere. The second commissure to develop is the fornix, which runs along the inferior border of the hemispheres. Because the fornix connects the cortex of the hippocampus to each hemisphere, it is also called the hippocampal commissure. The third tract, appearing late in embryonic development but destined to become the important and massive intercerebral connection, is the corpus callosum. At first, its fibers connect only the frontal lobes, but it later connects the parietal lobes as well. The corpus callosum undergoes tremendous growth, paralleling that of the neocortex. It is pulled along as the neopallium as it first grows forward then backward, arching over the third ventricle. The remaining lamina terminalis—lying between the corpus callosum and the fornix—is stretched into a thin membrane by the anterior movement of the corpus callosum, forming the septum pellucidum between the lateral ventricles.

GROSS ANATOMY

It is common practice to study the brain in terms of structures derived from the primary brain vesicles—the forebrain, the

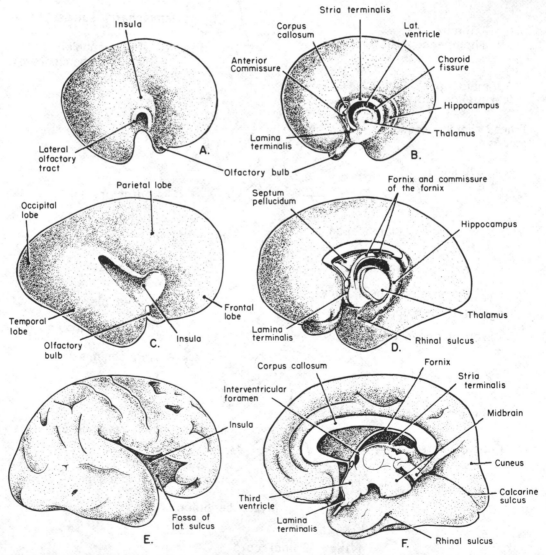

FIGURE 9. Development of human cerebral hemisphere. *A* and *B*. Lateral and medial surfaces of the hemisphere in a fetus of 3 months. *C* and *D*. Lateral and medial surfaces of the hemisphere in a fetus at the beginning of the fifth month. *E* and *F*. Lateral and medial surfaces of the hemisphere at the end of the seventh month. (From Carpenter, M. B. *Human Neuroanatomy*, ed. 7. Williams & Wilkins, Baltimore, 1976.)

midbrain, and the hindbrain.

Forebrain. The external surface of an intact brain is represented by the cerebral hemispheres. Their removal exposes the brain stem to view. Numerous furrows—sulci or fissures—are present on the cerebral surface, along with elevated regions called gyri. On the basis of those landmarks, the cerebral hemispheres are divided into five areas—frontal, parietal, occipital, temporal, and insular lobes. With the exception of the insular lobe, which is buried beneath the lateral fissure, each lobe is visible on the surface of the brain (see Figure 11). The two cerebral hemispheres are almost completely separated by the longitudinal fissure; they communicate with each other primarily through the corpus callosum, which forms the floor of the fissure. The outer covering of the hemispheres is formed by the cerebral cortex, which consists of some 14×10^9 nerve cells. Beneath the cortex are several areas of white matter and nuclear masses. Prominent are the basal ganglia, made up of the caudate, lenticular, and amygdaloid nuclei and the claustrum (see Figure 12). Below the basal ganglia, structures derived from the diencephalon are seen. They are the thalamic and hypothalamic nuclei. They are closely associated with the ventricular system, representing the floor and the lateral walls of the third ventricle.

Midbrain. Internally, the midbrain can be divided into three parts—the tectum, the tegmentum, and the crura cerebri. The crura cerebri contain numerous descending fibers. The tegmentum, which runs into the midbrain from the spinal cord, contains a diffuse aggregate of cells and fibers called the reticular formation. The tectum forms the roof of the midbrain.

Externally, the mesencephalon is characterized by the superior and the inferior colliculi, nuclei involved with the relay of visual and auditory impulses, respectively.

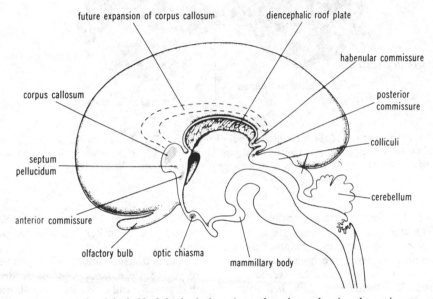

FIGURE 10. View of the medial surface of the right half of the brain in a 4-month embryo, showing the various commissures. The *broken line* indicates the future expansion of the corpus callosum. The hippocampal commissure is not indicated. (From Langman, J. *Medical Embryology*, ed. 3. Williams & Wilkins, Baltimore, 1975.)

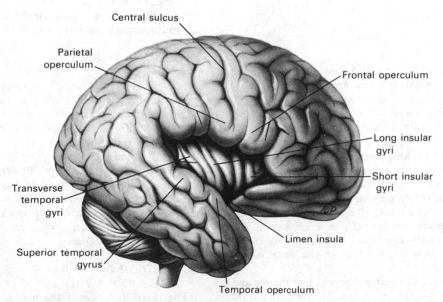

FIGURE 11. View of the right cerebral hemisphere with the banks of the lateral sulcus drawn apart to expose the insula. (From Carpenter, M. B. *Human Neuroanatomy*, ed. 7. Williams & Wilkins, Baltimore, 1976.)

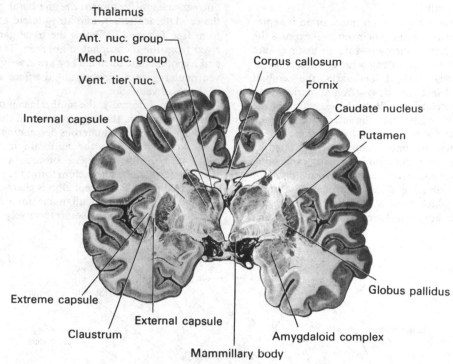

Thalamus
Ant. nuc. group
Med. nuc. group
Vent. tier nuc.
Internal capsule
Corpus callosum
Fornix
Caudate nucleus
Putamen
Extreme capsule
External capsule
Claustrum
Mammillary body
Globus pallidus
Amygdaloid complex

FIGURE 12. Photograph of a frontal section of the brain at the level of the mammillary bodies. In this section the main nuclear groups of the thalamus are identified and portions of all components of the basal ganglia are present. The amygdaloid nuclear complex lies in the temporal lobe internal to the uncus and ventral to the lentiform nucleus. (From Carpenter, M. B. *Human Neuroanatomy*, ed. 7. Williams & Wilkins, Baltimore, 1976.)

Hindbrain. The medulla, the pons, and the cerebellum constitute the hindbrain. The medulla and the pons are rich in discrete ascending and descending tracts and in cranial nerve nuclei. In addition, the pons provides connections to the cerebellum and other parts of the nervous system. The cerebellum is markedly different from other brain stem parts; it is structurally similar to the cerebrum in that it has a cortex of gray matter and an interior composed of both white matter and nuclei.

Neurophysiology

NEURON

The neuron is the anatomical and functional unit of the nervous system. Individual neurons, arranged in simple or complex circuits, exist in a wide variety of sizes and shapes throughout the peripheral and central nervous systems. However, 90 per cent of all neurons are found in the brain. Despite their diverse morphology, all nerve cells have three common parts—cell body, dendrite, and axon (see Figure 13).

The cell body (soma, cyton, perikaryon) contains the machinery essential to cell life. That machinery includes the nucleus, the nucleolus, the mitochondria, the Golgi apparatus, and other structures. It is from the cell body that the embryonic outgrowth of all portions of the neuron takes place. The integrity of the cell body is crucial to the maintenance of the entire nerve cell; its destruction results in the death of the neuron.

Dendrites are branch-like neuron processes that receive and conduct impulses toward the cell body. Most neurons have multiple dendrites, although some cells may have none at all. Dendrites within the central nervous system generally divide

into multiple branches close to the cell body. Such a structure provides an exquisitely sensitive receptor surface for incoming impulses.

Axons transmit impulses away from the cell body. In that respect they are the opposite of dendrites. Axons also differ in that usually only one of those processes is found in each neuron. The axons occupy a prominent position in the transmission of nervous impulses, for they carry excitatory information to receptor sites. That is done through a series of events that occur at the terminal of the axon; at the synaptic knobs, which contact the cell bodies or dendrites of other neurons; or at effector organs, such as muscles.

NUCLEI AND TRACTS

Masses of nerve cell bodies are gray in appearance and are called gray matter. When they occur outside of the central nervous system, such concentrations of cell bodies are called ganglia. Within the brain and the spinal cord, they are called nuclei. The term "nucleus" in this instance and the term "nucleus" used in discussing the architecture of an individual cell have different meanings. Bundles of fibers within the central nervous system, usually subserving special sensory or motor functions and existing in discrete regions, are commonly termed tracts or fasciculi. Since fibers in those tracts are covered by myelin, they take on a white color, giving those areas the designation white matter.

CONDUCTION OF IMPULSES

The prime function of the nervous system is to transmit excitatory messages from one point in the body to another. Initial stimulation may be electrical, thermal, chemical, or

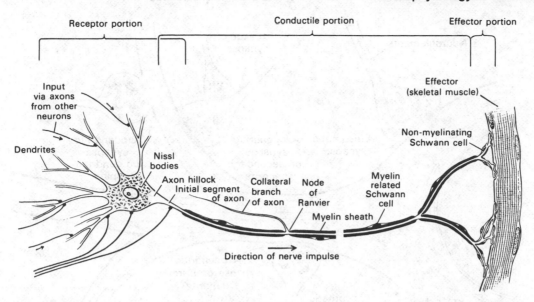

FIGURE 13. This diagram illustrates the receptor, conductile, and effector portions of a typical large neuron. The effector endings on skeletal muscle identify it as a somatic motor neuron; in many neurons the effector endings are applied to the receptor portions of other neurons. The presence of the myelin sheath on the conductile portion of the neuron (the axon) increases conduction velocity. The axon is shown to be interrupted, because it is much longer than can be illustrated here. Note the numerous axons communicating with the dendritic zone. *Arrows* indicate the unidirectional nature of the impulse. (From Copenhaver, W. M., Bunge, R. P., and Bunge, M. B. *Bailey's Textbook of Histology*, ed. 16. Williams & Wilkins, Baltimore, 1971.)

mechanical. If the stimulus reaches a threshold value, it creates an excitatory state, initiating a propagated impulse within the neuron. That process is called conduction and is accomplished by the movement of ions into and out of the nerve cell. The movement creates alterations in the electrical charge on the axon membrane. In the normal intact nerve cell, impulses are transmitted in one direction—away from the cell body and toward the synaptic knobs at the end of the axon.

SYNAPTIC TRANSMISSION

Once the propagated nerve impulse reaches the terminal end of the axon, it initiates a series of events that transfer that impulse to a second neuron. That event takes place at a structure called the synapse. The synapse is composed of the presynaptic axon terminus and, at a distance of 200 Å, a postsynaptic membrane. Thus, there is a discontinuity, termed the synaptic cleft, between communicating neurons (see Figure 14). As noted by Schwartz (1973),

the postsynaptic component of the synapse may be formed by any part of the surface of the second neuron with the exception generally of the axon hillocks; it usually is a dendrite but it may be part of the cell body or part of the membrane of another axon. A single neuron may be involved in many thousands of synaptic connections but in every case the impulse transmission can occur only in one direction.

If there is a gap between presynaptic and postsynaptic membranes, how is impulse transmission effected? Electrical depolarization of the presynaptic membrane permits the release of chemical transmitters stored in presynaptic vesicles. Those substances cross the synaptic cleft and combine with a postsynaptic receptor system. The action of the mediators may either cause a depolarization of the postsynaptic membrane, resulting in excitation of the second neuron, or cause a hyperpolarization, resulting in an inhibitory situation. In that fashion, chemicals mediate the transmission of impulses.

CHEMICAL MEDIATORS

Many substances influence activity at the synapse. Hormones, electrolytes, drugs, and metabolic products are among the compounds that modify neuronal response. However, the primary chemical mediators of synaptic communication are the neurotransmitters, a class of endogenous substances that are grouped together on the basis of biological function, rather than molecular structure.

To be considered a neurotransmitter, a compound must be associated with a complex of features and events. They include synthesis within a neuron; storage close to the synaptic cleft, release from the axon terminal after neuronal depolarization, movement across the synaptic cleft, combination with a receptor site on the postsynaptic membrane, resulting change in ionic permeability of the postsynaptic membrane, and rapid removal or deactivation of the transmitter so that the receptor is free for another communication.

Some compounds act as both neurotransmitters and hormones. In contrast to transmitters, hormones are secreted by specialized nonneuronal cells, usually ductless glands. Released in trace amounts, they are transported in the blood to sites that may be distant from their sources. Once at those target tissues or organs, a hormone tends to have longer-acting effects than neurotransmitters, sometimes initiating biological responses that last for hours or days. Peripheral hormones are mainly steroids, peptides, substituted amino acids, and modified fatty acids. Most hormones originating in the brain are peptides.

Just as some compounds exhibit qualities of hormones and transmitters, certain neurons possess gland-like features. Those neurons are termed neurosecretory cells and their products are described as neurosecretions.

Acetylcholine. One of the earliest neurotransmitters to be identified, acetylcholine is still poorly understood with respect to its role in the regulation of behavior. It is the acetyl ester of choline and is present in the peripheral neurons and in the brain. Neurons that release acetyl-

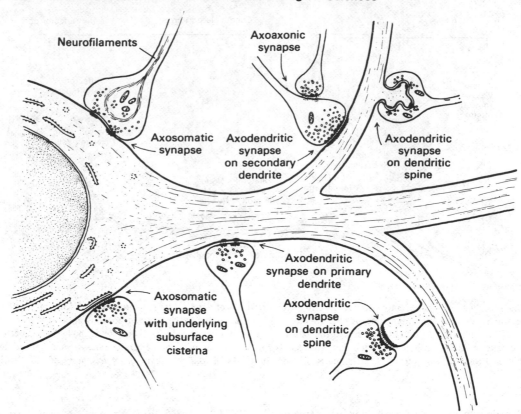

FIGURE 14. Schematic representation of the types of synapses occurring on various parts of a single neuron. (From Copenhaver, W. M., Bunge, R. P., and Bunge, M. B. *Bailey's Textbook of Histology*, ed. 16. Williams & Wilkins, Baltimore, 1971.)

choline are termed cholinergic. In the peripheral nervous system, acetylcholine and norepinephrine are by far the most important neurotransmitters. Within the brain, that situation is altered, and the agents are of quantitatively minor importance. Acetylcholine has an uneven distribution, having its lowest concentration in the cerebellum and its highest concentration in the brain stem. Connections within the corpus striatum are acetylcholine mediated. The injection of the compound into either the ventricles or the gray matter produces excitatory effects and profound behavior alterations. The excitatory role of the cholinergic neurons in the corpus striatum has led to speculation about their role in tardive dyskinesia.

Dopamine. The neurotransmitter dopamine is synthesized in dopaminergic neurons from the amino acid tyrosine. Dopamine is manufactured in other neurons as well, but in those neurons it is merely an intermediate compound in the synthetic pathway leading to norepinephrine and epinephrine. The enzyme dopamine β-hydroxylase catalyzes the transformation of dopamine to norepinephrine. Since dopamine, norepinephrine, and epinephrine all contain a catechol nucleus, they are termed catecholamines.

Dopamine and other catecholamines act as inhibitory agents in the control of hormone secretion. Their influence is primarily on the hypothalamus. Central dopamine activity is measured indirectly through the determination of cerebrospinal fluid levels of homovanillic acid (HVA), the principal metabolite of dopamine.

Three distinct dopamine systems or tracts have been described—the nigrostriatal, the tuberoinfundibular, and the mesolimbic pathways.

Fibers of the nigrostriatal system arise in the substantia nigra of the midbrain and terminate in the caudate nucleus and the putamen. Collectively, the caudate nucleus and the putamen form the corpus striatum or simply the striatum. Striatal dopamine, thus, originates in cells of the substantia nigra. The major afferent system of the substantia nigra is formed by fibers that originate in the striatum. Those neurons contain the neurotransmitter γ-aminobutyric acid (GABA). Together the nigrostriatal and strionigral fibers form a closed feedback loop.

Nigrostriatal dopamine neurons have long been known to be in-

volved in the regulation of fine motor activity. Degeneration of those tracts is associated with Parkinson's disease, and treatment of that disorder involves the administration of the exogenous dopamine precursor levodopa.

The tuberoinfundibular system originates in the hypothalamic arcuate nucleus and terminates in the median eminence. Neurons of that pathway influence the release of hypothalamic peptides, which, in turn, regulate pituitary activity.

Included in the mesolimbic system are the septal region, the olfactory tubercle, the nucleus accumbens, and the medial, prefrontal, cingulate, and entorhinal areas.

Another dopamine pathway, with terminals in the frontal and the cingulate cerebral cortex, has been elucidated (Snyder, 1978).

Pharmacological research has led to the observation that dopamine neurons in different areas of the brain are physically distinct, each exhibiting unique responses to dopamine agonists and antagonists. Those differences may correlate with the presence or the absence of dopamine-sensitive adenylate cyclase in the receptors. Clinical experience with the drug clozapine, an effective antipsychotic agent that does not produce concomitant extrapyramidal symptoms, has led to speculation that clozapine has a selectively greater effect on dopamine turnover in limbic areas than in the nigrostriatal system. That supports a current view that the mesolimbic system is an important site of neuropathology in schizophrenia (Stevens, 1973).

Norepinephrine and epinephrine. Norepinephrine is essentially a peripheral transmitter, synthesized and stored in sympathetic neurons. Those postganglionic neurons are morphologically similar to the chromaffin cells of the adrenal medulla—the most primitive nerve cells in the human body. In the central nervous system, norepinephrine is most highly concentrated in the hypothalamus but is also found in the cerebellum, the hippocampus, the cerebral cortex, the reticular formation, and the spinal cord. Neurons, originating in the locus coeruleus, contain high concentrations of norepinephrine. Central nervous system concentrations of epinephrine are low, and the functions of the substance are poorly understood.

Methoxyhydroxyphenylethyleneglycol (MHPG) is a major metabolite of brain norepinephrine and is believed to reflect the functional activity of central noradrenergic neurons. With urinary MHPG used as a marker, the inference has been made that a relationship exists between changes in norepinephrine activity and the symptom of depression.

Serotonin (5-hydroxytryptamine). Serotonin was first recognized in cells of the intestine and in blood platelets. Later, the biogenic amine was also described as a central neurotransmitter. The pineal gland, the hypothalamus, and the raphe nuclei, a group of mesencephalic and pontine nuclei, are especially high in serotonin content. The substance is synthesized from tryptophan. Dietary intake of tryptophan may affect central serotonin levels. Degradation of the compound is catalyzed by monoamine oxidase, and inhibitors of the enzyme cause an increase of serotonin in the brain. Actually, less than 2 per cent of the total body serotonin is found in the brain. Since the neurotransmitter does not cross the blood-brain barrier, all central nervous system serotonin originates within the system.

Serotonin is an inhibitory transmitter, although it seems to activate neurons in some areas, such as the limbic system. Currently, many studies link serotonin to the regulation of sleep, appetite, temperature, and arousal. It has also been associated with migraines, depression, schizophrenia, and Gilles de la Tourette's disease. The injection of serotonin into the lateral ventricles of animals has produced somnolence, catatonia, and fever. Lesions of the raphe nuclei, which act as an important sleep synchronization center, result in insomnia. Inhibition of serotonin synthesis produces similar effects.

The major metabolite of serotonin, 5-hydroxyindolacetic acid (5-HIAA) is used as an indirect measure of central serotonin activity.

γ-Aminobutyric acid (GABA). GABA is formed through the removal of the carboxyl group from the amino acid glutamate. Neither GABA nor glutamate can enter the central nervous system from the periphery, and thus they must be synthesized in the brain. GABA may represent 40 per cent of all synapses. GABA is an inhibitory transmitter, and several forms of induced convulsions have been shown to result from its decreased concentration in the brain. When cats are injected with GABA receptor antagonists, as has been done in the nucleus accumbens, the animals exhibit withdrawal, hyperalertness, approach avoidance, and motor stereotypes. The highest concentrations of GABA are in the substantia nigra, the globus pallidus, and the hypothalamus.

Enkephalins and endorphins. In late 1975, Hughes and his co-workers succeeded in isolating a brain peptide with opiate-like properties. The substance was later determined to be two separate but structurally similar pentapeptides that differ only in a terminal amino acid. Together those compounds are termed the enkephalins. Another class of opiate-like peptides, subsequently discovered in extracts of the pituitary gland, are called endorphins. The pituitary peptides are larger than the enkephalins. Both the enkephalins and the endorphins have been shown to act as neurotransmitters, mediating the central response to pain. The enkephalins, most highly concentrated in areas where opiate receptors are present, are destroyed by the enzyme carboxypeptidase A. Inactivation of that enzyme produces increased enkephalin levels. Initial studies have suggested that higher pain tolerance is associated with the phenomenon. The agent used to inhibit carboxypeptidase A is a synthetic compound similar to the amino acid D-phenylalanine.

All those substances produce analgesia in pharmacological doses. Naloxone, a pure narcotic antagonist, partially reverses the analgesia.

An intriguing feature of enkephalin distribution is their occurrence in areas that mediate not only pain but emotional and stress reactions as well. The limbic and the hypothalamic regions are rich in both enkephalins and opiate receptors.

One outgrowth of enkephalin and endorphin research are theories that acupuncture may produce analgesia through the release of one or both peptides; another is that psychoses may be related to some peptide abnormality.

Evidence suggests that the enkephalins work through inhibition of a second compound, possibly a pain-specific sensory transmitter. Substance P, a spinal cord afferent sensory transmitter that is also concentrated in the hypothalamus, is a likely candidate as that compound.

Neurosecretions. Two neurosecretory centers, the supraoptic and the paraventricular hypothalamic nuclei, are the sites of synthesis for vasopressin (antidiuretic hormone) and oxytocin. Those peptide hormones are transported axonally from the hypothalamus (bound to the carrier protein neurophysine) to the posterior lobe of the pituitary gland, where they are finally secreted. Once thought to act exclusively as a regulator of renal water retention, vasopressin has recently been implicated as a mediator of certain learning processes (DeWied, 1971; Walter et al., 1975). Clinical trials have suggested that vasopressin is effective in restoring memory loss caused by trauma or presenile disorders. DeWied's studies with animals indicate that vasopressin improves learning retention. There is further speculation that altered memory function observed in severe mental disorders may involve underlying abnormalities of vasopressin synthesis or secretion.

Amino acids. Aspartic acid (aspartate), glutamic acid (glutamate), cysteric acid, and homocysteric acid are amino acids currently believed to serve as neurotransmitters. Each of those compounds seems to act as an excitatory transmitter. Another amino acid, glycine, has been shown to act as an inhibiting transmitter in the spinal cord.

Reticular Activating System

Soon after World War II, Moruzzi and Magoun (1949) reported that direct electrical stimulation of medial portions of the medulla, the tegmentum of the pons and the midbrain, the hypothalamus, and the subthalamus produced generalized electroencephalogram (EEG) pattern alterations that appear identical to those observed in animals aroused from sleep or called to attention. Corresponding to those EEG changes were overt behavioral patterns indicating increased alertness or arousal on the part of the animal. Subsequent observations confirmed that similar changes in human EEG patterns—from high-voltage slow waves to low-voltage fast waves—occurred when a person was startled or merely opened his eyes. On the basis of changes in EEG activity, it was suggested that those areas of the brain stem and diencephalon that produce arousal or altered consciousness on stimulation be called the reticular activating system (RAS). The term RAS, therefore, refers to a functional unit made up of several morphological segments. The most extensive portion of that system is the reticular formation.

ANATOMY

The examination of sections under the light microscope, noted Carpenter (1976), shows the central portion of the brain stem to be made up of

a wealth of cells in various sizes and types, arranged in diverse aggregations and enmeshed in a complicated fiber network.

Early neuroanatomists, unable to discern any specificity of structure within the core region, simply described it according to its appearance as the reticular formation. Further research provided a better understanding of the reticular formation, making it possible to describe various paths and nuclei. Nevertheless, the interconnections between circumscribed regions are profuse, and evidence of major differences in function between areas has only recently been demonstrated. It is thus common practice to consider the reticular formation as a single unit. It is defined as that region of the brain stem, extending from the caudal medulla to the diencephalon, occupying a central location and characterized structurally by numerous diffusely arranged neurons. If the RAS were to be divided into both anatomical and physiological portions, the reticular formation would represent its caudal segment, and the diencephalon centers would be at the cephalic pole.

STRUCTURE-FUNCTION RELATIONSHIPS

All aspects of RAS function derive from the structure of the system's neurons and their connections. Individual cells are able to send impulses rostrally into the brain, caudally into the spinal cord, and collaterally to other RAS neurons and are able to do so with marked variations in the speed of impulse conduction. In that fashion any specificity is quickly lost in a chain reaction of impulses between the branching neurons.

The RAS differs from classical sensory pathways in two respects. The first difference relates to the routes taken by sensory impulses to the cerebral cortex. For example, a direct pathway system, such as the spinothalamic tract, converges on the thalamus before going to other areas of the brain (see Figure 15). The RAS represents an indirect route, with many of its fibers bypassing the thalamus as they diffusely project to the cortex. The second difference involves specificity of sensory input. Because of the complex neuron network, any specificity of sensory input is quickly abolished, so that different sensory stimuli produce equal activation. In that respect, too, the RAS differs from other sensory systems.

CONNECTIONS

The central role of the RAS as an integrating system is evident in the multiplicity of sources providing afferent impulses to the system. In broad terms, it may be said to receive all afferent sensory paths, receiving and sending fibers to the cerebral cortex, the cerebellum hypothalamus, and neurons at all levels. Even the spinothalamic and spinocerebellar tracts give off collaterals to the RAS. Similarly, impulses are received from sensory components of the various cranial nerves and peripheral nerves. Thus, touch, pain, temperature, and other superficial sensibilities; muscle and deep tendon sensations; and afferent impulses from the viscera and other internal structures of the body contribute to the RAS input. Only certain areas of the cerebral neocortex provide sensory tracts into the RAS. Those areas include the orbital, oculomotor, sensorimotor, and parietal cortices; parts of the cingulate gyri; and the temporal pole.

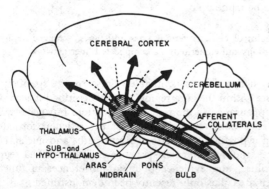

FIGURE 15. Outline of the brain of the cat, showing general location of the activating mechanism in the tegmentum of the brain stem and its relation to principal afferent systems and projections via thalamus to cerebral cortex. (From Brobeck, J. R. Neural control systems. In *Best and Taylor's Physiological Basis of Medical Practice*, J. R. Brobeck, editor, ed. 9, sect. 9, p. 1. Williams & Wilkins, Baltimore, 1973.)

FUNCTIONS

Experimental studies have shown that stimulation of the RAS can have both facilitory and inhibitory effects. All forms of movement can be affected, muscle tone altered, and respiration increased or decreased, and the circulatory system can experience pressor or depressor effects. The most provocative findings, however, have been reported with experiments relating to behavior. Besides playing a central role in sleep and arousal, the RAS seems to be involved with attention, memory, and habituation. Through disorders of those functions, several documented clinical syndromes have arisen.

Attention. Brain (1958) observed that the RAS is responsible for a 2-fold process:

> The reduction of other sensory information which might compete for attention and the integration of the sensory information being attended to with the continuously changing background of environmental sensory data.

That function is evident when a sleeping mother wakes to the sound of her crying baby but not to louder noises. Similarly, a person is able to hear his name called in the midst of a noisy crowd.

Memory. A model for RAS participation in memory and learning was outlined by Penfield (1954). The RAS and its cortical connections, he suggested, form the centrencephalic system, which integrates sensory input. A selected portion of that information is then somehow projected upward to the temporal cortex.

> As it is thus projected, a comparison is made with past similar experiences, thanks to records of the past which are held there, and a judgment with regard to familiarity, or significance is made.

Sensory habituation. Closely related to attention focusing is habituation to sensory stimuli, which may be defined as the method by which the nervous system reduces or prevents response to inconsequential repeated stimuli. Livingston (1959) reported brain stem reticular formation involvement in such adaptive processes. A series of experiments revealed that animals treated with drugs that depress reticular neuronal activity could not be habituated. In animals previously habituated,

> A lesion restricted to the pontine or mesencephalic brain-stem reticular formation is followed by permanent "release" from the habituated pattern.

Among the conclusions drawn from those findings: The RAS is more active—that is, it inhibits more—when sensory impulses are not novel or when habituation is present.

CLINICAL SYNDROMES

Most hypotheses of RAS dysfunction as a cause of pathological behavior, wrote Millon (1969)

> are highly inferential and are based on indirect clinical and experimental data.

Yet a knowledge of RAS functions and available evidence of mental disorders permit certain conclusions.

Hyperkinetic syndrome in children. First described by Bradley (1937), the hyperkinetic syndrome in children is characterized by attention weakness, distractibility, overactivity, irritability, impulsiveness, low frustration tolerance, and poor school performance. Although no single cause of the syndrome has been shown, Frederiks (1969) noted that

the symptomatology of the condition and the specific effect of amphetamine lead us to see in the hyperkinetic syndrome of children a manifestation of some disorder in the function of the reticular formation.

Narcolepsy. Even when no structural disease is found, it is presumed that some disorder of the reticular system produces the characteristic behavior seen in narcolepsy (Matthews and Miller, 1972). One piece of evidence directly implicates the reticular formation in that disorder. Victims of von Economo's encephalitis early in this century displayed acute symptoms resembling narcolepsy, and patients who presented with narcolepsy later in life reported having once suffered from encephalitis. Moreover, necroscopic examination of victims of the encephalitis revealed evidence of reticular formation degeneration.

Schizophrenia. Numerous researchers have suggested mechanisms of schizophrenia based on failure of the RAS integrating activities. Rosenzweig (1955) outlined a possible scheme in which

functions of selective conation and emotional associations break ... affect is no longer coordinated with idea, and the ideas themselves are reduced to a chaotic avalanche of thoughts or impressions, which often intrude themselves upon the patient's consciousness out of context, without order, sense or meaning.

Kornetsky and Eliasson (Kety, 1971) proposed a model based on RAS overarousal. Rats with electrodes implanted in the reticular formation were stimulated

with current so mild as not to produce a change in gross behavior.

During that stimulation, measurement of attention was made

by counting errors of omission and commission in response to brief signals which the animals had learned to call for particular responses.

Through variations of stimulation strength and the administration of psychoactive drugs, the following observations were made:

With very weak stimulation of the reticular formation, the animals showed fewer errors of omission than in the normal state—evidence that attention was improved.

With stronger stimulation, errors of omission increased, with no change in errors of commission.

Amphetamines produced effects similar to those of reticular stimulation, but barbiturates produced quite different effects, increasing the errors of commission.

The administration of chlorpromazine to a rat showing increased errors of omission under reticular formation stimulation decreased those errors and improved performance. The same drug given to an animal without reticular formation stimulation had no effect.

Limbic System

Papez (1937) attempted to point out that emotion is not a magic product but

a physiologic process which depends on an anatomic mechanism.

A group of structures associated with an arcuate convolution on the medial surface of the cerebral hemisphere known as the limbic lobe, he suggested,

deal with the various phases of emotional dynamics, consciousness, and related functions.

That seat of emotion included a portion of the cerebral cortex—the septal region, the amygdaloid complex, and the hippocampus—that connects with the anterior thalamic nuclei, mammillary bodies, and the hypothalamus. They

form part of a circuit by which impulses are transferred from the hypothalamus to the cortex and returned by the cortex to the hypothalamus.

That interconnecting network of nuclei and tracts, involving separate structural areas, can be viewed as a circuit that permits the projection of impulses to and from higher cortical centers. It provides pathways through which regions in the neocortex influence events in the limbic structures and, conversely, permit processing by those structures between components of the limbic system before relaying emotionally colored impulses into the cortex.

The Papez hypothesis is remarkable in the context of what little functional neuroanatomy relating to behavior and emotion was known at the time. In the years since 1937, evidence in support of the proposal has grown, and another element of the Papez theory—that emotional experience and emotional expression are separate phenomena—has gained general acceptance. Many workers have built on the initial suggestion of Papez and have clarified the role of structures regulating emotional behavior. MacLean (1952) suggested that an expanded group of structures related to emotional functions be termed the limbic system. That system, also known as the visceral brain because of its intimate relationships to visceral function through the hypothalamus, is composed of several structures—the subcallousal, cingulate, and hippocampal gyri and the hippocampus proper. Collectively, they are designated the limbic lobe (see Figure 16). Also included are associated subcortical nuclei, such as the amygdaloid complex, septal

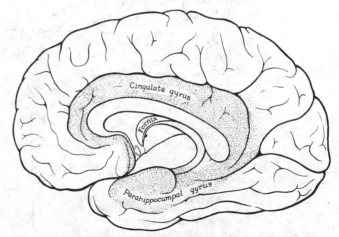

FIGURE 16. Drawing of the medial surface of the hemisphere. *Shading* indicates the limbic lobe, which encircles the upper brain stem. Although the cortical areas designated as the limbic lobe have some common structural characteristics, the extent to which they form a functional unit is not clear. (From Carpenter, M. B. *Human Neuroanatomy*, ed. 7. Williams & Wilkins, Baltimore, 1976.)

nuclei, the hypothalamus, the epithalamus, anterior thalamic nuclei, and parts of the basal ganglia (see Figure 17). For the purpose of organization, it is helpful to conceptualize the limbic system as consisting of three parts: one part in the temporal lobe, another outside of the temporal lobe, and a third made up of the major tracts connecting the system. However, various authors do differ as to the precise definition of the limbic system.

STRUCTURE-FUNCTION RELATIONSHIPS

Precise functional relationships among elements of the limbic system have not been defined, but it is possible to ascribe dominant control of specific functions to parts of the system. No component of the limbic system seems to exert a single effect. As a unit, the system exerts a restraining force on the cortex. That force is demonstrated in experiments in which the neocortex is totally removed, resulting in extreme rage reactions. If the cortex is partially resected, with the limbic cortical areas left intact, behavior is markedly placid. The importance of the limbic system lies in its role of regulating affective response to danger and the discrimination as to what is safe or dangerous.

Amygdaloid nuclear complex. The amygdala consists of a group of nuclei occupying a dorsomedial position in the temporal lobe. In the experiments of Klüver and Bucy (1939), portions of both temporal lobes, including the entire amygda-

loid complex, were destroyed. Profound disturbances in emotional behavior resulted. However, because of the generalized destruction of many structures, it was impossible to attribute any specific emotional function to the amygdalae. Subsequent work clarified the role of those nuclei. A study by Rosvold and his co-workers (1954) demonstrated that removal of the amygdalae in dominant male monkeys transformed them into submissive animals. Similar experiments have consistently produced placidity and lack of fear, rage, and aggression. No amount of provocation evokes retaliation. Threats are not answered. The characteristic fearlessness seen in amygdalectomized animals is exemplified by monkeys playing with and eating snakes, which normally terrify them (Ganong, 1971).

There have been reports of stereotactic lesions in the amygdaloid nuclei of humans that have produced marked reductions in emotional excitability, normalization of social behavior, and adaptations in patients with severe behavior disturbances (Carpenter, 1976). Those findings support the concept of the amygdala as an excitatory influence in the expression of emotion. Stimulation of the amygdala in humans produces a subjective sense of danger.

Hippocampal formation. The dentate gyrus, the hippocampus proper, and the parahippocampal gyrus are commonly termed the hippocampal formation. The rostromedial portion of the parahippocampal gyrus is called the uncus. The hippocampus is also called Ammon's horn (CA), and areas of the structure are subdivided as hippocampal fields CA 1 to CA 4.

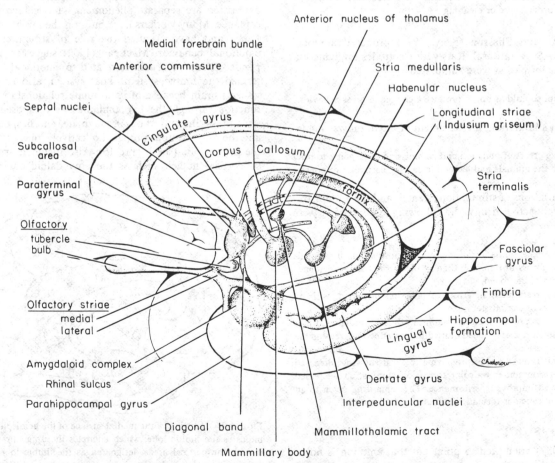

FIGURE 17. Semischematic drawing of rhinencephalic structural relationships as seen in medial view of the right hemisphere. Both deep and superficial structures are indicated. (Modified from a drawing by Krieg. From Carpenter, M. B. *Human Neuroanatomy*, ed. 7. Williams & Wilkins, Baltimore, 1976.)

Lesions and stimulation of the hippocampus in cats have induced behavioral changes similar to those observed in psychomotor epilepsy. There is abundant evidence that the area has an extremely low seizure activity threshold. States of hyperarousal, anxiety, and stress are produced by hippocampal stimulation.

Contrary to early beliefs, the hippocampus has no olfactory function. It does play a major role in memory functions. Bilateral hippocampal damage results in permanent arrest of recent memory and is related to several amnestic syndromes. The manifest disorder is in the registration of memories.

The disturbance of memory is marked by the lack of any major degree of retrograde amnesia. There is no disorder of recent memory, and attention is normal. However, all recollections of events disappear within minutes after their occurrence.

Cingulate gyrus. Stimulation of the cingulate gyrus produces an arrest reaction. Animals in such experiments immediately stop other activities and appear attentive or surprised, their head and eyes moving to the opposite side.

Localized stimulation of the posterior cingulate areas has been shown to produce sexual and pleasurable reactions. Spontaneous changes in behavior result from lesions in the anterior cingulate region of monkeys. Previously aggressive animals become placid, and anxious animals become calm.

Septal region. The septal region is commonly described as consisting of the medial septal nucleus and lateral septal nucleus. Similarly, it has been divided into medial and lateral regions, with lateral septal regions including the nucleus accumbens septi. The region derives its name from its association with the septum pellucidum.

Behavioral investigations with animals have demonstrated diverse changes associated with septal lesions and stimulation. Lesions generally cause increased emotional reaction—such as aggression, rage, or overreaction to normal handling—and decreased response to punishment. Hyperdipsia has also been observed (De Frank, 1976).

Researchers have consistently demonstrated that activity of the septal region correlates with the emotion of pleasure, a fact that has led to the concept of the septal region as a pleasure center. Experiments by Olds (1960) showed that animals with electrodes implanted in the area delivered as many as 5,000 self-stimulatory shocks within 1 hour. Heath (1972) used a modification of the Olds technique as part of a treatment program for patients with severe mental illness. One patient had stimulatory electrodes placed in the septal region. Moan and Heath (1972) reported:

Allowed free access to the buttons of the self-stimulator—[the patient] stimulated himself to a point that, both behaviorally and introspectively, he was experiencing an almost overwhelming euphoria and elation and had to be disconnected, despite his vigorous protest.

On one such occasion, he stimulated himself 1,500 times within 3 hours. Each time the unit was removed, he protested and pleaded to "self-stimulate just a few more times." The localization of a sexual function to the septal region was confirmed by deep, cortical, and scalp electroencephalograms obtained from the patient during a session in which he reached orgasm. MacLean (1957) showed that septal stimulation in cats could produce penile erection.

In human beings, electrical stimulation has halted epileptic seizures, dulled intractable pain, and brought relief from anger and frustration. It is suggested that the septum exerts an inhibitory influence on emotion, thus opposing the effects of the amygdala.

CLINICAL SYNDROMES

Several clinical syndromes have been shown to correlate with underlying limbic pathology.

Klüver-Bucy syndrome. The effects in monkeys of bilateral temporal lobe destruction—involving total destruction of the amygdaloid complex and destruction of major sections of the parahippocampal gyrus, the hippocampus proper, and the temporal neocortex—were described by Klüver and Bucy in 1939. The pathological features manifested by such lesions are collectively termed the Klüver-Bucy syndrome and include: (1) Psychic blindness—vision is physically intact, but there is an inability to discriminate between objects in a meaningful fashion; there is a similar response to objects as diverse as food and a menacing animal. (2) Oral activity—it includes compulsive licking and biting and the examination of all objects by mouth. (3) Hypermetamorphosis—the patient demonstrates an inability to ignore any stimulus, with exploration of all objects regardless of their novelty. (4) Placidity—docility is shown, without evidence of reactions associated with fear or anger. (5) Altered sexual behavior—hypersexuality is manifest without regard to gender or species of partner. (6) Altered dietary habits—hyperphagia is seen.

Examples of the Klüver-Bucy syndrome in human beings have been described. Terzian and Dalle-Ore (1955) reported the manifestation of bilateral anterior temporal removal in a 19-year-old epileptic. Initially, the patient displayed psychic blindness and was unable to recognize anyone. A catatonic-like state persisted for 2 weeks after surgery; then it was replaced by hypermetamorphosis. Other changes included the development of an insatiable appetite, sexual exhibitionism, a loss of emotional behavior—including indifference and amimia—and disorders of both remote and short-term memory.

Shraberg and Weisberg (1978) presented a detailed account of the Klüver-Bucy syndrome in a 23-year-old woman. The complete expression of the syndrome in that case emphasized the importance of the limbic system to emotional and intellectual functioning. Psychic blindness and memory loss were ascribed to the interruption of connections with the primary memory storage areas, the hippocampus and the temporal neocortex, and damage to the hippocampus itself. Oral tendencies and sexual behavior were attributed to temporal lobe lesions. Hypermetamorphosis was associated with the disruption of connections involving visual integration and memory.

Korsakoff's psychosis. Patients with Korsakoff's psychosis suffer from profound amnesia, which the patient denies and is, in fact, unaware of. The condition is disguised by confabulation and pseudoremembrance. Apathy, indifference, poor initiative, and inertia are also present. The syndrome is believed to be caused by thiamine deficiency and to represent late changes of Wernicke's encephalopathy seen in chronic alcoholics. If untreated, the process may progress to irreversible dementia. Response to thiamine therapy is dramatic. It has long been held that the pathophysiology of the disorder involves the destruction of the mammillary bodies. However, recent studies suggest that loss of dendritic spines of neurons in the hippocampal formation and dentate gyrus may account for the characteristic mnemonic disturbance of the disorder (Riley and Walker, 1978).

Violent behavior. The limbic system is involved in the regulation of anger and rage. The hippocampus and the amygdala, as well as other components of the limbic system, seem to play important roles in those behaviors. A wide range of clinical conditions—including explosive personality disorder, antisocial personality, and pathological intoxication—have been correlated with EEG abnormalities localized in the temporal limbic area.

Limbic dementia. Damage confined to portions of the limbic system is not a commonly recognized cause of dementia. Corsellis and his associates (1968) suggested that a demented condition results from damage to limbic structures. In a patient with damage exclusively to the limbic system, Gascon and Gilles (1973) reported behavioral alterations identical to those seen in classic demented states. They suggested that the syndrome be termed "limbic dementia."

Uncinate fits. A constellation of changes seen in temporal lobe epilepsy arises from involvement of the uncus and is collectively grouped as uncinate fits. The characteristic olfactory aura, involuntary movements, and sensations of *déjà vu* and *jamais vu* are accompanied by the changes of behavior seen in schizophrenia. Rage, fear, and depression may be present. Penfield and Jasper (1954) reported such changes during electrical stimulation of limbic structures in patients undergoing neurosurgery.

Schizophrenia. The limbic system has been implicated as a possible site of underlying pathology in schizophrenia. The septal nuclei have been postulated to be attacked by toxic antibodies characteristic of schizophrenia (Heath, 1972). On the basis of the link between antipsychotic and antiparkinsonism drugs, as well as certain histochemical findings, Stevens (1973) implicated the limbic striatum—the nucleus accumbens septi, the bed nucleus of the stria terminalis, and the deep portion of the olfactory tubercle—in the schizophrenic process.

Limbic leukotomy. Psychosurgical relief of mental illness has been aimed primarily at the frontal lobe. On the basis of reciprocal relationships between the frontal cortex and the limbic system, a team of English physicians (Kelly et al., 1973) performed stereotactic surgery in patients with intractable psychiatric illness. Those operations interrupted connections between the frontal cortex and the limbic system and destroyed a portion of the system itself by placing a lesion in one of the main circuits in the anterior cingulate gyrus. It was reported that over-all improvement resulted in patients suffering from obsessive-compulsive disorder, depression, chronic anxiety, and schizophrenia.

Hypothalamus

The question of whether emotional experience and emotional expression are mutually exclusive assumes added importance in considering the hypothalamus, because the hypothalamus is directly or indirectly involved in the physiological changes associated with fear, anger, hunger, thirst, pleasure, and sex. Hypothalamic secretions control the release of anterior pituitary hormones, thus modulating the endocrine system. Many of the hypothalamic hormones and factors exert direct behavioral effects and are themselves influenced by dopamine, serotonin, and norepinephrine—neurotransmitters involved in mediating behavior.

Controversy revolves about which comes first, the emotional experience or the visceral reaction. Does one feel sorrow because he cries or cry because he feels sorrow? If one were to remove the visceral and somatic changes manifest in emotion, would emotion still exist? When one reviews the results of behavioral changes produced by hypothalamic destruction and stimulation, its interpretation, as suggested by MacLean (1969), must necessarily

be a matter of the observer's identification with it on the basis of his own subjective experience and introspective reasoning.

TOPOGRAPHY

The hypothalamus is a mass of gray matter in the anterior portion of the diencephalon (see Figure 18). Although it occupies a relatively small area in the human brain, the hypothalamus has important relationships and connections to structures mediating visceral, somatic, and emotional functions. The

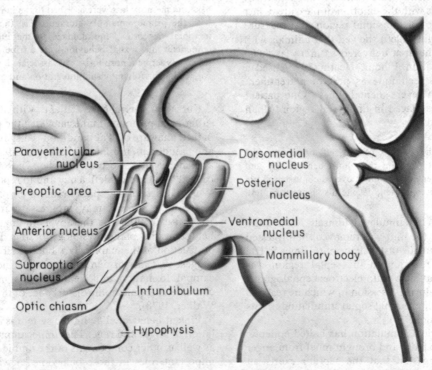

FIGURE 18. Schematic diagram of the medial hypothalamic nuclei. (From Carpenter, M. B. *Human Neuroanatomy*, ed. 7. Williams & Wilkins, Baltimore, 1976.)

hypothalamus helps to form the floor and the lateral walls of the third ventricle. Dorsally, it is bounded by the thalamus. Laterally and caudally, it is bounded by the subthalamus and the internal capsule. From anterior to posterior, it extends from the region of the optic chiasma to the mammillary bodies. Directly anterior lies the preoptic area, a portion of the forebrain ultimately related to the hypothalamus. The infundibulum, which connects to the posterior hypophysis, projects from the ventral portion of the hypothalamus.

CONNECTIONS

The richness of fiber connections between hypothalamic nuclei and other brain structures reflects its pivotal role in emotional expression. Several afferent pathways connect the hypothalamus with parts of the limbic system. The medial forebrain bundle, for example, arises from the periamygdaloid region and septal nuclei, passes to lateral portions of the hypothalamus, then out into the mesencephalic tegmentum. Similarly, fibers from the hippocampal formation and amygdaloid complex project to portions of the hypothalamus. Other afferent fibers project directly from the frontal lobe.

Efferent hypothalamic fibers from the mammillary bodies travel cephalically and caudally as the mammillothalamic and mammillotegmental tracts (see Figure 19). The mamillothalamic tract is important, since it connects with the anterior thalamic nuclei, which then form part of a hypothalamic-thalamic-cingulate circuit. Other important tracts emerge from the periventricular nuclei, which establish connections with the dorsomedial thalamic nuclei and the midbrain reticular formation. The supraoptic hypophysis tract conducts fibers from the supraoptic and paraventricular nuclei to the posterior lobe

of the hypophysis. Cells of those nuclei are involved in the production of vasopressin (antidiuretic hormone) and oxytocin.

BEHAVORIAL CHANGES

Fear and rage. The most dramatic behavioral changes associated with hypothalamic function are the related expressions of fear and rage. Both responses are closely tied to the visceral and somatic processes evident during periods of danger or stress and represent the organism's instinctive efforts at self-preservation. The familiar concept of flight-or-fight reactions refers to those fear-induced or defensive changes. Confronted with danger, animals flee, but, if retreat is not possible, they fight. In both instances there is a discharge of epinephrine, accompanied by sympathetic autonomic phenomena, such as dilation of the pupils, increased heart rate, elevated blood pressure, increase in respiration, and muscle vasodilation. That the hypothalamus is involved in such reactions is evidenced by the fact that both selective destruction and stimulation of the structure produce all the above symptoms.

Removal of the cortex or lesions in the ventromedial hypothalamic nuclei produce characteristic episodes of rage. Cats exhibit hissing and growling, spitting, baring of claws, pupillary dilation, biting, arching of the back, clawing, and horripilation. The term "sham rage" was initially used to describe such expressions in decorticate animals because the anger lacked direction, and with no cortex to feel anger, noted Walsh (1964), it merely represented "the motor concomitants of an emotion the animal cannot experience," thus representing a pseudoaffective reflex. For many years it was common practice to describe the fury seen in animals with hypothalamic lesions as manifestations of sham rage, but it was subsequently observed

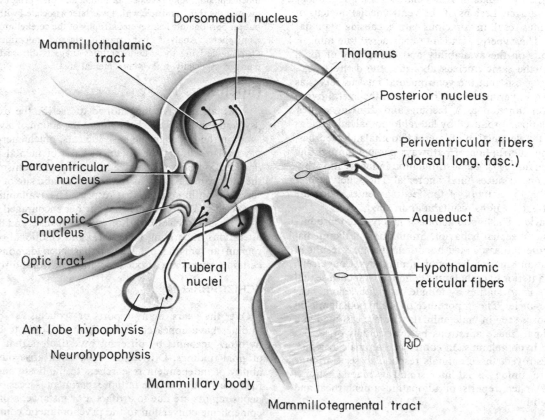

FIGURE 19. Diagram showing some of the efferent hypothalamic pathways. (From Carpenter, M. B. *Human Neuroanatomy*, ed. 7. Williams & Wilkins, Baltimore, 1976.)

that, in those animals, the savage behavior was quite specific in its focus. Indeed, the animals seemed to possess full sensory and motor cortical function, thus suggesting that they experienced the emotions they expressed. In one series of experiments (Flynn, 1967), cats persistently attacked anesthetized or stuffed rats instead of styrofoam or foam-rubber blocks. In human beings, lesions of the posteromedial nucleus have reduced anxiety in patients with behavior disturbances. Stimulation and manipulation of the hypothalamus in the course of neurosurgery caused outbreaks of manic behavior, and the patients were reported to feel fear, rage, or tranquility. Those findings are of value in understanding hypothalamic activity, since they suggest the involvement of the cerebral cortex and the thalamus in the rage responses. Rather than being a simple effector organ, the hypothalamus influences and is subject to influence by other neural structures, a fact that is most clearly seen in the interaction of hypothalamic neuroendocrine cells and the central neurotransmitters.

Passivity. The hypothalamus also seems to influence passive behavior. In 1937 Ranson reported that lesions in the lateral hypothalamus transformed "very wild and excitable rhesus monkeys" into "emotionally unreactive . . . free from fear" animals.

> Their faces were blank and free from wrinkles . . . and failed to register the play of emotions so characteristic of the wild monkey in captivity.

Studies by Hess (1969) similarly revealed adynamia in cats with destruction of the middle and posterior hypothalamus. The loss of affective response is especially marked by lesions restricted to the posterior regions (Ingram, 1959).

Appetitive behavior. Both the frontal lobe and the amygdala connect with the hypothalamus and share with it a regulatory function over hunger. Lesions of the ventromedial nucleus of the hypothalamus result in voracious eating, causing hypothalamic obesity. The hyperphagia is not considered true hunger, since it depends on the availability and desirability of food. Stimulation of the same nucleus abolishes the desire to eat. That finding suggests that the ventromedial nucleus serves as a satiety center. Experiments also reveal that the lateral hypothalamic nuclei function as a feeding and drinking center. Aphagia and adipsia produced by lateral hypothalamic lesions are related to the destruction of lateral hypothalamic neurons, rather than the interruption of pathways passing through the region (Grossman, 1977). Their stimulation induces eating, but their destruction produces fatal anorexia. The satiety center seems to inhibit the activity of the feeding center, since the destruction of both regions results in anorexia.

Sexual behavior. The hypothalamus is involved in reproductive functions and sexual behavior. Stimulation of the medial forebrain bundle and associated hypothalamic areas results in penile erection and mating behavior in monkeys. Conversely, lesions in the anterior hypothalamus completely abolish sexual interest. There is no mating by female cats with lesions near the supraoptic nuclei. The importance of the hypothalamus in sexual behavior is seen in male animals who are castrated and in female animals made anestrous by ovariectomy or lesions that spare the hypothalamus. In contrast to animals in which the area is destroyed, those animals respond to sex hormone injections by regaining sexual interest and by mating activity. Ingram (1959) cited reports of idiopathic amenorrhea and frigidity caused by

emotional disturbances which may possibly interfere with hypothalamic activation of the pituitary.

Sleep. The hypothalamus is but one of many parts in the sleep-waking mechanisms of human beings. On the basis of early animal experiments, it has been theorized that the hypothalamus contains primary centers controlling somnolence. Posterior hypothalamic lesions induced prolonged sleep and emotional lethargy, and tumors of the pineal, with involvement of the hypothalamus, were described in association with abnormal somnolence. On the basis of extensive experimentation, it is presently believed that such pathological behavior is a consequence of widespread neural activity involving parts of the thalamus and the RAS.

HYPOTHALAMIC ATROPHY

Lesions in specific hypothalamic nuclei inevitably produce dramatic alterations of behavioral or endocrine function. Indeed, the deliberate production of discrete lesions in animals has been a major research strategy in hypothalamic investigations. However, the strategic and global position of the diencephalic region in the regulation of emotional and physiological homeostasis is best observed in persons with disease of the hypothalamus. Kelts and Hoehn (1978), for example, documented the 13-year course of a patient with progressive hypothalamic atrophy:

> A patient, who has been followed for thirteen years, developed the first symptoms of progressive hypothalamic atrophy at the age of 39. The diagnosis was confirmed by pneumoencephalography five years after onset. Hypothalamic dysfunction was manifested clinically by loss of libido, impotence, obesity, polydypsia, somnolence, and rage attacks. Assessment of endocrinologic function demonstrated low serum levels of testosterone, FSH, and LH, a diabetic glucose tolerance curve, decreased basal and hypoglycemic stimulated levels of HGH, and progressively increasing levels of serum prolactin. Repeated pneumoencephalography revealed an initial, and then progressive, enlargement of the third ventricle which was later associated with generalized, but proportionately less severe, atrophy of the cerebellum and cerebral hemispheres. Analysis of the physiologic and endocrinologic mechanisms underlying these abnormalities suggests diffuse hypothalamic damage, especially in the ventromedial area.

Biochemistry

Psychiatrists have long hoped to ascribe the expression of psychotic and affective behavior to the action of a well-defined agent in the brain. In the past 30 years, much energy has been devoted to finding the chemical basis of mental illness. The introduction of psychoactive and antiparkinsonism drugs and the attendant curiosity as to their mode and site of action have served as an impetus in that respect. The availability of newly perfected study techniques has further encouraged work in the area. Despite such efforts, however, the causes and the chemical alterations underlying behavioral and emotional disturbances remain an enigma. At best, it has been demonstrated that certain changes are associated with behavioral disorders.

SCHIZOPHRENIA

Over the years, many reports of "conclusive" biochemical findings have appeared in the literature, only to be followed by other accounts by different investigators that dispute the original findings. Difficulties most often arise out of the inability of independent researchers to duplicate and thus confirm the validity of the initial experiment. Occasionally, erroneous reports are due to artifact. For instance, a proposal that epinephrine conversion to the psychomimetic compounds adrenochrome and adrenolutin produced psychosis was eventually discounted after it was discovered that suspicious metabolites were, in fact, the result of low blood ascorbic acid levels. Once widely discussed reports of correlations between schizophrenia and elevated serum copper, ceruloplasmin, creatine phosphokinase, rheumatoid factor, and taraxein remain poorly understood.

Dopamine hypothesis. The dopamine hypothesis of schizophrenia relates the specific behavioral symptoms of the disorder to a functional excess of structurally normal dopamine. Clinical and laboratory evidence supporting the concept is abundant and compelling.

The idea that schizophrenia is associated with dysfunction in the dopamine system was first presented by Carlsson and Linqvist (1963). It was based on their observation that all clinically effective antipsychotic drugs increase dopamine metabolite levels and thus, it was inferred, cause a central elevation of dopamine activity. The mechanism responsible for the phenomenon, it was speculated, is a drug-induced blockade of dopamine receptors, which triggers an increased production of the transmitter.

Later studies repeatedly demonstrated an acceleration of dopamine turnover and dopamine neuron firing rate after the administration of phenothiazines or other neuroleptics. It was further demonstrated that those drugs inhibit dopamine-sensitive adenylate cyclase in certain receptor membranes. Normally, cyclase activity increases when dopamine stimulation provokes biological activity.

Antipsychotic agents have been shown, through the use of X-ray crystallography, to assume molecular configurations similar to that of dopamine. It has also been shown that those drugs do, in fact, compete with dopamine and exhibit an affinity for stereospecific dopamine-binding sites. That ability has been correlated with their clinical potency.

The long-known ability of amphetamines to induce clinical symptoms identical to those seen in schizophrenia has also been linked to the dopamine system. Dopamine and dopamine agonists, such as apomorphine, produce symptoms that resemble the amphetamine-induced psychosis. When the dopamine tracts are lesioned, however, high doses of both amphetamines and dopamine-like drugs fail to produce stereotyped behavior.

As convincing as that evidence is, the precise nature of the underlying defect of the dopamine system has not yet been elucidated. Many researchers think that the hyperdopaminergia is merely the most evident expression of another pathophysiological defect.

Transmethylation hypothesis. Harley-Mason (Osmond and Smythies, 1952) originally proposed that schizophrenia may result from abnormal transmethylation—specifically, aberrant *O*-methylation—of catecholamines, yielding dimethoxyphenylethylamine (DMPEA), a compound closely related to mescaline. Ten years later, Friedhoff and Van Winkle (1962) reported finding DMPEA in the urine of schizophrenics and not in normal control subjects, and they were also able to demonstrate the conversion, in vitro and in vivo, of dopamine in schizophrenic patients to the urinary excretion product of DMPEA.

Research conducted by other workers has failed to confirm the initial findings of a relationship between urinary DMPEA and schizophrenia. Perhaps the most serious challenge to the proposed mechanism has been the observation that DMPEA in the urine is closely related to diet, raising the question as to whether it is an endogenous metabolite or an artifact of exogenous origin. The pink spot seen in chromatographic studies reported to represent DMPEA has similarly been implicated as an artifact, being produced by the ingestion of phenothiazines or tea drinking.

A defect in the methylation of indolamines, most notably serotonin, has also been investigated for the possible significance of their role in schizophrenia. The theory has been referred to as the psychedelic model of schizophrenia. It is based on the observation that two substances, bufotenine and dimethyltryptamine (DMT)—the *N*-methylated derivatives of serotonin and tryptamine, respectively—both have hallucinogenic properties. Early investigations demonstrated increased blood and urine levels of methylated indolamines in schizophrenic patients and showed that an enzyme that mediates the methylation of tryptamine to DMT—indolamine-*N*-methyltransferase—is present in the human brain. The feasibility of the hypothesis was enhanced by clinical studies that demonstrated that normal persons given large doses of the two amino acids tryptophan and methionine or a combination of the two experience an excited state. The same regimen in schizophrenics produces a recurrence and exacerbation of psychosis, with the disorder being more severe if there is concurrent administration of a monoamine oxidase (MAO) inhibitor. That experimental technique, termed precursor loading, is of particular value in elucidating the biochemical reactions underlying observed behavioral changes. Methionine, for example, is a methyl donor that can combine with either tryptophan or serotonin. The provision of exogenous tryptophan or the accumulation of endogenous serotonin, through the action of MAO inhibitors, produces an excess of substrate with which methyl groups can combine. The enzyme described may then divert synthesis toward the pathway that results in bufotenine or DMT. Mandell and Morgan (1970) showed that inhibition of the enzyme in rabbits results in decreased conversion of *N*-methyltryptamine to DMT.

Contradictory reports have appeared. Some workers have encountered difficulty in replicating the early findings.

Cottrell and his associates (1977) described a bufotenine-like substance in the urine of many schizophrenic patients, especially in acutely ill, unmedicated patients.

The concept of low platelet MAO activity, which raises plasma tryptamine levels and leads to increased DMT, is also compatible with the indolamine hypothesis.

Baldessarini and his associates (1979) restudied the process of transmethylation. Their findings failed to support the methylation hypothesis, in that they were unable to demonstrate increases of methylated metabolites of the amine transmitters. Nevertheless, the administration of methionine consistently worsened psychoses. The authors speculate that the effect of methionine in schizophrenia may involve other metabolic pathways than those currently recognized or that methionine may have toxic effects unrelated to its role as a methyl donor.

Monoamine oxidase hypothesis. In 1972, Murphy and Wyatt reported a

somewhat lower mean activity of monoamine oxidase (MAO) in blood platelets of chronic schizophrenic patients than in normal control subjects.

Subsequent attempts to replicate the original observations have produced conflicting results. Indeed, some investigations have suggested higher values of platelet MAO values in certain groups of schizophrenic patients (Groshong et al., 1978). At present, low MAO activity does not seem to be a specific feature of schizophrenic disorders or of vulnerability to the development of schizophrenia.

Electrolyte hypothesis. Carman and Wyatt (1977) reported a relationship between malignant catatonia and high calcium levels. Describing the clinical course of one patient over a 25-

year period, the authors noted concurrent hyperthermia during catatonic episodes, a phenomenon they linked to increased muscle calcium levels.

Calcium affects neurotransmitter activity and competes with neuroleptic drugs at the neuronal membrane site. Calcium and magnesium levels are decreased by antipsychotic treatment.

Alexander et al. (1978) investigated serum calcium in schizophrenia, focusing on its relationship to clinical events. It was found that serum calcium levels increased markedly at the onset of catatonic episodes. It has been hypothesized that elevations of serum calcium levels are temporally involved in the switch process of affective state changes (Carman and Wyatt, 1977).

AFFECTIVE DISORDERS

Studies of biochemical derangements associated with affective disorders have been among the most extensive and productive areas of psychiatric research. Investigators have uncovered specific alterations of monoamine neurotransmitter activity in some forms of depression and have been able to elucidate a relationship between abnormalities of those biogenic amines and neuroendocrine dysfunction. At present, research efforts continue to focus on changes in neurotransmitter activity and brain peptide physiology. But attention is also directed at elaborating an understanding of neuronal membrane permeability, monoamine enzyme activity, fluid electrolyte balance, and adenylate cyclase function in affective disorders. Accumulated evidence increasingly suggests that the many observed changes in mood disorders are separate manifestations of a complex interaction involving events at different levels of neural and endocrine organization.

Biogenic amine hypothesis. Some, if not all, depressions are associated with an absolute or relative deficiency of catecholamines, particularly norepinephrine, at functionally important receptor sites in the brain. Elation, conversely, may be associated with an excess of such amines.

Schildkraut (1965) thus described the relationship between biogenic amines and affective or behavioral states. That theory, the biogenic amine hypothesis, has, since the early 1960's, been regarded as the central dogma of biological psychiatry.

The biogenic amine hypothesis is based, in part, on the observations that drugs such as the MAO inhibitors and tricyclic antidepressants, which potentiate or increase brain catecholamines, cause behavior stimulation and excitement and have an antidepressant effect. Conversely, drugs that deplete or inactivate central amines produce sedation or depression. Lithium carbonate, effective in the treatment of mania, decreases the release and increases the reuptake of norepinephrine.

Although attention has been directed to the role of norepinephrine in affective disorders, there is also interest in possible abnormalities of indolamine metabolism. Evidence linking the central action of serotonin to depression, for example, has come from studies that demonstrate below-normal concentrations of the principal serotonin metabolite, 5-hydroxyindolacetic acid (HIAA), in the lumbar spinal fluid of depressed patients. The use of probenecid, which prevents the acid from leaving the cerebrospinal fluid, has shown that the accumulation of HIAA is less in depressed patients than in normal controls. Another piece of evidence that suggests the involvement of serotonin in depression is the observation that tryptophan, a serotonin precursor, relieves depression in some patients.

Studies by Wirz-Justice and Pühringer (1978) revealed possible altered serotonin rhythmicity, rather than an absolute deficiency, in particular subgroups of depression. It was reported that platelet serotonin, which shows a normal diurnal rhythmicity, was desynchronized in unipolar depressives, especially among postmenopausal women.

Endocrine model. Congruent with the available knowledge of biogenic amine activity in depression is the newly developed endocrine model of affective disorders. According to the endocrine model, behavioral and physiological abnormalities manifest in certain dysphoric states are a direct consequence of altered neuropeptide activity.

Involvement of the endocrine system in depression has been suspected for many years. Among the observed somatic symptoms suggestive of endocrine changes in affective disorders are decreased appetite, weight loss, insomnia, diminished sex drive, gastrointestinal dysfunction, and predictable diurnal variations of mood. Newly developed, highly sensitive assay techniques have been able to detect marked alterations of hormone activity concurrent with depressive events, leading to an elaboration of the biogenic amine hypothesis—the endocrine model. In that scheme, the monoamine transmitters regulate the release of hypothalamic compounds through the discharges of dopaminergic, seratoninergic, and noradrenergic neurons in the hypothalamic-pituitary region.

Growth hormone. Basal secretions of growth hormone (GH) by the pituitary gland are normally augmented in response to a drop in blood sugar, starvation, stress, exercise, and estrogens. A conventional test of GH activity involves the administration of insulin, followed by the measurement of the expected rise in plasma GH levels. Using that method, investigators have repeatedly demonstrated that, in many instances of depression, there is a diminished response to such insulin-induced hypoglycemia. The phenomenon is noted most often in unipolar depressions. In bipolar and neurotic depressions the response is normal or enhanced. GH release is impaired in a significant percentage of postmenopausal women with diagnosed unipolar depression. A number of clinical and laboratory investigations have demonstrated an association between maternal deprivation and inhibition of GH secretion. It is noted among human infants with the failure-to-thrive syndrome. Similar findings have been noted in rat pups who are removed from their mothers soon after birth. When the pups are returned to their mothers, there is a rapid reversal of the deprivation-induced GH abnormality (Kuhn et al., 1978).

Control of GH release seems to reside in catecholinergic neurons. GH release is increased by dopaminergic stimulation.

Cortisol. Many depressed patients exhibit hypersecretion of cortisol. The sequence of events leading to the elevation of the adrenal steroid hormone probably begins with an increase of hypothalamic corticotropin-releasing factor (CRF) discharge. Normally, noradrenergic tracts inhibit CRF release. In depressed states, diminished activity by those neurons results in disinhibition of CRF. With the absence of restraint, CRF levels rise, sparking the function of the adrenal cortex and the resulting release of adrenocorticotrophic hormone (ACTH).

Some depressed patients fail to exhibit dexamethasone suppression of cortisol, and the normal circadian rhythm of cortisol is disturbed. In normal persons, cortisol levels decrease in the late evening and stay low through the early morning period.

Other hormones. A significant proportion of depressed patients exhibit an absent or diminished thyroid-stimulating hormone (TSH) response to thyrotropin-releasing hormone (TRH) challenge (Kastin et al., 1972; Prange et al., 1972).

Additional changes in neuroendocrine activity have been discerned. Prolactin levels may exhibit irregular circadian rhythm, and luteinizing hormone (LH) secretion is often diminished in depressed postmenopausal women.

Learning and Memory

Brain activity during the performance of common mental activities, with respect to both normal and abnormal functions, represents another important area of scientific investigation. The related phenomena of learning and memory have generated particular interest.

Many of the early contributions to the understanding of the physical aspects of learning and memory came as a consequence of anatomically oriented research. It was shown, for example, that disorders of remote and short-term memory result from bilateral temporal lobe destruction. It was also shown that the hippocampus is involved in the registration of recent memories. Numerous attempts to locate neural regions that act primarily as learning centers or memory centers have, nevertheless, been unsuccessful. It is currently held that learning and memory functions are performed in a diffuse fashion in many areas of the cortex, with many areas of overlapping activity.

The concept of diffuse cortical involvement in learning and memory was described as the law of mass action. That theory states that impairment of memory is primarily a result of the amount of tissue destroyed and not the result of ablations of specific regions.

Anatomical investigations of learning and memory functions are presently using newly developed histochemical techniques. However, the most significant recent advances have come in the fields of biochemistry and physiology. Several models—involving molecular, chemical, and electrophysiological events—have been proposed.

RIBONUCLEIC ACID (RNA)

Early biochemical experiments of memory involved worms. Planarians were trained, then they were killed and fed to untrained planarians. The untrained worms, when trained identically as the worms they had eaten, learned more readily.

Moreover, when RNA was extracted from trained worms and injected into untrained worms, the untrained worms were observed to possess the conditioned behavior of the trained worms. Subsequent findings have also suggested RNA involvement in long-term memory. It has been found that nerve stimulation increases RNA turnover, that interference with RNA synthesis impedes learning, and that the facilitation of RNA synthesis or the increased availability of RNA results in more rapid learning.

CHOLINERGIC AGENTS

Deutsch (1969) and his associates have used diisopropyl-phosphorofluoridate, an anticholinesterase, to study the role of cholinergic drugs in memory. One finding that suggests such a role is that rats injected with diisopropylphosphorofluoridate suffer from memory losses. Those losses involve recently learned tasks and seem to be concerned with the process of memory retrieval. Eserine, another anticholinesterase, has similarly been found to inhibit the learning of passive avoidance reactions in rats. *0,0*-Diethyl-*S*-ethylmercaptothiophosphate, an insecticidal anticholinesterase, increases problem-solving errors in rats.

McEntee and Mair (1978) reported that norepinephrine metabolite levels are decreased in the cerebrospinal fluid of patients with Korsakoff's syndrome, a disorder characterized by retrograde and anterograde amnesia. Citing recent evidence that implicates the ascending catecholamine pathways in learning and memory consolidation, the investigators speculated that there is a correlation between the disorder and brain noradrenergic activity.

PROTEINS

It is difficult to separate concepts of protein synthesis from RNA activity. That is especially true of ribosomal RNA, a nucleic acid that is primarily involved in the formation of proteins. Rats that are being trained to perform new tasks, for example, are found to have increased amounts of nervous system ribosomal RNA, indicating that protein synthesis is occurring. Direct evidence of protein involvement in learning and memory comes from two recently isolated compounds, S-100 and scotophobin. Inhibitors of protein synthesis, such as acetoxycycloheximide and puromycin, provide indirect evidence of a role for proteins. Under certain conditions, those compounds have decreased memory functions.

ELECTROPHYSIOLOGY

Spontaneous or evoked brain electrical activity has been explored as a reflection of previous experience. That research has been reviewed by John and his associates (1973). Neural electrical activity during learning and memory activities has been intensively investigated by John (1972).

Electrophysiological brain research is highly complex and combines the techniques of EEG recording with mathematics and computer technology. Using those methods, investigators have analyzed cerebral electrical rhythm and EEG wave shapes. Several findings related to learning and memory have been reported.

By using evoked potential techniques, for example, workers have found that released patterns of electrical activity may reflect the activation of specific memories.

It has also been observed that cerebral potentials normally elicited by a specific event are recorded even when the specific event fails to occur. That phenomenon has been interpreted as representing the electrical events of past memories or imaginary stimuli.

Another important finding relates to the fact that evoked response wave shapes are identical for identical stimuli. Moreover, when a novel stimulus is presented, a wave shape similar to the initial evoked response is recorded. As both stimuli are repeatedly presented, the similarity between the wave shapes decreases. The early responses represent the phenomenon of generalization. That phenomenon decreases after differential training of the subject has taken place.

CEREBRAL LATERALIZATION

Cerebral lateralization refers to the specialization of function characteristic of each cerebral hemisphere. The left side of the brain, for example, dominates language function in most people. It specifically seems to be concerned with the registration and the comprehension of language. The left hemisphere is also more strongly involved than its counterpart in the process of abstract and symbolic thinking.

The right hemisphere shows greater efficiency in the processing of spatial perception and emotional material. In fact, the differences of function between the hemispheres seem to be not absolute but, rather, to result from one side's performing certain activities with great efficiency than does the other side.

Much evidence regarding the phenomenon of cerebral lateralization has come from split-brain patients—patients who have undergone surgery, usually for the treatment of severe epilepsy, in which the corpus callosum and anterior commissure have been sectioned. As a result, the two cerebral hemispheres become disconnected.

Hoppe (1977) reported that a number of psychological changes accompany the split-brain procedure. For instance, commissurotomy may result in a qualitative paucity of dreams, fantasies, and symbolization.

Conclusion

Recent advances in biological psychiatry have exceeded the expectations of even the most optimistic researchers and clinicians. Yet, the new understanding is accompanied by the realization that brain function, especially as it relates to psychic function and behavior, is far more complex than had been suspected. Moreover, purely physical explanations of mental disorders do not satisfy or serve to answer all the questions that surround the disorders.

Nevertheless, the knowledge already gained is impressive and over the past decade has had a profound impact on the practice of psychiatry. Romano (1973) stated:

There has been a renaissance of biochemistry, of pharmacology, and of genetics as these relate to the field of psychiatry.... There is a greater concern for accuracy and precision in diagnosis, because it is now necessary to distinguish carefully between schizophrenia, mania, several types of depressions, and other psychotic behavior to prescribe the appropriate medication.

What are the implications of such developments for psychoanalytic theory? Perhaps an appropriate answer to that question was offered by an educator, Silberman (1970), in reference to the radical changes evident in all fields of endeavor:

No approach is more impractical than one which takes the present arrangements and practices as given, asking only "How can we do what we are doing more effectively?" or "How can we bring the worst institutions up to the level of the best?" These questions need to be asked to be sure; but one must also realize that the best may not be good enough and may, in any case, already be changing.

The validity of psychological concepts is not diminished by newly gained scientific data. The data merely serve as an impetus for new efforts to construct diagnostic and therapeutic modalities that take into account the interplay between genetic, psychological, environmental, anatomical, and biochemical factors.

Suggested Cross References

The neurochemistry of behavior is discussed in Section 2.4. The basic science of psychopharmacology is discussed in Section 2.2. Neurology is discussed in depth in Chapter 3. Schizophrenia is discussed in Chapter 15 and affective disorders in Chapters 18 and 19. Aggression is discussed in Section 4.5.

The authors wish to thank Norman Sussman, M.D., who collaborated on the preparation of this section.

REFERENCES

Alexander, P. E., Van Kammen, D. P., and Bunney, W. E. Serum calcium and magnesium in schizophrenia: Relationship to clinical phenomena and neuroleptic treatment. Br. J. Psychiatry, *133:* 143, 1978.
Angelergues, R. Memory disorders in neurological disease. In *Handbook of Clinical Neurology*, P. J. Vinkin and C. W. Bruyn, editors, vol. 3, p. 268. American Elsevier, New York, 1969.
Baldessarini, R. J., Stramentinoli, G., and Lipinski, J. F. Methylation hypothesis. Arch. Gen. Psychiatry, *36:* 303, 1979.
Ban, T. *Psychopharmacology*. Williams & Wilkins, Baltimore, 1969.
Bradley, C. The behavior of children receiving benzedrine. Am. J. Psychiatry, *94:* 577, 1937.
Brain, W. R. The physiological basis of consciousness: A critical review. Brain, *81:* 426, 1958.
Brobeck, J. R. Neural control systems. In *Best & Taylor's Physiological Basis of Medical Practice*, J. R. Brobeck, editor, ed. 9, sect. 9, p. 1. Williams & Wilkins, Baltimore, 1973.
Brodie, K. H., and Sabshin, M. An overview of trends in psychiatric research: 1963–1972. Am. J. Psychiatry, *130:* 1309, 1973.
Brown, D., Tomchick, R., and Axelrod, J. The distribution and properties of a histamine methylating enzyme. J. Biol. Chem., *243:* 2048, 1959.
Carlsson, A., and Lindqvist, M. Effect of chlorpromazine or haloperidol on formation of 3-methoxytryptamine and norepinephrine in mouse brain. Acta Pharmacol., *20:* 140, 1963.
Carman, J. S., and Wyatt, R. J. Alterations in cerebrospinal fluid and serum calcium with changes in psychiatric state. In *Neuroregulators and Psychiatric Disorders*, E. Usdin, D. A. Hamburg, and J. D. Barchas, editors, p. 186. Oxford University Press, New York, 1977.
* Carpenter, M. B. *Human Neuroanatomy*, ed. 7. Williams & Wilkins, Baltimore, 1976.
Copenhaver, W. M., Bunge, R. P., and Bunge, M. B. *Bailey's Textbook of Histology*, ed. 16. Williams & Wilkins, Baltimore, 1971.
Coppen, A., Shaw, D. M., and Farrell, J. P. Potentiation of the anti-depressive effect of a monoamine oxidase inhibitor by tryptophan. Lancet, *2:* 527, 1963.
Corsellis, J. A. N., Goldberg, G. J., and Norton, A. R. "Limbic encephalitis" and its association with carcinoma. Brain, *91:* 481, 1968.
Cottrell, A. C., McLeod, M. F., and McLeod, W. K. A bufotenin-like substance in the urine of schizophrenics. Am. J. Psychiatry, *134:* 322, 1977.
DeFrank, J. F., editor. *The Septal Nuclei*. Plenum Publishing Corp., New York, 1976.
Deutsch, J. A. The physiological basis of memory. Annu. Rev. Psychol., *20:* 85, 1969.
DeWied, D. Long-term effect of vasopressin on the maintenance of conditioned avoidance response in rats. Nature, *232:* 58, 1971.
Eckstein, G. *The Body Has a Head*. Harper & Row, New York, 1970.
Everett, N. B. *Functional Neuroanatomy*. Lea & Febiger, Philadelphia, 1971.
Flynn, V. P. The neural basis of aggression in cats. In *Neurophysiology and Emotion*, D. C. Glass, editor, p. 40. Rockefeller University Press and Russell Sage Foundation, New York, 1967.
Frazer, A., Ghanshyam, P. N., and Mendels, J. Metabolism of tryptophan in depressive disease. Arch. Gen. Psychiatry, *29:* 528, 1973.
Frederiks, V. A. M. Disorders of attention in neurological syndromes. (Sensory extinction syndromes: The hyperkinetic syndrome.) In *Handbook of Clinical Neurology*, P. J. Vinkin and G. W. Bryun, editors, vol. 3, p. 187. American Elsevier, New York, 1969.
Friedhoff, A. J., Park, S., Schweitzer, J. W., Burdock, E. I., and Armour, M. Excretion of 3,4-DMPEA by acute schizophrenics and controls. Biol. Psychiatry, *12:* 643, 1977.
Friedhoff, A. J., and Van Winkle, E. Isolation and characterization of a compound from the urine of schizophrenics. Nature, *194:* 897, 1962.
Ganong, W. F. *Review of Medical Physiology*. Lange, Los Altos, Calif., 1971.
Garfinkel, P. E., Warsh, J. J., Stancer, H. C., and Sibony, D. Total and free plasma tryptophan levels in patients with affective disorders. Arch. Gen. Psychiatry, *33:* 1462, 1976.
Gascon, G. G., and Gilles, F. Limbic dementia. J. Neurol. Neurosurg. Psychiatry, *36:* 421, 1973.
* Goodwin, F. K., and Bunney, W. E. A psychobiological approach to affective illness. Psychiatr. Ann., *3:* 19, 1973.
Goth, A. *Medical Pharmacology*, C. V. Mosby, St. Louis, 1972.
Groshong, R., Baldessarini, R. J., Gibson, D. A., Lipinski, J. F., Aexelrod, D., and Pope, A. Activities of type A and B MAO and catechol-*O*-methyltransferase in blood cells and skin fibroblasts of normal and chronic schizophrenic subjects. Arch. Gen. Psychiatry, *35:* 1198, 1978.
Grossman, S. P. The neuroanatomy of eating and drinking behavior. Hosp. Practice, *12:* 45, 1977.
Heath, R. G. Schizophrenia: Biochemical and physiologic aberrations. Int. J. Neuropsychiatry, *2:* 597, 1966.
Heath, R. G. Pleasure and brain activity in man: Deep and surface electroencephalograms during orgasm. J. Nerv. Ment. Dis., *154:* 3, 1972.
Hess, W. R. *Hypothalamus and Thalamus: Experimental Documentation*. Thieme, Stuttgart, 1969.
Himwich, H. E., and Shimizu, A. Neurophysiological correlates of psychotropic drug action: Animal studies. In *Drugs and the Brain*, P. Black, editor, p. 75. Johns Hopkins University Press, Baltimore, 1969.
Hoppe, K. D. Split brains and psychoanalysis. Psychoanal. Q., *46:* 220, 1977.
Horn, A. S., and Snyder, S. H. Chlorpromazine and dopamine: Conformational similarities that correlate with the antischizophrenic activity of phenothiazine drugs. Proc. Natl. Acad. Sci. U. S. A., *68:* 2325, 1971.
Ingram, W. R. Central autonomic mechanisms. In *Handbook of Physiology*, sect. 1, vol. 2, *Neurophysiology*, J. Field, editor, p. 951. American Physiological Association, Washington, D.C., 1960.
Janowsky, D. S., El-Yousef, M. K., Davis, J. M., and Sekerke, H. J. Antagonistic effects of physostigmine and methylphenidate in man. Am. J. Psychiatry, *130:* 1370, 1973.
John E. R. Switchboard versus statistical theories of learning and memory. Science, *177:* 850, 1972.
John, E. R., Bartlett, F., Shimokochi, M., and Kleinman, D. Neural readout from

memory. J. Neurophysiol., *36:* 893, 1973.

Kastin, A. J., Ehrensing, R. H., Schalch, D. S., and Anderson, M. S. Improvement in mental depression with decreased thyrotropin response after administration of thyrotropin-releasing hormone. Lancet, *2:* 740, 1972.

Kelly, D., Richardson, A., and Mitchell-Heggs, N. Stereotactic limbic leucotomy: Neurophysiological aspects and operative technique. Br. J. Psychiatry, *123:* 133, 1973.

Kelly, D., Richardson, A., Mitchell-Heggs, N., Greenup, J., Chen, C., and Hafner, R. J. Stereotactic limbic leucotomy: A preliminary report on forty patients. Br. J. Psychiatry, *123:* 141, 1973.

Kelts, K. A., and Hoehn, M. M. Hypothalamic atrophy. J. Clin. Psychiatry, *39:* 357, 1978.

Kety, S. Commentary. J. Nerv. Ment. Dis., *153:* 323, 1971.

Klüver, H., and Bucy, P. C. Preliminary analysis of functions of the temporal lobes in monkeys. Arch. Neurol. Psychiatry, *42:* 979, 1939.

Kuehl, F. A., Ormond, R. C., and Vandenheuvel, W. J. A. Occurrence of 3,4-dimethoxyphenylacetic acid in urines of normal and schizophrenic individuals. Nature, *211:* 606, 1966.

Kuhn, C. M., Butler, S. R., and Schanberg, S. M. Selective depression of serum growth hormone during maternal deprivation in rat pups. Science, *201:* 1034, 1978.

* Langman, J. *Medical Embryology,* ed. 3. Williams & Wilkins, Baltimore, 1975.

Livingston, R. B. Central control of receptors and sensory transmission. In *Handbook of Physiology,* sect. 1, vol. 1, *Neurophysiology,* J. Field, editor, p. 471. American Physiological Association, Washington, D.C., 1959.

MacLean, P. D. Some psychiatric implications of physiological studies on frontotemporal portion of limbic system (visceral brain). Electroencephalogr. Clin. Neurophysiol., *4:* 407, 1952.

MacLean, P. D. Chemical and electrical stimulation of hippocampus in unrestrained animals. II. Behavioral findings. Arch. Neurol. Psychiatry, *78:* 128, 1957.

* MacLean, P. D. The hypothalamus and emotional behavior. In *The Hypothalamus,* W. Haymaker, E. Anderson, and W. J. Nauta, editors, p. 659. Charles C Thomas, Springfield, Ill., 1969.

Mandell, A. J., and Morgan, M. Human brain enzyme makes indole hallucinogens (abstract). In *Proceedings of the 1970 American Psychiatric Association Meeting, San Francisco, May, 1970,* p. 228. American Psychiatric Association, Washington, D.C., 1970.

Matthews, W. B., and Miller, H. *Diseases of the Nervous System.* Blackwell, Oxford, 1972.

McEntee, W. J., and Mair, R. G. Memory impairment in Korsakoff's psychosis: A correlation with brain noradrenergic activity. Science, *202:* 905, 1978.

Millon, T. *Modern Psychopathology: A Biosocial Approach to Maladaptive Learning and Functioning.* W. B. Saunders, Philadelphia, 1969.

Moan, C. E., and Heath, R. G. Septal stimulation for the initiation of heterosexual behavior in a homosexual male. J. Behav. Ther. Exp. Psychiatry, *3:* 23, 1972.

Moruzzi, S., and Magoun, H. W. Brain stem reticular formation and activation. Electroencephalogr. Clin. Neurophysiol., *1:* 455, 1949.

Murphy, D. L. L-dopa behavioral activation and psychopathology. In *Neurotransmitters,* I. J. Kopin, editor, p. 472. Williams & Wilkins, Baltimore, 1972.

Murphy, D. L., and Wyatt, R. S. Reduced monoamine oxidase activity in blood platelets from schizophrenic patients. Nature, *238:* 225, 1972.

Nemeroff, C. B., and Prange, A. J. Peptides and psychoendocrinology. Arch. Gen. Psychiatry, *35:* 999, 1978.

Olds, J. Differentiation of reward systems in the brain by self-stimulation techniques. In *Electrical Studies on the Unanesthetized Brain,* S. R. Ramey and D. S. O'Doherty, editors, p. 17. Hoeber Medical Division, Harper & Row, New York, 1960.

Osmond, H., and Smythies, J. Schizophrenia: A new approach. J. Ment. Sci., *97:* 725, 1952.

Papez, J. W. A proposed mechanism of emotion. Arch. Neurol. Psychiatry, *38:* 725, 1937.

Penfield, W. Mechanisms of voluntary movement. Brain, *77:* 1, 1954.

Penfield, W. Centrencephalic integrating system. Brain, *81:* 231, 1958.

Penfield, W., and Jasper, H. H. *Epilepsy and the Functional Anatomy of the Human Brain.* Little, Brown, and Co., Boston, 1954.

Prange, A. J., Wilson, I. C., Lara, P. P., Alltop, L. B., and Breese, G. R. Effects of thyrotropin-releasing hormone in depression. Lancet, *2:* 999, 1972.

Ranson, S. W. *Harvey Lecture.* Williams & Wilkins, Baltimore, 1937.

Riley, J. N., and Walker, D. W. Morphological alterations in hippocampus after long-term alcohol consumption in mice. Science, *201:* 647, 1978.

Romano, J. Psychiatry and medicine, 1973. Ann. Intern. Med., *79:* 582, 1973.

Rosenzweig, N. A mechanism in schizophrenia. Arch. Neurol. Psychiatry, *74:* 544, 1955.

Ross, S. B., and Reny, A. L. Accumulation of tritiated 5-hydroxytryptamine in brain slices. Life Sci., *6:* 1407, 1967.

Rosvold, H. E., Mirsky, A. F., and Pribram, K. H. Influence of amygdalectomy on social behavior in monkeys. Comp. Physiol. Psychol., *47:* 173, 1954.

Sachar, E. J., Frantz, A. G., Altman, N., and Sassin, J. Growth hormone and prolactin in unipolar and bipolar depressed patients: Responses to hypoglycemia and L-dopa. Am. J. Psychiatry, *129:* 1362, 1972.

Salvador, R. A., and Burton, R. M. Inhibition of the methylation of nicotinamide by chlorpromazine. Biochem. Pharmacol., *14:* 1185, 1965.

Schildkraut, J. J. The catecholamine hypothesis of affective disorders: A review of supporting evidence. Am. J. Psychiatry, *122:* 509, 1965.

Schwartz, I. L. General physiological processes. In *Best & Taylor's Physiological Basis of Medical Practice,* J. R. Brobeck, editor, ed. 9, p. 1-1. Williams & Wilkins, Baltimore, 1973.

Shore, P. A. Release of serotonin and catecholamines by drugs. Pharmacol. Rev., *14:* 531, 1962.

Shraberg, D., and Weisberg, L. The Klüver-Bucy syndrome in man. J. Nerv. Ment. Dis., *166:* 130, 1978.

Silberman, C. E. *Crisis in the Classroom.* Random House, New York, 1970.

Smythies, J. R. Psychiatry and the neurosciences. Psychol. Med., *3:* 267, 1973.

Snyder, S. Antipsychotic drugs and the dopamine receptor. Drug Ther., *3:* 29, 1978.

Stein, L., and Wise, D. Possible etiology of schizophrenia: Progressive damage to the noradrenergic reward system by endogenous 6-hydroxydopamine. In *Neurotransmitters,* I. J. Kopin, editor, p. 298. Williams & Wilkins, Baltimore, 1972.

Stevens, J. R. An anatomy of schizophrenia? Arch. Gen. Psychiatry, *29:* 177, 1973.

Szara, A. Behavioral correlates of 6-hydroxylation and the effect of psychotropic tryptamine derivatives on brain serotonin levels. In *Comparative Neurochemistry,* D. Richter, editor, p. 245. Pergamon Press, Oxford, 1964.

Tanimukai, H., Ginther, R., Spaide, J., Bueno, J. R., and Himwich, H. E. Occurrence of bufotenin (5-hydroxy-*N,N*-dimethyltryptamine) in the urine of schizophrenic patients. Life Sci., *6:* 1097, 1967.

Terzian, H., and Dalle-Ore, G. Syndrome of Klüver and Bucy reproduced in man by bilateral removal of the temporal lobes. Neurology, *5:* 373, 1955.

Thudichum, J. W. L. *A Treatise on the Chemical Constitution of the Brain.* Balliere, Tindall, and Cox, London, 1884.

Walsh, E. G. *Physiology of the Nervous System.* Longmans, London, 1964.

Walter, R., Hoffman, P. L., and Flexner, J. B. Neurohypophyseal hormones, analogs, and fragments: Their effect on puromycin-induced amnesia. Proc. Natl. Acad. Sci. U. S. A., *72:* 4180, 1975.

Wirz-Justice, A., and Pühringer, W. Seasonal incidence of an altered diurnal rhythm of platelet serotonin in unipolar depression. J. Neural Transmission, *42:* 45, 1978.

2.6 Biological Rhythms in Psychiatry

CHARLES F. STROEBEL, Ph.D., M.D.

Introduction

The concept of periodicity in behavior and physiology has been a significant aspect of medicine and psychiatry since their earliest foundations. Some 2,400 years ago, Hippocrates (Luce, 1970) advised his colleagues that

regularity is a sign of health, and that irregular body functions or habits promote an unsalutary condition. Pay close attention to fluctuations in a patient's symptoms, his good and his bad days in times of health and illness.

In an indirect fashion, Freud became fascinated with periodic manifestations of neurotic behavior through his extraordinary friendship and correspondence with Wilhelm Fliess in the 1890's. Fliess's theory, still currently popular with the lay public and known as biorhythm, interrelates the concepts of inherited bisexuality, subsequently developed by Freud, with intrinsic 23-day physical (male) and 28-day emotional sensitivity (female) rhythms, which are set in motion at the moment of birth. Subsequent biorhythm theories also claim evidence for a 33-day mental performance rhythm. Fliess's (1906) theory and his major work, *The Course of Life*, which is mathematically incomprehensible, probably would have faded into obscurity had not Freud credited him with a "great breakthrough in biology," as documented in Sigmund Freud's (1954) letters. Fliess observed a confluence of a patient's 23-day and 28-day rhythms as critical days, associated with changes in the mucosal lining of the nose and subsequently related nasal irritation to neurotic symptoms and sexual abnormalities. Fliess treated his patients by applying cocaine to the nasal mucosa, a procedure that Freud himself underwent. Freud rejected Fliess's theory in 1900 and severed their close relationship. According to Jones (1953):

> If all the changes in neurotic manifestations—their onset and cessation, their improvements and exacerbations—were strictly determined, as Fliess held, by the critical dates in life revealed by his periodic laws, then all Freud's dynamic and etiological findings were *de facto* irrelevant and meaningless, even if correct. This is so plain that it is really astounding how the two men managed for 10 whole years to interchange their ideas at length in such apparent harmony.

Biorhythm Theory versus Biological Rhythms

Fliess's biorhythm theory is also anathema to modern biological rhythm investigators, who view it as pseudomathematical and as astrological folklore. In fairness, modern science has only recently begun to document quantitative possible relationships among birthdates, planetary periodicities, daily rhythms, sexual rhythms, and behavior—a miniscule observation period compared with the centuries of data collected by the ancient Babylonian priests who founded astrology.

Unfortunately, widespread promotion of biorhythm as fact (Thommen, 1968) by the lay media, including readily available personalized computerized predictions and pocket calculators, has tended to obscure the distinction between the speculative theory of biorhythm and the sound empirical foundations underlying the study of biological rhythms. No single proof of biorhythm predictions advanced to date has withstood scientific scrutiny. Case selection bias, inappropriate statistics, and failure to control the Hawthorne or expectancy factors are common defects cited by Persinger et al. (1978), who, using a sound experimental design, found no evidence for a relationship between biorhythm and industrial accidents.

Clinical Background

Periodicities in the clinical manifestations of psychiatric illness have been intuitively recognized as a defining characteristic of certain diagnoses, such as periodic catatonia and manic-depressive illness, circular type. The introduction to *Lectures on Clinical Psychiatry* by Emil Kraepelin (1913) cited the

> importance of observing the periodicity of nervous diseases through long periods of time.

Kraepelin (1913) went on to describe periodic states of excitement in his patients as follows:

> Very marked low spirits have, however, been also observed here. Especially after the disappearance of the excitement the patient was often downcast and quiet for days, thought that he had no longer any friends left—it was misery to be in his position. There are also hours of intervening in the maniacal excitement when he weeps bitterly and deplores his sad fate, soon to fall back into the old boisterous mood. It appears to me that not only the deep inward relationship of such apparently contradictory states, but also the clinical unity of all those cases, which one generally tries to distinguish as the different forms of simple and periodic mania and of circular insanity, are distinctly marked in these fluctuations, which are hardly ever absent, even in the most hilarious mania. The tendency to repeated relapses, as well as the

usually favourable termination of a single attack, is common to all of them, even if the indications are very severe and of very long duration.

In discussing Kraepelin's findings, Bleuler (1950) made the following observations, which are still relevant today:

> Kraepelin's "periodic psychosis" has closed many a door which was open to the term "manic-depressive insanity" because there were psychiatrists who under no circumstances could bring themselves to designate as "periodic" a disease which under certain conditions manifests itself only in a few attacks, or perhaps even as only one isolated attack in the course of a whole life time. Kraepelin has explained that French psychiatrists, among them mainly Falret and Baillarger, had in addition to mania and melancholia described, on the basis of the course of illness, various subvarieties of the manic-depressive psychosis, *manie* and *melancholie intermittente, type régulier et irrégulier, folie alterne, folie à double forme, folie circulaire continue.* Kraepelin felt that such tendencies for grouping necessarily must fail "because of the irregularity of the disease."

Bleuler's uncertainty about the diagnosis of manic-depressive illness continued in the American Psychiatric Association's (1968) second edition and (1980) third edition of the *Diagnostic and Statistical Manual of Mental Disorders.* Application of the concepts of unipolar versus bipolar or circular depends on whether a periodicity is apparent clinically or historically. If the observation period is comparatively short and the underlying periodicity relatively long, the periodicity may be missed, creating diagnostic uncertainty. Since some psychiatric illnesses are clearly periodic and disturbances in the intrinsic rest-activity cycle are a common manifestation of many other illnesses, it is possible that observation techniques have been so crude that they overlook the role of underlying hidden periodic factors. The field of chronopsychophysiology is exploring that possibility (Stroebel, 1974). Important contributions to the field have already been made by Richter (1965) and Gjessing and Gjessing (1961) in documenting physiological correlates of periodic catatonia, by Jenner et al. (1968), by Bunney and Hartmann (1965) with manic-depressive patients with 48-hour cycles, and by Wever (1977), Kripke et al. (1978), and Wehr and Goodwin (1979) in studying bipolar patients with cycles longer than 48 hours.

Chronopsychophysiology

Implicit in much of the current research in chronopsychophysiology is the hypothesis that disturbances in periodic processes contributing to psychopathology may not be apparent at the surface level of clinical description and observation and that measurement and elucidation of such latent periodic processes may be crucial in advancing psychobiological understanding of psychiatric illness, just as insight into latent unconscious mental processes was crucial for the development of psychodynamics. The rationale for that hypothesis is the observation that virtually every physiological process, when studied with repeated measurements of sufficient accuracy over time, has demonstrated a 24-hour periodicity. It is inconceivable that human behavior could be totally independent of those pervasive rhythmic fluctuations. The orderly sequence of crest and trough of those component rhythms, not all in phase, creates a unique succession of internal physiological states that is repeated once every 24 hours. That orderly sequence—an internal temporal coordination of interlocking metabolic functions—can be viewed as the body's own timing mechanism or biological clock. In the normal organism the over-all sequence of internal rhythms may be synchronized with laboratory clock time by means of a light-dark cycle, permitting precise manipulation and study.

In fact, rhythms underlie much of what is assumed to be in the range of constant homeostasis in people and the world. In health, a human being has an appearance of stability that cloaks an inner symphony of biological rhythms—a spectrum covering microseconds for biochemical reactions, milliseconds for unit nerve activity, about a second for the heart rhythm, the 90-minute rapid eye movement cycle of dreaming, the major 24-hour rest-activity cycle, the 27-day menstrual cycle, and, finally, the single life-span cycle. Lieber (1978 a, b) has been accumulating impressive evidence implicating a 27.5 day lunar rhythm in emotional behaviors, with homicides and aggravated assaults clustering around the time of the full moon and psychiatric emergency room visits clustering around the first quarter, with a decreased frequency around the new moon and the full moon. Similarly, an annual biological rhythm, with a period of about 1 year, is emerging as a rationale for the initial observations by Tramer (1929) that an excessively large proportion of schizophrenics are born during the winter and early spring in both the northern and the southern hemispheres (Dalén, 1975; Parker and Neilson, 1976; Ødegard, 1977). A schematic spectrum of bioperiodicities is shown in Figure 1. The normally unconscious regularity of those inner rhythms becomes apparent only when there is discord caused by trauma, disease, chronic stress, or erratic external synchronization.

An example of erratic external synchronization that has dramatically drawn attention to chronopsychophysiology is the 4- to 5-day period of fatigue and adjustment needed after a transcontinental flight to resynchronize the inner clock system with the activity cycle of the new time zone. Diplomats and athletes are beginning to anticipate that circadian resynchronization syndrome through one of several techniques: artificially adopting the destination's time schedule 1 week before departure, incorporating intermediate stopovers into transcontinental travel, or allowing for an adjustment period at the destination point before performing or making critical decisions. Most healthy persons in experimental studies prefer east-to-west travel, rather than the reverse, because they find it easier to retire later and later each night (Klein and Wegmann, 1974; Aschoff et al., 1975). A related new clinical entity is the jet fatigue experienced by flight crews, a varying combination of headaches, burning eyes, blurred vision, gastrointestinal problems, loss of appetite, shortness of breath, excessive sweating, insomnia, and, occasionally, nightmares.

Until the comparatively recent advent of convenient artificial illumination and jet travel, humans remained at a fixed longitude and worked when the sun was out and slept when it became dark. An intrinsic inner clock—the circadian (circa, around; dies, day) 24-hour cycle—apparently became embedded in human physiology through evolution (Halberg, 1960). A contrary view is held by Brown (1969), who maintains that an extrinsic cosmic-electromagnetic influence is the time giver. The phenomenon of free running makes that position tenuous, but the question may not be finally settled until adequate satellite experiments are completed (Luce, 1970). Circadian rhythms are believed by most scientists to be intrinsic in every cell and to persist under constant conditions (Sollberger, 1965).

Diurnal rhythms (which are not inherent but entrained by the environment) on the other hand tend to damp out under constant conditions. Given normal environmental conditions, there is a high correlation between an adaptive organism's circadian rhythms and light-dark, eating, drinking, sleeping, and reproductive times; however, the terms circadian and diurnal are confused when those correlations are mistakenly assumed to have a causal relationship (Stroebel, 1967).

External cues—light cycle, social regimen—serve to synchronize circadian rhythms through the hypothalamic-pituitary axis and adrenal steroid hormone system. Recent experiments (Zucker et al., 1976; Moore, 1978) suggest that the suprachias-

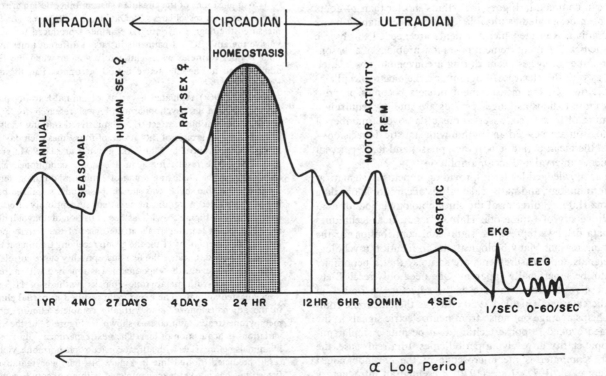

FIGURE 1. Schematic spectrum of biological periodicities along a continuum, with more reactive rhythms on the right. (From Stroebel, C. F. Behavioral aspects of circadian rhythms. In *Comparative Psychopathology*, J. Zubin and H. F. Hunt, editors. Grune & Stratton, New York, 1967.)

matic nucleus of the hypothalamus is the apparent master oscillator in rodents. Night people differ from day people in simply using a different set of cues to synchronize their rhythms with their environment. Without such cues, the rhythms approximate a 24-hour period, keeping neither a precise solar-day cycle (24 hours) nor a precise lunar cycle (24.8 hours). In the complete absence of external synchronizers, a rhythm drifts, gaining or losing a few minutes each day, a condition known as free running. The free-running condition has been advanced as one possible explanation for certain forms of insomnia that may be associated with symptoms of depression (Stroebel and Glueck, 1965; Stroebel, 1969). For example, if a person consciously or unconsciously, because of stress or conflict, has begun to ignore important external cues, as in certain neurotic states, his underlying rhythm structure may begin to free run, so that his body is eventually prepared for day activity during the night and for night rest during the day. When the rhythm progressively drifts by consistently gaining a few minutes each day, insomnia is first experienced at bedtime, subsequently during the night, and finally in the early morning. The opposite progression is observed when the free-running rhythm consistently loses a few minutes each day. In the absence of a consistent trend, virtually any insomnia pattern can be explained by that mechanism. The condition has been documented in behaviorally stressed monkeys, who simultaneously demonstrated a variety of psychosomatic symptoms (Stroebel, 1969).

Some persons have the ability to set an awakening time with their inner biological clocks, consistently awakening 1 or 2 minutes before their bedside alarm rings. It is not understood at present whether that capacity is genetic or acquired, but it may become recognized as an important variable in evaluating the personality style and defense mechanisms used by a person, conceivably correlating with perceptual coping patterns—field independence-dependence, kinesthetic enhancing or reducing, intolerance of sensory isolation (Stroebel and Glueck, 1973).

As can be noted in Figure 1, rhythms shorter than 24 hours have been designated as ultradian, those longer than 24 hours as infradian. Repeated measurements are needed to observe periodicities. That requirement poses few problems if a reasonable number of cycles occur during a convenient observation span, as with the electrocardiogram and the electroencephalogram. However, the measurement process becomes progressively more tedious as longer periods are studied, requiring a minimum of four to six observations a day over a number of days to estimate a circadian rhythm with statistical precision—that is, the mean period length (acrophase) and its 95 per cent confidence interval and mean amplitude.

An acknowledged leader in providing impetus, systematization, terminology, and statistical analysis of chronobiology data is Franz Halberg, director of the chronobiology laboratories at the University of Minnesota. Halberg's statistical techniques and data displays represent a significant contribution for the following reason: Many biological, not to mention psychological, signals and measurements are so noisy that a periodicity may not be superficially apparent. One need only recall Bleuler's observation about the use of the adjective "periodic" in periodic catatonia (Bleuler, 1950). Just as the electronic computer helps average out noise from neuroelectric signals in the averaged evoked response technique, it permits a similar microscopic clarity in resolving periodicities. In a real sense, the modern computer is the microscope of the chronobiologist (Halberg et al., 1972). Luce (1970) presented an introductory description and Halberg (Halberg, 1966; Halberg et al., 1972) a definitive description of those computer procedures.

Although documentation of human circadian rhythms is tedious for both subjects and experimenters, the list of body functions identified as circadian is steadily growing, making possible circadian rhythm maps or norms under conditions of health and disease. Figure 2 is an example of such a map, as analyzed by Halberg and his colleagues (Luce, 1970).

In view of documented circadian fluctuations in levels of consciousness, temperature, and liver, adrenal, pituitary, and kidney function (Unger and Halberg, 1962a; Halberg, 1966, 1969; Luce, 1970), it is not unreasonable to think that the body also varies cyclically in its ability to tolerate stress or to detoxify and excrete toxins, poisons, and drugs. Numerous studies have identified circadian susceptibility rhythms to such agents, usually in animals in which death is the end point.

Figure 3 shows the outcome of a study in which four identical groups of rats synchronized by a 12-on-12-off light-dark cycle were each given identical intraperitoneal injections of the phenothiazine mesoridazine (Serentil) at the times marked by the arrows (Stroebel, 1967). The acrophase (peak) of sensitivity occurred at the onset of the normal rest period; by implication, a smaller dose of the drug, with fewer attendant side effects, could be given at the onset of the rest period, as compared with other times in a 24-hour span. That finding apparently anticipated the increasingly widespread practice of giving a single dose of an antidepressant or neuroleptic drug at the hour of sleep. Chronobiologists are actively investigating a wide variety of chemotherapeutic agents, particularly anticancer drugs, to determine whether an optimal time exists for administering the drug each day to maximize its therapeutic principle and to minimize its undesirable side effects (Reinberg and Halberg, 1971; Halberg et al., 1973b).

The circadian peaks for a number of human susceptibility variables have been analyzed by Halberg and his colleagues (Luce, 1970), as shown in Figure 4.

CIRCADIAN SUSCEPTIBILITY TO ECT AND CONDITIONED FEAR

Two applications of the circadian susceptibility design are of particular interest for psychiatry. McGaugh and Stephens (Luce, 1970) measured the degree of retrograde amnesia produced by electroconvulsive therapy (ECT) treatments in rats at different times over a 24-hour period. Amnesia was significantly greater when the ECT was administered during the active period, as opposed to the quiescent period.

Stroebel (1967) evaluated a variety of animal-learning paradigms commonly used in psychopharmacological research for a possible circadian susceptibility effect. He administered training trials to each of four identical groups of rats at one of four times each day (group 1 at 8:00 A.M.; group 2 at 2:00 P.M.; group 3 at 8:00 P.M.; group 4 at 2:00 A.M.). The results for acquisition of a conditioned emotional response in which a clicking sound of 2 minutes' duration, terminated by an unavoidable shock, was superimposed on a stabilized bar-pressing habit revealed a significant circadian susceptibility effect (see the control curve in Figure 5), with faster acquisition of unavoidable fear— a median of six learning trials at the onset of the activity period, as opposed to a median of 11 for the group receiving training at the onset of the rest period. Because the fear-susceptibility curve correlated with serum cortisol levels, the experiment was repeated with adrenalectomized and also with metapyrone- (blocks synthesis of 11-β-steroids) premedicated animals. The experiment resulted in partial elimination in the adrenalectomized and virtually complete elimination in the metapyrone-treated animals, as shown in Figure 5, in the circadian variations in acquisition of fear. The next experiment—premedication of animals before trials with adrenocorticotropic hormone, yielding the result predicted (dotted line in Figure 5)—has been tentatively confirmed but has not yet been completed with an adequate sample size.

The same experimental design was repeated with five additional learning paradigms widely used in psychopharmacology, using new

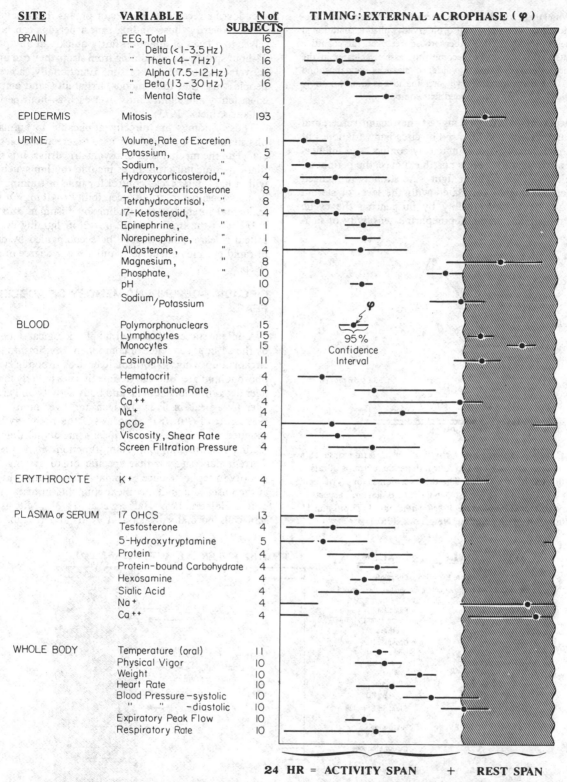

SITE	VARIABLE	N of SUBJECTS	TIMING: EXTERNAL ACROPHASE (φ)
BRAIN	EEG, Total	16	
"	" Delta (<1-3.5 Hz)	16	
"	" Theta (4-7 Hz)	16	
"	" Alpha (7.5-12 Hz)	16	
"	" Beta (13-30 Hz)	16	
"	" Mental State		
EPIDERMIS	Mitosis	193	
URINE	Volume, Rate of Excretion	1	
	Potassium, "	5	
	Sodium, "	1	
	Hydroxycorticosteroid,"	4	
	Tetrahydrocorticosterone	8	
	Tetrahydrocortisol, "	8	
	17-Ketosteroid, "	4	
	Epinephrine , "	1	
	Norepinephrine, "	1	
	Aldosterone, "	4	
	Magnesium, "	8	
	Phosphate, "	10	
	pH	10	
	Sodium/Potassium	10	
BLOOD	Polymorphonuclears	15	
	Lymphocytes	15	
	Monocytes	15	
	Eosinophils	11	
	Hematocrit	4	
	Sedimentation Rate	4	
	Ca++	4	
	Na+	4	
	pCO2	4	
	Viscosity, Shear Rate	4	
	Screen Filtration Pressure	4	
ERYTHROCYTE	K+	4	
PLASMA or SERUM	17 OHCS	13	
	Testosterone	4	
	5-Hydroxytryptamine	5	
	Protein	4	
	Protein-bound Carbohydrate	4	
	Hexosamine	4	
	Sialic Acid	4	
	Na+	4	
	Ca++	4	
WHOLE BODY	Temperature (oral)	11	
	Physical Vigor	10	
	Weight	10	
	Heart Rate	10	
	Blood Pressure –systolic	10	
	" " –diastolic	10	
	Expiratory Peak Flow	10	
	Respiratory Rate	10	

95 % Confidence Interval

24 HR = ACTIVITY SPAN + REST SPAN

FIGURE 2. Map of human circadian rhythms, as analyzed by the chronobiology laboratory at the University of Minnesota. The rhythm peak acrophase is indicated by a *dot* surrounded by lines indicating the 95 per cent confidence interval. (From Luce, G. *Biological Rhythms in Medicine and Psychiatry*. United States Public Health Service, Bethesda, 1970.)

groups of naive rats for each experiment. The results are shown in Figure 6, indicating a rank order (highest to lowest) of circadian susceptibility for acquisition as follows: CER (P ≤ .01), escape (P ≤ .07), Sidman avoidance (P ≤ .11), classical avoidance (P ≤ .30), punishment (P ≤ .45), and discriminative lever-pressing task (P ≤ .50) (Stroebel, 1967).

The following rationale is advanced to explain the outcomes: The conditioned fear associated with Sidman avoidance, classical avoidance, and punishment becomes avoidable with learning. The conditioned fear associated with the conditioned emotional response is unavoidable, even under criterion-learning conditions. Hunt and Brady (1955) labeled that unavoidable fear "intercurrent anxiety." A greater degree of sympathetic nervous system activation—piloerection, micturition, defecation, freezing—is also observed with the conditioned emotional response than in the other procedures. And the cognitive cues associated with avoidance become progressively clearer in the rank sequence of escape, Sidman avoidance, classical avoidance, and punishment. The discriminative lever-pressing task is almost entirely cognitive, with little or no conditioned fear component.

Those experiments strongly suggest that cognitive cerebral behaviors are minimally influenced by circadian variations but that emotional behaviors dominated by conflict—no intellectual or cognitive solution seems possible; hence, the peripheral autonomic arousal for flight or fight—are strongly influenced and, further, are highly correlated with the level of steroid hormones in the blood, possibly by influencing the cyclic adenosine monophosphate-norepinephrine sensitivity of neu-

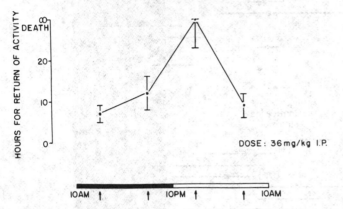

FIGURE 3. Circadian susceptibility rhythm for the same dose of a phenothiazine drug administered to four independent groups of rats at the times indicated by the *arrows*. The dose was lethal for 75 per cent of the animals in group 3. (From Stroebel, C. F. Behavioral aspects of circadian rhythms. In *Comparative Psychopathology*, J. Zubin and H. F. Hunt, editors, Grune & Stratton, New York, 1967.)

roendocrine receptors on effector organs. Personal experience seems to verify those findings; most persons can bring themselves to a level of attention fairly quickly at any point in the 24-hour span, even awakening from sleep; they can intelligently converse, abstract, and reason. Emotionally, however, most people sense that their moods, irritability, and empathy vary consistently and significantly over each 24-hour period (Stroebel and Glueck, 1973).

Those findings are directly applicable to animal psychopharmacology and are widely used to screen and biochemically elucidate the mechanisms of psychiatric drugs. It is mandatory that experimental procedures include rhythm synchronization with a light-dark cycle, control for time of training trials, and designs sensitive to drug-susceptibility rhythms. Of more than incidental interest is the finding by Fishman and Roffwarg (1972) that the traditional 12-on-12-off lighting cycle used in rodent research may, in fact, be accompanied by deprivation of rapid eye movement sleep and a lesser degree of slow-wave sleep.

CIRCADIAN-DEPENDENT MEMORY OF ACQUIRED FEAR

A unique succession of internal physiological states is created by the 24-hour sequence of component rhythms. In the mouse, circadian upswings in cortisol, liver deoxyribonucleic acid, and phospholipid are followed in time by rises in body temperature, liver deoxyribonucleic acid, and body activity and are followed later by a peak in liver glycogen and liver mitoses (Halberg, 1969; Luce, 1970). It is almost as if the body rhythm system assigned a sequence of priorities, a metabolic time table, directing resources to important functions in a preset order. Current data suggest that specific organ systems are given priority to replicate once each day—for example, liver mitoses at the onset of activity, corneal epithelial mitoses at the onset of rest (Halberg, 1969; Halberg et al., 1973b). Mitosis of human skin cells normally peaks at 1 A.M. and troughs at 1 P.M.

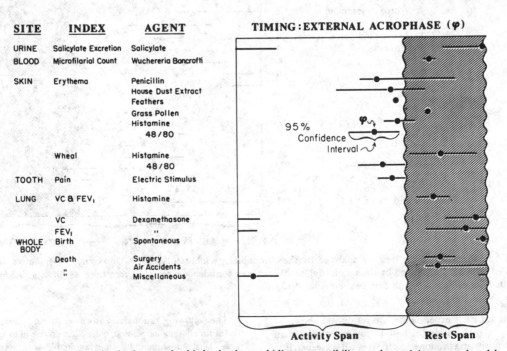

FIGURE 4. Map of circadian rhythms in the human for birth, death, morbidity, susceptibility, and reactivity, as analyzed by the chronobiology laboratory at the University of Minnesota. (From Luce, G. *Biological Rhythms in Medicine and Psychiatry*. United States Public Health Service, Bethesda, 1970.)

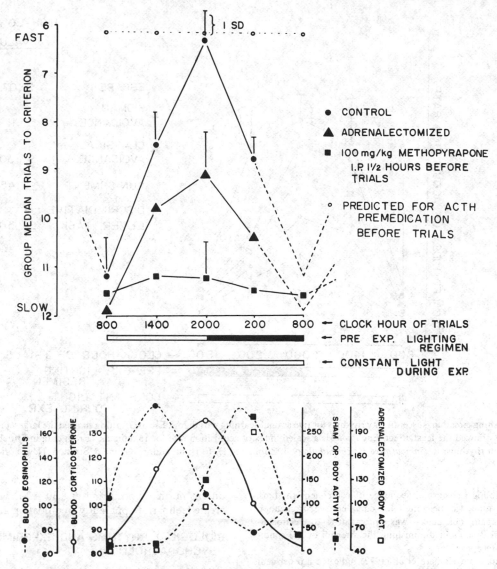

FIGURE 5. Results correlating the circadian rhythms of adrenal steroids with susceptibility to learning fear, as measured by the conditioned emotional response. Each *point* is the median of 16 animals. The *upper panel* presents behavioral data. The *lower panel* presents physiological measures at corresponding time points for untrained animals. (From Stroebel, C. F. Behavioral aspects of circadian rhythms. In *Comparative Psychopathology*, J. Zubin and H. F. Hunt, editors, Grune & Stratton, New York, 1967.)

Mitotic frequency observed in skin cancer biopsies showed a 5-fold elevation over the normal peak at both 1 A.M. and 1 P.M. (Zagula-Mall et al., 1978). Whether the rhythm was lost or shifted cannot be determined from sampling only two time points, but it is different from the normal circadian rhythm. It is possible that the escape of a cell or organ from the endocrine-circadian priority system may be one of the mechanisms involved in cancer, since the cells could presumably replicate repeatedly, out of control as body clock outlaws. Although highly speculative, abnormal rhythm functioning may provide a link to explain the frequent, usually retrospective, reports of a personality change in a family member months before a malignancy manifested itself clinically.

CIRCADIAN RHYTHMS AS AN EMOTIONAL MEMORY SUBSTRATE

Several experiments (Stroebel, 1967) suggest that emotional memory, previously demonstrated to be circadian dependent,

may be directly linked to specific body clock times, much like the vault of a bank that opens only at preset hours.

Rats who received conditioned emotional-response training trials at 8:00 P.M. (onset of dark and activity) each day demonstrated full retention of the response when tested (clicker but no shock) at 8:00 P.M.; when tested at 8:00 A.M., a significant reduction in the response was noted. In a second experiment, the animals received conditioned emotional response training each day at 8:00 P.M.; however, after training, the light-dark cycle was inverted, so that the light and dark periods were reversed (equivalent to traveling halfway around the earth by jet); after a 3-week period for readjustment of the circadian rhythms to the new schedule, the animals were again tested and showed the strongest response at 8:00 A.M. and a much weaker response at 8:00 P.M., the original time of training. Memory of the conditioned emotional response was apparently linked to the biological clock time of training. The novel internal milieu unique to a specific biological clock time is apparently an important part of the total stimulus complex in emotional learning and memory (Stroebel, 1972). A third experiment demonstrated that four weekly inversions of the light-dark cycle—

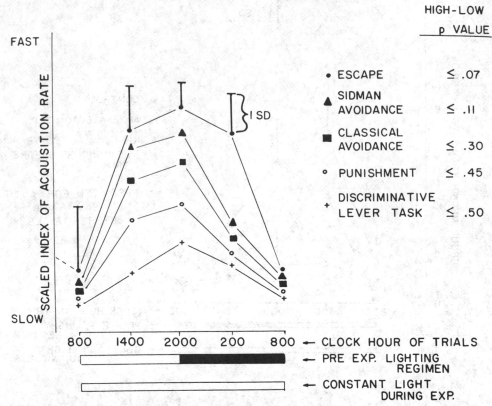

FIGURE 6. Diminishing circadian susceptibility rhythms for five animal-learning paradigms. Escape learning showed the largest effect; a discriminative lever-pressing task showed the least effect. Each *point* is a scaled index of acquisition rate for 16 animals. (From data in Stroebel, C. F. Behavioral aspects of circadian rhythms. In *Comparative Psychopathology*, J. Zubin and H. F. Hunt, editors. Grune & Stratton, New York, 1967.)

essentially, scrambling the normal sequence of component rhythms, since inadequate time was permitted for complete synchronization before inversion again took place—was equivalent to 10 electroconvulsive therapy treatments in diminishing the strength of the conditioned emotional response.

Preliminary data from Halberg et al. (1972) indicated a 6 per cent reduction in the life-span of mice who repetitively experienced light-cycle inversion once weekly (Luce, 1970). Further, Halberg and Haus (Luce, 1970) demonstrated that mice on light schedules incompatible with a 24-hour world—for example, lights on 8 hours and off 8 hours—were significantly more susceptible to alcohol toxicity. The issue of natural work-rest schedules, in a world in which communications encourage 24-hour-a-day activity, is a significant one.

The extension of those findings to clinical psychiatry, with proper precaution, suggests that emotional responses acquired at the same time each day—for example, the indigestion and frustration felt by a secretary when her tyrannical boss storms into the office each day at 8:30 A.M.—are optimally accessible to conscious memory and to deconditioning only at that time. Furthermore, those findings suggest that emotional behaviors randomly acquired at many points in the biological rhythm cycle are particularly resistant to behavior therapy procedures unless the therapy sessions are conducted at many points in a 24-hour span. And those findings suggest that daily repetition of the internal states associated with the memory of an emotional behavior may serve as unconscious practice of that behavior, even in the absence of the usual external cues—that is, even on Saturday and Sunday, when the secretary is not confronted by a boss, the biological rhythms are cycling through the same circadian-determined internal stimulus con-

ditions normally occurring at 8:30 A.M. each day, serving to create feelings of apparently free-floating anxiety.

BIOLOGICAL RHYTHMS AND EXPERIMENTAL PSYCHOPATHOLOGY

Various models of experimental psychopathology have been developed in which animals are placed in conflict with regard to response alternatives, forced to make difficult discriminations, restrained, or deprived of some aspect of their social environment—object loss, mother deprivation, peer separation, loss of escape security. Most of the symptoms of human neurosis and psychosis, except language-thought disorders, have been produced in a varying and unpredictable degree by one of those procedures.

However, probably the most common denominator among various behavioral models is a disturbance in the rest-activity cycle, indicative of a basic malfunction in the normal biological rhythm system. That finding is strange, since the normal biological rhythm system is profoundly resistant to change from physical stresses. For example, Richter (1965), in an exhaustive variety of experiments, tried without success to alter the circadian cycle of rat activity by subjecting animals to shock and drugs and by exposing them to prolonged danger, a variety of forced abnormal environmental schedules, freezing, cardiac stoppage, brain ablation, and blinding.

In a report that directly addressed the issue of behavioral versus physical stress in producing rest-activity cycle abnormalities, Stroebel (1969) accidentally observed and then studied two forms of psychopathology in chronically instrumented, isolated monkeys that resulted from a behavioral stress—removal of an operant lever that the monkeys had used to escape noxious situations. Psychopathology occurred after loss of the lever, even though the noxious stimuli were never again presented. Hence, in a sense, that stress was unconscious. The finding in that study was a virtually parallel relationship of circadian-rhythm abnormalities with exacerbation or amelioration of psychopathology. Monkeys stressed with loss of their security lever developed one of two brain temperature rhythm abnormalities used to classify them into group 1 or group 2. Brain temperature and other physiological measures were recorded every 12 minutes over a period of months from chronically implanted transducers monitored by an online computer (Stroebel, 1970).

Group 1 animals developed free-running brain temperature rhythms, seemingly ignoring the normal synchronizing effect of the 12-on-12-off light cycle, which was always present. Psychosomatic symptoms of abnormality—asthmatic breathing, duodenal ulcers, gastrointestinal disturbances, neurogenic skin lesions, excessive water consumption—resolved when the temperature rhythm was resynchronized, either by the return of the security lever or after the animals resynchronized, having gained or lost an entire 24-hour period through free running.

Group 2 animals, as well as a maternally deprived female, developed abnormal infradian periodicities of predominantly 48 hours in length, despite the 12-on-12-off light-dark cycle—a startling result in view of the imperturbability of the 24-hour cycle in Richter's (1965) studies. Richter's stresses, however, were physical in nature, while these were emotional. Regressed behavioral symptoms observed in the animals included lassitude and weakness, poor grooming, frequent brief naps, compulsive hair pulling, loss of appetite, and movement stereotypy alternating with total disinterest in their environment. Neither the behavior nor the rhythms of the group 2 animals ever returned entirely to normal, although significant behavioral improvement was noted in most subjects receiving a phenothiazine through a chronic intraperitoneal catheter, closely paralleled by a significant suppression of previously prominent, abnormal, longer-than-24-hour rhythms. The 48-hour cycles seen in group 2 subjects were apparently similar to those documented in psychiatric patients by Richter (1965), Gjessing and Gjessing (1961), and Jenner et al. (1968).

To summarize the two patterns: Syndrome one includes free-running circadian rhythms (insomnia) associated with psychosomatic symptoms and the ignoring of normally important environmental cues. Syndrome two includes abnormal infradian rhythms associated with severely maladaptive regressed behavior, in which both the behavioral abnormalities and the rhythm abnormalities partially responded to phenothiazine medication.

Although a great deal remains to be explored in evaluating the comparability of animal models of mental illness with the human condition, the striking parallel between behavioral abnormalities and rhythm abnormalities cannot be ignored. Had the animals in those studies not been involved in a repeated-measures design sensitive to periodicities, it is likely that the rhythm abnormalities would not have been identified.

For example, Kripke's (1972) finding suggested that the 90- to 100-minute REM cycle associated during sleep with enhanced dream recall continued during the waking state. Kleitman (1963) called this basic rest activity cycle the BRAC rhythm. Recent studies have shown, among other things, that daytime fantasy activity and oscillations between verbal-analytic and spatial-wholistic cognitive styles appear to follow a 90- to 100-minute ultradian rhythm (Kripke and Sonnenschein, 1978; Klein and Armitage, 1979). It is possible that some of the dream-like hallucinations characteristic of the schizophrenic process represent a breakthrough into consciousness of REM-type activity which is normally inhibited during waking.

REPLICATION PROBLEM IN NEUROPSYCHIATRY

The replication status of most physiological correlates or explanations of mental disorders is uncertain at present. Findings in the original laboratory are only rarely confirmed in a second setting (Kety, 1965; Stroebel, 1972).

Some major source of previously unidentified variance must be present in those studies to account for the discrepant findings. The ubiquitous nature of rest-activity disturbances in human emotional illness, coupled with their appearance as a common denominator in most models of psychopathology, clearly make biological rhythm variation a possible candidate for the missing variance.

Practical factors for studying that possibility may include differences in social regimen and schedules of patients or animal subjects in various replication centers, variations in the time of day when biochemical or other physiological samples are collected, and the distinct possibility that an underlying desynchronization—that is, uncoupling of rhythms—or abnormal rhythm period length associated with a hardly homogeneous diagnostic entity may make control of either of the two previous possibilities irrelevant.

The replication problem potentially attributable to rhythm effects might be even more elusive were the situation as follows: Most neurophysiological functioning seems to be a balance of at least two countering forces; examples are sympathetic and parasympathetic components of the autonomic nervous system and neurotransmitters and their destruction mechanisms, such as acetylcholine and acetylcholinesterase.

With just a two-variable system—and the situation is undoubtedly more complex, as in the conditioned emotional response susceptibility rhythm, which involves both autonomic balance and an interaction with steroids—unless the rhythms of each variable remain exactly balanced with the other over time, their difference generates potentially complicated beat-frequency effects, much like the subharmonics and overtones of an organ pipe. If—because of trauma, behavioral stress, or drugs—a balanced autonomic nervous system were altered so that the population of sympathetic neurons shifted its period from 24 hours to 21 hours 20 minutes while the parasympathetic neurons retained a circadian period, a panoramic beat of 9 days would be superimposed on measures of autonomic balance (sympathetic minus parasympathetic difference scores). Rank reversals of varying magnitude in balance would occur over each 24 hours. Even if two investigators were studying the same subject, one sampling 12 hours apart from the other, their findings could be in exactly opposite directions over the entire 9-day period of the beat (see Figure 7).

The foregoing situation would provide a more than adequate missing variance to explain the replication problems in neuropsychiatry. The only solution for detecting the variance is repeated measurements within each day, as well as over a period of days, a duration several magnitudes longer than the longest beat that may be modulating the rhythm structure. That solution may be a clinical impossibility, akin to keeping a psychiatric patient catheterized and instrumented in an intensive care unit for months at a time. Radiotelemetry, portable recorders, and innovative new biochemical sensors may facilitate the repeated measurement problem but will bring about new complications—for example, increased recording artifact due to physical motion, difficulty in simultaneous objective recording of changing behavioral and mental states that may have produced spurious physiological changes and vice versa, and the uncertainty principle—as in quantum mechanics, in

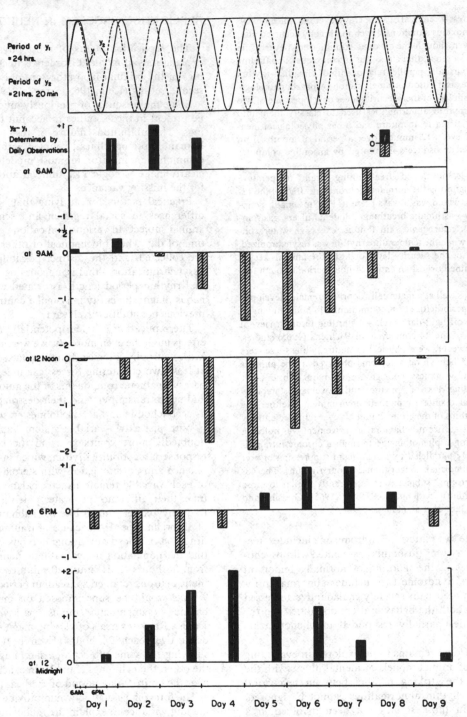

FIGURE 7. Illustration of a 9-day beat between two rhythms, y_1 with a period of 24 hours and y_2 with a period of 21 hours 20 minutes. As a result of the beat, y_1–y_2 difference scores can change dramatically (rank reversal) within a single day, as well as over several days. A scientist sampling at 12 noon each day would obtain diametrically opposite results from those obtained by a scientist sampling at 12 midnight. (From Reinberg, A., and Halberg, F. Circadian chronopharmacology. Am. Rev. Pharmacol., *11*: 455, 1971.)

which the process of measurement itself changes the basic state one is attempting to measure. Conscious or unconscious awareness by the subject of measurement, monitoring, and its related apparatus changes the subject's natural condition, which one is trying to measure. Ideally, chronopsychophysiology would be sensitive to the entire spectrum of human experience—mental, behavioral, physiological, pathological—as viewed longitudinally. That sensitivity would resolve periodic changes over time and the effects of past life stresses on subsequent

functioning. Unfortunately, practical considerations—cost, limited laboratory facilities, and the endurance of subjects and experimenters—have tended to limit psychophysiological investigations to several occasions for each subject. For example, the discipline has experienced its greatest success in the study of correlates and sequences of sleep stages, a situation in which subjects are easily confined to a fixed location and are relatively unaware of the considerable instrumentation that must be worn; the instruments often include an electroencephalograph, an electromyograph, an electrooculograph, an electrocardiograph, and galvanic skin response electrodes and penile and respiration strain gauges.

Biological Rhythms and Bipolar Affective Disorders

The beat-frequency model illustrated in Figure 7 provides a paradigm for the periodic recurrence of endogenous depressions or manic-depressive symptoms in bipolar illness. The model requires that the circadian rhythms of at least two interacting neurophysiological variables underlying affect become uncoupled in phase so as to provide alternating augmentation (mania or hypomania) and cancellation (depression) to produce beat intervals longer than 24 hours. Slight uncoupling would produce relatively long intervals (months or years) between bipolar symptoms, whereas significant decoupling would produce rapid cycling. Within the context of the catecholamine hypothesis of affective disorders, the decoupling of norepinephrine from its precursor, dopamine, through the enzyme dopamine β-hydroxylase, for which a circadian rhythm was demonstrated by Van Cauter and Mendlewicz (1978), would produce a norepinephrine excess (mania) or deficiency (depression), with the interval between the occurrences of symptoms dependent on the degree of the uncoupling.

A growing body of data supports that hypothesis, which was first proposed by Halberg (1960, 1968) and later refined by Stroebel (1969, 1975), Wever (1977), Kripke et al. (1978), and Wehr and Goodwin (1979). Crucial experiments were performed by Aschoff (1969) and Pittendrigh (1974), showing that at least two distinct internal circadian oscillators in the human body are capable of desynchronizing either from one another or from environmental cues. Phase shifts leading to such decoupling of biochemical circadian rhythms have been suggested—for example, stress (Stroebel, 1969; Regal, 1975; Calhoun, 1977), steroids (Halberg et al., 1968), electrolyte rhythms (Lobban et al., 1963; Moody and Allsop, 1969), neurohumoral metabolites (Reiderer et al., 1974), and social factors (Wever, 1975a). In clinical studies Pflug et al. (1976) and Kripke et al. (1978) demonstrated faster than circadian free-running rhythms in manic patients that responded to lithium carbonate therapy, with a slowing of the fast rhythm to achieve circadian synchrony. In the study by Kripke et al., two manic patients with slower than circadian free-running rhythms were nonresponsive to lithium therapy, as might be predicted. Data to substantiate the hypothesis that lithium may be effective by slowing or delaying fast free-running circadian rhythms were documented in plants by Engelmann (1973). In contrast to the effect of lithium in slowing fast rhythms in manic conditions, Wehr and Goodwin (1979) demonstrated that the administration of tricyclic antidepressants produces more rapid cycling in bipolar patients. Recognizing the cyclicity phenomenon in depression, the role of sleep disturbances as symptomatic of depression, sleep as a primary diurnal rhythm, and recent findings that sleep deprivation in major depressions showed a dramatic but transient (less than 1 day) improvement, Wehr and Goodwin (1979) advanced two hypotheses concerning the role of biological rhythms in affective disorders.

First, that daily rhythms of activity, sleep, mood and neuroendocrine function, which are regulated by a biological clock, are altered in depression and mania so that the patient's internal daily cycles are no longer synchronized with the 24-hour environmental cycle. Also, that from animal studies evidence suggests that antidepressants and lithium may work in depression and mania in part through their almost unique ability to speed up and slow down, respectively, the clock in the brain. The second hypothesis is that the long-term cyclicity of the illness is itself a pathological example of a biological rhythm.

Data relating genetic and age-related features of biological rhythms also have common features with manic-depressive illness. In fruit flies Konopka and Benzer (1971) demonstrated that various alleles on the X chromosome control circadian frequency with an incomplete dominance pattern. Although possibly not fully comparable, manic-depressive disease also seems to be X-linked (Mendlewicz et al., 1972). Similarly, in animals circadian oscillators seem to free run faster with greater ease with increasing age (Pittendrigh and Daan, 1974), just as humans are more likely to experience internal desynchronization (Wever, 1975b) and a greater incidence of manic-depressive illness as they age.

Additional data may be advanced to support the relatively new model of bipolar illness, which emphasizes timing of neurotransmitter chemical rhythms, rather than absolute serum levels. Human beings can arbitrarily shift their daily times of sleep and schedules of working with uncomfortable side effects, but their circadian rhythms of body temperature, steroids, mitoses, and other functions require as long as 3 weeks to shift their circadian phases to resynchronize with the arbitary timing of the environment (Weitzman et al., 1968; Aschoff et al., 1975). Experimental shifts in the hours of sleep cause a dysphoric mood and poor performance, producing symptoms with a striking resemblance to retarded depression, as shown by Kripke et al. (1970) and Hauty and Adams (1966). Derangements of circadian rhythms also cause a characteristic early awakening and shortened rapid eye movement (REM) sleep latency (Kripke et al., 1970; Weitzman et al., 1970) similar to sleep patterns thought to be specific for primary depression (Kupfer, 1976).

Biological Rhythms and Behavioral Medicine

Biofeedback and related techniques for achieving voluntary self-regulation of unconscious body processes previously thought to be involuntary have fostered a new awareness of a large domain of physiological functioning that is normally under the adaptive control of behavior. Psychosomatic or stress-related disorders develop when that normal range of homeostatic functioning becomes restricted, whether through stress, isolation, helplessness and hopelessness, or unconscious conflict.

An estimated 50 to 70 per cent of all symptoms presenting in general medical and gynecological practice are in that category, with the symptoms either induced by stress or exacerbated by a stressful bracing against the symptom—the latter termed dysponesis—faulty effort—by Whatmore and Kohli (1974). Acute activation of symptoms through the sympathetic nervous system—adrenal medulla-mediated emergency fight-or-flight response (Cannon, 1929; Rado, 1969) produces psychosomatic symptoms—such as a tension headache, hyperventilation, and irritable colon—in rather consistent patterns, known as psychophysiological response specificity, within a given person. With more chronic perception of stress, the hypothalamic-pituitary-adrenal cortex-steroid system is activated in an alarm-resistance-exhaustion defense sequence, described as the general adaptation syndrome by Selye (1950). Selye and others have demonstrated that the consequences of chronic activation of the general adaptation syndrome include renal impairment, renal hypertension, atherosclerosis leading to coronaries and strokes, duodenal ulcer, and immunosuppression against potential pathogens and mutagenic (cancer) cells. Many of those consequences of behaviorally perceived stresses fall into the domain of traditional medicine, which uses the treatment modalities of medication and surgery. Those illnesses, such as coronaries, seem to be increasing and occurring at earlier and earlier ages as modern humans increasingly perceive stress inappropriately in regard to time, place, and person.

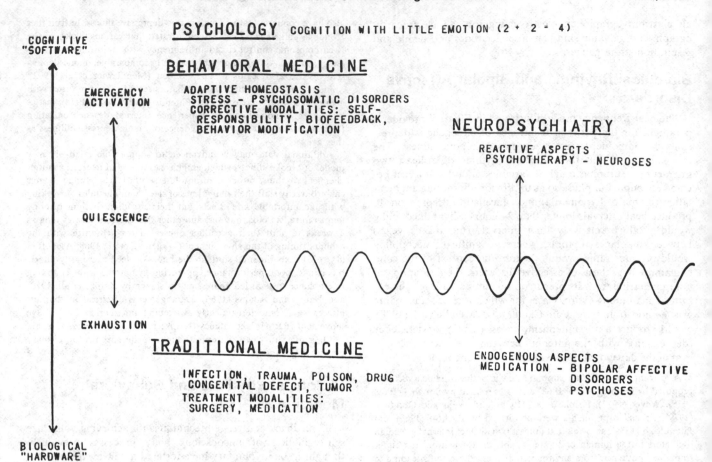

FIGURE 8. Schematic illustration demonstrating that biological rhythms are an important interface between the cognitively accessible and the biologically accessible domains of behavioral medicine, neuropsychiatry, and traditional medicine. (Redrawn with alterations from Stroebel, C. F., and Glueck, B. C. Passive meditation: Subjective, clinical, and electrographic comparison with biofeedback. In *Consciousness and Self-regulation*, G. E. Schwartz and D. Shapiro, editors. Plenum Publishing Corp., New York, 1978.)

Behavioral scientists are beginning to adopt a new holistic paradigm wherein about 95 per cent of all medical illnesses are viewed as derived from behaviorally driven stress mechanisms. That conceptual framework recognizes that a significant domain of physiological functioning is responsive to behavioral stimuli, is potentially adaptive, and is vulnerable to dysregulation (Schwartz, 1977), as well as voluntary reregulation, particularly before tissue pathology occurs. That behaviorally modifiable domain is becoming designated as behavioral medicine, a formal recognition of the interaction between physiology and behavior. The major tools of behavioral medicine include self-awareness, self-responsibility, self-regulation, and the prevention of inappropriate stress states. Once tissue pathology has occurred—whether through infection, trauma, poison, congenital defect, or tumor—external intervention by modern medicine to patch the defect is often impressive and largely beyond the subjective control of the patient. Even there, behavioral medicine plays a role in altering stress reactions and the tendency to brace against the organic pathology, which only serves to exacerbate its symptoms. Figure 8 schematically delineates the domains of psychology, behavioral medicine, neuropsychiatry, and traditional medicine, summarizing the foregoing discussion and postulating that biological rhythms modulate the interfaces among the domains. For example, the rat experiment (Stroebel, 1967) cited earlier in Figures 5 and 6 demonstrated that emotionality, in the domain of neuropsychiatry, was most easily conditioned at the onset of the activity cycle; and in Figure 3 it was shown that a drug, in the domain of physical medicine, was more potent at the onset of the rest cycle.

The circadian steroid rhythm is apparently the messenger of a superchiasmic master clock in synchronizing biological rhythms located in each cell in the body. Alteration of the steroid rhythm—as in iatrogenic steroid therapy, Cushing's syndrome, Addison's disease, or chronic activation of the general adaptation syndrome—has profound behavioral and physical consequences. For example, for many years a clinical association has been noted between affective disturbances and diseases of the adrenal gland, especially Cushing's syndrome and Addison's disease. Studies by Carrol et al. (1976) and Shulman and Diewold (1977) clarified the role of abnormal limbic system activation of the hypothalamic-pituitary-adrenal axis in primary depressive illnesses.

The modern human is apparently still equipped with a Stone Age body that uses the circadian steroid rhythm as a signal system for recharging physiological energy stores of both the brain and the body. When the periodicity of the steroid signal system becomes obscure because of feelings of helplessness and hopelessness or chronic stress activation of the general adaptation syndrome, illness ensues. In the years ahead, the holistic perspective of behavioral medicine, sensitive to the role of body time in regulating health and illness, may eventually help prevent 90 to 95 per cent of all illnesses—emotional and physical.

Psychophysiological Chronotography

The preceding discussion has strongly implicated biological rhythm processes in the acquisition, extinction, and memory of emotional behaviors. The failure to resolve biological rhythm influences, including potential beat frequencies, may be viewed as a major impasse in attempts to elucidate the psychobiology of emotional disorders. Clearly, the application of present knowledge about rhythms and emotions requires repeated measures of some type. For all but relatively short periodicities, as shown by electroencephalograms and electrocardiograms, the acquisition of a statistically adequate series of physiological measures is tedious for both patients and clinicians and is biased by a number of other problems that have been cited. Are there alternatives to repeated physiological measurements by clinicians?

Halberg et al. (1972, 1973a) strongly advocated the daily measurement of a number of biological rhythm variables as a focal tool for preventive medicine. Significant changes in body timing are sensitive early-warning signs of pathology and could be used to alert the patient and the clinician that a careful medical examination was warranted. For example, Halberg et al. (1958) observed rhythm variation significantly in advance of obvious pathology in mice injected with a transmittable mammary tumor. Halberg et al. (1972) recognized the impossibility of preoccupying half the population in making measurements on the other half and vice versa about six times each day. Hence, they developed a new concept, called autorhythmometry, in which persons are trained to make computer-scorable measurements—such as blood pressure, pulse, temperature, mood scale, grip strength, and time estimation—on themselves with relatively inexpensive instruments. They have encouraged educators to teach autorhythmometry to children, beginning in the second grade, so that it becomes a routine of life, like brushing one's teeth (Halberg et al., 1973a). Autorhythmometry will provide an enormous prospective data base on the population who cooperate, willingly carrying their instruments and scoring sheets with them wherever they go. It may also produce a new population suffering from heightened hypochondriasis. Another problem with current autorhythmometry procedures, were they to be applied in psychiatry, is their relative insensitivity to the richness of psychic life—that is, unreported feelings of love on a beautiful spring day may account for variations in the measured variables.

In a practical attempt to make rhythm measurement palatable to as large a segment of the population as possible in the interest of preventive medicine and psychiatry, Stroebel et al. (1973) developed a computer-scored daily record of moods, body changes, and life events called the psychophysiological diary. They observed that bodies provide a significant amount of information about periodic functioning each day—sleep patterns, time of bowel movements, hunger times, sense of time, recurrence of minor physical complaints (Stroebel, 1974). Usually, however, most people forget that information as trivial on a day-to-day basis. The psychophysiological diary, recorded on awakening and at bedtime each day, captures that trivial information, making possible the use of a computer's memory to detect subtle rhythms fluctuations, and patterns of daily routine that precede changes in living style and health. The 1978 version of the diary provides a single new diary scoring sheet each day on a tear-off pad in a plastic binder. The sheet for each day of the week is a different color. Every 2 weeks, diary users send their completed sheets to a data-processing center, where time series and sequential analyses are performed to detect significant variations, as compared with the user's

accumulated data file. At the present time, correlations with illness are retrospective; however, a number of predictive indices are emerging that will eventually permit prospective notification of the user and his physician of a potentially adverse pattern.

Although the psychophysiological diary is still in the early stages of development, previous successes in automating behavioral observations have already demonstrated the potential power of repeated behavioral observations as a means for detecting underlying periodic functioning. One example is the automated psychiatric nursing note.

The procedure for routine charting of psychiatric nursing notes was computerized at the Institute of Living in 1967 (Glueck, 1965; Rosenberg et al., 1967; Glueck and Stroebel, 1969). Nursing reports are made on each patient twice daily—reports could be made as often as desired, were extra staff available—by routine nursing personnel on a special IBM 3881 mark-sense form that is designed for computer scoring. Eleven areas of noninferential patient behavior are rated on the front side of the form, which is shown in Figure 10. Temperature, pulse, blood pressure, the nature of the patient's daily activities, and his physical complaints are reported in a similar fashion on the reverse side of the form. The computer produces two types of output from each report: The first is a narrative summary to be filed in the patient record as a legal document; the second is a set of 20 daily factor scores, describing the patient's behavior numerically, as compared with his hospital residence unit (normalized in T-score units, in which the mean for each factor = 50 and the standard deviation = 10). The original factor loadings and normalization were obtained from factor analysis-varimax rotation of 2,325 reports. Each factor possesses independence, since no single item loads on more than one factor. Further, nursing personnel are not required to make complicated inferences about such behavior as depression, since they are unaware of which items load on which factor.

Among the 20 factors are measures of acceptable behavior, disorganization, depression, and anxiety. Figure 11 shows a longitudinal display of those four factors over a 60-day period in a manic-depressive patient undergoing psychiatric treatment; the patient's 6-day cycle of behavioral change is dramatically apparent, as is her response to medication over time. Of special interest are the phase relationships among the factors, which indicate a possible factor sequence in that patient's illness as follows: Increased depression is followed by increased anxiety, which is followed by increased disorganization, which is followed by an increase in unacceptable behavior. The reverse sequence is also possible, depending on one's cause-and-effect rationale.

A superficial inspection of similar graphs collected on 2,400 patients since 1967 with runs of from 3 weeks to 4 years reveals obvious—that is, not requiring statistical analysis for resolution, a procedure currently being implemented for routine use—abnormal infradian periodicities in 30 per cent of the patients. The majority of those rhythms have been noted to change in response to clinical improvement.

Relatively crude quantitative evaluations of behavior—combined with repeated measurements, factor analysis, and computer technology—can use a routine nursing staff procedure to provide new information that previously escaped clinical awareness, except in blatantly obvious cases. The psychophysiological diary, a self-report variant, should prove to be especially powerful with all but the sickest inpatients and will also have applicability to the general population.

Those procedures, called psychophysiological chronotogra-

PSYCHOPHYSIOLOGICAL DIARY

IDENTIFICATION ☐☐☐ — ☐☐ — ☐☐☐☐   MON TUE WED THU FRI SAT SUN

AWAKENING DIARY   DATE TODAY ☐☐ - ☐☐ - ☐☐

WAKING TIME ☐☐ : ☐☐ AM PM
ALARM TIME ☐☐ : ☐☐ AM PM
TIME TO REALLY WAKE UP ☐☐ MINUTES
BEDTIME WAS ☐☐ : ☐☐ AM PM
TIME TO FALL ASLEEP ☐☐ MINUTES
PULSE RATE IN 20 SEC. ☐☐
AWAKENING TEMPERATURE ☐☐☐.☐ DEGREES

AMOUNT OF DREAMING	VH	HIGH	MOD	LOW	VL
DREAM EXPERIENCES	VG	GOOD	MOD	FAIR	BAD
SLEEP QUALITY	VG	GOOD	MOD	FAIR	POOR
SLEEPING CONDITIONS	VG	GOOD	MOD	FAIR	POOR
SLEEPING PILLS	MORE	3	2	1	NONE
NUMBER OF AWAKENINGS	MANY	4-5	3-2	1	NONE
ENERGY FOR TODAY	VH	HIGH	MOD	LOW	VL
EXPECTATIONS FOR TODAY	VH	HIGH	MOD	LOW	VL

BEDTIME WAS [PLANNED] [OTHER]
COMMENTS:

BEDTIME DIARY

DIARY TIME ☐☐ : ☐☐ AM PM   PULSE RATE IN 20 SEC. ☐☐

[WORK DAY] [LEISURE DAY] [VACATION] [AWAY FROM HOME] [AT SCHOOL] [NON ROUTINE DAY] [SICK]
[AIR TRAVEL] [ON DIET] [IN HOSPITAL] [SAW M.D.] [LATE PARTY] [LATE DATE]

	VH	HIGH	MOD	LOW	VL
TIREDNESS NOW					
TIREDNESS DURING DAY					
WORK PRESSURE TODAY					
PHYSICAL ACTIVITY TODAY					
MENTAL ACTIVITY TODAY					
INFLUENCE OF WEATHER					
PERSONAL HAPPINESS					
PUNCTUALITY					
SOCIABILITY					
FUN ACTIVITIES					
FEELING OF BEING RUSHED					
GUILTY FEELINGS					
ANGER EXPRESSED TODAY					
ANGER HELD IN TODAY					
CRITICISM OF OTHERS					
REMINISCENCES TODAY					
SEXUAL THOUGHTS					
INNER CALMNESS					
ORDERLINESS					
SENSE OF ACCOMPLISHMENT					
FEELINGS OF LOVING					
SENSE OF FREEDOM					
THINKING EFFICIENCY					
NEED FOR VACATION–REST					
MOODINESS					
FEELING OF HELPLESSNESS					
DEPRESSED FEELINGS					

	VF / VG	FAST / GOOD	MOD / MOD	SLOW / FAIR	VS / POOR
SENSE OF TIME TODAY					
PERFORMANCE AT WORK					
PERSONAL LIFE TODAY					
EMOTIONAL STATE					
GENERAL STATE OF HEALTH					
FEELINGS ABOUT FUTURE					
FEELINGS ABOUT DIARY					

	EXCESS	MORE	NORM	LESS	NONE
ACCIDENTALS					
ABDOMINAL FULLNESS					
ALLERGIES					
INDIGESTION					
COUGH					
SNEEZING					
THIRST					
URINATION					
CRAMPS					
BLEMISHES					
GAS					
BELCHING					
SMOKING					
ALCOHOL					
DRUGS					
ANNOYANCES					
APPETITE					
SNACKS					

HEADACHE SEVERITY	V BAD	BAD	MOD	SOME	NONE
FOOT TEMPERATURE	HOT	WARM	COMF	COLD	ICY
SKIN OILINESS	EXCESS	MORE	NORM	DRY	PEEL
NUMBER OF BOWEL MOVTS.	MORE	3	2	1	NONE

BM TYPE [LIQUID] [LOOSE] [NORMAL] [CONSTIP.] [NONE]

BM URGE ONSET TIME ☐☐ : ☐☐ AM PM

BEDTIME TEMPERATURE ☐☐☐.☐ DEGREES

SPEC. RATING A
SPEC. RATING B
SPEC. RATING C
SPEC. RATING D

WOMEN: MENSTRUAL FLOW	EXCESS	MORE	AVE	LESS	NONE

WEATHER TODAY: [COMF] [HOT] [COLD] [HUMID] [CLOUDY] [FOG] [RAIN] [SNOW] [WINDY] [ICY] [OTHER]
MEDICATIONS TODAY: [ASPIRIN] [COLD PILL] [ANTACID] [LAXATIVE] [TRANQUILIZERS] [ANTIBIOTIC] [OTHER]
LIFE EVENTS TODAY: ☐☐ ☐☐   BEDTIME COMMENTS ON REVERSE SIDE ☐
PHYSICAL SYMPTOMS OR ILLNESS TODAY:

FIGURE 9. Facsimile copy of the computer-scored *Psychophysiological Diary*, showing the awakening portion recorded on the top and the bedtime portion at the bottom. Fortran IV computer programs for scoring the diary and analyzing it for periodicities are available from the authors for the cost of reproduction. (From Stroebel, C. F., Luce, G., and Glueck, B. C. *The Psychophysiological Diary*. Institute of Living, Hartford, Conn., 1973.)

phy (Stroebel, 1974), represent an apparently practical means for extending the knowledge of rhythmic processes clinically as they relate to emotional functioning. Like the revelation of the paper chromatogram, which separates an organic com-pound into its components and makes them visible by colors, a psychophysiological chronotogram, as in Figure 9, helps identify those specific components of behavior and physiology that progressively evolve over time in health, in psychic devel-

PATIENT NAME   CASE NUMBER   UNIT   DATE

```
0   1   2   3   4   [ ]   5   6   7   8   9
OBSERVER STAFF IDENT NUMBER
0   1   2   3   4         5   6   7   8   9
0   1   2   3   4         5   6   7   8   9
0   1   2   3   4         5   6   7   8   9

0   1   2   3       [ ]   DAY OF MONTH
0   1   2   3   4         5   6   7   8   9

0   1   2   3   4   [ ]   5   6   7   8   9
REPORTING AREA
0   1   2   3   4         5   6   7   8   9
```

```
0   1   2   3   4   [ ]   5   6   7   8   9
PATIENT CASE NUMBER
0   1   2   3   4         5   6   7   8   9
0   1   2   3   4         5   6   7   8   9
0   1   2   3   4         5   6   7   8   9
0   1   2   3   4         5   6   7   8   9
```

SHIFT   1   2
DAY NIGHT

INSTITUTE OF LIVING

PATIENT BEHAVIOR INDEX ● NURSING

PERSONAL HABITS
- WITHDRAWN
- HAS TO BE REMINDED WHAT TO DO
- ANNOYS PERSONNEL BY TOUCHING THEM
- SMOKES INCESSANTLY
- SLOW TO FOLLOW ROUTINE
- RESENTS UNIT ROUTINE
- FOLLOWS ROUTINE ACCEPTABLY
- NEEDS HELP WITH PERSONAL HYGIENE
- REFUSES TO DO ROUTINE THINGS EXPECTED OF HIM
- DOES ODD, STRANGE THINGS
- SEE NARRATIVE
- UNABLE COMMENT

APPEARANCE
- FUSSY, FASTIDIOUS
- LOOKS TIRED, WORN OUT
- INAPPROPRIATELY, INFORMALLY DRESSED
- CAREFULLY DISORDERED
- CLEAN, NEAT, APPROPRIATELY DRESSED
- SLOPPY, UNKEMPT
- OVERDRESSED FOR THE OCCASION
- DRAMATIC, THEATRICAL
- BIZARRELY DRESSED
- LOOKS YOUNGER THAN IS
- SEE NARRATIVE
- UNABLE COMMENT

SLEEPING AND EATING HABITS
- SLEEPS DURING DAY
- COMPLAINED OF NOT BEING ABLE TO SLEEP
- SKIPPED MEAL
- RETIRED EARLY
- NOT UP FOR BREAKFAST
- SLEPT WELL
- EATS WELL
- SLEEPS RESTLESSLY DURING NIGHT
- FOOD INTAKE INADEQUATE
- WAKES EARLY
- SEE NARRATIVE
- UNABLE COMMENT

UNIT RELATIONSHIPS
- PREFERS COMPANY OF PERSONNEL
- ENJOYS SADISTIC HUMOR
- COMPLAINS ABOUT BEING IN HOSPITAL
- SUSPICIOUS OF ACTIONS OR MOTIVES OF PERSONNEL OR OTHER PATIENTS
- SPENDS GREAT DEAL OF TIME IN ROOM
- SATISFACTORY ADJUSTMENT TO UNIT
- RARELY GOES OFF UNIT ON HIS OWN INITIATIVE
- MUST BE REMINDED TO ATTEND CLASSES
- PRANKISH
- HAS TO BE TOLD TO COME OUT OF HIS ROOM
- SEE NARRATIVE
- UNABLE COMMENT

SOCIAL BEHAVIOR
- SECLUSIVE
- CANNOT TOLERATE DELAYS OR DENIAL OF HIS WISHES
- MEMBER OF "CLIQUE"
- FORMAL, RESERVED
- QUIET
- BOISTEROUS
- MAINTAINS A CLOSE RELATIONSHIP WITH ONE OTHER PATIENT
- FRIENDLY AND COOPERATIVE
- RELAXED, AT EASE
- RESTLESS, FIDGETY
- SEE NARRATIVE
- UNABLE COMMENT

SOCIAL INTERACTION
- EXCESSIVELY FAMILIAR WITH MEMBER OR MEMBERS OF OPPOSITE SEX
- IS SEDUCTIVE
- CONVERSES ONLY ON APPROACH
- OVERLY FAMILIAR WITH SAME SEX
- UNPOPULAR
- IMPULSIVE
- AVOIDS OPPOSITE SEX
- TEASES
- IMPOLITE
- PARTICIPATES IN GROUP ACTIVITY
- SEE NARRATIVE
- UNABLE COMMENT

MOOD
- SAD
- IRRITABLE
- MOODY, CHANGEABLE
- SMOOTH, EVEN DISPOSITION
- SHOWS LITTLE FEELING
- SEEMS AFRAID OF SOMETHING
- IS PLEASED WITH HIMSELF
- ANGRY
- TEARFUL
- PREOCCUPIED, OFTEN SEEMS TO BE DAYDREAMING
- SEE NARRATIVE
- UNABLE COMMENT

ATTITUDE
- SEEMS PLEASANT, YET IS OBSTRUCTIVE
- MAKES EXCUSES FOR HIS ACTIONS
- PLEASANT
- HOSTILE TO ONE PERSON IN PARTICULAR
- OFTEN DEMANDS ATTENTION OR PRAISE
- DEMONSTRATES FEELINGS OF INADEQUACY
- ARGUMENTATIVE OR UNCOOPERATIVE
- CAN'T MAKE UP MIND, INDECISIVE
- MANIPULATIVE
- FEELS REJECTED
- SEE NARRATIVE
- UNABLE COMMENT

VERBALIZATION
- USES STRANGE WORDS, PHRASES
- LOGICAL, CLEAR
- RAMBLES
- VOICE FLAT, MONOTONOUS
- VULGAR LANGUAGE
- SPEAKS SLOWLY, HESITANTLY
- SAYS THINGS ARE HOPELESS; HE IS NO GOOD
- SARCASTIC
- TALKATIVE
- REPEATS THOUGHTS, WORDS OR PHRASES OVER AND OVER
- SEE NARRATIVE
- UNABLE COMMENT

INTELLECTUAL BEHAVIOR
- EXPRESSES FEW THOUGHTS
- INAPPROPRIATE LAUGHTER
- CONFUSED
- STATEMENTS OR THOUGHTS INAPPROPRIATE TO MOOD OR SITUATION
- MOSTLY SELF-CENTERED
- FORGETFUL
- ALERT AND RESPONSIVE; CONCENTRATES WELL
- STATES PEOPLE ARE UNFAIR OR MEAN TO HIM
- GIDDY, CHILDISH
- DOESN'T PROFIT FROM MISTAKES
- SEE NARRATIVE
- UNABLE COMMENT

MISCELLANEOUS
- STATES NEED FOR LEAVING HOSPITAL
- HELPFUL
- OVERACTIVE
- WELL-MANNERED
- TENSE
- SLUGGISH OR DROWSY
- PACING
- UNREALISTIC IDEAS ABOUT HIMSELF, OTHERS OR HIS SURROUNDINGS
- NEGLECTS RESPONSIBILITIES
- UNUSUAL FACIAL EXPRESSIONS, GRIMACES
- BECOMES UPSET EASILY
- ENGAGES IN SOLITARY ACTIVITIES ON UNIT

INSTRUCTIONS
1. MAKE YOUR MARKS WITH A NO 2 BLACK LEAD PENCIL
2. FILL EACH MARK POSITION COMPLETELY.
3. ERASE COMPLETELY ANY MARKS YOU WISH TO CHANGE.
4. DO NOT STAPLE OR FOLD THIS SHEET.
5. PRINT NARRATIVE STATEMENT(S) ON REVERSE WHEN "SEE NARRATIVE" IS MARKED IN ANY CATEGORY.

IOL FORM 1232-1 P-C 7-66

FIGURE 10. Front side of the automated nursing note form for ratings by psychiatric personnel on each shift. (Reprinted by permission of the Institute of Living.)

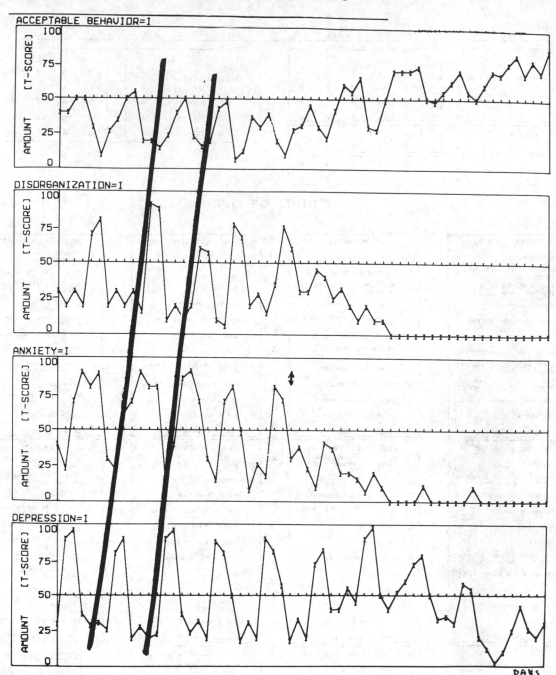

FIGURE 11. Computer-produced longitudinal graphs of four automated nursing note factors over a 60-day period in a manic-depressive inpatient. The phase relationships of the individual factors (the *slanted lines* clarify them) and the gradual damping of the 6- to 7-day periodicity in each of the factors shortly after medication was initiated *(arrow)* are evident. The graph is an example of a psychophysiological chronotogram.

opment, and in disease. It provides a new kind of laboratory precision to prospective analysis in psychiatry and preventive medicine, perhaps complementing and improving on the traditional retrospective approaches.

Suggested Cross References

Sleep is discussed in Section 2.3. Ethology is discussed in Section 4.6. Biofeedback is discussed in Section 4.9. Computers and clinical psychiatry are discussed in Section 6.2. Experimental disorders are discussed in Section 6.3. The applications

of statistics to psychiatry is discussed in Chapter 7, and factor analysis is discussed in Section 11.1.

REFERENCES

Aschoff, J. Desynchronization and resynchronization of human circadian rhythms. Aerosp. Med., *40:* 44, 1969.

Aschoff, J., Hoffmann, K., Pohl, H., and Wever, R. Re-entertainment of circadian rhythms after phase-shifts of the zeitgeber. Chronobiologia, *2:* 23, 1975.

Bleuler, E. *Dementia Praecox or the Group of Schizophrenias.* International Universities Press, New York, 1950.

Brown, F. A., Jr. A hypothesis for extrinsic timing of circadian rhythm. Can. J. Botany, *47:* 207, 1969.

Bunney, W. E., and Hartmann, E. Study of a patient with 48-hour manic-depressive cycles. Arch. Gen. Psychiatry, 12: 611, 1965.

Calhoun, J. B. Social modification of activity rhythms in rodents. In International Society for Chronobiology: XII International Conference Proceedings, p. 83. The Publishing House, Il Ponte, Milan, 1977.

Cannon, W. B. Bodily Changes in Pain, Hunger, Fear, and Rage, ed. 2. Appleton, New York, 1929.

Carrol, B. J., Curtis, G. C., and Mendels, J. Neuroendocrine regulation in depression. Arch. Gen. Psychiatry, 33: 1039, 1976.

Dalén, P. Season of Birth. American Elsevier, New York, 1975.

Engelmann, W. A slowing down of circadian rhythms by lithium ions. Z. Naturforsch., 28: 733, 1973.

Fishman, R., and Roffwarg, H. REM sleep inhibition by light in the albino rat. Exp. Neurol., 36: 166, 1972.

Fliess, W. Der Ablauf des Lebens [The Course of Life]. Deuticke, Leipzig, 1906.

Freud, S. The Origins of Psycho-Analysis: Letters to Wilhelm Fliess, Drafts and Notes: 1887–1902. Basic Books, New York, 1954.

Gjessing, R., and Gjessing, L. Some main trends in the clinical aspects of periodic catatonia. Acta Psychiatr. Scand., 37: 1, 1961.

Glueck, B. C. A psychiatric observation system. In Proceedings of the Seventh Medical Symposium, H. D. Steinbeck, editor, p. 317. IBM Press, Yorktown Heights, N. Y., 1965.

Glueck, B. C., and Stroebel, C. F. The computer and the clinical decision process. Am. J. Psychiatry, 125: 2, 1969.

* Halberg, F. Temporal coordination of physiologic function. In Biological Clocks, Cold Spring Harbor Symposia on Quantitative Biology, vol. 25, p. 289. Cold Spring Harbor Labs, Cold Spring Harbor, N. Y., 1960.

Halberg, F. Resolving power of electronic computers in chronopathology: An analog of microscopy. Scientia, 101: 412, 1966.

Halberg, F. Physiologic considerations underlying rhythmometry with special reference to emotional illness. In Cycles Biologiques et Psychiatrie, J. de-Ajuriaguerra, editor, p. 73. Masson, Paris, 1968.

* Halberg F. Chronobiology. Annu. Rev. Physiol., 31: 675, 1969.

Halberg, F., Bittner, J. J., and Smith, D. Mitotic rhythm in mice, mammary tumor milk agent, and breast cancer. Proc. Am. Assoc. Cancer Res., 2: 305, 1958.

* Halberg, F., Halberg, J., Halberg, F., and Halberg, E. Reading, 'riting, 'rithmetic—and rhythm: A new "relevant" "R" in the educative process. Perspect. Biol. Med., 17: 128, 1973a.

Halberg, F., Haus, E., Cardoso, S. S., Scheving, L. E., Kuhl, J. F. W., Shiotsaka, R., Rosene, G., Pauly, J. E., Runge, W., Spalding, J. F., Lee, G. K., and Good, R. A. Toward a chronotherapy of neoplasia: Tolerance of treatment depends on host rhythms. Experientia, 29: 909, 1973b.

* Halberg, F., Johnson, E. A., Nelson, W., Runge, W., and Sothern, R. Autorhythmometry: Procedures for physiologic self-assessment and their analysis. Physiol. Teach., 1: 1, 1972.

Halberg, F., Vestergaard, P., and Sakai, M. Rhythmometry on urinary 17-ketosteroid excretion by healthy men and women and patients with chronic schizophrenia: Possible chronopathology in depressive illness. Arch. Anat. Histol. Embryol. Norm. Exp., 51: 301, 1968.

Hauty, G. T., and Adams, T. Phase shifts of the human circadian system and performance deficit during the periods of transition. I. East-West flight. II. West-East flight. Aerosp. Med., 37: 668, 1966.

Hunt, H. F., and Brady, J. V. Some effects of punishment and intercurrent "anxiety" on a simple operant. J. Comp. Physiol. Psychol., 48: 305, 1955.

Jenner, F. A., Goodwin, J. C., and Sheridan, M. The effect of an altered time regime of biological rhythms in a 48-hour periodic psychosis. Br. J. Psychiatry, 114: 215, 1968.

Jones, E. The Life and Work of Sigmund Freud. Basic Books, New York, 1953.

Kety, S. S. Biochemical theories of schizophrenia. Int. J. Psychiatry, 1: 409, 1965.

Klein, K. E., and Wegmann, H. M. The resynchronization of human circadian rhythms after transmeridian flights as a result of flight direction and mode of activity. In Chronobiology, L. E. Scheving, F. Halberg, and J. E. Pauly, editors, p. 564. Igaku Shoin, Tokyo, 1974.

Klein, R., and Armitage, R. Rhythms in human performance: 1½-hour oscillations in cognitive style. Science, 204: 1326, 1979.

Kleitman, N. Sleep and Wakefulness. University of Chicago Press, Chicago, 1963.

Konopka, R. J., and Benzer, S. Clock mutants of Drosophila melanogaster. Proc. Natl. Acad. Sci., 68: 2112, 1971.

Kraepelin, E. Lectures on Clinical Psychiatry, ed. 3. William Wood, New York, 1913.

Kripke, D. F. An ultradian biologic rhythm associated with perceptual deprivation and REM sleep. Psychosom. Med., 34: 221, 1972.

Kripke, D. F., Cook, B., and Lewis, O. F. Sleep in night workers: EEG recordings. Psychophysiology, 7: 377, 1970.

* Kripke, D. F., Mullaney, D. J., Atkinson, M., and Wolf, S. Circadian rhythm disorders in manic-depressives. Biol. Psychiatry, 13: 335, 1978.

Kripke, D. F. and Sonnenschein, D. In The Stream of Consciousness, K. Pope and J. Singer, editors. Plenum, New York, 1978.

Kupfer, D. J. REM latency: A psychobiologic marker for primary depressive diseases. Biol. Psychiatry, 11: 159, 1976.

Lieber, A. L. Human aggression and the lunar synodic cycle. J. Clin. Psychiatry, 39: 385, 1978a.

Lieber, A. L. The Lunar Effect. Anchor Press/Doubleday, Garden City, N. Y., 1978b.

Lobban, M., Tredre, B., Elithorn, A., and Bridges, P. Diurnal rhythms of electrolyte excretion in depressive illness. Nature, 199: 667, 1963.

* Luce, G. Biological Rhythms in Medicine and Psychiatry. United States Government Printing Office, Washington, D. C., 1970.

Mendlewicz, J., Fleiss, J. S., and Fieve, R. R. Evidence for X-linkage in the transmission of manic-depressive illness. J. A. M. A., 222: 1624, 1972.

Moody, J. P., and Allsop, M. N. E. Circadian rhythms of water and electrolyte excretion in manic-depressive psychosis. Br. J. Psychiatry, 115: 923, 1969.

Moore, R. N. Central control of circadian rhythms. In Frontiers of Neuroendocrinology, W. F. Ganong and L. Martini, editors, vol. 5, p. 185. Raven Press, New York, 1978.

Ødegard, O. Season of birth in the population of Norway, with particular reference to the September birth maximum. Br. J. Psychiatry, 131: 339, 1977.

Parker, G., and Neilson, M. Mental disorder and season of birth—a southern hemisphere study. Br. J. Psychiatry, 129: 355, 1976.

Persinger, M. A., Cooke, W. J., and Janes, J. T. No evidence for relationship between biorhythms and industrial accidents. Percept. Mot. Skills, 46: 423, 1978.

Pflug, B., Erikson, R., and Johnsson, A. Depression and daily temperature. Acta Psychiatr. Scand., 54: 254, 1976.

Pittendrigh, C. S. Circadian oscillations in cells and the circadian organization of multicellular systems. In The Neurosciences: Third Study Program, F. O. Schmitt and F. G. Worden, editors, p. 437. MIT Press, Cambridge, Mass., 1974.

Pittendrigh, C. S., and Daan, S. Circadian oscillations in rodents: A systematic increase of their frequency with age. Science, 186: 548, 1974.

Rado, S. Adaptational Psychodynamics: Motivation and Control. Science House, New York, 1969.

Regal, P. J. Social synchronization and desynchronization of biological rhythms in the fitness and pathology of vertebrates. Chronobiologia, 1 (Suppl.): 57, 1975.

Reiderer, T., Birkmayer, W., Neumayer, E., Ambrozi, L., and Linauer, W. The daily rhythm of HVA, VMA (VA), and 5-HIAA in depression syndrome. J. Neurol. Trans., 35: 23, 1974.

* Reinberg, A., and Halberg, F. Circadian chronopharmacology. Am. Rev. Pharmacol., 11: 455, 1971.

Richter, C. P. Biological Clocks in Medicine and Psychiatry. Charles C Thomas, Springfield, Ill., 1965.

Rosenberg, M., Glueck, B. C., and Stroebel, C. F. The computer and the clinical decision process. Am. J. Psychiatry, 124: 595, 1967.

Schwartz, G. E. Psychosomatic disorders and biofeedback: A psychobiological model of disregulation. In Psychopathology: Experimental Models, J. Maser and M. E. P. Seligman, editors, p. 270. W. H. Freeman & Co., San Francisco, 1977.

Selye, H. The Physiology and Pathology of Exposure to Stress. Acta, Montreal, 1950.

Shulman, R., and Diewold, P. A two-dose dexamethasone suppression test in patients with psychiatric illness. Can. Psychiatr. Assoc. J., 22: 417, 1977.

Sollberger, A. Biological Rhythm Research. American Elsevier, New York, 1965.

* Stroebel, C. F. Behavioral aspects of circadian rhythms. In Comparative Psychopathology, J. Zubin and H. F. Hunt, editors, p. 158. Grune & Stratton, New York, 1967.

* Stroebel, C. F. Biologic rhythm correlates of disturbed behavior in the rhesus monkey. In Circadian Rhythms in Nonhuman Primates, F. G. Rohles, editor, p. 91. S. Karger, New York, 1969.

Stroebel, C. F. Computer techniques for studying biological rhythms: Quantitative chronobiology. Behav. Res. Meth. Instru., 2: 79, 1970.

Stroebel, C. F. Psychophysiological pharmacology. In Handbook of Psychophysiology, N. S. Greenfield and R. A. Sternbach, editors, p. 787. Holt, Rinehart and Winston, New York, 1972.

Stroebel, C. F. Autorhythmometry methods for longitudinal evaluation of daily life events and mood: Psychophysiologic chronotography. In Chronobiology, L. E. Scheving, F. Halberg, and J. E. Pauly, editors, p. 379. Igaku Shoin, Tokyo, 1974.

* Stroebel, C. F. Chronopsychophysiology. In Comprehensive Textbook of Psychiatry, A. M. Freedman, H. I. Kaplan, and B. J. Sadock, editors, ed. 2, p. 166. Williams & Wilkins, Baltimore, 1975.

Stroebel, C. F., and Glueck, B. C. The biologic rhythm approach to psychiatric treatment. In Proceedings of the Seventh Medical Symposium, H. D. Steinbeck, editor, p. 215. IBM Press, Yorktown Heights, N. Y., 1965.

Stroebel, C. F., and Glueck, B. C. Biofeedback treatment in medicine and psychiatry: An ultimate placebo? In Biofeedback: Behavioral Medicine, L. Birk, editor, p. 379. Grune & Stratton, New York, 1973.

Stroebel, C. F. and Glueck, B. C. Passive meditation: Subjective, clinical, and electrographic comparison with biofeedback. In Consciousness and Self-regulation, G. E. Schwartz and D. Shapiro, editors, p. 401. Plenum Publishing Corp., New York, 1978.

Stroebel, C. F., Luce G., and Glueck, B. C. The Psychophysiological Diary: A Computer-scored Record of Moods, Body Changes, and Life Events. Institute of Living, Hartford, Conn., 1978.

Thommen, G. Biorhythm. Universal, New York, 1968.

Tramer, M. Über die biologische Bedeutung des Geburtsmonates, insbesondere für die Psychoseerkrankung [Concerning the biological significance of the month of birth, particularly for psychotic illnesses]. Schweiz. Arch. Neurol. Psychiatr., *24:* 17, 1929.

Unger, F., and Halberg, F. Circadian rhythms in the *in vitro* response of the mouse adrenal to ACTH. Science, *137:* 1058, 1962.

Van Cauter, E., and Mendlewicz, J. 24-hour dopamine-beta-hydroxylase pattern: A possible biological index of manic-depression. Life Sci., *22:* 147, 1978.

Wehr, T. A., and Goodwin, S. K. Rapid cycling in manic-depressives induced by tricyclic antidepressants. Arch. Gen. Psychiatry, *36:* 555, 1979.

Weitzman, E. D., Goldmacher, D., Kripke, D. F., MacGregor, P., and Nogeire, C. Reversal of sleep-waking cycle: Effect on sleep stage pattern and neuroendocrine rhythms. Trans. Am. Neurol. Assoc., *93:* 153, 1968.

Weitzman, E. D., Kripke, D. F., Goldmacher, D., MacGregor, P., Kream, J., and Hellman, F. Acute reversal of sleep-waking cycle in man. Arch. Neurol., *22:* 480, 1970.

Wever, R. Autonomous circadian rhythms in man: Singly versus collectively isolated subjects. Naturwissenschaften, *62:* 443, 1975a.

Wever, R. The meaning of circadian rhythmicity with regard to aging man. Verh. Dtsch. Ges. Pathol., *59:* 169, 1975b.

Wever, R. Quantitative studies of the interaction between different circadian oscillators within the human multioscillator system. In *International Society for Chronobiology: XII International Conference Proceedings*, p. 525. The Publishing House, Il Ponte, Milan, 1977.

Whatmore, G., and Kohli, D. *The Physiopathology and Treatment of Junctional Disorders.* Grune & Stratton, New York, 1974.

Zagula-Malley, Z. W., Cardoso, S. S., Simpson, H., and Reinberg, A. Selected time point differences of observed skin mitosis frequency in 18 patients suffering from actinic keratoses and skin cancer. Chronobiologia, *5:* 217, 1978.

Zucker, I., Rusak, B., and King, R. G. Neural bases for circadian rhythms in rodent behavior. Adv. Psychobiol., *3:* 35, 1976.

2.7 Sociobiology

DAVID P. BARASH, Ph.D.
JUDITH E. LIPTON, M.D.

Introduction

Sociobiology has been defined by E. O. Wilson (1975) as "the systematic study of the biological basis of all social behavior." Since sociobiology integrates principles of evolutionary biology, population and behavior genetics, ecology, and ethology, it has become a distinctive new discipline, with demonstrable applicability to the study of animal behavior. At present, the field of human sociobiology does not formally exist, but it seems likely that sociobiology's relevance to human behavior will be systematically explored and evaluated in the near future. It is tempting to speculate extensively about the possible connections between sociobiological theory and data on the one hand and psychiatry on the other. However, in view of the unfamiliarity of most psychiatrists with sociobiology and the tentative and largely unexplored relevance of the discipline to psychiatry, such speculation seems inappropriate in the present context.

In the following pages the basic principles and findings of sociobiology are outlined, emphasizing those areas that seem to have special potential for human relevance. More detailed information can be found in Wilson (1975) and Barash (1977a). Material oriented toward social science appears in Chagnon and Irons (1979), DeVore (1978), and Silvers and Gregory (1979). Interactions between sociobiology and other disciplines are explored in Barlow and Silverberg (1980) and Barash et al. (1980). A popularized account, with speculations on human applicability, occurs in Barash (1979).

Basic Principles

Two principles underlying sociobiology are the interaction principle and the central postulate of sociobiology. The interaction principle states that all phenotypes, including behavior, derive from the interaction between the organism's genotype and its environment—learning, impinging stimuli, social situation, and so on. Although a given proportion of the phenotypic variance in any population may be attributed to genotypic variance, it is absolutely impossible to discriminate environmental from genetic factors in an individual. Statements about any individual phenotype, including behavior, must take both genetic tendency and environmental influences into consideration, although the extent of their contributions varies with the organism and the behavior. The nature-nurture, instinct-learning controversy is resolved by recognizing that both factors operate and that no one factor is deterministic (Hinde, 1970; Lehrman, 1970).

As a general rule, organisms with complex nervous systems such as mammals, tend to rely less on genetically mediated behavioral factors than do simpler organisms, such as insects. Behaviors that must be done correctly the first time, such as escape from predators, tend to be under more genotypic influence than behaviors that are linked less directly to survival or reproductive success. Further, those organisms that inhabit relatively stable environments or that participate in relatively little social interaction are likely to be under more genetic influence than are those for which rapid adaptations to fluctuating environments or social situations are necessary. For example, plant behavior tends to be more genetically mediated than animal behavior, although both can be considered to use behavioral strategies (Janzen, 1977). Behavior in this context is not considered qualitatively distinct from any other biological function of an organism. Indeed, organisms need not have a brain at all in order to behave.

The field of behavior genetics has demonstrated substantial proof of the genetic basis of numerous complex behaviors in insects, birds, and mammals. Classic experiments have demonstrated single-gene effects (Rothenbuhler, 1964), responses to selective pressure (Tolman, 1924), and specific hybridization effects (Sharpe and Johnsgard, 1966). However, there are no cases in which genes determine behavior in the absence of environmental influence, just as there are no cases in which environment alone determines behavior without the organism's contribution. Since sociobiology is largely based on the application of evolutionary biology to social behavior and since natural selection is effective only when it acts on a genetic substrate, this connection between genotype and behavior is crucial for the sociobiological enterprise. However, the connection implies only some above zero genetic influence, not genetic determinism (Dobzhansky, 1976).

The central postulate of sociobiology (Barash, 1977a) states that, insofar as a behavior reflects some component of genotype, individuals should behave so as to maximize their inclusive fitness. Fitness may be defined as a measure of evolutionary success or the rate at which an individual passes on its genes to succeeding generations, compared with the mean rate in its population. More exactly, it is a number that, when multiplied by the proportion of members in one generation, gives the proportion in the next. Inclusive fitness (Hamilton, 1964) is the sum of an individual's reproductive success or personal fitness and that of his relatives, with each relative devalued in proportion to its coefficient of relationship with the individual in question. Coefficient of relationship refers to the proportion of genes that any two individuals share by virtue of their common descent or, equivalently, the probability that an allele, or one of a number of alternative forms of a gene, present in one individual will be present in another because of their common descent. Accordingly, the coefficient of relationship between parents and offspring is ½, full sibs ½, grandparents and their grandchildren ¼, half sibs ¼, and cousins ⅛.

The central postulate is exemplified by the following oversimplification. Two alternative alleles, A and a, are both competing for the same genetic locus. Allele A influences its carrier to perform behavior X, and allele a influences its carrier toward behavior Y. Furthermore, the evolutionary fitness of individuals performing behavior X is greater than that of individuals performing behavior Y. In other words, X-behaving individuals produce a greater number of reproductively successful offspring or other relatives than do Y-behaving individuals. As a result, allele A spreads in the population, at the expense of allele a. Eventually, the population comes to be made up of individuals carrying allele A and performing behavior X.

A sociobiological approach to behavior accordingly involves the expectation that each individual will tend to behave in a manner that maximizes his or her inclusive fitness, since each individual is composed of many genes, each of which functions to maximize the likelihood that it will be projected into future generations (Dawkins, 1976). The genes that are recognized as constituting any individual are present because their ancestors were of sufficient fitness to project copies of themselves into succeeding generations. Sociobiology analyzes the behavior of individuals by considering them as fitness-maximizing organisms or, alternatively, as the sum of various fitness-maximizing entities—the genes.

Evolution is any change in the genetic make-up of a population. It occurs largely through natural selection—differential reproduction of genes ultimately produced by mutation. Natural selection should be distinguished from Lamarckian evolution, which occurs through the inheritance of acquired characteristics. For example, it is widely believed that future human beings will have large heads and small bodies, presumably because they have been using their brains so much and their bodies so little. However, the flow of biological information is from DNA to somatic tissues, not vice versa. Accordingly, future *Homo sapiens* will be small bodied and large headed only if persons with genes promoting these phenotypes are more fit than alternatives. Although cultural evolution proceeds in a Lamarckian fashion, biological evolution is exclusively Darwinian.

The central postulate, then, is a statement of the evolution of behavioral tendencies in accord with the understanding of natural selection, first proposed by Darwin (1859). Any alleles that confer differential reproductive success are expected to spread in a population, whether these alleles pertain to morphology, physiology, or behavior. The proximate mechanisms by which they act—that is, the DNA or RNA structures, protein and enzyme formation, and so on—are not the domain of sociobiology. Rather, evolutionary biology and sociobiology are primarily concerned with distal causation, the adaptive significance of the traits (Barash, 1977a).

In addition, confusion and controversy have surrounded the units of selection. Advocates of group selection (Wynne-Edwards, 1962) have proposed that alleles exist that confer group adaptive advantage or an increase in group fitness, in spite of detrimental effects on individual reproductive success. Despite a few exceptions that have been found in nature (Lewontin, 1962) and a few theoretically possible computer models (Boor-

man and Levitt, 1972, 1973; Gadgil, 1975; D. S. Wilson, 1977), it is generally agreed that group selection is relatively unimportant in nature, since it can occur only in extremely small, isolated populations that face the possibility of rapid extinction. However, many eminent social scientists (Montagu, (1968), ethologists (Lorenz, 1965), and psychiatrists (Bowlby, 1969) have been misled into believing that natural selection operates for the good of the species. In most cases the unit of selection can be considered to be the individual or the individual gene (Lewontin, 1970; Dawkins, 1976); this recognition has given rise to much of sociobiology's conceptual vigor (Alexander, 1975).

The central postulate, focused on natural selection operating at the level of individuals or genes, is largely responsible for sociobiology's distinctiveness from ethology, another behavioral discipline that also uses concepts from evolutionary biology. But whereas classic European ethology typically uses evolution in a historical perspective, sociobiology uses natural selection in an analytic and often predictive mode (Barash, 1980), with the postulate that behavior will be directed toward the maximization of inclusive fitness.

Competition and Conflict

Conflict can be predicted to occur whenever two individuals differ over the strategy necessary to maximize the inclusive fitness of each. In sexually reproducing species, conflict seems inevitable because each individual has a unique genotype. By contrast, among asexual reproducers, individuals are genetically identical and, therefore, noncompeting (E. O. Wilson, 1975). Indeed, the remarkable cohesiveness and cooperation among the cells of multicellular organisms may be sociobiologically attributed to their genetic identity. This novel approach is also consistent with the speculation that both aging and cancer are associated with somatic mutations that decrease the coefficient of relationship between the affected cells and the rest of the organism; competition occurs because the cells are not identical, and the result may be detrimental to the organism as a whole.

A behavioral perspective, however, is concerned with conflict between individuals. Because evolution occurs when limited resources prevent unlimited population growth, differential reproduction occurs; some individuals project more genes into future generations than do other individuals. One individual's success may be considered to be at the expense of another individual. Consequently, sociobiology predicts a great deal of conflict and competition between individuals, more so as the individuals are unrelated and, therefore, unlikely to share genes.

There are essentially two ways in which individuals can compete: scramble competition and contest competition (MacArthur, 1972). In scramble competition, each individual attempts to accumulate a maximum number of reproductively relevant resources without regard to the activities of any other individual. In contest competition, individuals vie with one another, with resources distributed as a function of the social encounters between them. Many examples of contest competition have relevance to human behavior, particularly territoriality and aggression.

Territory has been defined as "any defended area" (Carpenter, 1958) and as "an area of exclusive use" (Pitelka, 1959). Natural selection should favor the maintenance of territories when doing so enhances inclusive fitness—that is, when the cost of territorial behavior is less than the benefit, with both measured in units of inclusive fitness. Territoriality is most likely when the reproductively relevant resources are in short supply and considerations of time, energy, and resource distribution make the resource in question economically defendable (Brown, 1964). There is abundant literature in support of this proposition among animals (Brown, 1975; E. O. Wilson, 1975; Barash, 1977a) and among humans as well (Dyson-Hudson and Smith, 1978). Such emphasis on the adaptive significance of territoriality seems more useful than facile and often acrimonious debate over whether it is instinctive (Ardrey, 1966; Montagu, 1968).

Aggressive behavior is a related phenomenon that can be analyzed in similar economic terms, with inclusive fitness as the ultimate currency. The costs of aggression include the expenditure of time and energy and the risks of injuring oneself or a relative. Possible benefits include increased territory, or the possible elimination of competitors. The ultimate effects of these behaviors can be translated into effects on fitness. Insofar as the behaviors evolved through natural selection, they can be analyzed as strategies for increasing inclusive fitness (central postulate). Accordingly, game theoretic models have been developed with the goal of identifying evolutionarily stable strategies. These strategies are defined as behaviors that, once practiced by the majority of members of a population, cannot be replaced—that is, exceeded in fitness maximizing—by any other strategies (Maynard Smith and Price, 1973; Parker, 1974; Maynard Smith and Parker, 1976). The crucial difference between this approach and earlier efforts to understand aggressive interactions is that evolutionarily stable strategies recognize that the payoff resulting from a behavior is a function of the probability of encountering others who engage in alternative, predictable strategies—for example, a threatening, highly aggressive stance would be more successful against easily intimidated opponents than against others who are likely to respond in kind.

By contrast, ethologists have often emphasized the tournament-like nature of aggressive displays between individuals, generally interpreting them as benefiting the species. There appears to be a relative absence of bloodshed and killing associated with much animal aggression in natural settings (Eibl-Eibesfeldt, 1961; Lorenz, 1963). Sociobiology suggests several explanations based on individual benefit. Bluff and threat are less expensive than serious fighting. The cost of aggressive behavior is decreased if there is less chance of injuring oneself or a relative. Even when a rival is clearly subordinated, the cost of killing it may be personal injury, although the benefit is decreased competition. Accordingly, aggressive restraint may be mediated by considerations of personal and inclusive fitness.

A sociobiological view of aggression is not necessarily incompatible with the more traditional approach of the behavioral sciences, which emphasize the role of experience. Indeed, learning itself may be seen as an adaptive strategy that maximizes fitness by providing an appropriate modifiability for behavior. This approach is receiving increased recognition in both ethology (Hinde and Stevenson-Hinde, 1973) and psychology (Seligman and Hager, 1972). Aggression in response to frustration (Dollard et al., 1939) may well be adaptive insofar as a violent behavioral response may overcome a resistance to ongoing behavior that constituted the frustration in the first place. Furthermore, it is now well known that animals learn to fight by fighting, just as they learn to win by winning (Scott, 1958). If fighting is a means of enhancing fitness by increasing access to reproductively relevant resources, it is appropriate that individuals learn to fight when they have a high expecta-

tion of success. Correlations of early social learning with aggressiveness (Bandura et al., 1961) also fit this conceptual scheme.

A sociobiological view of aggression suggests several alternative strategies for the defeated individual. In particular, it can emigrate or disperse (a common response in many solitary species), or, if sociality conveys sufficient compensations to the fitness of a defeated contestant, it can remain in the social group but as a subordinate individual. This is the sociobiological explanation of social dominance hierarchies. In view of the previously described advantages to inhibited aggression on the part of the victor, the maximally fit response by the vanquished may be to assume the role of subordinate. Such a strategy may be advantageous if the cost of solitude is great and if the subordinate individual retains the chance of bettering himself or herself in the future. Genetic relatedness between subordinate and dominant may increase the benefit of remaining in the group for the subordinate if the behavior sufficiently enhances the fitness of relatives because of the presence of a larger social group (West Eberhard, 1975). A large group may provide increased protection from predators, increased territory, and increased sexual opportunity. In sum, sociobiology suggests that normal patterns of aggression may be seen as adaptive strategies that confer increased fitness on the individual concerned.

Reproductive Strategies

All genetically mediated biological functions should ultimately affect reproductive function. However, evolutionary theory predicts that those structures or behaviors dealing directly with reproduction are those subject to the most intense selective pressure; indeed, these structures and behaviors have proved to be especially susceptible to sociobiological analysis. Furthermore, the principles of conflict and competition should be applicable to all sexually reproducing species in which genetic asymmetry is the rule, whether one is considering relationships between mates, parents and children, or sibs. Human family structure has been analyzed in sociobiological terms (van den Berghe and Barash, 1977), and there has been much speculation on the human relevance of natural selection operating on reproductive behaviors (Alexander, 1975, 1977; Hartung, 1976; Barash, 1977a, 1979; Weinrich, 1977). The central postulate is the paradigm by which each of these relationships is evaluated; insofar as behavior is influenced by heredity, individuals are predicted to behave so as to maximize their inclusive fitness.

MATE SELECTION AND MALE-FEMALE DIFFERENCES

Biologically, male is defined as the sex that produces a large number of small gametes; female is defined as the sex that produces a small number of large gametes. The implications of these definitions are profound. A single ovum must represent more investment to the female than a single sperm does to a male, simply measured by the number of gametes produced by each sex. In most species the discrepancy between male and female parental investment is increased by even further reproductive burdens on the female. This discrepancy has been most cogently analyzed by Trivers (1972), who defined parental investment as any behavior by the parent toward the offspring that increases the chances of the offspring's survival and, hence, reproduction at the cost of the parent's ability to invest in future offspring. Because the sex investing more becomes a limiting resource for the sex investing less, members of the latter sex are selected to compete among themselves for the sexual attentions of members of the former sex. Similarly, the sex that is more limited by the number of gametes produced or the amount of energy required to support the young is selected to be more discriminating about the choice of mates, place of reproduction, and time of reproduction, whereas the sex investing less, generally the male, tends to be sexually aggressive and easily aroused.

Accordingly, the usual pattern is for males to compete with other males, and the females—and increased fitness—are the ultimate goal. This male-male competition may take various forms. For example, sperm can be thought of as competing for access to ova. The most successful sperm are those that swim fastest and resist chemical degradation or predation longest. At the organismic level a small number of males can fertilize a large number of females. In any given society a large number of males could, therefore, be sexually inactive while a few males monopolize all the sexual opportunities. Those few males would enjoy enormous fitness, but the majority represent an evolutionary loss. Sea elephants represent one such species, and physical size seems to be a major factor in determining reproductive success. Consequently, male infant sea elephants compete vigorously and at much risk for extra milk (Reiter et al., 1978). Males in most vertebrate species seem selected to engaged in aggressive, showy, or otherwise risky reproductive strategies. If they are successful, they may win substantial advantages. Although they may lose their lives, males in most species are by definition playing for higher stakes than are females. In addition, there is little risk associated with male promiscuity and much advantage to be gained by inseminating as many females as possible. Thus, evolutionary theory predicts that males are selected to engage in behaviors that produce a maximum number of sperm that are dispersed as many times as possible. Various species-specific behaviors represent adaptive consequences of the usual ecology of each species and the evolutionary biology of male-female differences.

Williams (1966) pointed out that there are important examples of role reversal, which indicate that the biological definitions of maleness and femaleness are not strictly predictive. For example, in seahorses (Syngnathidae family), females are not inseminated by males; instead, the female transfers her eggs to a brood pouch in the male. The young develop to an advanced stage with the aid of a placental connection to the male. Males are thus the limiting resource, and they are more cautious and discriminating than the females, who tend to be both aggressive and promiscuous (Fiedler, 1954). Several bird species show pronounced predominance of paternal investment; in these cases the females are more brightly colored, more aggressive, and more promiscuous than the males (Kendeigh, 1952). Sexual dimorphism, in both behavior and structure, is a function of the economics and of the biology of the species under consideration.

However, among mammals, initial female investment is invariably greater than male investment, since fertilization must be followed by a long period of both prenatal and postnatal care. The cost of pregnancy and lactation is inevitably greater than the cost of sperm production. Therefore, female mammals are selected to be particularly careful comparison shoppers, and males are selected to be promiscuous, easily aroused sexually, and competitive for females. Monogamy is in the female interest, since she may then gain exclusive rights to the male's attention and territory, which can be transformed into enhanced fitness by the increased success of her offspring. However, males are selected to favor those social arrangements that provide maximum access to receptive females. The ensuing conflict is often resolved by an apparent compromise (Downhower and Armitage, 1971).

Among human beings the signs of male-male competition and male-female differences seem quite clear; males tend to be larger than females, with a higher proportion of muscle and hormonally mediated inclinations toward greater aggressiveness and activity beginning early in life (Money and Eberhardt, 1972). Furthermore, sexual maturation in boys occurs later than in girls, a pattern found in species characterized by male-male competition, in which male fitness is higher if maturation and, therefore, competition is delayed until greater size, strength, and experience are attained.

An advantage that the female enjoys is confidence that her offspring are genetically her own. Male paternity is necessarily less certain, and, accordingly, male courtship strategies for increasing confidence of paternity seem to occur in those species in which biparental investment is required (Barash, 1976b, 1977b). The formation of harems that provide females with access to wealthy males and males access to a number of faithful females is a predicted strategy in mammals. In fact, monogamy is exceedingly rare among mammals (Kleiman, 1977), although it is predominant among birds, in which it correlates with the necessity of both parents' cooperating in the care of the young (Lack, 1966). Females may assess the quality of a male by his status in relationship to other males or by the size and quality of the reproductively relevant resources he controls. In either case the females can judge the males and choose those that seem most fit.

Many examples of resource-based mating systems have been described, usually with the common denominator that mating privileges are accorded males who are able to provide reproductively relevant resources to their females (Wolf, 1975; Cronin and Sherman, 1977). There seems to be a general correlation between the economic monopolizability of environmental features and the degree of polygamy found in any species (Emlen and Oring, 1977). Females may choose males who control quality territory, as in red-winged blackbirds (Orians, 1969); they may incite competition among males, copulating with the victors (Cox and LeBoeuf, 1977); they may prefer males who provide maximum food resources—sometimes even their own bodies—during courtship (Thornhill, 1976); or the females may simply accept the victors of aggressive male-male competition, as in deer (Darling, 1937) and mountain goats (Geist, 1971). The equivalent of divorce occurs among at least one species of gull; it is strongly associated with failure to produce successful young the previous year (Coulson, 1966). Sociobiology predicts that mate selection is a careful process of appraisal and choice, with individuals of either sex selected to mate with others that maximize the fitness of the chooser.

In all considerations of this sort, behavioral strategies that appear to require insight or conscious assessment of fitness differentials can always be translated into evolution acting on genes. For example, among females, a genetically influenced tendency to mate preferentially with males who control good resources is more successful over evolutionary time than an alternative tendency to be less discriminating, as mediated by an alternative allele. Accordingly, such behavior evolves without regard to conscious intent; individuals are selected to maximize their fitness and that of their genes without necessarily realizing it.

PARENTING

A sociobiological perspective suggests that inclinations toward parental investment vary with confidence of genetic relatedness. Support for this hypothesis is generated by the fact that neither sex invests postzygotically in teleost fish with pelagic eggs or in most marine invertebrates in which neither sex has assurance of genetic relatedness to the offspring. By contrast, biparental care is found in those species in which confidence of relatedness is high—for example, such monogamous birds as warblers, sparrows, and hawks and such monogamous mammals as gibbons, beaver, and certain foxes. Males bear greater parental responsibility when they have greater confidence of parenthood, such as when several females have laid eggs in the nest of a single male. Examples are demersally spawning fish, such as the pomacentridae, and certain birds, such as rheas and tinamous. The most common pattern among mammals is for females to have the primary parenting role, presumably because internal fertilization guarantees them an exceptional degree of confidence in their parenthood. For the same reason, the females lactate, not the males. Similar considerations also suggest an evolutionary explanation for menopause (Alexander, 1974; Barash, 1977a).

Differential confidence in genetic relatedness may help provide an evolutionary explanation of why, in some species, parents are able to recognize their offspring, but in others they are not. For example, ground-nesting gulls that have nesting sites in close proximity to one another and whose young are able to intermingle socially are able to discriminate their young. Gulls that inhabit solitary cliff ledges and rear their young in isolation are not able to distinguish their offspring from substituted strangers of the same age (Cullen, 1957). Elephant seals raise their young in large groups that are populated by many adult females and juveniles and by one or a few adult males. The females are able to recognize their own offspring, and they reject orphans and the offspring of other females.

Avoidance of incest seems almost universal among free-living nonhuman animals, despite the fact that the products of incestuous pairings have an increased coefficient of relatedness to each parent. However, there are decrements to fitness resulting from inbreeding (Cavalli-Sforza and Bodmer, 1971), presumably because of increased homozygosity. Consideration of the adaptive significance of heterozygosity can be found in Haldane (1932), Fisher (1958), and Wright (1969). Social mechanisms that seem to perpetrate outbreeding include dispersal before sexual maturation and play patterns developed during infancy that interfere with sexual activity at maturity (Hill, 1974). The biological disadvantages of incest and the cultural advantages of exogamy, such as making social alliances (Lévi-Strauss, 1968), may explain the ubiquity of the human incest taboo (Ember, 1975).

Living things generally do not care for offspring that are not their own (Power, 1975). Species with precocial young tend to reject infants to whom they have not been imprinted (Klopfer and Gamble, 1966), and infanticidal strategies have been reported in lions (Schaller, 1972), ground squirrels (Steiner, 1972), African wild hunting dogs (Van Lawick-Goodall, 1973), and langur monkeys (Hrdy, 1977). In the langurs, infanticide occurs when a bachelor male supplants a dominant harem leader; the new leader then kills the nursing infants that were sired by the ousted male. The lactating females rapidly come into estrus and mate with the new leader, thus propogating his genes. Female langurs occasionally cooperate with each other to defend their offspring (Hrdy and Hrdy, 1976). Furthermore, deception may occur, as when pregnant females undergo false estrus at the time of a coup, during which they copulate with the new male and then give birth to the previous leader's offspring. As with each case of deceptive strategies, one can predict counterstrategies for detecting cheating and then increasingly refined capacities for deception.

The most parsimonious explanation of each of these examples is that selfish concern for successful reproduction promotes a wide variety of adaptive strategies that are increasingly complex as the social structure becomes more complex. Mate selection, patterns of parenting, and family structures are all behavioral strategies that seem to promote maximization of individual inclusive fitness.

PARENT-OFFSPRING CONFLICT

Ethological studies of nonhuman primates have fascinated those interested in maternal-infant behavior and have led to many studies of human attachment and bonding processes (Bowlby, 1969, 1973; Klaus and Kennell, 1976). Emphasis has usually been on the processes by which mother and offspring adjust to one another, including recognition and signaling mechanisms that enhance the mutually gratifying aspects of the relationship. Both Freudian and post-Freudian developmental models have described normal periods of conflict and conflict resolution during ontogeny that occur both intrapsychically in the infant and interpersonally between parent and child. Sociobiological theory predicts a special kind of parent-offspring conflict, one based on the inherent genetic asymmetry of the related individuals. Much of the following discussion is based on the pioneering work of Trivers (1974); possible human implications beg for exploration.

Sociobiological theory predicts that newborn mammals are selected to engage in behaviors that enhance their fitness by encouraging parental investment on the part of the mother. Similarly, mammalian mothers are selected to engage in behaviors that enhance the fitness of their offspring, thus increasing the fitness of the mother. Such behaviors include lactation, defense against predators, and various patterns of solicitous attention. Early in the life of the infant, the interests of the parent and child coincide, and one predicts very little conflict. However, as the infant matures, it makes increasing demands on the mother that can ultimately be measured as costs to her fitness. Initially, the costs include calories expended on lactation, risks taken to defend the offspring, and time and energy expended on the care of the infant. Ultimately, the greatest cost to the mother is that she may do well to reproduce again and invest in another offspring, rather than continue to invest in the more mature juvenile. The mother is equally invested in each of her offspring; she shares half her genes with each and her fitness is maximized by reproducing an optimal number of times. The offspring, however, is related to its mother and to each of its full sibs by a coefficient of ½; by contrast, it "shares" all its genes with itself. Accordingly, the offspring should be selected to devalue considerations of maternal and sibling fitness by 50 per cent relative to the optimum from the viewpoint of the mother or the other sibs. In other words, a given child is only one-half as interested in the sibling as it is in itself, whereas the mother is equally interested in each of her children. The conflict may be the biological basis for sibling rivalry, which can be viewed as competition for parental investment.

Evolutionary considerations suggest that parent and offspring do not conflict early in the life of the infant, when the benefit of continuing to invest in the infant outweighs the cost of postponing investment in another infant, as measured in units of maternal fitness (see Figure 1). Similarly, when the ratio of benefit to cost exceeds 2, parent and offspring should agree on terminating the initial investment and initiating parental investment in a sib. The interval in which cost-benefit exceeds 1 and yet is less than 2 is predicted to be one of parent-

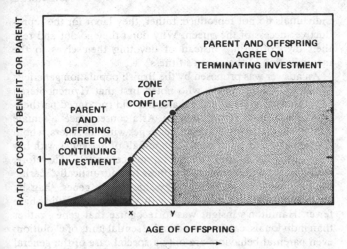

FIGURE 1. Predicted parent-offspring conflict over the time of termination of parental investment. When the offspring is relatively young, both parent and offspring benefit from continued parental investment, and the cost of postponing reproduction to the mother is low; hence, parent and offspring are predicted to agree on continued investment. Similarly, when the offspring is more mature, it benefits in inclusive fitness from gaining siblings, and the cost to its own fitness is low, so no conflict is predicted. However, the parent is selected to terminate investment in any given offspring when the cost-to-benefit ratio of terminating investment to reproducing again is 1 (x). The offspring is predicted to devalue the cost to parental fitness by a factor of 2 because its coefficient of relationship to a full sib is ½. Consequently, the offspring is selected to prolong parental investment until the cost-to-benefit ratio for the parent is 2 (y). Cost and benefit are measured in units of maternal fitness, and the cost-to-benefit ratio refers to the value of terminating investment and subsequently reproducing from the parent's point of view.

offspring conflict, with the parent selected to terminate investment and the offspring selected to induce the parent to provide more investment than is in the parent's best evolutionary interest.

A similar argument can be made for parent-offspring conflict over the amount of maternal investment during any one episode of interaction. If the mother behaves so as to maximize her inclusive fitness, she is predicted to try to optimize the amount of her investment, with costs and benefits measured in units of inclusive fitness. However, the offspring will devalue the maternal costs by a factor of 2, again because parent and offspring share only half of their genes. The offspring is selected to try to obtain more than the parent is selected to want to give (see Figure 2).

Similarly, parents are selected to encourage altruism between sibs whenever the benefit to the recipient exceeds the cost to the altruist—that is, when the total benefit to all offspring exceeds the total cost of the behavior. However, the offspring themselves are expected to view things differently and to behave altruistically only when the benefit to the recipient exceeds twice the cost to the altruist, since each offspring devalues its sib by one-half, compared with a parent who is equally related to each of its offspring. Sibs, therefore, are selected to be more selfish than parents wish, and full sibs are expected to be more altruistic toward one another than are half sibs. Older juveniles are predicted to show more solicitous behavior and less rivalry toward infant siblings than are those who are more dependent on parental input. Parents are predicted to encourage more altruism toward the extended family than the offspring are selected to favor, since parents share

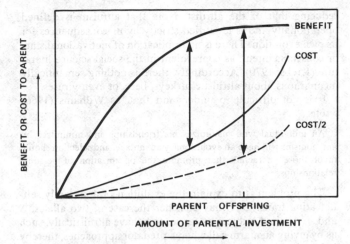

FIGURE 2. Parent-offspring conflict predicted over the amount of parental investment in any single episode of interaction. Parents are predicted to try to maximize the difference between benefit and cost to their own fitness to provide an optimal amount of parental investment. The offspring is also selected to try to obtain an optimal amount of parental investment, but its view of an optimal amount is different from and greater than the parent's view. The conflict occurs because the offspring shares only half its genes with its parent; therefore, it devalues all costs to parental fitness by a factor of 2. Again, cost and benefit are measured in units of parental fitness.

more genes with nieces and nephews, for example (¼), than offspring share with cousins (⅛).

Trivers (1974) emphasized that offspring are unable to force parental investment. As he said, "An offspring cannot fling its mother to the ground at will and nurse." He postulated that offspring are selected to engage in various psychological manipulations designed to increase the amount and duration of parental investment. For example, the offspring may exaggerate their degree of neediness or strive to give the impression of exceptional reproductive potential so as to elicit more parental investment. Parents are selected to detect these deceptions and to try to manipulate their offspring to maximize parental inclusive fitness (Alexander, 1974).

Parent-offspring conflict has been observed to occur over weaning in many mammals, including baboons (DeVore, 1963), langurs (Jay, 1963), rhesus macaques (Hinde and Spencer-Booth, 1971), and other macaques (Rosenblum, 1971). In dogs (Rheingold, 1963) and cats (Schneirla et al., 1963), postnatal maternal care can be observed to pass through a sequence of increasing offspring demands accompanied by increasing maternal avoidance and aggression. Barash (1974) observed increasing maternal aggression toward weaning infants in captive woodchucks. These findings are consistent with Trivers's model, although quantitative verification of the detailed predictions is lacking.

Altruism and Cooperation

Evolution is quintessentially selfish, since natural selection is blindly opportunistic (Dobzhansky, 1951), favoring any genetic variants that contribute to enhanced personal fitness. In view of this relentless self-centeredness, altruistic behaviors seem paradoxical; some of the major breakthroughs in sociobiology were stimulated by interest in the evolutionary rationale for seemingly altruistic behaviors among animals.

Altruism can be defined biologically as behavior that enhances the personal fitness of another (the recipient) while reducing that of the altruist. Note that altruism is defined operationally and is identified strictly by its consequences for its own evolution. There is no implication of motivational state or conscious intent, as is prevalent in the social science literature (Krebs, 1970). Accordingly, there is nothing semantically incongruous about altruistic turkeys, bees, or even viruses.

It is not difficult to understand that, as Williams (1966) wrote:

An individual who maximizes his friendships and minimizes his antagonisms will have an evolutionary advantage, and selection should favor those characters that promote the optimization of personal relationships.

The problem is to explain the evolution of apparently self-defeating traits. One may consider the case of two alleles, S and A. Allele A induces its carrier to behave altruistically, such as by giving an alarm call when a predator approaches, thereby helping others but revealing its position to the predator, or by sharing significant resources, such as food or a mate. By contrast, allele S induces its carrier to behave selfishly—refraining from an alarm, not sharing, and so on. Insofar as the bearers of allele A are less successful reproductively than the bearers of allele S, one can expect S to increase in the population at the expense of A, so that altruism should not occur in nature. But, in fact, naturalists have long been aware of apparently altruistic behavior among animals. Hunting dogs share food, baboon males may sacrifice themselves in defending the troop, and, among many bird species, juveniles help adults rear additional offspring, rather than reproducing themselves. Classical Darwinian selection does not explain these behaviors, since individuals should be selected to maximize their own reproduction, rather than that of another.

There are several explanations for apparent altruism, the simplest being that it is not altruism at all but actually selfishness misidentified by the human observer. Thus, parental solicitude toward offspring may involve substantial costs in terms of the personal survival of the parents, since they expend precious calories and may run substantial risks in provisioning and nourishing their young, as well as more direct risks incurred by defending them from predators. However, parents share one-half their genes with their offspring; and selection operates very strongly on any behavior with direct consequences for reproductive success (Barash, 1976a). A genetic basis for childlessness has a dim evolutionary future, so the converse—bearing and caring for children—is consistent with the traditional understanding of natural selection and is not altruism at all.

Selfishness may actually provide the ultimate explanation for much apparent altruism, even beyond the parent-offspring nexus. For example, even alarm calling may be selfish if the callers manipulate the behavior of other flock members so as to increase the likelihood that they, rather than the caller, will be taken by a predator (Charnov and Krebs, 1974). Similarly, assistance toward a mate may rebound to selfish advantage insofar as the mate is then able to invest in offspring, in whom both parents have a vested genetic interest.

In some cases, however, simple selfishness does not apply, and the behavior in question appears to enhance the reproductive success of another individual, with no benefit in fitness derived by the altruist's offspring. A major breakthrough in sociobiology was the recognition that such instances can still be explained by selfishness but that it must be selfishness at the level of the gene, rather than the individual and its offspring. The classic case is sterility in the female worker classes of the social Hymenoptera—the wasps, bees, and ants. These individuals do not reproduce; rather, they labor for the reproductive success of the queen. Why don't they go out and rear their own offspring, instead of devoting themselves to the maximization of the queen's fitness?

An answer was proposed by the British population geneticist W. D. Hamilton (1964), who noted first that Hymenopteran females are diploid and the males haploid (produced parthenogenetically from fertilized eggs). As a consequence, a female worker shares three-fourths of her genes with her sisters, whom she helps to rear, as opposed to one-half of her genes with her own offspring, if she were to reproduce herself. Therefore, sterile workers maximize their fitness by "altruistically" caring for their sisters, with whom they share more genes, than by producing their own offspring, with whom they would share fewer. Hamilton's insight was to recognize that genes, rather than individuals, can be considered essential units of evolution; even parental behaviors are only a special case of the general phenomenon, wherein individuals care for others in proportion as those others are closely related. Hamilton's simplified formula describes the necessary conditions for altruism of this sort to evolve: br ⟩ c, where b = benefit to recipient, c = cost to altruist, and r = the coefficient of relationship between any two parties. In this case, as in virtually all sociobiological considerations, benefits and costs are measured in units of inclusive fitness.

To reiterate, the term "inclusive fitness" is now used to include the sum of Darwinian fitness (simple reproductive success) and the reproductive success of all relatives, with the importance of each devalued in proportion as each is more distantly related—that is, as it shares fewer genes with the prospective altruist. Since kin, rather than offspring per se, are now identified as relevant to selection, the term "kin selection" has found common use (Maynard Smith, 1964) in describing the pattern of selection whereby inclusive fitness is maximized. Predictions based on Hamilton's original concept have been strikingly verified in the ants (Trivers and Hare, 1976; see also Alexander and Sherman, 1977, and Noonan, 1978, for alternative views). Inclusive fitness has been refined and applied with great success to vertebrates, in which it provides a cogent underlying explanation for much of vertebrate sociality (Hamilton 1975; West Eberhard, 1975) and a possible biological basis for human nepotism as well (Alexander, 1977; Barash, 1979).

For example, birds that serve as helpers at the nest turn out to be helping their parents rear additional siblings (Brown, 1974; Wolfenden, 1975). Their behavior represents a gain to their own inclusive fitness through altruism evolved by kin selection. A field study of social behavior among Japanese monkeys showed that the expectations of kin selection predict a wide range of both affiliative and agonistic behaviors (Kurland, 1977). Similarly, Sherman (1977) showed that Belding's ground squirrels varied their alarm-calling frequency as a predictable function of the likelihood that they would benefit close relatives.

Inclusive fitness considerations also help explain observations that would otherwise be anomalous, such as wife sharing in the Tasmanian native hen, a situation in which two males share one female (Maynard Smith and Ridpath, 1972). Significantly, the two males are likely to be sibs, so each is guaranteed to be at least an uncle, if not a father, thereby enhancing its inclusive fitness more than if nonrelatives shared the same mate. A similar pattern has also been reported for North American turkeys (Watts and Stokes, 1971). Inclusive fitness also provides insights into human family arrangements (van den Berghe and Barash. 1977) and may help explain the apparent cross-cultural universal of social organization based on kinship and the extraordinary importance of relatives and family networks to human beings.

There are other possible mechanisms for the evolution of altruism—group selection and reciprocity. Group selection was first proposed as an explanation for the observed tendency of many animals to restrict reproduction to a level below that which would damage the carrying capacity of their habitats (Kalela, 1957; Wynne Edwards, 1962). The idea is simple and appealing: If groups containing altruists are more successful than those composed entirely of selfish members, these altruistic groups succeed at the expense of the selfish ones, and altruism evolves. However, there is a serious problem. Within each group, altruists would be at a severe disadvantage relative to selfish individuals, however well the group as a whole was able to do (Williams, 1966, 1971). As mentioned earlier, group selection is now believed to be rare under natural conditions. On the other hand, models for limited altruism have also proved successful, based on a mix of kin and group selection (D. S. Wilson, 1975, 1977; Wade, 1977). Indeed, social groups often consist of kin, thus confounding the mechanism of one with the other (E. O. Wilson, 1975; Barash, 1977a).

A final biological mechanism for the evolution of altruism is reciprocity. Originally labeled "reciprocal altruism" (Trivers, 1971), this system explains the evolution of apparently altruistic traits in the absence of group selection and without any assumptions of genetic relatedness between altruist and beneficiary. The basic requirements for the evolution of reciprocity are that the act itself involves a small risk to the donor and a large gain to the recipient and that at some time in the future the situation will be reversed, with the previous beneficiary in a position to render assistance and the previous donor in need of such aid. If reciprocity occurs under such circumstances, the tendency to behave altruistically in the first place is selected.

However, reciprocity is susceptible to the evolution of cheaters, individuals who receive benefits from others but then fail to repay them when the appropriate circumstances occur. Such a trait experiences an advantage in fitness over the honest reciprocators, since practitioners of the cheating strategy profit from the altruism of others, just as honest reciprocators do, but the cheaters avoid the costs incurred by returning the favor. As a consequence, reciprocity cannot be a stable strategy, unless there is some way to distinguish cheaters from honest reciprocators. This could occur in long-lasting social systems in which individuals are recognized, categorized on the basis of previous behavior, and remembered. Human social structures seem to provide an optimal situation for the evolution of reciprocity.

The occurrence of cheaters within a reciprocating system selects for ability to discriminate honest reciprocators from cheaters, which selects for greater deception and then greater means of counter detection. Trivers (1971) proposed that humans may keep each other in line within reciprocating systems by visiting moralistic aggression on nonreciprocators. Indeed, the compulsion to repay a favor or gift is very powerful and prevalent cross-culturally; it forms the basis of primitive economics and exchange (Mauss, 1967).

An apparent example of reciprocal altruism has been described for the olive baboon, *Papio anubis* (Packer, 1977). In this species an adult male commonly forms a short-lived coalition with another male, often for the purpose of gaining sexual access to a female who is associating with a third male. When successful, this coalition results in the initiating male's copulating successfully with the female (a presumed increment to his fitness), concurrent with some cost of time, energy, and risk of injury on the part of the successfully recruited partner,

who is not immediately rewarded. However, when that partner, the initial altruist, solicits and receives aid from another adult male, he is significantly more likely to do so with the male who previously solicited him. Further indication of evolutionary self-interest in this system is shown by the fact that adult males do not solicit the help of juveniles; in turn, they are more likely to refuse the solicitations of juveniles, since juveniles are unlikely to be capable of effective reciprocity.

In summary, the sociobiology of altruism suggests that all seemingly altruistic behavior is founded on a bedrock of selfishness, interpreted most parsimoniously as acting on individuals or genes. The paradox is real. Furthermore, insofar as human inclinations are molded by natural selection to favor biological selfishness, psychology and psychiatry may do well to reexamine the currently fashionable glorification of natural motivations as against societal constraints. There may be an ultimate evolutionary wisdom in moral prohibitions that function to restrain what may otherwise be socially destructive selfishness (Campbell, 1975).

Implications for Psychiatry

There is a long history of attempts to use evolutionary theory in elucidations of human nature, as well as theories of the instinctive basis of behavior. Unfortunately, many of these attempts were marred by misunderstandings of natural selection and the mechanisms of evolutionary adaptation. Freud, for example, attempted to refute the popular theories of Charcot and Janet that heredity was

the only true and indispensable cause of nervous disease. Other aetiologic factors may aspire only to the title of precipitating causes (1962).

However, long after biologists had abandoned Haeckel's misleading simplification that ontogeny recapitulates phylogeny, Freud remained a recapitulationist:

Each individual somehow recapitulates in an abbreviated form the entire development of the human race, into phylogenetic prehistory too (1963).

Bowlby (1973) reviewed Freud's evolutionary perspective and emphasized that Freud's commitment to Lamarckian theories is reflected in all subsequent psychoanalytic thought, to the exclusion of Darwinian concepts of differential reproductive success and natural selection. Bowlby made an eloquent plea for psychoanalytic theory to be recast in the light of modern concepts of evolution; as yet, this has not been done.

In the following discussion, the authors shall attempt to explore several areas in which predictions of behavior, based on principles of evolution by natural selection, could be formulated so as to apply to human beings. It is tempting to speculate broadly, yet it is difficult to design and execute experiments demonstrating conclusively that any specific human behavior has a strong genetic component. Nonetheless, the authors feel that this approach may eventually make a significant contribution to models and theories of human mental function and behavior.

NORMALITY

Sociobiology suggests that insofar as natural selection influences the behavior of *Homo sapiens*, it does so by promoting inclinations toward behaviors that promote maximization of individual inclusive fitness. This is a very different conception from the innate releasing mechanisms and fixed action patterns of classical Lorenzian ethology (Eibl-Eibesfeldt, 1975). By contrast, human behavior is not expected to show the stereotypy or automaticity of response that characterizes, for example, the agressive display of a male stickleback fish to the appearance of another male's red belly (Tinbergen, 1951). The genetic influences postulated by sociobiology are subtle, diffuse, and rather unspecific—more like vague inclinations than strident demands. Just as most human infants find sugar sweet, so sociobiology predicts that most humans will find certain behaviors sweet. Those behaviors that directly contribute to reproductive success— such as sex, romantic love, childbearing and nurturance, and family formation—are selected to feel good to most people. On the other hand, one need not reproduce directly to promote one's inclusive fitness, and social behaviors that enhance the reproduction, status, or territory of close relatives are also selected to feel sweet. No biological mandate or imperative is postulated; rather, each person possesses a unique genotype and unique experiences and can be expected to try to make the best adaptation to his or her personal situation.

Analyses of human sexual behavior have emphasized its reproductive function rather than its psychodynamic components (Shepher, 1971; Kaffman, 1977; Weinrich, 1977). The structure and functions of human consciousness may, at least in part, also be the result of natural selection. Thus, humans may be selected to enhance consciously their own reproduction, so that reproductive usefulness becomes the ultimate intentional arbiter of much cultural behavior (Durham, 1976a). Aggression and even primitive war may also subserve fitness maximization, with or without the conscious intent of the perpetrators (Durham, 1976b). Further studies of human emotion and behavior that adopt the quantitative, observational methods of ethology can be used to test these and other sociobiological hypotheses. In addition, existing cross-cultural data can be used to test these predictions.

PSYCHOPATHOLOGY

Genetic research has played an increasingly important role in modern biological psychiatry. Twin and adoptive studies have revealed significant genetic concordance in schizophrenia (Rosenthal et al., 1969; Kety et al., 1971), manic-depressive illness (Winokur, 1978), and alcoholism (Goodwin et al., 1973). However, there have been relatively few analyses of the adaptive significance of the heritable psychological disorders. For example, a high fertility rate in patients with Huntington's chorea is doubtless relevant to the persistence of the gene at levels exceeding that attributable to mutation alone; the social disability that afflicts these patients occurs when they are postreproductive and apparently does not significantly diminish the enhanced fitness due to the trait (Bruyn, 1968). Similarly, a variant of kin selection may be directly involved in the maintenance of schizophrenia. The lower reproductive success of process schizophrenics may be balanced by increased fitness in their nonpsychotic, schizoparanoid relatives, particularly under conditions of social instability (Jarvik and Deckard, 1977). Demographic studies that include fertility rates, particularly differences in male-female reproductive rates, would be useful in determining the mechanisms and magnitudes of selective forces that maintain psychopathological traits in the population.

At a more individual level, it is possible that both the recognition and the nosology of psychological dysfunction may be related to perceiving biologically maladaptive behavior patterns. For example, spite can be defined as behavior that

decreases the fitness of a recipient either at cost or with no benefit to the initiator. Spiteful behavior has never been reported in free-living animals and is perceived as pathological in human beings. Human behavior that threatens other humans senselessly—that is, with no benefit to the perpetrator—is seen as insane, but conflict in regard to property or kin is perceived as justifiable. Intuitively healthy behavior may be that which is in accord with evolutionary considerations. Thus, further insight into psychopathology may be gained in the future by evaluating behavior vis-à-vis fitness maximization, both by using natural selection as a model against which deviant behavior may be assessed and by considering that psychopathologies may occur when efforts to achieve fitness maximization by behavior are unsuccessful because they are excessive, insufficient, or inappropriate. In addition, the suggestion has been made that by delineating normal behavior patterns and by providing a framework for a functional analysis of interpersonal relationships, sociobiological theory may have implications for psychotherapy (Weisfeld, 1977).

Fear of biological determinism and Social Darwinism has caused many scientists and political groups to advocate a cessation of research in sociobiology, both human and nonhuman, on the grounds of adverse political implications (Science for the People, 1975). Sociobiology is not racist. It emphasizes cross-cultural behavioral universals that can be found in all *Homo sapiens*. Furthermore, understanding human tendencies does not imply condoning them. Rather, it may provide the intellectual leverage to change aspects of human behavior through therapeutic, cultural, and environmental means.

In sum, sociobiology may provide insight into both normal and abnormal psychology. A real strength of the theory lies in its value as a predictive and analytic paradigm that could be applied in a quantitative fashion to the study of human behavior.

Suggested Cross References

Genetics is discussed in Section 2.1. Ethology is covered in Section 4.6, aggression in Section 4.5. The family is discussed in Section 5.3, sexuality in Chapter 24, child development in Section 34.2, and parent-child problems in Section 44.4. Freud is reviewed in detail in Chapter 8. Normality is discussed in Section 6.6.

The authors wish to thank Leslie Becker, Phillip Berger, Roland Ciaranello, Kenneth Davis, Morris Lipton, Joseph Maggliozi and Isabel Paret for their helpful comments and suggestions.

REFERENCES

Alexander, R. D. The evolution of social behavior. Annu. Rev. Ecol. System., *5:* 325, 1974.

Alexander, R. D. The search for a general theory of behavior. Behav. Sci. *20:* 77, 1975.

Alexander, R. D. Natural selection and the analysis of human sociality. In *The Changing Scenes in the Natural Sciences, 1776–1976,* C. Goulden, editor, Academy of Natural Sciences, Philadelphia, 1977.

Alexander, R. D., and Sherman, P. W. Local mate competition and parental investment in social insects. Science, *196:* 494, 1977.

Ardrey, R. *The Territorial Imperative.* Atheneum, New York, 1966.

Bandura, A., Ross, D., and Ross, S. Transmission of aggression through imitation of aggressive models. J. Abnorm. Soc. Psychol., *63:* 575, 1961.

Barash, D. P. Mother-infant relations in captive woodchucks (*Marmota monax*). Anim. Behav., *22:* 446, 1974.

Barash, D. P. Some evolutionary aspects of parental behavior in animals and man. Am. J. Psychol., *89:* 195, 1976a.

Barash, D. P. The male response to apparent female adultery in the mountain-bluebird, *Sialia currucoides:* An evolutionary interpretation. Am. Naturalist, *110:* 1097, 1976b.

* Barash, D. P. *Sociobiology and Behavior.* Elsevier, New York, 1977a.

Barash, D. P. Sociobiology of rape in mallards (*Anas platyrhynchas*): Responses of the mated male. Science, *197:* 788, 1977b.

Barash, D. P. *The Whisperings Within*. Harper & Row, New York, 1979.

Barash, D. P. Predictive sociobiology. In *Sociobiology: Beyond Nature/Nurture?* G. Barlow and J. Silverberg, editors, American Association for the Advancement of Science, Washington D. C., 1980.

Barash, D. P., MacCluer, P. J., and Schlesinger, K., editors. *Encounters with Sociobiology*. W. H. Freeman & Co., San Francisco, 1980, In Press.

Barlow, G., and Silverberg, J., editors. *Sociobiology: Beyond Nature/Nurture?* American Association for the Advancement of Science, Washington, D. C., 1980.

Boorman, S. A., and Levitt, P. R. Group selection on the boundary of a stable population. Proc. Natl. Acad. Sci. U.S.A., *69:* 2711, 1972.

Boorman, S. A., and Levitt, P. R. Group selection in the boundary of a stable population. Theor. Pop. Biol., *4:* 85, 1973.

Bowlby, J. *Attachment*. Basic Books, New York, 1969.

Bowlby, J. *Separation*. Basic Books, New York, 1973.

Brown, J. L. The evolution of diversity in arian territorial systems. Wilson Bull. *76:* 160, 1964.

Brown, J. L. Alternate routes to sociality in jays—With a theory for the evolution of altruism and communal breeding. Am. Zool., *14:* 63, 1974.

Brown, J. L. *The Evolution of Behavior*. W. W. Norton, New York, 1975.

Bruyn, G. W., Huntington's chorea: Historical, clinical and laboratory synopsis. In *Handbook of Clinical Neurology*, Vinken, P. S., and Bruyn, G. W. editors, vol. 6, p. 298. Wiley-Interscience, New York, 1968.

Campbell, D. T. On the conflict between biological and social evolution and between psychology and moral tradition. Am. Psychol., *30:* 1103, 1975.

Carpenter, C. R. Territoriality: A review of concepts and problems. In *Behavior and Evolution*, A. Roe and G. Simpson, editors, p. 224. Yale University Press, New Haven, 1958.

Cavalli-Sforzsa, L. L., and Bodmer, W. F., *The Genetics of Human Populations*. W. H. Freeman, San Francisco, 1971.

Chagnon, N. and Irons W., editors. *Evolutionary Biology and Human Social Behavior*. Duxbury, North Scituate, Mass., 1978.

Charnov, E. L., and Krebs, J. R. The evolution of alarm calls: Altruism or manipulation? Am. Naturalist, *108:* 107, 1974.

Coulson, J. C. The influence of the pair-bond and age on the breeding biology of the kittiwake gull, *Rissa tridactyla*. J. Anim. Ecol., *35:* 269, 1966.

Cox, C. R., and LeBoeuf, B. J. Female initiation of male competition: A mechanism in sexual selection. Am. Naturalist, *111:* 317, 1977.

Cronin, E. W., and Sherman, P. W. A resource-based mating system: The orange-ramped honeyguide. Living Bird, *15:* 5, 1977.

Cullen, E. Adaptations in the kittiwake to cliff-nesting. Ibis, *99:* 275, 1957.

Darling, F. F. *A Herd of Red Deer*. Oxford University Press, London, 1937.

Darwin, C. *On the Origin of Species by Means of Natural Selection*. Murray, London, 1859.

Dawkins, R. *The Selfish Gene*. Oxford University Press, London, 1976.

DeVore, I. Mother-infant relations in free-ranging baboons. In *Maternal Behavior in Mammals*, H. Reingold, editor, p. 305. John Wiley & Sons, New York, 1963.

DeVore, I., editor. *Sociobiology and Human Social Behavior*. Aldine Publishing Co., Chicago, 1978.

Dobzhansky, T. *Genetics and the Origin of Species*. Columbia University Press, New York, 1951.

Dobzhansky, T. The myths of genetic predestination and of tabula rasa. Perspect. Biol. Med., *19:* 156, 1976.

Dollard, J., Miller, N. E., Mowrer, O. H., Sears, G. H., and Sears, R. R. *Frustration and Aggression*. Yale University Press, New Haven, 1939.

Downhower, J., and Armitage, K. The yellow-bellied marmot and the evolution of polygamy. Am. Naturalist, *105:* 355, 1971.

Durham, W. H. Resource competition and human aggression. I. A review of primitive war. Q. Rev. Biol., *51:* 385, 1976a.

Durham, W. H. The adaptive significance of cultural behavior. Hum. Ecol., *4:* 89, 1976b.

Dyson-Hudson, R., and Smith, E. Human territoriality: An ecological reassessment. Am. Anthropol., *80:* 21, 1978.

Eibl-Eibesfeldt, I. The fighting behavior of animals. Sci. Am., *205:* 112, 1961.

Eibl-Eibesfeldt, I. *Ethology, the Biology of Behavior*. Holt, Rinehart & Winston, New York, 1975.

Ember, M. On the origin and extension of the incest taboo. Behav. Sci. Res., *10:* 249, 1975.

Emlen, S. T., and Oring, L. W. Ecology, sexual selection, and the evolution of mating systems. Science, *197:* 215, 1977.

Fiedler, K. Vergleichande Verhaltensstudien av Seenadeln, Schlargennadeln, und Seepferdchen (*Syngnathidae*). Z. Tierpsychol., *11:* 358, 1954.

Fisher, R. A. *The Genetical Theory of Natural Selection*. Dover, New York, 1958.

Freud, S., Heredity and the aetiology of the neuroses. In *Standard Edition of the Complete Psychological Works of Sigmund Freud*, vol 3, p. 142. Hogarth Press, London, 1962.

Freud, S. Introductory lectures on psychoanalysis. In *Standard Edition of the Complete Psychological Works of Sigmund Freud*, vol 15, p. 199. Hogarth Press, London, 1963.

Gadgil, M. Evolution of social behavior through interpopulation selection. Proc. Natl. Acad. Sci., U.S.A. *72:* 1199, 1975.

Geist, V. *Mountain Sheep*. University of Chicago Press, Chicago, 1971.

Goodwin, D., Shulsinger, F., Hermansen, L., Guze, S., and Winokur, G. Alcohol problems in adoptees raised apart from biological parents. Arch. Gen. Psychiatry, *28:* 238, 1973.

Haldane, J. B. S. *The Causes of Evolution*. Longman's Green, London, 1932.

Hamilton, W. D. The genetical theory of social behavior. J. Theor. Biol., *7:* 1, 1964.

Hamilton, W. D. Innate social aptitudes of man: An approach from evolutionary genetics. In *Biosocial Anthropology*, Fox, R. editor, p. 133. John Wiley & Sons, New York, 1975.

Hartung, J. On natural selection and the inheritance of wealth. Curr. Anthropol., *17:* 607, 1976.

Hill, J. L. *Peromyscus*: Effect of early pairing on reproduction. Science, *186:* 1042, 1974.

Hinde, R. A. *Animal Behaviour*. McGraw-Hill, New York, 1970.

Hinde, R. A., and Spencer-Booth, Y. Effects of brief separation from mother on rhesus monkeys. Science, *173:* 111, 1971.

Hinde, R. A., and Stevenson-Hinde, J. *Constraints on Learning*. Academic Press, New York, 1973.

Hrdy, S. B. *The Langurs of Abu*. Harvard University Press, Cambridge, 1977.

Hrdy, S. B., and Hrdy, D. B. Hierarchical relations among female Hanuman langurs. Science, *193:* 913, 1976.

Janzen, D. A note on optimal mate selection by plants. Am. Naturalist, *111:* 365, 1977.

Jarvik, L. F., and Deckard, B. The Odyssean personality. Neuropsychobiology, *3:* 179, 1977.

Jay, P. Mother-infant relations in langurs. In *Maternal Behavior in Mammals*, H. Reingold, editor. John Wiley & Sons, New York, 1963.

Kaffman, M. Sexual standards and behavior of the kibbutz adolescent. Am. J. Orthopsychiatry, *47:* 207, 1977.

Kalela, O. Regulation of reproductive rate in subarctic populations of the role *Clethrionomys rufocanus*. Ann. Acad. Sci. Fenn., *34:* 1, 1957.

Kendeigh, S. R. Parental care and its evolution in birds. Ill. Biol. Monogr., *22:* 1, 1952.

Kety, S. S., Rosenthal, D., Wender, P. H., and Schulsinger, F. Mental illness in the biological and adoptive families of adopted schizophrenics. Am. J. Psychiatry, *125:* 302, 1971.

Klaus, M. H., and Kennell, J. H. *Maternal-Infant Bonding*. C. V. Mosby, St. Louis, 1976.

Kleiman, D. Monogamy in mammals. Q. Rev. Biol., *52:* 39, 1977.

Klopfer, R. H., and Gamble, J. Maternal imprinting in goats: The role of chemical senses. Z. Tierpsychol., *25:* 862, 1966.

Krebs, D. Altruism: An examination of the concept and review of the literature. Psychol. Bull., *73:* 258, 1970.

Kurland, J. A. Kin selection in the Japanese monkey. Contrib. Primatol., *12:* 1, 1977.

Lack, D. *Population Studies of Birds*. Oxford University Press, Oxford, 1966.

Lehrman, D. C. Semantics and conceptual issues in the nature-nurture problem. In *Development and Evolution of Behavior*, L. Aranson et al., editors. W. H. Freeman & Co., San Francisco, 1970.

Lévi-Strauss, C. *The Elementary Structures of Kinship*. Beacon Press, Boston, 1968.

Lewontin, R. C. Interdeme selection controlling a polymorphism in the house mouse. Am. Naturalist, *96:* 65, 1962.

Lewontin, R. C. The units of selection. Annu. Rev. Ecol. System., *1:* 1, 1970.

Lorenz, K. Z. *On Aggression*. Harcourt, Brace and World, New York, 1963.

Lorenz, K. Z. *Evolution and Modification of Behavior*. University of Chicago Press, Chicago, 1965.

MacArthur, R. H. *Geographical Ecology: Patterns in the Distribution of Species*. Harper & Row, New York, 1972.

Mauss, M. *The Gift*. Mouton, the Hague, 1967.

Maynard Smith, J. Group selection and kin selection. Nature, *201:* 1145, 1964.

Maynard Smith, J., and Parker, G. A. The logic of assymetric contests. Anim. Behav., *24:* 159, 1976.

Maynard Smith, J., and Price, G. R. The logic of animal conflict. Nature, *246:* 15, 1973.

Maynard Smith, J., and Ridpath, M. G. Wife sharing in the Tasmanian native hen, *Yribonyx mortierii*: A case of kin selection? Am. Naturalist, *106:* 447, 1972.

Money, J., and Eberhardt, A. A. *Man and Woman, Boy and Girl*. Johns Hopkins University Press, Baltimore, 1972.

Montagu, M. F. A., editor. *Man and Aggression*, Oxford University Press, Oxford, 1968.

Noonan, K. M. Sex ratio of parental investment in colonies of the social wasp, *Polistes Fuscatus*. Science, *199:* 1354, 1978.

Orians, G. H. On the evolution of mating systems in birds and mammals. Am. Naturalist, *103:* 589, 1969.

Packer, C. Reciprocal altruism in olive baboons. Nature, *265:* 441, 1977.

Parker, G. A. Assessment strategy and the evolution of animal conflicts. J. Theor. Biol., *47:* 223, 1974.

Pitelka, F. A. Numbers, breeding schedule and territoriality in pectoral sandpipers of northern Alaska. Condor *61:* 233, 1959.

Power, H. Mountain bluebirds: Experimental evidence against altruism. Science, *189:* 142, 1975.

Reiter, J., Stinson, N. L., and LeBoeuf, B. J. Northern elephant seal development: The transition from weaning to nutritional independence. Behav. Ecol. Sociobiol. *3:* 174, 1978.

Rheingold, H. Maternal behavior in the dog. In *Maternal Behavior in Mammals*, H. Reingold, editor. John Wiley & Sons, New York, 1963.

Rosenblum, L. A., The ontogeny of mother-infant relations in macaques. In *The*

Ontogeny of Vertebrate Behavior, H. Moltz, editor. Academic Press, New York, 1971.

Rothenbuhler, W. Behavior genetics of nest cleaning in honeybees: Responses of F 1 and back-cross generations to disease killed brood. Am. Zool. *4:* 111, 1964.

Rosenthal, D., and Kety, S. *The Transmission of Schizophrenia*, Pergamon Press, New York, 1969.

Schaller, G. B. *The Serengetti Lion*. University of Chicago Press, Chicago, 1972.

Schneirla, T. C., Rosenblatt, J. S., and Tobach, E. Maternal behavior in the cat. In *Maternal Behavior in Mammals*, H. Rheingold, editor. John Wiley & Sons, New York, 1963.

Science for the People: Against sociobiology. N. Y. Rev. Books, Nov. 13, 1975.

Scott, J. P. *Aggression*. University of Chicago Press, Chicago, 1958.

Seligman, M., and Hager, J. *Biological Boundaries of Learning*. Appleton-Century-Crofts, New York, 1972.

Sharpe, R., and Johnsgard, P. A. Inheritance of behaviorial characters in F2 mallard and pintail hybirds. Behaviour, *27:* 259, 1966.

Shepher, J. Mate selection among second-generation kibbutz adolescents and adults: Incest avoidance and negative imprinting. Arch. Sex. Behav., *1:* 293, 1971.

Sherman, P. W. Nepotism and the evolution of alarm calls. Science, *197:* 1246, 1977.

Silvers, A., and Gregory, M., editors. *Sociobiology and Human Values*. Jossey-Bass, San Francisco, 1978.

Steiner, A. L. Mortality resulting from intraspecific flighting in some ground squirrel populations. J. Mammal., *53:* 601, 1972.

Thornhill, R. Sexual selection and parental investment in insects. Am. Naturalist, *110:* 153, 1976.

Tinbergen, N. *The Study of Instinct*. Oxford University Press, London, 1951.

Tolman, E. C. The inheritance of maze-learning ability in rats. J. Comp. Psychol., *4:* 1, 1924.

* Trivers, R. L. The evolution of reciprocal altruism. Q. Rev. Biol., *46:* 35, 1971.

Trivers, R. L. Parental investment and sexual selection. In *Sexual Selection and the Descent of Man*, B. Campbell, editor, p. 136. Aldine Publishing Co., Chicago, 1972.

Trivers, R. L. Parent-offspring conflict. Am. Zool., *14:* 249, 1974.

* Trivers, R. L., and Hare, H. Haplodiploidy and the evolution of the social insects. Science, *191:* 249, 1976.

van den Berghe, P. L., and Barash, D. P. Inclusive fitness theory and human family structure. Am. Anthropol., *79:* 809, 1977.

Van Lawick-Goodall, J. *The Innocent Killers*. Houghton-Mifflin, Boston, 1973.

Wade, M. J. An experimental study of group selection. Evolution, *31:* 134, 1977.

Watts, C. R., and Stokes, A. W. The social order of turkeys. Sci. Am. *224:* 112, 1971.

Weinrich, J. D. Human sociobiology: Pair-bonding and resource predictability. Behav. Ecol. Sociobiol., *2:* 91, 1977.

Weisfeld, G. E. A sociobiological basis for psychotherapy. In *Ethological Psychiatry*, M. T. McGuire and L. A. Fairbanks, editors, p. 11. Grune & Stratton, New York, 1977.

West Eberhard, M. J. The evolution of social behavior by kin selection. Q. Rev. Biol., *50:* 1, 1975.

* Williams, G. C. *Adaptation and Natural Selection*. Princeton University Press, Princeton, N. J., 1966.

Williams, G. C. editor, *Group Selection*. Aldine Publishing Co., Chicago, 1971.

Wilson, D. S. A theory of group selection. Proc. Natl. Acad. Sci., U.S.A., *72:* 143, 1975.

Wilson, D. S. Structured demes and the evolution of group-advantageous traits. Am. Naturalist, *111:* 157, 1977.

* Wilson, E. O. *Sociobiology*. Harvard University Press, Cambridge, 1975.

Winokur, G. Mania and depression: Family studies and genetics in relation to treatment. In *Psychopharmacology: A generation of progress*. M. A. Lipton, A. DiMascio, and K. S. Killam, editors, p. 1213. Raven Press, New York, 1978.

Wolf, L. L. Prostitution behavior in a tropical hummingbird. Condor, *77:* 140, 1975.

Wolfenden, G. E. Florida scrub jay helpers at the nest. Auk, *92:* 1, 1975.

Wright, S. *Evolution and the Genetics of Populations*. University of Chicago Press, Chicago, 1969.

Wynne-Edwards, V. C. *Animal Dispersion in Relation to Social Behavior*, Hafner Press, New York, 1962.

chapter

3

Science of Human Behavior: Neurology

3.1 Anatomy and Physiology of the Central Nervous System

SEYMOUR SOLOMON, M.D.

Introduction

The inclusion of a chapter on neurology in a psychiatric textbook is unusual but appropriate, for organic disease of the central nervous system may cause psychiatric, as well as neurological, symptoms. Understanding of the function and dysfunction of the mind must be based on knowledge of the structure and diseases of the brain. This chapter is an outline of those features of neurology essential to the psychiatrist's understanding of the complex structure where psychiatric illnesses arise. With rare exceptions the spinal cord and peripheral nerves and muscles have been excluded from this presentation.

This chapter is divided into five sections. The first section reviews, in elementary form, the anatomy and physiology of the central nervous system. The neurological evaluation described in the second section includes the history and examination of the patient, with special attention to the aphasias; laboratory techniques useful in establishing a diagnosis, particularly electroencephalography, are then discussed. In the third section, clinical neurology is correlated with neuropathology. The fourth section reviews other neurological syndromes, including those diseases that do not present well-defined pathology; special attention is paid to epilepsy and the common symptoms of pain and dizziness. In the fifth section, the mental and emotional syndromes associated with lesions of different parts of the brain are discussed, as are those phenomena commonly encountered in both neurology and psychiatry. This chapter is not intended as a substitute for a neurological text, for the data presented here must necessarily be brief. Only basic facts are recorded in the section on anatomy and physiology. Similarly, only the highlights of neurological diseases can be included in the subsequent sections. The diseases have been outlined to enable the physician to approach the neurological differential diagnosis in a systematic, logical manner.

Many areas of the brain are clinically silent—that is, recognizable symptoms or signs need not result from a lesion of those parts. The following sites are associated with specific functions, and, when diseased, specific signs occur.

Cerebral Cortex

Table I is a chart of cerebral functions, and the cytoarchitectural map of the cortex after Brodmann is presented in Figure 1. Figure 2 outlines the chief landmarks of the surface of the brain. The specific areas described here are not as sharply demarcated physiologically as the anatomical borders suggest.

FRONTAL LOBE

The frontal lobe is anterior to the central sulcus or Rolandic fissure.

Motor area. This area is in the most posterior portion of the frontal lobe and occupies the precentral convolution. The motor area contains the greatest number of Betz pyramidal cells and gives rise to corticobulbar and corticospinal pathways. Impulses from this area initiate volitional movement on the opposite side of the body. The lower extremity is represented over the medial portion of the contralateral cortex, and the remainder of the body is represented over the adjoining convexity. Those parts requiring greater complexity of function, such as the fingers, are represented over a disproportionately wide area. Loss of function in this area results in contralateral weakness or paralysis. In monkeys, apes, and perhaps human beings, the paresis or palsy is first flaccid and later spastic.

Premotor area. Anterior to the motor area, the premotor area controls complex motor functions of the opposite parts of the body, paralleling the functions of the motor area, and such complicated activities as locomotion, eating, and speaking. The contralateral weakness or paralysis associated with a lesion in this area is spastic in primates.

Frontal motor eye field. This area is anterior to the premotor area and is the center of volitional control of conjugate eye movement. A destructive lesion in this field is associated with initial but transient deviation of the eyes to the side of the lesion and palsy of conjugate gaze to the opposite side, whereas an irritative lesion causes conjugate gaze toward the opposite side.

Motor speech area (Broca's area). This area is located anterior and inferior to the motor and premotor areas in the dominant hemisphere. It is the center for expressive speech. A lesion in this area is associated with expressive nonfluent aphasia.

Less well-defined areas within the frontal lobe. A transitional area between the motor and premotor zones is believed to be inhibitory in its action, and lesions affecting this area are primarily responsible for contralateral spasticity.

In or about the middle frontal convolution is the origin of fibers giving rise to the corticopontocerebellar tract. This area permits smooth voluntary and automatic skeletal muscle movement. Loss of function is manifested by contralateral ataxia. A lesion in this area of the dominant hemisphere (anterior and superior to Broca's area) may result in transcortical nonfluent aphasia.

TABLE I

Functions of the Cerebral Cortex

The numbers referred to below are those corresponding to Brodmann's cytoarchitectural map of the cerebral cortex (see Figure 1). These numbers are used only for simplicity of identification. The functions cited are not as precisely localized as indicated by the map. The defects described in the last column are due to destructive unilateral lesions unless otherwise stated. As a rule, an irritative lesion evokes a focal seizure, augmenting or altering the function of the affected area.

Lobe	Area	Function	Effect of Lesion
Frontal	Primary motor area (4)	Initiate voluntary movement on opposite side	Initial contralateral flaccid palsy of skeletal muscles; later, spastic paresis
	Secondary or premotor area (6)	Organize and control voluntary movement	Contralateral spastic palsy or paresis of skeletal muscles
	Transitional area between 4 and 6 (4S)	Inhibit motor activity, extrapyramidal functions	Spasticity of contralateral somatic musculature
	Motor eye field area (8) and area 19 of occipital lobe	Control voluntary conjugate eye movement	Initial but transient deviation of eyes to side of the lesion and palsy of gaze to the opposite side (deviation of eyes away from irritative lesion)
	Speech area—Broca's area (44), (dominant hemisphere)	Control expressive speech	Motor, Broca's, nonfluent aphasia
	Association areas or prefrontal lobe (9, 10) and adjacent areas	Govern highest intellectual processes and emotions	Intellectual and emotional impairment, such as psychomotor retardation, lack of concern, *witzelsucht,* alteration in moral and social spheres
	Cingulate region (24, 25)	See temporal lobe	See temporal lobe
	Areas 4, 6, 10 and adjacent zones give rise to frontopontocerebellar pathways	Permit smooth voluntary and automatic skeletal muscle movement	Contralateral ataxia, predominantly truncal ataxia
	Areas throughout the frontal cortex and adjacent areas have connections: (a) to basal ganglia (areas 4, 6, 8, 9, 24, 45)	Elaborate voluntary and automatic movement with cerebellar centers	Areas too diffuse for focal lesions to cause specific dysfunctions
	(b) from thalamus and to hypothalamus (areas 4, 6, 8, 9, 11, 12, 45, 46, 47)	Integrate and elaborate stimuli for highest prefrontal functions	Mental and emotional symptoms as for association areas of prefrontal lobe
Parietal	Primary sensory area (1, 3, and minimally, 2)	Discriminate, appreciate, and localize somatic sensory stimuli from opposite side	Contralateral impairment of somatic sensory modalities
	Secondary sensory association area (5 and, especially, 7)	Further integrate, synthesize, and elaborate somatic sensory impulses	Slight contralateral impairment of somatic sensory modalities, spatial disorientation, contralateral astereognosis, extinction phenomena, trophic lesions
	Areas 39 (angular gyrus) and 40 (supramarginal gyrus)	Integrate visual and auditory stimuli with somatic sensory impulses	Dominant hemisphere: alexia and agraphia or anomia (area 39); with area 40, transcortical and conduction aphasias
	Gustatory area (43)	Receive gustatory impulses	No deficit because of bilateral representation
	Cingulate region (23 and 31)	See temporal lobe	See temporal lobe
	Subcortical: optic radiations deep within the parietal lobe	Carry visual impulses	Contralateral homonymous inferior quadrantanopsia or hemianopsia
Temporal	Primary auditory receptive area—Heschl's gyrus (41, 42)	Receive auditory impulses	No deficit because of bilateral cortical representation

TABLE I—*Continued*

Lobe	Area	Function	Effect of Lesion
	Auditory association areas (22, 42)	Discriminate sounds; form memory patterns, especially for symbolic sounds; may receive vestibular impulses	Dominant hemisphere: receptive, Wernicke's, fluent aphasia
	Olfactory areas (28 and 35)	Receive olfactory impulses	No deficit because of extensive bilateral representation; uncinate fits and psychomotor seizures with irritative lesions
	Association areas (20, 21, 36, 37, 38) make connections with cortical areas of frontal, parietal, and occipital lobes	Form memories and take part in other intellectual and emotional phenomena	Little or no deficit because of extensive cerebral representation; bilateral disease of medial temporal lobes (hippocampal areas) causes loss of recent memory
	Cingulate region: areas 29, 30-temporal; 23, 31-parietal; 23, 25-frontal; subcortical structures of the limbic system	Control visceral phenomena, sexual activities, and emotions	With extensive bilateral lesions: personality changes, especially disinhibition; impairment of recent memory; Klüver-Bucy syndrome; (psychomotor seizures with irritative lesions)
	Subcortical: optic radiations in the temporal lobe	Carry visual impulses	Contralateral homonymous superior quadrantanopsia
Occipital	Primary visual receptive area (17)	Receive visual impulses from opposite side	Contralateral homonymous hemianopsia with macular sparing; cortical blindness with bilateral lesions
	Parareceptive area (18) and preoccipital area (19)	Perceive and interpret visual impulses; form visual associations: orientation, recall; both areas 18 and 19 take part in optically induced reflexes	Disturbance of spatial orientation and discrimination, visual agnosia, illusions, and hallucinations; transient conjugate deviation of eyes toward the side of the lesion

There are intimate but poorly defined connections between the frontal lobe and the basal ganglia. With cerebellar centers, these connections elaborate voluntary and automatic movement. Cortical lesions do not usually cause basal ganglion symptoms because the cortical connections are too widespread.

Frontal association areas or the prefrontal lobe. In this most anterior portion of the frontal lobe, neurons are interconnected with sensory areas of the cortex. In addition, connections, predominantly afferent, are made with the thalamus, and predominantly efferent impulses are sent to the hypothalamus. The prefrontal lobe governs higher intellectual functions (judgment, reasoning, abstract thinking) and restrains emotional impulses. Associations take place that allow appropriate complex responses to the environment; here is the highest level of motor integration. It is in this area that psychomotor activity is initiated. Lesions in this area may result in mental and emotional symptoms.

PARIETAL LOBE

The parietal lobe is posterior to the Rolandic fissure.

Primary sensory area. This area includes the postcentral gyrus and immediately adjacent areas. It receives and identifies somatic sensory stimuli, particularly touch and position sensations, relayed from the nuclei ventralis posterolateralis and posteromedialis of the lateral nuclei of the thalamus. The pattern of cortical representation roughly corresponds to that of the motor cortex. A lesion in this area is associated with contralateral somatic sensory impairment but not complete analgesia or anesthesia.

Secondary sensory association area. This area is located posterior to the primary sensory area. It synthesizes and elaborates somatic sensory impulses and permits such fine perceptions as stereognosis.

Other parietal areas. The posterior parietal cortex has to do with discrimination of somesthetic and visual signals, making connections with motor systems for the purpose of directing responses to targets. In addition, other complex perceptual functions are carried out.

Lesions of this area and the secondary sensory association area frequently result in only slight contralateral sensory impairment or astereognosis. Inattention to stimuli (extinction of the contralateral stimulus during bilateral simultaneous stimulation) is often noted with these lesions. Sometimes trophic changes occur in the contralateral extremities, particularly the upper extremity.

The area inferior and posterior to the primary sensory area and the sensory association area contains the angular and supramarginal gyri. In this zone there occurs integration of visual and auditory stimuli with somatic sensations. A lesion in this area of the dominant hemisphere may cause alexia with agraphia, anomia, or conduction and transcortical fluent aphasias. A defect in body scheme may occur. Gerstmann syndrome (agraphia, acalculia, finger agnosia, right-left disorientation) may also be seen with lesions here, but this syndrome cannot be precisely localized with consistency. A deep parietal lobe lesion may affect the optic radiations and cause contralateral homonymous inferior quadrantic or hemianopic visual-field defects.

OCCIPITAL LOBE

The occipital lobe is the posterior tip of the cerebrum.

Primary visual receptive area. This area (Brodmann's area 17) is located along the lips of the calcarine fissure on the medial aspect of the occipital lobe and extends to adjacent areas around the lateral surface. This zone receives impulses relayed by the lateral geniculate body from the ipsilateral half of each retina. There is point-by-point representation of retinal segments in the calcarine cortex. A lesion in this area causes contralateral homonymous hemianopsia with macular sparing.

Parareceptive area. The parareceptive area (Brodmann's area 18) is

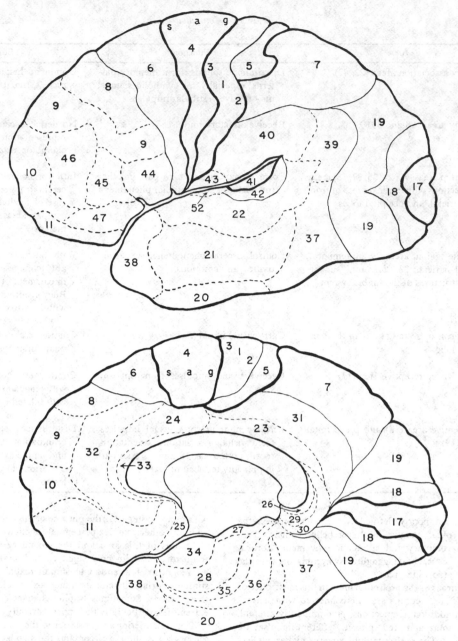

FIGURE 1. Cytoarchitectural map of the human cortex, modified after Brodmann. (From Elliott, H. C. *Textbook of Neuroanatomy*, p. 357. J. B. Lippincott, Philadelphia, 1969.)

immediately adjacent to the primary visual receptive area. In the parareceptive area, visual impulses are interpreted so that they may be recognized and identified. Perhaps visual memory engrams are stored here.

Preoccipital area. The preoccipital area (Brodmann's area 19) is immediately adjacent to the parareceptive area. Area 19 connects the visual receptive and parareceptive areas with other parts of the cortex. Its function is complex and has to do with perception, recall, visual association, and orientation.

Areas 18 and 19 are also centers for optically induced reflexes, such as fixation, through corticofugal fibers to the midbrain, medial longitudinal fasciculus, and nuclei of the ocular nerves. Lesions of the parareceptive and preoccipital areas are associated with disturbed spatial orientation, impaired visual discrimination, visual agnosia, illusions, and hallucinations. Cortical blindness occurs with lesions of both occipital lobes.

TEMPORAL LOBE

The temporal lobe is below and behind the lateral, Sylvian, fissure.

Auditory receptive area. This area is in the transverse temporal gyrus (Heschl's convolution) located on the posterior aspect of the superior temporal convolution. The auditory association area receives auditory impulses relayed by the medial geniculate body.

Auditory association area. This area is adjacent to the auditory receptive area but is poorly defined. It is in this zone that memory patterns for symbolic sounds are stored; here auditory impulses are differentiated and interpreted as words. This area may also receive vestibular impulses. A lesion of this area in the dominant hemisphere is associated with receptive fluent aphasia (Wernicke's aphasia) and often alexia and agraphia as well.

Gustatory and olfactory areas. The olfactory area is in the medial portion of the temporal lobe corresponding to the uncus and adjacent

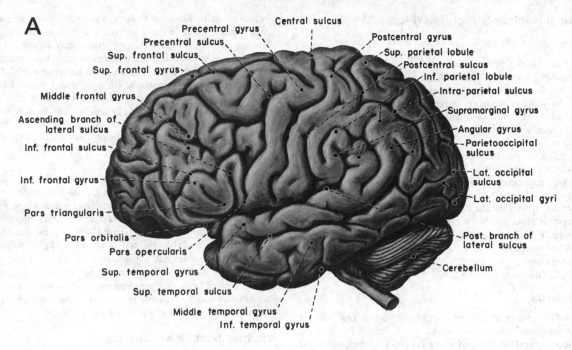

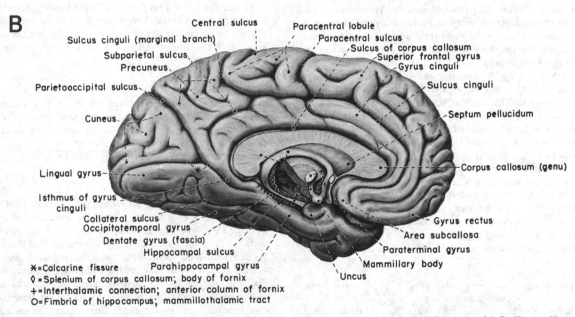

FIGURE 2. *A*. Lateral surface of left hemisphere showing principal gyri and sulci. (From Truex, R. C., and Carpenter, M. B. *Human Neuroanatomy*, ed. 6, p. 47. Williams & Wilkins, Baltimore, 1969.) *B*. Medial surface of left hemisphere showing principal gyri and sulci. The ependyma and part of the thalamic nuclei were removed to expose the relations of the anterior column of the fornix and the mammillothalamic tract. (From Truex, R. C., and Carpenter, M. B. *Human Neuroanatomy*, ed. 6, p. 49. Williams & Wilkins, Baltimore, 1969.)

portion of the hippocampal gyrus. The gustatory area, deep in the Sylvian fissure at the lower tip of the postcentral gyrus of the parietal lobe, is more functionally related to the temporal lobe.

Unilateral lesions of the temporal lobe do not cause auditory, gustatory, or olfactory impairment because these sensations have an extensive bilateral cerebral representation. Subcortical lesions of the temporal lobe may affect optic radiations and cause contralateral homonymous superior quadrantanopsia.

The functions of the temporal lobe are varied and complex. Al-

though the physiology of memory is poorly understood, it is more closely associated with the temporal lobe than with any other area of the brain. Stimulation of the temporal lobe may evoke past memories, and bilateral lesions of the medial aspects of the temporal lobe (hippocampus) cause loss of recent memory. This lobe is probably associated with sexual function and other visceral phenomena. The temporal lobe, as a major part of the limbic system, is intimately associated with psychological phenomena. Irritative lesions of the temporal lobe may cause psychomotor epilepsy or other mental and emotional symptoms.

Subcortical Nuclear Structures (Figure 3)

THALAMUS

The thalamus is the principal relay center for sensory pathways. These nuclei receive many different afferent impulses and relay them to the cerebral cortex and to lower centers for further integration. The anterior nuclei of the thalamus are important parts of the limbic system and are linked closely with the cingulate gyrus. The medial nuclei are associated primarily with the prefrontal area of the brain. The lateral group of nuclei are further subdivided into an anterior portion and a posterior portion; the pulvinar may be considered the most distal aspect of the posterior portion. The anterior nuclei of this lateral group are concerned with connections between the motor cortex, the basal ganglia, and the cerebellum. The posterior nuclei of the lateral group (the nuclei ventralis posterolateralis and ventralis posteromedialis) receive sensory impulses from the body and the face to be relayed to the parietal cortex. Visual and auditory impulses received by the pulvinar are relayed to visual and auditory association areas of the cortex. A lesion of the thalamus is associated with peculiar contralateral sensory phenomena, the thalamic syndrome.

HYPOTHALAMUS

The hypothalamus is the center controlling visceral functions. It governs the peripheral autonomic nervous system and, by its influence on the pituitary, regulates the endocrine glands. It is responsible for maintaining normal homeostasis. Vital functions are controlled in this area: temperature stability; cardiovascular and respiratory activity; the sleep cycle; metabolism of fat, carbohydrates, and protein; water and electrolyte balance; sphincter activity; and sexual activity. The posterior and lateral nuclei of the hypothalamus are primarily sympathoadrenal in their function. The anterior and medial nuclei are mainly associated with parasympathetic activity.

The hypothalamus regulates neural and humoral mechanisms of emotional activity and may be regarded as an effector organ of emotional expression. The cerebral cortical representation of autonomic functions is poorly defined, but areas in the prefrontal lobe are known to be connected to the hypothalamus. These cortical autonomic centers probably act as inhibitory influences on the more rudimentary visceral responses arising in the hypothalamus. As might be expected, many clinical syndromes are associated with lesions of the hypothalamus. Disease of the supraoptic nucleus causes diabetes insipidus. A lesion of the anterior nuclei, including the tuber cinerium, may be associated with prepubertal adiposity and genital dystrophy (Frölich's syndrome) or with postpubertal amenorrhea or impotence. On the other hand, less well-defined hypothalamic lesions may result in precocious puberty, and widespread disease of these nuclei is associated with emaciation. Lesions in the ventromedial nuclei of human beings cause bulimia, and in lower animals the resultant voracious appetite is associated with savagery. Hyperthermia may follow a lesion of the anterior or ventromedial hypothalamic nuclei. Less commonly, hypothermia is associated with disease of the posterior nuclei. Disorders of sleep, especially hypersomnia, are seen with lesions of the posterior nuclei and adjacent structures of the upper brain stem. Convulsive disorders manifesting visceral phenomena may be due to dysfunction of the hypothalamus, and more common generalized seizures may arise in the hypothalamic portion of the centrencephalic system.

BASAL GANGLIA

The basal ganglia consist primarily of the caudate, putamen, and globus pallidus; functionally related groups of neurons are the subthalamic nucleus, red nucleus, and substantia nigra. These structures are essential parts of efferent pathways and modify impulses from the motor cortex and interrelated cerebellum-thalamic relays. This complicated system elaborates and integrates complex voluntary motor activity to allow smooth actions. In addition, the basal ganglia take over motor skills that have become automatic. Lesions of the basal ganglia cause involuntary movements; alterations in muscle tone; loss of associated and automatic movements, with resultant impairment of postural reflexes; and loss of facial expression.

Subcortical Fiber Bundles

CORPUS CALLOSUM

The corpus callosum is the major commissural system of the brain, connecting the two cerebral hemispheres and facilitating the integration of their functions. On the other hand, surgical section or congenital absence of the corpus callosum need not be associated with any symptoms or signs.

INTERNAL CAPSULE

This is the major afferent and efferent pathway connecting the spinal cord and brain stem to the cerebral hemispheres. It also contains association fibers of the cerebellum, thalamus, and basal ganglia. A small lesion in this tightly packed area causes profound contralateral defects of motor, somatic sensory, or visual modalities.

Limbic System

The limbic lobe is the large arcuate convolution of the medial surface of the cerebrum, consisting of the cingulate and hippocampal gyri, the subcallosal and parahippocampal areas, the posterior orbital cortex of the frontal lobe, and the anterior aspects of the insula and of the temporal lobe. The limbic system includes all the above, plus associated nuclei—the amygdala, septal nuclei, preoptic area, anterior thalamus, and nuclei of the hypothalamus, epithalamus, and portions of the basal ganglia; the medial aspects of the tegmentum of the midbrain may also be included. This system, the so-called visceral brain, is the substrate of emotions.

A broad functional division has been postulated. The amygdala and frontotemporal areas are said to be concerned with self-preservation, particularly with regard to food and other visceral functions. The hippocampus, cingulate gyrus, and septal region are thought to be concerned with emotional states pertaining to interpersonal relations, particularly those of a sexual nature.

Cerebellum

The afferent aspects of the cerebellum, traveling mainly through the inferior peduncle (restiform body) and the middle peduncle (brachium pontis), are primarily concerned with proprioceptive and vestibular impulses. Its efferent functions, traveling mainly through the superior peduncle (brachium conjunctivum), play essential roles in activities under the control of the motor cortex. The cerebellum integrates and coordinates motor impulses, both voluntary and involuntary. Equilibrium is attained by cerebellar functions that maintain orientation of

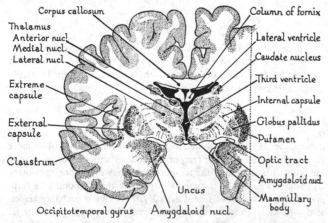

FIGURE 3. Frontal section of brain, passing through mammillary bodies. (From Truex, R. C., and Carpenter, M. B. *Strong and Elwyn's Human Neuroanatomy*, ed. 5, p. 435. Williams & Wilkins, Baltimore, 1964.)

the person in space and regulate muscle tone and posture. A lesion of the midline, vermis areas of the cerebellum causes truncal ataxia. A lesion of a cerebellar hemisphere results in ipsilateral incoordination of the extremities, more than of the trunk.

Brain Stem

The brain stem consists of the medulla, the pons, and the midbrain. Efferent and afferent impulses pass through and are relayed in the brain stem. The cranial nerve nuclei are located in this vital area. Unilateral lesions of the brain stem are characterized by a combination of ipsilateral cranial nerve signs and contralateral long-tract motor or sensory signs.

The reticular formation is a poorly demarcated group of neurons within the tegmentum of the brain stem. This complex network receives impulses from all parts of the peripheral and central nervous system and sends impulses to the spinal cord, the thalamus, the basal ganglia, and the cerebral cortex. The reticular formation exerts both inhibitory and facilitory influences on the peripheral motor system. In the opposite direction, its effect is that of maintaining the arousal or vigilant state, and, by its influence on the threshold of the various stimuli, it has a large role in establishing the level of attention. It also takes part in regulating visceral, vascular, and endocrine activities. Lesions of the reticular formation may affect motor tone, state of consciousness, and any or all vital functions. Dysfunction of the reticular formation is probably associated with many psychological alterations, but these alterations have yet to be documented.

Diencephalic Area

The diencephalon is made up of the thalamus, the hypothalamus, the epithalamus (which includes the pineal body), the subthalamus (including the corpus luysi), and portions of the substantia nigra, red nucleus, and reticular formation of the midbrain. It is thought to be the primary integrating system. Here the sensorimotor impulses of the occipital-parietal-central areas of the cortex are integrated with functions of the temporal cortex and probably the frontal cortex, subserving those intellectual mechanisms essential to perception and memory.

Spinal Cord

The spinal cord is made up of long axons, carrying efferent and afferent impulses, surrounding a core of nerve cells. On cross-section, the core of neurons appears as a gray "H" within the white matter, the latter formed by myelin sheaths of the axons. The cell bodies of sensory neurons are located in the dorsal root ganglia. Nerve fibers carrying proprioception, vibration, and touch sensations ascend in the ipsilateral posterior column of the cord to nuclei in the medulla. These sensory impulses are then relayed to the opposite side of the brain stem, where they ascend in the medial lemniscus to the thalamus. Fibers carrying superficial pain and temperature sensations terminate near the posterior horn of the gray "H" soon after entering the cord. These sensations are then relayed to the opposite lateral aspect of the cord and ascend to the thalamus in the lateral spinothalamic tract. Some fibers carrying touch sensation follow a similar course and form the ventral spinothalamic tract. The pyramidal, corticospinal tracts descend from the brain, decussate at the caudal end of the medulla, and take up the major portion of the lateral columns of the spinal cord, terminating at the anterior horn cells of the gray "H." Axons of the latter lower motor neurons then leave the cord, through the ventral roots, to innervate muscles. Short, intercalated neurons abound in the central gray matter and are integral parts of reflex arcs.

Disease of the posterior column causes ipsilateral loss of proprioception and vibration below the affected level. A lesion of the lateral column results in ipsilateral upper motor neuron (spastic) paralysis and contralateral loss of pain and temperature sensitivity below the level of injury (Brown-Séquard's syndrome). Disease affecting the anterior horn of the gray matter causes ipsilateral lower motor neuron (flaccid) palsy within the distribution of the diseased segment.

Autonomic Nervous System

The autonomic nervous system consists of all the efferent neurons innervating the viscera and involuntary muscles. Impulses descend from the hypothalamus and from autonomic centers in the brain stem through the brain stem and the spinal cord by short axons and numerous synaptic relays. The afferent neurons transmitting impulses from the viscera are carried cephalad as visceral afferent components of spinal and cranial nerves.

The autonomic neurons in the spinal cord are located in the lateral portion of the intermediate zone (between the anterior and the posterior horns) of the gray matter and in cranial nerve nuclei of the brain stem. These preganglionic neurons make synaptic connections with ganglionic neurons that arise from cell aggregates (autonomic ganglia). The sympathetic ganglia are incorporated in a pair of cords ventral to the vertebrae, and thoracolumbar preganglionic neurons make connections with postganglionic neurons within these chains. The parasympathetic ganglia are located in the walls of the effector organs or in plexuses near these organs, and the cranial and sacral preganglionic neurons form synaptic links with postganglionic neurons within these plexuses.

Suggested Cross References

The neurochemistry and neurophysiology of behavior are discussed in Section 2.4 and Section 2.5, respectively. Sections 3.2, 3.3, 3.4, and 3.5 cover other aspects of neurology. Organic mental disorders are discussed in Chapter 20.

REFERENCES

* Bourne, G. H., editor. *The Structure and Function of Nervous Tissue.* Academic Press, New York, 1969.
Brazier, M. A. B., and Pelsche, H. *Architectonics of the Cerebral Cortex.* Raven Press, New York, 1978.
* Carpenter, M. B. *Human Neuroanatomy,* ed. 7. Williams & Wilkins, Baltimore, 1976.
Chusid, J. G. *Correlative Neuroanatomy and Functional Neurology,* ed. 16. Lange, Los Altos, Calif., 1976.
* Curtis, B. A., Jacobson, S., and Marcus, E. M. *An Introduction to the Neurosciences.* W. B. Saunders, Philadelphia, 1972.
Elliot, H. C. *Textbook of Neuroanatomy.* J. B. Lippincott, Philadelphia, 1969.
Guyton, A. C. *Textbook of Medical Physiology.* W. B. Saunders, Philadelphia, 1976.
Haymaker, W. *Bing's Local Diagnosis in Neurological Diseases,* ed. 15. C. V. Mosby, St. Louis, 1969.
* House, E. L., and Pansky, B. *A Functional Approach to Neuroanatomy,* ed. 2. McGraw-Hill, New York, 1967.
* Mountcastle, V. B., editor. *Medical Physiology,* ed. 13. C. V. Mosby, St. Louis, 1974.
* Peele, T. L. *The Neuroanatomical Basis for Clinical Neurology,* ed. 3. McGraw-Hill, New York, 1977.
Ruch, T. C., Patton, H. D., Woodbury, J. W., and Towe, A. L. *Neurophysiology.* W. B. Saunders, Philadelphia, 1965.
Towers, D. B., editor. *The Nervous System.* Raven Press, New York, 1975.
* Willis, W. D., and Grossman, R. G. *Medical Neurobiology: Neuroanatomical and Neurophysiological Principles Basic to Clinical Neuroscience,* ed. 2. C. V. Mosby, St. Louis, 1977.

3.2 Neurological Evaluation

SEYMOUR SOLOMON, M.D.

Introduction

In making a neurological diagnosis, one must first decide whether the illness is psychogenic, pathophysiological, or organic. If the last, the anatomical location and then the main cause must be established. Finally, the precise name of the disease may be appended.

Evaluation of the Adult

HISTORY

An adequate history is probably the most important step in establishing a diagnosis. The source and the reliability of the history should be recorded. The patient's age, sex, and handedness are best noted at the outset. A detailed and chronological résumé of the present illness is the essential feature of the history. Each complaint should be evaluated with regard to onset, duration, and frequency of occurrence. Note should be made of both aggravating and alleviating factors. Specific qualities of the complaint must be evaluated. For example, if pain is a chief complaint, the type of pain and its location and radiation are important. The exact meaning of the symptom to the patient must be elicited. The term "dizziness," for example, should mean a spinning sensation or a sensation of imbalance, but many patients use the term to denote such symptoms as nausea, malaise, and faintness. Other symptoms associated with the prime complaint must be sought. The course of the disease should be established.

To be sure that the patient has not omitted pertinent information, one should review a set of neurological symptoms. Thus, the patient should be specifically questioned with regard to the occurrence of headaches, dizziness, episodes of fainting or faintness, fits or convulsions, shaking or trembling, unsteadiness or incoordination. He should be asked about past or present weakness, stiffness, paralysis, aches, pains, and numbness or tingling, either focal or generalized. The patient should be queried as to symptoms referrable to the special senses. Was there a history of double vision, spots before the eyes, temporary blindness, or blurring of vision? Did the patient experience ringing in an ear or hearing impairment in one or both ears? Was the sense of taste or smell impaired? Perversions of these special senses may be neglected by the patient unless specifically questioned: "Do you ever smell or taste anything peculiar? Do you ever hear or see things out of the ordinary?" Visceral symptoms may be important neurological phenomena. Has there been a history of disturbance of swallowing or speech, an alteration of bladder or bowel control? In female patients the history of pregnancy and menstruation may be significant. Sexual potency and recent change in sexual activity are important features of the history. An alteration in sleep pattern may be pertinent. Symptoms of mental illness should be sought. Indications of organic disease manifested by memory impairment or confusion are as important as symptoms of psychological disturbance manifested by personality change, anxiety, or a past history of delinquency or "nervous breakdown."

The past medical history should include queries as to trauma, surgery, and medical illness, particularly diabetes and hypertension. Was there a history of allergy, of exposure to toxins, or of weight gain or loss? The use of medication or drugs, particularly in the recent past, should be noted. Sometimes, defects in the patient's memory for past illnesses may be overcome by inquiring about all past hospitalizations.

The patient's social history should include occupation, home environment, and drinking and smoking habits. The family history should note not only the diseases that may cause death but the presence of epilepsy, migraine, and other diseases, both mental and neurological. The question of consanguinity should be raised.

PHYSICAL EXAMINATION

A general physical examination need not be considered a part of the neurological examination, but findings in such an examination are often the chief clue to the neurological diagnosis. Many brain tumors are metastatic from the lung or the breast. Infectious disease within the head may be secondary to subacute bacterial endocarditis or to infections of the ear or lung. Metabolic encephalopathies are often associated with hepatic or renal failure, and toxic encephalopathies may be due to drug overdose. Hypertension predisposes to cerebral atherosclerosis or cerebral hemorrhage. Differences in the pulse or blood pressure

readings of the two arms suggest subclavian stenosis, which may give rise to vertebrobasilar artery insufficiency.

NEUROLOGICAL EXAMINATION

Mental status. An evaluation of the patient's mental state should include tests for intellectual functioning and emotional status. It is essential to note the patient's level of consciousness. His language can then be carefully evaluated.

INTELLECTUAL FUNCTIONS. If the patient is alert, the degree of his attention or distractibility and of his cooperativeness is pertinent. It is important to establish the degree of the patient's orientation to place, time, and person. More than one answer to these queries is necessary. For example, does the patient know not only that he is in a hospital but also the name of the city and state? Does he know the month, season, and year? Can he correctly identify the nurse and the doctor, as well as his wife? Calculation can be judged by asking the patient to subtract sevens from 100 in serial fashion. Reasoning can be evaluated by noting the patient's ability to deal with abstract concepts. For example, he may be asked the similarities between a bicycle and a train and asked to interpret a common proverb. Asking the patient what he would do if he were in a theater and saw smoke coming from one corner of the room is one way of evaluating his judgment. The patient's memories are tested in different ways. Retention and immediate recall are examined by asking him to repeat three, four, or five digits in sequence both forward and backward; normally, one is able to repeat four digits in reverse sequence. Recent memory is tested by asking the patient to recall three items after 3 to 5 minutes. If one lists the items at the beginning of the mental status examination and asks the patient to recall them at the end of the examination, the 3 to 5 minutes will usually have elapsed. Both remote memory and fund of information can be tested by asking the patient to recall recent past Presidents of the United States.

EMOTIONAL STATUS. The patient's emotional status should be noted, particularly with regard to his perception of reality and to the presence of delusions, illusions, or hallucinations. The production of his thought processes and their progression, preoccupation, and content are important observations. His affect and its appropriateness, his depression or euphoria, his emotional lability, and his degree of anxiety are pertinent. Behavior, neatness, mannerisms, and other forms of motor activity can be seen. Determination of the patient's insight, motivation, and special appetites may require more prolonged evaluation.

LANGUAGE DISTURBANCES

The aphasias. A disturbance of language is in itself a manifestation of organic mental disease. The term "dysphasia" is usually more appropriate than the term "aphasia," because rarely is communication completely lost, as connoted by "aphasia." Defects in language can best be evaluated by dividing those that are mainly disturbances in reception and understanding from those that are primarily impairments of expression. Language defects may also be divided into impairments in spoken language and in written language. The fluency or nonfluency of speech is the chief feature dividing the motor nonfluent expressive dysphasias from the sensory/fluent/receptive dysphasias. When expression is impaired, very little spontaneous speech is evident, and the words are uttered nonfluently—that is, slowly, in short phrases, and with effort; dysarthria is common. When the reception and understanding of language are impaired, speech is fluent, with normal or increased rate of output and length of phrases, but the content may be nonsense, jargon, or neologisms. The other differences between expressive-nonfluent aphasia and receptive-fluent aphasia are listed in Table I.

Evaluation of spontaneous speech is the first step in the examination for aphasia. In addition to listening for truly spontaneous speech, the physician should attempt to elicit speech by asking conversational questions "How are you? What is your name? What kind of work do you do? What brings you to the hospital?" and asking the patient to explain a picture presented to him. One should next test comprehension. The patient's inability to understand instructions must be clearly differentiated from the physical inability to carry them out. Thus, the physician should request "yes" or "no" responses, verbal, by gesture, or by a nodding or shaking of the head. ("Is your name Jones? Do you live in New York? Is this a hotel? Am I a doctor?") Then one should ask the patient to point to or show named objects or body parts. Right and left parts of the examiner's or the patient's body further bring out right-left dissociations or autotopagnosias. Finally, the physician should ask the patient to perform increasingly difficult tasks, from "Close your eyes" to "Touch your nose with your hand" to "Put your left thumb on your right ear."

The patient's ability to repeat, further helps differentiate specific types of aphasia within the major categories of nonfluent and fluent aphasias. The examiner should ask the patient to repeat single words, then phrases, a long sentence, and a nonsense sequence ("no ifs, ands, or buts"). Finally, the physician should ask the patient to name objects; a small number of patients, those with amnestic aphasia, falter only in this task.

Most language dysfunctions occur with lesions of the dominant hemisphere. In about 99 per cent of right-handed persons and in 60 to 70 per cent of left-handed persons, the left cerebral hemisphere is dominant. Signs of aphasia or dysphasia may be exceedingly difficult to differentiate from signs of dementia. Table II shows the differential features and the site of lesion of the aphasias.

Alexia and agraphia. The inability to understand the meaning of written symbols is termed "alexia." The term "dyslexia" is now reserved for particular difficulty in learning to read. The physician should ask the patient to read out loud and then question him for comprehension. A defect of expression in written language is called agraphia. Alexia usually occurs with agraphia, and the responsible lesion is in the dominant angular gyrus. In a few cases, alexia occurs

without agraphia; the pathology in such cases is within the dominant medial occipital lobe.

AGNOSIA. Inability to recognize objects or symbols by specific senses is called "agnosia." Visual agnosia is the inability to recognize a familiar object by sight. Patients with prosopagnosia are unable to identify familiar faces. This phenomenon is caused by bilateral but predominantly nondominant parietooccipital lesions. Auditory agnosia is the loss of ability to identify familiar sounds. Other complex defects of cortical integration are impairment of right and left discrimination and the inability to recognize body parts. Gerstmann syndrome consists of finger agnosia, agraphia, right-left disorientation, and acalculia. When seen in its pure form, which is rare, this syndrome is associated with dominant parietal lobe disease.

APRAXIA. Defective cortical motor integration results in apraxia, the incapacity to carry out purposeful acts while maintaining the motor strength and coordination abilities to perform those acts. Ideomotor apraxia is the inability to carry out motor activity on command while retaining the ability to do so spontaneously. In the testing of a patient, commands are given referable to the extremities (for example, "Pretend to comb your hair. Make a fist."), to the facial musculature (for example, "Whistle. Show your tongue."), and to the whole body (for example, "Stand up. Walk."). Often, apraxia of limb and face occurs, but commands regarding trunk musculature can be carried out. Less common ideational apraxia refers to the inability to carry out a complex multistep command while able to perform each step individually. These forms of apraxia are manifestations of lesions of the dominant hemisphere.

Impairment of visual spatial integration results in constructional apraxia. This defect may be uncovered by asking the patient to copy geometric figures and to draw objects, such as a clock or a cube. Apraxia in dressing often accompanies constructional apraxia. These forms of apraxia are usually associated with lesions mainly in the nondominant hemisphere, but disease usually affects both left and right sides of the cerebrum. Other phenomena commonly associated with nondominant hemisphere lesions are anosognosia (denial of illness) and motor impersistence (the inability to maintain a static posture, such as a protruded tongue or a fixation of gaze).

Examination of the head and neck. Inspection may reveal asymmetries of the head and unusual postures of the neck. On palpation of the scalp, one may note exostosis, such as that overlying a meningioma. The temporal, carotid, and radial pulses should be palpated and cervical lymph nodes noted. Direct percussion of the skull, comparing the right side with the left side, sometimes reveals dullness overlying a subdural hematoma. Auscultation over each eyeball (allowing the opposite eyelid to open greatly diminishes adventitious muscle sounds) may reveal bruits of a vascular malformation or of collateral circulation associated with carotid artery stenosis. Bruits over the carotid arteries or subclavian arteries may also be indicative of stenosis of these vessels. The loudness of a bruit does not have a direct relationship to the

TABLE I

Aphasias: Nonfluent versus Fluent

Qualities of Speech	Nonfluent	Fluent
Rate of output	Decreased (less than 50 words a min.)	Normal or excessive (100 to 200 words a min.)
Rhythm-inflection	Poor (dysprosody)	Normal
Articulation	Dysarthric	Normal
Effort-initiation	Difficult	Normal
Press of speech	Decreased	Normal or logorrhea
Phrase length	Decreased (2± words)	Normal or increased (8 to 10 words)
Word content	Nouns and verbs	Clichés and circumlocutions
Paraphasia	Slight	Moderate

TABLE II

Aphasia: Differential Features and Site of Lesion

	Fluency	Comprehension	Repetition	Site of Lesion
Global	Poor	Poor	Poor	Extensive lesion affecting anterior and posterior areas and their connections
Broca (expressive nonfluent)	Poor	Good	Poor	Posterior third frontal gyrus
Isolation	Poor	Poor	Good	Wide border zone of frontal, parietal, and temporal lobes, isolating the perisylvian speech area
Transcortical (motor)	Poor	Good	Good	Anterior border zone: frontal lobe (anterior and superior to Broca's area)
Wernicke's (receptive fluent)	Good	Poor	Poor	Posterior superior temporal gyrus
Transcortical (sensory)	Good	Poor	Good	Posterior border zone parietotemporal lobes (angular gyrus and posterior inferior temporal lobe)
Conduction	Good	Good	Poor	Posterior sylvian region
Anomic (impairment in naming)	Good	Good	Good	Angular gyrus but often not well localized

degree of stenosis. Mobility of the neck to passive movement may be diminished after cervical injuries. Restriction of neck flexion as an indication of meningeal irritation may be associated with Brudzinski's sign—characterized by pain in the neck and back, with flexion of the thighs on an attempt to flex the neck passively—or Kernig's sign—manifested by pain of the back and neck, with tendency to flex the neck slightly on passive straight leg raising.

Examination of the cranial nerves

Olfactory nerve (1). The patient is asked to identify familiar odors, such as coffee and tobacco. Each nostril is individually tested. The most common causes of defects in olfactory sensation are due not to disease of the first cranial nerve but, rather, to obstruction of the nasal passage or disease of the nasal mucous membranes—for example, allergic rhinitis. Thus, bilateral impairment of the sense of smell is usually not significant. Loss of the sense of smell on one side, in the absence of local causes, may be due to an olfactory groove meningioma.

Optic nerve (2). The patient's visual acuity is determined either by using a Snellen chart or, more crudely, by having the patient read ordinary newsprint. Each eye should be tested individually, both with and without the patient's corrective lenses. Testing the visual acuity by having the patient read through a pin hole is an excellent substitute for corrective lenses. Ophthalmoscopy is then performed, noting the optic disc and retina, with its arteries and veins. Retinal hemorrhages and exudates may be seen in a large variety of diseases, particularly those of a vascular nature. Pallor and sharpness of an optic disc may be due to optic atrophy. Hyperemia of the disc, blurring of its margins, disappearance of the physiological cup, venous engorgement, and absence of venous pulsations are indications of papilledema.

Papilledema. The most common causes of increased intracranial pressure and papilledema are intracranial masses (neoplasm, hematoma, abscess), block of cerebrospinal fluid outflow or absorption, and swelling of the brain due to traumatic, inflammatory, toxic, or metabolic factors—for example, water intoxication and pseudotumor cerebri. Papilledema may also be due to optic neuritis or to other lesions within the orbit. Extracranial factors sometimes cause papilledema. This sign may be due to carbon dioxide toxicity or increased venous pressure, as seen in cardiopulmonary diseases, or to increased arterial pressure or flow—for example, malignant hypertension or arteriovenous fistula. Papilledema rarely occurs with acute polyneuritis or spinal cord tumors. Other extracranial diseases that may be associated with papilledema are anemia, polycythemia, and other blood dyscrasias; toxins such as lead and arsenic, gentamycin, and tetracycline; vitamin abormalities (excess of vitamin A or D, paucity of vitamin A or C); and endocrinopathies, especially dysfunction of the adrenal and parathyroid glands but rarely hypothyroidism.

The visual field of each eye can be tested by confrontation—that is, by having the patient cover one eye, look at one of the examiner's eyes, and note the examiner's moving fingers at the periphery of the field. Each quadrant and each half of the right and left visual fields are tested. When more precise information is required, standard perimetry and the tangent screen examination are necessary to determine the exact peripheral and central visual fields.

An irregular central scotoma within one visual field is usually a residual of retrobulbar or optic neuritis, as seen in multiple sclerosis. Enlargement of the blind spot occurs in papilledema. Constriction or loss of the visual field in one eye is due to a lesion of the optic nerve. Bitemporal hemianopsia is caused by a lesion of the optic chiasm. Homonymous hemianopsia is associated with a lesion of the opposite optic tract or optic radiations. Homonymous superior quadrantanopsia is found with a lesion of the opposite temporal lobe. Homonymous inferior quadrantanopsia is associated with a lesion of the opposite parietal lobe. Homonymous hemianopsia with macular sparing is due to a lesion of the opposite occipital lobe.

Oculomotor, trochlear, and abducens nerves (3, 4, and 6). These nerves are tested together, because they supply the muscles of eye movement and, in the case of the oculomotor nerve, the constrictors of the pupil and the elevator of the eyelid. The size, shape, and symmetry of the pupils are noted. The response of the pupil to accommodation is tested by noting the pupillary constriction as the patient focuses from a distant object to a close object. The reaction of the pupil to light is seen by shining a light into each eye from the side. (Direct approach of the light may cause the pupils to constrict because of accommodation.) Both direct and consensual pupillary reactions should be tested. A unilaterally dilated pupil may be the first sign of oculomotor nerve compression. Conversely, the pupil is usually spared when the oculomotor nerve is affected by diabetic neuropathy. Constriction of a pupil associated with ptosis and impairment of sweating over the ipsilateral forehead are manifestations of Horner's syndrome, indicative of an ipsilateral sympathetic nerve pathway lesion. The range of extraocular movements is noted by asking the patient to follow the movement of the examiner's finger in all directions of gaze. The examiner should pause briefly in every direction to look for nystagmus. Ptosis of the lid is one sign of involvement of the oculomotor nerve, but the palpebral fissures may be asymmetrical from other causes. For example, disease of the facial nerve, causing weakness of the orbicularis oculi muscle, results in a larger palpebral fissure on the side of the facial involvement.

A complete loss of function of the oculomotor nerve is manifested by the patient's inability to deviate the eye up, down, or medially, with associated ptosis of the lid and dilation of the pupil. In lesions of the trochlear nerve affecting the superior oblique muscle, the patient has difficulty looking down and out. As a consequence, the head is tilted toward the shoulder of the opposite side. As the name implies, disease of the abducens nerve prevents abduction of the eye. In all cases, the patient complains of double vision.

Involvement of the third, fourth, or sixth cranial nerves may be due to direct or indirect compression of the nerve fibers within the cranial cavity or to lesions of the cranial nerves in the brain stem. In patients with conjugate gaze palsy, the eyes are deviated away from the side of an irritative cerebral lesion or toward a destructive cerebral lesion.

Nystagmus is due to disease of the vestibular apparatus ranging from the inner ear to the brain stem and cerebellum. Inner ear disease may evoke nystagmus that is horizontal or rotatory. These types of nystagmus may also be noted with disease of the brain stem, but vertical nystagmus and monocular nystagmus are pathognomonic of disease of the brain stem. Nystagmus of vestibular origin is predominant when fixation is eliminated, as by strong lenses or with the eyes closed, but nystagmus of cerebellar disease is most marked on fixation. Electronystagmography may help in differentiating disease of the labyrinth from that of the brain stem.

Trigeminal nerve (5). Sensation of the face and cornea is first tested by observing the patient's blink response when a wisp of cotton lightly touches the edge of the cornea. The same wisp of cotton can then be used to test touch over the three divisions of the trigeminal nerve (forehead, cheek, and chin), comparing the right side with the left side. Response to a light pin prick is tested in a similar distribution. When hypalgesia is mild, temperature impairment over the same distribution confirms the objective nature of the defect. Loss of corneal reflex may be the first sign of trigeminal nerve compression by an ipsilateral acoustic neuroma, and analgesia over one side of the face may be seen in brain stem infarction—for example, the lateral medullary syndrome. The masses of the temporal and masseter muscles are palpated with the jaws tightly closed. An open jaw deviates toward a weakened external pterygoid muscle. A jaw jerk is elicited by tapping the middle of the chin with a reflex hammer while the patient's jaw is loosely open. Hyperactivity of this reflex may be a manifestation of pyramidal tract disease. The trigeminal nerve carries pain and touch sensations from the mucous membranes of the nose and mouth, but sensations of these areas need not be routinely tested.

Facial nerve (7). The muscles innervated by this nerve are observed at rest and after asking the patient to show his teeth and wrinkle his forehead. Sometimes minimal asymmetries noted on movement of the face to command are exaggerated during the expression of emotion or other spontaneous activity; at other times the reverse is true. The strength of the orbicularis oculi muscle is tested by attempting to open the patient's eyes against his resistance. Paralysis or weakness of all the facial muscles on one side, including the forehead, is indicative of ipsilateral lower motor neuron disease, as seen in Bell's palsy. If the muscles of the forehead are spared, the facial weakness is presumed to be due to a contralateral lesion affecting corticobulbar pathways, such as a cerebral infarct. The sensory portion of the facial nerve carries taste from the anterior two-thirds of the tongue. Sugar or salt in solution is placed on the left or right anterior portion of the protruded tongue. The patient is asked to indicate the presence of taste by raising his hand. The rapidity of responses on one side is compared with the rapidity on the other side. Taste is often unilaterally lost in a patient with Bell's palsy but not in a patient with central nervous system disease.

Acoustic nerve (8). This nerve is composed of two portions, the cochlear and the vestibular nerves. During a routine neurological examination, only the cochlear nerve is examined. Auditory acuity may be determined by noting how far from his ear the patient is first able to hear a watch tick; the examiner may use himself as a control. Weber's test is performed by placing a vibrating tuning fork on the midline of the patient's skull. If the sound is referred to one ear, the test is considered positive. When air conduction deafness is present because of otitis media or an accumulation of wax in the canal, Weber's test lateralizes to the affected ear; if there is nerve deafness, the sound is heard in the normal ear. Rinne's test is performed by placing the vibrating tuning fork on the mastoid portion of the skull behind the patient's ear. When the patient can no longer hear the sound, the fork is then placed next to the ear. Under normal circumstances, air conduction of sound is better than bone conduction. Bone conduction, as well as air conduction, is impaired on the side of nerve deafness, but bone conduction is preserved in the presence of an air conduction defect. Audiometry is of value in precisely quantitating the hearing loss. When nerve deafness is suspected, the caloric test should be performed to evaluate the vestibular portion of the acoustic nerve. With the patient supine and his head raised 30 degrees, injection of 4 ml. to 15 ml. of ice water into the external auditory canal normally evokes, within a few seconds, vertigo, nystagmus (with fast component to the opposite side), and past pointing to the stimulated side. When the acoustic nerve is compromised, loss of auditory acuity and of caloric response is evident on the side of the involvement. Many refinements of audiometry and other tests of the vestibular system may assist in differentiating lesions of the inner ear, of the acoustic nerve, and of the brain stem.

Glossopharyngeal and vagus nerves (9 and 10). These two nerves are tested together. The gag reflex is tested by touching each side of the pharynx. Bilateral impairment of the gag reflex need not be abnormal, but loss of the gag reflex on one side and pulling up of the soft palate toward the opposite side are indicative of involvement of the ninth nerve. Hoarseness may be an indication of weakness or paralysis of a vocal cord. Difficulty in swallowing (dysphagia), when of neurological origin, is noted earliest with liquids and is indicative of bulbar (medullary) or pseudobulbar disease. Dysarthria may be due to a motor disease affecting the tongue or other portions of the vocal mechanism, but more often it is due to neural defects in coordination of the speech mechanism. The glossopharyngeal nerve carries taste from the posterior third of the tongue, but this sensation is not routinely tested. The autonomic functions of the vagus nerve, having to do with cardiopulmonary activity, are usually noted during the general physical examination.

Spinal accessory nerve (11). The trapezius muscle is tested by having the patient shrug his shoulder against resistance. The sternocleidomastoid muscle is examined by having the patient turn his head against resistance. These muscles are affected by lesions compressing the nerve at the jugular foramen or, less often, by lesions in the lower medulla. The trapezius and, less often, the sternocleidomastoid may also be weakened or paralyzed by a contralateral cerebral lesion. The sternocleidomastoid muscle is often uncrossed in its supranuclear innervation. Thus, a lesion in a cerebral hemisphere may affect the ipsilateral sternocleidomastoid muscle.

Hypoglossal nerve (12). The protruded tongue is normally in the midline. It deviates to the weakened side—that is, ipsilateral to the lesion—if the lower motor neuron is involved, and it deviates contralateral to the lesion in upper motor neuron disease. If lower motor neuron disease is present, atrophy or fine fasciculations of the tongue may be seen on the side of the involvement.

Cranial nerve signs of cerebral disease. The following is a summary of cranial nerve signs that may be found in a lesion of one cerebral hemisphere—for example, cerebral infarct or tumor. The numerals refer to the cranial nerves, but it is their supranuclear innervation that is affected.

Contralateral homonymous hemianopsia (2).

Conjugate deviation of eyes away from the side of the irritative lesion or toward the side of the destructive lesion (3, 4, and 6).

Contralateral impairment of pain and touch over the face and diminished corneal reflex (5).

Contralateral paresis of the face, not including the forehead (7).

Contralateral weakness of the trapezius muscle and ipsilateral weakness of the sternocleidomastoid muscle (11).

Contralateral weakness of the tongue (12).

Pseudobulbar palsy. This syndrome is characterized by symptoms implicating the brain stem but due to bilateral disease of supranuclear corticobulbar fibers—most often, multiple small cerebrovascular lesions. Because most bulbar musculature has a bilateral cerebral representation, a unilateral supranuclear lesion does not cause bulbar signs. Dysarthria and dysphagia are most common. The patient's speech has a nasal, slurring, and often explosive quality, and his voice volume is diminished. Chewing and swallowing are impaired, and food may accumulate in the mouth, with drooling of saliva and frequent choking. The patient's gait is often impaired, particularly because of disequilibrium. All movements may be slow and poorly performed. The facies may be flattened, as in parkinsonism. Exaggerated emotional responses are prominent. Spontaneous laughing and crying frequently occur, but they are involuntary and unassociated with appropriate emotions. Gag reflexes are preserved, and deep reflexes, including the jaw jerk, are often hyperactive.

Motor examination. Voluntary muscle strength is impaired in certain patterns, corresponding to the site of the disease. Weakness of the distal portions of the extremities suggests neuropathy, whereas proximal weakness is characteristic of myopathy. If there is suspicion of nerve root or peripheral nerve involvement, individual muscles of the extremities are specifically examined. With spinal cord involvement, weakness of the lower extremities is common but may initially be masked by associated spasticity. In the presence of minimal unilateral upper motor neuron disease—for example, a lesion in a cerebral hemisphere —slight weakness of the contralateral extremities may be manifested first in the extensor and supinator muscles of the upper extremity and in the flexor and internal rotator muscles of the lower extremity. Thus, when the patient's eyes are closed and his arms extended, one may see a slight downward drift, flexion, and pronation of the affected upper extremity. With the patient prone, a slight downward drift of the affected flexed lower leg may occur (Barré's sign), and, with the patient supine, slight external rotation of the leg and a slight foot drop may be noted. Documentation of the degree of weakness is an important parameter in establishing the course of the patient's illness. The muscle strength is graded as follows: normal—grade 5; able to resist the examiner—grade 4, good; able to resist gravity but not the examiner—grade 3, fair; able to move only when gravity is eliminated—grade 2, poor; only a flicker of movement discernible—grade 1, trace; total paralysis—grade 0.

Posture and contractures and deformities of the extremities or trunk should be noted. The muscles are inspected and palpated; symmetry, atrophy, fasciculations, and tenderness are noted. Accurate measurement of circumferences of the extremities documents the degree of atrophy. Fasciculations may be evident in lower motor neuron disease but are not pathognomonic. Muscle tenderness is frequently present in a patient with myositis. The consistency of the muscle may be fibrous or rubbery in myopathies or myositides. A prolonged depression occurs when a myotonic muscle (thenar eminence or tongue) is briskly tapped.

The hand grip of a myotonic is slow to relax. Muscle tone, the resistance to passive movement, is characterized by flaccidity in lower motor neuron disease, knife-clasp spasticity or simple increase in tone with an upper motor neuron lesion, and rigidity (often of the cogwheel type) in certain extrapyramidal diseases, such as parkinsonism.

Involuntary movements

Extrapyramidal diseases. The involuntary movements associated with disease of the basal ganglia occur mainly at rest, in contrast to the intention tremor of cerebellar disease. These involuntary movements are invariably increased by emotional stress and disappear during sleep.

Parkinsonism is characterized by a resting rhythmic tremor affecting the extremities, particularly distal parts, and, in the hands, by a pill-rolling quality. Cogwheel rigidity and bradykinesis are other features of the parkinsonian syndrome. Akathisia, the inability to sit or stand still, may be seen in this condition.

Athetosis is manifested by slow, writhing, twisting movements affecting predominantly the distal portions of the extremities; associated similar movements of the face cause grimacing. Spasticity is present more often than is hypotonicity. It is usually due to anoxia at birth, kernicterus, or some other congenital defect.

Chorea is characterized by rapid, irregular, asymmetrical jerks of the extremities. The movements are purposeless but may be turned into semipurposeful movements. Hypotonicity is usually present. In childhood, Syndenham's chorea is usually a manifestation of rheumatic fever; in adult life, the movements are signs of Huntington's chorea or senile diseases.

Dystonia musculorum deformans or torsion spasm is manifested by slow, writhing torsions of the trunk and the pelvic and shoulder girdles. Scoliosis and lordosis are common.

Hemiballism is characterized by unilateral violent, flail-like movements of the extremities. The patient appears to be trying to throw his extremities away from his trunk. A lesion, usually vascular, of the subthalamic nucleus causes this condition.

Buccal lingual dyskinesias are choreiform movements of the head and neck, mouth, jaw, and tongue often associated with levodopa toxicity or psychotropic therapy.

Paroxysmal dystonic choreoathetosis is a familial disease; the bursts of activity last from minutes to hours, recurring several times daily. Paroxysmal kinesigenic choreoathetosis, as the name implies, is precipitated by voluntary activity and, thus, occurs frequently (100 times a day).

Diseases of the liver and brain. Wilson's disease is manifested by one or a combination of irregular resting or intention tremors or choreoathetoid movements. The basal ganglia, the cerebellum, and the cerebral cortex are implicated in this disease.

Asterixis is a flapping motion of the hands, demonstrated with the hands and arms extended. It is characteristic of impending hepatic coma.

Tics (habit spasms). Tics are sudden, repetitive, irregular muscle contractions. They usually consist of grimacing, blinking, or other facial movements; twisting of the head and neck; or shrugging of the shoulders.

Torticollis, the involuntary turning of the head to one side, may be the first sign of dystonia musculorum deformans or a fragment of similar mechanisms.

Gilles de la Tourette's disease is manifested by multiple tics and coprolalia.

Other movement disorders. Restless legs syndrome is a nocturnal phenomenon wherein peculiar sensations—cramp-like, paresthesia, vague pain—of the lower extremities evoke their restlessness.

Cerebellar outflow tremor, rarely seen with lesions affecting the pathways of the dentate nucleus or the brachium conjunctivum, are severe, coarse, rhythmic tremors occurring almost continuously at rest static against gravity, and on intention.

Myoclonus is a sudden brief jerk or contraction of a muscle or muscle groups. The activity may be almost imperceptible, or it may be gross, as when the entire body is affected. Myoclonic activity may arise from disease or dysfunction of any part of the central nervous system. It may occur spontaneously or may be evoked by activity (intention myoclonus). Cerebral ischemia and Creutzfeldt-Jakob disease are among the common causes of myoclonus.

Essential tremor affects the upper extremities and is both postural with the arms outstretched, and present on action. It is sometimes hereditary. Alcohol and propranolol ameliorate the tremor.

Epilepsia partialis continua is manifested by continuous clonic movements of a portion of one extremity—for example, the thumb—lasting for hours or days.

Status epilepticus is rarely a difficult diagnostic problem, except for those rare cases of petit mal status, wherein slow, clonic movements of the trunk and upper extremities occur.

Coordination examination. Coordination may be divided into equilibratory functions and nonequilibratory functions.

Equilibratory functions. These functions are noted by observing the patient stand and walk. A tendency to drift to one side, as in ipsilateral cerebellar disease, may be exaggerated by having the patient walk with his eyes closed or in tandem fashion, touching the heel of one foot to the toe of the other. The associated movements of arm swing may be lost in ipsilateral cerebellar or contralateral extrapyramidal or pyramidal tract disease. The patient should be asked to stand erect with his feet together, first with his eyes open and then with his eyes closed. Romberg's sign is an inability to maintain an erect posture with the eyes closed and is usually indicative of posterior column disease of the spinal cord, but the sign may also be present with a cerebellar lesion. Impairment of truncal equilibrium may be noted by the awkward manner in which the patient arises from a supine position or gets up from or sits down in a chair. These manifestations of truncal ataxia suggest midline cerebellar disease. Impairment of postural reflexes in Parkinson's disease is evident by the *en bloc* movements and associated difficulties in changing position.

Nonequilibratory functions. Coordination of the extremities is tested by having the patient touch the heel of one foot to the knee of the other leg and then run the heel down the shin of the leg, first with his eyes open and then with his eyes closed. The patient is asked to touch his nose and then the examiner's finger, first with his eyes open and again with his eyes closed. The ability to alternate movements rapidly is tested by having him tap his foot on the floor or alternately pat his thigh with his palm and then with the dorsum of his hand. A defect in rapid alternating movements is called dysdiadochokinesis. Rebound phenomenon occurs with the inability to check a movement quickly. This phenomenon may be tested by suddenly and without warning releasing an extremity that has been forcefully restrained. Fine skills are noted by observing the patient write and button his clothes.

Defects in any of the above coordinative functions suggest ipsilateral cerebellar disease. Coordination is also impaired in extrapyramidal disease, but the intention tremor on heel-to-knee and finger-to-nose tests of cerebellar disease is in contrast to the resting tremor of Parkinson's disease. Rebound phenomenon is seen with cerebellar disease but not with Parkinson's disease. Ataxia may also be caused by position-sense impairment or weakness, and one must always note whether the degree of ataxia is commensurate with the weakness or out of proportion to it.

Signs of cerebellar or cerebellar pathway disease. Defective equilibrium and posture are associated with tendencies to deviate toward the side of the lesion. Associated movements are impaired on the affected side. Ipsilateral lack of coordination is manifested by ataxia of the extremities, with intention tremor, dysmetria, past pointing, dysdiadochokinesis, and rebound phenomenon. There is ipsilateral decrease in muscle tone, and pendular reflexes may result. Fatigability and slowness of movement are common. Dysarthria, especially of the scanning (staccato) type, and nystagmus may be present.

Gait disturbances

Neurogenic alterations of gait. Upper motor neuron disease is characterized by a spastic gait. In a hemiplegic, the lower extremity is extended and circumducted while walking. In paraparesis of spinal cord disease, the gait is stiff legged and wide based. In paraparesis of cerebral palsy (diplegia), adductor spasm causes a scissors gait, in which extended lower extremities are alternately crossed.

Lower motor neuron disease causes a steppage gait. The leg of the flaccid foot is raised higher than usual, and the foot is slapped down to prevent stumbling over the toe.

Diseases of the basal ganglia impair movement. In parkinsonism, the gait is characterized by shuffling, small steps, and festination—that is, a tendency to accelerate. Choreoathetotic gait is intermittently irregular and jerking. Dystonic gait is characterized by pelvic and truncal torsion. In Wilson's disease, both cerebellar ataxia and extrapyramidal features may be present.

Cerebellar disease is characterized by a staggering gait, with a tendency to fall toward the site of the lesion.

Proprioceptive defect, particularly when due to disease of the posterior columns of the spinal cord, is manifested by an ataxic, wide-based gait that is worse at night or with the eyes closed.

Gait apraxia is the inability to walk, in spite of intact motor power and coordination. The patient does not know what to do with his feet; they seem to be glued to the floor. The defect involves cortical motor integration; therefore, the patient may be unable to perform other complex tasks with his lower extremities—for example, draw a figure eight with his foot.

Gait disturbances not associated with neurological disease. A limping gait may be due to pain or an orthopaedic defect of the leg, low back, or hip. A mincing gait is often seen in patients with spinal rheumatoid arthritis and in senile patients. A waddling gait is associated with bilateral dislocations of the hip and with muscular dystrophy.

The gait of hysteria is bizarre and variable. The disability is often so great that, if the disturbance were organic, one would expect the patient to fall frequently, but the contrary is the case. Astasia-abasia is the inability to stand or walk in spite of adequate muscle strength and coordination.

Sensory examination. This portion of the examination is often the most difficult and frustrating. Both patient and examiner must be alert and cooperative. Inasmuch as it is not practical to stimulate every square centimeter of the body, the examiner must have an idea of the location of the neurological lesion for which he is searching. Only gross lesions are found by asking the patient to differentiate pain from touch sensations. In almost all instances one must ask the patient to differentiate a stimulus applied to a normal portion of the body from the same stimulus applied to a portion of the body that is presumably affected. Thus, in searching for a peripheral nerve defect, the examiner asks the patient to compare a stimulus in the area of presumed deficit with a similar stimulus over the opposite extremity. When searching for polyneuropathy manifested by distal sensory impairment, one asks the patient to compare the sensation over the toes and feet or fingers and hands with a similar sensation over the more proximal portions of the extremity. In the search for a spinal level, the examiner asks the patient to compare a stimulus below the presumptive sensory level with a stimulus above that level. When dealing with an intracranial lesion, one asks the patient to compare a sensation over the affected side of the body with a similar sensation over the presumably unaffected side.

During all sensory testing, it is preferable that the patient's eyes be closed. Superficial touch sensation is examined by means of a wisp of cotton, superficial pain by a pin or a pinwheel. Sensitivity to temperature may be tested by using test tubes containing hot and cold water; if test tubes are not readily available, the handle of the reflex hammer may be used. In an attempt to quantitate the degree of sensory impairment, one may ask the patient to estimate the degree of impaired sensation as a percentage of the 100 per cent normal stimulus. Inconsistencies in the patient's response and minor impairments—for example, "90 per cent of normal"—can usually be ignored. Vibration sense is evaluated by means of a tuning fork, preferably one with a frequency of 236 cycles a second, placed on bony prominences of the extremities. Position sense is examined by passively and slowly moving the distal phalanx of the patient's finger or toe, asking him to indicate promptly the direction of movement. The examiner should take care that pressure on the skin of the finger or toe cannot be used by the patient in interpreting the direction of movement; this precaution is best taken by grasping the sides of the digit. Deep pain can be tested by squeezing the Achilles tendon or by hyperflexing the distal phalanx of a finger or toe.

Vibration, position, and deep pain sensations are carried by the posterior columns of the spinal cord, whereas superficial pain, touch, and temperature sensations are carried by the spinothalamic tracts. Any modality may be impaired by a lesion of its pathway from the peripheral nerve through the spinal cord and brain stem to the thalamus and parietal lobe.

Fine discriminatory sensations require the cerebral cortex for interpretation. In cerebral defects, especially defects of the parietal lobe, extinction of the stimulus on the opposite side of the body may occur when the right and left sides of the body are simultaneously stimulated by touch or pin pricks with the patient's eyes closed. Two-point discrimination is tested by simultaneously applying two stimuli in close proximity and asking the patient whether he feels one or two points; this discrimination is best in the fingers. Stereognosis is tested by asking the patient, with his eyes closed, to identify familiar objects placed in his hand. One tests graphesthesia by asking the patient to recognize letters or numbers written on his skin. The patient may be asked to differentiate the textures of cotton, silk, and wool. It is obvious that defects of these cortical sensory phenomena do not implicate the cortex or cerebrum if more peripheral sensory pathways are affected.

Examination of reflexes. Again, one must compare symmetrical areas and apply the stimulus with equal intensity to relaxed extremities.

Tendon and periosteal reflexes are elicited by tapping the tendon or the bony prominence associated with a specific muscle. Contraction of the muscle may be graded from slight to hyperactive—or 1, 2, 3, or 4 plus. In the upper extremities, the reflexes most commonly tested are the biceps (C5-6), triceps (C6,7,8), radial (C5-6), and ulnar (C6-7). In the lower extremities, the patellar (L2,3,4) and the Achilles (S1-2) tendons are tapped. Ankle clonus may be elicited by briskly dorsiflexing the foot and maintaining sustained pressure. Clonus is a manifestation of hyperreflexia. Hyperreflexia is seen in upper motor neuron disease, and hyporeflexia is a manifestation of lower motor neuron disease or myopathy. These reflex alterations are not, in themselves, pathognomonic of disease unless striking asymmetry is present.

The superficial reflexes are tested by stroking the skin with a semisharp object. The four quadrants of the abdomen should be tested (D7,8,9 upper; D11-12 lower). The cremasteric reflex (D12-L1) is elicited by stroking the medial aspect of the thigh. Stimulation of the perianal area evokes the anal reflex (S2,3,4,5)—that is, contraction of the anal sphincter.

Certain pathological reflexes are indicative of pyramidal tract disease. Babinski's sign is elicited by stroking the lateral aspect of the sole from the arch to and across the ball of the foot with a semisharp object. Flexion of the toes is the normal response; dorsiflexion of the big toe and spread of the other toes are the abnormal responses. The Chaddock sign (stroking the lateral aspect of the dorsum of the foot), the Oppenheim sign (forcefully stroking the anterior surface of the shin), and the Gordin sign (squeezing the calf muscle) show toe responses like that of Babinski's sign but are not pathognomonic of upper motor neuron diseases, as is Babinski's sign. Hoffmann's sign is elicited by forcefully flicking downward the distal portion of the patient's middle finger. In a positive response, flexion and adduction of the thumb occur. An alternate method of obtaining the same response, by abruptly tapping the volar surface of the distal portion of the middle finger, is Tromner's sign. Both the Hoffmann and the Tromner signs have the same significance as tendon reflex hyperactivity.

Examination of the autonomic nervous system. Observation of the patient often provides valuable information about his autonomic nervous system. Evaluation of vital signs should be part of the general physical examination. Signs of autonomic defects or endocrinopathies may be evident on inspection. Obesity and other alterations of fat metabolism are readily seen. In an examination of the patient's skin, the physician should note its color, temperature, perspiration, pilomotor activity, and texture. Trophic changes of the skin, mucous membranes, hair, and nails, as well as alterations, of the vasomotor tone of the extremities, may give many clues of autonomic dysfunction. Certain diseases of the bones and joints may be of a trophic nature—for example, the Charcot joint of tabes dorsalis. In evaluating cranial nerves, the examiner should look for Horner's syndrome and defects of tearing and of saliva. Determining the function of the urinary bladder may require cystometric examination, but the sphincter tone of the rectum can easily be determined by palpation.

There are many special tests of autonomic function. Most common is the test for localized disturbance in perspiration, performed by sprinkling a starch and iodine powder over the skin; moisture reveals the iodine pigment.

Evaluation of the Child

HISTORY

A child's history is obtained in a manner similar to that outlined for the adult but with different emphasis. A review of systems proves to be less helpful in children. In the child, a past history of trauma, encephalitis, meningitis, or neonatal seizures is particularly important, because these conditions may more seriously effect the developing brain than the brain of an adult. The social history concentrates on environmental factors. The family history must be more thorough than in the evaluation of an adult.

The importance of the prenatal, perinatal, and postnatal history cannot be overemphasized. Was the mother's pregnancy normal, or was there a history of vaginal bleeding? Did the mother experience illness during the pregnancy, and what drugs, if any, were taken by her? Was the pregnancy full-term, or was the delivery premature? Was the labor unusually prolonged or in any other way abnormal? Was the delivery of the infant difficult or in any other way potentially traumatic? Was the infant of good color, and did he cry immediately? The neonatal history should include the weight of the infant.

The assessment of the neurological status of the infant and child is primarily a measurement of the maturation of the nervous system. The developmental history is essential. Figures 1 and 2 indicate milestones in the maturation of a child. The parents may not be aware of all the features in the infant's development, but they can often remember some of the following events.

The infant should begin to lift his head while prone from the time of his birth and lift it well by 4 months of age. He should begin to smile at 2 months of age and laugh, as well as recognize his mother, by 4 months of age. The baby should sit unsupported by 8 months of age and begin to crawl or creep between 10 and 12 months of age. He should wave "bye-bye" at 10 to 11 months of age. At 11 months of age, he should pull himself up to the standing position, and he should begin to walk with support at 1 year. The word "mama" becomes meaningful at 10 months of age, and by 1 year an additional one- to three-word vocabulary should be evident.

There is a wide range of normal, of course, and slow development of one or two features should not be taken as evidence of significant retardation. For example, although the average child walks without assistance soon after 1 year of age, retardation of gait is not considered present before 18 months of age.

In addition to these landmarks, other history during the first year of life may be pertinent. Was the baby colicky, or were there other feeding problems? Did the infant sleep excessively—that is, was he an unusually "good" baby? Or, on the other hand, was evidence of hyperactivity manifested during the first year of life? The course of the patient's symptoms helps to differentiate a static encephalopathy, such as one due to birth injury, from a progressive disease, in which an initial period of normal development precedes the evidence of disease and deterioration.

PHYSICAL EXAMINATION

Even more important than in the adult is the child's general physical examination, for often it reveals the major clue to the diagnosis. For example, the child may exhibit the skin manifestations of a phacomatosis, the skeletal characteristics of mongolism, or the hepatosplenomegaly of a lipidosis.

NEUROLOGICAL EXAMINATION

An essential objective of the neurological examination of the infant is an assessment of the maturity of the patient as related to his chronological peers. Repeated observations are often necessary before drawing conclusions. Tremulousness, for example, may disappear after the hungry child is fed. The patient is often too young for the examiner to conclude that a lesion is static or progressive without reexamination weeks or months later.

The neurological examination of the infant differs from that of the adult in that one must first evaluate those features that least disturb the child and then progress to those parts of the examination that may require restraint. For example, the ophthalmological evaluation is performed early in the neurological evaluation of an adult but last when examining an infant.

Observation of the young child may reveal asymmetries of the face or head, asymmetry of limb size or movement, or abnormal posture of the trunk or head and neck. In performing the neurological examination, one observes the social adaptability and language of the child, his motor activity, his perception, and his postural reactions and reflex activity. These features are outlined in Figures 1 and 2. Other tests, as discussed for the adult, are integrated into this general pattern of examination wherever applicable.

Special reflexes

Moro reflex. This reflex is elicited by a sudden mild extension of the neck or any stimulus that suddenly changes the plane of the supine body. In response to such stimuli, there is extension of the trunk and extension with abduction of the upper and lower extremities, then flexion with adduction of the upper extremities. This reflex is normally present at the time of birth, diminishes by 2 to 3 months of age, and should be absent after 6 months of age.

Tonic neck reflex. Turning of the head to one side when the infant is supine results in extension of the arm and leg of that side, with flexion of the opposite extremities. This reflex, normally present at the time of birth, diminishes after 4 to 6 months of age, but fragments of this reaction may be present during the remainder of the first year.

Traction response. When the infant is pulled up by his hands from the supine position to the sitting position, the degree of flexion of the elbows increases from birth to 5 months of age, at which time the

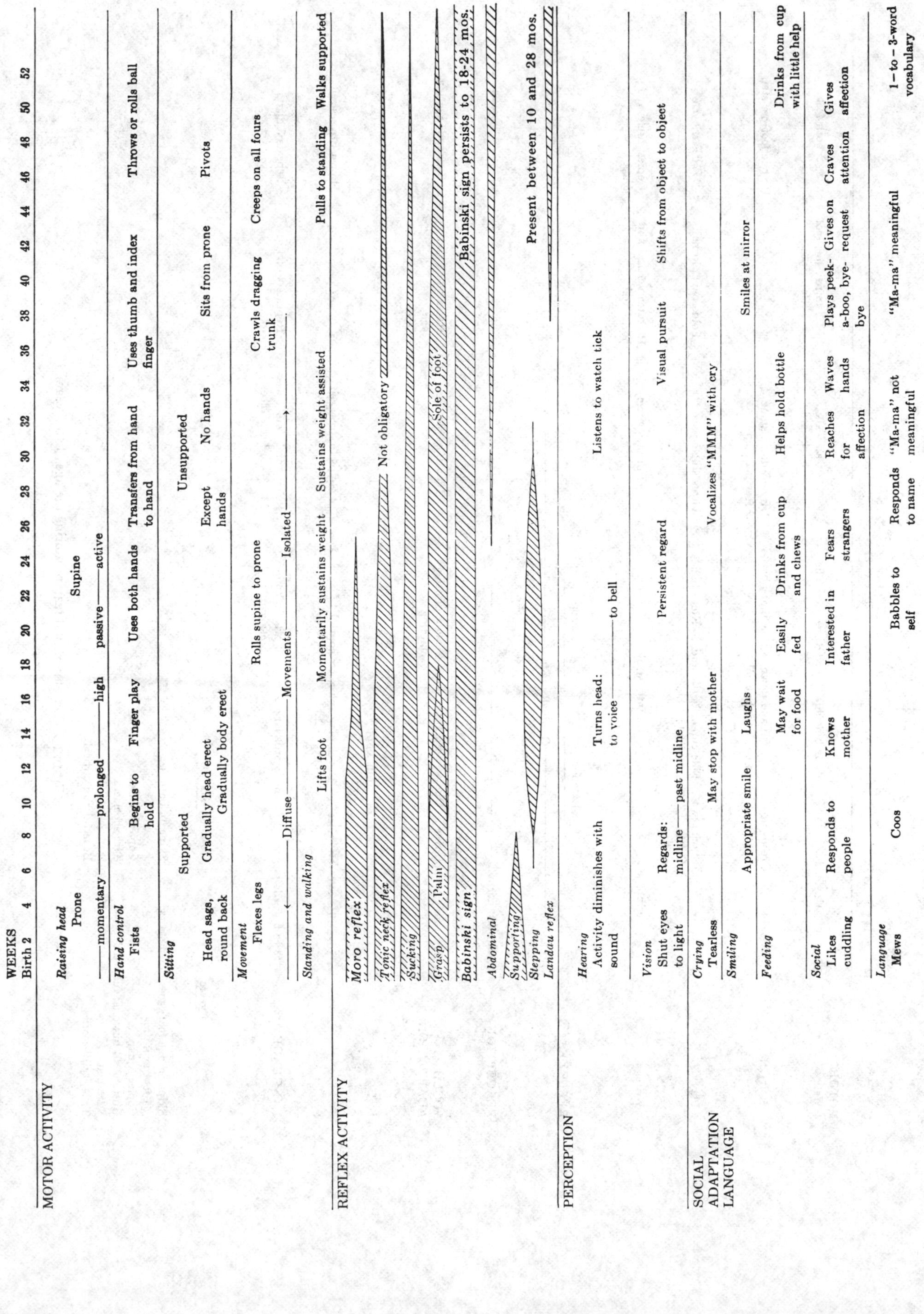

WEEKS: Birth 2 · 4 · 6 · 8 · 10 · 12 · 14 · 16 · 18 · 20 · 22 · 24 · 26 · 28 · 30 · 32 · 34 · 36 · 38 · 40 · 42 · 44 · 46 · 48 · 50 · 52

MOTOR ACTIVITY

Raising head
Prone — momentary ———— prolonged ———— high
Supine — passive ———— active

Hand control
Fists — Begins to hold — Finger play — Uses both hands — Transfers from hand to hand — Uses thumb and index finger — Throws or rolls ball

Sitting
Supported — Gradually head erect — Gradually body erect
Unsupported — Head sags, round back — Except hands — No hands — Sits from prone — Pivots

Movement
Flexes legs — Diffuse — Rolls supine to prone — Movements — Isolated — Crawls dragging trunk — Creeps on all fours

Standing and walking
Lifts foot — Momentarily sustains weight — Sustains weight assisted — Pulls to standing — Walks supported

REFLEX ACTIVITY

Moro reflex
Tonic neck reflex — Not obligatory
Sucking
Grasp — Palm — Sole of foot
Babinski sign — Babinski sign persists to 18–24 mos.
Abdominal
Supporting
Stepping
Landau reflex — Present between 10 and 28 mos.

PERCEPTION

Hearing
Activity diminishes with sound — Turns head: to voice — to bell — Listens to watch tick

Vision
Shut eyes to light — Regards: midline — past midline — Persistent regard — Visual pursuit — Shifts from object to object

SOCIAL ADAPTATION LANGUAGE

Crying
Tearless — May stop with mother — Vocalizes "MMM" with cry

Smiling
Appropriate smile — Laughs — Smiles at mirror

Feeding
May wait for food — Easily fed — Drinks from cup and chews — Helps hold bottle — Drinks from cup with little help

Social
Likes cuddling — Responds to people — Knows mother — Interested in father — Fears strangers — Reaches for affection — Waves hands — Plays peek-a-boo, bye-bye — Gives on request — Craves attention — Gives affection

Language
Mews — Coos — Babbles to self — Responds to name — "Ma-ma" not meaningful — "Ma-ma" meaningful — 1- to 3-word vocabulary

FIGURE 1. Developmental landmarks during the first year of life.

MONTHS

	12	13	14	15	16	17	18	19	20	21	22	23	24	30	36
MOTOR Walk		Unsteady			Runs but falls			Runs, rare falls				Can walk backward		Can tiptoe	Jumps: one foot..........both feet
Stairs	Assisted		Creeps up alone		Up and down alone, but holding		Climbs better			Up and down 2 feet per step					Up one foot per step
Play			Stacks two blocks		Fills cup or bottle and stacks 3 to 4 blocks		Kicks ball			Turns single pages			Folds paper in half		Rides tricycle
Write		Scribbles			Imitates stroke							Imitates circle	Imitates vertical and horizontal		Copies circle and cross
REFLEXES	Landau		Extensor — Plantar — Flexor Gradually fades												
PERCEPTION	Toward normal														
SOCIAL ADAPTATION	Demands by pointing				Obeys commands			Jealous of other children				Identifies pictures	States name and age		Understands sharing
					Feeds self but sloppy										
	Identifies eyes and nose					Developing sphincter control						Helps to dress self		Almost dresses self	
LANGUAGE	3 to 6 words jargon					6+ words jargon		12 words, combines words				"You" and "me"; uses 2 to 3-word sentences	Repeats 2 digits	Repeats 3 digits	

4 years
Skips on one foot; goes down stairs, 1 foot at a time
Copies square
Buttons all buttons; fully toilet-trained
Tells "tall" stories

5 years
Skips on both feet
Copies triangle
Ties shoelaces
Boastful and critical

FIGURE 2. Developmental features during the ages 1 to 5 years.

infant actively assists in the process and maintains good head control.

Sucking reflex. Touching a finger to the infant's lips elicits the sucking reflex. This reflex diminishes after a few months and is absent after 1 year.

Grasp reflex. The infant's hand and fingers flex when the examiner's finger is placed in the palm of the hand; similarly, the foot and toes flex when the examiner's finger is pressed to the ball of the foot. The palmar grasp reflex diminishes after a few months and disappears after 4 months of age, but the flexion reaction of the plantar surface of the foot does not usually disappear until the tenth month.

Plantar reflex. Stimulation of the lateral aspect of the sole of the foot elicits an extension of the big toe (Babinski's sign). This sign may be normally present from the time of birth until 18 months of age or, at the most, 2 years of age.

Abdominal reflex. Contraction of the abdominal wall results from stroking the overlying skin. The abdominal reflex may not be easily elicited until 6 to 12 months of age.

Supporting reflex. With the infant held upright, extension of the legs occurs when the infant's feet touch the table. This reflex, present at birth, ends after 1 to 2 months of age.

Stepping reflex. With the infant held in a position similar to that described for the supporting reflex, stepping movements should be noted between 2 and 6 months of age, and proper walking movements should be evident after 10 to 11 months of age.

Landau reflex. With the infant held prone, he assumes the position of hyperextension of the spine and neck. Flexion of the head in that position results in flexion of the spine and extremities. The reverse phenomena are observed with the patient held supine. The Landau reflex occurs normally between 10 and 28 months of age.

Examination of the head, eyes, and ears. The posterior fontanel should be closed by 6 weeks of age. The anterior fontanel should close between 9 and 18 months of age.

Measurement of the head size is important, particularly serial measurements for evidence of increasing hydrocephalus.

Percussion of the skull may elicit a cracked-pot sound as evidence of suture separation due to increased intracranial pressure.

Transillumination of the skull may aid the diagnosis of hydrocephalus, porencephalic cyst, or subdural hematoma.

Bruits over the eyeballs are commonly heard in infants and young children and should not be considered abnormal.

Eye muscles may be tested by rotating the infant's head and noting the movement of the eyes in the orbits (doll's eye or oculocephalic maneuver). Testing for opticokinetic nystagmus is of aid in evaluation of visual pathways.

Hearing is essential for normal language development and must always be tested.

Movement, posture, and motor tone. Movements are diffuse, rather than isolated, and voluntary movements are not evident until 4 to 6 months of age.

By 9 months of age, certain alterations in motor tone, posture, or use of the extremities can be considered abnormal: (1) Abnormal alteration of muscle tone is manifested by asymmetry of tone, generalized hypotonicity, or generalized hypertonicity. (2) Abnormal posture of the extremities is revealed by persistence of abduction, adduction, flexion, or extension of the arms; persistence of extension or scissoring of the legs; or persistence of fisted hands or other abnormal hand postures. Abnormal postures of the trunk or head and neck are noted by a rounded back when sitting or by the head's sagging forward, tilting, or retracting. Abnormal posture when standing is manifested by the infant's attempting to stand on an unusually narrow base, failing in the attempt to support the body while standing with assistance, or standing on his toes. (3) Abnormality of an arm or hand is revealed by the tendency to avoid use of the extremity, difficulty in retaining a grasped object, persistence of grasp, other impairment of grasp, or maldirection in reaching for an object.

Electroencephalography (EEG)

This topic is discussed in greater detail than are other diagnostic measures not because it is a more useful test in the neurological evaluation of the patient but because it is a test very commonly used by psychiatrists.

In obtaining the electroencephalogram (EEG), 16 electrodes are placed in standardized positions equidistantly over the scalp and additional reference electrodes are placed on the ears and at the vertex. The tracing consists of 8 or 16 channels, each simultaneously printing out the difference in electrical potential transmitted by a pair of electrodes. This electrical activity of the cerebrum represents postsynaptic potentials of apical dendrites in the cerebral cortex. Only the sum of inhibitory and excitatory potentials of large groups of neurons is recorded. Great amplification is required for purposes of recording; a 7-mm. deflection of the recording pen is usually calibrated to correspond to 50 μv. In interpreting a tracing, the electroencephalographer scans the entire page as a single picture, rather than evaluating each individual wave. The interpretation is, therefore, in large part subjective.

ANALYSIS OF THE EEG

In analyzing the EEG, one must consider three major components: (1) The individual waves are evaluated with regard to their frequency, form, and amplitude. (2) Series of waves—that is, their rhythmic qualities—are analyzed. (3) The locations of waves are studied, particularly with regard to differences between one cerebral hemisphere and the other (see Figure 3).

Probably the most important feature of the EEG is the frequency of the electrical activity. The frequencies of an adult record normally range from 8 to 13 hertz (Hz.) alpha (α) rhythm. (One Hz. corresponds to one cycle a second.) Other frequencies are often abnormal. Frequencies of 4 to 7 Hz. are termed theta (θ) activity; less than 4 Hz., delta (δ) activity. Activity faster than α-rhythm—that is, 14 to 30 Hz. of voltage, averaging 20 μv or more—is called beta (β) activity.

The wave forms are normally those of a sinusoidal pattern, although complex forms with faster rhythms superimposed on slow frequencies may also be noted. Fast waves have sharp contours. Cycles less than 1/12 second in duration that are distinct from the background activity and represent abrupt change in electrical potential are spikes and are usually abnormal.

The amplitude of a normal adult EEG is usually moderate—that is, it averages 50 to 75 μv. Considerable variation in voltage may normally occur.

In summary, the cerebral electrical activity of a normal awake adult consists of moderate-voltage sinusoidal waves occurring at 8 to 13 (predominantly 9 to 10) Hz. These waves occur in rhythmic series that form spindle patterns and are seen best over the occipital areas of the head (see Figure 3A). Low-voltage fast activity may also be normal (see Figure 3B).

The normal cerebral electrical activity is altered with changes in the conscious state of the patient and in response to stimuli and varies from childhood to adult life.

EFFECT OF STATE OF CONSCIOUSNESS ON EEG OF ADULTS

The conscious state of the patient has a tremendous influence on the EEG. In an adult, during drowsiness, α-rhythm decreases in amplitude and slightly in frequency, becomes intermittent, and, finally, α-rhythm is gradually replaced by low-voltage activity. This pattern is termed stage 1 sleep (see Figure 4A). With the advent of light sleep (stage 2), θ-activity appears within the low-voltage activity, and intermittent series of 14-Hz. sleep spindles are seen (see Figure 4B). As stage 3 evolves, δ-activity occurs in 20 to 60 per cent of the record, with

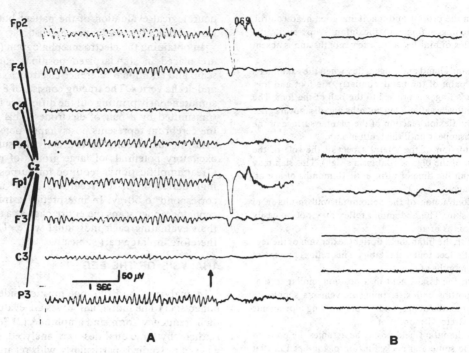

FIGURE 3. *A*, the normal adult EEG. At the *arrow* the eyes of the patient were open: note the "blocking" of α-rhythm. *B*, the normal low-voltage fast adult EEG. The designation of electrode positions is that adopted by the International Federation of Societies for Electroencephalography and Clinical Neurology: F$_p$ (frontal pole), F (frontal), C (central), P (parietal), O (occipital), T (temporal), C$_z$ (vertex), A (ear). Even numbers as subscripts indicate the right hemisphere, odd numbers the left.

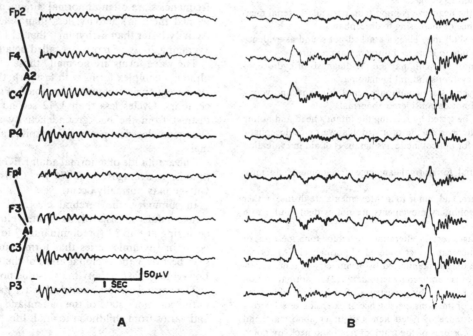

FIGURE 4. *A*, the normal adult drowsy EEG. Note the dropping out of α-rhythm and its replacement by low-voltage activity. *B*, the normal sleeping EEG with θ-activity, 14-per-second sleep spindles, and bilaterally synchronous sharp waves of predominantly central origin (K-complexes).

decreasing amounts of θ-activity, and the frequency of sleep spindles diminishes from 14 to 12 to 10 Hz. In the deepest degree of sleep (stage 4), δ-activity grows slower and of higher amplitude and forms more than 60 per cent of the tracing; sleep spindles no longer occur. Vertex transients are random, sharp waves arising from the central areas of the cortex and are evoked by stimulation during sleep stages 1 and 2. K-

complexes (see Figure 4*B*) are high-voltage waves followed by faster spindle activity, predominantly from the anterior cerebrum, and are evoked by stimulation in sleep stages 2 and 3.

Periods of rapid eye movement (REM) sleep occur at approximately 90-minute intervals during a normal night's sleep (see Figure 5). The EEG pattern of REM sleep is similar to that of stage 1 sleep, with low-voltage activity of mixed fre-

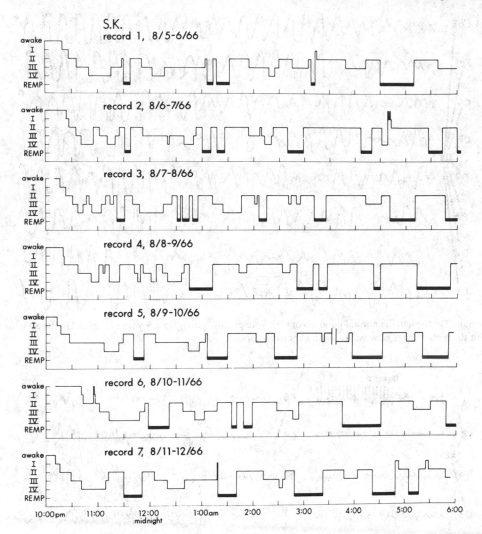

FIGURE 5. The ordinates represent stages of sleep during 7 nights. *REMP*, rapid eye movement periods. (Courtesy of Dr. Elliot D. Weitzman.)

quencies, but, in addition, saw-tooth waves representing eye movement activity are superimposed. Dreaming and inhibition of motor tone throughout the body, except for eye and sphincter muscles, are among the most dramatic events that occur during REM sleep.

RESPONSE TO STIMULI

The response of the cerebral electrical activity to stimuli is routinely tested. The α-rhythm normally disappears during stimuli. The EEG is performed with the patient's eyes closed, and opening of the eyes interrupts α-rhythm. Mental stimulation—asking the patient to perform a complex mathematical task—blocks the α-rhythm. Emotional tension often obliterates α-rhythm, and the normal EEG of an unusually tense person may consist of nothing more than low-voltage fast activity.

Lambda (λ) waves are sharp or saw-tooth waves over the occipital areas and are evoked by visually scanning an object or a picture. MU-rhythm is a series of waves within the 7- to 11-Hz. range that appear as the written letters "M" or "U" over the central areas of the head and is abolished by intended or actual movement, particularly of the contralateral limbs.

During the EEG, hyperventilation is performed for 3 minutes. A build-up of slow activity—decrease in frequency and increase in voltage, more commonly seen in children than in

adults (see Figure 6, *left side*)—may persist for as long as 100 seconds after the cessation of hyperventilation. A relatively low blood sugar and the erect posture increase the response to hyperventilation. The slow activity during hyperventilation is probably due to cerebral vasoconstriction evoked by hypocapnia.

Photic stimulation is attained by means of a bright, flashing stroboscope held close to the patient's closed eyes. A driving response can often be evoked over both occipital areas. This normal response consists of bilaterally symmetrical activity, synchronous with the flash frequencies, usually near or within the α-range (see Figure 7A). Sometimes the evoked response is a subharmonic or a multiple of the flash stimuli. Photic stimulation may evoke a photomyoclonic response characterized by twitches of the face and eyes, with associated muscle artifact in the EEG. This response should not be interpreted as a manifestation of epilepsy.

EEG CHARACTERISTICS OF CHILDREN

In the premature and the newborn. The EEG of a premature child manifests low-voltage, slow activity of 1 to 3 Hz. over the occipitotemporal areas, with superimposed low-voltage, faster activity. These features alternate with long periods of electrical silence. No difference can be discerned between the waking and the sleeping state.

The newborn, while awake, exhibits a pattern similar to that of the

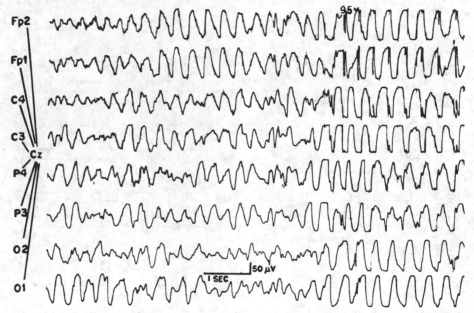

FIGURE 6. Hyperventilation. On the *left*, the normal build-up of high-voltage slow activity in a 9-year-old child. On the *right* the superimposed spike activity, alternating with the high-voltage slow waves, is an abnormal response.

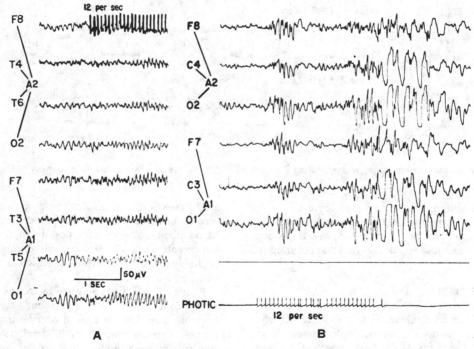

FIGURE 7. Photic stimulation. *A*, the normal response. Photic stimulation has been superimposed on the F[8] recording. Note the change from a slower background pattern to a 12-cycle-per-second rhythm synchronous with the photic flash. *B*, an abnormal response to photic stimulation. Polyspike-and-slow-wave activity is evoked and persists after cessation of the photic stimuli.

premature infant. The most common state in the newborn is that of drowsiness. The EEG of this transitional state consists of θ- and δ-activities, increasing in voltage with age. Activities of 4 to 6 Hz. may be noted over the central areas and are sometimes saw-toothed. These transitional state patterns closely resemble those of REM sleep, and the percentage of time spent in these states decreases as the infant grows older. When the newborn is asleep, the record reveals high-voltage (150 μv) 1- to 3-Hz. activity alternating with relatively low-voltage activity (*tracé alternant*).

During the first year of life. During the first year of life, the waking record shows the gradual development of occipital rhythm, beginning with random low-voltage, slow activity. By 3 to 4 months of age, frequencies of 4 to 6 Hz. are noted and can be interrupted when the eyes are opened. Toward the end of the first year, the activity further increases in frequency.

A great many changes occur in the maturation of sleep activity during the first year of life. By the sixth to the eighth week of age, well-defined sleep spindles (series of 14-Hz. activity) are seen over the frontocentral areas of the head. At 3 to 6 months of age, sharp waves over the central areas of the head occur during light sleep. After 3 to 6 months of age, long series of high-voltage, slow activity are noted during drowsiness; and beyond 6 to 8 months of age, paroxysmal series of high-voltage, slow activity occur during drowsiness, particularly over the central areas of the head. There is little arousal response in the newborn, but after the second month, especially by 6 to 8 months of age, K-complexes are seen and are followed by series of moderate- to high-voltage, slow activity.

After the first year of life. The waking EEG after the first year of life reveals a gradual increase in frequency, especially over the occipital areas. Between 2 and 9 years of age, the background activity is polyrhythmic, with an increasing proportion of frequencies within the α-range as the child grows older (see Figure 8). Waves as slow as 2 Hz. may be seen throughout youth; however, this activity is either of low voltage or occurs as single waves. Between 10 and 16 years of age, stable and dominant frequencies within the adult α-range of 8 to 13 Hz. are seen. Fewer and fewer slow frequencies are noted within the fast rhythms as age advances. Particularly between the age of 8 and 15 years, MU-rhythms often appear.

Drowsy EEG activity in children after the first year of life is characterized first by disorganization of the record. Increases in voltage and in diffuse slow activity are noted with 1- to 3-Hz. frequencies over the posterior portions of the head. The steady, slow activity of drowsiness usually disappears after 6 years of age. Paroxysmal bilaterally synchronous high-voltage, slow activity during drowsiness rarely persists after 15 years of age.

The EEG of children during light sleep reveals intermittent central sharp waves occurring in a bilaterally synchronous fashion. The second stage of sleep is manifested by 14-Hz. sleep spindles. With moderately deep sleep, there is an increase in 4- to 6-Hz. activity and then in 2- to 3-Hz. activity, and 12-Hz. sleep spindles are noted. In deep sleep, very high-voltage, very slow activity is seen without further evidence of spindles or central sharp waves. Continuous slow activity occurs in children after the K-complex of arousal, but such slow activity usually disappears by the fifteenth year or earlier. Between the tenth and the fifteenth years, paroxysmal slow activity may normally follow the K-complex.

ABNORMAL CHARACTERISTICS OF THE EEG

The following features are abnormal only when not accounted for on the basis of youth, a change in the conscious state of the patient, or in response to stimulation.

Frequency. Activity slower than 8 Hz.—that is, θ- or σ-activity, particularly if occurring in series—is abnormal. Generalized slow activity is suggestive of diffuse organic disease or of a metabolic cerebral disturbance. Focal slow activity (see Figure 9) is indicative of underlying organic disease, although small amounts of θ-activity over the bitemporal areas are of doubtful significance. Activity faster than α-rhythm (β-activity) is abnormal if focal, excessive, or of high amplitude. Generalized fast activity is seen in some drug intoxications. Particularly if intermittent, β-activity may be noted in records of patients with convulsive disorders. Focal fast activity is usually indicative of an underlying organic disease that may be epileptogenic.

Voltage. Low-voltage, diffuse slow activity may be a manifestation of the suppression of cerebral electrical activity seen in severe cerebral disease. Low-voltage activity of a focal nature indicates an underlying disease that may be interposed between the cerebral cortex and the electrodes—for example, a subdural hematoma. Activity progressively increasing in amplitude may precede a seizure.

Epileptiform activity. Anterior temporal spike activity is most commonly associated with complex partial, psychomotor, seizures (see Figure 10). Other spike activity or spike-and-wave activity may be indicative of an underlying epileptogenic lesion. Multiple spike foci in children suggest seizure activity or mental or physical retardation. Spikes in children's EEG's may change location from one time to another. Fourteen- and 6-per-second positive spikes (see Figure 11A) may be associated with visceral phenomena or behavioral symptoms but are most often normal variants.

Bilaterally synchronous paroxysmal slow activity is seen in patients with generalized convulsive disorders and in disease or dysfunction of deep midline structures. Generalized nonconvulsive, petit mal, epilepsy is characterized by 3-per-second spike-and-slow-wave bilaterally synchronous paroxysmal bursts (see Figure 12). Spike-and-slow-wave bursts of faster frequencies are often indicative of grand mal epilepsy (see Figure 13).

The determination of EEG abnormality depends on a large

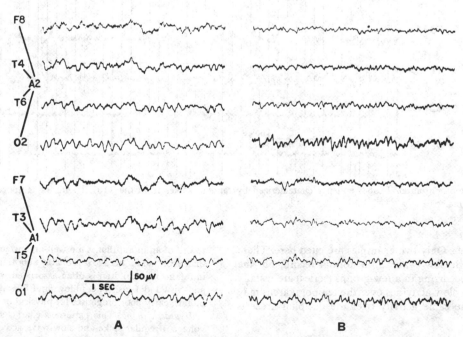

FIGURE 8. *A*, the normal child's EEG, age 3 years. *B*, the normal child's EEG, age 9 years. Note the increase in frequency, but with persistence of scattered and underlying slow activity.

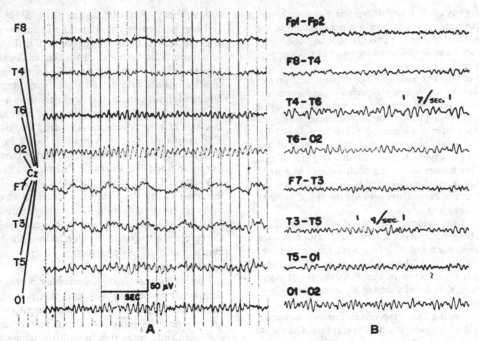

FIGURE 9. *A*, focal 2-cycles-a-second δ-activity from the F7 and T3 electrodes, indicative of a left anterior temporal lobe lesion, in this case a glioblastoma multiforme. *B*, slightly slow activity of 7 cycles a second, predominantly from the T6 electrode, indicative of a right posterior temporal lobe lesion, in this case an infarct.

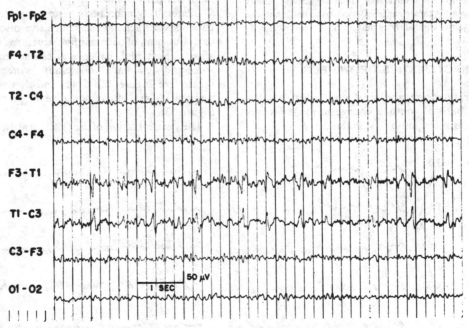

FIGURE 10. Psychomotor (temporal lobe) epilepsy characterized by random spikes from the Tl (left anterior temporal) electrode. Note phase reversals from this area.

number of variables. Only two examples are cited here. There may be many single slow waves in a normal record, but the same slow waves occurring in a few groups (series) are usually abnormal. Slightly slow activities over the temporal areas may be normal, but the same activity over the occipital areas is often abnormal.

Abnormal EEG patterns in the first year of life. Abnormal slow waves, fast activities, and spikes may occur in infants. In addition, the record of an infant that is too well-organized or appears more mature than expected for his age is probably abnormal. Occipital spike activity in infants and children is often associated with seizures, prematurity, and visual defects. The following EEG abnormalities, peculiar to infants, carry poor prognoses for physical or mental development.

Hypsarrhythmia. This pattern is characterized by multifocal high-voltage, irregular spike-and-slow-wave activity occurring on a markedly disorganized background (see Figure 14). This pattern is seen in patients with infantile spasms. The EEG abnormality usually clears

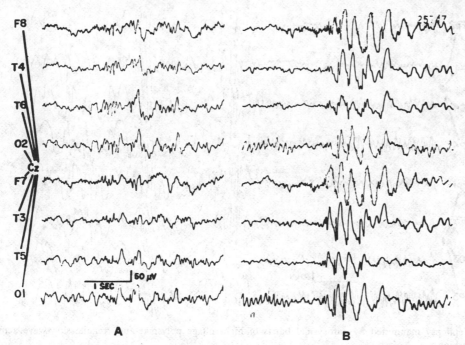

FIGURE 11. *A*, 14-per-second positive spikes seen in a 10-year-old child with behavior disorder and intermittent episodes of abdominal pain. *B*, paroxysmal irregular spike-and-slow-wave bursts occurring in a bilaterally synchronous fashion at approximately 4 cycles per second, seen in another 10-year-old child with sudden paroxysms of abdominal pain (abdominal epilepsy).

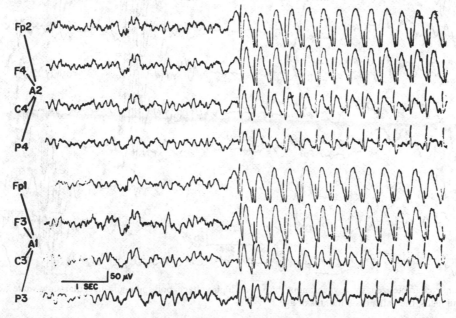

FIGURE 12. Petit mal epilepsy characterized by bilaterally synchronous, 3-cycles-per-second spike-and-slow-wave activity.

after 2 years of age and is rare after 4 years, but physical and mental retardation is almost invariable.

Extreme spindles. These are sleep spindles of higher voltage, occurring in a wider distribution and more continuously than normal sleep spindles. They are usually seen after 6 to 7 months of age and before 5 years of age. This pattern is associated with mental retardation and often with cerebral palsy, particularly of the extrapyramidal type.

DIAGNOSTIC VALUE OF THE EEG

The EEG may be normal in the presence of organic brain disease. This is particularly true if the lesion is deep, small, or

old. For example, the EEG is often normal early in the course of multiple sclerosis, when the lesions are small, scattered, and subcortical. The EEG may be normal in epilepsy because the duration of the record was not long enough to catch intermittent paroxysmal activity. The EEG may be normal because of the attenuation of voltage when recording from the scalp. A tremendous increase of abnormal electrical activity can be seen from electrodes placed directly on the cerebral cortex at the time of surgery, in contrast to simultaneous recordings from the scalp.

EEG patterns are not pathognomonic of specific disease,

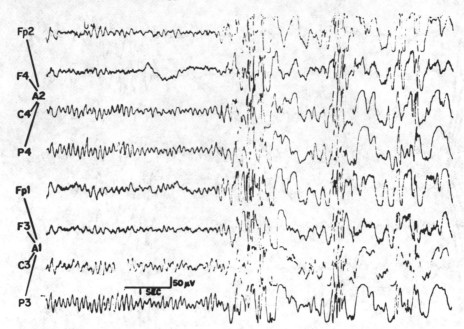

FIGURE 13. Grand mal epilepsy manifested by paroxysmal bursts of high-voltage polyspike-and-irregular-slow-wave activity occurring in a bilaterally synchronous fashion.

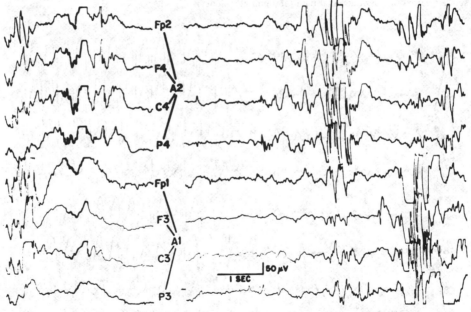

FIGURE 14. Hypsarrhythmia characterized by asynchronous bursts of high-voltage polyspike-and-irregular-slow-wave activity occurring in a haphazard fashion from all leads; the patient is 8 months of age.

with the possible exception of petit mal epilepsy. The response of cerebral electrical activity to injury or disease of any type is relatively limited. The initial response of the EEG to cerebral disease is slow activity or depression of voltage or both. As a rule of thumb, the slowest frequencies correspond to the most severe lesions. Spike or sharp activity is often a manifestation of the sequela of injury. Focal spike activity may indicate that an old or relatively old lesion has become epileptogenic. Focal slow activity is indicative of an underlying anatomical lesion or, less often, a functional defect, but the disease does not always exactly underlie the site of maximum EEG abnormality. A lesion within a cerebral hemisphere may be associated with

slow activity that is reflected predominantly over the occipital lobe in children or over the temporal lobe in adults.

Neoplastic cerebral disease. A cerebral tumor is usually manifested by focal δ-activity (see Figure 9A). If the tumor is deep or causes increased intracranial pressure, diffuse activity, especially frontal intermittent rhythmic delta activity (FIRDA), may occur. This pattern (FIRDA) may be seen with other diseases affecting deep frontal or diencephalic structures. Infratentorial lesions in adults may similarly project FIRDA, whereas such tumors in children are often associated with biooccipital slow activity. The EEG is often normal in slowly growing extracerebral intracranial tumors, such as meningiomas. Sometimes focal δ-activity may be found in a relatively silent area of the brain, giving the clinician the only clue or the major clue to the presence of an underlying neoplasm. On the other hand, an EEG focus is not sufficiently reliable to allow surgery without more definitive study.

Vascular lesions. Cerebral infarction is usually associated with focal slow-wave activity (see Figure 9B). If the cerebral infarct is recent, large, or superficial or if a hematoma is present, focal δ-activity may occur. Scattered small-vessel disease often results in diffuse or scattered θ-activity. A subarachnoid hemorrhage is often associated with diffuse slow activity, but in some instances focal slow waves may be the clue to the site of a ruptured aneurysm. Serial studies are extremely valuable in differentiating neoplastic disease from vascular disease.

Inflammatory disease. Inflammatory diseases affecting the cerebrum as a whole, such as meningitis and encephalitis, usually manifest diffuse slow activity (see Figure 15A), with occasional focal qualities. An abscess, on the other hand, causes high-voltage focal δ-activity. In children, the EEG is useful in differentiating encephalitis associated with convulsive seizures from benign febrile seizures; the EEG is usually normal in benign febrile seizures, but it may take 2 or 3 days for the postictal changes to clear. Serial studies may be helpful in evaluating meningitis of children; if improvement in the EEG does not occur after 2 weeks, one should suspect the development of sinus thrombosis, subdural empyema, or subdural effusion. Subacute sclerosing panencephalitis is often characterized by an unusual EEG pattern of sharp and slow-wave complexes occurring periodically every 2 to 8 seconds on a background pattern of abnormally slow activity. In patients with Creutzfeldt-Jakob disease, the EEG rapidly evolves from diffuse slow activity to generalized spike or sharp activity, occurring characteristically in periodic fashion at about 1-second intervals. In the early stages of herpes simplex encephalitis, pseudoperiodic lateralized epileptiform discharges (PLEDS) occur from a temporal or frontotemporal area with a background pattern of diffuse slow activity. Periodic discharges, whether generalized or PLEDS, may also occur in a variety of other diseases, particularly vascular and traumatic diseases.

Cerebral trauma. Injury to the brain may produce focal or diffuse EEG abnormality (see Figure 15B) and sometimes paroxysmal slow activity. The paroxysmal slow activity may be due to the shearing effect of the brain on its pedestal, the brain stem, with associated dysfunction of the diencephalon. In children, the response of the EEG to trauma is more severe than in an adult, but the return to normal is faster. A comatose patient manifesting waking α-rhythm or sleep spindles probably has severe brain stem injury, with its concomitant poor prognosis. Diffuse slow activity soon after severe cerebral trauma may obscure focal slow activity overlying an area of contusion. Focal depression of amplitude in a patient with head trauma raises the suspicion of an underlying subdural hematoma. Because a spike focus is usually the result of an old injury, such a focus seen on the day of the cerebral trauma or a few days later suggests that the focus is not related to the recent trauma. The incidence of posttraumatic epilepsy in those patients who develop a persistent spike focus after a closed-head injury is estimated to be 10 to 15 per cent.

Metabolic or degenerative diseases. These illnesses usually cause diffuse slow activity in the EEG. Hepatic and other encephalopathies are manifested by bilaterally synchronous slow waves predominant over the anterior cerebrum, often accompanied by sharp and slow-wave forms called triphasic waves. The EEG is not a precise guide to the activity or severity of metabolic cerebral disease, because clinical changes often precede changes in the EEG. On the other hand, the occurrence of triphasic activity and burst suppression patterns correlate well with depression of consciousness.

Drugs and toxic substances. Toxins have a nonspecific effect on the EEG, causing either diffuse slow activity or diffuse fast activity or sometimes both. The drugs that may cause fast activity in the EEG are the sedatives (barbiturates, chloral hydrate, glutathimide), minor tranquilizers (meprobamate, chlordiazepoxide, diazepam), tricyclic antidepressants, and stimulants (amphetamine). The anticonvulsants usually have

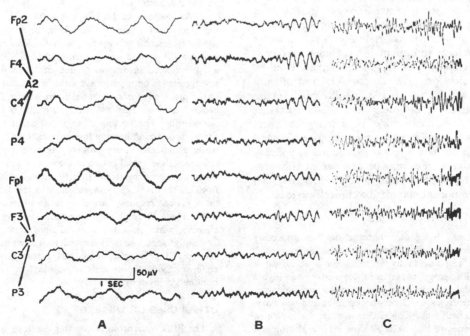

FIGURE 15. A, diffuse moderate- to high-voltage very slow (δ) activity seen in a patient with severe encephalitis. B, diffuse θ-activity seen in a patient soon after cerebral trauma. C, diffuse fast (β) activity seen in a patient with barbiturate intoxication.

little effect on the background pattern of the EEG, but primidone may be associated with either fast or slow activity. Anesthetic agents induce fast activity before the slow activity associated with unconsciousness. The phenothiazine derivatives may cause fast activity at low dosages but, as with most major tranquilizers and antidepressants, usually evoke slow activity, and these drugs also potentiate EEG and clinical seizure activity in susceptible persons. Analgesics, narcotics, and hallucinogens have little effect on the EEG, unless consciousness is depressed or an organic mental disorder is evoked. Other drugs and noxious agents, if they affect the EEG, do so by evoking slow activity. The patient in deep coma with diffuse fast activity in the EEG raises the strong suspicion of barbiturate narcosis (see Figure 15C). With a stuporous patient who has been taking anticonvulsant medication, the EEG helps to differentiate subclinical—that is, electrical—status epilepticus, manifested by almost continuous paroxysmal activity, from drug intoxication, with resultant diffuse fast or slow activity.

Other extracerebral factors may change the EEG, particularly in children. Alterations in electrolytes and fluid balance (water intoxication) and endocrine disturbances are all associated with diffuse slow activity in the EEG. In children, mild fever, stress of surgery, and systemic illness, especially leukemia, often cause diffuse slow activity.

Epilepsy. The EEG is of greatest value in epilepsy. After the history, the EEG is the most important factor in the diagnosis of epilepsy. The classical characteristics are paroxysmal abnormality or focal spike abnormality. The EEG is most often abnormal in generalized nonconvulsive, petit mal, epilepsy; almost all such cases reveal an abnormal EEG before treatment. The EEG may be normal in from 30 to 50 per cent of other forms of epilepsy during the interictal period. The percentage of records that reveal abnormalities in epileptic patients depends to a great extent on the EEG laboratory, because abnormalities are found in a greater percentage of patients who have had tracings of long duration or repeated tracings and who have been recorded during drowsiness and light sleep. Generalized nonconvulsive, petit mal, epileptic activity (see Figure 12) is characterized by generalized bilaterally synchronous, symmetrical 3-per-second spike-and-wave bursts. Petit mal variant is an EEG pattern of spike-and-wave bursts slower than 3 cycles per second; it is associated with minor motor seizures that usually have an organic basis. Generalized convulsive, grand mal, epilepsy (see Figure 13) is manifested by diffuse paroxysmal slow or spike activities or, most often, a combination of the two; this activity is bilaterally synchronous. Focal or partial convulsive disorders reveal focal spikes or sharp waves, often associated with slow activity; the most common example is a spike focus over an anterior temporal lobe in patients with partial complex, psychomotor, epilepsy (see Figure 10). Partial seizures may become secondarily generalized when focal discharges lead to diffuse paroxysmal activity; the focal component may not be clinically evident.

ACTIVATION AND OTHER TECHNIQUES

Certain techniques may bring out abnormalities not previously evident or may exaggerate abnormalities noted in the resting record.

Hyperventilation. A response to hyperventilation is abnormal if spikes are associated with paroxysmal series of slow activity (see Figure 6, *right side*) or if a focal spike or focal slow-wave pattern is evoked. Hyperventilation frequently evokes 3-per-second spike-and-wave paroxysms in patients with petit mal epilepsy. On the other hand, even an unusually prolonged series of high-voltage, slow activity during and after hyperventilation is of indeterminate significance.

Photic stimulation. The response to photic stimulation is considered abnormal if bilaterally synchronous or focal paroxysmal spike-and-slow-wave activity is evoked or if suppression of the normal driving response occurs over one hemisphere. Brief paroxysmal series during photic stimulation are of equivocal significance, but paroxysmal activity can be considered definitely abnormal if the response persists after the cessation of the photic stimuli; this is the photoconvulsive response (see Figure 7B).

Metrazol activation. Pentylenetetrazol (Metrazol) activation, either with or without photic stimulation, is of value only if a focal EEG abnormality is demonstrated, because the normal threshold for convulsion may be unusually low, and bilaterally synchronous paroxysmal activity may be evoked in both normal and epileptic persons. Metrazol activation is also of some value in differentiating hysterical seizures from true epilepsy; the test can be used to precipitate a seizure and allow first-hand observation under EEG and video control. Because of its limited value and danger, this form of activation is rarely used.

Special electrode placements. Epileptogenic activity is often buried within the medial anterior temporal lobe, relatively far from scalp electrodes. Nasopharyngeal electrodes or, less often used, sphenoidal electrodes may be placed much closer to the anterior temporal lobes and thus pick up electrical abnormality that otherwise may be too attenuated to be observed by means of standard electrodes.

In patients being evaluated for surgical treatment of refractory seizures, electrodes may be implanted in the brain. Recordings may be carried out for hours or days in an attempt to precisely define the site and extent of the epileptogenic tissue.

Intracarotid Amytal. This technique is used in the study of patients before surgical resection of an epileptic focus. The test is valuable in establishing the side of cerebral dominance and in confirming the site of primary epileptogenic focus. Intracarotid amobarbital (Amytal) injected in a patient who manifests bilateral seizure activity causes obliteration of that activity in both hemispheres if its primary site of origin is in the hemisphere ipsilateral to the injection, but only the epileptogenic activity on the side of injection is obliterated if the primary focus is in the contralateral hemisphere.

Carotid compression. Carotid compression under EEG, electrocardiographic, and blood pressure controls has been used to establish the site of major arterial stenosis or occlusion. Compression of a normal carotid artery in the presence of occlusion of the opposite carotid artery or disease of the vertebrobasilar arteries usually evokes diffuse slow activity in the EEG. The dangers of the test generally outweigh its limited diagnostic value.

Evoked potentials. Linking the EEG to a computer that extracts repeated stimulus-related events from the background activity permits the determination of evoked potentials. This technique is applied to visual, auditory, and somatosensory stimuli. Visually evoked potentials are diminished in amplitude and of longer latency when there is involvement of optic pathways within a diseased hemisphere, especially in the presence of homonymous hemianopsia. Impairment of visually evoked potentials may be the only evidence of a past bout of retrobulbar neuritis. The finding of impaired auditory-evoked potentials is useful in detecting hearing loss in infants and in other uncooperative patients. Somatosensory-evoked potentials are carried by the dorsal columns of the spinal cord and the medial lemnisci of the brain stem. Potentials occurring in the first 10 milliseconds after a stimulus arise from the brain stem. Abnormalities in the latency or amplitude of those evoked responses are clues to disturbances of brain stem pathways. These findings may be present in diseases, such as multiple sclerosis, when no other residual signs exist. Visually evoked and, especially, somatosensory-evoked responses may be of higher than normal voltage in epileptic patients, particularly in cases of myoclonic epilepsy. Evoked potentials are normal in patients with hysterical blindness or hysterical sensory loss.

OTHER USES OF THE EEG

The EEG is useful in monitoring depth of anesthesia and has been used to note changes in cerebral electrical activity during cardiac and carotid surgery. Depth electrode recordings from nuclear structures within the brain are well-recognized techniques in the study of brain physiology in lower animals and have been used to limited degrees in humans. Computerized frequency analysis of the EEG and computerized topography of the EEG for pictorial display of abnormal cerebral activities are additional research tools.

The same techniques of monitoring astronauts' body functions by telemetry have been used to monitor patients with convulsive disorders. Rarely occurring abnormal EEG discharges can be found that are not otherwise revealed during standard EEG recording. Using telemetry while observing the patient directly or by videotape for a prolonged period of time as he moves about has been valuable in differentiating psychomotor epilepsy from hysterical seizures.

The EEG is an important research tool. It has been valuable in the study of the 24-hour sleep-wake cycle. Patients who have primary depression exhibit a shorter time between the onset of sleep and the first REM period than do patients with reactive depression. Because penile erection is an almost invariable phenomenon during REM sleep, this observation eliminates organic causes of sexual impotency in differential diagnosis. Polygraphic recordings, coupled with frequent blood sampling, have determined temporal episodic patterns for neuroendocrine secretions. In female patients with anorexia nervosa and amenorrhea, a prepubertal pattern of luteinizing hormone secretion has been found.

The determination of brain death has been necessary to permit the use of organs for transplantation and for other medicolegal purposes. With clinical neurological criteria of brain death, the complete absence of EEG activity over a defined period of time is part of the determination. Specific guidelines for EEG recording under these circumstances must be followed to exclude technical causes of a seemingly flat tracing. Extreme care must be taken to exclude such causes of a flat EEG as metabolic encephalopathy, especially the toxic encephalopathies associated with severe barbiturate narcosis and other drug narcoses.

ABNORMAL EEG'S IN NORMAL PEOPLE

What percentage of the normal population have abnormal EEG's? Most electroencephalographers agree on a figure of 10 to 15 per cent.

The difference in statistics is due in large part to differences in the interpretation of those EEG's that lie on the borderline of normal—that is, diffuse slightly fast and diffuse slightly slow activity. Those so-called normal people who have unequivocally abnormal EEG's probably experienced, at some time in their lives, a subclinical disease or injury that caused persistent cerebral electrical changes—for example, birth trauma without obvious signs or encephalitis manifested by no more than a headache and a common cold.

ARTIFACTS

It may seem to be a simple task to analyze the EEG with respect to its wave form, frequency, and voltage, relating these factors as they occur in rhythms over the two hemispheres. Unfortunately, because of the great amplification of electrical activity (50 million times), artifacts are frequently present and form a major pitfall in the interpretation of the EEG. Examples of artifacts are seen in Figures 16 and 17. Muscle contraction and movement cause a great variety of artifacts (see Figure 16A) but are usually easily distinguished. Swallowing may cause a paroxysmal burst of muscle spikes (see Figure 16B). A defective electrode may cause artifacts resembling focal spikes or focal slow activity (see Figure 16C). The electrocardiogram, when superimposed on the EEG, may sometimes simulate spike-and-wave patterns (see Figure 17A). The almost imperceptible tremor of parkinsonism may cause paroxysmal spike-and-slow-wave artifact (see Figure 17B). Eye movement is a common source of artifacts that need not be limited to the bifrontal areas (see Figure 3A).

In summary, except in epilepsy, the EEG is usually not a definitive test; but, then, few tests are. The EEG should be used as any other laboratory tool and judged only in association with all other factors in the clinical evaluation of the patient in order to establish as wide a base as possible for appropriate diagnosis and treatment.

EEG IN PSYCHIATRY

The EEG is a relatively crude method used to record the sum effect of the electrical activity of millions of neurons. It is

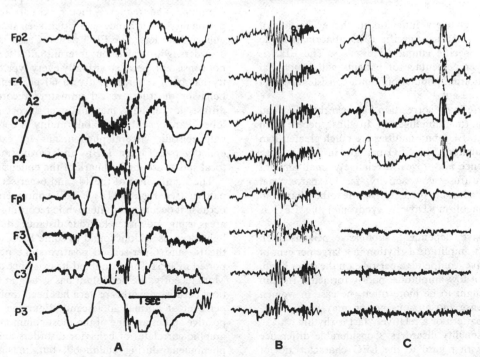

FIGURE 16. Artifacts. *A*, a combination of movement and muscle artifact manifested by high-voltage irregular slow waves and very fast activity, respectively. *B*, swallowing artifact, causing paroxysmal series of spikes followed by lower voltage very rapid activity. *C*, right ear electrode artifact, producing a random irregular slow wave, a random spike, and an irregular spike-and-slow-wave complex.

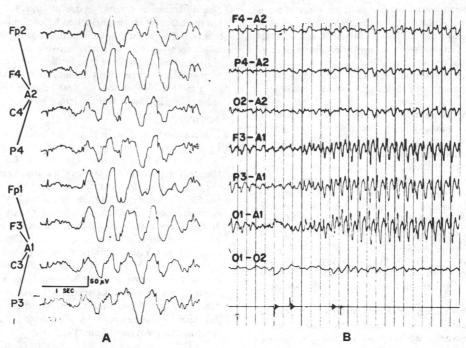

FIGURE 17. *A*, electrocardiographic spike artifact superimposed on the normal high-voltage slow activity evoked by hyperventilation in a child, causing an irregular spike-and-slow-wave pattern. *B*, a burst of spike-and-slow-wave activity occurring at a rate of 5 to 6 cycles a second, seen in a patient with parkinsonism and an almost imperceptible tremor.

too much to ask this test to measure psychological phenomena that represent the highest integrative function of the brain. The normal EEG patterns are best recorded when the cortex is least integrated—that is, when the patient is resting comfortably with his eyes closed and his mind unstimulated. Activation of high cerebral function tends to disrupt the well-formed EEG pattern.

The EEG is of relatively little aid in the evaluation of psychological illness, because specific EEG abnormalities do not correlate with specific emotional diseases. The EEG is abnormal in a larger percentage of patients with emotional illness than in the normal population, but a consistent type of abnormality is not present.

Intelligence. There is no correlation between the EEG and normal or above-normal intelligence. In those people with intellectual deficits, EEG abnormalities are much greater than in the normal population. The EEG patterns in persons with subnormal intelligence may reveal a relatively small amount of α-rhythm and diffuse slow activity; fast or paroxysmal abnormalities may also be present. On the other hand, in uncomplicated mongolism (Down's syndrome) the EEG is usually normal.

Personality. Passive, dependent, submissive persons often show relatively high-amplitude α-rhythm in a large per cent of the record. Aggressive, competitive persons, on the other hand, often have EEG's of low-amplitude, poorly formed α-rhythm (this pattern is thought to be more often the case in women than in men). A tense and anxious person may have a low-voltage, fast EEG pattern or a relatively fast α-rhythm.

Behavior or personality disorders. Considerable difference of opinion exists with regard to the EEG characteristics of persons with behavior disorders. The European schools stress slow-wave EEG abnormalities as evidence of immaturity, and Americans have stressed the association of EEG's with the 14-

and 6-per-second spike pattern. This pattern, however, is now most often considered to be a normal variant.

Behavior disorders of childhood. The behavior disturbances most likely to be associated with EEG abnormalities are those of aggressive, impulsive types. Sometimes children with episodic visceral complaints have accompanying psychological symptoms, and frequently their EEG's are abnormal. Similarly, personality disturbances are often seen in patients with convulsive disorders. The EEG patterns associated with behavior disorders, with or without intermittent visceral symptoms, are not consistent, because virtually every type of EEG abnormality has been reported. Fifty to 60 per cent of children with behavior disorders reveal immature records, manifested by diffuse slow activity, maximal over the occipital and temporal lobes. Paroxysmal EEG abnormality is commonly associated with episodic visceral phenomena—for example, abdominal epilepsy (see Figure 11*B*)—and paroxysmal abnormality or focal spikes are the hallmark of the epilepsies.

The significance of the 14- and 6-per-second positive spike pattern (see Figure 11*A*) is still controversial. This activity, because it occurs most often while recording from the temporal areas using wide interelectrode distances during drowsiness or light sleep, is seldom found in some EEG laboratories. When the 14- and 6-per-second positive spike pattern was first reported in 1951, some doubted its existence as a specific entity. More recently, the pendulum has swung in the opposite direction, because now this pattern has been found in more than 50 per cent of normal adolescents. Fourteen- and 6-per-second positive spikes are one of the most common electroencephalographic correlates of behavior disorders and episodic visceral phenomena during childhood, but, inasmuch as the EEG pattern may be a normal variant and behavioral disorders are not precisely defined, this relationship is of dubious validity. Heredity plays some part in the 14- and 6-per-second spike pattern of children, because abnormalities in the EEG are seen in a greater percentage of these children's parents than in the normal population.

Personality disorders in adults. Adults with personality disorders, particularly those with aggressive characteristics, often reveal prominent temporocentral θ-activity or 3- to 5-Hz. posterior temporooccipital slow activity over one or both hemispheres. A prominent increase in slow-wave activity occurs during hyperventilation. These adults have a higher percentage of 14- and 6-per-second positive spikes than is seen in the normal population. Six-per-second spike-and-wave complexes may be a variant of 14- and 6-per-second positive spikes, and the clinical significance of these patterns is similar, but the 6-per-second spike-and-wave complexes are more common in adults. When spikes or other abnormal activities are seen from the anterior temporal lobe in adults with personality disorders, it is likely that many of these patients have psychomotor epilepsy or behavioral disturbances due to a mechanism operative in this type of epilepsy. In criminals the highest incidence of EEG abnormalities is found in aggressive psychopaths.

Neuroses. Anxiety causes a decrease in α-rhythm and an increase in low-voltage, fast activity (see Figure 3*B*), especially over the central areas. Maturational defects in the EEG, such as increased per cent time of bitemporal θ-activity, may also be present.

Those persons who manifest obsessional phenomena and patients with psychosomatic complaints reveal EEG characteristics no different from those of the normal population.

Patients with hysteria often have immature records. Usually, the cerebral electrical activity of hysterical patients and of persons who have been hypnotized reacts exactly the same as that of normal people. Evoked potentials can be recorded in the EEG after pain stimulation of the hysterically analgesic extremity. Similarly, the α-rhythm of the EEG may be blocked on visual stimulation in a patient with hysterical blindness.

Functional psychoses

Affective disorders. Patients with manic-depressive psychosis reveal a somewhat greater percentage of abnormal EEG's than does the general population; β-activities are especially prominent. The α-frequency is often increased in those who are predominantly manic and decreased in those who are predominantly depressed. The sedation threshold test is valuable in differentiating endogenous depression from reactive depression. Reactive depression seems to be more often associated with temporal lobe abnormalities than would be expected on the basis of chance.

Schizophrenia. It is not surprising that the reports of EEG characteristics in this disorder are as variable as is its definition. Certainly, a consistent pattern is not present. Most schizophrenic patients have normal EEG's, but the percentage of abnormal EEG's in patients with schizophrenia is 2 or 3 times that found in the normal population. The majority of autistic children have abnormal EEG's. Abnormality in the EEG is more likely to be present when there is a family history of psychosis or when the onset of the disease is early, the duration long, and the severity great. Paradoxically, the prognosis has been reported to be worse for schizophrenics with normal EEG's than for those having EEG abnormalities. EEG abnormalities are most often seen in catatonics, least often in paranoiacs. In schizophrenics, α-rhythm may not respond to visual or emotional stimuli, and, conversely, α-rhythm is absent during hallucinations. β-Activity and paroxysmal abnormalities are more frequent in schizophrenics than in the normal population. The threshold to photic Metrazol stimulation is often unusually low in schizophrenia. Many schizophrenic patients show marked reduction in sleep stage 4 and, to a smaller extent, stage 3, as well as reduction in REM sleep. Low-voltage, slow activity is often seen in catatonic stupor, and paroxysmal patterns are seen more often in catatonics than in patients with other forms of schizophrenia. These paroxysmal activities are maximal over the posterior cerebrum, are faster than 4 cycles per second, and are of lower voltage than patterns characteristic of epilepsy. The B-mitten complex is a sharp and slow-wave complex forming the last part of a 10- to 12-Hz. sleep spindle over the frontoparietal areas of an adult. This pattern was reported to be associated with psychoses, but most authorities believe the pattern to be a normal variant.

Organic psychoses. The EEG abnormality corresponds to the nature of the underlying lesion in the organic psychoses. Patients in the early stage of dementia due to cerebral degenerative diseases—for example, Huntington's chorea and Alzheimer's disease—reveal a slowing of the α-frequency and decreased per cent time of α-rhythm. (These are also normal manifestations of the aging process.) As the disease advances, diffuse θ-activity or, less often, diffuse δ-activity may occur, sometimes with focal components. The severity of dementia does not necessarily correlate with the severity of the EEG abnormality, but the degree of EEG abnormality seems to be most severe in those cases of dementia showing rapid progression.

The EEG is helpful in establishing the diagnosis of psychosis secondary to drug or metabolic encephalopathy, psychosis of brain tumor, psychosis with epilepsy, and dementia associated with Creutzfeldt-Jakob disease. The EEG may be particularly useful in differentiating organic delirium from paranoid agitated behavior and in differentiating severe dementia with associated psychomotor retardation from the withdrawal and mute states of depression and schizophrenia.

Additional techniques of EEG study in psychiatry

Sedation threshold. This is the amount of amobarbital sodium (Amytal) required to produce a maximum degree of fast activity in the EEG. Unfortunately, there is not a sharp end point, and the degree of variation is too great for most diagnostic purposes. The sedation threshold is highest in patients with anxiety states, but it is also high in obsessive-compulsive patients, those with reactive depression, and chronic schizophrenics. The sedation threshold is lower than normal in persons with organic psychoses. It has its greatest practical value in differentiating endogenous depression, which has an unusually low sedation threshold in spite of agitation, from reactive depression, with its high threshold.

Contingent negative variation. After conditioning a patient to a warning signal several seconds before a stimulus to which the patient is to react, one can record electrically negative activity from the vertex between the first signal and the second stimulus. Many neurotic and most psychotic patients reveal a prolongation of this negative wave beyond the response to the second stimulus; however, the procedure is not clinically useful.

Photic Metrazol stimulation. This form of stimulation evokes, at some stage, a paroxysmal response in every person, but the threshold is often unusually low in schizophrenics and epileptics.

Depth electrode studies. Such studies have shed light on the anatomical and physiological substrate of emotion. Spike discharges and slow-wave activity in the septal region, the hippocampus, and the amygdala have been recorded in patients with schizophrenia and other psychoses. Bilateral bursts of high-voltage 2- to 5-Hz. slow activity have been noted from deep ventromedial frontal areas in psychotic patients, but most of these patients had been tested after electric shock therapy. High-voltage, fast spindles have been recorded from the hippocampus of patients during periods of strong emotion. The significance of these recordings with regard to psychological phenomena is by no means certain.

Electroconvulsive therapy. Slow activity after electroconvulsive therapy (ECT) is presumed to be due to the same mechanism as that after seizures of other origins. This initial postictal EEG change is due to secondary activation of inhibitory interneurons with hyperpolarization of neural membranes. More prolonged EEG abnormalities and prolonged clinical changes are probably due to neuronal loss or dysfunction associated with failure of the vascular supply to meet the increased metabolic demands of the hyperactive electrically discharging brain. The severity of the EEG abnormality after ECT is a highly individual factor. With the first electrical shock there is usually quick return of the EEG to normal. After successive treatments slow activity decreases in frequency, increases in voltage, and becomes more diffuse. The increasing slow-wave abnormality is often associated with organic mental signs. Slow EEG activity usually persists after several treatments; the EEG usually returns to normal after days, weeks, or months, but sometimes it never returns to normal. Even when the EEG does not return to normal, clinical evidence of organic cerebral disease usually does not persist. The number and the frequency of shock treatments are important factors in the severity of EEG abnormality, but there are too many variables to correlate these features with the rapidity of disappearance of slow activity. The major factors are the underlying cerebral metabolic and cerebrovascular states of the patient.

There is some evidence that organic changes, manifested in part by an abnormal EEG, must occur for success in ECT; when slow activity in the EEG fails to persist or is relatively slight, the outcome of the therapy is often unfavorable. Delta slow-wave activity may be revealed at an early stage in the course of therapy by intravenous barbiturate-induced sleep 3 to 4 hours after ECT. This method has been calibrated and used in determining the effectiveness of such treatment.

Examination of the Cerebrospinal Fluid (CSF)

Significant complications of a lumbar puncture are rare. Papilledema and other evidence of increased intracranial pressure, especially with signs of a mass lesion in the temporal lobe or in the posterior fossa, are the major contraindications for this procedure. A sudden change in intracranial pressure may occur as a result of a spinal tap in the presence of increased intracranial pressure. This change may cause herniation of the medial portions of the temporal lobe through the incisura of the tentorium of the cerebellum, with resultant compression of the upper brain stem and the oculomotor nerve, or it may cause a shift of the tonsils of the cerebellum through the foramen magnum and associated compression of the medulla. These complications are grave, and their possible occurrence must be weighed against the potential benefits of a lumbar puncture.

The spinal tap is performed by inserting a needle into the spinal canal below the spinal cord, which ends at vertebral level L1 or L2. Usually, the tap is made at the level of the iliac crest, corresponding to the interspace of L3–4 or L4–5.

PRESSURE

The initial spinal fluid pressure must always be measured with the patient horizontal and relaxed. Pressure of more than 180 mm. to 200 mm. is elevated. The causes of increased intracranial pressure are discussed above. Manometrics, as tested by compression of the jugular veins, may be performed when a spinal lesion is suspected but must not be carried out when there is suspicion of an intracranial lesions.

COLOR AND CLARITY

The color and the clarity of the cerebrospinal fluid are normally indistinguishable from water, with which it should be compared. Bloody spinal fluid may be due to a traumatic lumbar puncture. If this is so, the amount of blood in the spinal fluid decreases in successive collecting test tubes, the red blood cells are not crenated, and the supernatant spinal fluid after centrifugation is clear. Blood in the spinal fluid is usually due to a subarachnoid hemorrhage or, less often, to an intracerebral hemorrhage that has ruptured into the ventricles or out to the subarachnoid space. Cerebral trauma and a subdural hematoma may be associated with blood in the spinal fluid. Xanthochromic spinal fluid is seen as the residual pigment of blood after a subarachnoid hemorrhage or with a subdural hematoma, but it may be evident when the spinal fluid protein is unusually high. Severe jaundice may cause a yellow discoloration of the spinal fluid. Turbid CSF may be due to meningitis, a slight amount of blood in the spinal fluid, or a highly elevated protein content.

CELL COUNT

Spinal fluid should be routinely examined for red and white blood cells, protein, and glucose. A serological test for syphilis should also be performed. An elevated white blood cell count—that is, more than three lymphocytes per mm.[3]—is indicative of inflammation or irritation of the meninges. If the cell count is elevated, the spinal fluid should be smeared and stained, as well as cultured, for infecting organisms. A low-grade infection such as central nervous system syphilis or aseptic meningeal irritation—for example, a brain tumor near the meninges—may be manifested by 5 to 50 white blood cells, especially lymphocytes, per mm.[3]. Chronic meningitis, as caused by torula, results in an elevation of white blood cells, predominantly lymphocytes, ranging from 50 to 500 per mm.[3]. An acute purulent meningitis is usually associated with pleocytosis of 1,000 to 15,000 white blood cells per mm.[3], predominantly (90 per cent) polymorphonuclear leukocytes. Tumor or yeast cells may resemble white blood cells in the routine white cell count of the spinal fluid. If a search for exfoliative tumor cells is to be made, the spinal fluid must be immediately preserved in an equal volume of 50 per cent ethyl alcohol.

PROTEIN

Protein elevation of the spinal fluid—more than 50 mg. per 100 ml.—may be seen in any organic neurological disease. If the spinal tap has been traumatic, the amount of protein added to the spinal fluid by the blood can be roughly calculated by subtracting 1 mg. per cent of protein for every 750 red blood cells per mm.[3]. As a rule of thumb, an elevation of protein of more than 100 mg. per cent is much more indicative of a cerebral neoplasm than of a cerebrovascular lesion. Fluid drawn below a spinal block usually contains protein elevated beyond 100 mg. per cent, and the CSF of meningitis may reveal similar findings. In multiple sclerosis, neurosyphilis, and subacute sclerosing parencephalitis, the CSF γ-globulin is usually elevated—that is, beyond 12 to 15 per cent of the total protein.

GLUCOSE

The glucose content of spinal fluid is normally 50 to 65 mg. per cent and corresponds to a value two-thirds that of the blood glucose drawn at the time of the spinal tap. Spinal fluid glucose of less than 40 mg. per cent or less than half that of the simultaneously drawn blood glucose is definitely abnormal and is found in meningitis of bacterial or fungal origin, but it may sometimes occur in noninfectious diseases that irritate the meninges, such as meningeal carcinomatosis, sarcoidosis, and subarachnoid hemorrhage.

SEROLOGICAL TEST FOR SYPHILIS

A positive finding of a spinal fluid serological test is indicative of active central nervous system syphilis if the test is accompanied by an elevated white blood cell count and elevated protein in the cerebrospinal fluid. The colloidal gold test is performed only if central nervous system lues is suspected.

Evaluation of spinal fluid chlorides is of little value, although chlorides may be low (less than 120 mEq. per liter) in tuberculous meningitis.

INFUSION TEST

This test is used to determine the CSF absorptive ability in patients suspected of having normal-pressure hydrocephalus, an uncommon but treatable cause of dementia. Normally, a solution of artificial CSF or saline can be infused into the spinal canal through a lumbar puncture at the rate of 0.75 ml. per minute without significantly raising the CSF pressure. In patients with communicating hydrocephalus and absorptive block of CSF, as in dementia associated with normal-pressure hydrocephalus, a progressive rise in CSF pressure occurs at the above rate of infusion.

Roentgenograms of the Skull

Standard roentgenograms of the skull should include a posterior-anterior view, a lateral view, and a Towne's view (anterior-posterior projection with the chin flexed on the chest). Other special views, stereoscopy, and tomography may be necessary to visualize specific structures, such as the optic foramina, the base of the skull, and the internal acoustic meati. Polytomography permits minute roentgenographical sections of any part of the skull, revealing defects that might otherwise be obscured.

NORMAL LANDMARKS

In the skull films one studies the appearance of such normal landmarks as the sella turcica, the petrous pyramids, and the calcified pineal gland. The shape and integrity of the skull are observed for evidence of developmental anomalies and fractures. Both abnormal and normal calcifications must be recognized, as well as evidence of erosion and exostoses.

CALCIFICATIONS

Normal or benign calcifications include those within the dura, especially the falx cerebri, the pineal body, the choroid plexus, the petroclinoid ligament, and the habenula. Sometimes the basal ganglia calcify either secondary to parathyroid disease or from an unknown cause. Abnormal calcifications may be found in certain tumors. Calcification can be roentgenographically visualized in 50 per cent of oligodendrogliomas, 25 per cent of ependymomas, 15 to 20 per cent of meningiomas, and 70 per cent of craniopharyngiomas. Teratomas and astrocytomas may also present calcifications. The most common vascular lesion is atherosclerosis, but the often seen calcification in the siphon of the internal carotid artery is of little clinical significance. Calcifications may be visualized within aneurysms, in chronic subdural or intracerebral hematomas, and underlying the angioma of Sturge-Weber syndrome. Those infectious processes that may reveal multiple calcifications include toxoplasmosis, cytomegalic inclusion body encephalitis, and cysticercosis. Calcification is noted within tuberculomas and other chronic abscesses. An uncommon disease in which calcifications may be seen is tuberous sclerosis.

EROSION

Increased intracranial pressure may be manifested in roentgenograms of the skull by erosion of the clinoid processes and dorsum sellae, increased convolutional markings, and, in children, separation of the sutures. Large channels due to increased vascular markings may lead to an area occupied by a meningioma. Enlarged foramina of cranial nerves are often indicative of associated tumors; the most common example is the enlarged internal acoustic meatus due to an acoustic neuroma. Metastases to the skull, commonly causing erosion, are most often from carcinoma of the breast.

EXOSTOSES

A localized area of exostosis is often seen overlying a meningioma. Hyperostosis frontalis interna is an insignificant finding, in spite of syndromes associated with it in the past.

Computerized Tomography (CT)

The most revolutionary diagnostic concept in recent decades has relegated many of the older diagnostic techniques to ancillary procedures. The equipment records minute variations in the density of brain tissue by means of an X-ray source and opposing sensitive detectors arrayed around the head. Tens of thousands of readings are computer processed, and the relative tissue densities of thousands of areas within one plane are then printed out and displayed on a cathode ray tube. The picture of one plane of the brain thus presented is photographically recorded by Polaroid or X-ray film. Enhancement of the densities, especially within lesions, may be achieved by performing the study during an intravenous infusion of diatrizoate meglumine (14 per cent iodine per 300 ml.).

Most lesions larger than 1.5 cm. on cross-section can be visualized by computerized tomography. In addition, ventricular size and displacement can be seen, as well as the subarachnoid space and adjacent cortex, with or without atrophy. In some instances, the disease is more striking than would be seen by gross inspection of the cut brain (see Figure 23). In other instances, lesions may not be demonstrated by computerized tomography, either because the size is too small—for example, an aneurysm—or because the density is not distinguishable from the density of the brain—for example, the midstage in the evolution of a subdural hematoma from high to low density. Figures 18 through 24 are examples of computerized tomograms picturing a cerebral neoplasm, a cerebral abscess, a subdural hematoma, a cerebral infarct, a cerebral hemorrhage, acute multiple sclerosis, and cerebral atrophy.

Diagnostic Nuclear Medicine

RADIOISOTOPE BRAIN SCANNING

Abnormal tissue within the head, in contrast to normal brain tissue, tends to retain radioisotopic compounds. This tendency is due to the breakdown of the blood-brain barrier associated with organic disease. By means of scanning equipment, markedly improved in recent years, the gamma-energies emitted by the radioisotope retained in a lesion can be mapped on X-ray film (photoscan).

The radioisotope—such as pertechnetate labeled with technetium (^{99}Tc)—is intravenously injected from 30 minutes to 2 or 3 hours before the scanning. The scanning equipment most useful is the Anger scintillation camera, which projects signals to an image-read-out oscilloscope, and the image, in turn, may be recorded by Polaroid or conventional film. Other instruments, especially the rectilinear scanner, and

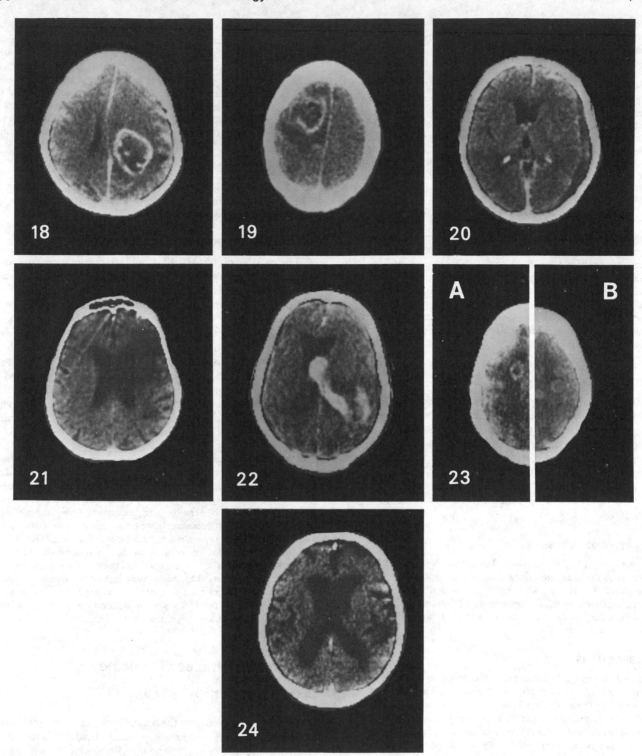

FIGURES 18 THROUGH 24. Computerized tomograms of the head are presented as if looking down on a coronal cross-section, with the frontal area at the top and the occipital area at the bottom of the picture; the left and right sides are the same as the viewer's right and left. In the pictures, the least dense substances, such as air and cerebrospinal fluid, are the darkest; the densest areas, such as the skull and blood clots, are the lightest. Although air and clear fluid may appear equally dark and bone and blood clot may appear equally light, the great differences in the densities of these materials can be determined with the aid of the computer. (Figures 18 through 24, courtesy of Dr. Norman Leeds, Montefiore Hospital and Medical Center, New York, New York.)

FIGURE 18. Cerebral neoplasm. A large mass, glioblastoma multiforme, is present within the right hemisphere. Circumferential density is enhanced by intravenous contrast, and there is adjacent edema, as manifested by rarefaction.

FIGURE 19. Cerebral abscess. A large left frontal abscess is enclosed by a hypervascular capsule (density enhanced by intravenous contrast) and surrounded by a zone of edema (decreased density). The tiny markedly lucent zones within the lesion represent gas produced by bacteria and indicate that this mass is an abscess, rather than a neoplasm.

other radioisotopes, such as chlormerodrin labeled with ^{197}Hg, have been used extensively in the past and are still being used. The isotope gallium (^{67}Ga) tends to be picked up in inflammatory and lymphomatous lesions. The interval between the injection of the radioisotope and scanning allows the kidneys to clear the radioisotope from the blood and thus diminish the background radioactivity in the blood stream of the head. Because this background radioactivity is particularly prevalent over dense muscles and draining vascular structures, it often obscures lesions of the posterior fossa, sella turcica, and sphenoid ridge. In cases of suspected posterior fossa lesion, a 24-hour interval between the injection of the radioisotope and scanning is sometimes advisable to allow more complete clearing of the radioisotope from the blood. On the other hand, only a few minutes' interval is used when searching for a suspected vascular malformation.

Dynamic brain scanning is an important additional procedure used to evaluate circulation through the carotid arteries and their major intracerebral branches. Nine to 12 seconds after the intravenous injection of the radioactive isotope, serial pictures are taken in rapid sequence. Asymmetry in the flow of blood containing the radioisotope is indicative of stenosis or occlusion of the major artery or ischemia within the zone of the artery. There is usually delayed perfusion in an area of ischemia and increased perfusion to a neoplasm. The rapid filling and emptying of an arteriovenous malformation can be seen by this technique.

The brain scan is most consistently positive in mass lesions—neoplasms, abscesses, hematomas—but increased uptake is also noted in arteriovenous malformations. A cerebral infarct picks up the radioactive isotope only after 1 to 4 days have elapsed since onset; the zone of infarction often has a wedge-shaped appearance. The brain scan is as accurate in localizing a lesion as any test now available, for the radiographical abnormality is seen within the lesion, rather than inferred by displacement of vessels or ventricles, as is often the case in angiography and pneumography. Brain scans, on the other hand, are frequently negative when the lesion is small (less than 2 cm. in diameter), avascular (such as a cyst), or obscured by a muscle mass or a confluence of blood vessels. A major drawback of brain scanning is the inability to differentiate mass lesions from other abnormal tissue, such as an infarct, definitely.

RADIOISOTOPE CISTERNOGRAPHY

This is a test to determine the rate of absorption of CSF in normal-pressure hydrocephalus. This same testing method may be used to trace leakage of CSF. When indium (^{111}In) is injected through a lumbar puncture, the isotope diffuses through the spinal canal and into the basal cisterns in 2 to 4 hours. It is seen over the convexity of the brain in 24 hours, is predominantly parasagittal in 48 hours, and is minimally detectable at 72 hours. In patients with normal-pressure hydrocephalus, which is most often due to a chronic defect impairing absorption of CSF, the radioactive isotope diffuses into the ventricles of the brain, and, most important, the isotope is still seen in the ventricles after 24 hours.

Cerebral Angiography

After the introduction of a radiopaque solution—meglumine iothalamate (Conray) or meglumine diatrizoate (Hypaque)—into arteries supplying the brain, arteries and veins can be seen in serial roentgenograms.

In recent years there has been a trend to study selectively the carotid or vertebral arteries and their branches by femoral catheterization. The radiopaque solutions may also be injected percutaneously into the common carotid artery to visualize vessels of the ipsilateral cerebral hemisphere, as supplied by the internal carotid, anterior cerebral, and middle cerebral arteries. Right brachial arteriography allows visualization of the right carotid arterial tree and the right vertebral, basilar, and posterior cerebral arteries; left brachial arteriography opacifies the left vertebrobasilar and posterior cerebral circulation. Serious complications of arteriography occur in fewer than 2 per cent of patients and are manifested primarily by ischemia or infarction of the brain with convulsions, focal signs, and (very rarely) death. These events are caused by inadvertent embolic phenomena (air or calcific plaques), manual or hemorrhagic occlusion of the punctured artery, prolonged carotid sinus effect, or idiosyncratic or allergic reaction of the nervous tissue to the injected contrast material; hemorrhage from the punctured artery may also occur.

As a rule, angiography is performed when a focal lesion is suspected, except when the focal lesion is thought to be atrophic, or when an aneurysm or vascular malformation is sought.

Neoplasms may be angiographically demonstrated by the displacement of adjacent blood vessels or the presence of a tumor stain. A tumor stain is seen as retained contrast material in a zone of new or abnormal vessels within the tumor. Glioblastomas and meningiomas usually have characteristic tumor stains. A hematoma or an abscess displaces vessels in a manner like that of a neoplasm, but the mass usually appears avascular. A subdural or epidural hematoma displaces the cortical vessels from the inner table of the skull and is best seen in the anterioposterior views. Occlusion or stenosis of major arteries can be angiographically demonstrated. Right and left carotid, vertebral, and basilar arteries must be visualized before surgery for carotid stenosis or for a cerebral aneurysm.

Pneumoencephalography and Ventriculography

Roentgenographical visualization of areas normally containing cerebrospinal fluid can be attained when air is substituted for cerebrospinal fluid. With the advent of computerized tomography this test is rarely necessary.

Pneumoencephalography is accomplished by the injection of air, usually 30 ml. to 75 ml., through the route of a lumbar puncture, performed with the patient seated. Air is allowed to rise into the head and to fill the ventricles, the subarachnoid spaces of the basal cisterns, and the sulci over the convexity of the brain. Pneumoencephalography is contraindicated in patients with increased intracranial pressure; instead, ventriculography is performed by the direct instillation of air into a lateral ventricle through a burr hole in the posterior parietal area of the skull. Serious complications of pneumoencephalography are rare—less than 1 per cent. They are due to shift and herniation of the brain or to precipitation of cerebrovascular lesions.

FIGURE 20. Subdural hematoma. A chronic subdural hematoma over the right convexity has caused a ventricular shift from right to left. A small rim of increased density between the surface of the brain and the hematoma represents the membrane enclosing the hematoma. The hematoma has, for the most part, changed from dense blood clot to a less dense fluid.

FIGURE 21. Cerebral infarct. An old right frontal infarct is manifested by a zone of decreased density. The adjacent right lateral ventricle is, if anything, larger than the left lateral ventricle.

FIGURE 22. Cerebral hemorrhage. A right parietal hemorrhage has broken into the posterior horn of the right lateral ventricle. There is swelling of the right hemisphere and a shift of the ventricles from right to left.

FIGURE 23. A and B, acute multiple sclerosis. With intravenous contrast, multiple circular densities are seen on both the right and the left sides at slightly different levels in a patient with acute multiple sclerosis. These lesions might be mistaken for metastases were it not for the absence of mass effect. This picture is not an invariable finding in multiple sclerosis but the lesions are even more prominent here than are those seen on sectioning of the brain at autopsy.

FIGURE 24. Cerebral atrophy. Cerebral atrophy is manifested in this case by both ventricular dilation and widened cortical sulci.

Atrophic brain diseases are best studied by means of pneumoencephalography. Focal atrophy, as in posttraumatic epilepsy, is seen as large air-filled sulci. Diffuse cerebral degeneration, such as Alzheimer's disease, is manifested by dilated ventricles and scattered areas of widened sulci. On pneumoencephalography, normal-pressure hydrocephalus is suspected by the presence of dilated ventricles and the paucity of air over the convexity of the brain.

These air studies are well suited to the evaluation of congenital hydrocephalus, sometimes manifesting hugely dilated ventricles with only a small rim of cerebral cortex. Aqueductal stenosis and other blockages of CSF flow are the few examples of the advantage of pneumoencephalography over computerized tomography. In tuberous sclerosis, small multiple nodules along the walls of moderately dilated ventricles are seen. A mass—such as a neoplasm, hematoma, an abscess, or a cyst—deforms or displaces the walls of the adjacent ventricles. The sulci of the cerebral hemisphere containing a mass are usually less well filled with air than are those of the normal side. If the mass is near midline structures, obstruction to the outflow of cerebrospinal fluid results in ventricular dilation.

Carotid and Cerebral Blood Flow

Several tests are useful in estimating blood flow through the carotid artery. Ophthalmodynamometry is a measurement of retinal artery pressure. A difference in pressure of 20 per cent between right and left eyes suggests carotid artery stenosis or occlusion on the side of the lower pressure. By means of thermography, the temperature of the skin above and medial to the orbits is measured; asymmetry between the two sides suggests carotid artery disease. Doppler ultrasonography is used to study the flow of blood in the carotid artery and its orbital or periorbital branches.

Regional cerebral blood flow can be measured by the clearance curves after intracarotid arterial injection of radioactive xenon (^{133}Xe), but these studies are, thus far, limited to research.

Electronystagmography (ENG)

The cornea is electrically positive, relative to the retina, and surface electrodes near the eyes transmit differences in corneoretinal potentials to a strip recorder. Nystagmus of labyrinthine end-organ disease is enhanced by eye closure and loss of fixation; the opposite is true in cerebellar nystagmus. This difference is most easily detected by ENG. The test also permits precise records of induced and spontaneous nystagmus. Ocular dysmetria of brain stem or cerebellar disease can be recorded.

Echoencephalography

The recorded echo of a very high-frequency sound (ultrasound) is used to measure the location of intracerebral structures. The test is no longer used if computerized tomography is available.

The A-scan records the location of the brain's midline structures—falx cerebri, third ventricle, septum pelicidum. A shift of midline structures has the same significance as a shift of the pineal gland and most often indicates a mass lesion on the side opposite the direction of shift. Because the procedure is harmless and painless, it can be used as a screening procedure in cases of suspected intracranial mass lesion, such as subdural hematoma. It is particularly helpful in those patients who do not have localizing neurological signs, as may be the case in comatose patients.

The B-scan roughly outlines the ventricles or an intracerebral mass that has a density different from that of the cerebral parenchyma. The equipment and the technique required for the B-scan have not yet been perfected, but the B-scan has been useful in establishing the diagnosis of hydrocephalus.

Myelography

The configuration of the spinal subarachnoid space can be visualized in roentengrams after a radiopaque liquid is injected through a lumbar puncture.

The radiopaque solution, which is heavier than the spinal fluid, is maneuvered through the spinal canal by tilting the patient on the X-ray table under fluoroscopic control. Mass lesions—neoplasms and herniated intervertebral discs—are precisely located by their indentation of the radiopaque column. Less common causes of complete or partial block of the subarachnoid space, as visualized myelographically, include arachnoiditis, spinal abscesses, syringomyelia, and diseased and fractured vertebrae. Vascular malformations of the cord may also be recognized by a typical configuration within the radiopaque column. (The more recent development of selective spinal angiography has permitted precise visualization of spinal vascular malformations.) The spinal needle used for the injection of the contrast material in myelography is maintained in place throughout the procedure, so that at the completion of the test the radiopaque solution—iophandylate (Pantopaque) may be removed. A new compound recently introduced, metrizamide, does not require removal for it is absorbed from the cerebrospinal fluid into the blood stream. Arachnoiditis as a complication of myelography is extremely rare.

Electrodiagnosis of Peripheral Nerves and Muscles

Several procedures are most helpful in confirming the diagnosis of lower motor neuron disease or myopathy.

Testing the responses of a muscle to stimulation at motor points by direct galvanic current or by faradic tetanizing current was the chief electrodiagnostic method until the adaptation of the cathode ray oscilloscope. A sluggish response to galvanic stimulation or a decreased or absent response to faradic stimulation is indicative of denervation.

NERVE CONDUCTION VELOCITY

Nerve conduction velocity is determined with the use of two electrodes placed over the skin of the nerve and muscle to be tested. The time (as a measure of distance on the cathode ray oscilloscope) required for the impulse to travel between the stimulating proximal electrode and the distal recording electrode is tabulated. The speed of conduction between the known distance of the two electrodes is then calculated. Normal conduction velocities range from 40 to 50 meters per second for the ulnar, median, and peroneal nerves. Slower velocities are indicative of disease of the peripheral nerve. The conduction time through a simple, monosynaptic reflex arc, similar to that of the knee jerk, can be measured and recorded as the H-reflex. Motor diseases of the central nervous system influence the reactivity of the lower motor neuron and may be evaluated by changes in the H-reflex.

ELECTROMYOGRAM (EMG)

The EMG is a record of electrical activity transmitted from a muscle by a needle electrode to a cathode ray oscilloscope and a loudspeaker for purposes of visual and auditory evaluations. A normal muscle is electrically silent at rest. During contraction, normal action potentials are manifested by fast, moderate-voltage, well-modulated bursts of activity. Ten to 20 days after nerve injury, evidence of denervation can be found. A partially denervated muscle produces complex polyphasic arrhythmic, high-voltage potentials during contraction. With total denervation, spikes of low-voltage, fast, random potentials (fibrillations) are noted at rest; these sound like drops of rain on a tin roof. Resting denervated muscle may also give rise to spontaneous, brief motor-unit contractions (fasciculations), seen as high-voltage complex potentials. Tests of a patient with muscular atrophy due to disease of the anterior horn cells in the spinal cord reveal fibrillation potentials with normal nerve conduction velocity. These studies in a patient with lower motor neuron disease of peripheral nerve origin show delayed conduction velocity and fibrillation potentials. In muscular dystrophy, electrical activity during muscle contraction is faster and of lower voltage than normal action potentials. The EMG of a patient with myositis may reveal activities indistinguishable from fibrillations, and dystrophic electrical patterns are also seen. The contraction of a myotonic muscle or stimulation of this muscle by needle insertion is manifested by prolonged electrical activity that slowly fades away (decreases in amplitude). In myasthenic patients, abnormal fatigability of muscles activated by repetitive electrical stimuli is seen by the rapidly progressive decrease in amplitude of electrical activity. Hysterical weakness is suspected when irregular contractions of varying strengths are poorly sustained.

Cystometric Examination

In the cystometric examination, intravesicular pressures, transmitted to a manometer attached to a catheter, are recorded after specific amounts of saline have been introduced into the urinary bladder. The patient's sensations of fullness and desire to void are also noted.

Normally, a powerful voiding contraction occurs at a volume of 400 ml. to 500 ml. A spastic (reflex) bladder, as may occur with a lesion of the pyramidal tracts in the spinal cord, produces a relatively high pressure with a small volume. An atonic bladder, associated with lower motor neuron disease or a lesion of sensory pathways, reveals relatively low pressure with a large volume. A complete, usually traumatic, lesion of the conus medullaris or adjacent structures often results in autonomous bladder activity, with muscle tone partially preserved. The demented, incontinent patient usually has normal cystometric responses, whereas urinary retention of psychological origin often presents evidence of an atonic bladder.

Suggested Cross References

Other tests and techniques used in evaluating and diagnosing psychiatric patients are described in Chapter 12. Sections 3.3, 3.4, and 3.5 contain more information about neurological syndromes. Organic mental disorders are discussed in Chapter 20; of special interest are the sections devoted to epilepsy (Section 20.9), brain trauma (Section 20.5), and intracranial neoplasms (Section 20.8). Mental retardation is discussed in Chapter 36, schizophrenic disorders in Chapter 15, affective disorders in Chapters 18 and 19, personality disorders in Chapter 22, unusual psychiatric disorders (such as Gilles de la Tourette's disease) in Section 27.1, and developmental and speech disorders in children in Chapters 37, 39, and 40. The neurological evaluation of children is also described in Section 35.2. The convulsive therapies are discussed in Section 31.5. The stages of sleep are described in detail in Section 2.3.

REFERENCES

Barber, H. O., and Stockwell, C. W. *Manual of Electronystagmography.* C. V. Mosby, St. Louis, 1976.
Baum, S., and Bramlet, R. *Basic Nuclear Medicine.* Appleton-Century-Crofts, New York, 1975.
* DeJong, R. N. *The Neurologic Examination,* ed. 3. Harper & Row, New York, 1969.
Geschwind, N. Aphasia. 'N. Engl. J. Med.', *284:* 654, 1971.
Gesell, A., and Amatruda, C. S. *Developmental Diagnosis: Normal and Abnormal Child Development.* Harper & Row, New York, 1969.
* Gibbs, F. A., and Gibbs, E. L. *Atlas of Electroencephalography.* Vol. 1: *Methodology and Controls,* ed. 2; Vol. 2: *Epilepsy;* Vol. 3: *Neurological and Psychiatric Disorders.* Addison-Wesley, Reading, Mass., 1974.
* Goodglass, H., and Kaplan, E. *The Assessment of Aphasia and Related Disorders.* Lea & Febiger, Philadelphia, 1972.
Kellaway, P., and Peterson, I., editors. *Neurological and Electroencephalographic Correlative Studies in Infancy.* Grune & Stratton, New York, 1964.
* Kiloh, I. G., McComas, A. J., and Osselton, J. W. *Clinical Electroencephalography,* ed. 3. Butterworth, London, 1972.
* Mayo Clinic and Mayo Foundation for Medical Education and Research. *Clinical Examinations in Neurology,* ed. 4. W. B. Saunders, Philadelphia, 1976.
Peterson, H. O., and Kieffer, S. A. *Introduction to Neuroradiology.* Harper & Row, New York, 1972.
* Taveras, J. M., and Wood, E. H. *Diagnostic Neuroradiology,* ed. 2. Williams & Wilkins, Baltimore, 1976.
Weisberg, L. A., Nice, C., and Katz, M. *Cerebral Computed Tomography.* W. B. Saunders, Philadelphia, 1978.

3.3 Clinical Neurology and Neuropathology

SEYMOUR SOLOMON, M.D.

Histopathology

Cells of the nervous system react in certain general patterns to many different types of injury and stress. Neuroglia or interstitial cells follow one pattern; neurons, the cells that conduct impulses, react in another.

NEUROGLIA

Astrocytes form the basic matrix of the brain. They are either protoplasmic with prominent cytoplasm, found predominantly in the gray matter, or fibrillary, located mainly in the white matter. They may be considered functionally similar to fibroblasts of other body tissues. Oligodendroglia, small cells with prominent nuclei, are responsible for myelin formation around neuronal axons of the central nervous system. Ependyma is the layer of ciliated columnar cells lining the ventricles and its function is the transfer of substances between the cerebrospinal fluid and the brain. Microglia are small cells when inactive, but they hypertrophy during their function as phagocytes.

NEURONS

The neuron is made up of a cell body, dendrites to receive impulses, and an axon to send impulses. The cell body consists of cytoplasm or perikaryon; its nucleus contains dye-staining material (chromatin) consisting of deoxyribonucleic acid (DNA) and a nucleolus, predominantly ribonucleic acid (RNA). Within the cytoplasm are glycogen, the cell's fuel, and the pigment lipofucsin, which increases in amount with age; melanin pigment is also found in certain neurons. The cytoplasm also contains a number of organelles. Mitochondria, made of complex lipoproteins, are the site of oxidative phosphorylation and, as such, are the main energy source of cell metabolism. Nissl bodies are aggregates of linked nucleoprotein and RNA molecules forming the endoplasmic reticulum. On the framework of endoplasmic reticulum are clustered ribosomes, tiny granules of RNA that subserve protein synthesis.

Other parts of the endoplasmic reticulum are involved in protein transport. Protein molecules form neurotubules or neurofilaments that, with the light microscope, are seen as neurofibrils; their function is unknown. The Golgi apparatus is seen as granular material on light microscopy. It forms part of the endoplasmic reticulum and probably plays a role in neurosecretion or lysosome formation. The lysosomes are packets containing the cell's acid phosphatase and hydrolytic enzymes and are thought to be the cell's catabolic agents by aiding the digestion of macromolecules.

NEUROGLIAL REACTION TO INJURY

If severe, injury results in degeneration of the interstitial cells, as manifested by swelling of the cell bodies, fragmentation of the cell processes, and shrinking with hyperpigmentation (pyknosis) of the nuclei. If injury is less severe, reactive gliosis occurs. The astrocytes proliferate and hypertrophy to replace destroyed tissue. The astrocyte divides by amitosis, and, in the early phase of reactive gliosis, cell bodies are numerous. Eventually, a gliotic scar is formed by a dense network of astrocytic fibers.

Demyelination is manifested by swelling of the myelin sheath, then fragmentation of the myelin into lipoid globules. The axis cylinder within the sheath may remain relatively intact. Phagocytosis occurs after brain injury. Microglia proliferate, as in an inflammatory reaction, and move toward the affected area while changing their shape and increasing in size to globular structures devoid of cell processes. After ingesting degenerated tissue consisting in large part of myelin breakdown, these fat-laden granule cells migrate to blood vessels and discharge their products into the perivascular (Virchow-Robin) spaces. Corpora amylacea (amyloid bodies) are round, often laminated, amorphous bodies representing the cellular debris found especially around old areas of degeneration.

NEURONAL REACTION TO INJURY

Acute injury to the neuron is manifested by swelling of the cytoplasm; chromatolysis of the Nissl substance (fragmentation and dissolution); swelling and degeneration of the neurofibrils; dissipation of the Golgi apparatus; swelling, hyperpigmentation, and fragmentation of the nucleus; and detachment and fragmentation of the cell processes. The loss of staining properties of the cell eventually leaves a ghost cell. After injury to the cell body, the axon (seen with silver stains) first swells and then fragments. The surrounding myelin sheath degenerates when loss of the axon occurs, but, as noted above, the reverse need not apply. Chronic injury to the nerve cell is characterized by shrinkage of the cytoplasm, coalescence of the Nissl substance, shrinkage and increased tortuosity of cell processes, shrinkage and pyknosis of the nucleus, and eventual destruction of the nucleus, with death of the cell. The degenerated nerve cell then undergoes phagocytosis—that is, neuronophagia.

The ultrastructure of the nervous system, as revealed by the advancing techniques of electron microscopy and progress in histochemical and biochemical studies, has shed much light on old diseases and has permitted the recognition of new ones. During the past century, scientists have been concerned with cellular pathology. The new methods cited above have opened the door to the understanding of molecular pathology.

Neoplasms of the Brain

The classical clinical manifestations of brain tumor—headache and papilledema—are no longer to be regarded as criteria for diagnosis. These features often occur late in the course of the disease, if at all. The chief manifestation of brain tumor is the progressive nature of the patient's neurological symptoms and signs, whether they be generalized or focal.

Generalized symptoms may include an organic mental disorder, personality changes, convulsive seizures, headache, lethargy, and other symptoms of increased intracranial pressure. An organic mental disorder and personality changes are particularly prevalent in frontal brain tumors but may be seen with neoplasms in any area of the brain. A tumor must be a primary consideration when convulsions originate during adult life, and seizures are the presenting symptom of tumors in 15 to 20 per cent of all cases. The incidence of brain tumors with adult onset of seizures is 25 to 35 per cent if the seizures or the electroencephalogram have focal qualities or if the seizure begins after the age of 50 years; the incidence is as high as 50 per cent if neurological signs are found. Increased intracranial pressure is usually manifested by headache, vomiting (not necessarily projectile), lethargy, and papilledema. The headaches are often most prominent on awakening in the morning and are increased by coughing or straining. Similarly, vomiting is more common in the early morning. Visual acuity is impaired only late in the course of papilledema due to increased intracranial pressure, in contradistinction to optic neuritis, which may present an almost identical funduscopic picture but with early blindness. During the terminal stage of increased intracranial pressure, the pulse becomes slow and bounding, respirations decrease in rate and become irregular, and blood pressure rises. Roentgenograms of the skull in patients with increased intracranial pressure first reveal decalcification of the dorsum sellae and, later, digital impressions of the inner table of the skull. In children, separation of the cranial sutures almost always occurs, and cracked-pot resonance may be noted on percussion of the skull. It is of little value to discuss the incidence of organic mental disorders or increased intracranial pressure in patients with brain tumors, for they invariably occur if the tumor is allowed to follow its natural course.

Focal signs of a neoplasm within a cerebral hemisphere consist of progressive contralateral hemiparesis, hemisensory impairment, homonymous hemianopsia, or aphasia. A cerebellar tumor, on the other hand, manifests progressive symptoms and signs of ataxia of the trunk or the extremities on the same side as the lesion.

Intracranial neoplasms are discussed with regard to incidence, age of onset, sexual predominance (if significant), site of origin, clinical characteristics (if the site of origin is other than the cerebral hemisphere or cerebellum), degree of malignancy, clinical course (if different from that expected on the basis of degree of malignancy), probability of complete surgical excision, response to radiotherapy, and gross and microscopic appearance.

The approximate incidence of intracranial neoplasms is listed in order of decreasing frequency:

Gliomas: 45 per cent of all intracranial neoplasms
Metastatic tumors: 15 per cent
Meningiomas: 15 per cent
Hypophysial tumors and tumors of embryonic rests: 10 per cent
Tumors of nerves (acoustic neuromas): 8 per cent
Vascular tumors: 2 per cent
Other tumors: 5 per cent

GLIOMAS

Most primary brain tumors arise from glial (interstitial) cells. Few primary neoplasms of the brain are of other neuroectodermal origin. In the following classification only the most common neoplasms are listed:

A. Tumors of glial origin
   1. Glioblastoma multiforme
   2. Astrocytic
      a. Astrocytoma
      b. Astroblastoma
      c. Spongioblastoma polare
   3. Oligodendroglioma
   4. Ependymal
      a. Ependymoma
      b. Papilloma of choroid plexus
      c. Colloid cyst
B. Tumors of the pineal gland
   1. Pinealoma
   2. Teratoma
C. Tumors of neuronal or retinal origin
   1. Medulloblastoma
   2. Retinoblastoma

Glioblastoma multiforme. This tumor accounts for 55 per cent of all gliomas. It is a tumor of adult life and arises within a cerebral hemisphere. This neoplasm is the most malignant of all primary brain tumors, and the duration of life is less than 1 year after onset. Response to radiotherapy or surgery is poor. The gross appearance (see Figure 1) is that of a soft, hemorrhagic, necrotic, infiltrating mass that often spreads from one hemisphere to the other across the corpus callosum. Under the microscope (see Figure 2), both the cells and their nuclei show great variation in size and shape, with giant ameboid cells and numerous mitoses. The cells may form a pseudopalisade pattern around areas of necrosis. Endothelial proliferation is evident; necrosis and hemorrhage are marked.

Astrocytoma. This tumor makes up 20 per cent of all gliomas.

In adults the tumor occurs within a cerebral hemisphere; in children it is found within the cerebellum. The tumor is benign, can be extensively excised, and responds moderately well to radiotherapy. It appears as a rubbery, infiltrating, poorly defined mass, with a tendency to pseudocyst formation, particularly in the cerebellum, where the tumor may present as a mural nodule in the pseudocyst. Microscopically, the tumor appears either as a tangle of glial fibrillae (see Figure 3) or as prominent large protoplasmic astrocytes. Sometimes degenerative changes in the cell bodies form ameboid or gemästete cells. Vascular proliferation is noted from both endothelial and adventitial cells; cyst formation is evident.

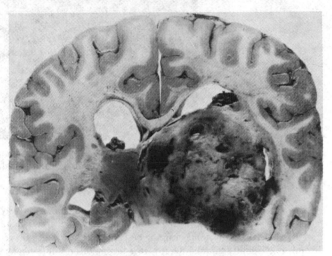

FIGURE 1. Glioblastoma multiforme. The massive tumor extends from the area of the basal ganglia. (From Russell, D. S., and Rubenstein, L. L. *Pathology of Tumors of the Nervous System*, ed. 3, p. 170. Williams & Wilkins, Baltimore, 1971.)

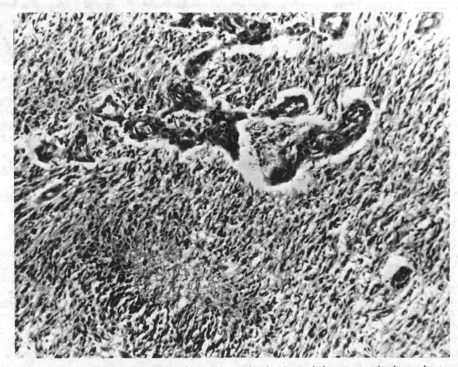

FIGURE 2. Glioblastoma multiforme. Cells, with hyperchromatic nuclei, varying in size and shape, grow in dense sheets or form pseudopalisades around an area of necrosis. Vascular proliferation is also present. Hematoxylin and eosin, low power. (From Slager, U. T. *Basic Neuropathology*, p. 281. Williams & Wilkins, Baltimore, 1970.)

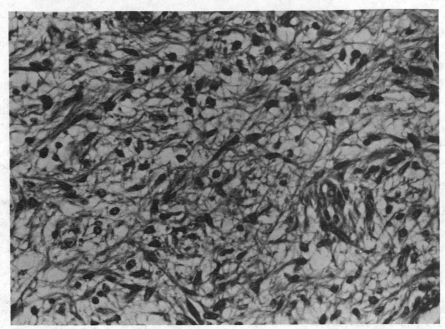

FIGURE 3. Astrocytoma. These fibrillary astrocytes form an irregular meshwork. Hematoxylin-phloxin-saffron; 350 X. (From Robertson, D. M., and Dinsdale, H. B. *The Nervous System,* p. 183. Williams & Wilkins, Baltimore, 1972.)

Astroblastoma. The astroblastoma is an uncommon tumor of early adult life that occurs within a cerebral hemisphere. It grows more rapidly than an astrocytoma, cannot be completely excised, and responds only slightly to radiotherapy. It is firm and sometimes hemorrhagic and may appear fairly well defined. On microscopy, the tumor is seen to have a loose texture, with cells arranged around blood vessels in a pseudorosette formation. Long processes extending from the cell bodies to the blood vessel wall are seen with gold stains.

Spongioblastoma polare. This is a rare tumor, often beginning in childhood or adolescence, with its origin in the area of the third or fourth ventricle or midbrain. There may be early signs of increased intracranial pressure, due to blockage of ventricles, and signs implicating the midbrain. Its rate of growth is slow to moderate, but the course of disease may be relatively rapid, due to the tumor's location. The site of origin precludes surgery, and response to radiotherapy is minimal. The tumor appears as a firm mass, only fairly well-demarcated. Microscopic examination reveals spindle-shaped cells, often arranged in parallel, irregular bands with elongated nuclei and long processes extending from one or both poles of the cells.

Oligodendroglioma. The oligodendroglioma accounts for 5 per cent of all gliomas and usually begins in adult life within a cerebral hemisphere. The tumor is benign, can be completely removed, and has slight to moderate response to radiotherapy. It appears as a solid, well-demarcated mass, sometimes containing cysts, hemorrhages, and, usually, areas of calcification. The calcification can often be seen in roentgenograms of the skull. Microscopically (see Figure 4), one sees densely packed cells in uniform distribution. The scanty cytoplasm of the cell forms a halo-like zone around the conspicuous dark nucleus. Calcium deposits are prominent.

Ependymoma. The ependymoma constitutes 6 per cent of glial tumors and is predominantly a tumor of childhood and adolescence but often occurs in adults as well. It arises from the lining of the ventricles, particularly the fourth ventricle. The tumor is benign but usually causes increased intracranial pressure, due to blockage of the ventricular system, and its course may, therefore, be subacute. It can be only partially excised, but there is moderate response to radiotherapy. The tumor appears as an infiltrating mass. Under the microscope

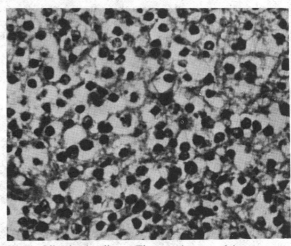

FIGURE 4. Oligodendroglioma. The prominent nuclei are surrounded by unstained cytoplasm. Hematoxylin and eosin, 400 X. (From Russell, D. S., and Rubenstein, L. L. *Pathology of Tumors of the Nervous System,* ed. 3, p. 148. Williams & Wilkins, Baltimore, 1971.)

(see Figure 5) there is a dense mass of cells with large oval nuclei. Many cells form perivascular rosettes or papillary tufts.

Papilloma of choroid plexus. This type of tumor makes up about 2 per cent of glial tumors. It is predominantly a tumor of children, especially boys. The tumor arises within the ventricles, most often the fourth ventricle, and causes increased intracranial pressure with hydrocephalus. The tumor is benign, can be completely removed by surgery, and responds somewhat to radiotherapy. It appears as a relatively small nodule within the ventricle. Microscopically, one sees columnar or cuboidal cells covering papillae with vascular cores.

Colloid cyst. The colloid cyst accounts for about 2 per cent of glial tumors and usually occurs in early adult life. It arises from the rostral portion of the roof of the third ventricle, is often mobile, and may cause intermittent increased intracranial pressure, due to occlusion of the foramen of Munro. The tumor is benign and can be completely

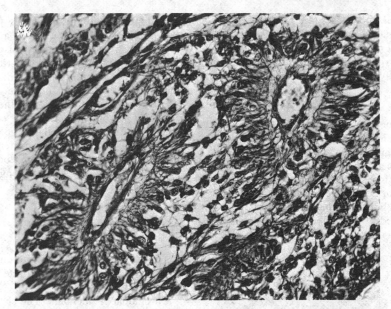

FIGURE 5. Ependymoma. Ependymal cells grouped around blood vessels form true rosettes. Phosphotungstic acid-hematoxylin, low power. (From Slager, U. T. *Basic Neuropathology,* p. 284. Williams & Wilkins, Baltimore, 1970.)

excised, but it does not respond to radiotherapy. It appears as a smooth cyst, and microscopically the cyst wall is lined by a single layer of columnar or cuboidal cells.

Pineal neoplasms. About two-thirds of these tumors are germinal tumors, such as teratomas and germinomas; one-third are tumors of pineal parenchyma, usually pineoblastomas. These rare tumors of the pineal gland usually occur during the first two decades of life, mostly in boys. By compressing the quadrigeminal plate, the tumor causes paralysis of upward gaze (Parinaud's syndrome); compression of the underlying Sylvian aqueduct results in symmetrical hydrocephalus. Precocious puberty, rarely seen with this tumor, is due to its compression of the hypothalamus, rather than to secretion of an occult hormone. Even if the tumor is histologically benign, the course is affected by its vital location. It cannot be surgically removed, but there is often excellent response to radiotherapy. The benign tumor appears as a smooth encapsulated mass; the malignant tumor is invasive. On microscopy, the pineoblastoma reveals many lymphoid cells and clusters of large cells with prominent nuclei containing one or two nucleoli, all within a stroma of connective tissue. Sometimes gliomas and cystic tumors arise from this site.

Medulloblastoma. This tumor accounts for 6 per cent of all neuroectodermal neoplasms. It occurs in childhood, more frequently in boys than in girls. The tumor usually arises in the midline of the cerebellum and causes increased intracranial pressure by expanding from the roof of the fourth ventricle and blocking cerebrospinal fluid outflow. The neoplasm is highly malignant, and cells may exfoliate and disseminate through the cerebrospinal fluid, becoming implanted in other parts of the cerebrospinal axis. It can be extensively excised, and there is usually an excellent initial response to radiotherapy. Unfortunately, recurrence is rapid, and the course is usually 6 to 9 months in duration. The tumor appears as a friable invasive mass. Under the microscope (see Figure 6), it is very cellular, with small pear-shaped cells containing prominent dark-staining nuclei, frequently in mitoses. Some cells may be grouped into pseudorosettes.

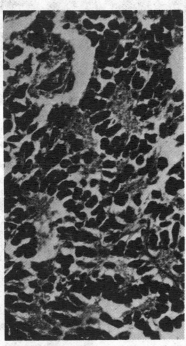

FIGURE 6. Medulloblastoma. Small cells with hyperchromatic nuclei and scanty cytoplasm occur in masses or are arranged in pseudorosettes. Phosphotungstic acid-hematoxylin, 420 X. (From Russell, D. S., and Rubenstein, L. L. *Pathology of Tumors of the Nervous System,* ed. 3, p. 186. Williams & Wilkins, Baltimore, 1971.)

METASTATIC TUMORS

Fifteen per cent of all intracranial neoplasms are metastatic malignancies. The lesions usually occur in adults and arise from carcinoma of the lung or breast; much less often, they arise as malignant melanomas or from malignancies of the kidneys and other organs. Death usually occurs within the first year, but radiotherapy with steroid therapy often prolongs useful life. Surgical excision of a single metastasis is rarely associated with long survival. Metastases (see Figure 7) appear as firm, well-demarcated masses within the parenchyma, but one-third of all intracranial metastases are meningeal. Microscopically, the tumors often resemble the primary lesion, but sometimes they are markedly altered and anaplastic.

MENINGIOMAS

Meningiomas account for 15 per cent of all intracranial tumors and usually occur in adults. These neoplasms arise from the meninges of the sagittal sinus, the sphenoid ridge, and over the convexity of the cerebrum and less often from any other site covered by meninges. The clinical characteristics depend on the specific site or origin. Meningiomas often cause hyperostosis of the adjacent bone that may be seen or palpated on examination or visualized in roentgenograms of the skull.

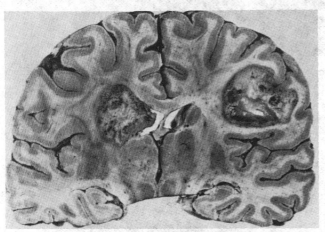

FIGURE 7. Metastatic carcinoma (from the lung). The well-circumscribed masses contain necrotic cysts. (From Russell, D. S., and Rubenstein, L. L. *Pathology of Tumors of the Nervous System,* ed. 3, p. 267. Williams & Wilkins, Baltimore, 1971.)

The tumor is benign and grows slowly, although meningeal sarcomas occur in rare cases. If accessible, the tumor can be completely removed, but response to radiotherapy is slight. The tumor appears as a firm, gritty, encapsulated mass, extending from the inner surface of the dura and compressing the underlying tissue. Under the microscope (see Figure 8A and B) one or a combination of the following features may be seen: (1) fibroblastic elongated cells forming reticulin and collagen; (2) meningothelial large cells with vesicular nuclei, often arranged in whorls, the centers of which may be replaced by calcium to form psammoma bodies; (3) mesenchymal bipolar or multipolar cells, with long processes intertwined into a loose network; (4) angioblastic, endothelial cells lining the vascular spaces.

TUMORS OF THE PITUITARY

Tumors arising from the pituitary or from embryonic rests adjacent to the pituitary constitute about 10 per cent of intracranial neoplasms.

Chromophobe adenoma. The chromophobe adenoma is the most common tumor of this group. It occurs in adult life from nonendocrine-producing cells of the pituitary. The tumor's expansion from the pituitary fossa causes compression of the optic chiasm and resultant bitemporal hemianopsia. Compression of endocrine-secreting cells of the pituitary results in hypopituitarism. The tumor is benign, and response to radiotherapy is usually good to excellent. The recent surgical approach through the nose and sphenoid sinus has been so successful that many consider it to be the treatment of choice. The tumor appears as a soft, circumscribed mass. Under the microscope, alveolar clusters of cells are seen with poorly staining cytoplasm but deeply staining nuclei.

Eosinophilic adenoma. This rare tumor occurs much more often in adults than in children and results in acromegaly or in gigantism, respectively. It is benign and responds to radiotherapy; transphenoidal

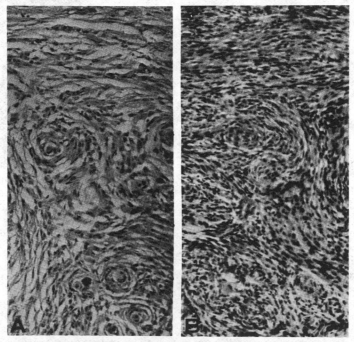

FIGURE 8. Meningioma. *A.* Whorl formations are prominent in this section. *B.* Interlacing sheets of fibroblastic cells are seen. Hematoxylin and eosin, 130 X. (From Russell, D. S., and Rubenstein, L. L. *Pathology of Tumors of the Nervous System,* ed. 3, p. 57. Williams & Wilkins, Baltimore, 1971.)

surgery is rarely recommended. The tumor consists of a small circumscribed mass within the pituitary fossa. Microscopically, one sees groups of cells in alveolar patterns. The cytoplasm surrounding a vesicular nucleus is filled with eosinophilic granules.

Basophilic adenoma. A basophilic adenoma of the pituitary is a rare tumor. Cushing's syndrome, associated with hyperplasia of the adrenal cortex, is usually due to this tumor of the pituitary. The neoplasm is benign and appears as a small, sometimes microscopic nodule made up of cells with basophilic granules in the cytoplasm.

Craniopharyngioma. These tumors occur one-half or one-third as often as chromophobe adenomas and are somewhat more frequent in childhood and adolescence than during adult life. The tumors arise above the pituitary fossa and usually compress the optic chiasm, causing bitemporal hemianopsia. Symptoms of hypothalamic disease and hypopituitarism often occur. Calcification frequently present within the tumor may be seen in roentgenograms of the skull. The tumor is benign, but complete removal by surgery is rare; a moderate response to radiotherapy may occur. It appears as an irregular grapelike mass of encapsulated cysts that contain thick oil-like fluid. On microscopic examination (see Figure 9), the cysts are lined by stratified squamous epithelium, forming papillary masses. Other forms of epithelial tissue may be seen. Calcification is frequently present.

Other tumors arising from embryonic rests in the midline at the base of the brain include teratomas, dermoid cysts, epidermoids, chordomas, and lipomas.

TUMORS OF CRANIAL NERVES

Schwannoma. Arising from the sheath of the acoustic nerve, the acoustic neuroma of schwannoma is the most common tumor of cranial nerves. This tumor accounts for 8 per cent of all intracranial tumors. It occurs in adults, women more often than men. The tumor is located in the cerebellopontine angle,

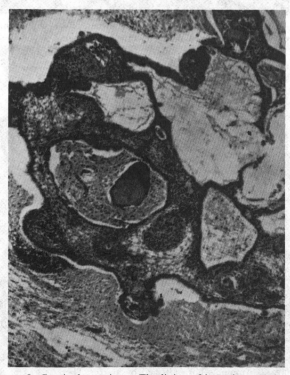

FIGURE 9. Craniopharyngioma. The lining of irregular cysts is composed of columnar cells forming a base for stratified squamous epithelium. Hematoxylin and eosin, 90 X. (From Russell, D. S., and Rubenstein, L. L. *Pathology of Tumors of the Nervous System*, ed. 3, p. 21. Williams & Wilkins, Baltimore, 1971.)

and symptoms result from involvement of the acoustic nerve and compression of adjacent trigeminal and facial nerves and cerebellum. The tumor is benign and can often be completely excised, but it does not respond to radiotherapy. The neuroma appears as an irregular, encapsulated, firm mass surrounding the acoustic nerve. Microscopically (see Figure 10), elongated fibroblastic cells with dark nuclei are seen in palisading interlacing rows associated with a great deal of collagenous tissue. The schwannoma may be part of a more generalized neurofibromatosis, the congenital often hereditary, Recklinghausen's disease.

Optic nerve glioma. The optic nerve glioma is a rare tumor of the first decade of life that arises from glial elements of the optic nerve. There is associated blindness and sometimes exophthalmus. Although the tumor is histologically benign, it infiltrates the optic chiasm and adjacent tissue, eventually causing death. In the early stage, however, it can be completely excised, and there may be good response to radiotherapy. The tumor appears as a bulb-like swelling around the nerve. Under the microscope, astrocytes and spongioblasts are the predominant cells.

VASCULAR TUMORS

Tumors of vascular origin are mainly hemangioblastomas. They account for only 1 or 2 per cent of all intracranial tumors and may be seen in adults as well as children, occurring more often in males than in females. Polycythemia is often evoked by the tumor. The most frequent site is the cerebellum. When this cerebellar tumor is associated with cystic disease of the kidneys, pancreas, or other organs and with angiomatosis of the retina, the clinical picture is called von Hippel-Lindau disease. The benign tumor can be totally removed, and it may also respond well to radiotherapy. It appears as a small red nodule within a cyst, and, on microscopy, small immature blood vessels or large endothelial cells are seen within a prominent reticular network.

Vascular Diseases of the Central Nervous System

The physiology of cerebral blood flow (CBF) has been more clearly documented during the past decade. Two major factors are autoregulation and metabolic control of CBF. Autoregulation refers to the maintenance of stable CBF in the presence of blood pressure alterations by cerebral vasodilation, with drop in blood pressure, and vasoconstriction, associated with blood pressure rise. The major metabolic factor regulating CBF is blood carbon dioxide levels. Increased cerebral metabolism generates more CO_2, and the subsequent increase in hydrogen ions evokes vasodilation and associated increase in CBF; decreased metabolism is associated with an opposite series of events. A less important factor is oxygen concentration; its effect on the arteries is the converse of the effect of CO_2.

Regional CBF is altered in association with acute cerebrovascular disease and with other cerebral lesions. Autoregulation is lost in the areas of diseased brain and sometimes in other areas as well. Hypotension under these circumstances is not compensated by vasodilation; instead, decrease in CBF occurs. Carbon dioxide accumulates in areas of acute infarction, and there is resultant local vasodilation, with loss of normal reactivity to further metabolic change. Although the above factors are relevant to small arteries and arterioles, they do not affect capillaries. Block of capillary microcirculation due to ischemically induced local cellular edema may result in infarction, even though the occlusion within the more proximal arterial tree has been transient.

Vascular lesions are the major cause of organic brain disease, yet the number of different diseases under this classification is

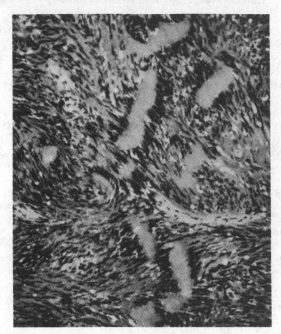

FIGURE 10. Schwannoma. Spindle-shaped fibroblasts are arranged in interlacing palisades. Hematoxylin and eosin, 110 X. (From Russell, D. S., and Rubenstein, L. L. *Pathology of Tumors of the Nervous System,* ed. 3, p. 289. Williams & Wilkins, Baltimore, 1971.)

relatively small. The lesions and their associated signs may be focal or scattered. Abrupt onset is most characteristic of sudden occlusion or rupture of an artery. With atherosclerosis of many small cerebral vessels, the onset of generalized symptoms may be insidious, and progression may be slow.

STENOSIS OR OCCLUSION OF ARTERIES: CEREBRAL INFARCTION OR ISCHEMIA

Causes. Atherosclerosis is the most common vascular disease. On examination of the affected vessel, one sees irregular yellow plaques projecting into the lumen, with stenosis or occlusion often due to superimposed thrombosis. In the early stages, fat-containing cells are deposited in the intima of the vessel, and there is an associated build-up of connective tissue. Later, degeneration with hyalinization and calcification occurs.

Hematological causes of thrombosis include sickle-cell anemia, thrombotic thrombocytopenia, and polycythemia vera. Arteritis, characterized by the mononuclear cell infiltration of all arterial layers, causes fibroblastic proliferation and subsequent stenosis or occlusion. These changes may be seen in syphilis and toxic encephalitis and as the result of infected emboli. Temporal arteritis and collagen diseases cause similar vascular occlusions.

Pathogenesis. Infarction is due to reduced blood supply to a local area. Complete arterial occlusion need not be present, for ischemia or hypoxia of sufficient duration and severity may cause irreparable damage. The rate of reduction in blood flow is an important factor in the development of infarction, as slow reduction allows collateral circulation to develop within the ischemic zone and may prevent the damage that almost invariably occurs with sudden major occlusive disease. Neurons are much more susceptible to ischemic damage than are astrocytes, and there are considerable differences in the vulnerability of nerve cells. Neurons of the cerebral cortex, particularly Ammon's horn, and Purkinje's cells of the cerebellar cortex are most vulnerable to ischemia (see Figures 11 through 14). An

infarct (see Figures 15 and 16) appears as a pale, often wedge-shaped zone of softening—first swollen, then shrunken. Embolic infarcts are frequently multiple and more often hemorrhagic than are infarcts of thrombotic origin. The microscopic reactions of neurons and glial cells to these and other injuries are described above.

Transient ischemic attacks (TIA's). TIA's are bouts of central nervous system symptoms or episodes of monocular blindness (amaurosis fugax) lasting for minutes or hours. These attacks are usually due to minute emboli that break away from atheromatous plaques within the carotid, vertebral, or basilar arteries. Less often, changes in the cardiovascular system, such as arrhythmia or hypotension, may induce a TIA. The transient attacks are followed by infarction (completed stroke) at a rate of 25 to 30 per cent during the first few months, then about 5 per cent a year.

TIA's within the vertebrobasilar system are usually mani-

FIGURE 11. Normal Ammon's horn—the portion of the hippocampus that projects into the temporal horn of the lateral ventricle. A layer of large pyramidal cells curves into the nerve cell layer of the dentate gyrus. Thionin, 9 X. (From Blackwood, W., Dodds, T. C., and Sommerville, J. C. *Atlas of Neuropathology,* ed. 2, p. 25. Williams & Wilkins, Baltimore, 1964.)

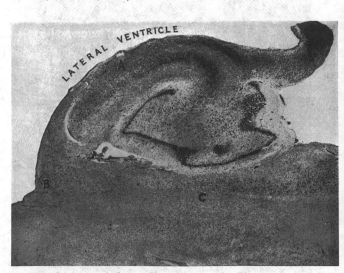

FIGURE 12. Ammon's horn affected by anoxia. There is loss of the pyramidal cell layer from *A* to *C.* That section between *A* and *B* (Sommer's sector) is particularly vulnerable to anoxia. Thionin, 10 X. (From Blackwood, W., Dodds, T. C., and Sommerville, J. C. *Atlas of Neuropathology,* ed. 2, p. 25. Williams & Wilkins, Baltimore, 1964.)

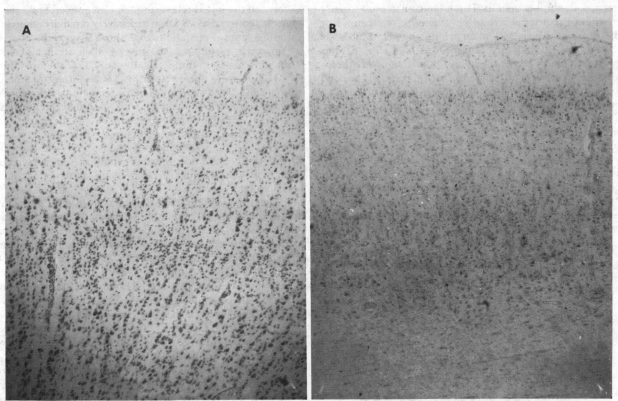

FIGURE 13. *A.* A portion of normal cerebral cortex. Nissl stain. 52 X. *B.* Cerebral cortex affected by anoxia. The cortex has shrunken in depth. Loss of neurons accounts for the decreased quantity of cell bodies, especially in the third layer of the cortex. Nissl stain, 60 X. (Courtesy of Dr. H. M. Zimmerman, Montefiore Hospital and Medical Center, New York, New York.)

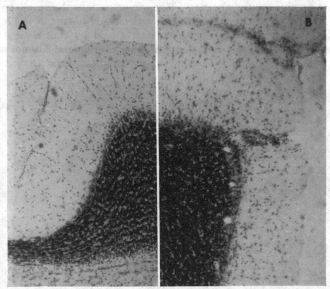

FIGURE 14. *A.* A section of normal adult cerebellar cortex. Note the layer of Purkinje's cells between the outer molecular layer and the inner granular layer of cells. Nissl stain, 68 X. *B.* Cerebellar cortex affected by anoxia. Loss of Purkinje's cells leaves empty spaces in their place. Nissl stain, 55 X. (Courtesy of Dr. H. M. Zimmerman.)

fested by one or more of the following: vertigo, diplopia or blurring of vision, perioral numbness, unsteadiness, or dysarthria; loss of consciousness or loss of body tone (drop attack) may also occur. In the subclavian steal syndrome, occlusion of the subclavian artery, proximal to the branching of the verte-

bral artery, causes brain stem ischemia when blood flows retrograde from the basilar and vertebral arteries into the distal subclavian, axillary, and brachial arteries. A decrease in the ipsilateral radial pulse or in the brachial blood pressure and a subclavian bruit are the chief clues to the condition. This lesion of the subclavian artery can be surgically corrected, but other atherosclerotic disease causing vertebrobasilar artery insufficiency is usually not amenable to surgery.

TIA's within the carotid arterial tree are manifested by bouts of ipsilateral amaurosis fugax with or without associated contralateral hemiparesis, hemisensory impairment, or homonymous hemianopsia; aphasia may occur if the dominant hemisphere is affected. There may be associated ipsilateral throbbing headache. Carotid stenosis or an ulcerating atheromatous plaque may cause none, one, or any combination of these symptoms. Examination may reveal bruits over the orbits or carotid arteries in the neck, diminished pulsation of the carotid artery or its temporal branch, or evidence of microemboli in the retinal arteries. There may be an ipsilateral partial Horner's syndrome. Decreased retinal artery pressure as measured by ophthalmodynamometry, decreased arterial perfusion as seen in the dynamic isotope brain scan, and changes found by Doppler and thermographic tests may support the diagnosis of carotid artery disease. Only arteriography is definitive, however, and visualization of all the cervicocephalic and cerebral vessels is necessary before endarterectomy is attempted.

Thrombotic infarction. Most cerebrovascular diseases are due to thrombotic infarction. Embolic infarction and cerebral hemorrhage are less common. The symptoms and signs of cerebral artery thrombosis usually occur rapidly—within minutes or hours. Sometimes the signs slowly progress. However, progression for more than 48 hours requires primary consideration of a cerebral neoplasm. Thrombotic infarctions usually occur within the arterial tree of an atherosclerotic carotid or middle cerebral artery, less often within the vertebrobasilar arterial system. Stenosis or occlusion of the internal carotid artery is a common cause of cerebral infarction. The atherosclerotic lesion on which thrombosis occurs is usually located just beyond the bifurcation of the common carotid artery.

Embolic infarction. Embolic infarcts are sudden in onset and often multiple. Emboli usually occur from a mural atrial thrombus in rheumatic heart disease with arrhythmia or from valvular vegetations of subacute bacterial endocarditis or marantic endocarditis. Emboli occur infrequently from the endocardium recently damaged by a myocardial infarct and in association with other cardiac disease. Fat emboli result from crushing injuries to the bone or other manipulation of fatty tissue; characteristically, a time lapse of 2 to 5 days occurs

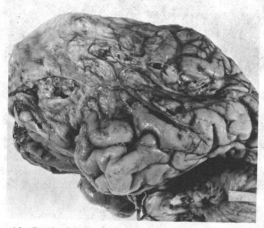

FIGURE 15. Cerebral infarction. The infarct and associated encephalomalacia affect predominantly the frontal lobe (and extend down to the external capsule). The lesion was caused by thrombotic occlusion of the left common carotid artery. (From Slager, U. T. *Basic Neuropathology,* p. 46. Williams & Wilkins, Baltimore, 1970.)

between the initial injury and the onset of cerebral symptoms. Air embolism may occur in excessively rapid decompression or during surgical operations that allow air into the arterial system, such as surgical abortion. Emboli from atheromatous plaques of major arteries usually cause TIA's before infarction.

Hypertensive encephalopathy. This is an uncommon condition caused by a sudden severe rise in blood pressure (diastolic pressure above 140 mm. Hg), with associated cerebral vasoconstriction. Headache, seizures, and obtundation are common, but any variety of generalized more than focal signs may occur. Severe hypertensive retinopathy is invariably present. Petichial hemorrhages and edema occur within the parenchyma of the brain as well. The use of rapid-acting antihypertensive agents is mandatory.

Focal signs of infarction. The classical syndrome of internal carotid occlusion is that of blindness of the ipsilateral eye (supplied by the ophthalmic branch of the internal carotid artery) and contralateral hemiparesis, hemisensory impairment, homonymous hemianopsia, and (if the dominant hemisphere is affected) aphasia. Usually, only fragments of the complete syndrome are seen. Occlusion of the main trunk of the middle cerebral artery causes the contralateral signs listed above. Occlusion of the anterior cerebral artery is associated with contralateral paresis of the lower extremity, and occlusion of the posterior cerebral artery results in contralateral homonymous hemianopsia. Sudden occlusion of the basilar artery is incompatible with life. More often, stenosis within the vertebral or basilar arteries causes ischemia or infarction of the brain stem, with a variety of ipsilateral cranial nerve signs and ipsilateral cerebellar signs, coupled with contralateral motor signs or sensory signs or both. The most common infarct of the brain stem is within the distribution of the posterior inferior cerebellar artery and is usually due to thrombosis of the adjoining vertebral artery. The resultant lateral medullary syndrome is characterized by vertigo and nystagmus, with ipsilateral ataxia and facial analgesia, and by contralateral analgesia of the trunk and extremities; ipsilateral Horner's syndrome and paresis of the soft palate, pharynx, and larynx

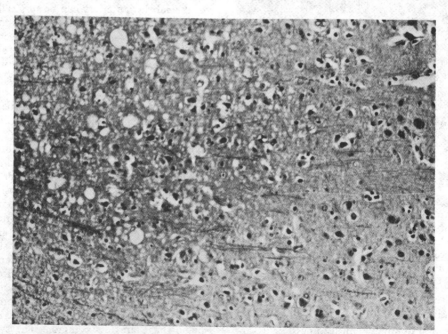

FIGURE 16. Cerebral infarction. The *upper left* area reveals necrosis and edema. The infarct is recent, and cellular reaction is not yet prominent. Luxol fast blue-hematoxylin-eosin, 130 X. (From Robertson, D. M., and Dinsdale, H. B. *The Nervous System,* p. 94. Williams & Wilkins, Baltimore, 1972.)

are usually present. In elderly hypertensive patients, multiple occlusions of small arterioles gradually occur deep in the cerebrum. The resolution of the resultant minute infarctions leaves lacunae. One of the associated lacunar syndromes is manifested by the insidious development of dementia, psychomotor retardation, and pseudobulbar signs, with gait impairment and incontinence. Frequently, however, the lacunae are clinically silent.

Treatment. Specific treatment of a completed cerebral infarct is still unsatisfactory; supportive therapy, especially of the patient's cardiovascular status, continues to be essential. Vasodilating agents have not proved to be of value and may, indeed, hinder local cerebral blood flow in the area of the infarction where vessels are already maximally dilated. Agents such as mannitol and steroids, used to reduce edema in the hope of opening blocked capillary circulation, have not been successful. Anticoagulants have been effective in reducing TIA's but are of doubtful value in preventing infarction. Antiplatelet agents—such as aspirin, dipyridamole, and sulfinpyrazone—may prove to reduce the chances of both stroke and TIA's. A completed infarct may sometimes be prevented by treating a stroke in progression with intravenous heparin. Anticoagulant therapy is particularly indicated in the prophylaxis of embolic infarction, except when the process is septic. Carotid endarterectomy is of definite value in preventing cerebral infarction in those patients who present with the warning TIA's. The ideal candidate for carotid surgery is a relatively young person with a single arterial lesion that has caused TIA's with little or no residual neurological deficit, but not all patients are good, let alone ideal, surgical candidates. A new surgical approach to stroke prophylaxis is that of enhancing the brain's collateral circulation by microvascular anastomosis between a branch of the superficial temporal artery in the scalp and a cortical branch of the middle cerebral artery or, for the vertebrobasilar circulation, joining the occipital artery in the scalp to the posterior inferior cerebellar artery.

INTRACRANIAL HEMORRHAGE

Cerebral hemorrhage. Long-standing hypertension not only hastens atherosclerosis but causes microaneurysms of arterioles, especially the deep perforating vessels, usually in the area of the putamen or less often the thalamus. When one or more of these lesions blows out, hemorrhage results. Cerebral hemorrhage may also be due to rupture of an aneurysm or an arteriovenous malformation. Petechial hemorrhages are small, scattered lesions and may be associated with severe infections or toxic reactions. Much less common causes of hemorrhage include blood dyscrasias and vascular malformations.

A large cerebral hemorrhage is manifested by the sudden onset of loss of consciousness and focal neurological signs; it is often catastrophic, and the prognosis is poor. Cerebellar and brain stem hematomas account for 10 per cent of all parenchymal hemorrhages and are usually associated with hypertension or a cryptic arteriovenous malformation. Depression of consciousness and progressive ataxia, which may be solely truncal, are the chief clues to a remediable cerebellar hematoma. As the disease progresses, gaze palsies with small pupils and hemiparesis or quadriparesis occur.

Surgical evacuation of the hematoma may be indicated only if the hematoma acts as an expanding, relatively superficial cerebral mass or if it is within the cerebellum. Computerized tomography of the head is the best method of establishing the diagnosis of hemorrhage.

Subarachnoid hemorrhage: aneurysm. Ruptured aneurysms

in or near the circle of Willis are the most common causes of subarachnoid hemorrhages. The mortality rate of this disease is close to 50 per cent for each bleeding episode. The hemorrhage is manifested by the sudden onset of severe headache and, usually, loss or alteration of consciousness; nuchal rigidity is found on examination. If blood from the ruptured aneurysm breaks into the parenchyma, focal neurological signs occur (see Figure 17). Aneurysms may also cause signs by their pressure on adjacent structures, such as the oculomotor nerve. Blood is found on lumbar puncture, with xanthochromia of the supernatant cerebrospinal fluid. Computerized tomography often confirms the diagnosis before the lumbar puncture. Angiography is necessary to define the vascular anatomy.

Most aneurysms are due to congenital defects in the media of the arterial wall, especially at the bifurcation of vessels. Mycotic aneurysms are secondary to infection, often spread from subacute bacterial endocarditis. Atherosclerosis or trauma may weaken an arterial wall and lead to aneurysmal formation. A carotid cavernous sinus fistula is due to rupture of the carotid artery within the cavernous sinus and causes pulsating exophthalmus, ophthalmoplegia, and bruit. Dissecting aneurysm of the aorta may occlude or extend into the carotid artery.

The treatment of choice for a cerebral aneurysm is surgical ligation of the neck of the aneurysm, if accessible. Less satisfactory is the ligation of the common carotid artery supplying the aneurysm. Bed rest, control of blood pressure, and prevention of clot lysis within the aneurysm by means of the antifibrinolytic agent aminocaproic acid are the major features of initial conservative therapy. The ideal time for surgery after the onset of subarachnoid hemorrhage has not been established.

OTHER CONGENITAL VASCULAR LESIONS

Arteriovenous malformation. An arteriovenous malformation consists of a tangle of abnormal arteries and veins within the cerebrum. After aneurysms, this lesion is the most common intracranial vascular anomaly. Seizures may occur, and a bruit is frequently heard, but often the first clinical manifestation is bleeding, with resulting neurological defect. An intracerebral or subarachnoid hemorrhage caused by an arteriovenous malformation is usually less serious than a hemorrhage associated with a ruptured aneurysm.

Sturge-Weber syndrome. This syndrome is manifested by a facial wine-colored nevus, contralateral neurological signs, epilepsy, and glaucoma. Roentgenograms of the skull reveal curvilinear calcifications

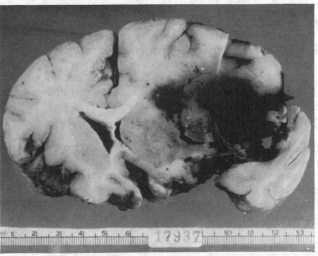

FIGURE 17. A ruptured aneurysm and associated massive cerebral hemorrhage. (Courtesy of Dr. H. M. Zimmerman.)

that have developed in an atrophic cortex underlying a meningeal angiomatous malformation, most often over the occipital area. Angioma of the choroid of the eye is often present.

Telangiectasis. Familial telangiectasis (Rendu-Osler-Weber disease) is a condition manifested by multiple telangiectases of the skin and mucous membranes. Similar involvement of the brain rarely results in small hemorrhages. Ataxia telangiectasis adds cerebellar signs to oculocutaneous telangiectases, and immune defects lead to recurrent respiratory infections.

VENOUS OCCLUSION

Primary aseptic thrombosis of dural sinuses is sometimes seen in children who suffer from malnutrition or who have serious systemic illnesses. Thromboses of dural sinuses are more often secondary to pyogenic infections. These lesions are manifested by increased intracranial pressure and congestion in the area of the head or face normally drained by the affected sinus and its contributory veins. Venous thrombosis, especially of cortical veins, may be a postpartum complication; convulsive seizures and focal signs are due to passively congested cerebral tissue.

ARTERITIS OF CEREBRAL VESSELS: COLLAGEN DISEASES

These diseases affect predominantly connective tissue. Degeneration of connective tissue is associated with inflammatory cell infiltration and fibroblastic proliferation. These illnesses are discussed here under diseases of the vascular system because most of the related central nervous system symptoms and signs are due to multiple small-vessel occlusions. The resultant zones of ischemia gradually coalesce to form infarctions. All organ systems may be affected, and virtually any symptom or sign referable to the central or peripheral nervous systems may occur. The diseases in the arteritis-collagen family usually respond to steroid therapy, and prompt treatment is particularly essential in cases of temporal arteritis.

Temporal arteritis (giant-cell arteritis) occurs in elderly patients and is manifested by headache in the area of a swollen, hard, and tender temporal artery of the scalp. The disease often involves other cranial arteries, and inflammation of the retinal arteries results in blindness in about 25 per cent of untreated patients.

Polymyalgia rheumatica is closely related to giant-cell arteritis. This disease of the elderly is manifested by muscle pains and malaise, but a paucity of objective signs often falsely raises the question of psychogenicity. An elevated sedimentation rate is the chief laboratory sign, short of temporal artery biopsy.

In systemic lupus erythematosus, central nervous system involvement may occur early, and 75 per cent of patients develop neurological or psychological problems in the course of their illness. Convulsive seizures and toxic psychosis are common.

Peripheral neuropathy develops in 30 to 50 per cent of patients with polyarteritis nodosa, but central nervous system involvement is much less common.

Arteritis of the aorta and its major branches (pulseless disease or Takayasu's disease) is most common in young women, and neurological symptoms are due to ischemia of the brain stem or the cerebrum.

Thrombotic thrombocytopenic purpura often causes multiple infarcts or hemorrhages in the cerebrum and in other organs.

Other collagen diseases include dermatomyositis, sclero-

derma, and rheumatoid arthritis, but these diseases do not usually affect the central nervous system. Rheumatic fever is considered by some to be a collagen disease.

DISEASES OF THE HEMATOPOIETIC SYSTEM

Sickle-cell anemia is a hereditary disease affecting young blacks. In addition to anemia, the course is characterized by multiple thrombotic infarcts of bones and viscera. Neurological features occur in 25 per cent of all cases and are due to cerebral thrombosis or hemorrhage. Roentgenograms of the skull reveal a ground-glass appearance of the bone, with spicules projecting through the outer table.

Hemophilia is a hereditary disease of abnormal blood coagulation. It affects males but is transmitted by women. The neurological complications are associated with intracranial bleeding.

Polycythemia vera is characterized by an excess of red blood cells and all other cellular elements of the blood. There is associated increased blood viscosity and splenomegaly. It usually begins after the age of 50 and affects men more often than women. Headaches and other nonspecific neurological symptoms are so common that patients are often labeled neurotic. More serious features are associated with thrombosis of cerebral vessels, either arteries or veins. Venous congestion may cause increased intracranial pressure. Cerebellar hemangioblastoma is sometimes associated with this disease.

Thrombotic thrombocytopenic purpura and, less often, disseminated intravascular coagulation may cause cerebral symptoms ranging from transient ischemic attacks to frank infarction, with either focal or generalized brain dysfunction.

Macroglobulinemia, Waldenström's syndrome, is considered a neoplasia of the reticuloendothelial system. It usually occurs in middle or late adult life, affecting men more often than women. Its course is relatively chronic. Hemorrhagic diatheses occur in two-thirds of these patients. Cerebral involvement may be acute and focal, due to hemorrhage; or multifocal or diffuse, due to lymphocyte and plasma cell infiltration. Peripheral nerve lesions may also occur.

Multiple myeloma and other dysglobulinemias affect the central nervous system as a result of blood hyperviscosity. Tumor may infiltrate the brain.

Leukemia causes cerebral disease because of hemorrhage more often than thrombosis. There may be leukemic infiltration of the meninges or the parenchyma. Associated impairment of the patient's immune defenses may result in infections, such as fungal meningitis, herpes zoster, and progressive multifocal leukoencephalopathy (papova-virus). Other lymphomas, Hodgkin's disease, lymphosarcoma, and reticulosarcoma involve the central nervous system about 25 per cent of the time, and their complications are similar to those just noted.

Subacute combined system disease of pernicious anemia and kernicterus may also be considered under diseases of the hematopoietic system but are discussed later.

Trauma to the Central Nervous System

In most cases these disorders can be diagnosed on the basis of history, but unrecognized trauma may be associated with convulsive seizures or alcoholic intoxication and may occur in the elderly, especially those with dementia. Neurological signs of cerebral trauma may be focal or diffuse and, with the exception of dural hemorrhages, usually show evidence of gradual improvement. Recovery is not always complete, and focal signs, as well as mental and personality changes, may be permanent sequelae. Posttraumatic epilepsy and other neurological lesions occur more often after open-head injuries than after closed-head injuries.

Cerebral injury need not underlie the site of trauma but may be *contrecoup*—opposite the point of trauma—due to a shift of the brain against the confines of the skull. This shift occurs particularly when the trauma is directed to the frontal or occipital portions of the head.

Fractures of the base of the skull are notoriously difficult to detect in roentgenograms but are often clinically evident by ecchymoses over the postauricular area (Battle's sign) or around the orbits (raccoon-eyes sign) or by blood behind the ear drum or in the outer ear canal. Fractures through the cribriform plate or the middle ear may cause rhinorrhea or otorrhea, respectively—a leak of cerebrospinal fluid (CSF) through the skull, with associated risk of intracranial infection. Rhinorrhea of CSF can be distinguished from the secretion of nasal mucosa by the presence of glucose in the CSF.

DEGREES OF CEREBRAL TRAUMA

Cerebral concussion. This clinical term denotes unconsciousness with rapid recovery and lack of residual cerebral signs. Repeated cerebral concussions, on the other hand, may eventually lead to irreversible brain damage, as seen, for example, in the punch-drunk boxer. Experimental studies and those few cases that have come to autopsy have revealed petechial hemorrhages and associated edema.

Cerebral contusion. In a patient with cerebral contusion, residual signs of cerebral injury are noted after recovery of consciousness, but these signs usually show extensive improvement or complete clearing. The inferior aspects of the frontal (see Figure 18) and temporal lobes are particularly subject to contusion. The injured areas of the brain appear discolored because of the confluence of small hemorrhages and associated maceration of the parenchyma.

Cerebral laceration. The patient with cerebral laceration has severe and often permanent signs of cerebral damage after prolonged unconsciousness. The lesion is often associated with a depressed skull fracture, and bony fragments may cause gross tears of the brain tissue.

Intracerebral hemorrhage, usually superficial, is frequently associated with severe head injury—that is, contusion or laceration of the brain. The symptoms may simulate that of a subdural hematoma, and surgical therapy may be warranted.

POSTCONCUSSION SYNDROME

As the name implies, this condition follows relatively minor, rather than major, head injuries. The syndrome is characterized by one or a variety of neurological symptoms, most often headache and dizziness. Other symptoms that are impossible to document are fatigue and impairment of concentration. Personality changes most often include irritability and depression, often with associated insomnia or impotence. Postconcussion syndrome is difficult to evaluate because there usually are no accompanying objective neurological signs. It is often impossible to decide whether the symptoms have an occult neurophysiological mechanism or whether the condition is solely an emotional phenomenon.

DURAL HEMORRHAGES

Dural hemorrhages may be cured by prompt diagnosis—verifying the clinical suspicion by computerized tomography or angiography—and surgical evacuation.

Epidural hemorrhage. An epidural hemorrhage is acute because of arterial bleeding, most often from a rupture of the middle meningeal artery in its course through a fractured temporal bone. After an initial loss of consciousness caused by trauma, the patient awakens for a short time. He then lapses into stupor and coma.

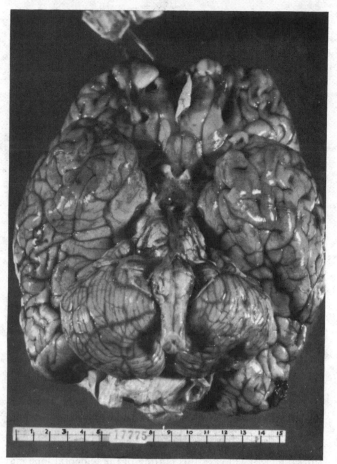

FIGURE 18. Severe contusion of the frontal poles has resulted in their atrophy and distortion. (Courtesy of Dr. H. M. Zimmerman.)

Subdural hematoma. A subdural hematoma is usually subacute or chronic (see Figure 19) and due to bleeding from traumatically sheared veins in the subdural space. A history of trauma need not be present; particularly in infants and the elderly, this diagnosis should be suspected when a deteriorating neurological course is evident. Generalized cerebral symptoms of depressed consciousness, organic mental disorder, headache, and other symptoms of increased intracranial pressure are common. The most accurate lateralizing sign is ipsilateral pupillary dilation when the oculomotor nerve is compressed in the course of herniation of the medial temporal lobe through the tentorium of the cerebellum. Focal signs need not be present or may be falsely localizing—for example, a shift of the contralateral cerebral peduncle against the tentorium of the cerebellum may cause hemiparesis ipsilateral to the intracranial mass. Subdural hematomas are located predominantly over the frontal and parietal areas of the brain.

In the early stages, liquid blood or a black clot is present, but soon organization occurs. New capillaries and fibroblasts grow from the dura and enclose the hematoma with a false membrane that grows increasingly dense. The new vessels within this membrane may exude serum or may rupture and cause additional bleeding, thus enlarging the total size of the mass. When fully encapsulated, the hematoma changes to brown fluid; eventually, the fluid turns yellow, although it still contains blood elements.

Subarachnoid hemorrhage and arteriovenous fistulas may result from trauma. Their manifestations are noted above.

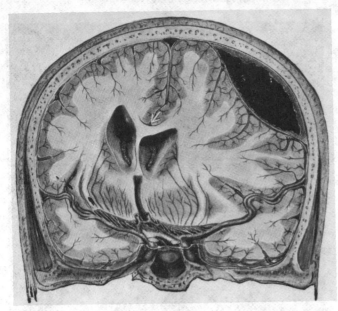

FIGURE 19. Chronic subdural hematoma. The mass displaces the brain toward the opposite side. (From Blackwood, W., Dodds, T. C., and Sommerville, J. C. *Atlas of Neuropathology*, ed. 2, p. 167. Williams & Wilkins, Baltimore, 1964.)

BIRTH TRAUMA

Trauma at the time of birth may result in cerebral palsy or intellectual retardation. Cerebral edema associated with the birth process sometimes causes herniation of the uncus of the temporal lobe through the tentorium of the cerebellum. The subsequent ischemia of this portion of the temporal lobe may result in a small glial scar that later becomes epileptogenic and produces psychomotor (temporal lobe) seizures.

OTHER FORMS OF TRAUMA

Electric shock. Electric shock occurs by accidental contact with lines of moderate voltage and high amperage. Coma and almost any variety of central and peripheral nervous system signs may be noted. Electric convulsive therapy rarely causes permanent organic mental disorder. The brain reveals small hemorrhages, perivascular edema, zones of necrosis, and scattered neuronal degeneration.

Heat. Heat exhaustion is related to loss of water and chlorides. It is manifested by generalized weakness, headache, muscular cramps, nausea, and vomiting; sometimes loss of consciousness occurs. Heat stroke secondary to a high environmental temperature with dehydration, and malignant hyperthermia as a complication of general anesthesia are serious diseases with high mortality rates. Weakness, dizziness, stupor, sometimes delirium or convulsions, and eventually coma occur. High fever is associated with the cessation of sweating. The fever must be quickly reduced to save the patient's life. Both the brain and the meninges are edematous, petechial hemorrhages are present, and degeneration of nerve cells is seen.

Cold. Severe cold may be associated with peripheral neuritis, but disease of the brain does not occur. On the contrary, hypothermia lowers oxygen consumption and cerebral metabolism, facts that may be therapeutically applicable.

Radiation. Neurological symptoms and signs referable to an area of former radiotherapy are most often correctly attributed to recurrent malignancy. Occasionally, however, the clinical features are caused by radiation injury. The effects of such injury usually begin from 6 to 18 months after radiation. The necrosis of the central nervous system caused by radiation is progressive.

Burns. Burns may cause lethargy, disorientation, seizures, and a variety of other mental and focal neurological signs. These phenomena seem to be due to an alteration of cerebral blood flow; toxic and metabolic factors probably play large roles. Cerebral edema and petechial hemorrhages are the chief pathological features.

Degenerative Diseases (Including Deficiency States) of the Central Nervous System of Adults

The term "degenerative diseases of the central nervous system" is often a euphemism for illnesses of unknown cause. One by one, the pathophysiological mechanisms of these diseases are being understood. Subacute combined degeneration is now known to be related to a vitamin B_{12} deficiency, and hepatolenticular degeneration has been found to be associated with defective copper metabolism. Other metabolic causes will probably be found for many other so-called degenerative diseases.

In many diseases a definite hereditary pattern has been discerned. There have been great advances in the understanding of inherited enzymatic deficiencies that cause metabolic defects and associated degenerative changes in children. Autoimmune reactions are currently thought to be an important mechanism in multiple sclerosis, but this and other demyelinating diseases have been particularly baffling. Occult infectious processes with a mechanism akin to that of postencephalitic parkinsonism may be the underlying basis of some illnesses. A slow virus infestation has now been proved for diseases formerly classified as degenerative, such as Creutzfeldt-Jakob disease and kuru.

The degenerative diseases remain the most frustrating in the search for underlying causes and the most resistant to treatment. These diseases usually begin insidiously and progress slowly, and there is tremendous variability in their courses.

DISSEMINATED DEMYELINATING DISEASES

In this group of diseases, the lesions may occur in small scattered zones or may involve large areas. In any one case, all stages in the process of demyelination may be seen (see Figure 20), from early breakdown of myelin sheaths and removal of debris by fat-laden phagocytic microglia to glial proliferation and resultant scar. Sometimes extensive degeneration causes cavity formation within the glial scar. The degeneration of axis cylinders usually depends on the severity of the demyelination.

Demyelinating disorders may be classified into those of unknown cause, those associated with known inborn errors of metabolism, and those presumed to be immunologically mediated, with or without associated viral induction. Multiple sclerosis and progressive mutifocal leukoencephalopathy are diseases predominantly of adults; all the others are, with rare exceptions, diseases of children and are discussed later.

Multiple sclerosis. This, the most common demyelinating disease, usually begins between the ages of 20 and 40 years. The disease is most prevalent in those who have spent their childhoods in the northern latitudes. It is postulated that a viral illness in childhood induces an autoimmune reaction many years later. Antibodies against measles have been found in the

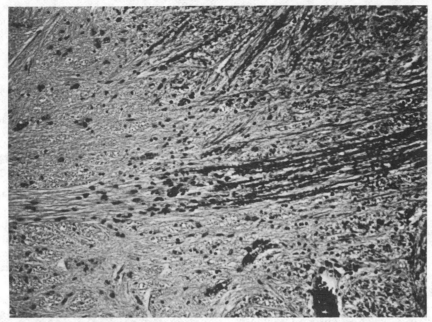

FIGURE 20. Demyelination of multiple sclerosis. The horizontal bundles of axons lose their myelin sheaths at the edge of a plaque of demyelination (the *left half* of the field). Luxol fast blue-Bodian, 125 X. (From Robertson, D. M., and Dinsdale, H. B. *The Nervous System,* p. 111. Williams & Wilkins, Baltimore, 1972.)

serum and the cerebrospinal fluid of many patients with multiple sclerosis but not in control subjects.

The disease is mutiple in space (central nervous system) and in time. Involvement of the optic nerve by retrobulbar neuritis causes unilateral blindness. Disease of the brain stem is often manifested by diplopia and nystagmus; internuclear ophthalmoplegia, with nystagmus of the abducting eye and palsy of the adducting eye on lateral gaze, is almost exclusively due to multiple sclerosis affecting the medial longitudinal fasciculus. Cerebellar demyelination is manifested by ataxia, with intention tremor and scanning (staccato) speech. Spinal cord involvement results in paraparesis, with impaired sphincter control and impaired sexual potency. A lesion of the pyramidal tract anywhere along its course from the cerebrum to the spinal cord may cause monoparesis or hemiparesis. Such signs as hemiparesis and an organic mental disorder occur infrequently; seizures, aphasia, and homonymous hemianopsia are rare. The symptoms often outnumber the signs, and at the onset of the disease may be mistaken for a neurosis. Conversely, signs may be found without associated symptoms. Euphoria, often present in these patients, may be similarly misinterpreted as *la belle indifférence* of hysteria. The course is characterized by exacerbations and remissions of unpredictable severity, duration, and frequency.

Optic nerve disease, not otherwise evident, may be established by the finding of a cecocentral scotoma in the visual field examination. Cortical-evoked potentials may also verify disease of the visual or somatosensory pathways when signs are not present on neurological examination. The other laboratory aid in the diagnosis is an elevated γ-globulin content of the spinal fluid, found in about 65 per cent of cases. Adequate treatment is not available, but steroids are considered of value in ameliorating the acute attack, and long-term steroid or immunosuppressive therapy is believed by some to decrease the frequency of exacerbations.

Gross examination of the brain (see Figure 21) reveals scattered gray, sharply demarcated plaques of demyelination

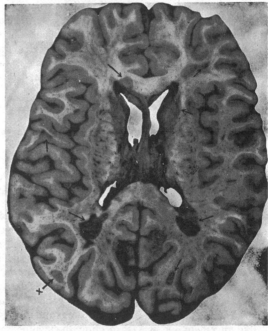

FIGURE 21. Multiple sclerosis. The *arrows* indicate plaques of demyelination. Note their predominance in the ventricular area and near the cortex. *X* indicates the section of a deep gyrus, not an abnormal plaque. (From Blackwood, W., Dodds, T. C., and Sommerville, J. C. *Atlas of Neuropathology,* ed. 2, p. 81. Williams & Wilkins, Baltimore, 1964.)

variable in size and shape, most numerous in the areas adjacent to the ventricles. In recent areas of demyelination, microscopic examination shows destruction of myelin, swollen axis cylinders, and many fat-laden phagocytic cells. Old areas of demyelination (see Figure 22) reveal complete myelin loss, with fragmentation of axis cylinders and the formation of a dense

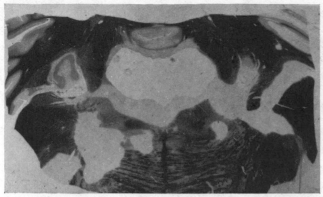

FIGURE 22. Multiple sclerosis. Irregular, seemingly punched-out zones of demyelination are evident in this section through the level of the fourth ventricle. Myelin stain, 2.6 X. (Courtesy of Dr. H. M. Zimmerman.)

glial scar. Often, there is remarkable preservation of nerve cells within the demyelinated plaques.

Neuromyelitis optica (Devic's disease). This is probably a variant of multiple sclerosis in which lesions are fortuitously limited to the spinal cord and the optic nerves.

Progressive multifocal leukoencephalopathy. This disease occurs in late adult life and causes death in 2 to 6 months. It is due to papova-virus infiltration after immune mechanisms have been impaired, most often by a malignant lymphoma. The disease is manifested by lethargy, progressive dementia, and multifocal cerebral signs. Under the microscope, one sees zones of demyelination scattered throughout the cerebrum. At the periphery of the demyelinated areas are monster-sized astrocytes and oligodendroglia, with enlarged nuclei; inclusion bodies may be found in some of the glial cells.

DISEASES AFFECTING PREDOMINANTLY THE CEREBRAL CORTEX

Alzheimer's disease. The division of dementias into senile and presenile varieties is no longer considered appropriate, for the only clinical feature that distinguishes the two is the age of onset; there are no pathological differences. Alzheimer's disease accounts for half of all cases of dementia. It is manifested by chronic progressive deterioration of intellect and personality, beginning after the fifth decade. Minor focal neurological signs may occur but, with the exception of aphasia, not gross defects. In any case of progressive dementia, a brain tumor in the frontal lobe or other silent area must always be considered, as well as other treatable causes. There is not very good correlation between the severity of the pathological findings and the degree of clinical involvement. On gross inspection, the meninges may appear thickened and opaque. The underlying brain, particularly the frontal lobes, exhibits generalized or scattered atrophy, manifested by narrow convolutions and wide sulci. Ventricular enlargement is seen in the cut section, and small cavities within the parenchyma may be noted. Microscopic examination (see Figure 23) reveals neural degeneration with Alzheimer's neurofibrillary changes (fusion of neurofibrils into small tangled masses), ghost cells, and altered lamination of the cortex. Senile plaques, characterized by large extracellular silver-staining masses with radiating fibrils, are prominent in the cerebral cortex and the basal ganglia, maximal in the area of major cell damage. Granulovacuolar degeneration of neurons is noted, particularly in the pyramidal cells of the hippocampus.

Pick's disease. Pick's disease is a rare form of dementia. The age of onset and the clinical manifestations are similar to those in Alzheimer's disease. On inspection of the brain (see Figure 24), there is marked localized, asymmetrical atrophy of all or part of the frontal lobe or temporal lobe. Under the microscope, severe neuronal loss is seen, with destruction of normal cortical layers. Characteristic but not invariable are Pick cells—neurons with large argentophilic inclusions in the cytoplasm that may displace the nucleus. Severe demyelination and glial proliferation are associated microscopic features.

DISEASES AFFECTING PREDOMINANTLY THE CEREBRAL CORTEX AND THE BASAL GANGLIA

Huntington's chorea. Huntington's chorea is inherited as an autosomal dominant trait, thus affecting 50 per cent of every generation. The disease usually begins between 30 and 50 years of age, but much earlier onset is not rare. A change in personality is the first sign in half the cases, and psychoses are manifest during the course of the illness in 50 per cent of all

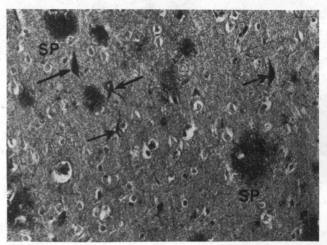

FIGURE 23. Alzheimer's disease. Senile argyrophilic plaques (*SP*) and Alzheimer's neurofibrillary degenerations (*arrows*) are seen in this section of the cerebral cortex. Modification of Bielschowsky's silver stain, 250 X. (Courtesy of Dr. H. M. Zimmerman.)

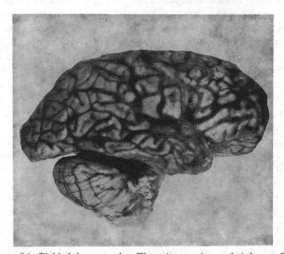

FIGURE 24. Pick's lobar atrophy. There is prominent shrinkage of the temporal lobe with generalized atrophy of the middle and anterior aspects of the hemisphere. (From Blackwood, W., Dodds, T. C., and Sommerville, J. C. *Atlas of Neuropathology*, ed. 2, p. 113. Williams & Wilkins, Baltimore, 1964.)

patients with the disease. Dementia slowly develops, with the psychological symptoms; months or years later, chorea insidiously begins. Sometimes the two begin together; less often, chorea precedes dementia. The mental, emotional, and motor defects slowly progress, leading to death in about 15 years. The chorea often causes multiple injuries. The knowledge of the disease and its consequences and the associated personality changes are associated with a high suicide rate. Only symptomatic therapy is available.

The biochemical defects are the converse of those in Parkinson's disease. In Huntington's chorea there is a heightened response of striatal receptors to dopamine. Impairment of acetylcholine and other neurotransmitters is also present. It has been said that 3 gm. a day of levodopa may precipitate chorea in potential victims, thus allowing early diagnosis and genetic counseling. At autopsy there is neuronal loss and atrophy of the caudate and putamen, as well as of the cerebral cortex, but these features are not pathognomonic.

Wilson's disease (hepatolenticular degeneration). This familial disease of adolescence more often has a chronic course than an acute course. It is characterized by dementia and a combination of cerebellar and extrapyramidal signs. Kayser-Fleischer rings (gray-brown-green in color) are noted along the outer zone of the corneas. Portal cirrhosis of the liver is invariably present. In this disease of defective copper metabolism, excessive copper deposits in tissues cause the clinical and pathological features. The findings of high copper output in the urine, aminoaciduria, and low ceruloplasmin (the copper-carrying plasma protein) confirm the clinical diagnosis. Although the basic metabolic defect is unaffected, treatments with dimercaprol (BAL) to hasten copper excretion and penicillamine to decrease copper absorption are beneficial in prolonging life beyond the average 5 to 10 years. On gross inspection of the brain, wasting of the lenticular nuclei, especially the putamen, and other basal ganglia is seen. Under the microscope, neuronal loss is predominant in the putamen, other basal ganglia, the frontal cortex, and the dentate nucleus of the cerebellum. Large phagocytic cells containing hemosiderin (Opalski cells) are characteristic of Wilson's disease. Proliferation of astrocytes with large nuclei and demyelination of the subcortical white matter are usually seen.

Creutzfeldt-Jakob disease. Formerly classified as degenerative, this disease is now known to be due to a slow virus and is discussed later.

Parkinsonism-dementia complex. This peculiar disease, characterized by a combination of dementia and parkinsonism, is found in 7 per cent of the native population of Guam. Most of the pathological features of parkinsonism and of Alzheimer's dementia are found, but argyrophilic plaques and Lewy bodies are usually absent.

DISEASES AFFECTING PREDOMINANTLY THE BASAL GANGLIA

Parkinson's disease. This disease occurs in about 1 per cent of the population over the age of 50 years. It is usually of unknown cause (idiopathic), arteriosclerosis no longer being considered a significant factor. The condition may also occur as a sequela of encephalitis, as in the cases after the pandemic in the early decades of this century, or it may be the result of toxins, such as manganese and carbon monoxide, or of drugs, such as the phenothiazines and butyrophenones.

Parkinsonism is characterized by resting tremor (usually beginning with the pill-rolling type), rigidity (with cogwheeling quality), bradykinesis, and the impairment of postural reflexes, which affect such simple acts as arising from a chair and rolling over in bed. Mask-like facies and flexed posture are common. The clinical features may occur individually or together. Akathisia, the inability to remain still, rarely occurs. Oculogyric crises, the involuntary fixation of the eyes in one position for

minutes or hours, is an occasional manifestation of postencephalitic parkinsonism. The intimate relationship of this disease to the patient's emotional state is evidenced when organic clinical features, such as tremor, are invariably aggravated by mild emotional stress. Dementia is common in disease of long duration.

Parkinsonism is the most recent example of a degenerative disease of adult life whose pathophysiological clarification has led to major therapeutic benefits. The major site of dopamine, a neurotransmitter, is in the substantia nigra, putamen, and caudate nuclei. In the normal basal ganglia, there is a balance between dopanergic inhibition and cholinergic excitation. In parkinsonism the dopamine stores are depleted.

In the past, anticholinergic agents—belladonna, trihexyphenidyl, benztropine, and others—were primarily used in the treatment of Parkinson's disease. These drugs are now considered adjuvants. Levodopa, which redresses the dopamine deficiency, is now the treatment of choice. It is usually administered with carbidopa, a peripheral dopa decarboxylase inhibitor that allows a higher percentage of levodopa to enter the brain and so permits a 4-fold decrease in levodopa dosage. Amantadine also has dopanergic properties and is useful. Bromocriptine and lergotrile are other dopanergic compounds that have been found to be useful in some patients who do not respond to levodopa. If an antidepressant is required, the tricyclic compounds are most useful. Exercise is important in maintaining mobility. Surgical destruction of the lateral thalamus (thalamotomy) often eliminates the contralateral tremor or rigidity, but this procedure has been virtually eliminated since the advent of levodopa therapy. Thalamotomy may also benefit other dyskinesias.

Unfortunately, all the dopaminergic agonists may cause side effects. Gastrointestinal and cardiovascular complications are no longer common problems, but orthostatic hypotension and arrhythmias can be troublesome. Choreiform movements of the neck, face, mouth, jaw, and tongue are frequent at high doses. The on-off phenomenon is the abrupt occurrence, then remission, of akinesia that lasts for minutes or hours; it is associated with rapid alterations of plasma dopamine levels. Psychological side effects occur in from 10 to 40 per cent of patients taking dopanergic medication. The most common manifestations are confusion (disorientation or delirium), depression or restlessness to agitation, and psychoses (hallucinations, delusions, paranoid ideations). Less common are hypomania, anxiety, lethargy, and hypersexuality.

At autopsy, loss of pigment and atrophy of the substantia nigra are seen on gross examination of the brain (see Figure 25) as well as under the microscope. Neuronal disease with hyalin intracytoplasmic inclusions (Lewy bodies) and associated gliosis are most prominent in the substantia nigra; there is less involvement of the globus pallidus, other basal ganglia, and the cerebral cortex.

Dystonia musculorum deformans. This condition begins before or soon after puberty, is predominant in Jews, and is sometimes familial. The course is usually slowly progressive, but in some cases deterioration stops or remissions occur. Slow writhing movements of the trunk, shoulders, and pelvic girdle characterize the disease. Bizarre postures and torsion spasms also occur. The few pathological studies of this condition have revealed neuronal loss in the caudate and putamen nuclei and sometimes in the pons and dentate nucleus of the cerebellum as well. Torticollis may be a *forme fruste* of dystonia musculorum deformans.

Senile chorea. Senile chorea is a slowly developing dyskinesia unassociated with dementia or other neurological signs.

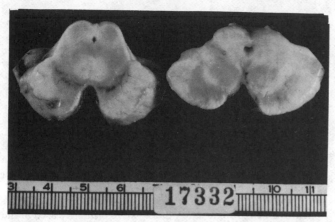

FIGURE 25. Parkinsonism. The substantia nigra is well pigmented in the normal section of the midbrain (*left*). Neuronal loss in the substantia nigra is manifested by depigmentation of this area in the section (*right*) from a patient with parkinsonism. (Courtesy of Dr. H. M. Zimmerman.)

Buccal, lingual dyskinesias manifested by grimacing and athetoid tongue movements are predominant. Such involuntary movements are also seen as toxic effects of levodopa therapy for parkinsonism.

Other degenerative diseases affecting the basal ganglia. Progressive supranuclear ophthalmoplegia (Steele-Richardson-Olszewski syndrome) is manifested by extraocular muscle pareses, especially in the downward gaze. There are associated signs of pseudobulbar palsy, dystonic rigidity of the neck and trunk, and dementia. Cerebellar or pyramidal signs may also develop.

Primary autonomic insufficiency (Shy-Drager syndrome) usually begins with orthostatic hypotension. Extrapyramidal and cerebellar features occur later, associated with impotence, hypotonic urinary bladder and the impairment of perspiration. Atrophy of the iris, extraocular muscle palsies, and peripheral neuropathy may occur. The disease is due to degeneration of autonomic neurons.

In delayed postanoxic encephalopathy, progressive neurological deterioration occurs days or weeks after recovery from a severe bout of cerebral anoxia. This disorder is manifested by progressive dementia or parkinsonian features or both. Other motor defects may also occur. Cerebral demyelination is seen at autopsy.

Creutzfeldt-Jakob disease and olivopontocerebellar atrophy may have parkinsonian signs as part of their clinical pictures.

DISEASES AFFECTING THE CEREBELLOSPINAL SYSTEM

Heredodegenerative spinocerebellar ataxias are the predominant group under this classification. These slowly progressive diseases form a spectrum with maximum involvement ranging from the cerebellum to the spinal cord or the peripheral nerves. In addition to disease of these sites, defects may include optic atrophy or retinitis pigmentosa; atrophy of the cerebral cortex; and degeneration of the red nucleus, the cochlear nucleus, or other brain stem nuclei. Thus, signs of blindness, seizures, dementia, deafness, and pupillary and extraocular muscle palsies sometimes accompany heredodegenerative spinocerebellar diseases.

Diseases predominantly cerebellar

Cerebellar degeneration or cerebelloolivary degeneration. This condition is often familial and usually occurs in men in their sixth or seventh decade. The disease is manifested by cerebellar ataxia and dysarthria. There is gross atrophy of the cerebellum. Under the microscope, loss of Purkinje's cells with preservation of basket cells is noted. Some reduction of the granular cell layer of the cerebellar cortex is also seen.

Olivopontocerebellar atrophy. This disease is often familial and begins in the second and third decades. It is characterized by cerebellar ataxia, and parkinsonian features may occur later in the course of the disease. The pathological manifestations are neuronal degeneration of the olivary and dentate nuclei, with less involvement of Purkinje's cells of the cerebellar cortex. Demyelination of fibers interconnecting the olivary nuclei, pons, and cerebellum causes gross atrophy of these parts. Involvement of the spinal cord is common.

Diseases predominantly spinal

Friedreich's ataxia. This is a familial disease of late childhood. Its clinical manifestations are ataxia of all extremities associated with position-sense loss, areflexia, and bilateral Babinski's signs. There is microscopic evidence of degeneration of the dorsal nuclei of the spinal cord, with demyelination of the posterior and lateral columns, the latter affecting both spinocerebellar and pyramidal tracts. Some involvement of the posterior nerve roots is also evident. Cerebellar cortical degeneration often occurs, and there are many other variations of this disease.

Hereditary spastic paraplegia. This condition is characterized by spastic weakness, then paralysis, affecting predominantly the lower extremities. Microscopic study reveals demyelination in the lateral columns of the spinal cord.

Amyotrophic lateral sclerosis. This is the only disease in this group not commonly hereditary, except among the natives of Guam and the other Mariana Islands, where the disease is strikingly familial and occurs in 10 per cent of the population. The illness begins in middle or late life, and, in contrast to the chronic courses of other diseases discussed above, amyotrophic lateral sclerosis ends in death after 2 to 4 years. Spastic or flaccid progressive weakness, with atrophy and fasciculations, affects the extremities and bulbar musculature. Under the microscope, degeneration of the anterior horn cells, the motor cells of the medulla, and the Betz cells in the cerebral motor cortex is evident. Demyelination of the pyramidal tracts is a concomitant feature. More chronic variants of this disease are progressive spinal muscular atrophy, with major involvement of the anterior horn cells, and primary lateral sclerosis, with maximum involvement of the pyramidal tracts.

Diseases predominantly of the peripheral nerves. Charcot-Marie-Tooth disease or peroneal muscular atrophy is a hereditary, slowly progressive disease beginning in the first three decades of life. It is manifested by weakness and atrophy of the lower legs and lower third of the thighs, with distal sensory impairment. Similar but less marked features affect the upper extremities. The pathological characteristics are myelin and axonal degeneration of the peripheral nerves. Degeneration in the spinal cord is probably secondary to the peripheral nerve disease. Charcot-Marie-Tooth disease is often associated with Friedreich's ataxia, just as Friedreich's ataxia may blend into the cerebellar degenerations.

There are several other hereditary neuropathies; chronic interstitial hypertrophic polyneuropathy (Déjérine-Sottas disease) is the next best known of this group. Hereditary sensory radicular neuropathy and neuropathies associated with defects of lipoid metabolism rarely occur.

DISEASES ASSOCIATED WITH NUTRITIONAL FACTORS

Vitamin deficiency. Vitamins, especially of the B complex group, are essential for neuronal metabolism.

Vitamin B complex. Thiamin deficiency may result in beriberi and in peripheral neuropathy. Cerebral disease is rare, but, in severe forms, mental symptoms and cerebral edema have been noted. Thiamin deficiency is a major factor in the cause of Wernicke's encephalopathy.

Niacin deficiency is an important factor in the causation of pellagra, but pellagra is truly a polyavitaminosis. The combination of dementia, diarrhea, and dermatitis is the familiar triad of this disease, which may also be manifested by delirium and convulsive seizures early in its course. Motor signs implicating the peripheral nerves, pyramidal tracts, cerebellum, or extrapyramidal system occur later, if at all. Pellagra is associated with neuronal loss in the cortex and other areas of the central nervous system. In addition, there may be posterior and lateral column demyelination of the spinal cord.

Pyridoxine (vitamin B_6) deficiency may cause convulsions in infants, but its pathological characteristics in adults are obscure.

Vitamin B_{12} deficiency causes pernicious anemia. It is a disease of middle or late adult life. The neurological syndrome of subacute combined degeneration may develop within a few weeks or months, sometimes before clinical evidence of the hematological disorder. Achlorhydria is present, the B_{12} level in the serum is depressed, and the Schilling test is diagnostic. The neurological signs implicating the spinal cord are spastic weakness and ataxia due to demyelination of the lateral and posterior columns of the cord. Peripheral neuropathy is common. Cerebral manifestations are either neurotic symptoms or dementia, but associated neuronal degeneration, perivascular demyelination, and petechial hemorrhages are rare.

Vitamin A. Vitamin A deficiency in infants may cause mental retardation and hydrocephalus with papilledema.

Vitamin C. Deficiency of vitamin C (scurvy), when severe, is sometimes associated with intracranial bleeding.

Vitamin D. Vitamin D deficiency (rickets) may result in tetany or convulsions late in its course.

Alcoholism. The harmful effects of alcoholic beverages are 2-fold: They tend to be ingested to the exclusion of food, with resultant nutritional deficiencies, and alcohol has direct toxic effects on the nervous system. Nutritional factors account for more disease than do toxic factors. The alcoholic intoxications are discussed later, with delirium tremens and degeneration of the corpus callosum. The nutritional deficiencies, especially of the vitamin B complex group, may cause devastating encephalopathies.

Wernicke's encephalopathy. This disease is characterized by (1) eye signs (oculomotor or conjugate gaze palsies and nystagmus); (2) ataxia, especially of gait; and (3) mental aberrations (delirium or, more often, a confused apathetic state or Korsakoff's syndrome). Consciousness may be depressed, and convulsions sometimes occur. Thiamin deficiency is the predominant cause, and prompt intravenous administration of this vitamin with glucose may be lifesaving. On examination of the brain (see Figure 26), petechial hemorrhages and necrosis are found in the upper brain stem and diencephalon, particularly the mamillary bodies and periventricular hypothalamic nuclei.

Korsakoff's syndrome. This condition is characterized by recent short-term memory loss. Other manifestations of an organic mental disorder and confabulation may occur. Delirium tremens frequently precedes the psychosis; polyneuropathy and Wernicke's encephalopathy are usually superimposed. Korsakoff's syndrome may be due to diseases other than nutritional deprivation—most often, ischemic lesions affecting memory centers in the dorsal medial thalamic nuclei, the medial pulvinar, and, to a lesser extent, the mamillary bodies. Even when Korsakoff's syndrome is associated with alcoholism, treatment with thiamin and glucose is less strikingly beneficial than in Wernicke's disease. Both neuronal disease and demyelination are found in the brain when alcohol is the major cause of the syndrome.

Central pontine myelinolysis. This acute and fatal disease occurs primarily in adults and has many different presentations—most often, mental signs, ocular defects, other brain stem signs, and quadriplegia. Usually, a history of chronic alcoholism is noted, but other causes of nutritional deprivation are also associated with this disease. Pathological examination reveals a focus of demyelination in the center of the basilar portion of the middle and upper pons, with preservation of nerve cells, axis cylinders, and vascular structures.

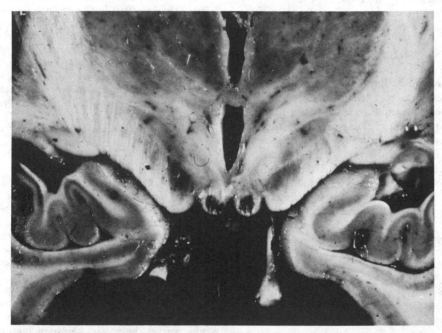

FIGURE 26. Wernicke's encephalopathy. Bilateral hemorrhagic necrosis is seen in the mammillary bodies and necrotic zones are scattered in the hypothalamus near the third ventricle. (From Robertson, D. M., and Dinsdale, H. B. *The Nervous System,* p. 71. Williams & Wilkins, Baltimore, 1972.)

DISEASES ASSOCIATED WITH SYSTEMIC MALIGNANCY

Subacute cortical cerebellar degeneration. This condition is manifested by progressive cerebellar signs and dementia. Death occurs within a few months. The disease is associated with carcinoma, most often of the bronchus or the ovary. Frequently, the neurological symptoms antedate evidence of the primary malignancy. Microscopic examination reveals loss of Purkinje's cells of the cerebellar cortex, and there may be additional neuronal degeneration of the olives and subthalamic nuclei. Demyelination of the long tracts of the spinal cord sometimes occurs.

Progressive multifocal leukoencephalopathy. This disease occasionally occurs in patients with malignant lymphoma that impairs immunological mechanisms and allows papova-virus infiltrations.

Encephalomyelitis rarely occurs as a remote effect of oat cell carcinoma of the lung. In a few cases the disease has affected predominantly the limbic system, with associated recent memory loss. Both neuronal degeneration and inflammatory changes are seen.

A toxic psychosis sometimes occurs in patients with metastatic carcinoma of the lung but without metastases to the brain.

Neuromyopathy, demyelination, and neuronal degeneration within the spinal cord and medulla may also occur as remote effects of malignancy.

Toxic Diseases Affecting the Brain

The brain is affected in different ways by different toxins. Anoxic poisons evoke vasodilation and increased capillary permeability, with petechiae or hemorrhages. Heavy metals and organic compounds are protoplasmic poisons that cause neuronal degeneration. An inflammatory response may occur, particularly if the clinical course is acute; and degenerative (demyelinating) changes are found in both acute and chronic lesions. The addicting drugs and bacterial toxins alter cell metabolism, and death may occur without appreciable microscopic cerebral changes.

The toxic encephalitides present evidence of generalized cerebral dysfunction. In adults, symptoms of headache and dizziness are accompanied by lethargy, confusion, delirium, and other evidence of toxic psychosis. Convulsive seizures may occur, but focal signs are usually minimal. Fever may or may not be present. Systemic signs depend on the offending agent. Acute toxic encephalopathy in children is manifested by the sudden onset of fever, nausea, vomiting, stupor, delirium, or convulsions. The child may be flaccid but more often manifests increased muscle tone, with meningismus. The deep reflexes are hyperactive, and bilateral Babinski's signs may be present. Pupils are often dilated, and papilledema may occur. The severity of the disease and its sequelae are variable. In adults and particularly in children, multiple factors may contribute to the acute toxic encephalopathy. The effect of the toxin itself, the high fever and its associated dehydration, the changes in serum electrolytes, other alterations in blood chemistry, and the anoxia secondary to a convulsion or to respiratory deficits must all be considered. In the case of infection, such as pneumonia in a child, the neurological features are often obscured by the systemic effects of the disease. Other disturbances of electrolytes and endocrinopathies may cause encephalopathy.

ENDOGENOUS TOXINS

Endogenous toxins are most often associated with uremia, diabetic acidosis, hepatic failure, eclampsia, and rarely, porphyria.

Diabetic or uremic coma. Lethargy and stupor precede coma. Delirium and seizures commonly occur in acute uremia; signs of meningeal irritation may occur. Kussmaul respirations are noted most often in patients with diabetic coma. The comatose states associated with diabetes and uremia may be clinically distinguished by the odor of the patient's breath (acetone and urea, respectively). Determination of the blood sugar and urea nitrogen establishes the diagnosis. Both diabetes and uremia may be associated with distal polyneuropathy.

Hepatic coma or hepatic encephalopathy. This disorder is characterized by the insidious impairment of mental processes, leading to stupor and coma. Sometimes delirium and other evidence of toxic psychosis occur. Asterixis is characteristic of impending hepatic coma, and hyperventilation is often associated. The findings of liver function tests are abnormal, and blood ammonia is elevated, but the level of the blood ammonia does not necessarily coincide with the severity of the encephalopathy. The electroencephalogram often shows diffuse slow activity, with bilaterally synchronous triphasic waves. The treatment is aimed at decreasing nitrogenous metabolites by a low-protein diet, oral nonabsorbable antibiotics (neomycin or kanamycin) to reduce bowel flora, and the administration of lactulose, an inert sugar that acidifies colonic contents.

Eclampsia. Convulsions and coma during the last trimester of pregnancy or in the immediate postpartum period may be due to toxins of indeterminate nature or to hypertension and renal failure.

Porphyria. Porphyria is an inherited disorder of porphyrin metabolism; enzyme deficiency prevents the inhibition of porphyrin synthesis. The most common form affects young and middle-aged adults, more often women than men. The disease is characterized by episodic bouts of abdominal pain, other visceral symptoms, and peripheral neuropathy; mental and emotional symptoms and convulsive seizures are common. Exacerbations may be precipitated by the ingestion of many agents, including alcohol and barbiturates. Porphobilinogen is found in the urine. Treatment with hematin has been beneficial; the compound suppresses hepatic production of porphyrin precursors.

EXOGENOUS TOXINS

These toxins may be grouped into those elaborated by bacteria, alcohol, drugs, heavy metals, and organic poisons.

Bacterial toxins

Tetanus. Tetanus is caused by the toxin of the *Clostridium tetani.* The toxin disinhibits inhibitory impulses within the central nervous system. Symptoms usually occur 5 to 15 days after the patient has suffered a contaminated wound. There is first stiffness of jaw and neck muscles, with tonic spasm (trismus), retraction of the corners of the mouth (risus sardonicus), and dysphagia. Rigidity gradually develops, with severe and painful extensor spasms, especially of the trunk musculature. Convulsions may occur. Consciousness is usually preserved. Recovery is likely if the incubation period has been long and the patient has survived the first week of illness. Tetanus-immune globulin (human) should be administered, and penicillin is recommended. Subsequent treatment consists of supportive measures with appropriate sedatives, muscle relaxants, and respiratory maintenance; tracheostomy is sometimes necessary.

Botulism. The toxin of *Clostridium botulinum* blocks synaptic transmission, causing weakness of skeletal and cranial nerve musculature and respiratory paralysis. Symptoms begin 18 to 36 hours after eating contaminated food. Botulism antitoxin should be administered.

Diphtheria. Corynebacterium diphtheriae toxins frequently cause weakness of the palate, paralysis of accommodation of the pupils, laryngopharyngeal weakness, and more generalized polyneuritis.

Alcohol. The most common of all toxins, of course, is ethyl alcohol, although methyl alcohol is much more toxic. Methyl alcohol, particularly, affects the ganglion cells of the retina and optic nerve fibers, with resultant blindness. Acute (ethyl) alcoholic intoxication, simple drunkenness, is an all too well recognized entity. In its extreme form it may lead to coma.

Encephalopathy secondary to alcoholic liver disease must also be considered.

Delirium tremens occurs in chronic alcoholics, either associated with intercurrent infection or injury or 8 to 48 hours after sudden withdrawal from alcohol. Restlessness, sleeplessness, tremulousness, or coarse tremors occur with vivid visual hallucinations, and convulsions may appear. A more severe and potentially fatal form of delirium may evolve or occur de novo 2 to 4 days after alcohol withdrawal. Extreme psychomotor activity and autonomic dysfunctions of fever, tachycardia, and diaphoresis require prompt treatment. The treatment is directed to restoring fluid and electrolyte balances with vitamin supplementation while controlling hyperactivity with minor tranquilizing agents, such as chlordiazepoxide in high dosage; phenytoin may be advisable as an anticonvulsant. The brain of a patient who has died of delirium tremens or, rarely, of acute alcoholic intoxication appears edematous and hyperemic, with diffuse petechial hemorrhages.

Chronic alcoholic intoxication is manifested by one or a combination of the following: dementia with disintegration of personality, cerebellar ataxia affecting the trunk and legs, tremulousness, restlessness, convulsions. Peripheral neuropathy is common, optic atrophy less so. Gross atrophy of the brain is evident, and cortical neuronal loss in the cerebrum and the cerebellum is seen under the microscope. These changes may well be more nutritional than toxic.

Marchiafava-Bignami disease is clinically indistinguishable from chronic alcoholic intoxication except that the former progresses to death in 4 to 6 years. It is most often associated with chronic alcoholism, especially with Italian wines, and nutritional deficiencies. The pathology is characterized by demyelination of the medial portion of the corpus callosum.

Acute alcoholic hallucinosis is manifested by accusatory or threatening hallucinations, chiefly auditory, accompanied by fear and apprehension. This condition may be a psychogenic reaction liberated by alcohol, rather than a toxic reaction.

Drugs

Habituating and addicting drugs. Morphine and heroin cause miosis, respiratory depression, and stupor progressing to coma. The antidote for acute narcotic poisoning is 0.4 mg. to 0.8 mg. of naloxone (Narcan) given intravenously. Cocaine and the amphetamines produce excitement and delirium. Marihuana and lysergic acid diethylamide (LSD) evoke hallucinations. In the remarkably few pathological studies that have been carried out in cases of morphine poisoning, the changes are similar to those described under the anoxic poisons.

Anoxic toxins—barbiturates. Anoxic toxins prevent oxygen from reaching or being used by nerve cells. The chief offenders are anesthetics and hypnotics (such as barbiturates), carbon monoxide, cyanide, and war gases.

Intoxication by barbiturates is manifested by the gradual development of coma, occasionally preceded by delirium. Depressed respiration is a prominent sign. The duration of coma has greater prognostic significance than does its depth. Diffuse, fast activity in the electroencephalogram may be an important clue in establishing the diagnosis; the determination of barbiturate levels in gastric contents, blood, or urine is definitive. Support of vital functions, particularly respiration, is the cornerstone of treatment. In severe cases, peritoneal dialysis may be warranted. The chief pathological feature of barbiturate and other anoxic poisoning is neuronal degeneration, particularly in those areas of the central nervous system most vulnerable to ischemia.

Psychotropic drugs. Psychotropic drug intoxication may cause neuronal damage, most pronounced in the basal ganglia, hypothalamus, and mesencephalon. The following outline refers for the most part to major tranquilizers, as exemplified by the phenothiazines; the butyrophenones have similar but usually fewer side effects. Most of the signs may also be associated with antidepressant drugs, either tricyclic derivatives or monoamine oxidase inhibitors.

I. Toxic effects on the nervous system
  A. Neurological phenomena
    1. Dyskinesias or muscle spasms; parkinsonism, akathisia, dystonia; tetanus-like syndromes
    2. Convulsive seizures
    3. Lethargy, somnolence, fatigue
    4. Other neurological symptoms (headache, dizziness, weakness)
    5. EEG slow-wave or paroxysmal abnormality
    6. Peripheral neuropathy*
  B. Mental and emotional reactions
    1. Impaired psychomotor function
    2. Restlessness and excitement
    3. Confusion and delirium
    4. Insomnia and bizarre dreams
    5. Increase in schizophrenic symptoms or in depression
  C. Autonomic and endocrine disturbances
    1. Alteration of vital signs
      a. Disturbed temperature regulation, both hypothermia and heat stroke
      b. Tachycardia (more often than bradycardia) or other cardiac arrhythmias*
      c. Depression of respiration
      d. Hypotension, especially orthostatic*; hypertension with other compounds*
    2. Anticholinergic symptoms
      a. Dry mouth and skin
      b. Tachycardia and fever
      c. Dilated pupils
      d. Paresis or paralysis of the bladder or bowel
      e. Mental and motor signs (as above)
    3. Altered sexual function
      a. Inhibition of ejaculation and impotence in men or, paradoxically, increase in libido in women
      b. Gynecomastia in men or lactation and menstrual irregularity in women
      c. False-positive pregnancy test
    4. Other effects
      a. Hyperglycemia or hypoglycemia
      b. Nasal congestion, excessive perspiration*
      c. Weight gain, peripheral edema
II. Systemic toxic reactions
  A. Primary reaction
    1. Cholestatic jaundice and xanthomatous biliary cirrhosis, liver cell disease*
    2. Eosinophilia, hemolytic anemia, agranulocytosis, pancytopenia, thrombocytopenia
    3. Contact and other dermatitis, skin photosensitivity
    4. Pigmentary retinopathy, melanin pigmentation of the cornea and lens
    5. Gastrointestinal disturbances
    6. Questionable teratogenic effects
    7. Vagolytic quinidine-like effect in electrocardiogram
    8. Shock after electroconvulsive therapy
    9. Death due to overdosage
  B. Secondary effect on other modalities
    1. The potentiation of other drugs, such as sedatives, narcotics,

---

* Features peculiar to or predominant with the antidepressants

anesthetics, amphetamines, hypotensive agents, digitalis, insulin*; the potentiation of alcohol and its complications
2. Sedation leading to hypostatic pneumonia and trophic ulcers
3. Inflammation or infection of the injection sites

The most frequent complications of the antidepressant drugs are hypotension (especially of the orthostatic type), anticholinergic phenomena, and the potentiation of other drugs (especially those causing hypertension). Extrapyramidal disorders are some of the most common side effects of the major tranquilizers.

Of the extrapyramidal side effects, acute dystonia and akathisia usually appear at the onset of therapy, and signs of parkinsonism appear after therapy is in progress. Both of these phenomena are reversible and respond to drug withdrawal and anticholinergic medications. Tardive dyskinesia (buccal-lingual-masticatory movements), on the other hand, occurs especially after long-term therapy or after the discontinuation of such therapy; the disorder is often irreversible. Tardive dyskinesia is noted particularly in the elderly who have received high doses of neuroleptic agents, especially the phenothiazines and haloperidol. The disorder seems to be due to a relative excess of cerebral dopamine, the chronic blockade of dopamine receptors by the tranquilizer having resulted in a state of denervation hypersensitivity. Acetylcholine precursors, such as deanol and choline, appear to be of some therapeutic benefit.

The first signs of lithium intoxication are nausea, polyuria, thirst, and tremor; there may be a predisposition to heat stroke. Later, vomiting, diarrhea, dizziness, ataxia, weakness, dysarthria, and blurred vision are associated with changes in conscious and mental states. Finally, stupor progresses to coma, with or without associated convulsions. In the early stages, drug withdrawal and sodium chloride with fluid replacement are indicated. In severe cases, hemodialysis is the treatment of choice, but damage to the cerebellar and basal ganglion pathways may be permanent.

Other drugs. Drugs frequently encountered in toxic dosages are the hydantoins, atropine and its related compounds, and bromides. The hydantoins in toxic dosages cause ataxia by their effect on Purkinje's cells of the cerebellum. Atropine and its congeners produce a central anticholinergic effect with mental symptoms of amnesia, hallucinations, illusions of unreality, or delirium and motor signs of weakness, ataxia, restlessness, excitement, or choreiform activity. Bromide intoxication causes mental and emotional disturbances, ranging from memory impairment to delirium; tremors and cerebellar signs occur; a skin rash is common. Very high doses of penicillin may cause convulsions. Levodopa toxicity is discussed above. Most of the drugs used in medical practice—for example, cardiovascular agents, hormones, and anti-inflammatory agents—may have toxic effects on the brain, manifested by alterations in behavior and mentation.

Heavy metals. Poisoning by mercury, arsenic, or lead may cause symptoms and signs affecting the optic nerves and all portions of the central and peripheral nervous systems. In mercury toxicity, cerebellar signs are often predominant. Encephalopathy, neuropathy, or myopathy may be associated with arsenic poisoning. Chronic manganese poisoning may result in parkinsonism.

Lead poisoning is one of the most frequent exogenous poisons encountered in children; it usually occurs when infants chew the paint off furniture. This activity in infants is not abnormal, but its persistence in older children is an expression of perverted taste, sometimes seen in the mentally retarded. The clinical features of acute lead encephalopathy are the same

as those discussed under toxic encephalopathy of children. The diagnosis of chronic lead intoxication can be made from roentgenograms of long bones, where dense radiopaque bands are noted below the proliferating zone of the epiphysis. Chelating agents (edathamil calcium dysodium) are judiciously used in treatment. Supportive therapy is vital, and symptomatic measures, including anticonvulsants, may be required.

Organic toxic compounds. These include carbon tetrachloride, certain mushrooms, and insecticides. Carbon tetrachloride affects both the central and the peripheral nervous systems, but the primary changes in the central nervous system are difficult to differentiate from the effects secondary to severe liver and renal disease. Mushroom poisoning may cause extensive cerebral damage. The insecticides containing organic phosphate derivatives and the drugs taken by patients for myasthenia gravis produce their toxic effects by cholinesterase inhibition. This inhibition is manifested by muscarinic effects of abdominal cramps, lacrimation, and incontinence; nicotinic effects of fasciculations followed by generalized muscle weakness and paralysis; and central nervous system effects of headache, dizziness, ataxia, lethargy, convulsions, and psychic phenomena varying from excitation to depression.

Inflammatory Diseases of the Brain

Intracranial infection may occur from infected paranasal sinuses, ears, or mastoids through emissary veins or from organisms in the blood stream. With the increasing use of immunosuppressive therapy, infection by opportunistic organisms has become more and more frequent. Cerebral infection is, nevertheless, relatively uncommon because of the blood-brain barrier. The barrier consists of the arachnoid, which forms the adventitia of the blood vessels, and the contiguous glial membrane, composed of the sucker-like feet of astrocytes. This barrier is much more than an anatomical structure; it is primarily a neurochemical homeostatic mechanism. Focal breakdown in the blood-brain barrier may lead to the spread of infection from blood to brain, with abscess formation. Meningitis usually causes a more generalized disturbance of the blood-brain barrier and allows infection to spread to superficial areas of the brain.

SUPPURATIVE INFECTIONS

Brain abscess. Sources of infection in the development of a brain abscess are the blood stream, carrying organisms from a distant site, such as a chronic pulmonary infection or subacute bacterial endocarditis; infected paranasal sinuses, mastoids, or ears; and fractures of the skull, either through infected sinuses or penetrating injuries. Patients receiving immunosuppressive drugs and children with congenital cyanotic heart disease are particularly prone to develop brain abscess. The symptoms and the signs of a brain abscess are similar to those of a neoplasm of the brain. Fever is often conspicuous by its absence. Inflammatory cells are usual but need not be present in the cerebrospinal fluid; however, cerebrospinal fluid protein is almost always elevated. The brain abscess may seal off and resolve; it may rupture to the surface or into a ventricle, causing meningitis; or it may result in sinus thrombosis. Antibiotics are necessary, but surgical extirpation is the treatment of choice. The acute brain abscess appears as a pus-filled cavity surrounded by soft necrotic brain tissue and, beyond that, localized edema (see Figure 27). More chronic abscesses are walled off by thick, firm, fibrous tissue. On microscopy, necrosis and inflammatory cells are obvious. The abscess is bordered by a wall of collagenous tissue built of fibroblasts, rather than glial cells, and new capillaries.

Dural abscess. Abscesses adjacent to the dura usually produce focal cerebral signs and signs of increased intracranial pressure. The patient shows clinical evidence of infection, but the spinal fluid reaction is that of an aseptic meningitis. These diseases require intensive antibiotic therapy and surgical evacuation.

Subdural abscess. A subdural empyema is most often secondary to middle-ear or paranasal sinus infections but may follow a dural sinus thrombophlebitis. Subdural empyema appears as a purulent exudate over the surface of the brain. Under the microscope, polymorphonuclear inflammatory cells make up a fibrous exudate.

Extradural abscess. An extradural abscess is usually secondary to frontal sinusitis or mastoiditis. It is more localized than a subdural abscess. Its gross and microscopic appearance is similar to a subdural abscess.

Sinus thrombosis. Sinus thrombosis is most often caused by the extension of an infection, particularly from the ears or paranasal sinuses, to the cranial venous sinuses. Cavernous sinus thrombosis usually arises from an infection of the face, nose, eye, or sphenoid or ethmoid paranasal sinuses. Transverse sinus thrombosis is secondary to middle-ear infection or mastoiditis. Superior longitudinal sinus thrombosis most often occurs from frontal sinusitis or is secondary to debilitating disease in the very young or the very old. Edema and congestion in the areas of the head and the face drained by veins filling these sinuses are accompanied by fever and increased intracranial pressure. Antibiotic therapy is vital, but the role of anticoagulants is still in doubt. All forms of sinus thrombosis cause extensive venous congestion of the adjacent brain, with scattered hemorrhages and softening of the parenchyma.

MENINGITIS

It is best to consider the meningitides under two large classifications: purulent or acute meningitis and nonpurulent or chronic meningitis.

Purulent or acute meningitis. Purulent meningitis is manifested by the sudden onset of headache, usually with nausea and vomiting. Examination reveals an acutely distressed patient with high fever and nuchal rigidity; depression of consciousness soon occurs. The spinal fluid is turbid; contains 1,000 to 15,000 white blood cells per cubic millimeter, predominantly polymorphonuclear leukocytes; and has elevated protein and low glucose. The gross appearance of purulent meningitis (see Figure 28) is characterized by hyperemia of the meninges and, first, the development of a fibrinous exudate and, later, a purulent exudate within the subarachnoid space. The exudate follows cerebral sulci or vessels or both along the base and over the convexity of the brain. There may be associated blockage of absorptive surfaces of the meninges or obstruction of the foramina of the fourth ventricle, with resultant hydrocephalus. If recovery is delayed, the purulent exudate

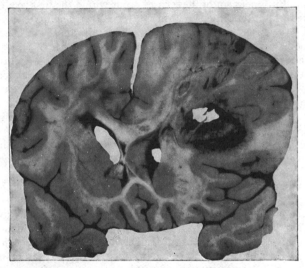

FIGURE 27. Cerebral abscesses. Surrounding edema has displaced midline structures. (From Blackwood, W., Dodds, T. C., and Sommerville, J. C. *Atlas of Neuropathology,* ed. 2, p. 51. Williams & Wilkins, Baltimore, 1964.)

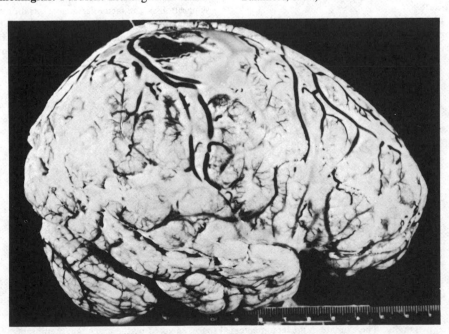

FIGURE 28. Acute bacterial meningitis. The convexity of the brain is covered by a purulent exudate which fills the sulci. Superficial veins have thrombosed. (From Robertson, D. M., and Dinsdale, H. B. *The Nervous System,* p. 124. Williams & Wilkins, Baltimore, 1972.)

may organize into a thick, gray membrane. On microscopic examination (see Figure 29), one sees numerous polymorphonuclear leukocytes and large mononuclear cells within the exudate. In the brain, perivascular infiltration of inflammatory cells is predominantly within the Virchow-Robin spaces. These spaces surround the arteries and the veins but not the capillaries and may be considered an invagination of the subarachnoid space along the vessel walls. The exudate may follow the blood vessels into the cortex, causing small microabscesses.

The most common organism causing acute purulent meningitis is the meningococcus (a Gram-negative diplococcus). Seventy-five per cent of these cases occur before the age of 10 years. Associated infection of the adrenal glands is rare but causes the Waterhouse-Friderichsen syndrome, with adrenal hemorrhage, shock, and death. The pneumococcus (a Gram-positive diplococcus) is associated with the highest mortality rate. Fifty per cent of these cases occur within the first year of life or after the fiftieth year of life. The *Hemophilus influenzae* (a Gram-negative bacillus) cause a disease primarily of childhood, 90 per cent of cases occurring before the age of 5 years. Children recovering from this disease may develop subdural effusions. The streptococcus (a Gram-positive coccus) is almost always secondary to a distant focus and causes a small percentage of purulent meningitides. Even less common organisms causing purulent meningitis include the staphylococcus (Gram-positive), usually associated with a localized abscess; *Escherichia coli* (Gram-negative), usually found in diseases of the newborn or young children; and *Pseudomonas aeruginosa* (Gram-negative), rarely a contaminant of a spinal tap.

Often the organism is not seen on initial staining of the spinal fluid, and sometimes an organism cannot be cultured. Treatment must then be started on the basis of probability, using the patient's age as the chief factor. If the patient is under 6 years of age, the organism is likely to be *Hemophilus influenzae,* pneumococcus, or meningococcus (in that order of probability), and treatment with chloramphenicol (100 mg. per kilogram a day) is recommended. In older patients, more than 90 per cent of meningitides are due to meningococcus or pneumococcus, and they should be treated with 20 million units of penicillin-G a day.

Chronic meningitis. The chronic meningitides are manifested by the gradual development of headache, stiff neck, malaise, and fever. Cranial nerve involvement is often present because of exudate at the base of the brain. Arteritis with thrombosis and infarction is another frequent complication, especially of tuberculous meningitis. The spinal fluid usually contains 50 to 500 white blood cells per cubic millimeter (predominantly mononuclear leukocytes), elevated protein, and low glucose. Some organisms, such as the Cryptococcus, may be difficult to find in the cerebrospinal fluid. The fluid can be additionally tested for cryptococcal antigen.

Tuberculous meningitis. Tuberculous meningitis is by far the most common form of chronic meningitis. The gross appearance of this disease is characterized by a pale, glistening, web-like exudate at the base of the brain. Sometimes miliary tubercles (gray-white nodules) may be seen in the cerebral sulci and fissures. Under the microscope, fibroblasts, lymphocytes, epithelioid cells, and giant cells are seen to be present in and around the zones of necrosis. Large granulomas, tuberculomas, may act as slowly growing brain tumors. Treatment of tuberculous meningitis consists of 1 gm. a day of streptomycin, 300 mg. a day of isoniozid, and 25 mg. per kg. a day of ethambutol; 600 mg. a day of rifampin, may replace streptomycin in the above regimen. Steroid therapy is recommended if the disease is severe.

Torula meningitis. Cryptococcus neoformans produces an exudate similar to that of tuberculosis at the base of the brain. In addition, foreign-body giant cells contain torula organisms that appear as small bodies surrounded by a thick, clear capsule. Granulomatous nodules of torula in the cerebrum may act as solid or cystic masses. Torula meningitis and other fungal meningitides, once invariably fatal, often respond to amphotericin B, administered by intravenous and intrathecal or intraventricular routes. An antifungal agent, 5-fluorocytosine, is less potent than amphotericin but can be administered by mouth.

Other forms of chronic meningitis are distinctly less common. They are associated with other fungi or nonbacterial organisms. Sarcoidosis and carcinoma may invade the meninges and present a picture similar to that of a chronic infectious meningitis.

Sarcoidosis. Sarcoidosis is a systemic disease of uncertain origin characterized by granulomata composed of large epithelioid cells, unassociated with necrosis. The most striking neurological involvement is paralysis of the facial nerve in association with uveitis and parotitis (uveoparotid fever). Optic neuritis and peripheral neuritis may occur. Granulomatous meningeal infiltration can cause an aseptic meningitis but with low levels of spinal fluid glucose. Involvement of the base of

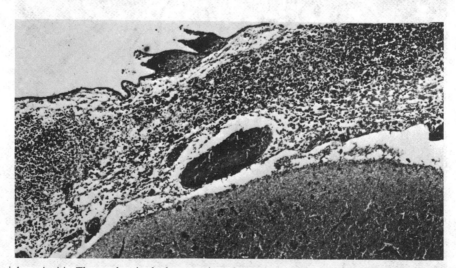

FIGURE 29. Acute bacterial meningitis. The exudate in the leptomeningeal space, enclosed by the arachnoid membrane above and the pial surface below, is composed predominantly of neurophils. (From Robertson, D. M., and Dinsdale, H. B. *The Nervous System,* p. 124. Williams & Wilkins, Baltimore, 1972.)

the brain is associated with diabetes insipidus, and diffuse infiltration may cause a variety of diffuse or focal cerebral signs. Steroid therapy is beneficial.

Virus meningitides. These diseases are usually benign. Lymphocytic choriomeningitis and the meningitides of mumps, Coxsackie, and ECHO viruses are the most common.

Opportunistic infections. These infections occur in patients with lymphoma and in those requiring immunosuppressive drugs. The infections are often manifested as a chronic meningitis due to otherwise unusual fungi; brain abscess may occur, especially with aspergillosis. Encephalitis in these patients may be caused by toxoplasmosis or viruses (cytomegalovirus, papova-virus, herpesvirus).

ENCEPHALITIS

The nonsuppurative encephalitides induce a slight to moderate meningeal congestion, and the underlying edematous, hyperemic brain tissue often reveals small hemorrhages. On microscopic examination (see Figure 30), an inflammatory cellular infiltrate is seen within the tissue and perivascular spaces. Arteritis and petechial hemorrhages are present. There is demyelination and neuronal degeneration of varying degrees, with microglial hypertrophy and proliferation. Inclusion bodies within neurons or glial cells suggest a virus origin. The diseased brains affected by slowly incubating viruses may reveal degenerative changes, rather than an inflammatory reaction.

Neurotropic viruses. Neurotropic viruses cause encephalitis that may be manifested by no more than headache and fever. The more severe, typical cases cause additional features of seizures, somnolence, confusion, and, sometimes, delirium, coma, and death. Ocular signs and other focal signs may occur. Stiffness of the neck is common. Systemic involvement is manifested by malaise and upper respiratory tract or gastrointestinal symptoms. The spinal fluid reveals a leukocytosis of 25 to 250 cells per cubic millimeter, mostly lymphocytes.

Infections caused by neurotropic viruses include those borne by arthropods: the equine encephalitides, St. Louis encephalitis, and Japanese B encephalitis. These diseases do not have distinguishing clinical, focal, or pathological characteristics.

Some viruses are predisposed to affect one particular area of

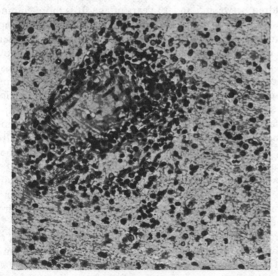

FIGURE 30. Encephalitis. Polymorphonuclear and mononuclear leukocytes infiltrate and surround a blood vessel within an area of disintegrating white matter. Hematoxylin and eosin, 250 X. (From Blackwood, W., Dodds, T. C., and Sommerville, J. C. *Atlas of Neuropathology,* ed. 2, p. 77. Williams & Wilkins, Baltimore, 1964.)

the central nervous system much more than other areas. Economo's encephalitis in the 1920's injured the basal ganglia, and postencephalitic parkinsonism resulted. Poliomyelitis attacks the anterior horn cells.

Herpes simplex encephalitis. This disease is the most common severe, sporadic encephalitis in the United States. Generalized cerebral signs associated with focal signs, often stimulating a temporal lobe tumor, develop and rapidly progress. The electroencephalogram reveals periodic sharp waves from a temporal area on a background of diffuse slow activity. The cerebrospinal fluid is often hemorrhagic. Craniotomy has been advocated to establish the diagnosis by isolating the virulent type 1 virus from the brain biopsy, as well as to decompress the swollen cranial contents. (The type 2 herpes simplex virus causes a more benign meningitis in adults and, in contrast to type 1, can be isolated from the cerebrospinal fluid or from blood leukocytes.) Treatment with adenine arabinoside has shown promising results. Mortality rates were once considered to be close to 100 per cent, but recoveries of untreated patients have been increasingly reported. At autopsy, severe, often hemorrhagic necrosis accompanies an inflammatory reaction that especially affects the inferior medial portions of the temporal lobes (see Figure 31). Intranuclear inclusion bodies are seen under the microscope.

Rabies. Rabies occurs from 30 to 70 days after the bite of a rabid animal. In addition to the usual features of encephalitis, rabies causes extreme agitation and severely painful spasms of the throat, with inability to swallow. Seizures, coma, and death are invariable in untreated cases. Treatment with antirabies vaccine after rabies is found or strongly suspected in the attacking animal prevents the disease in most cases, and postvaccinal complications have diminished with the use of the new vaccines. In the brain infected by rabies, Negri bodies (see Figure 32)—oval acidophilic inclusion bodies—are seen in the cytoplasm of neurons, particularly in Ammon's horn and in Purkinje's cells.

Slow viruses. In recent years, some diseases formerly classified as degenerative have been found to be due to viruses having an extremely slow incubation period, often years. Kuru, which affects an isolated people in New Guinea, was the first disease in humans found to be due to a slow virus.

Creutzfeldt-Jakob disease has been transmitted from humans to chimpanzees after prolonged incubation and, accidentally, has been transmitted from human to human. This illness begins in the fourth or fifth decade and is manifested by progressive dementia and motor signs of pyramidal, extrapyramidal, cerebellar, and lower motor neuron disease, with myoclonus, spasticity, tremors, atrophy, and fasciculations. The electroencephalogram shows periodic generalized spike activity. Death occurs within 3 to 12 months. The pathology is that of subacute spongiform encephalopathy. Neurons are affected predominantly in the cerebral cortex, basal ganglia, and other areas of the central nervous system, including the anterior horn cells of the spinal cord. Vacuolation affects the dendrites and axons; extensive astroglial hypertrophy and proliferation are also seen. An inflammatory response is not evoked.

Conventional viruses causing slow infections. Other viruses cause slow but progressive degeneration of the brain. The papova-virus causes progressive multifocal leukoencephalopathy after immune mechanisms have been impaired (see Demyelinating Diseases).

Subacute sclerosing panencephalitis begins insidiously in childhood or adolescence, with progressive deterioration of the intellect and of behavior. Within weeks or months, a variety of

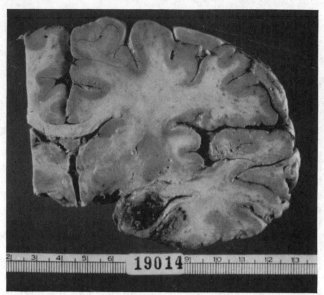

FIGURE 31. Encephalitis, in this case due to herpes simplex virus. Edematous brain tissue has compressed the ventricles. Hemmorrhagic necrosis is seen in the inferior medial aspect of the temporal lobe. (Courtesy of Dr. H. M. Zimmerman.)

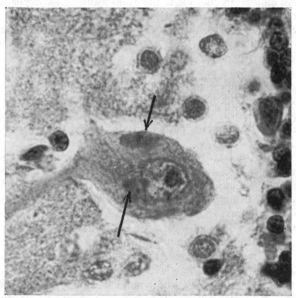

FIGURE 32. Rabies. In a Purkinje cell of the cerebellum are rounded intracytoplasmic inclusions, Negri bodies (*arrows*). Hematoxylin and eosin, 1,000 X. (Courtesy of Dr. T. Poon and Dr. A. Hirano.)

central nervous system phenomena occur involving, especially, motor and visual modalities; seizures and myoclonic jerks are common. Decerebration, coma, and death occur after a course of months to years. The clinical diagnosis is established by the findings of periodic sharp activities in the diffusely slow electroencephalogram and elevated γ-globulin, representing immune globulins to measles virus in the cerebrospinal fluid. On microscopic examination, intranuclear and intracytoplasmic eosinophilic inclusion bodies (Dawson bodies) are found in cortical neurons. Other features of encephalitis affect both gray and white matter. Highly increased measles antibody titers implicate the measles virus, which somehow has been altered and eventually evokes this disease.

Cytomegalic inclusion disease causes neonatal jaundice, thrombocytopenia, and pneumonia; there is microcephaly and cerebral calcifications. The disease is often fatal, and survival is associated with cerebral palsy, including mental retardation, hydrocephalus, and epilepsy. Cytomegalic inclusion disease may also occur in older children, causing systemic illness, and on rare occasions, in adults who have received immunosuppressive medications or who are otherwise debilitated. The cytomegalic viruses cause swelling of cells and form intranuclear and intracytoplasmic inclusions in the viscera and in glial cells and neurons. Findings of such inclusions in large cells of urinary sediment establish the diagnosis during life. In the brain, multifocal zones of necrosis are seen, with glial proliferation, perivascular infiltrations, and calcifications, especially around the ventricles.

It is intriguing to consider how many other degenerative diseases may be due to a virus incubating for many years and frustrating to consider how long it may take to prove or disprove this concept.

Postinfectious or postvaccinal encephalitis. Some encephalitides are a reaction of the brain to vaccination, exanthemata (such as measles and chicken pox), rheumatic fever, and other systemic inflammations.

Acute disseminated encephalomyelitis occurs either during an infectious disease or a few days to 3 weeks after an infectious illness or vaccination. Recovery may occur. Acute hemorrhagic leukoencephalitis, as the name implies, affects white matter predominantly but is probably a fulminating form of disseminated encephalomyelitis. This disease often follows a febrile illness and ends in death after a few days. These two illnesses are probably acute allergic demyelinating diseases with secondary reactive inflammation.

Reye's syndrome is an acute encephalopathy associated with fatty degeneration of the liver and other viscera. It occurs 2 or 3 days after a mild flu-like illness, mainly in children from 5 to 14 years of age, and is usually fatal. Vomiting is rapidly followed by delirium and coma. Cerebral edema is present, and hypoglycemia may also be operative.

Sydenham's chorea may occur in young adolescents or young primiparas (chorea gravidarum), but it most frequently occurs in children between 5 and 13 years of age. It is more common in girls than in boys. The onset may be manifested by no more than irritability or unusual restlessness. Choreiform movements of the extremities increase in prominence, and similar movements affect the face and the tongue. Hypotonic weakness is common. Sometimes emotional symptoms increase to psychotic delirium. Bed rest in a quiet environment, with judicious use of sedatives, is the treatment of choice. The relationship to rheumatic fever is well known, and prophylactic penicillin is warranted. The pathogenesis of Sydenham's chorea is still in doubt, for vascular and immunological mechanisms have been implicated, as well as inflammatory disease.

Acute cerebellar ataxia of childhood is probably of virus origin. The abrupt onset of truncal ataxia, incoordination of the limbs, and ocular dymetria occurs in preschool children. Recovery takes place in 1 week to 6 months.

Viscerotropic organisms. Most other organisms causing encephalitis are viscerotropic and involve the nervous system as part of a generalized systemic infection.

The following is an incomplete list of organisms that may infect the central nervous system:

1. Viruses: Coxsackie, ECHO, mumps, and the Epstein-Barr (EB) virus of infectious mononucleosis cause generalized encephalitis.

2. Bacteria: Most bacteria cause cerebritis associated with meningitis or cerebritis before abscess formation. Typhoid may cause generalized cerebral inflammatory changes, but associated arteritis sometimes results in focal infarctions. Tetanus, diphtheria, and botulism produce their effects by elaborating toxins.

3. Rickettsia: Typhus and Rocky Mountain spotted fever produce generalized encephalitis, and associated arteritis may cause focal signs.

4. Spirochetes: The leptospira of Weil's disease may cause meningitis, usually mild. Syphilis is the most notorious organism infecting the nervous system.

Syphilis may affect predominantly the vascular and interstitial tissue of the central nervous system or cause maximal disease in the neurons, but these conditions are not mutually exclusive.

Parenchymal neurosyphilis is characterized by two major diseases, tabes dorsalis and general paresis. Both diseases occur many years after the primary infection. In both, miotic pupils unreactive to light (Argyll Robertson pupils) are found, although less often in paresis than in tabes. The cerebrospinal fluid reveals elevated protein and increased numbers of lymphocytes, a positive finding in the serological test, and abnormal colloidal gold curves, although in burnt-out tabes the cerebrospinal fluid is sometimes normal.

General paresis occurs in 2 to 3 per cent of all patients with untreated syphilis. Symptoms of progressive dementia—with agitated, expansive, or depressive qualities—occur 5 to 20 years after the primary infection. Slurred speech and minor tremors are common. On gross inspection of the brain, old meningitis is manifested by thick opaque meninges, particularly over the convexity. The underlying brain is small, and wide sulci are further evidence of atrophy, predominantly in the frontal lobes. The microscopic appearance of general paresis is primarily that of neuronal degeneration within the frontoparietal cortex. There is associated long-tract and patchy demyelination. Hypertrophied microglia are seen as elongated rod cells, often filled with iron granules that stain brilliantly with Prussian blue.

Tabes dorsalis is chiefly characterized by demyelination of the posterior columns of the spinal cord and of the dorsal roots. The resultant position-sense loss causes ataxia, and the associated loss of deep pain sensation may lead to the development of painless traumatic arthropathies (Charcot joints). Sometimes degeneration of the optic nerves causes blindness, and oculomotor nerve paresis frequently occurs. Pains are a prominent symptom. Lightning-like pains, usually in the extremities, and girdle pains or paresthesias are common, and crises of severe pain may arise from visceral areas.

In leutic arteritis, parenchymal involvement is secondary to thrombosis and infarction. Leutic meningitis presents the features of a chronic meningitis, with thickening of the meninges at the base of the brain. Mononuclear cell infiltration is evident in arteritis and meningitis due to syphilis. The leutic granuloma (gumma) acting as a brain tumor is virtually extinct.

The therapy of choice for neurosyphilis is penicillin. A total dose of 6 to 9 million units is administered by intramuscular injection in divided doses over a period of 2 to 3 weeks.

5. Protozoa: Cerebral malaria due to occlusion of capillaries often causes delirium and other psychic manifestations, as well as other signs of general and focal cerebral disease.

Toxoplasma infects infants in utero and causes hydrocephalus, convulsions, chorioretinitis, and intracranial calcifications. On microscopy, miliary granulomas of large epithelial cells and chronic inflammatory cells are seen. Intracellular and extracellular parasites appear as small acidophilic masses.

6. Fungi: Torula (cryptococcosis) is the most common fungus causing chronic basilar meningitis; but coccidioidomycosis, histoplasmosis, norcardiosis, actinomycosis, candidiasis, mucormycosis, aspergillosis, and other fungi also invade the cranium on rare occasions.

7. Helminths: In patients with trichinosis and schistosomiasis, granulomata occur; with cysticercosis and echinococcosis, cysts develop. All result in focal signs and seizures, and cysts frequently cause increased intracranial pressure.

Other inflammatory syndromes. These syndromes may affect the brain, but the causes are unknown.

Behçet's syndrome is manifested by recurrent uveitis and ulcers of mucous membranes. Meningoencephalitis occurs, and sometimes there is involvement of the brain stem or the spinal cord.

Vogt-Koyanagi-Harada syndrome is characterized by uveitis, deafness, and depigmentation of the skin and hair. Neurological manifestations are predominantly those of meningitis or encephalitis.

Reiter's syndrome is characterized by urethritis, conjunctivitis, and arthritis. Meningoencephalitis, cranial neuropathy, or peripheral nerve involvement occur on rare occasions.

Diseases of Early Life

The process of embryonic maturation is so complex that one must marvel at the relative rarity of congenital disorders, classified in Table I. Many defects are due to abnormalities of the germ plasm, but trauma, infection, and biochemical stimuli during embryonic life account for a large number of malformations. Defects vary with the embryonic stage at which alteration in the maturation process occurs, with the site of neural involvement, and with the severity and type of the underlying disturbance. The process of birth is fraught with potential hazards, particularly traumatic and anoxic phenomena. Infections and other illnesses in the neonatal period may cause irreparable damage.

TABLE I
Congenital Disorders

Developmental deformities
  Cerebrum
  Cervicocranial
  Ventricles or central canal
Chromosomal anomalies
Phakomatoses
Endocrinopathies
Infections
Metabolic diseases

There has been a rapid growth of knowledge in neurochemistry and genetics. Elevation of α-fetoprotein in maternal blood and in amniotic fluid obtained by amniocentesis leads to the prenatal diagnosis of neural tube defects, such as anencephaly and spina bifida. Cells of fetal origin obtained by amniocentesis can be cultured and permit the diagnosis of chromosomal anomalies. Many inborn errors of metabolism responsible for physical and mental retardation and death are now detectable in the fetus and in the carrier. Recently, the prenatal diagnosis of muscular dystrophy has been accomplished by fetal blood sampling from the placenta. Genetic counseling is now based on more accurate predictions. The prenatal diagnosis of crippling and fatal diseases now permits the consideration of therapeutic abortion.

CEREBRAL PALSY

Cerebral palsy may be due to prenatal factors, such as developmental anomalies and infections in utero, or to postnatal factors, such as kernicterus, infections, and injuries; but most often the condition is due to perinatal events, especially asphyxia and mechanical trauma at the time of birth. The premature infant is particularly vulnerable to these stresses, and the correlation of cerebral palsy with prematurity is high. There are many opportunities for the development of asphyxia during the birth process; breech delivery is the most common example. Trauma may cause intracerebral, subdural, subarachnoid, and intraventricular hemorrhages; contusions and lacerations of the brain; and tears of the dural sinuses and tentorium. Some think that venous congestion is a significant causative factor in cerebral palsy, and others believe that arterial compromise during the birth process is a more important mechanism.

The manifestations of cerebral palsy depend on the site of maximum damage. Disease of the cerebral hemispheres and cortex causes bilateral spastic weakness. Lesions of the basal ganglia result in dyskinesias (athetoid or choreiform movements). Defects of the cerebellum are associated with hypotonia and ataxia. The severity of the neurological signs is extremely variable, and mental retardation is an associated feature in a third of all children with cerebral palsy; a seizure disorder is present in a similar fraction of all cases.

After the initial insults to the brain have healed, the pathological characteristics of birth injury are noted. Ulegyria is manifested by shrunken gyri, with maximum atrophy of their walls deep within the sulci and relative sparing of their crowns (see Figure 33). These gyri are found particularly in zones of the brain between main arterial territories or within one arterial distribution. Sclerosis, rarification, or cavitation of the white matter adjacent to the lateral ventricles is another distinctive feature of cerebral palsy. Atrophy of the basal ganglia, especially the caudate nucleus, is frequently seen in these brains.

Kernicterus. Kernicterus is caused by severe neonatal hyperbilirubinemia, usually due to maternal-fetal blood (especially Rh group) incompatibility and associated erythroblastosis fetalis. It is manifested during the first 2 weeks of life. Jaundice, lethargy, opisthotonos, and seizures are common. If the infant survives, cerebral palsy with mental retardation, extrapyramidal signs, and deafness usually results. Exchange transfusions with Rh-negative blood during the first 4 to 5 days of life are the best prophylaxis. The chief pathological features are bile pigmentation of nerve cells and their associated destruction. The disease affects predominantly subcortical nu-

clear structures, particularly the subthalamic nucleus, Ammon's horn, and the globus pallidus. There is associated patchy demyelination and gliosis.

FAILURE TO THRIVE

This term is used to denote the lack of normal physical growth and mental development during infancy. The cause is often obvious, for gross congenital malformations, severe feeding problems, and chronic infections are almost invariably associated with failure to thrive. Sometimes more subtle defects may be the cause. Poor care by the mother, emotional or social deprivation, poor nutrition, chronic intoxication, and low-grade infection may be underlying factors. A specialized examination may be required to find genetic factors, enzyme defects, or metabolic deficiencies, such as the malabsorption syndromes and endocrinopathies. Last but not least, any disease of the brain may result in failure to thrive; occult chronic subdural hematoma secondary to trauma and subdural effusion after meningitis are prime examples.

DEVELOPMENTAL DEFORMITIES

Defects of the cerebrum. Anencephaly is the absence of the calvaria and the cerebral hemispheres; it is not compatible with life. Microcephaly is the reduction in the size of the cerebral hemispheres; this condition—along with anomalies of face, limbs, and heart—may occur in the offspring of chronic alcoholic mothers. Porencephaly is characterized by a cavity within a cerebral hemisphere; the condition need not manifest clinical signs. Patients with agenesis of the corpus callosum usually do not show evidence of this lesion.

Cervicocranial deformities. These malformations include craniostenosis (premature closure of cranial sutures), basilar impression (elevation of the rim of the foramen magnum into the cranial cavity), and Arnold-Chiari malformation. There are several types of Arnold-Chiari malformation; the most common defect is the extension of the medulla and the cerebellum through the foramen magnum, with the cerebellum overlapping the upper cervical spinal cord, and associated meningomyelocele. Hydrocephalus is often associated with these and other defects of the occipitocervical junction.

Dilation of the ventricles or the central canal

Hydrocephalus. Hydrocephalus is the abnormal dilation of the ventricular system; in the infant, it is associated with head enlargement. It is usually due to congenital obstruction of the ventricular channels, such as stenosis of the Sylvian aqueduct. In patients with Dandy-Walker syndrome, atresia of the foramina of the fourth ventricle causes a cyst-like dilation of the fourth ventricle and lesser hydrocephalus of the other ventricles. Hydrocephalus is often seen in paranatal inflammatory diseases that prevent reabsorption of the cerebrospinal fluid into the blood stream and in neoplastic diseases that obstruct the outflow of the cerebrospinal fluid. In addition to the cervicocranial deformities noted above, hydrocephalus is often associated with congenital defects of the meninges, such as meningocele (failure of the envelope of the meninges to close fully at the midline) and meningomyelocele (failure of the neural tube to close fully, with splitting of the spinal cord and the meninges). The prognosis of hydrocephalus is related to its cause and severity. The process may stabilize with little or no clinical cerebral deficit. Surgery to shunt ventricular fluid around an obstruction or to drain cerebrospinal fluid out of the cranial cavity is often indicated but may do no more than prolong a tragic vegetative state.

Syringomyelia and syringobulbia. These conditions are characterized by cavitation within the central portion of the spinal cord and the medulla. Although one basis for this disease is congenital, symptoms may not begin until the second or third decade of life. In the typical case, loss of pain but with preservation of touch sensations in the hands precedes other signs of neuraxial involvement.

CHROMOSOMAL ANOMALIES

These genetic defects can be diagnosed in utero by culturing cells obtained through amniocentesis. A decision can then be made regarding therapeutic abortion.

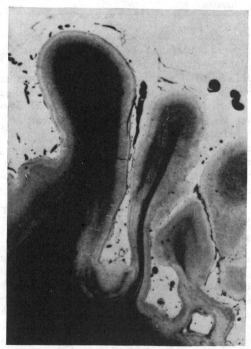

FIGURE 33. Cerebral palsy. Ulegyria, *right,* next to a relatively intact gyrus on the *left.* Note that maximum shrinkage affects the deep aspects of the convolution. (From Blackwood, W., McMenemy, W. H., Meyer, A., Norman, R. M., and Russell, D. S. *Greenfield's Neuropathology,* ed. 2, p. 387. Williams & Wilkins, Baltimore, 1963.)

Mongolism (Down's syndrome). Mongolism is due to a chromosomal defect (trisomy of chromosome 21) occurring in the fetus, most often when the mother is beyond the age of 35 or 40. The condition is characterized by idiocy and alterations of the head and face, as revealed by brachycephaly, flattened nose, large tongue, slanting and widely spaced eyes, and small ears. The bones, especially of the fingers, are shortened, and other deformities are common. Death is due to the effect of associated congenital anomalies, especially of the heart, or of intercurrent infections. The gross configuration of the brain is more diagnostic than is its microscopic appearance. There is a reduction in the size of the entire brain, with large simple convolutions. Under the microscope, alterations in nerve cells and their stratified architecture are seen.

Sex chromosomal defects. Klinefelter's syndrome is manifested by gynecomastia and aspermatogenesis in males. Turner's syndrome is characterized by retarded growth and retarded sexual development and by webbed neck in females. Patients with these syndromes may exhibit mild mental retardation. An extra X chromosome is present in Klinefelter's syndrome; an X chromosome is missing in Turner's syndrome.

PHAKOMATOSES

Phakomatoses are diseases affecting ectodermal tissue, primarily neurocutaneous structures. They are usually inherited as autosomal dominants with variable penetrance. The lesions become manifest in childhood and slowly progress.

Neurofibromatosis (Recklinghausen's disease) is manifested by spots of hyperpigmentation (*café-au-lait*) and by cutaneous and subcutaneous tumors that become increasingly prominent in late childhood. Tumors may also arise from the sheaths of spinal nerve roots or of cranial nerves, especially the acoustic nerves. Meningiomas and, less often, gliomas may affect the central nervous system, and glial hypertrophy may cause hydrocephalus. Bones and other organs may be involved. The nerve tumors are composed of fibroblasts and Schwann's cells.

Tuberous sclerosis is sometimes inherited as a dominant factor. It is characterized first by convulsive seizures and mental retardation; later (about 4 years of age), sebaceous adenomas, depigmented spots, and other lesions of the skin occur. On inspection of the brain, numerous pale nodules are seen projecting from the cortex or into the ventricles, like the gutterings of a candle (see Figure 34). These nodules may be evident in air encephalograms or computerized tomograms and their calcifications may be seen in plain roentgenograms of the skull. On microscopy, the nodules reveal an alteration in the normal neuronal pattern, with many giant-sized nerve cells. Demyelination is seen, and fibrillary glial proliferation is especially prominent, with astrocytes forming large multinucleated giant cells. Brain tumors may occur; adenomas and myomas are found in other organs of the body.

Several vascular anomalies of the skin are associated with neurological abnormalities. In Sturge-Weber syndrome a congenital craniofacial vascular nevus is seen, and double-contoured calcifications within an ipsilateral atrophic cerebral cortex underlie a meningeal angioma. The cerebral lesion is often associated with seizures and focal neurological signs.

von Hippel-Lindau disease is manifested by hemangioblastoma of the cerebellum and retina and sometimes the spinal cord or nerve root as well, with associated polycythemia and cystic disease of other organs. The clinical onset may occur in children or adults, most frequently during the second decade of life.

Ataxia telangiectasia (Louis-Bar syndrome) is a hereditary ataxia that becomes evident at about 4 years of age. Ataxia is

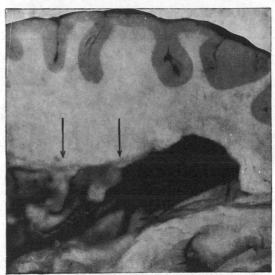

FIGURE 34. Tuberous sclerosis. The *arrows* indicate nodules of glial tissue projecting into the lateral ventricle. (From Blackwood. W., Dodds, T. C., and Sommerville, J. C. *Atlas of Neuropathology,* ed. 2, p. 221. Williams & Wilkins, Baltimore, 1964.)

caused by degeneration of the cerebellar cortex and by demyelination of the posterior and spinocerebellar tracts of the spinal cord. Degenerative changes also occur in peripheral nerves and sympathetic ganglia. After the onset of ataxia, telangiectatic lesions develop over the conjunctivae and the face. Impairment of immunoglobulin accounts for recurrent respiratory tract, paranasal sinus, and pulmonary infections.

Familial telangiectasis (Rendu-Osler-Weber disease) affects the skin, mucous membranes, other organs, and occasionally the central nervous system. The telangiectases appear in childhood and may cause bleeding later in life, but only rarely in the brain.

ENDOCRINOPATHIES

Hypothyroidism during fetal life, cretinism, results in severe mental retardation. The infant is sluggish and excessively lethargic. His infantile development is slow, and deaf mutism may be present. The habitus is that of small body, short extremities, large head, thickened facies, open mouth, and large protruded tongue. Neonatal diagnosis now permits prompt corrective therapy.

Abnormalities of parathyroid function may result in tetany, choreiform activity or seizures, and mild mental retardation.

INTRAUTERINE INFECTIONS

Viruses may reach the fetus through the placental barrier at an earlier stage than do larger organisms. Maternal rubella causes cataracts, deafness, mental retardation, and congenital heart disease in the offspring. Congenital neurosyphilis causes clinical and pathological changes in the infant similar to those syndromes in the adult. These children develop stigmata of interstitial keratitis, dental deformities, and, later, saddle nose. Syphilis and the effects of the cytomegalic inclusion virus and of the protozoan causing toxoplasmosis are discussed above.

METABOLIC AND DEGENERATIVE DISEASES

These diseases are classified in Table II. The diseases are listed according to the type of tissue and the area of the nervous

TABLE II
Metabolic and Degenerative Diseases of Early Life

I. Diseases of white matter
  A. Central nervous system
    1. Metabolic diseases due to enzyme deficiencies
      a. Lipid diseases
        (1.) Metachromatic leukodystrophy
        (2.) Globoid cell leukodystrophy (Krabbe's syndrome)
      b. Amino acid diseases
        (1.) Phenylketonuria
        (2.) Other aminoacidurias
    2. Unknown pathogenesis
      a. Merzbacher-Pelizaeus disease
      b. Adrenoleukodystrophy (Schilder's disease)
      c. Other sudanophilic leukodystrophies
      d. Spongy leukodystrophy (Canavan's sclerosis)
      e. Multiple sclerosis
      f. Central pontine myelinolysis*
    3. Immune or viral-induced demyelinations
      a. Postvaccinal and postinfectious diseases
      b. Subacute sclerosing panencephalitis
      c. Progressive multifocal leukoencephalopathy*
  B. Peripheral and cranial nerves: spinal cord
    1. Metabolic diseases
      a. Refsum's disease
      b. Primary familial amyloidosis
      c. Fabry's disease
    2. Unknown pathogenesis
      a. Peroneal muscular atrophy (Charcot-Marie-Tooth disease)
      b. Hypertrophic interstitial neuritis (Déjérine-Sottas disease)
      c. Hereditary sensory neuropathy
      d. Leber's optic atrophy
      e. Congenital deafness
      f. Hereditary spastic paraplegia
II. Diseases of gray matter: neuronal disease
  A. Cerebrum
    1. Metabolic diseases due to enzyme deficiencies
      a. Lipid diseases
        (1.) Cerebromacular degeneration (Tay-Sachs disease)
        (2.) Niemann-Pick disease
        (3.) Gaucher's disease
        (4.) Other lipid storage diseases
      b. Mucopolysaccharidoses
        (1.) Hunter's syndrome
        (2.) Hurler's syndrome
        (3.) Other mucopolysaccharidoses
      c. Carbohydrate diseases
        (1.) Galactosemia
        (2.) Gierke's disease
        (3.) Other diseases of complex carbohydrates
    2. Other metabolic diseases
      a. Subacute necrotizing encephalomyelopathy (Leigh's disease)
      b. Alpers' disease
      c. Copper malabsorption disease (Menkes' kinky-hair disease)
      d. Familial myoclonus
  B. Basal ganglia
    1. Metabolic disease
      a. Wilson's disease
    2. Unknown pathogenesis
      a. Dystonia musculorum deformans
      b. Hallervorden-Spatz disease

* Included for the sake of completeness but not diseases of childhood.

TABLE II—*Continued*

  C. Spinal cord
    1. Unknown pathogenesis
      a. Progressive infantile spinal muscular atrophy (Werdnig-Hoffmann disease)
      b. Wohlfart-Kugelberg-Welander disease
III. Diseases of gray and white matter
  A. Spinocerebellar diseases
    1. Metabolic diseases
      a. Ataxia telangiectasis
      b. Bassen-Kornzweig syndrome
    2. Unknown pathogenesis
      a. Friedreich's ataxia
      b. Other spinocerebellar degenerative diseases
  B. Other diseases previously listed (examples)
    1. Krabbe's disease
    2. Copper malabsorption disease
    3. Amino acid diseases

system predominantly affected. Obviously, some diseases affect more than the tissues under which they are listed—for example, Krabbe's disease and the aminoacidurias affect neurons, as well as white matter—or affect areas of the nervous system in addition to their predominant sites.

Enzyme deficiencies, usually inherited as autosomal recessive diseases, have been found to be responsible for most of the diseases formerly considered degenerative diseases of childhood. It has been customary to classify these diseases according to their respective defects of fat, protein, or carbohydrate metabolism (see Table III). There are now dozens of different inborn errors of metabolism, and the list is expanding yearly.

For want of the degradative enzyme, metabolites accumulate in excessive amounts in cells or may be excreted in excessive amounts in the urine. The diseases are now diagnosed by quantitative analysis of specific metabolites or their enzymes. Enzyme systems present in skin fibroblasts can be assayed by cell culture, and enzymes can also be measured from blood serum, leukocytes, or amniotic fluid. Prenatal diagnosis, made by tissue culture of cells obtained by amniocentesis or by analysis of noncultured amniotic cells or fluid, allows time for therapeutic abortion. The finding of deficient or absent enzymes in the blood or in skin biopsies, or analysis of the blood or the urine for excess metabolites, permits diagnosis in affected patients. Detection of carriers has revolutionized genetic counseling. Some regions now routinely perform newborn screening tests for congenital metabolic disorders of phenylketonuria, galactosemia, homocystinuria, maple syrup urine disease, and hypothyroidism. Thus, diagnosis and treatment can be instituted within the first few weeks of life.

In the establishment of a clinical diagnosis, the most crucial aspect of the history is that of developmental regression or lack of development. There are many clinical manifestations of these diseases. Failure to thrive, mental retardation, seizures, and failure of neurological and physical development are common. Blindness is more frequent than is deafness. As a general rule, those diseases affecting the white matter begin with motor deficits, such as spastic weakness and paralysis. Diseases affecting primarily the gray matter of the cerebrum present with seizures, especially myoclonic seizures, and loss of cognitive functions soon occurs.

Diseases of white matter. In children, disease of white matter is often termed leukodystrophy, implying faulty myelin formation, rather than the myelin degeneration of demyelination, but this distinction is

TABLE III
The Most Common Metabolic Diseases Due to Enzyme Deficiency

Disease	Deficient Enzyme
Lipid diseases	
Tay-Sachs disease	Hexosaminidase A
Gaucher's disease	Glucocerebrosidase
Niemann-Pick disease	Sphingomyelinase
Krabbe's disease	Galactocerebrosidase
Metachromatic leukodystrophy	Aryl sulfatase
Mucopolysaccharidoses	
Hurler's syndrome	α-L-Iduronidase
Hunter's syndrome	Iduronate sulfatase
Carbohydrate diseases	
Galactosemia	Galactose 1-phosphate uridyl transferase
Gierke's disease*	Glucose-6-phosphatase
Amino acid diseases	
Phenylketonuria	Phenylalanine hydroxylase
Maple syrup urine disease	Decarboxylasing enzymes
Histidinemia	Histidase
Homocystinuria	Synthase, methyltransferase, reductase

* Affects central nervous system secondarily.

not always valid. Similarly, these diseases of white matter are usually distinguished from the lipoidoses by degeneration of lipids (myelin) in diseases of white matter and the accumulation of abnormal lipids in the lipoidoses. This distinction is not sharp, for in some diseases, such as metachromatic leukoencephalopathy, both processes occur. Most of the diseases of white matter begin in infancy, are inherited in a recessive mode, and are fatal. Weakness progresses to paralysis and terminally to decerebrate rigidity. Optic atrophy is common. The primary pathological lesion is diffuse and symmetrical degeneration of myelin; loss of axis cylinders is usually commensurate with the degree of demyelination.

Metachromatic leukodystrophy (leukoencephalopathy, sulfatide lipidosis). This illness often begins between 1 and 4 years of age and has a course of 2 to 5 years; when it begins in late childhood or, on rare occasions, in young adults, its duration is somewhat more prolonged. The progressive impairment of motor function is usually spastic or ataxic, but involvement of peripheral nerves is associated with lower motor neuron signs as well. Regression of mental function and of vision occurs later. Prominent metachromatic staining (staining a tint different from that of the stain used) lipids occur in irregular granular masses, both intracellular and extracellular, within demyelinated white matter. An excess of sulfatides accounts for this staining reaction and is due to a deficiency of the enzyme aryl sulfatase. The metachromatic lipids are also found in the epithelium of renal tubules and in peripheral nerves. The diagnosis can be made during life by an examination of the urinary sediment for metachromatic lipids, by measuring the metabolite or its enzyme in the urine and in blood leukocytes, and by sural nerve biopsy.

Globoid cell leukodystrophy (Krabbe's disease). This disease begins in infancy and runs a course of 1 or 2 years. The motor defect is manifested by rigidity progressing to opisthotonos. The spinal cord and peripheral nerves are affected, as well as the cerebrum. Within demyelinated areas are groups of mononuclear epithelial-like cells and large multinucleated globoid cells. Both types of cells occur most often near or around small blood vessels. Galactocerebroside accumulates in the globoid cell because the enzyme of this complex lipid is deficient.

Phenylketonuria. This familial disease is most common in blond, blue-eyed babies. During the first year of life, physical and mental retardation become evident. Mental deficiency is usually severe, and a large variety of motor defects become obvious during the preschool years. In 25 per cent of all affected children, convulsive seizures occur.

This disease is caused by a defect in the enzyme required for oxidation of phenylalanine to tyrosine. One of the alternate metabolites, phenylpyruvic acid, can be detected by the green color produced when acidified urine is tested with 5 per cent ferric chloride. If diets designed to lower blood phenylalanine are instituted during the first few months of life, prognosis for near-normal intelligence is good. On microscopic examination of the brain, defective myelination and associated gliosis are noted.

Other aminoacidurias. Many diseases are caused by abnormalities of protein metabolism, with resultant elevation of amino acids in the urine or the blood. Mental and motor retardation and seizures are the most common sequelae. Most diseases are named for the amino acid abnormality—for example, histidinemia. Clinical features that help to distinguish some of the aminoacidurias include abnormalities of the skin (red, scaly rash of Hartnup disease), abnormalities of the eyes (dislocated lens of homocystinuria), and abnormalities in the odor of the urine or the body (maple syrup urine disease). The neonatal diagnosis of maple syrup urine disease permits treatment by the restriction of foods containing branched-chain amino acids and allows normal mental development. Similarly, the restriction of methionine in the diet after the early diagnosis of homocystinuria may be of benefit.

Merzbacher-Pelizaeus disease. This illness is more common in boys than in girls; it often begins during the first 1 or 2 years of life. It has a chronic course of several years, and patients may survive into early adult life. Pendular nystagmus and titubation of the head occur early; cerebellar ataxia usually precedes spastic weakness. Sudanophilic neutral fat is found in the myelin breakdown products.

Adrenoleukodystrophy (sudanophilic leukoencephalopathy). This disease shows a sex-linked male inheritance and begins between 5 and 10 years of age, although it may occur anytime within the first three decades of life. The course ranges from a few months to 3 years. Blindness is common, along with deafness and physical and mental retrogression; seizures often occur. Adrenal insufficiency may be clinically obvious or noted only by laboratory studies. Sudanophilic neutral fat is prominent in the products of severe demyelination. The demyelination is subcortical, sparing the U. fibers, and the occipital lobe is most severely affected.

The term "Schilder's disease" was once used synonymously with sudanophilic leukodystrophy. With rare exceptions, the cases classified as Schilder's disease were either adrenoleukodystrophy or subacute multiple sclerosis.

Spongy leukodystrophy (Canavan's sclerosis). This condition begins in infancy, results in death after 6 to 36 months, and affects mainly Jews. Macrocephaly is present, as well as progressive motor deterioration and blindness. In this disease the normal white matter is replaced by a meshwork of axons and glial fibers that surround cystic areas.

Multiple sclerosis may begin in childhood. This disease is discussed above. Similarly, the demyelinating processes after vaccination and infections and those induced by viruses are noted above.

Diseases of gray matter. The largest group of diseases in this category are the so-called storage diseases, in which metabolites are stored in excessive amounts in nerve cell bodies. Secondary demyelination often occurs. The lipid storage diseases, lipidoses, are the best known. Recent studies have revealed many different degrading enzyme deficiencies that are now classified at the molecular level as the sphingolipidoses. Less common than the lipidoses are storage diseases of mucopolysaccharides and defects of carbohydrate metabolism. Deterioration of physical and mental faculties and seizures are the most common clinical characteristics of these diseases. Most of these illnesses are genetic and caused by autosomal recessive genes.

Cerebromacular degeneration. Tay-Sachs disease begins between the fourth and eighth month of life and usually occurs in Jews. It is characterized first by an exaggerated startle reaction to acoustic stimuli and a regression of development; hypotonia is followed by spasticity and, finally opisthotonos. Blindness occurs as a cherry red spot replaces the macula. Seizures and head enlargement are late signs. Death occurs in a few months to 3 years. Deposition of fine fat granules in the cytoplasm (see Figure 35) is responsible for the swelling of nerve cells, particularly in the cortex of the cerebrum and the cerebellum. Similar but less prominent changes are noted in microglia. The enzyme hexosaminidase A is absent in Tay-Sachs disease, allowing the excessive deposition of ganglioside G_{m2}.

Several other gangliosidoses are neurologically similar to Tay-Sachs disease, some with, and some without visceral involvement.

Ceroid lipofuscinosis. Another group of diseases clinically resemble Tay-Sachs disease but are biochemically dissimilar, for the storage material appears to be ceroid or lipofuscin, rather than a ganglioside. These degenerative diseases include a late infantile form with onset at 3 to 4 years of age (Bielschowsky's disease), a juvenile form beginning between 3 and 10 years of age (Batten-Spielmeyer-Vogt disease), and an adult form (Kufs disease.) These diseases differ clinically from Tay-Sachs disease in that predilection for Jews is not evident, their courses are chronic, and retinal lesions may be absent or show pigmentary degeneration, rather than a cherry red macular spot. Myoclonus is prominent.

Niemann-Pick disease. About 50 per cent of the infants with this disease are Jewish, and its neurological features are similar to or indistinguishable from Tay-Sachs disease. In Niemann-Pick disease, however, systemic involvement (hepatosplenomegaly) is present. The fatty products of abnormal metabolism are stored in the reticuloendothelial system of the body and in the neurons of the central nervous system. The resultant large foam cells can be seen in the bone marrow. These cells are filled with sphingomyelin, and lack of a sphingomyelin-cleaving enzyme has been demonstrated.

Gaucher's disease. Gaucher's disease usually begins in the fourth to sixth month of infancy, but some forms occur in later life. It is characterized by developmental retrogression, retroflexion of the head, strabismus, bulbar palsy, and spasticity. Enlargement of the spleen and the liver occurs. The affected infants die during the first year. The lipid glucocerebroside is stored in the cells of the reticuloendothelial system (spleen, liver, and bone) much more than in nerve cells, but neuronal degeneration is, nevertheless, a common feature. The diagnosis can be made by liver or bone marrow biopsy. The enzyme that hydrolyzes the glucocerebroside is deficient. The other lipid storage diseases rarely occur.

Mucopolysaccharidoses. The ground substance component of connective tissue is composed of complex molecules called mucopolysaccharides. Inherited diseases of these compounds become evident during the first years of life. Growth retardation and mental retardation—often associated with corneal opacities, coarse facies, and skeletal deformities—are features of gargoylism. The illnesses last for one or more decades. Hurler's syndrome and Hunter's syndrome are the two most common illnesses of this group. The metabolic deposits of gangliosides, as well as mucopolysaccharides, accumulate in the central nervous system and in the viscera.

Galactosemia. Galactosemia is a familial disease seen in infants soon after birth. The illness is first manifested by vomiting, diarrhea, and a failure to thrive. Jaundice, hepatomegaly, and cataracts develop. Survivors are mentally and physically retarded. An increase in galactose in the blood and the urine is due to an enzyme deficiency that prevents the infant's utilization of the breakdown products of milk digestion. Withdrawal of milk at the earliest age is beneficial.

Patients who have enzyme defects within the glucose-to-glycogen metabolic pathway accumulate excessive amounts of glycogen. The glycogen storage diseases usually affect the nervous system secondarily. These diseases may be manifested by hypoglycemia, seizures, mental retardation, and myopathies. There are almost a dozen such diseases; Gierke's disease is the best known.

Subacute necrotizing encephalomyelopathy (Leigh's disease). This familial disease usually begins during the first year or two of life and results in death within a few years. The chief clinical features are vomiting and dysphagia, psychomotor retrogression, hypotonic weakness, seizures, and eye signs of ophthalmoplagia, abnormal eye movement, and blindness. The pathological lesions resemble Wernicke's disease, with necrosis, vascular proliferation, and gliosis, affecting predominantly the thalamus and brain stem; however, in Leigh's disease the mamillary bodies are spared. Several biochemical abnormalities have been reported; some are related to disordered thiamin metabolism.

Alpers' disease. Alpers' disease is a rare illness of infancy, and it is sometimes familial. Convulsions, mental impairment, spasticity, and extrapyramidal and cerebellar signs progress to death within a few years. The characteristic pathological feature is degeneration of cerebral and cerebellar gray matter.

Copper malabsorption disease (Menkes' kinky-hair disease). This rare, sex-linked disease affects male infants and is manifested by seizures and developmental retardation. Scalp hair is coarse and fragile. Death occurs within a few years. The brain pathology is manifested by neuronal loss more than by glial disease and is associated with certain protein deficiencies containing copper linkages. Failure of gastrointestinal copper absorption can only be ameliorated by parenteral administration.

Familial myoclonus. There are rare familial diseases manifested in large part by myoclonus, lightning-like arrhythmic muscle twitches. The illnesses are often autosomal dominant and occur in adolescence more often than in childhood. The metabolic defects underlying these conditions are as yet unknown. Lafora body polymyoclonus is probably the familial myoclonic epilepsy formerly termed Unverricht's disease. Myoclonic jerks or convulsive seizures or both are eventually followed by dementia and ataxia. Death occurs after one or two decades. Neuronal degeneration is widespread, and affected neurons contain basophilic intracytoplasmic round inclusion bodies (Lafora bodies), consisting of protein-bound mucopolysaccharides. Juvenile cerebroretinal degenerations are probably diseases of lipid metabolism clinically similar to infantile Tay-Sachs disease, with myoclonus as a prominent feature. The course is less acute than the infantile disease, but the outcome is nevertheless fatal. In dyssynergia cerebellaris myoclonia (Hunt's syndrome) cerebellar ataxia is added to the myoclonic phenomena, but the course is much more chronic than the other familial myoclonic diseases.

Wilson's disease. Hepatolenticular degeneration usually begins in adolescence and is discussed above. The abnormalities of copper metabolism primarily affect the basal ganglia and neurons of the cerebellum and cerebral cortex.

Dystonia musculorum deformans. This condition begins in middle childhood and is associated with degenerative changes, primarily in the putamen and caudate nuclei. It is discussed above.

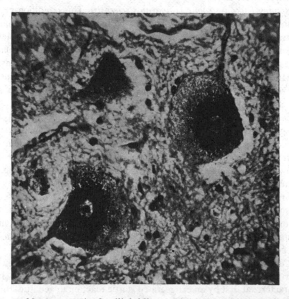

FIGURE 35. Amaurotic familial idiocy. Lipid deposition swells the cytoplasm of neurons (in this case, anterior horn cells of the spinal cord) and crowds the Nissl substance around the nucleus. Thionin, 350 X. (From Blackwood, W., Dodds, T. C., and Sommerville, J. C. *Atlas of Neuropathology,* ed. 2, p. 9. Williams & Wilkins, Baltimore, 1964.)

Hallervorden-Spatz disease. This rare familial illness is characterized by progressive rigidity, choreoathetosis, other extrapyramidal signs, and mental deterioration. It begins between 6 and 12 years of age and progresses to death after one or two decades. After autopsy, one sees brown pigmentation, caused by iron deposits, in the globus pallidus, substantia nigra, and red nucleus.

Werdnig-Hoffmann disease (infantile spinal muscular atrophy). This inherited disease is manifested by progressive spinal musculature atrophy, with flaccid weakness, beginning during the first year of life. Death usually occurs within a few months or years, but on rare occasions the disease becomes static, and the patient may live to adulthood. Loss of anterior horn cells is the major pathological finding.

Wohlfart-Kugelberg-Welander disease. The term "juvenile proximal spinal muscular atrophy" characterizes the chief features of this condition. It is not necessarily fatal, but pathologically and genetically it resembles Werdnig-Hoffmann disease.

Diseases of gray and white matter

Bassen-Kornzweig syndrome (acanthocytosis, lipoproteinemia). This rare familial disease begins between 6 and 12 years of age and has a chronic course of two or three decades. It is neurologically manifested by weakness and areflexia, sensory and then cerebellar ataxia, and retinal degeneration. Steatorrhea is due to an absorptive block in the intestines. The diagnosis is made by observing the characteristic thorny red blood cells (acanthocytes) and by finding a decrease in the serum lipoproteins. The pathological changes consist of neuronal loss in the cerebellar cortex and the spinal cord, with demyelination of the posterior and spinocerebellar tracts of the spinal cord.

Other diseases of gray and white matter. Ataxia telangiectasia is discussed with the phakomatoses and Friedreich's ataxia is discussed with the degenerative diseases. Several other diseases affect the spinocerebellar pathways and cause ataxia in children. Some are of known metabolic origin—for example, the amnioaciduria Hartnup disease, which manifests a scaly rash and episodic cerebellar ataxia. Other heredospinocerebellar degenerations are linked with lesions in different systems of the neuraxis or eyes; their biochemical mechanisms have yet to be discovered.

DISEASES OF CHILDHOOD AND ADOLESCENCE DISCUSSED UNDER OTHER CATEGORIES

Neoplasms. Brain tumors in children differ from those in adults in several ways. About 75 per cent of all childhood brain tumors affect midline structures, and more than half are in the posterior fossa— the cerebellum, the brain stem, and the fourth ventricle. Above the tentorium the most common sites are the third ventricle, the adjacent diencephalon, and the optic chiasm. Gliomas are even more common in children than in adults, particularly meduloblastoma and astrocytoma. Craniopharyngiomas and optic nerve gliomas occur most often in childhood. Ependymomas, papillomas of the choroid plexus, and pinealomas are seen predominantly in the young. The clinical manifestations are similar to those previously noted in adults, but, because of their midline predominance, increased intracranial pressure is an early sign in children with brain tumors. In children less than 6 years of age, there may be separation of the sutures of the skull, with cracked-pot resonance to percussion and head enlargement.

Vascular disease. The cause of cerebrovascular disease in childhood is likely to be congenital. Sturge-Weber syndrome is noted above. Congenital heart disease causes embolic cerebral infarction in 10 to 25 per cent of all cases. An arteriovenous malformation is much more likely to cause subarachnoid hemorrhage in childhood than is an aneurysm. A cerebral hemorrhage in a child is most often associated with a blood dyscrasia;

for example, such hemorrhages occur in 50 per cent of children with leukemia. A debilitated child is more likely to develop sinus thrombosis than is an adult. Acute infantile hemiplegia is probably of vascular origin and occurs in infants and preschool children; febrile illness is often the precipitating event; convulsive seizures are common.

Toxic and inflammatory diseases. Lead toxicity causes encephalopathy in children but not in adults. Hemophilus meningitis, toxoplasmosis, cytomegalic inclusion body disease, and subacute sclerosing panencephalitis are almost exclusively seen in children. Acute cerebellar ataxia is thought to be of viral origin. Those diseases associated with childhood systemic infection include Sydenham's chorea and Reye's syndrome. The postvaccinal and postexanthemata encephalitides are usually childhood phenomena.

Other syndromes beginning in childhood. Of the epilepsies, infantile spasms, febrile convulsions, and petit mal are invariably diseases of children. Familial dysautonomia is congenital; Gilles de la Tourette's disease and Kleine-Levin syndrome begin in childhood and adolescence, respectively. All the most common muscular dystrophies begin in childhood. The periodic palsies usually begin in childhood or adolescence.

Suggested Cross References

Other neurological syndromes are discussed in Section 3.4 and Section 3.5. Neurological evaluation is discussed in Section 3.2 and central nervous system anatomy in Section 3.1. The organic mental disorders are discussed in detail in Chapter 20. Mental retardation is discussed in Chapter 36. Drug dependence is discussed in Chapter 23.

REFERENCES

* Baker, A. B., and Baker, L. H. editors. *Clinical Neurology.* Harper & Row, New York, 1978.
Blackwood, W., and Corsellis, J. A. N. *Atlas of Neuropathology,* ed. 2. Churchill Livingstone, New York, 1970.
Calne, D. B. *Therapeutics in Neurology.* Lippincott/Blackwell, Philadelphia, 1975.
Carter, S., and Gold, A. P. *Neurology of Infancy and Childhood.* Appleton-Century-Crofts, New York, 1974.
Escourolle, R., and Poirier, J. *Manual of Basic Neuropathology,* ed. 2. W. B. Saunders, Philadelphia, 1978.
Feiring, E. H. , editor. *Brock's Injuries of the Brain and Spinal Cord and Their Coverings,* ed. 5. Springer, New York, 1974.
Ford, F. R. *Diseases of the Nervous System in Infancy, Childhood, and Adolescence,* ed. 6. Charles C Thomas, Springfield, Ill., 1973.
* Gilroy, J., and Meyer, J. S. *Medical Neurology,* ed. 2. Macmillan, New York, 1975.
Grinker, R. R. , and Sahs, A. L. *Neurology,* ed. 6. Charles C Thomas, Springfield, Ill., 1966.
Marshall, J. *The Management of Cerebrovascular Diseases,* ed. 3. Lippincott/Blackwell, Philadelphia, 1976.
* Menkes, J. H. *Textbook of Child Neurology,* ed. 2. Lea & Febiger, Philadelphia, 1979.
* Merritt, H. H. *A Textbook of Neurology,* ed. 6. Lea & Febiger, Philadelphia, 1979.
Robertson, D. M., and Dinsdale, H. B. *The Nervous System: Structure and Function in Disease,* A. Golden, editor. Williams & Wilkins, Baltimore, 1972.
Russell, D. S., and Rubinstein, L. J. *Pathology of Tumors of the Nervous System,* ed. 4. Williams & Wilkins, Baltimore, 1977.
Slager, U. T. *Basic Neuropathology.* Williams & Wilkins, Baltimore, 1970.
Spillane, J. D. *Atlas of Clinical Neurology,* ed. 2. Oxford University Press, New York, 1976.
* Stanbury, J. B., Wyngarden, J. B., and Friedrickson, D. S. *The Metabolic Basis of Inherited Disease,* ed. 3. McGraw-Hill,New York, 1972.
Swaiman, K. F., and Wright, F. S. *The Practice of Pediatric Neurology.* C. V. Mosby, St. Louis, 1975.
Thompson, R. A., and Green, J. R., editors. *Infectious Diseases of the Central Nervous System.* Raven Press, New York, 1976.
* Walton, J. N., editor. *Brain's Diseases of the Nervous System,* ed. 8. Oxford University Press, New York 1977.

3.4 Clinical Neurology and Pathophysiology

SEYMOUR SOLOMON, M.D.

Introduction

Many diseases are characterized by pathophysiological phenomena, rather than by well-defined or consistent neuropathology. These illnesses are due to biochemical abnormalities, the intricacies of which are only beginning to be discovered. Those diseases that cannot be confirmed by the microscope are often misdiagnosed as psychogenic.

Dysfunctions of the Motor System

MYASTHENIA GRAVIS

Myasthenia gravis occurs most often between the ages of 20 and 40 years, and it affects women more often than men. It is an autoimmune disease, and recent evidence points to the inactivation of acetycholine receptors at the myoneural junction by antibodies binding those sites. There is an increased incidence of diseases of the thymus and thyroid glands in myasthenia, suggesting that those organs are involved in the causative mechanism. The disease is characterized by excessive fatigability and weakness, predominantly of the muscles innervated by the cranial nerves. The extremities, especially the upper extremities, are involved to a lesser extent. Double vision, ptosis, dysphagia, and difficulty in chewing are common initial symptoms. Spontaneous remissions sometimes occur, but usually intermittent progression is noted, with eventual respiratory paralysis. The diagnosis is established when brief disappearance or improvement of signs occurs within 30 seconds of an intravenous injection of edrophonium (Tensilon).

Maintenance therapy consists of neostigmine (Prostigmin) or pyridostigmine (Mestinon), but some of the toxic effects of these cholinesterase inhibitors may simulate an exacerbation of myasthenia. As the disease progresses, the need for increasing medication raises the therapeutic dose to the level of the toxic dose. Withdrawal from the anticholinesterases and obligatory artificial respiration for 2 to 3 days usually permit reinstitution of medication at a lower dosage.

Two major therapeutic measures have been appreciated in recent years. Thymectomy, now recommended for virtually all patients below the age of 50 years, is associated with improvement or remission in most cases, but the benefits may be delayed for years. Steroid therapy usually permits reduction in the dosage of anticholinesterase drugs and may induce complete remission, particularly in the elderly; therefore, titrated alternate-day steroids are almost always indicated after 60 years of age. Therapeutic doses of curare or succinylcholine may cause fatal paralysis in patients with myasthenia gravis; weakness may also be potentiated by cardiac antiarrhythmic drugs, local anesthetic agents, and some antibiotics, particularly the aminoglycosides.

PERIODIC PARALYSIS

Hypokalemic (familial) periodic paralysis. This condition begins in adolescence and affects men more than women. It is manifested by recurrent bouts of flaccid weakness or paralysis of somatic musculature, usually sparing the muscles innervated by the cranial nerves and the muscles of respiration. The symptoms persist for 2 to 24 hours. The episodes usually occur during rest after exercise and may be precipitated by a high carbohydrate meal, alcohol, or adrenocortical hormones. The paralysis is associated with a drop in the serum potassium and corresponding electrocardiographic changes (depressed S-T segment and diminished amplitude of T-wave). Treatment consists of the administration of potassium during the attack and prophylactically. Hypokalemic paralyses may also be associated with thyrotoxicosis, hyperaldosteronism, and potassium loss through the kidneys or gut.

Hyperkalemic periodic paralysis (adynamia episodica hereditaria). As differentiated from familial (hypokalemic) paralysis, the hyperkalemic bouts of paralysis usually begin in the first decade of life, affect both sexes equally, are of short duration, and are associated with paramyotonia. The distinction can be made with certainty by a determination of the serum potassium level during an attack. The electrocardiogram affords the most rapid evaluation of hyperkalemia (prolongation of the Q-R-S interval and T-wave elevation). The episodes are treated by the administration of intravenous calcium. Acetazolamide and other diuretics are useful prophylactic agents.

Periodic paralysis may occur without a change in serum potassium levels and may be associated with spontaneous episodes of hyponatremia.

MYOTONIA

Myotonia is characterized by prolonged muscle contraction, with delay of muscle relaxation. It is most often seen as part of myotonic muscular dystrophy (myotonia dystrophica). Myotonic muscular dystrophy is a hereditary disease, beginning in young adults, manifested by myotonic impairment of motor function and by dystrophic muscle wasting of the face, neck, and extremities. Associated features include premature baldness, cataract formation, testicular atrophy, other endocrinopathies, and mental deterioration. Myotonia congenita is a more benign variant of myotonia dystrophica. Paramyotonia is the occurrence of this peculiar muscular reaction in association with cold; it occurs with hyperkalemic periodic paralysis. Treatment with procainamide, phenytoin, or quinine helps to diminish the myotonic phenomena.

McARDLE'S DISEASE

This familial myopathy is due to phosphorylase deficiency. The deficiency results in persistent muscle contraction, with pain and stiffness (cramp) after exercise.

STIFF-MAN SYNDROME

This syndrome is characterized by bouts of severe spasm of the somatic musculature that last hours or days. It is often precipitated by minimal physical or emotional stimuli. The musculature spasm may or may not be painful. Trunk and abdominal wall musculature is particularly involved; when generalized, the syndrome resembles tetanus. The mechanism of this condition is unknown, but diazepam (Valium) decreases the severity of the muscle contractions.

TORTICOLLIS

Torticollis is the unilateral contraction of cervical muscles, predominantly the sternocleidomastoid, twisting the head to one side. This disease may be a manifestation of drug toxicity, especially from phenothiazine derivatives, but most cases are fragments of a pathophysiological process akin to dystonia musculorum deformans. Psychogenic mechanisms are no longer thought to be the predominant cause. The results of medical and psychiatric therapy are poor, but spontaneous remissions are common. Surgical therapy, ranging from denervation of the cervical muscles to the placing of bilateral lesions in the ventrolateral thalamic nuclei, is warranted only in severe and intractable cases.

GILLES DE LA TOURETTE'S DISEASE

Beginning before puberty, multiple tics, especially those affecting the upper extremities, and grunting noises occur. The tics increase in complexity, and the vocalizations progress to scatologic words, coprolalia. The condition had been considered psychogenic because of the absence of objective neurological disease, but excellent response to haloperidol and the poor results with other compounds or psychotherapy indicate a pathophysiological mechanism.

RESTLESS LEGS SYNDROME

The patient experiences peculiar, uncomfortable (sometimes painful or crawling) sensations in the muscles or "bones" of the lower legs. These sensations evoke almost constant movement of the legs. The phenomena occur at rest, especially at night. The cause is not known.

Disorders of Sleep and of the Diencephalon

NARCOLEPSY

The narcolepsy syndrome begins in youth or early adult life. The syndrome has four main features, although some patients never exhibit more than one. Narcolepsy, the most common feature, is manifested by a sudden irresistible desire to sleep, usually while sedentary. Sleep may last from a few minutes to a half hour. Cataplexy is a brief impairment of muscle tone precipitated by a sudden emotional stimulus; it may be manifested by no more than a slight buckling of the knees, or it may affect the entire body. Total flaccid paralysis—occurring immediately on awakening from sleep or, less often, during the transition from drowsiness to sleep—is termed sleep paralysis. This condition lasts only a few seconds but is, nevertheless, frightening. Hypnagogic hallucinations are usually vivid but brief. The disease is presumably due to dysfunction of the diencephalic reticular system. The majority of narcoleptic patients reveal rapid eye movements (REM) at the onset of sleep, in contrast to normal sleep, in which REM occur about 1½ hours after the onset of sleep. Treatment with amphetamines or methylphenidate benefits narcolepsy, but patients with this syndrome may need much more than the average dose. Imipramine is most useful in counteracting cataplexy.

SLEEP APNEA

Normally, minor respiratory pauses for less than 15 seconds occur during REM sleep. Bouts of prolonged apnea, lasting from half a minute to 2 or more minutes, occur in some persons and briefly awaken them periodically throughout the night, with resultant complaints of insomnia or hypersomnia. The first reported cases were associated with obesity (Pickwickian syndrome), but obesity is no longer considered the primary factor. The apnea is of two types: central apnea, due to the cessation of diaphragmatic contractions, and obstructive apnea, either due to anatomical defects of the nasopharynx (for example, large tonsils and adenoids) or due to physiological defects of the pharyngeal wall. There may be hundreds of such bouts each night, and the associated hypoxia evoked by the apnea may have a profound effect on the cardiovascular status. Vigorous weight loss helps when obesity is a factor, but a tracheostomy may be necessary.

SLEEP DISORDERS OF CHILDHOOD

Several sleep disorders are predominant in childhood. Somnambulism, sleepwalking, lasts from 1 to several minutes and occurs during deep (non-REM) stages of sleep. Night-terrors also occur in deep non-REM sleep, unlike the dreams associated with REM sleep, and are often associated with somnambulism. There is severe anxiety, with hyperactivity and screaming. Psychopathology is not found in children with somnambulism or night-terrors, but adults manifesting these traits usually have serious psychological problems. Enuresis is a common failure of urinary continence during deep non-REM sleep in boys; it occurs less often in girls. Only rarely are organic causes found, and psychogenic mechanisms are usually secondary. Imipramine at bedtime is often beneficial.

KLEINE-LEVIN SYNDROME

This is a rare disorder of males 10 to 25 years of age. It is characterized by periods of ravenous appetite alternating with many (18) hours of sleep. An acute illness or fatigue may precede the episodes, which may occur three or four times a year. During an attack, behavior is disturbed; hyperirritability and uninhibited sexual activity occur. There may be impaired thought processes and hallucinations. On recovery, days or weeks later, depression of spirits is occasionally noted. The pathophysiological site of this disease is presumed to be the hypothalamic or prefrontal regions or both.

RILEY-DAY SYNDROME (FAMILIAL DYSAUTONOMIA)

This rare condition is noted during the first year of life, usually in Jewish children. The disease is characterized by blotchy skin, defective lacrimation, and excessive perspiration and salivation. Further dysfunction of the autonomic nervous system is manifested by intermittent hypertension, with postural hypotension and defective temperature control. The affected infants feed poorly and frequently vomit. A neurological examination often reveals evidence of motor retardation and emotional instability. Incoordination and indifference to pain may be present. Corneal ulceration and systemic illness are common. The site of disturbance is uncertain. This condition may be due to a defect of catecholamine metabolism affecting hypothalamic centers, the reticular formation, or peripheral autonomic ganglia.

AKINETIC MUTISM

In this condition, the patient is mute and immobile, but his eyes may follow people about the room or may be diverted by sound. A painful stimulus sometimes evokes reflex withdrawal or feeble movements but without manifestations of pain or other emotion. The patient may swallow when fed, but he does not always chew food. Duration of sleep is greater than normal, but the patient is easily aroused. In contrast to psychotic withdrawal, akinetic mutism is not characterized by negativism or catatonia, although during recovery, if it occurs, the patient may show these symptoms. Akinetic mutism is associated with organic disease of the diencephalon, especially the caudal hypothalamus, and is presumably due to incomplete interruption of the reticular activating system.

Cerebral Edema and Ventricular Dilation

Many diseases discussed under the major etiological categories cause increased intracranial pressure or ventricular dilation or both, either by the involvement of the brain parenchyma or by the blockage of cerebrospinal fluid (CSF) flow or absorption. Two conditions warrant special mention.

BENIGN INTRACRANIAL HYPERTENSION (PSEUDOTUMOR CEREBRI)

Cerebral edema causes increased intracranial pressure and resultant headache and papilledema but without focal signs. There is frequent association of this condition with youth, females, menstrual irregularities, and obesity, but a specific endocrine dysfunction has not been discovered. All causes of increased intracranial pressure without focal signs must be considered, such as extracranial causes of papilledema and occult intracranial masses. Mass lesions are ruled out by computerized tomography that reveals normal but small ventricles. This disorder usually undergoes spontaneous remission, but treatment with steroids and such dehydrating agents as glycerol is warranted to decrease intracranial pressure.

NORMAL-PRESSURE HYDROCEPHALUS

This condition is an unusual but correctable cause of dementia in adults. Gradual ventricular dilation occurs as the result of chronic impairment of absorption of CSF due to residual inflammatory changes of past subarachnoid bleeding or past meningoencephalitis or due to partial obstruction of CSF outflow through the Sylvian aqueduct or from the basal cisterns to the convexity of the brain. Often, the underlying cause is not evident. The clinical features are slowly progressive dementia, urinary incontinence, and gait difficulties, such as gait apraxia. The diagnosis can be made by noting the lack of diffusion over the convexity of the brain of radioactive indium after its intrathecal injection, the rapid rise of intracranial pressure during the saline intrathecal infusion test, and the lack of air over the convexity of the brain in the presence of dilated ventricles at the time of pneumoencephalography. The configuration of the ventricles and the periventricular areas, as seen in the pneumoencephalogram and on computerized tomograms, may also be of aid. The reversal of dementia and associated signs is sometimes dramatic after the ventricular fluid is surgically shunted into the pleural cavity or into the atrium of the heart, but not any one or combination of the diagnostic studies is certain to predict response to therapy.

FLUID-ELECTROLYTE AND ENDOCRINE DISORDERS

WATER AND SODIUM ALTERATIONS

Dehydration may cause personality changes progressing to delirium. Lethargy, convulsions, and coma may occur. Hypernatremia is usually associated with dehydration.

Overhydration also evokes the above symptoms. In addition, increased intracranial pressure, generalized weakness, and muscular cramps or twitching may be noted. Sodium depletion, often associated with water intoxication, frequently causes nausea, vomiting, and signs of shock. Inappropriate antidiuretic hormone secretion occasionally occurs with deep-seated cerebral lesions; it is manifested by water retention, with associated hyponatremia, and sodium wasting, with relatively hypertonic urine.

ACIDOSIS AND ALKALOSIS

Respiratory acidosis (CO_2 narcosis), due to hypoventilation, results in drowsiness and weakness. Increased intracranial pressure due to vasodilation may occur.

Metabolic acidosis is most often associated with diabetic coma and uremia. The hyperpnea of Kussmaul's respiration accompanies lethargy, progressing to stupor and coma.

Respiratory alkalosis, caused by hyperventilation, frequently produces symptoms of lightheadedness, feelings of unreality, paresthesias, palpitation, drowsiness, tremulousness, tremors, and, finally, tetany. Tetany is manifested by carpopedal spasm, laryngospasm, and neuromuscular irritability, as demonstrated by Trousseau's and Chvostek's signs. If tetany is severe, convulsions may occur.

Metabolic alkalosis, often due to excessive vomiting, is associated with hypoventilation, apathy or delirium, generalized weakness, and tetany.

POTASSIUM DISORDERS

Excessive serum potassium, hyperkalemia, causes flaccid paralysis (see hyperkalemic periodic paralysis, above), paresthesias, and lethargy. Arrhythmias and cardiac arrest may occur.

Hypokalemia results in flaccid paralysis of somatic musculature (see hypokalemic periodic paralysis, above) and paralytic ileus; lethargy may be prominent. Sometimes cardiac arrhythmias and heart failure occur.

MAGNESIUM ALTERATIONS

Excess serum magnesium is associated with lethargy, decreased neuromuscular responsiveness, respiratory failure, and, finally, coma.

Magnesium depletion causes paresthesias, irritability, and delirium. Muscular weakness, twitching, coarse irregular tremors, tetany, and convulsions may occur; cerebellar and basal ganglion signs have been reported. Cardiac arrhythmias may develop.

COMPLICATIONS OF HEMODIALYSIS

The disequilibrium syndrome occurs during dialysis when an osmotic gradiant develops between the brain and the blood, causing a shift of water into the brain and resultant cerebral edema. Most patients undergoing dialysis complain of headache, and a small percentage of patients also experience nausea, muscle cramps, and changes in mentation ranging from irritability to delibrium or stupor, with or without convulsions.

Progressive encephalopathy associated with long-term hemodialysis for chronic renal failure is of uncertain origin. The standard serum chemistries are not significantly changed, but a disorder of central nervous system metabolites is postulated. The condition begins after 2 or 3 years of hemodialysis. It is characterized by dementia, dyspraxia of speech, and abnormal motor activities—myoclonus, asterixis, grimacing, seizures. The abnormalties are, at first, transient and associated with the dialysis; then they become permanent and progress to death in 3 to 15 months.

Patients requiring chronic dialysis are also subject to other neurological complications. Vitamin depletions may cause Wernicke's encephalopathy. Subdural hematomas may occur without obvious trauma.

HYPERALIMENTATION

This term refers to the maintenance of nutrition solely by parenteral means, and hypophosphatemia is its most common complication. Neurological side effects range from motor signs of weakness or paralysis to ataxia and seizures; numbness of hands and feet and diffuse sensory impairment may occur. Coma with cerebral hemorrhage and death may supervene.

PARATHYROID AND CALCIUM DISORDERS

Hyperparathyroidism is associated with hypercalcemia and resultant hypotonic weakness and bone and muscle pains. Personality changes, delirium, dementia, and coma may occur. Osteomalacia is seen in roentgenograms of bones.

Hypoparathyroidism causes hypocalcemia, with hyperreflexia, muscular weakness, tetany, or convulsions. Paresthesias are common. Mental changes may range from nervousness to frank psychosis. Cataracts form when the disease is chronic, and cerebellar or basal ganglia signs may be noted. Osteoblastic changes in bones and sometimes calcifications in basal ganglia are evident in roentgenograms.

PANCREAS ABNORMALITIES

Hyperinsulinism causing hypoglycemia is initially manifested by anxiety, hunger, weakness, palpitation, shortness of breath, and perspiration. Then tremor, irritability, increasing confusion, delirium, or frank psychosis may occur. Muscular twitching or spasms, convulsive seizures, decerebrate rigidity, and coma are the final signs.

The cerebral symptoms of diabetes are related to premature atherosclerosis. Diabetic coma (acidosis) is noted above.

Pancreatic encephalopathy is manifested by agitation and confusion progressing to delirium and coma. It is said to occur in association with acute pancreatitis, especially in alcoholics. There is doubt as to whether it represents a specific entity, in contrast to the combinations of the effects of alcoholism, shock, and metabolic defects that accompany pancreatitis.

THYROID DYSFUNCTIONS

Hyperthyroidism causes dyspnea and tachycardia. Myopathy and, especially, eye signs—exophthalmos, lid swelling, lid lag, and ophthalmopareses—are common. Tremor is noted, and choreiform movements or convulsions may develop. The disease is associated with emotional symptoms of anxiety, lability of affect, irritability, and agitation; apathetic hyperthyroidism rarely occurs and may lead to coma. Thyroid crisis may result in acute delirium and other symptoms of toxic psychosis.

Myxedema is associated with lethargy and weakness. The skin, especially of the face, is dry and puffy; the hair is thin and brittle. There is decreased psychomotor activity, and personality changes are common—most often depression but sometimes paranoid symptoms and frank psychosis. Memory and perceptual impairments are the chief signs of dementia; hypothermia and coma may be terminal events. Headache, dizziness, dysarthria, and hoarseness are often present; truncal ataxia sometimes occurs. Myopathies, carpal tunnel entrapment neuropathy, and, less often, peripheral neuropathies may affect the extremities, and pseudomyotonic reflexes can frequently be elicited.

ADRENAL GLAND DISEASES

Primary aldosteronism (hyperaldosteronism), a dysfunction of the adrenal cortex, causes hypertension with potential cardiac and cerebral complications. Muscular weakness or cramps, paresthesias, and headaches are common symptoms. Polyuria and polydypsia may occur. There is associated hypokalemia, hypernatremia, and metabolic alkalosis.

Cushing's syndrome (hyperadrenocorticism) causes symptoms of weakness and fatigability. Personality changes are common. Obesity of the face, neck, and trunk, with purplish striae, are characteristic of this condition. Amenorrhea, hirsutism, and loss of libido also occur. Patients with this disease frequently develop diabetes mellitus and hypertension.

Pheochromocytoma is a tumor of the adrenal medulla that causes paroxysms of hypertension, with associated symptoms of anxiety, tremulousness, perspiration, palpitation, and headache. In addition, there may be dizziness, paresthesias, pallor, coldness of extremities, nausea, and vomiting. Cerebral hemorrhage is a potential complication.

Addison's disease, decreased function of the adrenal cortex, is manifested by progressive fatigue, asthenia, and weakness. Syncope and shock are associated with hypotension, and sometimes tremors or convulsions occur. Irritability, apprehension, and personality changes are common. Abdominal distress and pigmentation of the skin and mucosa are characteristic of this disease.

Adrenogenital syndrome, adrenal hyperplasia, is associated with virilization in children (congenital form) and with virilization in women and sometimes feminization in men (acquired form, such as adenocarcinoma). There are no primary neurological symptoms.

PITUITARY DISORDERS

Hyperpituitarism due to an eosinophilic adenoma in an adult causes acromegaly, characterized by bone overgrowth—especially of the hands, feet, and mandible—and enlargement of the nose, lips, and tongue. Muscular weakness and personality changes frequently occur. The tumor in children is manifested by gigantism. Very rare basophilic adenomas are associated with Cushing's syndrome.

Hypopituitarism causes apathy and asthenia, lethargy, and fatigue. The facies is often bland; the skin is waxen, pale, and dry; the body is free of hair. There is associated hypofunction of other endocrine glands (especially the ovaries and testes), hypothermia, and hypotension. This condition in children results in dwarfism. Minor emotional symptoms are common, but depression and frank psychosis sometimes occur. Crises of hypopituitarism, pituitary apoplexy, as may occur in pituitary infarction secondary to postpartum uterine hemorrhage or other systemic stresses, may cause coma and death.

Epilepsy

Epilepsy is a recurrent paroxysmal disturbance of cerebral function manifested by somatic, visceral, or psychic phenomena or all three; it is usually associated with loss or alteration of consciousness. It has been useful to name the convulsive disorders by their clinical manifestations, hence the terms "grand mal," "petit mal," and "psychomotor." Recently, epileptic seizures have been classified by correlating pathophysiological (electroencephalographic) phenomena with clinical phenomena. Under this system of classification, epilepsy is divided into two major groups, partial or focal seizures and generalized seizures.

PARTIAL OR FOCAL SEIZURES

These seizures are manifested in the electroencephalogram by discharges that are more or less localized to one cerebral hemisphere and arise in cortical or subcortical regions. Organic cerebral diseases usually cause these convulsive disorders, although constitutional factors may be important. Seizures of this type may occur in children, but the incidence increases with age.

Partial seizures are divided mainly into those with elementary symptoms and those with complex symptoms.

Seizures with elementary symptoms. Partial seizures with elementary symptoms are usually focal motor in character and unassociated with loss of consciousness. They often consist of focal clonic movements involving all or part of the musculature on the side contralateral to the discharging cerebral focus. Adversive seizures are manifested by a turning of the head, eyes, and body away from the side of the discharging lesion. Less common focal motor seizures include inhibitory seizures, characterized by focal loss of tone and strength, and seizures that involve speech, either arrest of speech or forced vocalization. Other partial seizures of an elementary type are of a sensory nature and usually occur as an aura of a motor seizure, rather than as an isolated seizure state. These may be somatosensory phenomena, such as local pain over some part of the contralateral face, body, or extremities. Seizures with special sensory symptoms include visual, auditory, olfactory, and gustatory experiences. Vertiginous phenomena are sometimes of epileptic origin, arising from the insula or medial temporal lobe. Autonomic symptoms, occurring in a paroxysmal fashion, are also classified as partial seizures with elementary symptoms; the epileptogenic focus is in the insular or orbitofrontal cortex. Episodic abdominal pain (abdominal epilepsy) is the most common form.

Seizures with complex symptoms. Complex partial seizures reveal electroencephalographic abnormalities of unilateral or asynchronous bilateral discharges, primarily involving the temporal or frontotemporal areas. These seizures may begin with some of the sensory phenomena described above or with auras of uncinate phenomena and lip and tongue movements. Alteration of consciousness or mental status invariably occurs. Some seizures may be manifested only as impaired consciousness. Others involve mental and psychological symptoms and may include intellectual alteration; amnesia or forced thinking; illusions or hallucinations, including altered awareness of self and *déjà vu* phenomena; affective symptoms, such as fear or forced laughing; and, most often, psychomotor manifestations (automatisms)—psychomotor seizures. These phenomena may occur individually or in various combinations.

Partial seizures with either elementary or elaborate symptoms may spread from the initial discharging site to adjacent areas or to noncontiguous zones and thus progress to generalized seizure activity—that is, they may become secondarily generalized. Jacksonian seizures begin as focal motor activity in one extremity, spread over the entire side, and, finally, become generalized (grand mal). Sometimes this progression is so rapid that the focal qualities may not be apparent. Similarly, the electroencephalographic focus during a seizure may rapidly become secondarily generalized.

GENERALIZED SEIZURES

Seizures that are generalized from the onset are presumed to arise in the diencephalon because the electroencephalographic discharges appear from all areas of the cerebral cortex in a bilaterally symmetrical and synchronous fashion. Loss or alteration of consciousness is almost invariable. These seizures have been most often termed "idiopathic," for frequently an organic defect cannot be found. On the other hand, toxic or metabolic disturbances and diffuse or scattered organic cerebral disease may cause generalized seizures. Those seizures for which an organic cause cannot be found usually occur in children, but at any age seizures may be due to an organic or metabolic defect.

Generalized seizures are subdivided basically into nonconvulsive and convulsive seizures.

Nonconvulsive seizures. Generalized nonconvulsive seizures are usually manifested as simple loss or impairment of consciousness, petit mal absence. The seizure is brief, often momentary, and begins and ends abruptly without aura or sequelae. Petit mal usually begins between the ages of 5 and 10 years and subsides after puberty. The electroencephalogram reveals rhythmic bilaterally synchronous and symmetrical 3-cycles-per-second spike-and-wave discharges. The typical absence is manifested by abrupt interruption of consciousness and movement. Slight clonic activity; lip, mouth, and head movements; and blinking—all rhythmic and corresponding to the 3-per-second cerebral discharges—are usually associated, especially if the seizure persists for more than 10 seconds. Brief automatism and decreased postural tone may occur. Hyperventilation often induces an absence, and these seizures may occur many times a day. Typical absences are only rarely associated with organic disease. Petit mal status is characterized by a semistuporous state and, in the electroencephalogram, by more or less continuous activity of rhythmic 3-cycles-per-second spike-and-wave forms or similar but less characteristic activity.

Other forms of generalized seizures are minor motor seizures. Children with these disorders have serious cerebral disease and are relatively refractory to treatment. The electroencephalographic patterns of these minor motor seizures show slower and less rhythmical spike-and-wave complexes than do those of petit mal absence. Bilateral myoclonus may occur in some patients with petit mal; one or two generalized myoclonic jerks occur without loss of consciousness. Almost half the children with this disorder also develop generalized tonic-clonic convulsive seizures. Atonic or akinetic seizures are associated with loss of postural tone and resultant drop attacks. Tonic seizures may later occur, and the incidence of mental retardation is high.

Infantile spasms are clusters of brief myoclonic jerks affecting predominantly the head, neck, and extremities, usually in flexion. The electroencephalogram reveals high-voltage polyspike-and-slow-wave activity occurring in a haphazard fashion from all areas of the head (hypsarrhythmia). The clinical and electrical phenomena disappear after the first few years of life, but signs of cerebral disease are usually permanent. Fragmentary myoclonic jerks may occur at any age; they are similarly associated with polyspike-and-irregular-slow-wave activity in the electroencephalogram and with severe organic cerebral disease.

Convulsive seizures. Tonic and then clonic generalized seizures, grand mal seizures, show bilaterally synchronous polyspike-and-slow-wave bursts in the interictal electroencephalogram. An aura of peculiar visceral sensation or other nonfocal symptoms may precede the tonic and clonic phenomena. Loss of consciousness is invariable, and tongue biting or incontinence may occur. After the seizure there may be muscle aches or pains, sometimes related to fractures that have occurred; headache and drowsiness are common. Grand mal seizures may be seen at all ages, except in early infancy.

NEONATAL SEIZURES

Seizures in the newborn are not classified as focal or generalized. Focal clonic seizures in the neonate are, curiously, not associated with a focal cerebral lesion but are most often of metabolic origin and

usually have a good prognosis. Generalized fragmentary seizures of the newborn are erratic tonic or clonic movements or both, rapidly fleeting from one side to another. Minor seizures are easily overlooked, for they may consist of nothing more than slight tremors of the mouth or brief apnea.

OTHER SEIZURES

As examples of the diverse mechanisms associated with convulsive disorders, the following are of interest.

Febrile convulsions. Always generalized, febrile convulsions occur before the age of 3 years. The high familial incidence (25 per cent) and normal interictal electroencephalogram help to establish the benign nature of this condition, but 20 per cent of the children with these disorders later have seizures unrelated to fever.

Withdrawal seizures. The so-called rum fit occurs in the alcoholic from 6 to 48 hours after abstinence from alcohol. About a third of the patients with withdrawal seizures develop delirium tremens. Seizures may occur after withdrawal from many types of drugs, most often after barbiturate withdrawal. The seizures occur on the second or third day after discontinuation of a short-acting barbiturate and on the seventh or eighth day after stopping a long-acting barbiturate. Seizures rarely occur as late as 2 or 3 weeks after drug withdrawal.

Posttraumatic epilepsy. These seizures occur within 4 years of the date of a cerebral trauma, most often within the first year. The incidence of seizures after head trauma largely depends on the severity of the cerebral injury. Table I gives approximate statistics.

SEIZURES WITH PSYCHIC PHENOMENA (COMPLEX FOCAL SEIZURES)

These psychic phenomena are often perceptual, characterized by illusions. Sensory illusions may be manifested by a distortion of any of the special senses, such as by floors tilting or sounds echoing. Or there may be somatosensory distortions, with an alteration in self-awareness; *déjà vu* phenomena are common. Hallucinations, usually formed and complex, may be evoked by seizures. In contradistinction to schizophrenic hallucinations, these hallucinations are usually recognized as such. When an olfactory hallucination occurs as the aura of a seizure, there is a 90 per cent probability of an underlying low-grade glioma. Alterations in mood or affect, most often fear and depression, sometimes occur. Anger or sexual sensations are not associated with seizures; if laughter occurs, it is not accompanied by appropriate affect. Disturbance of thought, especially forced thinking, may be a seizure manifestation. Automatisms are the most common type of psychomotor phenomena associated with convulsive disorders. Automatic behavior may follow, may be part of, or may constitute the seizure itself, psychomotor epilepsy.

The anatomical sites of the psychic states noted above have been evaluated by surgical exploration and electrical stimulation. Although repeated stimulation at the same point in the same patient does not always evoke the same response, the

TABLE I
Incidence of Epilepsy after Head Trauma

Type of Injury	Post-traumatic Epilepsy
	%
Closed-head injury	
Cerebral concussion	5–10
Cerebral contusion	25
Penetrating head injury	
No loss of consciousness or neurological signs	15
Cerebral laceration	33
Gross cerebral defect	50

following correlations have been most consistent. Illusions of an olfactory nature may be evoked from the uncus, auditory illusions from Heschl's gyrus, illusions of taste from the circular sulcus of the temporal lobe, and visual illusions from the posterior aspect of the temporal lobe. Stimulation of the superior lateral zones of the temporal lobe or the adjacent parietal cortex may produce hallucinations. Feelings of unreality may be evoked from the supramarginal gyrus. Other emotional phenomena may be experienced during stimulation of the temporal lobe deep in the Sylvian fissure or its undersurface. Forced thinking may occur on stimulation of the frontal and the temporal lobes. The insula is associated with intestinal and other visceral symptoms. Automatisms may be evoked by stimulating the circuminsular cortex, the amygdaloid nucleus, the anterior hippocampal gyrus, the hippocampus itself, the termination of the anterior commissure, or the anterior portion of the frontal lobe. Automatic activity seems to be associated with epileptic interference of connections between the midbrain-diencephalic centers and those parts of the cerebral cortex that are related to memory and other intellectual functions. The most common automatisms are those associated with psychomotor seizures. They usually arise in the cortex of the anterior portion of the temporal lobe, but they may originate in other areas of the limbic system. Sometimes small foci may trigger diencephalic (generalized) epileptogenic activity.

Psychomotor seizures often start as visceral discomfort within the abdomen or the head or as emotional phenomena, such as anxiety. Uncinate symptoms—illusions or hallucinations of taste or smell—may occur as auras. During the seizure there is alteration of consciousness and thought processes; amnesia is invariable. The seizure may be simple and consist of a syncopal-like episode or of staring blankly into space. Autonomic features are often manifested by chewing, swallowing, or smacking of the lips. Automatic stereotyped behavior is most characteristic. This behavior is often bizarre, semipurposeful, and partially or totally inappropriate, but usually the activity has some relationship to the environment. Simple automatisms may consist of fumbling with clothing, manipulation of the hands, or aimless stumbling about. More complex activities may be manifested by the pursuit of a previous line of action of habitual activity, such as boarding a bus to work. During the seizure the patient may obey simple commands; on the other hand, he may be antagonistic or assaultive.

DIFFERENTIAL DIAGNOSIS

The distinguishing clinical characteristics of the most common forms of epilepsy can be briefly summarized. The diagnosis of a generalized, convulsive, tonic-clonic (grand mal) seizure is supported by evidence of an aura, tongue biting, or incontinence during the seizure and subsequent somnolence or muscular aches, although none of these features need be present. Generalized, nonconvulsive (petit mal) epilepsy, on the other hand, is not associated with an aura or subsequent symptoms, and it never begins in adult life. Complex partial seizures (psychomotor seizures) may be preceded by an aura of uncinate phenomena or by licking and smacking of the lips, and amnesia of the seizure is invariable; although these seizures, usually automatisms, may be extremely variable from one patient to another, they tend to be stereotyped for each patient. All the above symptoms are associated with loss or alteration of consciousness, which is most profound in grand mal seizures, may be so brief as to be indiscernible in petit mal, and may be obscured by the complex automatism of a psychomotor seizure. Partial seizures with elementary symptoms are not associated with loss of consciousness unless the seizure

spreads to deep cerebral structures and becomes secondarily generalized.

In older children and adults, the differential diagnosis of epilepsy includes syncope, severe vertigo, cataplexy-narcolepsy, and cerebrovascular insufficiency. The distinguishing features of these phenomena are discussed elsewhere in this section. A normal myoclonic twitch during the transition from drowsiness to sleep is sometimes misdiagnosed as a minor seizure. Psychogenic phenomena, particularly hysteria and attacks of anxiety, may be difficult and sometimes impossible to differentiate from psychomotor epilepsy.

Epileptic seizures in young children must be differentiated from several nonconvulsive phenomena: (1) Breath-holding spells occur from 6 months to 3 years of age and are provoked by crying. At the onset of crying, expiration is prolonged; the cry is held or breath lost for about 15 seconds. Then loss of consciousness occurs for a few seconds, with flaccidity, rigidity, tonic spasm, or, sometimes, brief clonic activity. Children given to breath-holding spells often have a hypersensitive oculovagal reflex—that is, ocular compression causes brief apnea and syncope. (2) Spasmus nutans occurs between 6 months and 2 years of age, especially in children living in a dark environment. It consists of rhythmic nodding or tremor of the head, with rapid pendular nystagmus. These features can be stopped by closing the child's eyes, but forceful control of the tremor increases the nystagmus. (3) Very young girls may masturbate by squeezing their extended legs together in a tonic fashion. The child may be poorly responsive during this time and fall asleep afterward. (4) Tics are usually more complex and less stereotyped than are myoclonic jerks. Tics can be voluntarily controlled for a short time. (5) Paroxysmal behavioral disturbances and temper tantrums may be difficult to differentiate from psychomotor seizures, but the seizures are more stereotyped. (6) During and briefly after somnambulism and night-terrors, the child may be unresponsive. These sleep disorders are discussed above.

EVALUATION OF THE EPILEPTIC

In the evaluation of patients with a convulsive disorder, several laboratory studies are advisable in addition to the electroencephalogram. The blood count, urinalysis, serological test for syphilis, fasting blood sugar, and serum calcium may be diagnostic. For example, several anemia or leukemia, uremia, lues, hypoglycemia, and hypocalcemia may all present seizures as the initial symptom.

Computerized tomography is indicated for every patient with onset of seizures after the age of 20 years. About 50 per cent of all epileptics show changes in the computerized tomogram, usually of an atrophic nature, but the incidence of brain tumor increases if the onset of seizure is after the age of 50 and especially if there are focal electroencephalographic or focal clinical manifestations. The computerized tomogram is also of diagnostic value in childhood epilepsy, with the exception of generalized nonconvulsive, petit mal, seizures. Atrophy and malformations may be seen, as well as calcifications not seen in skull roentgenograms (tuberous sclerosis, toxoplasmosis, cytomegalic inclusion disease). Mass lesions are less common in children than in adults. When the index of suspicion of remediable organic disease is high, further studies are warranted, including radioisotope brain scan and evaluation of the cerebrospinal fluid.

THERAPY

Drugs. Most patients with epilepsy can be completely or adequately controlled by medication. Seizure control is often attained only after trial and error. One drug should be used, and the dosage should be increased from the average dosages listed below to the point of toxicity before adding or substituting another drug. It takes about five elimination half-lives for the anticonvulsant to build up to its steady-state blood level. Phenytoin has a half-life of 1 day, phenobarbital a half-life of 4 days; thus, phenytoin reaches a steady state in 5 days, and phenobarbital reaches a steady state only after 20 days. One must allow the drug to reach its plateau before judging its efficacy. When a second anticonvulsant drug is added to a therapeutic regimen, it may inhibit or stimulate the metabolism of the first drug. This drug interaction may decrease or increase the formerly stable therapeutic blood level, and there may then occur increased seizures or drug toxicity. When discontinuing an anticonvulsant, gradual withdrawal is mandatory.

In the treatment of status epilepticus, diazepam (10 mg.) is the drug of choice; 240 mg. of phenobarbital or 500 mg. of phenytoin are favored by some. All are intravenously administered—very slowly, phenytoin no faster than 50 mg. a minute. Attention to an open airway is a primary concern. If the initial dose of anticonvulsant is ineffective, intubation may be necessary before repeating the dose.

A large number of drugs have been made available since 1938, when phenytoin (Dilantin) was introduced. The administration of Dilantin given to an adult in doses of 0.3 gm. to 0.4 gm. a day, or phenobarbital (0.1 gm. to 0.12 gm. a day) or both is still the most common treatment of generalized tonic-clonic grand mal and complex partial psychomotor seizures. Carbamazepine is particularly effective for complex partial seizures and for generalized tonic-clonic seizures as well. Dosage starts with 200 mg. twice a day and, if necessary, is increased to 800 mg. to 1,200 mg. a day in divided doses. Mephenytoin may be somewhat more potent than phenytoin in similar dosages, but it is more toxic. Primidone is at least as effective as phenytoin; the average adult dose of 0.25 gm. three to four times daily must be attained by gradual increments of smaller amounts. Trimethadione, introduced in 1945, was the first preparation effective in generalized nonconvulsive petit mal epilepsy. The average dose for a child is 0.3 gm. three to four times a day. Paramethadione is somewhat less effective than trimethadione in similar dosages. Ethosuximide, administered to the child in doses of 0.25 gm. three to four times daily, has become the drug of choice for generalized nonconvulsive petit mal seizures. In recent years clonazepam has been found useful in petit mal absence and akinetic seizures; it is particularly beneficial for myoclonic seizure activity that has been and still is most resistant to therapy. The dose of clonazepam is 0.01 to 0.03 mg. per kg. a day for the young child and 1.5 mg. a day in divided doses after age 10 years. Valproic acid is the most recent drug introduced for the treatment of petit mal absence and myoclonic seizures. The average dose is 250 mg. from one to four times a day. Other succinimides—phensuximide, 0.5 gm. three times a day, and methsuximide, 0.3 gm. three to four times daily—are also of benefit in petit mal; methsuximide is also useful for psychomotor and grand mal seizures.

The most recent advance in seizure control is the use of gas chromatography to measure the serum levels of anticonvulsant agents. Therapeutic levels of the most commonly used drugs are as follows: phenytoin, 10 to 20 μg/ml.; phenobarbital, 15 to 40 μg/ml.; primidone, 8 to 12 μg/ml.; ethosuximide, 40 to 100 μg/ml.; trimethadione, 20 to 40 μg/ml.; carbamazepine, 6 to 10 μg/ml.; clonazepam, 5 to 50 μg/ml.; valproate, 50 to 60 μg/ml.

The anticonvulsant drugs are relatively safe, but many toxic reactions have been recorded. Drowsiness, dermatitis, and gastrointestinal symptoms are common to all. Depression of the bone marrow is rare but obviously serious. Certain toxic reactions are characteristic of a specific drug. Nystagmus, ataxia, and drowsiness occur in that order with increasing blood levels of phenytoin; gum hypertrophy, megaloblastic anemia, and hirsutism are common; occasionally, syndromes simulating lupus erythematosus or lymphoma are evoked. Adolescents and, especially, adults taking trimethadione may experience photophobia. Vertigo and nystagmus may occur with many anticonvulsants but are most prominent with primidone overdosage. Hematological and hepatic toxicity with carbamazepine is rare but occurs more often than with other anticonvulsants. Both phenobarbital and clonazepam, in addition to causing drowsiness and ataxia, may cause hyperkinetic behavior in children.

Ancillary measures. Several other agents may be appropriate in the treatment of patients with convulsive disorders. The amphetamines are useful in counteracting the drowsiness that may be a side effect of anticonvulsant medication. Meprobamate, chlordiazepoxide, and diazepam have some anticonvulsant properties and, as tranquilizers, are preferred to the phenothiazine derivatives, which tend to lower the convulsive threshold. Carbonic anhydrase inhibitors, such as acetazolamide, have direct anticonvulsant action, and other diuretics may be helpful, particularly for those women who experience an increase in seizure frequency associated with the menstrual period. A ketogenic diet, recommended only as a last resort for children with akinetic seizures, can rarely be maintained. Infantile spasms may be ameliorated by clonazepam, and adrenocorticotropic hormone often decreases or abolishes these seizures. Because pyridoxine deficiency in infants may cause seizures, a therapeutic trial with this vitamin is always indicated. General hygienic measures are important. People with epilepsy should avoid alcoholic beverages, overhydration, fatigue, and emotional stress.

Surgery. Surgical resection of an epileptogenic scar or other lesion should be considered under the following circumstances: All conservative measures have failed. There is clinical and electrical evidence that focal seizures arise from a resectable area of brain, usually the temporal lobe. Seizures should be of at least several years' duration, thus allowing all potentially epileptogenic areas of the brain to mature and become active and, conversely, permitting time for spontaneous regression, as may occur in the transition from adolescence to adult life or after trauma. In properly selected cases, such as patients with a single anterior temporal lobe focus, surgery has been about 65 per cent successful in significantly decreasing the frequency of seizures or in completely halting seizures. About 15 to 20 per cent of patients have shown a small decrease in seizure frequency after surgery; in another 15 to 20 per cent, surgery has proved to be ineffective or has caused significant morbidity. The mortality rate of temporal lobectomy is only 1 to 2 per cent.

Less conventional surgical procedures include commissurotomy, with sectioning of the corpus callosum, and more radical hemispherectomy of the scarred shrunken cerebral hemisphere. Recently, periodic cerebellar electrical stimulation by means of implanted electrodes has been associated with improved seizure control.

Pain and Dizziness

Pain and dizziness are the two most common neurological symptoms.

PAIN

Pain, mainly a subjective phenomenon, is difficult to evaluate, but there are several factors to be considered. The threshold of pain varies greatly from one person to another. At one end of the spectrum is the entity of congenital indifference to pain. There are no consistent anatomical alterations in this condition, but autonomic dysfunctions may be present; it is considered a pathophysiological disease, rather than a psychological disease. At the opposite extreme are those persons with little tolerance for pain; in this group, psychogenic elements are predominant. Attention and distraction are the most important factors influencing the appreciation of and reaction to pain. The attenuation of response to painful stimuli by placebo therapy and the disappearance of pain with hypnosis are two well-recognized examples of the power of suggestion.

The difference between real and imagined pain is more semantic than physiological. Often, however, there may be great difficulty in differentiating pain of organic or physiological origin from pain manifested as part of a psychological illness. Pain caused by an organic disease is usually accompanied by objective signs of the disease, such as malignancy, ischemic phenomena, or peripheral neuritis. Neuralgias, on the other hand, are not usually associated with organic disease; nevertheless, they usually have a neurophysiological mechanism. These pains follow the anatomical course of a peripheral nerve, nerve root, or nerve plexus, and neuralgias affecting the head and face are the most common. Other pain syndromes do not follow specific somatic nerve distributions but should be distinguished from pain as a manifestation of neurosis.

The patient with a chronic pain syndrome presents one of the most difficult therapeutic challenges. Of course, elimination of the source of pain is the ideal therapy, but this elimination can rarely be accomplished. Analgesics are invariably administered and sometimes fail to effect relief because the physician is too timid to prescribe sufficiently high dosages or narcotics—narcotics, however, are best reserved for the terminally ill. Psychotropic medications are often of more benefit than are analgesics and narcotics. The combination of an antidepressant and a phenothiazine seems to have a distinct physiological effect in ameliorating chronic pain that is unrelated to its mood-lifting and tranquilizing actions. In some instances, interruption of the pain pathways is necessary, either by a chemical block of the nerve or nerve root or by a surgical sectioning of the nerve, root, or spinothalamic tract. Tractotomy is usually performed in the spinal cord (cordotomy) and rarely at higher centers. Psychotherapy may be of value in helping the patient cope with his illness. Other modalities—such as hypnosis, biofeedback, cutaneous electrical stimulation, and acupuncture—have been beneficial in selected cases.

Pain in the head and face is, of course, often due to organic disease. Trigeminal neuralgia in youth is often a symptom of multiple sclerosis. Postherpetic neuralgia often follows herpes zoster. Involvement of a sensory nerve by an aneurysm, tumor, of infection is associated with pain. Other pain syndromes that do not follow a specific peripheral nerve distribution and may be confused with pain of psychological origin are related to disease or dysfunctions of the autonomic nervous system or the central nervous system.

Cranial neuralgias. The cranial neuralgias are characterized by brief bouts of paroxysmal lancinating pain recurring within the anatomical distribution of a cranial nerve. These illnesses occur most commonly in old patients. Often, the pain is triggered by external stimuli, and it can usually be relieved by interrupting the affected nerve. The involved nerve does not manifest objective defects on neurological examination. Gross pathology is not seen, but recent evidence suggests that a tortuous artery has come to lie on and irritate the nerve at its exit from the brain stem.

Trigeminal neuralgia. Trigeminal neuralgia (tic douloureux) is characterized by pain within the distribution of the fifth cranial nerve, most often in the second and third divisions.

Pains may be precipitated by touching the affected side of the cheek, by chewing, and by swallowing. This illness is often benefited by anticonvulsant medication, such as phenytoin, or carbamazepine, but medical therapy may not be permanent in its effect. Surgical interruption of the nerve usually produces lasting relief. The less traumatic procedure of surgically shielding the nerve from the adjacent irritating artery has shown great promise.

Glossopharyngeal neuralgia. This condition is manifested by bouts of sharp pain in the tonsillar and aural areas, spreading to the base of the tongue and throat. The pains may be precipitated by yawning or swallowing. Superior laryngeal neuralgia is probably a fragment of glossopharyngeal neuralgia. The pain in this disease extends from the larynx to the ear, sometimes along the angle of the jaw, and is precipitated by talking or swallowing.

Geniculate neuralgia. Geniculate neuralgia is characterized by pain deep in the ear and adjacent structures. It is due to dysfunction of the geniculate (sensory) ganglion of the facial nerve.

Other craniofacial neuralgias of uncertain origin. In some cases, these pains have a pathophysiological mechanism; in other cases, the pains are neurotic manifestations.

Occipital neuralgia. This type of neuralgia is characterized by pain over the occipital nuchal areas. The pain may extend over adjacent areas of the head and is predominantly unilateral. Pains of this nature implicate the greater occipital nerve; chemical blocks and surgical section are beneficial.

Temporomandibular neuralgia. This condition is manifested by pain in the temporomandibular joint, with radiation of pain beyond that area. This syndrome is due to disease or dysfunction of the temporomandibular joint; when objective signs cannot be demonstrated by physical or roentgenographic examinations, psychogenic mechanisms are usually predominant.

Sphenopalatine neuralgia. Sphenopalatine neuralgia is characterized by pain behind the eyes, in the cheeks, in the roof of the mouth, at the root of the nose, and in the upper jaw and teeth. Sometimes this pain radiates to an ear, to the occipital nuchal areas, to the shoulder, or to the arm. Most often, pains of this nature are psychogenic, rather than due to a dysfunction of the sphenopalatine ganglia.

Atypical facial pain. Atypical facial pain is not a neuralgia as defined above. Instead, this term refers to a constant and often bizarre pain in any part of the face, head, or neck, not confined to the anatomical distribution of a trigeminal or other cranial nerve. This syndrome is most common in women in their late thirties and forties. There is often a long past history of discomfort in the face. The pain may be completely disabling in that the symptom becomes the patient's only concern. These patients eagerly submit to unnecessary dental work and other types of surgery in an attempt to find relief. Although this disease is thought to be psychogenic, psychotherapy has not been any more beneficial than medical or surgical treatments.

Pain originating in the autonomic nervous system

Causalgia. Causalgia is due to dysfunction of sympathetic nerve fibers, usually associated with partial peripheral nerve injury. It is characterized by a peculiar burning hyperpathia affecting a poorly demarcated zone of a hand or foot. Associated autonomic and trophic changes in the affected part consist of smoothened and reddened skin, excessive perspiration, swelling, and tapered digits. Sympathectomy is usually beneficial.

Reflex dystrophies. Other reflex (sympathetic) dystrophies follow minor trauma. They cause not only pain but also muscle contracture and atrophy (with paralysis or weakness), vasomotor changes (hypothermia, cyanosis, edema), and trophic changes of the bones, skin, hair, or nails. Sudeck's atrophy—posttraumatic osteoporosis—is considered in this category.

Shoulder-hand syndrome. The shoulder-hand syndrome is a form of reflex sympathetic dystrophy of nontraumatic origin. It is usually associated with coronary heart disease, although it may be seen with diseases of other viscera. This condition is manifested by pain and restricted mobility of the affected extremity. Trophic and vasomotor changes take place in the skin, muscles, bones, and joints. The shoulder-hand syndrome can be prevented by activation of the extremity; physical therapy is required once the symptoms have begun.

Pain originating in the central nervous system

Thalamic syndrome. This condition is characterized by continuous, often indescribable pain or discomfort over one part or one side of the body. There is often a paucity of objective signs on neurological examination, and psychogenic mechanisms may be falsely invoked. The threshold of superficial pain is slightly raised, but, when the stimulus is appreciated, it is unusually painful or disagreeable, and the zone of pain may spread from the area of the stimulus over ever-widening adjacent zones. There may be delay in appreciation of the stimulus, but the resultant sensation may persist for an unusually long period of time. The thalamic syndrome is usually due to an infarction of the contralateral thalamus after occlusion of the thalamogeniculate branch of the posterior cerebral artery. Many characteristics of the thalamic syndrome may occur in other lesions affecting sensory pathways within the central nervous system. Pain of central nervous system origin is extremely resistant to all forms of medical, surgical, and psychiatric treatment. Psychotropic medications using combinations of major tranquilizers and antidepressants afford the best relief.

Phantom-limb pain. Pain of a phantom limb is a poorly understood, complex, psychophysiological phenomenon. Awareness of a phantom limb is common after amputation. In a small number of patients (2 to 5 per cent), the phantom may not disappear or may become painful. The pain appears to be initiated at the amputation stump and perpetuated in sensory cerebral centers.

Epilepsy. Pain as an epileptic manifestation is rare and is discussed above.

Pains of poorly understood mechanism

Acroparesthesias. These are unpleasant, crawling, tingling, sometimes painful sensations, usually in the hands and arms. The symptoms occur predominantly at rest at night and are diminished by rubbing or moving the extremities. The restless legs syndrome is probably related to this condition.

Postherpetic neuralgia. Pain may persist for months after the initial infection of herpes zoster. It is not benefited by surgical section of the affected nerve.

Posttraumatic neck pain. Pain in the neck musculature often persists for many months after a head and neck injury (whiplash effect). Demonstrable changes are often not evident in the muscles, joints, or vertebrae.

Visceral pain. Pain of visceral origin and pain referred from distant sites may be extremely difficult to diagnose and to differentiate from psychogenic pain.

Headache. Headache is the most common neurological symptom. Most headaches are not associated with organic disease, but, when certain features are associated with a headache, the probability of organic disease is sufficiently high to warrant investigation. The sudden onset of an excruciating headache, often precipitated by stress and associated with a brief loss of consciousness, is typical of a subarachnoid hemorrhage. If a migraine headache is invariably localized to the same side of the head, there may be an underlying aneurysm or arteriovenous malformation. When an elderly patient complains of unilateral temporal headache of recent origin, temporal arteritis must be considered and promptly treated. The headache caused by a brain tumor is most likely to be predominant on awakening in the morning. The physician must always consider meningitis when fever accompanies a headache.

Table II lists the chief differentiating features of the most common types of headache. Of necessity, the features outlined in Table II are not complete, and wide variations may occur. In particular, the symptoms of vascular headache and muscle-contraction headache often coexist. Many causes of headaches are not listed in Table II, but their diagnosis is usually not difficult if associated factors are considered. The severe headache of meningitis is associated with fever and nuchal rigidity. Headaches may be caused by diseases of the eye, ear, nose, paranasal sinuses, teeth, and musculoskeletal structures of the head and neck. Headaches, often with vascular qualities, may occur in response to systemic diseases or toxins, such as an alcoholic hangover. The postconcussion headache may have several mechanisms, not the least of which is psychogenic. In other cases a headache may be a delusional, conversion, or hypochondriacal symptom.

DIZZINESS

The symptom of dizziness has different meanings for different people. Unfortunately, patients not only use the words "dizziness" and "vertigo" interchangeably but also use the term "dizziness" as synonymous with such feelings as faintness, malaise, and headache. It is essential to determine the patient's meaning of "dizziness." The word should indicate a sense of movement or a disturbance of equilibrium, such as imbalance or unsteadiness, or, more specifically, vertigo—that is, spinning sensation. Although it is customary to attempt to distinguish vertigo from less specific forms of dizziness, this differentiation, in the author's opinion, is not crucial, because localization of a disease cannot be made on the basis of a single symptom. More important is the differentiation of dizziness or vertigo of labyrinthine or peripheral origin from dizziness or vertigo of central nervous system origin by the criteria listed in Table III.

Diseases of the ear. Dizziness may be caused by obstructions in the external or middle chambers of the ear. The most common lesions are wax or a foreign body in the external canal, block of the Eustachian tube, and disease of the middle ear, particularly inflammation or injury. Diseases of the internal ear are the most common causes of dizziness.

Labyrinthitis is of unknown origin but, as the name implies, is a disease or dysfunction of the labyrinth or the adjacent vestibular nerve. Many causes have been implicated, including infection, allergy, vascular disease, trauma, and tumor (cholesteatoma). Drugs and toxins often associated with labyrinthine defect include streptomycin, other antibiotics, quinidine, salicylates, anticonvulsants, nicotine, and carbon monoxide. In most cases, the cause of the dysfunction is indeterminate. Labyrinthitis is characterized by sudden dizziness or vertigo lasting minutes or hours and often associated with nausea and vomiting. The attacks usually recur with decreasing frequency and severity over a period of days or weeks. Between the acute bouts a slight insecurity when moving, a poorly described sense of ill-being, or difficulty in mental activity is often present. These vague symptoms may be mistaken for neurosis. Two types of labyrinthine dysfunction have been described. Benign paroxysmal positional vertigo is of a few seconds duration and is precipitated by sudden movement of the head. Repeated movements to evoke this symptom are associated with increasing delay and exhaustion of the response. Vestibular neuronitis is of longer duration, not necessarily precipitated by sudden movement, and associated with unilateral vestibular paresis (absent or decreased response to caloric stimulation). Labyrinthitis is not progressive but often recurrent.

Ménière's disease is probably caused by hydrops, rarely hemorrhage, of the labyrinth. The pathogenesis of this syndrome is unknown, but all the causative factors listed under labyrinthitis may also be operative here. This condition is clinically distinguished from labyrinthitis by the additional symptoms of auditory impairment, especially tinnitus and

Differentiating Features of the Most Common Types of Headache

	Muscle Contraction (Tension) Headache	Vascular Headaches — Migraine	Vascular Headaches — Cluster Headache	Giant Cell (Temporal) Arteritis	Intracranial Mass (Tumor)	Hemorrhage — Subarachnoid	Hemorrhage — Intracerebral	Aneurysm or Arteriovenous Malformation	Hypertension
Sex	Male = female	Female > male	Male ≫ female	Male = female	Male = female	Male = female	Male = female	Male = female	Male = female
Age of onset	Not specific	Puberty to menopause	After 25 years	After 60 years	Not specific	Adults	Adults	Adults	Adults
Family history	Not specific	Often familial	Not familial	Not specific	No family history	Not specific	Not specific	Occasionally familial	Not specific
Quality of pain	Pressure, tightness, band-like, or not specific	Throbbing	Excruciating, boring, piercing	Unilateral throbbing or severe and not specific	Steady ache, increasing severity	Very severe	Ache or throbbing — Severe	None or occasionally migraine	Not specific
Location of pain	Bilateral, occipital > frontal	Unilateral, often temporal	Unilateral medial orbit or adjacent head or face or both	Temple; jaws or tongue, especially when eating	Generalized or on side of mass	Frontal and occipitonuchal or generalized or not specific		If migraine, always on same side	Not specific or occipital
Time of onset	Afternoon or evening	Early morning, often on weekends	Soon after onset of sleep	Not specific, worse at night	Morning	Not specific		Not specific	Sometimes on awakening
Mode of onset	Gradual	Abrupt or gradual, often prodromata*	Abrupt	Not specific	Not specific	Very sudden	Rapid — Loss of consciousness	Not specific	Sudden rise in pressure causes sudden headache
Duration	Hours, days, or weeks	Hours, days	From 20 minutes to 2 hours	Days or weeks	Hours, then days, then constant	Hours, days, or weeks		Not specific	Not specific
Frequency	Not specific	Not specific	Cluster, such as one or more a day for 2 to 8 weeks	Not specific; continuous or episodic	Not specific but increasing	Continuous		Not specific	Not specific
Precipitating aggravating factors	Emotional stress or not apparent	Emotional stress, premenstruation, vasodilators; certain foods, such as those containing tyramine	Alcohol, lying down	Not specific or horizontal position; chewing may cause jaw pain	Cough, sneeze, strain; change in posture	Stress, strain, increased by neck flexion	Hypertension	Not specific	Emotional > physical stresses, alcohol
Ameliorating factors	Not specific; Rx: analgesics, tranquilizers	Rest, compression of scalp arteries; Rx: ergotamine, propranolol	Activity; Rx: methysergide steroids, propranolol	Not specific; Rx: steroids	Not specific; Rx: surgery, radiotherapy, steroids	Rx: bed rest, hypotension, surgery	Rx: bed rest	Rx: blood pressure control, surgery	Rx: hypotensive agents
Associated symptoms or signs	None or not specific symptoms—tenderness of scalp or neck muscles	*Prodromata; scintillating scotomata, hemianopsia, other cerebral signs. During attack: malaise, nausea, vomiting, photophobia, red and tearing eyes; depression and irritability; tender scalp; rarely ophthalmoplegia	Ipsilateral redness and tearing of eye, stuffiness and discharge of nostril, photophobia; no scalp tenderness. Ptosis and myosis are common, bradycardia less so	Systemic disability (malaise, weight loss), blindness (common but preventable; brain stem infarction; scalp tenderness, induration, and redness of scalp over temporal artery	Generalized CNS dysfunction (drowsiness, change in personality, organic mental syndrome, seizures). Focal CNS dysfunction (hemiparesis, focal seizures; progressive deterioration)	Depressed consciousness. Increased intracranial pressure ++++ Nuchal rigidity + Subhyaloid retinal hemorrhages. When cerebral hemorrhage is added + oculomotor palsy — {focal CNS signs} Flame-shaped — Invariable unless comatose		Aneurysm may compress cranial nerves especially oculomotor; arteriovenous malformation > aneurysm may cause seizures and bruit	Hypertensive encephalopathy is associated with severe retinopathy, including papilledema and generalized > focal cerebral dysfunction. Eclampsia, glomerulonephritis, pheochromocytoma. Hypertension itself is a doubtful cause of headache.
Personality traits	Competitive, sensitive, conscientious > perfectionistic	Perfectionistic, neat, efficient, restrained, ambitious > compulsive	Not specific > perfectionist	Not specific	Not specific	Not specific		Not specific	Not specific

TABLE III
Differentiation of Dizziness of Labyrinthine Origin from Dizziness of Central Nervous System Origin

Labyrinthine Disease	Central Nervous System Disease
There may be a history of past bouts of dizziness or ear disease	There may be a history of central nervous system disease, such as old symptoms of multiple sclerosis.
Episodes of dizziness are paroxysmal.	Dizziness is less acute and more prolonged.
Dizziness is precipitated or aggravated by movement of the head, as when suddenly lying down or rolling over in bed.	Dizziness need not be aggravated by head movement. Dizziness due to vertebrobasilar artery insufficiency may be precipitated by arising from the horizontal position or by neck movement.
There may be associated symptoms or signs of tinnitus, hearing impairment, difficulty in multiple-voice discrimination, or hyperacusis. Nausea and vomiting often accompany dizziness.	There are often associated symptoms or signs of disease implicating the brain stem, such as diplopia and sensory or motor signs.
Nystagmus, when present during an attack, is horizontal more than rotary and increases when fixation is eliminated, as by strong lenses.	Nystagmus may be of any variety but, when vertical, is pathognomonic of brain stem site. Nystagmus increases on fixation and may persist after dizziness has gone.
Ataxia, if present, occurs only during the attack.	Ataxia may be present without dizziness.
Tests:	*Tests:*
The caloric test may be normal or reveal decreased reactivity of the labyrinth.	The caloric response is usually normal but may evoke nystagmus of perverted or incongruent type.*
On repeated stimulation, there is delay and exhaustion (decreasing duration and degree) of response.	Repeated stimulation evokes a consistent response.
Electronystagmography reveals increased nystagmus with eyes closed.	Electronystagmography reveals increased nystagmus with eyes open.
Audiometry often reveals defective acuity and, in Ménière's disease, recruitment of loudness of pure tones but impaired intelligibility of amplified speech.	Audiometry is usually normal.†
Roentgenograms of the skull may reveal evidence of old mastoiditis or cholesteatoma.	Roentgenograms may reveal intracranial pathology.‡
Other laboratory features are usually normal.	The electroencephalogram, spinal fluid, angiography, or pneumoencephalography may reveal abnormality.§

Acoustic neuroma is usually associated with:
* Absent caloric response
† Nerve deafness and severe impairment of speech discrimination
‡ Enlarged acoustic meatus
§ Elevated cerebrospinal fluid protein
Special audiometric measurements—such as recruitment phenomenon, von Békésy test, and short-increment sensitivity index—help to differentiate cochlear from retrocochlear (nerve) lesions.

hearing loss. These symptoms are present during acute bouts of dizziness but persist intermittently or continuously thereafter and usually grow progressively severe. There is impaired intelligibility of amplified speech, and audiometry reveals recruitment phenomena.

Treatment of labyrinthitis and Ménière's disease, when of unknown cause, consists of rest and such antihistaminic agents as dimenhydrinate, meclizine, or cyclizine, 25 to 50 mg. three or four times a day. If the vertigo recurs so frequently as to cause prolonged disability, surgical destruction of the labyrinth or of the vestibular nerve may be necessary to effect relief.

Diseases of the eighth cranial nerve or brain stem. The auditory nerve may be affected by meningitis, trauma, or, most often, tumor (acoustic neuroma). In the brain stem, involvement of the vestibular nuclei is particularly associated with dizziness, but lesions in other areas of the brain stem also cause this symptom. All causes must be considered. Vascular diseases (vertebrobasilar insufficiency and the lateral medullary syndrome) are usually secondary to atherosclerosis. Degenerative diseases, such as multiple sclerosis and syringobulbia, are to be considered in the young age group. Inflammation, trauma, and intrinsic tumor are less common causes of brain stem disease.

Diseases of the cerebellum or cerebrum. The symptom of dizziness with lesions of the brain is often likely to be faintness or lightheadedness poorly described. Vertigo of cerebral origin is most often secondary to disease of the temporal lobe, but any anatomical or metabolic disease of the cerebrum or cerebellum, especially of an acute nature, may cause dizziness. The toxic effect of alcohol is the most common example. Vascular diseases, posttraumatic conditions, and cerebellar tumors are more frequent causes of dizziness than are deficiency states and inflammatory disease.

Physiological dysfunctions. Dizziness sometimes occurs before syncope. Vertigo may be associated with epilepsy and in rare instances is the only manifestation of epilepsy. Dizziness occasionally accompanies migraine. After headache, dizziness is the most common symptom of the postconcussion syndrome.

Proprioceptive impairment. Imbalance due to position-sense defects may be interpreted by the patient as dizziness. Diseases affecting the posterior columns of the spinal cord and peripheral neuropathies are the major considerations.

Diseases of the eye. Intrinsic eye muscle imbalance or extraocular muscle paresis sometimes causes dizziness. Refractive error and glaucoma may be associated with this symptom.

Systemic diseases. Virtually any generalized illness may cause dizziness. Endocrine disturbances are sometimes associated with dizziness, particularly hypocalcemia, hypoglycemia, hypothyroidism, hypoadrenalism, and hyperadrenalism. Systemic infections, hematological diseases, deficiency states (especially pellagra), and allergic and toxic phenomena often present dizziness as a prominent symptom.

Mental and Consciousness Syndromes

UNCONSCIOUSNESS

The distinction between different degrees of the depressed conscious state is not precise. As a rule of thumb, stuporous patients require vigorous and frequent verbal or noxious stimuli to evoke a response that may be briefly mumbled or briefly purposeful. Semicomatose patients respond only to superficial or deep pain stimuli, without verbal or purposeful activity. Patients in coma reflexly respond only to deep stimuli or do not respond at all.

SYNCOPE

Syncope is a brief loss of consciousness—less than 1 minute and usually no more than 15 seconds in duration. The most frequent causes of syncope are vasovagal mechanisms, orthostatic hypotension, cardiac arrhythmia, and vertebrobasilar artery insufficiency.

Differential diagnosis of syncope should consider these disorders:

I. Primary cerebral mechanisms
    A. Vascular causes
        1. Transient ischemic attack, especially within vertebrobasilar arteries
        2. Small cerebral infarct or hemorrhage
        3. Subarachnoid hemorrhage
        4. Hypertensive encephalopathy
        5. Carotid sinus reflex (direct cerebral effect)
        6. Migraine
        7. Hyperventilation (causing vasoconstriction)
    B. Other transient cerebral dysfunctions
        1. Epilepsy
        2. Concussion
        3. Vertigo (severe)
    C. Psychological factors
II. Cerebral ischemia caused by cardiovascular factors (Note that mechanisms under A and B are often associated with diseases under C and D)
    A. Cardiac arrhythmia
        1. Bradycardia or heart block
            a. Complete block—Adams-Stokes syndrome
            b. Partial heart block
            c. Vagal reflexes—vasovagal (carotid sinus), vagovagal (swallowing), oculovagal (eyeball pressure), viscerovagal (intrathoracic or intraabdominal)
        2. Tachycardia
            a. Atrial arrhythmias
            b. Ventricular arrhythmias
    B. Hypotension
        1. Orthostatic hypotension
            a. Pathophysiological—after prolonged bed rest, pregnancy, exhaustion, prolonged standing, drugs
            b. Pathological—idiopathic autonomic disease, diabetes mellitus, adrenal insufficiency, postsympathectomy, malnutrition
        2. Vagal reflexes of a vasodepressor nature
            a. Carotid sinus reflex
            b. Severe pain
            c. Emotional stimuli
        3. Shock of any cause, such as dissecting aneurysm of the aorta, gastrointestinal hemorrhage
    C. Primary decrease in cardiac output
        1. Valvular disease—especially aortic stenosis (also hypertrophic subaortic stenosis, mitral insufficiency and stenosis)
        2. Myocardial infarction
        3. Other cardiac causes of heart failure
        4. Atrial myxoma
    D. Secondary decrease in cardiac output
        1. Changes in intrathoracic pressure
            a. Physiological—cough (tussive syncope), Valsalva maneuver, positive pressure breathing
            b. Pathological—pulmonary embolism, pneumonia
        2. Changes in peripheral resistance
            a. Physiological—micturition, hyperventilation, vasodilator drugs
            b. Pathological—sodium loss, hypovolemia, anemia
III. Impairment of brain metabolism
    A. Hypoxia—hypoventilation, lack of environmental oxygen, toxins
    B. Hypoglycemia
    C. Other causes of metabolic encephalopathy

COMA

Coma of acute onset is most likely due to trauma, cerebrovascular or cardiovascular disease, intoxication, heat stroke, or allergic reactions. Gradually developing coma is probably due to meningoencephalitis or some other infectious process, cerebral neoplasm, metabolic disease, or ischemic or hypoxic phenomena.

Management. In the unconscious patient, the immediate primary concern is maintenance of vital functions—respiration, blood pressure, pulse, and temperature. An obstructed air passage or alterations in the rate and the depth of respiration require correction—if necessary, by means of tracheal intubation and artificial respiration. Shock is the most common cardiovascular factor requiring treatment. Tachycardia or bradycardia may require corrective medication or a cardiac pacemaker. High fever must be brought down by ice packs. Hypothermia is a clue to hypoglycemia or hypothroidism. Metabolic factors cannot be immediately evaluated, but a major concern is hypoglycemia. Blood should be drawn for analysis, and then 50 ml. of 50 per cent glucose should be intravenously administered. If there is suspicion of narcotic overdosage, a narcotic antagonist, naloxone (Narcan), should be given intravenously. Nutrition, hydration, and electrolyte balance must be maintained. Attention to the bladder and the bowels is necessary, and a retention catheter is usually required. The patient should be turned frequently to prevent pneumonia and decubiti. Sedatives are to be avoided; but, if extreme restlessness occurs, paraldehyde or one of the phenothiazines may be used.

Examination. During attention to the vital functions, the heart, the lungs, and the abdomen are evaluated. The odor of the patient's breath and the quality of his skin may give important diagnostic clues. The breath may smell of alcohol, or its odor may be indicative of diabetic coma, uremia, or hepatic failure. The skin may be discolored (pale, cyanotic, jaundiced), or it may show signs of altered hydration (edema, dehydrated) or of vascular changes (petichiae, bruises).

The neurological examination of the comatose patient allows a determination of the site of the disease affecting the brain, if not its cause.

Respiratory rate and rhythm. Cheyne-Stokes respiration is usually due to disease or dysfunction deep within the cerebral hemispheres. Central (neurogenic) hyperventilation is due to lesions between the lower midbrain and the lower pons. Intermittent prolonged periods of apnea are associated with lesions of the mid and lower pons. Ataxic respirations occur when respiratory centers in the medulla are affected.

Mental status. The physician should document, particularly for future reference, the degree of responsiveness to stimuli (light, sound, superficial and deep pain). The depth of coma may be gauged by the patient's type of response. In a semicomatose state the patient may make purposeful movements to ward off the stimulus. The comatose patient may withdraw the part stimulated, but at a deeper state only decorticate or decerebrate activity may be evoked.

Head and neck. Nuchal rigidity may be evidence of meningitis or subarachnoid hemorrhage, but this sign may disappear in deep coma. Battle's sign or periorbital ecchymoses are indicative of a basilar skull fracture.

Cranial nerves. Of all the cranial nerves, those to the eyes are of chief concern in the comatose patient. The optic fundi may reveal hemorrhages or papilledema. A record of the size and reactivity to light of each pupil is essential. A unilateral dilated and fixed pupil is often indicative of oculomotor nerve compression by herniation of the medial portion of the temporal lobe through the tentorium of the cerebellum. When all other signs of neurological life are absent, reactive pupils are characteristic of metabolic or toxic coma. Important exceptions to this rule are hypoxia and such drugs as the belladonna compounds, opiates, and glutethemide, as well as local eye disease and eye medication.

Pupillary signs are important clues to the site of neurological disease. The pupils are unaffected by superficial cerebral disease; they become small (2 to 3 mm. in diameter) but remain reactive in diseases of the diencephalon. When a lesion involves the midbrain or medulla, the pupils are usually in midposition and fixed, whereas a pontine lesion is associated with pinpoint pupils. The extraocular movements are tested by moving the patient's head and noting changes in the position of the eyes relative to the orbits (oculocephalic maneuvers). Absence of such eye movement is suggestive of brain stem disease, which can be confirmed by the absence of response to cold caloric stimulation of the inner ear. If the brain stem is intact, such stimulation in a comatose patient evokes tonic conjugate deviation to the side of the injection.

Motor and sensory systems. The examiner should note decerebrate or decorticate posturing, especially their provocation by stimuli. Asymmetry of the facial muscles or of the extremities in reaction to painful stimuli or asymmetry of muscle tone may reveal the side affected by the central nervous system disease. Similarly, asymmetry of corneal reflexes may be the chief clue to unilateral sensory impairment.

Reflexes. Asymmetry of reflexes is more important than is the presence of pathological reflexes, which are common in comatose patients, no matter what the cause or prognosis.

Laboratory evaluation. In the comatose patient, laboratory studies should include blood count, urinalysis, serum electrolytes, blood glucose, blood urea nitrogen, serum calcium, liver-function tests, serum T_4, and the other blood chemistries. Vomitus or gastric analysis and stool examination may be diagnostic. Toxicological studies of the blood, especially for barbiturates, are appropriate. Evaluation of arterial blood gases may be helpful. A spinal tap is essential if there is suspicion of meningitis; otherwise, the tap is best deferred until after skull roentgenograms or other studies have ruled out a mass lesion with a shift of midline structures. Roentgenograms of the chest and an electrocardiogram are essential.

Differential diagnosis of coma

I. Toxic-metabolic diseases
  A. Exogenous toxins
    1. Addicting or habituating drugs
    2. Hypoxia-producing drugs
    3. Psychotropic drugs
    4. Organic compounds
    5. Heavy metals
  B. Endogenous metabolites
    1. Diabetes
      a. Ketosis
      b. Hyperosmolar, nonketotic
    2. Uremia
    3. Hepatic encephalopathy
    4. Other endocrine and electrolyte disorders
    5. Other less well-defined mechanisms
      a. Eclampsia
      b. Heat stroke
II. Infections
  A. Systemic
    1. Pneumonia
    2. Septicemia
  B. Intracranial
    1. Meningitis
    2. Encephalitis
III. Vascular diseases
  A. Systemic
    1. Cardiovascular
    2. Pulmonary
  B. Intracranial
    1. Hemorrhage
    2. Ischemia or infarction
IV. Other etiological categories affecting the brain
  A. Trauma
  B. Tumor
  C. Degenerative disease
V. Pathophysiological mechanisms
  A. Postconvulsion
  B. Electric shock
  C. Hyperthermia > hypothermia
VI. Spurious coma
  A. Hysteria or catatonia
  B. Mutism—akinetic or aphasic
  C. Akinetic parkinsonism
  D. Locked-in syndrome (except for eye movement, inability to move or respond: brain stem lesion)

DELIRIUM

Delirium is an acute or subacute alteration in mental, motor, and autonomic function; it is usually reversible. Intellectual function is impaired, particularly recent memory and orientation for time. There is decreased awareness of the environment or interest in society. Behavior may be apathetic and withdrawn, but, more often, the patient is hyperactive and agitated. Fear and panic, illusions, and visual hallucinations often occur. Motor abnormalities may include coarse tremor, asterixis, multifocal myoclonus, and convulsive seizures. Fever with tachycardia and increased sweating is often present, although in some cases the patient is hypothermic. Similarly, hyperventilation or hypoventilation may occur. The autonomic changes depend on the underlying cause. The symptoms fluctuate markedly and tend to be most severe at night. Delirium may last for hours or for several days, even after the cause is corrected.

Cause. Almost any organic brain disease may result in delirium. Most common are intoxications by endogenous metabolites or exogenous agents, especially alcohol and drugs. Febrile illnesses, vitamin deficiencies, and exhaustive states are frequent causative factors. Cerebral trauma, intracranial inflammation, cerebral ischemia, and hypoxia are less common causes. Patients with senile cerebral disease are particularly predisposed to the development of delirium.

Certain clinical manifestations of delirium may be clues to the cause of the toxic state. The classical delirium tremens, especially when associated with Korsakoff's syndrome, leaves little doubt about the diagnosis of chronic alcoholic intoxication. If depression of consciousness follows delirium, the toxic effects of sedatives, hypnotics, or narcotics must be suspected. Amphetamine intoxication often produces euphoria preceding delirium. The toxic effects of alkaloids of the belladonna group are manifested by parasympatholytic reactions and sometimes choreiform movements. The phenothiazine derivatives and other tranquilizers may cause dyskinesias with delirium as manifestations of toxicity. Cocaine intoxication results in extreme excitement. In addition to excitement, hallucinations and illusions are particularly prominent with mescaline and lysergic acid diethylamide (LSD) toxicity.

Differential diagnosis. Delirium must be differentiated from nonorganic psychogenic states. Neither the manic nor the young depressed patient shows intellectual impairment. Psychotic hallucinations are more often auditory than visual. Amnesia of psychological origin is manifested by disorientation for place and person much more than for time. Neurotic tremors are usually fine and not accompanied by asterixis or myoclonus. Ganser's syndrome may superficially resemble delirium, but the consistency of inconsistent responses of the patient with Ganser's syndrome is the differential clue. Abnormally slow electroencephalographic activity in delirium is not seen in psychogenic diseases.

Management. With a delirious patient, force must be avoided. The patient can usually be moved by gentle means. For example, several people gathering around the patient can gradually crowd him into his room, which should be quiet but lit and bare of decoration. Someone should be in attendance to calm, reassure, and repeatedly orient the patient. Restraints should be avoided, and sedation should be used sparingly. Paraldehyde, 10 cc. in iced fruit juice, is still favored by many physicians. Chlordiazepoxide in doses ranging from 25 mg. to 100 mg. may be orally or parenterally administered. If more potent therapy is required, intramuscular chlorpromazine, 50 to 400 mg., or trifluoperazine, 2 mg., or haloperidol, 0.5 to 2.0 mg., may be necessary every 4 hours. The underlying cause must be determined and corrected. Prompt therapy of hypoxia, hypoglycemia, meningitis, or Wernicke's encephalopathy may be lifesaving. Hydration with vitamin supplementation and electrolyte balance must be maintained. Oral or intravenous administration is preferred to the nasogastric tube because of the hyperactivity that the tube often evokes.

ORGANIC MENTAL DISORDERS IN ADULTS

Memory. Memory impairment is the most common feature of an organic mental disorder. Loss of recent memory, as exemplified by Korsakoff's syndrome, is due to lesions of the medial thalamus and mamillary bodies. Diffuse cortical lesions—especially those affecting the frontotemporal lobes, as in Alzheimer's disease—are associated with the loss of remote memories; with difficulty, these patients may be able to retain new material.

Transient global amnesia is the loss of transitional recent memory, lasting from half an hour to several hours and associated with varying degrees of retrograde amnesia; remote memory is preserved. As the condition clears, the retrograde amnesia shrinks, but amnesia for the episode itself is permanent. The lesion is presumed to affect the right and left hippocampi. This condition occurs in middle or late life and is probably of vascular origin.

Dementia. The impairment of cognitive function is also associated with personality deterioration: the process is usually chronic and progressive. Even when dementia becomes obvious, vocabulary and past memory remain adequate, and these factors help to differentiate recent organic mental disorders from congenital or educational defects.

Manifestations. The first sign of organic mental disorder is a change in personality, a reduction in adaptive function. There is decreasing interest in social activities. The patient becomes less emotionally stable. Mental processes are slower, and physical activity is also diminished. With the patient's awareness of these changes, depression and anxiety may occur. As the above factors increase, the patient becomes more self-absorbed and less sensitive to others. Memory for recent events becomes impaired, the patient finds it difficult to deal with abstract concepts, and judgment is defective. Sedatives and alcoholic beverages may cause unusually marked lethargy.

Further deterioration is manifested by loss of inhibition. Dress becomes less orderly. Behavior and language are irrelevant, facetious, or circumstantial. Affect is flattened, or emotional lability is prominent. All intellectual factors are further impaired, with particular difficulty in calculation and in orientation for time. Premorbid personality factors often become prominent, and psychotic behavior may then occur. Lethargy and inappropriate sleep alternate with restlessness. The patient no longer recognizes his deficiencies, and the anxiety of the past is lost. Sedatives, tranquilizing medication, alcoholic beverages, intercurrent illnesses, or a change in the environment (such as hospitalization) exacerbate mental symptoms and may provoke delirium.

Disorientation in all spheres is finally evident, with severe impairment of all intellectual functions. Confabulation or perseveration of speech and activity occurs. Passivity or catatonic posturing may be noted; on the other hand, hyperactivity is often present. The patient becomes relatively indifferent to noxious stimuli, but sometimes these evoke excessive infantile responses of crying or rage. There may be neurological signs of a focal or generalized nature. These signs include grasp, snout, and suck reflexes; flexion of trunk and extremities; and irregular stiffening of the limb against passive movements (*gegenhalten*).

Finally, the patient is totally incapable of caring for himself. He is incontinent of urine and feces and unable to walk or talk. He is seemingly unaware of visual, auditory, or noxious stimuli. If he reacts to such stimuli, it is a generalized reaction, rather than a focal reaction. Terminally, the patient becomes stuporous and lapses into coma.

Attempts to correlate these defects in intellectual function with specific areas of the brain have been unsuccessful. However, certain features suggest subcortical location—as occurs with Huntington's chorea, Parkinson's disease, and hydrocephalus—in contrast to disease predominantly of the cerebral cortex, as exemplified by Alzheimer's disease and Creutzfeldt-Jakob disease. In subcortical dementias, psychomotor retardation is prominent, with apathy slowly progressing toward an akinetic mutism state. The cortical dementias, on the other hand, frequently manifest aphasic phenomena and Korsakoff-like recent memory impairment; cortical blindness may occur.

Differential diagnosis. It may be difficult if not impossible to differentiate dementia from global aphasia, and the two may coexist. Because dementia is more likely to be associated with diffuse disease, rather than focal disease, the following signs are more often associated with dementia than with aphasia: inappropriate behavior, emotional lability or irritability, inability to deal with new concepts, depression of consciousness, urinary or fecal incontinence, release signs of snout or grasp reflexes. The aphasic patient may show evidence of faulty understanding by incorrectly carrying out a requested activity or by perseveration of speech; focal signs implicating the dominant cerebral hemisphere are most helpful. The important differentiation between dementia and pseudodementia associated with depression of spirits is discussed later (Chapter 3.5).

Causes. Alzheimer's disease accounts for about half of all cases of dementia. The next most frequent cause is cerebral vascular disease with small multiple infarctions (20 per cent). Brain tumors account for 5 per cent of the dementias. Dementia may be the sequela of many other acute and chronic diseases and injuries to the brain, but the incidence of these is only 1 or 2 per cent each.

The following diseases are to be considered when dementia is the chief presenting sign:

I. Degenerative diseases
    A. Alzheimer's disease
    B. Pick's disease
    C. Normal-pressure hydrocephalus
    D. Huntington's chorea
    E. Myoclonus epilepsy
II. Metabolic diseases
    A. Endocrinopathies
        1. Myxedema
        2. Hypoglycemia
        3. Parathyroid disease
        4. Hypopituitary disease
        5. Adrenal disease
    B. Deficiency states
        1. Vitamin B complex—Wernicke's syndrome, Korsakoff's syndrome
        2. Niacin—pellagra
        3. Vitamin B_{12} and folic acid—pernicious anemia
    C. Other diseases
        1. Chronic liver disease
        2. Chronic renal disease
        3. Lipoidoses

4. Wilson's disease
5. Remote effect of malignancy
6. Porphyria
III. Toxins
   A. Exogenous toxins
      1. Alcohol
      2. Drugs
      3. Heavy metals
      4. Organic toxins
   B. Endogenous metabolites (see II above)
IV. Vascular disorders
   A. Multiple small infarcts and lacunae
      1. Atherosclerosis and hypertension
      2. Emboli of endocarditis
      3. Arteritis-collagen diseases
   B. Subarachnoid hemorrhages
   C. Repeated effects of hypoxia or ischemia of pulmonary or cardiovascular disease
V. Trauma
   A. Subdural hematoma
   B. Repeated concussions and contusions (punch-drunk)
VI. Tumors
   A. Neoplasm in a silent area of the brain, such as the frontal pole
   B. Neoplasm causing increased intracranial pressure without focal signs, such as in deep midline areas
VII. Inflammations
   A. Chronic (fungal) meningitis
   B. Neurosyphilis
   C. Creutzfeldt-Jakob disease
   D. Progressive multifocal leukoencephalopathy
   E. Occult brain abscess
   F. Encephalitis

Diagnostic evaluation. About 10 per cent of all patients with dementia have treatable diseases, but half of this number have brain tumors, which are not always remediable. Establishment of the cause of the dementia is essential to find the remediable diseases. The neurological evaluation may reveal evidence of an occult intracranial mass or chronic meningitis, but in most cases these diseases are found by laboratory studies. A general physical examination with chest roentgenograms and electrocardiogram gives clues to the presence of cardiopulmonary and other systemic diseases, as do the blood count, urinalysis, and serum serological test for syphilis. The serum chemistries, serum thyroxine (T_4), and serum level of vitamin B_{12} determinations help to establish the diagnosis of most of the metabolic and endocrine causes of dementia. Computerized tomography of the head can find a mass lesion, such as a subdural hematoma, and evidence of hydrocephalus. If ventricular dilation is found with little or no cortical atrophy, further studies or a ventricular shunt may be advisable for normal-pressure hydrocephalus. The cerebrospinal fluid is evaluated for evidence of chronic infection (cryptococcal meningitis or syphilis). The physician should consider and search for chronic alcohol and drug intoxication, such as barbiturate and bromide intoxication, and deficiency states, such as pellagra. Roentgenograms of the skull, electroencephalograms, and isotope brain scanning are also useful, but if the studies up to this point were normal, diseases discovered at this end of the diagnostic work-up are likely to be irremediable.

Management. In the treatment of the demented patient, one must preserve and enhance what functions remain. But first there may be the task of correcting past neglect. Dementia may follow a superimposed delirium, which must be treated before management of the dementia is undertaken. Adequate nutrition, including all the necessary vitamins and fluids, is essential.

Physical therapy may allow the ignored person to recover ambulation and other activities of daily living.

The correction and prevention of systemic disease is important, because pain, fever, toxins, metabolic abnormalities, and associated dehydration have exaggerated effects on the demented brain. Similarly, psychological stresses more readily disturb the demented personality than that of the normal person. Thus, one must reduce the demands on the patient who can no longer adequately perform former tasks at work or at home. Stressful contact with people and other environmental factors should be avoided. Instead, the familiar should be preserved, and the surroundings should be calm; alteration of routine activities is to be avoided. One should encourage activity and social contact. The services of a visiting nurse, a social worker, and an occupational and physical therapist should be used and integrated into family life.

Finally, medications may be necessary for symptomatic relief, but the physician must remember that the demented patient is often unusually sensitive to psychotropic and sedative drugs. Anxiety is best treated with diazepam or chlordiazepoxide. For paranoid agitation, thioridizine or haloperidol may be necessary. Amitriptyline or imipramine are the drugs of choice for depression. Insomnia is difficult to treat, but promethazine, diphenhydramine, and flurazepam are recommended.

BRAIN DAMAGE OR DYSFUNCTION OF CHILDHOOD

The extent of neurological disability depends on the size, location, activity, focal or diffuse nature, and age of onset of the cerebral lesion. Age is a particularly important variable. Brain injury in the prenatal or neonatal period may cause severe and permanent damage, whereas a similar injury in an older child may be tolerated to a marked degree and with much greater recuperation.

Mental retardation. "Mental retardation" is a general term that includes all forms of intellectual impairment with onset at birth or early age. Virtually all the diseases of early life affecting the brain may cause mental retardation. The affected patients range from idiots, those human beings who survive on an almost vegetative level, to the children who have difficulty in school but who lead a normal life and are able to carry out customary social functions and perform simple work.

Many neurological features may be associated with intellectual impairment. Most common is speech retardation and subsequent speech disturbance, particularly indistinct speech. In addition, neuromuscular development is often retarded. Obvious motor defects—such as paresis, dyskinesia, and ataxia—may be present. In patients with these defects, cerebral palsy and mental retardation coexist, but the two disorders often occur independently. Sensory function is sometimes impaired, and defects of hearing and vision are common. Other abnormal signs may be noted in the neurological examination.

Visceral defects or dysfunctions may be manifested by unusual susceptibility to upper respiratory tract infections or infantile feeding problems. Defective regulation of vital signs is often revealed by excessive responses of temperature, pulse, or respiration to relatively minimal stress. Convulsive seizures are common in the mentally retarded.

Emotional symptoms are almost invariable and are related to the type and extent of the cerebral lesion and to environmental stresses. Those patients with mild retardation are more capable of appreciating failure, feeling rejection, and experiencing frustration and insecurity than are patients with more severe retardation.

Difficulty in making the diagnosis of mental retardation is inversely proportional to the age of the patient. The diagnosis may be impossible in the newborn, unless there are obvious signs of cerebral disease. Neonatal infants who are comatose, have bulging fontanels indicative of increased intracranial pressure, or are in the opisthotonic position with dilated fixed pupils almost always have some residual cerebral defect if they survive. In other newborns, abnormal signs are only suggestive of brain damage. The most common of these signs are an abnormal cry, altered autonomic function, cranial nerve palsies, and motor abnormalities. The motor abnormalities may be manifested by myoclonus; defects in posture, muscle tone, or movement; or asymmetry of motor power, muscle tone, or reflexes. Analgesia or anesthesia is sometimes noted. Lack of blinking, sucking, and grasping reflexes or absent Moro's reflex in the newborn is suggestive of cerebral disease.

Minimal brain dysfunction. The term "minimal brain dysfunction" is preferred to "slight brain damage," which falsely connotes a poor prognosis. The category of minimal brain dysfunction includes those children of normal intelligence or just below or above average intelligence with behavioral or learning disabilities or both and often with minor neurological abnormalities, usually in the realm of impaired coordination. Neurological defects and evidence of socioeconomic or emotional deprivation are not present or are too slight to be obvious. The condition is much more common in boys than in girls.

Behavioral alterations. Behavioral alterations are usually manifested as deviations in motor activity and interrelated defects in attention. Hyperactivity is the most common characteristic of minimal brain dysfunction, but caution should be exercised in making the diagnosis solely on this factor. The hyperactive child is constantly active and shows lack of inhibition and of impulse control. He touches everything and speaks and acts impulsively; his behavior is in other ways disruptive, inappropriate, or antisocial. Emotional lability is often present. The child cries with minimal provocation; temper tantrums and panic are easily evoked. Paradoxically, there is an increase in activity after the administration of phenobarbital, and there is an amelioration of hyperactivity after taking amphetamine. In a small percentage of cases, a decrease in physical activity may be a manifestation of minimal brain dysfunction.

Attention defects. Most children with minimal brain dysfunction have difficulty in focusing and sustaining their attention, for they are distracted by everything. Like the immature, they cannot discriminate unimportant from important stimuli in the environment. The degree of impairment of attention changes from time to time, causing the uninformed observer to suspect psychological mechanisms. Defective attention impairs the ability to deal with abstract concepts and interferes with the learning process.

In a small percentage of children with minimal brain dysfunction, a phenomenon opposite to the above is present; these children are preoccupied with details. They show markedly decreased response to different stimuli; perservation of speech or actions may be noted.

Learning disabilities. Learning disabilities, either generalized or specific, are common in patients with minimal brain dysfunction. Perceptual motor deficits often occur. The child may be poor in writing, in drawing, and, particularly, in copying geometric figures. Concept formation is frequently disturbed. Specific learning deficits may be present in only one sphere, such as reading, spelling, or calculation. Scatter of performance on psychometric tests and differences from one test to another are often seen.

Dyslexia is the most common learning defect. There are three major types of this disorder. In many patients, a specific language disorder is present in which anomia is the chief factor. In other patients, the problem is associated with the impairment of speech articulation and defective graphomotor coordination. The smallest group of patients has a disorder of visual-spatial perception. Differentiation of these phenomena has therapeutic implication. The language disorder dyslexia responds best to a phonics program, but those patients with defects of speech articulation and graphomotor coordination learn best by whole word recognition.

Neurological signs. Children with minimal brain dysfunction often have equivocal or minimal (soft) neurological signs. Defects in coordination are most common and may be manifested by a generalized awkwardness (maladroitness), poor finger coordination, or dysdiadochokinesia. Speech defects, such as retarded speech, may be noted. Confusion of right and left often occurs. Sometimes transient strabismus is seen. Mild somatic sensory defects or slight impairment of hearing or vision may be present. Occasionally, physical defects are evident.

History. The history is of some value in establishing the diagnosis of minimal brain dysfunction. Sometimes slightly abnormal factors in the prenatal, perinatal, or neonatal history can be elicited. Defects in the developmental history, such as retarded speech, or abnormal socioeconomic factors are occasionally noted. Impaired academic progress is most common. There is often a history of similar symptoms in a parent or a sibling.

Laboratory studies. Additional studies are of relatively little value. The electroencephalogram may be abnormal or borderline abnormal. Fourteen- and 6-per-second positive spikes are sometimes associated with minimal brain dysfunction, and many other slight electroencephalographic abnormalities have been noted. Psychometric studies are valuable but require expert interpretation.

Early diagnosis. The diagnosis of minimal brain dysfunction is particularly difficult to establish during the first few years of life, but there may be many clues.

During the first month of life, difficulty in sucking or other feeding problems, alteration in expected muscle tone, cranky behavior, or unusual docility may be evidence of brain dysfunction.

At 9 months of age, better criteria exist for the diagnosis of minimal brain dysfunction. The degree of cerebral defect roughly corresponds to the quality and quantity of abnormal signs. In the motor sphere, alteration of muscle tone; abnormal posture of the extremities, trunk, head, or neck; or altered use of an arm or hand are usually significant. Eye signs of strabismus, nystagmus, or failure to fixate may be meaningful. Other neurological signs of importance are reflex alteration and persistence of the tonic neck reflex. Retardation in adaptive and social factors is often significant.

In the preschool years, minimal brain dysfunction may be indicated by a delay in walking, in speaking, or in toilet training. Impaired coordination and other failures to attain expected landmarks of development are important signs. Simplicity of play, choice of younger playmates, and lack of imagination are further clues to this disorder.

Differential diagnosis of organic brain disorder of children
Deprivation. Deprivation may cause reversible symptoms and signs of organic brain disorder. Malnutrition, avitaminosis, and anemia are well recognized examples of this fact. Emotional deprivation, as occurs with the absence of the mother or mother figure or lack of affection, may cause growth hormone deficiency and resultant retardation. The deprivation of social

stimuli and of contact with other human beings may similarly cause mental retardation. Early correction of these factors leads to a normal course of mental development.

Autism. An autistic infant is unable to make contact with his environment. There is resultant extreme aloofness. The child does not respond to external stimuli; when picked up and cradled, he does not cuddle or adapt himself to the person holding him. An attachment to and fascination with inanimate objects is in contradistinction to the child's relationship to people. There is often an obsessive insistence on sameness and a corresponding aversion to new things. This marked inflexibility of personality may be strongly defended by temper tantrums or rages. The onset of walking and, especially, speaking is delayed.

Schizophrenia. Childhood schizophrenia may be first manifested as autism. Although the diagnosis of schizophrenia is being made as early as the third and fourth years of life, it may be equivocal before 8 years of age. The schizophrenic child, in concert with the autistic child, does not respond to the environment, other children, or adults. Sometimes activity is diminished, but more often hyperactive behavior is noted. Repetitive movements, such as rocking and swinging, are common. Speech may be retarded or develop in bursts. Regression, in contrast to retardation, of mental and physical development occasionally occurs.

Communication defects. Speech retardation is sometimes the result of overindulgence; the child finds that verbal communication is not required, because his needs are anticipated and immediately fulfilled. Deafness as a cause of speech retardation and associated behavioral impairment must always be considered. Unrecognized visual impairment may retard mental development. Dyslexic and dysgraphic children may be falsely considered brain damaged unless the reading and writing impairments are appreciated as specific and isolated phenomena.

Physiological defects. Hysteria and other psychogenic phenomena are occasionally misinterpreted as physical or mental retardation. The postictal state is associated with a dulling of mentation, and frequent seizures often prolong this condition. During petit mal status epilepticus, the patient may appear awake, with marked impairment of intellectual functions. Prolonged systemic illnesses in children are frequently associated with mental retardation.

Suggested Cross References

Other neurological syndromes are discussed in Sections 3.3 and 3.5. Neurological evaluation is discussed in Section 3.2 and anatomy and physiology of the central nervous system in Section 3.1. The organic mental disorders are discussed in Chapter 20. Mental retardation is discussed in Chapter 36. Developmental disorders of childhood are discussed in Chapters 37 and 39. Attention deficit disorders are discussed in Chapter 38. Maternal deprivation is discussed in Section 43.1.

REFERENCES

*Adams, R. D., and Victor, M. *Principles of Neurology.* McGraw-Hill, New York, 1977.
*Baker, A. B., and Baker, L. H., editors. *Clinical Neurology.* Harper & Row, New York, 1978.
Baloh, R. W., and Honrubia, V. *Clinical Neurophysiology of the Vestibular System.* F. A. Davis, Philadelphia, 1978.
Barlow, C. F. *Mental Retardation and Related Disorders.* F. A. Davis, Philadelphia, 1978.
Dalessio, D. J. *Headache and Other Head Pains,* ed. 3. Oxford University Press, New York, 1972.
Davidson, A. N. *Biochemistry and Neurological Disease.* J. B. Lippincott/Blackwell, Philadelphia, 1976.

*Himwich, H. E., editor. *Brain Metabolism and Cerebral Disorders,* ed. 2. Halsted Press, New York, 1976.
Johnson, R. H., and Spalding, J. M. K. *Disorders of the Autonomic Nervous System.* F. A. Davis, Philadelphia, 1974.
*Katzman, R., Terry, R. D., and Bick, K. L., editors. *Alzheimer's Disease: Senile Dementia and Related Disorders.* Raven Press, New York, 1978.
Laidlaw, J. P., and Richens, A. *A Textbook of Epilepsy.* Churchill Livingston, New York, 1976.
Lipton, S., ed. *Persistent Pain: Modern Methods of Treatment.* Academic Press, London, 1977.
Martin, J., Reichlin, S., and Brown, G. M. *Clinical Neuroendocrinology.* F. A. Davis, Philadelphia, 1977.
Penfield, W., and Jasper, H. *Epilepsy and the Functional Anatomy of the Brain.* Little, Brown, and Co., Boston, 1954.
* Plum, F., and Posner, J. B. *The Diagnosis of Stupor and Coma,* ed. 2. F. A. Davis, Philadelphia, 1972.
Spector, M. *Dizziness and Vertigo: Diagnosis and Treatment.* Grune & Stratton, New York, 1967.
Terry, R. D., and Gershon, S., editors. *Neurobiology of Aging.* Raven Press, New York, 1976.
Victor, M., Adams, R. D., and Collins, G. H. *The Wernicke-Korsakoff Syndrome.* F. A. Davis, Philadelphia, 1971.
Wells, C. E. *Dementia,* ed. 2. F. A. Davis, Philadelphia, 1977.
Woodbury, D. M., Penry, D. K., and Glaser, G. H., editors. *Mechanisms of Action of Antiepileptic Drugs.* Raven Press, New York, 1978.

3.5 Application of Neurology to Psychiatry

SEYMOUR SOLOMON, M.D.

Introduction

This section presents a discussion of those phenomena common to both neurology and psychiatry. The first part of this section is a résumé of the different mental and emotional syndromes that result from disease affecting specific sites within the brain. There follows a discussion of syndromes common to neurology and psychiatry. Finally, there is a discussion of the symptoms of neurological diseases that often cause diagnostic error.

Mental and Emotional Syndromes Related to Site of Organic Disease

Mental and emotional symptoms have certain characteristics dependent on the site of organic involvement. All the syndromes described below are both physiologically and anatomically interrelated.

FRONTAL LOBE SYNDROME

The frontal lobe syndrome is particularly associated with lesions of the prefrontal and basilar cortex of the brain, and the clinical features are most striking when the disease is bilateral. These illnesses are characterized by changes in personality. One form may simulate the personality of the sociopathic-antisocial person or the hypomanic but without the feeling of happiness associated with euphoria. The patient's behavior is inappropriate, silly, and child-like, and his responses are boastful, jocular, or facetious (*witzelsuch*). There is a lack of concern, and the loss of self-consciousness and o inhibition may result in erotic behavior, such as exhibitionism. There may be bursts of irritability and sometimes violence. Another form of this syndrome simulates depression. Patients with this syndrome are apathetic and abulic, with lack of interest and indifference to and lack of concern for their environment. What may superficially appear as depression is not accompanied by sadness or morbid preoccupation. There may be alterations between these two forms of behavior, but, in both, affective responses are impaired, and lack of concern is evident, with loss of social awareness.

Motor activity in frontal lobe syndrome is diminished. There is lack of spontaneity and loss of initiative, with associated decrease in activities having to do with personal habits of washing, dressing, and toilet. Motor impersistence and perseveration are noted.

Finally, cognitive functions that effect predominantly abstract thinking and memory are impaired. Some of the errors in the mental status examination may be due to inattention and unconcern; initially, the over-all I.Q. need not be subnormal. The patient cannot easily adjust to change. Eventually, orientation for time and place become disturbed, and there may be varying degrees of impairment in the other cognitive functions. The mute state of expressive aphasia due to a lesion of Broca's area of the dominant hemisphere may be mistaken for psychosis.

The most important factor in supporting the organic nature of the personality and motor phenomena described above is the history of change from the patient's previous personality. Sometimes the change is an exaggeration of the former personality. Thus, a woman who was parsimonious and reserved may become miserly and paranoid. Sometimes the change is opposite that of the lifelong personal traits. For example, a quiet and introverted man may change to one who is garrulous and grandiose. The development of cognitive defects, incontinence, or dysphasia firmly establishes the organic nature of this disease.

PARIETAL LOBE DISEASE

Parietal lobe lesions may be associated with agnostic, apraxic, or aphasic phenomena; the differentiation of patients with these signs from demented patients may be extremely difficult or impossible. Lesions of the nondominant hemisphere, especially those affecting the parietal lobe, may cause anosognosia (denial of illness) and impairment of spatial integration, with associated constructional apraxia or autotopagnosia—the inability to relate the individual parts of the body to one another or the inability to recognize body parts.

The clinical manifestations of lesions of the parietal lobe may be difficult to differentiate from hysteria, and it is more common for signs of parietal lobe disease to be erroneously considered hysterical than vice versa. Bizarre symptoms, such as distortion of body image and other spatial disorders, may initially suggest the diagnosis of hysteria. The patient with a parietal lobe lesion may seem apathetic and indifferent. There is sometimes variability of performance, especially at the hands of different examiners.

OCCIPITAL LOBE DISEASE

Occipital lobe lesions may cause visual illusions and hallucinations. Metamorphopsia, distortion of images, may be simple—for example, the illusion of objects' appearing to be larger than they really are (megalopsia)—or may be complex—for example, the illusion of objects' taking on strange affective qualities. Visual hallucinations may occur within one visual field, either in a hemianopic field or in the normal field, or they may be generalized. Suggestion may influence the type of formed hallucination—for example, the hallucination of seeing Santa Claus at Christmas time. The intellectual and emotional background of the patient is an important factor in the type of hallucination experienced. Visual hallucinations are not limited to lesions of the occipital lobe but rarely occur with lesions of the frontal lobe or retina and are as common with disease of the temporal lobe as with lesions of the occipital lobe. It was once thought that formed hallucinations were of temporal lobe origin and that unformed or crude hallucinations were of occipital lobe origin. This differentiation is certainly not invariable and cannot be used as a localizing sign.

Just as hallucinations may suggest psychosis, other occipital lobe phenomena may simulate hysteria. Patients with cortical blindness are usually indifferent to their illness. Such patients often deny blindness and confabulate. Visual agnosias, such as the inability to recognize familiar faces (prosopagnosia), may be falsely considered psychogenic; concentrically reduced fields of vision of organic origin may be misinterpreted as hysteria. Visual disorientation may be difficult to differentiate from disorientation of more diffuse organic disease.

DISEASE OF THE TEMPORAL LOBE

Irritative lesions of the temporal lobe evoke mental and emotional symptoms with or without associated psychomotor seizures. Disturbances of behavior—usually automatisms if part of seizure activity—are often difficult to differentiate from impulsive nonorganic behavioral disorders. Organic phenomena, in contrast to hysterical seizures, are usually of short duration and are stereotyped for each patient, and there is amnesia for the event. Illusions and hallucinations of any of the special senses may be the only manifestation of temporal lobe seizures. When the hallucinations are olfactory or gustatory, they are usually unpleasant and may occur as the aura of a temporal lobe seizure. Auditory hallucinations are rare and vague, rather than specific. Visual hallucinations tend to be formed, and the patient is usually aware of their unreality.

Disease of the temporal lobe may alter conscious, mental, and emotional states. Disorders of consciousness are manifested by dreamy states. Organic mental disorders are characterized by impairment of recent memory. Abnormalities of thought and behavior range from obsessions and compulsions to sensations of unreality or depersonalization to frank psychoses, especially manifestations of paranoia. Affective symptoms most frequently include anxiety, depression, rage, and fear.

Receptive fluent aphasia, alexia, and agraphia due to lesions of the dominant hemisphere may be mistaken for psychogenic phenomena.

The Klüver-Bucy syndrome occurs in monkeys after bilateral temporal lobectomy. These animals become unusually tame and demonstrate severe memory loss, hypersexuality, bulimia, and visual agnosia, with hyperreactivity to all visual stimuli. Bilateral temporal lobe lesions in human beings may be associated with symptoms similar to the above but considerably modified. More often, patients with lesions of the medial aspects of both temporal lobes manifest Korsakoff's syndrome, loss of recent memory.

DISEASES AFFECTING OTHER CEREBRAL STRUCTURES

The limbic system is, in large part, made up of the medial portions of the temporal lobe. The diencephalon is intimately related to the limbic system, and the thalamus and the rostral reticular formation form a major part of the diencephalon. Lesions in one of the above structures affect the functions of others, and disease of one area cannot always be differentiated from disease of another.

Disease of the limbic system. Irritative lesions within the limbic system may evoke psychomotor seizures. The disagreeable olfactory or gustatory hallucinations and associated lip, tongue, and swallowing activities are specific for cortical areas of the limbic system. Genital and sexual responses may be evoked by irritative lesions of the limbic system. The autonomic aspects of emotional expression—especially those of rage, fear, and defense phenomena—may be similarly evoked.

Lesions of the right and left hippocampus and hippocampal gyri result in severe loss of recent memory. Bilateral lesions of the cingulate gyri cause apathy, akinesis, and mutism. Lesions of the septal area result in the reduction in or absence of emotional expression.

Diencephalic disease. Lesions of the diencephalon, even more clearly than those of other structures, produce their effects by the release of facilitating or inhibiting mechanisms necessary for balanced human behavior. Disease of this area is often associated with emotional lability or spontaneous laughing or crying. In lower animals, lesions of the anterior diencephalon are associated with sham rage—that is, sympathetic motor activity of rage, probably without appropriate change of affect. Extreme excitement, savageness, and increased feeding drive are also evoked with experimental lesions of the anterior diencephalon. In human beings a mania-like syndrome may be seen with disease in this area. Lesions of the posterior diencephalon in animals are associated with unusual tameness, sometimes to the degree of severe apathy. In humans, disease in this area is associated with apathy, hypersomnia, and akinetic mutism. Conscious sensory perception is affected in disease of the ascending reticular formation that interrupts the sensory input to the cerebral cortex.

Disease of the thalamus. The thalamic syndrome is due to unilateral disease, usually infarction, of the thalamus. Much more disturbing than the impairment of sensation on the opposite side of the body is the extreme hypersensitivity to all forms of stimuli. This hypersensitivity evokes unpleasant sensations, often of an agonizingly painful nature, that tend to be constant and intractable. These sensations are often aggravated not only by such minor stimuli as the touch of clothing but also by visceral and affective stimuli. On the affected side of the body, stimulus below the raised pain threshold may be perceived as less than normal, but a stronger stimulus above the pain threshold is perceived as unusually severe and often distorted in quality. There may be a delay in the appreciation of the stimulus and a spread of the evoked sensation far beyond the point of stimulation. These peculiar features and the frequent paucity of objective signs sometimes lead to a mistaken psychogenic diagnosis. Surgical thalamic lesions are sometimes complicated by confusion, amnesia, or confabulation. Bilateral thalamic lesions cause emotional lability or spontaneous laughing or crying without the associated emotional feeling, and dementia may occur.

Disease of the reticular formation. Lesions within this complex system necessarily affect the multiple functions that include motor activity and sensory conduction; arousal, alerting, and awareness; and neuroendocrine functions—all of which influence behavior and emotions. Special clinical syndromes of these lesions are not present except for akinetic mutism and generalized convulsive disorders.

Disease of the basal ganglia. Lesions of these structures and the related extrapyramidal systems primarily cause disturbances of motor function. Dyskinesias are sometimes mistaken for psychogenic tics, especially in their early stages—for example, the restlessness of the child with Sydenham's chorea. The tics, grunts, and coprolalia of Tourette's disease were, until recently, considered psychogenic.

Several of the features of Parkinson's disease may be mistaken for psychological disturbance. The early tremor of parkinsonism may be considered nervousness, particularly because slight emotional stress invariably aggravates the tremor. The sudden freezing of activity may wrongfully be considered catatonia. Conversely, akathisia, the inability to sit still or maintain a resting posture, is sometimes a feature of parkinsonism. The bradykinesia of parkinsonism—with slowness and decreased spontaneity of movement and speech, coupled with loss of facial expression—is frequently misinterpreted as withdrawal and depression.

Patients with disease of the basal ganglia may become depressed and irritable. Emotional lability and spontaneous laughing or crying sometimes occur. Compulsive and obsessive features are common. Slowness of mentation may parallel slowness of movement, and intellectual deterioration occasionally progresses to severe dementia.

Disease of the corpus callosum. Because the corpus callosum may be congenitally absent without obvious signs, the clinical manifestations seen with lesions of this area are probably due to disease or dysfunction of neighboring structures. Disease of the corpus callosum, such as Marchiafava-Bignami disease, is associated with personality changes or intellectual defects, drowsiness and apathy, and symptoms of delirium; apraxia is more common than is aphasia.

Syndromes Common to Neurology and Psychiatry

One is frequently presented with symptoms that cannot be immediately differentiated as due to organic disease of the brain, due to identifiable pathophysiology of the nervous system, or of psychogenic origin. (Perhaps the metabolic mechanisms of the diseases of psychogenic origin will eventually be discovered, and psychiatry will become the biochemical branch of neurology.) When confronted with a clinical problem that could be either neurological or psychiatric, it is wise to err in favor of organic disease. The patient with headache suffers least from an assumption and search for a brain tumor that is not present than from the presumption and treatment of a psychiatric disorder that turns out to be due to a brain tumor. The major exception to that rule is dementia. Dementia caused by depression of spirits is often more remediable than is dementia of organic brain disease.

As a paradoxical rule of thumb, the patient who has multiple symptoms and who insists on their organicity often has a psychological basis for the symptoms. Conversely, the patient who denies his illness or who searches for a psychological cause for his symptoms often has organic disease.

HYSTERIA

Hysteria, conversion disorder, is the occurrence of symptoms or signs that the patient erroneously believes to be of organic origin. Usually there is a history, dating back to youth, of multiple and complex symptoms that do not conform to disease entities.

The hysterical patient usually appears bland and indifferent to his defect, *la belle indifférence*. But some patients are anxious, or their attitude is evocative of sympathy. The marked suggestibility of the patient with hysteria is manifested by contradictory responses and changes in and disproportion between symptoms and signs. The history of an emotional disturbance that has acted as a precipitating factor or a past history of psychosomatic phenomena can often be elicited.

In differentiating hysteria from malingering, one notes less tangible evidence of secondary gain in hysteria. For example, the symptoms may allow the hysterical patient to escape from responsibility, whereas the malingerer may seek the settlement of a lawsuit. The only absolute proof of malingering, however, is the patient's confession. The signs of hysteria discussed below can usually be applied to malingering. Hysteria occurs most frequently in women; malingering occurs most often in men.

Sensory. Pain is the most difficult symptom to evaluate because of its subjective nature, whether organic or psychogenic. Psychogenic pain may be poorly described as to quality and site or elaborately depicted with unusually graphic qualities—for example, "like someone pounding a nail in my head." Psychogenic pain need not disturb sleep, but it may be the major focus of the patient's waking hours.

Psychogenic sensory phenomena are commonly manifested by analgesia; analgesia, in contrast to hypalgesia, is rare as an organic phenomenon. On the other hand, extreme hypersensitivity to examination may be found in hysterical patients, and responses may not vary with the intensity of the stimulus. A psychogenic glove or stocking distribution of sensory loss has a sharp border and usually affects all modalities. But hypalgesia and hypesthesia, found in a similar distribution with peripheral neuropathy, have less distinct borders and have gradations of increasing sensitivity in the distal to proximal direction that may be different for pain, temperature, and touch. The sensory impairment in hysteria does not conform to the anatomical zone of a peripheral nerve or dermatome, and in an extremity the defect may extend only over the medial or lateral side. Inconsistencies in sensory responses are frequently noted. The patient may profess loss of superficial sensation and yet be able to identify objects placed in his hand. He may deny superficial abdominal sensation, and yet abdominal reflexes can be elicited. Complete loss of position sense may seem to be present on direct testing, and yet the patient is well able to use the extremity with his eyes closed and does not show the pseudoathetosis of organic position sense loss.

Autonomic changes normally associated with pain are useful in testing the patient with hysteria. The involuntary responses of tachycardia, hypertension, hyperpnea, and mydriasis may be evoked, even though the patient claims to be insensitive to the painful stimulus. Several tricks are used to foil the malingerer and detect the hysteric. A dull patient may be asked to say "yes" when he feels the pin prick and "no" when he does not. With the patient's hands crossed behind his back and fingers interlaced, quickly testing the sensation of right and left fingers may evoke inconsistent responses. The patient with a hemisensory impairment often orients the defective side to his environment, such as the wall next to the examining table. As a result, the hysteric may reveal a hemisensory defect on one side when supine and on the opposite side when prone. Over the trunk, the change from normal to impaired sensation is usually in the exact midline with a nonorganic hemisensory defect, in contrast to the overlap of normal sensation beyond the midline with a hemisensory lesion of organic origin. Vibration sensation in hysteria may be experienced differently over the right and left halves of the same bone, such as the sternum or skull. A hemisensory defect that includes the penis, vagina, or rectum is rarely of organic origin.

Motor. Psychogenic weakness usually varies with the effort of the examiner testing the strength of the affected part, thus producing a variably collapsing type of weakness. The patient may contract antagonist muscles in an attempt to simulate weakness of protagonist muscles, and resistance of "weak" muscles to passive movement is sometimes found. Covert observation of the patient may reveal withdrawal from unexpected pain stimuli or some other use of "paralytic" muscles, as when dressing. Inconsistencies may be found in the patient's responses when he is asked to move those fingers that are touched while his hands are crossed behind his back with fingers interlaced. In hysterical hemiplegia, the face and tongue muscles are spared, and a circumducting gait may not be evident. Hoover's sign is present when downward movement of the hysterically paralyzed leg occurs while the patient lifts his normal leg. Downward drift of a hysterically weak upper extremity is not associated with pronation of organic weakness. Paralysis of wrist extension is noted as false by the synergistic extension occurring while making a fist. There may be lack of resistance on testing dorsiflexors of the feet, and yet the patient may be able to walk on his heels. In psychogenic paraplegia, the urinary and rectal sphincters are usually unaffected.

Coordination. Defects of coordination seen in hysteria are often gross and bizarre. The hysterical ataxic gait often has a bouncing quality, and, when falling, the patient may show normal dexterity in preventing the fall or may conveniently fall so as to prevent injury. In spite of marked ataxia on finger-to-nose and heel-to-knee tests, the patient may be able to write and perform fine movements normally. During the Romberg test, the patient may sway only from the hips or fall *en masse* without attempting to catch himself; distracting the patient during the test sometimes prevents falling. Associated movements are often normal in these patients, such as the normal swing of a "paralyzed" arm while walking.

Reflexes. Reflexes are usually normal in patients with hysteria, but absent gag reflexes and decreased corneal reflexes may occur. Symmetry of reflexes—whether diminished or hyperactive—lessens the likelihood of organic disease.

Special senses. With the exception of vision, the special senses are usually not impaired on a hysterical basis. Occasionally, hearing loss is psychogenic, and then it is usually bilateral and complete; a patient with psychogenic hearing loss makes no attempt to read lips. Rarely is the loss of sense of taste or smell hysterical; such defects are very difficult to differentiate from organic lesions. Psychogenic blindness is usually bilateral. When a patient is asked to look at a close object, convergence occurs in the organically blind but not in the hysteric. Opticokinetic nystagmus can usually be evoked in patients with hysterical blindness. Hysterical amblyopia is often associated with tubular constriction of the visual fields, and the size of the retained visual field does not increase as the testing distance increases, as is the case with organic disease. In unilateral hysterical blindness the pupillary reaction is preserved.

Other modalities. A large variety of other symptoms may be psychogenic. Dysphonia is the most common speech disorder of this nature; patients with dysphonia may be able to cough loudly. Dysphagia, globus hystericus, may accompany dysphonia or may occur independently, and the symptom of a "lump in the throat" is usually not organic. Respiratory dysfunctions, particularly hyperventilation, are often hysterical. Urinary retention may have a psychological mechanism; urinary incontinence rarely does. Tics and habit spasms were readily classified as psychogenic, but there is growing belief that they are metabolic in origin. Gilles de la Tourette's disease, once thought to be psychogenic, is now considered a neurological disease. Fits or fainting of a hysterical nature may also be difficult to differentiate from psychomotor epilepsy or syncope. The differences between hysterical seizures and psychomotor seizures are discussed later. Major hysterical convulsions are rare but often simulate coitus.

Memory (amnesia). Amnesia is often of hysterical or psychological origin, and its differentiation from memory loss of organic disease may be difficult. Amnesia due to organic disease is frequently abrupt (posttraumatic, postictal) and has both retrograde and anterograde components. These components gradually shrink as recovery occurs; the retrograde shrinks more than the anterograde. The memory loss of psychological origin is often of vague onset and termination; if there is a retrograde component, it may be of inappropriately long duration. Recovery from organic amnesia is often incomplete and followed by confusion for hours or days; there is no recall of events during the illness. After the hysterical patient has recovered his memory, complete return to normal mentation occurs, and he may remember isolated events during the past period of amnesia. In organic disease, precipitating factors may be obvious, such as trauma, or the cause may be occult— for example, ischemia is postulated as the cause of transient global amnesia. A traumatic emotional experience may precipitate hysterical amnesia, which serves a psychological need.

The behavior of a patient with organic loss of memory is often abnormal, and delirium is common. But the behavior of a patient with psychogenic amnesia is frequently purposeful, and he is usually in excellent contact with his surroundings. Amnesia of organic disease is most often generalized in that it affects all intellectual spheres, whereas in hysteria there may be selective loss of certain psychologically stressful topics, and the forgotten painful events may, nevertheless, influence actions. Amnesia of one's identity while maintaining other orientation and intellectual skills is always a hysterical dissociation. Organic amnesia is frequently accompanied by objective neurological signs; psychogenic memory loss is often accompanied by hysterical signs.

Special tests. Examination of the patient while he is asleep may reveal sensory or motor reactivity not evident when he is awake. Tests may be of aid in making the diagnosis of hysteria. The electroencephalograms of patients with hysterical blindness usually reveal normal suppression of α-rhythm when the eyes are opened and driving response to photic stimulation. The electroencephalogram K-complex during sleep is a reaction to an auditory stimulus. More sophisticated equipment that measures evoked responses belies patients' claims of blindness, deafness, or somesthetic sensory loss. During an amobarbital (Amytal) test, psychogenic signs tend to disappear or diminish, whereas organic signs are exaggerated. The test is administered by infusing amobarbital intravenously at a rate of 100 mg. every 30 seconds until nystagmus is evoked, usually at a dose of 250 mg. to 300 mg. Psychometric tests and hypnosis are also useful in evaluating the hysterical patient.

PSYCHOSOMATIC DISORDERS

Psychological factors affecting physical conditions (psychosomatic disorders) are distinguished from hysterical symptoms by mode of expression and degree of symbolism. Hysterical symptoms are mediated by the voluntary sensorimotor system, and they symbolically express an unconscious concept. Psychosomatic symptoms are autonomic responses to an unconscious process, and symbolism is not present. As with many classifications, this dichotomy is not always precise. Often, a patient presents with a symptom that could be classified as hysterical or as psychosomatic. Such a patient is usually an adolescent or young adult, and the history is unusually complex, with many symptoms. The examination does not reveal evidence of disease. The clinical picture does not conform to well-recognized organic disease.

The psychosomatic disorders are discussed in detail in another chapter of this textbook. Only two aspects are mentioned here—pain and hyperventilation.

Pain. Virtually every neurological symptom may be psychologically evoked. Pain is the most common symptom and the one least able to be quantified. It is a psychophysiological phenomenon. Individual variability ranges from congenital indifference to pain to little or no tolerance to minor discomfort. The fact that pain may be ameliorated by suggestion (placebo therapy) or distraction does not mean that the pain is imagined. It is a common and disturbing fact that pain is often present without obvious cause and yet is due to organic dysfunction, rather than psychological dysfunction.

Headache is usually unaccompanied by objective signs. When sudden and severe, headache may be the only clinical evidence of subarachnoid hemorrhage; when occurring for the first time in an elderly person, headache may be the first clue of cranial arteritis; when headache awakens the patient in the morning, it may be the first warning of increased intracranial pressure. Brief lightning-like pains, especially in the elderly, are manifestations of neuralgia; although the pain is in the anatomical distribution of a cranial nerve, there are no associated signs on examination. The thalamic syndrome evokes spontaneous pain over one-half of the body, yet signs of this syndrome are subtle, if present at all. The pain of a phantom limb and other somesthetic illusions and hallucinations after amputation are poorly understood pathophysiological phenomena. Pains due to muscle trauma—for example, whiplash injury of the neck or low back strain—and pains of visceral origin are often unassociated with objective physical signs. In patients with a reflex dystrophy, such as the shoulder-hand syndrome, the examination may be negative.

Hyperventilation. Anxiety and other psychological phenomena may evoke hyperventilation, which, in turn, may cause a large variety of symptoms. This syndrome occurs most often between 15 and 30 years of age and is more common in women than in men. There is often a past history of complex multiple symptoms, conversion disorder, or hypochondriasis.

Cranial phenomena as a result of hyperventilation include faintness or impairment of concentration, headache or fullness in the head, vague dizziness or vertigo, and visual disturbances. The most frequent systemic symptoms are fullness of the chest or epigastrium, shortness of breath or palpitations, nausea and occasionally vomiting, sensations of heat or cold sweat, and paresthesias, especially of hands or feet or mouth. These symptoms are due to decreased cerebral blood flow caused by hypocarbia, respiratory alkaloses and associated tetany, or the swallowing of air.

DENIAL OF ILLNESS (ANOSOGNOSIA)

In this state either the patient denies his physical defect, or there is lost or impaired perception or conception of the affected part. The patient may deny the existence of the affected part of his body or may experience a feeling of depersonalization toward the affected part. Any type of defect may be denied, especially motor loss (hemiplegia) and blindness.

There are many degrees of denial of illness. Anosognosia may be explicit, with associated confabulation, or it may be implicit and manifested by withdrawal, inattention, or other psychological mechanisms. Denial may assume various forms of disturbed orientation. For example, autotopagnosia is a disorientation of body parts or a defect in body schema, and finger agnosia of the Gerstmann syndrome is one of its manifestations. Reduplication of parts of the body or place or time may occur. Paraphasia, the substitution of a partially incorrect term for the proper word, is common. The patient may refer to himself in the third person. Often, the patient ascribes his inability to move or get out of bed to some external interference.

Anosognosia is most often associated with lesions of the nondominant hemisphere, with resultant left hemiparesis and impairment in spatial orientation, especially constructional apraxia. However, denial of illness may occur with lesions in the dominant cerebral hemisphere. The site of the brain damage determines the disability that is denied and the perceptual symbolic structure or language in which the denial is expressed. The mechanism of denial, on the other hand, is much more complex. It includes the integration of environmental factors, past experiences, premorbid personality, symbolic values, type of disability, and the degree of brain damage or dysfunction. Rarely are denial reactions psychological. When they are psychological, they are almost always in reaction to some catastrophic event.

ORGANIC MENTAL DISORDER AND PSYCHIATRIC ILLNESS

An organic mental disorder is an impairment in cognitive function, in the thought processes of perception, memory, and information processing. But behavior is also affected in this condition, and sometimes, as in frontal lobe disease, behavioral changes precede intellectual deterioration. The terms "acute brain syndrome" and "chronic brain syndrome" had been used to connote reversible and irremediable cerebral diseases, respectively, but these relationships are not valid, and the terms are not prognostically useful. For example, the acute syndrome of Wernicke's encephalopathy often causes permanent intellectual defects, and the chronic brain syndrome of hypothyroidism is eminently remediable.

There are three major factors in the pathogenesis and manifestation of organic mental disorder. First, the type of organic disease is most important. Second, the severity of its effect on the brain is a factor of the location and extent of the disorder, its duration and course, and the differences between a static lesion and one that progresses. With regard to progressive lesions, the rate of change is important. And, third, the state of the patient is a major factor in the pathogenesis of mental symptoms. His age and personality are important determining elements. Not only is the patient's previous personality to be considered, but his emotional state at the time of the illness. The presence of systemic disease and the preexistence of other cerebral disease are influential. In addition, there is an ill-defined variation in the susceptibility of different persons to the same noxious stimulus. Finally, environmental factors may be operative. Isolation and unfamiliar surrounding may be destabilizing factors. Conversely, excessive environmental stimulation or sleep deprivation or both may have similar untoward effects. The stresses of recent interpersonal relationships may modify the patient's reaction to organic disease. All the above factors must be considered in planning the patient's management.

Acute mental syndromes. Organic or metabolic cerebral disease of sudden onset may be impossible to differentiate at first from psychological illness. The most common of these psychological illnesses are the affective disorders, the manic state, and the agitated or stuporous state of manic-depressive disorder. Certain symptoms may be common to both acute organic syndromes and acute psychogenic syndromes. Changes in personality with loss of interest in self and in the environment, and decreased attention and awareness are common. Conversely, the patient may be aggressive, hostile, and accusatory. Behavioral changes may be manifested by restlessness, irritability, agitation, and excitement. Disturbances of intellect may be manifested by impairments of memory, judgment, and orientation; speech disorders may occur. Sleep disturbances may be present, and consciousness may be altered or depressed. The neurological evaluation and the initial laboratory studies usually establish the diagnosis of organic disease.

Several clinical features support the diagnosis of acute organic cerebral disease, rather than psychogenic illness. A past history of systemic illness is sometimes elicited. Patients may give a history of failing memory, especially of recent memory impairment, but with adequate recall of events before the acute onset. Disorientation for time or date precedes disorientation for place and person. Hallucinations, if they occur, are likely to be visual. The change in personality is often abrupt, and there may be rapid fluctuations in mental state, behavior, or consciousness. Dishevelment of the patient and his surroundings suggests abuse of alcohol or drugs. The patient with a toxic psychosis usually manifests simple, poorly systematized thought processes; his mood is often labile. Asterixis or myoclonus may occur. The condition is likely to be worse at night and tends to improve with repeated reorientation. The course of acute organic cerebral disease is also diagnostically helpful, for either recovery or deterioration toward coma and death usually occurs within a few days.

Certain characteristics of acute psychogenic disorder differ from features of organic disease. Rarely is the onset of psychological illness abrupt and *de novo*. The past history usually reveals a former personality disturbance or some prodromal phenomena, such as loss of interest, anorexia, and sleep disturbance. A mild depression frequently precedes a manic state. The history often reveals a precipitating psychologically stressful event. Sociability is lost early in the course of acute psychosis. Schizophrenic hallucinations tend to be more auditory than visual; delusions are elaborate, thought processes bizarre, and mood inappropriate. Disorientation is more likely to be for place and person, rather than for time or date. The poor judgment of a neurotic is likely to be due to feelings of anger or fear. If tremors are present, they are likely to be fine. With the passage of time, additional evidence of psychological disorder appears. In contrast, patients with acute organic disease either improve or deteriorate toward coma.

Chronic mental syndromes (dementia and pseudodementia). The term "pseudodementia" is based mainly on symptoms of impaired memory and disorientation, formerly thought to be pathognomonic of organic disease. These features, plus speech and sleep disturbances, are the chief features of the dementia and pseudodementia syndromes but may be seen with both acute and chronic mental syndromes, both organic and psychogenic.

The initial symptoms of these mental syndromes of gradual onset may be similar to the symptoms in syndromes of acute onset. Apathy with loss of interest and decreased concentration and attention are frequent, but irritability may also be noted. In dementia and pseudodementia, somatic complaints and delusions occur more often than in the acute mental syndromes.

It is often difficult to differentiate dementia caused by organic or metabolic cerebral disease from pseudodementia due to depression of spirits. Both impair psychological and cognitive functions. Affect is flat or depression evident, and both thought and action are slow in the dementia and pseudodementia syndromes. A major difficulty is that of evaluating thought content, for communication may be impossible because of the absence of verbal expression, or because of inaccessibility associated with the patient's agitation or hostility. The differential features between dementia and pseudodementia are listed in Table I.

The differentiation of dementia from pseudodementia has

TABLE I
Comparison between Dementia Caused by Organic Disease and Pseudodementia Caused by Depression*

Dementia of Organic Disease	Pseudodementia of Depression
Patient adult, but age is nonspecific	Patient always elderly—60 years or older
Onset slow—months, years	Onset rapid—days, weeks
Past history of systemic illness or of drug or alcohol abuse	Past history of depression or mania
Often unaware of cognitive defect and unconcerned	Often complains of cognitive loss and distressed
Organic signs of neurological disease, such as dysphasia, dyspraxia, agnosia, incontinence	Psychological symptoms of sadness or somatic symptoms of depression, self-accusation, preoccupation, anxiety, delusions
Greater impairment of cognitive features, such as memory, especially recent, and orientation, especially for time and date	Greater impairment of personality features, such as confidence, drive, interests; impairment of attention
Mental status examination shows spotty responses, with some features poor and other modalities better; consistent on repeated exams	Mental status examination tends to show variabilities of impairment of different modalities on repeated exams
Behavior consistent with degree of cognitive defect	Behavior incongruent with degree of cognitive impairment
Responses to queries erroneous, confabulated, or perseverated	Responses to queries often "I don't know"; little effort to do well
Responses to funny or sad situations normal or exaggerated; lability of mood	Little or no response to funny or sad circumstances; flattening of mood
Neurological studies (computed tomogram and electroencephalogram) usually abnormal	Neurological studies usually normal

* The differences listed above are not mutually exclusive, and there is considerable overlap between the two categories.

great therapeutic implications, because patients with pseudodementia often respond well to treatment of depression, with restoration of more normal mood and with clearing of memory, orientation, and other seemingly organic signs.

Finally, one should remember the frequent occurrence of depression in reaction to organic cerebral disease. Patients who have experienced a stroke or Parkinson's disease, as two common examples, are often depressed. The presence of organic disease is not necessarily a contraindication to treatment of depression with psychotropic drugs or electroconvulsive therapy.

DISORDERS OF SPEECH AND LANGUAGE

Impairment of speech production. Speech production refers to fluency and articulation of speech and to voice volume. Disturbances of these factors lead to phenomena that are often incorrectly diagnosed as psychogenic. Usually, other features of the neurological examination establish the neurological diagnosis. Several conditions, however, have no known organic or pathophysiological mechanism. That does not mean that they are due to psychological disturbances.

Stuttering is the interruption of speech flow by the tendency to repeat the initial syllable of a word. It is aggravated by emotional stress. The mechanism of this disorder is unknown.

It is usually a pathophysiological phenomenon, but stuttering may be the sequela of organic cerebral disease that has affected both hemispheres.

Palilalia is the tendency to repeat the last word or words of a sentence. The repetition increases in frequency but fades out in volume. This rare condition may occur with diseases of the basal ganglia, as in postencephalitic parkinsonism, and with bilateral cerebral lesions causing dementia, but it may also be a manifestation of schizophrenia.

Cluttering is an uncommon disorder manifested by such rapid speech that words are run together and syllables within words may be omitted. The result may be incomprehensible. The cause of this condition is unknown.

Dysarthria is an impairment of enunciation, the articulation of words. Slurring dysarthria refers to indistinct articulation and the tendency to run together both syllables and words. In speech of scanning dysarthria, each syllable tends to be pronounced individually in a staccato fashion. Dysarthria is usually due to organic disease, ranging from diseases of the muscles of articulation to diseases of the highest cortical centers, but slurring speech is also common in the emotionally disturbed.

Dysphonia or aphonia is an impairment or loss of voice volume. The disturbance in phonation may be due to local diseases affecting the respiratory system or vocal cords or due to neurological disease affecting the speech musculature or its innervation. Whispered speech is sometimes a neurotic manifestation. Hoarseness is usually due to structural changes of the vocal cords or paralysis of a vocal cord; rarely is this sign psychogenic.

Spastic dysphonia is a peculiar phenomenon caused by the contraction of speech musculature. After normally speaking a few words or sentences, the patient sounds as if he were being strangled during attempts to continue conversational level speech. Whispering is unaffected, and shouting is easier than quiet speech. The condition begins in middle or late life. Because organic causes cannot be found, the condition is often assumed to be psychogenic. Neither medical therapy nor psychotherapy is beneficial, but surgical section of the recurrent laryngeal nerve affords considerable relief.

Mutism is the lack of verbal or vocal expression. It is seen in a variety of organic lesions, especially those affecting the diencephalon. Mutism is commonly the result of expressive aphasia and may occur during petit mal status epilepticus. The absence of vocal output is also a common manifestation of psychological illness. It occurs during the acute phase of catatonic schizophrenia, in association with paranoid distrust, and in the chronic schizophrenic who is relegated to the isolation of a back ward. Mutism is also seen in severe depression but rarely during a manic state. In these conditions there is a preceding history of psychosis. Transient mutism is less often a manifestation of hysterical aphonia. The neurological and physical examinations almost always quickly differentiate organic mutism from psychological mutism, although on rare occasions a catatonic-like stupor is caused by disease of the brain—for example, catatonia has been reported in herpes encephalitis, tumors of the corpus callosum, and hyperparathyroidism. The elective mutism of a child who speaks only to his mother does not present a problem in differential diagnosis.

Disorders of language. Usually, the neurological examination reveals other signs of organic disease associated with lesions of the dominant cerebral hemisphere in patients who have aphasia or dysphasia. Occasionally, however, aphasia occurs without other signs, and then it may be mistaken for psychological illness.

Nonfluent dysphasia. Slight word-finding difficulties are normal experiences and vary with education, speech habits, and many other factors. However, word-finding difficulty is the major feature of nonfluent expressive dysphasia and may occur with such diverse psychological phenomena as anxiety, depression, and catatonic schizophrenia. Careful evaluation usually reveals that thoughts are blocked in schizophrenia, in contrast to the word blocking of dysphasia. The schizophrenic is undisturbed and unconcerned by this change in language, but the dysphasic patient is often distraught in his inability to express himself adequately. The circumstantiality of speech as the dysphasic gropes for expression may simulate the circumlocution of schizophrenia, but schizophrenic circumlocution is associated with inattention and lack of concern regarding responses. The verbal output of the schizophrenic is characterized by bizarre content, rather than by the defective language production of the aphasic.

The patient with expressive dysphasia makes unaccustomed errors in grammar, avoiding adjectives and adverbs; this is not the case with psychological illness, in which syntax and vocabulary are intact. The patient with expressive aphasia usually shows a decrease in rate of speech and in length of phrase and impairments in rhythm and in inflection; dysarthria may also be present. All or some of these features may be manifestations of depression, but the depressed patient appears sad, and the expressed thought content is morbid, self-deprecatory, and negative. The schizophrenic responses are longer than those of the dysphasic patient.

Fluent aphasia. Fluent, receptive aphasia, in which the patient is unable to understand speech, results in a verbal output that has been appropriately called "word salad." Such meaningless jumbles of words may be spoken with a rapid output, and the speech often contains clichés, circumlocutions, neologisms, and other paraphasic errors. This "crazy" speech, if unassociated with other neurological signs, may be mistaken for schizophrenic behavior. Almost always, the sudden onset of such speech in a previously healthy person is indicative of a cerebral infarct affecting the posterior speech areas. In schizophrenics, on the other hand, this type of speech is seen only in chronic cases. As with expressive nonfluent aphasia, the patient with fluent aphasia shows some awareness of his difficulties and is often disturbed by them, in contradistinction to the schizophrenic, who is unconcerned and often presumes that the listener understands him. Thus, the aphasic patient may attempt nonverbal communication and may pause to allow the examiner to help him; not so with the schizophrenic patient. The patient with aphasia is more attentive to the examiner than is the schizophrenic. Paraphasic words and neologisms are more common in fluent aphasia than in schizophrenia. The patient with fluent aphasia has difficulty in the comprehension of spoken language. The severely disturbed schizophrenic may seem to have such difficulty, but he usually shows some understanding of speech by carrying out some commands, by incorporating some of the examiner's words into his own speech, or by echoing the examiner. The content of verbal output, those pieces of language that can be understood, may reveal several different ideas attempting to be expressed by the aphasic, whereas the schizophrenic tends to repeat the same bizarre theme during one examination period.

APRAXIA AND AGNOSIA

Occasionally, an apraxia or agnosia results in bizarre behavior or responses that may be misinterpreted as psychogenic. Apraxia of gait, wherein the feet seemed glued to the floor, and prosopagnosia, with inability to recognize familiar faces, are but two examples of such phenomena.

ABNORMALITIES OF MOVEMENT

Both hyperkinetic activity and hypokinesis may be seen in organic diseases and in psychological illnesses. The underlying mechanism of abnormal movements or the abnormal paucity of movement is poorly understood, and controversy exists as to the classification of some activities. For example, are tics a manifestation of neurological or of psychological illness?

Before the turn of the century, many considered parkinsonism to be a psychiatric illness. A tremor that was precipitated or markedly aggravated by minimal stress and disappeared when the patient was alone or asleep seemed to fulfill the criteria for nonorganic disease. Moreover, the bradykinetic patient immobilized in a wheelchair could, nonetheless, quickly move his arms to protect himself from a ball thrown at him and had been known to run out of his wheelchair when the house was on fire. Did not such brief spontaneous activities belie the organicity allegedly responsible for his immobility? Many parkinsonism patients find that their feet seem to be glued to the floor when they attempt to walk, but, once movement has begun, their gait may be close to normal. Some must perform a peculiar act, such as tapping the head with the hand, before walking can begin. Many other peculiar idiosyncratic activities have been reported in patients with Parkinson's disease. Similarly, peculiar sudden immobility of the body or the eyes (oculogyric crises) occurs in parkinsonism. These bizarre changes in activity, once attributed to the psyche, are now known to be associated with metabolic abnormality of dopamine metabolism in the nigrostriatal system of the brain.

Hyperkinesis. Slight tremor is a normal physiological phenomenon and can be recorded by amplifying instrumentation, but tremor is not usually seen with the naked eye. Such a tremor is predominantly static, with the extremities extended against gravity, or postural, as when the head is supported by the neck in the erect position. These slight tremors may become more prominent and, therefore, visible without instrumentation by such physiological states as fatigue, anxiety, and fear and by such pathophysiological states as thyrotoxicosis and alcoholic intoxication. Benign essential familial tremor is probably no more than an exaggeration of these normal tremors but, in addition, there may be an increase in tremor during precise movement. The resting tremor of parkinsonism and most tremors associated with activity are due to organic neurological disease. Action tremor and intention tremor, which grow worse as the goal of the action is approached, are associated with cerebellar disease. Tremors of brain stem origin may have resting, static, and intention qualities. Hepatic encephalopathy is associated with finger tremors and flapping tremors (asterixis). Patients with Wilson's disease may have a combination of several tremors.

The involuntary movements of chorea, athetosis, dystonia, and ballismus were once thought to be psychogenic because of their bizarre pattern, aggravation by emotional stress, amelioration during tranquility, and disappearance during sleep. Ballismus, almost always hemiballismus, is rarely misdiagnosed as psychogenic because of its stroke-like onset in mid or late adult life. Similarly, athetosis is usually recognized as the organic sequela of birth anoxia, kernicterus, and other congenital disorders. Chorea and dystonia, however, are frequently mistaken at their onset for restlessness or nervousness. On the other hand, 50 per cent of patients with Huntington's chorea present with psychological symptoms. A similar percentage develop a frank psychosis during the course of the illness, and 25 per cent of the psychoses are characterized as schizophrenic. There is still debate with regard to the mechanism of torticollis. Certainly, torticollis is a sign of dystonia, and many neurologists believe that all instances of torticollis are *forme frustes* of the full-blown dystonia musculorum deformans.

Buccal-lingual dyskinesias have become well-recognized pathophysiological complications of psychotropic therapy but may occur spontaneously in the elderly. Some rare diseases, such as familial paroxysmal choreoathetosis, were thought to be hysterical until other families were reported with identical symptoms and signs.

Myoclonic activity may range from the single contraction of a muscle to the synchronous contractions of the entire somatic musculature. Because consciousness is not lost, some of these activities may be incorrectly diagnosed as tics or psychogenic phenomena. Frequently, the myoclonic activity is evoked by movement; this relationship is particularly true of the hypoxic encephalopathies. Sometimes it is only a specific movement or a certain posture—for example, attempting to sit—that precipitates the myoclonic activity. When this stereotyped sequence occurs, psychological interpretations may be falsely applied. Occasionally, myoclonic jerks occur with increasing frequency, and a convulsive seizure ensues.

Because of their uncertain pathogenesis, tics are still in the borderland between neurology and psychiatry. On the one hand, tics are so common in children—in one series, 25 per cent of children from 1 to

13 years of age had tics—that they are considered of little consequence. On the other hand, tics are an integral part of Gilles de la Tourette's disease, which neurologists and many psychiatrists believe to be a pathophysiological disease of yet-to-be-discovered metabolic origin. Moreover, tics may be a fragment of most other organic hyperkinetic syndromes; for example, a tic may be the first sign of Sydenham's chorea. A further indication of their organic origin is the finding of abnormal electroencephalograms in a high percentage of people with tics. In contrast to other involuntary movements, tics are somewhat easier for the patient to voluntarily suppress, but doing so is associated with great tension. Whatever their mechanism, a consistent psychological profile or set of psychodynamics has not been found in patients manifesting tics.

Not all movement disorders are of neurological origin. Psychological disturbances may evoke activity ranging from slight simple tics to complex behavioral disorders. Occasionally, the movements of such patients simulate the oral-facial dyskinesias, chorea, athetosis, or dystonia. When the schizophrenic patient has a movement disorder, it is usually stereotyped and repetitive. Although such movements may appear purposeless, they frequently enact a specific mannerism. Psychotic movements often include the handling of body parts or of other objects.

Hyperactive behavior of organic origin is sometimes mistaken for the euphoria or mania of the manic-depressive. Such behavior, when seen with organic disease of the orbital frontal lobes or the medial temporal lobes, is characterized by lability, volatility, and lack of inhibition. There is often associated tremor, impairment of skilled acts, or apraxia, and neurological signs of frontal lobe disease are present (snout or suck reflexes). Hyperactivity may also be a manifestation of generalized cerebral dysfunction, as in toxic delirium. When neurological disease evokes hyperactivity, signs of cognitive and intellectual impairment are present. The bizarre and sometimes hyperkinetic behavior of a patient in a psychomotor seizure is discussed later. Restlessness and akathisia may be manifestations of parkinsonism. The restless legs syndrome is a nocturnal phenomenon associated with sensations of fatigue, cramps, and paresthesia in the lower legs; its pathogenesis is unknown.

Hypokineses. At the other end of the spectrum are the hypokineses and akinesias. Bradykinesia and hypokinesia are common features of parkinsonism. Rarely is akinesia of such severity that it simulates coma or schizophrenic catatonia. With patience, the examiner is eventually able to evoke some slight response from the patient with parkinsonian akinesia to indicate that his mind is alert and rational. Akinesia may be part of an oculogyric crisis or part of the on-off phenomenon associated with levodopa therapy in parkinsonism, but these bursts of akinesia are of short duration. Inertia may be part of the apathy seen in patients with disease of the frontal lobes, especially the paramedian areas, or the diencephalon. Akinetic mutism is discussed above. Paucity or slowness of movement in brain disease is usually associated with similar slowness of thought, other signs of dementia, and other neurological signs of cerebral disease, such as pseudobulbar palsy, gait apraxia, and other types of gait impairment.

Hypokinesis is often seen in psychological illness. Catatonic schizophrenia is the prime example of such a phenomenon. In contrast to the hypokinesis in organic disease, the inert posture of the catatonic is awkward and sometimes bizarre. The muscle tone has a variable waxy flexibility, rather than cogwheeling or rigidity; and the catatonic tonicity is less generalized than that seen in parkinsonism. Abrupt changes in tone may occur in the catatonic, but such changes in parkinsonism are seen only with oculogyric crises or the on-off phenomenon. Depression may simulate parkinsonism. In both conditions there may be slowing and paucity of movement, small-stepped or shuffling gait, expressionless face, and weak voice. Such features as constipation and sleep disturbance may occur in both Parkinson's disease and depression. The mood and the thought content clearly define the depressed patient, but, of course, Parkinsonism may evoke depression. Psychotic withdrawal of schizophrenia or depression may simulate true stupor, coma, or akinetic mutism. Usually, the negativism of schizophrenia can be found in the resistance to eyelid opening or withdrawal from

the examiner, and catatonic positioning may be demonstrated. Oculocephalic reflexes are not evoked, and the caloric response is that of the awake patient in psychotic pseudocoma. At the onset, laboratory studies may be necessary to establish the presence of organic disease. In time, if the problem is psychological, verbal responses appear. Then the disordered thought of the schizophrenic and the sad mental content of the depressed patient are evident.

SEXUAL PROBLEMS

Most problems of a sexual nature are psychological, rather than due to organic disease.

Hyposexuality. When organic illness affects sexual function, the effect is usually that of inhibiting sexual drive or function. Impairment of libido may be associated with many systemic or cerebral diseases. It is a common sequela of temporal lobe diseases, including epilepsy. Impairment of sexual potency also occurs with hypothalamic lesions, perhaps because of hormonal dysfunction. Sexual impotence may be the first sign of diabetic or other autonomic neuropathy, and it may be an early sign of spinal cord disease. Most causes of impotence are psychological. The differentiation between organic impotence and psychological impotence can now be established with certainty. Nocturnal erection of the penis is an invariable occurrence with rapid eye movement (REM) sleep. The documentation of nocturnal erection in a man complaining of impotence is clear evidence of the nonorganic nature of this symptom.

Hypersexuality. Although hypersexuality is a rare result of organic disease, it may be seen in association with temporal lobe epilepsy, either as a postictal event or after the seizures have been controlled by temporal lobectomy or with medication. On rare occasions, deviant sexual behavior—for example, exhibitionism—may follow a temporal lobe resection. Hypersexual activity has occurred after recovery from encephalitis. Frontal lobe lesions may cause loss of inhibition and a resultant increase in sexual activity that is often inappropriate. On rare occasions, disease of the parietal lobe or thalamus may heighten pleasurable genital sensations. Those rare young men with Kleine-Levin syndrome may manifest uninhibited sexual activity during bouts of ravenous appetite. An increase in sexual desire is associated with some medications, such as amphetamines; it has also been imputed to such drugs as marihuana, and it may occur in women who require androgen hormone therapy. Other agents touted as aphrodisiacs probably achieve their effects either by removing the person's inhibitions or by relieving anxiety or depression.

DRUG TOXICITY

Of the many facets to the problem of drug toxicity, two interrelate psychiatry and neurology. On the one hand, one must consider the possibility of inducing a psychotic reaction when using drugs to treat neurological and other systemic diseases. On the other hand, one must be aware of the neurological and other medical reactions evoked by drugs used to treat the psychosis.

Drug-induced psychological syndromes. The psychological syndromes associated with drug intoxication may be mild (nonpsychotic), as manifested by slight impairments in sleep, alertness, and memory or by slight changes in mood, such as euphoria, mild depression, anxiety, or irritability. More severe reactions are classified as psychoses and include hallucinations, illusions or delusions (especially paranoid delusions), and alterations of mood so marked as to greatly disturb the patient's functioning. In addition, cognitive defects may be manifested in the patient's perception, memory, orientation, and language. There may be depression of consciousness or agitation. The differentiation between these phenomena and schizophrenia and psychotic depression are discussed above.

Sedatives and hypnotics are the most frequently prescribed drugs in the United States, with mild tranquilizers replacing barbiturates in popularity. Abrupt withdrawal of barbiturates may result in a grand mal convulsion or delirium, with other signs of acute severe psychosis. When discontinued, stimulants, especially the amphetamines and methylphenidate, may cause severe depression, sometimes to the degree of suicidal ideation. Psychosis simulating paranoid schizophrenia is easily induced by an overdosage of amphetamines. The anticonvulsants are more likely to produce neurological side effects than psychological side effects. The anticholinergic agents, including the belladonna alkaloids used for symptomatic treatment of dizziness and for parkinsonism, have long been known for their psychosis-inducing properties; symptoms of stimulation are more common than symptoms of depression of the nervous system. Levodopa evokes a psychological reaction in from 15 to 30 per cent of patients treated for Parkinson's disease. The most common reactions are confusion, delirium, depression, agitation, and delusions (often paranoid) or hallucinations (usually visual, anthropomorphic, and menacing). Levodopa may occasionally exacerbate or precipitate schizophrenia. Corticosteroids and adrenocorticotropic hormone (ACTH) often produce an elevation in mood and less often produce euphoria or restlessness and agitation. High dosages may cause severe psychosis, especially manic behavior or paranoid thoughts or both. These phenomena are usually dose dependent; a decrease in dosage, rather than a discontinuation of the medication, may alleviate the toxic reaction. Nonnarcotic analgesics, even aspirin, may produce agitation and delirium.

Psychotropic drug-induced neurological syndromes. There are many neurological side effects of antipsychotic drugs. All these drugs may cause extrapyramidal side effects. Haloperidol and fluphenazine are among the most troublesome in this respect; thioridazine is least likely to evoke an extrapyramidal reaction. Acute dystonia may occur so early in the course of treatment, especially in children after an initial dose of prochlorperazine for nausea, that the history of such therapy may be omitted and the diagnosis made more difficult. The acute dyskinesias may be relatively mild, with face, tongue, and neck movements simulating the bizarre mannerisms of schizophrenia. They may also be severe, with oculogyric crisis or opisthotonos sometimes suggestive of catatonia. The parkinsonian symptoms associated with psychotropic medication may be indistinguishable from idiopathic Parkinson's disease. The bradykinesia and mask-like facies cause the appearance of apathy and lifelessness that may be mistaken for the emotional withdrawal of depression or schizophrenic apathy. Akathisia may be misinterpreted as psychotic agitation. Tremor is likely to be a later feature of drug-induced parkinsonism than is bradykinesis; if the tremor is asymmetrical, it is unlikely to be drug related. Dystonia and akathisia are usually early manifestations of antipsychotic medications, parkinsonism is a later complication; all respond to antiparkinsonism medication (the anticholinergic drugs, such as benztropine and trihexyphenidyl).

The tardive dyskinesias manifested by bizarre buccolingual movements occur late in the course of high-dosage psychotropic therapy, especially in the elderly. Few physicians fail to differentiate this activity from the mannerisms of the psychotic but may make the mistaken diagnosis of early Huntington's chorea, which shows more gait impairment and fewer abnormal oral movements.

The major antipsychotic medications lower the convulsive threshold, but seizures are a rare complication of such therapy, and one can usually continue the treatment at the same or a slightly lowered dosage by adding an anticonvulsant drug. The psychotropic agents may evoke drowsiness, but this effect usually occurs early in the course of treatment and is soon tolerated by the patient. Alterations in sleep physiology—insomnia, bizarre dreams, somnambulism—are sometimes seen. Psychomotor retardation may simulate bilateral or diffuse cerebral disease.

The autonomic side effects of the potent antipsychotic drugs may cause neurological symptoms. Orthostatic hypotension may cause syncope or some other manifestation of cerebral ischemia. Urinary retention or paralytic ileus may be mistaken for primary urological, colonic, or neurological disease. Sexual impotence, beginning with the impairment of ejaculation, is thought to be an autonomic complication of psychotropic medication. The toxic confusional states sometimes seen with these drugs may be related to their anticholinergic properties, which may cause mydriasis and blurring of vision; the adrenergic properties of some drugs may cause miosis. Compounds such as thioridazine occasionally provoke retinitis pigmentosa, with associated impairment of visual acuity.

Psychiatric Phenomena and Specific Neurological Diseases

EPILEPSY

Interictal personality. Is there an epileptic personality? The high incidence of interictal psychological disturbances in patients with convulsive disorders has long been noted, but controversy continues with regard to the mechanism of these changes in personality. There are unquestionable psychological consequences of having to deal with long-standing seizures or the threat of seizures. In addition, most people believe that personality changes are caused by the disease or dysfunction that evokes the seizures. This is especially true of seizures arising in the temporal lobe or other parts of the limbic system. It has been postulated that the discharging temporal lobe, over a period of years, forms new bonds (hyperconnections) to the special sensory association cortical areas; thus, enhanced emotional associations are made with what would ordinarily be emotionally neutral stimuli. The behavioral and mental abnormalities in epileptic patients are believed to be due to a pathophysiological process, rather than being secondary to life stresses. In support of this concept is the fact that these behavioral traits are stable, rather than episodic, and their severity correlates with the duration of epilepsy, rather than with the frequency of seizures. Moreover, the mental abnormalities are more common in patients with bitemporal lobe electroencephalographic abnormalities than in those who have a consistently unilateral temporal lobe focus.

Many behavioral traits have been seen in patients with chronic temporal lobe (psychomotor) seizures. The most common traits are aggressive impulsive activity, hyposexuality, hyperreligiosity, and hypergraphia. The aggressive behavior may be manifested as hostility, with a tendency toward rage attacks; anger and temper tantrums are often associated. Suspiciousness and paranoid ideations have been noted. There is often a deepening of all emotions and emotional lability, so that the patient may exhibit great warmth yet experience bursts of aggressiveness. Alteration of mood is noted, with irritability most common. Depression, helplessness, self-recrimination, and self-deprecation occur more often than does elation. Hyposexualism with loss of libido is common, but occasionally deviant sexual behavior occurs. Hyperreligiosity, often idiosyncratic, may be seen in these patients. They may have fixed metaphysical or cosmological theories or believe in specific divine guidance. A high moral tone is often accompanied by humorlessness. Such patients may be unable to distinguish significant from minor infractions of the law, and they desire to punish all offenders severely. Hypergraphia, the writing of detailed notes or extensive diaries, is a peculiar obsessional phenomenon, and other rituals or compulsive qualities may be present. The careful consideration of minute details may also be a manifestation of viscosity, with associated slowness of thought and circumstantiality.

Some believe that schizophrenia-like psychosis is induced by epilepsy. The clinical features of such psychosis are indistinguishable from schizophrenia without epilepsy, but in schizophrenia without epilepsy there is usually a past history of schizophrenic behavior or other severe personality disturbance, and there may be a family history of schizophrenia.

A temporal lobectomy for intractable seizures usually diminishes traits of aggressiveness and impulsivity and often ameliorates the patient's hyposexuality. However, there is usually no change in the hyperreligiosity and viscosity phenomena or in those patients manifesting schizophrenic-like psychoses. Sometimes, the suppression of seizure activity with an anticonvulsant medication paradoxically increases the psychological abnormalities that are often present in these patients.

Seizure activity. In addition to the interictal disturbances of personality, complex partial seizures—psychomotor seizures—are difficult and often impossible to differentiate from similar brief behavioral disturbances of psychological origin. Hysterical reactions are particularly difficult to distinguish from psychomotor seizures. The chief differentiating features of this form of epilepsy are the aura (especially of an uncinate nature), the postictal depression of mentation, and amnesia for the event. Although the automatisms of the psychomotor seizure may be as bizarre as the psychogenic seizure, the epileptic seizures tend to be stereotyped for each patient. Occasionally, the psychomotor seizure takes the form of schizophrenic-like behavior and may lead to the mistaken diagnosis of psychosis, rather than epilepsy. The epileptic has greater fluctuation of mental status, spotty loss of associations, and makes attempts to maintain contact with reality; dysphasia or impaired perception may also be evident. The autisms, withdrawals, bizarre thought content, and symbolic processes seen in schizophrenia are usually absent in the person with seizures. Moreover, analysis of the activity during psychomotor seizures reveals a stereotyped sequence and a fixed pattern, occurring episodically and lasting less than 24 hours (usually much less) before spontaneously terminating—all in contradistinction to the activity in schizophrenia. The epileptic maintains a relatively intact affect and ability to relate to others. The gustatory or olfactory aura of temporal lobe seizures should not be mistaken for psychotic hallucinations or illusions, which are more likely to be auditory, to be of longer duration, and to have meaning to the patient.

Extreme violence is rare as a seizure manifestation. The legal term "temporary insanity," if at all applicable to medicine, should be limited to acts during temporal lobe seizures. The proof should be neurological, not psychiatric, because there must be electroencephalographic evidence of epileptogenic abnormality of the temporal lobe.

Other seizures are less likely to be confused with psychological events. Hysterical seizures rarely simulate grand mal epilepsy; the hysterical movements are more likely to affect the trunk than the extremities, and they often mimic coitus. Occasionally, a child's inattention may be mistaken for petit mal epilepsy, but the reverse error is more frequent. What seems to be syncope may be either a minor seizure or a hysterical phenomenon. The fugue state of temporal lobe status epilepticus may resemble the stuporous appearance of a patient having petit mal status or the amnesia of psychogenic origin. One should not confuse abnormal behavior during a temporal lobe seizure with postictal psychosis—a confused and delirious state that may follow other types of epiletic seizures, especially generalized convulsions, and may last for minutes, hours, or days. Overdosage of anticonvulsive medication may also cause a toxic psychosis.

DISEASES CAUSING SYMPTOMS WITHOUT SIGNS

Probably the most common error in medicine is the assumption of psychological illness when the physician cannot find objective signs to explain the patient's symptoms. In addition, the psychological reaction of the patient to the initial symptoms of organic disease may be depression, conversion disorder, or some other phenomenon that may mislead the physician. This error occurs with diseases that cause anatomical lesions, as well as with pathophysiological illnesses.

Symptoms of short duration. Diseases in the pathophysiological category, because of the transient nature of their symptoms and the lack of evidence of anatomical lesion, may be mistakenly diagnosed as psychological. The dysphagia of myasthenia gravis may be mistaken for globus hystericus; dysphonia and other fleeting and variable weaknesses of the cranial nerve musculature may be similarly misinterpreted. The more generalized weakness of periodic potassium abnormalities and of cataplexy or sleep paralysis also may be misdiagnosed as of psychological origin. Pitfalls in the diagnosis of epilepsy and syncope are discussed above.

Diseases that affect the structure of the nervous system may present diagnostic problems when their initial symptoms are of short duration. Vascular diseases causing transient ischemic attacks are the most common examples of such phenomena, but brief focal or generalized symptoms may also be the first signs of brain tumors. Transient sensory symptoms, such as numbness, are most difficult to evaluate, but one is also hard put to interpret brief weakness described as "heaviness," momentary blurring of vision, and fleeting speech impairment. Subarachnoid hemorrhage may be manifested only by headache.

Occult site of disease. Other problems in differentiating organic neurological disease from psychiatric illness occur when the site of the organic disease is occult. Although this problem may arise with diseases of every etiological category, it is most common with cerebrovascular diseases and with brain tumors (neoplasm, abscess, hematoma). Diseases of the brain may be relatively silent in anterior aspects of the frontal or temporal lobes, in parts of the parietal lobe, over the surface of the brain, or affecting deep midline structures, including extensions into ventricles. Such lesions cause generalized symptoms, rather than specifically focal signs. Headache, dizziness, lethargy, and personality changes associated with such diseases are often unaccompanied by objective signs. Probably the most common intracranial mass producing such symptoms without signs is a chronic subdural hematoma, which is often present without a history of trauma. Meningiomas over the convexity of the brain, ependymomas growing into a ventricle, and infiltrating diencephalic gliomas are other examples of mass lesions affecting silent parts of the brain. An infarct or a neoplasm of the temporal lobe or other part of the limbic system may be manifested solely by a disturbance of behavior. Cortical blindness resulting from an infarction of the occipital lobes may simulate psychogenic blindness, because in both conditions the pupillary reactions and optic fundi are normal, and in both instances the patient may be indifferent to his defect.

The psychomotor retardation associated with hydrocephalus and pseudobulbar palsy may be misinterpreted as depression of spirits. Pseudobulbar palsy, which is usually the result of a small bilateral cerebral infarcts, evokes spontaneous laughter or crying, but the emotional basis for these activities is lacking in this organic syndrome. Lesser gradations of the emotional release phenomenon of pseudobulbar palsy include emotional lability and crying or laughter with minimal provocation. All are subject to misinterpretation with regard to psychogenic versus organic illness. Other diseases that cause multiple small infarcts, such as lupus erythematosis, may present with an acute psychotic disorder.

Encephalopathies. Those diseases that affect the brain as a whole often begin by disrupting the personality. Encephalitis and metabolic or toxic encephalopathies may, therefore, be initially mistaken for psychosis or neurosis. For example, psychotic reactions are associated with acute porphyria, schizophrenic behavior is seen in Wilson's disease, and autism is seen in children with neurolipidosis.

In addition to the psychological manifestations of acute encephalitis, one must be aware of postencephalitic personality disorders, which are often noted in association with postencephalitic parkinsonism and which sometimes antedate the motor abnormalities. Behavioral abnormalities may be the only residual effect of encephalitis. Occasionally, the encephalitis was not clinically obvious, but day-night sleep reversal or oculogyric crises are clues to the postencephalitic nature of the patient's symptoms.

Trauma. Head trauma may result in a variety of symptoms without signs. Such effects of a subdural hematoma are noted above. After a cerebral concussion, symptoms may occur without clinical or laboratory evidence of disease. The postconcussion syndrome is associated with symptoms of headache, dizziness, easy fatigability, anorexia, loss of libido, and impairments of concentration and of memory. These symptoms often last for many months, and compensation neurosis may complicate and prolong the clinical picture. Many consider the postconcussion syndrome to be a neurotic reaction to injury. But the paradoxical occurrence of these symptoms more often after minor trauma than after major trauma, the similarity of symptoms from one patient to another, and the frequent absence of appropriate psychodynamics lead most people to agree that this is a pathophysiological disruption of brain function, rather than a psychological phenomenon.

Degenerative diseases. The so-called degenerative diseases of the central nervous system are often confused with psychological illnesses. Those diseases characterized by movement disorders are discussed above. Many of these diseases also manifest disturbances of personality and of mentation. The cortical blindness associated with some of the metabolic diseases of the central nervous system may simulate hysteria, as noted before.

Multiple sclerosis is a common disease of youth that is characterized by multiplicity of symptoms and signs. The relative euphoria often seen in patients with multiple sclerosis may be mistaken for *la belle indifférence* of hysteria. Often, symptoms outnumber signs, and sometimes symptoms precede objective evidence of disease. This is true not only for blindness of retrobulbar neuritis without evidence of disease on ophthalmoscopic examination but also for other symptoms. Sensations of numbness and tingling may be particularly difficult to document objectively, whether the sensory defect is due to a central nervous lesion or an early peripheral neuropathy, because methods of measuring sensation during a neurological examination are many times less sensitive than are the fine perceptual discriminatory powers of the brain.

Those diseases causing dementia may start with changes in personality. Huntington's chorea may manifest mental changes, including psychosis, before the onset of dementia or chorea. In patients with Huntington's chorea there may be schizophrenic-like delusions and hallucinations or manic behavior, but much more common is depression—both spontaneous and, later, reactive to the other aspects of the illness. In a child with Sydenham's chorea, the abnormal movements may be mistaken for restlessness.

Diseases of the spinal cord, cauda equina, and peripheral nerves. Lesions at these sites may suggest a psychological illness in their initial presentation. Loss of sexual potency may be the first sign of cord disease in a man. Urinary retention is sometimes the only sign of cauda equina compression, especially in women. The glove-and-stocking sensory impairment of peripheral neuritis may be mistaken for a similar defect of hysteria. The pain of herpes zoster and the sense of weakness in the Guillain-Barré syndrome usually precede overt signs of these diseases. Diseases of the muscles often begin with pain as the chief or only symptom. Patients with muscle injuries—for example, whiplash injury of the neck and low back strain— and those with illnesses such as McArdle's disease and myoglobinemia may be falsely accused of malingering or incorrectly diagnosed as neurotic. The stiff-man syndrome, which causes tetanic-like contractions of the trunk without obvious clinical or laboratory evidence of disease, has led to the erroneous diagnosis of hysteria. The vague aches, pains, and malaise of the patient with polymyalgia rheumatica are unassociated with objective signs. These elderly people are often labeled "crocks," yet their symptoms clear dramatically with the onset of steroid therapy.

Suggested Cross References

The anatomy and physiology of the central nervous system are described in Section 3.1, and neurological evaluation is discussed in Section 3.2. Many neurological diseases and syndromes are discussed in Sections 3.3 and 3.4; for example, myoclonus is discussed in Section 3.3, and pain and minimal brain dysfunction are discussed in Section 3.4. Diagnosis is discussed at length in Chapters 12 and 13. Schizophrenia is discussed in Chapter 15, and organic mental disorders are discussed in Chapter 20. Sexual problems are discussed in Chapter 24. Psychological factors affecting physical conditions are discussed in Chapter 26. Drug therapy is discussed in Chapter 31. Speech and language disorders in children are discussed in Sections 39.3, 39.4, and 40.2; movement disorders are discussed in Section 40.1.

REFERENCES

* Adams, R. D., and Victor, M. *Principles of Neurology.* McGraw-Hill, New York, 1977.
Baker, A. B., and Baker, L. H., editors. *Clinical Neurology.* Harper & Row, New York, 1978.
* Benson, D. F., and Blumer, D. *Psychiatric Aspects of Neurologic Disease.* Grune & Stratton, New York, 1975.
Bruens, J. H. *Psychosis in Epilepsy.* In *Handbook of Clinical Neurology,* P. J. Vinken and G. W. Gruyn, editors, vol. 15, p. 593. North Holland Publishing Co., Amsterdam, 1974.
* Carpenter, M. B. *Human Neuroanatomy,* ed. 7. Williams & Wilkins, Baltimore, 1976.
Delgado, J. M. R., and DeFeidus, F. V., editors. *Behavioral Neurochemistry.* Halsted Press, New York, 1977.
* Guyton, A. C. *Textbook of Medical Physiology.* W. B. Saunders, Philadelphia, 1976.
Pincus, J., and Tucker, G. J. *Behavioral Neurology,* ed. 2. Oxford University Press, New York, 1978.
Waxman, S. G., and Geschwin, J. The interictal behavior syndrome of temporal lobe epilepsy. Arch. Gen. Psychiatry, *32:* 1580, 1975.
Weinstein, E. A., and Friedland, R. P. *Hemi-inattention and Hemisphere Specialization.* Raven Press, New York, 1977.
Wells, C. E. *Dementia,* ed. 2. F. A. Davis, Philadelphia, 1977.

4

Science of Human Behavior: Contributions of the Psychological Sciences

4.1 Perception, Cognition, and Attention

MITCHELL L. KIETZMAN, Ph.D.
BONNIE SPRING, Ph.D.
JOSEPH ZUBIN, Ph.D.

Processing and Psychopathology

In his review of information processing, Haber (1974) pointed out that the origins of processing models in psychology can be traced back to Freud's psychoanalytic theory of motivation and personality, in which energy undergoes various kinds of processing in the form of cathexes and shifts as a function of development and experience. The next development was due to Heinz Werner and his colleagues at Clark University, who argued that the processing of visual stimuli should be characterized as a temporal growth process—a growth in clarity. That is the basis for Werner's microgenetic approach to perceptions covering the first few hundred milliseconds after stimulation. However, the full development of information processing in its modern form did not begin until the communication theory of Shannon and Weaver in 1949. Since then, as Haber pointed out, there has been a veritable explosion of models of information processing. Thus, information processing, although stemming originally from Freud's work in psychopathology, is now a term borrowed from experimental psychology. In the past decade the term has come into use in experimental psychopathology without receiving a universally acceptable definition.

The central nervous system is the matrix in which information processing takes place. It acts like a complex computer that receives the vast variety of energies with which a person is continually bombarded both externally and internally. The manner in which those energies are selected, transduced, encoded, and decoded is what is called information processing. In more specific terms, by information processing is meant the route that the energy of a given stimulus follows in entering the central nervous system; how it travels through the various stations from the physiological substrate engendered by the input to the sensory, perceptual, and conceptual processes; how those processes are propagated as the message from the stimulus energy; and how the message finally arrives at the appropriate centers and is absorbed or dissipated. Thus, once the energy of a specific stimulus impinges on a specified receptor, it is encoded and decoded along certain paths in the central nervous system. The nature of those paths is governed by wired-in propensities, neural patterns produced by experience, and temporary circuitry established during certain psychological states.

In this section it is assumed that the energy processing and the information processing that take place in mental patients are in some way deviant from those that characterize normal persons, and the authors' purpose is to discuss where, when, and how the deviation takes place. In that approach the focus is primarily on the findings from controlled laboratory investigations of information processing. Often those studies seem rather arid and removed from meaningful contexts in the lives of psychiatric patients. In fact, one often wonders why those investigations were ever begun, since they seem to reveal deviant responses far removed from those presented as the patient's chief complaint. It is the authors' premise here that the deviant responses patients display in laboratory testing underlie some of the symptoms they present clinically.

The description of deviant behavior in humans goes back at least 34 centuries to the observations contained in the *Ayurveda*, reflecting the clinical acumen of the ancient Hindus. That descriptive literature is rich in clinical impressions and interpretations that antedate the recent application of scientific methods for establishing the reliability and the validity of interviewing methods. But the experimental approach to those phenomena would never have been launched if the phenomena had not been carefully described. Indeed, the initial endeavors to establish the source of behavioral deviances in psychiatric patients arose directly out of clinical observations and patients' descriptions of their sensations, images, thoughts, and associations. Those behavioral deviances may be very subtle, and it would be only too easy to miss them if one leaped too quickly from observation to interpretation of what the patient was saying. The following example appears in Sechehaye's (1951) *Autobiography of a Schizophrenic Girl*:

One day we were jumping rope at recess. Two little girls were turning a long rope while two others jumped in from either side to meet and cross over. When it came my turn and I saw my partner jump toward me where we were to meet and cross over, I was seized with panic: I did not recognize her. Though I saw her as she was, still it was not she. Standing at the other end of the rope, she had seemed smaller, but the nearer we approached to reach each other, the taller she grew, the more she swelled in size. I cried out, "Stop, Alice, you look like a lion; you frighten me."

From what is known about the social isolation and interpersonal difficulties of the schizophrenic, it is easy to cast that passage in terms of the psychodynamics of the patient. For example, her anxiety about intimacy and interpersonal closeness caused her to lapse into a state of derealization as she was about to approach her partner. Indeed, she might even be described as nearing a state of ego disintegration in which she dreaded being merged with and devoured by her "lioness" partner. However, there is a much simpler, if less dramatic, explanation of the passage, an explanation based on a possible disturbance of the young girl's size constancy—the phenomenon that makes two objects that are equal in size and presented at different distances appear to have the same size, despite the differences in the size of the retinal image cast by the objects at the two distances. To be sure, one is left with the need to explain why and how the disturbance in size constancy developed, but at least one is dealing with a precise and testable hypothesis.

Patients' subjective accounts have provided a great richness of detail about the way in which the experiences of daily events are altered in psychopathology. Those accounts have been well chronicled by McGhie and Chapman (1961), Freedman (1974), and Freedman and Chapman (1973). Far from being removed from life, those accounts of disturbed attention and perception are closely linked with various types of symptoms. It is easy to understand schizophrenic loosening of associations in relation to an inability to filter relevant from irrelevant percepts and thoughts. Even the experience of auditory hallucinations may reflect an inability to discriminate ongoing events in the environment from ongoing thought processes.

In spite of the obvious possible relationship between such clinical manifestations and deviations in attention and information processing, those disturbances in processing have generally not captured the interest of those studying psychopathology. Why? Cromwell (1978) suggested that psychopathology has traditionally been described and defined primarily in terms of deviations from the norms and expectancies of society. Many patients, especially those characterized as schizophrenics, may manifest symptoms that are threatening or intolerable to those around them. Cromwell contended that the long-standing emphasis on clinical symptoms in psychopathology research is not because those symptoms are more important etiologically, prognostically, or therapeutically but because they are intolerable; they create problems for the patient and for the community. Cromwell (1978) stated:

Perhaps the reason why deviations in attention and information processing have not been viewed as a dramatic or exciting feature of schizophrenia is that they are tolerable. No one has ever been arrested for a reaction time crossover deficit. No one has been committed to an institution for velocity arrests in his eye-tracking. No one has been taken into psychiatric treatment because of overestimating the size of visual stimuli.

Even though those behaviors may well underlie the more dramatic symptoms, Cromwell suggested that for 8 decades

primary consideration has been given to the dramatic, disturbing, or intolerable clinical symptoms, and that emphasis has produced little genuine understanding, prevention, or amelioration.

That may not be an entirely balanced assessment of the situation, and the contrast between the dynamic and the scientific approaches is a philosophical issue that has produced considerable controversy. Savodnick (1978) designated the two contrasting views as the objective-descriptive (neo-Kraepelinian) and the dynamic; he regarded the dynamic approach as yielding a manifest image and the objective-descriptive approach as yielding a scientific image. The manifest approach is the everyday approach, involving the manifest appearance of psychiatric behavior—the dramatic, disturbing, and intolerable behaviors—and the scientific approach is the reductionist approach. In this section the authors combine the two approaches through the application of both types of explanation to the same phenomena and in this way permit an interaction between them.

For example, clinicians have usually attempted to explain the origin of behavioral eccentricities on the basis of psychodynamic principles or as attempts to escape from undesirable thoughts or situations. An alternative approach is to attribute the behavioral eccentricities to fundamental disturbances in information processing. Thus, in schizophrenia, Kraepelin (1913) described difficulties in shifting attention, a kind of perseverative behavior influenced by the patient's rigid fixity of focus on some trivial portion of the environment relevant to a preoccupation or delusion. Cameron (1938) and Payne (1962) described a pattern of overinclusion or difficulty in selective attention, a breakdown of the ability to filter relevant from irrelevant information. Sullivan (1962) and Silverman (1964) suggested that, whereas acutely ill patients may be unable to filter out irrelevant thoughts and sensations, chronically ill patients may have learned the defense of selective inattention, narrowing their focus down to a small sphere.

Harrow et al. (1972) developed a Perceptual Experiences Inventory, which elicits self-report statements that are excerpted from patients' accounts of overinclusive attention. Consistent with Sullivan's (1962) and Silverman's (1964) predictions, Harrow found scores to be elevated in a variety of acutely ill patients and to diminish over time as the patients recovered.

Some theorists (McGhie and Chapman, 1961; Hoffer and Osmond, 1966; Ornitz, 1969; Maher, 1972; Rochester, 1978) have proposed that basic disturbances in attention and information processing may constitute a fundamental component of vulnerability to psychopathology. Those disturbances may antedate and postdate the onset of psychopathology and provide the mechanism by which the experience of daily events assumes the bizarre and terrifying characteristics observed in psychosis. The incidence of subjective disturbances in perceptual experience declines as patients recover from their episodes of illness. However, it is necessary to determine whether subtler, objectively measurable information-processing deviances are stable traits of the patient that persist after the episode ends. It is also essential to determine the precise nature and extent of those disturbances. Although disruptions in attention have been emphasized in the discussion above, it is possible that those deviations are the most flagrant or observable ones to both patient and clinician. Certainly, disturbances in sensation, perception, and cognition other than those involved with attention have also been observed clinically.

Information Processing

Haber (1974) referred to the information-processing approach to the study of perception as a "revolution"—one that has caused a fundamental change in the way research is done and the way ideas are formulated. That revolution has had major repercussions in the areas of perception, but it has also influenced research in such areas as cognition, memory, learning, thinking, and problem solving. Introductory psychology textbooks (Lindsay and Norman, 1977) regard information processing as an organizing principle, a way of conceptualizing some of the dynamic complexities that are known to characterize human behavior. The appeal of the approach is that it offers a welcome relief from the stifling rigor of the static stimulus-response paradigm that characterized much of academic psychology from Watson's behaviorism through World War II.

Whatever the reason for its popularity, there is little doubt that information processing in psychology has come of age and is vigorously being extended to all avenues of psychological knowledge and research. Noteworthy are the theoretical articles that are appearing in the psychological literature (Turvey, 1973, 1977, 1978; Breitmeyer and Ganz, 1976). The impact of the approach was illustrated by the experience of Schneider and Shiffrin (1977), who received more than 2,000 reprint requests for the second half of a theoretical paper on information processing (Shiffrin and Schneider, 1977). Most of those models are highly sophisticated and quantitatively explicit, which encourages readers to interpret their data in similar ways. Concomitant with the theoretical models are numerous empirical studies designed either to explicitly test hypothetical models of information processing or to interpret results—often post hoc—in terms of their implications for information processing. In short, information processing is here, and its application to psychopathology has already begun (Cromwell and Spaulding, 1978).

Although information processing is dominating explanation in psychology, there have been few attempts to systematically present a broad portrayal of the approach to the problem of studying or understanding abnormal populations. The situation is not surprising; understanding abnormal behavior characteristically awaits a clearer understanding of the principles of normal behavior. The reasons for delay are particularly clear in this case, since progress has been so rapid that the major models of information processing are always undergoing substantial revisions. Empirical reports of the information-processing approach for studying abnormal populations usually do not discuss the systematic basis of the concept and seem to be little concerned about its validity.

The few theoretical papers that have discussed information processing in relation to abnormal populations have generally attempted to demonstrate that a particular aspect of processing is disordered among a specific clinical subgroup. Generally, data collected for a variety of purposes and from widely varying theoretical perspectives are assembled and interpreted in terms of a new, unique theoretical formulation (Giora, 1975). That type of approach is problematic in that the studies reviewed were generally not designed to bear on the theory under discussion and thus permit a variety of interpretations. Difficulties of interpretation are quite pronounced in the study of information processing, since the researcher's interest is generally in drawing inferences about precise changes that occur in the encoding and decoding of stimulus energies over brief periods of time. Unless converging operations (Garner et al., 1956) have been built into an experiment to allow the selection or elimination of specific alternative hypotheses, it is difficult to determine exactly what changes and processes have occurred. Indeed, Haber (1969) suggested that it is virtually impossible to apply post hoc information-processing interpretations to data collected for other reasons or within the context of other points of view.

SURVEY

Processing as a general term. Sometimes in the literature the terms "process" and "processing" are simply used to modify terms used to describe traditional topics of psychology. Thus, it is fashionable to call sensation, perception, cognition, and memory by different names, such as sensory processes, perceptual processes, cognitive processes, and memory processes. Such a general, unspecified use of the terms is not employed in this section.

Processing and information theory. The term "information" in information processing can be traced to an early attempt to apply a theory from communication engineering to problems in psychology. Mathematical information theory (Shannon and Weaver, 1949) attempted to define the transmission of information in terms of bits in relation to the reduction of uncertainty. The formal definition of information was independent of both the stimulus and the response and was focused merely on transmission; it may be that its disembodied independence explains in part why the bit concept of information transmission never became particularly fruitful in either psychological or biological research (Gilbert, 1966; Johnson, 1970; Haber, 1974). Despite several vigorous attempts to apply the theory to problems in psychology (Attneave, 1959; Garner, 1962), relatively little research using formal information theory and the transmission of information in bits currently appears in the literature.

One major exception is a group of researchers in psychopathology (Lhamon and Goldstone, 1973; Crain et al., 1975; Goldstone et al., 1977) who, with some success, are applying information theory to their time-judgment tasks. There is a controversy over whether time-judgment studies can be considered perceptual research, since the exact definition of the adequate stimulus is vague. It may be that the information-theory approach becomes of value in circumstances in which the stimuli are not readily specifiable, as in time-judgment research.

Processing and computers. The emergence and the growing use of electronic digital computers after World War II was another major influence in the development of information-processing research, especially for those aspects in the cognitive domain involving complex behaviors, such as problem solving and thinking (Simon, 1979). Early attempts to simulate on the computer such complex functions as visual-pattern recognition and artificial intelligence gave way in the period of 1956 to 1972 to well-developed models dealing with such diverse topics as problem solving, rote verbal learning, and performance on different induction tasks, such as concept attainment and sequence extrapolation. Today, computer technology is an intricate part of information-processing research.

Processing as a sequence of events over time. As used here, the processing approach specifies that the processing of stimuli involves an ongoing series of events that occur over time. It is assumed that the time from the stimulus to the response can be divided into a sequence of discrete stages. During each stage different operations are performed to transform and transmit energy and information. The objective of research is to devise methods by which the flow of stimulus energy and information can be sampled at various time points to determine which operations occur at which times, which operations occur sequentially (serially) and which occur simultaneously (in parallel), how and when the energy and information are transformed or recoded, and where they are lost. Those stages correspond only roughly to the traditional areas of experimental psychology: sensation, perception, memory, and cognition.

ADVANTAGES AND DIFFICULTIES OF A PROCESSING APPROACH

In what follows, an emphasis is placed on having independent and dependent variables specified temporally in order to study processing. The emphasis is not intended to exclude nontemporal variables completely. Obviously, if certain nontemporal measures have repeatedly been found to differentiate between normals and patients or among types of patients, those variables remain of potential importance and should continue to be investigated (Lewine, 1978). Such variables may prove even more valuable if they are investigated as process measures—that is, in studies in which the independent variable or the dependent variable or both are varied in time. For example, perceptual constancy differences between patients and normals (Weckowicz, 1957, 1964) may be more effectively measured in terms of processing differences. Previously obtained differences may be even larger, or slight differences may become significant. Of course, it is also possible that phenomena measured as processes will not reveal differences that had been observed when measured with nontemporal variables. Studying phenomena as processes provides several advantages: time as a common metric, the opportunity to group phenomena according to that common temporal metric, and the possibility of comparing independent and dependent variables in terms of time.

The major advantage of applying a processing approach to psychopathology is that the approach makes possible far more precise specification than has previously been possible of the exact nature of the impairments in psychopathological populations. Until now, most research on patient groups has been devoted to demonstrating the existence of gross deviations—for example, in perception, attention, motivation, and thinking. The widespread use of such constructs as attention dysfunction and thought disorder illustrates the global and nonspecific nature of the inferences that can be drawn from such research. The fact that such widely divergent and essentially uncorrelated tasks can be selected to measure a presumably unitary deviation (Kopfstein and Neale, 1972) is indicative of the diffuse and relatively uninformative nature of the hypotheses about psychopathological deficits that have prevailed to date. However, by virtue of the explicitly detailed and quantitative models of information processing that have been proposed, as well as the sophisticated research techniques for measuring various parameters of those models, it is now possible to obtain fine-grained knowledge of areas of intact and deviant processing in psychiatric patients.

Progress in the processing approach to understanding psychopathology depends in large part on knowledge about processing obtained by studying normal persons. If, as Broen (1968) contended, progress in understanding processing in psychopathology depends on advances in basic knowledge about processes, one strategy is to focus on data that can be clearly related to aspects of sensory, perceptual, and cognitive processing that are already well established at the forefront of research with normals. Furthermore, it is a good strategy to use data that can be referred to with considerable confidence because the research from which they were obtained displays adequate concern with experimental design and the elimination of possible confounding factors. In that case the most valid data provide the strongest possible building blocks for the development of models of processing in psychopathology.

To be sure, a processing approach to psychopathology also presents some difficulties. One is the difficulty of specifying what is meant by key concepts like information. Generally, the term is loosely used to refer to those aspects of the stimulus with which the experimenter is concerned. Further, many processing experiments, especially those concerned with sensory processing, involve primarily stimulus energy, not stimulus information. To use the term "information processing" to describe the approach would misrepresent what is actually being processed. Thus, the authors try to use both terms, "energy processing" and "information processing," whenever it is appropriate to do so.

ANALYSIS OF PROCESS AND PROCESSING

In the scientific literature the term "process" has been used in a number of technical and nontechnical ways. A good general definition (Boring, 1963) is that a process is something other than time that changes over time. The point is that process is closely related to time and to changes over time. In science the term usually refers to specific operations or procedures. For example, in perception, the field of psychology that has perhaps emphasized processing more than any other, reference is made to perceptual processes—specific, observable events occurring over time in relation to some precipitating or evoking stimuli. A process is not a specific ostensive event, observable by itself. In any processing experiment the only elements that can be directly observed and measured are the initiating stimulus and the resulting response. The important intervening processes that are of primary concern are hypothetical constructs; often they cannot be directly measured but must instead be inferred. The nature of the inference is heavily influenced by the stimuli that are administered and the responses that are measured. As Underwood (1957) pointed out, concepts can be defined at levels of abstraction that differ from the operations used to measure them. The intention is to refer to processes that have meaning beyond the simple stimulus-response operations used to measure them.

One can describe and analyze processing in terms of several general questions about the characteristics of processing. The first question is *what* is being processed? What is the nature of the stimulus material being presented for processing, and how do differences in stimuli influence the types of processing that occur? Second, *where* is the processing occurring? Although that is basically a physiological question having to do with structure within the nervous system, the "where" question can be approached purely on the basis of behavioral data in at least two different ways. The first concerns the level of processing, which loosely translates into gross distinctions, such as peripheral and central levels, input and output levels. Methodological strategies and theoretical strategies allow one to make those behavioral distinctions about levels. Another way in which the *where* question can be approached experimentally concerns the locus of processing. Where within the nervous system do particular processes occur or, at least, display a major focus of activity? Here, that question translates into a more specific question about the presence of lateralized functional hemispheric asymmetries for different measures and types of processing. Again, numerous behavioral techniques allow researchers to attempt to localize types of processing as being primarily associated with right or left hemispheric functioning.

The next basic question is, *when* does a particular process occur? At what time after the stimulus presentation does a given process occur? That question has to do with the sequence of processing events. If one knew when the different processes occurred between the stimulus and the response, it would be possible to reconstruct the sequence of processing or the temporal order of events between stimulus and response—the flow of processing.

The last two questions are related to each other and are discussed here in terms of the construct of attention. One question pertains to *how much* of the presented material is being processed by a person. That question relates both to the nature of the stimuli themselves and to the capacities and organismic state of the person to whom the stimuli are presented. The other question is *how* does processing occur? What are the mechanisms of processing? That question concerns the actions or operations of the processes and the possible interrelationships between processes. In that context one can discuss the control strategies—the operations by which processing is modified or regulated, especially by complicated and diverse attentional mechanisms.

To bring a single organizational schema to bear on aspects of processing that do not actually occur in isolation, one can divide and discuss the processing literature in three diverse domains: sensory processing, perceptual processing, and cognitive processing. Those domains are defined largely in terms of what is being processed and where and when processing occurs. General issues regarding how much is processed and specifically how the processing operations are carried out apply across all three domains.

Not all behavioral experiments deal with processing. The key components of processing studies are a stimulus that changes in time or a response measured in time or both. Stated differently, processing experiments have either or both their independent and their dependent variables specified in temporal units. The magnitude of the time manipulated or measured provides an indication of which type of process—sensory, perceptual, or conceptual—is being studied. Those important characteristics of processing studies mean that not all research can be regarded as studying processing directly. For example, a detection threshold study may or may not be a processing study. It is not a processing experiment if the sound stimulus is fixed in duration or is presented continuously while the intensity of that stimulus is increased until the subject reports that he hears it; in that case, time has not been varied or measured. It is a processing experiment when the duration of the stimulus is varied.

Since it is postulated here that deviations or impairments in psychopathology are most clearly understood from processing experiments, the distinction between experiments that do or do not measure processing becomes crucial. Only by manipulating over time or measuring in time can conclusions begin to be made about the nature of the processes being investigated. Each true processing study provides a temporal referent that can contribute to a processing analysis of behavior. Such temporal referents also make possible the grouping and the comparing of otherwise diverse experimental studies on the common variable of time. Several important questions about processing are now considered.

What? Variations in the nature of the stimuli presented relate to the differences in what is being processed for the three different domains of processing. In general, two things are processed—energy and information (Miller, 1975). Both factors are always involved in processing, since energy is the carrier of information. Energy stimuli are those that can be adequately defined completely with reference to their physical characteristics—for example, frequency and amplitude for sound or wavelength and intensity for light. The description of informational stimuli is more complicated. In the professional literature, "information" is a term used loosely to mean something akin to stimulus

complexity or the amount of stimulus patterning. Informational stimulus displays are generally rather complicated; they are configurational or have sign or symbolic significance. There have been attempts to refine the meaning of information (Attneave, 1954), but various authors (Eriksen and Spencer, 1969; Garner, 1970) have commented on the inadequate objective specification of information and how more adequate specifications are needed. One of the difficulties arises from the fact that the quality of information depends not only on the stimulus but also on the person's prior experience. Despite reservations about the vagueness of the term "information," it is used here to indicate some undefined or unspecified component of the stimulus.

Across the different domains of processing, there are differences with respect to the relative importance given to energy and information. Thus, sensory processing is predominantly concerned with measuring the effects of precisely varying stimulus energies, as in classical psychophysics, although the stimuli still carry information, albeit information of a rather primitive or limited nature—for example, the stimulus is amorphous, or the stimulus is simply present or absent, as in absolute threshold research (Jenness et al., 1975).

At the other extreme, in cognitive processing, the major emphasis is on the information content of the stimuli, which may be quite complicated. In cognitive research relatively little attention is given to the energy aspects of the stimulus, except perhaps to attempt to keep the energy constant, so that energy changes do not confound the major interest—the effects of information on the response measures.

With respect to energy and information, perceptual processing falls somewhere between sensory processing and cognitive processing, depending on the particular perceptual study. Some perceptual studies are primarily concerned with controlling and measuring the response in relation to variation in the energy aspect of a stimulus; other perceptual studies are notable in that they demonstrate perceptual differences with constant energy (illusions), or they display perceptual constancies in the face of changing stimulus energies (size and brightness constancies). Of course, even cognitive processing measures must to some degree entail sensory processes, which are dependent on energy, and perceptual processes, which are guided by both energy and low-level information. For example, the response to a visually presented word may progress through the sensory processing of contrast and color; then the perceptual processing of lines, angles, and letter forms; and, finally, the cognitive processing of the meaning of the word.

Where? Any systematic discussion of processing necessarily introduces questions about the underlying physiology or the physiological correlates of processing. Although several processing models describing central nervous system functioning have been proposed (Leibovic, 1969), those models usually do not attempt to relate both physiology and behavior (Broadbent, 1965, is an exception). This section does not directly include physiological investigations but does touch on the question of physiological localization in two ways. First, the authors consider the level of processing, which roughly means whether the processes occur more or less peripherally or centrally in the nervous system. Various experimental paradigms (Weiss, 1965; Sternberg, 1969) and testing procedures, such as dichoptic stimulation, allow one to make rough inferences about the peripheral and central balance for given processes. Second, the authors discuss the loci of processing, which refers to where in the nervous system the processing is most likely to be centered. Actually, here the locus question is related only to the issue of hemispheric laterality or hemispheric asymmetry of function. By selected testing procedures—for example, dichotic listening and tachistoscopic hemifield presentations—it becomes possible to obtain estimates of the relative efficiency or speed of processing of the right and left cerebral hemispheres.

When? Processing approaches assume that a sequence of events takes place between the presentation of the stimulus and the subsequent response. Broadly, several stages of processing are postulated, but the exact number and the type of stages that occur and the order in which they occur differ for various models. Also, there are numerous complexities to the stages, since several channels of processing may occur simultaneously, and those channels may influence each other through negative and positive feedback loops. In some models, several processes or events are assumed to occur within each stage. Thus, the listing of stages between stimulus and response can provide only a rough indication of what is happening during the processing chain of events.

In a nontechnical way, the stages can be described as follows (Zubin and Kietzman, 1966): (1) the input stage, at which there is action on the energy and information components of the stimulus; (2) the interpretation of what has been acted on; (3) the classification of the components; (4) the organization of the classified components; and (5) the output stage, which culminates in the response. That description assumes a simple linear direction in time, but the picture is actually much more complicated. The number and the types of stages involved may differ for different types of stimuli, for different tasks, and for the person at different phases of practice, experience, and organismic states.

In view of the difficulty of definitively specifying the number or even the order of stages of processing, one can imagine the complexity of attempting to specify exactly when, after the stimulus, a certain stage or a certain process has occurred. However, certain theoretical developments in basic information-processing studies hold promise for eventual answers to such questions with psychiatric patients (Wasserman and Kong, 1979).

Processing domains. The processing research literature can be classified into three general domains: sensory processing, perceptual processing, and cognitive processing. Cognitive processing can be further subdivided into two types: short-term cognitive processing—for example, short-term memory—and long-term processing—for example, long-term memory.

Those three domains of processing can be characterized and distinguished in several ways. First, they relate roughly to a traditional division among psychological topics. Second, each domain relates to a different time period after the presentation of the stimulus. Thus, sensory processing refers to the briefest periods of time after the stimulus presentation, usually periods up to a maximum of 1 second (Zubin and Kietzman, 1966). Perceptual processing refers to slightly longer periods of time after the stimulus presentation, periods of up to about 5 seconds (Bartley, 1958). Cognitive processing refers to even longer periods of time after the stimulus presentation, and the exact type of cognitive processing depends in part on the duration of the phenomenon under consideration. For example, short-term cognitive processing refers to investigations of phenomena that occur within the first few minutes after the stimulus presentation; long-term cognitive processing refers to the investigation of events that are measured in many minutes or even hours or days after the stimulus presentation. Such specific temporal distinctions are, of course, only approximate and are subject to modification. Subsequent research should help to clarify which phenomena should be grouped together or what time periods are believed to represent similar phenomena.

The three domains of processing can also be distinguished according to the nature of the stimulus material. The applied stimulus can be of either the energy type—in which case the response of the organism depends on the physical characteristics of the stimulus, such as its intensity—or the signal type, in which case the response depends more on the accrued meaning or significance of the stimulus. Studies of sensory processing usually entail the simplest stimuli, such as flashes of light and noise bursts. Experiments on cognitive processing usually entail the most complicated stimulus displays, involving words or sentences with sign or symbolic significance. The nature of the stimuli associated with perceptual-processing experiments generally lies between the simple sensory stimuli and the more complicated cognitive stimuli. For example, shapes, dot configurations, or patterns of notes may be used in experiments on perceptual processing.

How and how much? In the above description of the three domains of processing, sensory processing, perceptual processing, and cognitive processing were implicitly characterized along a structural dimension. The discussion of the "where" of processing assumed that the structures responsible for processing in each domain can be localized more or less centrally or peripherally in the nervous system and, moreover, that more precise localization of the relevant physiological loci involved in each domain is possible. And the discussion of the "when" of processing assumed that the processing activity in the key loci is greatest at certain specifiable time points after an applied stimulus. Thus, one can hypothesize that the underpinnings of each domain are wired-in structures that are basically invariant from one organism to the next within a given species and from one situation to the next. Such structures may be analogized to the hardware of a computer that performs the input processing operations (Atkinson and Shiffrin, 1968).

In addition to the structural dimension, processing activity may also be described in terms of certain control processes (Schwartz, 1978). Control processes describe what is done to the incoming information, what operations are performed, or *how* processing is carried out. Some examples of control processes are searching, filtering, pigeonholing, categorizing, and rehearsing. Control processes are analogous to computer programs or software that govern specifically what actions are to be performed on incoming information. Control processes are more ephemeral than processing structures. They vary from one person to the next, from one situation to the next, and from one moment to the next. Some control processes are more costly than others in terms of the time required to carry them out and probably also in terms of the demands they place on processing structures. To extend the computer analogy, one may think of control processes as varying in their requirements for capacity of computer memory.

The concept of processing capacity refers to the "how much" question of processing. Out of the myriad amounts of energy and information to which the organism is continuously subjected, how much can be processed, or how much is being processed? Some limitations on processing are imposed by limits on the capacity of the information-processing structures (Miller, 1956). Just as there is no computer with hardware adequate to handle all the simultaneous jobs that could be entered in it, no organism is structurally equipped to process all the information-processing tasks that life imposes simultaneously. Similarly, further limitations are imposed by the execution of single-control and multiple-control processes that place demands on the processing structures or hardware. Thus, limitations in processing capacity reflect not only the constraints of structure but also the constraints imposed by the functioning of ongoing control processes.

Numerous theorists have proposed that, in some psychopathological disorders, patients may experience information overload because processing demands exceed available processing capacity. Overload may result because of too much information input, because of deficiencies in information-processing structures, because of the inept use of certain control strategies or processes, or because of the inefficient allocation of processing activities among simultaneous control processes. Those formulations of information overload came from a wide variety of research approaches representative of the sensory, perceptual, and cognitive processing domains (Miller, 1960, 1964; Korboot and Damiani, 1976; Weingartner et al., 1980).

Two modes of processing. To further understand the relationships among sensory processing, perceptual processing, and cognitive processing, one may find it useful to adopt the distinction made by Lindsay and Norman (1977) between two modes of processing: data-driven processing and conceptually driven processing. Data-driven processes are most closely related to the stimulus components of energy and information. Those processes are thrown into motion by the arrival of an input of energy and information from the stimulus. The processing of the stimulus then progresses through an increasingly sophisticated sequence of analyses until the stimulus is recognized or interpreted. Data-driven processing is also described as bottom-up processing, since activity in the system begins with the arrival of the input, progresses directly to the early and relatively simple sensory processing of the stimulus, and finally proceeds to the later and more complex cognitive interpretation of its meaning. In contrast, conceptually driven or top-down processing begins with the person's expectation or interpretation of what stimulus may be present. The expectation guides the processing throughout the system to test whether the interpretation of the stimulus is correct. Whereas data-driven processing begins with the stimulus and ends with the interpretation of the stimulus, conceptually driven processing begins with the expectation and interpretation and goes in the opposite direction.

One may also use the phrase "externally driven processing" to refer to what was above called data-driven processing. The term "externally driven" implies that the processing is initiated and controlled by external stimulus components. Similarly, conceptually driven processing may be described as internally driven. That term emphasizes initiation and control from within the organism based on the organism's expectancies and interpretations.

In most processing of everyday events, it is clear that the data-driven system and the conceptually driven system operate together. However, for the sake of simplicity, much of the discussion here of sensory and perceptual processes relates to the data-driven system, and most of what is emphasized in cognitive processing relates to the conceptually driven system. The concept of attention represents a bridge between the two types of processing and helps to describe how the two systems operate in unison.

To clarify and measure the distinction between those two modes of processing, one may use the theory of signal detection (McNicol, 1972; Swets, 1973). That theory is currently being used extensively in the area of experimental psychopathology. Its chief virtue is that it provides two theoretically orthogonal response measures—a measure of the sensitivity called d' and a measure of response criterion or bias called *beta*. The theory is actually an extension of statistical decision theory.

Although signal-detection theory was originally concerned with the problems of threshold—how much energy is needed to see or hear the stimulus?—the model is completely generalizable to a wide variety of phenomena. It has been applied to problems in the areas of perception, memory, learning, personality, and social and clinical psychology. The major requirement for devising an experiment in the signal-detection theory framework is that the responses required from the organisms—both animals and humans have been tested—be difficult enough to cause some doubt or uncertainty. If stimuli are never discriminable or are always discriminable, then the theory is not appropriate.

What is the relationship between signal-detection theory and the two modes of processing? It is possible to conceptualize the two major measures of signal-detection theory—d' for sensitivity and *beta* for response criterion—as measures of the data-driven processing system and the conceptually driven processing system, respectively. Since the value of the d' measure of sensitivity is affected by manipulations of the stimulus characteristics, it seems appropriate to relate that measure to the data-driven system. In contrast, the value of *beta* is not influenced by alterations of the stimulus but is influenced by manipulations of the subject's attitudes toward responding, as modified by instructions, motivating payoffs, and expectancies about how often the stimulus will be presented. Such factors seem to be adequately described as conceptually driven. The application of the signal-detection model to the domain of attention (Swets and Kristofferson, 1970; Broadbent, 1971) to study such topics as vigilance illustrates the potential value of using signal detection to separately measure data-driven and conceptually driven aspects of attentional control processes.

Attention and processing. Despite James's (1950) 19th-century claim that "everyone knows what attention is," the subsequent years have not brought a consensus on the meaning of the term. Moray (1969) listed 6 different definitions of attention, and Boring (1970) described 10. A thorough review of the literature would undoubtedly reveal hundreds of different usages of the term, to say nothing of the myriad theoretical models that have been advanced to explain the phenomenon of attention. Nonetheless, in the past 2 decades the concept of attention dysfunction has come into widespread use to describe and explain various characteristics of psychopathology (McGhie, 1969). The rapid growth of the literature on attention is

rivaled only by that on theories of memory. Moreover, it is a literature characterized by healthy scientific controversy among theories, rather than by consensus on a single theory or model of attention.

With some exceptions, the empirical research on attention in psychopathology has not been guided by any single theory of attention or by an effort to determine the exact nature and locus of a processing impairment. Rather, the approach taken has been somewhat reminiscent of the orientation of faculty psychology. Attempts have been made to determine whether a global faculty of attention is impaired in certain patient populations. The tools used to answer that question are techniques borrowed from experimental psychology. It is not surprising that the intercorrelation among the various putative measures of attention is minimal (Payne et al., 1970; Kopfstein and Neale, 1972; Asarnow and MacCrimmon, 1978) and suggests that it is untenable to speak of a unitary attention deficit. Instead, one must refer to the series of histories that has grown up around each measuring instrument of attention. It is really a moot question to ask why all those experimental tasks are called measures of attention. Their lack of intercorrelation indicates that they are not measures of the same kind of attention. The only common thread among the separate measures is that all attempt to appraise two key elements in the construct of attention. The first element is limitation; since not all simultaneous incoming stimuli can receive processing, how much can be processed, and what governs those constraints on processing? The second element is selectivity; of all possible incoming stimuli, some will be selected for processing, and others will not be processed.

Processing capacity. The phenomenon of attention is intimately bound up with the concept of processing capacity. With a multiplicity of stimuli impinging on the organism at any one time, it may not be possible to process and respond to all the inputs. Therefore, the organism's behavior cannot be predicted directly from the stimuli, and attention describes the phenomenon by which some stimuli and not others command processing and behavioral responses.

Involuntary and voluntary control. In a variety of different ways, most contemporary models of attention make a distinction between voluntary and involuntary attention. William James (1950) offered a subjective description of the difference by describing involuntary attention as passive or effortless processing in which attention is gripped, captured, or arrested by some object or event despite the intentions of the subject. Voluntary attention, by contrast, refers to the ability to direct the focus of attention in accordance with current expectations, plans, or goals. There are parallels between involuntary attention and data-driven processing and between voluntary attention and conceptually driven processing.

Involuntary attention is automatically initiated by stimuli that have some significance in terms of the organism's enduring dispositions. Different kinds of stimuli can initiate involuntary attention. Research on the orienting response (Pavlov, 1927; Sokolov, 1963; Lynn, 1966) has demonstrated that the nervous system is biased to preferentially respond to novel stimuli. Stimuli that are relevant to an aroused motivational or drive state will also automatically initiate attention. When a person is hungry, his attention is automatically gripped by the smell of dinner cooking. The examples thus far have described stimuli that are significant largely in terms of wired-in neural propensities. However, other stimuli involuntarily grip attention because, over a long period of time, one has learned that they are important and require a response. One's own name is an example of a learned stimulus that automatically commands attention. So is a red light when driving. Schneider and Shiffrin (1977) and Shiffrin and Schneider (1977) demonstrated that one can learn to attend and respond automatically and involuntarily to many categories of stimuli, some of them quite complex, if one is consistently trained to respond to them.

The process by which one learns to attend and respond automatically to certain stimuli was described by La Berge (1975) as the development of automaticity. After much practice, certain stimuli command attention and lead directly to a response, without requiring any conscious awareness. Schneider and Shiffrin (1977) described such data-driven processing as automatic processing. In automatic processing, certain stimuli lead directly to interpretation and response, independently of the subject's control. Such processing is described as veiled or hidden from conscious awareness largely because it occurs rapidly and is virtually impossible to manipulate through conscious intention. The greatest advantage of automatic processing for the organism is that it places few demands on a limited processing capacity. When a variety of processing sequences are well learned, it is possible to automatically process and respond to a range of events simultaneously without effort or voluntary attention. Thus, automaticity frees one's limited processing capacity to deal with other events in the environment that require conscious effort and voluntary attention.

Voluntary attention is a form of conceptually driven processing that describes the allocation of attention to stimuli that are relevant to current plans, expectations, and intentions. Voluntary attention is analogous to controlled processing, as described by Schneider and Shiffrin (1977). In that form of top-down processing, the person controls the types of stimuli for which he is searching. He is conscious of his intention to select some stimuli for processing and response and to ignore others. That type of attentional activity proceeds slowly, requires effort, and is highly demanding of processing capacity.

To understand the development of automatic processing and its relationship to controlled processing, one may think of a person learning to ski. The new skier has to devote controlled processing to many aspects of the task at hand. He has to exert concerted effort to pay attention to keeping his knees slightly bent and his hands slightly before him and to the negotiating sequence of shifts in weight that are necessary to carry out a turn. In addition, he is likely to be distracted by automatic attention responses that are difficult to suppress. His attention is involuntarily drawn to the precipitous drop of the slope before him—a stimulus that is well learned to be a sign of the danger of falling. The new skier very likely feels somewhat overwhelmed by the number of events to which he has to attend; in fact, it seems impossible to carry out all those processing tasks at once. But after long practice, all those component events are processed smoothly and without awareness. It is even possible to add other processing tasks to the array, such as watching for other skiers and carrying on a conversation. Indeed, attention to all the relevant elements has become so fully automated that it is nearly impossible for the skilled skier to describe what stimuli are monitored.

Selective attention and filtering. Much contemporary research on attention has concerned the problem of selective attention. Given one's limited processing capacity, how does one allocate processing to relevant stimuli and avoid becoming overloaded by irrelevant stimuli? Many theories have postulated the existence of a filter, a selection device or a bottleneck at some point in the information-processing sequence. Bottleneck models of attention imply that a large number of stimuli can be processed simultaneously or in parallel up to the point of the bottleneck. Thereafter, stimuli must be processed serially, one at a time, so that some selection is necessary. Controversy has ranged over the location of the bottleneck stage and the characteristics of the filtering mechanism.

The attentional filter was originally described as a processing structure. Investigations were undertaken to determine the "where" of the filter—that is, its localization at a peripheral or central level (Hernández-Péon, 1975) and whether it is part of the sensory, perceptual, or cognitive domain. More extensive research was carried out to answer "when" questions about the filter. At what period of time after the delivery of a stimulus is the filter most actively operating? In recent years, theoretical models of selective attention have shifted from reified structural conceptualizations of the filter to active processing models that describe selection and filtering as control processes or operations. Although the original hypotheses about the filter as a structure have proved to be inadequate, the descriptions of the separate operations thought to be performed by the different filters have been retained.

Originally, Broadbent (1958) proposed that the attentional filter be described as a structure in the sensory domain. That filter operates to filter out some stimuli even before the stage of perceptual analysis. In contrast, Deutsch and Deutsch (1963) and Norman (1968) localized the filter in the conceptual domain, arguing that the only bottleneck in the system occurs late in the processing sequence, after the meanings of all incoming stimuli have been extracted in parallel. Broadbent (1971) later modified his model to include two filters, one in the sensory domain and the other in the cognitive domain. The second filter operates on the input from a cognitive analysis of the stimuli. The bottleneck models describing the location of a filtering structure generated some correct predictions and some erroneous ones. The existence of an early-stage filter is disputed by the fact that some irrelevant inputs that are clearly discriminable from relevant inputs in physical characteristics nonetheless receive processing. The exclusive existence of a late-stage filter is implausible because of the extensive amount of processing capacity that would be needed to analyze the meaning of all incoming stimuli. Moreover, increasing the number of stimuli that must be processed simultaneously does produce impairments in performance. That finding would not be expected if it were possible to extract the meaning of all incoming stimuli in parallel before any selection occurs.

Instead of referring to early and late filter structures, contemporary researchers tend to discuss the selective operations that were initially attributed to those hypothetical filter structures. Thus, one can describe filtering, also called "stimulus set" by Broadbent (1971), as a data-driven control process by which some stimuli are selected to receive further processing because they display certain physical properties. A different kind of control process called "pigeonholing" is a conceptually driven operation that selects inputs that correspond to expectations. Those expectations specify an allowable category of responses—for example, the members of a conceptual category. For that reason, pigeonholing is also called "response set." The pigeonholing control process, based on the conceptual analysis of stimuli, was originally thought to be carried out by a late-stage filter. Broadbent (1970) suggested that the d' and *beta* indices of the signal-detection theory could serve as measures of stimulus selection and response set, respectively.

The following example may clarify the distinction between filtering and pigeonholing. Two messages are presented, and someone is asked to listen to the message spoken by the female voice and to ignore the message spoken by the male voice. In that case, selection can be accomplished by filtering out the message that has the inappropriate physical characteristics associated with the sound of a male voice. If, however, the person is asked to detect the names of animals spoken in either voice, there is no simple physical distinction between relevant and irrelevant target stimuli, so stimulus set is not helpful. The control strategy used in that case is pigeonholing—detecting a match between an input and cognitive templates for all members of the target's conceptual category.

In general, filtering is considered less demanding of processing capacity than is pigeonholing. To the extent that the processing of some inputs is governed by data-driven, automatic, or involuntary attention, people generally have considerable processing capacity to spare. However, to the extent that voluntary attention requiring controlled, conceptually driven processing is necessary, as in pigeonholing, the processing capacity is more fully taxed. When a task is highly practiced or requires simple physical discriminations among stimuli, performance may become automated, and selective attention should operate efficiently. However, an exception should arise when irrelevant, distracting events generate automatic processing that the person must attempt to suppress by voluntary attention.

In summary, the most recent discussions of attention (Kahneman, 1973; Norman, 1976; Schneider and Shiffrin, 1977; Shiffrin and Schneidcr, 1977) dispute the need to postulate any critical stage of attentional bottleneck. The question of how many inputs can be processed at any one time seems to depend on the control strategies that are used to select among stimuli and the demands they place on the total processing capacity afforded by the processing structures.

Focused and divided attention. In the discussion of attentional control processes, a distinction is made between two modes of attention that may be required of a person. In some tasks the person is asked to divide his attention among two or more inputs. Studies concerned with determining how much can be processed (the limitation aspect of attention) generally require divided attention. The objective of such investigations may be to determine how many simultaneous inputs can be processed accurately, or it may be to determine the extent to which the addition of further relevant inputs impairs the speed or the accuracy of processing. Other tasks require the person to attend to a particular input while ignoring competing inputs. Those tasks may require focused attention. Such tasks are generally used to investigate the selective aspect of attention. For example, they may inquire how efficiently stimuli sharing a common physical attribute may be filtered out from a nexus of stimuli. Or they may pose the problem of how easily stimuli belonging to a common conceptual category may be pigeonholed out from all incoming information.

Arousal and attention. The relationship between arousal and attention has often been discussed, and a general tendency toward hyperarousal has frequently been invoked to explain attentional anomalies in psychiatric patients, particularly schizophrenics (Mednick, 1958; Venables, 1964; Broen and Storms, 1967; Kornetsky and Eliasson, 1969). Arousal is a psychophysiological concept pertaining to the activation of the nervous system, and there is an enormous experimental literature relating arousal to psychopathology (Alexander, 1972). The relationship between arousal and attention is most easily understood in the case of voluntary or conceptually driven attention. Kahneman (1973) proposed that the degree of effort devoted to attentional processing is reflected in measures of arousal. On the other hand, most studies of psychopathological populations begin with the hypothesis that patients have an altered basal level of arousal, for whatever reason, and attempt to determine the consequences of that state for attentional processing. With a condition of low arousal, the case is clear enough. The patient is drowsy, rather than alert; he is poorly motivated to perform the task; and he does not allocate much processing capacity to it. Kahneman (1973) proposed that the underaroused person actually has a reduced amount of processing capacity at his disposal to allocate to any task. However, one may also suspect that the available processing capacity is allocated to the least demanding tasks and perhaps given over preferentially to daydreaming.

At more moderate levels of arousal, it becomes important to distinguish between different states of arousal, since that notion is not a unitary construct. Lacey (1967) described two important states of moderate arousal. In one state, the various measures of sympathetic arousal show a pattern that has been described as directional fractionation. The diameter of the pupil increases, as expected in sympathetic dominance, but the pulse rate and the heart rate slow down. The subject seems to be in a pattern of relaxed acceptance of external stimulation or waiting for something to happen. Motor responses are inhibited, and conditions are ideal for data-driven processing. In the second state of moderate arousal, the indicators of sympathetic arousal cohere as the heart rate accelerates. Lacey (1967) originally proposed that the latter pattern of generalized sympathetic dominance occurs when the subject resists stimulation, but subsequent research has indicated that the pattern occurs whenever the subject exerts an effort in problem solving or prepares to make a response. Performance on an experimental task is enhanced in moderate arousal conditions, as opposed to low arousal conditions; but at very high levels of arousal, performance most often deteriorates. The Yerkes-Dodson law describes the general observation that task performance is an inverted U-shaped function of arousal. The deterioration of behavior at high levels of arousal is thought to result from the fact that the subject tends to narrow his attention down to the dominant stimuli in the task but simultaneously becomes impaired in the ability to discriminate relevant from irrelevant aspects of the situation at hand (Easterbrook, 1959). Broen and Storms (1967) presented data suggesting that the disorganization of response tendencies in chronic schizophrenia follows precisely that pattern.

PROCESSING AND PSYCHOPATHOLOGY

Although processing research is too new to definitively describe what happens to processing in instances of psychopathology, there is no shortage of theories or models. Many of the models come from quite divergent areas of research and are described by investigators who are apparently unaware of the similarities among their viewpoints. Those different models can be conceptualized in relation to the earlier distinction between data-driven processing and conceptually driven processing. The models take different forms, varying primarily in their complexity. Some are simple models that posit a unitary deficit; others are more complicated, involving explanations about the balance or imbalance between the two modes of processing.

In unitary models, different types of patients are characterized as displaying impairments or disruptions of one of the two major modes of processing. Some patients may show predominant deviations in tasks in which data-driven processing is paramount; other patients may show deviations primarily in conceptually driven tasks. A few models focus primarily on the functioning of the data-driven mode of processing.

Johnson (1975) proposed a theory of depression based on information processing that states that depression is a defense reaction mounted to cope with anxiety that arises as a result of a defect in the patient's information-processing mechanism. Because of mounting anxiety, the patient stops analyzing incoming sensory information and, instead, evokes a sleep-like mechanism, as is shown by his becoming lethargic and unresponsive to stimuli. The clinical status of the patient correlates with that type of information-processing dysfunction. In mania, data-driven processing is accentuated, and information is said to be overprocessed. That, in turn, leads to depression. In depression, data-driven processing is suppressed, and information is underprocessed. Johnson tentatively suggested that the locus of the dysfunction in data-driven processing is at the sensory input stage. However, he admitted that research has not ruled out the possibility that affective disorders may also be characterized by changes at the output stage—that is, changes in the motor mechanisms.

Buchsbaum (1979) has been involved in a line of research investigating the relative influence of stimulus control with respect to psychopathology. His emphasis is on individual differences in subjects' responses to simple stimuli varying in intensity. Subjects are believed to differ in their perceptual-cognitive styles, a personality dimension; the reducers tend to inhibit or attenuate physical stimulus inputs; the augmenters accentuate the same stimulus inputs. On the basis of earlier work reported by Petrie (1967) in the area of pain perception (Silverman, 1972), Buchsbaum and colleagues (Landau et al., 1975) investigated whether there are correlations between the tendencies to respond selectively to simple stimuli (augmenters versus reducers) and patient diagnosis.

To summarize the results, acute schizophrenics tend to be reducers, presumably as a protective device against excessive flooding of stimulus inputs. In comparison, chronic schizophrenics are augmenters, but the explanation is unknown. Paranoid schizophrenics are augmenters, and that finding is hypothesized to be related to their tendency to vigilantly scan the environment. Bipolar depressed patients are extreme augmenters in that they augment even more than normal persons do. However, a subsequent report (Gershon and Buchsbaum, 1977) found that there were no differences between patients with bipolar affective disorders and patients with unipolar affective disorders. Most of the research involved the average evoked response—a physiological measure. Unfortunately, the most common behavioral measure of stimulus intensity modulation, the kinesthetic figural aftereffect procedure (KAE) has been found to be unreliable, even with normal persons. Schooler et al. (1976) argued that the optimum research strategy is to measure both the KAE and the average evoked response, since they do correlate but probably measure different phenomena.

Augmentation and reduction of stimulus intensity are obviously characteristics of the data-driven processing system, and the body of research using the average evoked response and the kinesthetic figural aftereffect illustrates how it can become possible to experimentally clarify aspects of data-driven processing. Similarly, research can be designed to investigate characteristics of conceptually driven processing.

As shown above, some models simply describe processing deviances within one of the two modes of processing—for example, an anomaly in the data-driven processing system. More complex models describe deviances in the balance or integration between the two processing modes. Those models suggest that in psychopathology the normal interrelationship between the two modes of processing is altered or modified, so that one mode of processing becomes more frequent or dominant, with a corresponding change or even inhibition of the other mode.

A clinically derived hypothesis that has persisted for some time suggests that many persons with psychiatric disorders display disruptions of the balance between data-driven processing and conceptually driven processing and that conceptually driven processing predominates. For example, Freud (1966) suggested that the interest or cathexis of schizophrenic patients is withdrawn from the external world and refocused on internal preoccupations. To some degree, that observation may merely reflect the fact that the patient is not motivated to participate in most of the tasks the therapist gives him. It was suggested in the discussion of arousal that, at low levels of motivation, the person does not have much processing capacity to invest and tends to allocate his available capacity to the least demanding activities, such as daydreaming. Alternatively, the patient may simply be more interested in inner events, rather than outer events, and may voluntarily direct attention toward his own mental processes. In any event, the hypothesized reorientation of attention inward implies that conceptually driven or internally directed processing tends to prevail over data-driven, externally directed processing.

The best examples of an imbalance in which conceptually driven processing overrides data-driven processing come from clinical observations and patients' subjective descriptions. Here is one such patient account (McGhie, 1969):

> I'm not sure of my own movements any more. It's very hard to describe this but at times I'm not sure about even simple actions like sitting down. It's not so much thinking out what to do it's the doing of it that sticks me. I found recently that I was thinking of myself doing things before I would do them. If I'm going to sit down for example, I've got to think of myself and almost see myself sitting down before I do it. It's the same with other things like washing, eating or even dressing—things that I have done at one time without even bothering or thinking at all. . . . I take more time to do things because I am always conscious of what I am doing. If I could just stop noticing what I am doing, I would get things done a lot faster. I have to do everything step by step now, nothing is automatic. Everything has to be considered.

In the earlier example of learning to ski, it is as if the experienced skier had to learn to ski all over again. In the example above, highly overlearned processing sequences have become deautomatized. It is now necessary for the patient to voluntarily direct his attention to the relevant stimuli; processing is driven top-down, effortfully, by the conceptual image of what is to be achieved. Processing should be slowed accordingly, since conceptually driven sequences take longer to execute. If that hypothesis is correct, one may predict that schizophren-

ics display particular difficulty in acquiring automatized, data-driven sequences or that automatic processing, once acquired, tends to break down and be rapidly replaced by controlled, serial, conceptually driven processing strategies.

A model by Cancro et al. (1978) also suggested a predominance of conceptually driven processing in schizophrenia. Their experimentally investigated hypothesis was that schizophrenics attend preferentially to mental stimuli over external visual stimuli. Their research was based on the hypothesis that the proportions of time spent blinking versus fixating are indices of internal and external attentional deployment, respectively. That distinction was supported by earlier research demonstrating that both psychiatric patients and normal controls showed a reduction in blinking during visual tasks and an increase in blinking during mental tasks. The results showed that schizophrenics spent more time blinking and less time fixating than did normal controls. There were no significant differences between schizophrenics and depressed patients or between depressed patients and normal controls on the blinking and fixation measures. Those data have been interpreted to indicate that schizophrenics tend to pay attention to internal conceptual events in preference to external stimuli. They consequently assimilate less information about the environment than do normal persons.

It is possible that the Cancro et al. (1978) findings can be explained by the schizophrenics' poor level of motivation to attend to external events. However, another possible interpretation of the data is based on the information-processing model outlined here. In many situations in which normal processing is guided by the efficient operations of data-driven or even automatic processing, it seems necessary for the patient to resort to the more demanding system of conceptually driven, controlled processing.

Most of the theories reviewed thus far suggest that in psychopathology, conceptually driven processing is favored over data-driven processing. However, at least two theories propose that the imbalance goes in the opposite direction—to favor data-driven processing.

Salzinger (1971) presented an immediacy hypothesis of schizophrenic behavior; it postulates that schizophrenic patients are more controlled than are normals by stimuli that are immediate in their temporal and spatial environment, even when they are irrelevant to the behavioral context. The key concept is the compelling control of the immediate stimulus over behavior for schizophrenics. Presented with two stimuli, one past and one present, the schizophrenic finds the present stimulus more influential than does a normal person. To the extent that present stimuli are data external to the person, whereas past stimuli are internally or conceptually represented, the immediacy hypothesis suggests that processing in schizophrenia is disproportionately data driven.

Rimland (1978) suggested that an imbalance favoring data-driven processing is also characteristic of some forms of childhood psychopathology. On the basis of clinical observations of autistic and idiot savant children, Rimland proposed that processing in those children is locked in to the exact physical dimensions or qualities of the stimulus. Rimland suggested that autistic children have great difficulty with conceptually driven processing in which attention is directed to the meaning of incoming stimuli.

In another model describing processing in schizophrenia, Magaro and colleagues (McDowell et al., 1975) suggested that the direction of the imbalance—toward data-driven or conceptually driven processing—depends on the diagnostic subtype of the schizophrenic patient. They also attempted to relate different types of psychopathology to the domain of processing and to whether or not the processing is automatic or controlled. Paranoid patients show a greater than normal tendency to display primarily controlled, cognitive processing; nonparanoid schizophrenic patients are more likely to use automatic, perceptual (icon-directed) processing. To the extent that perceptual processing is more data driven than is cognitive processing, this model may be a variation on the distinction made above between patients who rely primarily on data-driven processing and those who primarily use conceptually driven processing.

Magaro, in an unpublished 1978 paper, extended his model to suggest the possibility of hemispheric asymmetries that parallel the types of processing associated with each form of psychopathology. He postulated that, if automatic processing is mainly a right-hemisphere function, then nonparanoid schizophrenics are predominantly right-hemispheric processors. Since controlled processing is thought to be a left-hemispheric function, then paranoid patients are primarily left-hemispheric processors.

GENERALIZED PATIENT DEFICITS

A major source of confusion permeates almost all research in experimental psychopathology. It is shown by the ubiquitous, experimental finding that patients invariably perform more poorly—more slowly, less accurately—than do normal persons. Explaining differences in which patients do poorly is a problem because those differences may be due to several general factors, such as the patients' lower motivation or cooperativeness or inability to understand instructions, rather than to the postulated specific deficit. Reports of patient-normal differences of that general type are not helpful in processing research, since they do not elicit particular differences that can provide some answers to the specific questions about the "where," "when," and "how" of processing that were asked earlier. This methodological problem is the generalized deficit problem. Several researchers have described the problem and its manifestations (Bannister, 1968; Chapman and Chapman, 1973, 1978; Sutton, 1973; Spring and Zubin, 1978).

There are several ways, experimentally and methodologically, to approach the generalized deficit problem. The best approach is to devise experiments in which at least some of the patients do better than the normal controls. In that way, the obtained patient-normal differences cannot be described as artifactual. Patient-doing-better experiments are not always easy to design, however, and sometimes the doing-better aspect is a relative improvement, rather than an absolute improvement. Thus, in one study (Bruder et al., 1975), psychiatric patients had, as expected, slower reaction times than normal controls, but the reaction time improvements as a function of stimulus manipulations were relatively better for the patients than for the controls.

Another approach to the generalized deficit problem is to design functional experiments in which several stimulus values are tested for all groups. Then a comparison of the functional curves for each group provides maximum information about the performance of the subjects and about their cooperation, motivation, and willingness to participate. If the functions are very similar but simply displaced upward or downward, that strongly suggests that the subjects were actively participating in the task. If the subjects were not participating, the functional curves would be not simply displaced but irregular and quite variable. That strategy is especially effective if the shape of the function for normal subjects is well established. For example, Granger (1961) compared the dark-adaptation threshold curves of psychiatric and normal subjects—based on well-established data from numerous previous investigations of normal subjects. He found both groups of subjects generated similar functions, except that patients required about 0.3 log unit more intensity than did normals across the function. Granger suggested that patients performed as if they were wearing sunglasses or neutral-density filters.

Other strategies can be used to eliminate the generalized deficit as an explanation of patients' deviant performances. Chapman and Chapman (1973, 1978) suggested that before a given deviation in patient performance on a task or a condition can be attributed to their psychopathology rather than to a generalized deficit, it is necessary to introduce a control task or condition. The control task or condition must be so calibrated as to be equivalent to the experimental task with regard to reliability, discriminating power between persons, difficulty, and similarity in the distribution of scores or measures. The calibration

must be based on the normal group only. It is expected that normals give results that do not differentiate between the two tasks. If the patients give a different result on the experimental task, as compared with the control task, that difference relates to their specific psychopathology and not to their generalized deficit. That conclusion holds even if the patients' general level of performance is poorer than that of the normals. The basis for the conclusion is the difference between the experimental tasks and the control tasks and not the patients' difference in level of performance from the normals.

The general psychometric approach to dealing with such confounding variables is univariate or multivariate analysis of co-variance. That approach, however, can be called into question in this context because analysis of co-variance was developed for the case in which the two groups under comparison are random samples of the same population, rather than naturally occurring groups, such as patients and normals.

A strong but complicated approach to the generalized deficit problem is a theoretical one advocated by Underwood (1957) and Underwood and Shaughnessy (1975). They discussed the problem in the context of how to avoid confounding by subject variables (such as age and sex) when manipulating other subject variables. In the typical study comparing patients and nonpatients, the intent is to obtain behavioral differences that are caused by some theoretically meaningful difference between the two groups. For example, one hypothesis might be that patients tend to use filtering operations when nonpatients use pigeonholing operations, and that the difference explains the patient deficit on the task under investigation. However, in addition to the hypothesized difference in control processes, patients also generally differ from nonpatients on a host of possibly confounding variables that may also explain their poorer performance. Numerous subject variables—for example, age, intelligence, and cooperation—generally co-vary with the patient-nonpatient diagnostic distinction.

The approach Underwood and Shaughnessy (1975) suggested to handle the problem is difficult to explain briefly, but its essential ingredients are to compare groups with respect to thoroughly investigated measures, to postulate a possible theoretical explanation for the differences, and to design a series of experiments involving several variables to test the validity of the postulated process. The outcome of that testing takes the form of obtaining significant interactions that are consistent with the postulated explanatory process. In the example given above, one might design a task in which the postulated preference of patients for filtering strategies yields a pattern of patient performance that is superior to the normal performance. Or one might manipulate normal subjects to use filtering operations in a task situation in which pigeonholing is the optimum strategy. In the latter case one would test the prediction that normals perform like patients in that context, since they do what patients do ordinarily without the added inducement of the experimental manipulation.

By suggesting and testing an explanatory process to explain the patient-normal differences, one essentially handles the generalized deficit problem and, more important, tests the effects of postulated mechanisms or processes. Such testing over several experiments constitutes a form of the converging operations strategy (Garner et al., 1956) mentioned earlier as essential for investigating processes and their interrelationships.

Sensory and Perceptual Domains

Three separate domains of processing—sensory, perceptual, and cognitive—were described earlier and given operational definitions. Although ideally it should be possible to categorize processing research into those three domains, for the purpose of this section and for the description of the existing processing data, the sensory and the perceptual processing domains are presented together for several reasons. Surprisingly, relatively few published studies are uniquely sensory or perceptual and also distinctively concerned with processing, as those concepts are described here. Even fewer of those studies of psychiatric patients have ever been replicated. Further, the sensory and perceptual domains are traditionally considered together. For example, in the autobiographical reports of patient disturbances, both sensory and perceptual disturbances are reported interchangeably. Also, both domains share many methodological problems, such as the need for refined methods and the possible contamination by drugs. Thus, it is efficient and adequate to discuss those issues only once. Finally, certain substantive topics, such as the levels of processing and functional hemispheric asymmetries, can be appropriately discussed with reference to both their sensory and their perceptual components; since those topics have relatively little solid data, to attempt to discuss them separately for each domain would be unrealistic.

Processing research in the sensory and perceptual domains usually involves relatively simple stimuli that are varied primarily along energy dimensions. The general purpose of research in the sensory and perceptual domains is to assess a person's discriminatory powers for sensory stimulation. More specifically, research in those domains has several possible objectives: (1) to determine the conditions under which a stimulus is reported as present (the detection threshold); (2) to establish which stimulus is different from several similar stimuli (the discrimination of differences, as in the forced-choice procedure); (3) to determine whether two stimuli seem to be the same or different (a matching procedure); (4) to measure a response that is based on some instructions that require the person to respond to a designated stimulus (a recognition procedure); and (5) to measure a response about some specified quality of the stimulus, such as: Is the stimulus flickering or fused (an identification procedure)? Those are basic psychophysical questions that can be answered by verbal reports or by psychomotor responses, such as reaction-time responses (Kietzman and Sutton, 1977). Experimentally, those questions are not always asked in ways that permit one to assess the various aspects of processing, but the intention here is to focus primarily on those studies that can be considered to measure processing. The one exception to that plan is in the area of detection threshold research, which is considered broadly, since it is basic to all other phenomena.

PSYCHIATRIC PATIENTS AND SENSORY AND PERCEPTUAL DEVIATIONS

In an earlier edition of this textbook, Jenness et al., (1975) discussed the question of whether there are genuine sensory and perceptual differences between psychiatric patients and nonpatients. They concluded that, although autobiographical reports (Silverman, 1969; Gross and Huber, 1972) by former patients strongly suggest that sensory and perceptual differences do exist, their clear experimental demonstration is difficult for several reasons. Such differences, if present, are probably quite small, which means that the experimenter needs precise equipment to adequately control the stimulus, well-designed experiments, and subjects who are able and willing to participate in what are often boring or uninteresting tasks. In short, even though sensory-perceptual differences may be present, demonstrating those differences is not easy, since they are probably small effects.

Furthermore, sensory and perceptual studies share certain common methodological problems. First, since those studies report less sensitive or poorer performances for patients, there is a possibility that the patient-normal differences do not relate to differences in sensory-perceptual performance at all but are simply due to differences in motivation or cooperation—that is, due to the generalized deficit described earlier. Second, the sensory-perceptual differences may be the result of medications being taken by the patients. That potential source of confound-ing can be reduced somewhat by comparing different types of patients taking similar drugs, if one assumes that there is no interaction between the drug and the type of patient. Also, some investigations have shown that, taken in therapeutic dosages, the usual psychotropic drugs do not seem to modify certain sensory response measures, such as reaction time (Held et al., 1970). Other studies (Spohn et al., 1974) suggest that psychotropic drugs do modify sensory and perceptual performance, sometimes in a complex interaction with patient diagnoses (Rappaport and Hopkins, 1971). Therefore, none of the drug "control" procedures completely disposes of the possibility of confounding.

Clinical psychophysics. An important methodological consideration in the field is the possibility that patients do not really differ in sensory or perceptual capability but actually differ only in their willingness to accept the task and to respond as required by the experimental task (Grossberg and Grant, 1978). Emphasis on methodology in the area of psychophysics is not new; indeed, a major contribution of psychophysics has been the development of precise, objective response-measurement techniques. It was no coincidence that the application of a sophisticated signal-detection theory to problems of psychology began in the area of sensory psychophysics. Clinical psychophysics is simply an attempt to apply many of the highly developed techniques of psychophysics to clinical problems and to the field of experimental psychopathology.

One aspect of the signal-detection theory that seems to hold promise for clinical psychophysics is its potential for measuring a person's response bias, the *beta* measure of signal detection. Since that measure is largely a measure of the person's attitudes and readiness with respect to making the positive response under investigation, it follows that patients may differ systematically from normals in that respect. The measurement of *beta* is a topic that should be systematically investigated.

Several investigators have discussed the possibilities of research that explores response-bias tendencies in psychiatric patients (Clark, 1966; Price, 1966; Price and Eriksen, 1966; Grossberg and Grant, 1978; Lewine, 1978). Over the years, numerous signal-detection studies have reported on the response-bias characteristics of different types of patients. However, those reports are scattered, and the results are by no means consistent. For example, in two auditory threshold studies, Rappaport and his colleagues (Rappaport et al., 1972 a, b) reported that paranoid schizophrenics displayed a stricter or more conservative criterion than did nonparanoid schizophrenics and normal persons. In comparison, in a visual two-flash study, Gruzelier and Venables (1974b) reported that paranoid schizophrenics had more lenient criteria than did nonparanoid schizophrenics, who, in turn, were more lenient than normal persons. Those results are seemingly opposite to Rappaport's conclusions. How are those discrepancies explained? Were they due to the difference in modalities (visual versus auditory) or to the difference in tasks (detection threshold versus two-flash threshold)? Were the subjects not comparable? Or were the differences related to the way the criteria were calculated? Rappaport's studies used the conventional signal-detection model and formulae to obtain *beta*; Gruzelier and Venables used a signal-detection procedure developed from the method of constant stimuli (Treisman and Watts, 1966).

Some of the complexities of measuring and interpreting the values of response bias are illustrated by the above example. At the most elementary level, even within the signal-detection theory there are several different response-bias measures, and some of the difficulties of measuring response bias have been brought out in a technical review (Dusoir, 1975). An investigator is faced not only with the problem of determining which one of several possible measures of response bias to choose but also with the interpretation of what any particular measure means. Even the empirical interrelationships between the diverse measures of response bias are largely unknown. The difficulties of making comparisons are further increased when two models, such as the signal-detection model and the Treisman and Watts model, are used to derive measures of response bias.

Since response bias is largely a measure of idiosyncrasy, it is to be expected that persons differ with respect to response bias under different experimental conditions or tasks. Also, the same person may even differ from himself at different times. Some additional complexities of the response-bias or response-criterion problem were discussed by Kahneman (1968), who distinguished between two types of response criteria—the criterion-level factor, which relates to the willingness of the subject to respond (this is the response-criterion or response-bias problem of the signal-detection theory), and the criterion-content factor, which relates to the basis on which the subject decides to respond (the cues being used, for example). Clearly, several types of criteria can influence responding, and attempts must be made to distinguish between them and to develop separate research strategies to measure them.

Response bias is simply part of the larger problem of the influence of different response factors in measuring behavior. There seems to be increasing evidence that response factors can be of crucial importance in psychiatric research. Lewine (1978) reviewed the influence of different response factors for a large number of psychiatric studies, all of which involved untimed psychophysical tasks. He concluded that such response factors as response complexity and the social interaction required in making the response are of key importance in distinguishing between chronic schizophrenics and paranoid schizophrenics. By considering those two response factors, Lewine was able to clarify previously discrepant or apparently inconsistent results. The performance of chronic schizophrenic patients seemed to be impaired greatly in experiments using complicated responses. The performance of paranoid schizophrenics particularly differed from normals when the required response involved a social interaction—that is, when the response had to be spoken.

Lewine (1978) deliberately excluded timed psychophysical tasks, such as reaction time, because they "are ultimately a measure of the temporal limits of information processing." However, he did refer to one particular signal-detection study that used a timed task and produced data that did not support his major thesis about paranoid manifestations. To explain the apparent discrepancy between the data and his thesis, Lewine pointed out that the particular study involving the timed task may be subject to influences different from those affecting the other untimed studies he described. Lewine apparently believed, as the present authors do, that it is important to distinguish between timed and untimed tasks, since the distinction can lead to important interpretative differences. In this section the authors have largely limited their selection of studies to timed tasks, since those studies provide the best measures of processing.

The topic of clinical psychophysics is developing rapidly, but, so far, the development has been scattered and uncontrolled. Individual studies report results that include response-bias measures, but there has been little attempt to standardize measures of response bias. Typically, only a single response-bias measure is obtained for each group; few studies report trying to measure bias at several values or trying to manipulate bias for different clinical groups. Only by such a systematic empirical thrust, with the concomitant development of theoretical explanations as to why and how psychiatric patients may be expected to differ with respect to response bias, can one expect the potential of clinical psychophysics to be realized.

Sensory studies. Sensory processing topics include (1) the detection threshold, (2) temporal resolution, and (3) temporal integration. Detection-threshold research with patients has usually not involved time as either an independent variable or as a dependent variable; therefore, such threshold studies do not usually provide direct measures of processing but may indi-

rectly reflect processing differences. However, the two sensory phenomena of temporal resolution and temporal integration always provide measures of sensory processing, since they are operationally defined in terms of temporal changes of the stimuli.

Detection threshold. Many scattered reports suggest that psychiatric patients are less sensitive than nonpatients in a variety of threshold-type tasks.

Those reports were for auditory thresholds (L. E. Travis, 1924; R. C. Travis, 1926; Levine and Whitney, 1970) and visual thresholds (Granger, 1957 a, b; Rubin and Stein, 1960), although Bartlett (1935) questioned the conclusion in audition. Originally, the reports simply compared normals with large groups of patients given a single global diagnosis, frequently a hospital diagnosis, such as schizophrenia. Relatively little effort was made to obtain refined classifications of patients, and even fewer attempts were made to relate thresholds to specific symptoms or syndromes. In retrospect, it is obvious that in such research there was a marked imbalance in that they compared precise behavioral threshold estimates with global clinical judgments that were frequently unreliable (Vaughan, 1975). It is not surprising, therefore, that the conclusions from those early studies, considered as a whole, are not convincing.

More recently, threshold investigations have emphasized more refined classification procedures for grouping patients. The use of the semistructured interview (Spitzer et al., 1964) has given more reliable diagnoses and has provided, for research purposes, detailed analyses of patients' clinical symptoms and syndromes. Several investigators have reasoned that not all psychiatric patients should be expected to show the same sensory differences (Levine and Whitney, 1970; Bruder et al., 1975). In fact, they have suggested that it may be of interest to group patients according to their sensory performance to see whether those showing a particular pattern of sensory deviation, for example, also show unique patterns of symptoms or syndromes. Perhaps a limited subgroup of patients selected from a larger group of patients with a particular global diagnosis, such as schizophrenia, may be the patients who display the elevated thresholds.

The dual emphasis on more objective and, therefore, more reliable diagnoses and on more refined and detailed clinical information has provided renewed interest in the possibility of finding sensory-threshold differences (Emmerich and Levine, 1970; Rappaport et al., 1972 a, b; Bruder et al., 1975, 1979; Mannuzza et al., 1980). Several of those studies have also combined the refined classification techniques with more sophisticated psychophysical methods in an attempt to handle the response-bias problem.

In one study (Bruder et al., 1975) that used a forced-choice technique to measure the auditory threshold, higher thresholds were found for the patients with affective disorders than for others tested; the schizophrenics and normals did not differ significantly in their auditory thresholds; that result was replicated by Bruder et al. in 1979. Significant correlations were reported in both studies between the clinical symptom of speech retardation and the auditory threshold (in the first study, $r = 0.56$; in the second study, $r = 0.41$). For both of those studies, the right-ear threshold was the discriminating measure; the left-ear threshold, measured only in the second study, was not significantly different across the groups of subjects. Speech retardation is a symptom frequently associated with the diagnosis of psychotic or endogenous depression. Malone and Hemsley (1977) found that depressed patients displayed lowered motor responsiveness during depression than when their clinical state improved. When depressed, the patients also displayed reduced auditory sensitivity to tones. Motor responsiveness—in that case, an attitudinal, response-bias measure—and its exact relationship to speech retardation were unclear.

In studies of the thresholds of psychiatric patients, inevitably some patients show thresholds in the same range of performance as the normals show, and other patients have markedly higher thresholds than do the normals.

Mannuzza et al. (1980) reported on two visual-threshold experiments. In a preliminary study of 23 patients and 13 nonpatients, 40 per cent of the patients had higher thresholds than did any of the nonpatients; there was also a significant positive correlation between the total number of symptoms displayed by the patients and their visual thresholds ($r = +0.58$, $P < .01$). In the second experiment, visual thresholds were obtained for 32 hospitalized psychiatric patients, 15 siblings of patients, and 18 nonpatient controls. That threshold study also obtained extensive clinical information about all the subjects by the use of a semistructured psychiatric interview schedule. Analyses of the data for all 65 subjects indicated that 55 per cent of the patients had higher thresholds than did any of the nonpatient controls.

To evaluate the relationship between psychiatric symptoms and visual sensitivity of the patients, the researchers combined data from both studies and computed correlations between visual-threshold scores and scores on 20 factorially derived clinical scales obtained from a semistructured interview (Gurland et al., 1976). Only 1 of the 20 factors of psychopathology significantly and positively correlated with high visual thresholds; the factor was auditory hallucinations.

None of the detection-threshold studies mentioned above directly measured sensory processing, since no temporal measures were used. One auditory-threshold study did combine threshold and temporal integration measurements (Babkoff et al., 1977). Temporal integration refers to a very brief basic sensory process in which the energy of the stimulus determines the characteristics—such as the magnitude, speed, or accuracy—of the response, regardless of how that energy is distributed in time. That auditory investigation illustrated the potential power of using refined diagnostic and classificatory strategies.

The experiment used noise-burst stimuli of three different durations. An initial analysis of data compared the temporal-integration function of the psychiatric patients, considered together, with the function obtained from normal controls. The analysis indicated that the psychiatric patients had a 5-decibel higher threshold for all stimulus durations than did the normal controls (Bruder et al., 1975, 1979; Babkoff et al., 1977). A subsequent analysis compared the normal controls with subgroups of patients formed from symptom profiles based on clinical information obtained from a semistructured interview. Interview data were scored to obtain the symptom profiles that had been derived from a factor analysis. From the data, two groups of patients were identified—a depressed group and a schizophrenic group. Patients with the highest factor loadings of depression showed the highest thresholds; patients with schizophrenic-like profiles of symptoms also had thresholds that were higher than those of the normal controls, but their thresholds differed from those of the depressed patients according to the duration of the stimulus—that is, there was a significant interaction between the groups of subjects and the stimulus durations. By dividing the patients into two more homogeneous groups on the basis of similarities in clinical symptoms, the researchers made the interpretation of the threshold data more meaningful.

Temporal resolution. Temporal resolution refers to the ability of the organism to resolve successively presented stimulus inputs as discrete events. At slow input rates the subject is able to resolve (process) the inputs as discrete and successive—that is, temporal resolution is demonstrated. As the rate of successively presented inputs, such as flashes of light, increases, resolution is no longer possible, and the successively presented inputs merge; the light no longer flickers but is seen as continuous—that is, resolution is absent. Temporal resolution is possible for all types of inputs, and there are numerous ways of measuring resolution, such as the critical-flicker-frequency threshold, the two-flash threshold, and the temporal-order threshold. Those different measures of temporal resolution

may not be correlated (Lindsley and Lansing, 1956; King, 1962).

In the domain of sensory-processing research with psychiatric patients, studies of temporal resolution have been the most popular and the most frequent. The critical-flicker-frequency technique, for example, has been used extensively to measure the effects of stress, anxiety, and other arousing and activating stimuli. Bibliographies of the critical-flicker-frequency literature (Landis, 1953; Ginsberg, 1970) list more than 2,000 references, many of which have clinical, organismic, and psychopharmacological significance.

The two-flash threshold is another sensory measure of temporal resolution. It has been used extensively to study clinical populations. Venables (1964) engaged in a series of studies using the two-flash-threshold technique as a measure of cortical activation, a hypothetical concept related to central nervous system functioning. He reported that the two-flash threshold correlated with an electrodermal (skin potential) response, which served as his measure of arousal of the autonomic nervous system. Furthermore, the direction of the correlation differed for different groups of subjects (patients and normal persons). Generally, normals and paranoid schizophrenics showed a positive correlation between the two measures; the relationship was negative for nonparanoid schizophrenics. Venables's theory postulated that chronic schizophrenic patients display a breakdown in the mechanisms regulating the balance between cortical and autonomic arousal, and that breakdown explains their distinctive negative correlation.

In a follow-up study to test Venables's theory, Gruzelier et al. (1972) used a more sophisticated forced-choice method and experimentally manipulated arousal by having subjects pedal a bicycle ergometer under different loads. Their results showed that the two-flash thresholds of paranoid and nonparanoid schizophrenics were, in general, negatively related to skin potential and to a related measure, skin conductance, but only for nonactivated (low-arousal) conditions; when activated, the paranoid schizophrenics showed the same changes as did the normals, and the nonparanoid schizophrenics showed raised two-flash thresholds and lowered skin-conductance levels. Hieatt and Tong (1969) also investigated the effects of experimentally increasing arousal on the two-flash threshold for normals and schizophrenics. The normals showed increased sensitivity (lower two-flash thresholds) with increasing arousal, but the schizophrenics' sensitivity decreased. Again, the data suggested that the patients may have been overaroused initially and that the additional arousal led to a reduced level of performance, as might be inferred from the Yerkes-Dodson law. Obviously, the relation between the two-flash threshold and psychopathology is not a simple one.

There are also several methodological reasons why those results must be considered tentative. First, the results were always based on correlations between the two-flash thresholds and other physiological measures; the groups of subjects themselves showed no significant differences in the threshold measures (Borinsky et al., 1973). Second, other investigators have failed to replicate the results (Hume and Claridge, 1965), and methodological studies of the two-flash threshold procedure (Pearson and Tong, 1968) showed it to be sensitive to numerous variables—such as age, sex, and method of measurement—that were not adequately controlled in the earlier patient studies. A potential problem with much of that early research is the inadequacy of the psychophysical methods used. Generally, the two-flash thresholds were obtained by using an abbreviated method of limits based on relatively few trials. This method does not separate the resolution sensitivity of the subjects from their response bias, and that failure may have contributed to an undermining of the entire area of research, as was the case of research using the critical-flicker-frequency technique with psychiatric patients.

In recent years interest in testing patients for critical-flicker-frequency differences has greatly diminished, largely because a series of studies (Clark, 1966; Clark et al., 1967) indicated that previous differences in critical-flicker-frequency threshold displayed by psychiatric subjects (Goldstone, 1955; McDonough, 1960) may actually have been response-bias differences and not sensory differences. When Clark and his colleagues (1967) used a forced-choice technique to measure the critical-flicker-frequency threshold (that procedure eliminates opportunities for response-bias contamination), the previously reported higher thresholds for patients (less temporal-resolving capacity) as compared with normals was eliminated. It was concluded that the previous critical-flicker-frequency studies were actually measuring only response-criterion differences and not differences in temporal resolution.

Two problems remain. One: Why not design studies to measure directly the response criterion of patients in order to begin to determine how they may differ? Perhaps different types of patients show systematic types of response bias; direct measurement of response bias may provide important correlates of psychopathology.

The second problem is that it is possible that the conclusion that there are no genuine differences in temporal resolution for psychiatric patients based on the work of Clark et al. (1967) was premature. Perhaps response-criterion differences are not the only factor accounting for patient-normal differences in critical-flicker frequency; numerous investigations using diverse measures of temporal resolution—critical-flicker frequency, two-flash threshold, temporal-order judgments—have concluded that there are large differences in temporal resolution for brain-damaged subjects (Swisher and Hirsh, 1972; Lackner and Teuber, 1973) and for normal subjects taking various psychotropic drugs (Smith and Misiak, 1976). To the extent that psychiatric illness is conceptualized in terms of central nervous system impairment or biochemical impairment, sensory-processing measures would be expected to reflect such dysfunctions. The researcher who originally brought into question the genuineness of the critical-flicker-frequency differences in patients (Clark, 1966) has suggested, on the basis of some unpublished data on psychiatric patients in a forced-choice experiment, that an unfortunate result of his studies may have been to lead people to throw out the baby with the bath water; with refined methods, resolution differences may still be obtained. In summary, the possibility remains that psychiatric patients display both temporal-resolution differences and response-bias or response-criterion differences.

Temporal integration. The concept of temporal integration refers to the way in which stimulus energy is processed in the period immediately after the presentation of the stimulus. Complete temporal integration is said to occur when the stimulus is very brief. Then all the presented stimulus energy is used in determining the response, regardless of how that energy is distributed in time—for example, two equal-energy stimuli, one stimulus brief and intense and the other stimulus longer but less intense, produce the same response because they have the same total energy. However, for longer duration stimuli there is a breakdown of that complete integration; for a given response not all the stimulus energy presented is processed by the organism. Temporal integration has several characteristics, each of which can be measured separately. It is a general concept that has been measured for numerous behavioral and physiological responses by using several different techniques and procedures. The brevity of the time constants of integration place the measure primarily in the sensory-processing domain, although under some conditions integration has been demonstrated for periods of time of up to several seconds.

For numerous reasons (Boynton, 1961), temporal integration is viewed not simply as a peripheral or receptor phenomenon. The fact that it can be demonstrated in several modalities with minor differences between modalities presents a strong argument that temporal integration is most correctly interpreted as reflecting central processing. Also, there may be an empirical relationship between temporal integration and temporal resolution. Piéron (1965), among others, suggested that possibility and even used the critical-flicker-frequency threshold, a resolution measure, to estimate the critical duration of temporal integration.

There have been relatively few temporal-integration studies of psychiatric patients, despite a long history of extensive physiological and behavioral integration research with both animals and humans dating back almost 100 years (Brown, 1965). Because of its basic nature, disorders of the central nervous system may be expected to reflect changes in the characteristics of temporal integration. Indeed, Wilson (1967) reported that subjects with postgeniculate brain lesions displayed changes in integration, but those with pregeniculate lesions displayed integration functions that did not differ from those of normal controls.

Two studies with psychiatric patients, one in audition and one in vision, reported similar results, despite the fact that they differed in modalities, in the energy levels of the stimuli tested, and in the use of different response measures. The auditory study used a verbal report (Babkoff et al., 1977) to measure the detection threshold, and the visual study used a simple reaction-time response (Collins et al., 1978) to estimate critical duration. The detection-threshold results of the audition study were described above in the discussion of detection thresholds. When the patients were grouped into factorially derived diagnostic categories of schizophrenic and affective disorders, two distinct auditory integration functions were obtained for them. For the stimulus durations tested, the integration function for the normal controls was what has been reported previously in audition for normals—a linear function relating changes in stimulus intensity and duration in order to maintain a constant threshold response. Specifically, an increase in the duration of the noise burst by 1 log unit (10 decibels) allowed a corresponding 0.8-log-unit decrease in the stimulus intensity. Patients with affective disorders displayed integration functions with greatly reduced slopes; for each log duration increase they showed a corresponding intensity reduction of only about 0.3 log intensity, suggesting that changes in those patients' processing of energy were much slower than in normals. The schizophrenics' integration functions were unique; for the two briefest stimuli, they displayed a steep integration function, steeper than for normals; but for their longest duration stimulus, the function became flat, indicating that they had reached critical duration and were no longer using the total energy of the stimulus. The functions for the normals and the patients with affective disorders at the longest duration continued to decrease, suggesting that integration was still occurring for them, even for the longest stimulus. Thus, in that auditory study, schizophrenics seemed to have the shortest critical duration.

The visual temporal-integration study (Collins et al., 1978) also reported that schizophrenics—especially those who clinically displayed speech disorganization, a dimension related to thought disorder—showed shorter critical durations than did other psychiatric patients and normal controls. In that study the stimuli were just above the threshold level, and the subjects lifted their fingers in a simple reaction-time response as quickly as possible when they saw a flash of light. Here again, as in the audition study, some schizophrenics showed shorter periods of complete integration. That result is opposite to what Wilson (1967) reported for his brain-damaged (postgeniculate lesioned) group.

The fact that two studies of temporal integration, done in separate laboratories in different countries with two different modalities, found similar results should encourage further follow-up research.

Perceptual studies. Finding relevant perceptual studies of psychiatric patients, especially processing studies, is not easy. Most of the perceptual studies with patients have not been replicated or were not distinctively concerned with measuring processing. For example, many perceptual studies of illusions and constancies have not been done in a way that allows for the measurement of processing. Other perceptual studies, such as those of spiral-figural aftereffects and kinesthetic aftereffects, are known to have methodological difficulties. Although studies of the relationship between perceptual performance, cognitive styles, and psychopathology are still of some interest (Schooler and Silverman, 1969), research in that area has clearly declined in recent years (Eriksen and Eriksen, 1972). Studies of subliminal perception and perceptual defense also have been severely challenged on methodological grounds (Goldiamond, 1958, 1962; Eriksen, 1960). However, in a theoretical article, Erdelyi (1974) defended the body of new-look research in perception on the grounds that the empirical evidence in the area is too incomplete to reach a final judgment about its validity. Instead, he argued that there is a need to approach the issues in an information-processing framework in order to do justice to the complex factors that may influence performance at all stages between the stimulus input and the response output.

The section on perception in the second edition of this textbook (Jenness et al., 1975) included relatively little material that was purely perceptual in nature and stressed sensory data instead. Other reviewers have done the same. For example, the chapter on abnormalities of sensory perception in the first edition of Eysenck's *Handbook of Abnormal Psychology* (Granger, 1961) was actually a chapter dealing primarily with sensory phenomena. In the second edition, Frith's (1973) chapter, published 12 years later, emphasized a cognitive approach to perception. As Frith (1973) pointed out, there has been "a recent movement in psychology to consider perception as a cognitive process." No doubt the movement is due—in part, at least—to the rapid development of information-processing research, with its heavily cognitive emphasis. Spivack (1963) noted a similar problem when he reviewed the area of perceptual processes with reference to mental deficiency. Regretfully, nowhere in the literature of psychopathology does one find a review of relevant perceptual materials similar to that undertaken by Teuber (1960) to describe basic perceptual phenomena and their relationship to neurological impairments.

Two research topics that can be considered as perceptual are reaction time and visual masking. Those topics illustrate the type of perceptual-processing research prevalent in the field today.

Reaction time. The time between the presentation of a stimulus and the subject's response to that stimulus is called reaction time. Simple reaction time is measured when the same single response is produced to a stimulus on each and every trial. Other types of reaction-time measures—such as one stimulus-multiple responses and multiple stimuli-one response—are called choice-reaction times and are interpreted as measuring different types of processing (Snodgrass, 1975) or different stages of processing (Taylor, 1976; Simon and Pouraghabagher, 1978).

Historically, the reaction-time technique was one of the earliest experimental procedures used in psychology, and the founders of experimental psychology, used the technique to "time mental events." In the past 20 years, with the growing interest in information processing, the reaction-time technique has undergone a renaissance. In fact, it has become a primary technique of measurement in the laboratory. A series of books entitled *Attention and Performance* (Requin, 1978) provided documentation of some of the innovative and pacesetting research developments in reaction-time measurement.

In the areas of sensory and perceptual processing, considerable knowledge exists about the reaction-time measure both empirically and theoretically (Nissen, 1977). Several sophisticated, quantified models of reaction-time behavior exist (McGill and Gibbon, 1965; Luce and Green, 1972; Teichner and Krebs, 1972), and those models relate to the nature of the changes occurring as simple stimulus manipulations are made. As a result, the effects of changing stimulus parameters can be predicted with considerable precision. Such baseline data are a valuable source of information against which to compare the reaction times of patient populations. Researchers who have conducted sensory-

perceptual reaction-time studies with psychiatric patients include, among others, Venables (1965, 1968) and King (1975).

Reaction-time studies of abnormal subjects are not concerned with actual skill in lifting the finger from the response key; it is assumed that all subjects are about equal in performing the motor act itself (Yates, 1973). Of interest are the changes in speed and accuracy of the response as indicators of central nervous system functioning. As a measure of the speed of processing, reaction-time studies of patient populations generally report that patients respond slower than do normals, but the exact reasons for the difference are not known. Since reaction times are known to change as a result of numerous factors, there are several possible reasons for the difference in the speed of reaction times of patients and normals (King, 1975).

In the area of experimental psychopathology, a special issue of the *Schizophrenia Bulletin* (Nuechterlein, 1977) was devoted entirely to reaction-time studies of schizophrenia. In that issue, major bodies of reaction-time literature were critically analyzed and defended by several investigators. One area was the work pioneered by Shakow and his colleagues (Shakow, 1963) having to do with reaction time as a measure of segmental set, an aspect of attention.

Steffy and his colleagues (Bellissimo and Steffy, 1972, 1975; Steffy and Galbraith, 1974) extended the work of Shakow and his investigations of the effects of preparatory interval manipulations on reaction time. Steffy's model provided an alternative interpretation of some of the earlier set reaction-time data and, in some instances, helped to clarify apparent inconsistencies among results across studies in which variations of the Shakow set paradigm were used.

Another area of reaction-time work mentioned in the Nuechterlein (1977) review was that of Sutton and Zubin and their colleagues having to do with cross-modality reaction time. Although that technique is also related to attentional components, it can be treated as a perceptual phenomenon, since it involves simple stimuli and simple reaction-time responses. A typical paradigm for the cross-modality reaction time is that the subject is told to respond on each and every trial to either of two stimuli—for example, a flash of light and a brief tone. The general finding of several cross-modal reaction-time studies with patients conducted in the past 2 decades is that schizophrenics show a significantly greater lengthening of simple reaction time than do controls when the stimulus in the preceding trial was in the different modality. That effect has been referred to as the cross-modal retardation or modality-shift effect.

Cross-modal retardation has been found in both acute schizophrenics (Spring, 1979) and chronic schizophrenics (Sutton et al., 1961) and in process and reactive schizophrenics (Sutton and Zubin, 1965). The modality-shift effect persists when patients and controls are informed what the forthcoming stimulus on each trial will be (Waldbaum et al., 1975; Spring, 1979); thus, it seems unlikely that an expectancy hypothesis can explain the cross-modality effect. Further, the modality-shift effect persists when patients and nonpatients are statistically equated on reaction-time speed by using an adaptation of the analysis of covariance method (Sutton and Zubin, 1965; Waldbaum et al., 1975). In addition, in three independent studies of drug-free schizophrenics, cross-modal-retardation effects were obtained (Sutton et al., 1961; Sutton and Zubin, 1965; Waldbaum et al., 1975). The results from a study using a nonschizophrenic psychiatric control group (Spring, 1979) suggested that the modality-shift effect is not unique to schizophrenics; patients with major affective disorders also displayed cross-modal retardation.

Visual masking. Visual masking is a complicated perceptual phenomenon that takes several forms and has been interpreted in various ways. Reviews of the extensive visual-masking literature describe some of the complexities (Kahneman, 1968; Turvey, 1973; Breitmeyer and Ganz, 1976). One stimulus paradigm to study masking is to present two brief stimuli separated by a short interval of darkness. One stimulus, the masking stimulus, may simply be a visual "noise" pattern; the other stimulus, the test stimulus, can be an identifiable word, letter, or geometric form. In one form of masking, both stimuli are presented successively to the same retinal region—that is, they overlap in space but are separated in time. If the two stimuli are presented close enough in time—say, 20 milliseconds apart the masking stimulus interferes with the perception of the test stimulus, and the subject cannot report its contents. As the interval between the light pulses is increased, the test stimulus gradually becomes visible and is reported with greater frequency or accuracy. Longer interpulse intervals produce less and less masking until masking is said to have ended.

Visual masking of that type has been investigated by Saccuzzo and his colleagues with schizophrenic patients. In their initial study, Saccuzzo et al. (1974) reported that, under masking conditions, normals and nonschizophrenic psychiatric patients did not differ in performance, but both of those groups showed less masking than did two schizophrenic groups, a group with delusional symptoms and a group without delusional symptoms.

In a follow-up study, Saccuzzo and Miller (1977) measured the critical interstimulus interval, the minimum interval between the presentation of a masking stimulus and the presentation of a test stimulus at which the masking stimulus no longer interferes with the processing of the test stimulus. The results indicated that a longer critical interstimulus interval was needed for the schizophrenics than for the other subjects. That finding is consistent with the interpretation of more masking for the schizophrenic patients—that is, more time between stimuli was needed to overcome the masking effect. Also, all subjects showed less masking with practice, but there were no differential practice effects between patients and normal controls.

Saccuzzo and Miller (1977) interpreted those differences in masking between schizophrenics and normals and nonschizophrenic patients as being due to a slowness in processing (encoding) the information from an iconic store (visual short-term memory). That slowness was assumed to affect both the quality and the quantity of the information reaching the higher brain centers. They also noted that the measurement of the speed of processing using the visual-masking technique gave different conclusions from those arrived at by other researchers on the speed of processing (Yates, 1966; Korboot and Yates, 1973; Korboot and Damiani, 1976). For example, the masking technique failed to differentiate between the different types of schizophrenics, something that the other processing studies had done. Perhaps, Saccuzzo and Miller (1977) suggested, masking measures an "earlier and more finely grained stage of processing" than was tested by Yates and Korboot. The notion apparently is that schizophrenic patient differences manifest themselves at a later stage of processing.

There are several similarities between the visual-masking procedure and the two-flash procedure described above in the discussion of temporal resolution. Both techniques involve successive inputs separated in time; even the durations of the interstimulus intervals are about the same, in the low millisecond range. The major difference in the procedure is that masking involves a configural stimulus—a patterned test stimulus—and thus is a perceptual task; but the two-flash-threshold technique simply involves an energy stimulus—flashes of light—and is, therefore, more sensory in nature. If patients were tested on both procedures, predictions of the performance from one technique to another might be possible.

Unfortunately, in evaluating the masking research with patients, one can also explain the results on the basis of the generalized-deficit hypothesis, since in those studies the schizophrenics always performed worse than did the normals and the other patients. As an initial approach to dealing with the problem, visual-masking studies using signal-detection or forced-choice techniques could be done. Then, at least, differences in d' (the signal-detection measure of sensitivity) would not be contaminated by response-criterion factors. However, the use of signal detection does not solve all problems; subjects who are not adequately motivated or who are not able to attend to the task

fully may simply obtain lower d' values. Of course, those patients may also display more variable data than do the normals.

RESEARCH STRATEGIES

Visual masking and reaction time can be examined in relation to two questions posed earlier about the "where" of processing: First, at what level of processing are the masking and reaction-time responses occurring? Second, what are the loci of those behavioral responses, and is there any evidence that they display hemispheric asymmetries of function? In both cases—the level of processing and the locus of processing—the fundamental interest is whether psychiatric patients characteristically differ from one another and from normals.

The levels and loci questions can be explored physiologically; then it would become a question of localizing where in the nervous system particularly significant activity is being displayed in connection with the behavior under investigation. Physiological correlates of measures of behavioral processing can be obtained. However, this section has focused largely on behavioral responses, but even those measures, used with certain techniques, can give rough answers to the question as to where between the stimulus and the response the crucial processing occurs.

Levels of processing. An important question to investigate experimentally for different measures of processing is the level at which the phenomenon under consideration is occurring. The general idea is to use methods or strategies that help localize a particular processing phenomenon as more or less peripheral or central. A lower level of processing refers to a peripheral stage; a higher level of processing is one that occurs more centrally in the nervous system.

At least two general strategies can be used in the attempt to ascertain the different levels of processing, and those strategies are illustrated here with reference to visual masking and reaction time: (1) procedural or methodological strategy and (2) theoretical strategy.

Visual masking. Methodologically, estimates of the level of processing for masking can be obtained by the use of selected stimulating conditions that are known to be associated with particular anatomical connections. For example, in vision, the use of dichoptic stimulation provides a behavioral way of estimating the level of processing. Dichoptic stimulation refers to the technique in which corresponding points of the retinas of both eyes are stimulated independently in such a way that each eye receives no input from the stimulus presented to the other eye. Independence can be obtained, for example, by separating the two stimulus fields with a partition. In visual masking, the test stimulus is presented to one eye, and the masking stimulus is presented to the other eye. The stimulation of the corresponding points is achieved by the use of prisms to fuse the fixation point of each independent, visual-stimulus field. The subject sees the two visual fields as a single, fused field.

The strategy in the dichoptic approach is to compare the results obtained by dichoptic stimulation with the results obtained by either monocular or binocular stimulation or both. If the visual effect under investigation—masking, for example—is the same for both the dichoptic and the monocular conditions, the interpretation is that the obtained effects are not peripheral; they must be occurring at least retrochiasmally. Why? Because the anatomy of dichoptic stimulation is such that interactions between the two eyes must occur beyond the chiasma, since there are no known anatomical connections directly across the retinas. Such an experimental outcome would mean that the phenomenon under investigation has to be occurring more centrally. However, if there are marked differences in the magnitude of visual masking produced by monocular and dichoptic stimulation, such results would lead to different interpretations about the level of processing. If the dichoptic condition shows little or no visual masking but the monocular condition shows a full-masking effect, then masking would seem to be largely a peripheral phenomenon. Thus, the use of selected stimulating conditions enables one to make interpretations about the level of processing.

To date, the visual-masking studies with patients have been conducted binocularly, and that condition does not allow conclusions about the level of processing. Future patient studies comparing binocular and dichoptic conditions could strengthen conclusions about Saccuzzo and Miller's (1977) interpretation that masking is measuring earlier processing. For example, dichoptic masking comparable in magnitude to binocular masking would argue against a more peripheral interpretation.

A theoretical approach to levels of processing was provided by Turvey (1973) with a theoretical model of visual-information processing that predicted different quantitative outcomes for visual masking, depending on whether the masking was primarily central or peripheral. The two distinct quantitative statements can be tested by the obtained data. Specifically, peripheral masking was described by the following relationship: Target stimulus energy *multiplied by* the minimal interstimulus interval necessary to escape masking (the critical interstimulus interval) is equal to a constant ($TE \times ISI = K$). In comparison, central masking was identified by this relation: Target stimulus duration *plus* the critical interstimulus interval equals a constant ($TD + ISI = K$). By determining which quantitative relation best fits the data, one can infer whether the visual masking is peripheral or central.

Walsh (1976) applied Turvey's (1973) backward dichoptic masking experimental paradigms to investigate the effect of the age of the subject on visual masking. His data supported the interpretation that older subjects are slower in processing than are younger ones. The data displayed the additive quantitative relationship, supporting the hypothesis that what he was investigating was central masking. Walsh (1976) pointed out that other investigators with apparently discrepant results may actually have been investigating peripheral masking, rather than central masking. His study illustrated the importance of considering distinctions between peripheral and central masking such as Turvey's in interpreting results. In that regard, as mentioned previously, it is not known if Saccuzzo and his co-workers (Saccuzzo et al., 1974; Saccuzzo and Miller, 1977) were, in their investigations of schizophrenia, studying peripheral masking or central masking. They interpreted their data as if they were peripheral, and it would be of interest to establish if, according to Turvey's model, the masking they obtained displayed the multiplicative relationship associated with peripheral masking. Those distinctions and the methodological and theoretical referents associated with them illustrate the potential power of information-processing research and provide a challenge to researchers in psychopathology to use as many of those refinements as possible in analyzing and interpreting their patient data.

Reaction time. A theoretical approach for investigating the question of the level of processing with reaction time was offered by Sternberg (1969) for normal subjects and was tested by Wishner et al. (1978) for psychiatric patients.

Sternberg's (1969) additive method assumed that the interval between the stimulus and the response can be depicted as a sequence of independent stages or events. Each stage receives an input from a previous stage, transforms that input, and passes it to the next stage. The total reaction time is simply a sum of those individual stages. As the reaction time is changed by experimental manipulation, the duration of one or more of the stages also changes. If two separate variables affect different stages, they should produce additive effects on the final reaction time. That outcome is reflected in the absence of statistical interactions between the experimental variables. By designing experiments in which interactions can be demonstrated, one can determine whether the experimental variables are affecting either the same or different stages of processing. If interactions are present, the same stages are influenced by the variables. If interactions are absent, different stages are influenced. The exact variables or procedures used can indicate whether the stages under consideration are more or less peripheral. For example, stimulus variables are considered more peripheral than are response variables.

Wishner et al. (1978) applied the Sternberg (1969) paradigm to schizophrenia. They reasoned that, if schizophrenics show an impairment in one or more processing stages, they should respond differently from normals to the manipulations affecting a particular stage. In other words, there should be an interaction between the subject variable (schizophrenics versus controls) and the variable specifying the manipulation that affects a particular stage. In the Sternberg task the subject was asked to remember a set of digits that served as target stimuli. Those digits were called the positive memory set. On each trial a single digit was presented, and the subject was required to respond in one way if the digit was part of the positive set and in a different way if it was not. The measure taken was reaction time. The parameters of the task were varied to place more or fewer demands on each processing stage. During the first stage, encoding, the subject formed a representation of the stimulus. That process took longer than usual if degraded stimuli were presented, so that reaction time was lengthened in the degraded condition relative to the intact condition. If schizophrenics suffered an impairment in data-driven encoding such that stimulus images were degraded to begin with or such that filtering based on physical stimulus properties was impaired, the reaction time for degraded images should be slowed for the patients disproportionately to the slowing shown by the normals. Thus, an interaction between subject group and the encoding-stage manipulation was predicted.

The second stage, serial comparison, involved the sequential comparison of the stimulus with each member of the memory set to see whether a target was present. That stage took longer as the number of items in the positive (target) set was increased. Serial comparison was particularly sensitive to divided-attention deficits, since processing was conceptually driven to search for a variety of different targets. The next stage, binary decision, should be particularly sensitive to pigeonholing difficulties. That stage took longer when the response was to the absence of a target (negative response) than when it was to the presence of a target (positive response). Difficulty in pigeonholing the match between a stimulus and a cognitive template for the target should be reflected by abnormalities of binary decision. The final stage, translation and response organization, was influenced by such variables as the relative frequency of the response. Interference between competing response tendencies has often been implicated in schizophrenia (Broen and Storms, 1967) and should be manifested by abnormalities in the final stage.

Wishner et al. (1978) reported the results of their own study of manipulating serial comparison, binary decision, and response organization. They also reported the results of a study by Chekosky of manipulating encoding, serial comparison, and binary decision. Neither study revealed a specific schizophrenic deficit at any processing stage. The reaction times of schizophrenics were lengthened to the same degree as were those of normals by manipulations affecting the processing demands at each stage. In all cases the reaction times of schizophrenics were simply slower than were those of normals. The data suggested that schizophrenics perform the operations at each stage in the same manner as do normals but require a longer time to complete each phase of processing.

In reaction-time research, it is also possible to introduce methodological strategies for evaluating the level of processing.

For example, Weiss (1965) and Botwinick and Thompson (1966) made a distinction between premotor time and motor time by measuring both the reaction time and the latency of the electromyographic response to the same stimulus. The time between the onset of the stimulus and the first noticeable change in the electromyographic record is the premotor time; that latency was interpreted as reflecting the central component of the over-all reaction time. The total reaction time minus the premotor time is the measure of the motor time, which was interpreted as the peripheral, output component of the total reaction time.

The results from the studies of those investigators strongly supported the notion that changes in total reaction time are primarily associated with changes in the premotor (central) component and that the motor component is not an important factor in evaluating reaction-time results. However, Schneider, in an unpublished report, suggested that for certain psychiatric subjects, such as those who are very anxious, the motor-time component may be of increasing magnitude, thereby accounting, at least in part, for the ubiquitous reaction-time slowing displayed by such patients.

Additional support for the contention that changes in reaction time as a function of increases in the intensity of the stimulus are largely due to central factors were provided by Rosenblith and Vidale (1962). They concluded, on the basis of data from several human and animal studies, that simple reaction time, even to sensory stimuli, reflects changes in the speed of central processing mechanisms (Nissen, 1977).

Loci of processing. In recent years there has been a renewed interest in the possibility of an asymmetry of function (a functional lateralization) for the two cerebral hemispheres. Currently, an extensive amount of research is underway in the field (Milner, 1975; Kinsbourne, 1978). Clinically, neurologically lesioned or commisurectomized (split-brain) patients have been investigated. The consensus of the evidence suggests that the left hemisphere is most specialized for analytic, sequential, and verbal processing and that the right hemisphere is specialized mainly for holistic, spatial, and nonverbal processing. For intact normal persons and patients without known neurological problems, such hemispheric specialization would be only relative, since, in those persons, excitations from stimuli project to both hemispheres, and both hemispheres are involved in the processing.

That strategy for establishing the locus of function involves many complexities; numerous organismic and experimental factors are known to modify, in varying degrees, the overly simplistic depiction of the asymmetry of functioning outlined above. The age, the sex, and the handedness of the subjects are a few of the important subject factors. Experimental factors of importance include the amount of practice given the subjects and the implicit interpretations the subjects give to the instructions provided them about how the experimental task should be done.

In behavioral studies of that type, the most frequently used techniques are, in audition, the dichotic listening procedure, which involves presenting separate messages to each ear, and, in vision, the brief presentation of visual stimuli to the right or the left of the fixation target. The visual apparatus usually used is called a tachistoscope, and the research strategy is based on the known anatomy of the visual system; stimuli presented to the right of the fixation stimulus (the right visual field) project directly to the left hemisphere, and stimuli presented to the left of the fixation stimulus (the left visual field) project directly to the right hemisphere. Combined with reaction-time measure-

ments, those hemifield presentations with the tachistoscope or its equivalent provide an excellent technique for the assessment of possible hemispheric differences in latency, frequency of report, and accuracy of discrimination.

Precise investigations of the relationship between functional brain asymmetries and psychopathology are comparatively recent, but several investigators (Gruzelier and Venables, 1975a; Flor-Henry, 1976) have described theoretical possibilities supported by some clinical data. The most frequent hypothesis is that schizophrenics display left-hemispheric impairment; a less-mentioned hypothesis is that the affective disorders reflect right-hemispheric impairment or dysfunction (Gruzelier and Flor-Henry, 1979). Clinically, those postulations seem reasonable, given the language-related disturbances seen in schizophrenia and the mood or affective disturbances characteristic of depressive disorders. Considerable physiological evidence and some behavioral evidence support the schizophrenic model (Shimkunas, 1978). And some developing evidence indicates that the right hemisphere is specialized for the processing of emotional or affective material, so its postulated relationship to the affective psychoses has a certain apparent validity. Recent data lend support to those interpretations (Bruder and Yozawitz, 1979; Yozawitz et al., 1979).

An overview of sensory-perceptual processing research shows that in that domain, with the possible exceptions of the topics of temporal resolution and reaction time, there has been no extensive or systematic exploration of processing and processes. Occasional positive results in a single study are either not replicated on being retested or are not explored further. Thus, it becomes essential for investigators to do research with well-defined measures of processing and to repeat studies to clarify and extend positive results. For example, research with patients in the area of hemispheric asymmetries is one topic worthy of further extensive investigation.

And what of the future? Clearly defined sensory-perceptual processing operations, combined with detailed and objective diagnostic material, would do much to improve the quality of the research. Research that directly measures response-bias differences in patients is badly needed. Under some circumstances, researchers should analyze their data for more than group differences; individual functions and reports of how many persons do or do not show the group trend are examples of other types of analyses. Several stimulus values should be tested, if possible, so that functions of the data can be generated and the mathematical techniques of functional analysis be applied. On the other hand, psychophysical researchers should recognize the need to develop or adapt procedures and strategies that enable most patients to be tested and to obtain a large enough patient sample so that results can have some generality. To combat the ever-present possibility that patients differ from normals only because of a generalized patient-deficit factor and not because of sensory-perceptual differences, researchers must design more experiments in which some patients are able to do "better" than the normal controls. As more facts are learned about processing and about the deviations or differences in processing displayed by patients, it should become possible to combat the generalized-deficit interpretation of differences.

Cognitive Domain

In the sensory and perceptual studies described above, the response required to an incoming stimulus occurred immediately after stimulus presentation. In the measures to be discussed here, a period of time elapses between the presentation of the stimulus and the response. Because more time is required for processing the stimulus, one can infer that processing progresses through a greater number of stages in cognitive responses.

Unlike sensory and perceptual processing, which depend only minimally on the organism's prior learning experience, cognitive processing is highly dependent on prior experience as it is encoded in stored memories. Cognitive processing can be described as involving a response to signal stimuli—stimuli to which prior learning has been attached—whose interpretation involves the retrieval of short-term and long-term memories.

One of the most important aspects of cognition is the thought process and its deviations. Disorders of thinking have been described for centuries in relation to a number of forms of psychopathology; indeed, thought disorder still serves as the hallmark of the most recalcitrant of the functional psychoses, schizophrenia. However, little persuasive experimental work has been done on abnormal cognitive functioning, particularly in psychosis, because of the inaccessible nature of cognition, the difficulties of working with the mentally ill, and the enormous and unstable range of signs and symptoms evinced in the various conditions and syndromes. Many examples of what has been claimed to be essential cognitive malfunctioning in schizophrenia, for example, have proved to be unreliable (that is, not always elicitable in a given patient), distinctive but not widely present among patients taken as groups (for example, echolalia), or overlapping with other diagnostic categories (like unusual word associations in neuroses and depressive disorders). In this domain, as in others, it has often proved to be impossible to separate cognitive malfunctioning from impaired motivation, the effects of treatment or management of patients, and the understandable inability of the patient to comprehend or engage fully in the experimental task. All those aspects, for example, present serious problems in experimental work with long-term chronic schizophrenics.

Cognitive behavior is characteristically refractory to explanation, unless the entire past history of the patient is taken into account. At the same time, the tremendously variegated manifestations of illness, even within one diagnostic category, reflect to a large degree inevitably different courses of illness. Those two considerations suggest that progress in the study of cognitive functioning in relation to psychopathology may depend largely on the provision of longitudinal and prospective studies.

This discussion deals only with schizophrenia and to a large extent follows the organization of relevant material by Broen (1968). Although cognitive performance is impaired in other disorders—for example, in anxiety neurosis and depression—that impairment seems to be less fundamental and less long lasting or, at least, more comprehensible in those other contexts.

Classical descriptions of cognitive behavior in schizophrenia are found, from different theoretical points of view, in Bleuler (1950) and Jaspers (1963) and in impressive detail in a psychoanalytic case history by Sechehaye (1951). Those and the clinical and quasiexperimental studies to date show that the most attention has been paid to difficulties in the schizophrenic's memory, his categorizing behavior, his simple word associations, and the quality of his speech in spontaneous connected discourse.

SHORT-TERM MEMORY

There are numerous measures of cognitive processing, some of them highly complex. All the more sophisticated measures of cognition require short-term memory processing. Short-term memory is measured by processing tasks in which the response occurs in a matter of minutes after the stimulus is presented. Measures of long-term memory, in which responses are required hours or days after stimulus presentation, are not discussed here. However, that distinction does not mean that short-term memory and long-term memory entail different processes or that processing in short-term memory is carried out independently of the influence of events in long-term store.

The study of memory is one of the oldest areas in psychopathology. Aside from organic psychoses, dementia, and Korsakoff cases, memory functioning in mental patients has not been generally faulted, although a variety of categories for classifying memory deficits have been proposed. Especially noteworthy in that connection are the alleged effects of electroconvulsive therapy and tranquilizers. But even in electroconvulsive therapy, the alterations in memory were generally found to be transient (Zubin, 1948; Janis, 1950 a, b, c).

Short-term memory in normal persons. Until 10 years ago, models of human memory emphasized the existence of several storage systems, sometimes called sensory memory, short-term memory, and long-term memory. Sensory memory has already been described as a sensory-perceptual phenomenon, rather than a cognitive one. Sensory store operates to preserve an image of the stimulus for several hundred milliseconds—long enough to permit the encoding of its meaningful components. The output of that encoding process is preserved in short-term store. At least for verbal materials, regardless of whether they are presented visually or in spoken form, stimuli are encoded primarily in terms of their acoustical properties in short-term memory. Some limited amount of semantic information from the stimulus also seems to be contained in short-term memory (Shulman, 1972). A particular processing operation, rehearsal, is performed on material in short-term memory and is related to the limited storage capacity of that system. Rehearsal is a kind of inner speech that occurs serially, one item at a time, and slowly, at a rate of three to six items a second (Norman, 1976). Many theories of schizophrenic deficit predict that a consequence of slowed processing is an overload of short-term memory because only a limited number of items can be rehearsed at one time. Rehearsal seems to serve two functions. The first is to maintain information in short-term storage by essentially re-presenting it. Material that is not rehearsed simply decays from storage and is lost. The second function of rehearsal is to help transfer information from short-term memory to long-term memory. That is essentially the model of memory proposed by Waugh and Norman (1965).

In recent years, models of memory have changed dramatically and no longer postulate separate memory stores. The new models point out that the characteristics of memory for an item depend on the way it has been rehearsed, how it has been encoded, and how much processing it has received. That formulation is a depth-of-processing approach and has been articulated most clearly by Craik and Lockhart (1972). Although at least one author (Baddeley, 1978) has suggested that the depth-of-processing approach is not fruitful, it is the model of memory in widest use today. As stimuli undergo the sequence of processing stages, they are encoded and represented in different ways. At early sensory stages, stimuli are encoded in terms of images of physical features. Those types of encodings display the retention characteristics associated with sensory memory. That is, they can be preserved only briefly. At intermediate stages, stimuli are represented through matching or pattern recognition with familiar templates—for example, words are remembered as acoustic patterns. Such representations display the degree and the duration of retention associated with short-term memory. At later stages of analysis, memory templates are modified, enriched, and reorganized on the basis of semantic associations and abstractions from past experience. Those traces persist longest and display properties associated with long-term memory.

Greater depth of processing implies that more semantic and cognitive analyses have been used to encode stimuli. Stimuli that have received the greatest depths of processing are encoded and organized most efficiently and persist longest. In sum, stimuli that are structured and encoded in terms of deep, cognitively enriched traces are remembered longest. But how does that structuring occur? Craik and Lockhart (1972) postulated that there are two types of processing or rehearsal operations. Type I processing involves maintenance rehearsal, which recirculates stimuli at a given level of encoding without reorganizing them. Maintenance rehearsal simply maintains stimuli in conscious awareness and affords effective temporary storage but does not lead to long-term storage of the input. Thus, contrary to the Waugh and Norman (1965) model, rote rehearsal in the absence of deeper semantic processing and reorganization of the input, does not facilitate long-term memory. Type II processing elaborates the input in terms of meaningful cognitive associations and does facilitate long-term persistence of the memory trace.

In examining short-term memory, therefore, one is concerned with two rather different sets of operations. First, one is concerned with the encoding operations performed on the memory test stimuli, a process clinicians refer to as registration. If stimuli are not encoded or are not encoded deeply enough, their traces may decay before the memory test is administered. Second, one is concerned with retrieval operations governing the manner in which the memory trace is relocated and brought to consciousness.

Memory deviations in psychiatric patients. With those distinctions in mind, one can pose several different questions about the short-term memory of psychiatric populations: (1) Do patients have normal mnemonic structures to organize the encoding of stimuli? (2) Do patients generally use normal mnemonic organization when given a memory task? (3) Can patients be induced to use normal encoding strategies if they do not generally do so? (4) If normal encoding can be induced, does deeper encoding facilitate recall in the same manner for patients as for normals?

Before reviewing the relevant literature for schizophrenia, one must distinguish between the retrieval processes used in recognition and those used in recall memory. Recognition memory entails data-driven processing, in which a memory test item initiates the attempt to identify a matching template in memory. That process is one elsewhere described as pigeonholing. It essentially involves pattern recognition and a decision about whether two patterns—one a stimulus, the other a memory trace—are identical. The matching process can be performed accurately when stimuli are encoded at a fairly shallow depth in terms of physical features or acoustic properties. Thus, factors enhancing the discriminability—for example, the imagery-inducing value—of memory items also enhance recognition memory. Recall memory, by contrast, requires conceptually driven processing to initiate a search for some class of templates in memory. An active search requiring conscious, strategic efforts must be initiated by the person. The search operates most efficiently if memory items have been encoded efficiently and deeply into meaningful cognitive categories.

One self-evident observation is that recall is much more difficult than recognition. Recall, as compared with recognition, makes much more extensive demands on the voluntary execution of controlled processing activities and, accordingly, more greatly taxes the person's motivation and processing capacities. In studies that endeavor to compare the recognition and recall performances of patients and normals, it is particularly important to match both memory tasks on difficulty for normals. If the performance of patient groups is different on the two tasks, that difference can be attributed to psychopathology and not to any irrelevant factor, such as lack of interest or motivation. Unfortunately, that matching has not been done. Bauman and Murray (1968), Traupman (1975), and Koh and

Peterson (1978) all reported that schizophrenics displayed recall but not recognition deficits relative to normal controls. Traupman found that process schizophrenics but not reactive schizophrenics also displayed impairments in recognition. On the basis of those findings, it has been proposed that most schizophrenics display deficits in search or retrieval but not in pigeonholing or decision. Process schizophrenics are hypothesized to suffer an input dysfunction that impairs organized encoding. An alternative hypothesis is that process schizophrenics suffer generalized deficits reflected on any task. Nonprocess schizophrenics suffer less severe generalized deficits that are revealed on more difficult or more discriminating tasks.

Although the authors have proposed that recognition memory depends primarily on data-driven processing, certain attitudinal factors may affect recognition performance. In one experiment with electroconvulsive therapy, Zubin (1948) compared preshock and postshock recognition for newly learned meaningless material. At first, patients showed much poorer recognition in postshock periods than in preshock periods. Since those patients served as their own controls, that difference could not be explained by recourse to individual differences in age, sex, and prior learning. In searching for an explanation of why the retention was poorer postshock than preshock, Zubin scrutinized the postshock performance and noted a new phenomenon. The patients seemed to be much more uncertain and tentative in the recognition task after the shock than before the shock, and some of them verbalized that hesitation by disclaiming ever having seen or learned the material before. To circumvent that *jamais vu* phenomenon, Zubin urged the patients to guess, even if they felt that the material was brand new. The rate of recognition then went up considerably and approximated the preshock rate, indicating that the reluctance of the patients to try to recognize the material or their uncertainty stood in their way. That experiment was done in the early 1940's, before the signal-detection theory became popular. Today one would recognize the difference between preshock and postshock test results as due to a criterion difference, rather than to a sensitivity difference.

The first question above was: Do patients have normal mnemonic structures? Weingartner et al. (1980) investigated that question by asking patients to categorize stimuli in word lists to determine whether patients could organize stimuli in a manner that would facilitate recall. For word lists devised for easy sorting into categories, schizophrenics sorted stimuli into the same number and types of categories as did normals. For random, unrelated words, schizophrenics imposed less structure of organization on the list than did normals. Normals grouped the list into approximately three categories, whereas schizophrenics formed more than eight categories. Those data suggest that schizophrenics can perform the necessary deep, cognitive analyses that encode material for long persistence in memory; however, they tend to perform such organization not on their own initiative but only when stimuli readily suggest the organization. Since tasks requiring subjects to actively impose an organization on memory stimuli generally facilitate deep processing, that lack of initiative may lead to an impairment in schizophrenic long-term memory.

The next question was: Do patients use normal mnemonic organization when given a memory task? The answer to that question seems to be that schizophrenics do to some degree, particularly when the organization is inherent in the stimuli. Nidorf (1964), Truscott (1970), and Bauman (1971) found that schizophrenic recall improved when memory lists provided an easy organization, and the schizophrenics' degree of improvement in recall with increasing list organization was only slightly less than that shown by normals, confirming the expectation based on Weingartner et al. (1980). Traupman (1975) found that reactive schizophrenics but not process schizophrenics profited from increases in the degree of interitem association (categorization) of memory lists. However, Weingartner et al. (1980) found that, whereas normals recalled many more words from categorized than from random lists, schizophrenics remembered similar numbers from both lists.

It is important to ask whether the structure inherent in the memory list is preserved in the subject's own structuring of recall. Traupman (1975) found that the degree of intertrial repetition, an index of clustering or categorization of items in recall, was greatest for normals, smaller for reactive schizophrenics, and smallest for process schizophrenics. Weingartner et al. (1980) found no difference in the degree to which schizophrenics and normals recalled items in sequential or clustered order. However, their data also suggested an important drawback for schizophrenics who attempt to organize recall by clustering. Schizophrenics displayed more than the normal number of intrusion errors, recalling nonlist words in the same superordinate categories as list words. That observation suggests that, even when schizophrenics impose sufficient organization to deeply process the memory list, the usual recall advantage observed with deep processing may be lost. That loss seems to be due to the phenomenon described as loosening of associations—the fact that the likelihood of response is increased by generalization to the entire class of semantic associates for the encoded stimulus, rather than simply to the target stimulus. Although the pigeonholing process or match between a list item and a memory template may be intact for stimuli encoded at fairly shallow depth, pigeonholing may be more problematic for stimuli encoded at a greater depth. Chapman and Chapman (1973) demonstrated that schizophrenics experience difficulty in discriminating identical stimuli from associated stimuli when matching is done on the basis of semantic features.

Can patients be induced to use normal encoding strategies, and does deeper encoding facilitate recall in the same manner for patients as for normals? Koh and Peterson (1978) reasoned that, if schizophrenic recall difficulties reflect problems in encoding stimuli at sufficient depth to permit retrieval, then recall difficulties may be overcome by inducing subjects to perform deeper, semantic encoding of stimuli during input. In a task preceding the memory test, Koh and Peterson induced subjects to process list words at different depths of encoding. Subjects were asked questions about words to induce graphemic processing (questions about word letters), phonemic processing (questions about rhyme words), semantic-conceptual processing (questions about synonyms), or semantic-propositional processing (using the word in a sentence). A surprise memory test was then administered. In a separate study, subjects were forewarned of the memory test and asked to produce their own memory test words in response to similar questions inducing different depths of processing. Schizophrenic recognition for presented words was not inferior to normal recognition and was improved by greater depth of processing in the same manner as was normal recognition. Contrary to previous findings (Koh et al., 1976) that the schizophrenic recall deficit was overcome by inducing subjects to semantically process target words, the study found an over-all deficit in schizophrenic recall for presented words. However, on closer inspection, the recall deficit was evident only for words that had been processed at the rhyme level and not for words processed at the semantic level. For schizophrenics, encoding for rhyme may be particularly likely to induce competition among clang associates during recall. Induced semantic processing does, therefore, overcome the schizophrenic recall deficit. Moreover, the different depths of processing seemed to operate in the same manner for schizophrenics and for normals. As processing became deeper, memory was enhanced at the same rate for both groups. However, self-generation of semantic processing by producing memory words did not overcome the schizophrenic recall deficit.

Weingartner et al. (1980) proposed that schizophrenics' mnemonic processing may be impaired on tasks requiring them to use conscious strategic efforts to organize the task. In other words, although schizophrenics may be perfectly able to use mnemonic organization, they have difficulty in generating the effort to do so. Already noted was the fact that recall requires greater self-generated organizational efforts than does recognition and is correspondingly more impaired in schizophrenics than is recognition. A list of random words requires more effort to organize than does a list of categorized words, and Weingartner et al. (1980) showed that schizophrenics impose less organization on random word lists than on categorized word lists. Intentional recall of self-generated words requires greater strategic processing effort than does incidental recall of presented words, and schizophrenic performance suffers accordingly.

The observation that schizophrenic short-term memory seems to be most impaired on tasks requiring self-generated processing efforts is problematic. Such effortful tasks are likely to be more difficult than control tasks, even for normals. Unless the various kinds of memory tasks—recognition versus recall, categorized versus uncategorized lists, experimenter-presented words versus subject-generated words, semantic processing versus processing of physical features—are matched for their discriminating power with normals, the Chapman strategy, one can only conclude that schizophrenic deviations on more effortful tasks may reflect generalized deficits. In addition, general slowness of processing may be particularly likely to yield defects on more effortful, conceptually driven tasks. Schizophrenics take longer to complete any processing operation than do normals, and, if they are deprived of time, they may not be able to demonstrate their capacities, particularly on tasks that require the longest processing time, even in normals. Koh and Peterson (1978) found that the time taken to answer questions requiring greater depth of processing increased proportionately for schizophrenics and normals and did not differ significantly between the groups for presented words. However, for self-generated words, schizophrenics required significantly longer time than did normals to complete each level of processing operations. Since the recall task in that study was time limited, it is possible that schizophrenics were simply not given enough time to complete their retrieval operations.

LANGUAGE AND COGNITION

Categorizing and conceptual behavior. According to Whitehead (1925), abstraction has two general meanings. In one sense it refers to the analysis of actual objects, events, and relations into attributes, like redness or sphericity. That he called "abstraction from actuality." He suggested the expression "abstraction from possibility" for the process by which an abstractive hierarchy is erected from attributes by a consideration of possible relations among attributes. Abstraction from possibility is the recognized method for extracting implications from assumptions, as in logic, law, philosophy, and mathematics. Whitehead (1925) pointed out:

Simple eternal [universal] objects represent the extreme of abstraction from an actual occasion, whereas [they] represent the minimum of abstraction from the realm of possibility. It will, I think, be found that, when a high degree of abstraction is spoken of, abstraction from the realm of possibility is what is usually meant—in other words, an elaborate logical construction.

Many schizophrenics can evolve rather elaborate logical constructs (abstractions from possibility) but fail on conceptual tests because they are unpredictable in abstraction from actuality, often defining category boundaries in an unusual fashion or selecting an incidental attribute, rather than a commonly recognized property, as a basis for classification. In that respect, their behavior shows high eccentricity but not necessarily low abstract ability.

In an experiment by Chapman and Taylor (1957), schizophrenics were asked to sort cards bearing the names of fruits, vegetables, and birds. The correct category, as established by the first card shown to the patient by the experimenter, was fruits—that is, fruits were to be separated from vegetables and birds, which together made up the complementary category. The patients sorted fruits into the experimentally designated category but also included vegetables—though not birds—to a far greater extent than did normal subjects. Thus, the schizophrenics were overinclusive in their categorizing but in a manner that showed that they were responding to commonalities across stimulus classes (fruits, vegetables) that are conceptually and culturally of high probability but in that case irrelevant. In a second part of the experiment, schizophrenics were given the same cards and asked to sort edibles together—that is, to include fruits and vegetables in the same category and to exclude birds. The first trial, performed by the experimenter, showed only a fruit being so categorized, thus potentially biasing the patients' performance toward including only some edibles, falsely excluding vegetables; but the schizophrenics performed about as well as did normal subjects.

The experiment showed several important aspects of schizophrenic conceptual behavior. First, it showed the patients' conceptual ability to be adequate under certain nontrivial conditions, and it showed their ability to think abstractly. The second task, with its basis in edibility, was at least as demanding in that regard as was the first task. Second, it showed the often-noted tendency of schizophrenics toward a loosening of conceptual boundaries and toward overinclusion. The results were evidence for the overinclusive pattern, first offered by Cameron (1938) as typical of schizophrenics, rather than the corresponding claim for overexclusion, put forth by Goldstein (1939), who suggested that schizophrenics, like brain-damaged patients, are stimulus bound, rigid, and overconcrete in their thinking. Most experimental evidence in schizophrenia argues against the notion of concreteness; as for the issues of inclusive-exclusive, a number of authors (Broen, 1968; Chapman and Chapman, 1973) have pointed out that the issue depends on the content of the negative category or categories and the kind of linguistically or culturally mediated response interference—that is, logical equivalence or similarity of attributes—created in the experiment, as well as on recent life experience. The experiment also showed errors that were far from random, either in the sense of being sporadic in a given subject or in the sense of being uninterpretable. However, schizophrenics do vary in their propensity toward overinclusion, and it appears that the behavior is most typical of acute, reactive, early schizophrenics. Chronic schizophrenics generally appear normal, narrow focused, and underinclusive on tasks like those. But it is difficult to separate conceptual from motivational factors or those involving task comprehension (Payne, 1962).

What is the likely basis for the kind of overresponsiveness, response interference, loosening of conceptual boundaries, or the like that may be demonstrated here? Bleuler (1950) suggested that in schizophrenia the psychic functions are split or fragmented, that associations are loosened in their stability and influence, and that thinking becomes unguided. Loss of total context means an interference with the proper selection of appropriate associations from all existing or potential associations. In general, Bleuler's theory and the work of his followers are in accord with finding errors of schizophrenics to be associative errors and with the idea that schizophrenics as a group and as individuals are more variable than are normal subjects. It focuses, that is, on response disorganization and the loosening of boundaries. Cameron's (1938) somewhat similar theory, which particularly stressed social disarticulation, predicted that conceptual looseness is most noticeable with socially toned or socially experienced tasks and materials. There is much evidence that that is so but no proof that only socially governed experience is most susceptible. Neither theory, however, suggested why particular patterns of associative error, such as overinclusion, should occur.

Chapman and Chapman's (1965) more recent theory emphasized the predictability as to the content or form of schizophrenic errors, which amounts to saying that, far from all associations being haphazardly weakened, some are relatively strengthened. Their view was that schizophrenic errors are an exaggeration of normal association biases and, in particular, reflect or are mediated by the dominant meaning at the expense of subordinate but contextually more appropriate meanings. Chapman and Chapman's theory was, thus, a semantic one, and most evidence for it comes from experiments with verbal materials. However, the importance of words as mediators and the close relation in conceptual behavior between habit-family hierarchies and meaning or verbal-association hierarchies offer a potentially rich field of application for the theory.

The hypothesis of dominant-meaning responses as an interpretation of observed schizophrenic errors in language and language-mediated behavior is a difficult notion to specify. It does not refer to statistically most-probable word associates or verbal responses; if it did, schizophrenic behavior would be described as statistically predictable or even stereotyped, which it is not. The notion has to encompass overdetermined or formulaic responses (black: white; father: son: Holy Ghost), responses that are easily available but too loose or at too high a level of superordination for the situation (a bicycle is the same as an airplane because one can go places on both of them). That is the sense that best accommodates the evidence of overinclusion studies—for example, the semantic compound "fruits and vegetables" predominating over the narrower category; meaning responses that reflect, quite dramatically, the special mental experience of the subjects involved (obsessions, distortions, *idées fixes*). The suggestive power of the theory can best be put negatively: The associative hierarchies or lattices of normals' and schizophrenics' meaning responses are substantially the same, but normal persons, unlike schizophrenics, take into account the total context. Thus, normal persons are able to bypass the dominant (most probable or most readily available) response or mediator and use the weaker but more appropriate one; they are able to assess the necessary level of generality or abstraction more appropriately than do schizophrenics, to separate personal or situation-bound meanings from those in the common cultural realm.

Chapman and Chapman's (1965) theory seems to account for a number of observed behaviors—for example, schizophrenics' tendency to call similar things identical or synonymous, overlooking fine distinctions or shades of meaning; to fail to understand the difference between literal and metaphorical meanings; to fail to comprehend puns or other verbally ambiguous material; and to make antonym substitutions ("hot" for "cold"; each is a highly probable covert-meaning response for the other, but only in some circumstances is one a suitable replacement for the other. The theory can correctly predict both overinclusion (grouping things together inappropriately when the dominant meanings are the same) and overexclusion. In the case of overexclusion, when the basis for inclusion is mediated by a relatively weak meaning response, it is not so classified. For example, in a study by Chapman and Chapman (1973) that required things with heads to be grouped together, schizophrenics, apparently attending to animate meaning responses predominantly, failed to include pins, hammers, and so on. The weakness of the theory seems to be the difficulty of reliably specifying dominant or weak meaning responses in specific contexts. Also, the theory fails to deal with the greater variability across and within schizophrenic subjects than in normal persons.

Other modern theorists, like Broen and Storms (1967), have offered explanations of schizophrenics' classificatory behavior that emphasized not the effect of dominant response tendencies but the complement—the heightening of interfering or incompatible response tendencies. Both types of theory assumed an ordered response hierarchy that is essentially the same in both normal subjects and schizophrenics. However, Broen and Storms proposed a partial collapse of such hierarchies, thus raising the probability of alternative or competing responses, which in normal people would be improbable or elicited only after the more probable responses had been rejected. Thus, schizophrenic behavior takes on its particular wayward character. Although that theory seems not much progress on Bleuler's (1950) original formulation, especially in predicting the patterning of schizophrenic behavior, it does handle more readily than the Chapman and Chapman theory the improbable and vacillating aspects of that behavior. Also, there is evidence from learning-theory experiments and comparable studies in psychopathology that, under conditions of high drive, such as anxiety, ordinarily low-probability responses are raised toward or above threshold. Extrapolations to schizophrenics' behavior, involving the notions of abnormally wide perceptual scanning (overinclusiveness?) or the altering of relative response strength, have been made by Silverman (1969) and Mednick (1958), respectively, although in both cases, as with most hypotheses in experimental psychopathology, the evidence is by no means consistent.

Word association. As stated above, idiosyncratic word associations are among the most striking and most noted aspects of schizophrenic behavior. Systematic studies over many years have demonstrated that, compared with responses in normal persons, schizophrenics' responses in word association tests are unusual (but not meaningless) and variable from test to test in the same subject and in schizophrenics taken as groups compared with normal groups. Their clinical value aside, those phenomena by themselves are of little more than descriptive interest until they are related to theoretical models, such as those dealing with categorizing and concept usage—both of which take such phenomena into account in one way or another—or until they are related to a broader behavioral context. Such a context is provided by the connected speech of schizophrenics, in which it has long been noted that seemingly unnatural verbal associations and intrusions break into the progress of directed discourse.

Schizophrenic speech. The disordered speech of schizophrenics is unmistakable yet elusive. Transcribed samples of such speech—and by no means the most bizarre examples—can be reliably identified as seriously abnormal by university students. Yet schizophrenic speech is not frequent; many patients rarely or never show disordered speech, and those who do by no means do so in all their utterances but only in connection with certain situations or topics, often those that are emotionally toned. The most dramatic and oft-recorded forms of schizophrenic speech—such as echolalia and word salad and, for that matter, muteness—are rare in modern times; in view of the ease with which particular speech patterns can be operantly conditioned in psychotics and normals, one can reasonably suspect that those forms owe much to special circumstances, including the interest and the attention historically paid to such speech by others.

Salzinger (1973; Salzinger et al., 1978) and others have reviewed the objective characteristics of schizophrenic speech emitted in situations approximating sustained natural discourse—interviews, monologues, unstructured interpersonal colloquy. Schizophrenic speech is repetitious, frequently interrupted—that is, nonfluent—occasionally studded with neologisms, somewhat impoverished in breadth of vocabulary, and, in general, less comprehensible than the speech of normal persons. For example, schizophrenic speech, compared with normal speech, is less accurately reconstructed by judges presented with speech samples with every n^{th} word deleted. Neologisms aside, those characteristics are not sufficient to define the peculiar quality of schizophrenic speech; much normal speech, if analyzed objectively, is nonfluent, repetitious, lexically constrained, and barely understandable. The basic discriminating aspect of schizophrenic speech that observers report—that is, the basis on which judges identify such speech as that of psychotics—is its communicatively and culturally unusual referential range. What is odd about schizophrenic speech is not how it is produced but what it is about.

Brown (1973), in considering the matter, went so far as to suggest that there is nothing wrong with schizophrenic speech, only with schizophrenic thinking. He said that schizophrenic speech is recognizable as such because the speaker says things that others in the language community know cannot be true, even metaphorically or hypothetically, and that in such speech others recognize a profound failure of reality testing and knowledge of the world. The overriding difficulty seems to lie in the semantic realm, dealing with the meaning and content, but one must not ignore the stable structural aspects of the speech itself. For example, schizophrenic speech is said, above all, to be tangential, and that characteristic is objectively verifiable. Sentences emitted by schizophrenics are referentially less well knit than are those of normal people. Schizophrenics begin dealing with one subject matter but never do quite deal with it, and they end dealing with another one entirely. The facts that their speech is sequentially unpredictable,

relative to normal speech, and that the dependency from speech unit to unit seems to be lessened suggest that some of the factors discussed earlier—intrusions, loosening of conceptual boundaries, interference of competing responses or mediating tendencies, overinfluence of dominant meaning responses—can fruitfully be brought to bear on even so presumptively complex a matter as schizophrenic speech. Speech, after all, is an important class of human behavior, needs no special instruction to perform, is fairly easily recorded and analyzed, and can be elicited in a wide range of natural settings. For further experimentation on cognitive processes in schizophrenia, it is perhaps the behavior of choice.

Schizophrenic language. Language was defined by Carroll (1953) as

a structured system of arbitrary vocal sounds and sequences which is used or can be used, in interpersonal communication by an aggregation of human beings, and which rather exhaustively catalogs the things, events, and processes in the human environment.

Schizophrenic language seems to suffer in regard to two aspects of that definition: (1) arbitrary vocal sounds and (2) interpersonal communication. The arbitrariness of the relationship between sounds and their referents requires that those relationships be learned through social interaction with the things, events, and processes in the human environment, a requirement in which the schizophrenic seems to fail. Furthermore, the very arbitrariness of the relationship often focuses too much attention on the sound itself in the schizophrenic, leading to echolalia, clang associations, and garbled speech. Furthermore, the tendency for schizophrenics to have less interpersonal communication than do normals also militates against the development and maintenance of communicative ability. Because language is such a natural type of behavior, it is easy to use it as a means of detecting schizophrenia, and for that reason it has become an important field of investigation. However, the earlier work in language was directed at intrapsychic processes—thinking and association—and only recently has the focus shifted to its interpersonal, social, and communicative aspects (Ostwald, 1978).

Deviations in language observed in the mentally ill are rather gross and reflect some of the overt spontaneous natural history of deviant behavior observed freely in uncontrolled fashion in the mentally ill. Just what goes wrong in a given instance, what is the contingency in which the deviation occurs, and just where in the process of cognitive behavior the deviations spring up are unknown.

It is not sufficient to indicate that schizophrenic language is noncommunicative or that it suffers from thought disorder. To arrive at a satisfactory knowledge of what is wrong with schizophrenic language, one must approach it systematically and discover the specific stage in processing that upsets the integration or balance of language.

Deviations in the communicability of speech. One of the most striking characteristics of schizophrenic behavior is the fact that conversation with schizophrenics is often very difficult. In extreme cases the lack of clarity in schizophrenic speech is regarded as pathognomonic (Jaspers, 1963). Just what goes wrong in such conversations is often difficult to analyze, but it has become generally recognized that it is a disturbance not in language itself but in its communicability to the listener. It is as if the schizophrenic did not take into consideration the immediate needs of the listener (Rochester, 1978). That difficulty in communicability has a variety of sources, and one of them is that the listener often finds the referents in the schizophrenic's conversation elusive—that is, when the schizophrenic refers to an object or event, it is not always clear to the listener which event or object is being referred to. Although that is not the only difficulty that characterizes schizphrenics' conversation, it is, according to Cohen (1978), a major problem and may explain much of the misunderstanding experienced in conversation with schizophrenics.

Cohen (1978) suggested that there are two possible sources for the disorder in referent communication: (1) disorders in the speaker's repertoire of associations to meanings or descriptions of a referent and (2) disorders in the selection mechanism through which the speaker edits out contextually inappropriate (cryptic, ambiguous, or misleading) responses before they intrude into overt speech. There is still a third possibility: The schizophrenic speaker fails to heed the listener's immediate needs insofar as the referents he refers to remain obscure.

To test out which of those possibilities explain the actual behavior of the schizophrenic, Cohen (1978) applied the following basic experimental paradigm: (1) An explicit set of stimulus objects—the display— was presented to a subject (the speaker). (2) The speaker was instructed to provide a verbal description of one of the objects (referent) in the display in such a manner that (3) the listener, given the verbal description, was able to pick the correct referent out of the display.

The purpose of such an investigation was not merely to demonstrate the poorer communicability of the schizophrenic utterances but to determine just where in the communicative process the deviation occurs. If it could be demonstrated that, up to a certain point in the communication act, the process was quite similar to the way the normal person proceeds, one could conclude that, at least up to that point, the schizophrenic's motivation and interest was not lagging and that the subsequent verbal behavior was probably not attributable to the generalized lack of motivation and interest that usually characterizes schizophrenia.

The first question that needed to be answered was whether the deviation in the communication act was the result of some disturbance in the schizophrenic's repertoire of words, concepts, and associations. To test that hypothesis, Cohen (1978) asked the schizophrenics to listen to a normal speaker's performance of the task. The schizophrenics were able to select the correct referent, indicating that they comprehended the speaker's communication and that they, therefore, possessed the required repertoire of words, concepts, and associations necessary to carry out the task. It was only when a schizophrenic served as the speaker that he failed to communicate the referent appropriately.

In an attempt to discover why the schizophrenic was unable to communicate appropriately, Cohen (1978) hypothesized that there was a failure in editing the variety of utterances that were sampled from the repertoire of possible available utterances. That failure may have been due to either a neglect to consider the nonreferents from which the referent was to be discriminated, thus leading to an impulsive response, or a difficulty in dismissing an inappropriate utterance—that is, a perseverative difficulty.

To discriminate between the impulsive hypothesis and the perseverative hypothesis, Cohen et al. (1974) conducted the following experiment. After demonstrating that, when the two referents in the display are readily distinguishable objects, schizophrenics perform as well as normals in the role of speaker, the researchers considerably reduced the discriminability of the two objects in the display so as to make the task of communicating the cue for identifying the correct referent more difficult. That was done by using Munsell color disks that were quite similar on the scale of hues.

Under those conditions both patients and normals showed increases in the latency of the response and in length of utterance. Cohen et al. (1974) proposed the hypothesis that there are two stages to the process: (1) the sampling stage, in which the repertoire of possible descriptions of the referents is sampled, and (2) the editing stage, in which the appropriateness of the selected sample is examined, the inappropriate response is rejected, and further sampling of other possible responses follows. It became clear from the experiment that it was in the editing

stage that the schizophrenic's difficulty lay.

If it were true that schizophrenics react in an impulsive manner, without editing, then the strongest associate, regardless of its appropriateness, should win out immediately, and there should be no increase in latency and length of utterance. Even if there were an increase in latency as similarity between the referents increased, there should be no increase in utterance length if no editing took place. Actually, there was an inordinate increase in both latency and length of utterance. An examination of the utterances indicated that, after the initial response, the schizophrenic's referent was no longer the color referent but the immediately preceding word in his utterance. Instead of responding to the stimulus situation, he began responding to the words in his own utterances. As Cromwell (1975) described that result:

> It is as if once he discovers his dominant association does not meet the task demand, he pulls the windowshade down on the outside world and starts associating to his own associations.

Salzinger's (1971; Salzinger et al., 1970) immediacy hypothesis seems to be exemplified in that act of the schizophrenic. Cohen (1978) dubbed that phenomenon "perseverative chaining." The phenomenon seems to characterize primarily acute schizophrenics; chronic schizophrenics seem to be more impulsive in their responses, giving even shorter latencies than do normals and, of course, less accurate responses, so that listeners make many more errors in identifying the referent.

Cohen's (1978) study dealt with adult schizophrenics. Goldfarb et al. (1973) dealt with referent communication in schizophrenic children and their mothers, based on the Krauss-Glucksberg experiments (Glucksberg et al., 1966; Glucksberg and Krauss, 1967). In contrast to Cohen's study, the Goldfarb et al. study was unidirectional—the mother being the speaker and the child being the listener, never the speaker. In an earlier experiment, Goldfarb et al. (1966) found that the mothers of schizophrenic children were judged to be inferior to the mothers of normal public school children in speech and language, thus serving as poorer models of communication for their children. That was found to be true despite the fact that more of the schizophrenics' mothers were from upper-class families than were the control group mothers.

To determine just where and how in the referent communication process the mothers of schizophrenic children deviated from the mothers of normal children, Goldfarb et al. (1973) carried out a referent communication experiment following the Krauss-Glucksberg paradigm. The display of the referent objects consisted of six novel graphic forms printed on four vertical faces of a small wooden block. The mother and her child each had a set of six blocks. The mother's task was to describe the chosen block in such manner that her child could find it in his duplicate set. There were 14 dyads of schizophrenic children and their mothers and 14 dyads of normal public school children and their mothers; all the children were about 9 years old. The results indicated that the mothers of the schizophrenic children were inferior in at least three aspects: (1) mutuality (her responsiveness to the child's request for help), (2) content (the level of information in the mother's message), and (3) style (evidence of cognitive fragmentation, tentativeness, and ambiguity).

The inferior quality of referent communication in the mothers of schizophrenics may be in response to the extreme behavioral deviances of the children. Nevertheless, the impact on language development in the children seems inevitable. If the child incorporates his mother's referent communicative style as his model, he cannot help but become a poor speaker in referent communication later in life.

Rochester (1978) pointed out that it was generally assumed that schizophrenics could not produce or perceive normal speech until Gerver (1967) found that schizophrenics could distinguish between normal sentences, sentences syntactically adequate but semantically anomalous ("Trains steal elephants around the highways"), and random strings of words. The subjects in that experiment repeated the sentences read to them and then were tested for recall. Although schizophrenics recalled fewer words than did normals, they recalled more of the normal sentences than of the other two types, and the rate of increase across the three types of sentences as meaning increased was about the same in schizophrenics as in normals.

It is now generally accepted that, even though the recall of sentences is poorer in schizophrenics, it is not due to an inability to use the organization inherent in language.

If it is true that schizophrenics can and do use language adequately, what is the source of their communicative difficulty—that is, their failure to account for the listener's immediate needs? According to Rochester (1978), that failure is based on providing misleading or unclear cues about the location of referents. Normals gave only 2 per cent of unclear referents in their noun phrases in their speech, thought-disordered schizophrenics gave 19 per cent of such unclear referents, and the nonthought-disordered gave 12 per cent.

To summarize, acute schizophrenic speaker-listeners use language adequately but fail to account for their listeners' immediate needs; they fail to provide a referent after it is promised or to facilitate the transition from clause to clause.

The language system used to account for listeners' immediate needs—the so-called informational system (Rochester, 1978)—demands unusually complex information processing from the speaker so that he can continually update and retrieve information from a short-term memory store. Since schizophrenics probably have difficulty in short-term encoding and retrieval operations, they experience difficulty in the rapid shifting of attention required between a prior clause and the clause being produced, and that is what produces the incomprehensibility noted in their referential utterances. That characteristic is what makes their referents so elusive. Rochester (1978) did postulate a lack of capacity not in the schizophrenic speaker's short-term memory but in the way he uses his memory system.

Attention and the Control of Processing

Attentional studies can be divided into two large groups: studies that are most relevant to sensory-perceptual processing and studies that are most relevant to cognitive processing. Although such a bifurcation is somewhat artificial, it is based on several parameters of difference between the two types of studies.

Attentional studies relevant to the sensory-perceptual domain are generally concerned with examining the nature of the limitations of how much can be processed and how fast it can be processed. Attentional studies related to the cognitive domain are generally aimed at determining what is selected for processing and what is not selected, as well as how such selectivity is achieved. Partly as a consequence of those different objectives, sensory-perceptual studies of attention usually require divided attention among many inputs, whereas cognitive attentional studies require focused attention to one input out of an array of competing inputs. In addition, the "when" aspect of processing varies across the two types of studies. Sensory-perceptual attentional studies examine processing that occurs within seconds after a stimulus is received, whereas cognitive-processing attentional studies examine processing activities that are maintained over a considerable time span. It can be argued that such maintenance of alertness over prolonged periods of time is achieved by conceptually driven operations. Therein lies another difference between the two kinds of attentional studies: Sensory-perceptual attentional experiments chiefly concern data-driven processing; in cogni-

tive attentional studies, conceptually driven processing is the prevailing influence.

ATTENTIONAL CONTROL PROCESSES RELATED TO THE SENSORY AND PERCEPTUAL DOMAINS

The first set of studies to be described can be considered as being of greatest relevance to the sensory- and perceptual-processing domains. To be sure, there is overlap with the cognitive-processing domain, particularly with reference to visual-search tasks. But these studies are discussed in relation to sensory and perceptual processing for several reasons. First, they share the objective of investigating limitations at the input end of processing—the sensory-perceptual end, as opposed to the conceptual or response end of the processing spectrum. In other words, they attempt to determine how much simultaneous input can receive sensory or perceptual processing. Second, they use brief stimuli and examine control processes occurring with rapid latency after an input is received. The "when" of what is investigated is consistent with the temporal parameters of the sensory- and perceptual-processing domain. Finally, these studies generally concern data-driven processing. They examine processing initiated by the arrival of the stimuli and minimally guided by conceptual expectations. The search tasks to be discussed represent something of an exception in that the subject's expectation of a particular target introduces the element of conceptually driven processing. However the concept that guides the search for a target on these tasks is a rudimentary one. Subjects are asked to search for either of two letters, and their search entails primarily physical discriminations between distinctive perceptual features of these letters, as opposed to other letters. If the search were guided by a more elaborate conceptual category—for example, animal names or prepositions—such studies would be of greater relevance to the cognitive-processing domain.

Although all these tasks are often described as measures of attention or attention dysfunction, the intercorrelations among them are minimal. They do not seem to measure any unitary faculty of attention, nor do the authors think that any unitary domain or structure of attention can be validly hypothesized. Instead, they prefer to describe attention in terms of various operations that modulate the amount of information intake and the nature of the intake across the processing domains.

Span of apprehension. The span test was developed to determine how many stimuli can be perceived simultaneously in one glance. According to Woodworth and Schlosberg (1954), the logician Jevons in 1871 commented that it was one of the few issues in psychology that could actually be submitted to an experimental test. The span test can be construed as an attempt to measure the basic capacity limits on data-driven processing. Processing capacity is measured over brief durations of time corresponding to those usually associated with sensory-processing experiments. A tachistoscope is generally used to present visually a variable number of stimuli for some duration of time less than 100 milliseconds. Eye movements cannot occur with such rapid latency, so that the reception of stimuli must literally be accomplished within a single glance. However, the information present in the stimulus display persists in a sensory (iconic or echoic) store for at least several hundred milliseconds after the display terminates. The quality of information in that brief sensory store is degraded over time.

Cash et al. (1972) administered displays of four or eight stimuli lasting 70 milliseconds to schizophrenic patients and to nonschizophrenic psychiatric patients. When asked to report all the stimuli in the display (full-report procedure), the schizophrenics performed as accurately as did the controls. However, Sperling (1960) pointed out that the accuracy of apprehension under full-report conditions reflects limitations of memory capacity to a greater degree than limitations of data-driven sensory or perceptual-processing capacity. That conclusion is based on the observation that, if subjects are instructed to report any given row in the display (partial report) immediately after the stimulus offset, they can do so with a high degree of accuracy, even though they cannot fully report all the letters in the display (full report). That finding suggests that much of the information in the display has been processed perceptually but that the subjects may not be able to remember all the information that was perceptually processed. The demands on memory capacity are reduced in the partial-report condition because the stimuli can be gathered directly from the short-term sensory store. In contrast, to remember stimuli under full-report conditions, one must verbally encode the display stimuli and later retrieve them from short-term memory.

The adequate performance of schizophrenics under full-report conditions permits two interpretations. The first interpretation is that schizophrenics resemble normals in their perceptual-processing capacity and their memory capacity. In other words, schizophrenics are adequate in perceptually processing a normal amount of stimulus information in the display and in verbally encoding that information into short-term memory. However, Davidson and Neale (1974) suggested an alternative interpretation. Schizophrenics may perceptually process fewer letters in the display than do controls, and, therefore, the schizophrenics do not overload short-term memory. With less information in short-term memory, the task of retrieval for a full report is easier for schizophrenics than for controls. In other words, whereas schizophrenics may recall nearly all the limited amount of information that has been apprehended, controls may have apprehended more information but be unable to demonstrate that fact because of memory limitations.

The design of the Cash et al. (1972) study does not permit a selection between those two alternative hypotheses. That study investigated whether the faculty of attention (in that case apprehension) was intact or deficient in schizophrenic patients. It did not investigate the "how" of processing by asking how the limitations in processing capacity come about. Questions of how and how much can be approached in a more informative manner by processing studies that measure the stimulus or the response in temporal units.

A study by Knight et al. (1977) illustrated a processing approach to the study of capacity limitations. Knight et al. reasoned that a partial report should yield a performance superior to a full report when tests are conducted immediately after the display presentation, when the icon is still intact. However, a performance on partial report should be no better than a full-report performance after the iconic image decays and retrieval must depend on short-term memory. Stimulus displays were administered for 100 milliseconds. In the full-report condition, subjects reported all that they recalled of the matrix immediately after its offset. In the partial-report condition, a bar presented 0, 300, or 600 milliseconds after the stimulus offset indicated which line was to be reported. To the extent that the subjects could use iconic storage to enhance their apprehension, their performance on the partial report, zero-delay condition should have been superior to their full-report performance. In addition, since the partial report depends on the icon, accuracy should rapidly decrease with increasing delays between the stimulus offset and the presentation of the bar, because the icon decays over time. Knight et al. (1977) found that nonpsychotic patients and overinclusive schizophrenics showed the expected superiority of partial-report performance over full-report performance. That finding suggests that both patient groups had an adequate iconic store that facilitated partial-report performance. In addition, partial-report performance in those groups deteriorated as the delay increased between the stimuli and the bar, suggesting that in nonpsychotic patients and overinclusive schizophrenics the icon displays decay characteristics similar to those seen in normals. In contrast, minimally and moderately overinclusive schizophrenics showed no superiority of partial-report

performance over full-report performance, and partial-report performance did not deteriorate with increasing delays after stimulus offset. Therefore, those subgroups of schizophrenic patients seemed to have deficiencies in the iconic store. Since the icon extended the time during which incoming information was available for perceptual processing, deficiencies in the icon among minimal and moderately overinclusive schizophrenics should have severely limited processing capacity in those groups. Therefore, attentional capacity in minimal and moderately overinclusive subjects does not seem to be assisted by a normal icon.

Visual search. The procedure in a visual-search task is the same as that in a span-of-apprehension task with one important exception. The number of elements in the display is still varied, so that search tasks also investigate limitations in how many inputs can be processed at once. The new element in the search procedure, as compared with the span procedure, is that, before the brief stimulus display is presented, subjects are given the job of determining which of two target stimuli—for example, T or F—is present in the display. That slight variation in instructions changes the nature of the task in two important ways. First, selective processing is now required. Whereas in the span task, all display stimuli are relevant to the response, in a search task only target stimuli are relevant; nontarget stimuli are irrelevant distractors. Second, the search-processing task requires conceptually driven processing, as well as data-driven processing. Since the subject knows which stimuli are relevant before the display comes on, his expectations guide the allocation of processing efforts.

Neale et al. (1969) and Asarnow and MacCrimmon (1978) found that schizophrenics performed as accurately as did normals when identifying a single target stimulus presented tachistoscopically in an array. However, when the display contained a variety of distracting letters in addition to the target, the performance of the schizophrenics deteriorated relative to that of the normals. Asarnow and MacCrimmon found that remitted schizophrenics and children of schizophrenics were as impaired as ill schizophrenics at detecting the targets in arrays that included distracting elements.

Again, the two studies demonstrating schizophrenics' impairment on visual-search tasks exemplify the faculty psychology approach to attention, and the conclusions that can be drawn from them are limited accordingly. Although one can state with certainty that ill and remitted schizophrenics and their children are impaired at detecting targets amid briefly presented arrays, including a target and distractors, one cannot determine why that deficit arises. In fact, the search task requires a variety of capacities and processing operations, and impairment in any one may explain the observed deficiency.

Filtering impairment. One possible explanation for schizophrenics' impairment in search is that schizophrenics are impaired in their ability to filter or exclude some display stimuli from further processing on the basis of inappropriate physical characteristics. Such a problem reflects an anomaly of data-driven selection or filtering. Davidson and Neale (1974) tested that possibility. They hypothesized that, if schizophrenics cannot filter out irrelevant stimuli on the basis of physical characteristics, their search performance should be unaffected by manipulations of the physical similarities between target and distractor stimuli. They found that, although schizophrenics performed less accurately than did controls at all levels of target-distractor similarity, their performance did improve as distractors became more different from targets. Thus, a complete absence of filtering ability cannot explain the schizophrenics' search deficit.

Slowness of processing. Another possible factor in schizophrenic patients' search deficiencies is over-all slowness in processing. Schizophrenics may perform the scanning and filtering of the display normally, but they may carry out those functions more slowly than do normals. Thus, they perform processing operations on the icon for a longer period of time than do normals and may not have completed encoding all the stimulus information before the icon fades. If the icon is impaired or degraded in some subgroups of schizophrenics, as Knight et al. (1977) suggested, then only a limited amount of stimulus information can be processed at a snail's pace before the stimuli are no longer available. There is considerable evidence to support the hypothesis of slow processing speed in schizophrenia (Yates, 1973).

The evidence supports the hypothesis that slowness is one of the factors responsible for a schizophrenic impairment in search performance. Russell and Page (1976) found that the time needed to detect a target amid distractors increased disproportionately for schizophrenics relative to normal controls as the number of distracting elements was increased. In that reaction-time study, schizophrenics were able to identify the correct target as accurately as did normals, but they required considerably more time to do so, especially when many stimuli had to be searched. Whereas Russell and Page varied the duration of the stimulus arrays to study the speed of processing, Saccuzzo and Miller (1977) presented brief (6-millisecond) stimuli of constant duration but varied the duration of the icon by presenting a masking stimulus at varying intervals after the stimulus. They found that schizophrenics required a longer use of the icon—a longer time between stimulus and mask—to attain a level of accuracy comparable to that of normals. Again, the patients could perform as accurately as did the normals but required a longer processing time to achieve that result.

Pigeonholing impairment. Another processing deficit that may be involved in the schizophrenic impairment of search involves an anomaly in pigeonholing. Pigeonholing is a conceptually driven selection process involving the allocation of effort to determine whether an expected target is present or absent. The subject must keep in mind the members of the searched-for category and must inspect each incoming stimulus to determine whether it matches the target category—that is, whether it fits into the conceptual pigeonhole. Pigeonholing can occur in search tasks but not in span-of-apprehension tasks because only in the search task can the subject formulate a hypothesis or cognitive template to guide his search for the expected target. A deficit in pigeonholing may lead to difficulty in determining whether a display stimulus in a search task constitutes an appropriate match to the cognitive template for an expected target. Several theorists have suggested that schizophrenics experience particular difficulty in performing pigeonholing operations (Hemsley, 1975; Schwartz, 1978).

ATTENTIONAL CONTROL PROCESSES RELATED TO THE COGNITIVE DOMAIN

Whereas the studies discussed with reference to the sensory and perceptual domains were most concerned with the limitation aspect of the attention construct, those discussed below are most concerned with the selective aspects of attention. In other words, they consider focused attention in the presence of distractors. The authors' suggestion that this research is most relevant to the cognitive processing domain is based primarily on the criterion of the "when" of processing. The processing examined in these studies takes place over an extended time span, and conceptually driven control processes are brought into play to maintain processing activities. It is possible to divide this literature in other ways. For example, it would be appealing to say that studies examining filtering or selection by physical discriminations belong appropriately in the sensory and perceptual domain, whereas those examining pigeonholing or selection by conceptual discriminations belong in the cognitive domain. Any single organization is basically arbitrary and unsatisfactory since control processes that operate across the processing spectrum, rather than structures that can be clearly localized, are being discussed.

Divided attention versus focused attention. There is an important difference between the attentional tasks just described and those about to be discussed. In terms of the distinction proposed earlier between divided and focused attention, all the tasks above require some degree of divided attention. Those tasks measure the extent to which performance is impaired—for example, accuracy suffers or reaction time is slowed—when processing capacity must be divided between two or more events. The requirement for divided attention is consistent with the objectives of the studies that use those tasks. They aim to determine how much can be processed or how well processing capacity can be divided.

Treisman (1969) proposed a distinction between attention to competing inputs and attention to competing targets. An input is simply a stimulus or a set of stimuli that can be grouped together on the basis of some common dimension, usually a physical characteristic. A target is a particular input expected by the subject. The span-of-apprehension task is a direct measure of the ability to divide attention among competing inputs. Each letter or digit presented on a display is an input, a piece of sensory data that must be processed. Evidence suggests that the accuracy of the report suffers and reaction time is lengthened when the stimulus-display size is increased to include more competing inputs. Although divided-attention deficits occur for normal subjects, they may be more pronounced for some schizophrenics. Attention to competing targets is exemplified by tasks in which the subject must use conceptually driven processing to expect and test for one or more inputs, each characterized by some set of critical features. Divided attention to competing targets is exemplified by visual-search tasks in which the subject must test for two possible targets. It is also illustrated by the Sternberg paradigm, in which the size of the positive memory set can be increased to include more targets. The search tasks described above require divided attention to both inputs and targets. First, the multiple inputs in the display must be processed; then either of two targets must be searched. The only task discussed above that seems to require focused attention is that of Knight et al. (1977). In the partial-report condition, subjects are required to search the icon for an input or channel (stimuli in the same spatial location or row) while ignoring competing inputs from elsewhere in the icon.

The tasks to be discussed below are measures of the ability to focus attention on a single sensory input or target while ignoring competing stimuli. Vigilance tasks require the subject to respond to a single target event that occurs intermittently. Responses to interspersed environmental and mental events must be suppressed. Vigilance tasks are commonly described as measures of sustained attention. In dichotic listening tasks, responses are required to one category of inputs—for example, words presented to one ear or spoken by a particular voice—and responses to simultaneous competing inputs must be suppressed. The dichotic listening task is considered to measure the ability to sustain selective attention.

Maintenance of alertness. In addition to requiring focused attention, vigilance and dichotic listening tasks require another element not found in divided-attention tasks. They require that processing efforts be maintained at a high level over relatively prolonged periods of time. Posner and Boies (1971) described that aspect as the maintenance of alertness. Alertness must be maintained whenever performance must be paced to stimuli occurring at a fairly rapid rate over time. The demands on maintaining alertness are particularly pronounced when initially slow or poor performance can interfere with the efficient processing of stimuli later in a sequence. Alertness can also be required on tasks presenting discrete stimuli on a single trial—for example, when subjects are given a warning signal and must prepare themselves to respond to a stimulus on a reaction-time trial. In that case alertness must be maintained for a relatively brief period throughout the duration of the preparatory interval.

There is no reason why alertness or sustained attention should be more relevant to a discussion of focused attention than it is to a discussion of divided attention. Rather, it seems to be simply a matter of chance that those tasks chosen to illustrate the assessment of divided attention only require responses to briefly presented discrete stimuli not requiring sustained attention. The concept of arousal is particularly germane to the problem of how subjects maintain alertness. Indeed, Broadbent (1970) speculated that it is necessary to postulate two arousal systems, a lower one concerned with executing well-established decision processes and an upper one that modulates the lower system to maintain a constant degree of alertness. That distinction is similar, although not identical, to the one proposed by Claridge (1972) and by Mirsky and Rosvold (1960) between subcortical and cortical arousal. One might describe the maintenance of alertness as a process by which arousal is modulated and held at a constant level by conceptually driven operations.

Vigilance. Nowhere have deficits in schizophrenics' information processing been more clearly demonstrated than on tasks requiring vigilance.

The most widely used measure of vigilance for psychiatric populations is the Continuous Performance Test originally proposed by Rosvold et al. (1956) as a measure of brain damage. In that task a sequence of single letters or digits is continuously flashed on a screen, and subjects are required to depress a lever whenever a particular target stimulus or sequence of stimuli occurs. Performance is scored for reaction time to target stimuli or for errors of omission (failing to detect a target) and errors of commission (responding to a target stimulus when none is present). Increased errors relative to controls have been found in chronic schizophrenics, particularly those with a family history of mental illness (Orzack and Kornetsky, 1971), remitted schizophrenics (Wohlberg and Kornetsky, 1973; Asarnow and MacCrimmon, 1978), and children of schizophrenic parents (Rutschmann et al., 1977; Asarnow and MacCrimmon, 1978). More recently, Buchsbaum et al. (1978) modified the Continuous Performance Test to obtain a more direct measure of processing speed. The rate of stimulus presentation was adjusted and monitored to preserve an optimal level of accuracy. In conjunction with the numerous findings indicating that impaired vigilance seems to be a stable trait of schizophrenics and persons at risk for schizophrenia, the Continuous Performance Test used by Buchsbaum should make it possible to determine the pacing of environmental events that is necessary to compensate for deficits in vigilance.

A simple measure of sustained attention was described by Kay and Singh (1974). Subjects were given a page filled with X's and were asked to circle each X. The span of attention was measured by the amount of time that elapsed until the subject discontinued work on the task for at least 10 seconds. Consistent with the hypothesis that the ability to maintain alertness is related to arousal, span-of-attention scores have been found to correlate significantly with clinical ratings of distractibility, pulse rate, sleeplessness, and resistance to chloral hydrate sedation. In addition, schizophrenics show shorter attention spans than do normal adults.

The other major paradigm that has been used to study sustained attention in psychiatric patients is the set reaction-time procedure originally proposed by Shakow (1962). In that technique, reaction time to simple energy stimuli is measured as a function of the duration and regularity of the preparatory interval between a warning signal and the stimulus to respond. The set technique has generated an enormous amount of research in schizophrenia (Nuechterlein, 1977), most of it consistent with the hypothesis that diverse groups of psychiatric patients display deficits in vigilance.

Although pathologies of sustained attention are clearly and reliably demonstrable in psychiatric patients, there are numerous possible explanations of the deficit. Obviously, the tasks described above are difficult. Many of them require conceptually driven pigeonholing operations. Moreover, they require that an optimal level of processing be sustained over time, a task made more difficult by the manifestly boring nature of the procedures. Such procedures are, therefore, particularly likely to reflect a wide range of generalized deficits in the patient populations studied (Chapman and Chapman, 1973) without being particularly revealing of the specific nature of the deficit. Problems in maintaining motivation or modulating arousal loom large as potential explanations of poor performance on the Continuous Performance Test and span-of-attention tasks.

Since tasks of sustained attention are particularly difficult, it is necessary to compare performance on them to a control task matched on discriminating power (Chapman and Chapman, 1973) to be certain that performance does not simply reflect the generalized patient deficit described previously. A related problem involves the need to determine whether subjects are sufficiently motivated to pay voluntary attention to the procedure and perform the task requested of them. If those two nuisance factors can be ruled out, there are at least two possible explanations for deficits in sustained-attention performance. The first suggests that deficits in sustained processing can be explained simply by slowness in processing each individual stimulus event in the sequence. Findings from Buchsbaum et al. (1978) with the modified Continuous Performance Test procedure bear directly on that hypothesis. The second hypothesis suggests that deficits are caused by involuntary shifts in the focus of attention away from the major task and toward distracting events. Rappaport and Hopkins (1969) proposed that some schizophrenics undergo periodic defocusing of attention, during which they simply tune out and undergo an elevation of thresholds to external stimulation. The Rappaport and Hopkins position bears some resemblance to Cancro et al.'s (1978) proposal that schizophrenic attention may be devoted preferentially to mental events, rather than external events. However, Rappaport and Hopkins predicted that the turning inward would be periodic, rather than persistent. Shakow (1963) suggested that schizophrenic attention is drawn away from the task at hand and toward the adoption of minor sets to distracting mental or environmental events. Cromwell and Dokecki (1968) suggested that, once distracted, schizophrenics have difficulty in disengaging from or disattending to irrelevant events. The hypothesis that sustained-attention deficits in psychiatric patients are caused by distraction by external events is clearly an indirect inference from vigilance tasks. That hypothesis is tested directly by dichotic-listening experiments.

Dichotic listening. In dichotic-listening tasks, subjects are generally asked to shadow or repeat a single message or channel, word by word, while ignoring a simultaneous message. Deviations in the ability to maintain focused or selective attention are generally inferred from errors in shadowing performance and from enhanced memory for stimuli presented on the distracting channel.

In one of the earliest studies of that kind with psychiatric patients, Rappaport et al. (1966) compared the processing of a single message and the processing of a main message presented simultaneously with three, five, and seven distracting messages. Two presentation conditions were compared: one in which the main message was presented to both ears (a procedure that seems to localize the source of the message at the center of the head) and competing messages were presented dichotically (separately to each ear) and one in which all messages were presented diotically (to both ears) in different voices. The subjects were asked to write down the main message continuously. Schizophrenics made more reporting errors than did normal controls for all conditions in which messages seemed to be spatially separated, except for the condition in which only a single message was presented. However, when all messages were presented to both ears and discrimination among messages was based on voice quality alone, accuracy was much poorer, and the patients did not differ from the controls. Even in the condition in which schizophrenics made a greater number of errors, patients performed similarly to normals in the proportions of errors they made involving the omitting of main channel elements and the reporting of elements from the distracting channel. Moreover, the performance of the patient group was unaffected by the administration of acute doses of phenothiazines. Except when floor effects were encountered, as they seemed to be when all messages were presented diotically, this study suggests that schizophrenics do experience more difficulty than do normals in maintaining filtering operations over time. However, there is no direct evidence that they shift the focus of attention to distracting stimuli, since they do not shadow proportionally more distractors than do normal controls.

Payne et al. (1970) studied a single main channel and a single distractor channel presented separately to each ear. They compared drug-free schizophrenics described as clinically overinclusive or non-overinclusive with normal controls. The groups did not differ significantly on shadowing errors without distraction. However, all three groups differed significantly in total shadowing errors with distraction; overinclusive patients made the greatest number of errors, followed by nonoverinclusive schizophrenics and controls. However, the groups did not differ in errors involving the shadowing of words from the distracting channel. If schizophrenics process more distractors, they might be expected to show enhanced memory for distracting stimuli. The data for recognition memory for distractors were inconclusive. Overinclusive schizophrenics, compared with the other groups, claimed to recognize more words previously presented as distractors; however, they also claimed to recognize more words that had never previously been presented. Technically, enhanced memory for distracting words can be considered to provide a measure of the ability to divide attention, rather than to focus attention.

Wishner and Wahl (1974) administered a task similar to Payne et al.'s (1970) task but varied the rate of stimulus presentation and the instructional set to maintain focused or divided attention. For the slow-presentation condition, two-syllable words were presented at the rate of 25 words a minute; for the fast-presentation condition, one-syllable words were presented at 50 words a minute; the number of syllables a minute was actually the same at both presentation rates. Without distraction, schizophrenics shadowed as well as did alcoholic controls. When distraction was present, schizophrenics made significantly more shadowing errors than did alcoholics under the fast-presentation condition. At the slow-presentation rate, schizophrenics made more errors than did controls only when they were instructed to try to remember the distracting words. When instructed to ignore the distracting channel, patients did not make more errors than did controls in shadowing the slow tape. Schizophrenics omitted significantly more main channel words than did controls only when shadowing the fast tape, and they shadowed more distracting-channel words only when instructed to remember them. In terms of memory for distractors, whether tested by recall or tested by recognition, alcoholics remembered more distractor words than did schizophrenics.

On the basis of those findings, Wishner and Wahl (1974) concluded that schizophrenics' dichotic listening performance is affected both by their slowness and by inefficiencies in filtering irrelevant stimuli. It is apparent that schizophrenics possess the capacity to filter irrelevant stimuli that are clearly separated from the main inputs by a physical cue (spatial location). Indeed, filtering is performed normally when stimuli are presented at a slow rate that allows added time for processing. In fact, although schizophrenic performance deteriorates to a greater degree than does the performance of controls when distraction

is introduced, the data provided little evidence to support the hypothesis that the impairment is due to a breakdown in data-driven filtering. Since schizophrenics did not display increased shadowing of distractors, except under instructions encouraging divided attention, and remembered fewer distractors than did controls, there is no good evidence to suggest that the distracting stimuli were processed when they should not have been. Instead, it seems that schizophrenic performance deteriorated whenever the demands on their processing capacity were increased by adding distractors, by increasing the rate of stimulus presentation, or by requiring divided attention.

Wahl (1976) replicated the Wishner and Wahl (1974) study on a new sample, including nonschizophrenic psychiatric controls. He found that the increased frequency of shadowing errors under distraction was not unique to schizophrenics, since nonschizophrenic psychiatric controls also made more errors than did normals, although the nonschizophrenic patients made fewer errors than did the schizophrenics. Wahl's study was the first to find that schizophrenics shadowed significantly more distractors than did controls, thereby indicating that distracting stimuli were processed excessively by schizophrenics. Wahl also attempted to determine whether distracting mental events were processed to a greater extent by schizophrenics than by other subjects. He quantified a type of shadowing error called an importation, which occurred when the subject's response was neither a main channel word nor a distractor word. Importation errors were believed to represent the interpenetration of personal thoughts into the ongoing performance. Schizophrenics tended to make more importation errors than did controls only when distraction was present. The schizophrenics' increased rate of importation shadowing errors and the increased recall of nonpresented words led Wahl to hypothesize that under distraction schizophrenics show an increased tendency for attention to wander to personal thoughts.

Schneider (1976) pursued a hypothesis similar to Wahl's, suggesting that perhaps the ability to selectively attend is intact in schizophrenics but that attention is allocated to unusual events. Schneider compared delusional schizophrenics, nondelusional schizophrenics, nonschizophrenic psychiatric patients, and medical patients—all of whom were inpatients at a Veterans Administration hospital. The distracting material on the dichotic listening tapes consisted of three kinds of content: material from a physics text, discussion about the hospital, and discussion of delusional material. A different tape was prepared for each delusional patient, so that the content of the distractor pertained to the patient's specific delusional system. Each delusional tape was also administered to a matched control in each of the remaining three groups. In the study, schizophrenics did not generally make more shadowing errors than did controls when shadowing with distraction. However, when delusion-related distraction was present, delusional schizophrenics made significantly more errors than did any other group. The shadowing performance of the other groups was not significantly affected by the topic of the distractor. Even the personally relevant hospital distractor did not produce a significant excess of errors. Schneider concluded that schizophrenics may allocate greater processing effort to unusual events, rather than to those deemed relevant by the experimenter. He suggested that the impairment in schizophrenic dichotic-listening performance may reflect those unusual allocation policies, rather than a deficit in filtering operations.

The Schneider (1976) finding may illustrate a principle described earlier in this section. The authors proposed that focused attention should operate efficiently and even automatically when selection between relevant and irrelevant inputs is data driven and prompted by a simple physical cue. However, divided-attention deficits may appear when distractors generate automatic processing that the subject must attempt to suppress. In that case the highly salient delusional material may have compelled automatic processing for the delusional schizophrenics. Comparable deficits might have been observed for controls in the presence of highly salient distractors. The Schneider finding differs from the previous ones in revealing the selection of relevant inputs on the basis of conceptually driven processing, rather than data-driven processing. Both forms of processing may always occur simultaneously, and conceptually driven selection may entail the performance of tests on incoming stimuli to determine whether certain salient targets are present. In the Schneider study the targets were relevant to inner preoccupations. In the study to be discussed next, they were based on an analysis of the input and formulation of expectancies for what category of words might occur.

Dykes and McGhie (1976) compared the shadowing performance of schizophrenics with that of high-creative normals and low-creative normals. Words on the distracting channel were varied to display high association or low association to words on the main channel. Unlike the normals, the schizophrenics tended to shadow distractors, even when those distractors were minimally associated with the main-channel words. When distractor and main-channel words were highly associated, schizophrenic shadowing of distractors was enhanced still further. In addition, under high-association conditions, creative normals shadowed more distractors than did noncreative normals, although both groups shadowed fewer distractors than did schizophrenics. When recognition of distractors was tested, all groups showed an equal tendency to recognize more distractors under the high-association conditions. Under the low-association conditions, high-creative normals recognized significantly more distractors than did low-creative normals, and the performance of the schizophrenics fell in between. The enhanced shadowing and recognition of distractors under high-association conditions indicates that conceptually driven processing operated to examine the entire class of associates, and sometimes it led to the selection of the erroneous input. In addition, Dykes and McGhie concluded that the creative normals' minimal shadowing of distractors but high recognition of them under low-association conditions indicated that attention was allocated as broadly across a range of inputs in that group as in schizophrenics but was voluntarily controlled so as not to disrupt performance. The findings, therefore, suggest that unusual policies for the distribution and allocation of processing efforts are found within some range of the normal population and are not unique to schizophrenics.

Korboot and Damiani (1976) conducted a dichotic-listening study that was clearly within a processing framework: The rate of stimulus presentation was varied, and the response was measured in temporal units. Korboot and Damiani measured the vocal response time to the onset of each shadowing response for digits presented simultaneously with distracting digits or letters. They also superimposed a signal-detection task in which subjects were required to detect consecutive identical digits on the main channel. They found that the shadowing response times of chronic nonparanoid schizophrenics were significantly slower than those of acute nonparanoids, paranoids, and neurotics. In addition, paranoids performed significantly more slowly than did normals. The subjects made few shadowing errors, and there were no differences in shadowing accuracy between groups. Moreover, there were no group differences in sensitivity (d') or bias for the main-channel detection task. That finding is similar to Rappaport and Hopkins's (1969) failure to demonstrate a schizophrenic reduction in sensory sensitivity to signals on the main channel during distraction. Korboot and Damiani (1976) concluded that schizophrenics do not display a deficit in filtering, since they exclude distractors sufficiently to avoid errors in shadowing and since they display no reduction in sensitivity to the main-channel task. Additional evidence suggests that schizophrenics' filtering effectively attenuates the distracting channel, since Broen and Nakamura (1972) found reduced sensitivity (d') to a secondary task in schizophrenics. On the basis of the shadowing-response times, Korboot and Damiani suggested that schizophrenics process the dichotic stimuli at an extremely slow rate. However, although reduced processing speed would be expected to disrupt the accuracy of schizophrenic processing at rapid presentation rates, such an impairment was not found. On the other hand, disruption of schizophrenic shadowing performance at fast presentation rates was found in the Wishner and Wahl (1974) study cited earlier.

On the basis of all those findings, it seems apparent that schizophrenics do generally show deficits in sustained selective processing when distractors are present. One can, therefore, conclude that focused-attention deficits do appear when selection between inputs must be sustained over time. However, it is far from certain that such deficits reflect an inability to filter out irrelevant inputs on the basis of a physical cue. In all but two studies (Dykes and McGhie, 1976; Wahl, 1976), schizophrenics did not display an increased tendency to respond to or shadow the distracting channel. Nor did schizophrenics display enhanced recall or recognition of distracting elements unless memory enhancement was also found for nonpresented words, suggesting criterion differences between patients and nonpatients. Moreover, sensitivity to targets on a secondary channel was reduced in schizophrenics, suggesting that appropriate attenuation of the distracting channel does occur. That is not to say that attenuation of elements on the basis of physical cues cannot be overridden by conceptually driven alteration of the allocation of attention. Indeed, Schneider's (1976) and Dykes and McGhie's (1976) findings demonstrate that such alterations in allocation policy can occur and yield divided-attention deficits. However, similar alterations in selectivity can also be induced in normals by comparable manipulations.

The fact remains that schizophrenics do generally make an excessive number of shadowing errors under distraction relative to normals and relative to their own performance without distraction. Just as there is no clear evidence to suggest that those shadowing errors reflect shifts of attention to distracting external stimuli, there is no clear evidence to suggest that they reflect the processing of distracting mental events, since they cannot be adequately observed. Instead, the disruption of shadowing performance may reflect the disorganization of verbal-response selection instead of or in addition to disorganization in selection of relevant stimuli. The only conclusion that can be drawn with certainty is that schizophrenic shadowing performance becomes increasingly inaccurate as the demands on processing are progressively increased by presenting stimuli at a faster rate, by requiring selection between relevant and irrelevant inputs, or by requiring the processing of two simultaneous inputs. Korboot and Damiani (1976) demonstrated that increasing the rate of stimulus presentation slows the rate of stimulus processing in all subjects. They also demonstrated that schizophrenics tend to process incoming information at a slower rate than do normals. It is likely that the baseline slow processing in schizophrenics places them at a special disadvantage when faced with additional processing demands that slow the speed of processing still further. Although the hypothesized slow processing in schizophrenics can account for a general disruption in shadowing under increased processing demands, it cannot predict the specific nature of the errors that are made. Those errors do not seem to reflect enhanced processing and response to distracting external events, but they may reflect attention to ongoing distracting mental events. Alternatively, they may reflect deviant response selection, rather than deviant allocation of attention.

Implications of Deviations in Information Processing

The application of information-processing procedures to psychopathology has as its goal the probing of the integrity of the central nervous system for deviations in processing that may underlie the grossly aberrant and dramatic deviations in behavior that are generally recognized as the earmarks of mental disorder. The assumption underlying the effort is that the basic deviations on which psychopathology feeds are to be found somewhere in the central nervous system, especially in the brain, where the control of behavior in general and information processing in particular resides.

For that reason, the progress being made in information processing research was reviewed. Experimental psychologists are providing means for probing the intactness of the sensory domain by investigating the manner in which energy stimuli are transduced by the receptors and processed through the iconic stage. From there they proceed to an examination of the perceptual domain by picking up the process from its iconic or echoic stage through the immediate-memory storage. Finally, they pass on to cognitive processing, which culminates in the long-term memory store. In addition to examining the structural domains described above, experimentalists are interested in examining any deviations in the action of mechanisms controlling processing, such as attention, arousal, and motivation. In the course of those analyses, the impact of new techniques for examining information processing, such as signal detection and forced choice, are discussed.

Besides focusing on how information processing in its various stages takes place in normals, experimental psychopathologists also focus on applying the basic knowledge gained on normals to the determination of how mental patients deviate from normal expectancy. In doing so, they are often called on to investigate normal information processing in order to determine baselines that have not been previously assessed. For example, there has been little work done on the problem of how stimulus energy is converted into information. Psychophysicists devote themselves to the study of the impact of stimulus energy impinging on the central nervous system, but cognitive psychologists deal with the processing of the information contained in the energy of their complex stimuli. Still, the details of the nature of the transformation from stimulus energy to information remain unclear. Even an adequate specification of exactly what is meant by the term "information" is missing. Those questions, which underlie the entire information-processing approach, are in need of further development. In addition, the recent development in experimental psychology of behavioral techniques that can provide answers to questions about the loci of processing, such as the hemispheric asymmetry question, or the levels of processing, such as the peripheral versus central question, have barely begun to be applied to psychopathology. Those strategies, perhaps ultimately applied in conjunction with psychophysical measures, offer great potential for answering the important questions about the relationship between central nervous system functioning or malfunctioning and psychopathology.

The following selection of tentative findings illustrates how the cutting edge of information-processing research may enhance the detection and understanding of psychopathology: In the sensory and perceptual domains, detection thresholds are generally higher in mental patients than in normals, temporal resolution (critical-flicker-fusion and two-flash thresholds) are higher, critical duration for sensory integration is shorter, visual masking is greater, reaction time is generally slower, and special reaction-time indices (cross-over index and cross-modality effects) are highly differential for psychopathology, with special reference for schizophrenia.

In the cognitive domain, short-term memory is not used effectively by schizophrenics, but it can improve under training; referent communication suffers when the schizophrenic is the speaker, but he does as well as normals as a listener; and the cloze technique provides a measure of the communicability of schizophrenic speech.

In the attentional control of processing, the following techniques are found to be differential: (1) In span of apprehension, the iconic storage on which the task depends seems to be deficient in minimally or moderately overinclusive schizophrenics. (2) In visual search, schizophrenics perform poorly because of slower than normal processing in the iconic stage, thereby losing items in the display that are not processed for lack of time; they also show impairment in pigeonholing. (3) In dichotic listening, as the difficulty of the shadowing task increases, performance becomes poorer in schizophrenics than in normals, possibly because of the schizophrenics' slowness in processing.

The generalized-deficit problem is the one omnipresent stumbling block that potentially interferes with systematic research. That interference inheres in the fact that mental patients almost invariably do less well than do normals in any task. Before an observed difference in performance can be attributed to a specific mental disorder, it is necessary to rule out, as a possible source of confounding, the general lethargy and the lack of motivation and interest that characterize most patients and prevent them from exerting their capacities, even though those capacities may be intact. Several techniques have been developed to deal with the generalized deficit of patients, including (1) the signal-detection technique; (2) the forced-choice technique; (3) the selection of tasks in which patients perform unexpectedly better than do normals insofar as they excel relatively in one task with regard to another, but the normals show no such advantage; and (4) the use of control tasks calibrated for equivalence to the experimental task on normals. The use of those sophisticated techniques, it is hoped, can provide relatively reliable indicators of psychopathology.

Anecdotal and careful phenomenological observations made by astute clinicians over the centuries have created a literature regarding sensation, perception, and cognition that is fascinating and dramatic but difficult to establish on a scientific basis. Not all patients in a given category show the alleged deviations in behavior, and even the same patient may cease to exhibit it or do it only from time to time, so that the conclusions based on that literature are hardly dependable.

Beginning with the impetus to the application of techniques borrowed from the psychological laboratory by Kraepelin, who had studied with Wundt, psychological and physiological experimentation has gradually spread into psychopathology. It was overshadowed at first by the wave of psychoanalysis that dominated the American psychiatric scene until recently and stressed internal dynamics often not accessible to experimentation and measurement. The rise of clinical psychology after World War II, with its stress on applied clinical work, found greater usefulness in the dynamically oriented projective and cognate techniques than in the experimental laboratory techniques. As a result, the earlier thrust of experimental psychologists who entered psychopathology—Shepherd Ivory Franz, Frederick Lyman Wells, and Boris Sidis, for example—did not flourish. The only centers where experimental approaches flourished before the end of World War II were Worcester State Hospital in Massachusetts and the New York State Psychiatric Institute. However, the few experimentally minded psychologists working in clinics and hospitals readily seized on the new developments in psychology as they came on the scene. Reaction time entered the clinic soon after its introduction by Helmholtz in the 1850's. Similarly, sensory thresholds, constancy phenomena, sensory resolution (flicker), fatigue measures, autokinetic effects, and a host of other techniques were adopted by the clinical researchers. That borrowing by the clinical researchers was not a one-way street. The clinic, in turn, provided experimental psychology with phenomena that challenged experimenters. Thus, brain function in brain-damaged cases, retrograde amnesia, registration of memory, loss of familiarity (*jamais vu*), and false familiarity (*déjà vu*)— all proved challenging to researchers and led to some exciting investigations in experimental laboratories, not to mention the attempts to use animal models for investigations of neurosis and other mental conditions.

As a result of the interaction between clinic and laboratory, many of the clinical beliefs were challenged and found wanting. Thus, the belief that schizophrenics showed considerable perceptual distortions led to the assumption that the sensory thresholds of schizophrenics were different from those of normals. In the early experiments in the laboratory, that was found to be true. However, as time brought new and better techniques, the threshold question was reopened. Similarly, the patient's sensory and perceptual behavior and cognitive behavior were not always found to be deviant in all cases. With the improvement in diagnosis, the introduction of signal-detection theory, and forced-choice methods, the entire status of sensory, perceptual, and cognitive functioning in the mentally ill has taken on a new vitality in the attempt to find just how sensation, perception, and cognition are affected by mental disorders.

Perhaps the most striking recent development in experimental psychology that promises to be of greatest use in psychopathology is the recent rapid development of information processing, which deals with the problem of how the sensory systems take in external energies and transform them into behavior. In a sense, the problem of how the central nervous system provides for the intake, dissemination, and use of the energy provided in information processing is like the intake, dissemination, and use of nutritional substances provided by the circulatory system. The organization of the circulatory system and its various functions have been studied for so long a period that any deviations that interfere with functioning are readily detected and frequently remedied. By studying the processing of information by the central nervous system, researchers may arrive at a similar level of sophistication in which deviation leading to behavioral dysfunction can be readily detected and remedied if possible.

This section has indicated the progress in experimental psychopathology that the new developments in experimental psychology have made possible and what still lies ahead. One of the most difficult obstacles in the way of making progress is the general lack of interest and motivation that characterizes mental patients. It is partly responsible for the observation that in nearly all tasks placed before schizophrenics, for example, they do worse than do normals; furthermore, that situation is not a constant feature but varies with level of interest and motivation. Consequently, most of the research with schizophrenia is redundant and predictable in outcome. Information processing, with its stress on determining just where and when in processing the deviation takes place, makes it less probable that future findings can be attributed to a generalized deficit. Furthermore, it has become possible to find some tasks in which the response of schizophrenics seems to be better than that of normals, and that would eliminate the generalized deficit as an explanation.

Another problem that current research suffers from involves the ever-present effects of drug treatment. That, too, can perhaps be resolved by investigating information-processing capabilities to see just where the deviation occurs and whether it is at a juncture at which drug effects can be implicated.

In a sense, the problem in determining the presence or absence of cognitive dysfunction is not different from the larger problem of determining the presence or absence of physical or mental disorder. As Wooton (1978) wrote:

Drawing a parallel between physical and mental illness, Lewis argued that the former always involves the disturbance of a system or organ in relation to its norm, and that, when this disturbance of "part-function" upsets the integration of balance of the whole organism, "illness is certain." In mental illness likewise Lewis maintains that "for illness to be inferred, disorder of function must be detectable at a discrete or differentiated level that is hardly conceivable when mental activity as a whole is taken as the irreducible datum." From this he further concludes that "if non-conformity can be detected only in total behavior, while all the particular psychological functions seem unimpaired, health will be presumed, not illness."

Similarly, it is not sufficient to indicate that schizophrenic language is noncommunicative or that it suffers from thought disorder. To arrive at a satisfactory knowledge of what is wrong with schizophrenic cognition, one must approach it more systematically and discover the part-function that upsets the integration or balance of language.

In a recent incisive review of cognitive disorders, Venables (1978) concludes that deficits in the more complex cognitive processes are probably due to disturbances of attention and perception rather than thought itself. This being the case, research efforts in the future should perhaps concentrate on the abnormalities of the physiological substrates of sensory, perceptual, and attentional processes rather than on further explorations of complex cognitive phenomena.

While the experimentalists were busy with their investigations, the character of schizophrenia and, to a smaller extent, the character of some of the other disorders have changed from being persistent conditions leading inevitably to chronic states of either deterioration or unremitting impairment to being more benign in status. The older view has recently been challenged by a more hopeful view, which regards schizophrenia as occurring episodically in a vulnerable person (Spring and Zubin, 1978). The earlier experiments dealt with chronically ill patients, but the number of those chronically ill patients has dwindled to no more than 5 to 10 per cent, according to Bleuler (1978), and in some of them the episode may have long since passed, but they remain in the hospital for social, economic, and iatrogenic reasons (Zubin and Spring, 1977). The bulk of the mentally ill are now living in the community, and the entire approach to diagnosis and experimentation has had to be revised. Much of the behavior studied earlier has been shown to be characteristic of the patients only when they were undergoing an episode of mental disorder; that behavior disappeared with the lifting of the episode. Those have been designated episode markers. Some behaviors seem to persist in and out of episodes, and those have been referred to as vulnerability markers. Even during the episode, behavior varies, depending on the development of miniepisodes, which seem to elicit and exacerbate deviant behavior. That may be the reason for the intraindividual variability exhibited by many schizophrenics. Consequently, one must begin to classify the behavior and the responses of patients to experimental situations in accordance with whether the behavior characterizes a miniepisode, a maxiepisode, or vulnerability (Zubin and Spring 1977).

Granted that the information-processing approach to sensory, perceptual, and cognitive deviations in psychopathology establishes specific markers of miniepisodes, maxiepisodes, and vulnerability, the question arises whether those deviations are antecedent or consequent to the development of the episode or the development of vulnerability to episodes. Furthermore, regardless of their position in the causal chain, how do those subtle, mild laboratory-discovered deviations play a role, if they do, in the development of the gross dramatic behavioral deviations noted in psychopathology.

As to the position of the vulnerability markers in the causal chain, it is possible to determine an answer to that question by investigating first-degree blood relatives to see whether any of the unaffected family members also show the laboratory-discovered deviation. If they do, there is presumptive evidence that the marker in question antecedes the episode.

As to episode markers, only the monitoring of behavior in the ward or in the home can answer that question. If the marker in question appears before the miniepisode or the maxiepisode becomes noticeable, it seems to anticipate the episode. Although that question may not be of great significance scientifically, it is of extreme importance clinically, since objective markers of the beginnings and the ends of episodes and of anticipated exacerbations in the form of miniepisodes would be of great importance to the clinician in guiding his or her treatment of the patient.

The relation of episode markers to symptoms is an important question. Is it possible to connect specific markers to specific symptoms? For example, can the response to verbal reinforcement with regard to affective utterances be regarded as a basis for estimating the communicability of schizophrenic speech? Perhaps the finding that the higher effect of reinforcement on schizophrenic utterances is related to outcome underlies the clinical judgment that such patients are ready for discharge (Salzinger et al., 1966).

The relation of vulnerability markers to gross deviant behavior is a little more problematical. What possible connection can there be between a higher visual threshold, a slower reaction time, a cross-over effect, or a slower cross-modality shift in reaction time and hallucinatory delusional behavior or autistic and communication disturbances? Perhaps the connections are no more intrinsic here than those between the allele for color-blindness and the gene for depression, except that they coexist in close proximity on the same chromosome. On the other hand, the gross deviations in behavior do not bloom forth instantaneously. They take time to develop. Perhaps the slow reaction time, the awkwardness in shifting attention from one sensory modality to another, the hypersensitivity to critical duration in integrating sensory inputs, and the other findings tend to gang up on the developing youngster or adult and render him a maverick among peers. Gradually, he begins to feel that there is something the matter with him, and his self-image, communication abilities, and general interaction with others begin to falter. In that way, the gross deviation in behavior may be an epiphenomenon built on the deviations in information processing that can now be discovered only in the laboratory. That possibility, too, may offer an opportunity for intervention before the full-blown episode develops.

Although the information-processing approach holds much promise in pinpointing the locus where the deviation in processing occurs, the results reported in this section are still tentative, and many of them must be replicated before they can enter the corpus of certitude. Their promise inheres in the fact that they are aimed at specific targets in the processing procedure and tend to eliminate the more general deficit explanation for deviation in behavior.

At the present time, the diagnosis, causes, and treatment of the mental disorders are at about the same stage that characterized the physical disorders at the beginning of the 19th century, before the first diagnostic instrument—the stethoscope—was invented. Up to then, the diagnosis of physical disorders was based on patients' verbal accounts of their illness, through interviewing for symptoms, and the physician's observation of signs—skin color, tongue, breathing, and so on. The astute clinician of those days had to contend with the fact that patients with the same disorder often exhibited different symp-

toms and signs and that patients with different disorders often appeared alike (Reiser, 1979). That situation is similar to the current scene in psychopathology. In this section the authors have begun to provide, through information processing, the objective indicators that may eventually free diagnosis from total dependence on clinical symptoms and signs alone.

Suggested Cross References

Clinical manifestations of psychiatric disorders are described in Chapter 13, and the examination of the psychiatric patient is discussed in Chapter 12. Normality is discussed in Section 6.6. Schizophrenia is discussed in Chapter 15. General living systems theory is discussed in Section 1.2, and factor analysis is discussed in Section 11.1.

We are indebted to Dr. David Jenness for his substantive contributions to this chapter, which are from the second edition of this textbook. We appreciate greatly the able assistance of Dr. P. Collins, B. Bienstock, B. Krooss-Glover, V. Maschio, and L. Weeks in the preparation of this manuscript.

REFERENCES

Alexander, A. S. Psychophysiological concepts of psychopathology. In *Handbook of Psychophysiology*, N. S. Greenfield and R. A. Steinback, editors, p. 925. Holt, Rinehart and Winston, New York, 1972.

Asarnow, R. F., and MacCrimmon, D. J. Residual performance deficit in clinically remitted schizophrenics: A marker of schizophrenia? J. Abnorm. Psychol., 87: 597, 1978.

Atkinson, R. C., and Shiffrin, R. M. Human memory: A proposed system and its control processes. In *The Psychology of Learning and Motivation: Advances in Research and Theory*, K. W. Spence and J. T. Spence, editors, vol. 2, p. 85. Academic Press, New York, 1968.

Attneave, F. Some information aspects of visual perception. Psychol. Rev., 61: 183, 1954.

Attneave, F. *Applications of Information Theory to Psychology*. Holt, Rinehart, and Winston, New York, 1959.

Babkoff, H., Sutton, S., and Zubin, J. *Auditory Research in Experimental Psychopathology*. United States-Israel Binational Science Foundation, Jerusalem, 1977.

Baddeley, A. D. Trouble with levels: A re-examination of Craik and Lockhart's framework for memory research. Psychol. Rev., 85: 139, 1978.

Bannister, D. The logical requirements of research into schizophrenia. Br. J. Psychiatry, 114: 181, 1968.

Bartlett, M. R. The auditory threshold in reverie: A study of normal and psychopathic individuals. Arch. Psychol., 27: 182, 1935.

Bartley, S. H. *Principles of Perception*. Harper & Brothers, New York, 1958.

Bauman, E. Schizophrenic short-term memory: The role of organization at input. J. Consult. Clin. Psychol., 36: 14, 1971.

Bauman, E., and Murray, D. J. Recognition versus recall in schizophrenia. Can. J. Psychol., 22: 18, 1968.

Bellisimo, A., and Steffy, R. A. Redundancy-associated deficit in schizophrenic reaction time performance. J. Abnorm. Psychol., 80: 229, 1972.

Bellisimo, A., and Steffy, R. A. Contextual influences on crossover in the reaction time performance of schizophrenics. J. Abnorm. Psychol., 84: 210, 1975.

Bleuler, E. *Dementia Praecox or the Group of Schizophrenias*. International Universities Press, New York, 1950.

Bleuler, M. E. The long-term course of schizophrenic psychoses. In *The Nature of Schizophrenia*, L. C. Wynne, R. L. Cromwell, and S. Matthysse, editors, p. 631. John Wiley & Sons, New York, 1978.

Boring, E. G. *The Physical Dimensions of Consciousness*. Dover, New York, 1963.

Boring, E. G. Attention: Research and beliefs concerning the conception in scientific psychology before 1930. In *Attention: Contemporary Theory and Analysis*, D. I. Mostofsky, editor, p. 5. Appleton-Century-Crofts, New York, 1970.

Borinsky, M., Neale, J. M., Fox, R., and Cromwell, R. L. Two-flash threshold in normal and subclassified schizophrenic groups. Percept. Mot. Skills, 36: 911, 1973.

Botwinick, J., and Thompson, L. W. Premotor and motor components of reaction time. J. Exp. Psychol., 7: 9, 1966.

Boynton, R. M. Some temporal factors in vision. In *Sensory Communication*, W. A. Rosenblith, editor, p. 739. M.I.T. Press, Cambridge, Mass., 1961.

Breitmeyer, B. G., and Ganz, L. Implications of sustained and transient channels for theories of visual-pattern masking, saccadic suppression, and information processing. Psychol. Rev., 83: 1, 1976.

Broadbent, D. E. *Perception and Communication*. Pergamon Press, London, 1958.

Broadbent, D. E. Information processing in the central nervous system. Science, 150: 457, 1965.

Broadbent, D. E. Stimulus set and response set: Two kinds of selective attention. In *Attention: Contemporary Theories and Analysis*, D. Mostofsky, editor, p. 51. Appleton-Century-Crofts, New York, 1970.

* Broadbent, D. E. *Decision and Stress.* Academic Press, New York, 1971.

Broen, W. E. *Schizophrenia: Research and Theory.* Academic Press, New York, 1968.

Broen, W. E., and Nakamura, C. Y. Reduced range of sensitivity in chronic nonparanoid schizophrenics. J. Abnorm. Psychol., *79:* 106, 1972.

Broen, W. E., and Storms, L. H. A theory of response interference in schizophrenia. In *Progress in Experimental Personality Research*, B. Maher, editor, vol. 4, p. 269. Academic Press, New York, 1967.

Brown, J. L. Flicker and intermittent stimulation. In *Vision and Visual Perception*, C. H. Graham, editor, p. 251. John Wiley & Sons, New York, 1965.

Brown, R. Schizophrenia, language, and reality. Am. Psychol., *28:* 395, 1973.

Bruder, G., Spring, B., Yozawitz, A., and Sutton, S. Auditory sensitivity in psychiatric patients and non-patients: Monotic click detection. Psychol. Med., *9:* 1979.

Bruder, G. E., Sutton, S., Babkoff, H., Gurland, B. J., Yozawitz, A., and Fleiss, J. L. Auditory signal detectability and facilitation of simple reaction time in psychiatric patients and non-patients. Psychol. Med. *5:* 260, 1975.

Bruder, G. E., and Yozawitz, A. Central auditory processing and lateralization in psychiatric patients. In *Hemisphere Asymmetries of Function in Psychopathology*, J. H. Gruzelier and P. Flor-Henry, editors. Elsevier, Amsterdam, 1979.

Buchsbaum, M. S. Psychophysiology and schizophrenia. Schizophr. Bull., *3:* 6, 1977.

Buchsbaum, M. S. Neurophysiological reactivity, stimulus intensity modulation, and the depressive disorders. In *The Psychobiology of Depressive Disorders: Implications for the Effects of Stress*, F. A. Depue, editor, p. 221. Academic Press, New York, 1979.

Buchsbaum, M. S., Murphy, D. L., Coursey, R. D., Lake, C. R., and Zeigler, M. G. Platelet monoamine oxidase, plasma dopamine-beta-hydroxylase and attention in a "biochemical high risk" sample. In *The Nature of Schizophrenia*, L. Wynne, R. Cromwell, and S. Matthysse, editors, p. 387. John Wiley & Sons, New York, 1978.

Cameron, N. Reasoning, regression, and communication in schizophrenics. Psychol. Monogr., *50:* 1, 1938.

Cancro, R., Glazer, W., and Van Gelder, P. Patterns of visual attention in schizophrenia. In *Cognitive Defects in the Development of Mental Illness*, G. Serban, editor, p. 304. Brunner/Mazel, New York, 1978.

Carroll, J. B. *The Study of Language: A Survey of Linguistics and Related Disciplines in America.* Harvard University Press, Cambridge, Mass., 1953.

Cash, T. F., Neale, J. M., and Cromwell, R. L. Span of apprehension in acute schizophrenics: Full-report technique. J. Abnorm. Psychol., *79:* 322, 1972.

Chapman, L. J., and Chapman, J. P. Interpretation of words in schizophrenia. J. Personal. Soc. Psychol., *1:* 135, 1965.

Chapman, L. J., and Chapman, J. P. *Disordered Thought in Schizophrenia.* Appleton-Century-Crofts, New York, 1973.

Chapman, L. J., and Chapman, J. P. The measurement of differential deficit. J. Psychiatr. Res. *14:* 303, 1978.

Chapman, L. J., and Taylor, J. A. Breadth of deviate concepts used by schizophrenics. J. Abnorm. Soc. Psychol., *54:* 118, 1957.

Claridge, G. S. The schizophrenias as nervous types. Br. J. Psychiatry, *121:* 1, 1972.

Clark, W. C. The psyche in psychophysics: A sensory-decision theory analysis of the effect of instructions on flicker sensitivity and response bias. Psychol. Bull., *65:* 58, 1966.

Clark, W. C., Brown, J. C., and Rutschmann, J. Flicker sensitivity and response bias in psychiatric patients and normal subjects. J. Abnorm. Psychol., *72:* 35, 1967.

Cohen, B. D. Referent communication disturbances in schizophrenia. In *Language and Cognition in Schizophrenia*, S. Schwartz, editor, p. 1. Erlbaum Associates, Hillsdale, N. J. 1978.

Cohen, B. D., Nachmani, G., and Rosenberg, S. Referent communication disturbances in acute schizophrenia. J. Abnorm. Psychol., *83:* 1, 1974.

Collins, P. J., Kietzman, M. L., Sutton, S., and Shapiro, E. Visual temporal integration in psychiatric patients. In *The Nature of Schizophrenia*, L. C. Wynne, R. L. Cromwell, and S. Matthysse, editors, p. 244. John Wiley & Sons, New York, 1978.

Craik, F. I. M., and Lockhart, R. S. Levels of processing: A framework for memory research. J. Verbal Learn. Verbal Beh. *11:* 671, 1972.

Crain, P., Goldstone, S., and Lhamon, W. T. Temporal information processing and psychopathology. Percept. Mot. Skills, *41:* 219, 1975.

Cromwell, R. Assessment of schizophrenia. In *Annual Review of Psychology*, M. R. Rozenzweig and L. W. Porter, editors, vol. 26, p. 593. Annual Review, Palo Alto, Calif., 1975.

Cromwell, R. L. Attention and information processing: A foundation for understanding schizophrenia? In *The Nature of Schizophrenia*, L. C. Wynne, R. L. Cromwell, and S. Matthysse, editors, p. 219. John Wiley & Sons, New York, 1978.

Cromwell, R. L., and Dokecki, P. R. Schizophrenic language: A disattention interpretation. In *Developments in Applied Psycholinguistics Research*, S. Rosenberg and J. H. Koplin, editors, p. 209. Macmillan, New York, 1968.

Cromwell, R. L., and Spaulding, W. How schizophrenics handle information. In *The Phenomenology and Treatment of Schizophrenia*, W. E. Fann, I. Karakan, A. D. Pokorny, and R. L. Williams, editors, p. 127. Spectrum, New York, 1978.

Davidson, G. S., and Neale, J. M. The effects of signal-noise similarity on visual information processing of schizophrenics. J. Abnorm. Psychol., *83:* 683, 1974.

Deutsch, J. A., and Deutsch, D. Attention: Some theoretical considerations. Psychol. Rev., *70:* 80, 1963.

Dusoir, A. E. Treatments of bias in detection and recognition models: A review. Percept. Psychophysics, *17:* 167, 1975.

Dykes, M., and McGhie, A. A comparative study of attentional strategies of schizophrenic and highly creative normal subjects. Br. J. Psychiatry, *128:* 50, 1976.

Easterbrook, J. A. The effect of emotion on cue utilization and the organization of behavior. Psychol. Rev., *66:* 183, 1959.

Emmerich, D. S., and Levine, F. M. Differences in auditory sensitivity of chronic schizophrenic patients and normal controls determined by use of a forced-choice procedure. J. Dis. Nerv. Syst., *31:* 554, 1970.

Erdelyi, M. H. A new look at the new look: Perceptual defense and vigilance. Psychol. Rev., *81:* 1, 1974.

Eriksen, B. A., and Eriksen, C. W. *Perception and Personality.* General Learning, Morristown, N. J., 1972.

Eriksen, C. W. Discrimination and learning without awareness: A methodological survey and evaluation. Psychol. Rev., *67:* 279, 1960.

Eriksen, C. W., and Spencer, T. Rate of information processing in visual perception: Some results and methodological considerations. J. Exp. Psychol. Monogr., *79:* 1, 1969.

Flor-Henry, P. Lateralized temporal-limbic dysfunction and psychopathology. Ann. N. Y. Acad. Sci., *280:* 777, 1976.

Freedman, B. J. The subjective experience of perceptual and cognitive disturbances in schizophrenia. Arch. Gen. Psychiatry, *30:* 333, 1974.

Freedman, B. J., and Chapman, L. J. Early subjective experiences in schizophrenic episodes. J. Abnorm. Psychol., *82:* 46, 1973.

Freud, S. *Introductory Lectures on Psychoanalysis.* W. W. Norton, New York, 1966.

* Frith, C. D. Abnormalities of perception. In *Handbook of Abnormal Psychology*, H. J. Eysenck, editor, ed. 1, p. 284. R. R. Knapp, San Diego, 1973.

Garner, W. R. *Uncertainty and Structure as Psychological Concepts.* John Wiley & Sons, New York, 1962.

Garner, W. R. The stimulus in information processing. Am. Psychol., *25:* 350, 1970.

Garner, W. R., Hake, H. W., and Eriksen, C. W. Operationalism and the concept of perception. Psychol. Rev., *63:* 149, 1956.

Gershon, E. S., and Buchsbaum, M. S. A genetic study of average evoked response augmentation/reduction in affective disorders. In *Psychopathology and Brain Dysfunction*, C. Shagass, S. Gershon, and A. J. Friedhoff, editors, p. 279. Raven Press, New York, 1977.

Gerver, D. Linguistic rules and the perception and recall of speech by schizophrenic patients. Br. J. Soc. Clin. Psychol., *6:* 204, 1967.

Gilbert, E. N. Information theory after 18 years. Science, *152:* 320, 1966.

Ginsberg, N. Flicker fusion bibliography, 1953–1968. Percept. Mot. Skills, *30:* 427, 1970.

Giora, Z. *Psychopathology: A Cognitive Review.* Gardner Press, New York, 1975.

Glucksberg, S., and Krauss, R. M. What do people say after they have learned to talk? Studies of the development of referential communication. Merrill-Palmer Q., *13:* 309, 1967.

Glucksberg, S., Krauss, R. M., and Weisberg, R. Referential communication in nursery school children: Method and some preliminary findings. J. Exp. Psychol. *3:* 333, 1966.

Goldfarb, W., Goldfarb, N., and Scholl, H. The speech of mothers of schizophrenic children. Am J. Psychiatry, *122:* 1220, 1966.

Goldfarb, W., Yudkovitz, E., and Goldfarb, N. Verbal symbols to designate objects: An experimental study of communication in mothers of schizophrenic children. J. Autism Child. Schizo., *3:* 281, 1973.

Goldiamond, I. Indicators of perception. I. Subliminal perception, unconscious perception: An analysis in terms of psychophysical indicator methodology. Psychol. Bull., *55:* 373, 1958.

Goldiamond, I. Perception. In *Experimental Foundations of Clinical Psychology*, A. J. Bachrach, editor, p. 280. Basic Books, New York, 1962.

Goldstein, K. *The Organism.* American Book Company, New York, 1939.

Goldstone, S. Flicker fusion measurements and anxiety level. J. Exp. Psychol., *49:* 200, 1955.

Goldstone, S., Lhamon, W. T., and Nurnberg, H. G. Temporal information processing by alcoholics. J. Studies Alcohol, *38:* 2009, 1977.

Granger, G. W. Night vision and psychiatric disorders: A review of experimental studies. J. Ment. Sci., *103:* 48, 1957a.

Granger, G. W. Effect of psychiatric disorder on visual thresholds. Science, *125:* 500, 1957b.

Granger, G. W. Abnormalities of sensory perception. In *Handbook of Abnormal Psychology*, H. J. Eysenck, editor, ed. 1, p. 108. Basic Books, New York, 1961.

Gross, G., and Huber, G. Sensorische störungen bei schizophrenien. Arch. Psychiatr. Nervenkr., *216:* 119, 1972.

Grossberg, J. M., and Grant, B. F. Clinical psychophysics: Applications of ratio scaling and signal detection methods to research on pain, fear, drugs, and medical decision making. Psychol. Bull., *85:* 1154, 1978.

Gruzelier, J. H. Bimodal states of arousal and lateralized dysfunction in schizophrenia: Effects of chlorpromazine. In *The Nature of Schizophrenia*, L. C. Wynne, R. L. Cromwell, and S. Matthysse, editors, p. 167. John Wiley & Sons, New York, 1978.

* Gruzelier, J. H., and Flor-Henry, P., editors. *Hemisphere Asymmetries of Function in Psychopathology*. Elsevier, Amsterdam, 1979.

Gruzelier, J. H., Lykken, D. T., and Venables, P. H. Schizophrenia and arousal revisited: Two-flash thresholds and electrodermal activity in activated and non-activated conditions. Arch. Gen. Psychiatry, *26:* 427, 1972.

Gruzelier, J. H., and Venables, P. H. Bimodality and lateral asymmetry of skin conductance orienting activity in schizophrenics: Replication and evidence of lateral asymmetry in patients with depression and disorders of personality. Biol. Psychiatry, *8:* 55, 1974a.

Gruzelier, J. H., and Venables, P. H. Two-flash threshold, sensitivity and β in normal subjects and schizophrenics. Q. J. Exp. Psychol., *26:* 594, 1974b.

Gurland, B. J., Fleiss, J. L., Goldberg, K., Sharpe, L., Copeland, J. R. M., Kelleher, M. J., and Kellett, J. M. The Geriatric Mental State Schedule. 2. A factor analysis. Psychol. Med., *6:* 451, 1976.

Haber, R. N. Introduction. In *Information Processing Approaches to Visual Perception*. Holt, Rinehart and Winston, New York, 1969.

Haber, R. N. Information processing. In *Handbook of Perception*, E. C. Carterette and M. P. Friedman, editors, vol. 1, p. 313. Academic Press, New York, 1974.

Harrow, M., Tucker, G., Himmelhock, J., and Putnam, N. Schizophrenic "thought disorders" after the acute phase. Am. J. Psychiatry, *128:* 58, 1972.

Held, J. M., Cromwell, R. L., Frank, E. T., and Fann, W. E. Effect of phenothiazines on reaction time in schizophrenics. J. Psychiatr. Res. *7:* 209, 1970.

Hemsley, D. R. A two-stage model of attention in schizophrenia research. Br. J. Soc. Clin. Psychol., *14:* 81, 1975.

Hernández-Péon, R. Some neurophysiological models in psychopathology. In *Experimental Approaches to Psychopathology*, M. L. Kietzman, S. Sutton, and J. Zubin, editors, p. 15. Academic Press, New York, 1975.

Hieatt, D. J., and Tong, J. E. Differences between normals and schizophrenics on activation-induced change in two-flash fusion threshold. Br. J. Psychiatry, *115:* 477, 1969.

Hoffer, A., and Osmond, H. Some psychological consequences of perceptual disorder and schizophrenia. Int. J. Neuropsychiatry, *2:* 1, 1966.

Hume, W. I., and Claridge, G. S. A comparison of two measures of "arousal" in normal subjects. Life Sci., *4:* 543, 1965.

James, W. *Principles of Psychology*. Dover, New York, 1950.

Janis, I. L. Psychologic effects of electric convulsive treatments: Posttreatment amnesias. J. Nerv. Ment. Dis., *111:* 359, 1950a.

Janis, I. L. Psychological effects of electric convulsive treatments: Changes in word association reactions. J. Nerv. Ment. Dis., *111:* 383, 1950b.

Janis, I. L. Psychologic effects of electric convulsive treatments: Changes in affective disturbances. J. Nerv. Ment. Dis., *111:* 469, 1950c.

Jaspers, K. *General Psychopathology*. University of Chicago Press, Chicago, 1963.

Jenness, D., Kietzman, M. L., and Zubin, J. Cognition and perception. In *Comprehensive Textbook of Psychiatry*, A. M. Freedman, H. I. Kaplan, and B. J. Sadock, editors, ed. 2, p. 266. Williams & Wilkins, Baltimore, 1975.

Johnson, F. N. Depression: Some proposals for future research. Dis. Nerv. Syst., *36:* 228, 1975.

Johnson, H. A. Information theory must be modified for the description of living things. Science, *168:* 1545, 1970.

Kahneman, D. Method, findings, and theory in studies of visual masking. Psychol. Bull., *70:* 404, 1968.

Kahneman, D. *Attention and Effort*. Prentice-Hall, Englewood Cliffs, N. J., 1973.

Kay, S. R., and Singh, M. M. A temporal measure of attention in schizophrenia and its clinical significance. Br. J. Psychiatry, *125:* 146, 1974.

Kietzman, M. L., and Sutton, S. Reaction time as a psychophysical method in psychiatric research. Schizophr. Bull., *3:* 429, 1977.

* Kietzman, M. L., Sutton, S., and Zubin, J. *Experimental Approaches to Psychopathology*. Academic Press, New York, 1975.

King, H. E. Two-flash and flicker fusion thresholds for normal and schizophrenic subjects. Percept. Mot. Skills, *14:* 517, 1962.

King, H. E. Psychomotor correlates of behavior disorders. In *Experimental Approaches to Psychopathology*, M. L. Kietzman, S. Sutton, and J. Zubin, editors, p. 421. Academic Press, New York, 1975.

Kinsbourne, M., editor. *Asymmetrical Function of the Brain*. Cambridge University Press, New York, 1978.

Knight, R., Sherer, M., and Shapiro, J. Iconic imagery in overinclusive and nonoverinclusive schizophrenics. J. Abnorm. Psychol., *86:* 242, 1977.

Koh, S. D., Kayton, L., and Peterson, R. A. Affective encoding and consequent remembering in schizophrenic young adults. J. Abnorm. Psychol., *85:* 156, 1976.

Koh, S. D., and Peterson, R. A. Encoding orientation and the remembering of schizophrenic young adults. J. Abnorm. Psychol., *87:* 303, 1978.

Kopfstein, J. H., and Neale, J. M. A multivariate study of attention dysfunction in schizophrenia. J. Abnorm. Psychol., *80:* 294, 1972.

Korboot, P. J., and Damiani, N. Auditory processing speed and signal detection in schizophrenia. J. Abnorm. Psychol., *85:* 287, 1976.

Korboot, P., and Yates, A. J. Speed of perceptual functioning in chronic nonparanoid schizophrenics: Partial replication and extension. J. Abnorm. Psychol., *81:* 296, 1973.

Kornetsky, C., and Eliasson, M. Reticular stimulation and chlorpromazine: An animal model for schizophrenic overarousal. Science, *165:* 1273, 1969.

Kraepelin, E. *Psychiatrie: ein Lehrbuch für studiernan de und Arzte*, vol. 3, ed. 8. Barth, Leipzig, 1913.

LaBerge, D. Acquisition of automatic processing in perceptual and associative learning. In *Attention and Performance V.*, P. M. A. Rabbitt and S. Dornic, editors, p. 50. Academic Press, London, 1975.

Lacey, J. I. Somatic response patterning and stress: Some revisions of activation theory. In *Psychological Stress*, M. H. Appley and R. Trumbull, editors, p. 14. Appleton-Century-Crofts, New York, 1967.

Lackner, J. R., and Teuber, H. L. Alterations in auditory fusion thresholds after cerebral injury in man. Neuropsychologia, *11:* 409, 1973.

Landau, S. G., Buchsbaum, M. S., Carpenter, W., Strauss, J., and Sacks, M. Schizophrenia and stimulus intensity control. Arch. Gen. Psychiatry, *32:* 1239, 1975.

Landis, C. *An Annotated Bibliography of Flicker Fusion Phenomena Covering the Period 1740–1952*. University of Michigan Press, Ann Arbor, 1953.

Leibovic, K. N. *Information Processing in the Nervous System*. Springer Verlag, New York, 1969.

Levine, F. M., and Whitney, N. Absolute auditory threshold and threshold of unpleasantness of chronic schizophrenic patients and normals. J. Abnorm. Psychol., *75:* 74, 1970.

Lewine, R. R. L. Response complexity and social interaction in the psychophysical testing of chronic and paranoid schizophrenics. Psychol. Bull., *85:* 284, 1978.

Lhamon, W. T., and Goldstone, S. Temporal information processing in schizophrenia. Arch. Gen. Psychiatry, *28:* 44, 1973.

* Lindsay, P. H., and Norman, D. A. *Human Information Processing*, ed. 2. Academic Press, New York, 1977.

Lindsley, D. B., and Lansing, R. W. Flicker and two-flash fusional thresholds and the EEG. Am. Psychol., *11:* 433, 1956.

Luce, R. D., and Green, D. M. A neural timing theory for response times and the psychophysics of intensity. Psychol. Rev., *79:* 14, 1972.

Lynn, R. *Attention, Arousal, and the Orientation Reaction*. Pergamon Press, Oxford, 1966.

Maher, B. The language of schizophrenia. Br. J. Psychiatry, *120:* 3, 1972.

Malone, J. R. L., and Hemsley, D. R. Lowered responsiveness and auditory signal detectability during depression. Psychol. Med., *7:* 717, 1977.

Mannuzza, S., Spring, B. Gottlieb, M. D., and Kietzman, M. L. Visual detection threshold differences between psychiatric patients and normal controls. Bull. Psychon. Soc., *15:* 1980.

McDonough, J. M. Critical flicker frequency and the spiral after-effect with process and reactive schizophrenics. J. Consult. Clin. Psychol., *20:* 150, 1960.

McDowell, D., Reynolds, B., and Magaro, P. The integration deficit in paranoid and nonparanoid schizophrenia. J. Abnorm. Psychol., *84:* 629, 1975.

McGhie, A. *Pathology of Attention*. Penguin Books, Baltimore, 1969.

McGhie, A., and Chapman, J. Disorders of attention and perception in early schizophrenia. Br. J. Med. Psychol., *34:* 103, 1961.

McGill, W. J., and Gibbon, J. The general gamma distribution and reaction times. J. Math. Psychol., *2:* 1, 1965.

McNicol, S. *A Primer of Signal Detection Theory*. Allen & Unwin, London, 1972.

Mednick, S. A. A learning theory approach to research in schizophrenia. Psychol. Bull., *55:* 316, 1958.

Miller, G. A. The magical number seven, plus or minus two: Some limits on our capacity for processing information. Psychol. Rev., *63:* 81, 1956.

Miller, J. G. Information input overload and psychopathology. Am. J. Psychiatry, *116:* 695, 1960.

Miller, J. G. Adjusting to overloads of information. Dis. Commun., *42:* 87, 1964.

Miller, J. G. General systems theory. In *Comprehensive Textbook of Psychiatry*, A. M. Freedman, H. I. Kaplan, and B. J. Sadock, editors, ed. 2, p. 75. Williams & Wilkins, Baltimore, 1975.

Milner, B., editor. *Hemispheric Specialization and Interaction*. M.I.T. Press, Cambridge, Mass., 1975.

Mirsky, A. F., and Rosvold, H. E. The use of psychoactive drugs as a neuropsychological tool in studies of attention in man. In *Drugs and Behavior*, L. Uhr and J. G. Miller, editors, p. 181. John Wiley & Sons, New York, 1960.

Moray, N. *Attention: Selective Processes in Vision and Hearing*. Hutchinson Educational, London, 1969.

Neale, J. M. Perceptual span in schizophrenia. J. Abnorm. Psychol., *77:* 196, 1971.

Neale, J. M., McIntyre, C. W., Fox, R., and Cromwell, R. L. Span of apprehension in acute schizophrenics. J. Abnorm. Psychol., *74:* 593, 1969.

Nidorf, L. J. The role of meaningfulness in the serial learning of schizophrenics. J. Clin. Psychol., *20:* 92, 1964.

Nissen, M. J. Stimulus intensity and information processing. Percept. Psychophysics, *22:* 338, 1977.

Norman, D. A. Toward a theory of memory and attention. Psychol. Rev., *75:* 522, 1968.

Norman, D. A. *Memory and Attention*, ed. 2. John Wiley & Sons, New York, 1976.

* Nuechterlein, K. H. Reaction time and attention in schizophrenia: A critical evaluation of the data and theories. Schizophr. Bull., *3:* 373, 1977.

Ornitz, E. M. Disorders of perception common to early infantile autism and schizophrenia. Compr. Psychiatry, *10:* 259, 1969.

Orzack, M. H., and Kornetsky, C. Environmental and familial predictors of attention behavior in chronic schizophrenics. J. Psychiatr. Res. *9:* 21, 1971.

Ostwald, P. R. Language and communication problems with schizophrenic patients: A review, commentary, and synthesis. In *Phenomenology and Treatment of Schizophrenia*, W. E. Fann, I. Karacan, A. D. Pokorny, and R. L.

Williams, editors, p. 173. Spectrum, New York, 1978.

Pavlov, I. P. *Conditioned Reflexes.* Dover, New York, 1927.

Payne, R. W. An object classification test as a measure of overinclusive thinking in schizophrenic patients. Br. J. Soc. Clin. Psychol. *1:* 213, 1962.

Payne, R. W., Hochberg, A. C., and Hawks, D. V. Dichotic stimulation as a method of assessing disorder of attention in overinclusive schizophrenic patients. J. Abnorm. Psychol., *76:* 185, 1970.

Pearson, L. A., and Tong, J. E. Two-flash fusion threshold: The influence of age, psychophysical method, instructions, viewing conditions, sex, and subject variability. Br. J. Psychol., *4:* 407, 1968.

Petrie, A. *Individuality in Pain and Suffering.* University of Chicago Press, Chicago, 1967.

Piéron, H. Vision in intermittent light. In *Contributions to Sensory Physiology,* W. D. Neff, editor, vol. 1, p. 180. Academic Press, New York, 1965.

Posner, M., and Boies, S. Components of attention. Psychol. Rev., *78:* 391, 1971.

Price, R. H. Signal-detection methods in personality and perception. Psychol. Bull., *66:* 55, 1966.

Price, R. H., and Eriksen, C. W. Size constancy in schizophrenics: A reanalysis. J. Abnorm. Psychol., *71:* 155, 1966.

Rappaport, M., and Hopkins, H. K. Drug effects on auditory attention in paranoid and nonparanoid schizophrenics. J. Nerv. Ment. Dis., *148:* 597, 1969.

Rappaport, M., and Hopkins, H. K. Signal detection and chlorpromazine. Hum. Factors, *13:* 387, 1971.

Rappaport, M., Hopkins, H. K., and Hall, K. Auditory signal detection in paranoid and nonparanoid schizophrenics. Arch. Gen. Psychiatry, *27:* 747, 1972a.

Rappaport, M., Hopkins, H. K., Silverman, J., and Hall, K. Auditory signal detection in schizophrenics. Psychopharmacologia, *24:* 6, 1972b.

Rappaport, M., Rogers, N., Reynolds, S., and Weinmann, R. Comparative ability of normal and chronic schizophrenic subjects to attend to competing voice messages: Effects of method of presentation, message load, and drugs. J. Nerv. Ment. Dis., *143:* 16, 1966.

Reiser, S. J. The medical influence of the stethescope. Sci. Am., *240:* 145, 1979.

Requin, J. *Attention and Performance.* Erlbaum Associates, Hillsdale, N. J., 1978.

Rimland, B. Savant capabilities of autistic children and their cognitive implications. In *Cognitive Defects in the Development of Mental Illness,* G. Serban, editor, p. 43. Brunner/Mazel, 1978.

Rochester, S. R. Are language disorders in acute schizophrenics actually information processing problems? In *The Nature of Schizophrenia,* L. C. Wynne, R. L. Cromwell, and S. Matthysse, editors, p. 320., John Wiley & Sons, New York, 1978.

Rosenblith, W. A., and Vidale, E. B. A quantitative view of neuroelectric events in relation to sensory communication. In *Psychology: A Study of a Science, Biologically Oriented Fields,* S. Koch, editor, p. 334. McGraw-Hill, New York, 1962.

Rosvold, H., Mirsky, A., Sarason, I., Bransome, E., and Beck, L. A continuous performance test of brain damage. J. Consult. Psychol., *20:* 343, 1956.

Rubin, L. S., and Stein, G. H. Scotopic visibility in normals and psychotics. J. Clin. Exp. Psychopathol. Q. Rev. Neurol. Psychiatry, *21:* 231, 1960.

Russell, P. N., and Page, A. E. Comparison of schizophrenics and normals on a visual search task. Percept. Mot. Skills, *42:* 399, 1976.

Rutschmann, J., Cornblatt, B., and Erlenmeyer-Kimling, L. Sustained attention in children at risk for schizophrenia: Report on a continuous performance test. Arch. Gen. Psychiatry, *34:* 571, 1977.

Saccuzzo, D. P., Hirt, M., and Spencer, T. J. Backward masking as a measure of attention in schizophrenia. J. Abnorm. Psychol., *83:* 512, 1974.

Saccuzzo, D. P., and Miller, S. Critical interstimulus interval in delusional schizophrenics and normals. J. Abnorm. Psychol., *86:* 261, 1977.

Salzinger, K. The immediacy hypothesis and schizophrenia. In *The Future of Time,* H. M. Yaker, H. Osmond, and F. Cheek, editors, p. 272. Doubleday Doran, New York, 1971.

Salzinger, K. *Schizophrenia: Behavioral Aspects.* John Wiley & Sons, New York, 1973.

Salzinger, K., Portnoy, S., and Feldman, R. S. Verbal behavior in schizophrenics and some comments toward a theory of schizophrenia. In *Psychopathology of Schizophrenia,* P. H. Hoch and J. Zubin, editors, p. 98. Grune & Stratton, New York, 1966.

Salzinger, K., Portnoy, S., and Feldman, R. S. Communicability deficit in schizophrenics resulting from a more general deficit. In *Language and Cognition in Schizophrenia,* S. Schwartz, editor, p. 35. Erlbaum Associates. Hillsdale, N. J. 1978.

Salzinger, K., Portnoy, S., Pisoni, D., and Feldman, R. S. The immediacy hypothesis and response-produced stimuli in schizophrenic speech. J. Abnorm. Psychol. *76:* 258, 1970.

Savodnick, I. The manifest and the scientific images. In *Schizophrenia: Science and Practice,* J. C. Shershow, editor, p. 21, Harvard University Press, Cambridge, Mass. 1978.

Schneider, S. J. Selective attention in schizophrenia. J. Abnorm. Psychol., *85:* 167, 1976.

Schneider, W., and Shiffrin, R. M. Controlled and automatic human information processing. I. Detection, search, and attention. Psychol. Rev., *84:* 1, 1977.

Schooler, C., Buchsbaum, M. S., and Carpenter, W. T. Evoked response and kinesthetic measures of augmenting/reducing in schizophrenics: Replications and extensions. J. Nerv. Ment. Dis., *163:* 221, 1976.

Schooler, C., and Silverman, J. Perceptual styles and their correlates among schizophrenic patients. J. Abnorm. Psychol. *74:* 459, 1969.

* Schwartz, S. Language and cognition in schizophrenia: A review and synthesis. In *Language and Cognition in Schizophrenia,* S. Schwartz, editor, p. 237. Erlbaum Associates, Hillsdale, N. J., 1978.

Sechehaye, M. *Autobiography of a Schizophrenic Girl.* Grune, New York, 1951.

Shakow, D. Segmental set. Arch. Gen. Psychiatry, *6:* 1, 1962.

Shakow, D. Psychological deficit in schizophrenia. Behav. Sci., *8:* 275, 1963.

Shannon, C. E., and Weaver, W. *The Mathematical Theory of Communication.* University of Illinois Press, Urbana, 1949.

Shiffrin, R. M., and Schneider, W. Controlled and automatic human information processing. II. Perceptual learning, automatic attending, and a general theory. Psychol. Rev., *84:* 127, 1977.

Shimkunas, A. Hemispheric asymmetry and schizophrenic thought disorder. In *Language and Cognition in Schizophrenia,* S. Schwartz, editor, p. 193. Erlbaum Associates, Hillsdale, N. J., 1978.

Shulman, H. G. Encoding and retention of semantic and phonemic information in short-term memory. J. Verbal Learn. Verbal Behav., *11:* 221, 1972.

Silverman, J. The problem of attention in research and theory on schizophrenia. Psychol. Rev., *71:* 352, 1964.

Silverman, J. Perceptual and neurophysiological analogues of "experience" in schizophrenic and LSD reactions. In *Schizophrenia: Current Concepts and Research,* D. V. S. Sankar, editor, p. 182. PJD Publications, Hicksville, N. Y. 1969.

Silverman, J. Stimulus intensity modulation and psychological disease. *Psychopharmacologia, 24:* 42, 1972.

Simon, H. A. Information models of cognition. Ann. Rev. Psychol., *30:* 369, 1979.

Simon, J. R., and Pouraghabager, A. R. The effect of aging on the stages of processing in a choice reaction time task. J. Gerontol., *33:* 553, 1978.

Smith, J. M., and Misiak, H. Critical flicker frequency (CFF) and psychotropic drugs in normal human subjects: A review. Psychopharmacology, *47:* 175, 1976.

Snodgrass, J. G. Psychophysics. In *Experimental Sensory Psychology,* B. Scharf and G. S. Reynolds, editors, p. 16. Scott, Foresman, Glenview, Ill., 1975.

Sokolov, E. N. *Perception and Conditioned Reflex.* Pergamon Press, Oxford, 1963.

Sperling, G. The information available in brief visual presentations. Psychol. Monogr., *74:* 1, 1960.

Spitzer, R., Fleiss, J., Burdock, E. I., and Hardesty, A. The mental status schedule: Rationale, reliability, and validity. Compr. Psychiatry, *5:* 384, 1964.

Spivack, G. Perceptual processes. In *Handbook of Mental Deficiency,* N. R. Ellis, editor, p. 480. McGraw-Hill, New York, 1963.

Spohn, H. E., Lacoursiere, R. B., and Williams, R. O. The effect of chlorpromazine on visual information processing in normal subjects. J. Nerv. Ment. Dis., *159:* 198, 1974.

Spring, B. Shift of attention in schizophrenics, depressed patients, and siblings of schizophrenics. J. Nerv. Ment. Dis., *168:* 129, 1980.

Spring, B. J., and Zubin, J. Attention and information processing as indicators of vulnerability to schizophrenic episodes. J. Psychiatr. Res., *14:* 289, 1978.

Steffy, R. A., and Galbraith, K. A. A comparison of segmental set and inhibitory deficit explanations of the crossover pattern in process schizophrenic reaction time. J. Abnorm. Psychol., *83:* 227, 1974.

Sternberg, S. The discovery of processing stages: Extensions of Donders' method. Acta Psychol., *30:* 276, 1969.

Sullivan, H. S. *Schizophrenia as a Human Process.* W. W. Norton, New York, 1962.

Sutton, S. Fact and artifact in the psychology of schizophrenia. In *Psychopathology,* M. Hammer, K. Salzinger, and S. Sutton, editors, p. 197. John Wiley & Sons, New York, 1973.

Sutton, S., Hakerem, G., Zubin, J., and Portnoy, M. The effect of shift of sensory modality on serial reaction time: A comparison of schizophrenics and normals. Am. J. Psychol., *74:* 224, 1961.

Sutton, S., and Zubin, J. Effect of sequence on reaction time in schizophrenia. In *Behavior, Aging, and the Nervous System,* A. T. Welford and J. E. Birren, editors, p. 562. Charles C Thomas, Springfield, Ill., 1965.

Swets, J. A. The relative operating characteristic in psychology. Science, *182:* 990, 1973.

Swets, J. A., and Kristofferson, A. B. Attention. Ann. Rev. Psychol., *21:* 339, 1970.

Swisher, L., and Hirsh, I. J. Brain damage and ordering of two temporally successive stimuli. Neuropsychologia, *10:* 137, 1972.

Taylor, D. A. Stage analysis of reaction time. Psychol. Bull., *83:* 161, 1976.

Teichner, W. H. and Krebs, M. J. Laws of the simple visual reaction time. Psychol. Rev., *79:* 344, 1972.

Teuber, H. L. Perception. In *Handbook of Physiology-Neurophysiology III,* J. Field, H. W. Magoun, and V. E. Hall, editors, p. 1595. American Physiological Society, Washington, D.C., 1960.

Traupman, K. L. Effects of categorization and imagery on recognition and recall by process and reactive schizophrenics. J. Abnorm. Psychol., *84:* 307, 1975.

Travis, L. E. Suggestibility and negativism as measured by auditory threshold during reverie. J. Abnorm. Soc. Psychol., *18:* 350, 1924.

Travis, R. C. The diagnosis of character types by visual and auditory threshold. Psychol. Monogr., *36:* 18, 1926.

Treisman, A. M. Strategies and models of selective attention. Psychol. Rev., *76:* 282, 1969.

Treisman, M., and Watts, T. R. Relation between signal detectability theory and the traditional procedures for measuring sensory thresholds: Estimating d' from results given by the method of constant stimuli. Psychol. Bull., *66:* 438, 1966.

Truscott, I. P. Contextual constraint and schizophrenic language. J. Consult. Clin. Psychol., *35:* 189, 1970.

Turvey, M. T. On peripheral and central processes in vision: Inferences from an information-processing analysis of masking with patterned stimuli. Psychol. Rev., *80:* 1, 1973.

Turvey, M. T. Contrasting orientations to the theory of visual information processing. Psychol. Rev., *84:* 67, 1977.

Turvey, M. T. Visual processing and short-term memory. In *Handbook of Learning and Cognitive Processes*, Vol. 5: *Human Information Processing*, W. K. Estes, editor. p. 91. Erlbaum Associates, Hillsdale, N. J., 1978.

Underwood, B. J. *Psychological Research.* Appleton-Century-Crofts, New York, 1957.

Underwood, B. J., and Shaughnessy, J. J. *Experimentation in Psychology.* John Wiley & Sons, New York, 1975.

Vaughan, H. G., Jr. Physiological approaches to psychopathology. In *Experimental Approaches to Psychopathology*, M. L. Kietzman, S. Sutton, and J. Zubin, editors, p. 351. Academic Press, New York, 1975.

Venables, P. H. Input dysfunction in schizophrenia. In *Progress in Experimental Personality Research*, B. Maher, editor, vol. 1, p. 1. Academic Press, New York, 1964.

Venables, P. H. Slowness in schizophrenia. In *Behavior, Aging, and the Nervous System*, A. J. Welford and J. E. Birren, editors, p. 598. Charles C Thomas, Springfield, Ill., 1965.

Venables, P. H. Experimental psychological studies of chronic schizophrenia. In *Studies in Psychiatry*, M. Shepherd and D. L. Davies, editors, p. 83. Oxford University Press, New York, 1968.

Venables, P. H. Cognitive disorder. In *Schizophrenia: Towards a New Synthesis*, J. K. Wing, editor, p. 117. Academic Press, London, 1978.

Wahl, O. Schizophrenic patterns of dichotic shadowing performance. J. Nerv. Ment. Dis., *163:* 401, 1976.

Waldbaum, J. K., Sutton, S., and Kerr, J. Shift of sensory modality and reaction time in schizophrenia. In *Experimental Approaches to Psychopathology*, M. L. Kietzman, S. Sutton, and J. Zubin, editors, p. 167. Academic Press, New York, 1975.

Walsh, D. A. Age differences in central perceptual processing. J. Gerontol., *31:* 178, 1976.

Wasserman, G., and Kong, K. L. Absolute timing of mental activities. Behav. Brain Sci. *2:* 243, 1979.

Waugh, N. C., and Norman, D. A. Primary memory. Psychol. Rev., *72:* 89, 1965.

Weckowicz, T. E. Size constancy in schizophrenic patients. J. Ment. Sci., *103:* 475, 1957.

Weckowicz, T. E. Shape constancy in schizophrenic patients. J. Abnorm. Soc. Psychol., *68:* 177, 1964.

Weingartner, H., Van Kammen, D. P., Docherty, J., and White, R. The schizophrenic thought disorder: Structure, storage, and retrieval of information from memory. J. Abnorm. Psychol., 1980, In Press.

Weiss, A. D. The locus of reaction time change with set, motivation, and age. J. Gerontol., *20:* 60, 1965.

Whitehead, A. N. *Science and the Modern World.* Macmillan, New York, 1925.

Wilson, M. E. Spatial and temporal summation in impaired regions of the visual field. J. Physiol., *189:* 189, 1967.

Wishner, J., Stein, M. K., and Peastrel, A. L. Stages in information processing in schizophrenia: Sternbergs paradigm. In *The Nature of Schizophrenia*. L. C. Wynne, R. L. Cromwell, and S. Matthysse, editors, p. 23. John Wiley & Sons, New York, 1978.

Wishner, J., and Wahl, B. Dichotic listening in schizophrenia. J. Consult. Clin. Psychol., *42:* 538, 1974.

Wohlberg, G. W., and Kornetsky, C. Sustained attention in remitted schizophrenics. Arch. Gen. Psychiatry, *28:* 533, 1973.

Woodworth, R. S., and Schlosberg, H. *Experimental Psychology.* Holt, Rinehart and Winston, New York, 1954.

Wooton, B. *Crime and Penal Policy: Reflections on Fifty Years Experience.* George Allen and Unwin, London, 1978.

* Wynne, L. C., Cromwell, R. L., and Matthysse, S. *The Nature of Schizophrenia.* John Wiley & Sons, New York, 1978.

Yates, A. J. Psychological deficit. Ann. Rev. Psychol., *17:* 111, 1966.

Yates, A. J. Abnormalities of psychomotor function. In *Handbook of Abnormal Psychology*, H. J. Eysenck, editor, p. 261. R. R. Knapp, San Diego, 1973.

Yozawitz, A., Bruder, G., Sutton, S., Sharpe, L., Gurland, B., Fleiss, J., and Costa, L. Dichotic perception in psychiatric patients and nonpatients: Evidence for right hemisphere dysfunction in affective psychosis. Br. J. Psychiatry, *135:* 224, 1979.

Zubin, J. Objective studies of disordered persons. In *Methods of Psychology*, T. G. Andrews, editor, p. 595. John Wiley & Sons, New York, 1948.

Zubin, J., and Kietzman, M. L. A cross-cultural approach to classification in schizophrenia and other mental disorders. In *Psychopathology of Schizophrenia*, P. Hoch and J. Zubin, editors, p. 482. Grune & Stratton, New York, 1966.

Zubin, J., and Spring, B. Vulnerability: A new view of schizophrenia. J. Abnorm. Psychol., *86:* 103, 1977.

4.2 Developmental Structuralism of Jean Piaget

DAVID ELKIND, Ph.D.

Introduction

Jean Piaget is the Swiss psychologist whose discoveries concerning children's thinking have earned him a permanent place among the first rank of psychologists and social scientists. Like Freud, Piaget and his work have had effects outside the boundaries of social science. In fields such as chemistry, physics, mathematics, and philosophy, Piaget's work is well known and is being applied, particularly in designing new curriculums for high school and college courses in those subjects. Jean Piaget has shown that developmental psychology is a true science, because it has significance for many different domains of research investigation.

Piaget's Life

Jean Piaget was born in a small village near Lausanne, Switzerland, in 1896. His father was a historical scholar known for his fine literary style. Piaget's mother was a deeply religious woman whose piety often came into conflict with her husband's more liberal thinking. Growing up in that environment, Piaget learned quite early to discriminate between arguments based on faith and those that were grounded in reason and evidence. In his own life, Piaget clearly opted for arguments based on reason and evidence, and he eschewed faith as a valid basis for scientific argument.

Like many men of genius, Piaget showed his talents early. When he was 10 years old, he happened upon an albino sparrow and reported his observations in a brief note that he submitted to a Swiss journal of nature studies. The note was published, and so, at the age of 10, was launched a career of publishing that has had few, if any, equals in scientific annals. While in his early teens, Piaget became interested in

FIGURE 1. Jean Piaget. (By permission of the Jean Piaget Society, Temple University, Philadelphia.)

mollusks and became a pupil of the curator of the mollusk collection at a museum near his home. When that man died, he willed Piaget his collection. Piaget began his first systematic research investigations, which resulted in a series of papers on mollusks, all of which were published before he was 16. His early publications won Piaget a considerable reputation as a conchologist. As a consequence of his publications, Piaget was offered, sight unseen, the curatorship of a museum in Geneva. He had, of course, to refuse the offer, inasmuch as he had not yet finished high school.

During his adolescence Piaget was attracted to philosophy, as well as biology. That tension between his talents and curiosity as a naturalist and his genius for philosophical understanding and insight was the major dynamic for his revolutionary theories and observations. But in his adolescence, all that was future, and Piaget read widely in search of answers to his questions regarding the relationships of biology to knowledge. He was attracted to Bergson and the notion of *elan vital*, but that dualism of life and knowledge did not really please him. Aristotle—who found logic in nature, as well as in knowledge—was much more to his liking. Piaget took from Aristotle the notion that logic can unite biology and knowledge, man and nature.

Piaget's concerns and involvement in those issues led to a mild case of exhaustion. To recover, Piaget went to a resort in the mountains. Once there, however, he proceeded to write a romantic novel, *Recherché* (Piaget, 1918). In that novel Piaget, like many other European youths, was really writing a life plan, a blueprint of accomplishments to come. He outlined some of the problems he hoped to solve and anticipated some of the solutions. It is remarkable the extent to which Piaget did accomplish the goals he set for himself before the age of 20.

After receiving a doctorate at the University of Lausanne with a dissertation on mollusks, Piaget began, at the age of 21, to find his metier. He went first to the Burghölzli Hospital in Zurich, where he studied psychiatry and undertook a didactic analysis. But he found it not to his liking. Then he went to Paris, where he got a position in Alfred Binet's former laboratory school. His job was to test children with Sir Cyril Burt's reasoning tests in order to establish French norms for them.

In the course of administering those tests, Piaget became fascinated with children's wrong responses because they revealed much more about children's thinking than did the right answers. The wrong responses seemed to reveal ideas and modes of thought quite different from those encountered in adults, and Piaget's curiosity was aroused. The naturalist in him wanted to explore and categorize those new modes of thinking, and the philosopher-biologist wanted to understand their origins and logical structure. In studying children's thinking, Piaget found a way to combine his talents as a naturalist with his theoretical and philosophical concerns.

As a result of some papers written about children's thinking and based on his testing experiences, Piaget was offered a teaching position at the Jean Jacques Rosseau Institute in Geneva. The institute was the teacher-training facility for the University of Geneva. At the time Piaget arrived, in the mid-1920's, it was under the direction of Eduard Clapredé, the famed Swiss educator. Clapredé became Piaget's mentor and encouraged him to follow up the research ideas that he had developed during his stay in Paris. Some of those studies Piaget undertook at the Maison des Petits, the children's school attached to the institute, and other studies were conducted in the public schools by him and his teachers.

In those early investigations Piaget wanted to follow up in a systematic way some aspects of children's language and thinking with which he had been impressed while standardizing Burt's reasoning tests. The resulting work, carried on over several years in the mid-1920's, was published in a series of five books. Those books—*The Language and Thought of the Child* (Piaget, 1952b), *The Child's Conception of Physical Causality*, (Piaget, 1930), *The Moral Judgment of the Child* (Piaget, 1948), *The Child's Conception of the World* (Piaget, 1951b), and *Judgment and Reasoning in the Child* (Piaget, 1951c)—were well received and made Piaget world famous before he had reached the age of 30.

Piaget's first books not only disclosed a great deal about what may be called the hidden side of the child's mind but also revealed a method of investigation uniquely adapted to exploring children's thinking. That method has come to be called the semiclinical interview. It is a creative combination of the two methods Piaget had learned in his apprenticeship years—namely, the clinical interview and the mental test. Like the mental test, the interview began with several more or less standard questions, but, like the clinical interview, it pursued the child's answers wherever they went. Except in his studies of infants and perception, the semiclinical interview has been the mainstay of Piaget's research work.

Those early books not only introduced new knowledge and new methods but also introduced a new method of reporting—new, at least, to the annals of psychology. In that method of reporting his findings, Piaget's biological training was clearly evident. He carefully classified the responses he obtained to the questions he asked and supported those classifications, often into sequential stages, by illustrative examples from the children's protocols. Although Piaget sometimes reported numbers and statistics, they were not a prominent part of his research reporting. Indeed, a major criticism of his research has been just that absence of experimental design and statistics. Other investigations, however, have since demonstrated that Piaget's findings hold true when rigorous methods are used.

Those initial studies of children's concepts led Piaget to question their origins. Were they preformed and innate, were they entirely learned, or were they constructed by the child out of his or her experiences with the environment? The only way to answer those questions, or so it seemed to Piaget, was to study the development of thinking in infants, in whom the preformed, learned, or constructed nature of ideas can be most clearly seen. That is true because the infant is more or less unblemished by experience and hence his role vis-à-vis maturation can be more clearly seen than at later points in development.

Of course, the study of infants poses enormous methodological problems. It is a measure of Piaget's genius that he was able to overcome those difficulties and to devise experiments to test the origins of children's thinking. Those experiments were so successful that they have since been incorporated into infant tests of mental development (Uzgirus and Hunt, 1966). Piaget used his own three children as subjects, and the resulting investigations were published in three books that have become classics—*Play, Dreams, and Imitation in Childhood* (Piaget, 1951a), *The Origins of Intelligence in Children* (Piaget, 1952c), and *The Construction of Reality in the Child* (Piaget, 1954).

Those studies of infancy confirmed Piaget in his view that children construct their knowledge of the world and that their knowledge is neither preformed nor copied. He then proceeded—with the assistance of many gifted colleagues, notably Barbel Inhelder and Alina Szeminska—to conduct a long series of investigations into how children go about constructing the world of space, time, and quantity concepts that adults use in their everyday living. He also undertook a series of investigations dealing with the development of perception. Those investigations were begun before World War II and continued into the 1950's. They resulted in many books, including *The Child's Conception of Number* (Piaget, 1952a), *The Child's Conception of Space* (Piaget and Inhelder, 1956), and *The Origins of the Idea of Chance in Children* (Piaget and Inhelder, 1975).

In the late 1950's Piaget and his co-workers began to study the figurative processes of perception, imagery, and memory. Those studies, too, resulted in new books, entitled *The Mechanisms of Perception* (Piaget, 1969a), *Mental Imagery in the Child* (Piaget and Inhelder, 1966), and *Memory and Intelligence* (Piaget and Inhelder, 1973). More recently, Piaget and his colleagues have begun to explore such issues as consciousness and causality, and books on those subjects have been published (Piaget, 1974, 1976). Piaget has also written on education (1970b), structuralism (1969b), biology and knowledge (1976), genetic epistemology (1970a), and his continuing biological work with a species of plant, the sedum (1966).

In addition to his research work, Piaget became director of the Jean Jacques Rousseau Institute on Clapredé's retirement, and he retained that post until his own retirement in 1975. He was also a visiting professor at the Sorbonne and for many years served as director of the Bureau of International Education supported by the United Nations Educational, Scientific, and Cultural Organization. He has won many honors, including more than 25 honorary degrees—the first was from Harvard in 1936—and many distinguished prizes. In the 1950's Piaget established the International Center for the Study of Genetic Epistemology; each year the center invites scholars from different disciplines and different parts of the world to come together for discussion and joint research work. The center has now published more than 30 books of research and theoretical discussion.

Piaget's Theory

Although Piaget's theory of mental development is extraordinarily rich and varied, it starts from a fairly straightforward set of premises. The first and perhaps the most important of the premises is that human intelligence is an extension, albeit at a higher level, of biological adaptation. Second, Piaget argued that adaptation—at whatever level of organization, from protozoa to humans—has a logical substructure. And, third, he assumed that human intelligence evolves in a series of stages that are related to age. At each successive stage, intellectual adaptation is more general and shows a higher level of logical organization than at the previous stages.

INTELLIGENCE AS BIOLOGICAL ADAPTATION

At first reading, the idea that intelligence is an extension of biological adaptation seems rather far from revolutionary. Psychologists, at least since the time of Binet, have spoken of intelligence as the capacity to adapt to new situations. In that definition, however, adaptation referred to processes such as learning and problem solving that were defined in psychological terms, rather than in biological terms. The relationships of those processes to biological processes of adaptation were left implicit and not dwelt on. Indeed, one of Binet's great achievements was to establish truly psychological scales of measurement. Although such scales had great practical usefulness, they had the negative consequence of giving support to the theoretical assumption of a discontinuity between psychological and biological processes of adaptation. Animals, for example, cannot take intelligence tests.

Piaget, however, insisted on the continuity between biological and psychological processes of adaptation. In his view, the processes of adaptation are the same from the lowliest organisms, such as protozoa, to humans. The process of assimilating knowledge has parallels to the processes of assimilating nutriments. Likewise, intellectual accommodation to new information is directly parallel to biological accommodations to physical changes in the environment. However, Piaget's assertion of that continuity was not reductionistic. Quite the contrary. What Piaget recognized was the extraordinary complexity of even the simplest biological adaptation. To assert the continuity between biological and psychological adaptations is, thus, not a simplification of the psychological processes but, rather, an assertion of their profound intricacy.

It is in that respect that Piaget's position differed from that of much of psychological learning theory. Learning theory, for the most part, also postulates a continuity between biological and psychological processes of adaptation. But those processes are seen as elementary connections between measurable behaviors and stimuli. For Piaget, however, the stimulus and the response are abstractions made for the benefit of the investigator. From the earliest moment of life, the infant seeks to transform the stimulus—for example, by making everything an object to be sucked—by his or her own actions. From a Piagetian position, the stimulus and the response are constructed by the child's mental activity, and they cannot be defined, as learning theory defines them, objectively and without reference to the child's own mental activity.

Piaget's assertion that intelligence is an extension of biological adaptation went beyond the postulation that the processes of assimilation and accommodation operate at all levels of biological functioning. Piaget also asserted that there is a developmental continuity in the formation of intellectual and biological structures. In the formation of the embryo, for example, genetic programs are sequentially executed in coordination with environmental inputs. The same is true in intellectual development, in which new mental structures are formed in a regular sequence of stages—the genetic program—and the rate at which the sequence appears depends on environmental circumstances.

The notion that intelligence is an extension of biological adaptation informed all of Piaget's work and set it apart from much contemporary theorizing to which it seemed similar. For example, much of the use of information-processing models to explicate human intelligence has a common failing. Although such models recognize the complexity of human mental processes, the model itself is essentially mechanical. However, only when such models can account for biological structure and functioning can they account for human intelligence. For Piaget, the test of any viable model of psychological functioning was whether it made sense biologically.

Biology, in its turn, is far from being without theoretical controversy. Thus, Piaget, by asserting the continuity of intelligence and biology, did not avoid theoretical controversy; he simply confronted it on a different plane. That explains why Piaget was more likely to discuss biological theories than to discuss psychological theories. From a Piagetian point of view, one's choice of a biological model necessarily determines the character of one's psychological theory.

Of the various biological models, Piaget advocated a sophisticated version of epigenesis. In biology, epigenesis is the position that growth and development are not preformed but, rather, are sequentially created. At each stage in development, the preceding structure writes the program for the next succeeding structure. In some ways epigenesis is like the act of creative writing. Many times, in the act of writing, new ideas are generated as a consequence of the activity itself and were not previously entertained by the writer. Accordingly, epigenesis says that growth and development are emergent phenomena that are, nonetheless, tied to past history and to immediate experience.

Piaget's was a sophisticated epigenesis because he went beyond a descriptive acceptance of the concept and tried to understand its mode of operation. The question for epigenesis, as well as for human intelligence, is how is it possible for anything new to come about? Biologically, that question has been answered with the concepts of variation, natural selection, and mutation. Psychologically, the question has traditionally been answered with the concepts of learning and problem solving. For Piaget, however, neither the biological nor the psychological answers sufficed. At the biological level, behavioral and structural changes occur too quickly and too nonrandomly to be accounted for by selection and mutation. Within a few generations, for example, fruit flies inherit enlarged anal papillae, even after being removed from the high salt diet that originally produced them.

On the plane of human psychology, similar objections hold true. Learning accounts for how persons acquire what other persons already know, but it does not explain how new knowledge itself comes into being. Likewise, problem solving, which is a little like mutation, can hardly account for the directionality of human knowledge acquisition. Solving problems is perhaps less critical than finding the problems and deciding which ones are important to be solved. The growth of human knowledge cannot be explained by learning, and its directionality cannot be explained by problem solving.

What, then, was Piaget's answer. Oddly enough, it harked back to behavior, to the activity of the organism. But Piaget read behavior quite differently than did behaviorists—at least, behaviorists of the old stamp. For Piaget, behavior was the means by which new phenomena in biology and in psychology come about. A child building with blocks learns how to stack them so that they stay upright. But he or she learns from that activity on the blocks, not just from the blocks themselves. Such discoveries are not fortuitous, however, but derive from an underlying directionality in the child's developing thinking capacities.

Something similar happens at the biological level. When the fruit fly develops enlarged anal papillae as a function of a high salt diet, there is a change in the internal environment of the genome. In Piaget's view, behavioral adaptations result in phenocopies or translations into the genetic programs that make possible a kind of selection at the genetic level that parallels selection at the behavioral level. That internal selection process, triggered by the organisms behavioral adaptations, helps to account for behavioral progress.

Piaget was not a Lamarckian—at least, not in the strict sense. Lamarck argued that morphological changes could be transmitted directly through the genome. The usual example of Lamarckism is that of the giraffe whose ancestor would be assumed to have acquired his long neck by stretching it in order to reach tender upper leaves on trees. In Piaget's view this acquired length would be passed on to progeny not simply because the giraffe's neck had lengthened but, rather, because that change had produced a corresponding change in the genome that made selection within the internal environment possible. Genetic change can be brought about by phenotypic change (the phenocopy) but not directly and only through an internal equilibrating process.

In summary, Piaget asserted that psychological processes are continuous with biological processes, that even the simplest of those processes are extraordinarily complex, and that mental growth, like physical growth, is epigenetic.

LOGICAL SUBSTRUCTURE OF BEHAVIOR AND KNOWLEDGE

One of Piaget's abiding philosophical concerns was the issue of the whole and its parts. But in Piaget's thinking the whole is the whole of human knowledge, and the parts are the various divisions of that knowledge—science, history, mathematics, and so forth. Is there a unity, despite the diversity of human knowledge? If so, it must of necessity be at the genotypic level, rather than at the phenotypic level, because phenotypically, the methods and the concepts of diverse disciplines are so disparate that specialists in those disciplines can rarely talk to one another about anything other than the weather.

For Piaget, however, knowledge was first and foremost human. Whether the discipline is mathematics or sociology, the accumulation of information is carried on by human minds. If there is a unity to human knowledge, therefore, it must be sought not in the resulting knowledge—although that can

provide guidelines—but in the processes of human knowing. It is when one looks at the processes involved in constructing knowledge that one begins to discern the unity of the sciences.

In that regard, Piaget was a structuralist. He argued that, in any domain of human knowledge, one can find three principles in operation—wholeness, self-regulations, and transformations. In Piaget's view those characteristics hold true both for human thought and for the various disciplines of knowledge. That parallelism is not accidental or fortuitous but a direct consequence of the fact that any system of knowledge must reflect, in some ways, the intellectual system of those who created it.

Before talking in detail about the characteristics of structuralism, one might do well to say how that position differs from Kantianism. In his *Critique of Pure Reason*, Kant (1943) argued that reason is not pure because it requires experience but always categorizes it, so that one can never know it in the raw. Thus, Kant saw that all human knowledge bears the imprint of human knowing. But the imprint that Kant perceived was dictated by the physics and mathematics of his time. He mistook some of what was known for categories of knowing. He had no method, other than reflection, for separating the knowing process from the content known.

Piaget, by creating a genetic epistemology—an experimental epistemology—was able to arrive at an empirical separation between the processes of knowing and the content known. By studying children, who lack knowledge of the world, he was able to explore how they reconstruct the world. He was able to separate out what was contributed by the child from what was contributed by experience in a more exact way than Kant was able to. Piaget's structuralist position resulted from his work on genetic epistemology. The principles enunciated earlier are characteristic of children's thinking as they approach any area of knowledge but also characterize those areas of knowledge themselves. Structuralism, however, permits new reorganizations and new knowledge and is, therefore, more flexible and open than the Kantian categories.

Wholeness. The structures or systems that characterize human knowledge, as well as human thinking, are organized wholes. Piaget distinguished between a whole and an aggregate. Although the aggregate is a mere collection of parts, the whole has parts that are dynamically related one to the other. The difference is a little bit like that between 100 or so people in a restaurant who are unrelated and the same number in a restaurant who are relatives and having a family reunion. In the one case there is merely an aggregate, in the other case there is a whole, a group that is organized according to principles of kinship.

The universality of wholes in that sense is easy to demonstrate. In mathematics, the system of whole numbers is but one of the many wholes dealt with by that dicipline. In physics, too, there are macrowholes, such as the planets and the gravitational forces that hold them in orbit. At the micro level, there are the elements and the forces that operate within atoms. In chemistry, too, one can observe wholes—chemical compounds organized according to the principles of valence and equilibrium. In sociology there are groups that have different organizations, and in anthropology there are kinship systems. Organized wholes, then, are to be found in every discipline—and in children's thinking as well.

Transformation. What distinguishes wholes from aggregates is that the system can undergo transformations without losing its identity. If, for example, the population of people eating at a restaurant changes, the aggregate changes as well. The group eating there one day has no systematic relationship to the group eating there the next day. In contrast, the kinship group remains a group, even after they have dispersed: spatial transformations do not destroy the group's wholeness. Other transformations, such as birth and death, do not alter the kinship system in any fundamental way.

A true whole, then, embodies principles of transformation that permit changes to occur within the system that do not, at the same time, destroy the system. In mathematics the system of whole numbers includes the operations of arithmetic that allow numbers to be transformed within the system. In physics wholes are governed by the principles of conservation, which say that, regardless of the transformation, matter can be neither created nor destroyed. In chemistry a similar principle holds true; when liquid is transformed into gas, the results are reversible, which means that gas and liquid are part of the whole.

In the social sciences, too, wholes are regulated by principles of transformation. Kinship systems are a case in point. They permit transformations—say, by marriage—but also include the results of those transformations within the system. Sociology, when it discusses organizations or social institutions, also describes the principles that permit those institutions to persist across transformations in the specific people who hold certain roles. Indeed, the concept of social role means that certain functions are performed across transformations of the people who perform them. Principles of transformation are, then, present in the wholes postulated by all the sciences.

Self-regulation. The third property of structured wholes is that of self-regulation. What that means is that the transformations that characterize a whole are such as to keep the system intact. Although the transformations permit changes to occur, they do not permit changes that would produce new elements that could not be incorporated into the system. In mathematics, for example, the operations of arithmetic yield only new numbers that are again subject to the operations of arithmetic. In physics the principle of entropy operates within a defined system and results not in a new system but only in a dynamically altered one.

Piaget argued that self-regulation takes many different forms in different disciplines. Piaget (1971a) suggested, for example, that biological rhythms are a form of self-regulation. He also suggested that the feedback systems in information processing described by cybernetics are a kind of self-regulation. And homeostatic systems are still another example. At the ethological level, migratory patterns of birds and the mechanisms that prevent a particular species from getting too large—such as scarcity of food—are other examples of self-regulation.

Piaget's structuralism made patent the parallelism between the structures of knowledge and the structures of knowing. In effect, Piaget's structuralism was an analytic argument to support his view that the structure of human intelligence is isomorphic with the structure of knowledge.

STAGES IN THE DEVELOPMENT OF INTELLIGENCE

In his extensive studies of children's thinking, Piaget found four major stages leading to the attainment of adult thought. In keeping with Piaget's biological orientation, each stage is a necessary prerequisite for the one that follows. On the other hand, the rate at which different children move through the stages varies with their native endowment and environmental circumstances. Likewise, in keeping with Piaget's structuralist position, each stage is characterized by a system of operations that has the characteristics of all true structures—namely, wholeness, transformation, and self-regulation.

For heuristic purposes, it is useful to describe the Piagetian stages not only in terms of the structural system that marks that stage but also in terms of the facets of reality that are constructed during that period. The infancy period, for example, may be said to be concerned with the construction of the object world and with questions of space, time, and causality that are centered on concrete objects. In other words, at each stage of development, the child acquires a structural system that enables the child to construct a reality that is isomorphic with his or her intellectual abilities.

Sensorimotor period (birth to 2 years). At birth the infant has a limited behavioral repertoire—a small number of simple reflex reactions, such as sucking and rooting. Even those simple reflexes, however, are far from automatic. The infant, for example, attempts to suck many different things, like a rattle, and could be said to be trying to transform objects into elements to be sucked. In the same way, the infant varies the sucking response in order to adjust to the size and the shape of the nipple. Even the newborn infant, then, is actively accommodating to and assimilating from his or her environment.

The critical achievement of that period, however, is the construction of object concepts. To the adult, objects such as balls, cars, houses, and other people have an existence that is independent of the adult's own immediate experience. The adult believes that objects are there, even though he is not able to see them. He assumes that the Eiffel tower is present now, even though it is some 4,000 miles away. That belief is not innate; it could hardly have been part of his biological heritage. Nor was the idea simply learned, because object permanence is not taught. When a parent shows his or her child the Eiffel tower, the parent does not say, "Remember that the tower will still be here when we get back to Peoria."

Objects and one's sense of their permanence are constructed during the first year or so of life by the progressive coordination of sensorimotor schemata—elementary concepts—that result from the infant's actions on the world and from his or her growing mental abilities and motor skills. For example, as children gain better control over their heads, eyes, and hands, they can begin to coordinate touching and seeing. They can begin to look at objects they touch and touch objects they see. In that way they begin to coordinate visual and tactile schemata to form elaborate object concepts that are both seeable and touchable.

As the infant becomes more mobile, he or she can elaborate new schemata as the spatial, visual, and tactile world expands. In addition, new motor and mental abilities permit new and more elaborate coordinations. For example, toward the end of the first year, infants begin to use one object to attain another. Such attempts reflect not only a beginning sense of objects and their relations but also a sense of intentionality. By the end of the first year the child's sense of objects as permanent has advanced to the point at which he or she will look for them even when they are hidden.

Toward the end of the second year of life, the child's object world is fairly well elaborated, as is the sensorimotor system of intelligence. The structural nature of that system is reflected in the infant's behavior. When the child touches one object to get another, those actions are part of an organized whole and are not random, isolated acts. Likewise, at the end of the second year, the infant can look for and find an object that was displaced two times—say, a sweet that was put first under a cup and then under a handkerchief. The concealment and the displacements are transformations, and the young infant's ability to deal with those transformations is indicative of the fact that his or her mental system is a transformed one.

As far as self-regulation is concerned, that, too, is evident in the child's behavior vis-à-vis objects. Indeed, the 2-year-old's ability to follow a double displacement—to look first under the handkerchief and then under the cup—indicates that the child sees the act of hiding the object as reversible. For every act of putting an object under, there is a compensatory act of taking out. Those understandings are at the sensorimotor level, not the verbal level. Nonetheless, the young child's understanding that actions or objects are reversible is evidence that his or her mental system has the characteristic of self-regulation. Even at the sensorimotor level, therefore, there are reciprocal operations.

One dynamic consequence of the construction of object permanence has to do with the development of attachment. The attachment of a child to a parent presupposes object permanence—the object will continue to exist when it is no longer present to the senses. True attachment to parents apparently does not happen until the last trimester of the first year of life. For example, a young infant separated from his parents for a few days shows no untoward signs. On the other hand, a 9-month-old infant under the same circumstances shows anxiety and clinging on his return to his parents that persists for weeks (Schaffer and Emerson, 1964).

A second consequence of the construction of object permanence has to do with the child's self-concept. Just as the infant begins to construct object concepts, so does he or she construct a concept of the self as object. That object self, however, is primarily a body self, consisting of the parts of the body the child can see, activate, and manipulate. Thus, the infant's initial concept of self as object is distorted because of limited information, and those distortions must be corrected as the child grows older and is able to construct a more veridical body schema. It may be that some schizophrenics retain the distorted body schema they constructed in early infancy.

Preoperational stage. During the second year of life, children begin to give evidence of having attained a new, higher order level of mental functioning that manifests wholeness, transformations, and self-regulation at a higher level. Those characteristics are shown not only in the child's language but in his or her play, dreams, and imitative behavior as well. All those behaviors are symbolic in the sense that they are processes by which the child re-presents objects and activities in their absence. The attainment of object permanence, which involves representation of an imaginal variety, marks the transition from sensorimotor to preoperational or intuitive intelligence.

The progressive elaboration of language offers one example of the structures of the period. With respect to wholeness, the young child's verbal utterances quickly begin to show grammatical regularities that suggest that they are not generated at random (Brown, 1973). After the child's initial one-word utterances, his two-word utterances are usually noun-verb or noun-adjective constructions. Those utterances also reflect transformations in the sense that the child can substitute words in his or her constructions. A child may say "Bobby up" and "Bobby eat." Self-regulation is shown by the fact that the child's new linguistic constructions, such as the words children make up, are speakable within the language system that he or she is operating in.

Children's play during the period shows the same features. In block construction and in painting, for example, the child's product is not a set of unrelated pieces or strokes. Blocks are put together to make a tower or a space, and the child's brush strokes are not unrelated but, rather, constitute a pictorial whole. Transformations are also in evidence. The same blocks can be used to make different constructions and thus show a certain reversibility. In the same way, children paint a variety of patterns that are limited not only by their motoric skill but also by an internal set of regulations that governs what are acceptable and what are unacceptable productions. Those regulations may not be shared by adults, but they arc always there. The same is true in block play. Self-regulation is evident in the limited range of play variations that children allow themselves to engage in.

With respect to thought processes and reasoning, children at this stage have a system of mental regulations and functions that anticipate a true logical system. Functions operate much as do the functions of arithmetic—namely, x is a function of y. In other terms, children represent things—the semantic dimension of language and symbolic activity—in terms of their functions. That is why children define a hole as "to dig" and a bike as "to ride." Once again, the functional mode of thought constitutes a structural system.

With respect to wholeness, the fact that young children define almost everything in terms of functions suggests that there is a principle operating and that the definitions are not given at random. With respect to transformations, the child's definitions of objects in terms of functions are, in effect, symbolic transformations. To say that a bicycle has wheels and is red is not a transformation. Likewise, to say that it is a vehicle is a classification, not a transformation. But to say that a bike is "to ride" is to transform it into something defined not by itself but, rather, by one's activity on it. The child who says that a bike is "to ride" does what the infant does when he attempts to convert everything his lips touch into something to be sucked.

The functional transformations engaged in by the preschool child also show self-regulation. The transformations children perform on objects are bounded by an internal system of constraints. The child does not say, for example, that a bike is "to fly," even though that is well within his or her verbal repertoire. The functional system manifests self-regulation, as well as wholeness and transformations.

From a clinical point of view, the preoperational period bears witness to the constructions of a symbolic self. The child symbolizes not only the world but also the self. "Me" and "mine" and the child's name becomes a powerful foci of feelings and emotions. Like the body self-constructed in infancy, the symbolic self constructed in early childhood is distorted. The boundaries are unclear, as are the functions of self vis-à-vis the functions of others. Much of the symbolic and verbal play of the period has, as one of its aims, a better delineation of the symbolic or representational self.

In addition, the modes of thinking at this stage—phenomenalistic causality (events that happen together cause one another), animism, and nominal realism (belief that words partake of the object or quality they represent)—pertain to the self as well. The symbolic self has loose boundaries and has a closer participation with the immediate world than is true for adults. The young child feels more at the mercy of external forces and also feels that he or she has more control over them (magical participation) than is true at later stages of development.

Concrete operational stage. Toward the age of 5 or 6, children give evidence of having attained another, higher level system of mental structures that Piaget called concrete operations. Those operations resemble, in their mode of functioning, the operations of arithmetic. Concrete operations enable children to engage in syllogistic reasoning, which in turn permits them to acquire and to follow rules. In addition, concrete operations enable young people to construct unit concepts (a unit, such as a number, is both like and different from every other number) and thus to quantify their experience. It seems reasonable, then, to say that this period of development is characterized by the construction of what may be called the lawful world.

Like the mental structures of the previous stages, concrete operations manifest the characteristics of wholeness, transformation, and self-regulation. Indeed, in concrete operations those characteristics are prominent; one can discern them even in the child's verbal behavior. Take, for example, the matter of wholeness. A child who knows that in a given classroom there are 15 boys and 10 girls knows also that there are more boys than girls, more children than either boys or girls, and that the number of boys in the class is equal to the number of children in the class minus the number of girls. Once a child grasps the concept that boys and girls make up the class of children, he or she also knows a group of relationships. A true understanding of classification, therefore, is, in effect, a coordinated set of understandings that constitute a conceptual whole.

Concrete operations also provide the prime example of transformations. By means of concrete operations, children are able to discover the various conservations of quantity. Conservations have to do with the discovery that a quantity remains the same despite a change in its appearance. In the traditional paradigm, children are shown two quantities—two balls of clay, two glasses of orangeade, two sets of six pennies—and are asked if the two quantities are the same. Then one of the quantities is transformed—rolling one of the balls of clay into a sausage, pouring one glass of orangeade into a tall narrow container, spreading apart one row of pennies—and the children are asked if the two quantities are still the same in amount.

Although young children say that a quantity changes in amount when it changes in appearance, older children do not. They are able to deal with the transformation by means of syllogistic reasoning. $A = B$; B transformed into B^1 is still equal to B; therefore, $A = B^1$. Thanks to concrete operations, children are able to grasp the idea that a quantity transformed in appearance remains the same in amount. Concrete operations, therefore, make possible the understanding of the reversibility of transformations in the physical world, much as preoperations made possible the understanding of transformations in the symbolic world.

Concrete operations also show the property of self-regulation. When children use their reasoning powers, they do so on the basis of knowledge that they already have within their own conceptual frameworks. For example, if one asks a concrete-operational child to assume that snow is black, he or she may argue that it is white and refuse to make the contrary-to-fact assumption. Such assumptions are outside the child's conceptual system, and the child will not reason from them. That is but one example of how the concrete-operational child's mental structures regulate themselves so that children use them only on conceptual materials that are within the system.

From the dynamic point of view, the child at the concrete-operational stage arrives at a concept of a lawful self as one who can make and follow rules. Children who become overly invested in that facet of themselves may show obsessive-compulsive symptoms. Children who resist that facet of themselves often seem willful and immature. The most desirable outcome is for the child to develop a healthy respect for rules but to come to understand that there are legitimate exceptions.

Formal operational period. At about the age of 11 or 12, most children begin to give evidence of having attained a new system of mental structures that Piaget called formal operations. It seems that formal operations are not as universally attained as are concrete operations. The attainment and the use of formal operations is probably much more variable than is the case for concrete operations.

The formal operations are more abstract than are the concrete operations and, in effect, constitute a second-order system that operates on the first. Put differently, concrete operations enable children to reason about things; formal operations enable young people to reason about reasoning or thinking. It may be said that formal-operational thinking is to concrete-operational thinking what algebra is to arithmetic. Arithmetic is still tied to content in the sense that 2 plus 2 must equal 4. But algebra separates content from form, and $(a + b)^2 = a^2 + ab + b^2$ regardless of the content, the specific numbers involved.

Because formal-operational thought is, to a considerable extent, freed from content, it can soar. With formal operations young people can conceive of ideal worlds, ideal people, and many possible careers. An ideal, by definition, does not take concrete limitations into account and assume that they do not exist. Formal operations thus account for the idealism of youth, for their intellectualism, and for their capacity to reflect on their own and other people's thinking.

Formal operations, like the other systems of mental structures, show the characteristics of wholeness, transformation, and self-regulation but at a higher, more abstract level. With respect to wholeness, for example, in order to deal with abstractions and ideals in many different domains, young people construct ideal parents and criticize their own parents, they construct ideal governments and find their own government deficient, and they discover new religions that seem less material than their own religion. Those new discoveries and disenchantments are related; they reflect the work of formal-operational thought. In each case form has been separated from content, and young people, without really knowing it, are saying that they like the form but not the content. They approve of the idea of parents, the idea of government, and the concept of religion, but they do not approve of the specific contents of those forms that they know from their own experience.

Formal operations also manifest the property of transformation. That is most evident in the formal-operational young person's skill in dealing with permutations and combinations. Adolescents, for example, can tell all the possible combinations that will result from taking four different colored chips one, two, three, four, and none at a time. In generating combinations, the young person is, in effect, transforming the elements. At the same time, however, each new combination remains within the set, which shows that the system encompasses not only transformations but self-regulations as well.

From a clinical perspective, formal operations make possible the construction of a reflective self. Thanks to formal operations, young people are able to distinguish between the ideal self and the real self—both facets of the reflective self. Just as young people can find fault with real parents in relation to the ideal, so can they find fault with themselves for the same reason. If they do not conform to the stereotypic ideal in terms of height, dimensions, or body build, they become critical of themselves. Self-criticism is a phenomenon of the reflective self and is rare in childhood.

Because young people can reflect on their own and other people's thinking, they can become secretive and can engage in strategic interactions to conceal, reveal, or distort information. They also confuse their own self-centeredness with that of others and construct an imaginary audience that is constantly observing and monitoring their behavior. The audience helps to account for adolescent self-consciousness. Young people's self-centeredness also leads to the construction of a personal fable, a belief that the young person is unique and special—for example, will not grow old. Strategic interactions, the imaginary audience, and the personal fable are but some of the constructions made possible by formal operations, constructions that must be taken into account when dealing with adolescents (Elkind, 1978).

Conclusion

For Piaget, intelligence had to be regarded as an extension of biological adaptation; as a structural system that manifests wholeness, transformations, and self-regulation; and as appearing in a necessary sequence of stages that are related to age. At each of the stages, the structural system makes possible new modes and levels of adaptation. They also make possible new concepts of self that form the bridge between adaptation to the physical world and adaptation to the social world. The significance of Piaget's discoveries for that form of adaptation is only now beginning to be explored.

Suggested Cross References

Information processing is discussed in Section 4.1 and learning theory in Section 4.3. Normality is discussed in Section 6.6, normal child development in Section 34.2, and normal adolescent development in Section 34.3. Intelligence tests are described in Section 12.5.

REFERENCES

Brown, R. *A First Language.* Harvard University Press, Cambridge, Mass, 1973.
Elkind, D. *The Child's Reality: Three Developmental Themes.* Erlbaum Associates, Hillsdale, N. J., 1978.
Kant, I. *Critique of Pure Reason.* John Wiley & Sons, New York, 1943.
Piaget, J. *Recherché.* Concorde, Lausanne, 1918.
Piaget, J. *The Child's Conception of Physical Causality.* Kegan Paul, London, 1930.
Piaget, J. *The Moral Judgment of the Child.* Free Press of Glencoe, New York, 1948.
* Piaget, J. *Play, Dreams, and Imitation in Childhood.* W. W. Norton, New York 1951a.
Piaget, J. *The Child's Conception of the World.* Routledge and Kegan Paul, London, 1951b.
Piaget, J. *Judgment and Reasoning in the Child.* Routledge and Kegan Paul, London, 1951c.
Piaget, J. *The Child's Conception of Number.* Routledge and Kegan Paul, London, 1952a.
Piaget, J. *The Language and Thought of the Child.* Routledge and Kegan Paul, London, 1952b.
* Piaget, J. *The Origins of Intelligence in Children.* International Universities Press, New York, 1952c.
* Piaget, J. *The Construction of Reality in the Child.* Basic Books, New York, 1954.
Piaget, J. Observations sur le mode d'insertion et al chute des rameaux secondaires chez les Sedum. Candollea, *21:* 137, 1966.
Piaget, J. *The Mechanisms of Perception.* Basic Books, New York 1969a.
* Piaget, J. *Structuralism.* Basic Books, New York, 1969b.
* Piaget, J. *Genetic Epistemology.* Columbia University Press, New York, 1970a.
Piaget, J. *Science of Education and the Psychology of the Child.* Orion Press, New York, 1970b.
* Piaget, J. *Biology and Knowledge.* University of Chicago Press, Chicago, 1971a.
Piaget, J. *Psychology and Epistemology.* Orion Press, New York, 1971b.
Piaget, J. *Understanding Causality.* W. W. Norton, New York, 1974.
Piaget, J. *The Grasp of Consciousness.* Harvard University Press, Cambridge, Mass., 1976.
Piaget, J., and Inhelder, B. *The Child's Conception of Space.* Routledge and Kegan Paul, London, 1956.
Piaget, J., and Inhelder, B. *Mental Imagery in the Child.* Routledge and Kegan Paul, London, 1966.
Piaget, J., and Inhelder, B. *Memory and Intelligence.* Routledge and Kegan Paul, London, 1973.
Piaget, J. and Inhelder, B. *The Origin of the Idea of Chance in Children.* W. W. Norton, New York, 1975.

Schaffer, H. R., and Emerson, P. E. The development of social attachments in infancy. Monog. Soc. Res. Child Dev., *29:* 1, 1964.
Uzgirus, I. C., and Hunt, J. McV. *An Instrument for Assessing Infant Psychological Development.* University of Illinois Press, Urbana, 1966.

4.3   Learning Theory

ARTHUR J. BACHRACH, Ph.D.

Introduction

Basic to every form of behavioral interaction—therapy and teaching in particular—is the concept that a change takes place in the person's behavior and that this change is, in large measure, a result of learning. What factors contribute to the success of learning as a behavioral change and how they can be measured, improved, and applied become crucial enterprises for researchers and clinicians.

This interest in learning is reflected in many ways. Statistically, the importance of learning is demonstrated by the total of 21,678 abstracts on learning in the *Psychological Abstracts* from 1967 to 1977. Learning as modifiability of behavior is basically a laboratory focus, yet it is clearly central to clinical questions about the possibilities of learning in the aged, which, like many similar questions, are intensely addressed but are lacking current clear resolution. Resolution or no, it is an important question: Can aging persons modify their behavior? Is behavior always a plastic process? Similar questions of clinical import can be posed: How do drugs affect learning? Do they enhance learning or retard it? Does the administration of a tranquilizing agent such as diazepam (Valium) prepare a patient better for the learning experience of therapeutic modification, or could it actually retard learning? Do the same principles of learning studied in individuals hold when groups or dyads are involved in the behavioral change process? These questions are raised, but, at present, there are few hard data on which one can base anything remotely approaching a definitive answer. Nonetheless, they illustrate the centrality of learning to the study of behavior and its modification, and the theories underlying the learning process become more than an academic nicety. As Hilgard (1956) observed:

Psychologists with a penchant for systems find a theory of learning essential because so much of man's diverse behavior is the result of learning. If the rich diversity of behavior is to be understood in accordance with a few principles, it is evident that some of these principles will have to do with the way in which learning comes about.

When Hilgard asserted that learning theory is critical "if the rich diversity of behavior is to be understood in accordance with a few principles," he was stating an assumption completely in keeping with a scientific method designed for explanations of events in terms of lawfulness and a striving for a minimal set of rational, demonstrable principles to account for these events. In a laboratory science such as experimental psychology, the search for laws of learning has been carried on with just such methods. The leaders in formulating theories of learning—Hull, Tolman, Skinner, Spence, Thorndike, Pavlov, and Guthrie—have all been, to a large degree, laboratory scientists committed to research. A major part of their efforts and those of their colleagues has been the definition of learning variables.

Definition

The definition of learning has always been a difficult problem. Kimble (1961) suggested that there are two roads to definition—factual and theoretical. The factual definitions relate learning to observable events in the physical world. The theoretical definitions are concerned with descriptions of basic processes that the learning theorist believes to be necessary for learning to occur. Hebb (1966) illustrated the theoretical definition when he discussed central nervous system (CNS) activities, the neural messages that occur in the CNS pathways:

> Learning means a change in the direction of messages in the CNS.

Skinner (1953a) discussed response probability as a basic datum in the learning process and offered a factual definition:

> We may define learning as a change in the probability of response, but we must also specify the conditions under which it comes about.

Hebb was postulating changes in the CNS that may be difficult to observe. Skinner concentrated on the frequency and altered probability of a specific observable response under specified observable conditions.

There is a general agreement that somehow learning is a change in behavior that results from practice, with learning representing an intervening process or variable that links organismic states before and after a change in behavior occurs. As Kimble (1961) observed, the definition of learning always assumes a permanent change in behavior, excluding changes resulting from such factors as maturation, sensory adaptation, and fatigue.

LEARNING VERSUS PERFORMANCE

The central question has always been that of differentiating learning from performance. Learning is inferred from observed performance. Kimble saw learning as a change in behavior potentiality. The organism may acquire capabilities to perform some act through learning, but the act itself may not occur. Kimble (1961) stated:

> *Learning* refers to long-term changes of the organisms produced by practice. *Performance* refers [to the] translation of learning into behavior.

At this point Kimble introduced another aspect of the definition in observing that practice alone does not produce learning; it is necessary for some maintaining event to occur, and so it is necessary to add reinforcement. Sidman (1960) defined reinforcement as:

> any event, contingent upon the response of the organism that alters the future likelihood of that response.

REINFORCEMENT

Learning, then, may be defined as a change in behavior potential resulting from reinforced practice. Reinforcement, as so considered, becomes an example of an empirical law of effect that is basic to much of contemporary learning theory. The law of effect, as stated by Thorndike (1931) says:

> Acts followed by a state of affairs which the individual does not avoid, and which he often tries to preserve or attain, are selected and fixated, while acts followed by states of affairs which the individual avoids or attempts to change are eliminated.

The following year, 1932, Thorndike modified his law and indicated that rewarded responses are always strengthened but that punished responses do not always diminish in strength, thus leading to an emphasis on reward as a primary determinant of behavior.

The "rich diversity of behavior" of which Hilgard spoke underscores the necessity for and problems attendant on developing theories of learning. Most of the carefully designed research done in learning is found in the laboratory situation, and most of this research is reported on a limited number of animal species, predominantly the ubiquitous white rat and the pigeon. Species-specific behavior is also a consideration if a restricted number of types of animals is used.

Most of the field research on animals has been of an ethological sort dealing largely with naturalistic observation (Tinbergen, 1958). Recently, however, researchers have applied learning techniques to wild animal research—for example, bait shyness, the avoidance of bait reported for a long time in nonscientific field and stream journals, by studying the effects of toxic agents in conditioning food aversion (Gustavson et al., 1974, 1976). These investigators found that food treated with lithium chloride encased in hides (mutton-lamb carcass and dog food-rabbit) conditioned wolves and coyotes to avoid live sheep and rabbits, even though the bait had only flavor and textural stimuli, with no physical resemblance to an intact animal. Food-illness association has been demonstrated in wild rats by Rzoska (1953) in studies on rat eradication; he found that survivors of a rat colony, most of which was killed by poisoned food, refused to eat the food again.

Studies such as these have implications for learning theory. Learning occurred rapidly, even in one trial. It also occurred after delay, inasmuch as the illness resulting from consuming the bait did not occur until long after the eating. Thus, there was no immediate association contiguous in time between the food and the consequences. And in the case of the wolves and coyotes, there was generalization from one set of cues to an intact prey, resulting in aversion. The learning theorist has much to learn from laboratory and field research; he must be careful to incorporate relevant studies into theorizing, without oversimplification. Garcia et al. (1977) subtitled their paper on food-aversive conditioning in wild animals: *Caveant canonici*, "Let theoreticians beware!"

Conditioning

It is fairly traditional to view conditioning as a case of learning. Hull, in many of his writings, described the classical Pavlovian conditioned reflex as a special case of the law of effect, assuming reinforcement to be operative in such simple learning examples, as well as in higher order learning. Most theorists accept a rough dichotomy between two types of conditioning: classical (Pavlovian) and instrumental (operant).

A recent symposium (Davis and Hurwitz, 1977) attempted to explore the interactions between these two types of conditioning. For the most part, they appeared to recognize potential relationships but emphasized the differences in procedure existing in the two approaches, assuming that procedure is clearer than process. In the discussion that follows, emphasis is placed on procedure in experimentation and analysis for optimal clarity.

CLASSICAL CONDITIONING

Ivan Pavlov, the Russian physiologist, observed in his work with gastric secretions in dogs that stimuli that were often present at the time the dogs were offered food came to evoke salivation in the animals even in the absence of food. For example, the footsteps of the experimenter as he entered the room came to evoke salivation in dogs, even though the dogs could not see or smell food. Pavlov assumed that the stimulus of the footsteps came to be associated with food. His research was directed toward an analysis of this event, which he called the "conditional reflex"—the reflex that would occur, given certain conditions—later somewhat mistranslated as the more familiar "conditioned reflex" or "conditioned response."

In a typical Pavlovian experiment, a stimulus that, before training, had no capacity to evoke a particular type of response becomes able to do so. For example, under normal circumstances, a bell sounded near an animal probably does no more than evoke exploration, such as a turning of the head toward the sound or, perhaps, at most, a startle response. Also, under normal circumstances, a hungry animal may be expected to salivate in the presence of food. Pavlov's conditioned reflex experiment was a training experiment in which the previously neutral stimulus of a bell was made, by pairing it with the food, to evoke the response of salivation, which it normally would not do. To diagram this:

Preconditioning: $S \rightarrow R$
               (bell) (exploration)
               $S \rightarrow R$
               (food) (salivation)
Conditioning: S (bell) $\rightarrow S$ (food) $\rightarrow R$ (salivation)

Bell sounds are followed by the presentation of food. The animal salivates at the sight of the food and ultimately pairs S (bell) and S (food).

Postconditioning: S (bell) $\rightarrow R$ (exploration)
                  conditioned

               S (food) $\rightarrow R$ (salivation)
               (unconditioned stimulus)
               (unconditioned response)

Because the food naturally produces salivation, it is referred to as an unconditioned stimulus. Because the bell was originally unable to evoke salivation but came to do so when paired with food, it is referred to as a conditioned stimulus.

STIMULUS GENERALIZATION AND DISCRIMINATION

In the process of conditioning, Pavlov noted that animals would respond to stimuli similar to the stimulus to which they were conditioned. This event, noted by other experimenters, was called by Thorndike "response by analogy" and by Pavlov "generalization." Primary stimulus generalization, in which physical stimuli similar to the one conditioned are generalized, is illustrated in a classic experiment conducted more than 40 years ago by Hovland (1937), working with human subjects. Immediately after sounding a pure tone of 1,000 cycles a second, he delivered an electric shock to his subject. He recorded the reaction to the shock by the psychogalvanic reflex (PGR) and found that the subjects were conditioned to the tone, giving a PGR to the conditioned tone (CS) without shock. As he ran along a range of tones above and below 1,000 cycles

a second, Hovland discovered that the PGR was lessened more and more as the tones were distant from the original. Pavlov conducted similar experiments, using drops of saliva as a variable to measure the generalization of conditioning. Such generalization has also been referred to as a "spread of effect."

Generalization is at the basis of higher learning, inasmuch as it is possible through stimulus generalization to learn similarities. For example, one need not learn individual street sign characteristics (on a curb, on a pole, on a building). There is sufficient stimulus similarity in such events to allow for generalization to occur. However, for a balance in learning, stimulus discrimination must also occur. To learn differentiation of similar stimuli is also the beginning of higher learning. For example, a child may refer to any quadruped as "doggie," but he learns to discriminate among quadrupeds so that he can differentiate a dog from a cow from a cat and, ultimately, as finer discrimination occurs, a boxer from a beagle from a basset.

A good deal of disordered behavior illustrates problems of this balance between generalization and discrimination. A patient may have negative affective reactions to a person with a moustache, presumably based on a traumatic earlier experience. To have a faulty generalization to all men with moustaches shows that discrimination training, presumably in therapeutic experience, has not been successful.

In sum, learning becomes a balance of generalization and discrimination, with conditioning leading to generalization of similar stimuli to the one conditioned and with discrimination leading to an extinction of responses to those stimuli similar to the original but not the actual conditioned stimulus.

INSTRUMENTAL CONDITIONING

In contrast to classical conditioning, in which the organism is usually restrained—in a Pavlovian harness, for example—and in which the response is elicited by the experimenter, instrumental conditioning is an experimental technique in which a freely moving organism emits behavior that is instrumental in producing a reward. For instance, a cat in a Thorndike puzzle box must learn to lift a latch in order to escape from the box; a monkey in an experimental chair must press a lever to effect the presentation of food.

Sanford (1965) listed four kinds of instrumental conditioning:

The simplest kind is called *primary reward conditioning.* The learned response is instrumental in obtaining a biologically significant reward, such as a pellet of food or a drink of water. In *escape conditioning* the organism learns a response that is instrumental in getting him out of some place he prefers not to be. *Avoidance conditioning* is the kind of learning in which a response to a cue is instrumental in avoiding a painful experience. A rat on a grid, for example, may avoid a shock if he quickly pushes a lever when a light signal goes on. *Secondary reward conditioning* is that in which there is instrumental behavior to get at a stimulus which has no biological utility itself but which has in the past been associated with a biologically significant stimulus. For example, chimpanzees will learn to press a lever to obtain poker chips, which they insert in a slot to secure grapes. Later they will work to accumulate poker chips even when they are not interested in grapes.

Generally, it is assumed that most learning occurs as a result of instrumental responding, rather than as an elicited consequence of classical conditioning. But both classical and instrumental conditioning techniques have begun to occupy a central place in the theoretical and practical behaviors of a growing group of clinicians who consider their methods to be clearly based on experimental laboratory procedures, therapists who derive their techniques and principles from learning theory as based in the laboratory. The clinicians—represented by such theorists as Mowrer, Wolpe, and the followers of methods developed by Skinner—refer to themselves as "behavior therapists," "learning therapists," and "conditioning therapists," such appellations being virtually interchangeable and synonymous.

The most influential contemporary theories of learning have been advanced by Hull, on whose theoretical structure much of Wolpe's work is based, and Skinner, whose methods are basic to operant conditioning techniques in treatment. These theorists fall within the group of learning theorists espousing a reinforcement model of learning. The two-factor learning theory espoused by Mowrer, in which classical conditioning and reinforcement theory are considered, has also been influential.

Hull's Learning Theory

Hull's approach to learning theory is strongly mathematical and neurophysiological. He sought to establish a theory of behavior, which he equated with learning, that could be quantified and tested in accordance with scientific method. In 1943 Hull described the learning process this way:

Just as the inherited equipment of reaction tendencies consists of receptor-effector connections, so the process of learning consists in the strengthening of certain of these connections as contrasted with others, or in the setting up of quite new connections.

These connections occurred internally and were mediated by nervous system stimulation. The establishment of a connection occurs as:

$$S \rightarrow s \rightarrow r \rightarrow R$$

An external stimulus, S, has as its function the stimulation of an efferent system, s, which, in turn, effects a motor impulse, r, within the nervous system. The final response, external R, does not have to occur for learning to take place. The critical connection is the s-r connection, leading to a habit.

HABIT FAMILY HIERARCHY

The habit, for Hull, is an established connection within the nervous system, but these connections are not limited. The concept of the habit family hierarchy allows for the transfer of learning or generalization to occur. Thus, a given stimulus, S, may evoke a number of different responses in varying levels of strength, but this stimulus evokes a response or set of responses within the nervous system that anticipates a goal response. For Hull, the goal response is antedated by fractional responses in the establishment of a habit. Thus, r may become a fractional response, an element of R, called a "fractional anticipatory goal response," or r_G, which in itself is stimulating. As Hull (1942) wrote:

A fractional anticipatory goal situation s_G becomes a guiding stimulus leading to its own realization, to the final complete act of which it is a part. As such, the fractional goal reaction (r_G) is a *pure stimulus act*, i.e., an act whose only biological or survival function is that of producing a stimulus for the control of other action of a more direct adaptive value.

The fractional response, r_G, then becomes a mediating element between S and R. An example of this is salivation occurring before the consummatory goal response to eating.

Because there is variability in response sequences leading to a goal as a result of varying environmental conditions, Hull (1943) postulated that:

since all the alternative behavior sequences have led to the same goal, all of the component acts of all the sequences will alike be conditioned to the same fractional anticipatory goal-reaction stimulus (s_G), and in this sense will constitute a *family*.

The habit family hierarchy, noted Bugelski (1956), proposes that:

any of a number of S's can eventuate in the same R_G goal response.

There is a common fractional goal reaction (r_G) to all the elements in the series and hence in the habit family, but some of these reactions are weaker than others in excitatory potential. (Hull suggested that this difference results from being more remote from the final R_G at the beginning of the sequence.) Therefore, the reactions form a hierarchy of strength. This conceptualization forms an important basis for the therapeutic application of this learning theory, inasmuch as it allows for an analysis of behavior clearly in terms of adaptation through alternative response conditioning.

HULL'S CONCEPT OF DRIVE

Thorndike's law of effect used the concept of satisfaction to account for reinforcing effects of certain responses. Hull (1942) attempted to make the satisfying element less subjective by stating the law of effect as he understood it:

If the central afferent receptor discharge (s_c) of a stimulus element (S_c) of a stimulus compound is active in the central nervous system at the same time that a reaction (r_u) is evoked and if at about this time there occurs a "reinforcing state of affairs," there will result from this conjunction of events an increment to a habit (sHr).

The "reinforcing state of affairs," Hull believed, represented the "diminution in a need (and the associated diminution in the drive [D])."

This principle of primary reinforcement is clearly a drive reduction approach. Attaining the goal response reduces the drive associated with the aroused need, strengthening the behaviors that led to the reduction in tension. This strengthened sequence becomes the habit.

INHIBITION

Hull (1942) postulated that neural impulses (afferent receptor discharges) "occurring at about the same time interact and so modify each other." He called this afferent interaction and viewed it as a basis for the reduction or elimination of a response through the presence of an

extra or alien stimulus in a conditioned stimulus compound which can reduce the excitatory potential.

An example is the interference of "irrelevant stimulations resulting from an emotional upset" that may disrupt a child's classroom performance.

Hull saw this as equivalent to Pavlov's external inhibition. Pavlov's concept of internal inhibition is similar to Hull's conditioned inhibition (sIr), which resulted from reactive inhibition, a negative drive state similar to fatigue or physiological impairment resulting from activity. Hull's conditioned inhibition is an interfering set of events.

This brief summary of salient features of Hullian learning theory indicates that Hull's theoretical position was largely based on neurophysiological postulates and concerned itself with drive and drive reduction as basic to reinforcement. A paper by Eccles (1975) reviewed neurophysiology in learning.

Wolpe's Conditioning Theory

In 1950 Wolpe defined neurotic behavior as behavior that

consists of persistent habits of learned (conditioned) unadaptive behavior acquired in anxiety-generating situations.

It is no coincidence that Wolpe invoked the term "habit" to describe neurotic behavior in this regard. The Hullian influence becomes clear again in the following observation by Wolpe about anxiety responses:

They necessarily produce anxiety drive (with concomitant central neural excitation) as an antecedent.

Wolpe also reflected this neural approach to learning when he noted that:

learning is subserved by the development of conductivity between neurons in anatomical apposition.

Here one sees the Hullian concepts of learning as being mediated by central nervous system activity, the neurophysiological basis of drive, and anxiety as a drive leading, presumably, to activity at drive reduction.

RECIPROCAL INHIBITION

Wolpe (1958, 1962) also reflected a Hullian orientation in his important principle of reciprocal inhibition, which may account for anxiety drive reduction. In 1962 Wolpe stated:

If a response inhibitory to anxiety can be made to occur in the presence of anxiety-evoking stimuli, it will weaken the connection between these stimuli and the anxiety responses.

Relaxation, for example, is considered to be incompatible with anxiety and, therefore, inhibitory to it.

ANXIETY HIERARCHY

Wolpe also used Hull's concept of habit family hierarchy in an interesting clinical fashion when he established anxiety hierarchy relationships among anxiety-evoking stimuli. Assuming that varying stimuli may evoke the response of anxiety, Wolpe asked his patient to imagine, usually under hypnosis, the least disturbing item of a list of potentially anxiety-evoking stimuli, then to proceed up the list to the most disturbing stimuli. For example, a patient with a fear of death might rank the sight of a coffin lower in the hierarchy than a corpse (highest intensity), with perhaps a tombstone ranked somewhere in between.

Wolpe's technique of desensitization is a counterconditioning technique in which responses designed to inhibit the anxiety response are evoked at each level along the hierarchy. Reciprocal inhibition of the fear response is thus conditioned.

Skinner's Learning Theory: Operant Conditioning

Proponents of an experimental analysis of behavior based on operant conditioning techniques and reinforcement theorists form a group of behaviorists who tend largely to minimize theoretical considerations and to concentrate on an analysis of the functional relationships among events. For example, instead of dealing with the repression of unacceptable thoughts, as psychoanalysts do, Skinner (1953b) suggested that it is more important to avoid the inner causes and to emphasize the questions that ask

why the response was emitted in the first place, why it was punished, and what current variables are active.

The term "operant" refers to a class of responses that is emitted by the organism, rather than elicited by some known stimulus. Operant responses are also frequently referred to by such terms as "voluntary," as opposed to "involuntary" or reflex behavior. Reflex responses are elicited as in classical conditioning and are called "respondents." Thus, respondents, such as pupillary reflexes, are differentiated from operants. An example of an operant response is reaching for a telephone. An operant has some effect on the environment. Keller (1969) observed:

Respondents, right from the start, are evoked by their own special stimuli. Food in the mouth will bring salivation . . . In the case of operants, however, there are at the beginning no specific stimuli with which we can evoke them. Rather, we are compelled to wait until they appear before we can do anything about them . . . It is for this reason we may speak of operant behavior as *emitted* ("sent out") rather than elicited.

Skinner, in his first major work, *The Behavior of Organisms* (1938), differentiated two types of conditioning, which he called type *S* and type *R*. Type *S* conditioning

is defined by the operation of the simultaneous presentation of the reinforcing stimulus and another stimulus.

In type *R* conditioning, the reinforcing stimulus "is contingent upon a response." This distinction between classical (respondent, involuntary, type *S*) and instrumental (operant, voluntary, type *R*) conditioning is not entirely accepted by many learning theorists, on the grounds that the criteria are too ambiguous. Psychophysiological interactions, for example, are not clearly differentiated into operant or respondent. For most purposes, however, the distinction can be useful if one avoids the tendency to let theoretical niceties restructure the nervous system.

REINFORCEMENT

A key concept in operant conditioning is that of reinforcement, which, as noted earlier, Sidman defined as

any event, contingent upon the response of the organism that alters the future likelihood of that response.

In operant conditioning the term "positive reinforcement" is used to describe an event consequent upon a response that increases the probability of that response recurring. A "negative reinforcement" is an event likely to decrease the probability of that response's recurrence. A negative reinforcement is an event that strengthens the response that removes it; for example, if a punishing consequence attaches to a response, any behavior that avoids or escapes the punishment will be strengthened—that is, increased in probability.

RESPONSE FREQUENCY

Another important concept is the use of response frequency as a basic datum. The frequency with which a response is emitted is a clear, observable measure of behavior. Skinner (1953 a,b) observed that personality descriptions are couched in frequency terms; to say that a person is "an enthusiastic skier," "an inveterate gambler," or "hostile" reduces to a statement of a perceived frequency with which a certain class of behavior is emitted, presumably with some normative conceptualization in mind. Aggressive behavior is emitted by most people; to say that a person is hostile suggests that this class of response occurs with a higher level of frequency than is usually expected.

SHAPING BEHAVIOR

A fundamental concept in operant conditioning is that of shaping, by which the experimenter, having specified the response he desires from the organism, successfully brings the organism closer to the chosen terminal behavior. In establishing this behavior, he begins with the mass of responses available to

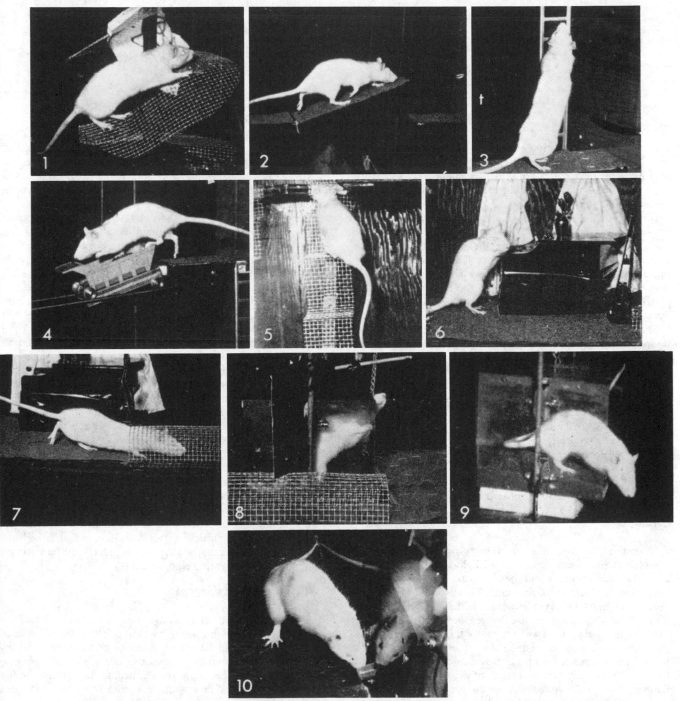

FIGURES 1 to 10. Demonstration of chained responding. (From Bachrach, A. J. Some applications of operant conditioning to behavior therapy. In *The Conditioning Therapies: The Challenge in Psychotherapy*, J. Wolpe, A. Salter, and L. J. Reyna, editors. Copyright 1964 by Holt, Rinehart and Winston, Inc. Reprinted by permission of Holt, Rinehart and Winston, Inc.)

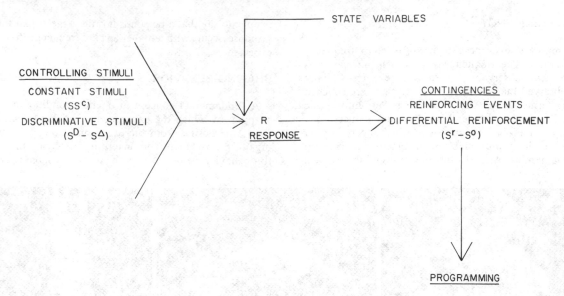

FIGURE 11. A paradigm of operant conditioning.

the organism he is manipulating. By clearly defining the terminal response, the experimenter must then identify the steps by which this terminal response will be shaped. By successive approximation—that is, leading the organism to the desired behavior—shaping occurs.

For example, if an experimenter wishes a pigeon to peck at a translucent plastic key on a wall of an experimental box, he most likely starts by reinforcing the pigeon for facing the particular wall on which the key lies. Then he reinforces the pigeon when he moves toward the wall, when he ultimately pecks at the wall, and, finally, when the pigeon pecks at the plastic key. The terminal response of key pecking was shaped from a large number of possible responses.

Shaping derives in large measure from exploratory responses in which the animal moves in the experimental box and the experimenter selects those responses to be reinforced. By presenting the food hopper with the food available at each successive approximation, the experimenter has an active animal working toward the ultimate response. When the key pecking occurs, the reinforcement may then be programed by having the pellets delivered automatically by the machine, rather than hand activated by the experimenter. It is critical in shaping that the reinforcement occur immediately after the response, inasmuch as a delay in reinforcement may be accompanied by other responses that are not desired, and these responses, in turn, may be reinforced adventitiously.

CHAINING

Responses can be built on other responses to develop a complex chain. A demonstration of behavioral chaining in a white rat was set up a number of years ago by a team of psychologists, Pierrel and Sherman. This procedure was modified by Bachrach (1964) to demonstrate that complex behavior may be conditioned response by response. The rat in the experiment by Bachrach was originally trained at the University of Virginia and was named Rodent E. Lee. He was first trained to eat from a food tray, then to press a lever to obtain food that was delivered by means of a solenoid activating a hopper. Once his bar-pressing response for food reinforcement was established, it was possible to shape a number of responses chained in a complex fashion.

Figures 1 through 10 illustrate the steps Rodent E. Lee went

through to reach the final reinforcement of bar pressing and food. It was necessary for him to climb a spiral stairway, run across a draw bridge, climb a ladder, enter a cable car and pull himself across a gap a few feet above the floor of his experimental box, climb another stairway, and play a toy piano by hitting two keys of the eight that activated a switch that opened a crossing gate for a model railroad. He then ran through the crossing gate tunnel when the crossing gate was open, climbed into an elevator, pulled the chain to release the elevator, rode down to the bottom floor, and pressed the bar to receive his food pellets. This complex chain of behavior was shaped, as noted, beginning with pressing the bar for food. In this sense he was trained backward. After the food response, he was trained to ride the elevator to get to the bar to press it for the pellet. The next response shaped was to pull the chain to release the elevator so he could ride to the bottom of the box and so on. At each stage of the shaping, the responses were achieved by successive approximation techniques. For example, the difficult task of getting him to pull the elevator chain to release the elevator was accomplished by shaping him to make movements toward the chain in a fashion similar to that described earlier for the pigeon pecking. Any response initially—to sniff, to approach the chain, to touch it with his nose, then his paws, and, finally, the terminal response, to pull it—was reinforced. Each action was an approximation toward the final desired response of pulling. In chaining, each response becomes the reinforcing event for the previous response and the stimulus for the succeeding response. In this manner all complex behavior, particularly in skills that appear to be fluid responses, may actually be shaped and perceived as a chain of individual stimulus and response units.

AN OPERANT PARADIGM

A clear way of visualizing the operant situation is through a paradigm originally presented by Goldiamond (1962). Goldiamond stated that Dollard and Miller listed the four variables of learned behavior as drive, response, cue, and reinforcement, and he suggested that these are identical to the variables in his operant paradigm. The schema in Figure 11 is modified from Goldiamond.

To understand the procedure, one must first recognize the state variables, which are usually referred to as needs, motives, and the like. The state variables make the consequences of the response effective in the control of the response, but they are difficult to determine. In a real sense, state variables are always inferred from the subject's history. The experimenter then presents a discriminative stimulus—that is, a stimulus to which the experimenter wishes the organism to respond, which occasions a response (R). Other stimuli present in the situation may be referred to as constant stimuli (SS^c). Those stimuli that appear but to which the organism does not respond are referred to as $S^\triangle$ (S delta). Thus, the experimenter wishes the organism to select from the stimulus complex of constant stimuli the discriminative stimulus to which he has been presumably shaped to respond. Once the response occurs, the reinforcing contingencies (consequences) strengthen the response and later the probability of its recurrence. A consequence (S^r) can be positive, negative, or punishing.

Positive reinforcement presumably increases the probability of the response recurring. A negatively reinforcing stimulus event, as Keller observed, is one that strengthens the response that takes it away, but it is also a stimulus that weakens the response that produces it; that is, a response that removes the organism from an aversive situation is reinforced positively, but a response that evokes an unpleasant consequence is weakened by the contingency. Punishment is distinguished from negative reinforcement in that a punisher (aversive stimulus) is presented specifically to suppress an undesired response. Punishment reduces response frequency. Negative reinforcement, in a manner related to positive reinforcement, increases frequency of response (Ferster and Perrott, 1968). It is possible that no consequence may be apparent to the organism responding. This is noted in the paradigm as S^0.

The concept of constant stimuli from which discriminative stimuli are drawn is not unlike the topological approach of Kurt Lewin. In vector analysis of behavior, Lewin (1935) described a life-span that included a physical or geographical environment containing all stimuli to which the organism might respond and a behavioral environment that included those stimuli to which the organism is actually responding. The experimenter's or therapist's task is to understand clearly those stimuli that evoke certain kinds of behavior under specified conditions, recognizing the different types of events to which the individual may respond.

STIMULUS CONTROL

Basic to the question of stimulus complexity and stimulus presentation is the concept of stimulus control. There is reason to assume that, although behavior is established through reinforcement in a stimulus situation, the maintenance of once-established behavior is more a function of stimulus control than of continuing reinforcement. Stimulus generalization and stimulus discrimination are powerful aspects of maintaining behavior once conditioned—the control of behavior by stimuli is something taken for granted. A rudimentary example of stimulus control is one familiar to most people. Assume for the moment that you have been sitting in room A and need an object that is located in room B. You go to room B to secure the object and, when you enter the room, forget what it was you went to get, whereupon you return to room A, where the object is not but where the stimuli that evoked the searching behavior are.

Stimulus control emphasizes the importance of environmental stimuli in the study of behavior. In recent years the interest in architectural psychology in analyzing the impact of such environments as hospital wards and classrooms on human behavior reflects an important application of stimulus control.

PROGRAMING (SCHEDULES OF REINFORCEMENT)

A final important concept of the operant paradigm is that of programing or schedules of reinforcement. Behavior is developed to specification by these schedules of reinforcement, which are centered on the contingent relationship between response and reinforcement. Because these programed schedules of reinforcement are quantifiable procedures, man-made attempts to duplicate environment-learning interactions, they are discussed here in some detail. In the research setting, the responses on these schedules are recorded on a cumulative recorder, providing a pen-and-ink record of the organism's responding (see Figure 12).

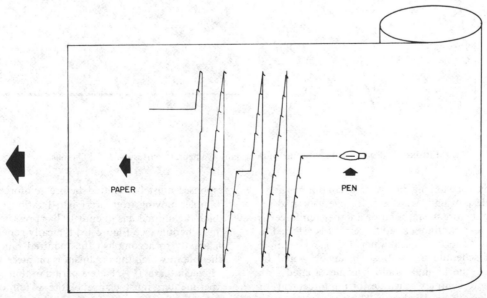

FIGURE 12. Diagram of a cumulative record. The pen moves up one step each time the subject responds, and the paper moves from right to left at a rate of about 1 inch every 5 minutes. The higher the rate of responding, the steeper the slope recorded by the pen, which resets after excursion to the top.

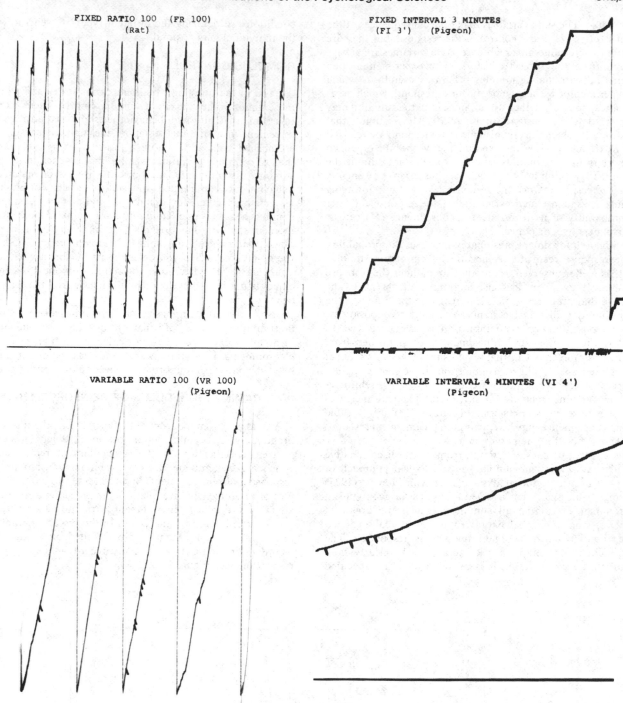

FIGURE 13. Four schedules of intermittent reinforcement. (Courtesy of J. R. Thomas.)

Under conditions of shaping behavior a continuous rein-forcement schedule is usually in effect; for every desired re-sponse emitted by the organism, food or another reinforcer is presented. This 1-to-1 continuous reinforcement is referred to as the "crf schedule" (Ferster and Skinner, 1957). To continue shaping on a crf schedule to establish behavior would be impossible, because the animal would become satiated with food; therefore, more complex schedules of reinforcement for specific purposes have been developed. The main intermittent schedules are as follows.

Fixed ratio (FR). In this schedule a certain number of responses must be emitted before reinforcement occurs—for example, moving from a crf 1-to-1 ratio to a 10-to-1 ratio, in which the animal has to emit 10 bar presses to receive a pellet. This schedule (see Figure 13) typically generates a rapid burst of activity to accomplish the required ratio. It is a counting schedule in which the organism is on piece work.

Fixed interval (FI). Here a period of time, determined by the experimenter, must elapse before a reinforcement becomes available. Until the fixed interval elapses, no responses can be reinforced. The time interval is fixed not between reinforce-ments but between availability of the reinforcement, and the first response reinforced is the one made by the animal after the elapsed interval. This schedule generates a typical scallop (see Figure 13) in which, after a reinforcement, there is a diminution of responding that gradually accelerates as the interval between reinforcements approaches its end. An everyday example of this schedule is study behavior. After a weekly Friday examination, the chances are high that books will be put away after the test, with study behavior accelerating to a height of activity just before the next examination.

Variable ratio (VR). In this schedule a range of ratios around a determined mean value is programed. For example, a variable ratio of 50 means that, on an average of every 50 responses, the animal is reinforced, but reinforcement could occur after 4 responses, then perhaps not again until 100 or more responses have been emitted. This type of schedule (see Figure 13) generates a fairly constant rate of responding, inasmuch as the probability of reinforcement at any given time remains stable. This is the schedule used in the slot machines in Las Vegas.

Variable interval (VI). Similar to the VR, the VI is often substituted for a fixed-interval schedule; it also generates stable responding. Again, the unpredictability of the reinforcement tends to generate a fairly constant response rate. In a fashion similar to the fixed-interval and variable-ratio schedules, the variable-interval schedule may have a predetermined average interval of 5 minutes; but, once again, the appearance of the reinforcement is uncertain (see Figure 13).

Differential reinforcement of low rates (DRL). This is a timing schedule in which the organism is reinforced for spaced responding. Under the schedule the organism is reinforced for a response that follows a preceding response by a specified time interval. A DRL of 16 seconds, for example, means that, if the organism responds before 16 seconds have elapsed, the timer is reset, and he is, in effect, punished for responding. A more precise timing behavior can be established by producing a limited hold (LH) with the DRL schedule. Limited hold permits a specified time period in which the reinforcement is available; for example, on a DRL 16 LH 6, the organism is not reinforced for any response occurring before 16 seconds or after 22 seconds. Any response falling outside of this band again resets the timer, making reinforcement unavailable.

An example of a DRL schedule that illustrates the slow rate of responding is taken from a study of adaptation to narcosis in diving (Walsh and Bachrach, 1974) (see Figure 14). The surface control is at the bottom right of the composite profile of response patterns. After control on the surface, the experimental rat was subjected to 200 feet of hyperbaric pressure in a chamber in a sequence of dives, spaced several days apart. When the record for the first dive is compared with the record for surface control, it is seen that the timing behavior was extremely disrupted. Adaptation occurred by dive 5, in which the response profile closely resembles the surface control. This schedule has been very useful in drug assessments; in this paper the authors compare the effect of hyperbaric pressure and narcosis to a similar amphetamine reaction as reported by Sidman (1955).

Differential reinforcement of other behaviors (DRO). This is a somewhat less structured programing of reinforcement in which the undesired response is selected by the experimenter or therapist and is ignored, with the reinforcement of other behaviors programed. This schedule is designed to extinguish undesired responses by nonreinforcement (Reynolds, 1961).

Multiple schedules. These are a combination of schedules of reinforcement. The timing behavior of the DRL may be paired with the counting behavior of the FR to provide another type of discrimination, so that when one colored light (red) is on, the DRL is operative; when a green light is on, the FR is in effect. This alternation of schedules (see Figure 15) is valuable in that it requires yet another discriminative behavior on the part of the subject.

Repeated acquisition of behavioral chains. An extension of the chaining procedure discussed previously, which is not properly a schedule, has been developed in recent years (Boren and Devine, 1968). It allows the investigation of the learning process on a daily basis. The procedure is referred to as the repeated acquisition of behavioral chains. Typically, in this schedule an animal is trained to respond on multiple levers, which must be operated in a predetermined sequence to produce reinforcement. A continuing state of acquisition or transition is achieved by periodically changing the reinforced sequence. As a result, the subject eventually learns to acquire a

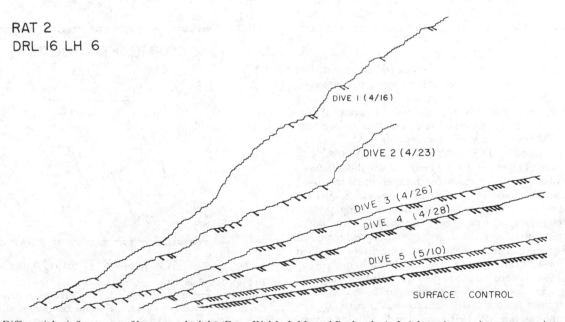

RAT 2
DRL 16 LH 6

DIVE 1 (4/16)

DIVE 2 (4/23)

DIVE 3 (4/26)

DIVE 4 (4/28)

DIVE 5 (5/10)

SURFACE CONTROL

FIGURE 14. Differential reinforcement of low rate schedule. (From Walsh, J. M., and Bachrach, A. J. Adaptation to nitrogen narcosis manifested by timing behavior in the rat. J. Comp. Physiol. Psychol., *86*: 883, 1974.)

RAT 14

MULT FR 40 DRL 18 (LH6)

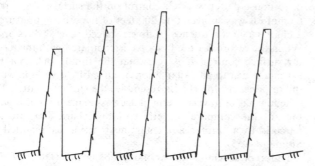

FIGURE 15. Multiple schedule of reinforcement. (Courtesy of J. M. Walsh.)

number of different response sequences. Various aspects of the performance reach a stable state after a period of training. The baseline may then be used to investigate variables affecting the learning process.

This procedure circumvents a long-standing problem in experimental psychology—that an organism is naïve only once. Traditionally, this difficulty has been dealt with by exposing groups of animals to a problem under differing circumstances and comparing the groups to obtain an estimate of a variable's effect on the learning process. The repeated acquisition procedure requires an organism to learn a new problem daily. Therefore, variables affecting learning can be studied with an individual subject over extended periods of time.

For example, the effects of cocaine on this schedule can be seen through the alteration in cumulative response records shown in Figure 16. In these records the pen steps with each incorrect response and resets after the completion of each block of 20 sequences. Sequence completion is indicated by the downward deflection of the response pen. In this schedule the animals were responding to avoid electric shock; shock delivery is indicated by the downward deflection of the lower (event) pen. Each sequence completion resulted in a discriminated period of time, 30 seconds, during which the animal was never shocked.

The baseline or control record at the top of the figure demonstrates the normal pattern of repeated acquisition. The initial segment of the session is characterized by numerous incorrect responses and periodic pauses in responding; as a consequence, shocks are delivered relatively frequently. As the animal acquires the behavioral chain, incorrect responding, pausing, and shock delivery are greatly diminished.

At this point the chain is established, and it is possible to study effects of other events on the behavior—in this situation, the effects of cocaine hydrochloride. Intraperitoneal injections of cocaine administered 5 minutes before the session alter the established pattern of behavior. With a dose of 10 mg. per kg., incorrect responding and pausing diminished after the initial block but did not achieve the degree of stability evidenced in the baseline record. The frequency of shock delivery remained relatively constant throughout the session. With 30 mg. per kg. the acquisition pattern was completely abolished. Incorrect responding was consistently high throughout the session, alternating with brief pauses; shock delivery was consistently elevated over the baseline. Obviously, cocaine disrupts the normal acquisition process.

ADVENTITIOUS REINFORCEMENT

There are times when responses are reinforced adventitiously or accidentally by coincidental pairing of response and reinforcement. An early experiment by Skinner illustrates this. Skinner placed a pigeon in an experimental box and left it there for a brief period every day. Every 15 seconds, no matter what the bird was doing, a food hopper appeared, allowing the bird access to food. The appearance of food was completely independent of the bird's actions. Despite this, certain well defined responses of a stereotyped nature, such as turning counterclockwise in a box two or three times between reinforcements, began to appear in the bird's behavior. Skinner (1958) noted:

the bird happens to be executing some response as the hopper appears; as a result, it tends to repeat this response.

217

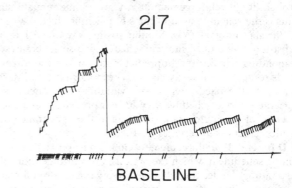

BASELINE

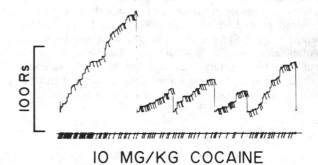

100 Rs

10 MG/KG COCAINE

10 MIN

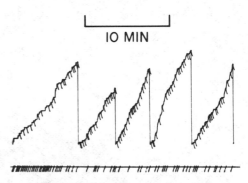

30 MG/KG COCAINE

FIGURE 16. Cumulative records for one rat, showing the effect of cocaine on repeated acquisition. Incorrect responses stepped the pen; downward deflections indicate sequence completion; the pen resets with the completion of blocks of 20 sequences. Deflections of the lower (event) pen indicate shock delivery. (Courtesy of J. F. Schrot.)

Most of the responses were observed to occur in a specific area of the experimental box, suggesting that somehow the geographical space was also associated with the response. Because the response of the bird bore no causal relationship to the appearance of food but persisted nonetheless, Skinner referred to this behavior as "superstitious." The incidental occurrence of a reinforcer, which was not a contingent reinforcement, has been referred to as "adventitious reinforcement."

In a second kind of experimental situation, Skinner and Morse (1957) placed pigeons on a variable-interval schedule of 30 minutes, during which they pecked at a translucent key behind which an orange light appeared. For 4 minutes out of each hour, at a time unpredictable to the pigeon, an incidental stimulus appeared—the color of the light changed from orange to blue. On occasion, the appearance of the blue light adventitiously coincided with the presentation of the food. A type of sensory superstition developed in which the sensory stimulus (blue light), adventitiously associated with the reinforcing appearance of food, took on properties of behavior control. Skinner and Morse further experimented by presenting the blue light intermittently in the absence of food and found that the bird's pecking dropped to a low rate or actually ceased—a type of negative superstition.

Thus, adventitious reinforcement can be linked to responses of the organism accidentally paired with reinforcing contingencies, as well as with incidental stimuli. The incidental stimuli may play a role in the development of phobic responses (Bachrach, 1962). Adventitious association of sensory stimuli with punishing or rewarding events appears to be closely related to the type of superstitious responding illustrated by the experiments described. The adventitious association of certain consequences to responses may be at the basis of much of what is referred to as neurotic behavior, which persists as though it were contingent on certain responses and events. A major contribution to this neurotic behavior appears to be the unpredictability of reinforcement on a variable-interval schedule, which, as noted above, produces a stability of responding because of the uncertainty involved in the appearance of the reinforcement. An anthropological example of superstitious behavior in the face of unpredictable consequences was described by Malinowski (1925):

An interesting and crucial test is provided by fishing in the Trobriand Islands and its magic. While in the villages on the inner Lagoon fishing is done in an easy and absolutely reliable manner by the method of poisoning, yielding abundant results without danger and uncertainty, there are on the shores of the open sea dangerous modes of fishing and also certain types in which the yield varies greatly according to whether schools of fish appear beforehand or not. It is most significant that in the Lagoon fishing, where man can rely completely upon his knowledge and skill, magic does not exist, while in the open-sea fishing, full of danger and uncertainty, there is extensive magical ritual to secure safety and good results.

The easy and reliable fishing situation suggests a continuous reinforcement schedule, and the dangerous and uncertain open-sea fishing is clearly an intermittent, unpredictable schedule. As Malinowski observed, magical ritual occurs only with uncertainty. It is perhaps in the learning of superstitious behavior that a key to understanding certain neurotic responses may lie.

The importance of adventitious reinforcement in the development of avoidance behavior is illustrated in a case dealing with sensory association of phobic objects (Lief, 1955). This case portrayed a woman whose presenting symptoms included an inability to drive her car and difficulty in sleeping. Lief's analysis of her difficulties in the course of a therapeutic interaction appeared to relate the symptoms to an earlier incident involving her husband when he was hospitalized (Lief, 1955):

One particular Sunday she decided to visit her husband earlier than usual—he was in the hospital recuperating from an illness—and so she attended an early church service that morning. When she walked into the hospital room, about two hours sooner than she was expected, she saw a young woman—a pretty redhead—holding her husband's hand. The girl got up and left hurriedly with a murmured apology. Upon the wife's insistent demands, the husband confessed a two-year's intimate relationship with the girl, a waitress in a drugstore. The wife fainted and had to be carried to another room and put to bed.

Following this episode, the wife developed a profound depression, and she also developed a phobic avoidance of many things adventitiously associated with the traumatic experience. The time of the original experience was involved in that she woke up with panicky feelings on Sunday mornings for months after what she termed the "shock." The places were also involved: Going to church upset her so that for a while she actually remained away, although she was ordinarily a conscientious, almost compulsive, churchgoer. The hospital where the trauma had occurred was avoided like the plague, and she would suffer unbearable anxiety if she came within blocks of it. Various accessory cues also became significant: Although the dress she was wearing that day was an expensive one, she threw it out. She likewise threw out all drugs bearing the label of the drugstore where the redhead worked, and she ordered her husband never to buy anything from, much less frequent, that drugstore. If she came anywhere near the store she would become panicky, and so she made wide detours to avoid it. The delivery wagons of the drugstore gave her the same frightened feeling. She also began to develop a phobic avoidance of all places where she learned her husband had taken the girl—motor courts, restaurants, even particular streets and highways. For a time it was almost impossible for her to drive her car.

The behaviors reported in this case may be discussed as symbolic behaviors, but they may also be viewed as consistent with principles of learning theory. There were three major events: (1) a noxious event (the hospital encounter), (2) a lowering of response (profound depression), and (3) a generalization of an avoidance response, with a spread of effect from the original traumatic stimulus. As Bachrach and Quigley (1966) observed in discussing the learning aspects of this case:

The spread of effect, in learning terms, from the original noxious stimulus took three chains, one generalizing from the church and two generalizing from the hospital:

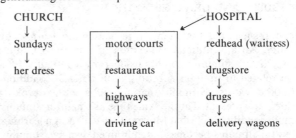

Superstitious behavior is also in evidence in the association of previously neutral events (objects and times) with traumatic events.

Although this case may, indeed, be illustrative of the faulty generalization described earlier, it clearly illustrates the adherence to known principles of learning of what is described as abnormal behavior. It also illustrates one of the more important types of learning that theorists and researchers find of interest, that of avoidance. Earlier, the rapid conditioned food aversion in wild animals was discussed. Avoidance is central to much of the theorizing of psychopathology, and experimentation over the years by learning researchers continues to reflect a model presented by Schoenfeld (1950), in which an avoidance paradigm characterizes the events as follows:

$$S_1 ------ S_2$$

in which S_1 is followed by S_2, a noxious or painful event. Thus, S_1 becomes, in effect, a discriminative stimulus or a warning stimulus, which indicates that the temporally or spatially noxious S_2 will occur. This leads to an avoidance response:

$$S_1 ------/------ S_2$$
$$R_{T\,(av)}$$

where $R_{T\,(av)}$ becomes a response that terminates the situation leading to S_2 by avoidance. This clearly characterizes much of what is found in patients described as neurotic. Other experimenters in avoidance research have followed leads by Solomon et al. (1953), whose early work on traumatic avoidance learning remains of interest. These investigators conditioned avoidance responses in dogs trained to avoid a shock by jumping over a barrier. Once this conditioned response was established, it was difficult, if not impossible, to extinguish. They suggested that the only truly successful way in which extinction of the avoidance response in these dogs could be accomplished was by forced reality testing, making the animal test the situation to learn whether or not the shock was still on. Their findings suggest that this is not unlike the behavior of a neurotic whose reality testing of previously traumatic events is not likely to occur as long as the $R_{T\,(av)}$ continues to work, no matter how limiting the behavior may be to other aspects of his life.

Mowrer's Two-Factor Learning Theory

In a paper in 1939, Mowrer offered, as Hilgard (1956) has observed:

> the first clear statement of the anxiety-reduction or fear-reduction theory of reinforcement.

Mowrer (1947, 1956, 1961) then theorized that much learning can be explained on the basis of acquired fear (anxiety) and that responses that reduce this anxiety are learned and maintained.

CONTIGUITY AND DRIVE REDUCTION

Mowrer suggested that anxiety responses are learned by contiguity. An adventitious association of a neutral stimulus with a painful stimulus conditions fear by contiguity in a fashion related to stimulus substitution in classical conditioning. In other words, a stimulus that in itself is not fear evoking is accidentally presented at the same time as a painful stimulus; by simple conditioning, what Mowrer then called sign learning, the neutral stimulus becomes a conditioned aversive stimulus.

Any response that results in the avoidance or elimination of such a conditioned aversive stimulus, as an anxiety-producing event, is reinforced, even in the absence of other reinforcement, because the response reduces anxiety (drive). Once learned, these avoidance responses persist.

Mowrer thought that these were different from other types of conditioned responses in that there was no need for contin-

ued reinforcement to maintain the response. Other conditioned responses extinguish in the absence of reinforcement; Mowrer felt that conditioned anxiety responses do not need the reinforcement of repetition of the original trauma. Although the responses were conditioned by contiguity, they are maintained by the reinforcing effects of drive reduction. Classical conditioning of fear by contiguity is maintained by the subsequent conditioning (instrumental) of avoidance behavior by drive reduction.

AUTONOMIC RESPONSES

Another differentiation Mowrer assumed in his two-factor theory was that fear responses are entirely autonomic. Emotional responses are involuntary and largely autonomic; instrumental responding is voluntary and largely under the control of the central nervous system. The classically conditioned fear response learned under contiguity (sign learning) was, therefore, physiologically differentiated from the instrumentally conditioned avoidance responses maintained by anxiety reduction, what Mowrer came to call "solution learning." The operant-respondent, type S-type R dichotomy is clearly in evidence here.

Operant and Pavlovian procedures with respect to autonomic conditioning were brought into focus in an article by Miller (1969), in which the author presented research on the operant conditioning of autonomic responses, such as heart rate. This paper gave rise to a considerable amount of research, which, to date, has not been successful in this type of conditioning, except in occasional situations (Black et al., 1977). Replication of the earlier work has not been achieved.

Some experimental evidence supported Mowrer's position that drive reduction is important in solution learning (instrumental conditioning) but that it is not crucial in the autonomically controlled anxiety response. Studies such as those reported by Mowrer and Solomon (1954) tended to support such a position, although Solomon and Wynne (1954) suggested that fear responses are more than autonomic, involving such events as visceral and neuroendocrine responses, as well as skeletal motor discharge. Thus, central nervous system functions and voluntary behavior are also involved.

Mowrer also invoked a model in which the stimuli conditioned to the onset of painful events acquire certain drive (anxiety) characteristics, but those stimuli associated with the avoidance of or escape from pain become positively reinforcing. Mowrer described these two events as responses of fear and hope. In recent years, Mowrer's theorizing has centered largely on the development of neurosis and, in particular, the centrality of guilt and anxiety in emotional disorders.

Cognitive Learning Theory

The learning theorists so far discussed have all been essentially S-R associationists, no matter what differences existed between and among them. In recent years there has been a resurgence of interest in an approach that, according to many of its proponents, goes beyond a mechanistic view of learning and behavior and takes into account the cognitions, thoughts, and expectations of the individual organism. This cognitive psychology derives, in the main, from Tolman (1951), whose influence in the period around World War II was significant but waned as more sophisticated laboratory techniques and instrumentation made a more experimental S-R approach more attractive.

TOLMAN

Tolman's learning theory was very much a sign-learning approach, and he believed that what an organism learns is not simply an *S-R* association, no matter how conditioned, but, rather, an expectancy of signs. His organism is goal directed and purposive. (Tolman's major work, published in 1932, was entitled *Purposive Behavior in Animals and Men.*) "Purposive," for Tolman, describes a behavioral pattern and, as Bolles (1975) wrote, states that learning

> consists of the acquisition of information about the environment, rather than the attachment of particular responses to particular stimuli.

This acquisition of information about the environment considers a stimulus, for example, as a sign for food and thus creates an expectancy that food is in its environment. The Pavlovian model of bell-food conditioning, therefore, is viewed in a cognitive fashion as a sign learned to produce an expectancy for food. Another crucial abstraction is that of demand. The need for food creates a demand that, coupled with the signs acquired as information about the environment, enables the individual to engage in the purposive behavior of food seeking. Finally, a concept unique to the cognitive approach is that of a cognitive map, by which Tolman meant a learned representation of the environmental situation. In the words of Bolles (1975), describing a cognitive map:

> It is as if the rat learns where it is, where food is, where the blind alleys are, and where the open pathways are.

Although it is clearly possible to develop a rapprochement between much of Tolman's cognitive theory and *S-R* associationists, many modern cognitive theorists believe associationist behaviorists are entirely too mechanistic. Wolpe (1978) discussed Bandura's (1974) cognitive approach, noting that Bandura

> declared that "the fabled reflexive conditioning in humans is largely a myth" and contended that an adequate account of human learning must recognize that "contrary to the mechanistic metaphors, outcomes [i.e., reinforcing events] change human behavior through the intervening influence of thought."

This is a position with which Wolpe strongly disagrees; he believes that thought and cognition are no different from other motor responses and behave according to conditioning procedures (Wolpe, 1978):

> Thoughts are responses, whether they are perceptions or imaginings. Like other responses, they are evoked when the relevant neural excitations occur. They are a subset of learnable responses and, inasmuch as they have stimulus aspects, may be conditioned to other thoughts and to responses in other categories.

No theorist, of whatever persuasion, would deny that there are inner events in an individual and that perceptions of events color actions. The behaviorist learning theorist—and this is by far the dominant group, owing to the history of experimentation—does not gainsay such events but declares that all such behaviors are susceptible to an experimental analysis and that to declare them as separate from other cognitive and motor events is not adequate.

COMPUTER MODEL OF COGNITION

Recent developments in cognitive theory seem more related to the computer model of information processing than to any other model. Indeed, the computer has allowed for a more sophisticated approach to the model offered by Tolman that learning is the acquisition of information about the environment. For example, consider the simplified model of decision making in Figure 17. Bachrach (1972) described this diagram as follows:

> An ordinary person making a decision or solving a problem tries to get as much information as possible (in computer language he scans), evaluates this information in terms of the present situation and his past experiences (memory), decides on a course of action in which he makes a prediction (or hypothesis) that one course of action will be better than another, and following the action, verifies his hypothesis. The final operation is one of storing this experience for future reference in a feedback to memory.

What makes such an approach different from the behavioral orientations described is that it uses everyday language: He *decides* on a course of action or predicts that one course will be *better* than another. Operational definitions require that such descriptive terms be replaced by less subjective terms in experimentation, but, over-all, learning theorists—*S-R* associationists and cognitive theorists alike—are concerned with how the individual learns and how his behavior can be modified. Consider the cognitive-computer model of decision processing portrayed above. The learning theorist interested in avoidance, using a Schoenfeld paradigm, would invoke a

$$S_1 ------/------ S_2$$
$$R_{T \text{ (av)}}$$

explanation for avoidance and describe it as an event in which a response terminates the situation after S_1 (the warning stimulus) and before S_2 (the noxious stimulus), thereby avoiding S_2. The traumatic-avoidance-learning researchers suggest that such avoidance does not allow for reality testing; therefore, the

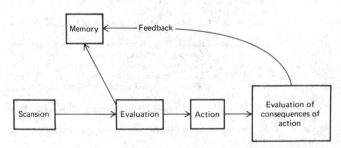

FIGURE 17. Simplified model of decision making.

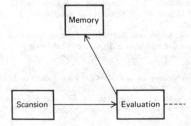

FIGURE 18. Avoidance pattern, as explained by cognitive-computer model.

response of avoidance after S_1 will persist, appropriate or not. The cognitive-computer theorist could invoke the decision model and cover the same territory, perhaps saying that the avoiding, neurotic subject who had been punished by S_2 can be described in terms of the left half of the model portrayed by Bachrach (1972) shown in Figure 18.

In other words, acquiring information about the environment takes place (S_1 is perceived); this information is evaluated in terms of the present environmental situation and past experience (memory), but the action that follows is avoidance and not action carried through to test. The action is, in a fashion, stereotyped—always avoidance in these events and not modified by possibly changing environmental conditions, such as the modification or absence of S_2.

Conclusion

Despite the differences that may exist among the various learning theories and between the cognitive and behavioristic approaches, learning theory is basic to an understanding of the acquisition, continuation and modification of behavior. The laboratory work in learning experiments has provided a body of data of exquisite complexity, and questions remain that are as yet unanswered. Nevertheless, the combination of field experience and laboratory experimentation seems to be the most fruitful means of solving the important question of integrating learning theory research and clinical practice.

Suggested Cross References

Behavior therapy is discussed in Section 30.2. Section 4.9 describes the applications of learning and biofeedback to psychiatry and medicine.

REFERENCES

Bachrach, A. J. An experimental approach to superstitious behavior. J. Am. Folklore, *75:* 1, 1962.

Bachrach, A. J. Some applications of operant conditioning to behavior therapy. In *The Conditioning Therapies: The Challenge in Psychotherapy*, J. Wolpe, A. Salter, and L. J. Reyna, editors, p. 62. Holt, Rinehart and Winston, New York, 1964.

Bachrach, A. J. *Psychological Research: An Introduction*, ed. 3. Random House, New York, 1972.

Bachrach, A. J., and Quigley, W. A. Direct methods of treatment. In *An Introduction to Clinical Psychology*, I. A. Berg and L. Pennington, editors, ed. 3, p. 482. Ronald Press, New York, 1966.

Bandura, A. Behavior theory and the models of man. Am. Psychol., *29:* 859, 1974.

Black, A. H., Osborne, B., and Ristow, W. C. A note on the operant conditioning of autonomic responses. In *Operant-Pavlovian Interactions*, H. Davis and H. M. B. Hurwitz, editors, p. 27. Erlbaum Associates, Hillsdale, N. J., 1977.

Bolles, R. C. *Learning Theory*. Holt, Rinehart and Winston, New York, 1975.

Boren, J. J., and Devine, D. D. The repeated acquisition of behavioral chains. J. Exp. Anal. Behav., *11:* 651, 1968.

Bugelski, B. R. *The Psychology of Learning*. Holt, Rinehart and Winston, New York, 1956.

Davis, H., and Hurwitz, H. M. B. *Operant-Pavlovian Interactions*. Erlbaum Associates, Hillsdale, N. J., 1977.

Eccles, J. C. Under the spell of synapse. In *The Neurosciences: Paths of Discovery*, F. G. Worden, J. P. Swazey, and G. Adelman, editors. Colonial Press, Cambridge, Mass., 1975.

Ferster, C. B., and Perrott, M. C. *Behavior Principles*. Meredith, New York, 1968.

Ferster, C. B., and Skinner, B. F. *Schedules of Reinforcement*. Appleton-Century-Crofts, New York, 1957.

Garcia, J., Rusiniak, K. W., and Brett, L. P. Conditioning food-illness aversions in wild animals: *Caveant canonici*. In *Operant-Pavlovian Interactions*, H. Davis and H. M. B. Hurwitz, editors, p. 273. Erlbaum Associates, Hillsdale, N. J., 1977.

Goldiamond, I. Perception. In *Experimental Foundations of Clinical Psychology*, A. J. Bachrach, editor, p. 280. Basic Books, New York, 1962.

Gustavson, C. R., Garcia, J., Hankins, W. G., and Rusiniak, K. W. Coyote predation control by aversive conditioning. Science, *184:* 581, 1974.

Gustavson, C. R., Kelly, D. J., Sweeney, M., and Garcia, J. Prey-lithium aversions. I. Coyotes and wolves. Behav. Biol., *17:* 61, 1976.

Hebb, D. O. *A Textbook of Psychology*, ed. 2. W. B. Saunders, Philadelphia, 1966.

* Hilgard, E. R. *Theories of Learning*. Appleton-Century-Crofts, New York, 1956.

Hovland, C. I. The generalization of conditioned responses. I. The sensory generalization of conditioned responses with varying frequencies of tone. J. Gen. Psychol., *17:* 125, 1937.

Hull, C. L. Conditioning: Outline of a systematic theory of learning. In *The Psychology of Learning*, 41st Yearbook, National Society for the Study of Education, Part II. University of Chicago Press, Chicago, 1942.

Hull, C. L. *Principles of Behavior: An Introduction to Behavior Theory*. Appleton-Century-Crofts, New York, 1943.

* Keller, F. S. *Learning: Reinforcement Theory*. Random House, New York, 1969.

* Kimble, G. A. *Hilgard and Marquis' Conditioning and Learning*, ed. 2. Appleton-Century-Crofts, New York, 1961.

Lewin, K. *A Dynamic Theory of Personality*. McGraw-Hill, New York, 1935.

Lief, H. I. Sensory association in the selection of phobic objects. Psychiatry, *18:* 331, 1955.

Malinowski, B. Magic, science, and religion. In *Science, Religion, and Reality*, J. Needham, editor, p. 32. Macmillan, New York, 1925.

Miller, N. E. Learning of visceral and glandular responses. Science, *163:* 434, 1969.

Mowrer, O. H. A stimulus-response analysis of anxiety and its role as a reinforcing agent. Psychol. Rev., *46:* 553, 1939.

Mowrer, O. H. On the dual nature of learning: A reinterpretation of "conditioning" and "problem-solving." Harvard Educ. Rev., *17:* 102, 1947.

Mowrer, O. H. Two-factor learning theory reconsidered, with special reference to secondary reinforcement and the concept of habit. Psychol. Rev., *63:* 114, 1956.

Mowrer, O. H. *The Crisis in Psychiatry and Religion*. D. Van Nostrand, Princeton, N. J., 1961.

Mowrer, O. H., and Solomon, L. N. Contiguity vs. drive-reduction in conditioned fear: The proximity and abruptness of drive-reduction. Am. J. Psychol., *67:* 15, 1954.

Psychological Abstracts. American Psychological Association, Washington, D.C., 1967–1977.

Reynolds, G. S. Behavioral contrast. J. Exp. Anal. Behav., *4:* 57, 1961.

Rzoska, J. Bait shyness: A study in rat behavior. Br. J. Anim. Behav., *1:* 128, 1953.

Sanford, F. *Psychology: A Scientific Study of Man*. Belmont, Wadsworth, Calif., 1965.

Schoenfeld, W. N. An experimental approach to anxiety, escape, and avoidance. In *Anxiety*, P. J. Hoch and J. Zubin, editors, p. 70. Grune & Stratton, New York, 1950.

Sidman, M. A technique for assessing the effects of drugs upon timing behavior. Science, *122:* 925, 1955.

Sidman, M. *Tactics of Scientific Research*. Basic Books, New York, 1960.

* Skinner, B. F. *The Behavior of Organisms*. Appleton-Century-Crofts, New York, 1938.

* Skinner, B. F. *Science and Human Behavior*. Macmillan, New York, 1953a.

Skinner, B. F. Some contributions of an experimental analysis of behavior to psychology as a whole. Am. Psychol., *8:* 69, 1953b.

Skinner, B. F. "Superstition" in a pigeon. J. Exp. Psychol., *38:* 168, 1958.

Skinner, B. F., and Morse, W. H. A second type of "superstition" in the pigeon. Am. J. Psychol., *70:* 308, 1957.

Solomon, R. L., Kamin, L. J., and Wynne, L. C. Traumatic avoidance learning: The outcomes of several extinction procedures with dogs. J. Abnorm. Soc. Psychol., *48:* 291, 1953.

Solomon, R. L., and Wynne, L. C. Traumatic avoidance learning: The principles of anxiety conservation and partial irreversibility. Psychol. Rev., *61:* 353, 1954.

Thorndike, E. L. *Human Learning*. Appleton-Century-Crofts, New York, 1931.

Tinbergen, N. *Curious Naturalists*. Basic Books, New York, 1958.

Tolman, E. C. *Purposive Behavior in Animals and Men*. Century, New York, 1932.

Tolman, E. C. *Behavior and Psychological Man*. University of California Press, Berkeley, 1951.

Walsh, J. M., and Bachrach, A. J. Adaptation to nitrogen narcosis manifested by timing behavior in the rat. J. Comp. Physiol. Psychol., *86:* 883, 1974.

Wolpe, J. The genesis of neurosis. S. Afr. Med. J., *24:* 613, 1950.

* Wolpe, J. *Psychotherapy by Reciprocal Inhibition*. Stanford University Press, Palo Alto, Calif., 1958.

Wolpe, J. The experimental foundations of some new psychotherapeutic methods. In *Experimental Foundations of Clinical Psychology*, A. J. Bachrach, editor, p. 554. Basic Books, New York, 1962.

Wolpe, J. Cognition and causation in human behavior and its therapy. Am. Psychol., *33:* 437, 1978.

4.4 Motivation and Affective Arousal

ROBERT B. MALMO, Ph.D., LL.D.

Motivation

Many subjects that are of interest from the psychiatric point of view are included under the general topic of motivation. This section focuses on some of these subjects instead of attempting to touch on all points in the general area. For example, drug dependency in animals has been selected not only because it is relevant for theories of motivation but also because these observations on animals have proved invaluable in placing the human problems of drug dependency in clearer perspective.

ANIMAL MOTIVATION

One of the most fundamental bases of human behavior is need. In the science of human behavior, therefore, one of the most pressing problems is to understand how need systems operate.

The approach taken here is neuropsychological, and the experimentation dealt with in this section is with animals, whose behavior can be observed under carefully controlled conditions, including surgical and other interventions not possible with humans.

Homeostatic mechanism for water regulation. The mechanisms for water regulation serve perhaps the most basic need. Everyone knows that for the mammal to survive it must have water. But the problem of water regulation requires analysis at two levels—physiological reflexive and behavioral levels.

At the physiological reflexive level, water deprivation causes a release of the antidiuretic hormone, vasopressin, which, in its action on the kidneys, reduces urine flow to a minimum, thus conserving water. Crucial for understanding this mechanism and other fluid-regulating homeostatic mechanisms is the *milieu intérieur* concept of Claude Bernard. In the case of water regulation, *milieu intérieur* refers to critical physicochemical relations between internal conditions of certain cells (called receptor cells or sensors) and the extracellular fluids surrounding them.

Three questions are generally raised when the detailed workings of any homeostatic mechanism are being sought: (1) What critical changes in physicochemical conditions represent a significant departure from the optimal *milieu intérieur* or other steady state? (2) What sensors detect this departure from the optimum? (3) What is the line of transmission from sensors to the mechanisms responsible for effecting return to more optimal conditions?

These questions will be considered first with respect to the reflex mechanism for vasopressin release and afterward the same questions will be considered in relation to the problems of thirst and water-seeking behavior.

What critical changes in physicochemical conditions represent a significant departure from the optimal milieu intérieur? The critical physicochemical changes are increment in osmotic pressure in extracellular fluids and intracellular volume changes.

In a mammal who has had continuous access to water and consequently is in a normally hydrated state, the percentages of sodium chloride in the extracellular fluids and in the intracellular fluids are nearly identical, 0.9 per cent. When the animal is deprived of water, the sodium chloride concentration is increased in the extracellular compartment, but the intracellular sodium chloride concentration remains at 0.9 per cent. The cause of this disequilibrium is the semipermeable cell membrane, which blocks the passage of the sodium chloride molecule into the cell but allows water molecules to pass through. The excess pressure necessary to prevent water from flowing into a solution through a semipermeable membrane is called the osmotic pressure of the solution.

There is general agreement that there are central receptors, although the kind of receptor is currently at issue. Mention of the sensors and their function in eliciting release of the antidiuretic hormone anticipates answers to the second and third questions, which will be dealt with later in greater detail.

Apparently, the putative central receptors are stimulated not by a rise in total body fluid osmolarity per se but, rather, by changes in the extracellular fluid, changes involving substances like sodium salts, whose molecules have low mobility through the semipermeable cell membranes. In support of this point, Andersson et al. (1967) cited Verney's (1947) finding

that intracarotid infusions of hypertonic Na salts are much more effective in eliciting a release of antidiuretic hormone than infusions of hypertonic K salts, urea or glucose which are transferred much more readily into the cells.

On a putative central receptor as starting point in a sequence leading to antidiuresis. Verney's idea was that there are osmoreceptors that swell or shrink under the influence of extracellular osmolarity and that, in doing so, stretch the dendrites of neighboring neurons and thus signal osmolarity. However, as P. M. Milner (1970) has pointed out, Verney's microstretch detector may not be necessary, because

the neurons themselves undergo changes as a result of variations in extracellular fluid concentration, and these changes may have a direct effect upon the neurons' firing rates.

During the past 30 years a considerable body of evidence has been accumulated to support the osmoreceptor concept, especially in relation to the supraoptic nucleus, the posterior pituitary, and the antidiuretic reflex. However, Andersson (1977) argues that the concept of osmoreceptors should be replaced by the concept of sodium receptors in the anterior wall of the third ventricle. This radical change in the theory of central receptors for water balance was proposed on the basis of experiments in his laboratory in which hypertonic solutions were infused into the ventricles of goats. In these experiments sodium chloride infusions were far more effective in causing antidiuresis and in causing goats to drink than were equiosmolar infusions of sugars. Hence the attractiveness of the sodium receptor concept for Andersson, who nevertheless is cautious enough to suggest other possibilities. In referring to the putative juxtaventricular sodium-sensitive receptors, Andersson (1977) says:

Since knowledge about their exact location and morphology is still lacking, the possibilities that cerebral receptors regulating body fluids to a great extent are also stimulated directly via the blood-brain barrier, or that they are located in parts of the brain which are devoid of this barrier, can by no means be excluded.

There may also be central receptors that respond chiefly to

reduction in intravascular fluid volume (Fitzsimons, 1972).

There is considerable evidence, much of it electrophysiological, to support the concept of osmoreceptors in and around the supraoptic nucleus (Malmo and Mundl, 1975). Most of this work has focused on the supraoptic nucleus and its role in the neuroendocrine hypothalamo-pituitary mechanism of the antidiuretic reflex.

Some pertinent findings follow: (1) To demonstrate that neurons in the supraoptic nucleus are central receptors—that is, not synaptically driven by neurons outside the nucleus—Sundsten and Sawyer (1961) and Ishikawa et al. (1966) studied small islands of supraoptic nucleus cells that had been separated by cuts from adjacent neural tissue. These isolated neurons reacted to intracarotid injections of hypertonic saline, thus behaving like first-order neurons. (2) After intracarotid infusions of hypertonic D-glucose, Hayward and Jennings (1973) observed changes in the firing rate of supraoptic neurons that were too rapid to be due to a slow change in sodium ions in the cerebrospinal fluid of the third ventricle. (3) Durham and Novin (1970), recording slow potential changes from the rabbit's supraoptic nucleus, found that intracarotid injections of sucrose were as effective as equiosmolar sodium chloride solutions. (4) The slow depolarizing potential that Durham and Novin (1970) observed to spread outward from the region of the supraoptic nucleus with osmotic stimuli is characteristic of receptor function in general. (5) According to Hayward (1975), Eggena and Polson's (1974) exposures of a cultured toad hypothalamo-neurohypophyseal system to hypertonic sodium chloride, mannitol, and urea supported the osmoreceptor concept, rather than the sodium detector concept. (6) Morphological studies of the supraoptic nucleus based on light and electron microscopy have revealed increases in over-all cell and nuclear size (Rechardt, 1969), nucleolar dry mass and neuronal nucleic acid (Watt, 1970), and nucleolar RNA (Edström and Eichner, 1958) that occurred with dehydration. Hatton and Walters (1973) studied the sensitivity of supraoptic nucleus cells to the conditions of acute progressive dehydration and the effects of subsequent rehydration. Cell size increases were measurable early in dehydration, and they continued as long as the deprivation conditions persisted. Rehydration for 10 days did not completely return the cells to the size of those in nondeprived animals. Multiplication of nucleoli in the supraoptic nucleus during water deprivation was also observed.

On the basis of his recent research, Hatton (1976) now believes that the nucleus circularis, dorsomedial to the supraoptic nucleus, is the major site of osmoreceptors for the antidiuretic reflex. A substantial, short latency, enduring antidiuresis was produced by electrical stimulation of this nucleus. Changes in the number of nucleoli and in cell sizes were induced by water deprivation, and the multiplication of nucleoli in this nucleus during water deprivation was greater than that previously observed in the supraoptic nucleus. A quantitative ultrastructural investigation by Tweedle and Hatton (1976) revealed that the normal nucleus circularis is made up of only one ultrastructurally identified cell type (monopolar), which the authors regarded as probably indicative of its sensory function.

Hayward and Vincent (1970) recorded from osmoreceptors in the supraoptic nucleus of awake monkeys. The precise specialization of these cells was demonstrated. They responded strongly to small injections of hypertonic sodium chloride into the carotid artery, but they showed little or no response to arousing sensory stimuli—for example, sounds and touches. Hayward and Vincent reviewed earlier positive findings with unit recording from the supraoptic nucleus during intracarotid

hypertonic saline injections. These earlier experiments by others were with anesthetized animals.

What is the line of transmission from sensor to the mechanisms responsible for effecting return to more optimal conditions? There is now little doubt that central receptors are involved in the production and release of the antidiuretic hormone, vasopressin, from the posterior lobe of the pituitary. Whether the osmoreceptor cells have a neurosecretory function is not certain, although there is strong presumptive evidence that they do. But the end result of the reflexive chain, beginning with discharge of the osmoreceptors, is conservation of water by the kidneys, effecting return to more optimal physiological conditions.

At the reflex level, then, a chain of events from central receptor to effector is clearly visible. But renal water conservation is only a temporary measure, and, of course, the animal must ingest water, usually having to seek it, in order to avoid fatal dehydration. What is known about neurophysiological mediation of these behavioral mechanisms?

Neurophysiological approach to thirst-related behavior. The patterns of neuronal activity underlying thirst-related, drinking-related behavior are certain to be enormously more complicated than the reflex chain. Nonetheless, the research on central receptors for the antidiuretic reflex provides a key starting point for this undertaking.

Neuropsychological evidence indicates that receptors for thirst-related behavior are located outside the supraoptic region. The loss of cells after the pituitary stalk has been cut is sufficiently heavy to conclude that the cells in and around the supraoptic nucleus project mainly to the posterior pituitary (Daniel, 1966; Smialowski, 1966; Nauta and Haymaker, 1969).

In addition to the anterior wall of the third ventricle, the lateral preoptic area has been considered as a probable site of putative central receptors for thirst (Blass and Epstein, 1971; Peck and Novin, 1971; Blank and Wayner, 1975; Malmo and Mundl, 1975; Weiss and Almli, 1975). Malmo and Malmo have multiple-unit activity data from the lateral preoptic area suggesting that extracellular osmolarity, not merely sodium concentration, is the physicochemical condition of key importance in producing changes in multiple-unit activity.

A number of lines of evidence suggest that rejection of the osmoreceptor theory as obsolete is premature. As a move in the direction of resolving the issue, it seems possible to entertain the concept of multiple receptors: osmoreceptors in the supraoptic and preoptic areas, sodium receptors in the anteroventral wall of the third ventricle, and, on the basis of research by Emmers (1973, 1977) and Niijima (1969), peripheral receptors and their projections to the brain. As the research findings from Mogenson's (1977) laboratory and elsewhere clearly demonstrate, the neuronal structures involved in thirst are widely distributed, and the possible neural relations are exceedingly complex. It seems plain, therefore, that one should avoid oversimplistic models.

In working toward a theory about thirst, one does well to take careful note of the gate-control theory of pain (Melzack, 1973), which holds that one is never aware of receptor activity as such. Each different sensation depends on brain patterns, which *involve* inputs from receptors. In line with Melzack's arguments, it is also plain that any theory about behavior that is based on direct transmission from a receptor to a specific brain area is bound to be oversimplistic, although a simple formulation of this kind comes close to being adequate for a reflex such as the antidiuretic reflex. Research on this reflex has been useful in suggesting the kinds of receptors that may be involved in thirst and drinking behavior. Physicochemical shifts in the extracellular environments due to water loss selectively change the firing rates of these central receptors to produce distinctive patterns of neural activity that represent the initial stage of a complex process that greatly increases the probability that the animal will drink.

Although it is merely an analogy, the distinctive neural patterns suggested above may represent an internal push that, in interaction with an external pull from environmental stimulation, instigates drinking behavior. "Incentive" is the term for this external pull. For a comprehensive discussion of incentive-motivation theory, the reader is referred to Bolles (1967). The importance of this interaction can hardly be overemphasized. Researchers have observed 48-hour water-deprived rats that have lost 20 per cent of their body weight but that fail to drink water placed directly under their noses in an observation box to which they had not become thoroughly habituated. The internal push was surely there, but the external pull was insufficient to initiate drinking behavior. Conversely, a water-replete rat may fail to drink water in a familiar cage because it lacks the internal push. However, the drinking behavior of animals is determined more by external factors than is generally recognized. For instance, it has been reported that rats drank significantly more in their home cages when experimenters went in and out of their room frequently than when entrances into the room were relatively infrequent. Fitzsimons (1972) has gone as far as to say that normally animals keep ahead of change in fluid balance by drinking more water than they need, and there is some evidence for this (Mogenson, 1977). This secondary drinking bypasses the central receptors, so that some drinking is accounted for by pull factors only. Whether or not secondary drinking is more normal than primary drinking, in view of the vital importance of water for mammals, it is not surprising that such a mechanism is found in animals.

Finally, contrary to some old notions about drive, the water-deprived animal does not necessarily become more active. In fact, in the absence of relevant cues, the animal usually becomes even less active than normal. Again, push is not to be taken too literally.

Some cells in the lateral preoptic area, one of the sites where putative central receptors for thirst are thought to be located, are inhibited by hypertonic challenge (Malmo and Mundl, 1975), as are some cells in the dorsal midbrain (Malmo, 1976). Inhibitory mechanisms undoubtedly play an important role in the control of behavior in the thirsty animal when environmental conditions are discouraging with respect to prospects for finding a watering hole. Of course, even activated neurons may have an inhibitory influence on other neurons with which they synapse.

Psychology went through a long period in which various attempts were made to endow drive with energizing properties. This theoretical approach generated an enormous body of experimental data, which on balance showed that the drive-energy conceptualization is oversimplistic (Bolles, 1967).

Behavioral reaction, then, is the product of an interaction between internal and external instigators. The problem for psychology is to determine in detail the nature of these instigators and eventually to reach an understanding of their neural substrates. This is not to depreciate in any way the continuous gaining of new knowledge at the behavioral level, which, as Skinner (1977) points out, is propaedeutic to advancing toward a theory of behavior at the neurophysiological level.

From this discussion it is clear just how timely are the recent neurophysiological advances on the problem of central receptors for detecting changes in water balance. These advances have progressed further than those for other mechanisms, such as those for regulating food intake and body temperature, and that is one reason for selecting thirst as the need system to discuss in this section.

Drug addiction as an acquired need. The concept of central receptors as mediators of internal push is heuristic in approaching the problem of acquired needs, such as morphine addiction, from the neuropsychological point of view.

Suppose one adopts the working hypothesis that the morphine addict in need of a fix has his internal push mediated by brain cells that act in principle like central receptors for thirst. Just as the pattern of neural firing of central receptors for thirst was assumed to be distinctive, one may assume that another pattern of neural responses, distinguishable from that associated with changed water balance, is associated with lowered morphine levels in the blood stream of the addict.

On the behavioral side, animal experiments have been useful in sharpening the focus on the important questions to ask. Weeks (1964) showed that rats can easily be made dependent on morphine over a period of time; then, when deprived of morphine, they would press a bar to inject themselves in their jugular veins by means of an indwelling injection device. Rats addicted to morphine also learn to drink bitter morphine solutions, which normally they reject (Stolerman and Kumar, 1970).

Behavioral descriptions of morphine-dependent chimpanzees (Spragg, 1940) impress one with the human-like character of the behavior, although one also sees the close similarity between the rodent and the higher primate in the way they develop drug dependence.

In Spragg's (1940) investigation of morphine addiction in chimpanzees, when a dose was skipped or delayed for a few hours, some early signs of mild withdrawal were noted: slight rhinorrhea, drops of perspiration on the face, an unusually large quantity of feces in the cage, heightened irritability, and yawning. (The physiological changes in withdrawal are generally opposite those changes seen during acquisition of dependence.) Animals differed in the time required to produce the first clear withdrawal signs of dependence from as early as 2½ weeks in one animal to 7 weeks in another.

When the animal sought out the injection on his own initiative, which happened after as long as 5 months of injections, Spragg called the animal "addicted." Examples of such purposeful goal-seeking behavior, usually after some break in the continuity of dosing with the drug, were: showing eagerness to be taken from the living cage by the experimenter when doses were needed, in clear contrast to behavior exhibited when taken from the living cage at other times; tugging at the leash and leading the experimenter toward and into the room in which injections were regularly given; exhibiting frustration when led away from the injection room and back to the living cage without having been given an injection; showing eagerness and excitement when allowed to get up on the box on which injections were regularly made; cooperating eagerly in the injection procedure; choosing a syringe-containing box, whereupon the injection was given, in preference to a food-containing box.

The chimpanzee, needing an injection and seeing Spragg approaching the cage, acted like a hungry chimpanzee at feeding time when it sees the attendant approaching with food: an excitement shown in activated motor behavior and vocalizations with orientation toward the attendant. However, the excitement of the morphine-deprived addicted chimpanzee in the morning was not removed by breakfast, as in the case of the nonaddicted animals. This agitated behavior continued after breakfast and ceased only after the injection.

The foregoing descriptions provide clear examples of interactions between the two factors of internal push and external pull, which were discussed earlier in relation to thirst. One may now direct attention to the question of neural mediation of the internal push that is involved in morphine addiction.

According to Snyder (1975), opiate receptor binding varies dramatically throughout the monkey brain and the human brain.

> The amygdala binds most, but only slightly more than the periaqueductal grey of the midbrain, hypothalamus, and medial thalamus.

There seems to be no overlap between these brain areas and sites of putative receptors for detecting changes in water balance.

On the neuropsychological side, there are a number of parallels between addictive phenomena and those of thirst. After repeated morphine administration there is either a change at the level of the opiate receptor or some other kind of effect on neuronal activity (Snyder, 1975). In any event there must be an alteration in the nervous system such that low levels of morphine in the blood stream are now detected much as central sensors for water balance detect extracellular hypertonicity.

Compared with the amount of brain-recording research done with nonaddicted animals given opiates, there has been relatively little done with dependent animals. However, Kerr et al. (1974) have shown that, during withdrawal phases in addicted rats, firing rates of units in the lateral hypothalamus were greater than rates recorded in the same area of nonaddicted rats. This is the kind of evidence that supports the concept of neural signaling of low levels of morphine in the blood stream of dependent animals, although the observed changes may not have been in primary sensor neurons, since the lateral hypothalamus is not listed as one of the major sites of opiate receptors (Snyder, 1975). Obviously, there is a need for more electrophysiological work of this kind, especially recording from brain areas that biochemical studies have pointed to as sites where opiate receptors are concentrated. In this projected research one sees the possibilities for determining the distinctive patterns of neural firing in withdrawal as the basis for the craving that addicts describe and for gaining facilitation on the motor system mediating drug-seeking behavior.

Morphine addicts retain a residual craving for the drug after withdrawal, predisposing them to relapse, which, according to the Interim Report of the Canadian Commission of Inquiry into the Non-Medical Use of Drugs (1970), is the major problem in opiate addiction. An internal push appears to remain after withdrawal; although weaker than before withdrawal, in interaction with external sources of pull, it is strong enough to cause a relapse. Physiological consequences of previous physical dependence have been observed to persist long after thorough withdrawal treatment (Wikler, 1968; Jaffe, 1969).

The importance of the external pull factor in relapse has been experimentally demonstrated. It is easier to readdict rats in the same environment where they were originally addicted than in a different environment (Thompson and Ostlund, 1965; Weeks and Collins, 1968). Stimuli in the familiar environment most likely exert pull on the rat—the same kind of interaction that occurs when a thirsty animal is pulled in the direction of water by stimuli in a familiar watering place.

This fundamental concept of interaction between neuronal activity patterns instigated internally and the neural patterns instigated externally is useful in overcoming the mind-body dichotomy inherent in the distinction between physical and psychological dependence. In rejecting this artificial distinction, one sees the real problems more clearly. For instance, what are the residual biochemical conditions that remain after withdrawal? How do they interact with the perceptual cues in the postaddict's environment? Surely these questions are propaedeutic to further comprehensive study of the postaddict.

Experimental alcoholism in animals. Richter (1957) succeeded in producing dependence in three wild rats by restricting their fluid intake to a 10 per cent alcohol solution for a period of about 40 days. At the end of the period of force-feeding with alcohol, the rats continued to drink large quantities of alcohol, even though plain water was made available to them. One animal drank progressively more alcohol and less plain water, ate less and less, and died 30 days later. The course was one that closely parallels that of some human alcoholics.

In domesticated rats, however, Richter states that, even with more prolonged periods of force-feeding of alcohol, no such clear signs of dependence were ever observed. It is possible that dependency in the domesticated rat can be demonstrated with still longer periods of exposure to alcohol. But Richter found no such difference between wild and domesticated rats when force-fed for 3 to 6 months on diets supplemented with increasingly higher concentrations of morphine sulfate. Wild and domesticated rats showed very similar withdrawal symptoms when the morphine sulfate was removed from the diet. (Other workers reported clear-cut dependence on morphine in domesticated rats.) The available evidence from animals is in line with clinical knowledge that dependence on morphine is much more readily established than is dependence on alcohol. That dependence is much more common in the case of tobacco than of alcohol has been commented on by Brain (1965).

From research on human alcoholism (Isbell et al., 1955; Mendelson and LaDou, 1964), it is known that large quantities of alcohol must be drunk over a prolonged period to produce severe withdrawal symptoms. Special measures are needed to make most animals drink ethanol in sufficient volumes to drive their blood-ethanol concentrations to intoxicating levels.

Ellis and Pick (1970a) gave ethanol by gastric intubation to rhesus monkeys.

> Termination of ethanol administration after 10 to 18 days of treatment resulted in the emergence, during the withdrawal periods, of a series of hyperexcitability signs which could be classified into tremulous, spastic, and convulsive stages.

Declining blood-ethanol concentrations showed correlations with the progressive severity of symptoms, and it was possible to reverse these symptoms by the administration of ethanol. Subsequently, these investigators obtained similar results with dogs (Ellis and Pick, 1970b).

Pieper et al. (1972) put alcohol in the formulas of six infant chimpanzees, who drank the alcohol and liquid diet mix in their baby bottles at scheduled feeding times. At first, the chimpanzees refused to drink the solution if it contained alcohol. However, by commencing with weak solutions and gradually increasing the alcohol concentration, the experimenters contrived to get the animals to drink large quantities of alcohol in concentrations high enough to produce high blood-alcohol levels.

After 6 to 10 weeks, when the alcohol was abruptly removed from the diet, all six chimpanzees showed withdrawal symptoms. Extremely severe symptoms, including convulsions, were observed in three animals, one of whom died after prolonged and repeated convulsions. In the course of these studies, tolerance to ethanol was also observed. Pieper and Skeen (1972) obtained positive results in similar experiments using young rhesus monkeys as subjects. Falk et al. (1972) found that rats maintained on an intermittent food schedule with an available ethanol solution drank to excess. They found that removal of the ethanol produced dependency symptoms, including death from tonic-clonic seizures. Earlier investigators had failed to produce these effects in rats. The success of Falk and co-workers may be attributed to their ingenious use of the schedule-induced polydipsia technique.

The classic syndrome that is generally meant when the term "alcoholism" is used depends, then, on the repeated ingestion of large quantities of ethanol over a considerable period of time. In general, two hypotheses are guiding research in this area at the present time. The first hypothesis suggests that the continuous ingestion of large quantities of ethanol may cause deviations in the normal metabolism of alcohol, resulting in the formation of compounds capable of producing physical dependence. According to the second hypothesis, sudden abstinence after heavy and continuous ethanol intake produces a state of disuse or denervation supersensitivity (Jaffe and Sharpless, 1968). This pharmacological hypothesis does not necessarily imply the invalidity of the other hypothesis. That is, they are not mutually exclusive.

There is wide agreement that moderate drinking is safe—that is, that a biochemical chain of events will not lead to dependence. Ethanol in small quantities metabolizes readily, leaving the cellular environment the same as before. But taking morphine in comparable amounts—that is, enough to produce pleasurable effects—initiates tissue changes that stand a good chance of producing dependence.

The results of experiments on chimpanzees by Fitz-Gerald (1972) at the Yerkes Regional Primate Research Center suggest that chimpanzees resemble humans in their enjoyment of alcohol. Unlike most lower mammals, some chimpanzees drink alcohol voluntarily, even to intoxication in some cases. As with humans, chimpanzees show wide variations in voluntary intake. It would be interesting if it turned out that there is something about a larger brain, with a relatively higher proportion of cerebral cortex, that predisposes toward the enjoyment of ethanol and its voluntary intake.

THE PROBLEM OF GENERAL DRIVE, ACTIVATION, OR AROUSAL

Students of animal motivation are becoming somewhat more specialized in area of study than was formerly the case. From the earlier discussion of thirst it is clear, for example, that there are a host of important research questions that, like those pertaining to central receptors, are specific to mechanisms of thirst.

On the other hand, writers like Miller (1967) and Valenstein

(1968) caution against swinging too far in the direction of narrowness. There is undoubtedly a need for general denotative constructs such as drive, motivation, and the like. The need stands out more clearly perhaps in the case of human motivation, but an overspecific approach to animal motivation is also a danger. It is clear that important general behavioral questions are common to specific drives; in addition, concepts denoting interactions between specific instigators are needed.

Research in the area of activation. As explained elsewhere (Malmo, 1966, 1972), the term "activation" is useful chiefly in referring to an area of psychophysiological research in which the level of physiological activation is studied in relation to interacting factors. These are the internal and external factors, which were discussed earlier. The changes in the *milieu intérieur* produced by water deprivation are examples of internal factors; the external cue factors interacting effectively with the internal ones to raise the level of activation are perception of water or other cues associated with the procurement of water.

Bélanger, Ducharme, and co-workers at the Université de Montréal have found that the heart rate increases progressively with hours of water deprivation or food deprivation when the recordings are made under appropriate conditions of cue stimulation (Malmo and Bélanger, 1967). They reported that heart rates in rats bar pressing for water showed progressive increments as a function of increasing hours of water deprivation. They also reported that the heart rate increment could regularly be produced by depriving the animal of food. But they found that food deprivation and cues associated with food had to be operative together for the heart rate to show a rise. Even though the animal was deprived of food or water, the heart rate did not increase in the absence of appropriate external cues. This observation provides important clues to the kind of neural mechanism that mediates goal seeking motivated by deprivation of a basic need. It is also related to the concept of incentive motivation (Campbell and Misanin, 1969).

The Montreal workers found that the relation between hours of deprivation and frequency of bar pressing in a Skinner box took the form of an inverted U. This finding is consistent with the principle that there is a level of activation that is optimal for performance and that, on either side of this optimum, there is a performance decrement—the greater the departure from the optimum, the greater the decrement in performance.

According to the activation or arousal concept, the kind of neural activity considered here feeds impulses into organized neural cell assemblies, supporting the firing of their units in delicately timed sequences. According to this conception, the optimal level of activation is that level of background firing that provides the optimal facilitations of the organized neural activities. It follows that too little or too much background firing of cells in the arousal system is deleterious with regard to organized neural firing (mediating performance).

There are other ways in which overarousal can be deleterious. Furthermore, in animal experiments there are complexities that must be taken into account. In the Université de Montréal laboratory and elsewhere, under certain conditions—such as running down a straight alley for water—the inverted U curve does not appear. Furthermore, from Hokanson's laboratory there is a report that the heart rate rise correlated with degree of food deprivation did not occur until later in the bar-pressing session than would have been expected on the basis of the principle stated earlier (Campbell and Misanin, 1969).

Malmo (1962) suggested that understanding of the arousal system could probably be greatly advanced by experiments using direct recording of discharge from the reticular system.

The point is that indirect and remote reflections of arousal system activity in autonomic measures are less satisfactory than are more direct neural recordings. An experiment by Goodman (1968) supported this conception.

Goodman (1968) was apparently the first to publish a quantitative description of spontaneous multiple-unit activity in the brain stem of an animal while its performance efficiency was being measured. The results of this experiment are, therefore, of considerable interest. Goodman trained three rhesus monkeys to press a bar for obtaining water in response to visual stimuli. Averaged multiple-unit activity from the mesencephalic reticular formation was compared with reaction time performance. In accordance with the inverted U hypothesis, Goodman found that, for best performance (shortest reaction times) to occur, it was necessary for reticular neural activity to be of moderate intensity at the onset of the stimulus. When the level of neural activity was outside this optimal range, either too low or too high, reaction times were in every instance relatively long. In other words, moderate background reticular activity was a necessary condition for best performance.

It was not particularly surprising to learn that reticular activity in the moderate range was not a sufficient condition for best performance. Even with favorable background neural activity, long reaction times were sometimes observed—another illustration of the principle that background neural activity should never be viewed as the only independent variable determining the level of performance.

A recent development is the increasing attention being paid to the monitoring of skeletal-motor activity in brain-recording experiments (Vanderwolf, 1971; Schwartzbaum, 1975; Malmo and Malmo, 1977).

Figure 1 shows the dramatic drop in multiple-unit activity (MUA) from the dorsal midbrain reticular formation coinciding with a cessation of ongoing activity observed by Malmo and Malmo (1977). This kind of correlation between midbrain activity and head and body movements was a typical finding

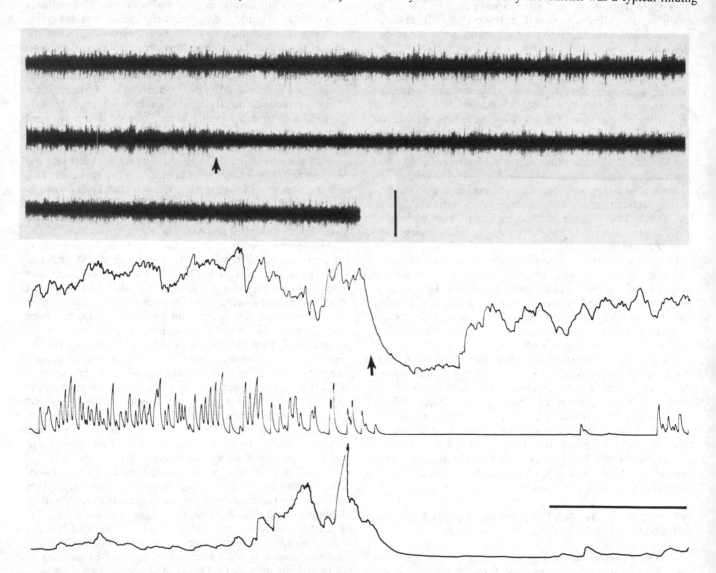

FIGURE 1. Decline in midbrain multiple-unit activity (MUA) during period that was free of head and body movement. *Top three lines:* photographic recording of reticular formation MUA (from oscilloscope); *fourth line:* integrated MUA; *fifth line:* head movement; *bottom line:* body movement. *Arrows* indicate same moment in time. *Horizontal line:* 2 seconds for film and 5 seconds for other three traces. *Vertical line:* 200-microvolt calibration for film. Quiescent period was preceded by walking. (From Malmo, H. P., and Malmo, R. B. Movement-related forebrain and midbrain multiple unit activity in rats. Electroencephalogr. Clin. Neurophysiol., *42:* 501, 1977. Copyright 1977 by Elsevier/North-Holland Biomedical Press and reproduced by permission.)

in this study of 16 rats with MUA electrodes implanted in forebrain and midbrain areas. In addition, correlations of this kind, although not as striking, were even found between forebrain MUA and skeletal-motor activity. It was established that none of these correlations was due to muscle or other artifacts.

Reticular formation MUA frequently appeared uncoupled from skeletal-motor activity. A rise in reticular formation MUA preceding movements (a common observation) may be seen in Figure 1. Even more impressive were observations of a marked rise in reticular formation with a return to the baseline in the absence of any movement whatever under conditions—such as the dispensing of sucrose into a dish—that had on previous occasions elicited immediate and energetic approach reactions.

This focus on motor activity in brain-recording research represents a reversal of the usual approach, in which the focus is on sensory input. The desirability of such a reversal was stated by Evarts (1973):

It seems possible that understanding of the human nervous system, even in its most complex intellectual functions, may be enriched if the operation of the brain is analyzed in terms of its motor output rather than in terms of its sensory input.

As Evarts pointed out, Sperry stated this principle a quarter century ago in maintaining that the sole product of brain function is muscular coordination. A more detailed discussion of Sperry's principle appears in Malmo (1975).

Nonhomeostatic mechanisms of motivation. When an animal is hungry or thirsty, its behavior is largely dominated by cues associated through learning with these organic needs. However, when the animal's basic needs are satisfied, its behavior is often directed by cues that have nothing whatever to do with seeking food or water or escaping from painful stimulation. Thorough experimental documentation of this point comes from extensive work on the so-called curiosity drive in monkeys in Harlow's laboratory. Harlow and co-workers demonstrated that monkeys work for hours on mechanical puzzles with no reward other than solving them. Butler's (1954) experiments in the same laboratory showed that monkeys work hard, hour after hour, just to have a small door open, allowing them the opportunity to look at objects in another room. They worked hardest to see another monkey there, but they worked nearly as hard to see an electrical train running.

This finding, is one conclusive disproof of the drive-reduction theory in its monolithic form. As a matter of fact, these and other findings, such as Hebb's (1946) show that, far from seeking a reduction in the level of activation or arousal, animals look for excitement. Even lower mammals like the rat manifest exploratory behavior that seems to have little or nothing to do with food seeking.

Recently, Malmo and Malmo discovered a cued alternation behavior in rats that is maintained over a long series of trials in the absence of reinforcement with food or water. In observing a rat in an exercise cage on one occasion, they noticed that it came to a window where one of the experimenters was and promptly followed her to the opposite window and so on in rapid alternation, following the experimenter back and forth with no sign of ceasing this alternation. The same kind of results were obtained with two other rats that were tried in this preliminary way. It occurred to the experimenters that this was a remarkable kind of behavior, considering the fact that the rat's alternation behavior was not being rewarded with food, water, or any of the usual reinforcements.

Figure 2 shows the results of the systematic study of one rat

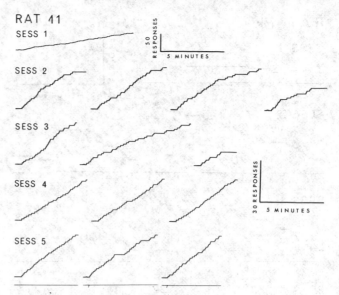

FIGURE 2. Cumulative-response records for a rat that had been in the colony for a long time. The graphs show the number of responses on the *ordinate* against time on the *baseline. Steeper curves* (when the scale is the same) indicate more rapid alternation. The scale for the *first curve* is different from that of all the other *curves.* Note that alternation-following of the experimenter commenced immediately.

in cumulative curves that are graphs showing the number of responses on the ordinate against time on the baseline (Skinner, 1938; Ferster and Skinner, 1957). On 5 different days (sessions 1 through 5) the alternation response persisted, without experimental extinction. As a matter of fact, the last curve in session 5 was the steepest of all, which means that those 30 alternations were the most rapid of all, so that, far from showing signs of weakening, the alternation response was stronger than ever before. The only reinforcement offered throughout the five sessions was verbal ("Good boy"), but, when the animal failed to achieve 30 alternations, it was petted briefly before the rest period. For rats, whose behavior is generally thought to be dependent on primary reinforcement, this behavior, which was typical of the several adult rats tested, was truly remarkable, much more so, it appears, than exploratory behavior, which is not related to interaction with the experimenter. With respect to the effectiveness of experimenter-animal interaction as reinforcement, the nearest parallel may be Falk's (1958) demonstration that allowing a chimpanzee to groom him could be used as reinforcement in the chimpanzee's learning a visual discrimination.

This remarkable behavior in rats appears to be related to the special day-to-day treatment that rats receive in the Malmos' laboratory, especially regular gentling and handling of animals and the practice of hand feeding preferred foods (usually raw carrots) 6 days a week in the late afternoon. The male rat whose data are shown in Figure 2 had been in the colony for nearly 2 years.

Figure 3 shows curves for a 36-day-old male rat that had been in the colony only 15 days when the cumulative curves for session 1 (Figure 3) were taken. During these 15 days the rat, Bk, was handed a preferred food (lettuce and spinach at first, carrot later), and this special hand feeding was continued each afternoon in the home cage. Figure 3 shows that in contrast to the immediate alternation of the older animals, Bk's alternation developed only later. On the whole, this kind of

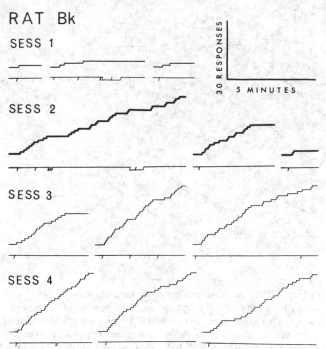

FIGURE 3. Cumulative-response records for a rat that had been in the colony for a short time. Note that alternation-following of the experimenter did not commence immediately but required some time for development. Compare with Figure 2.

development was typical of these young animals, especially so of the females. For this kind of development or learning to take place in the absence of any primary reinforcement in the test cage where the alternations took place is contrary to what would have been expected of rats. Apparently, when newly arrived young rats receive this special day-to-day treatment, they soon develop the capacity for being reinforced in this unusual way and fail to show experimental extinction. These observations appear to be particularly important in cautioning against an experimental psychology of animal motivation that is too rigid in its insistence on the absolute necessity for primary reinforcements while disregarding day-to-day interactions between the animals and their experimenters. In none of these tests were the animals ever deprived of food or water. Although some remote connection between feeding outside the experimental cage and the data shown in Figures 2 and 3 is not ruled out, the alternation behavior and its failure to extinguish cannot be accounted for by any simple formulation.

Another strongly motivated activity that does not depend on the animal's being in a deprived state is the Olds-Milner phenomenon of intracranial self-stimulation. Electrical stimulation of certain areas of the brain is clearly rewarding. Much remains to be learned about the mechanisms responsible for this phenomenon, which is the subject of a recent *Neurosciences Research Program Bulletin* (Hall et al., 1977). In another area of brain-stimulation experiments of particular interest to psychiatrists are the experiments by Flynn et al. (1963), Glusman (1974), von Holst and von Saint Paul (1962), and others on offensive-defensive behavior (Malmo, 1972).

The importance of viewing motivated behavior as the product of complex, though potentially decipherable, interactions between external stimulation, hormonal influences, and neural influences is clearly illustrated in the work of Lehrman (1964) on the reproductive behavior of ring doves. Normally, external

stimuli are effective in eliciting a particular behavior only if the bird's reproductive cycle has progressed sufficiently far. But the behavior can be induced much earlier in the cycle by injecting a hormone, provided the hormone is selected with knowledge of the succession of hormone secretions during a normal reproductive cycle. For example, if eggs are introduced into the cage before the doves have engaged in courtship behavior for 5 to 7 days, the birds will not sit on the eggs. Instead, they ignore the eggs while they engage in courtship. However, injecting both members of the pair with the ovarian hormone progesterone almost always elicits incubation behavior within 3 hours after the eggs' introduction into the cage, instead of 5 to 7 days later.

An important key to an understanding of the neurophysiological aspect of these interactions lies in the fact that the activity of the pituitary gland, which secretes gonad-stimulating and other hormones, is largely controlled by the nervous system through the hypothalamus.

In the higher mammals, especially in the chimpanzee but to some extent even in the dog—as shown, for example, in the work of Beach and LeBoeuf (1967)—copulatory behavior is more complicated than the stimulus-bound subcortically mediated behavior in lower mammals. The relative importance of the cerebral cortex in mating behavior increases in the mammalian series from rat to man.

HUMAN MOTIVATION

Extremes of motivation and overarousal. Broadbent (1966) wrote:

It is one thing to walk along a narrow plank a foot above the ground, and quite another to carry out the same task between the roofs of two high buildings. Yet we often assume that a rise in the rewards or punishments involved in a situation will make a man work more efficiently.

Broadbent goes on to describe how the United States Army has studied efficiency levels of men performing skilled tasks, such as mending telephones, in situations in which they felt they were in real danger. They were led to believe that they were being fired on accidentally by artillery or that they were almost surrounded by a forest fire. Under these conditions, performance declined.

A related finding from the same laboratory came from research on the effects of noise on performance. It was found that noise reduced efficiency only when the men were working under high incentive and not if they were relatively bored and unmotivated. Thus, the factors of noise and incentive interacted to impair performance. On the other hand, Broadbent cited other experiments with unstimulating, boring tasks in which better work was obtained under noisy conditions, rather than under quiet conditions.

These and other experiments that he refers to provide evidence for the inverted U hypothesis. The theoretical problem for Broadbent is not the improvement in performance associated with increasing arousal up to some optimal point. This part of the curve he accounts for in conventional terms, along the lines that the arousal system provides more and more facilitation for response up to the optimal point. The problem for Broadbent is to account for decrements in performance associated with increases in arousal beyond the optimal point.

The earlier discussion of impairment produced by overactivation was concerned mainly with the impairment of response manifested in slow performance or failure to respond at all. Apparently, this is the most prevalent kind of impairment in disaster situations. A relatively simple neural model based on Lorente de No's classic work and on observations of Penfield and Rasmussen has been suggested to account for this kind of impairment, which is generally manifested in errors of omission (Malmo, 1962). This model still seems reasonable as far as it goes. But Broadbent points out that under conditions producing overarousal

the effects of noise appear to be largely in the form of positive actions which happen to be wrong, rather than failures to act at all.

To account for this kind of error, one needs a different neural model, a model that increases the probability of a wrong response. Looking at the problem this way brings to mind the writings of the Spences (1966). In their terminology, increasing the level of drive increases the advantage of a strong response over a weaker one in the competition for control of overt expression. If the strongest response happens to be wrong, an error of commission will be made. The Spences make it quite clear that their theorizing is in no way based on physiological consideration, their concepts being

convenient mathematical fictions rather than speculations about physiological facts.

The example taken from Broadbent's (1966) article on noise and incentive is one of many that could be used to point up the need for some concept like that of general arousal or activation to deal with interacting factors like incentive and noise in relation to performance.

An experiment by Wood and Hokanson (1965) runs parallel to the previously described experiments with rats. The human subjects squeezed a hand dynamometer, applying a different force under each of several conditions. Heart rates varied directly with the strength of pull. While squeezing on the dynamometer, the person was performing a digit-to-symbol translation task. While the curve plot for heart rate against strength of pull was a steadily rising one, the plot for performance took the form of an inverted U. Earlier experiments by Courts (1939) without physiological measures had yielded inverted U curves for performance on mental tasks as a function of induced tension.

Other means have been used in Hokanson's laboratory and elsewhere to produce changes in performance and in physiological measures when they were recorded. Systematic variation of incentives has perhaps been the most effective means of producing these changes. Average performance scores on various tasks for groups of subjects have been found to change significantly as a function of these incentives. In psychophysiological studies, muscle potentials, heart rates, and respiration rates have consistently reflected differences between incentive conditions. These are tonic physiological values—that is, measures of levels of function over relatively long time intervals. Phasic changes in heart rate, usually involving only a few heart beats, are associated with the orienting reaction (Graham and Clifton, 1966), which is a different kind of phenomenon (Malmo and Bélanger, 1967; Malmo, 1972).

Overarousal in schizophrenia. The concept of overarousal is in the focus of various studies of chronic schizophrenia. According to Shagass (1969), one of the most prevalent interpretive ideas about certain schizophrenic disorders is that they involve a chronic state of cerebral overstimulation or hyperarousal.

In a review of the effect of centrally acting drugs on behavior, Mirsky and Kornetsky (1968) refer to a series of articles from their laboratory bearing on these problems. In attempting to account for the effects of certain drugs like chlorpromazine, they found the inverted U curve formulation useful. Their particular formulation was as follows:

Since the [arousal] level is higher, and consequently on the less steep portion of the [inverted U] curve, chlorpromazine-like drugs which presumably act via effects on the [ascending reticular activating system] ... produce less apparent effect in schizophrenics than in normal subjects on attention-demanding tasks. This relationship does not hold with other drugs or tasks.

This formulation was stated earlier by Kornetsky and Mirsky (1966) in an article urging caution in applying their formulation. King (1969), in pursuing a similar line of thinking, stated that one might expect that relaxing and sedating drugs, which slow down the fine psychomotor performance, would paradoxically improve the performance of schizophrenics. He cited five studies that showed that this is just what these drugs seem to do. Further documentation for the hypothesis of overarousal in chronic schizophrenics is provided in the review of autonomic and somatic reactivity in relation to psychopathology by Sternbach et al. (1969).

The treatise of Tecce and Cole (1972) represents a significant theoretical advance in the psychophysiology of schizophrenia. They present a two-process theoretical model. In essence, their theory holds that the performance of schizophrenics is nonmonotonically (inverted U) related to arousal but positively and monotonically related to attention.

Collative variables. Berlyne (1960) used the term "collative variables" to refer to novelty and change, complexity, conflict, surprise, and uncertainty. The majority of writers have used the terms "arousal" and "activation" as synonymous. However, Pribram and McGuinness (1975) applied the term "arousal" to effective collative inputs. By "effective" they meant that the input change produced a

measurable incrementing of a physiological (single-unit recording of neural potentials; galvanic skin response) or behavioral (response amplitude of a single reflex; frequency of a locomotor response) indicator over a baseline.

"Activation" is defined in terms of tonic physiological readiness to respond. Pribram and McGuinness view arousal and activation as distinct systems involving different brain structures. According to their schema, arousal and activation are coordinated by means of a third system involving effort.

Electromyographic and other physiological gradients. The results from a number of studies (Malmo, 1965, 1972, 1975) have revealed electromyographic gradients from certain muscles, depending on the task, commencing with the onset of the behavior sequence and terminating at its conclusion. Gradients of this kind have been found in other physiological measures, but the gradients seem to be most prominent and most consistent in recordings of muscle potentials. Gradients have not been found in electroencephalograms.

Evidence from a number of studies indicates that the steepness of the rise in muscle tension is an indication of degree of motivation, interest, and the like. The gradients do not appear to reflect increasing motivation mounting steadily during the task or other sequence. The gradients appear to reflect some supportive central mechanism that is required to ensure the steady running off of a behavioral sequence. For the behavioral sequence to proceed without breaking down, its central mechanism must receive an ever-increasing facilitation from the supportive central mechanism, whose peripheral facilitation is reflected in the electromyogram and other physiological gradients.

Whatever the mechanisms are that furnish the support for continuous productive mental activity, they seem to depend partly on normal exteroceptive sensory stimulation, since, under prolonged conditions of sensory isolation, mental activity suffers markedly. To this extent, at least, the peripheral components, sensory and motor, are critically important for the operation of central activities.

Other motivational phenomena

Achievement motivation. There are individual differences in human plans. What are the conditions that make one person determined to achieve certain goals in a lifetime, and how are these conditions different from those that operate to make another person content with a low level of achievement?

The hypothesis that the strength of achievement motivation can be gauged in a meaningful and useful way by analyzing the content of stories told from pictures, like those in the Thematic Apperception Test (TAT), underlies the extensive investigative work of McClelland et al. (1953). The research began with a demonstration that college students, given instructions designed to heighten their intensity of motivation to perform well on certain tests, produced in the stories they wrote from the TAT pictures more responses having to do with future achievement than did students who were in a relaxed state at the time of writing TAT stories. The next stage in the experimental program was guided by the general hypothesis that persons who obtain high TAT need (*n*) achievement scores under controlled conditions are normally more intensely motivated to achieve than are persons who obtain low (*n*) achievement scores under the same conditions.

From the results of investigations so generated, it was concluded that intensity of motivation to achieve at any task in any particular situation is determined by at least two factors: (1) the achievement motive—that is, the desire to achieve—and (2) expectancy of probable success or failure. McClelland has been engaged in field research, including some in underdeveloped countries, that has demonstrated that it is possible to teach businessmen to acquire (*n*) achievement and thereby to advance in business.

Expectancy X value. The further development of this general line of attack has been pursued by Atkinson (1964) in the expectancy X value approach to motivation. The value factor refers to the common observation that there are marked individual differences with respect to values placed on certain objects or goals. Some students strive for A's, for example, and others depreciate the importance of grades, placing high values mainly on intellectual satisfactions or on extracurricular activities. The expectancy factor refers to the subjective probability that, with the expenditure of sufficient effort, the object may be acquired or the goal reached.

It is of interest to consider what an aphysiological theory such as this may gain from observations in the neurological clinic. B. Milner (1964) has found that frontal lobe patients break test rules more often than do other patients. For example, in performing a stylus maze test, they push ahead, instead of going back to the point where they made an error, or they move along diagonals, which is against the rules. It was not that they did not realize these things were wrong; it seemed that they just could not control their impulsiveness. When progress toward the goal came into conflict with the rules, the value system that normally respects rules was shown to be abnormally weak in the frontal lobe patients. What is there about frontal lobe mechanisms that make them essential for such value systems to have normal control over behavior? This question seems relevant for the expectancy X value theory of motivation.

Level of aspiration. This term has been used by Kurt Lewin and his students and involves a procedure in which the subject is asked to say how he will do on the next trial of a task. For example, a person engaged in a dart-throwing task may be asked before his first throw what number he expects to hit. After the throw and before the next trial, he is asked again to predict his performance, and so on for several trials. The relation of level of aspiration to achievement motivation is discussed in detail by Atkinson (1964).

Cognitive dissonance. According to Festinger (1957), "cognitive dissonance" means incongruity or disharmony with respect to such matters as expectation and actuality. An A student who makes a B experiences a tension not experienced by a B student who makes the same grade. In general, dissonance occurs when there is a palpable disparity between two experiential or behavioral elements. It is postulated that cognitive dissonance produces a tension state, like hunger, that is motivating. The kinds of experimental investigations generated by the theory are illustrated by the following questions: How does dissonance in different degrees affect the person's inclination to seek out or to avoid new information? What are the reactions of persons who are forced to consider information or propaganda they would normally have avoided?

The chief distinguishing feature of a cognitive approach to motivation is that the cognitive motivation theorists focus on perceptual and informational aspects of the total stimulating situation (Weiner, 1972). They tend to deal with physiological arousal in terms of stimuli generated by the physiological processes. The research of Schachter and Singer (1962), described below, is an example of a cognitive approach to emotion.

A review of research on cognitive dissonance (Greenwald and Ronis, 1978) reveals a shift away from Festinger's original focus on logical inconsistency to

cognitive changes occurring in the service of ego defence, or self-esteem maintenance, rather than in the interest of preserving psychological consistency.

Attribution theory. Attribution theory is also a cognitive approach, and in essence it is concerned with how people perceive the motivations of others. It is generally acknowledged that Fritz Heider is the founder of attribution theory. According to Kelley (1967), the basic assumption here is that a person is motivated

to attain a cognitive mastery of the causal structure of his environment.

Psychoanalytic motivation theory. From the historical point of view, Freud's contribution to the psychology of human motivation should come first, of course. Freud's writings were probably the most powerful single influence initiating scientific investigations of human motivation. The whole course of experimental psychology was changed by the combined attack of Freud and the behaviorists on structural psychology, which had become lost in sterile introspective exercises. From Freud's observations it was plain that a full understanding of the causes of human behavior cannot be gained from conscious intro-spections. Clearly, much of behavior is determined by uncon-scious mental activities, activities that the person is unaware of and consequently cannot report on. Hebb (1967) put it this way:

> Objective behavior theory may seem unpalatable to the analytical psychiatrist, but he must realize that psychoanalysis itself is the great forerunner of objectivism. The whole theory of the unconscious tells us that verbal report is unreliable as an index of mental content, and that one can learn more about the presence of hostility or anxiety as an inference from a person's nonverbal behavior (and some of his verbal behavior) than one can by simply asking for a subjective report. Freud anticipated Watson as a behaviorist.

Physiological Concomitants of Affective Arousal

EMOTIONAL AROUSAL AND THE SITUATION

Careful physiological recordings made with sensitive instru-ments invariably show measurable changes concomitant not only with reaction to an emotion-producing situation but with reaction to any significant change in the environmental situa-tion. For example, working under conditions of high incentive is generally reflected in appropriately selected physiological measures. For reasons such as this, Duffy (1962) proposed that the distinction between emotion and motivation is relatively dispensable. However, this point of view, if carried too far, is unacceptable, as Duffy realized. An overly rigid physiological emphasis runs the risk of neglecting the perceptual or cognitive factors whose importance for emotion has been so convincingly argued by Schachter. An experiment by Schachter and Singer (1962) illustrates the approach. When subjects were injected with adrenalin, which produced a state of physiological arousal, but were given an inappropriate explanation of the effects by a physician, their reactions were determined by the environ-mental situation, whereas with an appropriate explanation there was no such dependence on the environmental events. When given an inappropriate explanation of the effects ("You feel numb"), the subjects reported that they disagreed but began feeling like the euphoric stooge in the waiting room. When given an appropriate explanation ("You are trembling, and your heart is racing"), they agreed with the explanation, did not identify with the stooge, and were annoyed by him.

Hebb's (1946) classic paper, "On the Nature of Fear," also points up the critical role played by perception in emotional response, but it goes beyond this in drawing on his observations of chimpanzees to sketch the nature of central organizational events that must be involved in fear.

There is some evidence that the physiological pattern of reaction during fear is different from that during anger, al-though control for the intensity factor was inadequate (Malmo, 1972). It is clear, however, that the degree and consistency of physiological differentiation between two such states as fear and anger are not nearly as clear as the differentiation between the feeling states that are reported by the persons who experi-ence these emotions nor between the overt behavior patterns generally elicited.

On this basis, it seems unlikely that subjective differences between emotions can be based mainly on differentiation between autonomic nervous system patterns of reaction, as some early writers thought. This is not to say that sensory feedback from the autonomic nervous system does not ever enter significantly into the picture. Indeed, in the case of some psychiatric patients with somatic symptoms, when stress evokes

a symptom reaction such as tachycardia or palpitations, the sensations associated with this physiological reaction can be frightening, in some cases even terrifying if, as in some in-stances, there is fear of impending death. Lacey's concept of visceral afferent feedback from the cardiovascular system to the brain (Valenstein, 1968) is also related to the points under consideration. This feedback can have inhibitory effects, rather than excitatory effects, on the central nervous system.

PHYSIOLOGICAL MEASUREMENTS WITH PSYCHIATRIC PATIENTS

There are distressing sensations from muscles tensing under stress in patients prone to muscular discomfort in specific muscular groups. Figure 4 provides a typical illustration of this phenomenon.

Data for the graphs in Figure 4 were obtained from a 42-year-old female psychiatric patient who complained of muscular discomfort localized in the left thigh. While the patient was engaged in a tracking task, electromyograms (EMG's) were recorded from various muscles over the body; only those from the left and right thighs are shown in the illustration. Figure 4 shows that, when a loud distracting noise was presented during tracking, tension in the left thigh rose to a much higher level than that recorded from the right thigh. As a matter of fact, tension in the thigh muscles on the right (nonsymptom) side of the body actually fell slightly under the activating condition. When tracking was performed under distraction-free conditions, no tensional difference between right and left thighs was observed.

Figure 5 shows the reactions in a second patient.

A depressed single woman of 28 complained of a painful tightness on the right side of her neck. At the time the EMG recordings were made, the patient had been suffering from this tension for some weeks.

The young woman feared contact with men, a fear that may have been caused in part by severe punishment that she received as a child from her mother, who believed that the patient and her brother had been engaging in sex play. The patient had considered marriage but only under the condition that there would be no sexual intercourse. In fact, she stated these conditions to a man who had proposed to her just before her admission to a psychiatric institution.

In view of her fear of contact with men, the results of an unplanned incident during EMG recording are of special interest. The EMG tracings in Figure 5 were recorded soon after the patient had finished her tracking test. She was resting quietly while a male research assistant began to remove cloth electrode holders from her arm. In so doing, he happened to take her hand in his, whereupon, as Figure 5 shows, the EMG's from her right neck muscles suddenly increased in level, and the EMG's from the opposite side of her neck showed little or no change. It was established that the rise in right neck muscle tension was not an artifact of head turning or of any other kind of head movement. By taking her hand in his, the male assistant evidently embarrassed her by an unintended act of intimacy, triggering her specific tensional reaction.

EMG's were recorded from this patient while she was being inter-viewed by her therapist. During the interview, right neck muscle tension rose to more than double left neck muscle tension and to 10 to 20 times the level of tension in her arm muscles. Again, there was specific activation of the symptom mechanism, this time in reaction to topics discussed in interview.

This patient also took the tracking test. At the beginning of tracking, right neck muscle tension was much higher than the tension recorded from the other muscles. After some minutes of quiet tracking, her neck tension fell gradually. However, like the first patient, she reacted specifically with her symptom-related muscles when the loud distract-ing sound was turned on. When the noise came on, right neck muscle tension increased markedly, whereas tension in the other muscles, including those on the left side on her neck, showed no rise whatever.

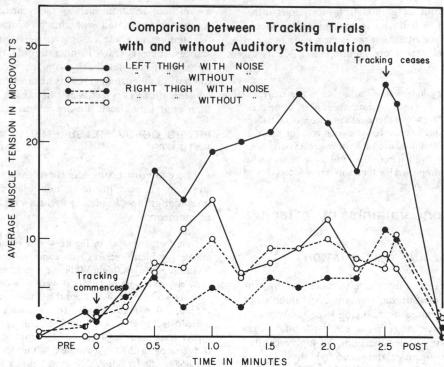

FIGURE 4. Case 1. Cramping feelings in muscles of left thigh. Turning on loud noise while the patient is tracking causes muscle potentials from her left thigh (symptom area) to rise high, far exceeding those for her symptom-free right thigh. (Compare the two graphs with *closed circles*.) When tracking was done under more favorable (distraction-free) conditions, tension in the symptom muscles (left thigh) was about the same as tension in the muscles of the right thigh. (Compare the two graphs with *open circles*.) (From Malmo, R. B. Activation: A neuropsychological dimension. Psychol. Rev., *66:* 367, 1959. Copyright 1959 by the American Psychological Association and reproduced by permission.)

Specific Muscle – Tension Reaction in Symptom Area

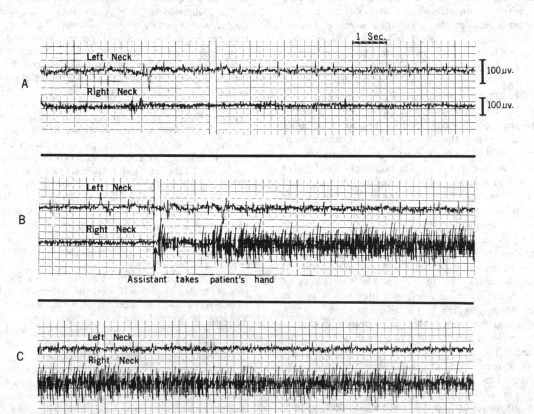

FIGURE 5. Case 2. Painful tightness on right side of neck. Shy and fearful of men, the patient, a 28-year-old single woman, was evidently embarrassed by the male assistant's taking her hand. The muscle tension reaction to this emotional experience was specific to the muscles involved in her symptom. The electromyographic reaction was not due to some movement artifact, such as head turning.

Figure 6 shows the reactions in a third patient.

A 45-year-old typist had strong feelings of inadequacy and insecurity. There was also an undercurrent of hostility, directed mainly toward men. Her therapist found her to be extremely tense and rigid. The patient felt so inadequate in trying to talk to another person that conversation was a great strain for her. She was most tense when she was trying hard to think of something to say and the words would not come. Associated with these personality weaknesses were a number of bodily complaints; the most troublesome disorder was the occurrence of severe headaches, band-like across her forehead. She reported that these headaches seemed to wax and wane according to the intensity of stresses that she encountered.

EMG's from the patient's forehead and right forearm were recorded in 12 psychiatric interviews, which were conducted while the patient lay on a bed in the experimental room. The tape recording of the interview content was synchronized with the EMG tracings (Davis and Malmo, 1951).

The seventh interview was conducted in a special way. Soon after the beginning of the interview, the therapist put the patient much more on her own than hitherto. He realized that, because of her difficulty in communicating, forcing her to take the initiative for the material to be discussed would be tension producing. But he hoped that this experience would help the patient work better in psychotherapy.

Figure 6 shows the effects of this procedure on the EMG's. Her forehead muscle tension climbed high, and as it was reaching a peak after about 8½ minutes of this special session, the patient spontaneously complained of headache. When the doctor resumed his usual supportive role, the patient's forehead muscle tension dropped, despite the fact that she was talking more.

Physiological recordings that have been successfully taken from patients under test conditions or during psychiatric interview include the following: cardiovascular, respiratory, skin conductance, gastrointestinal, electromyographic, and electroencephalographic (Greenfield and Sternbach, 1972). Physiological changes, especially cardiovascular reactions, are generally polyphasic in character; a change in one direction is followed by a compensatory change in the opposite direction. In some cases the compensatory reaction may predominate over the initial reaction. A striking example of this kind is vasovagal (vasodepressor) fainting (Graham et al., 1961), in which the faint itself, characterized by low blood pressure and bradycardia, is the second phase of a diphasic response, the first phase being characterized by a rapid or rising heart rate and by a rising blood pressure, especially the diastolic readings. Vasovagal fainting has been observed in persons donating blood, in persons having a simple venipuncture, and in patients undergoing pneumoencephalography. In the absence of careful physiological monitoring, the brief initial sympathetic (fear?) reaction was not observed.

Individual differences. Individual differences in physiological reactions are of considerable importance. Some people tend to show what has been called sympathetic dominance, and others tend to show parasympathetic dominance. This trait of autonomic balance has been quantified by Wenger and Cullen (1972). The distribution seems about normal; the majority of persons show a fairly equal balance, a few persons show extremely high sympathetic dominance, and a few show extremely high parasympathetic dominance (Sternbach, 1966).

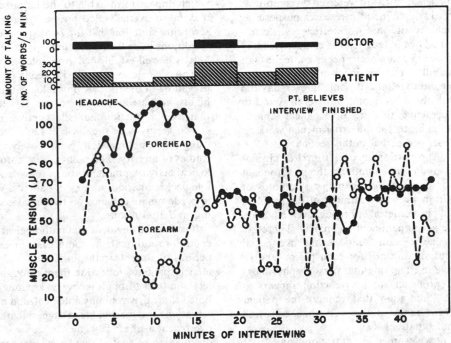

FIGURE 6. Case 3. Band-like headaches across forehead. The patient, a 45-year-old woman, complained of headache during interview at the point shown in the graph. The patient was under stress at this point because her therapist was forcing her to take the initiative: He was trying unsuccessfully to get her to produce meaningful topics for discussion. During the first 5 minutes, the doctor explained how he wanted the interview to be conducted, and the patient asked him questions about the procedure. In the second 5 minutes, the doctor said as little as he could (drop in his amount of talking shown in *bar graph*), but the patient was still unproductive. She talked less and less, and what she said was superficial and repetitious. Her forehead muscle EMG's rose. Her forearm muscle EMG's fell during this period, probably because, with less and less talking, the patient's habitual use of her hands in talking was reduced more and more. When the doctor resumed his facilitative role, her forehead muscle EMG's fell, and her forearm muscle EMG's rose. Later in the interview, when the patient believed that the interview was finished, her forehead muscle EMG's dropped and then rose again when she realized that the interview would continue. (From Davis, F. H., and Malmo, R. B. Electromyographic recording during interview. Am. J. Psychiatry, *107:* 906, 1951. Copyright 1951 by the American Psychiatric Association and reproduced by permission.)

Another kind of individual difference is determined by particular physiological measures that show the greatest relative changes under standard conditions of stimulation. Specificity of physiological reactions to stress is observed with remarkable clarity in patients with complaints of bodily discomfort, such as tachycardia, palpitations, precordial pain referred to the cardiovascular system, and tensional discomfort, including muscular pains and tension headache, referred to the skeletal-motor system. Electromyographic (EMG) recordings from various muscular areas over the body, for example, show highly specific correlations between sites of peak EMG reaction to stress and sites of muscular discomfort. This phenomenon is illustrated in Figure 4. The term "symptom specificity" was introduced by Malmo and Shagass (1949) to refer to these correlations. The parallel work of the Laceys on individual differences in normal persons has drawn attention to the importance of looking for individual response specificities in psychophysiological studies.

The principle of symptom specificity has been confirmed by a number of other research workers, and there is general agreement that the principle is sound (Buss, 1966; Sternbach, 1966; Engel, 1972; Goldstein, 1972). Engel and co-workers brought the principle of symptom specificity to bear on rheumatoid arthritis and hypertension.

Pathological anxiety. The term "anxiety" is often used colloquially and in laboratory parlance to refer to acute emotional states, such as fear and apprehension. Here the term refers to pathological anxiety, the emotional responses of pathologically increased intensity and duration that may be observed in certain neurotic patients.

Pathological anxiety (henceforward referred to simply as anxiety) has been objectively defined for research purposes as a tensional state of such severity that work efficiency is interfered with and medical advice is sought. It is characterized by one or more of the following complaints: persistent feelings of tension or strain, irritability, unremitting worry, restlessness, inability to concentrate, and feelings of panic in everyday life situations. Patients with these symptoms have been found to be physiologically hyperactive; this group of patients constituted a major source of subjects for the experimental work on symptom specificity described earlier in this section.

With regard to the disproportionately high level of physiological activation in everyday life situations, the symptoms of anxiety are possibly unique among the major symptoms of psychiatric disorder. From Freud's treatment of the problem of anxiety to the present physiological approach, overactivation is cited as an objective accompaniment of anxiety. There are undoubtedly particular cues, certain situations that have special meaning or unconscious significance for each person and so are particularly effective in triggering that person's physiological overreaction. But proneness to overreaction appears to involve a physiological alteration that renders the patient overly sensitive to a wide range of relatively innocuous and insignificant stimuli and situations.

Because of the current widespread use of tranquilizing drugs in the treatment of anxiety, it is now extremely difficult to obtain valid psychophysiological data from anxiety patients. For this reason, the reliable physiological investigations that were carried out before the widespread use of these drugs are particularly valuable in providing relatively artifact-free data.

Startle induced by a strong auditory stimulus was found to be an effective form of stimulation for physiological differentiation of anxiety patients and normal persons. EMG recordings under these circumstances revealed no differences between patients and controls in the immediate reflex reactions to the startling sound; the differences in the EMG reactions of patients and controls came after the primary period of reflex startle (see Figure 7). In view of the results from neurophysiological experiments, a likely explanation of the abnormally high after-reaction observed in anxiety patients is that the sustained tension is due to the failure of some central homeostatic mechanism, possibly located in the reticular systems. Experiments with animals have demonstrated that, by stimulating certain parts of the thalamic reticular system, the researcher can inhibit motor afterdischarge.

Examples of other kinds of physiological dysfunction that were observed in anxiety patients compared with controls under experimental conditions are the following: irregularities in motor action, such as finger tremor and respiratory irregularity, and autonomic nervous system overreactivity, such as reactions of blood pressure and heart rate. Interpretations of the vast and conflicting literature on the galvanic skin reaction have benefited greatly from a critical review by Edelberg (1972).

The high-anxiety patients in the Montreal studies were more physiologically uncontrolled than all other psychiatric-patient groups except for early schizophrenics. Psychophysiologists agree that regulatory mechanisms are defective in anxiety, a point that Lader (1969) clearly establishes in his review.

It is important to take into account the precise laboratory conditions under which the physiological recordings were made. For instance, it makes considerable difference whether or not the recording crew tried to reassure the patient and took the precaution of habituating him to the laboratory procedures, which appear formidable to the uninitiated. Indeed, a patient may be so overactivated physiologically by the impact of the recording situation that the subsequent controlled stimulating conditions have little additional effect.

It is a well-established principle in psychophysiology that any phasic reaction must be judged in relation to the tonic level prevailing at the time. A physiological function that is already highly activated generally reacts less to further stimulation than does a function that is less activated at the outset.

This seems to be the sense of Lader's (1969) caution against using the term "reactivity" too loosely in psychophysiological studies of anxiety. The point is that chronic, excessive physiological activity, phasic or tonic, is evidence for defective physiological regulation in anxiety patients. Which action happens to predominate depends on the precise conditions before, during, and after testing.

It is clinically evident that pathological anxiety is a reversible condition, although in some cases it may persist over long periods of time. Careful longitudinal physiological studies of anxiety patients, following them through periods of high anxiety and later through recovery, are much needed. From combined clinical, psychophysiological, and neurophysiological observations, it is reasonable to suggest tentatively that the general overreaction in anxiety may be caused, in part, by reversible dysfunction of central regulatory mechanisms.

Pitts (1969) refers to the fact established by work in the McGill laboratory and elsewhere that patients with pathological anxiety show excessive and abnormally prolonged contractions of their skeletal muscles under conditions of controlled observation that use thermal or auditory stimulations and that record muscle potentials continuously from patients and control subjects.

Muscular exercise produces lactate as the end product of anaerobic glycolysis, the process by which glucose is broken down by cells in the absence of oxygen, as in the case of muscle cells during exercise. Pitts demonstrated in carefully controlled studies that he could bring on anxiety attacks in patients by 20-minute infusions of lactate. Nonpatient controls had many fewer and less severe symptoms in response to lactate. It was clear that the patients were responding to a specific effect of the lactate, not to any psychological aspects of intravenous infusion.

No anxiety attacks occurred when calcium was added to the lactate infusion. According to Pitts's (1969) theory, which is still in a preliminary stage:

Anxiety symptoms may ultimately be expressed through a common biochemical mechanism: the complexing of calcium ions by lactate ions. If this binding occurs in the intercellular fluid at the surface of excitable membranes such as nerve endings, an excess of lactate could interfere with the normal functioning of calcium in transmitting nerve impulses.

The difference between patients and nonpatients is nothing so simple as impaired ability to clear lactate from the blood. In patients, the excess lactate from infusions was removed normally by the liver. According to the theory, an excessive flow of adrenalin in patients is probably a key factor in accelerating lactate production.

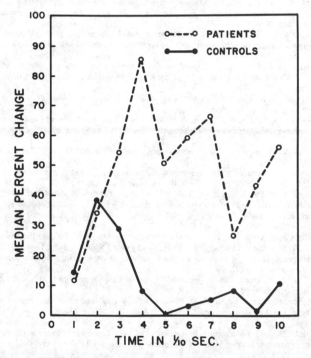

FIGURE 7. Muscle tension reaction to startling auditory stimulus. The difference between anxious patients and controls occurs in the period after the immediate startle reaction. *Curves* show the median percentage change in EMG. (Zero per cent represents the level preceding the stimulus.) Patients and controls show nearly identical responses (EMG changes) during the first ²⁄₁₀ second. But from ²⁄₁₀ to ³⁄₁₀ second the controls' *curve* falls while the patients' *curve* continues to rise. The patients' *curve* reaches a peak at a time when the controls' *curve* is down to almost the prestimulus level. (From Malmo, R. B., Shagass, C., and Davis, J. F. A method for the investigation of somatic response mechanisms in psychoneurosis. Science, *112:* 325, 1950. Copyright 1950 by the American Association for the Advancement of Science and reproduced by permission.)

According to Pitts, the

anxiety neurotic would be someone particularly subject to this [hypothetical] mechanism because of chronic overproduction of adrenalin, overactivity of the central nervous system, a defect in metabolism resulting in excess lactate production, a defect in calcium metabolism or a combination of these conditions.

His reference to overactivity of the central nervous system is of interest in relation to indications of defective regulatory mechanisms in psychophysiological findings.

The chronic character of pathological anxiety, its persistence for months or longer after stress has been removed, must be due to a breakdown, for a time, in certain parts of these complexly interacting mechanisms. Such a pathological state could develop in a number of different ways—for instance, by chiefly constitutional metabolic and neural deficiencies or by an extraordinarily stressful life situation, which could start the pathological chain of physiological events by, perhaps, causing a greatly increased flow of adrenalin over a long period of time.

The anxiety-patient group, perhaps because it has been most thoroughly studied, stands out with respect to the clear correlations between subjective pathology and objective physiological changes. These remarkably positive findings are in contrast to the relatively negative findings from patients in whom depression is the primary symptom, not patients with depression that is secondary to anxiety—they are placed in the anxiety-patient group. An exception is salivary output, which is decreased in psychotic depression and in schizoaffective disturbances and is increased in depressed patients after electroconvulsive therapy. From the physiological evidence, primary anxiety and primary depression appear to involve quite different mechanisms. Certainly, the evidence is opposed to thinking that they are on the same continuum.

It seems likely that an objective study of depression would profit greatly from further cinematographic analysis of postures and bodily movements in depressed patients. On clinical grounds it appears that objective somatic deviations specifically characteristic of depressives may be found in careful analyses of how the patient walks, turns his head and body, and so on, rather than in measurements of autonomic nervous system changes. However, this matter is far from being settled.

Prospects for a rich yield from these combined attacks on disorders of affect appear excellent. With coordinated efforts from specialists in different fields, there are sure to be significant advances in scientific knowledge and, consequently, in the treatment of psychiatric patients.

Suggested Cross References

The anatomy and function of brain structures such as the limbic system and hypothalamus are described in Section 2.5. The clinical aspects of alcoholism and drug dependence are discussed, respectively, by Selzer (Section 23.3) and Freedman (Section 23.1). Further discussion of human motivation, especially its behavioral aspects, may be found in Chapters 8, 9, 10, and 11 on current theories of personality and psychopathology.

REFERENCES

Andersson, B. Regulation of body fluids. Annu. Rev. Physiol., *39:* 185, 1977.
Andersson, B., Jobin, M., and Olsson, K. A study of thirst and other effects on an increased sodium concentration in the 3rd brain ventricle. Acta Physiol. Scand., *69:* 29, 1967.
Atkinson, J. W. *An Introduction to Motivation.* D. Van Nostrand, New York, 1964.

Beach, F. A., and Le Boeuf, B. J. Coital behaviour in dogs: I. Preferential mating in the bitch. Anim. Behav., *15:* 546, 1967.

Berlyne, D. E. *Conflict, Arousal, and Curiosity.* McGraw-Hill, New York, 1960.

Blank, D. L., and Wayner, M. J. Lateral preoptic single unit activity: Effects of various solutions. Physiol. Behav., *15:* 723, 1975.

Blass, E. M., and Epstein, A. N. A lateral preoptic osmosensitive zone for thirst in the rat. J. Comp. Physiol. Psychol., *76:* 378, 1971.

Bolles, R. C. *Theory of Motivation.* Harper & Row, New York, 1967.

Brain, L. Drug-dependence. Nature, *208:* 825, 1965.

Broadbent, D. E. How noise affects work. New Society. March 12, 1966.

Brown, J. S. *The Motivation of Behavior.* McGraw-Hill, New York, 1961.

Buss, A. H. *Psychopathology.* Wiley, New York, 1966.

Butler, R. A. Curiosity in monkeys. Sci. Am., *190:* No. 2, 70, 1954.

Campbell, B. A., and Misanin, J. R. Basic drives. Annu. Rev. Psychol., *20:* 57, 1969.

Cofer, C. N., and Appley, M. H. *Motivation: Theory and Research.* John Wiley & Sons, New York, 1964.

Courts, F. A. Relations between experimentally induced muscular tension and memorization. J. Exp. Psychol., *25:* 235, 1939.

Daniel, P. M. The anatomy of the hypothalamus and pituitary gland. In *Neuroendocrinology,* L. Martini and W. F. Ganong, editors, vol. 1, p. 15. Academic Press, New York, 1966.

Davis, F. H., and Malmo, R. B. Electromyographic recording during interview. Am. J. Psychiatry, *107:* 908, 1951.

Duffy, E. *Activation and Behavior.* John Wiley & Sons, New York, 1962.

Durham, R. M., and Novin, D. Slow potential changes due to osmotic stimuli in supraoptic nucleus of the rabbit. Am. J. Physiol., *219:* 293, 1970.

Edelberg, R. Electrical activity of the skin: Its measurement and uses in psychophysiology. In *Handbook of Psychophysiology,* N. S. Greenfield and R. S. Sternbach, editors, p. 367. Holt, Rinehart and Winston, New York, 1972.

Edström, J. E., and Eichner, D. Quantitativ Ribonukleinsäure-Untersuchungen an den Ganglienzellen des Nucleus supraopticus der Albino-Ratte unter experimentellen Bedingungen (Kochsalz-Belastung), A. Zellforsch., *48:* 187, 1958.

Eggena, P., and Polson, A. X. Osmotic stimulation of vasotocin secretion by the toad's hypothalamo-neurohypophyseal system in vitro. Endocrinology, *94:* 35, 1974.

Ellis, F. W., and Pick, J. R. Experimentally induced ethanol dependence in rhesus monkeys. J. Pharmacol. Exp. Ther., *175:* 88, 1970a.

Ellis, F. W., and Pick, J. R. Evidence of ethanol dependence in dogs. Fed. Proc., *29:* 2, 1970b.

Emmers, R. Interaction of neural systems which control body water. Brain Res., *49:* 323, 1973.

Emmers, R. Tonic control of water intake via the thalamic taste nucleus. Ann. N. Y. Acad. Sci., *290:* 124, 1977.

Engel, B. T. Response specificity. In *Handbook of Psychophysiology,* N. S. Greenfield and R. S. Sternbach, editors, p. 571. Holt, Rinehart and Winston, New York, 1972.

Evarts, E. V. Brain mechanisms in movement. Sci. Am., *229:* No. 1, 96, 1973.

Falk, J. L. The grooming behavior of the chimpanzee as a reinforcer. J. Exp. Anal. Behav., *1:* 83, 1958.

Falk, J. L., Samson, H. H., and Winger, G. Behavioral maintenance of high concentrations of blood ethanol and physical dependence in the rat. Science, *177:* 811, 1972.

Ferster, C. B., and Skinner, B. F. *Schedules of Reinforcement.* Appleton-Century-Crofts, New York, 1957.

Festinger, L. *A Theory of Cognitive Dissonance.* Stanford University Press, Palo Alto, Calif., 1957.

Fitz-Gerald, F. L. Voluntary alcohol consumption in apes. In *The Biology of Alcoholism.* Vol. II. *Physiology and Behavior,* B. Kissen and H. Begleiter, editors, p. 169. Plenum Publishing Corp., New York, 1972.

Fitzsimons, J. T. Thirst. Physiol. Rev., *52:* 468, 1972.

Flynn, J. P., Wasman, M., and Egger, M. D. Behavior during propagated hippocampal afterdischarges. In *EEG and Behavior,* G. H. Glaser, editor, p. 134. Basic Books, New York, 1963.

Glusman, M. The hypothalamic "savage" syndrome. Res. Publ. Assoc. Res. Nerv. Ment. Dis., *52:* 52, 1974.

Goldstein, I. B. Electromyography: A measure of skeletal muscle response. In *Handbook of Psychophysiology,* N. S. Greenfield and R. S. Sternbach, editors, p. 329. Holt, Rinehart and Winston, New York, 1972.

Goodman, S. J. Visuo-motor reaction times and brain stem multiple-unit activity. Exp. Neurol., *22:* 367, 1968.

Graham, D. T., Kabler, J. D., and Lunsford, L., Jr. Vasovagal fainting: A diphasic response. Psychosom. Med., *23:* 493, 1961.

Graham, F. K., and Clifton, R. K. Heart-rate change as a component of the orienting response. Psychol. Bull., *65:* 305, 1966.

*Greenfield, N. S., and Sternbach, R. A., editors. *Handbook of Psychophysiology.* Holt, Rinehart and Winston, New York, 1972.

Greenwald, A. G., and Ronis, D. L. Twenty years of cognitive dissonance: Case study of the evolution of a theory. Psychol. Rev., *85:* 53, 1978.

Grossman, S. P. *A Textbook of Physiological Psychology.* John Wiley & Sons, New York, 1967.

Hall, R. D., Bloom, F. E., and Olds, J. Neuronal and neurochemical substrates of reinforcement. Neurosci. Res. Prog. Bull., *15:* 141, 1977.

Hatton, G. I. Nucleus circularis: Is it an osmoreceptor in the brain? Brain Res. Bull., *1:* 123, 1976.

Hatton, G. I., and Walters, J. K. Induced multiple nucleoli, nucleolar margination, and cell size changes in supraoptic neurons during dehydration and rehydration in the rat. Brain Res., *59:* 137, 1973.

Hayward, J. N. Neural control of the posterior pituitary. Annu. Rev. Physiol., *37:* 191, 1975.

Hayward, J. N., and Jennings, D. P. Osmosensitivity of hypothalamic magnocellular neuroendocrine cells to intracarotid hypertonic D-glucose in the waking monkey. Brain Res., *57:* 467, 1973.

Hayward, J. N., and Vincent, J. D. Osmosensitive single neurones in the hypothalamus of unanaesthetized monkeys. J. Physiol., *210:* 947, 1970.

Hebb, D. O. On the nature of fear. Psychol. Rev., *53:* 259, 1946.

Hebb, D. O. Cerebral organization and consciousness. Res. Publ. Assoc. Res. Nerv. Ment. Dis., *45:* 1, 1967.

Interim Report of the Commission of Inquiry into the Non-Medical Use of Drugs. Information Canada, Ottawa, 1970.

Isbell, H., Fraser, H. F., Wikler, A., Belleville, R. E., and Eisenman, A. J. An experimental study of the etiology of "rum fits" and delirium tremens. Q. J. Stud. Alcohol, *16:* 1, 1955.

Ishikawa, T., Koizumi, K., and Brooks, C. McC. Activity of supraoptic nucleus neurons of the hypothalamus. Neurology, *16:* 101, 1966.

Jaffe, J. H. Pharmacological approaches to the treatment of compulsive opiate use: Their rationale and current status. In *Drugs and the Brain,* P. Black, editor, p. 351. Johns Hopkins University Press, Baltimore, 1969.

Jaffe, J. H., and Sharpless, S. K. Pharmacological denervation supersensitivity in the central nervous system: A theory of physical dependence. In *The Addictive States,* A. Wikler, editor, p. 226. Williams & Wilkins, Baltimore, 1968.

Kelley, H. H. Attribution theory in social psychology. In *Nebraska Symposium on Motivation,* D. Levine, editor, p. 192. University of Nebraska Press, Lincoln, 1967.

Kerr, F. W. L., Triplett, J. N., Jr., and Beeler, G. W. Reciprocal (push-pull) effects of morphine on single units in the ventromedian and lateral hypothalamus and influences on other nuclei: With a comment on methadone effects during withdrawal from morphine. Brain Res., *74:* 81, 1974.

King, H. E. Psychomotility: A dimension of behavior disorder. In *Neurobiological Aspects of Psychopathology,* J. Zubin and C. Shagass, editors, p. 99. Grune & Stratton, New York, 1969.

Kornetsky, C., and Mirsky, A. F. On certain psychopharmacological and physiological differences between schizophrenic and normal persons. Psychopharmacologia, *8:* 21, 1966.

*Lader, M. H. Psychophysiological aspects of anxiety. In *Studies of Anxiety,* M. H. Lader, editor, p. 53 (Br. J. Psychiatry, Spec. Publ. No. 3). Headley Brothers, Ashford, Kent, 1969.

Lehrman, D. S. The reproductive behavior of ring doves. Sci. Am., *211:* No. 5, 48, 1964.

*Malmo, H. P., and Malmo, R. B. Movement-related forebrain and midbrain multiple unit activity in rats. Electroencephalogr. Clin. Neurophysiol., *42:* 501, 1977.

Malmo, R. B. Activation: A neuropsychological dimension. Psychol. Rev., *66:* 367, 1959.

Malmo, R. B. Activation. In *Experimental Foundations of Clinical Psychology,* A. J. Bachrach, editor, p. 386. Basic Books, New York, 1962.

Malmo, R. B. Physiological gradients and behavior. Psychol. Bull., *64:* 225, 1965.

*Malmo, R. B. Studies of anxiety: Some clinical origins of the activation concept. In *Anxiety and Behavior,* C. D. Spielberger, editor, p. 157. Academic Press, New York, 1966.

Malmo, R. B. Overview. In *Handbook of Psychophysiology,* N. S. Greenfield and R. A. Sternbach, editors, p. 967. Holt, Rinehart and Winston, New York, 1972.

*Malmo, R. B. *On Emotions, Needs, and Our Archaic Brain.* Holt, Rinehart and Winston, New York, 1975.

Malmo, R. B. Osmosensitive neurons in the rat's dorsal midbrain. Brain Res., *105:* 105, 1976.

*Malmo, R. B., and Bélanger, D. Related physiological and behavioral changes: What are their determinants? Res. Publ. Assoc. Res. Nerv. Ment. Dis., *45:* 288, 1967.

Malmo, R. B. and Malmo, H. P. Responses of lateral preoptic neurons in the rat to hypertonic sucrose and NaCl. Electroencephalogr. Clin. Neurophysiol., *46:* 401, 1979.

Malmo, R. B., and Mundl, W. J. Osmosensitive neurons in the rat's preoptic area: Medial-lateral comparison. J. Comp. Physiol. Psychol., *88:* 161, 1975.

Malmo, R. B., and Shagass, C. Physiologic study of symptom mechanisms in psychiatric patients under stress. Psychosom. Med., *11:* 25, 1949.

*Malmo, R. B., Shagass, C., and Davis, J. F. A method for the investigation of somatic response mechanisms in psychoneurosis. Science, *112:* 325, 1950.

McClelland, D. C., Atkinson, J. W., Clark, R. A., and Lowell, E. L. *The Achievement Motive.* Appleton-Century-Crofts, New York, 1953.

*Melzack, R. *The Puzzle of Pain.* Harmondsworth, Middlesex, England, 1973.

Mendelson, J. H., and LaDou, J. Experimentally induced chronic intoxication and withdrawal in alcoholics: Part 2. Psychophysiological findings. Q. J. Stud. Alcohol, *2* (Suppl.): 14, 1964.

Miller, N. E. Laws of learning relevant to its biological basis. Proc. Am. Philos. Soc., *111:* 315, 1967.

Milner, B. Some effects of frontal lobectomy in man. In *The Frontal Granular*

Cortex and Behavior, J. M. Warren and K. Akert, editors, p. 313. McGraw-Hill, New York, 1964.

Milner, B. Visually-guided maze learning in man: Effects of bilateral hippocampal, bilateral frontal, and unilateral cerebral lesions. Neuropsychologia, *3:* 317, 1965.

Milner, P. M. *Physiological Psychology.* Holt, Rinehart and Winston, New York, 1970.

Mirsky, A. F., and Kornetsky, C. The effect of centrally-acting drugs on attention. In *Psychopharmacology: A Review of Progress 1957–1967*, Public Health Service Publication No. 1836, p. 91. United States Government Printing Office, Washington, 1968.

*Mogenson, G. J. *The Neurobiology of Behavior: An Introduction*, Erlbaum Associates, Hillsdale, N. J., 1977.

Nauta, W. J. H., and Haymaker, W. Hypothalamic nuclei and fiber connections. In *The Hypothalamus*, W. Haymaker, E. Anderson, and W. J. H. Nauta, editors, p. 136. Charles C Thomas, Springfield, Ill., 1969.

Niijima, A. Afferent discharges from osmoreceptors in the liver of the guinea pig. Science, *166:* 1519, 1969.

Peck, J. W., and Novin, D. Evidence that osmoreceptors mediating drinking in rabbits are in the lateral preoptic area. J. Comp. Physiol. Psychol., *74:* 134, 1971.

Pieper, W. A., and Skeen, M. J. Induction of physical dependence on ethanol in rhesus monkeys using an oral acceptance technique. Life Sci., *11:* 989, 1972.

Pieper, W. A., Skeen, M. J., McClure, H. M., and Bourne, P. G. The chimpanzee as an animal model for investigating alcoholism. Science, *176:* 71, 1972.

Pitts, F. N., Jr. The biochemistry of anxiety. Sci. Am., *220:* No. 2, 69, 1969.

Pribram, K. H., and McGuinness, D. Arousal, activation, and effort in the control of attention. Psychol. Rev., *82:* 116, 1975.

Rechardt, L. Electron microscopic and histochemical observations on the supraoptic nucleus of normal and dehydrated rats. Acta Physiol. Scand., *329:* 1, 1969.

Richter, C. P. Production and control of alcoholic cravings in rats. In *Neuropharmacology*, H. A. Abramson, editor, p. 39. Josiah Macy, Jr. Foundation, New York, 1957.

*Schachter, S., and Singer, J. E. Cognitive, social, and physiological determinants of emotional state. Psychol. Rev., *69:* 379, 1962.

Schwartzbaum, J. S. Interrelationship among multiunit activity of the midbrain reticular formation and lateral geniculate nucleus, thalamocortical arousal, and behavior in rats. J. Comp. Physiol. Psychol., *89:* 131, 1975.

*Shagass, C. Neurophysiological studies. In *The Schizophrenic Syndrome*, L. Bellak and L. Loeb, editors, p. 172. Grune & Stratton, New York, 1969.

Skinner, B. F. *The Behavior of Organisms.* Appelton-Century-Crofts, New York, 1938.

Skinner, B. F. The experimental analysis of operant behavior. In *The Roots of American Psychology: Historical Influences and Implications for the Future*, R. W. Rieber and K. Salzinger, editors, p. 374. New York Academy of Science, New York, 1977.

Smialowski, A. The myeloarchitectonics of the hypothalamus in the dog. Acta Biol. Exper. (Warsaw), *26:* 99, 1966.

Snyder, S. H. Opiate receptor in normal and drug-altered brain function. Nature, *257:* 185, 1975.

Spence, J. T., and Spence, K. W. The motivational components of manifest anxiety: Drive and drive stimuli. In *Anxiety and Behavior*, C. D. Spielberger, editor, p. 291. Academic Press, New York, 1966.

Spragg, S. D. S. Morphine addiction in chimpanzees. Comp. Psychol. Monogr., *15:* 5, 1940.

Sternbach, R. A. *Principles of Psychophysiology.* Academic Press, New York, 1966.

Sternbach, R. A., Alexander, A. A., and Greenfield, N. S. Autonomic and somatic reactivity in relation to psychopathology. In *Neurobiological Aspects of Psychopathology*, J. Zubin and C. Shagass, editors, p. 78. Grune & Stratton, New York, 1969.

Stolerman, I. P., and Kumar, R. Preferences for morphine in rats: Validation of an experimental model of dependence. Psychopharmacologia (Berlin), *17:* 137, 1970.

Sundsten, J. W., and Sawyer, C. H. Osmotic activation of neurohypophysial hormone release in rabbits with hypothalamic islands. Exp. Neurol., *4:* 548, 1961.

Tecce, J. J., and Cole, J. O. Psychophysiologic responses of schizophrenics to drugs. Psychopharmacologia, *24:* 159, 1972.

Thompson, T., and Ostlund, W., Jr. Susceptibility to readdiction as a function of the addiction and withdrawal environments. J. Comp. Physiol. Psychol., *60:* 388, 1965.

Tweedle, C. D., and Hatton, G. I. Ultrastructural comparisons of neurons of supraoptic and circularis nuclei in normal and dehydrated rats. Brain Res. Bull., *1:* 103, 1976.

Valenstein, E. S. Biology of drives: A report of an NRP work session. Neurosci. Res. Prog. Bull., *6:* 1, 1968.

Vanderwolf, C. H. Limbic-diencephalic mechanisms of voluntary movement. Psychol. Rev., *78:* 83, 1971.

Verney, E. B. The antidiuretic hormone and the factors which determine its release. Proc. R. Soc. Lond. (Biol.), *135:* 25, 1947.

von Holst, E., and von Saint Paul, U. Electrically controlled behavior. Sci. Am., *206:* No. 3, 50, 1962.

Watt, R. M. Metabolic activity in single supraoptic neurones and its relation to osmotic stimulation. Brain Res., *21:* 443, 1970.

Weeks, J. R. Experimental narcotic addiction. Sci. Am., *210:* No. 3, 46, 1964.

Weeks, J. R., and Collins, R. J. Patterns of intravenous self-injection by morphine-addicted rats. Res. Publ. Assoc. Res. Nerv. Ment. Dis., *46:* 288, 1968.

Weiner, B. *Theories of Motivation.* Markham, Chicago, 1972.

Weiss, C. S., and Almli, C. R. Lateral preoptic and lateral hypothalamic units: In search of the osmoreceptors for thirst. Physiol. Behav., *15:* 713, 1975.

Wenger, M. A., and Cullen, T. D. Studies of autonomic balance in children and adults. In *Handbook of Psychophysiology*, N. S. Greenfield and R. A. Sternbach, editors, p. 535. Holt, Rinehart and Winston, New York, 1972.

Wikler, A. Interaction of physical dependence and classical and operant conditioning in the genesis of relapse. Res. Publ. Assoc. Res. Nerv. Ment. Dis., *46:* 280, 1968.

Wood, C. G., Jr., and Hokanson, J. E. Effects of induced muscular tension on performance and the inverted U function. J. Pers. Soc. Psychol., *1:* 506, 1965.

Wright, J. W. Deviations in food and water consumption and urinary electrolytes with frequency of measurement in rats. Psychon. Sci., *29:* 32, 1972.

Zubin, J., and Shagass, C., editors. *Neurobiological Aspects of Psychopathology.* Grune & Stratton, New York, 1969.

4.5 Aggression

ROBERT A. BARON, Ph.D.

Introduction

Lebanon, Angola, Bangladesh, terrorism in Italy, violence on the streets of major cities, murder, rape, child abuse—the list of examples of human cruelty goes on and on. Indeed, so common do instances of violence appear to be that it seems impossible to pick up a newspaper, leaf through a magazine, or tune in the evening news without learning of the occurrence of some frightening new atrocity. It sometimes seems that this is a period when the evil side of human nature is stronger than at any time in the past. Yet history reveals a long and unbroken record of war, invasion, torture, and destruction stretching back to the shadowy beginnings of organized society. With such evidence, it seems reasonable to conclude that the 20th century in general and the current decade in particular hold no monopoly on widespread violence.

Why, it may be asked, do human beings aggress? What causes men and women to turn on others with a brutality unmatched by even the fiercest of predators? What steps can be taken to prevent or control such behavior? For many years, attempts to answer such questions focused on the needs and conflicts of individual aggressors. It was widely believed that human beings engage in such actions because they are somehow driven or impelled in this direction by dark forces within their own nature. More recently, though, it has become apparent that violence, like many less dramatic forms of behavior, is strongly influenced by social and environmental conditions. In fact, it now appears that the occurrence, form, and direction of aggressive acts are as much a function of the external context in which they occur as of the motives and needs of individual aggressors. In short, growing evidence suggests that the roots of human violence must be sought in prevailing and often complex social and situational conditions, as well as within the psyches of violent men and women.

As the complex nature of aggression has become more and more apparent, growing attention has been devoted to this topic. Because of the volume of this research, it is impossible to present anything even approaching a complete summary of it here. Therefore, the scope of the present discussion is limited in two important ways. First, because it is human, rather than animal, aggression that currently threatens humanity's survival, attention is focused primarily on this topic. Second, rather than attempting to examine all lines of current investigation, the author has selected a smaller number of central issues for detailed discussion.

Aggression: A Formal Definition

Although many different definitions of aggression have been offered, none has been universally adopted. However, one that would probably be acceptable to many researchers in this area is as follows: Aggression is any form of behavior directed toward the goal of harming or injuring another living being who is motivated to avoid such treatment. At first glance, this definition may seem quite straightforward. However, closer examination reveals that it actually involves several complex features.

First, it suggests that aggression is a form of behavior—not an emotion, need, or motive. As such, it must be distinguished from emotions that may or may not accompany it (such as anger), motives that may or may not underlie it (such as the desire for vengeance), and negative attitudes that sometimes enhance its occurrence (such as ethnic and racial prejudice).

Second, this definition limits application of the term "aggression" to acts in which an aggressor intends to harm the victim. The inclusion of such a criterion raises a number of difficulties. As pointed out by several experts in this field (Buss, 1971; Bandura, 1973) intentions are private, hidden events not open to direct observation. As a result, they must be inferred from events that precede and follow alleged acts of aggression. In some cases, establishing the presence of an intention to harm others is simple. For example, aggressors often admit their desire to injure their victims and express regret if their attacks have failed. Similarly, the social context within which harm-producing behavior occurs often provides strong grounds for assuming the presence or absence of such intentions. In other situations, though, it is much more difficult to establish the presence of aggressive intent. For example, while hunting, one person may shoot and kill another. If the person who did the shooting expresses deep remorse about the victim's death, it may at first appear that intention to harm was lacking. However, if further evidence reveals that he had quarreled with the victim immediately before the so-called accident, the presence of a strong motive for aggression may be suspected.

Despite the difficulties involved in determining the presence or absence of aggressive intent, there are several compelling reasons for retaining this criterion in the definition of aggression. First, if all reference to such intent were eliminated, it would be necessary to classify accidental harm or injury to others as aggression. In view of the fact that people do sometimes harm others purely by accident, it seems important to distinguish between such actions and overt aggression. This distinction can be made only through reference to the intentions behind such behaviors. Second, if the notion of intent were excluded from the definition of aggression, instances in which attempts to harm or injure others are made but fail would not be labeled as aggression. After all, no harm is produced. But since the availability of better weapons, more accurate aim, or greater physical strength on the part of aggressors would result in serious injury to others, it seems crucial that these instances be viewed as aggressive in nature. In short,

just as accidental harm to others should be distinguished from aggression, accidental failure to harm should be included within its domain. For these and other reasons, it seems essential to define aggression not simply as behavior that inflicts harm or injury on others but, rather, as actions directed toward this goal.

A third major aspect of the above definition that requires some comment involves the contention that only actions that harm or injure living beings be viewed as aggressive in nature. It is obvious that people often strike or seek to destroy various kinds of inanimate objects, such as furniture and dishes, but such behavior is not considered aggression unless it causes some form of harm to another living organism. In many instances, of course, this is actually the case. For example, the proud owner of a priceless painting is certainly harmed when another person destroys his or her loved possession. In many other cases, however, attacks against inanimate objects cause no harm or injury to other persons—for example, throwing rocks against a brick wall or into a lake or repeatedly punching one's pillow. Although such actions often closely resemble aggressive behavior in physical form, they are best viewed as primarily emotional or expressive in nature. Thus, they are not considered instances of aggression in this section.

Finally, the definition of aggression suggested above notes that such behavior takes place only when the recipient—that is, the victim—is motivated to avoid such treatment at the hands of the aggressor. Obviously, this is often true. For example, the victims of harmful physical or verbal assaults usually wish to avoid such unpleasant experiences. In other cases, however, the persons on the receiving end of such actions are not motivated to avoid them. For example, some persons seem to enjoy being hurt in various ways by their lovers and make no effort to shun such treatment. Indeed, they may actually invite it. Similarly and in a more dramatic manner, persons who either attempt or actually commit suicide actively seek the injuries they suffer. Although of considerable importance, such events are not viewed as instances of aggression within the present context because there is no apparent motivation on the part of the victims to avoid the harm inflicted.

In summary, then, aggression is defined throughout the present discussion as any form of behavior directed toward the goal of harming or injuring another living being who is motivated to avoid such treatment. Such actions take many different forms and are directed against a wide variety of targets, but all are similar in one crucial sense: They represent intentional efforts to inflict unpleasant, harm-inducing consequences on unwilling victims.

Theoretical Perspectives

That human beings frequently engage in harmful acts of aggression is hardly open to question—the record of history leaves little room for doubt on this score. The question of why they engage in such actions, however, has long been the subject of serious debate. Over the years, sharply contrasting views concerning the nature of aggression, the factors affecting its occurrence, and the forces from which it stems have repeatedly been proposed. These different theoretical perspectives have taken many forms, but most seem to fall into one of three distinct categories, in which aggression is attributed primarily to (1) innate urges or dispositions, (2) externally elicited drives, or (3) present social and environmental conditions, coupled with previous social learning.

AGGRESSION AS INSTINCTIVE BEHAVIOR

The oldest and probably best-known theoretical perspective on aggression is the view that such behavior is mainly instinctive in nature. According to this approach, aggression occurs because human beings are genetically or constitutionally programed for such behavior. Many scientists have supported this general view, but the most famous proponents of the position have been Sigmund Freud and Konrad Lorenz.

Aggression as instinctive behavior: The Freudian view. In his early writings, Freud held that all human behavior stems either directly or indirectly from *Eros*—the life instinct—whose energy or libido is directed toward the enhancement or reproduction of life. Within this framework, then, aggression was viewed simply as a reaction to the blocking or thwarting of libidinal impulses. As such, it was neither an automatic nor an inevitable part of life.

After the violent events of World War I, Freud (1963) gradually came to adopt a somewhat gloomier position regarding the nature and origins of aggression. Briefly, he proposed the existence of a second major instinct—*Thanatos,* the death force—whose energy is directed toward the destruction or termination of life. All human behavior, he held, stemmed from the complex interplay of this instinct with Eros, and the constant tension between them.

Since the death instinct, if unrestrained, would result in the rapid end of life, he further reasoned that through other mechanisms, such as displacement, the energy of Thanatos is redirected outward and serves as the basis for aggression against others. In Freud's view, then, aggression stems primarily from the redirection of the self-destructive death instinct away from the person himself and outward toward others (see Figure 1).

Freud's proposals regarding the origins and nature of aggression are quite pessimistic. Not only is such behavior innate, but it is inevitable. That is, if Thanatos is not turned outward on others, it soon results in the destruction of the person himself. In brief, human beings essentially face the following choice: aggress against others, or face self-destruction at the hands of their own death force. This is a pair of bleak and gloomy options, to say the least. Of course, it should be noted that Freud held out at least a ray of hope through the process of cartharsis. He suggested that a discharge of the destructive energy of Thanatos may be obtained through the expression of aggression-related emotions, such as anger. In general, though, he seemed to feel that such effects are quite minimal and short-lived in nature (Zillmann, 1979). Thus, he was far from optimistic with respect to the possibility of preventing or controlling human aggression.

Aggression as instinctive behavior: Lorenz's view. A second

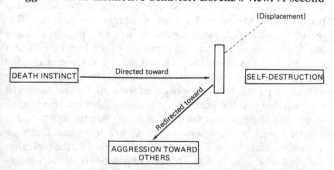

FIGURE 1. Freud's view concerning the origins of human aggression. As shown above, he held that aggression stems from the redirection, through displacement, of the self-destructive death instinct.

and in some ways similar view concerning the nature of human aggression has been proposed by Konrad Lorenz (1966, 1974). According to Lorenz, aggression springs primarily from an innate fighting instinct that human beings share with many other organisms. Presumably, this instinct developed during the long course of evolution because it provided many benefits. For example, fighting often helps to disperse animal populations over a wide area, thus ensuring maximal use of available food resources. Similarly, since it is often closely linked to mating, such behavior may help to strengthen the genetic make-up of various species by assuring that only the most vigorous manage to reproduce.

Although Freud was less than specific regarding the generation and release of instinctual aggressive energy, Lorenz has been quite precise about these issues. Briefly, he has proposed that aggressive energy, deriving from the fighting instinct, is spontaneously produced within the organism in a continuous manner at a constant rate. Moreover, it accumulates regularly with the passage of time. The elicitation of aggressive actions, then, is primarily a joint function of (1) the amount of accumulated aggressive energy and (2) the presence and strength of aggression-releasing stimuli in the immediate environment. Thus, the greater the amount of aggressive energy present, the weaker the stimulus that releases overt aggression. Indeed, if enough time has passed since the performance of the last aggressive act, such behavior may erupt in a spontaneous manner in the total absence of releasing stimuli. As Lorenz himself remarked in an interview (Evans, 1974):

In certain animals, aggressivity follows all the rules of threshold lowering and appetitive behavior. You can see an animal looking for trouble, and a man can do that too.

Lorenz, like Freud, holds that aggression is inevitable, stemming in large measure from innate forces. However, he is somewhat more optimistic than Freud regarding the possibility of reducing or controlling such behavior. In particular, Lorenz has suggested that participation in many noninjurious aggressive actions may prevent aggressive energy from accumulating to dangerous levels and so serve to reduce the likelihood of more harmful outbursts of violence. Further, he has suggested that greater feelings of love and friendship for others may prove incompatible with the expression of overt aggression and thus tend to block the occurrence of aggression. In these ways, he feels, aggression can be redirected and so controlled.

Instinct views of aggression: Some implications. Various instinct theories of aggression differ sharply in terms of specific details. But in an important sense they all involve similar implications. Specifically, the suggestion—central to each—that aggression stems largely from instinctive, innate factors leads logically to the conclusion that it is probably impossible to eliminate such reactions entirely. Neither the satisfaction of all material needs nor the elimination of all social injustice nor any other positive changes in human society will succeed in preventing the generation and expression of aggressive impulses. The best that can be attained is a temporary prevention of such behavior or a reduction in its intensity when it occurs. According to such theories, then, aggression will always be present. Indeed, it is an integral part of basic human nature.

AGGRESSION AS AN ELICITED DRIVE

The instinct views proposed by Freud, Lorenz, and others continue to receive support in some quarters, but they have been challenged in recent decades by another approach. This view—generally known as the *drive theory of aggression*—

rejects the suggestion that aggressive actions stem primarily from innate and spontaneously generated aggressive energy. Instead, it proposes that such behavior derives mainly from an externally elicited drive to harm or injure others (Feshbach, 1970; Berkowitz, 1974, 1978). The most famous statement of this general perspective was offered some years ago by Dollard et al. (1939) in their book *Frustration and Aggression*. The theory they proposed at that time is quite broad in scope and deals with many different issues. The most crucial portion for purposes of the present discussion is the frustration-aggression hypothesis. This hypothesis can be summarized as suggesting that frustration—the blocking of ongoing, goal-directed behavior—leads to the arousal of a drive whose primary goal is that of harm to some person or object. The arousal of the aggressive drive, in turn, leads to the performance of overt aggressive acts. In short, aggression is assumed to stem from exposure to a particular environmental condition—frustration—that elicits strong motivation to engage in aggression.

Other drive theories of aggression share this basic perspective. Regardless of the specific source of aggressive drive they propose, it is assumed that (1) the drive is elicited by external, situational conditions and (2) its arousal then leads to overt forms of aggression (Feshbach, 1970; Zillmann, 1979).

Drive theories of aggression: Some implications. Because the drive theories of aggression, such as the one proposed by Dollard et al. (1939), attribute aggression to the arousal of an externally elicited motive, they seem, at first glance, to be somewhat more optimistic with respect to the prevention or control of aggression than various instinct theories. That is, they seem to imply that the removal of all external sources of aggressive drive from the environment may well eliminate—or, at least, greatly reduce—the occurrence of human violence. Unfortunately, though, the conditions serving to elicit the aggressive drive, such as frustration, are ones it would prove difficult, if not impossible, to remove entirely. For this reason, then, drive theories, too, seem to leave human beings burdened with a continuous and largely unavoidable source of aggressive impulses. In these theories, aggressive urges stem mainly from external sources, rather than innate sources, but they still seem too common in the world to allow much room for optimism.

AGGRESSION AS LEARNED SOCIAL BEHAVIOR

In recent years a third distinct theoretical perspective regarding the nature of human aggression has been developed. Briefly, this perspective regards aggression primarily as a specific form of social behavior that is both acquired and maintained in much the same manner as many other forms of activity. According to the supporters of this position, human beings do not aggress either because of built-in urges toward such behavior or because of aggressive drives aroused by frustration or other conditions (Bandura, 1973; Baron, 1977). Rather, human beings engage in aggression toward others because (1) they have acquired aggressive responses through past experience, (2) they either receive or anticipate various forms of reward for performing such actions, and (3) they are directly instigated to aggress by specific social or environmental conditions.

The social learning theory of aggression represents a marked departure from previous views, but it is supported by several important considerations. First, it is clear that human beings are not born with a large repertoire of aggressive responses at their disposal. Rather, these responses must be acquired in a manner similar to the way in which other complex forms of behavior are acquired. In this respect, certainly, the process of learning plays an important role. Second, it is equally apparent that both children and adults often receive important material and social rewards for aggressing against others. For example, during a time of war, soldiers gain medals and special privileges for killing large numbers of enemy troops. Similarly, professional athletes win both widespread admiration and lucrative contracts by competing in a highly aggressive manner. The rulers of organized crime reap huge fortunes through the expert use of violence. Of course, aggression does not always lead to such rewards. In many cases, it actually yields negative outcomes, such as fines and prison sentences, rather than positive outcomes. But aggression does seem to bring rewards with sufficient frequency for it to become a strong behavioral tendency on the part of many persons. In view of this and other facts, the proposal that aggression be viewed, at least in part, as a learned form of social behavior seems quite reasonable.

Social learning view: Some implications. The social learning perspective is much more optimistic with respect to the possibilities of preventing or controlling human aggression than either the drive or the instinct view already considered. This is the case for two important reasons. First, according to the social learning perspective, aggression is a learned form of social behavior. As such, it is open to direct modification and can be readily reduced through many procedures. For example, the removal of those conditions tending to maintain its occurrence should be quite effective in this respect. Aggressive behaviors would still be present in a person's repertoire of responses, but there would be little reason for their use.

Second, in contrast to the drive and instinct theories, the social learning theory does not view human beings as continuously driven toward violence by built-in forces or ever-present external stimuli, such as frustrating events. Rather, it suggests that human beings aggress only under appropriate social or environmental conditions that tend to encourage such behavior. Alter these conditions, it is suggested, and aggression may be readily prevented or reduced. Of course, accomplishing such ends may often prove quite difficult. Societies do not, as a rule, alter their structure or reinforcement contingencies at the request of social scientists. However, the social learning view does suggest that, if appropriate changes could be instituted, the incidence of dangerous acts of aggression would decrease sharply. In this sense, at least, it does offer grounds for considerable hope.

The Systematic Study of Aggression

Attempts to study aggressive behavior in a systematic manner involve a puzzling dilemma. On the one hand, researchers wish to investigate human tendencies to harm or injure others. On the other hand, they cannot, of course, permit actual harm to the participants in their research. The major solution to this predicament has generally been a straightforward one. Research is conducted under conditions in which participants are led to believe that they can harm another person in some manner when, in fact, they cannot. Many variations on this basic theme have been used. For example, in a large number of studies, participants have been informed that their ratings of a researcher or the assistant on a special form may have important implications for that person. Specifically, they are told that negative ratings of the researcher or the assistant may adversely affect his or her chances of obtaining further research support or a scholarship. In such experiments, then, participants are led to believe that they can inflict considerable harm on another person through verbal or written comments (Zillmann, 1979).

In many other investigations, participants have been informed that they can inflict harm on another person in a different manner. Specifically, they have been led to believe that they can cause that person to experience actual pain or discomfort. In some cases the experiment has involved electric shocks (see Figure 2), in others unpleasant heat, and in still others loud and painful noises. However, in all these instances, no painful stimuli were ever delivered to the supposed victim. The participants were simply led to believe that they could inflict pain or discomfort (Baron, 1977).

Through the use of such procedures, much interesting and potentially valuable information about the causes and control of human aggression has been obtained. However, one crucial question involving such techniques concerns their validity. Do the findings obtained in such experiments actually indicate anything about human aggression outside, as well as within, the laboratory? This complex question can be answered on several different levels. Most research directly concerned with this issue has yielded positive evidence. That is, in most experiments the findings have suggested that laboratory techniques of the type under discussion do yield valid information concerning the participants' tendencies to engage in overt aggression. For example, it has been found that persons known from their previous behavior to be highly aggressive—for example, violent prisoners—are also more aggressive in standard laboratory situations than unselected college students (Wolfe and Baron, 1971). Similarly, it has been repeatedly found that persons who are angered immediately before participating in such research show a higher level of aggression—that is, greater willingness to inflict harm or discomfort on others—than persons who have not been so angered (Donnerstein and Barrett, 1978; Dyck and Rule, 1978). Finally and perhaps of greatest importance, findings uncovered in laboratory studies using such techniques have often been found to generalize to aggression in extralaboratory settings. For example, several laboratory studies concerned with the effects of heat on aggression—the so-called long, hot summer effect suggested that, contrary to popular belief, aggression is maximum in the presence of moderate, rather than extreme, environmental warmth—that is, temperatures in the mid to upper 80's, as opposed to those in the mid to upper 90's (Baron, 1978a). This finding was then

FIGURE 2. In many laboratory studies of human aggression, participants are led to believe that they can harm another person in some manner when, in actual fact, they cannot. A number of such studies have used the type of apparatus shown above. Participants are informed that, by pushing the 10 buttons on this device, they can deliver electric shocks of varying intensity to a victim. In reality, however, no shocks are ever received by that person.

confirmed in a study of the incidence of violent riots. As predicted, such events were found to be much more common at temperatures in the mid to upper 80's than at temperatures above these levels (Baron and Ransberger, 1978).

These and other findings suggest that laboratory methods for the study of aggression do, in fact, yield reasonably valid information about this important topic. This is not to say, of course, that an immediate leap from laboratory findings to actual instances of aggression is always justified. On the contrary, such generalization is, in part, an empirical question, and a degree of caution seems best. However, the weight of existing evidence does seem to suggest that laboratory research using the methods described above often yields valid evidence concerning human aggression. Thus, the findings obtained in such experiments serve as the basis for much of the discussion that follows.

Determinants of Human Aggression

SOCIAL DETERMINANTS

Detroit (AP)—No one will ever know why David Harrell drove past the exits. A co-worker who wanted to stop at a restroom allegedly slit Harrell's throat when he refused to pull off the highway. . . .

Ronald Lee Barnes, 26, told police Harrell drove past the exit on the Fort Freeway and made a derisive comment when Parker asked him to get off at another exit.

Police say that is when Parker reached over the seat and cut Harrell's throat with a small pocket knife.

News accounts of incidents such as that one often give the impression that violence is a random event—one that strikes innocent victims without warning or cause. That is certainly true in some instances, but it is more often the case that aggression stems from important social factors. Violence, in short, does not usually take place in a social vacuum. Rather, it often seems to spring from specific conditions that pave the way for its occurrence. A very large number of factors seem to play a role in this regard. Three that have often been viewed as among the most important are frustration, physical or verbal provocation, and exposure to the actions of live or filmed aggressive models.

Frustration. More than 40 years ago, a group of social scientists (Dollard et al., 1939) proposed a sweeping theory of aggression, which was mentioned earlier. At the heart of their view were two suggestions that have come to be known as the frustration-aggression hypothesis. Briefly, these suggestions indicated that (1) frustration always leads to some form of aggression and (2) aggression is always the result of frustration. In short, Dollard et al. suggested that thwarting others—preventing them from reaching goals they are seeking—always causes them to aggress and that this is the only cause of such behavior.

These proposals quickly won widespread acceptance and are still widely cited today. In a sense, this is far from surprising. The frustration-aggression hypothesis is, after all, highly appealing in its boldness. If it is accepted, a highly complex form of social behavior is explained in one daring stroke. Unfortunately, though, it now appears that there are strong grounds for doubting both parts of the hypothesis.

First, it is now clear that frustrated persons do not always turn to aggressive actions in their thoughts, words, or overt deeds. Rather, they may actually show a wide variety of reactions, ranging from despair and resignation on the one hand to attempts to overcome the source of their frustration on the other. In many cases it appears that depression—not aggression—is the most likely reaction to strong frustration (Bandura, 1973).

Second, it is also apparent that all aggression does not result from frustration. People aggress for many different reasons and in response to many different conditions. For example, boxers hit and occasionally injure their opponents because it is part of their job to do so, not because they are frustrated. Hired assassins cold-bloodedly murder persons they have never met, even when they are in high spirits, simply because they are paid to perform such actions. Clearly, then, aggression can stem from many other factors aside from frustration. To suggest that it is always the result of such treatment, then, is quite misleading.

In the face of these criticisms, the frustration-aggression hypothesis has recently been revised (Berkowitz, 1974, 1978). In its more modern form, the hypothesis now states only that frustration sometimes leads to aggression and is only one of many factors causing such behavior. Such proposals are, of course, far easier to defend than the original, sweeping suggestions. Moreover, they have been supported by experimental findings suggesting that frustration can, indeed, enhance aggression under some conditions (Geen, 1968; Zillmann and Cantor, 1976). However, even these more limited proposals have been called into question by other recent findings. Specifically, several experiments have reported that frustration often fails to enhance aggression (Buss, 1966; Pisano and Taylor, 1971). And others have reported that frustration may actually tend to reduce aggression in some circumstances (Gentry, 1970). A completely satisfactory resolution of these contradictory results has not yet been obtained. However, a careful comparison of studies yielding positive results and those yielding negative results suggests that whether frustration increases or fails to increase aggression may depend mainly on two important factors.

First, it appears that frustration leads to heightened aggression only when the frustration is quite intense. When it is of low or even moderate strength, little or no effect on aggression is observed (Harris, 1974). Second, the results of several studies suggest that frustration leads to increased aggression only when it is perceived as arbitrary or unreasonable. When frustration is viewed as justified or reasonable, little or no aggression may result (Worchel, 1974). In sum, it appears that thwarting others—that is, blocking their goal-directed behavior—may, indeed, be one of the social conditions tending to elicit aggression. However, the effects of such treatment appear only under relatively specific conditions and do not seem to be nearly as strong or as general as was once believed.

Physical and verbal provocation. Although there is currently some uncertainty regarding the effects of frustration on aggression, the impact of another factor—direct physical or verbal provocation—is well established. Indeed, existing evidence suggests that physical abuse or verbal taunts from others may often serve as a very powerful elicitor of aggressive actions. Further, once it begins, aggression often shows an unsettling pattern of escalation (Goldstein et al., 1975). As a result, even mild taunts or glancing blows may start a process in which stronger and stronger provocations are exchanged; and, of course, this type of escalation is visible not only in relations between individuals but in dealings between nations as well. Growing spirals of tension, threat, and counterthreat often lead to incidents or even wars that neither side really wants but that both seem powerless to prevent.

Direct evidence for the strong influence of physical provo-

cation on aggression has been obtained in many laboratory experiments (Kimble, et al., 1977; Dengerink et al., 1978). In these studies, persons exposed to physical provocation, usually in the form of increasing electric shocks, have not been found to turn the other cheek to such treatment. Rather, they usually retaliate in kind, aggressing against the persons who provoke or anger them. Further, they seem to act in this manner even when they do not actually receive physical provocation but simply learn that others intend to treat them in this manner (Greenwell and Dengerink, 1973; Dyck and Rule, 1978).

Similar findings support the view that verbal provocation, too, may have strong aggression-eliciting properties. In several experiments, verbal insults or taunts have been found to elicit strong retaliation from the recipients (Geen, 1968; Wilson and Rogers, 1975). Indeed, in some cases, persons exposed to such treatment have been quite willing to respond with physical, rather than similar verbal, assaults (Wilson and Rogers, 1975). Given the frequency of cutting and sarcastic remarks in the normal course of social interaction, such findings seem to have important implications.

In view of all these findings, the following conclusions seem justified. Aggression, like many other forms of social behavior, is strongly influenced by a rule of reciprocity. In general, people tend to treat others as they have been treated by those persons. Aggression is no exception to this over-all pattern.

Exposure to aggressive models: The effects of televised violence. A classic finding of social psychology—perhaps *the* classic finding—is that people are often strongly affected by the actions or words of the persons around them. A large body of research conducted over several decades indicates that persons can often be induced to alter their attitudes, feelings, or behavior as a result of social influence from others. Until recently, it was widely assumed that such influence must be intentional in order to be effective. Within the past decade, however, it has become increasingly clear that social influence can also be unintentional. A growing body of evidence suggests that simple exposure to the actions and outcomes of others is often sufficient to produce important alterations in the feelings or behavior of observers (Bandura, 1977).

As awareness of the powerful impact of such unintentional influence—generally termed "modeling"—has grown, a question relevant to the present discussion has taken shape. Can aggression, too, be affected through this process? Specifically, can exposure to the behavior of others who act in a highly aggressive manner serve to elicit similar actions on the part of observers? Interest in this issue has stimulated two distinct yet closely related lines of research.

The first has sought to determine whether exposure to live aggressive models plays an important role in the occurrence and spread of collective violence. That is, it has been concerned with the possibility that the presence of persons who behave in a highly aggressive manner can serve to trigger similar actions on the part of others on the scene. The findings of a large body of research suggest that this may well be the case (Baron, 1974a, 1978b). That is, in many studies persons exposed to the actions of highly aggressive models later demonstrate stronger levels of aggression against others than do persons not exposed to such models.

The second line of research has been concerned with the possible impact of violence in the mass media—especially television—on the behavior of children. This research has focused on the question of whether continued exposure to media violence can induce similar behavior on the part of young viewers.

Research findings on televised violence. Over the past 20 years, literally hundreds of experiments have been performed to determine the impact of televised violence on the behavior of young viewers (Liebert and Schwartzberg, 1977). The methods used in this research have varied greatly. For example, in many early studies children were first exposed to specially prepared films of adults attacking plastic toys (inflated Bobo dolls); the children were then placed in a room with similar toys (Bandura et al., 1963). Not surprisingly, they often imitated the actions of the adult models and attacked the toys in a similar fashion. Further, they engaged in such imitative behavior to a much greater extent than did children who had never witnessed the adult models' aggressing. In many later experiments markedly different procedures were used. Often, children were exposed to either a violent segment from an actual television show or a nonviolent episode of similar length. Then they were given the opportunity ostensibly to harm another child in some fashion. (In reality, of course, no harm was ever permitted to the victim.) Again, the results generally showed that children exposed to the violent segments directed stronger attacks against the victim than did the children exposed to the nonviolent episodes (Liebert and Baron, 1972). In several recent studies youngsters have been exposed to a steady diet of violent or nonviolent programs or movies for several weeks, and their actual aggression toward others during this period has been observed (Parke et al., 1977). Once again, the findings suggest that those who witness media violence tend to behave in a more aggressive fashion than do those who witness nonviolent films or programs. Regardless of the methods used, therefore, similar results have generally emerged: Exposure to media violence often seems to encourage similar behavior on the part of young viewers.

However, not all the results have pointed to such effects. In fact, at least one large-scale study has found that exposure to a steady diet of aggressive television programs may reduce, rather than increase, the level of aggression shown by children (Feshbach and Singer, 1971). The weight of existing evidence, though, seems to suggest that, after watching violent films or television shows, some children, at least, are more willing to engage in aggressive actions than they are after watching nonviolent films or shows. The social implications of this conclusion are too obvious to require further comment.

The effects of televised violence: Underlying mechanisms. In addition to examining the effects of media violence on children's behavior, researchers have also attempted to specify the mechanisms underlying these effects. Basically, three crucial processes have come to light. First, it appears that viewers can often acquire new aggressive responses—new ways of harming others—through exposure to scenes of violence. That is, through the process of observational learning, they widen or enlarge their repertoire of specific aggressive actions (Bandura, 1977). Second, persons exposed to media violence often seem to experience a sharp reduction in the strength of internal restraints against overt aggression. In many cases, they seem to reason as follows: "If the characters in these shows or films can behave in this manner, then I can, too!" As a result of such disinhibitory effects, their willingness to aggress against others may be greatly enhanced. Third, persons exposed to a steady diet of televised or filmed violence seem to experience a gradual desensitization to aggression and signs of pain or suffering on the part of others. That is, their initial, negative emotional reactions to such stimuli decrease and may entirely vanish (Thomas et al., 1977). This reduced or blunted responsivity to

scenes of violence may remove still another internal restraint against engaging in such actions.

Together, these three processes, which are summarized in Table I, seem to account for the effects of filmed or televised violence on the behavior of children. That is, they help explain why repeated exposure to such materials can often stimulate increased aggression on the part of young viewers. However, a word of caution is probably in order. Although exposure to media violence does seem to exert such effects on the behavior of children and perhaps adults as well, this does not mean that, after watching such materials, they are likely to rush out and launch blind attacks against anyone unfortunate enough to be in their paths. The effects observed in most research conducted to date have been too small in magnitude to warrant such a conclusion. What existing evidence does seem to suggest is simply this: Exposure to a steady diet of televised violence over a period of years may contribute, along with many other factors, to the occurrence of overt aggression.

ENVIRONMENTAL DETERMINANTS OF AGGRESSION

Anyone who has ridden on crowded subways, worked near a noisy construction project, or lived through intense heat waves without air conditioning knows from his or her own experience that behavior can often be strongly affected by the physical environment. Persons' physiological states, the way in which they feel, and even their performances on many tasks are often strongly influenced by various aspects of the physical world around them (Bell et al., 1978). It seems possible that aggression, too, is affected by the physical environment. This suggestion has been confirmed by a growing body of empirical research. Many different factors, ranging from darkness (Page and Moss, 1976) to phases of the moon (Lieber and Sherin, 1972), have been investigated in this regard. But by far the greatest amount of attention has been focused on the impact of three variables: noise, crowding, and heat.

Effects of noise. Noise levels in many major cities have risen sharply in recent years. In response to this trend, many authorities have reacted with stern warnings regarding the potential health hazards that noise may pose (Kryter, 1970). In fact, it now appears that the levels of noise commonly encountered in many locations within urban areas may, over a period of time, induce permanent hearing loss or even deafness. Certainly, this is a serious result in and of itself. Unfortunately, though, it may not be the only type of harmful effect produced. The findings of several recent experiments suggest that, under some conditions, loud and unpleasant noise may also exert a

TABLE I

Mechanisms Underlying the Impact of Televised or Filmed Violence on the Behavior of Viewers

Mechanism	Description of Effects
Observational learning	Viewers acquire new means of aggressing not previously present in their behavior repertoires.
Disinhibition	As a result of observing other persons, especially adults, participating in aggressive actions, viewers' own inhibitions against performing similar behaviors are reduced.
Desensitization	As a result of repeated exposure to aggressive actions, viewers gradually show reduced emotional responsivity to such events—that is, they are no longer upset by violent acts or their consequences.

less obvious effect: It may facilitate the occurrence of interpersonal agression (Donnerstein and Wilson, 1976; Konečni, 1975b). In these studies persons exposed to loud but not physically harmful noise have been found to direct stronger levels of aggression against others than do persons not exposed to such environmental stress. Moreover, this seems to be the case regardless of whether aggression is expressed while such noise is present or after its cessation (Donnerstein and Wilson, 1976). There does seem to be one important restriction on this finding. Such results seem to occur only when research participants have been angered or annoyed in some manner by the target of their aggressive acts. When they have not been exposed to such treatment, even loud and irritating noise fails to enhance overt aggression (Konečni, 1975b). Thus, it appears that unpleasant noise may facilitate interpersonal violence only when such behavior is a strong or prepotent response tendency among potential aggressors. Unfortunately, annoyance or provocation from others is an all too common experience, especially in the type of urban settings in which loud noise is most likely to be encountered. In view of this fact, it appears that the high levels of noise present in most major cities play an important role in enhancing, if not actually initiating, harmful instances of interpersonal aggression. It appears that the growing noise pollution of recent decades may be exacting a high social cost.

Effects of crowding. Despite all efforts to slow its growth, world population continues to increase at an alarming rate. At the same time, of course, the amount of physical space available for human habitation remains unchanged. The result is all too obvious: In the closing decades of the 20th century, crowding has become a very common state of affairs (see Figure 3).

The presence of large number of human beings within a limited area raises many problems. Natural resources are strained, and irreversible damage may be inflicted on the environment. But what precisely is the impact of such conditions on social behavor? Does crowding exert adverse effects? Do such conditions affect the incidence of overt aggression? Systematic research on these questions has yielded a complex picture.

With respect to the possibility of a relationship between crowding and social disorder, recent investigations have yielded largely negative findings. For example, in one well-known study, Freedman et al. (1975) related two separate measures of crowding to such signs of social decay as the frequency of venereal disease, infant mortality, and frequency of illegitimate births in 338 different neighborhoods within New York City. When such factors as income, educational level, and ethnic background of the persons living in those areas were statistically controlled, no link between crowding and signs of social disorder was found.

In regard to the possibility of a link between crowding and aggression, the results have been quite mixed. On the one hand, some studies—both those conducted in the laboratory and those based on systematic observation—suggest that crowding may, in fact, be associated with elevated levels of aggression (Freedman et al., 1972; Altman, 1975). On the other hand, additional studies have failed to find evidence for a link between crowding and aggression (Hutt and Vaizey, 1966). Indeed, in at least one experiment high levels of crowding were found to reduce aggression, rather than enhance it (Loo, 1972).

One possible explanation for these contradictory findings has recently been proposed by Freedman (1975). He suggested that crowding acts primarily as an intensifier of behavior, strengthening or enhancing a person's typical reactions to any situation. If these reactions are negative, then crowding will

FIGURE 3. As human population has grown, crowding has become increasingly common. Recent research suggests that the link between such conditions and overt aggression is quite complex.

magnify their unfavorable nature, and aggression may well be increased. If the typical reactions are positive, crowding will make them even more favorable, and tendencies toward aggression may be reduced.

Such intensification of typical reactions is a familiar occurrence. For example, consider a somewhat unpleasant situation—riding on a noisy and jarring subway car. Freedman's theory predicts that persons will find this experience even more unpleasant under crowded than under uncrowded conditions. In contrast, consider an intrinsically pleasant situation—eating a good meal in a fine restaurant. Here, Freedman's theory suggests that this experience will be more enjoyable under crowded than under noncrowded circumstances.

If one applies Freedman's proposals to the effects of crowding on aggression, relatively straightforward predictions may be derived. Under conditions in which initial reactions to a situation or to other persons are unfavorable, crowding may increase the likelihood of overt aggression. Under conditions in which typical reactions are basically favorable, the opposite may be true. Careful examination of past research in the light of these suggestions suggests that they may well be accurate. In studies in which crowding has been found to increase aggression, conditions do seem to be ones that induce unfavorable reactions (Freedman et al., 1972). In studies in which crowding has been found to exert no effect on aggression or to reduce its occurrence, conditions seem to be ones that induce neutral or positive reactions (Loo, 1972). Thus, Freedman's intensification hypothesis seems capable of accounting quite well for the results of previous investigations. However, until the theory is subjected to more direct, independent assessment, it is best viewed as only tentative in nature. Regardless of whether Freedman's theory is confirmed or refuted by further research, existing evidence does seem to point to the following conclusions: Crowding does not exert any simple or global effects on aggression. Rather, crowding seems capable of both facilitating and inhibiting such behavior under appropriate but as yet not fully understood conditions.

Effects of heat. During the late 1960's and early 1970's a wave of dangerous riots swept through the U.S. and other nations. Several different factors were suggested as possible causes for these events, but one that received major attention in the mass media was ambient temperature. Newspaper, radio, and television accounts of these events often suggested that uncomfortable heat played a crucial role in their initiation. Specifically, such accounts often suggested that prolonged exposure to temperatures above 90° F had shortened tempers and increased irritability and so set the stage for the outbreak of collective violence.

At first glance, such suggestions seem quite reasonable. Informal observation suggests that most persons do become irritable and tense when exposed to uncomfortable heat. Further, these proposals are supported by the results of several laboratory studies in which subjects were found to report greater discomfort and to react more negatively to others in the presence of excessive environmental heat than in its absence (Griffitt, 1970; Griffitt and Veitch, 1971). On the basis of these considerations, it may well be expected that exposure to high ambient temperatures will, in fact, facilitate human violence. Surprisingly, however, this prediction has not been confirmed by systematic research.

In a series of laboratory studies conducted by the author (Baron, 1972; Baron and Bell, 1975, 1976; Bell and Baron, 1976), it has been consistently observed that high temperatures—that is, temperatures in the mid to upper 90's F—do not enhance overt aggression by research participants. In fact,

the results of such experiments indicate that extreme environmental conditions of this type may actually reduce the tendency of many persons to aggress against others. This finding may at first appear somewhat paradoxical, but the psychological mechanisms underlying it seem to be straightforward. Briefly, a curvilinear relationship exists between negative affect (unpleasant emotions or feelings) and aggression. Up to some point, increments in such negative feelings—whether induced by excessive warmth, negative evaluations from others, or any other factor—may cause persons to feel irritated and tense and so increase their willingness to aggress against others. Beyond this point, however, further increments in negative affect may lead persons to feel so uncomfortable and unpleasant that other responses—including responses incompatible with aggression, such as escape or attempts to reduce discomfort—become dominant. As a result, persons may shift their efforts in this direction, and aggression may actually decrease.

Relatively direct evidence for these suggestions has been obtained in recent studies (Baron and Bell, 1976; Bell and Baron, 1976). In this research, subjects have been exposed to conditions designed to induce varying levels of negative affect among them. For example, low levels of such reactions are induced by a combination of pleasantly cool temperatures (the low to mid 70's F) and positive evaluations from a stranger. Very high levels of negative affect, in contrast, are induced by a combination of excessive heat (temperatures in the mid to upper 90's F) and a negative evaluation from a stranger. As predicted, the results have conformed to the curvilinear relationship outlined above. Aggression has been enhanced by moderate levels of negative affect, but it has actually been reduced by very high levels of this factor. It appears that the influence of ambient temperature on aggression may be understood within this general framework.

The implications of this proposed curvilinear relationship for the occurrence of riots and other forms of collective violence should be specified. It seems to suggest that, contrary to common sense and comments in the mass media, such events are not most likely to take place when temperatures rise to extremely high levels. Rather, it appears that they are most likely to occur in the presence of more moderate—but still uncomfortable—readings. Evidence indicating that this is, in fact, the case has been obtained in a study by Baron and Ransberger (1978). These researchers examined weather bureau records to determine the temperatures prevailing on days when 102 serious riots took place during the years 1967–1971. It was found that these dangerous events were most likely to occur when temperatures were in the mid 80's F. Beyond that level, the frequency of riots dropped off quite sharply (see Figure 4).

In conclusion, existing evidence concerning the effects of ambient temperature on aggression does not support the suggestion of a simple and straightforward link between these variables. Environmental warmth does seem to influence both individual and collective violence, but it interacts with several other factors. Thus, it exerts its impact on social behavior in a far more complex manner than that suggested by such phrases as "the long, hot summer."

SITUATIONAL DETERMINANTS

As noted earlier, social and environmental variables often play important roles in the initiation of overt aggression. However, additional factors, not directly related to the words or deeds of other persons or aspects of the physical environment, also exert crucial effects. Such factors are quite diverse in nature and do not seem as closely related to one another as

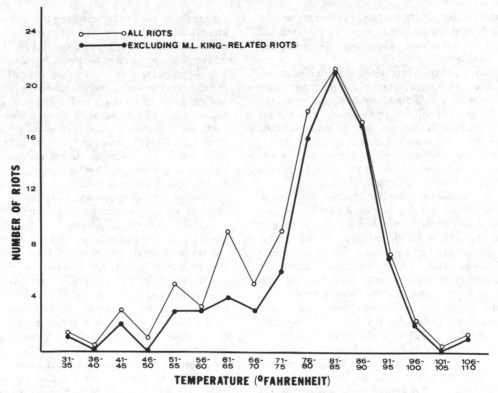

FIGURE 4. Contrary to informal observation but consistent with the findings of laboratory experiments, dangerous riots seem most likely to occur when temperatures reach the mid to upper 80's F. Beyond this level, the frequency of such events decreases sharply. (From Baron and Ransberger, Ambient temperature and the occurrence of collective violence: The "long, hot summer" revisited. J. Pers. Soc. Psychol., *36:* 351, 1978.)

either social or environmental variables, but they are often considered under the heading of situational determinants of aggression, since they relate to various aspects of the general context within which such behavior takes place. Two variables of this type are heightened physiological arousal and the impact of various drugs.

Heightened physiological arousal. Since aggression, especially when it takes physical forms, is quite effortful in nature, it seems reasonable to expect that the occurrence of such behavior is sometimes enhanced by heightened physiological arousal. That this is, indeed, the case is suggested by the findings of a number of experiments (Rule and Nesdale, 1976). Such research indicates that heightened arousal stemming from such diverse sources as participation in competitive activities (Christy et al., 1971), vigorous exercise (Zillmann et al., 1972), and exposure to arousing films (Zillmann, 1979) can facilitate aggression under some conditions. The words "under some conditions" should be emphasized however, for it is also clear that heightened arousal stemming from situational factors exerts such effects only under certain specific circumstances.

First, it appears that heightened arousal enhances aggression only when such behavior represents a strong or dominant response tendency on the part of the persons involved. If, in contrast, aggression is not a strong or prepotent response, increased arousal may fail to enhance its occurrence. If other responses that are incompatible with aggression are dominant, they may be facilitated, with the result that aggression is reduced. Evidence pointing to these conclusions has been obtained in several different studies (Zillmann et al., 1972; Konečni, 1975b). For example, in the experiment conducted by Zillmann et al. (1972), male subjects were first provoked or not provoked by a male confederate; next, they engaged in

either 2.5 minutes of strenuous physical exercise on a bicycle ergometer or performed a nonstrenuous, cognitive task; finally, they obtained an opportunity to deliver electric shocks to the accomplice. In line with the view that heightened arousal facilitates aggression only when such behavior is a strong or dominant response, physical exercise was found to enhance electric "assaults" only by participants who had previously been strongly angered.

A second factor that seems to determine whether heightened physiological arousal leads to increased aggression involves the manner in which persons label or interpret such feelings. A series of studies conducted by Zillmann and his associates (Zillmann and Bryant, 1974; Zillmann et al., 1974; Zillmann, 1979) suggests that heightened arousal does facilitate later aggression when persons label or interpret such feelings as anger but does not exert such effects when they correctly attribute such reactions to their original source—that is, exercise or competition. Apparently, the crucial factor in such cases is the extent to which persons are uncertain about the source of the arousal they are experiencing. If it is clear that such feelings stem from sources unrelated to aggression—exercise, unpleasant noises—heightened arousal fails to increase aggression. However, if the source of such feelings is no longer readily identified because, for example, some time has elapsed since the arousing event, the persons may be uncertain as to its origins and may label it as feelings of anger. In such cases heightened aggression may result (Zillmann, 1979).

In sum, it appears that increased arousal stemming from diverse sources can, indeed, facilitate subsequent aggression under certain circumstances. In order for such effects to occur, however, two conditions must usually be met. First, aggression must be a relatively strong or dominant response among the persons in question. Second, those persons must interpret their feelings of arousal as anger or annoyance.

As noted above, arousal stemming from many different sources seems to influence the occurrence of aggressive behavior. One particular type of arousal that has been of special interest to researchers for several years is the sexual excitement stemming from exposure to erotic stimuli. Interest in this topic stems, in part, from repeated suggestions regarding the existence of a special link between sexual and aggressive motives. For example, Freud (1963) proposed that desires to hurt or to be hurt by one's lover form a normal part of heterosexual relations. Similarly, Berne (1964) suggested that the arousal of aggressive motives or feelings often serves to increase sexual pleasure for both men and women. Such proposals seem to imply that sexual arousal often encourages the occurrence of overt aggressive actions, especially if these are linked in some manner to the fulfillment of sexual desires. A number of investigations have been conducted to examine this possibility; somewhat surprisingly, they have yielded inconsistent results.

On the one hand, several researchers have reported that heightened sexual arousal may, indeed, facilitate overt attacks against others by angry persons (Zillmann, 1971; Jaffe et al., 1974). In contrast, several other studies have indicated that increased sexual arousal may actually serve to reduce later aggression (Baron and Bell, 1973; Baron, 1974b, 1974c; Frodi, 1977).

At first glance, these findings seem both contradictory and puzzling. Fortunately, though, a resolution to this seeming puzzle has been provided by further research. The first hint was suggested by a careful comparison of the procedures used in the two sets of studies mentioned above. This comparison revealed that those reporting an increase in aggression after exposure to erotic stimuli used explicit materials of a highly arousing nature, such as films of young couples engaged in lovemaking and highly explicit erotic written passages. In contrast, studies reporting a reduction in later aggression generally used much milder stimuli, such as *Playboy* and *Playgirl* nudes and pictures of attractive men and women in bathing suits or other revealing outfits. In short, it appeared that highly arousing erotic materials may well enhance overt aggression but that milder stimuli of this type may actually inhibit such behavior.

Direct evidence for this suggestion was then obtained in several further studies (Donnerstein et al., 1975; Baron and Bell, 1977; Baron, 1978e). In these experiments persons exposed to mild erotic stimuli generally showed lower levels of aggression than did those exposed to such nonerotic materials as pictures of scenery and abstract art. In contrast, persons exposed to explicit erotic stimuli often showed higher levels of aggression than did those who viewed more neutral materials. Thus, it appeared that the relationship between overt aggression and sexual arousal, as induced by erotic stimuli, may be curvilinear in nature. Mild levels of arousal may inhibit aggression, but stronger levels may enhance it.

Additonal findings have also cast light on the psychological mechanisms underlying this relationship. It appears that many persons find exposure to mild erotic stimuli and the minimal levels of sexual arousal so induced quite pleasant. Such positive reactions counter the effects of past annoyance or provocation and in this manner tend to reduce later aggression (Zillmann and Sapolsky, 1977). In contrast, many persons seem to find exposure to explicit erotic stimuli and the higher levels of arousal so produced quite unpleasant. This may be due in part to disgust at the acts portrayed (Byrne and Byrne, 1977), and in part to the fact that strong sexual arousal that cannot be quickly reduced is intrinsically frustrating or annoying (Baron, 1977). Regardless of the precise source of such feelings, they are compatible with both anger and overt aggression and may, therefore, facilitate such behavior.

It appears that, as often suggested in the past, there is an important link between sexual arousal and aggression. But the nature of this bond seems to be somewhat more complex than was at first assumed.

Drugs. The fact that various drugs exert profound effects on human behavior has been known for centuries and requires no further comment here (Leavitt, 1974). The existence of such effects, however, suggests that some biologically active agents may well influence the occurrence of overt aggression. In fact, many drugs, such as a number of tranquilizers, have been found to exert such effects. However, two substances—alcohol and marihuana—have been the subject of special attention in recent research because of their widespread and often uncontrolled use.

Alcohol has long been viewed as a stimulator of aggressive actions. Consume too much of this drug, informal knowledge suggests, and the chances of becoming involved in hostile interactions with others are increased. In contrast, marihuana has sometimes been held to be an inhibitor of overt aggression, presumably because it places its users in such a relaxed and pleasant state that aggression is difficult to elicit.

Although not all existing evidence is consistent in this respect, a series of studies conducted by Taylor and his colleagues suggest that both of these beliefs are generally accurate (Taylor and Gammon, 1975; Taylor et al., 1976). In these studies male subjects were provided with special cocktails consisting of ginger ale, peppermint oil, and either a small dose or a large dose of one of two drugs—alcohol or THC (the active substance in marihuana). (Persons in corresponding control groups received only the ginger ale and peppermint oil mixture.) After receiving these special drinks, the subjects were provided with an ostensible opportunity to deliver electric shocks of varying intensity to another person. (Needless to say, the supposed victim never received any shocks.) The results of such research have been relatively clear. With respect to alcohol, small doses (0.5 ounce of vodka or bourbon per 40 pounds of body weight) tend to inhibit aggression, but larger doses (1.5 ounces of these beverages per 40 pounds of weight) tend to facilitate such behavior. Thus, as suggested by informal observation, one cocktail or a couple of beers may put people in a happy state of mind and so reduce the likelihood of aggression. However, larger quantities of alcohol may reverse such effects and increase the probability of aggressive episodes.

With marihuana, a different pattern of findings emerged. Small doses of this drug (1.82 mg. per 40 pounds of body weight) seemed to have little impact on aggression. Larger doses (5.44 mg. per 40 pounds of body weight) tended to inhibit such behavior. Considered together, the findings of Taylor's research suggest that both alcohol and marihuana are capable of exerting important effects on the tendency of human beings to aggress against others. But the direction and the size of these effects seem to differ greatly between the two drugs (see Table II).

Prevention and Control of Human Aggression

Aggression is, by definition, a harmful form of behavior. Further, as noted earlier, its incidence in human relations is alarmingly high. In view of these facts, it might be expected that, over the years, researchers would have devoted consider-

TABLE II

Effects of Alcohol and Marihuana (TIIC) on Physical Aggression by Adults

Drug and Dose	Effects on Aggression
Alcohol: Small dose (0.5 ounce/40 pounds of body weight)	Aggression is reduced.
Alcohol: Large dose (1.5 ounces/40 pounds of body weight)	Aggression is increased.
THC: Small dose (1.82 mg./40 pounds of body weight)	No effect; aggression is neither increased nor reduced.
THC: Large dose (5.44 mg./40 pounds of body weight)	Aggression is reduced.

able attention to procedures for preventing or controlling such behavior. Surprisingly, though, this has not been the case. A careful survey of the existing literature on aggression reveals that many studies have focused on the social, environmental, and situational antecedents of violence, but a much smaller number have examined techniques for preventing or controlling its occurrence (Kimble et al., 1977). Several factors have probably played a role in this unsettling state of affairs, but two seem to be of greatest importance.

First, there appears to have been an implicit assumption on the part of many researchers that aggression can be controlled in a largely negative fashion—through the removal of factors that stimulate its occurrence. This view seemed quite reasonable in the past, when only a small number of variables were assumed to affect human violence. Its persuasiveness has been sharply diminished in recent years, however, by the ever-growing list of social, environmental, and situational antecedents of such behavior.

Second and perhaps of greater importance, it was widely assumed until quite recently that the best means for preventing or controlling human aggression were already known. Specifically, it was believed that two factors—punishment and catharsis—are highly effective deterrents to human violence. This was a comforting view. Unfortunately, though, this is a view that has been called into serious question by recent findings. In particular, it now appears that neither punishment nor catharsis is quite as effective in controlling overt agression as was once believed.

PUNISHMENT AS A DETERRENT TO AGGRESSION

Over the course of several decades, scientific opinion concerning the impact of punishment on human behavior has swung from one extreme to the other. Initially, such procedures were viewed as providing a highly effective means for modifying behavior. But because several early studies seemed to suggest that the impact of punishment is only temporary in nature, it soon fell into general disfavor (Estes, 1944). More recently, the pendulum has swung the other way once again, and it is now generally agreed that, provided certain conditons are met, punishment may produce relatively permanent changes in overt behavior (Tarpy, 1978).

In contrast to these wide swings in scientific opinion concerning the over-all influence of punishment, the views of most researchers regarding the impact of this factor on aggression have remained surprisingly stable. Punishment has generally and consistently been assumed to act as a powerful deterrent

to such behavior. For example, in their famous monograph, Dollard et al. (1939) stated:

The strength of inhibition of any act of aggression varies positively with the amount of punishment anticipated to be a consequence of that act.

Some 27 years later Walters (1966), a developmental psychologist, remarked:

It is only the continual expectation of retaliation by the recipient or other members of society that prevents many individuals from more freely expressing aggression.

That punishment is sometimes quite effective in deterring overt aggression is obvious. Indeed, the results of many studies conducted with both children and adults suggest that the frequency or the intensity of such behavior can often be sharply reduced by even such mild forms of punishment as social disapproval (Deur and Parke, 1970). However, does punishment always or even usually produce such effects? There seem to be strong grounds for doubting such conclusions.

First, it is clear that the recipients of actual punishment often interpret it as an attack against them. To the extent that this is so, they may respond with heightened aggression, rather than lessened aggression. In fact, severe punishment, either physical or psychological, is often more likely to instill a desire for revenge or retribution than permanent restraints against violence among its recipients. Second, the persons who administer punishment may often serve as aggressive models for those on the receiving end of such discipline. For example, consider the case of a parent who spanks his or her child as punishment for striking other children. What the youngster may learn in such cases is that it is appropriate to aggress against others but that one should always choose a victim smaller than one's self. Third, there is some indication that, because of the conditions under which it is usually administered, punishment induces only temporary reductions in the strength or the frequency of aggressive behavior. Once the punishment is discontinued, such acts quickly reappear with all their previous force and vigor (Baron, 1977). For all these reasons, it seems quite likely that direct punishment often backfires and actually tends to enhance, rather than inhibit, the aggressive actions it is designed to prevent.

A number of recent studies suggest that threats of punishment may also be of only limited effectiveness (Donnerstein et al., 1972, Baron, 1973). Specifically, it appears that the success of threats of punishment in deterring later aggression may depend to an important degree on several mediating variables. For example, the deterrent impact of such procedures may be strongly influenced by the level of anger experienced by potential aggressors. When such persons have been exposed to mild annoyance or provocation, threats of punishment may be quite successful in preventing overt aggression. When they have been subjected to more powerful annoyance, even threats of severe punishment may be relatively ineffective in inhibiting such behavior (Baron, 1973). An extreme example of this fact is provided by the following description of events occurring during the Bengali-Pakistani war (Leamer, 1972):

Some of the Bengalis were so fierce in their fury . . . that they could not be held back, and they ran forward into the cantonment until they were cut down by machine-gun bursts, a few . . . rising again to throw spears.

Here, the degree of anger experienced by the persons involved was so intense that they literally threw themselves into the guns of their foes, seemingly oblivious to the fact that, by such actions, they were courting certain death.

Two other factors that also seem to mediate the success of threats of punishment in deterring later violence are (1) the apparent probability that such treatment will actually be delivered and (2) the magnitude of the rewards that aggressors can gain through assaults against others. Only when the likelihood of punishment is high and aggressors have relatively little to gain by engaging in such behavior are threats of punishment effective in deterring later violence. When, in contrast, the likelihood of punishment is low and aggressors have much to gain through such actions, threats of aversive treatment are often much less successful (Baron, 1971b, 1974d).

In sum, evidence gathered in recent studies suggests that the influence of punishment on aggression is quite complex. Punishment may sometimes serve as an effective deterrent to such behavior, but this is not always the case. Further, its use may often involve several consequences or side effects that largely counter its deterrent influence. Thus, it does not seem to be as useful in this regard as some researchers have assumed.

CATHARSIS

For many years it has been widely assumed that providing angry persons with an opportunity to engage in expressive but noninjurious behaviors (1) causes them to experience reductions in tension or arousal and (2) weakens their tendency to engage in overt and potentially dangerous acts of aggression.

Together, these suggestions are generally termed the *catharsis hypothesis*. They can be traced to the writings of Aristotle, who held that exposure to stirring stage drama could produce a vicarious purging of the emotions. Aristotle himself did not refer directly to the reduction of aggressive impulses or emotions in this manner, but such views were expressed by Freud, who suggested that such reactions can be lessened through the expression of aggression-related emotions and perhaps through exposure to aggressive actions. Although Freud accepted the existence of such effects, he was not optimistic regarding their usefulness in deterring overt aggression. Rather, he seemed to regard them as both minimal in scope and short-lived in nature (Freud, 1963). Popular acceptance of the usefulness of catharsis, therefore, seems to stem primarily from certain statements by Dollard and his colleagues (1939) in their book on frustration and aggression. According to those authors:

> The expression of *any act of aggression* is a catharsis that reduces the instigation to *all other acts of aggression* [italics added].

In short, Dollard et al. held that the performance of one aggressive act, whatever its nature, reduces an aggressor's tendency to engage in all other forms of aggression. Thus, inducing an angry person to engage in verbal or fantasy aggression against an enemy may reduce the probability that he or she will later engage in direct attacks against that person.

Largely on the basis of this and related suggestions, both portions of the catharsis hypothesis have obtained widespread acceptance. That is, it has been assumed that the performance of expressive but noninjurious acts can both lower the emotional arousal stemming from provocation and reduce the likelihood of more dangerous forms of aggression. Both of these suggestions seem quite reasonable, but the evidence gathered in recent research suggests that only the first may actually be valid.

Tension reduction through catharsis. Evidence for the ten-sion-reducing properties of various types of aggression, including noninjurious forms, has been obtained in a series of studies conducted by Hokanson and his colleagues (Hokanson and Burgess, 1962; Hokanson et al., 1963). In these studies subjects were first angered by the experimenter, who treated them in an insulting fashion, and then provided with an opportunity to aggress against that person or another person physically (by means of electric shock), verbally (on a questionnaire), or in fantasy (on a projective psychological test). Measures of physiological arousal (heart rate, systolic and diastolic blood pressure) were taken throughout the study to determine whether and to what extent various actions by the subjects (shocking the experimenter, rating him negatively on a special form, and so on) were successful in reducing the heightened arousal induced by provocation. The results in several experiments generally indicated that both physical assaults and verbal derogation of the anger instigator were effective in reducing such arousal. However, other actions, such as imagining harm to that person, failed to produce similar effects. Thus, there was some evidence for the view that even noninjurious forms of aggression can reduce physiological tension, but it was clear that not all behaviors of this type can produce such reductions.

In further experiments Hokanson and his colleagues have demonstrated that cathartic-like reductions in arousal can often be induced by many different behaviors, including ones that deliver neither real nor imagined harm to anger instigators (Stone and Hokanson, 1969; Hokanson, 1970). Thus, taken as a whole, the existing evidence seems to suggest that a wide range of activities can, in fact, counter the heightened arousal that often follows direct provocation or annoyance from others.

Catharsis as a deterrent to later aggression. Empirical evidence offers some support for the first portion of the catharsis hypothesis, but it is much less encouraging with respect to the second. Contrary to widespread belief, the performance of safe aggressive actions does not seem to reduce the likelihood of more dangerous forms of aggression in many situations in which such effects have been assumed to occur.

First, a growing body of research suggests that angry persons cannot be restrained from aggressing through exposure to scenes of violence (Berkowitz and Alioto, 1973; Parke et al., 1977). Indeed, as noted earlier, exposure to such materials often enhances, rather than reduces, later aggression.

Second, allowing angry persons to aggress against inanimate objects—such as dolls, inflated clowns, and punching bags—does not seem to be effective in reducing their tendencies to direct such actions against persons who have provoked them. In fact, there is some indication that subsequent aggression is actually facilitated by such activities (Mallick and McCandless, 1966).

Third, it appears that verbal aggression against others often fails to reduce the tendency to harm them on later occasions. Again, several experiments suggest that quite the opposite may be true (Ebbesen et al., 1975). The opportunity to criticize or derogate others in their absence may sometimes increase, rather than reduce, the likelihood of aggressing against them on subsequent occasions.

Together, such findings suggest that the performance of many so-called cathartic activities is less effective in deterring overt aggression than was once believed. It should be noted, however, that the performance of one type of action does seem to reduce the tendency of angry persons to harm the sources of their annoyance. Specifically, such effects are often observed when angry persons are provided with an opportunity to directly harm the anger instigator in some manner (Konečni, 1975a). The occurrence of catharsis under such conditions is of little practical significance. Present violence is simply substituted for later mayhem. Further, the duration of even those effects is open to question and may well be quite brief. Thus, it seems reasonable to offer the following conclusion: Participation in cathartic activities may sometimes succeed in reducing tendencies toward overt aggression, but the potential benefits of such procedures have probably been overstated in the past (Geen and Quanty, 1977).

AGGRESSION-INHIBITING INFLUENCE OF INCOMPATIBLE RESPONSES

It is a well-established principle in the study of behavior that all organisms, including human beings, are incapable of engaging in two incompatible responses at once. Recently, attempts have been made to extend this basic dictum to the control of human aggression. Specifically, it has been suggested that any conditions serving to induce responses or emotional states among aggressors that are incompatible with either anger or the performance of violent acts are often effective in deterring such behavior (Baron, 1977; Zillmann and Sapolsky, 1977). Although many different responses may prove inconsistent with anger or aggression, two have been the subject of increasing interest in recent years: Empathy and feelings of amusement. (A third, mild sexual arousal, was considered in an earlier portion of this section.)

Empathy as a deterrent. When aggressors attack other persons in a face-to-face confrontation, they are often exposed to signs of pain and suffering on the part of their victims. For example, the target may groan, cry out, or even beg for mercy as he or she is harmed by the aggressor. It seems possible that one reaction to such feedback is sometimes a reduction in further aggression. That this is, in fact, the case is suggested by the findings of several experiments (Baron, 1971a, 1971c, 1974a; Rule and Leger, 1976). In these studies exposure to signs of pain or discomfort on the part of the victim were found to inhibit further aggression by male participants. Apparently, the subjects in such research experienced negative emotional reactions when confronted with the simulated pain of their victims and so ceased or reduced their attacks in order to lessen such feelings.

Such findings are quite encouraging, but further studies suggest that signs of pain on the part of the target of aggression are not always successful in producing such effects. In particular, it appears that, when aggressors have previously suffered strong provocation at the hands of their victims, signs of pain on the part of those persons may fail to reduce aggression. Indeed, in cases in which provocation was intense, it may actually serve as a form of reinforcement for aggressive actions and so enhance its occurrence (Hartmann, 1969; Baron, 1974a, 1978d; Swart and Berkowitz, 1976). Thus, exposure to cries of pain or pleas for mercy cannot always be counted on to inhibit further assaults by enraged aggressors.

Taken as a whole, therefore, the existing evidence concerning the ability of empathy to inhibit human aggression presents a somewhat mixed picture. In the absence of strong provocation, such reactions are readily induced and do seem effective in deterring further violence. In the context of strong and unendurable provocation, however, their occurrence is blocked by the aggressor's existing state of anger. Thus, the induction of empathy may tend to inhibit overt aggression but only, it appears, under relatively specific conditions.

Humor as a deterrent. A second form of activity that appears to be incompatible with aggression is that of laughter or feelings of amusement. Informal observation suggests that anger can often be reduced through exposure to humorous materials or statements, and the results of several laboratory studies lend support to this proposal (Baron and Ball, 1974; Leak, 1974; Mueller and Donnerstein, 1977; Baron 1978c). In these studies angry persons exposed to various forms of humor have been found to direct lower levels of aggression against the persons who provoked them than did angry persons exposed to neutral stimuli of a nonhumorous nature. Thus, exposure to various cartoons, comedy monologues, or written jokes has been found to be effective in reducing overt aggression on some occasions.

It should be noted, however, that not all types of humor seem capable of producing such effects. In particular, jokes or cartoons possessing hostile content do not seem to reduce aggression by previously angered persons. Indeed, in several studies exposure to such materials has actually been found to enhance such behavior (Berkowitz, 1970; Baron, 1978d). Apparently, the characters depicted in such humor can serve as aggressive models and so tend to stimulate, rather than reduce, later aggression. Aside from this one exception, however, it does appear that several types of humor presented in several different formats, such as spoken and written, may induce reactions or emotional states incompatible with aggression among the persons who observe them.

Conclusion. Although attention has been focused on empathy and humor in this discussion, it is apparent that many other reactions may prove to be incompatible with anger or overt aggression. For example, as noted earlier, the mild titillation stemming from exposure to certain types of erotic stimuli may sometimes exert such effects. Similarly, feelings of guilt concerning the performance of aggressive actions may often reduce such behavior. There is some indication that even participation in absorbing cognitive tasks, such as attempts to solve mathematical problems, may induce reactions incompatible with anger or aggressive actions (Konečni, 1975a).

In view of the wide range of responses that may prove inconsistent with feelings of annoyance or aggression, it seems possible that useful control techniques based on this general strategy may ultimately be developed. For example, it may prove possible to train persons suffering from an inability to inhibit aggressive impulses to self-generate incompatible reactions at times when they are provoked. Procedures of this type may well prove far more effective in deterring subsequent aggression than the oft-recommended strategy of counting to 10. Many practical problems obviously remain with respect to translating the principle of response incompatibility into effective and specific treatment programs. At present, though, an approach to the control of human violence based on this general principle seems quite promising.

Suggested Cross References

Social violence and aggression are discussed in Section 56.6. Aggression in animals is discussed in Section 4.6. Personality disorders are discussed in Chapter 22. Disorders of impulse control are discussed in Section 25.2. Conduct disorders in children are discussed in Section 41.7. Forensic and correctional psychiatry are discussed in Chapter 54. Child maltreatment and battered child syndromes are discussed in Section 43.2.

REFERENCES

Altman, I. *The Environment and Social Behavior.* Brooks-Cole, Monterey, Calif., 1975.
* Bandura, A. *Aggression: A Social Learning Analysis.* Prentice-Hall, Englewood Cliffs, N. J., 1973.
Bandura, A. *Social Learning Theory.* Prentice-Hall, Englewood Cliffs, N. J., 1977.

Bandura, A., Ross, D., and Ross, S. Imitation of film-mediated aggressive models. J. Abnorm. Soc. Psychol., *66:* 3, 1963.

Baron, R. A. Aggression as a function of magnitude of victim's pain cues, level of prior anger arousal, and aggressor-victim similarity. J. Pers. Soc. Psychol., *18:* 48, 1971.

Baron, R. A. Exposure to an aggressive model and apparent probability of retaliation as determinants of adult aggressive behavior. J. Exp. Soc. Psychol. *7:* 343, 1971b.

Baron, R. A. Magnitude of victim's pain cues and level of prior anger arousal as determinants of adult aggressive behavior. J. Pers. Soc. Psychol., *17:* 236, 1971c.

Baron, R. A. Aggression as a function of ambient temperature and prior anger arousal. J. Pers. Soc. Psychol., *21:* 183, 1972.

Baron, R. A. Threatened retaliation from the victim as an inhibitor of physical aggression. J. Res. Pers., *7:* 103, 1973.

Baron, R. A. Aggression as a function of victim's pain cues, level of prior anger arousal, and exposure to an aggressive model. J. Pers. Soc. Psychol., *29:* 117, 1974a.

Baron, R. A. The aggression-inhibiting influence of heightened sexual arousal. J. Pers. Soc. Psychol., *30:* 318, 1974b.

Baron, R. A. Sexual arousal and physical aggression: The inhibiting influence of "cheesecake" and nudes. Bull. Psychonom. Soc., *3:* 337, 1974c.

Baron, R. A. Threatened retaliation as an inhibitor of human aggression: Mediating effects of the instrumental value of aggression. Bull. Psychonom. Soc., *29:* 217, 1974d.

* Baron, R. A. *Human Aggression.* Plenum Publishing Corp., New York, 1977.

Baron, R. A. Aggression and heat: The "long, hot summer" revisited. In *Advances in Environmental Psychology,* A. Baum, S. Valins, and J. Singer, editors, p. 57. Erlbaum Associates, Hillsdale, N. J., 1978a.

Baron, R. A. Aggression, empathy, and race: Effects of victim's pain cues, victim's race, and level of instigation on physical aggression. J. Appl. Soc. Psychol., *9:* 103, 1978b.

Baron, R. A. Aggression-inhibiting influence of sexual humor. J. Pers. Soc. Psychol., *36:* 189, 1978c.

Baron, R. A. The influence of hostile and nonhostile humor upon physical aggression. Bull. Pers. Soc. Psychol., *4:* 77, 1978d.

Baron, R. A. Sexual arousal, physical aggression: An extension to females. J. Res. Person, *4:* 10, 1978c.

Baron, R. A., and Ball, R. L. The aggression-inhibiting influence of nonhostile humor. J. Exp. Soc. Psychol., *10:* 23, 1974.

Baron, R. A., and Bell, P. A. Effects of heightened sexual arousal on physical aggression. Proc. Am. Psychol. Assoc., 171, 1973.

Baron, R. A., and Bell, P. A. Aggression and heat: Mediating effects of prior provocation and exposure to an aggressive model. J. Pers. Soc. Psychol., *31:* 825, 1975.

Baron, R. A., and Bell, P. A. Aggression and heat: The influence of ambient temperature, negative affect, and a cooling drink on physical aggression. J. Pers. Soc. Psychol., *33:* 245, 1976.

Baron, R. A., and Bell, P. A. Sexual arousal and aggression by males: Effects of type of erotic stimuli and prior provocation. J. Pers. Soc. Psychol., *35:* 79, 1977.

Baron, R. A., and Ransberger, V. M. Ambient temperature and the occurrence of collective violence: The "long, hot summer" revisited. J. Pers. Soc. Psychol., *36:* 351, 1978.

Bell, P. A., and Baron, R. A. Aggression and heat: The mediating role of negative affect. J. Appl. Soc. Psychol., *6:* 18, 1976.

Bell, P. A., Fisher, J. D., and Loomis, R. J. *Environmental Psychology.* W. B. Saunders, Philadelphia, 1978.

Berkowitz, L. Aggressive humor as a stimulus to aggressive responses. J. Pers. Soc. Psychol., *16:* 710, 1970.

* Berkowitz, L. Some determinants of impulsive aggression: The role of mediated associations with reinforcements for aggression. Psychol. Rev., *81:* 165, 1974.

Berkowitz, L. Whatever happened to the frustration-aggression hypothesis? Am. Behav. Sci., *21:* 22, 1978.

Berkowitz, L., and Alioto, J. T. The meaning of an observed event as a determinant of its aggressive consequences. J. Pers. Soc. Psychol., *28:* 206, 1973.

Berne, E. *Games People Play.* Grove Press, New York, 1964.

Buss, A. H. Instrumentality of aggression, feedback, and frustration as determinants of physical aggression. J. Pers. Soc. Psychol., *3:* 153, 1966.

Buss, A. H. Aggression pays. In *The Control of Aggression and Violence,* J. L. Singer, editor, p. 7. Academic Press, New York, 1971.

Byrne, D., and Byrne, L. *Exploring Human Sexuality.* Holt, Rinehart, and Winston, New York, 1977.

Christy, P. R., Gelfand, D. M., and Hartmann, D. P. Effects of competition-induced frustration on two classes of modeled behavior. Dev. Psychol., *5:* 104, 1971.

Dengerink, H. A., Schnedler, R. W., and Covey, M. V. The role of avoidance in aggressive responses to attack and no attack. J. Pers. Soc. Psychol., *36:* 100, 1978.

Deur, J. D., and Parke, R. D. Effects of inconsistent punishment on aggression in children. Dev. Psychol., *2:* 401, 1970.

Dollard, J., Doob, L., Miller, N., Mowrer, O. H., and Sears, R. R. *Frustration and Aggression.* Yale University Press, New Haven, Conn., 1939.

Donnerstein, E., and Barrett, G. Effects of erotic stimuli on male aggression toward females. J. Pers. Soc. Psychol., *36:* 180, 1978.

Donnerstein, E., Donnerstein, M., and Evans, R. Erotic stimuli and aggression: Facilitation or inhibition. J. Pers. Soc. Psychol., *32:* 237, 1975.

Donnerstein, E., Donnerstein, M., Simon, S., and Ditrichs R. Variables in interracial aggression: Anonymity, expected retaliation, and a riot. J. Pers. Soc. Psychol., *22:* 236, 1972.

Donnerstein, E., and Wilson, D. W. The effects of noise and perceived control upon ongoing and subsequent aggressive behavior. J. Pers. Soc. Psychol., *34:* 774, 1976.

Dyck, R., and Rule, B. G. The effect of causal attributions concerning attack on retaliation. J. Pers. Soc. Psychol., *36:* 150, 1978.

Ebbesen, E. B., Duncan, B., and Konečni, V. J. Effects of content of verbal aggression on future verbal aggression: A field experiment. J. Exp. Soc. Psychol., *11:* 192, 1975.

Estes, W. K. An experimental study of punishment. Psychol. Monogr., *57:* 1944.

Evans, R. I. Lorenz warns: "Man must know that the horse he is riding may be wild and should be bridled." Psychol. Today, *8:* 82, 1974.

Feshbach, S. Aggression. In *Carmichael's Manual of Child Psychology,* P. H. Mussen, editor, p. 159. John Wiley & Sons, New York, 1970.

Feshbach, S., and Singer, R. D. *Television and Aggression.* Jossey-Bass, San Francisco, 1971.

Freedman, J. L. *Crowding and Behavior.* W. H. Freeman & Co., San Francisco, 1975.

Freedman, J. L., Heshka, S., and Levy, A. Population density and pathology: Is there a relationship? J. Exp. Soc. Psychol., *11:* 539, 1975.

Freedman, J. L., Levy, A. S., Buchanan, R. W., and Price, J. Crowding and human aggressiveness. J. Exp. Soc. Psychol., *8:* 528, 1972.

Freud, S. Introductory lectures on psycho-analysis. In *Standard Edition of the Complete Psychological Works of Sigmund Freud.* J. Strachey, editor. Hogarth Press, London, 1963.

Frodi, A. Sexual arousal, situational restrictiveness, and aggressive behavior. J. Res. Pers., *11:* 48, 1977.

* Geen, R. G. Effects of frustration, attack, and prior training in aggressiveness upon aggressive behavior. J. Pers. Soc. Psychol., *9:* 316, 1968.

Geen, R. G., and Quanty, M. B. The catharsis of aggression: An evaluation of a hypothesis. In *Advances in Experimental Social Psychology,* L. Berkowitz, editor, p. 2. Academic Press, New York, 1977.

Gentry, W. D. Effects of frustration, attack, and prior aggressive training on overt aggression and vascular processes. J. Pers. Soc. Psychol., *16:* 718, 1970.

Goldstein, J. H., Davis, R. W., and Herman, D. Escalation of aggression: Experimental studies. J. Pers. Soc. Psychol., *31:* 162, 1975.

Greenwell, J., and Dengerink, H. A. The role of perceived versus actual attack in human physical aggression. J. Pers. Soc. Psychol., *26:* 66, 1973.

Griffitt, W. Environmental effects on interpersonal affective behavior: Ambient effective temperature and attraction. J. Pers. Soc. Psychol., *15:* 240, 1970.

Griffitt, W., and Veitch, R. Hot and crowded: Influence of population density and temperature on interpersonal affective behavior. J. Pers. Soc. Psychol., *17:* 92, 1971.

Harris, M. B. Mediators between frustration and aggression in a field experiment. J. Exp. Soc. Psychol., *10:* 561, 1974.

Hartmann, D. P. Influence of symbolically modeled instrumental aggression and pain cues on aggressive behavior. J. Pers. Soc. Psychol., *11:* 280, 1969.

Hokanson, J. E. Psychophysiological evaluation of the catharsis hypothesis. In *The Dynamics of Aggression,* E. I. Megargee and J. E. Hokanson, editors, p. 74. Harper & Row, New York, 1970.

Hokanson, J. E., and Burgess, M. The effects of status, type of frustration, and aggression on vascular processes. J. Abnorm. Soc. Psychol., *65:* 232, 1962.

Hokanson, J. E., Burgess, M., and Cohen, M. E. Effects of displaced aggression on systolic blood pressure. J. Abnorm. Soc. Psychol., *67:* 214, 1963.

Hutt, C., and Vaizey, M. J. Differential effects of group density on social behavior. Nature, *209:* 1371, 1966.

Jaffe, Y., Malamuth, N., Feingold, J., and Feshbach, S. Sexual arousal and behavioral aggression. J. Pers. Soc. Psychol., *30:* 759, 1974.

Kimble, C. E., Fitz, D., and Onorad, J. The effectiveness of counteraggression strategies in reducing interactive aggression by males. J. Pers. Soc. Psychol., *35:* 272, 1977.

Konečni, V. J. Annoyance, type and duration of postannoyance activity, and aggression: The "cathartic effect." J. Exp. Psychol. Gen., *104:* 76, 1975a.

Konečni, V. J. The mediation of aggressive behavior: Arousal level versus anger and cognitive labeling. J. Pers. Soc. Psychol., *32:* 706, 1975b.

Kryter, K. D. *The Effects of Noise on Man.* Academic Press, New York, 1970.

Leak, G. K. Effects of hostility arousal and aggressive humor on catharsis and humor preference. J. Pers. Soc. Psychol., *30:* 736, 1974.

Leamer, L. Bangladesh in mourning. *Harper's Magazine,* 84, August 1972.

Leavitt, F. *Drugs and Behavior.* W. B. Saunders, Philadelphia, 1974.

Lieber, A. L., and Sherin, C. R. Homicides and the lunar cycle: Toward a theory of lunar influence on human emotional disturbance. J. Psychiatry, *129:* 69, 1972.

Liebert, R. M., and Baron, R. A. Some immediate effects of televised violence on childrens' behavior. Dev. Psychol., *6:* 469, 1972.

Liebert, R. M., and Schwartzberg, N. S. Effects of mass media. In *Annual Review of Psychology,* M. R. Rosenzweig and L. W. Porter, editors, p. 141. Annual Reviews, Palo Alto, 1977.

Loo, C. M. The effects of spatial density on the social behavior of children. J. Appl. Soc. Psychol., *2:* 372, 1972.

Lorenz, K. *On Aggression.* Harcourt, Brace, and World, New York, 1966.

Lorenz, K. *Civilized Man's Eight Deadly Sins.* Harcourt, Brace, Jovanovich, 1974.

Mallick, S. K., and McCandless, B. R. A study of catharsis of aggression. J. Pers. Soc. Psychol., *4:* 591, 1966.

Mueller, C., and Donnerstein, E. The effects of humor-induced arousal upon aggressive behavior. J. Res. Pers., *11:* 73, 1977.

Page, H. A., and Moss, M. K. Environmental influences on aggression: The effects of darkness and proximity of victim. J. Appl. Soc. Psychol., *6:* 126, 1976.

Parke, R. D., Berkowitz, L., Leyens, J. P., West, S. G., and Sebastian, R. J. Some effects of violent and nonviolent movies on the behavior of juvenile delinquents. In *Advances in Experimental Social Psychology*, L. Berkowitz, editor, p. 136. Academic Press, New York, 1977.

Pisano, R., and Taylor, S. P. Reduction of physical aggression: The effects of four strategies. J. Pers. Soc. Psychol., *19:* 237, 1971.

Rule, B. G., and Leger, G. J. Pain cues and differing functions of aggression. Can. J. Behav. Sci., *8:* 213, 1976.

Rule, B. G., and Nesdale, A. R. Emotional arousal and aggressive behavior. Psychol. Bull., *83:* 851, 1976.

Stone, L. J., and Hokanson, J. E. Arousal reduction via self-punitive behavior. J. Pers. Soc. Psychol., *12:* 72, 1969.

Swart, C., and Berkowitz, L. Effects of a stimulus associated with a victim's pain on later aggression. J. Pers. Soc. Psychol., *33:* 623, 1976.

Tarpy, R. M. *Foundations of Learning and Memory.* Prentice-Hall, Englewood Cliffs, N. J., 1978.

Taylor, S. P., and Gammon, C. B. Effects of type and dose of alcohol on human physical aggression. J. Pers. Soc. Psychol., *32:* 169, 1975.

Taylor, S. P., Vardaris, R. M., Rawitch, A. B., Gammon, C. B., Cranston, J. W., and Lubetkin, A. I. The effects of alcohol and delty-i-tetrahydrocannabinol on human physical aggression. Aggress. Behav., *2:* 153, 1976.

Thomas, M. H., Horton, R. W., Lippincott, E. C., and Drabman, R. S. Desensitization to portrayals of real-life aggression as a function of exposure to television violence. J. Pers. Soc. Psychol., *35:* 450, 1977.

Walters, R. H. Implications of laboratory studies of aggression for the control and regulation of violence. Ann. Am. Acad. Pol. Soc. Sci., *364:* 60, 1966.

Wilson L., and Rogers, R. W. The fire this time: Effects of race of target, insult, and potential retaliation on black aggression. J. Pers. Soc. Psychol., *32:* 857, 1975.

Wolfe, B. M., and Baron, R. A. Laboratory aggression related to aggression in naturalistic social situations: Effects of an aggressive model on the behavior of college students and prisoner observers. Psychonom. Sci., *24:* 193, 1971.

Worchel, S. The effect of three types of arbitrary thwarting on the instigation to aggression. J. Pers., *42:* 301, 1974.

Zillmann, D. Excitation transfer in communication-mediated aggressive behavior. J. Exp. Soc. Psychol., *7:* 419, 1971.

* Zillmann, D. *Hostility and Aggression.* Erlbaum Associates, Hillsdale, N. J., 1979.

Zillmann, D., and Bryant, J. Effects of residual excitation on the emotional response to provocation and delayed aggressive behavior. J. Pers. Soc. Psychol., *30:* 782, 1974.

Zillmann, D., and Cantor, J. R. Effect of timing of information about mitigating circumstances on emotional responses to provocation and retaliatory behavior. J. Exp. Soc. Psychol., *12:* 38, 1976.

Zillmann, D., Johnson, R. C., and Day, K. D. Attribution of apparent arousal and proficiency of recovery from sympathetic activation affecting activation transfer to aggressive behavior. J. Exp. Soc. Psychol., *10:* 503, 1974.

Zillmann, D., Katcher, A. H., and Milavsky, B. Excitation transfer from physical exercise to subsequent aggressive behavior. J. Exp. Soc. Psychol., *8:* 247, 1972.

Zillmann, D., and Sapolsky, B. S. What mediates the effect of mild erotica on hostile behavior by males? J. Pers. Soc. Psychol., *35:* 587, 1977.

4.6 Ethology

HARRY F. HARLOW, Ph.D.

Introduction

Definitions of ethology are varied enough to encompass a vast range of behaviors or a multitude of sins. The psychological and biological definition refers to the systematic study of animal behavior. Originally, ethologists were primarily interested in the detailed analysis of the behavior of intact animals in their natural or closely related environments, using direct observation as the basic technique for behavioral assessment. However, with the passage of time, ethologists added experimental modification to the natural environment and even initiated experimental laboratory investigations.

During the 20th century, research in animal behavior followed directions in England and Europe different from those in the United States. In England and Europe animal behavior research became formalized under the name of ethology, and the leaders of ethological research were, on the continent, Lorenz and Tinbergen and, in the British Isles, Hinde. In Europe and England the ethologists systematically investigated the behaviors of birds, fish, and to a lesser extent insects. Probably for practical reasons and availability, the first choices were fish, such as the stickleback, and birds, such as the greylag goose and the crow.

The American animal behaviorists became first obsessed with rodents—in particular, the white rat. Since *Mus norvegicus albinus* is a rodent as diverse from humans as any mammal that could possibly be chosen, rodentology had little chance to make any great contributions to facts and theories relating to human primate behavior. Even more bizarre is the fact that the American rodentologists seriously believed that the rat was the ideal subject for analyzing learned behaviors. They assumed that basic learning facts and theories acquired in studying rat learning could be generalized to human learning, even though those facts and theories were obtained from highly specialized, atypical animals. Even the most primitive of primate forms are highly visual animals, whereas rats are primarily oriented by the olfactory sense. Primates are also manually motivated, and they keep their noses to the ground only in allegory. The less said about the neocortex of rodents the better, whereas the neocortex represents the primates' crowning glory.

Just as the ethologists' original primary interests lay in the behavior of submammalian forms, the primary interests of psychologists have traditionally related to mammalian behavior. Bitter criticism was leveled at psychologists by ethologists some decades ago to the effect that psychologists were imprinted on the rat, which is a very unhuman mammal. Indeed, it differs enormously from almost any and all other mammals except the mouse. However, the ethologists ignored the fact that the psychologists had already made an effective beginning in analyzing subhuman primate behavior. It is for others to judge whether or not fascination with fish and birds is more restrictive biologically than interests in rodents or primates.

Animal behavior in America, fortunately, had also developed in a manner that was diverse and entailed interest and research in the subhuman or simian primate forms. Great credit for this specific interest in primate research, the study of subhuman primates, goes to Yerkes, who created the first official primate laboratory in America at Orange Park, Florida. This laboratory led indirectly to the formation of many other primate laboratories. The second formal primate laboratory originated in the 1930's at the University of Wisconsin and was followed in the 1960's by seven national and regional primate laboratories subsidized by official congressional action. Scientific study of animal behavior in America was guaranteed representation by primate research.

Another basic distinction between European ethology and American animal behavior lies in the emphasis, even overemphasis, given by the European ethologists to field research. The ethologists studied animal behavior in its natural environment, whereas in America for many decades the animal behavioral studies were concentrated on laboratory investigations. Actually, the ethologists, while verbally extolling the natural environment, never entirely deserted the laboratory. Von

Frisch produced magnificent studies on color vision in bees and wasps. Similarly, the sensory capabilities of the simians have been effectively analyzed by many ethologists and psychologists. The classical investigations by Grether on color vision in monkeys and apes showed that New World or platyrrhine monkeys are woefully weak at the red end of the visual spectrum but otherwise are very similar to humans. The Old World or catarrhine monkeys are slightly weak at the red end of the spectrum, and the chimpanzee color vision is almost identical to that of humans.

The American animal researchers developed an early interest in correlating brain function with behavior. The exploratory researches by Franz were followed by Lashley's brilliant investigations and then by extensive, prolonged primate studies by Jacobsen at Yale and Harlow at Wisconsin analyzing frontal lobe functions. Pribram and Chow at Orange Park and Harlow and co-workers at Wisconsin defined the temporal lobe syndrome in monkeys and related both the frontal and the temporal lobe syndromes in monkeys to the appropriate human and clinical researches.

The ethologists have now become interested in primate behavior. Instead of human beings influencing the behavior of monkeys, the behavior of monkeys is now influencing the behavior of human beings, here used as a synonym for ethologists.

Morris's book, *Primate Ethology,* includes 10 chapters, all written by authors with ethological knowledge and biases. Here ethological fixed-action patterns are no longer fixed but flexible, determined not by a single bond but by multiple variables. The behaviors chosen for study are facial displays, sociosexual symbols, allogrooming, various patterns of play, social organization, communication, mother-offspring relations, infant relations in monkeys, mother-offspring relations in chimpanzees, and the social behavior of human children. Both field researches and laboratory researches are cited, and they are not regarded as dichotomous. Reunification has followed the civil war, and the least civil differences are disregarded.

Ethological Contributions to Psychiatry

The primary contribution of a section on ethology to psychiatry is or should be to describe the contributions of research on subhuman animals to human psychiatric problems.

However, ethological data and theory have allegedly been used to support basic constructs of psychoanalysis. Freud postulated psychic energy as the basic motivating force underlying human behavior, and psychic energy is a tenuous and possibly untestable hypothesis. It has been suggested that an objective explanation or description of psychic energy may be provided in terms of Lorenz's action-specific energy hypothesis, which implies that external inhibition of instinctive behavior patterns acts as a powerful intrinsic motivational factor insofar as the behavior is concerned. Once an animal's specific reservoir of energy is completely drained or depleted as a result of continuous activation of a particular response, a time interval is required for the energy supply to be replenished.

According to Hess, the action-specific energy hypothesis is illustrated by the phenomenon of displacement, in which a conflict between two instinctive behavior patterns results in the release of a third instinctive behavior pattern. Thus, in the stickleback, conflict between attack and flight is often resolved by nest-building behavior. According to Kaufman, the transition from the purely physical behavior patterns for animals to the physical and psychic relationships characterizes the developmental motivational differences between the animal and the

human level. Furthermore, at the human level the psychic energy that may be invested in the sexual and aggressive drive may be cathected to the mental representations of these objects, as determined by individual experience.

A complex interpretation of displacement activity has been presented by Ostow (1962). Comparing psychoanalytic and ethological concepts of instinct, he used displacement activity to explicate a logical progression of human development. He hypothesized that the gratification of sexual instincts takes different forms during different periods of development and that the mechanism that leads from one form to another functions in the same way that displacement activities function in lower animals. As one form of gratification is inhibited, the instinct accepts another form of gratification. In this way Ostow traces the sexual aims in psychic development through oral, anal, phallic, and genital stages. This thesis represents an interesting analogy, whether or not it is acceptable to all or even only a few psychoanalysts.

Since psychoanalytic theory ascribes more than love to the importance of early experience, Hess (1959) has strongly indicated that Freudian theory is closely related to ethology by way of the concept of imprinting, which places an enormous emphasis on the importance of early learning. Imprinting refers to the early, rapid, specific, and persisting learning, seen particularly in birds, by which the neonatal animal becomes attached to the mother and, by generalization, to members of the animal's own species. The term imprinting was given to this behavior by Lorenz (1935), although this or a similar phenomenon had been described previously by Spalding in 1873 and centuries ago by Sir Thomas More. In Utopia the poultrymen hatched chickens by the dozens through heat application to the eggs. Once out of the shells, the chicks regarded the poultryman as their mother and followed him everywhere (Figure 1A).

Hess believed that imprinting contrasted to associative learning, since imprinting can be acquired only during a circumscribed critical period; is not blocked by muscle-relaxant drugs; is most efficiently learned by massed, rather than spaced, practice; and is primarily contingent on early experience, rather than recency of experience. Finally, unlike most learning, imprinting is facilitated by punishment or pain. It can be argued that all or most of these phenomena characterize affectional learning in many mammalian infants, including the human infant.

Hess's thesis is correct in that the laws for efficient imprinting are different from those of serial or nonsense learning, but imprinting may not differ fundamentally from positive, affectional emotional development in mammals. The following response in fledglings, like the body-contact responses in infant monkeys and other mammals, are prepotent unconditioned responses that are incorporated with learned responses early, readily, and semipermanently. Furthermore, the mother or caretaker rapidly becomes the infant's security figure; if the infant is injured or frightened, it contacts the mother for security. No doubt there is a phylogenetic basis for these responses, but it is not necessary to assume that the mechanisms are operating at an unconscious level.

Extensive study of the variables operating in the onset and, even more significant, the wane of the critical age period of sensitivity for imprinting has disclosed possible relationships between imprinting and the development of fear responses. Numerous investigations suggest that only after imprinting has sufficiently familiarized young birds with their environment do they become aware of strangeness (Hinde, 1974). One of the complex, unlearned behaviors is fear of strange objects and

FIGURE 1. *A.* The chicks followed the poultryman everywhere. *B.* In a famous experiment, Lorenz demonstrated that goslings would respond to him as if he were the natural mother. (Reprinted by permission from Hess, E. H. Imprinting: An effect of early experience. Science, *130:* 133, 1959.)

places, and, of course, familiarity with some objects and with some places is a prerequisite to the concept of strangeness. The interrelationship of the familiarity with the environment and the developing fear responses may be reflected in the varied lengths of the sensitivity period.

An affectional learning problem that has attracted broad attention by both analytic and nonanalytic investigators is that of the mechanism binding the baby to the mother. The classical derived drive or cupboard theory is in disrepute for both

nonanalysts, such as Zazzo, and analysts, such as Duykaerts. Body contact or some similar mechanism is now generally accepted as a vital primary, if not *the* primary, mechanism. However, beyond this basic fact, analysts are unwilling to accept any further ethological-psychological affectional theory, since it contradicts or does not relate to Freud's motivational theory of libido.

There is no reason why ethology should have made any great theoretical contribution to psychoanalytic theory. Even if one should concede that ethology made the greatest contribution to animal behavior theory during the early half of the 20th century and that psychoanalysis made a similar contribution to psychiatric theory during the same period of time, the basic goals and theoretical positions of the two diverse disciplines were at that time far apart.

Ethologists were primarily interested in analyzing the variables guiding the behaviors of nonmammalian forms, with great emphasis on the grey-lag goose and the stickleback. The ethologists gave great emphasis to imprinting, since they were imprinted on nonmammalian models. The ethologists apparently did not read the vast primate literature that was being accumulated while they worked on the pisces and the grey-lag goose.

Furthermore, the ethologists were primarily interested in t. behaviors of normal animals—a perfectly legitimate position but not one designed to lead to psychiatric insights. The basic new constructs achieved by the psychiatrists evolved from the study of abnormal members of a particular primate—the human being—by the use of highly specialized techniques of verbal report. These methods, of course, are inadmissible for the study of any nonhuman animal, and they particularly limit generalization of behavioral facts and theories that depend on distant relatives in the phyletic kingdom.

Psychologists, not ethologists, carried out the first studies of intact, normal monkeys and apes in their normal environment. These studies, initiated by Yerkes, were conducted by Carpenter, Nissen, and Bingham, and the techniques were later modified and exploited by anthropologists and zoologists, particularly Washburn and DeVore, Jay, and Goodall (Jolly, 1972). The early psychological studies were probably less imaginative, less colorful, and usually less prolonged than the subsequent field investigations. Suffice it to say that the passage of time and international seminars have dampened the characteristic invectives that once sharply separated the ethologist from the comparative psychologist.

As far as the author knows, no ethologist has attempted to analyze variables producing subhuman or human psychopathologies. Psychopathologies seldom appear in normal animals in their normal environments, since abnormal animals do not survive in the savannahs. However, an ethologist's interest in ethological methods and human psychopathology has been presented by two world-famous ethologists—Niko Tinbergen, who was one of the two founders of the modern ethological movement, and his wife, E. A. Tinbergen (1972). On the basis of observation and study of normal and autistic children, the Tinbergens explicated basic rules, long used in ethological practice, that they felt should be observed in socially contacting and subsequently treating the autistic human infant.

Social approach and contact with the child should be achieved by aversion of the face, since facing the child is a biologically threatening gesture. Also, any successful gestural approach should be followed and extended by cautious step-by-step procedures. The Tinbergens believed that every attempt should be made to avoid overintimidation of the autistic child, that intense observation and attention should be given to nonverbal interactions, and that intense social bonding should be achieved without extreme or sudden intrusion. Few would question the Tinbergens' injunctions, since they doubtless represent valuable techniques for achieving social relationships with the disturbed child or, for that matter, with the normal child. Whether or not these ethological techniques represent new methods for child psychiatry may be open to question. The Tinbergens' injunctions represent and describe essential observational practices in the study of nonhuman animals under naturalistic or seminaturalistic conditions, as well as in the study of children in the clinic.

History of Induced Subhuman Psychopathology

The use of subsimian animals for the analysis of human-type psychiatric problems has a long and honorable history. The first scientist to study induced psychopathology in a laboratory animal was the eminent neurophysiologist Pavlov in Russia. Pavlov (1927) inadvertently produced the abnormal phenomenon, which he labeled "experimental neurosis," by use of a conditioning technique. He taught dogs to discriminate between a circle and an ellipse and then progressively diminished the ratio between the diameter of the circle and the diameter of the ellipse. When the difference was reduced to about 10 per cent, the neurotic symptoms of extreme and persistent agitation with continual struggling and howling appeared and apparently remained for a long period of time in most dogs. Pavlov attributed the neurosis to a collision in time or space of the processes of excitation or reinforcement and inhibition or nonreinforcement. Pavlov's theory was not particularly surprising, since he attributed many conditioning phenomena to excitation, inhibition conflict, or spreading cortical waves.

Countless other investigators have since trained carnivores and primates to achieve far more precise liminal discriminations without inducing notable neurosis. It is true that forcing the achievement of liminal discriminations may produce some emotional stress, but Pavlov's success may have stemmed from the fact that he wished to produce experimental neurosis, whereas most animal laboratory investigators want to avoid it when studying the liminal phenomena. These scientists, wishing to avoid stress, develop a greater sense of security in their animals before experimentation. For example, at Wisconsin, extensive and intensive adaptation procedures were formalized. To assure a complete sense of security, the researchers trained the animals until they achieved 50 responses within a required period of time.

Elder (1934) achieved auditory pitch discriminations with chimpanzees. Grether (1940) and Weinstein (1940) obtained visual acuity limens with monkeys. With both chimpanzees and monkeys, color discrimination limens comparable to those of human beings were obtained (DeValois and Jacobs, 1968). None of the chimpanzees, monkeys, or human subjects developed experimental neuroses.

Gantt (1944) and Liddell (1938) in America subsequently used similar techniques to produce behavior disorders in subhuman animals forced into conflictual learning situations. Gantt used the term "behavior disorders" to describe his dogs' complex and variegated autonomic responses. Liddell described the stress responses he obtained in sheep, goats, and dogs as "experimental neurasthenia," and this condition was obtained in some cases by merely doubling the number of daily test trials in an unscheduled manner. It was also achieved by conflict between food and pain. Liddell believed that the experimental neurasthenia represented a primitive, relatively undifferentiated state, rather than mimicking any human psychopathological condition.

Bijou (1943) produced experimental neurosis in albino rats by training them to differentiate between the location of two light bands as the size of the gap between the two bands was progressively reduced from 12 inches to 1 inch. The narrowing of the gap led to an increase in squealing, food-cup biting, resistance to being placed in the animal-holding device, and excessive urination and defecation. The apparatus is cleverly designed to delineate behavioral changes objectively during the differentiation of stimuli.

A fundamental question is that of what kind of human psychopathic and psychotic problems can be achieved or approximated with the use of subhuman animal subjects. It is unlikely that human adult psychoses will ever be adequately achieved because of the enormous personality and intellectual differences between adult human beings and subhuman animals. It is much more likely that human infantile psychoses can be illustrated and implemented by simian and subsimian researches.

Nurturance of Normality

LABORATORY ENVIRONMENT

The only way to demonstrate induced psychopathic behavior in laboratory animals is to compare the abnormal animals with others that are normal or at least as normal as can be achieved. However, production of socially normal subhuman monkey laboratory subjects is a task of enormous difficulty and one seldom achieved. Indeed, the common techniques of raising monkeys and even lower mammals in laboratories are so limited that many zoologists have insisted that the only normal

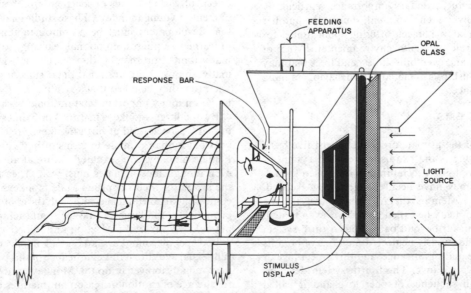

FIGURE 2. The six light bands of the positive stimuli are presented to the right of the animal's head, the six bands of the negative to the left.

environment is a feral environment and that all laboratory animals are raised in an abnormal environment. Nevertheless, serious attempts have been made to raise socially normal laboratory animals by Rosenzweig with rats and the Harlows with monkeys.

The strongest argument against the position that normal animals cannot be raised in a laboratory environment is that provided by humans. The human being is no longer a feral animal; humans are laboratory animals raised from birth to death in a laboratory or laboratory-like environment. As long as humans were reared in a feral environment, they were merely another type of animal living in an animal world. However, when humans became civilized and were reared in a laboratory world, they ceased being animals and became human beings. If modern humans were returned to a feral environment, all their cultural credentials would rapidly disappear. Even more dramatic, the human being would probably disappear. The primatologists would view this phenomenon with dismay. The ethologists might well be charmed—as long as they lasted.

The normal mammalian social-cultural environment is replete with physical facts and artifacts providing its inhabitants with environmental protection, provender, and even playthings. However, physical objects do not make and do not create a normal laboratory environment or normal feral environment.

On the basis of prolonged and profound study, the Harlows have defined the social, as contrasted to the physical, essentials that create a normal environment—laboratory or feral. These essentials are provided not by palaces and provender but by people—particular people. These are gifts of love or, if this is an inadmissible word, gifts of affection. The number and nature of the affectional forces doubtless came about through evolution, even though their exact form and finesse have been modified by learning, particularly by social learning.

Although in theory there are very few normal environments, there are an almost unlimited number of abnormal environments in which animals, in our case particularly monkeys, can be raised. An obvious criterion for the social inadequacy of any particular environment is the degree to which it prohibits or limits social interactions, particularly affectional interactions, between or among its inhabitants during or throughout any or all stages of social development. Doubtless there are many other variables of secondary importance, particularly those relating to the physical environment, such as the number and niceties of manipulatable objects offering opportunities for play by infants and pride by adults, environmental rhythm of daylight and darkness and even hills, holes, and trees that may facilitate social relationships associated with behaviors ranging from flight to dominance.

AFFECTIONAL SYSTEMS

Throughout most of the primate order there exist five basic affectional systems. One is the exquisitely exalted system of mother love, a system of great social importance, even though its vigor and virtues may have been exaggerated. A second, closely synchronized system is that of infant love for the mother. It may for simplicity be called baby love, even though it persists in some form far beyond babyhood. A third system is one that has been enormously neglected, in terms of both its power and its social-sexual significance, and this is peer love or age-mate love or playmate love. The fourth system develops from and is a normal sequence of peer love and is called

heterosexual love. In primates—probably somewhat unlike rodents, including rats and rabbits—heterosexual love in normal form depends on the establishment of the antecedent affectional systems. Actually, this sequence may be true in limited form for many mammalian species. The fifth love or affectional system is that of paternal love. Paternal love is a very difficult system to analyze since it is hard to determine the unconditioned responses that underlie it and difficult to see its total operation, even in the feral environment.

NUCLEAR FAMILY ENVIRONMENT

Most feral environments provide opportunities for the development of all of these forms of love or affection to the members of the primate order. No monkey laboratory environment made all these forms of love available to all monkey participants until the creation of the nuclear family apparatus by Margaret K. Harlow. This apparatus achieves the sociologists' dream of producing nuclear families of rhesus monkeys with a single father and a single mother and their infants and having the family members live in such a manner that both parents are accessible to their own infants, and all infants are accessible to each other and to all of the parental groups.

The structure of the nuclear family apparatus is illustrated in Figure 3. Four nuclear families are housed in each apparatus, and a nuclear family group is shown in Figure 4. The nuclear family apparatus provides all family members full opportunity for social and sexual expression, and the primary missing feral variable is the elimination of predators. Thus, the nuclear family environment retains all that is good and eliminates what is evil in the world of the wild.

The creation of a normal environment makes possible the comparison of the behavior of animals raised in a normal social environment with the behavior of animals raised in various abnormal or debased environments. On the assumption that normality, like abnormality, is a syndrome, one may facetiously state that nuclear family-reared monkeys have a normality syndrome, a syndrome found in some but not all human beings.

MONKEY MATURATION

Over a period of a decade the Harlows have studied the effects of various forms of social environment on social development of young monkeys. These studies have convinced them that development must be a combined function of complex unlearned responses, emotional learning, social learning, and maturation. Fortunately, they accumulated a wealth of normative monkey maturational data, since, unlike many social scientists, they believed that yearning, as well as learning, was based on many important maturational variables.

By and large, monkeys mature 4 or 5 times as fast as humans in many aspects, and at birth monkeys are comparable to a 1-year-old human primate in terms of body and bone structure. Female monkeys are sexually mature at about 3 years of age, even though most females must wait at least 1 more year for the advent of their offspring. Male monkeys are spermatically competent at an equal age, although the anatomical adornment of maturity, the large canine teeth and temporal muscles, do not achieve pubertal perfection until 6 or 7 years.

Like people, monkeys attain full intellectual age at about full sexual age, albeit the significance of this positive correlation may remain forever in doubt. Monkey curiosity does not wait for the age of caution or reason but matures by 30 days of age.

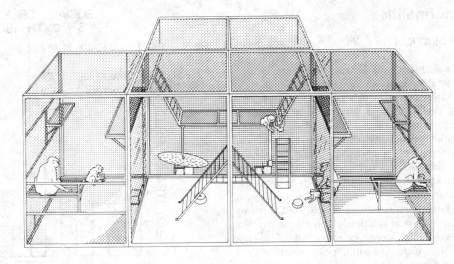

FIGURE 3. Nuclear family living apparatus.

FIGURE 4. Nuclear family father with children.

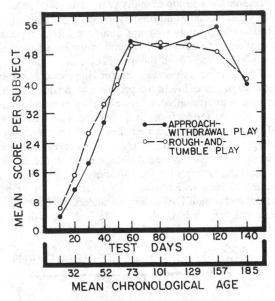

FIGURE 5. Maturation of social play.

Early curiosity is regulated and restrained by maternal ministrations.

The all-important primate behavior pattern of play, the primate prerogative of personal peregrinations, matures at about 90 days of age, as shown in Figure 5. Play makes or breaks social roles and rules in age-mate associations, and the absence of play is an enormously powerful indicator of social maladjustment. Fortunately, play persists for a long time, merely awaiting the appearance of proper social stimuli for its release. Of course, any native play patterns become modified

by learned or cultural components in monkeys and, more dramatically, in humans.

Fears mature at various appropriate periods of time, but social fears appear at about 80 to 100 days of age in monkeys, similar to Spitz's 9-month anxiety in human beings—an anxiety that actually matures somewhere between 6 and 13 months of age. Ninety-day anxiety in monkeys may briefly interfere with play development if they are in a strange environment or with strangers, but it does not override play. It is probably more fun to frolic than to fear. Of course, playmates are usually familiar and not unfamiliar objects.

Only a few of the complex behavior patterns with important unlearned components are described here, but they should be recognized to interpret properly basic mechanisms involved in the experimental induction of psychopathological stages. Leaving the exposition on maturation and turning to social isolation, one can describe the effects of social developmental obliteration in terms of maturational data, as well as learning variables.

Advent of Abnormalities

TOTAL SOCIAL ISOLATION

Probably the most dramatic and destructive abnormal environment is that of total social isolation. Monkeys have been raised from birth onward under such conditions. Here, for some predetermined period of time, an animal has no social partners and can consummate no social interactions. This worst of all possible social worlds or antisocial worlds has never, or almost never, been tested on humans. It would have been totally improper to deliberately raise human beings in such an environment in order to study them, but it is not improper to do this with subhuman subjects—monkeys and apes. Few, if any, human beings have been socially isolated from birth by their parents; had this occurred faultlessly and frequently, the population explosion would have been averted. Although rarely experienced from birth on, total social isolation does occur with sufficient frequency and with drastic enough results to be of critical consideration. Children are tied to bedsteads and locked in closets or bedrooms and left completely alone. Prisoners, criminal or convenient, are placed in solitary confinement, some for a period of many years. The social problems entailed by total social isolation may, however, be studied with both profit and propriety by using simian subjects, especially since recent research has succeeded in finding therapeutic relief for the simian subjects from the drastic effects.

One of the primary advantages of studying psychopathology in subhuman primates lies in the precision with which animate and inanimate environmental variables may be manipulated. Monkeys may be raised from birth onward under conditions of total social isolation in which they have no capability of interacting in any way with any other living form throughout all or any specified part of their developmental sequence, while still maintaining faultless physical health.

Three-month total social isolation. Two studies conducted at the Wisconsin Primate Laboratory on the effect of total isolation in monkeys from birth through the first 3 months of life

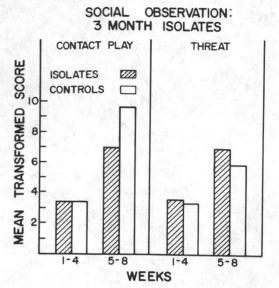

FIGURE 7. Contact play and social threat after 3 months total social isolation.

yielded highly similar results. When removed from their early world of social nothingness and exposed to the world of monkeys and manipulanda, some of the infants went into a state of deep shock. One died of self-imposed anorexia, and another was on the verge until saved by forced feeding. Another 90-day-old monkey died of self-imposed anorexia because he was born at a time when no trained staff members were available.

The infants that survived, and most did, made a remarkable social adjustment subsequently, as shown in Figure 6, by the development of play. When allowed to interact with equal-age normally reared rhesus monkeys, the isolates were playing effectively within the first week or so. By the end of the first month and throughout the second month, the behavior of the 90-day isolates was normal, as indicated by both the frequency of play and the threat gestures depicted in Figure 7.

The normal or relatively normal nature of the threat gestures in the 90-day-old isolate monkeys is particularly surprising, since monkey infants raised with inanimate surrogate mothers are gesturally inadequate. Probably, if the isolates were relaxed enough to learn play along with the normal monkeys who were also just beginning to play, they could learn the threat gestures that were also being incorporated into the behavior repertoire of the normal 3-month-old playmates.

Six-month total social isolation. Raising monkeys in total social isolation from birth throughout the first 6 months of life produced dramatic developmental differences in the isolated monkeys. The early infantile responses of self-clasp and huddle remain consistently low in socially raised monkeys. Conversely, these infantile behaviors increased progressively in the isolated rhesus monkeys, as shown in Figure 8. The maladaptive behaviors attained a level that was clearly abnormal and significantly higher than the level of infantile responses made by the controls.

Similar results were obtained for the level of rocking responses and stereotypy responses, as illustrated in Figure 9. Rocking responses remained at a near-normal level throughout the first 4 isolation months and then exploded upward with increasing frequency. Stereotypy progressively increased from the second month onward. Neither rock nor stereotypy are

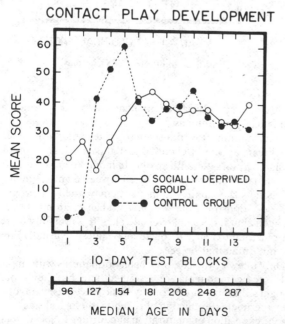

FIGURE 6. Contact play development after 3 months total social isolation.

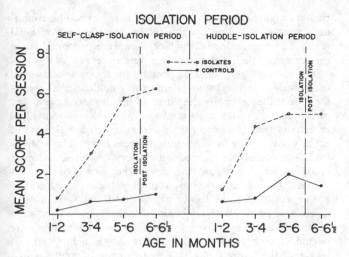

FIGURE 8. Self-clasp and huddle in 6-month total social isolates.

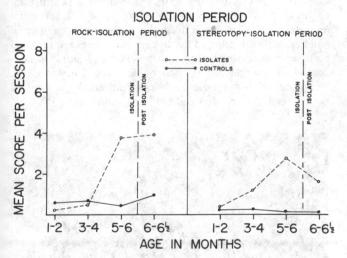

FIGURE 9. Rock and stereotypy in 6-month total social isolates.

normal infant responses but apparently depend on prolonged maternal or other deprivation.

The data presented make it clear that grossly abnormal behaviors developed during the half-year isolation period. It is not surprising to find, therefore, that the total-isolate monkeys were completely unable to interact socially with normal or near-normal age-mates.

When removed from the isolation chambers these 6-month isolates were terrified by relatively normal social age-mates. Representatives from the normal and the abnormal groups were then tested 5 days a week for 2 months in social groups of two isolates and two controls in a standardized playroom situation. Situational and social fears had clearly matured, and the monkeys raised in isolation were foredoomed to suffer a terrible social toll, foreshadowed by the abject animal pictured in Figure 10.

As is illustrated in Figure 11, the monkeys isolated for 6 months exhibited a very low level of threat responses, whereas the controls showed a high incidence of threat. Because of the monkeys' age it is obvious that situational and social fears would ordinarily have matured in all the animals, but the isolates had had no opportunity to learn from mother or confrere the use of social threat in the face of fear. They knew only the fear of the strange environment and of the monkeys

who, though age-mates, were fully fearful to them. Being paralyzed with fear, they acted strangely to the normal monkeys, who then threatened them and caused further escalation of the maladaptive behaviors. One cannot learn in a social vacuum. Threat responses were essentially nonexistent in the isolate monkeys, and the levels of threat behavior remained practically unchanged for both groups during the second, as well as the first, month.

The differences between the two monkey groups in frequency of play data are at least as striking as the differences in threat responses. As is shown in Figure 12, play is, for all practical purposes, nonexistent in the first weeks and begins to show improvement only toward the fifth month of playroom sharing. This finding cannot be explained in maturational terms, since the capability for monkey play is present in normal monkeys half this age.

Play does not thrive in strange environments, and play does not go hand in hand with fear. Each factor by itself delays play, and the degrees of both strangeness and fear in the case of the isolates are sufficient to explain prolonged persistent

FIGURE 10. Six-month total social isolate just removed from isolation chamber.

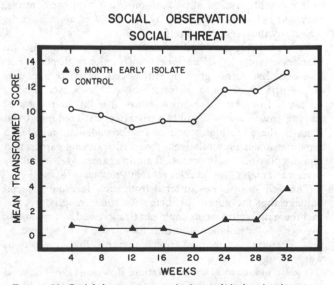

FIGURE 11. Social threat responses in 6-month isolate in playroom.

SOCIAL OBSERVATION
CONTACT PLAY INITIATION

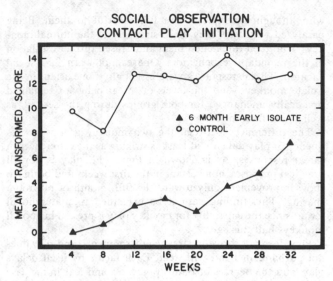

FIGURE 12. Contact play initiation in 6-month isolate in playroom.

SOCIAL OBSERVATION
ROUGH & TUMBLE PLAY

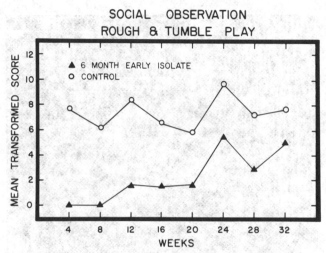

FIGURE 13. Rough-and-tumble play in 6-month isolate.

effects (see Figure 13). In addition, although there was no visible actual physical aggression on the part of the controls, play can be further inhibited by the threat of aggression, as well as by the aggression itself.

Fear of strangeness had matured long before these isolate monkeys were allowed any social interaction with peers, and monkeys that do not grow up with social threat are undoubtedly a prize package for threat by normal associates. Studies on normal monkeys demonstrate how true this injunction is. In play groups composed of two pairs of equal-aged males and females, there is a high tendency for the males and females to separate; males play relatively rough, threatening games, and females play relatively genteel, feminine games. Male monkeys threaten females, but females seldom threaten males.

The 6-month isolates suffered from such devastating social damage that the author predicted for some months or years that these maladjustments could not be increased by prolonging the periods of isolation and that they could not be cured by any technique of monkey psychotherapy. Both predictions were wrong.

Twelve-month total social isolation. Rowland (1964) isolated a group of macaque monkeys for the first 12 months of life, a

period roughly equivalent to 5 or 6 human years. These monkeys were totally unresponsive to the new physical or social world (see Figure 14) with which they were presented when the screens of their isolation world were raised.

The researchers hunted desperately for social or semisocial measures of any remaining latent or fragmented social behaviors. Since they properly despaired of finding social play, they measured play of the most nonsocial type—that of individual or activity play. The control monkeys showed a high level of activity play throughout the entire 10-week test period, whereas the 12-month isolates started with a very low level, and even that languished as far as it could with the passage of time.

Since the isolates were devoid of play, the investigators did not expect them to be full of passion, and they were correct. There may be play without passion, but there is seldom passion without play as a precursor. In fact, these isolate monkeys were devoid of both ploys and plays, as is shown in Figure 15. It was as if they were living in a social prison of total vacuity. Undaunted, the researchers looked for data on another measure—that of social biting. Biting in bitterness is antisocial aggression, but gentle biting is a sign of significant social importance. However, as is illustrated in Figure 16, the normal monkey, after adapting to the test situation, engaged in social biting with increasing frequency, whereas the 12-month isolates never had a single bite in their bodies—social or antisocial. The 12-month isolates did not bite control monkeys, they did not bite isolates, and they did not bite themselves.

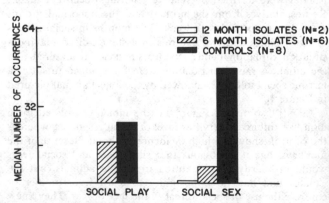

FIGURE 14. Twelve-month isolate on removal of isolation screen.

FIGURE 15. Social play and social sex in isolate monkeys.

SOCIAL OBSERVATION BITING

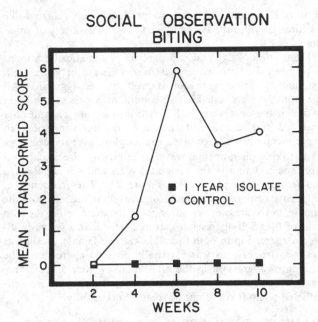

FIGURE 16. Biting in 12-month total social isolate.

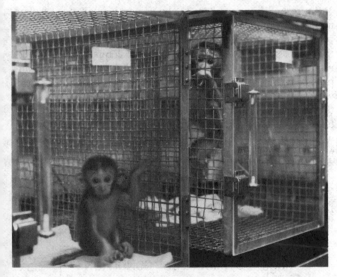

FIGURE 17. Partial isolates in individual wire cages.

PARTIAL SOCIAL ISOLATION

The socially destructive power of total social isolation results from readily apparent reasons, since the confined subject has little or no chance to acquire any social learning. Compared with total social isolation, partial isolation sounds relatively innocent or benign. Under partial social isolation each animal lives in a wire cage, usually one arranged in a rack of several cages, as shown in Figure 17. Actually, monkeys and doubtless many other animals in zoos, in pet shops, and in laboratories have been housed in this manner for many decades without thought being given to the fact that these animals were being severely socially deprived. Indeed, before the researchers at Wisconsin became aware of the social predicament of monkeys raised in partial social isolation, the monkeys were described as control subjects or even normal subjects for various experimental groups.

Monkeys raised in partial social isolation can see and hear

and doubtless smell other monkeys. But partially socially isolated monkeys can never make any physical contact with other monkeys, and, without physical contact, monkeys can experience none of the normal affectional or love sequences. Doomed to a wire cage, monkeys can receive no love from a mother nor give love in return. Partially isolated monkeys have absolutely no opportunity to develop affection for age-mates through play, and the concept of sex behavior is a mockery in total physical isolation.

Frequency of representative behaviors in the first and after the second year of life by partially isolated monkeys is shown in Figure 18. Totally infantile responses of rock and huddle

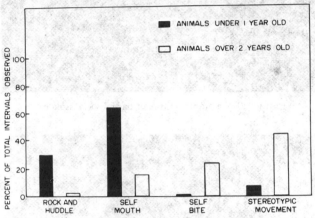

FIGURE 18. Frequency of selected behaviors on increase of duration of partial social isolation.

FIGURE 19. Staring vacantly into upper space.

FIGURE 20. Catatonic posture of partial social isolate.

FIGURE 21. Partial social isolate attacking offending appendage.

and self-mouth wane with age, whereas self-bite and stereotypy wax. In other words, the extremely infantile responses drop out and are superseded by more complex responses.

Even early in life, the postures of monkeys raised in total social isolation differ qualitatively from the postures of partially isolated rhesus monkeys. Total social-isolate monkeys tend to exhibit a depressive-type posture, including such patterns as self-clutch, rocking, and depressive huddling. Partially isolated monkeys assume with increasing frequency postures that are more schizoid-like. These postures may include extreme stereotypy and sitting at the front of the cage and staring vacantly into space, as illustrated in Figure 19. Occasionally, the arm of a monkey starts to rise, and, as it extends, the wrist and fingers flex (see Figure 20). While this takes place, the monkey ignores the arm, but, when it is extended, the monkey may suddenly respond to the arm, jump as if frightened, and even attack the offending appendage (see Figure 21). Unfortunately, the inves-

tigators have not been able to produce these schizoid-like postures at will but have produced them in a variety of situations.

Maturation of aggression progresses systematically in monkeys raised in bare wire cages over a period of years, both externally directed aggression and self-directed aggression. All the monkeys were tested in two conditions, a passive condition in which the observers sat 8 feet from the subjects and only observed and scored, and an active condition, in which an experimenter ran a large black rubber glove over the cage top.

A striking phenomenon was that externally directed aggression was apparent in the male at 2 years and not apparent in the female until year 4 (see Figure 22). The frequency of aggressive responses matured progressively in the male and the female, but aggression was stronger in the male before the fifth year of life. Self-aggression matured later than externally directed aggression in both the male and the female, and it was never as frequent as was externally directed aggression. The waning of aggression in the male monkey after 5 years may have stemmed from the loss of some monkeys whose self-inflicted wounds could not be treated successfully.

SIX-MONTH TOTAL SOCIAL ISOLATION FOLLOWED BY PARTIAL ISOLATION

Representative members of the 6-month total social-isolate monkeys were maintained in the laboratory under conditions of partial social isolation for 3 or more years, and, even when they were socially tested under these inadequate social conditions, their social responses to each other became more impaired, rather than improved. When these long-term isolates were paired with equal-aged macaques or even monkeys half their age, they assumed violent and grotesque postures of terror, such as the monkey lying on its back supine and frozen with terror (see Figure 23). This is a posture never assumed by a normal monkey. Similarly, a group of isolates is shown in Figure 24.

It is common to think of fear and aggression as antithetical emotions. Aggression is for the bold, and fear is for the frightened. But 6 months of total social isolation paradoxically

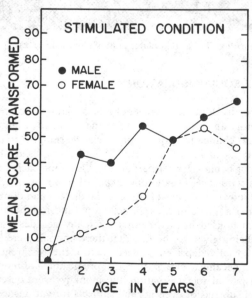

FIGURE 22. Maturation of externally directed aggression in male and female partial isolates.

FIGURE 23. Frozen fear posture in 6-month total plus partial isolate.

FIGURE 24. Abnormal fear postures in isolates.

created adolescent monkeys that were both abnormally aggressive and abnormally fearful, and these exaggerated emotional states sometimes appeared almost simultaneously.

The total and partial isolates aggressed or attempted to aggress against all other monkeys. They aggressed or threatened infants—an activity beneath the dignity of any normal rhesus monkey. Furthermore, during these acts of threat or assault, the isolates indicated, by their gestures, feelings of fear and apprehension. The isolates aggressed against age-mates who were far more physically adept. These aggressions were fraught with fear, and well they might have been, since the actual physical encounters were massacres little exceeded by the Battle of the Little Big Horn. Even worse, the 6-month isolates often made one suicidal aggressive assault against a member of a group of large, mature aggressive males, illustrating the ultimate combination of paradoxical fear and hate. Such aggressions seldom occurred twice, since even the isolate monkeys could learn in this situation to compensate for their emotional deficiencies or hypersufficiencies.

LACK AND LOSS

The phenomena of isolation may be classified in terms of lack and loss of social interaction. In lack or absence, the animal experiences no social companionship from birth until some predetermined period. Loss results when the animal is isolated or separated after social relationships have been established. Harlow and Novak (1973) have completed many studies in which subjects lived normal or relatively normal lives before being placed in total social isolation or occasionally in partial social isolation for some prescribed time. Rowland (1964) delayed isolating one group until the seventh month, and other groups were not socially isolated until they were 6, 9, 12, or 22 months of age. Invariably, these deprived or late-isolate groups have shown far less behavioral deficit than the early-isolate or privation animals. Furthermore, when the late-isolate deprivation monkeys returned to social living, they often appeared to be meaninglessly hyperaggressive, a behavior that has been described as sociopathic.

INDUCTION OF ANACLITIC DEPRESSION IN MONKEYS

Isolation of the types just described represented no direct or deliberate attempt to mimic or approximate any human psychopathological syndrome, regardless of the results obtained. The author's first deliberate approach to the study of comparative psychopathology lay in the production of anaclitic depression in infant monkeys.

Mother-infant separation. In the late 1950's the author separated infants from inanimate cloth surrogate mothers and obtained data similar to that of Spitz (1946) and Bowlby (1969) with mother-infant separation, followed by subsequent despair—which, in fact, is depression—and ending in reunion, when the infant was returned to the mother. Unfortunately, the study was marred by technical flaws, since the infants were separated from the cloth surrogate mothers for an hour a day since birth for purposes of surrogate sanitation, and many of the infants had partially adapted to transient maternal loss. Furthermore, the periods of separations—usually measured in hours, not days—were doubtless too brief. Disturbed by the fact that they did not obtain significant behavioral differences between the experimental group and the control group in all cases, the researchers withheld the data.

The first formal Wisconsin study on induced nonhuman anaclitic depression was conducted by Seay et al. (1962). The test situation illustrated in Figure 25 was designed so that each of two mother-infant pairs lived in home cages, with an infant play area in between. The infants were free to wander at will from the home cages to the mutual play area, but the mothers were restrained in the home cages by the size of the apertures into the play area. Play by these infants, like all rhesus infants, matured at about 90 days of age and was near maximal at 180 days, which was the age chosen to begin maternal separation. This separation was achieved by dropping transparent Plexiglas screens in front of both home cages while the two infants were

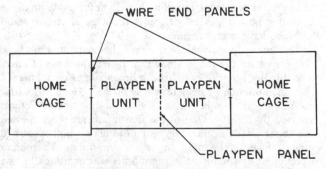

FIGURE 25. Mother-infant separation apparatus.

PROTEST STAGE OF SEPARATION

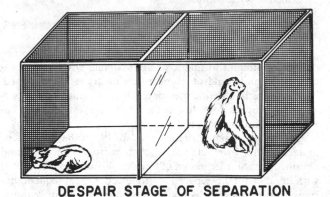

DESPAIR STAGE OF SEPARATION

FIGURE 26. First two stages of mother-infant separation.

romping in the play area. The researchers had designed this apparatus and chosen the maturational age of the subjects so that they could measure play behavior during separation, on the proper assumption that play is a complex social behavior and that loss of complex social behaviors would be highly effective indicators of personal-social distress.

All the monkeys tested in this situation exhibited a complete or near-complete picture of human anaclitic depression; if one makes allowance for the fact that monkeys mature 4 or 5 times as fast as humans, the variable of age of onset was comparable. At initial separation the rhesus infants exhibited a protest stage, as shown by violent attempts to regain maternal contact, plaintive vocalization, and a persistent high level of random behavior (see Figure 26). The protest stage changed to despair during the next 48 hours. Despair was characterized by a drastic reduction in vocalization and movement and the frequent assumption of prone postures with the head and body wrapped in the arms and legs. The most dramatic measure of the despair stage was that of the near-total suppression of play, as the researchers had surmised. Play was almost abolished during the 3-week period of maternal separation and then rose rapidly after maternal reunion. It was unfortunate that the separation period was so brief, since the stage of despair could doubtless have been extended.

When many human children are reunited with their mothers, their responses toward the maternal figure are those of rejection; Bowlby actually called this reunion stage "detachment." This phenomenon of detachment is far less common and far less intense in monkey infants than in the human infants reported by Bowlby. One of the first infant monkeys showed some maternal detachment on reunion, and one mother showed some transient reluctance to accept her infant. Temporary detachment by the infant to the mother was exhibited by one

out of four infants in a replication study. However, the separated monkey infants typically reattached to the monkey mother vigorously and rapidly when the separation phase ended. Bowlby (1969) has more recently expressed doubts about the universality of the detachment stage in human infants. Furthermore, even allowing for maturational differences in comparison with the monkey studies, Bowlby dealt with a much wider age range of human children and much longer separation periods, and the human children were doubtless subjected to a great variety of new social arrangements during the period of maternal loss.

Variables influencing separation effects. The effects of maternal separation in macaque monkeys were replicated by a second study, differing only in that the partitions separating mother and infant were opaque instead of transparent, and each stage was measured for only 2 instead of 3 weeks. The infant's distress was slightly less when the view of the mother was totally obscured—perhaps a case of out of sight, out of mind. Play was again dramatically and significantly reduced during the depression stage.

From a purist's point of view, the study was confounded in that a playmate was always available to ameliorate social loss. The surprising fact is the devastating distress on the part of the monkeys, even when the playmate was available to offer surcease from sorrow. Playmate loss, as well as maternal loss, can produce anaclitic depression.

In the majority of early studies of mother-infant separation, the age of the infants at the time of separation was not found to have qualitative influence on the nature of the infant's reaction to separation. These separations occurred after 4 months of age, during the middle months of the infant's first year. In a recent study of permanent separations from the mother (Suomi et al., 1973), the monkeys were separated at 60, 90, and 120 days of age. The first separation occurred before the normal 70- to 90-day-old maturation of the fear response in the rhesus monkey. Some investigators have associated maturation of the corresponding fear response in human infants with qualitative changes in the nature of the infant attachment reactions. However, in the rhesus monkey no qualitative changes occurred in the separation responses between the 60-day separation and the 90- and 120-day separation groups.

However, there was in this experiment a quantitative difference in the reactions of the 90-day monkeys that supports previous findings that major environmental changes adversely affect infants to a greater degree immediately after maturation of the fear response. The type of housing condition after the separation also produced varying effects. Infants housed alone evinced much higher levels of self-directed behaviors, such as self-clasping and huddling, than did infants housed in pairs. Postseparation, as well as preseparation, variables do influence the separation responses.

Species differences in anaclitic depression. After the early Wisconsin studies were published, most primatologists with laboratories did one or more maternal separation studies. The results are in accord with the Wisconsin data, allowing for interspecies differences in mother-infant attachment.

Hinde and Spencer-Booth (1971) studied social separation in macaques by removing a mother from a spacious cage and leaving the infant to associate with the remaining female, an adult male, and assorted infants. Hinde had previously described the fact that some female macaques serve as aunts in this situation with the mother present. Hinde removed the mothers at about 200 days of age for either one or two 6-day periods or one 13-day period. The results were very similar to those previously obtained by the Wisconsin studies, with a protest period characterized by distress vocalizations and hyperactivity or by despair and depression, indicated by hunched postures, decreased activity, and social withdrawal. On reunion, three of the monkey infants rapidly returned to preseparation activity levels, but the fourth did not. The less the monkeys had been attached to the mothers before separation, the more quickly normal behavior appeared after maternal return. The longer the total separation period, the more profound and prolonged the depression was.

These separated infants were tested 12 and 30 months later, and few, if any, abnormalities were disclosed in home cage behaviors. However, the isolated monkeys showed less approach and exploration of strange objects in a strange cage, and these differences may possibly have persisted for 2 years.

In a series of studies, Kaufman and Rosenblum (1967) compared the separation reactions of infant pigtail monkeys (*Macaca nemestrina*) with infant bonnet macaques (*Macaca radiata*). In their studies they departed from the conventional model of removing the infant from the mother and, instead, removed the mother from the infant and from a relatively large housing group consisting of several adult females, an adult male, and infants of assorted ages. Most of the pigtail infants went through a conventional protest and despair stage, which began to lift after a week and fluctuated during the next month. But, the comparably treated bonnet infants showed little indication of anaclitic depression. Instead, the separated bonnets found surcease from sorrow by attaching to the remaining adults, particularly the females, who reciprocated their affectional advances and thus became substitute mothers.

The behaviors of the infant and mother pigtail and bonnet monkeys were totally in keeping with the normal behaviors for their species before any separation procedures had been instituted. Bonnet macaque mothers are born to be receptive to group maternal administrations. From the first month of life onward, bonnet mothers allow their infants to wander forth and accept female social advances from other female members of the bonnet group. Thus, removal of the biological mother produced only extenuated maternal loss. But pigtail mothers are physically demanding and restrict the social adventures of their infants for at least several months. Lacking experience with other mothers, the maternally separated pigtail infants suffered intense pigtail-type anaclitic depression. Anaclitic depression is not produced by mere physical manipulations; it is produced by social loss.

Schlottmann and Seay (1972), using a modification of the original Seay and Harlow apparatus and a modification of their experimental design, measured the effects of mother-infant separation in Java macaques. One out of three groups of Java infants was given no mother figures during the 3-week separation period, another was given adult mother substitutes, and the third group was separated and immediately reunited with their mothers. The last group suffered virtually no reduction in amount of contact play during maternal separation, indicating that the trauma of separation was not a variable of great importance. The infants totally deprived of mothers and those given substitute mothers showed significant decreases in infant play and related behaviors and significant changes in some nonsocial behaviors. Maternal reunion revealed an intensification of mother-infant relationships in the mother-deprived and substitute-mother groups.

Preston et al. (1970) studied patas infants after maternal separation shortly after 6 months of age and found a slight, nonsignificant increase in contact play during the separation period. They explained this unusual phenomenon by pointing out that patas mothers are overprotective of their infants and threaten other infants during close-quarter play. Thus, during maternal separation the patas infants had more freedom to engage in natural and normal play than they had in the laboratory and probably in the feral world.

As indicated, there already exists an extensive literature on the effects of maternal separation on various species of Old World (catarrhine) monkeys. Unfortunately, there are only two reports of maternal separation in New World (platyrrhine) primates. In an exploratory study using squirrel monkeys, Kaplan (1970) observed that separation of the infant from the mother at 100 to 150 days of age gave rise to a severe protest stage, characterized by extreme activity and intense shrieking. Furthermore, reduction in the two measures of play and sex behavior provided evidence of a profound or prolonged period of depression. Kaplan suggested that this behavior may be a function of maturational stage. Although the squirrel monkey infants were younger than the half-year-old catarrhine monkeys commonly separated from their mothers, they were probably older in their stage of behavioral maturation, since Kaplan's squirrel monkey infants spent only 10 per cent of their time in maternal affiliative behaviors before the study was initiated. The most surprising and probably most important finding by Kaplan was the fact that the depression of play and allied social behaviors extended into the reunion period, after the depression period had theoretically ended.

In a brilliant and apparently definitive paper, in spite of the small number of subjects tested, Jones and Clark (1973) showed that maternal separation enormously depressed activity play and the social behaviors of contact play and sex play in squirrel monkeys. Mixed play was nonexistent throughout this period. However, simple affiliative behaviors of approach and huddling were augmented. This was doubtless a compensatory function for maternal body contact loss.

The squirrel monkey is one of the intellectual weaklings within the primate order, but this lamentable learning lack does not prevent it from developing severe and presumably prolonged anaclitic-type depression. A consideration of all nonhuman primate data to date would substantiate the hypothesis that the squirrel monkey is the primate prototype for the demonstration and investigation of the anaclitic depression phenomenon, in terms of both the severity of social behavior loss and the range of social behavior loss, including play and sex.

Repetitive separation of infant monkey peers. Almost by definition, anaclitic depression involves separation of mother and child. This phenomenon has now been demonstrated in many monkey species. The affectional ties between mother and child of most monkey species are strong and enduring, as described by Harlow and Harlow (1969).

In experiments subsequent to maternal-infant separation studies, infants living with mothers and peers were first separated from the mothers at about 180 days of age and then separated from their peers at 205 days. This procedure produced a double despair syndrome, first elicited by maternal separation and then by playmate or peer separation. It is clear that anaclitic depression may be induced by the loss of any social object to which the animal has become deeply attached and not by loss of the mother alone. Since age-mate affectional ties are also very abiding, age-mate separation of itself should produce profound emotional distress. This thesis was tested experimentally by Suomi et al. (1969, 1970, 1971, 1974), who were able to measure the effects of repetitive separation of infant pairs that had been separated from their mothers and raised in a spacious cage as part of a group of eight infants. At 90 days of age, the first of a series of 20 separations was begun, with monkeys being separated for 4 days and reunited for 3 days for 20 separations completed over a 6-month period.

These infants had become so attached to each other that, together, they were overclinging, sharing the ever-close contact comfort of each other (see Figure 27). Surrogate-raised infants pursue their exploratory urges at will, unrestrained, and mother-raised monkeys are aided in breaking too-close ties by the mother's urging it, at the ripe time, to leave her side, but peer together-raised infants have only their immature selves and are much less inclined to relinquish their togetherness.

During the course of every separation, the separated age-mate pairs displayed the three conventional stages of anaclitic depression—protest, despair, and reattachment (detachment). However, a completely new phenomenon appeared during the course of multiple separations—a phenomenon of induced behavioral infantalism. Infantile behaviors of self-mouth and self-clasp, which normally drop out by the fourth month, persisted in undiminished frequency and remained throughout the 9-month test period. Furthermore, complex social behaviors of environmental exploration and, particularly, play, which should become progressively more frequent and precise from 3 to 6 months and on to 9 months remained unchanged in its formlessness and remained at a near-nonexistent frequency throughout the entire 9-month period. Multiple peer separations did more than cause distress and depression. The separations eradicated the entire normal behavioral maturational process. Without each other, the infants had absolutely nothing. It is as if the infants had walked through the fountain of youth of Ponce de Leon and had achieved unending infancy.

Vertical chamber researches. Animal research (Seligman and Maier, 1967) has shown that a habit of helplessness may be learned and generalized from one situation to another. Dogs who had learned in one situation that they could in no way escape experiencing punishing electric shocks later did not avail themselves of chances to escape or avoid pain and punishment in other situations. In reverse, animals who had first learned to avoid punishment successfully could cope with the next situation as well.

Since depressed human patients often report feelings of

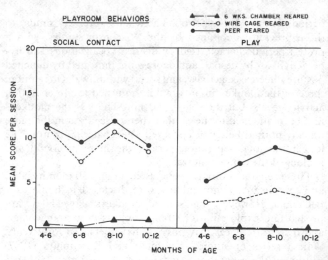

FIGURE 28. Persistent depression of social behaviors after vertical chamber confinement.

hopelessness and helplessness, the author sought the possibility of creating an apparatus that imparts just such a feeling in monkeys and contributes another dimension to the depression induced through social separation or isolation from loved ones.

In an effort to create an apparatus that produces this feeling rapidly and persistently, the author created the vertical chamber. This apparatus is, basically, a stainless steel chamber, open at the top, that measures 18 by 12 to 16 inches. The depth is 28½ inches, and the sides slope downward and inward to a half-cylinder at the base 18 inches in length, with a diameter slightly more than 3 inches. Sanitation, as well as food and water intake, are all admirably anticipated.

As far as could be ascertained, the vertical chamber apparatus did not induce any physiological deficits, since the monkeys ate a normal amount of food, drank a normal amount of water, and showed no abnormal tendencies toward infection or disease. However, the monkeys placed in the vertical chambers for 30 to 90 days exhibited pervasive and persisting depressive states (Harlow and Suomi, 1971; Suomi and Harlow, 1972a). The monkeys showed abnormally high frequencies of depressive posturing, including self-clasp, rock, and huddle. The more complex behavioral processes of locomotion and environmental exploration were depressed, social contact was enormously depressed (see Figure 28), and play responses were eradicated. Even the monkeys placed in the vertical chambers for relatively brief periods of time exhibited pervasive and persisting depressive states.

Trends on all measures were exaggerated and not alleviated with time, as graphed in Figure 29. Since there was no tendency for recovery of such behaviors as locomotion and a persistence of self-directed maladaptive behaviors for months after chambering, the goal of producing depression relatively rapidly and permanently seems to have been achieved.

HUMAN INFANTILE PSYCHOSES

As the topic or theme of childhood psychoses attracts progressively more acceptance, three theories or theses have appeared in the literature. Kanner's syndrome of early infantile autism has created wide interest, and Kanner (1973) himself has written a book describing the syndrome, giving illustrative cases, case studies, and summaries of the researches on infantile autism, particularly those at the Linwood Childrens' Center.

FIGURE 27. Choo-choo phenomenon in together-raised rhesus.

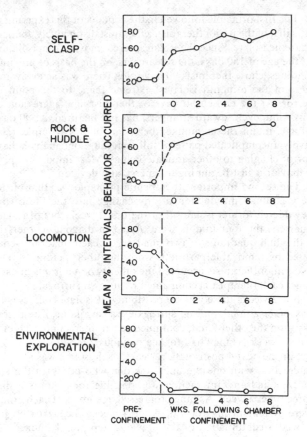

SELF-CLASP

ROCK & HUDDLE

LOCOMOTION

MEAN % INTERVALS BEHAVIOR OCCURRED

ENVIRONMENTAL EXPLORATION

PRE-CONFINEMENT   WKS. FOLLOWING CHAMBER CONFINEMENT

FIGURE 29. Behaviors of monkeys before and after chambering.

There are, unfortunately, few if any cues as to how this syndrome can be simulated by using subhuman animal subjects.

Two other theories of childhood psychoses may be researchable. These are the double-bind theory of Bateson et al. (1956) and Mahler's (1952) theory of symbiosis. The double-bind theory assumes that persistent, contradictory maternal communication with the child leads to schizoid behaviors, including social withdrawal. Symbiotic psychoses, presumably arising from the mother's overprotection and limitations of activity to suit her own demands, make it impossible for the child to progress to later developmental stages of socialization, particularly to what are called peer or age-mate affection and play.

At the University of Arizona, Wooley (1977) has conducted researches designed to simulate the double-bind and symbiotic behavior forms. Wooley produced inconsistent mothers by raising squirrel monkey infants on a standard cloth surrogate, which was covered intermittently with a spiked wire frame. The symbiotic mother was a standard cloth surrogate surrounded by a rotating Plexiglas sheet that emitted a strong air blast at the infant anytime it left the surrogate. This blast lasted for 2 minutes and was then repeated if the infant did not return and cling to the surrogate.

The double-bind infants showed greatly depressed amounts of self-motion play, excessive locomotion, and little or no depression after surrogate separation. However, when offered an opportunity at the appropriate age to play with age-mates, the double-bind infants failed to respond socially and exhibited a pathological degree of aggression.

The symbiotic group after 6 months developed no abnormal aggression toward playmates but an extremely high level of both contact and noncontact play when left alone with age-mate playmates, behaviors that persisted unabated throughout the entire 6-week period of testing.

These infant monkey syndromes, both differential and consistent, relate with total propriety to the behaviors of human double-bind infants and symbiotic infants. Strong presumptive evidence is presented that monkeys appropriately treated early in life simulate the syndromes of double-bind and symbiotic psychoses described for human children. These data support the human researches of induced double-bind and symbiotic infantile psychoses. Such admirable human analogues produced through the exploratory monkey research support both the human theories and the likelihood of effective further studies using simian subject simulation.

Behavioral Rehabilitation

The production of abnormal syndromes is in no sense the ultimate goal of subhuman psychopathology. If syndromes are created, they should also be curable and cured. Psychiatric syndromes can be produced in various animals by diverse factors and forces. A primary goal of subhuman psychopathological research is to analyze the nature of these many variables and, by the use of this knowledge, to produce behavioral rehabilitation. Three basically different strategies may be used to assess the nature and number of these psychopathological variables.

TIME AS A PSYCHOPATHOLOGICAL TREATMENT

An approach to psychopathology that may be considered either a method or a control is the manipulation of no variable other than time. It is said that time works wonders, whether or not this holds true for psychotherapy. Probably, time operates differently in ways ranging from useful to dangerous, depending on the behavioral disorder involved.

It is doubtful whether time is ever the therapeutic method of primary choice. Time's efficacy is a function of the disorder, and, even if it may be useful in some psychological disturbances, it is useless or worse than useless in others. Finally, time's efficacy may be an illusory factor, since in many cases it is the natural and normal or unidentified social forces acting on the animal during the temporal interval that facilitate any cure rather than time itself.

The effects on monkeys of 6 months of social isolation have already been assessed when these animals were placed with normal peers. By any and all measures, the isolates were socially inadequate. Subsequently, they lived alone for 3 or more years. Time, compounded by partial isolation, had worked wonders for these animals in a negative direction, since the original behavioral deficits not only remained but were exaggerated. There is no record of a monkey psychopathology being cured by time.

TREATMENT OF SPECIFIC SYMPTOMS

A theoretically interesting type of therapy lies in the deliberate treatment of one or more abnormal symptoms, whether or not this treatment achieves rehabilitation of the total organism.

All the basic affectional patterns of mother love, infant love, peer love, heterosexual love, and paternal love are based on responses involving bodily contact. Social isolation denies the monkey any contact comfort during all its personal and social development. When social contact became accessible to the isolated monkeys after isolation had ended, they did not make systematic attempts to achieve or maintain bodily contact with their simian associates. In fact, they went out of their way to avoid contact with fellow species members.

If acceptance of contact comfort stimulation can be achieved after prolonged social isolation, it may operate in one of two ways—each of almost equal therapeutic interest. Passive contact comfort may be a first step, which may then be expanded by supplementary procedures to attain total therapy; or contact comfort therapy may alleviate predictable or unpredictable components of a pathological syndrome, such as that of isolation. Partial therapy is of theoretical interest; complete social rehabilitation is of practical, personal interest.

To test contact comfort rehabilitation, Suomi first placed a group of rhesus monkeys in total isolation for a half-year period. The isolates were then put in individual cages with a heated, simplified surrogate. Subsequently, six pairs of isolates and their surrogates were placed in a large group living cage for 8 weeks. The data showed that the monkeys that were given surcease from social sorrow by surrogate satisfaction later showed a marked decrease in self-directed disturbance activities, including self-clasp, self-mouth, rock, and stereotypy. There was evidence that, contingent on the reduced frequency of display of these behaviors, there was an increase in frequency of environmental exploration and peer contact. Obviously, increased frequency of environmental exploration and peer contact is not total rehabilitation, which should involve multiple peer interactions, various forms of peer play, and real or, at least, attempted heterosexual behavior. It appears that experience with the warm surrogate imparted considerable social security to the isolated monkey, as it can impart security during the social development of the normal infant. Contact with surrogates changed the isolated monkeys from animals devoid of security when with their confreres to animals capable of maintaining some social contacts. This behavioral change obviously represented some psychiatric gain. Surrogate contact training, nevertheless, failed as a therapy even approaching a total rehabilitation process. The isolated monkeys never achieved the full gamut of monkey behaviors involving active, sex-typed play and appropriate sexual responsiveness. The one-step specific goal of the designed experiment was accomplished. The monkeys were rehabilitated to accept contact comfort, and from this they gained a modicum of social security. No serious attempt was made to rehabilitate these socially isolated monkeys totally, and total social rehabilitation was not achieved. The acceptance of the contact comfort of a surrogate mother is even more passive and less interactive than the acceptance of bodily contact from another animate body.

SOCIAL BEHAVIOR THERAPY

No one expects to resolve complex problems by way of a pair of explanatory studies, but two attempts to rehabilitate socially isolated monkeys by behavior therapy have been conducted, and the results are extremely encouraging.

Six-month isolate therapy. The first successful Wisconsin study on the psychiatric rehabilitation of monkeys rendered socially abnormal by social isolation for the first 6 months of life was conducted by Suomi and Harlow (1972b). Four males, reared for the first 6 months of life in total isolation, became the patients, and the four normal and available monkeys of the desired age, the only four available, were female. Without prior design, the four male patients were to receive therapy from four very young female therapists.

The first principle followed in the conduct of this experiment was that of the junior therapist, a therapist distinctively younger than the isolate. Since the isolates were removed from isolation at the age of 180 days, the researchers, on the basis of previous findings, chose therapists 90 days old. There was acute awareness of the 6-month isolates' extreme fears, to the point of terror. At the chosen 90 days of therapist age, aggression of any kind, even toward strangers, has not matured. At 90 days of age, infant rhesus monkey behavior follows a simple, relatively uncomplicated pattern, still including some baby behavior of clinging to other animate beings. Most important, play behavior is just beginning to emerge and develop.

The second important therapeutic principle was that of the very gradual introduction of any change into the life of the bewildered former isolates. For the first 2 weeks out of isolate quarters, the four infants were placed in diagonal corners in individual quadrants of two quad cages, each quadrant separated by removable partitions from the other quadrants. The two junior therapists occupied the other two quadrants of each cage, each therapist accompanied by its own surrogate.

For 2 weeks there was no possibility of isolate contact with any other animal, and no surrogate was available. The therapists, on the other hand, continued social interaction each of 5 days a week, as they had for the previous 2 months.

For the next 4 postisolation weeks, each isolate was allowed interaction with one therapist, the one who occupied the adjacent quadrant. Interaction was possible for 2 hours a day three times a week. As time progressed, members of each group were systematically rotated. After 4 weeks the next step involved a continuation of the previous step plus 1 hour a day the other 2 weekdays of interaction in the strange playroom between two pairs consisting of one patient and one therapist each.

The same very gradual increase in length of time, number participating, and playroom versus quad cage continued until all four in each quad cage were allowed constant interaction in the quad cage and pair-play by isolates and therapists in the playroom. The entire period of adaptation and therapy covered 28 weeks.

As had been postulated but not positively assumed, the gentle, younger therapists did not pose a threat to the unhappy isolates, as had the same-aged monkeys. Although the isolate cowered in corners at first, it did allow the soft, tentative clinging of the therapist, as shown in Figure 30. Physical contact became acceptable, and the first stage of the therapy was successful.

Successful therapy in the home cage and in the playroom was indicated by the progressive reduction of abnormal behaviors, such as self-clasp, huddle, rocking, and stereotypy (see Figures 31 and 32). All these infantile, maladaptive behaviors were progressively reduced under behavior therapy, and the frequency of these deviant derelictions fell to a normal level in the relatively strange playroom.

Although the decrease in frequency of abnormal behaviors is an indicator of rehabilitation, the most important measure of successful behavior therapy is that of the development of adequate, positive social behaviors, such as contact and, particularly, play. As illustrated in Figures 33 and 34, social contact and play by the 6-month isolates had approached normal levels in the quad cage environment by the end of the preplanned period of rehabilitation. Although frequency of play progressively increased throughout the planned 6-month period, it did not quite attain normal levels in the playroom.

Since there had been no rationale for the optional or necessary period of therapy, an additional 6-month period of behav-

FIGURE 30. Therapist monkey maintaining bodily contact with isolate.

Twelve-month isolate rehabilitation. The author had felt extremely skeptical that the severe social deficits created by 6 months of isolation living could be replaced by social graces. Even when the seemingly impossible had been accomplished, he felt that the obliteration of social behavior in 12-month isolate rhesus monkeys was so much more complete and devastating that rehabilitation was too much to expect.

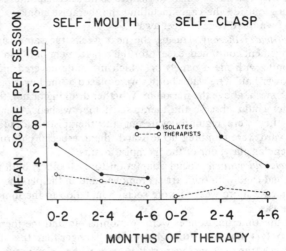

FIGURE 32. Playroom 6-month isolate therapy.

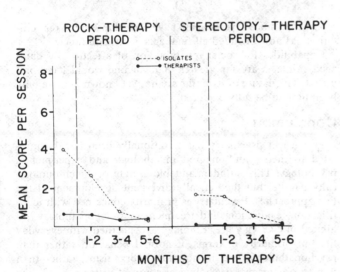

FIGURE 31. Quad cage 6-month isolate therapy.

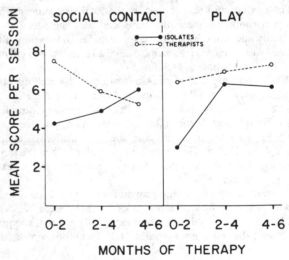

FIGURE 33. Quad cage 6-month isolate social behavior therapy.

ior therapy was instituted. At the end of the 12-month period of therapy, highly experienced observers could not distinguish behaviorally the isolates from the therapists while they played (see Figure 35), nor were there any statistical differences in their play behaviors.

Through accidents of time of birth and no fault of the experimenters, the four therapists were females and the four isolates were males. Normative monkey studies have shown that males and females play differently. Male play is rough, tough, and contactual; female monkey play is gentle, chasing, and basically noncontactual. The only play the female therapists could have taught the isolates was gentle, noncontact play, but, when the male monkeys were rehabilitated, their play was masculine contactual monkey play. Thus, when the males were converted to behavioral normality, they achieved their full heritage of monkey masculinity.

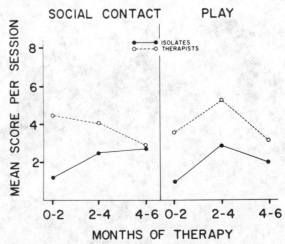

FIGURE 34. Playroom therapy, social contact, and play.

However, Novak and Harlow (1975)—through patient extension of the gradual adaptation to the new environment, use of a junior therapist even more relatively junior than heretofore, and the introduction of self-paced therapy—accomplished the feat beyond all expectations.

Cage adaptation. The first 2 postisolation weeks were spent in individual quadrants of a quad cage with outer walls of masonite. The newly emerged isolates could see each other but nothing outside the cage, including the therapist monkeys in their own quad cage 3½ feet away.

Self-paced therapy. During the next weeks the same cage arrangement continued, except for the replacement of the solid masonite with mesh panels on which masonite covered only the lower half. The water bottles were placed at the lower part of the mesh, above the masonite. Whether drinking or not, the isolates could observe the therapists if they wished. After a time they were regularly watching the therapists and soon afterward were climbing up to watch them, especially during the regular play hour of the therapist infants.

Social adaptation. Social adaptation to each other, both in the quad cage with the barriers removed and in the playroom, occupied 2 more weeks before social adaptation to the junior therapists.

At this time the isolates were 16 months old and the therapists only 4 months. Although 1 month younger than the first therapists, the new ones were still at an age when play was just beginning to burgeon.

The anxiety and fear caused by the total strangeness of the new environments, both the nonsocial and the social, were gradually alleviated by slow and separate familiarization of the isolates with each environment. Active adaptation was encouraged by the self-pacing technique.

When climbing walls, drinking water, and watching other monkeys play, the isolates found it difficult to indulge in self-directed maladaptive behavior, such as self-clasping, huddling, and rocking. Even before therapist interaction, positive adaptive responses began to replace the undesirable behaviors. Further acquisition of social behaviors evolved when the junior therapists led the way out of lonely retreat into the paths of play (see Figure 36).

The remaining prime requirement for completely convincing rehabilitation is the development of normal sexual behavior. In 14- to 20-month-old rhesus monkeys, isolate or not, adequate adult sex behavior is not assessible, but the author is pleased to

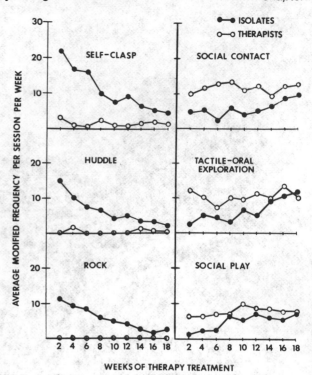

FIGURE 36.   Behaviors during total therapy period of 12-month isolates.

report that, since several years have now elapsed, the rehabilitation has now included all final acts, facts, and fancies.

Capabilities for social rehabilitation of affectionally damaged primates are far greater than anyone would have predicted. The nature of its limits are not yet known and are only beginning to be fully explored.

Conclusion

Practice in psychiatry has traditionally been largely unrelated to theory and method in ethology and experimental psychology. This is understandable in light of the chronologically parallel but theoretically divergent development of the two approaches. Psychiatry is primarily concerned with identification, evaluation, and treatment of psychopathology exhibited in everyday life. Ethology is concerned with everyday life but primarily in terms of normal behavior, rather than psychopathology, and in nonhuman organisms, rather than human organisms. Psychological study of primates may, like psychiatry, choose to focus on aberrant behavior but, unlike psychiatry, is more suited to laboratory settings.

The primate literature indicates that human psychotic infantile states can be simulated or produced with monkey or anthropoid subjects. This finding is interesting in view of the fact that at their intellectual maturity monkeys attain a human mental age of about 4 years in a comparison of their scores on Wisconsin General Test Apparatus learning tests with the scores of retarded human children.

Probably by coincidence, monkeys become intellectually mature, by monkey standards, at 4 years of chronological age, at about the same time that they are becoming sexually mature. In other words, from a maturational point of view, humans and monkeys become both intellectually mature and probably sexually mature at about the same time. Also coincidentally, the ratio is then reversed. Monkeys mature 4 times as fast, but the human primate reaches a level 4 times as great.

Psychiatry has now officially or unofficially accepted the

FIGURE 35.   Play pervades.

reality of childhood psychopathology. There is now an acceptance of anaclitic depression, symbiotic psychosis, and the double-bind syndrome. All these maladaptive behaviors are well within the human-type mental age of the macaque monkey.

It is a fundamental scientific rule that all developmental behaviors should be traced ontogenetically and even phylogenetically if possible. This is exactly what has not been done consistently in the creation of psychotic theories of many diverse types and by many diverse psychiatrists. These psychotic theories emerged from classifications made on human adults and adolescents. The analysis of senile gerontological, adult, and adolescent symptoms is not the way to create theoretical developmentally ordered psychiatry. The desired basis of pathological description is totally reversed and produces an ontogenetically oriented theory with time seen backward.

One may assume, as if it were a fact, that these childhood psychoses and some behaviors, such as parental child abuse and learned helplessness, for which psychiatry has as yet not appropriated specific names are among the basic psychoses. The long-accepted adolescent and adult psychotic disorders of Bleuler (1951) may be outgrowths of these or other childhood psychotic states. When considering the adult psychoses, one would then be looking at the fruit and not the seed.

Closer examination of the ethological and psychological data obtained from subhuman subjects reveals numerous areas of potential interest to psychiatric theory and practice. The ethologist's concern with basic social response patterns may point out relevant nonverbal components of any human interaction session, therapeutic sessions included. More important, careful experimentation using species closely related to humans may afford the therapist a better understanding of the variables that are capable of causing, characterizing, and ultimately curing a wide variety of psychopathologies not unrelated to the syndromes he faces daily.

Suggested Cross References

For a detailed discussion of the principles of learning, see Section 4.3. Normal child development is discussed in Section 34.2 and maternal deprivation in 43.1.

REFERENCES

Bateson, G., Jackson, D. D., Haley, J., and Weakland, J. Toward a theory of schizophrenia. Behav. Sci., *19:* 251, 1956.
Bijou, S. W. A study of "experimental neuroses" in the rat by the conditioned response technique. J. Comp. Psychol., *36:* 1, 1943.
Bleuler, E. P. *Textbook of Psychiatry.* Dover, New York, 1951.
* Bowlby, J. *Attachment and Loss,* Vol. I: *Attachment.* Basic Books, New York, 1969.
DeValois, R. L., and Jacobs, G. H. Primate color vision. Science, *162:* 533, 1968.
Elder, J. H. Auditory acuity of the chimpanzee. J. Comp. Psychol., *17:* 157, 1934.
Gantt, W. H. *Experimental Basis for Neurotic Behavior.* Paul B. Hoeber, New York, 1944.
Grether, W. F. A comparison of human and chimpanzee spectral hue discrimination curves. J. Exp. Psychol., *26:* 394, 1940.
Harlow, H. F., and Harlow, M. K. Effects of various mother-infant relationships on rhesus monkey behaviors. In *Determinants of Infant Behavior,* B. M. Foss, editor, vol. 4, p. 15. Methuen, London, 1969.
Harlow, H. F., and Novak, M. A. Psychopathological perspectives. Perspect. Biol. Med., *16:* 461, 1973.
Harlow, H. F., and Suomi, S. J. Production of depressive behaviors in young monkeys. J. Autism Child. Schizo., *1:* 246, 1971.
Hess, E. H. Imprinting: An effect of early experience. Science, *130:* 133, 1959.
Hinde, R. A. *Biological Bases of Human Social Behavior.* McGraw-Hill, New York, 1974.
Hinde, R. A., and Spencer-Booth, Y. Effects of brief separations from mother on rhesus monkeys. Science, *173:* 111, 1971.
* Jolly, A. *The Evolution of Primate Behavior.* Macmillan, New York, 1972.
Jones, B. C., and Clark, D. L. Mother-infant separation of squirrel monkeys living in a group. Dev. Psychobiol., *6:* 259, 1973.
Kanner, L. *Childhood Psychosis.* Winston & Sons, Washington D.C., 1973.

Kaplan, J. The effects of separation and reunion on the behavior of mother and infant squirrel monkeys. Dev. Psychobiol., *3:* 43, 1970.
Kaufman, I. C., and Rosenblum, L. A. Depression in infant monkeys separated from their mothers. Science, *155:* 1030, 1967.
Liddell, H. S. The experimental neurosis and the problem of mental disorder. Am. J. Psychiatry, *94,* 1938.
Lorenz, K. Der Kumpan in der Unwelt des Vogels. J. Ornithol., *83:* 137, 289, 1935.
* Mahler, M. S. On child psychosis and schizophrenia: Autistic and symbiotic infantile psychosis. Psychoanal. Study Child, *7:* 286, 1952.
More, T. *Utopia.* W. & J. Mackay, Chatham, 1965.
Morris, D., editor. *Primate Ethology.* Aldine, Publishing Co., Chicago, 1967.
* Novak, M. A., and Harlow, H. F. Social recovery of monkeys isolated for the first year of life. Dev. Psychol., *11:* 453, 1975.
Ostow, M. *Drugs in Psychoanalysis and Psychotherapy.* Basic Books, New York, 1962.
Pavlov, I. P. *Conditioned Reflexes: An Investigation of the Physiological Activity of the Cerebral Cortex,* G. V. Anrep, translator and editor. Oxford University Press, London, 1927.
Preston, D., Baker, R., and Seay, B. M. Mother-infant separation in the patas monkey. Dev. Psychol., *3:* 298, 1970.
Rowland, G. L. The Effect of Total Social Isolation upon Learning and Social Behavior in Rhesus Monkeys. Unpublished doctoral dissertation. University of Wisconsin, 1964.
Ruppenthal, G. C., Arling, G. L., Harlow, H. F., Sackett, G. P., and Suomi, S. J. A 10-yr. perspective of motherless-mother monkey behavior. J. Abnorm. Psychol., *85:* 341, 1976.
Schlottmann, R. S., and Seay, B. M. Mother-infant separation in the Java monkey (*Macaca irus*). J. Comp. Physiol. Psychol., *79:* 334, 1972.
Seay, B. M., Hansen, B. W., and Harlow, H. F. Mother-infant separation in monkeys. J. Child Psychol. Psychiatry, *3:* 123, 1962.
Seligman, M., and Maier, S. Failure to escape traumatic shock. J. Exp. Psychol., *74:* 1, 1967.
Spalding, D. A. Instinct with original observations on young animals. Br. J. Anim. Behav., *2:* 2, 1873.
* Spitz, R. A. Anaclitic depression. Psychoanal. Study Child, *2:* 313, 1946.
Suomi, S. J., Collins, M., and Harlow, H. F. Effects of permanent separation from mother on infant monkeys. Dev. Psychol., *9:* 376, 1973.
Suomi, S. J., and Harlow, H. F. Apparatus conceptualization for psychopathological research in monkeys. Behav. Res. Methods Instru., *1:* 247, 1969.
Suomi, S. J., and Harlow, H. F. Abnormal social behavior in young monkeys. In *Exceptional Infant: Studies in Abnormalities,* J. Hellmuth, editor, vol. 2, p. 483. Brunner/Mazel, New York, 1971.
Suomi, S. J., and Harlow, H. F. Depressive behavior in young monkeys. J. Comp. Physiol. Psychol., *180:* 11, 1972a.
Suomi, S. J., and Harlow, H. F. Social rehabilitation of isolate-reared monkeys. Dev. Psychol., *6:* 487, 1972b.
Suomi, S. J., Harlow, H. F., and Domek, C. J. Effect of repetitive infant-infant separation of young monkeys. J. Abnorm. Psychol., 76, 1970.
Suomi, S. J., Harlow, H. F., and Novak, M. A. Reversal of social deficits produced by isolation rearing in monkeys. J. Hum. Evol., *3:* 527, 1974.
* Tinbergen, E. A., and Tinbergen, N. Early childhood autism: An ethological approach. J. Comp. Ethol., *10* (Suppl.): 9, 1972.
Weinstein, B., and Grether, W. F. A comparison of visual acuity in the rhesus monkey and man. J. Comp. Psychol., *30:* 187, 1940.
White, N. F. *Ethology and Psychiatry.* University of Toronto Press, Toronto, 1974.
Wooley, M. J. The Effect of the Double Bind and Symbiotic Types of Surrogate Mothers on the Development of Infant Squirrel Monkeys (*Saimiti sciureus*). Unpublished doctoral dissertation. The University of Arizona, Tucson, 1977.

4.7 Communication and Psychiatry

JURGEN RUESCH, M.D.

Introduction

Communication is an organizing principle of nature that connects living creatures with one another. When a biological or social entity is equipped to register the impact of signals, to react selectively, and to emit signals in return, it is prepared to enter into communication with other entities. Communication is mediated through three basic properties of living matter: input (perception), central functions (decision making, memory), and output (expression, action). Each small unit, such as a cell, may combine with other units to make a larger entity; this larger organization, such as an organ, may combine with other organs to become an organism; several organisms may cluster together to form a social organization, such as a family; and different organizations make up a society. At each level of organization, one finds that input, central, and output functions of the larger system restrict the autonomy of the smaller system.

Definitions

The processes of communication are implemented through signals, signs, and symbols. A signal is an impulse in transit; when it impinges on sensory end organs, it serves as a stimulus that may generate a response. Signals have to be arranged in a certain order to be understood; this order, which must be shared by both sender and receiver, is called a code. Unwanted, randomly arranged signals are referred to as noise and are usually eliminated from consideration. When a receiver can attribute referential properties to a signal, it becomes a sign with problem-solving qualities. If vocal sounds—that is, speech—are used for communication, the code is referred to as language. The body of knowledge contained in the referential properties of signs is called information. A symbol is a physical mark, the referential property of which has been publicly agreed on; paintings, statues, and architectural structures are examples of such symbols.

The study of communication is shared by many different disciplines. Linguistics is concerned with speech and language; semantics is concerned with the referential property of signs and symbols; syntactics is concerned with the relationship of signals, signs, and symbols to each other; and the relationship of a sign to its user is the domain of pragmatics. The whole field related to signals, signs, and symbols has been summarized under the heading of semiotics. In the 19th century the study of language and communication was considered a humanistic field, but in the 20th century the development of electrical engineering led to the construction of sophisticated communication machinery, with the result that by the end of the century the subject of communication began to dominate science, engineering, and public life. However, millenia of slow evolution preceded these events.

Evolution of Human Communication

PALEONTOLOGY

The development of language has been intimately tied to the invention of writing. But before writing could develop, there had to be speech; and before speech there had to be organized action. The first evidence of human organization is based on the discovery of human skeletons buried together with implements of various kinds. These earliest remains of human material culture are made up almost entirely of crude articles of stone. Although some doubts exist as to the identification and dating of these early findings, those attributed to the Pleistocene, around 600,000 B.C., preclude the possibility that they are accidental freaks of nature. In the middle Paleolithic, roughly between 150,000 and 75,000 B.C., appeared Neanderthal man, whose remains are associated with outspoken flint points, a developed bone industry, burial grounds, and evidence of the use of fire. From findings in burial mounds, anthropologists concluded that Neanderthal man of the Mousterian culture could talk, although the limited space near the floor of the jaw where the tongue muscles are attached indicates that he could not talk very well. In the past 50,000 years, finally emerged *Homo sapiens*, who hunted with a bow, engraved tools, lived in caves, and decorated the walls with drawings and paintings known today as the Ice Age art or the Arctic and Spanish Levant art.

ARCHEOLOGY

Between the appearance of cave art and the invention of writing, centuries of careful observation and painstaking recording of the rising and setting of the sun must have occurred. In Egypt, Karnak's principal avenue was laid out in such a way that at the time of the summer solstice the setting sun shone directly into it; in Stonehenge, England, the alignment of shadows cast by certain stones indicated the beginning of the new year. The Mesopotamian moon timekeepers, with their 360-day year and twelve 30-day months, and the Egyptian sun timekeepers, with their 365½-day year, must have had ways of noting down their observations, otherwise these structures could not have been erected. Unfortunately, the records of these early astronomers have not come down to us.

HISTORY OF WRITING

However, one can infer that tens of thousands of years must have elapsed between the beginning of speech and the first appearance of the cuneiform writing of the Sumerians, a people who lived in the Mesopotamian valley between 4000 and 300 B.C. Almost as old are the records of the Akkadian language of the Babylonians and Assyrians who invaded the Sumerian territory around 3000 B.C. Of somewhat more recent origin are the scriptures of the ancient Chinese and the hieroglyphics of the Egyptians, that date back to about 2000 B.C., and those of the Mayas and Aztecs that have been placed around the 1st century A.D.

Primitive systems of writing originally consisted of simple pictorial designs denoting an object or person. But because such a pictograph could not satisfactorily denote actions or ideas, several pictographs were combined into an ideograph to signify more abstract notions. Regardless of the language spoken, pictorial writing enabled ancient people of different cultures to communicate with each other. Pictographs and ideographs are by no means defunct. Contemporary Chinese script developed from pictorial representation, much as did some of the modern technical denotation systems, such as the floral diagrams of botanists, the wiring diagrams of electricians, and the action symbols used in modern comic strips.

The limitations inherent in pictorial writing must have induced ancient scholars to look for better denotation systems. Thus, the people living near the Euphrates, the Tigris, and the Nile discovered that the vocal sounds used for the designation of persons, objects, and actions provide a more convenient basis for writing. The step from pictorial to phonetic denotation probably was taken after 2000 B.C., and the perfection of the phonetic alphabet was left to the Phoenicians and the Hebrews; the system was later adopted by the Greeks and the Romans. Early phonetic writing consisted of engravings on stone or metal; at the time of Moses, tablets of wood or of lead coated with wax were used; thereafter came writing with liquid inks on such surfaces as papyrus, linen, and vellum. Although phonetic systems of writing are generally accurate, simple, and fast, they have a limitation in that they can be understood only by the people who speak the same language. As phonetic denotation became generally accepted, it began to exercise a controlling influence on language and thinking in that the word defined the manner in which events were dissected. In the early days of the phonetic era, the art of writing was practiced by scribes and priests, who thus controlled the cumulative body of knowledge of mankind. This monopoly continued until the invention of the printing press in 1440 A.D. which marked the beginning of a more universal literacy.

EMERGENCE OF THE MASS MEDIA

Print was the first among the mass media, but its use required the ability to read. Thus, it was in the interest of the publisher to foster literacy. From the 16th to the 18th centuries, books were still largely written for the educated few. The introduction of compulsory education in the 19th century, however, enlarged the number of readers. In the 19th century the invention of telegraphy (1832), photography (1839), telephone (1876), motion pictures (1889), and, in the 20th century, television (1926) completed the list of communication devices making up the mass media. Together with the printing press, these gadgets facilitated the separation of the word from its author, and any text or recorded speech could now be edited or altered by third parties at will. This opportunity gave the image-making industry new powers and served as a political tool in exerting influence and control over the population.

CYBERNETICS AND THE INFORMATION SCIENCES

The theoretical advances made in electrical engineering significantly influenced other fields; although servomechanisms were known since 1868, when Maxwell published his treatise on the governor of the steam engine—a device that keeps the speed of the machine constant—it was not until 1943 that this principle was applied to biological processes. In 1948 Wiener published his book entitled *Cybernetics, or Control and Communication in the Animal and the Machine,* and in the same year Shannon contributed his mathematical theory of communication, which laid the foundations for a quantitative formulation of the concept of information. These theoretical contributions cleared the way for the introduction of the digital computer—a machine that can perceive, scan, retain, and process information; deliver computations; control other machines; and make decisions. The unprecedented growth of the computer sciences in the past 25 years has established the computer's position as an auxiliary brain.

Theory

HUMAN COMMUNICATION APPARATUS

The human communication apparatus is composed of sense organs that serve as receivers; of effector organs that constitute the sender; of the brain, which processes information, including the functions of scanning, memory, computation, and decision making; and of the body, the shelter of the communication apparatus. Sensory end organs are stations of signal transformation. Phylogenetically oldest are the chemical and mechanical end organs (smell, taste, touch, pain, temperature, vibration), which serve as proximity receivers. Phylogenetically younger are the more complex distance receivers found in the visual and auditory end organs. The proximity receivers serve as exteroceptors and proprioceptors, and the distance receivers function primarily as exteroceptors. Signal transformation occurs in the sensory end organs when outside stimuli are transformed into muscular contractions. Stations of transformation are also located at the boundaries of cells and organs, where signals are transformed for transmission within a given tissue. The organism possesses a dual communication system: In the nervous system, impulses move quickly to their destination through specialized pathways; in the humoral system, chemical impulses travel more slowly through the vascular system; cells and tissues selectively retrieve chemical compounds out of the content of the blood stream, and these compounds serve as signals for the regulation of bodily functions.

CODIFICATION

Codes are devices that embody signals. There exist two fundamentally different systems: The analogue system rests on some similarities in shape, color, or proportion to the events it purports to represent; the digital system is purely arbitrary in that a number or letter is assigned to a given event and a legend has to indicate what these signs refer to. Nonverbal communication rests on the analogue principle and verbal codification on the digital principle. The inner experience of

what is going on at any moment involves nonverbal images that in some way reflect the total situation. Bodily movements and spontaneous, immediate reactions require an analogical appreciation of events. The human being thus develops internally a small-scale model of the world based on the recognition of similarities or differences. This method is used for gaining a bird's-eye view of events and for implementing quick reactions necessary for survival. But when a person has time to analyze a situation, words or numbers are assigned to complex events, specifying details without recourse to analogies. In complex human encounters, both verbal and nonverbal communication are used; the objective parts of the message tend to be expressed in words, and the subjective parts tend to be expressed nonverbally.

In right-handed people, digital codification has been localized primarily in the left hemisphere of the brain, where the speech centers are located. Because of the characteristics of the ear, words and numbers can be perceived only one after another. In a more abstract sense, then, the left hemisphere of the brain has been said to control successive order. Analogue codification, in contrast, has been assigned to the right hemisphere. Here, pattern recognition is based on the simultaneous perception of many features involving primarily visual functions. Simultaneous order hence is said to be controlled from the right hemisphere in right-handed people (Galin, 1974).

METACOMMUNICATION

The term "metacommunication" refers to the instructions and interpretative devices that indicate the ways in which a message ought to be interpreted. Metalanguage is more subtle, the rules governing its application are more open ended, and its effectiveness varies with the skill of the participants. Drama students are trained to read the same passage first as a comedy, then as a tragedy, and finally as a reportage. These variations of interpretation are modulated through nonverbal expressions that go along with the words. A child masters the variations of metacommunication when there exists consistent contact with family members through the different contexts and situations to which he is exposed. Patients with brain disease, depressed persons, schizophrenics, and compulsive characters have difficulty with the variations of metacommunication, and, therefore, their human relations suffer.

FEEDBACK

The output of the organism consists of verbal or gestural expressions and of silent action. When the effects of a statement or an action are observed and the information is incorporated at the source, the process is referred to as feedback. Both the behavior of organisms and the performance of machines are regulated by feedback. Whereas the process of negative feedback reduces the magnitude and the direction of the ongoing process, positive feedback increases the existing tendencies of the system. Steady states are achieved when change is kept to a minimum. Feedback thus exercises control—a function that is not localized in any particular part of the network but depends on the circular relay of messages. It equips people with an informational model of internal and external events that is the basis for decision making and for the control of action.

SUCCESSFUL COMMUNICATION

The establishment of concordant information between participants can be conceived of as successful communication, whereas the establishment of discordant information can be viewed as unsuccessful communication. The pleasure that persons derive from well-functioning communication constitutes the driving force that induces them to seek and maintain human relations. Frustrating communication, in contrast, manifests itself by increasing symptom formation and frequently induces persons to withdraw from the ill-functioning network. The processes of communication, hence, have to be conceived of in circular terms; they are characterized by self-corrective devices, the establishment of repetitive patterns, the presence of purposive or seeking aspects, and the maximization or minimization of certain features bearing on the maintenance of a steady state at a fairly high level of orderliness. In such systems, part functions are always functions of the systems as a whole, and the chains of causation are at least circular if not more complex. For source material bearing on the history and theory of communication, see Table I.

Nonverbal Communication

GENERAL CHARACTERISTICS

Nonverbal communication includes all the silent movements used for signaling and the traces of movements left on objects and those incorporated in sketches, paintings, and sculptures. Nonverbal denotation is the method of choice for indicating simultaneous order and for outlining boundaries, contiguities, overlaps, and similar relationships. It is also ideal for indicating the timing of action at any given moment, but it is inadequate for describing elapsed time. Because nonverbal denotation is based on self-evident analogies, it is suitable as an international, intercultural, interracial, and interspecies language. It can be used for communication with the out-group when agreed-on meanings have not been established.

COGNITION

Nonverbal denotation can be appreciated by distance and proximity receivers alike. For example, action may be seen, heard, and perceived by the other senses as well; it influences individual perception, decision making, and expression, but it does not have a significant impact on language. The understanding of nonverbal denotation is based on the participant's empathic assessment of similarities and differences; thus, pain, anxiety, rage, pleasure, excitement, and most other emotions of humans and animals can be appreciated without further explanations.

TABLE I
General References on Communication

Topic	Description	Source
Early contributions	Anthologies, including mathematical, linguistic, social, and technical aspects of communication	Smith, 1966 Matson and Montagu, 1967
Later contributions	Review articles on various aspects of the communication sciences	Miller, 1973
Textbook	The study of human communication with bibliography	Lin, 1973
	Interpersonal communication	Patton and Giffin, 1974
Perspective	The functions of human communication	Dance and Larson, 1976
Moral issues	Ethical and moral considerations	Thayer, 1973
Social issues	Communications technology and social policy	Gerbner et al., 1973
Cognition	Image formation and cognition	Horowitz, 1970
	Perception, decision making, and stress	Broadbent, 1971
Memory	Short-term and long-term memory	Klatzky, 1975 Cofer, 1975
Neurosciences	Languages of the brain	Pribram, 1971
	Physics and mathematics of the nervous system	Conrad et al., 1974
	Hemisphere specialization	Weinstein and Friedland, 1977
Theory	The social matrix of psychiatry	Ruesch and Bateson, 1968
	Theoretical contributions	Bateson, 1972
	Semiotic approaches to psychiatry	Shands, 1970
	Axioms, premises, and paradoxical communication	Watzlawick et al., 1967
	Feedback	Wiener, 1961
Communication engineering	Evolution of computers	Davis, 1977
	Computer models and artificial intelligence	Weizenbaum, 1976
	Systems analysis and planning	Ackoff and Sasieni, 1968

EXPRESSION

Nonverbal expressions are mediated by both smooth and striated muscles. In contrast to verbal communication, which involves only the vocal apparatus, nonverbal communication may be carried out by a large number of skeletal muscles, such as those used in controlling body posture, movements of the extremities, and secretions of glands. Studies of behavior in patients with brain lesions point to separate neuronal pathways for nonverbal and verbal expressions, as evidenced in certain cases of aphasia and apraxia. The semantic, lexical, grammatical, and syntactical aspects of nonverbal communication are not rigidly controlled; therefore, nonverbal codification permits redundancy. For these reasons, it is used for emotional appeal and for the expression of feelings and sentiments, allowing for a great range of individual variation. Nonverbal codification does not refer to isolated or abstract aspects of events. It is not based on a subject-predicate dichotomy, with all its analytic features, but always refers to the totality of an event.

SIGN LANGUAGE

Not all bodily movements serve as analogue codification devices. The sign language of the American Indians, of the deaf, and of construction workers have the same arbitrary and discrete characteristics that words and numbers have. These signals have previously agreed-on meanings, the participants have a dictionary or legend for their interpretation, and, although the signals are nonvocal, they have all the lexical characteristics of verbal or digital codification. For source material bearing on nonverbal communication, see Table II.

Verbal Communication

GENERAL CHARACTERISTICS

The biological foundations of verbal denotation are mostly associated with the phylogenetically young structures of the brain, particularly the cortex. A person learns verbal communication only after nonverbal denotation has been mastered. The spoken or printed word is perceived by the distance receivers. Words can only be heard or seen; they cannot be touched, smelled, or tasted. Verbal codification lends itself to information storage, facilitates information retrieval, influences thinking, and is essential for planning. Thus, logic is inconceivable without digital or verbal denotation. Mastery of verbal communication requires decades of training, particularly because the referential property of words is based on prior agreements that differ from culture to culture and from group to group.

SERIAL ALIGNMENT

No number or letter can be broken down further. For example, there does not exist a meaningful subdivision of the printed letter A or the digit 7. Verbal and digital codifications are arbitrary and discontinuous, and the printed marks have a discrete beginning and end. Inasmuch as verbal denotation consists of a serial alignment of signals, simultaneous events must be listed successively. In addition, words have to be spoken at a given speed; when produced too slowly or too quickly, they become unintelligible. Written words, however, may be reproduced in large or small print and may be read

TABLE II
References on Nonverbal Communication

Topic	Description	Source
History	The origins of language	Revesz, 1956
	Gesture language	Tylor, 1964
	From cave painting to comic strip	Hogben, 1949
Paralinguistics and kinesics	Research guide and bibliography	Key, 1977
Anthology	The rhetoric of nonverbal communication	Bosmajian, 1971
Facial expression	A century of research	Ekman, 1973
	Interpretation of facial expression	Ekman and Friesen, 1975
Gesture	Varieties of gestures	Critchley, 1975
Kinesics	Communication by means of movements	Birdwhistell, 1970
Body language	Communication as behavioral control	Scheflen, 1972
	Interaction	Scheflen, 1974
	Bodily communication	Argyle, 1975
Human sounds	Communication of emotions	Ostwald, 1973
Technology	Nonverbal thought in technology	Ferguson, 1977
Action	Knowledge preparatory for action	Ruesch, 1975
Theory	Gesture, posture, situational context, and traces of action	Ruesch and Kees, 1972

slowly or rapidly. Verbal denotation is clumsy when used to indicate spatial arrangements, except for the description of boundaries. It is also unsuitable for indicating timing and coordination, but it is excellent for indicating elapsed time and for referring to the past or the future.

REFERENTIAL PROPERTY OF WORD OR NUMBER

Since words have no other function than to serve as signs or symbols, the intent of those using words to communicate is unmistakable. However, verbal codification is not economical and often requires long-winded statements. Words exert an intellectual appeal and are suitable for reaching agreements. Most words refer to things that can be heard and seen or about which humans can think. Words and their definitions are listed in the dictionary of any language. But those events that are perceived by means of the mechanical and chemical proximity receivers—that is, touch, smell, taste, pain, and temperature—have hardly any verbal representation at all. For example, there are no specific words for the designation of smell, and only four words—sweet, sour, salty, and bitter—for describing taste. Because verbal codification is best suited for distance communication, it has a vocabulary that primarily refers to events that occur in the world around us. The vocabulary for events occurring inside the organism and referring to bodily experiences, in contrast, is considerably smaller. For these reasons, artists often resort to nonverbal expression to represent inner experience. The poet relies on the rhythmical and sound qualities of words in addition to their lexical meaning, and the painter uses color and shape to convey feelings and emotions. For source material bearing on verbal communication, see Table III.

Development of Communication

Ontogeny repeats phylogeny, and the history of communication of the human race is repeated in the development of the child. When the baby gets familiar with the breast, the bottle, or the rattle, the first appreciation of the thing itself occurs. With the development of vision and hearing and, later on, of locomotion, comes the appreciation of space. Corresponding to the historical period of pictorial writing, the 2- or 3-year-old child looks at picture books and realizes that the images stand for something that is not there. Soon the first attempts at writing take the place of drawing. When the child enters school, digital codification, phonetic writing, and the syntactical rules of grammar are taught. But the learning of communication and interaction takes almost two additional decades to master completely.

INFANCY

In utero the fetus is in a state of contiguity with the mother and is shielded from external stimuli, but at birth the newborn is suddenly exposed to all the stimuli emanating from the surroundings. At first, the baby does not react to sounds of minimal intensity; however, almost every external stimulus of more than minimal intensity tends to produce defensive reactions—for example, the head may be thrown back and turned, the hands of the mother may be pushed away, the nipple may be forced out of the mouth, or screaming or crying may prevent feeding. Auditory stimuli, in particular, produce negative movements of expression that may continue throughout the first 3 months of postnatal life. Gradually, a more positive

TABLE III
References on Verbal Communication, Language, and Speech

Topic	Description	Source
History	The story of language	Pei, 1965
Biology	The biological foundations of language	Lenneberg, 1967
Human development	Infant speech	Lewis, 1975
	The language and thought of the child	Piaget, 1962
Perception	A procedural approach to word meaning	Miller and Johnson-Laird, 1976
Semiosis	Signals, signs, and symbols	Morris, 1971
Speech	Speech communication	Dance, 1972
General semantics	The meaning of language	Hayakawa, 1972
Mass media	The understanding of radio, television, and other media	McLuhan, 1973

response sets in. At 4 weeks of age the infant quiets down when picked up; at 8 weeks he smiles at the sight of a face; and at 16 weeks he recognizes his mother. Expression occurs through nonverbal means, but specialized movements are still very limited; the child speaks with his whole body. As long as sucking, biting, and clutching are the only available expressions, communication by necessity is interpersonal and is carried on at close range. By movements of her hand, through rocking motions of the whole body, and by manipulation of the nipple, a mother conveys messages to her baby; through sucking, biting, crying, and smiling, the baby responds. In the first few months of life, the infant changes from a sensory reactor to a social organism. In the third month of life, positive expressional movements—such as glowing eyes, arms outstretched toward an object, and smiling—and such vocalizations as crowing, shouting, babbling, and laughter show a marked increase. By the time the child is 5 months old, he dislikes being left alone and cries when people leave; toward the end of the first year, the relationship to the mother has become highly personalized.

In early infancy the child depends on the muscular assistance of the adult, and his incomplete and undifferentiated movements are interpreted and complemented by the parents. A crying baby sets in motion a whole sequence of supportive, parental actions. Conversely, the adult creates the situations in which the infant can practice his limited movements. In the early stages of communication, the mother interprets silence, sleep, and expressions of satisfaction as affirmative responses and crying as a negative response. Although speech gradually takes on more and more importance, communication mediated through action continues to predominate. When locomotion develops, the child's statements may be expressed through creeping, walking, and running. In this concrete and immediate type of communication, one message follows another, reception alternates with transmission, impact is immediately observed, and feedback or correction follows closely.

DEVELOPMENT OF SPEECH

The first infant sounds use only large muscle groups and do not require any particular shaping of the tongue. Later, specialized movements require use of the mandible, the lips, and the tip of the tongue; subsequently, movements develop that involve the soft palate and the back of the tongue. The child first learns to produce sounds that range in pitch and intensity with the words or phrases used; only later does the infant learn to add meaningful plosive, sibilant, and fricative noises produced by articulation. The first words to be developed are primitive interjections, followed by nouns, action verbs, and adjectives. Most normal children, even those who develop late, have begun to speak by the time they are $3^1/_2$ years old; all speech sounds have developed by the time the child is 7. The 8-year-old uses language fluently, is interested in reading, listens to verbal accounts, begins to use codes and secret languages, experiences ideas, and is capable of verbally localizing bodily complaints. The development of speech and the coordination of sensory and motor components are more or less completed within the first decade of life, together with mastery of bodily balance and the execution of fine muscular movements. At the age of 18, most anatomical structures of the body have reached a point of maturation beyond which they will not noticeably progress, except for the hardening of the cartilaginous parts of the larynx, which process continues well into the adult years.

CHILDHOOD

During the third, fourth, and fifth years of life, the child goes through the oedipal period, in which the old dyadic relationship with the mother is replaced by a triadic relationship with both parents. When the child enters nursery school, kindergarten, or the first grade, an entirely new situation has to be mastered; now the child has to learn to get along with the peer group. Almost all of the next 10 years are spent in mastering the art of communicating in a group, learning the rules that govern the organization, and becoming familiar with the multiple roles that have to be assumed. During the grade-school years, the child gets used to the fact that correction of information may be delayed and that replies are sometimes completely missing. This transition from interpersonal to group communication is gradual. At first, the child's participation in group activities occurs for only brief periods of time. Children under 5 have been observed associating in groups of two or three other children for anywhere from 10 to 40 minutes. With children between 5 and 7, the time span may range from 1 to 3 hours, increasing as they get older. Gradually, the assistance given by the adult involves more and more information and less and less direct action. Thus, around the time of adolescence, the gradual switch from nonverbal to verbal communication seems to have been completed. Communication through silent action is being relinquished; instead, verbal, gestural, and symbolic means of communication predominate.

ADOLESCENCE AND YOUNG ADULTHOOD

In adolescence one-half to two-thirds of all youths between 11 and 17 belong to groups. Although group communication reaches its peak during this period, interpersonal communication reminiscent of the first few years of life is resumed with new vigor; however, instead of involving one parent, the adolescent now relates to members of the opposite sex and to slightly older members of the same sex. When the adolescent becomes a young adult, a new procedure of communication must be learned. This time, inclusion into the working process involves communication with persons of differing ages, statuses, backgrounds, and occupations. It may take several more years to learn these varied approaches, and only after the person has become a parent and has learned to understand the infant's and the child's way of relating may communicative maturity be reached. In adult life, nonverbal communication is retained to denote events for which words are inadequate or for metacommunicative instruction of the other person. Matters pertaining to the emotions of the participants, their state of health, or the urgency of the situation are particularly suitable for nonverbal expression.

MIDDLE AGE AND OLD AGE

In the fourth and fifth decades of life, another change in relationships occurs. At this age, persons do not strive so much for the acquisition of information as for the use of communication to solidify their position of control. From roles concerned with input and output, they switch to roles that involve decision making for other people. In the sixth and seventh decades, people begin to protect themselves from excessive stimulation, fatigue, and exhaustion; positions of responsibility are gradually relinquished; and reminiscences of past events become more significant than is planning for the future. The mastery of new symbolization systems at this age is unlikely, but the use of previously learned systems is at its peak. Those who possess communicative skills can enjoy relationships well into the eighth and ninth decades of life.

Analysis of a Communication System

In the analysis of a network, the expert focuses on the following features.

COMMUNICATING PERSONS

A communication system is made up of at least two persons who are equipped to receive and send messages. Technically, each person is characterized by input facilities involving perception and cognition; by central functions involving scanning (recognition), data processing (thinking), and information storage (memory), enabling the person to make decisions; and by output facilities involving verbal and nonverbal expression and action.

CONNECTING PROCESSES

The paths along which messages travel define the network. The language used indicates the way the messages are encoded. The metacommunicative instructions are used by the participants to indicate how the messages are to be interpreted. The content analysis indicates what the messages refer to. Feedback consists of the observation of the impact that a message or an action has had and subsequent correction of the body of information. Finally, repetitive communicative processes weld the various persons into small groups, which can be combined into larger groups.

SCIENTIFIC OBSERVER

The analysis of an ongoing exchange is not complete unless the observer is included in the system. If he is a basic scientist, he may engage in unobtrusive observation; if he is a manager, he focuses primarily on the effects achieved; if he is a therapist, he focuses on breakdowns and their prevention. Treatment involves interference with the bodily integrity of a person, an activity that requires a university degree and a license; management, in contrast, may be learned on the job and, though requiring experience, is not subject to licensing.

ANALYSIS OF A FUNCTIONING NETWORK

The analysis of a small group network can be accomplished by finding answers to the following questions (Ruesch, 1972a):

Who says or does...?	Position, identity, role, status
What...?	Content of message or specification of action
For which reasons...?	Motivation, rewards
With what intent...?	Anticipated response or effect
Under what rules...?	Regulated by law, agreed on, improvised
To whom...?	Position, identity, role, status
By what means...?	Face-to-face, discussion, written, telegram, telephone, public address system, silent action
In what code...?	Type of language, form of speech, nature of action
Where...?	Context or location of exchange
When...?	Present or future
For how long and how often...?	Duration, frequency
With what intensity...?	Magnitude, dimension
With what effect...?	Reversible and irreversible changes

ASSESSMENT OF A NONFUNCTIONING SYSTEM

Many professionals are called on to consult with, make decisions for, and render practical help to persons, groups, and organizations. They are called on when a crisis arises, when a person has a behavioral problem, and when a group disintegrates. In other words, they are called in when a network has become nonfunctional. The assessment of a nonfunctional system has been outlined by Ruesch (1975) and focuses on the following points:

Step 1. The problem: Who has become a problem, for whom, in what matter, when, and where? What kind of assistance is being asked for?

Step 2. The label: What label should be placed on the problem at hand, and what consequences does such a decision entail?

Step 3. The problem population: What are the characteristics of the persons who need assistance?

Step 4. The problem situation: What features characterize the problem situation, and what brings about, stabilizes, or resolves the existing situation?

Step 5. The tolerance limits: What is the range of acceptable behavior in this particular social system, and what are its tolerance limits?

Step 6. The resources: What kinds of physical, institutional, economic, and manpower resources are available for remedial action?

Step 7. The expectations: What kind of help is acceptable to the victims, and what kind of help is the social system ready to give?

Step 8. The intervention: What kind of help is relevant, and who should administer it, when, where, and for how long?

Step 9. Instruction and preparation: How should the personnel be instructed to give the required help? How should the problem population be prepared to accept the help?

Step 10. Preventive measures: Can a recurrence of such a situation be prevented by medical, psychotherapeutic, or organizational means?

Once the observer has gained an overview of the network, knows the participating persons, and understands the message exchange, he can proceed with the remedial task of improving the communications of the participants.

The psychiatrist normally deals with small networks, composed of two or more people up to perhaps eight or 10 (family size), but the engineer and the business manager have to cope with networks of corporate size, as do the military commander and the government official. Operations research, which is based in part on general systems theory, is aimed at establishing computer models of these large systems.

Disturbed Communication

DISTURBANCES ASSOCIATED WITH DISEASES OF THE ORGANS OF COMMUNICATION

Disturbances of communication are detected through medical examination of the sensorium, of the cranial nerves, of mobility, and of coordination. A psychiatric mental status examination reveals disorders of consciousness, perception, expression, speech, and judgment.

Conditions affecting input functions. The sensory end organs and the afferent nerve fibers mediate the input functions of human communications. Therefore, infectious, toxic, degenerative, traumatic, and neoplastic conditions and congenital malformations can alter or obstruct input. Among these disturbances one finds defects of the sensory end organs, primarily the ear and the eye, leading to partial or complete deafness or blindness; afflictions of the sensory cranial nerves—particularly of the olfactory (I), optic (II), trigeminal (V), facial (VII), and acoustic (VIII) nerves— leading to difficulties of sensation and perception; afflictions of the peripheral nerves and of the long, afferent fibers of the spinal cord and brain, which may affect the sensations of touch, pain, temperature, and vibration.

Conditions affecting output functions. The output of the human communication apparatus is mediated by the motor system, with its efferent neurons, muscles, and glands. Among the disorders that alter output are afflictions of the motor cranial nerves, particularly of the oculomotor (III), trochlear (IV), abducens (VI), facial (VII), glossopharyngeal (IX), vagus (X), accessory (XI), and hypoglossal (XII) nerves. These nerves control, among other things, the movements of the eye, the face, the pharynx, the tongue, and the vocal cords. Output is also altered by disorders of the efferent fibers of the central and peripheral nervous systems. These disorders alter muscle tone and motor strength and occasionally give rise to involuntary movements. The disorders may interfere with the ability to carry out voluntary movements.

Both sensory and motor defects influence a person's ability to speak, to express self through silent movements, to react promptly and appropriately, and to behave in a coordinated fashion.

Conditions affecting central functions. The central part of the human communication system serves to connect input with output, to regulate the magnitude of excitation, to accelerate or retard responses, to store and recall information, to process data, and to make decisions. Among the integrative functions are (1) the reflex, the impairment of which interferes with prompt reaction to external and internal stimuli; (2) the cerebellar functions that control body balance and coordination; afflictions of the cerebellum and its afferent and efferent pathways produce abnormalities of muscle tone and speech, nystagmus, ataxia, tremor, and difficulties in alternating movements; (3) the cortical functions that control the interpretation of sense data in the area of sight, hearing, and touch; afflictions of these functions result in visual, auditory, and tactile agnosia; the cortical functions that control purposive movements, when affected in the absence of paralysis, lead to apraxia; (4) the cortical functions that control spoken or written language and gesture and coordinate auditory and visual input with vocal and other skeletal movements; central disturbances of these functions lead to aphasia.

In acute afflictions of the cortex, the over-all responsiveness of the person diminishes; he loses alertness, cannot follow instructions, may become drowsy or stuporous, and may fall into a coma. Under these circumstances his consciousness is said to be altered. Cortical impairment also affects the regulation of emotional responses in that previously restrained expression may come to the fore in an uninhibited way.

In the presence of diffuse brain lesions, the intellectual functions suffer. Recall of recent events (short-term memory) is more affected than is the recall of events of earlier years (long-term memory). Performance in terms of reaction time, speed, and accuracy is impaired. The ability to make sound decisions deteriorates inasmuch as information processing becomes defective.

Aphasia, agnosia, and apraxia. The classical examples of language disorders are the aphasias, in which a variety of sensory and motor functions are disturbed. On the input side, the understanding of words may be affected, as in word deafness; on the output side, there may exist an inability to express words, as in Broca's cortical motor aphasia; or the difficulty may involve the ability to recall words, as in amnestic or nominal aphasia. More involved lesions may produce a central aphasia, in which both receptive and expressive disturbances are involved. In agnosia there exists a failure of recognition. This failure may involve the tactile sense, hearing, vision, and the appreciation of space, object, or color. In agnosic alexia the patient fails to recognize written language, although he retains the ability to write; in alexia with agraphia the ability to write is also lost. In apraxias the ability to perform purposive movements is impaired. In ideomotor apraxia the idea of a movement cannot be translated into action; in constructional apraxia the spatial disposition of action is disordered.

DISTURBANCES ASSOCIATED WITH LANGUAGE AND SPEECH DISORDERS

The mind is located in the head, and speech and language are considered the royal road to the mind. Consequently, deviant usage of language has for centuries been used as an indication of mental derangement. However, speech and language do not stand in a simple one-to-one relationship to intrapsychic processes; the relationship is far more complex. Although abnormal behavior may be expressed through an unusual vocabulary, more often than not it is the sequential order and the quantitative features that betray the presence of pathology; timing and spacing are as much a function of language and speech as they are a function of silent action.

Speech therapists and speech clinics encounter a wide variety of disturbances. Among these are central nervous system-related speech difficulties (aphasia, apraxia, agnosia); reading and writing disorders subsumed under the heading of dyslexia; peripheral nervous system-related speech difficulties (dysarthria); vocal cord disorders (dysphonia, aphonia); cleft palate and other congenital malformations affecting speech; stuttering and stammering. Interpersonal communication is seriously interfered with if words cannot be pronounced or articulated. When accessory noises, mannerisms, or unusual intonations call attention to the production of speech sounds, the attention of the participants is deflected from the content and focuses on the mechanics of speech of the handicapped person; as a result, interaction slows down, the exchange loses spontaneity, and corrective feedback suffers.

Those who are afflicted by diseases of the speech apparatus and who cannot express themselves can now be helped by specific prostheses. Stroke victims suffering from certain forms of aphasia and people suffering from diseases affecting the vocal cords can avail themselves of machines that translate typed words into speech. The patient types the desired words on an electronic keyboard; these words are then displayed on a video screen and read by a microcomputer that activates a speech synthesizer. One such machine is being developed by Kenneth Colby of the Neuropsychiatric Institute at the University of California, Los Angeles. A commercially available speech synthesizer, the Phonic Mirror HandiVoice, which has a self-contained vocabulary of 500 to 1,000 words and is portable, is made by the American Hospital Supply Corporation in Evanston, Illinois.

Those who have visual difficulties are usually cut off from input that derives from printed sources. Indeed, inability to read is one of the great handicaps of the blind. But modern electronics can now compensate for this particular disability. A television camera is used to scan the print along a page; the input is fed to a minicomputer that analyzes the words and activates a mechanical voice device capable of speaking up to 200 words a minute. One of these machines is made by Telesensory Systems, Inc., in Palo Alto, California. For the latest information on these prostheses, one can write to the U.S. Department of Health, Education, and Welfare.

DISTURBANCES ASSOCIATED WITH DEFICIENT INFORMATION PROCESSING

If a person does not have the information necessary to carry out an action, is inept at obtaining information from others, has not tested the correctness of information in action, or has an emotional problem regarding certain subjects, disturbances of communication may develop. The professional does best to observe these disturbances in the social situation in which they occur. He may discover any of the following difficulties: (1) inaccurate or faulty observation of self and others, with the result that erroneous information is fed into the decision-making process; (2) difficulties with the use of printed information (reading difficulties, inability to scan, attitudinal mistrust of written or printed words); (3) inability to follow spoken instructions or to take orders; (4) inability to combine information derived from the proximity receivers with information derived from the distance receivers, usually resulting in a disregard for one or the other set of information; (5) inability to cope with contradictory information arising from different external sources, resulting in pluralistic views or ambivalence that interferes with decision making; (6) fixation of certain sets of information associated with intense experiences of either pleasure or frustration; in this case the information is held together by intense emotions that render it immune to correction—a feature central to the neurotic process; (7) threatening information that endangers the person's safety, human relations, plans, or action in progress; such information alarms the person, may produce anxiety later on, and interferes with proper information processing.

A special difficulty arises when people have to organize future action. For example, everyone has to apportion time, space, energy, and money to cope with the tasks of everyday life. But most of these tasks are cyclical; they have to be abandoned at one point and taken up again the next day, week, or month, with time in between to rest, eat, or do something else. This discontinuity poses problems for some people. Short-term programing seldom constitutes a major difficulty as long as people can react to the situation at hand. Thus, when people are employed, the institution or organization delivers schedules and takes over the burden of apportioning time and resources. But long-term programing is more difficult, particularly in family and social life. Here, personal and interpersonal difficulties may arise in the setting and implementing of priorities.

DISTURBANCES ASSOCIATED WITH DEFICIENT EXPRESSION AND ACTION

The connection between disturbed communication and abnormal behavior is not always easy to trace. If the feedback processes operate properly and the person is capable of correcting information, he is eventually able to engage in action that is both gratifying and tolerated by the group. But if the feedback devices do not operate effectively, he is stuck with a distorted body of information, leading to unrewarding, ineffective or possibly deviant action that is not tolerated by the group. Repetitious communicative exchanges that provide for an erroneous body of information perpetuate failure in action. Such experiences may induce the person to withdraw from social contact, to doubt the ability of self to engage in realistic thinking, and to give up the testing of assumptions in action. Instead, the person may rely on fabricated or imagined responses of others, on a body of information that has not been tested, and on action behavior that is unacceptable to others. As a result, the link between initial assumption, the perception of the response of others, and subsequent action is broken.

If the derangement involves language, violations of norms pertaining to word and gesture are easily recognizable. In any society there exist rules that govern accepted usage, and in extreme cases the laws of libel and slander reinforce good taste. Paradoxically, the inhibited person who has difficulties in expressing or asserting himself and who cannot act decisively rarely runs afoul of the law. The world bypasses such a person, but he or she pays the price of social isolation, with the concomitant feeling of loneliness or pent-up rage. Aggressive persons are rewarded for socially competitive behavior in peacetime and for physically aggressive behavior in wartime. Because action behavior is so varied, most civilizations avoid establishing norms but, instead, prescribe in their criminal codes the actions that are prohibited. By deduction, then, people infer what actions are permitted. In modern court

procedures it is assumed that persons who repeatedly engage in prohibited actions and violate the criminal laws suffer from some sort of mental derangement.

DISTURBANCES ASSOCIATED WITH QUANTITATIVE VARIATIONS OF INPUT AND OUTPUT

Humans, animals, and machines have a finite capacity for processing information. When the load exceeds this capacity, the machinery or the organism breaks down; when the load is too small, the machinery or the organism may deteriorate for lack of use. Overload is a well-known source of disorganization. To protect self from the fatigue resulting from excessive input, the person learns to disregard certain classes of stimuli; but in the process the person may also disregard vital information. Underload in the form of simple neglect may lead in mild cases to retarded development and in severe cases of sensory deprivation to disorganization of behavior, confusion, and hallucinatory syndromes. Excessive output, as in overwork, results in fatigue, whereas output below par leads to poor physical fitness, decline in intellectual functioning, and possibly to premature aging. Because the homeostasis of the organism requires that input be quantitatively adapted to the output and vice versa, changes in one function always affect the other functions; imbalance between input and output results in frustration, overt anxiety, and, eventually, disorganized behavior.

Ill-timed messages likewise have a quantitative impact in that they have to be delivered with greater intensity and have to be repeated more often than those messages that are well timed and, therefore, are likely to be readily received. The speed of delivery of a message is likewise significant. Too fast or too slow a delivery and poor separation from preceding and following statements can render interpretation impossible. Recorded messages, for example, have to be played back at a given speed to remain intelligible. In interpersonal and group communication, responses to initial statements have to follow in reasonably short time if they are to be correctly understood. The art of proper timing is the specialty of the military man, the politician, the athlete, the businessman, and, in brief, of the well-functioning person in action.

DISTURBANCES ASSOCIATED WITH FRUSTRATING INTERACTION

The human being is a herd animal linked to other human beings by means of communication. If the message exchange is gratifying, anything that threatens this linkage upsets the individual and the group. If a communicative exchange is frustrating, the regulatory mechanisms that control the exchange bring about a weakening or dissolution of the network. Disturbed communication is characterized by the fact that these regulatory processes do not operate; in spite of frustration, the people continue to participate in the nonfunctioning network—sometimes because separation is too painful, sometimes because they are unable to find new connections. Thus, disturbed or pathological communication is stabilized by mutually inflicted frustration. In the process the participants become dependent on the other members of the group; they find it hard to partake in networks that do not observe the paradoxical rules that revolve around frustration.

If a person wishes to remain a member of a group in spite of frustrating human relations, he or she has to neglect the needs of self and has to overadapt. The behavior of such a person is diagnosed as a neurosis, a personality disturbance, or a character disorder. If, in contrast, the person refuses to adapt, resists, or rebels, the group may use coercive measures to bring him or her into line; this behavior is called psychopathic or sociopathic. In such cases the psychological and social therapies aim at restoring the connection between the patient and other people; the therapies are designed to restore those maintenance processes that enable a person to acquire the correct information, to establish a workable model of self and of the world, to respond to the message and actions of others, and to partake in group enterprises that cannot be carried out alone.

The secret of devious interaction lies in the manner in which the message or the action of the first person is connected with the message or the action of the second person. An appropriate response amplifies, attenuates, or corrects the information contained in the initial message; inappropriate or tangential responses are more likely to exert a disorganizing effect. For example, inappropriate responses are frequently given by mentally deranged persons; acknowledgment may be inadequate, exaggerated, or omitted. Often, the response simply introduces a new topic, as in the case of the tangential reply to a peripheral aspect of the initial message, disregarding the intent of the sender.

The processes of human interaction are based on three elementary responses: understanding, acknowledgment, and agreement. Understanding indicates that the other person's behavior has been considered within a larger framework and that some insight has been gained. Acknowledgment indicates that the intent to communicate has been perceived, without necessarily implying understanding. Agreement refers to the establishment of concordance of information between two or more people about a limited topic. To be understood is pleasant; to be acknowledged reaffirms one's sense of existence and indicates that the other is ready to enter into a message exchange; to reach an agreement paves the way for group action. A fitting reply to one's intent produces a feeling of satisfaction; the lack of a reply is discouraging. Anticipated satisfaction in communication is the motor that drives people to relate to others; dissatisfaction weakens the linkage between humans beings and leads to a rearrangement or a dissolution of the network. Table IV lists references on disorders of communication and their treatment.

Communication and Psychiatric Disorders

ORGANIC CONDITIONS

Disorders of communication are almost always present in mental retardation; acute brain syndromes caused by trau-

TABLE IV

References on Disorders of Communication and Their Treatment

Topic	Description	Source
Overview	Disturbed communication	Ruesch, 1972a
Anthology	Various aspects of disturbed interaction	Ostwald, 1977
Interviewing	Talking with patients	Bird, 1973
Mannerisms	Speech and gesture in everyday life	Feldman, 1969
Written language	The psychopathology of the written word	Rosenthal, 1977
Stress	Stress-response syndromes	Horowitz, 1976
Neurophysiology	The biological basis of hearing and speech disorders	Eagles, 1976
Deafness	Impaired hearing and mental retardation	Lloyd, 1976
Dyslexia	Developmental dyslexia	Duane and Rawson, 1975
Communication disorders	Remedial principles and practices	Dickson, 1974
Vocal prostheses	Phonic Mirror HandiVoice, simulating voice for nonvocal persons	JAMA, 1977
Visual prostheses	Electronic scanning of print and transformation into verbal sounds	White and Meindl, 1977
Stuttering	Voice disorders, stuttering, stammering	Weston, 1972
Aphasia, apraxia, agnosia	Clinical and theoretical aspects	Brown, 1974
Schizophrenia	Computer model	Callaway, 1970
	The double bind	Bateson, 1972
	Communication difficulties	Ostwald, 1978
	Family relations	Wynne et al., 1977
	Scoring communication defects in Rorschach and TAT	Singer and Wynne, 1966
Childhood autism	Echolalic speech	Simon, 1975
Depression	Various models of depression	Akiskal and McKinney, 1975
	Linguistic analysis of depressive speech	Andreasen and Pfohl, 1976
Personality disorders and psychosomatic conditions	Anxiety, duodenal ulcers, thyroidectomies, vasospastic syndromes, and the infantile personality	Ruesch, 1972b
Therapeutic communication	The remedial aspects of communication	Ruesch, 1973

matic, infectious, toxic, neoplastic, metabolic, or vascular conditions; and chronic brain syndromes associated with degenerative and senile conditions.

The nature of the condition may selectively involve the input, the output, the central functions, or, more likely, all these functions. Naturally, feedback and correction are seriously impaired; scanning, recall, and judgment also suffer. Slurred speech and articulatory difficulties and a variety of symptoms related to aphasia, agnosia, and apraxia may appear in the course of the disease.

FUNCTIONAL PSYCHOSES

The functional psychoses are characterized by disturbances of perception, decision making, and expression. Cognition is distorted; judgment is clouded; the ability to make decisions is impaired; expression is idiosyncratic and often inappropriate to the circumstances. Because of disturbed attention, the perspective of present events seen in the light of past or future experiences is deficient; also, feedback and correction are disturbed, leading to an erroneous model of self and of the world.

Schizophrenia. Patients diagnosed as schizophrenics frequently show aberrations of verbal behavior. These aberrations were described in a systematic way by Eugen Bleuler at the beginning of the 19th century. He mentioned neologisms, stilted language expression, echolalia, verbigeration, verbal mannerisms, and many other features. At that time schizophrenia was viewed primarily as a thought disorder, and the formulations were concerned not as much with language as with an analysis of intellectual and affective functions. Among the disorders studied were disturbances of association, ambivalence, sense deceptions, delusions, exaggerated symbolism, and excessive concreteness. By the middle of the 20th century, the emphasis had shifted to a more complex analysis of schizophrenic logic, as exemplified in the contributions of von Domarus (Kasanin, 1944). He called attention to the fact that Western thought, including scientific logic, has been largely based on the Aristotelian approach, which is rooted in Greek grammar and its subject-predicate language structure. Within such a structure, the subject of discourse must be stated and the level of abstraction defined. The subject is usually indicated by a noun or a pronoun, sometimes modified by an adjective; the predicate is indicated by a verb, sometimes modified by an adverb. The subject thus labels and names; the predicate specifies and indicates what the subject does. The structure of our Indo-European languages is the basis on which our Western science, engineering, and technology are built. In the evolution of language, the separation of the subject (noun) from what it does (verb) was a necessary precursor for the development of the notion of process; likewise, the separation of adjectives from nouns and of adverbs from verbs prepared the ground for scientific analysis. However, the verbal dissection of various aspects of an event is also responsible for some serious distortions. If a word exists, some people are inclined to attribute body and substance to it. However, through this process of reification, people forget that some words used in the sciences reflect abstractions or intervening constructs that do not refer to real events but have been created solely for human convenience.

The average person's logic is essentially subject oriented, but the schizophrenic's logic is predicate oriented. An example of predicate logic runs as follows: Trees are green; curtains are green; therefore, trees are like curtains, and the two nouns may be used interchangeably. The unifying principle around which the schizophrenic collects information is the process and its qualifying features. The predicate orientation of the schizophrenic frequently gives his reasoning a superconcrete character; for example, the concept of trees or curtains is more concrete than the percept of green. In addition, the schizophrenic uses words as a tool for self-expression, rather than as a device for conveying messages to others.

Around 1950 Ruesch and Bateson first called attention to the significance of communication for the understanding of psychiatric disorders. Later on, Bateson formulated his double-bind theory of schizophrenic communication. This concept refers to the observation that in certain families the child is exposed to two or more messages that cancel each other out. Caught between the devil and the deep blue sea, the child withdraws from the parents with whom communication is such a problem, becomes autistic and self-centered, and exhibits a variety of schizophrenic symptoms.

Affective disorders. In depressions, communication is also seriously disturbed. Psychomotor retardation slows reaction time; the percepts of the depressive patient emphasize the difficult, the heavy, and the impossible. The self is seen as incapable, unworthy, and in need of help, and the lighter side of life and the pursuit of pleasure are absent. The manic patient, in contrast, sees only the optimistic, joyful, and expansive features of life. But in both states, interpersonal communication is disturbed because the patient's perception is selective, self-interest displaces concern for other persons, and the use of information coming from the outside is minimized.

PSYCHOSOMATIC CONDITIONS

The autonomic nervous system and the smooth muscles of the body participate in the processes of communication in the first year of life. This involvement of the whole body is gradually abandoned between the second and the third years of life when special groups of striated muscles involved in speech take over the communicative task. People who suffer from psychosomatic conditions have, on the whole, retained some of the earlier, infantile ways of communication. This tendency is reflected in the evaluation of events; information received from the chemical and the mechanical sensory end organs is unduly weighted. The maturational shift in emphasis from the proximity receivers (touch, taste, smell, pain, temperature, vibration) to the more complex distance receivers (vision and hearing) is delayed. Signals that impinge on the proximity receivers, therefore, remain more significant than those relating to the distance receivers. Because of their limitation in communicative skills, these patients often engage in symbiotic relationships; some aspects of perception, decision making, or expression are delegated to the other person.

Reliance on proximity receivers and insufficient mastery of the higher symbolic processes result in an incomplete or arbitrary delineation of physical, psychological, and social boundaries. These patients believe that the physical or mental state of other people is identical with their own and that messages are to be understood as if they were traveling within one and the same neuronal network. Lacking the propensity to make independent decisions, these patients depend on the actual, protective actions of others. In their delayed maturation, the protective actions of others are not replaced by reliance on information, as is the case in the normal person.

NEUROSES AND PERSONALITY DISORDERS

The neuroses and personality disorders are characterized by the fact that, although perception and cognition are functioning satisfactorily, systematic biases affect the person's cognition and reasoning, his judgment may not always be the best, and the person may have difficulty in coping with his affairs. Expression is usually not affected, except for occasional inefficient implementation of speech, expressive movements, and gestures. Feedback and correction operate well except in the area of the bias, which has been referred to as a conflict or complex. Whereas the psychosomatic patient's expressions are devoid of fantasy, the neurotic patient exhibits a prolific fantasy life. Action takes place in fantasy, and these fantasies are often expressed in words; the involvement in doing may remain minimal. With personality disorders, the person of action shows the opposite tendency. All inner emotions are expressed through action, which serves as a vehicle to convey messages to others. Action is well developed, but verbal sophistication may often be rudimentary.

In the field of psychopathology, three levels of language development can be observed. The first, which may be called organ language, uses primarily the smooth muscles and the glands for purposes of expression. It is a form of ostensive communication, letting the thing speak for itself. This type of language is used by the infant and by some psychosomatic patients who rely on the self-evident perception of the other person to understand the bodily manifestations they exhibit. The second level of language development, which may be called action language, uses the striated skeletal muscles to engage in action. Such action can be observed by others and also has a physical impact on the surroundings. This is the language of the child and the adolescent, and it is used by some psychosomatic patients and sociopathic patients. The third level, which may be called symbolic language, uses words and gestures to convey messages to others. This is the language of the adult, and psychopathology is expressed through syntax and content.

Most people have a spectrum of all three types of language, but the healthy adult emphasizes the symbolic or third type. In the personality disorders and psychosomatic conditions, the spectrum may shift toward the first and second types.

Therapeutic Communication

Therapeutic communication is a skill practiced by professionals to help people overcome temporary stress, get along with other people, adjust to the unalterable, and overcome psychological blocks that stand in the path of self-realization. Educationally, these procedures have three facets: The psychological aspects deal with the development of certain cognitive or motor skills; the medical aspects consist of interventions with the bodily integrity of the patient to restore the organs of communication to a better level of functioning; and the social aspects deal with decision making, communication, and interaction with people. In therapeutic communication the following processes are likely to be exercised.

SHARPENING OF PERCEPTION AND COGNITION

To increase the patient's awareness of physical, psychological, and social events, the therapist must be trained to select those percepts that have problem-solving properties. These percepts may bear on the self, on other people's behavior, or on the total situation. Many of the relevant cues are embedded in sensations and actions emanating from the patient's own body, or they originate in the posture, facial expression, vocal intonation, and bodily movements of others. Every person should be able to recognize subtle hints hidden in a gesture, interpret roles that have not been explicitly stated, and know the extent to which rules can be stretched. The person must also learn to tolerate perceptions that are at odds with what he

or she presumes to exist, so that the perceptions that do not fit the expectations need not be distorted or repressed.

RECAPTURE OF INFORMATION

The absence of certain types of information bearing on significant others or on a period in a patient's life appears as gaps or as impoverishment of memories. Heightened awareness and accessibility to the person's stored body of knowledge, thus reestablishing a full spectrum of memories and gradually eliminating the lacunae in the patient's consciousness, is the goal of most insight-producing therapies.

DEVELOPMENT OF SELF-EXPRESSION

Varying forms of acknowledgment on the part of the therapist immediately after the patient's attempts at self-expression eventually induce him or her to speak more freely. As time goes on, the patient discovers that self-expression induces others to do likewise, a process that keeps communication going. Self-expression can be practiced outside the therapeutic situation through discussions with friends or through more formal speaking exercises or acting classes.

FACILITATION OF DECISION MAKING

To many patients the systematic procedure of decision making is unknown. But people can learn. The therapist facilitates decision making by verbalizing all pertinent information on which a choice is based. The information is elicited by seeking answers to such questions as: What kind of a problem are we faced with? What is the range of procedures available for solving the problem? What is the most fitting approach for this particular situation? Are you comfortable in seeing such a task through? What kind of technical, financial, social, or professional resources do you need in order to cope with the problem? What other problems will have to wait for a solution if you devote yourself fully to the task at hand? What do you expect the outcome will be?

MASTERY OF METACOMMUNICATION

Each message is accompanied by a subsidiary message that indicates how the principal message ought to be interpreted. These metacommunicative instructions guide the recipient in deciphering the content of what has been said. Frequently, the metacommunicative instructions are given nonverbally, but the principal content is spelled out verbally. Instructions may be hidden in the context of a social situation expressed in its label, the roles and identities of the participants, the bodily appearance and the nonverbal sound behavior of the participants, or the silent movements of the participants.

The patient is made aware of these features when discussing his or her recent experiences, particularly those experiences that led to misunderstandings or otherwise unsuccessful communication.

PROGRAMING ACTION

Action is steered by information. Preceding any action, therefore, the individual or the group has to make certain assumptions that are tentative at first and subject to subsequent modifications. To practice the process of making viable, a priori assumptions, the patient is encouraged to verbalize his initial assumptions, even if there is insufficient evidence to back them up; to correct these assumptions as more information becomes available; to detect resistances in himself and in others that defy correction, in spite of information to the contrary; to understand the assumptions made by others and to help others correct such assumptions if they prove to be wrong; and to resolve differences in assumptions on a concrete level rather than on an abstract level, by considering the evidence pertaining to the situation in question.

Inasmuch as the therapist has little opportunity to engage in action with the patient, planning and analysis of the actual effects achieved are the principal topics that bear on action in the therapeutic situation. In preparation for a systematic activity, the therapist must first understand the patient's cognitive and motor patterns and his or her ways of proceeding. The therapist has to find answers to such questions as: How does the patient cope with personal-private space, communal space, and public space? How does the behavior vary in these situations? How does the patient time action to coincide with, precede, or follow other events? Is the patient slow or fast to react? How does the patient cope with energy in terms of exercise, rest, diet, and so forth? Is the patient tenacious, or does he give up easily? How does the patient cope with financial, technical, and social resources? Is the patient skilled and does he learn easily? Or is the patient unskilled and slow to learn?

Once these and other features have been worked out, the therapist can help the patient to program action in holding with his cognitive and motor patterns, as well as with his major or minor disabilities.

OBSERVATION OF EFFECTS AND CORRECTIVE FEEDBACK

Each action and each message have an impact, both on the self and on the other. The observation of such effects and the correcting of the initial body of information is called feedback. A mentally healthy person possesses the ability to correct erroneous information and, therefore, to improve his performance. A mentally ill person has usually lost the ability to correct information, or perhaps he never possessed it in the first place. This inability may reside in faulty perception, in inept decision making, or in deficient expression or action. Improvement in these cases depends on reinstatement of corrective feedback as the guiding principle of behavior. Corrective feedback is more likely to be reacquired when a person is exposed to a crisis that involves survival. Schizophrenics, for example, act quite normally when faced with injury or illness but return to their bizarre behavior as they recover physically. Correction also occurs when another person gently rewards the acceptance of tested and proved information and the giving up of the erroneous body of information.

SMALL-SCALE MODEL OF SELF AND OF THE WORLD

Corrective feedback plays a central part in establishing an appropriate model of the self and of the world. Together with a therapist, parent or teacher, the physical and social realities that constitute the underpinnings of a person's life can be reviewed and certain central questions answered. In these circumstances the therapist acts as a catalyst; he raises the questions and lets the patient find the answer. On the whole, the experienced therapist asks questions that can be answered, bringing the problems down from the lofty heights to manageable levels. Topics to be touched on are:

Internal sense of identity: What is my occupational, family, and social role? What role do I feel comfortable with?

External sense of identity: What impression do I make? What do others see in me? Does the concept of myself coincide with the one that others have of me?

Support group: Whom can I count on in my family? Who are my friends? Who will support me in case of illness or adversity?

Expectations: Do I have reasonable expectations of myself and of others?

Fit into the world: How well do I fit into the world that surrounds me?

INCREASING TOLERANCE FOR HOMOGENEITY OR HETEROGENEITY

People who are members of a homogeneous group may feel safe and accepted, but they also seek novelty through travel and contact with different persons. People who live in a heterogeneous environment may long for the simplicity and clarity of groups that are composed of persons like themselves. In either case the therapist can help the patient learn to tolerate both homogeneity and heterogeneity of groups. If the therapist perceives that excessive differences may produce tensions, these tensions can be decreased (1) through equal exposure of group members to persons, things, and situations; this exposure leads to the establishment of similar experiences, a process that has been referred to as communization; (2) through the exchange of messages, thereby establishing correspondence of information; this procedure is referred to as communication; (3) through explanations to justify the existence of differences; every social system has available ready-made interpretations that explain exceptions to the rule and exempt a person from conforming, as in the case of illness; (4) through coercive action or threat of coercive action; this coercion is achieved through confinement, hospitalization, or social exclusion. If the therapist perceives that insufficient differences may produce tensions, these tensions can be increased (1) through isolation from the group and exposure to self (solitude); (2) through exposure to new groups, thus forcing persons to undergo some degree of adaptation and change; (3) through the acquisition of knowledge and skill not possessed by others, a process referred to as achievement; (4) through unusual life experiences not shared by others; these experiences may fall into the category of adventure, illness, or adversity.

DEFINITION OF MENTAL HEALTH

Appropriate cognition and perception, the ability to correct information, readiness to make decisions and to implement these decisions in action, self-expression in words or gestures, and the ability to respond to the messages of others are the prerequisites of mental health.

Conclusion

Certain disorders of communication originate in the person and are the result of malformations, illness, trauma, deficient learning, or one-sided exposure to people and situations. Other disorders of communication originate in the processes that connect people with each other. Among these disorders are faulty networks of organization, inappropriate codes, language systems that are not shared, deficient metacommunicative devices, and poorly matched responses. All these difficulties interfere with the feedback processes and the chance to establish an appropriate informational model.

Questions as to the causal connection between mental disease and disordered communication are not always easy to answer.

Mental disease is caused by the coincidence of a multiplicity of factors. Illness may impair, or it may affect the speed and the quality of the human response in a functional way. Thus, particularly stressful situations interfere with communication; in extreme cases—for example, in solitary confinement—the relationship between the disruption of communication and the external situation that exerts a direct and continuous stressful impact on the person is easy to recognize. However, where stress is discontinuous, evaluation is more difficult. An initially innocuous message may have a prolonged and, therefore, significant impact. This frequently occurs in children, who, depending on the verbal and nonverbal elaborations of the adults, may maximize or minimize an experience they have had.

The significance of communication for animals and humans is that of a connective function that coordinates the various parts of the organism and relates the individual to other individuals and to the group. In this way communication serves as an integrative system. The better it works, the better the person is protected; the worse it works, the more vulnerable the person becomes. Once a person is faced with an illness or a social problem, the chances of adequately coping with the difficulties greatly increase if the person can relate to others. Such communication has a corrective, attenuating, or aggravating impact, which triggers corresponding action. But in disordered communication the steering qualities of communication are lost. Such disturbed communication can be recognized by considering the quantity, timing, appropriateness, and sequence of messages. The following ditty may help one remember these facts:

> Too much, too little; too early, too late;
> At the wrong place, is the disturbed message's fate.

Repeated communicative exchanges leave their imprint on the person, not only in terms of content but also in terms of interpersonal procedures in which message or action sequences are joined together. What is called personality is, in effect, the result of a person's genetic endowment modified by a large number of communicative exchanges. This innate body of information, modified by later experiences, steers the actions of the person required for the implementation of daily life. Correct and appropriate information about the organism, its component parts, and the world surrounding it greatly enhances the person's chances to cope successfully with his or her life. In psychiatric treatment all the somatic, psychological, and social therapies have as their central aim the establishment or reestablishment of communicative functions. Therapists attempt to modify the communicative patterns of the patient in the expectation that once the exchange of messages and the expression of thoughts and emotions operate satisfactorily, corrective feedback can exert its regulatory effect on the central body of information that guides the patient's overt behavior.

Suggested Cross References

In this section, human behavior and psychiatric treatment were discussed from the viewpoint of communication. The other sections in Chapter 4 offer discussion of subjects bearing on communication, particularly Section 4.3, on learning theory, Section 4.8, on psycholinguistics, and Section 4.9, on biofeedback. See Section 6.2, on computers and clinical psychiatry, for a more detailed discussion of the application of computer technology to psychiatry. See Section 1.2 for a discussion on general living systems theory which relates to communication.

REFERENCES

Ackoff, R. L., and Sasieni, M. W. *Fundamentals of Operations Research.* John Wiley & Sons, New York, 1968.
Akiskal, H. S., and McKinney, W. T. Overview of recent research in depression. Arch. Gen. Psychiatry, *32:* 285, 1975.
Andreasen, N. J. D., and Pfohl, B. Linguistic analysis of speech in affective disorders. Arch. Gen. Psychiatry, *33:* 1361, 1976.
Argyle, M. *Bodily Communication.* International Universities Press, New York, 1975.
* Bateson, G. *Steps to an Ecology of Mind.* Ballantine Books, New York, 1972.
Bird, B. *Talking with Patients,* ed. 2. J. B. Lippincott, Philadelphia, 1973.
Birdwhistell, R. L. *Kinesics and Context: Essays on Body-Motion Communication.* University of Pennsylvania Press, Philadelphia, 1970.
Bosmajian, H. A. *The Rhetoric of Nonverbal Communication.* Scott, Foresman, Glenview, Ill., 1971.
Broadbent, D. E. *Decision and Stress.* Academic Press, New York, 1971.
Brown, J. W. *Aphasia, Apraxia, and Agnosia: Clinical and Theoretical Aspects.* Charles C Thomas, Springfield, Ill., 1974.
Callaway, E. Schizophrenia and interference. Arch. Gen. Psychiatry, *22:* 193, 1970.
Cofer, C. N., editor. *The Structure of Human Memory.* W. H. Freeman & Co., San Francisco, 1975.
Conrad, M., Guttinger, W., and Dal Cin, M., editors. *Physics and Mathematics of the Nervous System.* Springer, New York, 1974.
* Critchley, M. *Silent Language.* Butterworth, London, 1975.
Dance, F. E. *Speech Communication.* Holt, Rinehart and Winston, New York, 1972.
Dance, F. E., and Larson, C. E. *The Functions of Human Communication.* Holt, Rinehart and Winston, New York, 1976.
Davis, R. M. Evolution of computers and computing. Science, *195:* 1096, 1977.
Dickson, S., editor. *Communication Disorders: Remedial Principles and Practices.* Scott, New York, 1974.
Duane, D. D., and Rawson, M. B., editors. *Reading, Perception, and Language.* York Press, Baltimore, 1975.
Eagles, E. L., editor. *Human Communication and Its Disorders.* Raven Press, New York, 1976.
Ekman, P., editor. *Darwin and Facial Expression.* Academic Press, New York, 1973.
Ekman, P., and Friesen, W. V. *Unmasking the Face.* Prentice-Hall, Englewood Cliffs, N. J., 1975.
Feldman, S. S. *Mannerisms of Speech and Gestures in Everyday Life.* International Universities Press, New York, 1969.
Ferguson, E. S. The mind's eye: Nonverbal thought in technology. Science, *197:* 827, 1977.
Galin, D. Implications for psychiatry of left and right cerebral specialization: A neurophysiological context for unconscious processes. Arch. Gen. Psychiatry, *31:* 572, 1974.
Gerbner, G., Gross, L. P., and Melodey, W. H., editors. *Communications Technology and Social Policy: Understanding the New Cultural Revolution.* John Wiley & Sons, New York, 1973.
Hayakawa, S. I. *Language in Thought and Action.* Harcourt, Brace, Jovanovich, New York, 1972.
Hogben, L. *From Cave Painting to Comic Strip: A Kaleidoscope of Human Communication.* Chanticleer Press, New York, 1949.
Horowitz, M. J. *Image Formation and Cognition.* Appleton-Century-Crofts, New York, 1970.
Horowitz, M. J. *Stress Response Syndromes.* Jason Aronson, New York, 1976.
Journal of the American Medical Association. Electronic devices give voice to speechless. J. A. M. A. *238:* 2589, 1977.
Kasanin, J. S., editor. *Language and Thought in Schizophrenia.* University of California Press, Berkeley, 1944.
Key, M. R. *Nonverbal Communication: A Research Guide and Bibliography.* Scarecrow Press, Metuchen, N. J., 1977.
Klatzky, R. L. *Human Memory.* W. H. Freeman & Co., San Francisco, 1975.
Lenneberg, E. H. *Biological Foundations of Language.* John Wiley & Sons, New York, 1967.
Lewis, M. M. *Infant Speech: A Study of the Beginnings of Language.* Arno Press, New York, 1975.
Lin, N. *The Study of Human Communication.* Bobbs-Merrill, New York, 1973.
Lloyd, L. L., editor. *Communication Assessment and Interaction Strategies.* University Park Press, Baltimore, 1976.
Matson, F. W., and Montagu, A., editors. *The Human Dialogue: Perspectives on Communication.* Free Press, New York, 1967.
McLuhan, M. *Understanding Media: The Extensions of Man.* New American Library, New York, 1973.
* Miller, G. A., editor. *Communication, Language, and Meaning.* Basic Books, New York, 1973.
Miller, G. A., and Johnson-Laird, P. N. *Language and Perception.* Harvard University Press (Belknap Press), Cambridge, 1976.
Morris, C. *Writings on the General Theory of Signs.* Mouton, The Hague, 1971.
Ostwald, P. F. *The Semiotics of Human Sound.* Mouton, The Hague, 1973.
* Ostwald, P. F., editor. *Communication and Social Interaction.* Grune & Stratton, New York, 1977.

Ostwald, P. F. Language and communication problems with schizophrenic patients: A review, commentary, and synthesis. In *Phenomenology and Treatment of Schizophrenia*, W. Fann, I. Karacan, A. Pokorny, and B. Williams, editors, p. 163. Spectrum Publications, New York, 1978.

Patton, B. R., and Giffin, K. *Interpersonal Communication: Basic Text and Readings.* Harper & Row, New York, 1974.

Pei, M. *The Story of Language*, rev. ed. J. B. Lippincott, Philadelphia, 1965.

Piaget, J. *The Language and Thought of the Child*, ed. 3. Humanities Press, New York, 1962.

Pribram, K. H. *Languages of the Brain: Experimental Paradoxes and Principles in Neuropsychology.* Prentice-Hall, Englewood Cliffs, N.J., 1971.

Revesz, G. *The Origins and Prehistory of Language.* Longman's, Green, London, 1956.

Rosenthal, J. H. *The Neuropsychopathology of Written Language.* Nelson-Hall, Chicago, 1977.

Ruesch, J. *Disturbed Communication*, ed. 2. W. W. Norton, New York, 1972a.

Ruesch, J. *Semiotic Approaches to Human Relations.* Mouton, The Hague, 1972b.

Ruesch, J. *Therapeutic Communication*, ed. 2. W. W. Norton, New York, 1973.

* Ruesch, J. *Knowledge in Action: Communication, Social Operations, and Management.* Jason Aronson, New York, 1975.

Ruesch, J., and Bateson, G. *Communication, the Social Matrix of Psychiatry*, ed. 2. W. W. Norton, New York, 1968.

Ruesch, J., and Kees, W. *Nonverbal Communication*, ed. 2. University of California Press, Berkeley, 1972.

Scheflen, A. E. *Body Language and the Social Order.* Prentice-Hall (Spectrum), Englewood Cliffs, N.J., 1972.

Scheflen, A. E. *How Behavior Means.* Jason Aronson, New York, 1974.

Shands, H. C. *Semiotic Approaches to Psychiatry.* Mouton, The Hague, 1970.

Shannon, C. E. The mathematical theory of communication. Bell System Tech. J., July and October, 1948.

Simon, N. Echolalic speech in childhood autism. Arch. Gen. Psychiatry, *32:* 1439, 1975.

Singer, M. T., and Wynne, L. C. Principles for scoring communication defects and deviances in parents of schizophrenics: Rorschach and TAT scoring manuals. Psychiatry, *29:* 260, 1966.

Smith, A. G., editor. *Communication and Culture.* Holt, Rinehart and Winston, New York, 1966.

Thayer, L., editor. *Communication: Ethical and Moral Issues.* Gordon and Breach, New York, 1973.

Tylor, E. B. *Researches into the Early History of Mankind.* University of Chicago Press, Chicago, 1964.

Watzlawick, P., Beavin, J. H., and Jackson, D. D. *Pragmatics of Human Communication.* W. W. Norton, New York, 1967.

Weinstein, E. A., and Friedland, R. P., editors. *Hemi-inattention and Hemisphere Specialization.* Raven Press, New York, 1977.

Weizenbaum, J. *Computer Power and Human Reason.* W. H. Freeman & Co., San Francisco, 1976.

Weston, A. J., editor. *Communicative Disorders: An Appraisal.* Charles C Thomas, Springfield, Ill. 1972.

White, R. L., and Meindl, J. D. The impact of integrated electronics in medicine. Science, *195:* 1119, 1977.

Wiener, N. *Cybernetics, or Control and Communication in the Animal and the Machine,* ed. 2. MIT Press, Cambridge, 1961.

Wynne, L. C., Singer, M. T., Bartko, J., and Toohey, M. L. Schizophrenics and their families: Recent research on parental communication. In *Developments in Psychiatric Research*, J. M. Tanner, editor. Hodder & Stoughton, Sevenoaks, Kent, 1977.

4.8 Psycholinguistics

NANCY C. ANDREASEN, Ph.D, M.D.
RICHARD R. HURTIG, Ph.D.

Introduction

Psycholinguistics as a discipline attempts to explore the psychology of language. That is, it attempts to characterize the psychological factors, perceptual and cognitive, involved in the development and use of language. Most psycholinguistic research has emphasized investigation of the psychological factors governing language in normal individuals. Increasingly,

however, insights gained from the discipline of psycholinguistics have also been applied to psychiatric populations.

In order to follow the development of the research into those psychological factors, one needs to be familiar with the level of formal analysis of language proposed by linguists. Language as a complex behavior can be characterized as being rule governed. Its rules are fundamental and define regular properties of all human languages. The scope of its rules ranges from the physical properties of the acoustic wave form to the psychosocial aspects of interpersonal interaction. The grammar of a language is defined as the set of rules that characterizes the given language and, more important, characterizes the means by which the correlation between sound and meaning necessary for communication is established. The grammar is composed of the discrete yet interrelated components (subsets of rules) that represent the levels of linguistic analysis.

Structuralists (Sapir, 1921; Bloomfield, 1933; Harris, 1951) have proposed the following characterization of the levels of description of components of the grammar:

The phonological component—the set of rules governing the combination and the distribution of individual speech sounds (phonemes).

The morphological component—the set of rules governing the construction and distribution of minimal meaning units (morphemes), such as word and meaningful grammatical particle.

The syntactic component—the rules governing the sequencing of words and the establishment of relations between them, such as subject-verb-object.

The semantic component—the rules governing the interpretation of the meaning of individual words and the structural relations in which they occur.

In addition to those four basic components, discourse-level linguistic structure has been increasingly studied recently. Thus, one can characterize at least two additional components or subsets of rules:

The discourse component—the set of rules governing the manner in which the propositional content of sentences or utterances may be combined to construct an idea set or story.

The pragmatic component—the set of rules governing the use of sentences to accomplish specific intents (such as request, inform, and demand) and the rules governing the use of sentences as a function of social interaction setting.

Historical and Theoretical Background

TAXONOMIC AND EMPIRICAL APPROACHES

Concurrent with the adoption of logical positivism and British empiricism by the American behaviorists, the American linguists Bloomfield (1933) and Sapir (1921) attempted to introduce an empiricist orientation to the study of language. That move to empirical description underlies all investigation up until the work of Noam Chomsky (1957). Like the behaviorists, the linguists of that era attempted to construct linguistic theories in terms of observable units of behavior, with description proceeding from the most basic elements (sound-phonetic units) to successively higher levels of structure (morphology, syntax, and semantics). That taxonomic approach had much currency up through the 1950's.

With the advent of the information theory, considerable interest developed in analyzing spoken speech samples and written texts in terms of the distributional properties of various linguistic units. Attempts were made to explain the rules of language in terms of statistical probability. Attempts to characterize the structure of language in terms of Markov processes or finite state grammars are characteristic of the period. In principle, psychologists attempted to demonstrate that sentence perception and production proceed simply from the analysis of the probabilities of cooccurrence of various linguistic units. Examples of the approach include Yngve's (1960) depth hypothesis and Johnson's (1968) transitional error probability models of sentence processing and production. Miller (1951) and Neisser (1967) extensively reviewed that approach to the study of language.

Within psychology it soon became apparent that there were limitations to the strict observational methods of behaviorism and single-stage (stimulus-response) learning theory when attempts were made to account for human linguistic behavior. Attempts to account for semantic properties within the learning theory framework led away from single-stage models and to the adoption of the two-stage or mediational models that developed out of the work in classical conditioning and held that there may be intermediate unobservable events involved in the growth and structure of meaning (Mowrer, 1954; Osgood, 1963). The most notable work to come out of that mediational paradigm was Osgood's semantic differential (Osgood et al., 1957). That technique proposed that knowledge or understanding of the meaning of an item is represented as a set of scale values on a set of dimensions in which each dimension is defined by the opposition of a pair of attributive adjectives (such as good-bad, hot-cold). However, Fodor (1965) argued that mediation theory is reducible to a single-stage theory and, as such, not capable of overcoming the problems associated with that theory.

The writings of Chomsky (1957) eventually led to a major revolution in the study of language. Chomsky proposed an alternative as an attempt to deal with some of the problems and failures of the various taxonomic, behavioral, and empirical approaches to the study of language. Chomsky argued that the basic unit of analysis is the sentence (utterance) and not the atomic acoustic elements. He furthermore proposed that the relevant data base is not derived from purely behavioral observations but, rather, from the intuitions about sentences of native speaker-hearers. To a large extent that view shifted or expanded the goals of linguistic theory from accounting for performance (actual utterances) to competence, the knowledge of the rules governing the structure of the utterance. Chomsky argued that the shift is necessitated by the desire to meet conditions of explanatory adequacy, as well as those of descriptive adequacy. Chomsky proposed that his theory (grammar) should account not only for the structural properties of a language sample but also for the way linguistic knowledge is represented in the brain of a speaker-hearer. Furthermore, he believed that his theory is capable of accounting for language acquisition in children. He emphasized that the study of language by empirical means alone, without drawing on native speakers' introspection about language, would not lead to an adequate linguistic theory (grammar).

George Miller's (1965) American Psychological Association presidential address may well be taken as the major public introduction to concerns of modern psycholinguistics. It was also the call to consider the Chomskian approach to the study of language when one does, in fact, study the psychology of language. In that address, Miller proposed seven points that must be kept in mind by anyone interested in investigating language in the post-Chomsky era. Those points make it clear that a simple taxonomic approach is incapable of providing an adequate account of linguistic behavior. Those points are:

1. Not all the physical features of the speech signal are relevant to the study of language, and some significant features may have no physical representation. For example, in an acoustic signal various features may be due to vocal tract or transmission channel noise. Further, in the sentence "Mary was loved" there is no physical representation of the actor, yet native speakers always interpret the sentence as "Some X loved Mary."

2. Meaning cannot be solely defined in terms of reference. It is clear that, even though the expressions "morning star" and "evening star" refer to the same heavenly sphere, they mean different things. Likewise, everyone knows the meaning of the word "unicorn" but cannot find a real-world referent for it. The expression "Can you pass the salt?" in terms of its semantic meaning is a request for information, but it is more commonly used as a request for an action.

3. The meaning of a sentence cannot be derived solely by some Boolean summation of the meaning of the individual words. If knowing the meaning of "John," "loves," and "Mary" were sufficient for an interpretation of the sentence "John loves Mary," then it would have to be the case that "Mary loves John" means the same thing. In addition, memory of the meaning of a sentence seems not to be dependent on the memory of the individual words.

4. The syntactic structure governs the combination of the meanings of words in a sentence. Thus, the structural description that defines John as the actor of the first sentence in point 3 above and Mary as the actor in the second sentence leads to the different semantic interpretations of those two sentences. The underlying syntactic structure accounts for the ability to distinguish the different roles in which the doctor finds himself in the following two sentences: "The doctor is easy to treat." (object) "The doctor is eager to treat." (subject)

5. Language seems to have infinite capacity. There seems to be no limit on the number of possible sentences. Given any sentence, one can always construct a longer one. Natural languages seem to have recursive properties that allow sentence, clause, and phrasal embedding. Any linguistic or psychological theory must be able to handle the recursive nature and infinite capacity of language in order to adequately reflect the competence of a speaker-hearer.

6. A distinction must be made between the structure or constraints of the language (grammar) and the structure and constraints of the user (speaker-hearer). Thus, a theory must be able to distinguish a constraint due to limits on the formal structure of language (competence) from one due to limits on the perceptual, cognitive, or storage capacities of users (performance). Thus, a simple sequence like "John loves Mary" might be judged unacceptable if each word was followed by a silent interval of indeterminable length. The unacceptability would not be caused by a violation of any grammatical principle or rule but, rather, would be caused by temporal limits on the immediate memory buffer involved in sentence perception.

7. Language seems to be species specific. That is, only human beings seem to perform the verbal communicative behaviors that characterize language. That point need not be construed as a theologically based conception; rather, it should be reviewed as part of the nativist view, which holds that the human brain is genetically endowed with a certain tacit knowledge of linguistic universals. The point is supported by considerable evidence about similar patterns of language acquisition across languages, cultures, and intelligence levels.

By presenting those seven points, Miller brought the competence-performance issue back to psychology and, more specifically, to the investigation of the psychology of language. Miller cautioned against analysis that proceeded solely on the basis of physically recorded signals.

CHOMSKY AND TRANSFORMATIONAL-GENERATIVE GRAMMAR

Chomsky's transformational-generative grammar provides a useful theoretical model for the psychologist. The general form of Chomsky's grammar can be seen in Figure 1. In that characterization the base component, which is composed of phrase structure rules, specifies the underlying relationships of subject-verb-object. That is, who does what to whom? Those underlying descriptions are then transformed by a second class of rules called transformations into the surface sequences that correspond to the surface spoken forms. Thus, a given physical sentence that is ambiguous, such as "Visiting relatives can be a nuisance," would be characterized as a single-surface structure derived from two independent deep structures—"Visiting relatives is a nuisance" and "Visiting relatives are a nuisance"—by a set of transformations. Analogously, two sentences with radically different surface forms, such as "John loves Mary" and "It is Mary whom John loves," would be derived from the same underlying representation by different transformational histories. The grammar can be seen as a model of the iterative process of sentence derivation, beginning with the application of the phrase structure rules of the base, and followed by the transformational rules that permute the sentence constituents into their eventual surface order.

In the standard transformational-generative theory (Chomsky, 1965) the meaning of a sentence is obtained by the interpretation of the deep structure relationships and the semantic features assigned to each of the constituents by the lexicon (dictionary). The rules of the semantic component are not conceived of as generative (iterative) in the manner in which the syntactic rules are. Recently, some linguists have proposed an alternative theory (generative semantics), in which the distinction between syntactic and semantic rules is abandoned (McCawley, 1968; Lakoff, 1972). Other linguists have argued against the alternative theory (Bever et al., 1976; Katz and Bever, 1976).

Similarly, in the standard theory the phonetic form of a sentence is obtained by the application of a distinct set of phonological rules that are also interpretive in nature (Chomsky and Halle, 1968). Those rules interpret the structure derived by the application of the transformation. That is, they apply to the surface order of the constituents.

That iterative nature of the grammar was very seductive to those concerned with speech perception and production. Early application of Chomskian linguistics assumed the grammar to be the psychological generative device. Research in psycholinguistics during the 1960's was centrally concerned with the empirical demonstration of the psychological reality of transformational analysis. It was assumed that speech perception could be characterized by an analysis-by-synthesis device that consisted of a transformational grammar. That is, during perception an internal grammar attempts to generate a match for an input sentence. Comprehension occurs when the grammar has generated a match for the input sentence. Similar proposals have been made for speech production. In that case, production occurs when the grammar generates a sentence that is somehow judged to match the underlying idea-message.

The analysis-by-synthesis model and its corollary, the analysis-by-analysis model, form the basis of the derivational theory of complexity. That theory assumes that a linguistic rule is a characterization or a reflection of a psychological operation and, therefore, that the complexity of an individual sentence is a function of the number of linguistic rules involved in its derivation. A sentence with N number of rules in its derivation should be easier to process or remember or learn than a sentence with N + 1 rules in its derivation. A series of early studies seemed to give initial support to the derivational theory of complexity and to the notion that transformational grammar has psychological reality. If comprehension involves a decomposition of a sentence in terms of its transformational history, then it should be the case that storage (memory) of sentences may also reflect the transformational nature of sentences. That model of sentence memory has been termed the coding hypothesis. It assumes a coding in memory of the specific transformations in a discrete form apart from the underlying proposition of the sentence. Thus, sentences with more transformations in their histories require more storage capacity. That model was initially proposed by Miller (1962) and Mehler (1963) and received extensive examination and initial support in a variety of studies (Miller and McKean, 1964; Savin and Perchonock, 1965; Clifton and Odom, 1966). However, on further investigation (Watt, 1970) it became clear that, in fact, the psychological reality of transformations and, by extension, the derivational theory of complexity and the analysis-by-synthesis and analysis-by-analysis models are inadequate accounts of speech or sentence perception.

By and large, the concentration of psycholinguistic research in the early period was on syntax processing, following the similar emphasis in linguistics itself. However, research on semantics did continue, and in more recent times interest in semantics has overtaken interest in syntax. Within the framework of transformational grammar as proposed by Chomsky, the semantic component is an interpretive component, as opposed to a generative component, and as such is not easily incorporated into the earlier versions of the derivational theory of complexity. One might argue that constructs involving more semantic features would be more complex than those requiring fewer semantic features. Such a proposal has, in fact, been made by H. H. Clark (1970, 1973). Specifically, he argued that the acquisition of lexical items is determined, in part, on the basis of the semantic features. Thus, two words that differ in only one feature, as is the case in certain pairs of polar adjectives—such as tall and short, hot and cold, more and less—demonstrate an acquisitional pattern in which such antonyms are first treated as if they meant the same and only subsequently become differentiated as the additional feature necessary to distinguish the two ends of the polar dimension is acquired. Some data supporting that notion exist (E. V. Clark, 1973).

However, it has become clear that the relationship between the transformational grammar and the psychological theory cannot be characterized as a simple one-to-one relationship between psychological operations and linguistic rules. What has emerged is an alternative conception of the relationship. The alternative conception derives from a series of studies on sentence processing.

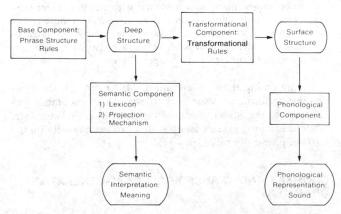

FIGURE 1. Schematization of Chomsky's transformational-generative grammar.

Investigators hypothesized that they could examine the psychological reality of sentence structure by constructing tasks that would require a response from subjects at various points during the processing of speech. One experimental paradigm, which developed out of the work of Broadbent (1958) on selective attention, required subjects to attend to a linguistic message and simultaneously monitor for an embedded noise burst (click) (Fodor and Bever, 1965). It was assumed that the subject's ability to detect or locate the click would vary as a function of its location vis-á-vis the structure of the sentence, with detectability lowest at points where attention might be directed away from the incoming signal and toward the internal cognitive processing of sentence structure. A large number of studies have used that paradigm with a variety of response measures (location, Fodor and Bever, 1965; reaction time, Abrams and Bever, 1969; detection, Bever and Hurtig, 1975; galvanic skin response, Bever et al., 1969; auditory evoked response, Seitz and Weber, 1974). The general finding is that the clause boundary seems to function as a processing point. That finding fits with Bever's (1970) notion that speech is processed clause by clause and that the perceptual segmentation strategy attempts to isolate a noun-verb-noun sequence and assign it the propositional representation of subject-verb-object.

A second experimental paradigm examined the processing of ambiguity. The paradigm addressed two issues. The first issue involves the alternative readings of an ambiguous clause, phrase, or word that are available during the processing of speech. The second issue involves examining at what point in the processing of speech the alternatives are available and at what point a choice is made between the alternatives. Bever et al. (1973) and Hurtig (1978) showed, in a sentence fragment completion task, that the alternative readings are available during the on-line processing of speech for an ambiguous sequence like "The shooting of the Indians upset the agent." Furthermore, the choice point corresponds to the clause boundary. Hurtig (1978) further demonstrated that the availability of alternative readings during on-line processing is not affected by the presence of an antecedent ambiguating context.

Both the click and the ambiguity paradigms, in demonstrating an effect of clause boundary, seem to support the notion that the distinction between deep structure and surface structure proposed in the transformational grammar has psychological validity. The behavioral results seem to indicate that subjects are sensitive to the relationship between the underlying deep-structure constituent and its surface realization.

In many respects the more recent period of investigation has been concerned with the validity of the levels of linguistic description and the psychological validity of the levels of description proposed by a generative grammar. It has become clear that the goals of psycholinguistics are not to discover the psychological reality of any given set of rules proposed by linguists but, rather, to uncover those sets of heuristics used by perceivers and, in turn, producers to properly encode any given propositional content. What has emerged is the growing interest in the set of perceptual and cognitive strategies required to map a surface phonetic sequence onto an underlying representation in semantic memory and likewise to characterize the set of strategies required to convert the propositional content or intent into a surface spoken sequence. Evidence of the existence of such strategies comes not only from the work on adult sentence perception—from experiments like those with clicks and ambiguous fragments—but also from the examination of universals of language acquisition (Slobin, 1973) and from the investigation of the relation of the development of sentence-perception strategies to the development of other cognitive abilities and cerebral organization (Bever, 1970, 1971). In addition, some attempts have been made to formalize those strategies in the form of heuristics in a computer simulation of comprehension (Kaplan, 1972).

What has emerged is an interactionist model (Bever, 1970; Bever et al., 1976). The model has, on the one hand, moved away from the earlier strict dependence on a linguistic basis for sentence processing. On the other hand, it has reexamined

the basic theoretical tenet proposed by Chomsky (1957) and later by Miller and Chomsky (1963) concerning the relation of grammaticality and acceptability (competence versus performance).

STUDY OF DISCOURSE

Interest has shifted from the study of the perception, production, and retention of individual sentences to the broader investigation of properties of discourse. That shift has had several consequences in terms of the content of study. It has brought psycholinguistic research closer to the general problems being dealt with in information processing and cognitive psychology. Specifically, research has moved toward a reexamination of the relationship of language and the internal representation of knowledge (thought).

The traditional problem of the relation of language and thought posed by Whorf (1956) contains two propositions. The first, linguistic relativity, claims that speakers of different languages have different perceptions and conceptions of the world. The second proposition, linguistic determinism, claims that the structure of a language places constraints on the possible cognitive representations (thought). Whorf proposed that the semantic, morphological, and syntactic distinctions marked by a language determine the limits of one's conceptions of reality: One sees what one can name.

Considerable data have been collected over the years both supporting and contradicting the Whorfian hypothesis (Hurtig, 1977). Most damaging to the hypothesis is the work on linguistic universals, specifically Osgood et al.'s (1957) work on the semantic differential, which attempts to demonstrate the universality of the underlying semantic content of lexical items. However, Osgood noted that support for the hypothesis comes from studies examining denotative functions of language (the arbitrary referential naming of objects), while the contradictory data come from studies concerned with connotative functions of language (the representational mediational process). Bever (1972) reformulated the Whorfian hypothesis in terms of the interaction of conceptual organization and linguistic structure. Specifically, he has drawn on the psycholinguistic research, which has indicated that one's perceptual system puts limits on the output of the grammar and also that specific linguistic constructions place constraints on the type of processing heuristics that one must develop in order to communicate with sentences. Thus, the relation of language and thought can be seen as dynamic interaction, rather than the unidirectional relation proposed by Whorf.

The general memory and problem-solving literature (Norman and Rumelhart, 1975) has been centrally concerned with how the propositional content of successive utterances (a discourse) is integrated into a unified internal representation (Freedle, 1977). Various models of text-story interpretation have been proposed. Most have taken a semantic interpretive orientation. That is, they have taken the form of a descriptive model, rather than a generative model. The central element to most of those models is a thematic analysis of the discourse that specifies the presupposed (given) and the asserted (new) elements. Quite often, those models present the propositional content in the form of a tree diagram (Kintch, 1974; Mandler and Johnson, 1977). By and large, the models have been derived from and verified by text-recall studies in which recall performance is assumed to reflect properties of the internal representation of the text (Shepard and Chipman, 1971). It is as yet unclear to what extent the proposed models can be differentiated formally or whether empirical evidence can be found to support one over the other. However, the general technical developments have proved useful for text or discourse analysis. Research on discourse and cognitive representation is still in its formative years, yet the payoff in terms of relating language and thought processes is already being realized in that the research is providing the empirical tools for the study of representational schemas. It will undoubtedly be invaluable to those interested in the study of thought disorders.

Most recently, there has been a considerable amount of research on sentence use (pragmatics). The research has developed along three major lines: the theoretical discussion of speech acts (the study of the intentional or performative force of utterance) by Austin (1962) and Searle (1969); the work on conversational implicature (the study of the cooperative principle governing the normal interpretation of both the conventional and the conversational meanings of an utterance) by Grice (1967); and the work on conversational devices (the study of the stylized verbal and sometimes nonverbal cues used in the management of a dyadic interaction) by Sachs et al. (1974). The research in the area has been largely observational in nature. Many papers have appeared in the past few years on the acquisition of pragmatic skill in children. However, the most significant outcome of research in the area has been the development of elaborate coding schemes for the analysis of dyadic interactions. Since the pragmatic rules govern the use of language in the social-communicative setting, those codes provide an excellent tool for the analysis of social interaction, specifically intention on the part of an individual. The application of those codes to the analysis of defective communication and asocial behavioral patterns may provide, through the analysis of the linguistic behavior, a greater understanding of the cognitive aspects of those disorders.

Psycholinguistic Studies in Psychiatric Populations

Investigators interested in understanding the relationship between language and psychopathology have drawn on the discipline of psycholinguistics in a variety of ways. Methods for studying language in psychiatric populations have developed and changed in response to changes within the discipline of psycholinguistics. The earliest studies of language in psychiatric populations drew from the empirical tradition and used a variety of taxonomic approaches. More recently, investigators have attempted to examine syntactical and semantic aspects of language by using methods that derive from the transformational-generative tradition of Chomsky. Because psychiatrists and psychologists have had a long-standing interest in language as a manifestation of thought and thought disorder, interest in discourse-level analysis has also been prominent for a number of years. Studies of language in psychiatric populations have tended to focus on schizophrenia, since language disorder can be considered a manifestation of thought disorder. Investigators have also studied language in mania, depression, and childhood disorders.

EMPIRICAL AND TAXONOMIC APPROACHES

Early empirical approaches to the study of language tended to be descriptive and atheoretical. They stressed the importance of studying language because it is public and directly observable, while thought is private and can only be examined inferentially either through the observation of language behavior or through the observation of a person's performance on some type of cognitive test. Within the empirical tradition,

several different approaches have been applied to the study of language in psychiatric populations.

Lexical diversity and the type-token ratio. The type-token ratio, originally described by Johnson (1944), has been widely used as a measure of lexical diversity or vocabulary range. The measure is determined by dividing the total number of words or tokens into the total number of different words or types in a given passage of speech or writing. Whitehorn and Zipf (1943) were the first to suggest that schizophrenic language may be characterized by a decrease in lexical diversity. Since their suggestion, the type-token ratio has been used to compare the lexical diversity of schizophrenic language to that of normals, manics, and depressives.

Various studies are summarized in Table I. As those studies indicate, a wide range of values can be obtained using the type-token ratio. Spreen and Wachal (1973) pointed out that the type-token ratio tends to be highly dependent on sample length and on whether the sample is written or spoken. The topic of conversation may also influence the measure. It has become increasingly clear that the type-token ratio is not a particularly promising method for studying language in psychiatric populations, since it has not been useful in differentiating pathological groups either from one another or from normals.

Taxonomic approaches. Several investigators have attempted to relate older taxonomic grammatical categories—that is, parts of speech—to psychopathology. Busemann (1925) first developed the verb-adjective ratio as a means of developing a quantitative score that may be useful in studying speech in psychiatric patients. It was originally considered to be an action quotient or index of emotional instability. A large number of investigators have applied that measure to psychiatric populations (Balken and Masserman, 1940; Fairbanks, 1944; Mann, 1944; Benton et al., 1945). Schizophrenics, manics, hysterics, and highly anxious persons have all been found to have higher quotients than do comparison groups. However, few studies have been able to replicate the figures of others. For example, the quotient in normals has been variously reported as 1.07, 1.98, and 3.43. Such variability is probably due to differences in definition of terms—that is, verb and adjective—and to the factors mentioned above that may affect the type-token ratio. Like the type-token ratio, the verb-adjective ratio has been largely abandoned as newer methods have been developed for studying language.

Other investigators have attempted a more detailed analysis of parts of speech in the language of various patient groups. Lorenz (1953) and

TABLE I
Type-Token Ratios in Psychiatric Patients and Normals

	Normals	Schizo-phrenics	Manics	Depres-sives
Salzinger et al. (1964)	.64 (N = 13)	.61 (N = 13)		
Andreasen-Pfohl*		.4169 (N = 14)	.4280 (N = 16)	.4098 (N = 14)
Fairbanks* (1944)	.64 (N = 10)	.57 (N = 10)		
Pavy et al.* (1969)	.71 (N = 24)	.66 (N = 24)		
Mann† (1944)		.6088 (N = 17)		

* Speech samples.
† Written samples.

Cobb (Lorenz and Cobb, 1952, 1953) examined speech in both manic and neurotic patients. After determining the number of words spoken a minute and the distribution of parts of speech, they found both neurotics and manics to differ from normal controls. Andreasen and Pfohl (1976) produced a relatively close replication of Lorenz and Cobb's findings with respect to frequency of taxonomic categories in manic speech. Comparing the frequency of taxonomic categories in manics and in depressives, Andreasen and Pfohl concluded that manic speech tends to be more colorful and concrete and that depressive speech tends to be vague, more personalized, and more qualified. They also noted that manics and depressives tend to resemble one another more than they resemble normals, suggesting that mania and depression may be different expressions of the same underlying phenomenon.

Other investigators have examined the frequency of taxonomic categories in schizophrenic speech (Fairbanks, 1944; Mann, 1944). Those studies indicated a greater difference between spoken language and written language than between schizophrenic language and normal language. They also indicated that findings concerning the frequency of taxonomic categories in schizophrenia can be replicated from one study to another, just as they can be replicated in mania.

Even though those taxonomic approaches to examining language have yielded relatively similar data from one study to another, they suffer from a serious defect: They observe language behavior at the level of single words, rather than at more complex syntactical, semantic, pragmatic, and discourse levels. Consequently, that method for studying language in psychiatric populations has only a descriptive value; it does not lend itself to an examination of the psychology of language—that is, to the cognitive processes underlying the perception, processing, and production of language.

STUDIES DERIVING FROM THE TRANSFORMATIONAL-GENERATIVE TRADITION

Concurrent with the development of methods for studying language at the syntactical and semantic levels within the discipline of psycholinguistics, investigations of psychiatric populations began to shift their emphasis from a taxonomic approach to a transformational-generative approach. Studies have moved from the level of the word to the level of the sentence. They have also shifted from examining actual performance to evaluating the underlying linguistic competence of psychiatric patients. Those studies recognize that the implementation of competence in the perception and the processing of language must be distinguished from the implementation of competence in language production. To date, however, most studies have focused primarily on the perceptual and processing dimensions.

Studies of contextual constraint. During the 1960's, a number of investigators examined the ability of schizophrenics to recall sentences that varied in contextual constraint. The sentences presented ranged from random word strings to sentences that were syntactically and semantically coherent and normal. Random word strings are considered to have the least amount of contextual constraint, and semantically and syntactically normal sentences are considered to provide the greatest amount of contextual constraint (Miller and Selfridge, 1950). The ability of patients to perceive and recall sentences with varying contextual constraint is considered to be an index of their sensitivity to the structure of language. Indirectly, therefore, the ability to use contextual constraint may be considered an index of linguistic competence.

Lewinsohn and Elwood (1961) were the first to use the contextual constraint paradigm to study schizophrenic language. They found that chronic schizophrenics tended to benefit less from increasing contextual constraint than did normals, but those differences tended to disappear when vocabulary was controlled. Their study was later replicated by Lawson et al. (1964). Raeburn and Tong (1968) determined that psychomotor retardation and vocabulary were both potential contaminating variables, because in their study schizophrenics with good vocabulary scores and no psychomotor retardation did benefit from increasing contextual constraint, but those with poor vocabulary and significant psychomotor retardation did not. Levy and Maxwell (1968) found schizophrenics to be impaired in comparison with a control group, but depressives to be even more impaired, indicating that the finding may be comparatively nonspecific.

Several other investigators have modified the contextual constraint paradigm in an attempt to map deficiencies in linguistic competence more specifically. One refinement has been to provide sentences that vary in syntactical and semantic constraints. Four different types of sentences have been used: normal (snug rings bind chubby fingers), anomalous (snug olives spread splintered subdivisions), semantically related (rings snug fingers chubby bind), and random word strings (olives snug subdivisions splintered spread). The normal sentences are both syntactically correct and semantically meaningful. The anomalous sentences use normal syntactical patterns but are not semantically meaningful. The semantically related sentences have syntactical disarray but a meaningful semantic component. Random word strings are completely unstructured.

Gerver (1967) found both schizophrenics and normals to have progressively greater recall of normal sentences than of anomalous sentences and random word strings. The schizophrenics, compared with the normals, were able to recall a smaller percentage of sentences of all types but had an over-all curve similar to that of the normals. On the other hand, Truscott (1970) compared the ability of schizophrenics and normals to recall all four different types of sentences. Again, the schizophrenics performed more poorly than the normals under all conditions but showed the greatest difference from normals in the recall of normal sentences. Because schizophrenics had their greatest difficulty in remembering normal sentences, she concluded that schizophrenics showed less sensitivity to the structure of language than did normal subjects. However, Chapman and Chapman (1973) pointed out that her results may have been an artifact of her experimental design. Because her tasks were difficult, they tended to get relatively low scores on all tasks and, consequently, relatively poor discrimination between schizophrenics and normals on all tasks except the easiest, the recall of normal sentences. They suggested that, had her tasks all been in the middle range of difficulty, she might have obtained the opposite results—a greater deficit in recalling random word strings than in recalling sentences.

Thus, to date, studies of contextual constraint have yielded relatively inconclusive results concerning the linguistic competence of schizophrenics. Schizophrenics consistently show a poorer ability to recall sentences than do normals, but the reasons for that difference are not clear. Some studies have suggested that the deficit may be attributed primarily to such factors as inattentiveness and psychomotor retardation. Consequently, most of those studies may have tapped a performance dimension and been unsuccessful in their efforts to evaluate underlying linguistic competence. The attempt to map syntactical versus semantic competence initiated by Gerver (1967) and Truscott (1970) is also inconclusive because of defects in the experimental designs.

Studies of syntactical competence. In the 1970's several investigators attempted to correct the defects in the earlier contextual constraint studies and to achieve a purer evaluation of the syntactical competence of schizophrenic patients. Although the investigators recognized that it is probably impossible to totally isolate syntactical components from semantic components, those studies used experimental techniques developed for the study of normal speech that focus on syntactical components. They suggested that schizophrenic listeners process sentences syntactically in the same manner as normal listeners.

Rochester (1973), Rochester et al. (1973), and Carpenter (1976) used the embedded-click paradigm developed by Fodor and Bever (1965) to study syntactical processing by the schizophrenic listener. Fodor and Bever showed that normal subjects, when asked to recall the location of clicks embedded in sentences, tended to displace the clicks in the direction of syntactical boundaries. Their work suggested that normal persons tend to process sentences by chunking them into syntactical units. Both Rochester and Carpenter showed that schizophrenics had generally poorer recall than normals but tended to displace clicks to syntactical boundaries, just as the normals did. That relatively rare instance of independent replication in studies of schizophrenic language seems to argue strongly that schizophrenics function normally in syntactical processing. Those studies have, therefore, provided some relatively hard data concerning the mapping of language abnormalities in schizophrenia. When those studies are combined with the clinical fact that schizophrenic speech is often impaired, they suggest that the defect in schizophrenic language is in output, rather than in input. That is, schizophrenics can perceive and process language normally, but they are impaired in some aspects of language production. Further, the impairment is probably not at the syntactical level but, rather, at the semantic, discourse, or pragmatic level.

Although most investigators have been concerned with language behavior in schizophrenia, several investigators have suggested that language and thinking are disrupted in other psychiatric disorders, especially in mania. Durbin and Martin (1977) examined syntactical aspects of speech in mania from the perspective of transformational grammar, looking specifically at linguistic competence. They concluded that basic speech capacities are well preserved in mania, so that manics are able to comprehend and generate grammatical sentences and to make complex grammatical transformations. However, they also observed a disruption in the manics' ability to use ellipsis and discourse anaphora (i.e., problems with reference). They suggested that the disruption may be the phenomenon that characterizes the manic flight of ideas.

STUDIES OF DISCOURSE AND COMMUNICATION

Although psycholinguists have become interested in the analysis of units larger than the sentence only recently, psychiatrists and psychologists have examined language at the discourse level for a number of years. Studies of disordered schizophrenic speech grew naturally from an interest in an underlying schizophrenic thought disorder considered by Bleuler and his followers to be a primary and pathognomonic symptom of schizophrenia. Speech and language behavior were seen as the objective means through which an underlying deficit in thinking can be studied empirically. Early approaches to the study of discourse derived primarily from behavioral and empirical traditions. A wide range of methods have been applied to the study of schizophrenic speech, and a number of those methods have also been applied to patients with other diagnoses. More recently, psycholinguists have also attempted to study schizophrenic discourse in terms of communication strategies.

Cloze analysis. Cloze analysis is one of the earliest methods developed for examining language at the discourse level. It was originally developed by Taylor (1953) as a measure of the effectiveness of communication. As ordinarily used, cloze analysis involves the deletion of every nth (usually fifth) word from a passage of written or spoken discourse. The mutilated passage is then given to normal decoders, who are asked to guess which words have been deleted. A cloze score is derived from the ratio of the number of correct guesses to the total number of words deleted. That score may be considered a measure of the clarity or the redundancy of the passage of discourse. The higher the score, the greater the clarity and the redundancy. If schizophrenic speech communicates poorly and has a decreased redundancy because of idiosyncratic language usage, it should have a lower cloze score than the speech of normal persons.

Salzinger (1971) developed an immediacy hypothesis that accounts for the lower cloze scores observed in schizophrenic patients (Salzinger et al., 1964). That hypothesis derives primarily from a behavioral tradition that emphasizes the importance of stimulus-response conditions and stands in opposition to Chomsky and transformational approaches. The hypothesis states that schizophrenic behavior is primarily controlled by stimuli that are immediate in the environment. As compared with normal persons, schizophrenics tend to respond to immediate stimuli at the expense of more distant ones. Consequently, in their speech schizophrenics are responding to the stimulus of the words they have spoken recently and are not taking into account the words they have spoken that are further removed from the present. That tendency causes their speech to have less redundancy and less contextual constraint than the speech of normals.

A series of studies using the cloze procedure is summarized in Table II. All those studies used normal decoders to guess the missing words in schizophrenic speech with every fifth word deleted. The studies indicated some difficulty in replicating Salzinger's original findings. They indicated that there may be greater variability of schizophrenic speech from study to study than there is between schizophrenic speech and normal speech. Furthermore, when schizophrenics are compared

TABLE II
Cloze Scores of Speech from Psychiatric Patients and Normals

	Salzinger et al. (1964) (15–17 decoders)	Honigfeld (1967) (37 decoders)	Cheek and Amarel (1967) (10 decoders)	Silverman (1972) (4 decoders)	Rutter et al. (1975) (4 decoders)	Andreasen and Pfohl (5 decoders)
Newspaper article		50.7% (N = 1)				53.8% (N = 4)
Normal speech	49% (N = 13)		44.0% (N = 10)		41.7% (N = 12)	62.5% (N = 11)
Schizophrenic speech	40% (N = 13)	50.5% (N = 1)	37.6% (N = 10)	55.96% (N = 7)	43.3% (N = 12)	59.6% (N = 15)
Manic speech						57.5% (N = 13)
Depressed speech						59.6% (N = 15)

with manics and depressives, there is little difference between the three patient groups. That result suggests that, if there is a defect, it is not specific to schizophrenia.

Cloze analysis is a technique that has many methodological problems, despite its apparent simplicity. As Table II indicates, considerable variability may be produced, depending on whether the passage of discourse is written or spoken. Other major factors that may influence the cloze score are the topic of conversation, the number of decoders, the intelligence of the decoders, and, perhaps most important of all, the care with which the decoders perform their task. The cloze technique involves so many contaminating variables that it is probably not the most powerful technique available for the study of language in psychiatric populations.

Content analysis. One approach to examining discourse in psychiatric populations has been to evaluate various aspects of its content. The theoretical base for that approach has frequently been the psychoanalytic tradition, rather than the psycholinguistic tradition. The goal has usually been to use word choice or topic choice as a guide to understanding the underlying dynamics of thinking. Working independently, investigators have developed several different methods for analyzing the content of discourse. None of those independent methods has been widely replicated or generally accepted.

Weintraub and Aronson (1964, 1965, 1967, 1969, 1974) developed a method of using word choice as a reflection of various psychological defense mechanisms. Although their purpose was to illuminate psychodynamics, their method was taxonomic. By counting the number of words and phrases in particular predefined categories—such as negators, qualifiers, and words that reflect a value judgment—they found differences between normal controls and patients suffering from a wide range of psychiatric disorders—delusional behavior, impulsive behavior, compulsive behavior, and depression. Their method requires individual scoring in transcribed samples of speech. It is, therefore, necessarily time consuming and somewhat dependent on the subjective judgment of the scorer and the sampling error of the sample.

Stone et al. (1966) were responsible for developing computerized approaches to the content analysis of discourse. Their method, developed primarily to study the speech of normal persons, analyzes the content of discourse through the use of content-analysis dictionaries, sets of word categories that group together words considered to share a similar psychological significance. For example, all words dealing with the concept of failure are enumerated in a dictionary under that general category. The computer is used to scan passages of discourse and report the number of words used in the various categories under investigation. Tucker and Rosenberg (1975) introduced the use of that technique to psychiatric populations. They reported that it was possible to differentiate schizophrenic speech from normal speech on the basis of content or thematic material alone. Andreasen and Pfohl (1976) piloted the technique on speech in affective disorders and in schizophrenia. They were unable to replicate Tucker's findings concerning the usefulness of content-analysis dictionaries.

Gottschalk (1967) and his associates (Gottschalk et al., 1958, 1961) developed an elaborate weighted scoring system designed to evaluate anxiety, social alienation, uncertainty, and feelings of being controlled. Most of their work focused on schizophrenic patients, and they reported a schizophrenic scale derived from discourse analysis that correlates well with clinical state and that can be used to distinguish schizophrenic patients from patients with brain damage. Recently, Gottschalk et al. (1975) attempted to develop computerized methods for the study of discourse, but the schizophrenic scale requires hand scoring.

Discourse analysis. Recently, investigators have begun to shift their emphasis from examining the content of discourse to examining the structure of discourse. Studies that derive from a psychiatric and phenomenological tradition have attempted to define formal thought disorder and associative loosening more precisely than in the past. Those investigations have attempted to document the existence of structural disorganization in the speech of psychiatric patients. Other studies, drawing from more purely psycholinguistic traditions, have attempted to define the precise nature of the structural defect.

Siegel et al. (1976) described a set of categories for analyzing the structure of discourse and used the method to compare the speech of chronic schizophrenic inpatients and chronic schizophrenic outpatients. They documented that inpatients manifest more severe disruption than do outpatients, tending to show shifts from topic to topic both within and between sentences. Andreasen (1979) developed a more detailed set of definitions to describe the structural abnormalities observed in the language of psychiatric patients. Many of those definitions and descriptions, which have good to excellent reliability, have been incorporated into the third edition of the American Psychiatric Association's (1980) *Diagnostic and Statistical Manual of Mental Disorders*. Andreasen's studies—using those definitions to examine the language of manics, depressives, and schizophrenics—indicated that nonschizophrenic patients, especially manics, may also manifest severely disorganized speech.

Rochester and her associates (1977) did several studies that examined the structure of schizophrenic discourse in terms of the burden it places on the listener. They used a quantitative approach to examine various aspects of structure, such as the use of reference, cohesive ties, and retrieval strategies. They concluded that the schizophrenic complicates the listener's task by asking the listener to search for information that is never clearly given and by providing relatively few cohesive links between clauses. They hypothesized that the schizophrenic speaker fails to account for a listener's immediate needs because of limitations in the schizophrenic's short-term memory, since many of the communication problems in schizophrenic speech are due to problems of reference. Theirs are the only studies that draw directly from the psycholinguistic tradition and apply methods developed for the study of normal discourse to discourse produced by schizophrenic patients.

Studies of communication strategies. Although psycholinguists have only recently become interested in the rigorous examination of pragmatic aspects of language, investigators interested in psychiatric populations have examined language behavior in terms of its social and communicative functions for a number of years. Many of those studies examined communication and language behavior in the families of schizophrenic patients. They derived from a concern that schizophrenic thought disorder and schizophrenic breakdown may be induced by pathological communication styles within the family.

The earliest attempts to study communication styles within the family were developed by Wynne and Singer (1963 a, b; Singer and Wynne, 1965 a, b). Their method emphasized the use of projective techniques to identify communication and thinking patterns considered to be pathological. They defined several different communication styles they considered to be related to premorbid history, severity, and prognosis. Patients with amorphous styles, which are impoverished and flat, tended to have a poorer premorbid history and prognosis than did patients with fragmented styles, which are productive but disorganized. Using their approach, a blind rater was able to study responses to projective tests and to identify the parents of schizophrenic patients with a high degree of accuracy.

Wild et al. (1977) combined the use of projective tests with the study of family interactions. They studied family members both alone and as a group. In that approach, familial power patterns are operationalized by coding who speaks to whom and for how long. They found evidence that schizophrenic families tend to have different patterns of communication and dominance than do control families. That body of research on language and communication strategies and schizophrenic families may argue for the importance of the interaction between familial communication patterns and a genetic substrate.

Another approach to examining the communication skills of schizophrenics has been to study their skills in performing a communication task. Cohen and Camhi (1967) and later Putterman (1975) studied communication skills in schizophrenia, using a word-communication task in which a speaker must attempt to provide a listener with a clue that will help the listener select a correct response. They found schizophrenics to perform more poorly than did normals in the speaker's role but not in the listener's role. Cohen and Camhi interpreted that finding in terms of traditional associational psychology; they saw it as reflecting a faulty selection from the schizophrenic's associational repertoire. However, it can also be interpreted as providing further evidence for some kind of deficit in language production, as opposed to perception and processing. It provides further evidence that schizophrenic speakers are unable to take the needs of their listeners into account to communicate clearly with them.

Schizophrenic language and aphasia. A tradition growing from German psychiatry, in particular the Frankfurt school, sees the language disturbance in schizophrenia as organic in origin. Kleist (1960) saw schizophrenia as a neurological disorder that was related conceptually to the dementias and aphasias. He developed a classification system and a terminology for describing thought and language disturbances in schizophrenia, and he believed that the differing clinical pictures in schizophrenia were due to different focal lesions in the brain. One such subtype was schizophasia, a form of schizophrenia characterized primarily by disorganized speech.

During recent years a number of investigators have become interested in exploring again the relationship between schizophrenia and the aphasias. Interest has been spurred by a number of studies that suggest left-hemisphere abnormalities in schizophrenia (Flor-Henry, 1969; Galin, 1974). Documentation of a relationship between schizophrenia and the aphasias may aid in the further localization of the language abnormalities in schizophrenia.

Although it is clear that not all schizophrenics manifest disorganized speech, a small subset definitely do (Gerson et al., 1977; Rochester and Martin, 1978; Andreasen and Grove, 1980). Chaika (1974, 1977) was the first to describe features of schizophrenic speech that link it to the aphasias. She described a variety of disruptions in ability to follow phonological, syntactical, semantic, and discourse rules. She argued that those abnormalities reflect a true break in linguistic competence in schizophrenia. Some investigators have argued in response that the abnormalities Chaika noted also occur in normal speech (Fromkin, 1975) or that they reflect an underlying thought disorder, rather than a break in linguistic competence (Lecours and Vanier-Clement, 1976). Andreasen and Grove (1980) supported Chaika's position by observing that schizophrenics with severely disorganized speech make paraphasic-like substitutions, have difficulty in naming, and show other abnormalities similar to those found in fluent or Wernicke's aphasia.

Conclusion

Psycholinguistics is a relatively young discipline that has grown and changed rapidly during its brief life-span. In its beginnings it emphasized descriptive and empirical approaches, but its major emphasis at present is to examine underlying psychological processes, using a variety of experimental designs. Although initially allied with behaviorism, the Chomskian revolution has made psycholinguistics a discipline that

advocates, instead, a philosophical rationalism and mentalism. Psycholinguistics has moved from examining language at the level of the phoneme or word to the study of the sentence and to the current emphasis on the examination of discourse, dyadic interactions, pragmatic aspects of language, and communication strategies.

The rapid and creative growth of psycholinguistics is no doubt caused in part by the fact that it is a discipline that borders on many others. In examining language, psycholinguistics interfaces with the disciplines of cognitive psychology, psychopathology, developmental psychology, speech and hearing science, speech pathology, and linguistics itself. Its interaction with each of those related disciplines tends to raise new questions and to create a need for new methods. Its interaction with psychiatry has grown increasingly close and productive, particularly for the field of psychiatry. Applying the new methods of psycholinguistics to psychiatric populations, investigators have added significantly to the understanding of language behavior in schizophrenia, mania, depression, and some neurotic disorders.

Suggested Cross References

Learning theory is discussed in Section 4.3. Communication is discussed in Section 4.7. Schizophrenic disorders are discussed in Chapter 15, affective disorders in Chapters 18 and 19, and language and speech disorders of childhood and adolescence in Sections 39.3 and 40.2.

REFERENCES

Abrams, K., and Bever, T. G. Syntactic structure modifies attention during speech perception and recognition. Q. J. Exp. Psychol., *21:* 280, 1969.
American Psychiatric Association. *Diagnostic and Statistical Manual of Mental Disorders,* ed. 3. American Psychiatric Association, Washington, D.C., 1980.
Andreasen, N. C. The clinical assessment of thought, language, and communication disorders: The definition of terms and evaluation of their reliability. Arch. Gen. Psychiatry, 1980a, In Press.
Andreasen, N. C. The diagnostic significance of thought, language, and communication disorders. Arch. Gen. Psychiatry, 1980b, In Press.
Andreasen, N. C., and Grove, W. The relationship between schizophrenic language, manic language, and the aphasias. In *Hemisphere Asymmetries of Function and Psychopathology,* P. Flor-Henry and J. Gruzelier, editors. Elsevier, New York, 1980, In Press.
Andreasen, N. C., and Pfohl, B. Linguistic analysis of speech in affective disorders. Arch. Gen. Psychiatry, *33:* 1361, 1976.
Austin, J. L. *How to Do Things with Words.* Oxford University Press, Oxford, 1962.
Balken, E. R., and Masserman, J. H. The language of the phantasies of patients with conversion hysteria, anxiety state, and obsessive-compulsive neurosis. J. Psychol., *10:* 75, 1940.
Benton, A. L., Hartman, C. H., and Sarason, I. G. Some relations between speech behavior and anxiety level. J. Abnorm. Soc. Psychol., *5:* 295, 1945.
Bever, T. G. The cognitive basis for linguistic structures. In *Cognition and the Development of Language,* J. R. Hayes, editor, p. 279. John Wiley & Sons, New York, 1970.
Bever, T. G. The nature of cerebral dominance in speech behavior of the child and adult. In *Mechanisms of Language Development,* R. Huxley and E. Ingram, editors, p. 231. Academic Press, New York, 1971.
Bever, T. G. Perception, thought, and language. In *Language Comprehension and the Acquisition of Knowledge,* R. O. Freedle and J. B. Carroll, editors, p. 99. Winston & Sons, Washington, D.C., 1972.
Bever, T. G., Carroll, J. M., and Hurtig, R. Analogy or ungrammatical sequences that are utterable and comprehensible are the origins of new grammars in language acquisition and linguistic evolution. In *An Integrated Theory of Linguistic Ability,* T. G. Bever, J. J. Katz, and D. T. Langedon, editors, p. 149. Crowell, New York, 1976.
Bever, T. G., Garrett, M. F., and Hurtig, R. The interaction of perceptual processes and ambiguous sentences. Mem. Cognition, *1:* 277, 1973.
Bever, T. G., and Hurtig, R. Detection of a nonlinguistic stimulus is poorest at the end of a clause. J. Psycholing. Res., *4:* 1, 1975.
Bever, T. G., Lackner, J. R., and Kirk, R. The underlying structures of sentences are the primary units of immediate speech processing. Percept. Psychophysics, *5:* 225, 1969.
Bloomfield, L. *Language.* Holt, Rinehart and Winston, New York, 1933.
Broadbent, D. E. *Perception and Communication.* Pergamon Press, London, 1958.
Busemann, A. *Die Sprache der Jugend als Ausdruck der Entwicklungsrhythmik.* Fisher Verlag, Jena, 1925.

Carpenter, M. D. Sensitivity to syntactic structure: Good versus poor premorbid schizophrenics. J. Abnorm. Psychol., *85:* 41, 1976.

Chaika, E. A linguist looks at "schizophrenic" language. Brain Language, *1:* 257, 1974.

Chaika, E. O. Schizophrenic speech, slips of the tongue, and jargonaphasia: A reply to Fromkin and to Lecours and Vanier-Clement. Brain Language, *4:* 464, 1977.

Chapman, L. J., and Chapman, J. P. Problems in the measurement of cognitive deficit. Psychol. Bull., *79:* 380, 1973.

Cheek, F. E., and Amarel, M. Some techniques for the measurement of changes in verbal communication. In *Research in Verbal Behavior and Some Neurophysiological Implications*, K. Salzinger and S. Salzinger, editors, p. 327. Academic Press, New York, 1967.

Chomsky, N. *Syntactic Structures*. Mouton, The Hague, 1957.

Chomsky, N. *Aspects of the Theory of Syntax*. MIT Press, Cambridge, Mass., 1965.

Chomsky, N., and Halle, M. *The Sound Pattern of English*. Harper & Row, New York, 1968.

Clark, E. V. What's in a word? On the child's acquisition of semantics in his first language. In *Cognitive Development and the Acquisition of Language*, T. E. Moore, editor, p. 65. Academic Press, New York, 1973.

Clark, H. H. The primitive nature of children's relational concepts. In *Cognition and the Development of Language*, J. R. Hayes, editor, p. 269. John Wiley & Sons, New York, 1970.

Clark, H. H. Space, time, semantics, and the child. In *Cognitive Development and the Acquisition of Language*, T. E. Moore, editor, p. 28. Academic Press, New York, 1973.

Clifton, C., and Odom, P. Similarity relations among certain English sentence constructions. Psychol. Monogr., *80:* 1, 1966.

Cohen, B. D., and Camhi, J. Schizophrenic performance in a word-communication task. J. Abnorm. Psychol., *72:* 240, 1967.

Durbin, M., and Martin, R. L. Speech in mania: Syntactic aspects. Brain Language, *4:* 208, 1977.

Fairbanks, H. The quantitative differentiation of samples of spoken language. Psychol. Monogr., *56:* 19, 1944.

Flor-Henry, P. Psychosis and temporal lobe epilepsy: A controlled investigation. Epilepsia, *10:* 363, 1969.

Fodor, J. A. Could meaning be an r_m? J. Verbal Learning Verbal Behav., *9:* 73, 1965.

Fodor, J. A., and Bever, T. G. The psychological reality of linguistic segments. J. Verbal Learning Verbal Behav., *4:* 414, 1965.

Freedle, R. O., editor. *Discourse Production and Comprehension*. Ablex, Norwood, N. J., 1977.

Fromkin, V. A. A linguist looks at "A linguist looks at 'schizophrenic language.'" Brain Language, *2:* 498, 1975.

Galin, D. Implications for psychiatry of left and right cerebral specialization. Arch. Gen. Psychiatry, *31:* 572, 1974.

Gerson, S. N., Benson, F., and Frazier, S. H. Diagnosis: Schizophrenia versus posterior aphasia. Am. J. Psychiatry, *134:* 966, 1977.

Gerver, D. Linguistic rules and the perception and recall of speech by schizophrenic patients. Br. J. Soc. Clin. Psychol., *6:* 204, 1967.

Gottschalk, L. A. Theory and application of a verbal behavior method of measuring transient psychological states. In *Research in Verbal Behavior and Some Neurophysiological Implications*, K. Salzinger and S. Salzinger, editors, p. 299. Academic Press, New York, 1967.

Gottschalk, L. A., Glesner, G. C., Daniels, R. S., and Block, S. The speech patterns of schizophrenic patients: A method of assessing relative degree of personal disorganization and social alienation. J. Nev. Ment. Dis., *127:* 153, 1958.

Gottschalk, L. A., Glesner, G. C., Magliocco, E. B., and D'Zmura, T. L. Further studies on the speech patterns of schizophrenic patients. J. Nerv. Ment. Dis., *132:* 101, 1961.

Gottschalk, L. A., Hausmann, C., and Brown, J. S. A computerized scoring system for use with content analysis scales. Compr. Psychiatry, *16:* 77, 1975.

Grice, H. P. *Logic and Conversation*, William James Lectures. Harvard University Press, Cambridge, Mass., 1967.

Harris, Z. S. *Methods in Structural Linguistics*. University of Chicago Press, Chicago, 1951.

Honigfeld, G. Cloze analysis in the evaluation of central determinants of comprehensibility. In *Research in Verbal Behavior and Some Neurophysiological Implications*, K. Salzinger and S. Salzinger, editors, p. 345. Academic Press, New York, 1967.

Hurtig, R. Language and thought: The question of linguistic relativity and linguistic universals. In *International Encyclopedia of Psychiatry, Psychology, Psychoanalysis, and Neurology*, B. Wolman, editor, vol. 6, p. 349. Van Nostrand Reinhold Aesculapius, New York, 1977.

Hurtig, R. The validity of clausal processing strategies at the discourse level. Discourse Proc., *1:* 195, 1978.

Johnson, N. F. Sequential verbal behavior. In *Verbal Behavior and General Behavior Theory*, T. R. Dixon and D. L. Horton, editors, p. 421. Prentice-Hall, Englewood Cliffs, N. J., 1968.

Johnson, W. Studies in language behavior. I. A program of research. Psychol. Monogr., *56:* 1, 1944.

Kaplan, R. Augmented transition networks as psychological models of sentence comprehension. Artif. Intelligence, *3:* 77, 1972.

Katz, J. J., and Bever, T. G. The rise and fall of empiricism. In *An Integrated Theory of Linguistic Ability*, T. G. Bever, J. J. Katz, and D. T. Langendon, editors, p. 11. Crowell, New York, 1976.

Kintch, W. *The Representation of Meaning in Memory*. Erlbaum Associates, Hillsdale, N. J., 1974.

Kleist, K. Schizophrenic symptoms and cerebral pathology. J. Ment. Sci., *106:* 246, 1960.

Lakoff, G. Linguistics and natural logic. In *Semantics of Natural Language*, D. Davidson and G. Harman, editors, p. 545. Reidel, Dordrecht, Holland, 1972.

Lawson, J. S., McGhie, A., and Chapman, J. Perception of speech in schizophrenia. Br. J. Psychiatry, *100:* 375, 1964.

Lecours, A. R., and Vanier-Clement, M. Schizophasia and jargonaphasia: A comprehensive description with comments on Chaika's and Fromkin's respective looks at "schizophrenic" language. Brain Language, *3:* 516, 1976.

Levy, R., and Maxwell, A. E. The effect of verbal context on the recall of schizophrenics and other psychiatric patients. Br. J. Psychiatry, *114:* 311, 1968.

Lewinsohn, P. M., and Elwood, D. L. The role of contextual constraint in the learning of language samples in schizophrenia. J. Nerv. Ment. Dis., *133:* 79, 1961.

Lorenz, M. Language as expressive behavior. Arch. Neurol. Psychiatry, *70:* 227, 1953.

Lorenz, M., and Cobb, S. Language behavior in manic patients. Arch. Neurol. Psychiatry, *69:* 763, 1952.

Lorenz, M., and Cobb, S. Language behavior in psychoneurotic patients. Arch. Neurol. Psychiatry, *69:* 684, 1953.

Mandler, J. M., and Johnson, N. S. Rememberance of things parsed: Story structure and recall. Cognitive Psychol., *9:* 111, 1977.

Mann, M. B. The quantitative differentiation of samples of written language. Psychol. Monogr., *56:* 41, 1944.

McCawley, J. D. The role of semantics in grammar. In *Universals in Linguistic Theory*, E. Bach and R. T. Harms, editors, p. 125. Holt, New York, 1968.

Mehler, J. Some effects of grammatical transformations on the recall of English sentences. J. Verbal Learning Verbal Behav., *2:* 346, 1963.

Miller, G. A. *Language and Communication*. McGraw-Hill, New York, 1951.

Miller, G. A. Some psychological studies of grammar. Am. Psychol., *17:* 748, 1962.

Miller, G. A. Some preliminaries to psycholinguistics. Am. Psychol., *20:* 15, 1965.

Miller, G. A., and Chomsky, N. Finitary models of language users. In *Handbook of Mathematical Psychology*, R. D. Luce, R. R. Bush, and E. Galanter, editors, vol. 2, p. 419. John Wiley & Sons, New York, 1963.

Miller, G. A., and McKean, K. A. Chronometric study of some relations between sentences. Q. J. Exp. Psychol., *16:* 297, 1964.

Miller, G. A., and Selfridge, J. A. Verbal context and the recall of meaningful material. Am. J. Psychol., *63:* 176, 1950.

Mowrer, O. H. The psychologist looks at language. Am. Psychol., *9:* 660, 1954.

Neisser, U. *Cognitive Psychology*. Appleton-Century-Crofts, New York, 1967.

Norman, D. A., and Rumelhart, D. E. *Explorations in Cognition*. W. H. Freeman & Co., San Francisco, 1975.

Osgood, C. E. On understanding and creating sentences. Am. Psychol., *18:* 735, 1963.

Osgood, C. E., Suci, G. J., and Tannenbaum, P. H. *The Measurement of Meaning*. University of Illinois Press, Urbana, 1957.

Pavy, D., Grinspoon, L., and Shader, R. I. Word frequency measures of verbal disorders in schizophrenia. Dis. Nerv. Syst., *30:* 553, 1969.

Putterman, A. H. Referential speaker processes in male and female process-reactive schizophrenics. J. Nerv. Ment. Dis., *160:* 354, 1975.

Raeburn, J. M., and Tong, J. E. Experiments on contextual constraint in schizophrenia. Br. J. Psychiatry, *114:* 43, 1968.

Rochester, S. R. The role of information processing in the sentence decoding of schizophrenic listeners. J. Nerv. Ment. Dis., *157:* 217, 1973.

Rochester, S. R., Harris, J., and Seeman, M. V. Sentence processing in schizophrenic listeners. J. Abnorm. Psychol., *82:* 350, 1973.

Rochester, S. R., and Martin, J. R. *Discourse of the Schizophrenic Speaker*. Plenum Publishing Corp., New York, 1978.

Rochester, S. R., Martin, J., and Thurston, S. Thought process disorder in schizophrenia: The listener's task. Brain Language, *4:* 95, 1977.

Rutter, D. R., Wishner, J., and Callaghan, B. A. The prediction and predictability of speech in schizophrenic patients. Br. J. Psychiatry, *126:* 571, 1975.

Sachs, H., Schegloff, E. A., and Jefferson, G. A simplest systematics for the organization of turn-taking for conversation. Language, *50:* 696, 1974.

Salzinger, K. An hypothesis about schizophrenic behavior. Am. J. Psychother., *25:* 601, 1971.

Salzinger, K., Portnoy, S., and Feldman, R. S. Verbal behavior of schizophrenic and normal subjects. Ann. N. Y. Acad. Sci., *105:* 845, 1964.

Salzinger, K., Portnoy, S., Pisoni, D. B., and Feldman, R. S. The immediacy hypothesis and response-produced stimuli in schizophrenic speech. J. Abnorm. Psychol., *76:* 258, 1970.

Sapir, E. *Language*. Harcourt, Brace, New York, 1921.

Savin, H., and Perchonock, E. Grammatical structure and the immediate recall of English sentences. J. Verbal Learning Verbal Behav., *4:* 348, 1965.

Searle, J. R. *Speech Acts*. Cambridge University Press, Cambridge, 1969.

Seitz, M. R., and Weber, B. A. Effects of response requirement on the location of clicks superimposed on sentences. Mem. Cognition, *2:* 43, 1974.

Shepard, R. N., and Chipman, S. Second-order isomorphism of internal representations: Shapes of states. Cognitive Psychol., *1:* 1, 1971.

Siegel, A., Horrow, M., Reilly, F. E., and Tucker, G. J. Loose associations and disordered speech patterns in chronic schizophrenia. J. Nerv. Ment. Dis., *162:* 105, 1976.

Silverman, G. Psycholinguistics of schizophrenic language. Psychol. Med., *2:* 254, 1972.

Singer, M. T., and Wynne, L. C. Thought disorder and family relations of schizophrenics. III. Methodology using projective techniques. Arch. Gen. Psychiatry, *12:* 187, 1965a.

Singer, M. T., and Wynne, L. C. Thought disorder and family relations of schizophrenics. IV. Results and implications. Arch. Gen. Psychiatry, *12:* 201, 1965b.

Slobin, D. I. Cognitive prerequisites for the development of grammar. In *Studies of Child Language Development*, C. A. Ferguson and D. I. Slobin, editors, p. 175. Holt, New York, 1973.

Spreen, O., and Wachal, R. S. Psycholinguistic analysis of aphasic language: Theoretical formulations and procedures. Lang. Speech, *16:* 130, 1973.

Stone, P. J., Dunphy, D. C., Smith, M. S., and Ogilvie, D. M. *The General Inquirer: A Computer Approach to Content Analysis*. MIT Press, Cambridge, Mass., 1966.

Taylor, W. L. "Cloze procedure": A new tool for measuring readability. Journalism Q., *30:* 415, 1953.

Truscott, I. P. Contextual constraint and schizophrenic language. J. Consult. Clin. Psychol., *34:* 189, 1970.

Tucker, G. J., and Rosenberg, S. D. Computer content analysis of schizophrenic speech. Am. J. Psychiatry, *132:* 611, 1975.

Watt, W. C. On two hypotheses concerning psycholinguistics. In *Cognition and the Development of Language*, J. R. Hayes, editor. p. 137. John Wiley & Sons, New York, 1970.

Weintraub, W., and Aronson, H. The application of verbal behavior analysis to the study of psychological defense mechanisms. II. Speech pattern associated with impulsive behavior. J. Nerv. Ment. Dis., *139:* 75, 1964.

Weintraub, W., and Aronson, H. The application of verbal behavior analysis to the study of psychological defense mechanisms. III. Speech associated with delusional behavior. J. Nerv. Ment. Dis., *141:* 172, 1965.

Weintraub, W., and Aronson, H. The application of verbal behavior analysis to the study of psychological defense mechanism. IV. Speech pattern associated with depressive behavior. J. Nerv. Ment. Dis., *144:* 22, 1967.

Weintraub, W., and Aronson, H. Application of verbal behavior analysis to the study of psychological defense mechanism. V. Speech pattern associated with overeating. Arch. Gen. Psychiatry, *21:* 739, 1969.

Weintraub, W., and Aronson, H. Verbal behavior analysis and psychological defense mechanisms. VI. Speech pattern associated with compulsive behavior. Arch. Gen. Psychiatry, *30:* 297, 1974.

Whitehorn, J. C., and Zipf, G. K. Schizophrenic language. Arch. Neurol. Psychiatry, *49:* 831, 1943.

Whorf, B. L. *Language, Thought, and Reality: Selected Writings of Benjamin Lee Whorf*. John Wiley & Sons, New York, 1956.

Wild, C. M., Shapiro, L. N., and Abelin, T. Communication patterns and role structure in families of male schizophrenics. Arch. Gen. Psychiatry, *34:* 58, 1977.

Wynne, L. C., and Singer, M. T. Thought disorder and family relations of schizophrenics. I. A research strategy. Arch. Gen. Psychiatry, *9:* 191, 1963a.

Wynne, L. C., and Singer, M. T. Thought disorder and family relations of schizophrenics. II. A classification of forms of thinking. Arch. Gen. Psychiatry, *9:* 199, 1963b.

Yngve, V. H. A. A model and a hypothesis for language structure. Proc. Am. Philosophical Soc., *104:* 444, 1960.

4.9 Applications of Learning and Biofeedback to Psychiatry and Medicine

NEAL E. MILLER, Ph.D.

Introduction

Certain simple applications of the principles of learning and behavior theory are believed to be particularly relevant to psychiatry and to other branches of medicine. This section discusses how neurotic maladjustment and symptoms may be learned or unlearned, how repression can interfere with problem solving; it discusses conflict behavior, ways in which learning may influence such emotions as fear, the bodily effects that these emotions can produce, habituation to stress, visceral learning, and what is popularly called biofeedback.

To the extent that neuroses and psychoses are functional—in other words, instrumental in serving a need—they must be learned either by the laws of learning and behavior that have already been discovered in the laboratory or by new laws yet to be discovered. The laws of learning and behavior studied in the laboratory are useful to the psychiatrist, and the clinical observations of the psychiatrist are useful as points of departure for new experimental studies of learning and behavior. Putting the emphasis on learning does not denigrate genetic and other organic factors; all behavior is a result of an interaction among genetic, organic, and learned factors. Conversely, emphasizing the organic factors does not eliminate the learned factors. For example, paresis caused by brain damage in the late stages of syphilis produces delusions, but the specific content of these delusions varies with the history of the times and hence must be learned.

Role of Animal Models

In psychiatry, clinical experience is often too convincing to the person experiencing it and not convincing enough to the person reading about it. The experimental method has the advantage of correcting the investigator when he is wrong and of convincing others when he is right. It also allows the relationships among variables to be dissected analytically in detail. But in some of the strongly emotional situations involved in psychiatry, it is often impossible or, at least, unethical to perform relevant controlled human experiments. In these cases the experiments that ultimately help relieve human misery must be conducted on animals. Such experiments are particularly relevant in dealing with some of the primitive emotional and motivational processes that humans and other mammals share in common. Animal experiments may be irrelevant, of course, in dealing with language and higher cognitive functions. In any case, the human applicability must be checked; but agreement between rigorous animal experiments and relevant clinical observations can greatly increase the probability that the conclusions are correct.

Fear in Symptom Formation

One can start with a simple animal model. At different times various laboratory rats are put into the left side of the apparatus illustrated in Figure 1. Most of them wander casually about, sniffing and exploring various parts of the apparatus. If by chance they happen to rotate the little wheel that causes the door below to drop, they wander through to explore the other side and then back to the left side with the grid. However, the behavior of one particular rat is unusual; it immediately walks up to the wheel, turns it, and walks through to the other side. It performs this stereotyped behavior every time it is put in. If the apparatus is changed so that rotating the wheel no longer causes the door to drop, the rat becomes agitated and turns it vigorously. If the wheel remains nonfunctional long enough, the rat eventually chances to press the bar, which now causes the door to drop, and rather quickly learns to substitute that new form of behavior. One might say this rat had a wheel-turning compulsion that eventually changed to a bar-pressing compulsion. The behavior seems bizarre.

But, if one knows the rat's history, this particular behavior is understandable. The bizarrely behaving rat has been a subject in an

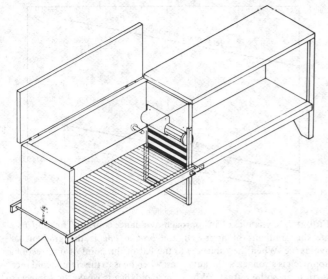

FIGURE 1. Apparatus for demonstrating that fear functions as a learned drive and a reduction in fear as a reward. (From Miller, N. E. Studies of fear as an acquirable drive. I. Fear as motivation and fear reduction as reinforcement in the learning of new responses. J. Exp. Psychol., *38:* 89, 1948.)

experiment on fear as a learnable drive (Miller, 1948). On a number of trials, it has been dropped into the left side of the apparatus and there given strong electric shocks, which it has learned to escape by running through the open door into the right side. On subsequent trials, all without electric shock, it has continued to run. To determine whether this behavior was the mere persistence of an automatic habit or whether some drive was involved, the experimenter closed the door, but it could be made to fall open by rotating the little wheel. With its escape blocked, the rat performed a variety of responses, one of which finally happened to rotate the wheel, allowing it to escape. By trial and error it gradually learned to perform immediately only the correct response, even though no shocks were administered. The learning was exactly as if the rat had been motivated by the drive of hunger and rewarded by food. But in this experiment it is reasonable to assume that the electric shocks have taught the animal a learned drive of fear in the left compartment and that the escape from fear when the animal runs into the right compartment functions as a reward analogous to food for a hungry animal. The previous experience produced the learned drive of fear, and the rewarding value of escape accounts for the peculiar behavior of this rat.

The fact that fear can be learned quickly, can be a strong drive, and can motivate the learning of new habits allows it to be responsible for behavior in one rat that is different from that of the others. Clinical evidence (Freud, 1936; Wolpe, 1958) also indicates that fear—or anxiety, as it is called when its source is vague or unknown—can play an important role in a considerable range of abnormal behavior. In fact, such clinical observations led to the development of the foregoing animal model.

As this particular rat becomes skillful during repeated trials of performing the coping response that allows him to escape, the relaxation that first begins to appear in the safe compartment gradually begins to appear earlier and earlier in the sequence of responses, until he seems to be performing the entire sequence mechanically in an unmotivated way, analogous to *la belle indifférence* of the hysteric. Because the cues produced by performing the successful coping are never followed by electric shock, they become safety signals (Miller,

1951). But if the coping response is interfered with, the fear and agitation reappear, and the rat may learn a new habit.

With the history known, the rat's behavior is completely understandable. But, merely from closely observing the rat mechanically performing the skilled habit, someone who observed the behavior in detail might infer that the motivation was fear and that, if he interfered with the coping response, he might see behavior—such as agitation, urination, and defecation—that would confirm his inference. Then the history would be unnecessary.

If one continues to give the rat trials without electric shock, it may continue to perform for as many as 500 trials (Miller, 1951), and a higher organism, such as a dog, may persist for thousands of trials (Solomon et al., 1953). But eventually, if one does extinguish or countercondition the fear, not only does the performance of the original habit disappear, but so also does the tendency to learn a substitute habit. In some cases the substitute habit may be socially unacceptable or otherwise not adaptive in the long run; learning it is called symptom substitution. In other cases it removes the danger and fear and is called a coping response. The removal of fear or learning a more adaptive response to it is a goal of various types of psychotherapy, psychoanalytic and behavioral. As behavior therapists are getting experience with more serious problems, they are finding that it is sometimes necessary to locate and deal with the patient's real phobia, rather than with subsidiary symptoms, and that the process of discovering the real phobia can be described as like peeling the successive layers off an onion. Psychoanalysts are now placing more emphasis on ego strength and getting well in real life. Perhaps the facts of nature are forcing these two types of therapy to converge (Porter, 1968).

As Dollard and Miller (1950) pointed out, the animal model just described appears to be quite applicable to phobias and also to certain compulsions whose interruption induces anxiety. The model also seems to be readily applicable to combat neurosis, in which the source of fear is usually quite clear, and the fear-reducing value of the symptom that allows escape from combat provides a clear explanation of the reinforcement of that symptom. The impaired depth perception of a pilot or the hysterical paralysis of the trigger finger or the legs of an infantryman are examples.

Studies of combat show that the average person's response to extreme fear runs the gamut of virtually all neurotic and many psychotic symptoms. These reactions are a pounding heart and rapid pulse, a strong feeling of muscular tension, trembling, exaggerated startle response, dryness of the throat and mouth, a sinking feeling in the stomach, perspiration, a frequent need to urinate, irritability, aggression, an overpowering urge to cry or run and hide, confusion, feelings of unreality, feeling faint, nausea, fatigue, depression, slowing down of movements and thoughts, restlessness, loss of appetite, insomnia, nightmares, interference with speech, the use of meaningless gestures, the maintenance of peculiar postures, and sometimes stuttering, mutism, and amnesia (Miller, 1951). Presumably, most of these reactions are innate responses to fear.

Once strong fear is learned, any of the foregoing symptoms can appear as a direct consequence of it. But, if one of these symptoms is followed by a decrease in fear, one may expect it to be rewarded and hence to become relatively more dominant. Indeed, the first stages of combat neurosis are likely to be characterized by a kaleidoscopic array of diverse symptoms that come and go. With the passage of time, one type of symptom usually becomes predominant (Grinker and Spiegel,

1945 a, b); it is exactly what one would expect if the patient were showing trial-and-error learning (Dollard and Miller, 1950).

Innate Factors in Fear

Virtually all experimental studies have used pain, primarily from electric shock, as the unconditioned stimulus to elicit fear. But Fuller (1967) found that suddenly plunging puppies reared in isolation into the complex normal environment elicited traumatic fear from which they virtually never recovered. Clinical observations indicate that fear can be elicited by strange situations, by sudden unexpected strong stimuli, by the removal of social supports and safety signals, by helplessness, by threats of bodily harm or death, and of the loss of love, respect, prestige, or money. It is easier to condition and then harder to extinguish fear to a potentially phobic stimulus, such as a snake, than to a more neutral object (Miller, 1951; Öhman et al., 1975). Some people may be more susceptible to fear than are others, and a given person may be more susceptible at one time than at another. Some situations may innately counteract fear. A monkey or a child is more difficult to frighten when clinging to his mother than when alone (Miller, 1951, 1979).

Other Drives

Dollard and Miller (1950) advanced the hypothesis that other functional symptoms are learned in exactly the same way as are those of combat neuroses. They emphasized fear because a great deal is known about how it can be learned as a strong drive that, in turn, motivates further learning. But any other strong drive could be the basis for similarly reinforcing the learning of a symptom. Indeed, there is evidence that the reward for a given symptom often comes from a number of drives. An incomplete list of such drives includes guilt (which seems to be closely related to fear and is perhaps a special kind of fear), disgust, anger, sex, and the needs for self-esteem, dominance, love, and social approval. Most of these drives have not been studied in any detail and are not yet accurately defined (Miller, 1959).

Conflict and Displacement

Both clinical and experimental evidence show that conflict plays a key role in many forms of mental disorder (Pavlov, 1927; Freud, 1943; Gantt, 1944; Weiss, 1971b). Thus, a theoretical and experimental analysis of conflict behavior is relevant to psychiatry. A common form of conflict is that in which a subject is motivated both to approach and to avoid a given desired but feared goal.

The analysis of such conflicts is based on a number of assumptions, each of which has been verified separately in simple experiments; the principal deductions from these assumptions have also been experimentally verified (Miller, 1944, 1959, 1964b; Brown, 1948). These assumptions are illustrated in Figure 2. The assumptions are: (1) The tendency to approach a goal is stronger the nearer the subject is to it, so there is a gradient of approach, as represented by the *solid lines* in the figure. (2) The tendency to avoid a feared stimulus is stronger the nearer the subject is to it, so there is a gradient of avoidance, as represented by the *broken line.* (3) The strength of avoidance increases more rapidly with nearness than does the strength of approach. (4) The strength of the tendency to approach or to avoid varies directly with the strength of the drive on which it is based; increased drive raises the height of the entire gradient, as illustrated by the various *solid lines.*

Looking first at the weak approach and avoidance in Figure 2, one can see that, when the subject is to the left of point *N*, at which the

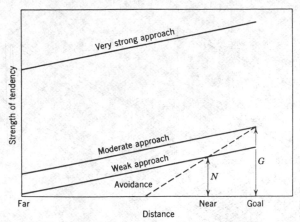

FIGURE 2. Dynamics of an approach-avoidance conflict. The *solid lines* are the gradients of approach; the *broken line* is the gradient of avoidance. When the subject is to the left of the point of intersection, approach is stronger, so he advances; when he is to the right, avoidance is stronger, so he retreats. When the avoidance is weak, the subject is able to approach near to the goal, and a small increase in the strength of approach (from weak to moderate) causes him to reach it and produces only a small increase (from *N* to *G*) in the amount of fear elicited. Throughout, linear gradients are used for clarity, but similar deductions can be made from any curves with a continuous slope steeper for avoidance than for approach at each point above the *abscissa.* (From Miller, N. E. Some implications of modern behavior theory for personality change and psychotherapy. In *Personality Change*, P. Worchel and D. Byrne, editors, p. 149. John Wiley & Sons, New York, 1964b.)

gradients intersect, the approach is stronger than the avoidance, so that he moves nearer. But, if he moves beyond the point of intersection, avoidance is stronger than approach, so that he retreats. Therefore, the subject tends to approach partway and then stops, remaining in the general region of the point of intersection, being unable either to achieve or to leave his goal. Such behavior is characteristic of a wide variety of approach-avoidance conflict situations.

Furthermore, when the avoidance is relatively weak, the subject approaches near to the goal, even under weak motivation to approach. Then a slight increase in the strength of approach from weak to moderate causes the subject to reach the goal.

The amount of avoidance and presumably also of fear actually elicited depends on where the subject is, which is in the region of where the two gradients intersect. This fear elicited is represented by the *vertical double-headed arrows.* The increase from weak to moderate approach that causes the subject to go ahead the short additional distance to reach the goal is expected to produce only a moderate increase (from *N* to *G*) in fear. But after the subject reaches the goal, further increases in the strength of approach are not expected to produce any further increases in fear, because the subject is already at the dangerous goal and cannot move any nearer. In the case of a relatively weak conflict based on unrealistic fears, it presumably is relatively easy to produce therapeutic changes by moderate increases in the strength of the drive to approach, so that the subject can reach the goal, be rewarded for achieving it, and begin to extinguish and countercondition his fear. Thus, therapy can come about readily by natural increases in the drive to approach or can be facilitated by associates who use various means to enhance the attractiveness of the goal and to encourage the subject. Most subjects whose avoidances of important goals are so weak that they can respond to such therapy do not reach a professional psychotherapist.

By contrast, the situation represented in Figure 3 is one in which strong avoidance is motivated by strong fear, so that the subject with moderate motivation to approach remains far from the goal. In this case it takes a very strong approach drive to bring him to the goal, and inducing such motivation produces a great increase (from *F* to *G*) in

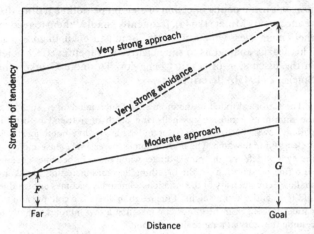

FIGURE 3. When strong avoidance keeps a subject with moderate motivation far from the goal, very strong motivation is required to cause him to reach it and produces a great increase (from *F* to *G*) in the amount of fear elicited. (From Miller, N. E. Some implications of modern behavior theory for personality change and psychotherapy. In *Personality Change*, P. Worchel and D. Byrne, editors, p. 149. John Wiley & Sons, New York, 1964b.)

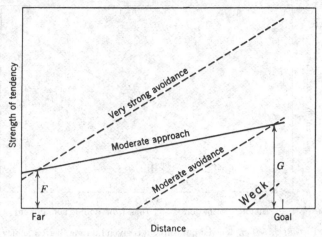

FIGURE 4. When very strong avoidance keeps the subject far from the goal, decreasing the strength of avoidance as he reaches the goal increases the strength of fear but not as much as when the same advance is produced by increasing the strength of approach, as shown in Figure 3. (From Miller, N. E. Some implications of modern behavior theory for personality change and psychotherapy. In *Personality Change*, P. Worchel and D. Byrne, editors, p. 149. John Wiley & Sons, New York, 1964b.)

fear. If the motivation to approach is not strong enough, the subject may never reach the goal, where he would have the most effective opportunity for extinguishing fear, but he may be near enough to it to suffer intolerable fear and conflict. The procedure of forcing a patient to remain in a frightening situation is called flooding. For a person with a severe conflict, it is extremely painful and perhaps impossible. It certainly does not work unless the therapist has powerful enough control over his patient to prevent him from escaping by fleeing from therapy. For a person with a weaker conflict or a therapist with strong control over the patient, it does work, often in combination with other procedures.

In the same strong conflict, Figure 4 shows what happens when the same amount of approach to the goal is produced by lowering the gradient of avoidance. As he considers the goal to be less dangerous and moves nearer to it, one may expect a paradoxical increase (from *F* to *G*) in the strength of the fear actually elicited. Such increases have been observed by clinicians and are called negative therapeutic effects. But, by comparing Figures 3 and 4, one can see that the increase produced in this way is much less than the one produced by inducing exactly the same advance by increasing the strength of motivation to approach. This difference supplies a rationale for concentrating therapeutic efforts with severe neurotics on lowering unrealistic fears—in other words, on analyzing the resistances first. After the fears have been reduced enough so that the patient is near to achieving his goal, he is in the situation of weak avoidance represented in Figure 2. A minor increase in the strength of approach may bring him to his goal.

Many strong fears are realistic. In these cases a person either suffers severe punishment if he achieves a dangerous goal or strong fear and conflict if the punishment just barely keeps him away from it. In such a situation, attempting to decrease fear and avoidance produces a negative therapeutic effect; conversely, a positive therapeutic effect may be produced by increasing the strength of fear and avoidance to the point at which the subject remains far enough away from the dangerous goal so that he is not tempted and hence not in any conflict. Certain psychopaths should benefit by such treatment.

In certain situations the punishment is likely to occur only some time after a goal has been achieved. Figure 5 diagrams such a situation. The subject is free to advance toward or to retreat from the goal along the dimension of distance represented by the left part of the diagram, but, once he achieves the forbidden goal, he is carried forward inexorably on the irreversible dimension of time until he reaches the point at which punishment occurs. Such a subject is expected to experience

moderate fear before he achieves the goal but strong fear—commonly called guilt in such a situation—afterward. This situation is made still worse if the strong punishment occurs only on certain unpredictable occasions and with unpredictable delays, so that one cannot learn when one is safe. In all these cases, increasing the strength of avoidance enough so that the subject no longer tries to approach produces a great reduction in fear.

In the analysis of conflict, one is dealing with distance from the dangerous goal object. A similar analysis applies to displacement, in which the relevant dimension is similarity to the original dangerous goal object (Miller, 1959). In many cases, changes in the stimulus situation or in the goal object reduce the generalized fear more than the generalized approach, so that the subject may be able to achieve the same goal under altered conditions or a somewhat similar goal under the same conditions. In behavior therapy the construction of hierarchies is often based on the principle of a stimulus-generalization decrement in fear as the stimulus conditions are altered. The therapeutic value of a change in scenery has a similar basis.

Although the foregoing analysis applies to many situations, there are apparently some in which the gradient of approach is steeper than the gradient of avoidance. In this case at a distance the behavior is consistent avoidance, but, if the subject can be brought near enough to the goal, the behavior shifts to complete approach. This same pattern is also expected if the punishment occurs partway along the path to the goal. Such experimental evidence as is available indicates that—when the drive is elicited by stimuli in the environment, as fear usually is—the strength of the tendency is affected more by changes in distance and similarity and hence is steeper. Conversely, when the drive is dependent mainly on factors within the subject that are carried by him into the different situations—near and far, similar and dissimilar—the effect of any change is less, and hence the gradient is flatter (Miller and Murray, 1952; Miller, 1959; Hearst, 1969).

Motivational Effects of Words and Thoughts

Experiments have shown that fear and thus, presumably, other motivations can be conditioned to saying and hearing words and that it generalizes with little if any decrement from external cues to thoughts (Miller, 1951). Such generalization, which can also occur in the reverse direction, appears to

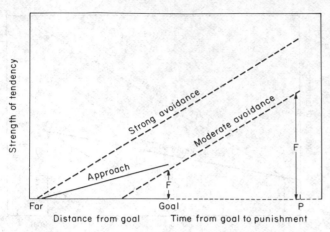

FIGURE 5. When delayed punishment is given (at time *P*) after achieving the goal, fear mounts rapidly during the delay. The strongest fear actually encountered is greatly reduced (from *P* to *Far*) when the strength of avoidance is increased (from *Moderate* to *Strong*), so that the subject is prevented from starting toward the goal. (Modified from Miller, N. E. Some implications of modern behavior theory for personality change and psychotherapy. In *Personality Change*, P. Worchel and D. Byrne, editors, p. 149. John Wiley & Sons, New York, 1964b.)

provide the basis for the effectiveness of using hierarchies of thoughts and images in behavioral techniques of desensitization. There is abundant clinical evidence for the motivational power of words and thoughts. Learning a new thought, "He is a friend," may immediately elicit motivations and responses that have been slowly learned during the patient's life (Dollard and Miller, 1950; Miller, 1951). Cognitive approaches to psychotherapy are making increasing use of the power of labels and thoughts (Wachtel, 1977; Murray and Jacobson, 1978). But, if the patient has not learned to respond to thoughts with the necessary motivations and responses, effective use cannot be made of them. A patient may say, "I understand exactly what I am doing wrong and what I must do right, but I don't seem to be able to change." Furthermore, strong fear, disgust, or guilt aroused by a thought can lead to repressing that thought.

Functional Amnesia and Repression

The most easily understood type of repression is the combat amnesia produced by extremely terrifying circumstances without any head injury. Dollard and Miller (1950) pointed out that learning theory predicts that the intense fear aroused by the terrifying memories should motivate the victim to stop thinking about them, and the consequent relief should reinforce the inhibition of such thoughts. If someone who has a mild fear of heights were offered $1,000 to jump across a 4-foot gap from the roof of a skyscraper to a ledge 2 feet wide, he might well run up to the edge and suddenly find himself physically unable to jump. The hypothesis of Dollard and Miller was that a train of thought is a sequence of responses, just like running, and that stopping a specific train of thought is a response, just like stopping running. To carry the analogy further: If one were given a drug that reduced his fear enough, it is conceivable that he would be able to jump to the precarious ledge but that, once there, the stimuli confronting him would elicit far more fear than he was experiencing when he was unable to jump before taking the drug.

As would be predicted from the foregoing analysis, Grinker and Spiegel (1945b) found that giving victims of combat am-

nesia an intravenous injection of sodium pentothal, a drug that reduces fear (Miller, 1964a), frequently enabled them to recover their memories, which acted as stimuli to elicit intense fear. This fear is analogous to the negative therapeutic effect noted in the discussion of conflict behavior. To quote Grinker and Spiegel's (1945b) description:

> The terror exhibited in the moments of supreme danger, such as at the imminent explosion of shells, the death of a friend before the patient's eyes, the absence of cover under a heavy dive-bombing attack, is electrifying to watch. The body becomes increasingly tense and rigid, the eyes widen and the pupils dilate, while the skin becomes covered with fine perspiration . . . the breathing becomes incredibly rapid and shallow. The intensity of the emotions sometimes becomes unbearable; and frequently, at the height of the reaction, there is a collapse and the patient falls back in bed and remains quiet a few minutes, usually to resume the story at a more neutral point.

The terrifying memories that occur when the fear-motivating combat amnesia is reduced by a drug may be related to the terrifying thoughts that sometimes occur to certain patients whose fears are reduced by deep relaxation and to the Makyo (manifestations of devils) that can occur in certain stages of Zen meditation (Miller, 1978).

According to the hypothesis of Dollard and Miller (1950), other forms of repression are motivated and reinforced in much the same way as combat amnesia is.

Cognitive Defect Maintains Maladjustment

When the subject loses his ability to remember and to think about certain topics, he loses his ability in the area of repression to make discriminations, including those between realistic and unrealistic dangers. He also loses the ability to use his higher mental processes in achieving creative thought, foresight, and sophisticated problem solving. Similarly, the social and voluntary controls involving language and thought are lost. In short, the patient's behavior in the area affected by repression becomes more child-like (Dollard and Miller, 1950). The cognitive loss can severely interfere with adjustment and lead to consequences that further reinforce the fear. Wachtel (1977) showed how other people's reactions to the clumsy behavior caused by conflict, repression, or lost opportunities for learning can maintain the fear motivating the neurotic behavior.

Methods of Reducing Fear

One way of reducing fear is by drugs. Although drugs may be useful, a number of difficulties should be borne in mind. One expects the reduction in fear to reinforce the taking of the drug, and there is good experimental evidence that this can occur (Davis et al., 1968). Furthermore, one does not expect a drug to differentiate between realistic and unrealistic fears. Thus, a person who uses alcohol to reduce his unrealistic fear of normal self-assertiveness at a party may not be cautious enough in driving home. And there is the problem of transfer from the drugged state to the nondrugged state, so that it may be desirable to reduce the dose gradually and take special steps to help the patient cope after withdrawal (Miller, 1966).

In contrast to the effects of a drug, learning can be made very specific. A patient can be taught the discrimination of not being afraid of appropriate self-assertiveness but of being cautious about inappropriate aggression. Learning a discrimination of when it is dangerous and when it is safe can reduce chronic fear. But one needs to discover by further empirical research those circumstances under which it is most efficient to concentrate on forming discriminations in the present and those circumstances under which it may be more efficient to recover memories of the origins of a currently unrealistic fear in order to contrast those dangerous conditions with the different current safe ones.

One way of getting rid of an unrealistic fear is to expose the subject to the fear-inducing cues without having the fear be reinforced by any aversive event. Students of learning call this procedure experimental extinction. But the extinction is often slow. Researchers do not yet know for sure the relative advantages of exposing the subject so gradually to a hierarchy of fear-arousing cues that virtually no fear is aroused (crowding the threshold) versus the advantages of trying to expose the subject to as much fear as he can endure (flooding).

There is some evidence that the process of extinction can be hastened by the procedure of counterconditioning—namely, by pairing a fear-inducing stimulus with some stimulus that has a stronger tendency to elicit a response incompatible with fear (Pavlov, 1927). Giving food to a hungry child and giving specific training in relaxation to an adult have been used as counterconditioning measures. The calm example of the therapist (Dollard and Miller, 1950) and expressions of love and support from an important person or group can produce a strong fear-reducing effect. In spite of the extensive theoretical and practical use made of the procedure of counterconditioning (Wolpe, 1958), there has been relatively little experimental study of the most effective means of producing it.

Effects of Learning on Fear

Observations of people in dangerous situations, such as combat, suggest that two of the factors reducing fear are learning exactly what to expect and learning exactly what to do about it (Miller, 1959). These observations have been confirmed by experiments showing that, when the physical strength of painful electric shock is held constant, these purely psychological factors of learning when to expect the shock and how to cope with it can produce a great difference in chronic fear, as measured by a variety of indices, including gastric lesions.

Myers (1956) established the experimental design of holding the electric shock current constant by wiring in series the electrodes on the tails of two or more rats. He showed that, when the rats had a signal to enable them to learn when the electric shock was coming and hence when it was safe, they showed much less generalized fear between trials than did rats who had no signal and could not learn this discrimination. He measured fear by its interference with the thirsty rats' response of drinking. In subsequent experiments Weiss (1970) used a similar design to show that the signaled shock produced a reduction in fear, as measured by body temperature and weight loss during the experiment and by plasma corticosterone and food intake afterward. This purely psychological variable also produced a 6-fold difference in the length of stomach lesions, as illustrated in Figure 6.

In other experiments, Weiss (1968, 1971a) showed that rats that have the opportunity to learn a simple coping response, such as rotating a little wheel in order to escape shock and to avoid it if they perform quicky enough, have far fewer stomach lesions than do their yoked partners who receive exactly the same shocks through the tail electrodes wired in series. This difference is illustrated on the left side of Figure 7. One plausible interpretation of this result is that the cues involved in performing the successful coping response become conditioned inhibitors of fear—in other words, safety signals—because they are never followed by shock. As would be expected from this interpretation, giving the avoidance-coping rats a tone as additional feedback whenever they have performed a correct response reduces the length of their stomach lesions still more (Weiss, 1971c).

Conversely, if the safety-signal value of performing the coping

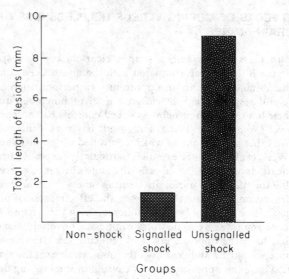

FIGURE 6. The amount of gastric lesions produced by signaled (predictable) as compared with unsignaled (unpredictable) electric shocks of equal physical intensity. (From Miller, N. E. Interactions between learned and physical factors in mental illness. Semin. Psychiatry, *4:* 239, 1972a.)

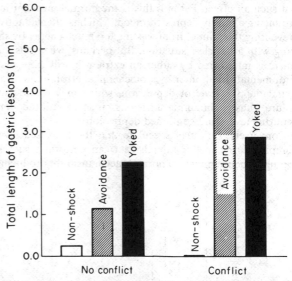

FIGURE 7. Being the executive rat that learns the avoidance coping response reduces gastric lesions when the task is clear-cut and involves no conflict but increases the lesions when the task involves conflict. (From Miller, N. E. Interactions between learned and physical factors in mental illness. Semin. Psychiatry, *4:* 239, 1972a.)

response is destroyed by causing it to deliver a brief shock, so that the rats have to take a shock in order to escape a longer train of shocks, their stomach lesions are greatly increased, as shown by the right side of Figure 7. In this condition, the avoidance-coping rats have many more stomach lesions than their yoked controls that receive exactly the same shocks (Weiss, 1971b). In short, having to perform the response that controls the situation is greatly beneficial if the task is simple and straightforward but can be greatly detrimental if the task is difficult and produces conflict. These results illustrate the extreme importance of psychological factors. Furthermore, the fact that such factors can interact, so that the opportunity to perform a simple coping response is an advantage but performing a conflict-inducing response has the exact opposite effect, illustrates the necessity for a careful experimental analysis of the relevant factors before making any sweeping generalizations.

EFFECTS OF COPING VERSUS HELPLESSNESS ON BRAIN AMINES

In the situation with a simple, clear-cut coping response, Figure 8 shows that, compared with the nonshocked controls, the animals that had an opportunity to perform such a successful response had an elevated level of norepinephrine in their brains, but their helpless yoked controls had a depressed level (Weiss et al., 1970). This result has been confirmed by two other studies, one of which controlled for physical activity (Weiss et al., 1976). The result is particularly suggestive because the drugs and even the superficially quite different electroshock therapy that are useful in treating many clinical cases of depression are those that increase the effectiveness of norepinephrine and possibly other monoamines at the synapse where these amines serve as neurotransmitters. Conversely, the drugs that have the opposite effect of reducing the effectiveness of norepinephrine and possibly other monoamines at the synapse also have the opposite effect of causing or intensifying depressions if they are given to the wrong patient.

Schildkraut (1969) advanced the hypothesis that situationally produced depressions may involve a similar reduction of the effectiveness of norepinephrine at the synapse; the foregoing experiment has produced evidence showing that a hopeless situation, which one might expect to be depressing, may have just such an effect. Perhaps this is the normal mechanism for producing a mildly depressed mood, which is often adaptive in preventing the animal from wasting too much energy by struggling with a hopeless situation. But perhaps, when this mechanism is intensified by either an extraordinarily hopeless environmental situation or by a biochemical error, it may lead to a maladaptive level of depression, which may create further failure, thus maintaining a vicious circle of reduced norepinephrine levels and continued depression.

Conversely, one may speculate that the increased level of norepinephrine in the animals that can perform a successful coping response may be a normal mechanism for producing an elevation of mood that helps to keep successful responses going at a high level. One may even speculate that meeting and overcoming a certain number of difficulties may be essential for maintaining a normally cheerful mood.

EFFECTS OF BRAIN AMINE DEPLETION

The vicious-circle hypothesis advanced above assumes that depletion of norepinephrine in the brain can interfere with behavior for a while afterward. Indeed, a series of experiments demonstrated that treatments that depleted norepinephrine in the brain—strong, unpredictable, unavoidable, electric shocks; swimming in cold water; injections of the drug tetrabenazine—seriously interfered with rats' ability immediately afterward to learn and perform a shuttle-avoidance task. The fact that the drug produced the same effect as the other two treatments ruled out learned helplessness (Glazer et al., 1975; Weiss and Glazer, 1975).

Habituation to Stress

From the mechanism of enzyme induction, one might expect exposure to an appropriate series of stresses to increase the synthesis of norepinephrine in the brain and thus to protect the rats from subsequent stress. Indeed, rats exposed to similar unpredictable, unavoidable shocks once a day for 15 days had in their brains greater activity of tyrosine hydroxylase, the enzyme that synthesizes norepinephrine, than did those exposed for the first time on the fifteenth day. They also had higher brain levels of norepinephrine and, as an additional unpredicted result, slower rates of reabsorption of norepinephrine into the presynaptic terminals, a change—like that produced by tricyclic antidepressants—that would be expected to increase the effectiveness of norepinephrine and other monoamines in the synapse. As would be expected from these results, the rats with prior exposure resisted the behavioral depression produced by the stress much better than did those exposed for the first time. That the depletion of norepinephrine was the critical factor in producing the foregoing results is shown by the fact that similar resistance to the stress of electric shock was produced by 14 prior injections of the norepinephrine-depleting drug tetrabenazine.

Yet other tests showed that prior exposure to electric shock reduced the behavioral aftereffects of exposure to a cold swim, and prior exposure to a cold swim reduced the behavioral aftereffects of electric shock. The electric shock effect seemed to be produced primarily by a reduced rate of reabsorption of norepinephrine. Prior exposure to stress also reduced the levels of corticosterone induced by a subsequent stress (Glazer et al., 1975; Weiss et al., 1975).

The foregoing effects of severe stress were primarily physiological. Other experiments with weaker electric shocks have shown that animals can learn to resist the stress of fear and pain (Miller, 1960; Feirstein and Miller, 1963). Presumably, helplessness can also be learned (Seligman, 1975), but its status in animal experiments is controversial (Glazer and Weiss, 1976 a, b; Weiss et al., 1976).

SOME IMPLICATIONS FOR MEDICINE

As noted above, if animals are given exactly the same physical strength of painful electric shock, purely psychological factors can make a great difference in the amount of fear elicited, as indicated by a number of behavioral and physiological measures. These animal experiments confirm clinical ob-

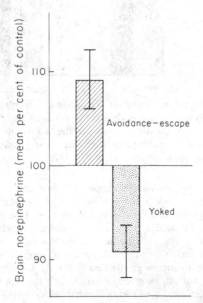

FIGURE 8. Compared with nonshocked control rats, those that are able to perform an avoidance-escape coping response have an increased level of norepinephrine in their brains, but their helpless yoked partners have a decreased level of norepinephrine. (From Weiss, J. M., Stone, E. A., and Harrell, N. Coping behavior and brain norepinephrine level in rats. J. Comp. Physiol. Psychol., 72: 153, 1970.)

servations; they are also in line with tests on people performing stressful tasks. Studies summarized by Frankenhaeuser (1977) show that psychological factors, such as the availability of a coping response to control the situation, can play a significant role in physiological and psychological measures of the amount of stress produced by working in a mechanized industry and by commuting to work. A study of pilots by Blix et al. (1974) showed that increases in heart rate and blood pressure, which can reach clinically dangerous levels depend not only on the actual task or on the physical exertion as measured by oxygen consumption but also on the experience level of the pilot himself.

The foregoing animal experiments also confirm the clinical observation that psychological factors can play a significant role in the production of stomach lesions (Stewart and Winsor, 1942; Weiner et al., 1957). Such psychological factors interact with organic ones. Additional clinical evidence suggests that the effects of such psychological factors may not be limited to the types of disease frequently considered to be psychosomatic. For example, a study by Kraus and Lilienfeld (1959) showed that the death rates from a variety of diseases of people between the ages of 25 and 34 who have suffered the loss of a spouse by death are markedly higher than those of a group who have not suffered such a loss. The ratios are presented in Table I. For many people, the loss of a spouse is a psychological trauma for which there is no immediately effective coping response. Additional evidence for the importance of coping responses comes from a study in which Rodin and Langer (1977) compared the effects of two types of intervention designed to improve the lives of patients in nursing homes. In one case the interventions were designed to help the patients do things actively for themselves; in the other case the interventions were designed to have more things done for the patients. There were twice as many deaths in the latter group than in the former group.

Epidemiological investigations and studies of life changes indicate that psychological stress can increase the probability of a wide range of adverse medical consequences (Rahe, 1972; Cassel, 1973; Levi and Andersson, 1975; Wolf and Goodell, 1976; Jenkins, 1977; Klerman and Izen, 1977). But in such clinical evidence it is difficult to rule out all other possible contributing factors. However, Stein et al. (1976) and Miller (1980) summarized not only additional clinical evidence but also a number of experiments in which stresses like fear-inducing electric shocks increased the mortality of animals exposed to standardized doses of specific viruses or given

transplants of malignant tumors. They also summarized experiments in which avoidance learning and other psychosocial variables, such as the housing arrangements of the animals, affected the antibody level after a challenge by a specific foreign protein. Other aspects of the immune response, such as asthmatic attacks, can also be affected. Some progress is being made toward analyzing the brain and hormonal mechanisms responsible for the foregoing effects.

Another clinical observation is that fear or other strong emotions can contribute to the sudden death of patients who are subject to premature ventricular contractions. Lown et al. (1973) secured evidence supporting this observation in controlled experiments on dogs, in which premature contractions were elicited by electrodes chronically implanted in the ventricle. They found that a series of such contractions greatly reduced the threshold for fatal fibrillation. Then, either stimulating the stellate ganglion of the sympathetic system or placing the dog in an environment that induced fear because of previous association with electric shocks greatly reduced this threshold further, bringing it down to the point at which sudden death could be induced by stimulation within the physiological range. Buell and Eliot (1979) have summarized both clinical and experimental evidence for a variety of adverse effects of stress on various aspects of the cardiovascular system.

Evidence of the foregoing type indicates the desirability of further controlled and analytic investigations of the roles of psychological factors in a variety of medical problems. One important question to be answered is whether the type of illness is solely a function of the amount of stress and of constitutional weaknesses or whether it can also be affected by the specific type of behavioral situation involved—for example, suppressed anger predisposing to hypertension and chronic fear to ulcers. Another question concerns the circumstances under which the proper timing or proper strength of a stress, such as fear, can have a medically beneficial effect (Miller, 1979).

SOME IMPLICATIONS FOR PSYCHOTHERAPY

The first experiments on the effects of learning on fear demonstrated the degree to which learning a discrimination can reduce the amount of chronic fear and its psychosomatic effects. In this case, the discrimination was between when it is dangerous and when it is safe. A similar effect apparently comes from learning what is dangerous and what is safe. The experiments have also shown the beneficial effects of learning a simple, clear-cut coping response to reduce the danger. In practice, the discrimination and coping are often closely linked because one has to locate the danger first, converting a vague anxiety into a specific fear, before one can figure out or learn the coping response that will reduce that danger and thus transmute worry into effective action.

But turning away from danger and suppressing or repressing thoughts about it is a natural type of response, which is rewarded by a temporary reduction in fear. This type of habit may be useful when there is nothing at all that can be done about the danger. But it often interferes with a more adaptive response when something can be done about the danger. Thus, for a student who fears an examination, the sight of the book may arouse fear, which causes him to shy away from the book, perhaps going to the movies instead of studying. This act produces a momentary relief but in the long run increases the danger of failing. Such short-sighted maladaptive behaviors are maintained because immediate rewards or punishments are more effective than delayed ones.

TABLE I

Ratios of Death Rates, Widowed to Married, of Men and Women Aged 24 to 34*

Cause of Death	Men	Women
Tuberculosis	12.7	4.9
Cancer	2.3	2.5
Diabetes	3.3	2.5
Stroke	8.1	4.2
Coronary heart disease	4.9	5.9
Hypertension with heart disease	10.8	4.7
Renal disease	2.6	2.8
Influenza and pneumonia	7.7	5.0
Cirrhosis of the liver	5.6	—
Automobile accidents	4.5	3.3
Suicide	6.9	—

* Abstracted from Kraus, A. S., and Lilienfeld, A. M. Some epidemiologic aspects of the high mortality rate in the young widowed group. J. Chronic Dis., *10:* 207, 1959.

In the foregoing example, going to the movies instead of studying might be thought of as a symptom. If the symptom is blocked, the drive, in this case fear, continues to mount, so that the patient is likely to learn another maladaptive response, such as daydreaming, to avoid the fear-inducing books. On the other hand, a therapist may help him learn the adaptive habit of effective studying, a coping response that reduces the danger and also the fear.

If the fear of examinations is extremely strong, it may be necessary to reduce that fear by counterconditioning or by teaching the student a discrimination between the only moderately dangerous examination and the more dangerous situations from which the fear is generalizing. With the fear reduced, the student should be able to face his books but may need training in techniques of effective studying.

The foregoing analysis also applies to drives other than fear. Thus, a patient frustrated in his work may let his anger motivate him to perform sly types of maladaptive sabotage. The task may be to teach him to remove the frustration by standing up for his reasonable rights.

Although a theoretical prescription of teaching a more adaptive response is simple, one needs to discover more powerful practical techniques for achieving it. A number of techniques discussed by Dollard and Miller (1950) are: classical conditioning, imitation (recently renamed "modeling"), verbal instruction (once the relevant units have been learned), reasoning, and trial and error. Students of Skinner (1938) have powerfully improved on trial and error by emphasizing the process they call "shaping," which consists of producing successively better approximations of the desired behavior by closely observing and immediately rewarding small spontaneous variations in the desired direction. Another contribution of this group has been the study of schedules of reinforcement, which enable behavior to be maintained when rewarded only occasionally. Such schedules of reinforcement can account for the maintenance of either maladaptive behavior or adaptive behavior.

Placebo Effects

The experiments noted above showed the potent effects that purely psychological factors can have on the physical well-being of the subject. Additional evidence for such potent effects of psychological factors comes from clinical observations on the effects of a placebo—in other words, a pill containing a therapeutically inert substance, such as sugar, or a type of treatment that has no specific effects on the particular illness involved. Some but not necessarily all of the effects of a placebo may be related, perhaps by stimulus generalization, to the fear-reducing effects of coping responses and of safety signals that have been demonstrated in the experiments already described. Other reassuring effects of the doctor-patient relationship may come from innately programed fear-reducing mechanisms, analogous to those that cause primate and human infants to be less fearful when clinging to their mothers. Indeed, anxiety is one of the conditions believed to predispose patients to placebo effects (Shapiro, 1971). Whatever their mechanisms, placebo effects are not limited to verbal testimonials; they can produce clinically significant changes in physiological functions. For example, Ayman (1930) summarized 35 papers in which therapeutic results were reported from agents ranging from mistletoe to watermelon seed extract; he believed the only common element was enthusiastically doing something for the patient. Beecher (1961) showed that some types of surgery that were widely performed turned out to have only placebo effects.

To avoid the placebo effect in evaluating the therapeutic action of drugs, scientists have evolved the double-blind technique. In it, neither the physican nor the patient knows whether the coded medication is a presumably active agent or an inert placebo. Using a double-blind procedure, Grenfell et al. (1963) studied a variety of antihypertensive drugs. Under somewhat different conditions, four placebo control groups of 12 patients each were used. In each of these groups receiving inert medication, both the systolic and the diastolic blood pressure decreased, with the systolic showing more change than the diastolic in each of the four groups, the average decreases being, respectively, 25 and 12 mm. Hg. In each of the four placebo groups, the decrease was progressive, with the maximal effect not being reached until at least 7 weeks into the experiment. It is possible that habituation to the procedure of taking blood pressure and regression toward the mean played some role in these results; but, after about 50 weeks in the test that was continued for the longest time, the blood pressures started to drift slowly up toward the initial level.

That the physician's attitude, as well as the idea of taking a drug, can contribute to the results is illustrated in a study by Shapiro et al. (1954). In this study, doses of the drug and a placebo were administered alternately by a double-blind procedure. After a period of initial enthusiasm, the young physician administering the medications returned from a brief vacation to finish up the project but had considerably less enthusiasm for it because analysis of the results to date indicated that the drug was less effective than had been hoped and because his fellowship had been cut short by a call to report to the Army in a little over 2 months. The effects of this reduction in enthusiasm showed up in a sharp increase in the blood pressure of the patients under both the drug and the placebo conditions. This result confirms in an especially clear-cut way the general observation that the effectiveness of drugs—including those that subsequently are discovered to be, in fact, placebos—depends on the enthusiasm of the physician administering them. Applying these results in reverse, one can assume that, if an investigator knows the time at which patients are being shifted from a baseline procedure to what he hopes is an effective treatment, his unconsciously communicated increased expectations may initiate a placebo effect that progressively increases after that time.

Placebo effects can be quite specific. For example, Luparello et al. (1970) showed that the effects on airway resistance of a drug that produced bronchial dilation were about twice as great when asthmatic patients were told that it was going to produce this effect than when they were told it would have the opposite effect. Similar effects of expectation occurred with a drug that produced bronchial constriction. Furthermore, isotonic saline produces the appropriate effects when it was described as a drug that produces bronchial dilation on some administrations and as a drug that produces constriction on other administrations. In another study, Sternbach (1964) found that, when subjects were given a pill containing nothing but a little magnet used to measure their stomach motility, this activity increased, decreased, or remained constant according to the effects they were led to expect the pill would produce. The results of these two studies indicate that Alexander (1950) underestimated the autonomic nervous system when he claimed that, because psychosomatic symptoms are under its control, they necessarily cannot be subject to the higher type of symbolic control involved in other symptoms.

It is only in the past 80 years that physicians have been able to use an appreciable number of treatments with specific therapeutic effects. During thousands of years of prescribing what are now known to be useless and often dangerous therapies—blood letting and puking and medicines such as the eye of a newt, crocodile dung, fly specks, flesh of vipers, the ground-up sole of a worn-out shoe, and the spermatic fluid of frogs—physicians nevertheless maintained their position of honor and respect. Shapiro (1960) argues that this was possible primarily by virtue of the powerful placebo effect and the ability of the human body to produce its own recovery.

Placebo effects can be highly beneficial to a patient. Nevertheless, there are a number of excellent reasons for wanting to find out whether a given treatment has primarily a placebo effect. If the treatment acts as a placebo, it may be possible to achieve the effect in a far more economical way. Furthermore, placebo effects are often transient. Shapiro (1960) noted that about 100 years ago Trousseau was credited with the admonition:

You should treat as many patients as possible with the new drugs while they still have the power to heal.

A scientific understanding of the mechanism by which a treatment produces its effects often leads in the long run to significant improvements and new applications. It is a waste of time to investigate the mechanism of a treatment as though the effects were specific to its rationale when, in fact, its effects are the quite different ones of a placebo. But placebo effects are so powerful that their mechanism should be a fruitful subject for further research.

Visceral Learning

Learning can affect the strength and the duration of an emotion such as fear, which can lead, through presumably innate physiological mechanisms, to visceral effects, such as stomach lesions and fibrillation of the heart. But learning can also have more direct effects on visceral functions. Pavlov (1927) and his students (Gantt, 1944; Bykov, 1957; Razran, 1961) showed that a large number of visceral responses can be classically conditioned. In the gastrointestinal tract, secretion of saliva in the mouth, digestive juices in the stomach and by the pancreas, bile by the liver, and contractions of the gall bladder, stomach, and intestines, can each be conditioned to previously neutral stimuli that are followed by unconditioned stimuli that elicit such responses. It seems unreasonable that the ability to form such conditioned reflexes could have evolved if it had not proved to be adaptive, and it is plausible that being prepared for food by anticipatory conditioned reflexes facilitates the processes of digestion, absorption, and elimination. Such conditioning may be the basis for the healthy effects of regular habits of eating and elimination and the unfavorable effects of drastic changes in such routines. Booth et al. (1976) showed that conditioning is involved in the adjustment of the amount of food consumed to changes in the caloric density of the diet.

Changes in heart rate, blood pressure, and vasomotor responses; contractions of the spleen; secretion of adrenaline and corticosterone; antidiuresis; and inhibition of gastrointestinal activity—all can be conditioned. These responses appear to be parts of the flight-or-fight pattern. Nausea elicited by morphine and defecation elicited by an enema can also be conditioned.

The traditional concept of classical conditioning is that a response elicited by the unconditioned stimulus, such as salivation to food, is transferred to the preceding neutral stimulus, such as the dinner bell. But a number of responses learned by the classical conditioning procedure do not seem to fit this pattern. For example, atropine produces a dry mouth, epinephrine decreases gastric secretion, morphine produces hyperthermia, insulin produces hypoglycemia, and an electric shock produces tachycardia; but the conditioned responses may be the opposite effects—salivation, increased gastric secretion, hypothermia, hyperglycemia, and bradycardia, respectively (Siegel, 1978; Miller and Dworkin, 1980). Are they reinforced by the reductions they may produce in the disturbance caused by the unconditioned stimulus? If so, these effects may be more like the instrumental learning of the rat rotating the wheel or pressing the bar (see Figure 1). Siegel (1977, 1980) showed that habituation to the hyperthermic and analgesic effects of repeated moderate doses of morphine are learned compensatory responses.

In classical conditioning a learned response is reinforced by an unconditioned stimulus that elicits a response similar to the one that is conditioned. But in many situations—for example, learning to sink a 10-foot putt—no unconditioned stimulus elicits the correct response on a novice's first try. The skill is gradually acquired by trial and error, with the success of seeing the ball sink into the cup being the reward that reinforces the successful sequence of responses. This type of learning, also called instrumental learning and operant conditioning, is more flexible than classical conditioning because a given reward can be used to reinforce a number of different responses—for example, food is used to teach a dog to sit up, lie down, speak, or roll over—or a given response may be reinforced by a number of different rewards. The strong traditional view has been that visceral responses are not subject to modification by this type of learning, which is generally thought to be responsible for the acquisition of voluntary control. However, recent experiments, with both animal and human subjects have shown that instrumental training procedures can be used to produce either increasees or decreases in salivation, heart rate, cardiac arrhythmias, blood pressure, vasoconstriction, and the galvanic skin response (Kimmel, 1974; Miller, 1978). But there is controversy about how these changes are produced (Dworkin and Miller, 1977).

1. The subject may learn a skeletal response that has a direct mechanical effect on the transducer used to measure the visceral response. This is an artifact to be avoided.

2. The subject may learn a skeletal response that has a genuine mechanical effect on a visceral process. For example, some Yogis perform an exaggerated Valsalva maneuver—contracting the chest muscles and diaphragm, with the outflow of air stopped by the glottis—that builds up enough pressure in the thoracic cavity to collapse the veins returning blood to the heart, thus stopping both heart sounds and pulse. But an electrocardiogram shows that the heart is beating rapidly. Passing a stool or emptying the bladder may be facilitated by similar mechanical effects.

3. The subject may learn a skeletal response that stimulates the receptive field of an innate reflex. Such a response can be involved in the causation of a symptom, as when a hysterical person hyperventilates, which reduces the pCO_2 level of the blood and thus stimulates tachycardia. Case histories suggest that, if the tachycardia is rewarded by a diagnosis of illness that allows the patient to escape from some problem, this symptom may be rewarded (Pickering, 1974). Such mediated changes may also have therapeutic value, as when certain patients can arrest an attack of paroxysmal tachycardia by taking a sudden deep breath or by plunging the face into cold water. In one case, attacks of paroxysmal bigeminy were elicited by a Valsalva maneuver and terminated by exercise that speeded up the heart rate (Pickering and Miller, 1977).

4. Skeletal and visceral responses may be inextricably linked together as parts of a centrally integrated pattern that can be elicited by learning. Inasmuch as one of the functions of the cardiovascular system is to supply blood to the muscles, the functional value of skeletal-cardiovascular patterning is apparent. The classic example of a large pattern is the flight-or-fight response, in which the muscles become tense, the heart rate increases, and adrenaline is released, which increases stroke volume, helps mobilize stores of energy, and increases the clotting action of the blood to reduce bleeding; in addition, antidiuretic hormone is released to preserve water for use in cooling, and many other associated responses occur. But work by Lacey and Lacey (1974) and by Mason et al. (1976) and physiological evidence summarized by Smith (1974) indicated that there are many other patterns.

5. A learned specific visceral response may be elicited directly without any necessary skeletal links. Many skeletal responses occur as

part of a larger pattern, as when a person swings his arms while walking. But smaller, far more specific patterns can be learned—for example, the movement of a single finger, combined into novel combinations, as in playing a Beethoven sonata. Evidence suggests that visceral responses have some of these capabilities, but the matter is still controversial.

In an attempt to rule out possibilities 1 through 3, a series of experiments were performed in the author's laboratory on rats paralyzed by curare. In an attempt to rule out possibility 4, some of the responses were made highly specific (Miller, 1969). At first, these results were confirmed in three other laboratories, but later the size of the effects in similar experiments declined progressively down to zero, so that it became impossible to repeat them (Miller, 1978). Until this puzzling matter is cleared up, it is wise not to rely on the results of experiments on curarized animals.

Pickering et al. (1977) showed that patients whose skeletal muscles were extensively paralyzed by polio or muscular dystrophy but whose autonomic responses were left relatively intact could learn to produce small but statistically highly reliable changes in blood pressure without changing the tension of their nonparalyzed skeletal muscles, as measured by electromyography, or the pCO_2 level of expired air, as measured by a capnograph. The possibility of a centrally integrated pattern, however, was demonstrated by the fact that asking the patients to try to contract completely paralyzed muscles produced an increase in both blood pressure and heart rate. The fact that the learned responses were specific, involving changes in blood pressure but not heart rate, shows that they were not elicited by this particular central pattern and provides further evidence that they were not elicited by changes in pCO_2 or by muscular work that would be expected to produce changes in both heart rate and blood pressure.

More recent work on patients paralyzed by spinal lesions has shown that they have an unusual ability to produce large increases in blood pressure (15 to 70 mm. Hg systolic) that, after sufficient practice, do not involve appreciable changes in heart rate, as would be expected if they were being produced by changes in volume of respiration or by commands to tense intact or even paralyzed muscles. Direct measurements and control tests also seem to rule out the latter possibilities (Miller and Brucker, 1979). Further tests are being made to check more subtle possibilities.

Experiments on normal human subjects also show specificity. By discriminative training, subjects have been trained to either increase or decrease heart rate independently of blood pressure and vice versa and to change these functions in the same direction or in opposite directions. However, the training periods have been relatively brief, and the changes produced have been quite small (Schwartz, 1977). Taub (1977) and Roberts et al. (1975) reported highly specific learned changes in skin temperature, but Lynch and Schuri (1978) had difficulty repeating such results.

Although additional work is needed, the evidence for the specificity of learned visceral responses and their capability of being acquired in a variety of patterns has already advanced the field beyond Cannon's (1953) notion that the sympathetic part of the autonomic nervous system always fires in undifferentiated mass action.

Considerable evidence suggests that changes in visceral responses produced by instrumental learning may play an important role, like that of the classically conditioned ones already discussed, in supplementing and in adjusting the priorities among the innate autoregulatory processes involved in maintaining homeostasis (Miller and Dworkin, 1979). A better understanding of such a role may have basic significance for medicine. It may also suggest more effective ways of producing and using visceral learning. For example, physiological studies have demonstrated that stimulation of the carotid sinus by increases in blood pressure by electrical stimulation or by inflation of a balloon lead to inhibition of the activity of the reticular formation which can be strong enough to inhibit sham rage or induce sleep. In the light of these data, Lacey et al. (1963) advanced the hypothesis that by stimulating the carotid sinus, elevated heart rate and blood pressure can lead to decreased sensory sensitivity. Dworkin has extended this hypothesis by assuming that in an aversive situation such inhibition can reduce the functional strength of aversive stimulation and hence serve to reinforce the learning of the increased blood pressure that produced this reduction (Miller and Dworkin, 1977). Dworkin and Miller have secured experimental evidence showing that an increase in blood pressure can indeed reduce the functional strength of aversive stimulation.

Biofeedback

In instrumental learning, also called operant conditioning and trial-and-error learning, the performance and learning of a response is determined by whether that response is followed by a reward or by a punishment. For the person who wants to improve, the information that he has succeeded serves as a reward. If a novice golfer were blindfolded so that he could not see where his putts went, he would not learn. With many visceral responses and some cases of muscular tension and neuromuscular disorders, the patient has a poor perception of what he is doing; he is in the position of the blindfolded golfer and cannot learn. With modern measuring devices, however, it is possible to provide moment-to-moment information about the patient's responses and thus, figuratively, to remove the blindfold. In the language of servomechanisms, such information is called feedback; when the information is about a biological function, it has been called biofeedback (Miller, 1978).

Theoretically, biofeedback should be most useful when the medically desirable direction of change is clear, a response that can produce that change is learnable, the desirable learning has been prevented by poor or wrong perception of natural feedback, and moment-to-moment measurement can provide better feedback.

APPLICATION OF BIOFEEDBACK

As frequently happens with a new form of therapy, biofeedback has been taken up with considerable enthusiasm by the mass news media, in which some practitioners have made extravagant claims. Almost 200 clinical studies were cited in a recent comprehensive review (Ray et al., 1979). Most of these were uncontrolled case studies, but a fair number contained enough information to show that the patient improved for some reason. This information makes it clear that it will be worthwhile to proceed to the next step of conducting the difficult and rigorously controlled studies that are necessary to rule out the factors that have led to a gross overestimation of the value of many other forms of treatment, from blood letting, puking, and purging to the extraction of the tonsils and the tying off of the mammary arteries (Beecher, 1961; Shapiro, 1960, 1971). The factors causing such overestimation are (1) the remarkable capacity of the body to heal itself; (2) selection errors, with patients suffering from fluctuating chronic conditions coming to treatment when they are feeling unusually ill and being discharged when they are feeling unusually well; and (3) the powerful placebo effects already described.

Some studies that are better controlled for the foregoing factors and some studies directly comparing the effectiveness of biofeedback with other techniques are beginning to appear, but the number of cases involved in these studies is still too small to provide a definitive evaluation. Thus, biofeedback must still be considered an experimental, rather than a rigorously evaluated, form of treatment. On the other hand, the therapeutic value of other widely used forms of therapy, including some surgical procedures (Bunker et al., 1977), is still being debated.

In the light of the foregoing facts, biofeedback should not be used when there is any danger that it will distract patients from a form of treatment that they may need and that is known to be effective. But it may be useful to try biofeedback when successful alternatives are not available or when it seems to be the best available adjunct to some other form of treatment. One of the appealing features of biofeedback is that, instead of having something done to or for him, the patient learns to do something for himself.

In general, two types of biofeedback application may be distinguished. The first is a direct type, in which the patient is provided feedback about the primary condition that needs to be controlled, such as blood pressure or contraction of the anal sphincters. If it can be demonstrated that voluntary control— that is, the ability to perform the desired response promptly on request—is absent before training but clearly present after training it seems unlikely that such acquired specific control is a nonspecific placebo effect. However, in such cases it remains to be demonstrated whether the necessary control can be transferred from the protected environment of the clinic to the more stressful and distracting environment of everyday life. If such a transfer does not occur, the patient being trained to lower his blood pressure, for example, may inadvertently use his voluntary control to lower the pressure whenever it is being measured and thus to fool the physician into taking him off medication that he really needs. In other cases, such as fecal incontinence, the evidence of transfer from the laboratory or clinic to life may be obvious.

In successful cases of the direct type of biofeedback application, the patient learns during training to perceive the natural feedback from the correct response. This perception and the prompt curative effect are often rewarding enough, so that further practice with the feedback-augmenting equipment is unnecessary.

The second type of biofeedback application is an indirect type; the symptom or condition itself is not directly measured on a moment-to-moment basis, but the patient is taught a skill that seems to produce a desirable effect on the symptom. For example, learning to warm the hands may be used to reduce the frequency of migraine headaches. In cases of the indirect type of biofeedback application, continued frequent practice with or without the feedback equipment seems to be necessary to maintain the therapeutic gain. In cases of the indirect type, the results are more convincing when a strong immediate relationship can be established between the performance of the learned voluntary control and the relief of the condition. If such a relationship or, at least, a correlation between the progress in learning the control and the relief cannot be established, one should be especially alert to the possibility that the results are due to nonspecific placebo effects or to other factors that can lead to an overestimation of therapeutic value.

In the long run, more rigorous evaluation of any therapeutic technique has cash value for the general public. With the growing role in the payment for treatment by the government and insurance companies, which increasingly insist on rigorous evaluation, it also has cash value for the professional therapist.

Some examples of specific applications of biofeedback are discussed separately below; for a more detailed review, see Miller (1978) and Ray et al. (1979) and their references. Reprints of selected studies of visceral learning, biofeedback, and related topics are gathered together in a series of annuals (Barber et al., 1971; Stoyva et al., 1978).

Neuromuscular rehabilitation. Biofeedback has been applied to a wide range of neuromuscular disorders, such as peripheral nerve-muscle damage, spasmodic torticollis, cerebral palsy, and stroke hemiplegias. In some cases the feedback has been from special mechanical devices for detecting specific head or finger movements, but in most cases it has been from electromyographic measurement of electrical activity of muscles, displayed to the patient as a series of clicks that vary in frequency with the activity of the muscle. In most cases the feedback is directly from the response that needs to be changed and the transfer of the response to life; for example, restoration of enough use of the hand and forearm to help in eating or dressing is fairly obvious. A fair number of the case studies are impressive because they include long histories of behavior that has not improved in spite of considerable efforts by other techniques that would have been expected to produce cures if the conditions had been responsive to placebo effects (Brudny et al., 1976). But there are still no well-designed, completely conclusive studies.

In one of the better-designed studies using the indirect approach, Finley et al. (1977) trained four children with spastic cerebral palsy to relax in order to improve speech and motor functions. Feedback was from the electromyogram recorded by electrodes on the frontalis muscle. An ABAB design was used; measurements were made A_1 before training, B_1 after a period of 6 weeks of training, A_2 after 6 weeks of no training, and B_2 after 4 weeks of additional retraining. During the initial training, the muscle tension measured by the electromyogram was reduced, and improvements in speech and motor function occurred. During the 6 weeks without training, muscle tension increased, and speech and motor function declined. In the retraining period, these trends were reversed. Children showing the greatest decreases in electromyogram level also showed the most improvement in speech and motor function. This study definitely merits replication on a more adequate number of cases.

In a study of an application of the direct type that is a model of general design, Basmajian et al. (1975) used 20 patients suffering from foot-drop after stroke to compare the effects of 40 minutes of traditional physical therapy with the effects of 20 minutes of such therapy supplemented by 20 minutes of training aided by feedback from the electromyogram. A variety of objective measures and some ratings of improvement were used. Unfortunately, the two groups of patients were not initially well matched on a number of relevant variables. With the small number of cases, the differences in results, which were in favor of the feedback group, were not statistically reliable (Fish et al., 1976).

From the reports of case studies of between 100 and 200 patients, it seems clear that patients with neuromuscular disorders are benefiting from the use of biofeedback. Thus, it is desirable—indeed, mandatory—that controlled studies be performed to determine how much of the benefit is due to the specific information and motivation provided to both the patient and the therapist by the more perspicuous feedback and how much is due simply to paying more attention to patients whose potential for recovery by traditional methods has not been fully exploited. Inglis et al. (1976), Basmajian (1978), and Ray et al. (1979) wrote excellent, detailed reviews of the work on neuromuscular rehabilitation.

Enuresis and fecal incontinence. A precursor of biofeedback was the development of a device by Mowrer and Mowrer (1938) to treat bed wetting by causing the first traces of moisture to sound a buzzer. Lovibond (1964) summarized extensive evidence that this technique definitely has value but that retraining is often necessary. Finley et al.

(1973) showed that, as would be expected from the effects of partial reinforcement on experimental extinction, a 70 per cent schedule of reinforcement produces more resistance to relapse than does a 100 per cent schedule of reinforcement and that both schedules are superior to an ingenious placebo control in which, after a 20-minute delay, a bell wakes up the parents to arouse the child and change the bedclothes. Finley and Wansley (1977) also showed that with deep sleepers a 105-decibel alarm produces better learning than an 80-decibel alarm. Baker (1969) found that, far from producing symptom substitution, the use of the Mowrer technique produces a general reduction in symptoms of maladjustment, as rated blindly by the teachers in the child's classroom.

In treating fecal incontinence, Cerulli et al. (1976) provided patients with feedback on the way that their internal and external sphincters respond to pressure produced by inflation of a balloon in the lower colon. Of 40 patients, 28 were either cured or virtually cured of this extremely troublesome symptom, with 20 of these 28 showing great improvement after one brief session. For a number of these patients, the length of their previous histories of unsuccessful treatment and the follow-up data on the successful results are impressive.

Cardiac arrhythmias. In studies of cardiac arrhythmias summarized by Blanchard (1978) and one subsequent study by Pickering and Miller (1977), 14 of 17 patients given direct feedback on the performance of their hearts as recorded by the electrocardiograph improved. Some of the studies summarized by Engel (1977) are rather convincing because the previous history and follow-up are extensive and the patients demonstrated a learned voluntary control, turning the arrhythmias on or off on request, that scarcely could have been a placebo effect. The results on the control of premature ventricular contractions probably have the greatest medical promise. Further research into the behavioral mechanisms by which these effects are produced is desirable, as indicated by the fact that Benson et al. (1975) found that the regular practice of the relaxation response produced a considerable reduction in the premature ventricular contractions in 6 of 11 patients. Because of the possibility of using portable electrocardiographic tape-recording equipment to secure records, to be scored by a computer, of the behavior of the heart in the daily life situation both before and after treatment, the study of the effects of various treatments on the frequency of premature ventricular contractions provides an especially good opportunity for rigorous research.

Hypertension. In a review of behavioral methods of treating hypertension, Shapiro et al. (1977) reported that a wide variety of procedures—biofeedback, relaxation, psychotherapy, environmental modification, hypnosis, and placebo effects—all produced modest (5 to 25 mm. Hg) but not necessarily insignificant reductions in mean blood pressure. These reductions are variable enough in different patients and studies so that no clear-cut differences have appeared to date among the results of these various procedures.

In a promising pair of studies, Patel and North (1975) and Patel and Datey (1976) used a combination of indirect methods—autogenic phrases, relaxation, meditation, and feedback for increased skin resistance—with consistent home practice on all but the last, to reduce the average blood pressure of the 17 patients in the first study and the 27 patients in the second. This procedure produced average reductions in pressure of 26/15 and 17/12 in the two studies. The reductions were maintained during follow-ups of 3 and 6 months, respectively. These decreases in pressure occurred in spite of some decreases in medication. A control group, adequate for regression to the mean and habituation to the situation but scarcely for placebo effects was merely told to spend time relaxing while reclining. These control patients showed initial reductions in blood pressure that were not maintained. In the first experiment, the control patients were given subsequent training, during which lasting reductions in blood pressure occurred. That Patel's procedures produced some effect is reasonably clear, but it is not clear what role the various components, including the placebo effect, played in the reductions in pressure. No relationship between increases in skin resistance and decreases in blood pressure was reported. Therefore, it is impossible to determine what role any increase in skin resistance, presumably indicating a decrease in sympathetic activity, may have played in the results.

In a few cases in which direct feedback was used to train both increases and decreases in blood pressure (Miller, 1972b; Kristt and Engel, 1975), the specific voluntary control that was learned could scarcely have been a placebo effect, but one wonders whether the decreases in baseline blood pressure that were observed were the results of using this voluntary control to bring the blood pressure down only when it was being measured or whether the reductions were transferred to the stressful conditions of everyday life. Very little is known about the natural history of blood pressure or the effects of drugs on it except from the brief readings taken during visits in doctors' offices. It is remarkable that such readings have as much predictive value, at least with untrained patients, as they do. Detailed summaries of studies on the effect of biofeedback on hypertension are given in reviews by Engel (1977), Blanchard (1978), and Ray et al. (1979).

Hypotension. Brucker (1977) worked on patients with spinal lesions that had produced a history of more than 2 years of severe postural hypotension that severely limited their activities. Giving them feedback of their systolic blood pressure, Brucker trained all three patients to produce large (20 to 70 mm. Hg) voluntary increases. That this direct, specific control was transferred to daily life was shown by the fact that these patients were later able to tolerate, for hours at a time, postures that previously caused their blood pressure to fall so low that they fainted. For a period of at least 2 years after training, this control enabled them to participate in a wider range of daily activities. (See also Brucker and Ince, 1977, and Pickering et al., 1977.) In these cases it is clear that learning was able to play a role in maintaining the homeostasis of blood pressure during postural changes. In how many other cases does learning have a similar homeostatic function not yet discovered because circumstances have not made this function perspicuous and researchers have not looked for it (Miller and Dworkin, 1980)?

Raynaud's disease. Blanchard (1978) summarized eight studies in which 17 of 19 patients showed appreciable improvement, but these results must be treated with caution because symptoms of this condition vary with the weather and because there is no way of finding out how many negative results are unpublished. More impressive are the results by Stroebel (personal communication) on 70 patients with primary idiopathic Raynaud's disease. They were trained by means of electromyography and thermal feedback to produce a quieting response—that is, a prompt decrease in the forehead electromyogram and an increase in hand temperature. Different subjects were assigned to waiting periods of different lengths in a variable baseline design. Measures were the subjective reports of symptoms and the temperature responses of the dominant hand to a cold pressor test (plunging into ice water) of the nondominant hand. At the end of a 2-year follow-up, 7 of the 70 patients showed complete remission—that is, no indication of Raynaud's disease by either measure. Another 41 patients were markedly improved; they could avoid symptoms if they had a chance to anticipate either environmental cold stresses or the experimental cold stress. Still another 10 patients were slightly improved, and 12 were unimproved but these 12 tended to have either physical stigmata of Raynaud's phenomenon—scleroderma, rheumatoid arthritis, systemic lupus—or depressive reactions. In view of the uncertain success and the drastic nature of other modes of treatment, such as sympathectomy, it seems reasonable to try biofeedback on patients with Raynaud's disease.

Migraine headaches. After a serendipitous discovery that a patient being trained to warm her hands had sudden relief from a migraine headache, Sargent et al. (1973) used the indirect approach of giving 32 migraine patients training, first in the laboratory and then in the home, to warm their hands by use of a biofeedback temperature trainer and a series of autogenic-type phrases that they repeated to themselves to help them relax. The investigators reported that 29 of the 32 migraine patients were rated improved on the basis of a global assessment. Since then, this technique has been widely applied to cases of migraine headache, with about 60 per cent of the patients judged to show moderate to very good improvement (Miller, 1978). But such results are not completely beyond the range of placebo effects (Shapiro, 1960, 1971).

To date, most of the studies of the effects of hand warming on migraine headaches have been of the uncontrolled, case history type. Better-controlled studies are beginning to appear, but they are still on relatively small numbers of patients. Most of these better-controlled studies are not supporting the unique value of warming the hands. In a study with a model design, Kewman (unpublished data, 1977) used a double-blind procedure to train 11 migraine patients to raise finger temperature and 12 to lower it; another 11 patients remained in an untreated group. Detailed diaries of headache activity were kept during 6 weeks of pretraining, 9 weeks of training, and 6 weeks of post-training. All three groups of patients improved, and there were no reliable differences among them. In a study of 13 migraine patients given hand-warming biofeedback and autogenic training and 13 patients given progressive relaxation, both groups with home practice, Blanchard et al. (1978) found that the patients given progressive relaxation improved slightly but not statistically reliably more than those given hand warming.

A few recent studies, involving too few patients to be conclusive, suggest that a more direct type of feedback—for reduced dilation or pulse amplitude in the temporal artery—may be useful in treating migraine (Friar and Beatty, 1976; Feuerstein and Adams, 1977).

Relaxation. The favorite feedback for teaching patients to relax has been from electrodes widely spaced on the forehead. Frequently, it is assumed that such electrodes record primarily the activity of the frontalis muscle. But, as Basmajian (1976) pointed out:

The integrated EMG from the forehead surface electrode generally reflects the total or global EMG of all sorts of repeated dynamic muscular activities down to about the first rib—along with some postural activity and nervous tension over-activity.

This wide sampling, of course, may be an advantage when the effort is to teach general relaxation. Although a number of studies seem to indicate that such feedback from the electromyogram does help to produce relaxation, a study by Alexander et al. (1977) raises questions about these results by showing that, when control subjects without feedback are adequately motivated, they can achieve levels of relaxation equal to those of subjects aided by feedback. However, there is some evidence (Stoyva and Budzynski, 1974) that, although most subjects are already able to relax quite well, a subgroup of unusually tense subjects may be initially unable to relax and are especially benefited by electromyographic feedback. There is no good evidence on whether or not this subgroup would benefit equally well by other methods of relaxation training. Furthermore, Shedivy and Kleinman (1977) and Alexander (1975) failed to find generalization of electromyographic training of frontalis relaxation to other muscles. In short, for many patients, training in relaxation without the use of biofeedback machines (Jacobson, 1938) is as effective as training with the electromyogram, but in most cases the practice has to be continued on a daily basis; it is often as effective as apparently more direct forms of feedback (Silver and Blanchard, 1978).

Tension headaches. In the treatment of tension headaches by using electromyographic feedback from widely spaced electrodes on the forehead to aid training in relaxation, a considerable number of studies reviewed by Budzynski (1979) and by Ray et al. (1979) show a 50 to 70 per cent reduction in headache frequency. These figures are not completely outside the range of placebo effects for this type of symptom. Studies on small numbers of patients suggest that the effects of true feedback are greater than those of false feedback (Wickramasekera, 1972; Kondo and Canter, 1977) or of a placebo pill (Cox et al., 1975). Inasmuch as the false feedback was not given double blind, one cannot rule out a possible effect of the differential enthusiasm of the therapist; furthermore, a pill may not be an effective placebo for patients who have a history of unsuccessful medication. And three studies suggest that traditional training in progressive relaxation may be as effective as is relaxation aided by electromyographic feedback (Cox et al., 1975; Haynes et al., 1975; Chesney and Shelton, 1976).

Dental problems. Bruxism, a tendency to grind the teeth, and the related temporal mandibular dysfunction syndrome have been treated by using the electromyogram to train relaxation of the jaw muscles in about half a dozen uncontrolled preliminary case studies summarized by Miller (1978) and Ray et al. (1979). In these patients, between 60 and 70 per cent success is reported. In some cases, favorable results have been on patients with considerable histories of previous treatment failures. On the other hand, these disorders are known to respond to placebo treatments of various kinds (Miller, 1978); in one study in which the dentist said he was detecting and correcting an unevenness in the surface of the teeth so that the jaws could come together more normally but he actually did only a conspicuous grinding in irrelevant places, 64 per cent of the 25 patients reported total or nearly total remission of their symptoms (Goodman et al., 1976).

Asthma. Studies indicating that asthmatic children can benefit from training in relaxation are summarized by Kotses et al. (1976), who reported a study of their own in which true feedback for relaxation recorded from forehead leads produced greater relaxation and improvement in flow rate than did false feedback or no training. Because of the small number of patients involved, these studies are at best suggestive.

Neurosis and anxiety. The effectiveness with psychiatric patients of three different methods of producing general relaxation, presumed to be incompatible with the flight-or-fight response, was studied by Glueck and Stroebel (1975) with 225 patients. After giving 26 patients biofeedback training for producing α-waves and 12 patients modified autogenic training, the lack of promising results and resistance by the patients caused these two treatments to be dropped. The investigators reported that training in enhancing the α-component of the electroencephalogram did not, in general, prove to be effective in helping the patient to relax or in relieving anxiety. In contrast, they reported that transcendental meditation yielded more promising results and was used with 187 patients.

Patients who had been troubled by anxiety for at least 2 years were trained by Raskin et al. (1973) in deep muscle relaxation aided by feedback from electromyographic leads on the forehead. They reported that one patient improved markedly and that three improved moderately but that six were unimproved, two of whom experienced great anxiety that ultimately disrupted the sessions, in spite of the fact that they maintained deep muscle relaxation. Orne and Paskewitz (1974) showed that patients could simultaneously have high α and high anxiety. These results contradicted the idea that low electromyogram or high α are always incompatible with anxiety.

Gatchel et al. (1977) found that equal decreases in anxiety about public speaking were produced by training in progressive relaxation, by training in reducing heart beat by true feedback, and by the control procedure of training in reducing heart rate by false feedback. The improvement of the last group is yet one more indication of the fact that studies that do not include effective placebo controls may yield misleading results.

Epilepsy. In testing the seizure-producing effect of a drug, Sterman made the serendipitous observation that cats that had been trained to produce a sensorimotor rhythm (10 to 15 Hz.) required a higher dose of the drug to produce a seizure. He then started to test the effects of such training on patients with epilepsy. He summarized the data from six laboratories, showing that 25 of 30 epileptic patients treated with electroencephalographic feedback improved (Sterman, 1977). Most of those patients had proved to be unresponsive to other forms of treatment. During periods when training was abruptly stopped, the seizures tended to increase, in some cases to higher levels than the initial baseline. Giving feedback that was not dependent on the electroencephalogram—that is, noncontingent—without the patient's knowledge did not produce any reduction in seizures in a total of seven patients, five of whom improved with contingent feedback. These results suggest that the reduction in seizures is the result of the electroencephalographic training (Finley, 1976; Wyler et al., 1976). Furthermore, Sterman (1977) reported that training three patients to suppress 2 to 7 Hz. activity and five others to increase 6 to 9 Hz. activity did not produce a reduction in seizures. He concluded that a reduction in seizures and in abnormal electroencephalogram activity can be produced by training in a band ranging from 9 to 20 Hz. But there is still controversy over the degree to which therapeutic results are correlated with specific changes in the power spectrum of the electroencephalogram (Miller, 1978; Ray et al., 1979). With the increasing availability of less expensive and better electronic equipment, larger-scale studies should provide more definitive evidence of the effects of electroencephalographic training on epilepsy.

INTEGRATION OF BIOFEEDBACK WITH OTHER TECHNIQUES

In some cases the patients' problems may arise from a difficulty in perceiving the feedback from the correct response or even from a complete misperception. For example, some of the patients with premature ventricular contractions could feel the abnormal beats but not the normal beats and were afraid that their hearts had stopped beating during the normal condition (Engel, personal communication). Some patients reported a tension in the region of the jaws that could be relieved by clenching the teeth (Ball, personal communication). With these patients the feedback from the heart or the jaw muscles could be used to correct the misperception, and this correction seemed to be an important part of the treatment. In one case of rehabilitation (Brucker, personal communication), the muscles for lifting the shoulder recovered from paralysis before the muscles for lifting the arm recovered. Therefore, the patient developed the bad habit of trying to raise her arm by lifting her shoulder. After the other muscles had recovered, this bad habit prevented her from using them properly. But when she was told to increase the signal from the electromyogram of the proper muscles to lift the arm, she had no interference from the bad habit and learned to contract the proper muscles for raising her arm.

A symptom that is produced in one of the ways just described does not need to be reinforced by serving some important functional need. Therefore, getting rid of the symptom can be a pure gain. On the other hand, a symptom whose origin was organic or from some failure in learning may secondarily become instrumental in achieving some need, such as escaping responsibility or collecting insurance money.

If the symptom is originally learned or secondarily maintained because it produces a strong rewarding gain, biofeedback will not be successful unless the patient can learn or the therapist can teach him some other way of achieving the goal that was achieved by the symptom. For example, in cases in which a headache is used by a submissive person as a means of escape or of controlling others, the therapist may have to discover its function and give the appropriate assertive or other social training.

Sometimes, after a person has first achieved deep relaxation, he suddenly tenses up again. If the therapist can find out what caused him to do this and if the patient can see the connection between a certain fear or fantasy and his tension, a significant step in the therapy may be achieved. One of the frequent negative effects of deep relaxation is a feeling of disorientation, lack of control, or the emergence of a frightening image. Adler and Adler (1976) are among those who have observed that deep relaxation can help uncover unresolved grief, repressed rage, fear of death, and other emotions and that muscular tension can be one of the ways certain patients suppress these emotions. The Adlers found that it is useful to arouse the patient's curiosity about the emotions, ideas, and images that are correlated with sudden shifts in functions measured by the biofeedback instrument. In dealing with all the foregoing problems, the biofeedback therapist needs the experience and skills of the psychotherapist. More research is needed on the effec-

tiveness of integrating biofeedback with psychotherapy, including various forms of behavior therapy. These problems are discussed in detail by Glueck and Stroebel (1975), Budzynski (1979), and Miller and Dworkin (1977).

In dealing with any organ system, the biofeedback therapist needs considerable knowledge about the functions and clinical problems of that system, and in many cases the therapist also needs the collaboration of a relevant medical specialist. As Basmajian (1976) pointed out, to use the electromyogram effectively in rehabilitation, it is necessary to know not only the basic principles of electromyographic recording but also the specific anatomy, functions, and reflexes of muscles. In all cases, an adequate physical examination is essential to avoid the neglect of any condition, such as an infection or a malignancy, that is subject to successful treatment by conventional medical techniques if dealt with early enough.

Suggested Cross References

Learning theory is discussed in Section 4.3 and behavior therapy in Section 30.2. Ethology is discussed in Section 4.6. Traumatic war disorders are discussed in Section 25.3. Psychological factors affecting physical conditions (psychosomatic disorders) are discussed in Chapter 26.

REFERENCES

Adler, C. S., and Adler, S. M. Biofeedback-psychotherapy for the treatment of headaches: A 5-year follow-up. Headache, *16:* 189, 1976.

Alexander, A. An experimental test of assumptions relating to the use of EMG biofeedback as a general relaxation training technique. Psychophysiology, *12:* 656, 1975.

Alexander, A. B., White, P. D., and Wallace, H. M. Training and transfer of training effects in EMG biofeedback-assisted musuclar relaxation. Psychophysiology, *14:* 551, 1977.

Alexander, F. *Psychosomatic Medicine: Its Principles and Applications.* W. W. Norton, New York, 1950.

Ayman, D. An evaluation of therapeutic results in essential hypertension. J. A. M. A., *78:* 57, 1930.

Baker, B. Symptom treatment and symptom substitution in enuresis. J. Abnorm. Psychol., *74:* 42, 1969.

Barber, T. X., DiCara, L. V., Kamiya, J., Miller, N. E., Shapiro, D., and Stoyva, J., editors. *Biofeedback and Self-Control 1970.* Aldine Publishing Co., Chicago, 1971.

Basmajian, J. V. Facts vs. myths in EMG biofeedback. Biofeedback Self-Reg., *1:* 369, 1976.

Basmajian, J. V. Biofeedback for modification of skeletal muscular dysfunctions. In *Clinical Applications of Biofeedback: Appraisal and Status,* J. Gatchel and K. P. Price, editors, p. 47. Pergamon Press, New York, 1978.

Basmajian, J. V., Kukulka, C. G., Narayan, M. G., and Takebe, K. Biofeedback treatment of foot-drop after stroke compared with standard rehabilitation technique: Effects on voluntary control and strength. Arch. Phys. Med. Rehabil., *56:* 231, 1975.

Beecher, H. K. Surgery as placebo: A quantitative study of bias. J. A. M. A., *176:* 1102, 1961.

Benson, H., Alexander, S., and Feldman, C. L. Decreased premature ventricular contractions through use of the relaxation response in patients with stable ischaemic heart-disease. Lancet, *2:* 381, 1975.

Blanchard, E. B. Biofeedback and the modification of cardiovascular dysfunctions. In *Clinical Applications of Biofeedback: Appraisal and Status,* J. Gatchel and K. P. Price, editors p. 22. Pergamon Press, New York, 1978.

Blanchard, E. B., Theobald, D. E., Williamson, D. A., Silver, B. V., and Brown, D. A. Temperature biofeedback in the treatment of migraine headaches. Arch Gen. Psychiatry, *35:* 581, 1978.

Blix, A. S., Stromme, S. B., and Ursin, H. Additional heart rate: An indicator of psychological activation. Aerosp. Med. Assoc., *45:* 1219, 1974.

Booth, D. A., Lee, M., and McAleavey, C. Acquired sensory control of satiation in man. Br. J. Psychol., *67:* 137, 1976.

Brown, J. S. Gradients of approach and avoidance responses and their relation to level of motivation. J. Comp. Physiol. Psychol., *41:* 450, 1948.

Brucker, B. S. Learned voluntary control of systolic blood pressure by spinal cord injury patients. University Microfilms, Ann Arbor, Mich., 1977.

Brucker, B. S., and Ince, L. P. Biofeedback as an experimental treatment for postural hypotension in a patient with a spinal cord lesion. Arch. Phys. Med. Rehabil., *58:* 49, 1977.

Brudny, J., Korein, J., Grynbaum, B. B., Friedmann, L. W., Weinstein, S., Sachs-Frankel, G., and Belandres, P. V. EMG feedback therapy: Review of treatment of 114 patients. Arch. Phys. Med. Rehabil., *57:* 55, 1976.

Budzynski, T. H. Biofeedback strategies in headache treatment. In *Biofeedback: A Handbook for Clinicians,* J. V. Basmajian, editor, p. 80. Williams & Wilkins, Baltimore, 1979.

Buell, J. C., and Eliot, R. S. Stress and cardiovascular disease. Mod. Concepts Cardiovasc. Dis. *48:* 19, 1979.

Bunker, J. P., Barnes, B. A., and Mosteller, F., editors. *Costs, Risks, and Benefits of Surgery.* Oxford University Press, New York, 1977.

Bykov, K. M. *The Cerebral Cortex and the Internal Organs.* Chemical Publishing, New York, 1957.

Cannon, W. B. *Bodily Changes in Pain, Hunger, Fear, and Rage,* ed. 2. C. T. Branford, Boston, 1953.

Cassel, J. The relation of the urban environment to health: Implications for prevention. Mt. Sinai J. Med. N. Y., *40:* 539, 1973.

Cerulli, M., Nikoomanesh, P., and Schuster, M. M. Progress in biofeedback treatment of fecal incontinence. Gastroenterology, *70:* 869, 1976.

Chesney, M., and Shelton, J. A comparison of muscle relaxation and electromyogram biofeedback for muscle contraction headache. J. Behav. Ther. Exp. Psychiatry, *7:* 221, 1976.

Cox, D. J., Freundlich, A., and Meyer, R. G. Differential effectiveness of electromyographic feedback, verbal relaxation instructions, and medication placebo. J. Consult. Clin. Psychol., *43:* 892, 1975.

Davis, J. D., Lulenski, G. C., and Miller, N. E. Comparative studies of barbiturate self-administration. Int. J. Addict., *3:* 207, 1968.

* Dollard, J., and Miller, N. E. *Personality and Psychotherapy.* McGraw-Hill, New York, 1950.

Dworkin, B. R., and Miller, N. E. Visceral learning in the curarized rat. In *Biofeedback: Theory and Research,* G. E. Schwartz and J. Beatty, editors, p. 243, Academic Press, New York, 1977.

Engel, B. T. Biofeedback as treatment for cardiovascular disorders: A critical review. In *Biofeedback and Behavior,* J. Beatty and H. Legewie, editors, p. 395. Plenum Publishing Corp., New York, 1977.

Engel, B. T., and Bleecker, E. R. Application of operant conditioning techniques to the control of the cardiac arrhythmias. In *Cardiovascular Psychophysiology,* P. A. Obrist, A. H. Black, J. Brener, and L. V. DiCara, editors, p. 446. Aldine Publishing Co., 1974.

Feirstein, A. R., and Miller, N. E. Learning to resist pain and fear: Effects of electric shock before versus after reaching goal. J. Comp. Physiol. Psychol., *56:* 797, 1963.

Feuerstein, M., and Adams, H. E. Cephalic vasomotor feedback in the modification of migraine headache. Biofeedback Self-Reg., *2:* 241, 1977.

Finley, W. W. Effects of sham feedback following successful SMR training in an epileptic: Follow-up study. Biofeedback Self-Reg., *1:* 227, 1976.

Finley, W. W., Besserman, R. L., Bennett, L. F., Clapp, R. K., and Finley, P. M. The effect of continuous, intermittent, and "placebo" reinforcement of the effectiveness of the conditioning treatment for enuresis nocturna. Behav. Res. Ther., *11:* 289, 1973.

Finley, W. W., Niman, C. A., Standley, J., and Wansley, R. A. Electrophysiological behavior modification of frontal EMG in cerebral-palsied children. Biofeedback Self-Reg., *2:* 59, 1977.

Finley, W. W., and Wansley, R. A. Auditory intensity as a variable in the conditioning treatment of enuresis nocturna. Behav. Res. Ther., *15:* 181, 1977.

Fish, D., Mayer, N., and Herman, R. Biofeedback. Arch. Phys. Med. Rehabil., *57:* 152, 1976.

Frankenhaeuser, M. Quality of life: Criteria for behavioral adjustment. Int. J. Psychol., *12:* 99, 1977.

Freud, S. *The Problem of Anxiety.* W. W. Norton, New York, 1936.

Freud, S. *A General Introduction to Psychoanalysis,* ed. 3. Garden City Publishing, Garden City, N. Y., 1943.

Friar, R., and Beatty, J. Migraine: Management by trained control of vasoconstriction. J. Consult. Clin. Psychol., *44:* 46, 1976.

Fuller, J. L. Experiential deprivation and later behavior. Science, *158:* 1645, 1967.

Gantt, W. H. *Experimental Basis for Neurotic Behavior.* Hoeber Medical Division, Harper & Row, New York, 1944.

Gatchel, R. J., Hatch, J. P., Watson, P. J., Smith, D., and Gaas, E. Comparative effectiveness of voluntary heart-rate control and muscle relaxation as active coping skills for reducing speech anxiety. J. Consult. Clin. Psychol., *45:* 1093, 1977.

Glazer, H. I., and Weiss, J. M. Long-term and transitory interference effects. J. Exp. Psychol.: Anim. Behav. Processes, *2:* 191, 1976a.

Glazer, H. I., and Weiss, J. M. Long-term interference effect: An alternative to "learned helplessness." J. Exp. Psychol.: Anim. Behav. Processes, *2:* 202, 1976b.

Glazer, H. I., Weiss, J. M., Pohorecky, L. A., and Miller, N. E. Monoamines as mediators of avoidance-escape behavior. Psychosom. Med., *37:* 535, 1975.

Glueck, B. C., and Stroebel, C. F. Biofeedback and meditation in the treatment of psychiatric illnesses. Compr. Psychiatry, *16:* 303, 1975.

Goodman, P., Greene, C. S., and Laskin, D. M. Response of patients with myofascial pain-dysfunction syndrome to mock equilibrium. J. Am. Dent. Assoc., *92:* 755, 1976.

Grenfell, R. F., Briggs, A. H., and Holland, W. C. Antihypertensive drugs evaluated in a controlled double-blind study. South. Med. J., *56:* 1410, 1963.

Grinker, R. R., and Spiegel, J. P. *Men under Stress.* McGraw-Hill, New York, 1945a.

Grinker, R. R., and Spiegel, J. P. *War Neurosis.* McGraw-Hill, New York, 1945b.

Haynes, S., Griffin, P., Mooney, D., and Parise, M. Electromyographic biofeed-

back and relaxation instructions in the treatment of muscle contraction headaches. Behav. Ther., *6:* 672, 1975.

Hearst, E. Aversive conditioning and external stimulus control. In *Punishment and Aversive Behavior,* B. A. Campbell and R. M. Church, editors, p. 235. Appleton-Century-Crofts, New York, 1969.

Inglis, J., Campbell, D., and Donald, M. W. Electromyographic biofeedback and neuromuscular rehabilitation. Can. J. Behav. Sci., *8:* 299, 1976.

Jacobson, E. *Progressive Relaxation.* University of Chicago Press, Chicago, 1938.

Jenkins, C. D. Epidemiological studies of the psychosomatic aspects of coronary heart disease. Adv. Psychosom. Med., *9:* 1, 1971.

* Kimmel, H. D. Instrumental conditioning of autonomically mediated responses in human beings. Am. Psychol., *29:* 325, 1974.

Klerman, G. L., and Izen, J. E. The effects of bereavement and grief on physical health and general well-being. Adv. Psychosom. Med., *9:* 63, 1977.

Kondo, C., and Canter, A. True and false electromyographic feedback: Effect on tension headache. J. Abnorm. Psychol., *86:* 93, 1977.

Kotses, H., Glaus, K. D., Crawford, P. L., Edwards, L. E., and Scherr, M. S. Operant reduction of frontalis EMG activity in the treatment of asthma in children. J. Psychosom. Res., *20:* 453, 1976.

Kraus, A. S., and Lilienfeld, A. M. Some epidemiologic aspects of the high mortality rate in the young widowed group. J. Chronic Dis., *10:* 207, 1959.

Kristt, D. A., and Engel, B. T. Learned control of blood pressure in patients with high blood pressure. Circulation, *51:* 370, 1975.

Lacey, J. I., Kagan, L., Lacey, B. C., and Moss, H. A. The visceral level: Situational determinants and behavioral correlates of autonomic response patterns. In *Expression of the Emotions in Man,* P. H. Knapp, editor, p. 161. International Universities Press, New York, 1963.

Lacey, B. C., and Lacey, J. I. Studies of heart rate and other bodily processes in sensorimotor behavior. In *Cardiovascular Psychophysiology,* P. A. Obrist, A. H. Black, J. Brener, and L. V. DiCara, editors, p. 538. Aldine Publishing Co., Chicago, 1974.

Levi, L., and Andersson, L. *Psychosocial Stress: Population, Environment, and Quality of Life.* Spectrum, New York, 1975.

Lovibond, S. H. *Conditioning and Enuresis.* Pergamon Press, Oxford, 1964.

Lown, B., Verrier, R., and Corbalan, R. Psychological stress and threshold for repetitive ventricular response. Science, *182:* 834, 1973.

Luparello, T., Leist, N., Lourie, C. H., and Sweet, P. The interaction of psychologic stimuli and pharmacologic agents on airway reactivity in asthmatic subjects. Psychosom. Med., *32:* 509, 1970.

Lynch, W. C., and Schuri, U. Acquired control of peripheral vascular responses. In *Consciousness and Self-Regulation: Advances in Research,* G. E. Schwartz and D. Shapiro, editors, vol. 2, p. 100. Plenum Publishing Corp., New York, 1978.

Mason, J. W., Maher, J. T., Hartley, L. H., Mougey, E. H., Perlow, M. J., and Jones, L. G. Selectivity of corticosteroid and catecholamine responses to various natural stimuli. In *Psychopathology of Human Adaptation,* G. Serban, editor, p. 147. Plenum Publishing Corp., New York, 1976.

Miller, N. E. Experimental studies of conflict. In *Personality and the Behavior Disorders,* J. McV. Hunt, editor, p. 431. Ronald Press, New York, 1944.

Miller, N. E. Studies of fear as an acquirable drive. I. Fear as motivation and fear reduction as reinforcement in the learning of new responses. J. Exp. Psychol., *38:* 89, 1948.

Miller, N. E. Learnable drives and rewards. In *Handbook of Experimental Psychology,* S. S. Stevens, editor, p. 435. John Wiley & Sons, New York, 1951.

* Miller, N. E. Liberalization of basic S-R concepts: Extensions to conflict behavior, motivation, and social learning. In *Psychology: A Study of a Science,* S. Koch, editor, study 1, vol. 2, p. 196. McGraw-Hill, New York, 1959.

Miller, N. E. Learning resistance to pain and fear: Effects of overlearning, exposure, and rewarded exposure in context. J. Exp. Psychol., *60:* 137, 1960.

Miller, N. E. The analysis of motivational effects illustrated by experiments on amylobarbitone sodium. In *Animal Behaviour and Drug Action,* H. Steinberg, A. V. S. de Reuck, and J. Knight, editors, p. 1. J. & A. Churchill, London, 1964a.

Miller, N. E. Some implications of modern behavior theory for personality change and psychotherapy. In *Personality Change,* P. Worchel and D. Byrne, editors, p. 149. John Wiley & Sons, New York, 1964b.

Miller, N. E. Some animal experiments pertinent to the problem of combining psychotherapy with drug therapy. Compr. Psychiatry, *7:* 1, 1966.

Miller, N. E. Learning of visceral and glandular responses. Science, *163:* 434, 1969.

Miller, N. E. Interactions between learned and physical factors in mental illness. Semin. Psychiatry, *4:* 239, 1972a.

Miller, N. E. Learning of visceral and glandular responses: Postscript. In *Current Status of Physiological Psychology: Readings,* D. Singh and C. T. Morgan, editors, p. 245. Brooks-Cole, Belmont, Calif., 1972b.

Miller, N. E. Biofeedback and visceral learning. Annu. Rev. Psychol., *29:* 373, 1978.

* Miller, N. E. Effects of learning on physical symptoms produced by psychological stress. In *Guide to Stress Research,* H. Selye, editor, p. 100. Van Nostrand Reinhold, New York, 1980.

Miller, N. E., and Brucker, B. S. Learned large increases in blood pressure apparently independent of skeletal responses in patients paralyzed by spinal lesions. In *Biofeedback and Self-Regulation,* N. Birbaumer and H. D. Kimmel, editors, p. 112. Erlbaum Associates, Hillsdale, N. J., 1979.

Miller, N. E., and Dworkin, B. R. Critical issues in therapeutic applications of biofeedback. In *Biofeedback: Theory and Research*, G. E. Schwartz and J. Beatty, editors, p. 129. Academic Press, New York, 1977.

Miller, N. E., and Dworkin, B. R. Homeostasis as goal-directed learned behavior. In *Neurophysiological Mechanisms of Goal-directed Behavior and Learning*, R. F. Thompson, editor, 1980. In Press.

Miller, N. E. and Murray, E. J. Displacement and conflict: Learned drive as a basis for the steeper gradient of avoidance than of conflict. J. Exp. Psychol., *43:* 227, 1952.

Mowrer, O. H., and Mowrer, W. M. Enuresis: A method for its study and treatment. Am. J. Orthopsychiatry, *8:* 436, 1938.

Murray, E. J., and Jacobson, L. I. Cognition and learning in traditional and behavioral therapy. In *Handbook of Psychotherapy and Behavior Change*, S. L. Garfield and A. E. Bergin, editors. John Wiley & Sons, New York, 1978.

Myers, A. K. The *The Effects of Predictable vs. Unpredictable Punishment in the Albino Rat*. University Microfilms, Ann Arbor, Mich. 1956.

Öhman, A., Eriksson, A., and Olofsson, C. One-trial learning and superior resistance to extinction of autonomic responses conditioned to potentially phobic stimuli. J. Comp. Physiol. Psychol., *88:* 619, 1975.

Orne, M. T., and Paskewitz, D. A. Aversive situational effects on alpha feedback training. Science, *186:* 458, 1974.

Patel, C., and Datey, K. K. Relaxation and biofeedback techniques in management of hypertension. Angiology, *27:* 106, 1976.

Patel, C., and North, W. R. S. Randomised controlled trial of Yoga and biofeedback in management of hypertension. Lancet, *2:* 93, 1975.

Pavlov. I. P. *Conditioned Reflexes*. Oxford University Press, London, 1927.

Pickering, G. W. *Creative Malady*. Oxford University Press, New York, 1974.

Pickering, T. G., Brucker, B., Frankel, H. L., Mathias, C. J., Dworkin, B. R., and Miller, N. E. Mechanisms of learned voluntary control of blood pressure in patients with generalised bodily paralysis. In *Biofeedback and Behavior*, J. Beatty and H. Legewie, editors, p. 225. Plenum Publishing Corp., New York, 1977.

Pickering, T. G., and Miller, N. E. Learned voluntary control of heart rate and rhythm in two subjects with premature ventricular contractions. Br. Heart J., *39:* 152, 1977.

Porter, R., editor. *The Role of Learning in Psychotherapy*. J. & A. Churchill, London, 1968.

Rahe, R. H. Subjects' recent life changes and their near-future illness susceptibility. Adv. Psychosom. Med., *8:* 2, 1972.

Raskin, M., Johnson, G., and Rondestvedt, J. W. Chronic anxiety treated by feedback-induced muscle relaxation. Arch. Gen. Psychiatry, *28:* 263, 1973.

* Ray, W. J., Raczynski, J., Rogers, T., and Kimball, W. *Evaluation of Clinical Biofeedback*. Plenum Publishing Corp., New York, 1979.

Razran, G. The observable unconscious and the inferable conscious in current Soviet psychophysiology: Interoceptive conditioning, semantic conditioning, and the orienting reflex. Psychol. Rev., *68:* 81, 1961.

Roberts, A. H., Schuler, J., Bacon, J. G., Zimmerman, R. L., and Patterson, R. Individual differences and autonomic control: Absorption, hypnotic susceptibility, and the unilateral control of skin temperature. J. Abnorm. Psychol., *84:* 272, 1975.

Rodin, J., and Langer, E. Long-term effects of a control-relevant intervention with the institutionalized aged. J. Pers. Soc. Psychol., *35:* 897, 1977.

Sargent, J., Walters, D., and Green, E. Psychosomatic self-regulation of migraine headaches. Semin. Psychiatry, *5:* 415, 1973.

Schildkraut, J. J. *Neuropsychopharmacology and the Affective Disorders*. Little, Brown, and Co., Boston, 1969.

Schwartz, G. E. Biofeedback and patterning of autonomic and central processes: CNS-cardiovascular interactions. In *Biofeedback: Theory and Research*, G. E. Schwartz, and J. Beatty, editors, p. 183. Academic Press, New York, 1977.

Seligman, M. E. P. *Helplessness on Depression, Development, and Death*. W. H. Freeman & Co., San Francisco, 1975.

Shapiro, A. K. A contribution to a history of the placebo effect. Behav. Sci., *5:* 109, 1960.

Shapiro, A. K. Placebo effects in medicine, psychotherapy, and psychoanalysis. In *Handbook of Psychotherapy and Behavior Change: Empirical Analysis*, A. E. Bergin and S. L. Garfield, editors, p. 439. John Wiley & Sons, New York, 1971.

Shapiro, A. P., Myers, T., Reiser, M. F., and Ferris, E. B. Comparison of blood pressure response to Veriloid and to the doctor. Psychosom. Med., *16:* 478, 1954.

* Shapiro, A. P., Schwartz, G. E., Ferguson, D. C. E., Redmond, D. P., and

Weiss, S. M. Behavioral methods in the treatment of hypertension. I. Review of their clinical status. Ann. Intern. Med., *86:* 626, 1977.

Shedivy, D., and Kleinman, K. Lack of correlation between frontalis EMG and either neck EMG or verbal ratings of tension. Psychophysiology, *14:* 182, 1977.

Siegel, S. Morphine tolerance acquisition as an associative process. J. Exp. Psychol.: Anim. Behav. Processes, *3:* 1, 1977.

Siegel, S. The role of learning in the development of tolerance to the hyperthermic effect of morphine. J. Pharmacol. Exp. Ther., 1980. In Press.

Silver, B. V., and Blanchard, E. B. Biofeedback and relaxation training in the treatment of psychophysiologic disorders: Or, are the machines really necessary? J. Behav. Med., *1:* 217, 1978.

Skinner, B. F. *The Behavior of Organisms*. Appleton-Century-Crofts, New York, 1938.

Smith, O. A. Reflex and central mechanisms involved in the control of the heart and circulation. Annu. Rev. Physiol., *36:* 93, 1974.

Solomon, R. L., Kamin, L. J., and Wynne, L. C. Traumatic avoidance learning: The outcomes of several extinction procedures with dogs. J. Abnorm. Soc. Psychol., *48:* 29, 1953.

Stein, M., Schiavi, R. C., and Camerino, M. Influence of brain and behavior on the immune system. Science, *191:* 435, 1976.

Sterman, M. B. Effects of sensorimotor EEG feedback training on sleep and clinical manifestations of epilepsy. In *Biofeedback and Behavior*, J. Beatty and H. Legewie, editors, p. 167. Plenum Publishing Corp., New York, 1977.

Sternbach, R. A. The effects of instructional sets on autonomic responsivity. Psychophysiology, *1:* 67, 1964.

Stewart, D. N., and Winsor, D. M. DeR. Incidence of perforated peptic ulcer: Effect of heavy air-raids. Lancet, *1:* 259, 1942.

Stoyva, J., Barber, T. X., Kamiya, J., Miller, N. E., and Shapiro, D., editors. *Biofeedback and Self-Control, 1977-1978*. Aldine Publishing Co., Chicago, 1978.

Stoyva, J., and Budzynski, T. Cultivated low arousal: An anti-stress response? In *Limbic and Autonomic Nervous System Research*, L. V. DiCara, editor, p. 369. Plenum Publishing Corp., New York, 1974.

Taub, E. Self-regulation on human tissue temperature. In *Biofeedback: Theory and Research*, G. E. Schwartz and J. Beatty, editors, p. 265. Academic Press, New York, 1977.

Wachtel, P. L. *Psychoanalysis and Behavior Therapy: Toward an Integration*. Basic Books, New York, 1977.

Weiner, H., Thaler, M., Reiser, M. F., and Mirsky, I. A. Etiology of duodenal ulcer. I. Relation of specific psychological characteristics to rate of gastric secretion (serum pepsinogen). Psychosom. Med., *19:* 1, 1957.

Weiss, J. M. Effects of coping responses on stress. J. Comp. Physiol. Psychol., *65:* 251, 1968.

Weiss, J. M. Somatic effects of predictable and unpredictable shock. Psychosom. Med., *32:* 397, 1970.

Weiss, J. M. Effects of coping behavior in different warning signal conditions on stress pathology in rats. J. Comp. Physiol. Psychol. *77:* 1, 1971a.

Weiss, J. M. Effects of punishing the coping response (conflict) on stress pathology in rats. J. Comp. Physiol. Psychol., *77:* 14, 1971b.

Weiss, J. M. Effects of coping behavior with and without a feedback signal on stress pathology in rats. J. Comp. Physiol. Psychol., *77:* 22, 1971c.

Weiss, J. M., and Glazer, H. I. Effects of acute exposure to stressors on subsequent avoidance-escape behavior. Psychosom. Med., *37:* 499, 1975.

Weiss, J. M., Glazer, H. I., and Pohorecky, L. A. Coping behavior and neurochemical changes: An alternative explanation for the original "learned helplessness" experiments. In *Animal Models in Human Psycho-Biology*, G. Serban and A. Kling, editors, p. 141. Plenum Publishing Corp., New York, 1976.

Weiss, J. M., Glazer, H. I., Pohorecky, L. A., Brick, J., and Miller, N. E. Effects of chronic exposure to stressors on avoidance-escape behavior and on brain norepinephrine. Psychosom. Med., *37:* 522, 1975.

Weiss, J. M., Stone, E. A., and Harrell, N. Coping behavior and brain norepinephrine level in rats. J. Comp. Physiol., Psychol., *72:* 153, 1970.

Wickramasekera, I. Electromyographic feedback training and tension headache: Preliminary observations. Am. J. Clin. Hypn., *15:* 83, 1972.

Wolf, S. G., and Goodell, H. *Behavioral Science in Clinical Medicine*. Charles C Thomas, Springfield, Ill., 1976.

Wolpe, J. *Psychotherapy by Reciprocal Inhibition*. Stanford University Press, Palo Alto, Calif., 1958.

Wyler, A. R., Lockard, J. S., Ward, A. A., Jr., and Finch, C. A. Conditioned EEG desynchronization and seizure occurrence in patients. Electroencephalogr. Clin. Neurophysiol., *41:* 501, 1976.

chapter

5

Science of Human Behavior: Contributions of the Sociocultural Sciences

5.1 Anthropology and Psychiatry

ARMANDO R. FAVAZZA, M.D., M.P.H.
MARY OMAN, M.A.

Introduction

The concept of culture, like that of mind, is complex, subtle, and sometimes elusive. Unlike psychology, biology, and sociology, it has not been well integrated into psychiatric theory and practice. That does not mean that psychiatrists have neglected some consideration of culture. English-language mental health journals from 1925 to 1974 contain more than 3,600 articles with anthropological or cross-cultural themes (Favazza and Oman, 1977). From the contents and the bibliographies of those articles, however, it is evident that many authors are either not familiar with anthropological and social-psychological work on the same topics or are not able to integrate the information in the most meaningful manner.

From clinical experience, current research, and reviews of the psychiatric and anthropological literature, it is evident that no culture is free of mental disorder. The experience of mental illness and the different causative models, diagnostic techniques, and therapeutic approaches to mental disorder cannot be divorced from the complex interrelationships found in cultural and social settings.

Culture

A well-known definition of culture (Kroeber and Kluckhohn, 1952) includes the following points: Culture consists of values, explicit and implicit behavioral patterns, and historically derived and selected ideas; distinctive symbols mediate the acquisition and transmission of those values, patterns, and ideas; culture systems are the products of action, as well as conditioning elements of further action. More recent formulations of culture emphasize abstract elements, such as cognition, that lie behind observable behavior.

Thus, a culture may be studied through observable behavior and through the organizing values, beliefs, ideas, and principles

of its members. Culture has been viewed in terms of causal interrelationships and configurations. It has also been studied from ecological, biological, psychological, historical, evolutionary, utilitarian, and instrumental standpoints. General characteristics of culture that have been proposed include: (1) Culture does not exist apart from society. (2) Culture is learned. (3) Culture is shared or may be seen as the organization of diversity. (4) Culture is based on symbols transmitted through communication. (5) Culture is integrated.

The concept of culture is not synonymous with that of social class. The broad concept of social class does not take into account the important cultural differences among groups of people within a given social class. Thus, terms such as "the culture of poverty" and "mental health of the poor" assume an invariance that is unrealistic (Spiegel, 1976). As shown in the Stirling County study (Leighton, 1963), poverty itself was not necessarily linked to high rates of mental illness. However, high rates of mental illness were found in impoverished areas characterized by sociocultural disintegration at a community level, as exemplified by fragmented communication networks, weak leaders, the high frequency of crime and delinquency, and few patterns of recreation.

Culture affects the social order, individual and group psychology, and biological adaptation (Chapple, 1970). Gene pools, for example, are established through culturally defined mating preferences. The relationship between sickle cell anemia and malaria in West Africa is related to cultural adaptations to the environment, such as agricultural practices, settlement patterns, and population movements. Decisions about diet may affect mental status; pellagra and its associated dementia may be prevented by selecting certain foods to eat. Cultural priorities affect the handling of environmental pollutants. Even some fundamental operations of the brain, such as the cognitive functions of the right and left cerebral hemispheres, may differ according to cultural background (Paredes and Hepburn, 1976). In stressful environments various human physiological responses may affect and be affected by culturally defined behavior patterns.

Anthropology has classically regarded humans as largely products of the cultural milieu and only recently has taken an interest in culture itself as part of human biological survival equipment. The argument for viewing humans as cultural animals contains the notion that, despite their great degree of behavioral flexibility and ability to manipulate symbol systems, humans have a basic repertoire of common behavioral units that limit the organization of social relationships. In ethological studies, culture can be seen to do for humans what instincts did for early hominids. Analogies are often drawn from non-human primate ethological studies to support propositions on the evolutionary basis for human behavior, although the variability and the complexity of territorial and aggressive patterns in primates precludes simplistic "instinctive" interpretations (Alland, 1973). Ethological and ethnographic approaches have been combined in the examination of aggression, dominance relations, attachment behavior, and sex roles.

Applications of ethology to psychiatry are seen in some propositions concerning the biological and evolutionary bases for the Oedipus complex, neurotic behavior, and schizophrenia (Jonas and Jonas, 1974; 1975 a, b). If the Oedipus complex is viewed as having a biological foundation in terms of developmental stages, attachment behavior, and dominance hierarchy, then a broader psychotherapeutic approach to sexual problems may be formulated. Neurotic behavior may result from the retention of archaic survival responses no longer adaptive, and certain features of schizophrenia may be identified as representations of earlier biological norms.

CULTURE, MENTAL HEALTH, AND MENTAL ILLNESS

The psychiatrist's perception of reality, of human nature, and of the natural order of things is intimately linked to the dominant suppositions of Western culture. In Western culture, at least until recently, the typical sex-role behaviors of men and women were well defined and seemed natural and proper. A person who behaved differently was usually thought of as eccentric, maladjusted, or sick. Freud noted that "anatomy is destiny," but Margaret Mead (1935) showed that, although anatomy imposes some limitations on sex-role behavior, it is not destiny. Within a 100-mile area of New Guinea, she was able to observe three tribes, each of which had strikingly different patterns of appropriate sex-role behavior for men and women. She thought that society could create cultural deviants by connecting a person's sexual orientation with specific, approved behaviors. For example, a person who is homosexual may be regarded as sick in a culture that accepts only heterosexuality as normal. It took more than 40 years for American psychiatry to accept Mead's findings and to remove homosexuality from the nomenclature of mental disorders. Mead, however, also dealt with psychological deviants—homosexuals and others whose behavior results from psychological pathology and not from innate temperament.

Modern deviance theory, with its emphasis on behavioral relativism, has deep intellectual roots in the concepts of cultural relativism expressed by Benedict (1934) and Kroeber (1944). The relativistic approach has had a beneficial impact on all the behavioral sciences yet, when carried to excess, may have deleterious social implications. The ultimate extreme of the relativistic approach in psychiatry is expressed in Szasz's contention that mental illness is a myth. A more logical development of that approach—one in keeping with the data—is the conclusion that mental illness exists and is recognized in all cultures from the most structurally simple to the most structurally complex, although its expression and its identification may vary. Cultures with a magical configuration may mask latent delusional thinking, but cultures with a rational, scientific orientation may expose the psychotic person (Murphy and Leighton, 1965).

Primary prevention mechanisms by which culture exerts a positive influence on mental health have been outlined (Du-breuil and Wittkower, 1976): (1) Culture synchronizes individual differences and provides persons with a meaningful world view. (2) Culture provides mechanisms to lessen the stressses created by ecological adaptation and social rules. (3) Culture provides emotional outlets and cathartic strategies, such as carnivals and status-reversal rituals (Turner, 1969). (4) Cultures provide methods for curing, isolating, or killing persons perceived as sick, marginal, or criminal. (5) Socioeconomic organization, political control, and leadership may help create a gratifying environment.

Culture has also been described as causative of mental disorders (Leighton and Hughes, 1961). Culture may produce and maintain mental disorder (1) by creating basic vulnerable personality types; (2) by establishing pathogenic child-rearing practices; (3) by fostering sanctions against selected behaviors; (4) by rewarding certain maladjusted deviants; (5) by creating stressful roles; (6) by creating change, such as immigration, acculturation, and detribalization; (7) by indoctrinating persons with particular sentiments; (8) by establishing mating patterns; and (9) by allowing practices that result in poor physical hygiene. Recent critics, however, note that there is no definitive evidence that cultural factors cause mental disorder.

The molding influence of culture is evident in the "culture-bound" syndromes. However, all syndromes are culture bound, and it is conceptually misleading to perpetuate the notion that some syndromes are influenced by culture, and others are not. Traditionally a culture-bound syndrome is one in which an observer with a Western frame of reference imputes the impact of culture on mental symptoms. As might be expected, those syndromes are recognized most often in exotic locales and are characterized by flamboyant symptoms. Examples are amok in Malaysia and windigo psychosis among the Cree Indians. Some culture-bound syndromes appear in diverse cultural groups; koro, a condition characterized by a feeling of penile shrinkage, has been described in Chinese, Malaysian, British, American, and Canadian patients. The closeness of the Western psychiatrist to his own culture undoubtedly makes it difficult for him to apprehend the influence of Western culture on mental illness. Foulk's (1972) monograph on Arctic hysteria demonstrates how biological, psychological, sociological, and cultural variables can be meaningfully integrated to elucidate a syndrome prevalent in a structurally simple society.

PSYCHOANALYSIS AND CULTURE

Freud believed that culture creates repression and that repression creates culture. He was an armchair anthropologist, as evidenced by the vast collection of artifacts in his office and his wide reading in anthropology. Among his major sources for *Totem and Taboo* (1913) were Bachofen's *Mother-Right* (1861), Frazer's *Golden Bough* (1911), Lang's *Secret of the Totem* (1905), Morgan's *Ancient Society* (1877), Spencer's *Principles of Sociology* (1893), and Tylor's *Primitive Cultures* (1891). Freud believed that he could reconstruct past epochs of human behavior and thought through the analysis of patients' neuroses. He described a fanciful scenario set in the childhood of the human race in which a group of brothers kill and devour their violent, primal father. That criminal deed and totem meal, which may have occurred only in the brothers' fantasy, was supposed by Freud to be the beginning of social organization, moral restrictions, and religion. In *The Future of an Illusion* (1927) Freud described religion as a neurotic relic born from the human need to make helplessness tolerable. In *Civilization and Its Discontents* (1921–1930) Freud considered the evolution of civilization as the struggle between the instinct of life and the instinct of destruction as it works itself out in the human species. He concluded that the superego was created by civilization to control the dangerous human desire for aggression. In *Moses and Monotheism* (1934–1939)

Freud postulated that Moses was really an Egyptian who was murdered. Remorse for that murder, Freud asserted, stimulated the wishful fantasy of the messiah who would return and lead his people to redemption and the promised land.

The psychoanalysts Otto Rank and Theodor Reik also published cultural studies similar to Freud's. Rank (1971) agreed with Freud's concept of a primal horde, the totemic parricide, and the original state of matriarchy that evolved to patriarchy. He emphasized the importance of the normal trauma of birth, and he developed the idea that the origin of totemism was the desire to return to the mother's womb, which represented a belief in collective immortality. Reik (1946) specialized in psychoanalytic interpretations of myths, such as the mythic basis for the couvade, Kol Nidre, and the shofar. Carl Jung (1967), after his break with Freud, published *Symbols and Transformations* (1912). His commentary included copious references to anthropological studies, especially in the areas of archeology and mythology. In that book Jung claimed to have traced the origins of a patient's fantasies back to the earliest recorded artifacts of mankind.

Geza Roheim (1950) was a psychoanalyst-anthropologist with extensive field experience. He published widely in both disciplines although he was not well received by either. He carried many of Freud's cultural theories to extreme conclusions and seemed to enjoy irritating his anthropological colleagues; he accused them of rejecting the obvious proofs of the oedipal complex because of their own repressed conflicts. One of Roheim's most enduring accomplishments was the founding of the series now known as *The Psychoanalytic Study of Society.* Erik Erikson, another psychoanalyst-anthropologist, published his enormously popular *Childhood and Society* in 1950. He thought that, just as embryology focuses on epigenetic development—that is, the step-by-step growth of fetal organs, time factors, and critical periods—psychosexual development can be understood epigenetically. The varieties of cultural conditioning for Erikson contain an intrinsic wisdom or an unconscious planfulness. Many of his conclusions were based on field work among the Dakota and Yurok Indians. George Devereux, a psychoanalyst-anthropologist, is best known for his field work among American Plains Indians (1951, 1957, 1969). He noted that shamans did not cure patients but rather helped to create a "social remission" through the repatterning of ethnopsychologically suitable defense mechanisms. In his therapeutic endeavors with Mohave Indians Devereux produced many insights into the unique problems, such as dream interpretation and transference-countertransference, which arise in dealing with patients from diverse ethnic backgrounds.

Abram Kardiner (1939) pioneered in bringing psychoanalysts and anthropologists together to observe their respective techniques in operation and to exchange observations on the efficacy of the working concepts used by each. He believed that a culture acquires its conformation and specificity from the uniqueness of its institutions; primary institutions form individual basic personality structure and create the needs and tensions which are satisfied by secondary institutions. With a small but impressive group of anthropologists Kardiner (1935, 1945) produced psychocultural analyses of Tanala (Madagascar), Marquesas Islands (Oceania), Alorese, Comanche, and "Plainsville, U.S.A." cultures. He found it difficult to apply his concept of institutions to complex societies and eventually produced a list of key situations which influence personality formation and which could be utilized in a psychocultural analysis. Among the key situations he identified were maternal care, induction of affectivity, early discipline, institutionalized sibling attitude, induction into work, puberty, marriage, character of participation in society, factors that keep the society together, projective systems (such as religion), reality systems, crafts, and techniques of production. He believed that each society must be studied as an entity in itself because social evolution has not followed a unilinear course. He felt that psychoanalytic methods of investigation can be used to relate social institutions to the individual and his genetic inheritance, and that the interactions of individuals in a society create new institutions which may promote cooperation or stimulate anxiety or rage. "Unfortunately," he wrote (1961), "this particular approach to culture-personality investigation has ground to a halt." The main reasons for

this were the academic resistance of anthropologists to an invasion of their field by psychiatrists, the limited number of collaborators who possessed an expert knowledge of psychodynamics, and the attitude of fellow psychoanalysts who regarded his work as "sociology" and hence not worthy of attention.

Freud's influence on anthropology was great. His major contributions to anthropology derived from his clinical studies that affected the development of culture and personality. Among the anthropologists who have worked with psychoanalytic concepts are Sapir, Mead (1952), Benedict (1934), Du Bois (1944), and La Barre.

The current trend in anthropology is to reject traditional psychoanalytic cultural studies as reductionistic. In fact, much psychoanalytic anthropology has been based on superficial field work. Recently, LeVine (1973) pioneered in developing new ideas and techniques for using psychoanalytic methods and concepts in cultural studies. *Tahitians* (Levy, 1973) is a fine example of the application of psychodynamic principles in an ethnographic study. The renewed, albeit limited, interest in psychoanalysis among anthropologists is evidenced by the founding of the *Journal of Psychological Anthropology* in 1977. *American Imago* is a psychoanalytic journal which publishes articles with a cultural theme. *Psychiatry,* a journal which has fostered collaborative work, was founded by the psychoanalyst Harry Stack Sullivan, with the assistance of the cultural anthropologist, Edward Sapir.

CULTURE AND PERSONALITY

National character. The idea that culture and individual adult personality are interrelated is an old one. Anecdotes about group differences and national character abound in the work of historians, travelers, essayists, and novelists. Aristotle, for example, in *Politics* described Europeans as spirited but not particularly intelligent or skillful and Asians as intelligent and inventive but not particularly spirited. The Hellenic race, however, was described as intermediate in character, being high spirited and intelligent, and, consequently, free and well governed.

The scientific study of culture and personality began with Franz Boas. He greatly influenced a host of prominent anthropologists, including Ruth Benedict, Ruth Bunzel, Alexander Goldenweiser, Jules Henry, Melville Herskovits, Alfred Kroeber, Robert Lowie, Margaret Mead, Ashley Montagu, Paul Radin, and Edward Sapir. In studying American immigrants and their children, Boas found that the head forms of second-generation children were more like those of dominant, established Anglo-Saxon Americans. For Boas that proof of the plasticity of physical traits clearly contradicted biological theories that claimed that racial groups had fixed physical, psychological, and personality characteristics.

Early culture and personality studies were attracted to psychoanalytic interpretations of personality as an open system embedded in social relationships. Ruth Benedict (1934) developed the idea of cultural *configurations,* namely that

cultures . . . are individual psychology thrown large upon the screen, given gigantic proportions and a long time span.

She described three prototypical cultures, the Zuni of New Mexico, the Dobu Islanders of Melanesia, and the Kwakiutls of Vancouver, which she categorized respectively as having Apollonian, Faustian, and Dionysian configurations. She thought that individual personality types reflected a culture's configuration, and she postulated that people assume a society's expected behavior patterns because most people are enormously malleable, rather than because a society's particular institutions reflect an ultimate and universal sanity.

In the late 1930's Abram Kardiner, a New York psychoanalyst, organized a series of psychocultural seminars with anthropologists. He thought that a culture acquires its conformation and specificity from the uniqueness of its institutions, which shape individual basic personality structure. The most important publication of the seminar group was Du Bois' (1944) *The People of Alor*. Through independent analyses of psychological tests, historical biographies, and field observations, Du Bois claimed she could identify central personality tendencies that constitute the modal personality for any given culture. In 1951 Kardiner and Ovesey interviewed 25 American Negroes. These in-depth interviews (from 20 to 100 sessions per subject) were used in conjunction with projective psychological tests to portray a modal Negro personality in terms of adaptation to a discriminating culture. In later years Inkeles and Levinson (1969) equated modal personality with national character; thus, certain limited sets of relatively enduring personality traits may be found in groups of from 10 to 30 per cent of a nation's population, a multimodal distribution.

A controversial study by Gorer and Rickman (1949) attempted to correlate the personality of Russian adults with child-rearing practices. Depression in the adult was linked to the childhood experience of impotence in struggling against swaddling bandages, and mania—orgiastic Russian feasts and drinking bouts—was linked to the feeding and love that accompanied the removal of the bonds.

The concept of national character is fraught with difficulties (Favazza, 1974a). Benedict's cultural configurations were based on selective data; she neglected information that might refute her arguments. Kardiner's concept of basic personality structure neglected the importance of data imparted to a child through direct learning and through consciously inducted systems. The Alorese study has prompted criticisms: The life histories that were analyzed were not representative of Alor society, and the analysis of Alorese infancy and its sequelae focused exclusively on children born during one season of the year. Gorer and Rickman's arguments for childhood determinism have been criticized for their reductionism. That sort of reductionism was clearly evident in the national-character studies of allied enemies in World War II, in which Japanese brutality was explained on the basis of toilet-training practices. The modal personality concept is problematic because a multimodal distribution of personality patterns can characterize a population but not an individual person. Such a distribution refers not to a national character but, rather, to the characters of a nation (Duijker and Frijda, 1960).

Stereotyping is inherent in the concept of national character, even though some stereotypes may contain a kernel of truth. Such stereotyping became pronounced in many studies of World War II. Germans were described as paranoid or neurotic. Their harsh language was said to manifest a crude mentality. On the basis of those distorted ideas in 1944, a group of noted psychiatrists and anthropologists proposed to solve the "German problem." In the name of mental health, they developed a plan to transform German culture (Favazza, 1977). Subsequent studies have shown that what was conceived as peculiarly German was, in reality, generally human or Occidental or continental European.

The current consensus is that the concept of national character has little scientific merit and that many such studies may tell more about socioeconomic or vocational groups than about cultures or nations. It is impossible to make a clinically meaningful prediction about a person's personality on the basis of nationality alone.

Child rearing. In psychoanalytic theory the childhood years are considered crucial to the development of adult personality and mental functioning. One of the first anthropologists to examine psychoanalytic theory in a non-Western culture was Bronislaw Malinowski. His report on the Trobriand Islanders (Malinowski, 1923) led to a lively and significant exchange between psychiatrists and anthropologists. He noted that Trobrianders were ignorant of the role of semen in creation and that the mother's brother represented the principle of discipline, authority, and executive power in the family. Malinowski claimed that Freud's description of the Oedipus complex was not universal because in the matrilineal Trobriand society the child's wish was to marry his sister and to kill his maternal uncle. Ernest Jones (1925) retorted that Trobriand boys unconsciously deflected their hatred toward the father onto the uncle, thus protecting both the father and the son from their mutual rivalry and hostility. Some critics felt that Malinowski's findings shattered psychoanalytic claims for the universality of the Oedipus complex but, Roheim (1950) led a counterattack. When he told Freud of Malinowski's finding that there was no anal eroticism among Trobrianders, Freud responded, *"Was, haben denn die Leute Keinen anus?"* (What! Don't those people have an anus?) Roheim declared that, due to human neoteny, symbolism and certain universal human traits are autogenic and not conditioned by culture. A more moderate approach came from Hartman et al. (1951), who agreed that cultural conditions may produce variations of behavior during the oedipal-conflict situation. Over the years the oedipal debate has lost its sting (Favazza, 1974b), and most observers agree with Mead's (1952) statement that

the oedipal situation, in the widest meaning, is a way of describing what any given society does with the fact that children and adults are involved in the growing child's sexual attitudes, especially toward the parent of the opposite sex.

Many studies have attempted to link child-rearing patterns to a culture's menstrual taboos, beliefs in supernatural figures, female and male initiation ceremonies, the couvade, alcohol-drinking behavior, pictorial arts, folktale aggression, dreams, and adult stature. *Child Training and Personality* (Whiting and Child, 1953) was an especially influential study that correlated ethnographic data from diverse societies. It demonstrated that excessive childhood deprivation but not excessive childhood indulgence or gratification could be correlated with psychopathological reactions in later adult life. Standardized field work techniques have resulted in more meaningful studies of child rearing, such as the Six Cultures Project (Whiting, 1963; Minturn and Lambert, 1964).

Barry (1969) summarized the conclusions drawn from cross-cultural studies of child rearing in this way: (1) Indulgence in early infancy is an extremely important determinant of adult mental health. (2) The diffusion of nurturance among caretakers, in addition to the mother, is beneficial. (3) A functioning society, most of whose members are well adjusted, is compatible with a wide variety of child-rearing practices. (4) Conditions assumed to maximize the conflicts between love and hatred and between masculine and feminine identification are almost identical. (5) Personality development seems to be influenced more by conflicts between love and hatred and between dependence and independence than by conflicts over bladder and bowel control or by punishments for sexual behavior.

Critics of cross-cultural survey studies, however, point to the lack of direct measures of children and adults and to the inability of a correlational approach to prove a hypothesis. Among the cross-cultural studies that have attempted to prove a causal relationship between child training and subsequent behavior are those on achievement motivation, father absence, and attachment behavior. Whiting (1977) developed a model for psychocultural research that accommodates sophisticated, modern approaches to the study of infancy and culture.

The relationship between adult personality and cultural patterns has been studied from two functional perspectives. One view holds that personality serves society's needs. The other view holds that cultural patterns such as rituals and religious movements serve personality needs—for example, the reduction of stress and the clarification of roles. Those functional (instrumental) approaches, however, are problematic (Honigmann, 1973) for several reasons: (1) A focus on consequences of an event results in teleological explanations, rather than causal explanations. (2) A useful function for any item of human behavior or cultural pattern can be claimed if an investigator is imaginative enough. (3) Dysfunctional patterns and behavior are more difficult to establish than are eufunctional patterns.

Honigmann (1973) devised a flow chart representing the general formula followed by researchers in culture and personality: General social and cultural conditions—such as economy, technology, and cultural maintenance systems—and biological human features, such as infant dependency and sexual instincts, are antecedent inputs that influence socially patterned childrearing experiences and socially patterned later-life experiences. They result in the outputs of adult personality and culture and society such as patterns of culture, social roles, and secondary institutions. Further outputs may occur through feedback—for example, social and cultural conditions may reinforce or validate personality and maintain socialization procedures.

The study of culture and personality is refocused today in psychological anthropology, which examines the fate of persons in specific cultural settings through the use of psychological theory. The earlier emphasis on motivation is now balanced by an emphasis on patterns of cognition. The relationship between culture and personality may be approached along a continuum from the cultural determinants of personality formation and operation to the cultural patterns manifested in individual human behavior. The basic relationship between child-rearing patterns and subsequent adult personality in complex societies has not yet been elucidated clearly.

CROSS-CULTURAL STUDIES

Brislin et al. (1973) defined cross-cultural psychology as

the empirical study of members of various culture groups who have had different experiences that lead to predictable and significant differences in behavior. In the majority of such studies, the groups under study speak different languages and are governed by different political units.

The psychiatric literature, unfortunately, is burdened with the anecdotal reports of authors who spent a brief period of time in an often exotic locale and then commented on differences from Western culture. Some observers with ethnocentric biases may make sweeping generalizations about such topics as the African personality. Africa is a vast continent with so many diverse cultures that simplistic, stereotypical notions about a pan-African mentality or personality or cultural pattern are totally unfounded.

Cross-cultural research may prove profitable in several ways (Strodtbeck, 1964). One may study (1) the culture as an experimental treatment for individual subjects; a specific culture can be regarded as an independent variable that would be irreproducible in a laboratory; (2) the differential incidence of selected traits, such as schizophrenia or suicide; detected differences may lead to research on the reasons for the different rates; (3) the culture as a locus for the development of a new category of experience; behavior patterns not found in the researcher's own country can be studied; (4) the comparative content of published ethnographies. One well-known study compares how people in 25 cultures understand different concepts (Osgood, 1965).

Many assessment instruments have been widely used in cross-cultural studies. Cognitive-intellectual instruments include concept formation, classification, and object-sorting techniques, Culture-Fair Intelligence Test, Goodenough-Harris Drawing Test, Kohs Blocks, Porteus Maze Test, and Ravens Progressive Matrices. Personality-interest instruments include the California Personality Inventory, the Eysenck Personality Inventory, the Minnesota Multiphasic Personality Inventory, Rotter's Locus of Control Scale, Semantic Differential, and Zung's Self-rating Depression Scale. The State-Trait Anxiety Inventory has recently been calibrated for use in different cultures. Current methodological approaches in psychological anthropology include in-depth interviews, projective tests and devices, the observation of family interactions, the analysis of dreams, and the recording of life histories.

Special problems are associated with cross-cultural research. Those problems include translation inadequacies, the experience of the subjects with paper-and-pencil tests, the skewed selection of subjects (cooperative and talkative subjects may not be representative of a group), the selection of a culture on the basis of convenience instead of scientific interest, the willingness of subjects to participate in more than one interview, the differential ability of subjects to learn certain tasks over the course of the project, the tendencies of subjects to please the experimenter, and the meaningfulness of measures in all the cultures under examination (Campbell, 1969). Studies with multiple variables are especially difficult to compare crossculturally. Cross-cultural studies of the incidence and the prevalence of mental disorders must cope with the additional difficulty of establishing bona fide diagnoses in disparate cultural settings.

Psychiatric Disorder among the Yoruba is the best-known cross-cultural psychiatric-epidemiological study (Leighton et al., 1963). By replicating the methods of the Stirling County (Canada) study in Nigeria, Leighton hoped to compare the findings from two disparate cultures. Unfortunately, the Yoruba study was not totally successful. The study has been criticized for skewed sampling; for failing to distinguish psychophysiological symptoms from symptoms associated with infections, parasites, and nutritional diseases; and for assuming that the indicators of sociocultural disintegration are culture free (Kennedy, 1973).

The controlled experiment is the best method for proving a point, and Naroll (1973) championed holocultural or worldwide correlational studies as the second best method. Holocultural studies consider data from all described cultures, assume that irrelevant factors vary randomly, and are designed to consider inconsistent, discrediting evidence, as well as consistent, supporting evidence.

The development of the human relations area file (HRAF) at Yale University by George Murdock led to the professionalization of holocultural studies. Materials contained in the HRAF and in associated books—such as the *Outline of World Cultures, Outline of Cultural Materials*, and *World Ethnographic Sample*—form the largest categorized data bank of cultural information in the world. Almost all holocultural studies include four principles developed by Murdock (1965): (1) a representative sample of world cultures, (2) a statistical correlational test of a prestated hypothesis, (3) a test of a null hypothesis, and (4) a formal set of concept definitions and objective codings.

A serious problem with cross-cultural surveys of psychiatric topics is that significant psychiatric data are unavailable for many societies. Of the 4,000 to 5,000 human societies that have existed in the past century, only 100 to 150 have been adequately described for inclusion in holocultural research. One study of HRAF data determined that the suicide rate seems to be the best measure of culture stress.

Because of the many problems associated with cross-cultural studies of psychiatric topics, general reviews cannot do more than indicate trends. A recent review of depression from a transcultural perspective (Singer, 1975) made the following general points: (1) Reports that depression is infrequent in non-Western cultures may be due to unrepresentative samples and differences in diagnostic criteria. (2) The reported high incidence of somatization and hypochondriasis in non-Western depressives may be due to self-selection for treatment. (3) Culture does not seem to influence the morbidity of depressive disorders. (4) The Western concept of depressive disorder—depressive mood, fatigue, insomnia, loss of interest, weight loss, and periodicity—seems to be universally valid. However, Singer's data are primarily etic; observers have looked for evidence of what constitutes the Western category of depression, itself a confusing concept, in non-Western cultures. In that regard the International Pilot Study of Schizophrenia is not what anthropologists would consider to be a cross-cultural study because, although it examines schizophrenia in nine cultural settings, cultural variables are excluded from the research protocol.

EMICS AND ETICS

Phon*emics* refers to a system of describing sounds in a culture, but phon*etics* refers to a general system of describing the phenomenon of human-generated sounds. On the basis of that distinction, emic and etic approaches were proposed for the study of cultural phenomena, (Pike, 1966). The emic approach focuses on the informant's point of view—the informant's meanings and interpretations of his behavior, thoughts, attitudes, and motives. The underlying assumption of the emic approach is that knowledge of a person's principles of classification and conceptualization provide a new, descriptive, and productive basis for understanding his culture. The etic approach refers to the investigator's classification and conceptualization of what is observed. The investigator creates a structure of interpretation. In an emic study the investigator must abandon his own stereotypes and preconceived notions in order to understand reality as it is perceived by the informant. In an etic study the investigator establishes his own conceptual framework of reality and records and interprets his observations in relation to that framework.

Awareness of the emic-etic distinction has practical conse-

quences. If a test standardized in one culture is given to subjects in a different culture, the researcher may impose an etic approach and may fail to recognize the emically meaningful aspects of the phenomena to be tested and the impact of the testing situation for the subjects. In a clinical interview the underlying Western medical etic, the order, and the phraseology of questions may bias responses. Even seemingly innocuous, open-ended questions may represent a subtle, artificial etic. The emic-etic distinction thus suggests the potential for misinterpretation of a therapist's behavior by a patient and vice versa. One difficulty with the logical, analytic consequences of the emic approach is that behavior and concepts that are uniquely meaningful to members of a particular culture may be difficult to compare with similar behavior and concepts in other cultures. The second volume (1975) of the *American Ethnologist* was devoted to the question of intracultural and intercultural emic variability. The embedded emic and imposed-derived etic are attempts to balance emic and etic approaches (Silverman, 1966; Goodenough, 1970).

ETHNOGRAPHY

In the anthropological tradition, ethnography refers to a method of describing cultural forms inductively through the examination of a series of cases. Ethnographers document phenomena by various methods, such as the examination of written records, folk tales and myths, linguistic analysis, interviews with key informants, collections of life histories, questionnaire surveys, psychological tests, and, most important, participant observation. Among the best-known life-history ethnographies are those of native Americans.

A modern ethnographic approach in Western subcultures is demonstrated by Valentine and Valentine's (1971) controversial study of a predominantly black ghetto in a large northern American city. The researchers studied the community by living in it and by experiencing ghetto life directly. They progressed from observer-participants to active participants in community life, becoming partisans who openly identified with the population under study. The scientific motivation for their study was to examine the patterns usually ascribed to persons living in a culture of poverty. Contrary to expectations, they found that 83 per cent of the Afro-American families were conventional, male-headed households and that the social structure beyond the family level consisted of a multiplicity of local institutions, such as churches, social clubs, and political organizations. The culture of poverty is usually thought to be characterized by institutional nonparticipation, yet Valentine and Valentine found rather high participation in ethnically distinct versions of mainstream institutions. Although Valentine and Valentine studied an entire community, other researchers have focused on a residential city block, a network of black street-corner men, and a gang.

Medicine has also been considered as an ethnographic category. Frake's (1961) emic study of the diagnosis of disease in a Filipino tribe has become a minor classic. He regarded diagnosis as a cognitive process, rather than a purely sociocultural process, and was able to discern the process and the criteria used by the members of that culture for diagnosing disease. A study of illness and healing in the Mayan community of Zinacantan is an excellent example of modern medical ethnography (Fabrega and Silver, 1974). Topics of interest to psychiatrists were dealt with in recent, high-quality ethnographies of Japanese (Reynolds, 1976), Moroccan (Crapanzano, 1973), and New Guinean (Lewis, 1975) cultures. Detailed psychiatric case studies and psychiatrists' observations of patients, usually in an institution, may be considered partial ethnographies if the cultural background of the patients is taken into account. Important information about cultural influences on the causes and the course of mental illness may be provided by ethnographies of noninstitutionalized patients.

Ethnicity is an important concept, but difficult to operationalize; as Giordano and Giordano (1977) noted:

It involves conscious and unconscious processes that fulfill a deep psychological need for security, identity and a sense of historical community.

Ethnography is one approach to portraying the ethnic experience, as seen in Lewis's ethnographies of Mexican (Lewis, 1959) and Puerto Rican (Lewis, 1965) families. Autobiographies, although less objective than true ethnographic studies, often provide poignant protrayals of ethnic experiences.

SUBJECTIVE CULTURE

Subjective culture, the characteristic ways in which a cultural group perceives its social environment, focuses on cognitive structures that mediate between stimuli and responses in different cultural settings (Triandis, 1972). Among the concepts used to delineate subjective culture are cognitive map, life space, world view, behavioral environment, and mazeway.

The basic strategy of subjective culture studies is to present members of a cultural group with different stimuli. A pattern of similar responses constitutes one aspect of the group's subjective culture and can be compared with the response patterns of groups in other cultures. Among the most important concepts for study are associations, attitudes, beliefs, categorizations, evaluations, expectations, memories, opinions, percepts, role perceptions, stereotypes, and values (Campbell, 1963).

Subjective culture deals with the way people categorize experience. Experience is categorized at several levels, beginning with discriminable stimuli and progressing to meaning categories, concepts, elemental cognitive structures (beliefs, norms), major cognitive structures (such as attitudes), values, and value orientations. Language is clearly important to the process of categorization, and one of the primary instruments for determining the meaning of verbal concepts is the semantic differential (Osgood et al., 1957). With that instrument persons use a series of bipolar scales to rate concepts that can then be located in a three-dimensional meaning space through the use of statistical analysis.

The study of attitudes and values has a special importance for psychiatry. An effective, primary-prevention program for alcoholism assuredly would involve changing attitudes and values toward drinking. The literature on values is enormous, and values have been associated with such concepts as central cultural themes, environmental sensitivity, ways of life, achievement needs, human adjustment, self-sufficient satisfaction, ideal types, and activity-passivity. The Human Value Survey is an instrument that measures 18 terminal values and 18 instrumental values (Rokeach, 1973). That instrument, which only requires a subject to rank order values, may be adaptable to psychiatric research. A useful approach for the study of values (Kluckhohn and Strodtbeck, 1961) is an instrument that examines five basic value orientations. The instrument limits choices and can distinguish 2,688 patterns that can be used to differentiate cultures.

Mazer (1976), in his cultural psychiatric study of Martha's Vineyard, gathered data by recording the responses of islanders to the presentation of 12 different human situations and by recording the consensus estimation of 18 local, knowledgeable observers. Mazer used Kluckhohn and Strodtbeck's (1961) instrument to determine the dominant values of the islanders: (1) Is human nature evil, good, or a mixture of both? (2) Is man in subjugation to nature, in harmony with her, or master over her? (3) Is the focus of human life generally on the past, the present, or the future? (4) Is being or doing more important? (5) Are the individuals in a society mainly concerned with their lineal relationships, with their collateral relationships, or with individualism? Knowledge of the value orientations greatly influenced the type of mental health programs established for the diverse cultural and age groups of the population.

Many public opinion studies regarding complex cultural problems use quantitative sampling and participant-observer or anecdotal recording. However, a small sample technique using Q-sort methodology has been developed that allows an investigator to compare and contrast attributes in different cultural settings, test the invariance of the factors, interpret consensus opinions, and determine in-depth, genuine segments of opinion about controversial matters. That method was used to study transcultural attitudes toward antisocial behavior. The study determined that a majority of people in each culture studied endorsed a traditional, moralistic, and punitive orientation to social control of crime but that upper-social class persons and experts, especially mental health professionals, tended to endorse preventive, rehabilitative, and therapeutic strategies (Weiss and Perry, 1977 a, b).

CULTURE OF MENTAL HOSPITALS

Until the 1950's the physical and sociocultural environment of mental hospitals was generally considered to be a static setting within which psychiatrists treated patients. Apart from the notion that a neatly landscaped, tightly ordered, and tranquil hospital somehow imparted a beneficial sense of neatness, order, and tranquillity to the patients, the impact of the hospital's sociocultural environment on patient care was hardly even considered.

Interest in various social aspects of mental hospitals developed gradually. Then Stanton and Schwartz (1954) published their study of institutional participation in psychiatric illness and treatment at Chestnut Lodge. They noted that patients usually improved during periods of effective collaboration on the part of personnel and concluded that the fact of organization itself seemed an important factor in the hospital's general therapeutic effects. They reported situations in which disagreements among staff members over a patient's management often resulted in an exacerbation of the patient's symptoms and in disturbances of staff behavior. Those situations were especially noticeable when staff disagreements were not discussed openly, thus permitting free-floating emotion to become manifest in secondary contexts. They clearly demonstrated that the hospital's administrative process was intimately linked with the patient-staff therapeutic process.

William Caudill (1958), an anthropologist influenced by Maxwell Jones's work in developing therapeutic communities on mental hospital wards, admitted himself as a patient to the Yale Psychiatric Institute in order to make around-the-clock observations about life on a ward; later on, he collected data openly. His analysis of the psychiatric hospital as a small society focused on role groups, communication flow about events that occurred in the hospital, and the compatibility of various hospital subsystems—the degree of fit between therapeutic and administrative programs. He proposed the development of clinical anthropology and thought that a psychiatric hospital was an advantageous place to study comparative or universal questions concerning the linked systems of human behavior, such as physiology, personality, small groups, and wider social structures.

Although clinical anthropology has never developed as a discipline, sociocultural research on mental hospitals has continued. One of the most devastating critiques of mental hospital culture was Goffman's (1961) *Asylums*. That work was especially influential because it supplied ammunition for community mental health advocates in their attempt to siphon power and funds away from state hospitals. With administrative approval Goffman posed as a student of recreation and community life at St. Elizabeth's hospital for a year. On the basis of his observations, he concluded that diagnoses were frequently based on ethnocentric bias and that therapy was based on political and moral, rather than scientific, considerations. He portrayed the institutionalized patient as a "serviceable object" whose basic humanity was debased by the hospital staff. He noted that patients adjusted to institutional life in various ways, such as by developing a barter system, establishing secret methods of communication, and stashing forbidden materials.

The idea that patients are helpless victims entrapped in the pathogenic web of hospital culture seems to overstate the case. Rosenberg (1970), for example, developed the concept that patients are full-system participants in hospital culture and that their needs and proclivities are strong determinants of the nature of the hospital's functioning and social structure. A patient's wish to be controlled may be transformed into the cultural belief that the institution is repressive.

Cultural studies of mental hospitals have led to major changes in psychiatric practice. Attention to the hospital environment has resulted in a decrease in "institutional neurosis," a form of cultural pathology that can superimpose itself on a patient's primary illness. Most wards now strive to establish a therapeutic milieu as a major treatment modality. Observations on the relationships between the mental functioning of patients and staff and the social organization and process of the hospital led to the community mental health focus on integrated and disintegrated communities, a link explored in the Stirling County study. Not all mental hospital environments are therapeutic, however, and Dunham (1976) suggested that the current state hospital culture will continue to be a liability until, in its forms and functioning, it more closely approximates the other institutions in the community.

Folk Beliefs and Rituals

Although disease occurs as a natural process with a biological and psychological reality, the experience of illness is a cultural or symbolic reality. Every culture has systems of symbolic meaning that may be overtly expressed and experienced through belief systems, such as those about mental illness.

Folk beliefs about mental illness fall outside of scientific tradition. The antiquity of some beliefs, such as soul loss and spirit intrusion, can be inferred from an examination of the few remaining hunting and gathering societies. The endurance of those beliefs, some relatively unchanged for thousands of years, is remarkable and differentiates them from popular beliefs. Folk beliefs are significant in both industrial and nonindustrial societies. Although some beliefs are unique to specific cultural groups, others are widely diffused throughout the world. In diverse cultures, for example, it is held that certain behavioral symptoms arise when a person's soul is separated from his body. Among Hispanic Americans a common name given to

the complex is *susto*, a condition characterized by restless sleep, anorexia, depression, fatigue, and loss of interest in dress and personal hygiene. But even in Hispanic America *susto* has many different names and affects people of different societal groups, regardless of race, social class, sex, or place of residency.

FOLK CLASSIFICATION AND CAUSES OF MENTAL ILLNESS

An understanding of folk causative theories has direct clinical relevance. A patient who believes in the supernatural causation of his mental illness may be able to discard the sick role in certain cases because he may not accept personal responsibility for his sickness state. In contrast, the sick role may be prolonged for a patient who believes that he is personally responsible for causing his illness (Waxler, 1974).

Folk classifications of mental illness are rarely found in written form. In a study of Mexican-Americans in the Southwest, Kay (1977) asked respondents to describe how a person feels when sick and to note the different kinds of sickness. Figure 1 illustrates the classification of emotional illness that emerged.

Although anthropologists have described many folk medical classifications, it is especially important for the psychiatrist to understand folk theories of causes (Glick, 1976). Folk theories of causes are as diverse as different cultural belief systems; among the many causes of mental illness are a disequilibrium of natural forces, such as yin and yang, dosha (Ayurvedic), cold, heat, winds, dampness, basic body elements, and the purposeful intervention of a human (witch or sorcerer), nonhuman (ghost, ancestor, or evil spirit), or supernatural (a deity) agent against a specific victim. Hexes and spirit possession are among the most prevalent examples of folk beliefs about the causes of mental illness.

Hexes. Sorcery and, less frequently, witchcraft are central to the concept of hexing. Although the terms "sorcery" and "witchcraft" are often used interchangeably, their meaning should be differentiated (Marwick, 1970). A sorcerer uses magic and rituals to alter natural and supernatural events. Anyone can be a sorcerer if he acquires certain powers through such means as apprenticeship, purchase, and theft. Sorcerers are often regarded ambiguously by the community because they may work toward either good or evil ends. Witches, in contrast, have an inherent potential to alter events and need not resort to magic. Witches almost invariably work toward evil ends and are regarded fearfully as deviants by the community. Among the Dobu islanders of the western Pacific, suspicion of sorcery pervades many aspects of life. A successful gardener, for example, is assumed to have used strong magic to his own advantage by seducing yams away from others and by socially trampling on weaker persons. The negative charisma associated with witchcraft is exemplified by the Chontal Indians of Oaxaca, Mexico, where witchcraft accusations may lead to the execution of the suspected person.

Often linked to sorcery and witchcraft is belief in the evil eye, a phenomenon widespread throughout Europe, the Near East, the Indian subcontinent, and Africa (Maloney, 1976). A study of a representative sample of cultures determined that 36 per cent possessed the belief in the evil eye. The belief was brought by immigrants to North America.

The evil eye is generally considered to be a sudden, destructive power emanating—sometimes unknown even to the person who possesses it—from the eye of a person or animal. Symptoms it may cause include headache, sleepiness or fitful sleep,

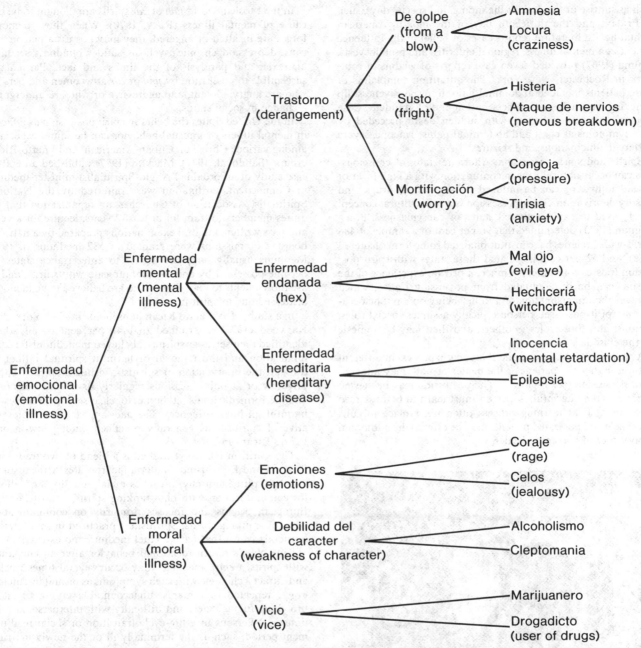

FIGURE 1. Southwest Mexican-American folk classification of emotional illness. (From Kay, M. Health and illness in a Mexican-American barrio. In *Ethnic Medicine in the Southwest*, E. H. Spicer, editor. University of Arizona Press, Tucson, 1977.)

exhaustion, depression, hypochondriasis, spirit possession, impotence, failure to thrive, anorexia, listlessness, diarrhea, vomiting, disrupted social relationships, and sudden death. It may also affect property, causing the death of animals, the destruction of cars and pots, the spoilage of food, and poor crops. A person affected by the evil eye is frequently unable to determine the source of the power, although the most highly suspect are persons with a physical deformity, strangers, kin and neighbors, marginal members of society, barren women, the poor and hungry, persons dissatisfied with their lot in life, children who return to the mother's breast after weaning (among Slovak-Americans), and, most important, anyone who utters a word of praise or compliment. The evil eye can strike anyone, but the most susceptible are wealthy, handsome, and weak persons;

children; and women, especially when pregnant. Foulks (1977) reported the case of a 27-year-old Italian-American living in Philadelphia who believed himself hexed and subsequently murdered six people whom he believed were sorcerers responsible for striking him with the evil eye.

Belief in root-work or voodoo can be found among some American blacks, especially those from rural backgrounds (Wintrob, 1973). Root-work, a probable derivative of voodoo, is essentially a hex most often administered by tampering with a victim's food or drink or by touch or an evil glance. Other techniques include sprinkling sand, salt, or pepper on a victim's front door step; burying a knife with its point toward a victim's house; and magically manipulating various items—household goods, blood, excreta, hair—in conjunction with special times, such as sunrise or the dark of the moon, and special days, such as Fridays and the thirteenth day of the month. American mental health literature reports cases of belief in the influence of hexes on mental illness, regional enteritis, and pseudocyesis. Tinling (1967) provided seven case reports of victims of rootwork in Rochester, New York. The admitting complaints of those patients included abdominal pain, unresponsiveness, lip smacking, and delusions of persecution and of grandeur. Case reports have linked hexing with sudden death preceded by such symptoms as chest and abdominal pains, syncope, severe anxiety, hallucinations, and seizures.

Spirits and spirit possession. Alternate states of consciousness can occur naturally, as in conjunction with a high fever or a head injury, or can be induced by suggestion, drugs, and sensory deprivation. Spirit possession is a folk cultural concept widely used to explain altered states of consciousness. Bourguignon (1973) determined that 90 per cent of a sample of 488 world-wide societies have institutionalized some form of altered states, and 52 per cent associated those states with spirit possession (possession trance). Trance, a private experience of the person, can be differentiated from possession trance, which involves the impersonation of another being on a public occasion. A spirit-possessed person typically assumes special roles, demonstrates those roles to others, and then may be amnesic for the episode.

As part of the diagnostic and therapeutic process in different cultures, either the patient or the healer or both may undergo spirit possession (see Figure 2). The possession may be viewed as beneficial or harmful. A person must learn to be possessed by a spirit. That learning process often takes place in cults where selected possessed patients may be offered the additional opportunity of becoming healers.

FIGURE 2. In New Guinea, among the Sepik, an initiate is shown during the skin-cutting ceremony. (Courtesy of Wolfgang Jilek, M.D., Vancouver, British Columbia.)

In the Moslem world *jinn* or *zar* spirits are thought to be one cause of mental illness (Racy, 1970). When those demonic forces are insulted or angered, they may possess a person and cause depression, chronic psychosis, sudden blindness, seizures, anorexia, and paralysis of the limbs and face. Particularly susceptible to possession by *jinn* or *zar* are women and persons who are angry, violent, and aggressive or who are undergoing a change in social status.

In the United States the belief in spirit possession as a factor in mental illness or unusual behavior can be found especially among various Christian, Cuban-American, and Puerto-Rican groups (Sandoval, 1977). Macklin (1977) published a detailed case study of an ordained Anglo-Spiritualist minister-medium in Connecticut. Ordination was conferred by the National Spiritualist Association of Churches, an organization that requires members to train for at least 2 years, lecture for a year, and pass written and oral examinations prepared by a national board. Commissions were granted to 532 mediums in 1975. Mediums usually have the ability to enter trance states, to become possessed by and to communicate with spirits, and to use those talents to help clients who are believed to be mentally distressed due to spirit intrusion.

In a study of 79 Puerto Rican households in New York City, Harwood (1977) determined that 47 per cent of all adults identified themselves as spiritists, believed in mediumistic communication and the removal of harmful spiritual influences through the intervention of spiritists, visited a spiritist either privately or at public sessions regularly or in times of crisis, and performed rituals at home to cleanse the premises of harmful spiritual influences. The data appear to be representative of spiritism as generally practiced among low-income Puerto Ricans in New York.

The spiritism Harwood studied is a blend of two traditions, Santeria and Espiritismo. Santeria incorporates African spirits into the spirit hierarchy, preaches racial equality, and allows for communication with high-ranking spirits. Espiritismo has European origins and focuses primarily on communication with low-ranking spirits. Spiritism is practiced in small neighborhood *centros* that have a chief medium and assistants who aid the chief's return to normal behavior after an encounter with spirits. *Centro* meetings may occur several times weekly and attract a clientele with such symptoms as insomnia, suicidal urges, repeated nightmares, unaccountable crying or silent brooding, fugue states, and difficulty with interpersonal relationships. Persons in a life-cycle transition or social readjustment period, such as the terminally ill or the newly married, may come to the *centro*, as may persons who fear a medical diagnosis of a fatal illness. Causative categories in spiritism are listed in Table I.

Other causes. Although hexes and spirit intrusion seem to be the most prevalent folk causes of mental illness, other purported causes, some of which are variations of those major themes, may be briefly described.

Object intrusion. An object, such as an animal, may enter a person's body and cause mental illness. Moth craziness (*iich' aa*) among the Navaho is thought to be caused by the presence of a moth within a person's cranial cavity.

Divine intervention. An angry god may cause illness if a person has not kept a sacred promise or has been disrespectful to a divinity. Among some American blacks, natural illness is thought to result from a failure to abide by God's behavioral rules; unnatural mental illness is due to the machinations of the devil (Snow, 1977). God may cause a person to become ill as a test of his faith. Among the Hutterites (south central Canada and north central United States) there is no shame associated with depression, since God may decide to test anyone.

TABLE I
Causes in Spiritist Diagnosis*

Causative Category	Implied Spiritual Cause
Envidia (envy)	The unexpressed envy of incarnate spirits in close association with the victim
Brujeria (sorcery)	A disembodied spirit sent to harm the victim by an enemy working in league with a spiritist
Mala influencia (evil influence) or mala corriente (evil current)	A disembodied spirit of low rank seeking to be given light
Facultades (faculties)	Spirits of various ranks who possess the body of a person insufficiently trained in controlling such seizures
Prueba (test or trial)	Protective spirits who test a person while he or she is developing faculties God-predestined trials in a person's life
Cadena (chain)	The spirit of a deceased relative or other associate from the past who has done some misdeed
Castigo (punishment)	Misguided spirits allowed to beset a victim who has neglected his relationship with his spiritual protectors

* From Harwood, A. *Rx: Spiritist As Needed.* John Wiley & Sons, New York, 1977.

Soul loss. Some Cuban-Americans believe that each person has an *eleda,* a spiritual double, who protects him. An enemy or a witch may capture a person's *eleda,* thus rendering him defenseless and susceptible to illness. The personal disasters that may result from soul loss in Western culture are clearly portrayed in stories about Faust. The *susto* complex is the most widespread soul-loss causative belief.

Dreams. Mental illness may result from a lack of dreams or may be the fulfillment of a frightening dream.

Prenatal influences. A pregnant woman who is unfaithful to her husband may cause damage to the embryo, who will suffer consequent behavioral abnormalities.

Heredity. Bad traits may be passed on to future generations through mechanisms that do not conform to scientific genetic theory; for example, a socially inadequate brother may cause similar traits to appear in the offspring of his sister.

Contamination. Lebra (1972) described a Japanese-American sect in Hawaii in which sickness is believed to be a punishment for religious or social misconduct. Other members of the sect avoid contact with the disturbed person for fear of catching and carrying away the spirit that has caused the illness. Among the Fipa (Tanzania) severe depression may result from social contact with a person who has had recent secret, adulterous sexual relations.

FOLK DIAGNOSIS

Folk diagnosis of mental disorders usually involves experienced diagnosticians with a repertoire of diagnostic tests. Some folk diagnosticians use astute psychological techniques to gather information from patients and members of their social network. Some diagnostic procedures are repetitive rituals that involve complex social negotiations and interactions. Diagnostic rituals set the scene for rituals of healing and cannot be divorced from treatment procedures.

Evil eye. Diagnosis of the evil eye in southern Italy is a simple procedure and reflects practices performed in many circum-Mediterranean and Hispanic-American cultures. A female specialist takes a bowl of water, puts three drops of oil in it, crosses herself, and recites ritual words, calling on God to remove the evil eye. If the oil mixes with the water, the patient's sickness is thought to be organic. If the oil coagulates, however, that is evidence of the evil eye. Symbolically, the water probably represents holiness, and the oil represents evil. The force of the Holy Trinity counterbalances the evil eye, thought, and desire.

Spirit possession. In some Moslem cultures *zar* spirits afflict women primarily. The patient is brought to a *sheikh,* who obtains psychosocial information, with special emphasis on dreams and disturbances of eating and sleeping. The patient may be asked to drink a special spicy beverage and may have incense passed under her clothing. Those procedures stimulate the possessing spirit, who then causes the patient to shake and dance. If the *sheikh* determines that a patient's symptoms are caused by spirit possession, he sets up a public or a more costly private *zar* ceremony. In the ceremony the *sheikh* goes into a trance, and his possessing spirit questions the patient to discover her spirit's name and the reason the spirit decided to possess her. Musicians play songs associated with particular *zar* spirits, and the patient goes into a trance and dances when the proper song is played. The diagnosis is thus complete, although several sessions may be needed to reach that point (Kennedy, 1967).

In Puerto Rican spiritist diagnostic procedures, the *centro* session begins with an invocation of good spirits. Cigar smoke is blown onto the patient while the medium fans the air to remove evil influences. By singing certain songs and drinking special beverages, such as black coffee with rum, the congregation is brought under the protection of the saints. The medium then goes into a trance, establishes communication with his spirit, and makes statements about the patient that the patient must answer truthfully. Initial statements may be quite general, touching on common problems, such as marital, sexual, and economic difficulties. Statements become more precise as the medium picks up cues from the patient. Typically, the process begins with an examination of the patient's mental status and then moves on to social relationships. Dream analysis is common; assistant mediums reinforce the more significant interpretations of the chief medium. A diagnosis, based on the categories in Table I, is often reached, although the medium may require several diagnostic sessions.

Other diagnostic methods. The potential for a wide range of folk diagnostic techniques in one culture is exemplified by the Nyoro tribe (Uganda). The procedures are, with local modifications, prevalent in many different cultures. A mechanical technique involves the interpretation of patterns displayed by cowry shells scattered on a mat by the ill client and the diagnostician. Diagnosis by augury—examining the entrails of a dead animal—and by spirit possession of client or diagnostician are also practiced among the Nyoro. A diagnostic technique used by native Americans of the Southwest is hand trembling, a ritual in which the diagnostician's hands magically tremble over a patient in order to point out the cause of the illness.

Not all diagnoses require a specialist. Very often a troubled person, his family, or friends may arrive at a diagnosis through the observation of complaints and behavior. Kay (1977) elicited nine signs and symptoms considered by Mexican-Americans to indicate mental illness: worry or fear (dwelling on unpleasant events, possibilities, or life problems), lack of equilibrium (disorientation and confusion), sadness (habitual depression with crying spells), rage, delirium (unrestrained irrational action), fainting, convulsions, hallucinations, and memory loss. Such popular or lay diagnostic processes undertaken by family, friends, and the community may generate expectations in the patient and in members of his social network that may not correspond with those of a psychiatrist. The result may be clinical noncompliance.

FOLK TREATMENT

Folk procedures for healing generally incorporate the patient and his social group as a whole into the treatment program. Dramatic healing rituals entail the active, public participation of the patient, the members of his social network, and the therapist. Through the use of powerful symbols and impressive, impersonal roles, the therapist conducts the healing ritual in a supernatural context. Those rituals contrast greatly with Western treatment techniques, which often take place in fairly secluded, quiet rooms.

Hexes. In some cultures the diagnostic test for the evil eye is thought to be curative in itself. The evil is dissolved during the diagnosis. Another method of curing the evil eye is to throw the diagnostic material of water and oil onto a pathway. The next person who walks by absorbs the evil eye and thus frees the original victim. Another method includes the recitation of special prayers:

> Go away, evil wind. You are banished by the Holy Trinity. All of you go away. Mother Mary banishes you.

Other curative methods are fumigation, burning alum (which pops like an eye bursting), and spitting. As with most disorders, prevention of the evil eye is easier than cure. Amulets against the evil eye are used throughout the world (see Figure 3). They include the horned hand and chili horn (Italian), the red plastic horseshoe with a small chili horn suspended from its arch (Italian-American), red ribbons (Eastern European Jewish), mirrors (Indian), and pieces of iron (world-wide). Other preventive measures include smudging a child's cheek to make him appear imperfect; avoiding ambition, perfection, and the display of wealth; avoiding suspicious persons; making palm prints on a doorway; displaying various hand signs; and wearing veils.

Spirits. Curative *zar* ceremonies differ in detail according to the *sheikh's* idiosyncrasies and the patient's mental illness. The curing ceremony for a chronic schizophrenic patient, for example, is apt to be longer and more elaborate than that for a patient with a hysterical neurosis. The ceremony—usually held in a large, hot (to stimulate the spirits) room or arena—may last from morning to evening for 7 days. Participants shake and dance when the appropriate spirit song is played. The *sheikh* changes costumes with each spirit that possesses him. He may sacrifice several animals during the ceremony and smear the animal's blood on the patient. He questions the patient's spirit. The patient finally becomes exhausted from dancing, but, before the *zar* consents to leave her body, it may demand special favors, such as jewelry, new clothing, or expensive foods. The patient's spouse, relatives, and friends feel duty bound to pacify the *zar*. Frequently, the patient may keep the items that her spirit has demanded, but sometimes they are returned after the ceremony. Although there is a social aspect to *zar* ceremonies, the membership of *zar* cults is composed primarily of chronic mentally ill persons. They participate in weekly, public *zar* ceremonies, dancing and placating the spirits that possess them. Thus, although it may be possible to exorcize some spirits, many permanently possess a patient. Therapy then consists of learning to live adaptively with a spirit. The Hamadsha, a Moroccan Islamic healing cult, requires the dancer to mutilate himself to please the spirit. The ultimate

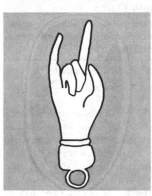

FIGURE 3. Amulets to ward off the evil eye: a chili horn; manus obscena; mano cornuto; and hunchback holding a horseshoe. (Courtesy of Dr. Foulks and Journal of Operational Psychiatry.)

goal is to transform the malevolent spirit into a benevolent one. That symbolic cure occurs only if the patient follows the spirit's orders to wear special colors, to burn incense, and to do a trance dance to certain tunes.

In Harwood's (1977) Puerto Rican study several principal therapeutic procedures for removing pathogenic spiritual influences emerge. In *despojo* (exorcism) the medium performs physical acts, such as fumigating a patient with cigar smoke or stroking his neck. In addition to attracting benign spirits to the patient, the medium may also attempt to draw off the evil spirits onto himself. *Trabajando la causa* (working the cause) is a technique used when specific pathogenic spirits have been identified. It is the treatment of choice for sorcery and requires the services of at least two mediums. The medium, possessed by his own spirit, interrogates the patient's spirit and tries to convince it to leave the patient. *Dando la luz al spiritu* (giving the spirit light) is a technique in which a patient follows a set of rituals in order to remove a spirit's harmful influence. A depressed patient, for example, may be ordered to purchase flowers or candles, to perform specified therapeutic tasks, and to attend *centro* meetings. *Desarollo* (spiritual development), which is indicated for persons with dissociative symptoms, is a process in which the patient is taught to display his symptoms at culturally and ritually appropriate times and places. In addition to all those techniques, mediums offer counseling that tends to be direct and reality oriented. Counseling focuses on the consequences of different decisions and attempts to build a patient's self-esteem and confidence.

Other folk treatment techniques. Plants, herbs, and weeds are ingested by many different cultural groups to treat mental illness. The best-known and probably the most effective folk remedy is the use of rauwolfia in Africa and India. Unscrupulous folk healers may deliberately administer poisons, such as scopolamine, to worsen a client's condition in the hopes of charging a higher fee to cure the client.

Coast Salish native Americans have developed a seemingly effective ceremonial for patients suffering from depression, anxiety, and antisocial personality disorders. A patient is symbolically "clubbed to death" and then subjected to immobilization, fasting, dehydration, rhythmic sensory stimuli, and didactic propaganda. The patient discovers his special song, is provided with new clothes and a new name, and finally is "reborn" with a healthy Indian identity. The Navaho have more than 50 major healing ceremonials, such as the Evil Way chant and the Holy Way chant, which are used to treat mental disorders. Patients are purified through emetics, sweating, and continence. The supernatural powers are forced to help the ill person, who need not examine his behavior, motives, or conscience.

FOLK HEALERS

Although folk healers may assume prestigious positions as priests, rulers, or university presidents, many specialize solely in healing. Some healers are sorcerers, but the vast majority work toward nonevil ends.

Landy (1977) listed major pathways through which a person may be recruited into a folk-healing role: (1) Inheritance from parent or child or through a hereditary priesthood. (2) Selection by parents, relatives, other healers, tribal elders, religious sodalities, or gods and spirits. (3) Self-selection by apprenticing oneself to a healer; by borrowing, buying, or stealing secret knowledge and rituals; by seeking entrance into a healing cult; and by study, observation, and practice. (4) Undergoing a profound emotional experience involving awe-inspiring symptoms that manifest spiritual power or receiving a divine call through a dream, a trance, or a hallucination, which may be the result of self-induced privation, torture, or drugs. (5) Self-dedication to a healing cult, often after having undergone a cult cure. (6) Miraculous self-recovery from a usually lethal disease or situation. (7) Possessing a physical or psychological disability, such as epilepsy, blindness, or various psychiatric symptoms. (8) Possessing exceptional personal traits, such as high intelligence, courage, storytelling ability, emotional control, and good judgment.

A shaman is a person who has followed a divine call to healing. He has received instructions directly from spiritual contacts, and he may be a medium to communicate those spiritual instructions. Shamans can be found in almost all cultural groups, such as the Haitian hungan (see Figure 4), West Indian Obeah men, and Western faith healers. Psychosocial profiles of shamans show that some are imposters, some are mentally disordered, and some are mentally healthy, mature persons with a special cognitive style. The last may be considered true shamans and the others pseudoshamans. True shamans possess a high tolerance for unconscious material and primary-process thinking and have an unusual ability to recognize and to organize unconscious needs and concerns both in themselves and in their cultural group. In many cultures those aspiring to be shamans undergo a formal didactic initia-

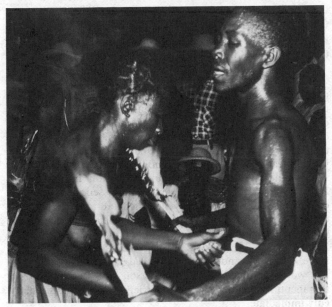

FIGURE 4. A voodoo shaman and shamaness, Houngan and Mambo, in Haiti, undergo an ordeal by fire while possessed by spirits in an altered state of consciousness. (Courtesy of Wolfgang Jilek, M.D., Vancouver, British Columbia.)

tion and an ecstatic initiation—a culturally formulated illness-like condition. The crazy witch doctor notion derived in part from observers who confused mental illness with initiatory, ecstatic sickness (Jilek and Jilek-Aall, 1978).

Murphy (1964) classified the therapeutic techniques of shamans among the St. Lawrence Eskimo. Many of her observations can be applied in whole or in part to other cultures, even to faith healers in Western society. The shaman gives objective reality to popular and emotionally accepted beliefs of the cultural group. Therapy takes place in a group context and is a public drama in which the patient and the shaman are given strong support by the group. The shaman, sometimes through the use of magical perception, focuses awe on himself as a truly extraordinary person. Through the mechanism of spirit possession, the shaman acts as an agent of a powerful spirit and is thus able to perform psychological "cures"; the spirit can declare that a patient's lost soul has been retrieved. More objective treatments—such as the use of medicines, surgery, chiropracty, and bandaging—may be therapeutic in themselves. In addition, by demonstrating objectively that a disease has been dispelled, the shaman may effect cures through suggestion. Finally, shamans prescribe steps through which the patient can stabilize the cure and demonstrate his healthy state. The patient may be told, for example, to perform acts of atonement and to adopt a new name or new manner of dress. The psychiatric concept of insight is of little importance in shamanistic approaches.

Although the ethnographic literature has emphasized the cultural conservatism of shamans, recent reports note new roles and new techniques of curing. *Curanderos*, Hispanic-American folk healers, have traditionally been described as providing mental health services that involve the patient's social network in lengthy diagnostic and curing rituals at low cost. Confession is used in therapy, and reintegration of the client into the community is a primary concern (Kiev, 1968). That peasant-derived stereotype holds true for some areas but contrasts sharply with an emerging, urban *curandero* style that focuses on dyadic process, patient self-reliance, and fee for service (Press, 1971).

CHRISTIAN BELIEFS ABOUT MENTAL ILLNESS

In the Old Testament sickness was portrayed as God's punishment, and God alone was the healer. In the New Testament, however, new ideas about sickness and healing emerged (Kelsey, 1973). Nearly 20 per cent of the Gospels are devoted to Jesus's healings and the discussions occasioned by them. The Gospels contain 41 instances of healing (72 including duplications). The most common ailment that Jesus healed was mental illness caused by demon possession. In Matthew 8: 28–32 Jesus meets two fierce, demon-possessed men and then commands the demons to leave the men and to inhabit a herd of swine, which immediately commit suicide by drowning. Other examples of demon possession are noted in Matthew 4: 24, 8:16, 15:22–28, Mark 1:23–27, 1:32, 1:39, 3:10–12, 6:13, and Luke 4:41, 7:21, and 8:2. Jesus healed primarily by saying a few words or touching the sick person with his hands. The therapeutic encounters were quite brief, and the results reportedly immediate.

In Luke 9:1–2, 10:1, and 10:8–9, Jesus not only granted healing powers to his disciples and other believers but also urged them to seek out and cure the sick. Indeed, healing was a central and natural function of early Christian tradition. Over the centuries, however, healing and demonology were deemphasized. In the *Book of Pastoral Care*, written in the 5th century by Gregory the Great, the sick were admonished because they were being chastized by God. When St. Jerome produced the Vulgate Bible in about 400 A.D., the only official church translation from Greek to Latin for nearly 1,500 years, he used the verb "to save" to translate the Greek verb "to heal." Thus, in the classic biblical healing text (James 5:12–16), the original reads

so confess your sins to one another, and pray for one another, and this will *cure* you.

Jerome's translation changed the last phrase to "and this will *save* you." An emphasis on spiritual salvation, rather than on healing, permeated Christianity until recent times. Sin and sickness became interrelated concepts and, for many, the suffering that resulted from illness was seen as a blessing. The neglect of healing in later Christian tradition is evidenced by the fact that St. Thomas Aquinas scarcely mentions it in his voluminous writings. Luther and Calvin thought that healing was a temporary power granted to the early Christians and that Christianity's greater task was to save men spiritually, although Luther did admit to curing a madman by prayer.

The concept of demon possession reemerged powerfully in the 15th century. Diagnostic criteria for demon possession included anorexia, impotence, great fatigue, and skin lesions. Both Catholic and Protestant ecclesiatics treated demon possession through exorcism.

In Catholic tradition, healing was relegated to monastic hospitals and holy shrines, such as the shrine of St. Dymphna in Gheel, Belgium. The most famous modern shrine is that of Lourdes. Although tens of millions of pilgrims have visited Lourdes since its founding in 1859, fewer than 100 miraculous cures have been recognized by the Church. A seemingly failsafe series of medical and ecclesiastical committees must give their consent before a cure can be judged miraculous. A British psychiatrist, D. J. West (1957), carefully examined the recorded miracle cases from 1925 to 1950. There were no reported cures

of mental illness. In fact, cures of chronic tuberculosis in women headed the list. West found that the records were poorly documented and contained instances of overenthusiastic interpretation. He concluded that the miracle cases could be explained medically.

During the 20th century Christian interest in healing was stimulated by the formation of the Pentecostal Church in 1900. Speaking in tongues is usually interpreted by Pentecostal sects as definitive evidence of the personal indwelling of the Holy Spirit. Through the power of the Spirit, both healing of illness and spiritual rebirth occur. The literature on neo-Pentecostal beliefs about physical healing is comprehensive, but that on mental illness is scant. Some Pentecostals have claimed remarkable success in healing drug addicts, such as a 70 per cent cure rate and a 30-second painless withdrawal from heroin. A popular concern is inner healing, a term associated primarily with Christian emotional well-being.

Among Christian Scientists, illness is considered an illusion, and, thus, healing is considered a mental phenomenon; healing occurs through the power of an intellectual, impersonal, spiritual force that allows the person to restructure his beliefs and to use self-reliant willpower. Current Christian Science publications still refer to the pathogenic properties of malicious animal magnetism.

The best-known contemporary healing ministry, that of Oral Roberts, focuses on physical healing—a publicly observable, dramatic phenomenon of considerable recruitment value. It is a far more difficult task in a public gathering to dramatize the healing of mental illness. Roberts claims that 85 per cent of all diseases are emotionally induced. He attributes personality disintegration to the fall of Adam and Eve; thus, sickness and suffering are sent by the devil. Spiritual wholeness is the key to healing, and Roberts outlines the steps to health, including the suggestion to plant a seed of faith and expect miracles. He claims that healing can be performed from afar; petitioners can send requests to the Tower at Oral Roberts University, where specialists pray for the healing of specific persons.

Interest in spiritual healing has spread among conservative American religious groups. More than 1,500 Episcopalian churches now have weekly healing services, as do more than 1,000 Catholic churches with charismatic groups. The shift in Catholic attitude is illustrated by official sacramental changes. The sacrament called "Annointing of the Sick" was originally administered to heal an ill person. When sickness came to be perceived as a blessing, the sacrament's purpose shifted to a spiritual one. It prepared a dying soul for entrance into heaven and was called "Extreme Unction." In 1974 the sacrament was retitled "Annointing of the Sick" and its original purpose reinstated. Healing, prophecy, and speaking in tongues are among the more manifest gifts of the spirit for charismatics.

Two leading figures in the Catholic charismatic movement are the priests Michael Scanlan and Francis MacNutt (1974, 1977). MacNutt's books present the most comprehensive and systematic formulations of the charismatic approach to illness and healing (see Table II). Although widely known among Catholic charismatics, MacNutt's formulations are those of a healing specialist. The beliefs of Catholic charismatics about mental illness and healing are more likely to appear as an unelaborated synthesis of popular, scientific, and religious concepts.

Thus, mental sickness may be caused by past emotional hurts, demonic oppression, and demonic possession. Demon possession is suspected if the patient confesses he is demon possessed, if the patient is unable to control self-destructive behavior—such as alcoholism or drug abuse—and if a prayer

TABLE II
Charismatic Concepts of Illness and Treatment*

Sickness	Cause	Prayer Remedy	Appropriate Sacrament or Sacramental	Ordinary Human Remedy

Of the spirit:
  Often contributing to emotional sickness
  Sometimes contributing to bodily sickness
	Personal sin	Repentance	Penance	

Of the emotions:
  Often contributing to spiritual sickness
  Often contributing to bodily sickness
	Original sin—that is, the person has been hurt by the sins of others	Prayer for inner healing	Penance	Counseling (psychiatric and spiritual)

Of the body:
  Often contributing to emotional sickness
  Sometimes contributing to spiritual sickness
	Disease, accidents, psychological stress	Prayer of faith for physical healing	Anointing of the Sick	Medical care

All or any of the above can, on occasion, be	Demonic in its cause	Prayer of deliverance (exorcism)	Exorcism	

* From MacNutt, F. *Healing.* Ave Maria Press, Notre Dame, Ind., 1974.

for inner healing fails to bring an improvement in the patient's condition.

The treatment setting must be private, unlike the treatment setting of organic illness, which may be treated publicly or even in the absence of the patient. Signs that one possesses the gift of healing include a sensation of heat or an electric current and a gentle trembling of power. Treatment involves the discussion of past emotional hurts and the childhood origins of the illness, prayer for inner healing, prayer of deliverance, or exorcism.

A prayer for healing is a petition addressed to God, but a prayer of deliverance or an exorcism is a command for evil demons to leave the patient. The person who exorcizes or makes prayers of deliverance must be secure, in control of his own aggression, experienced, and wise. He should work as a member of a small team and pray for the protection of everyone in the room, since the evil spirits once stirred up may redouble their attacks on the patient. As the power of the demons is bound up by the procedure, the patient may feel as if he were being choked by an invisible hand or being thrown to the ground. Next, the identity of the demon should be ascertained; the patient may discern the demon's name, or the exorcist may command the demon to identify itself. The patient himself then attempts to cast out the demon. If that effort fails, the team prays for deliverance:

In the name of Jesus Christ and of His Church, I command you, the spirit of _____, to depart without harming _____, and I send you straight to Jesus Christ to dispose of you as He will.

After the demon leaves, often after tormenting the patient, the patient reportedly feels better, free, and joyous. Follow-up care includes teaching the patient to change pathological behavior patterns, to adopt a regular schedule of prayer, to read the scriptures, to receive the sacraments, and to become part of a Christian community.

Healing by prayer may fail because of a lack of faith, a false high value on suffering by the patient, the continued presence of sin, the failure to unearth the root psychological cause of the

illness, a faulty diagnosis, the refusal to lead a healthy and balanced life or to use medical assistance, or a social environment that interferes with healing. In addition, the healer may not be the proper person for the particular task, and the time for healing may not be right.

MacNutt (1974) noted that for most people a single prayer for healing is not sufficient and that many people are improved but not completely healed by prayer. The extent of healing is proportionate to the time spent on prayer. Soaking prayers are those that are continued for months or years. They may result in the notable improvement or total healing of chronic ailments, such as mental retardation. Although miracles do occur, such as God's reportedly filling a person's teeth with gold, they are rare, and prayer healing most often works by speeding up the body's natural recuperative forces.

Resting in the spirit is a special phenomenon in which a person collapses or faints as God takes over his body. It is considered a welcome and beneficent state from which are generated the gifts of discernment, prophecy, speaking in tongues, miracles, and healing.

CONTEXTS OF FOLK BELIEFS AND RITUALS

The remarkable persistence of some folk beliefs about mental illness over thousands of years may be partly a result of their explanatory potency (Levi-Strauss, 1963; Pattison, 1977). In naturalistic, Western, scientific concepts, indeterminacy is accepted, and illness is viewed as a discrete entity that is possibly related to various systems. Folk beliefs of mental illness are often magical, integrative, and definitive. They offer explanations for the vagaries of human life and make more acceptable the capriciousness of pathology. Both the scientific and the magical world views are attempts to construct reality. The scientific view, in its attempt to be precise, is essentially a continuous quest for explanations; the magical view, in its attempt to be all-encompassing, accepts explanations that to the scientist are irrational. However, a belief in the magical origin of mental illness includes the inherent assumption that mental disease has a reversible nature. Both systems are ritualistic, and in regard to mental illness both have successes and failures. Both systems may function simultaneously within a culture and even within a person. A scientist may also be a firm believer in a supernaturalistic religion. A mentally disturbed person may seek psychiatric help and at the same time indulge in folk therapies.

The coexistence of scientific and folk medical traditions is clearly evident in the Far East (see Figure 5) and among Oriental-Americans. Although beliefs exist in China about spirit possession, ancestor vengeance, supernatural forces, and soul loss, the concept of yin-yang is central. In both scholarly and folk Chinese tradition, mental illness is thought to result from yin-yang imbalances. Those imbalances result when a person commits a moral transgression by deviating from the prescribed way, or tao, of nature and society. A study of the interplay between dual systems—Chinese and Western—in Boston's Chinatown identified four types of medical care: nonpure Western, nonpure Chinese, pure Chinese, and dualist.

Scholars have classified and proposed models of folk medical beliefs. Clements (1932) identified five major primitive disease concepts: sorcery, breach of taboo, disease-object intrusion, spirit-intrusion, and soul loss. But only soul loss and breach of taboo are efficient causes of illness; the other categories are mechanisms or instrumental causes. Despite that conceptual difficulty Ellenberger (1970) noted the relationship between some ancient beliefs and modern psychiatric practice. He suggested that the demonstration of a transference neurosis to a patient and its subsequent cure are akin to beliefs about disease-object intrusion. The psychiatrist who attempts to reconstruct the ego of a schizophrenic patient might be considered (Ellenberger, 1970):

The modern successor of those shamans who set out to follow the tracks of a lost soul, trace it into the world of spirits, and fight against the malignant spirits detaining it, and bring it back to the world of the living.

Other scholars have emphasized the relationship between folk medical beliefs and world views, cultural patterns, and

FIGURE 5. This photograph is of a psychotic woman in Laos. She was kept in stocks for several months to prevent her from running off into the forest, a well-known fatal outcome of psychosis in the area. (Courtesy of Joseph Westermeyer, M.D.)

personalistic-naturalistic systems. Psychiatrists have pointed out, however, that those abstract superstructures do not correspond with clinical reality. Patients often use multiple models to explain their illness (Kleinman, 1978). The psychiatrist must not assume that his own biomedical model can be used to understand folk models.

Sociological, psychological, historic, economic, and instrumental explanations have been offered for folk beliefs of mental illness. Belief in hexes, for example, may serve to reinforce behavioral roles. In a Guatemalan case study (Maloney, 1976) a child was struck by the evil eye, and the mother was blamed for not protecting the child adequately by keeping him away from crowds and strangers. For fear of the evil eye, women are expected to stay in or near home with their infants, thus reinforcing cultural restrictions on women's behavior. Also, the belief may be linked to economic action; a person may distribute his wealth and avoid conspicuous consumption, since prosperity attracts the evil eye.

Envy seems to be a central component of the evil-eye belief in many cultures. Other psychological interpretations of the evil-eye belief suggest that it is based on a paranoid defense mechanism, an autonomy-dependency conflict, or sibling rivalry in the context of paternal authority. Although the significance and the interpretation of the evil-eye belief may vary from culture to culture, both it and witchcraft beliefs persist in societies in which life is played as a zero-sum game (one player's advantage is at the expense of others). Cross-cultural evidence points to an increased prevalence of sorcery and witchcraft in societies that lack effective moral bonds and legitimate means of social control.

Although hexing beliefs are relatively neutral concepts to Western observers, spirit-possession beliefs are more threatening and psychologically loaded. The British psychiatrist Sargant (1974) wrote a vivid account of his experiences with spirit-possession ceremonies in American and other cultures. His explanation of spirit possession and of the power of faith healing was Pavlovian. He suggested that an intense emotional experience can abolish previous conditioned responses and create a state of hypersuggestibility, during which it is possible to redirect a person's basic drives and constitutional strengths.

The effective therapeusis that accompanies *zar* ceremonies may be the result of several factors (Kennedy, 1967): (1) The environment is emotionally charged. (2) Contact with dangerous spirits leads to intensified feelings of anxiety, fear, and guilt. (3) The patient undergoing the hypnotic trance is freed from social constraints and superego controls. (4) Emotional discharge takes place. (5) The patient never admits guilt but, rather, projects it onto spirit surrogates. (6) A safe setting is provided for the acting out and speaking out of repressed and suppressed material because the patient is blameless; it is the spirit who is acting and talking.

Spiritism can serve positive mental health purposes. The spiritist *centro* assists members in finding employment and acculturates them to the urban setting. Spiritism also allows for therapeutic status transformation. A patient's status increases if he becomes a therapist through control of his spiritual "faculties." Most of the patients in the spiritist system also receive crisis-intervention and short-term therapy, usually with a family focus. Social equilibrium may be restored by bringing the family members together in a series of symbolic, ritualistic sessions. Elements of psychodrama and abreaction are frequently used. Direct counseling is often quite perceptive. A depressed patient, for example, is forced to increase his social contacts by purchasing on his own the paraphernalia used in his curing ritual. Long-term therapy is achieved by integrating the patient into a curing society. That is such a common phenomenon in folk systems that Harwood (1977) noted:

> One must begin to question why psychiatric therapy has tended to stress independence from the therapeutic relationship as a goal rather than the cross-culturally more common practice of rehabilitating and socializing the sufferer into a long-term mutual aid group.

Spiritism reflects religious, especially Christian, beliefs. The resurrection of Christian interest in healing may be a result of several social trends. Medical advances have been so spectacular that patients may be developing an ever-increasing set of rising expectations. The increased life-span leads to a greater prevalence of chronic disorders that, by definition, cannot be cured by modern medical practice. Many turn to faith healing after receiving no results, no hope, or negative feedback from Western medicine.

Modern Christian healing is not a total return to supernaturalism; clients are usually urged to seek medical assistance. A person takes medicines, undergoes surgery, and participates in psychotherapy while he prays for the Holy Spirit to intervene. Faith healers generally acknowledge that mental illness is far more difficult to cure than are physical ailments. By continued participation in church activities, the patient is offered a lifelong aftercare program.

A study of Western faith healing was done in Seattle (Pattison et al., 1973). Forty-three fundamentalist Pentecostals with a high school education who had experienced faith healings of organic and psychosomatic conditions were studied. The subjects reported themselves healed or improved, even though symptoms persisted. Their perception of healing was related to participation in a healing ritual and not to a perception of change in their symptoms. The subjects viewed emotional distress and some organic illness in religious terms, rather than in scientific terms. In that context faith healing was sought after, since it dealt with the whole person and life style, rather than with a specific lesion. The authors concluded that, although faith healing does not reduce the patient's symptoms, it does reinforce magical belief systems, which range, on a continuum, from witchcraft to Christian Science.

How effective are folk mental health systems? The question is difficult to answer because magical and supernaturalistic systems do not lend themselves to scientific methods. It would be naive to accept the efficacy of folk systems, and it would be arrogant to dismiss them totally. In those instances in which folk approaches prove successful, it is clear that one-word explanations, such as suggestibility and brain washing, are much too simple. MacNutt (1977) estimated that 75 per cent of the emotionally or physically disturbed people for whom he prays experience either complete healing or noticeable improvement. Nolen (1974) however, failed to find any longlasting benefits to persons who were "healed" by one of America's most famous faith healers.

Psychiatric Treatment

Although universal themes may characterize the treatment of mental illness in cultures around the world, there are major differences in their intensity, quality, and depth (Wittkower and Warnes, 1974). Most of the medications prescribed by folk healers, for example, are placebos, but most medications prescribed by Western psychiatrists are pharmacologically active. And, although no one would deny the wisdom of prescribing phenothiazines instead of prayers in the treatment of most psychoses, scientific psychiatry may be enhanced by the application of cultural insights.

Because of the wide range of values, roles, and other important variables associated with ethnic backgrounds, the psychiatrist cannot treat all patients within a rigid framework. He must be aware of ethnic differences. A Chicano patient who is only 5 minutes late for a therapy session may be demonstrating a positive attitude toward therapy, rather than resistance. The age, sex, skin color, name, accent, dress, ethnic background, and degree of acculturation of both the patient and the therapist must be dealt with openly if a therapeutic alliance is to be formed. The psychiatrist should not assume that a patient who is acculturated in one sphere of life is acculturated in all spheres. A patient who has adjusted successfully to a culture's major economic system may still have beliefs about health and illness that are quite ethnocentric.

In dealing with patients with strong religious convictions, the psychiatrist should attempt to work within the patient's system, even though he does not agree with all the principles of that system. The majority of deeply religious patients find solace and support in their beliefs, even though those beliefs may inhibit the development of roles and talents prized by the larger, mainstream culture, as may be the case with some Mormon women. Attempts to undermine a patient's religious convictions often result in unsuccessful therapy. It must be recognized, however, that some modern cults, often of a quasireligious nature, engage in practices that imperil mental health. Those cults tend to attract youths with identity problems, social misfits, and mentally ill or psychologically distressed persons. Methods for treating the followers of such cults are controversial from the legal, political, and psychiatric viewpoints.

The psychiatrist who treats patients of differing ethnic backgrounds must be flexible in his approaches. The traditional indications for using behavioral or insight-oriented therapy may not prove useful for some patients. After discerning the patient's cultural background, the psychiatrist should be prepared to give advice and to be moralistic or authoritarian when necessary. The following case illustrates the point:

> A 58-year-old man living in a Midwestern city sought psychiatric help because of chronic depression. After the fifth session he broke into tears and sobbed, "I'm a no-good bastard!" He had been reared in a small Ozark town, where everyone knew that his father had not married his mother. Throughout his childhood he was constantly plagued by feelings of inferiority, and he felt that he was a horrible person. He told no one that he was a bastard, not even his wife, for fear of rejection. When he finally told his secret, the therapist offered consolation and acceptance. He called several clinic personnel into the room to share the patient's secret. As a group, they demonstrated tolerance and acceptance of the patient, who was astounded that no one laughed at him or ridiculed him. The patient learned that he was a victim of the cultural biases of the townspeople where he grew up. Relieved of his burden, he made rapid advances in therapy, much of which was spent in discussing cultural differences in values.

Special problems arise when the psychiatrist and the patient speak different languages. Patients who speak only a language different from the main language of the larger culture tend to possess more pronounced ethnic and cultural traits. A California study demonstrated that Mexican-Americans who spoke only Spanish tended to have stronger beliefs in fatalism and familism (Edgerton and Karno, 1971). They also exhibited strong attachment to formal religious values, patriarchal authoritarianism, and conservative morality regarding deviant behavior. Patients with a different primary language may be judged to possess more psychopathology when interviewed in English than when interviewed in their native tongue. Disturbances in the fluency, organization, and integration of language may be judged as indicative of a thought disorder. Slow speech and periods of silence may suggest depression (Marcos et al., 1973). Bilingualism in patients may facilitate therapy by promoting the verbalization of emotionally charged material through the protective process of linguistic detachment, or it may hinder therapy by reinforcing obsessive defenses and by blocking the expression of affect (Marcos, 1976). The bilingual patient who cannot verbally express or communicate his feelings toward the therapist in the therapist's language may manifest those displaced or blocked feelings through the acting-out process.

Sometimes patients seek help simultaneously from a psychiatrist and from a folk healer. A more common pattern is for patients to seek help on the basis of the perceived cause. A study in Connecticut discovered that Puerto Ricans generally sought psychiatric care for mental illness attributed to natural causes and spiritist care for mental illness attributed to supernatural causes (Gaviria and Wintrob, 1979).

Psychiatrists have become aware that some patients use the services of folk healers, and folk healers have come to realize that psychiatric therapy may benefit their clients. As a result, several modes of working relations are developing between the two groups (Pattison, 1977). In the cooperative mode both the psychiatrist and the folk healer maintain clearly separate boundaries and provide separate services to a mutual patient. In the syncretistic mode the psychiatrist cooperates with the folk healer by integrating him into the psychiatric mental health care system. In the collaborative mode the psychiatrist and the folk healer attempt to share each other's world view in providing services. There are many examples in the literature of the various modes of working relations (Lubchansky et al., 1970; Carstairs and Kapur, 1976; Harwood, 1977; Jilek and Jilek-Aall, 1978), as well as examples of psychiatric consultation with subcultural groups and agencies in Western countries and with groups and agencies in foreign countries (Kinzie et al., 1972; Westermeyer and Hausman, 1974; Young and Kinzie, 1974).

Conclusion

Psychiatry's lengthy flirtation with anthropology is finally ending, and a serious marriage of the two disciplines has emerged in the form of cultural psychiatry. A critical mass of psychiatrists now have formal and informal training in anthropology. Through a direct familiarity with the anthropological literature and through expertise in anthropological methods, psychiatrists are developing a sound theoretical basis for cultural psychiatry and are initiating attempts to apply cultural insights into psychiatric clinical practice. Journals such as *Social Science and Medicine; Culture, Psychiatry, and Medicine; Transcultural Psychiatric Research Review;* and the *Journal of Operational Psychiatry* regularly feature articles pertinent to cultural psychiatry.

The relationship between psychopathology and folk beliefs presents a difficult diagnostic problem. Some elements of psychopathology—such as the magical thinking of obsessive-compulsives, the dissociations of hysterical neurotics, and the reconstruction of reality by schizophrenics—may be integrative, normal elements of supernaturalistic belief systems. The folk, however, are not immune from mental illness in the forms defined by Western, scientific psychiatry. Although some psy-

chotic-like symptoms may be part of a patient's beliefs, in another situation a truly schizophrenic patient may incorporate cultural beliefs into his psychotic thinking process.

The United States is a nation of immigrants, and acculturation to a white, middle-class American norm may occur in a piecemeal fashion. Persons who seem fully acculturated may retain from their cultural heritage health beliefs that, for fear of ridicule, they may be loath to admit to health care professionals. In those situations the traditional mental status examination may prove insufficient to establish a diagnosis. One of the great challenges for cultural psychiatry is the development of a cultural status examination, akin to a mental status examination, that will allow the psychiatrist to understand better the significant cultural forces influencing a patient's condition.

Kleinman et al. (1978) expanded on the pioneering work of Fabrega (1974) in establishing an ethnomedical model that has vast implications for psychiatric practice. That model distinguishes illness—the personal, interpersonal, and cultural reactions to disease or discomfort—from disease—biological and psychophysiological malfunctioning or maladaptation in the patient. Both illness and disease are culture-specific, explanatory concepts as evidenced from cross-cultural, ethnic, social class, and historical studies. Folk healers and most patients focus on illness. Western-trained physicians focus on diagnosing and curing disease. The inattention of physicians to illness may result in patient and family dissatisfaction, noncompliance, and inadequate clinical care.

The psychiatrist should attempt to understand the patient's explanatory health model in regard to cause, onset, pathophysiology, course of illness, and treatment. Thus, it is important to ask the patient what he thinks caused his illness, why it started when it did, how the illness works within him, how severe it is, how long a course it will have, what type of treatment is expected, what results are hoped for from treatment, what major problems are being caused by the illness, and what fears he has about his illness (Kleinman et al., 1978). The psychiatrist should compare his clinical model with the patient's model. Discrepancies between the two may call for patient education, clear clinical explanations, or negotiation. A patient whose explanatory model includes the concept of hot and cold diseases, for example, may not be willing to take a hot or cold medication he deems inappropriate. Through negotiation the psychiatrist may be able to "neutralize" the medication, thus making it acceptable, or he may substitute an equally effective medication.

Clearly, the goal of the ethnomedical model and of cultural psychiatry in general is not to abandon science, to overculturalize mental illness, or to glorify folk wisdom. Folk healers have their fair share of therapeutic failures. A study of a peasant society in which there were no psychiatric facilities or psychiatrists revealed very low levels of social functioning among psychotic persons (Westermeyer, 1980). The goals of cultural psychiatry are to integrate significant cultural concepts into psychiatric formulations and to assist the psychiatrist in achieving his therapeutic potential as he deals with both mental illness and disease.

Suggested Cross References

Sociology and psychiatry is discussed in Section 5.2. Early cultural beliefs about mental illness are described in Section 1.1. Aggression is discussed in Section 4.5 and ethology in Section 4.6. Freud's theories are described in Chapter 8 and Jung's in Section 10.3. The mental status examination is described in Section 12.2 and the psychological testing of personality in Section 12.6. Unusual psychiatric disorders are discussed in Section 27.1. Hospitalization and milieu therapy are discussed in Chapter 32. Culture shock is discussed in Section 44.4. Community psychiatry is discussed in Chapter 45. Religion and psychiatry is discussed in Section 56.11. Parapsychology is discussed in Section 56.15, and nonprofessional psychotherapies, cults, and psychiatric quackery are discussed in Section 56.16.

REFERENCES

Abel, T. M., and Metraux, R. *Culture and Psychotherapy.* College and University Press, New Haven, Conn., 1974.

Alland, A. *Evolution and Human Behavior.* Anchor Press, Garden City, N. Y., 1973.

Barry, H. Cultural variations in the development of mental illness. In *Changing Perspectives in Mental Illness,* S. C. Plog and R. B. Edgerton, editors, p. 155. Holt, Rinehart and Winston, New York, 1969.

Benedict, R. *Patterns of Culture.* Houghton Mifflin, Boston, 1934.

Bourguignon, E. *Religion, Altered States of Consciousness, and Social Change.* Ohio State University Press, Columbus, 1973.

* Brislin, R. W., Lonner, W. J., and Thorndike, R. M. *Cross-cultural Research Methods.* John Wiley & Sons, New York, 1973.

Campbell, D. T. Reforms as experiments. Am. Psychol., *24:* 409, 1969.

Campbell, D. T. Social attitudes and other acquired behavioral dispositions. In *Psychology: A Study of a Science,* S. Koch, editor, p. 94. McGraw-Hill, New York, 1963.

Carstairs, G. M., and Kapur, R. L. *The Great Universe of Kota.* University of California Press, Berkeley, 1976.

Caudill, W. *The Psychiatric Hospital as a Small Society.* Harvard University Press, Cambridge, Mass., 1958.

Chapple, E. D. *Culture and Biological Man.* Holt, Rinehart and Winston, New York, 1970.

Clements, F. E. Primitive concepts of disease. U. Cal. Publ. Am. Archeol. Ethnol., *32:* 185, 1932.

Crapanzano, V. *The Hamadsha: A Study in Moroccan Ethnopsychiatry.* University of California Press, Berkeley, 1973.

Crapanzano, V., and Garrison, V., editors. *Case Studies in Spirit Possession.* John Wiley & Sons, New York, 1977.

Devereux, G. Three technical problems in the psychotherapy of Plains Indian patients. Am. J. Psychother., *5:* 411, 1951.

Devereux, G. Dream learning and individual ritual differences in Mohave shamanism. Am. Anthropol., *59:* 1036, 1957.

Devereux, G. *Reality and Dream,* ed. 2. Doubleday, New York, 1969.

Du Bois, C. *The People of Alor.* University of Minnesota Press, Minneapolis, 1944.

Dubreuil, G., and Wittkower, E. D. Primary prevention: A combined psychiatric anthropological appraisal. In *Anthropology and Mental Health,* J. Westermeyer, editor, p. 131. Mouton, The Hague, 1976.

Duijker, H., and Frijda, N. *National Character and National Stereotypes.* North-Holland Publishing Co., Amsterdam, 1960.

Dunham, H. W. *Social Realities and Community Psychiatry.* Human Sciences Press, New York, 1976.

Edgerton, R. B., and Karno, M. Mexican-American bilingualism and the perception of mental illness. Arch. Gen. Psychiatry, *24:* 286, 1971.

Ellenberger, H. *The Discovery of the Unconscious.* Basic Books, New York, 1970.

Erickson, E. *Childhood and Society.* W. W. Norton, New York, 1950.

Fabrega, H. *Disease and Social Behavior.* MIT Press, Cambridge, Mass., 1974.

Fabrega, H., and Silver, D. *Illness and Shamanistic Curing in Zinacantan Society.* Stanford University Press, Palo Alto, Calif., 1974.

Favazza, A. A critical review of studies of national character. J. Operational Psychiatry, *6* (1): 3, 1974.

Favazza, A. Oedipus interruptus: A psychiatric-anthropological interface. J. Operational Psychiatry, *5* (2): 37, 1974.

Favazza, A. A solution to the German problem. J. Operational Psychiatry *8* (2): 64, 1977.

* Favazza, A., and Oman, M. *Anthropological and Cross-cultural Themes in Mental Health.* University of Missouri Press, Columbia, 1977.

Foulks, E. *The Arctic Hysterias of the North Alaskan Eskimos.* American Anthropological Association, Washington, D. C., 1972.

Foulks, E. The Italian evil eye. J. Operational Psychiatry, *8:* 2, 1977.

* Foulks, E. F., Wintrob, R. M., Westermeyer, J., and Favazza, A. R., editors. *Current Perspectives in Cultural Psychiatry,* Spectrum, New York, 1977.

Frake, C. O. The diagnosis of disease among the Subanun of Mindinao. Am. Anthropol., *63:* 113, 1961.

Gaviria, M., and Wintrob, R. Spiritist or psychiatrist: Treatment of mental illness among Puerto Ricans in two Connecticut towns. J. Operational Psychiatry, *10* (1): ;40, 1979.

Giordano, J., and Giordano, G. P. *The Ethno-Cultural Factor in Mental Health.* American Jewish Committee, New York, 1977.

Glick, L. B., Medicine as an ethnographic category: The Gimi of the New Guinea Highlands. Ethnology, *6:* 31, 1967.

Goffman, E. *Asylums.* Doubleday Anchor, New York, 1961.

Goodenough, W. H. *Description and Comparison in Cultural Anthropology.* Aldine Publishing Co., Chicago, 1970.

Gorer, G., and Rickman, J. *The People of Great Russia.* Cresset Press, London, 1949.

Hartmann, H., Kris, E., and Loewenstein, R. M. Some psychoanalytic comments on "culture and personality." In *Psychoanalysis and Culture,* G. Wilbur and W. Muensterberger, editors, p. 15. International Universities Press, New York, 1951.

* Harwood, A. *Rx: Spiritist As Needed.* John Wiley & Sons, New York, 1977.

Honigmann, J. J. Personality in culture. In *Main Currents in Cultural Anthropology,* R. Naroll and F. Naroll, editors. Appleton-Century-Crofts, New York, 1973.

Inkeles, A., and Levinson, D. The study of modal personality and sociocultural systems. In *Handbook of Social Psychology,* G. Lindzey and E. Aronson, editors, p. 426. Addison-Wesley, Reading, Mass., 1969.

Jilek, W., and Jilek-Aall, L. The psychiatrist and his shaman colleague: Cross-cutural collaboration with traditional Amerindian therapists. J. Operational Psychiatry, *9* (2): 32, 1978.

Jonas, A. D., and Jonas, D. F. The evolutionary mechanism of neurotic behavior. Am. J. Psychiatry, *131:* 636, 1974.

Jonas, A. D., and Jonas, D. F. A biological basis for the Oedipus complex: An evolutionary and ethological approach. Am. J. Psychiatry, *132:* 602, 1975a.

Jonas, A. D., and Jonas, D. F. An evolutionary context for schizophrenia. Schizophr. Bull., *12:* 33, 1975b.

Jones, E. Mother-right and the sexual ignorance of savages. Int. J. Psychoanal., *6:* 109, 1925.

Jung, C. G. *Symbols and Transformations, Collected Works,* ed. 2, vol. 5, Bollingen Series XX, Princeton, Princeton University Press, Princeton, 1967.

Kardiner, A. *The Individual and His Society.* Columbia University Press, New York, 1939.

Kardiner, A., Linton, R., DuBois, E., and West, J. *The Psychological Frontiers of Society.* Columbia University Press, New York, 1945.

Kardiner, A., and Ovesey, L. *The Mark of Oppression.* W. W. Norton, New York, 1951.

Kardiner, A., and Preble, E. *They Studied Man.* World Publishing Co., Cleveland, 1961.

Kay, M. A. Health and illness in a Mexican-American barrio. In *Ethnic Medicine in the Southwest,* E. H. Spicer, editor. University of Arizona Press, Tucson, 1977.

Kelsey, M. T. *Healing and Christianity.* Harper & Row, New York, 1973.

Kennedy, J. G. Nubian Zar ceremonies as psychotherapy. Hum. Organization, *4:* 185, 1967.

Kennedy, J. G. Cultural psychiatry. In *Handbook of Social and Cultural Anthropology,* J. J. Honigmann, editor, p. 1128. Rand-McNally, Chicago, 1973.

* Kiev, A. *Magic, Faith, and Healing.* Free Press of Glencoe, New York, 1964.

Kiev, A. *Curanderismo: Mexican-American Folk Psychiatry.* Free Press of Glencoe, New York, 1968.

Kinzie, J. D., Shore, J. H., and Pattison, E. M. Anatomy of psychiatric consultation to rural Indians. Community Ment. Health J., *8:* 196, 1972.

Kleinman, A. What kind of model for the anthropology of medical systems? Am. Anthropol., *80:* 661, 1978.

Kleinman, A., Eisenberg, L., and Good, B. Culture, illness, and cure. Ann. Intern. Med., *88:* 251, 1978.

Kluckhohn, F. R., and Strodtbeck, F. L. *Variations in Value Orientations.* Row, Peterson, Evanston, Ill., 1961.

Kroeber, A. *Configurations of Culture Growth.* University of California Press, Berkeley, 1944.

Kroeber, A., and Kluckhohn, C. Culture. In *Papers of the Peabody Museum,* vol. 47. 1952.

* Landy, D. L., editor. *Culture, Disease, and Healing.* Macmillan, New York, 1977.

Lebra, T. S. Religious conversion and elimination of the sick role. In *Mental Health Research in Asia and the Pacific,* T. S. Lebra, editor, p. 288. University of Hawaii Press, Honolulu, 1972.

Leighton, D. C. *The Character of Danger.* Basic Books, New York, 1963.

Leighton, A. H., and Hughes, J. M. Culture as a causative of mental illness. Millbank Mem. Fund Q., *39:* 446, 1961.

Leighton, A. H., Lambo, T. A., Hughes, C. C., Leighton, D., Murphy, J., and Macklin, D. B. *Psychiatric Disorder among the Yoruba.* Cornell University Press, Ithaca, N. Y., 1963.

LeVine, R. *Culture, Behavior, and Personality.* Aldine Publishing Co., Chicago, 1973.

Levi-Strauss, C. *Structural Anthropology.* Basic Books, New York, 1963.

Levy, R. *Tahitians.* University of Chicago Press, Chicago, 1973.

Lewis, G. *Knowledge of Illness in a Sepik Society.* Athlone, London, 1975.

Lewis, O. *Five Families: Mexican Case Studies in the Culture of Poverty.* Basic Books, New York, 1959.

Lewis, O. *La Vida.* Random House, New York, 1965.

Lubchansky, I., Egri, G., and Stokes, I. Puerto-Rican spiritualists view mental illness: The faith healer as a para-professional. Am. J. Psychiatry, *127:* 312, 1970.

Macklin, J. A Connecticut Yankee in Summer Land. In *Case Studies in Spirit Possession,* V. Crapanzano and V. Garrison, editors, p. 41. John Wiley & Sons, New York, 1977.

MacNutt, F. *Healing*. Ave Maria Press, Notre Dame, Ind., 1974.

MacNutt, F. *The Power to Heal*. Ave Maria Press, Notre Dame, Ind., 1977.

Malinowski, B. *Sex and Repression in Savage Society*. Harcourt Brace, New York, 1923.

Maloney, C., editor. *The Evil Eye*. Columbia University Press, New York, 1976.

Marcos, L. Bilinguals in psychotherapy: Language as an emotional barrier. Am. J. Psychother., *30*: 552, 1976.

Marcos, L. R., Urcuyo, L., Kesselman, M., and Alpert, M. The language barrier in evaluating Spanish-American patients. Arch. Gen. Psychiatry, *29*: 655, 1973.

Marwick, M. G., editor. *Witchcraft and Sorcery in England*. Penguin Books, Harmonsworth, England, 1970.

Mazer, M. *People and Predicaments*. Harvard University Press, Cambridge, Mass., 1976.

Mead, M. *Sex and Temperament in Three Primitive Societies*. Morrow, New York, 1935.

Mead, M. Some relationships between social anthropology and psychiatry. In *Dynamic Psychiatry*, F. Alexander and H. Ross, editors, p. 411. University of Chicago Press, Chicago, 1952.

Minturn, L., and Lambert, W. *Mothers of Six Cultures*. John Wiley & Sons, New York, 1964.

Murdock, G. P. *Social Structure*. Free Press of Glencoe, New York, 1965.

Murphy, J. M. Psychotherapeutic aspects of shamanism on St. Lawrence Island, Alaska. In *Magic, Faith, and Healing*, A. Kiev, editor, p. 80. Free Press of Glencoe, New York, 1964.

Murphy, J. M., and Leighton, A. H. *Approaches to Cross-cultural Psychiatry*. Cornell University Press, Ithaca, N. Y., 1965.

Naroll, R. Holocultural theory tests. In *Main Currents in Cultural Anthropology*, R. Naroll and F. Naroll, editors, p. 309. Appleton-Century-Crofts, New York, 1973.

Nolen, W. *Healing: A Doctor in Search of a Miracle*. Random House, New York, 1974.

Osgood, C. E. Cross-cultural comparability in attitude measurement via multilingual semantic differentials. In *Current Studies in Social Psychology*, I. Steiner and M. Fishbein, editors, p. 95. Holt, Rinehart and Winston, New York, 1965.

Osgood, C. E., Suci, C. J., and Tannenbaum, I. H. *The Measurement of Meaning*. University of Illinois Press, Urbana, 1957.

Paredes, J. A., and Hepburn, M. F. The split brain and the culture-and-cognition paradox. Curr. Anthropol., *17*: 121, 1976.

Pattison, E. M. Psychosocial interpretations of exorcism. J. Operational Psychiatry, *8* (2): 5, 1977.

Pattison, E. M., Lapins, N. A., and Doerr, H. A. Faith healing. J. Nerv. Ment. Dis., *157*: 397, 1973.

Pike, K. *Language in Relation to a Unified Theory of the Structure of Human Behavior*. Mouton, The Hague, 1966.

Press, I. The urban curandero. Am. Anthropol., *73*: 742, 1971.

Racy, J. Psychiatry in the Arab east. Acta Psychiat. Scand. (Suppl.), *211*: 62, 1970.

Rank, O. *The Double*. University of North Carolina Press, Chapel Hill, 1971.

Reik, T. *Ritual: Four Psychoanalytic Studies*. International Universities Press, New York, 1946.

Reynolds, D. *Morita Psychotherapy*. University of California Press, Berkeley, 1976.

Roheim, G. *Psychoanalysis and Anthropology*. International Universities Press, New York, 1950.

Rokeach, M. *The Nature of Human Values*. Free Press of Glencoe, New York, 1973.

Rosenberg, S. Hospital culture as collective defense. Psychiatry, *33*: 21, 1970.

Sandoval, M. Santeria: Afrocuban concepts of disease and its treatment in Miami. J. Operational Psychiatry, *8* (2): 52, 1977.

Sargant, W. *The Mind Possessed*. J. B. Lippincott, Philadelphia, 1974.

Silverman, S. An ethnographic approach to social stratification. Am. Anthropol., *68*: 899, 1966.

Singer, K. Depressive disorders from a transcultural perspective. Soc. Sci. Med., *9*: 289, 1975.

Snow, L. Popular medicine in a black neighborhood. In *Ethnic Medicine in the Southwest*, E. H. Spicer, editor, p. 19. University of Arizona Press, Tucson, 1977.

Spiegel, J. P. Cultural aspects of transference and countertransference revisited. J. Am. Acad. Psychoanal., *4*: 447, 1976.

Stanton, A. H., and Schwartz, M. S. *The Mental Hospital*. Basic Books, New York, 1954.

Strodtbeck, F. L. Considerations of meta-method in cross-cultural studies. Am. Anthropol., *66*: 223, 1964.

Tinling, D. C. Voodoo, root work, and medicine. Psychosom. Med., *29*: 483, 1967.

Triandis, H. C. *The Analysis of Subjective Culture*. John Wiley & Sons, New York, 1972.

Turner, V. *The Ritual Process*. Aldine Publishing Co., Chicago, 1969.

Valentine, C. A., and Valentine, B. What the anthropologist does: Case study. In *Anthropology Today*, G. Berreman, C. A. Valentine and B. Valentine, editors, p. 84. CRM Books, Del Mar, Calif., 1971.

Waxler, N. E. Culture and mental illness: A social labeling perspective. J. Nerv. Ment. Dis., *159*: 379, 1974.

Weiss, J. M. A., and Perry, M. E. Transcultural attitudes toward antisocial behavior. In *Current Perspectives in Cultural Psychiatry*, E. F. Foulks, R. M. Wintrob, J. Westermeyer, and A. R. Favazza, editors, p. 51. Spectrum, New York, 1977a.

Weiss, J. M. A., and Perry, M. E. Transcultural attitudes toward antisocial behavior: Opinions of mental health professionals. Am. J. Psychiatry, *134*: 1036, 1977b.

West, D. J. *Eleven Lourdes Miracles*. Duckworth, London, 1957.

Westermeyer, J. Psychosis in a peasant society: Social outcomes. Am. J. Psychiatry, 1980. In Press.

Westermeyer, J., and Hausman, W. Cross-cultural consultation for mental health planning. Int. J. Soc. Psychiatry, *20*: 34, 1974.

Whiting, B. *Six Cultures: Studies of Child Rearing*. John Wiley & Sons, New York, 1963.

Whiting, J. A model for psychocultural research. In *Culture and Infancy*, P. H. Liederman, S. R. Tulkin, and A. Rosenfeld, editors, p. 29. Academic Press, New York, 1977.

Whiting, J., and Child, I. *Child Training and Personality: A Cross-cultural Study*. Yale University Press, New Haven, Conn., 1953.

Wintrob, R. The influence of others: Witchcraft and rootwork as explanations of behavior disorders. J. Nerv. Ment. Dis., *156*: 318, 1973.

Wittkower, E. D., and Warnes, H. Cultural aspects of psychotherapy. Am. J. Psychother., *28*: 566, 1974.

Young, B. B. C., and Kinzie, J. D. Psychiatric consultation to a Filipino community in Hawaii. Am. J. Psychiatry, *131*: 563, 1974.

5.2 Sociology and Psychiatry

JOHN A. CLAUSEN, Ph.D.

Introduction

A human being is at the same time an organism, a member of society, the bearer of a culture, and a person or personality. Human potentialities become manifest only in society, and the bent they take in any particular society is to be fully understood only in the context of the culture and social organization of that society. The self arises in the process of social interaction, and the formation of goals and motives in a person is likewise a product of interaction within a framework of norms and values basic to a culture. That being so, sociology—the systematic study of social organization and of group life—can hardly fail to have relevance for psychiatry.

Trends in Sociology

The range of sociological theory and research is extremely broad and its content heterogeneous. Political philosophers and others who have thought deeply about the prospects and dilemmas of humans in society have made many valid observations about the forms and processes of social life for at least two millenia, but the systematic study of society barely antedates the 20th century. Even within the short life-span of academic sociology, there have been a number of transformations in the style of inquiry and in the orientations enjoying the most prestige and influence. During the first half of the 20th century, for example, sociology went from a somewhat reformistic and humanistic tradition to one with a heavy emphasis on value-free empirical investigation, despite some dissenting voices. In the past 3 decades the dissenting voices have grown louder; young sociologists, like other students, have demanded relevance, especially relevance to social action. Sociological theory has to a great degree been functionalist—that is, inquiring into the functions served by particular organizational forms or social processes. But critics of functionalism assert that it inevitably tends toward a conservative approach to the study of social institutions. In recent decades, conflict theorists, largely drawing on Marxist formulations, have argued that conflicts of interest among groups and classes seeking to maintain or gain power are more typical of society than is the equilibrium posited by functionalists.

In modern industrial society, change, rather than stability, has been ubiquitous. With the end of colonial imperialism after World War II and the liberation of colonies, a large number of new nations have emerged through the coalescence of tribal societies and other populations. Those developing nations have afforded an unparalleled opportunity to study societies in change, and present-day sociology has itself undergone change as a consequence. Such broad trends in sociological thought provide a backdrop for a brief consideration of the sociological perspective.

Sociological Perspective

In seeking to understand the forms of human group life and the processes by which groups and organizations maintain themselves or change, the sociologist must achieve a measure of detachment from the prevailing beliefs and interpretations of everyday life. Those beliefs and interpretations are, of course, an important part of sociological data, but they must be viewed with skepticism. Just as there are often discrepancies between what individuals say and what they do, there are often wide discrepancies between official versions of organizational life and the patterns of behavior and belief that characterize the actual functioning of the organization.

One aspect of the sociological perspective, then, is to scrutinize the relationship between formal or official versions of the normative structure of social life and the ways that persons act within that structure. Another aspect is to ask how one's position within the social structure influences what one sees, experiences, and believes. In all societies but especially in large, complex societies, power and privilege are unequally distributed. Those who hold power are intent on maintaining as much of it as possible; those who are deprived are—potentially, at least—interested in gaining power. The uses of power and privilege, therefore, become focal points for sociological inquiry.

In examining the functioning of institutions and other social forms, sociologists seek to become aware of both manifest functions (those that are intended and constitute the ostensible reason for the existence of the particular social form) and latent functions (those that are unintended and of which most members of the society are not aware). Large public mental hospitals, for example, served the manifest function of caring for mental patients believed to be incapable of life in the community, but they served the latent function of isolating and hiding the mentally ill, thereby providing a form of institutionalized denial of the existence of mental illness while producing chronic patients incapable of functioning in the community.

The sociological perspective frequently results in calling into question some of the cherished beliefs of members of the society. All societies depend to some measure on myths to enhance solidarity and maintain existing social structures. Sociological theory and research may, therefore, be seen as threatening in much the same way that psychiatric theory and research are seen as threatening by persons who would prefer to remain unaware of their motivations. The potential to threaten is especially found in the realm of institutional and organization studies. It is perhaps less applicable to theory and research bearing on the relationships of the individual and

society, an area of study that offers some of sociology's most significant contributions to psychiatry.

Basic Formulations

The relationship of the individual to society and group life is the core problem of social psychology, a field shared by sociology and psychology. Sociological interest in the field has centered on such issues as the rise of the self in social interaction, the process of socialization (whereby the individual takes on the way of life of the society and becomes a competent participant in it), and the operation of processes of social control on the one hand and the genesis and stabilization of deviance on the other. The dominant perspective of sociologists working on those issues at present is that of symbolic interactionism, as derived from the formulations of the social philosopher George Herbert Mead (1934) and elaborated by such workers as Herbert Blumer (1969), Leonard S. Cottrell, Guy Swanson, Anselm Strauss, and Erving Goffman.

Symbolic interactionism rests on a few key premises. Central to it is the concept of the self, which comes into being through interaction between the small child and his caretakers. By virtue of language, gesture, and role taking in play and games, the child is able to get outside himself and to take the perspective of significant others toward himself. Once a symbol system has been mastered, the great bulk of human action is built up by noting and interpreting the actions of others in social situations. Behavior is not a release but a construction. Collective action always entails an aligning of individual actions, and, conversely, individual actions are a consequence of definitions and interpretations of social situations and the actions of others.

Symbolic interactionism focuses on the person's interpretation of his or her own behavior and the behavior of others. It tends, therefore, to give primary consideration to the rational, consciously purposive aspects of behavior. Nevertheless, it provides a framework for examining the subjective representation of interaction, a representation that can be analyzed from perspectives other than that of the actor. In much recent writing and research, that general perspective has informed the analysis of behavior in social roles.

ROLE

The concept of role has long been used to characterize coherent patternings in behavior, but its current use in the behavioral sciences focuses on behaviors expected of people because of their positions in groups or networks of social ties. The terms father, mother, son, and daughter designate not merely biological relationships but culturally defined sets of obligations, duties, and privileges between specified social positions. Similarly, the doctor-patient role relationship is defined in terms of general expectations that have been built up historically and that serve as guidelines for interaction. Each participant is expected by the other to know the guidelines and to follow them. However, role enactment tends to show considerable variation around the normative definitions of roles, largely because each enduring role relationship involves the construction of a new social reality through the give and take of interaction. Equally important, to the degree that any given social role increases in salience for the individual, his or her identity tends to be linked with that role and with the set of definitions by which it is sustained.

SOCIAL STRUCTURE, SOCIALIZATION, AND PERSONALITY

At every stage of life, a person is enmeshed in a structure of relationships and expectations that influence his or her formulations of goals and self-image. The infant is born into a matrix of social relationships and into an ongoing cultural order. They provide the child with its initial orientations and train it for expected performances (Clausen, 1968). Within that matrix the child develops characteristic ways of interpreting and responding to others. Position in society also carries an implicit social stereotype of attributed characteristics. Others define the child partly in terms of its family's reputation, social class, ethnic group, and religion.

As the child moves from the family into relationships in the larger community, he or she brings to each new situation or social role behavioral tendencies that are typical for him or her, most of which were built up in previous social roles with parents, siblings, or other salient caretakers. The child must somehow incorporate and integrate experience from one situation or setting to another, discerning what is expected by various co-participants and coping with conflicting demands. Sometimes it is possible to compartmentalize conflicting demands by varying roles across settings. At other times the child may be forced to choose between parties exerting claims on him or her—often before the child has either the knowledge of what a choice entails or the cognitive maturity to act on rational grounds.

Throughout life a person must cope with role strains and occasional role conflicts. By the adult years one has received a good deal of preparatory socialization for evaluating the claims on one and the potential costs and benefits of available choices. In childhood and adolescence, however, there are decided limits to the amount of conflict and dissonance that can be handled.

Few sociologists have focused their research on preadolescent children, except in the classroom or in research on deviant behaviors. The aims of parents for their children and the techniques and patternings of child care and child discipline have, however, received considerable attention. Of particular interest have been studies of the ways in which socialization practices differ by social class.

Social class. The concept of social class has been variously formulated in terms of economic power, social prestige, political identification, and patterns of association. In American society, class position is related to all of these factors, but it is most frequently characterized in terms of occupation and education. White-collar occupations, especially when coupled with education beyond high school, tend to place one in the middle class; blue-collar occupations tend to place one in the working class. Income differences between the classes may be minimal, but life styles, aspirations, and even, to a degree, cognition and modes of personality coping and defense tend to differ by class.

Kohn (1977) documented the ways in which social class and, especially, patterns of the father's occupation influence the values that parents hold for their children, the circumstances under which the children are punished, and the character of the parent-child relationship. In the working class parents tend to stress conformity to external standards, but in the middle class they place greater stress on self-direction and responsibility. Working-class parents seem to punish their children on the basis of the direct consequences of the children's actions, but middle-class parents seem to act more often on the basis of the child's intent. Praise and encouragement of the child also seem to be more prevalent in the middle class, especially with respect to the father-son relationship.

Other studies (Kerckhoff, 1972) have found a sharper differentiation of sex roles in the working class, less involvement of the father in child rearing, and a greater tendency toward authoritarian parental behaviors. Educational goals and cognitive skills are more emphasized in the middle class, and feelings of personal efficacy—of being in control of one's destiny, as against being subject to external controls—are more characteristic in the middle class than in the working class among both children and adults. Denial is more frequent as a working-class defense mechanism, and intellectualization and projection seem to be more common in the middle class.

Social class is just one source of contingent variations in the socialization process. Family size and authority structure, the homogeneity or heterogeneity of one's neighborhood in childhood, the consonance of values and goals presented to the child in home and school—these and many other aspects of socialization are influenced not only by class but by religion, ethnic background, community of residence, and parental personalities, to name only a few other categories.

Personality change. At each developmental stage, the socialization process entails changing goals, agents, and techniques. Although the tasks of early childhood socialization are basic to all later stages, both socialization and personality change continue throughout life. By adolescence, most persons are to a large extent selecting or, at least, modifying their own socialization opportunities, but they are also being selected or recruited for later roles. In Western societies—in which occupation is the most potent single predictor of attitudes, values, and life styles generally—educational attainment is the single most potent predictor of occupational status.

Substantial personality change is possible and, indeed, frequent beyond adolescence. The values and skills that ensure the popularity of the early-maturing, athletic, fun-loving boy in the high school years fade in significance a decade later. The less socially skilled boy or girl who struggles for acceptance by developing competence for adult life is likely to gain in self-confidence, assertiveness, and self-control over the years. Recently published reports of longitudinal research carried out over the past 40 years have documented both the ways in which early social experiences and identifications have influenced later development and the substantial amount of personality change that is associated with occupational success and changing networks of relationship in the adult years (Elder, 1974).

In societies in which occupational success and wealth are among the most salient criteria for evaluating people, it is not surprising that persons who fail to achieve occupational success have lower self-esteem, show more physiological symptoms, and, in general, exhibit many more forms of deviant behavior than do those who are highly successful in the occupational sphere.

SOCIAL CONTROL AND DEVIANCE

Behavior that contravenes the norms of the society gives rise to negative sanctions in all societies. Social control is maintained in part by the person's internalizing the norms and values of the society and in part by the institutionalization of mechanisms for punishing deviation. In complex societies, however, norms and values are themselves subject to variation among class strata and subcultural groups. Such differentiation is often associated with a good deal of mobility, both geographical and social. Some persons or groups may be marginal to the major social groupings of the society and, thereby, not incorporated into enduring social structures. Recent migrants, devalued ethnic groups, and persons alienated from the dominant way of life of the society are especially subject to stress, lacking in resources for dealing with such stress, and peculiarly vulnerable to being publicly defined or labeled as deviants.

The genesis of deviance has been of special interest to sociologists ever since Durkheim's (1951) classic demonstration that suicide rates vary inversely with degree of social integration. Merton's (1968) influential formulation noted that, in a society in which there is great emphasis on the goal of pecuniary success but in which many members do not have access to institutionalized means of attaining success, a high degree of anomie and deviance is to be expected. Further, to the degree that one subscribes both to the norms of the dominant groups in society and to patterns of behavior and association that contravene the dominant norms, a certain amount of tension and internal conflict is likely to be experienced.

Both the forms that deviance takes and the responses of others to the deviant are strongly influenced by social status and ethnic membership. For example, it seems that there are marked class and ethnic differences in the likelihood of being sent to prison for theft, of being hospitalized if one manifests psychotic behavior, and of being retained for a long period in a mental hospital, at least in those states where the law permits indefinite retention. Social class variations in the latter two respects and many others were impressively documented by Hollingshead and Redlich (1958).

Sociological concern with response to deviance has especially focused on the consequences of labeling the deviant. To be labeled delinquent, homosexual, or mentally ill is to be stigmatized. Regardless of the behaviors that led to one's being defined as deviant, to be so labeled is to be ascribed a stereotyped role. Being treated as one who is expected to make trouble may easily become a self-fulfilling prophecy.

Some sociologists have taken the position that deviance has no meaning except as a status conferred by labeling. Labeling does have important consequences, and the whole terminology of mental health and mental disorders must be considered in terms of the symbolic meanings conferred on behaviors and even on careers by actions taken toward the disordered person and labels attached to him or her as a consequence.

SOCIAL COMPETENCE

Mental health is often equated in popular thinking with personal adjustment; in the period before World War II, personal or social adjustment was a popular concept. Delinquency, divorce, and even efforts by social reformers to deal with injustice in the social order were seen by many psychiatrists and defenders of the status quo as reflections of faulty personal adjustment. Implicit in the use of the concept of adjustment is the assumption that existing social arrangements are either optimal or inevitable and that the person should accept them as such. But an examination of such phenomena as delinquency and drug abuse in urban areas and of the educational opportunities available to many minority-group children clearly reveals that those problems are group phenomena. Most juvenile delinquency in the city is learned behavior for which there is substantial social support in the preexisting peer culture. Indeed, the delinquent may be better adjusted to his or her milieu than is the nondelinquent if one takes the perspective of members of that milieu. However, the delinquent may be lacking in the kind of competence that is needed for successful functioning in conventional society.

The concept of competence stresses the societal referent:

Competence is the ability to attain and perform in social roles, both those to which one is assigned and those to which one aspires. The development of competence rests on the perception of the self as causally important and on at least moderately favorable levels of self-esteem. Its acquisition seems to be favored by early stimulation, enhancing cognitive development, the continuity of experience, and consistency in the presentation of valued goals. When gross discontinuities occur or there is a failure to provide the child with an adequate orientation and a preparation for expected roles, such as student, early difficulties with role performance are to be anticipated. Continuing research on the consequences of poverty and deprivation may be expected to illuminate both the knowledge of personality and cognitive development among the deprived and the most promising ways of dealing with persons who lack both competence and self-confidence. Such persons undoubtedly constitute part of the pool of persons with a high vulnerability to mental disorders.

Sociological Research on Mental Health and Disorders

In recent decades, many sociologists have been directly involved in the field of mental health, sometimes working in collaboration with psychiatrists and other mental health specialists and sometimes working independently and from perspectives markedly at variance with those of the psychiatric profession. Sociological contributions to mental health research fall into a number of areas, among them societal responses to mental disorder, pathways to and use of treatment facilities, sociocultural correlates of mental disorders, organization and operation of the mental hospital, needs assessment in community mental health, and research on deviance having a strong psychological component, such as suicide, drug use, and drinking patterns. In some of these areas, sociologists have teamed with psychiatrists, psychologists, and anthropologists; the discussion here makes no claims for the primacy of sociologists in any particular area but seeks, rather, to indicate how the methodological skills and theoretical perspectives of sociology have been brought to bear in mental health research and program planning and to summarize some of the major generalizations derived from such efforts.

SOCIAL RESPONSES TO MENTAL DISORDER

Although a few societies provide social roles for persons who show some forms of psychiatric disorder, the response to persons regarded as "crazy" is generally negative and derogatory at best. It seems a safe generalization to assert that in no society have a majority of those persons whom psychiatrists would classify as mentally ill been so regarded by most of their associates. Studies of public attitudes and reactions to mental disorder—whether they use hypothetical examples of mentally disturbed persons, as in the national survey developed by Star, or deal with persons who ultimately come into treatment— reveal that even profoundly deviant acts and gross thought disorder tend to be normalized or explained away. Only when other possible explanations have been exhausted do survey respondents or the families and associates of severely disturbed persons entertain the hypothesis of mental disorder (Clausen and Huffine, 1975).

A large number of studies support the proposition that whether or not a person receives treatment and the kind of treatment provided depend as much on social status and the roles occupied in social networks as on the seriousness of the symptoms. Insofar as involuntary commitment is concerned, persons represented by counsel are much more likely to escape involuntary hospitalization than are those who are not so represented. Rehospitalization of former patients tends to be related inversely to social status and occupational competence and directly to the duration and number of prior admissions and to intense emotional involvement, especially when critically tinged, in the setting to which the patient is returned (Brown et al., 1972).

Once labeled mentally ill, a person tends to be devalued or stigmatized, and labeling theorists have maintained that careers of mental disorder are thereby established (Scheff, 1966, 1975). This seems to be so as long as the person remains within the context of psychiatric settings, as attested to by a substantial body of research, of which perhaps the best known is that of Rosenhan (1973), but outside of mental hospitals it does not seem that having been labeled a mental patient is indefinitely stigmatizing. If a person performs effectively in major social roles and is able to relate intimately with significant others, feelings of stigma seem to drop away in a short time. To the extent that a person is not known intimately by others, however, to be characterized as a former mental patient or even as one who has seen a psychiatrist for personal problems still seems to be somewhat stigmatizing in the United States (Rabkin, 1974).

USE OF TREATMENT FACILITIES

Sociologists have delineated the pathways by which patients come into treatment and the many contingencies that determine who goes where (Clausen and Yarrow, 1955; Hollingshead and Redlich, 1958; Mechanic, 1969). They have repeatedly found that lower-class and minority members come into treatment through the police, the courts, and the welfare agencies, but upper middle-class persons come more often as a result of self-referrals or referrals by their families and family physicians. Only in the upper middle class is a knowledge of available mental health services widespread, and such knowledge is often accompanied by an understanding of the social and psychological processes entailed in mental disorders and their treatment.

As community mental health centers have been developed and charged with serving the needs of specified populations, sociologists have been involved in helping to plan methods of needs assessment, using survey techniques, analysis of social indicators, and studies of local social organizations and subcultural belief systems. Although still not widespread, the involvement of social scientists in mental health center program planning and assessment is increasing (Warheit et al., 1975).

SOCIOCULTURAL CORRELATES OF MENTAL DISORDER

Research on social responses to mental disorders and on pathways into treatment has documented the inappropriateness of using rates of treatment for mental disorders as an indication of the amount of mental disorders in various population groups. To the extent that segments of the population differ in their readiness to define a given symptomatic behavior as a mental or emotional problem, are differentially aware of or knowledgeable about potential treatment resources, or are not favorably oriented to using such resources, those segments are differentially represented in treatment. Awareness of the complexity of interpreting treatment data has led increasingly to efforts to assess directly the prevalence of acknowledged symptoms of anxiety (whether expressed in psychological or physi-

ological terms), of depression, and of aberrant behaviors in the general population. Such attempts confront other cultural and social realities; acknowledgement of one's psychological discomfort is itself socially patterned, as are the forms that the symptoms take. The literature on subcultural and cross-cultural efforts at assessment has been reviewed by Dohrenwend (1975), who summarized the main findings that emerged by the mid-1970's. Even with highly standardized psychiatric assessment techniques, it is clear that grossly variant results may be obtained from different ethnic groups and social status groups within the population.

Whatever the problems in assessing the incidence and the prevalence of mental disorders, the preponderance of evidence suggests that in urban America, at least, both treated mental disorders and the symptoms of psychological discomfort are more frequently found (1) in the lower class than in the upper and middle classes, (2) among persons who are not incorporated in meaningful social ties, (3) among those who do not have useful social roles, (4) among those who have suffered the traumatic loss of significant social ties, and (5) among those who experienced a great many stressful life events in the months before the assessment took place.

Social class and mental disorders. In their study of treated mental disorders in New Haven, Hollingshead and Redlich (1958) found the highest prevalence of inpatients in the lowest class, largely unskilled and semiskilled workers, and, in general, decreasing prevalence as one moves up the ladder of social status. In large part, the prevalence differences derived from the greater duration of hospitalization of lower status patients, who received the least treatment and were accorded the poorest prognoses. But even rates of initial hospitalization, which should come closer to reflecting the actual incidence of mental disorders, showed significant class differences. Entry into treatment for schizophrenia was 3 times as frequent in the lowest class as in the upper two classes. Outpatient care, on the other hand, was more frequent among persons of higher social status in New Haven in the early 1950's than among those of lower status. Since, however, the bulk of outpatient treatment at that time was available only to persons of means, that finding cannot be interpreted as an indication of the prevalence of mental disorders.

The Midtown Manhattan research of Srole and his associates (1962) was designed to assess the true prevalence of symptoms of mental disorder and of impairment, using a structured interview of a cross-section of the population. The investigators found that symptoms were much more widespread among persons of the lowest social status, of whom nearly half were rated impaired, than among the persons in the highest stratum. In the light of this study and a large number of other studies of symptoms that have followed, there can be no question that the frequency of emotional upset and other symptoms of mental distress is greater among the poor and deprived segments of the population than among those of higher socioeconomic status. It is less clear that diagnosable psychoses such as schizophrenia are as closely linked with social status, but evidence for a relationship is nevertheless strong (Kohn, 1973).

The Midtown Manhattan study also documented that upward and downward social mobility are highly related to the prevalence of symptoms. Persons who move up the ladder tend to show a lower prevalence of symptoms of emotional distress than do those who retain their initial social class placement, and persons who drop in status—that is, whose educational and occupational attainments are less than those of their parents—show a higher level of symptoms than do those who retain the class status of their parents. The meaning of social status is thus ambiguous, since it reflects both attainment and origins. Nevertheless, there are real differences in symptoms associated with childhood social class—that is, fathers' status. Attempts to explain such differences tend to focus on two sets of variables: (1) differences in childhood socialization experiences and in cognitive skills and social competence associated with childhood socialization and (2) the more stressful conditions of working-class life.

Certain differences in the socialization experiences of middle-class and working-class children have already been noted. The lower-class child encounters a much greater diversity of standards than does the middle-class child as he or she moves from the home to the school, the neighborhood, and the larger community. The lower-class child receives less coherent orientation to the nature of his or her world and, being less prepared for situations encountered, is more often likely to experience failure, rather than success. He or she is more often devalued and less often has available a competent and self-confident role model. Kohn (1973) hypothesized that

the constricted conditions of life experienced by people of lower social class position foster conceptions of social reality so limited and so rigid as to impair people's ability to deal resourcefully with the problematic and the stressful.

Social integration and mental disorders. Another line of sociological research has taken as its point of departure Durkheim's (1951) finding that rates of suicide are inversely related to the person's degree of integration into a network of enduring ties. In one of the earliest studies of the distribution of mental disorders, Faris and Dunham (1938) examined rates of first hospitalization for mental disorder from various areas of the city, with Chicago as their prime focus of research. Using data on first admissions of nearly 35,000 Chicago patients to state and private mental hospitals over a period of roughly a decade, the investigators found that rates of mental disorders were highest in areas in which the most recent migrants resided, areas with a high incidence of poverty, family disorganization, and social problems. Of particular interest was the great variation in rates of admission for schizophrenia, with the highest rates in areas that showed the greatest social disorganization. Faris and Dunham hypothesized that normal mental organization requires a reasonable stability of social ties and social supports. They suggested that isolation from normal social contacts in childhood, giving rise to vulnerable, seclusive personalities, may explain the distribution of schizophrenia in Chicago. Such isolation, they felt, was experienced most frequently in disorganized communities.

Subsequent attempts by Kohn and Clausen (1955) and by Dunham (1965) to examine the role of social isolation in schizophrenia have established that a significant proportion of schizophrenics do tend to have only tenuous relationships with peers in childhood and adolescence, but this seems to be characteristic of their premorbid personalities and not a cause of schizophrenia. Moreover, in the period before initial hospitalization, many schizophrenics move around a great deal, and unquestionably some drift into the areas in which they are hospitalized, rather than having been produced in those areas. Yet the absence of significant social ties cannot be dismissed as a contributing factor in the process of breakdown. A person who has no one to turn to for emotional support is much more likely to be devastated by life's stresses than is one who is integrated into a network of supportive social ties (Brown et al., 1976).

Social roles and mental disorders. Closely related to social integration is the meaningfulness of one's social roles for self

and others. Enforced retirement or unemployment may have devastating effects on identity, both because of the salience of occupational activities in the round of life and because of the feelings of powerlessness attendant on such a role loss. Much research on aging, such as that of Lowenthal and her associates (1967), suggests that old persons who fill roles salient in the lives of others have fewer symptoms and greater resilience than do those who do not fill such roles.

More recently, Myers et al. (1975) established that persons who display significant symptoms in the absence of recent stressful life events tend to be less socially integrated than are those who display few symptoms but report many stressful life events. Being employed and liking one's job or, for a homemaker, liking that role ranked with marriage and social class as a predictor of symptom change in the face of changing life events. The research of Brown et al. (1976) on life stress and depression among working-class women in London found that a wife and mother's being employed seemed to afford protection against depression, even though it often added to her daily pressures.

Also closely linked to general social integration is the loss of significant social ties through death or enforced separation. Bereaved spouses are subject to considerable excess mortality in the year after the loss of a mate and are subject to greatly increased psychological impairment. Individual migration may also sever ties that have helped to anchor the personality, and a large body of research attests to the greater incidence of symptoms of anxiety and depression among migrants.

Life stress and mental disorders. The stresses of modern urban life have been invoked as explanations of a high incidence of mental disorder for more than a century. The prevalence of superficial and segmental relationships among urban citizens, the regimentation of industrial workers, and the diversity and intensity of influences on the modern city dweller pose vastly different problems of adaptation than people confronted in the past. Have these changes increased the rates of mental disorders? To the extent that research has examined the effects of social change, especially urbanization and industrialization, it does not seem that the frequency of serious mental disorders has been much affected. The research of Goldhamer and Marshall (1953), using records of hospitals, jails, and almshouses to assess the amount of recognized mental illness in Massachusetts in the mid-19th century, established that, except for the aged, the rate of confinement for mental disorders was as high in 1850 as it was in 1950.

Studies of rural versus urban differences in rates of mental disorders (Dohrenwend, 1975) generally reveal only slight differences. Treated mental disorders are less frequent in rural areas with poor access to treatment facilities than in urban areas, but where facilities are comparable, functional psychoses seem to be equally prevalent in rural and urban areas. Treated anxiety, psychosomatic disorders, and personality disorders seem to be found more often in urban settings than in rural areas; on the other hand, symptoms of psychological distress, assessed through surveys, do not seem to vary appreciably by size of the community of residence.

As earlier noted, low social status has itself been invoked as a source of stress, but research findings have been surprisingly inconsistent. Langner and Michael (1963) found only slight differences between socioeconomic strata in their mean stress scores in the Midtown Manhattan study. Persons reporting no stress factors showed low levels of symptoms at all social status levels, but, if any stress factors were reported, they were differentially associated with the risk of poor mental health, which was highest in the lowest stratum.

Recent years have seen a great increase in research on the effects of specific life events as stressors (Dohrenwend and Dohrenwend, 1974). Several recent studies suggest that the greater prevalence of symptoms of psychological distress at the lower levels of status is directly related to higher levels of stressors that are negatively perceived. Thus, Myers and his collaborators at Yale (Dohrenwend and Dohrenwend, 1974) found, on the average, 4 or 5 times the level of psychological symptoms in the lower working class that they found in the upper middle class, and all of the difference in symptoms was explained by the greater number of intervening negative events, assessed at interviews 2 years apart, among members of the working class. Recent research by Brown et al. (1976) on depressive episodes among working-class women in London found a much higher incidence of depression among those who had been subject to severely stressful life events involving their husbands, children, or housing. Women who had several young children at home were especially vulnerable.

THE MENTAL HOSPITAL

In the decade after the end of World War II, a number of sociologists and other social scientists undertook studies of the organization and the functioning of mental hospitals. One of the earliest studies, by Stanton and Schwartz (1954), focused on the therapeutic implications of various aspects of formal and informal organization within a private, psychoanalytically oriented hospital. They documented such features as the role of staff tensions and disagreements as precursors of upsets in patients and the frequent tendency of staff members to interpret patients' motives, rather than to comply with simple requests.

Studies of large state hospitals revealed as a central feature the sharp dichotomy between the inmate world and its norms and the world of the attendants who made up the great bulk of the staff, who were often fearful of the patients and authoritarian in outlook. In such hospitals the attendants maintained a repressive control over the ward and even over the patients' access to physicians. In the decade after World War II, many state hospitals were just beginning to provide meaningful in-service training for their staff members.

The earlier studies of Belknap (1956), Weinberg, Bateman and Dunham (1965), and others served to inform Goffman's (1961) brilliant analysis of mental hospitals and similar institutions in *Asylums*. Goffman conceptualized social processes in mental hospitals and other total institutions in which persons live out the full round of their daily lives within the institution's confines. He examined the implications of the larger social structure and the mechanisms of social control, frequently involving the systematic stripping of the sense of selfhood and personal integrity, for the social role of the new patient and for his subsequent career. By focusing on the characteristics of the social organization as a processor of human beings—taking the patient's perspective, rather than that of the staff—Goffman irritated some psychiatrists but notably illuminated the problems of hospital operation for others.

Other sociological research on the mental hospital has dealt with the peculiarities of formal structure as a consequence of the splitting of the supervision of professional and maintenance operations, with the consequences of the limited access to advancement for attendants and aides, and with the different ideologies about mental illness and its treatment prevailing in different segments of the staff. More recent studies tend to focus more narrowly on particular screening and sorting processes, on the characterization of treatment milieus, on patient modes of adaptation to the hospital, and on the interaction of these features as determinants of hospital effectiveness. Collaborative studies between psychiatrists and sociologists have sought knowledge that could be used for planning and policy purposes, rather than primarily serving to extend the literature on organizational theory and operation. The effects of institutionalism as a product of long-term stay in an unstimulating environment and of programs designed to combat the debilitating consequences of inactivity in the mental hospital have been documented by Wing and Brown (1970), whose collaboration in several studies epitomizes the values of combining clinical psychiatric and sociological skills in the research team.

THE MENTAL PATIENT AND HIS CAREER

The stigmatization of mental illness seems inevitable in a society that puts heavy emphasis on instrumental achievement and devalues excesses of emotional expression. In such a society, immobilization through anxiety, depression, or psychotic episodes is likely to lead to ineffective performance of the occupational role and to the disruption of other role relationships. Hospitalization greatly accentuates the negative consequences of symptoms by symbolizing role failure. As already noted, a good deal of sociological research has focused on the processes by which mental disorders are processed through various relational and organizational channels and on the career contingencies that influence the patient's view of self and others, the duration of hospitalization or other treatment, and the probability of the patient's being retained in various community settings.

Even with the great increase in mental health education and the greater availability today of outpatient services in most communities, relatively few patients come into treatment with the directness that is found for most physical illness. Before the patient's initial treatment, one typically finds a high level of conflict in the family. Treatment comes only when other modes of attempting to cope—including consultations with clergymen, physicians, and lay confidants—have failed to produce a change in the patient's situation. Occasionally, of course, the mobilization of other resources does bring a remission of symptoms, but that has been a neglected area of research.

The mental disorders of old age present a particularly poignant problem. Hospitalization usually does not come until after a long period, during which the family has tried a number of alternative ways of dealing with the annoyances and disruptions caused by the older person's symptoms and confused behavior. Lowenthal (1964) delineated the pathways into treatment and the social processes involved. Changed social circumstances are perhaps more important precipitants of hospitalization than are changes in the symptoms of the disorder.

The patient career is usually not a permanent one. Follow-up studies have been undertaken by Freeman and Simmons (1963), Angrist et al. (1968), Brown et al. (1972), and others to ascertain the conditions leading to the retention of the patient in the community. Such studies have tended to examine the interaction of the patient's condition with characteristics of the home setting, the nature of role expectations held for the former patient, and the emotional involvement of other family members with the patient. In general, instrumental performance is strongly affected by continuing symptoms, and the level of manifest symptoms is more predictive of the retention of patients in the community than is the tolerance of deviance by significant others. However, several studies have found that the occupational performance of male patients after release from the hospital is more influenced by demonstrated competence before the initial breakdown than by symptomatic behaviors.

Research currently in process should add considerably to knowledge of the long-term adaptation of various segments of the population who have experienced symptoms of mental disorders or who have received psychiatric treatment. A number of the populations included in early studies of the distribution of symptoms of psychological distress and of the impact of mental illness on the family have recently been followed up a decade or two later, and early reports suggest that there is far less persistence of symptoms and impairment than had generally been expected (Simmons, 1979).

OTHER FORMS OF DEVIANCE

Much deviant behavior of interest to psychiatrists is viewed from quite a different perspective by social scientists. Suicide, alcoholism, and drug abuse, for example, have strong sociocultural correlates that may be examined either apart from or as they influence and interact with features of personality or psychopathology. A brief overview of the sociological perspective as applied to drug use may serve as an illustration.

The use of various drugs to achieve relaxation and pleasurable or transcendental states of mind has been a feature of many societies from antiquity to the present. Social norms determine the drugs used, the patterns of use, and larger societal responses to drug use (Josephson and Carroll, 1974). Social scientists have described and analyzed the group facet of drug use and the learning of subcultural patterns that support such use. Although the dynamics of personality undoubtedly influence willingness to experiment with illegal substances and susceptibility to psychological dependence on drugs, legal and illegal, sociological research on the problems of drug use and abuse suggests that those problems are no more soluble by dealing with them primarily under the rubric of medicine than by dealing with them primarily under the rubric of crime.

Of particular interest are recent studies that examine orientations to drug use and actual patterns of use in longitudinal perspective through the school years (Kandel, 1978). These studies reveal clear-cut development stages and sequences, beginning with the use of the legal drugs, tobacco and alcohol. In general, a constellation of attitudes and values conducive to various forms of deviance precedes involvement with illicit drugs. Among the most potent predictors of continuing drug use are low academic aspirations and motivation, peer attitudes and behaviors, and such evidences of personal maladjustment as rebelliousness, low self-esteem, and a low sense of psychological well-being.

Whereas psychiatric and social science perspectives on drug use tended in the decades immediately after World War II to be strongly oppositional, in the past decade or so there seems to be much more appreciation among both social scientists and psychiatrists that sociocultural and personality aspects are closely intertwined. Policies aimed at preventing the widespread use of potentially harmful substances must take into account both sociocultural orientations and personality dynamics.

Social Policy and Mental Illness

Apart from the light that sociological theory and research throws on the relationship of the individual to society, and its findings of social epidemiology, it seems that sociology has made its primary contribution to the field of mental health by analyzing how social processes influence the perception, use, and operation of services designed to provide psychiatric care or to prevent mental disorders. The effects of social stratifica-tion and of cultural heterogeneity cannot be ignored in planning services. Indeed, it has become increasingly obvious that the perceived needs of local populations, even when those perceptions directly conflict with the convictions of professional workers, cannot be ignored if services are to be accepted and used effectively. Only by close interaction in situations in which there is give and take and, in short, two-way learning can some of the policy issues be worked out. That seems to be the consensus of those social scientists and social psychiatrists who have been involved in both the development and the study of community mental health services in areas of cultural heterogeneity.

The rhetoric of the mental health movement has changed much in the 50 years since Kingsley Davis (1938) pointed out that the underlying ethic was adjustment to middle-class values—in other words, the striving after success in an individualistic, competitive society. Minorities have begun to assert their rights to hold alternative values, and much sociological research now documents that personal integrity is enhanced by the integrity of the system of beliefs and practices to which the person subscribes.

The community mental health movement was given great impetus by the demonstration that long-term stays in large mental hospitals led to incapacity and by the development of drugs that facilitated a consideration of alternatives to hospitalization. In the early blush of enthusiasm over the availability of federal support for the development of community mental health services, however, there was far too little consideration of social science knowledge and, in the view of many social scientists, a rather blithe tendency to assume that psychiatry had the answers to the population's needs. The diversity of problems that lead persons to feel despairing or anxious or unable to control their thoughts and impulses is such that many different psychological and social processes are implicated. As Mechanic (1969) pointed out, various forms of skill training may be more important than psychotherapy and drug therapy for dealing with the problems of some patients from deprived backgrounds. There seems to be a need for much more systematic study of alternative patterns in the attempt to assist different classes of patients, coupled with careful follow-up evaluation.

When one studies facilities in action, one almost always finds that both staff members and users hold beliefs about each other and about the facility that are, in fact, myths. Few professionals in the facilities know anything about the sifting and sorting processes that influence how people come to them or even those processes that determine what happens to patients when they get into the facility. Many businesses are more concerned with the assessment of their markets and of their customers' concerns than are most health facilities. Effective functioning requires such assessment.

Unfortunately, few administrators of community mental health programs are in a position to recruit adequately trained social researchers, and few social scientists are sufficiently aware of the potential theoretical significance and the practical value of large-scale systematic research on attitudinal, contextual, and organizational aspects of the provision of services to seek the level of support needed for such research. The extent to which the parts of the present system of services mesh is simply not known, although evidence of its inadequacies is abundant. What is the sequence of help seeking and help receiving in communities with or without a fully accredited community mental health center? Who gets referred where and with what consequences? Warheit and his associates (1975) spelled out some of the research approaches to evaluating mental health services, but much more ambitious, community-wide research efforts will have to be mounted if systematically obtained intelligence is to be applied to social planning and policy making.

As alternative living facilities are developed for chronically ill patients, what features maximize the level of daily functioning of their residents? A good start at identifying the relevant contextual and organizational features was made in Segal and Aviram's (1978) study of sheltered care in California.

Broader issues of social policy also need much more systematic study. When minimal data are lacking on the costs and the benefits of various policy decisions, such decisions will be made on the basis of political expediency. Not only sociologists and anthropologists but economists and political scientists will have potential contributions in that area.

Current Outlook

Some sociologists and other social scientists working in the field have shared the dominant premises of psychiatry with reference to the phenomena of mental health and mental illness, but others have questioned those premises. Most sociologists do not fully endorse the medical model of mental illness, and many have espoused the views of Scheff (1966) and Szasz (1961) that mental illness does not exist as such. Those who most vehemently question the premises of psychiatry and yet do research on mental illness are likely to aim primarily at contributing to sociological theory, rather than at contributing to the field of mental health. Yet they have frequently done both, largely because their alternative premises have a measure of validity. Dietz (1977) suggested that examinations by social scientists of psychiatry in the context of social structure and social processes have provided the impetus and the ammunition to those groups seeking to discredit psychiatry and have served to buttress class-action suits in behalf of patients' rights. Whether or not that has been the case, a perusal of psychiatric texts and psychiatric journals suggests that even the works of relatively unfriendly critics now receive far more attention than they did a decade or two ago.

More important, perhaps, is the great increase in the number of sociologists and other social scientists who are working collaboratively with psychiatrists and other professionals to learn how to deal more effectively with mental illness. It is not necessary that any particular set of premises be shared in order to carry out fruitful research; it is necessary that the participants in interdisciplinary efforts respect each other's integrity and entertain a degree of open mindedness about each other's approach. To the extent that mental disorders may result from an interaction between biological and social factors, an understanding of that interaction requires improved conceptualizations in both realms. Training programs at the postdoctoral level to prepare sociologists for mental health research—basic and applied—are in their infancy, but a new generation of sociologists who have a significant amount of sophistication with respect to psychiatric phenomena is in the making.

Psychiatrists in the United States and Great Britain have, in general, been more hospitable to sociologists who wish to study the phenomena of mental health and mental illness than have those of other countries. There is every reason to believe that the requirements of achieving a more rational public policy will bring the disciplines more closely into contact in the future.

Suggested Cross References

Anthropology and psychiatry is discussed in Section 5.1. Sociobiology is discussed in Section 2.7. Examination of the psychiatric patient is described in Chapter 12. Hospitalization and milieu therapy are discussed in Chapter 32. Conduct disorders in children and adolescents are discussed in Section 41.7. Community psychiatry is discussed in Chapter 45. Interracial relations and prejudice are discussed in Section 56.7.

REFERENCES

Angrist, S. S., Lefton, M., Dinitz, S., and Pasamanick, B. *Women after Treatment: A Study of Former Mental Patients and Their Normal Neighbors.* Appleton-Century-Crofts, New York, 1968.

Belknap, I. *Human Problems of a State Mental Hosptial.* McGraw-Hill, New York, 1956.

Blumer, H. *Symbolic Interactionism: Perspective and Method.* Prentice-Hall, Englewood Cliffs, N. J., 1969.

Brown, G. W., Bhrolchain, M. N., and Harris, T. Social class and psychiatric disturbance among women in an urban population. Sociology, *9:* 226, 1976.

Brown, G. W., Birley, J. L., and Wing, J. K. Influence of family life on the course of schizophrenic disorders: A replication. Br. J. Psychiatry, *121:* 241, 1972.

Clausen, J. A., editor. *Socialization and Society.* Little, Brown, and Co., Boston, 1968.

Clausen, J. A., and Huffine, C. L. Sociocultural and social psychological factors affecting social responses to mental disorder. J. Health Soc. Behav., *16:* 405, 1975.

Clausen, J. A., and Yarrow, M. R., editors. The impact of mental illness on the family. J. Soc. Issues, *11:* 3, 1955.

Davis, K. Mental hygiene and the class structure. Psychiatry, *1:* 55, 1938.

Dietz, P. E. Social discrediting of psychiatry: The protasis of legal disenfranchisement. Am. J. Psychiatry, *134:* 1356, 1977.

Dohrenwend, B. P. Sociocultural and social psychological factors in the genesis of mental disorders. J. Health Soc. Behav., *16:* 365, 1975.

* Dohrenwend, B. S., and Dohrenwend, B. P., eidtors. *Stressful Life Events: Their Nature and Effect.* John Wiley & Sons, New York, 1974.

Dunham, H. W. *Community and Schizophrenia: An Epidemiological Analysis.* Wayne State University Press, Detroit, 1965.

Durkheim, E. *Suicide.* Free Press of Glencoe, New York, 1951.

Elder, G. H. *Children of the Great Depression.* University of Chicago Press, Chicago, 1974.

Faris, R. E., and Dunham, H. W. *Mental Disorders in Urban Areas.* University of Chicago Press, Chicago, 1939.

Freeman, H. E., and Simmons, O. G. *The Mental Patient Comes Home.* John Wiley & Sons, New York, 1963.

* Goffman, E. *Asylums: Essays on the Social Situation of Mental Patients and Other Inmates.* Doubleday, New York, 1961.

Goldhamer, H., and Marshall, A. W. *Psychosis and Civilization: Two Studies in the Frequency of Mental Disease.* Free Press of Glencoe, New York, 1953.

Gove, W. R. Labeling and mental illness: A critique. In *The Labeling of Deviance: Evaluating a Perspective,* W. R. Gove, editor, p. 35. John Wiley & Sons, New York, 1975.

Hollingshead, A., and Redlich, R. C. *Social Class and Mental Illness.* John Wiley & Sons, New York, 1958.

Josephson, E. J., and Carroll, E. E., editors. *Drug Use: Epidemiological and Sociological Approaches.* Halsted Press, New York, 1974.

Kandel, D. B., editor. *Longitudinal Research on Drug Use.* Halsted Press, New York, 1978.

Kerckhoff, A. C. *Socialization and Social Class.* Prentice-Hall, Englewood Cliffs, N. J., 1972.

* Kohn, M. L. Social class and schizophrenia: A critical review and a reformulation. Schizophr. Bull., *7:* 60, 1973.

Kohn, M. L. *Class and Conformity: A Study in Values,* ed. 2. University of Chicago Press, Chicago, 1977.

Kohn, M. L., and Clausen, J. A. Social isolation and schizophrenia. Am. Sociol. Rev., *20:* 265, 1955.

Langner, T. S., and Michael, S. T. *Life Stress and Mental Health: The Midtown Manhattan Study.* Free Press of Glencoe, New York, 1963.

Lowenthal, M. F. *Lives in Distress: The Paths of the Elderly to the Psychiatric Ward.* Basic Books, New York, 1964.

Lowenthal, M. F., Berkman, P. L., and associates. *Aging and Mental Disorder in San Francisco: A Social Psychiatric Study.* Jossey-Bass, San Francisco, 1967.

Mead, G. H. *Mind, Self and Society.* University of Chicago Press, Chicago, 1934.

* Mechanic, D. *Mental Health and Social Policy.* Prentice-Hall, Englewood Cliffs, N. J., 1969.

Merton, R. K. *Social Theory and Social Structure,* ed. 2. Free Press of Glencoe, New York, 1968.

Myers, J. K., Lindenthal, J. J., and Pepper, M. P. Social integration and psychiatric symptomatology. J. Health Soc. Behav., *16:* 421, 1975.

Rabkin, J. Public attitudes toward mental illness: A review of the literature. Schizophr. Bull., *10:* 9, 1974.

Rosenhan, D. L. On being sane in insane places. Science, *179:* 250, 1973.

Scheff, T. J. *Being Mentally Ill: A Sociological Theory.* Aldine Publishing Co., Chicago, 1966.

Scheff, T. J. *Labeling Madness.* Prentice-Hall, Englewood Cliffs, N. J., 1975.

Segal, S. P., and Aviram, U. *The Mentally Ill in Community-based Sheltered Care.* John Wiley & Sons, New York, 1978.

* Simmons, R., editor. *Research on Community and Mental Health.* JAI Press, Greenwich, Conn., 1979.

* Srole, L., Langner, T. S., Michael, S. T., Opler, M. K., and Rennie, T. A. C. *Mental Health in the Metropolis: The Midtown Manhattan Study.* McGraw-Hill, New York, 1962.

Stanton, A. H., and Schwartz, M. S. *The Mental Hospital.* Basic Books, New York, 1954.

Szasz, T. S. *The Myth of Mental Illness.* Hoeber Medical Division, Harper & Row, New York, 1961.

Warheit, G. J., Bell, R. A., and Schwab, J. J. *Planning for Change: Needs Assessment Approaches.* Department of Psychiatry, University of Florida Press, Gainesville, 1975.

Wing, J. K., and Brown, G. W. *Institutionalism and Schizophrenia.* Cambridge University Press, London, 1970.

5.3 The Family and Psychiatry

STEPHEN FLECK, M.D.

Introduction

The family is the universal primary social unit and, therefore, must occupy a central position in any consideration of social psychiatry. As contemporary psychiatry and medicine encompass the study and understanding of the cell and its elements, of cellular organization and integration into organs and organ systems, and of their orchestration into a biopsychological whole that is the organism, so is that organism's behavior in and interaction with its environment important for the understanding of health and disease. Knowledge of the social elements and parameters of this environment is as essential to diagnosis and treatment as is reliance on laboratory data on body chemistry and the nature of food, water, and air supply.

The first social context for every human being is the biological family or its substitute. If a substitute, it consists ideally of adoptive parents who take over at the earliest possible time. Usually, however, one family provides offspring with both biological and cultural heritages and ensures the survival and the humanization of the infant.

The family is, therefore, an important sociocultural institution—the keystone of society. Every human group has devised traditional prescriptions and proscriptions to make sure that the family accomplishes not only the biological and developmental missions but also tends to enculturating tasks in the service of the society. In this way, the family is the link between generations that ensures the stability of the culture and is also a crucial element in culture change. The biological necessities of the infant are met in most societies, but not everywhere, by the nuclear family, especially the mother; the enculturating functions may be assigned to members of the extended family or even to unrelated persons in the community. In Western society both of these tasks have rested with the primary family, although not always with the nuclear family, as is usual today.

Scientific study and knowledge of the family, especially in the context of psychiatry, have a rather recent history, but preoccupation with the family as a sociocultural institution is as ancient as human history. Three of the Ten Commandments specifically concern family relations, and every religious doctrine contains many specific rules and taboos about family structure and family duties.

Equally ancient are concerns about family dysfunctions. Athenians deplored the alleged decline of family tradition and cohesion as endangering the state and society; the demise of the Roman Empire has been attributed, among other causes, to the family's failure to inculcate the earlier moral standards and discipline. Throughout history major social upheavals have been examined in the light of changes in family life. Today this age-old thesis finds expression in more scientific endeavors, such as the current interest in cross-cultural comparisons, which seek precise correlation between national characteristics and family practices, and in the studies of socioeconomic class variables and familial role structure and behavior. Also today, as probably always, one hears not only the age-old complaints or regrets about the dissolution of family traditions and predictions of its demise but also admonitions to sustain and nurture the family institution (Zimmerman, 1947).

As always, the family is changing, as are societies. The causal relationships between family characteristics and social change or human history are circular and complex, rather than linear. Because of the family's central importance in human development and in sociocultural continuity, not only historians and social anthropologists but also legal scholars, economists, philosophers, and sociologists have studied and written about the family. However, some of the most perspicacious insights derive from literature—for instance, *Oedipus Rex, Hamlet,* Strindberg's *The Father,* and O'Neill's *Long Day's Journey into Night.*

Psychiatric Studies

Although the medical profession has prided itself on its family physician, now elevated to the status of specialist, this designation is based on the physician's role with all members of the family and not until recently on any formal knowledge of group dynamics and their familial characteristics. Historically, such endeavors in Western medicine can be measured in decades. Freud, although aware that his discoveries pertained primarily to family processes, chose to study and treat family pathology only in individuals. He concentrated on the investigation and conceptualization of the psychic apparatus of his patients isolated from their usual environment in the stark setting of the analyst's office. He thereby limited the social parameters to the analyst-patient dyad, a situation in which a person can relive family experiences through the phenomenon of transference.

Not until 25 years after Freud's first accounts of family-related unconscious processes—such as his reinterpretations of Oedipus and Electra, of the family romance and incest—did the first psychoanalytic effort to conceptualize family processes appear in print (Flugel, 1921). At about the same time, investigation and clinical consideration of individual family members began in the American child guidance clinics. But, in clinical medicine and psychiatry, family histories have continued to focus mostly on familial incidence of disease and on hereditary patterns, not on family structure and dynamics. In psychiatry some investigation of sociocultural constellations in families of schizophrenic patients began in the 1930's (Midelfort, 1957) but systematic clinical study and research of the family as a group did not begin until the 1940's. Despite the existence during this century of an extensive sociological literature on family life, despite scholarly studies of family law, and despite anthropologists' preoccupations with non-Western family systems, medicine and psychiatry continued to focus on the individual patient and the doctor-patient relationship. Exploring, let alone treating, families as a group has been and still is considered nontraditional.

Only in the past 30 years has there been rapidly increasing clinical scientific interest in and appreciation of the family as the most significant social force in human development, specifically in personality development, and hence as a potential agent in personality disorders. The family, therefore, is not only the keystone of society but also a key to understanding the humanness of the human being and to failures—whether labeled psychopathology, social deviance, or alienation—to attain workable humanness. In line with scientific developments in other specialties, the study of the abnormal—that is, disturbed—families, forced consideration and study of the normal. The Lidzs's (1949) discovery of the frequency of abnormal family backgrounds of schizophrenic patients, Ackerman's (1958) findings that the families of disturbed children needed study and treatment as a group, Bruch and Touraine's (1940) observations of the mother's role in the obesity of children and the related unusual family frame, and other clinical data could not be ordered without some concept of normal or culture-typical family life. Sociologists such as Parsons (1954), Merton (1949), and Rainwater (1965) helped to elucidate some of the institutional characteristics of the family, as well as the differences of family behavior in different socioeconomic classes, whereas anthropologists contributed information about family structure in very different cultures—all of which pointed to certain core tasks and functions the family must perform or provide to ensure the health of its members. These key functions can usefully be considered in general systems terms.

A General Systems Viewpoint

The family constitutes or ought to constitute an open system with many subsystems; among these subsystems are the marriage as such, the marriage as a parental coalition, the triads of parents and each child, sibling coalitions, and possibly subsystems involving grandparents or other significant relatives or friends. The author has found it useful and clinically valid to consider the family as a system along five parameters derived from Rice's (1964) studies of the Enterprise, also a general systems approach. The five parameters are: (1) leadership or governance, (2) boundaries and their management, (3) affective forces in the system, (4) communication, and (5) system tasks and goals. The relevance of these five parameters will become obvious in the following discussion, although this consideration of the family and psychiatry is not limited to a systems viewpoint and these five parameters.

Some subsystems, especially the marriage, need to be considered in more detail than others, and family tasks and goals are of central concern within and without a general systems frame of reference. It may be noted, however, that the general systems viewpoint is the most useful for clinicians and when one needs to compare and comprehend different but interconnected systems, such as personality and family or the family and other human groups. Within the boundaries that differentiate the family system from its environment, each family must effect its own structure and organization. The boundary enables each family to become a distinct unit, sharing affection and tending to the nurturance, rearing, education, and enculturation of the children. Private and shared rituals serve to connect the family with the larger culture and to related lineal and collateral families. Such interactions require boundary management and regulation, in addition to governing internal familial subsystem relationships.

In earlier times the family was the primary unit for subsistence, and all family functions subserved the goal of survival. In industrial societies the family's economic role has become less critical, and the issues of the interpersonal and subsystem relationships—together with the everyday familial tasks of nurturance, education, work, and recreation—constitute the main mission of each family. Economic necessity has been superseded by affective bonds as the major cohesive force among family members.

Unlike other systems or groups, family goals and tasks are predetermined largely by biological givens and by the culture and society in which the family exists. Although family task and system goals cannot be as clearly defined as was possible when subsistence constituted an overriding task, the less tangible mission of guiding the younger generation into adulthood remains as vital as ever. Moreover, in modern developed societies the younger generation not only must be educated far beyond earlier levels in order to participate in societal processes but must also enter into a much more rapidly changing adult world and, therefore, cannot be guided into rigidly charted adult roles and functions. These system goals now change within the time span of a generation, as, for instance, role paradigms in the current realignment of gender relationships in Western countries. Already in this century the family as an institution has had to undergo a radical transformation by abrogating the major system paradigm of its own survival and continuance, at least as a tangible group. The nuclear family in industrialized nations usually begins as an isolated dyad in terms of living space, economics, and kinship supports and, after fulfilling its mission of guiding the younger generation into similarly isolated adult roles, again becomes a dyad.

These evolutionary changes also demand different boundary management by the family in contrast to that in its agricultural or nomadic past. The boundary must be not only expansible and contractible without undue trauma to the members but also more permeable. For instance, if women are to maintain extrafamilial roles and functions throughout most of their married state, small children must experience and master extrafamilial life in day care centers or nurseries. In intangible spheres there must be a parallel readiness and capacity for family members to separate and reunite. Until quite recently in the United States, only the breadwinner crossed the family boundary daily in this fashion, so that there was more opportunity for preschool children to establish relatively firm ego boundaries before having to negotiate the family boundary regularly with school entry. Interpersonal and intergroup boundary dynamics are a key element in social organization, of which the family is the basic unit. Investigation and elucidation of boundary functions and control, therefore, should lead to fruitful insights into intrapersonal and interpersonal functioning and malfunctioning and concomitantly to therapeutic and preventive applications.

Thus, there have emerged concepts of structural and functional essentials that, despite varying sociocultural factors, must be fulfilled to accomplish the family's institutional mission. These family tasks include the nurturance of the young, their enculturation into family life and the larger society, the teaching of the cultural tools of survival and communication, and preparing the young in general to assume adult gender-appropriate membership in their community.

For clarity of discussion, family structure and family functions are considered separately here, but it must be kept in mind that such a separation is as artificial in understanding an institution as it would be to treat cellular competence as if structure and function were not interdependent. As noted, effecting certain structural paradigms are basic parental and familial tasks.

Marriage

Because marriage, whether legally sanctioned or not, is usually basic to family formation and because marital functions are also to some extent independent of family issues—obviously so while there are no progeny—marriage is discussed first, to be followed by presentations of family structure, dynamics, and functions. Marriage and family leadership must be evaluated in each instance along a range of sociocultural and idiosyncratic contingencies.

PURPOSES OF MARRIAGE

A universal biopsychosocial need for completion and fulfillment of oneself through intimate life with another exists among humans and some other species, and two people may undertake marriage solely for their mutual satisfaction without intent or capacity to establish a family. In Western society today this definition of mutual satisfaction could be exclusively that of the two partners, although their definitions would necessarily reflect the cultural and psychological norms or deficiencies they have absorbed into their personalities during their respective developments. Western society does not actively interfere with a decision or plans not to produce offspring, the needs or demands of the spouses' parents or collateral relatives to the contrary notwithstanding. Other cultures may dictate in these matters. In extended family systems, parents may achieve neither full independence in these respects nor full authority over their own offspring, and in some societies failure to produce offspring can lead to dissolution of the marriage by either partner or by outsiders. On the other hand, marriage may also be undertaken solely for the purpose of procreation, and in some religions it is indeed so prescribed, even if not always practiced.

From the clinical vantage point, most marriages fall somewhere between these extremes of intent and purpose, one nonfamilial and the other 100 per cent family oriented. It is most important for the clinician to appreciate the implicit or subconscious intents and wishes that lead a couple to marriage. For instance, one spouse may agree to marriage determined not to have children, and the other spouse may accede to this condition quite prepared not to honor the agreement after marriage—or the other way around. Such behavior need not be a conscious or designed betrayal; both spouses may intend to honor their agreements but later find they cannot resist their own subconscious opposite desires, needs, or fears. For example, Catholics may have increasing guilt feelings over birth control, or one or more parents who aspire to the status of grandparents may exert pressure on the couple. In the United States in particular, subtle pressures operate to establish a family; childless couples are often pitied.

Depending on the partners' culture, they unite in marriage because they want to; because it has been arranged for them by their parental families, usually for economic reasons; or because of a combination of such mandates. In the West, partners choose each other by and large on the basis of their feelings and hopes, be they realistic or not. Among the less conscious motivations and unrealistic factors that lead to marriage are many neurotic tendencies or needs. Most common among these is probably the use of marriage to achieve the independence from the family of procreation that the young person cannot accomplish as an individual. This brings to the marriage dependency needs that are likely to result in expecting parental care from the spouse. Another factor is social pressure, especially on girls, from families or peers that marriage at a certain age is an essential earmark of success (see Figure 1).

Not all unconscious or external determinants need be unsound; the choice of a marital partner is a complex process, and a certain intuitive sense of personality fit between two people seems to operate effectively at times, even if neither spouse can account for it explicitly. There are many paths to marriage, sound and unsound foundations for family life, but spouses can build sound relationships even if they have united for ill-considered reasons or if the marriage was arranged for them. One of the chief criteria for a successful marriage is that it furthers individual growth and growth as a unit, especially as a parental team uniting for family leadership.

MARRIAGE IN INDUSTRIALIZED SOCIETIES

The personalities and the sociocultural values that two persons bring to marriage determine the nature of their relation-

FIGURE 1. A beginning. (From Steichen, E., *The Family of Man*, p. 17. Museum of Modern Art, New York, 1955.)

ship more than do their hopes, dreams, and intentions during courtship. This is particularly so now in industrialized societies, where marriage has shifted during this century from being an economic advantage and even a necessity (including having offspring) to being an economic responsibility, if not a liability. The basis for marriage and for marital continuity has changed from tangible issues to the intangible necessities and requisites of companionship, encompassing physical, intellectual, affectional, and social facets. Conventions and traditions no longer serve as behavioral and relational guideposts, as they did, for instance, in Victorian times. Although the partners can share economic burdens, they rarely can do so side by side, as they would have in working on complementary tasks on the farm. Maintaining a house and household can be reduced to a minimum of labors, leaving as the major shared goal family life itself, together with the care of the offspring. Work roles for women are important, therefore, especially if the family is to remain small in size.

Sharing family responsibilities, however, has been made more difficult by the absence of the husband during working hours; if he is ambitious, working hours may approach the entire waking hours of the family on many days. Hence, when there is concern in present-day America about the husband's declining role in the family, these sociocultural givens of an industrial society are probably more responsible and pertinent than are speculative clichés about the decline of masculinity or the ascendancy of masculine strivings on the part of women. It must be appreciated that a boy in this age, after a school day with women teachers, does not return to a home where a father works. Such a youngster may hardly ever see his father at work, the nature of which may be very difficult for a young child to comprehend. The burden of making an absentee husband a live and appropriate image for children often falls on the wife and depends, therefore, on the spouses' views of each other.

The interest in communes may, in part, represent an effort to reestablish synthetically an extended family system. The commune provides for wider familial task sharing and also for adult models in the family besides the child's parents. Although some regard communes as evidence of the demise of the family, they are yet another form of family constellation, neither new nor unknown in other parts of the world—for example, in Israel.

Another quasimarital phenomenon has increased in the past decade—couples living together indefinitely without being formally married. It is impossible to state how many of the estimated 750,000 couples living together intend to marry, let alone remain together permanently, or what they plan to do in case of pregnancy. Nor is it clear how many couples live in this manner for the sake of current tax advantages.

MARITAL COALITION

Marital coalition may be defined as those interactional patterns that the spouses evolve to provide at first for their mutual satisfaction. Later in the structure and dynamics of the family, this coalition must serve the age-appropriate needs of the children and still maintain an area of exclusive relationship and mutuality between the parents. One of these parental sectors is sexual activity, interdicted to children in this society. Mutuality denotes the spouses' interactive patterns on implicit and explicit levels, the sharing of feelings, and the conveying of respect and appreciation of the spouses to each other, as well as to outsiders about each other.

Marital roles. An important function of this coalition in family life is the mutual reinforcement of the spouses' complementary sex-linked roles. As parents, they represent culture-determined masculinity and femininity not only as individuals but through the other spouse's support and approval. Another facet of the coalition is the conjugal role divisions and reciprocities the spouses establish for themselves. These role allocations and the decision-making methods vary with each socioeconomic class. According to Bott (1957) and to Rainwater (1965), upper-class spouses believe that their role divisions are equal and complementary but that husbands make more decisions. Lower-class spouses, except for the lowest group, also state that their role allocations are joint and complementary but that wives make more decisions than husbands.

Currently, however, sex-linked roles and role paradigms are changing very rapidly in response to two significant sociodynamic forces. One of these is the women's liberation movement, and the other is the tendency toward small families. These factors reinforce each other because familial tasks tend to be shared more equitably, freeing women with few children for extrafamilial work and professional pursuits. Moreover, small families will eventuate as a prototype only if women have such opportunities for work and careers other than being housewives and mothers.

Effects of isolation. Industrialization, urbanization, and social and geographic mobility have isolated the nuclear family, adding to the critical importance of the marital coalition in the life of the family. Newlyweds may well seek isolation initially, but in the process of adjusting to married life, friends and relatives can be useful. Nowadays marriage is often followed by a move to new surroundings, strange for both partners. Whereas living apart from one's family of origin is considered desirable, letters are not the ideal forum in which one inquires about a recipe for tonight's supper or in which one reports and gains perspective about the first marital quarrel. These items may seem trivial, but professional experience with marital problems indicates otherwise; minor problems and disharmonies can accumulate and fester. Physicians can help as marriage counselors, but young people have few occasions to seek out health resources unless pregnancy occurs. Prenatal care, therefore, offers an important opportunity for remedial marital counseling and for the prevention of future marital and family disorders.

Because the marital partners usually become the sole or, at least, the major sources of identification for their young, the spouses' personalities and the marital coalition are much more critical today for the personality development of the children than in the past. In extended family systems a child has many adults of his or her sex to use for identification, and this is still true to some extent in subcultures in which grandparents and the parents' collaterals live nearby, albeit in separate households. Living isolated from close relatives deprives the spouses of the advantage of sharing parental functions with an extended family group and leaves children with little opportunity other than to view parents and their relationship as exemplary. Most offspring have no other adults as models in a continuing way at home to compensate for model deficits in one or the other parent. If fear and conflict dominate the parent-child relationship, these handicaps may govern the child's interaction with other adults.

Spouses must depend on each other in crises without ready availability of relatives to assume the tangible household or income-producing duties of a disabled partner. In this sense the demands for individual adjustment and maturity and for effective role complementarity are more stringent than in earlier times. Problems in the isolated nuclear family, therefore, are more encapsulated: Marital difficulties affect children adversely, and a difficult or ill child strains the marital coalition.

In a modern society spouses depend still more critically on their inner resources because, compared with other cultures, there are relatively few social rules or rituals concerning marriage. In the West, society and religion concern themselves primarily with the beginning of marriage and with death and divorce. Aside from the registration of the newborn, society intervenes with a family only if gross undercare or mistreatment of the young is made evident. Otherwise, marital partners are on their own to mesh their personalities into the kind of bond and coalition they desire and are capable of, but their capabilities may fall short of their desires. If this happens, they may seek help through counseling, which is available to only a very limited extent; they may live in conflict and disharmony; or they may seek divorce.

MARITAL PROBLEMS AND COUNSELING

Marriage in the United States now depends primarily on the personalities the spouses bring to it. Their personalities are shaped largely by their parents and by the marital modes to which they have been exposed, modes that often do not serve or suit a younger generation of newlyweds. From these circumstances, plus the greatly prolonged duration of the average marriage, derive some specific burdens on marriage in current industrial societies.

Whether the prevalence of marital maladjustment is absolutely greater or only proportionally so compared with other periods is uncertain. Because the marriage now depends greatly on the partners' personalities, the high prevalence of individual emotional maladjustment must be taken into account. If every tenth person spends some time in a mental hospital and if the prevalence of symptomatic personal maladjustment is still higher, marital adjustment, which depends greatly on personality factors, likely carries a commensurate incidence of instability. Of course, marriage can also lend support and stability to an unstable partner, but the doubling of the marriage lifespan also requires that the marital relationship be adaptable to more stages and meet the challenge of longer lives.

Because marital and familial maladjustment tends to be so encapsulated, the parents in need of help must seek it actively outside the family. In extended family systems, remedial influences may have arisen spontaneously from within the group through the efforts or the mere presence of one or more of the other adults. In this way the marital problem as such may have been contained and never have become quasipublic and statistical.

From the clinical standpoint a marriage should be evaluated as a singular undertaking of two people. It should be examined in the context of their respective personalities and the motivations for marriage and family and in the context of the family they have already created. Their sociocultural milieu must be taken into account and their coalition evaluated according to the class-specific modes of marital interaction.

Although a marriage between two disturbed partners can be satisfactory to them, it does not ensure a good prognosis for a healthy family. Furthermore, a marital coalition adequate for the nurturance of a few children may deteriorate if the family enlarges every year. Family planning through contraceptive control to avoid offspring, to plan and space them, or to limit family size is, therefore, an essential element of marital counseling and health care and of preventive psychiatry.

Extramarital sexual activity. Two topics relevant to marital problems deserve further discussion: one, sexual patterns within and without marriage, and two, divorce. Premarital and extramarital sexual intercourse is difficult to assess statistically and cannot be discussed meaningfully as a single phenomenon. In particular, these practices must not be confused with normality or morality, as societies that permit complete freedom of sexual activity after puberty are no less stable or less successful in living up to their cultural norms and preserving their continuity than is American society. The same is true of societies that condone extramarital sexual activity implicitly or explicitly.

The changes in premarital sexual activities in American society may be less marked in practice than are the attitudes toward such practice. In recent decades young people have gained freedom to know and talk about sexual matters; they also expect tolerance with regard to their activities. This has led to the present-day demand of adolescents for their elders to take an open and nondefensive stand about rules and guidelines for sexual behavior outside marriage. There are serious advocates of complete license in this respect, and there are equally serious advocates of Victorian rules of behavior and thought.

Physicians, however, should not take positions of generalities. When called on to advise or educate on matters of sex and marriage, they should inform about sexual matters and reproductive control, but it is incumbent on them to consider to whom they may be speaking and why. The patient's health needs, his or her life situation, and the capacity of the individual or couple for mature relationships, be the goal marriage or not, should concern physicians, who must be especially aware in this part of their work that the patient is apt to attribute to them a parental role. They must use such transference elements for the welfare of patients in these emotionally charged instances just as skillfully as in any other facet of doctor-patient interactions.

There is no clinical evidence that premarital sexual relationships either promote or detract from successful marital adjustment. However, one reason for early marriage seems to be the desire for legitimate sexual union, even though emotional and socioeconomic independence may not have been achieved by the couple. Early marriage can create special problems if the couple become parents while still dependent on others; also, they may not be as mature and certain in their identities as they may be a few years later, when they may seek different partners. In general, the younger marital partners are at the start, the less good is the prognosis for marital success and familial stability.

Sexual adjustment in marriage is a favorite topic and a new field for therapy. Like other aspects of marriage, it is not static or a single given or symptom but varies with the evolution of a marriage. In particular, the physician should know that sexual competence is not automatic and that two partners have to find their way. One of the important elements in satisfactory sexual relationships is that partners must learn how to communicate with each other about their sexual experiences, which is also an important preparation for the sex education of children. When sexual dissatisfaction becomes a complaint, it is rarely an isolated problem in the marriage, but, if so, it is readily remediable by appropriate discussion with both spouses and even by specific instruction (Masters and Johnson, 1966).

Divorce. The divorce rate is popularly considered as a kind of barometer of familial and societal stability, but divorce, too, must be understood in appropriate contexts. Marriages are dissolved, families persist. Divorce as a social phenomenon is susceptible to customs, to legalistic vogues and changes in the law, and to religious codes. It is fashionable to point out that the divorce rate in this country has risen 7-fold, from 0.7 in 1900 to 5.0 per 1,000 population in 1976, and that some 8 million divorced people have not remarried, although most do remarry eventually. These figures must be considered in the light of the changed bases for marriage, the modern risks to marital stability, and the freer attitudes toward the dissolution of marriages so beset by problems and suffering that present-day counseling or therapeutic agencies find them beyond salvage.

In particular, the marriage counselor must examine critically a common rationalization to avoid divorce for the sake of the children. Children's needs and how they are served by a particular marital pair must be carefully assessed without assuming a priori that two parents under the same roof are better than one, although neither the causes nor the consequences of divorce are of any benefit to children. In the past a very disturbed marriage may have been continued because there was no real avenue open or even known to the partners on how to dissolve it except through desertion, and economics often dictated the continuance of the marriage. Even today, severe economic liabilities are usually imposed on the divorcing parties by circumstances or the court or both.

An earlier peak divorce rate in the United States of 4.5 per 1,000 population occurred in 1945, when many hastily undertaken war marriages were dissolved, often by spouses whose life together could be counted in days or months. But, from the over-all statistical standpoint, the divorce-risk time has doubled, because with an increased life expectancy in this century from 47 to 70 years, the duration of marriages (more than 90 per cent of which take place before the age of 30) has risen by two to three decades. The real divorce rate for the population may have only tripled if the rate is corrected for risk, which has doubled in terms of duration, and if one considers the proportion of the population ever married, which has increased 20 per cent. The lowering of the average marriage age requires a further correction, so that the corrected rate increase may be only one-third of the gross 7-fold rate increment since 1900. Considering again that 10 per cent of the population will require temporary psychiatric hospital care and that many but not all divorces involve one or two emotionally unstable partners, the present divorce rate is not even commensurate with the estimated prevalence of emotionally disturbed persons. On the other hand, 95 per cent of all people over 15 years of age get married at least once, and one may wonder whether that high a percentage of men and women really find marriage, let alone parenthood, well suited to their interests in life and to those of their spouses and offspring.

Family Structure and Dynamics

In this section the term "family" refers to the Western nuclear family, the isolated family of industrial society, unless otherwise specified.

From the sociodynamic standpoint the family is a small group to which most small-group dynamics apply, but it is also a special group. The special group features pertain to the family's biosocial evolution in a particular culture and to its axial divisions into two generations and two sexes. These axes are important psychological and behavioral boundaries. The younger generation follows and learns from the parents as gender-typical models. The parents form the generation that leads, and they are implicitly obligated to relate sexually to each other. Sexual relations within the family are interdicted to all other members by the archetype of all taboos, the taboo against incest.

As a group, the family moves from the parental dyad to a triad or larger group and later contracts again. Because the family is divided into two generations, each child's relationship to the parents is to some degree exclusive and unique and can be represented by an inverted triangle. The family consists of a series of overlapping triangles, each child forming a unique subsystem with the parents, and these triangular relationships are not identical. It cannot be overemphasized that no two children live in the same family in a dynamic sense, sometimes tangibly so because of changing family fortunes (see Figure 2). Even identical twins are ascribed different roles and characteristics by parents, by siblings, and eventually by themselves, so that each has different relationships with parents and with the parental unit.

One important task of the family under the aegis of the marital coalition consists of mastering the family's evolutionary transitions or crises. Besides the arrival of children, such critical phases include each child's oedipal transition, school beginnings, puberty, adolescence, and eventual emancipation as children leave their families of origin physically and emotionally. Adversities such as illnesses and economic and political misfortunes may produce other crises and even temporary or permanent separations.

The evolutionary crises can also be viewed as a succession of separations that all family members must learn to master. These separations can be tangible or intangible; that is, they may be on only an emotional plane, as when a child in early adolescence withdraws from closeness to parents. The evolutionary expansion of the family also involves issues of emotional separation and lessened dependency gratifications for the older children in the family. Effective family life, therefore, requires the capacity to forego individual gratifications for the sake of the group, whose cohesion depends on the example being set by the parents' foregoing some degree of their individuality and some of their gratifications for the sake of leadership and family-wide needs. Each evolutionary step or crisis results in a new equilibrium and realignment of the family's emotional forces, and sometimes this realignment leads to role changes and different task distribution.

PARENTAL ROLE DIVISIONS

Compared with the Victorian prototype of the autocratic patriarch, the role of the father in present-day America has changed, but more in appearance than in substance. Typically,

FIGURE 2. Becoming a triad.

the father's role is still that of the leader; his activities, his productivity, and his education usually determine the position of the family in the community and larger society, and these same factors also influence the character of the marital coalition. He provides the instrumental model of how things are done in society in matters of acquisition and survival. It is true that he can be pushed by his spouse's ambitions and even be overshadowed by her accomplishments in all these respects, but such a family may be disadvantaged. The fact that the father's activities today occur mostly away from home, unshared and unobserved by the family, is also a disadvantage.

The mother's primary role usually concerns the affective life of the family, and she also tends to its biological needs in health and sickness. Her role is expressive in that she not only tends to affective needs but identifies them and helps the children to learn about and understand feelings and, therefore, is more responsible for their self-expressive communication and self-awareness. This is distinct from instrumental communication—how to get things done—which may be more the father's domain. Although such role differences are becoming more blurred, the basic biologically engendered infant-mother symbiosis persists.

Otherwise, role divisions are not absolute; they only indicate a dominant role for each parent. However, it must be appreciated that the mother's abilities to help a child gain self-awareness and body consciousness and to perceive and establish boundaries between himself and the world outside are more crucial than are the father's abilities to do this.

These role divisions are not only important examples but also essential in the children's acquisition of communicative skills. For instance, a father working away from home cannot be relied on to teach about intimate feelings in a detailed way, but he can bring to this and other family tasks a perspective that a mother harassed by the demands of young children throughout the day may not maintain for 7 days a week.

Parental role divisions should be flexible and complementary, rather than fixed, because in crises role complementarity may be essential and temporary role reversals even necessary. Permanent role reversal of the spouses occurs, too. It may be mutually satisfactory to the parents, but it provides offspring with difficult models for their future lives in society, unless society moves toward psychosocial gender equality to the greatest possible extent. Parental role reversals are particularly disadvantageous to children if the reversal is covert, although desired by both parents. Parents must provide gender-typical role models that are in some harmony with the larger society in which they live. Otherwise, children may fail to acquire and incorporate role attributes and expectations of themselves that have utility when they move into the community, even as a new generation may alter role stereotypes (see Figure 3).

FAMILY STRUCTURE AND PERSONALITY DEVELOPMENT

Dynamically, the triangular structure of the family is epitomized by each child's oedipal phase. Its adequate and appropriate resolution, which determines important salients of a child's psychic structure, depends more on the family structure and behavior than on biological determinants as postulated by Freud. This appears to be true of all phases of psychosocial development, although parental attitudes and behavior are both reactive and interactive with the child, so that a child's equipment at birth, his or her temperament, and the parents' capacity to cope with infantile needs all merge to establish the

"Pop, you've got to be more supportive of Mom and more willing to share with her the day-to-day household tasks. Mom, you have to recognize Pop's needs and be less dependent on him for your identity."

FIGURE 3. Role assignments. (Drawing by Koren; © 1978 by The New Yorker Magazine, Inc.)

family's interactional patterns. From these patterns derive much of what children learn and observe in terms of what kind of people their parents are—indeed, how they are human. Personality development proceeding through identifications and imitations depends as much on the parents' individual characteristics as on their correlated marital and familial interactive behavior. Children observe and absorb the defensive modes of those around them, and in this way the secondary processes evolve from familial examples and interaction modes.

After a child has learned body awareness and body management, including the correlated communicative facility, relational learning begins. The task for the family is to help each child establish his or her place in the family and to make each feel sufficiently secure in it so that he can begin to move beyond the family circle without undue anxiety. To attain this place of nearly equal emotional distance from both parents, the child not only must master body competence and competence in feeding, clothing, and toileting himself or herself but must also master the oedipal issues of having desexualized the close primary object relationships with the parents. Only then can children turn to peers as an increasingly important source for relationships. These integrating steps of achieving object constancy in one's mental life and of internalizing the incest taboo the family must accomplish with every child, verbally and even unconsciously. The personalities, especially the degree of security in sexual identity that the parents bring to their union, and their coalition are more crucial to this task than in any other phases of family life, most of which can be more explicit and verbally directed.

Further personality development of the child is less directly dependent on family structure and dynamics. But in subtle and not so subtle ways, the oedipal issues are relived in adolescence in terms of dependence-independence issues. These problems begin with the biological imbalances of puberty and continue into the prolonged path toward heterosexual competence and personal identity. The parental models play a role during this phase, often as an antipodal fulcrum for the offspring. To achieve a workable ego integration and identity, the adolescent must be able to overcome his negativistic stances, which serve the separation from his elders but do not serve in and of themselves the integration of an independent and inner-directed personality. A core of positive identification with one or the other parent or the family's image of that parent is essential in this structural development. If the antipodal position is intensely ambivalent and remains emotionally charged, it may become fixed. Young people then remain partially identified with a parent whom they also reject, a shaky foundation for ego integration and ego ideal.

Family System Functions

As stated before, it is artificial to separate structure, relationships, and functions, and, indeed, the formation of a family structure is one of its inherent functions for its own sake. It is also an implicit charge from the larger community. Society expects the family to prepare children for their lives as adults in the wider community, enabling them in turn to procreate and form their own families. Procreation is essential to the survival of any species, but the human species must also teach its heritage and thus ensure its continuity and future development. The family as the basic sociocultural unit is the embryo of social organization, and the parents are the sociocultural gametes.

The biological condition of the human infant demands a set of vital family tasks to be performed, such as feeding, sanitation, and the teaching of body management and the use of survival tools. All this many animals do for their young, and social organization is also a characteristic way of life of many species. For the human race another dimension is added through the development of the culture-typical symbols and their utility not only in the survival tasks but in planning for the future through an understanding of one's individual past and the group's collective past. Moreover, symbolic communication among humans does not require physical proximity of the communicators in time or space, a prerequisite to communication among animals.

For the purpose of discussion, family functions are here separated into marital, nurturant, relational, communicative, emancipational, and recuperative functions—keeping in mind that in vivo they overlap and to some extent are continuous. Only the predominance of one function over another may be discernible in actual life at a particular time. Also, all except the marital interaction itself involve educational tasks, even though formal education is assigned to extrafamilial institutions in many societies.

MARITAL FUNCTIONS

Marriage must serve the respective needs and satisfactions of the spouses and enable them to effect an appropriate family constellation in order to fulfill their leadership tasks. Beyond the familial obligations, the marital partners must jointly prepare to renounce their close ties to their children when they are ready to emancipate themselves physically and emotionally from the family. The family ultimately becomes a dyad again and must turn its concerns from productive engagement in the community to issues of retirement and the concomitant aging processes.

NURTURANT FUNCTIONS

The nurturant functions of the family encompass more than milk and food supply, although these are basic at first. Nursing includes the other forms of physical care that the helpless infant needs. Their performance requires the mother's motivation and some degree of security on her part in performing

these tasks. This security derives from her quasiinstinctual propensity for mothering, coupled with the almost symbiotic union with the newborn, such as the mutual and simultaneous relief of the baby's hunger and the mother's breast turgor, and from the support of her spouse and other family members if any. The less specific nurturant activities of the mother continue throughout the life of the family. They include weaning from breast or bottle, helping with locomotion and sphincter controls, and responding to the infant's many socializing behaviors, the anlagen for relationship and language. Eating together as a family at least once a day becomes not only a caloric ritual but a significant landmark in family life for communication, learning, interacting as a group, and relaxing together (see Figure 4).

The psychological and symbolic aspects and overtones of nursing and feeding grow from and with the earliest mother-infant interaction. Here the infant acquires initial trust in his human environment; therefore, nurturance is also the beginning of enculturation. Because the entire family is involved, their interaction with the mother-infant unit determines much of the nursing atmosphere. The broader nurturant tasks concern almost every aspect of young children's development as they acquire body awareness and learn body management, sphincter competence, and self-care with regard to feeding and clothing. All these myriad activities—feeding with its symbiotic and symbolic implications; caring for the baby; helping the child to walk and talk; getting things that the youngster cannot reach; supplying appropriate visual, auditory, and kinesthetic experiences—can at times be carried out by any family member or by other substitutes.

RELATIONAL FUNCTIONS

Weaning. Weaning is part of nurturing but entails more than withdrawing bottle or breast. The intimate physical closeness and attachment behavior with the mother must be weaned and an increasingly nonphysical intimacy established with all family members. Weaning involves still more, in that both the process of weaning and its accomplishment are foundation stones in the acquisition of ego boundaries. In reverse, a mother may fail to wean a baby adequately and at the appropriate age because her ego boundaries are blurred and because she overidentifies with the infant. She then also violates the generation boundary. In all these functions the mother plays the dominant role, but the entire family atmosphere and interaction are also crucial. For instance, parents already locked in an energy-consuming struggle with each other or with one child will necessarily neglect another child proportionally. It may be noted in passing that, in terms of ultimate mental health, the underattended child may fare better than the overinvolved one.

Weaning, the cessation of sucking in the narrow sense, has, therefore, important relational implications as the prototype of a succession of separation crises that characterize personal development and family life evolution. Nurturant competence on the part of the parents implies not only providing for needs and their satisfaction but also the capacity to frustrate and deny the child without provoking undue feelings of rejection and without undermining the natural propensity to grow and master problems, often painful problems. When frustrated or punished, children may find their anger and hostility quite overwhelming and temporarily lose faith in a parent. Nurturant and weaning competence in the family teaches the child that a temper tantrum does not overwhelm others in the family and that he or she is separate but not alone. In reverse, a parent's

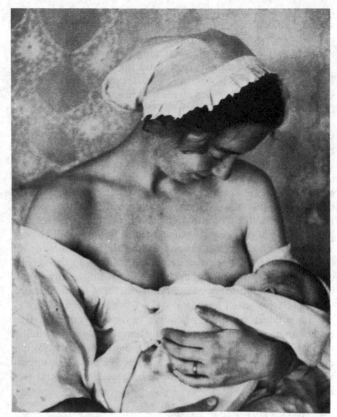

FIGURE 4. Biosocial nurturance. (From Steichen, E., *The Family of Man*, p. 24. Museum of Modern Art, New York, 1955.)

anger and frustration with a child teach the limits of provocative power and are another essential lesson in grasping limits between oneself and others and in establishing ego boundaries. Here the parental coalition counts. Ideally, the uninvolved and nonangry spouse supports both the upset parent and the child.

Mastery of separation can be defined as the child's experiencing the pain of acute loss of good feeling toward or dissatisfaction with another significant person—the parent—without losing faith and trust in the continuity of the relationship and the ultimate restoration of good feeling. Through these experiences children also learn and grow, becoming more able to avoid the same impasse and becoming less vulnerable to and threatened by subsequent separations or emotional distance. This mastery must be facilitated by the opportunity to observe, imitate, and eventually internalize how other family members cope with frustration and separation.

The relational issues involved in the feeding and weaning experiences culminate in each child's oedipal phase. Its successful passage includes the central issue of effecting the incest taboo as a rather unconsciously directed inhibitory force within the child and within the family. Conscious incestuous preoccupations beyond the oedipal phase interfere with subsequent successful personality integration and growth, especially in adolescence. The child's omnipotent sense of exclusive relationship with the mother must be curbed and frustrated, enabling the child to wish to grow up like the same-sex parent and to relate to both parents as individuals and as a unit.

Peer group relationships. After the child has been helped to find his place in the family, permitting him to feel comfortable and safe in intrafamilial relationships, relational learning turns to peer groups. Here familial guidance becomes more distant and indirect, but familial facilitation and support of peer

relationships are essential. After the age of 6 or 7, the child's relational learning depends increasingly on extrafamilial examples and on the family's social activities as a unit with relatives and friends.

Not only are the culture-typical distance and closeness to various people in differing situations learned that way, but extrafamilial persons are important as alternate figures for imitation and identification. Such experiences complement the parents' unique examples as members of their gender in their society and provide alternate and corrective models for parental shortcomings as people. Even if such shortcomings are not severe, teenagers often find their friends' parents or other adults superior and preferable as examples to follow in the service of emotional separation from the family (see Figure 5).

Parents and the family as a whole must be able to tolerate such "disloyalties," lest emancipating adolescents bear an undue degree of guilt, burdening them with intense conflicts between society's—that is, their peer group's—expectations that they be independent persons on the one hand and parental demands to conform to their standards on the other. Such an impasse may occur because of an adolescent's inner unresolved dependence-independence conflicts or because of parental resistance to such independence or both. The parents' respective values and expectations for their offspring must be in sufficient harmony so that the child can integrate parental objectives and standards, and parents and children must reconcile these values and goals with the realities both of the child's capabilities and of the community in which they live or wish to live.

COMMUNICATIVE FUNCTIONS

A central element in the family's educative mission concerns communicative competence. This competence includes non-

FIGURE 5. Separate, but not alone. (From Steichen, E., *The Family of Man*, p. 98. Museum of Modern Art, New York, 1955.)

verbal and verbal interchange, and there must be culture-typical congruence between the two; otherwise, messages are inconsistent and contradictory. Talking with young children about their earliest internal and external experiences is essential to their beginning to talk and to communicate meaningfully. What they say and what is said to them must make sense to them and others, so that through such validation they come to rely on the utility and consistency of language to express themselves and communicate with others. Only through language and the symbols basic to it does body awareness become body knowledge, and only through language can the basic trust of the mother-infant relationship be reinforced and broadened to include other family members and people outside. Without language or equivalent symbols, prediction and a grasp of the future are almost impossible; for instance, only by very rigid timing could infants feel assured that they will be fed when hungry. Language allows for flexibility—such as, "Supper will be late," or "After your bath tonight instead of before." Such communication is also essential in the development of object constancy.

Familial communication must, of course, be related to the communication styles and symbol usages of the family's community. Language plays a role in personality and concept formation beyond its communicative utility. Language reflects the culture's conceptual heritage and determines thought and concept organization across the generations—that is, the cultural system of logic and institutionalized beliefs. Without parental demonstration of abstract thinking children are handicapped in making the essential shift from concrete to abstract symbol usage (Piaget, 1968).

The jargon of any younger generation combines elements of both the emancipative striving for separateness and of evolutionary changes in language and culture. In some immigrant families special problems arise because school-age children surpass their parents in vocabulary and linguistic mastery, depriving both generations of certain communicative dimensions.

EMANCIPATIONAL FUNCTIONS

The ultimate goal for children is to grow up and become full-fledged members in the society into which their family has placed them. In Western industrialized society this usually means that offspring must attain physical, emotional, and economic independence from their families, being motivated and able to originate their own families.

In other societies emancipational tasks may not be as stringent and absolute, but the family still serves to guide the child toward the position society expects him or her to occupy as an adult. The process of emancipation of each child demands a compensatory reequilibration of the family after each departure until the spouses return to a dyadic existence, free to enjoy parental prerogatives as grandparents without the continuing responsibilities of a nuclear family. Obviously, each step toward emancipation poses the recurrent issue of separation until it is final and definitive, ideally without a rupture of emotional ties.

The degree of mastery of the earlier and more limited separations—beginning with weaning and later the beginning of school, separate vacations, and possible hospitalizations of members—indicates and to some extent determines the ease or difficulty experienced by the family when a child leaves for college, to get married, or for military service. But geographic separation is only a part of the issues to be mastered; more important are the emotional components, the sense of loss experienced by all involved and the inner capacity of each

member and the capacity of the family as a group to do the work of mourning appropriately without becoming pathologically depressed. The departing member must accomplish this alone or with a spouse; the remaining family group can work it out together, the parents demonstrating appropriate mourning, faith in everybody's ability to master separation, and faith in the continuity of life and altered yet rewarding relationships. Similar issues have to be mastered when a family member dies.

The modern family is handicapped with regard to total separation experiences, as the death of a parent or child within the life-span of the nuclear family is now rare, whereas it was rather usual only 50 years ago. Often now the four grandparents are still living at the time the young adults emancipate themselves from their families. And grandparents often live at a distance, so that the impact of their deaths on the nuclear family does not carry the immediacy and intensity of the permanent loss of a regular participant in family life. The time when the first child leaves may be the first occasion for all family members to mourn together, in contrast to the experience of a youngster of earlier generations who usually would have shared mourning with the family incident to the death of a close relative, often a sibling.

Family bonds continue, of course, beyond the emancipation of the young. Rejoining one's family temporarily is a mutually enjoyable and relaxing experience, provided the family has done its tasks well. Opportunities and needs for mutual support are likely to arise after parents have become grandparents (see Figure 6).

RECUPERATIVE FUNCTIONS

The family must provide for the relaxation of its members, relaxation of manners and behavior and even defenses essential to interaction in the community. Most mothers are familiar with the need of an elementary school child for strenuous physical activity, even for a fight, on his return from school, and the home must serve as a controlled environment for such socially nonadaptive, possibly regressive relaxation of behavioral standards.

In the family circle, parents also shed formal attire, actually and symbolically. If a man's house is his castle, his family is the one group in which he can be king or, at least, president but in which he can also exhibit dependency needs. The same is true for the wife, especially if she works outside the home. For such mundane reasons alone, the family might have to be invented if it did not exist, as no other living arrangements provide for so many individuals these opportunities to forego formal behavior and recover energy for the work in the community that requires more formal and defensive interpersonal demeanor.

To some degree the family also permits its members to engage in creative or other activities that afford relief by contrast with the monotony of many jobs. By setting limits on relaxing activities, the family as a group also demands and teaches impulse control—in games, for instance—and all members may have to defer individual interests and hobbies to family group activities at times. Children experience discipline in this way, as with other frustrating experiences, first as outer control and eventually as inner restraint.

Family celebrations, holidays, and birthdays are important events in promoting family unity and a sense of belonging. They are opportunities for the family to relate as a group with other families, related ones or neighbors or friends. Such events are particularly important and opportune with children beyond the oedipal passage and before adolescence, as are family unit vacations and trips when the children are this age.

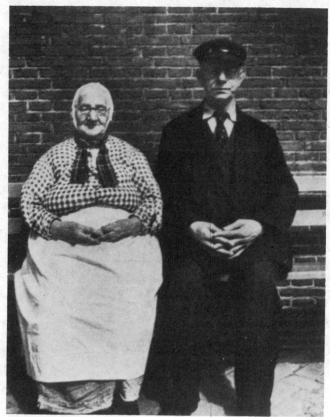

FIGURE 6. Grandparents: We two form a multitude. (From Steichen, E., *The Family of Man,* p. 182. Museum of Modern Art, New York, 1955.)

ADULT LIFE

Human growth and change do not stop with emancipation or the assumption of marriage and parenthood. All students of the human condition, including philosophers and religious teachers, have recognized the many seasons of life (Levinson, 1978). Familial changes tied to the personal, biological, and social evolutions are interwoven with each other. Continued individuation and personal growth—or decline—have become universal issues as the average life-span has increased. As a person moves through midlife toward his or her peak in power, effectiveness, and sense of accomplishment (sometimes failure) before declining faculties begin to prevail, the family also continues to change. The familial challenges of the later life periods vary greatly, depending primarily on how many of the three generations live in proximity or even in one household. Eventually, the paradigm of parents who lead and children who learn and follow becomes reversed as old age imposes increasing dependence on and even guidance and nurturance by the younger generation or generations. Thus, middle-aged people may often be and function as parents in two directions, besides having to attend to their own personal and marital growth and adjustment tasks (Neugarten, 1970).

EFFECTS OF IMPOVERISHMENT ON FAMILY FUNCTIONS

If the family is so burdened by its own tasks that relaxation and enjoyment as a group become jeopardized—either because of emotional conflicts or ill health or because the size of the family overtaxes its emotional, nurturant, educational, or tan-

gible resources and reserves—indications for family limitation through birth control and for outside assistance with family tasks are at hand (see Figure 7).

Besides exhaustion of family resources because of family size, any disproportion between essential resources and the magnitude of family tasks must lead to family dysfunction and distorted or inadequate task performance. If familial resources are limited in this way primarily through external social and economic circumstances, such families should be considered impoverished, as distinct from pathological, which is related primarily to deviant parental personalities or coalition or other intrafamilial distortions in relationships and interactions without undue exterior stresses or disadvantages. This somewhat arbitrary distinction between, on one hand, deviant family design and interaction modes that are more or less externally engendered and often characteristic of a class or minority group and, on the other hand, structural and functional deviances arising primarily from within the family has clinical value and leads to very different therapeutic measures. Both types of families may benefit from family group treatment, but the impoverished family needs many communal supportive and remedial measures, and treatment for tissue or metabolic abnormalities and defects may be as urgently needed as the restoration of family function competence.

One-parent families. Impoverishment in the form of one-parent families is of three origins, each leading to different problems. Widowed parents must cope with the loss of spouses, not only within themselves but also with the children's grief and sorrow. If not adequately resolved, the ensuing depression, whether masked or overt, may become pathological for that family member and a pathological focus for the family as a whole. Obviously, the problem varies, depending on the age of the children, the nature of the death, and other factors, such as support resources from outside the family, including possible remarriage. The crucial issue, however, is the surviving parent's mode of dealing with the loss and mourning and his or her representation of the deceased parent to the children.

Divorce or desertion presents a different problem, although the sense of loss may be equally intense. However, the feeling of abandonment may be quite realistic, and the likelihood for resentment is great. The remaining spouse may have great difficulty in representing the absent parent realistically, and opportunities abound for the children to be confused about what each parent is really like. The acme of such conflicts and confusion is custody fights between divorcing or divorced parents, often compounded by the introduction of stepparents.

Parenthood outside marriage is an increasing occurrence and is class related in that its prevalence is higher in the lowest socioeconomic class, although the incidence is increasing only in the middle and higher classes. The impoverishment, therefore, is often not only that of single parenthood but compounded by the characteristics of family life in the poverty sector of the population.

Poverty. Economically and educationally underendowed parents are obviously handicapped in their enculturating missions, and, because certain patterns are characteristically common in such families, the term "poverty culture" has been coined. This term seems incorrect and misleading, because the transmission of life on the welfare rolls is not the cross-generational passing on of a set of beliefs and values that have served well or are believed to have served preceding generations well. On the contrary, it is the transmission, if any, of deficiencies, such as undereducation for success in an industrial society, combined with pessimism about and resentment toward an environment that is or is perceived as hostile and repressive.

FIGURE 7. A family beyond its resources. (Courtesy Susan Perl.)

Nurturance in such families is often distorted by a literalness, in that all discomfort in infants is sought to be alleviated by feeding. This practice is often continued beyond infancy, and, instead of children's complaints or discomfort being explored, they are offered food or, if old enough, sent to the candy store or scolded. Thus, relational issues are met tangibly and often orally or by verbal or physical punishments. Neither type of interaction invites need consideration or thought development, thus interfering with emotional growth, communicative development, and the capacity to postpone need satisfaction, which are basic to the attainment of long-range goals, especially along educational lines.

Further enculturating deficiencies in poor families are the lack of toys and of play space and the common disinterest or inability of adults to interact meaningfully with children beyond infancy. In a one-parent family, that parent is often working, and the child is then left to the care of a grandmother or aunt or older sibling, none of whom is as motivated to stimulate and interact with the child as a mother can be if supported by a spouse who shares parental tasks. This set of familial deficiencies in enculturation leads to a circular handicap when formal education begins, and it has been demonstrated that even the Head Start program could compensate only partially for the earliest deprivations and understimulation of an impoverished family environment. Racial or other group discrimination may further impair the slim opportunities for developing self-esteem and hope for mastery over one's fate.

A second deficiency cycle then develops with formal education. Children ill prepared to begin school not only are hampered or discouraged by their own backwardness but are likely to be stamped as poor students from the beginning,

which leads to educational neglect in many school systems. The feedback from school to family then further depreciates an already underendowed family, enhancing their pessimism and probable apathy toward education and social betterment.

Such a family is likely to be beset by many problems—economic problems, conflicts with authority, health problems. It can be seen that these deficiencies, although largely externally engendered and reinforced, become internalized, especially as seen by mental health professionals, in the form of defective communication about inner experience and as so-called lack of motivation for treatment or education. The salient family dynamics are those of predominantly reactive interaction and defective development of thought and language because of disbelief and even mistrust in the utility of abstract and symbolic mentation and communication. Moreover, there is impaired capacity for pleasures that are not immediate, and generally such family members know—and exploit—how to make one another feel bad but can make each other feel good only by granting immediate gratification, regardless of the long-range consequences. Emancipation in one sense occurs early in such families because older children are usually left to be with their peers in school and out or are called on to tend to younger siblings or other small children in the neighborhood. However, such early emancipation occurs at the expense of further education and emotional and relational development and hence bodes ill for more mature family formation and parenthood when sexual activity begins, usually at an early age.

Impoverished families—all families whose tangible and emotional resources fall short of adequate family task performance—must be supported by the community through many agencies, among them day care centers for children, special school programs, and social and welfare services for the family as a unit.

The Family in Illness

There are two general familial aspects in any sickness—the family as care agent for a sick member and the question of the family's role in or contribution to ill health by virtue of neglect or through the transmission of some defect or by maintaining a sick member in that condition or role.

Aside from neglect or carelessness, which can lead to accidents or preventable infectious diseases, the role of the family as health educator and health promoter cannot be overstressed (Fleck, 1976).

The role of the family in the transmission of pathogenic or pathological conditions is complex because open systems and subsystems in motion must be dealt with. The relevant systems must be considered on at least five different levels:

1. Subcellular, chromosomal, and cellular defects due to intrauterine, mechanical, metabolic, or nutritional abnormalities can occur.

2. Postnatal maternal behavior, such as anxiety, can adversely influence autonomic system stabilization and integration, as well as feeding and bowel habits.

3. Body image, self-boundary, and self-awareness depend on parental inputs on weaning and helping children in their individuation, which may be faulty.

4. Relational guidance may be deficient, interfering with gender identity or culture-appropriate repression, so that intrafamilial relationships and peer relationships cannot be reconciled.

5. Socialization may be handicapped because of communicative deviance in the family, parental intolerance for individual growth and identity, especially adolescents' independency experiments and their eventual emancipation.

To relate one single item in such a complex series of pathogenic potentials in linear causal fashion to a symptomatically defined clinical condition and entity, such as schizophrenia, means disregarding the complexity and even the essentials of the human condition. Regardless of how determining a particular defect or deficiency of tissue or enculturation may be with regard to a particular illness, treatment should focus on persons and their context—the family.

The family physician, however, is generally not an expert in family dynamics and functioning, although the establishment of a specialty in family practice can fulfill its promise only if physicians of the future become family experts in this sense. The same holds for psychiatrists, who furthermore must become proficient in family treatment. Psychiatric illness does not occur in a vacuum, and whether or not the social environment, of which a patient's family is the most crucial vector, engenders psychiatric disturbances, psychiatric patients always interact with significant others, who in turn interact with them helpfully or pathogenically. Almost always these significant others are the family members, whether the family of origin or progeny. Spouses are, of course, the most significantly involved persons, but any significant relationship carries subterranean and prototypical elements of earlier familial relationships.

Another important aspect is the family's reaction to a member's serious illness of any type. If it is a psychiatric condition, especially if it requires institutionalization, the family deserves therapeutic attention for four general reasons. First, the family may be involved in the genesis of the illness, and this must be understood by clinicians who want to help patient and family. Second, if so, the patient should not return to the family unless its members are helped to change or unless it is ascertained that the family is supportive and helpful without major pathogenic impact. Third, the moment of hospitalization of a family member is a crisis that affects all members and that demands therapeutic or supportive attention. Fourth, the patient's return to the family may be unduly disruptive to the family, and psychiatrists must balance the advantages of returning patients promptly to the community against the possible pathogenic effects this return may have on them or their families or both. Some families may be so relieved by the removal of a sick member that they eagerly establish a new equilibrium that may interfere with the patient's early discharge from the hospital. This problem arises particularly often with disturbed elderly patients. In general, this divorcement between mental patients and their families (if extant) has been one important factor in the dismal subsistence and the frequent returns to the hospital of deinstitutionalized patients.

FAMILY PATHOLOGY IN CERTAIN PSYCHIATRIC ILLNESSES

Precise correlations between family pathology and psychiatric syndromes must comprise all the many levels of personal and social integration and the conceptualization of these processes, ranging from genetic coding to group dynamics. This is difficult and complex, even if a psychiatric entity is based on definite chromosomal and inborn defects, whether hereditary or not. These conditions are not considered here in detail. However, familial malfunctioning can ensue from severe guilt and other unrealistic reactions to the birth of a defective child. Because there is a need for further clinical investigation and standardization of diagnostic terminology and classification, specific correlations among family disorders and individual psychopathology and psychiatric syndromes are outlined only briefly. The new multiaxial diagnostic scheme of the American Psychiatric Association's third edition of *Diagnostic and Statistical Manual of Mental Disorders* (DSM-III) should be useful in further delineating clinically correlated familial and intrapersonal psychopathology.

Mental subnormality. This deficiency tends to run in families apart from hereditary factors. Below certain intelligence levels, parental functioning, especially the communicative performance, does not suffice to accomplish the enculturation of offspring. Educational inadequacies and inferior social position in a given subculture can also result in ineffectual family structure and dynamics, especially if the family belongs to a group against which the surrounding community discriminates actively.

Depression and manic-depressive illness. Parental overinvestment in the achievement of children, especially parents' social prestige aspirations, are commonly found in the backgrounds of these patients. Such parental attitudes are introjected, and they predispose the child to intense ambivalence and a sense of being loved and worthy only on the basis of superior performance and achievement. Resentment and punitive attitudes toward the self supervene when failure in terms of internalized overstringent expectations occur. Often, a parent is deceased at the time of the overt illness, and early loss of one parent has occurred in 10 per cent of psychotically depressed patients. This is only a fragmental sketch of the genesis of depression, disregarding other biological and intrapsychic phenomena related to familial and possible genetic transmission.

Psychopathy. Asocial behavior is often associated with family pathology when children have been found to carry out covert or overt needs or wishes of the parents. The young sociopath's behavior may express directly such propensities of a parent in exaggerated form; in other instances the child behaves like a sociopathic parental collateral, whom one parent secretly—or not so secretly—admires. Emphasis on surface appearance and denial of any problem in the face of evident malfeasance by a family member is often encountered in the families of psychopaths.

Addictive behavior, especially alcoholism, is also related to certain family problems. In general, parental examples of unrestrained indulgence in smoking or drinking or drug intake to alleviate habitually acute or chronic discomfort and stress are likely to be followed by offspring, although not necessarily in the identical form of overindulgence. Such habits may form a source of family conflict, but equally often they are used to bypass, instead of resolve, family stress. Evasion is also often involved in the current epidemic of drug abuse among the young, serving in general to avoid growth pains and emancipation anxieties, instead of mastering them.

Schizophrenia. Schizophrenia has long been known to show a specific correlation between incidence and the degree of biological relatedness. Geneticists have studied this correlation, but this psychosis has also been investigated most intensively with regard to psychosocial family pathology. According to Alanen (1966), Lidz et al. (1965), and Singer and Wynne (1963), the outstanding findings in this latter regard are that families with schizophrenic offspring evidence faulty structure and functioning in almost every parameter of essential family tasks. These faults include frequent and severe parental personality disorders resulting especially in gender model deficiency, deficient parental coalition, violation of generational and sexual boundaries, paralogical or dissimulating communication modes, and interference with a child's development of ego boundaries and individuation (Anonymous, 1972). In some cases the parental model paradigms are so irreconcilable that the offspring must fail in integrating a personal identity.

FAMILY SYSTEM DEFICIENCIES

A more promising approach to family pathology than the specificity search—that is, correlating phenomenological entities with a particular family constellation or dysfunction—is the study and discernment of how a family succeeds or fails in accomplishing the essential family tasks and how it operates as a system (Fleck, 1972). As stated above, family structure and functions or dysfunctions cannot be separated clinically as clearly as they can for the sake of discussion. For instance, a disturbed or immature parent may or may not satisfy the spouse but is apt to blur the generation boundaries, besides being a poor model for the same-sexed child. Faulty parental communication will likely pervade the family, distort its structure, and handicap the children, if not encourage them to continue a life in fantasy uncorrected by reality presentation from the older generation, without necessarily handicapping the latter in their communal activities.

Marital and parental dysfunction. This type of dysfunction impairs family leadership. Intrapersonal parental inadequacies cover a wide range of difficulties. For instance, severe immaturity may lead one spouse to seek a dependent position in the family akin to that of an offspring. Such a spouse expects parental care from the partner or even from a child. Almost any form of neurosis or psychosis in one parent is apt to produce defective parental coalitions, a situation which handicaps the nurturant and enculturating tasks on which children depend for their development.

Model deficit. Inability or failure of a parent to serve as an adequate gender model appropriate to the larger society leads to increased developmental vicissitudes for a child of the same sex, more so if the posture of such a parent is further weakened and undermined by the mate's critical or contemptuous attitudes. The insecure gender identity of a parent predisposes the same-sex child to gender uncertainty and confusion and to social ineptness, important elements in the development of perversions and schizophrenia. Parents with severe hysterical, obsessional, or other neurotic characteristics are apt to produce offspring with like defensive structures if not symptoms.

Nuclearity failure. This form of family pathology is due to emancipation failure of one or both parents. It can also be viewed as the surreptitious need for an extended family system. The pathology occurs overtly or covertly when one parent or both remains primarily attached to and dependent on his or her parents or a parental substitute, and the center of gravity for authority, decision making, and emotional investment rests outside the nuclear family group. This distorts family structure and functions, especially if both parents feel primarily beholden to their respective families of origin and no workable coalition for the younger family becomes established. An extended family system is quite workable with differential role assignments across three generations, but it is damaging to a nuclear family that intends or aspires to this designation, a family that lives geographically but not dynamically and emotionally as a nuclear family.

Incompetent boundaries. Family boundaries can be impaired in the form of undue rigidity, excessive porosity, or undue elasticity. The last, originally described by Wynne and colleagues in families of schizophrenic patients as a rubber fence, allows no real negotiation of the family boundary into the community. A departing member is somehow engulfed by an extension of the family, which allows no one to leave or emancipate from it. A father shadowing a daughter on her dates like a detective and a mother who accompanies a child on his or her honeymoon are pathological examples. Overly rigid boundaries are established by some pathological families, leading to isolation from and fear of the larger community. This impairment may occur in the form of physical and geographic isolation or through shared paranoidal suspiciousness of extrafamilial society or both. Obviously, such a family is overly isolated, deprived of friends and of other communal participation, and deficient in social training opportunities for children. Porous and inadequate boundaries are often found in ghetto and broken families. Frequently, such defective external boundaries coincide with or reflect chaotic internal organization of the family with faulty subsystem organization—for instance, a poorly defined generation boundary. Older siblings may be expected to function as parent figures for younger siblings. There may be age overlap between uncles or aunts and nephews and nieces in three-generation households, often a one-parent family for a particular child. Family boundaries may be blurred because kitchen and bathroom must be shared with other families, and there may be neither a pattern of nor room for family gatherings. Children of school age may often be left to their own devices if parents or the single parent are working during the day, which undercuts moving from the organized setting of the school to another supportive system— that is, a family home and atmosphere.

Parental break. Broken families are the grossest but not necessarily the psychiatrically most devastating form of family pathology. Broken families are disproportionally frequent in the backgrounds of sociopaths, unmarried mothers, and schizophrenics, regardless of whether the fracture is through death, desertion, or divorce.

Schism. Probably more pathogenic than actual parental separation is family schism. Here, the family is divided overtly or covertly into warring camps, usually because of chronic conflict and strife between the parents. The children are forced to take sides, to the detriment of their personality development and integration. This type of family pathology is found in the background of schizophrenic patients.

Skews. In a skewed marital relationship one spouse expects the other to be a parent to him or her, or one disturbed parent dominates the other and the family life absolutely and rigidly. Such a marital coalition often preempts parental functions and emotional resources, and the children's affective and psychological needs are neglected. A family may also be skewed because a dyad other than the parental one dominates the group emotionally and often tangibly. Most often, this is a symbiotic mother-child relationship.

In both schismatic and skewed families, violations of the generation boundary abound, and in both the intense relationship between one parent and one child may have seductive and incestuous components, an additional violation of sex role requisites, if not of the incest taboo.

Incest. Overt incest is evidence of gross parental psychopathology and of defective family structure. Father-daughter incest is commonest, but both parents are psychologically involved. Incest often bespeaks a tenuous equilibrium in a family that seeks to avoid overt disintegration. Frequently, the involved daughter has assumed many parental functions, while the parents maintain a facade of role competence. The family often breaks up after incest is brought into the open, usually by the involved child.

FAMILY TASK DEFICITS

Nurturant deficiency. In its grossest form this deficiency occurs because of parental neglect and disinterest. Infant victims of malnutrition are known to pediatricians in large municipal hospitals. The worst manifestation is the battered child syndrome, although such victims are not necessarily malnourished in the strict sense. More discrete nurturant disturbances occur because of maternal illness or because of anxiety and empathy failure, in that a mother fails to distinguish between an infant's hunger-borne crying and other bodily needs, discomforts, and pain. Such mothers may also tend to overfeed the baby or try to do so, thus coupling pain and discomfort with oral input. Such problems may have occurred in the backgrounds of psychosomatic patients, including obese ones. It is likely that the marital coalition is also deficient in such families.

Enculturation deficits

Failure in separation mastery. This failure may begin with a mother's inability to wean a child effectively, due to the mother's symbiotic propensities or, more generally, the parents' incapacity to effect inhibitions and adequate frustration tolerance in the child. This inability becomes crucial in the failure to help a child through his oedipal conflicts, a basic family task also in effecting the incest taboo. This does not mean that overt incest behavior will ensue; rather, the child is prone to develop one of the more classical neuroses. If coupled with other family function deficits, the defective separation competence may be

important in the development of schizophrenia and will be a handicap at all stages of personality development.

Aberrant communication. This is a common finding in families with psychiatric problems. Although usually secondary to parental psychopathology, notably thought disorders, faulty communication also builds up a pathogenic autonomy of its own. Young children learn the defective communication modes, which distort their cognitive and linguistic development, their perceptions, and concept formation. If communication is confusing within the family and ineffectual as an expressive and instrumental tool, children are deprived of a critical socializing element outside the family. They may never gain basic faith in and reliance on the utility of communication. The seeds of autism may be sown in this way.

Severely amorphous or fragmented modes of communicating have been found in families of schizophrenic patients and may be pathognomonic for schizophrenia (Wynne and Singer, 1963). Parental examples of paralogical thinking and of fear and mistrust of their social environment affect offspring by creating confusion and anxiety, and children may internalize the faulty ideation and the mistrust of the world and may externalize their problems by habitual projection. This is the familial counterpart of Cameron's (1963) pseudocommunity; paranoidal suspiciousness can be learned in this way and can also be viewed as the transmission of irrationality (Lidz et al., 1965).

Scapegoating. A special clinical problem in some families is the scapegoat phenomenon. This pathological family constellation is discernible only if the family as a unit is considered and studied, because the pathological character of the scapegoat's behavior and personality is usually blatant, and a diagnosis in traditional terms is warranted, although not identical from case to case. The scapegoat, the identified patient—regardless of whether he or she is schizophrenic, psychopathic, an underachiever, or shows neurotic trait disturbances—serves to bind family anxiety and to mask family deficiencies. "If it were not for him," it is contended, "this would be a happy family." However, it can often be demonstrated—for instance, by the scapegoat's institutionalization if this is required—that the family is unhappy or even more disturbed without the presence of the patient, unless another family member can be scapegoated soon. The scapegoat often serves to divert parents from their own conflicts or provides an alibi for deficient parenting of all offspring in terms of warmth and nurturant care. Scapegoated children suffer more because their needs are neglected and they are made to feel that it is all their fault, and siblings may also believe this. The siblings not only suffer insufficient care and attention but also either learn a distorted view of the scapegoat or must covertly oppose the parents' view, leading to conflict and a sense of guilt. In addition, the family as a whole does not escape unscathed, because the scapegoat may cause the family tangible harm and suffering, although such a patient may also save the family by leading it to therapy (Napier and Whitaker, 1978).

Affectivity deficiencies. Abnormalities in the affective climate of a family also do not occur in isolation. The parental relationship may be deficient in this respect or so overintense that feelings toward children are abrogated. As in scapegoating, one child may become the focus for negative feelings and conflicts.

Power abuse by parents is a manifestation of affective disturbances. The extreme of this process is child abuse, including fatal battering. Such children are not necessarily unwanted, but parental oscillations in feelings about themselves and others are extreme, including both overattachments and temper tantrum-like abuse of others (Gil, 1971).

A cold family climate is related to depressive illness, both engendering such an affective constitution and resulting in depression and low self-esteem among family members.

Clinical Evaluation

Besides the history of psychiatric disorders in the family, clinical assessment concerns family functions and structure. Observations about functioning and coping force inferences about structure and vice versa. Just as the clinician can draw inferences about lung structure or pathology from breathing patterns, so also can one infer on a statistical basis that chronic sociopathic behavior in an offspring is likely related to certain structural and functional family deficits, such as overemphasis on appearance of behaviors and relationships compared with substance.

Symptoms aside, the clinician seeks information about the basic elements of family structure, notably the maintenance of the generation boundary and the gender-linked role divisions and complementarities, and about the manner in which the family copes with its major tasks and functions. Clinicians pay special attention to familial communication modes.

Diagnostic investigation and therapeutic influences overlap in the establishment of family diagnosis, as they do in psychiatric examinations generally. Only the referential framework for evaluation through family history and direct observation is outlined here.

INFORMATION SOURCES

Ideally, the individual histories and statements of all family members are combined and examined for confluent and contradictory data, and these individual records are complemented by participant observation of the family as a group. There are many methods available for this observation, ranging from open-ended family interviews to more structured formats, including the possibility of having the family do specific tasks or tests together while being observed and preferably videotaped.

SPOUSES

The referential framework begins with an examination of the marital relationships, the pertinent data concerning the spouses' respective backgrounds, their personal developments, their educational levels, their socioeconomic class positions, and the cultural and ideological value patterns of their respective families of origin. Significant discrepancies in these parameters should alert examiners to potential conflict areas, and they should investigate the resolution of such discrepancies. For instance, one should explore differences with regard to religion, social class ambitions, desired family size, and rearing methods of and goals for the children and their resolutions or the absence thereof.

FAMILY ORGANIZATION

Data about family structure can be obtained through inquiries about living and sleeping arrangements, activities of the family as a group and as part groups, role divisions incident to various family tasks and crises, and the decision-making processes. As far as possible these items should also be examined directly through group observations, as should the possible existence and nature of dominant dyads other than that of the parents. In observing the family as a group, the diagnostician gains impressions about the extent and methods of parental leadership and whether it is united or not—that is, data about the effectiveness of the parental coalition and the integrity of generational division. For example, gender appropriateness in manners and conversational content can be established impressionistically in family interviews, or inappropriate seductiveness can be documented.

FAMILY COPING

This can be assessed by learning about crisis behavior. The normal crises of family evolution are important sources of understanding the family's coping patterns, coping reserves, and coping deficiencies. Among such crises are possible resistance or reservations of the spouses' families to the marriage and how this was resolved; the first pregnancy; the original triad formation; subsequent pregnancies and births; evolutionary separations, such as the first day of school; economic misfortunes or the deaths of relatives or friends. In psychiatric practice the examination often takes place in a crisis situation, such as that incident to the hospitalization of a family member as a mental patient.

SOCIAL NETWORK AND BOUNDARY COMPETENCE

The nature of the family's social network should be examined to establish social isolation or the nature of family relatedness within the community. The network must fit to some degree the class position and the patterns of the community and subculture of which the family is a part. The involvement with the spouses' families of origin and collaterals must also fit to some degree their cultural pattern, or conflict should be presumed and the resolution of it examined. A parent's intense attachment to either family of origin should alert the examiner to the possibility that a truly nuclear family has not been established.

Related to the issue of the family's social interactions is the issue of how family boundaries are managed. Properly permeable boundaries permit age-appropriate exit from and entry into the family circle without undue conflict. For instance, how do children and parents behave when the examiner wants to see the parents without the children or wants to interview a child alone? Kindergarten and school entries are items related to boundary adequacy or difficulties, as are emancipation events. Crisis coping also relates to boundary management. For example, can the family tolerate the introduction of a helper if needed? Does a potentially manageable problem spill into the larger community—for example, does a parental quarrel always end with neighbors' involvement?

CHILDREN'S DEVELOPMENTS

Evaluation of the children depends on their respective ages. Is their behavior age appropriate? Are their educational achievements and social participation within the range of community expectations for them? Pediatric histories, including well-child care data, may be the only source of information available from outside the family. For older children, kindergarten and school adjustments, records from recreational agencies, and, when indicated, information from neighbors and friends as to the socialization of a child can be used. School phobias are a classic manifestation of deficient separation mastery in the family, and school failures are a problem to families and may bespeak family problems.

In families with older children, attention must be paid to their emancipating efforts and the parents' reactions to these efforts. Adolescence, notoriously a stage of uneasy family truce in many respects, should be a family dissolution process, at least on an emotional plane. Adolescents must experiment with greater independence, and each step carries a potential for disagreement and conflict for all concerned. Also, adolescents' dissatisfaction with and opposition to parental standards are an intermittently necessary stance for them in their strivings for emotional distance and independence. Examining and evaluating the family with adolescent offspring are, therefore, especially difficult because of this evolutionary state of imbalance and conflict.

INTRAFAMILIAL COMMUNICATION

Here recordings or films are essential for detailed analysis. But, grossly or impressionistically, the clarity of communication or lack of it can also be seen and heard. Contradictory statements in the same verbal passage or discrepancies between verbal content and nonverbal signals may confuse, rather than convey meaning, or may have a double-bind effect. Scapegoating of a member becomes readily apparent, as do ambivalences, such as the more-or-less covert condoning of a member's behavior that also constitutes the family's complaint. Careful analysis of verbal passages or special tests given singly or to the group will disclose thought disorders and ideational defects.

EXAMINATION TOOLS

Questionnaires and schedules of family process items are available or can be composed for specific assessment modes, but, in general, they are ancillary diagnostic tools. They are most useful for the examiner who wants to standardize examinations for data retrieving purposes, for research, or for didactic purposes. Their major value, therefore, rests with the organization of data and not with the information-gathering segment for clinical evaluation, which depends primarily on the clinician's skill and art and his ability to order the data within conceptual frameworks such as those outlined here.

The scheme of five systems subdivisions serves as a grid for clinical family assessment:

1. Leadership and regulation involve the nature of the parental personalities, the parents' emotional emancipation from their families of origin, their marital adjustment and representation of each other, the role models and role complementarity they demonstrate, and their manner of power use, guidance, and discipline.

2. Boundary management can be examined with regard to age-appropriate parent-child proximity and children's development of ego boundaries, the formation of basic triads, the integrity of the generation boundary, and the age-appropriate permeability of the family-community boundary.

3. The affective climate in a family can be assessed by observing their interaction, the question of equivalency of the respective parent-child triads, evidence of tolerance of a wide range of feeling (or the opposite), and the record of the family's ability to celebrate and mourn together.

4. Communication must be evaluated in terms of clarity as to contents and syntax, speaking for oneself and not for others, listening as well as talking, verbal-nonverbal signal consistency, responsiveness with regard to content and feeling, and the possible discernment of thought disorder, abstraction deficiency, or failure to come to closure.

5. Family task and goal performances need to be reviewed historically, as well as examined in the present, and may be reiterated: the establishment of a marital coalition that can serve parental functions—nurturance, weaning, teaching body mastery and linguistic competence, peer relationship management, family-shared leisure, recreation, tangible crisis coping, role complementarity, and emancipation of the younger generation.

Suggested Cross References

Anthropology and sociology are considered in relation to psychiatry in Section 5.1 and Section 5.2, respectively. General living systems theory is discussed in Section 1.2. Communication is discussed in Section 4.7. Chapter 8 on Freudian theories discusses psychosexual development. Normal child development is discussed in Section 34.2, and normal adolescent development is discussed in Section 34.3. Chapter 24 discusses normal human sexuality and psychosexual disorders; particularly relevant to this section is Section 24.4 on gender identity disorders. Other psychiatric disorders are discussed in Chapters 15 to 19. Family therapy is discussed in Section 30.6.

REFERENCES

* Ackerman, N. W. *The Psychodynamics of Family Life.* Basic Books, New York, 1958.
Ackerman, N. W. Family diagnosis and therapy. In *Current Psychiatric Therapies,* J. Masserman, editor, vol. 3, p. 205. Grune & Stratton, New York, 1963.
Alanen, Y. O. The family in the pathogenesis of schizophrenia and neurotic disorders. Acta Psychiatr. Neurol. Scand., *24* (Suppl. 189): 75, 1966.
Anokhin, P. K. Functional system as unit of organism integrative activity. In *Systems Theory and Biology,* M.D. Mesarovic, editor, p. 376. Springer, New York, 1968.
Anonymous. Toward the differentiation of a self in one's own family. In *Family Interaction,* J. L. Framo, editor, p. 111. Springer, New York, 1972.
* Anthony, E. J., and Benedek, T., editors. *Parenthood: Its Psychology and Psychopathology.* Little, Brown, and Co., Boston, 1970.
Bell, N. W. Extended family relations of disturbed and well families. Fam. Proc., *1:* 175, 1962.
Bell, N. W., and Vogel, E. Toward a framework for functional analysis of family behavior. In *A Modern Introduction to the Family,* N. W. Bell, and E. Vogel, editors, p 1. Free Press of Glencoe, New York, 1960.
Benedek, T. Parenthood as a developmental phase. J. Am. Psychoanal. Assoc., *7:* 389, 1959.
Bibring, G., Dwyer, T. F., Huntington, D. S., and Valenstein, A. F. A study of the psychological processes of pregnancy and of the earliest mother-child relationship. Psychoanal. Stud. Child, *16:* 9, 1961.
Bott, E. *Family and Social Network.* Tavistock Publications, London, 1957.
Bowlby, J. *Maternal Care and Mental Health.* World Health Organization, Geneva, 1952.
Bowlby, J. *Child Care and the Growth of Love.* Penguin Books, Baltimore, 1965.
Bruch, H., and Touraine, G. The family frame of obese children. Psychosom. Med., *2:* 141, 1940.
Cameron, N. *Personality Development and Psychopathology: A Dynamic Approach.* Houghton Mifflin, Boston, 1963.
Christensen, H. T., editor. *Handbook of Marriage and the Family.* Rand McNally, Chicago, 1964.
Erikson, E. *Childhood and Society.* W. W. Norton, New York, 1950.
Erikson, E. *Insight and Responsibility.* W. W. Norton, New York, 1964.
Fishbein, M., and Burgess, E. W., editors. *Successful Marriage.* Doubleday, New York, 1948.
Fleck, S. Family welfare, mental health, and birth control. J. Fam. Law, *3:* 241, 1964.
Fleck, S. Some basic aspects of family pathology. In *The Manual on Child Psychopathology,* B. Wolman, editor, p. 189. McGraw-Hill, New York, 1972.
Fleck, S. Unified health services and family-focused primary care. Int. J. Psychiatr. Med., *6:* 501, 1975.
Fleck, S. A general systems approach to severe family pathology. Am. J. Psychiatr., *133:* 669, 1976.
Fleck, S. The family in the etiology of mental disorders. In *International Encyclopedia of Psychiatry, Psychology, Psychoanalysis, and Neurology,* B. Wolman, editor, vol. 4, p. 452. Human Sciences Press, New York, 1977.
Fleck, S., Lidz, T., Cornelison, A., Schafer, S., and Terry, D. The intrafamilial environment of the schizophrenic patient: Incestuous and homosexual problems. In *Individual and Familial Dynamics,* J. Masserman, editor, p. 142. Grune & Stratton, New York, 1959.
Flugel, J. *The Psychoanalytic Study of the Family.* Hogarth Press, London, 1921.

Frenkel-Brunswik, E. Differential patterns of social outlook and personality in family and children. In *Childhood in Contemporary Culture*, M. Mead and M. Wolfenstein, editors, p. 369. University of Chicago Press, Chicago, 1955.

Freud, S. Der Familieuroman der Neurotiker. In *Gesellschaff Werke*, vol. 7, p. 50. Imago, London, 1941.

Gil, D. Violence against children. J. Marr. Fam., *33:* 637, 1971.

* Howells, J. G. *Theory and Practice of Family Psychiatry.* Brunner/Mazel, New York, 1971.

Johnson, A. M. Sanction for superego lacunae of adolescents. In *Searchlights on Delinquency*, K. Eissler, editor, p. 225. International Universities Press, New York, 1949.

Keniston, K. *The Uncommitted.* Harcourt, Brace and World, New York, 1965.

Keniston, K. *All Our Children.* Harcourt, Brace, Jovanovich, New York, 1977.

Kluckhohn, F. *Variants in Value Orientations.* Row, Peterson, Evanston, Ill., 1957.

Kuebler-Ross, E. *On Death and Dying.* Macmillan, New York, 1969.

Leighton, A. H. *My Name is Legion.* Basic Books, New York, 1959.

Levinson, D. J. *The Seasons of a Man's Life.* Alfred A. Knopf, New York, 1978.

Lewis, J., Beaver, W. R., Gossett, J. T., and Phillips, V. A. *No Single Thread.* Brunner/Mazel, New York, 1976.

Lidz, R. W., and Lidz, T. The family environment of schizophrenic patients. Am. J. Psychiatry, *106:* 332, 1949.

Lidz, T. *The Family and Human Adaptation.* International Universities Press, New York, 1963.

* Lidz, T. *The Person*, ed. 2. Basic Books, New York, 1976.

Lidz, T., Fleck, S., and Cornelison, A. *Schizophrenia and the Family.* International Universities Press, New York, 1965.

Litman, T. J. The family as a basic unit in health and medical care: A sociological behavioral overview. Soc. Sci. Med., *8:* 495, 1974.

Masters, W., and Johnson, V. *Human Sexual Response.* Little, Brown, and Co., Boston, 1966.

Merton, R. K. *Social Theory and Social Structure.* Free Press of Glencoe, New York, 1949.

Midelfort, C. F. *The Family in Psychotherapy.* Blakiston, New York, 1957.

Minuchin, S. *Families and Family Therapy.* Harvard University Press, Cambridge, Mass., 1974.

Minuchin, S., Montalvo, B., Guerney, B., Rosman, B., and Schumer, F. *Families of the Slums.* Basic Books, New York, 1967.

Morris, G., and Wynne, L. Schizophrenic offspring and parental styles of communication. Psychiatry, *28:* 19, 1965.

Napier, A. Y., and Whitaker, C. A. *The Family Crucible.* Harper & Row, New York, 1978.

Neugarten, B. L. Dynamics of transition of middle age to old age: Adaptation and the life cycle. J. Geriatric Psychiatry, *4:* 71, 1970.

Parsons, T. The incest taboo in relation to social structure and the socialization of the child. Br. J. Sociol., *5:* 101, 1954.

Parsons, T., and Bales, R. F. *Family, Socialization, and Interaction Process.* Free Press of Glencoe, New York, 1955.

Piaget, J. *Six Psychological Studies.* Vintage, New York, 1968.

* Rainwater, L. *Family Design.* Aldine Publishing Co., Chicago, 1965.

Rice, A. K. *The Enterprise and Its Environment.* Tavistock Publications, London, 1964.

Richardson, H. B. *Patients Have Families.* Commonwealth Fund, New York, 1948.

Ridley, C. A., Peterman, D. J., and Avery, A. W. Cohabitation: Does it make for a better marriage? Fam. Coordinator, *27:* 129, 1978.

Riesman, D. *The Lonely Crowd.* Yale University Press, New Haven, 1950.

Rossi, A. S. Transition to parenthood. J. Marr. Fam. Living, *30:* 26, 1968.

Rossi, A. S. Family development in a changing world. Am. J. Psychiatry, *128:* 47, 1972.

Singer, M. T., and Wynne, L. C. Differentiating characteristics of parents of childhood schizophrenics, childhood neurotics, and young adult schizophrenics. Am. J. Psychiatry, *120:* 234, 1963.

Skynner, A. C. R. *Family and Marital Psychotherapy.* Brunner/Mazel, New York, 1976.

Strodtbeck, F. L. The family as a three-person group. Am. Sociol. Rev., *19:* 23, 1954.

Vogel, E., and Bell, N. W. The emotionally disturbed child as the family scapegoat. In *A Modern Introduction to the Family*, N. W. Bell and E. Vogel, editors, p. 1. Free Press of Glencoe, New York, 1960.

von Bertalanffy, L. *General Systems Theory*, ed. 2. Clark University Press, Worcester, Mass., 1968.

Vygotsky, L. S. *Thought and Language.* John Wiley & Sons and M. I. T. Press, New York, 1962.

Weinberg, S. K. *Incest Behavior.* Citadel Press, New York, 1955.

Whorf, B. L. *Language, Thought, and Reality: Selected Writings of Benjamin Lee Whorf.* John Wiley & Sons and M. I. T. Press, New York, 1956.

Winnicott, D. W. *The Family and Individual Development.* Tavistock Publications, London, 1965.

Wynne, L. C., Ryckoff, I., Day, J., and Hirsch, S. Pseudo-mutuality in the family relations of schizophrenics. Psychiatry, *21:* 205, 1958.

Wynne, L. C., and Singer, M. T. Thought disorder and family relations of schizophrenics. II. A classification of forms of thinking. Arch. Gen. Psychiatry, *9:* 199, 1963.

Zimmerman, C. *Family and Civilization.* Harper & Row, New York, 1947.

Zimmerman, C., and Cervantes, L. *Successful American Families.* Pageant Press, New York, 1960.

chapter

6

Science of Human Behavior: Quantitative and Experimental Methods in Psychiatry

6.1 Epidemiology

ERNEST M. GRUENBERG, M.D., D.P.H.

Introduction

Epidemiology is a science that studies the "mass phenomena of disease" (Greenwood, 1935) and analyzes "the distribution and determinants of disease prevalence in man" (MacMahon and Pugh, 1970). By relating the distribution, incidence, and duration of disorders to the physical, biological, and social environment in which people live, epidemiology results in what Gordon (1952) called "medical ecology." Both a basic science and an applied science, epidemiology helps to suggest, define, and evaluate strategies to prevent and control disease and disability.

Psychiatric epidemiology is that part of general epidemiology concerned with the pattern of occurrence of mental disorders, the ecological and human factors that influence those patterns, and the outcomes of attempts to alter them. Psychiatric epidemiology is the scientific basis of public health psychiatry and preventive psychiatry.

What Is Being Prevented?

GENERAL PARESIS INSANITY

New patients with a diagnosis of general paresis coming to hospital care each year can be taken as an index of the number of new cases arising in the population. There were 758 first admissions with general paresis to New York State hospitals in 1911 and 319 first admissions in 1951. If one divides those numbers by the state's population for those years, the drop in the annual first-admission rate was from 8.1 to 2.1 cases per 100,000 population. That decline was the result of technical advances—namely, the treatment of syphilis with arsphenamine (Salvarsan) and later with penicillin and other drugs. Figure 1 shows the sequence in which new therapies were instituted in relation to first-admission rates for syphilitic psychoses. The continual drop after 1939, which preceded the widespread use of penicillin, reflects the increased activity of venereal disease clinics, which systematically treated large numbers of patients with arsphenamine (Parran, 1937) during the long latency period (10 to 20 years) between the primary

and secondary stages and the tertiary stage that includes the general paresis. Today, psychiatrists hardly ever see a case of general paresis psychosis, not because of a decline in the annual incidence of syphilis but because of public health measures to monitor cases and to ensure effective treatment in the early stages of syphilis infection.

PELLAGRA PSYCHOSES

At one time, pellagra psychoses accounted for almost one-tenth of the admissions to mental hospitals in South Carolina (Group for the Advancement of Psychiatry, 1961). During the early 1920's, Goldberger and his associates showed that pellagra was associated with a nutritional deficiency, although they could not identify the specific item missing from the diet. However, their findings were not widely accepted, and no program of prevention was introduced. Yet, pellagra and its associated psychoses declined in frequency in the United States in the subsequent decades. It had already become rare before the exact nature of the nutritional deficiency was elucidated because of changes in eating habits and the nutritional value of food and, after 1939, the rising standard of living (Parran, 1939). Roe (1973) pointed out that pellagra persists in areas of the world where large communities of sharecroppers live on maize or millet. At present, pellagra is endemic in Egypt, India, and South Africa.

DOWN'S SYNDROME

Long before it was shown that Down's syndrome (mongolism) is often caused by an extra chromosome (trisomy 21), most often resulting from nondisjunction in oogenesis, the association of mongolism with the mother's age was so striking that it became evident as the result of clinical observation (Shuttleworth, 1909). Epidemiological studies have shown that other factors apparently associated with mongolism, such as the father's age (Penrose, 1933) and birth order (Penrose, 1934), have no independent effect when the mother's age is held constant.

Figure 2 shows how steeply the likelihood of a child being born a mongoloid rises after his mother reaches age 35. Amniocentesis in the 40-and-over age group is clearly justified, in spite of its dangers, because the risk in that age group is 1 in 50, compared with 1 in 1,000 in the youngest maternal age groups.

Although the preventable causes of trisomies are as yet

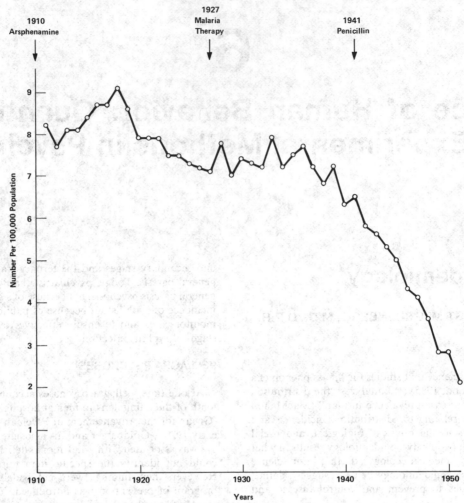

FIGURE 1. First admissions to New York State hospitals with a diagnosis of general paresis, 1911 to 1951. (From New York State Department of Mental Hygiene annual report, 1951.)

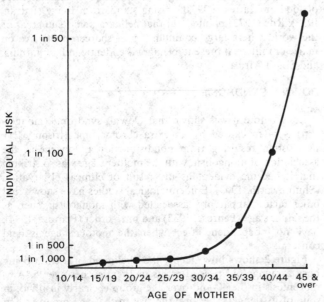

FIGURE 2. Individual risk of bearing a live Down's syndrome baby according to age of mother. (From Collmann, R. D., and Stoller, A. A survey of mongoloid births in Victoria, Australia, 1942–1957. Am. J. Pub. Health. *52:* 813, 1962.)

unknown, abortion after a diagnosis of Down's syndrome made by amniocentesis lowers the proportion of newborns who have that severe form of mental retardation. A similar effect can be obtained if pregnancies over the age of 35 are avoided. The proportion of Down's syndrome among newborns has declined somewhat during this century. There has been a small but consistent decrease in the proportion of newborns who are mongoloid since 1920 (Stein, 1975); that decline is probably attributable to a lowering in the age of pregnancy.

MEASLES AND RUBELLA

For many years, measles was regarded in medical circles as an inevitable, relatively benign disease of childhood. But those who had seen the tragedy of long-term brain damage resulting from measles encephalitis recognized that the measles virus is far from benign. The neurologic sequelae of measles are now well known (Litvak et al., 1943; Ford, 1960), and it has been demonstrated that the number of cases of brain damage after an attack of measles far exceeds the number with clinically obvious encephalitis (Gibbs et al., 1959).

Rubella (German measles) was regarded as an even more minor infection than measles until the Australian ophthalmologist Gregg in 1941 first observed an epidemic of congenital cataracts after an epidemic of German measles and connected the two. Later it was shown that a German measles infection during the first trimester of pregnancy not only produces cataracts in the fetus but many other congenital abnormalities, including a serious form of mental retardation. After an epidemic of German measles in 1963 in New York City, a group of investigators from New York University studied the mental consequences of congenital rubella in children through age 9. Of 210 children evaluated, about one-half had one or more psychiatric disorders, including mental retardation (26 per cent), reactive behavior disorder (18 per cent), cerebral dysfunction (12 per cent), autism (6 per cent), and neurotic behavior disorder (3 per cent) (Chess, et al., 1971; Cooper, 1975).

The annual incidence rate of a disease is the number of new cases beginning in the population during a year, divided by the average number of people in the population during that year. Since the licensure of live virus vaccines for measles in 1963 and for rubella in 1969, the annual incidence rates of reported cases of those diseases have declined substantially in the United States (Modlin et al., 1975; Center for Disease Control, 1978) and the transmission of those two viruses has been interrupted for considerable periods in many communities. In 1978 the goal of total eradication of measles by 1982 became official policy in the Department of Health, Education, and Welfare, and plans are currently underway to develop strategies for interrupting the transmission of the rubella virus as well.

Preventable Chronic Disability

Despite the intensification of scientific and technical energies devoted to understanding and altering the course of mental disorders since World War II, many mental disorders can be neither cured nor prevented. Too often, enthusiasm over new theories and techniques has obscured the reality that many of those suffering from severe mental disorders will be chronically ill for the rest of their lives unless some major new therapeutic discovery is made. Although the means to terminate many of the most serious mental disorders are lacking, psychiatrists know a great deal about how to prevent the most severe symptoms and disabilities associated with chronic psychotic illness.

Two classes of impairment are associated with chronic mental illness. The first class includes those stemming directly from the disease process. Today, various drugs are known to be effective in reducing the severity of such symptoms as depression, panic, paranoia, mania, and confusional states. The second class of impairment consists of disability that is not part of the disease process but is produced by the interaction between the disease, the ill person, and his social environment. The term "social breakdown syndrome" was devised by the American Public Health Association (1962) to describe the syndrome of withdrawal or hostile and angry behavior that seriously interferes with personal and social functioning and that is secondary to a wide range of psychotic disorders.

Social breakdown syndrome has a variable duration, lasting from minutes to decades. More than 90 per cent of all social breakdown syndrome episodes are acute and self-limiting— that is, they terminate within weeks, apparently in the absence of specific medical or psychiatric intervention. But about 10 per cent of social breakdown syndrome episodes become chronic—last for more than 1 year—representing wasted lives and a heavy burden to the disabled person and to his family and the community. Much of that burden can be reduced, however, with appropriate treatment and organization of psychiatric services and community supports. Those methods in-

crease the probability that a social breakdown syndrome episode will terminate in a few weeks or less and so reduce the number of episodes that become chronic (Gruenberg et al., 1969).

The appropriate methods were discovered in connection with the open-hospital movement in Britain in the late 1940's. Macmillan, Bell, and Rees, three young mental hospital directors, tried to give patients with severe mental disorders more humane care (Gruenberg, 1974b). First, doors were unlocked, and physical and chemical restraints were less often used. Second, patients were released early and treated at home. Third, readmission for a short-term stay in the hospital was acceptable at times of crisis.

That approach uses a unified clinical team to take responsibility for a set of patients in both their hospital and their community phases of treatment. A long-term treatment relationship is required, even though great intensity of attention is rarely needed. That long-term relationship permits the organization of a rapid relevant response to the first signs of decompensation. When the current crisis is defined in terms of a specific problem that the clinician will handle with the patient's active participation, a quick resolution of the crisis can be expected. The availability of acute treatment protects the patient's social support systems in times of crisis by helping to keep his family and friends from developing rejecting attitudes toward the patient and his illness. Short-term hospitalization must be available to assert that willingness to share responsibility and sometimes to speed the process of resolving a crisis in the course of the disorder.

The effectiveness of those methods was observed before the widespread use of neuroleptic drugs. Drugs do make hospital reforms and community care easier, but the decline in hospital censuses and the improvements in patient functioning due to what the British call "social treatments" were recorded before the introduction of the phenothiazines in 1955 (Wing, 1978).

The first systematic evaluation of those principles for reducing the frequency of chronic disability among the severely mentally ill took place in Dutchess County, New York, in the early 1960's. A preventive trial design was used in a demonstration service. The preventive trial is a study that determines whether a planned modification of circumstances actually lowers the incidence of a disorder. Although the benefits of community care programs had been observed in England before the advent of phenothiazines, the Dutchess County trial occurred after the phenothiazines were an established form of treatment and after many hospital wards had already been unlocked.

In January 1960 psychiatric services, excluding those for alcoholism and mental retardation, for Dutchess County residents aged 16 to 65 were reorganized to provide the type of unified community care program described above. The program increased the frequency of recovery during the first weeks after onset of an episode of social breakdown syndrome and reduced the annual number of new episodes of chronic social breakdown syndrome by one-half. That reduction represented an annual saving of at least 75 person-years of chronic disability for each 100,000 population getting the unified community care service. But even with the best services that could be provided, about 5 per cent of all social breakdown syndrome episodes did become chronic, and intense rehabilitation programs did not produce high recovery rates in those patients. Recovery rates fall with the square of time. Thus, the ability to provide a rapid relevant response to the first signs of social breakdown syndrome appears to be extremely important. Prevention of chronic disability is easier than rehabilitation.

At about the same time that the concept of chronic social breakdown syndrome was being introduced into the literature, Barton (1961) described institutional neurosis, a syndrome characterized by extreme apathy and passivity, occasionally punctuated by aggressive episodes.

Although fewer than 20 per cent of long-term institutionalized patients develop chronic social breakdown syndrome, institutional neurosis and chronic social breakdown syndrome are often described as equivalent syndromes (Zusman, 1966; Hinsie and Campbell, 1970; Kolb, 1973). That confusion leads to the damaging view that community care alone will prevent all episodes of chronic, secondary disability.

In 1963, of the 50 people with chronic social breakdown syndrome in Dutchess County who had become deteriorated after the community care pattern began, 17 episodes had begun before hospitalization, and 33 originated in an institutional setting. Most of the institution onsets (25 of the 33) fit Barton's description of institutional neurosis, but eight of them and all the community onsets did not. Hence, only about half of the episodes of chronic deterioration can be explained as a response to an institutional environment. About half of the savings in chronic social breakdown syndrome that occurred in Dutchess County when good community care programs were introduced were due to a quick termination of social breakdown syndrome episodes that began outside of hospitals (Gruenberg, 1977a).

Since psychiatrists must provide clinical assistance with only limited treatment techniques—which can, at best, be ameliorative and symptom reducing—and in a state of knowledge that leaves them unable to predict whether any given patient will become chronically disabled, the unified services described here need to be provided to all persons at risk of developing chronic social breakdown syndrome. If one adopts an attitude of acting on one's best hopes, backed up with readiness to act if one's worst fears become justified, patients do less badly than if psychiatrists permit themselves to act on their fears without giving hope a chance.

The above formula may strike the reader as being more like a sentiment extracted from the final paragraph of a minister's sermon than a scientific assertion, but the simple fact is that, regardless of such emotional reverberations, it is the best summary of the principles lying behind the community care of the severely ill mental patients that can be made in the light of today's knowledge, and it is based on empirical data and not on sentiment. In practice, when caring for patients in that type of situation, the clinician would much rather feel capable of being able to make a definitive sort of which patients will do well on release and which patients must be kept in the hospital. Emotionally, it is much harder to accept the suspended judgment that is exercised when each next step in the care of a patient must be taken with a readiness to have it succeed, together with a preparedness to have it fail.

What Is Disappearing? What Is Rising in Frequency?

Some mental disorders are sources of increasing concern, and others are on the wane. In 1961 the Group for the Advancement of Psychiatry reported the consensus of an expert panel of clinicians that general paresis, pellagra psychosis, and conversion hysteria were occurring with significantly decreased frequency. For general paresis and pellagra, one can document a decline in hospital admission for the treatment of those conditions. The conclusion that conversion hysteria has decreased in incidence is based solely on expert opinion, since it is not a condition usually treated by hospitalization.

Many declines are due neither to medical advances nor to public health efforts. Pellagra is disappearing because of improving standards of living. No one knows why the epidemic of von Economo's encephalitis occurred, with its neuropsychiatric sequelae, or why it disappeared. Chlorosis anemia, with its associated episodes of syncope among late adolescent and young adult females, appears to have disappeared along with the fashion for tight corsets. The dancing manias of late medieval times are also a thing of the past (Rosen, 1966).

Just as some psychiatric conditions disappear from populations, new conditions arise. Tardive dyskinesia is a new iatrogenic disorder produced by the long-term administration of phenothiazines. The often irreversible neurological symptoms of tardive dyskinesia can be observed in 30 to 50 per cent of patients who have been treated with those drugs for several years (Crane, 1974). Methadone addiction and psychoses associated with the use of angel dust (PCP) are new conditions in the psychiatric world. Greater foresight and planning can prevent many toxic reactions due to medically prescribed drugs, but clinicians must always expect to have to deal with new mental syndromes caused by newly discovered psychoactive agents. The designation of Munchausen syndrome—the repeated fabrication of illness, usually acute, dramatic, and convincing (Asher, 1951; Barker, 1962)—called attention to the special function that hospitals and doctoring play in the mental lives of some people. With the increasing availability of medical care at no cost to the patient, the capacity for simulating the need for medical and surgical procedures, combined with the determination to be the object of those procedures, has become a more conspicuous phenomenon.

From the above comments one can surmise that statistical data are helpful but not absolutely necessary in making judgments about the changing incidence of certain conditions. Statistical recording of the occurrence of diseases is a relatively recent phenomenon, although one can safely assume that diseases were changing their patterns of occurrence before the collection of data. Lepers, described as common in all the literature written from biblical times on, disappeared from Western Europe, probably because of the great plagues (Sigerist, 1943). The absence of statistical data does not mean that lepers did not exist; it only means that no one counted them systematically.

Even when data are available, interpretation requires awareness of changing styles in the use of diagnostic labels and treatment modalities (Penrose, 1952; Schimel et al., 1973). For example, the United States-United Kingdom diagnostic project on schizophrenia (Cooper et al., 1972) showed that in the United States some people admitted to mental hospitals were receiving diagnoses of schizophrenia who, if admitted to a United Kingdom mental hospital, would have received diagnoses of affective disorder. The widening spectrum of psychiatric treatment facilities in the United States in the past 30 years has extended the clinical horizon and has also led to the use of diagnoses once confined to severe disorders on very mild cases. The interpretation of epidemiological findings requires a judicious appraisal of such changes and how they affect the available data.

Regrettably, such a posture toward epidemiological findings is too infrequently applied, and the literature in the field of mental disorder epidemiology today contains much misinformation and improperly interpreted data. Each publication should be approached in the light of the simple facts that (1) there are many different mental disorders; (2) each mental disorder occurs at some rate in each population and (3) is distributed more or less differently in that population by age, sex, and social class from the distribution for the other mental disorders; and (4) the portion of those sick persons who come into contact with some aspect of the psychiatric services is relatively small. Those four propositions are quite simple. They assume that people were becoming mentally disordered before the profession of psychiatry developed, that in locations where there are no psychiatrists people become mentally ill, and that, if psychiatrists were wiped off the face of the earth, people would continue to become mentally ill. They take it for granted that the development of the profession of medicine in the last few thousand years and the specialty of psychiatry in the last few hundred years has occurred in response to people's distress about becoming ill and the assignment of specialty roles to help such people by making diagnoses and prognoses, prescribing treatment, and conducting research. If those simple ideas can be kept in the forefront of one's thinking, it becomes much safer to expose one's self to clinical publications that, because they ignore one or another of those simple propositions, are likely to be misleading.

Distribution of Mental Disorders

If one examines all members of a community or a random sample of a community and sorts them into sick and well, one is conducting what is called a morbidity survey.

The point prevalence rate of a particular mental disorder is the number of people with that mental disorder at a moment in time divided by the number of people in the population at that time.

VARIATIONS IN PREVALENCE RATES

The prevalence rates of disorders differ according to age, sex, and such social factors as class and marital status. Different mental disorders have different patterns of variation in prevalence rates according to those factors. That fact can be illustrated by contrasting the different shapes of the age-specific prevalence curves for mental deficiency (see Figure 3) and for psychoses (see Figure 4). In contrast to the prevalence rate of mental deficiency, which peaks at around age 14 and drops about 80 per cent in the next 10 years, the prevalence rate of psychotic disorders rises markedly with age.

The rates of mental disorder reported in morbidity surveys

depend both on the diagnostic criteria used to distinguish a case from other people and on how hard the investigators search for those cases. Those two factors vary so much between surveys that they can account for almost all the variations in the findings of different community surveys. Table I classifies the major morbidity surveys that have been conducted to date. The type of community in which the survey is conducted affects to a large extent the methods of case finding used and the nature of questions that can be investigated.

Communities that have been examined directly by psychiatrists (Bremer, 1951; Essen-Möller, 1956; Hagnell, 1966) are relatively small, homogeneous places where the clinician could obtain rapport with the population. In those communities, socioeconomic status does not vary as widely as it does in large metropolitan areas, hence such surveys provide little information on rates by socioeconomic status. By contrast, studies in large cities with great contrasts in socioeconomic status have relied on indirect methods of case ascertainment and diagnostic criteria that are too soft to relate socioeconomic status to standard diagnostic terminology. In the Srole et al. (1962) study conducted in midtown Manhattan in 1953–1954, the investigators reported a higher proportion of psychiatrically impaired persons in the low socioeconomic groups, but which nosologic or diagnostic categories the impaired belonged to is unknown.

The importance of obtaining data that can be classified into standard diagnostic categories cannot be overemphasized, since different mental disorders differ in kind, not merely in degree. For example, although prevalence rates for all mental disorders are higher for women than for men, the age-specific prevalence rates of organic syndromes are higher in men than in women. From the data available, severe mental disorders—organic syndromes and major psychoses—do appear to be more common in the lowest social class than in the higher social classes (Dohrenwend and Dohrenwend, 1969). However, suicide in the age group 20 to 64 is more common among the most affluent than among the poor (Dublin, 1963).

RISING AGE-SPECIFIC POINT PREVALENCE RATES

Medical advances have led to a paradoxical rise in the prevalence rates of certain chronic disorders. The discovery and widespread use of antibiotics resulted in an increase in the average duration of such disorders by curing complications of illness that earlier had been fatal. Since those lifesaving measures were disproportionately needed in people suffering from incurable diseases or disabilities, the increase in life expectancy has been greater for the chronically ill than for the population as a whole (Gruenberg, 1977b).

Since the widespread use of antibiotics began, the life expectancy of mongoloid (Down's syndrome) newborns has been extended much more dramatically than has the life expectancy of newborns as a whole. Carter (1958) estimated that the prevalence rate of mongolism at age 10 years doubled between 1929 and 1949 and doubled again in the next decade, reaching a level of more than 1 per 1,000 by 1958. Prevalence data from Victoria, Australia, in 1961 (Collmann and Stoller, 1962), and Salford, England, in 1974 (Fryers, 1975) show that the trend is continuing. The over-all prevalence rate increased by about 150 per cent between 1961 and 1974. For children aged 5 to 14, the prevalence rate per 1,000 was 1.3 in 1974, almost twice the 1961 rate of 0.7. Of the mongoloid children who survive to age 5 today, 50 per cent live on into their fifties (Øster et al., 1975). Even that situation is changing. As more and more cardiac and gastrointestinal lesions are being surgically corrected and as patients with leukemia and other cancers are receiving life-prolonging treatments, one can expect to see an even greater rise in the prevalence of Down's syndrome.

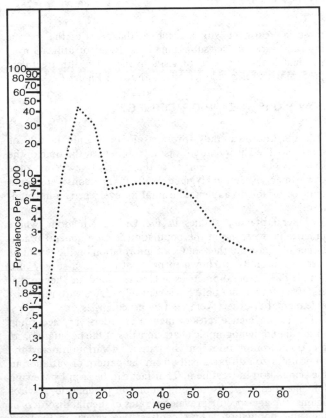

FIGURE 3. Age-specific prevalence rates of mental deficiency in Baltimore's eastern health district. (From Lemkau, P., Tietze, C., and Cooper, M. Mental hygiene problems in an urban district. Ment. Hyg., 25: 624, 1941.)

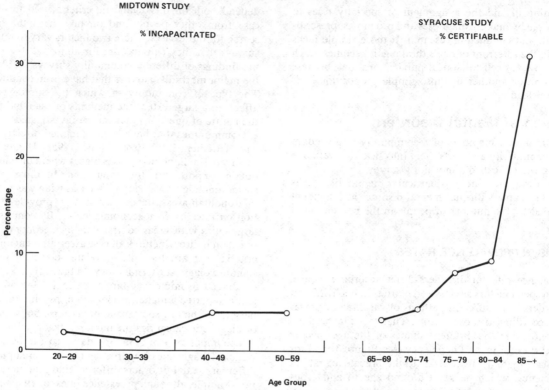

FIGURE 4. Age-specific prevalence rates of severe (psychotic) mental disorder—the incapacitated group in midtown Manhattan in 1954 (data from Srole, L., Langner, T. S., Michael, S. T., Opler, M. K., and Rennie, T. A. C. *Mental Health in the Metropolis*, vol. 1, *The Midtown Manhattan Study*. McGraw-Hill, New York, 1962) and people classed as certifiable to a mental hospital in Syracuse in 1952 (data from New York State Department of Mental Hygiene. *A Mental Health Survey of Older People*. State Hospitals Press, Utica, 1960).

The same medical advances are also extending chronic mental illness at the other end of life. Hagnell's longitudinal data on an entire Swedish community showed that between 1947 and 1957 the prevalence of senile dementia rose from 3.2 per cent to 5.7 per cent in women and from 2.3 per cent to 4.9 per cent in men more than 60 years old (Gruenberg and Hagnell, 1979). Figure 5, which shows the tops of two population pyramids, depicts the rising age-specific and sex-specific prevalence rates of senile dementia in the years after 1947–1949.

No evidence suggests that the age-specific incidence rates of senile dementia are either falling or rising. Rather, the increased prevalence is caused by a doubling in the average duration of senile dementia episodes. Because prevalence equals incidence times average duration, when the duration of a condition is increased, the prevalence of that condition also increases, even when the incidence rate remains unchanged. In Hagnell's population, all 24 of the people found to have senile dementia in 1947 were dead by 1953; but, of the 48 cases in 1957, five were still alive in 1967. Although medical advances and the changing age structure of the population have resulted in a greater proportion of elderly in the population as a whole, the lives of people with senile dementia have been extended longer than have the lives of people in the age groups at risk for developing that condition.

Use of Psychiatric Services

Epidemiologists have long known that the cases in clinical care represent something like the tip of an iceberg and that below the clinical horizon are several times as many cases that are not visible to the clinical facilities. Figure 6 shows that the two subpopulations—those with a specific mental disorder and those in treatment with a recorded diagnosis of the specific disorder—are distinct subpopulations. Rates of utilization of psychiatric facilities and of visits to mental health treatment professionals refer only to cells A and B in Figure 6.

HOW BIG IS THE TIP OF ICEBERG?

In the Midtown study (Srole et al., 1962) only 1 in 20 of those classified as impaired was in treatment at the time of the survey. In the Syracuse survey of the elderly (New York State Department of Mental Hygiene, 1960), four persons were found to be certifiable to a mental hospital for every person hospitalized.

General practice studies in the United Kingdom, where practically everyone in the population is on a general practitioner's list, are another source of information on the extent of mental morbidity unknown to psychiatrists. In a survey of a sample of 12 general practices in Greater London, Shepherd et al. (1966) found that only 5 per cent of patients with recognizable mental disorders were seen by psychiatrists.

Just as prevalence rates of mental disorders vary according to social and demographic characteristics of the population, so, too, do utilization rates; but the pattern of variation below the clinical horizon differs greatly from the pattern of variation in the population in treatment. That fact can be seen by viewing the age-specific rates of utilization of psychiatric services against the age-specific prevalence rates of mental disorders in the same population. Those contrasts are shown in Figure 7 with data from Hagnell's (1966) morbidity survey of an entire Swedish population and in Figure 8 from the Midtown Manhattan survey (Srole et al., 1962).

TABLE I

Mental Disorder Prevalence Rates per 1,000

Author	Site and Date	Total Mental Disorders	Psychoses	Schizo-phrenia	Affective Psychoses	Neuroses	Personality Disorders	Mental Retardation	Impaired	Comments
Treated cases plus identified through nonmedical records or key informants										
Cohen, Fairbank	Eastern Health District, 1933	44.5	8.18 (age over 15)							After Plunkett and Gordon table.
Lemkau et al.	Eastern Health District, 1936	60.5	6.6			3.10	4.61*			Age-adjusted rates. Population age over 10.
Same plus intensive survey of subsample population										
Rosanoff	Nassau County, 1916	13.74	2.39* (functional)			2.0		5.46		Intensively surveyed area's total mental disorder rate: 36.4.
Roth, Luton	Tennessee, 1938	69.4	6.32*	1.73*	1.65*	4.0*	37.8*	8.20*		Intensively surveyed area's total mental disorder rate: 123.7.
Lin	Formosa, 1946–48	10.8	3.8	2.1	0.7	1.2	0.5	3.4		Persons with more than one symptom pattern were counted for each, and diagnoses' specific rates exceed total rate.
Leighton	Bristol, 1952	690	10			570	290	110	420	
Surveys of total populations										
Bremer	Norway fishing village, 1939–1944	232.4	35.9			58.0	93.5	55.6	193.6 (chronic)	
Essen-Möller	Lundby, Sweden, 1947	Evident and probable 179.0 Conceivably ill 180.	19.5*	7	10.2*	58.8*	Major 64* Minor 210*	9.8		Lifetime prevalence rates calculated on total population.
Hagnell	Lundby, Sweden, 1957		17			131		12		Lifetime prevalence rates.
Eaton, Weil	Hutterites, 1950	46.5*	12.4*	2.1	9.3	16*		12*		Base population 15 and over. Lifetime prevalence.
Surveys of probability sample populations										
Leighton	Stirling County, 1948–50	570							240	Population over 18.
Rennie, Srole	Midtown Manhattan, 1953–54	815							234	Interviewed population's age: 20–59.

* Author's calculation.

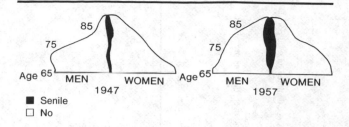

FIGURE 5. Age-specific and sex-specific prevalence of senile dementia, 1947 and 1957 in Lundby, Sweden. (From Gruenberg, E. M., and Hagnell, O. The rising prevalence of chronic brain syndrome in the elderly. In *Society, Stress, and Disease: Aging and Old Age,* L. Levi and A. R. Kagan, editors. Oxford University Press, New York, 1980.)

		Specific Mental Disorder Present	
		Yes	No
In Treatment for Specific Mental Disorder	Yes	A	B
	No	C	D
			N = A + B + C + D

FIGURE 6. Four-fold table to distribute *N* people according to whether they have a specific mental disorder and whether they are in treatment for that disorder at one point in time.

The variations in utilization rates by age shown in Figures 7 and 8 illustrate a fundamental principle: The proportion of young people in treatment is different from the proportion of middle-aged and elderly people in treatment, and those variations are quite different from the proportion of young, middle-aged, and elderly people who have mental disorders unrecognized by the treatment system. It is important to note the different shapes of the iceberg below and above the clinical horizon. The rate of being in treatment peaks in the middle years of life and tapers off and approaches nearly zero in the very old. But in the population of ill people outside of treatment, it is precisely in the oldest age groups that the most frequent manifestations of mental disorder can be found. Hence, variations in utilization rates are a poor index of variations in occurrence rates of mental disorders.

FACTORS THAT AFFECT UTILIZATION

Many studies of utilization rates have been done to understand service systems and their ability to meet the needs of defined populations. One of the earliest findings from such studies was Jarvis's law of distance. Jarvis (1866) showed that a community's rate of first admissions to a mental hospital is inversely proportional to the miles between the community and the hospital serving it. Even though the frequency of mental disorders is no lower in towns farther from the hospital, Jarvis showed that one hospital could not provide services equally to all communities in a single state. In the current literature such objective measures as travel time are rarely reported, even though the law of distance still has an effect on utilization rates not only of psychiatric facilities but of general hospitals and private practices as well. Today's concerns over accessibility and availability are reflected in National Institutes of Health policy that each catchment area of 100,000 should have a

comprehensive community mental health center. More than 2,000 community mental health centers would be required to meet that optimal availability of services. As of July 1975, however, the National Institute of Mental Health had awarded funds to only 603 comprehensive community mental health centers, of which 507 were in operation (Comptroller General of the United States, 1977).

Utilization rates are highly dependent on and sensitive to social and administrative policies. That fact can be illustrated by the enormous changes in the use of state mental hospitals in the past 20 years. From 1946 to 1955 the resident patient population in public mental hospitals was growing steadily at almost a constant rate of 2 per cent a year (Kramer et al., 1972). Figure 9 shows that the decline in the number of residents that began in 1955 accelerated rapidly after the mid-1960's. Because that dramatic decline coincided with federal legislation that stimulated the development of comprehensive community mental health centers and other community treatment programs, mental health personnel are accustomed to

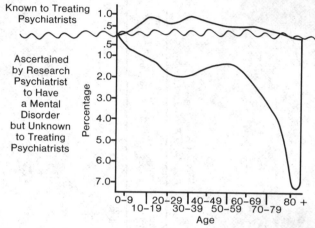

FIGURE 7. Age-specific prevalence rates (average of annual incidence rates, 1947–1957) of treated and untreated mental disorder, Lundby, Sweden. (From Hagnell, O. *A Prospective Study of the Incidence of Mental Disorder.* Svenska Bokförlaget, Norstedts, Lund, 1966.)

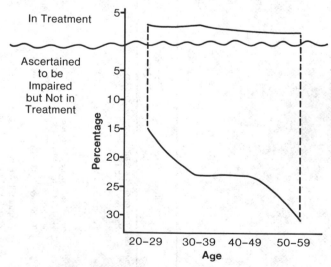

FIGURE 8. Age-specific prevalence rates of treated and untreated mental impairment, midtown Manhattan in 1954. (From Srole, L., Langner, T. S., Michael, S. T., Opler, M. K., and Rennie, T. A. C. *Mental Health in the Metropolis,* vol. 1, *The Midtown Manhattan Study.* McGraw-Hill, New York, 1962.)

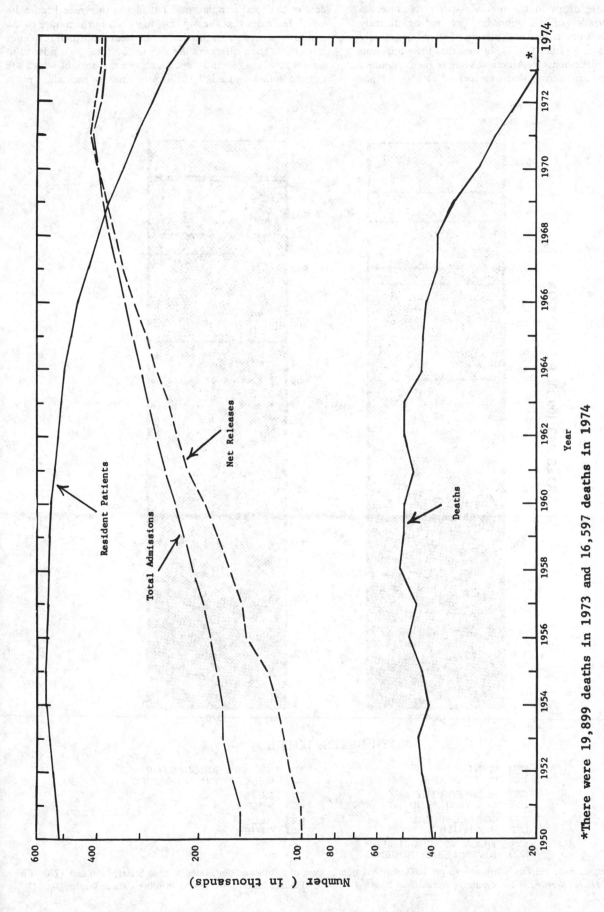

FIGURE 9. Number of resident patients, total admissions, net releases, and deaths, state and county mental hospitals, United States, 1950 to 1974. (From Kramer, M. *Psychiatric Services and the Changing Institutional Scene, 1950–1985*. United States Government Printing Office, Washington, D. C., 1977.)

*There were 19,899 deaths in 1973 and 16,597 deaths in 1974

pointing to those drops in the mental hospital censuses as though the utilization of institutions had declined significantly after 1955. That is not an accurate picture of what has actually been taking place. Kramer (1977) showed that the utilization of institutional placements by Americans has, in fact, remained remarkably constant during that time period at about 1 per cent of the total population. That fact is shown in Figure 10, which indicates that the big shift has been in the nature of the institutions used, with the decline in mental hospital residence rates more than offset by the rise in the rates of residence in homes for the aged and dependent, the majority of which are nursing homes. Indeed, the utilization rates for mental hospitals

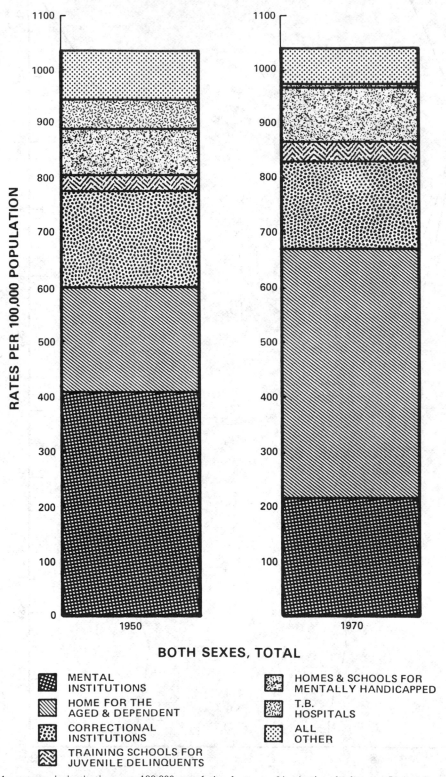

FIGURE 10. Distribution by persons in institutions per 100,000 population by type of institution, both sexes, United States, 1950 and 1970. (From Kramer, M. *Psychiatric Services in the Changing Institutional Scene, 1950–1985.* United States Government Printing Office, Washington, D. C., 1977.)

and homes for the aged and dependent combined rose from 600 per 100,000 in 1950 to more than 670 per 100,000 in 1970.

Hence, the drop in mental hospital censuses can be largely attributed to a shift in responsibility from mental hospitals to nursing homes after the 1966 amendments to the Social Security Act provided federal funds to pay for nursing home care. Because of those amendments, many mental hospitals made their services less available to the elderly and transferred many of the elderly they had to nursing homes. The use of the currently fashionable term "deinstitutionalization" to refer to the decline in the mental hospital census ignores the available facts on utilization rates, which show not a decline in institutionalization but a shift in locus from one type of long-term institution to another.

Figure 11 shows that rates of admission of the elderly to mental hospitals have gone through a remarkable transformation in the past century. It is interesting to note that the age-specific curve for 1885 parallels that for 1972. There has been a shift in the locus of care for the elderly mentally ill from the community to the state hospital and then to homes for the aged, mainly nursing homes.

Utilization rates are also influenced by treatment techniques and practices. Utilization rates of tuberculosis hospitals and infectious disease hospitals fell rapidly to almost zero between World War I and World War II as effective treatments and immunization techniques reduced the risk of cross-infection and hence the need for quarantine and isolation.

To some extent, the discovery and widespread application of chlorpromazine (Thorazine) and other psychotropic drugs that provide symptomatic relief for many patients has eliminated the need for inpatient care for many episodes of acute mental disorder. Simultaneously and even antedating the discovery of chlorpromazine, some mental hospital directors rediscovered the value of nonrestraint, formerly called moral treatment, for acute psychotic patients. Nonrestraint, combined with the principles of the open-hospital movement discussed earlier, reduced the use of long-term hospitalization (Gruenberg, 1974b).

Utilization rates are not solely a function of accessibility, administrative policies, and treatment practices. Utilization rates are also heavily influenced by the attitudes of people who become ill—by whether they define their problem as an illness and themselves as needing medical help and which treatment

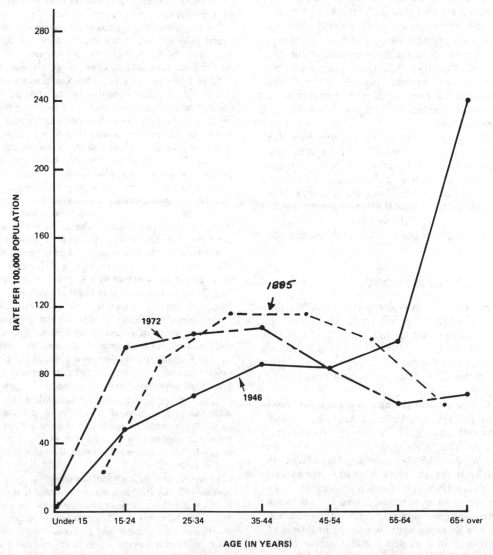

FIGURE 11. First admission rates per 100,000 population by age to state and county mental hospitals, Massachusetts, 1885 (data from Goldhamer, H., and Marshall, A. W. *Psychosis and Civilization.* Free Press of Glencoe, New York, 1949), and United States, 1946 and 1972 (data from Kramer, M. *Psychiatric Services and the Changing Institutional Scene, 1950–1985.* United States Government Printing Office, Washington, D. C., 1977).

settings they see as being suitable for providing the help they need. Those influences on utilization arise as much from the people close to the ill person—family, friends, and helping agencies—as from the ill person himself. Community authorities, such as police and school officials, similarly influence utilization rates.

Interrelated with the attitudes and practices of people who become ill and of their relatives and community authorities is the issue of stigma associated with a formal diagnosis of a mental disorder or with admission to a mental hospital. The extreme degree of stigma formerly attached to the person who accepted a patient role in psychiatry is hard for today's beginning practitioner to appreciate. Some notion of the stigma can still be seen in the extent to which families refuse to admit a severely handicapped child to a school for the retarded and the willingness of families to make great financial sacrifices to avoid the use of a state facility. But those currently observable behaviors should be seen as the last breath of what several decades ago was an extraordinary fear of mental disorders and of psychiatrists. Good objective data are not available, but much anecdotal evidence and many attitude surveys (Rabkin, 1974) bear out the increasing willingness of people to accept their mental illness and the decreasing rejection of the mentally ill by society. An indication that that is so comes from recent public statements made by prominent government leaders and their family members about their own experiences with psychiatric treatment, despite the notoriety surrounding the Eagleton affair in 1972. On the other hand, the exposés regarding the plight of former mental hospital patients dumped into hostile communities indicate how much more remains to be done regarding societal acceptance of responsibility for the mentally ill (Bachrach, 1976).

The current trend to mainstream psychiatric care, by which is meant a tendency to assign responsibility for diagnosis and treatment to nonpsychiatric health providers, will probably have a significant effect on societal attitudes toward mental illness. General practice studies in the United Kingdom (Shepherd et al., 1966) and general medical practice studies in the United States (Regier et al., 1978) showed that the majority of psychiatric diagnoses and prescriptions are already being made by nonpsychiatrists.

Ecology and Medical Ecology

The term "ecology" had a great vogue in the late 1960's and early 1970's, the period when the movement for the protection of the environment was first getting under way. Some of the national and international enthusiasm for the concept is reflected in a large amount of psychiatric literature, particularly literature relating to the distribution of mental disorders in American communities.

Although derived from ancient Greek roots, the term "ecology" was coined by the German biologist Ernst Haeckel in essays that tried to elaborate the evolutionary process after Darwin's publication of the *Origin of the Species* in 1859. The term was designed to describe the natural phenomenon in which plants and animals interact with one another in a natural habitat on the earth's surface and form a system of living organisms. That concept of systems of interaction between different species and their mutual interaction with the physical environment leads to a dynamic approach to the problems of living organisms. It was in that sense that Gordon (1952) described epidemiology as producing a kind of medical ecology in which human disease is studied in relationship to all the circumstances of human life. For example, does disease make

people poor, or does poverty lead to disease? That is an old question, and any experienced epidemiologist or one familiar with the literature will answer "Yes." There are abundant examples of diseases that are commoner among the poor than among the wealthier classes, and there are abundant examples of chronic debilitating diseases' incurring high costs for care that drive families into poverty. The willingness to look at that kind of dynamic interaction gives the concept of ecology its usefulness.

There are several conceptions of human ecology. They were best described by H. Warren Dunham (1966), who made distinguished contributions to the understanding of the social ecology of mental hospital admission rates for different mental disorders in the 1930's.

First, human ecology, from the perspective of medicine, tended to become medical ecology which emphasized the environmental relationships to disease and health of human beings. Thus, from this perspective, health was viewed as the maintenance of a delicate balance between a disease agent, organism, and the environment while disease results when this balance is shattered. Medical ecology developed a close affinity with epidemiological study of various diseases where the attempt was made to develop etiological hypotheses from any one of a number of theoretical frameworks to explain the concentration of a given disease in a particular environmental setting.

Second, human ecology has also been regarded as coterminous with human geography which was the discipline concerned with examining the role of climate, topography, and vegetation in relation to human behavior and various kinds of social organization.

Third, human ecology, in the hands of the sociologist, was developed as a discipline which focused upon the study of the settling, growth, and decline of human communities. In sociology, Robert Park, borrowing certain concepts from plant and animal ecologists, attempted to show their relevance to human society and, as in the case of animal and plant societies, to point to the consequences for human beings resulting from ecological processes. Consequently, human ecology became a study of man within a social system, locating his position within that system and examining his position in relation to the positions occupied by others in the system.

The difficulty with the classical statement of human ecological theory is that it posits man as being willy-nilly at the mercy of the inevitable and mechanical operation of ecological processes at the symbiotic level. The theory provided no postulate that would view man as an active cultural agent attempting to shape and remold the type of sociocultural environment that has evolved for and by him through time. Thus, what is natural in terms of biological ecology ceases to be completely natural, at least in a biological sense, when shifted to the human level. This is aptly noted by the hypothesis of drift as contrasted to the hypothesis of voluntary segregation both of which have been utilized to explain the differential distribution of schizophrenic rates in an urban setting. In the former hypothesis the person is pictured as rudderless and at the mercy of the impersonal ecological processes. The latter hypothesis depicts the person as actively searching and seeking the kind of environment that will maximize his chances for maintenance and survival. These two hypotheses . . . illustrate quite clearly the original conception of human ecology and the later difficulty it has encountered as a theoretical model for depicting man's involvement with his environment in order to explain both his maladaptations and adaptations.

However, this difficulty at the outset was not the concern of the human ecologist. Rather, it was only natural that within this theoretical model the many varieties of human behavior could be examined to determine the extent that they encouraged or discouraged the possibility of man's adjustment and survival. Within the framework many kinds of deviant behaviors which are evaluated as disruptive of the social order have been examined. It was only natural that the various diseases which man acquires, either through heredity or environment, should also be examined in relation to the ecological order. This was particularly true with respect to the various kinds of mental illnesses because here were instances of mental aberrations and distorted behaviors which, at first glance, almost seemed to grow out of the kinds of experiences in interpersonal relations that man had in selected subcultural environments.

What we have said already should indicate clearly the relationship between human and medical ecology. The human ecologist attempts a study of man in relation to his total environment, trying to ferret out those generalizations that explain the ease and difficulty of his adjustments and that explain the kinds of communities man develops in relation to the total conditions that surround them. There are, of course, difficulties in studying man from this perspective because man is both a highly mobile and a culture-bearing animal. In fact, from the viewpoint of human evolution it is perhaps worth noting that in man's earliest period the role of geographical factors in influencing and shaping culture were most marked. But as human culture has evolved, especially in relation to the development of technology, it has become so complex and overpowering that it becomes the dominant influence in shaping man's environmental setting. Medical ecology, as a specialized field of human ecology, focuses upon all classes of environmental factors as they cause, influence, and modify the development and spread of diseases in human societies.

That is by far the most lucid exposition of the human ecology or social ecology frame of reference. Dunham's (1966) exposition and critique point to the potential value of the social ecology model and to its tendency toward a one-sided, mechanistic approach, which sees human beings as victims of their social environment without understanding their role as its maker. The great value of that kind of perspective is that it opens our eyes to the dynamic intercomplexity of organisms with one another and of the two-way traffic of interaction. The ecological perspective does not say which flow of traffic is the most important or where intervention will be most helpful but is a necessary attitude toward complexity if one is to make rational choices.

Some ecologists have said that the basic lesson of ecology with respect to action is: "You can never do just one thing." A complex system is modified in manifold ways, even though one has undertaken to modify it in only one way. Many intended actions have unintended consequences that are unknown to the actor who does not understand the interaction processes with which he has interfered. A preoccupation with that issue can lead to passivity and a fear of taking any action at all. That attitude is sometimes expressed in the environmentalist movement when it automatically opposes any new industry or highway, disregarding the benefits and focusing only on the disruption of natural processes that is likely to ensue. When carried to an extreme, it becomes a worship of nature and is itself a choice.

The danger of discussions labeled "ecological" is that the lack of precision and exactness regarding the particular problem being discussed and the particular alternative solutions creates an atmosphere in which vague or even misguided propositions can be given the appearance of clear-headed, good-hearted rationality. For example, in a survey on sociocultural roots of mental disorders, Schwab and Schwab (1978) cited Alexander Leighton's description of an epidemic of typhus investigated by the German pathologist and founder of social medicine, Rudolf Virchow. Leighton's (1967) point was that Virchow recognized that the epidemic could be brought under control by eliminating poverty, overcrowding and lack of adequate food, even though the infectious agent had not yet been identified. Leighton (1967) wrote:

In putting his finger on the social conditions he was singling out for attention what he considered the most salient cause ... one that

is critical in terms of some particular orientation. In most of our concerns in preventive psychiatry this will be for the years to come the causes about which something can be done to improve health.

Although Leighton did not use the term "ecology" to describe that approach, it is the mechanistic variety of ecology that reduces the analysis of disease processes to a one-sided view of humans as only victims of social environment and ignores their technical achievements and ability to master natural processes. Leighton's description of what Virchow found and believed is correct, but not long afterward it became clear that the key factor was filth and that the typhus organism was carried by the body louse. Once that was understood, delousing programs were substituted for social change as a way to control that particular dread disease.

Epidemiology of the Future

As Frost wrote (Maxcy, 1941):

At any given time epidemiology is something more than the total of its established facts. It includes their orderly arrangement into chains of inference which extend more or less beyond the bound of direct observation. Such of those chains as are well and truly laid guide investigation to the facts of the future; those that are ill made fetter progress.

MORBIDITY SURVEY TECHNOLOGY

During the last decade major developments have been made in the techniques used to ascertain cases of mental disorders. Some of those developments have emerged from epidemiological questions.

The International Pilot Study of Schizophrenia (World Health Organization, 1975) raised the question of whether the diagnosis of schizophrenia was being used in a similar fashion in different societies and different cultures in nations in different stages of industrialization. Were the same kinds of cases being identified? Do they have the same course? That study was initiated by the World Health Organization in 1963 and mobilized research centers in nine countries throughout the world. Leading psychiatrists undertook to conduct comparable studies of schizophrenia in their own centers.

One aspect of that innovation in psychiatric collaboration was the development of a standardized form for gathering information on the mental status examination. That process became highly rationalized under the direction of John Wing of the Institute of Psychiatry at the Maudsley Hospital in London. His present state examination form has gone through nine editions (Wing et al., 1974).

In addition, the International Pilot Study of Schizophrenia took advantage of two new technical advances to achieve concensus observations by psychiatrists working in the different centers. One was the videotape recording of examinations, which was used extensively to unravel differences in linguistic use and in perceptions of different psychiatrists. The other crucial new technique was the jet airplane, which made it possible to repeatedly move groups of psychiatrists together to examine the same subjects on location and then reconcile their differences in the perception and recording of observations. Although the present state examination is not universally used in training psychiatrists throughout the world, there is a worldwide movement to use that method to improve the consistency and the reliability of the examinations conducted by psychiatrists in training. That development of a refined standardization of the psychiatrist's mental state examination, which emerged out of a need for epidemiological data, illustrates the interaction between epidemiological research on the one hand and the development of clinical teaching methods on the other.

A second group of data-gathering tools, which at present are having a large effect on psychiatric nosology and are beginning to be used in field studies on the distribution of mental disorders, developed out of clinical trials of psychopharmacological discoveries. The World Health Organization collaborators wished to find a concensus on the criteria they would use to distinguish patients that they would all regard as schizophrenics out of the heterogeneous stream of patients coming to their widely scattered clinical centers. In contrast, the clinical trials of new psychotropic medications were aimed at developing objectified methods of appraising the courses of two streams of patients who, because of random assignment, differed only in the treatment they were receiving. Therefore, such techniques as the schedule for affective disorders and schizophrenia (Spitzer and Endicott, 1973) were developed to obtain comparable information on both streams of patients in terms of the course of the key symptoms that had been used to select them for clinical trials. Since the two problems are different, it is not surprising that the solutions are different. In morbidity surveys of the future, the problem will be which of those approaches to use.

In some situations morbidity surveys will use the clinically trained observer who moves from the clinical setting into organized interaction with the general population. That is the type of method Essen-Möller (1956) and his colleagues used to survey Lundby in 1947 and which his successor, Hagnell has used to follow up, over a 25-year period, the development of mental disorders in that population. Such investigations can be greatly strengthened by taking advantage of the present state examination standardization of the interview and the interview record. In the United States clinically trained observers have rarely interacted directly with the population being studied in the conduct of morbidity surveys as did Roth and Luton (1943) in Tennessee. An intermediate method has more often been used in which the elements of information to be gathered were specified by the clinically trained investigators and selected interviewers were specially trained to gather particular classes of information, even though they had not been completely trained as clinicians. Subsequently, the clinicians reviewed the information gathered and formed judgments about the subjects' mental status (New York State Department of Mental Hygiene, 1960; Gruenberg et al., 1962; Srole et al., 1962; Leighton et al., 1963).

Neither of those two methods seems likely to be applied widely in the United States in the near future. Rather, in the next few years the objectified methods of appraisal will be used on a large scale in a series of National Institute of Mental Health-funded epidemiological catchment area surveys. The first such survey will be conducted in New Haven by Meyer, Weissman, and Tischler. They, in conjunction with the staff at the center for epidemiological studies, will develop a new structured schedule interview to be called the diagnostic interview schedule. That schedule will be an elaboration of the schedule for affective disorders and schizophrenia and will result in a new structured scheduled questionnaire for administration by lay interviewers to carefully sampled segments of populations. As yet, work on that type of interview schedule has not produced good data on the validation of the method. Such validation will require interviews of the subjects screened by the scheduled structured questionnaire and of people who are not patients but who are examined carefully by clinically trained psychiatrists. Another weakness of the type of scheduled structured interview so far developed is a lack of precision

regarding the identification and the classification of mental retardation and brain syndromes. However, mental retardation ascertainment technology is highly developed around the elements of the intelligence tests, and short versions, if refined for that particular purpose, could be used in surveys of adult populations. The identification of dementias can be greatly facilitated by use of the minimental status examination developed by Folstein and McHugh (1975). In addition, promising work with the portable tachistoscope may make field recognition of deliriums possible in the near future.

Numerous publications of epidemiological catchment area data will report prevalence rates of specific mental disorders during the next few years. But the reader should be careful to check for the evidence of validation and for evidence that the populations surveyed were large enough to produce usable measurements of prevalence rates. The attempt to make differential diagnoses on the basis of a structured scheduled questionnaire will remain debatable until adequate validation studies are made.

ESTIMATION OF SERVICE NEEDS

The planning of health services has always been based on epidemiological assumptions. There is no point in opening a general hospital in a city unless one is prepared to assume that people are sick and in need of the services it can provide. There is no point in opening a mental health center unless one assumes that a population is in need of its services. The fact that administrative and policy actions regarding the development of services are built on assumptions about the distribution of disorders in a population that could be benefited by the treatments to be offered does not mean that those assumptions are always grounded on good data. On the contrary, decision makers rarely have the appropriate, precise data. Very often, the argument turns on the simple fact that people are clamoring for a service that is not available. Maldistribution of services is used as an argument for making them available on a more even basis, as it was in Jarvis's (1866) work, discussed earlier. In the decade after World War II, there was pressure for more outpatient clinics and child guidance clinics. It was easy to show, for example, that areas in New York State had a full outpatient clinic team per 50,000 population and that those clinics had waiting lists 3 to 6 months long. That led to the argument that populations with no such clinics at all would show a similar demand once the services were made available. That is quite a different kind of reasoning from actually counting the number of people who could benefit from the service and more different still from actually counting the number of people who have specific illnesses.

Not everybody who has a recognizable mental disorder can benefit from an existing treatment technique. For example, many people who wear glasses to correct errors of refraction already have as much correction as anyone knows how to give them. But when a new technique is developed that can better correct certain kinds of visual defects than can present eyeglasses, some people will be benefited. Hence, the need for the availability of diagnostic and treatment services depends on the techniques that the treatment services can offer.

The most dramatic recent shifts in psychiatric techniques of treatment have been the introduction of antidepressive and antianxiety medications and the behavioral therapies for handicapping symptom formations. None of those techniques are truly curative; they are only palliative. But they are valuable, and, whenever a valuable treatment technique comes into existence, previous estimates of need have to be reevaluated. Although the new treatment technique does not always increase the number of people who will be suitable for it, it may eliminate an earlier, more cumbersome treatment technique. A dramatic example of that result occurred when the antimicrobial drugs practically eliminated mastoid surgery, which had been a subspecialty of surgery of growing importance up until that time. Psychiatry is currently going through a switch in technical skills that has apparently reduced the need for inpatient beds. The introduction of antihypertensive medications made it important to locate people in the early stages of hypertension. The effects on the frequency of death from stroke are already visible. The same drugs have probably also lowered the frequency of multiinfarct dementia.

The current period is one of health service planning on a large scale in the United States. One must be careful not to think that the long-term planning of health services can be highly rationalized. One can, at best, define the steps to take during the next few years. But a dramatic new finding, a dramatic new effective treatment, or even, more, a dramatic new preventive technique can totally transform the service needs of a population in a short period of time. Such major advances in preventive and treatment techniques are inherently unpredictable today; there is no soundly developed way to predict mankind's next important discovery.

CARE PATTERNS FOR THE LONG-TERM MENTAL PATIENT

The current crisis in the organization of services for people with mental disorders is in a highly fluid state. The increasing allowances by Blue Cross and Blue Shield for general hospital psychiatric care, the extension of financing mechanisms through Medicaid and Medicare, the integration of psychiatric services into health maintenance organizations, and the simultaneous extension of community support systems for the former mental hospital patient—all will interact with one another in the near future to produce a wide variety of service systems. Patterns of services that can be expected to emerge from the transition period of psychiatric service reorganization will provide opportunities for future investigations concerning (1) the potentiality for preventing chronic social breakdown syndrome and (2) the consequences of community neglect of long-term mental patients.

Prevention of chronic social breakdown syndrome. The potentiality for unified clinical services working in a constructive way to preserve the personal and social functioning of people with chronic mental disorders may develop in some general hospital psychiatric units. But that will occur only if (1) the psychiatric unit can overcome the general hospital's resistance to providing treatment for all comers in unlocked wards; (2) the general hospital can learn how to treat psychiatric patients with respect and with the minimum use of drugs, physical restraints, and involuntary certificates; and (3) the general hospital inpatient unit can integrate its staff with its own outpatient service and with community and family social support systems for the patients (Gruenberg, 1972).

Some general hospital psychiatric services may achieve such a good pattern of services, but many will not. That condition will offer an opportunity to restudy the effectiveness of the unified clinical team closely integrated with a pattern of preserving the patient's relationships with his normal environment—in contrast to less humane, more isolated and fragmented services—in lowering the incidence of chronic social breakdown syndrome.

Such a unified clinical service does not avoid using the hospital as part of its treatment equipment. At present, it is helpful to group the indications for hospital treatment under seven headings (Gruenberg, 1974a).

Safety. This indication is the legal justification for involuntary commitments. It is a good indication for admitting a patient to the hospital when no other safe location for care exists. Because most patients with this indication today will accept hospitalization voluntarily if a little work is done to reduce their fear of the hospital and because an excessive preoccupation with safety can be harmful to patients, at least one of the other six benefits can and should be emphasized in any decision to hospitalize a patient.

Diagnosis. Certain diagnostic procedures, some of which require close observation on a 24-hour basis, are done more safely in a hospital than outside. Psychiatric diagnosis can also be hastened by a short-term hospital admission. Diagnosis includes an appraisal of the patient's condition and familiarization with the patient's personal characteristics. Rapidity in appraising the patient accelerates the speed with which the optimal treatment plan is formulated.

Treatment. As with diagnosis, the use of the hospital for treatment is indicated to facilitate a rapid, relevant response to the presenting crisis. Treatments such as electroconvulsive therapy are safer and the speed with which higher doses of dangerous drugs can be safely achieved is greater in hospital than out. Retraining is also a form of treatment. Incontinence, noisiness, temper tantrums, and self-neglect are troublesome symptoms, and the hospital can provide intensive retraining programs unequaled outside.

Asylum. A protective, nurturing environment isolated from the patient's life situation provides a retreat from life's stresses when they become overwhelming. In the hospital the patient has the opportunity to remobilize his resources and assets in a context away from needs for immediate responses to demands that overwhelm him.

Burden sharing. The tendency to deteriorate in personal and social functioning is greatly reduced if the patient's fulfillment of ordinary living roles is systematically preserved. That is best facilitated by maintaining patients in their community lives as much as possible. However, modern community care always places some burden on families or neighbors, who are generally willing to accept the trouble. But if the burden becomes too prolonged or is too limiting on the lives of other household members, their attitudes toward the patient are likely to become more negative. Once rejection toward the patient occurs, it is almost impossible to reverse. If the hospital defines its relationship as one of burden sharing, it can make itself available to provide relief admissions for short periods and, hence, prevent rejection by families and friends.

Insight. If the patient is to use the clinician's help constructively, he must accept the patient role. A brief hospitalization can sometimes help resistant patients accept their need for help more quickly than does any other method. The switch from the normal person overwhelmed by insoluble conflicts and life problems to the patient on whom altered expectations are placed can, in itself, reduce tension sufficiently to terminate an episode of social breakdown syndrome.

Partnership. Patients with chronic severe mental disorders must be told that their future depends largely on what they do for themselves but that there is a role for clinical help and that it will be made fully available. Some patients have strong needs to test out the boundaries of that partnership; they go through periods when they fear that they will fall apart unless they can be hospitalized. Early in the course of their care and sometimes later, they present themselves for admission in such a state. Sometimes it is wise to admit them for a short time only, simply to assert the hospital's availability in time of need.

The free use of all those indications by a comprehensively unified clinical team has already been tested in a systematic trial to prevent chronic social breakdown syndrome (Gruenberg, 1966). However, because of institutional rigidities and professional opinions, in the next few years a great variety of more or less unified clinical teams may take responsibility for the defined populations of chronically mentally ill, and those teams will afford the opportunity for finding out, among other things, how important each of those indications is. The organization of rapid relevant responses to crises in the lives of chronically ill mental patients is developing rapidly on an outpatient basis, which is undoubtedly a good thing. However, the amount of community rejection and loss of functional abilities caused by failure to rehospitalize intermittently for all or some of the seven indications listed above still remains uninvestigated. The different clinical and administrative situations that arise cannot be regarded as planned social experiments to answer that question, but the resourceful investigator will recognize the opportunities that such variations in administrative flexibility offer in order to clarify which of the uses of inpatient care, listed above, play the most important roles, for which kinds of patients.

Consequences of community neglect. The other main group of patterns that should attract investigators is the spectrum of community neglect associated with the term "deinstitutionalization"—that is, the discharge from care of people with long-term illness without any organized plan to continue providing clinical services. The most severe form of the spectrum that will continue to call for research concerns the people in need of protective environments who will become killed through accidents, murders, and self-neglect because of serious psychoses that remain untreated and uncared for. The next most extreme form of mistreatment and neglect is the overincarceration of mentally ill people in prisons and jails on the basis of minor offenses against the law because of the lack of any other protective environment for them. Particularly in the current period of high unemployment, which seems likely to continue into the future, some magistrates will regard incarceration as the only way to prevent starvation.

A less severe form of neglect is the growing tendency to organize drug clinics for long-term follow-up of psychotic patients. When such clinics are isolated from appropriate social services, available inpatient care as indicated, and opportunities for frequent clinical reevaluations of the patients, those services offer an extraordinary opportunity for studying the isolated effect of psychopharmacological drugs in the presence of long-term psychoses. They also offer an opportunity to study the distribution of iatrogenic episodes of delirium and ineffective functioning caused by overdosage or extended dosage of psychotropic drugs. Clearly, not all such services are labeled "drug clinics." Some general hospital outpatient clinics carry many of their patients in that way, and some general hospital emergency rooms are the source of nothing but renewed psychotropic prescriptions for "nerves" in the absence of appropriate clinical evaluations.

PREVENTION

"Prevention" has several different meanings that must be distinguished from one another. There is a growing rhetoric regarding prevention in policymaking circles. According to many publications of the National Institute of Mental Health and according to the reports of the President's Commission on Mental Health (1978), "prevention" refers to information and education programs, to anticipatory guidance before life crises, and to providing extra community support systems during ordinary life crises. That concept of prevention is based on a theory that providing such anticipatory guidance and such support after ordinary life crises will reduce the frequency with which certain forms of deterioration arise. That is a believable theory, but it is remarkably unrelated to established facts. The lack of relationship between the theory and the fact is due largely to the absence of any systematically gathered relevant facts, rather than to good evidence that the theories are wrong. The advantage of that theory of prevention is that it provides a basis for extending employment opportunities to people

trained in one of the mental health professions and provides an almost infinite body of people to be given services. The disadvantage of the theory is that it loses sight of the fundamental meaning of prevention, which is to lower the incidence of mental disorders through planned interventions in the environment, people at risk of becoming ill or the interaction between people at risk and the environment. If the goal is to reduce the frequency with which disorders occur, the means must be suited to achieve that goal. Hence, it is an error to refer to information, education, and community supports as "primary prevention"; what is actually involved in those activities is an intent, not necessarily an effect, because it has been shown that those activities lower the incidence of disease. Ironically, measures of primary prevention of known effectiveness do exist but are not being applied as widely as they could be.

Another meaning of prevention that in the past was more common in psychiatric circles than it is today is the notion that early diagnosis and treatment is one form of prevention. For some disorders, effective treatments can arrest the disorder in its early stages. For example, in this country today the planned public health program to locate the enormously common syphilitic infections before the end of the secondary stage and to provide definitive treatment against the spirochete infection is, in fact, effectively preventing the third stage of syphilitic infection, which includes general paresis psychoses. In a similar fashion, in some countries where pellagra has not been completely eliminated, diagnosis based on the skin lesions leads to early dietary supplements, hence, the pellagra psychoses are becoming rare.

That method of preventing disorders, which has long been known as "secondary prevention," is based on the capacity to make an early accurate diagnosis of a condition for which an effective treatment is available. Without effective treatment, the early diagnosis only provides more work for clinicians without changing the prevalence of disorders in the population. The advantage of the epidemiological perspective is that it helps one to think about the prevalence of a given disorder in a population as a whole. Secondary prevention shortens the duration of the episodes and keeps the disorder from progressing to more severe stages and, therefore, reduces the prevalence of that particular disorder and reduces the number of people who reach the advanced stages.

The arguments about prevention as a matter of public social policy are two sided. Gori and Richter (1978) argued that prevention can have a regressive effect on the economy. A responding letter by Kramer and Gruenberg (1978) pointed out that, if that were correct, the sicker the population, the healthier the economy would be. Gori and Richter's error was to think that the diseases that may be prevented in the next decade were, in fact, fatal diseases attacking people late in life. As a consequence, their economic calculations figured that people would survive more often past the age of 65 and that, therefore, they would be a burden, not a resource for the economy. They took no account of such matters as the worldwide extermination of smallpox, which has significantly lowered childhood mortality rates in many countries. Nor did they take into account such potential for prevention as lowering the incidence of mongolism at birth through amniocentesis and selected abortions. Nor did they consider the potentiality of preventing such causes of long-term brain damage as measles and rubella.

Measles offers a particularly dramatic example of that feature of prevention for the mental health specialist because it is a virus infection that frequently causes encephalitis during the acute phase and is known to produce long-term brain damage in many children. It is completely eradicable with today's available techniques and resources. The measles virus survives only in humans. For the measles virus to take hold in a population, susceptible persons must be infected by a new case. A new case is infectious for only 10 to 12 days. Hence, the lowest frequency of new cases possible is one every 10 to 12 days. Therefore, when measles is introduced into a community, a new susceptible person must be infected at least once every 10 to 12 days if the virus is to be perpetuated. Hence, the density of susceptibles in the community is the decisive factor that determines whether an epidemic will take hold. Center for Disease Control (1978) data showed that, in each year between 1973 and 1976, the incidence rate of measles rose in children born between 1963 and 1967, when vaccines of unreliable effectiveness were in use. Even those vaccines were not universally distributed. Hence, the birth cohorts of that period contain many teenage susceptibles, who pose a hazard in two ways. First, they may fuel epidemics in school communities that have not been exposed to measles in recent years. Second, the proportion of measles patients who develop encephalitis increases with age of the victim. When that hazard and the mental health implications of the measles virus were brought to the attention of the Surgeon General, the priority for measles eradication was suddenly raised, and the goal of interrupting the transmission of the virus totally in the United States by 1982 became official policy in the Department of Health, Education, and Welfare.

If the lowering of disease prevalence is given high priority, there will be a future need for investigators able to conduct preventive trials. In the more familiar clinical trial the investigator starts with a small number of sick people, randomly assigns them individually to different treatments, and then observes the outcome. In contrast, in a preventive trial the investigator starts with a group of people who are not ill, exposes one portion of the population to a planned intervention, and withholds that intervention from the other portion to see what the differential risk of developing the disease will be. Sometimes, as in the polio vaccine trials, random individual assignment is possible. Even then, the political, organization, and ethical issues are substantially different from those involved in the clinical trial because the people being dealt with are not ill in a preventive trial at the time. As a rule, a larger number of subjects are required for a preventive trial than for a clinical trial. When the interventions cannot be assigned on an individual basis, random assignment, as is normally done in controlled clinical trials, becomes impossible, and comparison groups must be generated from the identification of whole communities, through a before-and-after type of design, or through some other method of obtaining comparison groups. Each preventive trial, therefore, cannot be based on some routine method—as the double-blind, randomized control clinical trial can be—but must be an active creation by the planners and organizers of the preventive trial, taking account of the concrete realities of the situation.

At present, a special group of prevention advocates share three critical assumptions about the interventions they advocate. They assume that the interventions are (1) harmless, (2) socially acceptable and not frightening to the subjects, and (3) able to prevent some disorders on some reasonable basis. Whether or not the interventions do prevent disorders is best found out by starting with a planned preventive trial. It is extraordinary that many of the fashionable mental health prevention programs have those characteristics, and yet none of them has produced a preventive trial. Such programs as widow-to-widow counseling to prevent extended depression, the correction of low self-esteem in pregnant women to prevent neurotic symptom formation in their daughters, and enhancing the coping skills of mentally retarded parents and of their children as a basis for special education of the parents and the

children to prevent mental retardation in the children are excellent examples of hypotheses that are best tested in the first instance by a carefully prepared preventive trial.

Suggested Cross References

For incidence and prevalence rates for specific mental disorders, see the sections that deal with those disorders. Psychopharmacology is discussed in Section 2.2. The application of statistics to psychiatry is described in Chapter 7. The mental status examination is discussed in Section 12.2. Classification of mental disorders is discussed in Section 14.1. Hospitalization and milieu therapy are discussed in Chapter 32 and community psychiatry in Chapter 45.

REFERENCES

American Public Health Association. *Mental Disorders: A Guide to Control Methods.* American Public Health Association, New York, 1962.

Asher, R. Munchausen's syndrome. Lancet, *1:* 339, 1951.

Bachrach, L. L. *Deinstitutionalization: An Analytic Review and Sociological Perspective.* United States Government Printing Office, Washington, D. C., 1976.

Barker, J. C. The syndrome of hospital addiction (Munchausen syndrome). J. Ment. Sci., *108:* 167, 1962.

Barton, R. Consideration, clinical features, and differential diagnosis of institutional neurosis. In *Third World Congress of Psychiatry Proceedings,* vol. 2, p. 890. University of Toronto Press, Toronto, 1961.

Brandon, S., and Gruenberg, E. M. Measurement of the incidence of chronic severe social breakdown syndrome: Has the Dutchess County Service been associated with a decline in incidence? Milbank Mem. Fund Q., *44:* 129, 1966.

Bremer, J. A. Social psychiatric investigation of a small community in northern Norway. Acta Psychiatr. Neurol., Scand. *62* (Suppl.): 27, 1951.

Carter, C. O. A life-table for mongols with the causes of death. J. Ment. Defic. Res., *2:* 64, 1958.

Center for Disease Control. Current status of measles in the United States, 1973–1977. J. Infect. Dis., *137:* 817, 1978.

Chess, S., Korn, S. J., and Fernandez, P. B. *Psychiatric Disorders of Children with Congenital Rubella.* Brunner/Mazel, New York, 1971.

Cohen, B. M., and Fairbank, R. E. Statistical contributions from the mental hygiene study of the eastern health district of Baltimore. II. Psychoses in the eastern district. 1. The incidence and prevalence of psychoses in the eastern health district in 1933. Am. J. Psychiatry, *94:* 1377, 1938.

Collmann, R. D., and Stoller, A. A survey of mongoloid births in Victoria, Australia, 1942–1957. Am. J. Pub. Health, *52:* 813, 1962.

Comptroller General of the United States. *Returning the Mentally Disabled to the Community: Government Needs to Do More.* General Accounting Office, Washington, D. C., 1977.

Cooper, J. E., Kendell, R. E., Gurland, B. J., Sharpe, L., Copeland, J. R. M., and Simon, R. *Psychiatric Diagnosis in New York and London.* Oxford University Press, London, 1972.

Cooper, L. Z., Congenital rubella in the United States. In *Infections of the Fetus and Newborn Infant,* S. Krugman and A. A. Gershon, editors. Allan R. Liss, New York, 1975.

Crane, G. E. Two decades of psychopharmacology and community mental health: Old and new problems of the schizophrenic patient. Trans. N. Y. Acad. Sci., *36:* 644, 1974.

Dohrenwend, B. P., and Dohrenwend, B. S. *Social Status and Psychological Disorder: A Causal Inquiry.* John Wiley & Sons, New York, 1969.

Dublin, L. I. *Suicide: A Sociological and Statistical Study.* Ronald Press, New York, 1963.

Dunham, H. W. Epidemiology of psychiatric disorders as a contribution to medical ecology. Arch. Gen. Psychiatry, *14:* 1, 1966.

Eaton, J. W., and Weil, R. J. *Culture and Mental Disorders.* Free Press of Glencoe (Macmillan), New York, 1955.

Essen-Möller, E. Individual traits and morbidity in a Swedish rural population. Acta Psychiatr. Neurol. Scand., *100* (Suppl.): 1, 1956.

Folstein, M. F., and McHugh, P. R. "Mini-mental state": A practical method for grading the cognitive state of patients for the clinician. J. Psychiatr. Res., *12:* 189, 1975.

Ford, F. R. *Diseases of the Nervous System in Infancy, Childhood, and Adolescence.* Charles C Thomas, Springfield, Ill., 1960.

Fryers, T. Life expectancy and causes of death in the mentally retarded. Br. J. Prev. Soc. Med., *29:* 61, 1975.

Gibbs, F. A., Gibbs, E. L., and Carpenter, P. R. Electroencephalographic abnormality in "uncomplicated" childhood diseases. J. A. M. A., *171:* 1050, 1959.

Goldberger, J., Wheeler, G. A., and Sydenstricker, E. A study of the relation of diet to pellagra incidence in seven textile-mill communities of South Carolina in 1916. Public Health Rep., *35:* 648, 1920.

Goldhamer, H., and Marshall, A. W. *Psychosis and Civilization.* Free Press of Glencoe (Macmillan), New York, 1949.

Gordon, J. E. The twentieth century—yesterday, today, and tomorrow. In *The History of American Epidemiology,* F. H. Top, editor, p. 114. C. V. Mosby, St. Louis, 1952.

Gori, B., and Richter, B. J. Macroeconomics of disease prevention in the United States. Science, *201:* 1124, 1978.

Greenwood, M. *Epidemic and Crowd Disease: An Introduction to the Study of Epidemiology.* Williams & Norgate, London, 1935.

Gregg, N. Congenital cataract following German measles in the mother. Trans. Ophthalmol. Soc. Aust., *3:* 35, 1941.

Group for the Advancement of Psychiatry. *Problems of Estimating Changes in Frequency of Mental Disorders.* Group for the Advancement of Psychiatry, New York, 1961.

Gruenberg, E. M. Epidemiology of mental disorders and aging. In *The Neurological and Psychiatric Aspects of Disorders of Aging,* J. E. Moore, H. H. Merrit, and R. J. Masselink, editors, p. 112. Williams & Wilkins, Baltimore, 1956.

Gruenberg, E. M. editor. *Evaluating the Effectiveness of Community Mental Health Services.* Milbank Memorial Fund, New York, 1966.

Gruenberg, E. M. Obstacles to optimal psychiatric service delivery systems. Psychiatr. Q., *46:* 483, 1972.

Gruenberg, E. M. Benefits of short-term hospitalization. In *Strategic Intervention in Schizophrenia: Current Developments in Treatment,* R. Cancro, N. Fox, and L. W. Shapiro, editors, p. 251. Behavioral Publications, New York, 1974a.

Gruenberg, E. M. The social breakdown syndrome and its prevention. In *American Handbook of Psychiatry,* G. Caplan, editor, vol 2, p. 697. Basic Books, New York, 1974b.

Gruenberg, E. M. Community care is not deinstitutionalization. In *New Trends of Psychiatry in the Community,* G. Serban, editor, p. 257. Ballinger Press, Cambridge, Mass., 1977a.

Gruenberg, E. M. The failures of success. Milbank Mem. Fund Q., *55:* 3, 1977b.

Gruenberg, E. M., and Hagnell, O. The rising prevalence of chronic brain syndrome in the elderly. In *Society, Stress and Disease: Aging and Old Age,* L. Levi and A. R. Kagan, editors. Oxford University Press, New York, 1980.

Gruenberg, E. M., Kasius, R. V., and Huxley, M. Objective appraisal of deterioration in a group of long-stay hospital patients. Milbank Mem. Fund Q., *40:* 90, 1962.

Gruenberg, E. M., Snow, H. B., and Bennett, C. L. Preventing the social breakdown syndrome. In *Social Psychiatry,* F. C. Redlich, editor, p. 179. Williams & Wilkins, Baltimore, 1969.

* Hagnell, O. *A Prospective Study of the Incidence of Mental Disorder.* Svenska Bokförlaget, Norstedts, Lund, 1966.

Hinsie, L. E., and Campbell, R. J. *Psychiatric Dictionary,* ed. 4. Oxford University Press, New York, 1970.

Jarvis, E. Influence of distance from and nearness to an insane hospital on its use by people. Am. J. Insanity, *22:* 361, 1866.

Kasius, R. V. The social breakdown syndrome in a cohort of long-stay patients in the Dutchess County Unit, 1960–1963. Milbank Mem. Fund Q., *44:* 156, 1966.

Kolb, L. C., *Modern Clinical Psychiatry.* W. B. Saunders, Philadelphia, 1973.

Kramer, M. *Psychiatric Services and the Changing Institutional Scene, 1950–1985.* United States Government Printing Office, Washington, D. C., 1977.

Kramer, M., and Gruenberg, E. M. Prevention of long-term and disabling disease. Science, *202:* 697, 1978.

Kramer, M., Pollack, E. S., Redick, R. W., and Locke, B. Z. *Mental Disorders/Suicide.* Harvard University Press, Cambridge, Mass., 1972.

Leighton, A. Is social environment a cause of psychiatric disorder? Psychiatr. Res. Rep., *22:* 337, 1967.

Leighton, D. C. The distribution of psychiatric symptoms in a small town. Am. J. Psychiatry, *112:* 716, 1956.

* Leighton, D. C., Harding, J. S., Macklin, D., Macmillan, A. M., and Leighton, A. H. *The Character of Danger,* Vol. 3, *The Sterling County Study of Psychiatric Disorder and Socio-cultural Environment.* Basic Books, New York, 1963.

Lemkau, P., Tietze, C., and Cooper, M. Mental-hygiene problems in an urban district. Ment. Hyg., *25:* 624, 1941.

Lin, T. A study of the incidence of mental disorder in Chinese and other cultures. Psychiatry, *16:* 313, 1953.

Litvak, A. M., Sands, I. J., and Gibel, H. Encephalitis complicating measles: Report of fifty-six cases with follow-up studies in thirty-two. Am. J. Dis. Child., *65:* 265, 1943.

MacMahon, B., and Pugh, T. F. *Epidemiology: Principles and Methods.* Little, Brown and Co., Boston, 1970.

Maxcy, K. F., editor. *Papers of Wade Hampton Frost, M. D.: A Contribution to Epidemiological Method.* Commonwealth Fund, New York, 1941.

Modlin, J. F., Brandling-Bennett, A. D., Witte, J. J., Campbell, C. G., and Meyers, J. D. A review of five years' experience with rubella vaccine in the United States. Pediatrics, *55:* 20, 1975.

New York State Department of Mental Hygiene. *A Mental Health Survey of Older People.* State Hospitals Press, Utica, 1960.

Øster, J., Mikkelsen, M., and Neilsen, A. Mortality and life-table in Down's syndrome. Acta Paediatr. Scand., *64:* 322, 1975.

Parran, T. *Shadow on the Land: Syphilis.* Reynal & Hitchcock. New York, 1937.

Parran, T. Nutrition: Its public health aspects in new light on old health problems. In *Proceedings of the Seventieth Annual Conference of the Milbank Memorial Fund,* p. 27. Milbank Memorial Fund, New York, 1939.

Penrose, L. S. The relative effect of paternal and maternal age in mongolism. J. Genet. *27:* 219, 1933.

Penrose, L. S. Method of separating relative aetiological effects of birth order and maternal age, with special reference to mongolian imbecility. Ann. Eugen., *6:* 108, 1934.

Penrose, L. S. *On the Objective Study of Crowd Behavior.* H. K. Lewis, London, 1952.

President's Commission on Mental Health. *Report to the President,* vol. 1, p. 76. United States Government Printing Office, Washingtion, D. C., 1978.

Rabkin, J. Public attitudes toward mental illness: A review of the literature. Schizophr. Bull., *10:* 9, 1974.

Regier, D. A., Goldberg, E. D., and Taube, C. A. The de facto U. S. mental health services system: A public health perspective. Arch. Gen. Psychiatry, *35:* 685, 1978.

Roe, D. *A Plague of Corn.* Cornell University Press, Ithaca, N. Y. 1973.

Rosen, G. *Madness in Society.* University of Chicago Press, Chicago, 1966.

Roth, W. F., Jr., and Luton, F. H. The mental health programs in Tennessee. I. Description of the original study program. II. Statistical report of a psychiatric survey in a rural county. Am. J. Psychiatry, *99:* 662, 1943.

Schimel, J. L., Salzman, L., Chodoff, P., Grinker, R. R., and Will, O. A. Changing styles in psychiatric syndromes: A symposium. Am. J. Psychiatry, *130:* 146, 1973.

Schwab, J. J., and Schwab, M. E. *Sociocultural Roots of Mental Illness: An Epidemiologic Survey.* Plenum Publishing Corp., New York, 1978.

Shepherd, M., Cooper, B., Brown, A. C., and Kalton, G. *Psychiatric Illness in General Practice.* Oxford University Press, London, 1966.

Shuttleworth, G. E. Mongolian idiocy. Br. Med. J., *31:* 661, 1909.

Sigerist. H. E. *Civilization and Disease.* University of Chicago Press, Chicago, 1943.

Spitzer, R. L., and Endicott, J. *Schedule for Affective Disorders and Schizophrenia.* New York State Department of Mental Hygiene, New York, 1973.

* Srole, L., Langner, T. S., Michael, S. T., Opler, M. K., and Rennie, T. A. C. *Mental Health in the Metropolis,* vol. 1, *The Midtown Manhattan Study.* McGraw-Hill, New York, 1962.

Stein, Z. A. Strategies for the prevention of mental retardation. Bull. N. Y. Acad. Med., *51:* 130, 1975.

Wing, J. K. *Reasoning about Madness.* Oxford University Press, Oxford, 1978.

Wing, J. K., Cooper, J. E., and Sartorius, N. *Measurement and Classification of Psychiatric Symptoms: An Instruction Manual for the Present State Examination and Catego Program.* Cambridge University Press, London, 1974.

World Health Organization. *Schizophrenia: A Multinational Study.* World Health Organization, Geneva, 1975.

Zusman, T. Some explanations of the changing appearance of psychotic patients: Antecedents of the social breakdown syndrome concept. Milbank Mem. Fund Q., *44:* 363, 1966.

6.2 Computers and Clinical Psychiatry

BERNARD C. GLUECK, M.D.
CHARLES F. STROEBEL, Ph.D., M.D.

Introduction

Some of the most extensive and sophisticated attempts at computerizing patient records have been undertaken by psychiatric hospitals. Because, to many observers, this may well seem to be the most difficult starting point, what are the reasons for the sizable number of energetic efforts currently under way to develop appropriate electronic capabilities for the collection, storage, analysis, and retrieval of information about the psychiatric patient? The multivariate nature of psychiatric illness, with its lack of specific causative agents and wide range of treatment techniques, certainly provides ample motivation for improved methods for dealing with the enormous mass of information represented by the record of even a single patient. The complexities of a patient's overt behavior, adaptational maneuvers, an increasing number of treatment alternatives, and the unique variations in each psychiatrist's training and experience result in marked disparities in the diagnosis, treatment, and eventual outcome in patients with apparently similar disturbances.

Means for cataloguing, storing, comparing, and weighing the

multiple variables were unavailable until recently. This unavailability prevented psychiatric data from being exposed to the comparative evaluation and recalibration seen in most fields of physical medicine. The pioneering attempts of experienced clinicians who were dissatisfied with the current state of affairs have given a strong impetus to the development of techniques for the effective use of the modern digital computer in the management of the psychiatric patient. They have proved that digital computer techniques can be devised to allow for the kinds of evaluation and comparison currently possible in physical medicine. This potential permits a more precise classification of the nature, progress, and outcome of each psychiatric patient. Every patient under treatment can be viewed as a research case, contributing to a massive storehouse of compatible information and simultaneously being evaluated and compared against information already accumulated.

The skilled clinician manages, on occasion, to ingest and process all this information successfully, arriving at appropriate conclusions about diagnosis and treatment, but the lack of specific causative agents in most instances of psychiatric illness and the large number of factors that can influence the course of the patient's illness make it impossible for the clinician to operate as consistently, accurately, and effectively as he would like. The modern computer, with its capacity for storing literally billions of bits of information and its unique ability to process these data in a variety of ways at extremely high speeds with almost infallible accuracy, is an extremely attractive potential assistant for the psychiatrist.

A second important stimulus to the development of standardized data bases and information systems came out of the collaborative studies that were organized in the Veterans Administration psychiatric facilities and by the Psychopharmacology Branch of the National Institute of Mental Health (NIMH) in the early 1960's. These studies were designed to determine the effectiveness of the many psychotropic drugs being made available to the field at that time. To develop a broad patient base, covering as many diagnostic and socioeconomic levels as possible, and to collect large enough amounts of information for adequate statistical significance, researchers designed multihospital and multiclinic studies. Initially, the lack of standardization of terminology across widely varying institutions resulted in the development of the concept of target symptoms for patient selection, instead of the diagnostic label. In addition, criteria of improvement that had been used in the past, such as a three-step scale of improvement or simply discharge from hospital as an index of improvement, were believed to be too unsophisticated. This belief resulted in the development of a variety of rating scales and other descriptive instruments that attempted to standardize and objectify the clinician's observations and judgments. These scales and instruments provided psychiatrists, for the first time, with quantified numerical statements about the condition of their patients.

To handle all this information, coming from many different sources, the researchers developed standardized information forms to cover the usual demographic identifying data about patients; in addition, rating scales and other standardized lists were used to provide for ready encoding of the data. In the NIMH collaborative studies, Dean Clyde was responsible for organizing the data collection and analysis efforts. He set up the first computerized programs to handle this information, using a computer facility developed jointly by the Psychopharmacology Service Center of the National Institute of Mental Health and by George Washington University.

Within the Veterans Administration system significant contributions were made in the standardization of personality descriptors and in the solution to the problems of data collection by Lorr (1960), Klett and Honigfeld (1965), Overall and Gorham (1962), and Hollister and Overall (1964).

History

In the field of psychiatry, the use of thinking machines—that is, the electronic computer and its predecessor, the electromechanical accounting machine—spans a brief 30 years. One of the first uses of accounting machines in psychology and psychiatry was the development of a Hollerith card (punch card) form of the Minnesota Multiphasic Personality Inventory (MMPI) by Stark R. Hathaway and Kenneth E. Clark at the University of Minnesota in the early 1950's. This punchcard version of the MMPI was processed on an accounting machine that tabulated the true and false responses to the various items and printed out a final tally of the raw scores for the various factor scales. This use marked a significant advance over the previous 15 years of hand scoring the inventory, with all the tedium and inaccuracy attendant on a repetitious clerical task. Although this was a significant forward step in the automation of the psychological assessment of personality, there still remained the translation of the scores obtained into a descriptive statement, for which the services of a skilled clinician were required.

The publication of *Clinical versus Statistical Prediction* by Meehl (1954) provided a convincing argument for the actuarial approach to the interpretation of the MMPI. This book gave a strong stimulus to the attempts that were already under way for producing a computer-derived interpretative comment about the MMPI test results.

The first of these systems was developed at the Mayo Clinic by Pearson et al. (1964), Swenson (1960), and Rome et al. (1962). This was the first operational system and was in use in the early 1960's. The Mayo group developed a computer program by means of which the MMPI could be scored and analyzed and a series of descriptive phrases and sentences could be printed out for use by the medical staff as part of the general medical evaluation. This was an attempt to meet the familiar problem of a large intake and a very small psychology staff. The program was highly successful in meeting the goals of its authors, and it provided an efficient means of screening large numbers of medical patients who otherwise might have had no psychological or psychiatric screening.

INDIVIDUAL HOSPITAL SYSTEMS

A modified interpretive system, which produced a somewhat longer and more detailed report for use with a psychiatric population, was developed in 1962 by Glueck and Reznikoff (1965) at the Institute of Living. The success of this system prompted this group to develop a project for computerizing all the functions of the psychiatric hospital. Early in 1965 the first real-time computerized psychiatric information system became operational at the Institute of Living. This system has served as a prototype working model for subsequent applications of computers in both psychiatric and general hospitals because of its early emphasis on clinical applications devoted to enhancing individual patient care, rather than on the automation of hospital business, administrative, and statistical functions. An IBM 1440 computer system serviced nine terminals that operated on a continuous on-line, real-time basis during an 8:00 A.M. to 5:00 P.M. working day.

Although this system was regarded as a remarkable operational achievement at the time, its many limitations—such as the relatively small, fixed format, patient record data base, and serial use of the computer, rather than true time sharing by the terminal user—limited the scope of its clinical usefulness. Nevertheless, it serviced a significant part of the hospital operations, including all admissions, transfers, changes in patient status, and discharges; a portion of the medication ordering and dispensing procedures; production of all nursing notes through the computer; and automation of several personality descriptors, such as the MMPI and the Minnesota-Hartford Personality Assay (MHPA) (Meehl, 1962).

Subsequently, a personnel file was developed that was the data base from which the payroll was managed and other types of significant employee information were produced. Patients' bills were also produced by the computer, with the information required for these bills coming, in part, from other automated parts of the system, such as the medication orders, where charges were automatically posted to the patient's bill. However, because of the limitations inherent in the system described above, a more modern system—using third-generation computers and the programing language MUMPS, which was developed at the Massachusetts General Hospital by Barnett and his colleagues—has been installed.

In this system the primary concerns were for the development of a totally integrated data base that would cover all patient information, all employee information, and all aspects of the business and administrative functioning of a typical institution. In the construction of the data base, much attention was focused on the development of a file structure that would permit fastest access directly to individual patient or employee information. Because the majority of activities involving patient care within the institution involve the entry of relatively simple pieces of data or an inquiry about specific data from a given record, the system design maximizes the speed of individual patient inquiry. Searching across patient files or employee files, recognized as one of the major uses of the system, usually does not require the same instantaneous response that a direct inquiry about a patient's current status does. When a search across a large number of patient or employee files is required to obtain information for research or administrative statistical purposes, the relatively slower response times are acceptable. Relative slowness is an important concept, however, because computers deal in fractions of a second for the individual patient inquiry and necessitate a wait of perhaps 20 to 30 minutes for a search across 400 patient records for up to 10 items of information, with a correlation of all these data. The obvious efficiencies of this electronic type of medical record system, when compared with the traditional medical record, hardly need elaboration.

In the development of this system, a major concern was the completeness of the record. To ensure as complete coverage as possible, the developers reviewed the requirements of the Joint Commission on Accreditation of Hospitals (Accreditation Council for Psychiatric Facilities, 1972) to make sure that the data base would cover all the principles and implementing procedures specified in the joint commission requirements. In addition, provision was made for the inclusion of all the specialized areas that may be encountered only in speciality hospitals, such as a psychiatric hospital.

The restriction of the one-user-at-a-time capability of the IBM 1440 system is met by the increase in the speed and capacity of the newer computer system and by the flexibility of the MUMPS programing language, which permits multiple users in a time-shared, real-time computer system. In this system each user, in effect, has the illusion of having the computer entirely to himself, even though he may be sharing the computer's activities with a number of other users simultaneously. An additional advantage of MUMPS is that it permits on-line programing, which adds a significant flexibility and ease to program development and programing changes.

The major advantages of the on-line, interactive, real-time system over all previous approaches lie in its flexibility and responsiveness to the needs of the individual clinician user, while simultaneously providing both the necessary standardization and the insistence on complete information required for good record keeping in both clinical and administrative areas. The system is user oriented and takes the approach of asking the clinician user what he would like to do and how he would like to do it. Within the inevitable constraints imposed by the particular computer hardware and even the most sophisticated of applications programs, attempts should be made to provide the clinician with exactly that sort of capability. This approach, to whatever extent it has been implemented, is an important component of the successful computer applications in psychiatry. This is in sharp contrast to most previous system approaches, in which the general attitude has been "This is what the computer can do, and this is the way you have

to do it; you do it our way, or you can't use the system." As might be expected, the reaction of the majority of clinicians to this take-it-or-leave-it approach has been to reject the system out of hand without ever trying it, let alone attempting to give it a careful and critical clinical trial.

Five years of successful experience with the first approach—namely, meeting the clinicians' needs as closely as possible—has confirmed the prediction made by the designers of the Institute of Living system. Use of the system by clinical and administrative staff has increased steadily, as they have tried various applications and found them meeting their needs and easy to use.

STATE-WIDE COMPUTER SYSTEMS

In contrast to the individual hospital system described above, the Missouri Department of Mental Health's automated mental health information system (Ulett and Sletten, 1969; Sletten and Ulett, 1972; Hedlund et al., 1977) was developed on a state-wide basis, linking 10 major facilities of the Missouri Department of Mental Health. This system, developed in collaboration with the Missouri Institute of Psychiatry of the University of Missouri-Columbia School of Medicine, was concerned from the outset with the completeness and appropriateness of the data base for storing patient information. The basic patient record includes the usual admission, demographic, and disposition information about each patient and, in addition, a number of specific types of clinical information that are normally filed in a manual medical record. The state-wide network operates through remote computer terminals located in the various state facilities, transmitting data over telephone lines to and from the central computer in St. Louis. Conceptualization of this system began in 1966, and, although development has been a continuous process up to the present time, its principal clinical components were fully implemented by early 1973. The system operates from a large IBM 370-155 central computer with 2 million bytes of fast core storage and 2 billion bytes of disk storage, with a capacity to store several hundred thousand patient records. The application systems run under the IBM Information Management System, which allows information from a variety of sources to be accumulated under a specific patient number and has automatic mechanisms to ensure that information is accurately maintained and stored. A commercial retrieval package is used for retrieving information from the system. This package requires the development of a dictionary, describing where the data are located in the computer file. One of the general principles in the development of the data base stipulates that only information that directly helps in making decisions about patient care needs to be in the system. Specific clinical applications include a 119-item mental status record, a detailed physical examination checklist, social functioning information at the time of admission, an emergency room or admission checklist that collects salient historical information concerning the current episode, alcohol history information, an inpatient behavior scale used by the nursing staff, and a sophisticated community adjustment scale that is used for systematically collecting information about the patient's community adjustment, both at the time of hospitalization and 3 months after discharge. Two psychological screening applications, involving the automated MMPI and the Peabody Picture Vocabulary Test, are also operational.

With the use of data already collected in the system, principally information from the mental status examination and the admission checklist, prediction models have been developed that indicate the likelihood of the patients' diagnosis, type of psychotropic medication, length of stay, dangerousness to self or others, and the likelihood of patient elopement (Altman et al., 1978). Evidence cited suggests that these computer-based prediction models are about as accurate as clinical judgments (Hedlund et al., 1978).

The strong computer applications central staff in the Missouri system, which combined a university department of psychiatry and the central office of the Department of Mental Health, was able to overcome many of the problems associated with the standardized language of standard checklists and rating forms. Despite some clinical resistance and a number of special problems (Hedlund et al., 1977), large amounts of standardized clinical information have been and are being collected and used in the Missouri system. Special or unique language systems that are often used by clinicians have been a major problem in the development of adequate computerized psychiatric data bases, whether within a single installation, within a state system, or across state systems. The relative success of the Missouri state system has been due in large part to at least the qualified acceptance of the use of a unified language and method for collecting data about psychiatric patients.

MULTISTATE SYSTEM

Under the guidance of Laska and his co-workers (Laska et al., 1967; Laska and Bank, 1975), a project, the Multistate Information System (MSIS), was developed at Rockland State Hospital in Orangeburg, New York. Its objective was a centralized computer system that would service a regional multistate area through communications lines and terminals located in institutions and central offices of the various state mental health departments. Over and above the many technical problems presented by the magnitude of this task, a major difficulty that is still only partially resolved has been the problem of obtaining the necessary agreement on the standardized input forms and the format of the data base from the representatives of six different state systems and the various institutions within each system. The limitations of a fixed format for the patient record, which has until recently been the basic technique for developing a computerized patient data base, were highlighted in the problems of the Rockland project. An additional difficulty has been the variable usefulness of the system to people in different institutions and state central offices, due, in part, to their unique requirements.

In spite of these initial difficulties, system complexity and sophistication of input modes have developed to the point at which more than 1,300 facilities—including community mental health centers, state hospitals, universities, and nursing homes—are using the system for information on individual patients and groups of patients. The larger number of standard input documents plus the option for any facility to design its own additional data collection instruments for clinical and administrative use are partly responsible for the increase in user acceptance of the system.

Most MSIS forms are multiple-choice checklists permitting the user to complete only those items that are appropriate for the individual patient. Moreover, the forms were designed as an integrated set, so that the same data need not be collected repeatedly. Once a data item, such as date of birth, has been recorded, it may be retrieved from the computer file to appear on any output report as needed.

Mental health programs and facilities may participate in MSIS by a telephone-linked terminal that transmits information directly to the computer, or it may be sent by mail or by courier service. Large facilities generally have terminals of their own. In some terminal locations, data are received by mail from other facilities and are then transmitted to a computing center.

Because of the great concern over the issues of privacy and confidentiality of the data stored in the computers at MSIS, safeguards have been instituted to limit access to the records. Technical precautions have been taken within the system to prevent unauthorized access to the files; internal programing checks and the use of identifying codes ensure to the greatest extent possible the integrity of the data. Physical security measures have been taken at MSIS and are in effect at terminal locations (Laska and Bank, 1975).

Computer Compared with Clinician

The digital computer differs from the clinician in many ways. It is virtually immune to fatigue and carelessness; it does not suffer memory loss with age; it works day and night, weekends and holidays, and without coffee breaks, fringe benefits, overtime, or human courtesy. It requires occasional maintenance, but, even in the absence of an extra backup machine, it is more likely than its human counterpart to be available during the moment of need. On the other hand, computer programs now available can hardly compete with an expert clinician working at peak efficiency in the performance of many of his tasks. Although the medical history and review of systems can now be collected through a computer terminal with relative sophistication, the computer cannot discuss the patient's condition with members of his family or make a physical, neurological, or mental status examination. Furthermore, the output that the computer generates is critically dependent on the accuracy of the information supplied by the physician, patient, nurse, laboratory technician, or laboratory instrumentation.

Of greater importance than these considerations, however, is the difference in the class of problems that the computer and the human brain solve best. Awareness of these differences may permit eventual optimization of the unique role of the clinician and the complementary role of the computer in providing a meaningful backup to save the clinician time and improve his efficiency.

Information is stored and used in computers as bits (a contraction of "binary digit"). A bit is defined as the standard unit of information, and it corresponds to a single binary alternative, such as on-off, zero-one, or true-false. Information stored by the computer can be located precisely. Under control of a program, the information may be moved from slower but less expensive areas of storage—such as a magnetic disk, drum, or tape—to areas of more rapid recall, such as magnetic core memory. By devoting six bits to code each character, the computer can represent up to 2^6 (or 64) different characters, providing for storage of letters, punctuation marks, and numbers. The rapid-access memory of the average medium-size computer available today is approximately 1.3×10^5 bits. Now becoming available are large random-access, mass-memory systems that provide storage capacity as high as 10^{12} bits at reasonable cost, with a retrieval time of less than 50 milliseconds. This memory capacity may be extended indefinitely with slower access disk or magnetic tape storage.

By contrast, the human brain has been estimated to possess a rapid, random-access memory capacity of approximately 10^{20} bits, a remarkable comparison when one recalls the size of the human brain as compared with the size of computers possessing potentially equivalent memories. Table I contrasts a medium-size PDP-9 computer with the human brain (Bleich, 1971).

The computer has a small number of exceedingly reliable and fast circuits and is designed to perform many simple tasks—one or perhaps a few at a time. Table I shows the time needed to perform serial subtractions by 7 from 100. The computer is immensely faster than the human brain. By contrast, the brain has a huge number of relatively slow circuits, operating in parallel, and is, therefore, better equipped to cope with large amounts of information presented for simultaneous processing. The human brain's clear superiority in pattern recognition can be noted in Table I.

TABLE I

Comparison of a Medium-size Computer with the Human Brain

	PDP-9 Computer	Human Brain
Number of circuits	10^4	10^{10}
Weight (pounds)	2,300	3
Size (cubic feet)	225	1/20
Memory (bits)	1.3×10^5	10^{20}
Speed (conduction rate)	10^7	10^3
Serial 7's (seconds)	3.0×10^{-5}	30
Pattern recognition	Minutes	Seconds

The remarkable cleverness of the brain when compared with the computer may, in part, be attributable to its capacity for global or holistic information processing. A computer must relate one piece of information to another along a prescribed serial or sequential path programed into its logic, but the human brain has the capacity to take any given piece of information and examine a virtually infinite number of simultaneous interrelations, selecting the relevant from the irrelevant. Not only does this ability allow the organism to orient itself in the complex stimulus field provided by the environment, but it allows a person to be creative and to discover meanings not otherwise apparent. One of the more remarkable distinguishing features of the human brain when compared with the brains of lower animals is that there has been a tendency for problem solving to be lateralized. The left hemisphere appears to specialize in logical analytic processes, and the right hemisphere seems to have developed special global information-processing abilities. The lateralization process in humans is not yet fully understood, but clearly the normal, intact human brain has the capacity not only to process data in two different modes but to do so in the somewhat independent hemispheres alternately and possibly even simultaneously.

Compared with the human brain, then, the computer lacks both the ability to solve problems in a truly global context and the capacity to integrate global with serial or sequential processing.

This lack of a global model has clearly been the problem, for instance, in attempts at computer translation of languages. The ambiguities of written text that remain after a word-for-word translation of the medical record into the computer can be resolved only by having at hand a common sense model of the world against which to test the semantic meaning of the phrase or sentence in question. Given the sentence "The pig is in the pen," the computer, with only an English dictionary and the rules of grammar in its memory bank, has no way to decide whether "pen" refers to an enclosure or a writing instrument.

The manner in which information may be most efficiently presented to the clinician in comparison to the computer provides another interesting contrast. Figure 1 shows the numerical results of a sequence of daily affect ratings on a psychiatric patient over a 15-week period; the information is presented in an effective and compact way for computer data input. With input in this form, the computer can assimilate the data, identify abnormal values, and perform other routine calculations very rapidly. But such a serial presentation is ineffective and confusing for the human diagnostician, who prefers a parallel type of presentation, commonly seen in the familiar bedside temperature chart. Figure 2 presents the same data as shown in Figure 1 but in familiar parallel form; it is now immediately apparent that affect varied in a cyclic fashion over the 15-week period, suggesting a fluctuating depressive illness.

Just as the clinician does poorly with serial presentation, the computer does poorly with the recognition of complex patterns, which implies parallel presentation of data. For example, a child easily identifies a letter or a number regardless of its size, position, color, or spatial orientation; on the other hand, the information required to recognize even such simple patterns is highly complex for a computer to ingest with its serial input. The single-accumulator computer must scan the pattern and translate the result into a stream of binary digits that can be assimilated serially. The task is not impossible for the computer and may become much easier as multiple-accumulator machines become more widespread, but the task has been only partially accomplished, using special pattern-recognition peripherals for tasks such as identifying postal zip codes and

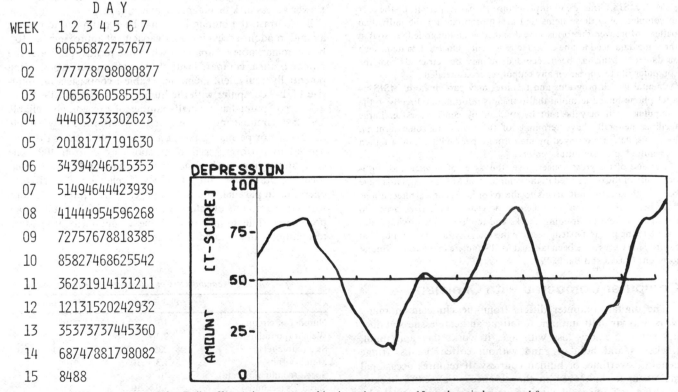

	D A Y
WEEK	1 2 3 4 5 6 7
01	60656872757677
02	777778798080877
03	70656360585551
04	44403733302623
05	20181717191630
06	34394246515353
07	51494644423939
08	41444954596268
09	72757678818385
10	85827468625542
11	36231914131211
12	12131520242932
13	35373737445360
14	68747881798082
15	8488

FIGURE 1 (*left*). Daily affect ratings on a psychiatric patient over a 15-week period, prepared for a computer.
FIGURE 2 (*right*). The same daily affect ratings on a psychiatric patient over a 15-week period, prepared in parallel fashion for a physician.

recognizing special character fonts, as in bank checks. Attempts to program computers to interpret patterns such as X-rays, electrocardiograms, and chromosomal patterns are at varying stages of development and are under intensive study by competent investigators.

The foregoing differentiation between serial and parallel processing has an interesting analogue with recent evidence and hypotheses about the lateralization of hemispheric functioning in the human brain; the left temporal cortex is viewed as a serial (language) processor in most persons, and the right temporal cortex may specialize in pattern recognition (Galin, 1977). Particularly provocative is the hypothesis that disturbances in communication between left brain and right brain may play an important role in some forms of psychopathology (Galin, 1977; Mirabile et al., 1978). A related model in which physical and neural analogies, such as computer versus brain, may have growing heuristic import is the hypothesis and evidence advanced by Pribram (1971; Ferguson, 1978) that the interference pattern of holograms, as produced by physicists with coherent laser light sources, has properties that are remarkably similar to the characteristics of human memory. Holographic computer memory systems, which should significantly enhance the computer's capability in pattern recognition, are already being developed.

If the recognition of a La Giaconda smile, myxedematous facies, parkinsonian gait, or abnormal shadows on a chest X-ray are, at least for the moment, human tasks, other medical and psychological problems are largely serial, and these are particularly amenable to solution by computer. In recent years two important developments have made it especially practicable to use the computer to assist the physician with a variety of medical decisions. One is the advent of programing languages that can manipulate strings of text according to the rules of syntax, just as the more widely used computer languages manipulate numbers according to the rules of arithmetic (Ruderman and Pappalardo, 1970). The other is the development of interactive or conversational computer programs that communicate with the user not through a batch of punched cards but through a suitable terminal, such as a teletypewriter-video-tube display that exchanges messages with the computer over ordinary telephone lines (Gordon, 1970; Greist et al., 1976). These video displays can be programed so that the responses required can be indicated on the face of the tube and can be activated by an electronic signal, by a light pen, or by simply touching the spot with one's finger, thus eliminating the need for typing responses. User acceptance of these terminals has been excellent.

Computer Applications in Clinical Psychiatry

Clinical applications of computers in psychiatry are being reported with increasing frequency. Most such applications can be classified into one of five general areas, as follows: (1) data collection about the patient, including numerous rating scales, automated history, and mental status procedures; (2) attempts to identify objectively symptom clusters that may be designated as syndromes or diagnoses; (3) formal assignment of diagnosis, treatment form, and prognosis; (4) evaluation of patient progress and treatment outcome; (5) treatment per se (Colby et al., 1975).

Within the traditional medical model, each of the first four areas may be viewed as a part of a diagnostic process undergoing continuous refinement. Conventional diagnoses are not logical, mathematical combinations of signs, symptoms, and premises. They are convenient labels, classifications of particular clusters of findings necessitated by the need for facile communication among clinicians and between clinician and patient. Stroebel and Glueck (1972) recommended that a diagnosis facilitates (1) choice of treatment alternatives, (2) evaluation of prognosis, (3) references to the therapeutic literature, (4) record keeping, and (5) feedback refinement of the diagnostic schema itself.

The results of clinical, as opposed to statistical, prediction studies by Sines (1970) show that, when adequately programed, computers can perform the diagnostic process as well as or better than skilled clinicians. Automation of diagnosis is of considerable value in freeing clinicians to devote their talents to other creative activities in which they clearly excel. But beyond considerations of the efficiency of automation, what are the possibilities of significantly improving clinical practice in other ways?

Because of natural limitations in human capacity, conventional diagnosis is a sequential process in which signs and symptoms are viewed one at a time or in small subsets. Subtle relationships between many variables, as in psychiatry, may go undetected by this approach. Through computer techniques, such previously unrecognized relationships can be detected, thus improving the science of diagnosis and not simply automating it (Stroebel and Glueck, 1972). Even with an abundance of clinical and laboratory information, the diagnosis of many diseases is difficult; for example, patients suffering from several ailments are often particularly difficult to diagnose with certainty. Preventive medicine is using mass-screening techniques with increasing frequency, such as the use of the MMPI for psychological screening. Many of these procedures necessitate analysis by clinicians or skilled technicians, and some method to minimize this work load, especially routine analysis, is desirable.

Before the computer can be used to significant advantage in diagnosis, precise procedures must be formulated to deduce the clinical state of the patient from observed signs and symptoms. Closer examination of this problem suggests several general strategies. One can try to use the processes the physician uses in a sufficiently precise manner to allow for their simulation by a computer program. Unfortunately, there are several drawbacks to this approach. According to Feinstein (1967), the most obvious drawback is the current lack of understanding of the processes used by physicians. The way in which a physician interprets clues from a patient may be exceedingly difficult to describe with the necessary precision. Even if this were not the case, the simulation of human diagnostic processes on a computer may fail to exploit the comparative advantages of the machine (Stroebel and Glueck, 1972). It seems highly unlikely that the diagnostic processes of doctors would be those most applicable for computers. Consequently, the study of the diagnostic process as performed by physicians may yield important insights into the general capabilities needed in a computer program; however, the actual strategies used in such a program should reflect the unique capabilities and limitations of the machine.

According to Lipkin et al. (1969) and Duckworth and Kedward (1978), many computer applications to the diagnostic process emphasize the reliability (consistency) of the computer in comparison with the clinical diagnostician; given the raw data describing a patient, the computer always arrives at the same diagnosis. Human diagnosticians—in, for example, videotape cross-cultural studies—do not command this degree of reliability and often come to different diagnoses. Of course, the computer diagnosis may be wrong, invalid—that is, not representative of the true state of affairs. A computer program that diagnosed every psychiatric case as schizophrenia would be 100 per cent reliable, but its validity would match only the base rate of actual schizophrenia in the population diagnosed by the computer. Both reliability and validity are important, but restrictions are usually imposed on the validity corresponding to the limitations of reliability. The reliability (consistency) of diagnoses is primarily an issue of method; validity (accuracy) reflects the achievement of an objective, the prediction of a real-life criterion.

Figure 3 presents four steps in the diagnostic process and illustrates conventional clinical approaches, as opposed to computer-compatible (objective or actuarial) approaches. Much of the difficulty in interpreting the literature on computer diagnosis arises from the confusion between steps 2 and 3 in this deceptively simple sequence.

STEP 1: MEASUREMENT-ASSESSMENT

Diagnosis starts with the identification of the historical and presenting signs and symptoms characteristic of a given patient. Conventional clinical methods that produce a history or a mental status summary in narrative form or both are usually not suitable for succeeding computer coding (Benfari et al., 1972). Spitzer and Endicott (1971) drew attention to the expanding interest in the substitution of semiobjective checklists, rating scales, and Q-sorts, which are more amenable to computer scoring to yield quantitative indices reflecting the patient's behavior, as well as a machine-generated narrative summary. Examples are the MMPI (Rome et al., 1962), MHPA (Glueck and Stroebel, 1969), Brief Psychiatric Rating Scale (Lyerly and Abbott, 1966), Current and Past Psychopathology Scales (Spitzer and Endicott, 1969), Automated Mental Status (Donnelly et al., 1970), Automated Psychiatric History (Maultsby and Slack, 1971), Automated Psychiatric Nursing Notes (Rosenberg et al., 1967), Clyde Mood Scale (Lyerly and Abbott, 1966), Psychophysiological Diary (Stroebel et al., 1971), Problem-oriented Record (Hayes-Roth et al., 1972), Present State Examination (Wing et al., 1974), and the Community Adjustment Profile System (Evenson et al., 1974). In addition to computer applicability, these semiobjective rating instruments are organized to ensure completeness and to augment reliability by requiring the observation of behavior in noninferential, phenomenologically small units; scored as numerical indices, they allow quantitative assessment of reliability and validity. Glueck and Stroebel (1969), Stroebel et al. (1967), and Leader and Klein (1977) observed that many clinicians find rating scales tedious, dull, and insensitive to the finer shadings of their clinical abilities. Recent developments in interactive video computer terminals, real-time computer systems, and branching logic may revive interest in using these instruments in routine clinical practice (Greist et al., 1976). One important capability of these techniques is their provision for immediate feedback of rating results.

STEP 2: DIAGNOSTIC SCHEMATA-MODELS

Clinicians gain knowledge of which signs, symptoms, and therapeutic modalities cluster together by way of training and experience. *Diagnostic and Statistical Manual of Mental Disorders,* third edition (DSM-III), the official American Psychiatric Association diagnostic system, is a formal basis for continuing empirical refinement of the diagnostic process (Feighner et al., 1972). Is the fundamental structure of this empirical schema optimal? Should it be subjected to drastic changes? Or will empirical refinement of the existing structure prove adequate—that is, by the addition of some new subcategories or combination of others to correspond more adequately with the prognosis and choice of therapeutic regimen? These are some questions being asked by investigators who used computerized clustering processes to pursue new diagnostic schemata for comparison with DSM-II (Spitzer and Endicott, 1974). Essentially, this is an endeavor to start with no a priori knowledge of current symptom-clustering to build a diagnostic schema. A large set of generally appropriate measurements and tests is made on a sizable number of patients, furnishing a multiple-variable data set of signs and symptoms, which is analyzed by a computer algorithm in an attempt to identify a latent organization by grouping patients into a diagnostic schema. In effect, the computer attempts to determine which patients seem to cluster together on the basis of available signs and symptoms, to which subsequent diagnostic labels may be applied. In the statistical literature this process is referred to as a taxonomy problem.

Various approaches have been taken for developing algorithms for clustering. The approach most extensively used in America is the generalized Euclidian distance between clusters, frequently referred to in the literature as a multivariate form of the Pythagorean theorem or Mahalanobis D (Benfari et al., 1972). The British (Jones, 1968; Paykel, 1971; Everitt et al., 1971; Everitt, 1972) have preferred multiple-correlation techniques, such as factor analysis. According to Maxwell (1971), the debate persists as to whether a typological (categorical or dimensional factor analytical) method is most propitious. Maxwell (1972) put forth persuasive arguments that the two processes should be combined; patients should first be classified according to a diagnostic cluster to specify type of pathology, followed by the application of dimensional analysis within each cluster to determine amount of pathology.

The diverse clustering procedures vary in (1) the selection of a measure of distance or similarity, (2) the choice of clustering subjects in attribute, or attributes in subject space, and (3) the choice of a search procedure for establishing maximum cluster constellations. Nilsson (1969) contended that available clustering techniques are logically optimal, but a survey of clinical applications of existing procedures is not reassuring. Two issues are notable. The average number of patients allocated to any identifiable cluster is rarely in excess of 50 per cent, and the identified sign-symptom clusters are often not reasonable clinically (Bonner, 1966; Glueck and Stroebel, 1969; Everitt et al., 1971). Lehman (1969) referred to an expanding number of computer-made psychopathological syndromes, clusters, and factors as "the new syndrome explosion."

Insofar as the clustering techniques can be specified as optimal, it must be inferred that some of the difficulty encountered in the application of the clustering or similarity algorithm techniques lies in the nature of the data provided. Logically, a classification system ultimately relies on those attributes, tests, signs, and symptoms that form its foundation. Patients who are alike in regard to one set of symptoms may appear quite disparate when viewed from another set. Currently applied sets may be inappropriate; a prevailing objection to nearly all computer-clustering or classification programs is that they seldom include any patient history data. Notable here is an investigation (Simon et al., 1971) in which the mental status examination was the sole basis for the initial diagnoses. Alter-

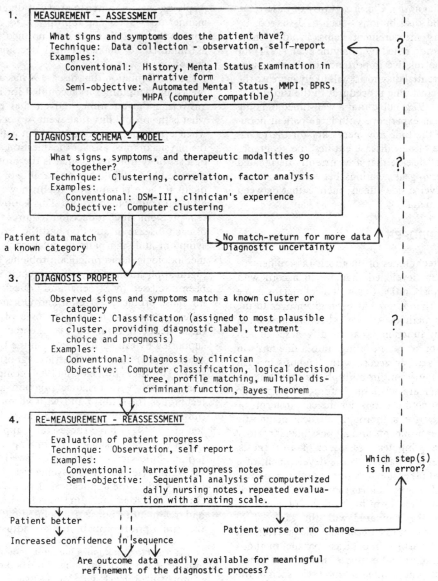

1. **MEASUREMENT - ASSESSMENT**

    What signs and symptoms does the patient have?
    Technique: Data collection - observation, self-report
    Examples:
        Conventional: History, Mental Status Examination in
                       narrative form
        Semi-objective: Automated Mental Status, MMPI, BPRS,
                         MHPA (computer compatible)

2. **DIAGNOSTIC SCHEMA - MODEL**

    What signs, symptoms, and therapeutic modalities go
            together?
    Technique: Clustering, correlation, factor analysis
    Examples:
        Conventional: DSM-III, clinician's experience
        Objective: Computer clustering

Patient data match   No match-return for more data
a known category   Diagnostic uncertainty

3. **DIAGNOSIS PROPER**

    Observed signs and symptoms match a known cluster or
            category
    Technique: Classification (assigned to most plausible
                cluster, providing diagnostic label, treatment
                choice and prognosis)
    Examples:
        Conventional: Diagnosis by clinician
        Objective: Computer classification, logical decision
                    tree, profile matching, multiple dis-
                    criminant function, Bayes Theorem

4. **RE-MEASUREMENT - REASSESSMENT**

    Evaluation of patient progress
    Technique: Observation, self report
    Examples:
        Conventional: Narrative progress notes
        Semi-objective: Sequential analysis of computerized
                         daily nursing notes, repeated evalua-
                         tion with a rating scale.

Which step(s)
is in error?

Patient better

Increased confidence in sequence   Patient worse or no change

Are outcome data readily available for meaningful
refinement of the diagnostic process?

FIGURE 3. Four steps in the diagnostic process.

ation of the diagnosis after history information was included occurred in only 15 per cent of the sample. Feinstein (1967) cited five components used by clinicians to determine the diagnosis, prognosis, and therapy of patients that are not now being included as assessment data in computer-clustering programs. (1) How the disease was detected: Did the patient go to the doctor with symptomatic complaints, or was he without symptoms and the illness discovered in some routine screening procedure? (2) Clusters of clinical characteristics: These included right lower quadrant abdominal pain, tenderness and muscle spasm on palpitation, and an elevated white blood cell count in appendicitis. (3) The succession in which symptoms appear: This is well exemplified in the development of paranoia by the series of changes in behavior called Magnan's progression. (4) Persistence of symptoms: If a patient presents with shortness of breath, is it a recent development, or has the condition existed over a period of years? (5) Co-morbidity: Is the patient suffering from other diseases in addition to the one being treated? Feinstein noted that these highly relevant distinguishing features are not designated in any current systematic fashion in the scientific investigations and statistics of therapy

because no method for classifying them has been adequately developed. He stated:

> One cannot expect the computer to develop such a taxonomy because the necessary data are not now included in the information we give the computer to play with.

Apparently, no general means exist for ascertaining either which or how various behavioral phenomena could most beneficially be denoted in numerical representation; this is still primarily an empirical matter, following a variety of rules and conventions found to be applicable in each particular circumstance. For this reason the design of a pattern-recognition algorithm for classifying electrocardiographic signals has necessitated the participation of competent cardiologists who know those aspects of an electrocardiogram wave form that are diagnostically critical. Nilsson (1969) suggested that for almost any automatic clustering problem 95 per cent of the design effort includes the pursuit of an appropriate numerical representation of the medical data to be categorized, basically the process of reaching genuinely appropriate measurement and assessment (step 1 in diagnosis). Closer scrutiny of base rates, dimensional scaling, and distributions—such as J-shaped, U-shaped, and normal—of measurement items, in addition to stepwise multiple regression noted by Forsythe et al. (1971) for the identification of the relative importance of various signs and symptoms for differential diagnosis, will likely increase the usefulness of objective clustering procedures in the future.

Stroebel and Glueck (1972) noted that a well-tuned ongoing cluster analysis of clinical experience with large patient populations could minimize the time now necessary for the recognition of the emergence of new disease entities, the geographically multifocal sites of disease that are currently designated as epidemics, and emerging associations between new therapeutic regimens and adverse side effects, such as that between thalidomide and phocomelia.

STEP 3: DIAGNOSIS PROPER

Objective computer techniques of diagnosis (assignment or classification) have been developed that are in accord with empirical clinical diagnosis, at least as well as clinicians agree among themselves. A prime effort has been given over to the development of parallel methods—Bayes's theorem, maximum likelihood, discriminant function—that modify a set of test results, measurements, or symptom ratings into a diagnosis in one stage. These models are in accord with diagnosis in such specialty areas as psychiatry and in multiphasic screening, in which all necessary data are available before the diagnostic formulation. However, one must consider the cost in terms of patient time and money for a thorough medical diagnostic system if all possible measurements and all possible laboratory tests were made before computer assessment of a diagnosis. Recognition of this dilemma has led to the development of a sequential approach that takes into account the relative cost of sign, symptom, and laboratory information and the cost of misdiagnoses, as does a clinician in his work-up of a patient. Sequential methods can be compared with the game of 20 questions, in which the answer to a question is the determinant of the next question to be asked. In contrast, parallel methods pose all 20 questions at once and evaluate the answers simultaneously to reach a decision. Sequential methods, such as the diagnostic tree, are gainfully used when each of the component questions is answered consistently for all members of a given category. However, when there is a scattering of answers, which is common when dealing with psychiatric data, sequential methods may take too many wrong turns. Klein et al. (1968) provide one answer to this problem by the use of a selective filter or sieve variation of the sequential diagnostic decision tree.

Parallel techniques. The two most often used versions of the parallel approach to computer diagnosis-classification of specific patients are Bayes's theorem and the multiple discriminant function. Bayes's theorem has been called the fundamental law of medical diagnosis, dating from the contribution of an English clergyman, Thomas Bayes, in the 18th century. Customary methods of the use of statistics to evaluate experimental outcomes—for example, the "t" statistic to test hypotheses, confidence intervals, and levels of significance—usually adopt a null hypothesis of "no prior knowledge"—for instance, whether a drug or a placebo will be superior in a therapeutic trial. Of course, investigators do use prior knowledge of their field to decide which drug is to be used, which hypothesis is to be tested, and what level of significance to use, but they never include this prior knowledge in the analysis of their results.

Applying the computer to arrive at diagnostic decisions in this manner does not seem appropriate to the logician because it implies that a statistician with no medical background is just as qualified to make medical decisions as an experienced doctor.

Prior information that disease X has a certain probability of preceding symptom Y is accounted for by Bayes's theorem by answering the question, "Given that event B has occurred, what is the probability that event A preceded it?" For example, when a physician examines a patient with a series of symptoms, the physician must answer the question, "Given the occurrence of a set of symptoms B, what is the probability that disease A preceded it?" What is the probability of the presence of appendicitis if there is pain over McBurney's point, nausea, and an elevated white blood count? This is obviously a Bayes's theorem problem. Such a decision requires the a priori probability of each disease in question and the provisional probability of symptom and sign patterns given each disease. A number of methodological and practical problems to be met in the meaningful application of Bayes's theorem to medical diagnosis have been discussed by Stroebel and Glueck (1972). Notwithstanding these problems, Overall and Gorham (1962) reported excellent consensus in the diagnoses of skilled clinicians and those deduced from Bayes's theorem (pattern probability), supported by ratings derived from the Brief Psychiatric Rating Scale (BPRS) for 13 psychiatric diagnostic types. In a following study, Hollister and Overall (1964) compared the Bayes's theorem solution with distance function and profile correlation techniques (favorably) and with vector product classification (unfavorable results). Greist and his colleagues (1973; Gustafson et al., 1977) have successfully applied a Bayes's theorem strategy to predict suicide risk in a pilot study, using computer terminal interviews, which were viewed as less threatening than being interviewed by a psychiatrist. In an overview, Kraus (1972) studied the application of Bayes's theorem in models of clinical decisions, including suicidal risk, differential diagnosis, and treatment response. He pointed out that, when the Bayes's theorem a priori probabilities are adjusted,

it is possible to minimize the most undesirable decision errors. For example, since misclassification of cerebral neoplasm or meningitis as schizophrenia is much more serious than a converse misclassification, the clinician could decide to minimize the former, notwithstanding a corresponding increase in the latter which would automatically result from the adjustment.

A second kind of parallel method, multivariate statistical classification procedures, has the capability of finding subtle connections among many variables that may be of diagnostic value. For this purpose the best-known technique is the linear multiple-discriminant function, which requires that groups of patients who have unequivocal diagnoses be grouped for each disease category included in the list of possible diagnoses. Then a designation set of variables is measured on each patient, and the classification rule is computed. The same variable set is measured for a patient of unknown diagnosis, and a diagnosis is made by using the derived rule. In essence, the unknown patient is placed in the diagnostic group he most closely approximates. Glueck and Stroebel (1969) summarized several basic steps in this classification process. Experienced clinicians first formulate a hypothesis about the number and the nature of anticipated groups sufficient for classification of the domain in question, such as diagnosis or prediction of treatment choices, and assign patients to them. Next, multiple-discriminant analysis, a statistical procedure, is applied to quantitative data in the patient files to minimize variability within each group and to maximize the distance among groups; this is accomplished by the calculation of a set of weights, which are then applied to the original data values. Frequently, a group is not distinctive enough to stand by itself and is deleted from the analysis.

The patients who are not properly classified into a valid group are also eliminated. The reasoning for this purification process, which adjusts the co-variance matrices to approximately equal size, is based on a cognizance of the uncertainties intrinsic in the original clinical decision about group membership and on the acknowledgment that the quantitative data used in the analysis may not be adequate for making the clinical decision in question, as when history information is not part of the analysis but is critical for group classification.

The last step is to repeat the discriminant analysis on the purified data to develop an optimal set of weights for subsequent classification. Only half of the cases in the original sample defined by the clinician are, in fact, used to arrive at the optimal weights; the other half are used to calculate the validity of the weights obtained. These weights are used to evaluate the probability of group membership for an individual patient in each of the groups.

This probabilistic output from the classification procedure is in keeping with clinical reality; it acknowledges that rarely is there a patient who exemplifies the classical textbook description of an illness. Probabilities further provide the intensity dimension frequently lacking in other computer classification approaches. Those patients without a high probability of membership in any of the available groups need additional clinical scrutiny to establish whether they are exceptional, rare, or highly deviant cases or if new group categories ought to be created to assimilate them in the future.

Sequential techniques. Various sequential computer methods have been developed to emulate the clinical diagnostic process in psychiatry. These methods include cookbook rules for sequential pattern matching, the logical decision tree, and the selective filter variation of the logical decision tree. The notion of deriving cookbook rules for sequential pattern matching may be attributed to Meehl's book *Clinical versus Statistical Prediction* (1954). In this procedure a list of empirically derived criteria or rules is applied in a sequential manner to sign and symptom information. When a pattern of sign and symptom data matches a set of criteria, the patient is placed in the associated diagnosis. Two such cookbook methods of diagnostic classification of the MMPI profile have been computerized by Glueck and Stroebel (1969). A set of 2,012 MMPI patient profiles was tried on each set of cookbook rules. The rules by Marks and Seeman successfully categorized 469 (23.3 per cent) of the 2,012 patients. When the Gilberstadt rules were applied, 805 (40 per cent) of the 2,012 profiles were successfully classified. When the 469 patients classified by the Marks and Seeman rules were tested on the Gilberstadt rules, 31 per cent passed. When the 805 patients classified by the Gilberstadt rules were tested on the Marks and Seeman rules, 54 per cent passed. These relatively low classification and agreement rates imply that the two populations used to make the rules were likely quite different from each other and also different from the sample against which they were compared. Careful study of the profiles that did not pass either set of rules showed that failure in most instances was due to an overly restrictive rule for one or another of the profile factors, despite the fact that the profile pattern was almost identical to others that passed the criteria. Because there was no consistent pattern as to which

rule was too restrictive, no easy means was obvious for loosening the restraints for this actuarial approach. Both the Marks and Seeman and the Gilberstadt rules are important contributions to the field of actuarially derived personality description. The expansion of their work to cover a higher percentage of personality types should receive precedence during the next several years.

The logical decision tree approach to psychiatric diagnosis resembles the logic used by most clinicians. At one point in this approach, all patients enter a branching decision tree and are then passed along different logic pathways, dependent on the result of a given test or measure. Good examples of the logical decision tree approach were the DIAGNO diagnostic classification systems devised by Spitzer and Endicott (1969) and their associates (Spitzer et al., 1974, 1978) for psychiatric patients. DIAGNO I was limited to current mental status and made one of 27 diagnoses. DIAGNO II also used current mental status, as well as some historical information, and increased the number of potential diagnoses to 46. The third version, DIAGNO III, used data from two major clinical intake forms of the Multistate Informational System: the Mental Status Examination Record (MSER) and the Psychiatric Anamnestic Record (PAR). By including the extensive coverage of both of these documents related to both present and historical information, the DIAGNO III program was sufficiently complex to make as many as 75 of the discrete psychiatric diagnoses listed in DSM-II. The rate of agreement between clinicians and the various versions of the DIAGNO programs approximated the agreement level reached among different clinicians when diagnosing the same patients. In several overview papers Spitzer et al. (1974, 1978) reviewed the logical constraints on the validity of computer diagnosis, as compared with expert clinicians, and reviewed their rationale for encouraging the use of the Kappa statistic, which corrects for the possibility of chance agreement among different evaluation sources. Their experience in developing the DIAGNO system and comparing it with alternative methods of computer diagnosis may be viewed as germinal in formulating the logical structure of the third edition of the American Psychiatric Association's *Diagnostic and Statistical Manual of Mental Disorders* (DSM-III), which requires that diagnoses be based on specific observational criteria, with provision for a multiaxial system sensitive to a number of other relevant physical and adaptational variables and for the evaluation of degree of severity. The rationale for the DSM-III criteria emerged from an analysis of the psychiatric diagnostic problem at Washington University conducted by Feighner et al. (1972), subsequently evolving into a system entitled Research Diagnostic Criteria (RDC) by Spitzer et al., (1975). It is anticipated that widespread adoption of the DSM-III rationale by the psychiatric community will improve the training of psychiatric residents, provide the potential for improved agreement rates among trained clinicians and computer approaches to diagnosis, and significantly improve the treatment of psychiatric patients.

By way of comparison of the logical decision tree approach and the parallel approach of discriminant function analysis, Melrose et al. (1970) compared the success rate of DIAGNO II with the stepwise multiple discriminant function classification of 443 patients. Seventy of the 94 Current and Past Pathology Scales variables that were found to be most instrumental in discrimination predicted the first criterion diagnosis about half as well as DIAGNO II; when second and third diagnoses were incorporated, the discriminant function worked moderately better than DIAGNO II. The superiority of the discriminant function method was in furnishing probabilities and providing increased perspective, particularly in cases assigned by DIAGNO II to "nonspecific conditions" or "no mental disorder," because it allows the clinician to determine his patient's inclination toward particular pathological states. In a somewhat comparable study, Altman and his colleagues (1978) at the Missouri Institute of Psychiatry, using a sample of 1,600 patients, found that the linear discriminant function approach actually performed somewhat better than the logical decision tree approach when two conditions were met: (1) when the derivation sample of patients was sufficiently large and (2) when patients being classified by the computer were similar to those used in the developmental sample for the discriminant function model.

One predicament arises with the logical decision tree approach when the measurement data are subject to scatter, thus allowing a given patient to be directed down an erroneous path in the logical decision tree. This issue has been resolved by designing a selective filter or sieve modification of the logical decision tree. In this variation, sequential nodal decision points function as filters, requiring that most but not all appropriate sign and symptom data be positive before they can be transmitted to the next point in the decision tree. This procedure was used by Klein and Davis (1969) for the classification of 13 psychiatric diagnoses, using a 36-item rating scale and Lorr's (1960) Multidimensional Scale for Rating Psychiatric Patients. Comparisons of this nonparametric method and discriminant function analysis indicated that the techniques are equally effective. However, Klein and Davis preferred the nonparametric approach because it does not chance violating multivariate suppositions needed by the discriminant function and because it makes prima facie sense in following traditional medical logic, whereas discriminant function weights do not.

Summary. The findings discussed here suggest that, regardless of the approach taken—whether an empirical model of diagnosis, as is provided by an expert clinician, or an objective clustering model of diagnosis—classification—assignment techniques are now at hand for diagnostic labeling of psychiatric patients with an accuracy (validity) that matches that of expert clinicians and with a reliability nearing 100 per cent. However, a disturbing fact is the lack of ability of any general

classification method—expert clinician or computer program—to accomplish more than 70 to 75 per cent interrater reliability in the prediction of psychopathological criteria. The systematic approach taken in the development of DSM-III may have a significant impact on these percentages and may change Sines's (1970) pessimism regarding the three factors that may contribute to this apparent limit of 75 per cent accuracy.

In any examination of the literature of prediction of human behavior, one cannot fail to note: (1) the wide variability in the accuracy with which individual clinicians are able to make predictions, (2) the existence of some types of patients about whom accurate predictions cannot regularly be made, and (3) the existence of some types of criterion characteristics that cannot be predicted by any method for any of our patients.

STEP 4: REMEASUREMENT-REASSESSMENT

Of the four steps in the diagnostic schema presented here, the last is likely to be of most consequence for refinement of the diagnostic system, because other external sources of validation—such as biopsies, laboratory tests, and postmortem examination—are seldom of use in psychiatry. Regrettably, this is the one step that is frequently omitted, especially in larger institutions, where there are not enough personnel, and in most discharges, where patients are not followed up.

Rating instruments have now become available that expedite routine quantitative measurement of treatment outcome. Examples are the Psychiatric Evaluation Form developed by Endicott and Spitzer (1972), Autorhythmometry developed by Halberg et al. (1972), and the Psychophysiological Diary, developed by Stroebel et al. (1971), which is a computer-scored record of moods, body changes, and life events sensitive to periodic or monotonic changes over time.

What is needed now are remeasurement-reassessment techniques that are routine, quantitative, and semiobjective. Toward this end, Stroebel and Glueck (1970) constructed a system in which factor scores secured on a regular daily basis for each patient from computer-scored nursing notes described by Rosenberg et al. (1967) and Glueck et al. (1978) were subjected to a graphic statistical process called sequential analysis to produce computer global decisions of "significantly better,"

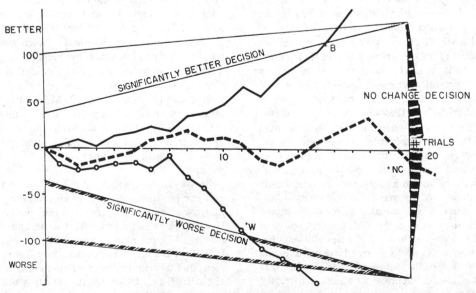

FIGURE 4. Computer global judgments.

"worse," or "unchanged" without special research techniques. The advantages of this approach are that it is automated and has built-in statistical guides for assessing patient progress over time on a daily basis. Figure 4 shows three possible outcomes for a patient's nursing note depression factor on a sequential analysis graph. When a significantly better decision is made, there is an increase in confidence in the whole diagnostic sequence, steps 1 to 3 (see Figure 3); when the patient remains unchanged or gets worse, there is uncertainty as to which of the preceding steps is wrong. Discrete quantitative data are available for feedback correction of the diagnostic sequence at a low price because automated nursing notes are already a part of the daily hospital routine, and the computer decisions become available without an additional commitment of time by psychiatrists in order to complete the periodic ratings. Because the result is in a numerical, computer-compatible state, meaningful purification of the diagnostic procedure is also possible on a routine basis, as it is in many other phases of medicine, such as morbidity-mortality conferences. With the more conventional techniques, which rely on narrative data and idiosyncratic models of diagnosis and classification, the result of the diagnostic succession is more uncertain and is usually lost for further refinement.

The development of the concept of the problem-oriented medical record (Weed, 1970) has led to the development of several automated approaches to the monitoring of patient progress. One of the best was described by Meldman et al. (1977). Most of the concerns about inadequate follow-up of patient progress expressed above seem to be answered in this system.

Other Clinical Uses of Computers

Several clinical applications of computers in fields closely related to psychiatry are attracting sufficient interest to warrant brief mention here.

PSYCHOPHYSIOLOGY

Psychophysiology has gained new relevance as a basic medical science of psychiatry (Sternbach and Greenfield, 1972) through the development of computer techniques making possible the analysis of multiple and complex variables approaching clinical reality. Historically noteworthy was the development in the 1960's at the Massachusetts Institute of Technology of the LINC (Laboratory Instrument Computer) class of computer, which could be interfaced relatively effortlessly with polygraphs and other psychophysiological devices. LINC-type computers (classic LINC, LINC-8, PDP-12, and subsequent variants using increasingly inexpensive and faster central processors) are now commonplace in psychiatry-neuroscience laboratories and have greatly enhanced the clinical relevance of laboratory investigations, permitting real-time interaction between a test subject and computations based on his ongoing physiology. The emerging technology of biofeedback is an especially relevant example of this real-time interaction, coupling physiological instrumentation with a microcomputer processor in portable form suitable for office treatment of a variety of psychosomatic and anxiety-related conditions.

NEUROLOGY AND PSYCHOPHARMACOLOGY

Bickford et al. (1972) developed a computer-based pictorial display technique that compresses electroencephalographic (EEG) frequency-spectrum information from a 30- to 40-minute clinical recording into one page. Similar computer techniques that examine the synchrony, calculated by measures of coherence and phase angle, between any two EEG electrode placements have been developed by Banquet (1973) and by Glueck and Stroebel (1978; Stroebel and Glueck, 1978). An example of the computer-produced compressed power spectrum array, coherence, and phase angle for 1 minute of recording of a patient having a seizure is shown in Figure 5. Figures 6 and 7 summarize the power spectral data for all eight electrode placements, with Figure 6 showing the power distribution for each frequency from 1 to 31 Hz., and Figure 7 showing the power distribution by five band widths—delta, theta, alpha, low beta, and high beta. These displays permit a more precise evaluation of EEG variations under conditions of normality, altered states of consciousness, and psychopathology and under drug conditions. Fink (1975 a, b) and Itil (1974) have been pioneers in developing techniques such as those shown in Figures 6 and 7 called "cerebral electrometry" (Fink) and "quantitative pharmacoelectroencephalography" (Itil) to assist in the clinical and preclinical evaluation of psychoactive drugs. Kupfer et al. (1976) developed similar procedures, with particular emphasis on psychophysiological sleep alterations, to assist in the diagnosis and treatment choice in depression. John and his colleagues (1977) developed an especially ambitious computer analysis involving power spectral and averaged evoked responses from up to 57 derived electrode locations in response to a variety of simple sensory and more complicated perceptual stimuli that they call the "neurometric test battery." With complicated multivariate statistical models and validation, the battery gave early results suggesting that the neurometric procedure may provide an objective, culture-free evaluation of a variety of soft and hard neurological deficits, including neurological subclasses of learning disabilities and minimal brain dysfunction.

Recent confusion surrounding attempts to correlate subtypes of depression with the most effective treatment alternatives has also been clarified by using computer technology. Schildkraut (1974) used the multiple-discriminant function to weight biochemical measures of urinary 3-methoxy-4-hydrohydroxyphenylglycol (MHPG), norepinephrine (NEP), vanillylmandelic acid (VMA), and normetanephrine (NMT) to yield a D-type score, which seems to correlate with diagnostic subtype better than do single measures alone. For example, recent data suggest that D-type scores can predict circular affective disorders responsive to lithium therapy before the clinical appearance of hypomania.

Computers as applied in neuroscience research (Brown, 1976) are beginning to provide a crucial degree of multivariate sophistication in keeping with the complexity of the brain itself. For example, a major breakthrough in the diagnosis of intracerebral pathology has already had dramatic clinical impact in psychiatry and neurology, using a technique known as computerized axial tomography. A review of the development of computerized X-ray scanning of the brain by Ambrose (1974) included Oldendorf's description in 1961 of an experimental system of producing a cross-sectional display of radiodensity discontinuities within the cranium. Independently of Oldendorf's findings, Hounsfield later devised a usable diagnostic system using X-rays. The transmission of X-ray photons across a slice of tissue can be measured by a system of crystal detectors using a scanning gantry, continuously operating X-ray tube, and a narrow collimated X-ray beam. The cranium may be scanned in 1.6-cm.- and 2.6-cm.-thick slices by paired crystal detectors, and the results of 1-degree readings over 180

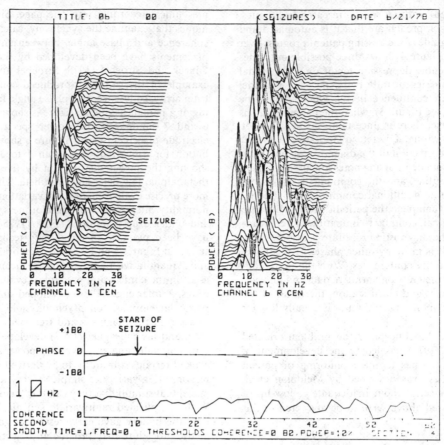

FIGURE 5. Isometric plot of electroencephalographic activity from the left and right central leads in a patient with seizure disorder.

degrees form the basis of 28,800 simultaneous equations, which are solved by a computer. The cathode ray tube picture is a visual presentation of an intensity display based on the relative densities of different tissue structures. The examination is both quantitative and qualitative and has contributed significantly to diagnostic insight into intracerebral tissue pathology.

User Acceptance of Automated Systems

Over the past dozen years, a number of attempts have been made to provide viable hospital information systems. The fact that most have failed is partially due to problems of user acceptance. A major factor in these difficulties has been the failure of the various parties involved to develop adequate lines of communication in the early stages of the project. Most attempts to develop hospital information systems have originated with the electronic engineers and systems technicians, primarily from computer manufacturing companies or as spin-offs from these companies. In addition, most hospitals that have started computer operations have done so through the medium of the business office, because the use of computers in a business office in industry is quite similar to the same use in the business and administrative offices of a hospital. As a result, business applications—such as payroll, patient billing, and inventory control—have been given priority in the development of hospital computer systems, and the system design has centered on these familiar applications, rather than considering, at the outset, changes that may have to be made for appropriate clinical use.

When clinicians have been approached about automation, the approach has usually been made by electronics experts, with the clinicians being told, "This is the way the system runs; now, how will you modify your procedures to fit the system?" The usual answer has been, "I won't" or "I can't, and, therefore, I'm not interested in the wonders of your computer system."

This attitude is in sharp contrast to that displayed by most clinicians when new medical devices are introduced that have an immediate impact on the treatment of the patient. If the devices seem to have any potential for improved patient care, they are usually accepted with enthusiasm and, if really effective, are rapidly adopted throughout the profession or specialty. It seems obvious, therefore, that in most instances the people who would develop an automated hospital or patient information system have failed in their initial attempts to convince the clinician that the system would, in fact, result in improved patient care. Generally, on installation of the computer system, all levels of the clinical staff initially see only a demand for a significant change in their traditional ways of doing their jobs, with the additional burden of voluminous new forms and added paperwork of all sorts, with almost nothing to show for this additional activity. The result is immediate and severe resistance to the entire idea, which may lead to a failure of the automation attempt at an early stage, or, if the project is pursued, inadequate and erroneous information is usually fed into the computer system. No one should be surprised when the output from such a system is greeted with little enthusiasm and, at times, outright scorn (Leader and Klein, 1977).

The hospital information systems that have survived have done so in large part because the clinical users of the system were consulted from the outset. The way they performed their tasks was carefully evaluated, and attempts, although not always successful, were made to try to modify the computer system to fit the clinical needs and usual mode of operation.

The direction of policy, planning, and evaluation should be vested in the competent administrative levels of the hospital, including the top clinical personnel. This procedure assures physicians and hospital personnel that the computer installation will be considered in relationship to the over-all objectives of the hospital and that matters that inevitably cross lines of responsibility will be dealt with effectively. The introduction of automation in any environment tends to provoke anxiety through its threat to personal security. This is certainly true in the hospital setting. There is not only the threat of job loss and the fear of losing identity as the machine takes over but also the belief, especially in psychiatry, that depersonalization as a result of using the machine will jeopardize the good relationship between patient and clinician and between patient and nurse that is essential to the therapeutic process. The development of a proper understanding of the capabilities of electronic equipment, including both its wonders and its limitations, lessens the unreasoning objections to automation founded on faulty premises or ignorance.

Any program designed to promote understanding of the computer project should include representatives from all departments of the hospital in the discussion of automation plans. The involvement of key personnel in the initial planning phases of the project can create tremendous interest, especially if deliberate attempts are made to show how automation of various hospital activities can, in fact, improve hospital efficiency and patient care. The development of automated pro-

cedures must include personnel from the various departments concerned, so that they can have an adequate say in the development of procedures, forms, and reports associated with each application. Equally important are the techniques developed for interfacing the clinical staff with the automated system. A basic philosophy governing the design of computer-based psychiatric information systems provides that all who require and are entitled to access to the data files are able to enter or receive appropriate information directly and without the need for special skills or extensive training. Hospital personnel are generally not familiar with the operation of conventional business machines and are certainly not familiar with the more sophisticated terminals that are coming into use in modern computer networks. The ideal set of terminals to satisfy all communications needs and user requirements has not yet been developed. However, various satisfactory techniques have been devised that allow hospital personnel, clinical staff, and, indeed, patients to communicate with the computer system with ease and with little discomfort. In some studies of computerized history taking, a majority of patients reported that they found the experience interesting and enjoyable. They were particularly impressed by the thoroughness of the questioning and the feeling that they could respond at their own pace, rather than being pressured to provide information to busy clinical staff members (Greist et al., 1977).

Another critical factor in determining acceptance of an automated system is the usefulness of the system to the clinical users. If the system requires large amounts of more or less precise information from the users but gives little in return, it

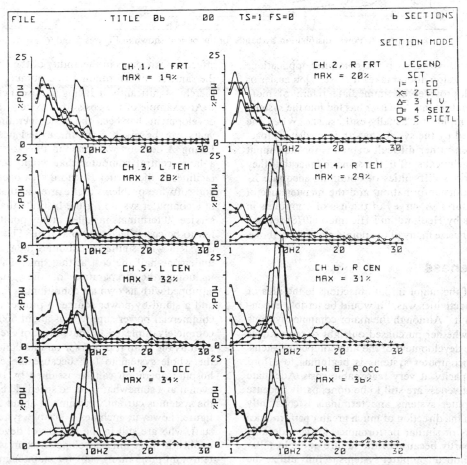

FIGURE 6. Percentage power distribution for frequencies from 1 to 31 Hz. in a patient with seizure disorder.

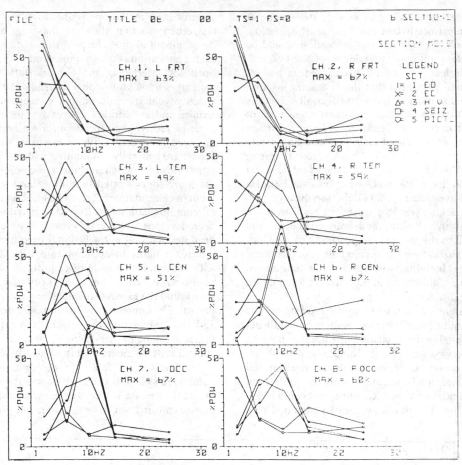

FIGURE 7. Power distribution by bands for the patient shown in Figures 5 and 6.

is quickly abandoned. However, if the computer applications are designed so that automation makes the user's job easier or more accurate and provides an immediate return of more sophisticated information than the user has fed into the system, then acceptance is rapid and usually enthusiastic. When the information provided by the system has an immediate impact on patient care, even rather difficult demands for data input are accepted by the clinical staff in the same manner that they now accept the various difficulties of obtaining adequate X-rays, clinical laboratory information, and the maintenance of strict asepsis procedures. A survey of the use of computers in psychiatric facilities by Hedlund and Hickman (1978) seemed to confirm and emphasize many of the points mentioned above.

Cost Effectiveness

In the past one of the major initial objections to the idea of automating clinical activities was, "It would be terribly expensive; we can't afford it." Although the major computer systems are still expensive, whether purchased outright or rented over a period of time, the development of the minicomputer systems and now the microcomputer systems is beginning to afford excellent system capacity at very reasonable costs. Adequate studies of cost effectiveness are still to be done, partly because the design of computer systems and terminals is constantly changing, usually in the direction of much greater performance for the same dollars or similar performance for considerably smaller costs, and partly because of the failure of the installations that have developed computer systems to fully utilize the system capability that has been installed. Much of the cost

effectiveness comes in the ability of the computer to distribute the same set of information to a number of application areas, thereby significantly reducing the usual clerical workload.

An example of the costs for a system that, while still under development, has been the basic operating system for several years can be given from the experience at the Institute of Living. A decision was made in 1969 to stop trying to develop a large central computer that would service various health facilities in the greater Hartford area because of the hardware and software problems that existed at that time. The purchase of a computer system for the Institute that had the capacity to service 40 terminals installed at key points in the hospital was felt to be cost effective at that time. The figures for acquiring a system with similar capabilities today would be somewhat under one-half the cost at that time. The cost of the system, including the preparation of the data processing center equipped with its own air conditioning for the computer room and a stand-by power source to protect against failure of the commercial power supply, was about $600,000. The system is completely duplexed, so that failure of even major components, such as the central processor on one computer, will not cause the whole system to fail, because the essential functions of hospital operation can be assumed by the second computer, even if at a somewhat reduced speed. The operating budget for the system is currently running at about $250,000 a year. This figure, however, includes a sizable systems and programing staff, who are still in the process of developing the computer applications. A fully developed system will require some systems and programing staff for maintenance of the system and for the development of new applications that will inevitably arise. However, the annual operating cost for a fully developed system can be reduced to $150,000. If the capital acquisition costs are spread over 5 years, the $370,000 a year cost for the system is about $1,000 a day, which, for a 400-bed hospital, is about $2.50 a patient a day (Glueck, 1974).

If computer technology develops to the point at which large central data systems, dedicated to the health care activities of the community, are built and shared by multiple users, some of the costs of the single hospital system described above can be reduced. None of the above figures tells the true final cost of the system, because many of the efficiencies that should be derived from a fully automated hospital are not yet available. These efficiencies are largely in the area of improved data communications, with a single transaction—for example, the ordering of a patient medication—having a simultaneous impact on the delivery of the proper medication to the patient, the appropriate charge being posted to the patient's bill, the pharmacy inventory being decremented for the amount of the medication dispensed, the medication being entered into the patient's record, and provisions for refill of the prescription, if required, being provided. The clerical and logistical costs of the above operation as presently done in a hospital can be figured and would be an essential part of the final determination of the net cost of the computer system to the institution.

The development of modern intelligent terminals—that is, terminals that have a minicomputer built into them—make it possible for sophisticated programs to be run at the terminals without communicating with the central computer. This increases the efficiency of the system, because much of the time consumed in processing information is involved in the access to and from the central computer and the data storage units.

As the pressure from third-party payers, federal agencies, and the various state agencies continues to grow for constant monitoring of patient care, length of patient stay, and professional competence, it is becoming ever more apparent that automation of both inpatient and outpatient psychiatric facilities, including the psychiatrist's private office, is no longer a question of an affordable luxury. In the opinion of many experts in the field, the only possible way to cut the staggering increase in costs, occasioned by the additional clerical work required to meet the demands for information before payment can be made and for the information required for continuing accreditation, is to fully automate these activities. It is increasingly apparent that "We can't afford the system" must change to "We can't afford *not* to have the system."

Medical-Legal Considerations

A major early concern of the developers of psychiatric computer systems, which were primarily located in institutions, was the question of meeting the accreditation requirements of the Joint Commission on Accreditation of Hospitals. With the passage in 1974 of the requirement for professional standards review organizations (PSRO's), it became obvious that automation of medical information was the only path for effective functioning of these review boards if they were to carry out their purpose of ensuring high-quality patient care and monitoring the use of hospital facilities. Various accrediting agencies have updated their standards to include electronic patient data storage, along with other forms of data storage, as providing adequate information. This change has increased the pressure for the development of adequate safeguards to ensure the accuracy and completeness of the information and to ensure confidentiality. Of immediate concern is the question of danger to the confidentiality of the doctor-patient relationship. The

issue of legal liability in the event of a serious system failure or a challenge to the adequacy of patient care has yet to be determined. The security of the storage of patient records against inadvertent or malicious invasion of their confidentiality and privacy is an important concern.

These concerns are not unique to the hospital field. Issues of confidentiality, signature confirmation, and backup in the event of system failure have been studied intensively in data processing applications in areas such as banking, airline reservations, military defense systems, Social Security, and income tax files. The unique responsibility assumed by medical personnel in caring for patients, however, makes these issues of particular concern when raised in regard to medical information systems.

A number of intricate coding schemes have already been devised to ensure a high degree of confidentiality and security for automated information systems. With time, however, any of these systems could be unscrambled by a determined expert. In an analysis of this problem, Glueck (1967) concluded that, ultimately, confidentiality in both automated and nonautomated procedures depends on trustworthy personnel. Viewing the specter of a national data bank, Glueck further suggested that psychiatrists and psychologists achieve much higher levels of sophistication in their selection of personnel who will have full access to and management of computer files. In fact, the number of persons with full access to the more complex systems actually may be reduced, because the complexity of the system permits a far more complex set of security codes, and it also forces specialization by programers to the point where no single person can unscramble the codes completely. The confidentiality of patient files is already much greater in the automated systems than in the usual record for many applications—such as demographic compilations, administrative reports, and research use of the data—because file access can be limited so that only the approved and required information is made available to the interrogator. These issues were discussed at considerable length by Laska and Bank (1975).

The most significant stumbling block at present is the lack of provision of some electronic alternative for the signature of medical and nursing staff members. The authorizing force of the signature is such an essential requirement in the traditional hospital record-keeping procedures that some electronic means of providing positive personal identification is essential if the automated systems are to develop to their full potential. Several approaches to the problem of positive personal identification are being investigated. These include devices to measure the geometry of the hand, thumb, or fingerprint comparison and voiceprint comparisons. All these devices try to provide the computer with a digitized interpretation of the various measurements that can be stored in the computer memory as the unique physical characteristics of a given person. Later access to the system by the same person requires comparison of the new digital input from these devices with the information on file, with access being provided only when an appropriate match is obtained. The fingerprint and the voiceprint of each person are unique and have been accepted by the courts as positive proof of identification, but current devices for converting the prints into computer-readable form are still much too expensive to be considered for use at every computer terminal. One of the devices for reading the hand measurements is considerably less expensive but does not have the unique identifying ability of the fingerprints and voiceprints. It is, in addition, still much too expensive for availability at every terminal in a multiterminal hospital system.

Conclusion

In trying to present the positive aspects of the use of computers in clinical psychiatry, the authors have also been forced to describe the many limitations of the present hospital information systems. It should be borne in mind, however, that the first of these systems began to be developed as recently as 1962. In a very short time, major advances have been made in the technology of computer design, with vast increases in the speed, computing power, and storage capability of the hardware, accompanied by a similar sophistication in the programing techniques and organization of the data base.

Although many of the pioneering efforts failed, significant progress has been made in developing a sound set of principles and techniques on which future systems can be developed. Each of these developmental efforts has seemed to be very costly, and exact figures are hard to obtain, but it is doubtful that, since 1962, more than $50 million nation-wide has gone into these efforts. This sum represents but a small fraction of the annual expenditures for health care and pinpoints a significant reason for some of the difficulties encountered in the development of psychiatric hospital systems to date—namely, inadequate financing. This inadequacy has resulted in numerous compromises being made in terms of the selection of hardware and the level of clinical and programing skills. By and large, because most hospitals are nonprofit organizations, they have not been able to compete with industry for the scarce, top-quality computer experts.

Because of various pressures mentioned above for greatly increased quality-control activity within the health care area, such as utilization review and professional standards review, the development of hospital information systems will have to be accelerated, with adequate financing being provided.

Suggested Cross References

The application of statistics to psychiatry is discussed in Chapter 7. Personality theory derived from quantitative experiment is discussed in Section 11.1. Diagnosis is discussed in Chapter 12, 13, and 14. Biofeedback is discussed in Section 4.9.

REFERENCES

Accreditation Council for Psychiatric Facilities. *Accreditation Manual for Psychiatric Facilities.* Joint Commission of Accreditation of Hospitals, Chicago, 1972.

Altman, H., Evenson, R. C., Hedlund, J. L., and Cho, D. W. The Missouri Actuarial Report System (MARS). Compr. Psychiatry, *19:* 185, 1978.

Ambrose, J. Computerized X-ray scanning of the brain. J. Neurosurg., *40:* 697, 1974.

Banquet, J. P. Spectral analysis of the EEG in meditation. Electroencephalogr. Clin. Neurophysiol., *35:* 143, 1973.

Benfari, R. C., Leighton, A. H., Beiser, M., and Coen, K. Case: Computer-assigned symptom evaluation. J. Nerv. Ment. Dis., *154:* 115, 1972.

Bickford, R. G., Billinger, T. W., Fleming, N. I., Stewart, L. The compressed spectral array (CSA): A pictorial EEG. In *Proceedings of the San Diego Biomedical Symposium,* University of California, La Jolla, 1972.

Bleich, H. L. The computer as a consultant. N. Engl. J. Med., *284:* 141, 1971.

Bonner, R. E. Cluster analysis. Ann. N. Y. Acad. Sci., *128:* 972, 1966.

Brown, P. B., editor. *Computer Technology in Neuroscience.* Halsted Press, New York, 1976.

Colby, K. M., Goldstein, A. P., and Krasner, L. *Artificial Paranoia: A Computer Simulation of Paranoid Processes.* Pergamon Press, New York, 1975.

Donnelly, J., Rosenberg, M., and Fleeson, W. D. The evolution of the mental status: Past and future. Am. J. Psychiatry, *126:* 121, 1970.

Duckworth, G. S., and Kedward, H. B. Man or machine in psychiatric diagnosis. Am. J. Psychiatry, *135:* 64, 1978.

Endicott, J., and Spitzer, R. L. What! Another rating scale? The Psychiatric Evaluation Form. J. Nerv. Ment. Dis., *154:* 88, 1972.

Evenson, R. C., Sletten, I. W., Hedlund, J. L., and Faintich, D. M. CAPS: An automated evaluation system. Am. J. Psychiatry, *131:* 5, 1974.

Everitt, B. S. Cluster analysis: A brief discussion of some of the problems. Br. J. Psychiatry, *120:* 143, 1972.

Everitt, B. S., Gourlan, A. J., and Kendell, R. E. An attempt at validation of traditional psychiatric syndromes by cluster analysis. Br. J. Psychiatry, *119:* 399, 1971.

Feighner, J. P., Robin, E., Guze, S. B., Woodruff, R. A., Jr., Winokur, A., and Munoz, R. Diagnostic criteria for use in psychiatric research. Arch. Gen. Psychiatry, *26:* 57, 1972.

Feinstein, A. R. *Clinical Judgment.* Williams & Wilkins, Baltimore, 1967.

Ferguson, M. Karl Pribram's changing reality. Hum. Behav., 28, May, 1978.

Fink, M. Cerebral electrometry in phase-1 assessment of psychoactive drugs. In *Current Developments in Psychopharmacology,* W. B. Essman and L. Valzelli, editors, vol. 1, p. 303. Spectrum, New York, 1975a.

Fink, M. Prediction of clinical activity of psychoactive drugs: Application of cerebral electrometry in phase-1 studies. In *Predictability in Psychopharmacology,* A. Sudilovsky, S. Gershon, and T. S. Beer, editors, p. 65. Raven Press, New York, 1975b.

Forsythe, A. B., May, P. R. A., and Engelman, L. Prediction by multiple regression. How many variables to enter? J. Psychiatr. Res., *8:* 119, 1971.

Galin, D. Lateral specialization and psychiatric issues: Speculations on development and the evolution of consciousness. Ann. N. Y. Acad. Sci., *299:* 397, 1977.

Glueck, B. C. Automation and social change. Compr. Psychiatry, *8:* 6, 1967.

Glueck, B. C. Computers at the Institute of Living. In *Progress in Mental Health Information Systems: Computer Applications,* J. L. Crawford, D. W. Morgan, and D. T. Gianturco, editors, p. 303. Ballinger Press, Cambridge, Mass., 1974.

Glueck, B. C., Gullotta, G. P., and Ericson, R. P. Automation of behavior assessments: The computer-produced nursing note. In *Technology in Mental Health Care Delivery Systems,* J. B. Sidowski, J. H. Johnson, and T. A. Williams, editors, p. 110. Ablex, Norwood, N. J., 1978.

Glueck, B. C., and Reznikoff, M. Comparison of computer-derived personality profile and projective psychological test findings. Am. J. Psychiatry, *121:* 1156, 1965.

Glueck, B. C., and Stroebel, C. F. The computer and the clinical decision process. Am. J. Psychiatry, *125* (Suppl.): 2, 1969.

Glueck, B. C., and Stroebel, C. F. Biofeedback and meditation in the treatment of psychiatric patients. Compr. Psychiatry, *16:* 303, 1975.

*Glueck, B. C., and Stroebel, C. F. Psychophysiological correlates of relaxation. In *Expanding Dimensions of Consciousness,* A. A. Sugarman and R. E. Tarter, editors, p. 99. Springer, New York, 1978.

Gordon, M. Graphic display for clinician-computer interaction in clinical management. Biomed. Eng., *5:* 539, 1970.

Greist, J. H., Gustafson, D. H., Stauss, F. F., Rowse, G. L., Laughren, T. P., and Chiles, J. A. A computer interview for suicide-risk prediction. Am. J. Psychiatry, *130:* 1327, 1973.

*Greist, J. H., Klein, M. H., and Erdman, H. P. Routine on-line psychiatric diagnosis by computer. Am. J. Psychiatry, *133:* 1405, 1976.

Greist, J. H., Klein, M. H., Gurman, A. S., and Van Cura, L. J. Computer measures of patient progress in therapy. Psychiatry Digest, *38:* 23, 1977.

Gustafson, D. H., Greist, J. H., Stauss, F. F., Erdman, H., and Laughren, T. A probabilistic system for identifying suicide attemptors. Comput. Biomed. Res., *10:* 1, 1977.

Halberg, F., Johnson, E. A., Nelson, W., Runge, W., and Sothern, R. Autorhythmometry procedures for physiological self-measurements and their analysis. Physiol. Teacher, *1:* 1, 1972.

Hayes-Roth, F., Longabaugh, R., and Ryback, R. The problem-oriented medical record and psychiatry. Br. J. Psychiatry, *121:* 27, 1972.

*Hedlund, J. L., Evenson, R. C., Sletten, I. W., and Cho, D. W. The computer and clinical prediction. In *Technology in Mental Health Care Delivery Systems,* J. B. Sidowski, J. H. Johnson, and T. A. Williams, editors, p. 110. Ablex, Norwood, N. J., 1978.

Hedlund, J. L., and Hickman, B. S. Computers in mental health: A national survey. J. Ment. Health Admin., *10:* 1, 1978.

Hedlund, J. L., Sletten, I. W., Evenson, R. C., Altman, H., and Cho, D. W. Automated psychiatric information systems: A critical review of Missouri's Standard System of Psychiatry (SSOP). J. Oper. Psychiatry, *8:* 5, 1977.

Hollister, L. E., and Overall, J. E. Computer procedures for psychiatric classification. J. A. M. A., *187:* 583, 1964.

Itil, T. M. Quantitative pharmaco-electroencephalography. In *Psychotropic Drugs and the Human EEG,* T. M. Itil, editor, vol. 8, p. 43. S. Karger, New York, 1974.

John, E. R., Karmel, B. Z., Corning, W. C., Easton, P., Brown, D., Ahn, H., John, M., Harmony, T., Prichep, L., Toro, A., Gerson, I., Bartlett, F., Thatcher, R., Kaye, H., Valdes, P., and Schwartz, E. Neurometrics. Science, *196:* 1393, 1977.

Jones, K. J. Computers in behavioral science: Problems of grouping individuals and the method of modality. Behav. Sci., *13:* 496, 1968.

Klein, D. F., and Davis, J. M. *Diagnosis and Drug Treatment of Psychiatric Disorders.* Williams & Wilkins, Baltimore, 1969.

Klein, D. F., Honigfeld, G., and Feldman, S. Prediction of drug effect by diagnostic decision tree. Dis. Nerv. Syst., *29:* 187, 1968.

Klett, C. J., and Honigfeld, B. Nursing Observation Scale for Inpatient Evaluation (NOSIE). J. Clin. Psychol., *21:* 65, 1965.

Kraus, J. Use of Bayes theorem in clinical decision: Suicidal risk, differential diagnosis, response to treatment. Br. J. Psychiatry, *120:* 561, 1972.

Kupfer, D. J., Foster, F. G., Reich, L., Thompson, K. S., and Weiss, B. EEG sleep changes as predictors in depression. Am. J. Psychiatry, *113:* 622, 1976.

Laska, E. The Multistate Information System. In *Progress in Mental Health*

Information Systems: Computer Applications, J. L. Crawford, D. W. Morgan, and D. T. Gianturco, editors, p. 231. Ballinger Press, Cambridge, Mass., 1974.

Laska, E., and Bank, R., editors. *Safeguarding Psychiatric Privacy: Computer Systems and Their Uses.* Wiley-Interscience, New York, 1975.

Laska, E., Weinstein, A., Logemann, G., Bank, R., and Breuer, R. The use of computers at a state psychiatric hospital. Compr. Psychiatry, *8:* 476, 1967.

*Leader, M. A., and Klein, D. F. Reflections on instituting a computerized psychosocial history in a clinical facility. Compr. Psychiatry, *18:* 489, 1977.

Lehman, H. E. The impact of the therapeutic revolution on nosology. Probl. Psychose, *34:* 136, 1969.

Lipkin, M., Engle, R. L., Jr., Flehinger, B. J., Gerstman, L. J., and Atamer, M. S. Computer-aided differential diagnosis of hemotologic diseases. Ann. N. Y. Acad. Sci., *161:* 670, 1969.

Lorr, M. Rating scales, behavior inventories, and drugs. In *Drugs and Behavior,* L. M. Uhr and J. G. Miller, editors, p. 579. John Wiley & Sons, New York, 1960.

Lyerly, S. B., and Abbott, P. S. *Handbook of Psychiatric Rating Scales (1950–1964),* Public Health Service Publication No. 1495. Department of Health, Education, and Welfare, Washington, D. C., 1966.

Maultsby, M. C., Jr., and Slack, W. V. A computer-based psychiatric history system. Arch. Gen. Psychiatry, *25:* 570, 1971.

Maxwell, A. E. Multivariate statistical methods and classification problems. Br. J. Psychiatry, *119:* 121, 1971.

Maxwell, A. E. Difficulties in a dimensional description of symptomatology. Br. J. Psychiatry, *121:* 19, 1972.

Meehl, P. E. *Clinical versus Statistical Prediction.* University of Minnesota Press, Minneapolis, 1954.

Meehl, P. E. *Minnesota-Ford Pool of Phenotypic Personality Items.* University of Minnesota Press, Minneapolis, 1962.

Meldman, M. J., Harris, D., Pellicore, R. J., and Johnson, E. L. A computer-assisted, goal-oriented psychiatric progress note system. Am. J. Psychiatry, *134:* 38, 1977.

Melrose, P., Stroebel, C. F., and Glueck, B. C. Diagnosis of psychopathology using stepwise multiple discriminant analysis. Compr. Psychiatry, *11:* 43, 1970.

Mirabile, C. S., Glueck, B. C., and Stroebel, C. F. Motion sickness: An index of sensory conflict relating to behavior. Neuropsychobiology *157:* 164, 1978.

Nilsson, N. J. Survey of pattern recognition. Ann. N. Y. Acad. Sci., *161:* 380, 1969.

Overall, J. E., and Gorham, D. R. Brief Psychiatric Rating Scale. Psychol. Rep., *10:* 799, 1962.

Paykel, E. S. Classification of depressed patients: A cluster analysis derived grouping. Br. J. Psychiatry, *118:* 288, 1971.

Pearson, J. S., Swenson, W. M., Rome, H. P., Mataya, P., and Brannick, T. L. Further experiences with automated MMPI. Mayo Clin. Proc., *39:* 823, 1964.

Pribram, K. H. *Languages of the Brain.* Prentice-Hall, Englewood Cliffs, N. J., 1971.

Rome, H. P., Swenson, W. M., Mataya, P., McCarthy, C. E., Pearson, J. S., Keating, F. R., Jr., and Hathaway, S. R. Symposium on automation techniques in personality assessment. Proc. Mayo Clin., *37:* 61, 1962.

Rosenberg, M., Glueck, B. C., and Stroebel, C. F. The computer and the clinical decision process. Am. J. Psychiatry, *124:* 595, 1967.

Ruderman, M., and Pappalardo, A. N. The hospital computer comes of age. Comput. Automation, *19:* 28, 1970.

Schildkraut, J. J. The current status of biological criteria for classifying the depressive disorders and predicting responses to treatment. Psychopharmacol. Bull., *10:* 5, 1974.

Simon, R. J., Gurland, B. J., Fleiss, J. L., and Sharpe, L. Impact of a patient history interview on psychiatric diagnosis. Arch. Gen. Psychiatry, *24:* 437, 1971.

Sines, J. O. Actuarial versus clinical prediction in psychopathology. Br. J. Psychiatry, *116:* 129, 1970.

Sletten, I. W., and Ulett, G. A. The present status of automation in a state psychiatric system. Psychiatr. Ann., *2:* 42, 1972.

Spitzer, R. L., and Endicott, J. DIAGNO II: Further developments in a computer program for psychiatric diagnosis. Am. J. Psychiatry, *125:* (Suppl.): 12, 1969.

Spitzer, R. L., and Endicott, J. An integrated group of forms for automated psychiatric case records. Arch. Gen. Psychiatry, *24:* 540, 1971.

Spitzer, R. L., and Endicott, J. Can the computer assist clinicians in psychiatric diagnosis? Am. J. Psychiatry, *131:* 523, 1974.

Spitzer, R. L., Endicott, J., Cohen, J., and Fleiss, J. L. Constraints on the validity of computer diagnosis. Arch. Gen. Psychiatry, *31:* 197, 1974.

Spitzer, R. L., Endicott, J., Robins, J. *Research Diagnostic Criteria.* New York State Department of Mental Hygiene, New York, 1975.

*Spitzer, R. L., Fleiss, J. L., and Endicott, J. Problems of classification: Reliability and validity. In *Psychopharmacology: A Generation of Progress,* M. A. Lipton, A. DiMascio, and K. F. Killam, editors, p. 857. Raven Press, New York, 1978.

Sternbach, R. A., and Greenfield, N. S. *The Handbook of Psychophysiology.* Holt, Rinehart & Winston, New York, 1972.

Stroebel, C. F., Bennett, W., Ericson, R. P., and Glueck, B. C. Designing computer information systems: Problems and strategy. Compr. Psychiatry, *8:* 491, 1967.

Stroebel, C. F., and Glueck, B. C. Computer-derived global decisions in psychiatry. Am. J. Psychiatry, *126:* 41, 1970.

Stroebel, C. F., and Glueck, B. C. Computers in medicine. In *Practice of Medicine,* G. J. Pace, editor, vol. 2, p. 1. Harper & Row, Hagerstown, Md., 1972.

*Stroebel, C. F., and Glueck, B. C. Passive meditation: Subjective, clinical, and electrographic comparison with biofeedback. In *Consciousness and Self-regulation: Advances in Research,* G. E. Schwartz and D. Shapiro, editors, vol. 2, p. 401. Plenum Publishing Corp., New York, 1978.

Stroebel, C. F., Luce, G., and Glueck, B. C. *The Psychophysiological Diary: A Computer-scored Daily Record of Moods, Body Changes, and Life Events.* Institute of Living, Hartford, Conn., 1971.

Swenson, W. M. A preliminary investigation of possibilities of application of computer devices to the scoring and interpretation of structured personality tests and their use in a medical center. In *Proceedings of the Second International Business Machines Second Medical Symposium,* M. D. Sternbuk, editor, p. 401. IBM Data Processing Division, White Plains, N. Y., 1960.

Ulett, G. A., and Sletten, I. W. A statewide electronic data processing system. Hosp. Community Psychiatry, *20:* 74, 1969.

Weed, L. *Medical Records, Medical Education, and Patient Care.* Year Book Medical Publishers, Chicago, 1970.

Wing, J. K., Cooper, J. E., and Sartorius, N. *The Measurement and Classification of Psychiatric Symptoms: An Instruction Manual for the PSE and Catego Program.* Cambridge University Press, London, 1974.

6.3 Experimental Disorders

CHARLES SHAGASS, M.D.

Basic Concepts

Experimental psychopathology attempts to investigate abnormal behavior systematically under conditions that are more or less known or controlled. Controlling conditions may be introduced in many ways. They include manipulations of physical and psychological aspects of the environment, administration of drugs and chemicals, and ablation of tissues by surgery. The studies discussed here involve mainly states produced by psychological manipulation.

The central assumption in experimental psychopathology is that laboratory models of clinical disorder can be created and that investigation of such models will yield information relevant to the nature of the disorders. The laboratory model concept has been successfully applied to many other areas of medicine, but its use in psychiatry involves serious difficulties and limitations. The major groups of chronic functional disorders—neuroses, personality disorders, psychoses, and psychophysiological reactions—about which new information is urgently required, are so complex in their symptomatic manifestations that they cannot be reproduced in convincing detail in any other species. With the possible exception of the psychophysiological reactions, which may be adequately defined by organ states, animal experimental models clearly limit the investigator to detection of behavioral changes that *seem* similar to those occurring in humans. Because the validity of the animal model cannot be proved by behavioral identity, in the way that anatomical identity gives relevance to tissue pathology, it must be confirmed by showing that laws governing the animal behavior are applicable to humans in an explanatory or predictive manner. However, despite their limitations, animal models of psychopathology offer significant advantages; perhaps the most important is that experimental procedures not permissible in humans, such as brain surgery, can be applied to the animal model to investigate intermediary mechanisms.

Experimentation in humans clearly provides possibilities for more convincing identification of the experimentally produced psychopathological states with those occurring naturally. However, human experimentation is ethically restricted to the induction of short-lasting and fully reversible psychopathology. Because the duration of mental disorders may be of crucial importance in determining their manifestations, the relevance of most human experiments is as open to question as the relevance of animal experiments. As with animal models, the validity of human experimental models depends on the predictions derived from their study that can be generalized to the clinical situation.

There are many kinds of laboratory models of psychopathology. These models can be grouped in various ways, such as species or organism, clinical state to be investigated, experimental manipulation—for example, induction of conflict, hypnosis—acute or chronic. Several forms of descriptive grouping have been used in organizing this section. Animal and human studies are considered separately; for each, the material has been subdivided either by the kind of clinical state studied—for example, psychosomatic disorders—or by the experimental method. It is possible, however, to classify laboratory models in a less descriptive and more generally applicable way by examining the kind of information provided by the model.

One useful approach is to ask whether the model focuses on replication of a state, on an intermediary process, or on essential causes. Clearly, a perfect model replicates all. These three kinds of information relate closely to three of the four criteria for validation of an animal model of psychopathology that were proposed by McKinney (1977): (1) similarity of behavioral states, (2) similar underlying neurobiological mechanisms (intermediary process), (3) similarity of inducing conditions (cause). McKinney's fourth validating criterion is reversal by clinically effective treatment techniques; for example, a valid animal model of depression should respond to antidepressant drugs. It is evident, however, that most available models of psychopathology deal mainly with one or the other kind of information and do not meet all validating criteria. In a consideration of the relevance of a particular model to clinical psychopathology, it is conceptually helpful to determine the level of information provided by the model. For example, a conflict-induced experimental disorder in the dog provides an unconvincing state replica of human neurosis, but the conflict model has considerable relevance to concepts of causes of disorders in humans. Drug-induced psychotic states in humans may differ descriptively from naturally occurring psychoses and certainly do not have the same causes as such psychoses, but they may involve common intermediary mechanisms, such as synaptic inhibition. Hypnotically induced anesthesia may provide an exact replica of a hysterical conversion state, but the model may be of low relevance with respect to either intermediary process or cause. Any given model should be examined for its significance at all levels—replication, intermediary process, and cause. Doing so may prevent a potentially useful intermediary process or etiological model from being rejected on the grounds that it fails to replicate the clinical state.

A laboratory model not only is a research technique but also represents a theory of naturally occurring psychopathology (Abramson and Seligman, 1977). Consequently, it should be subjected to the usual rules for proof of scientific theories. Such rules demand a high level of precision in the experimental analysis of the laboratory phenomenon; in particular, the essential causative factors must be specified. Even under laboratory conditions, it may be hard to identify the specific causes of behavioral change, because not all possibilities have been controlled. For example, when painful stimuli are applied during feeding with the aim of inducing conflict, the resulting avoidance behavior may reflect the animal's appropriate learned response, rather than psychopathology resulting from conflict. Ingenious controls may be needed to make the distinction.

Experimental Neuroses in Animals

ABNORMAL ANIMAL BEHAVIOR

Criteria of abnormality may be defined in many ways, and no attempt is made here to distinguish between neurosis and psychosis in the discussion of abnormal behavioral states in animals. Although some manifestations—waxy flexibility, for example—may appear to fall more clearly into one category than the other, there are no certain criteria for making the distinction.

From a psychiatric point of view, Hebb's (1947) approach seems highly relevant. Hebb began by defining human neurosis in behavioral terms, without use of verbal report of the subjective state, so that the definition can be used at the animal level. He distinguished between neurotic behavior and neurosis; neurotic behavior constitutes the signs of neurosis, the means by which it is recognized; neurosis is the concept of a central state. Proceeding in this way, Hebb's definition was:

> Neurosis is in practice an undesirable emotional condition which is generalized and persistent; it occurs in a minority of the population and has no origin in a gross neural lesion.

The six essential elements in this definition are as follows: (1) undesirable, evaluationally abnormal; (2) emotional, involving emotion activity; (3) generalized, implies manifestation in a number of ways; (4) persistent, chronic to some degree; (5) occurring in a minority of the population, statistically abnormal; (6) having no origin in a gross neural lesion.

Hebb listed three additional criteria that seem invalid to him but that have had some influence in determining what is called neurosis: (1) Neurosis has no physiological basis; (2) it produces a marked change of behavior from an earlier baseline; (3) it follows some theoretically traumatic experience, such as conflict or frustration. He regarded these criteria as "not essentially true." For example, to reject physiological causes of neurosis is to deny the possibility of anything but a psychological cause. It is conceivable that neurosis may be of lifelong duration, thus rendering the second criterion unessential. The third is considered unessential from the fact that neurotic behavior can result from nutritional or metabolic processes.

In his paper, Hebb described two chimpanzees with spontaneously occurring neuroses that appeared to meet his criteria.

Hebb's criteria have been criticized by Abramson and Seligman (1977). They pointed out that before one can apply the criteria to any animal behavior, Hebb's definition of human neuroses must be implicitly accepted and that more recent theorists have challenged Hebb's ideas. They cited Wishner's (1969) arguments in favor of the view that statistically deviant or socially unacceptable behavior may not necessarily be psychopathological. They asserted that Hebb's criterion of emotionality is vague and difficult to use and that the criterion of generalization may prevent one from accepting well-delimited phobias, based on specific experiences, as examples of psychopathology. They also contended that Hebb's persistence criterion rules out transient reactive depression from being considered a neurosis.

Abramson and Seligman's concerns about Hebb's criteria directed attention to their stringency and to the possibility that errors may result if they are applied in an absolute way. Their critical remarks also implied that Hebb's conception of neurosis as illness is not now acceptable. Broadhurst (1973), in reversing his previously positive view of Hebb's criteria (Broadhurst, 1961), also referred to "the demise of the disease model of neurosis." However, the concept of neurosis as disease retains validity for many psychiatrists. Furthermore, when evaluating experimental disorders in animals, clinical psychiatrists are especially likely to ask how well the models fit the illnesses with which they are familiar. To this writer, it is just because Hebb's criteria are so stringent that they are useful; a model that comes close to meeting them has a high probability of representing a clinically meaningful entity in humans. Consequently, Hebb's criteria are applied here.

PAVLOV AND HIS SCHOOL

The term "experimental neurosis" was introduced by the great Russian physiologist Pavlov (1927, 1941) to describe abnormal behavior of a more or less chronic nature that is produced experimentally.

Shenger-Krestovnikova (1921), in Pavlov's laboratory, produced perhaps the best known of Pavlov's experimental neuroses. It occurred in a dog that had been conditioned to differentiate between a circle associated with feeding (positive stimulus for salivation) and an ellipse not associated with feeding (negative or inhibitory stimulus). The original ratio of the semiaxes of the ellipse was two to one. Further differentiation was attempted by approximating the shape of the ellipse to that of the circle. Differentiation progressed as desired until an ellipse with nine to eight semiaxes was used. After 3 weeks of training with this ratio, the discrimination failed to improve and even became considerably worse, finally disappearing altogether.

Simultaneously, the general behavior of the animal changed abruptly. The previously quiet dog began to squeal in its stand, he kept wriggling about, with his teeth he tore off the apparatus attached to his skin, and he bit through tubes connecting his room with the observer's room. This behavior had never previously occurred. Also new was the violent barking of the dog on being taken into the experimental room. Pavlov interpreted the behavior changes as symptoms of acute neurosis.

Pavlov formulated three possible causes for experimental neurosis: (1) Excessive stimulation of inhibitory processes. This occurred in the experiment just described. (2) Overstrain of the excitatory process by extraordinarily strong or unusual stimuli. This is illustrated by the natural experiment occasioned by the Leningrad flood of 1924. All the animals had to swim for their lives through a storm. All their conditioned reflexes disappeared, and one of them developed a chronic neurotic condition. (3) Conflict between cortical inhibitory and excitatory processes. This mechanism is described in a dog that was able to discriminate between a positive tactile stimulus at the rate of 24 a minute and a negative one at the rate of 12 a minute. When one type of stimulus followed the other without a pause, the animal developed signs of a neurosis that lasted several weeks.

Pavlov's recognition of the potential significance of these observations for understanding abnormal behavior was to have a profound influence on the focus of investigation in his own laboratory and in conditioning laboratories elsewhere. However, Broadhurst (1961), who attempted to evaluate the Russian

research in the light of Hebb's criteria, was forced to conclude that the Russian findings provided insufficient information about the responses of the animal outside the experimental chamber. Because of this deficiency, the results on experimental neurosis originating in Pavlov's laboratory do not convincingly meet Hebb's criterion of generalization of abnormal behavior. It is also not clear that the behavior was statistically abnormal. In addition, as Abramson and Seligman (1977) pointed out, Pavlov failed to demonstrate close similarity between the laboratory phenomenon and natural human psychopathology; any resemblances were gross, at best. Consequently, the Pavlovian experimental neurosis is probably a model of general features of psychopathology—for example, the effects of conflict—rather than of any particular condition, such as anxiety neurosis.

GANTT AND HIS SCHOOL

The Pavlovian laboratory at the Johns Hopkins Medical School, directed by W. Horsley Gantt, was a principal American contributor to the study of experimental neurosis. An outstanding feature of the work is the provision of detailed case histories.

Case history of Nick. One mongrel dog, Nick, was studied for 12 years (Gantt, 1944). In 1932 he was about 3 years old, active, and playful. He appeared normal then but was more restless than most dogs during adaptation to feeding in the experimental room and slow in showing conditioned salivary response. When auditory differentiation was introduced (learning to respond to one tone and not to another), he refused food and showed a defense reaction. A rest restored food acceptance, but, with an increase in difficulty of the discrimination, he again refused food and continued to do so in the laboratory for most of his life (see Figure 1).

In the next year, all conditioned responses failed, and Nick ate more

FIGURE 1. Nick in camera, 1938, listening to tone that produced the conflict in 1933. Note the "anxious" facies, pulling on leash, tension in forelegs, sexual erection. (From Gantt, W. H. Experimental basis for neurotic behavior. *Psychosom. Med. Monogr., 3:* Frontispiece, 1944.)

readily the farther he was away from the experimental room. In the room, he showed a stereotyped restlessness whenever he was released from the apparatus. He rushed about, jumped up on the table and off it again, fumbled the uneaten food in his mouth, and dropped it.

As time went on, fresh abnormalities were observed. Disturbed respiration took the form of loud, forced breathing whenever he was excited, especially when approaching the experimental room or people connected with the experiment. Gantt repeatedly noted that Nick was friendlier toward strangers than toward anyone associated with the experiment.

From the end of 1936, Nick began urinating when brought to the experimental room, with a frequency as high as 25 times in 30 minutes. This behavior could not be inhibited by punishment. Concurrently, abnormal sexual excitation, as judged by penile erection, was observed during conditioning stimulation. These persistent sexual erections contrasted with the occasional short erections normally seen in young male dogs. Both the urinary and the sexual abnormalities occurred after a bitch in estrus had been used in the experimental situation in order to test the effect of normal sexual excitation on Nick's other abnormal signs.

Gantt observed wide generalization outside the experimental situation. He kept Nick on his farm in the country and found that the particular food given as reinforcement in the experimental situation was consistently refused there and that the signs of sexual erection, frequent urination, disturbed respiration, and a marked increase in heart rate were sometimes observed when people associated with the experiment or even members of their families approached the animal.

In relation to Hebb's criteria, Nick's behavior was frequently undesirable—for example, his refusal of food when hungry. It was markedly emotional, judging by overt signs. An autopsy report showed that he had no gross neural lesions. The persistence of the behavior pattern was strikingly well established, as was the generalization of the behavior to situations other than the experimental. The question of statistical abnormality is difficult to assess.

Schizokinesis and autokinesis. Gantt (1958) introduced two fundamental theoretical concepts: schizokinesis and autokinesis.

Schizokinesis implies a cleavage in response between the emotional and visceral systems and the skeletal musculature. The concept originated in observations suggesting that cardiac conditioned responses are formed more quickly than are motor responses, are of comparatively greater intensity, and are more resistant to extinction. Gantt considers schizokinesis to be a built-in unacquired mechanism, the function of the normal organism.

Autokinesis refers to the internal development of responses on the basis of old excitations without further external stimulation. This development is seen in the spontaneous restoration of extinguished conditioned responses and the appearance of signs of experimental neurosis long after the causal conflict has been removed. For example, new symptoms arose in Nick months or years after he was removed from the stressful laboratory environment. Moreover, although occurring much later than the original stress, the new symptoms were related to that stress, as could be seen by their ready evocation by the original environment or its elements. Gantt also distinguishes between negative and positive autokinesis. The development of new symptoms in a neurotic animal is negative, whereas improvement occurring some time after a specific therapeutic procedure, such as a drug, has been administered may be considered positive.

These concepts are primarily descriptive and rather broad; however, they draw attention to phenomena that may be of considerable importance to psychopathology.

LIDDELL AND THE CORNELL GROUP

The Cornell University group, led by H. S. Liddell (1944, 1953), succeeded in producing chronic abnormal states in several animal species, using conditioned reflex techniques. Single animals were observed for as long as 12 years.

Anderson and Parmenter (1941) described three types of procedure: (1) difficult differentiations, (2) experimental distinctions, and (3) rigid time schedules. The first procedure is similar to that used by Pavlov in the circle-ellipse differentiation. The second consists of following the positive (food) stimulus with an exceedingly long series of negative (no food) stimuli. The third involves the use of a monotonous, lengthy routine of alternating positive and negative stimuli.

Manifestations of experimental neurosis. The many manifestations of experimental neurosis included hyperirritability, tenseness, and restlessness during the experiment; inhibitory motor reactions; change in diurnal activity cycle; respiratory and cardiac changes recorded in the barn, as well as in the laboratory; changes in micturition and defecation patterns in the laboratory; social and emotional changes.

Some of these manifestations are of particular interest. The inhibitory motor reaction in some animals involved rigidity of the limbs; they could be placed in various abnormal positions, reminiscent of catatonia with waxy flexibility. Motor activity was measured by a pedometer; the daily total in neurotic animals was not significantly different from that in normal animals, but neurotic animals showed about as much activity during the night as during the day, whereas normal animals showed little or no activity during the night. This manifestation seems to parallel insomnia in humans.

With respect to social behavior, neurotic dogs and sheep exhibited shyness, tending to remain alone and lacking normal gregariousness. They went hungry when it was necessary for them to get their food from a common source. When cornered, the shy, neurotic animals became aggressive and would bite, struggle, or kick. Neurotic sheep and goats also appeared handicapped in their ability to cope with real danger. On several occasions, dogs invaded the pasture, and their victim was invariably one of the neurotic animals.

Causes of abnormal behavior. Liddell (1954) did not agree with Pavlov's hypothesis that the cause of the abnormal behavior is a clash between intense cortical excitations and inhibitions. He assigned considerable importance to the factor of restraint, introduced by negative conditioned stimuli, and showed that animals allowed to run at will in a maze while attempting to solve extremely difficult problems never developed disturbances. He thought the experimental neurosis was caused by the equivalent of a human conflict situation. The animal must decide whether or not to respond; if the decision is too difficult, there is a drastic change in nervous system functioning, resulting in signs of neurosis. Other workers found that restraint facilitated neurotic disturbances in the pig, cat, and rat.

Liddell also emphasized the importance of vigilance in experimental neurosis. The trained sheep or goat had initially struggled to escape from its restraining harness but had learned to restrict its movements to a precise limited response of the foreleg to electric shock. Its autonomic functioning, however, suggested a strong emotional undertow. On one occasion, a trained sheep was placed in the harness with electrodes attached to the foreleg and kept there for the customary hour without being given the usual signals or shocks. By the end of the hour, its breathing had become labored, and the respiratory rate had risen from 41 to 135 a minute (see Figure 2).

Observations such as these forced Liddell to conclude that the conditioned reflex described by Pavlov was not an example of ordinary learning. He saw it as an emotionally charged episode of behavior bracketed between two primitive stereotyped reactions, the vigilance reaction and the unconditioned reaction to the reinforcement of the conditioned stimulus by food or electric shock. He equated the conditioned reflex with the emergency reaction in response to danger, interpreting the waiting for the stimulus as a persisting apprehensive watchfulness in the animal (see Figure 3).

Relation to criteria of abnormality. How well do the results obtained by Liddell's group meet Hebb's criteria of abnormality? It seems clear that many examples of behavior were undesirable, emotional, and persistent, and there is no evidence that they may be attributed to a gross neural lesion. However, the criterion of generalization from the laboratory to other situations is not so easily met. The fact that change in pulse and respiratory rates could be recorded from the barn can be interpreted as a conditioned response to the apparatus used for measurement. The apparently decreased capacity to cope with actual danger seems more convincing, but the finding is derived from incidental and uncontrolled observation. The issue of statistical abnormality is also difficult to decide; apparently about 25 per cent of the animals developed experimental neuroses. The Cornell animal data thus approach but do not fully satisfy Hebb's criteria. Nor is it clear that the animal phenomena resemble any particular psychiatric disorder found in humans.

MASSERMAN'S EXPERIMENTS

Masserman's (1943, 1950, 1959) biodynamic approach is associated with a long series of experiments in which experimental behavior disturbances were produced in conditioning situations. In the basic experiment the animal learns to open a food box in response to a sensory signal. Various complexities were introduced into the experiments; for example, to obtain food, animals learned to press a series of switches a definite number of times in a required order or to differentiate between

FIGURE 3. Photographs showing the activity of normal and experimentally neurotic sheep on a special recording activity program. The normal animal shown in *A* stands quietly. The neurotic animal shown in *B* and *C* shows signs of extreme agitation. (From Anderson, O. D., and Parmenter, R. A long-term study of the experimental neurosis in the sheep and dog. Psychosom. Med. Monogr., *2:* 38, 1941.)

printed signs. The usual technique of inducing neurotic behavior in cats, dogs, or monkeys was to present a traumatically deterrent stimulus during the execution of the well-learned response. Stimuli were electric shock, a startling air blast across the food box, and, even more effective in the case of monkeys, the sudden appearance of the head of a toy snake when the food was about to be taken. If the traumatic stimulus was repeated several times (two to seven times in cats or dogs, generally more in monkeys), behavioral aberrations appeared.

Some of the symptoms of disturbance may be described under the interpretive headings used by Masserman.

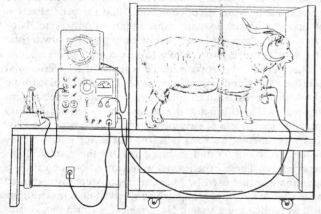

FIGURE 2. Conditioned reflexes were produced by means of this apparatus in the Cornell University Behavior Farm Laboratory. Attached to the right foreleg of the goat are two electrodes through which a mild electric shock can be administered after the click of the metronome at the *left*. After the animal has come to associate the two stimuli, it raises its leg in anticipation of the shock. (From Liddell, H. S. Conditioning and emotion. Sci. Am., *190:* 49, 1954.)

Pervasive anxiety was indicated by low threshold of startle, persistent hyperirritability, muscular tension, body postures, mydriasis, irregularly accelerated pulse rate, raised blood pressure, and increased coagulability of the blood.

Psychosomatic symptoms included, in some animals, recurrent asthmatic breathing, genitourinary dysfunction, anorexia, flatulence, and diarrhea.

Defensive reactions included inhibition of feeding, even outside the experimental apparatus, to the point of self-starvation and serious cachexia.

Phobic aversions were observed, first to stimuli directly associated with the traumatic experiences, then spreading to other situations.

Sexual deviations included diminished heterosexual interests and accentuated homosexual activity.

Sensorial disturbances were considered present on the basis of behavior ranging from extreme sensitivity to minor changes in the surroundings to recurrent episodes of apparent disorientation and confusion. Hallucinations were thought to be present in monkeys who, although refusing food readily available in their food box, could be observed picking up nonexistent pellets and appearing to chew and swallow these.

More recently, Masserman (1971) described severe but transitory emotional disturbances that were produced in monkeys by delayed auditory feedback of their own vocal productions or by varying the sequence and timing of the switches operated in a learned task. He also drew attention to species differences in symptomatic manifestations of experimental neurosis. For example, under similar stresses, spider monkeys showed infantile dependencies or catatonic immobility, but cebus monkeys developed various psychosomatic manifestations, including functional paralyses.

Masserman was particularly interested in procedures for ameliorating the manifestations of the disturbances induced in his animals. He found a number effective to some degree. They ranged from petting by the experimenter to neurosurgical operations.

From the point of view of Hebb's criteria, the behavioral disturbances produced by Masserman do not easily qualify as neuroses. The behavior was not statistically abnormal, and neither its persistence nor its generalization was satisfactorily demonstrated. With respect to the animal's adjustment, it is also not clear that the behavior was abnormal.

STROEBEL'S EXPERIMENTS

Stroebel (1969, 1975) and his associates (Stroebel and Luce, 1968) investigating circadian rhythms, had rhesus monkeys live on a rigid regimen of 12 hours light, 12 hours dark, and spend 6 hours in a problem cage. Two levers faced the animal. The right-hand lever, when pressed, provided rewards for correct responses in a variety of visual discrimination problems. The left-hand lever had the special purpose of relieving the animal from stressful or noxious stimuli. For example, the temperature of the cage would be increased until it was uncomfortably hot, but, if the animal pressed the left-hand lever, a gust of cool air was administered. Loud noises, uncomfortably bright lights, or electric shocks were presented at random times as the animal worked on the problems; by pressing the left-hand lever, he could rid himself of these unpleasant stimuli. After 2 to 4 weeks, the animals seemed to treat the lever as though it promised security; they often held onto it and refused to let it go. After this time the experimenters retracted the left-hand lever into a recess in the wall, so that the monkey could see it

but could not move it. Even though no further noxious stimuli were presented to the animals, they became frantic and would spend hours trying to get at the left-hand lever. At this time they began to show abnormal behavior patterns, which appeared to be of two distinct types, psychosomatic and psychotic.

The psychosomatic animals continued to perform their discrimination tasks, but poorly. They developed various symptoms, such as high blood pressure, asthmatic breathing, gastrointestinal disturbances, melena, and skin eruptions.

The psychotic animals began to perform very unpredictably on their discrimination tasks and often did not work at all. They stopped grooming themselves, pulled their hair for hours, masturbated, or caught imaginary insects. They showed stereotyped movements, such as rocking or continual hand gestures, and seemed to be abnormally unresponsive and excessively sleepy.

Stroebel was particularly interested in the alterations of circadian rhythm reflected in brain temperature measurements. The psychosomatic group developed a free-running brain temperature rhythm, which Stroebel associated with insomnia, but the psychotic group developed abnormally long brain temperature cycles.

From a behavioral perspective, the interesting feature of Stroebel's experiments is that, even though his animals were subjected to a long period of noxious stimuli, they did not become disturbed until the lever that signified their control over such stimuli was made unavailable to them. Disturbance was consequent upon loss of a control mechanism, which was actually no longer needed, since the unpleasant stimuli were no longer given. The symptoms appear similar to those produced by Masserman, but they were generated by removing a way of dealing with the traumatic stimuli, rather than by imposing such stimuli.

CONDITIONED EMOTIONAL RESPONSE VERSUS SPECIFIC STATE

It has been suggested that experiments of the Masserman type, involving inhibition of feeding responses by the introduction of fear-arousing stimuli, should be regarded as eliciting conditioned emotional responses. Such responses carry no implication of a specific abnormal state. Masserman has argued against this interpretation, contending that the generalization of anxiety reactions to many other situations only remotely or symbolically associated with the original one is characteristic of *human* neurosis and not of a simple conditioned response.

The crucial issue appears to be whether the experimental neurosis can be understood in terms of general laws of learning or whether it represents a specific state requiring special conditions, such as conflict and restraint, for its production and implying some form of susceptibility to breakdown. The view that experimental neurosis is learned behavior is favored by Wolpe (1958, 1967) and is supported by the results of his experiments. These experiments were carried out on cats in a situation like that used by Masserman but were distinguished by the use of a control group, which received no initial training to feed on hearing a signal. Nevertheless, electric shocks produced behavioral disturbances in all animals. These disturbances could be ameliorated by placing the hungry animal in a room enough unlike the experimental room to allow feeding and then gradually making the feeding environment more like the experimental room. Wolpe's animal studies led him to work out related procedures for the treatment of human neuroses. Wolpe's experiment could be criticized because those cats not subjected to conflict received more shocks than those that were subjected to conflict. Smart (1965) attempted to avoid this criticism by comparing three groups of cats, to each of which equal amounts of shock were administered but at different times in relation to eating. The animals were shocked either while approaching food, 1 second after starting to eat, or 30 seconds after eating in a given trial. The groups did not differ with respect to the amounts of disturbance produced. Smart's results were in agreement with Wolpe's view that conflict was not essential for the development of experimental neurosis.

More recently, Dmitruk (1974) proposed a different interpretation of the results of Masserman, Wolpe, and Smart in cats. He argued that any abnormal behavior observed in the conditioning situation may result from confinement, rather than from the experimental manipulation. To assess this possibility, one must know the normal activities of cats confined in a conditioning apparatus. Dmitruk's contention was that, after training for food reward, cats did not behave as they would if merely confined because the responses other than those connected with food reward would be extinguished during training. However, after aversive stimulation during feeding, these extinguished responses may be disinhibited and reappear. This hypothesis predicts that the behavior of cats in a conditioning apparatus before training for food reward will resemble that of cats made neurotic experimentally. Dmitruk then compared the behavior of cats exposed to a Masserman-type conflict experiment to that of cats confined in the apparatus for the same length of time but receiving neither food nor shock. All animals were observed on five occasions before the induction of conflict to assess base rates of the behaviors to be used as signs of neurosis. Dmitruk found that behaviors considered to be neurotic, such as hypersensitivity and bizarre responses, were present from the first baseline day. He concluded that experimenters using the Masserman procedure had not actually produced neurotic behavior and that the behavioral effects were artifacts of the experimental procedures.

Dmitruk's results suggest that the behavior of cats in the Masserman experimental situation can be viewed as a normal reaction to circumstances that are abnormal for cats. Unfortunately, Dmitruk did not also make his systematic behavioral observations in the animals' home cages; this failure leaves some doubts about whether the baseline behaviors in the conditioning apparatus were really different from usual, which they would have to be in order to be considered as reactions to confinement. However, if confinement did elicit behavioral disturbances, they can be interpreted not as symptoms of experimental neurosis but, rather, as reactions to a stressful environment. In addition to confinement, the Masserman procedure involves aversive or traumatic sitmuli—such as snakes, electric shocks, and air blasts—that augment stress. Indeed, the animals seemed to feed normally until exposed to stimuli that are universally disturbing to that species.

The interpretation of the Masserman experimental neurosis as either a conditioned emotional response or a stress situation is further supported by the fact that all the animals apparently displayed behavioral disturbances in the experiments of Masserman, Wolpe, and Smart. The uniform effectiveness of the Masserman procedure contrasts sharply with the results of the procedures used by Pavlov, Gantt, and Liddell, which elicited experimental neurosis in only a minority of the animals. One expects traumas to elicit more uniform reactions than stimuli that impose less obvious demands on the organism's adaptive reserves. Pavlov and Liddell postulated that the apparently innocuous requirements of their experimental situation for perceptual discrimination or delay of response generated conflict and strained the capacity of the nervous system. The occurrence of an experimental neurosis was apparently determined by the degree of susceptibility to the strain imposed by the need for inhibition or restraint. It seems reasonable that individual dfferences in susceptibility play a less important role in determining an animal's reaction to clearly traumatic stimuli. One may speculate about a possible parallel in human emotional disorders. The spontaneous neuroses of human life often seem to involve special susceptibilities to the strains imposed by intrapsychic and interpersonal conflicts. In contrast, the reactions elicited by gross stresses, such as war combat or natural disaster (explosion, fire), seem to depend less on individual susceptibility.

PERSONALITY TYPES

If susceptibility to experimental neurosis could be shown to depend on constitutional factors, this would reinforce the hypothesis that they reflect a specific central state. In his writings, Pavlov paid considerable attention to possible constitutional differences between dogs. He applied the humoral classification of Galen to his experimental animals, describing them as sanguine, phlegmatic, choleric, and melancholic. He noted the appearance of neurotic behavior only in dogs of the melancholic type—timid and docile with predominance of inhibitory process—or of the choleric type—aggressive and excitable with excitatory predominance. Initially well-balanced animals (the phlegmatic or sanguine type) did not develop chronic disturbances in behavior. The specific state issue might be resolved if other workers could confirm these observations with more exact methods of characterizing animal personality.

Pavlov did discover a pharmacological correlate of his neurotic types. He found that the temporary administration of bromides resulted in apparently permanent improvement of dogs with neuroses of the excitatory type. Treatment of the inhibitory type of neuroses was unsuccessful until he used a very small dose, only a fraction of that beneficial to the excitatory type. These observations indicate that the manifestations of a disorder are related to drug reactivity, and they favor Pavlov's theory of types, because it is easy to consider drug reactivity as an aspect of constitutional make-up. Of further interest is the fact that there are some consistent parallels between Pavlov's findings on reactivity to bromide in neurotic dogs and reactivity to amobarbital in psychiatric patients (Shagass, 1956).

EXPERIMENTS ON LEARNED HELPLESSNESS

The experiments of Seligman (1972, 1975) and his associates have provided an animal model that may be relevant to depressive reactions in humans. The model psychopathology is created by exposing a dog to unavoidable and uncontrollable electric shocks while restrained in a Pavlovian hammock. In each of two or more sessions, the dog receives 64 unescapable shocks to the hind feet; each shock lasts 5 seconds, and the intervals between shocks range from 50 to 110 seconds.

Testing of the lasting effects of this experience is performed several days later by placing the animal in a shuttle box for escape-avoidance training. The shuttle box is divided in two by a shoulder-high partition. A change in illumination signals that the floor of the box will give an electric shock; however, if the animal jumps over the partition, the shock will stop. Experimentally naive dogs, when first exposed to the shuttle box situation, run frantically about, defecating, urinating, and howling, until they accidentally scramble over the barrier and so escape the shock. They quickly learn to escape shock altogether.

Although the initial reaction of dogs previously exposed to inescapable shock is quite similar to that of the naive animal, their subsequent behavior is very different. The animals soon stop running and howling and sit whining quietly until the shock terminates. They do not cross the barrier and escape from the shock but seem to give up and passively accept it. Escape movements are absent on subsequent trials. Occasionally, the animal jumps the barrier in early trials, but this does not lead to escape learning; the animals revert to taking the shock. This behavior contrasts markedly with the behavior of naive dogs, in whom a successful escape response reliably predicts future successful shock-escape behavior.

Seligman (1972) reported that of more than 150 dogs subjected to inescapable shocks, two-thirds failed to learn to escape in the shuttle box, and only 6 per cent of the naive dogs exhibited such failure of escape learning. He called the phenomenon "learned helplessness" and drew attention to reports of similar findings in experiments performed with several other species, including rats, cats, fish, chickens, mice, and humans (Miller et al., 1977). The three basic effects of experience with uncontrollable trauma appear to be: (1) passivity in face of the trauma—that is, the animals take it, instead of doing something about it; their motivation to respond is reduced; (2) retarded learning of responses that may allow escape from trauma; ability to perceive success is diminished; (3) a higher degree of stress or emotionality in terms of such effects as defecation, fearful behavior, weight loss, and anorexia. The deficits in motivation and cognition are considered to be fundamental aspects of learned helplessness.

Seligman (1975) found that helplessness in the dog can be produced with a wide range of shock parameters—frequency, intensity, duration. It occurs when the inescapable shock is administered in the shuttle box instead of in the hammock. After uncontrollable shock, dogs seem to be unable to prevent or avoid it; when given a signal for shock, they did not use it to avoid shock (Overmier, 1968). Helpless dogs also act differently from other dogs outside of the shuttle box. Nonhelpless dogs resist handling by the experimenter when he comes to their cage; helpless dogs passively submit to handling.

Escape from shock is not the only form of adaptive behavior to be disrupted by the experience of being unable to control trauma. Seligman (1975) and Miller et al. (1977) reviewed a number of experiments that suggest rather widespread effects. Rats given inescapable shocks have been found to respond to pain with less aggression toward other rats and to be slower in learning to swim out of a water maze. Rats exposed to inescapable shock at the time of weaning showed impaired food-getting behavior in adulthood, even when very hungry. Exposure to uncontrollable events other than shock can produce effects like those following inescapable shock. Inescapable tumbling can produce escape deficits, as can unsolvable problems, loud noise, and defeat in fighting. The deficits in locomotion, exploration, and social behavior produced by confining neonatal monkeys to a narrow pit can also be viewed as learned helplessness (Suomi and Harlow, 1977).

Control experiments indicate that the essential condition leading to the learned helplessness effect is the experience of being unable to control the trauma by responding. If even a minimal degree of such control is provided, subsequent helplessness is avoided. It is also important that uncontrollable reward impairs responding for reward. When pellets of food were given to rats independently of their responses, their subsequent performance in learning to bar-press for food was poor. Seligman (1975) called this the spoiled-brat design; the organism is rewarded without having to exert special effort. Seligman believed that the animals learned that the outcome is independent of their responses, that responding and reinforcement do not go together. Consequently, it is futile to respond.

One way has been found to cure the dogs; treatment consists of dragging them by long leashes from side to side in the shuttle box until they eventually respond on their own (Seligman, 1968). The treatment reverses the inescapable shock experience and teaches that responses can control reinforcement. Similar treatment has been effective with rats (Seligman, 1975).

Dogs can be immunized against learned helplessness in the laboratory by giving them prior experience in escaping electric shock. Furthermore, it has been shown that cage-reared dogs, who are inexperienced with trauma, are more susceptible to helplessness than are mongrel dogs of unknown history; the interpretation is that the mongrels had a greater probability of previously encountering and escaping trauma.

Seligman (1975) contended that learned helplessness may parallel human depression, particularly reactive depression, in several ways. Depression is characterized by reduced response initiation and a hopeless attitude about the potential effectiveness of one's own responses. Seligman also drew attention to the probability that learned helplessness may play an important role in other forms of experimental neurosis, such as those of Pavlov, Liddell, Masserman, and Stroebel.

Learned helplessness does not meet the criteria of experimental neurosis in Hebb's sense, because the generalization of the maladaptive behavior is undetermined and the incidence is very high if preventive experience has not occurred. However, the concept has had a major influence on writings in the field of experimental neurosis (Maser and Seligman, 1977). Furthermore, the model of learned helplessness may be a valid one for conceptualizing the causes of some types of depressive reactions in humans. One thinks of the reaction to loss of a loved one either by rejection or by death. This means that one's responses can no longer bring about gratification through the loved person. Similarly, belief in one's helplessness may arise from failure in business or affliction with a serious disease. It also follows that an accumulation of experiences with unescapable trauma may increase susceptibility to depressive reactions, but experience in dealing effectively with trauma may be preventive.

Psychosomatic Disorders in Animals

Various physiological disturbances frequently accompany the behavioral manifestations of experimental neuroses. Often they are the most convincing signs of disturbance, as in the case of Liddell's sheep, whose respiratory rate rose to 135 a minute. It seems clear that psychophysiological reactions form an integral part of the picture of experimental neurosis. One could also argue that the experimental methods are essentially similar. This section considers some examples of experimental work more specifically directed to organ system pathology. These examples are among the most sophisticated and give some idea of the methods and problems.

GASTROINTESTINAL DISORDERS

There has been considerable work on the experimental induction of functional and structural changes in the stomach. The studies of Mahl (1953) were pioneering. He investigated the effects of chronic fear in dogs and monkeys and added some observations in humans.

Dogs were stimulated under control conditions day and night by a 20-second buzzer that occurred unpredictably at intervals of 5, 10, or 15 minutes. In the chronic fear condition the buzzer stimulation continued, but some buzzers were accompanied by a brief, painful electric shock, delivered to the animals through the grid floor of the cages. The dogs developed conditioned fear to the buzzer and the cage; this fear was manifested by motor withdrawal activity, paralysis, trembling, widespread autonomic changes, and intense vocalization. Measurements of free hydrochloric acid (HCl) and total acidity showed significant increases in both. The dogs were then allowed a recovery period, being removed to different cages in a rest room, with no buzzer or shock stimuli. Later they were returned to the experimental cages and were stimulated for 5 hours with only the buzzer. During this conditioned fear phase, there was an increase in gastric acidity. The results were similar in monkeys.

Mahl concluded that sustained fear is accompanied by increased HCl secretion in dogs, monkeys, and humans and that conditioned fear stimuli evoked increased HCl secretion in the absence of pain stimulation. By contrast, HCl secretion is inhibited during episodic fear stimulation. Mahl found no evidence of stomach lesions in his animals.

Other investigators were able to produce lesions and to study the relevant conditions. Porter et al. (1958) demonstrated that experimental psychological stress may produce gastrointestinal lesions in the monkey. In 11 of 19 animals, there were lesions that included gastric hemorrhage and erosion, duodenal ulceration, enteric intussusception, and chronic colitis; avoidance learning seemed to be particularly likely to produce duodenal ulceration. Brady (1958) investigated the critical conditions for the development of duodenal ulcers in monkeys during avoidance learning. His schedule involved shocking the animal every 20 seconds unless he pressed a lever. The lever-pressing response to avoid shock was quickly learned. To establish whether the amount of shock was a factor in producing the lesions, the researcher paired the experimental monkey with a control monkey who was shocked at the same time as the experimental monkey but who had no effective way of avoiding shock with his own lever (see Figure 4). After 23 days, the monkey that learned the avoidance response (the executive monkey) died suddenly and was found to have a large perforation in the wall of the duodenum. The control monkey had no lesion. This experience was repeated with the same outcome in three more pairs of monkeys. Further studies indicated that a time factor in the experiment was critical. In the lesion-producing experiment, the monkeys had alternated six-hour periods of shock avoidance and 6-hour periods of rest. When the shock frequency, with its required avoidance response, was increased or when the 6 hours on-6 hours off avoidance schedule was changed, the animals did not develop ulcers. Measurements of gastric acidity indicated that acidity increased not while the executive monkey was pressing the lever to avoid shock but during the rest period. The greatest period increase occurred on the 6-hour alteration schedule, which appears to have been the necessary condition for producing the lesions.

Although Brady's results place emphasis on the role of gastric acidity after stress and on the particular timing of the local factor, there is evidence that sustained central nervous system excitation can also produce lesions. French et al. (1957) showed that prolonged electrical stimulation to the hypothalamic region produced ulceration in monkeys. This finding suggests another mechanism whereby intense and long-lasting fear, conflict, and stress may bring about prolonged gastric hypersecretion and ulceration.

The failure of other investigators to replicate Brady's executive monkey phenomenon (Foltz and Millett, 1964) was hard to explain and diminished the great interest initially aroused by his demonstration. More recently, however, the theoretical formulation developed by Weiss (1977) to account for his results in experiments on gastric lesions in rats also helps to explain the executive monkey results.

Weiss (1968) had shown that rats able to control shock developed less severe gastric erosions than did yoked control rats that received the same shock but were without the capability of controlling it. Indeed, the extent of gastric erosions in the animals that could control shock was almost as low as in a second control group that was not shocked at all; this finding suggested that the control of shock is a more important factor than whether or not shock occurs. Weiss's results appeared to be directly opposite to the findings of the executive monkey study. The results were not due to differences in the warning signal given before shock (Weiss, 1971). Weiss postulated that gastric lesions were a function of two variables—the number of responses made by the animals and the informational feedback that animals received immediately after responses. He found that lesions increased in severity when there were more responses; conversely, there were fewer lesions when responses immediately produced appropriate feedback. Weiss (1977) used the model in subsequent experiments and obtained confirmatory results; for example, the introduction of a tone stimulus after a response in order to increase feedback resulted in reduction of gastric lesions.

Weiss's formulation appears to account for the executive monkey results. He points out that, in pretests, the monkey in each pair that was selected as the executive had shown a higher rate of responding than did its yoked partner; the executive was thus more likely to develop lesions. Also, the avoidance schedule used by Brady provided the executive animals with relatively little feedback, because no external warning signal had to be terminated by a correct response. The executive monkey was, thus, exposed to those conditions—high rate of responding and low level of relevant feedback—that were most favorable for developing lesions. In Weiss's opinion, the executive monkey situation was very unusual in that the normally beneficial effect of having control over a stressor was reversed by the combination of a high response rate and a low level of feedback.

As Weiss (1977) pointed out, his ability to arrive at an explanatory formulation of the factors influencing gastric lesion formation was favored by the availability of data from a large number of animals. Had he used larger animals than the rat, his sample size would almost certainly have been smaller. The advantages from being able to study relatively large groups have probably been responsible for the popularity of investigating gastric lesions in small animals. The methods used have involved inducing fear and conflict, as well as simply immobilizing the animals. Although gastric erosions, rather than ulcers, are more frequently produced, there is reason to believe that similar processes are involved in both kinds of lesion (Weiss, 1977).

Weisz (1957) divided 90 rats into six split-litter groups of equal size and placed each of these groups in a different experimental situation. Two situations involved an approach-avoidance type of conflict; two were fear-producing, with food and water deprivation present in one but not in the other; two were control situations, involving only food and water deprivation or food and water deprivation plus the facility to see

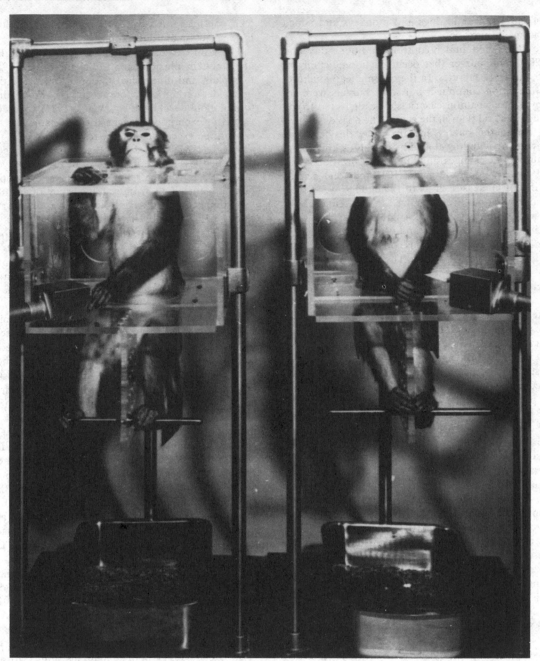

FIGURE 4. The monkey on the *left*, known as the executive monkey, controls whether or not both will receive an electric shock. The decision-making task produces a state of chronic tension. Note the more relaxed attitude of the monkey on the right. (United States Army Photographs.)

and smell food and water. Significantly more animals in the two conflict situations and in one fear-producing situation developed ulcers in the rumen of the stomach than did the comparable animals in control situations. The data suggested that severe food and water deprivation is a necessary prerequisite for the occurrence of the stomach lesions, although not sufficient in itself, and that both conflict and chronic fear can result in gastric lesions. The postulated chain of events is that stress due to fear, conflict, or immobilization leads to increased acidity; an excessive volume of unbuffered gastric juice then comes into contact with the upper portion of the stomach, which is not as well protected by mucosa as the remainder of the stomach.

Because stress does not lead to gastric ulceration in all animals, the factors governing variations in susceptibility are

of great interest. The data of Sines and McDonald (1968) suggested that more than half of the variability in stress ulcer responsiveness of the rat may be genetically determined. Many additional factors have been implicated. These include sex (females are more susceptible), prenatal maternal handling, the amount of handling in early life, whether the animal is housed alone or in a group, plasma pepsinogen level, and the phase of the activity cycle during which the animal is immobilized (Ader, 1963, 1970; Ader and Plaut, 1968). Early separation from the mother appears to have a powerful effect in bringing about predisposition to gastric lesions. Ackerman et al. (1975) found that rats separated before weaning (15 days after birth or earlier) had a nearly 100 per cent incidence of erosions after 24 hours of restraint, but the incidence was much lower in animals separated 21 or 25 days after birth. In addition, the early-separated animals frequently manifested severe gastrointestinal hemorrhage. Sines (1975) emphasized the importance of a multifactorial approach to the problem of gastric lesions. Using two different forms of stress—restraint and being forced to run in a drum—Sines demonstrated an interaction between the animal's activity level before stress and the type of stress, even though neither factor by itself was related to a different incidence of lesions. Whether or not a given stress will result in a gastric lesion seems to depend on interactions between the stress, constitutional factors (heredity, sex, intrauterine history), predisposing life circumstances (for example, early handling, separation, and housing), and current organismic state (nutrition, bodily activity cycle). Although complex and not understood in detail, this formulation of the pathogenesis of stress ulceration in the rat is in accord with the traditional multifactorial clinical approach to analysis of human illness.

Ackerman (1975) attempted to relate the findings on restraint ulceration in early-separated rats to what is known about peptic ulcer disease in children. Apparently, ulcers, particularly of the acute gastric type, occur relatively frequently during the first weeks of life and then become less frequent. Their causation is not really understood, but the most common presentation is massive hemmorhage. Also, the infants often fail to maintain body temperature, and chronic or acute malnutrition appears to be a frequent predisposing factor. There are, thus, many descriptive similarities between ulcer disease in young children and experimental rodent ulceration. Ackerman, in drawing attention to them, formulated a number of clinically important questions that the animal model may help to resolve. For example, what is the significance of interaction with the mother or lack of some critical aspect of it in bringing about ulcers in infants?

ASTHMA

It is possible to induce asthma experimentally in the guinea pig by sensitizing the animal to egg white; asthmatic attacks then occur in response to a spray of homologous antigen. The reactivity to antigen varies, but Ottenberg et al. (1958) found that consistently reactive guinea pigs displayed attacks when placed in the experimental chamber in the absence of the egg white spray. The asthmatic attacks of these animals appeared to be a conditioned response to the chamber.

The respiratory pattern associated with the pain-fear response to electric shock resembled that found in experimental allergic asthma but actually involves different mechanisms. Schiavi et al. (1961) determined this fact by measuring several respiratory characteristics and the mechanical properties of the lungs. Under both conditions, inspiration was shortened, and expiration was prolonged. However, there was evidence of bronchiolar obstruction in experimental allergic asthma, whereas no increased airway resistance was found in the animals exposed to electric shock. This study provides an example of the fact that detailed measurement and analysis of physiological functions can demonstrate that different mechanisms can be involved in an apparently similar bodily reaction pattern.

ARTERIAL HYPERTENSION

Systolic blood pressure increases with age in many but not all human populations. This increase is believed by some to be a response to repeated symbolic stimuli arising from the social environment. Henry et al. (1967) attempted to simulate these conditions in mice by playing on their inborn drives for terri-

tory, survival, and reproduction. Apparently, the experiments with mice were instigated after the observation that severe hypertension developed in young chimpanzees exposed to months of daily operant conditioning while immobilized in a seat as part of a training program for space flight. Henry et al. (1975) recounted that one chimpanzee had diastolic pressures as high as 130 mm. Hg, accompanied by reduced renal blood flow, and developed fixed hypertension, although he was apparently docile and unperturbed. In contrast, an untrained animal exposed to the situation for 14 days did not have hypertension but did display agitated behavior. In a series of long-term experiments, Henry and his associates mixed animals previously maintained in different boxes, brought them together in small boxes, subjected groups to threat from a predator, and induced conflict for territory by placing equal numbers of males and females in an interconnected box system. The most severe environmental conditions of psychosocial stimulation resulted in a mean arterial blood pressure rise from 126 mm. Hg to the range of 150 to 160 mm. Hg; the rise was sustained for 6 to 9 months.

Previous experience was a factor, because animals kept in groups from birth showed less pressure elevation (140 to 150 mm. Hg). Sex, probably in consequence of its relation to aggressive reactions, was also relevant. Female blood pressures were in about the same range as those of males that had been aggregated from birth, but castrates showed minimal effects. When the mice were returned to a less stimulating situation, the pressures usually subsided toward control levels. Autopsy revealed gross interstitial nephritis in a number of animals subject to both social isolation and aggression training; the systolic pressure of the males in this group averaged 190 mm. Hg. Gross pathology was not observed in other animals.

Henry et al. concluded that their results supported hypotheses that, in a constant external environment, systemic arterial pressure reflects the symbolic stimuli received during social interaction and that early experience plays a role in determining the arousal value of the stimuli received. They suggested that their data provide an experimental approach to the role of psychosocial stimuli and early environment that is relevant to the cause of human hypertension.

Henry et al. (1971) also demonstrated that mice exposed to a high level of social stimulation showed increases in adrenal weight and adrenal noradrenaline and adrenaline, as well as elevated blood pressure. Tyrosine hydroxylase, the rate-limiting enzyme for biosynthesis of noradrenaline, and phenylethanolamine N-methyltransferase, which catalyzes conversion of noradrenaline to adrenaline, were also both greatly increased in the socially stimulated animals. The data were interpreted to indicate long-sustained adrenal responses to acute episodes of social stimulation.

Further experiments by Henry's group documented the critical role of the duration of exposure to social stimulation in determining the reversibility of hypertensive changes (Henry et al., 1975). Different colonies of former isolated mice were exposed to periods of social interaction, ranging from 2 days to 9 months, and then returned to isolation. The longer the period of social stimulation, the less the restoration of normal values after the return to isolation. The 9-month colonies also manifested continued elevation of heart and adrenal weights and histological changes. Myocardial fibrosis, reflecting arteriosclerotic deterioration of the intramural vessels, appeared to be progressive during the 8 weeks' return to isolation in the 9-month colonies.

The work of the Henry group on experimental hypertension

emphasizes the role of social interaction factors, but other factors have received investigative attention elsewhere. The study by Friedman and Dahl (1975) is of interest because it focused on the interactions between chronic conflict and the genetic susceptibility to hypertension in rats. They exposed rats from a strain known to be genetically susceptible to experimental hypertension to several aversive environmental regimens. From greatest to least, the groups ranked as follows in degree of blood pressure elevation: (1) animals exposed to an approach-avoidance conflict between food and shock, (2) animals that received food and shock independent of their behavior, (3) rats food deprived but not given shock, (4) rats given shock but not food deprived, (5) controls (no shock or food deprivation). When the aversive conditions were removed, pressures usually returned to control levels, but some rats showed persistent elevations after removal of the stress. Because the blood pressure elevations found by Friedman and Dahl were greater than previously reported in other stress experiments, they concluded that the genetic component was involved in augmenting the effect of other stimuli leading to hypertension.

In a different experimental approach to experimental hypertension in rats, Falk et al. (1977) did not use a genetically susceptible strain or aversive and conflictful stimuli. They used a food schedule known to induce excessive drinking and other adjunctive behaviors, such as aggression and hyperactivity. They also generated a predisposition to develop hypertension by reducing renal mass (removing one kidney) and providing a high salt intake by means of a saline drinking fluid. Their experimental groups developed chronic hypertension; in addition to elevated blood pressure, heart weight increased, and the kidney showed minor pathological changes. Falk et al. contended that their experimental situation, schedule feeding leading to adjunctive behavior, when combined with somatic predisposing factors, may provide a more valid model of environmental situations conducive to hypertension than do situations involving pain or physical trauma.

As with the work on gastric lesions, the results of studies of experimental hypertension in small animals indicate that the pathology results from the complex interplay of many factors. To ascertain which may be relevant in a clinical situation obviously requires careful analysis.

Experimental hypertension has also been investigated in primates. Forsyth (1968, 1969) studied blood pressure responses in rhesus monkeys exposed to shock-avoidance conditioning according to various schedules. The monkeys were restrained in special chairs, and blood pressure was recorded from catheters implanted in the abdominal aorta. In 15-day experiments, all monkeys showed an initial increase of arterial pressures when the avoidance schedule was introduced. However, only those animals exposed to schedules longer or more complex than a 6 hours on-6 hours off design continued to display elevated pressures after the initial trials. It is significant that, when elevated, pressures remained high during the off hours. Behavioral observations suggested that the animals receiving avoidance conditioning were more excitable and anxious than were the controls.

In long-term experiments, lasting 7 to 14 months, Forsyth found that elevations of both systolic and diastolic blood pressures occurred in all but one of six animals after 4 to 6 months of normal pressure or even hypotension. However, autopsies revealed no consistent pathological findings, except for atheromatous plaques surrounding the catheter tip. The absence of gastric lesions was noteworthy, as these might have

been expected from the results of Porter et al. (1958). Also of interest were observations of acute increases in blood pressure lasting several days when the training schedule was interrupted by equipment failures during the normotensive period. Such interruptions did not produce hypertensive responses during the later phases, when blood pressure was consistently elevated.

Changes in arterial blood pressure were produced in the squirrel monkey by Morse et al. (1971). They used various reinforcement schedules that required key-pressing either to avoid shock or to obtain food. The pattern of systematic blood pressure changes associated with responding varied with the schedule; with one schedule, blood pressure was highest during key-pressing; with another, it was highest when the monkey was not responding. They found that four of six monkeys studied for several months developed sustained hypertension in the experimental situation and that this hypertension persisted after return to the home cage. They pointed to the similarities between behavioral hypertension in the squirrel monkey and essential hypertension in humans. In both cases, transient episodes of elevated pressures over a period of months are followed by sustained hypertension. They suggested that their experimental preparation may be used to study cardiovascular mechanisms during the hypertensive state.

INSTRUMENTAL LEARNING OF AUTONOMIC RESPONSES

The conditioning method introduced by Pavlov is called "classical conditioning." B. F. Skinner brought into prominence another type of conditioning called "instrumental" or "operant." In this type, learning is thought to occur because of the consequences of the response, rather than by virtue of pairing conditioned and unconditioned stimuli. For example, a rat placed in a cage with a bar that released food on being pressed quickly learns to press the bar after the initial, presumably accidental, discovery that pressing it brings about a reward. The avoidance conditioning experiments in monkeys described earlier used an operant approach. For a long time it was generally held that conditioning of autonomic responses could occur only in the classical and not in the operant paradigm. The demonstration that this is not the case was a key event in the development of the field now known as biofeedback. Instrumental learning of autonomic responses has been proposed as relevant for some mechanisms underlying symptom development in human psychosomatic disorders.

Neal Miller (1969) and his associates have conducted the most extensive series of studies on instrumental learning of autonomic responses. Because autonomic responses can be mediated by skeletal muscle activity, thus leaving open the possibility that the animals learned skeletal responses that had an unlearned tendency to elicit the visceral responses recorded, Miller and his colleagues performed most of the experiments on curarized, artificially respirated rats. In these preparations the reward was provided by electrical stimulation of the brain in the medial forebrain bundle or by avoidance of mild electric shock to the skin. They were able to show that the heart rate can be instrumentally conditioned to increase or decrease, depending on which spontaneous changes were reinforced. Rats also learned to respond discriminatively to light and tone stimuli signaling that cardiac changes would be rewarded. Other responses that have been instrumentally conditioned include increases and decreases in systolic blood pressure, vasoconstriction in one ear and vasodilation in the other ear of the same animal, intestinal contraction or relaxation, and electroencephalographic increased or decreased amplitude. These learned responses extinguished when the rewards stopped. The demonstrations of instrumental learning of visceral responses indicate that autonomic responsiveness can be highly specific as a consequence of reinforcement experience.

Aberrant autonomic responsiveness associated with human psychosomatic disorders could reasonably arise as a consequence of the reinforcement existing when variations in particular body responses occurred. Miller has given the hypothetical example of a child who fears to go to school and develops pallor and faintness. If the mother responds with concern and keeps her home, this response is reinforcing and, if repeated, the pallor and faintness may be instrumentally conditioned. Miller has also suggested that individual differences in autonomic responsiveness may depend on operant learning in addition to constitutional factors. At present, there is no information about how often, if at all, instrumental mechanisms may operate in human psychosomatic illness. Although likely examples of systematic reinforcement of variations in autonomic responses are hard to come by with respect to illness, one can think of some common instances that apparently do not lead to illness. For example, the cardiovascular changes associated with sexual arousal are frequently followed by significant gratification, but this does not seem to result in sustained hypertension or tachycardia.

The demonstration of instrumental learning of autonomic responses appears to be finding important applications in the area of therapy. No matter how deviant physiological responses may have come about, it may be possible to shift them toward normal by the application of instrumental learning techniques. A number of workers report success in applying biofeedback methods to clinical states. For example, Weiss and Engel (1971) trained patients with premature ventricular contractions to control heart rate voluntarily, and Welgan (1974) demonstrated that ulcer patients can learn to increase the pH of gastric acid secretions (reduce acidity).

Developmental Intervention in Animals

The proposition that the adult is significantly shaped by experience during infancy and childhood is generally accepted. There is also widespread belief in the related idea that experiential deprivation during development will result in abnormal behavior. However, although the deprivation hypothesis is supported by many clinical observations, their validity as proof of the hypothesis cannot fully withstand critical scrutiny. Because planned interference with normal development of human infants is not ethically permissible, animal experimentation provides a major source of scientific information. The general technique is to intervene in the normal course of development by removing some important factors from the environment. The later behavior of animals reared under specified conditions of experimental deprivation can then be observed and compared with that of undeprived controls. Two important groups of studies in this field involve sensory restriction and social, particularly maternal, deprivation.

SENSORY RESTRICTION

Animals reared under conditions of sensory deprivation generally show deficits in perceptual and learning performance. Although the perceptual deficits have been taken to reflect the role of perceptual learning, this interpretation has not gone unchallenged. For example, Riesen (1961) showed that cats, monkeys, and chimpanzees reared in darkness were impaired

in visual perceptual tasks. However, his conclusion that this finding indicated the importance of experience in patterned light for visual development was challenged on the grounds that the observed deficits could be due to oculomotor anomalies and neuronal degeneration produced by prolonged visual deprivation, to emotional disturbance on emergence from darkness, or to a deficit in the sphere of learning, rather than perception. To meet such criticisms, Wilson and Riesen (1966) deprived rhesus monkeys of pattern vision from birth to 20 or 60 days of age. They then tested the monkeys daily for various untrained visual responses and trained them on form, striation, and brightness discriminations. The results showed that deprived animals were similar to newborn monkeys in visual discrimination learning and in untrained visual behaviors, and they supported Riesen's earlier conclusion. However, because visual development of deprivates was quicker than that of newborns, it appeared that maturational, as well as experiential, factors contributed to visual development.

The deprivation strategy has been used by many investigators to study the role of experiential factors in perceptual functioning. The volume edited by Gottlieb (1976) provided a series of exellent reviews of the literature in this area. The general conclusion is that experiential factors do play important roles in the development of both neural and behavioral specificities. On the other hand, all is not experience; much order and specificity exists in the patterning of neural connections before they are involved in functioning. The basis of this neural order and specificity is thought to depend on unique biochemical labels acquired under genetic control early in the development of individual neurons; cells with similar labels develop selective interconnections (Meyer and Sperry, 1976).

In a pioneer demonstration of the effects of sensory restriction on learning, Hymovitch (1952) showed that problem-solving behavior in rats at maturity was superior when they were reared in a free-environment box than when their development took place in individual enclosures that severely restricted sensory input. He also found that the effects of environmental restriction were greater when it occurred during early life than when it occurred later on. He concluded that problem-solving activities at maturity depended on early opportunities for perceptual learning and that the impairments of the restricted animals appeared to be relatively permanent and possibly irreversible.

Melzack (1965) reared beagle dogs from 3 weeks of age under circumstances that drastically reduced the variety of patterned stimuli. The restricted dogs were released from their cages at about 10 months of age and compared with dogs of the same age raised normally on a farm. The restricted animals showed difficulty in performing simple visual discriminations between white and black cards and also failed to respond normally to auditory stimuli. They were unable to inhibit irrelevant response patterns; their rate of extinction when responses were not reinforced was slow, and they displayed stereotyped and nonadaptive behavior, such as nonrewarded position habits, in the testing box. They also showed abnormal responses to noxious stimulation—for example, one crashed violently into the wall of the large wooden test box every day for more than a month without ever giving any indication of pain, and several repetitively poked their noses into a flaming match.

In addition to deficits in perceptual and problem-solving ability, Melzack's restricted animals seemed to suffer some serious consequences in the sphere of emotional reactivity. They ignored a female in heat and continually avoided her approaches. They were clearly hyperexcitable. Most objects produced diffuse emotional excitement with rapid circling movements or vigorous dashing to and fro; sometimes the dogs had whirling fits. The restricted dogs were also socially submissive to normally reared dogs. Riesen also described several behavioral effects of an early deprivation period in mammals, which he felt could be separated from the obvious perceptual differences produced.

Fuller (1967) outlined three major theoretical interpretations of these changes in perception, learning, and emotional reactivity consequent on sensory restriction: (1) They reflect a need for perceptual learning. (2) Isolation has destructive or interfering effects on previously organized processes; this interpretation is supported by observations that, after isolation, dogs often perform more poorly than they did before. (3) The changes result more from competing emotional responses than from inferior behavioral organization during isolation or from loss of established patterns. Experiments conducted by Fuller and his colleagues appear to uphold the view that emphasizes the stressful effects of emergence from isolation. For example, they showed that the behavioral disturbances of puppies on release from isolation could be largely removed by stroking and handling them or by administering chlorpromazine. They also demonstrated that vulnerability to disturbance by isolation varies according to the breed of dog. Perhaps of greater importance from the standpoint of applying these animal observations to problems of human psychopathology is the observation that they could largely counteract the effects of isolation by introducing twice-weekly breaks of less than 10 minutes each and that an opportunity for the animal to look out of the isolation cage had some counteracting effect.

If isolation effects in dogs can be counteracted by only 20 minutes weekly of normal sensory experience, extreme caution must be exercised before attributing serious deficits in perceptual, motor, and learning abilities, together with disturbed emotional reactivity, to early experiential deprivation in humans. Few human infants are exposed to the severe continuous sensory restriction imposed on experimental animals. To extrapolate the animal findings, one would have to assume greater human vulnerability to lesser degrees of deprivation. Attention must also be paid to the fact that there are probably large individual differences in the persistence of postisolation deficits. This fact suggests that persistent psychopathological effects related to early experiential deprivation in humans may occur mainly in those who are rendered vulnerable for other reasons, such as genetic defect or nutritional deficit.

SOCIAL DEPRIVATION

The best-known studies of social deprivation in animals are those conducted under the direction of Harry F. Harlow (Harlow and Harlow, 1966, 1971). Rhesus monkeys were separated from their mothers at birth and brought up under conditions of total or partial social deprivation, with sensory deprivation held to a minimum. Some were given inanimate surrogate mothers made of cloth or wire, and some were raised with brutal, abnormal, live foster mothers (see Figure 5). Others were raised in the company of peers. The effects of these developmental interventions were tested in various ways, including observations of learning performance, play, aggressive behavior, sexual activity, and other kinds of social behavior. The duration of isolation was a critical determinant of later behavioral anomalies; animals isolated for 80 days would normalize after several months, but those isolated for 6 months or more would not normalize spontaneously.

FIGURE 5. Infant rhesus with cloth surrogate mother. (From Harlow, H. F., and Harlow, M. K. Psychopathology in monkeys. In *Experimental Psychopathology: Recent Research and Theory,* H. D. Kimmel, editor, p. 204. Academic Press, New York, 1971.)

In later life, monkeys reared in social isolation exhibited behavioral abnormalities rarely seen in wild-born animals brought to the laboratory as adolescents. The isolated monkeys sat in their cages and stared fixedly into space, repetitively circled the cages, clasped their heads in their hands or arms, and rocked for long periods. They frequently developed compulsive habits, such as pinching exactly the same patch of skin hundreds of times daily. Sometimes the animal chewed and tore at its body until it bled; this behavior was often precipitated by the approach of a human. This behavior contrasts markedly with the behavior of the wild-born monkey, who is aggressive toward the approaching person but not toward itself. The isolated monkeys were also extremely fearful of other monkeys and inappropriately aggressive toward them; they would threaten or assault infants and groups of larger mature males.

Perhaps the most striking deficit of the socially isolated monkeys was in sexual competence. At 2 years of age, the laboratory-born animals were not lacking in sex drive, inasmuch as the males frequently approached the females and the females displayed part of the pattern of sexual presentation. However, they did not orient themselves correctly, and they did not succeed in mating. As they grew older, the monkeys raised in partial isolation rarely interacted with cage-mates and avoided heterosexual behavior. A variety of therapeutic maneuvers, such as exposing males to females in estrus and letting the deprived males live as a group in the municipal zoo, was unsuccessful in bringing about normal sexual conduct. However, more recent studies have indicated that the behavioral deficits of isolated monkeys may not be as irreversible as originally supposed. Suomi et al. (1974) exposed socially incompetent isolates daily to younger normal monkeys and were able to demonstrate almost complete recovery in social contact and play after several months.

Turner et al. (1969) reported effects of early deprivation on the social behavior of adolescent chimpanzees that were similar to those observed in Harlow's monkeys. The animals were reared for the first 3 years in illuminated, covered, bare cribs. At about 10 years of age, they avoided social contact, played and copulated infrequently, and did not groom. These aberrations were resistant to modification by various maneuvers, including contact with normal social partners and various psychoactive drugs.

It is noteworthy that the damaging effects of early social isolation in monkeys do not seem to result specifically from maternal deprivation, because they may be overcome by the presence of peers. Furthermore, experimental observations on monkeys raised with their mothers but deprived of peer contacts revealed retarded play and social behavior in the peer deprivates.

The severe behavioral incapacity resulting from social isolation is accompanied by marked physiological abnormalities. Mirsky (1969) studied some of Harlow's monkeys that had been raised in isolation for 12 months. Although these animals had been in normal laboratory contact with other animals during the ensuing 3 years, they manifested minimal social interactions, and those that did occur were of an increasingly aggressive nature. The isolated monkeys were found to manifest polydypsia and polyuria; they drank and excreted nearly 3 times as much as wild-born controls. These symptoms were not due to a decrease in the secretion of antidiuretic hormone, because there was a normal response of decreased urinary output with restricted water intake. It appeared that the mechanism involved a derangement in regulation of the water satiety mechanism of the hypothalamus. The isolates also excreted larger quantities of uric acid than did the controls, but the excretion of creatinine was the same. Furthermore, the isolates excreted much smaller quantities of norepinephrine, although the excretion of epinephrine was the same in isolates and controls. The isolates also exhibited an increased rate of removal of glucose from the circulation and a more marked release of insulin by the pancreas after intravenous injection of a standard quantity of glucose. In Mirsky's opinion the biochemical aberrations exhibited by these socially isolated monkeys bore some similarity to chemical deviations observed in humans suffering from schizophrenia. One monkey, the isolate with the largest uric acid excretion, had to be maintained on chlorpromazine in order to inhibit his tendency to mutilate himself by chewing at various parts of his body.

Some behavioral experiments conducted in Mirsky's laboratory help to define the nature of the deficit in social behavior of monkeys reared in isolation. All monkeys, isolates and wild-born controls, were first taught to press a lever on exposure to a visual stimulus in order to avoid delivery of an electric shock that followed in 6 seconds after the onset of the stimulus. After acquiring the avoidance response, they were paired in a paradigm called "cooperative conditioning." One animal, the stimulus monkey, receives the conditioned stimulus but lacks the lever that would permit it to perform the required avoidance

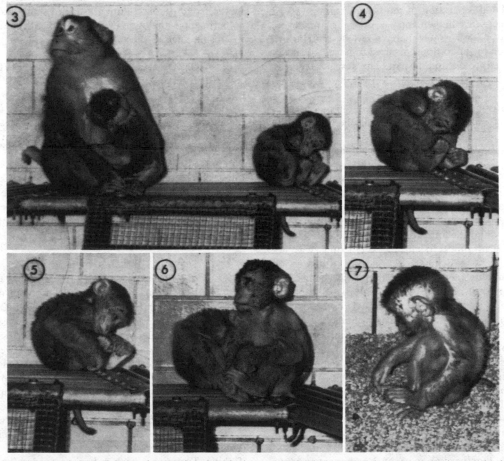

FIGURE 6. *3.* Depressed pigtail infant showing characteristic hunched-over posture with flexion throughout. He is completely disengaged from mother and infant nearby in ventral-ventral contact. *4.* Depressed pigtail infant showing characteristic posture including head between legs. Note slightly opened eyes as he sucks his penis. *5.* Depressed pigtail infant showing characteristic posture and dejected facies. *6.* Two depressed pigtail infants. The one in the rear shows characteristic hunched-over posture. The one in the front has lifted his head to look across the pen. Despite their passive contact, they are quite disengaged from each other. *7.* Depressed infant showing aimless, tentative exploration of bedding during early stages of recovery. (From Kaufman, I. C., and Rosenblum, L. A. The reaction to separation in infant monkeys: Anaclitic depression and conservation-withdrawal. Psychosom. Med., *29:* 655, 1967.)

response. The second, responder, monkey has the avoidance lever but does not receive the conditioned stimulus. Each monkey is located in a separate test room. The television camera focused on the head and face of the stimulus monkey is transmitted to a receiver located in front of the responder. Wild-born monkeys were easily able to develop such cooperative conditioning responses and functioned adequately as senders and receivers of nonverbal facial expressions when tested with other wild-born animals. The isolated monkeys, however, were totally incapable of responding either physiologically or instrumentally to the facial expressions of other monkeys. Furthermore, they were so impaired with respect to the nature of the messages that they sent to others that the wild-born monkeys had much difficulty in making appropriate responses to their facial expressions. The main impairment seemed to be in the area of responding to and transmitting social stimuli, such as facial expressions.

REACTIONS TO TEMPORARY SEPARATION

The effects on infant monkeys of being separated from their mothers for intervals ranging from a few minutes to several weeks have been studied by a number of workers. Very brief separations (5 minutes) produced strong emotional reactions, with agitation and continuous screaming by the infants and increased contact with the mother on reunion (Jensen and Tolman, 1962). Total separation of mother and infant (age, 7 months) for 2 weeks resulted in increased crying and severe depression of play and other social behavior (Seay and Harlow, 1965). The reaction to separation appeared to have two stages, described as violent protest and despair. The despair stage was characterized by less activity, little or no play, and occasional crying.

Kaufman and Rosenblum (1967) separated four pigtail monkey infants, about 5 months old, from their mothers for 4 weeks (see Figure 6). The initial severe emotional distress lasted 24 to 36 hours (protest stage). Then three of the four animals sat hunched over, almost rolled into a ball, with head often down between the legs; two were sucking their own penises in this position. The facial expression was one of dejection and sadness, and there was very little movement (despair stage). There were few social responses and no play behavior. Although the coat looked shaggy and the appearance gave the impression of sickness, no physical illness occurred, and eating was not impaired. After 5 or 6 days, the reaction akin to depression began to abate, activity increased, and there was engagement in play. However, the infant was still subject to periods of depression.

In their experiments Kaufman and Rosenblum (1969) noted that, in contrast to separated pigtail infants, infants of the bonnet species appeared to be immune to depression, although they manifested agitation when separated. They believed lack of depression resulted from an increased amount of contact between the infant and the remaining adults after the removal of the mother. In subsequent work they failed to induce depression in 17 bonnet infants. However, Kaufman and Stynes (1978) demonstrated that depression can be produced in the bonnet infant. They did so by having pregnant bonnet and pigtail females live together in one group; one bonnet and four pigtail babies were born. The bonnet infant was separated at 5 months from his mother and from all other bonnets. He manifested a depressive reaction indistinguishable from that illustrated in Figure 6 for pigtail infants. Apparently, the interpretation was correct that contact with other bonnet mothers had prevented depression after separation from the infant's own mother.

Kaufman and Rosenblum (1967) related the separation reaction of monkey infants to the anaclitic depression of human infants after separation, which was described by Spitz (1945). The view that the separated monkey infant provides a model of anaclitic depression appears to have gained acceptance by a number of workers (Suomi and Harlow, 1977). There is also experimental evidence that early separation experiences predispose to depressive-like reactions after later separations when the animal is older (Young et al., 1973).

The effects of separation in monkeys, particularly when brought about by confinement in a vertical chamber from which escape is impossible, can also be readily conceptualized as learned helplessness (Suomi and Harlow, 1977).

INFANTILE FRUSTRATION

Another type of experiment demonstrating a relationship between early experience and adult behavior involves the frustration of infant needs. For example, Hunt (1941) demonstrated that rats that suffered feeding frustration during infancy tended to display more hoarding behavior after periods of starvation in maturity than did rats that had not been so deprived. It has also been found that puppies that were deprived of the satisfaction of sucking needs later displayed a perverted type of continual sucking and oral behavior. An experimental analogue of the concept of fixation is suggested by results such as these.

RELATION OF DEVELOPMENTAL INTERVENTION STUDIES TO EXPERIMENTAL NEUROSIS

Although the experimental procedures used in the long-term developmental intervention studies clearly result in later behavioral abnormalities, these abnormalities are not experimental neuroses as defined by Hebb. They occur in virtually all animals subjected to the procedure and, as Mirsky's (1969) observations suggest, there may be neural lesions. However, the developmental intervention studies promise to shed considerable light on factors essential for normal behavioral development and on the psychopathology that may result when these factors are not present.

Studies in Humans

A number of experimental strategies have been used to obtain observations relevant to the problem of neurosis and psychophysiological dysfunction in humans. One obvious approach is to compare persons who clearly suffer from the condition now under examination with controls not so afflicted. However, although functional differences between sickness and health may be ascertained by this approach, the findings leave uncertain the antecedents of illness. For example, to show that neurotic patients have higher heart rates than do healthy controls does not reveal much about the genesis of neurosis, although it may help to clarify a symptom mechanism. Another approach is to attempt to reproduce the manifestations of illness in healthy persons in a temporary and fully reversible fashion. Techniques such as hypnotic induction of conflict and emotion and the application of controlled stressful stimuli have been used for this purpose. Conditioning techniques have also been applied. In addition, a number of investigators have availed themselves of naturally occurring stress or conflict situations, such as the time preceding college final examinations, to make observations of temporary disturbances in ordinarily healthy persons.

HYPNOTICALLY INDUCED CONFLICTS AND EMOTIONS

Before considering the use of hypnosis in various experimental procedures, one should keep in mind the fact that the status of the hypnotic trance as a special state is still under active investigation and remains controversial. The major difficulty arises from the fact that virtually all objectively observable changes that may be recorded during the trance state may also be elicited by verbal instructions or suggestions in unhypnotized persons. However, the uncertain status of hypnosis need not bar acceptance of the results of experiments using hypnotic methods, provided these methods are regarded merely as effective ways of instructing the person.

Luria method. The Russian psychologist Luria (1932) used hypnotic induction, together with a special method of recording motor effects, for the study of human conflicts. In a typical experiment a story was told to the hypnotized person; according to the story, he had committed a reproachable act, one that was contrary to his usual personality trend. A number of critical words were taken from this story and placed in a list of control words not specifically related to the story. The list was then presented as an association experiment. With each verbal response, the person was required to press on a tambour with his preferred hand. Control sessions were carried out before and after the hypnotic experiment in which the conflict was induced and later removed. In addition to the voluntary pressure curves, verbal reaction time to the words and, in some cases, involuntary movements from the nonpreferred hand and respiration were recorded. The signs of conflict consisted of irregular hand pressures, lengthened reaction times, and, when recorded, irregular respiration.

Luria derived several laws from his numerous experiments. He used concepts reminiscent of Pavlov. For example, in his law of the decreased action of the functional barrier, the functional barrier (a cortical property involving regulation of motor activities by inhibition) was weakened by excessive emotional excitation.

Huston et al. (1934) repeated one of Luria's experiments. They used hypnosis to induce a conflict in 12 normal persons. The story used for this purpose in one person follows. The young man met an attractive girl who was wearing a new, brown silk dress that was very important to her. He accidentally burned a cigarette hole in her dress and allowed her to believe that she had done it herself. Words such as silk, dress, brown, cigarette burn, and hole were selected as critical and placed in a long list of noncritical words. Apart from test responses, there appeared to be good evidence that strong conflict was produced by the procedure. The conflict was not removed in this subject for 24 hours after the hypnotic session. That night he slept poorly, awakened with a headache that persisted until the removal of the conflicts in the afternoon, had poor appetite, was resentful and antagonistic toward the hypnotist, and was somewhat uncooperative. He was unable to give any reason for these manifestations. Throughout the day, he gave away his cigarettes and apparently could not enjoy smoking. He rationalized this behavior by saying that he was giving up the habit.

In the group of 12 persons, nine appeared to accept the story told to them as something they had done, and it produced a profound reaction in them. In six of these nine persons, some motor aspect of the Luria technique revealed the presence of the conflict in either the hypnotic or the waking state. In the hypnotic state, they tended to give verbal responses definitely related to conflict, with few nonverbal disturbances; the reverse was found in the waking state, in which there was a relative increase of nonverbal disturbances over the verbal. This finding suggests that, if the excitation created by the conflict is not discharged verbally, there is a spread to the voluntary and involuntary motor levels.

Wittkower's experiments. The wide range of bodily functions that may be altered when hypnosis is used to produce emotional reactions is well illustrated in the monumental early report by Wittkower (1935). He was able to produce X-ray evidence of fluctuations in the size of the heart, with both enlargement and diminution of heart shadow occurring in different persons. Salivary secretions were altered both in quantity and in chemical constitution. Gastric motility and acidity were either increased or decreased; the nature of the gastric reaction was characteristic for the person, even with different emotions, but differed from one person to another. Wittkower demonstrated changes in the amount of bile and the chemical constitution of bile, alterations of leukocyte counts, and changes in the serum calcium, potassium, and chloride content. He also observed changes in the urine, in the blood iodine content, and in the galvanic skin response. Wittkower's main purpose was to demonstrate the profound bodily effects of psychological states. He drew attention to the need for integrating observations of multiple reaction systems if one is to understand the total emotional reaction.

The basic technique used by Wittkower has been used in a large number of experiments with various types of physiological recording. For example, one study of respiratory responses showed that increased ventilation and oxygen consumption followed meaningful hypnotic suggestions of situations eliciting anxiety, anger, exercise, and head pain (Kehoe and Ironside, 1963). Anger, anxiety, and exercise—all of which involve an orientation toward action—were contrasted with depression, the suggestion of which resulted in no respiratory changes. Depression is thought not to involve an action orientation. These results with respiration seem to parallel those obtained for secretion of gastric acid in studies of hypnotically induced depression; the highest gastric secretory rate was associated with suggested anger and the lowest with helplessness-hopelessness. There is also some similarity to the findings with plasma hydrocortisone level, which has been shown to be increased by hypnotically induced anxiety (Persky, 1962).

Specificity of attitudes in psychosomatic disease. Hypnotic techniques have also been used to provide evidence bearing on the specificity of attitude hypothesis in psychosomatic disease, which was proposed by Grace and Graham (1952). The hypothesis states that each attitude toward a disturbing situation is associated with its own specific disease or set of physiological changes. In one study, Graham et al. (1958) hypnotized normal persons, who were told to assume attitudes that the original study had found to be associated with hives and Raynaud's disease. With the hives attitude, the person sees himself as being mistreated and receiving injury, without developing even a wish to take any action himself. With the Raynaud's attitude, on the other hand, the person wishes to take some direct hostile action. Warming of the skin is part of the physiology of hives, whereas cooling is characteristic of Raynaud's disease. Skin temperatures, recorded during hypnotically induced attitudes, showed an average tendency for increase with the hives attitude and a tendency for decrease with the Raynaud's attitude. The results were taken to support the specificity of attitude hypothesis. There is evidence that similar effects can be obtained without hypnosis.

Use of suggestion in studies of asthma. Luparello and his co-workers (Luparello et al., 1968; McFadden et al., 1969) have used techniques based on suggestion to elucidate mechanisms influencing airway reactivity in asthmatic patients. In one study they compared measurements of airway resistance in normals and in patients with asthma, emphysema, and restrictive lung disease. All were led to believe that they were inhaling irritants or allergens that cause bronchoconstriction, although the inhaled substance was a nebulized solution of physiological saline. Nineteen of 40 asthmatics reacted with significant increase in airway resistance, and 12 developed attacks of bronchospasm. The attacks were reversed with saline placebo. Persons in the other groups did not react. The authors proposed the possibility that a conditioning mechanism, based on previous associations between a true allergen and bronchospasm, may have played a role in mediating the positive reactions. Subsequently, it was shown that intravenous atropine sulfate (1 to 2 mg.) can prevent the bronchospasm induced by suggestion in reactors. This indicates that the phenomenon is medicated through efferent cholinergic pathways.

In a third experiment, Luparello et al. (1970) demonstrated that bronchodilator and bronchoconstriction drugs exerted a greater effect when the pharmacological action was in accord with the expectations suggested to the person than when the drug action and the person's expectations were discordant.

CONDITIONING

Application of the method of conditioning to studies of children began in 1907. Krasnogorski (1925) reported observations in children that seemed to be analogous to the experimental neurosis in dogs. In one child, under conditions requiring a difficult discrimination between different rates of a metronome, latent periods of the positive conditioned reflexes first increased in length. At the same time the child, who had always been easy to deal with and quiet during the experiments, became irritable and refused to go to the laboratory. The ward reported that his behavior had changed—he had become rude, fought with other children, insisted on being discharged, and was disobedient. In the laboratory, previously accomplished differentiations were then lost, the negative stimulus was associated with yawning and sleepiness, and the child went to sleep for the first time in a period of 5 months of conditioning study. This child, presumably behaviorally healthy when the experiments began, thus became emotionally disturbed.

One may, of course, criticize interpretation of this reaction as experimental neurosis. It may be normal for a child required to undergo repeated exposure to a difficult laboratory situation to become upset. Furthermore, the generalization to the ward situation could have been determined mainly by anticipation of further exposure to the unpleasant laboratory situation.

Research in the Soviet Union has provided experimental demonstrations that most bodily functions obey Pavlovian laws of conditioning (Bykov, 1959). These experiments provide a basis for relating visceral dysfunctions to symbolic cues that have acquired meaning on the basis of previous experience. Furthermore, Razran's (1939) experiments on semantic conditioning indicate that bodily reactions may be elicited in response to verbal cues that are different in form from the initial stimuli but that have a similar meaning or a strong, previously formed, associational bond. For example, after establishing conditioned salivation to the word "black," just as much response will be obtained from its antonym "white," whereas another color name that has low associational relationship, such as "ocher," elicits much less response. Psychotherapeutic exploration is often concerned with working out specific examples of this phenomenon—for example, when the patient reports an attack of dyspnea under particular circumstances that have only an associational relationship to symbols of previous conflict or trauma.

The application of instrumental conditioning methods to humans has broadened the scope of mechanisms whereby bodily reactions may be linked to symbolic cues (Miller, 1969).

Investigators have continued to use conditioning techniques in comparative studies of psychiatric patients and normal persons. A detailed account of the results can be found in several books, like that of Ban (1964).

LEARNED HELPLESSNESS

The learned helplessness paradigm has been used in human experiments. Persons have been exposed to inescapable noise or insoluble problems; with proper control groups, tests were then performed to evaluate the effects. Hiroto (1974) used an analogue of the shuttle box, a finger shuttle, to test for evidence of learned helplessness. The finger shuttle is a box with a protruding handle that the person being tested can move from side to side to stop a stimulus, such as noise. Hiroto exposed two groups of persons to loud noise; one group could escape the noise, the other could not. A third group received no exposure to noise. Persons who had been exposed to inescapable loud noise demonstrated severe impairment in their ability to learn to move the handle to escape noise when compared with those exposed to escapable noise or no noise. Impairment in learning was also found to be greater among persons who were instructed that the task involved chance, rather than skill; one might expect the chance instruction to foster expectations that the situation could not be controlled. The inescapable noise condition caused persons to perceive reinforcement in a skill task independent of their responses, a finding consistent with the formulation that learned helplessness involves a dissociation between response and reinforcement (Klein and Seligman, 1976).

In several experiments, persons who had been exposed to inescapable noises or who had attempted to solve unsolvable problems were impaired both in learning to manipulate the finger shuttle to escape noise and in solving five-letter anagrams (Hiroto and Seligman, 1975; Miller and Seligman, 1975; Klein et al., 1976; Klein and Seligman, 1976). Klein and Seligman (1976) also demonstrated that the behavioral deficits associated with both depression and learned helplessness can be reversed by helping the person to experience success in solving discrimination problems.

Abramson and Seligman (1977), in reviewing the generally positive results obtained in human studies of learned helplessness, suggested that the model can provide a way of testing the effectiveness of any therapy for depression in the laboratory. They assumed that experimentally produced learned helplessness and depression are sufficiently similar to predict that a therapy that reverses learned helplessness will be effective for depression.

The important implications of the learned helplessness model for understanding depression and the development of techniques for studying the model in humans has generated a great deal of interest and stimulated much research. In February 1978 the *Journal of Abnormal Psychology* published a special issue, devoted entirely to 17 papers related to learned helplessness as a model of depression. Two papers, by Depue and Monroe (1978) and Costello (1978), were critical reviews that dealt with the problems involved in applying the laboratory data to clinical depression. Depue and Monroe focused on the heterogeneity of depressive disorders, the need for more precise specification of depressive subtypes that may fit the model, and the difficulties involved in assuming that depressed college students differ from clinical depressives quantitatively but not qualitatively. Costello's critique of six studies in humans by Seligman and his colleagues reached generally negative conclusions; he found that the evidence provided little or no support for the learned helplessness theory of depression. These and other critiques led to a reformulation of the learned helplessness theory of depression by Abramson et al. (1978).

Abramson et al. (1978) pointed out that the learned helplessness hypothesis was formulated before any studies were performed with humans. Studies with humans first attempted to replicate the animal findings. As time went on, however, it became evident that theoretical constructs based on animal helplessness were inadequate for understanding helplessness in humans. Two major inadequacies were identified: (1) The learned helplessness hypothesis did not distinguish between universal and personal helplessness, between cases in which outcomes are uncontrollable for all people and those in which outcomes are uncontrollable for only some people. (2) The hypothesis did not explain when helplessness is general and when it is specific, when it is chronic and when it is acute. The reformulated hypothesis of Abramson et al. used a version of what is known as attribution theory. The basic argument is that, when a person finds he is helpless, he asks why and attributes his state to a cause. The kind of cause to which attribution is made determines the generality and chronicity of his helplessness deficits and later self-esteem. Basic characteristics of the cause are stability (stable or unstable), generality (global or specific), and locus (internal or external). Different combinations of these characteristics give different effects. Consider the example of a student who fails an examination; he can make a stable, internal, and global attribution, such as, "I am stupid"; a stable, external, and global attribution could be, "The test was unfair"; an unstable, internal, and global attribution could be, "I was sick"; and so on.

Wortman and Dintzer (1978) reviewed the Abramson et al. reformulation of the learned helplessness model and found that it overcame many of the shortcomings of the original hypothesis. However, they pointed out that it is necessary to specify the conditions under which a given attribution is made in order to avoid circularity and lack of predictive power.

The learned helplessness model has had an enormous impact on theory and research in experimental psychopathology. The quick extension to human studies of the paradigms developed in animals is especially impressive. The controversies generated by the research can be regarded as a healthy indicator, foretelling vigorous growth of the field and significant advances.

EXPERIMENTAL STRESS

The idea that disturbed behavior and bodily reactions occur in response to severely taxing environmental conditions is in accord with general human experience and is widely accepted. Because environmental demands or stimuli that place strain on reserve capacities of the organism are relatively easy to produce in the laboratory, much experimental work has used this method. Unfortunately, investigators have used the word

"stress" to characterize a wide variety of experimental demands, from performing mental arithmetic tasks to exposure to severe temperature conditions and physical injury. Such indiscriminate use tends to deprive the term of its meaning.

Partial starvation. Among the most biologically meaningful procedures for studying stress are those that involve complete or partial frustration of basic organismic needs for food, sleep, or environmental stimulation. The effects of food deprivation are considered here.

Partial starvation over a prolonged period of time may result in various neurotic manifestations. The most systematic data come from the Minnesota studies conducted by Keys et al. (1950). Thirty-six apparently normal young men, after 3 months of control on a good diet, were subjected to 6 months of semistarvation, with provision of only half of their required caloric intake. Although tests of intellectual functioning and the Rorschach projective test demonstrated no significant change, the men became depressed, moody, and apathetic; felt that they were not alert mentally; and reported that they had lost ambition. The scores on the Minnesota Multiphasic Personality Inventory were in accord with these reports.

Nine of the 36 men were thought to develop specific neurotic behavior and ideas. Four of these showed character disturbances, with inability to maintain their former standards of morals or honesty. One man had sensory and motor disturbances of a hysterical character. One man mutilated himself twice. Bizarre behavior in connection with food was almost universal and often took the form of compulsive rituals. The men reported irritability and anger, which they were unable to express because of the effort involved. The disturbances were reversible with restoration of an adequate diet.

Sport parachuting. A dangerous sport provides a natural situation for studying the effects of stress and mechanisms used in coping with stress. The autonomic responses (galvanic skin response, respiration and heart rates) of sport parachutists have been studied before and after the jump. These measurements varied with their jumping experience. Novice parachutists showed a gradual increase in reactivity until the last point immediately before the jump; experienced jumpers showed their increase relatively early in the jump sequence, and their arousal had decreased nearly to normal at the time of the jump (Fenz and Epstein, 1967). Fenz and Jones (1972) demonstrated that actual jumping skill, apart from experience, was related to the autonomic reaction pattern. The good performers had patterns like those of the more experienced jumpers. The results were taken to indicate that all jumpers experienced fear and autonomic activation but that these reactions were more successfully reduced or inhibited in the experienced jumpers who performed well.

Brief laboratory stresses. The more commonly used laboratory stress procedures are probably less biologically significant because of their brief duration. Variants of pain stimulation have been used in several ways. Pain has proved to be particularly useful as a standardized stimulus to elicit differential physiological reactions in different types of psychiatric patients and healthy persons.

In general, it appears that persons with already established illnesses or proneness to anxiety tend to react to moderate pain stimulation with greater physiological disturbance in various organ systems than do persons who are free of illness (Shagass, 1962). Similar differentiations may be obtained by nonpainful stresses, such as those requiring the execution of difficult tasks. Furthermore, it has been demonstrated that the physiological system that is particularly responsive to experimental stress is more likely to be one habitually involved in the patient's illness—that is, one that produces symptoms. This has been called symptom specificity (Malmo and Shagass, 1949). For example, headaches frequently result from sustained contraction of head and neck muscles, whereas symptoms such as palpitations, dyspnea, and precordial pain involve altered functioning of the cardiorespiratory system. By subdividing psychiatric patients according to their complaint history into head and heart complaint groups and subjecting them to a standard pain-stress test, one can show significant differences in the affected response system. Increased neck muscle contractions were more often elicited in the head complaint group, and changes in pulse rate and respiration were more often found in the heart complaint group, even though very few of the persons reported actual symptoms during the stress procedure. Interesting as they are, findings such as these leave unanswered the important questions concerning the events leading to symptom choice—that is, the reason for the localization of dysfunction in particular organ systems.

A frequently used laboratory stress technique involves exposure to motion picture films, selected as being likely to induce particular kinds of emotional reactions. For example, people have been shown films of puberty rites in primitive tribes, involving incisions made in the genital area, while physiological reactions were recorded. The powerful effects of the films were reflected in the recordings. The investigators were able to relate the nature of the reactions to some personality variables and to the kind of psychological mechanisms used to deal with emotionally disturbing stimuli (Lazarus and Alpert, 1964). Comparative studies of psychiatric patients and nonpatients have demonstrated a higher frequency of disturbing emotional responses, such as fear, in the patients (Horowitz et al., 1973). Also, after viewing the film, patients manifested more intrusive thoughts, defined as thoughts they wished to dispel and not have again.

Another technique involves the manipulation of interpersonal events in a laboratory situation in order to arouse emotions the investigator wants to study. For example, Funkenstein et al. (1954) deliberately created a situation in which the person was required to carry out computational problems at a very rapid rate while the experimenter became critical and demanding. The person's behavioral reaction to this stress was classified as reflecting "anger in," "anger out," or "anxiety." Significant differences in various cardiovascular measures were found between the "anger in" and "anger out" groups.

Probing interviews. Interviews that deliberately focus on emotionally charged material so that related bodily reactions may be studied represent another variant of experimental stress. The interview is generally not standardized, although it can be made so. After a baseline interval, the topics considered emotionally relevant are introduced, and discussion centers on them. Usually, there is a phase of reassurance after the emotional arousal. At times, the material may be introduced after the person has been hypnotized (Dudley et al., 1964). Behavioral observations and physiological recordings are made, and the various responses are correlated with the ongoing stimuli. Although this procedure involves numerous methodological difficulties, it has yielded valuable data concerning the participation of physiological response systems in symptom mechanisms.

Role-playing simulations. Persons who have been asked to play particular roles in laboratory situations may show a remarkable degree of obedience in complying with instructions that are presumably discordant with their moral standards (Milgram, 1974). The experiment on a simulated prison conducted by Haney et al. (1973) provided a dramatic example of behavioral change emerging under conditions of simulation.

Haney et al. recruited 21 paid male volunteers from a larger pool of persons responding to a newspaper advertisement; the recruits were healthy college students. Half of the volunteers were randomly assigned to the role of prisoner, and the other half played the part of guards for 8 hours each day. Observations of several kinds provided a variety of data, all of which supported the conclusion that the simulated prison became a psychologically compelling prison environment. Many of the participants manifested reactions that were intense, realistic, and often pathological.

The prisoners were required to wear loosely fitting muslin smocks, with a number on front and back; they also wore a stocking cap to conceal their hair, and they were not permitted to wear underclothes. The guards wore khaki shirts and trousers; each carried a whistle and a wooden baton and wore reflecting eyeglasses that made eye contact impossible. The prisoners' clothing was designed to promote humiliation and subservience. The prisoners experienced a loss of personal identity; they became passive, dependent, depressed, and helpless. In contrast, most of the guards experienced a sense of increased social power, status, and group identification, and they thought the role playing was rewarding.

Four prisoners developed acute emotional disturbances, consisting of depression, crying, rage, and acute anxiety. The pattern of symptoms began as early as the second day of imprisonment. Another prisoner developed a rash over his body, thought to be of emotional origin. These disturbances made it necessary to terminate the experiment after 6 days, instead of the agreed-on maximum of 14 days. About one-third of the guards were judged to have become exceptionally aggressive and dehumanizing toward the prisoners. Although guards and prisoners were of equal physical size, the prisoners later expressed the belief that the guards were bigger than they were and were selected for larger stature.

Haney et al. (1973) interpreted their results to support the view that situational factors play a powerful part in determining behavior in a prison situation; this interpretation is in contrast to the tendency of many observers to attribute behavior to dispositional factors inherent in the involved persons. From the psychiatric point of view, the role-playing experiments teach that major behavioral changes and symptoms can emerge within a few days as a consequence of restructuring the social psychological characteristics of a situation. Furthermore, this change can happen even though the participants know they are engaged in an experimental simulation.

Conclusion

Experimental psychopathology has not yet developed methods that are truly satisfactory. However, there have been important advances in the past decade, and, even though limited, available techniques have contributed significant insights concerning relevant mechanisms. These insights are influencing clinical thinking. For example, the growth of behavior therapy was facilitated by laboratory models of learned emotional responses, and the investigations of learned helplessness have had an impact on concepts of the causation of depression and on the development of some new psychotherapeutic approaches. The increasing emphasis on careful experimental analysis of laboratory situations, with rigorous definition of variables, is encouraging, as is the increasing tendency to be cautious about generalizing across species. The investigation of models at the intermediary process level is benefiting greatly from computer technology, which has provided sophisticated instruments for measuring all kinds of bodily reactions. One can anticipate that the field will continue to develop its technology and expand the base of knowledge concerning mechanisms underlying psychopathology.

Suggested Cross References

Masserman discusses his biodynamic theories in Section 9.5. Harlow discusses his experiments in Section 4.6, Ethology. Learning theory, including various types of conditioning, is discussed in Section 4.3. Miller discusses biofeedback in Section 4.9. Psychosomatic disorders are discussed in Chapter 26. Behavior therapy is discussed in Section 30.2. Hypnosis is discussed in Section 30.4. Sensory deprivation is discussed in Section 6.5 and maternal deprivation in Section 43.1.

REFERENCES

Abramson, L. Y., and Seligman, M. E. P. Modeling psychopathology in the laboratory: History and rationale. In *Psychopathology: Experimental Models,* J. D. Maser and M. E. P. Seligman, editors, p. 1. W. H. Freeman & Co., San Francisco, 1977.

Abramson, L. Y., Seligman, M. E. P., and Teasdale, J. D. Learned helplessness in humans: Critique and reformulation. J. Abnorm. Psychol., *87:* 49, 1978.

Ackerman, S. H. Restraint ulceration as an experimental disease model. Psychosom. Med., *37:* 4, 1975.

Ackerman, S. H., Hofer, M. A., and Weiner, H. Age at maternal separation and gastric erosion susceptibility in the rat. Psychosom. Med., *37:* 180, 1975.

Ader, R. Plasma pepsinogen level as a predictor of susceptibility to gastric erosions in the rat. Psychosom. Med., *25:* 221, 1963.

Ader, R. Effects of early experience and differential housing on susceptibility to gastric erosions in lesion-susceptible rats. Psychosom. Med., *32:* 569, 1970.

Ader, R., and Plaut, S. M. Effects of prenatal maternal handling and differential housing on offspring emotionality, plasma corticosterone levels, and susceptibility to gastric erosions. Psychosom. Med., *30:* 277, 1968.

Anderson, O. D., and Parmenter, R. A long-term study of the experimental neurosis in the sheep and dog. Psychosom. Med. Monogr., *2:* 1, 1941.

Ban, T. *Conditioning and Psychiatry.* Aldine Publishing Co., Chicago, 1964.

Brady, J. V. Ulcers in "executive" monkeys. Sci. Am., *199:* 95, 1958.

* Broadhurst, P. L. Abnormal animal behavior. In *Handbook of Abnormal Psychology,* H. J. Eysenck, editor, p. 726. Basic Books, New York, 1961.

Broadhurst, P. L. Animal studies bearing on abnormal behavior. In *Handbook of Abnormal Psychology,* H. J. Eysenck, editor, ed. 2, p. 721. R. R. Knapp, San Diego, 1973.

Bykov, K. *The Cerebral Cortex and the Internal Organs.* Foreign Languages Publishing House, Moscow, 1959.

Costello, C. G. A critical review of Seligman's laboratory experiments on learned helplessness and depression in humans. J. Abnorm. Psychol., *87:* 21, 1978.

Depue, R. A., and Monroe, S. M. Learned helplessness in the perspective of the depressive disorders: Conceptual and definitional issues. J. Abnorm. Psychol., *87:* 3, 1978.

Dmitruk, V. M. "Experimental neurosis" in cats: Fact or artifact? J. Abnorm. Psychol., *83:* 97, 1974.

Dudley, D., Holmes, T., Martin, C., and Ripley, H. Changes in respiration associated with hypnotically induced emotion, pain, and exercise. Psychosom. Med., *26:* 46, 1964.

Falk, J. L., Tang, M., and Forman, S. Schedule-induced chronic hypertension. Psychosom. Med., *39:* 252, 1977.

Fenz, W. D., and Epstein, S. Gradients of physiological arousal in parachutists as a function of an approaching jump. Psychosom. Med., *29:* 33, 1967.

Fenz, W. D., and Jones, G. B. Individual differences in physiologic arousal and performance in sport parachutists. Psychosom. Med., *34:* 1, 1972.

Foltz, E. L., and Millett, F. F. Experimental psychosomatic disease states in monkeys. I. Peptic "ulcer-executive" monkeys. J. Surg. Res., *4:* 445, 1964.

Forsyth, R. P. Blood pressure and avoidance conditioning: A study of 15-day trials in the rhesus monkey. Psychosom. Med., *30:* 125, 1968.

Forsyth, R. P. Blood pressure responses to long-term avoidance schedules in the restrained rhesus monkey. Psychosom. Med., *31:* 300, 1969.

French, J. D., Porter, R. W., Cavanaugh, E. B., and Longmire, R. L. Experimental gastro-duodenal lesions induced by stimulation of the brain. Psychosom. Med., *19:* 209, 1957.

Friedman, R., and Dahl, L. K. The effect of chronic conflict on the blood pressure of rats with a genetic susceptibility to experimental hypertension. Psychosom. Med., *37:* 402, 1975.

Fuller, J. L. Experiential deprivation and later behavior. Science, *158:* 1645, 1967.

Funkenstein, D., King, S., and Drolette, M. The direction of anger during a laboratory stress-inducing situation. Psychosom. Med., *16:* 404, 1954.

Gantt, W. H. Experimental basis for neurotic behavior. Psychosom. Med. Monogr., *3:* 1, 1944.

* Gantt, W. H. Retrospect and prospect. In *Physiological Bases of Psychiatry,* W. H. Gantt, editor, p. 12. Charles C Thomas, Springfield, Ill., 1958.

Gottlieb, G., editor. *Studies on the Development of Behavior and the Nervous System,* vol. 3, *Neural and Behavioral Specificity.* Academic Press, New York, 1976.

Grace, W. J., and Graham, D. T. Relationship of specific attitudes and emotions to certain bodily diseases. Psychosom. Med., *14:* 243, 1952.

Graham, D., Stern, J., and Winokur, G. Experimental investigation of the specificity of attitude hypothesis in psychosomatic disease. Psychosom. Med., *20:* 446, 1958.

Haney, C., Banks, C., and Zimbardo, P. Interpersonal dynamics in a simulated prison. Int. J. Criminol. Penol., *1:* 69, 1973.

Harlow, H. F., and Harlow, M. K. Learning to love. Am. Sci., *54:* 244, 1966.

* Harlow, H. F., and Harlow, M. K. Psychopathology in monkeys. In *Experimental Psychopathology: Recent Research and Theory,* H. D. Kimmel, editor, p. 204. Academic Press, New York, 1971.

Hebb, D. O. Spontaneous neurosis in chimpanzees: Theoretical relations with clinical and experimental phenomena. Psychosom. Med., *9:* 3, 1947.

Henry, J. P., Ely, D. L., Watson, F. M. C., and Stephens, P. M. Ethological methods as applied to the measurement of emotion. In *Emotions: Their Parameters and Measurement,* L. Levi, editor, p. 469. Raven Press, New York, 1975.

Henry, J. P., Meehan, J. P., and Stephens, P. M. The use of psychosocial stimuli to induce prolonged systolic hypertension in mice. Psychosom. Med., *29:* 408, 1967.

Henry, J. P., Stephens, P. M., Axelrod, J., and Mueller, R. A. Effect of psychosocial stimulation on the enzymes involved in the biosynthesis and metabolism of noradrenaline and adrenaline. Psychosom. Med., *33:* 227, 1971.

Hiroto, D. S. The relationship between learned helplessness and the locus of control. J. Exp. Psychol., *102:* 187, 1974.

Hiroto, D. S., and Seligman, M. E. P. Generality of learned helplessness in man. J. Pers. Soc. Psychol., *31:* 311, 1975.

Horowitz, M. J., Becker, S. S., and Malone, P. Stress: Different effects on patients and nonpatients. J. Abnorm. Psychol., *82:* 547, 1973.

Hunt, J. M. The effects of infant feeding frustration upon hoarding in the albino rat. J. Abnorm. Soc. Psychol., *36:* 338, 1941.

Huston, P. E., Shakow, D., and Erickson, M. H. A study of hypnotically induced complexes by means of the Luria technique. J. Gen. Psychol., *11:* 65, 1934.

Hymovitch, B. The effects of experimental variations on problem solving in the rat. J. Comp. Physiol. Psychol., *45:* 313, 1952.

Jensen, G. D., and Tolman, C. W. Mother-infant relationship in the monkey, *Macaca menestrina:* The effect of brief separation and mother-infant specificity. J. Comp. Physiol. Psychol., *55:* 131, 1962.

Kaufman, I. C., and Rosenblum, L. A. The reaction to separation in infant monkeys: Anaclitic depression and conservation-withdrawal. Psychosom. Med., *29:* 648, 1967.

Kaufman, I. C., and Rosenblum, L. A. Effects of separation from mother on the emotional behavior of infant monkeys. Ann. N.Y. Acad. Sci., *159:* 681, 1969.

Kaufman, I. C., and Stynes, A. J. Depression can be induced in a bonnet macaque infant. Psychosom. Med., *40:* 71, 1978.

Kehoe, M., and Ironside, W. Studies on the experimental evocation of depressive responses using hypnosis. II. The influence of depressive responses upon the secretion of gastric acid. Psychosom. Med., *25:* 403, 1963.

Keys, A., Brozek, J., Henschel, A., Mickelsen, L., and Taylor, H. L. *The Biology of Human Starvation.* University of Minnesota Press, Minneapolis, 1950.

Klein, D. C., Fencil-Morse, E., and Seligman, M. E. P. Learned helplessness, depression, and the attribution of failure. J. Pers. Soc. Psychol., *33:* 508, 1976.

Klein, D. C., and Seligman, M. E. P. Reversal of performance deficits and perceptual deficits in learned helplessness and depression. J. Abnorm. Psychol., *85:* 11, 1976.

Krasnogorski, N. I. The conditioned reflexes and children's neuroses. Am. J. Dis. Child., *30:* 753, 1925.

Lazarus, R. S., and Alpert, E. Short-circuiting of threat by experimentally altering cognitive appraisal. J. Abnorm. Soc. Psychol., *69:* 195, 1964.

Liddell, H. S. Conditioned reflex method and experimental neurosis. In *Personality and the Behavior Disorders,* J. M. Hunt, editor, p. 389. Ronald Press, New York, 1944.

Liddell, H. S. A comparative approach to the dynamics of experimental neuroses. In *Comparative Conditioned Neuroses,* E. J. Kempf, editor, p. 164. Annals of the New York Academy of Science, New York, 1953.

Liddell, H. S. Conditioning and emotions. Sci. Am., *190:* 48, 1954.

Luparello, T. J., Leist, N., Lourie, C. H., and Sweet, P. The interaction of psychologic stimuli and pharmacologic agents on airway reactivity in asthmatic subjects. Psychosom. Med., *32:* 509, 1970.

Luparello, T. J., Lyons, H. A., Bleecker, E. R., and McFadden, E. R. Influences of suggestion on airway reactivity in asthmatic subjects. Psychosom. Med., *30:* 819, 1968.

* Luria, A. R. *The Nature of Human Conflict.* Liveright, New York, 1932.

Mahl, G. F. Physiological changes during chronic fear. In *Comparative Conditioned Neuroses,* E. J. Kempf, editor, p. 240. Annals of the New York Academy of Science, New York, 1953.

Malmo, R. B., and Shagass, C. Physiologic study of symptom mechanisms in psychiatric patients under stress. Psychosom. Med., *11:* 25, 1949.

Maser, J. D., and Seligman, M. E. P. *Psychopathology: Experimental Models.* W. H. Freeman & Co., San Francisco, 1977.

* Masserman, J. H. *Behavior and Neurosis: An Experimental Psychoanalytic Approach to Psychobiologic Principles.* University of Chicago Press, Chicago, 1943.

Masserman, J. H. A biodynamic psychoanalytic approach to the problems of feeling and emotions. In *Feelings and Emotions,* M. L. Reymert, editor, p. 49. McGraw-Hill, New York, 1950.

Masserman, J. H. The biodynamic approaches. In *American Handbook of Psychiatry,* S. Arieti, editor, p. 1680. Basic Books, New York, 1959.

Masserman, J. H. The principle of uncertainty in neurotigenesis. In *Experimental Psychopathology: Recent Research and Theory,* H. D. Kimmel, editor, p. 13. Academic Press, New York, 1971.

McFadden, E. R., Luparello, T., Lyons, H. A., and Bleecker, E. The mechanism of action of suggestion in the induction of acute asthma attacks. Psychosom. Med., *31:* 134, 1969.

McKinney, W. T. Behavioral models of depression in monkeys. In *Animal Models in Psychiatry and Neurology,* I. Hanin and E. Usdin, editors, p. 117. Pergamon Press, New York, 1977.

Melzack, R. Effects of early experience on behavior: Experimental and conceptual considerations. In *Psychopathology of Perception,* P. H. Hoch and J. Zubin, editors, p. 271. Grune & Stratton, New York, 1965.

Meyer, R. L., and Sperry, R. W. Retinotectal specificity: Chemoaffinity theory. In *Studies on the Development of Behavior and the Nervous System,* vol. 3, *Neural and Behavioral Specificity,* G. Gottlieb, editor, p. 111. Academic Press, New York, 1976.

Milgram, S. *Obedience to Authority.* Harper & Row, New York, 1974.

Miller, N. E. Learning of visceral and glandular responses. Science, *163:* 434, 1969.

Miller, W. R., Rosellini, R. A., and Seligman, M. E. P. Learned helplessness and depression. In *Psychopathology: Experimental Models,* J. D. Maser and M. E. P. Seligman, editors, p. 104. W. H. Freeman & Co., San Francisco, 1977.

Miller, W. R., and Seligman, M. E. P. Learned helplessness and depression in man. J. Abnorm. Psychol., *84:* 228, 1975.

Mirsky, I. A. Some comments on psychosomatic medicine. In *Psychiatric Research in Our Changing World,* G. F. D. Heseltine, editor, p. 107. Excerpta Medica Foundation, Amsterdam, 1969.

Morse, W. H., Herd, J. A., Kelleher, R. T., and Grose, S. A. Schedule-controlled modulation of arterial blood pressure in the squirrel monkey. In *Experimental Psychopathology: Recent Research and Theory,* H. D. Kimmel, editor, p. 147. Academic Press, New York, 1971.

Ottenberg, P., Stein, M., Lewis, J., and Hamilton, C. Learned asthma in the guinea pig. Psychosom. Med., *20:* 395, 1958.

Overmier, J. B. Interference with avoidance behavior: Failure to avoid traumatic shock. J. Exp. Psychol., *78:* 340, 1968.

Pavlov, I. P. *Conditioned Reflexes.* Oxford University Press, London, 1927.

Pavlov, I. P. *Conditioned Reflexes and Psychiatry.* International Publishers, New York, 1941.

Persky, H. Adrenocortical function during anxiety. In *Physiological Correlates of Psychological Disorder,* R. Roessler and N. S. Greenfield, editors, p. 171. University of Wisconsin Press, Madison, 1962.

Porter, R., Brady, J., Conrad, D., Mason, J., Galambos, R., and Rioch, D. Some experimental observations on gastrointestinal lesions in behaviorally conditioned monkeys. Psychosom. Med., *20:* 379, 1958.

Razran, G. A quantitative study of meaning by a conditioned salivary technique (semantic conditioning). Science, *90:* 89, 1939.

Riesen, A. H. Studying perceptual development using the technique of sensory deprivation. J. Nerv. Ment. Dis., *132:* 21, 1961.

Schiavi, R., Stein, M., and Sethi, B. Respiratory variables in response to a pain-fear stimulus and in experimental asthma. Psychosom. Med., *23:* 485, 1961.

Seay, B., and Harlow, H. F. Maternal separation in the rhesus monkey. J. Nerv. Ment. Dis., *140:* 434, 1965.

Seligman, M. E. P. Chronic fear produced by unpredictable shock. J. Comp. Physiol. Psychol., *66:* 402, 1968.

* Seligman, M. E. P. Learned helplessness. Annu. Rev. Med., *23:* 407, 1972.

Seligman, M. E. P. *Helplessness.* W. H. Freeman & Co., San Francisco, 1975.

Seligman, M. E. P., Maier, S. F., and Geer, J. H. Alleviation of learned helplessness in the dog. J. Abnorm. Psychol., *73:* 256, 1968.

Shagass, C. Sedation threshold: A neurophysiological tool for psychosomatic research. Psychosom. Med., *18:* 410, 1956.

Shagass, C. Explorations in the psychophysiology of affect. In *Theories of the Mind,* J. Scher, editor, p. 122. Free Press of Glencoe, New York, 1962.

Shenger-Krestovnikova, N. R. Contributions to the question of differentiation of visual stimuli and the limits of differentiation by the visual analyzer of the dog. Bull. Lesgaft Inst. Petrograd, *3:* 1, 1921.

Sines, J. O. The interaction of behavior and environmental conditions in the production of stomach lesions in the rat. Psychosom. Med., *37:* 492, 1975.

Sines, J. O., and McDonald, D. G. Heritability of stress-ulcer susceptibility in rats. Psychosom. Med., *30:* 390, 1968.

Smart, R. Conflict and conditioned aversive stimuli in the development of experimental neurosis. Can. J. Psychol., *19:* 208, 1965.

Spitz, R. A. Hospitalism: An inquiry into the genesis of psychiatric conditions in early childhood. Psychoanal. Study Child, *1:* 53, 1945.

Stroebel, C. F. Biologic rhythm correlates of disturbed behavior in the rhesus monkey. In *Circadian Rhythms in Nonhuman Primates,* F. H. Rohles, editor, p. 20. S. Karger, New York, 1969.

Stroebel, C. F. Chronopsychophysiology. In *Comprehensive Textbook of Psychiatry,* A. M. Freedman, H. I. Kaplan, and B. J. Sadock, editors, ed. 2, p. 166. Williams & Wilkins, Baltimore, 1975.

Stroebel, C. F., and Luce, G. The importance of biological clocks in mental health. Ment. Health Prog. Rep., *2:* 323, 1968.

Suomi, S. J., and Harlow, H. F. Production and alleviation of depressive behaviors in monkeys. In *Psychopathology: Experimental Models,* J. D. Maser and M. E. P. Seligman, editors, p. 131. W. H. Freeman & Co., San Francisco, 1977.

Suomi, S. J., Harlow, H. F., and Novak, M. A. Reversal of social deficits produced by isolation-rearing in monkeys. J. Hum. Eval., *3:* 527, 1974.

Turner, C. H., Davenport, R. K., and Rogers, C. M. The effect of early deprivation on the social behavior of adolescent chimpanzees. Am. J. Psychiatry, *125:* 1531, 1969.

Weiss, J. M. Effects of coping responses on stress. J. Comp. Physiol. Psychol., *65:* 251, 1968.

Weiss, J. M. Effects of coping behavior with and without a feedback signal on stress pathology in rats. J. Comp. Physiol. Psychol., *77:* 22, 1971.

Weiss, J. M. Psychological and behavioral influences on gastrointestinal lesions in animal models. In *Psychopathology: Experimental Models,* J. D. Maser and M. E. P. Seligman, editors, p. 232. W. H. Freeman & Co., San Francisco, 1977.

Weiss, T., and Engel, B. T. Operant conditioning of heart rate in patients with premature ventricular contractions. Psychosom. Med., *33:* 301, 1971.

Weisz, J. D. The etiology of experimental gastric ulceration. Psychosom. Med., *19:* 61, 1957.

Welgan, P. R. Learned control of gastric acid secretions in ulcer patients. Psychosom. Med., *36:* 411, 1974.

Wilson, P. D., and Riesen, A. H. Visual development in rhesus monkeys neonatally deprived of patterned light. J. Comp. Physiol. Psychol., *61:* 87, 1966.

Wishner, J. On deviant behavior, diagnostic systems, and experimental psychopathology. Int. Rev. Appl. Psychol., *18:* 79, 1969.

Wittkower, E. Studies on the influence of emotions on the functions of the organs (including observations in normals and neurotics). J. Ment. Sci., *81:* 533, 1935.

Wolpe, J. *Psychotherapy by Reciprocal Inhibition.* Stanford University Press, Palo Alto, Calif., 1958.

Wolpe, J. Parallels between animal and human neuroses. In *Comparative Psychopathology: Animal and Human,* J. Zubin and H. F. Hunt, editors, p. 305. Grune & Stratton, New York, 1967.

Wortman, C. B., and Dintzer, L. Is an attributional analysis of the learned helplessness phenomenon viable? A critique of the Abramson-Seligman-Teasdale reformulation. J. Abnorm. Psychol., *87:* 75, 1978.

Young, L. D., Suomi, S. J., Harlow, H. F., and McKinney, W. T. Early stress and later response to separation in rhesus monkeys. Am. J. Psychiatry, *130:* 400, 1973.

6.4 The Euphorohallucinogens

ARNOLD J. MANDELL, M.D.
MARK A. GEYER, Ph.D.

Introduction

Styles of research in biological psychiatry represent attempts to describe what may be invariants in the relationship between mechanisms regulating brain function and the subjective and objective aspects of human behavior. Heretofore, the anchoring variables in psychiatric pathophysiology have been the syndromes of diagnostic psychopathology—that is, what the clinicians "know." Such "facts," however, developed from historical accident, from the seductive writings of charismatic eccentrics, and from the field's professional politics—influences unlikely by chance to be concordant with the organizing principles governing brain function. That is not to say that direct clinical observation is not the final test of a biological model. As intuitive sources of biological hypotheses, the knowing of self and patients can be valuable. But damage is done when the degree of fit with sociopolitically determined diagnostic constellations becomes the final arbiter of the validity of a biological model. If studies of brain function are to be useful to psychiatrists, they must come with independently derived concepts that bring new dimensions to clinical work—images and thoughts that would not arise within the clinical situation and that are, in actuality, counterintuitive.

Glimpses of such visions in the past have included the limbic brain psychology of Papez, Nauta, and MacLean; the dimension of arousal-attention described by Magoun, Lindsley, and Sokolov; the spinal and cortical reflex cosmology of Pavlov, Sherrington, and Skinner; and the instinctual survival determinism of Darwin, Marx, and Freud. Although each of those positions summarized a great deal of important psychobiological research, the practicing psychiatrist could argue that they brought him nothing more than his listening and intuition had taught him already: that there is a brain seeking strong stimulation and sensual pleasure, which is capable of irrational thoughts and acts; that drive appears to be an inverted U-shaped function—that is, either too much or too little energy can impair normal functioning; that reinforcement both within and outside of awareness seems to fixate behavior; and that, when it comes to capturing the territories for eating and mating, things can get fearful—laboratory documentation of the known.

The next few years of brain research will bring characterizations of the machinery that will lead to a redefinition of most mental states and malfunctions, using concepts more resonant with the findings of neurobiology and perhaps somewhat more alien to present subjectivity. In place of descriptions of formal psychopathology, psychodynamic models arising from intuitive identification, descriptive clusters derived from psychological or psychophysiological instruments, and arbitrary diagnostic categories decided by committee and validated by post hoc multivariate studies, there will be new models derived from basic characteristics of human brain function.

In recent years the most productive research strategies have incorporated what Schildkraut (1969) named the "pharmacological bridge." A psychotropic drug as an independent and linking variable, a semistandardized piece of biological information, is given to an animal, after which its neurochemical effects are examined, and given to humans, whose responses are characterized in as many ways as possible—subjective reports, behavioral tasks, psychological assessments, chemistry of blood, urine, and cerebrospinal fluid—the instruments of psychophysiology and psychophysics. Relationships are speculated on, and neurochemically based concepts with clinical possibilities arise.

The group of drugs known as the euphorohallucinogens includes the indoleamines (dimethyltryptamine, 5-methoxydimethyltryptamine, psilocybin, and lysergic acid diethylamide (LSD)), the phenylethylamines (mescaline and its congeners, the methoxyamphetamines), and the tetrahydrocannabinols (marihuana and hashish). In spite of their chemical heterogeneity and the pervasive and complex character of the phenomena they induce, more may be known about their common neurochemical and neurophysiological mode of action than about those of many other more homogeneous classes of psychotropic drugs with apparently simpler behavioral effects in humans.

The field of single-unit neuropharmacology, in which drugs and neurotransmitters are manipulated either by local iontophoresis or systemic administration and spontaneous and evoked unit activities are monitored, has been combined with studies of neurochemical receptor binding to describe three sets of receptors for the biogenic amines—presynaptic inhibitory, postsynaptic inhibitory, and postsynaptic excitatory. Those that bind autoreceptor inhibitory agonists have the highest affinity

of the three sets and function by sensing the amount of transmitter produced and turning down the rate of discharge-related release.

In basic neurology one learns concepts first formalized by Sherrington and Jackson about regulation of brain function by inhibition. Freud's *Project for a Scientific Psychology*—the basis for the seventh chapter in *The Interpretation of Dreams*, which he later developed into an extensive metapsychology—contained diagrams that implied that descending and reciprocal inhibition were the major mechanisms of brain control. In that context, another interpretation can be made of the function of biogenic amine inhibitory autoreceptors. The concept of reciprocal inhibition may be of particular significance for the biogenic amine systems because noradrenergic and serotonergic cells appear to have axon collaterals that cross the midline. Those systems may operate so that, when aminergic cells on one side of the brain are on, those on the other side are off in an apparently regulable reciprocal oscillation of hemispheric biogenic amine inhibition. The classical work of Aghajanian (1972) first showed and others (Geyer and Mandell, 1979) confirmed that the three major families of euphorohallucinogens act, directly or indirectly, by turning off the firing of the brain's serotonergic systems.

Hallucinogen Structure and Function

INDOLEALKYLAMINES

One of the major categories of hallucinogens is made up of indolealkylamines, the simplest being N,N-dimethyltryptamine (DMT). Most of those compounds are active when given parenterally. Other derivatives include 5-methoxy-N,N-dimethyltryptamine, which is relatively potent in humans in the microgram dose range; the 4-hydroxy compound psilocybin, which is active in humans; and the N,N-dimethyl derivative of serotonin, bufotenine, which is not active in humans. Psilocybin is the active principal in the sacred mushroom of Mexico. Both bufotenine and DMT have been found in the hallucinogenic snuffs of South America. Other snuffs and drinks, such as parica, contain harmine or harmaline, β-carboline derivatives that are reported to be euphorogens of indoleamine (see Figure 1) origin. The β-carboline derivatives have three-ring aromatic systems that are similar to that of LSD.

PHENYLETHYLAMINES

Structurally, the simplest hallucinogens are substituted phenylethylamines (see Figure 2), of which the prototype is mesca-

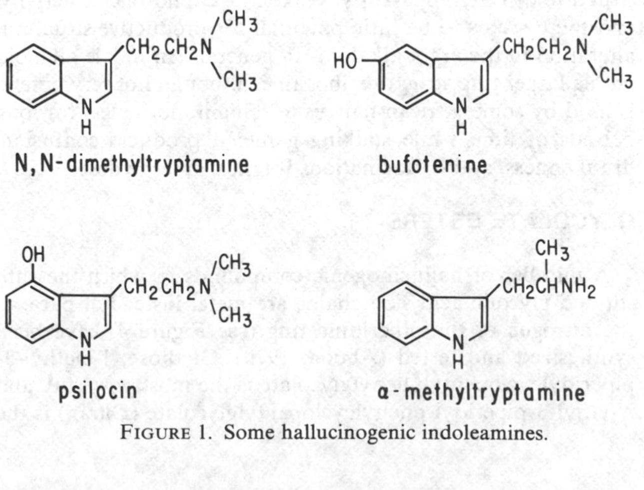

FIGURE 1. Some hallucinogenic indoleamines.

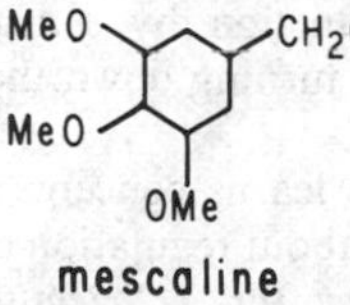

FIGURE 2. The major phenylethylamine hallucinogen.

line (3,4,5-trimethoxyphenylethylamine). Because mescaline is one of the least active drugs in the category, with an active dose range of about 200 mg. to 500 mg., behavioral pharmacologists usually designate the potency of related compounds in mescaline units. Mescaline's chemical structure is remarkably like that of the catecholamines and 3,4-dimethoxyphenylethylamine, one candidate for the role of endogenous hallucinogen. By shifting methyl and methoxy groups to different positions about the carbon ring, Shulgin (1973) and others such as Smythies (1970) created a number of exotic compounds, most notably the methoxyamphetamine series. Several of those compounds are natural constituents of the peyote cactus (*Lophophora williamsii*), although few of the naturally occurring derivatives are as potent as mescaline. Peyote has been widely used among American Indians in the Southwest and legally so under the auspices of the Native American Church.

TETRAHYDROCANNABINOLS

The active components of the cannabinols (see Figure 3) are characterized either by a three-ring system or by one easily convertible to three rings, a structure that differs significantly from the aromatic amine constellation of the other euphorohallucinogens. Δ-3-Tetrahydrocannabinol (THC) and Δ-9-tetrahydrocannabinol have been studied most extensively, but substitutions in the para position of the phenoxy ring increase the potency more than 1,000-fold. The dose-response characteristics of THC differ from those of LSD in one significant way: With increasing doses and over longer periods of time, subjects, instead of being stimulated, get sleepy and experience frequent bursts of dreaming during several hours of drug-induced sleep. The euphoric giggling and the uncontrollable laughter associated with THC are much more predictable than are similar phenomena produced on occasion by other hallucinogens.

ERGOT ALKALOIDS

Other hallucinogenic compounds are ergot alkaloids, and of those LSD, which is active in humans in doses of 25 μg. to 200 μg., is the most potent. Most experimental changes in the structure of LSD apparently weaken its euphorogenic activity, and there seems to be little potential for productive structural alteration in the ergot alkaloids in general. An indole alkaloid with a larger ring structure, ibogaine, although not very potent, is used by some African natives to remain motionless for long periods of time while stalking game; it produces confusion, drunkenness, and hallucinations if taken in large doses.

GLYCOLATE ESTERS

A number of hallucinogenic compounds in which the substituted glycolic acid side chains are meta, instead of para, to the nitrogen of the piperidine ring (see Figure 4) have been synthesized and tested (Abood, 1970). Of those, 1-methyl-3-piperidylcyclopentylphenylglycolate is the most powerful, and N-ethyl-3-piperidyl phenylcyclopentylglycolate (Ditran) is the

best known. They can cause delusional thinking, disorientation, and hallucinations. Another piperidine derivative is phencyclidine (PCP), which was originally thought to prevent sensory impulses from reaching nerve centers. Low doses of PCP produce the primary (Bleulerian) signs of schizophrenia—flattened affect, thought disorder, and emotional withdrawal—without the secondary signs—delusions and hallucinations. Psychotic reactions are frequent with large doses and have resulted in many emergency hospitalizations because PCP is widely available on the street.

ANTICHOLINERGICS

Anticholinergic compounds should also be mentioned in the context of hallucinogenic activity. However, some authorities exclude this group, of which atropine is representative, because at low doses atropine, unlike other hallucinogens, does not produce significant euphoria, and at high doses the hallucinations and delusions it produces are not later recalled—again, unlike other hallucinogens. Disruption of short-term memory is known with the cannabinols but not the permanent memory loss associated with the use of belladonna alkaloids. Psychiatrists are prone to label as organic psychosis the confusion, delirium, and hallucinations associated with anticholinergic administration. Anticholinergics, such as belladonna alkaloids, have been used for ages, most prominently by medieval witches and by the oracles of Delphi. Those compounds are common in the Solanaceae family, which includes mandrake (nightshade), and the Datura family, such as Jimson weed.

Structure-Function Studies

Attempts to understand the conformation of brain receptors relevant to hallucinogenic action are frustrated by the fact that the molecular structure of a drug also determines its distribution in the body, uptake in the brain, and vulnerability to detoxification mechanisms. Potency can be increased by impairing a site of detoxification, as with the substitution of a methyl group in the α position in the mescaline series to produce the methoxyamphetamines, precluding oxidative deamination. Shulgin (1973) placed a bromine atom in the para position and obtained a considerable increase in the potency of the methoxyamphetamine derivatives. Methoxy substitution in various positions probably alters the basicity or electron configuration of the benzene ring and interferes with metabolic hydroxylation of the ring. Amphetamine is a case in point. Without halogens or methoxy groups on the ring, para-hydroxylation and further substitutions to form sulfates or

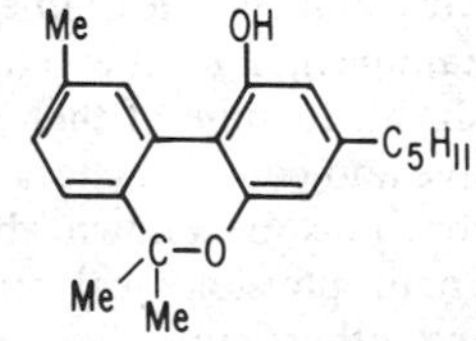

FIGURE 3. Cannabinol.

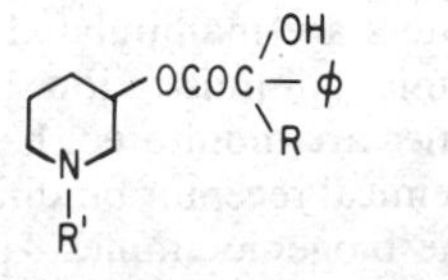

FIGURE 4. A model of the piperidine-derived glycolate series.

glucuronides are possible detoxification mechanisms. Theoretically, blocking of that common site for hydroxylation would change the configuration and detour the substance from the usual pathway for detoxification and excretion. In fact, para-methoxyamphetamine has appeared in the street drug traffic as a potent hallucinogen with effects like those of 3,4-methylenedioxyphenylisopropylamine (MDA). Only further investigation of the parahydroxylation pathway in humans will show whether those speculations are valid. At any rate, in addition to enhancing potency, certain substitutions on the mescaline ring may enhance the benignity or reduce the maleficence of the compound. The newest compounds derived from systematic variation of methyl, ethyl, and methoxy substitutions are potent in doses smaller than 1 mg., and their perceptual and sensory effects are spread over a wide dose range.

Alternatively, distribution and uptake of a drug may be delimiting, as in the case of bufotenine, in which the exposed polar group prevents its uptake into the brain. On the other hand, bufotenine's 5-methoxy derivative, which does not have the exposed 5-hydroxy group, is a potent hallucinogen in humans at 3 μg./kg. to 5 μg./kg. All told, dose-response curves, uptake, distribution, and detoxification mechanisms must be considered before relationships between structure and function can be attributed to the conformation of brain receptors.

Theorists in the past have approached hallucinogenic structure and function in four ways: (1) the indole hypothesis, (2) the phenylethylamine hypothesis, (3) molecular orbital models, and (4) discrimination of stereoisomers.

Viewed in planar representations, the indole nucleus is a common structural feature of hallucinogens. LSD has an indole nucleus, as do DMT, 5-methoxy DMT, psilocin, psilocybin, and the serotonin derivatives. Although phenylethylamine derivatives, mescaline and the methoxyamphetamines, can be represented as indole-like if the alkylamine side chain is bent around in juxtaposition to the substituted benzene ring, pseudoindole conformations are improbable. Such speculations lack analysis of the tertiary structures and accurate calculation of the forms requiring the least energy for stabilization. For instance, when bent around, the side chain would not be in the same plane as the single aromatic system, and in the methoxyamphetamine compounds the side chain is obviously less stable than the pyrrole component of the true indole nucleus. Although indole-like models may be made from phenylethylamines, there has been no evidence that such conformations occur at the tonicity, pH, or liquid biological environment of the brain.

In the phenylethylamine hypothesis mescaline is the reference compound. Systematically altering the position and kind of ring substitution and the length of the side chain in those series, Shulgin (1973) found maximal potency with 2,4,5-ring substitution and a side chain of three carbons leading to the amine nitrogen. Moreover, *N*-methylation of the substituted phenylethylamines reduces activity, whereas it does the opposite in substituted indoleamines.

The potency of those compounds may be a function of either the charge-transfer potential or the energy of the highest occupied molecular orbit of the ring; both are indices of the electron-donating capacity of the aromatic system. Some theorists associate hallucinogens that contain indole nuclei with the phenylethylamines on the basis of molecular orbital calculations demonstrating that the pyrrole component of the indole ring donates electrons to the π-system of the benzene in the same way that methoxy groups do in mescaline and the methoxyamphetamines. They suggest that the *N*-methyl substituent in the D ring of LSD could function as a terminal amine. Thus, the indole theorists claim to explain mescaline and the methoxyamphetamines, and the phenylethylamine theorists claim to explain LSD and the DMT derivatives.

Molecular orbital and other quantum mechanical calculations have their limitations as predictors of central activity, however. It is too easy to be impressed by efforts to predict drug activity by such means, which leave much to chance with compounds larger than three or four carbon rings; repeated passes through a computer program would be necessary to obtain self-consistent data, and such programs have not been run. Quantum mechanical calculations are not now specific enough to define tertiary structure except on an ad hoc basis, and no current mathematical models serve well here. The conceptual and qualitative contributions of the mathematical approach far exceed any hard data.

New analyses of hallucinogenic structure and function involve the resolution of optically asymmetrical stereoisomers. It is known, for example, that L-LSD and iso-LSD are inactive, whereas D-LSD is active. Working with the methoxyamphetamine series, Shulgin (1973) showed that the levorotatory form of 2,5-dimethoxy-4-methylamphetamine (DOM), with the α carbon as the asymmetric center, affects perceptual experience without sympathomimetic stimulation, whereas sympathomimetic stimulation does occur with the dextrorotatory form. The resolution of optical isomers and their clinical trials promise the possible fractionation of hallucinogenic compounds into agents that either expand perception and cognition or produce disruptive excitement, respectively, and more useful drugs may be the result.

As attempts to gain understanding of the relationships between the structure and the function of hallucinogens, the reports of small numbers of sensitive, experienced drug users have not gained much scientific credibility. A number of psychopharmacologists have found, however, that people who have had experience with many drugs can predict accurately the addictive, euphorogenic, and other effects of a new drug after an appropriate dose and that later parametric experiments confirm their impressions. Although similar dependent variables, such as Sidman avoidance, appear in animal models for screening drugs in the research of Smythies (1970) and others, the relationships between drug effects in animals and in humans have not been clearly established, and major difficulties confront pharmacological researchers. For example, of the methoxyamphetamines, 2,5-dimethoxy-4-ethylamphetamine (DOET) is reputedly more benign than DOM. Actually, their potencies differ slightly, but a full hallucinatory psychosis is possible with either agent if the doses are equalized properly. So full dose-response curves are the sine qua non of clinical drug research, just as they are of studies in animal pharmacology.

Neurophysiology

With the possible exception of the anticholinergics, hallucinogens have a number of physiological and neurophysiological effects in common, usually including mydriasis, elevated heart rate, elevated blood pressure, hyperreflexia, tachypnea, increased muscle tension, occasional ataxia, nausea and vomiting, salivation, lacrimation, leukocytosis, and increased sensitivity to internal and external stimuli. Most of those phenomena are concomitants of general physiological arousal, and stimulation of the autonomic nervous system is noted with almost all the mescaline and methoxyamphetamine derivatives at one dose or another, as well as with the ergot alkaloids and indolealkylamines.

After moderate doses of LSD, mescaline, or similar compounds, human and animal electroencephalograms are altered, although not dramatically, typically showing low amplitude and high frequency. Efforts to locate the primary sites of that general neurophysiological arousal were reviewed by Brawley and Duffield (1972). In animals the effect is maintained after cervical transection of the spinal cord but can be precluded by a postcollicular transection. As yet, the role of peripheral sensory input in central nervous system arousal produced by hallucinogenic drugs is not known. As originally suggested by Bradley and Key (1958), hallucinogens may increase the response of the reticular formation to collateral sensory input, with little direct influence on reticulocortical transmission. LSD lowers the threshold for electrocortical activation and retards habituation of responsive units to repeated stimuli but has little direct effect on the brain stem polysensory neurons. Possibly the serotonergic cells of the raphe nuclei, which extend from the midbrain to the medulla, are significantly involved in those phenomena. At low doses, LSD lowers the threshold for cortical arousal produced by noises or reticular stimulation, and the raphe neurons are inhibited. With larger doses, high-voltage slow rhythms often result, and the arousal threshold may be raised. LSD has also been reported to increase the duration of rapid eye movement (REM) sleep periods in humans; slow-wave sleep is often reduced and interrupted more frequently than usual by REM periods.

Hallucinogens have also been studied in relation to average evoked response. In cats anesthetized with barbiturates, LSD was found to suppress the late responses of sensory-evoked potentials. However, small doses of LSD have also been found to increase the later portion of sensory-evoked responses in unanesthetized, curarized animals (Bradley and Key, 1958). In humans, somatosensory and visual-evoked responses are suppressed by LSD, but long-latency discharges are often increased. Winters and Wallach (1970) suggested one of the more integrated descriptions of the cortical-evoked response to hallucinogens: a continuum that begins with high-frequency, low-voltage activity concomitant with heightened reticular unit activity and progresses to an eventual decrease in evoked responses.

In general, studies of evoked responses in specific sensory systems have been inconclusive, which supports the view that hallucinogens act primarily on the nonspecific reticular systems. Alterations in the electrical activity of limbic structures are more easily interpreted and have been related to the attentional, arousal, and affective functions currently attributed to those structures in the forebrain. Perhaps the most dramatic responses are the limbic cortex and hippocampal β-seizures observed in the cat after 25 μg./kg. to 100 μg./kg. of LSD (Adey et al., 1962). In most studies in which higher doses were used, hippocampal θ-rhythms were suppressed after LSD administration. Temporal lobe limbic cortex activity also seems to be altered in complex ways.

Working with microelectrodes, investigators have found that low doses of hallucinogens, particularly LSD, suppress the firing rates of the dorsal and median raphe neurons (Aghajanian et al., 1970), which include most of the serotonergic cells in the mammalian brain and may include other indoleamine transmitters as well. In peripheral systems, low doses of LSD have been shown to facilitate the actions of serotonin, although conflicting evidence has been reported. Excitation of reticular formation cells or cortical neurons by iontophoretic application of serotonin can be blocked by LSD, whereas electrophoretic depression of neural cells by serotonin is not antagonized by LSD. Generally, LSD has been reported to suppress the spontaneous firing of some neurons in most areas of the brain, including the lateral geniculate (Tebecis and DiMaria, 1972) and the ventral hippocampus (Haigler and Aghajanian, 1974). One notable exception is the spontaneous activity of the retinal ganglion cells, which increases after the administration of LSD and certain other hallucinogenic drugs. Haigler and Aghajanian (1973, 1974) systematically compared the effects of mes-

caline, LSD, and serotonin on cells of the raphe nuclei and cells receiving serotonergic input by iontophoresis and systemic administration. LSD and serotonin inhibited raphe neurons and cells normally innervated by serotonergic terminals; serotonin excited neurons in other regions in unanesthetized rats. When given intravenously in low doses, LSD still depressed raphe cell activity and caused a subtle increase in the tonic firing rates of cells normally receiving serotonergic input. Those results indicate that LSD acts primarily by inhibition of the raphe nuclei cell bodies, thus releasing the postsynaptic neurons from serotonergic inhibition.

Many efforts to explain hallucinogenic drug action are derived from the similarities between those compounds and endogenous neurotransmitters in the brain. The indolealkylamines and the indole moiety of LSD may act by blocking receptor sites or interfering with normal transmission in the serotonergic pathways. Methoxyamphetamines and phenylethylamines are related to dopamine, and the anticholinergic compounds resemble acetylcholine. However, attempts to relate specific transmission in those systems to neurophysiological responses have been far from satisfactory. For example, many of the phenylethylamine euphorogens seem to be as active as the indole alkaloids and the indoleamines in depressing the activity of serotonergic cells in the dorsal raphe if the doses are related to the differences in potency those agents manifest in humans.

Neurochemical Mechanisms

The serotonergic cell bodies of the midbrain, pons, and medulla (the raphe nuclei) project into the forebrain (striatum and limbic forebrain structures) and the lumbosacral cord. Serotonin, because its indole nucleus is identical to that of LSD, has been studied extensively in relation to hallucinogens. Gaddum (1953) and Woolley and Shaw (1954) demonstrated that LSD can block the agonistic actions of serotonin in gastrointestinal and clam heart neuromuscular junctions. Giarman and Freedman (1965) applied that model in the examination of the effect of LSD on serotonin and its major metabolite 5-hydroxyindoleacetic acid (5-HIAA) in the forebrain. Subcellular fractionation showed that LSD, DMT, and psilocybin increase serotonin and decrease 5-HIAA in nerve endings, whereas nonpsychoactive analogues of LSD do not. Subsequently, with the discovery by Aghajanian et al. (1970) that small doses of LSD inhibit the spontaneous firing of the cells of the dorsal and median raphe nuclei, the serotonergic system of the brain was established as one of the most sensitive to hallucinogens.

Major adaptive changes occur in the serotonergic system after the administration of narcotic drugs, and the responses of the system to psychoactive drugs are dampened by lithium—for example, the highs of marihuana or LSD are reduced or prevented by lithium. In general, most if not all hallucinogens reduce the rate of turnover of brain serotonin.

Various treatments that alter the activity of brain serotonergic pathways also influence the behavioral effects of hallucinogens. For example, pretreatment with reserpine or tetrabenazine, which release much of the vesicular store of serotonin and lead to depletion of the transmitter, enhances the effects of a threshold dose of LSD in rats. Similarly, a specific inhibitor of serotonin biosynthesis, parachlorophenylalanine (PCPA) potentiates the behavioral effects of LSD, but α-methyltyrosine, an inhibitor of catecholamine biosynthesis, does not (Appel et al., 1970). The potentiation may be related to the insomnia produced by PCPA and by raphe nuclei lesions. The serotonergic system has been implicated in the induction of normal sleep (Jouvet, 1969), and it is known that sleep deprivation by itself potentiates the effect of LSD (Safer, 1970).

The serotonin pathways in the brain relate to still other behavioral effects that may be relevant to the effects of hallucinogens. Electrical stimulation of the raphe nuclei impairs the habituation of startle responses in rats. That effect has been attributed either to an increase in the activity of serotonergic processes (Sheard and Aghajanian, 1968) or, alternatively, to tetanic stimulation resulting in functional impairment of serotonergic synapses (Brawley and Duffield, 1972). The latter interpretation is more consistent with the observation that PCPA attenuates habituation to auditory stimuli in rats (Connor et al., 1970; Carlton and Advokat, 1973). Swonger and Rech (1972) also reported that, in situations involving sufficient arousal, serotonin increases habituation or response inhibition. Electrolytic lesions of the raphe nuclei—particularly the median raphe nucleus, which contains the cells of origin of the mesolimbic serotonin pathway—induce a state of generalized hyperreactivity to sensory stimuli (Davis and Sheard, 1974b; Geyer et al., 1976b). Conversely, infusions of serotonin into the brain reduce both reactivity and activity (Geyer et al., 1975; Warbritton et al., 1978). Most hallucinogens increase reactivity in comparable startle-response paradigms (Davis and Sheard, 1974a; Geyer et al., 1978) but do not have consistent effects on measures of behavioral activity. Neurotoxin-induced lesions of the raphe nuclei—presumably more specific to serotonin than electrolytic lesions—increase startle responses but do not affect activity measures.

The effects of hallucinogens on catecholaminergic systems have yet to be studied thoroughly. Some evidence indicates that phenylethylamine hallucinogens may block noradrenergic transmission; other studies suggest that those drugs may specifically increase the turnover of brain norepinephrine (Leonard, 1973). Much more work is needed to assess the possible contribution of central norepinephrine and epinephrine to the effects of hallucinogens. Some recent work has revealed the mixed-agonist properties of LSD and other hallucinogens on brain dopamine receptors (Christoph et al., 1977). Hallucinogen-induced behavioral changes believed to be related to dopaminergic systems have been reported, although relatively high doses are required. Since the biogenic amine systems of the brain stem are complexly interrelated, it would be surprising if any of those fundamental systems were not involved in the actions of those drugs.

A controversy has evolved over whether LSD acts primarily as a blocker of postsynaptic serotonergic receptors or as an agonist. The commonly reported decrease in serotonin turnover in several brain regions has been thought by some to be a metabolic correlate of an apparent feedback inhibition of raphe unit firing. However, LSD inhibits raphe firing even when administered directly by iontophoresis or when the ascending projections from the raphe have been severed (Mosko and Jacobs, 1977). Those data indicate that LSD's effect on raphe firing is due either to a direct effect on the cell bodies or to short recurrent collaterals or dendrites. The inhibition of raphe firing produced by phenylethylamine hallucinogens seems to involve other mechanisms; it is not evident with iontophoretic application and can be blocked by a transection caudal to the raphe (Haigler and Aghajanian, 1973). Although electrophysiological data suggest that the effect of the phenylethylamine drugs is limited to the dorsal raphe nucleus, the origin of the mesostriatal serotonergic pathway, more recent cytofluorimetric studies, in which the scattered serotonergic cells can be readily distinguished from other cells, demonstrate that both indoleamine and phenylethylamine hallucinogens affect both the dorsal and the median raphe nuclei (Geyer and Mandell, 1979). That result is consistent with the observations that most behavioral changes related to serotonin involve the mesolimbic serotonin system originating in the median raphe.

Studies of the neurochemistry of chronic or repeated drug administration have become essential with respect to both the clinical phenomena and the neurobiological adaptive changes that may be involved in progressive and long-lasting changes in human beings. The hallucin-

ogens are perhaps the fastest inducers of tachyphylaxis of all centrally active agents, and that tolerance constitutes a formidable barrier to biochemical theories of psychosis that involve the notion of an aberrant metabolite. How could such a substance produce psychosis for days, weeks, or months on end when tolerance to analogous compounds develops so quickly? Bridger (1975) and Wyatt and Gillin (1975) demonstrated in animals that the excitatory component of the action of such hallucinogens as mescaline and DMT becomes more marked after repeated drug administration—that is, there is a reverse tolerance (increased sensitivity) to some of the features of the syndrome. Bridger suggested that the behavioral effects of hallucinogens that are found in stressful situations generally do not show tolerance and may provide the better animal models for the production of psychoses in humans. As in humans, the amount of environmental stress associated with the testing situation is an important factor governing the nature of the behavioral effects of hallucinogens in animals (Geyer and Light, 1979). In that context it should be noted that the depression of raphe firing produced by LSD does not exhibit tolerance in rats (Trulson et al., 1977). Work remaining to be done on the development and failure of tolerance may have important implications for the pathophysiology of psychosis and the peculiar intolerance of interpersonal disturbance manifested by heavy and chronic users of hallucinogens.

Animal Models for Behavioral Effects

In a literal sense most of the systematic research on hallucinogens is irrelevant or, at best, inferential if hallucinations are the subject of study. Most of that work has been done in animals, in which hallucinations cannot be directly observed or reported. Likewise, euphoric states are not readily amenable to study in animals. Siegel and Jarvik (1975) used sophisticated behavioral paradigms to study hallucinations in monkeys, but most animal behavioral models are designed more as assays of the drugs' effects than as analogues of the human phenomenology. The development of such animal models for the assessment of behavioral effects has been necessary for investigations of relationships between structure and function, the effects of dose on response, and pharmacological interactions. Investigators have used many species to screen new drugs and to study the biochemical, physiological, and psychological effects of hallucinogens—insects, spiders, fish, birds, amphibians, carnivores, rabbits, rodents, primates, and even elephants. Depending on dose and species, the drugs can produce hypoactivity or hyperactivity, aggression or docility, catatonia, peculiar postures, marked autonomic stimulation, incoordination, and hypersensitivity to sensory stimuli. In contrast to their exquisite potency in humans, the drugs must usually be administered in relatively large doses to produce readily observable effects in animals.

A few useful behavioral tests have evolved from systematic research with various forms of instrumental learning. LSD in sufficiently large doses impairs most psychomotor tasks that involve sustained, goal-directed responses. LSD reduces operant behavior maintained by positive reinforcement, such as food or electrical stimulation of the lateral hypothalamus. In rats trained to bar press for food on a fixed ratio schedule, a paradigm apparently more sensitive with respect to LSD than either variable or fixed-interval schedules, the relative potencies of various psychoactive drugs were roughly comparable to those reported for humans, and the alterations were often dependent on dose (Appel, 1968). Joseph and Appel (1976) suggested that the depression of response rate may be due to motivational variables. Perhaps distractibility and physiological arousal, as well as the usual increase in reaction time, also contribute to the decrement in performance. Motor inhibition is apparently not involved because similar behavior is maintained by different contingencies, even after high doses of LSD. That model, like most, is complicated by the fact that the time course of qualitatively different effects is influenced by both the dose and the route of the drug's administration.

The particular effect of hallucinogens on fixed-ratio responding that has received the most attention is the so-called hallucinogenic pause. A wide variety of such drugs produce characteristic intermittent pauses in responding, and rapid tolerance to that effect has been shown to occur with several hallucinogens (Rech et al., 1975). However, that pattern of responding is not unique to hallucinogens. On that and some other behavioral tests, the dopaminergic agonist apomorphine has effects similar to those of the hallucinogens (Silva and Calil, 1975; Geyer et al., 1978).

Generally, operant behavior maintained by aversive contingencies is relatively resistant to the actions of hallucinogens; results vary quantitatively and qualitatively with species and paradigms. Some dose-related effects have been measured in the Lashley III underwater maze, which is spatially complex, but tests in simpler mazes are less sensitive (Uyeno and Mitoma, 1969). Frustrated by the variability of shuttlebox measures, Smythies (1970) developed a fairly sensitive avoidance-response paradigm with rats based on the Sidman avoidance procedure and sophisticated analysis of data. He differentiated the effects of hallucinogens from the distinctive response patterns produced by other psychoactive agents, like chlorpromazine, reserpine, amphetamine, and imipramine. That model has been used successfully in some limited structure-function and drug-interaction studies. Bridger (1975) reported both excitatory and inhibitory effects of mescaline on shuttlebox avoidance behavior in rats. Both acute and chronic administration of mescaline improved acquisition, but acute administration inhibited previously acquired shuttle avoidance. Tolerance occurred only to inhibition of previously acquired shuttle avoidance.

Another approach to an animal model for hallucinogens, exemplified by the work of Jacobs et al. (1977), is the study of the elicitation by hallucinogens of unusual behavioral responses. Jacobs et al. found that cats given indoleamine hallucinogens exhibit limb flicks and abortive groomings, responses that rarely occur naturally or in response to other psychoactive drugs. Tolerance to those effects is extremely rapid and long lasting, and relatively low doses are sufficient to produce reliable effects.

Recent work by Gormezano and Harvey (1978) demonstrated that classical conditioning paradigms are quite sensitive to low doses of LSD. They suggested that LSD specifically affects the associational process relating the conditioned stimulus to the unconditioned stimulus during the acquisition phase. Further work with the paradigm may be fruitful both as an assay for hallucinogens and in the explication of the nature of the psychological changes produced by those drugs.

Because humans often report a variety of perceptual changes from hallucinogens, animal experiments have been designed to assess alterations in the visual and auditory modalities. Spatial disorientation and impaired visual discrimination of size have been noted in monkeys. Either increases or decreases in the accuracy of visual discrimination can be demonstrated, depending on the animal and the dose range. Visual thresholds are often raised, although responses to visual stimuli are typically exaggerated. Alterations in time perception, tactile discrimination, and auditory generalization, especially in the face of difficult tasks or complex stimuli, have been reported for several species. A pervasive effect of low doses of hallucinogens

in animals is an increased responsiveness to sensory stimuli in various modalities. Both indoleamine and phenylethylamine hallucinogens increase measures of behavioral reactivity, such as the startle response (Davis and Sheard, 1974a; Geyer et al., 1978). It is still not clear whether those compounds result in augmented sensitization to stimuli, impairment of the process of habituation, or a general change in reactivity. Similar findings have been obtained with a variety of psychophysical tests in humans. That heteromodal phenomenon may account for the distractibility and disorganized attentional mechanisms commonly reported to occur after hallucinogens are administered.

Drug Effects and Human Phenomenology

Research with hallucinogens has been curiously successful, for more often than not the hypotheses tested tend to be supported by the results obtained, although they may contradict other apparently reliable evidence. The experimental set uniquely complicates those studies because hallucinogens alter perceptual and experiential matrices. Bereft of the usual means of synthesis, subjects are influenced by their own expectations and those of the researchers as they seek to integrate what they are experiencing.

Despite the variability of particular effects, some general characteristics of hallucinogenic experiences can be described. After extensive observations of the effects of LSD and mescaline, Masters and Houston (1966) listed the following recurrent elements:

Changes in visual, auditory, tactile, olfactory, gustatory, and kinesthetic perception; changes in experiencing time and space; changes in the rate and content of thought; body image changes; hallucinations; vivid images—eidetic images—seen with the eyes closed; greatly heightened awareness of color; abrupt and frequent mood and affect changes; heightened suggestibility; enhanced recall or memory; depersonalization and ego dissolution; dual, multiple, and fragmentized consciousness; seeming awareness of internal organs and processes of the body; upsurge of unconscious materials; enhanced awareness of linguistic nuances; increased sensitivity to nonverbal clues; sense of capacity to communicate much better by nonverbal means; . . . and, in general, apprehension of a world that has slipped the chains of normal categorical ordering.

It seems clear that the lateral specialization of the human cerebral cortex provides two distinct and complementary modes of consciousness and that they function more or less in concert with one another. By virtue of its focal organization and sequential processing, the dominant (usually the left) side is best suited for verbal, mathematical, and analytic thought, whereas spatial orientation, artistic talent, visuoconstructive ability, and abstraction of part-whole relationships may well depend on the more diffuse organization that usually characterizes the right hemisphere. The startling perceptual experiences produced by hallucinogenic drugs may be more comprehensible in light of the capacity of the nondominant hemisphere for simultaneous integration of information. The heteromodal influx of perceptions produced by increased attentiveness and sensitization to sensory stimuli may overwhelm the systematic sequential processing of the language hemisphere and invoke the analogical integrative mode of the right hemisphere to consolidate the perceptual flood. However, with particular doses of hallucinogenic drugs, many subjects experience mind trips, bursts of ecstatic and sequentially logical thoughts, or the insight accompanying discovery.

Comparability of Drug-induced and Naturally Occurring Psychotic States

The introduction of hallucinogens into the armamentarium of experimental psychopathology brought the question of how the phenomena of experience induced by hallucinogenic drugs resemble the phenomena of naturally occurring psychotic episodes. The initial descriptions of drug-induced phenomena were taken at face value as similar to distortions of perception or psychological processes associated with such syndromes as schizophrenia (Masters and Houston, 1966). However, by the criteria of the classical primary signs of schizophrenia, many psychodiagnosticians think that primary thought disorder is absent in drug-induced hallucinosis, in spite of the superficial similarity of hallucinations and, with large doses of drug, delusional thinking. Others have argued that the episodes resembling psychotic states probably depend on some predilection in the experimental subject or patient that allows unique or idiosyncratic responses to that kind of drug. That is, hallucinogenic drug experiences that resemble schizophrenic episodes occur because the patients themselves have such a tendency or such an adaptive or defensive structure latent within them (Monroe et al., 1957; Grof, 1967). European and American studies in the late 1950's and 1960's were based on the premise that borderline schizophrenics and patients with schizophrenic episodes in their histories are more vulnerable to a standard dose or dose-response test of hallucinogenic drug vis-à-vis personality disintegration than are normal controls. However, the investigators failed to demonstrate the validity of that hypothesis (Cohen, 1964). Even among schizophrenic patient populations, so-called bad trips were idiosyncratic and unpredictable in occurrence. Clinicians who have participated in such research acknowledge that the people whose ego functions they expected to be the most disrupted by the hallucinogenic drug experience were often the least affected. Thus, the simplest of the potential relationships between the actions of hallucinogenic drugs and the syndromes of severe psychopathology appear in considerable doubt. That the acute effect of the drug mimics a type of schizophrenic episode (by means of a common biochemical mechanism?) or that hallucinogenic drugs can precipitate psychotic reactions in genetically prone persons is not documented in the literature.

Some clinicians attempt to refine the discrimination between hallucinogenic drug experience and naturally occurring psychosis by examining the drug experience from the standpoint of organic psychosis. In a general way, they emphasize distortions that can occur in perceptions of color, shape, and patterns, rather than the drug-induced changes involving highly personal imaginings of voices or persons intimately involved in the person's psychodynamic focus.

In fact, such discriminations are far from easily made (Cohen, 1967; Ungerleider and Fisher, 1967). For example, the expectation, the circumstances under which the drug is taken, and the set reported by the patient or his companions have become prominent parts of the clinician's matrix of comprehension. Once he ascertains that a drug has or has not been taken in an acute psychiatric emergency, it is difficult, if not impossible, to delineate post hoc what may or may not have been drug induced in the circumstance. Paranoid breaks have been diagnosed, for instance, in patients who felt that they had been given hallucinogenic drugs and who came to a doctor reporting such a circumstance, although later investigation revealed that no drug was involved. The reverse has also occurred—the blind administration of hallucinogens and associated diagnosis of functional psychiatric disease. From the literature and authors' experience, it becomes clear that the two phenomena have not been well differentiated. Such distinctions as more versus less organic, more perceptual versus more psychodynamic, and other commonly accepted clinical criteria are probably not as helpful as had been hoped. That is not to say that the primary pathology or the moving force of personality disintegration is the same in both cases; rather, the similarities may be the expression of the human being's limited armamentarium for coping with various degrees of ego disruption. In other words, the similarities in phenomenology may be due to similarities not in the primary causative agent or its neurobiological mechanisms but in the psychological, psychosocial, or psychobiological defenses used to handle that kind of central nervous system disruption.

Bowers (1973), using an assortment of objective descriptive scales—with and without drugs, as they may or may not have been suspected—reported that the premorbid adjustment scales he used were just as efficacious in predicting the outcome for drug-induced psychosis as they had been for naturally occurring schizophrenia. His examination focused on the phase after the acute episode, in which the drug use was associated with the disruption of function with or without later psychosocial regression in coping style after the severe psychotic episodes involving drugs. The patient with a poor premorbid condition often settled into a chronic pattern not discriminable from that seen in schizophrenic patients.

Thus, it may be informative to look for similarities between hallucinogenic drug experience and psychosis after severe acute episodes or after chronic use. The lethargy, flatness, tendency to interpersonal withdrawal, inertia, failure to thrive, disintegration of psychosocial coping mechanisms—the condition, in short, of the acid freak—may constitute a syndrome similar to that of chronic schizophrenia or process schizophrenia. Bower's (1973) results were consistent with the range of pathology seen in the emergency room of the University of California at Los Angeles Neuropsychiatric Institute during the years when hallucinogen overdoses provided many patients for observation (Ungerleider and Fisher, 1967).

In addition to the postacute phase, similarities between functional and drug-induced hallucinogenic phenomena may occur very early in a drug's course of action. The onset of action for most hallucinogens ranges from ½ hour to 2 hours after administration. Early in that period there are subtle and progressive changes in thought style and processes, withdrawal of focus to the self, highly personalized meanings, a gradual disintegration of psychological boundaries, and a number of other phenomena that resemble descriptions of early or primary signs of schizophrenia or the schizoaffective disorders (Rumke, 1923). Those disturbances of thought and feeling early in the drug's onset of action may resemble the real phenomena of schizophrenia more than the phenomena that occur under the maximal direct influence of the drug. Little relevant research is available in that area as yet.

Perhaps hallucinogenic drug-induced psychopathology and naturally occurring schizophreniform, schizophrenic, and schizoaffective disorders ought to be examined more systematically at those two times—that is, before the full-blown drug-induced distortions in affect, thought, and apperception and after, during the state of anergy following single or repeated administrations. The present supposition is that at those two times vulnerability may be assessed more easily than at other times. Furthermore, the criteria for describing the early drug effects could be derived from studies of the so-called fundamental thought disorders of the schizophrenic process and may even be useful in further refining them.

Interhemispheric Relating

To pursue the development of a theoretical relationship between the mechanisms of action of euphorohallucinogenic drugs and their manifestations in people—that is, to cross a pharmacological bridge toward a biological model of some aspects of human cognitive and emotional functioning—the authors return now to the notion, expressed in the introduction, of a regulable reciprocal oscillation of hemispheric biogenic amine inhibition. The concepts derived in this section lead toward a biological pathophysiology of the schizophrenias, affective disorders, and character disorders and to ideas regarding treatment with drugs and psychotherapy. The hope is that the reader will gain experience in an integrative style of thought, the use of neurobiological metaphors that are counterintuitive but have the capacity to infuse thinking about brain mechanisms with elements of subjective human experience. Every clinician is exhorted to develop for himself an experiential neurochemistry, a system connecting objectively known neurobiological fact with subjectively experienced clinical identification.

BIOGENIC AMINE ASYMMETRY

Evidence accumulates from many laboratories that all three biogenic amines—serotonin, norepinephrine, and dopamine—inhibitory neurotransmitters, are distributed asymmetrically in the brain hemispheres of animals and humans. Glick et al. (1977) showed that dopamine levels are bilaterally asymmetrical in rat brain and that amphetamine can alter the relative concentrations of that transmitter on the two sides of the brain. Serotonin levels are also different in the hemispheres. Lithium decreases the difference; tricyclic antidepressants increase the difference, as does cocaine; and LSD has no effect on the asymmetry, although it arrests serotonin cell firing and discharge-coupled serotonin release (Mandell and Knapp, 1979a). The enzyme that is rate limiting in serotonin biosynthesis, tryptophan hydroxylase, has active and less active kinetic forms; whereas lithium makes them similar on both sides of the brain, the tricyclics lead to the active form in one hemisphere and to the less active form in the other hemisphere (Knapp and Mandell, 1979b). Because submicromolar concentration of calcium, the level of that ion flux in discharging neurons, converts the less active to the more active enzyme form, the tricyclics appear to facilitate firing on one side and, perhaps through axon collaterals crossing the midline, to inhibit it on the other. Lithium increases serotonergic inhibition on both sides of the brain (Knapp and Mandell, 1979 a, b) and LSD appears to disinhibit it bilaterally. Psychotropic drugs altering hemispheric dominance through differential changes in biogenic amine inhibition become the first construct in this theoretical development.

ENDOGENOUS OSCILLATIONS IN BIOGENIC AMINE SYNTHESIS

Recently, two multienzyme complexes, groups of enzymes that function in concert, have been isolated from the caudate and the midbrain of the rat. The one from the caudate oscillates in its rate of dopamine biosynthesis at about 3 to 7 minutes a cycle, depending on temperature and other conditions (Yellin et al., 1979); the one from the midbrain, synthesizing serotonin, oscillates at 6 to 15 minutes per sine-wave cycle (Mandell and Knapp, 1979b). Because a similar oscillatory pattern is known in glycolysis and both biogenic enzyme systems require a reduced nucleotide generated by an 11-enzyme glycolytic complex, it may be that the oscillations are downstream metabolically from carbohydrate energy metabolism. What is important here is that each side of the brain is experiencing, diffusely and perhaps independently, an alternating on and off through the oscillatory production of biogenic amine brakes. Each hemisphere may be pictured as a light,

growing bright and dim at a rate determined by the rhythms of the biogenic amine biosynthesizing oscillators on either side. Certain factors, including drugs, have the capacity to alter the rates and the degrees of definition of those rhythms, and the existence of such parameters constitutes the second theoretical construct.

RECIPROCAL BILATERAL ORGANIZATION OF BIOGENIC AMINE SYNTHESIS

As noted, recurrent collaterals from biogenic amine cells cross the midline to end on similar amine cells in the homotypic nucleus on the other side. The neurotransmitters are generally inhibitory, and autoreceptors have high affinities for their own transmitters, so, when the two sides are coupled, one side is on and the other side is off. Unlike the oscillation of the cell-free multienzyme complex this oscillation manifests bilateral reciprocal organization. Glowinski's group (Nieoullon et al., 1978) demonstrated, by means of push-pull cannulae on both sides of the cat brain, that, when dopamine and serotonin synthesis are up on one side, they are down on the other side about 70 per cent of the time in an oscillation with periods of between 5 and 15 minutes. In view of the capacity for amine synthesis to oscillate independently in each hemisphere, that 70 per cent reciprocal coherence, which can be reduced by experimental manipulation, may indicate that there are degrees of reciprocal coupling. The third theoretical construct, then, is the notion of a variable amount of coupling—that is, bilateral coherence—between independent hemispheric oscillations.

COGNITIVE AND AFFECTIVE SPECIALIZATION OF THE HEMISPHERES

Beginning with the classical split-brain work of Sperry and Milner and culminating in a spate of investigations—psychoanalytic studies of split-brain patients; discrimination by means of sound psychological instruments of the personality changes in temporal lobe epileptics with right versus left tumor and spike foci, of personality differences in patients with left-side and right-side strokes, and of psychological changes induced by amobarbital injections differentially disinhibiting one or the other hemisphere; perceptual and cognitive studies using hearing, vision, problem-solving, and split-attention measures; and behavioral characterization of neurological syndromes—the literature makes it clear that humans have two relatively independent brains with contrasting thinking styles and feelings (Bear and Fedio, 1977; Desmedt, 1977; Harnad et al., 1977). The dominant lobe in most people is more syntactical, logical, categorizing, verbal, dysphoric, obsessional and paranoid; the other lobe is mute and is more visual, musical, intuitive, holistic, hysteric, and hypomanic. Although such a clear division of labor will, no doubt, be recognized as more complex with further work, the idea of two specialized brains in each living organism, descending the ladder of speciation at least to birds, suggests that a more fundamental dichotomy in function than verbal versus nonverbal remains to be penetrated. For example, each hemisphere probably controls the activity of the other in some way. What needs to be seen here, however, is that, whatever the specific characteristics are, one hemisphere seems to be more involved in what is commonly called thought and the other in what is construed as feeling. The fourth construct, then, is the concept of cognitive and affective specialization of the two hemispheres of the human brain.

PSYCHOBIOLOGICAL EVIDENCE OF BILATERAL OSCILLATION

Experimental animals that have been stimulated electrically in limbic sites or given drugs that affect biogenic amines and disinhibit high-voltage hypersynchronous activity in the limbic system manifest permanently lower than usual thresholds for the induction of limbic seizures; that process has been called kindling (Andy and Akert, 1955). There are two behavioral phases of kindling: In the cat, partial kindling causes facial twitching, motor movement, and clonic convulsions (Delgado and Selvillano, 1961). Kindled animals cycle every 5 or 10 minutes between attentional behavior and grooming and pleasure behavior (Wetzel et al., 1978) and that cycling can be viewed as reflecting the alternating dominance of the limbic system by the two hemispheres. Thresholds for the induction of limbic seizures oscillate about every 5 to 10 minutes on the two sides of the brain (Gaito et al., 1978). Temporal lobe epileptics have two kinds of seizures: (1) the classical psychomotor seizure of unpleasant affect, automatic movement, and sometimes violence and (2) what have been called interictal ecstasies, often interpreted as visitations from God (Waxman and Geschwind, 1975). Associated with long periods of good disposition afterward, the interictal ecstasies have been thought to be associated with prolonged periods of hippocampal-septal afterdischarge, which is likely to be right brain dominated, although perhaps tonically inhibited by the left brain-dominated amygdala component (Mandell, 1979b). The association of amygdala activation with the classical seizure phenomena in the temporal lobe epileptic has been established by depth-electrode studies. Although a spontaneous ecstasy has not been recorded, pleasure drugs and sexual thoughts have been associated with hippocampal slow waves in humans (Heath, 1972).

The sleep cycle has time parameters comparable to kindled animals' oscillations, and in humans slow-wave sleep with verbalization and no imagery and REM sleep with movie-like subjective experiences may represent the two hemispheres in oscillatory expression (Dement et al., 1969). Studies of awake humans have demonstrated a similar subjective cycling from preoccupation with reality to fantasy with a 100-minute rhythm resembling that seen in the sleep cycle (Kripke and Sonnenschein, 1973). Cycles of mania and depression can be seen as the sequential expression of the dominance of the distinct intrinsic affective properties of the two lobes. In 1902 William James (1929) described two phases of religious conversion, a period of suffering and rumination followed by the luminescence of transcendence.

Dopamine synthesis has a 24-hour rhythm that is 12 hours out of phase on the two sides of the rat brain, a fact that suggests a day brain and a night brain in terms of dopamine inhibition (Mandell et al., 1979). Pilot studies of the effects of increasing brain serotonin on food intake in the rat showed no relationship between appetite and whole-brain serotonin (Weinberger et al., 1978), but there was evidence of a relationship of the behavior to serotonin asymmetry. Perhaps many midline variables—such as hormone level, sexual excitement, and appetite—have oscillating systems of hemispheric influence. Complex neural programs underlying feeding and other functions in invertebrates can be turned on or off by the biogenic amines. It is probable that learning establishes the specific meanings attached to human behaviors; some people eat more when they are dysphoric, and others do so when they feel good. The feelings oscillate endogenously, but the meaning, the symbolic and functional accoutrements of each state, may be learned.

The dualistic oscillatory nature of the phenomena reviewed suggests two separable coherent organizations and a role for biogenic amine neurochemical variables in the regulation of the kind and the degree of their intercalation. Psychomotor epileptics, whose personality changes over 10 to 14 years make them resemble manic-depressive patients, as well as people with character disorders, were described by Geschwind (1965), who used the dimension of intensity. Fast bilateral oscillations of inhibition would be predicted to increase the likelihood that both sides of the brain are disinhibited at the same time and, thus, more likely to fuse a coordinate image of thought and

feeling than slower oscillations. If oscillation were too fast, the delaying function of thought might disappear, and the intensity of expression and impulsive action might be predicted. Slow oscillations would be predicted to be more characteristic of schizophrenic psychopathology, a disjunction of thought and feeling, a temporal distance between cognitive activity on one side and its homotypically represented conative aspects on the other. That dissociation of thought and feeling would be manifest in oscillations between flatness of affect and unexplainable excitements and the frozen conflict called ambivalence in classical Bleulerian terms. Thus, a descriptive parameter is conceived that would integrate neurochemical, neurophysiological, personality, and psychopathological variables: the dimensions of degree and kind of superimposition of two individually coherent hemispheric organizations of function in consciousness—the fifth construct.

A BIOLOGICAL MODEL FOR AN INTEGRATED PSYCHOPATHOLOGY

The next step in the development of this biologically based, counterintuitive system of psychiatric pathology is to try to classify some patients according to the constructs elucidated above—that is, (1) the bilateral asymmetry of biogenic amine inhibitory function expressed as hemispheric dominance in cognition and affect, (2) the independent oscillation of biogenic amine synthesis at varying rates on the two sides of the brain, (3) the bilateral oscillation of biogenic amine neuronal discharge with the properties of variable coherence and reciprocal inhibition, (4) the affective and cognitive specialization of the two sides of the human brain, and (5) evidence from psychobiological studies that oscillations in behavior represent more or less dominance of one side of the brain occurring under physiological circumstances. The general dimensions become personality style (degree of laterality), intensity (oscillatory rate), and (bilateral) coherence.

A 19-year-old man—tall, withdrawn, and a lifelong obsessional—was preoccupied with his "ugliness" and was having strange thoughts. He spoke very slowly in a flat voice and moved little in the chair. Answers to questions were slow in coming and were impoverished. His mother reported that he had outbursts of temper that were difficult to understand, often arising after hours spent trying to decide such apparently unimportant things as what color socks to wear or what television program to watch. He had become progressively less interested in things, giving up his hobbies and even his few friends. He complained of difficulty in concentrating.

If one visualizes the psychoanalytic personality dimension of obsessional-paranoid to hysterical-cyclothymic like a homunculus across the brain from left to right, the patient would be considered left lobe dominated. Because there appeared to be what the German psychopathologists have called a conative defect—a failure of emotional investment in thought and action, a volitional dysplasia—and because the likelihood of simultaneous disinhibition of the homotypic representations of ongoing processes in both left (thinking) and right (feeling) brains would increase as a function of oscillatory rate, the prediction would be that each hemisphere's biogenic amine oscillations were very slow. The history of episodic outbursts of strong feeling that made no sense—that is, that were independent of systematic relationships to thought structure—and other periods of flatness around material that appeared emotionally laden, what Kraepelin called "emotional blunting," would be accounted for on the basis of oscillations slow enough to be beyond the control of the bilateral neurophysiologically imposed coherence (serotonin cells discharge at a rate of one to three a second; dopamine cells are a little faster) or due to a defect in the reciprocating inhibitory system, a failure in coupling. Each of his brains seemed to operate independently. The patient would be described, then, as being left lobe dominated, with slow and uncoupled oscillations.

A 26-year-old woman had been married three times. Her one child had been placed for adoption after her last arrest for shoplifting, and she was referred for treatment by the probation department. In a clinging and provocative dress, she talked about how difficult her current boyfriend was and refused to speak much about her troubles with the law. Persistent inquiry revealed a belief that she had been set up for her trouble by her second husband, who, she suspected, was still trailing her. She spoke quickly and in colorful language, punctuating her talk with profanity. She had little memory of her childhood, denied sexual difficulties, and was without obvious feeling about her son, whom she had not seen in several months. She presented with a kind of impervious high mood and the attitude that she was without psychiatric difficulties. She mentioned drug use, but it was difficult to document. She said that for periods in her past she was without energy, characteristically sleeping and eating more than she would have otherwise; she denied, however, the experience of depression.

The patient would be seen as having a right lobe-dominated personality, with hysterical, impulsive, and cyclothymic features. The intensity of expression and the history of impulse disorder would suggest that she was a fast oscillator, probably with the emotional charge of a disinhibited right side occurring in synchrony with her thoughts. That would explain her quick intensity in conversation and her motor impulsivity. The coupling function would be strong enough to afford the possibility of paranoia, a felt-to-be appropriate attitude arising in conjunction with a cognitive possibility in emotionally dominated thought processes. She would be seen as a right lobe-dominated, fast and highly coupled oscillator. The two views normally available for accurately anticipating the future—a worried debate between the optimism of the right and the pessimism of the left—for her become one. That felt truth, an energized and singular possibility, could be seen as underlying her impulsive actions and paranoid thoughts.

A 42-year-old bookkeeper presented a history of several years of nervousness. Sweating, tremors, and a general fearfulness that was made worse in open spaces had restricted his life to his office and his home. He reported several episodes of fainting in doctors' offices. His associations were endless and detailed vacillations between desires and fears, recitations of somatic symptoms, and anticipations of future disasters. He had seen several psychiatrists for psychotherapy, to no avail. The only pleasure he was able to report was his work with an amateur acting troup. On stage he was without symptoms.

The patient would seem to manifest a mixed obsessional and hysterical style. His intensity would lead to a prediction of fast oscillations; his appropriate linkage of thought and feeling, adequate coupling. Here a failure of hemispheric dominance may be seen to lead to unresolved psychological positions. Unlike the first patient, whose indecision could be seen to arise from slow oscillations and a paralysis of the coherence function, this patient's two brains were too evenly matched, without usual biogenic amine asymmetry. Such patients, like this one, are often treated successfully with tricyclics which disinhibit one side of the brain and seem to make the hysterical-cyclothymic hemisphere dominant. One may suggest that the treatment could turn a neurosis into a character disorder. According to *The Upanishads*, fear comes from having two possibilities; Freud conceived of anxiety as being rooted in conflict.

A bizarre psychopath might be a manifestation of right-lobe domination, with fast, poorly coupled oscillations; a borderline hysteric schizophrenic might be predicted to have right lobe domination and slow oscillation, An obsessional depressed patient might be seen as left lobe dominated, with fast, well-coupled oscillations, and his depressive delusions, like those of the second patient above, might be made credible by the

intensity and the degree of associated feeling, in this case the dysphoria of the left lobe.

RELATION OF LATERALITY TO PERSONALITY AND PSYCHOPATHOLOGY

Evidence relating laterality to personality and psychopathology is accumulating in many quarters (Desmedt, 1977; Harnad et al., 1977). Medial temporal sclerosis in the left lobe appears to lead to depression and paranoia; in the right lobe it appears to lead to hypomania and impulsiveness. The clinical picture is one of high mood with denial in patients with strokes in the dominant hemisphere and one of low mood with exaggeration of problems in those with strokes in the nondominant hemisphere. Disinhibition of the left hemisphere with amobarbital results in fear; on the right, it results in joy. Intact right temporal lobes are necessary for the experience of euphoria and the psychedelic effects of LSD. Patients with electrical abnormalities on the left experience more negative feelings than do those with neurological foci on the right. Relatively more optimism and denial emerge in people with cerebral lesions on the right. Unilateral electroconvulsive treatment on the right influences pure mood variables more than left-sided treatment does. When persons are asked emotionally laden questions, they manifest more gazes upward to the left. More paranoid material is elicited from temporal lobe epileptics with foci on the left than with foci on the right. Perhaps the best-documented studies are those of Bear and Fedio (1977) in which ratings by self and others on most of 18 interpersonal dimensions showed that patients with temporal spikes on the left viewed themselves worse than close acquaintances rated them, and patients with spikes on the right viewed themselves better than they were rated by close acquaintances.

The obsessional-paranoid mode of dealing with others—characterized by general negativism, exaggeration of difficulties, preoccupation with difficulties, projection of rage, ruminative self-concern, mistrust, and emotional isolation—seems to be peculiar to the left lobe and has been documented in comprehensive interviews with split-brain epileptics who could relate only with their left hemispheres. A tendency toward bland denial (*la belle indifférence*), high mood, emotionality, impatience with detail, and impulsivity has been seen as characteristic of the personality disorder often called "hysterical-cyclothymic" by psychoanalytic and psychological researchers; it is a tendency apparently peculiar to the nondominant hemisphere (Hoppe, 1978).

The two lobes appear to have regulatory influence on each other. For example, in a recent study (Risse and Gazzaniga, 1978), amobarbital on the left produced in two patients periods of elation, inappropriate talk, and uncooperativeness and denial in the experimental situation; transcallosal reciprocal inhibition of bilaterally homotypic structures, each of the other, has been shown for many neocortical and nigrostriatal systems (Hull et al., 1974).

In the clinical realm it may be wondered whether the pattern of one hemisphere's inhibitory control over the other—the left lobe's mistrust and criticism of the fantasies of the right; the right lobe's dislike for the caution of the more fearful left—becomes the way a person deals with others. Depending on which lobe is dominant, a person's interhemispheric relations may serve as the biological matrix of his interpersonal style. Intervention in the struggle for control between the hemispheres may be a major dimension of psychiatric treatment in some disorders, whereas functional engagement of the hemispheres to normalize mutual interhemispheric regulation may be the theme in others. Perhaps an alteration in the relationship between the hemispheric brains is reflected by changes in the transference or the reverse. The effects of psychotropic drugs and psychotherapy can be brought into conceptual harmony by such a possibility.

RELATIONSHIP BETWEEN OSCILLATORY RATE AND PERSONALITY AND PSYCHOPATHOLOGY

Maps of the brain stem show that biogenic amine neural systems end on bulbar neurons regulating autonomic function, especially vasomotion (Bach, 1952). In view of the oscillatory character of biogenic amine enzyme function, with periods in the range of 3 to 15 minutes, the prediction might be made that the manifestation of such cyclic alternation in inhibition would appear in measures of autonomic nervous system function, and there is evidence of that. Using a measure of fingertip vasomotion, Burch et al. (1942) demonstrated three such rhythms independent of respiration rates, including one with periods in the range of 5 to 6 minutes. Lacey and Lacey (1958), measuring skin resistance and heart rate, found similar oscillations, and they showed that people with slow or less pronounced autonomic oscillations were quieter and more capable of the wariness and caution needed to slow their reaction time, as required by assigned psychomotor tasks. Those with faster, more pronounced oscillations, regardless of sympathetic tone—that is, the degree of general autonomic arousal was independent—were talkative, hyperkinetic, overreactive to environmental stimuli, and more impulsive.

The work of Doust (1960, 1962) perhaps best connects the rate of spontaneous oscillatory activity in peripheral indices of vasomotion with diagnostic psychopathology and drug treatment. Using the spontaneous rhythms in skin temperature, capillary blood pressure, capillary blood-oxygen saturation, and capillary blood flow in a large number of normal persons and psychiatric patients, he was able to associate mental health with rhythms in the range of 5 to 7 minutes. Epileptics—who, as noted above, show left lobe or right lobe personality intensification resembling the character and affective disorders—had cycles in the range of 1 to 2 minutes (manic-depressive disease was called "larval epilepsy" at the turn of the century), and schizophrenic patients manifested autonomic oscillations consistently in the range of 10 to 20 minutes. Phenothiazines consistently reduced cycle length in schizophrenic patients to the 6- to 8-minute range in association with clinical improvement, as did thyroid hormone, which is also effective in the treatment of some schizophrenics. Dibenamine, a β-blocker, also quickened the cycle, but other peripherally active vasomotor drugs did not. (In that regard recent studies suggesting the use of the β-blocker propranolol in schizophrenia may be relevant.) Several schizophrenic patients studied longitudinally could be titrated in and out of clinical remission in association with the predicted changes in cycle length. Thus, slow oscillations may be part of a syndrome characterized by functional dissociation of the two hemispheres, a separation in time of thought-dominated from feeling-dominated processes. Fast oscillations—that is, too close a relationship would lead to coherence and the possibility of dominance, capture, of one hemisphere by the other through underlying biogenic amine asymmetry and reciprocal interhemispheric inhibition.

Oscillating cell-free systems for biogenic amine biosynthesis in the brain, apart from biological clocks made of such intact neural systems as the pineal loop, suggest the existence of a fundamental brain timepiece. From the work cited above, it is possible to view schizophrenic patients, whose biogenic amine-autonomic neural machinery cycles slowly, as having a slower than normal neurological clock. Psychophysical studies of the temporal processing of bimodal signals posit an internal mechanism that generates a succession of equally spaced points in time, moments at which discriminations of the correct sequence of two stimuli can be made (A. B. Kristofferson, 1967). Research has shown that the temporal space between those hypothet-ical discrete, nonoverlapping units, moments of brain on, appears longer than usual in schizophrenic subjects, a finding consistent with those of Doust (M. W. Kristofferson, 1967).

STRATEGIES FOR PSYCHIATRIC TREATMENT

As instructions and rewards have been shown to change psychophysical time in normal persons and schizophrenic patients and antipsychotic drugs have been shown to normalize the rate of autonomic oscillations, so treatment using interpersonal strategies and biochemical agents can be used in efforts to change the relationships between the two hemispheres, mediated through shifts in lateral dominance, oscillatory rates, or coherence. According to the hypothetical model, the style of interpersonal relating between the therapist and the patient can be internalized. Psychotropic drugs are viewed as having their actions on the same dimensions, changing the oscillatory rates, asymmetry, and coherence of biogenic amine inhibitory systems.

Lateralization. As noted, cocaine and the tricyclic antidepressants increase the asymmetry in function of the brain's serotonergic system, whereas lithium decreases it. Lithium is effective against both mania and depression; cocaine has been shown to worsen both; tricyclics may precipitate mania. That model (Mandell, 1979a) can be applicable to vacillating neurotics without enough hemispheric dominance and to those with too much hemispheric dominance—for example, those grouped by Winokur (1974) as suffering from the genetically loaded affective spectrum disturbances, including some bipolar affective disorders, and character and impulse disorders, including hysteria and paranoia. The affective intensity of the thoughts of such people suggests fast oscillations and high coherence, a close relationship between hemispheres, and capture of one side of the brain by the dominant other side; the therapy would involve reducing the lateral dominance of one side by the other—that is, by reducing serotonin asymmetry with lithium or shifting dominance by disinhibiting the more euphoric side with tricyclics. In a phobic patient, tricyclics would be likely to create a lateral dominance when its previous absence had led to anxious ambiguity. Clinicians have complained about a loss of insight in depressed patients treated successfully with tricyclics; perhaps that loss indicates the functional absence of the verbalizing side.

In interpersonal operations, psychotherapy with that group involves aspects of dominance, submission, and control, as though the pathological degree of hemispheric dominance were externalized in the relation of the patient to the therapist. Here also, a better balance between the two is attempted through insight—for example, giving one side an empathic knowledge of the other in hopes of reducing the degree of polarization. Affective intensity, oscillatory rate, would not be changed; only the degree of interhemispheric conflict would be altered. Supportive psychotherapy, often an alliance between the therapist and only one of the patient's hemispheres based on a common enemy—doctor and patient agree that the mother is the villain—makes one side dominant, eliminating conflict by splitting, just as tricyclics exaggerate the influence of one lobe.

Reattachment. As the work of psychotherapy with the schizophrenic patient has as its major goal the establishment of a human relationship, the slow oscillations and an absence of bilateral coherence between the hemispheres, alternation between flat thoughts and inappropriate feeling, call for functional reattachment of the hemispheres. Thought blocking and perplexity may be the empty temporal space in consciousness where thoughts and feelings normally meet to create the subjective experience of knowing. Thyroid hormone, which depresses the synthesis of some glycolytic enzymes and has been used successfully in the past with some schizophrenic patients, and the phenothiazine antipsychotic drugs increase autonomic evidence of oscillatory rates. A fundamental biochemical oscillator made up of 11 enzymes acting together is the glycolytic system (Betz and Chance, 1965), turning glucose into energy or nicotinamide adenine dinucleotide (NADH) for use in the biosynthesis of compounds like dopamine. Dopamine uniquely mobilizes brain glycogen, an effect that is blocked by pimozide (Nahorski and Rogers, 1975). Dopamine alters the oscillatory rate of dopamine synthesis in the multienzyme complex that seems coupled to the oscillations in NADH generated by glycolysis. Thus, there appear to be some relationships among dopamine synthesis, dopamine effect on the oscillatory rates of its own synthesis, and the rates of glycolysis and brain energy metabolism. For example, citrate, an inhibitor of glycolysis, changes the rate of dopamine biosynthesis and its oscillation in vitro; whereas substantia nigra lesions do not change the discharge rates of caudate neurons (Hull et al., 1974), they markedly increase the glycogen content of those cells. The validity and the specificity of that approach remain open to question, but it seems possible that carbohydrate nutrition, dopamine as an effector, and oscillatory rates of glycolysis connected through NADH to the oscillatory rate of dopamine biosynthesis may be abnormally slow in some people and produce a functional hemispheric disconnection syndrome, to use Geschwind's (1965) term, which antipsychotic drugs active in dopamine systems repair. The bilateral oscillations in dopamine biosynthesis have been demonstrated in vivo by Glowinski's group (Nieoullon et al., 1978).

Psychotherapeutic work with those slow oscillators involves efforts to connect feelings and thoughts through the model of intimacy in the human relationship. If, in fact, there is a basic defect in oscillatory rate, so that interhemispheric coherence is impossible, it may help explain the frequently poor results obtained from psychotherapy alone.

Detachment. The chemical model of this treatment is the arrest of biogenic amine oscillations on both sides simultaneously by autoreceptor inhibitory agonists like apomorphine for dopamine cells, clonidine for norepinephrine cells, and LSD for serotonin cells. That is seen as reducing the rate of brain time, the biogenic amine oscillations, to zero. That transcendent timelessness, that insight (left) with ecstasy (right), that unity, seems to represent what has been called in psychoanalytic work the burst of energy of successful working through, both hemispheres disinhibited from the control of biogenic amines from below and from each other, the postambivalent capacity to see and feel on both sides of emotionally laden questions that used to elicit conflict, distort emphasis, or increase polarization. In Eastern metaphysics the state is described as "detachment with empathy." Unlike the disconnection of schizophrenia (slow oscillation, low intensity, lack of coherence), in this state each hemisphere runs free; since the oscillatory rate is normal, integrative moments occur as needed for normal thought. Whereas the slowly oscillating schizophrenic cannot reattach, the normal oscillator can detach reversibly. The sides can relate, but neither is dominated. In interpersonal terms that is the state praised by the existentialists, the gestaltists, and those trying to achieve a high-intensity disconnection syndrome by means of meditation, long-distance running, or the use of euphorohallucinogenic drugs. Either silence (meditation), which tends to reduce the firing rate of serotonergic cells

(Aghajanian et al., 1978), or the induced activity, which arrests firing through inhibitory autoreceptors (running or the hallucinogens), disinhibits both sides simultaneously.

RAPPROCHEMENT BETWEEN BIOLOGICAL AND PSYCHOANALYTIC THINKING

It is almost uncanny how one's attitude about whether the brain can know about itself determines the kind of science and psychiatry one practices. Logical positivism and the empirical tradition that have been the dominant philosophies of all science have, over the past century, taught mistrust of subjectivity. For the behavioral scientist the ritual has been to blind oneself to what one knows and then hope to discover it somewhere out there. Methods get contaminated, anyway, by silent inner voices, which configure research strategies and data management. Psychoanalytic data have been much maligned by harder scientists, perhaps in error. The verbal patterns and visual images of the human brain may spell out its biological state precisely—if they could be translated.

This already grand delusion of an integrated biological and psychodynamic psychiatry will stretch yet further. Freud and Abraham discussed the characterological relevance of the so-called anal dynamics to the problem of patients with affective and character disorders, who have been characterized here as experiencing an internal struggle for dominance and control between the hemispheres of their brains. The suggestion has been made that the degree of bilaterality is controlled by serotonergic asymmetry, which is sensitive to tricyclics and to lithium. Discipline, dominance, surrender, winning, losing, mania, depression, killing, and being killed may lie in the war between the hemispheres and the style of relating with others when it is externalized. Ferenczi, Fromm-Reichman, Sullivan, and Searles among others described the feelings of hopeless starvation and the oral incorporation fantasies of schizophrenic patients, and the suggestion has been made here that the slow oscillations of biogenic amines in the brains of schizophrenics may be related to the cyclic kinetic manifestations of the most primitive biochemical unit of energy nutrition, the glycolytic pathway; mention has been made of its interaction with the neurotransmitter dopamine, thought at present to be most relevant to the actions of the antipsychotic drugs controlling oscillation rate and bilateral coherence. Psychoanalytically, health can be reperceived as a state of independent but cordially cooperative relationships between the two brains, achieved by working through an ordeal that at crisis and turnabout yields a time of unconflicted bivalent vision.

Sophisticated and unpoliticized biologists working on brain function and undefensive psychiatric clinicians have an interesting future in prospect together, one that may be characterized neither by hemispheric capture nor by schizophrenic dissociation but by the high energy and free collaboration of two disinhibited hemispheres.

Suggested Cross References

Psychopharmacology is discussed in Section 2.2, the neurochemistry of behavior in Section 2.4, and the neurophysiology of behavior in Section 2.5. Biological rhythms in psychiatry are discussed in Section 2.6. Neurology is discussed at length in Chapter 3. The schizophrenic disorders are discussed in Chapter 15, paranoid disorders in Chapter 16, schizoaffective disorders in Chapter 17, affective disorders in Chapters 18 and 19, personality disorders in Chapter 22, and drug dependence in Chapter 23.

REFERENCES

Abood, L. G. Stereochemical and membrane studies with the psychotomimetic glycolate esters. In *Psychotomimetic Drugs*, D. H. Efron, editor, p. 67. Raven Press, New York, 1970.

Adey, W. R., Dennis, F. R., and Bell, B. J. Effects of LSD-25, psilocybin, and psilocin on temporal lobe EEG patterns and learned behavior in the cat. Neurology, *12:* 591, 1962.

*Aghajanian, G. K. Influence of drugs on the firing of serotonin-containing neurons in brain. Fed. Proc., *31:* 91, 1972.

Aghajanian, G. K., Sheard, M. H., and Foote, W. E. LSD and mescaline: Comparison of effects on single units in the midbrain raphe. In *Psychotomimetic Drugs*, D. H. Efron, editor, p. 165. Raven Press, New York, 1970.

Aghajanian, G. K., Wang, R. Y., and Baraban, J. Serotonergic and nonserotonergic neurons of the dorsal raphe: Reciprocal changes in firing induced by peripheral nerve stimulation. Brain Res., *153:* 169, 1978.

Andy, O. J., and Akert, K. Seizure patterns induced by electrical stimulation of hippocampal formation in the cat. J. Neuropathol. Exp. Neurol., *14:* 198, 1955.

Appel, J. B. The effect of psychotomimetic drugs on animal behavior. In *Psychopharmacology: A Review of Progress, 1957–1967*, D. H. Efron, editor, p. 1211. United States Public Health Service, Bethesda, 1968.

Appel, J. B., Lovell, R. A., and Freedman, D. X. Alterations in the behavioral effects of LSD by pretreatment with *p*-chlorophenylalanine and α-methyl-*p*-tyrosine. Psychopharmacologia, *18:* 387, 1970.

Bach, L. M. N. Relationships between bulbar respiratory, vasomotor, and somatic facilitatory and inhibitory areas. Am. J. Physiol., *171:* 417, 1952.

*Bear, D. M., and Fedio, P. Quantitative analysis of interictal behavior in temporal lobe epilepsy. Arch. Neurol., *34:* 454, 1965.

Betz, A., and Chance, B. Influence of inhibitors and temperature on the oscillations of reduced pyridine nucleotides in yeast cells. Arch. Biochem. Biophys., *109:* 579, 1965.

Bowers, M. B., Jr. LSD-related states as models of psychosis. In *Psychopathology and Psychopharmacology*, J. O. Cole, A. M. Freedman, and A. J. Friedhoff, editors, p. 1. Johns Hopkins University Press, Baltimore, 1973.

Bradley, P. B., and Key, B. J. The effects of drugs on arousal responses produced by electrical stimulation of the reticular formation of the brain stem. Electroencephalogr. Clin. Neurophysiol., *10:* 97, 1958.

*Brawley, P., and Duffield, J. C. The pharmacology of hallucinogens. Pharmacol. Rev., *24:* 31, 1972.

Bridger, W. H. Good trip or bad trip: The roles of tolerance and stress in hallucinogenic drug action. In *Neurobiological Mechanisms of Adaptation and Behavior*, A. J. Mandell, editor, p. 287. Raven Press, New York, 1975.

Burch, G. E., Cohn, A. E., and Neumann, C. A study by quantitative methods of the spontaneous variation in volume of the finger tip, toe tip and posterosuperior portion of the pinna of resting normal white adults. Am. J. Physiol., *136:* 433, 1942.

Carlton, P. L., and Advokat, C. Attenuated habituation due to parachlorophenylalanine. Pharmacol. Biochem. Behav., *1:* 657, 1973.

Christoph, G. R., Kuhn, D. M., and Jacobs, B. L. Electrophysiological evidence for a dopaminergic action of LSD: Depression of unit activity in the substantia nigra of the rat. Life Sci., *21:* 1585, 1977.

Cohen, S. *Drugs of Hallucination*. Secker & Warburg, London, 1964.

Cohen, S. *Beyond Within: The LSD Story*. Atheneum, New York, 1967.

Connor, R. L., Stolk, J. M., Barchas, J. D., and Levine, S. PCPA and habituation to repetitive auditory startle stimuli in rats. Physiol. Behav., *5:* 1215, 1970.

Davis, M., and Sheard, M. H. Effects of lysergic acid diethylamide (LSD) on habituation and sensitization of the startle response in the rat. Pharmacol. Biochem. Behav., *2:* 674, 1974a.

Davis, M., and Sheard, M. H. Habituation and sensitization of the rat startle response: Effects of raphe lesions. Physiol. Behav., *12:* 425, 1974b.

*Delgado, J. M. R., and Selvillano, M. Evolution of repeated hippocampal seizures in the cat. Electroencephalogr. Clin. Neurophysiol., *13:* 722, 1961.

Dement, W., Ferguson, J., Cohen, H., and Barchas, J. Non-chemical methods and data using a biochemical model: The REM quanta. In *Psychochemical Research in Man*, A. J. Mandell and M. P. Mandell, editors, p. 275. Academic Press, New York, 1969.

Desmedt, J. E., editor. *Language and Hemispheric Specialization in Man: Cerebral Event-Related Potentials*. S. Karger, Basel, 1977.

*Doust, J. W. L. Spontaneous endogenous oscillating systems in autonomic and metabolic effectors: Their relation to mental illness. J. Nerv. Ment. Dis., *131:* 335, 1960.

Doust, J. W. L. Consciousness in schizophrenia as a function of the peripheral microcirculation. In *Physiological Correlates of Psychological Disorder*, R. Roessler and W. S. Greenfield, editors. University of Wisconsin Press, Madison, 1962.

Gaddum, J. H. Antagonism between lysergic acid diethylamide and 5-hydroxytryptamine. J. Physiol. (Lond.), *121:* 15, 1953.

Gaito, J., Nobrega, J. N., and Gaito, S. T. Statistical evaluation of several aspects concerning the oscillation effect. Physiol. Psychol., *6:* 209, 1978.

*Geschwind, N. Disconnexion syndromes in animals and man. Part I. Brain, *88:* 237, 1965.

Geyer, M. A., and Light, R. K. LSD-induced alterations of investigatory responding in rats. Psychopharmacology, 1979, In Press.

Geyer, M. A., and Mandell, A. J. Similar effects of indoleamine and phenylethylamine hallucinogens on dorsal and median raphe neurons. In *Catecholamines: Basic and Clinical Frontiers*, E. Usdin, editor, p. 1304. Pergamon Press, New York, 1979.

Geyer, M. A., Petersen, L. R., Rose, G. J., Horwitt, D. D., Light, R. K., Adams, L. M., Zook, J. A., Hawkins, R. L., and Mandell, A. J. The effects of lysergic acid diethylamide and mescaline-derived hallucinogens on sensory-integrative function: Tactile startle. J. Pharmacol. Exp. Ther., *207:* 837, 1978.

Geyer, M. A., Puerto, A., Dawsey, W. J., Knapp, S., Bullard, W. P., and Mandell, A. J. Histological and enzymatic studies on the mesolimbic and mesostriatal serotonergic pathways. Brain Res., *106:* 241, 1976a.

Geyer, M. A., Puerto, A., Menkes, D. B., Segal, D. S., and Mandell, A. J. Behavioral studies following lesions of the mesolimbic and mesostriatal serotonergic pathways. Brain Res., *106:* 256, 1976b.

Geyer, M. A., Warbritton, J. D., Menkes, D. B., Zook, J. A., and Mandell, A. J. Opposite effects of intraventricular serotonin and bufotenin on rat startle responses. Pharmacol. Biochem. Behav., *3:* 687, 1975.

Giarman, N. J., and Freedman, D. X. Biochemical aspects of the action of psychotomimetic drugs. Pharmacol. Rev., *17:* 1, 1965.

Glick, S. D., Jerussi, T. P., and Zimmerberg, B. Behavioral and neuropharmacological correlates of nigrostriatal asymmetry in rats. In *Lateralization in the Nervous System*, S. Harnad, R. W. Doty, L. Goldstein, J. Jaynes, and G. Krauthamer, editors, p. 213. Academic Press, New York, 1977.

Gormezano, I., and Harvey, J. A. Analysis of hallucinogens by means of Pavlovian conditioning. In *The Psychopharmacology of Hallucinogens*, R. C. Stillman and R. C. Willette editors, p. 207. Pergamon Press, New York, 1978.

Grof, S. Use of LSD-25 in personality diagnostics and therapy of psychogenic disorders. In *The Use of LSD in Psychotherapy and Alcoholism*, vol. 3, p. 154. Bobbs-Merrill, Indianapolis, 1967.

Haigler, H. J., and Aghajanian, G. K. Mescaline and LSD: Direct and indirect effects on serotonin-containing neurons in brain. Eur. J. Pharmacol., *21:* 153, 1973.

Haigler, H. J., and Aghajanian, G. K. Lysergic acid diethylamide and serotonin: A comparison of effects on serotonergic neurons and neurons receiving a serotonergic input. J. Pharmacol. Exp. Ther., *188:* 688, 1974.

*Harnad, S., Doty, R. W., Goldstein, L., Jaynes, J., and Krauthamer, G., editors. *Lateralization in the Nervous System*. Academic Press, New York, 1977.

Heath, R. G. Marihuana: Effects on deep and surface electroencephalograms of man. Arch. Gen. Psychiatry, *26:* 577, 1972.

Hoppe, K. D. Split-brain: Psychoanalytic findings and hypotheses. J. Am. Acad. Psychoanal., *6:* 193, 1978.

Hull, C. D., Levine, M. S., Buchwald, N. A., Heller, A., and Browning, R. A. The spontaneous firing patterns of forebrain neurons. I. Brain Res. *73:* 241, 1974.

Jacobs, B. L., Trulson, M. E., and Stern, W. C. Behavioral effects of LSD in the cat: Proposal of an animal behavior model for studying the actions of hallucinogenic drugs. Brain Res., *132:* 301, 1977.

James, W. *The Varieties of Religious Experience*. Modern Library, New York, 1929.

Joseph, J. A., and Appel, J. B. Alterations in the behavioral effects of LSD by motivational and neurohumoral variables. Pharmacol. Biochem. Behav., *5:* 35, 1976.

Jouvet, M. Biogenic amines and the states of sleep. Science, *163:* 32, 1969.

Knapp, S., and Mandell, A. J. Conformational influences on brain tryptophan hydroxylase by submicromolar calcium: Opposite effects of equimolar lithium. J. Neural Transmission, *15:* 1, 1979a.

Knapp, S. and Mandell, A. J. Lithium and chlorimipramine differentially alter bilateral asymmetry in mesolimbic serotonin metabolites and kinetic conformations of midbrain tryptophan hydroxylase with respect to tetrahydrobiopterin cofactor. Neuropharmacology, 1979b, In Press.

Kripke, D. F., and Sonnenschein, D. A 90-minute daydream cycle. Sleep Res., *2:* 187, 1973.

Kristofferson, A. B. Attention and psychophysical time. Acta Psychol., *27:* 93, 1967.

Kristofferson, M. W. Shifting attention between modalities: A comparison of schizophrenics and normals. J. Abnorm. Psychol. *72:* 388, 1967.

Lacey, J. O., and Lacey, B. C. The relationship of resting autonomic activity to motor impulsivity. Res. Publ. Assoc. Res. Nerv. Ment. Dis., *36:* 144, 1958.

Leonard, B. E. Some effects of the hallucinogenic drug 2,5-dimethoxy-4-methylamphetamine on the metabolism of biogenic amines in the rat brain. Psychopharmacologia, *32:* 33, 1973.

Mandell, A. J. On a mechanism for the mood and personality changes of adult and later life: A psychobiological hypothesis. J. Nerv. Ment. Dis., *167:* 457, 1979a.

Mandell, A. J. Toward a psychobiology of transcendence: God in the brain. In *The Psychobiology of Consciousness*, J. M. Davidson and R. J. Davidson, editors. Plenum Publishing Corp., New York, 1979b.

Mandell, A. J., and Knapp, S. Asymmetry and mood, emergent properties of serotonin regulation: A proposed mechanism of action of lithium. Arch. Gen. Psychiatry, *36:* 909, 1979a.

Mandell, A. J., and Knapp, S. Brain protein fluctuations and personality asymmetries: Toward a field theory of the actions of lithium and the tricyclic antidepressants. In *Electrolytes and Neuropsychiatric Disorders*, P. E. Alexander, editor. Spectrum Publications, New York, 1979b, In Press.

Mandell, A. J., Stewart, K. R., Russo, P. V., and Tepper, J. V. Emergent wave phenomena in dopamine synthesis. V: Fluctuations in dopa decarboxylase and 3H-spiroperidol binding activity; in vitro and in vivo rhythms in striatal synaptosomes. Biochem. Pharmacol., 1979, In Press.

*Masters, R. E. L., and Houston, J. *The Varieties of Psychedelic Experience.* Holt, Rinehart and Winston, New York, 1966.

Monroe, R. R., Heath, R. G., Mickle, W. A., and Llewellyn, R. C. Correlation of rhinencephalic electrograms with behavior: A study on humans under the influence of LSD and mescaline. Electroencephalogr. Clin. Neurophysiol., *9:* 623, 1957.

Mosko, S. H., and Jacobs, B. L. Electrophysiological evidence against negative neuronal feedback from the forebrain controlling midbrain raphe unit activity. Brain Res., *119:* 291, 1977.

Nahorski, S. R., and Rogers, K. J. The role of catecholamines in the action of amphetamine and L-DOPA on cerebral energy metabolism. Neuropharmacology, *14:* 283, 1975.

*Nieoullon, A., Cheramy, A., and Glowinski, J. Release of dopamine in both caudate nuclei and both substantia nigrae in response to unilateral stimulation of cerebellar nuclei in the cat. Brain Res. *148:* 143, 1978.

Rech, R.H., Tilson, H. A., and Marquis, W. J. Adaptive changes in behavior after repeated administration of various psychoactive drugs. In *Neurobiological Mechanisms of Adaptation and Behavior*, A. J. Mandell, editor, p. 263. Raven Press, New York, 1975.

Risse, G. L., and Gazzaniga, M. S. Well-kept secrets of the right hemisphere: A carotid Amytal study of restricted memory transfer. Neurology, *25:* 950, 1978.

Rumke, D. H. *Phaenomen en Klinisch: Psychiatriche Studie oven Gelucksgevaal.* Proefschrift E. Idjo, Leiden, 1923.

Safer, D. J. The effect of LSD on sleep-deprived men. Psychopharmacologia, *17:* 414, 1970.

Schildkraut, J. J. Rationale of some approaches used in biochemical studies of the affective disorders. In *Psychochemical Research in Man*, A. J. Mandell and M. P. Mandell, editors, p. 113. Academic Press, New York, 1969.

Sheard, M. H., and Aghajanian, G. K. Stimulation of midbrain raphe neurons: Behavioral effects of serotonin release. Life Sci., *7:* 19, 1968.

Shulgin, A. T. Mescaline: The chemistry and pharmacology of its analogs. Lloydia, *36:* 46, 1973.

Siegel, R. K., and Jarvik, M. E. Drug-induced hallucinations in animals and man. In *Hallucinations, Behavior, Experience, and Theory*, R. K. Siegel and L. J. West, editors. John Wiley & Sons, New York, 1975.

Silva, M. T. A., and Calil, H. M. Screening hallucinogenic drugs: Systematic study of three behavioral tests. Psychopharmacologia, *42:* 163, 1975.

Smythies, J. R., editor. *The Mode of Action of Psychotomimetic Drugs.* MIT Press, Cambridge, Mass., 1970.

Swonger, A. K., and Rech, R. H. Serotonergic and cholinergic involvement in habituation of activity and spontaneous alternation of rats in a Y maze. J. Comp. Physiol. Psychol., *81:* 509, 1972.

Tebecis, A. K., and DiMaria, A. A re-evaluation of the mode of action of 5-hydroxytryptamine on lateral geniculate neurones: Comparisons with catecholamines and LSD. Exp. Brain Res., *14:* 480, 1972.

Trulson, M. E., Ross, C. A., and Jacobs, B. L. Lack of tolerance to the depression of raphe unit activity by lysergic acid diethylamide. Neuropharmacology, *16:* 771, 1977.

Ungerleider, J. T., and Fisher, D. The problems of LSD-25 and emotional disorder. Calif. Med., *106:* 49, 1967.

Uyeno, E. T., and Mitoma, C. The relative effectiveness of several hallucinogens in disrupting maze performance by rats. Psychopharmacologia, *16:* 73, 1969.

Warbritton, J. D., Stewart, R. M., and Baldessarini, R. J. Decreased locomotor activity and attenuation of amphetamine hyperactivity with intraventricular infusion of serotonin in the rat. Brain Res., *143:* 373, 1978.

Waxman, S. G., and Geschwind, N. The interictal behavior syndrome of temporal lobe epilepsy. Arch. Gen. Psychiatry, *32:* 1580, 1975.

Weinberger, S. B., Knapp, S., and Mandell, A. J. Failure of tryptophan load-induced increases in brain serotonin to alter food intake in the rat. Life Sci. *22:* 1595, 1978.

Wetzel, W., Ott, T., and Matthies, H. Periodic behavioral changes during hippocampal theta rhythm elicited by septal stimulation in rats. Neuroscience, *3:* 755, 1978.

Winokur, G. The division of depressive illness into depression spectrum disease and pure depressive disease. Int. Pharmacopsychiatr., *9:* 5, 1974.

Winters, W. D., and Wallach, M. B. Drug-induced states of CNS excitation: A theory of hallucinosis. In *Psychotomimetic Drugs*, D. H. Efron, editor, p. 193. Raven Press, New York, 1970.

Woolley, D. W., and Shaw, E. A biochemical and pharmacological suggestion about certain mental disorders. Proc. Natl. Acad. Sci. U.S.A., *40:* 228, 1954.

Wyatt, R. J., and Gillin, J. C. The development of tolerance to and dependence on endogenous neurotransmitters. In *Neurobiological Mechanisms of Adaptation and Behavior*, A. J. Mandell, editor, p. 47. Raven Press, New York, 1975.

Yellin, J. B., Russo, P. V., Bullard, W. P., and Mandell, A. J. Cell-free oscillations in striatal dopamine synthesis—arrest by micromolar lithium. FASEB Abstract No. 2742, 1979.

6.5   Sensory Deprivation

PHILIP SOLOMON, M.D.
SUSAN T. KLEEMAN, M.D.

History

Instances of aberrant mental behavior in explorers, shipwrecked sailors, and prisoners in solitary confinement have been known for centuries. Toward the end of World War II, startling confessions induced by brainwashing in prisoners of war caused a rise of interest in the psychological phenomena brought about by deliberate diminution of sensory input in the human being.

To test the hypothesis that an important element in brainwashing is prolonged exposure to sensory isolation, Hebb and his co-workers in Montreal (Bexton et al., 1954) brought solitary confinement into the laboratory and demonstrated that volunteer subjects—under conditions of visual, auditory, and tactile deprivation for periods of up to 7 days—reacted with increased suggestibility (see Figures 1 to 3 for a similar experiment). Some of the subjects also showed symptoms that have since become recognized as characteristic of the sensory deprivation state: anxiety, tension, inability to concentrate or organize one's thoughts, increased suggestibility, vivid sensory imagery—usually visual, sometimes reaching the proportions of hallucinations with delusionary quality—body illusions, somatic complaints, and intense subjective emotional accompaniment. The term "indeterminate stimulus experience" has been applied to this general group of symptoms and

FIGURE 1. A volunteer subject in a sensory deprivation experiment. The special room is soundproofed and pitch black. (The photograph was taken with the use of infrared light.) The subject wears gloves to blunt the sense of touch. (Yale Joel, Life Magazine, © Time, Inc.)

FIGURE 2. Just after his release, the subject tries in vain to hold a small rod in a hole without touching the sides. (Yale Joel, Life Magazine, © Time, Inc.)

has been defined as "a syndrome of experiences for which no appropriate environmental stimulus can be detected" (Ellis, 1972; Downs, 1974). In this section the term "sensory deprivation symptoms" is essentially synonymous with indeterminate stimulus experience.

Impressed by these results, Lilly (1956) at the National Institute of Mental Health and later Shurley (1960) went further and, in an attempt to reduce sensory excitation to as near zero as possible, immersed subjects in a tank of tepid water, having them breathe through a blacked-out head mask (see Figure 4). Symptoms occurred earlier and more intensely. At Boston City Hospital (Solomon et al., 1957) the tank-type respirator was used to produce sensory deprivation and monotony, with the advantage that polygraphic recordings from the subject became feasible. Soon many laboratories in the United States and in Canada were setting up similar experiments, and in 1958 a national symposium on the subject was held at Harvard. The proceedings were published in 1961 in book form (Solomon et al., 1961).

Papers in the professional journals appeared in spiraling profusion. A symposium entitled "Sensory Deprivation Research: Where Do We Go from Here?" was held at the annual meeting of the American Psychological Association in 1964. Facts were accumulating in awesome numbers, and theories were propounded by the dozens, yet little agreement could be reached regarding the significance of the findings or their proper place in understanding human behavior.

Experimentation

Interest in sensory deprivation became widespread for many reasons. It was intriguing to think that simply doing nothing and being cut off from the outside world could bring about a transient psychotic-like state. Heretofore, experimental psychoses could be produced only by drugs, toxic states, and other heroic measures. Theoretical considerations led to various hypotheses of basic psychological interest that could be tested by exposure to sensory deprivation. Among the parameters studied were physiological stress, biochemical changes, cognitive functioning, creativity, imagery, personality type, motivation, suggestibility, learning, and states of consciousness. Possible applications could be recognized in such fields as industry, architecture, military life, public health, clinical medicine, and psychiatry.

Psychiatrists began to lose interest in the subject when the early hopes faded for an experimental psychosis without drugs

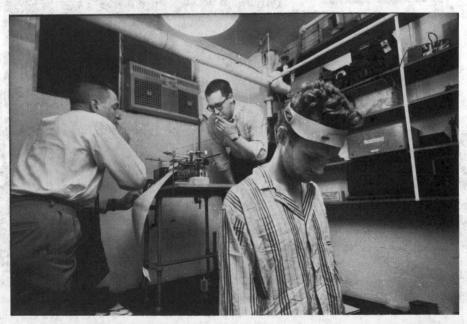

FIGURE 3. Immediately after his release, the volunteer was subjected to a battery of tests. Although most volunteers could perform simple memorization in confinement, tests showed their comprehension ability to be impaired just after release. It took most volunteers about a day to return to normal. (Yale Joel, Life Magazine, © Time, Inc.)

and for feasible therapeutic applications in clinical psychiatric practice. Psychologists continued to work vigorously in the field, using increasingly sophisticated and carefully controlled methods to tease apart the many interrelated variables.

Interest focused on choice of subjects (the covert selection factor and sampling bias in volunteers), motivations in subjects, instructions to subjects (the roles of suggestion and expectation), novelty and anxiety-provoking factors in the experimental setup, establishment of baseline, duration of isolation, extent of monotony and patterning of perceptive stimuli, breaks in sensory deprivation (feeding, toileting, talking, moving), type of deprivation (isolation room, iron lung, water immersion), methods of collecting data, parameters of observation, monitoring of drowsiness and sleep, strategies for control data, practice effects, and other variables and contaminating factors. Attempts were made to assess the effects on the subjects of concomitant immobilization and social isolation. In comparisons of the results of different investigators, using the same subject in different laboratories seemed a promising effort but proved to be of little avail. It was thought that quantification would somehow have to be introduced before it could be possible to standardize techniques and understand the discrepancies in the results of different investigators (Rossi and Solo-

mon, 1964). In 1969 Zubek edited a critical review of sensory deprivation and rendered a broad, dispassionate opinion of its scientific standing.

The serious student of sensory deprivation would do well to examine Zubeck's authoritative book—especially its first three chapters by Suedfeld, Rossi, and Zukerman—before exploring further in the periodical literature. He should not be dismayed by the controversies and dissensions among the researchers. More important than their differences are the facts that there are so many similarities and that, in the main, the discoveries of Hebb and his students in the early 1950's are still held valid and important today.

Sensory deprivation has now been studied not only in scores of laboratories in the United States and Canada but also to a lesser extent elsewhere in the world, notably in Japan, Czechoslovakia, France, England, Italy, Russia, the Netherlands, Denmark, Israel, Chile, and West Germany. In addition to experiments with human volunteers, work has been done with monkeys, dogs, cats, rabbits, hamsters, chicks, ducklings, chinchillas, pigs, crickets, crabs, rats, and mice. Publications number in the thousands, and scores are added every year. Thirty years after Hebb's pioneering work, interesting papers are still appearing, though at a noticeably slackened pace.

HYDROHYPODYNAMIC ENVIRONMENT

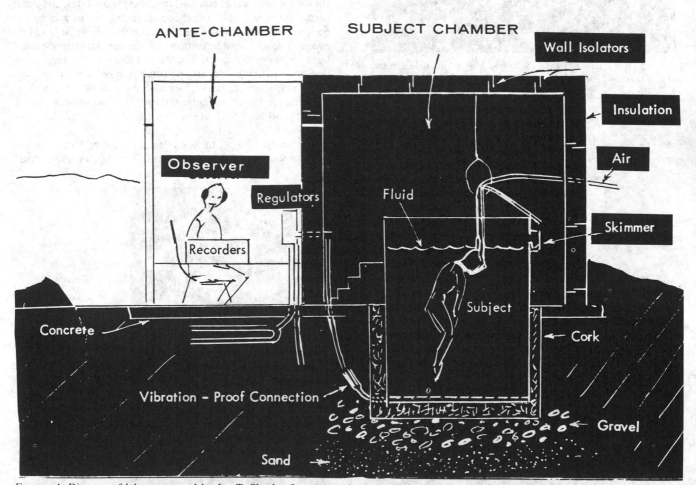

FIGURE 4. Diagram of laboratory used by Jay T. Shurley for sensory deprivation experiments. Volunteer subjects are immersed in tepid water, breathe through blacked-out head masks, and are observed and monitored. (Courtesy of Jay T. Shurley, M.D.)

Theoretical Explanations

The two most popular theories for the phenomenon of sensory deprivation are the psychological and the physiological.

PSYCHOLOGICAL THEORIES

Psychological explanations were anticipated by Freud, who wrote:

It is interesting to speculate what could happen to ego function if the excitations or stimuli from the external world were either drastically diminished or repetitive. Would there be an alteration in the unconscious mental processes and an effect upon the conceptualization of time?

This prophetic stab is an example of Freud's extraordinary and astonishing insight and intuitive faculty. Indeed, under conditions of sensory deprivation, abrogation of the ego's secondary process (perceptual contact with reality and with organized, logical thinking) brings about the emergence of the primary process—irrationality, regression, confusion, disorientation, fantasy formation, primitive emotional responses, hallucinatory activity, and wish-dominated, pseudopathological mental reactions.

A number of investigators have found it useful to use psychoanalytic terminology to make more understandable the results of their work. Thus, Rapaport (1958) stressed the concept of ego autonomy as crucial in a subject's ability to tolerate sensory deprivation and Goldberger and Holt (1961) agreed that ego strength as measured by them could predict individual tolerance in their experiments. Kris's concept of regression in the service of the ego was also used. Many pointed out that a patient being psychoanalyzed is in a kind of sensory deprivation mental room (soundproofing, dim lights, couch) and is encouraged to free associate and otherwise invite primary process mental activity. In the sensory deprivation situation, the subject becomes even more dependent on the experimenter and must trust him for the satisfaction of such basic needs as feeding, toileting, and physical safety. In water tank sensory deprivation there is also the similarity to the womb with its amniotic fluid.

Kammerman (1977) used a new variant of Shurley's sensory deprivation technique (a modification of water tank submersion), involving flotation of the subject in a strong epsom salt solution inside a lightproof ventilated Fiberglas tank. Kammerman preferred to explain his data in Jungian, rather than Freudian, terms, particularly with respect to the use of the designation "unconscious." He believed that sensory deprivation produces ego diffusion. His experimental results were suggestive of various personality modifications, but further research was considered necessary.

PHYSIOLOGICAL THEORIES

Physiological explanations are, as yet, equally speculative. Presumably the maintenance of optimal conscious awareness and accurate reality testing depends on a necessary state of alertness, which, in turn, depends on a constant stream of changing stimuli from the external world, mediated through the ascending reticular activating system in the brain stem. In the absence or impairment of such a stream, as occurs in sensory deprivation and in sensory monotony, alertness falls away, direct contact with the outside world diminishes, and the balance of integrated activity tilts in the direction of increased relative prominence of impulses from the inner body and the central nervous system itself. For example, idioretinal phenomena, inner ear noise, and somatic illusions may take on a hallucinatory character.

Reverberating circuits from the association areas and proprioceptive systems, previously inhibited and kept from greater spread by the exteroceptive and activating systems, find themselves released and able to dominate the brain. The result is an increased tendency to rehearsal of memory, meditative thought, reverie, excessive preoccupation with somatic stimuli, stimulus-bound thinking, and body image awareness and distortions. Material previously repressed and relatively unconscious is given an impetus to appear in consciousness. The breakthrough, when it occurs, is experienced as unwilled or spontaneous, because the material involved has been relatively inaccessible to willful utilization.

Schultz (1965) formulated a sensoristatic model of the nervous system in which the organism strives to maintain an optimal range of sensory variation, shifting it from time to time in response to several variables and monitoring it through the reticular activating system. The latter, serving as a homeostat, simply functions at lower sensory threshholds during sensory deprivation and, like a thermostat calling for heat, calls for stimulation in an attempt to restore balance. For more detailed explanations, see Lindsley (1961), Fiske and Maddi (1961), Schroder et al. (1967), and Zubek (1969).

OTHER THEORIES

Among the numerous other theories, those of particular interest are the following.

Personality. Personality theories attempt to explain not the phenomena of sensory deprivation but the variation in these phenomena from subject to subject. For example: Why do some volunteers in experiments quit sooner than others? Different approaches are offered by different investigations, and these approaches include introversion-extroversion, body-field orientation, and optimal stimulation level (inverted U curve) (Miyashiro and Russell, 1974).

Instinctual drive or need. These theories are based on hypothecated specific needs or drives built into the organism, allied to inquisitiveness, curiosity, investigative or search behavior, and information seeking, again with the inverted U curve (the "U-biquitous curve") for stimulus hunger, optimal satisfaction, and oversatiation (Butler and Harlow, 1957; Maddi, 1961).

Expectation. These hypotheses involve social influences, including the important role played by the experimenter. Modern researchers place great emphasis on anticipation, instructional set, and the demand characteristics of the experimental situation (tacit and overt suggestion) (Orne, 1962).

Cognitive. These theories, allied to the neurophysiological, lay stress on the organism as an information-processing machine whose purpose is optimal adaptation to the perceived environment. With insufficient information, the machine cannot form the cognitive map against which to match current experience, and there is resultant disorganization and maladaptation. Continuous feedback is necessary to monitor the organism's own behavior and to attain optimal responsiveness. Without this feedback, the person virtually lives inside a Rorschach inkblot, forced to project outward individually determined themes having little relationship to the reality situation. This is similar to what many psychotics do (Bruner, 1961; Kubzansky and Leiderman, 1961; Suedfeld, 1969).

Areas of Application

Although there are many unsolved problems regarding sensory deprivation—how it works and why it works—there can be little doubt that sensorily deprived, monotonous environments can produce serious and sometimes dangerous disruption of the mind. As this fact has become more widely known, numerous instances of its profitable application to problems of everyday experience have been found.

PUBLIC HEALTH

The dangers of long-haul trucking over monotonous superhighways have been recognized as being related to inherent sensory deprivation and its symptoms. Increased accident rates and errors in judgment in boring assembly-line work have been similarly implicated. It is becoming increasingly understood that automation for greater production, with the elimination of supposedly distracting stimuli on the remaining workers, carries its price in sensory deprivation symptoms and human fallibility.

Modern architecture applied to industrial and business plants sometimes has the deleterious effect of producing an environment devoid of adequate sensory stimulation for workers. A British writer (Keep, 1977) commented that, although the window tax was abolished in the last century, "Windows are still to a certain extent a financial burden on their owners" because of heat loss; thus, builders have a tendency to eliminate them. However, artificial light has been shown to disturb the performance of worsted weavers and of workers in munitions factories and in underground factories in Sweden. He recommended more windows to permit attention to the outer world, both to relieve the sense of enclosure and to provide muscular relief to the eye by allowing it to focus at a distance. Ideally, some portion of the ground, landscape, and sky should be in sight. Humanitarian protests have been made by Criminon, a prisoners' rights group in England, at the use of sensory deprivation screens—large boxes, cut in half on the diagonal plane and affixed to windows to shut out light but permit ventilation—to punish troublesome prisoners, as used in some English prisons, such as those at Wormwood Scrubs (Swaffield, 1977).

MILITARY

Reference has already been made to the pertinence of sensory deprivation in the brainwashing of prisoners of war. The possibilities for increasing human suggestibility and persuasibility have continued to attract investigators, largely from the disciplines of psychology and sociology (Myers et al., 1963; Smith et al., 1963) but also from psychiatry. Hölscher (1976) discussed the question of what former hostages may look forward to in the future after having been exposed to severe, long-enduring psychic sensory deprivation. In his reply he mentioned concentration camp syndrome and fear of annihilation as a person but finally hedged on the grounds that too many factors are involved.

Swaffield (1977) reported that the Irish Republic has recently appealed to the European Commission of Human Rights, protesting sensory deprivation hooding of prisoners by the British army in Northern Ireland.

Sensory deprivation has been recognized as an important causative factor in situations in which isolation and monotony are intrinsic to the military duty. Men assigned in small groups to constricted or remote stations—polar parties, radar watches, submarine duty, space vehicles, even fallout shelters—may develop temporarily distorted perceptions and disorganized thinking, such as a gray-out or break-off phenomenon in high-flying jet pilots, especially when the horizon cannot be seen; a kind of catatonic-like immobilization of the eyes or screen-fascination in radar observers; rapture of the deep, a form of space disorientation and confusion in deep-sea divers; white-out in polar bases (Clark and Graybiel, 1957; Lindemann, 1958; Ruff and Levy, 1959; Altman et al., 1960; Bennett, 1961; Nardini et al., 1962; Faubion and Tinnan, 1963).

NURSING

A relatively recent development in the field of nursing has been the discovery that sensory deprivation is a feature of ordinary hospital bed rest and, as such, plays an important part in the appearance of sensory deprivation symptoms. Ellis (1972) first became aware of the frequency and significance of sensory deprivation symptoms in her open-heart surgery patients; Downs (1974), using 80 male and 80 female volunteers, studied a simulated hospital bed rest situation and found that 20 per cent of her subjects experienced sensory deprivation symptoms. "One thought that we were cooking or burning eggs"—an olfactory hallucination. There were many vivid fantasies. One subject thought she had returned home: "I could swear I was there, yet my eyes were open all the time, and I knew I was here!" Another felt "like I was floating above the bed." Many could not concentrate or do any productive thinking. Downs concluded that the deliberate pretense of busy behavior on the part of the nurses and the avoidance of eye or verbal contact contributed greatly to the sensory deprivation results.

Bolin (1974) did her master's thesis on the study of 13 immobilized orthopaedic patients, all of whom had sensory deprivation symptoms. She arranged for remedial changes to counteract sensory deprivation—more responsive nursing, positioning the patients near windows, greater use of the telephone, making clocks and calendars more prominent, encouraging the use of the patient's own clothes and sleeping garments, and helping patients to talk about their sensory deprivation symptoms; talking about the symptoms was uniformly reassuring to them.

Woods and Falk (1974) pointed out, after a number of suitable measurements, that an excessive noise level often prevailed in hospital acute care units and that the masking effect (sensory overload) can be as disturbing to patients as is sensory deprivation. She urged the curtailment of professional consultations at the patient's bedside, especially, as was typical, when the patient was not included in the conversation. She made other valuable technical suggestions, such as positioning intermittent positive breathing machines as far as possible away from the patient and directing their outflow valves to face away from the patient; doing so made a difference of 10 decibels.

MEDICINE

Sensory deprivation is now frequently recognized as an important feature in the care of some patients with transient psychotic states or sensory deprivation symptoms, especially in hospitalized patients and in those with severe handicaps, such as blindness, deafness, and paralysis. Although it may be seen in all branches of medicine, it occurs more often and tends to show special aspects in the following fields.

Internal medicine. The so-called cardiac psychosis may be a form of sensory deprivation symptoms and may be quite unrelated to the actual state of the patient's hemodynamic physiology or medication. The well-meaning physician's hospital orders may turn out to be a sentence of sensory deprivation, with excessive or too long-enduring absolute bed rest, silence, and no visitors. The patient may be found wandering in the corridors—usually at night, when the wards have become quiet—confused, thinking he is at home, and being unable to find a familiar room. Sensory deprivation has loosened his hold on reality and has made him prey to fantasy.

Chronic arthritis patients and immobilized invalids generally may be found to be suffering in part from sensory deprivation symptoms, especially when they are being too carefully protected from environmental stimulation. For therapy, see the above discussion of nursing and the following discussion of geriatrics.

Geriatrics. Mental functioning in the elderly may deteriorate not only for organic neurological reasons but also because of pitiful social isolation and sensory deprivation. An increasing number of persons among the elderly live out their lives in single, desolate, barren rooms.

Boore (1977), a lecturer in nursing at the University of Edinburgh, wrote of her experience in preventing sensory deprivation in old people. She addressed herself to the special limitations of many old people—restricted visual fields and other visual faults, confinement in bed, tactile restriction to bedsheets, dulled taste and smell perceptions, unfamiliar hospital sounds, minimal kinesthetic stimulation, and restricted social environment. These patients need a great deal more light, including night lights, than most people realize, she said, those over 85 needing 8 times as much as normal. Their glasses should be cleaned frequently. Hearing aids should be more freely furnished and regular attention paid to their batteries. Food for the elderly should be spiced and seasoned more than usual. Their calendars and clocks should be large and prominent, and the clocks should chime. Rooms and corridors should be painted in attractive and different colors for better orienting value and to increase the pattern of sensory input. Television sets and radios are helpful. And nothing can match the value of attending people—the ministering nurse, friends, relatives, and hospital volunteers. As Boore wrote, "The methods for improving sensory input are limited only by one's imagination."

Wasmuth (1975) taught a 15-hour course in introductory gerontology at Ithaca College and emphasized much the same factors. She gave her students a vivid personal experience by having each of them spend 4½ hours in a simulated and exaggerated hospital atmosphere for elderly patients—darkened rooms, feeder chairs, stretchers, casts, dark goggles, rubber gloves, earplugs, hospital pajamas, and Posey chest restraints. All the students reported sensory deprivation symptoms. Wasmuth's recommendations were much like Boore's and included one interesting addition: The patients' signal cords, which they often have difficulty finding, should not be white on a background of white bedsheets.

Surgery. In recent years, postoperative psychosis has become an increasingly disturbing complication in surgery, largely in prolonged and especially dangerous operations, such as open-heart and organ transplant work. It is now felt that the extensive isolation and immobilization in postoperative recovery rooms

and intensive care units may play an important causative role by means of sensory deprivation (Prioleau, 1963; Kornfeld et al., 1965).

An example of valuable clinical research, done by an astute observer in El Dorado, a county seat in southern Arkansas, is pertinent here. Wilson (1972) noticed that, of two intensive care units in two general hospitals, one seemed to have many more psychiatric complications than the other. The hospitals and the units were about the same size, were in the same town, served the same class of patients, and were attended by the same group of doctors. However, one of the intensive care units had windows, and the other did not. In a carefully controlled prospective study, Wilson showed that the windowless unit incurred twice the organic delirium rate of the unit with windows, an emphatically significant result. In one category of patients—those with abnormal hemoglobin or blood urea nitrogen levels—the differential for delirium was almost 300 per cent. An editorial in the *Archives of Internal Medicine* at the time Wilson's article appeared was entitled "Windows for the Soul," and it contained the comment, "There is more to a window than glass." Apparently, sensory deprivation must be avoided assiduously, like wound infection.

Keep (1977) described an intensive care unit in a large hospital in Norwich, England, built in 1975. No windows were provided for the unit,

since it was thought that it would contain largely unconscious patients and if they recover they soon leave.

However, in the first year 84 per cent of the patients were substantially conscious for most of their stay. It was then recognized that the lack of windows contributed to the emotional stress of both the patients and the staff:

People will more readily accept a windowless environment only if some reason for it is obvious, as in subways, or department store basements. Some of the patients improved dramatically on a shift to a daylight ward.

Ophthalmology. The mental disturbance that sometimes follows operations for cataract or other eye disorders and that is characterized by confusion and disorientation has been known for years as cataract delirium. Weisman and Hackett (1958) preferred to call it black patch delirium, because they believed it is more related to the patching than to the cataract or the operation. Bandaging only one eye or allowing a central peephole in the patches has been found frequently corrective or preventive (McRae, 1964). However, there have been dissenting opinions as to whether the condition should be attributed in a major way to sensory deprivation (Stonecypher, 1963).

Orthopaedics. Patients with some forms of orthopaedic problems require long periods of immobilization in body casts, head tongs, and other severely restricting apparatuses. Some of these patients develop sensory deprivation symptoms, amounting at times to psychotic states that interfere seriously with orthopaedic treatment (Leiderman et al., 1958). Although immobilization alone can sometimes produce mental disturbances (Zubek and Wilgosh, 1963), it is reasonable to assume that the addition of other elements of sensory deprivation in the same patient can become additive. In any event, corrective sensory stimulation as part of the therapy in these cases has been found to be of practical value.

Neurology. In the days when poliomyelitis was a fearful and rampant illness, the bulbar form of it often required treatment in a respirator to sustain life. Some of the patients who had to remain in the respirator (iron lung) for long periods of time developed peculiar hallucinatory states that disappeared promptly when the patient was removed from the respirator. In these states the patient often imagined that he was traveling about in a strange vehicle resembling the respirator. The states were found to be due not to poor oxygenation, toxicity, fever, drugs, or progression of the poliomyelitis but to the condition of life in a tank-type respirator—staring at one spot on the ceiling, hearing little but the constant and monotonous drone of the motor, and being hardly able to move, even if one were not paralyzed—in fact, life in extreme sensory deprivation. Indeed, it was when volunteers placed in the respirator developed symptoms comparable to those of the patients that a program of experimental sensory deprivation was instituted at Boston City Hospital (Solomon et al., 1957).

Other neurological diseases sometimes requiring treatment in a respirator and thus being subject to sensory deprivation include polyneuronitis, myasthenia gravis, and bulbar palsy. Sensory deprivation has also been described in a patient with paraplegia (Jackson et al., 1962).

Mental hospital psychiatry. The element of sensory deprivation is surely important in delirium tremens, in which the best sedative is a sympathetic, attentive nurse. Sensory deprivation is probably also a vital factor in the deterioration of the chronic back-ward inmate. When this type of sensory deprivation is neutralized by the many attentions that accompany a new drug study, some previously neglected patients may seem to get well. Likewise, when wards for chronic patients are emptied by zealous physicians, sometimes at the behest of economy-minded authorities, the resultant flood of unaccustomed stimulation may have a nonspecific beneficial effect on these patients and on their sensory deprivation symptoms, the reaction being in addition to the usual favorable responses to the doctor's personal attention and expectations.

PSYCHOLOGY

Sensory deprivation not only is in itself a substantive area of research and theory in the field of psychology but also is a technique that can be used in many other substantive areas of psychology and related disciplines (Suedfeld, 1975). Sensory deprivation has influenced new research in areas as various as psychogalvanic skin reactions, electroencephalography, basic sensory and perceptual processes, infantile development, cognition, learning, motivation, conformity, creativity, attitude change, introspection, and personality types. The results have been universally interesting, often valuable, and sometimes surprising, especially those contributing to the fields of perception, clinical psychology, social psychology, and experimental design.

In addition to cutaneous stimuli, a variegated sensory environment is necessary for the normal development of the infant (Spitz, 1954). Mental retardation may be the result of sensory deprivation, as well as of biochemical and physiological factors (Hill and Robinson, 1929; Riesen, 1961). Animal studies have also shown that early sensory deprivation leads to lowered resistance to stress in later life (Zingg, 1940; Mandelbaum, 1943).

Psychoanalysis, in its theoretical aspects a branch of psychology, has also profited from sensory deprivation research. Rapaport (1958) drew from sensory deprivation work implications of value for his psychoanalytic ego psychology. Schmale (1974) and Freedman (1975) both used anecdotal data from sensory deprivation reports in their theoretical formulations regarding affect, a subject many psychoanalysts consider inadequately treated in psychoanalytic theory. References were made to "big eye" (pervading insomnia) and "long eye" (a state of mental blankness: "A 20-foot stare in a 10-foot room"), both encountered in South Pole expeditions and reported by Shurley (1970). Cited also were the reports of Schechter et al. (1969) on autistic children treated, in part, by 40 to 80 days of confinement in a dark environment with a minimum of intrusions or demands. The children were reported as markedly improved, but this work has not been duplicated. Harlow's well-known work with infant monkeys deprived of their mothers and raised on wire mesh or terry cloth surrogate mothers was discussed, as well as experiments of nature, such as the congenitally deaf or blind and the boy currently being raised in a germ-free plastic bubble because of a congenital defect in his immunological system. They concluded that sensory input in one modality can offset deprivation in another and that certain kinds of infant care—skin contact, embracing, cuddling—previously held essential are not critical for the development of a wide range of affective capacity.

PSYCHIATRIC TREATMENT

As might have been expected, the discovery and development of sensory deprivation, a new and in some ways fascinating technique for examining and influencing the human mind, quickly brought about efforts to use it for solving all the unsolved problems of clinical psychiatry. Mentally ill patients were placed in sensory deprivation and surprisingly, instead of the production of the usual sensory deprivation symptoms with negative feelings, most of these patients reported positive feelings, some persisting long after the study was completed. There were improvements in motivation, increased desire to socialize, loosening of defenses, subsidence of such pathological symptoms as depressive ruminations and hallucinations, and increased awareness of inner conflicts and anxieties. Presumably because of temporary regression and then improved ego functioning, these patients became more receptive to Azima's anaclitic psychotherapy (Azima et al., 1961). The same technique with three obsessive-compulsive neurotics, however, resulted in no improvement.

Sensory deprivation has also been used in combination with other psychotherapeutic techniques to treat patients with various neurotic disorders. Cooper and co-workers (1975) used sensory deprivation, followed by systematically planned role playing on the part of the therapist, in patients with intransigent hypochondriacal personality disorder. They felt that their results were good, compared with the lack of change in members of a control group (see also Adams et al., 1972).

Suedfeld at Rutgers has written voluminously on many aspects of sensory deprivation work. Recently, he has bent much of his energy toward the task of curing addicted smokers, using sensory deprivation, along with other psychotherapeutic measures (Suedfeld and Ikard, 1974). Taped messages about the hazards of smoking are read to the subjects during sensory deprivation, and their attitude structures are thus modified. Sensory deprivation is the unfreezer (a term attributed to Lewin). Permanence of no smoking then requires a refreezing in the new pattern, and this apparently is more difficult, depending as it does on many external factors.

Suedfeld (1975) believes that sensory deprivation of a sort is part of many effective psychotherapeutic processes—Morita in Japan, sleep therapy in Russia and elsewhere in Europe, primal therapy in the United States, and psychoanalysis everywhere—because they all involve reduced environmental stimulation. Suedfeld is confident that ways will be found to use sensory deprivation with modified psychotherapy in the treatment of stuttering, addictions of all kinds, infantile colic, anisophoria (cross-eyes), autism, mental retardation, hypertension, and sexual dysfunction. As yet, few investigators or therapists have sought to duplicate Suedfeld's work or take up his suggestions.

Conclusion

It has been said that mankind has suffered three major mortifications in its history: Copernicus forced the realization that the earth is not the center of the universe; Darwin stung man with the revelation that he was not created uniquely but evolved from lower animals; and Freud shook man's ultimate conceit, his mind, by showing that much of its vaunted value derives from unconscious elements. In a sense, the results of sensory deprivation studies may be considered a corollary of this last mortification, in that even man's conscious mind can now be seen to be intimately dependent on continuous changing stimuli from the outside world. Variety is the spice, even the staff, of life.

Suggested Cross References

Harlow discusses his work in the sensory deprivation of animals in Section 4.6. Experimental disorders are discussed in Section 6.3, and euphorohallucinogens are discussed in Section 6.4. Geriatric psychiatry is discussed in Chapter 53. Psychiatry and medicine is discussed in Section 28.1, psychiatry and surgery in Section 28.3, and psychiatric nursing in Chapter 50.

REFERENCES

Adams, H. B., Cooper, G. D., and Carrera, R. N. Individual differences in behavioral reactions of psychiatric patients to brief partial sensory deprivation. Percept. Mot. Skills, 34: 199, 1972.

Altman, J. W., Smith, R. W., Myers, R. L., McKenna, F., and Bryson, S. Psychological and Social Adjustment in a Simulated Shelter: A Research Report. American Institute for Research, Washington, D.C., 1960.

Azima, H., Vispo, R., and Azima, F. J. Observations on anaclitic therapy during sensory deprivation. In Sensory Deprivation, P. Solomon, editor, p. 143. Harvard University Press, Cambridge, Mass., 1961.

Bennett, A. M. H. Sensory deprivation in aviation. In Sensory Deprivation, P. Solomon, editor, p. 161. Harvard University Press, Cambridge, Mass., 1961.

*Bexton, W. H., Heron, W., and Scott, T. H. Effects of decreased variation in the sensory environment. Can. J. Psychol., 8: 70, 1954.

Bolin, R. H. Sensory deprivation: An overview. Nurs. Forum, 13: 240, 1974.

Boore, J. The elderly: A challenge to nursing. 4. Old people and sensory deprivation. Nurs. Times, 73: 1754, 1977.

Bruner, J. S. The cognitive consequences of early sensory deprivation. In Sensory Deprivation, P. Solomon, editor, p. 195. Harvard University Press, Cambridge, Mass., 1961.

Butler, R. A., and Harlow, H. F. Discrimination learning and learning sets to visual exploration incentives. J. Gen. Psychol., 57: 257, 1957.

Clark, B., and Graybiel, A. The break-off phenomenon: A feeling of separation from the earth experienced by pilots at high altitudes. J. Aviat. Med., 28: 121, 1957.

Cooper, G. D., Dickinson, J. R., Adams, H. B., and York, M. W. Interviewer's role-playing and responses to sensory deprivation: A clinical demonstration. Percept. Mot. Skills, 40: 291, 1975.

Downs, F. S. Bed rest and sensory disturbances. Am. J. Nurs., 74: 434, 1974.

Ellis, R. Unusual sensory and thought disturbances after cardiac surgery. Am. J. Nurs., 72: 2022, 1972.

Faubion, R. W., and Tinnan, L. M. Evaluation of Small Space Station Habitability: A Seven-Day Confinement Study. North American Aviation, Downey, Calif., 1963.

Ferrari, G. Pathology of sensory deprivation: Critical review. Riv. Sper. Freniatr., 95: 169, 1971.

Fiske, D. W., and Maddi, S. R., editors. Functions of Varied Experience. Dorsey Press, Homewood, Ill., 1961.

Freedman, D. A. Congenital and perinatal sensory deprivations: Their effect on the capacity to experience affect. Psychoanal. Q., 44: 62, 1975.

*Goldberger, L., and Holt, R. R. Experimental interference with reality contact:

Individual differences. In Sensory Deprivation, P. Solomon, editor, p. 130. Harvard University Press, Cambridge, Mass., 1961.

Hill, J. C., and Robinson, B. A case of retarded mental development associated with restricted movements in infancy. Br. J. Med. Psychol., 9: 268, 1929.

Hölscher, J. F. M. Effects of sensory deprivation on hostages, Ned. Tijdschr. Geneeskd., 120: 73, 1976.

Jackson, C. W., Jr., Pollard, J. C., and Kansky, E. W. The application of findings from experimental sensory deprivation to cases of clinical sensory deprivation. Am. J. Med. Sci, 243: 558, 1962.

Kammerman, M., editor Sensory Isolation and Personality Change, Charles C Thomas, Springfield, Ill., 1977.

Keep, P. J. Stimulus deprivation in windowless rooms. Anaesthesia, 32: 598, 1977.

Kempe, P., Schönberger, J., and Gross, J. Sensorische Deprivation als Methode in der Psychiatrie. Nervenarzt, 45: 561, 1974.

Kornfeld, D. S., Zimberg, S., and Malm, J. R. Psychiatric complications of open-heart surgery. N. Engl. J. Med., 273: 287, 1965.

*Kubie, L. Theoretical aspects of sensory deprivation. In Sensory Deprivation, P. Solomon, editor, p. 208. Harvard University Press, Cambridge, Mass., 1961.

Kubzansky, P. E., and Leiderman, P. H. Sensory deprivation: An overview. In Sensory Deprivation, P. Solomon, editor, p. 221. Harvard University Press, Cambridge, Mass., 1961.

Leiderman, H., Mendelson, J. H., Wexler, D., and Solomon, P. Sensory deprivation: Clinical aspects. Arch. Intern. Med., 101: 389, 1958.

Lilly, J. C. Mental effects of reduction of ordinary levels of physical stimuli on intact, healthy persons. Psychiatr. Res. Rep., 5: 1, 1956.

Lindemann, H. Alone at Sea. Random House, New York, 1958.

Lindsley, D. B. Common factors in sensory deprivation, sensory distortion, and sensory overload. In Sensory Deprivation, P. Solomon, editor, p. 174. Harvard University Press, Cambridge, Mass., 1961.

Maddi, S. R. Exploratory behavior and variation-seeking in man. In Functions of Varied Experience, D. W. Fiske and S. R. Maddi, editors, p. 253. Dorsey Press, Homewood, Ill., 1961.

Mandelbaum, D. G. Wolf-child histories from India. J. Soc. Psychol., 17: 25, 1943.

McClure, G., and Forgays, D. D. Human sex differences in extreme isolation. Percept. Mot. Skills, 40: 387, 1975.

McRae, R. I. Psychiatric reactions to eye surgery. J. Am. Osteopath. Assoc., 63: 1049, 1964.

Miyashiro, C. M., and Russell, D. L. Experimental participation as a source of stimulation in sensory and perceptive studies of stimulus-seeking behavior by introverts and extroverts. Percept. Mot. Skills, 38: 235, 1974.

Myers, T. I., Murphy, D. B., and Smith, S. The effect of sensory deprivation and social isolation on self-exposure to propaganda and attitude change. Am. Psychol., 18: 440, 1963.

Nardini, J. E., Herrmann, R. S., and Rasmussen, J. E. Navy psychiatric assessment program in the Antarctic. Am. J. Psychiatry, 119: 97, 1962.

Orne, M. T. On the social psychology of the psychological experiment with particular reference to demand characteristics and their implications. Am. Psychol., 17: 776, 1962.

Prioleau, W. H. Psychological considerations in patient isolation on a general surgical service. Am. Surg., 29: 907, 1963.

Rapaport, D. The theory of ego autonomy: A generalization. Bull. Menninger Clin., 22: 13, 1958.

Riesen, A. H. Stimulation as a requirement for growth and function in behavioral development. In Functions of Varied Experience, D. W. Fiske and S. R. Maddi, editors, p. 57. Dorsey Press, Homewood, Ill., 1961.

Rossi, A. M., and Solomon, P. Button pressing for a time-off reward during sensory deprivation: Effects of relatively comfortable and uncomfortable sessions. Percept. Mot. Skills, 19: 803, 1964.

Ruff, G. E., and Levy, E. Z. Psychiatric research in space medicine. Am. J. Psychiatry, 115: 793, 1959.

Schechter, M. D., Shurley, J. T., Sexaner, J. D., and Toussient, W. Perceptual isolation therapy: A new experimental approach in the treatment of children using infantile autistic defenses. J. Am. Acad. Child Psychiatry, 8: 97, 1969.

Schmale, A. The sensory deprivations: An approach to the study of the induction affects. J. Am. Psychoanal. Assoc., 22: 626, 1974.

Schroder, H. M., Driver, M. J., and Streufert, S. Human Information Processing. Holt, Rinehart, and Winston, New York, 1967.

Schultz, D. P. Sensory Restriction: Effects of Behavior. Academic Press, New York, 1965

Shurley, J. T. Profound experimental sensory isolation. Am. J. Psychiatry, 117: 539, 1960.

Shurley, J. T. Man on the South Polar Plateau. Arch. Intern. Med., 125: 625, 1970.

Smith, S., Myers, T. I., and Murphy, D. B. Conformity to a Group Norm as a Function of Sensory Deprivation and Social Isolation: Research Memorandum. U.S. Army Training Center, Monterey, Calif., 1963.

Solomon, P. Quantitative aspects in sensory deprivation. In The Psychodynamic Implications of Physiological Studies on Sensory Deprivation, L. Madow and I. H. Snow, editors, p. 28. Charles C Thomas, Springfield, Ill., 1970.

Solomon, P., Kubzansky, P. E., Leiderman, P. H., Mendelson, I. H., Trumbull, R., and Wexler, D., editors. Sensory Deprivation. Harvard University Press, Cambridge, Mass., 1961.

Solomon, P., Leiderman, P. H., Mendelson, J., and Wexler, D. Sensory deprivation: A review. Am. J. Psychiatry, *114:* 357, 1957.

*Solomon, P., and Rossi, A. M. Sensory deprivation. In *Modern Perspectives in World Psychiatry,* J. G. Howells, editor, p. 222. Oliver and Boyd, London, 1968.

Spitz, R. A. "Hospitalism": An inquiry into the genesis of psychiatric conditions in early childhood. Psychoanal. Study Child, *9:* 113, 1954.

Stonecypher, D. D. The cause and prevention of postoperative psychoses in the elderly. Am. J. Ophthalmol., *55:* 605, 1963.

Suedfeld, P. Theoretical formulations. In *Sensory Deprivation: Fifteen Years of Research,* Z. P. Zubek, editor, p. 433. Appleton-Century-Crofts, New York, 1969.

*Suedfeld, P. The benefits of boredom: Sensory deprivation reconsidered. Am. Sci., *63:* 60, 1975.

Suedfeld, P., and Ikard, F. F. Use of sensory deprivation in facilitating the reduction of cigarette smoking. J. Consult. Clin. Psychol., *42:* 888, 1974.

Sváb, I., and Gross, J. *Bibliography of Sensory Deprivation and Social Isolation,* ed. 2. Psychiatric Research Institute, Prague, 1966.

Swaffield, L. Behind the screens. Nurs. Times, *73:* 188, 1977.

Wasmuth, N. The value of experimental learning in long-term care education: Emphasis on simulated sensory deprivation in an institutional setting. Gerontologist, *15:* 548, 1975.

Weisman, A. D., and Hackett, P. Psychosis after eye surgery: Establishment of a specific doctor-patient relation in the prevention and treatment of "black-patch" delirium. N. Engl. J. Med., *258:* 1284, 1958.

*Wilson, L. M. Intensive care delirium: The effect of outside deprivation in a windowless unit. Arch. Intern. Med., *130:* 225, 1972.

Woods, N. F., and Falk, S. A. Noise stimuli in the acute care area. Nurs. Res., *23:* 144, 1974.

Zingg, R. M. More about the "baboon boy" of South Africa. Am. J. Psychol., *53:* 455, 1940.

*Zubek, J. P., editor. *Sensory Deprivation: Fifteen Years of Research.* Appleton-Century-Crofts, New York, 1969.

Zubek, J. P., and Wilgosh, L. Prolonged immobilization of the body: Changes in performance and the electroencephalogram. Science, *140:* 306, 1963.

6.6 Normality

DANIEL OFFER, M.D.
MELVIN SABSHIN, M.D.

Introduction

What constitutes mental health or normality has been a central issue in psychiatric theory and practice for decades. Impending national health policy decisions have made clarification and more open definitions of normality and mental health more essential than ever. There are new implications to accepting the classical definitions of mental health as the antonym of mental illness. With such an assumption, the absence of gross psychopathology is often equated with normal behavior. A number of recent policy trends have raised important questions about the usefulness of that assumption and have made it increasingly important for psychiatrists to become concerned with providing more precise concepts and definite definitions of mental health and normality.

Psychiatry still suffers from what Kaplan (1967) called "a trained incapacity." Trained to recognize the abnormal, the psychiatrist and his teacher have had difficulty in recognizing, let alone conceptualizing, normal behavior. Only recently has it been recognized that mental health has to be defined in positive terms. Writers on coping behavior, healthy defense mechanisms, and adaptation to life have made serious attempts to describe normal behavior with its own terminology.

Psychiatrists now realize that the best way to further enrich the theoretical understanding of what constitutes mental health and normality is to study a variety of different groups of mentally healthy populations. Various approaches, using similar methods when studying psychiatrically disturbed populations, would enhance the understanding of why some people can cope with their internal and external worlds and others can not.

Four Perspectives of Normality

Although each of the four functional perspectives of normality discussed below is unique and has its own definition, description, and problems, the perspectives complement each other; together they represent the total behavioral and social science approach to normality (Offer and Sabshin, 1974). The perspective of normality that an investigator subscribes to obviously influences the kind of population he chooses to study as normal or mentally healthy. Similarly, the perspectives of normality and what is meant by mental health and mental illness have serious implications for national mental health policies.

NORMALITY AS HEALTH

The first perspective is basically the traditional medical approach to health and illness. Most physicians equate normality with health and view health as an almost universal phenomenon. As a result, behavior is assumed to be within normal limits when no manifest psychopathology is present. If one were to put all behavior on a continuum, normality would encompass the major portion of the continuum, and abnormality would be the small remainder. That definition of normality correlates with the traditional role model of the doctor who attempts to free his patient from grossly observable signs of illness. To the physician, the lack of pathological signs or symptoms indicates health. In other words, health in this context refers to a reasonable, rather than an optimal, state of functioning. In its purest form, this perspective is illustrated by Romano (1950), Ludwig (1975), and Robins (1978). Ludwig stated:

> Mental illness [is] defined as any debilitating, cognitive-affective behavior disorder due primarily to known, suggestive, or presumed biological dysfunctions, either biochemical or neurophysiological in nature.

Disease, according to Ludwig, is sufficient deviation from the normal. Ludwig clearly subscribed to the normality-as-health perspective. That perspective on normality is at the heart of much of the debate concerning mental health policies. The medical model that subscribes to the alleviation of gross signs and symptoms is strongly advocated by many third-party payers. It is a condition that is easy to define reliably, and its limits are relatively clear.

NORMALITY AS UTOPIA

The second perspective conceives of normality as a matrix of highly integrated functions. It blends the diverse elements of mental (ego) function into idealized or optimal functioning. Such a definition often emerges when psychiatrists or psychoanalysts talk about mental health or when they grapple with the complex problem of defining criteria of successful treatment. The approach can be dated back to Freud (1937), who stated:

> A normal ego is like normality in general, an ideal fiction.

That approach is characteristic of a significant segment of psychoanalysts, but it is by no means limited to them. It can also be found among psychotherapists of quite different persuasions—for example, Rogers (1959).

The perspective of normality as Utopia is one of the specters of national health policymakers. They are afraid, without directly expressing it, that it is the perspective commonly adhered to by almost all psychiatrists and mental health specialists. Although many psychotherapists believe that the alleviating of signs and symptoms is only the first step in intensive, long-term individual psychotherapy, there is considerable debate within the mental health professions about whether helping people to become happier with themselves is a process that any insurance program should reasonably be expected to cover. Helping people achieve their potential is a laudable goal. It is also highly value laden and culture bound and seems to have almost no limits, hence, it is characterized in such terms as Utopian. Each culture has its norms and, hence, its ideals. The concept of normality as Utopia is, therefore, also related to the values of a particular culture.

NORMALITY AS AVERAGE

The third perspective is commonly used in normative studies of behavior and is based on the mathematical principle of the bell-shaped curve. This approach, when applied to psychological testing, conceives of the middle range as normal and of both extremes as deviant. One has either too many associations to the Rorschach Test or too few associations. Only the right number, in the middle range, is defined as normal. The normative approach based on that statistical principle describes each person in terms of general assessment and total score. Variability is described only within the context of groups and not within the context of one person. Although that approach is more often used in psychology and biology than in psychiatry, psychiatrists have also used the perspective in a number of projects. That approach to normality also has empirical implications in the understanding of people's behavior. Gross averages of behaviors in response to a variety of situations can be constructed. In addition, in developing model personalities for different societies, one assumes that the typologies of character can be statistically measured.

It is that perspective of normality that is often used by certain critics of psychiatry and the mental health professions. One could conclude from the above that, if to be normal is to behave like the majority of people within one's culture, then conformity becomes an ideal toward which one should strive. After all, both extremes of behavior or psychological responses are termed deviant. It also seems to suggest the labeling role that psychiatrists have undertaken at times. For example, if in a school setting a particular child behaves differently from the other children, he is often singled out by his teacher and, if the school has a mental health consultant, is sent to the school psychologist or psychiatrist for observation. The child may not have any signs and symptoms of mental illness; he may even feel well; but his behavior is different from that of the average child, and so he is seen as not normal.

That approach has direct implications in an illness such as manic-depressive disorder. Both extremes are obviously deviant. The difficult conceptual and practical problem is deciding exactly where the average or norm ends and where deviancy or psychopathology begins.

NORMALITY AS TRANSACTIONAL SYSTEMS

The fourth perspective stresses that normal behavior is the result of interacting systems over time. Temporal changes are essential to that definition of normality. In other words, the normality-as-transactional-systems perspective stresses changes or processes, rather than a cross-sectional definition of normality, which is characteristic of each of the other three perspectives. One cannot understand normality as transactional systems without tracing a full range of variables and factors back developmentally through time. Each of the three systems—biological, psychological, and social—feeds factors into it; each of the other three perspectives is part of the totality of the perspective.

Investigators who subscribe to that approach can be found in all behavioral and social sciences. Most typical are Grinker (1956) and Engel (1977), whose thesis of a unified theory of behavior encompasses polarities within a wide range of integration. The interest in general system theory (Von Bertalanffy, 1968; Gray et al., 1969) has further stressed the general applicability of general system research for psychiatry. Normality as transactional systems encompasses variables from all fields, all contributing to the functioning of a viable system over time. The integration of the variables into the final common pathway and the loading or significance assigned to each variable will have to be more thoroughly explored in the future.

From a scientific point of view, this perspective, although theoretically not as well thought through and conceptualized as the other three, is probably the soundest. It encompasses not only developmental issues in the biological, psychological, and social fields but also economics, political science, and the culture of health and illness. If the psychiatrist and his physician colleagues in the year 2080 will, indeed, be systematists, it will dramatically change the nature of medical practice and of health policies.

Research on Normal Behavior

Research on normal or nonpatient populations is of ancient origin and has been the province of many disciplines. Philosophers have been concerned with the functioning, behavior, feelings, and fantasies of the average or normal person. Anthropologists have been observing cultures other than their own for the past century. Social psychologists and child psychologists have worked with normal people in experimental and testing situations ever since psychology began functioning as a scientific discipline (Hall, 1906). Psychoanalysts, although primarily studying patients who come to see them in psychoanalytic therapy, have extended their theories to include concepts applicable to personality development in normal children and adults (A. Freud, 1936). Psychiatric and clinical studies of normal populations have been undertaken during the past two decades. What have been lacking in all the disciplines, however, are enough systematic studies by longitudinal and follow-up investigations of normal populations. The clinicians' experience and abilities need to be integrated with the researchers' skills and methods (Offer et al., 1972).

Two influential and typical works on normal behavior published after World War II were Grinker and Spiegel's (1945) *Men under Stress* and White's (1952) *Lives in Progress.* Both studies concentrated on coping mechanisms of nonpatient or normal populations but from different vantage points. Grinker and Spiegel studied the behavior and psychological functioning of soldiers under combat conditions. They were interested in finding out what can be learned from the way people cope with stress. On the other hand, White was interested in normal development. By following the lives of a selected group of college students with interviews, White was able to assess their adaptation to different normative crises that are part of everyday life. He studied how they coped with their internal and external environments and their over-all psychological competence. Like other brilliant innovative work, both pioneering studies raised a host of methodological problems, but they laid the groundwork for the more solid empirical work that followed.

The understanding of normal personality functioning and development must include studies of the behavior of normal or nonpatient populations. For too long behavioral scientists have extrapolated theories of normal development from studies of patients or deviant populations. That situation has changed in the recent past with the appearance of a host of psychiatric and clinical studies of nonpatient and normal populations (Grinker et al., 1962; Heath, 1965; Cox, 1970; Westley and Epstein, 1970; Block, 1971; King, 1971; Smith, 1972; Offer and Offer, 1975; Vaillant, 1977; Levinson, 1978).

Those studies helped behavioral scientists understand the complexities of the psychology and behavior of people without concentrating, as in the past, on populations of patients. They shifted the focus away from medical interest and concern with disease, maladaptation, and psychopathology. They showed that, in order to know more about problems in living, one needs to study well-adjusted persons in depth to better understand what went right. However, a few words of caution: Almost all the studies conducted in the past used middle-class and upper middle-class populations. There were comparatively few studies of normal minority-group populations and especially few longitudinal studies of normal minority-group populations. The danger is obvious. There may be a tendency to use the middle-class, white male as a model. There is an urgent need to study other nonpatient populations in order to broaden the understanding of the vicissitudes of normality and health. Adelson (1979) stated that, in editing *Handbook of Adolescent Development,* he asked that a chapter be written on the developmental psychology of adolescent girls. The invited author, after carefully studying the available data, stated that not enough data were available to justify writing the chapter. Obviously, a great need exists to study the normal development of persons other than white middle-class males.

CROSS-SECTIONAL STUDIES

It is relatively easy to undertake this kind of normative study. One can obtain reliable information concerning a limited number of behavioral variables. Most of those studies subscribe to the normality-as-average perspective. Relatively more studies use the cross-sectional approach than any other method. Two studies, one by Grinker et al. (1962) and another by Holmstrom (1972), typify the methods and the findings obtained from cross-sectional studies. Although the results from those studies have significantly enriched the understanding of normality and mental health, one major limitation has been the difficulty in obtaining reliable and valid data regarding background factors leading to the behavior described in the cross-sectional studies. One often wonders whether those young people will, indeed, stay mentally healthy in the future, or does their future mental health depend on their environment's staying the same? To answer those questions, one must understand longitudinal studies and undertake predictive studies.

LONGITUDINAL STUDIES

By definition, these investigations cover at least two different points in time. There have been a number of longitudinal studies on normal behavior. Those studies have presented valuable knowledge. One uses the data from a longitudinal study to find out which variables from year 1 of the study best predicted the behavior of the subjects in year 2, 3, or 10. Some valuable information has been obtained using the technique (Offer and Offer, 1975; Livson and Day, 1977; Vaillant, 1977). In the future, data from predictive studies will enrich the knowledge of human behavior.

The key finding in all the studies was the stability of psychological functioning over time. In many ways the studies confirmed the validity of the cross-sectional studies. They leave unanswered the question: How does this process take place? Does the process hinge on environments' staying stable, with social conditions relatively unchanged, or does it depend on biopsychological variables? More specific micropsychological analyses of behavior and feeling states of persons across time are necessary before one can begin to answer those perplexing questions. Longitudinal studies bring behavioral scientists one step closer to answering those questions, but the answers they provide are by no means definitive.

The study of normal adolescent boys (Offer, 1973; Offer and Offer, 1975) highlights some of the problems and the advantages of engaging in longitudinal studies. In that research program, the investigators use the normality-as-average perspective as the basis for their selection of the subjects. That process did, indeed, leave them with a middle-range group to study. The study itself used both the normality-as-health perspective and the normality-as-transactional-systems perspective. Offer studied overt behavioral phenomena and the interrelationships between the interpersonal, intrapsychic, and behavioral variables. Since Offer studied his subjects for 8 years, he also observed them temporally. The three groups described below were empirically derived by factor-and-cluster analysis. The boys were selected from among the incoming male freshmen in two suburban high schools near Chicago. One-third of those tested were selected and asked to participate in the study. The authors do not mean to imply that the other two-thirds were abnormal. The researchers' goal was to study one average group without implying pathology in the rest of the population. The boys were selected by using the normality-as-average perspective as one theoretical guide. The generalizations made from the study are, therefore, applicable to one-third of a number of middle-class, suburban male adolescents. Like King (1971), Block (1971), and Vaillant (1977), Offer demonstrated that, among a group of boys who were relatively uniform biologically and socially, one can decipher three psychologically distinct growth patterns—continuous growth, surgent growth, and tumultuous growth.

Continuous growth. Some boys had strong egos and were able to cope well with internal and external environments. They had active fantasy lives and the ability to postpone gratification. They accepted general cultural norms. Throughout the 8 years of the study, there was mutual respect, trust, and affection between the generations. They had no serious superego problems, and they developed meaningful ego ideals. When an external stress occurred, they used the defenses of denial and isolation to cope with the initial affect. By and large, their techniques of coping with situational stresses, such as moving to another city, and with developmental stresses, such as leaving home after graduating from high school, were handled without significant external signs of turmoil. Of the study population, 23 per cent belonged to this category. A question that needs to be raised here is: Will this group of young men continue with their continuous-growth pattern, even in a markedly changed environment?

Surgent growth. The surgent-growth group, although functioning as adaptively as the first group, was characterized by important enough differences in ego structure, in background, and in family environment to present a different cluster and be defined as a different group.

Developmental spurts were illustrative of the pattern of growth of the surgent-growth group. They differed from the continuous-growth group in the amount of emotional conflict experienced and in their patterns of resolving conflicts. There was more concentrated energy directed toward mastering developmental tasks than was obvious for members of the continuous-growth group. At times, surgent-growth boys were adjusting very well, integrating their experiences, and moving ahead; at other times, they seemed to be stuck at an almost premature closure and unable to move forward. A cycle of progression and regression is more typical of this group than of the continuous-growth group. The defenses used, anger and projection, represent more psychopathology than do the defenses used by the first group.

Some in the surgent-growth group were not able to cope smoothly with unexpected stress. Unlike the first group, they showed a slight tendency to use the defenses of projection, anger, and depression when things did not turn out well. In general, they were less introspective than either the first group or the third group. Relationships with their parents were not smooth. The mothers had difficulty in separating from their children. Neither the first group nor the second group had any observable identity crises in the usual Eriksonian sense, although they may have experienced a silent identity crisis (Erikson, 1968). One of the main differences between this group and the third group was that the periods of regression were circumscribed, both temporarily and psychologically, in the second group. Of the adolescent population 35 per cent belonged to this group.

Tumultuous growth. Some boys reacted to internal and external stresses as if they were major tragic events. They had a tendency to display the affects of anxiety, depression, and emotional turmoil. They were, in general, mistrustful of others. They were highly sensitive and introspective persons. One-third of this group had received psychotherapy or counseling. Separation was painful to their parents, who were unsure of their own value systems. Members of this group resembled the neurotic adolescents treated in outpatient clinics. Of the adolescent population, 21 per cent belonged in this category. Another 21 per cent had mixed scores (Offer and Offer, 1975).

Although the above examples focus on adolescent and young adult growth and development, longitudinal studies can obviously be undertaken at any stage of the life cycle. The major findings suggest that stability, rather than change, involves successive adaptation throughout the life cycle. That is not to say that people do not change as they grow older. However, the coping styles and psychological reactions in the different stages of development are similar. If a woman had a tumultuous adolescence, she is more likely to have a tumultuous menopause than are others who reacted differently in adolescence. That is true if one assumes relative constancy in the environmental variables—which, of course, is highly problematic. It stresses that the continuity model of development depends to a large extent on a stable environment. It is through predictive studies that one can better understand those interactions between nature and nurture.

PREDICTIVE STUDIES

Predictive studies are undertaken because, although one may know the questions that need to be asked, one does not know which variables need to be studied or how to conceptualize the problems well enough. The studies are also empirically time consuming to undertake because of the expense, commitment, and time involved. Such studies are particularly difficult to start because it is almost impossible to know which intervening variables will have the most influence on the functioning of persons in the future. At times, the intervening variables are not even in existence when the study begins; for example, the women's liberation movement has had an impact on the behavior and psychology of a segment of young adult women in the United States (Chesler, 1972).

Predictive studies are impressive if the predictions are borne out, despite the difficulties. Predictive studies of normal populations are nonexistent. However, there are some examples of short-term predictive studies on populations at risk, such as the parents of leukemic children (Futterman and Hoffman, 1973). Those successful predictions were made on selected individual cases. Ultimately, predictive studies will probably not be able to predict how persons cope under a variety of stressful and everyday life situations. The fact that many intrapsychic, interpersonal, and environmental factors and their interrelationships are involved makes it exceedingly difficult to undertake such a project. At this time, one can use retrospective studies for the purpose of separating crucial from noncrucial variables and identifying those variables with potential predictive power.

The better the empirical base, the more impact the findings will have on national health policy matters. Among potential services of information, predictive studies will supply the more exact data needed.

Health Policy and the Definition of Normality

The *Report to the President* by the President's Commission on Mental Health (1978) dramatically pointed to the importance of clearly defining what one means by mental illness and mental health. The report referred to "emotional disorder," "mental disorder," "psychiatric disorder," and "psychological distress" without stating the differences between those categories. Does that mean that those categories are all the same—interchangeable? That lack of clarity was also evident when the commission commented on what they meant by mental health. The report stated that 10 per cent of the population need some form of mental health services. That figure is currently used by some federal agencies in their assessments of what mental illness actually costs in terms of services and personnel. It is the base rate. Subsequently, it was stated that 15 per cent of the population carry diagnoses of mental disorder. In other words, 5 per cent should receive care but currently do not. Finally, it was stated that 25 per cent of the population are estimated to suffer from mild to moderate depression, anxiety, and other indicators of emotional disorders. Those additional 10 per cent, added to the baseline 15 per cent, are obtaining counseling from a variety of sources—marriage counselors, ministers, teachers, friends. That gray area is hard to define. Do the commissioners who wrote the report imply that those 10 per cent are not really mentally ill but suffer from transient disorders? Can moderate depression, if not attended to, become severe depression, which can even lead to suicide? The figure of 25 per cent was, according to the report, an estimate. Was the figure based on solid, sophisticated, epidemiological studies with follow-up information? The authors believe that it was, at best, an estimate, based on cross-sectional, pencil-and-paper survey studies. Those epidemiological studies have at their foundation the normality-as-health perspective. In other words, they set out to discover how many people suffer from mental illness after they had defined mental illness only in gross symptomatological terms. They did not deal with the gray areas, the boundaries between mental health and mental illness. The commissioners did not state who will decide when a person is suffering from mild to moderate anxiety or depression; nor did they state how to define emotional distress that does not fit conventional diagnoses.

The conceptual problems that arise when one attempts to distinguish between mental health and mental illness have major theoretical and scientific importance. They also have enormous significance for the economics of mental illness. Nowhere is that better illustrated than when national health insurance coverage for mental illness is discussed.

In the President's Commission on Mental Health report, it was suggested that there should be parity for psychiatric illness: Psychiatric illness should be treated the same way medical illness is treated. That sounds good and means that more psychiatric illness will be covered by insurance programs. The commission recognized the size of the problem; they were, of course, not expected to solve it. Although, in general, they made major strides forward, they left the central question: Who is going to decide when a disturbance or an illness is a disease? All the above seems to strongly suggest that, unless both mental health and mental illness are clearly defined, there will be a weakness in making fundamental health-problem decisions.

When one examines the current practices that insurance companies use on the national level in their reimbursement policies, one finds that the problems are numerous. No uniform policy states that a certain disease, problem, or disturbance is to be reimbursed when the coverage is identical. Recently, in Illinois, Blue Cross disallowed psychiatric hospitalization after the patient had been discharged because, the Blue Cross officials stated (Health Care Services Corporation Policy Rider CA-019-HCSC12, 1977),

> although the hospitalization was indicated for psychological, educational, and social reasons, we felt that medically it was not indicated and therefore it was not covered by medical insurance.

The insurance company in that case made a decision about what was medically indicated. A step back, they made a decision about what medical illness is or, in this case, what a psychiatric illness is. If their definition of a psychiatric illness does not coincide with the physician or the psychiatrist, who admits the patient, then their word is the last word, which in this case meant financial support for the medical-psychiatric care of the patient. The insurance companies and, ultimately, national health insurance programs want to help pay for the legitimate care of mentally ill patients. But they, like the presidential commission, are concerned that, if the definition of mental illness is too broad—such as "unhappiness" or "not living up to one's potential"—it will be financially impossible for any program to support such benefits.

The medical physician and the psychiatrist have been given the legal responsibility in diagnosing both health and illness. But neither has been given the right to determine what illness or problem is reimbursable. The length of a hospital stay is determined by an insurance company. What procedure is to be covered is often hotly debated in all branches of medicine.

It is little wonder, then, that the insurance companies have commented on the fact that psychiatrists cannot agree on what is a mental disease and what is mental health. The disagreements as to who should receive treatment for what is a direct consequence of that problem.

Because of the problems enumerated above, insurance companies—which are, after all, in the business of making money—have at times made unilateral decisions. The importance of establishing peer-review guidelines is very important. However, if the questions of what constitutes mental illness and who should be allowed to make that diagnosis are answered, the question will still remain: When is a patient mentally healthy? Is it when his overt signs and symptoms are under control? When his behavior is no longer disruptive? When he can function again in the community? When he can reasonably cope with his life situation? Or when he has become a relatively happy human being? Psychiatrists have not paid enough scientific attention to the question of what constitutes normality for a person within his own personal, familial, social, and cultural setting. Insurance companies have to worry about the costs of any particular program. From their point of view, a program has to be manageable, its outcome predictable, and its costs controllable in order for the program to work. The people in charge of insurance companies are afraid that the definitions of mental illness will become so broad that the companies will not be able to contain the costs. Ultimately, coverage will be better if there is agreement on the boundaries between health and illness.

For the above reasons, private and governmental insurance plans always opt for the more limited definition of normality—normality as health. Mental health is freedom from overt signs and symptoms. Mental illness is having gross observable problems. According to that theory, once the symptoms disappear, the patient is cured or should no longer be covered by insurance. According to that approach, it is difficult to conceptualize the treatment of underlying conditions that may lead more often than not to a recurrence of the signs and symptoms. One of the dangers of that limitation is that it will have a retrogressive effect and will lead to discrimination against those persons who are not hospitalized but are treated entirely on an ambulatory basis.

Where should one draw the line? Most psychiatrists recognize the fact that private and national health insurance programs cannot possibly cover all persons who receive counseling or treatment in order to optimize their capacity to work, love, and play. The normality-as-Utopia perspective would be inconsistent with any national health insurance program in any country. Those who take a normality-as-Utopia perspective have not proposed reasonable compromises. How to agree on what is mental health and mental illness is, therefore, still a major issue in psychiatry (Drucker, 1978).

Conclusion

It is incumbent on the psychiatrist to understand the implications of the four concepts of normality. Those four perspectives—normality as health, normality as Utopia, normality as average, and normality as transactional systems—are not mutually exclusive. They are also not independent of one another. There are, however, important differences among them, so that it becomes crucial for the psychiatrist to know which concept he uses in his research. Results must be interpreted differently if the basic premises of mental health are different. Most important, in the area of national health policy, a clear understanding of what constitutes mental health and mental illness has far-reaching consequences.

There has been a considerable increase recently in discussions and research on the concepts of normality. In debates on policy issues stemming from the President's Commission on Mental Health, and on proposed national health insurance programs, still greater attention needs to be paid to the issue: What can be done to better understand psychiatric disturbances? In the long run, greater clarification of the definitions and concepts of normality will lead to better solutions of national health policy problems.

Suggested Cross References

Nosology and the new official psychiatric nomenclature are discussed in Section 14.1. Normal child development is discussed in Section 34.2 and normal adolescent development in Section 34.3. Definitions of mental health and mental disease are discussed in Section 45.2. Contemporary comments relevant to mental health are presented in Section 56.4. Health insurance and psychiatric care are discussed in Section 56.10. Peer review is discussed in Section 56.20. General living systems theory is discussed in Section 1.2, and personality theory derived from quantitative experiments is discussed in Section 11.1. The women's movement is discussed in Section 56.8.

REFERENCES

Adelson, J., editor. *Handbook of Adolescent Development*. John Wiley & Sons, New York, 1979.

*Block, J. *Lives through Time*. Bancroft, Berkeley, Calif., 1971.

Chesler, P. *Women and Madness*. Doubleday, New York, 1972.

Cox, R. D. *Youth into Maturity*. Mental Health Materials Center, New York, 1970.

Drucker, P. F. The future shape of health care. Wall St. J., 15, July 19, 1978.

Engel, G. The need for a new medical model: A challenge for biomedicine. Science, *196*: 129, 1977.

Erikson, E. H. *Identity: Youth and Crisis*. W. W. Norton, New York, 1968.

Freud, A. *The Ego and the Mechanism of Defense*. International Universities Press, New York, 1936.

Freud, S. Analysis terminable and interminable (1937). In *Standard Edition of the Complete Psychological Works of Sigmund Freud*, vol. 23, Hogarth Press, London, 1964.

Futterman, E., and Hoffman, I. Crisis and adaptation in the families of fatally ill children. In *The Child and His Family*, E. J. Anthony and C. Koupernick, editors, vol. 2, p. 127. John Wiley & Sons, New York, 1973.

Gray, W., Duhl, F. J., and Rizzo, N. D. *General Systems Theory and Psychiatry*. Little, Brown, and Co., Boston, 1969.

Grinker, R. R., Sr. *Towards a Unified Theory of Human Behavior*. Basic Books, New York, 1956.

*Grinker, R. R., Sr., Grinker, R. R., Jr., and Timberlake, J. A study of "mentally healthy" young males (homoclites). Arch. Gen. Psychiatry, *6*: 405, 1962.

Grinker, R. R., and Spiegel, J. *Men under Stress*. Blakiston, Philadelphia, 1945.

Hall, S. *Adolescence: Its Psychology and Its Relation to Physiology, Anthropology, Sociology, Sex, Crime, Religion, and Education*. Appleton, New York, 1906.

Heath, D. H. *Exploration of Maturity*. Appleton-Century-Crofts, New York, 1965.

Holmstrom, R. On the picture of mental health. Acta Psychiatr. Scand., *231*: 1, 1972.

Kaplan, A. A philosophical discussion of normality. Arch. Gen. Psychiatry, *17*: 325, 1967.

King, S. H. Coping mechanisms in adolescents. Psychiatr. Ann., *1*: 10, 1971.

Levinson, D. J. *The Seasons of a Man's Life*. Alfred A. Knopf, New York, 1978.

Livson, N., and Day, D. Adolescent personality antecedents of completed family size: A longitudinal study. J. Youth Adol., *6*: 311, 1977.

Ludwig, A. M. The psychiatrist as physician. J. A. M. A. *234*: 603, 1975.

Offer, D. *The Psychological World of the Teen-ager: A Study of Normal Adolescent Boys*. Basic Books, New York, 1973.

Offer, D., Freedman, D. X., and Offer, J. B. The psychiatrist as researcher. In *Modern Psychiatry and Clinical Research*, D. Offer and D. X. Freedman, editors, p. 208. Basic Books, New York, 1972.

Offer, D., and Offer, J. B. *From Teenage to Young Manhood: A Psychological Study*. Basic Books, New York, 1975.

*Offer, D., and Sabshin, M. *Normality: Theoretical and Clinical Concepts of Mental Health*, ed. 2. Basic Books, New York, 1974.

President's Commission on Mental Health. *Report to the President*. United States Government Printing Office, Washington, D. C., 1978.

Robins, L. N. Psychiatric epidemiology. Arch. Gen. Psychiatry, *35*: 697, 1978.

Rogers, C. R. A theory of therapy, personality, and interpersonal relationships as developed in client-centered framework. In *Psychology: A Study of a Science*, S. Koch, editor, vol. 3, p. 184. McGraw-Hill, New York, 1959.

Romano, J. Basic orientation and education of the medical student. J. A. M. A. *194*: 409, 1950.

*Smith, M. B. Normality: For an abnormal age. In *Modern Psychiatry and Clinical Research*, D. Offer and D. X. Freedman, editors, p. 102. Basic Books, New York, 1972.

*Vaillant, G. E. *Adaptation to Life*. Little, Brown, and Co., Boston, 1977.

Von Bertalanffy, L. *General Systems Theory*. Braziller, New York, 1968.

Westley, W. A., and Epstein, N. B. *The Silent Majority*. Jossey-Bass, San Francisco, 1970.

*White, R. W. *Lives in Progress*. Dryden, New York, 1952.

chapter

7

Application of Statistics to Psychiatry

ANITA K. BAHN, M.D., Sc.D.

Introduction

Statistics is a basic tool in the scientific method in epidemiological and clinical investigation—both observational and experimental. The interface of statistics with psychiatry not only is concerned with tests of significance but involves all aspects of data collection and analysis. This chapter is intended both as an aid in the understanding of psychiatric research literature and as an elementary approach to the conduct of a research study. It provides an introductory overview of the following topics: methods of data collection, sampling, reduction (summarization) of data in the description of a population or sample of individuals, inference (generalization) from sample results, association of variables, evaluation of cause and effect, design of experiments, measures of disease frequency, and analysis of the fate of cohorts of patients.

Data Collection

In psychiatry, as in other fields, statistical aspects of a study must be considered in the early planning stages in order to (1) sharpen the question that the study is designed to answer; (2) appraise whether the question can be answered practically by valid and reliable data; (3) clarify the unit of population to be studied; (4) select the relevant aspects about the groups on which data should be sought; (5) help delineate the data essential for the objectives of the study; and (6) prepare an outline of the proposed tabulations of the data and of the methods of analysis to assure that the end result will be satisfactory.

The importance of clarifying the questions and of choosing the appropriate study groups and methods cannot be overemphasized. For example, an inappropriate study design would be the selection of a 1-day census of patients to answer questions about rates of psychiatric admission, length of stay, and probability of discharge. A cohort (group) of admitted patients with a high rate of turnover would be underrepresented in the patient census, and a cohort with a low rate of turnover would be overrepresented. Therefore, it is necessary to study cohorts of admissions for correct conclusions.

INSTRUMENTS AND METHODS

The instruments and methods of data collection require careful attention. Like the sphygmomanometer, the questionnaire and interviewing techniques must be standardized. For example, to the extent possible, open-ended questions should be replaced by categorical, objective choices, so as to assure precise, valid data.

Precision (reliability) is concerned with the repeatability or consistency of data. Validity, on the other hand, is directed to the question: Are the data measuring what is intended to be measured? For example, one may wish to record actual behavior but measure, instead, attitudes or anticipated behavior. Validity is also concerned with whether the instruments are measuring accurately and without bias.

Bias may be defined as systematic error—that is, the difference between the true value and the value obtained through data collection attributable to all causes other than sampling error or variability. Bias may enter the data through the manner in which the question is asked, by a leading question or tone of voice that prejudices the response consciously or unconsciously. Data relating to emotionally charged or stigmatized areas—such as previous mental illness, sexual activity, alcohol abuse, and income—are notoriously lacking in validity.

Bias enters not only in how the question is asked but also in how the response is judged. For example, in clinical trials, it is important to employ, wherever possible, double-blind techniques in which neither the patient nor the interviewer knows who has received the treatment and who has received the placebo in order to minimize conscious and unconscious influences. Standardized methods of asking the question and of probing for further information, categorical rather than open-ended questions, clear definitions of terms and of end points, and adequate training and supervision of interviewers with frequent checks on interviewer variation all help to reduce interobserver error and bias and to improve the quality of the data. A pilot study or trial run is a sine qua non for solving unforeseen difficulties before the data are amassed.

Bias may also enter the study through problems of recall. In retrospective studies, for example, patients and controls are compared as to antecedent events that may be of etiological significance in the development of the disease. A major difficulty is that the patients, under the influence or knowledge of their illness, may recall past events differently from the controls. Such bias is eliminated in prospective studies, where persons are followed over time to observe the differential risk of developing the disease. Here, the pertinent information as to the suspected risk factor is elicited at the start of the study before the subjects become differentiated into sick and not sick.

Bias also arises from nonresponse, inasmuch as nonrespondents may differ in health and other characteristics from those who do respond or can be readily traced. If a person randomly selected for study is not at home, the investigator cannot substitute the next-door neighbor but must make repeated recalls on the selected person. Similarly, educational efforts, mobile examining units, and various inducements may be necessary to elicit needed information from respondents who do not cooperate in replying to questions, who fail to come for examination, or who are lost to follow-up in a prospective (longitudinal) study. When the nonresponse rate is high, the entire study may be invalidated.

Another aspect of validity is the sensitivity and specificity of screening tests and procedures for detecting a disease or condition in the general population. A highly sensitive test is one that, when applied to a group, identifies as positive a large proportion of those with the disease; relatively few with the disease are labeled as not having the disease (false negatives). A highly specific test is one that identifies as negative a large proportion of those without the disease; relatively few without the disease are labeled as having the disease (false positives). These two characteristics of tests, sensitivity and specificity, are inversely related. Setting the cut-off point between normal and abnormal so as to increase the sensitivity of a test automatically decreases its specificity and vice versa. The test objectives and practical considerations, such as the cost of following suspected cases to confirm the diagnosis, determine the operational end points or definitions of normality.

In planning a community screening program for a genetic form of mental retardation, the prevalence of the condition in the population must be considered. If the condition is rare, then even with tests of high sensitivity and high specificity: (1) the yield of cases will be small; (2) a large number of false positives will result and a positive test will have a low predictive value. For these reasons, mass screening programs are directed toward high prevalence groups.

SELECTION OF SUBJECTS

A critical decision is the choice of the universe (population) appropriate for study. The selective factors that influence the admission of patients to a hospital reflect both societal forces (such as admission policies, geographic and referral patterns) and patient-determined forces (such as acceptance of care). Therefore, the patients in any one hospital are rarely representative of all such patients in the community. If it is appropriate to limit the study to hospitalized patients, the selection of study patients from all the hospitals in a defined area tends to reduce bias.

Additional bias or nonrandom selection enters into autopsy cases; conclusions based on autopsy series are suspect. Under some circumstances, however, autopsies can provide clues for further investigation.

After the universe or sampling frame of subjects is determined, a random sample may be selected from it. Random selection avoids personal prejudice, such as selecting the thickest or thinnest case folders from the file or the most attractive patients. A foolproof system (simple random sampling) is to number each case folder in sequence and then select a sample by use of a table of random numbers (see Table I).

Alternately, the terminal digit of the previously assigned case numbers may be used for selection, such as every case number ending in 3. This method is called systematic sampling. It is unbiased if the case numbers had been assigned sequentially to patients in turn, if the terminal digit bears no special significance (such as indicating that the patient is a child or his mother), and if there is no periodicity to the way patients turned up. Sampling on the basis of surname (alphabetical sampling) must be avoided, because surnames are highly correlated with ethnicity.

When the population is very heterogeneous—that is, when persons differ markedly from each other with respect to the characteristics being studied—the investigator may wish to stratify them into subgroups, such as short-term and long-term clinic cases, and sample from each stratum or subgroup separately. Stratified sampling assures that each subgroup is represented in the sample, thus tending to reduce sampling error.

Other types of sampling, such as multistage sampling and area sampling, can be employed to reduce travel costs or to increase efficiency.

In simple random sampling, all persons in the population have the same probability of selection. However, the investigator may choose to sample from different strata or subgroups at different sampling fractions (probabilities). In preparing the total estimates, he then compensates for these unequal probabilities by weighting the sample data inversely to the sampling fraction.

Before embarking on a survey, the investigator should estimate the minimum size of the sample needed to answer the question with a specified degree of precision or sampling error. He may find that a survey to detect a rare psychiatric disease or to estimate a population value requires an impractically large number of interviews.

Descriptive Statistics

After the data are collected, they must be summarized or reduced into a manageable and easily comprehended form. Tabulating devices varying in complexity from simple index cards to key-sort cards, electrical sorters and tabulators, and electronic machines (computers) are used, depending on the amount and complexity of the data and the analyses.

QUALITATIVE VERSUS QUANTITATIVE DATA

It is of help in discussing both descriptive and inferential statistics to classify data into two major types: qualitative and quantitative. Qualitative data deal with enumerative or categorical data, data that are readily divided into discrete groups or categories, such as those with or without a certain characteristic. Data of this type include "yes" or "no" responses, categories of "improved" or "not improved," and classification by sex. The data may be binomially distributed, consisting of only two categories, as in the above examples, or multinomially distributed, consisting of more than two categories, such as data collected in the form "improved," or "no change," or "condition worse." The hallmark of qualitative data is that the population is divisible into discrete categories.

In quantitative data, also referred to as measurement data, the data are usually continuous. That is, depending on the fineness of the calibrating instruments, there are an infinite number of points in the measurement of blood pressure, height, weight, hormone output; and so on. Occasionally, the data are discrete. The number of teeth is an example of a discrete quantitative variable.

Measurement data, however, can be condensed into qualitative (categorical) form. For example, in an ecological study of mental illness in Baltimore, census tracts were ranked into quartiles (categories) on a number of variables, such as psychiatric admission rate and median rent (see Table V).

It is simpler to describe distributions of qualitative data than of quantitative data. For example, a binomial population can be completely described by only one parameter. That parameter would be the proportion (p) with a certain attribute. The proportion (q) without that attribute is always ($1 - p$) (see Figure 1).

Populations of quantitative data, on the other hand, may assume any shape. Figure 2 illustrates: (A) a normal or Gaussian population, (B) a symmetrical non-normal population (in this case a bimodal distribution), (E) and (F) a log-normal population (that is, the logarithms of the data are normally distributed), and other skewed populations (C and D).

TABLE I
*Use of a Table of Random Numbers**

Problem:	Given a population of 90 cases, to select a random sample of 20 cases.	25 19 64 82 84	62 74 29 92 24
		23 02 41 46 04	44 31 52 43 07
Procedure:	1. Arbitrarily assign a number to each case from 01 to 90.	55 85 66 96 28	28 30 62 58 83
		68 45 19 69 59	35 14 82 56 80
		69 31 46 29 85	18 88 26 95 54

2. On the table of random numbers, arbitrarily pick a 2-digit column.	37 31 61 28 98	94 61 47 03 10
	66 42 19 24 94	13 13 38 69 96
3. With closed eyes, select a random start in that column.	33 65 78 12 35	91 59 11 38 44
	76 32 06 19 35	22 95 30 19 29
	43 33 42 02 59	20 39 84 95 61√

4. Beginning with the starting number, continue to sequentially select every 2-digit number in that column (and in the next 2-digit column, if necessary) until 20 cases have been selected.

28 31 93 43 94	87 73 19 38 47√
97 19 21 63 34	69 33 17 03 02√
82 80 37 14 20	56 39 59 89 63√
03 68 03 13 60	64 13 09 37 11√
65 16 58 11 01	98 78 80 63 23√

5. In the event a random number not included in the sequence 01 to 90 occurs (e.g., 98), skip that number and proceed to the next random number listed.

24 65 58 57 04	18 62 85 28 24√
02 72 64 07 75	85 66 48 38 73√
79 16 78 63 99	43 61 00 66 42√
04 75 14 93 39	68 52 16 83 34√
40 64 64 57 60	97 00 12 91 33√

6. Similarly, if a random number already used occurs again, disregard it and continue to the next random number listed.

06 27 07 34 26	01 52 48 69 57√
62 40 03 87 10	96 88 22 46 ~~94~~
00 98 48 18 97	91 51 63 27 ~~99~~
50 64 19 18 91	98 55 83 46 09√
38 54 52 25 78	01 98 00 89 85√

7. To assure that a number is not picked twice, keep some record in numerical sequence of numbers selected.

46 86 80 97 78	65 12 64 64 70√
90 72 92 93 10	09 12 81 93 ~~00~~
66 21 41 77 60	99 35 72 61 22√
87 05 46 52 76	89 96 34 22 37√
46 90 61 03 06	89 85 33 22 80√

Example: In the tenth 2-digit column, a blindfold random start is made with the number 61. The 20 numbers used to select the sample are shown by check mark. Numbers not used lie outside the sequence 01 to 90, or are repeats, and are crossed through.

11 88 53 06 09	81 83 33 98 29√
11 05 92 06 97	68 82 34 08 83√
33 94 24 20 28	62 42 07 12 63
24 89 74 75 61	61 02 73 36 85
15 19 74 67 23	61 38 93 73 68

(In this example we have moved down a column but we could have chosen to move in some other direction.)

05 64 12 70 88	80 58 35 06 88
57 49 36 44 06	74 93 55 39 26
77 82 96 96 97	60 42 17 18 48
24 10 70 06 51	59 62 37 95 42
50 00 07 78 23	49 54 36 85 14

*From Bahn, A. K., *Basic Medical Statistics*. Grune & Stratton, New York, 1972.

It is always desirable to graph a frequency distribution in order to inspect its shape. Most quantitative populations require a minimum of two parameters for adequate description: (1) a measure of central tendency (or average) and (2) a measure of variation or dispersion of individuals around that average.

MEASURES OF CENTRAL TENDENCY

The three most common measures of central tendency are the mean, the mode, and the median (see Figure 2):

The mean is the arithmetic average. (For example, the mean of 6, 6, 8, 10, and 15 = 45/5 = 9.)

The mode is the most frequent value (point of maximum concentration). (In the above example, the mode is 6.)

The median is the middle value of data ordered from the lowest to highest. (In the above example, the median is 8.)

In normally distributed populations the mean, the mode, and the median coincide, as shown in Figure 2A.

The mean is generally the most useful measure of central tendency. For skewed populations, however, the mean is misleading, inasmuch as it is greatly affected by extreme values.

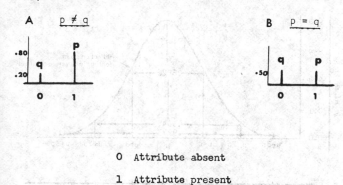

O Attribute absent

1 Attribute present

FIGURE 1. Binomial populations showing the proportions with an attribute present (*p*) or not present (*q*). *A*. The proportion with the attribute is greater than the proportion without the attribute. *B*. The proportion with the attribute and the proportion without the attribute are equal. (From Bahn, A. K. *Basic Medical Statistics*. Grune & Stratton, New York, 1972.)

In such cases as data on income, size of family, and many biological data, the median is more appropriate. For log-normal populations, the geometric mean (the antilog of the mean of the logarithms of the data) is a useful measure.

MEASURES OF VARIATION

The second parameter used to describe quantitative populations indicates how individuals vary among themselves. Such variation is an inherent property of a population or of a sample from it. It is unaffected by the size of the population or sample.

It is important to know how variable individuals in a population are because it indicates how useful the mean value is as a representative figure. Variability of individuals is important also because it affects the precision of sample estimates. For example, if all individuals in the population are of the same height, a sample of one is an adequate representation of it; but if they are of diverse heights, a larger sample is needed to assure that persons of various heights are selected.

A. Symmetrical Normal

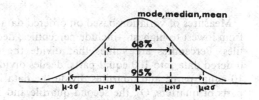

B. Symmetrical Non-Normal [1]
(in this case a bimodal curve)

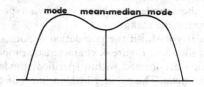

C. Non-Symmetrical with right tail skewness [2]

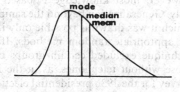

D. Non-Symmetrical with left tail skewness [3]

E. Non-Symmetrical Log Normal

F. Transformation of Log Normal

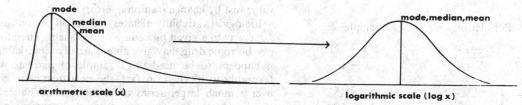

arithmetic scale (x)   logarithmic scale (log x)

[1] The bimodality of this population suggests that it is not homogeneous and should be divided into subgroups for analysis.

[2] Same as positive skewness.

[3] Same as negative skewness.

FIGURE 2. Hypothetical examples of continuous populations. (From Bahn, A. K. *Basic Medical Statistics*. Grune & Stratton, New York, 1972.)

Three common measures of variation are the range, the variance, and the standard deviation:

The range is the difference between the highest and the lowest values. (In the above example, the range is 15 minus 6 = 9.)

The variance is the average squared deviation of individual values around the mean value. (In the above example, the mean is 9, so the variance is $(6-9)^2 + (6-9)^2 + (8-9)^2 + (10-9)^2 + (15-9)^2 = 56/5 = 11.2$. This example assumes, for purposes of simplicity, that the data represent an entire population and, therefore, uses the formula for the population variance (see Figure 3).

The standard deviation (SD) is the square root of the variance. (In the above example, the SD is $\sqrt{11.2} = 3.3$).

Thus, to obtain the SD, one first computes the variance or average squared deviation of individual values around the mean. The SD, the square root of the variance, converts the unit of measure back into its original or unsquared form. The unit of measure, such as inches or grams, should always be specified.

A principle disadvantage of the range is that it is affected by sample size; it tends to be larger when the sample is larger, since then more extreme observations are likely to be selected. This disadvantage is not found in the SD, which is not systematically affected by the sample size, because it is a type of average deviation around the mean.

The SD is particularly useful if the population is normally distributed. Then, as shown in Figure 4, characteristic proportions of the population are located within specified standard deviations around the mean. The mean ±1 SD includes 68 per cent of the population. The mean ±2 SD includes 95 per cent of the population. The mean ±3 SD includes 99.7 per cent of the population.

Because of this property of the normal curve, if the SD or σ is known, any individual observation from the distribution can be located on the standard normal curve by the z transformation—that is, by the number of z units (SD or σ units) the individual (x) is from the mean (μ).

$$z = \frac{x \;\;\; \mu \;\leftarrow}{\sigma \;\leftarrow}$$

observed value
$\leftarrow$ center of normal curve
$\leftarrow$ standard deviation of normal curve

Another important property of the SD is that its square, the variance, can be partitioned into component parts, such as the variance between and within treatment groups. This property of the variance serves as the basis for the analysis of variance and experimental design. And if one knows the SD of the population or can estimate it from a sample, one can also estimate the standard error of any sample statistic.

A useful measure for comparing the variation of one group with that of another, irrespective of the unit of dimension, is

	Population	Sample
variance	$\sigma^2 = \dfrac{\Sigma(x - \mu)^2}{N}$	$s^2 = \dfrac{\Sigma(x - \bar{x})^2}{n - 1}$
standard deviation (SD)	$\sigma = \sqrt{\dfrac{\Sigma(x - \mu)^2}{N}}$	$s = \sqrt{\dfrac{\Sigma(x - \bar{x})^2}{n - 1}}$

FIGURE 3. Relationship of variance and standard deviation for a population and a sample where Σ = sum of, x is the value of the individual measurement in the population or sample, μ is the mean of the population, $\bar{x}$ is the mean of the sample, N is the number of individuals in the population (population size), and n is the number of individuals in the sample (sample size).

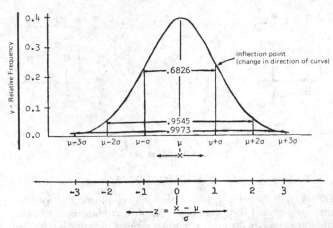

FIGURE 4. The normal frequency distribution and proportionate areas included within various multiples of σ. (From Bahn, A. K. *Basic Medical Statistics*. Grune & Stratton, New York, 1972.)

the coefficient of variation. This term relates the size of the SD to the size of the mean (in percentage):

$$\text{Coefficient of variation (C.V.)} = \frac{\sigma}{\mu} \times 100$$

Measures of variation based on ordered data—data arrayed from lowest to highest—include percentiles, deciles, and quartiles. Percentiles are values that divide the distribution of ordered data into 100 equal parts, deciles divide the data into 10 equal parts, and quartiles divide the data into four equal parts or quarters. Q_2, the second quartile and also the fiftieth percentile, is the middle value of ordered data and, therefore, the same as the median.

Inferential Statistics

The previous section outlines how populations of qualitative or quantitative data can be described. For practical reasons, however, most knowledge is based on sample observations only. Generalization beyond the sample to the population from which it was drawn is possible only if the sample was selected by appropriate random methods. If, however, the sampling technique excluded certain groups of persons—for example, those without telephones, as in the infamous *Literary Digest* survey for the 1936 presidential election—the sample is biased.

With random methods, inference to the population from a sample is possible, because the sample mean is then an unbiased estimate of the population mean, and the sample variance is an unbiased estimate of the population variance. "Unbiased" refers to the fact that the average of all such sample estimates equals the true (population) value. However, any single sample outcome may differ from the true population value just by chance (sampling error).

Biological variability dictates that not all persons react in the same way to a given procedure or treatment. Therefore, a new psychotropic drug may give an apparently remarkable result if it happens to be used on a sample of patients who react favorably to it when, in fact, the new treatment, considered over a much larger series of patients, is no better than the standard treatment. Two new drugs may be used on a sample of patients, and drug A may appear to give superior results; but, if applied to a very large number of patients, neither drug may be found to be superior, or drug B may actually be better.

Or one may wish to determine the relation between exposure to factor X and the risk of developing a certain psychiatric disorder. One may select a sample of men with the disorder and a group of healthy men (controls) of about the same age. One may observe that 28 per cent of the patients were exposed to factor X in their youth, whereas only 12 per cent of the controls were so exposed. This observed difference of 16 per cent is large and is of interest. However, before one can assert that a true difference exists between patients and controls in the percentage exposed to factor X, one must ascertain whether the sample difference could readily be explained by chance alone.

The evaluation of chance is often done intuitively. In the above example, if each sample contained only six or eight men one would be wary of asserting that a true difference exists; but if each sample contained 100 men, a true difference would seem much more likely. But what if the samples contained 50 men each? In the face of such uncertainty, a formal procedure is needed for the evaluation of chance. This procedure is called significance testing.

NULL HYPOTHESIS

In the general procedure for significance testing one sets up a straw man—the null hypothesis—and then determines whether it can be knocked down. One asserts that there is no true difference—that is, the difference is null or zero—between the two populations from which the samples were drawn. One then tests whether this hypothesis holds. That is, one asks: If the null hypothesis is true and the samples were, in fact, drawn from identical populations or the same population, how likely is one to obtain a sample difference as extreme as the one observed or more extreme? If very likely—that is, if the probability (P) of obtaining a sample difference as unusual as the one observed or more unusual, where there is no true difference, is greater than 5 in 100 trials (P > 0.05)—it means that the observed difference can be readily explained by chance. The null hypothesis is accepted, and the difference is declared not significant.

If on the other hand, the probability of finding a difference as extreme or more extreme than that observed (given no true difference) is relatively small (for example, P < 0.05), the null hypothesis is rejected. One then accepts the alternative hypothesis. That is, because of the rarity of such a chance event under the null hypothesis, one is willing to take the risk of saying that a true difference does exist, and the observed difference is called significant.

Thus P indicates the probability of finding a sample outcome as extreme or more extreme under the null hypothesis of no true difference. There are two steps in determining P: (1) generation of a sampling distribution under the null hypothesis—that is, a distribution of differences between two random samples drawn repeatedly from the same population; this can be done mathematically or experimentally; (2) location of the observed sample difference on this chance distribution to determine the probability of such an outcome or of one more extreme.

In the example used above, one observed that 28 per cent of a sample of 50 psychiatrically ill men had been exposed to factor X in their childhood but only 12 per cent of the 50 control subjects had been so exposed, a difference of 16 per cent. One could experimentally derive a distribution of chance differences against which to test this observed difference. One assumes that there is an infinite population of men exposed or not exposed to factor X. Such a population can be represented by an infinitely large jar of green and yellow beads in which a green bead represents a person exposed to factor X, and a yellow bead represents a person not exposed to factor X. Under the null hypothesis of no true difference, the best estimate of the proportion of exposed individuals (green beads) in this infinite population is the average of the two sample outcomes 28 per cent and 12 per cent (that is, 40 per cent ÷ 2 = 20 per cent). Thus, in terms of proportions, let p = the true proportion exposed (green beads) in the population = 0.20; and let $q = 1 - p$, the proportion not exposed (yellow beads) = 0.80.

If one draws two samples of 50 beads each from this infinite jar of beads repeatedly, for each sample the proportion exposed (green beads) can be represented by $\hat{p}$. After each draw from the jar or trial, one observes the difference in the proportion of green beads ($\hat{p}_1 - \hat{p}_2$) in the two samples. One conducts a large number of such draws and tabulates (see Table II) the frequency distribution of these chance differences in the proportions exposed ($\hat{p}_1 - \hat{p}_2$).

Although the two samples were drawn from the same population, in some trials sample 1 has, by chance, a larger proportion of green beads (a "+" difference). In other trials sample 2 has the larger proportion (a "−" difference). However, the average of all the sample 1 proportions and of all the sample 2 proportions is the true population proportion ($p = 0.20$) (see *curve A* in Figure 5). Therefore, the average difference between the sample proportions is the true difference (zero).

Because the samples were drawn from the same population, one has a distribution of chance differences or sample errors centered around a true difference of zero, the null hypothesis curve (see *curve B* in Figure 5).

The null hypothesis curve can be characterized further. Regardless of the shape of the population from which the samples were drawn (a binomial population in this instance), if the samples are of sufficiently large size, the null hypothesis distribution of sample outcomes (proportions, means, differences) is a normal curve (central limit theorem). Because this curve is a distribution of sample errors, its standard deviation is called a standard error (SE). The area of this normal curve included within the mean ±1 SE represents 68 per cent of the sample differences; within the mean ±2 SE, the area includes 95 per cent of the sample differences; and within the mean ±3 SE, the area includes 99.7 per cent of the sample differences. Therefore, using the z transformation, one can locate any of the sample differences on this null hypothesis curve of chance differences (see Figure 6) to determine how likely it is that a difference as extreme as that observed or more extreme will occur just by chance if the null hypothesis is true.

TABLE II

Frequency Distribution of Chance Differences in Proportions Exposed to a Factor for Repeated Samples from the Same Population, Where the True Proportion Exposed is 0.20.

Trial No.	Proportion Exposed in Sample 1 $\hat{p}_1$	Proportion Exposed in Sample 2 $\hat{p}_2$	Difference in Proportions Sample 1 − Sample 2 $\hat{p}_1 - \hat{p}_2$
1	0.24	0.18	+0.06
2	0.20	0.18	+0.02
3	0.20	0.28	−0.08
.	.	.	.
.	.	.	.
.	.	.	.
∞			
Average	0.20	0.20	0

A. Distributions of sample proportions around a
true proportion.

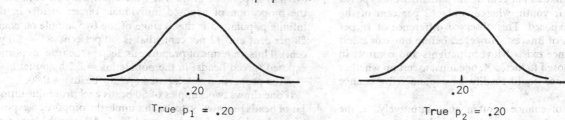

True $p_1 = .20$ True $p_2 = .20$

B. Distribution of sample differences between
two proportions around a *true difference* of 0.

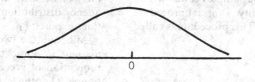

True $p_1 - p_2 = 0$

FIGURE 5. Samples from the same population. (From Bahn, A. K. *Basic Medical Statistics.* Grune & Stratton, New York, 1972.)

One can locate the sample difference in the above example on the null hypothesis curve. For this example the SE is:

$$SE\,\hat{p}_1 - \hat{p}_2 = \sqrt{\frac{(pq)}{n_1} + \frac{(pq)}{n_2}} = \sqrt{\frac{(0.20)\,(0.80)}{50} + \frac{(0.20)\,(0.80)}{50}} = 0.08$$

The observed sample difference ($\hat{p}_1 - \hat{p}_2$) is $(0.28 - 0.12)$ or 0.16. One then uses the z transformation to locate this observed difference on the standard normal distribution of sample (chance) differences. The general form for z, the standard normal deviate (assuming that n is sufficiently large) is:

standard
normal = $z = \dfrac{x - \mu}{\sigma}$
deviate

observed outcome
center of the normal curve
standard deviation of the normal curve

In this instance, x represents the observed difference ($\hat{p}_1 - \hat{p}_2$), μ is the center of the normal curve of chance differences, or 0, and σ is the standard error of the difference (SE $\hat{p}_1 - \hat{p}_2$).

Thus, the critical ratio $z = \dfrac{(\hat{p}_1 - \hat{p}_2) - 0}{SE\hat{p}_1 - \hat{p}_2}$

By substitution, $z = \dfrac{(0.16) - 0}{0.08} = 2$. Thus, one finds that the sample difference is located 2 SE from the center of the curve, 0 (see Figure 6).

From a table of the standard normal curve or z table (see Table III), one finds that for $z = 2$ the area from the center of the curve to the observation on either side $(1 - P)$ is 0.9545, and the total area in both tails representing more extreme observations (P), is only 0.0455. Arbitrarily, one may decide in advance that a probability (P) of 0.05 or less is a sufficiently rare event to rule out chance as a likely explanation of the sample observation. Therefore, one would reject the null hypothesis of no true difference between the samples and call the difference significant. If a priori one had set P = 0.01 (the 1 per cent level) as the dividing line between accepting and rejecting the null hypothesis, the difference would not be statistically significant.

Suppose the difference in proportions between the two samples had been only 0.08 instead of 0.16. Then:

$$z = \frac{(0.08) - 0}{0.08} = 1.$$

Therefore, one would find such a sample difference to be only 1 SE from the center of the normal curve. In this case the area in the tails or P would be about 0.32 (see Table III). Just by chance alone, then, in 32 of every 100 trials, a sample difference as extreme as that observed or more extreme would occur under the null hypothesis. This cannot be called a rare event. Chance may well be a likely explanation of the observed difference; the null hypothesis must be accepted. The difference is not statistically significant.

TYPE I AND TYPE II ERRORS

In the above example the arbitrary a priori decision was that if the probability of a difference as extreme as that observed or more extreme under the null hypothesis were less than 0.05 (P < 0.05), one would reject the null hypothesis, and the difference would be called significant. The arbitrary level of significance chosen a priori (in this case 0.05) is called alpha (α). If P were greater than 0.05, one would accept the null hypothesis, and the difference would be labeled not significant. In either case, whether one rejects or accepts the null hypothesis, he is at risk of making an error in the decision, depending on the actual situation (see Table IV).

Suppose that the actual situation is that the null hypothesis is true—there is no real difference between the two populations from which the two samples are taken—and the difference is due solely to chance. However, 5 per cent of the time such a difference will fall within the tail area of the null hypothesis

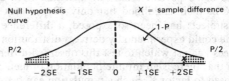

FIGURE 6. Location of an observed sample difference on the distribution of chance differences between two sample proportions.

TABLE III

Short Table of Areas of the Standard Normal Curve*

z	1−P	P	z	1−P	P	z	1−P	P	z	1−P	P
0.0	0.0000	1.0000	1.0	0.6827	.3173	2.0	0.9545	.0455	3.0	0.9973	.0027
0.1	.0797	.9203	1.1	.7287	.2713	2.1	.9643	.0357	3.1	.9981	.0019
0.2	.1585	.8415	1.2	.7699	.2301	2.2	.9722	.0278	3.2	.9986	.0014
0.3	.2358	.7642	1.3	.8064	.1936	2.3	.9786	.0214	3.3	.9990	.0010
0.4	.3108	.6892	1.4	.8385	.1615	2.4	.9836	.0164	3.4	.9993	.0007
0.5	0.3829	.6771	1.5	0.8664	.1336	2.5	0.9876	.0124	3.5	0.9995	.0005
0.6	.4515	.5485	1.6	.8904	.1096	2.58	.9901	.0099	3.6	.9997	.0003
0.7	.5161	.4839	1.64	.9000	.1000	2.6	.9907	.0093	3.7	.9998	.0002
0.8	.5763	.4237	1.7	.9109	.0891	2.7	.9931	.0069	3.8	.9999	.0001
0.9	.6319	.3681	1.8	.9281	.0719	2.8	.9949	.0051	3.9	.9999	.0001
			1.9	.9426	.0594	2.9	.9963	.0037			
			1.96	.9500	.0500						

$x - \mu$ = deviation of a variate from its distribution mean (+ or −)

σ = standard deviation of the distribution

$z = (x - \mu)/\sigma$ = the deviation expressed in standard units, the *normal deviate*

1−P = corresponding area under the normal curve between $-z$ and $+z$

= probability according to the normal curve of obtaining a deviation smaller than the absolute value of $x - \mu$

P = tail area of the normal curve or area beyond $\pm z$

= probability of obtaining a deviation equal to or larger than the absolute value of $x - \mu$

* Adapted from Fertig, John W. (mimeographed Lecture Notes, Columbia University School of Public Health and Administrative Medicine of the Faculty of Medicine). From Bahn, A. K. *Basic Medical Statistics.* Grune & Stratton, New York, 1972.

TABLE IV

Risk of Making an Error in Decision in Use of Null Hypothesis

		Decision Made	
		Null Hypothesis is *Accepted*	Null Hypothesis is *Rejected*
Actual Situation	Null hypothesis is *true*	No Error	Type I Error (α)
	Null hypothesis is *false*	Type II error (β)	No error

curve, that is more than 2 SE from the center. If the significance level had been set at 0.05 (alpha (α) = 0.05) then this is the rejection region of the curve and the chance difference will be called significant. It is a false claim of a true difference because the observed difference is due entirely to chance. This is called type I or α error (see Figure 7).

On the other hand, it is possible that an actual difference does exist between the two populations from which the samples are drawn (that is, the null hypothesis is false). However, by chance the sample difference is so small that it falls within the acceptance region of the null hypothesis curve (less than 2 SE from the center). In this case one falsely accepts the null hypothesis when, in fact, there is a true difference. This is called type II or β (beta) error.

Like sensitivity and specificity, these two error risks are inversely related. The risk of the type I error is established by the a priori level of significance (for example, α = 0.05 or 0.01). The risk of the type II error is more difficult to measure but can be minimized by sufficiently large sample sizes. Power curves can assist in estimating this risk for various assumed true differences (alternative hypotheses) and sample sizes.

FOUR BASIC CURVES

A major question to be asked when analyzing data is: Are the data qualitative (that is, categorical) or quantitative (that

is, measurement or continuous)? The distinction is of basic importance because, although there are many similarities in the approach to the two types of data, there are specific differences in method, with a larger number of parameters involved in most quantitative distributions.

A second major methodological question is: Do these data represent the distribution of individuals in a population (or sample), or do they represent the distribution of a statistic derived from samples, such as the distribution of sample means around a true mean or a distribution of sample differences around a true difference between population means?

With qualitative data, such as binomial data, the problem is almost always concerned with a sampling distribution because the population itself is readily described by one parameter, the proportion (p) with a certain attribute. With quantitative data, many problems are concerned with the description of the distribution of the population (or sample) of individuals because of the larger number of parameters involved, such as mean and standard deviation. Other problems are concerned with the sampling distribution of estimates of these parameters (such as sample means and sample differences) for the purposes of inference regarding the population (true) values and significance testing.

For comparison, one may consider four basic curves for qualitative and quantitative data (see Figures 8 and 9): the frequency distribution of a parent population of individuals (*curve A*); the frequency distribution of a random sample of

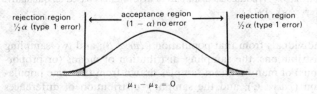

FIGURE 7. Actual situation: Null hypothesis, $H_0: \mu_1 = \mu_2$ is true. (From Bahn, A. K. *Basic Medical Statistics.* Grune & Stratton, New York, 1972.)

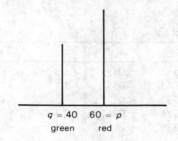

A. Parent population of individuals

$q = .40$ $.60 = p$
green   red

population proportion $= p$
population SD $= \sqrt{pq}$

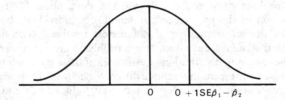

B. One random sample of individuals from population

$\hat{q} = .36$ $.64 = \hat{p}$

sample proportion $= \hat{p}$
sample SD $= \sqrt{\hat{p}\hat{q}}$

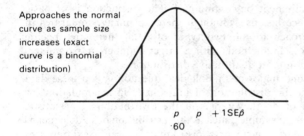

Approaches the normal
curve as sample size
increases (exact
curve is a binomial
distribution)

C. Sampling distribution of proportions ($\hat{p}$) of
many random samples like B

p p $+1SE\hat{p}$
$.60$

mean $= p$

SD $= SE\hat{p}$ or $\sqrt{\dfrac{pq}{n}}$

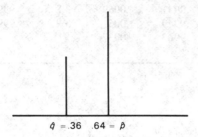

D. Sampling distribution of differences between
proportions ($\hat{p}_1 - \hat{p}_2$) of many two-random
samples like B

0 $0 + 1SE\hat{p}_1 - \hat{p}_2$

mean $= p_1 - p_2 = 0$

SD $= SE\hat{p}_1 - \hat{p}_2 = \sqrt{\dfrac{pq}{n_1} + \dfrac{pq}{n_2}}$

FIGURE 8. Hypothetical examples of distributions based on qualitative data. (Adapted from Bahn, A. K. *Basic Medical Statistics.* Grune & Stratton, New York, 1972.)

individuals from that population (*curve B*); and two sampling distributions: the sampling distribution of means (or proportions) of many random samples drawn from the same population (*curve C*); and the sampling distribution of differences between the means (or proportions) of a large number of two-random samples drawn from the same population (*curve D*). *Curve C* is similar to *curve A* in Figure 5, *curve D* is similar to

curve B in Figure 5 and to Figures 6 and 7. For quantitative data these four curves (*A, B, C,* and *D*) are shown for both a normally distributed parent population and for a skewed (log-normal) parent population.

Note the following from Figures 8 and 9:

1. A random sample (*curve B*) tends to be a replica of the parent population (*curve A*).

NORMAL   LOG NORMAL

A. Parent population of individuals

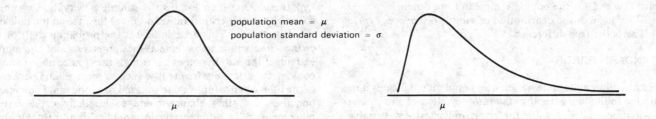

population mean $= \mu$
population standard deviation $= \sigma$

B. One random sample of individuals from population

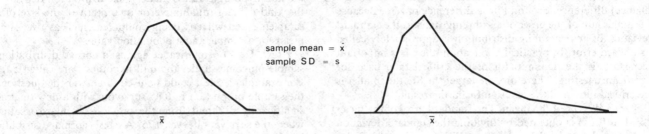

sample mean $= \bar{x}$
sample SD $= s$

C. Sampling distribution of means ($\bar{x}$) of many random samples like B

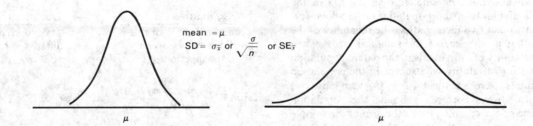

mean $= \mu$
SD $= \sigma_{\bar{x}}$ or $\sqrt{\dfrac{\sigma}{n}}$ or $SE_{\bar{x}}$

D. Sampling distribution of differences between means ($\bar{x}_1 - \bar{x}_2$) of many two-random samples like B

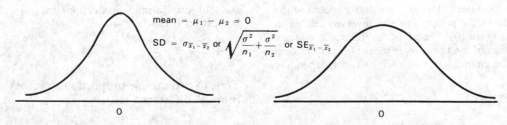

mean $= \mu_1 - \mu_2 = 0$
SD $= \sigma_{\bar{x}_1 - \bar{x}_2}$ or $\sqrt{\dfrac{\sigma^2}{n_1} + \dfrac{\sigma^2}{n_2}}$ or $SE_{\bar{x}_1 - \bar{x}_2}$

FIGURE 9. Hypothetical examples of distributions based on quantitative data. (Adapted from Bahn, A. K. *Basic Medical Statistics.* Grune & Stratton, New York, 1972.)

2. The sampling distribution of means (or proportions) (*curve C*) and of differences between means (or proportions) (*curve D*) is normally distributed if the samples are of sufficiently large size, regardless of the shape of the parent population (the central limit theorem).

3. The mean of the distribution of sample means (proportions) (*curve C*) is the population mean (proportion).

4. The mean of the distribution of sample differences (*curve D*) is zero, the true difference.

STANDARD ERROR

Just as the standard deviation of a population indicates how variable individuals are, the standard deviation of a sampling distribution, called a standard error, indicates how variable (reliable) the sample statistic is. Thus the standard error of the mean (SE $\bar{x}$) in *curve C* is a measure of the variability or error of the sample mean as an estimate of the true mean. Similarly, the standard error of the difference between two sample means (*curve D*) is a measure of the variation or error of sample (chance) differences around a true difference of zero. Because it is a measure of the error of a sampling statistic, the standard deviation of any sampling distribution is appropriately called a standard error. In practical application, the SE is important because it is the denominator of the critical ratio used for significance testing. Therefore, the larger the SE, the smaller is the critical ratio and the less significant the result.

Standard error of the mean. The standard error of the mean (SEM or SE $\bar{x}$) is obtained by dividing the standard deviation of the population by the square root of the number of individuals in the sample:

$$\text{SEM} = \frac{\text{SD}_{\text{pop}}}{\sqrt{n}} \left(\text{or } \text{SE}_{\bar{x}} = \frac{\sigma_{\text{pop}}}{\sqrt{n}} \right)$$

Therefore, the SEM, the standard deviation of the sampling distribution of means, must be smaller than the SD of the distribution of individuals in the population. The above formula indicates also that two factors affect the reliability of the sample mean—that is, the size of the standard error of the mean: (1) the variability of individuals in the parent population (σ); if there were no variability whatsoever in the population and all individuals were identical ($\sigma = 0$), then any one individual would always correctly estimate the population mean; (2) the size of the sample (n); as the size of the sample increases and n approaches N, the sample is more likely to include individuals from all parts of the population and, therefore, provide a better estimate of its parameters.

The corresponding formula for the standard error of the proportion is SE $\hat{p} = \sqrt{\frac{pq}{n}}$. SE $\hat{p}$ is largest where p and q are equal—that is, $p = q = 0.50$.

Standard error of the difference. The size of the standard error of the difference between two sample means (SE $\bar{x}_1 - \bar{x}_2$) or two sample proportions (SE $\hat{p}_1 - \hat{p}_2$) is directly related to the standard deviation of the population and inversely related to sample sizes (see Figure 10). The SE of the difference is larger than the SE of either of the two sample means (or proportions) because it involves chance error in each of two independent samples.

SIGNIFICANCE TESTS

Note that both *curves C* and *D* in Figures 8 and 9 represent distributions of results of samples from the same population. Therefore, they are distributions of chance outcomes under the null hypothesis—that is, these are null hypothesis curves used for significance testing.

Against this background one can now review the meaning of a significance test. In any test of significance, one uses a sampling distribution—such as a distribution of the means of many samples drawn from the same universe—under the null hypothesis. One then locates the sample observation on this curve by use of a critical ratio and notes the area in the tails of the distribution. This area indicates the probability (P) of a chance observation as extreme as that observed or of one more extreme if the null hypothesis is true. If the chance observation could occur relatively frequently, such as more than 5 per cent of the time when sample(s) are selected from the same universe, one then says that chance alone could likely explain the outcome, and the difference is declared not significant. On the other hand, if such a chance outcome occurs relatively rarely, one calls the outcome significant.

The form of the critical ratio to carry out the significance test depends on the type of sampling distribution against which the null hypothesis test is made. This distribution depends on the kind of data (qualitative or quantitative), the size of the sample(s), and what is being compared, such as two sample means or a sample and a population value.

z test. Tests of significance against a normal distribution of sample outcomes under the null hypothesis are called *z* tests. For example, a *z* test could be used to answer the question: Is the sample proportion of 0.85 survivors with a new treatment significantly different from the previous standard treatment where the survival rate was 0.75? A *z* test (normal distribution) would be appropriate if the sample size were sufficiently large. Similarly, a *z* test would be appropriate to answer the question: Do these two sample means (of 10 inches and 12 inches) differ significantly from each other (assume that the variance of the population is known)? (See Figure 11.)

t test. The use of the normal distribution and, therefore, the

Qualitative Data	Quantitative Data
Standard error of the difference between proportions.	Standard error of the difference between means.

$$\text{SE}\hat{p}_1 - \hat{p}_2 = \sqrt{\frac{pq}{n_1} + \frac{pq}{n_2}} \qquad \text{SE}\bar{x}_1 - \bar{x}_2 = \sqrt{\frac{\sigma^2}{n_1} + \frac{\sigma_2}{n_2}}$$

$$\text{and where } n_1 = n_2$$

$$= \sqrt{(\text{SE}\hat{p}_1)^2 + (\text{SE}\hat{p}_2)^2} \qquad = \sqrt{(\text{SE}\bar{x}_1)^2 + (\text{SE}\bar{x}_2)^2}$$

FIGURE 10. Standard error of difference for qualitative data and for quantitative data (independent samples).

Qualitative Data	Quantitative Data

Tests of one sample proportion (mean) with a population proportion (mean):

$$z = \frac{\hat{p} - p}{\text{SE}_{\hat{p}}} \qquad z = \frac{\bar{x} - \mu}{\text{SE}_{\bar{x}}}$$

Tests of two sample proportions (means) with each other (normal difference test):

$$z = \frac{(\hat{p}_1 - \hat{p}_2) - 0}{\text{SE}\hat{p}_1 - \hat{p}_2} \qquad z = \frac{(\bar{x}_1 - \bar{x}_2) - 0}{\text{SE}_{\bar{x}_1 - \bar{x}_2}}$$

FIGURE 11. Examples of *z* tests (critical ratios).

z test for quantitative data requires that the variance of the population be known. This is rarely the situation. Instead, one must estimate the population variance from the sample variance. One then must test against the t distribution.

The t distribution is similar to the normal distribution but for small samples has more area in the tails (see Figure 12). Therefore, the t ratio for a given sample size—for example, 20—must be larger than the z ratio to be significant. The t distribution approaches the normal distribution as the size of the sample increases. For samples greater than 30, the z ratio can be used in place of the t ratio.

Assumptions of the t distribution are (1) that samples are drawn from a normally distributed population and (2) that the variances of the populations from which the samples are drawn are equal.

As seen in Figure 12, the shape of the t distribution depends on the number of degrees of freedom (df). Here the df is the number of independent differences that enter into the sample variance, or the size of each sample minus one ($n - 1$).

χ^2 **test.** The χ^2 test is an alternative test for evaluating the significance of sample proportions. Most χ^2 tests can be called tests of association because they answer the question: Is there an association between a factor (or attribute) and an outcome? For example, in a test of two samples, one can visualize the data as a contingency table with two rows and two columns forming four cells:

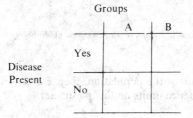

The test makes use of the χ^2 distribution, which, like the t distribution, requires specification of the number of degrees of freedom (independent differences) that contribute to the variance. For the contingency table the df are: (number of rows $- 1$) $\times$ (number of columns $- 1$). The formula for the χ^2 test is:

$$\chi^2 = \sum \frac{(\text{observed number - expected number})^2}{\text{expected number}}$$

That is, for each cell of the table, calculate the observed number minus the expected number, square this difference, divide by the expected number, and sum for all the cells of the table. The expected number or frequency is usually derived from the sample data under the assumption of the null hypothesis of no true difference between groups. For χ^2 with one degree of freedom (as in the 2×2 contingency table above) $\chi^2 = z^2$.

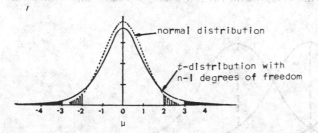

FIGURE 12. Relationship of t distribution to normal distribution. (From Bahn, A. K. *Basic Medical Statistics.* Grune & Stratton, New York, 1972.)

Therefore, identical results of P values are obtained by the χ^2 and the z tests.

The χ^2 test is important because of its versatility; it can be used for multinomial data—that is, for data classified into more than two categories, or for comparing more than two samples. An example of a χ^2 test applied to the Baltimore City ecology study referred to earlier is shown in Table V. Here the data for the two middle quartiles have been combined to form a 3×3 contingency table, with four degrees of freedom. The data show a significant association (P < 0.001) between census tract ranking on psychiatric admission rate and on proportion of persons on public assistance.

The χ^2 distribution can also be used to test whether a sampling distribution follows some theoretical distribution, such as the normal distribution or the binomial distribution, or a particular population distribution. Such tests are called χ^2 goodness of fit tests.

Paired test. In the two-sample tests discussed so far, the assumption is made that the samples are independent of each other. This is the situation, for example, when samples of patients from each of two psychiatric wards are compared with each other or when a sample of schizophrenic patients and a sample of manic-depressive patients are compared. The following types of samples, however, are not independent of each other but are most likely correlated: patients and control subjects matched individually on the basis of a large number of variables, such as age, sex, position in the family, and socioeconomic status; a sample of patients and a control sample composed of the patients' siblings; before and after measurements on the same persons; and littermates. In these situations, the significance test must take into account the nonindependence of the samples, or pairing.

The advantage of such pairing is that the heterogeneity (or variance) between the two groups is reduced. Because the groups are homogeneous (alike), they tend to differ only in the factor being tested, such as treatment effect. If successful pairing has been carried out, the reduced variance may make it possible to use a smaller sample size to demonstrate a significant difference, if one does exist.

The test for paired data requires a modification of the t test or of the χ^2 test. A nonparametric (distribution-free) method, such as the sign test, may also be used.

INTERVAL ESTIMATION

Up to now, the concern has been with questions of the type: Do these two samples come from populations with the same mean? In this case the null hypothesis was $H_0: \mu_1 = \mu_2$ (or $\mu_1 - \mu_2 = 0$). If the hypothesis of a zero difference is rejected, the next question posed is: What may be the true difference between μ_1 and μ_2? Thus, after one finds that a significant difference exists, one should like to know within what bounds the true difference may lie—that is, the problem is to estimate a confidence interval for the true population value. However, it is also possible to estimate a confidence interval for a population parameter without first conducting a test of significance. In this case, the interval itself is used to perform a significance test.

The sample provides a point estimate that is the most likely value. The interval estimate includes all possible values for the parameter that are consistent with the data at a specified probability or confidence level. This is comparable to estimating which of all possible population means or μ's (see Figure 13) are likely to have given rise to the observed sample mean

TABLE V

Distribution of Baltimore City Census Tracts by Quartile Ranking of 3-Year Psychiatric Admission Rate and Proportion of Persons on Public Assistance

No. of Tracts Ranked in Quartiles by 3-Year Total Psychiatric Admission Rate	No. of Tracts Ranked in Quartiles by Proportion of Persons on Public Assistance			
	I Lowest Quartile	II and III Middle Quartiles	IV Highest Quartile	Total No. of Tracts
IV. Highest quartile.................	2 (10.37)†	15 (19.73)	23 (9.90)	40
II and III. Middle quartiles......................	14 (20.50)	50 (39.00)	15 (19.50)	79
I. Lowest quartile	25 (10.13)	13 (19.27)	1 (9.60)	39
Total tracts	41	78	39	158

$$\chi^2 = \Sigma \left[\frac{(O-E)^2}{E} \right]$$

$$= \frac{(2-10.37)^2}{10.37} + \frac{(15-19.73)^2}{19.73} + \frac{(23-9.90)^2}{9.90}$$

$$+ \frac{(14-20.50)^2}{20.50} + \frac{(50-39.00)^2}{39.00} + \frac{(15-19.50)^2}{19.50}$$

$$+ \frac{(25-10.13)^2}{10.13} + \frac{(13-19.27)^2}{19.27} + \frac{(1-9.60)^2}{9.60}$$

$$\chi^2_{4\,df} = 63.2; \qquad P < 0.001.$$

† Numbers in parentheses are expected numbers: for example $10.37 = (\frac{41}{158}) \times 40$; $19.73 = (\frac{78}{158}) \times 40$.

From Klee, G., Spiro, E., Bahn, A. K., and Gorwitz, K. An ecological analysis of diagnosed mental illness in Baltimore. In *Psychiatric Epidemiology and Mental Health Planning*, Psychiatric Research Report 22, American Psychiatric Association, Washington, 1967.

of $\bar{x}$. It is possible that $\bar{x}$ came from a population with μ_1, but could it not also have come from a population with μ_2?

Researchers may prefer confidence interval estimation to a significance test because, essentially, it provides significance tests relevant for many null hypotheses rather than for a single null hypothesis.

In general, the confidence interval for any true (population) parameter can be constructed from:

Sample value or statistic ± [(factor) × (standard error of the statistic)]

The factor (such as 1.96 or 2.58) is determined by (1) the level of confidence (95 per cent or 99 per cent) that one wishes to achieve in including the true parameter within the interval estimate and (2) the appropriate sampling statistic (such as z or t).

The distinction between the term ($\bar{x} \pm 2$ SD) and ($\bar{x} \pm 2$ SEM) must be kept clearly in mind (2 is an approximation for 1.96). If a population or sample is normally distributed, then 95 per cent of individuals fall between the mean value and 2 SD on either side. On the other hand, if one is interested in the true mean value of the population, then $\bar{x} \pm 2$ SEM gives 95 per cent confidence limits on this parameter.

Miscellaneous Topics

TWO-VARIABLE ANALYSIS

Until now the discussion has been of the analysis of one variable. Regression and correlation are concerned with association among measurements of two variables. For example, suppose there are pairs of measurements x and y, such as caloric intake and the corresponding fasting blood sugar of diabetic patients or simultaneous measurements of the blood urea nitrogen and the creatinine for a number of persons. Regression and correlation attempt to answer the questions: Is there a relationship between the two variables? If a relationship exists, how can it be expressed? Can one variable be used to predict the other?

Linear regression. In regression, one variable is considered as the independent (x) (for example, caloric intake) and the

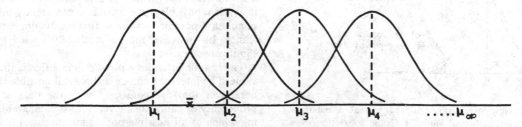

FIGURE 13. Distributions of sample means from populations with different μ's. (From Bahn, A. K. *Basic Medical Statistics.* Grune & Stratton, New York, 1972.)

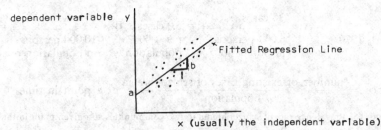

FIGURE 14. Fitted regression line in a linear relationship. (From Bahn, A. K. *Basic Medical Statistics*. Grune & Stratton, New York, 1972.)

other (for example, fasting blood sugar) as the dependent variable (*y*). If the relationship is that of a straight line, linear regression methods are used to obtain the best estimate of the dependent variable when the independent variable is fixed or is otherwise known. That is, a regression line is fitted to the data by inspection or mathematically (see Figure 14) so as to achieve a minimum sum of vertical squared deviations of the *y* values around that line—that is, minimum variance around the regression line. The fitted line is called the least squares regression line. The regression equation for the least squares regression line for sample data is $y_c = a + bx$. This equation relates the average *y* (the dependent variable) to the associated value for *x* (the independent variable); *a*, called the *y* intercept, is the point at which the sample regression line crosses the *y* axis (that is, where *x* is zero); *b*, the slope of the line or the average change in *y* per unit change in *x* (see Figure 14), is called the sample regression coefficient.

If each of the *y* values at a given *x* are distributed normally, significance testing on the true (population) regression coefficient (is the slope really different from zero?) can be carried out.

Correlation. Whereas in linear regression there are two types of variables, a dependent variable and an independent variable, in correlation neither variable is necessarily assumed to be the independent one. Correlation is used to measure the degree of linear relationship between two variables. The term that expresses this relationship is called Pearson's product moment correlation coefficient. For sample data the symbol is *r*; *r* is independent of any particular unit of measurement and thus indicates the strength of the association for any array of data in comparable terms; *r* can vary from 0 (for no linear relationship) (see Figure 15) to +1 (for a perfect positive) to −1 (for a perfect negative) linear relationship. An intermediate value indicates a less than perfect association, which is typical of most situations.

A positive *r* means that as one variable increases, the second variable also tends to increase in value; a negative correlation coefficient indicates an inverse relationship.

Of even more use than *r* is its square r^2, the coefficient of determination; r^2 measures the proportion of the total variance in *y*, which is associated with or can be explained by the variance in *x*.

There are important restrictions on the use of Pearson's product moment correlation coefficient *r*. If the populations cannot be assumed to be normally distributed and in certain other instances, such as nonlinearity, then alternative nonparametric (distribution-free) methods can be used, such as Kendall's τ and Spearman's rank order correlation coefficient. As with the population regression coefficient, there are significance tests on the hypothesis that the population correlation coefficient is really zero. Analogous to the distinction between an important difference and a significant difference for sample means, a correlation coefficient may be statistically significant because of a large sample size, yet be so weak (close to zero) as to be of no practical consequence. On the other hand, a correlation may appear to be strong (*r* close to +1 or −1) but because of the small sample size it may not be significant.

Cause and effect. Even if a correlation coefficient is large and significant, this does not prove a cause-and-effect relationship. Before a causal relationship is asserted, various alternative interpretations of a high correlation must be ruled out; for example, there may be a spurious correlation, or each variable may be independently related to a common third factor (indirect association). Six criteria may be used for judging the evidence for a causal association: strength of the association, consistency of the association in different places and study groups, temporally correct association, specificity of the association, coherence with existing knowledge, and reduction of disease incidence after elimination of the factor.

ANALYSIS OF VARIANCE (ANOVA)

The *t* test is applicable for the comparison of only two sample means. When more than two sample means are to be compared, it is necessary to use analysis of variance and the *F* test. (The *F* test for two sample means is equivalent to the *t* test, because $F = t^2$ and gives identical P values.)

In the simplest analysis of variance (ANOVA) model, the over-all variance of an experiment can be partitioned into the variance between treatment groups and the variance within treatment groups—that is, the variance between means and within means. Each of these variance terms is considered as an independent estimate of the population variance. The ratio of these two sample estimates is then compared with the *F* distri-

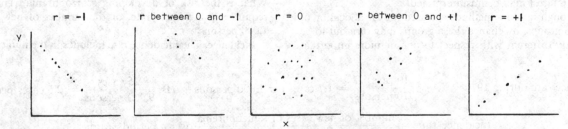

FIGURE 15. Correlation coefficient (*r*): a measure of the degree of linear relationship between two variables. (From Bahn, A. K. *Basic Medical Statistics*. Grune & Stratton, New York, 1972.)

$$\text{Point} \quad \text{prevalence} \quad \text{A:} \frac{30 \text{ cases}}{\substack{6,000 \text{ persons} \\ \text{in population}}} = \substack{5.0 \text{ cases} \\ \text{per 1,000} \\ \text{population}} \quad \text{B:} \frac{40 \text{ cases}}{\substack{10,000 \text{ persons} \\ \text{in population}}} = \substack{4.0 \text{ cases} \\ \text{per 1,000} \\ \text{population}}$$

as of January 1, 1970

$$\text{Point prevalence} = \frac{\text{number of existing cases of schizophrenia}}{\text{population}} \text{ at a point in time}$$

FIGURE 16. Prevalence rate of schizophrenia in two communities at a given point in time.

bution to determine the probability of finding by chance alone a ratio, between two sample variance estimates, of the observed magnitude or greater.

If the estimate between treatment groups is significantly greater than that within groups—that is, an *F* ratio significantly greater than 1—this suggests that not all the population means (treatment group means) are equal. One can then employ a multicomparison technique to determine which means are significantly different. Note that the *F* test requires specification of two degrees of freedom (df) terms—df for the numerator and df for the denominator of the *F* ratio—for the two variance estimates being compared.

DESIGN OF EXPERIMENTS

Although ANOVA can be used for observational data, it is particularly useful in analyzing the results of experiments. The design of experiments may vary from simple to highly complex models, depending on the kind of information that is sought and the practical clinical situation.

In evaluating a single factor intervention, such as treatment with only one drug and a placebo, one may randomly assign half of the subjects to each of two regimens. Alternatively, one arranges the subjects into clinically homogeneous groups, blocks, or pairs of individuals that are considered likely to respond in a similar manner to the intervention. Within such pairs, patients are allocated at random to the treatment or to the placebo. (Or the patient may serve as his own control in a cross-over study.)

In the first design, called completely randomized, the unpaired *t* test may be used. In the second, the randomized block design, where the subgroups are size two, the paired *t* test would be appropriate. Any extension of these models, however, including the cross-over design, or a comparison of the effects of two or more separate treatments and a placebo would require analysis of variance. Analysis of variance can take into account that there are more than two sample means or other factors such as carryover effects.

If several factors such as type of treatment, type of patient, day of test, technician or observer are to be investigated simultaneously then the experiment is multifactorial, and the design and analysis become more complex. The interaction between the factors also must be examined; otherwise the main factors of interest may be misinterpreted.

Even though random methods are used for the allocation of patients to groups, by chance these groups may turn out to be significantly different with respect to one or more important variables at the onset. Therefore, in order to assure alikeness at the start of the study, the experimenter should always compare the characteristics of the groups before the experiment is begun.

It is often desirable for ethical reasons to test for significance periodically during the course of an experiment. In this way any untoward added hazard experienced by a particular experimental group may be detected. Certain kinds of experiments are particularly suited for sequential tests. Sequential tests also permit termination of an experiment with the minimum number of patients after a significant result has been achieved.

Measures of Disease Frequency and Prognosis

RATE ANALYSIS

Measures of disease frequency are special forms of qualitative data, in which the number of cases enumerated is related to the denominator or population base in the form of a ratio or rate. There are two major types of morbidity rates: prevalence and incidence.

Prevalence. Suppose that it were possible to conduct a survey in two communities, A and B, and identify all persons who meet the diagnostic criteria for schizophrenia. Suppose, further, that 30 persons in A and 40 persons in B meet these criteria. Although the number of schizophrenics is of interest, fair comparison of the two communities requires that one relate the number of cases to the number of persons in the population (denominator) in the form of a prevalence rate. Thus, in Figure 16, although B has numerically more cases, A has the higher (point) prevalence rate.

Other prevalence measures may be used, such as (1) period prevalence—cases existing during a period of time, such as a year instead of on 1 day, and (2) lifetime prevalence—patients who have ever been ill at any time in their lives.

What does the point prevalence rate indicate? If the schizophrenics are classified by functional (psychosocial) capacity, point prevalence could indicate a great deal about the burden of this disease on the community in terms of sociomedical care requirements. It may also suggest whether the community has been able to prevent the more chronic forms of the disease. However, the prevalence rate does not answer the question: What is the risk of developing schizophrenia? That answer requires an incidence rate, or the number of new cases per 1,000 persons.

Incidence. The incidence rate includes in the numerator only

$$\text{Incidence rate during 1970} \quad \text{A:} \frac{10 \text{ cases}}{5,970 \text{ persons}} = 1.7 \text{ cases per 1,000 persons} \quad \text{B:} \frac{25 \text{ cases}}{9,960 \text{ persons}} = 2.5 \text{ cases per 1,000}$$

$$\text{Incidence rate} = \frac{\text{number of new cases of schizophrenia}}{\text{population at risk}} \text{ over a period of time.}$$

FIGURE 17. Incidence rate of schizophrenia in two communities over a period of time.

cases that have occurred for the first time during some defined period, such as 1 year, and includes in the denominator only those persons who do not already have the disease and, therefore, are at risk of developing it.

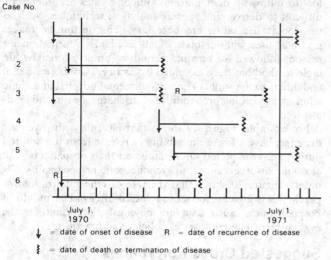

FIGURE 18. A diagrammatical representation of six cases of illness in a study group of 30 persons. From this diagram one calculates the following: Point prevalence on July 1, 1970: 4/30 (case numbers 1, 2, 3, and 6). Incidence rate for July 1, 1970 to June 30, 1971: 2/26 (numerator includes case numbers 4 and 5; denominator excludes case numbers 1, 2, 3, and 6). Period prevalence July 1, 1970 to June 30, 1971: 6/30. (From Mausner, J. S., and Bahn, A. K. *Epidemiology: An Introductory Text.* W. B. Saunders, Philadelphia, 1974.)

In Figures 16 and 17, one sees that, although A has the higher point prevalence rate, B has the higher incidence rate—that is, persons in B appear to be at greater risk of developing the disease than do persons in A.

Incidence indicates the rate at which new illnesses occur,

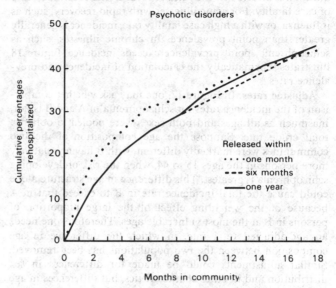

FIGURE 20. Cumulative percentages of psychotic patients rehospitalized after specified periods in the community, by length of initial hospitalization. (From Gorwitz, K., Bahn, A. K., Klee, G., and Solomon, M. Release and return rates for patients in state mental hospitals of Maryland. Public Health Rep., *81:* 1095, 1966.)

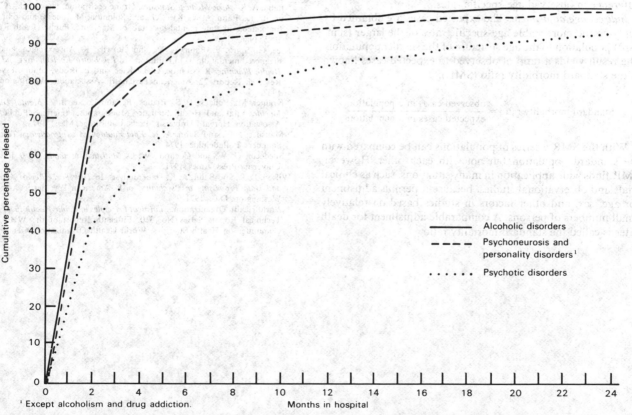

FIGURE 19. Cumulative patient release rates within specified periods in the hospital by diagnostic category. (From Gorwitz, K., Bahn, A. K., Klee, G., and Solomon, M. Release and return rates for patients in state mental hospitals of Maryland. Public Health Rep., *81:* 1095, 1966.)

whereas prevalence measures the residual of such illness, the amount existing at a point in time. The relation between incidence and prevalence is expressed by the formula: $P \sim I \times d$. That is, prevalence is proportional not only to the incidence rate but also to the duration of the disease. In turn, duration is affected by the rates of recovery, of recurrence, and of case fatality. For acute illnesses with rapid recovery, such as influenza, or with a high case fatality rate, incidence is generally greater than point prevalence. In chronic illnesses, such as schizophrenia, point prevalence exceeds incidence. Figure 18 illustrates schematically the calculation of incidence and prevalence rates.

Adjusted rates. In Figure 17, one may ask whether comparison of the incidence rates for schizophrenia in A and B is fair, inasmuch as all ages and both sexes were pooled to obtain a total crude rate. Suppose the age composition of the two communities were markedly different, with B having relatively more persons in the ages 15 to 44, when the risk of developing schizophrenia is greatest. This difference in age structure alone could cause the total incidence rate in B to exceed that in A because of the weighting effect of the large proportion of persons in B at the most vulnerable ages. Therefore, one needs an age-adjusted total rate, in which the difference in age composition between the two populations has been removed. Similar adjustments could be made for differences in sex distribution and in other characteristics, but differences in age are usually the most important. Two methods of age adjustments are used.

Direct age adjustment. A common age-structured population is used as the standard to which are applied the observed age-specific rates in A and B. One thus derives expected cases at each age. The resulting adjusted total rates reflect solely the difference in observed age-specific rates.

Indirect age adjustment. The expected cases are obtained by applying the more stable age-specific rates of the larger (standard) population to the age structure of the smaller population. The result yields a ratio of observed to expected cases known as the standard morbidity ratio (SMR):

$$\text{Standard morbidity ratio} = \frac{\text{observed cases in a population}}{\text{expected cases in a population}}$$

With the SMR a series of populations can be compared with the standard population but not with each other. However, SMR finds wide application in many situations, such as clinical trials and observational studies, because it permits adjustment for age, sex, and other factors in studies based on relatively small numbers of persons. A comparable adjustment for death rates is called the standard mortality ratio.

COHORT ANALYSIS

In the study of the prognosis of chronic diseases, such as schizophrenia, the long length of time that patients must be kept under observation may result in the attrition of cases from loss to follow-up or migration. Outcome rates are, therefore, difficult to derive, and special analytical techniques, such as the cohort life table, are necessary. This technique makes maximal use, without bias, of all available information on persons followed for unequal periods of observation. The life table method has been extended by Kramer, Goldstein, Bahn, and others to the study of cohorts of mental hospital and clinic admissions yielding probabilities of discharge, death, and readmission.

For example, Figure 19 shows that patients with psychotic disorders have a lower probability of release from the hospital during a 2-year period after admission than do patients with alcoholic disorders or with psychoneurotic or personality disorders. Figure 20 shows that the rate of rehospitalization for psychotics is greatest for those released after only 1 month of hospitalization. Such data are obviously important for the evaluation of mental hospital policies and practices.

Suggested Cross References

The use of statistics is exemplified in the sections on epidemiology (Section 6.1), computers and clinical psychiatry (Section 6.2), personality theory derived from quantitative experiment (Section 11.1), and psychiatric rating scales (Section 33.1).

REFERENCES

* Bahn, A. K. Some methodologic issues in psychiatric epidemiology and some suggested approaches. In *Psychiatric Epidemiology and Mental Health Planning*, R. Monroe, G. D. Klee, and E. Brody, editors, p. 69, Psychiatric Research Report 22. American Psychiatric Association, Washington, D.C., 1967.
* Bahn, A. K. *Basic Medical Statistics*. Grune & Stratton, New York, 1972.
  Gorwitz, K., Bahn, A. K., Klee, G., and Solomon, M. Release and return rates for patients in state mental hospitals of Maryland. Public Health Rep., *81:* 1095, 1966.
  Klee, G., Spiro, E., Bahn, A. K., and Gorwitz, K. An ecological analysis of diagnosed mental illness in Baltimore. In *Psychiatric Epidemiology and Mental Health Planning*. R. Monroe, G. D. Klee, and E. Brody, editors, Psychiatric Research Report 22. American Psychiatric Association, Washington, D.C., 1967.
* Kramer, M., Pollack, E. S., Redick, R., and Locke, B. Z. *Mental Disorders, Suicide*. Vital and Health Statistics Monographs, American Public Health Association. Harvard University Press, Cambridge, Mass., 1972.
* Mausner, J. S., and Bahn, A. K. *Epidemiology: An Introductory Test*. W. B. Saunders, Philadelphia, 1974.
* Snedecor, G. W., and Cochran, W. G. *Statistical Methods*, ed. 6. Iowa State University Press, Ames, 1971.
  Wilson, P. T., and Bahn, A. K. Data analysis. In *Task Force Report Automation and Data Processing in Psychiatry*, p. 8. American Psychiatric Association, Washington, D.C., 1971.
* World Health Organization. *Statistical Principles in Public Health Field Studies*. Technical Report Series No. 510. Fifteenth Report of the WHO Expert Committee on Health Statistics. World Health Organization, Geneva, 1972.

chapter

8

Theories of Personality and Psychopathology: Classical Psychoanalysis

WILLIAM W. MEISSNER, S.J., M.D.

Introduction

In the following pages the author attempts a more or less synthetic statement of psychoanalytic theory. It is a theory that in many ways remains the most comprehensive and most profound understanding of human behavior and experience. Despite the ferment of new discoveries, the breaking of new ground in the exploration of psychopathology, and the emergence of a plethora of contending points of view that have emerged since Freud's time, psychoanalytic theory remains the bedrock of psychodynamic understanding. Psychoanalytic concepts have so widely permeated the training and practice of modern psychiatry that they have come to be regarded as a fundamental part of the understanding and approach to mental and emotional disorders. One cannot, therefore, overstate the importance of a clear understanding of psychoanalytic theory in an approach to mental illness and, particularly, an understanding of the basic contributions of the founder of psychoanalysis, Sigmund Freud.

Such a synthetic formulation of psychoanalytic concepts as this carries with it certain risks and difficulties. The necessity for a concise and compressed statement of psychoanalytic ideas runs the risk of oversimplification and a loss of the greater nuance and sensitivity that analytic notions enjoy in application to clinical problems. Analytic theory tends to stultify when it moves away from the immediacy of clinical data, just as it tends to come alive when it finds its proper role in the clinical setting. The other major risk run is that the theory may present itself to the reader as a static entity. Although this is undoubtedly a risk, the reality is quite far removed from such sterile immobility. Rather, psychoanalytic theory has for more than three-quarters of a century undergone a process of continual growth and significant modification.

One of the purposes in this presentation is to preserve a sense of organic development and progressive enlargement of analytic theory. Therefore, the approach is in part historical, but it cannot be simply such. The approach must also be conceptual. This must be so, since psychoanalysis has undergone a continual remodeling and reorganizing of its basic concepts at almost every step of its progress. The ferment of rethinking and recasting was a dynamic manifestation of Freud's own struggles in bringing understanding to his ever-growing clinical experience. Since his passing from the scene, the struggle has continued. Consequently, as the reader moves from page to page, he has to keep one eye on the historical sequence and another eye on the conceptual progression that marks the development of psychoanalytic concepts.

One of the major impediments to the understanding and communication of psychoanalytic ideas—particularly when the discussion is aimed at residents, medical students, and other students of general psychiatry—is that the discussion depends to a significant degree on the familiarity with the basic investigative tool of classical psychoanalysis, free association. The student's basic lack of familiarity with free association and his limited contact with the kinds of data derived from the analytic process make it difficult to understand what it is that psychoanalysis is trying to understand and explain. It remains fundamentally true that the best place to learn the nature of free association and the nature of the psychoanalytic process is in psychoanalysis itself—that is, in the experience of being analyzed or of analyzing someone else.

An impediment of this nature obviously cannot be removed by a textbook presentation, but some observations are perhaps in order. The study of psychoanalysis substantially requires a fundamentally different orientation than the student is familiar with in the study of basic sciences or other medical sciences. The planned, organized pursuit of data is characteristic of most fields of medicine, but the psychoanalyst does not deliberately undertake to elicit specific information from his patient on any sort of organized plan. Rather, the psychoanalyst seeks to enable his patient to present verbal expressions of his own inner experiences and mental processes as spontaneously and in as completely uncensored a way as is possible.

The techniques of organized and systematic definition of variables and the search for data have their appropriate application when one is studying the phenomena of the external world. However, in the study of the inner world of subjective experience, an entirely different methodology and manner of thinking are required. Psychoanalysis has many links with the concerns and approaches of general medicine; nonetheless, the medical model of causal thinking plays only a minimal role in the study of psychoanalysis. In the course of this discussion, the author tries to define the specific methods and ideas that have become fundamental to classical psychoanalytic theory in an effort to avoid the usual sources of confusion and misunderstanding.

Freud's Early Years

SCIENTIFIC ORIENTATION

One of the important elements to remember in coming to understand Freud's work is that he was essentially a convinced empirical scientist of his era. His early training had been in the best scientific centers of his time. Consequently, he brought to his study of psychological processes a strong belief, which he shared with most of the scientists of his day, that scientific law and order would ultimately permit an understanding of the apparent chaos of mental processes. He believed that brain physiology is the definitive scientific approach to this objective. Even though, in the course of his experience, Freud had to modify and mitigate that basic scientific credo, he nonetheless maintained it throughout his long career. His own intense attempts to elaborate a physiology of mental processes were to prove disappointing and unsuccessful. But he continued to believe that, even though he was forced to work on a level of psychological consideration that did not seem to be immediately related to physiological processes, there is a close interrelationship between physical and psychic processes.

In the beginning of his theorizing, Freud gave considerable emphasis to physiological processes. For example, he felt that all information that reaches the mind begins in the form of physical excitation that impinges on the sensory apparatus. Such information can derive from excitation in the external world, which is then transmitted through the sense organs, or it can come from chemical stimuli, which are derived interiorly from the body. In his efforts to correlate mental processes with physiological processes, Freud noted many parallels and similarities in the way they operate. But he found the task of translating psychological processes into physiological terms a difficult and, in fact, an insurmountable one. Nonetheless, he made several attempts to describe mental phenomena in terms of the functioning of the nervous system. Finally, he suspended these efforts and decided that the integration of these levels of functioning was still beyond his grasp. He resolved to approach psychological problems on a level of investigation that did not depend immediately on the physiological parameters. After his most elaborate attempt to achieve the integration of the psychological and physiological, he wrote in discouragement to his friend Fliess in 1898:

> I have no desire at all to leave the psychology hanging in the air with no organic basis. But, beyond the feeling of conviction (that there must be such a basis), I have nothing, either theoretical or therapeutic, to work on, and so I must behave as if confronted by just psychological factors only.

FORMATIVE INFLUENCES

The formative influences on Freud's thinking and on his development stemmed from a variety of sources. One of the most significant influences on Freud's theories came from the Helmholtz school of physiology. The influence of Helmholtz's thinking dominated the empirical approach to physiology in European science of the time. It postulated a thoroughgoing determinism that stated that all processes, whether physical or physiological or mental, are determined by causal laws and sequences. Scientific laws, it held, can ultimately be reduced to the laws of physics. The relationships of the exchange and transformation of energy are governed by the principles of inertia and conservation.

Freud's neurological training and his experience in neurological research were also important influences. Freud's neurological background allowed him to understand psychological functioning in terms of a series of organizations that are hierarchically and topographically superimposed on each other. It also influenced his conception of the nervous system as composed of associative networks that are organized in terms of contiguity on one level and, more fundamentally, by drive influences. Also from this source came his basic approach to the understanding of neurodynamics in terms of the dynamics of the nervous system. Even when forced to abandon this point of view, he maintained the assumption in the form of a belief that psychodynamics could ultimately be placed on a more solid footing by an understanding of neurochemical or biochemical processes.

Another important influence in his thinking was the Darwinian heritage. Darwin's theories were very much in the air, and undoubtedly Freud had read Darwin. Darwin's influence

was reflected in the genetic aspects of Freud's own thinking, particularly in his concern for the relationship between phylogenesis and ontogenesis. Freud himself seemed to have maintained a peculiarly neo-Lamarckian view of the evolutionary process. Other important scientific influences came from the work of the psychologist Herbart and also, to a smaller extent, from Hering.

Another considerable influence that should not be passed over was Freud's immersion in and intense fascination with literature, particularly with the works of Shakespeare and Goethe. This aspect of Freud's mental life provides an interesting counterbalance to the image of the tough-minded, empirical scientist. It opens the door to the understanding of the romantic aspects of Freud's thinking. Freud was widely and intensely read in the literature not only of his own culture but of Western civilization as a whole. He became one of the outstanding masters of the German language and was awarded the Goethe Prize for literature.

Literature seems to have shaped in him a deep interest in and a sensitivity to the complexities of human nature, as well as a delicate sense of the subtlety of language and linguistic communication. It was Freud's readiness and capacity for discerning the meaning behind meaning and for unraveling the symbolic dimension of human cognitive functioning that laid the cornerstone for that aspect of psychoanalysis that is perhaps most characteristic of it, the emphasis on symbolic interpretation. Related to this influence, of course, is Freud's rooting in the Jewish tradition. It is possible that his deep interest in literature and religion comes from a long tradition of respect for the word. Perhaps more extensive and pervasive is the influence of the culture and *Zeitgeist* within which Freud lived and thought. Certainly, Darwin and Helmholtz were a significant part of that culture, but there was also the pervasive spirit of scientific inquiry and empirical methodology. One must also remember that Freud lived for the best part of his life in Victorian Vienna, where an emphasis on sexual conflicts and vicissitudes was a pervasive element in the life of that rich and vibrant city.

FREUD'S CAREER

Perhaps the easiest way to begin to appreciate the influence of these many formative factors on Freud's thinking is to see them in the context of his own emerging career. Sigmund Freud was born on May 6, 1856, in a little Moravian town called Freiburg. The territory has since been incorporated as part of Czechoslovakia. His father was a Jewish wool merchant who enjoyed moderate financial success. When Sigmund was only 4 years old, the family moved to Vienna. The rest of Freud's life and career was centered in Vienna, a city he both loved and hated. It was there he grew up, was educated, and practiced neurology and later psychoanalysis almost to the end of his life. It was not until he was forced to flee in the face of the impending Nazi persecution that he left Vienna and went with his family to England in 1938. He was to die there shortly afterward, in 1939.

Medical training. Freud's education followed a somewhat erratic course, with the result that it took him nearly 3 years longer than the average medical student of his day to earn his medical degree. The years of his medical apprenticeship, however, were years of intense intellectual ferment in which he was exposed to and assimilated some of the most profound influences that later revealed themselves in his thinking. It was during this period that the work of Darwin and his associates in biology and the physiological and physical investigations on the part of Helmholtz and his school were producing a new and vigorous scientific climate. Freud became a dedicated and convinced adherent of the new empiricism. The new empiricism dominated the scientific world of the day, since it emphasized natural laws, the unity

FIGURE 1. Freud with several of his early collaborators. *Top*, left to right: A. A. Brill, Sandor Ferenczi, Ernest Jones. *Bottom*, left to right: Freud, G. Stanley Hall, and Carl Jung. (Culver Pictures, New York, N. Y.)

of science, and scientific exactitude, specifically in terms of the importance of observation and measurement, and opposed these matters to the previously prevailing romanticism and mysticism that had characterized scientific thought in central Europe in the period after the Napoleonic wars.

During these years of medical study, Freud worked in the physiological laboratory of Ernst Brücke, who was one of the leading founders of the Helmholtz school of medicine. Helmholtz postulated that the only forces active in biological organisms are reducible to the physical chemical forces inherent in matter and are "reducible to the forces of attraction and repulsion." Thus, in Helmholtz's view, all biological organisms are to be counted as physical systems. They are composed ultimately of systems of atoms governed by physical forces, according to the principle of conservation of energy, which had been stated by Robert Mayer in 1842 and had been applied by Helmholtz and his followers in a thoroughgoing and vigorous manner a score of years later. Freud was strongly influenced by these basic principles and even more particularly by the man Brücke himself, who seemed to embody the qualities that Freud most admired, a capacity for scientific discipline and a thoroughgoing intellectual integrity.

The other figure who dominated Freud's early scientific world was the towering figure of Theodore Meynert. Freud looked up to and admired both Brücke and Meynert, and he was also strongly influenced by, even though somewhat more competitive with, Sigmund Exner, who also worked in Brücke's laboratory. These men—Brücke, Meynert, and Exner—formed a triumvirate that dominated physiological thinking and research in Europe at that time. They shared the idea that the nervous system operates by transmitting a quantitatively variable excitation from the afferent nerve endings to the efferent nerve endings. The nature of this neural impulse was not agreed on by any means, but it was referred to as "excitation." Brücke thought it to be basically electrical, and it had even been conceived of in hydraulic terms, as a sort of fluid carried in the nerve fibers, as if in a hollow pipe. At that time there was little understanding of the chemical aspects of nervous conduction.

One of Brücke's basic presumptions was that the mind and the body are organized along principles of psychophysical parallelism. This assumption allowed him to describe neural processes partly in physical and partly in psychological terms. This characteristic carried over into Freud's own research. Brücke also felt that there is no spontaneous central activity in the nervous system; he quite explicitly declared that the model of neural functioning is the reflex arc—that is, the whole

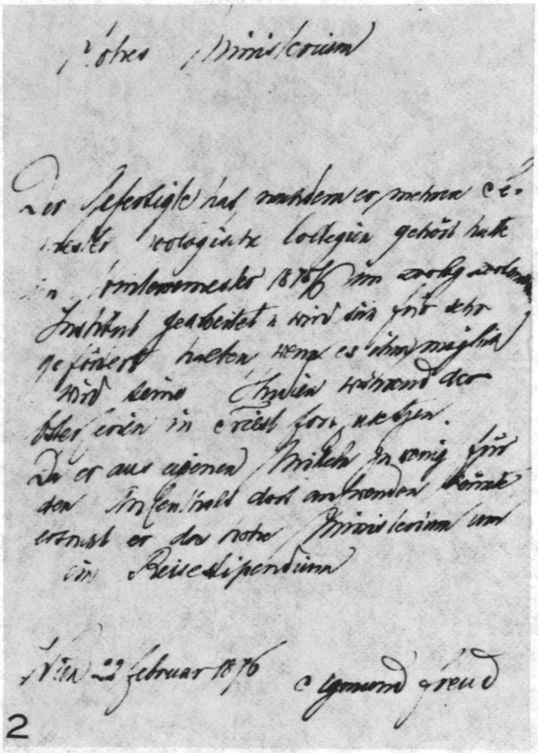

FIGURE 2. Sigmund Freud's handwriting. (Austrian Information Service, New York, N. Y.)

nervous system functions as a more or less passive instrument that remains at a state of rest until it is stimulated by exogenous energies and that the result of the stimulus is that the system is activated in such a way as to reduce the incoming irritation to a minimum. Brücke's physiology was a physiology of force and energies, and he strongly emphasized the doctrine of conservation of energy. Helmholtz gave this principle out as the ultimate foundation for the new physiology.

In 1894, Exner published a book on physiology that presented a synthesis of these same ideas. He regarded the excitation of nerve fibers as being without quality but varying only in quantity.

FIGURE 3. Sigmund Freud as a young man. (Austrian Information Service, New York, N. Y.)

FIGURE 4. Berggasse 19, the building in which Freud had his offices and which now houses the Freud Museum. (Austrian Information Service, New York, N. Y.)

Medical career. Freud graduated from medical school but continued to work in Brücke's laboratory for a year afterward. His experience in Brücke's laboratory allowed him to develop the physiological framework that played a prominent role in his casting of his psychological theories. Nor can it be said that Brücke's influence diminished during later portions of Freud's lifetime. His consistent, overriding goal was to apply the principles of Brücke and Helmholtz to the study of the nervous system and, ultimately, of the mind. Freud's early attempts at

theory were taken up with a continual struggle with this basic problematic—how to understand the workings of the mind and the clinical manifestations of psychopathology with which he was gradually becoming familiar through his clinical experience and how to explain them with the postulates and principles of neural functioning in terms of forces and energies and the principles that regulate them.

During the year Freud spent in Brücke's institute, his attention was primarily directed to neurological and neuroanatomical research, particularly on the histological investigation of the spinal ganglia of Petromyson, a primitive genus of Cyclostomata. His work there was of a high quality and made an important contribution that brought him to the threshold of a unitary theory of the neuron, a fundamental

FIGURE 5. Sigmund Freud and his father. (Austrian Information Service, New York, N. Y.)

FIGURE 6. Sigmund Freud and his mother in 1872. (Austrian Information Service, New York, N. Y.)

FIGURE 7. Sigmund Freud's office in Vienna. (Austrian Information Service, New York, N. Y.)

FIGURE 8. Sigmund Freud at his desk in his Vienna office. (Austrian Information Service, New York, N. Y.)

doctrine of neurological science that was only established a few years later by the work of Ramon y Cajal and Waldeyer.

Freud found such painstaking research work much to his liking and was ambitious to continue it, but financial considerations made this course increasingly difficult. In the meanwhile, he became enamored of Martha Bernays, and the prospects of marriage and family pressed themselves on him. He was forced to choose between the continuation of his research, with its life of economic deprivation, and the prospects of supporting a wife and family by way of medical practice. Despite his reluctance to surrender his beloved research, Freud made his choice and left Brücke's laboratory in 1882 to begin work as a general physician in the Vienna General Hospital.

He served first on the surgical service and later in Theodore Meynert's psychiatric clinic. Meynert had the reputation of being the most prominent brain anatomist of his time. Freud had been impressed by him in the lectures he had heard as a student, and his interest in neuroanatomy had been stirred by them. Freud did not respond quite so enthusiastically to Meynert's qualifications as a psychiatrist. He felt that Meynert's emphasis on neuroanatomy and neuropathology detracted from his clinical competence. But there is no question that Meynert's influence on the impressionable young physician was profound. Freud's study of Meynert's amentia (acute hallucinatory psy-

chosis) undoubtedly made a vivid impression on him and contributed to his own views on wish fulfillment, which later became a basic part of Freud's own theory of the unconscious.

Neurological work. Working on Meynert's service, Freud was directly exposed to the powerful influence of the great man, and his interest in neurology grew apace. His neurological knowledge of brain disorders grew by leaps and bounds. He obtained permission from Meynert to use his laboratory for an extensive study of neonatal brain disorders. Freud became more and more involved in neurological work and decided that—rather than engage in general practice, which he did not find particularly appealing—he would dedicate himself to specialization in neurology. In 1885 he received a coveted traveling grant that allowed him to visit Paris, where he studied for about 19 weeks in the neurological clinic of the great French neurologist, Jean-Martin Charcot, in the Salpêtrière, the famous French hospital.

Charcot's interests and his influence on Freud came at a very crucial period. Freud's own interests and his intellectual power were at a crucial phase of development. During his experience in Charcot's clinic, Freud was exposed to a fascinating variety of neurological syndromes, as well as to the charismatic personality of Charcot himself. The experience in Paris was also important for Freud, since it was the first time the young neurologist had been outside of the narrow cultural confines of Vienna and was exposed to the sophisticated culture of another great European capital. He saw that there was a great deal more to learn than he had come to know in Meynert's clinic.

Perhaps more than anything else, he was impressed by Charcot's radically different approach to hysteria. Under Charcot's influence Freud became deeply interested in the problem of hysteria and became firmly convinced that hysterical phenomena are a genuine form of pathology worthy of careful study and understanding. This view was not shared by Freud's Vienna colleagues.

In fact, the views about hysteria propounded by Charcot were markedly divergent from the attitudes toward hysteria that had been prevalent until that time. Hysterical phenomena were more commonly regarded as deliberate pretense, a form of malingering, or a product of an overly vivid imagination; as such, hysterical phenomena were not to be taken seriously as forms of pathology. As a result of Charcot's thorough and systematic study of the highly variable manifestations typical of hysteria, it was gradually recognized as a more or less legitimate disease of the nervous system and one worthy of scientific inquiry.

Charcot himself had not undertaken any specifically psychological explanation of hysterical phenomena, although he placed considerable emphasis on the role of hypnosis in treating hysterical disorders and,

FIGURE 9. Mrs. Paula Fichtl, Freud's last maid, with some personal items: hat, cane. (Austrian Information Service, New York, N. Y.)

FIGURE 10. A clinical lecture by Jean Charcot at the Salpêtrière. (Culver Pictures, New York, N. Y.)

consequently, opened the way to an appreciation of the similarities between hypnotic and hysterical phenomena. However, the possibility that hysterical phenomena might be psychological in origin was suggested to Freud by the fact that Charcot was able to precipitate and reproduce hysterical paralyses, seizures, and other characteristic hysterical manifestations through the use of hypnotic suggestion.

It was through his experiments in the use of hypnosis that Charcot was able to distinguish hysterical phenomena from organic, neurological disorders. Charcot firmly believed that the ultimate basis of hysteria is neurological, and he attributed it specifically to a congenital degeneration of the brain. But he also held that the form of the symptoms manifested in hysterical seizures is psychogenic in origin—that is, they are produced by specific ideas in the patient's mind. By the same token, he felt that hysterical symptoms can be cured by ideas. It was probably under the influence of Charcot that Freud began to suspect the connection between hysterical pathology and sexuality. Charcot even referred to hysteria as *une chose genitale.*

The use of hypnosis in the study of hysteria, which Freud had become familiar with in Charcot's clinic, was to provide one of the most significant points of origin for psychoanalysis. In a sense it can be said that psychoanalysis has its basic roots in hypnosis and that Freud's application of hypnosis in the study of his hysterical patients set his feet on the path of psychoanalytic discovery.

Hypnotism has a long, venerable, and obscure history that may stretch back to ancient times, but its modern origins are generally traced back to the Austrian physician Anton Mesmer. Mesmer was the discoverer of a special quality, which he called "animal magnetism," to cure people of afflictions that bear a striking resemblance to hyster-

ical phenomena. Mesmer used a powerful blend of charisma and suggestion to evoke the power of his magnetism, and his cures became a focus for both popular fervor and considerable opposition and debate toward the end of the 18th century. It was not until nearly a century later that Liébault, a kindly French country doctor in Nancy, began to use hypnotic induction to relieve the neurotic symptoms of large masses of peasants. The technique was basically one of hypnotic suggestion. Although it remained for Freud and psychoanalysis to provide a more rational explanation of the psychological mechanisms underlying such neurotic symptoms, psychotherapy, as a form of medical treatment, had its origins in Liébault's clinic.

Freud became particularly interested, after his exposure to Charcot's methods, in the work of Hippolyte Bernheim, who was associated with Liébault in the use of hypnosis as a therapeutic technique. Bernheim made a careful study of the characteristics of suggestibility and concluded that this phenomenon is not entirely confined to hysterics. It can be identified in patients with a wide variety of neurotic disorders, as well as in normal persons. Bernheim's attempt to account for a wide variety of normal and abnormal social reactions in terms of suggestion, specifically autosuggestion, provided a significant step in the direction of attempting to understand human behavior and its motivation on the basis of clinical study.

Freud had become quite deeply interested in the phenomenon of hypnosis and, consequently, spent several weeks during the summer of 1889 studying in Liébault's clinic in Nancy. He was profoundly impressed by the relationship that Liébault was able to establish with his patients, as well as the effects Bernheim was able to produce in hospitalized patients through the use of hypnotic suggestion. As Freud's familiarity with hysterical phenomena and his understanding of the uses of hypnosis grew, he became more profoundly impressed by the powerful nature of mental processes and by the possibility that such mental events may take place outside of the range of consciousness and may have powerful effects on human behavior and psychopathology. This awareness had been stirred by his experiences at the Salpêtrière, but it deepened and became more convincing by reason of his experience in Liébault's clinic.

When Freud returned to Vienna from Paris in 1886, his intention was to give up his laboratory studies and to devote his energies to the practice of clinical neurology. His interest in neurology had not waned. Not only had his imagination been stirred by his experience with Charcot, but he busied himself with translations of work by Charcot and Bernheim and even published a paper on hemianopsia in children. But his first major neurological work appeared in 1891. The book was entitled *Aphasia,* and in it he challenged some of the established localization schemata for aphasic disorders, particularly those of Wernicke and Lichtheim. Instead of minute localization of language functions, Freud offered a functional explanation that accounted for the subvarieties of aphasic disorders in terms of disruptions of the radiating associative pathways. Freud's was the only neurological work of the period to cite the genetic view of Hughlings Jackson.

Freud's work received little acclaim at the time, but it still stands as one of the important historical contributions to the understanding of aphasia. It is of interest that the book was dedicated to Josef Breuer, who in the ensuing years was to become an important figure in the origins of psychoanalysis. In the same year, 1891, Freud published a massive work in conjunction with his friend Oscar Rie, a pediatrician, on unilateral paralysis in children. This work received wide acclaim in neurological circles and is still considered a classic. Two years later, in 1893, Freud published another large monograph, this time on the central diplegias in children. His final important neurological contribution came in the form of a massive monograph on children's paralysis; the monograph was included in the great encyclopedia of medicine that was edited by Nothnagel. This work, too, has achieved the status of a major contribution in modern neurology and has been issued in English translation under the title of *Infantile Cerebral Paralysis* (1968). With this work, Freud brought to a close his specifically neurological labors.

SUMMARY OF THE NEUROLOGICAL PERIOD

In Freud's approach to the understanding of mental and emotional disorders during this early period, his thinking seems to have been determined by two principal influences. From the Helmholtz school and from his teachers—Brücke, Meynert, and Charcot—he had learned to emphasize rational scientific understanding, careful empirical study, and clinical observation. From the French hypnotists, Liébault and Bernheim, he had learned that the physician himself may play a significant role as an instrument of psychotherapeutic change. His experiences in the clinics of Charcot and later of Liébault gave him a profound impression that deep psychological forces, which are not immediately accessible to consciousness, are operative in ways that profoundly affect human motivation and behavior. In the beginning Freud was dominated by the empirical and scientific orientation of the Helmholtz school and its doctrine of radical physical empiricism. But, even more profoundly than these scientific doctrines, Freud's capacity as a clinical observer exercised a profound influence on his thinking. Ultimately, his ability to integrate these diverse influences, together with his extraordinary psychological sensitivity and insight, enabled him to create a new science that represented a unique approach to the study and resolution of human conflict.

The *Project*

The letter that Freud wrote to his friend Fliess, complaining that he would have to resign himself to thinking of his psychology as if it were suspended in midair without a physiological foundation, was born of his sense of frustration in being unable to bring his *Project* to successful completion. His *Project* represents the culmination and highpoint of Freud's neurological commitment.

At this time Freud was an established clinical neurologist and had made substantial contributions to that area of medical study. Moreover, he was intensely dedicated to the scientific ideals of the Helmholtz approach to physiology and psychology. He conceived the scheme of elaborating a complete psychology that would be based on the physicalistic supposition of the Helmholtz school. For nearly 2 years, from 1895 to 1897, Freud struggled with these ideas. Finally, in the white heat of intense inspiration, in a period of no more than 3 weeks, he wrote his *Project for a Scientific Psychology* (see Figure 11). When the white heat of his inspiration had begun to fade, Freud became increasingly discouraged with what he had written and finally, in disgust, threw it into a desk drawer, where it remained for years. It was his intention that it should be destroyed, but after his death his papers came into the hands of those who recognized the importance of this piece of writing, and it was finally published posthumously.

It would be a mistake to regard the *Project* as an aberrant interlude in the development of Freud's ideas. Quite the contrary. Even though Freud turned his back on an attempt to physiologize his psychology, the basic postulates and ideas that were built into the *Project* provided the basic foundations for his own thinking and provided the substratum on which the superstructure of psychoanalysis was raised. At those points in his thinking in which Freud was dealing with the economic and energic aspects of psychic functioning, the influence of the *Project* was apparent, and it is for this reason a document of supreme importance.

The influence of the *Project* permeates Freud's thinking and writing on many levels. During the period of his struggles with the ideas in the *Project,* he was working with Breuer on the problem of hysteria. In 1893 they published a "Preliminary Communication," in which they sketched some of their ideas about the nature of hysteria. Finally, they published *Studies on Hysteria* in 1895. In both the "Preliminary Communication" and the *Studies,* the influence of the ideas of the *Project* can be seen, particularly in the notions of cerebral excitation and discharge of affect. Later, in Freud's seventh chapter of *The Interpretation of Dreams* (1900), the model of the mind he proposed there has direct links to the concepts of mental functioning formulated in the *Project.* Still later, in his development of a theory of sexuality and in his elaboration of his instinct theory and even as late as *Beyond the Pleasure Principle* (1920), the influence of the *Project* is explicit and identifiable. It is now clear that many of the formulations that Freud reached in the writing of the *Project* were revived and found their way into his thinking, once again, in his later development of an ego theory.

Consequently, the *Project* must be seen as an extremely important and seminal work that, if it brought Freud's neurological period to a brilliant close, also opened the way to the broad vistas of psychoanalysis and, in extremely important and significant ways, determined the shape that psychoanalytic principles were to take. Freud stated his intention from the very beginning:

> The intention is to furnish a psychology that shall be a natural science: that is, to represent psychical processes as quantitatively determinant states of specifiable material particles, thus making those processes perspicuous and free from contradiction.

The *Project* was an ambitious attempt to be as scientific in the 19th-century sense of Helmholtz as possible. Freud based his thinking on two principal theorems. The first was a quantitative conception of neural activity that he referred to as Q.

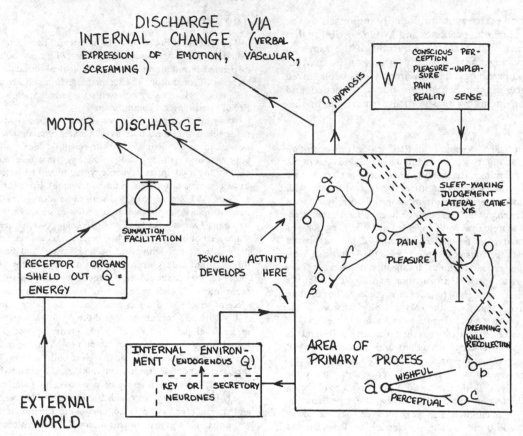

DISCHARGE VIA
INTERNAL CHANGE (VERBAL
EXPRESSION OF EMOTION, VASCULAR,
SCREAMING)

FIGURE 11. Diagrammatical summary of the theories in Freud's *Project for a Scientific Psychology*.

Q was a quantity of neural excitation which could be transmitted from cell to cell in the nervous system and from neural system to neural system. The second principal theory was the neuron doctrine, according to which the nervous system is composed of distinct and similarly constructed neurons that are separated from each other yet in contact with one another through contact barriers (synapses).

Freud postulated that there are at least two systems of neurons, which have different characteristics that affect psychological functions. The φ system of neurons consists of permeable elements, whose function is to transmit Q to other neuronal systems without any significant alterations of the φ neurons themselves. The ψ neurons are, by way of contrast, impermeable—that is, their function is not the transmission of Q but, rather, the reception of Q and the storing of it in such a way as to change the neuron and build up a level of internal charge. Freud saw these combined properties of the respective neuronal systems as explaining one of the pecularities of the neural system—namely, the capacity of retaining and storing excitations and, at the same time, remaining capable of receiving further excitatory input.

One of the fundamental principles of the operation of the nervous system Freud described as the principle of neuronic inertia. According to this principle, neurons tend to divest themselves of Q, the quantity of excitation. This property, by which the nervous system tends to keep itself free from excitation, leads to the process of discharge as one of the primary functions of neuronal systems. Freud called this the constancy principle, a principle more familiarly known today as homeostasis. In 1893 Freud had formulated the principle in these words:

If a person experiences a psychical impression, something in his nervous system, which we will for the moment call the sum of excitation, is increased. Now in every individual there exists a tendency to diminish this sum of excitation once more, in order to preserve his health.

The principle of constancy serves as the economic foundation stone for Freud's instinctual theory (see Table I).

Freud envisioned excitation not as arising spontaneously in the nervous system but, rather, as being put into it from the outside. Q is delivered to the nervous system from two sources. The first is external reality, which serves to excite the sensory organs by way of external physical excitation. The second is from the body itself, which provides endogenous stimuli that impinge on the mental apparatus and call equally for discharge. These endogenous stimuli are related to the major needs of the body, including hunger, respiration, and sexuality. Thus, Freud explicitly stated at the root of his thinking a theory of the nervous system as passively responsive to external sources of stimulation and a notion of motivation in terms of drive or tension reduction.

His view of the perceptual process was decidedly Helmholtzian—reality consists of nothing but material masses in motion and the roots of the perceptual process lie in the physical excitation of neural elements. But Freud was also careful not to leave his system exposed to the destructive impact of excessive excitation. He also postulated that excitation in the system is directly proportional to the amount of stimulation. When sums of excitation meet the sensory apparatus, they are broken up into portions of stimulation. This provides a preliminary threshold below which the quantities of excitation are barred from affecting the neuronal system. Consequently, the effectiveness of minor stimuli is minimized, and the system is restrictively responsive to more

TABLE I
Energic Principles Based on the Project for a Scientific Psychology

Entropy	Tendency for energy in physical system to flow from region of high energy to regions of lower energy. Tendency for system toward homogeneity. Tendency of system to diminish spontaneously the amount of energy available for work.
Conservation	The sum of forces (energy) in any isolated (closed) system remains constant.
Neuronic inertia	Neurons tend to divest themselves of quantities of excitation. Application of entropy and conservation to neuronal activity.
Constancy	The nervous system tends to maintain itself in a state of constant tension or level of excitation. Return to a level of constant excitation is achieved by a tendency to immediate energic discharge (through the path of least resistance).
Nirvana	The dominant tendency to reduce, keep constant, or remove the internal psychic tension due to the excitation of stimuli. The tendency to reduce the level of excitation to a minimum. Extension of constancy principle. Expressed in pleasure principle, ultimately in death instinct.
Pleasure-Unpleasure	Tendency of mental apparatus to seek pleasure and avoid unpleasure. Unpleasure is due to the increase of tension or level of excitation; pleasure is due to the release of tension or discharge of excitation. The pleasure principle thus follows the economic requirements of constancy.

or less medium quantities of excitation. Freud later referred to this threshold as a stimulus barrier, the primitive analogue of defense.

After excitation has penetrated to the φ system of permeable neurons, the qualitative characteristics of the stimuli are conveyed unhindered through the φ system to the level of the ψ system of impermeable neurons. Excitation is again processed in the ψ system and transmitted to the ω system, which is composed of perceptual neurons, where the functions of consciousness are carried out. The ψ nucleus is connected with those paths through which the endogenous quantities of excitation are derived. Endogenous stimuli are presumed to be intercellular in nature. As the ψ neurons fill with quantities of Q, there results an effort to discharge the quantity. The discharge is then effected through motor systems, autonomic discharge, and other effector mechanisms. The problem of how quantitative variation in excitation gives rise to the experience of quality reflects the underlying mind-body problem. The physical reductionism of the Helmholtz view did not admit qualities originating in external reality. Freud solved this difficulty by appealing to the special system of perceptual neurons, whose excitation gives rise to the experience of different qualities in the form of conscious sensations (ω).

With regard to the quantities of Q impinging on the neural systems, Freud did not differentiate between the energy from the outside and that from within the organism except in one important detail. The critical difference is that the organism can withdraw itself from external stimuli, but it cannot withdraw itself from the effects of endogenous stimuli. His theory of inner motivation, consequently, was based on a concept of drive energy and included a notion of discharge and reduction of energic inputs.

Freud then added that the success the nervous system experiences in discharging tension is equivalent to pleasure, just as pain is related

to the building up of excessive nervous excitation. Since discharge of excitation is the primary function of the neuronal system, the system was envisioned as ordered to the achieving of pleasure through discharge of excitation and, correspondingly, to the avoidance of pain. Thus, the principle of constancy can be seen to underlie the basic presumptions of Freud's instinctual theory and its relationship to the pleasure principle. The principle of constancy, further, has its roots in the principle of conservation of energy as proposed by Mayer and Helmholtz, according to which the sum of forces remains constant in every closed physical system. The principle also relates to Herbart's hypothesis that mental processes tend to strive for equilibrium, a notion similiar to Cannon's concept of homeostasis.

On the basis of these slender postulates, Freud elaborated a complex and ingenious account of mental functions. But he was unable to provide a satisfactory account of either defense or consciousness. In both cases he became embroiled in a continuing regress in which he seemed unable to stop. Despite a variety of ingenious feedback loops that he built into the system—Freud was many decades ahead of his time in envisioning informational servomechanisms—he was unable to complete the functioning of his system without violating the demands of his mechanical principles. He thus introduced into his system a major concession to vitalism, an observing ego. This observing ego is able to see the danger for the mobilization of defenses or is able to sense the indication of quality in conscious experiences. The ego remains as a sort of primary willer and ultimate knower—a personal center within the theory that cannot be reduced to the physicalistic terms of Freud's Helmholtzian postulates and that consequently enjoys a significant degree of autonomy.

Although the usefulness of these energic postulates is generally recognized insofar as they provided a useful heuristic basis for the development of Freud's early ideas and for the development of further psychoanalytic ideas, in the past few years these energic concepts have come under stringent methodological criticism. Freud's hypothetical psychic energy was assumed to be at work in the mental apparatus as the motivating force of mental operations but had no specified relationship to physical energies operating in the brain. Psychic energy is derived from instinctual drives and is subsequently modified and guided by psychic structures in the direction of discharge, whether directly or indirectly. The patterns of such discharge are governed by the economic principles already discussed. Nonetheless, Freud's idea that symptoms reflect such indirect patterns of discharge of quantities of energies that, without the presence of neurotic conflict, would have been more immediately and freely discharged was a fundamental and even revolutionary concept.

The most stringent forms of criticism of the notion of psychic energy propose that it fails to meet the most minimal criteria of accepted scientific methods. Specifically, it is internally contradictory and lacks consistency; it presents a logically closed system that misinterprets metaphor as fact; it involves tautological renaming of observable psychological phenomena in energic terms that masquerades as explanation; it is unable to explain all the revelant data; it tends to lead to a false sense of explanation, particularly insofar as it offers pseudoexplanations that are inconsistent with current knowledge of neurophysiology; and it promotes a form of mind-body dualism that prevents integration of psychoanalytic concepts with other related sciences. Thus, it tends to serve as a substitute for other forms of explanation—for example, neurophysiological—and becomes a barrier, rather than a bridge, between psychoanalysis and physiology.

Other more specific criticisms attack the concept of psychic energy. Such energy is essentially unmeasurable; in effect, one is unable to find ways to test quantitative assumptions specifically. This lack leaves psychoanalysts more or less in the position of providing descriptions that tend to be taken as explanations. Moreover, the imposition of the concept of psychic energy makes it difficult, if not impossible, to understand the connection between such energies and the physical energies known to be operating in neurological structures. Consequently, the laws of transformation from one to the other remain unspecified and unknowable. This deficiency also tends to make it difficult to generate testable hypotheses on the basis of psychoanalytic concepts that may be evaluated by other nonanalytic methods.

Another difficulty in this area arises in connection with the qualitatively different forms of psychic energy, such as libidinal energies, aggressive energies, various degrees of neutralized energies, bound and fused energies. The difficulty here has not so much to do with the varying manifestation of energies in different forms but, rather, with the idea that the differences are inherent in the energies themselves. At one time physiologists believed that specific nerve energies account for the differences in sensory perceptual experience—for example, that different sensory modalities, such as the auditory and the visual systems, operate on the basis of distinguishable forms of nervous energy specific to each modality. But more recent neurophysiological study of the nerve impulse indicates that there is no inherent differentiation on the level of neuronal energies and that the differences have to do with the central termination and organization of neuronal systems and the patterns of stimulus input. On this particular point the disparity between the hypothesis of psychic energy and more contemporary views of the functioning of the nervous system seems quite apparent.

Despite these criticisms and difficulties, a substantial number of analytic theorists are still unwilling to abandon the energic hypothesis. They argue, for example, that the attempt to integrate psychoanalytic findings with the discoveries and concepts of other related scientific fields may be premature. Freud's attempt to do so in the *Project* faltered because at the time too little was known of brain physiology to be useful in explaining his psychological observations. Consequently, he had to develop a rough working hypothesis of some sort of energy characterized by properties that were theoretically useful to him in developing his own ideas, leaving for the future the refinement of this hypothetical notion and its integration with other branches of science.

Despite the tremendous advance in the understanding of neurophysiology today, it remains questionable whether sufficient understanding of the function of the nervous system has been gained to allow a recasting of the energic and structural hypotheses in terms of these concepts. Consequently, such theorists argue that the best approach to these problems is to continue to elaborate psychoanalytic theory in whatever way seems to be most useful clinically without concern over its relation to or potential integration with data, observations, and theories from other related scientific fields. Further, the inability to measure quantitative dimensions continues to present a problem, but it is not a problem that is foreign to other scientific methods. Some years ago Rapaport (1960) pointed out that psychoanalysis shares such difficulties in quantification with certain of the biological sciences. Moreover, it is characteristic of the early development of many sciences to have relatively primitive forms of quantitative techniques. The difficulty in psychoanalysis is even more marked and understandable in view of the extraordinary complexity of variables, many of which are loosely defined and not specifically interrelated.

One of the difficulties inherent in the discussion of psychic energy is that, because of the original mode in which Freud expressed his economic views, the economic hypothesis has become overidentified with the hypothesis of psychic energy. This tendency has been reinforced by the classic formulation of the economic hypothesis by Rapaport and Gill (1959) specifically in terms of psychic energies. There is little doubt that psychoanalytic theory cannot do without a principle of economics. One must invoke the very concepts and issues of quantity and intensity that led Freud from the very beginning to postulate an economic point of view in order to express or understand matters of quantitative variation, degrees of intensity, and levels and intensity of motivation; to explain how a person is able to make choices among conflicting motivations and goals or bring about the resolution of conflict; to explain the whole range of affective, motivational, and structural concepts that form the backbone of psychoanalytic understanding.

What remains questionable, however, and what has essentially been the target of the sternest criticisms has been the hypothetical construct of psychic energy. Whether psychoanalysis can sustain a principle of economics without the energic encumbrances derived from late 19th-century physics and physiology remains a point to be argued and discussed. Many theorists have argued that the theoretical usefulness of an energy-force model has long been outlived and that the contemporary framework of scientific thinking calls much more for an informational-processing model of psychic functioning. The point to be emphasized is that such a model remains to be developed as a substitute for the theoretical implications of Freud's earlier energic views and that such a model cannot take its potential role in the complexities of psychoanalytic theory without embodying basic economic principles and an economic point of view. Informational and process concepts are no less inherently economic than their energic predecessors.

Beginnings of Psychoanalysis

In the decade extending from 1887 to 1897, the period in which Freud began to study seriously the disturbances of his hysterical patients, psychoanalysis can be said to have taken root. These slender beginnings had a 3-fold aspect: the emergence of psychoanalysis as a method of investigation, as a therapeutic technique, and as a body of scientific knowledge based on an increasing fund of information and basic theoretical propositions. These early researches flowed out of Freud's initial collaboration with Josef Breuer and then increasingly out of his own independent investigations and theoretical developments.

THE CASE OF ANNA O.

Freud had strong interests in the psychopathology of hysteria, and, by the time he returned to Vienna in the fall of 1889, he had been exposed to the teachings of Charcot, Liébault, and Bernheim. As soon as he opened his private practice, he began to become more familiar on a day-to-day basis with the pathological manifestations of hysteria. A fair proportion of the difficulties that patients presented in his office were psychoneurotic in nature, rather than strictly neurological.

Perhaps the decisive influence that drew Freud in the direction of the study of psychopathology came from Josef Breuer. Breuer was an older physician, a distinguished and established practitioner in the Viennese community. Freud had gotten to know Breuer and some of his work while Freud had been working at Brücke's Institute of Physiology. Knowing Freud's interests in hysterical pathology, Breuer told him about an unusual case of a woman he had treated for about a year and a half—from December 1880 to June 1882. This was the famous case of Fräulein Anna O., which proved to be one of the important stimuli in the development of psychoanalysis.

Anna O. was, in reality, Bertha Pappenheim, who later became quite famous as a founder of the social work movement. At the time that she began to see Breuer, however, she was an intelligent and strong-minded woman of about 21 years of age who had developed a number of hysterical symptoms in connection with the illness and death of her father. These symptoms included paralysis of the limbs, contractures, anesthesias, visual disturbances, disturbances of speech, anorexia, and a distressing nervous cough. Her illness was also characterized by two distinct phases of consciousness; one was relatively normal, but in the other she seemed to assume a second and more pathological personality. These latter states were called absences. The transition between these two states seemed to be brought about by a form of autohypnosis. Breuer became able to manipulate the transition between these two states by placing her in a hypnotic state.

Anna had been very close to and very fond of her father. She and her mother had shared the duties of nursing him on his death bed. During her altered states of consciousness, she was able to recall the vivid fantasies and intense emotions she had experienced while nursing her father. It was with considerable amazement, both to the patient and to Breuer, that, when she was able to recall with the associated expression of affect the scenes or circumstances under which her symptoms had arisen, the symptoms could be made to disappear. Anna vividly described this process as the "talking cure," also calling it "chimney sweeping."

Once the connection between talking through the circumstances of the symptoms and the disappearance of the symptoms themselves had been established, Anna proceeded to deal with each of her many symptoms, one after another. She was able to recall that on one occasion, when her mother had been absent, she had been sitting at her father's bedside and had had a fantasy or daydream in which she imagined that a snake was crawling toward her father and was going to bite him. She struggled forward to try to ward off the snake, but her arm, which had been draped over the back of the chair, had gone to sleep. She was unable to move it. The paralysis remained, and she was unable to move the arm until she was able to recall this scene under hypnosis. It is easy to see how this kind of material must have made a profound impression on Freud. It provided a convincing demonstration of the power of unconscious memories and of suppressed affects in the production of hysterical symptoms.

In the course of the somewhat lengthy treatment of Anna O., Breuer had become increasingly preoccupied with his fascinating and unusual patient and, consequently, spent more and more time with her and was more and more involved in the treatment. In the meanwhile, his wife had grown increasingly jealous and resentful. As soon as Breuer began to realize this, the sexual connotations of it frightened him, and he abruptly terminated the treatment. Only a few hours later, however, he was recalled urgently to Anna's bedside. He had felt that she was greatly improved as a result of the treatment, but he found her in a stage of acute excitement. She had never alluded to the forbidden topic of sex during the course of her treatment, but she was now experiencing hysterical childbirth. The phantom pregnancy was the logical termination of the sexual feelings she had developed toward Breuer in response to his therapeutic efforts. He had been quite unaware of this development, and the experience was quite unnerving to him. He was able to calm Anna down by hypnotizing her, but then he left the house in a cold sweat and immediately set out with his wife for Venice on a second honeymoon.

It is unlikely that the supposed cure of Anna O. was as successful as Breuer suggested. According to a version that comes from Freud through Ernest Jones, the patient was far from cured and had later to be hospitalized after Breuer's departure. It seems ironical that the prototype of a cathartic cure was, in fact, far from successful. But it must be remembered that Breuer's version was written mostly from memory about 13 or 14 years after the event, and at that it seems to have been published only reluctantly at Freud's insistence.

The case of Anna O. provided an important starting point and a crucial juncture in the development of psychoanalysis. If Freud had been threatened by the sexual feelings aroused by the cathartic treatment, psychoanalysis might have been aborted at its beginning. But it was Freud's unique capacity to treat these feelings and fantasies as facts of observation and to use them as the basis of a scientific theory that gave rise to the origins of psychoanalysis. Breuer, however, withdrew from the field, thereby surrendering his opportunity to advance the understanding of human behavior.

STUDIES ON HYSTERIA

During the early phases of his collaboration with Breuer, Freud seemed to vascillate between the views of hypnosis of the Nancy school, his allegiance to Charcot's ideas, and Breuer's cathartic method. The collaboration with Breuer finally brought about the publication of the *Preliminary Communication* in 1893. This was a first step in the direction of psychoanalysis. Essentially, Freud and Breuer extended Charcot's concept of traumatic hysteria to a general doctrine of hysteria. Hysterical symptoms were related to determined psychic traumata, sometimes clearly and directly and sometimes in a symbolic disguise. The observations based on these latter cases establish a connection between the pathogenesis of common hysteria and that of traumatic neurosis; in both cases the trauma is not followed by sufficient reaction and is thus kept out of consciousness.

The authors observed that the individual hysterical symptoms seemed to disappear immediately when the event that provoked them was clearly brought to life and the patient was able to describe the event in great detail and put the accompanying affect into words. The fading of a memory or the loss of its associated affect depends on various factors, including whether or not there has been an energetic reaction to the event that provokes the affect. Thus, memories can be regarded as traumata that have not been sufficiently abreacted. They observed that the splitting of consciousness that is so striking in the classical cases of hysteria is present to at least a rudimentary degree in every hysteria. The basis of hysteria is described in the *Preliminary Communication* as a hypnoid state—a state of dissociated consciousness. Psychotherapy was thought to achieve its curative effect on hysterical symptoms by bringing to an end the operative force of the idea that was not sufficiently abreacted in the first instance. Psychotherapy does this by allowing the strangulated affect to find a way of discharge by way of speech, thus subjecting it to an associative correction that introduces it to normal consciousness.

The *Preliminary Communication* created considerable interest, and it was followed in 1895 by the *Studies on Hysteria*, in which Breuer and Freud reported on their clinical experience in the treatment of hysteria and proposed a theory of hysterical phenomena. The book included the *Preliminary Communication*, a report by Breuer of his work with Anna O., a series of cases reported by Freud, a lengthy theoretical section written by Breuer, and, finally, a section on the psychotherapy of hysteria, which was contributed by Freud.

Freud's case discussions proved to be extremely significant, since they formed the original basis for much of his psychoanalytic thinking. The first case history was that of Emmy von N.

Emmy von N. was a woman of about 40 years of age whose treatment Freud undertook in 1889. She suffered from a variety of hysterical complaints, including mild deliria, hallucinations, anesthesia and pain in her leg, and an ovarian neuralgia. Freud had no doubt that her pathology was basically hysterical in nature. She also suffered from psychic symptoms, which included alterations of moods, phobias, and abulias. Freud became quite involved in her case, since her personality interested him, and he devoted a considerable amount of time to her treatment. She could be put into a state of somnambulism with considerable ease. Freud used hypnosis in this case and, for the first time, applied the cathartic technique, which Breuer had described to him and which Breuer had applied in the treatment of Anna O.

Freud used the hypnosis primarily for the purpose of providing Emmy von N. with maxims, which she could keep in mind and use to protect herself from relapsing into delirious states. Freud felt that the phobias and abulias in this patient were primarily traumatic in origin. The distressing affects connected with these traumatic experiences had remained unresolved. The lively activity of her memory brought these traumas and their accompanying affects little by little into her consciousness and gave rise to the hysterical symptoms.

The second case was Lucy R., whom Freud had treated toward the end of 1892.

Referred to Freud by another physician, Lucy R. suffered from a chronically recurrent suppurative rhinitis. At the time, she was also suffering from depression and fatigue and was tormented by subjective sensations of smell, particularly the smell of burnt pudding. Freud was able to determine that this hysterical symptom was related to an event in which the patient's employer had reprimanded her, thus dashing her romantic hopes. The smell was associated with a trauma and persisted in her consciousness as the symbolic representation of the trauma.

Freud concluded from these observations that an experience that had played an important pathogenic role, together with its subsidiary concomitants, was accurately retained in the patient's memory, even when it seemed to be forgotten and the patient was unable to recall it to mind. He postulated that as an essential condition for the development of hysteria, an idea must be repressed from consciousness and excluded from any modification by association with other ideas. At this early stage Freud felt that the repression was intentional and that it served as the basis for the conversion of a sum of neural excitation. This sum of excitation, when it was cut off from the more normal paths of psychic association, would find its way all the more easily along a deviant path that led to somatic innervation. The basis for such repression, he argued, must be a feeling of unpleasure that derived from the incompatibility between the idea to be repressed and the dominant mass of ideas that constituted the ego.

Moreover, as one symptom was removed, another developed to take its place. Freud regarded the case of Lucy R. as a model of one particular form of hysteria, in which the illness can be acquired even by a person of sound heredity as the result of the appropriate traumatic experiences. This view was quite different from the view proposed by Breuer, which ascribed the origin of hysteria to hypnoid states. The actual traumatic moment, in Freud's view, is the one in which the incompatibility of ideas forces itself on the ego and in which the ego decides on repudiation of the incompatible idea. This brings into being a nucleus for the crystallization of a psychic group that is somehow divorced from the ego. This resulted in a splitting of consciousness that is characteristic of acquired hysteria. The therapeutic process in Lucy R.'s case consisted of compelling this split-off psychic group to unite once more with the main mass of conscious ego ideas.

The case of Katharina is particularly interesting, since it is probably one of the shortest cases of psychoanalytic treatment on record.

Katharina was an employee at a mountain resort that Freud visited. She sought Freud out to seek his help with symptoms of anxiety that had first appeared about 2 years earlier. In the course of a few conversations, Katharina came to realize that her father had been making sexual advances to her and that he had also been sexually involved with her cousin. Freud related her anxiety to the sexual stimulation, which she had put out of her conscious awareness. He thus fitted the case into the schematic picture of an acquired hysteria. Katharina's anxiety was hysterical—that is, it was a reproduction of an anxiety that had appeared in the first instance in connection with earlier and even infantile sexual traumas.

In every case of hysteria based on such sexual traumas, Freud felt that the impressions from the presexual period, which produce little or no effect on the child, can attain a traumatic power at a later date as memories when the girl or married woman begins to acquire an understanding and exposure to sexual life.

Finally, Freud discussed the case of Elizabeth von R.

Elizabeth von R. was a woman of 24 who was afflicted with an impairment of her posture. She was unable to walk except with the upper part of her body bent forward and with some means of support (astasia-abasia). She also described a number of pains and hyperalgesias, which seemed to have a hysterical basis. Freud pointed out that the descriptions of her pain and the character of her pain were quite indefinite and that, if the hyperalgesic skin and muscles of her legs were touched, her face assumed a peculiar expression that seemed more akin to pleasure than to pain.

Freud was quite puzzled by the apparent lack of connection between the events in her history and her actual symptoms. Analysis seemed to point to the conversion of a psychic excitation into a physical pain. The conversion did not seem to take place when the impressions were fresh; rather, it seemed to take place in connection with memories of the impressions. Freud felt that such a course of events was not at all unusual and that it played a regular part in the genesis of hysterical symptoms.

He substantiated this theory by a description of the case of Rosalie H.

Rosalie H. was a woman of 23 who had been trained as a singer. She complained that in parts of her range she could not control her voice; she had a feeling of choking and constriction in her throat. The hysterical symptoms were found to be related to a sexual approach that had been made by an uncle of hers and that had badly frightened her. Freud was able to rid her of the hysterical symptom by getting her to reproduce the traumatic experiences and to abreact them.

Similiarly, Cecilie M. had suffered from an extremely violent facial neuralgia that appeared suddenly two or three times a year and lasted from 5 to 10 days. It had resisted any form of treatment but would abruptly cease after the 5- to 10-day period. The facial neuralgia was related to an argument with her husband in which he had insulted her, leaving her with a feeling that she had been "slapped in the face." The case seemed to involve conflicts over her hostile impulses toward her husband and the defenses against them. The neuralgia had come to be indicative of a particular psychic excitation, but afterward it could be reinstituted through associative reverberations or a form of symbolic conversion. This was the same phenomenon that had been observed in the case of Elizabeth von R.

Out of these cases Freud reconstructed the following sequence of steps in the development of hysteria:

1. The patient had undergone a traumatic experience, by which he meant an experience that stirred up intense emotion and excitation and that was intensely painful or disagreeable to the patient.

2. The traumatic experience represented to the patient some

idea or ideas that were incompatible with the "dominant mass of ideas constituting the ego."

3. This incompatible idea was intentionally dissociated or repressed from consciousness.

4. The excitation associated with the incompatible idea was converted into somatic pathways and resulted in the hysterical manifestations and symptoms.

5. What is left in consciousness is merely a mnemonic symbol that is connected with the traumatic event only by associative links, which are frequently disguised links. For example, in the case of Lucy R., the mnemonic symbol was the smell of burnt pudding. The pudding had burned when she and the children had forgotten about it during the episode when her employer had severely reprimanded her. The burnt pudding smell was the replacement for the heavy odor of cigar smoke from her employer's cigar during the traumatic episode.

6. If the memory of the traumatic experience can be brought into consciousness and if the patient is able to release the strangulated affect associated with it, the affect is discharged and the symptoms disappear.

There is little doubt that the patients Freud described in such detail would not be classified today as simply hysterical; they were probably somewhat sicker than that, as the states of dissociation, depersonalization, and forms of hallucinatory decompensation suggest. Some might be regarded today as borderline personalities or even schizophrenic. But they provided Freud with an abundance of clinical detail that served as the basis for his early thinking about psychodynamic processes. The pages of the *Studies on Hysteria* reflect the intense interest of Freud in these phenomena and his unique capacity for observation of relevant clinical detail. In his handling of the material in these cases, one can glimpse the first signs of Freud's divergence from Breuer's thinking about hysterical states. The small divergences in approach were soon to enlarge into a frank and irreparable rupture.

TECHNICAL EVOLUTION

One of the fascinating aspects of the *Studies on Hysteria* is the evolution in Freud's development of technical approaches to the treatment of these cases of hysteria. As a result of his early interest in hypnosis and his exposure to hypnotic techniques in Charcot's clinic and later at Nancy, Freud began to use hypnosis intensely in treating his patients when he opened his own practice in 1887. In the beginning, his use of hypnosis was primarily as a means of getting the patient to rid himself of his symptoms by means of hypnotic suggestion. It was quickly obvious, however, that even though the patient responded to hypnotic suggestion and acted under hypnosis as if the symptoms did not exist, the symptoms nonetheless asserted themselves during the patient's waking experience.

Freud found the contradiction and superficiality of this approach, as well as its relative ineffectiveness as a means of treatment, a source of increasing dissatisfaction. By this time, however, he had come under Breuer's influence, and the fascination of the case of Anna O. made him eager to learn what it was that lay at the root of his patients' symptoms. Freud's curiosity was stimulated, and his scientific mind felt the impulse to search out the reasons for these events and to learn their causes. This quality of restless and remorseless inquiry stamps the peculiar quality of Freud's mind—a quality that allowed him to seek out reasons and causes where others might have faltered and retreated. This same need to plumb the depths

characterizes the essential nature of psychoanalytic treatment today and serves to set it apart to some extent from those psychiatric techniques that seek merely to modify or relieve overt symptoms.

By 1889, then, Freud was sufficiently intrigued by Breuer's cathartic method to attempt to use it in conjunction with hypnotic techniques as a means of retracing the histories of neurotic symptoms, as Breuer had done to a striking degree with Anna O. The first time he used Breuer's method was in his treatment of Emmy von N. In treating her, he stayed quite close to the notion of the traumatic origins of hysterical symptoms. Consequently, the goal of treatment was restricted to a removal of symptoms through the recovery and verbalization of suppressed feelings with which the symptoms were associated. This procedure has since been described as abreaction.

However, as in the case of hypnotic suggestion, Freud was somewhat dissatisfied with the results of this treatment approach. The beneficial effects of the hypnotic treatment seemed to be transitory; they tended to last or seemed effective only as long as the patient remained in contact with the physician. Freud suspected that the alleviation of symptoms was, in fact, dependent in some manner on the personal relationship between the patient and the physician. In his account of Emmy von N., Freud had begun to feel that inhibited sexuality may have played a role in the production of the patient's symptoms. Freud's suspicion of a sexual aspect in the treatment of such patients was amply confirmed one day when a patient awoke from a hypnotic sleep and suddenly threw her arms around his neck. Freud suddenly found himself in the same position that Breuer had found himself in during his earlier treatment of Anna O. Perhaps bolstered by Breuer's experience and apparently able to learn from it, Freud did not panic or retreat in the face of this sexual advance. Rather, the peculiar observant quality of his mind was able to disengage himself sufficiently for him to treat this phenomenon as a scientific observation.

Freud began to understand that the therapeutic effectiveness of the patient-physician relationship, which had seemed so mystifying and problematical to him up until this time, could be attributed to its erotic basis. These observations were to become the basis of the theory of transference, which he later developed into an explicit theory of treatment. In any event, these experiences served to reinforce his dissatisfaction with hypnotic techniques. He became aware that hypnosis was masking and concealing a number of important manifestations that seemed to be related to the process of cure or in some cases to the failure of the patient to achieve a definitive resolution of the neurosis. Later on, his dissatisfaction with hypnosis became more specific, in that he could see that the continued use of hypnosis precluded the investigation of transference and resistance phenomena.

The decision to shift from the use of Breuer's cathartic method was based on somewhat less sophisticated and mundane considerations. Freud felt uncomfortable with the hypnotic technique because it increasingly became apparent that the hypnotic method was successful, in part, because of the patient's emotional attachment to the doctor. Often, the patient recalled traumatic experiences or feelings at the doctor's request and appeared to recover from the illness in order to please the doctor. Freud felt that a cure that did not involve some understanding on the part of the patient of the origins and significance of the symptoms and that did not base itself on some more scientific approach to the problem could not be expected to be a reliable cure but was, at best, only a temporary expedient.

There were other reasons for the abandonment of the cathartic method. Freud had discovered that many of the patients he treated in his private practice were refractory to hypnosis. Only gradually did he recognize that what seemed to be his inability to hypnotize a patient might be due to a patient's reluctance to remember traumatic events. He was later able to identify this reluctance as resistance.

The vagaries of the hypnotic method did not satisfy Freud, and he felt it necessary to develop an approach to treatment that could be usefully applied regardless of whether the patient was hypnotizable. Consequently, although Freud continued to use the hypnotic technique as a basic approach to the treatment of hysteria, he began to experiment and gradually succeeded in modifying the technique.

Concentration

One of the patients Freud found to be refractory to the hypnotic technique was Elizabeth von R. In this case Freud decided, for the first time, to abandon hypnosis as his primary therapeutic tool. He based his decision to alter his technique on the observation of Bernheim that, although certain experiences appeared to be forgotten, they could be recalled under hypnosis and then subsequently recalled consciously if the physician asked the patient leading questions and urged him to produce those critical memories. Freud thus evolved his method of concentration.

The patient was asked to lie down on a couch and to close her eyes. She was then instructed to concentrate on a particular symptom and to recall the memories associated with it. The method was substantially a modification of the technique of hypnotic suggestion. Freud would press his hand on the patient's forehead and urge her to recall the unavailable memories. Freud's graphic descriptions of this technique carry with them the unavoidable impression that he was struggling against a force he sensed in the patient and against which he found himself battling, as though in a hand-to-hand combat. He came slowly, by dint of this laborious experience, to realize that the separation of certain memory contents involved the operation of mental forces that generated considerable power and that operated to keep the complex of pathogenic ideas separate from the mass of conscious ideation. This realization substantially provided him both with the empirical notion of resistance and with his basic metapsychological perspective of the mind as operating in terms of psychic forces.

Free Association

The material presented in such graphic detail in *Studies on Hysteria* reflects in a dramatic way the evolution of Freud's technique in the direction of his more definitive approach to psychoanalysis. What is rehearsed there is the progression from the more hypnotically oriented and derived techniques of the original cathartic method introduced by Breuer to what was to become the staple of psychoanalytic technique, the method of free association. This evolution took place only gradually and with a slowly dawning realization in the mind of Freud over at least a 3-year period, from 1892 to 1895.

Freud's experience with Elizabeth von R. marked a decisive turning point in this evolution. At one point Elizabeth remarked that she had not expressed her thoughts to Freud because she just was not sure what Freud was expecting to hear. This observation made Freud realize the extent to which his interventions had been a form of suggestion akin to the basic suggestion involved in the hypnotic technique. Freud decided that he would not try to direct the patient's thinking but would, instead, encourage her to express every idea that occurred to her mind, no matter how insignificant, irrelevant, shameful or embarrassing it might seem to her and ignoring all censorship and suspending all judgment.

Moreover, Elizabeth complained to him at a number of points in the treatment process that Freud's continual attempt to question her and to push her persistently to respond only served to interrupt her train of thought. She even found his somewhat magical and suggestive technique of pressing his hand against her forehead more of a distraction than anything else. Slowly the awareness dawned on Freud that perhaps the most efficacious approach to dealing with the patient's resistances was not to try to engage them in struggle but to enlist the patient's cooperation in trying to get her to freely and uninhibitedly express whatever thoughts or feelings might come into her conscious awareness.

Freud became increasingly convinced by the late 1890's that the process of urging, pressing, questioning, and trying to defeat the resistances offered by the patient—all of which were part and parcel of the concentration method—rather than facilitating the overcoming of the patient's resistances actually substantially interfered with the free flow of the patient's thoughts. Piece by piece, Freud gave up the elements of the concentration method. Through this progressive evolution, the basic rule of psychoanalysis—the rule of free association— was articulated. Gradually, Freud surrendered his technique of forehead pressure, as well as the requirement that patients close their eyes while lying on the couch. The only remnant of this earlier procedure that now persists in the practice of psychoanalysis is the use of the couch.

The evolution of Freud's technique continued to progress until the free association technique had been perfected. The modification of technique that had originated in the case of Elizabeth von R. continued in this period, with an increasing reliance on the patient's capacity to manifest her mental content freely without the suggestive interference on the part of the therapist. By the end of the century, Freud had more or less established his free association technique. In *The Interpretation of Dreams* he described it in the following terms:

> This involves some psychological preparation of the patient. We must aim at bringing about two changes in him: an increase in the attention he pays to his own psychical perceptions, and the elimination of the criticism by which he normally shifts the thoughts that occur to him. In order that he may be able to concentrate his attention on his self-observation, it is an advantage for him to lie in a restful attitude and to shut his eyes. It is necessary to insist explicitly on his renouncing all criticism of the thoughts that he perceives. We therefore tell him that the success of the psychoanalysis depends on his noticing and reporting whatever comes into his head, and not being misled, for instance, in suppressing an idea because it strikes him as unimportant or irrelevant or because it seems to him meaningless. He must adopt a completely impartial attitude to what occurs to him, since it is precisely his critical attitude which is responsible for his being unable in the ordinary course of things, to achieve the desired unraveling of his dream or obsessional idea, or whatever it may be.

After a few more years the closing of the eyes was also abandoned, and thus free association became the definitive technique of psychoanalysis. The development of this technique opened the door to the exploration of dreams, which became one of the primary sources of data that bolstered the nascent psychoanalytic point of view.

THEORETICAL INNOVATIONS

Causes of Hysteria

The theoretical point of view propounded in *Studies on Hysteria* was relatively complex. The theoretical section of this work was provided by Breuer, but the fascinating aspect of this section is that it mirrors in striking detail the assumptions and even specific formulations that were made explicit by Freud in his *Project*. There seems little doubt that Breuer's theoretical formulations reveal in a profound manner the influence of Freud's thinking or, at least, a basic scientific orientation that profoundly affected both men. This aspect of the theoretical formulations in *Studies on Hysteria* was not appreciated until Freud's manuscript on the *Project* became available in 1950.

Breuer adopted the point of view that hysterical phenomena are not altogether ideogenic—that is, that they are determined simply by ideas. The phenomena of hysteria may be determined by a variety of causes; some of them are brought about by an explicitly psychic mechanism, but others are brought about without this mechanism. The so-called hysterical phenomena are not necessarily caused by ideas alone. However, it is specifically the ideogenic aspects of the phenomena of hysteria that are described as hysterical. The contribution of Freud and Breuer was that they focused on the investigation of these ideogenic aspects and discovered some of their psychic origins. Neuronal excitation, which was conceived of as subject to processes of hydraulic flow and discharge, was of fundamental importance in the understanding of hysteria and of neurosis in general.

A careful reading of Breuer's theoretical section in *Studies on Hysteria* makes it clear that what he proposed is a reworking of the ingenious ideas of Freud's *Project*, with a specific application to the explanation of hysterical phenomena. Breuer described two extreme conditions of central nervous system excitation—namely, a clear waking state and the state of dreamless sleep. When the brain is performing actual work, greater consumption of energy is required than when it is merely prepared to do work. The phenomenon of spontaneous awakening can take place in conditions of complete quiet and darkness without any external stimulus. This shows that the development of psychic energy is based on the vital processes of the neural elements themselves.

Speech can serve an important discriminating function. It distinguishes between those forms and degrees of the heightening of excitation that are useful for mental activity because they raise the level of free energy of all the cerebral functions uniformly and the forms and degrees that serve only to restrict mental activity insofar as they partly increase and partly inhibit psychic functions in a relatively nonuniform manner. The former processes are described as incitement; the latter are described as excitement. Excitement seeks to discharge itself in more or less violent ways that can be pathological. The psychic component of these aspects is composed of a disturbance of the dynamic equilibrium of the nervous system. Thus, acute effects are based on the disturbances of mental equilibrium that accompany such states of increased excitation. Such activated affects level out the increased intensity of excitation by means of motor discharge. If the affect cannot find a pathway of discharge of excitation, the level of intracerebral excitation is powerfully increased, even as it cannot be used in associative or motor pathways of discharge.

Breuer also provided an explanation of the process of hysterical conversion. The resistances in relatively normal people to the passage of cerebral excitation by way of the vegetative organs corresponds, after a fashion, to the insulation of electrical lines of conduction. At the point at which they are abnormally weak, they can be broken through when the tension of cerebral excitation is elevated. Thus, the affective excitation can pass over into the peripheral organs. The result is an abnormal expression of emotion based on two causal factors. The first is the high degree of intracerebral excitation, which has not been leveled down either by ideational association or by motor discharge. The second factor is described as an abnormal weakness of the resistances in particular paths of conduction. Thus, the level of intracerebral excitation and that of excitation in the peripheral paths are regarded as reciprocal. The level of intracerebral excitation increases if, and only if, no reflex action is elicited. The level, however, diminishes when it has been transformed into peripheral nervous excitation. Consequently, it follows that there can be no observable effect if the idea that gave rise to it immediately releases an abnormal reflex into which the excitation can flow as soon as it is generated. Under these circumstances hysterical conversion is complete.

The hysterical phenomena (the so-called abnormal reflexes) show little evidence of ideogenic origins, since the idea that gives rise to the reflex discharge is no longer colored with affect and no longer marked out among other ideas and memories in the mental content. The discharge of affect follows the principle of least resistance and takes place along the paths whose resistances have already been weakened. Thus, the genesis of hysterical phenomena that are related to trauma find a perfect analogy in the hysterical conversion of psychic excitation, which originates not simply from external stimuli or from the inhibition of normal psychic reflexes but from an inhibition of the course of association. In all such cases there must be a convergence of a number of factors before a hysterical symptom can be generated in a person who has previously been normal. Affective ideas can be excluded from such association either through defense or in situations in which the idea cannot be remembered, as in hypnotic states.

The basic explanatory concept that Breuer advanced—not originally, it might be noticed, since the concept had previously been a part of the thinking of French psychiatrists, particularly Janet—was the notion of hypnoid states. Such states were thought to resemble the basic condition of dissociation that obtained in hypnosis. Their importance lay in the amnesia that accompanied them and in their power to bring about a condition of splitting of the mind. The spontaneous origin of such states through a process of autohypnosis was identifiable relatively frequently in a number of fully developed hysterics. These states often alternated rapidly with normal waking states, as had been described by Breuer in the case of Anna O. The experience of the autohypnotic state was found to be subjected to a more or less total amnesia when the patient was in the waking state. The hysterical conversion seemed to take place more easily in such autohypnotic states than in waking states, similiar to the more facile realization of suggested ideas in states of artificial hypnosis.

Neither the hypnoid state during periods of energetic work nor the unemotional twilight states are pathogenic. On the other hand, the reveries that were filled with emotion and the states of fatigue arising from protracted affects did seem to be pathogenic. The occurence of such hypnoid states was important in the genesis of hysterical phenomena, since they somehow made conversion easier and served to prevent, by way of the resulting amnesia, the converted ideas from wearing away and losing their intensity.

Freud had little sympathy with Breuer's concept of hypnoid states, even though at the stage of *Studies on Hysteria* Freud had not been able to bring himself to reject it. The concept, in fact, did not explain very much. The hypnoid state was appealed to as an explanation for hysterical states, but the occurrence and the function of hypnoid states themselves were in no way explained or supported. They were merely postulated. The only explanatory attempt was made in terms of a hereditary disposition to such states. This unproved postulate was one that Freud's intensely scientific mind could not accept.

Breuer went on to describe the origin of unconscious ideas. Much of what falls under the heading of mood comes from ideas that exist and operate beneath the threshold of consciousness. The whole conduct of life is constantly influenced by such unconscious ideas. All intuitive activity is governed by ideas that are to a significant degree subconscious. Only the clearest and most intense ideas are available to self-consciousness; the great mass of current but less intense ideational content remains unconscious. Breuer related the occurrence of pathological phenomena to the persistence of such unconscious ideas. The existence of such ideas, which are inadmissible to conscious awareness, serves as a source of pathology.

Janet had proposed that a particular form of congenital mental weakness underlies the disposition to hysteria. The position adopted by Breuer and Freud, however, opposed that of Janet and denied that the splitting of the consciousness is based on an inherent weakness in the patient. Rather, their own hysterical patients seemed to be persons of high ideals, vivid and strong imaginations, and in many ways quite vigorous personalities. The appearance of weak-mindedness was simply due to the division in their mental activity that resulted in only a portion of their capacity being placed at the disposal of their conscious thought processes. The dissociation and splitting of the mind was, in fact, due to the coexistence of two heterogeneous trains of ideas. This splitting seemed also to be responsible for the apparent suggestibility of some hysterical patients, since the unconscious split was responsible for a relative poverty and incompleteness of ideational content.

The notion of an innate disposition served Breuer as a basic foundation on which he based the explanation of hypnoid states. He felt that the capacity to acquire hysteria was closely linked to this idiosyncrasy of innate disposition. A surplus of excitation that was liberated by the nervous system in a state of rest was thought to determine the patient's incapacity to tolerate a monotonous life and boredom and the patient's craving for sensations that would interrupt this monotony. Such a surplus of excitation can also give rise to pathological manifestations in the motor sphere as, for example, tic-like movements. Thus, a number of nervous symptoms, including pain and vasomotor phenomena and perhaps purely motor epileptic attacks, are the result not of pathogenic ideas but of a fundamental abnormality of the nervous system.

Closely related are the ideogenic phenomena, the simple conversion of affective excitation. Such phenomena are forms of purely somatic hysterical symptoms; the idea that is related to them and gives rise to them can be fended off and consequently repressed. The most frequent and intense of these fended-off and converted ideas have a specifically sexual content. The tendency to fend off such sexual ideas is intensified by the fact that, in young unmarried women, sensual excitation is accompanied by anxiety, fear, and apprehension of what is unknown and half-suspected. In addition to such sexual hysteria, there are hysterical states due to fright—the so-called traumatic hysterias, which constitute one of the major forms of hysterical manifestations. Basic to these hysterical states and a major constituent of them is the innate disposition that gives rise to the so-called hypnoid state, which manifests itself in a tendency to autohypnosis.

The spirit that moves through Freud's treatment of the psychotherapy of hysteria is quite different from that embodied in Breuer's theoretical treatment. The discussion of the treatment of hysteria in *Studies on Hysteria* gives a good sense of the extent to which Freud had moved away in his own thinking from the somewhat restrictive formulations of the *Project*. Freud pointed out that each individual hysterical symptom seemed to disappear more or less permanently when the memory of the traumatic event by which it was provoked was brought into conscious awareness, along with its accompanying affect. It was necessary for the patient to describe such traumatic events in the greatest possible detail and for him to put into verbal expression the affective experience connected with it.

Freud felt that the basic causes of neurosis had to be located in sexual factors. Different sexual influences operate to produce different pictures of neurotic disorders. Usually, the neurotic picture is mixed, and the purer forms of either hysterical or obsessional neurosis are relatively rare. Freud did not regard all hysterical symptoms as psychogenic in origin, and he felt that they could not all be effectively treated by a psychother-

apeutic procedure. In the context of his theory and technique at that time, he found that a significant number of patients could not be hypnotized, even when the diagnosis of hysteria seemed to be clearly established. In these patients Freud felt that he had to overcome a certain psychic force in the patient that was set in opposition to any attempt to bring the pathogenic idea into consciousness. In the therapy he sometimes engaged in forceful psychic work to overcome this intense counterforce.

But the pathogenic idea, despite the force of resistance, was always close at hand and could be reached by relatively easily accessible associations. The patient seemed to be able to get rid of such an idea by turning it into words and describing it. It was Freud's experience that in the cases in which he was able to surmise the manner in which things were connected and could tell the patient before the patient himself uncovered it, the therapist could not force anything on the patient about matters in which he was essentially ignorant, nor could the therapist influence the product of the analysis by arousing the patient's expectations.

Freud's development of the technique of free association illuminated a number of significant aspects of mental functioning that had never been previously observed. First, Freud discovered that the patient's train of memories extended well beyond the traumatic events that were responsible for precipitating the onset of illness. Indeed, he found that his patients were able to produce memories of childhood experiences, events, and scenes that had long been lost to memory. This finding led Freud to the conclusion that such memories had frequently been inhibited because they involved sexual experiences or other incidents in the patient's life that seemed painful or intolerable to hold in memory.

The recollection of such experiences could evoke intense affects of agitation, moral conflict, self-reproach, remorse, fear of punishment, and guilt. Freud concluded that since these childhood experiences retained such a vivid quality, they must exert a predisposing influence on the development of psychoneurotic manifestations. This point of view ran substantially counter to the prevailing attitude of the time, particularly to the point of view expressed by Breuer in his endorsement of hypnoid states as the explanatory basis for hysteria.

Freud, however, did not abandon the congenital point of view—namely, that heredity must be accorded a major role as a predisposing factor to neurosis. In fact, that point of view remains a significant part of the psychoanalytic understanding of neurosis today. But Freud did emphasize unfavorable childhood experiences. Essentially, he postulated that hysteria can also be acquired and that it is not simply a congenitally derived condition. Even further, he postulated that emotionally disturbing experiences can play a major causative role in acquired hysteria, in which hereditary factors seem to be of minor importance. Freud's views in this regard were a substantial and original contribution to the therapy of neurosis, particularly hysteria.

Resistance

The basic question that confronted Freud and Breuer had to do with the mechanism that makes the pathogenic memories unconscious. The divergence in their points of view was not simply a matter of theoretical differences. Freud's own thinking underwent a definite transition, and the transition seemed to be based primarily on his own experience in dealing with his patients. In the beginning, he and Breuer had agreed that their hysterical patients had suffered from traumatic sexual experiences. These traumatic experiences were not available to conscious recollection. They had also agreed, at least for a time, that the recovery of those forgotten experiences during a hypnotic state resulted in abreaction and the consequent symptomatic improvement.

Breuer's explanation for this state of affairs rested on the concept of the hypnoid state. The hypnoid state, he thought, is an altered state of consciousness in which part of the mind is split off from the rest of the mind in a state of dissociation. This splitting is a result of the stress of emotional arousal, so that the normal course of emotional reaction and expression is inhibited. The content of the dissociated part is isolated from associative links with the rest of consciousness, and these links can be reestablished through hypnosis. Breuer felt that the traumatic experiences must have occurred at a time when the patient was in one of these hypnoid states, so that the traumatic experience had been dissociated. To Breuer's mind, then, the therapeutic work consisted merely of reestablishing associative links.

The divergence between Breuer's viewpoint and Freud's viewpoint was apparent from the beginning of their collaboration. Even in the *Preliminary Communication*, they described two kinds of hysteria—dispositional hysteria and psychically acquired hysteria. The theory of dispositional hysteria was based on Breuer's notion of hypnoid states, but psychically acquired hysteria can be acquired only by the reaction of the personality to external trauma. This was essentially Freud's view. Freud's half-hearted endorsement of Breuer's notion of hypnoid states did not fade until he had analyzed the cases of Lucy R. and Elizabeth von R. It was only in the treatment of Elizabeth von R. that Freud came to a clear-cut formulation of his notion of defense. He recognized the conflict between her sexual impulses and her moral convictions. The hypnoid hypothesis was insufficient, since the sexual thoughts, Freud felt, were originally conscious and had to be excluded from the patient's consciousness. Thus, the two sides of the conflict seemed to coexist in the same system of consciousness. Freud moved toward understanding the basic meaning of hysteria in terms of conflict and a need for defense against repugnant thoughts and wishes.

Freud discovered that his patients were often quite unwilling or unable to recall the traumatic memories. He defined this reluctance of his patients as resistance. As his clinical experience expanded, he found that in the majority of patients he treated, resistance was not a matter of reluctance to cooperate; the patients willingly engaged in the treatment process and were willing to obey the fundamental rule of free association. The patients generally seemed to be well motivated for treatment; frequently, the patients who were most distressed by their symptoms seemed most hampered in treatment by the presence of resistance. Freud's conclusion was that resistance is a matter of the operation of active forces in the mind of which the patients themselves were often quite unaware and which resulted in the exclusion from consciousness of painful or distressing material. Freud described the active force that worked to exclude particular mental contents from conscious awareness as repression—one of the fundamental ideas of psychoanalytic theory.

Repression

The concept of repression, together with its related notion of defense, became Freud's basic explanation for hysterical phenomena. The notion of repression reflects one of the basic hypotheses of psychoanalytic theory—namely, the dynamic hypothesis, according to which the human mind includes in its operation basic dynamic forces that can be set in opposition and that serve as the basic source of powerful motivation and defense. Freud described the mechanism of repression in the following terms: A traumatic experience or a series of experiences, usually of a sexual nature and often occurring in childhood, were forgotten or repressed because of their painful or disagreeable nature. But the excitation involved in the sexual stimulation was not extinguished, and traces of it persist in the unconscious in the form of repressed memories. These memories can remain without pathogenic effect until some contemporary event—for example, a disturbing love affair—revives them. At this juncture, the strength of the repressive counterforce is diminished, and the patient experiences what Freud termed "the return of the repressed." The original sexual excitement is revived and finds its way by a new path, which allows it to manifest itself in the form of a neurotic symptom. Thus, the symptom results from a compromise between the repressed desire and the "dominant mass of ideas constituting the ego." The whole process of repression and the return of the repressed is conceived of in terms of conflicting forces—the force of the repressed idea struggling to express itself against the counterforce of the ego seeking to keep the repressed idea out of consciousness.

Freud's development of the notions of repression and resistance were based primarily on his studies of cases of conversion hysteria. In such cases he felt that the impulses that were not allowed access to consciousness were diverted into paths of somatic innervation, resulting in the hysterical symptoms—paralysis, blindness, disturbances of sensations, and other hysterical manifestations. Despite this early emphasis on conversion hysteria as the prototype of repression, Freud believed that the basic proposition, that symptoms are a result of a compromise between a repressed impulse and other repressing forces, could be applied to obsessive-compulsive phenomena and even to paranoid ideation. The logical consequence of this hypothesis is that the treatment process during this period focuses primarily on enabling the patient to recall the repressed sexual experiences so that the accompanying excitation can be allowed to find its way into consciousness and thus be discharged, along with the revivified and previously dammed-up affect.

Infantile Sexuality

One additional aspect of psychoanalytic theory emerged with striking clarity from Freud's early researches into hysteria. Invariably, in digging into the past histories of his hysterical patients, he found that the repressed traumatic memories that seemed to lie at the root of the pathology had to do with sexual experiences. Freud's attention became increasingly focused on the importance of these early sexual experiences, usually recalled in the form of a sexual seduction occurring before puberty and often rather early in the child's experience. Freud began to feel that these seduction experiences were of central importance for the understanding of the causes of psychoneurosis. Over a period of several years, he collected clinical material that seemed to reinforce this important hypothesis. He even went so far as to distinguish between the nature of the seductive experiences involved in hysterical manifestations and those involved in obsessional neurosis. In the case of hysteria, he felt, the seduction experience had been primarily passive—

that is, the child had been the passive object of seductive activity on the part of an adult or older child. In obsessive-compulsive neurosis, however, he felt that the seduction experience had been an active one on the part of the child—the child actively and aggressively pursued a precocious sexual experience.

The significance of all this is that Freud had taken literally the accounts his patients had given him in the form of forgotten but revived memories of sexual involvements. The patients provided him with tales of outrage committed by fathers, nursemaids, and uncles. Freud had devoted little attention to the role of the child's own psychological experience in the elaboration of these tales. But, little by little, he began to have some second thoughts about these so-called memories. Several factors contributed to his doubt. First, he had gained additional insight into the nature of pathological processes as a result of his clinical experience and his increasing awareness of the role of fantasy in childhood. Second, he simply found it hard to believe that there could be so many wicked and seductive adults in Viennese society. But the third influence, which undoubtedly was of major significance in this reconsideration, was his own self-analysis.

Freud had become increasingly aware of the importance of inner processes. While he was attempting to come to terms with the subjective experience of his own patients, he also found himself drawn to look inward and to find within his own introspective experience the reflections of what he had been able to identify in his patients. He began, therefore, the laborious and almost heroic process of his own self-analysis. He was able to survey his own history, to revive repressed memories from quite early levels of his childhood experience, and, particularly, to focus his attention on the content of dreams.

As this important process of self-analysis progressed, Freud began to have more and more reason to call the seductive hypothesis into question. During this time, from 1893 to 1897, Freud was still using the combined technique of pressure and suggestion with relatively great assurance. He would often insist that patients recall the seduction scene; therefore, much of the evidence on which the seduction hypothesis was based was open to the charge of suggestion. Consequently, as Freud became more aware of the role of suggestion in his technique, his doubts about the seduction hypothesis grew apace. In September 1897 his doubts came to a focus, and he wrote to his good friend Wilhelm Fliess as follows:

Let me tell you straight away the great secret that has been slowly dawning on me in recent months. I no longer believe in my *neurotica*. This is hardly intelligible without an explanation; you yourself found what I told you credible. So I shall start at the beginning and tell you the whole story of how the reasons for rejecting it arose. The first group of factors were the continual disappointment of my attempts to bring my analysis to a real conclusion, the running away of people who for a time had seemed my most favorably inclined patients, the lack of the complete success on which I had counted, and the possibility of explaining my partial successes in other, familiar ways. Then there was the astonishing thing that in every case . . . blame was laid on perverse acts by the father, and realization of the unexpected frequency of hysteria, in every case of which the same thing applied, though it was hardly credible that perverted acts against children were so general . . . . Thirdly, there was the definite realization that there is no "indication of reality" in the unconscious, so that it is impossible to distinguish between truth and emotionally charged fiction. (This leaves open the possible explanation that sexual fantasy regularly makes use of the theme of the parents.) Fourthly, there was the consideration that even in the most deep-reaching psychosis the unconscious memory

does not break through, so that the secrets of infantile experience are not revealed even in the most confused states of delirium. When one thus sees that the unconscious never overcomes the resistance of the conscious, one must abandon the expectation that in treatment the reverse process will take place to the extent that the conscious will fully dominate the unconscious.

It is obvious that at this period Freud was struggling with his own great reluctance to abandon the seduction hypothesis. The doubts and the clarifying realization that he expressed to Fliess were depressing. After all, he had put years of effort and had compiled a significant amount of evidence to bolster this seduction hypothesis. It was only with reluctance that he could surrender it. But he also sensed that in surrendering the seduction hypothesis, new possibilities for psychological exploration were opened up. In fact, this juncture in the development of Freud's thinking was crucial. The abandonment of the seduction hypothesis, with its reliance on actual physical seduction, forced Freud to turn with new realization to the inner fantasy life of the child.

This shift from an emphasis on reality factors to an attention to and an understanding of the influence of inner motivations and fantasy products marks the real beginning of the psychoanalytic movement. In this attempt to distinguish psychic reality and fantasy from actual external events and to distinguish psychoneurosis from perversion, psychoanalysis itself took on a new and highly significant dimension. What inevitably emerged from this shift in direction was a dynamic theory of infantile sexuality, in which the child's own psychosexual life played the significant and dominant role. This notion replaced the more static point of view in which the child represented an innocent victim whose eroticism was prematurely disrupted at the hands of unscrupulous adults.

The turning point was one of extreme significance for Freud himself. Increasingly, he turned his attention to his own self-analysis and put increasing reliance on it. He wrote to Fliess:

My self-analysis is the most important thing I have in hand and promises to be of the greatest value to me when it is finished.

Increasingly, he became involved in the study of dreams, all the more so as he developed the technique of free association, which provided him with a tool for exploring the associative content that underlies the dream experience. More and more, he concerned himself with the nature of infantile sexuality and the inner sources of fantasy and dream content, the unconscious instinctual drives. The abandonment of the seduction hypothesis was a crucial point in Freud's own development and in the development of psychoanalysis, for it brought to an end the period of initial exploration and opened up the way to the development of psychoanalysis as it is known.

SUMMARY OF THE BEGINNINGS

By 1897, when the hypothesis of actual seduction had fallen in the dust at Freud's feet, there had been a number of significant accomplishments. The fundamental concepts of psychic determinism and the operation of a dynamic unconscious were established, and a theory of psychoneurosis based on the idea of psychic conflict and the repression of disturbing childhood experiences had become clearly established. Sexuality, particularly in the form of childhood sexuality, had been unveiled as playing a significant role in the production of psychological symptoms—a role that had been previously underplayed or ignored. More significant, perhaps, Freud had arrived at a technique, a method of investigation that could be exploited as a means of exploring a wide range of mental phenomena that had been poorly understood before his time. Moreover, the horizons of psychoanalytic interest had begun to expand rapidly. Freud's attention was no longer focused on certain limited forms of psychopathology. It had begun to reach out, reflecting the wide-ranging curiosity and interests of Freud's mind, to embrace the understanding of dreams, creativity, wit and humor, the psychopathology of everyday experience, and a host of other normal and culturally significant mental phenomena. Psychoanalysis had, indeed, come to life.

The Interpretation of Dreams

Currently, the whole area of dream activity is one of the most exciting and intensely studied aspects of psychological functioning. The discovery of rapid eye movement (REM) cycles and the definition of the various stages of the sleep cycle have stimulated an intense and extremely productive flurry of research activity. A whole new realm of fresh and important questions has been opened up as a result of this activity, and researchers are drawing much closer to a more comprehensive understanding of the links between patterns of dream activity and underlying physiological and psychodynamic variables. As more is learned about this fascinating and complex problem, one comes much closer to understanding the nature of the dream process and the understanding of the dream experience itself.

In this context it is difficult to look back and to appreciate the uniqueness and originality of Freud's immersion in the dream experience. It was only when Freud's attention had been refocused to the significance of inner fantasy experiences, by reason of the abandonment of the seduction hypothesis and in the context of his development of the technique of free association, that the significance and value of the investigation of dreams impressed itself on him. Freud became aware of the significance of dreams when he realized that in the process of free association, his patients frequently reported their dreams, along with the associative material that seemed connected with them. He discovered, little by little, that dreams have a definite meaning, even though that meaning is often quite hidden and disguised. Moreover, Freud found that when he encouraged his patients to associate freely to the dream fragments, what they reported was frequently more productive of pertinent, repressed material than the associations to the events of their waking experience. Somehow the dream content seemed to be closer to the unconscious memories and fantasies of the repressed, and the association to dream material seemed to facilitate the disclosure of this content.

Also of central importance in this development of his thinking and in the focusing on dream processes as an area of investigation was Freud's self-analysis. Increasingly, in the work of his self-analysis, Freud relied on an examination and an associative exploration of his own dream experiences. Increasingly, through the years since the publication of *The Interpretation of Dreams,* public appreciation of the significance of Freud's self-analytic work has grown. Although they are frequently not reported as such, many of the significant and revealing dreams presented in the dream book were actually Freud's own and were the product of his self-analysis. This makes his monumental achievement of *The Interpretation of Dreams* all the more astounding.

THEORY OF DREAMING

The rich complex of data derived from Freud's clinical exploration of his patients' dreams and the profound insights derived from his own associated investigation of his own personal dreams was distilled into the landmark publication in 1900 of *The Interpretation of Dreams.* Basing his analysis on these data, Freud presented a theory of the dream that paralleled his analysis of psychoneurotic symptoms. The dream was viewed as a conscious expression of an unconscious fantasy or wish that is not readily accessible to conscious waking experience. Thus, dream activity was considered as one of the normal manifestations of unconscious processes.

Freud felt that the dreaming experience of any normal person in sleep bears a significant resemblance to the pathological conscious organization of the thought processes in psychotic patients. The dream images represent the unconscious wishes or thoughts disguised through a process of symbolization and other distorting mechanisms. This reworking of unconscious contents constitutes the dream work. Freud postulated the existence of a censor which was pictured as guarding the border between the unconscious part of the mind and the preconscious level. The censor functions to exclude unconscious wishes during conscious states. During the regressive relaxation of sleep, it allows certain unconscious contents to pass the border, but only after transformation of the unconscious wishes into a disguised form that is experienced in the form of dream contents by the sleeping person. Freud assumed that the censor works in the service of the ego—that is, he believed that it serves the self-preservative objectives of the ego. Although the mechanisms of the dream work were originally identified in connection with the censor—specifically, the processes of displacement, condensation, symbolism, and repression—they were later included among the functions of the waking ego and the superego. Freud became aware of the unconscious nature of these processes, but at this stage he thought of the ego more restrictively in terms of conscious processes of reasonable control and volition. Even in *Studies on Hysteria,* repression was envisioned in intentional terms.

Analysis of Dream Content

Freud's view of the dream material was that its content has been repressed or excluded from consciousness by the defensive activities of the ego. These activities during sleep are part of the functions of the censor. The dream material, as it is consciously recalled by the dreamer, is simply the end result of the unconscious mental activity that takes place during sleep. Freud felt that the upsurge of unconscious material is of such intensity that it threatens to interrupt sleep itself; he envisioned the function of the censor to be, in part, a guardian of sleep. Instead of being awakened by these ideas, the sleeper dreams. Freud regarded the conscious experience of such thoughts during sleep as dreaming.

From a more contemporary viewpoint the cognitive activity during sleep has a great deal of variety in it. Some of the cognitive activity follows the description Freud provided of dream activity, but much of it is considerably more realistic and more consistently organized along logical lines. The dreaming activity Freud analyzed and described is probably more or less restricted to the stage 1 REM periods of the sleep-dream cycle.

The so-called manifest dream, which embodies the experienced content of the dream and which the sleeper may or may not be able to recall after waking, is the product of the dream activity. The unconscious thoughts and wishes that, in Freud's view, threaten to awaken the sleeper, are described as the latent dream content. Freud referred to the unconscious mental operations by which the latent dream content is transformed into the manifest dream as the dream work. In the process of dream interpretation, Freud was able to move from the manifest content of the dream by way of associative exploration to arrive at the latent dream content, which lies behind the manifest dream and which provides it with its core meaning.

In Freud's view a variety of stimuli initiate dreaming activity. Contemporary understanding of the dream process, however, suggests that dreaming activity takes place more or less in conjunction with the psychic patterns of cental nervous activation that characterize certain phases of the sleep cycle. What Freud thought to be initiating stimuli may, in fact, not be initiating at all but be merely incorporated into the dream content and determine the material in the dream thoughts to that extent.

Nocturnal sensory stimuli. A variety of sensory impressions—including pain, hunger, thirst, and urinary urgency—may play a role in determining dream content. A sleeper who is in a cold room and who urgently needs to urinate may, instead of disturbing his sleep and leaving his warm bed, dream that he has awakened, voided, and returned to bed. Freud's view was that the activity of dreaming preserves and safeguards the continuity of sleep. Today it is known that the function of dreaming is considerably more complex and cannot be regarded simply as preserving sleep, although there is still room for this to be counted among the dream functions.

Day residues. Freud felt that one of the important elements that contribute to the shaping of the dream thoughts is the residue of thoughts, ideas, and feelings left over from the experiences of the preceding day. These residues remain active in the unconscious and, like sensory stimuli, can be incorporated by the sleeper into the thought content of the manifest dream. The day residue can be amalgamated with the unconscious infantile drives and wishes that derive from the level of unconscious instincts. The amalgamation of infantile drives with elements of the day residues can effectively disguise the infantile impulse and allow it to remain effective as the driving force behind the dream. These day residues coming from the day before or even from several days preceding the dream may in themselves be quite superficial or trivial, but they acquire their significance as dream instigators through unconscious connections with deeply repressed instinctual drives and wishes.

Repressed infantile drives. The essential elements of the latent dream content derive from one or several impulses emanating from the repressed part of the unconscious. The ultimate driving forces in Freud's schema behind the dream activity and the process of dream formation were the wishes that had their origin in the drives stemming from an infantile level of psychic development. These drives take their content specifically from the oedipal and preoedipal levels of psychic integration. Thus, nocturnal sensation and the day residue play only an indirect role in determining dream content. A nocturnal stimulus, however intense, must be associated with and connected with one or more repressed wishes from the unconscious in order to give rise to the dream content. Freud felt that, unless this strong link between the day residue and the repressed content is established, the concerns of waking life are unable of themselves to provide the impetus to dreaming activity, however compelling the claim on the sleeper's interests

and attention in the waking state. This point of view needs some revision, since it seems that in some phases of nighttime cognitive activity the mind is able to process the residues of daytime experience without much indication of connection with unconscious repressed content. However, in the phases of cognitive activity during sleep that bear the stamp of the dreaming activity, as Freud described and defined it, this essential link to the repressed probably still retains its validity.

By virtue of the fact that the psychic apparatus in early childhood is still relatively immature, the relationship between latent and manifest dream content is most aptly illustrated by the dreams of this stage of development. The distinction between infantile and current conflicts is not so easily made at this level, since they are equivalent. Nor can one distinguish sharply between conscious impulses and repressed impulses, since the ego of a young child has not sufficiently developed to a point where it is able to erect more or less permanent defenses against unconscious impulses. Consequently, the classification of dream content into latent and manifest material has less relevance with regard to the dreams of early childhood, particularly insofar as latent content is taken to refer to unconscious material and manifest content to more conscious material.

Significance of Dreams

Once Freud's attention had definitively shifted to the study of inner processes of fantasy and dream formation, the study of dreams and the process of their formation became the primary route by which he gained access to the understanding of unconscious processes and their operation. Consequently, even to this day, Freud's monumental work *The Interpretation of Dreams* remains the standard source for the documentation and explanation of unconscious processes, specifically those processes that come under the heading of primary process. In *The Interpretation of Dreams* he maintained that every dream somehow represents a wish fulfillment. He bolstered this hypothesis with a considerable amount of documentation, including an exhaustive analysis of one of his own dreams.

There is a more general tendency today to view dream activity as expressing a broader spectrum of psychological processes, keeping the aspect of wish fulfillment as one of the primary dimensions of dream activity but not maintaining it as an absolute principle, as it seemed to be in Freud's thinking. The manifest dream content seems to represent most clearly the imaginary fulfillment of a wish or impulse in early childhood, before such wishes have undergone repression. But in later childhood and even in adulthood, the ego acts to defend itself against the unacceptable instinctual demands of the unconscious. These demands remain repressed to a large extent during the waking state, but in the regressive relaxation of the sleep state the activity of the censor is somewhat more relaxed, so that the repressed impulses are allowed a greater degree of expression and become incorporated in a disguised and mutilated fashion in the manifest dream content. Nevertheless, the dream remains essentially a form of gratification of an unconscious instinctual impulse in fantasy form. In the state of suspended motility and regressive relaxation induced by the sleep state, the dream permits a partial and less dangerous gratification of the instinctual impulse.

This crucial aspect of wish fulfillment in the dream process is usually quite obscured by the extensive distortions and disguises brought about by the dream work, so that it often cannot be readily identified on a superficial examination of the manifest content. Inevitably, just as Freud's theory of neurosis has found an unsympathetic reception from those workers who have not accepted his findings concerning infantile sexuality, his theory of dreams has been rejected by those critics who tend to limit the focus of their investigations to the manifest elements of the dream content.

Dream Work

The theory of the nature of the dream work, which Freud developed in *The Interpretation of Dreams,* became the fundamental description of the operation of unconscious processes that stands even today, in regard to the basic mechanisms and the manner of their operation, as an unsurpassed and fundamental account of unconscious mental functioning. The focus of Freud's analysis was on the process by which the latent dream thoughts are disguised and distorted in such a fashion as to permit their expression and translation into the manifest content of the dream. The unconscious processes, however, which were part of the fruit of his investigation, found ready application and extrapolation not only to the understanding of the formation of neurotic symptoms but more broadly in their application to a more general range of expression of unconscious processes. The theory of dream work, consequently, became the basis for a more wide-ranging analysis of unconscious processes, which found its expression in his study of everyday experiences, processes of artistic creation, the analysis of jokes and humor, and a variety of other more culturally based activities of the human mind.

Dream formation. The basic problem of dream formation is to determine how it is that the latent dream content can find a means of representation in the manifest content. As Freud saw it, the state of sleep brings with it a relaxation of repression, and the latent unconscious wishes and impulses are permitted to press for discharge and gratification. Since the pathway to motor expression is blocked in the sleep state, these repressed wishes and impulses have to find other means of representation by way of the mechanisms of thought and fantasy. This representation is achieved in one of two ways. First, the thoughts, impressions, or memories that are suitable for representing these latent wishes and impulses in visual terms have to be provided. Individual experience in the course of the waking period provides an ample supply of such material. When the current psychological experience can be linked with the repressed urges, they are incorporated into the content of the dream thoughts in the form of day residues. Similarly, nocturnal stimuli can be associated with repressed impulses and wishes and give rise in the manifest content to representations in the form of auditory, tactile, olfactory, or gustatory elements.

The unconscious instinctual impulses that are continually pushing for discharge have been repressed because of their unacceptable or painful nature. The activity of the dream censor provides a continual resistance to the discharge of these impulses, with the result that the impulses have to be attached to more neutral or innocent images to be able to pass the scrutiny of the dream censor and to be allowed into conscious expression. This is made possible by selecting apparently trivial or insignificant images from the residues of the dreamer's current psychological experience and linking these trivial images dynamically with the latent unconscious images, presumably on the basis of some resemblance that allows the associative links to be established. In the process of facilitating the economic expression of latent unconscious contents and, at the same time, of maintaining the distortion that is essential for the contents to escape the repressing action of the censor, the dream work uses a variety of mechanisms that make it possible

for more neutral images to represent the repressed infantile components. These mechanisms include symbolism, displacement, condensation, projection, and secondary revision (see Figure 12).

SYMBOLISM. Symbolism is a complex process of indirect representation that in psychoanalytic usage has the following connotations: (1) A symbol is representative of or a substitute for some other idea, from which it derives a secondary significance that it does not possess itself. (2) A symbol represents this primary element by reason of a common element that they share. (3) A symbol is characteristically sensory and concrete in nature, as opposed to the idea it represents, which may be relatively abstract and complex. A symbol provides a more condensed expression of the idea represented. (4) Symbolic modes of thought are more primitive, both ontogenetically and phylogenetically, and represent a form of regression to an earlier stage of mental development. Consequently, symbolic representations tend to function in more regressed conditions—in the thinking of primitive peoples, in myths, in states of poetic inspiration, and particularly in dreaming. (5) A symbol is a manifest expression of an idea that is more or less hidden or secret. Typically, the use of the symbol and its meaning are unconscious. Symbols tend to be used spontaneously, automatically, and unconsciously. The use of symbols is a sort of secret language in which instinctually determined content can be reexpressed in terms of other images—for example, money can symbolize feces, and windows can symbolize the female genitals.

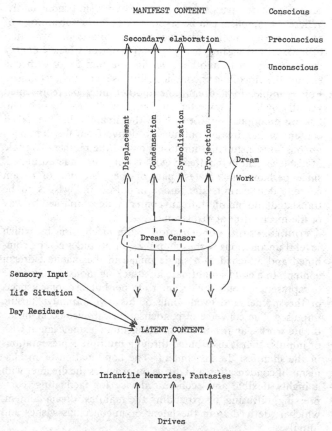

FIGURE 12. The dream process, as explained by Freud. (Modified from Ellenberger, H. *The Discovery of the Unconscious,* p. 491. Basic Books, New York, 1970.)

In his examination of dream content, Freud discovered that the ideas or objects represented in this way are highly charged with inappropriate feelings and burdened with conflict. The forbidden meanings of these symbols, derived from instinctual impulses and urges, remain unconscious. Freud toyed with the thought that symbols are somehow universal and inherited—following his notions of Lamarckian evolution—but he came gradually to attribute the use of such symbols to the basic similarities of interests and experiences in infancy. The common subjects dealt with in such forms of symbolic representations are usually body parts and functions, family members, birth, and death. Although the symbol disguises what is unacceptable, it can also offer partial gratification of underlying wishes or can signify and thus partially retain lost objects.

Many questions still persist about the origins of symbolic processes, the stage of development in which they become organized, the extent to which they require altered states of consciousness (such as the sleep state) for their implementation, and the degree to which symbolic expression is related to underlying conflicts. Current formulations regard the symbolic function as a uniquely human trait that is involved in all forms of human mental activity from the most primitive expression of infantile wishes to the most complex creative processes of literary, artistic, and scientific thinking.

DISPLACEMENT. The mechanism of displacement refers to the transfer of amounts of energy (cathexis) from an original object to a substitute or symbolic representation of the object. Because the substitute object is relatively neutral—that is, less invested with affective energy—it is more acceptable to the dream censor and can pass the borders of repression more easily. Whereas symbolism can be taken to refer to the substitution of one object for another, displacement facilitates the distortion of unconscious wishes through the transfer of affective energy from one object to another. Despite the transfer of cathectic energy, the aim of the unconscious impulse remains unchanged. For example, in a dream the mother may be represented visually by an unknown female figure or, at least, by one who has less emotional significance for the dreamer, but the naked content of the dream continues to derive from the dreamer's unconscious instinctual impulses toward the mother. The role of displacement in the dream work is not to be underestimated, since perhaps the greatest part of the distortion of dream content that permits the latent impulses and wishes to be translated into manifest dream content is accomplished by way of the mechanism of displacement.

CONDENSATION. Condensation is the mechanism by which several unconscious wishes, impulses, or attitudes can be combined and attached to a single image in the manifest dream content. In a child's nightmare an attacking monster may come to represent not only the dreamer's father but also some aspects of the mother and even some of his own primitive hostile impulses. The converse of condensation can also occur in the dream work—an irradiation or diffusion of a single latent wish or impulse that is distributed through multiple representations in the manifest dream content. The combination of mechanisms of condensation and diffusion provides the dreamer with a highly flexible and economic device for facilitating, compressing, diffusing, or expanding the manifest dream content, which is derived from the latent or unconscious wishes and impulses.

PROJECTION. The process of projection allows the dreamer to perceive his own unacceptable wishes or impulses as emanating in the dream from another person or independent source. Not surprisingly, the figure to whom these unacceptable impulses are ascribed in the dream often turns out to be the figure toward whom the dreamer's own unconscious impulses are directed. For example, the man who has a strong repressed wish to be unfaithful to his wife may dream that his wife has been unfaithful to him. Or a patient may dream that she has been sexually approached by her analyst, although she is reluctant to acknowledge her own repressed wishes toward him. Similarly, the child who dreams of a destructive monster may be unable to acknowledge his own destructive impulses and his fear of his father's power to hurt him. The figure of the monster is a result of both projection and displacement.

SECONDARY REVISION. The mechanisms of symbolism, displacement, condensation, and projection are all characteristic of relatively early modes of cognitive organization in a developmental sense. They reflect and express the operation of the primary process. In the organization of the manifest dream content, however, the operation of primary process forms of organization is supplemented by a final process, which organizes the absurd, illogical, and bizarre aspects of the dream thoughts into a more logical and coherent form. The distorting effects of symbolism, displacement, and condensation require a coherence. This rationality is required for acceptance on the part of the dreamer's more mature and reasonable ego, and it is supplied through a process of secondary revision. Secondary revision uses intellectual processes that closely resemble organized thought processes governing states of consciousness. Through the process of secondary revision, the logical mental operations characteristic of the secondary process are introduced into and modify dream work.

Aspects of dream work

AFFECTS IN DREAMS. In the process of displacement, condensation, symbolization, or projection, the energic component of the instinctual impulses is separated from its representational component and undergoes an independent variety of vicissitudes. These drive aspects are expressed in the form of affects or emotions. The repressed emotion may not appear in the manifest dream content at all, or it may be experienced in a considerably altered form. For example, repressed hostility or hatred toward another person may be modified into a feeling of annoyance or mild irritation in the manifest dream expression, or it may even be represented by an awareness of not being annoyed, a conversion of the affect into its absence. Or the latent affect may be directly transformed into an opposite in the manifest content, as when a repressed longing is represented by a manifest repugnance or vice versa. The vicissitudes of affect and the transformation by which latent affects are disguised thus introduce another dimension of distortion into the content of the manifest dream. The vicissitudes of affect, then, take place in addition to and in parallel with the processes of indirect representation that characterize the vicissitudes of dream content.

ANXIETY DREAMS. When Freud formulated his basic theory of dreams, he had by no means developed a comprehensive theory of the ego and its development and functions. Consequently, in his early studies of the dream process, he emphasized the role of the dream in discharging or gratifying instinctual wishes or impulses by the representation of wish fulfillments in the hallucinatory content of the dream. However, the same processes can be looked at in light of their function of avoiding tension or psychic pain. This is essentially a defensive function and is properly the domain of the ego. The dream thus affords an opportunity for studying some of the important, if more primitive, functions of the ego. Only gradually did

Freud realize that processes of symbol formation, displacement, condensation, projection, and secondary revision all serve a dual purpose. If they facilitate the discharge of unconscious drive impulses, they may also be regarded as primitive defense mechanisms that prevent the direct discharge of instinctual drives. They thereby protect the dreamer from an excessive discharge of unconscious impulses and from the excessive anxiety and pain that accompany it.

These mechanisms, however, have only a limited capacity to disguise and channel unconscious instinctual drive derivatives. When anxiety pervades the dream content or becomes so severe that it forces at least a partial awakening, some failure in the primitive defensive operations of the ego is suggested. An element of the latent dream content has succeeded, despite the dream work and the repressing efforts of the censor, in forcing its way into the manifest dream content in a form that is too direct, too little disguised, and too readily recognized for the ego to tolerate it. The ego reacts to this direct expression of repressed impulses with anxiety. However, even in *The Interpretation of Dreams* Freud foreshadowed a later development in his thinking about anxiety—namely, that the censor seems to serve a warning function that alerts the ego to the breakthrough of instinctual and repressed impulses. This warning function was later formalized in Freud's theory of signal anxiety.

PUNISHMENT DREAMS. The punishment dream is related to the anxiety dream. In the punishment dream the ego anticipates a condemnation on the part of the superego (conscience) if a part of the latent content, which derives from repressed impulses, finds its direct expression in the manifest dream content. In reaction to the anticipation and threat of the dire consequences of the loss of ego control in sleep and the threat of instinctual breakthrough, there is developed a compromise between the repressed wish and the repressing agency, specifically the superego. The demands of the superego for punishment are satisfied in the dream content by giving expression to punishment fantasies. In dealing with these various vicissitudes of dream functioning, Freud was formulating in a preliminary and as yet unself-conscious way some of the parameters of the mental apparatus that would find more explicit and sophisticated expression in his tripartite (structural) theory.

DREAMING AND THE REM CYCLE

Recent research on the physiological aspects of sleep and dream states has important implications for psychoanalytic theory. The pertinence of such studies has important implications for the understanding of dream processes. Perhaps the most fundamental finding to emerge from these experiments is that cognitive activity is a continuous process that extends throughout the sleep cycle and takes a variety of forms. The cyclic alternation of rapid eye movements (REM) with periods of lack of such patterns of eye movement (NREM) and the experimental relation of REM periods with dreaming have been well established and are described in detail in other sections of this textbook.

These two states are associated with considerably different patterns of electrical activity in the brain and have led to a description of two distinct phases of sleep. The NREM phase requires the presence and activity of neocortex activity and is thus described as telencephalic sleep; the REM period is triggered by activation of caudal pontine nuclei of the reticular formation and has been denominated rhombencephalic sleep. The form of mental activity that Freud described as dreaming seems to occur predominantly, although apparently not exclusively, in the REM phase of the sleep cycle.

Study of these respective phases of the sleep cycle indicates that there are identifiable differences between the mental activity of the REM period and that of the NREM period. NREM activity is generally less vivid, less visual, less well recalled, more conceptual, more plausible, less bizarre, more like thinking than dreaming, less emotional, more concerned with contemporary waking experience, and under greater volitional control. REM activity displays the opposite characteristics and is described as much more like the dreaming experience that Freud described. NREM activity, therefore, reflects a predominance of secondary process thinking, in contrast to REM activity, which represents the predominance of primary process thinking. The actual content of these respective processes seems to overlap to a certain extent; in fact, primary process characteristics can be identified to some degree in NREM sleep and vice versa. Many of the elements of NREM activity can be identified as representing preconscious day residues; NREM mentation may be the more or less conscious representation of preconscious processes containing the residues of the previous day's experience that form the point of contact for unconscious dream activity.

One of the basic questions that Freud raised about dreams is why they occur at all. Freud provided an answer to this question within a strictly psychological perspective in terms of endopsychic resistance. His answer is an example of the basic as-if presumption that he made from the beginning of his theorizing, leaving the potential connections with neurophysiological mechanisms in the air. In *The Interpretation of Dreams* Freud argued as follows:

> A consideration of the interplay of psychical forces in this case must lead us to infer that the dream would, in fact, not have occurred at all if the resistance had been as strong during the night as during the day. We must conclude that during the night the resistance loses some of its power, though we know it does not lose the whole of it, since we have shown the part it plays in the formation of dreams as a distorting agent. But we are driven to suppose that its power may be diminished at night and that this makes the formation of dreams possible. This makes it easy to understand how, having regained its full strength at the moment of waking, it at once proceeds to get rid of what it was obliged to permit while it was weak. Descriptive psychology tells us that the principal sine qua non for the formation of dreams is that the mind shall be in a state of sleep; and we are now able to explain this fact: the state of sleep makes the formation of dreams possible because it reduces the power of the endopsychic censorship.

In this account one can recognize beginnings of Freud's acknowledgment of a censoring agency in the mental apparatus that can be regarded as a precursor of the superego. However, if one translates this formulation into terms of the contemporary sleep-dream cycle, it seems that REM activity must represent the neurophysiological analogue of this relaxation of endopsychic censorship. The intrapsychic process Freud described lies between the more primitive, biologically based instinctual impulses of the id and the more elaborate, culturally determined resistances of the censorship mechanism. It is reasonable to suggest that activity dominated by rhombencephalic mechanisms, as seems to be the case with REM mentation, lies close to the biological roots of the organism and, correspondingly, that the pattern of activity controlled by telencephalic mechanism, as is the case in NREM mentation, is linked to more advanced and evolved patterns of integration within the neuraxis.

Consequently, one can suggest that REM activity represents a pattern of neuroactivation that is somehow correlated with the relaxation of endopsychic censorship and a pattern of mental activity that is characteristic of dreaming. Conversely, NREM activity may be taken to reflect a pattern of activity in which cortical mechanisms are relatively predominant in the interplay of patterns of activation. Freud's observation that the state of sleep makes the formation of dreams possible by a reduction of the power of censorship may have its neurophysiological equivalent in the activation of REM activity through the activation of rhombencephalic and associated limbic circuits in relation to the reduction of controlling influences flowing from the corticofugal inhibitory systems.

Freud also viewed the dream process as a form of regressive mental functioning in the sleep state. In 1933 he described this aspect of dreaming in the following terms:

> This unconscious impulse has to thank its link with the other, unobjectionable, dream-thoughts for the opportunity of slipping past the barrier of the censorship in an inconspicuous disguise. On the other hand, the preconscious dream-thoughts have to thank this same link for the power to occupy mental life during sleep as well. For there is no doubt about it: This unconscious impulse is the true creator of the dream; it is what produces the psychical energy for the dream's construction. Like any other instinctual impulse, it cannot strive for anything other than its own satisfaction; and our experience in interpreting dreams shows us too that that is the sense of all dreaming. In every dream an instinctual wish has to be represented as fulfilled. The shutting-off of mental life from reality at night and the regression to primitive mechanisms which this makes possible enable this wished-for instinctual satisfaction to be experienced in a hallucinatory manner as occurring in the present. As a result of this same regression, ideas are transformed in the dream into visual pictures: the latent dream thoughts, that is to say, are dramatized and illustrated.

This regressive form of mental functioning in the dream process can be connected to the rhombencephalic pattern of sleep that is both ontogenetically and phylogenetically the more primitive form of sleep activity. Jouvet (1961) referred to such REM activation as "archisleep."

The results of the analysis of dreaming from the point of view of the neurophysiology of dreaming activity make it clear that the function that Freud ascribed to the state of sleep is really a function of REM activity in the dream cycle. Consequently, one cannot apply Freud's analyses of dreaming activity to all mentation that takes place in the sleep state; rather, they must be seen as more appropriately applying to REM activity. In this understanding of the dream process, the sleeper passes through alternating phases of reworking the preconscious residues in terms of specific conflicts. This reworking process takes place in alternating phases of secondary process organization and phases of controlled binding of unconscious energies to preconscious elements, with subsequent discharge into dream consciousness.

The suppression of this activity (REM suppression) is economically followed by a build-up of pressure for REM discharge, which might be thought of in Freud's terms as a build-up of unconscious energies that increase the pressure for discharge in the dream state. This has certain parallels that are reminiscent of Freud's theory of repression and discharge in the genesis of neurotic symptoms. It may be that the dream process has a specific function in the psychic economy that is fulfilled by no equivalent mechanism. It binds and discharges unconscious instinctual energies in a manner that is neither psychologically overwhelming nor physiologically disruptive. The dream may represent a form of psychological regression that is phylogenetically derived and ultimately psychologically adaptive for the over-all functioning of the organism. If this regression has its adaptive uses—a form of regression in the service of the ego—it is at the same time a regression that is biologically organized in terms of the patterning of more or less spontaneous activity in specific and highly integrated neural circuits.

Freud's hypothesis regarding the role of the relaxation of endopsychic censorship in dreaming remains a limited if psychologically useful and heuristic hypothesis. But the evidence from study of the sleep-dream cycle suggests that REM states are produced by cyclically organized and specifically physiological influences, particularly the periodic activation of pontine level generator nuclei, whose activity brings about patterns of activation in rhombencephalic-limbic circuits. The activation of these specific integrating circuits and the mobilization of correlated REM phenomena may reflect the accumulation and release of transmitter neurochemical substances in these nuclei.

Researchers are still gathering data that may shed more light on the understanding of these basic mechanisms, but one may have to regard dreaming as a by-product of a basic physiological state in which certain neurological circuits subserving forms of cognitive organization in the dreaming state are activated. The correspondence between patterns of physiological activation and dreaming mentation is not unequivocal, since it seems clear that the REM pattern is not coextensive with dreaming activity and that it may even occur as a regular phenomenon when dreaming activity is out of the question—for example, in anencephalic defects.

Modern neurophysiological research has opened up new vistas in the understanding of the mechanisms of the dreaming process and has generated unique and significant opportunities for the study of the interrelationship between psychological phenomena on the one hand and activity in the central nervous system on the other. Two fundamental and apparently conflicting hypotheses remain: The first is Freud's basically psychological hypothesis of diminished endopsychic censorship; the second is a theory of spontaneous activation of neuronal circuits as the underlying cause of dreaming activity. Clearly, the choice is not either-or. Ample evidence suggests that modifications of psychological functioning can modify the basic patterns of physiological activation. At the same time, good evidence suggests that the manipulation of these spontaneous neural patterns may have significant psychological consequences. Making an effort to understand the shifting patterns of interaction between them and to explore the implications of those patterns seems to be a more fruitful avenue of further understanding and research than simply declaring them to be mutually exclusive alternatives.

Any explanation of complex psychological phenomena in terms of underlying neurophysiological systems is tenuous and hypothetical at this stage of knowledge, but such an explanation need not violate more dynamic approaches and understandings of the phenomena. The fact that the dream experience has a drive organization and that the dream content has meaningful associations to large complexes of significant previous life experiences needs more than a merely neurological construction to open it to understanding. Nonetheless, the physiologically determined organization of activity in the nervous system may set the stage in terms of patterns of cognitive organization for psychological drive influences to act as organizing principles in the elicitation of specific dream content. In this sense, then, neurological activation serves the psychological needs of the organism.

Psychic Apparatus

In the seventh chapter of *The Interpretation of Dreams*, Freud surveyed the copious information he had gathered about dreaming processes and focused his ideas on the nature of dream work. In addition, he provided a model of the psychic apparatus as he understood it at the turn of the century. Not only was the model he proposed a description of the functioning of the dreaming mind, but it also represented his broader conceptualization of the psychic apparatus as it functions in the broad range of human experience, both pathological and normal. What is most striking about this model today is that it represents an elaborate attempt to recast in more psychological language the basic model of the mind that Freud had formulated first in his *Project for a Scientific Psychology*. It seems clear that the economic model, on which Freud expended such intense effort in the 1890's and seemingly abandoned in frustration, came back to reassert itself in a new language and in a different setting. The lines of continuity and the parallels between the model of the *Project* and the model of the seventh chapter could not be appreciated until the manuscript of the *Project* was rediscovered after Freud's death.

The model Freud presented in 1900 was, taken schematically, an elaborate construction based on a basic notion of a stimulus-response mechanism (see Figure 13). In normal waking experience, the sensory input is taken into the receptor end of the apparatus and is then processed in a number of mnemonic systems of increasing degrees of elaborateness and complexity. After varying degrees of processing, the impulse is discharged through the motor effector apparatus. In the dream state the motor effector pathways are blocked, so, instead of discharge through motor effector systems, the excitation is forced to move in a backward or regressive direction in the mnemonic systems, leading back into the sensory systems.

During the daytime the path leading from the unconscious levels of the apparatus through the preconscious to conscious levels is barred by the activity of the censor. In sleep, however, this pathway is available, since the resistance of the censor is diminished in sleep. Unconscious memories and their instinctual determinants can press to discharge through the perceptual apparatus. This is particularly the case in hallucinatory dream experiences. Dreams can be described as having a regressive character. Regression consists specifically in the turning back of an idea into the sensory image from which it was originally derived in a waking state. Regression is an effect of the resistance opposing the discharge of energy associated with the thought into consciousness along the normal path. Regression is also contributed to by simultaneous attraction exercised on the thought by the presence of associated memories in the unconscious.

In the case of dreams, regression is further facilitated by the diminution of the progressive current, which flows from the continuing sensory input during waking hours. Regression, as Freud viewed it, is essentially a regression to the originating source of an impression, as he described it in the reversal within the mental apparatus, but it also was a regression in time. He commented:

Nor can we leave the subject of regression in dreams without setting down in words a notion by which we have already been repeatedly struck and which will recur with fresh intensity when we have entered more deeply into the study of the psychoneurosis: namely, that dreaming is on the whole an example of regression to the dreamer's earliest condition, a revival of his childhood, of the instinctual impulses which dominated it, and of the methods of expression which were then available to him.

Freud distinguished several forms of regression—a topographic regression, which involves a regression in the ψ systems within the mental model; a temporal regression, according to which the mental process refers back to older psychic structures, particularly those deriving from an infantile level of development; and formal regression, in which more primitive methods of expression and representation take the place of the more normal ones. He commented:

All these three kinds of regression are, however, one at bottom and occur together as a rule; for what is older in time is more primitive in form and in psychical topography lies nearer to the perceptual end.

Perhaps the most central aspect of Freud's envisioning of the functioning of this mental model, the aspect of it that comes strikingly close to the formulations of the *Project,* has to do with his notions of the primary and secondary processes. The impulses and instinctual wishes originating in infancy serve as the indispensable nodal force for dream formation. The energic conception of these drives follows the basic economic principles laid down by the *Project* (see Table I). They are elevated states of psychic tension in which the energy is constantly seeking for discharge, according to the principles of constancy and the pleasure principle that Freud had previously formulated.

However, the tendency to discharge is opposed by other psychic systems. Freud envisioned two fundamentally different kinds of psychic processes in the formation of dreams. One of these processes tends to produce a rational organization of dream thoughts, which is of no less validity in terms of contact with reality than is normal thinking. The second system, however, treats the dream thoughts in a bewildering and irrational manner. He felt that a more normal train of thought can be submitted to abnormal psychic treatment only if an unconscious wish, derived from infancy and in a state of repression, has been transferred onto it. As a result of the operation of the pleasure principle, the first psychic system is incapable of bringing anything disagreeable into the context of the dream thoughts. It is unable to do anything but wish. Operating in conjunction with the demands of this primary system, the secondary system can cathect an unconscious idea only if it can inhibit any development of unpleasure that may have proceeded from the bringing to awareness of that idea. Anything that evades that inhibition is equivalently inaccessible to the second system, as well as to the first, since it is promptly eliminated in accordance with the unpleasure principle.

The psychic process that derives from the operation of the first system is referred to as primary process, and it mirrors the primary process as described in the development of the *Project.* The process that results from the inhibition imposed by the second system is referred to as the secondary process, and it reflects the operation of the system of inhibition and delay sketched in the *Project.* The secondary system acts to correct and regulate the primary system. Among the wishful impulses derived from infantile impulses are some whose fulfillment would be a contradiction of the purposes and ideas of secondary process thinking. The fulfillment of these wishes could no longer generate an affect of pleasure but would be unpleasurable. This formulation was the basis for Freud's later elaboration of the pleasure principle as opposed to the reality principle.

The mental model of *The Interpretation of Dreams* was, in a way, a resumé and recasting of the original economic model that Freud had developed in the *Project.* Similarly, in a forward-looking perspective, the model opens the way to the development of the instinct theory and the associated topographic model, which dominated Freud's thinking for nearly the next quarter century.

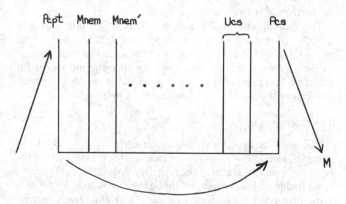

FIGURE 13. Freud's 1900 model of the psychic apparatus.

Topographic Theory

Beginning with the abandonment of the seduction hypothesis and the turning of Freud's interests to the inner processes of fantasy and dream formation and ending with the 1923 publication of *The Ego and the Id,* in which Freud propounded his structural model of the psychic apparatus, Freud's thinking was dominated by the topographic theory. The shift in emphasis, which directed his curiosity and attention to the inner products of instinctual drives, unavoidably involved him in a concerted effort to understand and grasp in theoretical terms the nature of the underlying instinctual drives that serve as the motivating force behind these phenomena and that are related to and driving unconscious processes. The period from the turn of the century until 1923 saw a gradual evolution and development of Freud's ideas about instincts and a continuing reworking and enriching of his theory of instinctual drives.

BASIC ASSUMPTIONS

A number of assumptions underlay Freud's thinking and served as the lines of continuity between the various stages of his thinking, thus connecting the successive models around which his thinking organized itself. The first assumption was that of psychological determinism, which holds that all psychological events—including behaviors, feelings, thoughts, and actions—are caused by—that is, are the end result of—a preceding sequence of causal events. This assumption was derived from Freud's Helmholtzian convictions and represents the applications of a basic natural science principle to psychological understanding. But it was also reinforced by Freud's clinical observation that apparently meaningless hysterical symptoms that had been attributed to somatic causes can be relieved by relating them to past experiences that had apparently been repressed. Apparently arbitrary pathological behavior can be tied into a causal psychological network. This observation served as the empirical point of departure for Freud's exploration into other aspects of psychic functioning. The connection of psychological events with explanatory causes does not specifically address the nature of psychological causes. Freud did not have in mind the distinction between causes and motives or reasons. His frame of reference was to an extent committed to nonpsychological events as the causes of all scientifically describable events, but he appealed to motives and meanings as part of the determinative sequence in explaining the origins of symptoms. The inherent determinism of psychoanalysis is generally accepted as resting on psychological causes involving motive and meaning, usually on an unconscious level.

The second assumption was that of unconscious psychological processes. This assumption was derived from a considerable amount of evidence that had been gathered through the use of hypnosis, but it was also consolidated by Freud's experience of the bringing to awareness of past experiences as the result of his patients' free associating. The unconscious material that survived and was able to influence present experience was found to be governed by specific rules, such as the pleasure principle and the mechanisms of primary process, which differed radically from those of conscious behavior and thought processes. Thus, the unconscious processes were brought within the realm of psychological understanding and explanation.

The third assumption was that unconscious psychological conflicts and forces form the basic elements at the root of psychoneurotic difficulties. This assumption was related to Freud's experience of the resistance and the drive to repression in his patients. The full realization of this aspect of psychic functioning came only with the realization that the reports of patients represented not unconscious memories of actual experiences but, rather, unconscious fantasies. The assumption that unconscious forces exist accounted for the process that creates those fantasies and brings them into consciousness during free association. The assumption also accounted for the agency that opposes the coming to consciousness of such fantasies. This counterforce, which clashes with the sexual drives and diverts them into fantasies or symptoms, is related to the function of censorship in the dream theory and to the operation of ego instincts that are set in opposition to the sexual instincts.

The final assumption of the topographic theory was that there are psychological energies that have their origins in instinctual drives. This assumption was derived from the observation that the recall of traumatic experiences and their accompanying affects results in the disappearance of symptoms and anxiety and suggested that a displaceable and transformable quantity of energy is involved in the psychological processes responsible for symptom formation. Freud originally assumed that this quantity is the affect, which becomes dammed up or strangulated when it is not appropriately expressed and is thus transformed into anxiety or conversion symptoms. After he had developed his notion of instinctual drives, this quantitative factor was conceived of as drive energy (cathexis). The assumption of psychic energies served Freud as an important heuristic metaphor. But the usefulness of the metaphor and its necessity as a basic assumption of analytic theory are now in question.

TOPOGRAPHIC MODEL

Freud's thinking about the mental apparatus at this time was based on a classification of mental operations and contents according to regions or systems in the mind. These systems were described in neither anatomical nor spatial terms but, rather, were specified in terms of their relationship to consciousness. Any mental event that occurs outside of conscious awareness and that cannot be made conscious by the effort of focusing attention was said to belong to the deepest regions of the mind, the unconscious region or system. Mental events that can be brought to conscious awareness through an act of attention were said to be preconscious and, consequently, were not to be regarded as derived from the deepest levels of the mind, as was the unconscious. The mental events that occur in conscious awareness were regarded as belonging to the perceptual-consciousness system and were conceived of as located on the surface of the mind.

The topographic model has essentially fallen into disuse in terms of its usefulness as a working model of psychoanalytic processes, largely because it has been surpassed and supplanted by the structural theory. However, the topographic viewpoint is still useful in terms of classifying mental events descriptively in terms of the quality and the degree of awareness.

The Conscious

The conscious system is that region of the mind in which the perceptions coming from the outside world or from within the body or the mind are brought into awareness. Internal perceptions include observations of thought processes and affective states of various kinds. Consciousness is by and large a subjective phenomenon whose content can be communicated only by means of language or behavior. It has also been regarded psychoanalytically as a sort of superordinate sense organ, which can be stimulated by perceptual data impinging on the central nervous system. It is assumed that consciousness uses a form of neutralized psychic energy, attention cathexis.

The nature of consciousness was described in less detail in Freud's early theories, and certain aspects of consciousness are not yet completely understood by psychoanalysts. Freud regarded the conscious system as operating in close association with the preconscious. Through attention, a person can become conscious of perceptual stimuli from the outside world. But from within the organism, only elements in the preconscious are allowed to enter consciousness. The rest of the mind lies outside awareness in the unconscious. Before 1923, however, Freud also believed that consciousness controls motor activity and regulates the qualitative distribution of psychic energy.

The Preconscious

The preconscious system consists of those mental events, processes, and contents that are capable of reaching or being brought into conscious awareness by the act of focusing attention. The quality of preconscious organizations range from reality-oriented thought sequences and problem-solving analysis with highly elaborated secondary process schemata all the way to more primitive fantasies, daydreams, and dream-like images, that reflect a more primary process organization. The term "preconscious" was originally applied by Freud to the mental contents capable of becoming conscious easily and under conditions that occur frequently. Preconscious content normally reaches consciousness by an increase in cathexis mediated by attention. Thus, it stands over and against unconscious processes, and the transformation to consciousness is accomplished only with great difficulty and by dint of the expenditure of considerable energy in overcoming the barrier of repression.

The preconscious region of the mind is not present at birth but develops in childhood in a manner that parallels the course of ego development, as described in the later structural theory. The preconscious is accessible to both the unconscious proper and the conscious. Elements of the unconscious can gain access to consciousness only by first becoming linked with words and thus reaching the preconscious. One of the functions of the preconscious is to maintain the repressive barrier or the censorship of wishes and desires. The secondary process organization of preconscious thinking is aimed at avoiding unpleasure, at delaying instinctual discharge, and at binding mental energy in accordance with the demands of external reality and the person's moral principles or values. Thus, the functioning of the secondary process is closely connected with the reality principle and for the most part is governed by the dictates of the reality principle.

The Unconscious

Unconscious mental events, namely those that are not within conscious awareness, can be described from one of several viewpoints. One can think of the unconscious descriptively—that is, as referring to the sum total of all mental contents and processes outside the range of conscious awareness at any given moment. This includes those aspects of the mind that Freud referred to as preconscious.

One can also think of the unconscious in dynamic terms—namely, as referring to those mental contents and processes that are incapable of achieving consciousness because of the operation of a counterforce, the force of censorship or repression. This repressive force or countercathexis manifests itself in psychoanalytic treatment as a resistance to remembering. The unconscious mental contents in this dynamic sense consist of drive representations or wishes that are in some sense unacceptable, threatening, or abhorrent to the person's intellectual or ethical standpoint. The drives are, nonetheless, regarded as continually striving for discharge in behavior or thought processes. This striving results in intrapsychic conflict between the repressed forces of the mind and the repressing forces. When the repressive countercathexis weakens, the result may be the formation of neurotic symptoms. Essentially, a symptom is viewed as a compromise between conflicting forces. These unconscious mental contents are also organized on the basis of infantile wishes or drives, rather than on logic or reality. They also strive for immediate discharge, regardless of the reality conditions. Consequently, the dynamic unconscious is thought to be regulated by the demands of primary process and the pleasure principle.

Finally, there is a systematic sense of the unconscious, referring to a region or system within the organization of the mental apparatus that embraces the dynamic unconscious and within which memory traces are organized by primitive modes of association, as dictated by the primary process. This systematic sense of the unconscious is considered in a specific topographic sense as a component subsystem within the topographic model.

Consequently, the systematic unconscious can be described in terms of the following characteristics:

1. Ordinarily, the elements of the systematic unconscious are inaccessible to consciousness and become conscious only through the access to the preconscious, which excludes them by means of censorship or repression. Repressed ideas, consequently, may reach consciousness only when the censor is overpowered (as in psychoneurotic symptom formation) or relaxes (as in dream states) or is fooled (as in jokes).

2. The unconscious system is exclusively associated with primary process thinking. The primary process has as its principal aim the facilitation of wish fulfillment and instinctual discharge. Consequently, it is intimately associated with and functions in terms of the pleasure principle. It disregards logical connections, permits contradictions to exist simultaneously, recognizes no negatives, has no conception of time, and represents wishes as fulfillments. The unconscious system can also be recognized to use those primitive mental operations that Freud identified in the operation of the dream process (see Figure 12). Thus, displacement and condensation permit rapid discharge of mental energies attached to repressive affects and ideas through the preconscious and conscious systems. As defined in the earlier consideration of dreams, displacement is the mechanism by which mental energy (cathexis) that is attached to one idea can be shifted to another idea that may encounter less censorship. Condensation is the process by which energy attached to more than one unconscious idea may be discharged through a single thought or image that embodies (symbolically) the characteristics of these several ideas. Condensation introduces a property of economy in unconscious operations. Moreover, the quality of motility, which is characteristic of primary process thinking and of unconscious energy, is frequently linked to the capacity for creative thinking.

3. Memories in the unconscious have been divorced from their connection with verbal symbols. Freud discovered in the course of his clinical work that repression of a childhood memory can occur if the energy is withdrawn from it and especially if the verbal energy is removed. However, when the words are reapplied to the forgotten memory traits, as during psychoanalytic treatment, it becomes recathected and can reach consciousness once more.

4. The content of the unconscious is limited to wishes seeking fulfillment. These wishes provide the motive force for dream and neurotic symptom formation. However, this view may be oversimplified.

5. The unconscious is closely related to the instincts. At this level of theory development, the instincts were thought to consist of sexual and self-preservative ego drives. The unconscious was thought of as containing the mental representatives and derivatives of the sexual instincts particularly.

Dynamics of Mental Functioning

Freud conceived of the psychic apparatus in the context of the topographic model as a kind of reflex arc, in which the various segments have a spatial relationship (see Figure 13). The arc consists of a perceptual or sensory end, through which impressions are received; an intermediate region, consisting of a storehouse of unconscious memories; and a motor end, closely associated with the preconscious, through which instinctual discharge can occur. In early childhood, perceptions are modified and stored in the form of memories.

According to this theory, in ordinary waking life the mental energy associated with unconscious ideas seeks discharge through thought or motor activity, moving from the perceptual end to the motor end. However, under certain conditions, such as external frustration or sleep, the direction in which the energy travels along the arc is reversed, and it moves from the motor end to the perceptual end. It thereby reanimates childhood impressions in their earlier perceptual forms and results in dreams during sleep or hallucinations in mental disorders. This reversal in the normal flow of energy in the psychic apparatus is the topographic regression previously discussed. Although Freud subsequently abandoned this model of the mind as a reflex arc, the central concept of regression was retained and applied later in a somewhat modified form in the theory of neurosis. The theory states that libidinal frustration results in a reversion to earlier modes of instinctual discharge or levels of fixation, which had been previously determined by childhood frustrations or excessive erotic stimulations. Freud called this kind of reversion to instinctual levels of fixation libidinal or instinctual regression.

FRAMEWORK OF PSYCHOANALYTIC THEORY

Throughout his long lifetime and in the course of the many twistings and turnings of the theoretical developments in his thinking, Freud's mind was dominated by a tendency to describe many of the aspects of mental functioning in terms of contrasting phenomena. He thought in terms of contrasting polarities. Some of the primary polarities were that of subject (ego) versus object (outer world), pleasure versus unpleasure, and activity versus passivity. Thus, his thinking about mental operations was dominated by a basic dualism. The fundamental dualism that dominated his thinking during the long period of the maturation of psychoanalytic ideas and that still constitutes one of the basic parameters of psychoanalytic thinking was the dualism between the forces and contents of the mind that were viewed as repressed and unconscious and the forces and mental agencies that were responsible for the activity of repression.

Although the persistence of such basic dualism in psychoanalytic thinking has clear advantages and undoubtedly helps one understand some fundamental aspects of the mind, one should not lose sight of the fact that such paradigms may prove to be restrictive. There is real question in the current state of psychoanalysis about whether some of these assumed basic parameters may not be limiting the capacity of psychoanalytic theory to grow apace with the expanding horizons of both clinical experience and experimental exploration. However, the historical role and the present vitality of the basic psychoanalytic dualism should not be undervalued, since it provides a powerful tool for understanding and treating clinical pathology.

In a basic sense psychoanalytic theory may be conveniently divided into a theory of the repressed on one hand and a theory of the repressing agency on the other. Both aspects of analytic theory underwent progressive delineation and evolution, and in each case the evolution was relatively independent. Early in his thinking about this duality and particularly focusing on the fundamental clinical fact of intrapsychic conflict, Freud envisioned the duality in terms of the conflict of opposing instinctual forces. He opposed the repressed sexual instincts to the repressing countercathectic force of the ego instincts. It was only gradually that his point of view shifted so that instead of thinking in terms of countervailing instinctual forces, he envisioned the repressing agency in terms of a regulatory psychic apparatus.

In the early years Freud's attention was taken up quite intently by the excitement of discovery and understanding of the instinctual processes and drives themselves. As the horizons of his clinical concern and theoretical interest broadened, he began to focus increasingly on the regulatory apparatus.

All human beings have similiar instincts. The actual discharge of these instinctual impulses is organized, directed, regulated, or even repressed by the functions of the individual ego, which serves as a mediator between the organism and the external world. Historically, the detailed exploration of the instincts in psychoanalysis preceded Freud's preoccupation with ego psychology. But there is also a logical sequence, since one would not try to investigate an apparatus whose function it is to organize, direct, regulate, and repress without having a prior understanding of the precise nature of the phenomena that are subjected to such organization, direction, and regulation.

To an increasing extent the study of the ego as a product of the interaction of unconscious instinctual demands and environmental influences has become a dominant concern not only of psychoanalysts but also of social scientists in allied disciplines. One of the dangers in this trend is that the increasing emphasis on ego psychology and its connections with more general psychological interests has been accompanied by an increasing theoretical separation between noninstinctual ego apparatuses and the unconscious motivating forces of the instincts. Thus, one runs the risk of deemphasizing the study of the deep instinctual forces of the mind and of isolating them from the concerns of ego psychology, which may not be to the ultimate advantage of psychoanalytic understanding.

Consequently, in a presentation such as this, in which the interests of pedagogy are served by dividing aspects of the theory and discussing their development separately, one needs constantly to remind oneself that these are aspects of an integrated psychic organism and that the various aspects of its functioning cannot be adequately understood without reference to other parts of the theory.

Instinct Theory

CONCEPT OF INSTINCTS

One of the first problems that must be dealt with in considering the theory of instincts is what is meant by the term "instinct." The problem is made more complex by the variation in usage of the term between a primarily biological use and the primarily psychological use employed by Freud. The difficulties are compounded by the complexities in Freud's own use of the term.

The term "instinct" was introduced primarily by students of

animal behavior. It refers generally to a pattern of species-specific behavior that is based mainly on the potentialities determined by heredity and is, therefore, believed to be relatively independent of learning. The term was applied to a great variety of behavior patterns, including patterns described in terms of a maternal instinct, a nesting instinct, and a migrational instinct. Such usage resisted successful physiological explanation and tended to introduce a strong teleological connotation, implying some sense of purposefulness, as in the use of a concept of an instinct of self-preservation. Freud adopted this usage unquestioningly, but its validity has been questioned even by strong proponents of instinctual theory among animal behaviorists.

The usefulness of a concept of instinct has been undermined from at least two directions. From the side of evolutionary change and the theory of genetics, evolutionary change is regarded as taking place primarily through mutation and natural selection. Mutations with a greater survival value are transmitted by the genetic code and result in the survival of those species members who bear the particular qualities resulting from mutation. The teleological import of instincts as serving the interests of species survival are consequently limited. The other inroads on instinctual theory derive from the increasing awareness from experimental study and extensive natural observation of the modification of instinctual patterns through experiential learning. The dichotomy of nature-nurture can no longer be simplistically or rigidly maintained. Instinctually derived patterns of behavior are seen to be increasingly modifiable in the interests of adaptation. Ethologists consequently prefer to speak simply of species-typical behavior patterns that are based on innate equipment but that mature and develop or are elicited through a certain degree of environmental interaction.

Freud, of course, took as the basis of his thinking the older concept of instinct, but, in adopting it for his purposes, he transformed it. Freud's own formulation of the notion of instinct underwent some shifting, and he actually offered a variety of definitions. Perhaps the most cogent was:

An instinct ... appears to us as a concept on the frontier between the mental and the somatic, as the psychical representative of the stimuli originating from within the organism and reaching the mind, as a measure of the demands made upon the mind for work in consequence with its connections with the body.

The basic ambiguity in the concept of instinct is that between its biological aspects and its psychological aspects. This ambiguity continued to influence Freud's thinking about instinctual drives, and it remains a latent ambiguity in subsequent psychoanalytic usage of the term.

Freud himself varied in the emphasis he placed on one or the other aspect of instinct, and the subsequent discussion of the concept of instinct in psychoanalysis has varied similarly between an emphasis on the biological aspects and an emphasis on the psychological aspects. The concept of instinct, then, standing on the borderline between the somatic and the psychic, embraces both the aspect of physiologically derived organismic drive components on one hand and the aspect of mental representation, which is specifically psychic, on the other. Psychoanalytic theorists, even on the contemporary scene, vary in the degree to which they think of these dual components as either integrated or separated. The instinct, then, is a psychic representation of internal stimuli, and the stimuli represent physiological needs. The physiological needs—for example, hunger, which can be described in terms of physiological processes of the lowering of blood sugar and the emptying of the stomach—cannot be confused with the psychic representation, whether that representation is conscious, preconscious, or unconscious. But Freud's notion of instinct embraces all these in varying degrees and with varying emphasis.

Another unfortunate source of confusion stems from the fact that the term used by Freud was the German word *Trieb*. The term has usually been translated into English, especially in the standard edition of Freud's writings, by the English term "instinct." Why was *Trieb* not simply translated as "drive"? The reluctance to do this was apparently based on the fact that the drive concept has been rather widely abused in the behavioral sciences. There was, presumably, a wish on the part of psychoanalytic theorists to maintain some distance between their own basic concepts and the notions of drive that were used by behavioral theorists. Moreover, Freud assumed that the *Triebe* were based on innate givens—that is, preformed biological potentials that are present at birth. This aspect of the concept is reflected in the English term "instinct." General usage currently prefers to use the term "instinctual drive" to express the Freudian notion of *Trieb* and, consequently, attempts to avoid the semantic pitfalls involved in the term "instinct."

CONCEPT OF LIBIDO

The ambiguity in the term "instinct" is reflected also in the term "libido." Briefly, Freud regarded the sexual instinct as a psychophysiological process that has both mental and physiological manifestations. Essentially, he used the term "libido" to refer to "that force by which the sexual instinct is represented in the mind." In its accepted sense "libido" refers specifically to the mental manifestations of the sexual instinct.

Freud recognized early that the sexual instinct does not originate in a finished or final form, as represented by the stage of genital primacy. Rather, it undergoes a complete process of development, at each phase of which the libido has specific aims and objects that diverge in varying degrees from the simple aim of genital union. The libido theory came to include the investigation of all these manifestations and the complicated paths they follow in the course of psychosexual development.

INFANTILE SEXUALITY

It had long been thought that Freud's thoughts on infantile sexuality constituted an assault on the cherished ideas of 19th century and Victorian thinking and that he was violently attacked for his views of the erotic life of young children. However, it seems that his significant contribution, *Three Essays on the Theory of Sexuality*, which appeared in 1905, came not as an exceptional work but as part of a flood of literature dealing with sexual problems. Contemporary sexual mores, particularly in the libertine atmosphere of Vienna, were quite lax, and there was hardly any aspect of sexual life, including the grossest perversions, that were not openly known and discussed. It is difficult to draw a line between Freud's sources and the parallel developments that were taking place in the intellectual climate around him. There was little in his psychosexual theory that was not already extant in the literature and usage of his time. The notions of infantile sexuality and the early phases of sexual development were by no means new. The notion of bisexuality had been anticipated by several decades. Freud's notion of anal eroticism seems to have been somewhat more original, but, even there, elements of it had been anticipated. Even the concept of narcissism had been described and argued about. Ellenberger (1970) commented on this aspect of Freud's theory:

> Current accounts of Freud's life state that the publication of his sexual theories aroused anger because of their unheard-of novelty in a "Victorian" society. Documentary evidence shows that this does not correspond to fact. Freud's *Three Essays* appeared in the midst of a flood of contemporary literature on sexology and were favorably received. Freud's main originality was to synthesize ideas and concepts, the majority of which lay scattered or partially organized, and to apply them directly to psychotherapy.

Nonetheless, Freud's clear and rather forceful presentation of these ideas about the development of sexuality did meet with some resistance. Some people have always found the undermining of the myth of childhood innocence to be difficult to accept. Even relatively sophisticated psychiatric residents today at times react with incredulity to the elucidation of sexual material in clinical cases of childhood neuroses. But, as is so often the case in figures of great genius, Freud's contribution was not so much in originating the ideas about psychosexual development as in his capacity to integrate them in a consistent and coherent theory that brought them to bear on the understanding of clinical phenomena with which he was dealing in his patients.

Freud had become convinced of the relationship between sexual trauma, in both childhood traumata and the genesis of psychoneurosis, and disturbances of sexual functioning as related to the so-called actual neuroses—hypochondriasis, neurasthenia, and anxiety neuroses. Freud originally viewed these conditions as related to the misuse of sexual function. For example, anxiety neurosis was thought to be due to the inadequate discharge of sexual products, leading to the damming up of libido, which was then converted into anxiety. Neurasthenia was attributed to excessive masturbation and a diminution in available libidinal energy. Freud's studies had led him to an awareness of the importance of sexual factors in the causation of psychoneurotic states.

As his clinical experience increased, Freud was able to reconstruct his patients' early sexual experiences and fantasies. These data provided the framework for a developmental theory of childhood sexuality, which, in the subsequent course of psychoanalytic exploration, has been amply corroborated in many respects by direct observation of childhood behavior. In addition to the data he derived from his clinical experience, perhaps an even more important source of information that contributed to Freud's thinking about infantile sexuality was his own self-analysis, which he had begun in 1897. Gradually he was able to recover memories of his own erotic longings in childhood and his conflicts in relationship to his parents, related specifically to his oedipal involvement. The realization of the operation of such infantile sexual longings in his own experience suggested to Freud that these phenomena may not be restricted to the pathological development of the neurosis but that essentially normal persons may undergo similiar developmental experiences.

Freud had essentially completed his basic theoretical notions about the essential phases of sexual development before the turn of the century, but the publication of his synthesis of views on psychosexual development was delayed until 1905. It was then that the first of many editions of *Three Essays on the Theory of Sexuality* was published. It was somewhat surprising that the detailed discussion of sexual development of children, including the notions of pregenital organization of the libido

and the libido theory itself, appeared for the first time in the third edition of *Three Essays* in 1915. Freud used the term "sexuality" in these essays in a more or less familiar sense to refer to the erotic life of the person, but he also extended the general concept to include those sensations and activities that can be described as sensual, in the sense that they are a source of pleasure and gratification but are not generally considered as sexual. Freud was able to show in terms of levels of development the connection between libidinal gratification and such sensual behaviors and activities.

The earliest manifestations of infantile sexuality, as Freud described them in *Three Essays*, arise in relation to bodily functions that are basically nonsexual, such as feeding and the development of bowel and bladder control. Freud divided these stages of psychosexual development into a succession of developmental phases, each of which was thought to build on and subsume the accomplishments of the preceding phases. He described the oral phase, the anal phase, and the phallic phase (see Table II). The oral phase occupied the first year to year-and-a-half of the infant's life, the anal phase the following period up until about the age of 3, and the phallic phase from the third until about the fifth year.

Initially, erotic activity in the phallic phase is linked with urination. Freud discussed in passing the urethral phase, which was subsequently elaborated by later writers. However, Freud postulated that, in boys, phallic erotic activity is essentially a preliminary stage for adult genital activity. In contrast to the male, whose principal sexual organ remains the penis throughout the course of psychosexual development, the female has two leading erotogenic zones, the clitoris and the vagina. Freud felt that the clitoris is preeminent during the infantile genital period but that the erotic primacy after puberty is transmitted to the vagina. Recent sexual investigations have cast some doubt on the transition from clitoral to vaginal primacy, but many analysts retain this view on the basis of clinical findings. The question for the moment remains unresolved.

Freud's basic schema of the psychosexual stages was modified and refined by the work of Karl Abraham, one of the most gifted of Freud's followers. Abraham further subdivided the phases of libido development, dividing the oral period into a sucking phase and a biting phase and the anal period into a destructive-expulsive (anal-sadistic) phase and a mastering-retaining (anal-erotic) phase. Abraham further hypothesized that the phallic period consists of an early phase of partial genital love, which he designated as the true phallic phase, and a later more mature genital phase.

For each of the stages of psychosexual development, Freud delineated specific erotogenic zones that, when stimulated, give rise to erotic gratification. Freud suggested that, in addition, there are at least three phases of genital masturbatory activity: during early infancy, at the high point of infantile sexuality in the phallic phase, and again during puberty. During the earliest months of life, the genital region is often stimulated as a natural part of parental caretaking activity. However, direct masturbatory activity—stimulation of the penis in boys and of the clitoris in girls—reaches a peak sometime during the phallic phase and continues until the end of the oedipal period. Table II provides a resumé of current more or less tentative views on psychosexual development.

THEORY OF INSTINCTS

When Freud began his investigation into the nature of unconscious drives, he strove consistently to base psychoana-

TABLE II

Stages of Psychosexual Development

Oral Stage

Definition	This is the earliest stage of development. The infant's needs, perceptions, and modes of expression are primarily centered in the mouth, lips, tongue, and other organs related to the oral zone.
Description	The oral zone maintains its dominant role in the organization of the psyche through approximately the first 18 months of life. Oral sensations include thirst, hunger, pleasurable tactile stimulations evoked by the nipple or its substitute, sensations related to swallowing and satiation. Oral drives consist of two separate components: libidinal and aggressive. States of oral tension lead to a seeking for oral gratification, typified by quiescence at the end of nursing. The oral triad consists of the wish to eat, to sleep, and to reach that relaxation which occurs at the end of sucking just before the onset of sleep. Libidinal needs (oral erotism) are thought to predominate in the early parts of the oral phase; they are mixed with more aggressive components later (oral sadism). Oral aggression may express itself in biting, chewing, spitting, or crying. Oral aggression is connected with primitive wishes and fantasies of biting, devouring, and destroying.
Objectives	To establish a trusting dependence on nursing and sustaining objects, to establish comfortable expression and gratification of oral libidinal needs without excessive conflict or ambivalence from oral-sadistic wishes.
Pathological traits	Excessive oral gratification or deprivation can result in libidinal fixations that contribute to pathological traits. Such traits can include excessive optimism, narcissism, pessimism (often seen in depressive states), and demandingness. Oral characters are often excessively dependent and require others to give to them and to look after them. Such persons want to be fed but may be exceptionally giving in order to elicit a return of being given to. Oral characters are often extremely dependent on objects for the maintenance of their self-esteem. Envy and jealousy are often associated with oral traits.
Character traits	Successful resolution of the oral stage provides a basis in character structure for capacities to give to and to receive from others without excessive dependence or envy, a capacity to rely on others with a sense of trust and with a sense of self-reliance and self-trust.

Anal Stage

Definition	This stage of psychosexual development is prompted by maturation of neuromuscular control over sphincters, particularly the anal sphincters, thus permitting more voluntary control over retention or expulsion of feces.
Description	This period, which extends roughly from 1 to 3 years of age, is marked by a recognizable intensification of aggressive drives mixed with libidinal components in sadistic impulses. Acquisition of voluntary sphincter control is associated with an increasing shift from passivity to activity. The conflicts over anal control and the struggle with the parent over retaining or expelling feces in toilet training give rise to increased recognizable intensification of aggressive drives mixed with libidinal components in sadistic impulses. Acquisition of voluntary sphincter control is associated with an increasing shift from passivity to activity. The conflicts over anal control and the struggle with the parent over retaining or expelling feces in toilet training give rise to increased ambivalence, together with a struggle over separation, individuation, and independence. Anal erotism refers to the sexual pleasure in anal functioning, both in retaining the precious feces and in presenting them as a precious gift to the parent. Anal sadism refers to the expression of aggressive wishes connected with discharging feces as powerful and destructive weapons. These wishes are often displayed in children's fantasies of bombing and explosions.
Objectives	The anal period is essentially a period of striving for independence and separation from dependence on and control by the parent. The objective of sphincter control without overcontrol (fecal retention) or loss of control (messing) is matched by the child's attempts to achieve autonomy and independence without excessive shame or self-doubt from loss of control.
Pathological traits	Maladaptive character traits, often apparently inconsistent, are derived from anal erotism and the defenses against it. Orderliness, obstinacy, stubbornness, willfulness, frugality, and parsimony are features of the anal character derived from a fixation on anal functions. When defenses against anal traits are less effective, the anal character reveals traits of heightened ambivalence, lack of tidiness, messiness, defiance, rage, and sadomasochistic tendencies. Anal characteristics and defenses are most typically seen in obsessive-compulsive neuroses.
Character traits	Successful resolution of the anal phase provides the basis for the development of personal autonomy, a capacity for independence and personal initiative without guilt, a capacity for self-determining behavior without a sense of shame or self-doubt, a lack of ambivalence, and a capacity for willing cooperation without either excessive willfulness or sense of self-diminution or defeat.

TABLE II—*continued*

Urethral Stage

Definition	This stage was not explicitly treated by Freud but is envisioned as a transitional stage between the anal and the phallic stages of development. It shares some of the characteristics of the preceding anal phase and some from the subsequent phallic phase.		or to what extent the objectives of urethral functioning differ from those of the anal period.
Description	The characteristics of the urethral phase are often subsumed under those of the phallic stage. Urethral erotism, however, is used to refer to the pleasure in urination and to the pleasure in urethral retention analogous to anal retention. Similar issues of performance and control are related to urethral functioning. Urethral functioning may also be invested with a sadistic quality, often reflecting the persistence of anal-sadistic urges. Loss of urethral control, as in enuresis, may frequently have regressive significance that reactivates anal conflicts.	Pathological traits	The predominant urethral trait is that of competitiveness and ambition, probably related to the compensation for shame due to loss of urethral control. In control, this may serve as the start for the development of penis envy, related to the feminine sense of shame and inadequacy in being unable to match the male urethral performance. This is also related to issues of control and shaming.
Objectives	The urethral stage involves issues of urethral performance, and loss of control. It is not clear whether	Character traits	Besides the healthy effects analogous to those from the anal period, urethral competence provides a sense of pride and self-competence derived from performance. Urethral performance is an area in which the small boy can imitate and match his father's more adult performance. The resolution of urethral conflicts sets the stage for budding gender identity and subsequent identifications.

Phallic Stage

Definition	The phallic stage of sexual development begins sometime during the third year of life and continues until approximately the end of the fifth year.	Pathological traits	The derivation of pathological traits from the phallic-oedipal involvement is so complex and subject to such a variety of modifications that it encompasses nearly the whole of neurotic development. The issues, however, focus on castration in males and on penis envy in females. The important focus of developmental distortions in this period derives from the patterns of identification developed out of the resolution of the oedipal complex. The influence of castration anxiety and penis envy, the defenses against both of these, and the patterns of identification that emerge from the phallic phase are the primary determinants of the development of human character. They also subsume and integrate the residues of previous psychosexual stages, so that fixations or conflicts that derive from any of the preceding stages can contaminate and modify the oedipal resolution.
Description	The phallic phase is characterized by a primary focus of sexual interests, stimulation, and excitement in the genital area. The penis becomes the organ of principal interest to children of both sexes, with the lack of a penis in the female being considered as evidence of castration. The phallic phase is associated with an increase in genital masturbation, accompanied by predominantly unconscious fantasies of sexual involvement with the same-sex parent. The threat of castration and its related castration anxiety arise in connection with guilt over masturbation and oedipal wishes. During this phase, the oedipal involvement and conflict are established and consolidated.		
Objectives	The objective of this phase is to focus erotic interest in the genital area and genital functions. This focusing lays the foundations for gender identity and serves to integrate the residues of previous stages of psychosexual development into a predominantly genital-sexual orientation. The establishing of the oedipal situation is essential for the furtherance of subsequent identifications that serve as the basis for important and enduring dimensions of character organization.	Character traits	The phallic stage provides the foundations for an emerging sense of sexual identity, of a sense of curiosity without embarrassment, of initiative without guilt, of a sense of mastery not only over objects and persons in the environment but also over internal processes and impulses. The resolution of the oedipal conflict at the end of the phallic period gives rise to powerful internal resources for regulation of drive impulses and their direction toward constructive ends. This internal source of regulation is the superego, and it is based on identifications derived primarily from parental figures.

Latency Stage

Definition	This is the stage of relative quiescence or inactivity of the sexual drive during the period from the resolution of the Oedipus complex until pubescence (from about 5 or 6 years until about 11 to 13 years).		functions allow for a considerably greater degree of control over instinctual impulses. Sexual interests during this period are generally thought to be quiescent. This is a period of primarily homosexual affiliations for both boys and girls and a sublimation of libidinal and aggressive energies into energetic learning and play activities, exploring the environment,
Description	The institution of the superego at the close of the oedipal period and the further maturation of ego		

TABLE II *continued*

and becoming more proficient in dealing with the world of things and persons around them. It is a period for development of important skills. The relative strength of regulatory elements often gives rise to patterns of behavior that are somewhat obsessive and hypercontrolling.

Objectives The primary objective in this period is the further integration of oedipal identifications and a consolidation of sex-role identity and sex roles. The relative quiescence and control of instinctual impulses allow for development of ego apparatuses and mastery skills. Further identificatory components may be added to the oedipal ones on the basis of broadening contacts with other significant figures outside the family—teachers, coaches, and other adult figures.

Pathological traits The danger in the latency period can arise either from a lack of development of inner controls or an excess of inner controls. The lack of control can lead to a failure of the child to sublimate his energies sufficiently in the interests of learning and develop-

ment of skills. An excess of inner control, however, can lead to premature closure of personality development and the precocious elaboration of obsessive character traits.

Character traits The latency period has frequently been regarded as a period of relatively unimportant inactivity in the developmental schema. More recently, greater respect for the developmental processes that take place in this period has been gained. Important consolidations and additions are made to the basic postoedipal identifications. It is a period of integrating and consolidating previous attainments in psychosexual development and of establishing decisive patterns of adaptive functioning. The child can develop a sense of industry and a capacity for mastery of objects and concepts that allow him to function autonomously and with a sense of initiative without running the risk of failure or defeat or a sense of inferiority. These are all important attainments that need to be further integrated ultimately as the essential basis for a mature adult life of satisfaction in work and love.

Genital Stage

Definition The genital or adolescent phase of psychosexual development extends from the onset of puberty in about the eleventh to thirteenth years until the adolescent reaches young adulthood. There is a tendency today to subdivide this stage into preadolescent, early adolescent, middle adolescent, late adolescent, and postadolescent periods.

Description The physiological maturation of systems of genital (sexual) functioning and attendant hormonal systems leads to an intensification of drives, particularly libidinal drives. This intensification produces a regression in personality organization, which reopens conflicts of previous stages of psychosexual development and provides the opportunity for a reresolution of those conflicts in the context of achieving a mature sexual and adult identity.

Objectives The primary objectives of this period are the ultimate separation from dependence on and attachment to the parents and the establishment of mature, nonincestuous, heterosexual object relationships. Related to these objectives are the achievement of a mature sense of personal identity and acceptance and integration of a set of adult roles and functions that permit new adaptive integrations with social expectations and cultural values.

Pathological traits The pathological deviations due to a failure to achieve successful resolution of this stage of development are multiple and complex. Defects can arise from the whole spectrum of psychosexual residues, since the developmental task of the adolescent period is in a sense a partial reopening, reworking, and reintegrating of all those aspects of development. Previous unsuccessful resolutions and fixations in various phases or aspects of psychosexual development produce pathological defects in the emerging adult personality. A more specific defect from a failure to resolve adolescent issues has been described by Erikson as identity diffusion.

Character traits The successful resolution and reintegration of prior psychosexual stages in the adolescent, fully genital phase sets the stage normally for a fully mature personality with a capacity for full and satisfying genital potency and a self-integrated and consistent sense of identity. Such a person has reached a satisfying capacity for self-realization and meaningful participation in areas of work and love and in the creative and productive application to satisfying and meaningful goals and values. Only in the last few years has the presumed relationship between psychosexual genitality and maturity of personality functioning been put in question.

lytic theory on a firm biological foundation. Only when this attempt was frustrated, as was apparent in his attempt to formulate a complete physiological theory in the *Project*, did he retreat from this idea. One of the most important parameters of this attempt to link psychological and biological phenomena came in the context of Freud's basing of his theory of motivation on instincts. He viewed the instincts as a class of borderline concepts that function between the mental and the organic spheres. Consequently, his use of the term "instinct" is not always consistent, since it emphasizes either the psychic aspect or the biological aspect of the term in varying degrees in varying contexts. Libido sometimes refers to the somatic proc-

ess underlying the sexual instinct; at other times it refers to the psychological representation itself. Freud's usage is quite divergent from the Darwinian implications of the term "instinct," which implies innate, inherited, unlearned, and biologically adaptive behavior.

The clearest formulation of the notion of instinct came in Freud's paper *The Instincts and Their Vicissitudes* (1915). "Instinct" is used there as a concept that functions between the mental and the somatic realms as a psychic representative of stimuli, which come from the organism and exercise their influence on the mind. They are a measure of the demand made on the mind for work as a result of its connection with the body. This concept plays an essential role in the psychoanalytic understanding of the function of the mind, but the concept remains somewhat ambiguous. The relationship between psychological and somatic processes is particularly difficult to elucidate. The difficulty is not diminished by simply affirming a conviction of the essential psychosomatic unity of mind and body.

Psychoanalysts today are forced, just as Freud was, to limit their theoretical constructs primarily to the psychological aspects of human behavior. Again and again in the course of the development of psychoanalytic thinking, there have been attempts to free psychoanalytic concepts from the cloying involvement with the somatic, biological organism. Most recently, for example, object relations theorists have been demanding an abandonment of instinctual theory as a biological aberration that was simply a peculiarity of Freud's thinking that only inhibits the development of a more purely psychological science. This is Freud's "as if" again. But the problem remains as to whether or not a disembodied psychology can be a psychology of human nature in any real sense. The tension remains in psychoanalytic thinking and was inherent in the very beginning of Freud's thinking about instincts and in the ambiguities over the formulation of the concept of instinct, ambiguities that he was never able to resolve.

Characteristics of Instincts

In Freud's description of instincts, he ascribed to them four principal characteristics: source, impetus, aim, and object. In general, the *source* of an instinct refers to the part of the body from which it arises, the biological substratum that gives rise to the organismic stimuli. The source, then, refers to a somatic process that gives rise to stimuli, which are represented in the mental life as drive representations or affects. In the case of libido, the stimulus refers to the process or factors that excite a specific erotogenic zone. The *impetus* or pressure is a quantitative economic concept that refers to the amount of force or energy or demand for work made by the instinctual stimulus. The *aim* is any action directed toward satisfaction or tension release. The aim in every instinct is satisfaction, which can be obtained only by reducing the state of stimulation at the source of the instinct. The *object* is the person or thing that is the target for this satisfaction-seeking action and that enables the instinct to gain satisfaction or to discharge the tension and thus gain the instinctual aim of pleasure.

Freud commented that the object is the most variable characteristic of the instinct, since it is appropriate only insofar as its characteristics make satisfaction possible. At times, the person's own body may serve as an object of an instinct—for example, in masturbatory activity. This early view of the instinctual object long held sway in psychoanalytic thinking, but it has recently come under some serious criticism. Considerably more weight is put on the significance of the objects of libidinal attachment, particularly by object relations theorists. Increasingly, the psychoanalytic concept of instincts is seen as meaningless unless it includes and derives from a context of object relatedness. Moreover, it cannot be said simply that the object of infantile drives is the most variable characteristic of the instinct, since attachment to the primary objects, particularly the mothering object, is of the utmost significance developmentally.

Vicissitudes of Infantile Sexuality

Part instincts. During infancy and early childhood, erotic sensation emanates for the most part from the mucosal surfaces of a particular body part or organ. Specifically, during the

earliest years of life, the mucous membranes of the mouth, anus, and external genitalia are the appropriate primary foci of the child's erotic life. The focus varies, depending on the phase of psychosexual development. Subsequently, the sexual activity in normal adults is dominated by the genital zone. Nonetheless, the pregenital or prephallic erotogenic functioning of the oral and anal zones still retains a place in sexual activity, specifically in preliminary mating activities or foreplay. Stimulation of such zones elicits preliminary gratification (forepleasure), which precedes coitus. In normal adults who have achieved a level of mature genital potency, the sexual act culminates in the pleasure (end pleasure) of orgasm.

Freud described the erotic impulses arising from the pregenital zones as component or part instincts. Kissing, stimulation of the area surrounding the anus, and biting the love object in the course of lovemaking are examples of activities associated with these part instincts. The activity of component instincts or early genital excitement may undergo displacement—for example, to the eyes in looking and being looked at (scoptophilia) and may, consequently, be a source of pleasure. Ordinarily, these component instincts undergo repression or persist in a restricted fashion in sexual foreplay. The young child is characterized by a polymorphous-perverse sexual disposition. His total sexuality is relatively undifferentiated and encompasses all the part instincts. However, in the normal course of development to adult genital maturity, these part instincts presumably become subordinate to the primacy of the genital region. The failure to achieve genital primacy may result in various forms of pathology. If, for example, the libido becomes too firmly attached to one of the pregenital erotogenic zones or a single part instinct becomes predominant, a perversion such as fellatio or voyeurism, which under ordinary circumstances is limited to the preliminary stages of lovemaking (foreplay), replaces the normal act of sexual intercourse, and orgastic satisfaction is derived from it. The persistent attachment of the sexual instinct to a particular stage of pregenital development is called a fixation.

Neurosis and perversion. Freud further discovered that in the psychoneuroses only a limited number of sexual impulses that are repressed and are responsible for neurotic symptoms are of a normal kind. Usually, the repressed and pathogenic impulses are the same impulses that are given overt expression in the perversions. He regarded the neurosis as the negative of a perversion. However, the relationship between the psychoneuroses and perversions is not nearly as simple as that. The situation is considerably more complex. For example, Freud's theory cannot account for the fact that in one case a part instinct is repressed and provides the stimulus for neurotic symptom formation and in another case the part instinct remains overt and dominates the person's sexual activity in the form of a perversion. In other words, although the theory of sexuality includes the concept of libidinal fixation insofar as it is limited to the description of various potential zones of libidinal stimulation and excitement, it is unable to explain the outcome of fixation in a particular case. The resolution of this problem had to await the development of later parts of the theory, particularly those concerning defense mechanisms, the functions of ego and the superego, and the nature and role of anxiety in mental functioning.

Development of Object Relations

Current theories in psychoanalytic psychiatry have increasingly focused on the importance for later psychopathology of early disturbances in object relationships—that is, disturbances in the relationship between the child's affect and the significant objects in the environment, particularly the mothering object. Students of development who emphasize the importance of cultural factors in development have criticized Freud for setting forth his notions of psychosexual development in a social vacuum, without taking into account the influence on the child's instinctual development of the adult objects with whom he comes into contact. The criticism does not seem to be altogether warranted. From his earliest writings on sexual development, Freud incorporated the basic notion of an object relationship as intimately connected to the functioning of the sexual instinct. He considered the aspects of drive discharge and object attachment as closely interwoven aspects of instinctual phenomena. From the beginning of the child's development, Freud regarded the sexual instinct as anaclitic, in the sense that the child's attachment to the feeding and mothering figure is based on the child's utter physiological dependence on the object. This is not surprising when one considers that the libido theory evolved from Freud's insight, which he acquired early in his clinical experience, that the sexual fantasies of even adult patients typically center on early relationships with their parents. In any event, throughout his descriptions of the libidinal phases of development, Freud made constant reference to the significance of the child's relationship with crucial figures in his environment. He postulated that the choice of a love object in adult life, the love relationship itself, and object relationships in other spheres of interest and activity depend largely on the nature and quality of the child's object relationships during the earliest years of life.

At birth, the infant's responses to external stimulation are relatively diffuse and disorganized. Even so, as recent experimental research on neonates has indicated, the infant is quite responsive to external stimulation, and the patterns of response are quite complex and relatively organized, even shortly after birth. Neonates a few hours of age respond selectively to novel stimuli and demonstrate remarkable preferences for complex, as compared with simple, patterns of stimulation. The neonate's responses to noxious and pleasurable stimuli are relatively undifferentiated. Even so, sensations of hunger, cold, and pain give rise to tension and a corresponding need to seek relief from painful stimuli. At the beginning of life, however, the infant is not responding specifically to objects. More development of perceptual and cognitive apparatuses and more differentiation of sensory impressions and integration of cognitive patterns are required before the child is able to differentiate between the impressions belonging to himself and those derived from external objects. Consequently, observations and inferences based on data derived from the first 6 months of life must be interpreted in the context of the child's cognitive functioning before self-object differentiation.

Oral phase. In the first months of life, the human infant is considerably more helpless than any other mammal, and his helplessness continues for a longer period of time than in any other species. He cannot survive unless he is cared for, and he cannot achieve relief from the painful disequilibrium of inner physiological states without the help of external caretaking objects. Object relationships of the most primitive kind begin to be established only when the infant first begins to grasp this fact of his experience. In the beginning, the infant cannot distinguish between his own lips and the mother's breast, nor does he initially associate the satiation of painful hunger pangs with the presentation of the extrinsic breast. Because he is aware only of his own inner tension and relaxation and is

unaware of the external object, the longing for the object exists only in the degree that the disturbing stimuli persists and the longing for satiation remains unsatisfied in the absence of the object. When the satisfying object finally appears and the infant's needs are gratified, the longing also disappears.

It is this experience of unsatisfied need, together with the experience of frustration in the absence of the breast and need-satisfying release of tension in the presence of the breast, that forms the basis of the infant's first awareness of external objects. The first awareness of an object in the psychological sense comes from the longing for something that is already familiar, for something that actually gratified his needs in the past but is not immediately available in the present. It is basically the infant's hunger that compels him to recognize the outside world. His first primitive reaction to objects becomes understandable insofar as he wants to put them all in his mouth. This reaction is consistent with the modality of the infant's first recognition of reality; he judges reality in terms of oral gratification—that is, whether something provides relaxation of inner tension and satisfaction and should, thereby, be incorporated and swallowed, or whether it creates inner tension and dissatisfaction and, consequently, should be spit out.

Early in this interaction the mother has served an important function, that of empathically responding to the infant's inner needs in such a manner as to become involved in a process of mutual regulation, which permits the homeostatic balance of physiological needs and processes within the infant within tolerable limits. Not only does this process keep the child alive, but it sets a rudimentary pattern of his experience, within which he can build the elements of a basic trust that allows him to rely on the benevolence and availability of caretaking objects. Consequently, the mother's ministrations and responsiveness to the child help to lay the foundations for the most rudimentary and essential basis for the subsequent development of object relations and the capacity for entering the community of human beings.

As the differentiation between the limits of self and object is gradually established in the child's experience, the mother is gradually acknowledged and recognized as the source of gratifying nourishment and as the source of the erotogenic pleasure the infant derives from sucking on the breast. In this sense she becomes the first love object. The quality of the child's attachment to this primary object is of the utmost importance. From the oral phase onward, the whole progression in psychosexual development, with its focus on successive erotogenic zones and the emergence of associated component instincts, reflects the quality of the child's attachment to the crucial figures in his environment and his feelings of love or hate or both toward these important persons. If a fundamentally warm, trusting, and affectionate relationship has been established between mother and child during the earliest stages of the child's life, then, at least theoretically, the stage is set for the development of trusting and affectionate relationships with other human objects during the course of his life.

It is only recently that psychoanalysts have developed any extensive awareness of the complexities of the oral stage of development and the vicissitudes to which the interaction between mother and child can be exposed. Increasingly, they are becoming aware of the multiple aspects of the mother's own personality and functioning that can impede or interfere with the normal pattern of development within the child. The nursing and caretaking interaction with the child can become the focus for a variety of conflicts and pathological influences deriving from disturbances in the mother-child relationship or from the mother's own personal inadequacies or psychopathology.

Aside from the adverse consequences typically associated with maternal rejection or undue frustration of the infant's needs, distortions in the early mother-child relationship may have more subtle if equally severe repercussions. The early stage of oral eroticism is succeeded by an increase of oral-sadistic impulses in the biting phase. Inevitably, the frustration associated with the biting part of the oral period—particularly with the weaning process, which to the child signifies the imminent loss of gratification and rejection—can evoke biting and cannibalistic impulses toward the object. When such impulses are excessive, as they may be under conditions of maternal rejection or unresponsiveness, they can serve as a prelude for later, more serious impairments of object relations.

A distinction should be made between the infant's biological relation to the mother in this early stage of life and his psychological relation to the mother. Even before the child's birth, in his prenatal dependence on the mother, there is a biological bond between mother and child that serves to satisfy the basic biological and physiological needs of the child. However, the psychological counterpart of this dependence is not externally evident in the early months of life and may, in fact, take many months to develop. Although some authors speak of a primitive emotional bond between mother and child in the first months of life, such an emotional relationship cannot develop before some degree of differentiation between self and object in the child's experience.

One can speak of primitive affective responses at this level of psychological organization, of pleasure and unpleasure, which may relate to states of physiological homeostasis. Such reactions are physiologically derived and do not imply awareness of the object as separately existing but may be regarded as providing the primitive basis for later psychological differentiation and for the emergence of affective ties to the object. Hartmann (1939) commented in this regard as follows:

> We should not assume, from the fact that the child and the environment interact from the outset, that the child is from the beginning psychologically directed toward the object as an object.

Thus, there is a distinction between the biological state of adaptedness or actual relatedness to the object that exists from birth and the psychological adaptation to the object that follows structural differentiation and the recognition of the object as separate from the self. This early stage of infantile adaptation has been described as undifferentiated, autistic, or objectless.

To the external observer the newborn infant seems to relate to the mother in a condition of unique dependence and responsiveness. However, this relationship is, at least at first, purely biological, based on physiological reflexes, and ordered to the fulfillment of basic biological needs. It is only as the child's ego begins to develop, along with the organization of perceptual capacities and memory traces that allow for the initial differentiation of self and object, that the infant can be said to experience something outside of himself to which he can relate as satisfying his inner needs. This dawning awareness of the external object is a most significant state in the child's psychological development and not only involves cognitive and perceptual developments but goes hand in hand with the organization of rudimentary infantile drives and affects in relation to emerging object experiences.

Freud's view in 1930 of this process was that the infant gradually learns to distinguish between his own bodily self and external objects by the repeated discovery that some sources of stimulus and gratification are always available, whereas others are not. The former become linked with his own body; the others are connected with the intermittently appearing and disappearing mother, initially with the mother's breast as a satiating and discomfort-relieving part object. The pleasure principle demands that sensations of pain or unpleasure be avoided and that sensations of pleasure or satiation be sought. In the beginning the sources of unpleasure are attributed to the world outside the self, thus creating what Freud called a "pure pleasure ego."

As the child's experience develops, the maintenance of the pure pleasure ego becomes more difficult as some of the unpleasurable experiences are found to be internally derived and as pleasurable experiences are also experienced as originating outside of the self. These early affective experiences in relation to the gratification or frustration of needs are put in the service of building up self and object representations as an initial phase of the organization of psychic structures. These representational components, deriving from affectively toned experiences, are initially organized at the rather crude level of differentiating pleasure from unpleasure. The child gradually learns to differentiate self from object in this representational sphere, and in this process his libidinal attachment to the object is specifically a function of the object's need-satisfying capacity.

Initially, these perceptual organizations may be created in the immediate context of need gratification and cease to function at those points in the infant's experience at which need gratification is no longer operative. These early fragmentary experiences of need gratification and their connection with the object are continually reinforced, and they begin to take on a constant structural organization that keeps them more continually available. This increasing differentiation is put in the service of the infant's adaptive needs; gradually, the functional differentiation of the perceptual and affective levels becomes increasingly autonomous and is consolidated as a structural acquisition of the infant's emerging ego.

As the infant's experience is amplified and reinforced, the attachment to and valuation of the object become relatively independent of the need-gratifying functions of the object. In the classical theory, it is at this point in the emerging experience of and attachment to the object that primary narcissism yields to secondary narcissism. Primary narcissism may be thought of as that infantile state in which the predominant feeling tone is one of self-contained pleasure. Such a primitive state can exist only before the differentiation of the self and the object and their respective representations. Consequently, primary narcissism is not a cathexis of the self, since the self is not yet structurally organized or experientially differentiated. At this stage of internal development, no self-representation is available, only a qualitative organization of the infant's experience. The child's early attachment to the need-satisfying object and the emerging psychological relationship to that object change the quality of the child's experience and begin to modify primary narcissism. Secondary narcissism, then, comes to mean a cathexis of emerging self-representations based on early internalization derived from these object relations.

The emergence of the psychological need-satisfying relationship to the object or part object occurs during the oral phase of libidinal development. However, the oral phase of development and the need-satisfying relationship are not equivalent. The oral phase is primarily concerned with libidinal development and stresses the predominance of the oral zone as the main erotogenic zone. The need-satisfying relationship is concerned not with drive development but, rather, with object involvement and object relationship.

In writing of this need-satisfying relationship, Anna Freud (1965) emphasized that the relationship is intermittent, existing only at times of need and ceasing to exist once the needs are gratified. The relationship is based on a:

part object (Melanie Klein), or need-fulfilling, anaclitic relationship, which is based on the urgency of the child's body needs and drive derivatives and is intermittent and fluctuating, since object cathexis is sent out under the impact of imperative desires, and withdrawn again when satisfaction has been reached.

In other words, the mother is perceived only in terms of her capacity to satisfy the infant's needs and not as a whole, separately existing object in her own right. This phase of development corresponds to Mahler's symbiotic phase (2 to 6 months of age) in which the child's awareness of the mother exists only as a need-satisfying quasiextension of the child's own self. These boundaries become temporarily differentiated in the state of affect hunger but disappear again as a result of need gratification. Only gradually does the child form more stable part images of the mother—breasts, face, hands, and so on. Consequently, Edgcumbe and Burgner (1972) concluded:

The crucial distinguishing characteristic of the state of need satisfaction (variously referred to also as the anaclitic or symbiotic phase) is that the subject is recognized as separate from the self only at moments of need; once the need is satisfied, we assume that—from the infant's (subjective) point of view—the object then ceases to exist until a need arises again. In other terms, cathexis is withdrawn from the object. Moreover, from the infant's point of view, the relationship is not to a specific object (or part object) but rather to the *function* of having the need satisfied and to the accompanying pleasure afforded by the object in fulfilling that function.

It is only when the specific object—that is, the whole object— becomes as important to the child as the need-satisfying function that it performs that the child's development moves beyond the level of need-satisfying relationship and toward the attainment of object constancy.

Although the oral phase of libidinal development and the need-satisfying relationship are not synonymous, there is a tendency to use the terms with overlapping significance They should be kept distinct. The need-satisfying relationship is specifically a mode or quality of interaction in which the object's need-satisfying functions assume prime importance to the subject. In contrast, demanding, greedy, passive, and dependent attitudes toward the object are often described as oral. The confusion of the terms "oral" and "need-satisfying" can give rise to considerable confusion, particularly if certain forms of character traits or other aspects of drive and ego organization are described as oral insofar as they represent persistent formations from the oral phase of drive development. But such developmental characteristics may not imply the persistence of need-gratifying relationships at all.

On the other hand, many of the behaviors toward objects that are clinging, egocentric, demanding, greedy, or selfish forms of behavior in relation to objects can be described as need-gratifying. However, such behaviors may be closely involved with underlying needs to satisfy narcissistic or even sexual drive pressures that may derive from multiple levels of development. This context of reference is quite different from that implied by developmental arrest or regression to a phase of need-satisfying relationships. This latter phenomenon is observed rarely, even in psychotic and borderline children. Consequently, care should be taken in the use of such terms as to what is implied specifically in

terms of the quality of object relationships and their developmental implications.

Psychological functioning can begin in rudimentary ways shortly after birth or even to some degree at birth, but the same cannot be said of the organization of psychological relationships. The emergence of such relationships requires the forming of at least a rudimentary representation of the external environment as external. The organization of the infant's psychological capacities and differentiating structures adequate to allow even primitive representations of need-gratifying objects probably requires several months and may only begin to emerge by about the third month of life. Even then, the organization of these capacities remains intermittent and unstable and is closely tied to states of need gratification. Nonetheless, they provide the beginnings of psychological relationships to objects and the rudimentary organization of these basic capacities.

The presence of certain identifiable perceptual capacities of primary autonomy cannot be regarded as proof that other aspects of psychic functioning have been elaborated. Even at birth, the child seems capable of organizing primitive perceptual formations that rapidly become more complex and sophisticated. But the presence of such perceptual structures does not imply that they are used by the infant in a context of psychological relationship to an object. The hungry infant may grow quiet and show signs of responding to the stimuli associated with feeding, but this reaction by no means implies that he is capable of recognizing the mother as a separate object or that he is capable of maintaining any connection or relationship with her once the hunger need has been satisfied. Even the development of stranger anxiety in the 8-month-old child does not necessarily indicate the establishment of such a constant relationship to the mother. It suggests no more than that the child has begun to distinguish between objects and has begun to invest in the representation of the mother. It does not yet imply that there is any cathectic attachment to or valuation of the mother as a whole person beyond her ability or function to satisfy certain specific needs.

It is useful to distinguish between need satisfaction as a stage of development in object relationships, related to but not synonymous with the oral phase of libidinal development, and need satisfaction as a determinant in object relationships at every level of development. The satisfaction of various kinds of psychological needs continues to play a role at all levels of object relatedness, but the satisfaction of such needs cannot be used as a distinguishing characteristic of the specific stage of need-satisfying object relationships. As objects become increasingly differentiated in the child's experience, their representations achieve increasing psychological complexity and value in a context of increasingly complex and subtle needs for a variety of inputs from objects. The development of object constancy implies a constant relationship to a specific object, but within that relationship the wish for satisfaction of needs and the actual satisfaction of those needs may be a significant component of the object relationship.

The attainment of object constancy marks a transition from the stage of need-satisfying relationships to a mature psychological involvement with objects. Object constancy implies a capacity to differentiate between objects and to maintain a meaningful relationship with one specific object, whether or not needs are being satisfied. Object constancy in the psychoanalytic sense must be distinguished from perceptual object constancy as described, for example, by Piaget. Perceptual constancy, which Piaget envisions as developing from the fifth month to the eighteenth month, implies the ability to differentiate between self and external objects, to organize relatively stable representations of both self and object, and to maintain a perceptual image of the object in its absence. This is only one component of libidinal constancy in the psychoanalytic sense, which also implies the stability of object cathexis and, specifically, the capacity to maintain positive emotional attachments to a particular object in the face of frustration of needs and wishes in regard to that object. This type of object constancy implies the capacity to tolerate ambivalent feelings toward the object and the capacity to value that object for qualities that it possesses over and beyond the functions that it serves in satisfying needs and in gratifying drives.

Consequently, the achievement of object constancy implies a complex and significant internal development in the child, particularly having to do with the consolidation of relatively autonomous ego functions and their harmonious integration with drive derivatives. In this connection separation anxiety suggests the beginning of the establishment of a libidinal object and the discrimination of that object from other humans. Similarly, the fear of loss of the love object and the fear of losing the love of that object are also related to the dynamics of object constancy. Ernst Kris (1975) commented:

> When in 1926 Freud entered into the discussion of typical danger situations to which the human child is exposed, he distinguished two—the two most archaic ones—which have a direct bearing on object relations: the danger of losing the love object and the danger of losing the object's love. The first represents the anaclitic needs; the second, the more integrated relationship to a permanent, personalized love object that can no longer easily be replaced. . . . Quite obviously, what is true of any other division into phases in the child's life is also true of this distinction: there are not only fluctuations from one type of object relation to the other, older one, but the two types normally overlap. The fear of object loss never quite disappears; the fear of loss of love adds a new dimension to a child's life and with it a new vulnerability.

The achievement of libidinal object constancy is a developmental attainment that is never superseded or outgrown but rather is expanded and amplified in the normal course of development. All subsequent developmental progress in the capacity for object relationships is really a deepening and extending of this original capacity for object constancy. Moreover, the developmental failure to establish object constancy has severe implications for all areas of psychic functioning, including drives, ego functions, affective experiences, and the capacity for human relationships.

In summary, then, object constancy involves a number of specific elements that are central to the further emergence of the meaningful capacity for relationships with objects. These elements include perceptual object constancy; the capacity to maintain drive attachment to a specific object, whether or not it is present; the capacity to tolerate both loving and hostile feelings toward the same object and to maintain a loving relationship with the object in the face of hostile and destructive impulses; the capacity to maintain significant emotional attachment to a single specific object; and the capacity to value the object for qualities and attributes that it possesses in itself, by virtue of its own uniqueness as individually and separately existing and as independent of any need-satisfying function it may serve.

Libidinal object attachment and object constancy provide the basic components for the emergence of significant object relationships in adult life, but they also contain the elements that lead to object relationships that transcend merely libidinal implications. Consequently, it is useful both theoretically and clinically to distinguish between a libidinal object and a love object. Although the libidinal object refers to the connection with libidinal drive organization, it is primarily concerned with diverse images of the object that may satisfy various drive needs and their associated states of libidinal satisfaction (pleasure) or dissatisfaction (unpleasure). By way of contrast, the love object implies an added dimension of the object, for it becomes valued over and above its need-satisfying functions. Consequently, the love object transcends the levels of libidinal drive organization and their satisfaction. This distinction applies with equal force to genital drive organization and to pregenital need-satisfying kinds of relationships. Thus, the concept of a mutually satisfying, reciprocally rewarding love relationship transcends the limits of libidinal attachment, even at the genital level. Such a mature love relationship must be responsive to a wide variety of human needs in both partners, including libidinal needs, but the regard and valuation of the love object are neither limited to nor wholly determined by those needs and their satisfaction. One can conceive of love relationships in which such needs are in some degree frustrated or denied, just as one can conceive of libidinal relationships that do not reach a level of love relationship. The libidinal object is not synonymous with the love object.

Anal phase. During the oral stage of development, the infant's role is not altogether passive, since he is caught up in a process of mutual interaction, in which he contributes by eliciting certain responses from the mother. The activity, however, is more or less automatic and dependent on physiological parameters, such as level of activity, irritability, and responsiveness to stimuli. Generally speaking, however, his control over the mother's feeding responses is relatively limited. Consequently, the primary onus remains on the mother to gratify or frustrate his demands.

In the transition to the anal period, this picture changes significantly. The child acquires a greater degree of control over his behavior, particularly over his sphincter function. Moreover, during this period the demand is placed on him to relinquish some aspect of his freedom for the first time. He is expected to accede to the parental demand that he use the toilet for the evacuation of feces and urine. The primary aim, however, of anal eroticism is the enjoyment of the pleasurable sensation of excretion. Somewhat later, the stimulation of the anal mucosa through retention of the fecal mass may become a source of even more intense pleasure. Nonetheless, at this stage of development, the demand is placed on the child to regulate gratification—to surrender some portion of the gratification at the parent's wish or to delay the gratification according to a schedule established by the parent. One of the important aspects of the anal period, therefore, is that it sets the stage for a contest of wills over when, how, and on what terms the child achieves his gratification.

The connection between anal and sadistic drives may be attributed to two factors. First, the feces themselves become the object of the first anal-sadistic activity. The pinching off and expulsion of the fecal mass is perceived as a sadistic act. Subsequent to this experience, the child can begin to treat objects as he had previously treated the feces. The sense of social power that evolves from sphincter control provides the second sadistic element. In his training for cleanliness, the child exerts his power over the mother by means of his control over evacuatory functions. He can exert power over her by yielding and giving up the fecal mass or by refusing to yield and withholding the fecal mass. The struggle can easily become one of who has whose way, and the child's sense of sphincter control gives him a sense of power that can easily be threatened. If his attempts to stubbornly withhold are excessively punished or his loss of control is excessively shamed, the child may regress to more primitive and oral patterns of relating to the mother.

The first anal strivings are autoerotic. Pleasurable elimination and, later, pleasurable retention do not require any outside help from an object. At this stage of development, defecation is accompanied by a sense of omnipotence, and the feces, which are the agency of this pleasure, become a libidinal object. The feces are invested with a high cathexis of narcissistic libido. Although they become external in the act of defecation, they have a high degree of narcissistic cathexis, since they represent an object that was once part of one's own body. The loss of highly cathected, powerful, narcissistically invested material is threatening to the child, who wishes to retain or regain the lost feces in order to restore the narcissistic equilibrium. In this way the feces become an ambivalently loved object; they are loved and retained or desired on one hand, and they are hated, pinched off, and expelled on the other.

During this period the ministrations of the mother, such as diaper changes, are also associated with pleasurable anal sensations. The quality of maternal care, in combination with conflicts surrounding toilet training, can alter the direction of object strivings. The combination of gratifying and punitive aspects of this interaction can contribute to and intensify the ambivalent strivings. There is a tendency for the attitudes toward feces to be displaced toward objects. For example, in an obsessive-compulsive neurotic, the compulsive neatness characteristic of this syndrome reflects the patient's regression to the anal phase of development and serves to express his wish to dominate. He exerts power over things and people and forces them into rigid and pedantic systems. At the same time, his feelings are characterized by the ambivalence of the anal strivings—that is, the desire to control and retain the object and the desire to expel and destroy it. The ambivalence characteristic of the obsessive is derived from the anal eroticism, which reflects itself in the child's developmental tendency to treat his feces in a contradictory manner. He alternately expels it from his body and retains it as a loved object.

In a sense, ambivalence is universal, and there is no object relationship of any significance or duration that does not contain elements of both love and hate. However, when the elements of the ambivalence are intensified and neurotically distorted, the conflict is usually resolved by the repression of one or the other aspect of the ambivalence. Usually, the hateful and destructive impulses toward the object are repressed, particularly in obsessive-compulsive conditions. However, the positive affect may also be repressed, as is often seen in paranoid conditions.

Phallic phase

OEDIPUS COMPLEX. In the normal course of development, the so-called pregenital phases are primarily autoerotic. The primary gratification is derived from stimulation of erotogenic zones; the object forms a significant, but secondary and instrumental role. A fundamental shift takes place in the phallic phase, since the direction of cathexis and the focus of libidinal intention falls primarily on the object. The fundamental task of the phallic phase is the finding of a love object. The establishment of genital love relationships in this period lays down the pattern for subsequent and more mature object choices. The phallic period is also a critical phase of development for the budding formation of the child's sense of his own gender identity as decisively male or female, based on the child's discovery and realization of the significance of anatomical sexual differences. The events associated with the phallic phase also set the stage for the developmental predisposition to later psychoneuroses. Freud used the term "Oedipus complex" to refer to the intense love relationships formed during this period between the child and his parents, together with their associated rivalries, hostilities, and emerging identifications.

Another significant dimension of the entrance into the phallic stage is that in the pregenital periods the child's relationships have been based primarily on one-to-one relationships with each of his parents, separately and individually. In the context of these separate dyadic relationships, the child has worked out important parameters of interpersonal relating, including trust, dependency, autonomy, and, to a certain extent, initiative. As the child emerges into the oedipal period, however, he achieves a new level in the complexity of object relationships in that his involvement with his parents is now specifically triadic.

Accompanying this important developmental step from a dyadic to a triadic level of involvement are other significant factors—an increased capacity for differentiation between internal and external reality and an increased capacity to tolerate the anxiety of the oedipal involvement. Consequently, the Oedipus complex represents the climax of the development of infantile sexuality. The transition from oral eroticism through anal eroticism to genitality and the various associated stages in the development of object relations from simple one-to-one dependency to the triadic oedipal situation culminate in the oedipal strivings. An overcoming of these strivings, which can then be replaced in the reworking of adolescence by a more mature and adult sexuality, is a prerequisite for normal development. Conversely, the psychoneuroses are specifically characterized by an unconscious fixation in the phallic phase and an unconscious clinging to oedipal attachments.

The Oedipus complex evolves during the period extending from the third to the fifth year in children of both sexes. There is some discrepancy between the sexes in the pattern of development. Freud explained the nature of this discrepancy in terms of genital differences. Under normal circumstances, he felt, the oedipal situation for boys is resolved by the castration complex. Specifically, the boy has to give up his strivings for his mother because of the threat of castration—castration anxiety. By way of contrast, the Oedipus complex in girls is evoked by reason of the castration complex. Unlike the boy, the little girl is already castrated; as a result, she turns to her father, as the bearer of the penis, out of a sense of disappointment over her own lack of a penis. The little girl is more threatened by a loss of love than by actual castration fears.

CASTRATION COMPLEX. In boys the development of object relations is relatively less complex than for girls, since the boy remains attached to his first love object, the mother. The primitive object choice of the primary love object, which develops in response to the mother's gratification of the infant's basic needs, takes the same direction as the pattern of object choice that will take place in response to opposite sex objects in later life experience. In the phallic period, in addition to the child's attachment to and interest in the mother as a source of nourishment, the boy develops a strong erotic interest in her and a concomitant desire to possess her exclusively and sexually. These feelings usually become manifest about the age of 3 years and reach a climax in the fourth or fifth year of life.

With the appearance of the oedipal involvement, the boy begins to show his loving attachment to his mother almost as a little lover might—wanting to touch her, trying to get in bed with her, proposing marriage, expressing wishes to replace his father, and devising opportunities to see her naked or undressed. Competition from siblings for the mother's affection and attention is intolerable. Above all, the little lover wants to eliminate his arch rival—the mother's husband and his father. His wishes may involve not merely displacing or superseding the father in the mother's affection but eliminating him altogether. The child understandably anticipates retaliation for his aggressive wishes toward his father, and these expectations give rise to a severe anxiety.

Specifically, the boy begins to feel that his sexual interest in his mother will be punished by the removal of his penis. Freud identified this idea of mutilation of the male organ in retaliation for incestuous wishes as the castration complex. He suggested in 1924 in *The Dissolution of the Oedipus Complex* that in the phallic period the narcissistic fear of injury to the penis is actually stronger than the erotic attachment to the mother. Any gratification of the boy's passionate love would endanger his penis and threaten him with severe narcissistic loss. Confronted with this threat of castration and the anxiety related to it, the boy must renounce his oedipal love for his mother. In renouncing his oedipal attachment to his mother and his oedipal ambitions, the boy identifies with the father and internalizes the father's prohibitions and restraints. In effect, the castration complex is internalized, freeing the child from the threat of external authority and retaliation, until such time as the internalization can be reexternalized under the regressive influence of puberty.

This somewhat simplified picture of the resolution of the Oedipus complex is considerably more complex in the actual course of development. Usually, the boy's love for his mother remains a dominant force during the period of infantile sexual development. However, that love is not free of some admixture of hostility, and the child's relationships with both parents are to some degree ambivalent. The boy also loves his father, and, at times, when he has been frustrated by his mother, he may hate her and turn from her to seek affection from his father. Undoubtedly, to some degree he both loves and hates both his parents at the same time. In addition, Freud's postulation of an essentially bisexual basis of the nature of the libido complicates matters further. On the one hand, the boy wants to possess his mother and kill the hated father-rival. On the other hand, he also loves his father and seeks approval and affection from him, and he often reacts to his mother with hostility, particularly when her demands on her husband interfere with the exclusiveness of the father-son relationship. The negative Oedipus complex refers to those situations in which the boy's love for his father predominates over his love of his mother, and the mother is relatively hated as a disturbing element in that relationship.

Under certain circumstances the reversal of the typical oedipal triangle may have serious implications for the child's future development. Homosexual development, for example, is often characterized by an unsatisfied longing for closeness with the father and a strong identification with the mother, derived from an unresolved negative oedipal involvement. The negative Oedipus complex is normally present to some degree, along with its positive counterpart, in normal and healthy development. Under normal conditions these conflicting feelings are able to coexist and can be integrated in a mature pattern of identifications without provoking undue conflict.

THE GIRL'S SITUATION. Understanding of the little girl's more complex oedipal involvement was a later development. Since her oedipal involvement could not be regarded as equivalent to the boy's development, it raised a number of questions that proved to be more difficult. Freud's views had to be elaborated and clarified by the researches of later psychoanalysts, particularly the clarifications provided by women like Helene Deutsch, Ruth Mack Brunswick, and Jeane Lampl-de Groot.

Like the little boy, the little girl forms an initial attachment to the mother as a primary love object and source of fulfillment of vital needs. For the little boy, the mother remains the love object throughout his development, but the little girl is faced with the task of shifting this primary attachment from the mother to the father in order to prepare herself for her future sexual role. Freud was basically concerned with elucidating the factors that influence the little girl to give up her preoedipal attachment to the mother and to form the normal oedipal attachment to the father. A secondary question has to do with the factors that lead to the dissolution and resolution of the Oedipus complex in the girl, so that the paternal attachment and the maternal identification serve as the basis for adult sexual adjustment.

The girl's renunciation of her preoedipal attachment to the mother cannot be satisfactorily explained as the result of ambivalent or aggressive characteristics of the mother-child relationship, for similiar elements influence the relationship between boys and the mother figure. Freud attributed the crucial precipitating factor to the anatomical differences between the sexes, specifically the girl's discovery during the phallic period that she lacks a penis. Up to this point, exclusive of constitutional differences and depending on the variations in parental attitudes in the treatment of a daughter in comparison with a son, the little girl's development parallels that of the little boy's development. However, fundamental differences emerge when she discovers during the phallic period that her clitoris is inferior to the male counterpart, the penis. The typical reaction of the little girl to this discovery is an intense sense of loss, narcissistic injury, and envy of the male penis. At this point the little girl's attitude to the mother changes. The mother had previously been the object of love, but now she is held responsible for bringing the little girl into the world with inferior genital equipment. The hostility can be so intense that it may persist and color her future relationship to the mother. With the further discovery that the mother also lacks the vital penis, the child's hatred and devaluation of the mother becomes even more profound. In a desperate attempt to compensate for her "inadequacy," the little girl turns to her father in the vain hope that he will give her a penis or a baby in place of the missing penis.

The second focus of Freud's concern was on the factors that lead to the dissolution of the Oedipus complex in girls. The little girl's sexual love for her father and her hope for a penis-child from him undergo a gradual diminution as a result of her continuing disappointment and frustration. The wish to be loved by her father may foster an identification with her mother, whom father loves and to whom he gives children. The threat to the little girl is not the loss of a physical organ, as it is for the little boy, but, rather, a loss of love—at the first level from the father, who is the object of her attachment, but at a deeper and more infantile level from the mother as well. Ultimately, the little girl must renounce her father in order to reattach her libido to a suitable, nonincestuous love object.

The Freudian model of feminine psychosexual development is currently undergoing considerable revision. The charge has been made, with some justification, that masculine phallic-oedipal development was the primary model in Freud's thinking and that feminine development was viewed as defective in consequence. Freud saw women typically as basically masochistic, weak, dependent, and lacking in conviction, strength of character, and moral fiber. He thought these defects were the results of a failure in the oedipal identification with the phallic father because of the fact of feminine castration. The resulting internalization of aggression, Freud felt, was both constitutionally determined and culturally reinforced.

These concepts must now be regarded as obsolete. Freud's hypotheses of a passive female libido, arrest in ego development, incapacity for sublimation, and superego deficiencies in women are outdated and inadequate. Differences in male and female ego and superego development may be defined, but there are no grounds for judging one sex to be superior or inferior to the other. They are simply different. As Blum (1976) observed:

Female development cannot be described in a simple reductionism and overgeneralization. Femininity cannot be predominantly derived from a primary masculinity, disappointed maleness, masochistic resignation to fantasied inferiority, or compensation for fantasied castration and narcissistic injury. Castration reactions and penis envy contribute to feminine character, but penis envy is not the major determinant of femininity.

Adequate conceptualization and understanding of feminine psychology and its development are still very much in progress. Much is poorly understood, and much more is hardly understood at all. Freud's views in this area cannot be simply jettisoned, since they served and still serve as important signposts along a difficult road. Current research has given partial support to and convincing refutation of his ideas. What is called for is scientific evaluation, theoretical reformulation, and modification, rather than rejection. Freud's views are heuristic and tentative formulations, rather than apodictic postulates. They can be tested, revised, reshaped, and adapted to fit the current realities of feminine psychological functioning. It is not at all clear that Freud was so much wrong. He may have simply expressed what he was able to observe in the women of his time and culture. But times change. The culture and the place of women in it have changed and are changing. To that extent, women today are different, and much of their psychology is different, too. Psychoanalytic understanding must inevitably lag behind these changing patterns of psychological experience, but a new view of feminine development is gradually emerging.

SIGNIFICANCE OF THE OEDIPUS COMPLEX. Freud regarded the Oedipus complex as the nucleus for the development of later neuroses and symptom formations. Furthermore, the various admixtures of libidinal fixations, object attachments, and identifications with which the child emerges from the oedipal situation exert a profound influence on the development of character and personality. The introjections that accompany the resolution of oedipal fixations provide the nucleus for the emerging superego.

This whole area is a focus of current concern in psychoanalytically oriented psychiatry. As such, the processes that bring about the resolution of the oedipal situation as the child emerges into latency clearly merit more detailed discussion than has been provided here. Those processes are intimately connected with the development of the psychic apparatus and its structural components. Their discussion, therefore, is deferred to another section where these areas of psychoanalytic theory are discussed. However, it should be emphasized here that with puberty and the onset of adolescence, there is a resurgence of incestuous oedipal feelings in both sexes. The task of separating libidinal attachments from parental figures and forming new, more appropriate adult, nonincestuous object attachments to suitable love objects becomes a critical task of the adolescent period. In young adulthood, with the advent of the biological reality of parenthood, both father and mother reexperience elements of their own infantile oedipal involvements in their relationships to and identifications with their own children.

Narcissism

The concept of narcissism holds a pivotal position in the development of psychoanalytic theory. It was Freud's dawning realization of the importance of narcissism that led him to important modifications in his understanding of libido and in his instinct theory. At the same time, Freud's examination of narcissism and its related clinical phenomena led him in the direction of an increasing concern with the origins and functions of the ego. Freud's first systematic discussion of the problem of narcissism appeared in a rather short paper published in 1914 under the title, *On Narcissism*. Freud's interest in the phenomenon of narcissism, however, had begun as early as 1909 and persisted through the period in which he produced some of his most important theoretical writings, including his analysis of the Schreber case.

The introduction and focusing on narcissism have had broad implications and reverberations in psychoanalytic thinking since Freud's day. The whole problem of narcissism remains a difficult and problematic one for psychoanalysis. The problem of pathological narcissism remains a focus of active interest, thinking, and clinical concern. The problem has special relevance with regard to certain forms of character pathology, which are relatively resistant to therapeutic intervention.

Theoretical basis. The notions of self-love, autoeroticism, and narcissism were not newly coined by Freud. The term "narcissism" is based on the reference to the classic myth of Narcissus, who is said to have fallen in love with his own reflection in the water of a pool and to have drowned in his attempt to embrace the beloved image. The incorporation of narcissism in Freud's perspective was extremely significant, in that it provided the first libidinal attachment directed toward the ego itself. This incorporation essentially violated the basic dualism of his instinct theory, which was based on the distinction between sexual-libidinal instincts and ego (self-preservative) instincts.

In 1908 Freud observed that in cases of dementia precox (schizophrenia), libido appeared to have been withdrawn from other persons and objects and turned inward. He concluded that this detachment of libido from external objects may account for the loss of reality contact that is typical of these patients. In his 1914 discussion of narcissism, he speculated that the detached libido is reinvested and attached to the patient's own ego. This attachment results in the megalomanic delusions of these patients; the libidinal investment is reflected in their grandiosity and omnipotence. Freud became aware at the same time that narcissism is not limited to these psychotic patients. It may also occur in neurotic and to a certain extent even in normal persons under certain conditions. He noted, for example, that in states of physical illness and hypochondriasis, libidinal cathexis is frequently withdrawn from outside objects and from external activities and interests. Similarly, he speculated that in sleep libido is withdrawn from outside objects and reinvested in the person's own body. He thought it could be that the hallucinatory intensity of the dream experience and the intensity of the emotional quality of the dream result from the libidinal cathexis of fantasy representations of the persons who compose the dream images. Freud also appealed to the basically narcissistic form of object choice in perversions, particularly homosexuality. Another manifestation of narcissism is the significant role it plays in the myths and beliefs of primitive people, who attribute the occurrence of external events to the magical omnipotence of their own thought processes. Particularly important is the narcissism of young children, which is relatively available even to casual observation.

Children are exclusively dedicated to their own self-interest and cling tenaciously and convincedly to the magical omnipotence of their own thoughts.

Development of object relations. Freud's observations on narcissism, particularly the behavior of very young children, provided strong evidence for the role of narcissism in development. The introduction of narcissism into his theory played a significant role, since it required that he reconcile his theory of libido with what now seemed to be a libidinal force operating within the ego.

Freud postulated a state of *primary narcissism*, which he said exists at birth. Primary narcissism is a hypothetical construct that Freud postulated to integrate certain observations and theoretical formulations. For obvious reasons, the hypothesis is not testable by direct observation. The postulate of primary narcissism, however, has been radically questioned in recent years, particularly under the pressure of increasing evidence that the neonate, even immediately after birth, can be quite responsive to environmental stimuli in quite complex and organized ways. Consequently, it is difficult to say whether such a postulated state as primary narcissism ever actually exists.

This is not to say that the neonate is not in a highly narcissistic state in terms of libidinal concentration. As Freud saw it, the neonate is entirely narcissistic. His libidinal energies are devoted entirely to the satisfaction of his physiological needs and to the preservation of a state of equilibrated well-being. This basic investment of libido in the infant himself Freud termed narcissistic or ego libido. Later on, as the infant gradually comes to recognize the person directly responsible for his care as a source of relief of tension or pleasure, narcissistic libido is released and redirected toward investment in that person, usually the mother. Freud called this transformed libido, which becomes available for attachment to external figures, object libido.

The development of object relations parallels this shift from primary narcissism to object attachment—that is, from early infancy, when narcissistic libido is preeminent, to later childhood, when object libido comes to dominate the libidinal organization. But some narcissistic libido is normally present throughout adult life. From the point of view of healthy development, a healthy and well-integrated narcissism is essential for the maintenance of a sense of well-being and a sense of self-esteem in the developing personality. Like the forms of object libido, narcissistic libido can also undergo fixation and undergo developmental vicissitudes, which direct it in the path of more pathological development. Freud observed that in a variety of traumatic situations, physical as well as psychological—for example, actual injury or the threat of injury, object loss, or excessive deprivation or frustration—object libido can be withdrawn from its attachment to objects and reinvested in the ego. He called this regressive renewal of libidinal investment in the person's own ego *secondary narcissism*.

Freud originally thought of the reinvestment of libido as directed to the ego as such. This has given rise to considerable confusion in the understanding of narcissistic libido. A decisive reorganization of the concept of narcissism was provided by Heinz Hartmann when he pointed out that it is more accurate to regard narcissistic libido as attached not to the ego as such but to the self. The proper opposition between object libido and narcissistic libido is that object libido is attached to objects and narcissistic libido is attached to the self. This important shift in the understanding of narcissism has opened up an area of theoretical reconsideration, which is still very much in flux, and has introduced into psychoanalytic thinking the concept of self as an important, although as yet ill-defined, intrapsychic structural component.

The development of a concept of object relations, following Freud's original view of the transformation of narcissistic libido into object libido, has classically been viewed in opposition to infantile narcissism. Extending Freud's view, classical analysts have always viewed the development of object relations as proportioned to the diminution in the titer of infantile narcissism. As the child develops, his attachment to objects, at first essential for the maintenance of life, calls on a basic shift of libidinal investment from the undifferentiated and self-contained sphere of primary narcissism to the form of object libido. As the child continues to develop, the quality and the nature of attachment to and involvement with objects undergo a progressive change, at each step of which the continued conversion of narcissistic libido is an essential aspect of the development of object relationships.

This perspective is able to provide a reasonable account of the transition from pathological narcissism to various degrees of object investment and development of object relationships, but it does not account very satisfactorily for the building of appropriate and adaptive degrees of narcissism into the developing psyche. Analysts generally agree today that a healthy degree of narcissism is required for adaptive human living and for the capacity to engage in mutually gratifying human relationships in psychologically healthy and adaptive ways. The mature love of the object in a loving relationship is sustained and supported by a degree of positive self-regard and a healthy narcissistic investment in one's own self. The deficits of such healthy narcissism in the pathological forms of exaggerated narcissistic grandiosity or its opposite sense of inferiority or depression can have a severely detrimental effect on the person's capacity for object relationships and on the vicissitudes of his particular love relationships.

A tension in points of view remains. On the one hand, the development of object relationships takes place only to the degree that infantile self-involvement and narcissistic self-investment can be surrendered. On the other hand, adult object relationships are possible only if one can enjoy and make a significant and meaningful narcissistic investment in one's own self and in one's own self-regard. These perspectives have led to differing analytic views about narcissism. For some analysts, narcissism is always clinically detrimental and must be regarded as pathological. Other analysts, adopting a view somewhat at variance with the classic Freudian theory, regard narcissism as undergoing a separate course of development; in certain degrees and within certain contexts not only is it not pathological, but its own inherent development is of extreme importance for the person's psychological growth.

This latter perspective has evolved in large measure from the contributions of Kohut (1966, 1971, 1977). In Kohut's account, the infant begins life in a state of self-contained, undifferentiated primary narcissism. His starting point, therefore, for the course of specifically narcissistic development is the same as Freud's—a primary state of undifferentiated, objectless, diffuse, and global energic containment. The first differentiation of this primitive narcissism comes in the form of two basic archaic narcissistic configurations, the grandiose self and the idealized parent image. This differentiation presumably takes place hand-in-hand with the emerging differentiation between self and objects that marks the passage out of the original state of primary narcissism.

Moreover, this earliest discrimination seems to take place because of the unavoidable conditions that make it impossible for the child to maintain his primary narcissistic state, conditions that are presumably contingent on the degree of frustration in maternal ministrations and responsiveness to the child's needs that brings with it the dawning realization that the child can no longer experience himself as a self-contained and self-sufficient entity capable of satisfying his own internal needs. Rather, the existential dependence on an external object for the satisfaction of needs and the consequent setting of limits on the child's sense of self-sufficiency and omnipotence are important developmental aspects of this process. Moreover, this earliest differentiation of archaic narcissistic states preserves an aspect of the undifferentiated narcissism as the internal possession around which the child preserves the residues of narcissistic omnipotence and grandiosity; the second component relocates these residues in the external object, which is viewed as powerful and idealized. From one point of view, the child's preservation of a sense of security requires the maintenance of some residue of infantile grandiosity; from another point of view, the maintenance of such security requires a situation of dependence and protective symbiosis with a powerful and idealized object.

As development proceeds, each of these basic narcissistic configurations undergoes progressive modification and gradual integration in the emerging and forming psychic structure that shapes the child's internal world. This narcissistic development takes place by the continual creation and recreation of a sequence of self-objects—that is, the child progressively relates to objects not merely as objects existing in themselves as independent and separate entities but, rather, as objects modified by the addition of specific components from the child's own emerging self-organization. Such objects differ from the classically conceived objects invested with object libido because they are invested with significant degrees of narcissistic cathexis proportional to the nature and the quality of the self-derived elements that are projected onto objects in the forming of such self-objects.

The relationship with such self-objects carries on the important function of maintaining the internal narcissistic equilibrium, which requires continual readjustment in the face of the sequence of narcissistic vulnerabilities arising at various phases of the developmental process. At the earliest infantile phase of development, the child may relate to the mother as a self-object in a quite symbiotic way; mother and child are merged as a psychic unit that allows only the faintest hint of distancing between mother and child as separate foci of psychic activity but in which the child's sense of continuing availability and lack of separateness between himself and the mother serves a stabilizing function in terms of the child's need to preserve an inner sense of narcissistic balance. In such a context, premature separation of the child and the essential self-object throws the child's fragile sense of self into a severe state of deprivation and fragmentation, whose implications are equivalent to psychic annihilation.

Gradually, the child's dependence on the mother and the quality of the self-object relationship shift; the vulnerability is concerned less with loss of the mother and more with loss of the mother's love. The connection with the mother, however, remains essential for the maintenance of the child's narcissistic equilibrium and coherence. At some point in development, the child reaches a state at which internal cohesiveness and the integrity of his evolving psychic structures allow him to preserve a sense of inner continuity and cohesiveness of his self-organization not only in the face of the potential loss of the object or even of the loss of the object's love but in the face of other narcissistic disappointments and vulnerabilities as well. The establishment of such inner narcissistic cohesion in the self-organization is an important developmental acquisition; it distinguishes between those conditions in which the child is capable of maintaining the integrity of narcissistic structures in the face of external threats and those forms of pathology in which regression and fragmentation of narcissistic structures take place in the face of narcissistic losses or traumata.

At each stage in this developmental progression, the original archaic narcissistic formations, the grandiose self and the idealized parent image, undergo progressive modifications. At each phase of the progression, the degree of narcissistic investment is modified in more modulated and realistic directions. At each stage there is a proportional transformation of these narcissistic structures into more constructive, stable, and autonomous psychic structures. Consequently, the grandiose self is gradually modified in more realistic directions that allow the child to maintain a sense of self-esteem and pride in accomplishment, even in the face of unavoidable disappointments and with the acknowledgment of given limitations. Ultimately, the grandiose self is modified in the direction of a mature sense of stable and secure self-esteem, pride in accomplishment, ambition, and the resilient capacity to maintain narcissistic balance in the face of severe losses and narcissistic disappointments. Similarly, the idealized parental image is modified progressively in the direction of a realistic and attainable ego ideal that is gradually internalized as a meaningful and sustaining set of personal values and ideals.

At any stage of this process, the reworking of the elements of archaic narcissism can be interfered with and undergo a variety of pathological vicissitudes. The results of such developmental impediments are a variety of narcissistic disorders, stretching from severe narcissistic vulnerability and the threat of disillusion and fragmentation of the self to higher orders of narcissistic vulnerability, in which the threat of loss of self-cohesion is minimal but in which various forms of pathological behavior can emerge as a result of narcissistic disappointment, threat, or trauma. Ultimately, the transformation of narcissism finds its most mature and realistic expression in a person's capacity for creativity, for empathy, for humor, for wisdom, and for the acceptance of transience and the inevitability of death.

Application to infantile sexuality. An important question raised by the consideration of narcissism is its difference from and relation to autoeroticism. In fact, the difference between the two is fundamental. In primary narcissism, there is no differentiation of self and object and no quality of object involvement in the infant's libidinal experience. Autoeroticism refers to eroticism in relationship to the person's own body or its parts. If the child cannot have the love object (mother) or the part object (breast) that he desires, he may seek to gratify his needs by use of his own body parts (thumb sucking, for example), as if they were objects. Any erogenous zone may be used for this purpose. The capacity to gratify sexual needs in this way is autoeroticism. Moreover, autoeroticism implies an absence of any specific object involvement. Secondary narcissism differs in that it refers specifically to the self, rather than to the person's body or its parts. Thus, there is considerable overlap between autoeroticism and primary narcissism, although they emphasize different aspects of the primitive libidinal condition. Autoeroticism, however, is quite distinct from secondary narcissism.

The vicissitudes of narcissism are mingled with and operating throughout the entire course of psychosexual development. Waelder (1960) made an initial attempt to apply the levels of self-love or narcissism to the developmental schemata of erotogenic zones within the framework of Freud's theory of infantile sexuality. Thus, in the oral period, narcissism is expressed as a wish for affection, a wish to be given to, and is defined as receptive narcissism. The narcissism of the phallic period designates a wish for admiration, which is said to characterize the phallic stage of psychosexual development.

At each stage of psychosexual development, the child is open to narcissistic insult of a kind that is phase specific and related both to the vicissitudes of object libido and to the state of internal development of the psychic apparatus. Oral deprivation can be envisioned in terms of narcissistic injury that contributes to the undermining of the infant's sense of inner value or worth. Similarly, the vicissitudes of the oedipal period open the child to narcissistic mortification by reason of the disappointment of oedipal wishes, which can leave him with a sense of inadequacy, inferiority, or lack of value. Narcissistic injury at these various points in the developmental program can leave the child with an emerging sense of shame and self-embarrassment and a variety of other vulnerabilities that can serve as the nidus of later character disorders or other psychopathology.

Choice of the love object. Early object relationships are crucial in the later choice of love objects. Freud found that a deepened understanding of the vicissitudes of narcissism made it easier to understand the basis for the choice of certain love objects in adult life. A love object may be chosen, as Freud put it, "according to the narcissistic type"—that is, because the object resembles the subject's idealized or fantasied self-image. Or the choice of object may be an anaclitic type, in which case the object may resemble someone who took care of the person during the early years of his life. Freud felt that certain personalities that have a high degree of narcissism, especially certain types of beautiful women, have an appeal over and above their esthetic attraction. Such women supply for their lovers the lost narcissism that was painfully renounced in the process of turning toward a love object. Another important category in which the narcissistic type of object choice plays an important role is that of homosexuality. In the homosexual object relationship, the person's choice of the object is predicated on the resemblance of the object to the person's own body, with its similarity of sexual organs.

In summary, the concept of narcissism occupies a central and pivotal position in psychoanalytic theory. With the introduction of the concept of narcissism, it became obvious that the concept of the individual, his body, and his ego could no longer be used interchangeably. It became clear that further understanding and advances in psychoanalytic theory depended on a clearer definition of the concept of self and its more adequate delineation from the concept of ego. Attempts to implement such understanding have brought into focus the ambiguities in the concept of the ego and underscored the need for the systematic study of its development, structure, and functions. Attention to narcissistic phenomena has also enlarged the understanding of a variety of mental disorders and various normal psychological phenomena.

Aggression

The aggressive drives hold a peculiar place in Freud's theory. His thinking about aggression underwent a gradual evolution.

Early in his thinking, Freud's attention was preoccupied by the problems posed by libidinal drives. He was quite aware of the aggressive components often expressed in the operation of libidinal factors, but he could not long avoid taking explicit account of the more destructive aspects of instinctual functioning. Undoubtedly, also, the horrors and destructiveness of World War I made a significant impression on him; he began to realize more profoundly the significance of destructive urges in human behavior.

In 1915, in *Instincts and Their Vicissitudes*, Freud arrived at a dualistic conception of the instincts as divided into sexual instincts and ego instincts. He recognized a sadistic component of the sexual instincts, but this aspect still lacked a sound theoretical basis. Oral, anal, and phallic levels of development all have their sadistic components. The sadistic aspects certainly have different aims from the more strictly libidinal, covering a wide range from sexual perversions to impulses of cruelty and destructiveness, which are devoid of any manifest eroticism.

Increasingly, Freud saw the sadistic component as independent of the libidinal, and he gradually separated the sadistic from the libidinal drives. Moreover, impulses to control, tendencies toward the acquisition and exercise of power, and defensive trends toward attacking and destroying—all manifest a strong element of aggressiveness. It seemed,

then, that sadism is associated with the ego instincts, as well as with the libidinal instincts. Freud once again followed the dualistic bent of his mind and postulated two groups of instinctual impulses, two qualitatively different and independent sources of instinctual impulses with different aims and modalities.

The problem, of course, was that in certain areas these two instincts seem to work in conjunction, but in other areas they seem to be in opposition. Thus, the notion of sadism was gradually broadened to include other characteristics under the heading of aggressiveness. At this point in his thinking, Freud attributed aggressiveness to the ego instincts and thus separated the sadistic components from the sexual instincts and preserved the duality. This new duality also served to assert the independent character of the ego instincts. Sexual sadism was then explained by the fusion between ego instincts and sexual instincts. This fusion is the converse of the admixture of libidinal impulses with the ego instincts in narcissism. There were some problems in this rearrangement of the instinctual theory. First, the criterion for distinguishing instincts had shifted from the source of the instinct to its aim. Second, the basic concept of instinct that regarded it as a mechanism for the discharge of energic tension, although still at least theoretically applicable to the sexual instincts, was difficult to apply to the ego instincts.

But putting the aggressive instinct in the category of ego instincts had further difficulties. The classification gave rise to still another problem. On the basis of clinical evidence of self-destructive tendencies in depressed patients and self-inflicted injury among masochistic patients, along with his observations of the wanton destructiveness normally manifested by small children, Freud concluded that in many instances aggression or aggressive impulses do not serve self-preservative purposes. Therefore, it seemed contradictory to assign them to the ego instincts. The difficulties made it necessary for Freud to take an additional step. The next step involved removing aggressiveness from the ego instincts and separating aggressive impulses from the ego.

With the publication of *The Ego and the Id* in 1923, Freud gave aggression a separate status as an instinct with a separate source, which he postulated to be largely the skeletomuscular system, and a separate aim of its own, destruction. Thus, libido and aggression were separated off into a separate stratum of the mind. Aggression was no longer a component instinct, nor was it a characteristic of the ego instincts; it was an independently functioning, instinctual system with aims of its own and was separately located in the vital stratum of the mind. Thus, the ego was left with its own ego instincts, the nature of which at this point remained unspecified.

The elevation of aggression to the status of a separate instinct, on a par with sexual instincts, dealt a severe blow to any lingering romantic notions of the essentially or exclusively good nature of humans. Aggression and destructiveness were seen as inherent qualities of human nature, such that aggressive impulses are elicited when a person is sufficiently thwarted or abused. Freud's new formulation also drew attention to the specific role of aggression in forms of psychopathology and to the understanding of the developmental processes through which aggression can normally be integrated and controlled.

Aggression remains a problem for psychoanalytic thinking even today. Although a great deal has been learned about the operation and vicissitudes of aggression since Freud originally struggled with it, there is still a great deal that remains to be learned about its nature, its origins, the conditions that produce and unleash it, the developmental factors that contribute to its pathological deviations, and its more constructive integration in the realm of human functioning.

The Pleasure Principle and the Reality Principle

From the very beginning, Freud envisioned the instincts as governed by certain regulatory principles that are applied to all stimuli impinging on the organism—both stimuli emanating from the external environment and stimuli emanating from within the organism (see Table I). Even at the time of the writing of the *Project* in 1895, Freud recognized the importance of the constancy principle—that is, the tendency of the organism to maintain a particular state or level of energic equilibrium. The Nirvana principle was a logical extension of the notions of entropy and constancy; it postulated a tendency on the part of the organism to discharge any internal tension in an effort to lower the levels of internal tension in the direction of seeking a state of complete cessation of stimuli or release of tension.

The pleasure principle was largely an application of these more fundamental regulatory principles. Freud viewed the pleasure principle as an inborn tendency of the organism to avoid pain and seek pleasure through the release of tension by way of energic discharge. However, the immediate discharge of tension is not always possible. Inevitably, then, the demands of the pleasure principle must be modified in order to meet the demands of reality. The reality principle modifies the pleasure principle to meet the demands of external reality. The demands of reality necessitate the capacity for delay or postponement of immediate pleasure or release of tension, with the aim of achieving even greater pleasure in the long run. The reality principle arises out of the organism's continual experience of the frustration imposed by the conditions of reality and, thus, is largely a learned function. Consequently, it is closely related to maturation of ego functions and may be impaired in a variety of mental disorders that are the result of impeded ego development. Here again one comes upon one of the theoretical propositions in Freud's middle period that underscores in a particularly striking way the deficiencies of an isolated, instinctual theory and the need for the operation of a systematic psychology of ego and its functions.

Life and Death Instincts

When Freud introduced his final theory of life and death instincts in 1920, he took what can now be seen as an inevitable and logical next step in the evolution of the instinct theory he had been developing. It was, nonetheless, a highly speculative attempt to extrapolate the directions in which his instinct theory was taking shape to the broad realm of biological principles. Freud's thinking about the instincts always cast its shadow in a dual modality. In the beginning he had distinguished sexual and ego instincts. This duality provided the basic dichotomy for the explanation of psychological conflict and the understanding of psychoneurosis.

The concept of narcissism, however, created a breach in the independent existence of the ego instincts and revealed the operation of libidinal instincts within the ego. Consequently, the dualistic character of the instinctual theory was undermined in favor of a monistic view of instincts as entirely libidinal. Moreover, the distinction of instincts with reference to their source was replaced by a reclassification of instincts according to their relations to objects. Freud tried to save the ego instincts by referring to the idea of ego interest, which he took to mean a form of nonlibidinal investment in the ego. The vacancy in the ego instincts, which resulted from the inroads of narcissism, was filled to a certain extent by the gradual separation of the aggressive instinct as a separate entity, which Freud could then locate in the ego and identify with ego instincts. The inconsistency, however, between the concept of aggressiveness and sadism, along with the alternate fusion and opposition between sadistic and libidinal impulses, led Freud to the next step of separating both libidinal and aggressive instincts from the ego

and locating them in the vital stratum of the mind, which is quite independent of the ego.

The introduction of the life and death instincts must be seen in the course of this development and as extending the inherent duality of instinctual theory to the level of ultimate and final biological principle. Freud had not divorced his notion from the underlying economic principles, which were derived from the principles of entropy and constancy. The constancy principle was extended to the Nirvana principle, whose objective is cessation of all stimuli or a state of total rest. A small, subsequent step led Freud from the Nirvana principle to the death instinct (Thanatos). Freud postulated that the death instinct is a tendency of all organisms and their component cells to return to a state of total quiescence—that is, to an inanimate state.

In opposition to this instinct he set the life instinct (Eros), which refers to the tendencies for organic particles to reunite, of parts to bind to one another to form greater unities, as in sexual reproduction. In Freud's view the ultimate destiny of all biological matter, driven by the inexorable tendencies of all life (with the exception of the germ plasm) to follow the principles of entropy and constancy, is to return to an inanimate state. He felt that the dominate force in biological organisms has to be the death instinct. In this final formulation, the life and death instincts were thought to represent abstract biological principles, which transcend the operation of libidinal and aggressive drives. The life and death instincts represent the forces that underlie the sexual and aggressive instincts. Consequently, they represent a general trend in all biological organisms.

In evaluating these general biological instinctual principles, one must realize that Freud was engaging in a somewhat exorbitant speculation. He in no way believed that the death instinct, for example, is clinically verifiable. He did think that certain clinical phenomena suggest that a more general principle like the death instinct may be operating, but he in no way thought that the observations can be used to demonstrate such principles. He pointed in particular to the tendency of persons to repeat past patterns of behavior (repetition compulsion), even when such behavior has proved to be ill advised or self-defeating. He also pointed to the evidence of strong masochistic needs in many neurotic patients.

Needless to say, Freud's extravagant speculation has been subjected to severe criticism. It is impossible to argue from the basis of clinical observation to such a general biological principle as a conclusion. If the inherent destructiveness of some states of psychopathology can permit the inference of destructive forces operating in the individual psyche, it by no means points to the existence of inherent and biologically determined forces of self-destructive potential. However one regards the argument as a biological speculation, it has little relevance as a psychological speculation. Consequently, the vast majority of contemporary psychoanalysts, although they strongly endorse Freud's dual instinct theory, either reject or pass over in silence the further extension of his theory to life and death.

One significant group of psychoanalytic theorists is a marked exception to this view. The school of analysts who have followed the lead of Melanie Klein base a considerable portion of their understanding of intrapsychic processes on the operation of the life and death instincts. In Klein's work with severely disturbed children, she ascribed the manifestations of aggressive instincts in such children to the operation of the death instinct. This point of view seems to collapse the intervening steps in the organization of instinctual theory and makes almost any manifestation of destructive aggression a direct expression of the death instinct. Although the contributions of Klein and her followers to the psychopathology of childhood disturbances are significant, other schools of analytic thinking have not followed their lead in this conceptualization of the primary instincts.

Moreover, the implicit parallelism in the organization and economy of separate instincts—libidinal and aggressive—that was embedded in Freud's systematic thinking about these instincts is currently under severe questioning and has been subjected to vigorous criticism. It is not at all apparent that the operation of aggressive instincts can be conceived of in terms analogous to that of libido (see Figure 14). Consequently, the whole understanding of the relationship between these separate instinctual drives, their relative economy, and their relationship and integration with the structures and functions of both ego and superego are currently undergoing considerable rethinking.

Anxiety

Parallel to the development of Freud's instinctual theory was the development of his thinking in relation to the theory of anxiety. The initial theory and its evolution and replacement by a subsequent formulation parallel the development that was taking place in other aspects of Freud's thinking. Particularly significant in relation to the theory of anxiety was his shift from a primarily physiological-energic-organismic basis of thinking about anxiety to a formulation that was specifically psychological. Accompanying this progression in his thinking was the movement from the rooting of his theory of anxiety in instinctual theory to the broader perspective of anxiety as an ego function.

INITIAL FORMULATIONS

Freud's initial theory of anxiety placed the emphasis on its biological genesis in the sexual instinct. As a result of his early clinical study in the 1890's, pathological anxiety was uniformly and univocally attributed to disturbances in sexual functioning. In the beginning of his theorizing about anxiety Freud's attention was focused on the causes of anxiety in specific clinical entities. He distinguished two important groups of pathology in which anxiety played a major role. On the one hand, he classified a group of syndromes that he denominated as the actual neuroses. This group included neurasthenia, hypochondriasis, and anxiety neurosis.

Neurasthenia is a state of chronic impoverishment and fatigue in which the patient is generally apathetic, disinterested, moody, suffering from a paralyzing fatigue due to an impoverishment of energy and from tension and restlessness due to warded-off impulses demanding discharge. The patient feels

the necessity for an outlet but lacks enthusiasm and interest in any outlet that may be offered.

Hypochondriasis is a form of organ neurosis that manifests itself in stressful and painful bodily sensations.

Anxiety neurosis is a state of restless agitation and perturbation in which the patient suffers from apparently unmotivated emotional attacks, chiefly anxiety spells, along with disturbances of physical function that are partly inhibition and partly anxiety equivalents.

In all the actual neuroses Freud felt that the causative factors have a physical basis. He contrasted those anxiety states to the psychoneuroses, such as hysteria and obsessive-compulsive neurosis, in which the basis of the symptoms is primarily due to psychological factors.

According to Freud, an increase in sexual tension as a purely physiological phenomenon leads to an increase in the mental representation of the sexual instinct, together with a variety of associated ideas and emotions. In the normal course of events, increased sexual tension seeks discharge somatically through sexual intercourse. Concurrently, there is a discharge of mental energy. However, in the actual neuroses, such as anxiety neurosis, abnormal sexual practices, including coitus interruptus and masturbation, prevent the proper somatic discharge of sexual tensions or toxins. The adequate expression of the psychic elaboration of these sexual tensions is also inhibited or distorted. Freud maintained that this interference with the adequate discharge of the psychic component of sexual tension—that is, its specifically libidinal aspects—gives rise to anxiety. Freud contrasted this situation to the causes of anxiety in psychoneurotic states, such as hysteria and obsessive-compulsive neurosis, which are due to psychological causes, specifically the interference with normal libidinal functioning due to psychic conflict or repression. The symptoms of the actual neuroses—anxiety accompanied by weakness, fatigue, rapid or irregular heart action, constipation, excessive sweating, and other vague somatic complaints—are often indistinguishable from those of psychoneurosis. They can be distinguished only in the light of the patient's history and the total clinical picture.

At this point, Freud held a dual theory of the causes of anxiety or, more accurately, two separate theories. One theory was a theory of toxic (physiological) origin, in which the anxiety is the result of dammed-up and undischarged libido, which is thereby forced to seek abnormal physiological dis-

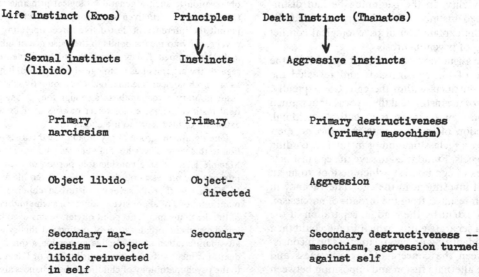

Life Instinct (Eros)	Principles	Death Instinct (Thanatos)
↓	↓	↓
Sexual instincts (libido)	Instincts	Aggressive instincts
Primary narcissism	Primary	Primary destructiveness (primary masochism)
Object libido	Object-directed	Aggression
Secondary narcissism -- object libido reinvested in self	Secondary	Secondary destructiveness -- masochism, aggression turned against self

FIGURE 14. Freud's theory of the life and death instincts.

charge in the anxiety symptom. The second theory is also related to the patient's sexual malfunction, but the cause lies at a more specifically psychological level—namely, in the repression of libidinal urges that are typically thought of as derived from unconscious infantile memories.

It is particularly striking that Freud maintained his toxic view of anxiety. However, he had a strong physicalistic bias and a powerful urge to root his study of the functioning of the mind and the pathological disturbances related to it in bodily functioning. Freud felt that in the actual neuroses he had identified a specific cause that explains the nature and origins of the anxiety symptoms. He maintained his view of the toxic cause of anxiety as at least one area of somatically based anxiety nearly to the end of his career. The basic notion of anxiety as transformed libido continued to be a part of his thinking. At the same time, however, there were subtle shifts in the concept of libido itself. The concept of libido had begun as a largely physiological concept but gradually shifted more and more until it became something of a border concept between the physiological and the psychological realms. It was not until 1933, in the *New Introductory Lectures,* that the hypothesis of anxiety as transformed libido was finally rejected altogether, even though Freud had radically revised and extended his theory of anxiety and had completely shifted and reoriented his thinking about instincts.

DIFFICULTIES WITH THE EARLY THEORY

Psychoanalytic investigators have differed rather broadly in their views about Freud's formulations on the actual neuroses. Some have considered the actual neuroses as valid and meaningful concepts; others have questioned not only the validity of Freud's toxic theory of anxiety but even the validity of the clinical entities themselves. For a long time, one of the main objections to Freud's toxic theory was that he postulated sexual substances related to the toxic aspects of sexual functioning. In the intervening years, however, endocrinological research has confirmed the existence of a surprising variety of sexual substances, the sex hormones. Freud's speculations were not so absurd, even though imbalances of sexual hormones may have little to do with anxiety as a psychological phenomenon. The role of norepinephrine and other hormonal and neurotransmitter substances in the elaboration of anxiety is yet to be determined.

Nonetheless, Freud's early theory of anxiety had certain inherent limitations. First, it contradicted a basic aspect of the psychoanalytic concept of psychoneurosis. Freud had postulated that in the psychoneuroses, anxiety is the result of sexual repression. If repression is the agency for the production of anxiety, repression must precede anxiety. What then is the cause of repression? Freud had also observed that repression arises in response to unbearable affects, which certainly include anxiety. Moreover, in certain clinical cases it was found that with the lifting or loosening of repression, the patients did not get better but became even more severely anxiety ridden and panicked. This unfortunate clinical outcome could not have been expected if repression were simply the cause of anxiety. The obvious alternative was that anxiety somehow preceded and was causally related to repression. The conflict between these two alternatives represented a source of considerable uncertainty and controversy in early analytic circles.

In addition, the theory did not take into account anxiety that arises in response to realistic danger—that is, objective anxiety. In certain situations the anticipation of external danger may cause somatic responses and subjective sensations of fear that are indistinguishable from those that occur in neurotic states. However, these conditions are entirely unrelated to the accumulation of sexual tension or of toxic sexual substances.

In struggling with these difficulties in his theory, Freud came to realize that anxiety can best be understood not in terms of its associated sensations or somatic expression but, rather, in terms of whether it is precipitated by an external danger or an internal danger. In other words, a comprehensive theory of anxiety must take into account its relationship to the self-preservative goals of the organism. The deficiencies involved in Freud's early theory of anxiety underscored the inevitable limitations of an approach that tries to account for a phenomenon as complex as anxiety entirely on the basis of consideration of the instincts and their vicissitudes, without reference to the functions of other levels and aspects of the psychic apparatus or its relationship to the outside world.

Freud's early theory was rooted in his early thinking about instinctual processes, specifically the sexual causes of psychopathology. The basically toxic and physiological rudiments of this theory reveal to a surprising degree the extent to which Freud's physicalistic bias influenced the entire tenor of his thinking. Even the emendations and extensions of his later theories of anxiety did not discard the important relationship between frustrated sexuality and anxiety in certain neurotic conditions. Nor did it rule out the possibility that there is a direct somatic relationship between sexual conflict and anxiety, the precise nature of which had not as yet been defined. However, in the modified theory Freud was able to incorporate these economic considerations within a broader and more meaningful theoretical framework.

Signal of Danger Theory

The new theory of anxiety was enunciated in Freud's *Inhibitions, Symptoms, and Anxiety,* which appeared in 1926. The date is important, since it means that the revision of the anxiety theory came a few years after the publication of *The Ego and the Id* (1923), in which Freud had presented his important theoretical reorientation, in which he abandoned the topographic model and put in its place the structural model. The revision in the theory of anxiety was prepared for by the gradual emergence of Freud's structural views and his increasing awareness of the importance and functioning of the ego. In contrast to the earlier theory, which approached anxiety from the standpoint of the drives, the new theory attacked the problem from the standpoint of the ego. It set aside the biological approach to anxiety. The physiological aspect of anxiety remained a subject of research chiefly in disciplines outside of psychoanalysis proper.

The new theory focused on the function of anxiety in relation to a variety of threats to the organism both from within and from without. Both real anxiety and neurotic anxiety were now viewed as occurring in response to a danger to the organism. In real anxiety the threat emanates from a known danger outside of the person. In neurotic anxiety the danger is precipitated from an unknown source, a source that is not necessarily external.

In his new theory Freud distinguished two kinds of anxiety-provoking situations. In the first, which takes as its prototype the phenomenon of birth, anxiety occurs as a result of excessive instinctual stimulation, which the organism does not have the capacity to bind or handle. In this type of situation, which arises because of the helpless state of the person, the excessive accumulation of instinctual energy overruns the protective barriers of the ego, and a state of panic or trauma results. These traumatic states are most likely to occur in infancy or childhood. when the ego is relatively immature. However, they may also occur in adult life, particularly in states of psychotic turmoil or in panic states, when the ego organization is overwhelmed by the threatening danger.

The more common situation, however, typically occurs after the defensive organization of the psyche has matured; in this situation, anxiety arises in anticipation of danger, rather than as its result. But the anxiety that is subjectively experienced may be similar to the anxiety that is caused by a danger that has already occurred. The affect of anxiety serves a protective function by signaling the approach of danger. The signal of danger may arise because the person has learned to recognize, at a preconscious or unconscious level, aspects of a situation that had once proved to be traumatic. Thus, the anxiety serves as a signal for the ego to mobilize protective measures, which can then be directed toward averting the danger and preventing a traumatic situation from arising. The danger may arise from external sources, but it may also arise from internal sources, such as the threatening of the ego or the potential overwhelming of its defenses by instinctual drives. The person may use avoidance mechanisms to escape from a real or imagined danger from without, or the ego may bring to bear psychological defenses within itself to guard against or to reduce the quantity of instinctual excitation. As Anna Freud pointed out, the defensive mechanisms of the ego may also, to a certain extent, serve the function of avoiding external dangers, as well as internal dangers.

According to this revised theory of anxiety, neurotic symptoms, such as phobias, indicate a partial defect in the psychic apparatus. Specifically, the defensive activity of the ego in phobias has not succeeded in coping adequately with the threatening drive manifestations. Consequently, mental conflict persists, and the danger that actually arises from within is now externalized and treated as though it had its origins in the external world, at least in part. Neurosis can be regarded as a failure in the defensive function of the ego, and this failure results in a distortion of the ego's relationship to some aspect of the outside world. In psychotic states the failure of defensive function is more complete, and the potential threat to the fragile ego and its permeable defenses is all the more overwhelming and annihilating. Greater portions of external reality are perceived as overwhelmingly threatening, and greater distortions of the ego become necessary to accommodate the distortions in the patient's view of the outside world.

Each stage of the child's development is accompanied by characteristic danger situations that are phase specific or appropriate to the issues pertinent to that particular developmental phase. The earliest danger situation, which occurs when the child is most immature and psychologically and physiologically vulnerable and helpless, is the loss of the primary object, the caretaking and nurturing person on whom the child is entirely dependent. Later, when the value of the object itself begins to be perceived, the fear of losing the object's love exceeds the fear of losing the object itself. The whole developmental effort of the child to separate himself physically and psychologically from his dependence on the primary symbiotic objects and the necessary developmental steps toward increasing individuation are all subject to the concomitant threats of loss of the object or loss of the object's love.

In the phallic phase of development, the fear of bodily injury or castration assumes a prominent influence. This fear may be thought of as a variation of fear of loss; in this instance, though, the loss is that of a narcissistically treasured part of the body. In the latency period the characteristic fear is that parental

representatives, in the internalized form of the superego, will be angry with, punish, or cease to love the child. In each of these phases, anxiety arises in the ego.

Freud noted that even though each of these determinants of anxiety is phase related and functions in reference to a particular developmental period, they can exist side by side in the contemporaneous ego. Furthermore, the person's anxiety reaction to a particular danger situation may occur after he emerges from the developmental phase with which that situation is associated. The persistence in later years of anxiety reactions that were appropriate to various pregenital phases of development has important implications for the understanding of psychopathology. The persistence of such early forms of anxiety in later stages of development is a reflection of neurotic fixations at earlier stages of development, as well as a persistence of the characteristic conflicts of such earlier stages.

IMPLICATIONS OF THE NEW THEORY OF ANXIETY

The first significant point relative to Freud's revision of his theory of anxiety is that it marks a decisive shift in emphasis away from a basically physiological perspective on anxiety to a perspective that is more decisively psychological. The theory of signal anxiety marks itself off from the earlier theory of toxic, dammed-up libido as the source of anxiety. Even though Freud still clung to his toxic theory, the new theory introduced a more meaningful concept of anxiety as related to anticipation of danger, a concept that has much broader application and much greater explanatory power.

The second important implication of the new theory is that it marked a decisive shift in the direction of Freud's thinking about the ego. When Freud introduced his structural theory in 1923, he defined the ego as an important regulatory agency in the psychic economy; it was a relatively weak and fragile ego that could survive only by more or less passively responding to the powerful drives of the id and the stringent demands of the superego. The introduction of the signal theory of anxiety, however, changed that picture of the ego in important if subtle ways. The new theory, which placed anxiety before the exercise of repression, signified that the ego enjoys a certain amount of control over the powerful instinctual forces of the id and that it enjoys a certain degree of autonomy in the exercise of some of its important functions. By implication, the ego has resources of its own that it can bring to bear in the management and direction of unconscious impulses and in the institution of defense against the threatening upsurge of instinctual drives.

The new theory of anxiety, then, was of great potential value in clarifying the understanding of a variety of psychological phenomena. At the same time, several fundamental questions remain unanswered. Further understanding is needed of the conditions or circumstances under which the ego becomes overwhelmed by anxiety, beyond its precipitation by the anticipation of danger. Similarly, little is known about the normal psychology of anxiety. More knowledge is needed about the quantitative and qualitative factors that determine whether a given amount of anxiety will spur ego development by mobilizing and stimulating the person's ego potential or whether the same quantity of anxiety will impede ego development by drawing the existing ego defenses into excessive conflict formations.

A subsequent implication of the signal theory of anxiety that has only begun to be explored by analytic theorists is the idea that anxiety is an important stimulus to structural growth and that an important index of intrapsychic development and integration is the increasing capacity to tolerate anxiety. The basic idea is that the ego must somehow learn to develop the capacity to use increasing degrees of anxiety to elicit its own inner resources for mastering anxiety and thus enlarging its capacity for internal mastery and control. By implication, the factors contributing to psychic growth that minimize, eliminate, or alleviate anxiety can undermine the important aspects of psychic development that contribute ultimately, in a healthy ego, to ego resourcefulness and strength. This aspect of the theory of signal anxiety has profound implications for the treatment process, particularly in regard to its concerns for stimulating the inner growth and development of the patient.

It was in relation to the signal theory of anxiety that Freud once again returned with renewed interest to the concept of defense. In his earlier dealings with psychic conflict in relation to the topographic model, Freud had minimized the notion of defense, reducing it somewhat simplistically to the notion of repression. However, his insight into the nature of anxiety as a signal function brought him back to a formulation of defense mechanisms as such. He began to see that the anxiety signal stimulates mobilization of a variety of defense forms. He began to see that repression serves as only one, although a very important, form of defense mechanism that the ego can use. The variety of defenses, he now saw, also include reaction formation, isolation, and undoing. With the development of the signal theory of anxiety, the ego was no longer a passive agency, helpless and vulnerable in the face of the demands of the id and the outside world. It was now credited as a kind of advance guard that can signal danger ahead of time and as having at its disposal a variety of possible responses to danger from without or within, responses that enable it to meet the demands and threats either from the drives or from the outside world. The ego had thus become a more forceful character on the stage of the intrapsychic drama, and the way was prepared for the elaboration of its autonomous function and capacities that was to follow.

Structural Theory

INADEQUACIES OF THE TOPOGRAPHIC THEORY

The topographic theory was essentially a transitional model in the development of Freud's thinking. It served an important function in providing the framework for the development of his basic instinctual theory, which was undergoing considerable revision and rethinking during this quarter century. However, the topographic theory underscores the need for a more systematic concept of psychic structure.

The main deficiency of the topographic model lies in its inability to account for two extremely important characteristics of mental conflict. Freud became aware of these aspects of mental life only by dint of a long accumulation of clinical experience with his psychoanalytic patients. The first important problem was that many of the defense mechanisms that Freud's patients used to avoid pain or unpleasure and that appeared in the form of unconscious resistance during the psychoanalytic treatment were themselves not initially accessible to consciousness. He drew the obvious conclusion that the agency of repression cannot be identical with the preconscious, inasmuch as this region of the mind is by definition easily accessible to consciousness. Second, he found that his patients frequently exhibited an unconscious need for punishment or an unconscious sense of guilt. However, according to the topographic model, the moral agency making this demand is allied with the

antiinstinctual forces available to consciousness in the preconscious level of the mind.

These new factors, the importance of which were gradually borne in on Freud out of his increasing clinical experience over the years, were of critical significance. They ultimately led him to discard the topographic theory, insofar as it was concerned with the assessment of specific processes related to specific regions of the mind. More precisely, Freud came to realize that what is more important is whether these processes belong to the primary system or to the secondary system. The divisions of the mind into unconscious, preconscious, and conscious levels of functioning were not adequate to account for the broader spectrum of clinical data. The concepts that were part of this early theory and that have retained their usefulness refer to the characteristics of primary and secondary thought processes, the essential importance of wish fulfillment, the tendency toward regression under conditions of frustration or stress, and the existence of a dynamic unconscious and the nature of its operation.

FROM TOPOGRAPHIC TO STRUCTURAL PERSPECTIVE

The germination of the shifting currents of Freud's thinking finally came to fruition in his abandonment of the topographic model and his replacement of it with the structural model of the psychic apparatus. The structural model was finally formulated and presented in *The Ego and the Id*, which appeared in 1923. The introduction of the structural hypothesis initiated a new era in psychoanalytic thinking. The structural model of the mind—the tripartite theory, as it is often called—is composed of three distinct entities or organizations within the psychic apparatus—the id, the ego, and the superego.

The terms have become so familiar and the tendency to hypostatize them so great that it is well to remember their nature as scientific constructs. The terms are theoretical constructs that have as their primary referents the specific mental functions and operations that they are intended to organize and integrate into higher order systems. Each refers to a particular aspect of mental functioning, and no one of them expresses or represents the sum total of mental functioning at any one time. If they often function as quasiindependent systems, they are, nonetheless, ultimately coordinated aspects of the operation of the mental apparatus. Moreover, unlike such phenomena as infantile sexuality and object relations, the id, ego, and superego are not empirically demonstrable phenomena in themselves but must be inferred from the observable effects of the operations of specific psychic functions.

The functional view of the systemic approach to ego psychology, which was responsible for much of the elaboration and systematization of the thinking about the ego and its functions, treats the ego as an organization of functions. This functional view presents the ego as an impersonal system composed of functions, thus giving the ego a highly mechanized and impersonal referent. This view is troublesome to some theorists, since the functional view bypasses and leaves open to question the role in psychoanalytic theory of the introspectively grasped, subjective experience of self. The objection is that the systematic and functional view of the ego seems to rule out of psychoanalytic theory the human person as the subjective source of action and behavior. This problem remains a basic one for psychoanalytic thinking even today.

Many writers have commented on the fact that Freud's attention was directed to the structural aspects of the mind and the functioning of the ego at a relatively late stage in the development of psychoanalysis. In fact, the structural concepts underwent a gradual evolution in the course of Freud's thinking. A careful review of even early formulations reveals that he clearly associated certain aspects of mental functioning with characteristics of the mind that were synthesized and attributed to structural mental entities only when he formulated the structural theory. In general, those aspects of the mind that he regarded as responsible in one way or another for the repressive activity of the mind were later seen to be attributable to the structural ego and superego. The censor in dream theory was a mental entity that carried the burden of certain ego and superego functions but was never explicitly recognized as a structural mental entity.

However, during the years of his early discoveries, Freud was interested primarily in establishing the existence of unconscious mental processes and in elucidating their nature. Concomitantly, he concerned himself with demonstrating the value of psychoanalysis as a potential technique for exploring the depths of the human mind. There is little surprise, then, that he was less concerned with a detailed study of aspects of the mental functioning that are normally more or less accessible to consciousness. Many of these aspects were already the object of psychological inquiry. The end of the 19th century saw the founding and early flourishing of experimental approaches to psychology. Only when Freud discovered that not all unconscious processes can be attributed merely to the instincts, that certain aspects of mental functioning associated with repressive activity are also unconscious, was he forced to turn to a more careful delineation and study of these mental structural components.

Freud unquestionably turned to an elaboration of a psychology of the ego as a result of the discrepancies and contradictions that seemed to arise out of the topographic model and so that the progress of psychoanalysis would not be impeded by a lack of understanding of specific phenomena associated with the ego aspect of mental functioning. There is no question that his efforts have had an important influence on the development and direction of psychoanalysis and the understanding of personality and human behavior in general.

Since the publishing of *The Ego and the Id*, ego psychology has continued to advance and enlarge the breadth and scope of its formulations and insights. The score of years after World War II saw a rapid emergence and elaboration of ego psychology. The ferment in ego psychology was triggered by Anna Freud's *The Ego and the Mechanisms of Defense* (1946) and slightly later by Heinz Hartmann's *Ego Psychology and the Problem of Adaptation* (1949). The contribution of the school of ego psychologists, following particularly on Hartmann's lead, has helped to refine psychoanalytic theory; more specifically, it has served to organize, to codify, to place in a systematic conceptual framework the vast amount of data derived from psychoanalytic investigation that have to do specifically with ego functions and operations. Such theoretical refinements have led to significant modifications of psychoanalytic treatment techniques.

HISTORICAL DEVELOPMENT OF EGO PSYCHOLOGY

The evolution of the concept of ego within the framework of the historical development of psychoanalytic theory parallels to a large extent the shifts in Freud's view of the instincts and, following Rapaport's organization, can be divided into four phases. The first phase ended in 1897 and coincided with the development of the early psychoanalytic formulations. The second phase extended from 1897 to 1923, thus spanning the development of psychoanalysis proper. The third phase, from 1923 to 1937, saw the development of Freud's theory of the ego and the gradual emergence to prominence of the ego in the over-all context of the theory. Parallel to this development was the evolution of Freud's thinking about anxiety. Finally, the fourth phase came after Freud's death and saw the emergence and systematic development of a general psychology of the ego at the hands of Hartmann, Kris, Rapaport, and their followers and a shifting of focus from the operation of ego functions themselves to the broader social and cultural contexts within which the ego develops and functions, particularly following the stimulus of Erik Erikson.

First Phase—Early Concepts of the Ego

In the initial phase of the development of psychoanalytic theory, the ego was not always precisely defined. Rather, the ego referred to the dominant mass of conscious ideas and moral values, which were distinct from the impulses and wishes of the repressed unconscious. The ego was thought to be concerned primarily with defense, a term Freud soon replaced with the notion of repression. At this stage, repression and defense were regarded as synonymous. In the neurophysiological jargon of the *Project*, the ego was described as "an organization ... whose presence interferes with passage of quantities [of excitation]." Translating this into the language of psychology, as in the *Studies on Hysteria* and *The Interpretation of Dreams*, Freud regarded the ego as an agent that erects a defense against certain ideas that are unacceptable to consciousness. These ideas were found to be primarily sexual in nature and were initially thought to have been engendered by premature sexual trauma and real seduction. Because the memory of such trauma led to the arousal of unpleasant and painful affects, they evoked a defensive response and a repression of the original thought content. However, this repression led to a damming up of energy and the consequent production of anxiety. The functioning of this early ego was to a degree contradictory, since its primary purpose was to reduce tension and thus avoid unpleasant affects connected with sexual thoughts, but in the process of repression it seemed to evoke an equally unpleasant affect state, that of anxiety.

It is important to note the role of reality in this early theory. Until 1897 it was Freud's firm belief that the accounts of traumatic sexual experiences provided by his patients as memories of early childhood experiences were real traumata. He envisioned the task of the ego as one of warding off the memories of those events. The ego was motivated in this task by considerations involving the person's relationship with the real world or, more accurately, with the ideational representations of real experiences. With the collapse of the seduction hypothesis, however, the investigation of this aspect of ego functioning receded into the background. The focus was on internal, instinctually derived, and fantasy-dominated experience. The role of reality in the influencing of behavior was minimized. It is only recently, with the increasing interest in ego psychology, that the important role of the ego in mediating the person's relationship with the outside world of events and human relationships has become a focus of increasing concern and study once again. The role of reality has particularly reasserted itself in relation to the vicissitudes of object relations in connection with the development and capacity for functioning of the ego. However, the implications of reality and its role in psychoanalytic thinking are considerably broader.

Second Phase—Historical Roots of Ego Psychology

The score and more of years that preceded the publication of *The Ego and the Id* were dedicated to the development of psychoanalysis proper. During this period the analysis of the ego as such received little direct attention, since Freud was concerned primarily with the instinctual drives, their representatives, and their transformations. Consequently, references to defense or to defensive functions were much less frequent. There were areas of confusion and contradiction in Freud's early theory of the instincts and in his more limited topographic conception of the mind. The clarification of these concepts required further elucidation of the ego, its functions, and the nature of its organization. During this second phase Freud grappled with these problems and gradually approached the more definitive resolution provided by the structural theory.

In 1915 in *Instincts and Their Vicissitudes*, Freud discussed the vicissitudes to which instincts are subjected as they seek expression. These vicissitudes include reversal into the opposite (a sadistic impulse may be changed to a masochistic impulse), turning on the person's own self (the love for the object may be turned toward the self), repression, and sublimation. When approached from the standpoint of the ego, each of these vicissitudes may be viewed as a defense mechanism. The ego's relationship to reality is particularly relevant in this connection. The concept of a secondary process implies the ability to delay discharge of the instinctual drives in accordance with the demands of external reality. The capacity for delay was to be ascribed later to the ego. The progression from the pleasure principle to the reality principle in childhood involves a similiar capacity to postpone gratification and, thereby, conform to the requirements of the outside world. The important relationship of libido to the self, which in this phase has not yet been completely defined, calls for a clearer understanding of the self. According to the topographic theory of the mind, the preconscious, which by definition is accessible to consciousness, is responsible for censorship. But in many instances censorship is an unconscious operation, thereby requiring a new formulation of the agency performing this function. Another problem arose in relation to the ego or self-preservative instincts that were held responsible for repression; presumably, the instincts are responsible for defense, but surely this task also belongs to the ego.

Finally, if neither the preconscious nor the ego instincts are solely responsible for repression or censorship, how is repression achieved? Freud tried to answer this question by postulating that ideas are maintained in the unconscious by a withdrawal of libido or energy (cathexis). In the manner characteristic of unconscious ideas, they constantly renew their attempt to become attached to libido and thus reach consciousness. Consequently, the withdrawal of libido must be constantly repeated. Freud described this process as anticathexis or countercathexis. But if such countercathexis is to be consistently effective against unconscious ideas, it must be permanent and must itself operate on an unconscious basis. An understanding of psychic structure—specifically of the ego, which can perform this complicated function—was clearly called for and constituted still another indication of the need for the development of ego psychology. Thus, the way was pointed toward the third phase, in which the ego was delineated as a structural entity and separated definitively from the instinctual drives.

Third Phase—Freud's Ego Psychology

With the publication of *The Ego and the Id* in 1923, the introduction and development of Freud's own theory of the ego was accomplished. The ego was presented as a structural entity, a coherent organization of mental processes and functions that is primarily organized around the perceptual-conscious system but that also includes structures responsible for resistance and unconscious defense. The ego at this stage is relatively passive and weak. Its functioning is still a resultant of the pressures deriving from the id, the superego, and reality. The ego is the helpless rider on the id's horse, more or less obliged to go where the id wishes to go. The assumption remains that somehow the ego is not only dependent on the

forces of the id but somehow genetically derived and differentiated out of the id. Freud had yet to recognize any real development of the ego comparable to the phases of libidinal development.

During this period the view of the ego underwent a radical transformation. In *Inhibitions, Symptoms, and Anxiety* in 1926, Freud repudiated the conception of the ego as subservient to the id. Signal anxiety became an autonomous function for the initiating of defense, and the capacity of the ego to turn passively experienced anxiety into active anticipation was underlined. The relatively rudimentary conception of the defensive capacity of the ego was enlarged to include a variety of defenses that the ego has at its disposal and that it can use in the control and direction of id impulses. Moreover, the elaboration of Freud's conception of the reality principle introduced a function of adaptation that allows the ego to curb instinctual drives when action prompted by them would lead into real danger.

The effect of this transformation of his theory of the ego was 3-fold. First, it brought the ego into prominence as a powerful regulatory force that is responsible for the integration and control of behavioral responses. Second, the role of reality was brought to center stage in the theory of ego functioning. Reality had been banished to the wings in the preceding quarter century, but the concern with the adaptive function of the ego again brought it back to prominence. Even so, the conception of adaptation here was rudimentary and limited to the ego's capacity to avoid danger. The notions that Freud was evolving during this phase provided the foundation for the concept of the autonomy of the ego that was to be developed by later theorists. Third, toward the end of this period, particularly in *Analysis, Terminable and Interminable* (1937), Freud finally made explicit the assumption of independently inherited roots of the ego that are quite independent of the inherited roots of the instinctual drives. This formulation was taken over by Hartmann and served as the basis for his notion of primary ego autonomy, which consequently stimulated the developments of the fourth phase.

Fourth Phase—Systematization of Ego Psychology

If the third phase can be thought of as culminating in Anna Freud's work on the defense mechanisms of the ego, the fourth phase can be seen as taking its initiation from the publication of Heinz Hartmann's work on the ego and adaptation. Hartmann's work focused primarily on two aspects of Freud's later notions of the ego, the autonomy of the ego and the problem of adaptation. The discussion of the apparatuses of primary autonomy served as the basis for a doctrine of the genetic roots of the ego and a development of the notion of epigenetic maturation. Hartmann's treatment of adaptation also brought the adaptational point of view into focus in such a way that it has become generally acceptable as one of the basic metapsychological assumptions of psychoanalytic theory.

The adaptational approach, however, also served a broader purpose—the consolidation of psychoanalysis as a general psychology, one that can communicate with, assimiliate, and theoretically integrate the experimental and clinical study of psychological phenomena from other allied scientific disciplines involved in the study of human behavior. One of the important consequences, therefore, of Hartmann's work was that the concentration on and elaboration of the theory of the ego gradually enlarged the areas of ego functioning in such a way that other aspects of the tripartite theory were somewhat shunted aside and were given only minor consideration. The process has been referred to as egotization of psychoanalysis.

Although the development of thinking about the ego was an important advance, many psychoanalysts began to feel that it created an imbalance in the theory and that by increasingly focusing on the mechanical and quantitative aspects of ego functioning, it left a picture of personality functioning and dysfunctioning that seemed relatively inhuman. Thus the more human aspects of psychic functioning and their correlative qualities seemed to be shunted off into the superego. Moreover, as the process of egotization took place, there developed a widening split between the id, the vital stratum of the mind and the dynamic source of psychic energies, and the noninstinctual, nondynamic, structural apparatuses of the ego. Consequently, the id increasingly came to be seen as the source of instinctual energies—the image of the seething cauldron—without the representational or directional qualities that so long characterized Freud's views of the instincts and their functions. These tendencies were to a large extent consolidated and crystallized in the systematizing work of David Rapaport, whose synthesis of structural theory followed hard on the heels of Hartmann's more exploratory work.

The other important aspect of the fourth phase is the re-emergence of the importance of reality in its broadest and most profound meanings as a significant dimension of psychoanalytic thinking. This is in many ways a direct extrapolation of Hartmann's thinking about adaptation, since the adaptive functioning of the organism has directly to do with its fitting in with the requirements of external reality and adaptively interacting with the environment, not only the inanimate but also the personal and social environment.

The concern with reality has led in two important directions. The first is the work of Erik Erikson, who has posed the question of the adaptation of the personality through the whole of the life cycle. He has viewed this progressive elaboration and integration of personality in terms of the resolution of life crises, as a progressive problem of adaptation to and resolution of the characteristic conflicts and crises that arise at various phases of human experience from birth to death. In Erikson's thinking, not only the human environment in which the human organism develops and with which it interacts but also the broader reaches of the social and cultural environment take on an increasing importance in psychoanalytic perspective.

The other important extension of the principle of adaptation has been in the direction of object relations theory. The major focus of concern for the object relations school has been between the child and the important figures who people the child's early environment and who give decisive direction to his personality development. The emphasis in the object relations approach, in considering the source of psychopathology, is on the deficiencies of the environment, rather than on the internal vicissitudes of the instincts or on more constitutional defects that impair the course of development. An important consideration in thinking about the contributions of the object relations theorists is that for the most part their theoretical concerns derive from the patient population with which they deal, who primarily have character disorders and forms of personality organization that are somewhat more primitive and show deeper levels of ego defect than the types of neurotic patients traditionally dealt with in psychoanalysis. One of the current leading concerns of psychoanalytic theorists has to do with the integration of these more recent approaches with traditional psychoanalytic theory.

ASSUMPTIONS OF THE STRUCTURAL THEORY

General assumptions

Empirical. The subject matter of psychoanalysis is behavior, broadly defined to include states of feeling and thought, as well as overt behavior, both normal and pathological. Hartmann was the first to state that psychoanalysis is a general psychology that embraces the study of normal behavior, as well as pathological behavior, although it is clear that Freud intended his theory to be a general psychology and not simply an explanation of specific psychopathological conditions. The principle of thoroughgoing psychological determinism of all behavior has been a cornerstone of psychoanalytic theory from the beginning. Psychoanalysis differs from other psychologies, however, in assuming specifically psychological determinism and in stressing latent behavior in general, along with unconscious determinants of behavior in particular.

Gestalt. Behavior is regarded as integrated and indivisible, such that the concepts constructed for its explanation pertain to different components of behavior and not to different behaviors. Concretely, no behavior can be described as id behavior or ego behavior or simply conscious behavior. Every behavior has conscious, unconscious, ego, id, superego, reality, and other components. Thus, all behavior is multiply determined (overdetermination).

Organismic. No segment of behavior can be taken in isolation. All behavior must be regarded as the product of an indivisible and integral personality. As Rapaport commented:

What this organismic point of view asserts is not that each behavior is a microcosm which reflects the macrocosm of the personality, but rather that an explanation of behavior, in order to have any claim to completeness, must specify its place within the functional and structural framework of the total personality and, therefore, must include statements about the *degree* and *kind* of involvement, in the behavior in question, of all the relevant conceptualized aspects of personality.

Topographic. The crucial determinants of behavior are unconscious. Enough has already been said about the unconscious determinants of behavior, but one can note here specifically that the psychoanalytic approach is characterized by its treatment of unconscious factors as specifically psychological entities that enter into the fabric of the theory as a psychological explanation. Other psychologies differ in that they tend to treat the nonconscious aspects of behavior in nonpsychological terms; psychoanalysis consistently treats them in psychological terms of motivations, affects, thoughts, and other psychic processes.

Metapsychological assumptions. The metapsychological assumptions hold a special place in psychoanalytic theory. They consist of a set of basic assumptions or points of view that state the minimum (both necessary and sufficient) independent assumptions on which psychoanalytic theory rests. They may be regarded as the basic postulates or perspectives from which any given psychoanalytic proposition or any given segment of psychoanalytic theory must be viewed and interpreted. They can be regarded also as the most general propositions in terms of which psychoanalytic thinking can be organized and integrated. In considering psychoanalytic theory, one must take into account and distinguish among, in the order of increasing generality, empirical propositions, specific psychoanalytic propositions, general propositions of psychoanalytic theory, and metapsychological assumptions. Metapsychological assumptions can be described in the following propositions.

Economic. The economic point of view has traditionally been conceptualized in terms of psychological energies and their distribution and transformation. This point of view has been interpreted in terms of the requirement that psychoanalytic explanation of any psychological phenomenon include propositions concerning psychological energies. It assumes, therefore, that psychological energies exist, follow a law of conservation, and are subject to the law of entropy (constancy,

Nirvana). It also assumes that these energies are subject to transformations that increase or decrease their entropic tendency.

The statement of the economic hypothesis in strictly energic terms seems no longer satisfactory or viable. However, the economic hypothesis does not rest on or require the notion of psychic energies, since this is, at best, a difficult and sometimes misleading metaphor. Any scientific account that involves quantitative intensity and any theory that allows for degrees of structural complexity, stability, hierarchical organization, drive motility, and structureless spontaneity cannot function without at least an implicit principle of economics. Even attempts to refocus analytic concepts and theoretical formulations in terms of principles of information transmission rest on an implicit economic basis. To this point, the energic metaphor, which has been mistakenly substituted for the economic metapsychological assumption, remains a viable if limited metaphor for the expression of economic issues, particularly in clinical terms. Such energic concepts will probably be replaced only by a more effective and less metaphorical statement of the economic dimensions of the theory.

Dynamic. The dynamic point of view demands that the psychoanalytic explanation of any psychological phenomenon include propositions concerning psychological forces. It assumes that psychological forces are defined by their direction and magnitude. The effect of simultaneously acting psychological forces may be the simple resultant of the work of each of these forces, or they may be set in opposition or may not follow the simple compositional laws of vectorial addition. The proposition concerning the genesis of discharge and overflow of affects from the conflict of drive forces and restraining (structural) forces and propositions concerning the origin and effects of signal affects imply an action of forces according to other laws than those of simple vectorial composition.

Structural. The structural point of view demands that psychoanalytic explanation include propositions concerning abiding psychological configurations (structures). It assumes that psychological structures are configurations of a slow rate of change that are hierarchically ordered. Mental processes are conceived of as taking place within, between, and by means of the organization of these structural configurations.

Genetic. The genetic point of view demands that psychoanalytic explanation include propositions concerning psychological origin and development. It assumes that all psychological phenomena have such origins and developmental histories and that they originate in innate givens that mature according to an epigenetic plan. Earlier forms of a psychological phenomenon remain potentially active, even though they may be superseded by later forms. At each point of psychological history, the totality of potentially active earlier forms co-determines all subsequent psychological phenomena.

Consequently, the psychoanalytic view of development postulates the gradual emergence of intrinsic maturational factors as innate givens that operate on a more or less preset time table. These intrinsic factors are influenced by a complex and continuing interaction with experiential factors during the course of development. Development is thus the outcome of nature and nurture and not the result of either to the exclusion of the other. The experiential aspects of development are not simply stimulus inputs in the sense implied by the rather impersonal designation "average expectable environment" but, rather, are provided by the specific context of object relationships within which the developmental experience takes place. There is an interplay between maturational factors and developmental learning, such learning taking place within the context of object relationships provided by the child's significant caretakers.

Freud alluded to the relationship between constitutional-maturational and environmental-experiential factors in his discussion of complemental series. He observed in 1905:

> It is not easy to estimate the relative efficacy of the constitutional and accidental factors. In theory one is always inclined to overestimate the former; therapeutic practice emphasizes the importance of the latter. It should, on no account, be forgotten that the relation

between the two is a cooperative and not a mutually exclusive one. The constitutional factor must awake experiences before it can make itself felt; the experiential factor must have a constitutional basis in order to come into operation. To cover the majority of cases we can picture what has been described as a "complemental series," in which the diminishing intensity of one factor is balanced by the increasing intensity of the other.

Hartmann and Kris (1945) added an important point by emphasizing that the genetic or developmental point of view concerns itself not simply with the recovery of past events but, rather, with the causal sequencing of developmental effects at various levels of the developmental experience. They put it in the following terms:

> The genetic approach in psychoanalysis does not deal only with anamnestic data, nor does it intend to show only "how the past is contained in the present." Genetic propositions describe why, in the past situations of conflict, a specific solution was adopted, why the one was retained and the other dropped, and what causal relation exists between these solutions and later developments.

There is a double emphasis in the psychoanalytic notion of development and in the genetic point of view that demands emphasis. From one point of view, the genetic hypothesis stresses the understanding of psychological processes in terms of antecedent determinants; from a second perspective, the genetic point of view stresses the role of developmental transformations—that is, the influence of progressive and regressive processes on the changing organization of the psyche. The view in terms of antecedent determinants, for example, asserts the direct effect of the past on current mental functioning, a point that Freud emphasized in his statement that "hysterics suffer from reminiscences." The role of antecedent determinants is also seen in the effect of infantile fantasies in determining later character and symptom formation. This view of antecedent determinants has clinical application in the understanding and interpretation of transference and in the use of genetic reconstruction.

On the other hand, the transformational view places the emphasis on the consequences of sequential genetic transformations, whether progressive or regressive, as determinants of current psychic functioning and behavior. Even though historical precursors have an inevitable influence on the course of such functioning, each phase in the developmental progression reflects a new organizational achievement that stands on its own without reference to specific antecedents. The genetic perspective within psychoanalysis embraces both genetic precursors as antecedent determinants and the capacity for genetic transformation as part of the ongoing process of the person's life history that expresses the continuing operation of causal antecedents in current adaptations.

The developmental viewpoint within psychoanalysis provides a far-reaching schema for the organization of analytical data and for the generation of specific explanatory schemata. The analyst is concerned not merely with establishing the current effects of antecedent contexts, circumstances, traumata, and affective fixations on the patient's current conflict and behavior but also with seeking a broader understanding of those causal determinants that have brought about one set of behaviors or responses at an earlier stage of developmental interaction and that correspondingly operate in similar or in modified ways to generate current conflicts and behavioral difficulties. The developmental viewpoint, therefore, provides a complex lens or frame of reference, through which it is possible to focus the interplay of important factors in the organization and functioning of the patient's personality. As such, it is capable of providing an integrative context for the understanding of the interaction of the rest of the metapsychological assumptions.

Adaptive. The adaptive point of view demands that psychoanalytic explanation include propositions concerning relationships to the environment. It assumes that psychological states of adaptiveness and processes of adaptation apply at every point of psychological experience. Adaptive processes are autoplastic or alloplastic and operate to maintain, restore, or improve existing states of adaptiveness, which thereby ensure fitting in with the environment and survival. Human adaptation is not merely environmental but also social, applying to both the physical and the human environments. Adaptational relationships are mutual in the sense that a person and the environment adapt to each other and in the further sense that a person and his significant objects adapt to each other. Rapaport (1967) commented:

> It is not yet possible to assess whether all these assumptions are necessary, and whether this set of assumptions is sufficient—when coupled with observational data—to yield the existing body of psychoanalytic propositions. Such an assessment could be achieved only by systematic study, by continuing to subject psychoanalytic propositions to an analysis, which would strip away their empirical content and establish whether or not their postulational (nonempirical) implications are accounted for by this set of assumptions. The future development of psychoanalysis as a systematic science may well depend on such continuing efforts to establish the assumptions on which psychoanalytic theory rests.

STRUCTURE OF THE PSYCHIC APPARATUS

The following more or less systematic survey of the tripartite theory is seen from the contemporary perspective, rather than from the historical perspective of the third phase. From a structural viewpoint, the psychic apparatus is divided into three provinces, which are designated as id, ego, and superego. They are distinguished by their different functions. The main distinction lies between the ego and the id. The id is the locus of the instinctual drives and is under the domination of the primary process. It operates according to the dictates of the pleasure principle, without regard for the limiting demands of reality. The ego, on the other hand, represents a coherent organization of functions, the task of which is to avoid unpleasure or pain by opposing or regulating the discharge of instinctual drives to conform to the demands of the external world. The regulation of id discharges is also contributed to by a third structural component of the psychic apparatus, the superego, which contains the internalized moral values, prohibitions, and standards of the parental imagos.

The Id

Freud separated the instinctual drives in his tripartite theory into a separate province, the vital stratum of the mind; in so doing, he reached the culminating point of the evolution of his theory of instincts. He borrowed and modified the term "id" from Georg Groddeck, an internist who became a somewhat enthusiastic apostle of the unconscious and who first used the term "it" in his own *The Book of the It*. Originally, the term stood for all that was ego-alien. In contrast to his concept of the ego as an organized, problem-solving agent, Freud conceived of the id as a completely unorganized, primordial reservoir of energy, derived from the instincts, that is under the domination of the primary process. However, it is not synonymous with the unconscious, since the structural viewpoint is unique in that it demonstrates that certain functions of the ego, specifically certain defenses against unconscious instinctual pressures, are unconscious; for the most part, the superego itself also operates on an unconscious level.

Freud postulated that the id is primarily a hereditary given, such that the infant at birth is endowed with an id with instinctual drives seeking gratification. The infant has no capacity to delay, control, or modify these drives. Consequently, in the beginning of life, the infant is completely dependent on the egos of the caretaking persons in his environment to enable him to cope with the external world.

Although separating instinctual drives into the id had the advantage of resolving certain observational and theoretical difficulties, it also left a residue of problems. Perhaps the most significant problem is that, in having separated the instincts, Freud left to the subsequent generations of psychoanalytic theorists the problem of dealing with ways in which instinctual components are effectively integrated with the functioning of the structural aspects of the psychic apparatus. The problem in many respects remains today and has become a focus of much contemporary controversy in psychoanalytic circles.

The other important problem that this separation left to be dealt with is the question of how much structure is involved in the functioning of the id. The tendency among systematic ego theorists has been to reduce progressively the id to terms of simple energic forces with a minimum of structure. This is the correlative aspect of the tendency to regard all organization or representational functioning as related to the ego. However, Freud was quite clear that the instinctual drives of the id have a vectorial and representational component and that they are organized in terms of the primary process. The primary process is not a process of random discharge but is, in fact, a modality of organization. The question of the characteristics and degree of id organization remains one on which psychoanalytic theorists differ; it remains an unresolved theoretical issue.

Partly in an attempt to resolve some of these difficulties, Hartmann and his followers proposed that the id and the ego do not have separate origins but that they both develop out of an undifferentiated matrix present at birth and that the separation into separate provinces defined as id and ego is a function of the developmental process.

The Ego

Those conscious and preconscious functions that are typically associated with the ego—for example, words, ideas, and logic—do not account entirely for its role in mental functioning. The discovery that certain phenomena that emerge most clearly in the psychoanalytic treatment setting, specifically repression and resistance, can themselves be unconscious pointed up the need for an expanded concept of the ego as an organization that retains its original close relationship to consciousness and to external reality and yet performs a variety of unconscious operations in relationship to the drives and their regulation. Once the scope of the ego had been thus broadened, consciousness was redefined as a mental quality that, although exclusive to the ego, constitutes only one of its qualities or functional aspects, rather than being a separate mental system itself.

No more comprehensive definition of the ego is available than the one Freud gave toward the end of his career in 1938 in *Outline of Psychoanalysis:*

> Here are the principal characteristics of the ego. In consequence of the pre-established connection between sense and perception and muscular action, the ego has voluntary movement at its command. It has the task of self-preservation. As regards external events, it performs that task by becoming aware of stimuli, by storing up experiences about them (in the memory), by avoiding excessively strong stimuli (through flight), by dealing with moderate stimuli (through adaptation), and finally by learning to bring about expedient changes in the external world to its own advantage (through activity). As regards internal events in relation to the id, it performs that task by gaining control over the demands of the instinct, by deciding whether they are to be allowed satisfaction, by postponing that satisfaction to times and circumstances favorable in the external world, or by suppressing their excitations entirely. It is guided in its activity by consideration of the

tension produced by stimuli, whether these tensions are present in it or introduced into it.

Thus, the ego controls the apparatus of motility and perception, contact with reality, and, through the mechanisms of defense, the inhibition of primary instinctual drives.

Origins of the ego. If one defines the ego as a coherent system of functions for mediating between the instincts and the outside world, one must concede that the newborn infant has no ego or, at best, the most rudimentary of egos. The neonate certainly has a rather complex array of capacities and both sensory and motor functions, but there is little coherent organization of these, so one must say that the ego is, at best, rudimentary. Developmental ego psychology is then faced with the problem of explaining the processes that permit modification of the id and the concomitant genesis of the ego.

Freud believed that the modification of the id occurs as a result of the impact of the external world on the drives. The pressures of external reality enable the ego to appropriate the energies of the id to do its work. In the process of formation, the ego seeks to bring the influences of the external world to bear on the id, substitute the reality principle for the pleasure principle, and thereby contribute to its own further development. Freud emphasized the role of the instincts in ego development and particularly the role of conflict. At first, this conflict is between the id and the outside world, but later it is between the id and the ego itself.

The work of Heinz Hartmann and his collaborators has expanded and modified this theory. Hartmann postulated the existence of primary autonomous ego functions, the development of which is independent of the drives and of conflicts. Specifically, Hartmann, Kris, and Loewenstein have suggested that the ego does not differentiate from the id as such but that both develop from a common undifferentiated matrix. It follows that the rudimentary apparatuses that underlie these primary autonomous ego functions—such as perception, motility, memory, and intelligence—are present from birth. This concept further implies that there may be congenital or genetically determined variations in ego functions. This hypothesis was actually advanced by Freud in 1937, but it was greatly expanded and elaborated on by Hartmann over a score of years, thus providing a more solid footing for his emerging concepts of ego autonomy. The elaboration of this view also contributed a genetic viewpoint to the theory of ego development.

In addition, Hartmann elaborated the role of rudimentary ego apparatuses in the infant's coordinations with the object and the environment for the satisfaction of instinctual needs and drives. These early coordinations are the basis for Hartmann's development of the adaptive functions of the ego; that is, the function it serves as mediator between external reality and the needs and demands of other psychic systems—id and superego. The adaptive functions of the ego are related to Hartmann's concept of ego development. The optimal functioning of the organism requires a balance of these controlling forces—ego autonomy from the demands of the id and ego autonomy from the demands of the environment.

Evolution of the ego

BODY EGO. At first, the infant is unable to differentiate his own body from the rest of the world. That is, he cannot distinguish between his own proprioceptive and other subjective perceptions and reality. Body and mind are one in the sense that perceptual stimulation is a prerequisite for somatic development. The ego begins with the child's ability to perceive his body as distinct from the external world. From this point on, the ego is concerned with the ordering of reality into subjective and objective phenomena and with the awareness of the relationship between these phenomena and of other complex relationships between current apperceptions and memories. These are the beginnings of what is termed self-object differentiation.

INSTINCTUAL ZONES AND MODES OF EGO DEVELOPMENT. A major contribution to the psychoanalytic concept of development has been made by Erik Erikson in terms of the relationship between instinctual zones and the development of specific modalities of ego functioning. Erikson's theory links aspects of ego development with the epigenetic time table of instinctual development.

Erikson postulated a parallel relationship between specific phases of ego or psychosocial development and specific phases of libidinal development. During libidinal development, particular erotogenic zones become the loci of stimulation for the development of particular modalities of ego functioning. The relationship between zones of instinctual stimulation and their corresponding modalities of ego functioning are easily specifiable in the pregenital levels of development, but Erikson projected this basic relationship and extended it to the limits of the life cycle.

The first modality of development is related to the development in the oral phase, specifically to the stimulus qualities of the oral zone. This early stage is called the oral-respiratory-sensory stage, and it is dominated by the first oral-incorporative mode, which involves the modality of taking in. This dominant modality is extended to include the whole skin surface and the sense organs, which also become receptive and increasingly hungry for proper stimulation. Other auxiliary modes are also operative, including a second oral-incorporative (biting) mode, an oral-retentive mode, an oral-eliminative mode, and an oral-intrusive mode. These modes become variably important according to individual temperament but remain subordinated to the first incorporative mode unless the mutual regulation of the oral zone with the providing breast of the mother is disturbed, either by a loss of inner control in the infant or by a defect in reciprocal and responsive nurturing behavior on the part of the mother. The emphasis in this stage of development is placed on the modalities of getting, getting what is given, thus laying the necessary ego groundwork for getting to be a giver.

The second stage, also focused on the oral zone but now in terms of the development of the teeth, is marked by a biting modality. This phase is marked by the development of interpersonal patterns, which center in the social modality of taking and holding onto things. Incorporation by biting dominates the oral zone at this stage, and the child's libido moves on to endow with power a second organ mode, which leads to the integration of the new social modality, taking. The interplay of zones and modalities that characterize this complex oral stage of development forms the springs of a basic sense of trust or, conversely, of a basic sense of mistrust, which remains the basic element in the most fundamental nuclear conflict in the development of personality.

Similarly, with the advent of the anal-urethral-muscular stage, the retentive and eliminative modes become established. The extension and the generalization of these modes over the whole of the developing muscular system enable the infant to gain some form of self-control in the matter of conflicting impulses, such as letting go and holding on. When this control is disturbed by developmental defects in the anal-urethral sphere, a fixation on the modalities of retention or elimination can be established, which can lead to a variety of disturbances in the zone itself (spastic), in the muscle system (flabbiness or rigidity), in obsessional fantasy (paranoid fears), in social spheres (attempts at controlling the environment by compulsive routinization). The second nuclear conflict that is derived from the development of these modalities related to the anal-urethral-muscular zones has to do with the establishment of a basic autonomy or, conversely, the establishment of a basic sense of shame or doubt.

Erikson's epigenetic theory of ego development describes the life task appropriate to the sequence of specific phases of development that encompass the life cycle. The characteristic successful or unsuccessful performance of these tasks has important implications for future development. If the task solution is successful in the oral period, basic trust is established. If it is unsuccessful, basic mistrust is the result, with a correlative impairment in ego functioning during the later stages of development. Autonomy versus shame and doubt are the issues to be resolved in the developmental crisis of the anal period. In the phallic phase the crisis is that of initiative versus guilt. In latency it is the crisis of industry versus inferiority. In adolescence it is the crisis of identity formation versus identity diffusion. In young adult life it is the crisis of intimacy versus isolation. In adulthood it is the crisis of generativity versus stagnation. And in the mature years of life it is the crisis of integrity versus despair.

DEVELOPMENTAL DETERMINANTS. Much of contemporary psychoanalytic research has been devoted to the elucidation of those factors that facilitate or impede the development of ego functions. Investigations in this area, including the direct observation of infants, have provided considerable evidence of the relationship between gratification and frustration of drives and needs in the early months of life and the future state of ego development. Concomitantly, the crucial importance for ego development of adequate satisfaction of the infant's libidinal needs by the mother or mother surrogate (good-enough mothering) has been repeatedly stressed. Although it is less clearly understood and appreciated, a certain amount of drive frustration in infancy and early childhood is equally important for the development of a healthy ego. There is considerable evidence that maternal deprivation at significant stages of development leads to the impairment of ego functions to varying degrees. But overindulgence of the child's instinctual needs interferes with the development of the ego's capacity to tolerate frustration and, consequently, with its ability to regulate the demands of the id in relation to the outside world.

SEPARATION-INDIVIDUATION. The awareness of the importance of these early developmental phases has been clarified and embellished by the work of Anna Freud and Margaret Mahler. Mahler's work has been particularly useful in conceptualizing the process of growing up in terms of the phases of separation-individuation. Mahler envisioned the infant in the beginning of life as related to the mother in a state of absolute primary narcissism, in which the infant has no awareness of the mothering object. She calls this stage "normal autism." At about the third month, the infant begins to perceive dimly need satisfaction as coming from a part object, the mother's breast, but perceives it as within the orbit of his omnipotent symbiotic unity. Growing up involves a gradual growing away from this state of intimate dependence on and involvement with the mother.

The child must separate himself out of this symbiotic state of oneness by a gradual process of separation and individuation, which is facilitated on one hand by the autonomous development of the ego and on the other by the operation of identificatory mechanisms. This growing-away process is a lifelong process of mourning. Inherent in every new step toward independent functioning is a threat of object loss.

The principal steps of the separation-individuation process, as Mahler described them, take place from the fourth or fifth months through the thirtieth to thirty-sixth months of age. The child is at first safely anchored within the symbiotic orbit of the mother's caring activities. Expansion beyond this symbiotic orbit takes place through a hatching process, which depends on the gradual maturation of the infant's

perceptual-conscious system. The child then begins to take his first tentative steps of breaking away from the passive lap-babyhood of the symbiotic phase. This period of differentiation is followed by a practicing period, in which the child experiences rapid body differentiation from the mother and establishes a specific bond with her that permits the growth and functioning of autonomous ego apparatuses in close proximity to and dependence on the mother.

At about the second year, the child moves into a subsequent phase of separation that involves the mastery of upright locomotion and an increasing capacity to tolerate periods of separation from the mother. The child becomes more and more aware and makes greater and greater use of his awareness of physical separateness. This increasing differentiation is accompanied by an increase of separation anxiety, a fear of loss of object at times when the child discovers that his mother is not immediately or automatically at hand. There is a tension between lack of concern about the mother's presence and a seemingly constant concern about her whereabouts. The increasing awareness of separation leads to an increased need for the mother to share with the toddler every new acquisition of skill and experience. This is a period of rapprochement. The individuation proceeds rapidly, and the child is exhilarated in the exercise of it, but he also becomes increasingly aware of and anxious about his separation and uses mechanisms to resist separation from the mother.

INTERNALIZATION. Within this framework, psychoanalysis has described two psychic mechanisms that are specifically involved in the development of ego functions. The loss of the loved object or of a particularly gratifying relationship with the object is a painful experience at any stage of life, but it is particularly traumatic in infancy and early childhood, when the ego is not yet strong enough to compensate for the loss. Yet in the early years of life, the child is constantly subjected to such deprivation, particularly through the process of separation and individuation. In the normal course of events, the young child does not suffer the actual loss of his parents, who are the primary objects at this stage of development, but he must endure constant alterations in his relationships with them. Moreover, at each stage of his development, he must endure the loss of the kind of gratification that was appropriate to the previous phase of his maturation but that must now be given up.

This developmental vicissitude involves not only the loss of specific forms of gratification but also narcissistic traumatization. The processes by which the internal world is thus built up and by which structure is consolidated within the ego are referred to under the heading of internalization. Increasing internalization, both phylogenetically and ontogenetically, permits an increasing capacity for delay and detour, increasing independence from the pressure of immediate stimuli, particularly instinctual stimuli, and a more developed capacity for flexibility of response. Internalization, therefore, increases the organism's range of adaptive functions and enlarges its resources for coping with environmental stresses. It includes those processes by which the inner psychic world is built up, including incorporation, introjection, and identification.

One can speak of internalization or its opposite correlative process, externalization, as primary or secondary. Secondary internalization refers to the internalization of something that was external; secondary externalization refers to the externalization of something that was antecedently internal. The secondary processes require the capacity for self-object differentiation and the recognition at least of what is internal and what is external. Without this capacity, internalization and externalization can refer only to processes by which the differentiation of internal and external are established. Primary internalization has to do with that aspect of differentiation that contributes to establishing the boundaries between the inner and the outer worlds, between the self and the object.

Incorporation. Incorporation was originally conceived of as an instinctual activity derived from and based on the oral phase and was considered as a genetic precursor of identification. However, even though incorporation fantasies are often associated with internalizing processes, they are by no means identical and may be quite independent. Some authors have envisioned incorporation as the mechanism of primary identification, aimed at a primary union with the maternal object.

Incorporation as a mechanism of internalization seems to involve a primitive oral wish for union with an object. The union has a quality of totality and globality, so that in the internalization of the object, the object loses all distinction and function as object. The external object is completely assumed into the person's inner world. Incorporation is thus operative in relatively regressive conditions. It can be regarded as the mechanism of primitive, primary internalizations and as probably operative in severely regressed psychotic states involving loss of self-object differentiation, permeation of ego boundaries, and so-called psychotic identifications. Incorporation is the most primitive, least differentiated form of internalization, in which the object loses its distinction as object and becomes totally assumed into the person's inner world.

Introjection. Perhaps the most central process in the development of the structural apparatus is the process of introjection. Introjection was originally described by Freud in *Mourning and Melancholia* as a process of narcissistic identification, in which the lost object is introjected and thus retained as a part of the internal structure of the psyche. Freud later applied this mechanism to the genesis of the superego, so that introjection becomes the primary internalizing mechanism by which parental imagoes are internalized at the close of the oedipal phase. The child tries to retain the gratifications derived from these object relationships, at least in fantasy, through the process of introjection. By this mechanism, qualities of the person who was the center of the gratifying relationship are internalized and reestablished as part of the organization of the self. Freud referred to this internalized product as a "precipitate of abandoned object cathexis."

Although the more or less traditional view of introjection describes it as a derivative of the mechanisms of oral incorporation, it seems unlikely that the model of oral incorporation can satisfy the functions or demands of introjection as now understood. The basic parameters of Freud's original formulation are still applicable—namely, that the mechanism implies abandonment of an object relation and the preservation of the lost object intrapsychically by way of internalization.

The earliest implementation of introjection and its correlative process of projection is involved in the vicissitudes of object relations and the early separation of the self out of the oneness with its object. These mechanisms originate in early infantile fantasies of incorporation and ejection but must be distinguished from them. They are psychic processes that result in the definition of self-images and of object images. These earliest introjections have a rudimentary, primitive, and disorganized form, since they are related to the more primitive levels of oral-libidinal and aggressive drives. The objects that frustrate the primitive instinctual demands mobilize infantile rage, which is both projected onto objects and introjected in the form of bad introjects. Similarly, good, pleasure-producing objects are internalized as good introjects.

At a primitive level, the good and bad introjects remain separate and continue to undergo the vicissitudes of introjection and projection. But in the course of development, the alternate cathexis of good introjects and the exclusion of bad introjects are modified in the direction of forming composite introjects. The child gradually achieves a more ambivalent and differentiated representation of the object and a more composite and differentiated self-representation. The earliest introjections are derived from primitive oral-sadistic instinctual drives, but later, more organized introjections derive from less primitive instinctual levels. The early introjects are gradually fused into more organized, more composite, and more highly differentiated introjects. In regressive states, however, these composite introjects can become defused into more primitive component elements.

The introject comes to exercise a particular influence on a person's inner state and behavior, and the relationships between the person and the introject are as varied as the relationships between two persons. The introject is the inner presence of an external object. Such a presence can be recognized only when it becomes conscious, but it may be active and effective when unconscious or subconscious. As a quasi-active presence, then, the introject provides a structural means for binding and mastery of basic instinctual energies.

The introject can be seen as serving a dual function. The early development of the correlative mechanisms of projection and introjection serves an important function in the development and gradual modification of object relations. They are the processes that contribute to the establishment of self-object differentiation and to the gradual modification and integration of object relations in terms of the respective contribution of internal drive derivatives and the real quality of the primary object figures themselves. When such object derivatives are internalized, they are not limited to the formation of superego, as Freud envisioned. Rather, they become components and foci of structural organization within the developing self.

However, since they are responsive to and derivative from instinctual drive components, introjects can also serve important defensive functions. Developmentally, their function is, in part, that of binding and mastering and thus modifying the impact of instinctual drives on the emerging ego apparatus. But they can become involved more deeply in the response to and modification of drive pressures, so that they become the foci of internal defensive functions, as well as channels for drive expression. This defensive function of introjective organizations within the psyche makes them highly susceptible to drive influences and relatively more susceptible to regressive drive pulls. When these defensive pressures predominate in the development of introjects, the results are an impediment to further consolidation and building of internal psychic structure, a susceptibility to regressive pulls, and a liability to projective forms of defense.

The process of introjection leads not only to the development of a pathological organization within the psyche but also to the development of internal structures that are compatible with the development of healthy object relationships. One of the classic examples of the pathological potentiality of the introjective mechanism was described by Anna Freud in terms of identification with the aggressor. Identification with the aggressor is a defensive maneuver based on the child's need to protect himself from the severe anxiety experienced in relation to the object. The child protects himself by introjecting the characteristics of the feared person, who is perceived by the child as his attacker and on whom the child is dependent. The perception of the object as attacking is usually due in part to the prior projection of the child's own hostile and destructive impulses onto the object by way of the defensive maneuver of projection. The child defends himself from his own hostile and destructive wishes by allying himself with the aggressor, rather than allowing himself to be the victim. Thus, he can share in the aggressor's power, rather than be helpless and powerless before him.

Such introjections, however, may impoverish the ego by burdening it with negative (aggressive, ambivalent) introjects. Such introjects, by reason of the susceptibility to projection, distort and impede the development of object relations and the subsequent capacity for more mature and meaningful relations and also impede the capacity for healthier and more constructive internalizations by way of identification. The increasing realization of the operation of such internalizing mechanisms and their possible pathological distortions directs attention to the importance of the characteristics and qualities of the object and their implications for the child's development. Freud did not investigate this aspect in detail, but it has been the focus for increasing attention in recent years, particularly in connection with the causes of childhood psychosis and other disorders of childhood.

The introject must be regarded as a quasiautonomous source of intrapsychic influence and activity that can substitute for the lost object as a source of narcissistic gratification or even aggressive impulse. The effect of the introject is to modify the self, so that it acquires characteristics of the internalized object, which functions intrapsychically as a quasiautonomous source of activity. The introject is, therefore, a center of functional organization, possessing its own relative autonomy in the economy of psychic function. Because of their tendency to regression and their susceptibility to drive influences, introjects must be considered as more structuralizing than structured, more feeble, less stable, and more transient than the less instinctually derived, secondary process organization of identificatory systems.

Identification. Identification has often been confused with introjection, partially because the two processes were treated in an overlapping and somewhat interchangeable fashion by Freud. There are, nonetheless, grounds for maintaining a distinction between them. Identification is, properly speaking, an active structuralizing process that takes place within the ego, by which the ego constructs the inner constituents of regulatory control on the basis of selected elements derived from the model. What constitutes the model of identification can vary considerably and can include introjects (internalized transitional-like objects), structural aspects of real objects, or even value components of group structures and group cultures. The process of identification, properly conceived, is specifically an intrasystemic ego activity and its effects are specifically structuralizing effects within the ego.

The lines that differentiate identification from introjection should be kept clear. Introjection operates as a function of instinctual forces—both libidinal and aggressive—so that in conjunction with projection, it functions intimately in the vicissitudes of instinctual and drive derivatives. Identification, however, functions relatively autonomously from drive derivatives. Introjection is indirectly involved in the transformation and binding of energies. Hence, introjection is much more influenced by drive energies, and its binding permits greater susceptibility to regressive pulls and to primary process forms of organization. The result of binding through identification, however, is more autonomous, more resistant to regressive pulls, and organized more specifically in secondary process terms. Identification, therefore, is specifically the mechanism for the formation of structures of secondary autonomy.

Both introjection and identification are involved in the formation of structure. But introjection is directly involved in the formation of structural modifications within the self. The introjective nuclei that constitute the core of the superego intrinsically modify psychic structure but do not directly affect ego structure as such. Identifications, however, are directly and specifically structural modifications of the ego and, as such, are integrated into the ego core of the personality.

Moreover, both processes play a role in the development of the psychic apparatus, but their functions are quite distinct. Introjection is taken up in the working through of instinctual vicissitudes; identification is specifically involved in the development of ego structures and functions. Development must be seen as a complex process in which introjection and identification are continually interacting with intrinsic maturational factors—introjection interacting more explicitly with instinctual factors and identification more with ego factors. Both are likewise subject to the laws of epigenesis, but they differ in their patterns of primacy—introjection exercising its developmental influence predominantly earlier in the course of development and identification assuming increasing importance in later phases of development.

Finally, from the point of view of adaptation, both identification and introjection serve adaptive processes. Both are essentially autoplastic processes but serve to increase the organism's capacity for adaptation. Both increase the capacity for internal regulation and thereby increase the adaptive capacity. Introjection and projection are involved in the modification and modulation of instinctual drives, thereby permitting an increasing tolerance and capacity for object relations. Although this aspect of introjection is important all through the early stages of development, it becomes particularly pertinent in the resolution of the oedipal situation. It is through identification, however, that ego development takes place. The capacity for mature object relatedness is correlative to and depends on the degree of ego development and integration. It is specifically through identification that a person's human adaptation to his environment—particularly to his social and cultural environment—becomes possible. Introjection serves the purposes of adaptation through instinctually derived self-modifications; identification can reach out to noninstinctual and conflict-free aspects of the human, social, and cultural environment and selectively internalize whatever serves the ego's adaptive needs.

Therefore, identification is clearly different from introjection or incorporation, which derive more from instinctual derivatives and defensive needs. Many of the forms of identification that Freud and subsequent analysts describe—the most important being narcissistic identification—are not identifications at all but, rather, modifications of introjective processes. Although such a clarification is useful for metapsychological understanding, it must be remembered that these processes are all involved in internalization and in the building of psychic structure but in different ways. Typically, they are found in conjoint operation clinically. Introjection may often dominate the pathological clinical picture, but it should not be forgotten that introjection also serves to induce further identificatory processes.

Thus, one can begin to appreciate the significance of internalizing processes for the building up of internal structures and the development of the ego. More particularly, one can begin to appreciate the importance of understanding the conditions of child rearing and early experience that contribute to the pathological distortions in development that allow introjective processes to predominate in the organization of internal structure, thus impeding the further positive constructive effects of healthy, ego-building identifications. Generally, the developmental vicissitudes described here regarding the development of instincts, problems of fixation, problems with ambivalence in object relations, and the incapacity of the developing ego to tolerate and neutralize aggression effectively—all contribute to the persistence of internal defensive conditions that call for the intensification and persistence of introjective patterns of internal organization.

Conversely, the conditions of adequate mothering, mutuality, optimal satisfaction of infantile needs without overindulgence or excessive deprivation and frustration, the conditions of parental interaction that allow for the establishment of trust, autonomy without shame or doubt, initiative without guilt, the conditions that allow for a satisfactory resolution of oedipal conflicts and a successful internalization of the positive aspects of parental imagos, the progressive neutralization of destructive drives that allow for the development of skills and capacities in the latency period, and the supportive interaction of intrapsychic and social processes in adolescence—all contribute to the successful history and evolution of identifications in the integration of any given personality. Furthermore, as Erikson made abundantly clear in his epigenetic considerations of the course of identity formation and its consequences in the life cycle, the essential processes of structural modification and internal building up of the ego do not come to a halt in the decisive identity formations characteristic of the adolescent phase of development. Rather, the process of resolution of life crises and the subsequent building up of ego strength through continuing processes of identification and identity modification continue through the whole of life experience.

Functions of the ego. This discussion of ego functions is based on the preceding definition of the ego as a substratum of personality, comprising an organization of functions that share the task of mediating between the instincts and the outside world. The ego is a subsystem of the personality and is not synonymous with the self, the personality, or character.

Any attempt to draw up a complete list of ego functions has to be relatively arbitrary. Invariably, the lists of basic ego functions suggested by various authors differ in varying degrees. This discussion is limited to several functions that are generally conceded to be fundamental to ego operation.

CONTROL AND REGULATION OF INSTINCTUAL DRIVES. The development of the capacity to delay immediate discharge of urgent wishes and impulses is essential if the ego is to assure the integrity of the person and to fulfill its role as mediator between the id and the outside world. The development of the capacity to delay or postpone instinctual discharge, like the capacity to test reality, is closely related to the progression in early childhood from the pleasure principle to the reality principle.

The progression from the pleasure principle to the reality principle parallels the development of secondary process or logical thinking, which aids in the control of drive discharge. The evolution of thought, from the initially prelogical primary process thinking to the more logical and deliberate secondary process thinking, is one of the means by which the ego learns to postpone the discharge of instinctual drives. For example, the representation in fantasy of instinctual wishes as fulfilled may obviate the need for urgent action that may not always serve the realistic needs of the person. Similarly, the capacity to figure things out or to anticipate consequences represents thought processes that are essential to the realistic functioning of the person. Obviously, the ego's capacity to control instinctual life and to regulate thinking is closely associated with its defensive functioning.

In this connection, it is important to highlight the role of the ego in the use of signal affects as part of its adaptive repertoire. Freud's original notion, derived from the signal theory of anxiety, has been enlarged to extend to a variety of signal affects. It seems clear that the ego can use the affects of anxiety and depression as signals of instinctual or other danger, and it may also have other affective states that it can exploit in the same manner—including, possibly, guilt and shame—as the means of adaptively mobilizing defensive capacities. The ego is in the position of exploiting the instinctual impulses as a means of organizing anticipatory signals, which then elicit more effective defensive alignments to prevent the disruptive and overwhelming breakthrough of threatening instinctual contents. The signal function of such affective states is in the service of mobilizing defense and is an essential part of the ego's emerging capacity to tolerate pain and frustration; thus they contribute to the building up and maintenance of structural apparatuses that, in turn, contribute to the regulation of instinctual drives. It is not yet clear what the relationship of this use of secondary or signal anxiety is to the internalizing processes discussed above, but it may be that the toleration of moderate amounts of anxiety or other dysphoric affects within manageable and relatively less threatening limits minimizes the defensive interference of introjective configurations and allows for the relatively nonconflictual and independent operation of ego-consolidating identifications and other synthetic processes.

RELATION TO REALITY. Freud always regarded the ego's capacity for maintaining relationship to the external world among its principal functions. The character of its relationship to the external world may be divided into three components: the sense of reality, reality testing, and the adaptation to reality.

Sense of reality. The sense of reality originates simultaneously with the development of the ego. The infant first becomes aware of the reality of his own bodily sensations. Only gradually does he develop the capacity to distinguish a reality outside of his body.

Reality testing. This function refers to the ego's capacity for objective evaluation and judgment of the external world, which depends, first of all, on the primary autonomous functions of the ego, such as memory and perception, but also on the relative integrity of internal structures of secondary autonomy. Under conditions of internal stress in which regressive pulls are effectively operating, introjective aspects of the inner psychic structure tend to dominate and thus become susceptible to projective distortions that color the person's perception and interpretation of the outside world. Because of the fundamental importance of reality testing for negotiating with the outside world, its impairment may be associated with severe mental disorder. The development of the capacity to test reality, which is closely related to the progression from the pleasure principle to the reality principle, to distinguish fantasy from actuality, occurs gradually. This capacity, once gained, is subject to regression and temporary deterioration in children, even up to school age, in the face of anxiety, conflict, intense instinctual wishes, or developmental crises. However, this temporary deterioration is not to be confused with the breakdown of reality testing referred to above, which occurs in adult forms of psychopathology.

Adaptation to reality. This function refers to the capacity of the ego to use the person's resources to form adequate solutions based on previously tested judgments of reality. It is possible for the ego to develop good reality testing in terms of perception and grasp but to develop an inadequate capacity to accommodate the person's resources to the situation thus perceived. Adaptation is closely allied to the concept of mastery in respect to both external tasks and the instincts. It should be distinguished from adjustment, which may entail accommodation to reality at the expense of certain resources or potentialities of the person. The function of adaptation to reality is closely related to the defensive functions of the ego. The mechanism that may serve defensive purposes from one point of view may simultaneously serve adaptive purposes when viewed from another perspective. In the obsessive-compulsive, intellectualization may serve important inner needs to control drive impulses, but from another perspective the intellectual activity itself may be serving highly adaptive functions in dealing with the complexities of external reality.

OBJECT RELATIONSHIPS. The capacity for mutually satisfying relationships is one of the fundamental functions of the ego. The significance of object relationships and their disturbance—for normal psychological development and a variety of psychopathological states—was fully appreciated relatively late in the development of classical psychoanalysis. The evolution in the child's capacity for relationships with others, which progresses from narcissism to social relationships within the family and then to relationships within the larger community, has been described. Focus has also been put on the early stages in the relationship to need satisfying and on the development of object constancy, which begins when the infant is about 6 months of age. The process of the development of object relationship may be disturbed by retarded development, regression, or inherent genetic defects or limitations in the capacity to develop object relationships. The development of object relationships is closely related to the concomitant evolution of drive components and the phase-appropriate defenses that accompany them.

DEFENSE. In his initial psychoanalytic formulations and for a long time thereafter, Freud considered repression to be virtually synonymous with defense. Repression was directed primarily against the impulses, drives, or drive representations, particularly against direct expression of the sexual instinct. Defense was mobilized to bring instinctual demands into conformity with the demands of external reality. With the development of the structural view of the mind, the function of defense was ascribed to the ego. However, only after Freud had formulated his final theory of anxiety was it possible to study the operation of the various defense mechanisms in terms of their mobilization in response to danger signals.

A systematic and comprehensive study of the defenses used by the ego was first presented by Anna Freud. In her classic monograph *The Ego and the Mechanisms of Defense,* Ms. Freud maintained that everyone, whether normal or neurotic, uses a characteristic repertoire of defense mechanisms but to varying degrees. Drawing on her extensive clinical studies of children, she described their essential inability to tolerate excessive instinctual stimulation and discussed the processes whereby the primacy of such drives at various developmental stages evokes anxiety in the ego. This anxiety produces a variety of defenses. With regard to adults, her psychoanalytic investigations led her to conclude that although resistance is an obstacle to progress in treatment insofar as it impedes the emergence of unconscious material, it constitutes a useful source of information concerning the ego's defensive operations.

Genesis of defense mechanisms. In the early stages of development, defenses emerge as a result of the ego's struggles to mediate between the pressures of the id and the requirements and strictures of outside reality. At each phase of libidinal development, associated drive components evoke characteristic ego defenses. For example, introjection, denial, and projection are defense mechanisms associated with oral-incorporative or oral-sadistic impulses, whereas reaction formations, such as shame and disgust, usually develop in relation to anal impulses and pleasures. Defense mechanisms from early phases of development persist side by side with those of later periods. When defenses associated with pregenital phases of development tend to become predominant in adult life over more mature mechanisms, such as sublimation and repression, the personality retains an infantile cast.

The repertoire that a person characteristically uses to deal with stress-evoking situations makes an important contribution to character formation. Character traits, such as excessive orderliness, are closely related to defenses but are distinguished from them by their greater role both in the over-all functioning of the personality and in situations that are not related to specific conflicts.

Although abnormalities in the development of the functioning of ego defenses or defense mechanisms may have a fundamental relationship to the causes of various forms of psychopathology, defenses are not of themselves pathological. On the contrary, they may serve an essential function in maintaining normal psychological well-being. Nonetheless, psychopathology may arise as a result of one of a variety of possible alterations in normal defensive functioning. For example, in hysteria the defense of repression is temporarily overwhelmed because of an excess of sexual stimulation. This revival of previously repressed wishes calls for more desperate and fragmented efforts at renewed repression, which themselves result in the formation of con-

version or phobic symptoms. On the other hand, the person may show an exaggerated development and overuse of certain defenses, as if the danger posed by infantile sexual and aggressive impulses were as great in adult life as it was perceived to be in childhood. This kind of hypervigilance is characteristic of obsessive-compulsive neurotics.

Or the development of the ego and its defenses may itself be faulty, with excessive reliance placed on the denial-projection-distortion modes characteristic of early oral or narcissistic phases of development. In that event, the defense mechanisms—although they permit limited functioning, particularly in the original family setting that may share these defensive patterns—cannot adequately equip the adult to meet the challenges of the external world. They can impede his capacity to form object attachments, to engage in heterosexual relationships, or to cope with vocational competition. When the defenses fail, there may be a breakthrough of direct instinctual expression and a regression in the ego's capacity to control instinctual motility. This breakthrough in defenses and accompanying regression is most graphically seen in states of acute schizophrenic turmoil.

Classification of defenses. It is possible to list the defenses used by the ego according to a variety of classifications, none of which is all-inclusive or takes into account all the relevant factors. For example, defenses may be classified developmentally—that is, in terms of the libidinal phase in which they arise. Thus, denial, projection, and distortion are assigned to the oral stage of development and to the correlative narcissistic stage of object relationships. However, certain defenses, such as magical thinking and regression, cannot be categorized in this way. Moreover, certain basic developmental processes, such as introjection and projection, may also serve defensive functions under certain specifiable conditions. The defenses have also been classified on the basis of the particular form of psychopathology with which they are commonly associated. Thus, the obsessional defenses include isolation, rationalization, intellectualization, and denial. But defensive operations are not limited to pathological conditions. Finally, the defenses have been classified as to whether they are simple mechanisms or complex, in which a single defense involves a combination or composite of simple mechanisms.

Table III presents a brief classification and description of some of the basic defense mechanisms that are most frequently used and that have been most thoroughly investigated by psychoanalysts.

SYNTHESIS. The synthetic function of the ego, which was described by Nunberg in 1931, refers to the ego's capacity to integrate various aspects of its functioning. It involves the capacity of the ego to unite, organize, and bind together various drives, tendencies, and functions within the personality, enabling the person to think, feel, and act in an organized and directed manner. Briefly, the synthetic function is concerned with the over-all organization and functioning of the ego and, consequently, must enlist the cooperation of other ego functions in its operation.

While it subserves the interests of adaptive functioning in the ego, it may also bring together various forces in a way that, although not completely adaptive, is an optimal solution for the person in his particular state at a given moment or period of time. The formation of a symptom that represents a compromise of opposing tendencies, although unpleasant in some degree, is preferable to yielding to a dangerous instinctual impulse or, conversely, to trying to stifle the impulse completely. Hysterical conversion, for example, combines a forbidden wish and the punishment for that wish into a physical symptom. On examination, the symptom often turns out to be the only possible compromise under the circumstances.

The operation of the synthetic function is closely involved in the process of structure formation and integration during the

TABLE III
Classification of the Defense Mechanisms*

Narcissistic Defenses

Projection. Perceiving and reacting to unacceptable inner impulses and their derivatives as though they were outside the self. On a psychotic level, this takes the form of frank delusions about external reality, usually persecutory, and includes both perception of one's own feelings in another and subsequent acting on the perception (psychotic paranoid delusions). The impulses may derive from the id or the superego (hallucinated recriminations) but may undergo transformation in the process. Thus, according to Freud's analysis of paranoid projections, homosexual libidinal impulses are transformed into hatred and then projected onto the object of the unacceptable homosexual impulse.

Denial. Psychotic denial of external reality. Unlike repression, it affects the perception of external reality more than the perception of internal reality. Seeing but refusing to acknowledge what one sees and hearing but negating what is actually heard are examples of denial and exemplify the close relationship of denial to sensory experience. However, not all denial is necessarily psychotic. Like projection, denial may function in the service of more neurotic or even adaptive objectives. Denial helps one avoid becoming aware of some painful aspect of reality. At the psychotic level, the denied reality may be replaced by a fantasy or delusion.

Distortion. Grossly reshaping external reality to suit inner needs—including unrealistic megalomanic beliefs, hallucinations, and wish-fulfilling delusions—and using sustained feelings of delusional superiority or entitlement.

Immature Defenses

Acting out. Direct expression of an unconscious wish or impulse in action in order to avoid being conscious of the accompanying affect. The unconscious fantasy, involving objects, is lived out impulsively in behavior, thus gratifying the impulse more than the prohibition against it. On a chronic level, acting out involves giving in to impulses in order to avoid the tension that would result from postponement of expression.

Blocking. Inhibition, usually temporary in nature, of affects especially but possibly also of thinking and impulses. It is close to repression in its effects but has a component of tension arising from the inhibition of the impulse, affect, or thought.

Hypochondriasis. Transformation of reproach toward others—arising from bereavement, loneliness, or unacceptable aggressive impulses—into self-reproach and complaints of pain, somatic illness, and neurasthenia. Existent illness may also be overemphasized or exaggerated for its evasive and regressive possibilities. Thus, responsibility may be avoided, guilt may be circumvented, and instinctual impulses may be warded off.

Introjection. In addition to the developmental functions of the process of introjection, it serves specific defensive functions. The introjection of a loved object involves the internalization of characteristics of the object with the goal of establishing closeness to and constant presence of the object. Anxiety consequent to separation or tension arising out of ambivalence toward the object is thus diminished. If the object is a lost object, introjection nullifies or negates the loss by taking on characteristics of the object, thus in a sense internally preserving the object. Even if the object is not lost, the internalization usually involves a shift of cathexis reflecting a significant alteration in the object relationships. Introjection of a feared object serves to avoid anxiety by internalizing the aggressive characteristic of the object, thereby putting the aggression under one's own control. The aggression is no longer felt as coming from outside but is taken within and used defensively, thus turning the person's weak, passive position into an active, strong one. The classic example is identification with the aggressor. Introjection can also arise out of a sense of guilt in which the self-punishing introject is attributable to the hostile-destructive component of an ambivalent tie to an object. Thus, the self-punitive qualities of the object are taken over and established within one's self as a symptom or character trait, which effectively represents both the destruction and the preservation of the object. This is also called identification with the victim.

Passive-aggressive behavior. Aggression toward an object expressed indirectly and ineffectively through passivity, masochism, and turning against the self.

Projection. Attributing one's own unacknowledged feelings to others; it includes severe prejudice, rejection of intimacy through suspiciousness, hypervigilance to external danger, and injustice collecting. Projection operates correlatively to introjection, such that the material of the projection is derived from the internalized configuration of the introjects. At higher levels of function, projection may take the form of misattributing or misinterpreting the motives, attitudes, feelings, or intentions of others.

Regression. Return to a previous stage of development or functioning to avoid the anxieties or hostilities involved in later stages; return to earlier points of fixation, embodying modes of behavior previously given up. This defense mechanism is often the result of a disruption of equilibrium at a later phase of development. It reflects a basic tendency to achieve instinctual gratification or to escape instinctual tension by returning to earlier modes and levels of gratification when later and more differentiated modes fail.

Schizoid fantasy. Tendency to use fantasy and to indulge in autistic retreat for the purpose of conflict resolution and gratification.

Somatization. Defensive conversion of psychic derivatives into bodily symptoms; tendency to react with somatic manifestations, rather than psychic manifestations. Infantile somatic responses are replaced by thought and affect during development (desomatization); regression to earlier somatic forms or response (resomatization) may result from unresolved conflicts and may play an important role in psychophysiological disorders.

Neurotic Defenses

Controlling. Excessive attempt to manage or regulate events or objects in the environment in the interest of minimizing anxiety and solving internal conflicts.

Displacement. Purposeful, unconscious shifting from one object to another in the interest of solving a conflict. Although the object is changed, the instinctual nature of the impulse and its aim remains unchanged.

Dissociation. Temporary but drastic modification of character or sense of personal identity to avoid emotional distress; it includes fugue states and hysterical conversion disorders.

* Compiled and adapted from Semrad, E. V. The organization of ego defenses and object loss. In *The Loss of Loved Ones,* D. M. Moriarity, editor, p. 126. Charles C Thomas, Springfield, Ill., 1967; Bibring, G. L., Dwyer, T. F., Huntington, D. S., and Valenstein, A. F. A study of the psychological processes in pregnancy and of the earliest mother-child relationship. II. Methodological considerations. Psychoanal. Study Child, *16:* 25, 1961; and Vaillant, G. E. Theoretical hierarchy of adaptive ego mechanisms. Arch. Gen. Psychiatry, *24:* 107, 1971.

TABLE III—*continued*

Externalization. A general term, correlative to internalization, referring to the tendency to perceive in the external world and in external objects components of one's own personality, including instinctual impulses, conflicts, moods, attitudes, and styles of thinking. It is a more general term than projection, which is defined by its derivation from and correlation with specific introjects.

Inhibition. Unconsciously determined limitation or renunciation of specific ego functions, singly or in combination, to avoid anxiety arising out of conflict with instinctual impulses, the superego, or environmental forces or figures.

Intellectualization. Control of affects and impulses by way of thinking about them, instead of experiencing them. It is a systematic excess of thinking, deprived of its affect, in order to defend against anxiety due to unacceptable impulses.

Isolation. Intrapsychic splitting or separation of affect from content, resulting in repression of either idea or affect or the displacement of affect to a different or substitute content.

Rationalization. Justification of attitudes, beliefs, or behavior that may otherwise be unacceptable by an incorrect application of justifying reasons or the invention of a convincing fallacy.

Reaction formation. Management of unacceptable impulses by permitting expression of the impulse in antithetical form. This is equivalently an expression of the impulse in the negative. When instinctual conflict is persistent, reaction formation can become a character trait on a permanent basis, usually as an aspect of obsessional character.

Repression. Expelling and withholding from conscious awareness of an idea or feeling. It may operate either by excluding from awareness what was once experienced on a conscious level (secondary repression), or it may curb ideas and feelings before they have reached consciousness (primary repression). The "forgetting" of repression is unique in that it is often accompanied by highly symbolic behavior, which suggests that the repressed is not really forgotten. The role of repression is central in the development of psychoanalytic theory; discrimination between repression and the more general concept of defense is particularly important.

Sexualization. Endowing of an object or function with sexual significance that it did not previously have or that it possesses to a smaller degree in order to ward off anxieties connected with prohibited impulses.

Mature Defenses

Altruism. Vicarious but constructive and instinctually gratifying service to others. This defense mechanism must be distinguished from altruistic surrender, which involves a surrender of direct gratification or of instinctual needs in favor of fulfilling the needs of others to the detriment of the self, with vicarious satisfaction only being gained through introjection.

Anticipation. Realistic anticipation of or planning for future inner discomfort; it implies overly concerned planning, worrying, and anticipation of dire and dreadful possible outcomes.

Asceticism. Elimination of directly pleasurable affects attributable to an experience. The moral element is implicit in setting values on specific pleasures. Asceticism is directed against all base pleasures perceived consciously, and gratification is derived from the renunciation.

Humor. Overt expression of feelings without personal discomfort or immobilization and without unpleasant effect on others. Humor

allows one to bear and yet focus on what is too terrible to be borne; in contrast, wit always involves distraction or displacement away from the affective issue.

Sublimation. Gratification of an impulse whose goal is retained but whose aim or object is changed from a socially objectionable one to a socially valued one. Libidinal sublimation involves a desexualization of drive impulses and the placing of a value judgment that substitutes what is valued by the superego or society. Sublimation of aggressive impulses takes place through pleasurable games and sports. Unlike neurotic defenses, sublimation allows instincts to be channeled, rather than to be dammed or diverted. Thus, in sublimation, feelings are acknowledged, modified, and directed toward a relatively significant person or goal, so that modest instinctual satisfaction results.

Suppression. Conscious or semiconscious decision to postpone attention to a conscious impulse or conflict.

---

course of development. The formation of introjects and their integration into progressive stages of personality development can be seen, in part, as a function of the ego's capacity for internal synthesis.

Autonomy of the ego

PRIMARY AUTONOMY. Although Freud referred to "primal, congenital ego variations" as early as 1937, this concept was greatly expanded and clarified by Hartmann (1949), who advanced a basic formulation about development—namely, that the ego and the id differentiate from a common matrix, the so-called undifferentiated phase, in which the ego's precursors are inborn apparatuses of primary autonomy. These apparatuses are rudimentary in nature and present at birth and develop outside the area of conflict with the id. This area Hartmann referred to as a conflict-free area of ego functioning. He included perception, intuition, comprehension, thinking, language, certain phases of motor development, learning, and intelligence among the functions in this conflict-free sphere. However, each of these functions may also become secondarily involved in conflict in the course of development. For example, if aggressive, competitive impulses intrude on the impulse to learn, they may evoke inhibitory defensive reactions on the part of the ego, thus interfering with the conflict-free operation of these functions.

With the introduction of the primary autonomous structure of the ego, Hartmann introduced an independent genetic derivation for at least part of the ego, thus establishing it as an independent realm of psychic organization that is not totally dependent on and derived from the instincts and the intrinsic patterning of instinctual development. This was an insight of major importance, since it laid the foundations for the emerging doctrine of ego autonomy and meant that the analysis of ego development has to take into consideration an entirely new set of variables quite separate from those involved in instinctual development.

This shift toward a consideration of autonomous factors followed a general functional tendency toward establishing psychoanalysis as a general psychology. Hartmann's emphasis was on the common factors that can be taken as underlying and influencing the process of development, since he related the emergence of the primary autonomous factors to what he called the "average expectable environment." This reflected a trend toward generality in theory and a movement away from the focus on specific environmental factors, especially those embedded in the person's object relationships, which are at work in the development of any given individual ego. This trend in Hartmann's work and the whole systematic school of ego psychologists has been objected to. Attempts to reverse and correct this abstractive tendency have recently been made in terms of object relations theory.

SECONDARY AUTONOMY. Hartmann observed that the conflict-free sphere derived from the structures of primary autonomy can be enlarged and that further functions can be withdrawn from the domination of drive influences. This was Hartmann's concept of secondary autonomy. A mechanism that arises originally in the service of defense against instinctual drives may in time become an independent structure, such that the drive impulse merely triggers the automatized apparatus. The apparatus may come to serve functions other than the original defensive function—for example, adaptation and synthesis. Hartmann referred to this removal of specific mechanisms from drive influences as a process of change of function. It has often been observed that this process is akin to Gordon Allport's concept of functional autonomy.

Along with the development of the notion of autonomy, Hartmann provided an economic basis for the support of autonomous functions. Obviously, the conflict-free functioning of these autonomous ego capacities cannot be maintained on the basis of unmodified instinctual drives, since the very notion of autonomy emphasizes the withdrawal of these functions from drive influence. He thus proposed that at least some of the ego's energies may derive from nondrive sources; he also proposed the concept of neutralization as an alternate explanation for the energy used in conflict-free functions of the ego. Neutralization is a generalization of Freud's concept of sublimation or desexualization. Neutralization involves the desexualization of libidinal drives or the deaggressivization of aggressive drives and thus provides the ego with independent energies that function without drive interference or dependence. The extent to which instinctual energy becomes neutralized is a measure of ego strength.

Hartmann made it clear that all autonomy is relative. The ego may lose its autonomy if the drive influences increase disproportionately. Autonomy can also be diminished if synthetic functioning is weakened by toxic effects, the influence of illness, or organic injuries. The loss or decompensation of defending or regulating structures can also lead to a process of deneutralization, so that instinctual drives come to influence the previously relatively autonomous functions. This may result in the undermining of secondary autonomous structures and can even influence the functioning of the apparatuses of primary autonomy. Such is the case, for example, in hysterical blindness.

Hartmann envisioned autonomy in terms of the autonomy of the ego from the influence of the id; another aspect of autonomy was added by Rapaport in focusing on the autonomy of the ego from external reality. By this he meant the capacity of the psychic apparatus to respond in relative independence from external stimulation—that is, the ego's response capacity is not stimulus-bound. The autonomy of the ego has to be safeguarded from both influences. Rapaport wrote:

While the ultimate guarantees of the ego's autonomy from the id are man's constitutionally given apparatuses of reality relatedness, the ultimate guarantees of the ego's autonomy from the environment are man's constitutionally given drives.

Although the appreciation of the autonomy in function and structure of the ego from drive and reality influences was a major contribution of the systematic ego school, there remain significant difficulties that need to be resolved. One of the important areas for thinking and investigation in psychoanalysis has to do with the influences and determining factors of the development of ego autonomy. One of the major areas of theoretical tension has to do with the emergence of autonomous functions and autonomous ego structures, along with the understanding of both their removal from and their involvement in instinctual sources of energy. There is a tendency in this area to follow Hartmann's lead in the direction of postulating independent sources of ego energy—independent, that is, of instinctual sources. This, however, raises the further problem of resolving and integrating the instinctual and the independent ego energies in the course of development of an integrated psychic apparatus.

The Superego

The origins and functions of the superego are, to a significant degree, involved with those of the ego, but they reflect different developmental vicissitudes. Briefly, the superego is the last of the structural components to develop, resulting from the resolution of the oedipal complex. It is concerned with moral behavior based on unconscious behavioral patterns learned at early pregenital stages of development.

The structural model provides a useful means of expressing the nature of neurotic conflict. Neurotic conflict can be explained structurally as a conflict between the forces of the ego on one hand and the forces of the id on the other. Frequently, the superego participates in the conflict by allying itself with the ego and thus imposing demands in the form of conscience or guilt feelings. Occasionally, however, the superego is allied with the id against the ego. This happens in cases of severely regressed reaction, when the functions of the superego may become sexualized once more or may become permeated by aggression, taking on a quality of primitive (usually anal) destructiveness, thus reflecting the quality of the instinctual drives in question.

Historical development. The concept of the superego, like the concept of the ego, has its historical origins in Freud's writings. The steps leading up to its formulations as a special agency of the mind can be traced to a paper written in 1896 entitled, *Further Remarks on the Defense Neuro-Psychoses,* in which he described obsessional ideas as

self-reproaches which have re-emerged in transmuted form and . . . relate to some sexual act that was performed with pleasure in childhood.

The activity of a self-criticizing agency is also implicit in Freud's early discussions of dreams, which postulate the existence of a censor that does not permit unacceptable ideas to enter consciousness on moral grounds.

Freud first discussed the concept of a special self-critical agency in 1914, when he published his exposition of narcissism. In *On Narcissism*, Freud suggested that a hypothetical state of narcissistic perfection exists in early childhood; at this stage, the child is his own ideal. But, as he grows up, the admonitions of others and his own self-criticism combine to destroy this perfect image of himself. To compensate for this lost narcissism or to recover it, the child "projects before him" a new ideal or ego ideal. At this point Freud suggested that the psychic apparatus may have still another structural component, a special agency whose task it is to watch over the ego, to make sure it is measuring up to the ego ideal. The concept of the superego evolved from these formulations of an ego ideal and a second monitoring agency to ensure its preservation.

In the following year, 1915, in *Mourning and Melancholia,* Freud wrote again of "one part of the ego" that "judges it critically and, as it were, takes it as its object." He suggested that this agency, which is split off from the rest of the ego, is what one commonly calls conscience. He further stated that this self-evaluating agency can act independently and become diseased on its own account and that it should be regarded as a major institution of the ego. In 1921 Freud referred to this self-critical agency as the ego ideal and held it responsible for the sense of guilt and for the self-reproaches that are typical in melancholia and depression. He had dropped his earlier distinction between the ego ideal, or ideal self, and the self-critical agency, or conscience.

In 1923 in *The Ego and the Id,* Freud's concept of the superego included both these functions—that is, the superego represented the ego ideal and conscience. He also demonstrated that the operations of the superego are mainly unconscious. Patients who are dominated by a deep sense of guilt lacerate themselves far more harshly on an unconscious level than they do consciously. The fact that guilt engendered by the superego may be eased by suffering or punishment is apparent in the case of neurotics who demonstrate an unconscious need for punishment. In later works Freud elaborated on the relationship between the ego and the superego. Guilt feelings were ascribed to tension between these two agencies, and the need for punishment was seen as an expression of this tension.

In one of his last discussions of the superego, in *Civilization and Its Discontents* (1930), Freud expanded on its relationship to his evolving conception of the aggressive instinct. When an instinct undergoes repression, its libidinal aspects may be transformed into symptoms, whereas its aggressive components are transformed into a sense of guilt.

On another level, Freud related the development of the superego to the evolution of culture and to the relation of human beings to one another in society. In such moral precepts as "Love thy neighbor," which are aimed at controlling aggression, the cultural superego makes demands on the person from without, much as his personal superego dictates to him from within. Freud believed that the cultural superego, which represents the ideals of civilization, evolved from the impression left by the personalities of great leaders,

men of overwhelming force of mind or men in which one of the human impulses has found its strongest and purest and, therefore, often its most one-sided expression.

Freud recognized that some limits on individual satisfactions are necessarily imposed by the demands of civilization, but he lamented deeply the degree to which the person must renounce instinctual gratification in order to conform to the social requirements of the larger group. These ideas—which Freud posed very tentatively, recognizing that his application of individual psychology to society was merely by analogy—have been adopted and greatly extended, often on a rather superficial level in various discussions of the neurotic culture of today.

Origins of the superego. The superego comes into being with the resolution of the Oedipus complex. During the oedipal period the little boy wishes to possess his mother; the little girl wishes to possess her father. However, each must contend with a substantial rival, the parent of the same sex. The frustration of the child's positive oedipal wishes by this parent evokes intense hostility, which finds expression not only in overt antagonistic behavior but also in thoughts of killing the parent who stands in the way, along with any brothers or sisters who may also compete for the love of the desired parent.

Quite understandably, this hostility on the part of the child is unacceptable to the parents and, in fact, eventually becomes unacceptable to the child himself. In addition, the boy's sexual explorations and masturbatory activities may themselves meet with parental disfavor, which may even be underscored by real or implied threats of castration. These threats and, above all, the boy's observations that women and girls lack a penis convince him of the reality of castration. Consequently, he turns away from the oedipal situations and enters the latency period of psychosexual development. He renounces the sexual expressions of the infantile phase.

Girls—when they become aware of the fact that they lack a penis, that they have come off badly—seek to redeem the loss by obtaining a penis or a baby from the father. Freud pointed out that although the anxiety surrounding castration brings the Oedipus complex to an end in boys, in girls it is the major precipitating factor. Girls renounce their oedipal strivings be-

cause, first, they fear the loss of the mother's love and, second, they are disappointed by the father's failure to gratify their wishes. However, the latency phase is not as well defined in girls as it is in boys. Girls' persistent interest in family relations is expressed in their play; throughout grade school, for example, girls act out the roles of wife and mother in games that boys scrupulously avoid.

Evolution of the superego. But what is the fate of the object attachments given up with the resolution of the Oedipus complex? Freud's formulation of the mechanism of introjection is relevant here. During the oral phase the child is entirely dependent on his parents. When he advances beyond this stage and must abandon his earliest symbiotic ties with his parents, he forms initial introjections of them; these introjections, however, follow the anaclitic model—that is, they are characterized by dependence on another. The dissolution of the Oedipus complex and the concomitant abandonment of object ties lead to a rapid acceleration of the introjection process.

One might think, following the model proposed above, that the child identifies with the parent of the opposite sex after he has been forced to renounce his oedipal object ties, and to some degree this may, in fact, occur. However, under normal conditions the striving toward masculinity in the boy and femininity in the girl leads to a stronger identification with the parent of the same sex. The problem is not simple; because of the bisexual potential of boys and girls, a child may emerge from the Oedipus complex with various admixtures of masculine and feminine introjections. Obviously, these introjections have a great deal to do with the child's ultimate character formation and later object choices.

Introjections from both parents become united and form a kind of precipitate within the self, which then confronts the other contents of the psyche as a superego. This identification with the parents is based on the child's struggles to repress the instinctual aims that were directed toward them, and this effort of renunciation gives the superego its prohibiting character. It is for this reason, too, that the superego results to such a great extent from an introjection of the parents' own superegos. Yet, because the superego evolves as a result of repression of the instincts, it has a closer relation to the id than does the ego itself. Its origins are more internal; the ego originates to a greater extent in the external world and is its representative.

Throughout the latency period and thereafter, the child continues to build on these early identifications through contact with teachers, heroic figures, and admired persons, who form his moral standards, his values, and his ultimate aspirations and ideals.

The child moves into the latency period endowed with a superego that is, as Freud put it, "the heir to the Oedipus complex." Its structures may, at first, be compared to the imperative nature of the demands of the id before it developed. The child's conflicts with his parents continue, of course, but now they are largely internal, between the ego and the superego. In other words, the standards, restrictions, commands, and punishments imposed previously by the parents from without are internalized in the child's superego, which now judges and guides his behavior from within, even in the absence of his parents.

Clearly, this initially punitive superego must be modified and softened, so that eventually it can permit adult sexual object choice and fulfillment. Adolescence poses a unique developmental hurdle in this regard. With the heightening of sexual and aggressive drives that is characteristic during this period, there is a threatened regressive revival of the abandoned incestuous ties to the parents and the undermining of the efforts of the superego. Often, the rebellious acting-out behavior of teenagers can be understood in terms of instinctual release that the superego has failed to curb. However, their behavior may be deflected from the more threatening attachment to the parents to their representatives in the external world. In contrast, the superego of the ascetic, oversubmissive, or intellectual adolescent has responded to the threat posed by these heightened drives with renewed vigilance and intensified instinctual renunciation. The task of adolescence is to modify the oedipal identifications with the parents. Ideally, such modification enables the choice of a love object that is not motivated entirely by the need for a parent substitute or based exclusively on the need to rebel against internalized parental imagos.

Current investigations of the superego. The exploration of the superego and its functions did not end with Freud, and such studies remain of active interest. Recent interest has focused on the difference between the superego and the ego ideal, a distinction that Freud periodically revived and abandoned. At present, the term "superego" refers primarily to a self-critical, prohibiting agency that bears a close relationship to aggression and aggressive identifications. The ego ideal, on the other hand, is a kinder agency, based on a transformation of the abandoned perfect state of narcissism, or self-love, that existed in early childhood and has been integrated with positive elements of identifications with the parents. In addition, the concept of an ideal object—that is, the idealized object choice—has been advanced as distinct from the ideal self. Many theorists regard the ego ideal as an aspect of superego organization derived from good parental imagos.

A second focus of recent interest has been the contribution of the drives and object attachments formed in the preoedipal period to the development of the superego. These pregenital (especially anal) precursors of the superego are generally thought to provide the very rigid, strict, and aggressive qualities of the superego. These qualities stem from the child's projection of his own sadistic drives and his primitive concept of justice based on retaliation that he attributed to his parents during this period. The harsh emphasis on absolute cleanliness and propriety that is sometimes found in very rigid persons and in obsessional neurotics is based to some extent on this sphincter morality of the anal period. Parenthetically, it should be noted that Melanie Klein's contention that the Oedipus complex, including the superego, is well established within the first year of life derives from another theoretical framework and is not to be confused with the concept of pregenital precursors of the superego, as postulated by classical psychoanalytic theory.

Object Relations Theory

Origins. One of the minor psychoanalytic currents, paralleling the main line of psychoanalytic development traced in the preceding pages, is the approach to psychoanalysis through object relations theory. Only recently have the parallel and somewhat independent courses of theoretical development begun to converge. The development of classical psychoanalytic theory through the elaboration of a systematic ego psychology has led inexorably in the direction of a better understanding of the adaptive functions of the ego, particularly the close involvement between the ego and reality in its functioning and development. One important dimension of the problem of reality in psychoanalytic theory is the whole question of object relations. The problem of integrating these two currents of analytic thinking remains a present theoretical concern within psychoanalysis.

The origins of the object relations view can best be traced from the

contribution of Melanie Klein. She had originally trained with Karl Abraham in Berlin, and during the late 1920's and subsequent decades she undertook extensive investigations of childhood pathologies in an attempt to document and refine some of Abraham's views about mental development and its pathological deviations. Klein's theorizing was based primarily on the death instinct as the main theoretical prop of her metapsychology. Her major emphasis fell on the developmental vicissitudes of the superego. She extended this approach to the study of the fantasies and behaviors of severely disturbed children into a full-scale analysis of the internal psychic world and its development.

She saw the superego as an endopsychic organization that develops independently of biological influences but that is determined entirely by the pattern of the child's relationship to his parents and the vicissitudes of the primary instincts. Klein's emphasis in the child's developmental experience fell on the processes of introjection and projection, derived from basic instinctual drives, and their interactions with the important and primary objects of the child's early experience. The emphasis on the relationship with objects and the careful delineation of the internal structuring of the child's inner fantasy world in terms of the vicissitudes of introjects provided the basis and the rudimentary content for an object relations view of development.

Klein's inner world is peopled by internal objects that are either good or bad and with whom the person is involved in intrapsychic interactions and struggles that are in many ways as real as those he carries on with the real objects outside himself. In fact, Klein saw external object relations as derived from and influenced by projective content derived from the internal object relations. Klein has been criticized for her almost blind interpretation of all forms of aggressive or destructive intent as manifestations of the death instinct, for her failure to distinguish among the various kinds of intrapsychic content (lumping object representations, self-representations, internal objects, fantasies, and psychic structures of various kinds together indiscriminately and treating them in a unitary fashion), for her tendency to substitute theoretical inferences for observations, and for her marked tendency to predate the emergence of intrapsychic organizations that are generally thought by other theorists to be achieved only in later developmental stages—locating the origin of the superego, for example, in the first year of life.

In any case, Klein's observations and formulations had a tremendous impact, particularly in bringing into prominence the role of aggression in pathological development, in making theorists of development much more aware of the early developmental precursors of later structural entities, and in providing the basic rudiments and foundations for an emergent theory of object relations. Although Klein's emphasis was primarily on the world of internal objects, rather than on the ego, and more strongly on the role of instincts in the intrapsychic dynamics, rather than on the objects themselves, subsequent theorists have followed her lead and have shifted the emphasis from the instinctual basis, which was more classically Freudian, to an emphasis on the objects and the external environment.

Ego and objects. Beginning about 1931, Ronald Fairbairn shifted the emphasis in his thinking to the problems of ego analysis. Fairbairn's contribution was to bring personal object relations to the center of the theory. Following Klein's analysis of the internalized psychic object, Fairbairn proposed a radical ego analysis. Whereas the ego in Freudian theory had been regarded as a superficial modification of the id, developed specifically for the purpose of impulse control and adaptation to the demands of reality, Fairbairn conceived of the ego as the core phenomenon of the psyche. He conceived of the ego in terms of real self—that is, as the dynamic center or core of the personality—rather than as an organization of functions. Instead of basing his theory on the instinctual drives as the basic concept, Fairbairn shifted the emphasis to the ego and saw everything in human psychology as specifically an effect of ego functioning.

With this reorientation there came a reformulation of the instinctual perspective. The libido or the instincts in general were regarded as essentially object seeking, rather than as mechanisms for energic discharge. Erotogenic zones are not the primary determinants of libidinal aims but, rather, channels that mediate the primary relationships with objects, particularly with objects that have been internalized during early life under the pressure of deprivation and frustration. Ego development itself is characterized by a process whereby an original state of infantile dependence, based on a symbiotic union with the maternal object, is abandoned in favor of a state of adult or mature dependence, based on differentiation between self and object. Thus, Fairbairn conceptualized the developmental process in terms of the vicissitudes of objects, rather than in terms of the vicissitudes of instincts.

The basis for much of Fairbairn's theorizing was his experience with schizoid patients. He contrasted the basic dilemma of the schizoid with that of more neurotic patients on whom classical psychoanalytic theory was based. He saw that the schizoid is not primarily concerned with the control of threatening impulses toward significant objects but that the issue for him is essentially whether he has an ego capable of forming object relations at all. This relationship to objects presents a difficulty not because of dangerous impulses arising in connection with them but because his ego is weak, undeveloped, infantile, and fragile. In the struggle to overcome this inner weakness, the schizoid's impulses become antisocial.

The schizoid's problem is, at bottom, a question of an infantile ego unable to cope with the world of objects. In his growing emotional life, the schizoid is split by the inconsistency in his primary objects and becomes a victim of the loss of internal unity and his own radical helplessness. His internalized objects are split into good and bad objects that cannot be amalgamated. Parallel to the split in objects, there is a split within the ego itself—a radical split that calls for a conception of intrapsychic structure different from that provided by the classical psychoanalytic model.

The schizoid experiences himself as empty, meaningless, worthless, lonely, isolated, and craving close contact with objects for the sake of preserving a sense of security. Such psychodynamic security can be achieved only by the adequate growth of the ego, fostered and initiated by what Winnicott calls "good-enough mothering." Fairbairn points out that the model for splitting of the ego was provided by Freud in his analysis of the superego, which he described initially as a "differentiating grade of the ego." But, whereas Freud's analysis of splitting was based on the phenomenon of depression and unconscious guilt, the object relations approach bases its analysis of splitting on the schizoid problem.

The object relations theory in its bare essentials contains a number of basic points that differentiate it from classical theory. First, the ego is conceived of as whole or total at birth, becoming split or losing inner unity as a result of early bad experiences in object relationships, particularly in relation to the mothering object. This point is contrary to the classical theory, according to which the ego begins as undifferentiated and unintegrated and achieves unity only through the course of development. Second, in object relations theory the libido is regarded as a primary life drive of the psyche, the energic source of the ego's search for the relatedness with good objects, which makes ego growth possible. Third, aggression is regarded as a natural defensive reaction to the frustration of the libidinal drive, rather than as an independent instinct. Fourth, the structural ego pattern that emerges when the pristine ego unity is lost involves a pattern of ego splitting and the formation of internal ego-object relations.

The shift in emphasis toward the primacy of the external environment and the influence of objects on the course of development has established a definite trend in psychoanalytic thinking and has been advanced primarily in the work of British theorists, among whom one can point particularly to the work of Michael Balint and Donald Winnicott. Winnicott has emphasized the importance of the early interactions between mother and child as determining factors in the laying down of important parameters of ego development. As things currently stand, there is ample room for overlap in the approaches and formulations of both the object relations theorists and the more classical psychoanalytic ego theorists.

Both Balint and Winnicott, in company with other object relations theorists, were concerned with levels of early developmental failure that are essentially preoedipal, are manifested in forms of personality disorders that are more primitive and more difficult to treat than the usual neurotic disorders, and do not fit well with the classical psychoanalytic structural theory, with its basic focus on issues of intrapsychic conflict.

Balint envisioned several layers of psychological functioning in analysis. The first is the familiar genital level, centering on triadic relationships and concerned with intrapsychic conflicts. These conflicts and relationships are the usual material of analysis and can be treated by adult language. However, there is a second, deeper level, at which the conventional meanings of words no longer have the same impact and at which interpretations are no longer perceived as meaningful by the patient. This is the level of preverbal experience. Balint recognized that an attempt to address or describe these experiences in adult language is bound to fail. Problems arise in analysis when efforts are made to interpret events from this preverbal level in adult terms.

Balint distinguished between phases of regression that he described as benign and malignant. The benign regression is more or less an extension of the basic notion of the analytic regression to a level of primitive relationship with the primary objects. Such a regression is gradual, tempered, and modulated according to the patient's capacity to tolerate and productively integrate the resulting anxiety. During this regression the analyst's empathic responsiveness and recognition make it possible for the patient to withstand this unstructured experience and to keep the anxiety within manageable limits. At the level of the basic fault, the lost infantile objects can be mourned, the quality of the relationships with them is open to reworking, and the patient's basic assumptions that govern his interactions with the object world can be reformed.

During phases of the benign regression to this preverbal and pregenital level of object relationship in the analysis, the analyst can usually provide not verbalized interpretations but an empathic acceptance and recognition, along with a tolerance of this level of the patient's unstructured experience without anxiety or the need to escape or the need to subvert this level of experience through interpretation. Balint referred to this level of impairment in object relations as the "basic fault." He felt that the dynamics at this level are more primitive than can be adequately expressed in terms of conflict, since they derive from the basic dual relationship involved in the early mother-child interaction.

In contrast, malignant regression tends to be precipitous and extreme; the ego is prematurely overwhelmed by traumatic and unmanageable anxiety. This anxiety prevents any effective reworking of fundamental disturbances in object relationships, and it recreates and reinforces the basic fault, rather than creating the conditions for its therapeutic revision.

At an even deeper level, beyond the reach of analytic resources, lies the area of creativity—an idiosyncratic, uncommunicable, and objectless area that lies beyond conventional expression.

Regression to the level of the basic fault is quite different and distinct from the more usual oedipal regressions experienced in the analysis of adult neurotics. In the oedipal regression the aim is gratification of infantile instinctual wishes. However, regression to the level of the basic fault seeks a basic recognition by the therapist and his protective support and consent to express the inner core of creativity that lies at the heart of the patient's being and that accounts for his capacity to become ill or well. Balint used the notion of primary love at this deepest level to describe the withdrawal of libido from the frustrating object in an attempt to reestablish a certain inner harmony in which it becomes possible to recover the conditions of early care and tranquility. He referred to a harmonious interpenetrating mix-up to describe the early, almost undifferentiated interaction of the infant and his environment. The analogy is that of breathing air; the organism cannot exist without air, so air and the organism are seemingly inseparable, but cutting off the supply of air reveals both the organism's need for it and the distinction between air and the organism. In terms of primary love, then, the patient seeks a basic form of recognition from the analyst, as he sought it from the significant objects in his life.

Winnicott was also concerned with the earliest phase of the mother-child relationship and the importance of what he described as "good-enough mothering" for the child's personality development. The course of development involves a movement from an early stage of total or absolute dependence, analogous to Mahler's symbiotic phase, toward a more adult phase of relative independence. As Winnicott saw it, the inherited native potential for growth is strongly influenced by the quality of maternal care. This potential for development is affected from the moment of conception. Even before the child's birth, he becomes invested by a strong narcissistic cathexis that allows the mother to identify with the child and to become empathically attuned to the child's inner needs, as if he were—as, indeed, he is—an extension of her own self. Winnicott called this early prenatal involvement of mother and child-in-the-womb a "primary maternal preoccupation." This sets the stage for the development of a holding relationship, in which the mother becomes sensitively attuned to the infant's needs and sensitivities and is both physically and emotionally responsive to them, thus providing physical, physiological, and emotional ambiance, protection, and security for the absolutely dependent infant.

As the infant moves from this early stage of absolute dependence toward a more relative dependence, he becomes more aware of his own needs and of the existence of the mother as a caretaking object. The optimal relationship at this stage involves a continuation of the protective holding, along with an optimal titration of gratification and frustration. As a result of this optimally attuned relationship between the patterning of infantile drives and initiatives and their harmonious fitting in with maternal sensitivities and responsiveness, there is a developing sense of reliable expectation that the infant's needs will be satisfied, without the threat of excessive withdrawal of the mothering object and without the threatening, overwhelming, and short-circuiting of the infant's initiatives as a result of excessive maternal impingements.

In the course of normal development, this allows for the emergence of a certain omnipotence, from which the child gradually retreats as he experiences tolerable degrees of frustration and separateness of the maternal object. The mother continues her holding at this phase, but she must allow enough separation between herself and the developing infant to permit the expression of his needs and initiatives that form the rudiments of his emerging sense of self. If she is too withholding, too unresponsive, too distant, or not sufficiently present, anxiety arises and is accompanied by the fading of the infant's internal representations of her. The upsurge of such anxiety provides the stimulus for the organization of a false self, based on the necessity for compliance with the demands of the external environment. The transition from a phase of absolute dependence to one of relative dependence represents a crucial development in the capacity for object relations. It is accompanied by a critical transition from total subjectivity to the capacity for objectivity in the perception of and relation to objects.

The transition from subjectivity to objectivity is accomplished by the development of Winnicott's transitional phenomenon, expressed in the first instance in the emergence of transitional objects. These are the child's first object possessions that are perceived as separate from his own emerging self, the first not me possessions. From the study of infant behavior, Winnicott argued that the object is a substitute for the maternal breast, the first and most significant object in the environment to which the infant relates. The transitional object exists in an intermediate realm that is contributed to both by the external reality of the object (the mother's breast) and by the child's own subjectivity. This intermediate realm is at once both subjective and objective without being exclusively either.

Winnicott referred to this as the realm of illusion, an intermediate area of experience that embraces both inner and external reality and may be retained in areas of adult functioning having to do with imaginative capacities, creativity, religious experience, and art. In its primitive form, however, the transitional object commonly experienced

in childhood development may take the form of a particular object—a blanket, a pillow, or a favorite toy or teddy bear to which the child becomes intensely attached and from which he cannot be separated without the stirring up of severe anxiety and distress. Attachment to this object is an immediate displacement from the figure of the mother and represents an important developmental step, insofar as it allows the child to tolerate increasing degrees of separation from the mother, using the transitional object as a substitute.

The mother participates in this intermediate transitional realm of illusion by her responsiveness to the infant's need to continually create her as a good mother. In her sensitivity and responsiveness, she functions as a good-enough mother. However, her failure to provide such adequate mothering, either by excessive withdrawal or by excessive intrusion and control, may result in the emergence of a false self in the child, a condition that reflects a developmental failure and results in a variety of often severe character pathologies.

When patients with character pathologies are seen as adults, they are neither neurotic nor psychotic but seem to relate to the world through a compliant shell that is not quite real to them or to others. They are mistrustful without being specifically paranoid; they seem withdrawn and disengaged and seem able to relate only by means of the protective shell, which seems apparently obsessive and compliant but which serves to separate and isolate them from meaningful contacts with their fellows, even as it provides their only basis for relationship. These disturbed personality types reflect a basic impairment in very early object relations, particularly in the mutuality and mutual responsiveness of the very early mother-child interaction.

Infants who develop in the direction of a false self mode have not experienced the security and mutual satisfaction of such a relationship. Their mothers are empathically out of contact with the child and react largely on the basis of their own inner fantasies, narcissistic needs, or neurotic conflicts. The child's survival depends on his capacity to adapt to this pattern of the mother's response, which is grossly out of phase with his needs. This establishes a pattern of gradual training in compliance with whatever the mother is capable of offering, rather than seeking out and finding what is needed and wanted. Consequently, the child's needs, instinctual impulses, wishes, and initiatives, instead of becoming a guide to satisfying growth experiences and the enlarging capacities to interact meaningfully with objects, becomes from the very beginning a threat to the harmony of the relationship with the mother, who remains unresponsive to any feedback from the child.

Winnicott's attempts to formulate principles of treatment of such basically impaired patients built on the model of good-enough mothering. This called for a capacity for holding, for empathic responsiveness, and for creatively playful exchange that allows the patient's capacities for growth to emerge and flourish and allows for the expansion of the patient's authentic sense of self, which remains hidden behind the external facade of false self-compliance.

Many contemporary analysts argue that Freud's instinct theory can in no way be conceived as excluding the importance of objects and the significance of the influence of objects as internal psychic development, but specific problems remain to be resolved. Particular theoretical issues that reveal some divergence in these approaches have to do specifically with the character of the ego. In the object relations approach, the ego seems to expand to encompass the whole of the internal psychic structure. Moreover, it is conceived of as a unitary structure in the beginning of the child's experience with objects. These propositions stand in direct opposition to the classical notion of the ego as a substructural organization within the psychic apparatus. It also stands in opposition to the basic Freudian notion of the infant's beginning life in a state of objectless primary narcissism and developing gradually in the direction of object libido and object attachment. Another critical area of divergence between these theories is between the concept of ego as an organization of functions (functional ego) in the classical approach and the concept of ego as more closely identified with the objectively experienced real self (personal ego), in the object relations approach.

Concept of Character

HISTORICAL DEVELOPMENT

The concept of character can vary widely in meaning, depending on whether it is used in a moralistic, literary, sociological, or general sense. The application of the concept in psychoanalysis has remained restrictive, despite the fact that theoretical propositions concerning the meaning of character have undergone an evolution that parallels the evolution in psychoanalytic theory, particularly in the theory of the ego. During the period when Freud was developing his instinctual theory, he noted the relationship between certain character traits and particular psychosexual components. For example, he recognized that obstinancy, orderliness, and parsimoniousness are associated with anality. He noted that ambition is related to urethral eroticism and that generosity is related to orality. He concluded in his paper *Character and Anal Eroticism* that permanent character traits represent

unchanged prolongation of the original instincts, or sublimation of those instincts, or reaction formation against them.

In 1913 Freud made an important distinction between neurotic symptoms and character traits. Neurotic symptoms come into being as a result of the failure of repression—the return of the repressed; but character traits owe their existence to the success of repression or, more accurately, of the defense system, which achieves its aim through a persistent pattern of reaction formation and sublimation. Later, in 1923, with increased understanding of the phenomenon of identification and the formulation of the ego as a coherent system of functions, the relationship of character to ego development came into sharper focus. At this point Freud observed that the replacement of object attachment by identification (introjection), which set up the lost object inside the ego, also made a significant contribution to character formation. In 1932, Freud emphasized the particular importance of identification (introjection) with the parents for the construction of character, particularly with reference to superego formation.

Several of Freud's disciples made important contributions to the concept of character during this period. A major share of Karl Abraham's efforts were devoted to the investigation and elucidation of the relationship between oral, anal, and genital eroticism and various character traits. Wilhelm Reich made an important contribution to the psychoanalytic understanding of character when he described the intimate relationship between resistance in treatment and character traits of the patient's personality. Reich's observation that resistance typically appears in the form of these specific traits anticipated Anna Freud's later formulation concerning the relationship between resistances and typical ego defenses.

CURRENT CONCEPTS OF CHARACTER

The development of psychoanalytic ego psychology has led to an increasing tendency to include character and character traits among the properties of the ego, superego, and ego ideal. However, character is not synonymous with any of these. Concomitantly, the emphasis has been extended from an interest in specific character traits to a consideration of character and its formation in general. Psychoanalysis has come to regard character as the pattern of adaptation to instinctual and environmental forces that is typical or habitual for a given person. The character of a person is distinguished from the ego by virtue of the fact that character refers largely to directly observable behavior and styles of defense, as well as of acting, thinking, and feeling. The clinical value of the concept of character has been recognized by psychiatrists and psychoanalysts and has become a meeting ground for the two disciplines.

EVOLUTION OF CHARACTER

The formation of character and character traits results from the interplay of multiple factors. Innate biological predisposition plays a role in character formation in both its instinctual and its ego fundaments. Id forces, early ego defenses, and environmental influences, particularly the parents, constitute the major determinants in the development of character. Various early identifications and imitations of objects leave their lasting stamp on character formation.

The degree to which the ego has developed a capacity to tolerate delay in drive discharge and to neutralize instinctual energies, as a result of early identifications and defense formations, determines the later emergence of such character traits as impulsiveness. A number of authors have stressed the particularly close association between character traits and the development of the ego ideal. The development of the ego ideal must be understood in the context of the developmental vicissitudes of narcissism. It is in this respect that the psychoanalytic concept of character begins to parallel the more common use of the word "character" in a somewhat moral sense. The exaggerated development of certain character traits at the expense of others may lead to character disorders in later life. At other times, such distortions in the development of character traits produce a vulnerability in personality organization or a predisposition to psychotic decompensation.

An important dimension in the study of character that has been elaborated in recent years is related to the development of the concept of narcissism as related to the self as an independent intrapsychic entity and, correlatively, to the emergence of a more global set of concepts having to do with identity formation. The function of the concept of identity in analytic theory, particularly in relation to the ego, remains to be defined. Erikson's own use of the term seems to vary between referring it specifically to the ego and referring it more globally to personality organization as such. In any case, the formulations regarding identity raise questions about its relevance to and integration with the concept of self. This whole aspect of psychoanalytic theory is in a very inchoate state of development, with many issues as yet unresolved. One of the primary aspects of the psychoanalytic theory of the self has to do with its relationship to narcissism and the vicissitudes of narcissistic development on the one hand and its relationship to aspects of the tripartite structural theory on the other. Nonetheless, this whole area of thinking has important implications for the psychology of character.

Psychopathology

THEORY OF NEUROSIS

Psychoanalytic theories concerning mental disorders have undergone extensive expansion and modification since Freud discovered the free association method of investigation. These theories have retained their emphasis on the investigation of causative factors, rather than on the mere description of symptoms. By 1906 Freud had succeeded in understanding the psychological processes underlying many mental disorders to a degree sufficient to permit him to classify them on the basis of psychopathology. At that point Freud's theory contained most of the major elements of current psychoanalytic concepts of psychopathology. He had advanced his initial hypotheses concerning the psychological mechanisms of the neuroses, character disorders, perversions, and psychoses.

Historical Evolution

Early concepts. Cases of hysteria treated by the cathartic method, Breuer's modification of hypnoid therapy, led Freud to conclude that hysterical symptoms are caused by unconscious memories of events in the past. These memories are accompanied by strong emotion that were elicited when these events actually occurred but that have not been expressed or adequately discharged. On the basis of this conclusion, Freud hypothesized that hysterical symptoms are the result of psychic traumata in persons congenitally or genetically predisposed to the development of such phenomena. This was Freud's modification of Breuer's hypothesis of hypnoid states. Although this theory differed somewhat from his earlier biological concept of neurasthenia in that it provided a purely psychological explanation, instead of an explanation based on toxic sexual factors, it also proved to be an oversimplification.

In his early formulations regarding the actual neuroses, Freud believed that excessive masturbation or nocturnal emissions give rise to the symptoms of neurasthenia—fatigue, listlessness, constipation, headache, and dyspepsia. He distinguished the syndrome of neurasthenia. Anxiety neurosis was related etiologically to states of activity that produce sexual stimulation or excitement but do not provide an adequate outlet for discharge. He thus cited coitus interruptus and lovemaking without sexual gratification as examples of such stimulation without adequate discharge. As late as 1906, Freud believed that symptoms of neurasthenia and anxiety neurosis represent the somatic effect of disturbances in sexual metabolism, which were thought to be biochemical in nature and referred to as "actual neuroses"—thus opposing them to hysteria and obsessional neurosis, which he described as "psychoneuroses." Of particular interest is the fact that these classifications stressed the causes of these disorders, rather than the symptoms. Freud assumed that drive energy that should have been discharged in the sexual climax creates a state of psychic stimulation that exceeds the ego's capacity to contain or master it and thus produces a state of anxiety.

Modifications. As the free association method continued to provide new insights into the origins of psychopathology, Freud revised and expanded his theories. Psychic conflict was recognized as an element in the production of psychoneurotic symptoms. This recognition required that he extend his earlier theory of hysterical and obsessional symptoms as caused by a forgotten past event and its inadequate discharge of the related emotion. Originally, Freud maintained that a psychic event or experience can be considered pathogenic if it is repugnant to the person's conscious self—that is, if it violates his ethical or moral standards to the degree that it may be consciously repudiated. Hysteria, most obsessions, and many phobias were understood in this way, although some phobias (agoraphobia) and some obsessions (doubting mania) were described as actual neuroses.

Theory of infantile sexuality. The fact that almost invariably in the course of treatment, Freud's patients recalled a previously forgotten sexual experience that had occurred in childhood led Freud to hypothesize that mental illness is the psychic consequence of a sexual seduction by a child or an adult at an early stage in the patient's development. His assumption that sexual seduction had actually occurred proved incorrect, but the basic proposition that the roots of psychoneuroses lie in a disturbance in early sexual development remains unshaken and is the cornerstone of the psychoanalytic theory of neurotic psychopathology.

Further clinical studies led to the conclusion that these memories of sexual seduction in childhood were actually fantasies, although the patients themselves seemed to believe in their reality. Reexamination of the data elicited through free association enabled Freud to formulate a theory of infantile sexuality, which states that sexual interest and activity are a normal part of human psychic life from the earliest stages of infancy and are not limited to traumatic episodes. Nevertheless, despite the psychological findings, Freud continued to stress the importance of the patient's sexual constitution and heredity in the etiology of the psychoneuroses. Progress in investigating the precise nature of such constitutional factors has been very slow. In contrast, knowledge of experiential causative factors has increased.

The discovery that infantile sexuality is a normal phenomenon narrows the gap between the normal and the psychoneurotic and enabled Freud to elucidate the origins of the sexual perversions and their relationship to both normal and psychoneurotic functions. The abnormal persistence in adult sexual life of some component of infantile sexuality may serve as the basis of a perversion. However, in the normal course of events, some components of infantile sexuality are repressed and others are integrated into the adult pattern of sexuality at puberty, with genital primacy. Other insights followed. Excessive repression creates instability, so that in later life there is a greater likelihood that precipitating events will cause a failure of repression. In that event, infantile sexual impulses emerge in the unconscious, at least to some degree, in the form of psychoneurotic symptoms.

Study of dreams. One of the major props of Freud's early thinking about psychoneurosis was that the process of symptom formation parallels the dynamic aspect of dream formation. Freud's study of dream processes showed him that the dream that the sleeper remembers—that is, the manifest dream—represents a compromise between one or more repressed impulses and those psychic forces that oppose the entrance of these impulses into conscious thought or behavior. Neurotic symptoms represent a similar compromise but with one exception: The latent, instinctual wish that underlies the manifest dream may or may not be sexual but the repressed impulses that produce the neurotic symptoms are always sexual. On the other hand, the meaning of neurotic symptoms, like the elements of the manifest dream, lies in their latent or unconscious content. They are disguised in distorted expressions of unconscious sexual fantasies, just as the manifest content of dreams is a disguised, distorted expression of the dream thought. All or part of the psychoneurotic patient's sexual conflict is expressed in his symptoms.

Current concepts of neurosis. The theory of neurosis in its traditional sense as referring to hysteria, obsessional neuroses, and phobias is central to the psychoanalytic concept of psychopathology. Neuroses develop under the following conditions: (1) There is an inner conflict between drives and fear that prevents drive discharge. (2) Sexual drives are involved in these conflicts. (3) Conflict has not been worked through to a realistic solution. Instead, the drives that seek discharge have been expelled from consciousness through repression or another defense mechanism. (4) Repression merely succeeds in rendering the drives unconscious; it does not deprive them of their power and make them innocuous. Consequently, the repressed tendencies fight their way back to consciousness, now disguised as neurotic symptoms. (5) An inner conflict leads to neurosis in adolescence or adulthood only if a neurosis or a rudimentary neurosis based on the same type of conflict existed in early childhood.

Developmental Schema of Causes

Early childhood. In the course of development, many vicissitudes may contribute to the future malfunctioning or malformation of the psychic apparatus. Maternal deprivation in the first few months of life may impair ego development in a manner that is particularly devastating to its integrated capacities. Failure to make necessary introjections and identifications, either because of overindulgence or because of obsessive deprivation and frustration, interferes with the ego's task of mediating between the instincts and the environment, with consequent limitations of drive discharge and restriction of the ego's capacity to obtain pleasure and to assert itself productively. A lack of the capacity for equitable expression of drives, especially the aggressive drive, may lead the person to turn them on himself and to become overtly self-destructive. Inconsistency, excessive harshness, or undue permissiveness on the part of the parent may result in disordered functioning of the superego. Similarly, instinctual conflict may impair the ego's capacity for neutralization or for sublimation, resulting in excessive inhibition of its autonomous functions. Severe conflict that cannot be dealt with through symptom formation may lead to severe restrictions in ego functioning and to impairment of the capacity to learn and to develop new conflict-free skills.

Puberty and adult love. When the ego has been weakened, a shock or a traumatic event later in life that threatens survival (or seems to)—especially when combined with external factors that further weaken ego resiliency, such as toxic conditions and exhaustion—may break through the ego's defenses. A large amount of libido is then required to master the resultant excitation. But the libido thus mobilized has been withdrawn from the supply normally applied to external objects and from the ego itself, and this withdrawal further diminishes the strength of the ego and produces a sense of inadequacy.

Precipitating factors in neuroses are experiences that disturb the balance between warded-off impulses and warding-off forces. An increase in the warded-off drive may be absolute, as in puberty or at the climacteric, due to the physiological intensification of sexual drives at these times. Or there may be a relative increase in a specific warded-off drive at the expense of other instinctual demands, as in the case of conscious or unconscious temptation or stimulation of a particular wish.

Disappointments, frustrations, and adult strivings can revive infantile longings, which may be dealt with through symptom formation or further regression. Decrease in the warding-off forces due to fatigue, intoxication, illness, or overexacting tasks may loosen previously effective defenses against drive derivatives and precipitate a neurotic or even a psychotic illness. As long as the warded-off instinct cannot be tolerated in consciousness, the ego has no choice but to form a symptom or to modify its aims so that the unfulfilled strivings become less urgent.

In addition to those more or less accidental conditions that induce regression, one must add to the list of conditions in which regression is a factor that of developmental crises. In the movement to any new developmental phase, progression is accompanied by regression. The reopening of old conflicts and areas of libidinal fixation makes possible a reworking in the interest of a more mature and developmentally sound resolution. This regressive reopening of developmental achievements may effectively induce a condition in which temporary neurotic solutions or even, in the developmental resolutions, more persistent neurotic disorders may be sought. Each developmental phase must be seen to possess an inherent dual potentiality. On the one hand, it has the potentiality for developmental progression and increasing maturity and integration; on the other hand, it possesses potential for regressive and neurotic resolution of the developmental crisis.

Secondary Gain

The reduction of tension and conflict through neurotic illness is the primary purpose or gain of the disorder. The ego, however, in making the best of it, may try to gain advantage from the external world by way of the illness by provoking pity in order to get attention and sympathy, by manipulating others to serve one's own end, or by receiving monetary compensation. Similarly, the patient may imply to others that his suffering somehow entitles him to a compensatory reward. These are referred to as the secondary gains of neurotic illness.

Each form of neurosis has its own characteristic and predominant form of secondary gain. In the phobias (anxiety hysteria), there is a regression to childhood levels of development, when the patient was still taken care of and protected. Gaining attention through dramatic acting out and deriving material advantages are characteristic of conversion hysteria. In compulsive neurosis there is frequently a narcissistic gain through pride in illness. In psychosomatic states (organ neurosis), psychic conflicts are denied by projecting them onto the physical sphere. And in the psychoses, warding off of a painful idea, experience, or frustration in the outside world leads to a severe regression, which requires that the patient be hospitalized, protected, and taken care of, thus satisfying the most extreme and infantile dependency needs.

Classification

Symptomatic neurotic states

HYSTERIA. Hysterical states are described in two major forms, depending on whether conversion symptoms or dissociative reactions are predominant in the pathology.

Conversion hysteria, which usually occurs in women but may also be seen in men, is characterized by bodily symptoms that resemble those of physical disease—paralysis, anesthesia, blindness, convulsions, pathological blushing, fainting, headaches, and other types of painful bodily experience—but that have no somatic basis. Unless these symptoms occur in very mild form in an otherwise well-adjusted personality, they may be positive indications for analysis. The typical course of treatment in such cases is the early alleviation of symptoms and the recognition of basic conflicts produced by genital wishes. Analysis of these conflicts usually leads to fundamental changes in the personality, in addition to permanent symptomatic relief. But a few cases of hysteria are difficult to analyze or may even be unanalyzable, particularly cases of hysteria in women whose personalities are exceptionally infantile and some chronic cases in which the pleasure derived over long periods of time from secondary gain is too great to be renounced.

The dissociative type of hysteria occurs in a variety of complex forms that are often difficult to distinguish sharply but that are characterized by the fact that a group of recent related mental events—which may consist of memories, feelings, or fantasies—are beyond the patient's power of conscious recall but still remain psychically active and ultimately capable of conscious recovery. The usual forms of dissociative hysteria are somnambulism, various forms of amnesia (which can be quite localized or general), a variety of fugue states, and the unusual condition of multiple personality. Other forms of dissociative phenomena that have been described include various trance states, automatic writing, Ganser's syndrome, and some forms of mystical states or experience.

Pathogenesis. Conversion hysteria provides a defense against overintense libidinal stimulation by means of a transformation or conversion of psychic excitation into physical innervation. As a result, various alterations of motor function or sensations may occur. The intervention is not haphazard; it represents a genitalization of the particular part of the body associated with repressed unconscious wishes directed toward a love object. Fixation of the phallic stage of psychosexual development, a tendency to libidinize thoughts and images, and frustration in external life in relation to strong, unconscious fantasies are causative factors.

The change in physical function gives expression in a distorted form to instinctual impulses that had been repressed. However, conversion symptoms are not simply somatic expressions of affect; they are very specific representations of thought that can be retranslated through the free association method from their somatic language into words. The syndromes of conversion are unique in every patient. In each instance the specific type of distortion is determined by the historical events that created the repression. The distortion mechanisms used in dreams are used in conversion hysteria as well—condensation, symbolism, displacement, and so on.

Freud's original thinking about the pathogenesis of neurosis was based on the study of such hysterical patients. With regard to the formation of symptoms, Freud's theory retains a certain validity; the mechanism of symptom production can be regarded as representing a defense against excessively intense libidinal stimulation and libidinal impulses by a transformation or conversion of psychic excitation into forms of physical innervation or expression. Consequently, the understanding of symptomatic hysteria is based on the conflict-related model of intersystemic conflict among structured psychic entities. Instinctual libidinal impulses may be in conflict with other areas of psychic function governed by the ego and the superego, setting up a conflict that results in repression of the instinctual impulse and its corresponding distortion and reexpression in somatic terms.

With that model of hysterical process, it was argued that the hysterical person must have gained developmentally sufficient access to the oedipal situation to allow for the internalization of relatively integrated parental imagos and the relatively stable consolidation of these psychic entities in the resolution of the oedipal attachments. However, greater experience with hysterical disorders has made analysts increasingly aware of the extent to which hysterical dynamics express a variety of pregenital determinants, particularly oral determinants. Moreover, analysts have become increasingly aware that hysterical symptoms themselves are not an adequate guide to the assessment of the underlying character structure. Consequently, hysterical symptoms in an otherwise reasonably well-functioning personality suggest that the person has successfully accomplished the developmental task leading up to the oedipal formation and that the basic conflicts lie at that level of psychic organization, but caution is called for and a more careful assessment of pregenital and other structural aspects of the personality must be made before any definite conclusions can be reached.

Critical issues in this regard are the susceptibility of the hysterical person to regression and the degree of vulnerability to depression (Zetzel, 1970). Although such persons may be thought of as having successfully negotiated the developmental issues of separation and individuation and the formation of a coherent and stable sense of self, analysts remain acutely aware that the hysterical façade may cover a variety of developmental defects and impediments affecting not only the organization and functioning of the patient's ego but a variety of possible narcissistic vulnerabilities as well. Consequently, it is not at all uncommon for patients who present as apparently hysterical to turn out to be considerably more infantile, depressive, and narcissistic than may have been apparent on brief acquaintance.

Symptoms. Hysterical spells or attacks, which are rarely encountered in current clinical practice, are usually pantomimic expressions of rather complicated fantasies relating to the child's concepts of his parents' sexual relations during the oedipal period. However, the hysterical seizure may also express pregenital actions that are regressive substitutes for the original oedipal fantasies. Some attacks are less specifically sexual and occur in the form of convulsions or as emotional outbursts or moods that appear to be entirely unmotivated or as screaming, laughing, or crying spells. Related to the seizures are various bizarre symptoms, including the sudden appearance or disappearance of physical needs, attacks of hunger or thirst, the urgent need to defecate or urinate, and difficulties in breathing.

In monosymptomatic conversions the somatic innervation expresses the memory of an event that took place in the forgotten situation. For example, Breuer's patient Anna O. had a paralysis of her arm whenever she was unconsciously reminded of her feelings for her father. When her father died, she had been sitting at his bedside with her arm pressed against the back of the chair while she was asleep; when she awakened, her arm was temporarily paralyzed. The motor disturbances thus represent a defense against an action, specifically an action that is associated with an objectionable, infantile impulse. Hysterical pain may represent a signal or warning not to yield to pleasant sensations associated with the memory of a painful episode. Pain originally experienced by the patient recurs in the conversion symptoms as a substitute for the pleasant excitement once connected with it.

At times the pain, imitated in the conversion symptoms, was experienced not by the patient but by another person with whom the patient identifies. Freud's patient Dora illustrated this sort of hysterical identification with a rival by developing a cough like that of Frau K., with whom she was unconsciously competing for the attentions of Herr K. The female patient whose hysteria is due to her unresolved Oedipus complex may make an identification not with her rival, her mother, but with her beloved father. In this case the girl struggles to free herself of the frustrating love for the father. She may then seek to satisfy negative oedipal wishes by taking her mother as her love object. A frequent form of hysterical identification takes place in an object with whom the patient has no genuine object relationship. It is formed on the basis of identical ideological needs. Freud used a hysterical epidemic in a girl's school to illustrate this phenomenon: A girl reacts with a fainting spell to a love letter, and the other girls in the school get fainting spells along with her. The unconscious meaning is, "We would like to get love letters, too." There may be multiple identifications by a single patient, as is exemplified in cases of multiple personalities.

Hysterical dream states are closely related to seizures. The daydreams, which represent derivatives of the repressed oedipal fantasies, involuntarily take possession of the personality, thereby removing the patient from reality. A mixture of hysterical spells and hysterical dream states is represented by the conversion symptom of sleepwalking. The typical aim is the wish to participate in the sexual nightlife of adults. Other alterations in states of consciousness, such as amnesic and dissociative states, also result from the repression of warding off an intolerable aspect of infantile sexual life that has been revived by current sexual stimuli. Hysterical disturbances of the senses, particularly hysterical blindness and deafness, may represent an attempt to reject upsetting sexual perceptions.

Choice of neurosis. Somatic compliance symptoms illustrate that the entire cathexis of the objectionable impulses appears to be condensed into a definitive physical function. The choice of the afflicted region may be determined by unconscious sexual fantasies and the corresponding erotogenicity of the afflicted part, by physical injury or change in part of the body that increases its susceptibility by the nature of the situation in which the decisive repression occurred, and by the ability of the organ to express symbolically the unconscious drive in question. As is well known, hysteria may imitate a wide variety of diseases, which complicates the clinical picture considerably.

PHOBIC STATES. Phobias, which are often referred to as forms of anxiety hysteria, are abnormal fear reactions that are caused by paralyzing conflict due to an increase in sexual excitation attached to an unconscious object. The fear is avoided by displacing the conflict onto an object or situation outside the ego system. After this displacement has occurred, the readiness to develop anxiety is bound to the specific situation that precipitated the first anxiety attack. When situations duplicate or represent the original event symbolically, anxiety becomes manifest. The ego fights off the anxiety through states of inhibition, such as impotence and frigidity, or through the avoidance of objects that have become connected with unconscious conflict, either through historical association or through their symbolic significance.

The manifestations of phobic anxieties can be quite varied, and often the connection between the fear situation and the original instinctual conflict becomes increasingly concealed as the degree of displacement from the original context increases. The feared situation or object may have a specific unconscious significance and may come to symbolize a forbidden gratification, a punishment for an unconscious impulse, or a combination of both. Phobic anxieties are relatively common in young children, particularly in connection with the stirring up of instinctual conflicts. In adults, however, the onset of phobic reactions usually occurs during times of sexual or aggressive crises and may be contributed to by fixations at the phallic stage, sexual frustrations, or the presence of external factors that weaken the ego's ability to manage anxiety or increases in libidinal excitement.

Symptoms. The patient's history, the nature of the drives warded off, and the mechanisms of defense used determine the clinical symptoms. Phobias about infection and touching often express the need to avoid dirt and show that the patient has to defend himself against anal-erotic temptation. Fear of open streets and stage fright may be a defense against exhibitionistic wishes. Anxieties about high places, closed places, falling, cars, trains, and airplanes are developed to fight pleasurable sensations connected with stimulation involving equilibrium.

Pathogenesis. The manifestations of phobias are protean. As the degree of displacement increases, the connection between the fear situation and the original instinctual conflict becomes more concealed. The feared situation or person has a specific unconscious significance and in a distorted way symbolizes a forbidden gratification or a punishment for an unconscious impulse or a combination of both. The advantage of the displacement is that the original offensive idea does not become conscious. In Freud's famous case of Little Hans, the boy's fear of the horse, instead of his father, helped him to avoid hating his father, by whom he felt threatened but whom he also loved. Projection from an internal danger onto an external one that exists in the imagination—such as a wolf, as in the case of the Wolf Man—has another advantage. Wolves are seen only in picture books, which need not be opened, or at the zoo, where one does not often have to go. Although the object or situation

from which the phobic person flees represents primarily the threatening parents, he is also in flight from his own impulses. Even the fear of castration, which is perceived as an external threat, arises primarily as a consequence of the child's own phallic impulses.

The conflict-related nature of the symptoms usually indicates that the phobic patient has achieved a reasonably coherent self-organization and that the internal psychic agencies have been reasonably well established. Consequently, the conflicts are usually regarded as phallic, although phobias about infection and touching often express the need to avoid contamination and suggest that the patient is defending against erotic impulses.

Another important factor in the assessment of phobias is the extent to which the ego is capable of tolerating and mastering anxiety. A reasonably strong ego may be able to manage the conflict-related anxiety by forming a single phobic symptom complex; but phobic anxieties can frequently be seen to generalize and become polysymptomatic. Agoraphobia, the fear of open or public places, may be particularly susceptible to such phobic generalization. This tendency may suggest in such patients a defect in ego development that may reflect impediments in the organization of the ego stemming from pregenital levels of development.

In recent years behavioral scientists have developed fairly sophisticated and useful techniques for dealing with symptomatic phobias. Freud himself noted that one of the important issues in the treatment of phobic patients is not only the resolution of their internal conflicts but enabling them to overcome their fear of objects or situations in the real world. From a psychoanalytic point of view, if the phobias are primarily symptomatic and limited to restricted contexts and do not reflect underlying defects in the structural organization of the psyche, behavioral intervention may be a reasonable and in many cases preferable approach. The genetic perspective may be of considerable use in helping to establish this difficult diagnostic discrimination.

Another difficulty with the phobic syndromes is that there can be a subtle shift from the level of externalization connected with phobic anxiety to a more frankly projective distortion of reality of a paranoid order. In this regard, consideration must be taken of the relationship between early phobic anxieties in children and the development of later adult forms of paranoid psychopathology. The history of adult paranoiacs often reveals an early childhood history of severe phobic anxieties and nightmares. The connections in this progression are not well established, but they seem to involve similar psychic mechanisms and defenses (Meissner, 1978). It is also interesting in this regard to compare Freud's two classic cases—that of Little Hans (1909), in which the conflicts were on a phallic level and related to oedipal fears of the castrating father, and that of the Wolf Man (1918), in whom the phobic symptoms were of a more primitive order, reflecting severe ego defects and narcissistic vulnerabilities that later issued in a full-blown paranoid psychosis (Gardiner, 1971; Blum, 1974; Meissner, 1977).

As a rule, the first neurotic reactions in children have the character of anxiety hysteria. In adults, the onset of phobic reaction typically occurs at a time of crisis in the sexual life. Fixation at the phallic stage, sexual frustrations, the presence of an external factor that may weaken the ego, increases in libidinal excitement, and a particular susceptibility to anxiety reactions are the most common causative factors.

OBSESSIONAL NEUROSIS

Symptoms. The obsessional or obsessive-compulsive neurosis is characterized by persistent or urgently recurring thoughts (obsessions) and repetitively performed behavior (compulsion) that bear little relation to the patient's realistic requirements and are experienced by him as foreign or intrusive. In addition, this syndrome is characterized by rumination, doubting, and irrational fears. All these symptoms can be accompanied by morbid anxiety when the intruding thoughts or the repetitive acts are prohibited or otherwise interfered with. Other major symptoms are a strong tendency to ambivalence, a regression to magical thinking (particularly in relation to the obsessional thoughts), and indications of rigid and destructive superego functioning. The conflicts involved in obsessional neurosis usually lie closer to the prephallic phase of psychosexual development than to the phallic-oedipal phase.

Pathogenesis. The obsessional neurosis comes about as a result of the separation of affects from ideas or behavior by the defense mechanisms of undoing and isolation, by regression to the anal-sadistic level, or by turning the impulses against the self. If hysterical syndromes can be roughly characterized as states of cognitive insufficiency, obsessional states can be characterized as states of affective insufficiency. As the defense against a painful idea in the unconscious, the affect is displaced onto some other, indirectly associated, more tolerable idea. This idea then becomes invested with an inordinate quantity of affect.

Freud described obsessional ideas as self-reproaches that have reemerged from repression in transmuted form. He also suggested that they relate to some sexual act that was performed with pleasure in childhood. Nevertheless, in early childhood there are few indications of the development of obsessional tendencies. Moreover, at the time such trends develop in latency, no self-reproach is attached to the memory of earlier pleasurable activities. However, at approximately this point a primary defense system—that is, the superego—develops, consisting of general conscientiousness, a sense of shame, and self-distrust, now referred to as character defenses. A period of apparent health or successful defensive functioning may occur before the onset of the illness. The period of illness proper is distinguished by the return of repressed memories in the form of obsessive-compulsive symptoms—that is, by the failure of the character defenses. The obsessional ideas that emerge are derivatives that express the warded-off drive. Sometimes they preserve their character as impulses. Sometimes the original drives cannot be readily discerned, and the patient is aware only of ideas that must be thought about, which indicates that the energy associated with the original impulse has been diverted to a more neutral idea.

Few well-defined obsessional traits can be established early in childhood before the oedipal period, but it is thought that occasionally such characteristics arise in the form of premature defenses or development and closure of structured aspects of psychic functioning earlier in the developmental time table than is normal or adaptive. As a rule, the obsessional structure arises out of the resolution of oedipal conflicts at a point at which the primary superego defensive system develops in the latency period. This consists of characteristics of general conscientiousness, a sense of shame and self-distrust, and unconscious guilt, usually attributed to oedipal transgressions, wishes, and fantasies.

The obsessional syndrome is seen as, in part, a regression to anal-sadistic levels as a defense against intolerable oedipal impulses and conflicts. This regression is classically thought to be motivated by castration anxiety. Consequently, many of the obsessional mechanisms and behaviors can be seen as secondarily defending against anal-sadistic impulses, and the general behavior of obsessional patients can usually be found to contain indirect sadistic expressions. The object relations of such patients generally tend to be sadomasochistic in quality. Developmentally, such patients usually have been found to have experienced severe conflicts during the anal stage of development, having to do primarily with toilet training but in a more general sense involving struggles with controlling parental figures over the child's emerging autonomy. Consequently, the issues of ambivalence and control and the need to establish and reinforce a fragile autonomy become predominant elements in the obsessional syndromes.

The obsessional patient is one in whom internal structure predominates and provides powerful and often regulatory control over drive impulses and their associated affects. However, in such patients the structure that has been established is often excessively rigid and fragile, having been established prematurely on an insecure basis. Defensively, in retreat from castration anxieties, and developmentally, in terms of fixations at the level of anal-sadistic impulses, the basic conflicts in these patients remain prephallic. The extent to which these fixations and conflicts have interfered with ego development determines the extent to which these patients can tolerate regression without severe consequences. If such ego capacities have been inadequately formed and established, the undoing of obsessional defenses may precipitate a rapid regression to near-psychotic levels in which obsessional thoughts become delusional, and compulsive behaviors may reach a level of severe incapacitation and self-destructiveness.

Compulsive and obsessive symptoms are a condensation of both instinctual and antiinstinctual forces. In some instances—the obsessions related to incestuous or murderous ideas, for example—the manifest clinical picture reveals the direct, instinctual aspect more clearly. In other instances—when symptoms obviously express the defensive or punitive demands of the superego—the antiinstinctual forces are predominant. Actually, the person tries to protect himself from the threatened loss of his self-respect; this threat is precipitated by the guilt feelings occasioned by the disapproval of the superego, rather than by the loss of love or castration. The onset of obsessive-compulsive neuroses occur relatively late in childhood because they depend on the formation of the superego. The introjections of the parental imagos into the superego explain the relative predominance of punitive and expiatory symptoms that affect the total personality of the patient.

A phobia may be transformed into an obsession. Certain situations must be avoided by the phobic person, and he exerts great efforts to ensure this avoidance, to the degree that in time these efforts assume an obsessive-compulsive character. Other obsessions may develop that are so remote from the original source of fear that the avoidance is assured. For example, touching rituals may replace taboos. Washing compulsions may take the place of the fear of dirt. Social rituals may supersede social fears. Or sleeping ceremonials may replace the fear of falling asleep.

In the obsessive-compulsive neurosis, fixation of libido at the anal-sadistic stage has taken place. Concomitantly, ego development has been arrested at the accompanying stage of omnipotence of thought. Factors that result in frustration of post-anal-sadistic impulses (usually of a phallic nature) or that impede more mature ego functioning lead to the precipitation of overt symptoms. Defenses are first directed against the phallic-oedipal drives, but, as regression occurs, they are directed against the anal-sadistic impulses themselves. External circumstances that remobilize the repressed, infantile sexual conflicts and disturb hitherto effective equilibrium between the repressing and the repressed forces may precipitate acute cases of obsessional neurosis. The more frequently chronic type continues more or less without interruption from adolescence. However, particular external circumstances may precipitate exacerbations from time to time if the defenses become less effective or if impulses defended against become more intense and unbearable. Freud's most important clinical study of this syndrome was his case history of the Rat Man.

If the hysterical disorders are more commonly identifiable in women, the obsessional neuroses are relatively more common in men. Treatment of obsessional neuroses is usually more difficult and protracted than the treatment of other neuroses. Frequently, such patients do not derive whole benefit from analysis. However, they have serious disturbances in total life adjustment, so that extended treatment is usually justified, even though the "cure" is not considered complete by the usual psychoanalytic standards.

DEPRESSIVE STATES. The basic psychoanalytic approach to depressive states was that laid down by Freud in *Mourning and Melancholia* in 1917. The basic mechanism he described there is the introjection of a lost object and a redirection of the ambivalence, originally directed to the object, against the internalized object, now an inherent part of the self. The effect of this mechanism is essentially a turning against the self of the aggressive impulses originally directed against the ambivalent object.

Further development in the understanding of depression was provided by Edward Bibring (1953). He pointed out that a common theme in depressive states is the undermining or diminution of self-esteem. Depressive patients feel helpless in the face of superior forces surrounding them or feel incapable of controlling or directing their inescapable fate. They see themselves as the victims of loneliness, isolation, and lack of love and affection. Moreover, they feel themselves to be inherently weak, inferior, or failures in life. They are helpless and powerless. Bibring defined depression as

the emotional expression (indication) of a stage of helplessness and powerlessness of the ego, irrespective of what may have caused the breakdown of the mechanisms which established his self-esteem.

Depression must be seen not merely in terms of the instinctual vicissitudes of object loss but also in terms of the inner weakness, vulnerability, and sense of helplessness and inferiority within the ego itself. Neurotic depressions usually involve a reactive component and are to be distinguished from more severe depressive syndromes, such as psychotic depressive states and manic-depressive states, in which the degree of regression is considerably more severe and in which the impairment of reality testing and of interpersonal functioning is much greater.

Symptoms. The patient in a depressive state often complains of disturbances of mood, which are described as involving sadness, unhappiness, and hopelessness. He usually experiences a loss of interest in his usual activities or complains of difficulties in concentration. The patient feels lonely, empty, guilty, worthless, inferior, or inadequate. His attitude toward himself is highly derogatory and critical. He often craves emotional support and affection or reassurance from the environment, and the depressive symptoms often serve the purpose of eliciting such sympathy and support. But at times his complaints are so hostile and demanding that he frustrates his own purpose by irritating or alienating potential sources of affection. Suicidal ideas are frequently a component of depressive syndromes, and it is often difficult to assess the intensity or severity of such thoughts. It is essential to distinguish clinically between occasional suicidal ideas and feelings and specific suicidal intentions. Usually, the level of suicidal intent is related to the degree of hopelessness the patient feels.

Pathogenesis. Depressive neurosis usually involves reaction to loss or failure. The loss may be the death of a loved person or a disappointment by a love object. A depression can also be triggered by failure to live up to one's own standards or to achieve specific personal or vocational goals. In any case, depression is characterized essentially by a diminution or loss of self-esteem. Important factors affecting self-esteem seem to be the following: First, the patient has a poor self-image, usually based on early pathological development of his self-concept in an unfavorable or rejecting family atmosphere. The self-concept is based on the poor quality of introjects, which form the basis of the organization of the inner self. Second, self-esteem can be lowered as a result of superego aggression. The discrepancy between behavior and the values maintained by the superego and the resulting punishment of the superego is experienced as guilt, but the guilt is associated with a lowering of self-esteem. If the superego is fixated in the archaic, infantile, or punitive form or if it regresses to this level of organization, the predisposition to depression and the damage to self-esteem is correspondingly increased. Third, self-esteem depends on the nature and level of integration of the ego ideal. The more realistic the organization of the ego ideal, the more possible it is for the person to satisfy its demands. If the ego ideal is excessively grandiose, it places excessive demands on the ego, and the result can be feelings of inadequacy on the part of the ego. Fourth, the maintenance of self-esteem depends in part on the capacity for effective functioning of the ego itself. The person's actual abilities and talents and the relatively harmonious integration of ego functions determine his capacity for successfully meeting the demands of the ego ideal and, consequently, partially determine the level of self-esteem.

Depressive patients, as a rule, have a considerable degree of oral instinctual and narcissistic underpinnings to their depression. This is particularly true when the excessive demands of the ego ideal are determined by primitive narcissistic wishes that tend to be excessive and sometimes even grandiose. The impossibility of meeting such expectations and ideals sets the stage for the punitive response of the superego. The failure in self-esteem, however, may reflect developmental difficulties and impairments from pregenital levels of development and may reflect difficulties from very early levels.

At the earliest levels of development, the infant's emerging concept of self depends on the quality of his introjected objects. In the beginning, the image of the good object and that of the bad object tend to be separated; it is only in the course of development that the child's inner psychic apparatus becomes more capable of complex functioning, so that the divergent good and bad images are gradually integrated and unified into a complex apprehension of the object that is essentially ambivalent. Along with the unification of object representations, there is an integration and unification of a more enduring and consistent self-representation. The union of the bad and good objects into an ambivalently held (usually maternal) object leads to what Melanie Klein has called the "depressive position." The essence of the depressive position is that the child can no longer direct his internalized aggression against the ambivalently held object, since this would threaten the child with the loss of the now loved object on which the child is excessively dependent. The only alternative is to reinternalize the destructive impulses and direct them against the self.

For the child to develop a positive and healthy sense of self-esteem, he requires an atmosphere of parental affection and interest that is able to tolerate the infant's aggressive impulses and that can expose him to tolerable levels of frustration in increasingly manageable amounts. A parental atmosphere that is accepting, tolerating, nonfrustrating, and mutually and reciprocally responsive to the infant's needs and desires tends to produce a sense of inner confidence that consolidates the child's sense of self-esteem. Particularly important in this regard is the process of separation and individuation, by which the child gradually establishes himself as a separate and autonomously functioning unit, no longer depending on such an intense degree on the ministrations or presence of the mother. If the child is able to accomplish this separation without a sense of precariousness, shame, or threatening loss of the mother, he is able to salvage and consolidate his sense of autonomous capacity and self-esteem.

The developmental vicissitudes that can undermine self-esteem and lay the foundations for depressed feelings are multiple. They include insufficient parental acceptance and affection, excessive parental devaluation, excessive frustration experienced prematurely, and a sense of ineffectiveness in the early social and independent performance of activities. Loss of the parent in childhood has long been established as a predisposing factor to depression. During and after childhood, self-esteem can be adversely affected by illness, disfigurement, unattractiveness, or poor social, vocational, or educational performance. The vicissitudes of self-esteem are dependent on and derived from the vicissitudes of narcissism.

The psychoanalytic treatment of depressive states is relatively successful but only when the depression is clearly reactive and does not reflect excessive fixations at pregenital (oral) levels. The presence of depression in a potential analytic patient is a matter for careful diagnostic evaluation. The treatment of depressed patients often evolves into more fundamental treatment of a narcissistic disorder, usually a narcissistic character disorder. Characterological factors that contribute to the undermining of self-esteem have to do primarily with the more latent aspects of narcissistic fixation and its correlative narcissistic entitlement. An excessively intense depression or a depressive state that has persisted over prolonged periods of time contraindicates strictly psychoanalytic treatment.

IMPULSE NEUROSES. The impulse neuroses, which are related to perversions, involve impulsive actions that, although not necessarily overtly sexual, serve the purpose of avoiding or mastering some type of pregenital anxiety that is intolerable to the ego. The strivings for security and for instinctual gratification are characteristically combined in the impulsive action. Running away, kleptomania, pyromania, gambling, drug addiction, and alcoholism are well-known examples of irresistible impulsive activities.

PSYCHOSOMATIC DISORDERS. Between the realm of organic disorders from known physical causes and the group of conversion (hysterical) disorders, there exist a large group of syndromes that are characterized by functional and even anatomical alterations. These were originally called "organ neuroses." They are presently referred to as psychosomatic disorders or psychological factors affecting physical condition. Peptic ulcer, asthma, and ulcerative colitis are typical examples of physical conditions affected by psychological factors.

These disorders are usually kept conceptually distinct from hysterical conversion disorders. Conversion disorders are regarded as due to transformations of psychic or symbolic conflicts into physical forms of expression that affect the peripheral sensory or motor nervous system or the special organs of sense. In the psychosomatic disorders, the transformations are regarded as affecting the vegetative nervous system and involve imbalances of sympathetic and parasympathetic regulation of organ systems. The influence on the functioning of organ systems can be both acute and chronic, producing both transient symptomatic attacks (migraine, asthmatic attacks) and chronic disease (ulcers, colitis).

Pathogenesis. Many theories have been advanced to explain the origins of psychosomatic disorders. The symptoms have been described as affect equivalents representing dammed-up emotions or their symbolic representations that cannot be discharged through behavior or speech and that find expression instead along somatic pathways in the form of a structural or functional alteration in an organ or organ system. One can recognize this theory as an extension of Freud's original ideas about the genesis of hysterical disorders. According to this theory, anger, sexual excitement, or anxiety may be supplanted by sensations and other changes in the intestinal, respiratory, or circulatory apparatus. For example, cardiac neurosis is thought to be an anxiety equivalent. Although the theory of affect equivalent has some validity, it is generally regarded as an oversimplified explanation of the complex interrelationships between psychological and somatic processes in these disorders, processes that are not as yet completely understood. Furthermore, although all affects are carried out by motor or secretory means, the physical manifestations of any given disease may occur without a clearly established causative relationship to specific mental or emotional experiences. The difficulties are compounded by the fact that the psychosomatic disorders themselves may bring about various pathological adaptive responses in the patient, such as the pathoneuroses described by Ferenczi. These responses make it more difficult to determine whether the emotional disorder preceded the physical disorder or vice versa.

Current issues. The normal interrelationship between hormonal physiology and instinctual phenomena is the subject of much current study and interest. The workers involved in these investigations maintain that with a predisposition or susceptibility to psychosomatic disorders in particular persons, the inhibition of specific affects may lead to certain hormonal secretions, to change in physical functions, and eventually to alterations in organ tissue. Different unconscious affects, as they occur in specific disorders, probably cause quantitative and qualitative differences in hormonal secretion and thereby bring about a complex combination in the vegetative nervous system of stimulatory (sympathetic) and inhibitory (parasympathetic) responses.

Prognosis. Psychosomatic illnesses are relatively resistant to successful psychoanalytic treatment. However, there is considerable variety in the types of illnesses and the degree of psychogenic involvement. Certain organic illnesses with reversible psychosomatic symptoms are so commonly an accompaniment of psychoneurosis that cures incidental to the major problems of the neurosis are a common experience among practicing analysts. Chronic and intermittent constipation, anorexia, and other minor digestive tract ailments are regularly relieved as a secondary consequence of the analysis of neurotic conflicts. The alleviation of a variety of menstrual disorders and sometimes sterility of even long duration are commonly experienced as a concomitant of the resolution of emotional conflicts surrounding sexuality.

Analysis frequently has a therapeutic effect on a variety of other common complaints—constant colds, headaches, pseudopregnancy, insomnia, frequence of urination, and skin eruptions. The effect of psychoanalysis on more severe conditions—such as asthma, thyroid dysfunction, disturbances of the stomach and the intestines, and some skin diseases—can vary considerably from case to case. Possible reversibility of psychosomatic disease is a major consideration. If the disease process is irreversible, psychoanalysis may still be recommended, with the aim of trying to slow the destructive process. However, the somatic process may be not only irreversible but also impossible to halt. In such cases, the misery produced by the somatic disease and the social incapacitation have become the major problems, so that the original neurosis is of secondary importance.

Another important consideration in the treatment of psychosomatic disorders is that the disease process often functions as a substitute symptomatic formation for an underlying psychotic process. When the psychogenic components and the personality organization lie at primitive levels, not only is psychoanalysis contraindicated, but the induced regression and attempts to undo defenses in psychoanalysis can have a positively harmful effect and can precipitate or uncover the underlying psychotic process.

PERVERSIONS. The perversions include such behavioral entities as homosexuality, fetishism, transvestism, exhibitionism, voyeurism, and sadomasochism. The general mechanism of the perversions is thought to be a defensive flight from castration anxiety connected with fears of oedipal retaliation. In homosexuality, there is a flight from the positive oedipal configuration, in which the opposite-sex parent is loved and the same-sex parent feared, to the negative oedipal constellation, in which the opposite-sex parent is feared and the same-sex parent loved. In fetishism, the anxiety is avoided by displacement of instinctual libidinal impulses to an inanimate object that symbolizes parts of the body of the loved person. Consequently, neurotic interest is attached to an object or body part that is inappropriate for normal sexual gratification. The transvestite finds sexual excitement in dressing in garments of the opposite sex. Other perversions can similarly be seen as avoidances of the threat of castration anxiety.

Perversions are manifestly sexual in character. When the pathological impulses are released, orgasm is achieved. The sexual aim in adult perversions corresponds to components of sexual drives in children. But the genesis of perversions cannot be attributed solely to the hypertrophy of infantile, partial instincts. Factors of anxiety at phallic (castration) and pregenital levels, bisexuality, identifications, structural considerations, and external circumstances—all play parts in determining the genesis of perversions.

The defense against castration anxiety in the perversions takes the form of a regression to pregenital instinctual levels; there is a failure of the normal developmental process by which early instinctual expressions become integrated in the normal heterosexual phallic adjustment. Greater appreciation of the developmental vicissitudes underlying various forms of perverted behavior, however, has impressed on analysts the variety of early developmental failures and fixations that can contribute to the development of perverted behavior. Homosexuality, for example, may be a reflection of genital level phallic conflicts, but it can also reflect a wide variety of much earlier and more primitive developmental difficulties, including early symbiotically based difficulties in separating from the mother, resulting in a relatively intense feminine identification or overwhelming anxiety related to fears of engulfment and loss of a sense of self in any attempts to establish intimate or sexual relations with a woman. Consequently, the diagnostic assessment of the perversions, as in other forms of psychopathology, requires a careful assessment of underlying ego strengths and earlier developmental achievements, particularly in relation to the problem of separation and individuation (Socarides, 1974).

Sexual perversions often seem to be quite intractable, and the results achieved in the psychoanalytic treatment of, for example, overt homosexuality, have been disappointing. On the whole, the indications for psychoanalytic treatment for patients whose homosexuality is accompanied by psychoneurotic difficulties are much the same as they would be for heterosexual patients with neurotic difficulties. The results of treatment with respect to the neurotic symptoms of the homosexual patient are quite similiar. The alteration of a neurotic preference for one's own sex is by no means assured. The more indications, either conscious or repressed, of some heterosexual interest in the past history of the patient and the less completely the patient has adopted the psychological traits and habits of the other sex, the better is the prognosis. Generally, patients who find their perverse behavior ego-alien and who are relatively well motivated to undertake therapy and to rid themselves of this behavior pattern have the best chance for modification of the perversion and its psychodynamic roots.

Homosexuality. Homosexuality may be considered a vicissitude of the Oedipus complex in that the resolution of the oedipal conflict is based on negative oedipal constellations. The child has identified with the parent of the opposite sex and chosen the parent of the same sex as the love object. Narcissistic factors also play an important role in that the choice of an object is based, in part, on its sexual resemblance to the person himself. However, homosexuals have with justification resented being labeled as pathological. Much research is needed to determine the extent to which homosexual life choices are psychopathological or, rather, alternative sexual orientations that are made maladaptive because of intolerance by a predominately heterosexual society.

Fetishism. Fetishism refers to the veneration of inanimate objects that symbolize parts of the body of an ambivalently loved person. It is essentially a mental state that leads the person to worship or love a material object that is supposed to possess magical power or to be of special neurotic interest. In the analytic context, this mental state involves the fixation of erotic interest on an object or body part that is inappropriate for normal sexual purposes but that is needed by the person for the attainment of sexual gratification. These objects may be part of the body—such as hair, hand, or foot—or perhaps a shoe or handkerchief or other object of personal apparel. The fetish usually symbolizes the female phallus, and its use represents part of the fantasy denying the danger of castration suggested by the anatomical difference between the sexes. The inner state of mind of the fetishist involves a splitting of the ego; one part of his mind is able to assess and accept the absence of the penis in the female realistically, but another part of his mind unconsciously adheres to and asserts the idea that the female does, in fact, possess a phallus.

Transvestism. The transvestite finds dressing in garments characteristic of the opposite sex a source of sexual excitement. For the male transvestite, doing so can represent an identification with the phallic mother; for the female transvestite, it can serve similar functions in addition to her wish to deny the lack of a penis (penis envy).

Exhibitionism. Exhibitionism is the deliberate exposure, usually compulsive, of sex organs under inappropriate conditions. Exhibitionism is usually performed by men and is regarded as a defense against castration anxiety because of the effect of shock or fright on the female object at the sight of the penis.

Voyeurism. The voyeur achieves sexual gratification by watching the sexual activities of others.

Sadomasochism. Sadism and masochism, in the early formulations of the theory, were regarded as partial instincts. They often appear early in childhood and represent a tendency to seek out or inflict physical or mental suffering as a means of achieving sexual arousal or gratification. The masochistic perversion is a condition that makes sexual gratification contingent on physical or mental pain, such as beatings, threats, humiliations, or subjugation at the hands of the sexual partner. Conversely, sadism gains sexual gratification by inflicting such torment on the sexual partner. The extension of sadomasochism into the formation of character can serve as the basis for neurotic dispositions. Moral masochism, for example, represents an unconscious or conscious need for punishment that can underlie anxiety states or self-destructive behavior. It may be related to an unconscious sense of guilt and can often be precipitated by situations that normally lead to gratification or an increase of self-esteem. Such masochistic inclinations can be involved in the frustration of therapeutic achievements, which is involved in a negative therapeutic reaction.

OTHER SYMPTOMATIC NEUROSES. Overt sexual symptoms, such as impotence based on psychic factors and impaired capacity for mature sexual love, usually represent the repression of fundamental conflicts in early object relationships and are often permanently relieved through psychoanalysis. However, other symptomatic psychoneuroses—such as adult enuresis, tics, and stammering—may be much more resistant to modification. Such symptoms are usually definite indications for psychoanalytic treatment, and treatment usually produces important alterations in basic personality problems, even though the chronically established abnormal muscle habits may not be entirely eliminated.

Character disorders. The psychoanalytic sense of character refers to the person's habitual mode of bringing into harmony the tasks presented by internal demands and the external world. When and how the person acquires the qualities that make it possible to adjust, first, to the demands of instinctual drives and of external reality and, later, to the demands of the superego and how this adjustment is accomplished in varying degrees and styles in terms of the functioning and adaptability of the ego could be the subject of a separate treatise. The description of pathological character types can be complex and confusing, since discrete personality types are rarely found in pure or discrete forms; there is considerable overlap with other character types.

Contemporary psychoanalysis is taken up with the diagnosis and treatment of character types more extensively than with any other aspect of psychopathology. When patients present with symptomatic complaints, these complaints are frequently relieved early in the treatment process, but, as treatment progresses, the problems of the underlying character structure increasingly become the focus of analytic treatment. There is a trend, often detectable in the course of therapy, from a focus on the issues of symptom formation to a focus on the problems of internal character structure, along with its concomitant issues of object relations. More prominently than in any other area of disability, the character disorders reveal their malfunctioning in the area of object relationships.

DEFINITION. A particular character pattern or type becomes pathological when its manifestations are exaggerated to the point that behavior destructive to the person or to others is the result or when the functioning of the person becomes so disturbed or restricted that it becomes a source of distress to him or to others. Characterological traits tend to be nearly life long and are usually deeply embedded in the organization of the person's personality. The character types are usually classified in terms of associated symptomatic expression. Character disorders are also known as personality disorders.

CLASSIFICATION

Hysterical character. Hysterical characters tend to sexualize all relationships. They tend toward suggestibility, irrational emotional outbreaks, chaotic behavior, dramatization, and histrionic activity. As Chodoff and Lyons (1958) wrote, the term can be applied

to persons who are vain and egocentric, who display labile and excitable but shallow affectivity, whose dramatic, attention-seeking and histrionic behavior may go to the extremes of lying and even pseudologia phantastica, who are very conscious of sex, sexually

provocative yet frigid, and who are dependently demanding in interpersonal situations.

Hysterical character need not be associated with hysterical symptoms, whether of conversion or dissociation. Hysterical characters may never experience conversion or dissociative reactions. On the other hand, hysterical reactions or symptoms may be found in a variety of character types—including passive-aggressive, schizoid, narcissistic, and borderline forms of personality organization—in addition to hysterical personalities.

Phobic character. These persons limit their reactive behavior to the avoidance of the situations that they wished for originally. Certain external situations are avoided, as in neurotic phobic behavior. In addition, however, internal reactions—such as rage, love, and all intense feelings—may be subjected to phobic avoidance.

Compulsive character. The obsessive-compulsive character, like his neurotic counterpart, tends to use defenses of reaction formation, isolation, and intellectualization in an attempt to control emotional conflicts. Typically, he attempts to overcome sadism by kindness and politeness and to conceal pleasure in dirt by rigorous cleanliness. He may show significant degrees of obsessional and compulsive ritualization or ritual actions. As a result of isolation, there is a lack of adequate affective response and a restriction in the number of available modes of feeling. Object relationships are usually of an anal-sadistic nature.

Depressive character. The depressive character may show the characteristics of the depressive neurosis on a more perduring and chronic, if more low-keyed, basis. Chronically low self-esteem and feelings of worthlessness are characteristic of this syndrome. Very often, there is a history of early object loss or severe deprivation, often involving the loss of one or the other parent. The depressive neuroses often have to do with object loss or narcissistic injury; the syndrome of depressive character relates more specifically to ego deficiencies and inadequacies.

Cyclical character. These persons exhibit periodic mood swings, from depression to varying degress of elation. Cyclical characters are particularly concerned with unresolved oral needs and conflicts. They are basically depressive characters who have been able to mobilize manic defenses, analogous to the cyclic alteration between depressive and manic phases in manic-depressive psychosis.

Passive-aggressive character. Passive-aggressive personalities are characterized by passive or submissive behavior as ways of expressing hostile or destructive feelings or intentions. Such behaviors are usually directed at others on whom they feel dependent or subordinate. They include disinterest, withdrawal, negativism, obstructionism, inefficiency, procrastination, sabotage, perfunctory behavior, errors of omission, indifference, foot dragging, lack of initiative, literalness in compliant behavior that frustrates the outcome, and a variety of other passive behaviors. Any hostile or negative intent is denied, although there may be angry outbursts from time to time.

Impulse-ridden character. The impulse-ridden character, who is frequently encountered in psychiatric practice, eventually discharges tension or avoids inner conflict by urgent activity, which is sometimes of a destructive or self-destructive nature.

The above group of character disorders can be regarded as the higher order of character pathology insofar as they generally reflect a reasonably well-organized ego and superego and have conflicts that pertain primarily to the phallic level of instinctual development. These higher order forms of character pathology provide the major area of effective psychoanalytic therapeutic intervention.

There is also a group of lower order character pathologies in which the developmental impediments and failures lie at a much more primitive and predominantly pregenital level. These patients generally show significant defects in ego and superego development and have significant difficulties in object relationships. This group of lower order character pathologies includes the narcissistic characters, the schizoid characters, and the borderline personalities.

The most useful division of character pathology has been provided by Kernberg (1970). He included the hysterical characters, obsessive-compulsive characters, and depressive-masochistic characters in his highest level of character pathology. He described this level in the following terms:

At the higher level, the patient has a relatively well integrated but severe and punitive superego. The forerunners of his superego are determined by too sadistic impulses, bringing about a harsh, perfectionistic superego. His ego, too, is well integrated; ego identity and its related components, a stable self-concept, and a stable representational world being well established. Excessive defensive operations against unconscious conflicts center around repression. The character defenses are largely of an inhibitory or phobic nature, or they are reaction formations against repressed instinctual needs. There is very little or no instinctual infiltration into the defensive character traits. The patient's ego at this level is somewhat limited and constricted by its excessive use of neurotic defense mechanisms, but the patient's overall social adaptation is not seriously impaired. He has fairly deep, stable object-relationships and is capable of experiencing guilt, mourning, and a wide variety of affective responses. His sexual and/or aggressive drive derivatives are partially inhibited, but these instinctual conflicts have reached the stage where the infantile genital phase and oedipal conflicts are clearly predominant and there is no pathological condensation of genital sexual strivings with pregenital, aggressively determined strivings in which the latter predominate.

At the intermediate level of character pathology, Kernberg emphasized the defective integration of the superego, which is unable to tolerate contradictory demands between sadistic, prohibitive superego nuclei on the one hand and rather primitive, magical, and somewhat idealizing nuclei on the other. Kernberg went on to say:

Deficient superego integration can also be observed in the partial projections of superego nuclei (as expressed in the patient's decreased capacity for experiencing guilt and in paranoid trends), contradictions in the ego's value systems, and severe mood swings.... The poor integration of the superego, which is reflected in contradictory unconscious demands on the ego, also explains the appearance of pathological character defenses combining reaction formations against instincts with a partial expression of instinctual impulses.... Repression is still the main defensive operation of the ego, together with related defenses such as intellectualization, rationalization, and undoing. At the same time, the patient shows some dissociative trends, some defensive splitting of the ego in limited areas (that is, mutual dissociation of contradictory ego states), and projection and denial. Pregenital, especially oral conflicts come to the fore, although the genital level of libidinal development has been reached.

Under this group Kernberg included the oral types of character pathology, including passive-aggressive personalities, sadomasochistic personalities, some infantile personalities, and some narcissistic personalities.

At the lower level of character pathology, structural deficits and their developmental consequences are even more severe. Kernberg wrote:

At the lower level, the patient's superego integration is minimal and his propensity for projection of primitive, sadistic superego nuclei is maximal. His capacity for experiencing concern and guilt is seriously impaired, and his basis for self-criticism constantly fluctuates. The individual at this level commonly exhibits paranoid traits, stemming both from projection of superego nuclei and from the excessive use of rather primitive forms of projections, especially projective identification as one major defense mechanism of the ego.... The synthetic function of the patient's ego is seriously impaired, and he uses primitive dissociation or splitting as the central defensive operation of the ego

instead of repression.... His pathological character defenses are predominantly of an "impulsive," instinctually infiltrated kind; contradictory, repetitive patterns of behavior are dissociated from each other, permitting direct release of drive derivatives as well as of reaction formations against these drives. Lacking an integrated ego and the capacity to tolerate guilt feelings, such patients have little need for secondary rationalizations of pathological character traits.... Their inability to integrate libidinally determined and aggressively determined self- and object images is reflected in their maintaining object-relationships of either a need-gratifying or a threatening nature. They are unable to have empathy for objects in their totality; object relationships are of a part object type, and object constancy has not been reached.... The absence of both an integrated world of total, internalized objects and of a stable self-concept determine the presence of the syndrome of identity diffusion. In fact, identity diffusion is an outstanding characteristic of this lower level of character pathology. The lack of integration of libidinal and aggressive strivings contributes to a general lack of neutralization of instinctual energy, and to a severe restriction of the conflict-free ego.

Included in this bracket of character pathologies are the infantile personalities, many narcissistic personalities, antisocial personalities, the more chaotic impulse-ridden characters, the as-if characters, other patients with multiple sexual deviations in combination with drug addiction or alcoholism and pathological object relationships, and other forms of schizoid and paranoid personality.

Narcissistic character. The narcissistic character presents a pathological picture that is characterized by an excessive degree of self-reference in interaction with others, an excessive need to be loved and admired by others, and apparently contradictory attitudes of an inflated concept of himself and an inordinate need for tribute and admiration from others. The emotional life of the narcissistic character is usually shallow. He experiences little empathy for others, and there is little reward in his activities beyond the admiration he receives from others. When the external glamour wears off and there are no new sources of reward to feed his self-regard, he becomes restless, bored, and disinterested. Envy is a strong characteristic of the narcissistic character. He often tends to idealize those from whom he expects narcissistic rewards and, conversely, depreciates, devalues, and treats with contempt those from whom he cannot expect such rewards. His relationships with other people are often exploitative and manipulative. He seems to feel that he has the right to control and possess others and to exploit them without guilt. Behind a façade that is often charming and engaging, there is a coldness and a ruthlessness that one senses, rather than sees. Although his need for admiration often makes him appear to be dependent, he characteristically has a deep distrust of others.

Some of these patients present strong conscious feelings of inadequacy and inferiority. The feelings of inferiority and insecurity may at times alternate with feelings of importance, specialness, and omnipotent fantasies. Especially after a period of analysis, unconscious fantasies of omnipotence and narcissistic grandiosity are evident. Such extreme contradictions of self-concept are often the first clinical manifestations of the level of pathology and structural impairment of ego and superego hidden beneath a veneer of smooth and effective social functioning.

In the course of analysis of such narcissistic characters, temporary regressive episodes may suggest an underlying psychotic process if one is not aware of the narcissistic organization of the patient's personality. Although the content, including paranoid suspiciousness or bodily delusions, may justify some apprehension, the regressions tend not to be viewed with alarm, either by the patient or by the analyst. Despite the transient regressions, the over-all picture of personality functioning remains much more coherent and reassuring.

Narcissistic personality disturbances must be distinguished from borderline and psychotic states. Insofar as narcissistic characters suffer from disturbances in the organization of the self and the archaic objects cathected with narcissistic libido, their pathology is based on narcissistic fixation to archaic self-images or representations. These narcissistically cathected introjects have not been integrated with the rest of the personality organization; the capacity for mature object relatedness and functioning is impoverished because of the intense investment of energy in the self. In addition, the reality orientation of such persons is interfered with by the intrusion of primitive narcissistic demands.

However, the narcissistic character disorders differ markedly from the borderline or psychotic states. Narcissistic character patients have attained a cohesive and organized self, and they are not threatened by the possibility of an irreversible decompensation of the organization of the self or of narcissistically cathected objects. Since the psychic organization is able to maintain cohesive and stable psychic representations, narcissistic characters are able to establish quite stable transferences, even though the transferences are of a highly narcissistic quality. The presence of such stable narcissistic configurations in the transference marks this area of psychopathology off from the borderline and psychotic states.

Narcissistic character disorders may seem to be affected by a fear of loss of the object or of the object's love and by castration anxiety. The primacy of these elements is quite opposite to what is usually found in the transference neurosis. In the transference neuroses, castration anxiety is the leading source of neurotic difficulty. Fear of the loss of the love of the object and fear of the loss of the object itself take secondary roles in frequency and significance. The order is reversed, however, in the narcissistic disorders, with fear of the loss of the object assuming a primary position and castration anxiety a secondary position. Thus, the narcissistic character displays a peculiar vulnerability.

If the object threatens punishment or abandonment or withdrawal of love and loss of the object, the result is a narcissistic imbalance or defect in the patient, for whom the maintenance of self-cohesiveness and self-esteem depends on the presence of a rewarding and approving object or on an object that provides some other form of narcissistic supply. In the transference neuroses, however, the object is cathected with object libido and the fear is a fear of punishment. The anxieties over object retaliation predominate, with only a secondary injury to narcissism or a diminution of self-esteem.

For the most part narcissistic character disorders are treatable by psychoanalysis, but they do not respond well to the classical technique; certain modifications of technique are necessary to bring treatment to a successful resolution. What must be taken into account in the treatment of such patients is the basically narcissistic nature of the transference, as distinguished from and opposed to the object-libidinal nature of the transference in the classical transference neuroses.

At the lowest level of character organization, the predominant forms are the schizoid personality and the borderline personality. In both of these personality configurations, conflict and developmental fixation tend to be at a very early pregenital level, and the basic conflicts are of a relatively primitive object relations type. The underlying conflicts for both personality types tend to be similar, but the pathological organizations of defenses tend to follow different lines. The schizoid personality tends to follow an obsessional pattern of defense; the schizoid may be regarded as a more primitive or genetically earlier form of obsessional pathology. Many schizoid personalities tend to use obsessional defenses and often present clinically as obsessive-compulsive personalities. Borderline patients tend to follow a hysterical form of defensive organization; the borderline patient may be regarded as a primitive form of hysterial pathology. Many borderline patients present with hysterical features, except that these manifestations are more poorly organized and chaotic and more readily susceptible to regression.

Schizoid character. The schizoid character often presents with a complaint of depression. He complains of feeling cut off, of being isolated and out of touch, of feeling apart or estranged from people and things around him, of feeling that things are somehow unreal, of diminishing interest in things and events around him, of feeling that life is futile and meaningless. Patients often call this state of mind "depression," but it lacks the inner sense of anger and guilt often found in depression. Depression is, moreover, often a struggle for the patient not to turn his aggression outward into overt angry and destructive behavior. Depression is essentially object related. But the schizoid character has renounced objects.

In the schizoid condition external relationships have been emptied by a massive withdrawal of libidinal attachment. The patient's ego is emptied of vital feeling and action, and it seems to have become unreal. The attitude to the outside world is one of noninvolvement and mere observation at a distance without any feeling. The schizoid state may alternate with depression and can be confusingly mixed with it. The schizoid's major defense against anxiety is to keep emotionally out of reach, inaccessible, isolated. The schizoid condition, then, consists of an attempt to cancel external object relations and to live in a detached and withdrawn manner. The depressive dilemma is that of anger directed toward a love object; the expression of anger against the object would destroy the loved object, so that anger must be turned against the self. The schizoid dilemma, however, is different; it is the dilemma of destructive love, the anxiety of destroying and losing the love object through being so devouring, hungry, greedy, and needy. The schizoid person can exist neither in a relationship with another person nor out of it without in various ways risking the loss of both the object and himself. Love relationships, consequently, are seen as mutually devouring and destructive.

The basic defect of the schizoid character lies at the earliest level of the introjection of primary objects. The schizoid condition is based on the internalization of hostile, destructive introjects. These internalized, unconscious objects remain locked away within the psyche, where they remain always rejecting, indifferent, or hostile. The resulting negative introject remains a focus for feelings of inner worthlessness, vileness, destructiveness, and evil and malicious power.

The schizoid character is not far removed from the narcissistic character disorder. They often overlap considerably in their clinical description and in their underlying psychodynamics. The schizoid pathology often shows markedly narcissistic characteristics. The cold and isolated self-sufficiency of the schizoid personality often expresses an inner grandiosity that reflects severe pathological roots in the grandiose self. This brand of grandiose self-sufficiency often makes such patients relatively inaccessible to therapeutic intervention. The core difference between the schizoid character and the narcissistic character may well be that the schizoid's character is taken up with a world of objects that are entirely within, and the narcissistic character is at least taken up with external objects, if only to the degree that they are invested with narcissistic cathexis. The schizoid character, consequently, must be regarded as the more severe and less treatable form of psychopathology.

Alcoholic and addictive personalities. Problems of alcoholism and addiction in general form a significant and perplexing proportion of contemporary character disorders. Such personalities tend to show a predominance of oral traits and can often be classified under the narcissistic or schizoid character disorders or the borderline personality organization, often showing a combination of characteristic qualities of these forms of character pathology. Because of the primitive nature of the addictive character and the predominance of orality, along with its attendant depressive pathology, alcoholic and addictive personalities are frequently poor risks for psychoanalytic treatment.

Delinquent and criminal personalities. Delinquent and criminal personality types are not specifically psychoanalytic categories. However, these personalities frequently show a high incidence of antisocial and even paranoid characteristics. The specific character pathology can reflect a broad spectrum of character disorders. Delinquency problems, particularly when they reflect developmental vicissitudes and are not reflections of severe ego pathology, can be readily and successfully treated by a psychoanalytic approach. However, these forms of pathology are complexly and intimately involved in social and environmental influences.

PROGNOSIS. The character disorders are treatable when they are allied to hysterical or obsessive-compulsive neurosis. Both hysterical and obsessive-compulsive characters manifest a variety of traits of definite neurotic origin. When these traits are a conspicuous and persistent source of tribulation for the patient and for the people in his environment, they constitute positive indications for psychoanalysis.

Some of the more common traits are uncontrollable temper, chronic nagging, constant complaints about others, excessive diffidence or feelings of inferiority, inclinations to change occupations repeatedly, recurrent unsolved work problems, a succession of unhappy love affairs, inability to concentrate at work, inability to derive pleasure from recreation or avocation, and inability to form friendships. Particularly common in these cases are complaints of marital discord, which is either the result of a neurotic choice of partner or a neurotic reaction to a more maturely selected spouse.

Today, neurotic character disorders are seen in treatment far more commonly than the symptomatic neuroses. The character disorders comprise a large portion of the population for whom analysis can be recommended.

Narcissistic characters can be significantly helped and even, to an extent, transformed by analysis, but the therapeutic prognosis is extremely variable and in many cases guarded. The more evidence there is in the narcissistic disorders of the presence of problems that are definitely psychoneurotic, in combination with the narcissistic traits, the more favorable is the prognosis for such patients. On the other hand, the prognosis is especially poor for extremely dependent personalities who are very unassertive and readily accept entirely dependent and passive relationships. This is often the case in primitive narcissistic disorders.

Mild schizoid characters can also be helped by analysis, but the analysis of such patients usually requires special parameters, and they should never be treated by analysts who lack general psychiatric experience. This caution is also advisable for patients who demonstrate even moderate degrees of paranoid symptoms. The more serious disturbances—such as alcoholism, drug addiction, psychopathic personality, and criminality—have occasionally been helped by analysis. But, all too often, the benefits of analytic therapy are limited by the infantile demands of these patients and their inability to tolerate frustration or to tolerate delay of gratification. Their ego functions are seriously impaired, and their reality sense is often defective.

Classical psychoanalysis is a completely appropriate treatment for the character neuroses. It can produce a far more complete and fundamental reorganization of the neurotic personality than other psychotherapeutic techniques currently in existence. But in other forms of psychopathology, the usefulness of psychoanalysis as a treatment is limited. The potential usefulness of the approach depends on the extent and the degree to which specifically neurotic elements are made part of the characterological condition.

Borderline personality organization. The diagnosis of borderline states has been gradually clarified in recent years. Such patients were often regarded as a variety of ambulatory schizophrenia and were frequently labeled as preschizophrenics or psychotic characters or pseudoneurotic schizophrenics. They were viewed as relatively compensated schizophrenics who tended to regress to psychotic levels as a transient reaction to stress or to toxic influences. The present view, however, is that they represent a stable form of personality organization that is intermediate between neurotic levels of integration and the more primitive psychotic forms of personality organization.

They have a typical constellation of symptoms and defenses and a typical pattern of defect in their object relations.

The borderline patient presents a variety of neurotic symptoms and character defects. Anxiety is usually chronic and diffuse. Neurotic symptoms are multiple and include multiple phobias, obsessive thoughts and behaviors, conversion symptoms, dissociative reactions, hypochondriacal complaints, and paranoid traits. Sexuality is frequently promiscuous and often perverse. Personality organization tends to be impulsive and infantile, and the imperative need to gratify impulses breaks through episodically, giving the borderline life style an acting-out quality. A turning to alcohol or drugs for relief of tension and gratification is a frequent feature of this character disorder, and addictive personalities often have a borderline structure. Narcissism is often a predominant element in the character structure, and the patient frequently looks clinically very much like a narcissistic character. Underlying these elements is often a core of paranoia based on the projection of a rather primitive oral rage. The underlying character dimensions may also take the form of severe depressive-masochistic pathology. The paranoid and depressive-masochistic traits are often closely related and may alternate in the patient.

The inner organization of the borderline personality reveals the weakness in the structure of the ego. The patient shows a marked lack of tolerance for even low degrees of anxiety, has poor capacity for impulse control, lacks suitable channels for sublimation, has a poor capacity for neutralization, and often shows a generalized shift toward primary process cognitive organization. The last aspect is not usually detectable in the usual mental status examination but may be revealed on projective test material.

It is difficult for the patient to engage in a productive therapeutic relationship. Frustration tolerance is low, and narcissistic expectations and entitlements are high. The therapeutic interaction is often distorted by attempts to manipulate the therapist in order to gain needed gratification. The manipulation often takes the form of a suicidal gesture aimed at getting the therapist to comply with the patient's wishes. Consequently, therapy with a borderline patient can often be very trying and difficult. Also characteristic of the borderline personality is the intensity and chaotic quality of the transference involvement, which can often alternate quickly between, on the one hand, excessive idealizing and dependence on the therapist and, on the other hand, devaluation of the therapist and impulsive withdrawal from therapy. This quality of the transference involvement is quite different from that found in the narcissistic personality, which is often much more remote and distant, particularly if the narcissistic personality is caught up in needs for grandiose isolation.

A characteristic defense of the borderline patient is splitting. This defense is also seen to a significant degree in the schizoid personality. Splitting involves the separation between the good introjects, derived from satisfying object experiences, and the bad introjects, derived from frustrating or rejecting object experiences. Splitting stems from a preambivalent level of development and prevents the child from integrating his objects into ambivalent (good and bad) objects and correlatively prevents him from achieving an integration of good and bad internalized objects. The operations of introjection and projection maintain the internal splitting and leave the ego with a poorly developed tolerance for ambivalence, whether internal or external. There is also a correlative intolerance for anxiety. The persistence of splitting has two important consequences: First, it prevents the neutralization of aggressive drive components, and second, it provides a persistent ego defect or weakness.

From the developmental point of view, the borderline patient has not successfully reached a level of triadic oedipal conflicts that is characteristic of psychoneurotic or higher order character disorders. The issues are more primitive and stem from preoedipal levels in which the developmental vicissitudes of affective one-to-one relationships with the parents have been ineffectively resolved. This inability to resolve the ambivalence toward separate parental objects prevents their being regarded as separate and whole objects, so the transition to the oedipal involvement is impeded. There is general agreement that the level of developmental defect in borderline patients lies somewhere in the area of separation and individuation. Mahler (1971) has suggested that the most likely phase in which the borderline fixations and defects occur is that of the rapprochement subphase. Among developmental theorists, the maintenance of separate and contradictory self-configurations is thought to reflect a failure of developmental integration and synthesis, rather than one of defensive splitting, as in Kernberg's view.

The importance of accurate diagnosis of borderline patients cannot be underestimated, since such patients often present as apparently normal or with symptoms that amply justify a more benign diagnosis of neurotic personality structure. Often, the borderline features reveal themselves only after a period of psychoanalysis or psychotherapy, when a certain amount of regression has taken place or when the distinctive quality of the patient's object relations and their relation to splitting mechanisms become more apparent.

It is important to distinguish between levels of borderline functioning. Some borderline patients with quite good levels of ego functioning tend to experience severe emotional difficulties in relatively restricted object-related contexts and regress to levels of borderline functioning quite slowly. These patients are the ones who may initially look neurotic or even normal and only begin to show borderline characteristics as a result of analytic regression. Their disorders may be regarded as higher order forms of character pathology within the borderline spectrum. These patients may well be analyzable, often with the introduction of parameters to the analytic situation. Other borderline patients have more diffusely disorganized ego functioning, manifest splitting more readily, are not able to tolerate anxiety or frustration, regress more easily, and tend to act out in destructive and self-defeating ways. Such patients represent a lower order organization within the borderline spectrum; they have poor tolerance for the regression and object relations conflicts inherent in analysis. Diagnosis in terms of potential analyzability in this group of patients is of primary importance.

Borderline patients are generally not regarded as suitable for psychoanalytic treatment. Such personalities cannot generally sustain their capacity for effective therapeutic work in the face of the induced regression of the analytic situation. However, they often do surprisingly well in a psychoanalytically oriented psychotherapeutic setting, in which they are able to establish a working alliance and that involves a capacity for firm limit setting on the part of the therapist.

From a developmental perspective, the borderline patient does not have to deal primarily with the triadic oedipal issues that are characteristic of psychoneurotic patients. Rather, the issues stem from a more primitive, preoedipal level, in which the developmental vicissitudes of a one-to-one relationship must be worked out. The primary prop of the therapy of borderline patients rests on the real one-to-one relationship that is established between the therapist and the patient. The context of such a firm and trusting relationship, the difficulties of magical expectations, impairments of the distinctions between fantasy and reality, episodes of anger and suspicion and excessive fear of rejection, and the conflicts stemming from the destructive, bad internalized objects can be gradually and productively worked through. The stability and solidity of the therapeutic alliance are important, since the borderline integration is fragile and somewhat precarious,

often subject to regressive pulls, and dependent on external support for its stabilization.

Perhaps the most telling and difficult area in the therapy of borderline patients is that of termination. Because of the developmental failure, the borderline patient has a limited and vulnerable capacity to internalize ego identifications. His internalizing capacity remains more or less on an introjective level, and he is unable to reach the healthier and more autonomous level of identification. This basic impairment in ego capacity sets a limit on the effectiveness of therapy. The patient may achieve a considerable degree of behavioral modification and stabilization of affect and may reach quite well-organized levels of psychic functioning and capacity for healthier and less conflicted relationships, but the capacity for regression to pretreatment levels of functioning remains a prominent element in the over-all picture. Moreover, the patient's markedly defective capacity for internalization impedes his capacity to separate effectively from the therapist. In analysis, treatment of such a patient seems to drag on interminably. In psychotherapy, the optimal course for such a patient is often a gradual attenuation of the therapeutic involvement, slowly spacing out therapeutic contact until the patient is in more or less minimal if, nonetheless, persistent contact with the therapist. In a real sense, such therapies often never end.

THEORY OF PSYCHOSIS

Early Concepts (1893–1923)

The most important findings to emerge from the psychoanalytic clinical investigations of the neuroses were the existence of an unconscious mental life and the description of its effects on conscious thought, symptoms, and behavior. On the basis of these data, Freud was able to demonstrate that the biological concept of adaptation has a valid application for all mental disorders. This notion led to Freud's insight into the purposefulness of psychosis. He suggested that psychosis may be best understood as the patient's mode of adapting to his emotional and realistic needs and to the environmental stresses with which he is confronted. Freud offered clinical evidence to support this hypothesis by demonstrating that a definite psychotic symptom—namely, hallucination—serves a useful restitutive purpose.

Freud's own experience with psychotic patients was relatively limited. He cited only a small number of cases from his own experience. His classic analysis of paranoid schizophrenia, the case of Daniel Paul Schreber, was based on the Schreber *Memoirs* and did not involve any direct clinical contact with the patient himself. Perhaps the greatest contribution that Freud made to the psychology of psychosis came from his study of dream processes. He pointed out that both the dream and psychotic thought are representative of a primitive cognitive organization, one characteristic of infantile levels of development and of animistic stages of thinking, which antedate the differentiation of autistic and objective experiences.

This application of the investigation of dream processes to schizophrenic thought was developed in detail by Carl Jung, and his formulations enabled other workers to demonstrate the validity of the basic concept—that delusions and hallucinations, like dreams, are prelogical (primary process) forms of thinking. In a number of his views, Freud was essentially dependent on the observations of those of his followers, like Abraham and Jung, who had more extensive general psychiatric experience, particularly with psychotic patients. Some of Freud's judgments about patients therefore, were misguided—for example, his view that schizophrenic patients are incapable of forming transferences due to a withdrawal of object libido. Psychoanalysts today are much more aware of the intensity of schizophrenic transference relationships and of the intensely ambivalent and destructive nature of the feelings generated within them.

Studies of Paranoid Psychosis

Freud originally directed his attention to paranoid symptoms as manifestations of psychotic processes. His understanding of the mental symptoms of paranoia was greatly facilitated by the discovery of unconscious homosexuality and the mechanisms of projection. His theoretical formulations regarding this form of psychopathology were based on clinical experience to only a limited degree. But he acquired considerable insight into these mechanisms as a result of his careful analysis of the Schreber *Memoirs,* an autobiographical account of Schreber's paranoid psychosis and his elaborate delusional system. Schreber, in fact, did not recover from his paranoid decompensation and finally died in a mental asylum. Freud had never met him and never had any contact with him.

In essence, Freud's analysis of the Schreber case was an elaborate attempt to impose the basic theory of repression and return of the repressed on the paranoid material contained in Schreber's *Memoirs.* Freud postulated that in paranoia, the need to project coincides with an unconscious impulse to homosexual love, which, though of overwhelming intensity, is unconsciously denied by the patient. Paranoid delusions represent sexual conflicts concerning persons of the same sex that have been projected onto some other object or force, which is then perceived as persecuting or threatening.

Other workers emphasized the close relationship of paranoid symptoms to infantile fantasies, in which feces are personalized and considered animistically as dangerous entities that are highly powerful and destructive and threatening to the person. In this connection the relationship between paranoia and a stage of development in which the emotions are centered on a particular part of the object's body, rather than on the total person, was demonstrated by Karl Abraham. Abraham also noted that paranoid psychosis resembles certain phases of melancholia in that the patient's fantasies indicate a desire to incorporate the object. However, paranoid psychosis differs from melancholia; in paranoia, the hostility is directed against part of the object, rather than the whole, and the paranoiac has fantasies that this incorporated part object can be destroyed and eliminated by defecation.

The concurrent demonstration of the relationship of primitive fantasies of aggression to overwhelming anxiety and the need to project facilitated further understanding of this clinical entity. One question, however, remained unanswered: Why had the homosexuality of the paranoid patient become so intense, threatening, and intolerable to the patient? This question was not examined or explained by Freud or his followers. Recent studies of paranoid psychosis and even of the Schreber case itself have tended to shift the emphasis away from homosexual dynamics and have emphasized broader and more complex issues relating to defects in ego development and dynamic conditions of primitive narcissistic traumatization and resulting narcissistic rage in the genesis of paranoid states.

Narcissism in the Psychoses

In his classic paper, *On Narcissism,* Freud stated that psychosis is characterized by the patient's incapacity for normal emotional interest in other people and things. He felt that the psychotic process does not represent a total depletion of libido but, rather, that it involves a redistribution of libido that is normally devoted to object love and to self-love. The energy withdrawn from impoverished object relationships produces an abnormally excessive interest in the self, increasing the degree of cathexis of both bodily functions and the psychic attributes of the self. The psychotic patient's use of language indicates a high cathectic interest in the verbal symbol, rather than in the object that the word represents. Many of the more obvious symptoms of psychosis can be considered secondary to this primary loss of the capacity for object attachment. As Freud saw it, they are essentially rudimentary and primitive efforts to reestablish and reconstitute some degree of relationship with external objects. The psychotic regression to earlier levels of mental functioning and development is manifested not only in prelogical thought patterns but also in the fact that the psychotic patient extracts pleasurable experience chiefly from his own sensory experience, without requiring reciprocal relationships between himself and another person.

Psychotic states represent conditions of extreme and archaic narcissistic disorganization. The narcissism of the psychotic patient is of an extremely primitive and oral variety, and the frustration of his intense narcissistic demands results in an extremely primitive and highly destructive and potent narcissistic rage. The conspicuous elements in the clinical picture in most psychotic states consist of fragments of the intact personality and incomplete phases of psychotic regressions, along with efforts at restitution. It was Freud's view that the delusions, hallucinations, and certain forms of disorganized behavior are secondary phenomena that represent rudimentary efforts on the part of the patient to restore some semblance or to substitute for lost object relations.

Current Concepts

Subsequent investigations have followed Freud's suggestion that the conflicts that result in psychotic adaptations occur primarily between the person and his environment. In contrast, the conflicts characteristic of the psychoneuroses are primarily within the personality, between unconscious infantile wishes and the constraining or controlling forces that adapt those wishes to the constraints and demands of reality. Recent work has focused in detail on the disturbances and disorganizations in ego functioning that impair the patient's relationship with reality. The psychoses are seen as resulting from defects in the ego's integrative (synthetic) capacities; from a defect in the ego's capacity for fusion and, consequently, from limitations in the ego's capacity to neutralize instinctual energies; from the ineffectiveness of those functions essential to the capacity for establishing real object relations; and from the impairment of functions essential for controlling intense infantile wishes by normal or neurotic mechanisms.

Investigations of the ego's adaptive capacities have shown that the psychotic, unlike the neurotic, needs to adapt in a way that enables him to avoid anxiety. However, the psychotic adjustment uses primitive types of defense that normally predominate at levels of development before more advanced degrees of personality organization. Psychotic defenses—particularly denial, distortion, and projection—tend to be of a more primitive and narcissistic type. The primitive defenses are reflected in flight, social withdrawal, and the simple inhibition of impulses (blocking) that is apparent in many psychotics. These defense mechanisms are much less highly organized than the higher order mechanisms of repression and reaction formation. The fear of detection by others, rather than the guilt of later childhood and maturity, is more conspicuous in the social reactions of the psychotic than in the neurotic. Limited patterns of imitation and introjection—that is, the adoption and organization of patterns with elements of behavior and affect that were originally perceived as details of other people's behavior—play important roles in the development of psychosis. These patterns derive from emotional relations and early reactions to other people that have played a conspicuous role in the development of the psychotic patient's ego capacities.

The pathology of psychosis is related to the primitive impairment of internalization processes. Certain forms of character pathology can be understood in terms of their structural components as involving an impairment of internalization processes and a failure of basic introjective mechanisms to reach levels of integration and organization that permit the establishment of solid ego structures through the implementation and induction of positive ego identifications. This form of pathology is frequently striking in the structural organization of the narcissistic character disorders, the schizoid disorders, and the borderline personalities. The essential defect in the psychotic disorders is related to this level of pathology, but in the psychotic process the level of fixation is considerably more primitive—deriving from a disruption and distortion in earliest context of mother-child interaction, the organization of introjects is more fragile and less coherent, the degree of instinctual diffusion is much more severe and primitive, the susceptibility to regressive pulls is much more profound and easily accomplished, the resultant splitting of the ego is considerably more profound and radical and leaves the ego in a severely fragmented, vulnerable, and weakened condition.

The development of greater understanding and of more effective therapeutic techniques that bear a more specific relationship to causative factors must wait for the accumulation of further knowledge regarding the primitive ego of the child and the phases and processes that influence its development. Recent approaches have focused on the defects of object relations at these earliest phases and their debilitating influence on ego development. Other studies of the development of the ego's capacity to transform primitive drives into socially useful functions (sublimation and neutralization) and of the factors that interfere with the development of this crucial ego capacity have enhanced the understanding of the pathogenesis of psychosis.

With respect to treatment, modifications in the basic free association method have made possible an approach to a variety of psychotic states and to the problem of vulnerability and the predisposition to psychosis. However, many of these initial concepts are still in a state of transition. Moreover, in addition to the psychodynamic factors that are the proper realm of psychoanalytic consideration, other constitutional and genetic factors influence the basic predisposition to patterns of psychotic development. These factors are being actively studied by students of genetics, and the findings of genetic psychiatry have important and significant implications for the basic understanding and ultimate capability for management of psychotic states. They do not, however, alter or minimize the significance of psychodynamic aspects of the psychotic process.

Classification

Hypochondriasis. The actual neuroses (Freud's term, which he used to describe hypochondriasis, neurasthenia, and anxiety neurosis) have ceased to be a significant part of psychoanalytic nosology. These clinical syndromes can now be recognized as phases of ego regression or phases in a return to optimal ego functioning. Yet they are rarely referred to in the literature. Hypochondriasis, which Freud originally included among the actual neuroses, and the pathoneuroses may well be indicative of phases of disorganization and reorganization of more integrated ego functioning. The consensus of psychoanalytic opinion is that this issue has not yet been determined. It is recognized that hypochondriasis is a form of organ neurosis, but the physiological factors involved are still unknown. It may be assumed that certain psychogenic factors—for example, a state of dammed-up libido or anxiety to which the person responds with narcissistic withdrawal—can create organic changes that give rise to hypochondriacal sensations.

Hypochondriasis rarely appears as an isolated neurosis. More frequently, it appears as a complication in the picture of some other psychopathological condition, such as a compulsion neurosis or depression, or it appears as a stage in the development of or recovery from a psychotic condition. Sadistic and hostile impulses withdrawn from objects and represented in the form of organic complaints may play a particularly pronounced role in hypochondriacal syndromes. The typical hypochondriac is a conspicuously narcissistic, seclusive, monomaniacal person who is often in a transitional state between reactions of a more hysterical character and those that are delusional and clearly psychotic. Hypochondriasis, with its excessive cathexis of bodily function and concern over organic states, has been regarded as one of the classic narcissistic neuroses. Further psychoanalytic study of infantile development may contribute more to the understanding of this frequently encountered clinical phenomenon.

Major depressive disorder (psychotic depression; melancholia). The initial insights into the internal origins of various forms of affective regressive states were provided by Freud as early as 1915. In *Mourning and Melancholia* Freud emphasized the topographic regions and systems of the psychic apparatus involved in melancholic states, the regression of libido, and the abandonment of the unconscious cathexis of objects. Freud's views differed in this respect from those of Abraham, who stressed the importance of anal sadism and maintained that its role in severe depressions is comparable to that of anal eroticism in obsessional neurosis. Abraham also pointed out that anal-sadistic impulses contribute to many other clinical syndromes as well. But Freud emphasized the fact that the pain in mourning is limited to loss of an external object. By way of contrast, in melancholia it is the ego itself that is impoverished because it has experienced an internal loss. Thus, melancholic depressions may or may not be precipitated by an actual loss. But, as a concomitant of loss, the melancholic suffers a shattering fall in self-esteem. The ego seems poor and empty, and, as such, it is deserving of reproach and attack from the superego. The early formulations of both Freud and Abraham concerning melancholia and depression emphasized the precipitating frustration in object love, accompanied by narcissistic traumata that reinforce early oedipal disappointments, and the introjection of an ambivalently loved parental image. These concepts still have a general validity.

Abraham's continued investigations within the framework of the infantile libidinal development, focusing particularly on the oral phase, led to further understanding of the mechanisms involved in depressive states. He suggested that the conflicts of depressed patients center on oral and anal-sadistic impulses. He pointed out that persons who are prone to depression often have a markedly obsessional underlying character structure.

SYMPTOMS. The symptom of depression is as ubiquitous as life itself, since it is a natural reaction to those events that must be counted among the normal vicissitudes of life. It is the excessive duration and domination of the organism by depressive affects, rather than its mere occurrence, that establishes the depressive state as pathological. The basic attributes of depressive states were discussed in considering depressive (reactive) neurosis. Psychotic depressions, however, are marked by their greater intensity and by the degree of fragmentation and helpless vulnerability that characterizes the ego response to the depressive affect. The intensity of the aggression released is more primitive in psychotic states, and psychotic depressions are almost universally accompanied by profound suicidal ideas or serious suicidal attempts. Both depressive states are characterized by a decrease in self-esteem, a sense of helplessness, an inhibition of ego functions to varying degrees, and a subjective feeling of sadness or loss of varying intensity. Psychotic depression has also been described as a basic affective state in which the ego feels totally incapable of fulfilling its aims or aspirations, although these aims persist as desired goals. The ego is thus thrown into a state of continuing and total hopelessness. Persons prone to depression often display a pseudoindependence and self-assurance, which is, in reality, a reaction to early severe deprivation and is intended to serve as a defense against the threat of further deprivation or rejection.

PATHOGENESIS. On the basis of his hypothesis regarding the oral and anal-sadistic basis of severe depressive states, Abraham formulated the concept of primary depression to designate severe narcissistic injury that had occurred in early childhood through disappointments in object relations. Later on, Rado studied the effect of various vicissitudes of the nursing situation on the infantile ego and postulated a relationship between the causes of depression and oral frustration on one hand and aggression, particularly at the oral level, on the other. Recently, Bowlby's studies of the relationship between early maternal deprivation and the susceptibility to severe depression documented some of these early trends. Also, Jacobson discussed the impact on the young child's ego formation of early disillusionment about parental omnipotence and the subsequent devaluation of parental images. Disillusionment and devaluation of the parents lead to a destruction of infantile self-esteem, which is based on the early introjection of the idealized, good parental objects, and give rise to a primary depression, which is repeated whenever the adult is similarly disappointed or disillusioned. Thus, early ambivalent relationships with the parental figures may play a decisive role in the causation of depressive states.

Other authors have expanded on this basic concept in a variety of ways. Fenichel ascribed the general predisposition to depression to an "oral fixation, which determines the later reaction to narcissistic shocks," and added that

the narcissistic injury may create a depressive disposition because it occurs early enough to be met by an orally orientated ego

—that is, an ego that depends on external oral-narcissistic supplies. Fenichel also discussed the possibility that shocks to the self-esteem in early childhood may secondarily create the decisive oral fixation in the sense that the ego may thus become fixated to orally based defense mechanisms. Much of the evidence cited by these authors in support of their hypothesis tends to confirm Melanie Klein's theory that the achievement of a whole object relationship is regularly accompanied by anxiety, together with a definite and specific vulnerability to depression in the event of object loss (the depressive position). Zetzel, however, argued that this view implies a greater incidence of infantile psychosis than can be shown to exist.

MECHANISM OF DEPRESSION. All human beings experience periods of depression in the face of real or fantasied disappointments or disillusionments. However, the orally dependent person (infantile dependence), who requires constant narcissistic supplies from external sources, is most likely to manifest this reaction in its severe form. The prototype of depression is deprivation, suffered by the infantile ego, of vital narcissistic supplies. The availability of such supplies in the form of love, affection, and care is most significant, in terms of future development, at the oral stage.

Later, with the internalization of the parental images that follows on and derives from the resolution of the oedipal situation, the struggle to secure love from the need-satisfying object takes place on the intrapsychic level—that is, the ego seeks the approval of the superego and seeks to live up to the ideal standards of the ego ideal. The struggle for gratification that took place on an external level now takes place intrapsychically. However, the child experiences this internalized need-satisfying object as initially frustrating and prohibitive, and his attitude toward the object displays a corresponding hostility. The quality of this early, crucial object relationship gives the superego a critical and aggressive dimension. Furthermore, the failure to abandon or modify early narcissistic expectations of the early ego may lead later to intransigent ego ideal expectations that, when unrealizable, result in depression. The severe self-reproaches of depressed persons are another concomitant of the infant's hostility toward the internalized object and also represent the ego's efforts to win the favor of the superego through devaluation of the self. In summary, then, when early object relationships were defective (excessively ambivalent), early intrapsychic conflicts may be revived in the face of object loss. Once the mechanisms described above are set into operation by frustration and loss in adult life, they give rise to the depressive response.

Bipolar affective disorder (manic-depressive psychosis). The manic-depressive manifests a particular kind of infantile, narcissistic dependency on his love object. To offset his feelings of worthlessness, he requires a constant supply of love and moral support from a highly valued and idealized love object. This object may be a person, an organization, or a cause that he feels he can attach himself to or to which he has a sense of belonging. As long as the object lasts, he is able to function with enthusiasm and effectiveness. But because of his strong self-punitive tendencies, the manic-depressive's object choice is masochistically determined and is bound to disappoint him. The patient himself sets the stage for his illness. All the ambitions and pursuits of the manic-depressive evolve from representations of the overvalued, idealized, parental love objects, which extend themselves to the whole world. Consequently, when the patient is disappointed by this idealized love object, his ego functioning is impaired at every level.

DEPRESSIVE PHASE. The depressive phase of manic-depressive psychosis often resembles paranoia, insofar as the patient's fantasies show a similar desire to incorporate the object. However, paranoia differs from depression in that hostility in paranoia is directed against a part of the object (breasts, penis, buttocks, hair, feces), rather than the whole, and also in the prominence in paranoia of fantasies that this incorporated part object can be symbolically destroyed and eliminated by defecation. From another point of view, however, the paranoid defense can be seen as a compensation for the inner sense of vulnerability and worthlessness that characterizes the basic depressive state. The paranoid mechanisms counter this underlying depressive condition by sustaining self-esteem in grandiose terms or by restoring the fundamental object loss through the paranoid delusional system. Thus, the paranoid posture can be seen as an alternative to the manic defense.

MANIC PHASE. The depressive phase subsides and gives rise to a state of temporary elation, which is referred to as mania. The transition to mania, psychodynamically considered, occurs under a variety of conditions: when the narcissistically important goals and objects appear to be within reach once again, when they have become sufficiently modified or reduced to be realistically attainable, when they are renounced completely, or when the ego recovers from its narcissistic shock and regains its basic self-esteem with the help of various recuperative agencies, with or without a change in the objects and goals. Theoretical efforts to grapple with the problem of mania in psychoanalysis have passed through various stages. Initially, mania was approached from the libidinal standpoint. But recent studies have stressed the role of structural components of the psychic apparatus and the importance of object relationships along with their intrapsychic representations. Since the purpose of manic flight is to avoid introspection, mania does not lend itself to fruitful psychoanalytic exploration. It is generally agreed, however, that mania represents a way of avoiding awareness of inner depression and includes a strong element of denial of painful reality and a flight into external reality. In other words, mania is essentially a denial of the underlying depressive affects by proclaiming the specific opposites. Since the manic person does not want to become aware of these inner painful feelings, he cannot permit himself to empathize with others, and he thus becomes emotionally isolated.

Lewin's work on elation focuses on the oral-libidinal and the oral-aggressive elements in mania, which he expanded into an oral triad. The oral triad consists of wishes to eat, to be eaten, and to sleep. These are all essentially linked with the infant's experience at the mother's breast. He described, in structural terms, the fusion of ego and superego (ego ideal) in elation and the prominent use of projection, denial, and introjection as major defenses. Lewin also emphasized the importance of ego regression as a concomitant of elation, insofar as there is a return to the pleasure principle. He also compared mania to a waking dream. In terms of the economics of elation, the abundance of energy characteristic of this phenomenon represents a concomitant depletion in the energy available for reality testing or for coping with superego demands.

Schizophrenias. Psychoanalytic concepts regarding the schizophrenias continue to undergo modification and revision. Originally, Freud postulated that the onset of schizophrenia signified a withdrawal of libido from the outside world. This libido, he thought, is subsequently absorbed into the ego, producing a state of megalomanic grandiosity, or it is returned to the outside world in the form of delusions.

Recent clinical interest in schizophrenia has centered on the intense ambivalence characteristic of schizophrenic patients, their retaliation (persecutory) anxiety, and the infantile ego mechanisms they typically use in their relationships with objects. The failure of these mechanisms results in the patient's decompensation or regressed state. Two stages are particularly conspicuous in the clinical picture of schizophrenic regression as emphasized by Freud and Fenichel: First, the break with reality; second, the attempts to reestablish contact with reality.

CLINICAL CONCEPTS. Object relationships in schizophrenia are based on the wish to possess the parental objects or their substitutes through fusion or merging. Primitive introjective mechanisms, fixation at the early oral stage of libidinal development, and multiple impairments of ego functions have been demonstrated repeatedly in this syndrome. Frustration of basic libidinal needs or factors that weaken ego resiliency, such as physical illness and increased demands on the patient's capacity for love or work, may precipitate the acute psychotic episode.

Poorly warded-off homosexual and pregenital impulses, particularly those of a sadistic and destructive nature, play an important role in schizophrenic regression. There is some argument as to whether such states of libidinal upheaval precede the schizophrenic regression or are, in fact, secondary to such regression. With the onset of the psychosis, however, these early sources of libidinal excitation cannot be mastered, and they flood the ego apparatus and overwhelm it. If the libido returns to the ego, a megalomanic picture results. But if the sadistic impulses are projected into the external world, as in the paranoid schizophrenic states, the once ambivalently loved person or his representative is perceived as the persecutor.

PSYCHOPHYSIOLOGICAL CONCEPTS. Several workers have approached these severe regressive states from the standpoint of a more unified concept of psychophysiological functioning. Mann and Semrad (1959) attempted to conceptualize schizophrenia as a psychophysiological entity. Basing their concepts on the work of Felix Deutsch, they conceived of the conversion process as the pathway that may shed light on the dynamic interrelationship between the mind and the body. They attributed schizophrenia to a defect in ego development that is, in turn, the consequence of the early failure of the conversion process to bind excessive instinctual excitation. People vary in the face of severe psychophysiological distress in their capacity to manage or absorb affect through somatic conversion processes. If the capacity of a person in this regard is exceeded, the need for further defenses arises, and these defenses are then regressively invoked. The immature or narcissistic ego defenses used in the schizophrenic psychosis are much more body oriented than are the more mature defenses. In the narcissistic defenses, affect is concentrated on the self to the marked exclusion of external objects. It is reasonable to assume, therefore, that the need for these defenses arises in inverse proportion to the success with which the conversion process can absorb affect.

PATHOGENESIS. Introjections, together with their correlated projections, following the pattern described in identification with the aggressor, are prominent aspects of the schizophrenic psychosis. These primitive introjects dominate the intrapsychic organization of the schizophrenic patient in such a way that the capacity for less defensive and more constructive identification is severely impaired. These patterns of introjection result in character traits that are related to the internalized aggressor or, alternatively, the internalized victim. In schizophrenia the aggressor may be experienced primarily as a foreign body within the patient's self. The defenses available to the ego at this point of its development—that is, the narcissistic defenses—may also be affected in that they become intensified and specialized, so that they emerge as a prominent series of executive patterns in the form of denial, projection, and distortion. Such prominence seriously compromises the capacity of the ego to function in its interpersonal negotiations, specifically because of the susceptibility of these primitive and unintegrated introjects to projection and the consequent distortion of object relations. This distortion eventually assures the frustration of the ego in its attainment of object gratification and its satisfaction of its basic needs for object relatedness.

Although the object with which the ego identifies is experienced as an aggressor and is perceived internally as a foreign presence, there is considerable ambivalence in this relationship. In this intense symbiotic relationship, the object becomes, in addition, a positive, pleasure-giving source. Indeed, these positive, pleasurable aspects become the source of narcissistic supply and the major factor in balancing aggression, making it possible for the ego to remain relatively intact. However, this stability is extremely vulnerable. It can be maintained only until such time as the person loses, in reality or in fantasy, the primary satisfying objects or, to a smaller extent, the secondary substitutes for these objects.

Once this sort of loss has occurred, the previously balanced destructiveness of the aggressively distorted introject is released. The ego is confronted anew with the problem of containing and controlling this malignant and destructive aggression, and libidinal problems assume a secondary position. At this point, the conversion process seems to have failed. The person is thrown once more into a disorganizing and exhausting state of intense psychophysiological pain, and he must soon reach toward another solution. The total process may be acute and overwhelming, or it may be slowly and gradually regressive. In any event, schizophrenic reactions invariably include distortions of the external world in the form of a series of frightening, confusing, and distorted body perceptions.

One may describe the predisposition to psychosis as due to the tenuous and delicate balance between positive introjections (contributing to the ego ideal) and the aggressive and destructive introjections (contributing to the punitive superego). The balance between these two is maintained by special ego defenses, by character disorders, or by disorders in psychophysiological functioning that permit the symbolic expression of the conflict, although the psychophysiological relationships are as yet poorly understood. Special narcissistic defenses used by schizophrenic patients are molded into organized patterns of denial, projection, and distortion. The ego is altered so that it operates in a self-saving manner. To do so, it must deny the presence of the painful sensations, deny any responsibility for the sensations, or lose the ability to distinguish between sensations emanating from internal stimuli and those emanating from external stimuli. Denial, projection, and distortion are themselves methods for altering sensory perceptions so that they can become ego-syntonic. The specialization of the narcissistic defenses becomes necessary because of the inadequacy of positive (ego ideal) introjections, which impairs the ego's capacity for repression and its ability to use and integrate more mature defenses to varying degrees.

In summary, schizophrenic regression is precipitated by loss or frustration of object needs. Dynamically, the effect of loss results too readily in the supremacy of negative affects, thus dislocating the delicate balance between introjective components in the patient's self-organization. There is a loss of equilibrium between the positive good introjects and the negative bad introjects that compose the structure of the self. The inundation with diffused and deneutralized destructive and negative feelings necessitates a regression to a point of deepest fixation—namely, the narcissistic position—at which the patient not only is a potential victim but also operates for self-consolidation. At this level, the patient's regressive disorganization is accompanied by a dedifferentiation of boundaries between self and object. Only in this position can the patient achieve release of the internal tension. The path of regression varies according to whether the losses are acute and overwhelming or slow and cumulative and according to the person's structural organization. When the illness is correctly diagnosed, its course can be plotted with relative accuracy, and it is possible to demonstrate conclusively, particularly in situations of chronic loss, a somewhat orderly progression or relinquishing of the more mature defense mechanisms.

Admittedly, the preschizophrenic ego is weak in terms of the development of mature defense mechanisms, but, with the onset of psychosis, elements of more mature mechanisms that have become established become admixed with more infantile patterns. This mixture may account for the clinical confusion surrounding the schizophrenias, which demonstrate not only many different kinds of mechanisms but also various shadings of these mechanisms, giving rise to a confusion of terms—such as schizoaffective components, hysterical components, hypochondriacal components, and neurasthenic components. In general, clinical evidence has shown that the acute onset of schizophrenia is related to an increased intensity of paranoid (persecutory) anxiety, feelings of omnipotence, and intolerable depressive anxieties—all of which had previously been warded off by narcissistic ego patterns of behavior. In addition, the patient typically demonstrates perceptual distortion, self-hatred, and a reliance on infantile and highly dependent patterns of object relatedness.

THERAPY. It is clear that classic psychoanalysis is contraindicated in the treatment of psychotic states. However, skillful and prolonged psychotherapy, based on essentially psychoanalytic principles, can ameliorate or even permanently remove the more morbid features in some cases and can help the patient establish a more stable and consistent life pattern.

But the question is still open as to whether psychoanalytic techniques can be specifically indicated for the treatment of schizophrenia, as they can be for the psychoneuroses and the character disorders. Some clinicians have argued for the application of psychoanalytic techniques to the psychoses, but these clinicians seem to be in the minority. For the most part, the experiences of psychoanalysts in attempts to apply psychoanalytic techniques to psychotic states have been consistently disappointing. In general, when paranoid elements are involved in the schizophrenic syndrome, the prognosis is even less optimistic, although in some cases, when the paranoid process operates in a minimal fashion or engages only a limited portion of the patient's energy, the prognosis may be somewhat better.

In general, the therapeutic climate in approaching the psychotic disorders has become considerably more optimistic in recent years. The psychoanalytic approach to psychotic patients has considerably deepened and broadened the knowledge of the psychodynamics involved in these disorders. However, the therapeutic approach through psychoanalytic perspectives is quite limited, and its value in recent years has been radically questioned. In general, comparative studies of treatment modalities of schizophrenia and other psychotic disorders suggest that the main parameter of treatment in these conditions remains organic, specifically the use of appropriate psychopharmacological regimes.

The evidence is not conclusive, however, that psychotherapeutic approaches to these disorders do not add an important component to a treatment program. At this stage of knowledge, much more knowledge is needed about the selective effectiveness of psychotherapeutic interventions, particularly in defining those patient populations in which the responsiveness to analytically based psychotherapy is greater. The general approach to psychotic states of the future may lie in the direction of increasingly effective drug management, but a subset of these patients may be able to profit from psychotherapeutic intervention added to drug management.

Treatment

Certain aspects of the therapeutic technique that Freud developed and that were later expanded by his followers bear a close relationship to the aspects of psychoanalytic theory discussed here. One of the distinctive aspects of the psychoanalytic approach to treatment in general is its consistent attempt to integrate therapeutic usages and approaches with the understanding of psychic functioning available from psychoanalytic theory. In its origins and in its special application, psychoanalysis is, in a special sense, a theory of therapy.

DIAGNOSIS

In any systematic approach to the treatment of emotional illness, diagnosis must hold a central place, since the decisions regarding the appropriate form of treatment depend on the accuracy and precision of the diagnostic process. This remains generally as true for psychoanalytic treatment as for any psychiatric or medical intervention.

However, the diagnostic process represents an attempt to impose categories on an underlying continuum of infinitely variable forms of illness. Consequently, no diagnostic system is definitive, and no diagnostic system answers all the decisional needs that relate to the treatment process. One important result of this state of affairs is that multiple diagnostic schemata have been evolved throughout the history of psychiatry. The kind of schema developed depends to a large extent on the purposes for which it is formulated and the objectives to which it is directed. Thus, the spectrum of psychiatric illnesses can be grouped and categorized in different ways, depending on the purposes and objectives of that set of categories.

Insofar as the objectives and purposes of psychoanalytic treatment are congruent with and overlap the objectives of general psychiatry, one expects a psychoanalytic diagnostic rationale to coincide with the psychiatric. A cursory glance through the previously described forms of psychopathology described from a psychoanalytic perspective suggests that there is a considerable degree of overlap with general psychiatric categories, as exemplified in the American Psychiatric Association's third edition of *Diagnostic and Statistical Manual of Mental Disorders* (DSM-III). However, there are significant differences. The objectives of DSM-III are to provide a set of discrete descriptive categories that can be more or less agreed on for categorization of types of mental disorder for purposes of consistency in record keeping, research evaluations, and statistical processing. The intent and purposes of psychoanalytic diagnosis share these concerns, but they have a quite different orientation. Psychoanalytic diagnosis is particularly concerned with issues of evaluation of potential analyzability, selection of appropriate patients for psychoanalytic treatment, predictive value for assessing the nature of the patient's conflicts and the predictable levels and areas of pathological impairment, and, finally, prognosis. Consequently, the diagnostic issues relate in an immediate and intimate way to the vicissitudes, whether actual or predictable, of the analytic process.

Traditionally, analysts have put themselves at odds with the merely descriptive and categorizing aspects of the traditional psychiatric approach. This represents a revolt against the rigidities and constraints of a descriptive form of diagnostic categorization that does not seem to fit well with the more dynamic orientation adopted by psychoanalysts. As a consequence, the attitude has grown up toward analysts and to a certain extent among analysts that diagnosis is ultimately irrelevant and that what really matters is the clinical understanding of psychodynamics. Paradoxically, however, analysts continue to be preoccupied with diagnostic issues, although not in the context dominated by the attachment of labels.

Thus, psychoanalysts have not been at pains to discriminate whether a patient is hysterical or obsessional or more of one than the other but, rather, have focused their attention more explicitly on the underlying motivation and dynamic considerations that enable the therapist to understand the nature of the patient's difficulties and to begin assisting the patient in dealing with them. Although the labeling of patients has received little emphasis, the refinements of psychoanalytic diagnosis have flourished on other grounds.

Analysts have concerned themselves increasingly over the years with sophisticated refinements in the assessment of levels of libidinal fixation and development, in growing competence in the evaluation and determination of the patterns and heterogeneity of ego development, and in evolving a sophisticated capacity for diagnostic assessment of the patient's strengths and weaknesses and the levels of developmental impairment, retardation, deficit, and regression. This process has led in the direction of the development of elaborate diagnostic assessment profiles, such as those developed by Anna Freud (1965) and others.

Historically, as analysts developed their capacity and sophistication in the recognition of structural and developmental deficits in the organization of personality, the diagnostic concern shifted from more or less symptomatic levels to forms of more complex personality evaluation, relying increasingly on structural and genetic data and less on symptomatic or dynamic issues. The work of Zetzel (1968) made it clear that traditional assumptions about the personality structure of patients presenting with a hysterical façade cannot be maintained, since other diagnostic issues indicated clearly that such patients have either not attained or only transiently attained a level of triadic oedipal conflict. Similarly, Kernberg's (1967) work on the diagnosis of borderline personalities indicated clearly that little of value can be judged on the basis of patterns of symptoms or psychodynamics; rather, one must resort to a level of structural and genetic diagnosis in order to evaluate

the extent and severity of the pathology and the potential prognosis of treatment.

Consequently, the basis for psychoanalytic diagnosis differs from that of a more general psychiatric approach. Descriptive psychiatry approached the patient in terms of external observations of behavior and patterns of descriptions, together with elements of the patient's history, including even elements of family history. That approach can be described as descriptive, observational, and extrinsic. The analytic approach, in contrast, has emphasized the patient's inner experience, particularly the quality of the patient's inner conflicts and related fantasies, as an important component of the diagnostic evaluation. As the psychoanalytic perspective has evolved, however, analytic diagnosis has extended its reach into such pertinent areas as assessment of the degree of autonomy of ego functions and their susceptibility to regression and the quality both historically and contemporaneously of the patient's object relationships. Assessments of the quality of object relationships can be derived in some degree from the history of the patient's relationships with significant others and can be evaluated in terms of the quality of relationships in the patient's present life situation.

Perhaps the most vital and meaningful place in which such evaluation can be made is in the context of the therapeutic relationship, specifically in the evaluation of the transference and other dimensions of the complex relationship that arise between analyst and patient. Many of the most critical aspects of evaluation of patients in a psychoanalytic perspective rest on this sensitive and delicate indicator. Obviously, the quality of object relations cannot be meaningfully assessed in short compass; it often requires lengthy periods of experience within the relationship to the patient before the analyst is able to gain an adequate sense of what the patient's capacity for object relationship is. One of the critical problems in evaluating patients for analysis is that the analyst is forced to make preliminary discriminations about such matters on the basis of relatively inadequate data. Consequently, it is not surprising that the patient selection process for psychoanalysis has its recognizable pitfalls.

It may be useful at this point to apply these issues to a particular diagnostic entity, such as hysteria. In DSM-III the terms "hysteria" and "hysterical disorder" do not occur as categories. Instead, the categories of hysterical disorder are distributed under the anxiety disorders, the somatoform disorders, and the dissociative disorders, and the hysterical personality has been designated as "histrionic personality." The descriptive and observable characteristics of each form are given so that a categorization of patients can be made on an observational basis.

The psychoanalyst, however, cannot remain comfortable with these categories. The distribution of these forms of behavior in terms of observable patterns of activity sets the categories in terms that are dissociated from the underlying fantasies and inner motivations that carry a central and significant impact to the psychoanalytic observer. What is important in establishing the diagnosis psychoanalytically is not so much the pattern of behavior as the underlying motivations and their significance. Thus, critical to the diagnosis is not the fact that the patient is frigid in sexual activity or tends to express affects in a ready or histrionic manner but, rather, what the underlying pattern of motivation and the unconscious meanings are. These may be related to specific fantasies that carry the unconscious derivatives or may be available only after significant periods of analytic work and regression.

Once one shifts the ground from external observation to the world of the patient's inner fantasy life and meaningful motivations, other significant dimensions of the problem are brought into focus. The analyst has additional questions regarding the organization of psychic structure, the quality and the nature of the patient's object relationships, the patient's capacities to tolerate anxiety and depression, the level and intensity of intrapsychic conflicts, and other indices of psychic integration and functioning. Important questions have to be settled as to the true level of the patient's inner conflicts—that is, whether they are effectively phallic-oedipal, as may be expected on the basis of hysterical manifestations, or whether they are contaminated by significant degrees of preoedipal instinctual derivatives. Other significant questions pertain to the level of ego development and integration obtained by the patient. Specific estimates have to be made of the patient's ego strengths—particularly the capacity to tolerate regression, anxiety, and loss—as important indices in the evaluation of the patient's capacity to undergo the stress of the analytic process and to provide some basis for the prediction of the capacity to terminate the relationship with the analyst effectively and to undergo the necessary mourning process in a productive and adaptive manner.

PATIENT SELECTION

The capacity for mature adjustment may be very limited in some persons, even though they may not have a particularly severe neurosis. An evaluation of their personalities indicates that no aspect of their function is really adult. Often, there is no evidence of a strong drive to combat the more infantile aspects of their personalities.

Analysis is contraindicated in extreme cases of this kind, since there is no element of personality that will strive to use the treatment for eventual maturity. The patient will continue to regard the analytic sessions as enjoyable hours during which he has someone's exclusive attention as long as the analyst will put up with it. The psychoanalyst regards the secondary gain not as a primary rationale for psychoanalytic treatment but, rather, as an important obstacle to be circumvented in his work. Frequently, secondary gain is so great as to impede seriously or entirely preclude successful analysis. In such instances the patient has learned to derive so much satisfaction from these secondary gains that the advantages of illness outweigh its suffering. However, this is a matter of degree, since the issue of secondary gain and gratification from the analytic process itself is frequently a component of most analyses, even those that are successfully completed.

During treatment the patient must continue to derive some gratification from life, even though these gratifications may perpetuate in certain ways his neurotic patterns of adjustment. Sometimes relationships that were conspicuous consequences of the neurosis cannot be renounced, even when the patient no longer requires the infantile gratification (or masochistic gratification) these relationships afford. No individual is a self-sufficient unit. His repressed impulses and his mature emotions constantly mingle with, stimulate, and respond to those of others. The infantile sadism of one partner responds to the infantile masochism of the other and demands it of him, despite the fact that after a successful analysis the masochist may desire a more mature relationship, unconsciously as well as consciously. In other circumstances, analytic results have a favorable effect on the neurotic problems of the patient's spouse, as well as on those of the patient, and there results a mutual improvement in marital adjustment.

Specific Criteria

Several factors must be kept in mind in judging a person's eligibility for psychoanalysis. Apart from the capacity for logical thought and a certain degree of ego strength, fundamental vigor of personality is a prerequisite. The analytic patient undergoes a difficult experience. From time to time he must be able to accept a temporary increase in unhappiness or anxiety in the expectation of eventual benefit. The capacity to undergo such stress is an excellent indication of the person's capacity to face the real vicissitudes of life after analysis. When there is some question as to the patient's qualifications in this regard, a short period of trial analysis may be recommended to evaluate the patient's problems and potentialities more completely. A youthful mind—less in terms of actual years than in terms of elasticity of functioning—is essential. Chronological age is a rough measure of total life experience. The more mature a person's experience has been, the more apt he will be to use the analysis. In general, however, treatment proceeds more quickly to an effective result when patients are in their twenties and thirties. But analysis can also be recommended in adolescence and middle age.

The capacity to fight the neurosis is as great an asset in psychoanalysis as it is in life crises, and this capacity varies as greatly as does the degree of neurosis itself. Often an important element in patients' lives is that they have been able to preserve and maintain some area of successful ego functioning in a consistent and productive manner. For example, if a person has a consistently good scholastic or work history, the probability of adequate ego capacity is much higher.

Honest skepticism about analysis is usually a good prognostic sign, as long as it is not so extreme as to prevent the patient from making a determined effort to use the unique advantages of the psychoanalytic approach. On the other hand, a naïve, exuberant conviction at the beginning of treatment that the omnipotent analyst will point the way to an existence that will remain forever untroubled, that analysis somehow offers a magic formula that will automatically and painlessly set everything aright, forbodes special difficulties after the treatment is underway.

Analyzability

The question of analyzability is one of central importance for contemporary psychoanalysis and psychiatry. The basic question is: For what patients is psychoanalysis a suitable form of treatment? As noted in the discussion of borderline personalities, it is not uncommon for patients to develop a treatment relationship that provides relief of symptoms. By retaining the relationship with the therapist, such patients can avoid serious regression and maintain a reasonable level of adjustment and functioning. The support of ego functions, however, requires the continuing availability of the therapist.

The more difficult aspect for the treatment of borderline patients is the surrendering of the relationship with the therapist in termination. The patient cannot tolerate the threat of loss and separation without regression. A crucial question is the extent to which such patients are capable of internalizing and identifying with the therapist. The capacity for such internalization requires a capacity for tolerating both depressive affects and regressive forms of anxiety that may be experienced in the face of the threatened loss. Borderline patients do not meet the criteria of analyzability.

Potentially analyzable neurotic patients have been able to reach a developmental level in which a genuine triangular conflict has been experienced. They have been able to sustain significant object relations with both parents through the latency years, after the resolution of the oedipal complex. Frequently, the postoedipal relationships between the developing neurotic and his parents are less satisfactory and more ambivalent than relationships during the preoedipal periods. Moreover, the relationship with one parent during the preoedipal years generally tends to be more ambivalent than the relationship with the other parent. When the degree of ambivalence in the early mother-child relationship has been excessive, this ambivalence proves to be a more severe handicap in the development of secure object relations than a highly ambivalent preoedipal relationship with the father. This distinction is applicable to children of both sexes. Classical psychoanalysis is the treatment of choice for potentially mature patients in whom the developmental difficulties lie on the level of the mastery of genuine internal conflicts. This implies that they have been able to establish meaningful one-to-one relationships with both parents and have been able to enter into and establish a triangular oedipal conflict. Patients who have not achieved this level of triangular involvement and conflict are, according to Zetzel and other analysts, generally unable to benefit from psychoanalysis.

The use of a therapeutic method that induces regression in patients who demonstrate more severe developmental failures is open to serious question. Patients who are unable to tolerate anxiety or depression are rarely able to work through a transference neurosis. The more significant difficulty for such patients is their inability to terminate any form of therapy successfully.

Patients who meet the criteria for analyzability fall into typical patterns of neurotic difficulty. The most common difficulty in analyzable women is in the area of capacities for heterosexual object relations. This difficulty is usually reflected in a hysterical form of personality organization. A common difficulty for analyzable men is likely to be in the area of work inhibitions. Men also predominantly present with symptoms of an obsessional nature, rather than hysterical nature. Patients with obsessional neurosis or obsessional character usually have little difficulty in establishing the analytic situation, but few of them are able to develop the overt and analyzable transference neurosis during the first year of analysis. When considering analyzability, one must distinguish between the capacity to establish and participate in the analytic situation and the capacity to establish a genuine transference neurosis.

Hysterical patients. Hysterical patients are either very good or very difficult patients. For them the development of a transference neurosis is relatively easy and quick, but it is more difficult to engage in and establish the analytic situation.

The presence of hysterical symptoms is not a sufficient index of analyzability. Hysterical symptoms are frequently seen in borderline personalities and in the closely allied category of primitive oral hysterics. Such patients desire basically an accepting one-to-one relationship with the father or the father surrogate and are not able to maintain a meaningful relationship with the mother. This contributes to the high incidence of intense and sexualized transference reactions in women treated by male therapists.

Analyzable hysterics have experienced a genuine triangular conflict developmentally and have been able to maintain significant object relations with both parents. They maintain a capacity to recognize and tolerate internal reality and internal conflicts, and they are able to distinguish adequately between internal reality and external reality. They have been able to develop a substantial mastery of ambivalence, particularly in the early relationship with the mother. This mastery provides a certain defensive organization, which can serve as the buffer against significant ego regressions during the analytic treatment. Many of the most analyzable hysterical patients reveal a combination of hysterical and obsessive characteristics described as mixed neurosis.

Less potentially analyzable hysterics differ in that they are often less mature, fail to demonstrate development of relatively stable and ego-syntonic obsessional defenses, and usually manifest less consistent achievement in their work efforts and in the maintenance of friendships. They tend to be more passive and more fearful of dependent wishes. These patients have greater difficulty is establishing a stable analytic situation.

They respond with a flight into health, or they plunge into a regressive transference neurosis before a therapeutic alliance can be established. If the pitfalls can be avoided in establishing the analytic situation, these patients can achieve a genuine therapeutic and analytic result.

Hysterics with underlying depressive character structures can generally be regarded as failing to mobilize their active resources during important developmental crises. Some of them may be analyzable, but long and difficult analyses must be expected. Usually, self-esteem is low, and they tend to devalue their own femininity. They may have experienced some genuine triangular conflict, often with excessive idealization of the father. They may also be able to recognize and tolerate considerable depression, but they have failed significantly in the area of positive mastery. They tend to be passive and to feel helpless and vulnerable. They tend to develop passive and dependent transference reactions, which interfere with their capacity to distinguish between therapeutic alliance and transference neurosis.

All these patients present serious problems in the terminal phases of analysis and present a serious risk of drifting into a relatively interminable analytic situation. The critical area in the evaluation and assessment of the analyzability of these patients is the intensity, depth, and chronicity of the depression. If it is excessive, the prognosis is less optimistic.

The primitive hysterics usually have a florid hysterical picture clinically and prove incapable of tolerating a genuine triangular conflict. Their transference fantasies are intensely sexualized, and they tend to regard this area of fantasy as offering the possibility of real gratification. They cannot distinguish between internal and external reality and, consequently, have considerable difficulty in establishing a therapeutic alliance and in distinguishing it from the transference neurosis. These patients do not meet the criteria for analyzability, since the major pathology reflects significant developmental failures in basic ego functions.

Obsessional patients. The criteria for analyzability of obsessional patients present somewhat different problems. Failure to resolve oedipal attachments in the male is much more likely to result in an obsessional pattern of symptoms or character structure than is the case in correspondingly analyzable women. The criteria for analyzability in obsessional patients do not depend on the content or the severity of the presenting symptoms. What is crucial in determining the analyzability of obsessional patients is the degree to which they can tolerate the instinctual regression necessary for the development of an analyzable transference neurosis without losing the capacity for distinguishing between fantasy and reality—that is, between transference and therapeutic alliance.

Freud originally noted that obsessional patients tend to develop conflicts in important areas—love versus hate, activity versus passivity, omnipotence versus helplessness. The resolution and mastery of such conflicts are crucial developmental tasks. The resolution of the conflict of love and hate, the tolerance for ambivalence, is one of the crucial developmental tasks. The resolution of the conflict of love and hate, the tolerance for ambivalence, is one of the crucial developmental tasks in the achievement of healthy self-object differentiation and early identifications. This resolution determines one of the basic criteria for analyzability.

The analyzable obsessional patient must have sufficient tolerance for conflicting emotions to allow him to endure the alteration between love and hate that emerges in the transference neurosis. Further, the patient must be able to distinguish such transference feelings from the analytic relationship. In other words, he must be sufficiently able to tolerate his ambivalence to allow himself to maintain a real therapeutic relationship. An important distinction must be made here between the developmental failure to integrate emotions and perceptions and the regressive impairment of previously established integration during neurotic symptom formation. Obsessional intolerance for conflict and ambivalence may reflect either developmental course. Analyzable adults, however, show basic achievement in one-to-one relationships with both parents, which allows the establishment of oedipal conflict to emerge without jeopardizing these important object relations.

Even so, the major unresolved conflict in analyzable obsessional men derives from the triangular oedipal conflict. One can be misled, however, since obsessive reaction formations can be established in obsessional development before the onset of the genital oedipal situation. Premature consolidation of obsessional defenses and the early crystallization of personality may form an impediment to the emergence of a genuine triangular conflict. The presence of obsessional systems in such patients is of much less importance in evaluating the potential for psychoanalysis than the degree to which certain major developmental steps have been accomplished and in the quality of object relations.

Tolerance of anxiety and depression. The capacity to tolerate anxiety and depression is another of the major concerns in evaluating analyzability. Obsessional characters are frequently more vulnerable to involutional depressions toward the end of active life, but, in general, depression, like hysteria, is more commonly observed in women than in men. Tolerance of depression involves a dual developmental task: the passive toleration of the painful reality that cannot be immediately modified and the subsequent mobilization of resources in available areas of achievement and mastery. The masculine ideal of competitive striving and mastery reinforces the second phase of this developmental task, so that it is hardly surprising that analyzable obsessional men have a relative intolerance for passivity and depression. For women, however, passivity, rather than activity, is central to the traditional image of femininity. Women may have more difficulty in dealing with the second phase of the developmental task, whereas men are more likely to have difficulty with the first phase.

Women may develop an exaggerated sense of passivity, helplessness, and vulnerability—characteristics found prominently in feminine depressive character structure. This passivity may also be frequently linked with hysterical symptoms. Such women can tolerate a considerable degree of passivity and depression, but their inability to mobilize active ego resources for mastery and growth leaves them vulnerable to regression and narcissistic injury. The basic conflicts for men relate to the recognition, toleration, and integration of passivity and dependence. The transference neurosis can unmask such feelings and severely threaten the patient. Conversely, the basic conflicts for women have to do with problems related to mastery, activity, and self-assertion.

The evaluation of depression and the patient's capacity to bear and master it are crucial aspects of the evaluation for psychoanalysis. Depression is a frequent presenting symptom in patients suffering from hysterical and obsessional neurosis. Such depressed patients often turn out to be potentially analyzable neurotics. But the evaluation of depression is difficult and often requires a preliminary course in psychotherapy aimed at reestablishing a sufficient level of self-esteem and the mobilization of coping resources to facilitate development of a positive therapeutic alliance. The patient's therapeutic response allows the therapist to evaluate more carefully the patient's capacity to tolerate depressive affects without significant regression and his capacity to respond to mobilizing resources for mastery and active coping.

ANALYTIC PROCESS

Modern psychoanalytic treatment procedures differ from those that Freud originally developed in one fundamental respect. Early in his approach to therapy, Freud felt that recognition by the physician of the patient's unconscious motivations, the communication of this knowledge to the patient, and its comprehension by the patient would of themselves effect a cure. This was his basic doctrine of therapeutic insight. But further clinical experience has demonstrated the fallacy of these expectations.

Freud found that his discovery of the patient's unconscious wishes and his ability to impart these findings to the patient so that they were accepted and understood were insufficient. Such insight might permit clarification of the patient's intellectual appraisal of his problems, but the emotional tensions for which the patient sought treatment were not effectively alleviated in this way. Freud began to realize that the success of treatment depended on the patient's ability to understand the emotional significance of an experience on an emotional level and depended on his capacity to retain and use that insight. Then, if the experience recurred, it would elicit a different reaction; it would no longer be repressed; the patient would have undergone a change in his psychic economy.

Freud continually refined his technique on the basis of his expanding clinical experience and his deeper theoretical understanding; psychoanalysis became recognized as a specific method for reaching and modifying unconscious phenomena that give rise to conflict. For a conflict to be considered a neurotic conflict, at least one aspect of it must be repressed. Psychoanalysis attempts to deal with repression and tries to bring the repressed material back into consciousness, so that the patient, on the basis of his greater understanding of his needs and motives, may find a more realistic solution to his conflict. Freud's formula for this process was, "Where id was, ego shall be."

Freud elaborated a treatment method that attaches minimum importance to the immediate relief of symptoms, moral support from the therapist, and guidance. The goal of psychoanalysis is to pull the neurosis out by its roots, rather than to prune off the top. To accomplish this, the analyst must break down the pregenital, deep crystallization of id, ego, and superego and bring the underlying material near enough to the surface of consciousness so that it can be modified and reevaluated in terms of reality. This distinguishes the classical psychoanalytic treatment from more psychodynamic forms of psychotherapy.

The repression of the forces of conflict is accomplished by design, and the patient is unaware of the psychic mechanisms that his mind uses. By isolating his basic problem, the patient has protected himself from what seems to him to be unbearable suffering. No matter how it may impair his functioning, the neurosis is somehow preferable to the emergence of unacceptable wishes and ideas. All the forces that permitted the original repression are mobilized once again in the analysis as a resistance to this threatened encroachment on dangerous territory. No matter how much the patient cooperates consciously with the therapist and in the analysis and no matter how painful his neurotic symptoms are, he automatically defends himself against the reopening of old wounds with every subtle resource of defense and resistance available to him.

In discussing the analytic process, one must clarify the basic distinction between the analytic process and the analytic situation. The analytic process refers to the regressive emergence, working through, interpretation, and resolution of the transference neurosis. The analytic situation, on the other hand, refers to the setting in which the analytic process takes place, specifically the positive real relationship between patient and analyst based on the therapeutic alliance. Obsessives have difficulty with the analytic process but have little difficulty with the analytic situation. That is to say, they can easily establish and participate in the therapeutic alliance, but they experience difficulty in tolerating the regression that is necessary for establishing and working through the transference neurosis. Hysterics, however, have no difficulty in relation to the analytic process but seem to experience difficulty in terms of the analytic situation. That is to say, they find it relatively easy to regress in the analytic situation and to allow the transference neurosis to form, but they have difficulty in establishing a meaningful and secure one-to-one relationship, which constitutes the therapeutic alliance.

The regression induced by the analytic situation (instinctual regression) allows for a reemergence of infantile conflicts and thus induces the formation of a transference neurosis. In the transference neurosis the original infantile conflicts and wishes become focused on the person of the analyst and are thus reexperienced and relived. In the analytic regression, earlier infantile conflicts are revived and can be seen as a manifestation of the repetition compulsion. Regression has a dual aspect. From one point of view, it is an attempt to return to an earlier state of real or fantasy gratification; from another point of view, it is as an attempt to master previous traumatic experience. The regression in the analytic situation and the development of transference are preliminary conditions for the mastery of unresolved conflicts. They can also represent regressive and unconscious wishes to return to an earlier state of narcissistic gratification. The analytic process must work itself out in the face of this dual potentiality and tension.

If the analytic regression has a destructive potentiality (ego regression) that must be recognized and guarded against, it also has a progressive potentiality for reopening and reworking infantile conflicts and for achieving a reorganization and consolidation of the personality on a healthier and more mature level. As in any developmental crisis, the risk of regressive deterioration must be balanced against the promise of progressive growth and mastery. The therapeutic importance of the criteria of analyzability can be easily recognized, since patients who are unable to achieve the progressive potentiality of the analytic regression cannot be expected to realize a good therapeutic result. The determining element within the analytic situation against which the regression must be balanced and in terms of which the destructive or constructive potential of the regression can be measured is the therapeutic alliance. A firm and stable alliance offers a buffer against excessive (ego) regression and also offers a basis for positive growth.

Phases of the Analytic Process

The analytic process can be usefully divided into three phases. The first phase involves the initiation and consolidation of the analytic situation. The second phase involves the emergence and analysis of the transference neurosis. The third phase involves the carrying through of a successful termination and separation from the analytic process. The three phases provide a framework for assessing the progress of the patient in analysis. Each phase of the analysis requires different capacities in the patient and focuses on different developmental aptitudes that are required if each of the phases is to be successfully accomplished. Moreover, in assessing the analyzability of a given patient, the analyst must determine the relative aptitude of the patient to meet the demands of each of the respective phases.

First phase. The first phase relates to the patient's capacity to enter into, establish, and sustain a therapeutic alliance. This alliance is essentially a one-to-one relationship between analyst and patient that imposes certain demands and exacts certain frustrations from the patient. The structure of the analytic situation is such that even the most mature and stable patients experience significant objective anxiety. Successful negotiation of this initial stage of the analysis involves the achievement of a special object relation that determines the nature and quality of the therapeutic alliance. The therapeutic alliance, therefore, involves both object relationship and, ultimately, ego identification. Both analyst and the patient are actively involved in this relationship, and it constitutes the essence of the analytic situation. The establishing of the therapeutic alliance, therefore, depends on and requires certain basic capacities in the patient. He must have a capacity to maintain basic trust in the absence of gratification; he must be able to maintain self-object differentiation in the absence of the object; he must retain a capacity to accept the limitations of reality, to tolerate frustrations, and to acknowledge his own limitations and lack of omnipotence. At the same time, he must be able to appreciate that the failure of the object to gratify wishes and demands may be due not to hostility or rejection but to realistic limitations that must be accepted. These capacities represent a mobilization of preanalytic ego resources and are essential in establishing the therapeutic alliance.

Second phase. The second phase of the analytic process relates to the patient's capacity to develop a genuine transference neurosis and to regress sufficiently to allow the transference neurosis to emerge, to be analyzed, and to work through its respective elements. The development of the transference neurosis involves a reopening and reworking of oedipal conflicts. These basic conflicts are then relived and reexperienced in the transference and become available to the patient for interpretation and understanding. The emergence, reworking, and resolution of these conflicts involve a number of therapeutic accomplishments, which are paralleled by the developmental attainments in the resolution of the original conflicts. Resolution involves development of a capacity to initiate and sustain intrapsychic defenses against instinctual wishes. It involves integration of both autonomous ego and ego ideal in a capacity for positive and constructive identification with the parent of the same sex. It involves renunciation of sexualized goals in regard to the parent of the opposite sex in favor of integration of a positive object relationship with that parent. It involves neutralization or sublimation of aggressive energies mobilized in the rivalry with the parent of the same sex. The working through of the transference aims at a resolution of these basic conflicts in order to gain the capacity for meaningful growth that is inherent in the resolution of the oedipal issues.

Third phase. The third phase involves the patient's capacity to tolerate separation and loss and to integrate these affects constructively in a pattern of positive identification with the analyst. This terminal phase of a successful analysis concerns itself directly with the issues of autonomy and independence. These issues have, to a degree, been operative through the entire course of the analysis, but they become particularly relevant in the final phase. As termination approaches, the patient's passive and dependent wishes are inevitably intensified and revivified.

The analytic task in this final phase is considerably different from that of the initial phase. In the initial phase the analyst was comparable to a parent who responded to the regressive, passive, and dependent aspects of the infantile neurosis. In the terminal phase, however, he becomes like the parent of a late adolescent who is more willing to foster and support the maturation and autonomy of the child. Passivity and dependence, which are essential to the analytic regression, become increasingly ego-alien as the process continues, until they come to be regarded as alien, infantile wishes in the terminal phase. The patient works toward more mature acceptance of realistic limits and mobilizes his resources to establish a more secure sense of autonomy and independence. The analyst, however, is retained as an object for continued positive identification. He remains an available object, much as the good parent, who remains an available and supportive object for the child, even after the separation involved in growth has been accomplished.

The work of termination involves the interpretation and integration of those relatively passive components in the therapeutic alliance that can facilitate the patient's future capacity for regression in the service of the ego. The patient must surrender his passive and dependent wishes. The analyst must be renounced. The patient must be able to tolerate and master the anxiety and depression involved in this renunciation. Termination is a form of mourning in which the analyst as a parent surrogate is renounced. To accomplish the work of the terminal phase, the patient must have sufficient ego resources to tolerate the pain of loss and to undertake the work of mastery that is necessary for a developmental gain. He must also have the important capacity to internalize the analytic situation and to identify with the positive and constructive aspects of the analyst-parent. The terminal phase of the analysis is parallel to the resolution of the oedipal situation, in which the parent must be surrendered and in which the resolution is based on the capacity for identification with the positive, ego-building aspects of the parental objects.

Treatment Techniques

The analytic technique is always adapted to the idiosyncrasies of the patient's developmental capacities, needs, and defensive constellation and to the stage of the analytic process at which the patient is at any given point. The technical work of the first phase in establishing the analytic situation differs considerably from what is required in the second phase, when the regression to the transference neurosis and its resolution are involved, and both differ considerably from the requirements imposed by the terminal phase of the analysis. The analytic techniques do not stand in isolation but are part of a living, dynamic process, which is intended to induce and achieve significant internal psychic growth.

Free association. The cornerstone of the psychoanalytic technique is free association. The patient is taught this method and instructed to use it to the best of his ability throughout the treatment. The primary function of free association, besides the obvious one of providing content for the analysis, is to induce the necessary regression and passive dependence that is connected with establishing and working through the transference neurosis. Free association is conjoined with the other techniques that induce such regression—namely, lying on the couch,

not being able to see the analyst, and conducting the analysis in an atmosphere of quiet and restful tranquility.

The use of free association in the analytic process is a relative matter. Although it remains the basic technique and the fundamental rule by which the patient's participation in the analysis is guided, there are multiple and frequent occasions in which the process of free association is interrupted or modified, according to the defensive needs or the developmental progression taking place within the analysis. The analyst is never in the position of simply passively listening to the endless free associations of his patient. The older model of the analyst as the passive mirror of the patient's associations is no longer functional and can now be recognized as an unrealistic and unproductive distortion of the analytic process.

Nor is the process of free association something that takes place in isolation in the patient. The process is more complex, more difficult to conceptualize, and increasingly must be seen in the context of and in reference to the more fundamental relationship between analyst and patient. The patient's free associating is a function of the more basic relationship. Moreover, much more is required of a patient than simply free associating. It is not enough for the patient to lie back and allow himself to sink back into a position of passive dependency within the analytic relationship. He must mobilize his basic ego resources in the service of mastery, gain insight, mobilize his executive and synthetic capacities, and ultimately assume a less passive and more active function within the analytic relationship. Obviously, the mobilization of these capacities in the patient varies from phase to phase of the analytic process.

Resistance. The most conscientious efforts on the part of the patient to say everything that comes into his mind are never completely successful. No matter how willing and cooperative the patient is in his attempts to free associate, the signs of resistance are apparent throughout the course of every analysis. The patient pauses abruptly, corrects himself, makes a slip of the tongue, stammers, remains silent, fidgets with some part of his clothing, asks irrelevant questions, intellectualizes, arrives late for appointments, finds excuses for not keeping them, offers critical evaluations of the rationale underlying the treatment method, simply cannot think of anything to say, or censors thoughts that do occur to him and decides that they are banal, uninteresting, or irrelevant and not worth mentioning.

The development of resistance in the analysis is quite as automatic and independent of the patient's will as is the development of the transference itself. The sources of the resistance are just as unconscious as the sources of the transference. However, the emotional forces that give rise to resistance are opposed to those that tend to produce the transference neurosis. The role of resistance in the analysis is particularly focused in the second phase, in which the regressive emergence of the transference is a central concern. The analysis becomes a recurring conflict between the tendencies toward transference and those toward resistance, manifested by the involuntary inhibition of the patient's efforts to associate freely. This inhibition may last for moments or days or may persist through the whole course of the analysis.

Resistance may take place in the other phases of analysis, but its quality and its significance are different in those phases, depending on the analytic task at hand. In any case, the resistance offered in the analysis enables the analyst to evaluate and become familiar with the defensive organization of the patient's ego and its functions. In this way the pattern of resistance not only offers valuable information to the analyst but also offers a channel by which he can approach the patient therapeutically. Part of the work of the second phase is the working through of resistance and defenses in the interest of facilitating the regression to a transference neurosis. As the patient gradually discovers and works through his defenses, the patient and the analyst inevitably come close to understanding what the patient must defend himself against.

The significance of this basic conflict is clear. It is a repetition of the same sexuality-guilt conflict that originally produced the neurosis itself. Transference may itself serve as a form of resistance, in that the wish for immediate gratification in the analysis can circumvent and postpone the essential goals of treatment. The wish for immediate gratification runs counter to the demands for tolerance of anxiety, delay of gratification, mastery, and growth, which are basic to the analytic process. Consequently, the analysis of resistance, particularly transference resistance, constitutes a primary function of the analyst. It also accounts in many cases for the extended time period required for successful psychoanalytic treatment.

No matter how skillful the analyst, resistance is never absent. The character of the resistance tends to change from phase to phase of the analysis. In the initial phase the patient's resistance may be directed toward establishing the analytic situation and entering into a real one-to-one meaningful relationship with the analyst. In the second phase resistance is usually more concerned with keeping the underlying conflicts unconscious and working against the induced regression of the analytic process. In this phase resistance tends to inhibit and postpone the emergence and development of a transference. In the terminal phase, however, resistance often takes an opposite tack; it works in the interest of clinging to the passive, dependent, and relatively regressed relationship with the analyst, thus resisting the demands of the terminal phase to activate resources for mastery and growth and the necessity for taking a more autonomous and independent stand in relationship to the analyst and the analytic process.

Interpretation. Interpretation is the chief tool available to the analyst in his efforts to reduce unconscious resistance. In the early stages of the development of psychoanalytic therapeutic techniques, the sole purpose of interpretation was to inform the patient of his unconscious wishes. Later, it was designed to help the patient understand his resistance to spontaneous and helpful self-awareness. In current psychoanalytic practice the analyst's function as interpreter is not limited simply to paraphrasing the patient's verbal reports; rather, the analyst indicates at appropriate moments what he is not reporting. As a general rule, analytic interpretation does not produce immediate symptomatic relief. On the contrary, there may be a heightening of anxiety and an emergence of further resistance.

If a correct interpretation is given at the proper time (mutative interpretation), the patient may react either immediately or after a period of emotional struggle, during which he offers new associations. These new associations often confirm the validity of previous interpretations and add significant additional data, disclosing motivations and experiences of the patient that the analyst could not previously have been aware of. Generally, it is not so much the analyst's insight into the patient's psychodynamics that produces progress in the analysis; rather, it is his ability to help the patient gain this insight for himself by reducing unconscious resistance to such self-awareness through appropriate, carefully timed interpretation. The most effective interpretation is timed so that it is given by the analyst in such a way as to meet the emerging, if hesitant

and half-formed, awareness of the patient. The analyst must gauge the capacity of the patient at any given moment to hear, assimilate, and integrate the content of a given interpretation.

Interpretations cannot be seen in isolation from the total context of the analytic situation and the analytic process. An interpretation, both as given by the analyst and as received by the patient, takes place within the context of the therapeutic relationship, including the elements of transference neurosis and therapeutic alliance. The giving and the receiving of interpretations are cloaked with a series of meanings that unavoidably influence the capacity of the patient to accept and integrate interpretations and the analyst's sense of offering and providing such interpretations. Experience has shown that, at best, the therapeutic benefits produced by virtue of the analyst's exortations or unilaterally provided insights are only temporary. Interpretations are most effective and of lasting therapeutic value when they are arrived at by the delicate dialectic that arises from the mutually facilitated and growing awareness of both patient and analyst.

Role of the Analyst

The role of the analyst in the analytic process can be seen specifically in relation to the phases of analysis and in terms of the developmental problems that are at issue in each of the respective phases. In the initial phase of the analysis, the analyst's task is to facilitate the establishing of the analytic situation and the therapeutic alliance. With relatively healthy patients, this is generally not a difficult feature of the analysis. These patients are generally capable of entering into a trusting and productive working relationship with the analyst without any great difficulty.

In the beginning the quality of the patient's interaction with the analyst is more a function of the dimensions of the patient's functioning personality and the interaction with characteristics of the analyst's personality than it is a function of regressive transference elements. In most analytic patients, transference elements are at work almost from the beginning, but other, more realistic aspects of the patient's personality and the interaction with the analyst must be taken into account and given consideration. In hysterical patients and in patients who develop a transference readiness before the beginning of the analysis itself, there may be a tendency to move more quickly into transference issues, in which case the analyst must help the patient build the foundations for a firm therapeutic alliance. The more severe the level of psychopathology, the more significant and important is the work of the first phase. When the therapeutic alliance is firmly and securely established, the more regressive aspects of the treatment situation can be faced with greater confidence and less risk of harmful regression. When the therapeutic relationship is not so established, the risks in regression are greater.

In the transition to the middle phase of analysis, which concerns itself directly with transference neurosis, the role of the analyst becomes closer to the traditional model of analyst in that he uses the approaches and techniques calculated to induce greater regression in the patient. The analyst's focus in the initial phases of analysis has been primarily on the real aspects of the patient's interaction and feelings, and he maintains a certain objectivity and distance in dealing with repressed instinctual derivatives. In the second phase the analyst must become more like the parent who can recognize the child's incestuous fantasies without gratifying them. The transference regression involves a recapitulation of crucial aspects of the mother-child relationship. In the beginning of the analytic process, the analyst is like a mother adapting to the innate dispositions of her child. His responses to the patient are intuitively adaptive and calculated to mobilize the patient's resources in the service of establishing a real relationship.

In the second phase of the analysis, the relative passivity of the analyst implies his avoidance of permissive and authoritative expressions and allows him to limit himself to interpretations, offered at the proper time, of the patient's mental dynamics as heard in his free associations. The analyst's passivity also allows him to clarify the way in which the patient's ego defense mechanisms operate to inhibit or preclude free association, preventing insight into unconscious wishes and impulses. In this respect, the passive role of the analyst reduces the realistic features of the patient-physician relationship, which has been the primary focus of the initial phase of the analysis.

The analyst's task in the second phase is to maintain the stabilizing therapeutic alliance but to facilitate the regression to a transference neurosis. The work of interpretation in this context has to do with the understanding of and working through of infantile conflicts derived from the infantile neurosis. One of the important aspects of this working through has to do with the differentiation between the therapeutic alliance and the elements of the transference neurosis. The therapeutic alliance enables the patient to differentiate between the objective reality of the alliance and the distortions and projections of the transference. The patient must be able to appreciate the difference between the reality of the personality characteristics of the analyst as a real object and the transference distortions that derive from the infantile neurosis. The therapeutic process involves a dual approach: The analyst must respond to the patient both in terms of the transference material and in terms of the therapeutic alliance. He must continue to respond intuitively to the patient's affect, particularly the basic need to feel accepted and understood as a real person, but he must also recognize and interpret the wishes and fantasies derived from the transference neurosis.

Dynamics of the Therapeutic Process

In the course of his analysis, the patient undergoes two processes, remembering and reliving, which constitute the dynamics of the treatment process. Remembering refers to the gradual extension of consciousness back to early childhood, at which time the core of the neurosis was formed, for this stage of development marked the onset of the interference and distortion of the patient's instinctual life. Making the unconscious conscious is accomplished, in part, by the recovery of important childhood experiences through the patient's actual memory of those events. More often, however, the recovery is made in other ways—through the use of fantasy, inference, and analogy. In successfully analyzed patients, recovery means more than mere verbal autobiographical reconstruction. Inevitably, inner convictions and values that were formed in early life are reevaluated and altered so that they can contribute to, rather than hinder, the patient's optimal functioning. Reliving refers to the actual reexperiencing of those events in the context of the patient's relationship with the analyst.

Transference. Through free association, hidden patterns of the patient's mental organization fixated at immature levels are brought to life, comparatively free from disguise. These free associations refer to events or fantasies that are part of the patient's private experience. When they are shared in the analytic setting, the analyst is gradually invested with some of the emotions that accompany them. The patient displaces the feelings he originally directed toward the earlier objects onto the analyst, who then becomes alternately a friend or an enemy, one who is nice to him or frustrates his needs and punishes him, one who is loved or hated as the original objects were loved or hated. Moreover, this tendency persists, so that to an increasing extent the patient's feelings toward the analyst replicate his feelings toward the specific people he is talking about or, more accurately, those whom his unconscious is talking about. The special type of object displacement that is an inevitable concomitant of psychoanalytic treatment is referred to as transference.

As unresolved childhood attitudes emerge and begin to function as fantasied projections toward the analyst, he becomes for the patient a phantom composite figure who represents various important persons in the patient's early environment. Those earlier relationships that remain unresolved are reactivated with some of their original vigor. Gradually, the patient sees himself as he really is, with all his unfulfilled and contradictory needs spread before him. The conscious, scientific use of transference as a dynamic therapeutic force through the analysis of its unconscious sources is unique to classical psychoanalysis. The combination of these two processes—remembering and reliving—enables the patient to gain deeper insights into the defects of his psychological functioning, in spite of himself.

Transference neurosis. The transference neurosis usually develops in the second phase of analysis. The patient who at first was eager for improved mental health no longer consistently displays such motivation during the treatment hours. Rather, he is engaged in a continuing battle with the analyst, and it becomes apparent that his most compelling reason for continuing analysis is his desire to attain some kind of emotional satisfaction from the analyst. At this point in the treatment, the transference emotions are more important to the patient than the permanent health he was seeking when he came to analysis. It is at this point that the major, unresolved, unconscious problems of childhood begin to dominate the patient's behavior. They are now reproduced in the transference with all their pent-up emotion. The patient is striving unconsciously to recapture what he was actually deprived of in childhood.

The transference neurosis is governed by three outstanding characteristics of instinctual life in early childhood: the pleasure principle (prior to effective reality testing), ambivalence, and repetition compulsion. The emergence of the transference neurosis in the analytic setting is usually a slow and gradual process, although, in certain patients with a propensity for transference regression, particularly hysterical patients, the elements of the transference and the transference neurosis may manifest themselves relatively early in the analytic process. The full comprehension and management of the transference neurosis are tests of skill that sharply differentiate those analysts who have received adequate training in classical psychoanalytic theory and technique from those who have not.

One situation after another in the life of the patient is analyzed until the original infantile conflict is fully revealed. Only then does the transference neurosis begin to subside. At that point the juncture between the second phase and the third phase of analysis is marked. Termination of the analysis begins from that point. But is a gradual process and is not even complete with the last visit to the analyst. However, if exposure of the unconscious source of the patient's major problem was fairly thorough, at times of emotional crisis the patient may resolve, through association and without assistance, those areas of conflict that were not entirely worked through with the analyst. Part of the patient's capacity to do this depends on his capacity for internalization and effective identification with the strength and objectivity of the analyst. After a variable period, the temporarily accentuated awareness of the unconscious diminishes. Useful repressions are then partially reestablished. The patient experiences less need for introspection and self-analysis, and he is gradually more able to deal with life on a more mature and satisfactory basis than was previously possible.

Therapeutic alliance. The therapeutic alliance is based on the real, one-to-one relationship that the patient established in the interaction with the analyst. This interaction is contributed to by the real personality characteristics of both the patient and the analyst. The distortions or misperceptions that the patient brings to this relationship may not all be due to transference but may be determined by the relatively stable aspects of the patient's personality structure that relate to his capacity to achieve and maintain a stable object relationship.

For this reason the analyst attempts to clarify the patient's anxiety, suspicions, fears, and unrealistic hopes and expectations or feelings about the analyst, particularly in the beginning of the analytic process, should not be regarded as transference interpretations. The purpose of such analytic interventions is to support and reinforce the patient's capacity to enter and establish a meaningful therapeutic alliance. The importance of the therapeutic alliance cannot be underestimated, since it provides the stable and positive relationship between analyst and patient that enables them both to engage productively in the work of analysis. The therapeutic alliance allows a split to take place in the patient's ego; the observing part of the patient's ego can ally itself with the analyst in a working relationship, which gradually allows it to identify positively with the analyst in analyzing and modifying the pathological defenses put up by the defensive ego against internal danger situations. The maintenance of this therapeutic split and the real relationship to the analyst involved in the therapeutic alliance requires the maintenance of self-object differentiation, tolerance and mastery of ambivalence, and the capacity to distinguish fantasy from reality in the relationship.

The analyst's own personality has an important influence in establishing the therapeutic alliance. The analyst enters the analytic process as a real person and not merely as a transference object. This aspect of the analytic situation should be clearly differentiated from excessive activity or inappropriate participation in the analytic relationship by the analyst. Nonetheless, the analyst's real characteristics can interfere with the achieving of a basic working relationship, and this impediment to the therapeutic alliance can interfere with the satisfactory working through in the analytic process. The maintenance of the therapeutic alliance requires that the patient be able to differentiate between the more mature and the more infantile aspects of his experience in his relationship to the analyst. The therapeutic alliance serves a double function: It acts, on one hand, as a significant barrier to regression of the ego in the analytic process, and it serves, on the other hand, as a fundamental aspect of the analytic situation against which the wishes, feelings, and fantasies evoked by the transference neurosis can be evaluated and measured. In many pathological conditions— some character neuroses, borderline personalities, and the more severe neurotic disorders—it may be impossible to maintain a clinical distinction between the transference neurosis and the therapeutic alliance as a real object relationship.

The therapeutic alliance derives from the mobilization of specific ego resources relating to the capacity for object relations and reality testing. The analyst must direct his attention toward eliciting the patient's capacity to establish such a relationship that will be able to withstand the inevitable distortions and regressive aspects of the transference neurosis. The ego capacities involved are closely related to the resolution of pregenital conflicts; the relationship that forms the basis of the therapeutic alliance must itself be included in the transference analysis.

The fundamental features of the therapeutic alliance must be carefully evaluated and understood and ultimately integrated with the analysis of the transference neurosis. This point is graphically displayed in the analysis of hysterical patients. The initial transference neurosis of such patients tends to present primarily oedipal material, but underlying oral factors are important in the genesis of hysterical disorders. In the terminal stages of the analysis of these patients, resolution of oedipal conflicts depends on the successful analysis of earlier conflicts stemming from the pregenital level of development. Specifically involved are conflicts, usually on an oral level, that are related to achieving early object relations and the acceptance of reality and its limitations. These elements form the developmental basis of the therapeutic alliance.

Modifications in Techniques

There are no short cuts in psychoanalytic treatment. Psychoanalytic treatment typically extends over a period of years and requires interminable patience on the part of both the physician and the patient. The classical analytic method, which best serves the aims of therapy, also constitutes the best experimental situation yet devised for studying the more complex features of human nature.

However, rigid adherence at all times to the fundamental mechanistic principles of psychoanalytic technique is an impossibility. For example, the immediate environmental situation may be so serious for the patient that the analyst must pay common sense attention to its practical implications. Those patient's whose early childhood was extraordinarily deficient in love and affection, so that they suffer from a basic developmental defect in their capacity for one-to-one relationship and, consequently, in their capacity to sustain a therapeutic alliance, must be given more support and encouragement than is advocated by strict psychoanalytic technique.

The analyst's role in the early stages of analysis in helping to establish the therapeutic alliance is of particular importance. With primitive patients, the establishment of a therapeutic alliance can be the more significant aspect of the treatment process and can even remain a problem through most of the analysis. The establishment of the therapeutic alliance for most patients is a significant aspect of the analytic process.

The nature and the degree of the analyst's active intervention in the opening hours of analysis are still matters of considerable discussion and controversy. The transference neurosis usually develops slowly and gradually, so that attempts at premature interpretation in the early hours may not be productive and may even be counterproductive. To forestall premature interpretation, the analyst may use prolonged silences, lack of responsiveness, rigidity, and relative lack of participation in the analysis, as if any reference to the analytic situation or to the person of the analyst or to the patient's feelings about the analyst were a transference interpretation and thus to be avoided. However, serious problems in the subsequent stages of analysis of the transference can often be due to a failure to establish a meaningful alliance in the initial stages of treatment. Thus, suitable interventions of the analyst in the early stages of treatment can be a help to the patient in establishing such a meaningful therapeutic alliance.

Particularly narcissistic and more borderline patients must establish a strong personal tie and strong feelings of attachment and relationship with the analyst before they can develop sufficient interest and motivation for treatment. Moreover, such a strong object tie and alliance with the analyst for these more primitive patients is an absolute necessity if the destructive effects of excessive regression are to be avoided. These are difficult problems, however, since experience also suggests that every deviation from strict analytic technique tends to prolong the length of treatment and considerably increases its vicissitudes and problems.

Modifications in analytic technique usually go under the heading of parameters, and they remain a considerable source of discussion and controversy among analytic therapists. A significant trend today is the increasing tendency of analysts to treat more difficult and complex cases; thus, the necessity for introducing modifications in various aspects of the treatment process correspondingly increases. The resolution of such difficulties in assessing and exploring modifications of techniques must ultimately rest on the basis of clinical experience.

RESULTS

The therapeutic effectiveness of psychoanalysis presents problems in its evaluation. Impartial and objective critics are handicapped in attempts to appraise therapeutic results by the fact that so many patients state that they have been analyzed when no such procedure was, in fact, undertaken or when it was undertaken by someone who used the title of analyst and who, in fact, had little understanding of analytic science and technique. Other patients have been in analysis for only a short time and then discontinued treatment on their own initiative or were advised that they were not suitable candidates for analytic treatment. Except for psychoanalysts themselves, professionals and laymen demonstrate varying degrees of confusion as to what psychoanalysis is and what it is not.

No analyst can ever eliminate all the personality defects and neurotic factors in a given patient, no matter how thorough or successful the treatment. On the other hand, mitigations of the rigors of a punitive superego is an essential criterion of the effectiveness of treatment. Psychoanalysts do not usually regard alleviation of symptoms as the most significant aspect in evaluating therapeutic change. The absence of a recurrence or of a further need for psychotherapy is perhaps a more important index of the value of psychoanalysis. However, the chief basis of evaluation remains the patient's general adjustment to life— his capacity for attaining reasonable happiness and for contributing to the happiness of others, his ability to deal adequately with the normal vicissitudes and stresses of life, and his capacity to enter into and sustain mutually gratifying and rewarding relationships with other people in his life.

More specific criteria of the effectiveness of treatment include the reduction of the patient's unconscious and neurotic need for suffering, reduction of neurotic inhibitions, decrease of infantile dependency needs, and increased capacity for responsibility and for successful relationships in marriage, work, and social relations. Another important criterion is the patient's capacity for pleasurable and rewarding sublimation

and for creative and adaptive application of his own potentialities. However, the most important criterion of the success of treatment is the release of the patient's normal potentiality, which had been blocked by neurotic conflicts, for further internal growth, development, and maturation to mature personality functioning.

Suggested Cross References

Classical psychoanalysis has a bearing on practically every other section of this book. But of particular interest are the discussions of historical and theoretical trends in psychiatry (Chapter 1), Erik Erikson (Section 10.1), Melanie Klein (Section 10.5), sleep and dreams (Section 2.3), neurosis, psychosis, and the borderline states (Section 14.3), psychotic disorders (Chapters 15 through 19), neurotic disorders (Chapter 21), personality disorders (Chapter 22), normal human sexuality and psychosexual disorders (Chapter 24), psychological factors affecting physical conditions (Chapter 26), psychotherapies (Chapter 30), evaluation of psychiatric treatment (Chapter 33), and the women's movement (Section 56.8).

REFERENCES

Abraham, K. *Selected Papers on Psychoanalysis.* Basic Books, New York, 1953.
Aichhorn, A. *Wayward Youth.* Viking Press, New York, 1965.
Alexander, F. *Psychoanalysis and Psychotherapy.* W. W. Norton, New York, 1956.
Alexander, F., and Ross, H. *The Impact of Freudian Psychiatry.* University of Chicago Press, Chicago, 1961.
Alexander, F., and Selesnick, S. T. *The History of Psychiatry.* Mentor, New York, 1966.
Amacher, P. Freud's neurological education and its influence on psychoanalytic theory. In *Psychological Issues,* G. S. Klein, editor, monograph 16. International Universities Press, New York, 1965.
Ansbacher, H. L., and Ansbacher, R. R. *The Individual Psychology of Alfred Adler.* Basic Books, New York, 1956.
Arlow, J. A., editor. *Selected Writings of Bertram D. Lewin.* Psychoanalytic Quarterly, New York, 1973.
Balint, M. *Thrills and Regressions.* International Universities Press, New York, 1959.
Balint, M. *Primary Love and Psychoanalytic Technique.* Liverwright, New York, 1965.
Balint, M. *The Basic Fault: Therapeutic Aspects of Regression.* Tavistock Publications, London, 1968.
Bibring, E. The mechanism of depression. In *Affective Disorders: Psychoanalytic Contribution to Their Study,* P. Greenacre, editor. International Universities Press, New York, 1953.
Bibring, G. L., Dwyer, T. F., Huntington, D. S., and Valenstein, A. F. A study of the psychological processes in pregnancy and of the earliest mother-child relationship. II. Methodological considerations. Psychoanal. Study Child, *16:* 25, 1961.
Blos, P. *On Adolescence: A Psychoanalytic Interpretation.* Free Press (Macmillan), New York, 1962.
Blum, H. P. The borderline childhood of the Wolf Man. J. Am. Psychoanal. Assoc., *22:* 721, 1974.
Blum, H. P. Masochism, the ego ideal, and the psychology of women. J. Am. Psychoanal. Assoc., *24:* 157, 1976.
Bowlby, J. *Child Care and the Growth of Love.* Penguin Books, Baltimore, 1965.
Bowlby, J. *Attachment and Loss.* Vol. I. *Attachment.* Basic Books, New York, 1969.
Brenner, C. *An Elementary Textbook of Psychoanalysis.* International Universities Press, New York, 1955.
Brill, A. A. *Lectures on Psychoanalytic Psychiatry.* Vintage, New York, 1955.
Burgner, M., and Edgcumbe, R. Some problems in the conceptualization of early object-relationships. II. The concept of object constancy. Psychoanal. Study Child, *27:* 315, 1972.
Burlingham, D., and Freud, A. *Infants without Families.* George Allen and Unwin, London, 1944.
Chodoff, P., and Lyons, H. Hysteria, the hysterical personality, and "hysteric*an*" conversion. Am. J. Psychiatry, *114:* 734, 1958.
Dalbiez, R. *Psychoanalytical Method and the Doctrine of Freud.* Longman's, Green, London, 1941.
Deutsch, H. *The Psychology of Women.* Grune & Stratton, New York, 1944.
Deutsch, H. *Neuroses and Character Types.* International Universities Press, New York, 1965.
Edgcumbe, R., and Burgner, M. Some problems in the conceptualization of early object-relationships. I. The concepts of need-satisfaction and need-satisfying

relationships Psychoanal. Study Child, *27:* 283, 1972.

Ellenberger, H. *The Discovery of the Unconscious.* Basic Books, New York, 1970.

Erikson, E. H. Identity and the life cycle. In *Psychological Issues,* G. S. Klein, editor, monograph 1. International Universities Press, New York, 1959.

Erikson, E. H. *Childhood and Society,* ed. 2. W. W. Norton, New York, 1963.

Fairbairn, W. R. D. *Psychoanalytic Studies of the Personality.* Tavistock Publications, London, 1952.

Fairbairn, W. R. D. *Object-Relations Theory of the Personality.* Basic Books, New York, 1954.

Federn, P. *Ego Psychology and the Psychoses.* Basic Books, New York, 1952.

* Fenichel, O. *The Psychoanalytic Theory of Neurosis.* W. W. Norton, New York, 1945.

Ferenczi, S. *First Contributions to Psychoanalysis.* Hogarth Press, London, 1953.

*Freud, A. *The Ego and the Mechanisms of Defense.* International Universities Press, New York, 1946.

Freud, A. *The Psychoanalytical Treatment of Children.* Schocken Books, New York, 1964.

Freud, A. *Normality and Pathology in Childhood: Assessments of Development.* International Universities Press, New York, 1965.

Freud, M. *Sigmund Freud: Man and Father.* Vanguard, New York, 1958.

Freud, S. *On Aphasia.* International Universities Press, New York, 1953.

* Freud, S. *Standard Edition of the Complete Psychological Works of Sigmund Freud.* Hogarth Press, London, 1953–1966.

Freud, S. Civilization and its discontents. In *Standard Edition of the Complete Psychological Works of Sigmund Freud,* vol. 21, p. 59. Hogarth Press, London, 1961.

Freud, S. *Infantile Cerebral Paralysis.* University of Miami Press, Coral Gables, 1968.

Fromm-Reichmann, F. *Principles of Intensive Psychotherapy.* University of Chicago Press, Chicago, 1950.

Gardiner, M., editor. *The Wolf Man by the Wolf Man.* Basic Books, New York, 1971.

Gill, M. M. Topography and systems in psychoanalytic theory. In *Psychological Issues,* G. S. Klein, editor, monograph 10. International Universities Press, New York, 1963.

Gill, M. M. *The Collected Papers of David Rapaport.* Basic Books, New York, 1967.

Glover, E. *The Technique of Psychoanalysis,* ed. 2. International Universities Press, New York, 1955.

Glover, E. *On the Early Development of the Mind.* International Universities Press, 1956.

Greenacre, P. *Trauma, Growth, and Personality.* International Universities Press, New York, 1952.

Greenson, R. *The Technique and Practice of Psychoanalysis,* vol. 1. International Universities Press, New York, 1967.

Guntrip, H. *Personality Structure and Human Interaction.* International Universities Press, New York, 1961.

Guntrip, H. *Schizoid Phenomena, Object-Relations, and the Self.* International Universities Press, New York, 1969.

Hale, N. G. *Freud and the Americans.* Oxford University Press, New York, 1971.

Hartmann, H. *Ego Psychology and the Problem of Adaptation.* International Universities Press, New York, 1949.

* Hartmann, H. *Essays on Ego Psychology.* International Universities Press, New York, 1964.

Hartmann, H., and Kris, E. The genetic approach in psychoanalysis. Psychoanal. Study Child, *1:* 11, 1945.

Hendrick, I. *Facts and Theories of Psychoanalysis,* ed. 3. Alfred A. Knopf, New York, 1958.

Holt, R. R., editor. Motives and thought: Psychoanalytic essays in honor of David Rapaport. In *Psychological Issues,* G. S. Klein, editor, monographs 18 and 19. International Universities Press, New York, 1967.

Horney, K. *New Ways in Psychoanalysis.* W. W. Norton, New York, 1939.

Horney, K. *Neurosis and Human Growth.* W. W. Norton, New York, 1950.

Jacobson, E. *The Self and the Object World.* International Universities Press, New York, 1964.

*Jones, E. *The Life and Work of Sigmund Freud.* Basic Books, New York, 1953–1957.

Jones, E. *Papers on Psychoanalysis.* Beacon Press, Boston, 1966.

Jouvet, M. Telencephalic and rhombencephalic sleep in the cat. In *The Nature of Sleep,* G. Wolstenholme and M. O'Connor, editors, p. 188. Little, Brown, and Co., Boston, 1961.

Jung, C. G. *Symbols of Transformation.* Harper & Row, New York, 1962.

Jung, C. G. *The Portable Jung.* Viking Press, New York, 1971.

Kernberg, O. Borderline personality organization. J. Am. Psychoanal. Assoc., *15:* 641, 1967.

Kernberg, O. A psychoanalytic classification of character pathology. J. Am. Psychoanal. Assoc., *18:* 800, 1970.

Klein, M. *The Psychoanalysis of Children.* Hogarth Press, London, 1932.

Klein, M. *Contributions to Psychoanalysis, 1921–1945.* Hogarth Press, London, 1952.

Klein, M. *Envy and Gratitude.* Tavistock Publications, London, 1957.

Klein, M., Hermann, P., Isaacs, S., and Riviere, J. *Developments in Psychoanalysis.* Hogarth Press, London, 1952.

Kohut, H. Forms and transformations of narcissism. J. Am. Psychoanal. Assoc., *14:* 243, 1966.

Kohut, H. *The Analysis of the Self.* International Universities Press, New York, 1971.

Kohut, H. *The Restoration of the Self.* International Universities Press, New York, 1977.

Kris, E. Notes on the development and on some current problems of psychoanalytic child psychology. In *Selected Papers of Ernst Kris,* L. M. Newman, editor, p. 54. Yale University Press, New Haven, 1975.

Kubie, L. S. *Practical and Theoretical Aspects of Psychoanalysis.* Praeger, New York, 1960.

Lewin, B. D. *Psychoanalysis of Elation.* Psychoanalytic Quarterly, New York, 1961.

Lorand, S. *Technique of Psychoanalytic Therapy.* International Universities Press, New York, 1946.

Mahler, M. S. *On Human Symbiosis and the Vicissitudes of Individuation.* Vol. 1. *Infantile Psychosis.* International Universities Press, New York, 1968.

Mahler, M. S. A study of the separation-individuation process and its possible application to borderline phenomena in the psychoanalytic situation. Psychoanal. Study Child, *26:* 403, 1971.

Mann, J., and Semrad, E. V. Conversion as process and conversion as symptom in psychosis. In *On the Mysterious Leap from the Mind to the Body,* F. Deutsch, editor, p. 131. International Universities Press, New York, 1959.

Meissner, W. W. The Wolf Man and the paranoid process. Annu. Psychoanal., *5:* 23, 1977.

Meissner, W. W. *The Paranoid Process.* Jason Aronson, New York, 1978.

Menninger, K. A. *Theory of Psychoanalytic Technique.* Basic Books, New York, 1958.

Modell, A. H. *Object Love and Reality.* International Universities Press, New York, 1968.

Nunberg, H. *Principles of Psychoanalysis.* International Universities Press, New York, 1955.

Nunberg, H. (1931). The synthetic function of the ego. In *Practice and Theory of Psychoanalysis,* p. 120. International Universities Press, 1955.

Nunberg, H. *Practice and Theory of Psychoanalysis.* International Universities Press, New York, 1961.

Rank, O. *Beyond Psychology.* Denver, New York, 1958.

Rank, O. *The Myth of the Birth of the Hero.* Vintage, New York, 1959.

Rapaport, D., editor. *Organization and Pathology of Thought.* Columbia University Press, New York, 1951.

Rapaport, D. *The Structure of Psychoanalytic Theory: A Systematizing Attempt.* International Universities Press, New York, 1960.

Rapaport, D. *The Collected Papers of David Rapaport,* M. M. Gill, editor. Basic Books, New York, 1967.

Reich, W. *Character Analysis.* Farrar, Straus, & Giraux, New York, 1949.

Ricoeur, P. *Freud and Philosophy: An Essay on Interpretation.* Yale University Press, New Haven, 1970.

Rieff, D. *Freud: The Mind of the Moralist.* Doubleday, New York, 1961.

Rochlin, G. *Griefs and Discontents: The Forces of Change.* Little, Brown, and Co., Boston, 1965.

Rochlin, G. *Man's Aggression: The Defense of the Self.* Gambit, Boston, 1973.

Sachs, H. *Freud: Master and Friend.* Harvard University Press, Cambridge, 1945.

Schafer, R. *Aspects of Internalization.* International Universities Press, New York, 1968.

Schilder, D. *The Image and Appearance of the Human Body.* International Universities Press, New York, 1950.

Schur, M. *The Id and the Regulatory Principles of Mental Functioning.* International Universities Press, New York, 1966.

Schur, M. *Freud: Living and Dying.* International Universities Press, New York, 1972.

Searles, H. F. *Collected Papers on Schizophrenia and Related Subjects.* International Universities Press, New York, 1965.

Semrad, E. V. The organization of ego defenses and object loss. In *The Loss of Loved Ones,* D. M. Moriarity, editor, p. 126. Charles C Thomas, Springfield, Ill., 1967.

Shakow, D., and Rapaport, D. The influence of Freud on American psychology. In *Psychological Issues,* G. S. Klein, editor, monograph 13. International Universities Press, New York, 1964.

Socarides, C. W. Homosexuality. In *American Handbook of Psychiatry,* ed. 2, vol. 3, S. Arieti, editor, p. 291. Basic Books, New York, 1974.

Spitz, R. A. *No and Yes.* International Universities Press, New York, 1957.

Spitz, R. A. *The First Year of Life.* International Universities Press, New York, 1965.

Stone, L. *The Psychoanalytic Situation.* International Universities Press, New York, 1961.

Vaillant, G. E. Theoretical hierarchy of adaptive ego mechanisms. Arch. Gen. Psychiatry, *24:* 107, 1971.

Waelder, R. *Basic Theory of Psychoanalysis.* International Universities Press, New York, 1960.

* Weisman, A. D. *The Existential Core of Psychoanalysis.* Little, Brown, and Co., Boston, 1965.

White, R. W. Ego and reality in psychoanalytic theory. In *Psychological Issues,* G. S. Klein, editor, monograph 11. International Universities Press, New York, 1963.

Whyte, L. L. *The Unconscious Before Freud.* Doubleday, New York, 1962.

Winnicott, D. W. *Collected Papers.* Tavistock Publications, London, 1958.

Winnicott, D. W. *The Child, the Family, and the Outside World.* Penguin Books, Baltimore, 1964.

Winnicott, D. W. *The Maturational Process and the Facilitating Environment.* International Universities Press, New York, 1965.

Yankelovich, D., and Barrett, W. *Ego and Instinct: The Psychoanalytic View of Human Nature,* ed. 2. Vintage, New York, 1970.

Zetzel, E. R. The so-called good hysteria. Int. J. Psychoanal., *49:* 256, 1968.

* Zetzel, E. R. *The Capacity for Emotional Growth.* International Universities Press, New York, 1970.

Zetzel, E. R., and Meissner, W. W. *Basic Concepts of Psychoanalytic Psychiatry.* Basic Books, New York, 1973.

Zilboorg, G. *A History of Medical Psychology.* W. W. Norton, New York, 1941.

chapter

9

Theories of Personality and Psychopathology: Cultural and Interpersonal Psychoanalytic Schools

9.1 Alfred Adler

HEINZ L. ANSBACHER, Ph.D.

Introduction

The work of Alfred Adler (1870–1937) has on numerous occasions been presented in straightforward expository form. But that presentation has not proved effective. One reason may be that the reader takes the widely accepted misconceptions about Adler as indubitable facts. When he finds those misconceptions ignored, he is likely to become distrustful and indifferent toward the new account and turn away from it. Therefore, it seems indicated to begin by dealing with those misconceptions.

The misconceptions are mostly based on taking Adler's early views for his final views.

Inferiority complex and overcompensation are thought to be the two key concepts of individual psychology. It is true that in 1907 Adler wrote on organ inferiority, compensation, and overcompensation. But later he virtually abandoned the concept of overcompensation, and a volume of his later writings (Adler, 1964c) has no index entry for it. As to inferiority complex, the situation is different. Adler (1963) began to use the term in 1930, in the phrase:

what in America . . . is called . . . the "inferiority complex," the feeling of inferiority,

indicating that the new term represented no new concept. But later Adler (1956) used the term in different meanings, confusing the matter. For the mature Adler the two key concepts were striving for superiority, as subjectively defined, and social interest.

Masculine protest is thought to have become the prime motivational force in normal and neurotic behavior in the Adlerian system. That was essentially true for the Adler of 1910. But by 1928 Adler had limited the masculine protest to a frequent special case of the general upward striving for superiority.

Adler and Jung, although dissidents, are thought to be best

FIGURE 1. Alfred Adler (print includes signature). (From The Bettmann Archive, New York, N. Y.)

categorized under psychoanalysis, together with Freud. That may be defensible from a certain viewpoint, yet it is a misconception leading directly to gross errors. Adler's unit of study was not elements and processes, nor was his preferred method free association. Rather, in those matters as otherwise, Adler fits well with the Gestalt psychology of Wertheimer, Koffka, and Köhler, whose unit of study was antielements (natural wholes or Gestalten), and whose preferred method was phenomenology and behavior observation.

A second phenomenon about Adler is the puzzling question, mentioned by Mora (1975):

> why Adler's work has not received more attention, considering the fact that many of his original ideas have found their way into psychiatry.

The following theories are positively related to Adler in some way that was original with him.

The theories of Karen Horney, Harry Stack Sullivan, and Erich Fromm are presented by Hall and Lindzey (1978) in one chapter, together with Adler's theories. Of Adler they said:

> Alfred Adler may be regarded as the ancestral figure of the "new social psychological look." . . . Fromm acknowledged that Adler was the first psychoanalyst to emphasize the fundamental social nature of humans.

Sandor Rado is identified with the adaptational psychodynamic viewpoint, which is based on the evolutionary biological principle. That had also been Adler's (1956) position:

> Individual Psychology stands firmly on the ground of evolution. . . . We must connect our thought with a continuous active adaptation to the demands of the outer world.

That common basic orientation gives rise to many essential similarities between Rado and Adler.

Jules Masserman's (1968) biodynamic considerations led him to ask:

> Can one really postulate simple conative entities called "drives" or "instincts"? And . . . what becomes of our artificial "localizations" and quasimethodologic distinctions between "conscious" and "unconscious" or "id," "ego," and "superego"?

Similar issues had been raised by Adler (1956; Ansbacher, 1974a). And where Masserman saw the essence of psychotherapy in rebuilding the patients' "confidences in themselves [and] in their fellow men," Adler saw it in encouragement and developing social interest.

Eric Berne (1972) stated:

> Of all those who preceded transactional analysis, Alfred Adler comes closest to talking like a script analyst,

and he added a 17-line quotation from Adler. Harris (1973), a transactional analyst, rightly equated the "I'm not O.K." of his "I'm O.K.—you're O.K." typology with Adler's concept of inferiority feeling.

Erik Erikson's relation to Adler is especially striking in his emphasis on ethics, including responsibility (Kaplan et al., 1975):

> If everything goes back to childhood, then everything is somebody else's fault, and trust in one's power of taking responsibility for oneself may be undermined.

Adler (1956) had asserted:

> The life plan of the neurotic demands categorically that if he fails it should be through someone else's fault and he should be freed from personal responsibility.

Erikson's (1974) dimension of actuality, a way of "relating to each other . . . in the service of common goals," is a characteristic of Adler's

(1964a) person with a well-developed social interest whose "goal . . . will be identified with ideas of serving the human race." He will overcome "common instead of private feelings of inferiority."

Adolf Meyer's emphases on psychobiological unity, the whole person and the whole situation, the soundness of common sense, prevention, the spreading of basic mental health principles to everyone, and the use of lay personnel were all shared by Adler.

Regarding Carl Jung (1979), a few lines by him of appreciation of Adler may be cited:

> Adler's meticulous elaboration of the psychology and phenomenology of the urge for significance . . . is vital for the etiology and structure of the neuroses in particular and the psychoses (especially schizophrenia) in general. . . . Adler's life work constitutes one of the most important keystones for the structure of a future art of psychotherapy.

Similarities between the existential psychoanalysts and Adler have often been pointed out by Rom and Ansbacher (1965), Stern (1967), and Van Dusen (1959). Kelman (1962) wrote:

> Of existentialism there is least in Freud, somewhat more in Jung and Rank, and the most in Adler and Ferenczi.

In the words of Frankl (1970):

> Alfred Adler may well be regarded as . . . a fore-runner of the existential-psychiatric movement.

The reader may magnify for himself the existentialistic quality of Adler's work by substituting each time for the term "life" the near-synonym "existence."

Jean Piaget's operational position on problems of cognition is in line with Adler's thinking. According to Piaget (1965), knowledge never proceeds "from ready-made structures innate in the subject, nor from a simple abstraction from objects" but supposes "interactions between the subject and object." Adler's interactionalism was well expressed by Kallen (1934) when he wrote:

> To Alfred Adler the metapsychologies of Jung and Freud are abhorrent. His inferential structures . . . are comparatively free from hypostases. . . . He sees psychology as an interpretation of the interaction of the individual with society

and, one may add, the world in general.

Other theories are essentially consistent with the humanistic point of view. Henry A. Murray, Kurt Goldstein, Andras Angyal, and Abraham Maslow were among the founding sponsors of the Association of Humanistic Psychology. But so was the present author, representing Adlerian psychology. Gordon W. Allport, in a personal communication, called Adler

> beyond doubt one of the wisest psychologists of this century.

Gardner Murphy (1970) credited him for his recognition of the social-science perspective. Kurt Lewin, closely related to the original Gestalt psychology, is reported to have found that Gestalt psychology confirmed experimentally the correctness of the Adlerian views. Parallels between Goldstein in particular and Adler have been shown by Alexandra Adler (1959).

Development of Adler's Work

Because misconceptions about Adler stem mostly from lack of knowledge of his development, a rather detailed presentation of it seems indicated. The development of Adler's work falls into four 10-year periods: 1898 to 1907, preliminary period; 1908 to 1917, inferiority-superiority dynamics; 1918 to 1927, social interest, phase 1; 1928 to 1937, social interest, phase 2.

Within that framework some of Adler's life events are also mentioned (Bottome, 1957; Orgler, 1963; Furtmüller, 1964; Ellenberger, 1970; Sperber, 1974).

1898 TO 1907: PRELIMINARY PERIOD

Social medicine and education. Adler was born in a Vienna suburb on February 7, 1870, and graduated from medical school there in 1895. His first publications in 1898 and 1902 refer to issues of social medicine: poor health conditions in the tailoring trade, the urgency for the medical profession to take a lead in social medicine, and the desirability of a chair in social medicine (Ellenberger, 1970). In the paper "The Physician as Educator" (Adler and Furtmüller, 1973), several later developments of Adler are foreshadowed—confidence in their own strength was presented as most important for children's intellectual development, and weak and pampered children were presented as being most in danger of losing their self-confidence.

Membership in Freud's circle. In 1902 Adler—together with Kahane, Reitler, and Stekel—was invited by Freud to meet at his apartment every Wednesday to discuss the psychology of the neuroses (Ansbacher, 1962). As to why Freud invited Adler, there is no documented explanation. In 1905 Adler (1978) acknowledged Freud's theory of sexuality, including infant sexuality, as his theoretical foundation. But Adler defined sexuality as a form of sensuality, thereby integrating it with a person's total interaction with his environment. In a paper on the ideas of numbers that was suggested by Freud's *Psychopathology of Everyday Life*, Adler (Ansbacher, 1962) concluded again in 1905:

> In none of these analyses do we find complete repression . . . . The large share of consciousness, of the unrepressed . . . can easily be proven.

Study of organ inferiority. Adler's (1917) often-cited monograph, written in 1907, is a physiological study. Organ inferiorities and their compensations through the nervous superstructure were considered as such. Any terms implying an individual person, such as "the patient," and psychological terms, such as "inferiority feeling," were carefully avoided. Persons were mentioned only in support of an abstract principle. Not until 1910 did Adler (1978) introduce the terms "inferiority feeling" and "masculine protest."

1908 TO 1917: INFERIORITY-SUPERIORITY DYNAMICS AND UNITY OF THE PERSONALITY

Aggression drive. In 1908 Adler presented his first dynamic principle on a psychological level, the aggression drive, a confluence of drives including but not dominated by the sex drive (Adler, 1956). The aggression drive combines with primary drives that have been blocked. Furthermore, drives in general may be transformed into their opposites, displaced to another goal, directed toward one's own person, or displaced to another drive. In 1915 Freud (1925) also wrote on the transformation of drives.

Neurotic disposition. The neurotically disposed person is characterized by lack of confidence in self and others, oversensitivity toward expected disparagement, guilt feelings based on "failures due to organ inferiority," and inhibition of aggression (Adler and Furtmüller, 1973). Not clearly distinguishing between neurotic disposition and actual neurosis, Adler considered those characteristics the uniform structure of most disorders. His report before the Vienna Psychoanalytic Society before publication of the paper in 1909 was entitled, "The Oneness [Unity] of the Neuroses" (Nunberg and Federn, 1967). Further characteristics that Adler soon added were reified thinking, depreciation tendency, and distance behavior; he dropped guilt feelings and inhibition of aggression.

Masculine protest. Masculine protest (Nunberg and Federn, 1967) was the striving for dominance and power as enjoyed by a "real man" according to the cultural stereotype of the time—a stereotype that, incidentally, Adler fought vehemently. In introducing this new concept in 1910, Adler explained (Nunberg and Federn, 1967):

> The aggression drive . . . suffered from . . . being biological . . . . One must consider a conception of the neurotic . . . only in psychological terms, or terms of cultural psychology.

Such an abrogation of drive psychology was intolerable for Freud and led to the break with Adler the next year, 1911.

Presidency of the Vienna Psychoanalytic Society. Meanwhile, certain organizational difficulties loomed so large for Freud that he overlooked the rift with Adler and suggested him for president of the Vienna Psychoanalytic Society, replacing Freud. Adler was elected president by acclamation on April 6, 1910. Around that time he, together with Stekel, also became editor of the newly founded *Zentralblatt für Psychoanalyse*, with Freud as editor-in-chief.

Meetings on suicide. The first scientific meetings under Adler's presidency, April 20 and 27, 1910, dealt with suicide, with Adler as chairman of the first meeting and Stekel as chairman of the second meeting. The proceedings were published as the first of a projected series, suggested by Adler and prefaced by him (Friedman, 1967). Four-fifths of the contents were by Adler and his later followers. Adler (Friedman, 1967) spoke of a social intention of suicide as an "act of revenge." Freud was reticent, commenting in conclusion (Friedman, 1967): "Let us suspend our judgment." Yet when the proceedings appeared in English in 1967, the editor, Paul Friedman, minimized Adler's part, named Freud as chairman, and inserted a page listing the participants, headed by Freud as chairman, without identifying this page as an insertion. Subsequently, the publicity for a 1968 conference on suicide featured Freud's "chairmanship" of the 1910 Vienna symposium on suicide, with no mention of Adler (Ansbacher, 1968). Those events illustrate the "puzzling phenomenon," noted by Ellenberger (1970), "of a collective denial of Adler's work."

Resignation from the Vienna Psychoanalytic Society. In 1911 Adler gave his critique of Freud's concepts, including sexuality, before the Vienna Psychoanalytic Society, an event that led to the resignation of Adler and nine other members.

Neurotic constitution. In 1912 Adler (1972, 1974a) published his historically most important book, *The Neurotic Constitution*, which introduced his school of individual psychology and replaced drives with values.

Finalistic thinking and goal orientation. Adler replaced thinking in terms of objective forces and past events—the causalistic, analytic thinking of the natural sciences—with thinking in terms of subjective goals and purposes—the finalistic thinking of daily life—a shift from a mechanistic to an organismic-humanistic conception. As Adler (1956) formulated the theory in 1914:

> The most important question of the healthy and the diseased mental life is not whence? but, whither? . . . In this whither? the cause is contained.

Unity of the personality and life plan. With respect to an assumed final goal, the personality is unified like a character by a good dramatist. That unity leads to the further assumption of a life plan, later called life style. In 1912 Adler (1972) wrote:

> Every smallest trait is permeated by a planful dynamic . . . every psychological process [carries] the imprint . . . of the uniformly oriented life plan.

Conscious-unconscious unity. In 1913 Adler (1974b) made it clear that consciousness and unconsciousness are both in the service of the self-consistent life plan. Thus, they are not in real conflict with each other and represent an "antithesis of means" only. Later Adler (1974b) added in a footnote:

> The contrast to the views of Freud and other authors is clear. Indeed the compulsion toward unity of the personality . . . dominates the extent of the conscious as it does that of the unconscious.

Subjectivistic approach. Although Freud listened to his patients, he took their statements as disguises for some causative-repressed primary processes. Adler took such statements as metaphorical samples of the patient's subjective reality. Symptoms were ways to cope with life problems in accordance with the patient's mistaken opinion of himself and the world—an opinion of which he was, however, not aware. Adler's motto for his book was the Stoic Seneca's, "Omnia ex opinione suspensa sunt."

Inferiority-superiority dynamics. In replacing drives with values, Adler also changed from a positivistic unipolar concept of dynamics to a dialectical, bipolar concept. When a car needs oil, nothing else will do—a unipolar concept. But the striving is always from a feeling of inferiority toward a goal of superiority or, in general terms, from a minus to a plus situation in which both poles are subjectively conceived and negotiable. In therapy such bipolarity affords scope and flexibility. Over the years Adler spoke of the plus situation variously as a goal of masculinity, power, superiority, success, perfection, completion, and overcoming difficulties. Any similar value term would also do.

Reified thinking of the neurotic. The striving—as from a minus situation to a plus situation, from inferiority to superiority—is actually a human construction in line with the general human tendency for practical reasons to dichotomize and categorize, whereas reality shows no such sharp distinctions. The normal person is somehow aware of deviation from reality, takes his categories as figures of speech, and sets them aside in the face of reality. But the neurotic and, even more so, the psychotic, wrote Adler (1956) in 1912, seeks greater security, "hypostasizes his fiction ... and seeks to realize it in the world." Similarly, Bateson et al. (1956) observed that, although all human communication involves metaphors, "the schizophrenic uses unlabeled metaphors," giving them reality value. In 1929 Adler (1964a), referred to rigid dichotomizing as:

> the neurotic formula of "all or nothing." ... When the hope of gaining *all* begins to fade, *nothing* is left.

Depreciation tendency. The neurotic is inclined to raise his self-esteem by depreciating others. That tendency is at the root of sadism, hatred, disputatiousness, intolerance, and envy. It is also generally directed against the therapist, what, Adler (1972) noted in 1912:

> Freud has called resistance and mistook for the consequence of the repression of sexual impulses.

Distance seeking. Another important device of the neurotic is the interposing of a distance between himself and an expected action or decision from which he fears defeat. In 1914 Adler, (1956) spoke of four such modes of distance seeking—moving backward, standing still, hesitation (the hesitating attitude), and constructing obstacles—and listed for each the various disorders for which it is typical. What is generally seen as a conflict was for Adler a device of assuring distance through a standstill.

A cheerless view of life? With vestiges of the aggression drive and striving for power and masculinity as Adler's main dynamic, Freud (1924) sarcastically wrote in 1914 of this "cheerless view of life, ... with no room in it for love." Although that statement seems absurd in the light of subsequent developments, at the time Freud had a point. Adler was, in his 1912 book, essentially concerned with the neurotic and had no positive specification of the normal person beyond more flexible thinking. Otherwise, the normal person was like the neurotic, only to a smaller degree. Obviously, Adler realized that shortcoming, for a few years later he added the concept of social interest, although quite unobtrusively and without ever admitting that there may have been a shortcoming.

Other developments. After his separation from Freud, Adler founded the Society for Free Psychoanalytic Research in 1911; in 1912 he changed the name to Society of Individual Psychology. Also in 1912 Adler founded a monograph series. And in 1914 he founded the

Zeitschrift für Individualpsychologie. That year he also edited with Carl Furtmüller (Adler and Furtmüller, 1973) a volume of collected papers (which was never translated); half the papers were his own, and half were by members of his group. In August 1914, of course, World War I broke out, with its great disruptions. In 1916 Adler was drafted into the Austrian army medical corps, where he served until the end of the war in 1918.

1918 TO 1927: SOCIAL INTEREST, PHASE 1

Social interest as counterforce. In 1918 Adler added the concept of social interest (*Gemeinschaftsgefühl*). He conceived it as an innate force, countering the striving for power or significance. This was not a satisfactory solution for a holistic theory stressing the unity of the personality. But it enabled Adler (1972) to counter criticisms of a completely self-seeking concept of a person. Adler (1972) asserted that he stood for

> the unconditional reduction of the striving for power and the development of social interest.

The concept was also sufficient for the other, mostly practical developments during that period.

Three relational systems. A main theoretical contribution of the decade was the 1924 conceptualization of the human-environment interaction as three relational systems (*Bezugssysteme*): human being-earth, individual-community, and male-female (Adler 1978). As a person does not respond to situations automatically or unconsciously, those relationships become tasks or problems (*Aufgaben*).

Three life problems. From the relational systems emerge the three problem clusters of work, communal life, and love and marriage. The neurotic leaves those problems unsolved and "puts us off with his symptoms and counterarguments" (Adler, 1974b). Adler (1974b) continued:

> Those are of course problems only if ... one takes the standpoint: There are no counterarguments against goodwill, work, and love! Our inexorable demand is to make life easier and more beautiful for the others! Instead, we hear the demand for exemption, and reasons for it.

Such arguments and demands sound like those of a preacher. In his last decade, Adler (1958) corrected that impression writing:

> There have always been men who ... tried to develop social interest and love. In all religions we find this concern. ... Individual Psychology arrives at the same conclusion in a scientific way..... All failures—neurotics, psychotics, criminals, drunkards, problem children, suicides, perverts, and prostitutes—are lacking in fellow-feeling and social interest ... All true "meanings of life" ... are common meanings ... in which others can share and ... which they can accept as valid.

Sexual problem. Adler gave particular attention to love and marriage in numerous papers on the subject, beginning in 1926 with "On Love Relationships and Their Disturbances" (Adler, 1978). The problem of the relationship between the sexes, Adler (1978) stated in 1927, can be solved only on the basis of equality, and the problem of marriage is a task for two equals of different sexes with responsibility to humanity in general. During that period Adler (1978) also wrote his major papers on sexual deviations, including homosexuality, all of which he understood as the seeking of psychological distance from a partner of the other sex.

Life style. Beginning in 1926, Adler replaced his "life plan" with "style of life," a term that today has virtually become a hallmark of Adlerian psychology (Ansbacher, 1967).

Child guidance centers. The particular characteristic of the decade was Adler's establishing of a system of child guidance centers—ultimately more than 30—in Vienna public schools and staffed by volunteer professionals and paraprofessionals. The basic idea was to replace personal power with cooperation and fellowship as ideals. As two procedural innovations, parents, teachers, and the children participated in the sessions, and the sessions were conducted before a disciplined audience of counseling trainees and other interested persons. In 1924 Adler was appointed lecturer (*Dozent*) at the Pedagogical Institute of the City of Vienna, giving courses on problem children. A volume of 20 child guidance cases, *The Problem Child* (Adler, 1963) was published in 1930.

Adlerian counseling in the United States was advanced mostly by Rudolf Dreikurs (1897–1972), who expanded it into family education centers and parent study groups. That aspect attracts by far the largest number of present-day Adlerians. It was described by Dreikurs (1973) and in the Dreikurs biography by Terner and Pew (1978).

During the 1918 to 1927 decade Adler also gave his well-received adult education courses, which resulted in the publication in 1927 of his most popular book, *Understanding Human Nature* (Adler, 1957).

1928 TO 1937: SOCIAL INTEREST, PHASE 2

During his last decade Adler made many important theoretical changes and innovations right up to his last year. Most important was the transformation of social interest into a cognitive process.

Social interest as cognitive process. Adler (1964c) equated social interest with identification in the general, non-Freudian sense and with empathy, both cognitive processes. With social interest, general intelligence becomes reason or common sense; without it, the outcome is private intelligence, the characteristic of all failures in life. Social interest is the criterion of mental health. Psychotherapy aims at bringing the patient's private view more in line with a common view of the world by developing his social interest.

Necessity of conscious development. As a cognitive process, social interest is not inborn as such. "It is an innate potentiality which must be consciously developed" (Adler, 1964a). That necessity is shared with all human aptitudes, such as for reading, skiing, and cooking. Without conscious development, they do not become effective abilities, skills, and interests.

Compatibility with holistic theory. Developed social interest becomes part of the person's goal concept, like any other ability or skill, and conflicts just as little with the central striving for success. With developed social interest, the striving is on the socially useful side; without it, the striving is on the socially useless side of private intelligence.

Nonconformist concept of adjustment. In 1933 Adler (1964c) extended the object of social interest to an ideal future society. The striving with social interest is then

> for a form of community . . . as . . . if humanity had reached the goal of perfection. It is never a present-day community or society, nor a political or religious form.

The truly socially interested, well-adjusted person strives for changes for a better future and is in this sense a nonconformist.

Creative power of the person. From at least 1913 onward Adler (1956) implied self-determination, as when he wrote of neurotic symptoms as "arrangements." But not until his last decade did he specify, in addition to heredity and environment as determiners, "still another force, the creative power of the individual" (Adler, 1964c). Hall and Lindzey (1978) considered it Adler's crowning achievement as a personality theorist.

Primacy of goal striving. Adler also saw his inferiority-superiority dynamics within a larger frame of life itself. "To live means to develop," Adler (1964c) wrote in 1933. "It is part of the structure of life . . . to overcome things" he said (in the *Daily Mail* of London) in 1936. "In comparison with unattainable ideal perfection the individual is continuously filled by an inferiority feeling," Adler (1956) wrote in 1933. Thereby, Adler advanced his theory from one of deficiency motivation to one of growth motivation, to use Maslow's (1968) terms.

Degree of activity. As the physicist movement has two variables, so Adler (1964c) added to his concept of life as movement a second variable, degree of activity. Social interest refers to the social space in which one moves; activity refers to the energy by which one moves. Heredity and environmental factors play a part but ultimately the life style is decisive. Adler (1964c) believed recognition of that second variable

> opens an entirely new and valuable perspective for psychiatric treatment, education, and prevention.

From these two variables Adler (1964c) outlined a two-dimensional personality theory with a 4-fold typology. For example, high social interest and high activity represent the socially useful type (the ancient sanguine temperament); low social interest and high activity represent the ruling type, including criminals, tyrants, and sadists (the ancient choleric temperament).

Interpretation as a device. Adler's last contribution, in 1937, was the understanding that the therapist's interpretations do not necessarily refer to actual facts but may be devices for the purpose of helping the patient reconstruct his perception of himself and the world. As Adler (1937) wrote:

> The inferiority complex has never been in the consciousness or unconsciousness of the patient but only in my own consciousness, and I have used it rather for illumination so that the patient could see his attitude in the right context.

Bringing psychology to the people. Adler intended to formulate a psychology for everybody and took pride in considering himself successful in achieving it. As he wrote (Adler, 1972):

> There may be more venerable theories. . . . There may be newer, more sophisticated theories. But there is certainly none which could bring greater gain to all people.

During his last decade particularly, he gave much time and energy to conveying his message to countless college and lay audiences in Europe and, especially, in the United States. He was considered a fascinating speaker. At a lecture series at Temple Emanu-El in New York, he drew an audience of more than 2,800 persons (*New York Times*, 1929). From a talk in Washington, D. C., before a Town Hall Club audience of 1,000, the *Washington Post* (1937) reported:

> Dr. Adler . . . charmed his audience and drew from it prolonged applause with his rapid-fire returns in a verbal duel with Dr. Harry Stack Sullivan.

That occasion, the only one known that Adler and Sullivan ever met, was reported in several newspapers.

Between 1929 and 1933 Adler published five books, of which the first four are based on English lecture series and appeared only in English: *Problems of Neurosis* (1964a), *The Science of Living* (1969), *The Education of Children* (1970), *What Life Should Mean to You* (1958), and *Social Interest* (1964b).

The last months. While lecturing in Europe early in 1937, Adler became increasingly concerned about his oldest daughter, Vali, who had fled from Nazi Germany to Russia in 1934 and was imprisoned there in February 1937 during the Stalin purges. All efforts to help her were unsuccessful, and Adler wrote in April to his youngest daughter, Nellie (Manaster et al., 1977): "Vali causes me sleepless nights, I am surprised how I can endure it." Several weeks later he wrote to his daughter, Alexandra, the psychiatrist (Manaster et al., 1977): "I cannot sleep and cannot eat. I do not know how much longer I can endure it." A few days later, on May 28, he succumbed to a sudden heart failure on a street in Aberdeen, Scotland.

Personality Theory

BASIC PREMISES

Organismic assumption: unity and purposiveness. Adler's theory is based on organismic biology. It assumes that (Nagel, 1961):

vital processes have a *prima facie* purposive character: organisms are capable of self-regulation . . . and their activities seem to be directed toward . . . goals that lie in the future. . . . Living things are organic wholes, not "additive systems."

Adler borrowed his basic metaphors from organic life, rather than from physics and chemistry.

Humanistic assumption: creative power. A person differs fundamentally from other organisms in being not only a creature but also a creator. "The circumstances make man, but man makes the circumstances." That dialectical sentence by Pestalozzi (1938), later taken up by Karl Marx, was also cited by Adler (1964c). It does away with hard determinism, assuming, in addition to heredity and environment, a third factor— the creative power of the human being. A person is ultimately "the artist of his own personality," as Adler (1956) wrote.

Phenomenological approach. Adler's approach was phenomenological, subjectivistic, or dialectical, rather than positivistic. As Adler (1956) wrote:

More important than disposition, objective experience, and environment is the subjective evaluation of these, which stands in a certain, often strange relation to reality. . . . Individual Psychology examines the attitudes of an individual.

Operational-pragmatic approach. Keenly aware of life as an ongoing process, Adler aimed his concepts at minimizing the danger of reification and maximizing the possibility of being operationalized, at least hypothetically—that is, if not at present, at some future time. Furthermore, when there is a discrepancy between a person's statements and his actions, credence is given to actions. Adler (1964c), like William James, accepted the Biblical maxim, "By their fruits ye shall know them."

BASIC CONCEPTS

Life style. The human organism, cited Adler (1974b) from Virchow, remains biologically

a unified community in which all parts cooperate for a common purpose.

Psychologically, all partial processes—such as drives, perception, memory, and dreaming—are coordinated to the person's unique, self-consistent, and relatively constant way of meeting the world—his life style, which is, within the limits of heredity and environment, of his own creation. Schema of apperception (cognitive style) and law of movement (response style) are aspects of the life style.

Goal striving. A concept of a human being as a unitary organism requires a unitary dynamic principle. As for life in general, it is characterized by movement toward growth and expansion. But beyond that, a human being is capable of anticipating his or her future, including his or her growth and decline, and of making choices. Thus, a person creates ideals and goals that provide him or her with criteria for making choices, values that function as guideposts. A person's movement is always toward an objective, a goal. When he or she is unaware of the goal or in error about it, the goal may be inferred from the consequences of his or her actions.

Inferiority-superiority dynamics. With regard to goals, the person has inferiority feelings about his or her present situation. The goal striving is a movement from a feeling of relative inferiority to a feeling of superiority, a dialectical conception. The goal always includes wanting and continuing to be a worthy human being. The supreme law of life, Adler (1956) wrote, is:

The sense of worth of the self shall not be allowed to be diminished.

Three life problems. A human being as a unified organism lives within larger relational systems. From those systems arise the life problems of occupation, social relations in general, and love and marriage.

Social interest. Adler (1937) wrote:

The degree of social interest is the main characteristic of each person and is involved in all his actions.

It is the main factor in the question of whether a person will be a success or a failure in solving his life problems. Objectively, social interest is expressed in cooperation; subjectively, it is expressed in an affirmative opinion of the world and in feeling at home in the world.

Degree of activity. Activity is the second most important personality variable after social interest; it is part of a two-dimensional personality theory with a 4-fold typology. Those types, however, are in no way meant to detract from the uniqueness of each individual life style. Going beyond Adler, one may note that, subjectively, activity goes with a better opinion of oneself, a higher self-esteem.

NORMAL PERSONALITY AND ADAPTATION

The ideally normal person has high social interest and activity, resulting in true courage; the essence of abnormality is low social interest and low activity, resulting in discouragement. In normality the inferiority-superiority dynamics still apply, but the poles are not reified or magnified, and the gap between them seems to be bridgeable. The goal is one of general validity on the socially useful side. The emphasis is on the striving itself. Normal inferiority feelings, wrote Adler (1956), "are the cause of all improvements in the position of humanity," the basis of all culture. Regarding the goal of superiority, Adler (1956) wrote:

We all have ambition to be successful; but so long as this striving is expressed in work, it does not lead to false valuations which are at the root of mental disorder.

Again, the pragmatic criterion prevails: The normal mode of life is so adapted, wrote Adler (1969), that whether the individual "wants it or not, society derives a certain advantage from his work."

Normal adaptation is active and contributive to a general better future. As Adler (1956) wrote:

An adaptation to immediate reality would be . . . an exploitation of the accomplishments of the striving of others, as the world picture of the pampered child demands. . . . [Such people] wish only to live like a worm in an apple.

PERSONALITY DEVELOPMENT AND CHILDHOOD SIGNIFICANCE

A holistic personality theory has little use for developmental stages. Dividing the life cycle into discrete steps raises self-fulfilling expectations for the steps as described. Personality emerges gradually, uniquely, and as a whole (Adler, 1964a):

In the first four or five years the child ... lays the irrevocable foundation of its style of life.

Heredity and environment offer only probabilities, alluring development in a certain direction.

Favorable and unfavorable factors. The important positive factor is the mother or her equivalent who, Adler (1964a) wrote, fills

the two-fold function of motherhood: to give the child the completest possible experience of human fellowship, and then to widen it into a life-attitude towards others.

Three negative factors endangering the child's development of self-esteem and social interest are: imperfect organs and childhood diseases, pampering, and neglect. Children with imperfect organs and childhood diseases easily become self-centered (Adler, 1956):

lose hope of playing a useful part in our common life, and consider themselves humiliated.

A pampered child

has been trained to receive without giving. ... He has lost his independence and does not know that he can do things for himself.

His social interest and self-esteem are low, making him prone to failure. The neglected, hated, or unwanted child strives (Adler, 1964a)

to escape and to get at a safe distance from others.

Under those circumstances the danger is increased of the child's developing a pampered life style, the predisposing condition for failure in life.

Family constellation. In all cases the family constellation is important. In developing his life style, the child takes his given position in the family, including his birth order, very much into account, with certain positions providing specific probabilities. The family constellation is "a sociogram of the group at home during the person's formative years" (Dreikurs, 1973) and has a lasting effect on the person. By contrast, Freud's oedipal situation overlooks the siblings and regards every childhood situation as that of an only child.

Regarding sexual development, Adler recognized two phases. In the primary phase, sex becomes manifest in a higher tickling sensation, and "the usual course is masturbation" (Adler, 1978). In the secondary phase, the social phase, the person (Adler, 1978)

has reached the right age for making the sexual function a task for two persons of different sexes.

Theory of Psychopathology

For Adler, functional disorders were the outcome of an erroneous way of living that the patient could change once he accepted the explanation offered to him (the educational model of psychotherapy).

MISTAKEN LIFE STYLE

The mistaken life style includes mistaken opinions about onself and the world and a mistaken goal of success, all strongly connected with underdeveloped social interest. Adler described it eventually as the pampered life style, the style of a person who is expecting from others, pressing them into his service, evading responsibility, and blaming the circumstances for his shortcomings, while actually feeling incompetent and insecure (Adler, 1956).

The pampered life style as a living phenomenon is the creation of the child, though its formation is frequently aided by others. Consequently, it can be found occasionally in cases where we cannot speak ... of pampering, but where, on the contrary, we find neglect.

But the pampered life style is not the disorder, only the disposition toward disorder, similar to the neurotic disposition.

EXOGENOUS FACTOR

A person with a mistaken life style may go through life without a crisis, provided he is spared any test of his social interest, "the proximity of a task that demands cooperation and fellowships" (Adler, 1956), always related to one of the three life tasks. The confrontation with such a task becomes the exogenous factor, which "sets the match to the fire" (Adler, 1956). Modern crisis intervention has partly followed that way (Ansbacher, 1972).

UNITY AND DIVERSITY OF MENTAL DISORDERS

Adler presented a unitary theory of mental disorders, within which each patient "arranges" his symptoms uniquely to serve as excuses for not meeting his life problems and to protect his self-esteem. Without changing this unity, Adler discriminated the failures in life along the dimensions of social interest and degree of activity.

The neurotic has more social interest than the psychotic. The neurotic follows the formula, "Yes—but" (Adler, 1956); in the "yes" he acknowledges his social obligations; in the "but" he weighs his symptoms that prevent him from realizing his intentions. The psychotic, on the other hand, cuts himself off completely from the common world. He represents, wrote Adler (1956):

the highest degree of isolation ... but ... is not incurable if the interest in others can be aroused.

As to activity, a low degree is found in neurosis and psychosis in general, with activity in compulsion neurosis and depression relatively higher than in anxiety neurosis and schizophrenia. Somewhat more activity is found in suicides and alcoholics than in others. The greatest activity is shown by criminals, with swindlers and pickpockets relatively low and murderers relatively high (Adler, 1964c).

Neurosis. Prototypical for Adler's understanding of the neurosis, even for all mental disorders, was the compulsion neurosis. The compulsion is "a secondary theatre of operations" (*sekundärer Kriegsschauplatz*) (Adler, 1978), which the patient opens to divert attention from the main life problem and provide him with an excuse for failing in that problem. Or the symptom is a device "to lose time in order to gain time" (Adler, 1956). Such understanding led Adler (1956) to the basic question, "What would you do if you were well?" In reply, the patient usually names the very problem from which he is excusing himself by his symptom. The initial therapeutic strategy might be to encourage the patient to work on the main problem the best he can under the circumstances of his disorder. Adler (1964a) described his approach on the basis of 37 case histories in *Problems of Neurosis*.

Psychosis. In psychosis an organic component cannot be ruled out. According to Alexandra Adler (personal communication, 1977), a daughter of Alfred Adler, an organic component must actually be assumed, as when a patient responds with a psychotic episode to a situation that does not seem to warrant such a violent reaction, even in view of his life style. But beyond that, the basic dynamics are still involved. Consequently, Adlerian psychiatrists have always accepted schizophrenic patients for office treatment (Alexandra Adler, 1966), having "devised various methods for keeping them out of hospitals and on an ambulatory basis" (Alexandra Adler, 1971).

The schizophrenic has abysmally low self-esteem, which is compensated by an extravagant reified goal of superiority, such as to be Jesus Christ or Napoleon. Most of the bizarre symptoms become meaningful in respect to the exalted goal. To safeguard his self-esteem, the schizophrenic exchanges the real world for a rigid, barren world of his private construction. That conception of schizophrenia is quite similar to Ludwig Binswanger's conception (Van Dusen and Ansbacher, 1960). It was described in some detail by Adler's son, Kurt (K. A. Adler, 1958). *Essays in Schizophrenia* from the Adlerian viewpoint have been published by Shulman (1968).

The manic-depressive was also well described by Kurt Adler (1961) as follows:

Mania is a frantic effort by the patient to force success in the service of his goal. ... He appears to take literally the "all" in the "all or nothing" proposition so typical of the neurotic. ... Both the manic and the depressed never really believe in themselves, do not appreciate others, and are always eager to exploit others for their own purposes. Both negate reality by the use of delusion about their prophetic gift: one, by foreseeing that everything will be wonderful and that he can do anything, the other, that everything will be dismal and he can do nothing.

Psychopathy. Adler considered the criminal, like all failures, lacking in social interest. But, unlike most others, he is relatively high in activity, albeit on the useless side of life (Adler, 1956).

Crime is a coward's imitation of heroism. ... The criminal is running away from the tasks of life in association. He feels himself incapable of normal success.

Thus, the criminal actually has an inferiority complex that he hides "by developing a cheap superiority complex" (Adler, 1956). According to Ellenberger (1970), Adler was, among the great pioneers of dynamic psychiatry, the only one who could write on criminals from his direct experience.

Regarding sexual disorders, Adler (1978) considered them "an expression of increased psychological distance between the sexes." His answer was equality and better cooperation between the sexes.

Psychotherapy

PATIENT-THERAPIST RELATIONSHIP

As Adler (1956) wrote:

Psychotherapy is an exercise in cooperation and a test of cooperation. ... We must cooperate with the patient in finding his mistakes, both for his own benefit and for the welfare of others.

The therapist's role. Adler (1956) wrote that the therapist's role is

to give the patient the experience of contact with a fellow man, and then to enable him to transfer his awakened social interest to others.

To accomplish that task, Adler (1956) held:

I must win the patient and take his part as far as possible. Every neurotic is partly right. ... I can bring him only very gradually to face the truth about what he is doing. ... The patient has to be brought into such a state of feeling that he likes to listen and wants to understand.

The patient's role. Adler (1956) wrote that the patient's role is to take

the responsibility for his cure ... for ... "You can lead a horse to water, but you can't make him drink." ... The actual change ... can only be the patient's own doing. ... He can't learn anything from me that he ... does not understand better, once he has recognized his lifeline [life style]. ... What the Freudians call transference ... apart from sexual implications ... is merely social interest.

Depreciation tendency. Adler (1956) wrote:

Since the physician obstructs the patient's neurotic strivings ... every patient will attempt to depreciate the physician. ... [It is the] depreciation tendency ... directed against the psychotherapist.

That is what Freud described as resistance. Fifty years later, Haley (1963) concurred about

the patient ... desperately trying to place the analyst one-down. [All such attempts] can be interpreted as resistance to treatment.

THERAPEUTIC PROCESS

The Adlerian therapy process has generally been described as involving four overlapping phases: (1) establishing and maintaining a good relationship with the patient; (2) gathering data from him to understand his life style; (3) interpreting the data to him, providing insight; and (4) reorientation and re-education (Alexandra Adler, 1946; Dreikurs, 1973; Papanek, 1975). Further comprehension may perhaps be afforded by dealing with those phases in terms of three factors involved in achieving change: affective factor (encouragement), included in phase 1; cognitive factor, included in phases 2, 3, and 4; and techniques, included in phase 4.

Affective factor (encouragement). Increased inferiority feeling is the core of psychopathology and "goes hand in hand with inadequate ... courage" (Adler, 1964b). Thus, encouragement becomes the essence of psychotherapy and includes all procedures not involved in the other two factors. Courage was defined by Adler (1956) as activity plus social interest—that is, socially useful striving. The patient strives on the socially useless side where successes, although pseudosuccesses, are easily and safely attained. Lack of courage applies even when on the surface no inferiority feelings can be discerned, as is generally the case in character disorders. Then the patient must be shown through his life history and recollections how he became discouraged from striving on the socially useful side.

Activation of social interest. When courage is equated with activity and social interest, encouragement includes the development of social interest (Adler, 1969):

Social interest is the most important part of our education, treatment, and cure.

When one feels solidarity with others, one has more courage in facing life problems than in isolation. For all forms of therapy-guidance, Adler (1964b) stated:

The task of the educator, teacher, physician, and clergyman is to raise social interest and thereby raise courage.

Successes of other schools are due less to their methods than to the fact that on occasion they also (Adler, 1956)

give the patient a good human relationship with the physician or, above all, encouragement.

The therapist's role, with its extension of social interest and its eliciting of social interest, is altogether that of encouragement.

Development of skills. A person's self-esteem and courage are raised also by a recognition of his or her existing competencies and training in further skills. That opens the door for dance, music, art, and work therapy.

Dealing with specific discouragements. Adler (1958) pointed out:

We must recognize the specific discouragement the patient shows in his life style; we must encourage him at the precise point where he falls short in courage.

For example, if a person is discouraged by his features, plastic surgery may be helpful (Adler, 1978).

Cognitive factor (insight). The therapist attempts to gain a conceptualization of the patient's life style, including his erroneous interpretations and goals and methods of attaining them, of which the patient may be quite unaware. The therapist lets the patient understand those errors so that he may then work on changing them. For that purpose Adler (1956) found it particularly helpful to investigate early recollections, position in the birth order, day and night dreams, and the exogenous factor.

Early recollections. It may seem strange that a psychology that does not look for causes in the past is interested in early recollections. The explanation is that the Adlerian is not so much concerned with the recollected event as with how the person responded to the described situation. The recollection itself is understood as being of the patient's choosing, an action of his, rather than merely an imprint he received passively. From that viewpoint it is unimportant to what extent a recollection is objectively true or not.

As a rather self-explanatory example, Marilyn Monroe—the sensationally successful film star who always described herself as a victim of circumstances, eventually put her career in jeopardy, and after three divorces and loneliness committed suicide—reported from the age of 1 year at her grandmother's (Ansbacher, 1974b):

I remember waking up from my nap fighting for my life. Something was pressed against my face. It could have been a pillow. I fought with all my strength.

That recollection could have been used, together with much similar evidence, to make her understand how she always saw herself as a victim of circumstances, as she did even at the height of her career.

Birth order position. From a person's birth order Adler (1964a) made certain inferences as to how that person may have chosen to respond to his original position. A first-born, dethroned from his original position as an only child, is often conservative, feeling that those in power should remain in power. The second child, wanting to equal the first, often does not recognize existing power but wants power to change hands. The youngest is in a favorable position in that he can never be dethroned. Although the birth order assigns a definite position in the family constellation, it can be played out in many different ways; the above are only some probabilities. In any case, the early response one has chosen to one's birth order position becomes part of one's life style. That insight is helpful to the patient in understanding his subsequent actions.

Dreams. For Adler (1956) the dream is a metaphorical expression, as in poetry, of thoughts about a problem with which the dreamer is presently concerned. The metaphors are in line with the dreamer's life style.

The following recurring dream has been selected as an example because the metaphors are so obvious that an interpretation is almost unnecessary.

I am standing at the top of a staircase with two other people—one male, one female. The male pushes me, and I tumble to the bottom and lie there helpless. The two at the top of the stairs stand there, pointing and laughing at me while I cry for help. Nobody helps me.

The dreamer, not a patient, is an outstandingly beautiful girl, a high school senior. She is oversensitive and considered unfriendly. An average student, she is supposed to have received, on account of her looks, many awards that she did not earn, others losing out to her. On the other hand, she had recently lost in becoming the beauty queen of her state and in becoming a member of an honor society. The dream reflects total helplessness in a hostile world when tumbled from her position at the top. It could well be used to get her to make a more realistic assessment of herself and her situation.

Exogenous factor. It is important to know the exact nature of the exogenous factor—which is always related to the three basic life problems of social living, occupation, and love and marriage. Adler said (1964b, new translation):

We must regard two sides—how this *unique person* moves in relation to and endeavors to master the [particular] *external problem* he or she is facing.

In the case of Marilyn Monroe the exogenous factor in her final crisis was her dismissal by the studio for unjustifiable absence during filming. This could have been used for discussing with her that in her notorious tardiness—she would be from 1 to 24 hours late for appointments—she was not the victim of uncontrollable forces, as she believed, but was making unreasonable demands on others. Her own response to the dismissal had been to blame the motion picture industry bitterly for not taking good enough care of its famous actors.

Techniques. Adler's special techniques were related to his general holistic and dialectical approaches. Although he used all the following techniques, he did not name them all.

Reframing. Technically, the process of psychotherapy can be described as one of reframing (Watzlawick et al., 1974). Adler introduced this concept, but mentioned it only on a few occasions, as in (Adler, 1956):

> The neurotic has a notion of the frame of reference (*Bezugssystem*) of normal life. . . . Yet . . . he behaves according to . . . a private frame of reference.

And (Adler, 1978):

> The task . . . is to replace the neurotic frame of reference with one of fellowmanship.

Concretely, the problem of reframing differs in each case.

Humor and reframing. Adler (1956) used jokes for their affective qualities and to demonstrate the possibility of changing a frame of reference and thereby finding the solution to a problem.

> The essential part of the joke is this dual frame of reference, and here we see the relationship with . . . the neurosis. . . . But . . . the neurosis is rather . . . a poor joke, because its particular frame of reference appears . . . invalid. . . . We have always been inclined to use jokes to clarify his error to the neurotic. . . . Here is a main point of attack of therapy.

Consideration of the context. With Adler, reframing was most often a consideration of the context (*Zusammenhangsbetrachtung*)—in the case of a particular symptom, the context of the patient's life style; in reference to the patient's situation, its larger social context. To regard a symptom in isolation, wrote Adler (1978):

> is like taking one note from a melody and regarding it by itself. To understand nervous phenomena, we must keep firmly in view their socially given and socially effective contexts.

As an illustration, when Freud read Goethe's early recollection of throwing dishes out the window, he waited with an interpretation until he found that isolated movement of throwing something out the window in the memories of two patients, where he thought it stood for sibling rivalry. Therefore, he searched in the case of Goethe for sibling rivalry. The Adlerian psychologist takes that movement in its context of having generated applause from boys across the street and of Goethe's continuing under applause until all the dishes were gone. The resulting understanding is consistent with Goethe the dramatist and stage director—giving a show.

Conflict resolution. Reference to another frame is the dialectical approach to the resolution of conflicts, intrapersonal and interpersonal. With the original thesis and antithesis left behind, synthesis is achieved within another frame. For example, Adler interpreted indecision and ambivalence by changing from the subjective to an objective frame. When a person is undecided, objectively, nothing happens. From that, Adler inferred that indecision, the hesitating attitude, was a disguised way to maintain the status quo, that being the hidden goal of success for the discouraged patient.

Dialectical interpretation. Adler (1972) noted that antithetical pairs, such as below-above, form one category, so that "the thought of each of the pair antithetically includes the other." Consequently, the therapist listens and observes dialectically—that is, he asks himself what opposites can be inferred from some of the patient's statements and actions. Considering oneself too good for any occupation may mean "not good enough." A woman's fear of being attacked may be an expression of pure vanity. Wearing shabby clothes may be an expression of conceit. Harm inflicted on oneself is linked by Adler with attempts to hurt others. When the patient complains about what others did to him, the therapist may ask, "And what did you do then?" For further examples, see Mosak and Gushurst (1971).

Paradoxical communication. The modern concept of paradoxical communication (Watzlawick et al., 1967) refers to the phenomenon in which a person overtly gives one message while giving, on another level and unknown to the person, the opposite message. Adler described that concept when he stated, for example, that in impotence the patient's words may express one intention, but "his sexual organ speaks another language" (Adler, 1978). He called that "organ dialect." Such paradoxical communication is likely to withstand direct attack but is amenable to paradoxical communication by the therapist. That technique is used by many therapists under many different names. Frankl's (1960) term "paradoxical intention" conveys the idea that the message intends the opposite of its overt meaning. It most often takes the form of "prescribing the symptom" (Haley, 1963). Adler would say to a patient complaining about indecision, "Above all, don't do anything rash!" (Wexberg, 1970). A review of the paradox in Adlerian psychotherapy was provided by Mozdzierz et al. (1976).

Survey of Adlerian practice. A survey of all aspects of therapy as practiced by contemporary Adlerians was published by Nikelly (1971). In 30 chapters it dealt with five kinds of group techniques, six kinds of special-syndrome techniques, and four kinds of educational techniques.

GOALS OF TREATMENT

Adler (1956) wrote about his treatment goals:

> All my efforts are devoted towards increasing the social interest of the patient. I know that the real reason for his malady is his lack of cooperation, and I want him to see it too. As soon as he can connect himself with his fellow men on an equal and cooperative footing, he is cured. . . .
> The neurotic regards his fictional world as the right one [and] finds the real objective world unbearable for his vanity.

If he can abandon his dream world, he will be able to

> feel himself an equal among equals. His courage will mount and his "common sense" increase and gain control where heretofore he has been under the sway of his private sense. . . . The cure of reorientation is brought about by the destruction of the faulty picture of the world and the unequivocal acceptance of a mature picture of the world.

When Freud (1933) expressed his goal of treatment as being: "Where id was there shall ego be," he actually agreed with Adler, because he was also talking of a maturation process, only Freud disguised the statement in his own metaphors, whereas Adler expressed himself in common language.

The Adlerian Movement

No account of Alfred Adler would be complete without a mention of the movement he spawned. Its growth during the last decades has been primarily along the lines of counseling and family education as developed by Rudolf Dreikurs (1964, 1968).

The North American Society of Adlerian Psychology—founded in 1952 as the American Society of Adlerian Psychology—as of 1978 had 1,100 members in the United States and Canada. It (1) publishes the *Journal of Individual Psychology*, the *Individual Psychologist*, and a newsletter; (2) holds annual, semiannual and regional meetings; and (3) sponsors workshops. Adlerian training institutes exist in New York, Chicago, and at Bowie (Maryland) State College. There are also scores of local organizations, training institutes, family education centers, and study groups.

Abroad, Adlerian groups exist in Austria, Denmark, France, Great Britain, Greece, Israel, Italy, The Netherlands, Switzerland, and West Germany. Together with the North American groups, they form the International Association of Individual Psychology which publishes a newsletter and sponsors international congresses every 3 years. The West German group is the largest. The German Society for Individual Psychology, reestablished in 1964, as of 1978 counted nearly 950 members. It provides training in four regional institutes, and since 1976 publishes the *Zeitschrift für Individualpsychologie*. Also noteworthy is the International Committee for Adlerian Summer Schools and Institutes (ICASSI), which has been active since 1968. It has been conducting a 2-week Institute every summer in various European countries and Israel, offering counselor training for 300 to 400 students.

Suggested Cross References

A general survey of historical and theoretical trends in psychiatry appears in Section 1.1. Chapter 8 presents Freud's theories and the early history of psychoanalysis. Other theorists mentioned in this section are discussed at length in Chapters 9, 10, and 11. Brief psychotherapy and crisis intervention are discussed in Section 30.9.

REFERENCES

Adler, A. *Study of Organ Inferiority and Its Psychical Compensation: A Contribution to Clinical Medicine.* Nervous and Mental Diseases Publishing Company, New York, 1917.
Adler, A. Answers during question period after Conway Hall lecture, May 11, 1936. *Daily Mail*, London, May 12, 1936.
Adler, A. Psychiatric aspects regarding individual and social disorganization. Am. J. Sociol., *42:* 773, 1937.
* Adler, A. *The Individual Psychology of Alfred Adler: A Systematic Presentation in Selections from His Writings*, H. L. Ansbacher and R. R. Ansbacher, editors. Basic Books, New York, 1956.
* Adler, A. *Understanding Human Nature*. Fawcett, Greenwich, Conn., 1957.
* Adler, A. *What Life Should Mean to You*. Capricorn, New York, 1958.
Adler, A. *The Problem Child: The Life Style of the Difficult Child as Analyzed in Specific Cases.* Capricorn, New York, 1963.
* Adler, A. *Problems of Neurosis: A Book of Case Histories*, P. Mairet, editor. Harper & Row, New York, 1964a.
Adler, A. *Social Interest: A Challenge to Mankind.* Capricorn, New York, 1964b.
* Adler, A. *Superiority and Social Interest: A Collection of Later Writings*, H. L. Ansbacher and R. R. Ansbacher, editors. Northwestern University Press, Evanston, Ill., 1964c.
* Adler, A. *The Practice and Theory of Individual Psychology.* Littlefield, Adams, Totowa, N. J., 1968.
Adler, A. *The Science of Living.* Doubleday Anchor, Garden City, N. Y., 1969.
Adler, A. *The Education of Children.* Regnery Gateway, Chicago, 1970.
Adler, A. *Ueber den Nervösen Charakter: Grundzüge einer Vergleichenden Individual-Psychologie und Psychotherapie (The nervous character: Outline of a Comparative Individual Psychology and Psychotherapy).* Fischer Taschenbuch, Frankfurt am Main, 1972.
Adler, A. *The Neurotic Constitution: Outlines of a Comparative Individualistic Psychology and Psychotherapy.* Arno Press, New York, 1974a.
Adler, A. *Praxis und Theorie der Individualpsychologie: Vorträge zur Einführung in die Psychotherapie für Ärzte, Psychologen und Lehrer (Practice and Theory of Individual Psychology: Introductory Lectures in Psychotherapy for Physicians, Psychologists, and Teachers).* Fischer Taschenbuch, Frankfurt am Main, 1974b.

* Adler, A. *Cooperation between the Sexes: Writings on Women, Love and Marriage, Sexuality and Its Disorders*, H. L. Ansbacher and R. R. Ansbacher, editors. Doubleday Anchor, Garden City, N. Y., 1978.
Adler, A., and Furtmüller, C., editors. *Heilen und Bilden: Ein Buch der Erziehungskunst für Ärzte und Pädagogen (Healing and Educating: A Book of the Art of Education for Physicians and Educators).* Fischer Taschenbuch, Frankfurt am Main, 1973.
Adler, Alexandra. Individual Psychology: Adlerian school. In *Encyclopedia of Psychology*, P. L. Harriman, editor, p. 262. Philosophical Library, New York, 1946.
Adler, Alexandra. The concept of compensation and over-compensation in Alfred Adler's and Kurt Goldstein's theories. J. Individ. Psychol., *15:* 79, 1959.
Adler, Alexandra. Office treatment of the chronic schizophrenic patient. In *Psychopathology of Schizophrenia*, H. Hoch and J. Zubin, editors, p. 366. Grune and Stratton, New York, 1966.
Adler, Alexandra. Present-day Adlerian psychiatric practice. J. Individ. Psychol., *27:* 153, 1971.
Adler, K. A. Life style in schizophrenia. J. Individ. Psychol., *14:* 68, 1958.
Adler, K. A. Depression in the light of individual psychology. J. Individ. Psychol., *17:* 56, 1961.
Ansbacher, H. L. Was Adler a disciple of Freud? J. Individ. Psychol., *18:* 126, 1962.
Ansbacher, H. L. Life style: A historical and systematic review. J. Individ. Psychol., *23:* 191, 1967.
Ansbacher, H. L. Adler and the 1910 Vienna symposium on suicide. J. Individ. Psychol., *24:* 181, 1968.
Ansbacher, H. L. Adlerian psychology: The tradition of brief psychotherapy. J. Individ. Psychol., *28:* 137, 1972.
Ansbacher, H. L. The first critique of Freud's metapsychology: An extension of G. S. Klein's "Two Theories or One?" Bull. Menninger Clin., *38:* 78, 1974a.
Ansbacher, H. L. Goal-oriented individual psychology: Alfred Adler's theory. In *Operational Theories of Personality*, A. Burton, editor, p. 99. Brunner/Mazel, New York, 1974b.
Bateson, G., Jackson, D. D., Haley, J., and Weakland, J. H. Toward a theory of schizophrenia. Behav. Sci., *1:* 251, 1956.
Berne, E. *What Do You Say after You Say Hello? The Psychology of Human Destiny.* Grove Press, New York, 1972.
Bottome, P. *Alfred Adler: Portrait from Life.* Vanguard, New York, 1957.
Dreikurs, R., and Soltz, V. *Children: the Challenge.* Duell, Sloan and Pearce, New York, 1964.
Dreikurs, R. *Psychology in the Classroom*, ed. 2. Harper & Row, New York, 1968.
Dreikurs, R. *Psychodynamics, Psychotherapy, and Counseling: Collected Papers*, ed. 2. Alfred Adler Institute, Chicago, 1973.
Ellenberger, H. F. *The Discovery of the Unconscious.* Basic Books, New York, 1970.
Erikson, E. H. *Dimensions of a New Identity.* W. W. Norton, New York, 1974.
Frankl, V. E. Paradoxical intention: A logotherapy technique. Am. J. Psychother., *14:* 520, 1960.
Frankl, V. E. Tribute to Alfred Adler. J. Individ. Psychol., *26:* 12, 1970.
Freud, S. On the history of the psychoanalytic movement. In *Collected Papers*, vol. 1, p. 287. Hogarth Press, London, 1924.
Freud, S. Instincts and their vicissitudes. In *Collected Papers*, vol. 4, p. 60. Hogarth Press, London, 1925.
Freud, S. *New Introductory Lectures on Psychoanalysis.* W. W. Norton, New York, 1933.
Friedman, P., editor. *On Suicide: Discussions of the Vienna Psychoanalytic Society.* International Universities Press, New York, 1967.
Furtmüller, C. Alfred Adler: A biographical essay. In *Superiority and Social Interest*, by A. Adler, p. 311. Northwestern University Press, Evanston, Ill., 1964.
Haley, J. *Strategies of Psychotherapy.* Grune & Stratton, New York, 1963.
Hall, C. S., and Lindzey, G., editors. *Theories of Personality*, ed. 3. John Wiley & Sons, New York, 1978.
Harris, T. A. *I'm O. K.—You're O. K.* Avon, New York, 1973.
Jung, C. G. *Word and Image.* Princeton University Press, Princeton, 1979.
Kallen, H. M. Psychoanalysis. In *Encyclopedia of the Social Sciences*, R. A. Seligman and A. Johnson, editors, vol. 2, p. 580. Macmillan, New York, 1934.
Kaplan, H. I., Sadock, B. J., and Freedman, A. M. Erik Erikson. In *Comprehensive Textbook of Psychiatry*, A. M. Freedman, H. I. Kaplan, and B. J. Sadock, editors, ed. 2, p. 566. Williams & Wilkins, Baltimore, 1975.
Kelman, H. Psychoanalysis and existentialism. In *Modern Concepts of Psychoanalysis*, L. Salzman and J. H. Masserman, editors, p. 115. Philosophical Library, New York, 1962.
Manaster, G. J., Painter, G., Deutsch, D., and Overholt, B. J., editors. *Alfred Adler as We Remember Him.* North American Society for Adlerian Psychology, Chicago, 1977.
Maslow, A. H. *Toward a Psychology of Being*, ed. 2. D. Van Nostrand, Princeton, N. J., 1968.
Masserman, J. H. The biodynamic roots of psychoanalysis. In *Modern Psychoanalysis*, J. Marmor, editor, p. 189. Basic Books, New York, 1968.
Mora, G. Historical and theoretical trends in psychiatry. In *Comprehensive Textbook of Psychiatry*, A. M. Freedman, H. I. Kaplan, and B. J. Sadock, editors, ed. 2, p. 1. Williams & Wilkins, Baltimore, 1975.
Mosak, H., and Gushurst, R. What patients say and what they mean. Am. J. Psychother., *25:* 428, 1971.

Mozdzierz, G. J., Macchitelli, F. J., and Lisiecki, J. The paradox in psychotherapy: An Adlerian perspective. J. Individ. Psychol., *32:* 169, 1976.

Murphy, G. Tribute to Alfred Adler. J. Individ. Psychol., *26:* 14, 1970.

Nagel, E. *The Structure of Science: Problems in the Logic of Scientific Explanation.* Harcourt, Brace and World, New York, 1961.

New York Times, November 6, 1929, p. 14.

Nikelly, A. G., editor. *Techniques of Behavior Change: Applications of Adlerian Theory.* Charles C Thomas, Springfield, Ill., 1971.

Nunberg, H., and Federn, E., editors. *Minutes of the Vienna Psychoanalytic Society,* vol. 2, 1908–1910. International Universities Press, New York, 1967.

Orgler, H. *Alfred Adler: The Man and His Work.* Mentor, New York, 1963.

Papanek, H. Alfred Adler. In *Comprehensive Textbook of Psychiatry,* A. M. Freedman, H. I. Kaplan, and B. J. Sadock, editors, ed. 2, p. 574. Williams & Wilkins, Baltimore, 1975.

Pestalozzi, J. H. *Sämtliche Werke,* vol. 12. De Gruyter, Berlin, 1938.

Piaget, J. Psychology and philosophy. In *Scientific Psychology: Principles and Approaches,* B. B. Wolman and E. Nagel, editors, p. 28. Basic Books, New York, 1965.

Rom, P., and Ansbacher, H. L. An Adlerian case or a character by Sartre? J. Individ. Psychol., *21:* 32, 1965.

Shulman, B. H. *Essays in Schizophrenia.* Williams & Wilkins, Baltimore, 1968.

Sperber, M. *Masks of Loneliness: Alfred Adler in Perspective.* Macmillan, New York, 1974.

Stern, A. *Sartre: His Philosophy and Existential Psychoanalysis,* ed. 2. Dell, Delta Books, New York, 1967.

er, J., and Pew, W. L. *The Courage to Be Imperfect: The Life and Work of udolf Dreikurs.* Hawthorn Books, New York, 1978.

Van Dusen, W. Adler and existence analysis. J. Individ. Psychol., *15:* 100, 1959.

Van Dusen, W., and Ansbacher, H. L. Adler and Binswanger on schizophrenia. J. Individ. Psychol., *16:* 77, 1960.

Washington Post, January 11, 1937, p. 13.

Watzlawick, P., Beavin, J. H., and Jackson, D. D. *Pragmatics of Human Communication: A Study of Interactional Patterns, Pathologies, and Paradoxes.* W. W. Norton, New York, 1967.

Watzlawick, P., Weakland, J. H., and Fisch, R. *Change: Principles of Problem Formation and Problem Resolution.* W. W. Norton, New York, 1974.

Wexberg, E. *Individual Psychological Treatment,* ed. 2. Alfred Adler Institute, Chicago, 1970.

9.2 Karen Horney

ALEXANDRA SYMONDS, M.D.
MARTIN SYMONDS, M.D.

Introduction

Karen Horney (1885–1952) was an outstanding woman pioneer in the field of psychoanalytic theory. She developed her innovative ideas after more than 17 years of clinical work, teaching, training, and research in classical psychoanalysis. Although she freely acknowledged her debt to Freud and accepted certain basic principles of psychoanalysis, her concept of human nature underlying her unique theoretical contributions to psychoanalysis differed from his. She stated (Horney, 1950):

Our philosophic premises had changed in decisive ways. These concerned above all our belief in the nature of man. Man for us was no longer an instinct ridden creature but being capable of choice and responsibility. Hostility was no longer innate but reactive. Similarly egocentric and anti-social cravings, like greed or the lust for power were not inevitable phases of man's development but the expressions of a neurotic process. Growing up under favorable conditions, we believed man would develop his inherent constructive forces and like every other living organism would want to realize his potentialities. Human nature was no longer unalterable but could change.

That constructive humanistic theme of seeing people as continually striving to evolve and realize themselves permeates the core of the theoretical system of psychoanalysis developed by Horney. That theme placed in proper perspective the importance of the culture, the family climate, and the environment as the major stresses that produce neurotic behavior.

Unlike other scientific theories, any theory concerning human behavior is inextricably woven with the philosophical beliefs of the individual theorist. To understand how Horney's orientation to life developed, one must know something of her background.

Life

Karen Horney was born in Hamburg, Germany, on September 16, 1885. She grew up in a comfortable, middle-class environment. Her father was a Norwegian sea captain, and her mother was of Dutch descent. It was her mother who actively encouraged her daughter to continue her education and study medicine. Karen Horney completed her medical studies in 1911. As was the custom in Europe, her medical degree was awarded after the completion of a doctoral thesis. Her early interest in psychiatry is evidenced by her doctoral thesis on traumatic psychosis. It was accepted, and she received her medical degree from Berlin University in 1915. While in medical school in 1911, she underwent a training analysis with Karl Abraham. She was considered an outstanding analyst and was soon appointed to the teaching staff of Abraham's psychoanalytic clinic in Berlin. Shortly afterward, she was assigned to develop the training program and curriculums of the clinic, which was renamed the Berlin Psychoanalytic Clinic and which received world recognition. It produced such eminent analysts as Sandor Rado, Franz Alexander, and Edith Weigert.

Horney left for the United States in 1932 at the invitation of Franz Alexander to be his associate director of the Chicago Psychoanalytic Institute. By that time she had achieved international fame and recognition as one of the foremost psychoanalysts in Europe. She had published her major papers on feminine psychology and had actively participated in and presented papers at many international psychoanalytic congresses.

During her stay in Germany, Karen Horney, then Karen Danielssen, married Oscar Horney in 1909. After separating from him in 1926, she was divorced in 1939. She maintained an amicable relationship with him until his death in Germany in 1948. She never remarried, and she maintained her married name. She had three daughters, one of whom is the eminent psychoanalyst Marianne Horney Eckardt.

Karen Horney arrived in the United States in 1932. Her searching, creative, innovative spirit, which paradoxically had been accepted in Berlin, quickly clashed with the traditional, autocratic attitudes of Franz Alexander, who, despite his admiration for her, felt that she was too revolutionary for his newly formed Chicago institute.

Horney moved to New York City in 1934. She was quickly accepted by the classical psychoanalytic societies and became a training analyst and lecturer. However, the seeds of creative insights and her doubts about a wholly biological and genetic base to psychoanalysis, seen in her earliest writing on psychoanalytic technique in 1917, took root and flowered in the lively American climate, which allowed the challenge of authoritarian behavior and dogma.

In 1937 Horney wrote *The Neurotic Personality of Our Time*, in which she clearly stated her belief in the crucial influence of the culture and the environment on the production of neurosis. Although the book met with substantial acceptance by the public, the classical analysts disapproved. In the subsequent work, *New Ways in Psychoanalysis*, published in 1939, she fully detailed her philosophical beliefs and psychoanalytic stand and her differences with Freud. As a result, there was a formal break with the transplanted dogmatic attitudes of organized psychoanalysis then prevalent in the late 1930's. She founded the American Institute for Psychoanalysis in 1941 and was its dean and guiding spirit until her death on December 4, 1952.

Evolution of Horney's Theory

During her lifetime Horney wrote 76 articles and five books and edited and contributed to a sixth book (Rubins, 1972).

Fifteen of her articles were posthumously published as a book under the title *Feminine Psychology* (Kelman, 1966). Her theory of neurosis and neurotic character structure, which represents her unique contribution to psychoanalysis, can be understood by studying her last two books, *Our Inner Conflicts* (Horney, 1945) and *Neurosis and Human Growth* (Horney, 1950). In those books she formulated her theory as it is taught, used, and practiced by analysts at the American Institute of Psychoanalysis in New York City. However, a fuller appreciation of her final theory and an understanding of the principles underlying the emerging humanistic concepts of psychoanalysis can be gained by a knowledge of her earlier works. Through her first two books one can trace her earliest thinking, her efforts to enlarge and enrich Freudian psychoanalysis, and, finally, in her later works her separation from the mechanistic thinking of Freud and the development of her own concepts and terminology. As was characteristic of Horney, her theory was never static but continually evolving. In each successive book she added to or made changes; each book is rich in clinical material and requires careful reading. Although she deliberately used plain language, her understanding was profound and her concepts were complex. In the introduction to her first book. *The Neurotic Personality of Our Time* (Horney, 1937), she said:

Technical terms have been avoided as much as possible because there is always the danger of letting such terms substitute for clear thinking. Thus it may appear to many readers that problems of the neurotic personality are easily understood. But this would be a mistake and even a dangerous conclusion.

The following is a brief outline of Horney's concepts as reflected in each of her books.

In Horney's first book *The Neurotic Personality of Our Time* (Horney, 1937), she introduced several basic premises that became the keystones of her later theory. In addition, she made a contribution to psychoanalysis that affected it significantly. Horney stated that neuroses are generated not by instinctual conflicts but by specific cultural conditions that lead to disturbed human relationships. The culture establishes values and standards, and those values and standards are in turn reflected in the family atmosphere of the growing child. Often, the parents' own neurotic problems influence and distort the child's evolving self. Freud thought that anxiety was mainly caused by the repression of sexual impulses, but Horney (1937) stated:

The frequency with which anxiety is generated by sexual impulses is largely dependent on the existing cultural attitude towards sexuality.

That understanding of the role of the culture was an important departure from the concepts of Freud, as it released analysts from the belief that biology is destiny and freed them to help their patients fulfill their potential in a more holistic manner. What Freud assumed to be universal human behavior, biologically and genetically predetermined, Horney recognized as culturally induced and shaped.

Another important principle stated by Horney (1937), one that became an important theme in all her work, was her focus on the ongoing neurotic process of the patient who presents himself for help. She did not consider the adult to be mechanically repeating childhood experiences, and she could not accept the focus of analysts at that time on recovering childhood memories, hoping thus to produce a cure. Horney stressed that the neurotic was in the grips of a dynamic, complex, self-perpetuating structure that caused him anxieties, fears, and blockages. Those ongoing neurotic patterns required careful

study and became the focus of her attention throughout her later works.

Those two concepts, the influence of the culture and the attention paid to the here and now, are commonplace today, but they were not acceptable to the psychoanalytic community at that time. Freud's theory of neurosis was entirely biological and instinctual, giving no weight to environmental factors.

In *The Neurotic Personality of Our Time* (Horney, 1937) are also important statements on masochism, a subject that Horney had long studied and written about, beginning with her early articles on feminine psychology. She could not accept Freud's premise that it was in the nature of healthy, normal women to get pleasure from suffering. Horney (1937) stated:

Masochistic drives are neither essentially sexual phenomenon nor the result of biologically determined processes, but originate in personality conflicts.

Again, Horney was indicating the importance of human relationships, rather than Freud's mechanistic instinctual concepts of biological predetermination.

In *The Neurotic Personality of Our Time* Horney (1937) first presented an early form of her theory of neurosis, which she later refined and developed. She stated that a child experienced anxiety in an unfavorable parental atmosphere that lacked warmth and love. The child attempts to relieve his anxiety by seeking affection, achieving power, or withdrawing. Those defensive adaptations or deformations of character are driven by his need to survive. They produce only temporary safety and eventually generate other long-lasting and disturbing consequences. In her later books Horney developed and elaborated on those basic defensive adaptations and showed the complexity of the complications that ensue.

In her second book, *New Ways in Psychoanalysis*, Horney (1939) devoted most of her energies to a detailed discussion of her theoretical position in relation to Freud. She felt that psychoanalysis could become of greater value if certain questionable theoretical postulates were recognized as inaccurate. Horney (1939) stated in her introduction:

The purpose of this book is not to show what is wrong with psychoanalysis, but through eliminating the debatable elements, to enable psychoanalysis to develop to the height of its potentialities.

Horney started with a discussion on what she considered the basic principles of Freud's psychology:

I regard as the most fundamental and most significant of Freud's findings his doctrines that psychic processes are strictly determined, that actions and feelings may be determined by unconscious motivations and that the motivations driving us are emotional forces.

She recognized the crucial importance of dreams and in her later works stressed the patient-analyst relationship as part of the analytic process. She was one of the earliest analysts to understand that the analyst had feelings in relation to the patient, and those feelings must be identified and worked with constructively. In 1939 Horney reappraised each concept of Freud's theory, showing in detail how his focus on sex as the driving force of human behavior was one sided and led to other distortions. The Oedipus complex, which Freud felt was universal, she pointed out as occurring only in disturbed parent-child relationships. Horney (1939) rejected the death instinct as

not only unsubstantiated, not only contradictory to facts, but positively harmful in its implications, since it implied that hostility and aggression are primary, rather than reactive to external provocation. That 1939 book is highly recommended to those who wish to understand the humanistic position in relation to Freud's theory that Horney carefully delineated.

In *Self-Analysis* Horney (1942) addressed herself to the large number of people who were then turning to analysis as a means of relieving their suffering. She recognized that motivated, intelligent people could help themselves overcome blockages to growth by the use of psychological knowledge, and she wrote *Self-Analysis* "to encourage endeavors towards a constructive self-examination." She felt that self-analysis was most applicable to those who had already experienced professional help and who wished to continue their own growth. However, she indicated that people who were highly motivated might be able to achieve considerable understanding of themselves with that process. In that book and in her contributions to *Are You Considering Psychoanalysis?* Horney (1946) expressed her belief that the patient contributes actively to his own growth and participates actively in analysis. That view laid the groundwork for her later focus on the important role of the analyst-patient relationship. It also reflected her abiding faith in the constructive aspects of human nature.

The major part of *Self-Analysis* (Horney, 1942) was a discussion of a self-effacing young woman named Clare that gave her background, her symptoms, and her efforts at self-analysis. Horney was careful to emphasize that self-analysis has limits, but the book is of interest to those seeking greater understanding of themselves by using psychological principles constructively. Of special interest to today's clinician is the chapter entitled, "The Driving Forces in Neurosis." There Horney succinctly presented a discussion on the nature of neurotic trends, their characteristics, their function, their genesis, and their effect. She pointed out that neurotic trends start out as a strategy for survival but become compulsive, indiscriminate, and insatiable and that anxiety ensues from their frustration. Once acquired, not only will they persist but in time will obtain a stronger hold on the personality, ultimately dominating the entire personality in the form of a neurotic character structure. At that point Horney postulated 10 neurotic trends as the driving forces in neurosis. Since each human being is unique and the product of almost limitless individual combinations of heredity, endowment, and environmental conditions, she emphasized that those trends are guides that can be helpful but are not to be applied as a rigid classification. Those 10 neurotic trends were the forerunner of her later theoretical formulation in which she grouped them into three main types. Her last two books, *Our Inner Conflicts* (Horney, 1945) and *Neurosis and Human Growth* (Horney, 1950), should be studied together to gain a full understanding of Horney's theory of neurosis, her approach to therapy, and, underlying it all, her optimistic feeling about human nature and the capacity for change.

Horney's Theory of Neurosis

Horney (1945) defined neurosis as a disturbance in one's relationship to self and others. As a clinician she saw that although some patients had specific symptoms—such as phobias, obsessions and compulsions, depressions, functional disorders, and anxiety states—many did not. Most patients came for help because they were unhappy, felt blocked and unfulfilled in their work, or were not able to form or maintain satisfactory relationships. Therefore, she specified early in her work that her theory applied to all neurotics and that one cannot restrict that understanding only to those with certain symptoms. A large number of people are plagued by feelings of hopelessness and despair and are driven to the empty pursuit of superficial values that, once attained, leave them dissatisfied and unfulfilled. Those feelings and symptoms, when they do occur, are the expression of a complex, self-perpetuating system of defensive patterns that started early in childhood, that the person developed in his efforts to survive, and that ultimately formed the neurotic character structure.

BASIC PRINCIPLES

From birth, each human being is a unique combination of biological endowments living in a specific, highly personal environment of family and culture. Horney (1942) felt that basic to all human development was the principle of growth, a powerful force that drives each person toward the development of his or her particular potentialities.

> You need not, and in fact cannot teach an acorn to grow into an oak tree . . . the human individual, given a chance will develop the unique alive forces of his *real self*—that central inner force, common to all human beings and yet unique to each, which is the deep source of growth (Horney, 1950).

Horney's concept of the real self is basic to her theory of neurosis. A person's real self is the source of his or her energy, aliveness, and spontaneity; it is his sense of who he is, the self that is referred to when he speaks of finding himself. That dynamic core of his being gives him his sense of identity. It enables him to make choices and to accept responsibility for the consequences. Although he is always changing and growing, there is an enduring inner sense of wholeness and integration that Horney called the real self. An outgrowth of the real self is the process of self-realization, a natural unfolding and development of the person's potential into actual, concrete activities and relationships. That process directs him into healthy activities, during which he moves toward others to express love and trust, against others to express healthy friction and mastery of the environment, and away from others to express his needs for autonomy and self-sufficiency.

Regardless of how alienated and out of touch a person becomes from his real self, the potential for healthy growth is always there as a constructive force if blockages are removed. Because of that potential, Horney (1945) had a deep conviction that people "can change and go on changing as long as they live." The strong, healthy core of the real self represents the force that makes survival possible in the face of almost insurmountable difficulties.

Unfortunately, however, conditions are often unfavorable to healthy growth, especially during the crucial years of childhood. When parents for various reasons do not provide the warmth and accepting atmosphere necessary for the child to trust, severe life-threatening anxiety occurs, and his energies are deflected toward survival. Under those conditions the child cannot develop in a healthy spontaneous way and a deformation of character or character neurosis develops. Horney called that basic anxiety.

BASIC ANXIETY

A fundamental concept in Horney's (1937) theory was basic anxiety:

> an insidiously increasing, all pervading feeling of being isolated and helpless in a potentially hostile world.

Although it has its roots in adverse childhood experience, it can also be experienced under stress at any time in life.

Basic anxiety has three aspects, and all must exist at the same time. Any one of those three feelings—isolation, helplessness, being surrounded by hostility—will produce anxiety. When all three are present and persistent, they create an emotional climate that is life threatening and must be alleviated at all costs. It is not a condition in which a child fears punishment or desertion because of specific forbidden drives; it is more inclusive (Horney, 1939):

> He feels the environment as a menace to his entire development and to his most legitimate wishes and strivings. He feels in danger of his individuality being obliterated, his freedom taken away, his happiness prevented. In an environment in which basic anxiety develops, the child's free use of energies is thwarted, his self-esteem and self-reliance is undermined, fear is instilled by intimidation and isolation, his expansiveness is warped through brutality—and the child is rendered helpless to defend himself adequately.

Horney found a wide variety of adverse conditions in the life histories of her patients that inhibited or distorted their growth in childhood. The conditions ranged from severe rejection and brutality to more subtle but equally destructive attitudes on the part of parents and other significant adults. Some parents were rejecting, critical, or controlling. Some were aloof, hostile, or punishing. In some families the child's individuality was not respected but ridiculed. Some parents used the child to relieve their own anxiety or fulfill their narcissism. Instead of warmth and acceptance, the child found an atmosphere that was cold, untrustworthy, and unpredictable and seemed dangerous for his survival. He became increasingly insecure and cut off from others and felt unworthy. When those conditions prevailed, basic anxiety developed.

SEARCH FOR SAFETY

Out of necessity, the child searches for methods to alleviate his intolerable condition and to make his life safer and more predictable and to achieve satisfaction (Horney, 1937).

Horney described three principal ways available to the child as he tries to protect himself against basic anxiety. He can search for affection and approval, he can become angry and hostile, or he can withdraw (Horney, 1950).

> He may try to cling to the most powerful person around him; he may try to rebel and fight, or he may try to shut others out of his inner life and withdraw emotionally from them. In principal, this means he can move toward, against or away from others.

Those three interpersonal ways of relating, present in all humans, become desperate strategies used by the child in his or her attempt to survive. Each one is an effort to deal with one of the aspects of basic anxiety. In moving toward people, he identifies with his feeling of helplessness; in moving against people, he accepts and takes for granted the hostility in his environment; and in moving away from people, he decides that it is impossible to communicate or get involved with others and tries to dissociate himself. The child tries all three strategies, searching for relief from the intolerable feeling of danger and vulnerability. Eventually, he finds that one way is rewarded or accepted by the environment, and he therefore emphasizes and exaggerates that move at the expense of his other needs. If clinging and helplessness succeed in appeasing the adults around him, the child is careful not to express any hostility or needs for separateness. If anger and rebelliousness succeed in gaining respect or a sense of power, then needs for closeness must not be acknowledged. If emotional withdrawal achieves

a sense of safety and is permitted by the adults, the child no longer makes attempts to gain closeness or express aggression.

A one-sided condition is produced in which only one aspect of the child's being is acknowledged and cultivated; the rest is ignored, neglected, or disapproved of. The first step has been taken away from healthy growth and self-expression. He can no longer explore or express his full range of feelings and impulses but must carefully limit himself to what is acceptable to those around him. Although he has gained a sense of safety, a new sense of precariousness has developed, with long-lasting intrapsychic repercussions. Instead of the security he needs in order to grow and develop, he finds himself in danger from within, requiring constant vigilance and leading to further and further restrictions on his genuine feelings and impulses. As long as those unfavorable external conditions persist, any feelings or impulses that would give rise to conflicting behavior must be repressed. Conflicting feelings are driven deeper and deeper until he is no longer consciously aware of them but is left with a diffuse sense of discomfort, anxiety, and apprehension and a generally shaky sense of self. He can no longer trust his own spontaneous feelings; he has shifted his center of gravity outside himself and is torn apart by the turmoil of conflicting needs and impulses. The patterns of behavior that began as ad hoc strategies ultimately become rigid, compulsive, indiscriminate, and insatiable. They are driven by anxiety and cause ever-increasing restrictions and blockages to growth. They crystallize into complex, relatively fixed attitudes toward himself and others that Horney called neurotic trends, and they come to dominate his life.

As Horney (1945) wrote:

> The neurotic is not flexible; he is driven to comply, to fight, to be aloof regardless of whether the move is appropriate in the particular circumstance, and he is thrown into panic if he behaves otherwise.... [Those attitudes] do not remain restricted to the area of human relationships but gradually pervade the entire personality. They end by encompassing not only the person's relation to others but also his relation to himself and life in general.

CHARACTER TYPES

Horney found that neurotic trends fall into three main groups, based on the person's predominant mode of relating to others (Horney, 1950).

> At the present state of knowledge the major solutions for intrapsychic conflicts seem to be the most appropriate basis for establishing types of neurosis.

Each move—whether toward, against, or away from—automatically generates characteristic attitudes, needs, taboos, and sensitivities to support and maintain it. As a result, identifiable character types evolve, each with a specific core attitude toward the self and others and each with a complex deeply rooted support system protecting the vulnerabilities and special needs that result. Moving toward others produces compliant behavior (interpersonal), and that behavior requires that the person diminish and efface himself (intrapsychic). Moving against others produces aggressive behavior, and that leads to an exaggerated expansion of his self-image. In moving away from others, the person detaches himself to make distance, and that causes him to resign from all conflict.

Compliant, self-effacing type. When the predominant solution to anxiety is moving toward others, the person is searching for approval to relieve his anxiety. He desperately needs to be accepted and gradually shapes his personality so that he will not provoke disapproval or rejection. He leans on others and turns to them for advice. He learns which qualities will be most acceptable and actively strives to develop them. Thus, he becomes sensitive to other people's needs, is agreeable, and tries to be unselfish. He subordinates himself to others, takes second place, and avoids the limelight. Any conflicting feelings and attitudes—assertiveness, giving orders to others, any expression of hostility or criticism—are rigidly suppressed. He values goodness, sympathy, and unselfishness, and he feels that all people can be won over if only you love them. He searches desperately for a partner and wishes to give over his life to that partner and to be taken care of. That type of person—who usually develops qualities of kindness, helpfulness, and sensitivity to others—lives a life of constant inner turmoil. He represses his true feelings to such an extent that he cannot speak up for himself and is often taken advantage of. He may work unceasingly for others but is fearful of reaching out for himself. Ordinary friction is almost unbearable, as he panics at the slightest possibility of rejection. He is terrified of being alone. In order to please others, he sees everyone else as better than him and more accomplished and considers himself a failure of no value.

Aggressive, expansive type. In moving against others, the person seeks to gain significance through power and mastery. He strives for control over others and mastery of himself and the environment. He needs to feel that he is superior to others—by achieving success and by outsmarting and exploiting other people's vulnerabilities. He sees the world as dog eat dog, and he rationalizes his aggressive behavior by saying such things as, "God helps those who help themselves." He tries to become a good fighter, and he develops the qualities of toughness and endurance. He equates tenderness with weakness and rigidly represses tender feelings. The expression of love from his partner is not important, but he does demand admiration and submission. He often achieves outward success because of his prodigious efforts at mastery and self-control.

Detached, resigned type. In moving away from others, the person attempts to remove himself from all conflict, and he tries not to be involved with either his dependency feelings or his aggressive feelings. He develops an inordinate need for privacy and becomes hypersensitive to any feelings or involvements. He becomes an onlooker at his own life, often dreaming that he is watching himself and others. He avoids competition and denies any need for help from others. That type develops a feeling of superiority based on his uniqueness. He stresses his self-sufficiency. For him the greatest value is what he calls freedom.

AUXILIARY METHODS TO RELIEVE INNER TENSION

When one rigidly develops and elevates into prominence one of the basic interpersonal moves, he submerges the other two basic directions of interpersonal behavior. However, those submerged and contradictory impulses are still active, and they produce stresses and strains that Horney called basic conflict. The person attempts to reduce his inner tension and conflict by using what Horney (1945) called "auxiliary approaches to artificial harmony." They consist of mental mechanisms—such as blind spots, compartmentalization, and rationalization—and the use of complex adjustment techniques, such as excessive use of self-control, arbitrary rightness, elusiveness, and cynicism. To further reduce the painful awareness of basic conflict, the person uses what Horney (1945) called the process of externalization.

He experiences internal processes as if they occurred outside oneself. Externalization is an active process of self-elimination and is an integral part of alienation from self. Although one of its functions is to place responsibility for the person's difficulties on to the outside world and thus relieve anxiety, it replaces inner conflict with external conflicts and aggravates his problems.

Idealized image. The methods to relieve tension and conflict leave the person vulnerable, since they are safety-oriented mechanisms primarily dependent on the satisfactory responses of others. As the growing need for personal meaning and personal identity increases and reaches its first peak in adolescence, the vulnerability and sensitivity to others is heightened, and self-confidence is markedly decreased. Horney made a crucial contribution to psychoanalytic theory by recognizing that the adolescent period of emotional turmoil stimulates the neurotic to develop a more comprehensive solution to reduce both the interpersonal conflict and the intrapsychic conflict and to provide personal meaning for his values and life style. The essence of that comprehensive solution is the use of imagination and fantasy to create an idealized image (Horney, 1945, 1950), which

promises not only a riddance from his painful and unbearable feelings (feeling lost, anxious, inferior and divided) but in addition an ultimately mysterious fulfillment of himself and his life.

The idealized image is formed creatively by harmonizing—through rationalization, enhancement, distortion and exaggeration—actual and imagined traits that the person admires and aspires to. Those personal qualities, traits, attitudes, and values, originally developed as survival techniques, forced the neurotic to override his genuine feelings, wishes, and thoughts, and they leave him more and more alienated from the inner core of his real self, with only a vague sense of identity. However, the imaginative creation of the idealized image smooths over all the contradictions, touches up the defensive nature of his behavior, and provides him with a model that magically restores a sense of wholeness to the conflicted person. Through the idealized image he can accept contradictions in himself without conflict. He shifts his energy, which heretofore was used for healthy self-realization, to the pursuit of actualizing his creation, the idealized self.

For example, the person who is love oriented and excessively dependent on others, who fears self-assertion and anxiously minimizes his own significance, who responds only to the expectations of others and is out of touch with his own wishes, who often finds himself in relationships in which he is abused and mistreated, rationalizes those neurotic needs and creates an image of a sensitive person, responsive to the needs of others, unselfish, always willing to extend himself. His fear of healthy self-assertion is experienced by him as humility, consideration of others, and the wish not to hurt their feelings. In effect, it is the image of a saint-like person. The power-oriented person rationalizes his aggressive exploitation of others as proof of his superior intelligence and capabilities. He creates an image of a knight in shining armor or a Robin Hood. He experiences himself as a natural-born leader, never indecisive or needing to consult others. The freedom-oriented person creates an image in which his fear of emotional involvement and the deadening of his feelings become serenity and self-sufficiency, making no demands on others and needing nothing from anyone.

At first, the image exists as a fantasy or as an idealized goal in the person's imagination. Eventually, however, a further stage in the neurosis develops. The person begins to experience that product of his imagination as though it were his actual self. He substitutes that glorified, pseudoself for his authentic feelings and capabilities, which he has habitually repressed and lost touch with. That identification is possible because the image is created by him from his preexisting behavior and values. From that point on, he identifies with his idealized image and believes that the image is really himself as he is in the world. He then attempts to actualize that idealized self and demonstrate it to others. That process of attempting to actualize his idealized self, which becomes his life plan, Horney (1950) called "the search for glory."

Since the idealized self is a personalized imaginative creation existing only in the imagination, it makes the neurotic readily vulnerable to interpersonal confrontation or contact with reality. To protect himself from that vulnerability, he is driven to prove that the image is really himself. He drives himself to actualize and demonstrate that idealized self through compulsive perfectionism, in which nothing short of flawless excellence is satisfactory. That neurotic perfectionism is reinforced by stringent inner demands that Horney (1950) called "shoulds." He is also obsessed and driven by neurotic ambition. He must be number one and must take revenge on others who he feels thwarted him, humiliated him, or prevented him from actualizing his idealized self.

Claims. As additional support of his idealized self, the neurotic expects others to treat him with the respect due his position. Horney (1950) called those external expectations and demands on others "claims." Neurotic persons believe that they are that glorified idealized self and feel that they deserve and are entitled to special benefits and considerations. Frustrations of neurotic claims produce disproportionate anger, righteous indignation, resentment, and vindictiveness.

The neurotic tenaciously holds on to his claims, continually asserting them because, through circular reasoning, the claims prove to him that his idealized self is real. If it were not real, it would not have claims; but, since he has claims, ergo, the idealized self exists.

Shoulds. At the same time as the person expresses his claims to the outside world, he demands from himself that he live up to his idealized self. Horney (1950) called those rigid inner dictates "shoulds." With a procrustean attitude he demands that he be perfect without blemish, regardless of any conditions. Those shoulds operate with dictatorial tyranny and with complete disregard for the person's psychic condition, since the premise in which they operate is that nothing is impossible for him. To reduce the unbearable inner pressure of shoulds, the person externalizes them. He experiences those inner coercive forces as arising from others. At the same time, he attempts to dilute the pressure of shoulds by insisting that others live up to the same unrealistic demands he makes on himself. The externalizations of shoulds then result in his becoming both hypercritical of others and hypersensitive to criticism, leading to further impairment of interpersonal relationships.

Self-hatred. The driving force that intensifies the shoulds is the self-hatred that is generated when the person experiences the terror of failing to fulfill those relentless inner demands. Self-hatred for Horney was a major source of psychic energy used to challenge, change, or even destroy any existing traits in the person that are in conflict with the idealized self. Self-hatred, shoulds, and claims are operative only because there is an idealized self. In a circular way they reinforce and support the neurotic's belief in the existence of the self that he has

created. Thus, the power of self-hatred is used to strip away all incompatible aspects of the person, to ensure realization of the idealized self. Horney (1950) described six modes of operation or expressions of self-hatred: relentless demands on one's self, merciless self-accusation, self-contempt, self-frustration, self-tormenting, and self-destruction.

Neurotic pride and the pride system. Although self-hatred serves the function of stripping away existing undesirable traits not compatible with the idealized self, the person also glorifies other aspects of his behavior. He invests that glorified behavior with neurotic pride, since he views that behavior as a confirmation of his idealized self. Neurotic pride is a substitute for healthy self-confidence and is based on glorifying aspects of his idealized image. It makes the neurotic extremely vulnerable to reality and confrontation by others. To protect that pride from being hurt, the neurotic may withdraw from others and even restrict his activities. When his pride is hurt by others, as when his idealized image is questioned, he responds with rage and seeks to avenge that injury to his pride by achieving vindictive triumph over the offender. It is not merely an act of getting even for his injured pride; rather, he actively seeks self-vindication and the restoration of his pride in his idealized self through those acts of revenge.

Neurotic pride and self-hatred, with their supporting forces of claims and shoulds, form an armor that protects the idealized self. Horney (1950) called that protective armor the "pride system." Just as cults defend their special beliefs by isolating their followers from free discussions with others, the pride system prevents any honest exploration of the idealized self. Any attempt to reduce the elements of the pride system is perceived as an attack on the person. Yet, despite the armor of the pride system, the neurotic is not at peace. He is still vulnerable and in inner conflict with the very forces that are protecting him. In therapy those unconscious inner conflicts are identified and worked through. Horney (1950) called the conflict between the forces of healthy self-realization and the pride system "central inner conflict."

Another major inner conflict is within the pride system itself. The forces of pride and self-hatred that are united to defend the idealized self serve difficult masters. Neurotic pride and claims directly identify themselves with the glorified idealized image; self-hatred and shoulds are involved with the weaknesses and unacceptable traits of the despised image. Conflict arises when the person tries to satisfy both forces at the same time. To relieve that inner tension and anxiety, he moves away from the center of the conflict and thus becomes alienated from both his actual self and his real self.

Alienation. These early solutions to intrapsychic conflict work only partially. While they give occasional relief of anxiety, they also set into motion other destructive processes which further weaken and undermine the individual's sense of self. One of the most serious consequences of neurotic development is the process of estrangement from self which Horney called "alienation." Alienation from self develops as a consequence of the individual's repeatedly and actively denying and repressing his genuine feelings and impulses. If this process continues, he gradually loses touch with the very core of his being and loses the ability and knowledge of what is right for him in any situation. Instead of a sure sense of himself he feels a diffuse sense of being lost, uncertain, and confused. If alienation is extreme, he may feel deadened and empty inside.

We cannot suppress or eliminate essential parts of ourselves without becoming estranged from ourselves. . . . The person simply becomes oblivious to what he really feels, likes, rejects, believes—in short, to what he really is. . . . Our real self, the alive unique personal center of ourselves . . . enables us to make decisions and assume responsibility for them (Horney, 1945).

Horney (1950) quotes the Kierkegaard (1941) who says:

The loss of self is sickness unto death, it is despair at not being conscious of having a self or despair at not being willing to be ourselves.

Horney saw the process of alienation as psychological anesthesia, numbing the person to conflict, feelings, aliveness, and his real inner self. The process of alienation is enhanced by externalization, psychic fragmentation, and other attempts to achieve artificial harmony. Alienation is one of the major consequences of the neurotic process, and the reduction of alienation is a major goal in therapy.

Analytic Therapy and Technique

Karen Horney's method of analytic treatment is derived from her theoretical framework. As early as 1917, Horney (1968) stressed the unity of theory and practice.

All psychoanalytic theories in their entirety have been formed out of observation and experiences which were made using the psychoanalytic method. These theories in turn exerted their influence on psychoanalytic practice. The intimate interrelationship of theory and practice makes it difficult to appreciate or understand one without the other.

She had a firm conviction of the inherent constructive forces in a person and his inborn capacity to make choices and change his way of life. That philosophy shaped her approach to treatment. She saw psychoanalysis as a cooperative venture enabling the person to liberate himself from his compulsive neurotic character structure and to mobilize his forces for creative living and self-realization. Horney felt that it was the analyst's responsibility to assist the patient in the process of liberation from the obstructive forces that retarded healthy growth and movement toward self-emancipation. She called those obstructive forces "blockages."

BLOCKAGES

Blockages are the neurotic's persistent attempts to resist change, maintain the status quo, and thwart the analyst's helping efforts. Although the patient has ostensibly sought help for the relief of his suffering, consciously or unconsciously he defends and maintains the precarious harmony of his neurotic character structure from perceived attack by the analyst, and he blocks his own healthy desires for constructive change.

In the initial phases of analytic therapy, blockages are to be identified and examined, so that the patient can become aware of their existence and make efforts to free himself from those obstructive forces. That first phase of self-awareness of blockages is part of what Horney (Zimmerman, 1956) called the "disillusioning process." In the first phase of the disillusioning process, the emphasis is on uncovering, identifying, and clarifying two major groups of blockages. Although all blockages are used for defensive purposes, some are used primarily for safety, and others are actively used to make the neurotic feel whole, since they are used in the service of the idealized image. Horney (1956) called the first group of safety-oriented defenses "protective blockages." Those defenses are activated by the patient to prevent the anxiety caused by self-awareness.

They are most often used to thwart and resist the analyst in exploring and clarifying the compulsive nature of the patient's present behavior patterns. Some of those protective blockages consist of silence, lateness, cancellation of sessions, narcotizing oneself through drugs or alcohol, expressed disappointment or deprecation of the analyst's values, pseudocompliance, and the use of the defense of self-accusation to prevent further insights and exploration by the therapist.

The second major group of defenses are called "positive-value blockages." They are actively used by the patient to prevent self-awareness and to make himself feel satisfied with himself. They are used to reinforce his personal philosophy, which sustains and supports his idealized image. The positive-value blockages affirm his behavior to himself. They are evident in the jingoistic slogans often expressed by the patient:

The world is a jungle. Good guys come in last. All's fair in love and war. If I'm miserable, why should everyone be happy.

The patient uses those concepts to reinforce his claims on people, to justify his exploiting behavior, and to permit acts of vindictiveness.

In the first phase of the disillusioning process, the analyst is quite active in identifying and clarifying either of those two groups of obstructive forces. Protective blockages can be explored with the patient early in the analysis without too many negative repercussions; however, those blockages that are used in the defense of the idealized image require much more careful handling. The neurotic has built up his entire comprehensive solution of well-being on that idealized image, and he responds to premature examination of his values with terror and feelings of being annihilated.

That crucial phase requires a good analytic relationship and special qualities in the analyst to enable the patient to free himself from the stranglehold of the positive-value blockages and the pride system, the major obstructions to self-realization, without the patient's feeling that his self-esteem and self-confidence are being destroyed.

QUALITIES OF THE ANALYST

Karen Horney (Azorin, 1957) stressed the importance of the patient-analyst relationship. She saw analysis as a human relationship, one in which the analyst helped the patient achieve liberation from his neurotic conflict and achieve mobilization of his constructive forces toward self-realization. To help the patient achieve those goals, the analyst should possess certain qualities. He should be a mature person who believes in the constructive resolution of conflict and who is able to communicate those feelings of hope to a patient who is overwhelmed by self-hatred and hopelessness. In the democratic atmosphere of the analysis, he should be able to communicate his feelings of respect for the patient's struggles. That respect is conveyed by listening, clarifying and illuminating, providing directions but not road maps, and thus helping the patient develop alternative solutions to conflict. An important goal is reducing alienation, so that the patient can own his feelings, and assisting him in regaining his spontaneity and in finding his own center of gravity.

Horney was flexible in the application of specific techniques of therapy. She recognized that each human being is a unique combination of hereditary endowments and environmental influences. Thus, rules and regulations regarding technique could not be rigidly applied. She stressed flexibility in technique based on the analyst's sensitive perception of where the patient is at any moment. Since the emphasis in analysis was always on the reduction of obstructive forces toward healthy growth, rigid adherence to the frequency of sessions and the use of the couch seemed less important than in Freudian analysis.

CHANGE IN ANALYSIS AND MOBILIZING CONSTRUCTIVE FORCES

Horney (1950) recognized that true durable change is not achieved by simple behavioral change in the patient. Behavioral change can occur coercively, through imitation or devotion, or from fear of the analyst's disapproval. But true attitudinal change can occur only through a reorientation of values in an open analytic atmosphere that permits the patient's reassessment as a free person with the choice to discover and select personal values consonant with his real self. That reorientation begins after the first phase, the disillusioning phase of analysis. When the patient begins to honestly question his present set of values and goals, when the idealizing process begins to fade in its intensity and compulsivity, he is ready to revise his values and to develop alternate sets of values that are less rigid and more appropriate to his life as it is in actuality. Dreams, which always played a prominent part in the early part of the analysis, are very useful in the latter phase. Horney (1950) stated:

In dreams we are closer to the reality of ourselves. They represent attempts to solve our conflicts either in a neurotic or healthy way, and in them constructive forces can be at work even at a time when they are hardly visible otherwise.

It is in that phase of the mobilization of the constructive forces that the patient experiences central inner conflict—that is, the struggle between the pride system and the real self. That inner conflict produces such psychic turbulence, pain, and rage that it requires the help of all the analyst's special qualities and expertise. When there is successful resolution of central inner conflict, the patient can move toward the final phase of analysis, the discovery and creative use of his spontaneous real inner self.

CLINICAL APPLICATION OF THE HORNEY THEORY

Hopelessness and sadism. Horney's (1945) concepts of neurotic hopelessness are particularly useful in understanding sadistic trends. She pointed out that, when a person experiences the despair of resolving his conflicts and feels hopeless that he will ever become his idealized image, he attempts to restore feelings of effectiveness and power by living vicariously through the control of others.

He externalizes his feelings of self-hatred by attacking others who are close to him and dependent on him. He plays on people's emotions—exploiting, enslaving, confusing, and frustrating them. Through those maneuvers he disparages and humiliates them. Horney saw sadism as an interpersonal act, not a sexual act, of making another pay for his suffering. Sadism is an act of revenge for the humiliation of injured pride. By making others miserable, the sadist restores to himself a feeling of power and thus achieves vindictive triumph, leaving him with a feeling of strength and omnipotence.

Disturbances at work. One is particularly rewarded with useful clinical insights when Horney's theory is applied to work disturbances. The person who is compulsively expansive generally overrates his capacities and the quality of his work. He

tends to underrate others and is oblivious of criticism. He accepts no limits to his ability and creativity, since he sees boundaries and hinderances as defeat and weakness. He starts many projects and generally loses interest before completion. If the expansive person is perfectionistic, he becomes quickly overworked and exhausted. The self-effacing person works well as long as he is working for others. In areas involving competition, he does very poorly since he experiences self-assertion as unacceptable aggression. Quite often he becomes depressed when he is promoted to a position of authority and command. The detached person, because of his hypersensitivity to coercion, finds it difficult to work in large organizations with rules and regulations. He often drops out to avoid becoming involved. That limits his potential for progress. He prefers working free-lance, with no deadlines.

Marital conflicts. Horney's concepts of the idealized image are quite useful in understanding the vindictiveness and explosive rage that is frequently observed in marital conflicts. When one partner attacks the idealized image of the other and dramatically confronts him with all the traits of his despised image, explosive and sometimes tragic acts of violence occur. Effective marital counseling helps each partner recognize and respect the existence of the idealized image in each person and the sensitivities and fragility caused by it. That new awareness aids in constructive communication between the two and prevents the outbreak of war with each other's pride system.

Karen Horney and Feminine Psychology

Horney's earliest contribution to psychoanalysis was in the area of feminine psychology. She experienced her first doubts of Freudian theory in questioning his belief that healthy women enjoyed suffering and were biologically predestined to be submissive and masochistic. Of her 33 articles published before her first book (Horney, 1937), 20 were on feminine psychology. She investigated each of Freud's concepts pertaining to women, carefully checking them out with her clinical experiences and her knowledge of herself as a woman. Those articles were written in the context and language of Freudian theory when she was trying to stay within the bounds of traditional psychoanalytic structure. Gradually, she recognized that classical theory could not support her clinical observations. That insight led her to a deeper understanding of all her patients, both male and female, and to the development of her theory as it exists today.

Horney's greatest contribution to the understanding of women was to see their behavior as the result of culturally enforced patterns. The character structure of both men and women can be fully understood only as the product of cultural forces, rather than as genetically determined. The application of Horney's theory in treatment has proved to be exceptionally useful in relieving women of the psychological complications of culturally induced submissiveness, self-effacement, and excessive dependency.

Suggested Cross References

Freud's theories are discussed in Chapter 8. Anxiety neurosis is discussed in Section 21.1a. Psychoanalysis is discussed in Section 30.1. The women's movement is discussed in Section 56.8.

REFERENCES

Azorin, L. The analyst's personal equation. Am. J. Psychoanal., *17:* 34, 1957.
Cantor, M. The initial interview. I. Am. J. Psychoanal., *17:* 39, 1957a.
Cantor, M. The initial interview. II. Am. J. Psychoanal., *17:* 121, 1957b.

Cantor, M. The quality of the analyst's attention. Am. J. Psychoanal., *19:* 28, 1959.

Cantor, M. Mobilizing constructive forces. Am. J. Psychoanal., *27:* 188, 1967.

* Horney, K. *The Neurotic Personality of Our Time.* W. W. Norton, New York, 1937.

* Horney, K. *New Ways in Psychoanalysis.* W. W. Norton, New York, 1939.

* Horney, K. *Self-Analysis.* W. W. Norton, New York, 1942.

* Horney, K. *Our Inner Conflicts.* W. W. Norton, New York, 1945.

Horney, K., editor *Are You Considering Psychoanalysis?* W. W. Norton, New York, 1946.

Horney, K. The value of vindictiveness. Am. J. Psychoanal., *8:* 3, 1948.

* Horney, K. *Neurosis and Human Growth.* W. W. Norton, New York, 1950.

Horney, K. On feeling abused. Am. J. Psychoanal., *11:* 5, 1951.

Horney, K. Human nature can change. Am. J. Psychoanal., *12:* 80, 1952a.

Horney, K. Paucity of inner experiences. Am. J. Psychoanal., *12:* 3, 1952b.

Horney, K. The techniques of psychoanalytic therapy. Am. J. Psychoanal., *28:* 3, 1968.

Kelman, H., editor. *Feminine Psychology.* W. W. Norton, New York, 1966.

Kelman, H. *Helping People: Karen Horney's Psychoanalytic Approach.* Science House, New York, 1971.

Kierkegaard, S. *Sickness unto Death.* Princeton University Press, Princeton, 1941.

Metzger, E. Understanding the patient as the basis of all technique. Am. J. Psychoanal., *16:* 26, 1956.

Rubins, J. L. *Developments in Horney Psychoanalysis.* Krieger, New York, 1972.

* Rubins, J. L. *Karen Horney: Gentle Rebel of Psychoanalysis.* Dial Press, New York, 1978.

Sheiner, S. Free association. Am. J. Psychoanal., *27:* 200, 1967.

Slater, R. Aims of psychoanalytic therapy, Am. J. Psychoanal., *16:* 24, 1956a.

Slater, R. Interpretations. Am. J. Psychoanal., *16:* 118, 1956b.

Slater, R. Evaluation of change. Am. J. Psychoanal., *20:* 3, 1960.

Weiss, F. A. Constructive forces in dreams. Am. J. Psychoanal., *9:* 30, 1949.

Weiss, F. A. Psychoanalysis and moral values. Am. J. Psychoanal., *12:* 39, 1952.

Weiss, F. A. Self-alienation: Dynamics and therapy. Am. J. Psychoanal., *21:* 207, 1961.

Willig, W. Dreams. Am. J. Psychoanal., *18:* 127, 1958.

* Zimmerman, J. Blockages in therapy. Am. J. Psychoanal., *16:* 112, 1956.

9.3 Harry Stack Sullivan

PATRICK F. MULLAHY, M.A.

Introduction

For Sullivan (see Figure 1), psychiatry is the study of interpersonal relations, real or symbolic or a blend of both. Hence, the unit of study is not the individual but an interpersonal situation at any given time. The rationale for this is that from the moment a person is born, he lives in a complex, dynamic series of interpersonal relations. Given a biological substrate, personality unfolds through time in conjunction with maturation and the person's interpersonal relations. More specifically, one is born with an indefinitely great number of capacities, although many of them rarely, if ever, develop to any important extent. But through the processes of maturation and learning during the long period of time from infancy to adulthood, in which a limited number of capacities are developed, one becomes a human, more or less mature being. This progression occurs in some given cultural context and within a broader historical framework. Any culture is always a network of interpersonal arrangements, organized in numerous and subtle ways into the institutions of a society. As he progresses from infancy to adulthood, every normal person develops a personality by learning select excerpts of his society's culture. In this connection Sullivan borrowed liberally from various philosophers (James, Peirce, Mead, Dewey), from various social scientists (Baldwin, Cooley, Lasswell, Sapir), and from psychiatrists (Freud, Kempf, Meyer). Given such an intellectual background, Sullivan, almost from the beginning of his career,

stressed the necessity of an interdisciplinary approach for a deeper and more comprehensive understanding of interpersonal relationships.

History

EARLY CAREER

It is noteworthy that at St. Elizabeth's Sullivan began his psychiatric career working with psychotics, chiefly schizophrenics, whereas Freud, for example, worked with people who suffered from hysterical, obsessive-compulsive, and other disorders. Apart from Adolf Meyer, virtually no psychiatrist in the United States regarded schizophrenics as either curable or treatable until Sullivan came along. This was in 1922, when, through a happy set of circumstances, he became, at the age of 30, a liaison officer for the Veteran's Administration, although he never became a staff member, apparently because there were no staff openings. He gave William Alanson White, the superintendent, major credit for furthering his research with schizophrenics.

Sullivan had entered the Chicago College of Medicine and Surgery in 1913 and was graduated in 1917. Sullivan publicly stated that he went through psychoanalysis in 1916–1917, during which he learned about transference and how to manage it. But in the course of his career, he showed little use for classical psychoanalysis. No one seems to know with certainty who his analyst was, though in certain places it has been a never-ending source of speculation. In 1917 he became medical officer in the National Guard in Mexico. He then, according to Crowley, became medical director for insurance companies in order to repay loans he incurred in medical school. When the United States entered World War I, he became a first lieutenant, a member of the Board of Medical Examiners for the Medical Corps. After the war, he secured the position of the medical executive officer in the rehabilitation division of the Federal Board for Vocational Education, dealing

FIGURE 1. Harry Stack Sullivan. (Courtesy of the New York Academy of Medicine.)

with war veterans. While in Washington, he drafted policies and procedures for handling soldiers disabled by neuropsychiatric conditions. In 1921–1922 he was a psychiatrist in the Public Health Institute. It was then he became a liaison officer for the Veteran's Administration at St. Elizabeth's, where, probably for the first time, he became acquainted with a mental hospital.

In 1923 Sullivan secured a position as assistant physician at Sheppard and Enoch Pratt Hospital in Towson, Maryland. The superintendent, Ross McClure Chapman, was, he said, "of every assistance." It was there he met Clara Thompson, his second analyst, who remained his friend until Sullivan died in 1949. While still connected with St. Elizabeth's he conducted diagnostic interviews with a large number of patients. His superiors quickly recognized his remarkable ability to reach patients who had been considered beyond the reach of therapy. According to Alfred H. Stanton, a former student and colleague, Sullivan became progressively convinced that the interviews he participated in as a consultant had important effects on the patient and, therefore, could not be sharply distinguished from treatment.

In 1925 Sullivan was made director of clinical research, a position he held until June 1930. Concurrently, he attended Johns Hopkins University's Phipps Clinic. While there, he came under the influence of Adolf Meyer, who conceived of mental disorders as reaction patterns to life situations confronting the sufferers. It was not long before Sullivan became an acknowledged master in his field and began to overshadow Meyer himself.

SPECIAL WARD

It was at Sheppard, probably during the last 12 months of his investigations there, that he set up, with the approval and support of Ross McClure Chapman, his almost legendary special ward for adolescent male schizophrenics. This was during 1929–1930, when psychiatry was still relatively primitive in the United States. The reader is referred to Mullahy (1970) for a full account of the therapeutic innovations that took place in this special ward under Sullivan's guidance. A summary of these accomplishments is presented here.

First, all those connected with the work of the special ward were trained by Sullivan to regard the patient as a person, rather than as a case, and to be at all times aware of and sensitive to the patient's fragile self-esteem. At the same time, they were taught to bear in mind that their purpose was to assist in redevelopment, or development de novo, of the patient's self-esteem. Second, Sullivan practiced a variant of psychoanalysis in which free association was subordinated to direct communication between patient and therapist. Interpretation according to the rules of classical psychoanalysis was modified and subordinated to timely occasions, as was free association. In other words, no attempt was made to put a disturbed patient on a couch, which Sullivan believed could not be achieved in any case. In fact, interpretation, when offered, was framed in an indirect hypothetical fashion. For example, if a patient seemed to be achieving insight at a considerable pace, the therapist might occasionally offer that thus-and-so had, in some patients, been found to be the result of this-and-that, with a request for the patient's associations to this comment. These techniques, among others, were directed to the maintenance and development of the patient's self-esteem or, in other words, his interpersonal security. Throughout his professional life, Sullivan held that this was the basic function of psychotherapy. From his experiences with schizophrenics, he reached two fundamental generalizations (later he added a third—sleep). First, he believed that the pursuit of security or the striving to maintain security, once the self begins to develop in late infancy and childhood, is one of the generic goals of human behavior. The other generic goal came to be labeled the pursuit of satisfactions or the fulfillment, basically, of physiological drives. What is often not fully realized is that the two (or three) are closely intertwined.

In his work with schizophrenics, Sullivan used certain mechanical means to assist him. For example he, unknown to the patient, made recordings of some of the interviews, which he could listen to and study at his leisure.

When Sullivan left Sheppard Hospital in 1930, he went into the private practice of his variant of psychoanalysis in New York City. By this time he had abandoned so many of Freud's ideas and techniques that he had largely abandoned psychoanalysis in the classical sense. He remained in New York for several years, until he returned to Washington before World War II. In his private practice he made a careful study of people suffering obsessive-compulsive disorders. His particular interest in these disorders resulted from his conviction that they often serve as a prelude to the graver set of disorders, schizophrenia.

Theory of Personality Development

Very early in his career, Sullivan abandoned Freud's pleasure principle and, along with it, most of Freud's ideas on psychosexual development. He gradually constructed a theory of personality that, in its main outlines, has stood up well over the years. Sullivan believed that a person's past history enters into his present behavior, not by way of a repetition-compulsion but by way of retention, recall, and recollection. This seems to be outstandingly true of those suffering from some functional mental disorder. Hence, he looked for arrests of development, more or less similar to Freud's fixation points. Apart from the limitations of the social order itself, which Sullivan thought were quite considerable, every patient who suffers a functional mental disorder manifests striking failure in development at some stage or stages of development because of the inadequacies of the development of his personal relations in the home, school environment, or other milieux. That is, apart from the idiosyncrasies of the person's family relationships, his inadequacies embody some of the limitations of institutional arrangements generally.

Because many psychiatrists no longer believe that the genetic functional method is of much help in the treatment of mental disorder, it is vital to understand Sullivan's orientation clearly. Human nature is its concrete history, the history of its interactions from birth onward (Randall, 1958). A life history is a career in time. In other words, we are our experience. Past, present, and prospective future must all be carefully examined or studied. For example, a person whose present existence is drab and without enjoyment, whose life is restricted to mechanical and meaningless routine, may anticipate a future as empty and worthless, something to be endured rather than enjoyed, hopeless almost to the point of despair. Therefore, past, present, and prospective future must all be carefully studied to understand and treat a patient, although the emphasis on one or another may differ from patient to patient or even in the case of one particular patient as the therapy proceeds. These concepts were made clear to Sullivan during the long, hard years he worked with schizophrenics.

In the case of any action or experience, four generic factors enter or influence it: biological potentiality, the level of maturation, the results of previous experience, and foresight. The present is not a knife edge; as John Dewey has said, it has thickness. Maurice Green (1962), paraphrasing Charles Peirce, has written that Peirce thought

that personality, like any general idea, cannot be appreciated in an instant, but must be lived in time, and that no finite time can embrace it in all its fullness. For Peirce, this reference to the future is an essential element of personality; for, in his opinion, were the ends of a person already explicit, there would be no room for development and growth, and consequently, there would be no personality.

The present is a focal point around which the generic factors revolve. Even though the present swiftly and imperceptibly flows into the past, it is the perdurable, dynamic point of reference for the understanding of any person. With this anchorage, therapy proceeds.

Sullivan, then, did not agree with Freud that the basic structure of personality is established during the first 5 years of a person's life, although he admitted that these years are critical in the career of any person. He held that organization of personality, including the subsystem called the self or self-dynamism, takes 15, 20, or even more years for its essential development. This development is primarily the ever-increasing elaboration and modification of the person's social relations in connection with the demands, limitations, and opportunities of his society or community. However, there is the given biological constitution of every person, which, in the course of maturation, interacts with environmental conditions. At any era or stage of development, favorable or unfavorable influences may significantly modify personality development.

For instance, the death of a normal boy's mother when he was 4 years old, followed a year later by the advent of a stepmother who treated him with indifference and neglect, almost inevitably destroyed his implicit faith in the goodness of the world, and predisposed him toward a lifelong insecurity. When he reached 12 or 13, he discovered that ethyl alcohol had a magic power to assuage his chronic insecurity. Soon, he discovered that more and more alcohol was needed to exert its potency. And so he began a lifelong journey down a sad and tragic road.

Thus, the quality and kind of interpersonal relations in the home, school, neighborhood, playground, and summer camps are crucial, as are relations with close friends and adolescent peer groups. In general, the older one is when disaster strikes, the less vulnerable one is to those devastating misfortunes. (The experiences of the ghetto child are often so different from this model of human development that they may require separate treatment. Still, as Sullivan was fond of saying, we are all much more simply human than otherwise. Minority groups are no more and no less vulnerable than are white youngsters to the slings and arrows of outrageous fortune.)

In human life nothing is static; everything changes. Some things change almost or entirely imperceptibly, while having a cumulative effect. Other things change quickly—some of them apparently too quickly. In the second half of the 20th century, social change is occurring at such a swiftly accelerating rate that interpersonal relations are often subject to conditions over which the person has little or no control. (Many Americans equate change with progress. This is peculiarly ironic, since there is no consensus as to the nature of progress.) Added to these problems is a lack of continuity in all walks of life. A person's lack of control over his life, the lack of continuity with what one has cherished for many years, such as the now-eroding city, the lack of understanding of complex institutions—all these things seem to be of profound psychiatric significance. The family, which is the basic institution of society, has been profoundly affected.

Significant personality change, for better or worse, may occur at various times in life with or without therapy. But so many variables enter into personality change that they need extensive discussion. Hence, from a Sullivanian point of view, social structure and social change are very significant in a person's life experience. Also important is one's position in the social order. The daily routines of a psychiatrist, a businessman, or any highly skilled professional are vastly different from those of a man who works as a construction worker, a miner, or an employee on an assembly line. For good or ill, the style of life of the two social groups is considerably different. The professional group generally seem to enjoy a life of superior quality, though there seem to be a few excessively addicted to dry martinis or Scotch whisky, rather than Bach, during their leisure time.

The Self

To understand interpersonal psychiatry, one must take up an explication of the self. An understanding of the self is notoriously difficult—so much so that many psychologists and psychiatrists seem to feel more at home with ego, which has its roots in French and German philosophy.

Psychoanalysts generally accept the ego of Freud, perhaps including the refinements introduced by Hartmann, Lowenstein, Kris, and Brenner. The traditional ego of psychoanalysis, at least until about 1920, is roughly what Sullivan called the personified self, that to which one refers when he says "I," "me," and "myself." The personified self is a subsystem of the self-dynamism. In other words, there are processes of the self that, because they have never been formulated or have been selectively inattended, are frequently not thought of as part of "me."

Sullivan's self is to a great extent in the pragmatic tradition of William James, whose theory of the self influenced a long line of philosophers. To a smaller extent he is indebted to the sociologist Charles Horton Cooley, who formulated the looking-glass concept of the self (Sullivan's reflected appraisals). Sullivan did not attempt to give a formal definition of the self, although he devoted much effort to the description of its development and functions. The self is not synonymous with personality. That is, the personality includes not only the self but those things that, in the course of development, failed to become meaningful or significant to the person or had to be excluded permanently from conscious awareness because of their great anxiety-provoking power. The part or the set of processes that is not of the self is said to be dissociated, functionally split off from the self and all meaningful life experience. It is theoretically possible that anything, short of the necessities for survival, may be dissociated if it is tabooed by the community in which one has lived during one's early formative years or made intolerable (extremely anxiety provoking) as a result of some peculiarity of one's individual upbringing.

The personality, according to Sullivan, is the relatively enduring pattern of recurrent interpersonal situations that characterize a human life. In his work with mentally disordered people, Sullivan discovered that some of these recurrent interpersonal situations were not meaningful to the person because of the peculiarities of his life experience. That is, they were generally dissociated. This is of profound psychiatric significance, since, it apparently makes the assimilation of new experiences more and more difficult. At any rate, they were generally dissociated. Hence, the self may be generally described as the person's dynamic organization of relatively enduring and meaningful patterns of interpersonal situations that characterize his life. Thus, the distinction between personality and self is chiefly characterized, operationally speaking, by the degree to which one's experiences are accessible to consciousness. Those that do not make sense are generally freighted with intense anxiety, which often progresses to horror or panic, with grave disintegration of personality.

There are, then, extraordinary integrations of total situations in which the self is not a part or toward which the self stands as an unwilling and detached observer, including phenomena of the whole organism (somnambulism, some trance phenomena, some hysterical behavior), of extensive neuromuscular units (automatic writing, mediumistic speech), of the projection field of one or more special senses (hallucinosis, crystal gazing, shell hearing), and of more or less limited parts of the expressive apparatus (tics and stereotyped movements). They are rather outstanding in that the traditionally unitary organism becomes the moving locus of two or conceivably more streams of total activity integrating and being integrated into two or conceivably more coexisting and mutually exclusive total situations.

Such phenomena usually appear at the beginning of the juvenile era, when the child first meets the world outside the home; as a result of morbid infantile and childhood experiences, he cannot handle the normal habits, games, and customs. So he is, perforce, compelled to adopt various abnormal situations. It is usually at preadolescence that these unfortunate youngsters progress into grave mental disorders.

Modes of Experience

For Sullivan, experience is anything thought, lived, or undergone. Experience is said to be, first of all, the inner component of events in which a living organism participates as such—that is, as an organizing entity. The limiting characteristics of experience depend on the quality and kind of experiences one has undergone or lived from early infancy, as well as on the quality and kind of the immediate event experienced. One may also express it as the outcome of the organism-environment complex. It has often been said that Sullivan ignores the inner or intrapsychic aspects of experience. This criticism rests on a false and popular metaphysics—a dualism usually credited to Descartes. In contrast, the author recommends Dewey's *Experience and Nature.*

The first mode of experience is the prototaxic, which is characteristic of infancy. It is assumed to be the rough basis of memory. Sentience in the experimental sense presumably relates to much of what Sullivan means by the prototaxic mode. At least in the very early months of life, the prototaxic may be regarded as the discrete series of momentary states of the sensitive organism, with special reference to the zones of interaction with the environment (mouth, nose, anus, and so on). Sullivan (1953) wrote that, by "sensitive," he was attempting to bring into the hearer's or reader's conception all those channels for being aware of significant events

from the tactile organs in, say, my buttocks, which are apprising me that this is a chair and I have sat on it about long enough, to all sorts of internunciatory sensitivities which have been developed in meeting my needs in the process of living. It is as if everything that is sensitive and centrally represented were an indefinite, but very greatly abundant, luminous switchboard; and the pattern of light which would show on that switchboard in any discrete experience is the basic prototaxic experience, if you follow me.

Analogously, a discrete series of stimuli form a momentary pattern in the infant's mind. These stimuli may come from within, as when a baby has a stomachache, or from without, as when the mother picks up the baby. Sullivan surmised that from the beginning of life until its end, the person undergoes a succession of discrete patterns of the momentary state of the organism, which implies that events of other organisms are moving toward or actually effecting a change in this momentary state. How one momentary state gets connected with another is not known; it is convenient to call whatever connection occurs as association—though it begs the question.

Any experience that can be discussed is in the parataxic or syntaxic mode. Any such experience, in either mode, is always interpenetrated by elements of the near past, sometimes of the distant past, and frequently, perhaps always, by elements of the anticipated future.

Sullivan thought that during infancy the ability to discriminate and identify objects occurs. But he wrote (1953a) that the identifying of differences is a precursor in all acts of recognition

because the differences evoke references to the past, in the process of which the experience of similar differences is effective in causing what we always lump under the term *I recognize.*

The parataxic mode follows—not in any strict logical sense but because nature and nurture have determined such a sequence.

Sullivan asserted that the infant's identifying eventually progresses to the point at which he is able to generalize experience marked with characteristics of several zones of interaction as experience pertaining to one recurrent pattern of sentience from the distance receptors, the eyes and the ears. When this occurs, the infant has begun to experience living in what is an elaboration beyond the prototaxic mode of experience. At this point one may say that he is experiencing the good (satisfaction-giving) mother, as well as the bad (anxiety-provoking) mother, in the parataxic mode. Thus the forms of experience are generalized. Generalizing is said to be a particular development in the identifying of differences. The forms of experience are generalized so that the things they hold in common, especially persons, as well as all their sundry differences, are in perception as useful experience. These influxes of experience are marked by one of several zones of interaction—taste, smell, or any one of several other zones provided by the oral, nasal, genital, and other zones. Other things follow the identifying of differences, such as forbidding gestures (mother's frowning) and encouraging gestures (mother's smiling and cooing). In general, the infant's experiences—of which many details are omitted—are in close cooperation with the mother as he gradually learns to detect the factors in common or in close connection with the mothering one.

As time goes on, recurrent patterns of sentience from various zones are elaborated. As the infant develops and maturation proceeds, the original undifferentiated or global form of experience becomes gradually replaced in the temporal sense by the recurrent patterns of sentience or experience. But the various kinds of experience are not related or connected for some time. The infant or child has to learn a great deal through his experiences and intellectual growth before he can connect the meaning of words and things. Consider Sullivan's illustration in *The Conceptions of Modern Psychiatry* (1953a): In this culture, most children have picture books that often have a little printed matter in them, and gradually the child learns to read. Suppose he learns that a certain colored or black and white pattern in a book is "kitty," although there is also a kitty that runs around the house. Sullivan wrote:

I am sure no child who can learn has not noticed an enormous discrepancy between this immobile representation in the book which, perhaps, resembles one of the momentary states that kitty has been in on some occasion. I am certain that every child knows there is something very strange in this printed representation being so closely connected with the same word that seems to cover adequately the troublesome, amusing, and very active pet. Yet, because of unnumbered, sometimes subtle, sometimes crude experiences with the carrier of culture, the parent, the child finally comes to accept as valid and useful a reference to the picture as "kitty" and to the creature as "kitty."

Thus, the child is said to learn some of the more complicated implications of a symbol in contradistinction to the actuality to which the symbol refers. However, this occurs before verbal formulation is possible. In this culture, from the picture book and the spoken word one progresses to the printed word and discovers that the combination of signs, c-a-t includes "kitty," and that it always works. Since the child is consistently exposed to this kind of experience, he gradually reaches a point at which printed words, with or without consensual validation, get to be very important in his growing acquaintance with the world. Normally, consistency in the use of language and its referents becomes so familiar that, at least for a great many children, the familiarity breeds indifference.

Gradually, the child, as he progresses into the juvenile era and beyond, learns the consensually validated meaning of language in the widest sense of language. With perhaps minor exceptions—for example, if the parents speak a different language in the home—the meanings of words—even among scientists, who make up a special group—have been gradually acquired from one's community. The various meanings of words involve an appeal that is accepted as true by one's hearers. This is the syntaxic mode of experience. Ordinarily, the hearer is a representative of the community.

Euphoria and Tension

There seems to be built into the human organism a striving or goal-directed process aimed at euphoria, which is simply an objective state of utter well-being. Of course, given the nature of the human organism and of the world, absolute euphoria can only be a construct. If the human organism had no need to limit his euphoria, he would have no requirement to satisfy needs, and he would have no necessity to strive or develop. This imaginary state of utter bliss is more suited to paradise, where everything is given without the asking. In short, he would not be a human being. But the actual human being, in fact, has an indefinitely great number of needs from birth to death, when all needs and functions cease forever.

Sullivan (1953b) formulated the notion of absolute euphoria in *The Interpersonal Theory of Psychiatry*. An ideal state is admittedly a construct. Relative states of well-being, of course, do exist. The qualifying adjective "objective" is added because euphoria is the outcome of the fulfillment of the need for satisfactions, such as for food, water, and security. Although certain agents, such as narcotics, may provide a temporary subjective feeling of euphoria, this state of affairs does not fulfill the ongoing requirements of the human organism. It cannot provide euphoria in Sullivan's sense.

Sullivan postulated two polar opposites: absolute euphoria and absolute tension. The two are inversely related. As has been pointed out in regard to euphoria, the two are ideal constructs and can never be reached by any person in his life. The two are reciprocally related. They may be approached at times, but almost all living is perhaps rather near the middle of the trail. In fact, some degree of tension is both normal and biologically necessary for life. Because of the necessities of the organism and of daily existence, the level of tension fluctuates, although it cannot be rigorously specified, since a number of variables are involved. For example, when a bodily need such as hunger is not satisfied, the level of tension ordinarily rises until satisfaction is achieved. Analogously, when one's interpersonal security is decreased, usually as a result of the disapproval of others or as a result of self-disapproval, the level of tension also rises and is designated as anxiety or anxiety tension. The bodily tension is an illustration of somatic needs. When the person experiences anxiety tension, he tends wittingly or unwittingly to modify his behavior, if feasible, to rid himself of this very unpleasant emotion. For example, infants try unwittingly to change their behavior when they undergo a considerable amount of empathized disapproval. As the self (also called the antianxiety system) begins to develop in late infancy or early childhood, the child experiences anxiety caused by the disapproval of significant others and soon caused by his self-disapproval because of some action, thought, fantasy, or feeling about himself. As time goes on, he incorporates the standards that are deliberately or otherwise taught in the home but more elaborately and intensively taught at school. A lowering of self-esteem is called anxiety tension, which by definition entails a lowering of euphoria. Physiological needs, if unfulfilled for any length of time, also lower euphoria. Thus, there is a marked difference in certain ways between somatic tension and the tension due to the disapproval of others or of oneself when one transgresses one's standards and ideals.

But there is a form of tension that needs a separate discussion—namely, night dreams. Recent psychological research has substantiated the hypothesis that dreams serve an important psychological function, regardless of one's interpretation of the dreams. Freud was, of course, the great pioneer of dream interpretation and perhaps the greatest book he ever wrote is *The Interpretation of Dreams*.

According to Freud, the function of dreams is to protect sleep. He thought sleep may be considered to be, among other things, a refusal to face reality; and there is a withdrawal of energy from the interests of life. In characteristic fashion, Freud believed that our relationships with the world, which we entered so unwillingly, seem to be withdrawn periodically and seem to be endurable only with intermission in order to make life endurable. Moreover, in sleep we withdraw periodically into a condition similar to that prior to our entrance into the world, namely, into a condition similar to that of intrauterine existence. As one withdraws from reality, one regresses to more primitive (infantile) modes of activity, and the controlling forces of the conscious mind are more and more reduced. Furthermore, since all the paths to mobility are (usually) blocked, less energy is needed for repression of instinctual drives, of internal drives, of internal excitations, which are active during sleep. In other words, there is (ordinarily) no possibility that one will give manifest expression to such drives by acting overtly. To anticipate somewhat, dreams are a reaction to stimuli, frequently though not always, originating in the unconscious (in the id). Dreams effect a discharge of excitation so that the stimuli are removed and sleep can continue (Mullahy, 1970).

What are the impulses and desires that express themselves in dreams? According to Freud, they are the evil, primitive, and infantile impulses and desires that remain in the id—the unconscious or the id of every adult. The unconscious is said to be the infantile in mental life. Incestuous wishes are apparently the most important. Hate rages unrestrainedly, as well as death wishes against parents and other relatives. In dreams all such wishes are shorn of all inhibition because the restrictions of morality are not operative in sleep.

Freud wrote that since the ego has the task of maintaining sleep in spite of the powerful unconscious drives that tend to disturb sleep, the sleeping ego resorts to the stratagem of allaying them by a seeming act of compliance. It provides an outlet for or satisfaction of a (hallucinated) fulfillment of those drives in the manifest dream or dream fragment. According to Freud, in the course of personality development, the ego and the superego reach a point at which they no longer countenance the forbidden drives because one has incorporated the values of society and learned that one must adjust to the modes of gratification, whether they are completely satisfactory or not. Thus, during the development of the person, forbidden impulses are repressed and forgotten. However irrational and nonsensical the remembered dream appears to be, it frequently if not always, according to Freud, ultimately represents unconscious processes, frequently infantile, stemming from a very early part of life and are usually repugnant to the waking ego, with its standards, values, and ideals and its conscious awareness of the demands and restrictions required by reality—that is, society. When one wakes up or as one is waking up, a powerful censorship comes into play and disguises the latent dream content.

An elaborate process of disguise called the dream work occurs between the latent dream thought and the dream one remembers—at least briefly. The dream work, in order to disguise the latent dream thoughts, uses certain stratagems, such as condensation and displacement, to make the manifest dream unrecognizably distorted and unintelligible. Even so, the ego attempts to shape the manifest dream content into a semblance of logic and coherence.

In Freud's view, the two aspects of a dream occur on two levels, one of which, the latent dream thoughts, are strictly an inferential construction. Whether or not the latent dream thoughts exist in a separate compartment of the mind is something that Sullivan believed constitutes an impassable barrier. This does not mean that Sullivan rejects the existence of unconscious processes. On the contrary, in *Personal Psychopathology* (1972) he devotes considerable space to dreams and symbols. However, Sullivan dispenses with Freud's topographic theory of the mind. The same unconscious content may be expressed in different kinds of symbols and in different ways. Sullivan claimed that the remembered dream undergoes falsification from hour to hour. Such falsifications suggest that the waking associations to the alleged latent dream are associations to the whole person, rather than to accessible and hypothetical latent dream thoughts.

According to Sullivan, sleep is necessary for the maintenance of the waking dissociation of powerful tendency systems. Its contribution to the success of the dissociative dynamics is said to take the form of the release and fantastic satisfaction of the dissociated systems in the activity of sleep. When an attempt at resolving a "conflict situation" suspends sleep, as it may be in the case of someone on the verge of schizophrenia, the psychiatric importance of sleep privation becomes evident. When the individual's preoccupation with a conflict situation is one concerning the gravest matters of his life, it "confirms" his sleeplessness. So his condition passes from bad to worse.

Therefore, the connection of a period of disordered sleep with the onset of a schizophrenic illness is intimate, and of a nature such that one might well believe that an intercurrent "good night's sleep" would often postpone the disaster (Mullahy, 1970).

Sullivan has said that on occasion he was able to stave off an incipient schizophrenic from catatonia by providing the patient with enough alcohol to enable him to have a good sleep. In such a case, when the patient awakened, he was sometimes able to talk about things that were impelling him toward disaster. Then there was a chance to save him from disaster, and the therapy could proceed.

In passing, it seems desirable to note that the tensions of needs and of anxiety are in opposition to the tensions of sleep. A brief but thorough account of Sullivan's ideas can be found in *The Interpersonal Theory of Psychiatry* (Sullivan, 1953b).

Phenomenological Analysis

Whatever the importance of biochemical and neurophysiological factors in the life of any person, they represent a level of analysis that, in the later years of his life, Sullivan preferred to leave to specialists. As long as one bears this in mind, there need be no quarrel with Sullivan's phenomenological level of analysis—the field of interpersonal relations.

In an interpersonal situation a transaction always occurs. Each person has his share to contribute to the situation, but it is the situation that governs the transaction. If one of the participants remains silent, that, too, is part of a transaction, since silence is a form of speech—sometimes an eloquent component. The almost infinite occurrences of life give rise to interpersonal situations.

One of the most profound aspects of a situation or of how the person tends to act in (integrate) a situation is the character of his self-esteem. If the person thinks highly of himself or believes he is of considerable worth, he tends to regard others, significant others, as people of worth also. On the other hand, if, because of unfortunate life experiences, he has a low opinion of himself and is seriously deficient in self-esteem and self-confidence, he consciously or otherwise tends to regard others as unworthy. He frequently has little success in life. Again and again, situations in which he is integrated rapidly dissolve (disintegrate). Such an unfortunate person may not even realize that he says or does things that repel others.

This leads to the theorem of reciprocal emotion. Sullivan (1953a) wrote:

> My initial theorem stated, approximately, that the evidence of needs, as manipulated by the infant, calls out tender cooperative behavior on the part of the mothering one.

This is true of the period of the infant's complete dependence, but in childhood the social responsibility of the mothering one begins to interfere with it. Thus, from early childhood onward another general statement may be applied to interpersonal relations, which Sullivan called the theorem of reciprocal emotion or reciprocal emotional patterns. Integration in an interpersonal situation is a reciprocal process in which (1) complementary needs are resolved or aggravated, (2) reciprocal patterns of activity are developed or disintegrated, and (3) foresight of satisfaction or of rebuff of similar needs is facilitated (Sullivan, 1953b). This formula applies from early childhood.

In regard to the first point, resolution or aggravation, the mother needs to act tenderly, and the infant or child needs tenderness. If the baby's need brings denial or anxiety, the youngster's need is aggravated. This aggravation can easily be generalized, since all life long people have complementary needs. As for the second point, development or disintegration, in late infancy or childhood the youngster has a need for activity, which may be facilitated by the parent or ignored or hindered, and in this case the need for activity, such as playing with pots and pans or pulling out drawers or dropping an expensive watch to the floor (after all, a thousand shining splinters are quite something) slows down or, in many respects, disintegrates. The destruction of curiosity is an excellent example. As for the third point, satisfaction or rebuff, reaching out for affection by a child may be consistently satisfied or consistently rebuffed. One could easily write a book using this great theorem and apply it to adolescents and adults, as well as children.

Stages of Development

From Sullivan's point of view, man is a social being. At the moment of birth or shortly after, his socialization begins. This socialization continues through several overlapping stages. Ideally, one continues to learn and to store up experience, so that one can, in the course of time, acquire more and more of the infinite riches of the world. But owing to innumerable factors, one may suffer a grave arrest of development, and personality development thenceforth may proceed at a greatly reduced rate or, given certain occurrences, may regress to an earlier stage.

Such persons suffer, in varying degrees, difficulties in living that are often collectively labeled mental disorder.

INFANCY

Sullivan began his exposition with an outline of the infant's needs and the activities of the other person required for their fulfillment. The activities pertain to the tender behavior of the mothering one, the affectionately predisposed impulsion to fulfill the infant's biochemical needs and the manner in which she or he does this. Certain other needs, such as the need for activity and the need to explore (curiosity) are not stressed. Normally, in the course of time, the infant experiences the mothering one's tenderness and then gradually develops a generic need for tenderness and, still later, a need to act tenderly. When the generic need is satisfied, the infant's euphoria remains high, apart from periodic discomforts caused by such needs as hunger and thirst. Psychiatric experience seems to indicate that if a person does not receive tenderness during the early years, he will not in later years know what it is and, therefore, will not have any need to behave tenderly. But if he is not gravely damaged and if he is intelligent, he may learn to act as if he felt tender. In this connection, the hysteric comes to mind.

Ideally, infancy is a period when one experiences a more or less blissful state. But reality intrudes, so that even the happy infant goes through some suffering due to illness and pain. What Sullivan stresses is the induction of a fear-like state—anxiety tension when the mothering one is anxious or, for a variety of reasons, upset, disturbed, or disapproving. Sullivan called the anxiety tension of the infant a fear-like state partly because at this time the infant cannot communicate his experiences or distinguish anxiety tension from what is thought of as fear. But Sullivan thought there were objective indications of infantile anxiety, such as feeding difficulties and marasmus. Sullivan thought that the roots of anxiety can be traced to this period of life. The infant's experiences of anxiety and his gradually developing ability to distinguish between increasing and diminishing anxiety canalize his behavior in various ways as he strives to avoid anxiety. The self-dynamism develops through various stages to avoid or minimize anxiety and gain approval, which ordinarily restores the youngster's security. As time goes on, not only parents but older brothers and sisters, an aunt, an uncle, and a grandmother become significant and may foster his security by the affection they may manifest. When the author was a little boy, he was impressed when an uncle explained to him that you cannot split a log into three halves.

The Interpersonal Theory of Psychiatry contains a meticulous description of Sullivan's views on how the infant gradually learns to discriminate his experience in relation to zonal needs that arise in connection with various zones of interaction or transaction, to general needs (hunger, thirst), and to his prehension (to prehend is to have potential information or misinformation about something) of the appearances, attitudes, and behavior patterns of significant others who satisfy those needs. Sullivan describes the beginning discrimination of the body from everything else, how the infant learns to distinguish phonemes and words from the continuum of available sound patterns that are articulated by the significant others, and how, chiefly by trial and error from human example, he gradually learns to reproduce sounds and words.

The notion of personification is portrayed. To personify is to attribute human characteristics to some fantasy, idea, or thing.

One personifies evil in the shape of the devil. The Greeks ascribed numerous human attributes, good and bad, to the gods of Olympus; Jove, for example, was forever chasing beautiful goddesses. Personification in infancy is the rudimentary perception or image of the mothering one. But only gradually do the rudimentary perceptions of the infant fuse into one unitary being. Sullivan inferred that the person who satisfies the infant's needs is prehended as the good mother, who symbolizes forthcoming satisfactions. But she is not the real mother as defined, say, by social consensus. Nor is the mothering one's perception of her baby the real infant. The mothering one perceives her infant in accordance with her own needs, previous experiences, current experiences with the infant, and what the baby symbolizes in relation to her social responsibilities. Moreover, the young infant also perceives or, rather, prehends a different sort of mother, who under some circumstances fails to provide the satisfactions or induces anxiety. In these situations the mother is perceived or prehended as the bad mother, the bearer of frustrating and anxiety-provoking experiences. Perhaps in late infancy but more definitely in childhood, the good mother and the bad mother personifications fuse into a rough approximation of the mothering one as she more or less actually is.

At all times, the infant strives to attain a state of euphoria. This striving for euphoria persists throughout life. The satisfaction of the infant's needs brings or restores euphoria, which is a condition of well-being. On the other hand, anxiety lowers one's euphoria and, if the anxiety is chronic, may result in disastrous consequences or, at the very least, a painful sense of insecurity, perhaps indefinitely.

Security is analogous to satisfaction. Security exists or comes into being when anxiety is assuaged or banished. Sullivanian psychiatry deals almost exclusively with the loss of security, which signifies a lowering of self-esteem and increasing anxiety tension. The self comes into being in order to minimize anxiety tension, which is experienced before the self-system—sometimes called the antianxiety system—has begun to develop. Insecurity (anxiety) and failure to achieve satisfaction of needs cause a loss or lowering of euphoria. It is possible to be well fed and dressed beautifully and still be more or less chronically anxious.

The distinction between fear and anxiety was important to Sullivan. Fear is characterized by any threat to the person's survival or by great newness or strangeness. Anxiety is provoked by the threat of a lowering or loss of self-respect. Anxiety is always interpersonal in origin and function.

Sullivan's attempt to reconstruct the infant's experiences of the mothering one into three sorts of personifications was designed chiefly to explain what often happens to people in later life when they suffer mental disorder, whether mild or severe. The third personification of the mother is called "not me" (not-of-me). This personification appears when the infant is exposed to intolerable anxiety and possibly abuse over a period of time. In any later period of life, a person undergoing anxiety may unwittingly misperceive a significant other to such a degree that the other becomes bad, evil, threatening, or dangerous. Such distortions do not arise from nothing. They have a history, which Sullivan thought could often be traced to the first year or two of life. Even in more or less normal people, such distortions are not rare, although they may differ in degree and frequency. Such parataxic distortions have also been called illusory me-you patterns.

The beginning development of the self is closely related to the experiences of infancy and early childhood. Apparently, the development of self starts with the infant's personifications of the mothering one. Within Sullivan's theoretical framework, there must be a significant correlation, but that is as far as one can safely go. It would be rash to formulate a one-to-one positive correlation. The infant is exposed to numerous and diverse experiences not only from the mother but also from the father, older siblings, and other relatives, such as an aunt, an uncle, and a grandmother. The self-system is never a function of or an identity with the mother. The infant does not incorporate a parent or her standards and norms. The self is an organization of experiences, extending over a period of years, for avoiding increasing anxiety between object and subject or, more accurately, for avoiding anxiety in the organism-environment complex. The act of sensing, perceiving, discriminating, understanding, and so on always intervenes from the beginning of the infant's development. As he grows physically and mentally, the young person is highly subject to past experiences and increasingly subject to foresight.

Personification of self. The beginnings of the self are closely related to three personifications—good me, bad me, and not me, which is closely bound up with dissociation. All three personifications arise in connection with the self-sentient character of "my body," an organization of experiences that is gradually distinguished from everything else. Good me is said to be the beginning personification; it organizes experiences in which satisfactions have been enhanced by rewarding increments of tenderness when the mothering one is pleased with her offspring and his behavior. Ordinarily, when one talks about "I" (the personified self), one is talking about good me, but not always, since residues of bad me may forever remain a part of the I, especially if the person has had to endure a great deal of disapproval during the early years of life. Increasing degrees of anxiety associated with the mothering one's behavior are gradually organized into the personification bad me. The increasing differentiation of tenderness, which induces euphoria, from the anxiety-laden attitudes and disapproving behavior that arouse interpersonal insecurity or anxiety tension (anxiety is always interpersonal in origin and function) are the source of bad me. The infant experiences the sources of bad me (and of good me) long before he can understand or formulate them. At best, he has not progressed beyond the parataxic mode in middle or late infancy when the self begins to develop.

The personification not me is difficult to formulate with precision. Apparently, Sullivan inferred its existence chiefly from observation of schizophrenic patients during periods when they had regressed or had reactivated certain kinds of experience that hardly progressed beyond the infantile level or stage. He also thought that most people probably have similar experiences in an occasional dream, such as a nightmare. Such experiences are dissociated. They ordinarily never become part of the self-dynamism. For most of his career, Sullivan had considerable difficulty in his attempts at formulation of dissociation. In any case, he surmised that from very early in life and possibly from the beginning, certain kinds of experience take on a separate organization, which is not integrated with the developing mainstream of the personality and is split off from the organization of meaningful experiences that become the self. Thus, they are dissociated experiences foreign to the self.

The organization of experiences called or labeled not me is said to evolve very gradually because it arises from experiences of ineffably intense anxiety. This personification is always relatively primitive (infantile) and, according to Sullivan's mature formulations, ordinarily occurs in the parataxic mode, when the global character of the infant's experiences gradually gives way to more particularized experiences that may be associated but not logically connected. The mothering one

distributes rewards and punishments—and anxiety, even if administered unwittingly, is a formidable kind of punishment—not only when the offspring is bad but when the mother is upset because of various individual and social circumstances. Not me embodies poorly grasped aspects of living or aspects of living that have never been grasped at all. These aspects gradually become regarded as dreadful and, still later, are differentiated into incidents attended by awe, horror, loathing, or the dread experiences that often bedevil schizophrenics. But, according to Sullivan, under certain special circumstances the not me may be encountered in everyone. One has only to think of the experiences of many young men who, convicted and jailed on a felony charge, are repeatedly gang raped by their fellow inmates.

The poorly grasped aspects of living that Sullivan is talking about have nothing to do with intellectual capacity or ignorance. They are not at all like the experiences of a man who once asked the author to explain how a telegram can go through the wires.

Self-system. Sullivan stated that there is some evidence that in the latter part of infancy good me and bad me become fused or assimilated in a rudimentary fashion into the unitary dynamism of the self or self-system. The purpose or function of the self-system is directed at how to live with the significant other person while avoiding or minimizing incidents of anxiety. However, this is only how it starts. All through life, the chief function of the self is to gain as much approval as possible from significant others—those who play an important role in one's life, either permanently or temporarily—while avoiding or minimizing disapproval, which arouses the unpleasant feeling of anxiety. From Sullivan's viewpoint, this function is absolutely necessary to obtain as much as one can of the things one wants from life and to avoid suffering, crushing defeats, and failures.

Since the mothering one is a product of her community, society, and social class, she embodies their irrational elements, as well as their rational elements—that is, their intelligent and humane elements. Hence, the origin of the self-system rests on the character of her social environment. No one can know or even imagine what sort of self-system, if any, a person would develop in a perfectly rational society. Presumably, the self-system would be co-terminus with personality, which in the real world includes both the self-system and the dissociated system. As things stand, the person makes his way from infancy to adulthood amid a network of social institutions that embody rational and irrational elements in an extremely complex organization.

Many psychiatrists have observed that their patients' efforts to maintain the self-esteem, however fragile, are the principle psychological stumbling blocks to favorable change. A psychiatrist encounters numerous resistances and security operations in patients. However paradoxical this resistance may seem, one must bear in mind that as it develops, the self-system becomes the instrumentality of all meaningful relationships to the world. The culture embraces one like a caul. From Sullivan's point of view, this can be understood only to the extent that one can learn how, from infancy onward, the person got to be what he is and the way he is. Ordinarily, therefore, reason can operate only within cultural limits. One is reminded of Americans who visit Athens and come back to the United States with as little understanding of Ancient Greek civilization as the grocer on the corner of the block. Selective inattention is the foremost dynamism that restricts the broadening of the self. It prevents one from seeing, hearing, perceiving, and understanding numerous things that, if one could surmount the limitations of the self, would enable one to learn many things that would not only be useful in the practical sense but contribute to a better and happier life.

CHILDHOOD

Childhood is roughly distinguished from infancy by the maturation of the capacity for language behavior, the foundations for which have been established in late infancy. The child begins to talk, however imperfectly, chiefly by means of trial and error and from human example. He gradually learns to imitate the speech of his parents or their surrogates. He also gradually learns to relate (associate) the meaning of words, phrases, and sentences with people, objects, and events. Of course, the elaboration and refinement of speech extend over a period of several years. Gradually, the youngster's speech—which is at first largely autistic, a species of the parataxic mode of experience—becomes consensually validated. He requires time and effort to grasp the meaning of words and sentences as defined by significant others. Parents who use a broad vocabulary may enhance this process by encouragement when the child starts to talk by helping him in the conventionally correct meaning and usage of words and sentences.

Around this time, the child has a whole world to discover and begins to ask numerous questions. This is a matter that Sullivan did not stress for a long time, though he mentions the experimentation of the infant in *Conceptions of Modern Psychiatry*. The uncluttered mind of an intelligent child has an almost infinite number of questions to ask. Some questions are so difficult and original, at least for the child, that they baffle or embarrass the parents, who, either overtly and plainly or subtly by frowns and changes in tone of voice, communicate to the infant that he is bad when he persists. And so, all too often, the marvelous curiosity of children gradually becomes dulled. The possible reason that Sullivan deemphasized curiosity may be that he believed parents who teach or encourage their children to be different will, very likely, cause their offspring to suffer and possibly be ostracized when they go to school. In any case, for Sullivan the achievement of self-respect was of overriding concern; everything else was subordinate.

In childhood, also, the youngster, because of maturation and learning, starts to acquire various habits and elaborates numerous individual-social skills that can be grouped under perception, manipulation, motor coordination, and cognition. Emotional development increases rapidly. That peculiar human ability that Sullivan calls the eduction of relations (a phrase borrowed from Spearman, 1927), which first begins to be elaborated in infancy, continues to grow during childhood and later stages with spectacular efficiency and refinement. Concomitantly, there is an increasing elaboration of the self, chiefly from the child's experiences of the reflected appraisals of significant others. If the child is valued and treated with tenderness, he experiences himself as someone who is valuable, capable, and good. For him the world is good, with associated experiences of ever-growing self-confidence and self-respect. If he is subjected to frequent or indiscriminate disapproval, he tends to regard himself as bad and unworthy, with accompanying experiences of anxiety, anger, and lack of self-confidence and self-respect.

Throughout childhood and later, communicative speech takes on more and more importance in the person's experiences and behavior patterns. Speech also greatly facilitates the syntaxic mode of experience, in which consensual validation is of its essence. This consensual validation, too, contributes greatly to the elaboration and refinement of the ever-growing self-system.

In *Personal Psychopathology,* Sullivan wrote:

Configurations that include other [significant] persons customarily ensue in one of three outcomes....

In one, the impulses of the child progress easily to complete satisfaction [and security]; the adult is compliant and pleased by the child; and the feeling tone of the child's related self-consciousness is pleasant....

In another sort of situation, the impulses of the child are directly thwarted; the adult is disapproving or displeased with the child; and the feeling tone is either a hateful feeling appearing as a tendency to

primitive rage, or one of antagonism originating by differentiation from the primitive rage....

In the third typical situation, the impulses of the child meet neither compliant facilitation nor direct active thwarting, but instead are met by accidental or studied indifference on the part of the adult.... The situation persists and its persistence, as in the case of all persisting motivations, is accompanied by a felt interest, in this case in the other self. At the same time, there is a new measure of awareness of the child's self, and of its needs for response by others. It is in such situations that there arises in the self-consciousness the need later to be manifested as the seeking of *status,* an enduring organization of the self and its appurtenances such that at least indifference will not be the outcome of situations including other persons, and preferably that the outcome will be favorable appraisal and approbation.

At this time, 1932, Sullivan had not fully recognized the importance of anxiety and its relation to self-esteem. Even though the child's status seeking often, if not always, has a negative social value, the drive for status is still urgently necessary. As Sullivan wrote:

In children whose impulses have evoked disapproval much more frequently or effectively than compliance, the pursuit of status by hateful or antagonistic activities is almost to be expected. To them "being bad" is at least being something.

In *Personal Psychopathology,* Sullivan emphasized status seeking in early life. He obviously borrowed freely from William James. Sullivan wrote that not only does the sentiment of self (self-dynamism) grow along the paths of assertion, domination, submission, and a variety of perhaps subordinate factors from all the experience in which an appraisal by another person has made its appearance in a social situation, but also it grows by a peculiar extravasation of selfhood on material and immaterial objects in varying degrees attached to or associated with the person. Sullivan might have added that to some degree status seeking is common among all groups.

To explain what Sullivan called the malevolent transformation of personality, one must first introduce some of his ideas on the parental teaching of *ought.* Normal authority figures are in varying degrees diligent in impressing on the child that he must learn to cooperate with them to take part in living, to carry out instructions, and to do various chores. Very often they try to teach him or instill in him the concepts of duties and responsibilities. According to Sullivan, that teaching is certainly good preparation for life in a social order; but, if the parents are uninformed or suffering from unfortunate peculiarities of personality, their training of the offspring in concepts and responsibility includes, among other things, the notion *ought.* Among such organizations as the military, there is a serious effort to provide rules that include *ought* and *must,* rules that can be understood by the comparatively uninitiated.

The prescriptions of the culture imposed on the child are often most glaringly contradictory on different occasions. So they necessitate complex discriminations of authority situations. For a good many years the child is incapable of comprehending the prescriptions in connection with their possible reasonableness. A child can rattle off the Ten Commandments long before he can comprehend them—if he ever does. He learns them according to rote learning principles. As Sullivan (1953a) wrote:

And more important than anything else, out of the irrational and impulse-driven type of education by anxiety, or by reward and punishment—that is, tenderness and fear—a great many children quite early begin to develop the ability to conceal what is going on in them, what actually they have been doing behind someone's back, and thus to deceive the authoritative figures.

Some of this ability to conceal and deceive is said to be literally taught by the authority-carrying figures, and some of it is said to represent trial-and-error learning from human example—that is, by observing and analyzing the performances, successes, and failures of siblings, servants, and other significant figures.

To a degree, in normal children the ability to conceal and deceive is perhaps almost universal. Some children become fairly skillful at concealing what might otherwise bring anxiety or punishment at the hands of the authority or authoritative figures who make more or less well-recognized demands. To escape anxiety or punishment, the offspring frequently has two successful patterns of evasion.

The first is to use verbalisms, frequently called rationalizations, wherein one offers a plausible series of words, regardless of its irrelevancy. When Cromwell was burning to the ground the town of Drogheda in Ireland and in the process killed every man, woman, and child, he loudly praised God and quoted the Bible for the opportunity to get rid of those rebellious, wicked Irish Catholics. In personal life, rationalizations often come in handy not only when a child is trying to escape anxiety but when an adult is trying to escape anxiety. Rationalization is also a potent instrument of the self when something threatens it with dreaded, however constructive, change. Rationalization is used when the possible change is not congruent with the current organization and direction of the self.

The second pattern of concealing and deceiving is even more unfortunate, the learning of as-if performances. As-if performances have two major subdivisions—dramatizations and preoccupations. The latter is a way of dealing with anxiety or the threat of punishment. One may become immersed in something which impresses the mother and thus sometimes even brings tenderness, however useless and irrelevant the activity is—a prelude to the obsessional. A great deal of learning by the child is said to be on the basis of human examples, which are in childhood authority-invested models. Inevitably, the child learns a good deal in this manner about the mother, as he does about the father personification. Ordinarily, the mothering one is the first and most important person or personification in the child's life. Trial-and-error learning by human example, according to Sullivan, can be observed in the child's playing at acting like and sounding like the parents and then acting as being them. It appears that the child first appears to act like and then to act as if he were. This formulation seems more intelligible than Freud's identification.

Sullivan believed that in the early half of childhood, dramatizations may become of serious concern, in terms of their consequences, only when these dramatizations become particularly significant in concealing violations of cooperation and in deceiving the authority-invested figures. For a variety of reasons, these dramatizations sometimes tend to become subpersonifications. Sullivan (1953a) wrote:

> The roles which are acted in this way that succeed in avoiding anxiety and punishment, or that perhaps bring tenderness when there was no performance based on previous experience to get tenderness, are organized to the degree that I think we can properly call them personae; they are often multiple, and each one later on will be found equally entitled to be called I.

Sullivan added that to describe this deviation from the ideal personality development, he once created the conception of me-you patterns, by which he meant often grossly incongruent ways of behaving or roles that one plays with someone else in interpersonal relations. That is one of the reasons Sullivan thought that under certain circumstances during childhood dramatizations can cause unfortunate consequences. All or most me-you patterns seem as close to the real thing—the personification of the self—as can be. But they do not make sense from the point of representing different aspects of durable traits. Furthermore, Sullivan added, although these dramatizations are

> very closely related to the learning to be human, they can even in these early days begin to introduce a very striking irrational element in the personification of the self.

One particular phase of learning is said to be related to playing at being father or mother—learning from the authority figures a peculiar way of avoiding or neutralizing a fear-provoking situation. Sullivan claimed that in punishment situations in which pain is to be inflicted, there is invariably an element of restraint of freedom of movement—that is, a particularly deliberate attempt on the part of the punishing person to interfere with the child's escaping the physically enforced pain. When the very young child had no previous disastrous experiences, it would lead to such fear that rage behavior would be called out. But in such a situation rage has no value. The possibility of analysis and discrimination does not exist, and the exercise of foresight is only developing. And so, instead of rage itself occurring, a frequent eventuality appears—anger. Most children learn to use anger forcibly and frequently. They use it when otherwise they would feel anxious, in some situations when there is no possibility of the child's learning why he was punished. In this sort of situation, anger aggravates the situation, and such unfortunate children develop resentment, which is more or less tolerated by the repressing, punishing mother. But this sort of an outcome seems to occur somewhat later in life. In certain homes, whether or not one has been trained or encouraged in the use of anger, children well into the school years have temper tantrums, which are essentially unmodified rage behavior. In other situations in which one's attempts to conceal even resentment, for fear of punishment, are unsuccessful, the consequences can be grave. As Sullivan wrote:

> In other words, in the concealing of resentment and in the gradual development of self-system processes which preclude one's knowing one's own resentment, one actually has to make use of distribution of tension in a fashion quite different from anything that we have touched on thus far.

Sooner or later everyone learns, though in varying degrees, the use of anger. Thus, children, as well as adults, learn that anger itself can bring a great deal of punishment. Children express a great deal of anger when they are playing with their toys. Subsequently, they become angry with their imaginary playmates. In some unhappy homes, Sullivan thought, all the more fortunate denizens of our culture get to use anger very forcibly and frequently and in some cases intimidate their peers as they grow older. (In these days, when child abuse seems rampant, Sullivan might have added something that the author has observed: A child who has tantrums may provoke so much anger in the mother that she beats him until he can scarcely breathe.)

In a great many other unfortunate homes, children often manifest a complex modification of anger and its use. A child of 2½ or 3 years who accompanies his mother to the grocery store observes all sorts of delicious candies, apples, oranges, and cookies. Since the child has little or no understanding of the rights of property, he proceeds to help himself to some of the goodies. Suddenly, to his consternation, he receives a hard slap from his mother, he's told to keep his hands off the candies and fruit, and he's scolded for being a bad child. Hence, the child suffers physical pain and anxiety. Or he may hide a dress that his mother is making or an unfinished sweater that his mother is knitting during her spare time. It may be that his mother is harried because of a recalcitrant husband. In this case the child knows what he is doing and, of course, gets punished. Such children know that anger will aggravate the situation and hence manifest resentment, though they are still repressing components of anger. In other words, there is a distribution of tension different from anything previously mentioned. If you have to swallow resentment, Sullivan used to say, it may give you indigestion.

The previous discussion of as-if performances and the modifications of attitudes and of interpersonal relations are not only significant in their own right but necessary to understand the evolution of malevolence or the malevolent transformation in interpersonal relations. Sullivan was absolutely convinced that no one is born with evil tendencies. It follows that he rejected Freud's destructive instinct. If given a fair chance, such as adequate care and affection, children can be wonderful people. In the juvenile era many are destined to suffer. The number of children who can be cruel, with or without reason, is great. But in all fairness youngsters of the childhood and juvenile eras are strictly amateur in comparison with many adults, who have enough knowledge and skill and finesse to be really nasty or worse. Sullivan mentions so-called timid children, whose malevolence shows in their being so afraid to do anything that they fail to do the things that are most urgently desired. Another group of malevolent children are the frankly mischievous, who become bullies and who take it out on pets and younger siblings.

According to Sullivan, many children have the experience that when they need tenderness, they meet with rebuff; when they do the things that once brought tender cooperation, they are not only denied tenderness but treated in a manner that provokes anxiety or, in some instances, pain. The more or less helpless child who is destined to become malevolent may discover that manifesting the need for tenderness toward the potent figures around him—his parents, first of all—frequently leads to his being disadvantaged, made anxious, ridiculed, and made to suffer pain, literal or otherwise. In such instances the developmental course changes to the point that the felt or perceived need for tenderness brings a foresight of anxiety or pain. In such cases the child is trapped in the nuclear family; the extended-family structure is dead. In any case, the child who consistently meets with rebuff when he needs tenderness learns that it is highly disadvantageous, wrote Sullivan, to

show any need for tender cooperation from the authoritative figures around him. When this occurs he shows something else. And that something else is the basic malevolent attitude, the attitude that one really lives among enemies.

This conviction becomes generalized. In school, he makes it practically impossible for anyone to feel tenderly toward him or to treat him with kindness. As Sullivan put it, he "beats them to it" by the display of his malevolent attitude. Generally, the convictions of the child toward the world around him

become a basic attitude toward life and a profound problem in interpersonal relations. This is clearly the greatest disaster in childhood. And it has set the stage for costly strategems in dealing with people as life goes on.

TRANSITION FROM CHILDHOOD INTO THE JUVENILE ERA

Arrest of development. Sullivan's conception of development has not been adequately developed so far. As-if performances and the transformations or modifications of attitudes and of interpersonal relations in the forming of malevolence contribute to an arrest of development. That they do so becomes more evident when one realizes that malevolence may become a barrier to subsequent developmental experience. Dramatizations and obsessional preoccupations (ritual avoidances) prevent rational discussion. If the child is encouraged by various influences to make use of a good deal of dramatization and obsessional substitution, healthy socialization is slowed down. However, Sullivan states that arrest of development does not imply that things have become static and will forever remain at the point in personality development reached when the arrest of development occurred. In human life and in human development, everything changes; some things change very fast, others very slowly. The conspicuous evidence of arrest of development and deviation of development is, first, in the manifestations that characterize the statistically usual course and, later, in the appearance of eccentricities in interpersonal relations, though they are often far from self-evident signs of what has been missed or sadly distorted.

Gender. Very early in his career, Sullivan rejected Freud's notion of the existence of a universal Oedipus complex and, more generally, Freud's ideas on psychosexual development. But he did have a good deal to say about what he thought does happen around the time that Freud called the phallic stage. Thus, Sullivan (1953) wrote:

Certain influences in childhood make for the growth of the personified self [I], the personifications "me" and "we," along what I choose to call gender lines.

He thought the child is influenced by the fact that normally, the parent who is of the same sex as the child has a feeling of familiarity with the child, of understanding him, and that the parent of the other sex has a surviving, justifiable feeling of difference and of uncertainty toward him. Thus, each authority figure treats the child of the other sex in a manner that tends to foster a more rational education of the child.

The additions to the personified self on the basis of gender are notably advanced by two influences. One is the child's play at being the authority figure of his own sex. The other is the influence of so-called rewards and punishments—particularly interest and approval, in contrast with indifference and disapproval—and sometimes the influence of shame and guilt—complex varieties of anxiety, though they are associated with other things also. Regarding the roles the child is playing, Sullivan wrote that these influences—approval, disapproval, praise, blame, appeal to shame, and the incubation of guilt—tend to educate the child with peculiar facility in the social expectations of his particular sex, in the sense of gender, and to incubate many of the cultural prescriptions. As Sullivan wrote:

Thus when the girl catches on in play to something that seems very feminine, this play gets a certain amount of applause, interest, and support from the mother—at least it does if the mother still happens to still endorse the feminine.

Sullivan does not mention that apart from play, the mother often gives a good deal of direct instruction in the art of being feminine for several years. And perhaps later on the girl learns from the other girls in school, directly or indirectly, by what is still often called imitation. Boys of comparable ages seem to spend more time learning to play sports, with the possible exception of those who plan to make a career in one of the natural sciences. Whether there is any inborn tendency to enjoy and excel in, say, traditional music or mathematics is still somewhat controversial. At all events, in the simplified language of Thorndike (1905), apart from certain biological imperatives, masculinity or femininity gets "stamped in."

Stories and their effect. Since Sullivan died in 1949, while television was in its infancy, it is difficult to know how much weight should now be given to bedtime stories in this age of semiliteracy. In any event, he thought that there is or was another strong influence in transmitting certain cultural prescriptions that foster the more rapid growth of personifications. At least in the past there was a widespread practice of telling or reading stories to the child. In general, the stories are said to be of two types. One type are culturally approved moral tales ingrained in the culture, since they embody ethical ideals in a manner that can be grasped by a child. There was a time when a parent read Bible stories to the child. The second type are inventions of the authority figure far different from the socially approved stories of the first kind and are or were a special function of the parental personality. These stories do not reflect conventional moral values. Thus, the parent may, under the guise of a fairy tale, recite stories in which the main character is frightening or wicked. At this time, the child's grasp of the distinction between reality and fantasy is tenuous.

Sullivan wrote that this is one of the ways in which children get the impression that they should be governed by influences called social values, judgments, or the ethical worth of certain types of behavior. (Sullivan seems to have forgotten the influences of parochial schools.) Ethical judgments are said to be in the parataxic mode. According to Sullivan, they do not necessarily have much to do with the observed behavior of the parents or the child's opinions of the parents. (Analogously, if one wishes his offspring to grow up to talk truthfully, he had better act truthfully himself.) These influences may appear years later in psychotherapy. These values are often said to continue to exist in notable magic detachment from the actual experience of the child himself. Sullivan (1953a) wrote:

They are apt to be particularly rich soil for the production of verbalisms; and these verbalisms, for the very reason that they are derived from moral stories or the like which are part of the cultural heritage, have an effect in impressing the other person which is quite magical.

Overt and covert behavior. The child develops an important discrimination between what can be expressed, demonstrated, shown, or said and what goes on in fantasy but must be treated as if it did not—what can be overt behavior and what must remain covert in the presence of authority figures. Sullivan claimed that a special instance of this discrimination is the pointless question. Once a child has grasped the fact that certain things about which he needs or wants some information

are taboo for any demonstration or discussion, he starts to ask irrelevant questions. Instead of getting the information he needs, he gets rebuffed and is prevented by anxiety and the threat of punishment in any one of numerous ways parents have at their disposal. The child tries to circumvent the taboo by asking the questions, but he adds an autistic element to replace what cannot quite be inquired into. Sullivan (1953b) wrote:

The older the child gets, the nearer these autistic elements are to word combinations that actually refer to something, so that the child may make perfectly rational, diligent inquiries about why mother and father are always doing this and that in the morning when he really wants to know why mother and father do not say a word to each other when they wake to join the day.

What the child really wants to know is why they're both morose and have nothing to do with each other except possibly in putting the food on the table and getting it eaten. To use a favorite phrase of Sullivan, this lack of communication between the parents leaves their offspring buffaloed. This field is mysterious and confusing as far as the child is concerned. If he is a normal, healthy child, he wants to greet the day, for it, like every day, promises new adventures and sometimes almost ecstatic experiences. Even if his ability to communicate is limited, he can express his desire for information clearly, but anxiety and the threat of punishment stand in his way. Not only is the child puzzled by his parents' moroseness, but he is intensely motivated for participant play with his parents and others who like to play with him. But it is scarcely possible for him to imitate morose behavior most of the time. In attempting to catch on to something that is, for him, not understandable, the child begins to ask pointless questions. The questions are not pointless to him, but the anxiety element requires that the child use words that conceal what he is really trying to find out. Sullivan wrote that in the child's apparently pointless and sometimes tediously repetitive questions, the question is actually an autistic combination of words which refers to what the child wants to know, and not what the parent supposes the question is. Questioning for questioning's sake, which can be at times a form of malicious mischief, may actually become rational. The reason is that the child offers an immense number of questions about a great many things which he really wants to understand. (It would appear that Aristotle was right when he said all men by nature desire to know.) But there is the additional impulse to question because there are still puzzling and disturbing elements in the interpersonal relationships around him which he is, or feels, prohibited from investigating. Sullivan might have added that eventually, in an indefinitely large number of cases, the child's curiosity dies.

Reality and fantasy. Throughout childhood, the youngster manifests an active imagination. He temporarily invests toys, for example, with human traits. He gradually develops a capacity to do so by purely referential processes. He does not need concrete objects to play with any more. The ability to have imaginary playmates has matured. Sullivan thought that a good deal of learning is attendant upon the parents' interest in these imaginary playmates and imaginary conversations. This use of imagination brings up something that is introduced to the child and often crops up in later years as a disturbing experience.

In infancy the child starts to make rudimentary distinctions. In childhood this ability is well advanced but far from perfect. As the child approaches the juvenile era, the distinction between reality and necessarily covert processes may at times be fairly clear. But it sometimes happens that what was intended to be covert—things that the child knows the parents ought not to hear, since they provoke anxiety or direct punishment—are nevertheless revealed to the parents because of the child's still limited grasp on many things. The child may speak aloud, for example, without intending to reveal anything or communicate anything to the authority figures, because this is exercise for his vocal abilities, which he enjoys, and is part of his imaginary play. Unhappily for the child, his rudimentary ideas are picked up by the parent who hears them, and rewards or punishments, especially the latter, "are poured out on the child to his profound mystification," as Sullivan put it. This experience is likely to give the child the idea that there is something violable about his covert process; the authority figures somehow know things he is trying to conceal, things that he does not wish to exhibit and that he knows are dangerous to show. Sullivan asserted that under some circumstances this kind of experience begins a group of processes in recall and foresight that, in later years, literally amount to a conviction that one's mind can be read or can, at least, be wonderfully suspected. These notions of the child may afterward show up in the content of a psychosis.

It has been pointed out or at least implied that there is a considerable need for the participation of the parents in the child's play, at least as an attentive audience and, if possible, as people who perform a role, unless siblings serve this purpose. Sullivan has related that in a good many instances circumstances do not permit much of this audience behavior by the authority figures, and loneliness at this stage is a foreshadowing of quintessential loneliness. The child who cannot secure the presence and participation, however passive, of adults and older teenagers, such as siblings, inevitably develops a rich fantasy life. He tries to compensate for the loss or lack of participation of authority figures by multiplying the imaginary personifications that fill his mind and influence his behavior. This process seems to be allied to the behavior of solitary people who, having no one else to talk to, develop the habit of talking to themselves. For example, a farmer living alone in some remote area where he rarely encounters other people may talk aloud to himself and continue to do so, just as a lonely child may talk to himself and create imaginary people whom he can talk to. One can hazard a guess that in hundreds of thousands of homes the children experience little participant play and are often neglected in other ways as well. As time goes on, the child, in order to gain attention, becomes a nuisance in the classroom. But when the teacher acquaints the mother with her offspring's misbehavior, she may tell the teacher that he has neglected his duties and failed to teach the child properly.

The young child probably does not recognize fantasy as a creation of his mind, having little or no direct relationship with the world. He knows a lot about the reality of a cup or a spoon, which he has directly experienced many times. But he has only a limited ability to distinguish between fantastic objects and those that have, for him, a degree of concrete reality. The child's fantasies have as much reality for him as do the perfectly concrete things—as long, at least, as the fantasies continue to be effective in covert processes and play. As a matter of fact, objects that adults regard as real—cups and saucers, postmen, policemen, food—are heavily invested by the child with autistic elements, so that this kind of reality and his fantasy life are indistinguishable to him—somewhat like certain Walt Disney creations. The objects and events that adults take for granted—the landlord, the President of the United States—have little or no significance for the child, since they are not part of his world, except perhaps peripherally. But the entire field of electronics is invested for most adults, barring a small group of specialists, with a certain magic that they accept because everyone else does.

Sullivan pointed out that by the end of childhood, the pressure toward socialization has almost invariably fixed a big premium on carefully sorting what can be agreed on by the authority figures. This is the first vivid manifestation in life of the role of consensual validation. What distinguishes syntax operations from everything else is that they work, under appropriate circumstances, quite smoothly with other people. Sullivan (1953b) wrote:

The only reason that they come to work quite precisely with other people is that in actual contact with other people there has been some degree of exploration, analysis and the obtaining of information.

Some ability to use consensual validation is vital. Otherwise, one makes mistakes and gets onself laughed at, ridiculed, or punished for reporting lively fantasy as real phenomena. (Sociologists have claimed that ridicule is a potent force in the achievement of conformity, whether one is young or not.) As the child begins to pass into the juvenile era, a time is reached when there is rapid acceleration of change in the character of fantasy. When circumstances, such as family life, do not contradict the possibility, there is the beginning of truly cooperative action with other youngsters of about the same age.

JUVENILE ERA

According to Sullivan, the importance of the juvenile era can scarcely be overlooked. It gradually appears at about the time children start going to kindergarten or the first grade in school. The juvenile phase is the time for becoming social. For the first time, the child encounters the world outside the home—except possibly for brief periods when he went on vacation with his parents, when he did not spend several hours every day in the company of his peers. People who bog down in the juvenile era are said to have conspicuous disqualifications for a comfortable life among their fellows. In this juvenile era, a vast number of important things happen, as Sullivan (1953) wrote:

This is the first developmental stage in which the limitations and peculiarities of the home as a socializing influence begin to be open to remedy.

There is continuity, especially in normal youngsters, from infancy onward. Everything that has been acquired and built into the personality becomes reasonably open to influence. The self, which is remarkably inclined to maintain its direction, becomes reasonably capable of modifying its organization at the thresholds of each era. Sullivan believed that in a society in which education is compulsory, it is the school milieu that rectifies or modifies a great deal of the unfortunate direction of personality evolution conferred on the young by their parents and other family members who may have acquired personality warp.

Sullivan held that the juvenile era is ushered in by a need for peers, people of about the child's own age and background. Already, a social segregation begins to appear. The need for compeers is fulfilled not only in the classroom but in the playground, park, and summer camp. During this stage, the juvenile enters a new world of experience—the world outside the home, with all its good and bad features. The self develops rapidly, partly because the school provides a range of experience not previously available. Apart from scholastic skills, the youngster normally learns or enhances the learning of numerous social skills and attitudes, including competition, cooperation, and compromise.

Competition. How much the school reflects the competitive society has been a matter of controversy. How much it is, in contemporary America, the cause of the impressive decline in standards, academic and otherwise, is heavily debatable. In any case, during the juvenile era a struggle for prestige among one's peers and for accomplishment in the classroom—at present, apparently much less important than a generation ago, with the possible exception of those who are science oriented—or on the athletic field has often been observed. Competition is strongly encouraged during the juvenile era and frequently throughout life. During childhood, competitiveness is often highly encouraged. From Sullivan's point of view, the significance of this attitude relates primarily to the person's over-all drive for satisfactions and security and to what extent competitiveness fosters or impedes their attainment.

Cooperation. It is almost axiomatic that every society, in order to function, must encourage at least a minimum of cooperation. In the United States, people take cooperation in all spheres of life almost for granted. Consider Italy as it now exists. In the New York Times on January 2, 1978, two scholars, Romeo and Urban, wrote:

You have to live in Italy to get the full measure of this [continuous agitation at the schools, universities, railways, airports, and post offices and in the press and the factories]: It has become practically impossible to manage public institutions or private enterprise, because the legitimacy of all authority has been challenged and defeated. We have examples of this every day. At the moment we are suffering from the suspension of the law in favor of terrorists. There are two principal left-wing terrorist groups in Italy: The Red Brigades in the north and the Proletarian Armed Guards in the south. Some members of these gangs have been arrested and put on trial in Turin and Naples. But when the arrested men's colleagues began attacking the police and the judges, the trials were halted and no more arrests followed.

To cooperate is to work with others for the achievement of common or shared ends not only in face-to-face interpersonal relations but in public life as well. It is doubtful if one can be, in fact, separated from the other. In any case, the juvenile learns, perhaps for the first time, that his prestige depends on how well he can cooperate with his peers. The degree to which institutional arrangements encourage cooperation varies from society to society. Normally, in a given sociocultural setup, the ability to cooperate grows stage by stage. To what extent a given society puts a brake on young people's tendencies toward cooperation is a topic best left to social scientists. However, the psychotherapist must recognize the extent to which cooperation is demanded in his or her patient's life and in his particular social station and how well or poorly the patient is equipped to fulfill this demand. How well or how poorly he can cooperate on suitable occasions almost always affects his strivings toward satisfactions and security.

Compromise. Compromise, unfortunately, often has pejorative connotations. It has frequently become associated with a sacrifice of one's moral or psychological integrity. In nearly all walks of life, from childhood on, compromise is required. According to Sullivan, to compromise is to give up part of what one wants or hopes to attain in order to obtain the rest in a given situation. Compromise is enforced by the juvenile society and to some extent by the school authorities. When it becomes a way of life, compromise, like competition, can become a troublesome, limiting trait. Some people emerge from the juvenile era willing to yield almost anything to maintain peace and quiet.

Social accommodation. One of the most important experiences of the juvenile era is the learning of social accommodation. It is, as Sullivan wrote:

a simply astounding broadening of the grasp of how many slight differences in living there are; how many of these differences seem to be all right even if pretty new and how many of them don't seem to be all right for reasons the juvenile cannot fathom, though how unwise one would be to attempt to correct them. When one is acquainted with people of the same age who have a variety of personal peculiarities, one must learn how to relate to them. As a result of morbidities in the home, the juvenile may start school with unrealistic appraisals, with exaggerated expectations, with their opposite if he has learned to be completely self-effacing and docilely obedient. His relations with new authorities may also require considerable modification since they are likely to be distributing rewards and punishment insofar as he is compliant, noncompliant, rebellious, or whatever. [One has to modify the statement about teachers in the light of what has happened to the once-great public educational system during the generation since Sullivan died.] The juvenile tends to learn that he no longer has a special place in the world and must adjust to the limitations and opportunities of the world outside the home. If the juvenile fails, his chances for a normal life are gravely diminished. Thus the juvenile era can provide an opportunity to remedy many of the parent's cultural limitations. However, if a person belongs to a special racial, ethnic, or religious group, he may encounter crippling experiences causing his faith in himself and the world to be undermined forever.

Consensual validation. In the school society, consensual validation is vigorously enforced. A major function of education is to extinguish the autistic thought from the expressed thought and to extinguish other idiosyncratic behavior in the juvenile. Many of the ideas and behaviors that were accepted in the home must be abandoned if one is to escape punishment from one's peers. But the learning of successful ways of expression and successful types of performance tends to earn one encouragement and rewards. Hence, one has the opportunity to learn about security operations (roughly, what Freud called defense mechanisms) and to learn ways of being relatively free from anxiety, frustration, and conflict. In this fashion the self usually learns to control focal awareness, so that what does not make sense in the juvenile world tends to get less and less attention.

It is during the juvenile era that the syntaxic mode of experience, because it includes more refined and powerful cognitive processes, is more effective in predicting the novel and offers some possibility of real interpersonal communication. The juvenile learns that there is no need to bother about things that do not matter. However, there is always the danger that he will resort to an unfortunate use of selective inattention, whereby he ignores things that do matter, excluding them from consciousness as long as possible, if he cannot find a way of being comfortable with them.

In his work with patients, Sullivan discovered that the misuse of selective inattention was a great enemy of therapy, since it is a great stumbling block on the road toward self-understanding, insight, and the learning of more healthy interpersonal relations. The tenaciousness of selective inattention in this sense is due to the fact that it is a function of the self-dynamism. The morbid use of selective inattention, which is an instrumentality of the self, may nevertheless serve as a shield against the eruption into consciousness of things, probably dissociated matters, that can be gravely disturbing.

This is a good example of what Sullivan (1953) meant by the theorem of escape.

[The] self-system from its nature—its communal environmental factors, organization, and functional activity—tends to escape influence by experience which is incongruous with its current organization and functional activity.

Because of his past experience, the patient lacks the ability to see that things may become better if he acts or thinks somewhat differently. Indeed, he may very well think that things will get worse, though this thought may be on an unconscious level. This thought is the major source of the resistance that has bedeviled many psychiatrists. Hence, a psychiatrist has to be alert at all times to what he says to his patient, how he says it, and when. Otherwise, he may discover one day that, for 6 months of treatment with a particular patient, he has been engaging in a long soliloquy.

Sublimation. Sublimation is the long-circuiting of the resolution of situations, chiefly those pertaining to zonal needs—a long-circuiting that proves to be socially acceptable. For example, during infancy the baby may derive pleasure from rubbing his anal region or tinkering with his genitals. But under certain circumstances, when the mother is present, these activities arouse intense anxiety, probably because of the empathic linkage. According to Sullivan, the infant may learn, first, that these pleasure-giving activities are not to occur when his mother is around, which is more or less learning by pure anxiety, and, second, that the peculiar circumstances of fiddling with these areas through a blanket, though the infant does not recognize the blanket as such, seems much less strikingly characterized by rapidly mounting anxiety. Soon, direct manipulation of the anus or genitals may be restricted to periods of somnolence; or, if the impulse is quite intense, some mediative performance may be discovered. The disapproval of the mothering one is due to her role as social censor, though some mothers can be quite morbid about such things. As Sullivan (1953) wrote:

[The infant] learns to chart a course by the anxiety gradient. Simple performances which would relax tension of some needs have to be made more complicated in order that one may avoid becoming more anxious. Before he is very many months of age, the child will be showing full-fledged sublimation, in the sense of quite unwittingly having adopted some pattern of activity in the partial, and somewhat incomplete satisfaction of a need which, however, avoids anxiety that stands in the way of the simplest completely satisfactory activity.

At no matter what time of life, sublimation is, unwittingly, not a matter of conscious thought of a communicable sort but, rather, the outcome of referential processes in the parataxic mode, whose goal is the avoiding or minimizing of anxiety.

Sullivan called the discrimination as to when euphoria is diminishing or increasing "learning by the anxiety gradient." He claimed that sublimation occurs when a way of behavior that is socially approved is unwittingly substituted for a part of the motivational pattern that is not acceptable to the authority figures and is not tolerated or regarded with esteem by one's fellows. When this happens, some remainder of unsatisfied need is worked off in a private reverie process, especially during sleep.

Sullivan believed that a great deal of one's education for living has to be this sort of sublimatory, strikingly unwitting catching on to how to get satisfaction, although not complete satisfaction. The sublimatory reformulation of behavior, when it is not overloaded, gives one great surety in what one is doing, though it has not been subject to rational analysis or valid information. A juvenile who acquires a pattern of relating himself to someone else that works and is approved of knows that what he is doing is right. This surety is due to the fact that during the juvenile era, the self-system has developed an increasing power to control the contents of consciousness and also because this process is unwitting. At least from childhood on, no one bothers to explain how he arrived at these formulations of behavior. Hence, most arrive at childhood with a great many beliefs and firmly entrenched ways of dealing with others that they cannot explain adequately. Sullivan said that even in adult therapy, it is fairly difficult for the psychiatrist to attract enough of the patient's attention to one of these sublimatory reformulations to get him to realize that there is something about it quite beyond explaining.

Supervisory patterns. An almost inevitable outcome of the most fortunate kind of juvenile experiences is the appearance of supervisory patterns of the self that embody value judgments of various kinds. Supervisory patterns are complex and subpersonifications of the self-system. They have a history, although Sullivan does not stress that fact directly. Freud's superego is one form of supervisory pattern, but there are many others. Thus if one writes, he has a reader, a sort of subpersonification who is very alert (when he is not very tired) to what the writer is putting down on paper, how well it is organized, its grammatical structure, its spelling, and its punctuation. If one has some self-confidence as a writer, he is convinced that some readers will give him a fair, interested hearing. Others will be inclined to be indifferent, perhaps because they belong to another "school." Still others will be inclined to be hostile.

Then there is the hearer. If one is a lecturer, the hearer will listen carefully to determine if what he is saying is clear, is coherent, and makes sense. Finally, there is the spectator. As Sullivan (1953) wrote:

The spectator diligently pays attention to what you show to others, and do with others; he warns you when it isn't cricket, or it's too revealing, or one thing and another; and he hurriedly adds fog or camouflage to make up for any careless breach.

Years ago, when America was less permissive, one might have observed a conservatively brought-up lady accept a second drink with reluctance (not to be a spoilsport) and drink it slowly, nursing it along for the rest of the evening. As Sullivan once said, a bit flippantly, quoting a colleague, the superego is the alcohol-soluble part of the personality.

Ideally, these supervisory patterns function suavely and skillfully, like a great lady or a great politician, so that, for the most part, one is barely conscious of them. They are said to come into being in the juvenile era and persist, with some refinements, from then on. Nevertheless, they are only a small part of the self-system developed for maintaining feelings of personal worth, for obtaining the respect of others, and for ensuring, if possible, the respect conferred by positions of prestige and preferment in American society.

Orientation in living. The conception of orientation in living sums up Sullivan's philosophy of psychiatry. This conception applies at the end of the juvenile era if the youngster has got this far with any good fortune. The conception reads as follows:

One is oriented in living to the extent to which one has formulated or has insight into data of the following types: the integrating tendencies (needs) that customarily characterize one's interpersonal relations, the circumstances appropriate to their satisfaction and relatively anxiety-free discharge, and the more or less remote goals for the approximation of which one will forgo intercurrent opportunities for the satisfaction or the enhancement of one's prestige.

To the degree that a juvenile has been denied an opportunity in living, he is so anxious for the approval and unthinking immediate regard of others that one may well think he lives to be liked. In some instances that is more or less true.

PREADOLESCENCE

Sullivan believed that, in general, Americans have little ability to love—a phenomenon not to be confused with sexual love or romantic love, which is aim-inhibited sexual love amid the moonlight and roses. He thought that Americans, generation after generation, had been so busy building an industrial society that they lacked the time and the energy to create a more refined, cultivated way of life. In *Conceptions of Modern Psychiatry* Sullivan (1953a) said that love exists only if the satisfactions and security of the other person, with whom one is integrated, are approximately as important as one's own satisfactions and security.

At about 8 or 9 years of age, a new type of interest in another person appears. This interest is an outcome of maturation and experience. The interest is focused on a particular member of the same sex who becomes a close friend or chum. In short, preadolescence is marked by the appearance of new integrating tendencies that, when they are completely developed, can be called love or the manifestation of the need for interpersonal intimacy. When fully developed, chumship is always a reciprocal relationship. Intimacy involves two people and permits validation of all components of personal worth. Of course, this kind of relationship takes time, like so much else in the world. Each chum relates to the other in such a fashion that he collaborates or makes clearly formulated adjustments to the other's pursuit of clearly identical satisfactions and maintains increasingly similar security operations. In the course of a successful preadolescence, one learns to relate to and communicate with another without the threat of anxiety or fear. For the first time and perhaps the last time, one can communicate freely with another human being without the threat of loss of integrity or individuality. Because of this closeness, a person becomes capable of seeing himself through another's eyes. Hence, he has an opportunity to correct autistic fantasies about himself and others. However, if a preadolescent has been warped, the ability for intimacy may be gravely limited or transitory. Loneliness that appears in full force at preadolescence may become an everyday companion.

No stage of the evolution of personality can be skipped without warp and arrest of development, which are likely to increase and become grave as the years pass by. In *The Interpersonal Theory of Psychiatry* Sullivan (1953b) discussed several types of warp and their remedies. Each phase of development must be successful before a person is ready for the next. Without this readiness, one can, at best, learn to act various roles on a very superficial level. In fact, unless one can acquire juvenile socialization, one's future career is usually imperiled. An important task of a therapist is to learn when, where, and how his patient failed and in what areas during his progress toward chronological adolescence (Sullivan, 1954). Otherwise, the patient's behavior may at times seem so bizarre that it is beyond the therapist's understanding.

EARLY ADOLESCENCE

Adolescence is ushered in by maturation of the genital lust dynamism. Early adolescence appears at an indefinite time, although it is observable at the end of several months. Of the important integrating tendencies lust is the last to mature.

Sullivan surmised that in the United States the age when adolescence appears varies by 3 or 4 years. Traditionally, adolescence has been regarded as a time of stress. In some other societies the extraordinarily stressful aspect of adolescence is not nearly as conspicuous as in America because the culture provides a great deal more real preparation for this great change. But even in Western society, the storm and stress of bygone days seem to have become so attenuated today that it is perhaps no more painful than the common cold. Television, magazines, and moving pictures, which provide a glamorous picture of romantic love, seem to make sex the greatest thing in the world—at least, until one is well on his or her way toward the third divorce. Of course, this sort of thing did not happen accidentally. The business of selling sex under the thin disguise of love is incalculably profitable. Contrary to the media and other sources of information, sexual relations provide no guarantee of love, happiness, or contentment. In themselves, sexual relations provide no guarantee of intimacy in Sullivan's sense. Sexual relations per se cannot ward off loneliness or fulfill the need for intimate exchange with a fellow human being.

Early adolescence extends from the eruption of true genital interest to the patterning of sexual behavior. Sullivan asserted that there is no necessarily close relationship between lust and the need for intimacy. The two are strikingly distinct. To complicate matters a bit, some men can maintain friendly, pleasant relationships with women without true intimacy or sexual relations. This works both ways. Sullivan held that in order to make sense of the complexities and difficulties that are experienced in adolescence and the later phases of life, one must be able to distinguish three generic needs, often intricately related and at the same time contradictory: personal security, intimacy, and sexual genital satisfaction.

Shift in intimacy need. During early adolescence there is normally a shift in the intimacy need. The boy begins to wonder how he can get to be on as friendly terms with a girl as he has been with his chum. This interest is usually ushered in by changes in his fantasy life and in covert processes generally. There may also be a broadening in the area of overt communication between the chums to include ideas, attitudes, and information about the opposite sex. If the chums belong to a gang, with some outstanding boy whom they can admire as leader, overt communicative processes regarding the information some members have already acquired may also be included. In any event, there must be a great deal of trial-and-error learning from human example. Junior high school and high school provide a rich source of observation of intersex behavior and opportunities for dating.

At all times, one must bear in mind not only the previous history of the person but the social class to which he belongs and the overarching cultural milieu. Preadolescent socialization subjects one to the great controlling, directing demands and opportunities of social arrangements. Within this milieu, adolescence normally progresses, barring earlier warps and arrests of development. Collisions of lust, security, and the need for intimacy may occur. Many people in early adolescence suffer much anxiety in connection with their newly developed motivation for sexual activity. On the basis of previous learning, one may regard genital activity of any sort as disgraceful, disgusting, and damned. In extreme instances, the genital area may become part of not me, something not quite of the body. An adolescent with this feeling about himself may endure frustration, loneliness, and other causes of restlessness. Masturbation may be taboo. His relations with others may become pointless and humiliating, since his peers are now progressing toward types of relationships and activities of which he is incapable. In such cases the mothering one may have incubated his morbid attitudes toward his body and possibly warned him of females' wiles as well. Such feelings and attitudes may generalize, and he may begin to believe he is inadequate in all areas. In such instances the boy may be in grave danger of a psychotic outbreak.

Collisions of intimacy and security. The shift in the intimacy need may also collide with the need for security. Perhaps because of jealousy, the mother may ridicule the young female adolescent who is reaching out toward a member of the other sex. In addition, there may be so much fear and anxiety on the part of the father regarding any date his daughter has with a boy, any relationship she may develop, that he literally patrols a nearby park. Or an adolescent boy's mother, the most potent symbol of womanhood, may be so warped and anxiety provoking that her son becomes crippled. One mother threatened to throw herself out the window when her son started talking to girls as a means of controlling him by fear. For such reasons, the chronologically early adolescent felt compelled to confine himself to preadolescent relationships of brief duration. The ultimate result was that he became isolated from both sexes, capable only of a friendly relationship with members of his family—two younger sisters who never married and a few other relatives.

Collisions of intimacy and lust. There may also be collisions between intimacy and lust, providing countless possibilities for failure. In fact, establishing collaborative intimacy with any-one, regardless of gender, may turn out to be an impossible task if social institutions are poisoned with an array of irrational elements. Several varieties of awkwardness are common, including embarrassment, diffidence, and excessive precautions. These are the flowers of unfortunate experiences. Still another kind of awkwardness, which has its origins in the past, is the not-technique, a swinging to the other extreme to get away from something that does not work. If one is diffident in his relations with the other sex, he may attempt something that is the opposite of diffidence—that is, the development of a bold approach in the pursuit of the genital objective. Such behavior tends to stamp on the sensitivities and insecurities of the other person, so that he or she becomes embarrassed and diffident. Hence, real intimacy becomes quite impossible, although one may develop great sexual virtuosity with some types of sex objects.

There are, therefore, many adolescent failures and misfortunes. One kind of adolescent failure pertains to the separation of lust from intimacy. For example, a person may place a member of the other sex on a pedestal, thereby effectively barring himself from any close relationship with such a superior, unapproachable being. Or an adolescent may integrate relationships with members of the other sex by striking up a pseudosibling friendship. In this case, a boy tries to act like a brother of a member of the other sex; a girl tries to act like a sister toward her boyfriend. Or the adolescent may regard all members of the opposite sex as unattractive, unsuited to anything but a hateful entanglement. Sullivan believed that sublimation, wherein one partially satisfies lust while connecting it with socially acceptable goals, is usually unfortunate. In *Conceptions of Modern Psychiatry,* Sullivan (1953a) related a young woman's encounter with a very attractive clergyman. The young woman was intensely envious of other women and even of her husband. The clergyman counseled her to engage in a life of good works. She took to looking after fallen women in the slums, and then she was able to live in relative happiness. Further details of this young woman's life seem unnecessary. Analysis would reveal that she experienced a powerful homosexual drive in dissociation. But the socially sanctioned activity provided, in part, for her

unconscious lust after women. However, this situation was not necessarily a secure solution, for it was always in danger of failing.

Sullivan claimed that in adolescence the genital lust dynamism usually tends to be too powerful and too compelling for even a partial sidetracking into indirect channels.

Another sort of misfortune is said to be a failure to change the preadolescent direction of the need for intimacy. In this situation there are, added to the impulse to cherish a friend of the same sex, all the forces of the genital lust dynamism. The result is either a transient or persistent homosexual organization of interpersonal relations, with the genital drive handled in various ways—from known or unconscious homosexual reverie to a frank, overt homosexual modus vivendi.

LATE ADOLESCENCE AND MATURITY

Late adolescence extends from the patterning of preferred genital activity through unnumbered educative and eductive steps to the establishment of a fully human or mature repertory of interpersonal relations, as permitted by available personal and cultural opportunities. Sullivan taught that the failure to achieve late adolescence is the last blow, the culminating defeat, for a great many warped, inadequately developed personalities. This kind of failure is often the presenting psychiatric difficulty, but it is not the real difficulty, which precedes the eruption of grave personality disorders.

The long stretch of late adolescence, if successful, gradually evolves into maturity, which cannot be characterized rigorously and which, at least in theory, may extend and grow for at least another generation. Wisdom, if one achieves it, seems to come during the middle years of life, and perhaps for most it is only an obscure promised land. At any rate, during the extended period of late adolescence, there is a great development in the syntaxic mode.

For the fortunate person who can attend a university and has the ability and motivation to profit from its educational resources, several years of truly extraordinary opportunity to learn lie ahead. He can observe his peers in various situations, learn about people in various parts of the world, and discuss what he and his fellows have observed within and outside the framework of university life. University life provides an opportunity for one to complete and round out what has been inadequately grasped in his past experience and serves as a springboard for grasping the new. Whether this sketch of university life is still entirely realistic may be open to doubt.

Within limits, those who do not attend a university have the same kind of experience as those who do, except for the probable lack of the broad cultural interests that characterize genuine higher formal education. How to make a living and how to get on with people in the same line of work are similarly sources of a great deal of observational data. These experiences provide great possibilities for an interchange of views and attitudes, for overcoming various limitations, and for validating information. At least in theory, Sullivan seems to have held a somewhat optimistic view of the working classes back in the New Deal days.

In late adolescence one increasingly refines personally limited experience into the consensually validated, which is much less limited and restricted. Late adolescents, if they are fortunate and not crippled or gravely handicapped by previous experience, continue to grow, observe, formulate, and validate more and more. Their foresight continues to expand, so that they can foresee their probable career lines, with perhaps provisions for disappointments. In general, late adolescents are legal adults, possessing the benefits of their new status. Ideally, they should be able to take on many responsibilities, ordained by sociocultural arrangements, although some people undoubtedly fall short of what is demanded or expected.

The influence of cultural change on Sullivan's thinking can be seen from the following, which appeared in *Personal Psychopathology* (1972):

> Marriage and other relatively durable interpersonal relations involving sexual adjustment are the test of personality. Their psychopathology is the psychopathology of personality.

The serious downgrading of marriage currently taking place seems ominous if the family is the basic unit of society.

Interaction and Transaction

Sullivan's theory and practice have always been hampered by his unfamiliar terminology. But his new terminology is a reflection of his vision of psychiatry. In other words, his terminology is a reflection of the substantive innovations he created over the years as his knowledge and experience grew. Like many others in the history of thought, he needed a new language to express his ideas. Until recently, Sullivan's theory was not well known. Fortunately, that barrier has been largely surmounted. More and more psychiatrists are becoming familiar with the theory and practice of Sullivan's psychiatry. Some psychiatrists seem to have borrowed liberally, while using a different vocabulary, knowingly or unwittingly, in some instances.

Transaction pertains to the conduct of inquiry and can be clarified by reference to the history of inquiry. Dewey and Bentley, in *Knowing and the Known* (1949), attempted to clarify the knowledge-getting process, what they called knowing and the known, by referring to the major turning points in the history of inquiry. They distinguished three levels of the organization and presentation of inquiry: the self-actual, the interactional, and the transactional. On the first level, the prescientific, things were regarded as possessing powers of their own, under which they acted. However, as Dewey and Bentley pointed out, something of the old, and often much of it, survived within or alongside the new. The second level of organization and presentation of inquiry, is interactional, contrasted with the prescientific procedure. Dewey and Bentley (1944) observed that the word "action" is a most general characterization of events where their durational aspect is being stressed.

> Where the older approach had most commonly seen "self-action" in the "facts," the newer approach took form under Newton as a system of interaction, marked especially by the third law of motion—that action and reaction are equal and opposite.

On the meaning of Newton's third law, a definition by two physicists, Holton and Roller (1958), is given as follows:

> In the interaction of any two objects—whether this interaction be by contact, by gravitational or electrical or magnetic means, or in any manner whatsoever—the first object exerts a force on the second and, at the same time, the second exerts a force on the first; these two forces have the same magnitude but opposite directions.

In a posthumous book, *Matter and Motion* (1877), Maxwell, as quoted in Dewey and Bentley (1949), had written that the

Newtonian conception of forces acting between one body and another

> has now fairly entered on the next stage of progress [the idea of transaction]—that in which the energy of a material system is conceived as determined by the configuration and motion of that system, and in which the ideas of configuration, and motion, and force are generalized to the utmost extent warranted by their physical definitions.

Dewey and Bentley (1949), in the main, confine themselves to a discussion of Faraday and Maxwell, especially the latter:

> Faraday's brilliant observation found that all which happened electrically could not be held within the condenser box nor confined to the conducting wire. Clerk Maxwell took Faraday's observations and produced the mathematical formulation through which they could be expressed.

Perhaps they might have mentioned Hertz, who, according to Einstein and Infeld (1942), proved for the first time the existence of electromagnetic waves. Maxwell's work furnished the structure, according to Dewey and Bentley, for the developments of Roentgen, Lorentz, Planck, and Einstein and for the more recent atomic exploration.

According to Einstein and Infeld (1942), the new field language, in which Maxwell pioneered, is the description of the field between the two charges and not of the charges themselves. This distinction is essential for understanding their action. Gradually, substance in the traditional sense was overshadowed by the field. A new reality was created.

Dewey and Bentley (1949) have sometimes been labeled behaviorists. They have, in truth, adopted a behavioral stand. For them a behavior is always to be taken transactionally,

> never as *of* the organism alone, anymore than *of* the environment alone, but always of the organic-environmental situation [what Sullivan called the organism-environmental complex] with organisms and environmental objects taken as its aspects. Studies of these aspects in provisional separation are essential at many stages of inquiry and are always legitimate when carried on under the transactional framework and through inquiry which is itself recognized as transactional.

Sullivan attempted early in his career to formulate his ideas in a transactional framework. Notice the following (Sullivan, 1926):

> Let us consider the beginning of anyone, the fecundated ovum in the uterus. This cell manifests the basic categories of biological process. The cell carries almost stupefying potentialities. It exists as a demonstrable entity. It lives, however, and starts the realization of its potentialities not as a unit organism surrounded by a suitable environment. It lives communally *with* the environment. Physico-chemical factors, substances, plentiful in the uterine environment, flow into the cell. They undergo changes while they are within the describable cell area. They return presently as other physico-chemical factors to the environment. The cell dies if the continuous exchange is interrupted. Progressive changes depend utterly on the communion; retrogressive changes appear swiftly on its restriction.

Clearly, according to Sullivan, the cell does not interact with a suitable environment; it lives communally *with* it. Nevertheless, it is a demonstrable entity. Sullivan (1953a) went on to say:

> From a relative position in time and space, the environment flows through the living cell, becoming of its very life in the process; and the

cell flows and grows through the environment, establishing in this process its particular career line as an organism. It is artificial, an abstraction, to say that the cell is one thing and the environment another. The two things refer to some unitary thing in which organism and environment are indissolubly bound—so long as life continues.

This is clearly a transactional point of view on a biological level. Quite early in his career, Sullivan for a time used the term "organism-environment complex," indicating that he was working toward a transactional point of view in psychiatry. Finally, as in *Conceptions of Modern Psychiatry* (1953a), he adopted the term "interpersonal situation."

Mental Disorder

An interpersonal situation is a transaction. But it is the action between the two or more people that defines the situation and the character of its integration. This is also true of one's emotions, as is made clear in *Clinical Studies in Psychiatry* (Sullivan, 1956). Emotions emerge from the situation. They cannot exist apart from one's interpersonal relations, whether real or symbolic or a blend of both. An emotion or a motive has no existence apart from the person experiencing it. Thus, emotions, motives, and other aspects of the inner life are relational. This is also true of reverie. It is well known that many people derive great comfort from their fantasy life. Reverie in many gifted people derives inspiration from night dreaming or waking reverie.

The self-dynamism has a suborganization called the personified self. But the entire self is the source of the personifications of others. How stable or erratic the self is depends on past experience. But when one personifies others, he is almost certainly operating in the parataxic mode. These personifications can be and often are multiple. Sullivan claimed that at the level at which communication is fairly easy, the critical opposition of anxiety (resistance) is manifested as inadequate and inappropriate personifications and is often impossible to understand without a retrospective survey, as is systematically revealed in *The Psychiatric Interview* (Sullivan, 1954). Early in Sullivan's career, he called these inappropriate personifications "me-you patterns." With a different me, there goes a different you, and conversely. Generally, me-you patterns of both Jones and Smith are not congruent.

In more popular language, one may say that as a result of unfortunate past experiences, people develop views, attitudes, and beliefs about themselves that often differ widely from the valid or more valid picture the expert has of them. These distorted views are forever trapping them or impelling them into incongruous and inappropriate situations, often with great harm to themselves and others. The person suffers the interference of anxiety, which hinders clear thought, accurate perception, and appropriate behavior. Severe anxiety fosters the misuse of selective inattention and, in extreme cases, dissociation. Partly because of such occurrences, the person may sometimes blindly stumble into destructive situations from which he can extricate himself only with great difficulty, if all.

With the exception of those who are badly crippled by hereditary defects or by birth injuries, Sullivan thought that persons suffering from mental disorder are not really very different from most other human beings. There are no peculiarities manifested by the mentally disordered, but there are differences in the timing and the intensity of what is manifested by everyone. Although Sullivan dropped the rubric "dynamisms of difficulty," which he used for a while when lecturing on mental disorders, he never abandoned the underlying conception that morbid processes are dynamisms pertaining to interpersonal relations. A generation later, when social disorganization has become an ever-increasing threat to the structure of American society and when demoralization affects large segments of the population, the older conception of difficulties in living seems more appropriate than ever.

What are dynamisms of difficulty or, if one prefers, mental disorders? They are processes of warped, frequently self-defeating transactions that hinder or undermine the pursuit of satisfactions and security. They are not to be confused with intrapsychic or interpsychic processes, since, according to Sullivan, every mental or psychological occurrence is an organism-environment complex. Whether a psychiatrist focuses on one or the other aspect of this continuum is entirely determined by the particular problem he is dealing with and by the assets and liabilities of the patient.

In *Clinical Studies in Psychiatry* (1956) Sullivan stated that dynamisms of difficulty can be studied by generally following the order in which they appear in the evolution of personality, as he shows in *The Psychiatric Interview* (1954). They are the processes of living, the particular parts of everyone's personal equipment, that are often so wrongly applied that they become self-defeating. This does not mean that the patient may not at times manifest several such dynamisms; he always does. But, in the main, a particular dynamism of difficulty emerges sooner or later as the major disorder. Nevertheless, the subordinate dynamisms, like all human dynamisms of difficulty, are also built into the self during the years of growth. Being functions of the self-system, they are always related to arrests of development or regressions to an earlier stage. Sullivan (1956) wrote:

First, we shall discuss sublimation, which appears quite early in life, and then we shall take up the obsessional dynamism, which comes into being with the learning of language. Both of these dynamisms have a relation to the protection of the self-system from the appearance in consciousness of types of referential processes, thought, or reverie closely related to the schizophrenic-like processes of late infancy and early childhood; and we shall pause from time to time to consider their relationship to these earlier referential processes. In the juvenile era, the vast body of processes for controlling awareness which I refer to as selective inattention first becomes an important dynamism. From there we shall consider a number of other dynamisms, all part of the human paraphernalia for protecting the self-system from the minor but effective manifestations of anxiety and the more threatening possibility of the collapse of the self-system. And finally, as the last steps in this survey of the dynamisms of difficulty, we shall consider the dissociative processes themselves and their relation to major personality disorder. We shall then be in a position to move on to the therapeutic implications and possibilities in terms of the major patterns of difficulties—the so-called clinical entities.

Dynamisms of difficulty, thus, are functions of the personality that are often misused. They go into action in fashions that do not achieve a goal or, at best, achieve only an unsatisfactory goal. It is their recurrence or their tendency to occupy long stretches of time that characterizes the mentally disordered from the comparatively well. It is also the extraordinary dependence of a person on a particular dynamism that appears to be fundamental to mental disorder. For example, a schizophrenic patient is one who, in the course of his life, persistently has the dynamism of dissociation as a means of resolving the conflict between powerful needs, such as lust, or failure to effect the adolescent change, which may or may not eventuate in a homosexual modus vivendi, due to the restrictions that the self imposes on such things as lust and intimacy. Failure to resolve such a conflict may be the last blow to the person's fragile self-esteem and may precipitate the onset of psychosis.

Developmentally, the schizophrenic process is of a piece with the referential processes—the primitive cognitive processes of very early life, infancy and early childhood. As a result, the schizophrenic suffers an extreme lack of clarity regarding actions that achieve goals or a particular goal.

In its simple, everyday manifestation, the obsessional dynamism can be completely described as the replacement of adjustive processes by autistic (parataxic) referential processes in the person's pursuit of security. (According to Sullivan, if the obsessional person failed in the sexual sphere, he would regard it as a calamity and would hasten to a psychiatrist.) Thus, the obsessional regresses in certain cognitive (referential) operations to early childhood. Much of the obsessional thinking and many of the obsessional rituals that serve as a prop to adjustment were fixed in childhood. But as the obsessional person progresses toward chronological adulthood, his magical thinking and his ritualistic behavior grow and proliferate. The self of the obsessional person was fixated during the childhood era. In times of stress, the self-system becomes preoccupied with strategems—such as autistic, uncommunicative speech and ritualistic behavior—in order to preserve what little security the person has. The obsessional dynamism has relatively little to do with the satisfaction of somatic impulses; it has to do with interpersonal security. In a sexual situation the obsessional person may cause a lot of trouble for his partner because of the former's needs, but he is relatively free insofar as the actual genital cooperation is concerned.

The Psychiatric Interview

According to Sullivan, the psychiatric interview is a situation or series of situations of primarily vocal communication in a two-member group consisting of the interviewer (the therapist) and the interviewee (the patient or client). The two people are voluntarily more or less integrated in a progressively unfolding expert-client relationship for the purpose of elucidating and clarifying the client or patient's characteristic patterns of living. These patterns of living are experienced by the patient as particularly troublesome or especially valuable. In the process of revealing them, with the therapist's help, he hopes to derive benefit. Sullivan carefully observed the nonverbal components of the situation, including the patterning of the patient's speech and its quality and the patient's facial expressions, bodily gestures, posture, and general demeanor.

When it suited his purposes, Sullivan had an extraordinary ability to interrogate, to ask questions without the patient's understanding the reasons or being clearly conscious of precisely what was happening—provided the patient was secure enough to talk freely. However, he would often, during the early part of the interview, ask direct "stupid" questions, a technique that is best described in his own words (Sullivan, 1954):

A patient tells me the obvious and I wonder what he means, and ask further questions. But after the first half hour or so, he begins to see that there is a reasonable uncertainty as to what he meant, and that statements which seem obvious to him may be remarkably uncommunicative to the other person. They may be far worse than uncommunicative, for they may permit the inexperienced interviewer to assume that he knows something that is not the case. Only belatedly does he discover that he has been galloping off on a little path of

private fantasy which clearly could not be what the patient is talking about, because now the patient is talking about something so obviously irrelevant to it. Thus part of the skill in interviewing comes from a sort of quiet observation all along: Does this, this statement, have an unquestionable meaning? Is there any certainty as to what this person means?

Clearly, Sullivanian therapy is very different from classical psychoanalysis. For Sullivan, the therapist is not a mirror. Nor does he sit passively, although he knew how to listen silently when the occasion or situation demanded it. He never forced interpretations on the patient.

Since the interview is a transaction, any striking emotion on the part of the interviewer is an unhappy artifact that may impede therapy by interfering with the therapist's objectivity and by encouraging the patient to act out. Sullivan also took a dim view of the Peeping Tom attitude. He taught that intense curiosity about the details of another person's life, particularly his sexual life, did not belong in a psychiatric interview. In due course the patient's sexual life, for example, may emerge as a significant factor in therapy, but an intense curiosity about the intimate details may be entirely uncalled for and unnecessarily embarrassing to the patient. On the other hand, an attitude of disdainful indifference about what the patient has to offer is equally inappropriate. Furthermore, Sullivan regarded an intense emotional involvement (entanglement) with a patient as dangerous to the therapeutic process. The interviewer seeks the data he needs without trying to gain satisfaction or prestige at the expense of the client.

As soon as possible, the psychiatrist must discover who the client is. He must review the course of events the patient has lived through to be who he is, as well as his background and experience. The psychiatric interviewer must learn what the patient conceives his problems and difficulties to be. Thus, the patient begins to realize quite early that he is going to learn something useful about the way he lives, which acts as a spur to a more communicative effort. Otherwise, the patient may proceed with a wary caution, withholding information that he believes may cause him harm if he reveals it.

MUTUAL PARTICIPATION

Sullivan's notion that psychiatry is peculiarly the field of participant observation has puzzled some psychiatrists. But if interpersonal relations are a form of transaction, one cannot be a detached spectator in the interview. Both interviewer and client are engaged in a task, a transaction, which by definition entails a form of participation, though the mutual roles are by no means identical. But one may question how one can observe the patient or client and also participate. First of all, the mutual participation stretches over time; sometimes it is almost instantaneous, and sometimes it takes an indefinitely longer stretch of time. Misunderstandings are just as much an aspect of the interplay as is perfect understanding and agreement. According to Sullivan, there is no other way to observe or study a person, unless one remains a detached spectator who imagines that he can intuitively interpret what the other person is experiencing and doing. In general, therapy is a temporal affair. Sometimes the interviewer or the client or both get bogged down, so that nothing is accomplished except that the client or patient has spent more of his money without observable benefit. Some psychological tests can augment participant observation, provided the investigator is expert in administering them and interpreting them, but Sullivan was essentially concerned with face-to-face social transactions. People generally acquire at least a superficial understanding of one another through such transactions; they cannot reveal their thoughts, attitudes, and feelings in social isolation.

The patient's productions are, within limits, meaningful to the therapist because they share a large body of similar experiences that have a public, conventional meaning. Sullivan taught that without this common background, the observer cannot deduce the meaning of the staggering array of human acts. The data of psychiatry are composed of events that pertain to the observer's own experiences in relation to the common culture, experiences that were common in the home of the observer, activities that are as meaningful to him as they are to the patient, and activities to which the observer responds as if he himself were directly concerned. Thus, the therapist, given his particular training and skill, can interpret the patient's actions and experiences on the basis of what he himself has experienced or observed under circumstances in which the purposes or intentions behind the action or experience were communicated to him. Without this common, shared background, there can be no interplay between psychiatrist and patient. That, in a sense, is why the therapist is a participant-observer. The more he is conscious of his participation, the more he can control the therapeutic situation. Of course, there are also differences between patient and therapist, differences due to native endowment and the peculiarities of each person's life in a given sociocultural framework. But Sullivan did not regard these differences as a significant obstacle as long as the interviewer applies his specialized knowledge and skill to the rules and techniques of the interview.

PARATAXIC DISTORTION

Perhaps the greatest stumbling block to communication in the two-member group is what Sullivan called parataxic distortion or an illusory me-you pattern, which is really a common but unfortunate instance of the parataxic mode of experience. In therapy, the parataxic mode—operating primarily as a result of immaturity, anxiety, and perhaps regression—facilitates illusory personifications of the therapist, which make the interview extremely complex. In a given therapy session or in many sessions, the patient substitutes for the psychiatrist an illusory person or persons, who are strikingly different from the actual interviewer. He addresses his actions, attitudes, and thoughts to this imaginary or quasi-imaginary person and interprets the psychiatrist's questions, statements, and behavior on the basis of the illusory personification. The astonishing misunderstandings and misconceptions that frequently characterize human relations are the result of this kind of parataxic distortion.

A certain lady had been in therapy with Sullivan for a good stretch of time. One day she entered his consulting room very excited. For 2 years she had been perceiving the therapist as a fat, white-haired old man. On further inquiry it turned out that the white-haired old man had some resemblance to her grandfather.

During the course of the interview situation, the psychiatrist must take precautions against parataxic distortions, including what Freudian psychiatrists call countertransference. It is through parataxic distortions that a person displays some of his gravest problems. The distortion may be manifested as an obscure attempt to communicate something that the therapist needs to grasp, and perhaps the patient as well, because it may be an oblique expression of a need. The psychiatrist must not allow such distortions to go unnoticed. He must expect them. If the possibility of their existence is ignored, some of the most important phenomena of the interview may be ignored by default.

PURPOSE OF INTERVIEW

In structuring the interview situation, Sullivan claimed that several considerations that affect the course of the interview as

a whole, as well as the detailed inquiry, have to be taken into account. The ostensible purpose of the interview is a major consideration. For example, a business executive may want help in overcoming problems he is having in a new position. A clergyman may seek enlightenment regarding difficulties he encounters with certain female members of his congregation. A competent engineer may try to discover why he loses one position after another. The psychiatric interview is by no means confined to those who have suffered from major difficulties for several years. However, the general assumptions regarding the therapy remain the same, regardless of the patient or the circumstances. The interview should convey to the patient more feeling of capacity, of adequacy to go on living, perhaps creating a brighter prospect as a result of the conference.

EXPLORING THE PATIENT'S LIFE

The interviewer has the task of discovering the major handicaps and major advantages in the patient's life, those liabilities and assets that are relatively enduring characteristics of his everyday, ongoing interpersonal relations. This discovery, if it occurs, happens when the psychiatrist experiences the ways that interpersonal occurrences follow one another during the interview situation, how these interpersonal events relate to one another, what striking inconsistencies occur, and so forth. The data of the interview are elicited not so much from the answers to questions as from the timing and stress of what the patient says, the slight misunderstandings here and there, the omission of important facts, the occasions when the patient gets off the subject while volunteering important information. The skilled, alert interviewer realizes with great clarity that he must watch the course of events and study how, as a pattern of progression from one topic to another, these events provide a wide field of data about the patient. The raw data thus obtained must be interpreted and inferences drawn from them.

PHASES OF THE INTERVIEW

Because of the continuing complexity of so many of the patient's communications, which in the early phase of the interview are often obscure, the skilled interviewer is unobtrusively methodical as well as constantly alert. In *The Psychiatric Interview* (1954), Sullivan mapped out four overlapping phases of the interview that serve as a guide, especially in prolonged intensive psychotherapy. The four phases are the formal inception, the reconnaissance, the detailed inquiry, and the termination.

Formal inception. Usually at the first physical encounter, the interviewee is a stranger and, as such, should be greeted as a stranger. There must be no social pretense wherein the client is greeted as if he were a distant cousin who has just returned from abroad. One greets the client by name, invites him in, and indicates the chair where he is to sit. While the patient is still at the door, the psychiatrist immediately takes a good look at him—perhaps he will never stare at him again. Then the interviewer should tell the client what he learned about him when the appointment was requested, although the data revealed at the time are probably irrelevant, mere excuses for making an appointment. Nevertheless, the interviewer has thus given the client an opportunity to revise the information if it is wrong. Thus, the client may say "Why, what on earth gave you that idea?" Without trying to justify himself, the interviewer may reply, "Well, now, tell me what really *is* the case." But if the client believes the psychiatrist has the correct information, he may say, "Yes, that's right, Doctor, and it's a great problem."

By immediately telling the client what he knows or has heard about him, the psychiatrist has made it easier for him to get started. The client believes he has communicated some notion of his problem or difficulty and some idea of himself. However, the therapist knows better. He realizes that he must know the patient before he can learn what ails him and that this is just the beginning of what may be a long and harrowing voyage of exploration and discovery.

There are several requirements as the therapeutic process starts. First, the interviewer must be aware that the patient's behavior and what he says are adjusted to what he guesses about the therapist. Throughout the inception period, the psychiatrist not only observes what seems to be going on vis-à-vis the client but must also find out how he—by his remarks, actions, and appearance—affects the client. He should know from past experience the usual impression he makes on strangers. The interviewer should also be conscious of the immediate impressions he has gained from his beginning observation of the client and what these impressions and resultant behavior are contributing to the interpersonal situation. Moreover, he must confine himself to what is feasible, not too difficult for him to sustain, that may baffle the client. The psychiatrist should also have some notion of how he facilitates or retards various things the stranger may have thought of doing. The psychiatrist should learn how to do nothing exterior to consciousness. Nor can he immediately know whether his first impressions are right or wrong. The variables in an interpersonal situation are multiple, and the best one can hope for during the inception is a reasonable probability of obtaining correct information, however limited. Until he achieves this conviction, he must continue to explore.

Reconnaissance. Sullivan asserted that the interviewer should be alert to what he is doing so that he can recall correctly all that he said and did in the formal inception of each interview and so learn to do better. As Sullivan (1954) wrote:

It is only when an interviewer can recall a course of events correctly, both as to movement and pattern of movement, that is, the timing of movement, which preceded what, what followed what, that he has the material from which to make a useful analysis of the processes which were involved, from which, in turn, he can synthesize an improving grasp of the particular aspect of living concerned.

A sort of watchful clarity is essential.

During the reconnaissance, the interviewer secures a rough sketch of the patient's life, not an extensive life history. Sullivan asserted that in intensive psychiatry he needed 7½ to 15 hours to complete the reconnaissance. During a single, unrepeated interview, he devoted 20 minutes of a 1½-hour consultation to the reconnaissance. He would start by saying, "Now, tell me, how old are you? Where were you born? Are your mother and father still living?" The client would become involved in answering an organized stream of questions. If one or both parents were dead, Sullivan would ask, "When did they die and of what?" If the patient does not know what his father died of, for example, this fact may lead to the discovery that the father had not lived in the home for his last 20 years and that, although the patient is pretty sure his father is dead, he does not know any of the circumstances. Sullivan also asked how many siblings there were in the home, including any who died. If a sibling died during the memory span of the patient, that fact may be quite significant, but it is also important to note those siblings who died before he could remember because they may have been of particular significance to his parents

and thus had a considerable effect on him. Sullivan would ask the patient about his place in the time order of siblings. Then he would ask who, besides the parents, was chronically or frequently in the patient's home during his first 7 years: an aunt or a grandmother may have left a permanent effect. If Grandma was the only bright spot in the patient's home during his first 7 years, he is glad to be reminded of that.

During the reconnaissance, a great many topics are covered. What did the father or the mother or whoever earned the money do for a living? Was there any sharp change in the economic circumstances at any time? Marked economic changes may have had marked effects on the course of personality and on the family generally. Those who lived through the Great Depression may recall what a nation-wide catastrophe it was, and how much suffering it caused. Readers who are too young to have experienced it, might read John Steinbeck's *The Grapes of Wrath* or Studs Turkel's *Hard Times*. Big adverse economic changes, Sullivan points out, may lead to tragic revisions of parental ambitions, with corresponding effects on the children's goals. Of course, if these adverse changes occurred after he had completed his education, they probably did not make much difference, except that other people may have become dependent on him.

Then Sullivan wanted to know what sort of person the patient's father was, sometimes to the amazement of the patient. If he becomes helpless in the face of such a question, the interviewer may say, "Well, how was he regarded in the community?" If the patient is still unable to think or to say anything useful, the interviewer may mention the pastor, the family doctor, the local druggist, the grocer, and others. Sullivan said he hurried a little over such questions. One may needlessly probe for a more complete biography of the father, causing the patient to be aggrieved because he is not in therapy for biographical purposes. And so, when the interviewer has obtained some idea of what sort of person the father was, he becomes curious to learn whether the patient's family was a happy one. For unstated reasons, Sullivan would ask the patient to describe his mother, not what sort of person she was. As a rule, the patient has only a vague idea of her. Then, what sort of people were those stray persons mentioned earlier who were around the house a great deal in the very early years? Often the client gives an account of a third person, the semiparent. This can be a clue to what role the therapist may play later on in the relationship.

The interviewer asks the client to tell him something about his education, although he is not much interested in it. The educational history may be so brief that it may be confined to the number of degrees the client or patient has accumulated. If he finally got a Ph.D., Sullivan said it merely tells him the client was lucky, as the average person goes.

Sullivan regarded the occupational history as much more important. He would want to know what the patient has done since leaving school, being rather curious about this. The sicker people are, the more they are said to omit from the occupational history. At this point Sullivan would do something he regarded as a very important part of the psychiatric history. He would tell the patient what he had heard and inquire whether that is the whole story. "Well, aside from these two jobs, you have had no other occupation?" Whereupon many people are said to reveal that they have had 25 other jobs, but they have not held them long. This is much more valuable information than the statements about the two jobs. What jobs? How long did the client hold them? Where? In this fashion, the interviewer gets an idea of whether the person was advancing in his work. The therapist also gets an idea of whether his client was so driven by a desire for money that he held a job only long enough to get one that paid more. Or, Sullivan (1954) wrote:

whether he held each job long enough to know what the work was about and then took another one, in a curiously thorough but superficially morbid pattern of learning something about life; whether he quarreled with everybody that he tried to work with ... I don't want details, but I do want a sketch of the facts.

Next Sullivan became curious as to whether the person has been married and, if so, for how long. "Quite happily?" If the marriage is not a happy one, the patient answers, hesitantly, "Yes." Sometimes Sullivan would look at him then and ask if there are any children; and he might ask if this is his first marriage. Frequently, the client may protest, "No, no. I was married before," despite his not having given a hint that he was previously married. In regard to the early marriage, the interviewer asks the essential question, "Was it your first love?" Should the client hesitate a little, then comes the question, "Why did you marry?" On occasion, the answer is "The family thought it was a great idea." This is approximately the point at which Sullivan completed the reconnaissance. He had not asked anything about the person directly. But he had picked up many clues about the person and the manner he got through life up to the time he entered therapy. On occasion, the patient may have suffered some dire problem that Sullivan would tackle at once in detail. Otherwise, the procedure outlined here was fairly consistently held to.

The interviewer may hear about some situation at some time in the patient's past that seems significant but unclear and is not accessible to the patient's consciousness. It has been repressed. When the patient is unable to recall whatever it is that is inaccessible, the interviewer may say, "Well, I wonder what may have been the case; tell me, what comes to your mind?" On being urged, the patient may talk more or less at random as things come to his mind; his thoughts begin to circle in a curious fashion toward the answer. But sometimes when the question is very significant, there are many starts and stops before the desired information becomes accessible.

Rather late in his career Sullivan recommended to his students a stratagem he had recently discovered—to conclude the reconnaissance with a summary statement. As Sullivan (1954) wrote:

In this summary statement, the psychiatrist tells the patient what he has heard and what he sees as a problem that seems well within the field of psychiatric competence. In my experience, such a statement has without exception proved extremely useful to the patient and gratifying to the therapist. In a long series of interviews, it is important to establish the justifiability of the patient's seeing [consulting] the psychiatrist; the relationship should not be left tacit as to its basic nature for very long. The psychiatric situation is formally established when there is a consensus—even if unwilling—that the patient and the psychiatrist might well talk further about the problem which has emerged from the reconnaissance.

Before he would start the summary, Sullivan would tell the patient what he was going to do and ask him to bear with him until he was through, so that he would be relatively uninterrupted. At the same time, the patient was informed that at the end of the summary he would be asked to amend and correct those things that the psychiatrist had misunderstood and to point out any important things the psychiatrist had missed.

The question of what to include in the summary is a most serious one. Sullivan (1954) wrote:

To be simply frank in psychiatric work would often result in a situation in which the psychiatrist was as cruel and destructive as possible. If the patient is deeply disturbed, with fragile self-esteem, such a procedure, entailing frank openness, would be simply disastrous.

In the summary the interviewer always strives to outline for a patient what he sees as a major difficulty in living, though not necessarily the major difficulty, which is more likely to show up during the detailed interview. Without the statement of a problem in living, treatment situations are apt to be quite defeating.

Detailed inquiry. Impressions of a patient by the psychiatrist are hypotheses that were gained during the first two stages. In the prolonged, detailed inquiry they are tested. In any life situation, Sullivan (1954) wrote:

when a person is asked a question his reply varies greatly in its appropriateness, significance, communicativeness, and so on, according to what area of reality the question seems to pertain to.

The work of the interviewer is largely concerned with evaluating statements—apologies for failure, extravagant exaggeration of successes, and studious minimization of errors. Anxiety enters here emphatically. For example, the patient may think, "If I tell the doctor the truth, he won't think well of me." Or, "I must put a good face on that; otherwise, I may make a bad impression." Everyone tries to put his best foot forward. The competent psychiatrist must accept this phenomenon and not get annoyed. Walking around the obvious is something that the patient's interviewer must be alert to. Of course, the patient does not have any real or true idea as to what the interviewer is thinking. One may say that anxiety is the general reason for the interviewee's trying to create a favorable impression. Anxiety rules. The self-system or the antianxiety system produces numerous stratagems or security operations to ward off anxiety. And so the therapist has his work cut out for him.

Nevertheless, the therapist has to deal with anxiety almost eternally. He knows that intense anxiety, if prolonged, almost certainly causes the psychiatrist to obtain data that are misleading and useless. Sullivan (1954) wrote:

This dealing with anxiety in relations with others is a work of exquisite refinement and crucial importance, at least until the patient sees a high probability that something useful is going to come of it.

Sullivan added that after that has happened, though the therapist must be judicious in judging when the almost paralyzing anxiety occurred, he may not have to worry quite as much about doing the wrong thing. Mild anxiety can be assuaged, usually by some sort of reassuring gesture. As Sullivan (1954) wrote:

Anyone who proceeds without consideration for the disjunctive power of anxiety in human relationships will never learn interviewing. When there is no regard for anxiety, a true interview situation does not exist; instead, there may be just a person (the patient) trying to defend himself frantically from some kind of a devil (the therapist) who seems determined (as the patient experiences it) to prove that the person (the patient) is a double-dyed blankety-blank.

To ward off anxiety—loss or lowering of self-esteem—the person in therapy, wittingly or otherwise, uses numerous strategies, which are called security operations. Anger is a frequent security operation. Something is said during the interview or perhaps by someone outside the formal session, and the patient becomes anxious. But he may show no overt evidence of it. Instead, he may manifest anger, partly because it is more tolerable, less painful. This displacement anger also mobilizes his energy, and so he has a feeling of power. Almost immediately after what arouses the anxiety, unwittingly succeeded by anger, he quickly develops an unfavorable estimation of the other person and reacts accordingly, whether he attacks, withdraws, or uses another strategy. The number of security operations in and out of therapy is legion, but the psychiatrist must be able to recognize them for what they are and look for the data they may reveal. Sullivan himself was markedly calm, objective, analytical in the face of bitter, furious, threatening behavior by disturbed patients. Early in his career he would enter the locked room of a violent, threatening patient and try to talk to him. If the psychiatrist does not recognize what lies behind the outbursts of certain patients—namely, anxiety—he will look in the wrong place for an explanation of the behavior. To react sadistically toward the patient was anathema to Sullivan. So was any sexual entanglement with a patient.

Several kinds of change occur in the interview as a process. One kind of change is in the client's attitude—favorable or otherwise. Sullivan (1954) also noted another difficult and significant kind of change:

> In the interview situation, these somewhat more recondite *changes* are changes in the *interviewer's attitude, as reflected by the interviewee.*

Sullivan said the interviewer should ask himself: What attitude of mine is being reflected by the interviewee? What does he think I am doing? How does he think I feel toward him? A great many useful clues to the complex processes making up the interview are said to appear when the interviewer begins to think in such terms. Sullivan said that there are two groups of processes directed to the interviewer: One is the direct attitude of the interviewee toward him and the other is that part of the interviewee's performances that are faithfully related to the supposed attitude of the interviewer.

> Since it is necessary to observe change, one must have a point of departure. The gross impressions obtained during the formal inception and the reconnaissance provide the point of departure when one begins the most difficult part of interview, the detailed inquiry. The gross impressions are data to be tested, not established facts. The therapist then begins to analyze them from several points of view. First, he considers the client in terms of his general alertness. How keen is he and in how many areas? The attention of clients varies considerably. Some people are said to be intent on everything the interviewer says and are very careful about what they say but are not guarded or suspicious; they are simply determined to get something out of the interview. Others are distracted by noises coming from outside or from their own minds. Distractions, of course, tend to get in the way of paying close attention to the work at hand. Occasionally, the patient's attention is vague, and he seemingly maintains only a casual, foggy contact with what the interviewer is trying to get at. Another characteristic that the interviewer tries to discover is the intelligence (in contrast to intellectual obtuseness) of the client—a very difficult matter. Verbal dexterity is often positively and highly correlated with intelligence but not always; consider some politicians. A man may be rather inarticulate but his record may show that he has made extremely rapid progress in handling complex machinery and thus show high general intelligence. One must consider the person's education and background in these matters.

Gross impressions are rough hypotheses that have to be tested continuously or recurrently so that, when warranted, they may be corrected. If the interviewer has been thorough in his checking and testing, he sometimes almost automatically is able to add up negative and positive evidence of this and that and so know that the patient is improving or not improving.

But, more frequently, the therapist acquires impressions, especially during the inception and reconnaissance, that, when scrutinized, may or may not be justified. Of course, then more or less specific testing operations should be applied with the idea of getting them nearly correct. One way is for the therapist to rely on more or less unnoted inferences. But this kind of testing is almost as risky as relying on intuition. Sullivan asserted that the testing of hypotheses cannot be safely left wholly to relatively unformulated referential operations. He said it is well for the interviewer now and then to think about the impressions he has obtained. The very act of beginning to formulate them throws them into two groups—those that the therapist has no reason to doubt and those that, when scrutinized, are open to question. There is another way of testing one's impressions or hypotheses—by clearly purposed exploratory activity of some kind. The interviewer asks critical questions so designed that the response indicates whether or not the hypothesis is correct.

Sullivan (1954) set up two general considerations:

> (1) that all interview situations fall under the theorem of reciprocal emotion and (2) that the processes in interview situations follow this general pattern of all interpersonal processes.

From these two relatively broad considerations, Sullivan said that it follows that the therapist shows his skill in his choice of a passive or an active role at particular junctures in the interview. He also said that one may work successfully in a deteriorating situation when things seem to be going from bad to worse—the patient is getting less communicative, for example—if the situation is not permitted to disintegrate. However, the best results are obtained most economically in a situation that is improving.

In the interview one can discern three sorts of communication. In the first, the interview appears to be more or less continuously improving or, at least, improving from period to period. Everything is going well. However, Sullivan said that for the inexperienced interviewer that can be a great misfortune, since he may fail to notice carefully and as completely as possible all the context—the operations, the remarks, and their patterns—that led to distinct improvements in the situation. If the therapist realizes how the situation came to be going so well in the sense that he knows when his operations coincided with the improving communicability of the patient, he has quite valuable clues to the patient's covert security operations, though they are only inferentially evident. On retrospection, the interviewer can discover the context in which things started to go well or seemed to. At that point the patient experienced relief from the feeling that he would make a bad impression, give away something disastrous, or something of the sort. Sullivan (1954) wrote:

> Looking back a little further, the interviewer can then begin to see the general pattern of the interviewee's precautions, the security operations by which he was warding off some particular area until the interviewer did something that seemed safe.

There is, second, the situation in which the communicative attitude is deteriorating. Not only is the patient getting less communicative, but he is acting as if he thought the interviewer were anything but an expert. Sullivan counsels any therapist, in such a case, first, to control his anxiety for the moment and, if possible, to try to study the deterioration in the relationship by retrospective survey, since a great deal can be learned in this way.

The deterioration may start with the inception; more often it begins during the reconnaissance. It may turn out that the interviewer has fallen over the patient's security apparatus while getting his gross social history. The retrospective survey may reveal that it was some time in the detailed interview, when he asked a particular question, which the patient answered, that everything seemed to go wrong. Yet Sullivan said that such a discovery is very useful, both as a basis for rectifying the deteriorating situation and, much more important, as data for achieving the purpose of the interview. Sullivan added that things do not have to be lovely for an interview to succeed. He also said that some quite unpleasant interviews may give the interviewer a pretty good impression of what ails the client.

Third, it is wise for the interviewer in a deteriorating situation to observe what relation the current situation has to his own attitude toward the client. Again, a retrospective survey is called for. Perhaps the therapist took a dislike to his patient when he came into his office the first time. Sullivan taught his students that one never gets angry at a patient, though for certain therapeutic reasons he may pretend to be irritated or angry at certain times.

Sullivan's theory of personality development is used extensively in *The Psychiatric Interview* (1954). Sullivan reiterated that it is important for the interviewer to pay close attention to anxiety, particularly his own anxiety. He said that anxiety is of such overwhelming and all but ubiquitous significance in the understanding of interpersonal relations that it is helpful to keep in mind during the entire interview a two-part schematization of the hypothetical personality of the interviewee. This two-part schematization is a useful way for the interviewer to organize his thinking, provided one does not take it too literally. Though this formulation has been extensively discussed in previous pages, it is worth repeating in this context.

The personality is divided into the self-system and the rest of the personality. Whenever a person is dealing with a stranger, both are seriously concerned with matters of appraisal, esteem, respect, deference, and prestige—all being manifestations of the self. Therefore, it is a rare moment in an interview situation, however prolonged, in which the interviewee's self-system is not centrally concerned.

The interviewer must always be alert to the fact that the interviewee is eternally showing efforts to avoid, minimize, and conceal signs of his anxiety from the therapist and from himself. The patient does not want to know that he is anxious, and he often exercises considerable ingenuity to conceal it from himself and the therapist, a form of resistance. Sullivan (1954) summed up these matters by what could be called a theorem of the psychiatric interview:

The interviewee's self-system is at all times, but in varying degrees, in opposition to achieving the purpose of the interview.

Hence, the person uses a plethora of security operations (very roughly, defense mechanisms). The skill of the therapist, therefore, is directed at circumventing the patient's security operations. This circumvention, in effect, amounts to the therapist's avoiding unnecessary provocation of anxiety, without at the same time missing data that are needed for a reasonably correct assessment of the person with whom he is dealing. Sullivan claimed that the developmental history of the self-system implies the circumstances under which the interviewee experiences anxiety, whether briefly or not in a given situation, and sets the general patterns of the security operations that are manifested.

The developmental history of the person, wrote Sullivan (1954), is accessible to the interviewer only in the form of

(1) experience formulated in the self-system—even if it is manifested

only in the form of *precautionary operations against* the clear recall and unmistakable showing of the effects of certain formative experience and (2) data which form an adequate basis for inference about experience—and deficiencies in experience—of universal developmental significance.

In other words, Sullivan claimed that, in one's dealing with an interviewee, one is provided with data that are fairly clearly related to the developmental history of the interviewee's self-system, which is manifested in his security operations, his precautions against anxiety; and these data form a reasonably good basis for inference as to his deficiencies in a good, basic experience for living.

Sullivan offered an outline for obtaining data. That is the reconnaissance. The psychiatrist first takes up disorders in toilet training, a phenomenon of late infancy or early childhood. He seeks information about such matters as disorders in learning toilet habits and also speech habits. Because of his skill and special orientation, he can ask pointed and ordinarily prohibited questions, but he also looks for direct clues to such information. For instance, the patient may reveal an extraordinary interest in personal cleanliness, or he may exhibit a revulsion toward dirty words. Hesitancy in speech, oral overactivity, or speech mannerisms during times of stress may provide clues to speech-learning disorders. By careful questioning, the interviewer can discover such difficulties in learning to speak, stuttering or lisping, peculiarities of vocabulary, and the continued use of autistic or neologistical speech. Speech difficulties are indications of personality distortions as far back as early childhood or late infancy, as are problems connected with toilet training.

The more obscure speech distortions are not disorders in acquiring speech behavior but defects in acquiring the skill of consensual validation. One must learn to use words in such a fashion that they mean the same thing to oneself and to the person one is about to address. Sullivan did not mention grammar, but it is far more important than he seemed to think. To formulate complex thoughts one needs a wide knowledge of vocabulary and a thorough knowledge of grammar. Alas, it seems that contemporary students are, for the most part, deficient in vocabulary and lacking in a knowledge of grammar.

Sullivan (1954) wrote:

We now move into the juvenile era, admittedly leaving a great deal of an exceedingly rich period, such as all the attitudes toward authority, which have their buttresses in childhood, in the gradual domination of the parents over certain unregenerate impulses of the child, and so on.

The juvenile era is the time when children are inducted into games. Games require cooperation, competition, and often a large element of compromise. The psychiatrist may ask direct questions about games. In the interview itself, he may discover that some patients are manifestly competitive; they show that they have to know more than the therapist, or they try to anticipate what he is driving at. Some people who have been relatively arrested in the juvenile era, while fiercely competitive, may sometimes be successful. In all fairness, academia is not without its competitive aspects. Nor are psychiatrists.

Other patients manifest a cooperative attitude in and out of therapy. As for compromise, Sullivan (1954) wrote:

Well what do you think of compromise—that is, what would be his opinion of other people who compromise? Would he easily compromise? Would he never compromise? What might he compromise about?

Still other patients may be unduly conciliatory; they try to show the therapist that they agree with everything he says.

Sullivan claimed that among the people who have been relatively, if not absolutely, arrested in the juvenile era are those who, from their competitive nature, develop an intense ambition, which is often richly rewarded. The culture itself is very rewarding of competition, and, as Sullivan (1954) wrote:

Within it anybody who sets his whole personality, tooth and nail, on a certain type of thing is apt to have experienced astonishing successes and failures.

Sullivan added that it is worthwhile to notice not only how intensely ambitious a person is but also the character of the goal that is the point of his ambition. Some people are ambitious about attaining one goal after another. One may call it a character trait. Many others—who are more significant, since they are likely to hold important positions in society—have been for all or most of their lives pursuing a more or less well defined goal, doing everything short of homicide to get it.

In regard to school, for those who start and keep on with it, day after day, it has a lot to offer, at least potentially. There one begins to learn social techniques rapidly in order to cover or disguise one's real feelings, so that what happens thereafter is often not very revealing. In general, the interviewer endeavors to know whatever may provide him with a notion of the way the patient felt toward grammar school.

The interviewer must not proceed from one developmental era to the next too closely and too clearly. To do so would be to risk suggesting to the client what answers or responses are expected of him. After asking something significant about the early years of the juvenile era, Sullivan would abruptly leap over high school to college. If the patient attended college, he would ask how he got along there, both scholastically and socially. Then he would return to the preadolescent era. Because the preadolescent era has much to do with one's social adaptation, the interviewer inquires whether the patient had a chum or close friend during the preadolescent era. Questions relating to puberty follow. Then come questions about risque stories, frankly sexual talk, the client's attitude toward his or her body, and so forth. Before becoming specific, the psychiatrist may ask general questions about his patient's sex preferences, often merely to bring this topic into the open. The patient's feelings about solitude are important because they reveal a good deal about his relationships with others. Hence the question, "Are you ever so lonely that you become restless?" If the answer is yes, another question may follow about what the patient does under such conditions.

Sullivan inquired extensively about the patient's use of alcohol, which he regarded as more revealing than eating habits. Although in his day few psychiatrists were concerned about the use of narcotics, Sullivan was aware of the problem of drug addiction and alert to any manifestation of it. Next, he would ask about the client's eating habits, since they are not isolated actions but occasions for social intercourse.

The interviewer must approach the topic of sleep and sleep functions gingerly. He may inquire, for example, about dreams, including nightmares.

Sullivan would ask about the patient's sex life—directly or obliquely as the situation demanded—although he emphatically rejected the idea that it is a mirror of personality. He asked such questions only after a proper groundwork had been established. He did, however, conduct a detailed inquiry about the patient's sex life, if only because it provides clues about the patient's development and important information about his relationships and attitudes toward both sexes. Questions about courtship, marriage, and parenthood follow under normal circumstances.

During a question-and-answer period at the end of a series of lectures delivered in 1944, Sullivan (1954) stated:

In general, in the treatment of personality there are three fields of events which are of very great relevance. The first of these is the field of current events in the patient's life outside the treatment situation—including his current employment. The second is his current relations in the treatment—that is, his relations with the psychiatrist; and the third field of relevant data is the events of the patient's past.

Although the vocational history pertains to the patient's past, it touches on current events indirectly, as do marriage and parenthood. The psychiatrist should find out what jobs the client has held from his first paid employment to the position he holds at present, his reasons for taking the jobs he has held, his attitudes toward them, how successfully he performed them, and whether he has moved up or down the socioeconomic scale during his occupational career. In considering these questions, the client reviews his career. Was he encouraged or discouraged doing this or that type of work? Did these jobs seem to have social usefulness? One reason for the latter question is to discover whether or not the patient's jobs enhanced his self-respect, as reflected by members of society.

An inquiry into his avocational and recreational histories follows next. Avocational and recreational fields are valuable and self-satisfying, but they also provide opportunities for meeting others and for establishing close relationships and casual acquaintances or for remaining aloof. Thus, these interests can reveal much about the sort of relationships the client has toward others and his attitudes toward them. In this context Sullivan (1954) asserted:

Do not overlook the application of vocational criteria to avocational activities. Again, don't believe that because something sounds familiar to you, you know exactly what a person is talking about. When I finally developed the idea that I should ask two or three additional questions to find out what a person was talking about, I discovered that the game of bowling actually means quite different things to different people.

Personified self. In contrast to overt occurrences, which can be observed, covert processes can only be inferred and are more inclusive than what one may discover by introspection. Primitive (protaxic and parataxic) referential operations frequently occur covertly, partly because Western society tends to discourage and punish by ridicule. There is a distinction between what an informant can tell an interviewer and what an interviewer can safely infer. The personified self, which is a substructure of the self-dynamism, is a source of overt communicated information, whereas other information about the self must be inferred. What one knows about oneself and can tell about oneself to the interviewer makes up the content of the personified self. Sullivan formulated a schematization of the personified self that is useful to the psychiatrist in the detailed inquiry, along with patient's various avocational interests from science to the arts. Sullivan suggested an inquiry into the following four types of information:

1. What does the interviewee esteem, and what does he disparage about himself?
2. To what experiences is the patient's self-esteem particularly, unreasonably vulnerable? [What kind of situation puts the patient at an acute disadvantage against all his reason?]
3. What are the characteristic righting movements—security operations—that appear after the patient has been discomposed, made consciously anxious?
4. How great are the interviewee's reserves of security?

In other words, how adequately can the patient state characteristics of his life that are indubitably estimable and worthwhile? Does he have exalted purposes in life that can be demonstrated in action? One must not be misled by rhetoric, the stock in trade of politicians and public relations persons. Does the patient possess secret sources of shame or enduring regret? If he does have them, how do they relate to his justification of his life? Some people cannot discover any justification of their lives. Has he a sense of humor—that is, can he maintain a sense of proportion about his life? Does he believe his position in life is insignificant or, on the other hand, exalted? Finally, how dearly does the client actually value his life? How steadfastly and for how long has he so valued it, despite the inevitable disappointments and sorrows of human existence? What, if anything, does the client consider to be worth more than himself? For what and under what sort of circumstances would he really sacrifice his life?

Termination or interruption. Sullivan asserted that in terminating the interview or in interrupting it for any length of time, the psychiatrist must consider what progress has been made and consolidate whatever durable gain has been achieved. He suggested that the psychiatrist adopt the following four steps:

1. The psychiatrist gives the patient a final statement in which he summarizes what he has learned during the interview(s). This statement serves more or less the same purpose as the summary at the end of the reconnaissance. In fact, this kind of summary statement is useful at various times during a series of interviews. Its repeated use serves as a test of the information the interviewer has gained at various intervals. However, if the prognosis is unfavorable, the therapist almost never reveals this fact, since he must never leave the patient deeply disturbed or hopeless about his future, perhaps the most destructive act any therapist can perform.

2. The therapist offers a prescription for action—that is, he outlines a course of events in which the patient may engage to improve his chances of success in life. This prescription may entail a change of jobs or advice about his marital status or a suggestion of situations to avoid.

3. The therapist gives the patient an assessment of the final statement and prescription for action, so that he gets a constructive picture of what he has been offered and its probable effects on his or her life course.

A highly educated woman, trained in economics, came to consult Sullivan. Some years previously, she had married and settled down to the life of a traditional housewife. Increasingly, life for her had lost its savor. After negotiating the interview in his usual fashion, Sullivan, in effect, told her: "Look here, you're a highly trained economist, but housework does not provide any outlet for your talents. Why not get a position in the area for which you were trained?"

4. In a formal leave-taking, the therapist detaches himself from the interview situation without awkwardness and without prejudicing the benefits that have been accomplished. For Sullivan, the formal leave-taking had to be a clear-cut, respectful, but unambiguous farewell.

Postscript. Genuine therapy is never restricted to the formal session in which the client is engaging in psychotherapy, a point about which some young psychiatric residents seem confused. Therapy also proceeds outside the formal interviews. In the course of his everyday living, the serious patient reflects on what he has been learning and sometimes even relives, during the final sessions, various problems that have come to light in his dreams during the formal sessions. Thus, therapy involves a modification of the client's design for living and a more constructive orientation toward interpersonal relations. Finally, some of the insights gained from therapy may remain as long as one is alive and in critical situations may stand one well.

Suggested Cross References

For a discussion of various comparative views of anxiety see Chapter 8 on Freud, and Sections 9.1 on Adler, 9.2 on Horney, and 9.4 on Rado. The clinical manifestations of mental illness are discussed in Chapter 13. For further discussion of the psychiatric interview see Section 12.1.

REFERENCES

Brenner, C. *An Elementary Textbook of Psychoanalysis.* Doubleday Anchor, New York, 1957.
Bridgeman, P. W. Some general principles of operational analysis. Psychol. Rev. *5:* 82, 1945.
Crowley, R. Harry Stack Sullivan. In *The Complete Bibliography.* Academic Press, New York, 1975.
Crowley, R. Harry Stack Sullivan. In *International Encyclopedia of Psychiatry, Psychology, Psychoanalysis and Neurology,* vol. 11, p. 23. Aesculapius, Boston, 1977.
Dewey, J. and Bentley, A. F. *Knowing and the Known.* Beacon Press, Boston, 1949.
Einstein, A. and Infeld, L. *The Evolution of Physics.* Simon & Schuster, New York, 1942.
Freud, S. *Standard Edition of the Complete Psychological Works of Sigmund Freud.* Hogarth Press, London, 1953–1966.
Green, M. The roots of Sullivan's concept of self. Psychiatr. Q., *36:* 271, 1962.
Holton, G., and Roller, D. H. D. *Foundations of Modern Physical Science.* Macmillan, New York, 1958.
Leif, A., editor. *The Commonsense Psychiatry of Alfred Meyer.* McGraw-Hill, New York, 1948.
Mullahy, P. *Psychoanalysis and Interpersonal Psychiatry.* Science House, New York, 1970.
Randall, J. H., Jr. *Nature and Historical Experience.* Columbia University Press, New York, 1958.
Spearman, L. *Abilities of Man.* Macmillan, New York, 1927.
Steinbeck, J. *The Grapes of Wrath.* Viking Press, New York, 1939.
Sullivan, H. S. The importance of symbols in psychiatry. Psyche, *1:* 81, 1926.
* Sullivan, H. S. *Conceptions of Modern Psychiatry.* W. W. Norton, New York, 1953a.
* Sullivan, H. S. *The Interpersonal Theory of Psychiatry.* W. W. Norton, New York, 1953b.
* Sullivan, H. S. *The Psychiatric Interview.* W. W. Norton, New York, 1954.
* Sullivan, H. S. *Clinical Studies in Psychiatry.* W. W. Norton, New York, 1956.
* Sullivan, H. S. *Schizophrenia as a Human Process.* W. W. Norton, New York, 1962.
Sullivan, H. S. *The Fusion of Psychiatry and Social Science.* W. W. Norton, New York, 1964.
Sullivan, H. S. *Personal Psychopathology.* W. W. Norton, New York, 1972.
Terkel, S. *Hard Times.* Avon, New York, 1970.
Thorndike, E. L. *The Elements of Psychology.* Macmillan, New York, 1905.

9.4 Sandor Rado

ROBERT A. SENESCU, M.D.

Introduction

Sandor Rado, born in Hungary in 1890, was an undergraduate studying law and political science when he made his first contact with Freud and psychoanalysis through reading a pamphlet by Sandor Ferenczi. Rado was profoundly impressed and, after reading all of Freud's available writings, introduced himself to Ferenczi, who recognized Rado's ability and encouraged him to study medicine and pursue a career in psychiatry and psychoanalysis. Rado helped Ferenczi, with whom he worked very closely, organize the Hungarian Psychoanalytic

Society and, while serving as its secretary, made the acquaintance of Freud.

In 1922, Rado was invited to join the faculty of the Berlin Psychoanalytic Institute after he had moved to that city to be analyzed by Karl Abraham. He participated actively in the development of the Berlin Institute's curriculum, which later served as the model for a number of other psychoanalytic institutes. In 1924 Freud appointed him managing editor of the *Internationale Zeitschrift für Psychoanalyse*, and, several years later, Rado was appointed to the same post on *Imago*. In 1931 the New York Psychoanalytic Society invited him to come to New York to assist in the establishment of a new psychoanalytic institute, which was to be based on that in Berlin. Rado served the institute for 10 years as educational director.

In 1945 Rado was appointed a professor of psychiatry in the department of psychiatry of Columbia University and became director of the first psychoanalytic institute established within a university medical school. The founding of the Columbia Psychoanalytic Clinic, originally called the Columbia University Psychoanalytic and Psychosomatic Clinic for Training and Research, met with considerable opposition from various psychoanalytic groups. Much of the antagonism was based on memories of the rejection of Freud and his ideas by academic medicine and psychiatry in Europe. As one knowledgeable in the history of the development of the Columbia Clinic put it (Klein, 1973):

> The voluminous correspondence between prominent psychoanalysts and between institutes within the Psychoanalytic Association makes fiery reading, [and] it is difficult to estimate the amount of acrimony and partisanship that existed for a number of years before and after the founding of the Columbia Clinic.

The establishment of the Columbia Psychoanalytic Clinic was the culmination of a lifelong interest of Rado's. In his first presentation to the Hungarian Psychoanalytic Society in 1914, he spoke of the potential contribution of psychoanalysis to medicine and biology. Rado (1956a) explored another major interest, the relation between psychoanalysis and scientific methods in his first published paper, "The Paths of Natural Science in the Light of Psychoanalysis."

After his retirement from Columbia in 1955, Rado, under the auspices of the New York State Department of Mental Hygiene, founded the New York School of Psychiatry, which was devoted chiefly to basic and advanced training of psychiatrists in the New York State hospital system. He served as both dean and president of this school until his retirement.

General Orientation

In describing Sandor Rado as belonging to the "second generation of psychoanalytic pioneers," Franz Alexander (1966) added:

> Rado is one of the few "reformers" who not only remained within the psychoanalytic fold, but also tried to advance psychoanalysis from within the fraternity.

Although Rado also saw himself working in the tradition of Freud, that opinion is not wholly shared by some of his colleagues and students, particularly those with more classical psychoanalytic backgrounds and interests. Many of them tend to regard him as divisive and rather contentious and as one whose scientific pursuits and interests carried him far out of the mainstream of classical psychoanalysis. For example,

Glover (1957), a reviewer of Rado's collected papers (Rado, 1956), questioned whether adaptational psychodynamics could be regarded either as an extension of psychoanalysis or "as psychoanalysis at all" and commented that he was "baffled by the author's orgies of paraphrase." To anyone who dealt directly with Rado, there is no question that Alexander (1966) engaged in a degree of understatement when he described Rado as a formidable debater—that quality is attributed to Rado's training in the law—and as one capable of "rapidly ferreting out the weak spots" in an opponent's presentation. Undoubtedly, his provocative style alienated many of his fellow psychoanalysts. It is unfortunate, however, that the dismissal of his work by a number of his colleagues—some on the basis of his polemical style, others on the debatable grounds that it departed from the psychoanalytic tradition—tends to obscure the fact that he constantly dealt in his writings with problems and issues of crucial importance to biology, medicine, and psychiatry, as well as to the future development of psychoanalysis.

As with many gifted teachers, Rado did not write as well as he lectured. One reason was his determined effort "to evolve a close-to-the-fact scientific language" that would "convey the most information in the fewest words," leaving him open to the criticism of creating unnecessary neologisms (Rado, 1956b). The reader must decide for himself to what degree Rado's reasons for attempting to substitute his own terminology for familiar and accepted terms were cogent—for example, "action-self" for "ego," "hedonic self-regulation" for "pleasure principle," "nonreporting" for "unconscious"—or whether there is not considerable truth in the observation that his thinking might have had greater effect on many of his colleagues if he had been content with sharpening definitions and classifications of traditional terms, rather than renaming them.

In commenting on the relation between his own work and that of Freud, Rado repeatedly referred to his theory of adaptational psychodynamics as "based on the Freudian methods of free association and interpretations of unconscious processes by contextual inference." Rado saw his theory as continuing the schema of motivational dynamics and, in accord with Freud's pleasure-pain principle, viewed the organism as a biological system operating under hedonic control. At other times, however, instead of stressing continuity, Rado spoke of retransforming psychoanalysis into a medical science by correcting a number of flaws, particularly in language and methods. On repeated occasions, Rado, at times quite admiringly, quoted Freud's remarks concerning instincts—

> The theory of instincts is, as it were, our mythology. The instincts are mythical beings, superb in their indefiniteness

—to reinforce his own arguments for more precise language and verifiable concepts.

Rado's interest in methods never waned, and his preoccupation with developing a unified and systematized theory of human behavior that he hoped would result in a truly psychoanalytic science is evident in all his work. There was never any question in Rado's mind that psychoanalysis, despite various methodological differences, should remain an integral part of general psychiatry, medicine, and biological science. He claimed that only the hostility of official German psychiatry toward psychoanalysis prevented the inclusion in the original Berlin curriculum of the opportunity for training in general psychiatry and work in mental hospitals. In a retrospective view of psychoanalytic education, (Rado 1961) stated his lifelong position as follows:

Psychoanalysis must seek to win its logical place in the system of medical sciences or else be uprooted from its native soil and float in mid-air.

Adaptational Psychodynamics

Apart from its value in establishing Rado's own biological orientation and differentiating his methodological approach from classical psychoanalysis, the concept of adaptation has some practical and clinical applications as well. First and foremost, it provides a meaningful and logical basis for defining psychological health and disease. In adaptational terms, the psychologically healthy person is one whose psychic apparatus (psychological equipment) is performing its adaptive functions effectively—namely, the facilitation of both physical and psychosocial survival and well-being. In adaptational terms, psychological illness or disordered behavior is defined as a failure of the organism's psychological equipment to perform its adaptive function, the severity of disorder being measured in terms of the threat to the person's physical and psychosocial survival and well-being. That aspect of the adaptational point of view may be best illustrated by using an analogy from biological science. The physiologist determines the adaptive functions of the heart, studies how it performs those functions, and then evaluates the health of the heart on the basis of its capacity to perform its adaptive function. Conversely, the diseased heart is defined as one that cannot perform its adaptive function, whatever the cause of the disease. Using that analogy, Rado first described what he regarded as the psychological equipment of the person, the "integrative apparatus," defined its adaptive function in terms of the evolution of both the species and the individual, and then attempted to classify psychiatric illness in those terms. Although not completely successful in his ambitious effort, Rado at least helped to identify a number of the obstacles in the way of developing a simple, more consistent and scientific understanding of maladaptive behavior.

LEVELS OF MOTIVATION AND INTEGRATION OF BEHAVIOR

In a term that he frequently used in his lectures, but that he did not use in his writings, Rado viewed the psychological blueprint of the human being as consisting of four hierarchically arranged levels of integration. Reminiscent of Hughlings Jackson, those levels not only show definite evidence of evolutionary encephalization but, in Rado's thinking, can also be conceived of as corresponding roughly to the phylogenetic evolution of the species in the direction of the increased cortical influence and control characteristic of humans. Figure 1 illustrates that evolutionary point of view and indicates how the levels relate to and are integrated by the ego or, as Rado preferred to call it, the action-self.

Hedonic level. Rado was in full agreement with Jeremy Bentham's (1939) oft-quoted statement concerning the hedonic level of behavior:

Nature has placed mankind under the government of two sovereign masters: pain and pleasure. It is for them alone to point out what we ought to do, as well as to determine what we shall do.

In adaptational language, pain signals to the organism that it is in the presence of damage and motivates it to move away, pleasure indicates to the organism that it is in the presence of a benefit and elicits moving-toward or clinging-to behavior.

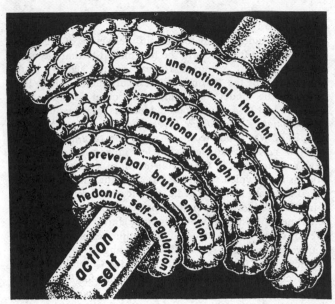

FIGURE 1. Integrative apparatus of the psychodynamic cerebral system. (From Rado, S. *Psychoanalysis of Behavior*, vol. 2, p. 46. Grune & Stratton, New York, 1962. By permission of Grune & Stratton.)

Rado spoke of the psychological effects of pain and pleasure on the human being as distinct from their more obvious adaptive value. Pain, as well as having a disorganizing effect if persistent, seems to indicate to the organism that it is failing and hence has a reductive effect on the self-esteem. Pleasure, on the other hand, is viewed as indicating to the organism that it is successful, thereby having the effect of raising self-esteem. In more metaphorical language, pleasure is seen as having three other effects: first, a food effect, serving as nourishment for the growth and development of self-esteem, confidence, or pride; second, a buffer effect, neutralizing the disorganizing or reductive effect of pain, failure, and frustration; and, finally, a glue or integrative effect, increasing the organism's resistance, as it were, to disorganization. Disturbances in the pleasure mechanism, the ability to obtain or use pleasure or do both, were increasingly viewed by Rado as playing a primary role in the pathogenesis of certain forms of disordered behavior, particularly drug dependence and schizophrenia.

Emotional level. Rado greatly admired the work of W. B. Cannon on the emotions, even though Cannon concentrated almost entirely on their peripheral manifestations. Rado frequently expressed the belief that Freud and Cannon would have recognized the significance of each other's work. In focusing on that central expression, Rado followed Cannon's lead and divided the emotions into two groups: the emergency emotions and the welfare or tender emotions. The emergency emotions, fear and rage, are defined as responses to actual or anticipated pain or damage; they prepare the organism psychologically and physiologically for flight or fight. The welfare emotions are responses to actual or anticipated pleasure or benefit; they prepare the organism psychologically or physiologically to cling to or to possess the pleasurable stimulus. Emotions may be pleasant or painful, have little or considerable thought content, and be expressed through either voluntary motor activity or the autonomic nervous system. The fact that emotional responses are frequently stimulated by symbolic or unconscious stimuli is a key factor in the development of emotional illness.

From the adaptational point of view, the human being, despite his capacity to think and reason, is essentially a hedonically and emotionally organized creature. That fact is particularly true when it comes to everyday living. Humans have the potential to be more reasonable and realistic in their behavior, but considerable effort is required to counteract the motivating force of various types of emotional thinking. From an evolutionary point of view, the emergency emotions—fear and rage, essentially equipment for adaptation or survival in the jungle—are far stronger than presumably civilized society requires, and the welfare emotions—motivating trust, cooperation, and affectionate exchange—are, as has been frequently noted over the centuries, far too weak.

In Rado's opinion, the nature and the significance of the emotional organization of the human organism were obscured by the instinct theory. Although Freud eventually recognized fear as a reaction to danger—whether real or imagined, internal or external, actual or symbolic—the same was not true of rage, which, along with pain, continued to be expressed in terms of the libido theory as a component of sadism and masochism.

Emotional thought. Emotional thought is primarily an intellectual expression of underlying feelings and, by definition, has little if anything to do with objective reality. Fantasies of all kinds, dreams, prejudices, biases, and a good deal of so-called everyday thinking are largely, if not entirely, manifestations of emotional thought. Illusions, delusions, and hallucinations are particularly pure examples of emotional thought. The principal characteristic of emotional thought is that it is selective and tends to justify and feed the emotion from which it springs.

Unemotional thought. This level acknowledges the human being's capacity to be rational and objective, to see things as they are. However, the motivating and integrating influence of unemotional thought in controlling everyday behavior is relatively weak. Insofar as this level makes it possible for the human being to delay action and gratification, tolerate pain, forgo present pleasure for future gain, and control his emotional responses, it is the equivalent of Freud's reality principle. If a human being were a computing machine, this level would be dominant, but, since a human is essentially a hedonic and emotionally organized animal, his behavior is always limited, modified, and controlled to some extent by nonobjective influences. To Rado, human emotional needs—trust, friendship, love, affectionate exchange—must be met if a human being is to function in a state of health and prosper.

CONSCIENCE

The conscience—the adaptive function of which is to facilitate cooperation and curb murderous competition by internal controls, rather than by external restraints—plays an important role in adaptational psychodynamics by influencing healthy development and by producing pathological behavior (Rado, 1956d). The development of conscience is based essentially on the dependent child's need and desire to remain in his parents'—usually his mother's—good graces or, conversely, on the fear of losing her loving approval and support, a terrifying threat to the dependent child. In Rado's language the child delegates his own omnipotence to his parents. The child believes that his parents see and know all, and that belief produces in the child a fear of inescapable punishment, the component of guilt that makes the conscience mechanism a powerful influence on behavior. The fully mature conscience operates unconsciously and automatically; it should facilitate and reward good behavior, thereby raising self-esteem, and should

restrain and punish bad behavior, which lowers self-esteem. Conscience is not foolproof; when the child inevitably misbehaves, he experiences an attack of painful guilty fear, a feeling of being bad plus the fear of inescapable punishment. Guilty fear has the reparative function of motivating the child to engage in expiatory behavior—to confess his wrongdoing and accept the punishment due as a means of getting back in the good graces (which relieves the painful guilty fear and raises self-esteem) of those on whom he is or feels totally dependent.

Pain-dependent behavior—Rado's term for masochistic behavior, sexual or otherwise—is conceived of as a maladaptive form of expiatory behavior based on strong guilty fears. Those fears motivate the person to seek punishment in advance, so that he is then permitted to attempt to satisfy the prohibited pleasurable desire.

An inescapable complication of discipline and the development of conscience is the inevitable build-up of rage that occurs when a child obeys or submits to parental prohibitions. That repressed rage, which constantly seeks discharge, obviously presents a serious problem both to the individual and to society. To Rado, conscience plays a crucial role in determining how much rage is built up and whether it is discharged and used constructively or destructively. In the person experiencing an attack of guilty fear, the repressed and retroflexed rage may break through, causing an attack of guilty rage, the essence of which is the persecuting idea: "I'm not bad; you are; furthermore, you are picking on me, and I must attack in self-defense." Since guilty rage externalizes the blame, it is temporarily less reductive and painful to the person's self-esteem than is guilty fear. That reparative function, however, is usually of little benefit, since bouts of guilty rage either elicit quick retaliation or, if sustained, give rise to painful feelings of persecution that may develop into full-blown delusions.

Rado considered conscience a special form of emergency behavior, and his conception of the development of conscience and the role it plays in human behavior, both healthy and pathological, provided a particularly good example of how the adaptational approach both developed out of and differed from the classical psychoanalytic concept of the superego.

CONCEPT OF SELF

The last time the term "ego" appears in a noncritical context in Rado's (1956c) writings is in his 1939 paper "Developments in the Psychoanalytic Conception and Treatment of the Neuroses," in which he states:

Clinical findings have demonstrated the validity of the following conception: *Neurosis is ego-functioning altered by faulty measures of emergency control.*

In the same paper he also spoke of the ego's lacking self-awareness and of being unaware of the true meaning of its neurotic manifestations. The term Rado substituted for ego is "action-self," which, as illustrated in Figure 1, is

located axially to the four levels of the psychodynamic integrative apparatus.

One of the functions of the action-self is integrating the conscious organism into a self-aware and intentionally acting whole. The integral action-self system, which functions unconsciously, as well as determining self-awareness, is regarded as the pivotal integrative system of the entire organism.

Along the line of Sherrington's comment that "mind is the manager of muscle," Rado saw the action-self originating in the proprioceptive sensations that the infant derives from the vigorous emotional muscular activity of sucking at his mother's breast (Rado, 1956f). To Rado, if the infant could speak, he would jubilantly paraphrase Descartes and announce "Succo, ergo sum"—"I suck; therefore, I am." The child's first or primordial concept of self is that of an omnipotent, magical being. When the child discovers the sad truth that his actual powers are limited, he is forced to give up or, more accurately, repress that highly satisfying picture of self. On the way to developing a more realistic concept of self, the child is seen as delegating his omnipotence and magical powers to his parents, who are then supposed to use those powers for his benefit. Both the concepts of primordial omnipotence, as in the pathogenesis of drug dependency or narcotic bondage, and delegated omnipotence, as in parentifying behavior, play important parts in Rado's attempts to clarify the mechanisms of disordered behavior and its treatment. In dispensing with the term "narcissism," Rado (1958) conceived of the organism as appreciating itself as a "proven provider of pleasure." That emotional appreciation of self is the basis of self-esteem or pride. The relation between pleasure and the increase or reduction of self-esteem and pride is then further developed in a clinically useful fashion.

Rado (1958) summarized his thoughts on the importance of pleasure to the growth and maintenance of a healthy concept of self as follows:

The organism esteems itself as a proven provider of pleasure. This emotional self-approval is the function of the action-self known as pride. Itself a derivative of sucking, the action-self continues to feed on pleasure. It absorbs the pleasure of all activity and success, above all the pleasure of loving, of being loved and respected, of loving and respecting oneself. As the action-self expands and contracts, concomitantly the pride of the organism rises and falls, in direct ratio to the amount of pleasure the action-self consumes—just as the bodily weight of the organism rises and falls with its intake of food. Thus pride, the organism's emotional stature, reflects the size of its action-self. By its dependence on pride, the action-self profoundly influences the organism's behavior in health and disease. For example, a paucity of pride may cause the organism to respond with rage when it would be prudent to respond with fear.

DISORDERED BEHAVIOR

How Rado used the adaptational frame of reference in his conceptualization of psychiatric illness is perhaps best illustrated in his formulation of the psychodynamic development of the neuroses (overreactive behavior) and of schizophrenia (schizotypal behavior), although his contributions to the understanding of the syndromes of depression, drug dependence, and obsessional behavior are also good examples of his clinical thinking. Some of Rado's (1956b) best work, especially that on the psychodynamics of depression and drug dependence (narcotic bondage), was done while he worked entirely within the classical or Freudian psychoanalytic framework. His writings on those subjects provide an excellent opportunity to evaluate how much the changes in his thinking over the years affected his clinical formulations.

To Rado, the failure of emergency adjustment, fundamentally an overproduction of fear and rage, is at the basis of all disordered behavior, the severity of the particular disorder being determined by the intensity, extent, and duration of the resulting adaptive failure. As might be expected, Rado (1956c)

disdained the use of such terms as "neuroses" and "psychoses." He also found the official diagnostic classification system both contradictory and inadequate. In 1953 he made an ambitious attempt to create his own classification system, necessarily based, as he put it, on "the psychodynamic aspect of etiology (or the "how" component in the etiology of maladaptive behavior) because "our knowledge of the genetic and physiologic phases of etiology" (presumably the "why" component of etiology) is too scant to serve as an ideal basis for etiological classification. In Rado's opinion, and he repeatedly cited Freud in support of his viewpoint, there is no question that the ultimate cause of disordered behavior must be sought through biochemical, physiological, and genetic investigations (Rado, 1956f).

When the initial excessive emergency responses either persist or recur, the organism has only a limited equipment with which to cope or adapt to the painful and threatening situation. The basic sequence that may be seen in all forms of disordered behavior is shown in Table I.

Miscarried prevention. In its simplest form, miscarried prevention is a reparative response after an attack of fear. Rado placed great emphasis on the painful, humiliating, reductive effect of fear. That response leads to (1) avoidance of the place in which the attack occurred, in which case it is called phobic avoidance; (2) avoidance of the activity being engaged in when the attack of fear occurred, in which case it is more likely to be called an inhibition; or (3) some combination of the two. Miscarried prevention is obviously maladaptive; even when displacement occurs or the danger is symbolically represented, there is some restriction of freedom of activity.

Miscarried repair. A critical element in Rado's conceptualization of the development of disordered behavior, miscarried repair, means essentially the maintenance of or revival of patterns of behavior of the helpless, dependent child. They may take a variety of forms. The forms most prominent in the production of pathological behavior are (1) further regression to helpless behavior; (2) attempts at breaking the inhibition by defiant, coercive rage or ingratiating behavior to obtain permission or regain approval or a combination of the two, as often seen in obsessional behavior; and (3) reliance on magical

TABLE I
Rado's Concept of the Development of Disordered Behavior

An array of fears of various forms of retaliation or punishment for assertive, angry, defiant, or sexual behavior or feelings lead to:

Inhibitions and losses of healthy function. These are essentially losses of adaptive utility, especially the capacity to work and the ability to obtain the minimal requirement of pleasure and to maintain healthy pride or self-esteem. Since those losses result in damage to functional capacity and to the child's pride and concept of self, they elicit:

Automatic mechanisms of repair 1. Healthy repair. If successful, the child outgrows the infantile neurosis. 2. Miscarried prevention and repair. Reparative efforts often miscarry for the obvious reason that the behaviorally causative factor, the excessive emergency response, is usually repressed to some degree, if not entirely.

or illusory fulfillment through wishful thinking, fantasy, or stature cosmetics, characteristic of the expressional (hysterical) behavior.

The two factors that Rado most strongly emphasized as having a primary or causative influence in the production of disordered behavior are the prolonged total helplessness and dependency of the infant and child and the inevitable battle for power that takes place between the mother and the child in such areas as feeding, toilet training, cleanliness, and matters of training or discipline in general. The child's response to education and discipline, the problem he faces in dealing with his rage at the inevitable frustrations of his desires and his need to assert himself, assumed ever-greater importance in Rado's thinking regarding the understanding of both healthy and disordered behavior. The child's fear of loss of approval or other punishment if he asserts himself was viewed as the fundamental problem. Those fears of self-assertion manifest themselves most damagingly in the areas of work (capacity to cooperate and compete) and of social and sexual behavior. Rado had strong and original ideas concerning the place of sexual motivation and behavior in the larger context of human behavior. A 1949 paper on the adaptational view of sexual behavior (Rado, 1956g) presented those ideas most concisely. In addition, it provided a particularly good example of what Rado meant by a biological and evolutionary approach to the study of human behavior.

Overreactive behavior. The essence of overreactive or neurotic behavior is emergency dyscontrol, characterized by essentially uncomplicated attacks of fear or rage that, depending on the degree of repression, may be expressed in dreams, phobias, inhibitions of motor behavior, or simple hypochondriac patterns in which the fear of punishment is expressed as a fear of illness. Descending dyscontrol or discharge of the emergency emotions through the autonomic nervous system and sexual disorders are each viewed as a separate subgroup of overreactive behavior.

In addition to including elements from the so-called simpler forms, more structured or symptomatic neurotic behavior, whatever its final form, is viewed as developing or occurring in persons whose basic pattern of behavior is characterized by some degree of social and familial overdependence and by significant inhibitions in self-assertiveness that interfere with performance in the social, sexual, and work areas in particular. That basic neurosis, although not acknowledged as such, in Rado's science is called common maladaptation. Expressive (hysteria), obsessive, and paranoid patterns of behavior are regarded as elaborations of that pattern of common maladaptation. What form the neurotic elaboration takes in a person depends on a number of factors affecting growth and development, such as the family constellation, the socioeconomic status, and cultural factors. The type of symptomatic behavior that develops depends also, to a considerable extent, on the severity and the extent of the early inhibitions in adaptive capacity, the degree of damage to self-esteem, and the degree to which reparative attempts were successful or failed.

Although Rado strongly emphasized the importance of learning, disciplinary, and cultural factors, as opposed to so-called instinctual factors in the production of disordered behavior, on occasion he stressed even more the significance of biological, especially genetic, factors. He and many of his colleagues at Columbia tended to emphasize the fundamental significance of the interaction of the person with his biocultural environment, but Rado himself, as his career progressed, expressed ever-greater interest in the physiological component of the psychophysiological correlation he regarded as the foundation of a basic or unified science of human behavior. That trend was particularly apparent in his approach to schizophrenia.

Schizotypal behavior. In his approach to the problem of schizophrenia (Gerty, 1953), Rado hypothesized the presence of an innate "integrative pleasure deficiency" and a "proprioceptive diathesis," probably also innate, as being characteristic of what he called schizotypal organization. Several years later (Rado, 1962a), he reported on a clinical study of a group of patients suspected of having a schizotypal organization. The purpose of the study was, first, to observe whether they possessed the postulated clinical traits and, second, to determine the distribution of the traits among the group of 37 patients studied.

In presenting his theory, Rado, in characteristic fashion, beclouded the issue somewhat at the beginning by implying in his hypothesis that schizophrenia is a definite disease entity and by asserting that the current genetic theory of the cause of schizophrenia as

> transmitted to the offspring from both parents by a Mendelian mechanism

is established fact, rather than a theory. Otherwise, his reasoning, except for a somewhat labored attempt to correlate his essentially dynamic theory with the descriptive concepts of schizoid behavior and pseudoneurotic schizophrenia, was quite consistent and was entirely based on clinical observation and clearly stated postulates. Using his own clinical experience with patients who had experienced schizophrenic disorganization (schizophrenic phenotypes), Rado was of the opinion that

> by subjecting the gross manifestations of the open psychosis to minute psychodynamic analysis, we discover an underlying ensemble of psychodynamic traits.

That ensemble of psychodynamic traits is what characterizes schizotypal organization and, according to Rado, is demonstrable in the patient throughout his entire life.

One of the most significant ways the integrative pleasure deficiency manifests itself is in a weakness in the motivating and organizing action of pleasure, resulting in a reduction in the welfare or tender emotions—affection, love, joy, pride, and pleasurable desire—which leads to a diminished capacity to deal with people on a warm, spontaneous, emotional level. The proprioceptive diathesis seems to manifest itself most directly in a profound disturbance of self-confidence and extreme self-consciousness. Both defects seem to contribute to the strong feeling of being irrevocably different—emotionally, psychologically, and physically.

Among the many clinical traits that may be seen as actively or potentially developing, three stand out particularly and are regarded as more general compensatory (reparative) maneuvers of adaptation. They are (1) overdependence on others to an extreme degree; (2) compensatory use of intellect—the patient attempts to think his way through life because of a lack of confidence in feelings—and (3) a scarcity economy of pleasure—the patient clings to scarce pleasure resources, even if self-damaging, and experiences any loss of pleasure as a severe blow. A failure or loss in any of those three compensatory areas may precipitate an episode of decompensation or disorganization.

Although his theory was never made as clear as it might or should have been, Rado's primary interest in defining schizotypal organization was to develop psychotherapeutic principles and techniques that were more effective in working with a person whose psychological organization was such that he seemed to be more prone than others to behavioral disorganization. Those patients not only require special treatment techniques but are too often misdiagnosed. Even though he stresses presumed innate or hereditary factors, Rado's approach does not deserve to be described as pessimistic, as it has been on several occasions.

TREATMENT

Rado's ideas concerning treatment are consistent with his notions regarding both emotional health and disordered behavior. As might be expected, he tended to define psychological health in terms of two criteria: first, the relative predominance of the welfare emotions—affection, pride, friendliness, optimism, and joy—second, the person's capacity to be reasonably independent and self-reliant. The emotionally healthy or happy person elicits similar pleasurable feelings in others that, by reinforcing his own pleasurable feelings, set up a benign cycle. In that idealized person, the emergency responses, always a potential problem, are still active but find nondestructive outlets, either in some form of activity or through dreaming. In any event they are not of sufficient intensity or duration to cause maladaptive behavior.

In those terms Rado saw the two primary goals of psychotherapeutic technique, from the simplest form of supportive psychotherapy to the most ambitious psychoanalytic or reconstructive therapy, to be, first, an alteration in the patient's emotional organization and, second, an increase in the patient's self-reliance. In the first instance, that emotional reeducation was designed to increase the motivating influence of the welfare emotions on behavior and to reduce the influence of the

emergency reponses; in the second instance, the goal was to encourage the patient to relinquish dependent patterns that are both the cause and the result of neurotic behavior and to assist him to learn to become as self-reliant as possible. Although it did not neglect the past, the adaptational approach strongly stressed the fact that the main reason for exploring the past, other than for research purposes, was to increase understanding of the present. As Ovesey and Jameson (1956) succinctly stated:

> The therapist is primarily concerned with failures in adaptation *today*, how they arose, and what the patient must do to overcome them.

Other major differences between the classical and the adaptational techniques centered mainly on what was felt to be the excessive importance the classical technique placed on the analysis and recovery of unconscious memories, the overestimation of the value of insight, and the relative neglect of the patient's present and actual behavior. In addition, Rado directed some of his sharpest criticisms at the whole concept of transference and its management. In Rado's opinion, the classical method actually infantilized the patient, instead of achieving Freud's stated goal of helping the patient achieve the highest level of maturity attainable. Preventing the patient, as much as possible, from developing a transference neurosis and frankly encouraging greater educational activity on the part of the therapist are two of the main points of difference between the two techniques. Actually, Rado believed that such reeducational activity was unavoidable and, furthermore, was of the opinion that classical analysts played the part of teacher far more than they acknowledged in their writings.

The fundamental significance that Rado attributed to the nature of the patient-physician interaction in determining the course and type of treatment is best illustrated by Table II. As

TABLE II*
Levels of Motivation in Treatment Behavior

ASPIRING LEVEL: Available only in the adult patient who is capable and desirous of self-advancement by extensive learning and maturation.	"I am delighted to cooperate with the doctor. This is my opportunity to learn how to make full use of all my potential resources for adaptive growth."
SELF-RELIANT LEVEL: Available in the average adult patient who knows or is capable of learning the simple adaptive patterns of daily life. ADULT, REALISTIC	"I am ready to cooperate with the doctor. I must learn how to help myself and do things for myself."
CHILD-LIKE, REGRESSIVE **PARENT-SEEKING LEVEL:** When the adult feels like a helpless child, he seeks parental help and, therefore, parentifies the physician.	"I don't know what the doctor expects of me. I couldn't do it anyway. He should cure me by *his* efforts."
MAGIC-CRAVING LEVEL: The completely discouraged adult patient retreats to the hope that the parentified physician will do miracles for him.	"The doctor must not only cure me, he must do everything for me—by magic."

* From Rado, S. *Psychoanalysis of Behavior*. 2, p. 114. Grune & Stratton, New York, 1962. By permission of Grune & Stratton.

can be seen, the nature and extent of the patient's ability to cooperate are the crucial elements.

Implied in that table is the fundamental point that a particular psychotherapeutic approach is selected not on the basis of a diagnostic label but, rather, because the particular method is best suited to the patient's capacity to work or cooperate with the therapist. If the patient is not able to move up the scale, at least regression downward should be prevented. The main purpose of what Rado called interceptive interpretation was essentially the prevention of such regressions downward, which he felt occurred all too often in psychotherapy.

In his treatment approach Rado made a sharp distinction between treatment behavior and life performance, being of the opinion that many unsuccessful psychotherapeutic attempts could be traced to a failure to discriminate between the two. Finally, not only did he stress the role of the therapist as educator, but he also continually emphasized the importance of successful doing on the part of the patient in the area of everyday practical living or in his life performance as the vital factor determining the patient's growth and, hence, the success of therapy.

Evaluation of Rado's Contributions

It is not easy to identify with any precision the influence that Rado's work had in the past or to predict how much influence it will have in the future. The task is made even more difficult by the fact that Rado, in at least one respect, resembled many of his productive and innovative psychoanalytic contemporaries in their tendency not to acknowledge their borrowings from or debts to one another—if, indeed, they were even aware of those borrowings except in the broadest terms.

Certain elements in Rado's work were handled in a unique and consistent fashion throughout his career. Foremost was his attempt to make psychoanalysis a branch of medical science and to keep it within the confines of the university and medicine. That ambition was best expressed by Rado's (1962a) statement that

adaptational psychodynamics proposes to lay the foundation for a unified science of human behavior.

Despite the success of the university-based training center that he directed from its inception, Rado's attempts to develop curriculums that reflected his goal of integrating psychoanalysis with the relevant basic sciences were not outstanding successes. His efforts to demystify psychoanalytic theory, eliminate jargon (when he did not yield to the temptation to develop his own), and create a discipline of psychoanalytic medicine were definitely more productive. A number of Rado's concepts have stimulated various types of research, both basic and clinical, in such diverse areas as schizophrenia, drug addiction, depression, psychosomatic medicine, homosexuality, and the role of the pleasure mechanism in the production of disordered behavior.

Another important aspect of Rado's work was the emphasis he put on human dependency. To Rado, human dependency was much more than simply a basic characteristic of the earliest stage of life. The fact that the human being is totally dependent on the loving care of others at birth and lives more or less in a dependent pattern on parents or parental substitutes for a significant portion of his or her life was regarded by Rado as the most critical factor in the development of any person. Human dependency was viewed by Rado as having the profoundest significance in determining the nature and the extent of whatever psychopathology developed. In addition, the manner in which the dependency needs or demands of the person were handled or mishandled in the treatment situation was regarded as the crucial element in the interaction between the patient and the therapist. The commonest neurosis to Rado was that seen in people who were emotionally still living in a dependent pattern—who, put even more simply, were not grown up. Failure to outgrow the dependent pattern of behavior was regarded as underlying most, if not all, disordered behavior, whatever the cause. Indeed, Rado's major criticism of most other therapeutic techniques was that they fostered dependency, with its concomitant magic seeking, an observation that has been more than verified with the enormous increase in recent years of various types of psychotherapies.

To Rado, the development of disordered behavior was literally the problem of anxiety. Rado regarded fear and anxiety as absolutely identical responses. The overproduction of fear—whatever the actual or presumed cause and usually, if not invariably, accompanied by rage—was seen as the primary element interfering with healthy functioning. To some clinicians, Rado's emphasis on the fundamental importance of the emergency emotions, fear and rage, in producing psychopathology and disordered behavior was of inestimable clinical and heuristic value; to others, it was the major manifestation of what has been regarded as Rado's tendency to oversimplify and to indulge in reductionism. Along those lines one critic charged Rado, along with French and Sullivan, with turning psychoanalysis into a combination of behaviorism and reflexology. Rado specifically, in his interpretations of sexual perversions, was accused of going back to the one-trauma theory abandoned by Freud. A further example of how extremely Rado could be misunderstood was contained in the criticism that, as a behaviorist, he failed to recognize that the human being still possesses wishes, drives, hopes, anxieties, and passions and that he is motivated by irrational forces that remain immune to purposive interpretations (Wyss, 1966).

Rado's discursive style of presentation and his intolerance of whatever he considered to be nonessential undoubtedly contributed greatly to his vulnerability to charges of being too positivistic, if not downright shallow. However, if Rado is read carefully, it is hard to avoid concluding that, rather than ignoring the irrational or so-called deeper forces, he perhaps overemphasized the significance of irrational elements—such as pain and pleasure, human dependency, fear, anger, and guilt—and the influence of the childish conscience in motivating behavior. There is more than a little irony in the fact that—in deemphasizing the motivating force of reason, intellect, and cognition in everyday behavior while stressing the importance of the physiological and biological substrata—Rado left himself open to the charge of being naive and lacking in depth. In his attempt to be logical, consistent, and scientific in his contributions to the deeper understanding of human behavior, his greatest strength lay in his capacity to describe what he considered to be most important in the motivation of human behavior in simple and exquisitely rational terms.

Suggested Cross References

Rado's theories may be compared with Freud's in Chapter 8. Section 6.6 discusses normality, and Section 34.2 discusses normal child development.

REFERENCES

Alexander, F. The adaptational theory. In *Psychoanalytic Pioneers*, F. Alexander, S. Eisenstein, and M. Grotjahn, editors, p. 240. Basic Books, New York, 1966.
Bentham, J. An introduction to the principles of morals and legislation. In *The English Philosophers from Bacon to Mill*, p. 791. Modern Library, New York, 1939.
Cannon, W. B. *Bodily Changes in Pain, Hunger, Fear, and Rage.* Appleton, New York, 1934.
Coyne, J. C. Toward an interactional description of depression. Psychiatry, *39:* 28, 1976.

Davidman, H. The contributions of Sandor Rado to psychodynamic science. In *Science and Psychoanalysis*. J. H. Masserman, editor, vol. 7, p. 17. Grune & Stratton, New York, 1964.

Frosch, J. The relation between acting out and disorders of impulse control. Psychiatry, *40:* 295, 1977.

Gerty, F. J. Discussion of Dr. Sandor Rado's academic lecture. Am. J. Psychiatry, *110:* 422, 1953.

Glover, E. Review of S. Rado, *Psychoanalysis of Behavior*, vol. 2. Psychoanal. Q., *26:* 251, 1957.

Heath, R. G. *The Role of Pleasure in Behavior.* Hoeber Medical Division, Harper & Row, New York, 1964.

Klein, H. R. Bull. Assoc. Psychoanal. Med., *12:* 1973.

Meehl, P. Schizotaxia, schizotypy, schizophrenia. Am. Psychol., *17:* 827, 1962.

Ovesey, L., and Jameson, J. The adaptational technique of psychoanalytic therapy. In *Changing Concepts of Psychoanalytic Medicine*, S. Rado and C. E. Daniels, editors, p. 165. Grune & Stratton, New York, 1956.

Rado, S. *Psychoanalysis of Behavior*, vols. 1 and 2. Grune & Stratton, New York, 1956, 1962.

Rado, S. The paths of natural science in the light of psychoanalysis. In *Psychoanalysis of Behavior*, vol. 1, p. 3. Grune & Stratton, New York, 1956a.

*Rado, S. The psychoanalysis of pharmacothymia (drug addiction). In *Psychoanalysis of Behavior*, vol. 1, p. 64. Grune & Stratton, New York, 1956b.

* Rado, S. Developments in the psychoanalytic conception and treatment of the neuroses. In *Psychoanalysis of Behavior*, vol. 1, p. 130. Grune & Stratton, New York, 1956c.

* Rado, S. Emergency behavior, with an introduction to the dynamics of conscience. In *Psychoanalysis of Behavior*, vol. 1, p. 214. Grune & Stratton, New York, 1956d.

* Rado, S. Dynamics and classification of disordered behavior. In *Psychoanalysis of Behavior*, vol. 1, p. 268. Grune & Stratton, New York, 1956e.

* Rado, S. Hedonic control, action-self, and the depressive spell. In *Psychoanalysis of Behavior*, vol. 1, p. 286. Grune & Stratton, New York, 1956f.

* Rado, S. An adaptational view of sexual behavior. In *Psychoanalysis of Behavior*, vol. 1, p. 320. Grune & Stratton, New York, 1956g.

Rado, S. Psychoanalytic education: Lessons of the past and responsibilities for the future. In *Psychoanalysis of Behavior*, vol. 1, p. 178. Grune & Stratton, New York, 1961.

* Rado, S. Schizotypal organization: Preliminary report on a clinical study of schizophrenia. In *Psychoanalysis of Behavior*, vol. 2, p. 1. Grune & Stratton, New York, 1962a.

Rado, S. On the retransformation of psychoanalysis into a medical science. Compr. Psychiatry, *3:* 317, 1962b.

Rado, S. Metapsychologic ego action self. In *Psychoanalysis of Behavior*, vol. 2, p. 46. Grune & Stratton, New York, 1968.

Rosenblatt, A. D., and Thickstun, J. T. Modern psychoanalytic concepts in a general psychology. Psychol. Issues, *11:* 20, 1977–1978.

Stein, L., and Wise, C. D. Progressive damage to the noradrenergic reward system by 6-hydroxydopamine. Science, *171:* 1032, 1971.

Wise, C. D., and Stein, L. Dopamine-beta-hydroxylase deficit in the brains of schizophrenic patients. Science, *181:* 344, 1973.

Wyss, D. *Depth Psychology: A Critical History*, p. 525. W. W. Norton, New York, 1966.

9.5 Biodynamics

JULES H. MASSERMAN, M.D.

Introduction

Biodynamics is not a separate school of psychiatry; indeed, the word "school," in the sense of cult, is best applied to fish swimming mindlessly in one direction, rather than to any aggregation of scientists. Instead, biodynamics connotes an integration of the biological and dynamic vectors of all animate behavior. It encompasses data from evolution, ethology, comparative animal research, anthropology, history, philology, ecology, sociology, and other sciences of behavior, as well as from clinical evaluations (diagnoses) and salutary transactions (therapy). From all these disciplines, biodynamics, developed by the author (see Figure 1), derives integrative premises and operative techniques asymptotically modifiable by further knowledge.

Research Studies

Investigations conducted by the author and his associates during the past three decades have led to the formulation of four basic biodynamic principles:

Motivational development. All behavior originates in variably emergent physiological needs for nutrition, environmental control, sexual and parental functions, and other conations toward individual and social survival.

Learned individuation. Each organism's evolving patterns of adaptation are the result of its genetic potentialities, their various modes and rates of maturation, and its unique experiences.

Versatile adaptability. Most dissatisfaction and frustrations are adequately met by a flexible repertoire of readjusted techniques or substitute goals.

Neurotigenesis. However, when an organism's coping capacities are overstressed by environmental uncertainties and adaptational conflicts, severe and persistent deviations of behavior are induced.

FIGURE 1. Jules H. Masserman is the originator of integrative biodynamic concepts of behavior. By inducing and treating behavioral deviations in animals, he has formulated comprehensive principles of motivation, individuation, adaptation, and neurotigenesis. By correlating these principles with clinical diagnostic, prognostic, and psychoanalytic concepts, he has arrived at effective modes of therapy.

Masserman has been trained in music, pharmacy, history, philosophy, and medicine. He studied psychobiology under Adolf Meyer and psychoanalysis at the Chicago Institute for Psychoanalysis under Franz Alexander. He is professor emeritus of psychiatry and neurology at Northwestern University, was president of the American Psychiatric Association in 1978–1979, and is president of the World Association of Social Psychiatry.

ANALOGOUS MOTIVATIONAL DEVELOPMENTS

Phases. Young animals pass through an orderly succession of stages during which sensory modalities are correlated, concepts of the environment are engrammed, manipulative skills are refined, early dependencies are relinquished in favor of exploration and mastery, and peer and sexual relationships are developed. Analogously a person matures and becomes socialized in his or her group.

Formative experiences. Young animals provided with the necessary nutritive, protective, and guiding presence of adults, supplemented by play and other contacts with peers, acquire self-confidence, motor skills, and effective group relationships. Conversely, animals deprived of appropriate parental, surrogate, or peer transactions during critical periods of growth and receptivity, though otherwise physically well cared for, do not develop normal initiative, physical stamina, or appropriate social behavior.

Unique early experiences may also leave peculiar characteristics that persist through adulthood. For example, if a young monkey is taught to work a pedal switch that administers increasingly intense but progressively acceptable electric shocks as signals for securing food, the adult animal may continue to seek such shocks, even in the absence of any reward, and may thus appear to be inexplicably masochistic to an observer unacquainted with its special history.

Adequate training in early life can in large part compensate for extensive brain damage in the newborn. On the other hand, in the absence of such special care, the effects of lesions in the thalami, amygdalae, and cerebral areas 13, 23, and 24 are more devastating in the young than in adult animals.

ANALOGUES OF SOCIAL TRANSACTIONS

Animal societies in the laboratory, as well as in the wild, organize themselves in hierarchies of relatively dominant and submissive members. Privileges are generally preempted not by size or strength alone but in accordance with special initiatives, aptitudes, skills, and other characteristics. Various relationships seen in animal societies help trace the biodynamic roots of collaboration, sit-down strikes, divisions of labor, automation, altruism, and hostilities as expressed with far greater complexity in human societies.

Cooperation. A cat or a monkey can be trained to operate a mechanism that produces food for a conspecific similarly trained, who then reciprocates in mutual service.

Parasitism. In most pairings, however, this pattern soon deteriorates into a situation in which both animals starve until one of them (the worker) operates the mechanism frequently enough to feed both himself and its dominant partner.

Technological solution. However, an occasional worker is sufficiently intelligent—that is, possessed of unusually high perceptive-manipulative capacities—to jam the feeding switch so that it operates continuously, rendering further effort by either animal unnecessary.

Altruism. Some animals exhibit self-sacrificing conduct without apparent reward other than that of preventing discomfort or pain to another member of the colony. This succoring behavior is apparently less dependent on the relative age, size, or sex of the two animals than on their respective characteristics and whether or not they had been mutually well-adjusted cagemates.

Aggression. Conversely, actual fighting among members of the same species to establish various relationships is minimal. Physical combat appears only under the following circum-

stances: (1) when an animal accustomed to a high position in its own colony is transferred to a group in which it comes into direct conflict with new rivals, (2) when a tyrannical monkey is subjected to an unexpected rebellion by an alliance of subordinates, (3) when a female monkey with increased status derived from mating with a high-ranking male punishes members of her group that had previously oppressed her, or (4) when a dominant animal, after being made experimentally neurotic as described below, expresses its frustration by physical attacks on both inanimate and living objects in its environment.

NEUROTIGENESIS

Aberrations of conduct analogous to human mental disorders can be induced by training an animal to work a switch that opens a food box and then subjecting it to randomly timed electric shocks during feeding (see Figure 2). In a more direct parallel to symbolically traumatic experiences, monkeys can be taught to respond to a sign reading *Fressen bitte* by lifting the lid of a food box in which, again at unpredictable intervals, it also sees a toy rubber snake—an object as representationally dangerous to the monkey as a live one would be. Yet, counter to classical Freudian and recent Wolpean doctrines, fear in the sense of dread of injury need not be involved at all. In accord with what may more generally be termed the Uncertainty Principle of neurotigenesis, equally serious and lasting disorganization of behavior can be induced by subjecting the animal to variously delayed feedbacks of its vocalizations, by sensorially confused cues that render its milieu seemingly beyond adequate control, or even by requiring difficult choices between mutually exclusive satisfactions (see Figure 3). Any of these stresses, when they exceed the organism's predictive and adaptive capacities, can induce physiological and mimetic manifestations of anxiety, spreading inhibitions, generalizing phobias, stereotyped rituals, somatic dysfunctions, addictions to alcohol or other drugs, impaired sexual and social interactions, regressions to immature conduct, cataleptic stupors, and, in monkeys, manifestations of hallucinatory and delusional behavior.

Animals closest to humans show symptoms most nearly resembling those in human neuroses and psychoses; however, the syndromes manifested depend less on the nature of the conflict than on the constitutional predisposition of the animal. For example, under similar stresses, spider monkeys revert to infantile dependencies or catatonic immobility, cebus develop various somatic and kinetic dysfunctions, and vervets become diffusely aggressive, persist in bizarre sexual patterns, or prefer hallucinatory satisfactions, such as chewing and swallowing purely imaginary food pellets while avoiding real ones to the point of self-starvation.

Laboratory Investigations of Modes of Therapy

Equally germane to human interests are the procedures that have proved to be most effective in ameliorating or eliminating the deviations of behavior induced by experiential stresses (see Figure 4). Methods analogous to those in clinical therapy can be summarized as follows.

SPONTANEOUS REEXPLORATION

In the absence of further deterrents, some animals retest the use of the switch and feeding mechanisms and dispel associated neurotic inhibitions and deviations at their own pace. So, also,

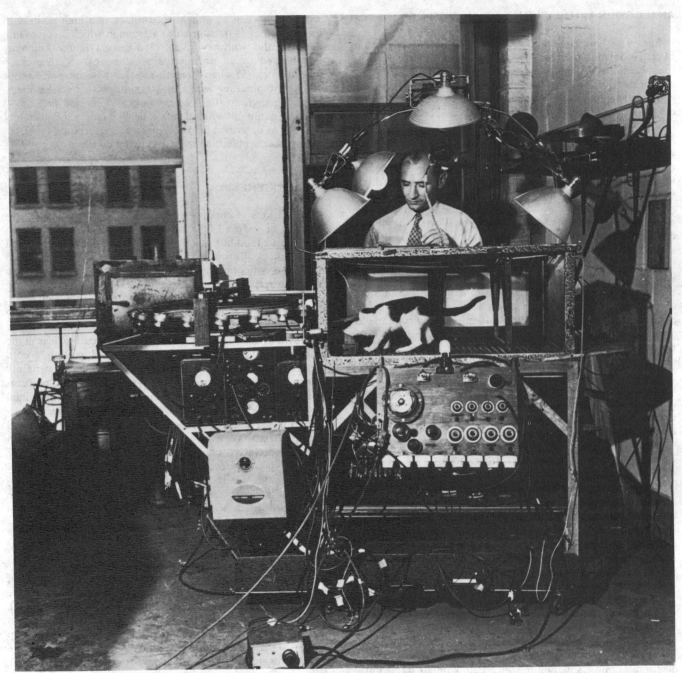

FIGURE 2. An apparatus for studying response behavior and experimental neuroses in cats. (Courtesy of Jules H. Masserman, M.D.)

most human beings spontaneously and providentially reexplore and reassert their mastery over the residues of traumatic physical or social experiences without need for therapy.

ENVIRONMENTAL PRESS

If autonomous readaptations do not occur, the hungry animal can be mechanically restricted ever closer to highly attractive food in the opened reward box until its feeding and related inhibitions are, in most instances, overwhelmed by an imperative need for nutrition. In some animals, however, the exacerbated conflicts between attraction and aversion induce a state of agitation and panic paralleling the adverse results of implosive behavior therapy in patients with coping capacities (ego strengths) inadequate to the rapid readaptations required.

SOCIAL INFLUENCES

An inhibited, phobic animal placed with others that respond normally to the feeding situation shows more expeditious amelioration of its neurotic inhibitions, as in exemplary group influences in humans.

REEDUCATION BY A TRUSTED MENTOR

The experimenter can retrain the animal by gentle steps: first, to take food from his hand; next, to accept food in the apparatus; then, to open the box while the experimenter merely hovers protectively; and finally, to work the switch and feed without further guidance. This procedure may be the paradigm for much dyadic psychotherapy. The patient channelizes his needs for help toward a therapist, who uses this transference with optimal patience and wisdom to reassure, guide, and support the patient as the latter reexamines his conflictful desires and fears, recognizes his previous misinterpretations of reality, and explores new ways of living until he is sufficiently successful and confident to proceed on his own. Whether this process is called reeducation, retraining, psychotherapy, psychoanalysis, or rehabilitation depends more on the context of the problem, the necessity for thoroughness in anamnestic review and symbolic analysis, and the skill and effectiveness in the use of the fantasied and actual interpersonal relationships involved than on any fundamental differences in the essential dynamics of the respective procedures.

PHARMACOTHERAPY

Preliminary tests of the effects of various sedative and narcotic drugs on normal animals show that, as in humans, alcohol, bromides, barbiturates, opiates, and, less effectively, various meprobamates or benzodiazepines disorganize complex skills, such as intricate switch manipulations, while leaving simpler behavior patterns relatively intact.

Protective effects. The various tranquilizing drugs, especially alcohol, so lull the perceptive and mnemonic capacities of animals that they are, while thus inebriated, relatively immune to the neurotigenic effects of experiential traumata. Many human beings are correspondingly tempted to take a bracer before bearding the boss, flying a combat mission, getting married, or facing other presumed dangers, including those of imposed social conviviality and the mystique of religious rituals.

Addiction. About half the cats whose inhibitions, phobias, and other complex neurotic responses are disorganized by alcohol begin to prefer Alexander cocktails (milk with 10 per cent alcohol) to other fluids and persist in this choice until their underlying neuroses are relieved by one or more of the methods herein described. Without such relief, monkeys made neurotic and alcoholic in reaction to environmental uncertainties revert to ethylated drinking even after 6 months of enforced abstinence in a stress-free environment, paralleling similar tendencies to recidivism in human alcoholics (Orloff and Masserman, 1974).

CEREBRAL ELECTROSHOCK

When a 35-volt, 60-cycle alternating current (equivalent to that usually used in clinical electrotherapy) is passed through

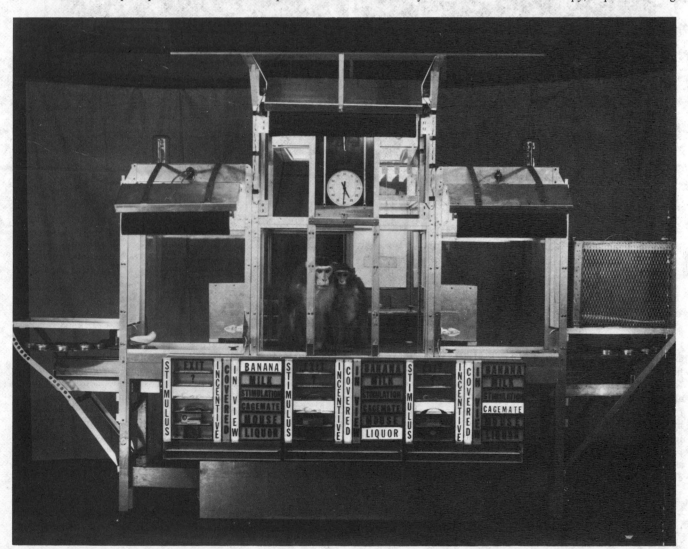

FIGURE 3. An apparatus for studying response and social behavioral phenomena and experimental neuroses in monkeys. (Courtesy of Jules H. Masserman, M.D.)

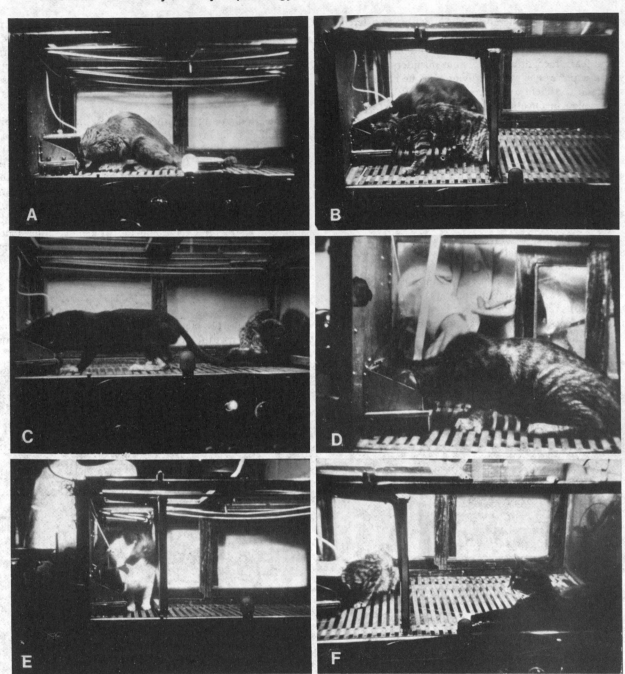

FIGURE 4. Experimental neuroses and therapy in cats. *A.* Control observations: A cat has been trained to pass a barrier at a signal light (center flash) and to open the food box for a pellet of food. The animal's behavior is goal directed and efficiently adaptive. *B.* Conflictful experience: At a later feeding signal, the cat is subjected to a mild air blast at the moment of food taking. The animal is shown recoiling from the traumatic situation. *C.* Neurotic behavior: After five such experiences at irregular intervals, the cat on the right refuses to approach the box and develops other neurotic aberrations of behavior. The animal, although starved for 48 hours, is here shown in a typical phobic response to a feeding signal crouched away from the food in cataleptic immobility against an impassable barrier. *D.* Transference retraining: After 4 months of neurosis, the cat is retrained by manual feeding and gentle guidance once again to feed from the box. At first, the animal does so only when being stroked by the experimenter; later, feeding responses may be reconstituted in response not only to the light but even to the air blast (nozzle shown in deep left corner). *E.* Therapeutic result: After 18 days of such retraining, the cat's neurotic reactions largely disappear, and it once again passes barriers for food at the light or air blast signal. *F.* Masochistic patterns: Another cat, trained to depress an electric switch for its feeding signals, was made experimentally neurotic by a mild electric shock at food taking and then retrained as above to take the food despite the trauma. The animal on the left once again manipulates the switch with spontaneous avidity to experience the shock with or without the food reward.

the brain of a cat or monkey for 2 seconds on 6 successive days, the resultant cortical diaschisis disorganizes recently acquired neurotic patterns more than previously established simpler ones, thus restoring approach and feeding responses. However, this procedure produces permanent impairment of more complex behavioral capabilities, even when the induced adaptational defects cannot be correlated with detectable pathological changes in the brain.

LOBOTOMY, TOPECTOMY, THALAMOTOMY

Circumscribed lesions in the thalamus, amygdalae, or cingulate gyri disintegrate experimentally induced neurotic patterns and overbalance the corresponding organic loss in adaptive skills by a sufficiently wide margin so that, from the standpoint of survival, the animal is manifestly benefited. However, the effects of apparently identical lesions in different animals vary widely not only as to species but also with each animal's previous experiences. For example, lesions in the dorsomedial nuclei of normal spider monkeys usually render them more otiose and gentle, whereas histologically identical lesions in neurotic conspecifics induce markedly increased irritability and aggressiveness.

Human Differences from Other Animals

These distinctions consist primarily of three illusory but indispensable and, therefore, ultimate Ur-beliefs on which humans base their highly intricate patterns of behavior. Briefly, these assumptions are as follows.

Physical invulnerability. Humans counter the threat of injury, disease, senescence, and death by many devices. All medicine is a quest for strength and longevity, and in other sciences and technologies humans seek to extend their power over the myriad chimeras that ever menace them—even though the robots they invent often turn into Frankenstein monsters.

Social security. Since humans live in an increasingly crowded and implicitly dangerous world, they mitigate social distrust by a wishful fantasy that their fellow beings are potential friends available for mutual service. Insofar as this hope has proved justified, they have indeed expanded their allegiances from the family through the clan, tribe, and nation to the hope of world brotherhood; insofar as this trust has failed, larger and larger alliances of frightened people have tried to exterminate each other—and may yet succeed.

Faith in a celestial order. Humans counter their anxieties not alone through their sciences and social systems but in various theologies, the essence of which is that humans are the sole concern of some omnipotent Deity Who devised all creation for humans' exclusive delectation and from Whom they can secure eternal bliss by the very techniques of appeal, bribery, or (as a last resort) obedience that once worked well on mortal parents. Michelangelo's greatest artistic subtlety may be that his Sistine Chapel painting can equally well be interpreted as Adam giving life to God.

In essence, then, everyone strives for physical survival, social belongingness, and cosmic identity, although each person's modes of seeking these elusive goals depend on his endowments, maturity, and unique experience in his milieu. Environmental frustrations, cultural conflicts, or poignant unpredictabilities in any of these three modes of Ur-adaptation—physical, interpersonal, and philosophical—correspondingly give rise to physiological dysfunctions, social maladaptations, and existential angst. These are variously tolerated or rejected by different cultures, which in their local idioms treat the aberrations of conduct as ranging from idiosyncratic (odd) through neurotic (troublesome) to psychotic (intolerable). Sufficiently alienated persons may then seek help from therapists in one or more of their triple Ur-roles as physicians, social ombudsmen, and philosophical mentors in restoring their health—a term significantly derived from the Anglo-Saxon root *hal* or *hol*, with the indissoluble connotations of bodily haleness, the special invitation "Hail, friend," and the metapsychological implication of wholesomeness or holiness.

Clinical Applications

INTERVIEW TECHNIQUES

The most productive exchanges of views occur when the patient, previously attracted by the reputation of the therapist, is further reassured by the therapist's warm reception and manifest interest and competence as physician, friend, and sage counselor. With rapport thus triply established, the initial survey should, by tactfully directed inquiry, elicit the patient's current disabilities, especially those requiring the most immediate care: toxic or organic dysfunctions; delusional, regressive, or aggressive tendencies; and threat of suicide. The past history can then survey the patient's genetic proclivities; the later vicissitudes of familial, sexual, and social experiences that induced various vulnerabilities; the special burdens that precipitated his present illness; and the assets and potentialities that can be constructively used in therapy.

DIAGNOSIS

Empathy. Any reflective survey of one's own life reveals the often irrational responses of suspiciousness, resentment, discouragement, and escapism to the stresses of past and current frustrations; the dependencies and poignant separations of childhood; the chaotic alienations, seekings, and rebellions of youth; the disjunctive economic, sexual, and cultural challenges of adulthood; and the wrenching disillusionments of middle and advancing age. Therapists can thereby empathize with their patients' more obsessive anxieties, phobic avoidances, and somatic dysfunctions when their individual modes of coping with physical, social, and metapsychological uncertainties fail. With regard to sensorial disturbances, many of us have had serious illnesses accompanied by toxic deliria and even hallucinatory episodes before a return to an intact sensorium. Also, when excessively pressed down (depressed) by physical, social, or philosophical Ur-disappointments, we may have reacted with loss of sleep, appetite, libido, and *elan vitale* or have become dolorous, bitter, demandingly preemptive, and intermittently preoccupied with melancholic thoughts of surcease or fantasies of posthumous revenge through suicide. Conversely, we may have tried to rationalize our failures by attributing our difficulties to the sinister plots of envious enemies nefariously organized to frustrate our genius—steps toward grandiosity and paranoia. And in our narcissistic reveries and dreams, we have, while immersed in alien affects, fancied ourselves independent of time, place, restraint, or logic and master of occult wisdoms and powers. Hence we have differed psychologically from the schizophrenic only in being less continuously divorced from a cultural consensus as to ambient reality. Finally, increasingly troublesome amnestic and communicative lacunae, gradually deteriorating skills, and affective labilities may have presaged cerebral syndromes or inevitable senility. The therapist's clinical appraisals should, therefore, be leavened by the empathetic "There but to a providentially milder degree, also go I."

Behavioral relativity. In line with the above, some clinical terminology should be carefully reconsidered in its philological and cultural context. Examples:

Factitious illness. By dictionary definition, is any mode of conduct to be characterized as artificial or unnatural?

Phobias. Does this category include so common an aversion as that to commercial flying or half a nation's McCarthyized fear of imminent engulfment by a Red tide?

Histrionic behavior disorder. Granted that hysterical patients no longer have wandering uteri, are they better understood as offering theatrical performances? Do therapists then function as dramatic critics?

Antisocial personality. Shall therapists resuscitate Prichard's notion of moral insanity?

Hallucinations. Should Bernadette have been hospitalized, burned, or beatified after she saw and spoke with the Virgin Mary and founded Lourdes?

Delusions and formal thought disturbances. In how inclusive a range? A nuclear scientist, who otherwise retained excellent social and occupational orientations, insisted that his luminescent healing powers had cured his wife of cancer; she agreed, and some of his professional friends confirmed that they had actually seen a therapeutic Krillian halo around him.

Paranoia. Freud—who also believed in thought transference, prescience, and various other occult phenomena—once wrote to Franz Alexander, in effect: "The paranoiacs are right, the rest of us are mercifully insensitive."

Grossly bizarre behavior. Does this apply to Holy Rollers somersaulting down a church aisle? Exclude naked Doukhobors in a protest march down a city street? Charismatic churchgoers speaking in tongues? A Hindu widow throwing herself on her husband's funeral pyre? A Kamikaze pilot joining his Emperor by way of a ship's funnel? Protestants and Catholics killing each other's wives and children in Ireland as do Moslems in Iran? How big, unsympathetic, and immediately influential need a jury of peers be to label such conduct grossly bizarre behavior?

Dynamic multivariate diagnoses. Philosophers from Empedocles through Auguste Comte to James Grier Miller have variously pointed out that sciences progress haltingly from occultism through taxonomic stereotypes to systems dynamics. Along these parameters psychiatry is gradually emerging from mysticism but is still partially immersed in a Linnean binomial nosology more appropriate to plant species than to the almost infinitely complex varieties of human behavior. To counter this cultural lag, therapists may consider eventually inevitable advances toward more dynamic diagnostic concepts along the following guidelines:

To modify terms (1) that have been retained merely because of outmoded traditions (example: conversion disorder, connoting either an unfortunate religious experience or Freud's early notions of displaced libidinal cathexes); (2) that have little import with regard to causes, current status, prognosis, or therapy (examples: depersonalization, psychasthenia); (3) that convey a false impression (borderline personality) that there really are topological or other borders between psychiatric diseases on which patients are precariously perched; (4) that still have pejorative connotations (dyshomophilia); (5) that are used merely to conform with their presumed usage abroad, under the false assumption that this uniformity leads to valid statistics of worldwide incidence (examples: recurrent depressions, atypical psychosis); or (6) that are semantically confusing (disorganized schizophrenia) or have serious forensic consequences (paranoia).

To develop a diagnostic system (Greek *diagnosis*, thorough knowledge, as opposed to mere classification) with the following polyvectorial features: (1) that it explore the etiological interplay of physiological, toxic, pathological, genetic, experiential, and sociocultural influences in the patient's past and current behavior; (2) that this review include an anamnestic assay not only of the patient's vulnerabilities but also of his adaptive capacities (ego strengths); (3) that the symptomatic

survey be inclusive, since every patient manifests behavior patterns that had previously been ascribed to ostensibly distinct categories ranging from neurotic through pharmacothymic and sociopathic to variably psychotic; (4) that the intensity, duration, and variability of these patterns be correlated with intercurrent stresses; (5) that there be an estimate as to the consequent extent of familial, occupational, and social disabilities; (6) that the above data indicate optimal modes of physical, environmental, dyadic, group, and community therapy and (7) an initial prognosis for individual and social recovery. It may be noted that child psychiatrists even now insist on essentially multidimensional approaches.

Admittedly, such a polyvectorial survey necessitates a diagnostic paragraph instead of an inadequate binome, requires more extended progress and discharge notes, and renders more rapidly obsolescent some current filing systems. However, the survey would obviate many of the pejorative terms or devious euphemisms now used in insurance and legal reports, would still be well within the differential capacities of relatively simple computers, and would extend psychiatric nosology toward the clinical validity demanded in other medical specialties. In those disciplines, no two-word diagnosis is regarded as prognostically or therapeutically significant unless it also indicates the nature and the extent of organic complications, forms of disability, prognostic and therapeutic implications, and other relevant considerations.

PROGNOSIS

Prognosis can be inferred from an evaluation of the origin, tenacity, and influenceability of all the patient's behavior tendencies and the probability of modifying or channeling them into new and more favorable patterns of adaptation by therapeutic means.

PSYCHIATRIC THERAPIES

To clarify the various claims and practices of the current welter of psychiatric cults, biodynamic therapists propose that insofar as any method alleviates the pathogenic, physical, social, and metaphysical Ur-anxieties of any patient, it is correspondingly effective; insofar as it does not, it fails. In pursuit of a desirable integration, one may reasonably hold that all modes of therapy (Greek *therapeia*, service) with or without medical components and whether brief (Wolberg, 1967) or deep (Waelder, 1960) and whether through suggestion (Bernheim, 1897), confrontation (Garner, 1970), or persuasion (Dubois, 1913) influence the psychoimagination (Schorr, 1972) or phenomenological orientation (Husserl, 1931) and psychosomatic functions (Mandell and Karno, 1972) of troubled patients or clients (Rogers, 1951) and thus favorably recondition (Skinner, 1971) their physical competence and environmental control. The concomitant behavioral learning (Bachrach, 1963; Hunt, 1971), corrective emotional experiences (Alexander, 1952), and experiential closures (Perls, 1966) then enhance the patient's group sensitivities (Goldberg, 1971), his social communication (Ruesch and Bateson, 1951), interpersonal transactions (Berne, 1964; Sullivan, 1964), and intersystemic adaptations (von Bertalanffy, 1962), thereby improving his familial (Ackerman, 1959; Laqueur, 1968), group (Bion, 1952), and community (Caplan, 1961; Greenblatt, 1961) adaptations and existential composure (Binswanger, 1963). Even if more eponymic catch phrases were included, the same fundamental parameters of all therapies would remain: to use every ethical physical, social, and psychological modality (1) to relieve the patient's immediate somatic, social, or psychological distress; (2) to help the patient realize that his former trepidations, escapisms, aggressions, and other deviant patterns are no longer necessary; (3) to guide the patient by every form of influence, including personal example, into new modes of conduct that he will ultimately adopt as more satisfactory and profitable; and (4) to assist him in evolving a philosophy of life in which he can find comfort, serenity, and creativity.

To accomplish these objectives, the therapist will find the following procedures expeditious:

Assurance of complete confidentiality, with, however, an explicit understanding that, if ever there are adequate reasons to believe that the patient may harm himself or others, the therapist will take action in the patient's best interests.

A flexible schedule of therapeutic sessions that realistically fit the patient's needs and resources.

Judicious combinations of all forms of therapy, including specific external guidance and ancillary use of drugs and physical modalities when indicated.

A pragmatic recognition that—whatever his convenient rationalizations as to his uncontrollable instincts, unconscious complexes, conditioning, or habits—the patient will be held responsible for his conduct by society and in one way or another be punished or rewarded. Ergo, therapy will deal not with polemics as to whether or not the patient *wants* to behave as he does but with *why*, and with the probability that improved patterns will be better rewarded by his associates and, therefore, ultimately more profitable to all concerned.

Prime concentration on the patient's physical, social, and attitudinal problems in the here and now with anamnestic tracings only sufficient to clarify retained but outmoded and inept childhood or adolescent behavior in and out of the therapeutic situation.

Joint sessions with family, friends, employers, and, when indicated, religious counselors to help clarify and improve the patient's interactions.

Emphasis on salutary and realistic behavioral changes as the only valid indication of progress, all other forms of "insight" being merely illusory verbal cliches temporarily shared by patient and therapist.

Open-end suspensions of treatment at optimum levels, the patient remaining, as elsewhere in medicine, free to communicate or to resume therapy should the need arise.

For mnemonic convenience, the essential parameters of psychiatric therapy may be subsumed alliteratively as reputation, rapport, relief, review, reorientation, rehabilitation, resocialization, and recycling.

The following highly condensed case vignettes illustrate various therapeutic techniques.

Rapport, reorientation, and resocialization. A 45-year-old socially prominent matron was referred for episodes of severe anxiety and depression, excessive intake of alcohol and tranquilizers, and intimations of suicide. Apparently conforming to her experiences with several previous therapists, she immediately launched into a melange of devastating criticisms of her parents, siblings, friends, and former therapists; fanciful childhood recollections; dream interpretations; and other such pseudoanalytic persiflage. To avoid encouraging these evasive tactics, the therapist made almost no comments until her fourth session. On that occasion she came in limping and, on inquiry, replied that she had stepped on the prongs of a rake in her rose garden that morning. She then again plunged into her gratuitous interpretations to the effect that this obviously signified her youthful relations with a brother who had been considered a sexually promiscuous rake; that, when the rake

handle rose up, it symbolized his penile erection; that the bleeding from her foot signified both her defloration and an incestuous abortion; and so on with other fantastic free associations. When this subtly derisive wordplay was finally interrupted by the therapist's request that he examine her foot, she professed to be shocked by his manifest voyeurism and further considered herself erotically impregnated when he tested and then administered tetanus toxoid gluteally to counter the dangers presented by an obviously dirt-contaminated wound. Nevertheless, this incident changed the whole course of her treatment. Reassured by the evidence of the therapist's concern and medical competence, she forsook the couch in subsequent sessions and simply and poignantly confided her many concerns as to her "change of life," her fading beauty, her faithless husband, her ungrateful offspring, and the social ostracism to which she had increasingly been subjected because of her defiantly flagrant sexual misadventures.

Therapy was correspondingly specific and direct: a period of disulfiram-reinforced abstinence from alcohol and a diminishing intake of drugs; a course at a beauty salon to restore much of her former attractiveness, which led to greater sexual satisfactions in and, more discreetly, outside her marriage; reutilization of her considerable artistic talents, resulting in a successful display of her sculptures in a prestigious gallery; and active participation in a successful political campaign, which helped restore her to a position of social prestige and influence. Within 3 months the patient was again an emotionally stable, creative, and fairly happy woman and maintained this status during 2 years of follow-up.

Familial and interpersonal modalities. A young wife was referred by her internist for compulsive mouth washing, sexual frigidity, and episodes of nausea and vomiting, which were especially severe on weekends. After rapport was established, she hesitantly related her symptoms to fellatio with her husband, a revulsion symbolically exacerbated on Sundays, when, as a devout Catholic, she swallowed the sacerdotal wafer symbolizing Christ's body, which she fantasied as "also His penis." The first difficulty was partially resolved by explanations as to the normal range of erotic techniques; the second conflict was resolved with the aid of an empathetic and benevolent priest, who assured her that the cloths that traditionally cover Christ's pubic region in religious paintings are there to conceal from profane eyes his ethereal and angelic asexuality. With further marital counseling as to related conflicts over contraception, in-law intrusions, and other familial tensions, the patient's obsessions and compulsions abated, and the placebos that had been substituted for her previous medications were discontinued.

Rehabilitation and resocialization in later age. A wealthy man still vigorous at age 67 had become a disruptive and obnoxious tyrant to his family after his retirement as chief executive of a tobacco firm 2 years previously. During his first interview he berated all concerned, including the therapist, because he had been sold stale cigars by a discourteous clerk at a tobacco stand in the therapist's office building. In response to a pointed query as to how such abuses could be prevented, he resolved that he would buy a chain of downtown tobacco stands and reorganize them for better service to humanity. He diverted his energies to this reapplication of his financial and managerial skills and, with some further politely indirect guidance, soon reverted to his former self as a busily officious, but relatively content and certainly more likeable business executive, friend, and capo de familia.

Conclusion

The ultimate Ur-anxieties or uncertainties of human beings are three: their abhorrence of physical injury and death, their doubts as to the reliability of their alliances, and their utter rejection of the concept that perhaps they are, after all, little more than a cosmic triviality. These triple trepidations also motivate their principal modes of presumed mastery. Their compensatory maneuvers are three: first, their attempts to subjugate their material milieu through various sciences and technologies, including medicine [Ur-defense 1]; next, their efforts to guarantee their social relationships by familial, economical, and political compacts [Ur-hope 2]; and, finally, their endeavors to encompass the entire cosmos in various philosophical and religious systems [Ur-faith 3]. Unfortunately, their strivings in all these modalities often fail, whereupon they become impatient patients and call upon psychiatrists as physicians, counselors, and ministers to serve them in corresponding modes of therapy. These modes are, predictably, tripartite: first, the restoration of their bodily strengths and skills; second, the recultivation of human companionships; and third, the reinvocation of their transcendent beliefs and protective idols. Can any mortal therapist do more?

Suggested Cross References

See Section 4.6 for a discussion of ethology, Section 6.3 on experimental disorders, and Chapter 21 on neurotic disorders.

REFERENCES

Ackerman, N. W. The psychoanalytic approach to the family. In *Science and Psychoanalysis,* J. H. Masserman, editor, vol. 2, p. 90. Grune & Stratton, New York, 1959.
Alexander, F., and Ross, H., editors. *Dynamic Psychiatry.* University of Chicago Press, Chicago, 1952.
Bachrach, A. J. Operant conditioning and behavior. In *The Psychological Basis of Medical Practice,* H. Lief and N. R. Lief, editors, p. 412. Harper & Row, New York, 1963.
* Berne, E. *The Games People Play.* Grove Press, New York 1964.
Bernheim, H. *Suggestive Therapeutics.* G. P. Putnam's Sons, New York, 1897.
Binswanger, L. *Being-in-the-World.* Basic Books, New York, 1963.
Bion, W. R. Group dynamics. Int. J. Psychoanal., *33:* 235, 1952.
* Caplan, G. *An Approach to Community Mental Health.* Grune & Stratton, New York, 1961.
Dean, S. *Psychiatry and Mysticism.* Prentice-Hall, Englewood Cliffs, N. J., 1975.
* Dubois, P. *The Psychological Origin of Mental Disorders.* Funk and Wagnalls, New York, 1913.
Freud, *Outline of Psychoanalysis.* W. W. Norton, New York, 1949.
Garner, H. H. *Psychotherapy.* Warren H. Green, St. Louis, 1970.
Goldberg, C. *Group Therapy.* Science House, New York, 1971.
Greenblatt, M. Formal and informal groups in a therapeutic community. Int. J. Group Psychother., *11:* 398, 1961.
Halleck, S. *Treatment of Emotional Disorders.* Jason Aronson, New York, 1978.
Hunt, H. Behavioral considerations in psychiatric treatment. In *Science and Psychoanalysis,* J. H. Masserman, editor, vol. 18, p. 36. Grune & Stratton, New York, 1971.
Husserl, E. *Ideas.* Macmillan, New York, 1931.
Laqueur, H. P. General systems theory and multiple family therapy. In *Current Psychiatric Therapies,* J. H. Masserman, editor, vol. 8, p. 143. Grune & Stratton, New York, 1968.
Lester, P. *Alternative Modes of Communication in Therapy.* Charles C Thomas, Springfield, Ill., 1942.
Mandell, A. J., and Karno, M. Isolation and neurochemical sensitization. In *Science and Psychoanalysis,* J. H. Masserman, editor, vol. 21, p. 18. Grune & Stratton, New York, 1972.
Masserman, J. H. *Practice of Dynamic Psychiatry.* W. B. Saunders, Philadelphia, 1955.
* Masserman, J. H. *Principles of Dynamic Psychiatry.* W. B. Saunders, Philadelphia, 1961.
Masserman, J. H. *Behavior and Neurosis.* Hafner Press, New York, 1963.
Masserman, J. H. *Biodynamic Roots of Human Behavior.* Charles C Thomas, Springfield, Ill., 1968.
Masserman, J. H. *A Psychiatric Odyssey.* Science House, New York, 1971.
Masserman, J. H. *Theories and Therapies of Dynamic Psychiatry.* Science House, New York, 1973.
Masserman, J. H. *Current Psychiatric Therapies.* Grune & Stratton, New York, 1980.
Maxmen, J. S. *The Post-physician Era.* John Wiley & Sons, New York, 1977.
Miller, J. G. *Living Systems.* McGraw-Hill, New York, 1978.
Orloff, E. R., and Masserman, J. H. Effect of uncertainty and ethanol self-selection. Biol. Psychiatry, *10:* 245, 1974.
* Perls, F. S. *Gestalt Therapy and Human Potentialities.* Charles C Thomas, Springfield, Ill., 1966.
Rogers, C. R. *Client-Oriented Therapy.* Houghton Mifflin, Boston, 1951.
Ruesch, J., and Bateson, G. *Communication, the Social Matrix of Psychiatry.* W. W. Norton, New York, 1951.

Schorr, J. *Psychoimagination Therapy.* Intercontinental Medical Books, New York, 1972.
Skinner, B. F. *Beyond Freedom and Dignity.* Alfred A. Knopf, New York, 1971.
Strupp, H. *Psychotherapy: Clinical, Research and Theoretical Issues.* Jason Aronson, New York, 1973.
* Sullivan, H. S. *Fusion of Psychiatry and Social Science.* W. W. Norton, New York, 1964.
von Bertalanffy, L. General systems theory. J. Gen. Systems, *7:* 1, 1962.
Waelder, R. *Basic Theory of Psychoanalysis.* International Universities Press, New York, 1960.
Wolberg, L. R. *The Techniques of Psychotherapy,* ed. 2. Grune & Stratton, New York, 1967.
Wolpe, J. *Psychotherapy by Reciprocal Inhibition.* Stanford University Press, Palo Alto, Calif., 1958.

9.6 Eric Berne

JOHN M. DUSAY, M.D.

Introduction

Eric Berne, the founder of transactional analysis, was, like many psychiatric innovators, trained in classical psychoanalysis and was particularly influenced by Paul Federn, a member of the early Vienna Psychoanalytic Society. His amiable parting from the psychoanalytic school occurred when he set aside the Freudian treatment modality in favor of more rapidly effective techniques. Transactional analysis was formally developed by Berne from the mid-1950's until his death in 1970, and it was originally used as a specific adjunct for application in group psychotherapy.

The history of the transactional analysis movement during that 15-year period is actually a history of the theory and techniques devised by Berne. Ego states, transactions, and games—basic components of Berne's system—facilitated a mutual understanding between the patient and the therapist that proved successful for the patient's rapid attainment of social control and treatment goals. Another component, which Berne called script analysis, came to the forefront between 1965 and 1970. It soon became apparent to members of the San Francisco Transactional Analysis seminars that a unique and total theory of personality was evolving. Berne posited to his followers a stimulating challenge as to whether or not the dynamic unconscious exists and is related to script theory. Berne's (1972) last book, *What Do You Say after You Say Hello?*, is his most complete elaboration on script theory and his final statement about why people do what they do to each other.

During his career, Berne was influenced by the innovative California group therapy milieu, including encounter, marathon, and, most important, the gestalt techniques of Frederick Perls. Those systems, which emphasized a here-and-now approach, were partially incorporated into transactional analysis because they aided perception and identification of ego states and game patterns. Indeed, many enthusiasts of various new psychologies have turned to transactional analysis because of its cohesive personality theory.

Contemporary social movements also influenced Berne. At his weekly seminars, Berne encouraged representatives of various struggling groups to present their problems, and he worked at developing theoretical and practical guidelines for resolution. He devoted discussions to school riots, the Haight-Ashbury drug culture, and the women's liberation movement. Those models paved the way for an exploration of the dynamics of oppressive systems.

The unique theoretical and practical characteristics of Berne's transactional analysis can be best comprehended in terms of the specific aspects of the system: intuition, ego states, transactions, games, strokes, scripts, and contracts.

Intuition

Berne studied the intuitive process throughout his career and assigned it primary importance in his system. As an army psychiatrist during World War II, he had to conduct psychiatric evaluations on more than 40,000 departing soldiers. Ninety seconds were allotted to perform each appraisal. In a playful manner, he experimented by trying to guess the prewar civilian occupations of the soldiers he examined. Although the men had been in the service for several years in various duties, Berne found that, with remarkable accuracy and consistency, he could guess which had been farmers and which had been mechanics. He was not as successful with other occupations. Expanding his curiosity, Berne devised objective, rational, and additive types of criteria that he applied to each soldier he examined. To his surprise, he found that his accuracy decreased sharply when he applied the scientific criteria. Later, Berne became intrigued by a carnival weight guesser, who was intuitively correct within 5 pounds. However, he missed by large margins when he attempted to become logical and rational about why he chose a particular weight. Berne formally studied intuition and published six important articles on the subject that contributed to the evolution of transactional analysis (Dusay, 1970).

DEFINITION

Berne (1949) initially defined intuition as:

Knowledge based upon experience and acquired through sensory contact with the subject without the "intuitor" being able to formulate for himself or others exactly how he came to his conclusions.

That knowledge was on a preverbal level. He also noted that intuition was facilitated by a state of awareness that required intense concentration directed toward the object of intuition. He distinguished intuition from the passive alert state used by many psychotherapists. He discovered that the intuitive process could be improved on with practice and that accuracy increased with experience. Fatigue tended to decrease intuitive powers; so did being put on the spot. He surmised that the intellect alone was not the dominant force in correct guessing or understanding life. Berne (1949) challenged the notion that logical and verbal abilities constituted knowledge:

This belief, still common since Freud, is the result of what happens to be an overdevelopment of reality testing which tempts some who are too interested in psychology to think too far from nature and the world of natural happenings. Dogs know things, and so do bees, and even the [protozoan] stentor. True knowledge is to know how to act rather than to know words.

NONVOCAL INDICATORS

Berne became interested in nonvocal indicators, such as facial expressions, voluntary and involuntary movements, tics, and gazes, and he paid particular attention to people's re-

sponses to different types of stimuli. Berne attempted to put those functions together into a meaningful mosaic, but categorical methods led to an additive process that was laborious and slow. He likened the process to the conscientiousness of new therapists as they look for the textbook signs and symptoms. Berne was impressed by the ability of small children, even at a preverbal age, to distinguish between friendly and unfriendly people. He also observed that people diagnosed as schizophrenic seemed to have the facility from time to time. He further observed the ability in artists, poets, actors, and other creative persons who occasionally operate on nonverbal levels.

PRIMAL IMAGES

In 1955, Berne reported the case of Belle, a 40-year-old housewife who behaved in two distinct ways toward the men in her life:

Belle would subtly mock and jeer at men whom she considered weak and tease and torment those men whom she felt were strong. She was continually intrigued and confused as to whether the therapist was weak or strong, and she confessed her fantasy that she could see the conformation of his genitals and then attempted to determine if his penis was flabby or erect. She remembered doing the identical thing with her father when she played on his lap as a child. She also recalled a conversation with a known exhibitionist, and how she experienced a jeering feeling of laughter when she fantasized him being nude with a flaccid penis. Her husband, however, reminded her of a strong man, implacable as stone, whose tremendous erections frightened her. She would taunt, tease, and lead him on sexually until he could not contain his passion, and then abruptly freeze him out with a ruthless frigidity. She became frightened and nauseated when her husband had an erection and could not bear to fantasize about it. She disclosed that she became nauseated and indisposed when her husband told her a graphic joke about an erection. "I could see that fellow's penis right in front of me, hairy, ugly, raw," she said. Belle could intellectually discuss the vagina but could not bear thinking of it as actually pictured, "a raw red slimy gash." The image terrified her, and she desperately avoided it. She said, "My images are too clear. It frightens me. I just can't bear to think of it." Smells also played a significant part in this type of imagery with her.

Berne called the type of images Belle experienced "primal images." They gave rise to primal judgments, which Belle used about men in her life: "This man is flaccid," and "That man is virile." Berne found that primal judgments occur in everyday life, and he researched them in the clinical setting. Statements such as, "She's a sucker," "He's a big asshole," or "He's a prick" are common phrases in day-to-day parlance. Other expressions—such as "gutless," "stinker," "jerk," "pushover," "old fart," "cock teaser," and "bleeding heart"— represent judgments that emanate from primal images. Berne found that the primal judgments were zonal and connected to oral, gastrointestinal, anal, genital, and excretory functions. People alter their actions toward other people because of these primal judgments; for example, some people avoid stinkers and gravitate toward heart throbs. Berne (1955) commented that "this is the stuff that long-term relations are made of," and noted that the bleeding heart and the jerk were prone to find each other.

Berne distinguished between primal images and ordinary memory images. Primal images have a pseudoperceptual quality and a superior clearness, richness, and accuracy of detail, with brilliant coloration. He compared his observations of primal images to similar phenomena described by others, mentioning Freud's observation of the "plastic image" in the case of Emmy von N. He noted that primal images were similar to Jaensch's description of eidetic imagery. Jung's primordial images came close to Berne's primal image, but Berne felt that Paul Federn's viewpoint was closer. Federn maintained that hypnosis, dreams, and psychosis proved that the ego configurations of early levels remained in potential existence in one's personality throughout life.

Berne made a monumental discovery when he recognized that the triad of primal images, primal judgments, and social response could be dealt with in the conscious and immediate sphere of the treatment setting when used in conjunction with his newly developed concept of ego states.

Ego States

DEFINITION

An ego state is a cohesive system of feelings and thoughts, with a related set of behavior patterns. Each person has a repertoire of ego states that can be broken down into (1) the Child ego state, which represents archaic elements that become fixed in early childhood but remain active throughout life; (2) the Adult, which is computer-like and is autonomously directed toward objective appraisals of reality; and (3) the Parent, which is derived from the person's actual parental figures (Berne, 1957).

An 8-year-old boy vacationing at a ranch in his cowboy suit helped the hired men unsaddle a horse. When they were finished, the hired man said, "Thanks, cowpoke." The assistant replied, "I'm not really a cowpoke; I'm just a little boy." The patient went on to remark, "That's just the way I feel. Sometimes I feel that I'm not really a lawyer. I'm just a little boy."

This story illustrates the separation of two ways of feeling, thinking, and behaving in this particular patient; everything he said was heard by two different people: one an adult lawyer and the other an inner little boy. This particular patient was in treatment for a compulsive gambling habit. Sometimes he used a rational, logical gambling system, which was occasionally successful, but more often he governed his behavior with superstitious and little-boy ways of explaining his losses. If he took $100 to the gambling table and came home with $50, he would reason to himself, "I made $50 and don't need to be upset." It became apparent that there were two types of arithmetic he employed. He would also go to a hotel room and take a shower after a winning streak and then meticulously avoid stepping on a sidewalk crack as he progressed from one casino to the next.

In the preceding case, both of the systems were conscious, deliberate, visible, and part of the patient's ego system. Berne labeled one of those classes of behavior the Child and observed that it was based on primal images and primal judgments and was, indeed, an active determinant in the person's behavior. The other he called the Adult, which encompassed thinking and behaving based on logical, rational, and computer-like data. Later Berne designated the Parent ego state as that part of a person that deals with morals, values, and prejudices derived from the actual parental figures. He portrayed the differences between the three ego states structurally by drawing three circles (see Figure 1*A*) and differentiated in his writings between the Child, Adult, and Parent ego states and actual children, adults, and parents by using capital letters for the ego states. The creation of the egogram (Dusay, 1972) provided a method for determining the intensity of individual ego states.

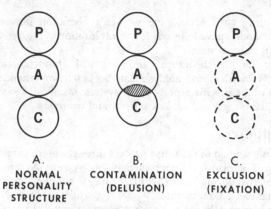

A.
NORMAL
PERSONALITY
STRUCTURE

B.
CONTAMINATION
(DELUSION)

C.
EXCLUSION
(FIXATION)

FIGURE 1. Ego states structures.

Thus, the complete theory of ego states evolved, integrating the concepts of structure and measurement.

EGO STATES AS CONSCIOUS FUNCTIONS

Berne parted ways with classical psychoanalysis because he found that it was not necessary to use the hypothetical concepts of the dynamic unconscious to explain his newly developing ideas. Berne ascertained that the Child ego state was not a direct manifestation of the id, defined by Freud as "a chaos, a cauldron of seething excitement," which lacked organization and direct relations with the external world. To Berne, the Child, quite to the contrary, was a dynamic and functioning part of the personality; it was a conscious, readily observable phenomenon, and it was involved as a determinant in behavior. Although the Parent, Adult, and Child ego states are observable phenomena, the id, superego, and ego remain hypothetical constructs. The part of the patient that is observable in the here-and-now situation is dynamic in that it influences behavior and governs relationships between people. It allows for the prediction of future events and inferences about past history.

EGO STATES AND INTUITION

Berne (1962) emphasized that the intuitive faculty, which is archaic and lodged in the Child, can be cultivated by the successful therapist. He agreed with Ferenczi, who remarked that education was not only the acquisition of new facilities but also the forgetting of others. Berne became critical when people were taught to think profusely at the expense of seeing. A potent therapist resurrects the dormant aspect of the imaginative child. Too much Adult, with its rational thinking, decreases the efficiency of the Child. The same holds true for ethical, moral, or prejudicial Parental thinking. A see-no-evil type of value, dwelling in the therapist's Parent, can hinder his intuitive powers.

Dynamically, intuition works best when the Child predominates and when the Adult and the Parent are decathected and decommissioned. A person uses intuitive faculties as he chooses his playmates at any age in life, and it becomes the most valuable tool of the therapist when diagnosing and treating patients. To Berne, creativity was the Child knowing and the Adult confirming.

EGO STATE PATHOLOGY

Certain types of pathology can be understood by astute attention to the structure of ego states (see Figure 1*B*). The structure of delusional thinking is exemplified by the break-down of the functional barriers between the Adult and the Child, in which fantasy and archaic imagery in the Child become mixed with the Adult. For example, "The programs on television have been created especially for me," is a Child statement of fantasy and archaic ideas of importance, contaminating the actual Adult observation of specific television programs. Another major type of ego state pathology is exclusion, which occurs when a person cannot freely cathect the different ego states (see Figure 1C). The fixed Parent of a prejudiced country preacher, who finds evil and sin under every bush, is an example. Berne described a case of an accountant who functioned with perfect Adult precision and computer-like accuracy but, because his Child and his Parent were excluded, had few ethical or moral concepts and, of course, little fun in his life.

Transactions

Berne defined a transaction as a stimulus from an ego state of one person and the corresponding response from an ego state of another person. He was cognizant of communication theories during the 1950's and was impressed by the cyberneticists, including Ashby, Weiner, and Brillouin. He became intrigued with the distinction between two different types of communication—the manifest and the latent. He gave as an example a radio: Manifest communication was the actual, specific, message-oriented sound being emitted. Latent communication was the distraction from the manifest, such as static and noise, which revealed the inner, mechanical functioning of the radio.

Applying those ideas to human interaction, Berne formulated a specific and concise definition of communication and developed three rules (see Figure 2). Figure 2A represents a complementary transaction in which the vectors (the *arrows* representing the stimulus and the response) are parallel. The first rule of communication is: "Whenever the vectors are parallel, communication can proceed indefinitely." In Figure 2B, the vectors form a crossed transaction, and the corresponding rule is: "Whenever the vectors cross, communication on that subject ceases immediately." In that example, a secretary and a boss are no longer discussing time but will likely have an argument about their relationship with each other and possible continued employment of the secretary. Figure 2C illustrates the complex use of both the manifest transaction, which Berne

called the social level, and the latent transaction, which he called the psychological level. That led to a third rule of communication: "Behavior cannot be predicted by the social level alone." Attention to the psychological message is the key to predicting behavior, and understanding of the dual transaction, the ulterior, is necessary for the understanding of games.

Games

Certain types of human behavior—predictable, stereotyped, usually destructive, and motivated by hidden desires—were clarified by Berne in his defiinition of psychological games. That term captured the public imagination and has become increasingly popular in everyday usage since the publication of Berne's (1964) best seller, *Games People Play*. A simple game played in a therapy group, which historically was the first type of game to be delineated, follows:

Patient S: "I wish we could fix the leak in our roof."
Respondent One: "Why don't you ask your husband to do it?"
Patient S: "That's a good idea, but he has to work this weekend."
Respondent Two: "Why don't you do it yourself."
Patient S: "I would but I don't have any tools."
Respondent Three: "Why don't you get some tools?"
Patient S: "Yes, but we overspent our budget this month."
Respondent Four: "Why don't you . . . ?"
Patient S: "Yes, but . . . ."

It becomes obvious that it is not a straightforward series of complementary transactions (see Figure 3). On the social level,

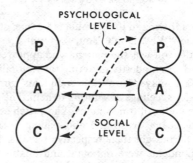

A GAME DIAGRAM

FIGURE 3. Typical game.

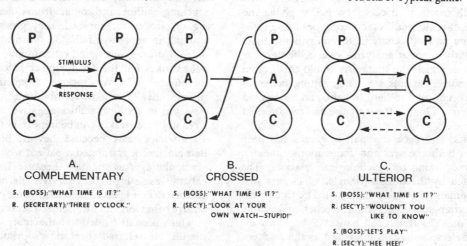

A.
COMPLEMENTARY

S. (BOSS):"WHAT TIME IS IT?"
R. (SECRETARY):"THREE O'CLOCK."

B.
CROSSED

S. (BOSS):"WHAT TIME IS IT?"
R. (SEC'Y):"LOOK AT YOUR
OWN WATCH—STUPID!"

C.
ULTERIOR

S. (BOSS):"WHAT TIME IS IT?"
R. (SEC'Y):"WOULDN'T YOU
LIKE TO KNOW"

S. (BOSS):"LET'S PLAY"
R. (SEC'Y):"HEE HEE!"

FIGURE 2. Transactions.

patient S provides an Adult stimulus by making a statement related to solving a specific problem, and the respondents reciprocated with straightforward advice. The dynamics are not expressed in the Adult-to-Adult social level, and the ulterior, psychological, broken-line level reveals that a Child-Parent transaction is occurring. The Child was saying to the helpful Parent, "Try to suggest some sort of change for me that I haven't already thought of myself (hee-hee)." The respondents rose to the challenge, tried to help, and ended up being frustrated. Berne looked for the psychological level in his treatment groups by observing the ego states in action. In the above example, the frustrated looks on the faces of the respondents and the triumphant, coy smile on the part of the patient tipped off the hidden meaning. Secretly, patient S proved, as she had so many times in the past, that others in her life were weak and ineffectual in suggesting things to her, and the frustrated respondents felt that she was ungrateful.

That conclusion or payoff, which is revealed in the game analysis, is related to each player's view of himself and others. People learn those game patterns in childhood and play them throughout their lives, changing such externals as place, persons, and time but not the principles of the game. People are inclined to have a small repertoire of games and to base their social relationships on finding suitable people to share them. The preceding game is colloquially entitled, "Why Don't You, Yes But ... " from the standpoint of the initiator, and those who enjoy playing the corresponding "I'm Only Trying to Help" are suitable partners.

Berne devised a game formula to which all games conform:

Con + Gimmick = Response → Switch → Payoff

All behavior adhering to the formula is a game; other behavior is not. In the "Why Don't You, Yes But ... " game just mentioned, the con was the patient who appeared needy, had potential, and was modestly flattering the restorative powers in the others. That played into the respondents' gimmick, which was their zealous feelings of wanting to help. The response was a predictable volley of transactions. The switch occurred when the rescuers became frustrated and patient S smiled triumphantly; all parties got their respective payoffs. Patient S felt that the respondents were impotent and unable to help. The respondents were irritated and felt that patient S was ungrateful. That particular game, which is common in consulting rooms, has resulted in "triumphant" patients being transferred from therapist to therapist, with each new helper giving the patient some vague, chronic, undifferentiated type of diagnosis, which lengthens the patient's chart in the outpatient clinic. Berne was particularly adept at analyzing case conferences at certain institutions in which the therapists would collaborate in justifying why some patients were not getting better in treatment after they had tried so hard to help, and he devoted one publication (Berne, 1963) to the structure and dynamics of organizations.

The switch, a vital and necessary part of games, has been well represented in both classical and contemporary theater, and it recurs in the drama of psychological relations. The switch is represented by the drama triangle, which was first delineated by Karpman (1968) (see Figure 4). The three positions of the drama triangle are persecutor, rescuer, and victim. In "Why Don't You, Yes But ... ," patient S began in the victim role, and the respondents commenced as the rescuers. After the switch, the rescuers went to the victim role with heightened frustration, and the patient, an ex-victim, delighted

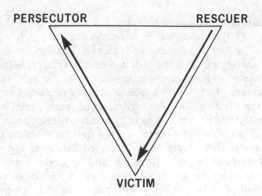

DRAMA TRIANGLE
(A Switch)
FIGURE 4. Drama triangle.

in watching the stymied victims as she moved to the persecutor role.

Games, therefore, contain ulterior transactions, conform to the game formula, and contain a dramatic switch that leads to the payoff. Game phenomena have predictive value for both the therapist and the patient, foretelling the outcome of treatment and perhaps the life course. The therapist proposes antithetical moves to block the games, disrupting the patient's pathological pattern. Awareness of those patterns allows a patient the opportunity to redecide whether to continue the game or to explore alternative growth possibilities and options. Berne distinguished between playing games and performing simple maneuvers. For example, there is no game if a patient asks for reassurance, gets it, says "thank you," and is told "You're welcome." People choose particular game patterns that structure their time and lives through early life programing. The payoff and the decisions that people make about themselves and others are formally considered in script analysis.

Strokes

Berne (1963) used the expression "strokes" to describe what he considered the basic motivating factor of human behavior. He was influenced by René Spitz's (1945) article, which researched the basic factors crucial to infant survival. Spitz found that the mortality rate decreased as infants received more touching, smiling, and contact from others. Infants need touching or strokes for survival; they gradually learn to obtain stroking in more symbolic or substitute ways as they grow older. Words, glances, and other human recognitions are symbolic strokes, and the developing child learns ways to maximize the number of strokes received from his mother, father, and siblings. Ideally, strokes are obtained in a loving and positive way, but in certain families negative strokes are exchanged. Even negative strokes can be important for survival, at least on a temporary basis, because they are better than none at all. Berne once congratulated a patient who was being accused of manipulating for attention because he recognized that the patient was struggling for survival. Berne (1964) observed that a stroke deficit leads to increased game playing and sometimes bizarre behavior, and he discussed sensory deprivation research in which persons tended to hallucinate in situations of limited stimuli. He referred to Harlow's primate research in which young animals raised without a mother developed unusual behavior patterns.

Scripts

Attention to scripts completes the theory of personality originated by Berne. One's success or psychopathology is determined by the degree of conformity to important early transactions. They are symbolized by the script matrix (see Figure 5), which was first constructed by Steiner (1971), a pioneering script theorist. A typical example of a script formation is illustrated by the case of Dabney, who was known as a momma's boy:

Dabney was 30 years old and had not left home in spite of several abortive attempts. Yet that failure appeared to conflict with the values given to him by his parents, as shown (see Figure 5*I*) in the matrix by messages given to him by his mother: "Go to college. Be successful. Make money. Get married." With those values clearly fixed in his head, Dabney started off to college, and, as he was leaving, his weeping mother said to him, "Everything will be OK . . . I hope (gulp)." Her facial expressions, inflections, and vocabulary conveyed the covert message to her son: "You won't make it." Similar transactions had occurred throughout his life. He had a school phobia in the first grade, could not stay a full week at Boy Scout camp, and was unable to marry his girlfriend. The broken lines on the script matrix (see Figure 5*II*) symbolize that message from Dabney's mother and expose the hidden nature of that transaction. When Dabney's mother was questioned in the consulting room, she reinforced her overt value message in words, yet again demonstrated anxiety in her muscular tone when her son discussed his desires to obtain distance from her. When Dabney was young, he looked to his father for guidance in how to live with two seemingly incompatible messages from his mother. Dabney noticed that his father's life was spent in nonchallenging employment, and that he whiled away most of the family hours by sitting passively in front of the television set, sipping beer. That was the here's-how message (see Figure 5*III*). Dabney, in conformity to those messages, decided that he was able to survive and get strokes from his mother by attempting to go to college, but he was able to remain at home by playing certain games, such as "Stupid" and "Alcoholic," to reinforce his position.

Berne noted that Dabney's basic life decisions were lodged in the Child ego state as a result of repetitive or especially strong injunctions. Goulding and Goulding (1976) emphasized a process of redecision to free the patient from the script.

Berne (1972) delved into folk and fairy tales that were passed down through the generations and found that various life styles were based on specific characters with whom the patients and their family members identified. Occasionally, they could be traced back to ancient myths, with their victims, villains, heroines, and heroes; but more frequently they were portrayed through the derivative popular folk tales—drama, movies, novels, and television. The script became lodged in the Child and was carried into his fantasy life. Berne differed from Jung and his theory of the collective unconscious because he felt that those influences and forces were passed on directly and transactionally from parent to child, from generation to generation. That explained why one family might have certain consistent game patterns and another family had different but also consistent game patterns.

Contracts

Berne (1966) used certain unique techniques in his groups. In one, the doctor and the patient formed a distinct contract, which was valid and acceptable and consisted of a clear and precise end point, colloquially called the cure. Berne asked the patients in his groups:

How will you know, and how will I know, when you achieve what you came here for?

If a specific answer to the question was not formulated, Berne did not consider that he and the patient were engaged in psychotherapy. He would not accept a contract from a patient unless it was antithetical to that person's usual game-playing and script-influenced behavior. He thought that the contractual nature of treatment served to break up games and that it gave both the therapist and the patient the necessary permission to be potent. He disliked "making progress" because that meant the patient was playing his game more skillfully.

Berne encouraged active participation by therapists and focused on the final common pathway: the transaction between the therapist and the patient. At his weekly seminars Berne would halt a hypothetical discussion of why a patient was in difficulty and ask each member in the seminar to state in one sentence what he would do with that particular patient at that moment.

The success of transactional analysis is, in part, due to the reduction of the complex maze surrounding human problems and distilling them to their simplest forms. Berne thought that arriving at simplicity was a complex matter, but he continually applied the rule of Occam's razor (it is vain to do with more what can be done with less) and admonished his colleagues to use readily understandable words of only one or two syllables. A simple vocabulary of easily defined words evolved in his treatment groups and eliminated the mysterious aura. That simplification helped the therapist and patients to talk straight to each other.

Current Status

Berne, a prolific writer, published 64 articles and eight books and started a bulletin that grew into the quarterly *Transactional Analysis Journal*. The San Francisco Transactional Analysis Seminars, which he founded in 1958, are the longest ongoing weekly seminars of group treatment in existence. From the original eight members, who met in Berne's home and office in the 1950's, the International Transactional Analysis Association has grown to include more than 10,000 formal members in the United States and foreign countries, and it is experiencing particularly rapid growth in Europe, South America, and India.

Berne taught that professionalism is not as important as curing patients. Although Berne's original seminar members

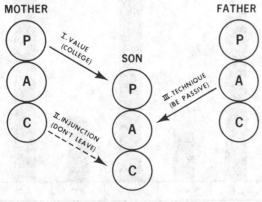

A TYPICAL SCRIPT MATRIX

FIGURE 5. Matrix.

were mental health professionals or recognized students who developed transactional analysis as an adjunct to their basic training, Berne himself, like many psychiatric innovators, invited a few select persons who were not traditionally trained to his seminars. Some of the best transactional analysis has been done by paraprofessionals and supervised lay persons, an extreme example being incarcerated prisoners trained as group leaders in prison. As an organization, the International Transactional Analysis Association has been struggling to resolve the question of who can be trained in and perform responsible psychotherapy. Although many professional associations face or have faced the same problem, the strength of transactional analysis, which is an easily learned theory with a noncomplex vocabulary, has fostered the problems of enthusiasts' prematurely assuming that familiarity is synonymous with competence. To resolve the dilemma of who is a therapist and who is a transactional analysis specialist even though not trained in the mental health field, a regularly convening training standards committee has established two different lines of training: (1) the clinical, limited to those whose basic training is as therapists, including psychiatrists, psychologists, social workers, and other recognized counselors, as well as paraprofessionals, such as psychiatric technicians who work under supervision, and (2) a line of training for behavioral scientists and scholars not formally interested in clinical concerns, including representatives of business, industry, and educational institutions. Under a highly advanced and rigorous training program, members formally train for a period of 2 to 5 years to attain competency and certification in the system.

Since 1958 the theories and the techniques of transactional analysis have gradually been applied to all areas of mental health issues and research concerned with the outcome of applied transactional analysis, and the validity of the theory itself is now evolving. A transactional analysis research index has been compiled and is regularly updated (Blair and McGahey, 1974, 1975). A comparison (McCormick, 1973) of the application of transactional analysis with the application of behavior modification was conducted with a population of 904 boys aged 15, 16, and 17 who had serious arrest records and were residents of two schools of the California Youth Authority. The advantage of the study is that transactional analysis, seeking the attainment of a treatment contract, and behavior modification, seeking distinct points, both had as their goals improved school performance records and improved recidivism rates—both hard data measurements. Although both methods achieved significant gains in both math and reading tests and improved recidivism rates compared with a control sample, the transactional analysis-treated population achieved their desired results in a shorter amount of time—that is, 7.6 months, compared with 8.7 months. In addition, the boys claimed that transactional analysis was more fun and more enjoyable than behavior modification.

Berne claimed that the ego states—Parent, Adult, and Child—the foundation of transactional analysis theory, are observable phenomena and not hypothetical constructs, like Freud's superego, id, and ego. Formal research on ego states has been conducted. Thomson (1972) demonstrated that transactional analysis professionals have a high interrater agreement as to which ego state is in operation in a given person and that naive observers can be trained to correctly identify ego states in agreement with experts.

Dusay (1972) demonstrated that not only can ego states be identified, but they can be measured. Those ego state measurements are symbolized by the egogram. An egogram represents

how much psychological energy emanates from each of the five functional ego states—Critical Parent, Nurturing Parent, Adult, Free Child, and Adapted Child—and they are symbolized on a linear bar graph. Trained observers have a high interrater agreement as to the relative amounts emanated when focusing on a given person. Those egogram profiles correspond with clinical problems.

Kendra (1977) constructed egograms of suicidal patients from Rorschach Tests and was able to delineate specific features of egograms that were common to that group of psychiatric suicidal patients. His findings confirmed the presence of high Critical Parent; Nurturing Parent and Free Child were extremely low (see Figure 6).

Heyer (1979) developed an objective questionnaire technique to measure the intensity of ego states and arrive at egogram profiles. His original research was based on a cross-section sample of the adult population of California conducted in September 1976. A sample of 1,044 persons rated themselves on items measuring ego states and also rated several major political figures (presidential and U.S. senatorial candidates). The study found that ego state energy is related to social and demographic characteristics and that perceived ego state images of candidates have an influence on voting intentions. The egogram questionnaire developed by Heyer is also being used for research on ego states in a variety of settings—including prisons, alcoholism outpatient clinics, growth workshops, and training programs—to examine the validity and the usefulness of some of Berne's theoretical formulations.

Berne encouraged his followers to organize and attend local seminars to sharpen their skills. After Berne's death in 1970, the International Transactional Analysis Association created the Eric Berne Memorial Scientific Awards, which are voted by the advanced membership each year to distinguished important advances in the field of transactional analysis. Each year persons using transactional analysis are nominated who have devised original and applicable concepts to further Berne's goal of curing patients faster. In 1971 Claude Steiner (1971) received the award for his development of the script matrix. In 1972 Stephen Karpman (1968) received the second award for the drama triangle. In 1973 John Dusay (1972) received the third award for his development

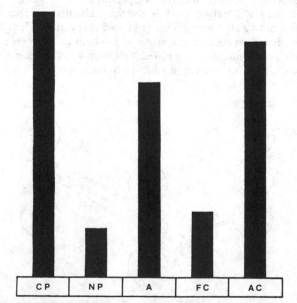

FIGURE 6. Suicide egogram. *CP,* Critical Parent; *NP,* Nurturing Parent; *A,* Adult; *FC,* Free Child; *AC,* Adapted Child.

of the egogram and the constancy hypothesis. In 1974 Jacqui Schiff and Aaron Schiff (1971) jointly received the award for their development of the reparenting techniques and passivity confrontation that they use in their residential treatment centers for schizophrenics. In 1975 Robert Goulding and Mary Goulding won the award for childhood decisions and redecisions. In 1976 Patricia Crossman (1966) won the award for recognizing the importance of permission, protection, and potency. In 1977 Taibi Kahler (1975) received the award for the miniscript. And in 1978 Fanita English (1972) won the award for her delineation of the distinction between authentic feelings and learned pathological rackets. The Eric Berne Scientific Award winners' theories are viewed as an integral part of developing transactional analysis theory and practices.

Berne's zest for expanding the theory encouraged a process of creativity among his followers and was consistent with his own career, which was continually in a process of evolution. His writings and methods have a wide appeal because they excite the reader's Child, and his simple vocabulary challenges intuitive minds. Berne quipped that anything written in the scientific literature or said to a patient in treatment should be understandable by at least two people: the professor of symbolic logic at the Massachusetts Institute of Technology, whom Berne exemplified as the most brilliant person in the world, and a farmer in Minnesota with a third-grade education.

Suggested Cross References

Freud's theories are discussed in Chapter 8 and Jung's theories in Section 10.3. Harlow discusses his findings in ethology, Section 4.6. Group therapy is discussed in Section 30.5.

REFERENCES

Berne, E. The nature of intuition. Psychiatr. Q., *23:* 203, 1949.
Berne, E. Concerning the nature of communication. Psychiatr. Q., *27:* 185, 1953.
Berne, E. Intuition. IV. Primal images and primal judgment. Psychiatr. Q., *29:* 634, 1955.
Berne, E. Intuition. V. The ego image. Psychiatr. Q., *31:* 611, 1957.
Berne, E. *Transactional Analysis in Psychotherapy.* Grove Press, New York, 1961.
Berne, E. Intuition. VI. The psychodynamics of intuition. Psychiatr. Q., *36:* 294, 1962.
* Berne, E. *The Structure and Dynamics of Organizations and Groups.* J. B. Lippincott, Philadelphia, 1963.
* Berne, E. *Games People Play.* Grove Press, New York, 1964.
* Berne, E. *Principles of Group Treatment.* Oxford University Press, New York, 1966.
* Berne, E. *Sex in Human Loving.* Simon & Schuster, New York, 1970.
* Berne, E. *What Do You Say after You Say Hello?* Grove Press, New York, 1972.
Blair, M., and McGahey, C. *Transactional Analysis Research Index,* vol. 1 and vol. 2. Florida Institute for Transactional Analysis, Tallahassee, 1974, 1975.
Crossman, P. Permission and protection. Trans. Anal. Bull., *5:* 152, 1966.
Dusay, J. Eric Berne's studies of intuition, 1949–1962. Trans. Anal. J., *1:* 1, 1970.
Dusay, J. Egograms and the constancy hypothesis. Trans. Anal. J., *2:* 3, 1972.
Dusay, J. *Egograms: How I See You and You See Me.* Harper & Row, New York, 1977.
Dusay, J., and Steiner, C. Transactional analysis in groups. In *Comprehensive Group Psychotherapy,* H. I. Kaplan and B. J. Sadock, editors, p. 198. Williams & Wilkins, Baltimore, 1971.
English, F. Rackets and real feelings. Trans. Anal. J., *2:* 1, 1972.
Goulding, R., and Goulding, M. Injunctions, decisions, and redecisions. Trans. Anal. J., *6:* 41, 1976.
Heyer, R. Development of a questionnaire to measure ego states with some applications to social and comparative psychiatry. Trans. Anal. J., *9:* 9, 1979.
Kahler, T. Scripts: Process and content. Trans. Anal. J., *5:* 277, 1975.
Karpman, S. Script drama analysis. Trans. Anal. Bull., *7:* 26, 1968.
Kendra, J. Suicide egograms. In *Egograms,* J. Dusay, editor, p. 56. Harper & Row, New York, 1977.
McCormick, P. TA and behavior modification: A comparison study. Trans. Anal. J., *3:* 10, 1973.
Schiff, J., and Schiff, A. Passivity. Trans. Anal. J., *1:* 1, 1971.
Schiff, J., Schiff, A., Mellor, K., Schiff, E., Schiff, S., Richman, D., Fishman, J., Wolz, L., Fishman, C., and Momb, D. *The Cathexis Reader.* Harper & Row, New York, 1975.
Spitz, R. Hospitalism: Genesis of psychiatric conditions in early childhood. Psychoanal. Study Child, *1:* 53, 1945.
Steiner, C. *Games Alcoholics Play: The Analysis of Life Scripts.* Grove Press, New York, 1971.
Thomson, G. The identification of ego states. Trans. Anal. J., *2:* 4, 1972.

chapter
10
Theories of Personality and Psychopathology: Other Schools

10.1 Erik Erikson

HAROLD I. KAPLAN, M.D.
BENJAMIN J. SADOCK, M.D.

Introduction

Erik H. Erikson (see Figure 1), America's most influential living psychoanalyst, has, throughout nearly 5 decades in the United States, distinguished himself as an illuminator and expositor of Freud's theories and as a brilliant clinician, teacher, and pioneer in psychohistorical investigation. He addresses himself to some of today's most critical issues, including the conflict between youth and authority, the problems of psychosexual identity, the status of women and minorities in American society, the function of psychoanalysis, and the place of nonviolence in a changing world. His books, articles, and monographs have been well received as original and thoughtful contributions to the study of psychology. Two of his psychosexual historical studies, *Young Man Luther* (Erikson, 1958b) and *Gandhi's Truth* (Erikson, 1969), were widely hailed as profound explorations of how crucial circumstances can interact with the crises of certain great persons at certain moments in time. The interrelationships of the psychological development of the person and the historical developments of the times were more fully explored in *Life History and the Historical Moment* (Erikson, 1975).

Life

Erik Homburger Erikson was born in Frankfurt, Germany, the son of Danish parents. His father abandoned his mother before he was born, and he was brought up in Karlsruhe in Baden by his mother and stepfather, Theordor Homburger, a German-Jewish pediatrician. Erikson's parents chose to keep his real parentage a secret from him, and for many years he was known as Erik Homburger. The man who introduced the term "identity crisis" into the language undoubtedly had his own identity problems. Compounding his parents' deception about his biological father—their "loving deceit," as he called it—was the fact that—as a blond, blue-eyed, Scandinavian-looking son of a Jewish father—he was taunted as a "goy" among Jews, at the same time being called a Jew by his classmates. His being a Dane living in Germany added to his identity confusion. Erikson was later to describe himself as a man of the borders. Much of what he was to study was concerned with how group values are implanted in the very young by culture-bearing mothers, how young people grasp onto group identity

FIGURE 1. Erik Erikson. (Courtesy of New York Academy of Medicine.)

in the limbo period between childhood and adulthood, and how a few persons, like Gandhi, transcend their local, national, and even temporal identities to form a small band of people with wider sympathies who span the ages.

The concepts of identity, identity crisis, and identity confusion are central to Erikson's thought. In his first book, *Childhood and Society*, Erikson (1950) observed that

the study of identity...becomes as strategic in our time as the study of sexuality was in Freud's time.

By identity, Erikson meant a sense of sameness and continuity "in the inner core of the individual" maintained amid external change. A sense of identity, emerging at the end of adolescence, is a psychosocial phenomenon preceded in one form or another by an identity crisis; that crisis may be conscious or unconscious, with the person being aware of the present state and future directions but also unconscious of the basic dynamics and conflicts that underly those states. The identity crisis can be acute and prolonged in some people.

The young Erikson did not distinguish himself in school, although at the Humanistische Gymnasium in Karlsruhe he did show artistic talent. On graduation, he chose to spend a year traveling through the Black Forest, Italy, and the Alps, pondering life, drawing, and making notes. After that year of roaming, he studied art in his home city of Karlsruhe and later in Munich and Florence.

In 1927 Peter Blos, a high school friend, invited Erikson to join him in Vienna. Blos, not yet a psychoanalyst, had met Dorothy Burlingham, a New Yorker who had come to Vienna to be psychoanalyzed; she had brought her four children with her and hired Blos to tutor them. Blos was looking for a fellow teacher in his new school for the children of

English and American patients and students of his new discipline of psychoanalysis. Erikson accepted his offer.

Blos and Erikson organized their school in an informal manner—much in the style of the so-called progressive or experimental schools popular in the United States. Children were encouraged to participate in curriculum planning and to express themselves freely. Erikson, still very much the artist, taught drawing and painting, but he also exposed his pupils to history and to foreign ways of life, including the cultures of the American Indian and Eskimo.

During that period Erikson became involved with the Freud family, friends of Mrs. Burlingham. He became particularly close to Anna Freud, with whom he began psychoanalysis. Anna Freud, who had been an elementary school teacher, was at that time formulating the new science of child psychiatry, trying to turn attention from the adult's corrective backward look at his childhood to a neurosis-preventive study of childhood itself. Under Anna Freud's tutelage Erikson began more and more to turn his attention to childhood, both his own and that of the children whom he saw in the classroom. Analysis was not then the rigidly structured procedure into which it later developed; Erikson met with Miss Freud daily for his analytic hour and frequently saw her socially as well, as part of the circle of Freud's followers and associates. Still undecided about his future, Erikson continued to teach school, at the same time studying psychoanalysis at the Vienna Psychoanalytic Institute. He also studied to become accredited as a Montessori teacher.

In 1929 he married Joan Mowast Serson, an American of Canadian birth, and was hastily made a full member, rather than an associate member, of the Vienna Psychoanalytic Society—unorthodoxy that allowed him to leave a Vienna threatened by fascism immediately after his graduation in 1933. Earlier, Erikson had met the Viennese Hanns Sachs, co-founder along with Otto Rank of the psychoanalytically oriented journal *Imago*. Sachs—who had settled in Boston, where he was associated with the Harvard Medical School—was sure that Erikson would be welcome at Harvard and suggested that he make Boston his home. After a brief stay in Denmark, the Eriksons moved to Boston, where he became that city's only child analyst. He held positions at the Harvard Medical School and at Massachusetts General Hospital, served as a consultant at the Judge Baker Guidance Center, and maintained a private practice.

Erikson was much influenced by Cambridge's circle of young social scientists, including anthropologists Margaret Mead and Ruth Benedict. Exposure to the views of those vigorous thinkers helped to shape his theories of child psychology and his cross-cultural approach to human development. Classical psychoanalysis had traditionally concerned itself with pathology and with treating disturbed people, but Erikson found himself more and more interested in the normal personality and in applying his own observations about how young people function and how childhood play affects character formation. Although he remained in the Boston area only 3 years, he established a solid reputation as a skilled clinician and researcher before moving to Yale University's Institute of Human Relations. There he furthered an interest sparked at Harvard in the work of American anthropologists. In 1938 he traveled to South Dakota to study the children of the Sioux Indians of the Pine Ridge Reservation. His observations about how communal and historical forces powerfully influence child rearing became an important contribution to psychology and to the study of humans in society.

In 1939 Erikson moved to a post at Berkeley, from which he studied the Yurok Indians, a group of salmon fishers. He left Berkeley in 1950 after refusing to sign what he called a vague, fearful addition to the loyalty oath. He resettled at the Austen Riggs Center in Stockbridge, Massachusetts, working with young people. In 1960 he was appointed to a professorship at Harvard, returning

in order to teach my whole conception of the life cycle—including identity crisis—to people normatively very much in it.

After his retirement from Harvard, Erikson in 1972 joined Mount Zion

Hospital in San Francisco as senior consultant in psychiatry. He has continued to focus on many of his earlier interests, examining the individual in this historical context and elaborating on concepts of the human life cycle.

Theory of Personality

THE HEALTHY PERSONALITY

Erikson brought Freud's psychoanalytic theory out of the bounds of the nuclear family, focusing his interest beyond the molding power of the child's early life and the oedipal family romance to the wider milieu of the social world, where the children interact with peers, teachers, national ethics, and expectations. He added to Freud's theory of infantile sexuality by concentrating on the child's development beyond puberty, thus rejecting the notion that childhood experience is the sole determinant of lifelong behavior patterns and personality. Said Erikson (1950):

If everything goes back into childhood, then everything is somebody else's fault, and trust in one's power of taking responsibility for oneself may be undermined.

Erikson maintained that a person grows throughout life, interacting with the environment. Conflict is therefore seen as a continuing and inexorable process between early, primitive values and later, more mature values. Later conflicts may open up earlier conflicts.

Freud had concentrated heavily on sexual conflict as the wellspring of neurosis—primarily because he lived in a time when sexual taboos were excessive—but he himself had been working in a more social direction late in life. He had begun to concern himself with the psychosocial development of the ego, but it remained for Erikson to take the focus of psychoanalysis from pathology to health, providing a picture of how the ego can usually develop in a healthy way if it is given the right environment. Erikson successfully brought Freud's theories out of the past, the home, and the hospital.

We have a name for the pressure of excessive wishes (the "id") and for the oppressive force of conscience (the "superego"),

wrote Erikson (1950), returning the labels of early psychoanalysis to the common language from which they had been transmitted. But the emphasis, he argued, should be on the ego. That emphasis had not been on the ego because psychoanalysis had evolved out of psychopathology, specifically out of the treatment of the personality made sick by repressed sexuality.

In considering the healthy personality, Erikson selected the ego as the tool by which a person organizes outside information, tests perception, selects memories, governs action adaptively, and integrates the capacities of orientation and planning. That is the positive ego, whose functioning produces a sense of self in a state of heightened well-being—an Indian "just calmly being an Indian," as Erikson (1950) put it. One is in that state of well-being when one is and does pretty much what one wishes and feels he ought to be and do.

The wishing and "oughtness" form polarities in Erikson's scheme. Excessive and barbaric wishes pull from one end of the horizontal axis, and the internalized restrictions of parents and society pull at the other end. Erikson's superego is as barbaric as the id, being that which turns the screw on the rack or punishes with mutilation. The image of Freud's superego, on the other hand, "the internalized sum of all the restrictions to which ego must bow" (Erikson, 1950), brings forth a vertical picture, with a wild id at the bottom, a defensive ego mediating in the middle height, and a judging superego high above.

With good functioning of the ego, the person is not neurotically crippled, wasting energy, or suffering. How does one come by the ego? The strong ego acquires its strength gradually through the expansive process of living, in a course that does not simply plow forward, picking up a permanent trust here and a never-to-be-lost industry there, but in stages during which the person meets a new situation with his accumulated make-up and, once again dealing in polarities, emerges from conflict with a certain ratio established of so much identity, for example, versus so much role confusion. That ratio is not stable; beneficient occurrences in the environment or corrective measures at home can change the ratio. Even a strong ego at 40 or 45 or 50 can face critical situations that thrust it back on the negative balance within and stir up infantile rages and anxieties that never entirely vanish.

Erikson is probably best known for his positing of eight stages of ego development, which cover the entire life-span from birth to death (see Table I). Those stages, which roughly parallel Freud's psychosexual stages, have both positive and negative aspects, are marked by emotional crises, and are very much affected by the person's particular culture and by his interaction with the society of which he is a part. Erikson conceptualized his stages of ego development as being governed by the epigenetic principle. He presented the stages in a diagrammatic form—the epigenetic chart (see Table I)—that shows the psychosocial stages in terms of an interplay of successive life events. Most important is Erikson's contention that personality continues to be molded throughout the eight stages. The stages are: oral-sensory, muscular-anal, locomotor-genital, latency, puberty, young adulthood, adulthood, and maturity. In each stage, psychosocial polarities war for ascendancy. Thus, in the first stage the infant learns to trust or mistrust; in the second stage the youngster faces the alternative basic attitudes of autonomy on the positive side and shame and doubt on the negative side. Throughout the stages of the life cycle, the growing person must deal with relative proportions of such interpersonal dimensions. And how he fares in one stage has much to do with his resolution of problems in the next. Fortunately, Erikson's polarities are not so firmly fixed that they cannot be modified from stage to stage. The baby who has learned to mistrust in his early months may reverse that feeling if his care becomes more positive and supportive later on.

Oral-sensory stage: trust versus mistrust. This first stage corresponds to Freud's oral stage and covers the first year of life. During this early stage the developing infant learns whether he can trust his own self and the world about him or whether his dominant feeling must be mistrust. When a person comes to stand on the continuum of trust, mistrust has to do with how well he is cared for. Although this stage is most characterized by the development of feelings of trust or mistrust, those emotions are misled and reestablished or changed in each successive stage.

The fetus develops sequentially, Erikson pointed out; each organ has its own time of origin, and they are all bound together in a standard time sequence. After birth, the infant continues to develop sequentially, mastering parts of his muscular and nervous systems at different times. During the first months the mouth is the most sensitive zone of the body, but one infant's oral sensitivities are not necessarily exactly like those of other babies. Furthermore, the oral stage is not really outgrown or left behind, since eating, drinking, and making sounds continue to be vital throughout life. The main action the infant performs with his mouth is incorporating—that is, taking in food, a nipple, a finger, or such. There is hunger for nourishment and for stimulation of the sense organs and the whole surface of the skin.

Basic trust, the positive social dimension of this period, begins with basic mothering, either by the parent or by another concerned caretaker. The mother welcomes the infant and reduces the discomfort of homeostasis with which he is born by giving him food and care. She smiles, and he smiles; mutuality of good feeling and warmth begins to develop. The infant comes to trust that his wants will continue to be satisfied, at least within the spectrum of his minimal needs and maximum tolerance for denial. Somewhere within that spectrum lie the expectations that the society has for the child. Although the mother adds her own opinions about satisfying the oral need of infants, she also transmits the reality orientation of the society. That orientation involves such things as the existence of plenty or scarcity, of peace or war, of limitation or fulfillment, of totalitarianism or democracy. The infant learns how to get his mother to give something; building on that base, he will later allow himself to be a giver.

Gradually, within the first 6 months, the infant learns to coordinate his vision and to attach meanings to specific sounds. His eyes pick out objects from the general background, and he learns to control his arms, fingers, and legs. He begins to sit or lean, giving his hands more freedom. The baby who stared longingly at a colorful toy is able to pick it up himself, although he sometimes drops it and sometimes finds it removed by his mother. He finds that in his environment he sometimes gets what he wants and sometimes not. Depending on what happens between the baby and the mother or other caretaker, who is also a bearer of the values of society, the baby develops a basic feeling of trust that his wants will be frequently satisfied or a sense that he is going to lose most of what he wants.

During the second 6 months of life, that ability to reach out and take the toy develops toward mastery of the taking gesture. At the same time, the teeth erupt painfully, filling the mouth, formerly a zone of pleasure, with a pain relieved only by biting. The teeth can bite on, through, and off, just as the eyes have begun to isolate individual items and the ears to attach significance to sounds. The dominant social mode moves from the getting of the first half year to the taking of the second, and taking manifests itself orally in biting. However, the nursing child finds the nipple removed if he bites. Weaning begins. Sorrow or nostalgia begins, too; it was with a bite, Erikson pointed out, that Eden was lost. The infant survives the rages of teething and weaning with (Erikson, 1950)

a residue of primary sense of evil and doom and of a universal nostalgia for a lost paradise.

TABLE I
Erikson's Developmental Stages and Psychosocial Crises

Developmental Stage	Psychosocial Crisis
I. Oral sensory (Infancy)	Basic trust versus mistrust
II. Muscular-anal (Early childhood)	Autonomy versus shame, doubt
III. Locomotor-genital (Play age)	Initiative versus guilt
IV. Latency (School age)	Industry versus inferiority
V. Puberty and adolescence	Identity versus role confusion
VI. Young adulthood	Intimacy versus isolation
VII. Adulthood	Generativity versus stagnation
VIII. Maturity	Ego integrity versus despair

But if his basic trust is strong, he has an inbuilt and lifelong spring of hope, instead of a well of doom.

Muscular-anal stage: autonomy versus shame and doubt. In the second and third years of life, the period Freud called the anal stage, the child learns to walk by himself, to feed himself, and to talk. Although the 1-hour-old infant can suck and swallow, it is 2 years or so before he can control the anal sphincter muscles to the point at which he can release waste material at will. He then has a choice of social modes—to keep or to let go.

Whether or not that choice becomes fraught with anxiety in the area of bowel and bladder retention or elimination depends on where within the spectrum of indoor, hygienic intolerance and outdoor informality the society is placed. Other meanings are, of course, involved in the idea of keeping or letting go; implications about the inside and the outside of the body—where the body ends and where the outside becomes the inside—and the differences between native and foreign become entwined. The two properly dominant modes must be mastered in alteration.

It is not only in anality that the struggle over keeping or letting go occurs. The walking and exploring child wants to practice and master his new accomplishments. If the parents are able to allow him to function with some autonomy, to rely on his own abilities to control himself, and if they are supportive without being overprotective, he gains a certain confidence in his autonomy by age 3. He feels a balance of love over hate, of cooperation over willfulness, or self-expression over suppression. He feels that he is good inside; he walks with confidence, uses his hands and eyes in a coordinated manner, and talks. He runs about independently and vigorously. Autonomy overbalances shame and doubt, and the child feels not only that he can control himself but also that he has some control over his world. But if his feces are called bad, if he is overrestrained, he feels enraged at his impotence, foolish, and shamed. Once shamed, he mistrusts his own rightness and comes to doubt himself.

Locomotor-genital stage: initiative versus guilt. This stage, corresponding to classical psychoanalysis's genital stage, goes through the fifth year. The child moves among peers and into the infantile politics of nursery school, street, and yard—out to the world itself, where his learning becomes intrusive, something he goes after and grabs with eagerness and curiosity. He is able to initiate activity on his own, both motor and intellectual, and whether or not that initiative is reinforced depends on how much physical freedom the child is given and how well his intellectual curiosity is satisfied. If he is made to feel bad about his behavior or his interests, he may emerge from this period with a sense of guilt about self-initiated activity. Erikson (1950) wrote about this period that

the child must now find out what kind of person he is going to be … he wants to be like his parents, who to him appear very powerful and very beautiful, although quite unreasonably dangerous. He "identifies with them," he plays with the idea of how it would be to be them.

In his desire to experience the world, the child takes the first initiative at home, where he involves himself in the so-called family romance by expressing passionate interest in his parent of the opposite sex. Of course, he is disappointed. The boy is refused intimacies with his mother; once refused, he has to deal with the sense that his not being welcome implies a wrong attempt on his part. If he did something wrong, he is bad. He feels guilt. He also knows that he is too small to rival his father effectively.

He may simultaneously be trying to wrest a place for himself, rather than just protect his autonomy, in the affection of his parents against his siblings. As he casts himself about, he develops a division between what he wants and what he is told he should do. The division increases until a gap grows between the infant's set of expanded desires, his exuberance at unlimited growth, and his parents' set of restrictions. He gradually turns those parental values into self-punishment. Gradually, he lessens his pregenital attachment to his parents and begins to think of the possibilities of becoming a parent and culture-bearer himself.

Usually, the child extracts more initiative than guilt from the conflict and turns happily outward from the home, where he knows he cannot act out sexual desires. Beyond getting, taking, peeking, and letting go, there is the excitement of being on the make, of attack and conquest for the boy, who becomes dominant in the intrusive mode, and of catching for the girl, who returns to the receptive mode of orality. All that takes place in a world that is gradually opening its mysteries to them.

Purposefulness—which Erikson (1976) defined as

the courage playfully to imagine and energetically to pursue valued goals, uninhibited by the defeat of infantile fantasies, by the guilt they aroused, and by the punishment they elicited

—emerges during the locomotor-genital stage.

Stage of latency: industry versus inferiority. This is the school-age period, the years from 6 to 11, Freud's latency period. The conflicts and turmoil of the family romance, dominant in the previous period, are laid aside for the moment. For the first time the child can really reason deductively, he can use the tools that adults use—language, implements, machines, objects of all sorts. Industry is the keynote of this period because the child of this age group is usually busy building, creating, accomplishing—initiating, executing, and completing tasks. Erikson (1950) described industry as a

sense of being able to make things and make them well and even perfectly.

If the child's efforts in that direction are thwarted, if he is made to feel that his goals or his accomplishments are not worthwhile, he develops a sense of inferiority about himself. He can become confident of his ability to use adult materials during this period of latency, when he, as a rudimentary parent, is waiting, learning, and practicing to be a provider. Or he can forsake industry itself and come to the conclusion that he is inferior and cannot operate the things of the world.

Competence—which Erikson (1976) described as

the free exercise of dexterity and intelligence in the completion of tasks, unimpaired by infantile inferiority

—emerges from the struggle of industry versus inferiority.

During these years, of course, it is not only the parents who help determine whether industry or inferiority is dominant. The child's teachers may enhance his sense of self-worth by supporting and encouraging him. Whereas Freud placed most of the blame or credit for a child's development squarely on the shoulders of the parents, Erikson is firm in emphasizing that sensitive social institutions may counteract nonsupportive parents and that a school environment that denigrates or discourages a child can diminish his self-esteem, even if his parents reward his industriousness at home.

Through play, alone or with other children, the child tries to make sense of the world and bring some part of it under his control. He makes models of experience and experiments with them, planning out of his memory and then producing the future he has chosen for his model. He learns to play and, later, work side by side with peers. He adjusts himself to the inorganic laws that govern the physical world. A sense of valuable industry results from achievement that has real meaning in the culture, not from artificial praise. The child of 8 or 10 must lay a groundwork of worthwhile achievement on which he can later base his sense of value.

Stage of puberty and adolescence: ego identity versus role confusion. During the fifth stage of development, the adolescent years, the teenager struggles to develop a personal identity. The youth cares a great deal about how he looks, since appearance helps commit him to a self. In the search for identity, the youth falls in love with heroes, ideologies, and members of the opposite sex. He talks a lot in his love affairs, his image reflecting off others to get a clearer picture of himself. Indecision and confusion often cause young people to cling to each other in a clannish manner; when individual identity is unknown, group identity becomes much more necessary. The adolescent strives to integrate what he knows of himself and of his world into a continuum of past knowledge, present experience, and future expectations. He is in suspension between (Erikson, 1950)

the morality learned by the child and the ethics to be developed by the adult.

That suspension Erikson called a moratorium.

How well the youth has fared in the psychosocial conflicts of the earlier stages—that is, how successful he has been in attaining trust, autonomy, initiative, and industry—has much to do with his developing a sense of personal identity. His particular position in his society also helps determine whether he emerges with a strong sense of ego identity, rather than role confusion. Ego identity is harder for certain groups of people to attain than for others. Girls look forward to reduced status; those whose lives have already seen rapid change between childhood and adolescence have trouble with the new change; and minority group members see possibilities narrowing in a limiting manner.

Successful resolution of the identity crisis, which is characteristic of the developmental period of adolescence and youth, depends on both psychological and social factors. The youth needs more than childhood identification to resolve the crisis. He or she must be able to experience new models in youth and have available workable roles in young adulthood. The process of gaining a sense of identity, therefore, depends on the support of parental and communal models. The subjective sense of an observable quality of sameness and continuity within the person and the large community occurs when the necessary physical, cognitive, and social conditions are present.

Stage of young adulthood: intimacy versus isolation. Classical psychoanalysis, with its emphasis on the early years of human development, was not overly concerned with this period, which extends from late adolescence through early middle age. But Erikson pointed out that an important psychosocial conflict can arise during this state and that, as in the previous stage, success or failure depends on how well the parents have laid the groundwork in earlier periods and on how the young adult interacts with his environment. If he has successfully resolved his identity crisis, he can involve himself with other people without having to fear losing his own identity. The intimacy of sexual relations, of friendships, of all deep associations do not frighten him, as they do the person who reaches his adult years in a state of continued role confusion. If a young adult is not

able to share himself in intense and long-term relationships, he may become self-interested and self-indulgent. Without a friend or a partner in marriage, a sense of isolation grows to dangerous proportions.

In true intimacy, there is mutuality. The word is reminiscent of the first stage of life. If a child achieves initiative in genitality, if the sensual pleasure of childhood merges with the idea of genital orgasm (rather than becoming an enemy to it), if love and sex become united (rather than separated), the young adult is able to make love that can be shared with another person. It is not only a love that is a sphere of isolated mutuality but one that goes back to the world through the children produced by love. Through the crisis of intimacy versus isolation, a person transcends the exclusivity of earlier dependencies and establishes a mutuality with an extended and more diverse social group.

Mutuality in heterosexual orgasm is hard to achieve in societies that do not devote a lot of leisure to its pursuit. Erikson's definition of ultimate genitality included orgasm with a partner of the opposite sex who is loved, trusted, and able and willing to regulate life's work, play, and procreation and to look to the healthy development of the offspring. That genitality must, of course, be mutual on all counts.

Stage of adulthood: generativity versus stagnation. During the all-important decades that span the middle years of life, the adult chooses between generativity and stagnation. Generativity means not a person's bearing or raising children but a vital interest outside the home in establishing and guiding the oncoming generation or in bettering society. The childless can be generative; it is the adults who are living only to satisfy personal needs and to acquire comforts and entertainment for themselves who are engaged in the self-absorption that is stagnation. The new generation depends on the adults and the adults on the young.

Stage of maturity: ego integrity versus despair. In Erikson's eighth stage of the life cycle, the conflict is between integrity, the sense of satisfaction one feels in reflecting on a life productively lived, and despair, for one who looks back on a life of little purpose and meaning and can only look ahead to the end of that life. It can be a contented period, a time to enjoy grandchildren, to contemplate one's major efforts, and perhaps to see the fruits of one's labors being put to good use by younger generations. As one aging scientist professed,

I can go on cheerfully so long as I remain convinced that cell division will continue indefinitely.

However, there is no peace in old age, no contented backward look, Erikson said, unless one has lived beyond narcissism, into intimacy and generativity. Without generativity, there is no sense of world order and, without world order, no conviction of the calming idea that one's single, accidental life has come at a time and in a segment of history when one developed exactly as one did. Without that conviction, there is a fear of death, a despair, and its mask, disgust.

ABNORMAL DEVELOPMENT AND FUNCTIONING

A person can veer off a normal course as a result of problems within himself, within his interpersonal relationships, or within the society to which he attempts to adapt. Erikson usually considered those three spheres simultaneously and attempted to unify them. The focus here is on interpersonal relationships.

To be human is to undergo a long childhood, and to be civilized and highly technological requires a further extension of that learning period. As long as the child is a controlled member of a partnership, he is unequal, and mutuality is lost. It is frightening just to be small in body or in capability. He lives a long time with infantile fears and finds them erupting at critical times during adult life.

Some anxiety is natural to all human beings. The infant is born helpless and uncomfortable; he has no knowledge of what is real and outer and what is imagined and inner, and so he cannot distinguish between fear and anxiety. The anxiety-fears of an infant that persist into adulthood can become neurotic anxieties.

Erikson (1950) spoke of five physical modes—passive and active, incorporation, retention, elimination, and intrusion—that underlie the social modes of getting, taking, holding, letting go, and being on the make or making. Those modes operate sequentially and relate to the zones of the body—oral-sensory, muscular-anal, and locomotor-genital—which also have a sequence. The oral zone, for instance, can get by simply opening to receive; or the jaws can clamp down and the teeth bite in a form of taking; then the lips can close and refuse to open, retaining what is inside the mouth; or things can be let go or spit out from the mouth; or the lips can become aggressive against the nipple, the head pushing in an attempt to press against the breast. If the mode and the zone are not matched correctly, a neurotic pattern can develop.

Erikson's theory of zones and modes forms the skeleton by which certain forms of malfunctioning can be understood. In a chart he organized the zones along a vertical axis and the modes along a horizontal axis. In the first zone, the oral, all modes are used, but simple incorporation should be dominant. If any other mode is dominant, trouble ensues. In the second part of the oral stage, the dominant mode should be biting, once the teeth develop. In the muscular-anal stage the dominant modes should be an alternating retention and elimination. In the locomotor-genital stage the dominant mode for boys should be intrusive and for girls a return to the two incorporative modes. Later, the boy works toward an image of masculinity that does not have intrusion as its dominant mode but a new behavior that is procreative and takes into account the fact that the boy will become the carrier of sperm and the provider for offspring. The girl works toward an image of femininity in which she will carry and bear the young and care for them.

A zone can become too prominent for a particular time. For example, an adult can be aware of the oral or the anal in a way that is inappropriate for his stage of life. Or a mode can become too habitual; elimination, for example, can start with spitting and move on to uncontrolled bowels and then to many but incomplete orgasms in women or to premature ejaculation in men.

Lying and sitting stage. Although, as has been pointed out, a number of auxiliary modes operate in addition to the dominant mode of passive incorporation, the dominance of another mode at this time can cause problems. For example, if the child is not fed when he is hungry—if, for instance, the mother withdraws the nipple because she is afraid of being bitten—the child may hang on and bite, thus moving into the mode of active incorporation (biting) too soon. The mother will naturally withdraw further, and the child will thus acquire a frustrating sense that he cannot get what he wants.

The infant fears not being fed. He may feel empty, as does the addict, who yearns to incorporate through his mouth or skin something to give him a sense of satiation. Manic-depressives can feel empty, as if there were nothing inside of them. The infant may feel starved not just for food but also for visual

or sensual stimulation. He may become, in a manic expression, a seeker after stimulating thrills that do not involve intimacy.

The newborn fears being manipulated, especially being interrupted while engaged in a pleasurable activity. Nursing is an activity of great warmth and mutuality, and anything that detracts from the reciprocal nature of the act can lead to distrust. The infant lives in a world where there is much more outer control than inner control; his resentment at being manipulated can make him compulsive and obsessive, and he may later turn his willfulness toward the manipulation of others.

If trust does not develop and mistrust does, fertile ground for schizophrenia exists. Trust involves mutuality. The mother enters the room and touches the infant, the infant smiles, his mother smiles, the infant reaches out, his mother strokes his hand. If, however, the infant's sending power is weak and he does not smile or touch in answer to his mother's overtures, she may cease to provide smiles and touches. If she does not show her feelings to her child, he may have nothing to respond to. If either partner is withdrawn, the gap widens. In the absence of mutual affect, the infant may begin a flight into a schizophrenic withdrawal. He is in pain, but he cannot, after all, distinguish what is inside himself from what is outside, and so he tries to push all the pain outside and live happily within, where there is pleasure.

At the weaning or biting stage, what Erikson (1950) called an "evil dividedness" can begin. The infant is enraged with his painful teeth, with his mother when she withdraws, and with himself for his powerlessness, developing a sadistic and masochistic confusion. A drastic, sudden weaning and loss of mother without a close substitute can lead to infantile and lifelong depression.

The infant's fear of manipulation becomes the baby's fear of loss of autonomy. At the time of bowel and bladder control, his fear becomes a fear of being robbed by outsiders or by inner saboteurs. A paranoid fear that evil lurks nearby or even within the body can originate at this time. If bowel and bladder training cannot be accomplished in an atmosphere of mutual regulation—if, for instance, control is demanded too early or is instituted too aggressively—the child may become so enraged against manipulation that he tries to control everyone and every event in a compulsion neurosis.

The crawling baby fears not only too much restraint but also too little; he is apprehensive of losing boundaries. Without boundaries, he has trouble in delineating autonomy.

Standing stage. When the child becomes upright, he experiences in a new way his sense of smallness. He is now vertically measurable and smaller than anyone else. He worries whether he will grow. The boy examining his genitals exposed from a new angle wonders whether they will grow or worries that he will lose them. On standing, the girl, according to Erikson (1950)

learns to hate him who so smugly has what it takes—and can take it with him.

Yet she is already aware of a "valuable inside" and returns to fears of an earlier stage with the new idea of inside value—she is afraid of being left empty or of being robbed. She may also develop a fear of being eaten into or being raped. The future female hysteric may find the receptive role undesirable and become obsessed with it.

He who stands upright experiences front and back as never before. He looks forward to see the eyes of others examining him. Feeling small, he may not be ready for that exposure. If he cannot force the other to cease examining him, he may want to become invisible. If he has been shamed and made to feel he is bad, he can ultimately develop extreme and sustained defiance after realizing that he cannot be all bad. Erikson considered the backside to be the area connected with doubt. The child cannot see his own buttocks, but others can. A feeling develops that others can dominate the backside, even invade and lay low one's autonomy. Paranoid fears of unseen and hostile people can come into being. If others condemn the feces that seemed acceptable when leaving the body, a doubt begins that what one produces and leaves behind is inadequate, bad. Paranoid fears of threats from within are based on that sense.

When the child finally walks, he fears losing that ability or becoming imprisoned or immobile. He also fears having no guidance. Like the crawling baby, he fears meeting no borders. Without being told when familiar ground ends, the child does not know against whom he must arm himself or when he can relax.

The child learns he cannot fulfill his sexual fantasies; he may punish himself for those fantasies by fearing harm to his genitals. Under the brutal assault of the developing superego, he may so repress his wishes that he cannot accept even having had them, thus engaging in hysterical denial. If that pattern is carried into late stages, paralysis, inhibition, or impotence can result. Or the child may turn to psychosomatic disease, rather than have to live up to his or others' expectations.

For boys, the dominant physical mode at this time is intrusiveness, but in the normal person by the time of true sexuality that aggressive intrusiveness has given way to mutuality. If it has not, a phallic-aggressive pattern results. Other neurotic boys may eschew the intrusive and prefer the physical modes of incorporation, retention, or elimination. A dominance of the physical modes of biting, rather than of phallic intrusiveness, at this period could indicate a tendency toward a form of male homosexuality in which the man who wants to be receptive to the penis does so in order to take male power. The dominance of an eliminative mode may later involve incomplete or premature ejaculation.

In girls, continued dominance of incorporation that does not give way to mutuality can lead to forms of frigidity, expressed with the passivity of simple incorporativeness or with the greed of the biting mode. Retentive dominance can make the vaginal muscles tighten up so much that the penis cannot enter, or it can prevent the vaginal muscles from relaxing, once the penis has been enclosed. The dominant eliminative mode can produce many small orgastic spasms that do not produce a satisfactory orgasm.

School stage. Erikson (1950) talked of two dangers during the elementary school years. One danger is that of considering oneself less a workman and provider than the next person. A child who acquired trust, autonomy, and initiative at home can come to school and find himself discriminated against or told that he is inferior. That treatment can cause him to draw away from identification with peers and go back to the personal scene in the home, where he will always remain small. The other danger is that of making work the whole of life. Although he has learned that producing things will gain him recognition, he must avoid the pitfall of concluding that work is his only obligation or that only what works well is worthwhile. That pitfall can be a real problem in technological societies.

Adulthood. The young man or woman who reaches adulthood without resolving his or her sexual identity or role finds it difficult to withstand the pressures of choosing a career and planning a future. If adult identity is not secure, a person may avoid intimacy and retreat into self-absorption or isolation.

Fearing the loss of what little ego identity he has managed to develop, he avoids intimacy, shunning friendships and all close associations.

The adult who has no interest in guiding or establishing the oncoming generation is likely to look obsessively for intimacy that is not truly intimate. Such people may marry and even produce children—but all within a cocoon of self-concern and isolation. Those persons pamper themselves as if they were the children, becoming prey to psychosomatic invalidism. Often, their narcissism results from severe struggles to acquire self-made personalities. Others may lack a belief in the species. Indeed, parents who do not truly believe life in the given society to be worthwhile may find that their children absorb that message only too well, the result being a lack of grandchildren.

If, looking back on his life, a person feels he never acquired the things he wanted, did not do anything meaningful, never found a sense that his life was integrated into a world order, he is open to a panic at seeing his time run out, his chances used up.

Treatment

One of the primary tasks for the therapist is to help the patient build the trust and confidence that he failed to acquire in infancy and childhood. Without that basic factor, the ego cannot develop healthily. Patients, to Erikson, are members of society who are most inactivated by the internal conflicts shared by all people.

Beginning as an analyst for children, Erikson tried to provide that mutuality and trust while he observed children re-creating their own worlds by structuring dolls, blocks, vehicles, and miniature furniture into the dramatic situations that were bothering them. Then he correlated his observations with statements by the children and other family members. He began treatment of a child only after eating an evening meal with the entire family. His therapy was usually conducted with much cooperation from the family. After each regressive episode in the treatment of a schizophrenic child, for instance, he discussed with every member of the family what had been going on with them before the episode. Only when he was thoroughly satisfied that he had identified the problem could treatment begin. He might provide corrective information to the child—for instance, telling a boy who cannot release his feces and has made himself quite ill from constipation that food is not an unborn infant. He might turn to play, which, along with specific recommendations to the parents, often proved fruitful as a treatment modality.

Play, for Erikson, is diagnostically revealing and thus helpful for the therapist who seeks to promote a cure, but it is also curative in its own right. Play is different from work, Erikson pointed out; it defies spatial and temporal restrictions, it is beyond the realms of fate and causality, and it allows one to toy with social reality.

Play is a function of the ego and gives the child a chance to synchronize social and bodily processes with the self. The child playing with blocks—or, indeed, the adult playing out an imagined dramatic situation—can manipulate the environment and develop the sense of control that the ego needs. However, play therapy is not the same for children and for adults. The child creates models in an effort to gain control of reality; he looks ahead to new areas of mastery. The adult, in a sense, uses play to correct the past and redeem his failures.

Erikson (1950) spoke of what he called "play disruption," the inability or unwillingness to continue playing, presumably when emotions of unbearable intensity enter the play situation. He likened the phenomenon to the familiar resistance of psychoanalysis and pointed out that it is an intrinsic part of therapy, often serving as a starting point for progress.

Mutuality, so important in Erikson's system of health, is also vital to the cure. He applauded Freud for the moral choice of abandoning hypnosis, since hypnosis heightened the demarcation between the healer and the sick, an inequality that Erikson compared to the inequality of child and adult. He urged that the relationship of the healer to the sick person be more of equals

in which the observer who has learned to observe himself teaches the observed to become self-observant.

In talk of cures, the familiar axis images are seen; Erikson (1950) discussed four dimensions of the psychoanalyst's job. The patient's desire to be cured and the analyst's desire to cure him run along an axis of cure research. It is to be a common research, there is mutuality in that patient and therapist are motivated by cure, and there is a division of labor in the guiding as to how to observe oneself and in the actual self-observation. The goal is always to help the patient's ego get stronger and cure itself.

The second dimension Erikson called objectivity-participation. The therapist must keep his mind open. "Neuroses change," said Erikson, and the therapist's knowledge must stay plastic, his mind fresh and able to deal with new information in a new way. New generalizations must be made and arranged in new configurations that must be abstracted into new models.

The third dimension runs along the axis of knowledge-participation. Combining those two, the therapist

applies selected insights to more strictly experimental approaches.

The fourth dimension is tolerance-indignation.

Identities based on talmudic argument, on messianic zeal, on punitive orthodoxy, on faddist sensationalism, on professional and social ambition,

which were involved in the new identity and profession of the early analyst, lent themselves, Erikson said, to a control of patients without a dedication to the enlightenment being produced. The expression of indignation by a controlling therapist is harmful. It widens the gap of inequality that makes more difficult the realization of that recurrent Eriksonian idea, mutuality.

Erikson thus saw psychiatric intervention as a process in which the therapist gains insight into the unconscious motivation of the patient and then shares that insight with the patient. The subsequent elimination of the unconscious sources of irrational anxiety frees the person to deal competently with the demands of living.

Suggested Cross References

Historical and theoretical trends in psychiatry are discussed in Chapter 1. Freud's theories are discussed at length in Chapter 8, and the developmental structuralism of Piaget is discussed in Section 4.2. Normality is discussed in Section 6.6, normal child development in Section 34.2, and normal adolescent development in Section 34.3. Adjustment disorders are discussed in Section 25.1. Geriatric psychiatry is discussed in Chapter 53.

REFERENCES

* Coles, R. *Erik H. Erikson: The Growth of His Work.* Little, Brown, and Co., Boston, 1970.
Erikson, E. *Childhood and Society.* W. W. Norton, New York, 1950.
* Erikson, E. Identity and the psychosocial development of the child. In *Discussion on Child Development,* vol. 30. International Universities Press, New York, 1958a.
* Erikson, E. *Young Man Luther: A Study in Psychoanalysis and History.* W. W. Norton, New York, 1958b.
* Erikson, E. *Insight and Responsibility.* W. W. Norton, New York, 1964.
Erikson, E. *Identity: Youth and Crisis.* W. W. Norton, New York, 1968.
Erikson, E. *Gandhi's Truth.* W. W. Norton, New York, 1969.
Erikson, E. *Dimensions of a New Identity.* W. W. Norton, New York, 1974.
Erikson, E. *Life History and the Historical Moment.* W. W. Norton, New York, 1975.
Erikson, E., editor. *Adulthood.* W. W. Norton, New York, 1976.
Erikson, E. *Toys and Reasons: Stages in the Realization of Experience.* W. W. Norton, New York, 1977.
Erikson, E., and Newton, H. *In Search of Common Ground.* W. W. Norton, New York, 1973.
* Evans, R. I. *Dialogue with Erik Erikson.* E. P. Dutton, New York, 1967.

10.2   Adolf Meyer

GEORGE MORA, M.D.

Background and Training

Adolf Meyer was born in Niederwenigen, in the outskirts of Zurich, on November 3, 1866, the son of a Zwinglian minister. While attending high school, he wrote an autobiography that was considered outstanding by his teacher—undoubtedly, it was an indication of his introspective urge and of his interest in individual psychology. In the medical school of the University of Zurich, he came under the influence of August Forel, director of the Burghölzli Hospital for the Insane. Forel was then quite involved in the study of hypnosis, in improving the methods of treatment of the mentally ill, and in disseminating principles of preventive mental hygiene, especially enlightening views on sex and the fight against alcoholism, through lectures, publications, and social action. Meyer maintained a father-son relationship with Forel, and, years later, in 1929, on the occasion of Forel's eightieth birthday, said:

Next to the interrelationship between parents and children, the association between teacher and pupil is potentially the most important in the development of a civilization.

After he passed the state examination in 1890, Meyer, contrary to the trend of the times of doing postgraduate work in Germany or Austria, chose to spend a year in Paris, London, and Edinburgh. In Paris, he attended Charcot's lectures and, a year later, studied under the neurologist J. J. Déjérine, who was also of Swiss origin. It was in England, however, that he was strongly influenced by the Darwinian, ecological orientation of Thomas Huxley, who based his philosophy on common sense, and by the teaching of Hughlings Jackson, who posited the functioning of the individual person on progressive levels of integration viewed in the context of the evolution and dissolution of the central nervous system. The British empirical orientation had probably been preceded by an educational and social influence stemming from Meyer's background. Through his paternal grandfather, Meyer's family considered itself the

Figure 1. Adolf Meyer, 1866–1950. (Courtesy of National Library of Medicine, Bethesda, Md.)

spiritual heir of the tradition initiated by Jakob Gujer (1716–1785), known as Kleinjogg (Little Joe), a farmer who taught an instrumental approach to farming, emphasized the importance of a healthy relationship between parents and children, and fostered community activity and teamwork. Consequently, he was held in high esteem by Goethe, Pestalozzi, and other great men of the times.

Early Career

Unable to find a university position, Meyer decided to emigrate to the United States, where he accepted a position as pathologist at the State Hospital in Kankakee, Illinois. At that time, the tradition of moral treatment, which had characterized American psychiatry in the 1830's and 1840's, had been completely forgotten. Under the impact of varying factors—such as immigration of large groups of uneducated and poor people from Europe, rapid urbanization and industrialization, and lack of labor and housing laws—mental hospitals had become overcrowded custodial places run by politically appointed administrators and served by untrained staff. The decision of the Kankakee hospital to appoint a pathologist was almost unique, so that young Meyer himself had to establish his role. Although he had had experience only in neurology and no real training in psychiatry, not unlike Freud, he soon turned his attention to the clinical significance of neuropathology by presenting patients at staff conferences and demonstrating the facts that could be observed.

Early in 1894, in a special report to the governor of Illinois, he wrote in regard to the responsibility of the state as the guardian of the mentally ill human beings:

One of the most important duties of the state is to see that every insane person has the benefit of treatment and supervision by a competent physician.

The year before, in a letter to Forel, he had expressed the following points concerning the teaching of psychiatry:

[We physicians] will always have to describe their clinical observations in concrete terms, without pseudopsychological and pseudophysiological circumlocutions. We shall then summarize the symptoms and clinical definition of the typical form, the definition of the deviating types, and the differential diagnosis.

At that time, his correspondence with Forel was particularly frequent. Meyer had referred his mother, Anna, to him, because she was suffering from depression and pathological ideation. He believed that her distorted notion that he (Meyer) was dead had been precipitated by his emigration. Thus, a personal problem may have contributed to his motivation to turn from neuropathology to psychiatry, especially in view of her unexpected recovery.

At any rate, the 28-year-old Meyer was then embarking on a program that in time radically changed American psychiatry. In that year, 1894, which marked the fiftieth anniversary of the founding of the Association of Medical Superintendents of American Institutions for the Insane (now called the American Psychiatric Association), the situation of psychiatry was far from encouraging. In his inaugural address, the neurologist S. Weir Mitchell severely chastised psychiatrists for their isolation from the medical community, for their unconcern with training and research, and for their involvement in politics to achieve personal gains.

The challenge brought forth by Mitchell's caustic remarks was soon to be met by Meyer. The next year, 1895, in three essays published for the Illinois Society for Child Study, he opposed the emphasis on heredity as "perfect fatalism" and stressed, instead, the "fundamental moral and intellectual characteristics" that could be traced back to childhood years. He wrote: "The child of abnormal parents is apt to be exposed from birth to irrational ways of life, and with a weak constitution is even more prone to acquire unconsciously habits of a morbid character . . . ." It was, indeed, an enlightening statement, forerunning dynamic psychology.

It is likely that around that time Meyer came to be influenced by the pragmatic trend of the leading American philosophers. Through the positivist Paul Carus, the editor of *The Monist*, he became acquainted with the writings of Charles Peirce and William James and later established personal relationships with John Dewey, George Mead, and Charles Cooley. Their disregard for abstract intellectualism and their emphasis on pragmatic, pluralistic thinking in a society that was optimistically viewed as a laboratory for natural experimentation did, indeed, present many similarities with Meyer's concrete and melioristic philosophy of psychiatry. From the practical perspective, his motivation for initiating reforms in the treatment of patients and for broadening his views on the social dimensions of psychopathology came from two remarkable women: Julia Lanthrop, one of the founders of the Hull House settlement in Chicago, and Jane Addams, perhaps the most famous woman of the time. With others, the National Child Labor Committee, the National Women's Trade Union League, and the National Association for the Advancement of Colored People were organized in the broader context of the progressive movement.

In 1895, Meyer accepted a position as pathologist at the Worcester State Hospital. This hospital, opened in 1833, had achieved renown in the two succeeding decades, during the era of moral treatment, under the leadership of Samuel Woodward. In the last three decades of the century, it had experienced a steady decline because of various factors. Hosea M. Quimby, the new superintendent appointed in 1890, had not remained insensitive to Mitchell's criticism, and, with his support, a position of pathologist had been established. This position offered considerable potential, especially for Meyer, who secured for himself an academic appointment at the nearby Clark University, a new graduate institution already famous for its department of psychology, then under the leadership of Stanley Hall, who had trained in Germany under Wundt.

There, the opportunity was offered to Meyer (at variance with what he called the "neurologizing fallacy") to carry on his ambitious project of organizing proper training for physicians, of developing a theoretical model based on the integration of neurology and psychiatry, and of expanding public awareness of the need for mental hygiene. To broaden his views further, Meyer visited some psychiatric centers in Europe—in Italy, Lombroso's institute of criminal anthropology and, in Germany, Kraepelin's clinic in Heidelberg, where he familiarized himself with the concept of dementia precox. In short time, Meyer introduced a series of important innovations at the Worcester State Hospital. He surrounded himself with intelligent and dedicated young physicians (Coriat, Dunlap, and Cotton), developed a close relation with Clark University, where he taught graduate students; introduced Kraepelin's nosology; and established standards for taking and recording detailed case histories for all psychiatric patients based on a special life chart. As he put it, "true medical study must begin before the patient is dead." In a few years, a new atmosphere was created in that institution, which came to enjoy national reputation.

In particular, Meyer's life chart came to be seen as the most tangible expression of his teaching. By graphically presenting the important data about the patient in chronological succession along a vertical dimension, it portrayed his life as a rocket or time capsule, starting at birth and shooting into the future. By that time, Meyer had rejected Kraepelin's deterministic view of the human personality as an unfolding of events related to constitutional endowment in favor of the emphasis on a relation between habit, situation, and pathology—that is, the disease process was viewed as the result of the habits or modes of adjustment and bad situations; as such, Meyer's theory offered a much more optimistic view of the disease's outcome. What Meyer accepted from Kraepelin's teaching was the objective method of gathering facts from and about the patient— a goal containing both positive and negative aspects to which he remained faithful to the end. A holistic biological concept of man, based on an integrated physiological and developmental approach, was slowly emerging in his mind.

Mature Stage

By the turn of the century, when Freud's *The Interpretation of Dreams* was to appear and represent the beginning of dynamic psychiatry, Meyer was already a famous person. It is, therefore, not surprising that in 1902 he was called as director of the Pathological Institute of New York State. This institute, founded in 1895 in New York City, had been run by Ira Van Gieson, a New York physician with an international reputation in neuropathology. After Van Gieson's resignation, Frederick Peterson, then professor of neurology at Columbia University and an early admirer of Freud, was instrumental in offering the appointment to Meyer. The institute was moved to Ward's Island in quarters immediately adjacent to the buildings of Manhattan State Hospital West.

As Meyer put it, "The aim of the Institute lies chiefly in the raising of the standard of the medical work in the [New York] State institutions," an intent that, in retrospect, he admirably accomplished. He advocated that hospital superintendents delegate authority to a clinical director, who would be responsible for maintaining standards, and he stressed that holding regular staff meetings was indispensable for the performance of medical duties and professional growth. He organized a 2-week course in clinical psychiatry for state hospital physicians, during which they were exposed to the florid psychopathology presented by the patients of the nearby hospital, which functioned very much as a psychopathic hospital—that is, it admitted patients for short-term intensive treatment. In 1907, Meyer was able to have the name of the institute changed from the Pathological Institute to the Psychiatric Institute. The next year, with Kirby and Peterson, he founded the *Psychiatric Bulletin*, a journal geared to presenting contributions even from outside of the state hospital service and to reviewing European and American psychiatric literature.

That period of Meyer's life was exceptionally active. From 1904 to 1907, as professor of psychiatry at the Cornell University Medical College, he organized the first psychiatric outpatient clinic in New York City. In regard to clinical psychiatry proper, in 1903, in an article entitled "An Attempt at Analysis of the Neurotic Constitution," he postulated that mental disorder often had its roots in a personality imbalance that, in turn, was caused by the disorganization of habits. The incomprehensible symptoms of mental illness were viewed as crude and inadequate attempts by the patient to cure himself, attempts that had to be guided rather than suppressed. Dementia precox, which was then the area of investigation of such outstanding psychiatrists as Kraepelin and Jung, was the testing ground for Meyer's concepts. Kraepelin stressed deterioration as the eventual outcome in dementia precox, but Meyer believed that personality traits, such as withdrawal, preceded the appearance of the disease, and he suggested that prevention, as well as recovery, might be possible. He conceived of schizophrenia as a twisted maladaptation that could be understood in terms of the patient's life experience and that was characterized by habit disorganization or deterioration.

In another paper, "Fundamental Conceptions of Dementia Praecox," read at the annual meeting of the British Medical Association in Toronto in 1906, Meyer argued that it was possible to classify patients according to a new system of reactions types—that is, typical ways of behaving in difficult or emergency situations.

Every individual is capable of reacting to a very great variety of situations by a limited number of reaction types, which we want to characterize briefly, without distracting ourselves . . . over the classifications and traditions of logical and analytical psychology with its sensations, feelings, and will.

Meyer believed that this approach could be very helpful for the early detection and prevention of faulty habits, thus leading to a much more hopeful outcome of the disease. He recommended that an attempt be made to intervene early in the development of the illness by the patient's school, family, and community. As he put it in a speech in 1907:

There is clearly a very potent stimulus of my interest in the schools in the fact that in all my work I am constantly confronted with the question: What has been the share of nature and of nurture and of the home and school, in the lives of patients who form the subject of my medical work?

Thus, his early interest in community psychiatry is noteworthy. Moreover, the first applications of the principles of social work to occupational and recreational therapy with convalescent patients and the organization of aftercare programs were inspired by Meyer's work during this period. As a matter of fact, his wife—Mary Potter Brooks, a Radcliffe graduate whom Meyer met in Worcester—began to visit discharged patients and their families in 1904, earning recognition as the first psychiatric social worker. On a broader scale, considerable support was given by Meyer to the National Association for the Protection of the Insane and the Prevention of Insanity, established in 1872.

In the meantime, psychoanalytic theories slowly came to be noticed in this country by a few philosophers, psychologists, therapists, broad-minded intellectuals, and social reformers. Meyer, too, accepted the importance of unconscious factors in psychopathology, although he opposed the term "unconscious" because, according to him, it mystified many physicians. While in New York, he came in personal contact with some of the earliest adherents of the psychoanalytic movement, notably Brill and Jones. In 1906, in discussing Freud's *Three Essays on the Theory of Sexuality* (1905), Meyer argued that Freud

opened the eyes of the physician to an extension of human biology which differs very favorably from the sensational curiosity shop of the literature on perversions [and was] especially illuminating on account of the pedagogically important study of the infantile period .... Freud's work is essential ... and is to the psychopathologists as important as the study of dietetics to the general physician.

Meyer warned against premature rejection of psychoanalysis, although he objected to Freud's emphasis on the pathological and hypothetical, rather than on the healthy and verifiable aspects of mental functioning.

Meyer's theory of psychobiology reflected this conflicting view: on the one side, in line with psychoanalysis, he recognized the importance of sexuality in the development of neuroses and psychoses and gave his support to the psychoanalytic movement. In 1911, he was elected an honorary member of the newly established New York Psychoanalytic Society; in 1919, he opposed the dissolution of the American Psychoanalytic Association and its incorporation into the American Psychopathological Association (as suggested by William Alanson White) on the ground that there was a definite need for a national organization geared to education and scientific exchange. On the other side, Meyer did not hesitate to criticize psychoanalysis for its lack of methodology and for its tendency to consider itself, especially during the period of popularization and uncritical acceptance in the 1920's and 1930's, as the theoretical framework and therapeutic method par excellence, rather than as only a specific field within psychopathology and psychiatry to be limited to especially talented physicians and well-chosen patients.

At any rate, invited by Stanley Hall to take part—with Freud, Jung, and others—in the twentieth anniversary celebrations at Clark University, Meyer had the opportunity of becoming personally acquainted with the pioneers of the psychoanalytic movement. It was there, in 1909, that he introduced the term "psychobiological interpretation" during his lecture on dementia precox in connection with the different types of

disorganizing personality reactions. In the broad context of psychobiological interpretation, stated Meyer, pathological personality reactions can be explained as regression to former, previously protective, phylogenetic reactions that are incompatible with adaptation at the later time.

Meyer's concrete approach to psychiatry and, in particular, the importance attributed to environmental factors in the etiology of emotional disorders naturally led him to become aware of the importance of prevention. Coincidentally, Clifford Beers, a young man from Connecticut and a Yale graduate, had finished in 1906 a manuscript in which, in a passionate way, he brought to the fore the deprivation, cruelty, and incompetence to which he had been subjected during his 3 years of hospitalization for a severe mental illness. Not unlike William James, Meyer immediately realized the potential that Beers presented for the cause of psychiatric prevention and helped him to launch his book, *A Mind That Found Itself*, in 1908. In the same year, the Connecticut Society for Mental Hygiene (a name suggested by Meyer) was incorporated, followed shortly thereafter, in 1909, by the National Committee on Mental Hygiene. Soon, however, substantial differences of opinion between Meyer and Beers began to emerge. Meyer insisted that example, not preaching, should be the standard—that is, the emphasis should be on specific tasks and on accurately and scientifically gathered data concerning psychiatry and mental hygiene, such as raising hospital standards, organizing practical work at the community and state level, and providing adequate courses of teaching. Beers, instead, continued throughout his life to draw rather grandiose plans and to rely on large distributions of material on mental health. In 1910, Meyer resigned from the board of the National Committee on Mental Hygiene, although, years later, after his retirement, he again became active in it, accepting the presidency from 1940 to 1943.

In 1908, while visiting William H. Welch—a Yale graduate and German-trained pathologist who, as dean, had organized, in 1893, the curriculum at the newly established Johns Hopkins Medical School, soon to become the most important in the United States—Meyer urged him to approach Henry Phipps, a wealthy former associate of the steel magnate Andrew Carnegie, about the possibility of funding a psychiatric center there. Within 60 days, the new psychiatric institute was in the planning stage, and Meyer was designated as its new director. Meyer, then 43, aware of the limitations of the New York state mental hospital system, decided to accept this challenging opportunity. The Johns Hopkins Hospital, opened in 1889, was already known for its efforts in integrating psychiatry into the mainstream of medicine. After the pioneering work of Stanley Hall, who had been professor of psychology and pedagogy from 1882 to 1889, the first superintendent of the department of psychiatry had been Harry M. Hurd, known for an encyclopedic work on mental hospitals in the United States and Canada that was published in 1916. Hurd was assisted by a number of other excellent physicians, notably Stewart Paton, Glanville Rusk, William Dunton, Jr., and Clarence Farrar, who was later the editor for many years of the *American Journal of Psychiatry*.

Officially appointed Henry Phipps Professor of Psychiatry in 1909, Meyer spent the rest of the year traveling in Europe to familiarize himself with the operations of that continent's psychiatric clinics. Slowly, he was preparing himself for the program to be inaugurated at the Phipps Clinic. In 1911, he first publicly urged that psychology be made part of the medical curriculum. The next year, in his presidential address to the American Psychopathological Association, he advocated a diploma testifying proficiency in psychological medicine. On April 16, 1913, the Phipps Clinic was finally opened. The 3-

day opening exercises included speeches by Welch, William Osler (the Canadian-born and European-trained physician, then a commanding figure in American medicine and later Regius Professor of Medicine in Oxford), Eugen Bleuler, August Hoch (like Meyer, he was Swiss born and succeeded him as director of the New York Psychiatric Institute), and Harvey Cushing (the neurosurgeon, then professor at Johns Hopkins).

After many years of preparation, the Phipps Clinic offered Meyer the opportunity to organize under university auspices a combined program of research, training, and therapy in a great hospital. His idea, however, was to reach out of the hospital into the community. In a paper read at the International Congress of Medicine in London in 1913, he outlined the program for an ideal psychiatric clinic. Such a clinic should serve a population of from 200,000 to 500,000 and should provide outpatient services for adults and children in school. It should be run by a psychiatrist, rather than by an administrator, and should become a mental health center, working in close association with adjacent mental hospitals. It would then be possible to carry on an integrated program of prevention, treatment, and aftercare of mental disorders, with the psychiatrist in the hospital working in concert with teachers, police officers, welfare workers, and general practitioners in the community. The family doctor should be involved in the treatment of his own patient, including participation at staff conferences, while the patient is in the mental hospital and should follow him after discharge. This continuity of care would help reduce the ignorance and fear of many general practitioners toward mental hospitals. Furthermore, by addressing many lay groups, the physician could help decrease the feeling of shame toward mental illness, and public support should lead to an improvement of community facilities for the mentally ill. Public education, it was hoped, would lead to improved methods of child rearing and to healthier ways of mastering life's problems. In essence, this was the outline of the program of community mental health that was going to be inaugurated in this country 50 years later.

In retrospect, it is clear that, being so much ahead of his time, Meyer's program could not succeed then. And Meyer never presented his philosophy of psychiatry in a clear and comprehensive way. His formal papers, which he prepared in a rambling Swiss-German English for various circumstances and audiences, make for very tedious reading. The following presentation, which does not necessarily follow a chronological order, is based on Meyer's salient points as he stressed them in the first Thomas W. Salmon Memorial lectures at the New York Academy of Medicine. The lectures were delivered in 1932 and published posthumously by Meyer's pupils in 1957.

Theory of Psychobiology

BASIC CONCEPTS

Psychobiology emphasized the importance of biographical study in understanding the whole person in the whole situation, in other words, the whole personality. The object of such study is the individual person, whom Meyer defined as a biological unit that always functions as a person, whether alone or in groups, and whose ultimate test of mental well-being was "adequate and efficient function." Although the person's experiment continuum changes constantly, it enables him to maintain an internal and external homeostatic equilibrium in coping with new situations. In addition, the person's plasticity allows him a wide spectrum of differentiation in capacity and function and a relatively high degree of spontaneity and re-

sponsiveness. Because of the complexity of human functioning, the psychiatrist who attempts to acquire a scientific understanding of his patients must have a combination of attributes: He must be a methodical investigator, biographer, artist, and educator.

In sketching the evolutionary development of the human mind, including its prehistory, largely through the process of symbolization, Meyer noted that the biographical study of man was the last discipline to pass from the stage of intuition and philosophical speculation to that of scientific investigation. This area of study, which he defined as objective psychobiology, consisted of the observation of objective facts, the formulation of predictable conditions in which these may occur, and the testing and validation of methods for their controlled modification. Instead of accepting predetermined hypothetical psychological or metapsychological constructs to account for these facts, he emphasized the soundness of common sense, a fact that justified involving all kinds of laymen—teachers, clergymen, and others—in working for community mental health.

Although an analysis of psychobiological assets may reveal the presence of a variety of factors in each person, Meyer emphasized the basic tendency toward integration that takes place. Because Meyer believed that multiple biological, social, and psychological forces contribute to the growth and development of the personality, he concluded that psychiatrists must study normal and abnormal behavior from many viewpoints.

Meyer conceived of the clinical value of the biographical approach to personality study as follows: It provides a practical and specific guide for eliciting individual data, a means of organizing that data, and a method for checking and reevaluating data elicited under varying conditions. Recognizing that only a fraction of the total personality can be understood at any particular time, he devised a biological-cultural formula. The denominator of the formula consisted of the total personality record or potentiality of the patient; the numerator was the particular sample of performance.

CLINICAL EXAMINATION

For Meyer, the clinical psychiatric examination included the following components: (1) identifying the motives or indications for the examination, with particular focus on presenting pertinent details in the patient's life history, elicited through biographical study; (2) listing the obviously related personality items, factors, and reactions; (3) careful study of the physical, neurological, genetic, and social status and the correlation between these variables and personality factors; (4) differential diagnosis; and (5) formulation of a therapeutic plan geared to each case. Meyer believed this to be the best way to reconstruct the "experiment of nature," which was defined as the reduction of events in the patient's life to the factors in a controlled experiment. In accordance with its common-sense approach, psychobiology began with the data that were accessible. Symptoms were viewed as compensatory phenomena. Because data selection was necessary in any examination, the study of all the factors in a person's life that played a significant role, whether favorable or unfavorable, in his adjustment was called "distributive analysis." The formation of better methods of adjustment by the patient, based on his understanding of past maladaptation, was termed "distributive synthesis."

In interviewing a patient, Meyer considered it better to begin by focusing on his chief complaint, which directed attention to the situation that required immediate therapeutic intervention. Later, the psychiatrist determined the nature and extent of the disturbance in the context of the patient's over-all functioning, his previous medical history, and the role played by such factors as constitution, development, and environment. Unconscious material elicited from the patient, as well as information supplied by his family, supplemented the psychiatrist's efforts and facilitated his understanding of the situation.

As a general rule, Meyer believed that one-word diagnoses were inadequate in a field as complex as human behavior. Initially, he used the terms "reaction set" or "reaction type" in diagnostic classification, stating that "all life is reaction, either to stimuli of the outside world or of the various parts of the organism." From the early 1920's on, however, he used the word "ergasia," derived from the Greek word for work, *ergon*, to describe the general concept of behavior and mental activity, and its plural, "ergasias," to denote specific behavioral units. Ergasias were the behaviorally conceived overt and implicit products of psychobiological integration. Of the many potentialities available for adaptation in the normal personality, various ergasias tended to prevail, depending on the internal and external needs of the person. Meyer defined the person's overt behavioral response to various situations as subject organization. He then listed the various ergasias, using a different prefix for each type. At the same time, he warned that these classifications in themselves were not to be regarded as diagnoses; they simply described phenomena that occur under various conditions.

The following ergasias are no longer in use but are listed here for historical reasons: anergasia (an = lacking or lost): an organic brain reaction, such as general paresis or senile brain disease, in which structural and functional brain deficit and pathology alter behavior; dysergasia (dys = difficult): syndromes resulting from an impairment of brain function, such as a toxic psychosis or delirium; thymergasia (thymo = affective): an affective psychosis, such as a manic-depressive reaction; parergasia (para = beside): the form of schizophrenia that is characterized by regression, abandonment of reality, and delusions; merergasia (mero = part): partial inability to work or function, as in a neurosis; kakergasia (kakos = bad): abnormal, poor, or faulty behavior, used synonymously with merergasia; and oligergasia (oligo = few or scant): mental deficiency.

THERAPY

Psychobiological treatment, which began with distributive analysis and terminated with distributive synthesis, was not considered apart from pathology. Meyer believed that the psychiatrist began to treat the patient at the time of their initial contact, with the patient's exposition of his problem. This did not mean that diagnosis was not essential. However, the first step in distributive analysis was the evaluation of the patient's assets and liabilities. This evaluation was best accomplished through the study of his life history, on the basis of current data initially provided by the patient and supplemented by his subsequent reconstruction of past experiences.

Meyer recognized the importance of the patient's cooperation for the success of the psychotherapeutic process. The cooperation of the patient's better self—that is, of the healthier part of the patient's ego—was considered essential. Meyer believed that these healthier aspects of the patient's personality should serve as the starting point for treatment. Therapy was thought of as a service performed on behalf of the patient; the therapist was obligated to use every available opportunity to assist the patient. The basic aim of psychobiological therapy was to help an organism, hampered by abnormal conditions, to make the best adaptation possible to life and change.

In the initial stage of treatment, the therapist's concern focused on the patient's sleep habits, nutrition, and the regulation of his daily routines. It was also important at this stage to induce the patient to describe his difficulties in a concrete way and for the therapist to use the patient's ideation and language to communicate his offer of help and advice.

Problems were approached on a conscious, rather than an unconscious, level. Thus, therapy was administered in the course of ordinary face-to-face conversation, in order to implement the psychiatrist's efforts to focus on the patient's current situation and his reactions to his everyday difficulties, as well as his long-term life adjustment. At the beginning of each therapeutic session, the patient was encouraged to discuss his experiences in the interval since the last interview, beginning with obvious and immediate problems. Eventually, when deeper relevant material had been elicited from the patient, these problems were explored in greater detail. This exploration was accomplished through the use of spontaneous association, a term used by Meyer in preference to "free association" to describe the overcoming of the patient's resistance to verbalizing his basic problems in the unbiased atmosphere of the psychiatrist's office.

The intensity and frequency of the treatment sessions depended on the needs of the individual patient. The psychiatrist permitted the patient to arrange his treatment schedule or asked him to agree to a specific therapeutic program. It was the psychiatrist's responsibility to reassure the patient, so that he could function adequately between interviews. This reassurance was conveyed through casual comments and sensitive questioning.

Under the guidance of the psychiatrist, the patient analyzed his personality problems and their relative importance (distributive analysis) and then reconstructed the origin of his conflicts and devised healthier behavioral patterns (distributive synthesis). The psychobiological therapist asked the patient to formulate his life story by means of a life chart, to demonstrate his understanding of the origin of his difficulties and the means that he might use to ensure their resolution and to prevent their repetition.

Meyer believed that the essential goal of therapy was to aid the patient's adjustment by helping him to modify unhealthy adaptations; these modifications would lead to personal satisfaction and proper environmental readjustment. He called this "habit training." In the process of habit training, the psychiatrist used a variety of techniques—for example, guidance, suggestion, reeducation, and direction—always with emphasis on the current life situation. Psychobiological therapy was especially valuable with psychotics, although it was also recommended for neurotic reactions. In regard to the treatment of the hospitalized patient, Meyer emphasized the importance of collaboration by the members of the therapeutic community—physician, patient, nurse, and ward group—and the patient's family in providing a setting to safeguard the integrity of the patient's personality functions.

Meyer emphasized that different criteria could be used to evaluate a patient's progress and his return to normality, according to the concepts of different schools of psychiatry. However, he preferred the criteria of the capacity of the person to follow a constructive regimen of work, rest, and play.

Contribution to Psychiatric Training

Meyer remained at the Phipps Clinic for 32 years, until he reached the age of retirement at 76. During that period, the

Phipps Clinic became the most important psychiatric center in the world for the training of psychiatrists. This does not mean that Meyer attempted to mold everyone according to his psychobiological theory. On the contrary, as early as 1916 he suggested migratory training, the exposure of students to various teachers and schools, possibly in an atmosphere of free interaction, to counteract the evils of the cult of personality.

In addition to psychoanalysis, Meyer advocated the teaching of Forel's hypnotism, Kraepelin's nosology, and Jung's symbolism to avoid a unilateral approach and to meet the distinct needs and temperaments of the various psychiatrists. At the opening exercises for the new building of the New York Psychiatric Institute and Hospital in 1929, he said:

> We have only to learn what kinds of facts we deal with and have in mind; the approach will come quite naturally, and without confusing perplexities and disturbing obstructions in a pluralism with intrinsic consistency, rather than on dogmatic dualism or monism.

Meyer himself set the tone for such a pluralism. At the Phipps Clinic, the director of the psychological laboratory until 1920 was John B. Watson, who, in 1913, published his manifesto, "Psychology as the Behaviorist Views It." And in 1930, the Pavlovian laboratory was established under W. Horsley Gantt, who had studied directly under Pavlov in Russia. Many others, especially those from Europe, were invited to teach there. Among them, Paul Schilder spent 3 months at Phipps Clinic in 1928, an experience that eventually resulted in his moving to the United States in 1930.

According to Meyer, psychiatric training should start with inspiring the student's confidence in his own common sense and should be carried through the 4 years of the medical curriculum, a concept that was implemented by some medical schools in the 1950's. The curriculum should include a personality study, including an autobiographical essay, in the first year; a study of psychiatric symptoms in the second year; a practice in methods of examination and diagnostic formulation, with the help of a life chart, in the third year; and a follow-up of six or more patients and their treatment in the fourth year. Regardless of how successful this system was, the fact remains that scores of prominent psychiatrists were trained at the Phipps Clinic. It is sufficient to mention here the names of Charles MacFie Campbell, David Henderson, Wendell Muncie, Oscar Diethelm, W. Horsley Gantt, Alexander Leighton, Franklin Ebaugh, Edward J. Kempf, John Whitehorn, Leo Kanner, Phyllis Greenacre, J. Masserman, and Theodore Lidz.

In 1937, on the occasion of his twenty-fifth anniversary as director of the Phipps Clinic, a tribute was paid to Meyer that included a map of the world, showing that 100 of his pupils, mostly in the United States, had become teachers of psychiatry. By that time, under Meyer's impetus, the American Board of Psychiatry and Neurology had been established in 1934. Meyer himself had received honorary degrees from Glasgow, Clark, Yale, and Harvard universities. From his retirement in 1941 to his death in 1950, he continued to work for strengthening psychiatric and related associations and for improving standards of psychiatric accreditation in the United States. In his last article, published in 1944, "The Rise of the Person and the Concept of Wholes or Integrates," he concluded:

> Let us hope that the next century will really be the century of those wholes which we obligatorily envisage as "persons" and "social group" and "political group" . . . for the study of health and also of diseases, but above all, a better hope for the varied cultures to respect each other's uniqueness and range of equity, so as to work towards a sound relativity for the individual and group.

ROLE IN PSYCHIATRY

Meyer's major contributions to psychiatry include his emphasis on the interactive nature of symptoms and the unity of the individual person's psychological and biological functioning, so that psychoses are described as "reactions," a definition that was reflected in the 1952 edition of the American Psychiatric Association's *Diagnostic and Statistical Manual, Mental Disorders;* his pioneering biographical and historical approach to the study of personality; his support of the psychotherapeutic treatment of schizophrenia, which made the Washington-Baltimore area the pioneering center for this endeavor through the work of Sullivan, Kempf, Hill, and Fromm-Reichmann; and his enthusiasm for social action, especially for community psychiatry. In fact, although community psychiatry has come to the fore only recently, Meyer predicted the establishment of the community mental health center as early as 1913.

In light of all this, it remains puzzling why so little is known today of Meyer's contributions; regardless of his writings, which are now almost virtually unknown and which, rather poorly organized and void of literary appeal, make for arduous reading, his name is hardly mentioned in most of the psychiatric literature. The reasons are rather complex and challenging for the historian. Perhaps most important is the fact that—in attempting to portray the always changing aspects of psychological life, especially the manifold etiological and symptomatic manifestations—Meyer shied away from any systematization of his thinking in favor of a rather provisional and pluralistic presentation, based on endless details and a variety of alternatives. In particular, he never outlined developmental stages and their critical tasks and, in contrast with Freud and his followers, never presented clear and comprehensive clinical histories of patients and thorough discussions of the therapeutic programs and techniques used. It is also likely that his common-sense philosophy, being so concrete and understandable to many, was incorporated into the mainstream of psychiatry without any mention of its originator. Moreover, not unlike Kraepelin's orientation, psychobiology focused almost exclusively on the individual and on the community at large but hardly at all on the family as the transmitter of symbolic functioning and communication. And Meyer's fundamental optimistic orientation of life was deeply challenged by the great depression of the early 1930's. A few years later, American psychiatry was to be influenced in the most pervasive and fundamental way by the arrival in this country of a great number of psychoanalysts; indeed, they were a well-organized group, in spite of unavoidable individual differences, who, in a relatively short time, achieved the widest acceptance in academic circles, in psychiatric settings, and in many segments of the population.

From the historical perspective, the importance of Meyer's psychobiology lies, in the first place, in its being a trend of thought that paved the way for the acceptance of psychodynamic concepts and, in the second place, in its representing a typical expression of American pluralistic thinking that is relevant today to the current movement of community mental health.

Suggested Cross References

Freud is discussed in Chapter 8. Community psychiatry is discussed in Chapter 45.

REFERENCES

Arch. Neurol. Psychiatry, *37:* 1, 1937.
Beers, C. W. *A Mind That Found Itself.* Longman's Green, New York, 1908.

Bleuler, M. Early sources of Adolf Meyer's concepts. Am. J. Psychiatry, *119:* 193, 1962.

Bull. Johns Hopkins Hosp., *89:* 1, 1951.

Cross, W. L., editor. *Twenty-five Years After: Sidelights on the Mental Hygiene Movement and Its Founder.* Doubleday, Garden City, N. Y., 1934.

* Deutsch, A. *The Mentally Ill in America.* Columbia University Press, New York, 1967.

* Diethelm, O. Adolf Meyer (1866–1950). In *Grosse Nervenärtze,* K. Kolle, editor, vol. 2, p. 129. Thieme, Stuttgart, 1959.

Feierstein, S. *Adolf Meyer: Life and Work.* Juris, Zurich, 1966.

Grob, G. N. Adolf Meyer on American psychiatry in 1895. Am. J. Psychiatry, *119:* 1135, 1963.

Grob, G. N. *The State and the Mentally Ill: A History of Worcester State Hospital in Massachussets, 1830–1920.* University of North Carolina Press, Chapel Hill, 1966.

* Hale, N. G. *Freud and the Americans: The Beginning of Psychoanalysis in the United States, 1876–1917.* Oxford University Press, New York, 1971.

* Lidz, T. Adolf Meyer and the development of American psychiatry. Am. J. Psychiatry, *123:* 320, 1966.

Lidz, T. Adolf Meyer. In *International Encyclopedia of Social Sciences,* vol. 10, p. 263, Free Press of Glencoe (Macmillan), New York, 1968.

* Lief, A., editor. *The Commonsense Psychiatry of Adolf Meyer.* McGraw-Hill, New York, 1948.

* Meyer, A. *Collected Papers of Adolf Meyer,* 4 vols. Johns Hopkins Press, Baltimore, 1948–1952.

Meyer, A. *Psychobiology: A Science of Man.* Charles C Thomas, Springfield, Ill., 1957.

Muncie, W. *Psychobiology and Psychiatry.* C. V. Mosby, St. Louis, 1939.

Muncie, W. Treatment in psychobiologic psychiatry: Its present status. In *Progress in Psychotherapy,* F. Fromm-Reichmann and J. L. Moreno, editors. Grune & Stratton, New York, 1956.

Muncie, W. The psychobiological approach. In *American Handbook of Psychiatry,* S. Arieti, editor, vol. 2, p. 1317. Basic Books, New York, 1959.

Quen J. M., and Carlson E. T., editors. *American Psychoanalysis: Origins and Development.* Brunner/Mazel, New York, 1978.

Schulman, J. *Remaking an Organization.* State University of New York Press, Albany, 1969.

Walser, H. H. Die wissenschaftlichen Anfängen von Adolf Meyer (1866–1950) und die Entstehung der "Zürcher psychiatrischen Schule." Gesnerus, *23:* 202, 1966.

Whitehorn, J. C., and Zilboorg, G. Present trends in American psychiatric research. Am. J. Psychiatry, *90:* 303, 1933.

Winters, E. E. Adolf Meyer's two and a half years at Kankakee. Bull. Hist. Med., *40:* 441, 1966.

Winter, E. E. Adolf Meyer and Clifford Beers, 1907–1910. Bull. Hist. Med., *43:* 414, 1969.

10.3 Carl Jung

DAVID ELKIND, Ph.D.

Introduction

Carl Jung was a Swiss psychiatrist who, early in his career, became an admirer and advocate of the then (1906) still heretical writings of Sigmund Freud. Jung's work on schizophrenia and his research with the word-association test won him Freud's admiration and respect. Indeed, Freud hoped that Jung would eventually assume the leadership of the psychoanalytic movement. But Freud's hope was never to be realized. Jung was too independent to be a follower and too devoted to research to become an administrator. But the major cause of the dispute between Jung and Freud was Jung's rejection of Freud's championship of sexuality as the root cause of all mental disorders. Jung recognized that sexuality could and did play a role in many mental maladies, but he believed that psychic forces other than sexuality were also inherent in the person and could lead to emotional and mental conflict.

Jung gradually elaborated his own theory of mental disorder and his own therapeutic techniques, which together he called

analytical psychology. Although Jung's analytical psychology has never had the wide popular appeal of psychoanalysis, it does have a substantial following in many different parts of the world. There are, for example, several Jungian training institutes in America. In addition, many of Jung's books and letters are now being published or republished, and there seems to be growing interest in his work among young people. Indeed, Jung's interest in Eastern religions, alchemy, and occult matters anticipated many contemporary interests and concerns in Western society.

Jung's contributions to modern psychiatry are practical, as well as theoretical. On the practical side, his brand of psychotherapy has been particularly helpful to those in the middle years of life. On the theoretical side, his conceptions of the symbol, of archetypes, of extroversion and introversion, and of the various psychological types have become part of the general psychiatric nomenclature and part of contemporary vocabulary.

Life

Carl Gustav Jung was born on July 26, 1875, in the country parish of Kesswill on Lake Constance in the Swiss canton of Thurgau. His father was a Lutheran minister of quite modest means who was well intentioned but somewhat strict and puritanical. As a poor but brilliant student, Jung became attracted, in his late adolescence, to the philosophical writers and avidly read Pythagoras, Heraclitus, Empedeocles, and Plato. But Schopenhauer was Jung's real discovery. Jung agreed with that philosopher's somber picture of the world, but he did not agree with Schopenhauer's solutions. At about the same time, Jung began to make his break with institutional religion and to arrive at a broader, more psychological conception of God.

At the university Jung studied medicine, partly because his great-grandfather and namesake had been a well-known physician in Basel.

FIGURE 1. Carl Gustav Jung, 1875–1961. (National Library of Medicine, Bethesda, Md.)

When he completed his medical studies, he was not sure which field to specialize in but chanced to read a text on psychiatry by Krafft-Ebing (perhaps a case of the synchronicity Jung was later to postulate in his theory of personality), and he discovered a field where he hoped he could work productively for the rest of his career. Thereafter, in 1900, he went to the Psychiatric Clinic of Bürgholzli in Zurich to work as an assistant under Eugen Bleuler, the well-known psychiatrist.

While at the Bürghölzli, Jung undertook studies of word association, wrote a classic textbook on schizophrenia, and became an advocate of Sigmund Freud. Jung was, however, never a blind devotee of Freud and always maintained his independence of thought. It was that very independence of thought which brought about the rift between the two men. Jung met Freud for the first time in 1907 and was greatly impressed by Freud's intelligence and insight, but he also felt that Freud was overly enamored of his sexual theories. It was on that point that the two men parted ways, despite Freud's hope that Jung would direct the psychoanalytic movement. When Jung (1967) was writing his *Transformations and Symbols of the Libido*, he knew that it would alienate Freud because he suggested that a large part of the unconscious was objective or collective and had nothing to do with the sexual instincts. The publication of the book ended Jung's association with Freud and with the psychoanalytic movement.

After his break with Freud, Jung went his own way. He entered private practice and began a long and arduous exploration of his own unconscious so as to discover as much as he could about the objective psyche. After concluding that voyage of discovery, Jung continued to develop his own analytic psychology, centered on the analysis of the symbols of the objective psyche and the realization of the self. Toward that end he explored areas as diverse as alchemy, flying saucers, and parapsychology. In all these endeavors he maintained an objective, comparative-analysis approach to the phenomena in question and did not slip into the mysticism of which he was so often accused. Jung died in 1961 at the age of 85.

The Symbol

At the heart of Jungian theory lies the concept of the symbol. Within Freudian psychology, symbols, particularly dream symbols, were assumed to reflect wishes and impulses that were repressed from conscious experience but then sought outlet in a disguised, symbolic form. Although Freud denied that there were fixed symbols (a cigar in a dream does not always signify a penis), he did believe that all symbols were related in some way to some hostile or sexual motivation. In the Freudian view, symbols allowed forbidden impulses to gain entry into consciousness, where they agitated the ego to work toward their satisfaction and fulfillment.

Jung agreed with Freud that many symbols did, indeed, represent what he called the personal unconscious. Symbols in the personal unconscious derived from the person's own life experiences and were, in effect, memory traces that were taken over and activated by socially prohibited thoughts and impulses. But Jung argued that such symbols were not the only ones that presented themselves to consciousness in dreams and reverie states. Some symbols originated in a deeper level of the unconscious, which Jung once called the "collective unconscious" but later called the "objective psyche." The symbols in the objective psyche do not derive from individual experience but, rather, from the collective experience of the race. They are, in a word, archetypical modes of thought.

Not surprisingly, the psychoanalysts insisted that Jung's interpretation of symbols was mystical and that, with the exception of a few archaic remnants admitted by Freud, all symbols were a construction of the personal unconscious. Also, not unexpectedly, Jung was attacked by the academic psychologists for, in effect, postulating the inheritance of ideas. To the new discipline of psychology, striving hard to be an experimental science, the possibility that ideas might be inherited, rather than derived from experiences, was something of an anathema.

Jung's evidence for archetypical symbols was, unfortunately, not always easy to appreciate. He first explored the depths of his own objective psyche and recorded all the themes and symbols he found in the nethermost regions of his own unconscious. Many of the symbols and themes Jung uncovered were impossible to trace to his personal experience but could be traced back to antiquity. Jung also found comparable symbols in the dreams and art productions of his patients that could, likewise, not be traced to personal experience. The weakness of those arguments is, of course, that it is difficult to prove the absence of personal experience without a complete record of the person's life history. Obtaining such a complete record is probably impossible.

Other evidence for the universality and, hence, the collective nature of some symbols came from comparative studies of different cultures, religions, and mythologies in geographically separated parts of the world. Presumably, if the natives of East Africa and the Eskimos of Alaska use comparable symbols and express common themes in their mythologies, those symbols and themes must derive from some common objective layer of consciousness, rather than from personal experience. In some ways, the contemporary work of Lévi-Strauss in anthropology, of Chomsky in linguistics, and of Piaget in psychology and epistemology gives partial support to the Jungian position. Each of those theorists postulates and provides evidence for the presence of universal structures, and personal experience is a necessary but not a sufficient condition for their realization.

Not only are the symbols of the objective psyche different in origin from those of the personal unconscious, but they are also different in their functions. In general, the function of symbols derived from the personal unconscious is to satisfy some unacceptable instinctual wish or impulse. But the symbols of the objective unconscious are much more closely tied to the total personality. Such symbols provide clues to hidden potentialities and qualities that the conscious mind would not otherwise be aware of. In addition, the symbols of the objective unconscious point toward the future and suggest the direction in which the person is moving in his own development. In other words, the symbols of the personal unconscious are basically in the service of the instincts, whereas the symbols of the objective unconscious aim at the fulfillment of the individual personality as a whole.

That conception of the origins and function of symbols in the objective unconscious suggests a theory of personality development and of personality disorder that complements, rather than supplants, the Freudian theory of personality growth and of neurosis. It suggests that there are nonsexual components of the personality that strive for realization and for expression and that mental disorder can ensue when such realization and expression are blocked or diverted. Ultimately, Jung argued that each man and each woman is born with a vast cultural heritage of propensities that need to find expression in their personal lives if they are ever to become whole and integrated personalities. But such wholeness and integration do not come about as a consequence of the absence of something, such as repressions and neurotic defenses; rather, they come about through an active search to discover one's potentialities and the various facets of one's own personality. Jung's theory of personality is not simple, since it suggests that personality growth does not come about because of fortunate external circumstances but, rather, from the person's own strength of will and his use of inner resources.

In a Jungian analysis, the realization of one's potentials comes about gradually through a laborious process of getting to know various facets of one's objective psyche. Ordinarily, that voyage of personal discovery goes through predictable stages, wherein more or less universal facets of the objective psyche come to the fore in many different guises. Only after those various facets have been confronted is the person free to realize the innermost part of himself that Jung called the self.

The Shadow

In many ways, the shadow is the objective counterpart of the personal unconscious in the sense that it represents some of the unacceptable aspects and components of the objective psyche. Indeed, the shadow can also include aspects of the personal unconscious. To illustrate some types of shadow phenomena: The man who thinks of himself as generous may discover that he has tendencies to be petty and cheap. To the extent that he can accept those tendencies as part of himself, he is able to further integrate his personality and work toward wholeness as a person. In contrast, the person who rejects the shadow parts of himself can never be totally honest with himself and never reach true integration as a whole personality.

The shadow consists, in part, of all the little sins and faults that one tends to ignore or forget about oneself because they do not fit with one's more flattering self-conceptions. Coming to grips with that aspect of the shadow requires a certain level of maturity and of perspective, which does not usually emerge until the second half of life. But the other parts of the shadow also begin to emerge in the second half of life, not because they were repressed or denied but because they were never given the opportunity to be realized. Those objective psyche components of the shadow can appear in dreams, in a person's artistic productions, or in his actions when he projects the contents of his shadow onto the external world.

Often the objective psyche components of the shadow reflect a side of the personality that was not realized in the first half of one's life. The scholar, for example, who immersed himself in his books and intellectual ruminations may, during the second half of life, find himself infatuated with an attractive young woman who has few if any intellectual pretensions. In such situations, the feeling side of the scholar's personality, so long suppressed in the service of the intellect, comes to the fore and begins to assert its power over the mind. The scholar, inexperienced in dealing with the world of feelings, often makes a fool of himself and can occasionally destroy himself by giving in to the undisciplined feelings of the shadow.

However, the shadow is not simply negative; it can have positive values. Dreams that reveal the shadow side of the personality can be used as guides to fulfilling functions that have been neglected. The businessman who dreams of visiting art galleries and museums and who experiences great admiration for the technical skill of artists may take the dream as a signal that he should begin some artistic work himself. Having given himself to the external world for the first part of his life, the artist hidden in the shadow now begins to press to the forefront of the businessman's consciousness. Intrusions of the shadow into dreams and reveries can, therefore, be important clues to the course that one's life should take.

Anima and Animus

After a person has come to grips with his shadow, in both its personal and its objective unconscious guises, he next meets his feminine side in the case of a man and her masculine side in the case of a woman. As was true for the shadow, the anima and the animus are combinations of personal and objective unconscious elements. The anima in a man, for example, reflects residues of experiences with his own mother and universal archetypal female patterns. Comparable to what pertained for the shadow, the anima and animus elements can have negative effects if they are ignored and repressed or positive effects if they are integrated within the personality and regarded as symbols of directions to be taken for further development of the personality.

The anima in a man involves many different psychological tendencies, such as moods, feelings, and intuitions that are usually characteristic of the opposite sex. Jung argued that the anima in a man often appears as receptivity to the irrational, openness to romantic love, and a feeling for nature. Aspects of the anima that derive from personal experience with the mother are colored by her qualities as a person. A man whose mother was complaining and bitter may experience moods in which he feels, "I am nothing; nothing makes any sense." Those feelings may be accompanied by obsessive ruminations and even thoughts of suicide. On the other hand, a man whose mother was happy, honest, and gay often experiences anima moods of elation and an enhanced sense of personal competence and personal esteem.

On a more universal plane, some archetypical anima forms are often projected onto the external world and are portrayed in art, dreams, and mythology. One such archetypical anima is the femme fatale, the beautiful woman who lures the man intoxicated by her charms into danger and frequently to death. The Lorelei of the Rhineland myth plays such a role, and Orpheus met his death because of such a woman's charms. Another prototypical anima figure is the witch or priestess, who often appears as the direct and undisguised embodiment of evil. The witch or high priestess in history and in fiction is often a projection of an archetypical figure onto the external world.

Jung suggested that the anima as it is constructed in the individual psyche has four stages. The earliest form of the anima is an Eve-like figure who is an earth-mother type and who represents primitive reproductive and sexual functions and pleasures. At the next stage, the anima is personified in a romantic ideal, such as Helen in the story of Faust. Helen represents purity and sexuality at a high and romantic plane. The next stage raises femininity to an even higher level and is embodied in the figure of the Virgin Mary. In Mary the sexual and maternal functions are no longer worldly; they have become spiritual. At the final stage, the anima transcends even the heights of spiritual purity and holiness and exists as a form of pure wisdom.

In dealing with those objective unconscious anima figures, the individual man must avoid two persistent dangers. One of those dangers is to think of the emergent anima figure as a fantasy, a made-up figure with no real meaning and no real function. In treating the anima in that way, the man fails to recognize the message that the anima carries and misses a chance for further personal growth. The opposite danger is to project the anima and to deal with it as real. The man who deals with the anima as the representation of some external verity, institution, or belief loses the personal value that the anima figure may have for him. Likewise, if the anima figure is projected onto a real woman, the man can never deal with her as the person she is but only as the anima that he wants her to be. The result is, at best, disappointment and, at worst, a disaster for both sides of the relationship.

In Jung's view the best way for a man to deal with his anima figures, as was true for his shadow, is to accept them as realities of his own psychic existence and to try to understand them as such. Once the man grasps the meaning of those animas for himself, they can be integrated into his personality and become functioning parts of it. But now they are no longer under their own volition but are, rather, under the control of the conscious personality, which can use them for creative and constructive purposes. Grasping the meaning of one's anima is, however, not a simple matter and requires much interpretative work. The path to personality realization and fulfillment through the experience and integration of the symbols of the objective unconscious is not an easy route and can be a tortuous road.

Like the anima of a man, the animus of a woman has its personal and objective components. On the personal side, the animus contains elements derived from experience with the woman's father. However, in contrast to the anima, which often appears in the form of an erotic fantasy, the animus most often emerges as an unchallengeable conviction of great personal importance. That conviction may appear directly in the woman's demeanor when she propounds it with ex cathedra pomp and circumstance, or it may appear indirectly in the coldness and obstinance of the woman whose conviction has been challenged. Animus opinions in women are most often overgeneralizations that may be true on a particular level of abstraction but that may not be true for the particular case in point.

The animus is also analogous to the anima of a man because it has both negative and positive propensities. When a woman, for example, feels guilty about not having met some obligation, she may dream of negative, destructive, murdering men. When, in addition, she begins to harbor the aggressive, destructive fantasies of the animus and project them onto her family, she can cause everyone involved untold anguish with her hawkish bitchiness. On the other hand, the animus can be of positive value because it embodies the positive masculine qualities of initiative, objectivity, and courage. If the woman can accept and work with the symbols of her animus, she can incorporate those positive qualities and subordinate the negative ones within her own personality and, paradoxically, become more completely feminine because of having integrated her masculine potentials.

In the development of the animus, there are four stages comparable to those found in the development of the anima. At the earliest stage, the animus is represented by athletic prowess, physical power, and strength, as embodied in a Samson or an Atlas. At the next stage, the animus figure displays qualities of initiative and efficiency and shows the ability to plan and carry out actions. At the third stage, the animus is embodied in the representatives of logos and mind, such as the scholar, the scientist, and the theologian. At the final stage, the animus takes the form of the wise old man and signifies the path through which a woman can renew herself and find new meaning in and for her life.

The animus and the anima represent, then, basic tendencies within each person that usually correspond to those manifested by persons of the opposite sex. Those tendencies are both positive and negative; the anima represents vengefulness and maliciousness, as well as tenderness and intuition; and the animus represents destructiveness and aggression, as well as initiative, objectivity, and reason. If those qualities are not recognized for what they are—intrinsic parts of the psyche that have to be dealt with—they can do untold mischief for the person who experiences them as foreign to his or her being. But if they are accepted as part of one's personality and are integrated into it, they can be brought under the control of the personality and used for constructive and creative purposes.

The Self

Within Jungian psychology, the term "self" is used quite differently from the way it is used in other personality theories. Freud, for example, used "self" to indicate the conscious part of the personality. For Jung, however, the self is at the very heart of the psyche and does not come into awareness until the person has succeeded in dealing with his shadow and his anima or animus. In many ways, the self, when it emerges, is experienced as a kind of rebirth, a renewal of life in a new, more integrated, and wise form. In some ways the self is a true cosmic man, in that he is omniscient when he appears symbolically in dreams and in myths. And, in Jung's view, the person who begins to realize the core of his psyche, his self, comes into possession of special psychic powers.

Other Jungian Concepts

THE PERSONA

Jung used the term "persona" in much the same way that sociologists use the concept of social role. The persona is the official social mask or pattern of behavior that the person uses in social situations. The role of doctor, teacher, or minister is defined socially and has prescribed values, orientations, and behaviors. The persona becomes a problem when the person either identifies too closely with it or becomes too distant from it. The doctor who plays the doctor role at home and with friends denies his true personality and is often a bore. The person who denies his social role or persona, like some alienated youth, loses touch with the larger society and may become totally self-serving. Personas are useful insofar as they are recognized as patterns that are necessary to but not identical with the true personality.

INTROVERSION-EXTROVERSION

When Jung broke with Freud, he looked back on his experience and the theories of Freud and Adler and tried to understand them as examples of general psychological phenomena. He argued that both Adler and Freud dealt with subject-object relationship but that each man looked at those relationships from a different perspective. Freud, Jung said, was most concerned with the objects in the external world to which the subject cathected or attached himself. Adler, on the other hand, was most concerned with the subject, with his power drives and security needs. Jung wondered whether Freud and Adler might not represent more or less universal types of persons. Freud would represent persons most concerned with the outer world, the extroverts; Adler would represent those persons most concerned with the inner world, the introverts.

Introversion and extroversion are, then, general human propensities, both of which are embodied in every person. Some persons emphasize their introversion most, and others emphasize their extroversion. There are objective psyche components to introversion and to extroversion; when a person goes too far in one or the other direction, the opposite pole of his personality begins to assert itself and to seek realization. The effective mother, to illustrate, finds in the second half of life that her children no longer need her and that life seems empty and without meaning. When such a woman begins to look inward to explore her artistic and creative potentials, she is often rejuvenated and finds new meaning to her existence.

Contrariwise, the person who has devoted the first part of his life to releasing his creative potentials may, in the second half of life, discover a new interest in the world of people and events. One often sees such transformations in scientists and professors who, in middle life, become involved in politics and in social movements. Having devoted themselves to the realization of their own abilities, they feel impelled to do something for other people and for the larger social group.

That phenomenon of opposites' seeking realization in their own right is fundamental to Jungian psychology and constitutes one of his major themes. Basically, all people are multifaceted, and many of those facets are archetypical in nature. When some of those facets are realized to the exclusion of the others, the unrealized abilities seek fulfillment in their own right.

PSYCHOLOGICAL FUNCTIONS

Introversion and extroversion are essentially more or less total orientations toward the subject or the object. But Jung also distinguished four basic psychological functions that are orthogonal to extroversion and to introversion. Two of those functions are rational, thinking and feeling; the other two, sensation and intuition, are irrational. As in the case of introversion and extroversion, a particular person may be characterized by a particular function, although he possesses all four. And since there is no direct connection with introversion-extroversion, there are eight possible combinations of functions and types. A thinking introvert may be exemplified in the absent-minded professor; the thinking extrovert may be exemplified in the politician or clergyman.

All the psychological functions have archetypal components and so obey the law of opposites. The overemphasis on the realization of thinking leads, at a certain point in life, to an eruption of intuition and sensation, and the person who realizes mostly his intuition and sensation finds that the rational functions of thinking and feeling eventually seek their due. These various functions are represented by universal and characteristic symbols that can be found in art, mythology, and dreams. If the person heeds the symbolic cues and works toward the total realization of his personality, those symbols can be helpful. But if he ignores them, if he continues to use the functions that worked for him in the first half of life in the hope that they will work for him during the second half, the result will be negative. The person will either engage in behaviors that he does not understand or feel empty and unfulfilled but not know where to turn. The denial of one's opposites, in Jung's psychology, is, in effect, a rejection of continued growth of self and personality.

SYNCHRONICITY

When Jung broke with Freud, one of the issues on which they differed was causality. Freud was a strict determinist in the sense that he believed nothing occurred by chance. Forgetting, slips of the tongue, and the vast array of errors of everyday life were all determined by unconscious motives, wishes, and fantasies. Jung, in contrast, believed that there were meaningful coincidences of events that were not caused in the strict sense of the word. The occurrence of such events Jung (1960) called "synchronicity."

He argued (Jung, 1960) that the events could be grouped into three categories:

The coincidence of a psychic state in the observer with a simultaneous, objective external event that corresponds to the psychic state or content, where there is no evidence of a causal connection between psychic state and the external event, and where considering the psychic

relativity of space and time, such a connection is not even conceivable. . . .

The coincidence of a psychic state with a corresponding (more or less simultaneous) external event taking place outside the observer's field of perception, i.e., at a distance and only verifiable afterward. . . .

The coincidence of a psychic state with a corresponding, not yet existent future event that is distant in time and likewise can only be verified afterward.

For Freud the determinism was intrapsychic in the sense that it was between a person's unconscious motives and his or her actual behavior. For Jung, synchronicity was extrapsychic in the sense that it dealt with the relation between inner states and outer events. Freud seldom dealt with such correspondences but, when he did, as in his discussion of the uncanny, he tended to reduce them to intrapsychic events. Jung, however, believed that meaningful coincidences were lawful and not just chance but that the laws were those that have yet to be discovered and understood.

To illustrate the first type of synchronicity, Jung told the story of a female patient with strong intellectual defenses that made treatment difficult. One day she recounted to Jung a dream of having been given a golden scarab, a costly piece of jewelry, as a gift. At that moment Jung heard an insect at the window apparently trying to get in. He opened the window, and, when the insect flew in, he caught it. It was a scarabed beetle (*Cetonia aurata*) with a gold-green color that made it look like a golden scarab. Jung held his closed hand near the patient, and, when he opened it, he said, "Here is your golden scarab." That experience broke through the patient's reserve and permitted treatment to proceed more productively.

The second type of synchronicity is reflected in dreams or fantasies that parallel concurrent events. There are many such dreams in folklore and mythology. Whereas Freud traced such dreams to unconscious desires, Jung saw connections between the psychic events and the physical events. He cited (Jung, 1960), for example, Swedenborg's vision of the great fire of Stockholm. He also cited (Jung, 1960) the report of Victor Goddard to the effect that an officer in his command dreamed that Goddard's plane would have an accident—an event that did, indeed, occur at about the same time.

Finally, to illustrate the third type of synchronicity, Jung (1960) related the story of a student whose father promised him a trip to Spain in the event that he successfully passed his examinations. Later, the student dreamed of walking down a street in a Spanish city and of seeing a Gothic cathedral and a carriage with two cream-colored horses. When he passed his exams, he went to Spain, and in one city he found the cathedral of his dream. As he left the cathedral and turned a corner, he saw the carriage with two cream-colored horses he had dreamed about as well.

Of course, it is easy to dismiss such incidents as being pure chance or overly fanciful. But in recent years some well-known scientists have been suggesting a scientific basis for synchronicity. Karl Pribram (1979), a Stanford neuropsychologist, has in the past few years proposed a holographic theory of memory. He argues that the brain acts like a holographic system to reconstruct the experience that impinges on it. The mental experience parallels that of the external world but is not a simple copy of it. That theory is close to the notion of a preestablished harmony between the physical and the psychic that was first espoused by Spinoza and that Jung described as the forerunner of synchronicity.

If the reality or experience one knows does not correspond point for point with the physical world, the physical world as one knows it is, perhaps, much more variable than it is thought to be. The possibility of multiple worlds and multiple realities cannot be excluded. Hence, synchronicity may relate to the fact that the relation between physical and psychic events is much more complex than it was previously supposed to be. The new work on holograms is tenuous, to be sure, but it does suggest that, with his concept of synchronicity, as with many of his other concepts, Jung was highlighting a phenomenon worthy of more serious attention than it had hitherto received.

Suggested Cross References

Freud's ideas are examined in depth in Chapter 8. Section 9.1 discusses Alfred Adler.

REFERENCES

Jung, C. G. *Psychology and Education.* Princeton University Press, Princeton, 1954.
Jung, C. J. *Synchronicity.* Princeton University Press, Princeton, 1960.
Jung, C. G. *Memories, Dreams, Reflections.* Vintage, New York, 1961.
Jung, C. G. *Man and His Symbols.* Dell, New York, 1964.
* Jung, C. G. *Two Essays on Analytical Psychology.* Princeton University Press, Princeton, 1966.
* Jung, C. G. *Symbols of Transformation,* ed. 2. Princeton University Press, Princeton, 1967.
* Jung, C. G. *Archetypes of the Collective Unconscious.* Princeton University Press, Princeton, 1968.
* Jung, C. G. *Psychological Reflections.* Princeton University Press, Princeton, 1970.
* Jung, C. G. *Psychological Types.* Princeton University Press, Princeton, 1971.
McGuire, W., editor. *The Freud-Jung Letters.* Princeton University Press, Princeton, 1974.
Pribram, K. Holographic memory. Psychol. Today, *12:* 71, 1979.

10.4 Otto Rank

ABRAHAM SCHMITT, D.S.W.

Introduction

Otto Rank was born in Vienna, Austria in 1884 and died in New York in 1939. He is known for two major contributions to psychology. First, as the only nonmedical philosopher in the Freudian inner circle, he brought a broad world view to the psychoanalytic movement during its early years of development (1905–1925). Second, he devoted the remainder of his life to developing a psychology and a psychotherapy method that eventually became known as the third force or humanistic psychology. Although he is not credited with being the forerunner in that movement, he was, in fact, its founder.

Of his early life, little is known apart from the few fleeting references in his *Daybook* (unpublished). He referred to his father as a drinker who bothered little with Otto or his brother. His mother found satisfaction primarily in the fact that the family had something to eat and was decently clothed. Otherwise, he was left to himself—without education, without friends, and without books. Rank made frequent references to his acute suffering and his feeling of the futility of his existence.

His deprived circumstances conflicted with his brilliant intellect, and he frequently contemplated suicide. Then, suddenly, at 19 years of age, he leaped forward to take hold of every resource he could to enact a transformation that became the key to his life philosophy and work. Nietzsche and Schopenhauer were his greatest inspirations, followed by Darwin and the novels of Stendhal and Dostoyevsky. He later discovered Kierkegaard, an existential philosopher. Rank was probably the first person to translate existentialism into a therapeutic technique. Thereafter, he was preoccupied with artistic creativity. He had truly translated his own life of futility into the life of an optimistic creative artist. Rank always advocated artistic creativity as the key statement of his belief.

Otto Rank (1907) synthesized his total life experience in the book *Der Kunster (The Artist)* while he studied all the writings of Freud as they were published and integrated them naturally into his own thought process. When he finally presented his writings to Freud, he was immediately taken into the inner circle. The event is recorded by Freud (1917) in *Collected Papers:*

> One day a young man who had passed through the technical training school introduced himself with a manuscript which showed very unusual comprehension. We induced him to go through the Gymnasium and the University and to devote himself to the nonmedical side of psychoanalytic investigation. The little society acquired in him a zealous and dependent secretary and I gained in Otto Rank a faithful helper and co-worker.

In Freud, Rank discovered a brilliant, caring, challenging, goal-oriented father figure—one he had never known before. It was with Freud that he learned the meaning of a union with another person; that experience facilitated his discovery of his self-worth as a person and as a therapist. Being a member of Freud's prestigious inner circle at the beginning of the psychoanalytic movement gave Rank confidence to develop an ideology that was, at first, in complete accord with Freudian doctrine. In this inner circle he matured as a therapist, as an editor of several psychoanalytic journals, and as a researcher. The meaning of union in the search for self-worth was later to become a key factor in his therapy.

As Otto Rank received deep affirmation from Freud for his novel contributions, his unique individuality emerged. As he gained a favored spot in Freud's sight, conflicts with other members of the inner circle increased. His own development turned more and more to the theoretical and philosophical base that he brought with him. Now it is hard to comprehend that neither he nor Freud understood the deep division between them. Rank was an existentialist philosopher to the core and could never yield to the fixed, reductionist theory of psychoanalysis. When Rank (1973) wrote *The Trauma of Birth* in 1923, he dedicated it to Freud, believing that he was adding a new dimension to the theory when, in fact, he was into another thought process. Although Freud never completed reading the book, he had full confidence that Rank would alter his view if really challenged or that Rank's contribution could be included in Freudian theory.

The other members of Freud's inner circle read the book with much keener insight and immediately saw it correctly as heretical. Because of pressure from those members, Freud had to ask his "beloved son," whom he had been grooming to become his successor, to recant or leave. At that point Freud had a dream of himself as Goliath being killed by the much smaller and younger Rank as David.

Rank then discovered another attribute in his growth psychology—that at every separation one must relive the trauma of birth in order to establish one's individuality and that the process evokes either the death fear caused by failing to separate—thus, death by suffocation—or the life fear caused by overasserting oneself—thus, abandonment. He knew that the creative artist had to be born in him as he chose to live by his belief at any price to himself. That is also the price that must be paid at the end of every therapeutic relationship. The concept is a key to his therapeutic method. He had to experience the traumatic ending that he later postulated as an integral part of his theory.

From 1925 until his death in 1939, the same year Freud died, Rank moved back and forth between Paris, New York City, and Philadelphia. He was under a lot of stress during most of that time, seeing an endless number of patients in psychotherapy in order to earn a living, continually lecturing along the Eastern seaboard at the request of professional groups and schools of social work, and inwardly yearning to develop his theory. His most influential contributions were (1) his writings; (2) seeing one particular patient, Anaïs Nin, in Paris; and (3) his affiliation with the University of Pennsylvania School of Social Work.

Theory of Personality

Rank's use of two sets of terms, "union-separation" and "likeness-difference," aid in understanding his total model of personality theory and therapy.

In union with another person or persons or with humanity, one discovers and affirms one's likeness. In the experience of separation, one discovers and affirms one's own and another's uniqueness or difference.

In union, one discovers one's self-worth. As one sees one's own reflection in a relationship with another person, one sees one's likeness and, thus, one's self-worth.

In separation, one discovers one's identity. That discovery is often experienced most abruptly as one is suddenly cut off from someone else because of an error or an impulsive act against another. Then one stands alone, and one has a chance to see oneself in clear relief and a chance to discover and affirm one's uniqueness.

Rank used those concepts and many other concepts as a dialectic, a state of being in which there is a harmony of opposites that are held in tension. Rank's theory is often described in terms of a duality; he played opposites against each other—black against white. They are not simply opposites, like the two colors; rather, the very existence of the one depends on its dialectic opposite.

Likeness and difference, union and separation are in dialectic relationship in Rankian theories. The degree to which any human being moves in any direction depends entirely on the degree to which he is certain of the opposite direction. One can move toward another human being only as one is certain of one's identity, which is discovered in separation. Simultaneously, one can move away from people only as one is internally certain of one's belonging.

Rank believed that the movement back and forth was not merely happenstance but an act of the will. As one chooses another and willfully engages with that other in an encounter, one meets the depth of one's need for belonging. Likewise, one chooses to cast out into the unknown to affirm and claim one's uniqueness. That act he described as negative-will assertion.

In the Rankian growth process, the will must overcome several inhibiting forces to move toward and away from people. The first inhibiting force is the problem of guilt. Every act of the will evokes guilt. The act of moving toward someone in union is laden with guilt for needing someone else or even needing to use someone for one's own growth. To move away evokes greater guilt for having to abandon someone whom one has used and may need again.

An even greater risk is involved in moving in any direction—the risk of going too far, of moving beyond the gravity pull of the dialectic opposite. Because of one's desperate need for union or the other's need for too great a union, one can get lost in the union. It is then a smothering, engulfing encounter, which Rank called the death fear—fear of dying by smothering. The more unsure one is of one's identity, the greater is the fear.

To move away from humanity carries the opposite danger and the concomitant fear. Separation carries with it the danger of moving so far that one overshoots one's orbit and the pull of the union no longer takes hold. Rank called that the life fear.

To Rank, the schizophrenic is the best example of the process. With next to no sense of self-worth, the schizophrenic is suddenly thrust out to claim his difference without first having belonged. He floats on into oblivion, far beyond the reach of humanity, and into isolation. He cannot discover his identity because he needed to have a firm grasp of his self-worth, his likeness to mankind, before he could engage in this venture as a growth experience.

The greatest trauma in the movement into union and into separation is even more intense in Rank's model. With each union, a person has to abandon his own will to another's

strange will to enjoy brief happiness, unaware of his difference. Each of those experiences must then be abandoned in a new rebirth experience. The fear of the unknown outcome of each movement must be borne as the price paid for growth. The problem of separation and union is the central drama of the Rankian growth process.

Rank's growth process of personality is a continuous movement into and out of relationships. Although one is always experiencing unions and separations, there are phases when major leaps forward occur in the growth process. Each phase begins with a major need for union and then moves toward a rebirth in the form of separation.

Rank divided the growth process into four major phases: familial, societal, artistic, and spiritual. Each phase has one or more major movements toward union with significant others or with the cosmos, and major rebirth experiences in the form of separation by will affirmation.

The two-sided nature of growth must be clearly understood. Each person needs to yield to a love relationship, to remove his difference in order to experience the unity of the self with others and the cosmos for the explicit purpose of briefly experiencing self-worth and a release from difference. That yielding to another's strange will terminates when the will needs to claim its separateness and renewed perception of difference. Another rebirth of the will and a new affirmation of individuality occur.

The movements are not repeated aimlessly; rather, they are direction oriented toward the ultimate goal of becoming the creative artist.

FAMILIAL PHASE

Life begins with union. In the intrauterine experience the organism experiences both physiological and psychological union to its cosmological perfection. Deep into the unconscious is written the meaning and the need for intimacy. It could be that the insatiable human longing for perfection, the longing for problem-free existence, or even the ability to anticipate the perfection of heaven comes as a result of having experienced all that before being born.

Rank questioned whether the numerous primitive accounts of the origin of human beings, including the biblical account, that begin with a state of perfection, the garden of Eden, are not written as a prototype of each human being's beginning. Rank's use of ancient literature, especially mythical writings, to support his theory clearly indicated that he believed the uncomplicated primitive mind was capable of comprehending intuitively and naturally what he and his colleagues were struggling to understand psychologically and rationally.

The nirvana of perfect belonging must come to an end. To stay is to die; to leave is to take a chance to live, at least for a while, and to open the possibility of growth toward wholeness again. Birth is a traumatic experience for the infant. Growth toward individuation is always bought with a price. Even the Edenic account of the creation tells of a traumatic expulsion from the garden—the price that needed to be paid for self-awareness.

The dialectic process moves on as both mother and infant choose to unite again. At the mother's breast, the deepest elected union is dramatically acted out between two people. Inscribed deeply in the infant's being is the message: "I belong; I belong because someone takes time to own me. I must be worthy because I am precious to someone."

The body develops, and there are new demands on the growing child—the discovery and the recognition of his autonomous anatomy and will: "I am not an extension of Mother. I may be part of a greater whole, but I am a separate self that needs to be identified and claimed." Making a venture toward separation and the discovery of the will is possible only because of the certainty that, once the task is completed for this phase of development, the child can return again to a union with the one who is waiting for it.

During the next 10 or more years, many small trips to discover one's separateness are made, but the predominant theme is closeness. The child stays close to his family as he learns the family's skills. He establishes his self-worth as he identifies with the values, habits, and ideals of his family, clan, community, and culture.

The success of discovering and claiming his self-worth in union with his family has prepared him for making the final and greatest journey in separation. The primary task of adolescence is to affirm for life one's psychological identity, and that affirmation can be done only in separation. That psychological birth process is painful for both the adolescent and his anxious family.

While on the venture for selfhood, the adolescent discovers his peer group, which is on the same trip. The mutuality of the experience develops into a new union with a partner of his own choosing. After clasping the hand of the new-found mate, he is ready to join the adult generation and find his place in the larger society.

SOCIETAL PHASE

Rank clearly defined three levels of development beyond the familial phase for the truly creative person. The first can be called the societal phase. A union comes first as the young adult internalizes the norms of universal humanity and civilization as his own. A rebirth occurs as he steps out from the crowd to declare his individual self as separate from the mass. He claims his psychic ideal. The neurotic is unable to make that affirmation, because he perceives the norms of society as external commands and wastes his life fighting them so as to make them correspond to his own self. The artistic type focuses his energy on the creation of his psychic self and thus rises above the mass.

For Rank, that rebirth occurred with the completion of the book *The Trauma of Birth* in 1923, when he paid the price of that step in his growth. As Progoff (1956) wrote:

The net effect of the book, and perhaps its unconscious intention, was to precipitate his separation from Freud, thus freeing the artistic side of his personality for creative self-expression.

To step out from the midst of the mass may result in the payment of a high price in guilt, remorse, and anxiety. For Rank, the price was so great that he momentarily abandoned the process to return to the fold. The pain of isolation and ostracism was great, but he reclaimed his growth and took his first major step beyond psychology.

ARTISTIC PHASE

The creative person is in close kinship with the outer world of the people to whom he belongs. He is in union with the cosmic reality, with nature, and with human nature about him. In the artistic act he listens to the voiceless voice of that reality and then articulates it through his words and deeds. He hears clearly what others have felt vaguely, although no less strongly, and their potential experiences are actualized by means of his work. Because of that, the artist is often regarded as a hero, for he is a living prototype of the human creative will. He experi-

ences creatively what is dormant or suppressed in others. They are thereby enabled to experience their own latent creativity through him.

SPIRITUAL PHASE

The highest form of creation is one's own ethical or spiritual ideal. That, too, is a rebirth process. At that stage, one no longer needs to create anything tangible. The self is its own art form.

The phase begins with a deep identification with an ideological, philosophical, or spiritual union. To claim it as one's own is a commitment of faith and, thus, a spiritual rebirth, because one is in touch with the eternal, the universal, or, for some, the personified God. It is a deeply religious rebirth.

To claim one's ethical ideal in its final form, one makes peace with the totality of existence, with one's life, with one's fate, and with death. Even the final separation by death has lost its pangs of fear; one has overcome the guilt for having lived because life was lived to its fullest. The fear of death is primarily the fear of failing to live.

To live at that level, one lives at the level of the soul, in tune with existence. Unions and separations are no longer in tension with each other. The human being is in union with the ultimate, even as he experiences himself as distinctively separate.

Rank reached that phase when he wrote the chapter "Psychology beyond the Self" in his final book, *Beyond Psychology* (Rank, 1941). In August 1939, in the preface, he wrote, "My work is completed." He proclaimed his freedom from psychoanalysis and was about to enjoy his liberated life in California when he died unexpectedly on October 31, 1939.

Treatment

To Rank, the successful therapeutic process was a rebirth experience in which the patient made drastic leaps forward in healing, rather than a slow process of gaining insight followed by adjustment or behavior modification. In the treatment experience, the patient moves into a relationship experience with the therapist that is a reenactment of all the past struggles with relationship, especially the problem of intimacy. In the actual encounter with the therapist, the patient experientially works through those feelings, especially the death fear, which is the innate fear of losing one's identity because of the suffocation in any relationship and, in particular, in the intensity of the therapeutic relationship. The rebirth occurs after the relationship between the patient and the therapist has affirmed the patient's innate self-worth. Then the patient has the inner strength to launch out in self-affirmation, separating himself from dependency on the therapist and claiming his own uniqueness as an individual. In that process, the patient overcomes the life fear as he dares to face up to his fullest potential and own it for himself.

In the process of therapy, the patient moves through phases that are identical to the personality growth process phases described earlier. He first moves into a relationship with the therapist as a person who is a prototype of a particular person in the patient's life and of universal humanity, with whom he must unite. The first rebirth occurs as the patient claims his own individuality as a person and as a unique part of universal mankind. The second phase begins as he discovers the physical universe and his likeness to it. After that phase, he claims his distinctiveness as a creator within the cosmic reality as the creative artist is born. In the emergence of the self, he moves to the final phase of growth as he unites with the ideological, philosophical, and spiritual reality. That phase is followed by the final birth of the ethical ideal—a self-fulfilled human being who no longer needs to create in order to prove his right to existence.

Current Assessment

Ironically, awareness of the contribution of Otto Rank is rapidly diminishing as the humanistic movement in psychology is growing. Few persons in or out of the movement know Rank or know the debt they owe to him.

Several recent events have contributed to Rank's receding. His most illustrious, influential, and articulate patient died in January 1977. Anaïs Nin embodied the best of what Otto Rank hoped to achieve in therapy, the birth of art and the artist. When she spoke, she always left the yearning to know more about her, about the process that made her a unique human being, and about the renowned therapist she called her mentor. Her death left no replacement to convey that feeling effectively.

The Otto Rank Association—at 35 West State Street, Doylestown, Pennsylvania 18901—has also lost a major direct tie to Otto Rank through the death of Virginia Robinson. That loss diminished the association's effectiveness in keeping the memory of Rank alive. Although the *Journal of the Otto Rank Association* continues to be published, one gets the feeling in reading the articles that strands tying it to Rank are being lost.

Unfortunately, the one location in America where Otto Rank made his greatest impact, the University of Pennsylvania School of Social Work, has abandoned him and his functional theory for a social action theory.

The major tie that keeps the legacy of Otto Rank alive is his writings. It is regrettable that most of Rank's voluminous writings are not published or not translated from the German. Those that are available in English are extremely difficult to read. His thought process was cyclical and often leaves the reader lost. Much of his writing is polemic against his former mentor, Sigmund Freud. Because that struggle belongs to another era, it leaves the reader uninterested.

Probably the single most influential reason that Rank is unknown to his heirs is the fact that psychologists feel he is not needed anymore. Many of the humanistic psychologists have gone past Rank to the great philosophers on whom Rank built his system: in their personalities and words, the psychologists have created Rank's message without ever mentioning his name. Thus, Rank remains forgotten.

Suggested Cross References

Chapter 8 contains a detailed discussion of the early years of Freudian psychoanalysis. Existential psychotherapy is discussed in Section 10.7. The third force in psychology is discussed in Section 11.2. Psychiatric social work is discussed in Chapter 51. Psychiatry and the creative process is discussed in Section 56.2, and psychiatry and the arts is discussed in Section 56.3.

REFERENCES

Freud, S. *Collected Papers.* Hogarth Press, London, 1917.
* Karpf, F. B. *The Psychology and Psychotherapy of Otto Rank.* Philosophical Library, New York, 1953.
Nin, A. *The Diary of Anaïs Nin,* vols.1–6. Harcourt, Brace, Jovanovich, New York, vol. 1, 1966; vol. 2, 1967; vol. 3, 1969; vol. 4, 1971; vol. 5, 1974; vol. 6, 1977.
* Progoff, I. *The Death and the Rebirth of Psychology.* Julian Press, New York, 1956.
* Rank, O. *Beyond Psychology.* Dover, New York, 1941.
* Rank, O. *The Trauma of Birth.* Harper & Row, New York, 1973.
* Rank, O. *Will Therapy and Truth and Reality.* Alfred A. Knopf, New York, 1952.
Taft, J. *Otto Rank.* Julian Press, New York, 1958.

10.5 Melanie Klein

OTTO F. KERNBERG, M.D.

Introduction

The psychoanalytic approach of Melanie Klein (1882–1960) and her followers constitutes a particular school of psychoanalytic theory and technique. Within the broad spectrum of classical and modified psychoanalytic theories and related clinical techniques, the Kleinian approach is closest to the constitutionalist, instinct-oriented pole; the culturalist approaches represent the opposite pole of stress on the psychosocial determinants of intrapsychic conflict. Between those poles, contemporary ego psychology occupies an intermediate position (Guntrip, 1961). Klein's theory of instincts is rooted in traditional psychoanalytic metapsychology, rather than in contemporary neurobiological approaches, which has led some critics to point to a pseudobiological orientation of the Kleinians. From the viewpoint of psychoanalytic object relations theory—that is, the general theory of the structures in the mind that preserve and organize interpersonal experiences and also constitute organizers of instinctual expression in the interpersonal realm—the Kleinians have important links with the culturalists, although Kleinian theory does not specifically acknowledge those links.

From a technical viewpoint, the Kleinian approach is very close to traditional psychoanalysis, with a heavy emphasis on the psychology of the id and on preserving a classical, non-modified psychoanalytic technique for all patients. However, Melanie Klein and other members of her school have made significant contributions to and modifications of that classical technique.

A psychoanalytic approach closely related to that of Melanie Klein is that of Fairbairn (1952) and his followers. Fairbairn and Melanie Klein influenced each other in their theoretical and clinical thinking. Fairbairn stressed even more than Melanie Klein the importance of internalized object relations as major organizers of the mind, but he rejected Klein's stress on inborn instincts as basic motivating factors. Jointly, the Kleinian and the Fairbairnian approaches tend to be called the British schools of psychoanalysis, in contrast to the contemporary ego psychological approach of Anna Freud (1936), Hartmann (1964), and Rapaport (1967), strongly represented in England and in the psychoanalytic work in this country.

Instinct Theory

Melanie Klein fully accepted Freud's dual-instinct theory involving the life instinct and the death instinct and particularly stressed the importance of inborn aggression as a reflection of the death instinct. The first manifestation of the death instinct is oral sadism, which constitutes the first source of diffuse anxiety of the ego. It is projected outward from birth on in the form of persecutory fears linked to the first objects and is experienced as fear of devouring objects, giving rise to the fantasies of a bad, destructive, devouring breast. Those fantasies reflect the projection of cannibalistic wishes that express oral sadism. Oral sadism is reinforced by the trauma of birth and, later, fantasied or real frustrations stemming from the mother. Both the death instinct and the life instinct express themselves mentally in the form of unconscious fantasy, which, for the Kleinians, exists from the beginning of life. Every instinctual impulse is represented by an unconscious fantasy, and the contents of those fantasies represent the self and objects under the influence of crude, primitive emotions, the prototypes of what will evolve as love and hate. The equation of various objects under the influence of the same instinctual drive derivative constitutes the origin of the capacity for symbol formation.

Envy, greed, and, later on, jealousy are specific emotions derived from oral aggression. Envy, the first manifestation of oral aggression, is expressed by the prototypical fantasy that the frustrating object, originally the breast, willfully withholds its supplies; oral envy expresses the hatred of that withholding object and the wish to spoil it in order to eliminate envy. Envy gives rise to greed and reinforces greed; oral envy also underpins later envy of the penis and of the other sex in general. Eventually, envy evolves into the envy of creativity in others and into a particular kind of guilt over one's own creativity because of the fear of the envy attributed to others. That unconscious guilt over creativity also predisposes to later types of oedipal guilt. Jealousy represents a later emotional development, characteristic of triangular situations typical of oedipal conflicts. A third person is hated because he preempts the love and general libidinal supplies from the desired object.

The death instinct, active from birth on and expressed in primitive emotions, particularly envy, is projected outward in the form of fears of persecution and annihilation. Melanie Klein postulated the existence of a functional ego from birth on, and the fear of persecution and annihilation refers to annihilation of the ego. All experiences of tension and unpleasure are expelled in an effort to preserve a purified pleasure principle within the ego and then projected into persecutory objects.

The life instinct or libido is expressed from birth on in pleasurable contacts with gratifying objects, primarily the good breast. Those objects are invested with libido and are introjected as internal objects infused with emotions representing libido. The breast constitutes the first stimulus activating the life instinct and is its first object; fantasies about the good, gratifying breast are introjected as the core ego identification or good inner object. The projection of the good inner object on new objects emerging in the perceptual field is the basis of trust, of the wish to explore reality, and of learning and knowledge. Gratifying experiences reinforce basic trust, shape the expression of libido, and influence the relative balance of life and death instincts. Cycles of projection and reintrojection of good objects foster growth, and good inner objects promote ego synthesis.

The predominant emotion linked with the expression of libido is gratitude. For Melanie Klein, gratitude expressed libido directed to external good objects that are also secured inside as good internal objects. Gratitude is closely connected with the emotion of trust based on the secure enjoyment of the good breast. Gratitude decreases greed—in contrast to envy, which increases it—because gratitude leads to satisfaction with what is received, in contrast to tendencies to spoil it. Gratitude is the origin of authentic generosity, in contrast to reactive generosity (a defense against envy), which eventually ends in feelings of being robbed. Guilt, a predominant emotion in later stages of development, reinforces feelings of gratitude but is not its origin.

Melanie Klein criticized the sequence postulated by Freud of an autoerotic phase to be followed by a narcissistic phase and finally by a phase of object investment. Melanie Klein thought that autoeroticism is based on gratifying experiences with the mother—on the first object relationship, therefore—

and that narcissism represents an identification with the good object. What Freud called hallucinatory wish fulfillment is represented by introjective fantasies of the good inner object—the breast.

For Melanie Klein, both life and death instincts were intimately linked with object relations. Although most of the death instinct is originally projected in terms of paranoid fears, part of it is fused with libido, giving origin to the development of masochistic tendencies.

Theory of the Ego

Melanie Klein agreed with Freud that the ego originates in the common matrix of the ego and the id in an effort to deal with reality, and she stated that the ego starts with the beginning of life (Klein, 1952b). She described four basic functions of the ego, all of which start with the beginning of life: (1) the experience of and defenses against anxiety, (2) processes of introjection and projection, (3) object relations, and (4) integration and synthesis.

ANXIETY

Anxiety is the first consequence of the operation of the death instinct. Melanie Klein considered the ego to be the seat of anxiety; anxiety constitutes the ego's response to the expression of the death instinct. She thought that constitutional factors determine the degree of anxiety tolerance. Although the death instinct, in the form of persecutory fears, constitutes the primary cause of anxiety, anxiety is also reinforced by the separation caused by birth and by the frustration of bodily needs. Anxiety becomes fear of persecutory objects and later, through reintrojection of aggression in the form of internalized bad objects, the fear of outer and inner persecutors. Inner persecutors constitute the origin of primitive superego anxiety. The content of paranoid fears varies according to the level of psychosexual development. At first, there are oral fears of being devoured, then anal fears of being controlled and poisoned; those early contents later shift into oedipal fears of castration. Basically, those fears represent aggressive wishes toward and fantasies about the mother, particularly about the contents of her body, and those primitive persecutory fears constitute the basis of persecutory delusions in schizophrenia and paranoid psychoses.

INTROJECTION AND PROJECTION

These are primary processes of growth, as well as defensive operations of the ego, and they constitute the basic defenses against anxiety. By their operation, they foster the integration of the ego and the neutralization of the death instinct. Both good and bad experiences are projected. The projection of inner tension states, reflecting basically the death instinct, and of external stimuli that are painful, constitutes the origin of paranoid fears, but the projection of pleasurable states, reflecting basically the life instinct, gives rise to basic trust. The introjection of good experiences gives rise to good internal objects, which constitute basic stimuli for ego growth. In the earliest stages of development, the paranoid-schizoid position, all aggression is projected outside; in a later stage of development, the depressive position, projection of aggression is only partially successful, and there is a reintrojection and tolerance of bad external objects as internal persecutors that now constitute the early superego.

OBJECT RELATIONS

External stimuli invested with libido or aggression become primitive objects. Objects are, at first, part objects—that is characteristic of the paranoid-schizoid position—and only later become total or whole objects. Melanie Klein used the term "part object" in two ways: first, in the anatomical sense she referred to partial aspects of real persons that are perceived by the infant as if they were the object with whom he is relating—such as, in his primary experience, the breast—the implication being that the breast is only one part of the real mother. In the second sense—and this is predominantly the way in which the term is used by Kleinian authors—as a result of splitting, part objects constitute either part of persons or total persons perceived in a distorted, unrealistic way under the influence of the projection of pure libido or aggression, so that those objects are either all good or all bad.

The tendency to perceive objects as either ideal (all good) or persecutory (all bad) is the consequence of the operation of another early defensive operation described by Melanie Klein—namely, splitting. Splitting consists in the active separation of good from bad experiences, perceptions, and emotions linked to objects; the good breast is kept separate from the bad breast, and the good internal object is kept separate from bad internal objects. For Melanie Klein, the predominance of part object relationships in earliest life was a consequence of the maximal operation of splitting mechanisms. Only later, when splitting mechanisms decrease, is a synthesis of good and bad aspects of objects possible and an ambivalence toward whole objects acknowledged. The good breast and the bad breast are the first objects involved in the earliest unconscious fantasies representing, respectively, libido and the death instinct. Because of processes of introjection and projection, there are both good and bad internal and external objects; splitting mechanisms keep both internal and external objects separate in terms of libido and aggression. Part object relations are characteristic of the earliest stage of development, the paranoid-schizoid position; whole object relationships characterize the depressive position.

INTEGRATION AND SYNTHESIS

The internalization of the good object constitutes the basis for growth of an integrative ego; the total projection of bad objects preserves a purified pleasure ego. Later, however, the synthesis of good and bad part objects into total or whole objects further contributes to ego growth and synthesis and to the integration of the experience of reality. The predominance of aggression over libido interferes with ego integration and synthesis; under those circumstances, there occurs an excessive development of idealization—a primitive defensive operation tending to preserve all-good internal and external objects. Excessive aggression also leads to an excessive development of splitting mechanisms in order to protect the good internal and external objects from contamination with badness. Insofar as pathological persistence of splitting interferes with the accurate perception of reality, splitting fosters denial of reality. Although she accepted the important influence of environmental factors in excessive development of aggression, Melanie Klein placed primary emphasis on the inborn strength of the death instinct expressed in sadistic impulses, reinforced by an excessive anxiety reaction and low anxiety tolerance of the ego; in short, while acknowledging environmental influences, she stressed the constitutional givens of severe psychopathology, of excessive development of aggression characteristic of the psychoses.

Paranoid-Schizoid and Depressive Positions

Melanie Klein (1948 a, b, c; 1952b) stressed how important the early internalized object relations are in determining the vicissitudes of instincts, intrapsychic conflicts, and psychic structures and how important pregenital aggression, especially oral sadism, is in determining the quality of primitive internal objects. She saw the vicissitudes of inborn aggression and libido as being intimately linked with, respectively, the bad and the good internal objects.

What follows is Melanie Klein's description of two major developmental constellations of object relations, their prevalent anxieties and conflicts, and, above all, the defensive operations characteristic of each constellation. Those two constellations are the paranoid-schizoid position and the depressive position, which are characteristic, respectively, of the first half and of the second half of the first year of life but capable of being reconstituted at various times or even from moment to moment in the course of a person's life. Although those positions develop originally in the context of the oral phase of libidinal development, they evolve as defensive constellations that are regularly activated later on. Thus, persecutory and depressive anxieties and mechanisms are involved in conflicts related to all psychosexual levels.

PARANOID-SCHIZOID POSITION

This is the earliest developmental stage, characterized by the predominance of splitting and other related mechanisms, by part object relationships, and by a basic fear about the preservation or survival of the ego; that fear takes the form of persecutory anxiety. Persecutory fears stem from oral-sadistic and anal-sadistic impulses, which, within certain limits of intensity, are a normal characteristic of the earliest phase of development. However, excessive persecutory fears determine a pathological strengthening and fixation at that level that underlies the development of schizophrenia and paranoid psychosis. If persecutory fears are not excessive, that phase evolves into the next developmental phase, the depressive position, in the second half of the first year.

The following defensive mechanisms, specifically directed against persecutory fears, are prevalent in the paranoid-schizoid position.

Splitting. Splitting constitutes a normal defensive operation characteristic of the early ego. Both objects and impulses are split, so that good and bad objects are maintained separately. Good objects are totally introjected, and bad objects are totally projected. When aggression is particularly strong and there is a related predominance of bad objects, a secondary splitting of bad objects into fragments may occur, and those fragments may be projected into multiple external objects, thus giving rise to multiple persecutors.

Bion (1967), one of the principal authors of the Kleinian school, described the development of bizarre objects, representing minute fragments of pathologically split and projected bad internal objects. The reintrojection of fragmented objects or, in more general terms, of an excessively split reality leads to states of internal confusion. Splitting mechanisms may persist pathologically and determine a general fragmentation of the affective experiences of the ego, leading to the depersonalization syndrome or to general affective shallowness, which is characteristic of schizoid personalities. Bion also described splitting processes affecting cognitive links that bring about a disorganization of formal thought processes characteristic of schizophrenia. Thus, pathological splitting may protect the ego from paranoid anxiety by means of a pathological destruction of internalized object relations, fragmentation and dispersal of emotions, and even disorganization of formal thought processes—all of which characterize severe types of psychopathology with loss of the relationship to reality and of reality testing.

Idealization. Idealization is another paranoid-schizoid operation that consists in an exaggeration of the all-good quality of internal and external objects linked with a denial and splitting off of any contradictory evidence regarding the real characteristics of the object. Idealization of external objects satisfies fantasies of unlimited gratification from them (the inexhaustible breast) as a protection against frustration and increments of aggression. Idealized external objects are also protections against persecutory objects. The flight toward an idealized inner good object may protect the person from an unbearable reality at the cost of loss of reality testing and may give rise to exalted or messianic states in the psychoses. The mechanism of idealization persists and evolves during the depressive position into an idealization of the good object, based not on splitting but on a defense against guilt feelings toward the object. In that case, the internal aggression toward the good external object is acknowledged, rather than split off, and the object is idealized so it will not be destroyed by the aggression. That later, depressive kind of idealization leads to overdependence on others.

Denial of inner and external reality. At the paranoid-schizoid position, there is denial of the existence of inner aggression and of the bad aspects of needed objects. Hallucinatory wish fulfillment is the prototype of denial, and, insofar as part of the reality of the ego and of the external world is denied, denial leads to a general impoverishment of reality experience and reality testing.

Stifling and artificiality of emotions. This is a pathological outcome of the paranoid-schizoid position, as well as a later defense derived from it; emotional dispersal secondary to excessive splitting persists, and, insofar as guilt and depression are denied or unavailable as part of the incapacity to reach the depressive position, in-depth development of emotions and broadening of the spectrum of normal emotions do not occur. That stifling of emotions and emotional artificiality protect the ego from awareness of its own aggression and persecutory anxiety.

Projective identification. This mechanism constitutes the prototype of projective mechanisms in general and consists of the projection of split-off parts of the ego or self or of an internal object into another person. Melanie Klein used the terms "ego" and "self" interchangeably. Although she did not fully clarify the relationships between the ego or self and internal objects, Melanie Klein implied, as Hanna Segal (1967) pointed out, that the ego identifies with and assimilates some of those objects, particularly the first good inner objects, whereas other objects remain as separate internal objects, and the ego maintains a relationship with them. One aim of the process of projective identification is the forceful entry into the external object and control of that object by part of the self. The clinical descriptions of projective identification by various authors of the Kleinian school convey the idea that the process contains both interpersonal and intrapsychic elements; an unacceptable internal object or the self is projected into an external object, which is forced, as it were, to acquire the unacceptable characteristics. That mechanism deals mainly with the projection of bad inner objects and bad parts of the self—in short, with primitive aggression. The object onto whom the projection has occurred (or "into" whom, as Kleinian writers prefer to say) is perceived as persecutory and needs to be controlled. Once the infant's own sadistic impulses are perceived as coming from the persecutory object, the need to control the object expresses simultaneously the defense against persecutors and the acting out of primitive sadism in the relationship with the object. Melanie Klein (1952b, 1957) suggested that—insofar as oral and anal aggression are the bases of the need for an awareness of power, strength, and, eventually, knowledge—the excessive activation of projective identification implies that all power is perceived as on the outside, and the self is perceived as impoverished and weak. Fantasies and delusions of being controlled from the outside, which are characteristic of the paranoid condition, stem from the pathological activation of that mechanism. Rosenfeld (1965) developed the Kleinian

approach to the psychoanalytic study and treatment of psychotic patients, centering his technical approach particularly on the interpretation of projective identification.

Psychopathology. Pathological fixation and predominance of paranoid-schizoid mechanisms determine various types of psychopathology. The psychoses present a combination of denial of reality, excessive projective identification, and pathological splitting, which leads to fragmentation, according to Kleinian theory. Escape into an idealized inner object leads to autistic exalted states; generalized splitting and reintrojection of multiple, fragmented objects lead to confusional states. The predominance of fear of external persecutors, derived from projective identification, is characteristic of paranoia; the projection of persecutors onto the patient's own bodily zones, organs, and functions determines hypochondriacal syndromes. Fear of poisoning and of pathological control from the outside may be a combined expression of persecutory fears of the paranoid and hypochondriacal nature.

Schizoid object relationships, characteristic of schizoid personalities, are characterized by shallowness of emotions, incapacity to tolerate guilt feelings in depth, a tendency to experience objects as hostile, and a combination of internal withdrawal from object relations and artificiality in surface social adaptation. Melanie Klein (1952e) suggested that obsessive traits may reflect a secondary defense against fears of external control by taking over such excessive control in dealing with external reality. The efforts to escape from feared persecutors by flights into excessive dependency on idealized external objects may give rise to pathological dependency, narcissistic object relations, and sexual promiscuity—a constant turning from one object that becomes bad to another object that is idealized. Melanie Klein stressed the consequences of excessive predominance of envy in terms of projection of such envy onto others, with consequent fear of success and inhibition in learning because the acquisition of knowledge is perceived as an expression of excessive greed and because of the spoiling of what is learned. Envy of the therapist as a giving mother is a basic source of negative therapeutic reactions related to the need to destroy the source of love and help. A synthesis of the theory of the paranoid-schizoid position can be found in Klein's 1952 paper (1952b).

DEPRESSIVE POSITION

Melanie Klein (1952e) stated that at about 6 months of age splitting processes begin to decrease, and the child's increasing sense of reality brings about a growing awareness that the good and the bad external objects are really one and that the mother as a whole object has good and bad parts. At that point, the infant begins to be able to acknowledge his own aggression toward the good object or to recognize the good aspects of the object he attacks and perceives at such times as bad. In other words, the full projection of aggression in the paranoid-schizoid position, which permitted all aggression to be deflected outward and to maintain a sense of lack of inner aggression and lack of guilt over such aggression, is no longer operant. Projection is then only partially successful. The infant's attack on the whole (good and bad) object also brings about an awareness of his own bad internal parts. In contrast to the persecutory fears characteristic of the paranoid-schizoid position, the predominant fear in the depressive position is no longer of external attack but of harming the good internal and external objects.

That basic fear about the survival of good inner and external objects constitutes depressive anxiety or guilt, the predominant emotional reaction of the depressive position. The preservation of good objects becomes more important than the preservation of the ego. Internal bad objects that are no longer projected constitute the primary superego, which attacks the ego or the self with guilt feelings; within the superego, bad internal objects may contaminate good internal objects that, because of their demanding or standard-setting nature, have also been internalized into the superego, bringing about cruel demands for perfection.

Working-through mechanisms. Under normal conditions, certain mechanisms characteristic of the depressive position permit the working through of that position.

Reparation. This is the normal effort to reduce the guilt over having attacked the good object by trying to repair the damage, express the love and gratitude to the object, and preserve it internally and externally. Reparation, in Klein's thinking, is the origin of sublimation.

Increase in reality testing. Although this is not a defensive mechanism in a strict sense, Melanie Klein (1952e) stressed the increase in awareness of reality that stems from the decrease of splitting mechanisms and from the growing capacity to evaluate whole objects and the total self—in contrast to the split self. As part of the unconscious fantasies characteristic of the depressive position, there is a fear that the good mother has been lost or destroyed because of the infant's greed and destructive fantasies. The sorrow and the concern over the mother and other objects with whom the infant repeats those processes bring about an increasing focus on the integration of reality and a reintrojection of objects then perceived as whole and alive, thus reassuring the survival and stability of good internal objects. Melanie Klein (1952e) considered that process of grief and mourning over one's own aggression and over the fantasied damage done to good objects a crucial part of development in the second half of the first year of life. That mourning period and its successful overcoming are influenced by the actual experience of weaning from the breast and the related, implicit loss of the mother while the realistic fact that the external mother continues to be alive, good, and available reassures the infant as to his inability to destroy his objects. The availability of the mother and the infant's reality testing reinforce each other. Melanie Klein stressed that the child, through being loved, is helped to preserve his faith in his inner goodness and to preserve his good inner objects.

Ambivalence. The infant's awareness of love and hate toward the same object brings about the capacity to experience ambivalence and, under optimal circumstances, a predominance of love over hate in combined emotional reactions to whole objects. The integration of love and hate brings about a deepening of emotions and emotional growth, reflected in increased self-knowledge and increased capacity for empathic perceptions of others. The perception of whole objects also leads to early oedipal developments; the infant is better able to differentiate the mother from the father and develops a capacity for deeper empathy with their specific sexual characteristics.

Gratitude. Although gratitude has an earlier origin than the capacity for experiencing guilt, guilt reinforces gratitude. Grief and gratitude activate the love for the object and strengthen reparative trends. Gratitude and reparation foster creativity, understanding, tolerance, and an increased capacity for trusting others and the self's capacity to give and receive love.

Pathological developments. Klein (1948b) described two additional mechanisms activated in the course of the depressive position that, to a limited extent, form part of the normal working through of that position. Excessive development of those mechanisms, however, forms part of a definitely pathological constellation—namely, that of the manic defenses. Those mechanisms are: (1) idealization, a paranoid-schizoid mechanism, which may be activated in the service of preserving the good internal and external objects in the face of ambivalence toward them; and (2) a sense of triumph over the lost object, reflecting the death wishes against the object, another typical manic defense that is part of normal mourning and that gives rise to and increases unconscious guilt.

The major pathological developments of the depressive position may take the form of either pathological mourning or excessive development of manic defenses. Pathological mourning is characterized by the loss of the good external and internal objects caused by their fantasied destruction by the hatred directed toward them. Melanie Klein (1948b) stressed that in pathological mourning there is a perception of death of both the external and the internal good objects as a consequence of excessive sadism. The bad internal objects constitute a primitive and sadistic superego, evoke excessive guilt, and determine the feeling that all good objects are dead and that the world is empty of love. That sadistic superego is characterized by cruelty, demands for perfection, and hatred of instincts. Efforts at compensation fail; the idealization of the object only increases further guilt and despair; and Melanie Klein considered the self-reproaches of the depressed patient as directed not against the object but against the self and the internal impulses. She thought that suicide often corresponds to the unconscious fantasy of destroying the bad self, thus preserving and protecting the good object from it. In depressive psychosis there are unconscious fantasies of a total destruction of objects of the inner world, represented by hypochondriacal delusions, or fantasies of destruction of the external world by means of projection; those fantasies give rise to delusions of emptiness or destruction of the world at large. In a general regressive defense against pathological, intolerable mourning, there may be a reinforcement of earlier paranoid-schizoid mechanisms—in other words, of paranoid fears as a defense against pathological guilt and depression. Neurotic depression and, particularly, psychotic depression are the clinical manifestations of the pathological development of all those defensive operations and the inability to work through the depressive position.

Hypomanic and manic syndromes reflect the pathological predominance of the constellation of manic defenses. Manic defenses, in addition to the idealization and manic triumph over the lost dead object mentioned earlier, include the following mechanisms.

Omnipotence. This is a mechanism based on identification with an idealized and powerful good object and the denial of other aspects of internal and external reality. What is denied is one's vulnerability, the need for objects, and the dreaded dependency on objects because dependency would imply the activation of the dreaded and denied internal badness as part of the closeness to an ambivalently loved object. The denial of the need for objects also permits the denial of attacks on such objects and by them. Omnipotence is characterized, at the same time, by the tendency to exert control and mastery of external objects, a control that provides reassurance that they are not in danger and not dangerous; a pathological sense of ego strength is thus generated. A mechanism related to omnipotence is that of contempt experienced or expressed toward objects.

Identification with the superego. This mechanism, originally described by Freud (1957) and Rado (1928), was characterized by Melanie Klein as an identification with the sadistic superego. Depressive guilt and aggression are denied and projected outward; external objects are considered and treated as the hated, depreciated, bad self.

Compulsive introjection. Pathological development of introjection may be expressed as an object hunger linked with the denial of the danger to and from objects. The implicit fantasy is that, since there are so many objects, a few less do not matter. The mechanism also implies disparagement of and contempt for objects. Manic patients' primitive fantasies of a cannibalistic feast are typical of the activation of the mechanism.

Manic triumph. This mechanism may become so intense that it is expressed clinically as conscious triumph over the world, an exalted state of power over an otherwise dead or dying universe.

Extreme manic idealization. The exaggeration of idealization of the self may be represented by purified exalted states reflecting fantasies of merging of the self with good, fantastically idealized objects.

Results. The extreme combination of those defensive mechanisms is characteristic of manic and hypomanic psychoses; less severe presence of those mechanisms characterizes the hypomanic personality. Hypomanic personalities tend to admire others excessively (idealization), to express contempt or devaluation, to think in large numbers, and to neglect details—that is, to neglect the real objects, about which there is a denial of guilt. Hypomanic personalities may also present dependency on idealized persons, narcissistic object relations, and sexual promiscuity—all of which reflect the flight into multiple relationships with external objects so as to deny and dispose of anxieties connected with unconscious guilt toward them. Joan Riviere (1936) and Rosenfeld (1965) developed that thesis in their studies of the narcissistic character.

Melanie Klein (1948 a, b) stressed that patients suffering from manic-depressive symptoms have in infancy been unable to establish securely a good inner object; they have not been able to work through the infantile depressive position. In contrast, in normal mourning, repetitive elaborations and working through of the normal infantile depressive position occur. It may be helpful at this point to compare Melanie Klein's theory of depression with the theories of Freud (1957) and Abraham (1911, 1927 a, b).

For Freud and Abraham, normal mourning was characterized by the real loss of the object and the work of mourning consisted in repeated reality testing of that loss and in gradually freeing the libido from the lost object. The narcissistic gratification of being alive contributed to coming to terms with the loss, and the mourning period was completed with the introjection of the lost object. In contrast, the fundamental process in melancholia for Freud and Abraham consisted in the loss of the loved object, with an inability or failure to introject that object because of the ambivalent relationship toward it that reflected excessive oral-sadistic impulses. A sadistic superego, also reflecting such an excessive sadism, determined excessive guilt over the aggression to the ambivalently and anaclitically loved and attacked object and directed the hostility inside, onto the introjected object, so that self-reproaches represented an attack of the superego not so much on the ego as on the introjected object. Suicide constituted the final consummation of such an attack.

For Melanie Klein (1948 a, b), normal mourning repeated the processes of the depressive position and reinforced the synthetic processes of the ego by which bad and good part objects were integrated into whole objects and by which the superego crystallized and determined the experience of guilt over the aggression toward the good, ambivalently loved object.

Therefore, for Freud (1957), normal mourning (1) did not contain guilt, (2) culminated in the introjection of the external object, and (3) was helped by the narcissistic gratification of being alive. But Melanie Klein (1948b) believed that normal mourning (1) always implied guilt (reactivating the guilt of the depressive position); (2) involved not only the introjection of the external object but also the internal good object, which was felt to be threatened and was reinstated; and (3) was characterized by a gratification over being alive, which included the activation of manic triumph and secondary guilt. In addition, there was also activation of idealization and, above all, of the normal processes that permit the working through of the depressive position. For Melanie Klein, the only difference in the depressive position of infancy and normal mourning later in life was that during the period of weaning the real, good mother was still there and helped the infant reinstitute and consolidate his good internal objects. In contrast, in later normal mourning there was a real loss of the object. One

practical implication is that a loving person can help the mourner work through the mourning period in the same way as the good mother helps the infant overcome his insecurity in the survival of his good internal objects. A general overview of the Kleinian approach to depression can be found in Rosenfeld's (1959) outline.

Superego Theory

Melanie Klein's stress (1949, 1952b) on the early developments of the superego and on the fundamental contribution of such a primitive superego on psychopathology is another major aspect of her theory. She thought the superego starts out in the first year of life as part of the depressive position—actually co-determining that developmental phase—and that excessive pathological superego pressures co-determine the incapacity to work through the depressive position and bring about a regression to the early paranoid-schizoid constellation. The superego derived, in Klein's thinking, from the reintrojected bad objects that earlier had been split off and projected outside, a reintrojection made possible by the mitigation of bad objects because of the introjection of whole or total objects as part of the depressive position. Thus, guilt derives from the reintrojection of projected sadism. The superego is the synthesis of bad inner objects with the demand aspects of introjected whole objects. As part of the depressive position and from then on, there occurs a simultaneous introjection of objects into the ego and the superego; the prohibitive and demanding aspects of those objects determine the internalization into the superego. Normally, the predominance of love over hate and the subsequent internalization of predominantly good, demanding whole objects into the superego neutralize the bad inner objects; however, even under ideal circumstances, there is a certain contamination of the predominantly good objects in the superego by the bad objects, giving rise to the following superego characteristics.

Superego pressures have a persecuting and demanding quality; the superego exerts strong demands to placate and preserve the good objects in the ego with the quality of cruel demands for perfection. The more idealized the quality of the good objects internalized in the superego, the more perfectionistic superego demands are. Under optimal circumstances, without excessive idealization of internalized good objects, superego pressures may have a protective function for the good inner objects of the ego, but under pathological circumstances those pressures are expressed as the unremitting harshness of infantile and childhood unconscious morality. Ultimately, the superego's hatred of the id stems from sadism.

Under normal circumstances, the superego brings about a certain degree of idealization of good inner objects and realistic demands for improvement and reinforcement of the reparative and sublimatory trends of the ego. It determines the crucial nature of the need to preserve the good inner objects and regulates ego functions by depressive anxieties reflecting the guilt or despair over dangers to the good internal objects.

Regression to the paranoid-schizoid position when the depressive position cannot be worked through may bring about a reprojection of the sadistic superego as part of an effort to deflect intolerable guilt outside. That reinforces persecutory—in contrast to depressive—fears, decreases the capacity to perceive reality and learning because of the fear of and rebellion against the projected superego, produces intellectual inhibition and omnipotent denial of reality, and reinforces the greedy absorption of supplies as a protection against the dangers of a threatening external attack.

Klein's concept of the superego was in contrast to Freud's (1961) assumption of the development of the superego as the heir of the Oedipus complex; Melanie Klein (1954), while stressing the early origin of the superego, in contrast to Freud's assumption that the superego comes into operation at the height of the Oedipus complex, agreed with the important contribution of oedipal fears and prohibitions to superego development. That may seem to be a contradiction; however, Melanie Klein found that oedipal conflicts in her child analytic patients started much earlier than had been assumed in the past. In the 1930's, she postulated (Klein, 1950 b, c) that oral frustration brings about a premature oedipal development, which she placed in the second or third year of life. However, in the 1940's, she stated (Klein, 1948c, 1949) that oedipal problems were already active, molded under the primacy of oral drives, from the first year of life on and that such early stages of oedipal development were the basis of the later, classical, oedipal constellation.

Early Stages of the Oedipus Complex

Melanie Klein (1948c, 1952c) stated that normally, in both boys and girls, the longing for oral dependency on the mother is displaced onto the father, determining longings for oral dependency on him. Basically, in unconscious primitive fantasy, the longing for the good breast is displaced toward the longing for the father's penis. In both sexes, that normal process is exaggerated when there is an excessive oral frustration, thus initiating prematurely the negative Oedipus complex or feminine position in boys and constituting the root for early development of positive oedipal striving in girls. Premature longing for dependent gratification from the father is an important determinant of homosexuality in men; premature development of oedipal striving in girls may foster hysterial developments.

There is also a displacement of oral-aggressive fantasies about the mother onto the father, so that, in terms of primitive fantasies, the bad breast is displaced to the bad penis. In both sexes, when there is a predominance of pregenital sadism, sexuality and the father's penis are experienced as bad and destructive. In contrast, when there is a predominance of good pregenital object relations, genitality and the father's penis have mainly a reparative function. Oral-sadistic fantasies may be reinforced by the envy over the parents' enjoyment of sex, determining the projection of sadistic fantasies onto the primal scene and distorting the sexual relations in terms of primitive aggressive oral fantasies. The consequences of that development are the elaboration of fantastic, primitive, combined father-mother images, the prototype of other related images, such as a devouring phallic mother (representing regressive castration fears in boys), a dangerous vagina (vagina dentata), or a dangerous penis.

In boys the predominance of the reparative, good images of the father's penis fosters the development of the positive Oedipus complex, a predominance of trust in a good oedipal father, rather than fear of him, and a reparative, sublimatory conception of sex, giving the mother a good penis. In contrast, when sadism predominates, there is an excessive development of castration anxiety, and boys tend to perceive the oedipal father as extremely dangerous and to perceive the mother also as dangerous. Under those circumstances, it is more difficult for the boy to achieve a positive oedipal identification with his father, and he is predisposed toward sexual inhibition and fear of women.

In girls the predominance of good oral experiences reinforces normal oedipal development and genital desires, the expectation of a good penis as a consequence of the experience of the good breast. The predominance of oral aggression in girls may bring about unconscious fantasies of robbing the mother of the father's love, penis, and babies and may bring on unconscious fears that the primitive oral-sadistic mother will retaliate, thus determining a renunciation of the positive oedipal relationship. Melanie Klein (1948c, 1952c) stressed that penis envy in women is normally of secondary importance to the wishes to receive the father's penis and replace the mother; in other words, penis envy stems from the predominance of sadistic elements of the oral relationship with both parents—ultimately, from oral envy—rather than being the primary feature of female sexuality. Klein also believed that objects reflecting persecutory mother images are the principal features of the feminine superego.

In both sexes there may be a premature flight into the oedipal stage as a defense against preoedipal conflicts. That flight attempts to deny pregenital aggression through genital love and may bring about a flight from depth in object relationships through sexual promiscuity or a defense against sadistic impulses infiltrating sexual urges through sexual inhibition.

For Freud the Oedipus complex succumbs to the castration threat mediated by the establishment of the superego. Guilt is predominantly linked with that oedipal superego. In girls the disappointment from the mother derived from penis envy, the main expression of the castration complex in women, triggers the Oedipus complex. Later, instead of wanting the father's penis the girl wants a child from the father. In contrast, Melanie Klein (1952c, 1958c) believed the oedipal developments start in early infancy under the primacy of oral drives and conflicts, so that oral and genital conflicts overlap. The superego develops during the oral phase, specifically the depressive position, and guilt reflects, first of all, guilt over oral conflicts. Castration fears in boys derive originally from oral-sadistic desires to destroy the father's penis, and the castration fear represents a projection of those impulses. The guilt over the aggression toward the father reinforces the repression of genital oedipal impulses. In girls the origin of the Oedipus complex derives not from disillusionment from the mother but, rather, from the mother's having taken possession of (incorporated) the father's penis. The oral and genital desires for the father's penis combine, and penis envy constitutes a derivative of early envy of the mother's breast. Penis envy thus derives from oral sadism and is not a primary envy of male genitals.

Melanie Klein (1948c, 1952e) stressed envy of the opposite sex in both sexes and traced it to the earliest sources of envy. In her later years, Melanie Klein (1957) assumed an inborn knowledge of the genitals of both sexes, so that the primitive oral and genital fantasies mentioned were assumed by her to characterize experiences and conflicts from the first year of life on, an assumption that most Kleinians seem to share.

Psychoanalytic Technique

Melanie Klein never wrote an overview of technique; her references to technique appear in her clinical case material, a book (Klein, 1961), and various papers. Hanna Segal, one of the leading members of the Kleinian group, published a book (Segal, 1973) that includes both a general outline of Melanie Klein's theories and clinical case material illustrating the Kleinian technical approach. Segal also wrote a brief summary of Melanie Klein's technique (Segal, 1967), in which she stressed the following features basic to their school.

Kleinians strictly adhere to the classical psychoanalytic setting and deal with the patient's material exclusively by means of interpretation. Interpretations are predominantly transference interpretations, and the same nonmodified psychoanalytic technique is used with patients along the entire spectrum from neurotic to psychotic or psychopathic disorders. The analysis focuses on the interpretation of unconscious fantasies representing, for Kleinian analysis, both the content and the defensive operations at primitive levels of the mind. Segal (1967) stressed that Kleinians interpret at the level of the patient's maximum unconscious anxiety, which in practice means interpreting material at deep levels from the earliest stages of treatment on. The interpretation of primitive fantasies and defenses related to the paranoid-schizoid and the depressive positions is a major focus of Kleinian analysts when dealing with material stemming from all levels of development. Melanie Klein (1952d) stressed that the transference originates in the earliest object relations and that the vicissitudes of the emotions expressing aggression, love, guilt, and anxiety derive from the early developmental positions she had outlined. Therefore, she considered the analysis of the transference as intimately linked to the analysis of the paranoid-schizoid and the depressive positions. Furthermore, she believed that all the anxiety situations a child goes through reactivate persecutory and depressive anxieties, so that primitive defenses and fears influence all interpretive work with the transference.

Kleinian authors have been particularly interested in the analysis of patients with severe types of character pathology, borderline cases, and psychoses, in whom primitive levels of conflicts and defenses predominate. Given their emphasis on the need to explore the splitting of love and aggression and the vicissitudes of integrative efforts to deal with them, Kleinians stress the interpretation of both negative and positive aspects of the transference, particularly the early interpretation of negative transference features.

The implication is that, generally speaking, paranoid-schizoid features have to be interpreted before depressive features, but all interpretation should combine negative and positive aspects of those features. Consistent with that approach, Melanie Klein (1950a) stressed that, particularly in the initial and termination stages of the analysis, careful exploration of early defenses and conflicts must be carried out. She suggested that a precondition for successful termination of analysis is a sufficient working through of the paranoid-schizoid and depressive anxieties related to termination. In later years, Melanie Klein (1957) stressed the importance of the analysis of envy and the relationship between envy and the negative therapeutic reaction.

Recent Developments

Hanna Segal (1957, 1962, 1967, 1973; Segal and Furer, 1977), Herbert Rosenfeld (1959, 1964, 1965, 1971, 1975), Donald Meltzer (1967, 1973; Meltzer et al., 1975), and Wilfred Bion (1959, 1962, 1963, 1965, 1967, 1970, 1974, 1975, 1977 a, b) are at present the leading representatives of the Kleinian approach to psychoanalysis. Although they essentially maintain their allegiance to the basic Kleinian theories and techniques just outlined, they have made significant theoretical and clinical contributions to that approach and have followed potentially divergent roads within the school.

SEGAL

Segal and Rosenfeld represent the mainstream of contemporary Kleinian thinking. Segal's (1973) summary of Kleinian theory is the clearest overview of Melanie Klein from within her school, and Segal's efforts to illustrate theoretical concepts clinically made it an eminently readable book; her brief surveys of psychoanalytic technique (Segal, 1962, 1967) and her brief summary of Kleinian contributions to

psychoanalysis (Segal and Furer, 1977) defined the essentials of Kleinian psychoanalysis today.

ROSENFELD

Rosenfeld applied psychoanalytic theory and technique first to the psychotherapeutic treatment of selected acute and chronic schizophrenic patients (Rosenfeld, 1965) and then to the study of severe character pathology, particularly narcissistic personality structures (Rosenfeld, 1964, 1971, 1975). In exploring psychoanalytically confusional states in the first group, he pointed to the pathological use of projective identification in those patients and their related tendency to project their selves and their internal objects so forcefully and completely into the analyst—and, by that same projective mechanism, to experience themselves as victims of a similar forceful invasion by the analyst—that the differentiation of the self from the external object dissolves, and a secondary mechanism of total, defensive withdrawal from the therapeutic relationship ensues. Rosenfeld differentiated that type of confusion of self and internal objects with external objects from another, more fundamental kind of confusion—when splitting mechanisms, separating good from bad impulses and good from bad aspects of the self and objects, fail and the schizophrenic patient experiences a fusion of libidinal and aggressive impulses that can no longer be sorted out. A decrease of that second type of confusion by reinforcement of excessive splitting, leading to fragmentation, may represent a further worsening of the patient's condition, decreasing his anxiety but increasing the psychotic reorganization of his total experience.

Psychotherapeutic intervention during such confusional states may, in certain cases, help the patient tolerate the integrating of love and hatred, achieve the depressive position with a heightened level of integration and ego strengthening, and relinquish the psychotic mechanisms of projective identification and pathological splitting. Rosenfeld found that the consistent interpretation of those mechanisms and experiences of the patient in the therapeutic interaction helps patients differentiate themselves from the therapist and reconstitute their ego boundaries.

In addition to the pathogenic operation of splitting mechanisms and projective identification in those cases, Rosenfeld pointed to the severely sadistic, persecutory nature of superego functioning of schizophrenic patients, leading to extreme forms of guilt over their aggressive impulses and, by means of projection, reinforcing their fear of punishment and persecution from external objects. Thus, those patients experience a dread of their internal impulses, a dread of external objects, and a withdrawal from receiving anything good from external objects because of their assumption that everything good will be destroyed inside of them.

Although Rosenfeld implied that the interpretation of those primitive defensive operations and object relations in schizophrenic patients may bring about their reintegration, he remained ambiguous regarding the extent to which he believed in the practical effectiveness of that psychotherapeutic approach with those patients.

Regarding the narcissistic personality, Rosenfeld (1964, 1971, 1975) detailed the structural characteristics and transference developments in the course of psychoanalysis of those patients. In the process, he linked, for the first time, a Kleinian approach to treatment with a descriptive and characterological analysis of a specific group of patients, and he developed an alternative theory of pathological narcissism to the current prevalent psychoanalytic formulations regarding those patients in this country (Kernberg, 1975, 1976; Kohut, 1971, 1977). Narcissistic personalities, Rosenfeld proposed, have omnipotently introjected an all-good, primitive part object (the breast) or omnipotently projected their own selves into such an object, thus denying any difference with or separation from the object. That tendency permits patients with narcissistic object relations to avoid any recognition of separateness between self and object and to deny any need of dependency on an external object. Any dependency would imply the need for a loved and potentially frustrating object that is also intensely hated, that hatred taking the form of extreme envy of the good object. Envy, Rosenfeld assumed, in following Melanie Klein, is a primary intrapsychic expression of the death instinct, the earliest manifestation of aggression in the realm of object relations. Narcissistic object relations permit the avoidance of aggressive feelings caused by frustration and of any awareness of envy. Such external objects as the patient realistically needs are often used for the projection of all undesirable parts of the patient into them, so that in treatment the analyst is used as a lavatory. The relation to a lavatory analyst is extremely gratifying because everything unpleasant is discharged into him, and the patient attributes to himself everything good that comes from the relationship.

Those patients, Rosenfeld went on, have a highly idealized self-image, and anything interfering with that picture is omnipotently denied. They may quickly assimilate other people's values and ideas and declare them to be their own; or else they unconsciously devalue and destroy what they receive from others because it would otherwise evoke unbearable envy and, therefore, have a chronic sense of dissatisfaction with what they are receiving from others.

Rosenfeld (1971) examined a further complication of those personality structures derived from the contamination of their self-idealization by the idealization of the omnipotent destructive parts of the self. The infiltration of the pathological grandiose self by primitive aggression and destructiveness gives a quality of violent self-destructiveness to those patients. Under those conditions, there is an unconscious hatred of everything that is good and valuable not only in external objects but in the patient's own potentially remaining good aspects of his normal dependent self. The patient's envy and resentment are directed not only against what others have but also against what may be good in himself. Under extreme conditions, such patients feel secure and triumphant only when they have destroyed everybody else, particularly the efforts of those who love them. The patient's sense of power seems to derive from his impenetrability to all usual human frailties. In short, severe cases of narcissistic personality may show a malignant fusion of libidinal and aggressive drives in which aggression strongly predominates, and the effort to rescue the dependent healthy parts of the self from their trapped position inside the narcissistic structure is extremely difficult.

Rosenfeld (1975) linked that theory with the most severe forms of negative therapeutic reaction. He also suggested that the unconscious grandiosity of those patients may take the form of fantasies that they have incorporated both the masculine and the feminine aspects of their internal and external objects, so that they are totally immune from any sexual needs, as well as any dependent needs. The breakdown of those narcissistic structures may bring about almost delusional experiences of a paranoid kind that need to be overcome by interpretation to permit the patient to advance toward a situation of true dependency, the depressive position, and the experience of oedipal conflicts. The pathological grandiose self of those patients reflects a more primitive, more severe, and more intractable resistance to the treatment than do unconscious guilt feelings stemming from a sadistic superego, which characterizes less severe forms of negative therapeutic reaction.

MELTZER

Meltzer (1967, 1973) attempted to spell out and classify unconscious fantasies as they determine, in his thinking, the nature of the transference development at various stages of psychoanalysis and the structure—in the sense of organizing fantasy—of infantile and adult polymorphous and perverse sexuality. The enactment of primitive object relations creates geographical confusions—that is, a patient's tendency to treat the analyst and his office as representations of the self and of internal objects. Geographical confusions refer both to confusion of self and object and to confusion of inside and outside. For example, a patient may try to cling to the analyst in an effort to deny any difference between him and the patient's own self; treat the office as if it represented the inside of an internal object (the mother's body); reverse the self-object relationship with the analyst, so that the analyst stands for the self, and the patient stands for the transference object; or exert

an omnipotent control over the analyst in an effort to avoid the enactment of alternative dangerous self and object interactions. Meltzer stressed the importance of the mechanism of projective identification and related severely paranoid transference dispositions in bringing about such geographic confusions.

Those developments, he suggested, take place particularly in early stages of child psychoanalysis under the impact of a child's intolerance of separation and his struggles with omnipotent control, envy, jealousy, deficiency of trust, and excessive persecutory anxiety. Meltzer suggested that the sorting out of those geographical confusions by the systematic investigation of the operation of massive projective identification and by the interpretation of those part object relations in the transference gradually brings about a more stable object relation—stable in the sense of a more definite identity enacted by the child—and the subsequent predominance in the transference of zonal confusions.

Those zonal confusions refer to fantasies related to the mother's body and to both parents in interaction—particularly in sexual intercourse—under the impact of early impulses of the oral, anal, and genital stages of development. Thus, the receptive qualities of mouth, anus, and vagina may lend themselves to condensation or confusion among them, expressed in fantasies influenced by the predominance of incorporative, retentive, expulsive, or penetrating modes; similarly, the protruding qualities of nipple, tongue, feces, and penis may also be condensed or confused in a feeding, retentive, expulsive, or penetrating mode. Meltzer thus borrowed the concepts of bodily zones and modes from Erikson (1963) and linked them with Kleinian interpretations of early fantasies about the mother's body. Erotic excitement, erotic possessiveness, and erotic idealizations, as well as various aggressive needs expressed in the infant's fantasies about his external and internal objects, are activated in unconscious fantasies about the analyst that incorporate such zonal confusions and, when structuralized, give rise to various fixations at the level of polymorphous infantile needs and sexual perversions. In differentiating polymorphous sexual tendencies in children and adults from sexual perversions, Meltzer (1973) considered a predominance of aggressive impulses condensed with libidinal impulses and expressed in zonal confusions as characteristic of perversions; he implied that the fusion of aggression and libido under the dominance of aggression, described by Rosenfeld (1971) as an aspect of certain narcissistic personalities, is the core aspect of perversions in general, rather than the descriptive characteristics of perverse behavior.

By means of analyzing zonal confusions during a psychoanalytic treatment, Meltzer went on, the therapist eventually sorts out the libidinal and aggressive impulses, as well as the masculine and feminine identifications and sexual functions, particularly regarding the internal image of the mother's body, where, eventually, feeding, anal, and genital functions are separated from each other, and their respective libidinal and aggressive drive derivatives are integrated.

The direct interpretation by Meltzer of children's play as reflecting unconscious fantasies of the kind mentioned stems from Melanie Klein's own technique but, in Meltzer's hands, seem to become an overriding, almost idiosyncratic concern, an impression heightened by his efforts to illustrate those zonal confusions by means of the dreams of adult patients. Meltzer's interpretations of the manifest contents of dreams, with only minimal information about the patient's associations and general clinical developments, and his interpretations of practically all unconscious fantasies as if they directly reflected contents of the first 2 years of life convey the impression that he has carried Melanie Klein's approach to an extreme.

Perhaps the most interesting application of all those considerations is to the psychoanalytic work with autistic and psychotic children (Meltzer et al., 1975). Meltzer incorporated a brief contribution by Esther Bick (1968) that has been quite influential among Kleinians. In it she suggested that the first function of the introjection of a good object is to provide the mental equivalent of a skin to the self; in other words, the first aspect of an object that is internalized is its containing function, which permits the various parts of the self to be experienced as contained by a sort of skin. Such a skin, in turn, permits the full internalization of an external object and the building up of an internal space within which internal self and object relate to each other. That earliest function precedes the other defense mechanisms and part object relations of the paranoid-schizoid position.

Bick's paper derived in part from Bion's work and has stimulated the application of his concepts to the psychoanalytic treatment of nonmentally retarded autistic children that Meltzer and his co-workers (1975) reported on. Frances Tustin (1972), in the psychoanalytic exploration of extreme failure or absence of internalized and external object relations in autistic children, applied some of the concepts of geographic and zonal confusions elaborated by Meltzer, perhaps more convincingly than Meltzer himself.

Tustin's work is not strictly Kleinian, and it incorporates, in addition to Meltzer's influence, the influences of Bion, Winnicott (1965), and Mahler (1968). The value of Tustin's book lies in the abundant clinical evidence for her psychoanalytic approach that permits the reader both to understand recent Kleinian conceptions of psychosis and autism and to evaluate them critically. Tustin illustrated how her autistic children were first unable to acknowledge the therapist's independent existence and later, in the process of a beginning relationship with her and her office, enacted fantasies that reflected confused and confusing primitive part object relations and geographic and zonal confusions as spelled out by Meltzer on the basis of Melanie Klein's work with children.

BION

Probably the most important development of Kleinian psychoanalysis at this time is represented by the conceptions of Wilfred Bion. Although Bion's writings are perhaps even more difficult to follow than are Meltzer's, he presents a logically cohesive argument that evolves in a series of extremely condensed and at times strange yet evocative writings. In *Attention and Interpretation* Bion (1970) stressed the essential unavailability of the ultimate knowledge about any patient's or person's intrapsychic processes and the need to acknowledge that the understanding reached by means of interpretation is at most an approximation of the ultimate truth of an intrapsychic experience. His recommendation to approach each session with a patient without memory or desire—that is, without preconceived theories or wishes to influence him into any direction—is, it would seem, an indirect attack on the authoritative style with which traditional Kleinian psychoanalysts seem to formulate their interpretations. In that regard, Bion has moved into the opposite direction from Meltzer's categorical interpretations of primitive mental contents and, in his most recent writings, may even represent a potential departure from the traditional Kleinian approach. However, there has also been a shift in Bion's latest writings (Bion, 1974, 1975, 1977 a, b) that reveals an emotionally charged attitude, an almost religious-mystical atmosphere, which seems uncomfortably directed against truly psychoanalytic method and approach.

After his basic contributions to the psychoanalytic understanding of small groups in the late 1940's and early 1950's—those articles were later brought together in the book *Experiences in Groups* (Bion, 1959)— Bion published a series of papers relating the pathology of thinking in borderline and schizophrenic patients to the activation of primitive defensive operations. Those papers, dating from the middle 1950's to the middle 1960's, were collected in *Second Thoughts: Selected Papers on Psycho-Analysis* (Bion, 1967). Three books dealt with a general psychoanalytic theory of thinking and of pathological distortions of thought processes in the psychoses (Bion, 1962, 1963, 1965). Bion's theories represent the introduction of a structural cognitive model into Kleinian thinking; it is unfortunate that he has not attempted to relate his theory of structural development to the work of others, such as Piaget (Bion rarely quotes other authors).

A basic theory of Bion's is the existence of early primitive elements of thinking, of thoughts that predate the capacity for thinking itself or what he called an apparatus for thinking thoughts. Bion (1962) called those earliest thoughts "beta elements" and related them to early sensory impressions and preconceptions. In that regard, he followed Melanie Klein's notion of some basic innate knowledge regarding good

and bad objects, genitality, and so on. Beta elements occur when a baby is seriously frustrated and when wishful hallucination breaks down in the face of continued frustration. At that point, primitive notions of bad objects occur (typical beta elements) and are evacuated in the form of primitive forms of projection simultaneously with efforts to get rid of the unpleasant emotional state by action (affective discharge). Bion linked his theory of thinking with Klein's theory of projective identification. If sufficient gratification occurs to allow the baby to tolerate some frustration, the mutually isolated, primitive, dispersed (sensorial, affective, and cognitive) beta elements, which were previously dealt with through evacuation, may be tolerated, integrated, and linked in the form of a higher thought process, which corresponds to the component elements of the dynamic unconscious and of dreams. Bion (1962) called the function by which beta elements are integrated into thoughts characteristic of primary-process thinking "alpha function" and the products of alpha functions "alpha elements." Alpha elements are sensorial impressions, affects, conceptions—in contrast to innate preconceptions—that can be stored in the form of memories, linked and elaborated, and giving rise to higher forms of thinking.

Intimately connected with Bion's theory of alpha function and alpha elements is his theory of a relationship between the baby and the mother by means of which the baby's projected primitive beta elements are absorbed, one might say, by the mother's intuitive understanding of the baby's predicament at points of frustration. The mother's intuitive daydreaming or reverie, in Bion's (1962) terms, permits her to incorporate the projected, dispersed, fragmented beta elements and to integrate them by means of her intuitive understanding of the total predicament of the baby at that point. The mother's intuition thus acts as a container, which organizes the projected content. The theory implies that the baby, by introjection of the mother, may identify with her function as a container and thus come to establish an internal apparatus for thinking thoughts. In other words, the mother's acting as an organizer of projected beta elements creates a model for alpha functioning (integration of thinking), with which the baby identifies and which the baby then uses to further transform beta elements into alpha elements.

Bion also linked those two stages of thinking—namely, the projection of beta elements and their subsequent integration by means of alpha function into alpha elements—with the Kleinian theory of the paranoid-schizoid and depressive positions. Projective identification, the mechanism dealing with beta elements, is a typical manifestation of the paranoid-schizoid position; the alpha function—integrative linking of sensorial, affective, and cognitive elements that belong together within a certain total situation of the baby—because of its implicit effort toward integration and acknowledgment of intrapsychic pain linked with the acceptance of knowledge, reflects the depressive position. In other words, as frustration, fear, and despair are no longer projected in the form of beta elements but accepted as an intrapsychic, affective, and cognitive reality, such consciousness reflects aspects of the depressive position.

Bion broadened the Kleinian analysis of the paranoid-schizoid position to include, as one more schizoid mechanism, active intrapsychic efforts to destroy cognitive functions. In his paper "Attacks on Linking" Bion (1967) pointed out that psychotic patients develop active efforts to destroy the links between their own associative processes, to destroy their alpha function, and also to destroy the capacity of the therapist to understand and empathize with what goes on in the patient by destroying the therapist's means of understanding the patient. Bion stressed that those active defensive processes occur in schizophrenic thinking. In that regard, his thinking contrasted with other psychoanalytic theories, which imply that the psychotic disintegration of cognitive processes is mainly a manifestation of failure or weakness of secondary-process thinking and a regression to primary-process thinking.

Bion (1962) also spoke of three essential links implicit in the integration of thought processes. Those three links are K (for knowledge), L (for love), and H (for hate). Those links refer both to the intrapsychic linkage of different thoughts and to the interpersonal processes related to those thought processes. For example, K, an essential link between cognitive elements, is also implicit in the relation between the baby and the mother. Bion referred to the sequence described earlier in which the baby projects split-off, isolated contents into the mother, who then acts as a container until the baby finally reintrojects the now-organized integration of previously split thought elements. In the psychoanalytic situation in which the patient is able to identify with the analyst's work in integrating the patient's material, a K-link is in action. The build-ups of good and bad inner and outer objects—a crucial aspect of Kleinian theory—are typical manifestations of what Bion described as L- or H-links. An important additional type of linkage is that determined by minus- K-links (−K), a form of pathological relation between the baby and the mother that can be observed in the relation between the patient and the analyst. The mother or the analyst is unable to experience the integrating reverie because of the aggressive threats implicit in massive projective identification, and the mother or the analyst replaces intuitive integration by an omnipotent effort to understand without empathy and to use such understanding as elements of control. The patient may, in turn, introject such a −K-link as a characteristic of the mother's or the analyst's functioning and thus perpetuate a false understanding that is split off from authentic emotional reality. The origin of such −K-processes usually lies in the patient himself and is especially related to intensive primitive envy and destructiveness that forces the patient to attempt to destroy the mother's or the analyst's capacity for creative thinking.

Bion (1963) described still another type of pathological distortion of thinking in the form of the reversed perspective. That terms refers to a pseudounderstanding between the patient and the analyst regarding certain cognitive interactions; the patient apparently agrees with the analyst's interpretation but is actually reorganizing all that the analyst is saying into a theory of his own, completely divorced from the theory responsible for the analyst's communications. Thus, the patient may be describing a dream that is really a hallucinatory experience, the analyst may interpret the dream for its meaning, and the patient then accepts that interpretation as a reassurance that he has not been hallucinating.

Returning to the basic theory of beta and alpha elements, Bion thus distinguished preconceptions (primitive innate elements and primitive sensorial experiences that are nonintegrated and cannot be linked directly to each other) from higher level linking processes that presuppose the development of integrating efforts of the baby's mind under the guiding principle of the mother's empathic understanding. In the case of preconceptions of a frustrating, frightening, and dangerous kind, there exists first an effort to discharge them through action or to expel them through projective identification and only later to accept the need to integrate cognitive elements in a painful but meaningful way by transforming beta elements into alpha elements, which can be stored and become part of thinking processes, which, in turn, can be used for further elaboration. The implication is that, in the case of psychotic regression, excessive fear, rage, and primitive persecutory preconceptions are so intense that the patient pathologically increases his efforts to discharge those beta elements through action and projective identification.

In several papers dealing with schizophrenic thinking, Bion (1967) stressed the functions of schizophrenic language as a mode of action, a mode of communication, and a mode of thinking. Under circumstances when a normal person would think, the schizophrenic patient acts; when a normal person would act, the schizophrenic patient acts in a primitive way by means of his language; and the dispersed, distorted, destroyed elements of his language are projected into the analyst in order to use him as an apparatus to think thoughts. The intensity of the patient's primitive envy and rage and the violence of his active efforts to prevent the development of knowledge about his own intrapsychic condition make it difficult for the analyst to empathize with the patient. Under such circumstances the analyst serves not only as the receptacle of dispersed, bizarre, primitive, chaotic elements but also as the victim of the patient's active

efforts to prevent the analyst from integrating what the patient himself cannot integrate because of his envy and destructive wishes toward the analyst. Thus, the patient's efforts to use the analyst as a container for clarifying his internal chaos are complicated by the patient's need to destroy the analyst's apparatus for thinking, as well as his own. The analyst's tolerance of the patient's projection and his capacity to experience in himself the panic, the dread, the confusion, the madness that the patient is trying to evade by means of general splitting and projective identification eventually permit the analyst to communicate to the patient what is really going on inside the patient and against which he is trying to defend himself. In the early stages of psychoanalytic psychotherapy with psychotic patients, the analyst has only his internal affective-cognitive processes as objective evidence to construct his theory regarding what goes on inside the patient.

Bion (1967) also postulated the simultaneous existence of nonpsychotic and psychotic parts of the personality in borderline patients; he described patients dominated by beta elements in whom violent projective identification develops to expel such beta elements. Because of those developments, borderline patients present what Bion (1967) called "bizarre objects"—that is, illusion-like or hallucination-like experiences of frightening, strange, sensorial material or cognitive elements that the patient experiences as existing in the external world. He considered those experiences the psychotic part of the personality, which may coexist with higher level neurotic parts; he implied that the presence of higher level defensive operations centering on repression defends the neurotic part of the patient against an awareness of his psychotic, primitive functioning. Bion suggested that there exists in each acute crisis of neurotic patients an activation of such primitive psychotic nuclei that need to be analyzed and resolved. He stressed that the schizophrenic patient must in the course of the treatment accept his chaos, confusion, and persecutory fears as belonging to himself; in other words, the schizophrenic patient must accept his own madness before real improvement can occur. Hallucinations occurring during psychoanalytic sessions are seen as particularly significant illustrations of projective identification, of violent expulsion and projection of bizarre objects, and Bion illustrated the clinical use of those concepts in his psychotherapeutic work.

The −K-link and the reversed perspective are two particular cases of a more general distortion or deterioration of the psychoanalytic process that Bion explored systematically in the extreme case of the psychoanalyst who treats a liar. The conscious and unconscious implications of such extreme distortions of the truth led Bion to postulate three over-all types of analytic relations in terms of the mutual influence of the container and the contained. Those three types are: (1) the establishment of a symbiotic link between analyst and patient in which there is a truly mutual relation and influence; (2) the parasitic link—typical of the liar—in which the patient consciously or unconsciously exploits the analytic relation for purposes other than those formally agreed on and assumed to exist by the analyst—in Bion's (1970) terms, "a relationship in which one depends on another to produce a third, which is destructive of all three"; and (3) the commensal link, a basic lack of emotional relation that is obscured by a pseudopsychoanalytic process.

Under optimal conditions, in a symbiotic link the psychoanalytic process can be characterized by the presence of transformations occurring within in each session—within the patient, as well as within the psychoanalyst—transformations in which the psychoanalyst's reality approaches the patient's reality without ever becoming identical with it. The analyst's point of view or vertex brings about a transformation, a new organization of the patient's material that is different from the organization initially assumed from the patient's vertex. The gradual approximation of their respective vertices reflects appropriate psychoanalytic work.

Therefore, the psychoanalyst needs to be extremely cautious in not confronting the patient with a predetermined, biased point of view and must approach each session with an honest willingness to be surprised by the patient's material. That is what Bion (1970) meant by the analyst's presenting himself without memory, and, insofar as he is determined not to influence or move the patient into any particular direction during that particular hour, he also meets the patient without desire.

It is regrettable that Bion has made little effort until now to relate his theories to the scientific mainstreams in the area of perceptive, cognitive, and psychosexual development. His cryptic style may discourage many readers. However, psychoanalysts working with borderline and schizophrenic patients may find his clinical observations and the technical implications of some of his theories intriguing, challenging, and stimulating. Grinberg et al. (1975) published an excellent summary of his work.

Critique

THEORY

The concept of an inborn death instinct—and its earliest expression as envy—the concept of an innate knowledge of the genitals of both sexes, and Melanie Klein's general lack of consideration of biological developments, both anatomical and physiological, have been sharply criticized in the non-Kleinian psychoanalytic literature (Waelder, 1937; Glover, 1945; Bibring, 1947; Zetzel, 1953, 1956a; Joffe, 1969; Kernberg, 1969; Yorke, 1971; Greenson, 1974). The telescoping of intrapsychic development, particularly that of complex relationships between oedipal and preoedipal conflicts, into the first year of life, appears unwarranted from present-day knowledge of neurophysiological and early psychological development and the accumulation of data stemming from direct observation of infants. In spite of the lip service given to the importance of environmental factors, there is a general neglect of the environment in the Kleinian approach.

Criticism has also been expressed by the above-quoted non-Kleinian authors of the neglect of the developmental analysis of ego and superego throughout later childhood and adolescence. Melanie Klein and other Kleinian authors have not considered the structural differences between various types of psychopathology, and they seem to neglect such differences, for they apply the same treatment technique to all patients along the entire spectrum of psychological illness. There has been a justified critique of the ambiguity of some Kleinian terminology—a major stumbling block that has prevented the correlation of Kleinian theory with other psychoanalytic formulations and findings. And non-Kleinian psychoanalysts who have become interested in the Kleinian approach (Brierley, 1961; Guntrip, 1961; Geleerd, 1963; Winnicott, 1965; Zetzel, 1966; Kernberg, 1969) object to the almost consistent neglect of findings stemming from other psychoanalytic orientations and other psychosocial sciences, of which the pseudobiological Kleinian orientation is only one symptom.

At the same time, certain aspects of Kleinian theory have significantly influenced and been incorporated into the mainstream of psychoanalytic thinking. The importance of early object relations in normal and pathological development has been generally accepted; the defensive constellations described by the Kleinians as paranoid-schizoid, depressive, and manic have been integrated by clinicians working with borderline and psychotic patients. The importance of aggression in early development, the evidence that superego formation occurs earlier than was originally assumed, and the importance of studying the mutual relation between genital and pregenital conflicts have been accepted by many non-Kleinians.

TECHNIQUE

One major criticism (Kernberg, 1969) of the Kleinian technique is of the application of the same, nonmodified, psychoanalytic technique to patients with all levels of illness, in spite of clinical experience indicating that at least a number of psychotic patients, some borderline patients, and patients with antisocial personality features do not respond well to a nonmodified psychoanalytic approach.

Another major criticism (Greenson, 1974, 1975) is that Kleinian analysts tend to neglect the reality aspects of the psychoanalytic situation with an almost exclusive focus on and overextension of the concept of transference. That seems to be particularly true regarding the opening phases of a Kleinian analysis. Kleinian technique has also been criticized (Zetzel, 1956a; Geleerd, 1963) because of the premature deep interpretations of unconscious fantasy and transference manifestations, interpretations that, by bypassing the ego's defensive structure, create the danger of an intellectual indoctrination of patients. That criticism is related to another of the peculiar terms related to early infantile development characteristic of many Kleinian analysts and the giving of interpretations in an atmosphere of excessive certainty and activity on the part of the analyst. Thus, Kleinian technique may have an indoctrinating quality that militates against the testing of specific hypotheses in individual cases.

All those criticisms converge into a general critique of the neglect of character analysis in Kleinian technique. Neglect of sufficient clarification of reality in the early stages of analysis and neglect of systematic working through of character defenses may cause an unnecessary prolongation of the analysis by driving character defenses underground, by fostering submission to the analyst's theories, and by losing the important function of monitoring the development of the patient's capacity for introspection and self-analysis. A recent review and summary of the ego-psychological critique of the management of the transference in Kleinian psychoanalysis can be found in Greenson's (1974) paper.

Some major contributions from the Kleinian school have gradually been integrated into psychoanalytic technique at large. First, the application of classical technique to the psychoanalysis of children is a generally acknowledged major contribution of Melanie Klein (1927). Second, there is an increasing technical use of the new understanding regarding early defensive operations provided by Melanie Klein and her followers. The understanding of the mechanisms of the paranoid-schizoid and the depressive positions have helped in psychoanalytic and modified psychoanalytic approaches to severe types of character pathology, particularly narcissistic character structures, the treatment of borderline conditions, and psychoanalytic psychotherapy with psychotic patients, including some autistic patients. Melanie Klein opened the door to the understanding of primitive defensive operations, fears, and fantasies, and those understandings have broadened the capacity to understand and help a wide variety of regressed patients.

CONCLUSION

Melanie Klein's work, in short, has provided major contributions to the understanding of borderline and psychotic conditions and to the understanding of early vicissitudes of aggression, defense mechanisms, and object relations.

Suggested Cross References

Freudian theories are discussed at length in Chapter 8, and Erikson's theories are discussed in Section 10.1. Paranoid disorders are discussed in Chapter 16, schizoaffective disorders in Chapter 17, and affective disorders in Chapters 18 and 19. Psychoanalysis and psychoanalytic psychotherapy are discussed in Section 30.1. Normal child development is described in Section 34.2, and psychotherapy with children is described in Section 42.1.

REFERENCES

Abraham, K. Notes on the psycho-analytical investigation and treatment of manic-depressive insanity and allied conditions. In *Selected Papers on Psycho-Analysis*, p. 137. Hogarth Press, London, 1927a.

Abraham, K. A short study of the development of the libido, viewed in the light of mental disorders. In *Selected Papers on Psycho-Analysis*, p. 418. Hogarth Press, London, 1927b.

Bibring, E. The so-called English school of psychoanalysis. Psychoanal. Q., *16:* 69, 1947.

Bick, E. The experience of the skin in early object-relations. Int. J. Psychoanal., *49:* 484, 1968.

Bion, W. R. *Experiences in Groups.* Basic Books, New York, 1959.

Bion, W. R. *Learning from Experience.* Basic Books, New York, 1962.

Bion, W. R. *Elements of Psycho-Analysis.* Basic Books, New York, 1963.

Bion, W. R. *Transformation: Changes from Learning to Growth.* Basic Books, New York, 1965.

Bion, W. R. *Second Thoughts: Selected Papers on Psycho-Analysis.* Heinemann, London, 1967.

Bion, W. R. *Attention and Interpretation.* Basic Books, New York, 1970.

Bion, W. R. *Brazilian Lectures. 1. Sao Paulo, 1973.* Imago Editora, Rio de Janeiro, 1974.

Bion, W. R. *Brazilian Lectures. 2. Rio de Janeiro/Sao Paulo, 1974.* Imago Editora, Rio de Janeiro, 1975.

Bion, W. R. Emotional turbulence. In *Borderline Personality Disorder*, P. Hartocollis, editor, p. 3. International Universities Press, New York, 1977a.

Bion, W. R. *Two Papers: The Grid and Caesura.* Imago Editora, Rio de Janeiro, 1977b.

Brierley, M. Problems connected with the work of Melanie Klein. In *Trends in Psycho-Analysis*, M. Brierley, editor, p. 57. Hogarth Press, London, 1961.

Erikson, E. *Childhood and Society*, ed. 2. W. W. Norton, New York, 1963.

Fairbairn, W. D. *An Object-Relations Theory of the Personality.* Basic Books, New York, 1952.

Freud, A. *The Ego and the Mechanisms of Defense.* International Universities Press, New York, 1936.

Freud, S. Mourning and melancholia. In *Standard Edition of the Complete Psychological Works of Sigmund Freud*, vol. 14, p. 237. Hogarth Press, London, 1957.

Freud, S. The ego and the id. In *Standard Edition of the Complete Psychological Works of Sigmund Freud*, vol. 19, p. 3. Hogarth Press, London, 1961.

Geleerd, E. R. Evaluation of Melanie Klein's "Narrative of a Child Analysis." Int. J. Psychoanal., *44:* 493, 1963.

Glover, E. Examination of the Klein system of child psychology. Psychoanal. Study Child, *1:* 75, 1945.

Greenson, R. R. Transference: Freud or Klein. Int. J. Psychoanal., *55:* 37, 1974.

Greenson, R. R. Transference: Freud or Klein: A reply to the discussion by H. Rosenfeld. Int. J. Psychoanal., *56:* 243, 1975.

Grinberg, L., Sor, D., and de Bianchede, E. T. *Introduction to the Work of Bion.* Clunie Press, Perthshire, Scotland, 1975.

* Guntrip, H. *Personality Structure and Human Interaction.* International Universities Press, New York, 1961.

Hartmann, H. *Essays on Ego Psychology.* International Universities Press, New York, 1964.

Heimann, P. Certain functions of introjection and projection in early infancy. In *Developments in Psychoanalysis*, M. Klein, P. Heimann, S. Issacs, and J. Riviere, editors, p. 122. Hogarth Press, London, 1952.

Heimann, P. A combination of defense mechanisms in paranoid states. In *New Directions in Psycho-Analysis*, M. Klein, P. Heimann, and R. E. Money-Kyrle, editors, p. 240. Tavistock Publications, London, 1955a.

Heimann, P. A contribution to the re-evaluation of the Oedipus complex: The early stages. In *New Directions in Psycho-Analysis*, M. Klein, P. Heimann, and R. E. Money-Kyrle, editors, p. 23. Tavistock Publications, London, 1955b.

Isaacs, S. The nature and function of phantasy. Int. J. Psychoanal., *29:* 73, 1948.

Joffe, W. G. A critical review of the states of the envy concept. Int. J. Psychoanal., *50:* 533, 1969.

Joseph, B. Some characteristics of the psychopathic personality. Int. J. Psychoanal., *41:* 526, 1960.

Kernberg, O. A contribution to the ego-psychological critique of the Kleinian school. Int. J. Psychoanal., *50:* 317, 1969.

Kernberg, O. Summary of two symposia on Bion. Bull. Menninger Clin., *35:* 363, 1971.

Kernberg, O. *Borderline Conditions and Pathological Narcissism.* Jason Aronson, New York, 1975.

Kernberg, O. *Object Relations Theory and Clinical Psychoanalysis.* Jason Aronson, New York, 1976.

Klein, M. The psychological principles of infant analysis. Int. J. Psychoanal., *8:* 25, 1927.

Klein, M. A contribution to the psychogenesis of manic-depressive states. In *Contributions to Psycho-Analysis, 1921–1945*, M. Klein, editor, p. 282. Hogarth Press, London, 1948a.

Klein, M. Mourning and its relation to manic-depressive states. In *Contributions to Psycho-Analysis, 1921–1945*, M. Klein, editor, p. 311. Hogarth Press, London, 1948b.

* Klein, M. The Oedipus complex in the light of early anxieties. In *Contributions to Psycho-Analysis, 1921–1945*, M. Klein, editor, p. 377. Hogarth Press, London, 1948c.

Klein, M. Early states of the Oedipus conflict and of superego formation. In *The Psycho-Analysis of Children*, M. Klein, editor, p. 179. Hogarth Press, London, 1949.

Klein, M. On the criteria for the termination of a psychoanalysis. Int. J. Psychoanal., *31:* 78, 1950a.

Klein, M. Early stages of the Oedipus conflict. In *Contributions to Psycho-Analysis, 1921–1945*, M. Klein, editor. Hogarth Press, London, 1950b.

Klein, M. The early development of conscience in the child. In *Contributions to Psycho-Analysis, 1921–1945*, M. Klein, editor. Hogarth Press, London, 1950c.

Klein, M. Discussion of the mutual influences in the development of ego and id. Psychoanal. Study Child., *7:* 51, 1952a.

* Klein, M. Notes on some schizoid mechanisms. In *Developments in Psycho-Analysis*, M. Klein, P. Heimann, S. Isaacs, and J. Riviere, editors, p. 292. Hogarth Press, London, 1952b.

Klein, M. On the theory of anxiety and guilt. In *Developments in Psycho-Analysis*, M. Klein, P. Heimann, S. Isaacs, and J. Riviere, editors, p. 271. Hogarth Press, London, 1952c.

Klein, M. The origins of transference. Int. J. Psychoanal., *33:* 433, 1952d.

Klein, M. Some theoretical conclusions regarding the emotional life of the infant. In *Developments in Psycho-Analysis*, M. Klein, P. Heimann, S. Isaacs, and J. Riviere, editors, p. 198. Hogarth Press, London, 1952e.

Klein, M. *The Psycho-Analysis of Children.* Hogarth Press, London, 1954.

* Klein, M. *Envy and Gratitude.* Tavistock Publications, London, 1957.

Klein, M. Symposium on child analysis. In *Contributions to Psycho-Analysis, 1921–1945*, M. Klein, editor, p. 152. Hogarth Press, London, 1958.

Klein, M. *Narrative of a Child Analysis.* Hogarth Press, London, 1961.

Klein, M. *Our Adult World.* Basic Books, New York, 1963.

Kohut, H. *The Analysis of the Self.* International Universities Press, New York, 1971.

Kohut, H. *The Restoration of the Self.* International Universities Press, New York, 1977.

Mahler, M. *On Human Symbiosis and the Vicissitudes of Individuation*, vol. I: *Infantile Psychosis.* International Universities Press, New York, 1968.

Meltzer, D. *The Psycho-Analytical Process.* Heinemann, London, 1967.

Meltzer, D. *Sexual States of Mind.* Clunie Press, Perthshire, Scotland, 1973.

Meltzer, D., Bremner, J., Hoxter, S., Weddell, D., and Wittenberg, I. *Explorations in Autism.* Clunie Press, Perthshire, Scotland, 1975.

Money-Kyrle, R. E. Normal countertransference and some of its deviations. Int. J. Psychoanal., *37:* 360, 1956.

Money-Kyrle, R. E. British schools of psychoanalysis. I. Melanie Klein and Kleinian psychoanalytic theory. In *American Handbook of Psychiatry*, S. Arieti, editor, p. 225. Basic Books, New York, 1966.

Racker, H. *Transference and Countertransference.* International Universities Press, New York, 1968.

Rado, S. The problem of melancholia. Int. J. Psychoanal., *9:* 420, 1928.

Rapaport, D. *The Collected Papers of David Rapaport*, M. Gill, editor. Basic Books, New York, 1967.

Riviere, J. A. A contribution to the analysis of the negative therapeutic reaction. Int. J. Psychoanal., *17:* 304, 1936.

Rodrigue, E. The analysis of a three-year old mute schizophrenic. In *New Directions in Psycho-Analysis*, M. Klein, P. Heimann, and R. E. Money-Kyrle, editors, p. 140. Tavistock Publications, London, 1955.

Rosenfeld, H. Notes on the psycho-analysis of the superego conflict in an acute schizophrenic patient. In *New Directions in Psycho-Analysis*, M. Klein, P. Heimann, and R. E. Money-Kyrle, editors, p. 180. Tavistock Publications, London, 1955.

Rosenfeld, H. An investigation into the psycho-analytic theory of depression. Int. J. Psychoanal., *40:* 105, 1959.

Rosenfeld, H. Notes on the psychopathology and psycho-analytic treatment of schizophrenia. In *Psychiatric Research Project 17*, H. Azima and B. C. Glueck, Jr., editors, p. 61. American Psychiatric Association, Washington, D.C., 1963.

Rosenfeld, H. On the psychopathology of narcissism: A clinical approach. Int. J. Psychoanal., *45:* 332, 1964.

* Rosenfeld, H. *Psychotic States: A Psycho-Analytical Approach.* International Universities Press, New York, 1965.

Rosenfeld, H. Infantile anxiety and psychosis. Int. J. Psychiatry, *4:* 549, 1967.

Rosenfeld, H. A clinical approach to the psychoanalytic theory of the life and death instincts: An investigation into the aggressive aspects of narcissism. Int. J. Psychoanal., *52:* 169, 1971.

Rosenfeld, H. Negative therapeutic reaction. In *Tactics and Techniques in Psychoanalytic Therapy*. Vol. 2: *Countertransference*, P. L. Giovacchini, editor, p. 217. Jason Aronson, New York, 1975.

Segal, H. Notes on symbol formation. Int. J. Psychoanal., *38:* 391, 1957.

Segal, H. The curative factors in psycho-analysis. Int. J. Psychoanal., *43:* 212, 1962.

Segal, H. Melanie Klein's technique. In *Psychoanalytic Technique: A Handbook for the Practicing Psychoanalyst,* B. B. Wolman, editor, p. 168. Basic Books, New York, 1967.

* Segal, H. *Introduction to the Work of Melanie Klein,* ed. 2. Basic Books, New York, 1973.

Segal, H., and Furer, M. Psychoanalytical dialogue: Kleinian theory today. J. Am. Psychoanal. Assoc., *25:* 363, 1977.

Tustin, F. *Autism and Childhood Psychosis.* Jason Aronson, New York, 1972.

Waelder, R. The problem of the genesis of psychical conflict in earliest infancy. Int. J. Psychoanal., *18:* 406, 1937.

Winnicott, D. W. A personal view of the Kleinian contribution. In *The Maturational Process and the Facilitating Environment,* D. W. Winnicott, editor, p. 171. International Universities Press, New York, 1965.

Wisdom, J. O. Comparison and development in the psycho-analytical theories of melancholia. Int. J. Psychoanal., *43:* 113, 1962.

Wisdom, J. O. Fairbairn's contribution on object-relationship, splitting and ego structure. Br. J. Med. Psychol., *36:* 145, 1963.

Wisdom, J. O. Freud and Melanie Klein: Psychology, ontology, and Weltanschauung. In *Psychoanalysis and Philosophy,* C. Hanley and M. Lazarowitz, editors, p. 327. International Universities Press, New York, 1971.

Yorke, C. Some suggestions for a critique of Kleinian psychology. Psychoanal. Study Child, *129:* 26, 1971.

Zetzel, E. R. The depressive position. In *Affective Disorders*, P. Greenacre, editor, p. 84. International Universities Press, New York, 1953.

Zetzel, E. R. An approach to the relation between concept and content in psychoanalytic theory (with special reference to the work of Melanie Klein and her followers). Psychoanal. Study Child, *11:* 99, 1956a.

Zetzel, E. R. Current concepts of transference. Int. J. Psychoanal., *37:* 369, 1956b.

Zetzel, E. R. Discussion of the paper by Herbert Rosenfeld, "Object Relations of the Acute Schizophrenic Patient in the Transference Situation." In *Recent Research on Schizophrenia*, P. Solomon and B. C. Glueck, Jr., editors, p. 75. American Psychiatric Association, Washington, D. C. 1964.

Zetzel, E. R. The analytic situation. In *Psychoanalysis in the Americas*, R. E. Litman, editor, p. 86. International Universities Press. New York, 1966.

10.6 Wilhelm Reich

DAVID ELKIND, Ph.D.

Introduction

Among the students of Freud's later years, the years after World War I, Wilhelm Reich was perhaps the most outstanding and the most controversial. He began as something of an *enfant terrible* and was treating patients referred to him by Freud before he had completed his medical training. But Reich's support of Marxian politics eventually alienated him from the analysts, and his efforts on behalf of sexual liberation eventually antagonized the Marxists. After being rejected by the political and professional movements to which he gave allegiance, Reich took an increasingly idiosyncratic path of research that led him, by the end of his life, to believe that society was the patient and that he was the therapist of its salvation.

Although much of Reich's later work was at the very least outlandish and scientifically unacceptable, his early achievements were a lasting contribution to psychiatry and social science. And even some of his later social psychological books and articles contain brilliant insights into human dynamics. Unfortunately, those insights were often embedded in a web of paranoid ideation. Reich was a brilliant but very troubled man who could not adapt to existing institutions and who was unable to create a viable alternative.

In describing Reich's contributions to contemporary psy-

chiatry, one must point out that he often came to the right conclusions for the wrong reasons. His theory of character structure, one of his most lasting achievements, grew out of his erroneous theory of the orgasm. Likewise, his theory of character formation, as a means of perpetuating the social status quo, was based on bad anthropology. To understand Reich's conceptions, therefore, one needs to look at the assumptions, however wrong and misguided, from which he began.

Life

Wilhelm Reich (see Figure 1) was born on March 24, 1897, in Dobrzynia, a part of Galicia that then belonged to the Austrian Empire. Shortly after his birth, the family moved, and Reich grew up on a kind of ranch in the Ukranian section of Austria. The family was well-to-do, and Reich and his younger brother engaged in pastimes of the outdoor life, such as hunting and fishing. Although the family was Jewish, it was well assimilated to German culture, and the Reich boys were not allowed to play with the Yiddish children any more than they were allowed to play with the peasant youngsters.

Reich's father was a rather stern, taciturn, dictatorial, and jealous man who completely dominated his wife and sons. During his adolescence, Reich was at least partly responsible for his mother's death. She was having an affair with her sons' tutor; Reich discovered the fact and revealed it to his father. Reich's mother committed suicide shortly thereafter. It is likely that Reich's sense of guilt in that matter played a part in his habitual unwillingness to face certain aspects of reality. Perhaps his insights into the character armor of neurotics grew out of an awareness of his own character armor in relation to his mother's death.

After World War I, Reich took up his medical studies in Vienna and became affiliated with the psychoanalytic group. He was at first very welcome, particularly because of his teaching and work on the therapeutic techniques. But his personal behavior (such as open affairs with former patients), his orgasm theories, and his political involvements eventually wore out the acceptance earned by his teaching and technical contributions. Reich's efforts on behalf of sexual liberation, birth control, and so on also lost him his good standing with the Communists.

From 1932 to 1939 Reich moved to several Scandinavian countries but settled in Oslo. In Norway, he continued his efforts on behalf of sexual liberation and also propounded his notions of a new form of living energy that could be created in a test tube. Reich soon became the target of a viscious newspaper attack, which charged him, among other things, with undermining the morals of the young. Ironically, the contemporary sexual freedom to be found in Scandinavian countries is probably, in part at least, a result of the influence of Reich and his followers.

In 1939 Reich moved to Forest Hills, New York, where he continued to teach, train students in his methods, treat patients, and write articles and books. He was exceedingly prolific but had the unfortunate habit of rewriting books and articles without adequate referencing for the reader. One can read an article by Reich written in the 1930's with insertions from the 1940's and 1950's but without any indication that new material had been added. For that reason many of his articles and books often jar the reader and have a somewhat bizarre quality.

Several years after his arrival in America, Reich bought some land in Rangeley, Maine, where he established a summer training workshop. Eventually, he built permanent buildings in Rangeley and moved his family and laboratories to Maine in the early 1950's. He tried to establish a work democracy at Orgonon, which was the forerunner of many contemporary communes. The commune effort failed, as did many of Reich's experiments on orgone energy. In the meantime, his ideas became more and more extreme, and even some of his closest followers, such as A. S. Neil, refused to follow him in his more outlandish theories.

Reich had difficulties in other areas as well. His claims that his orgone accumulators helped to cure cancer patients brought him under

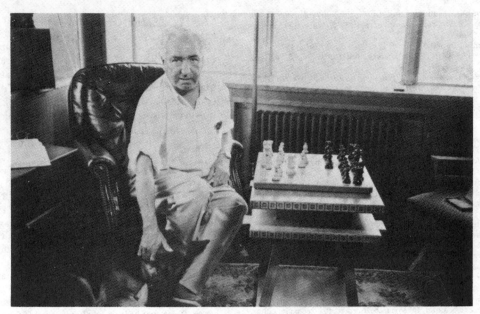

FIGURE 1. Wilhelm Reich at home. (Photo courtesy of Farrar, Straus & Giroux, Inc.)

the scrutiny of the United States Food and Drug Administration. A court order was eventually obtained, enjoining Reich not to publicize or distribute his orgone boxes. Reich refused to obey the injunction and, after a heated trial in which he defended himself, he was convicted and sent to prison. While in prison, Reich suffered the last of a series of heart attacks and died on November 3, 1957.

Theory of Neuroses

In Freud's early theorizing about the neuroses, he postulated that neurotic persons display two different patterns. One group of neurotic patients, those who are truly psychoneurotic, show symptoms such as hysterical blindness, impotence, and frigidity—all of which can be attributed to mental conflicts. Another group of neurotic patients, those who suffer from an actual neurosis, show symptoms of anxiety and its concomitants—palpitation, sweating, dizziness, and so on. In the actual neuroses, the symptoms can be attributed to physiological causes—namely, to the damming up of libido due to abstinence, coitus interruptus, and related practices.

In arguing for the actual neuroses as a clinical entity, Freud suggested that the dammed-up libido is converted or transformed into anxiety, the major symptom in that type of disturbance. Later in his career, however, Freud discarded the conception of the actual neuroses and argued that all neurotic persons are psychoneurotic in the sense that every one of their symptoms is produced by mental conflicts. According to that new conception, anxiety constitutes a general signal system that alerts the person to dangers from within himself and from without, in the social environment.

In contrast to Freud, who eventually subsumed the actual neuroses within the psychoneuroses, Reich went in just the opposite direction. He argued that every neurosis is an actual neurosis and results from the damming up of sexual energy. In Reich's view, that damming up has three possible outcomes. One outcome is the development of neurotic symptoms and character traits that are, in effect, maladaptive behavioral channels into which sexual energy flows when the normal outlet, orgasm, is blocked. The rigidity of neurotic symptoms and character traits derives from the fact that such symptoms and character traits do not fully discharge sexual energy, with

a resultant residual or stasis energy, which appears as bodily tension.

Reich also believed that sexual energy can alternatively be converted into anxiety, as in Freud's original theory of the actual neuroses. And Reich assumed that undischarged energy can be released as sadism or aggression. Sadism, in Reich's view, is the person's reaction to the frustration of his sexual desires. On the level of sociology, Reich argued that societies wherein sexuality is repressed are, of necessity, aggressive. The youth slogan "Make love not war" nicely expressed Reich's conception of, as well as his solution to, societal and individual psychopathology.

Reich was well aware of the arguments against the view that orgasms, in sufficient numbers, would solve individual and social problems. In response, he argued that ejaculation is not a measure of true orgastic potency. A truly orgastically potent person is totally involved with the other person and achieves total release of tension and pressure in the course of the orgasm. For Reich, such orgastic potency is rare in societies, such as those of Western Europe, that have excessive barriers against sexual expression. On the other hand, Reich did not advocate sexual license; he believed that the orgastically potent person is truly attached to his partner and that such relationships involve self-regulation of sexual desires. The orgastically potent person is, thus, moral in the highest sense because of his genuine regard and love for other people. But the majority of people in Western society are so armored against sexual expression that they manifest neuroses, anxieties, and character disorders. In his theory of character formation, Reich had to consider such formations in both the individual and the society.

Character Formation

Because Reich's theory of character formation, like his theory of psychopathology, was built on Freudian theory, it is necessary to start with Freud. The concept of character structure grows out of the Freudian structural model of id, ego, and superego as the basic apparatuses of the personality. The ego is the intermediary between the id (instinctual forces), the superego (internalized values and standards), and reality. To accommodate reality and the superego's restraints, the ego has to defend itself against the forces of the id, whose realization could result in either punishment or guilt.

In many persons, the defense system against the id impulses takes the form of habitual forms of interpersonal behavior or character traits. Such defensive character traits are like symptoms in the sense that they are involuntary, compulsive reactions to certain social situations that prevent the emergence of the repressed impulse. The ingratiating person, for example, may be defending against his hostile, self-assertive impulses, just as the hostile, self-asserting person may be defending against passivity and dependence. In contrast to symptoms, which are often experienced as alien and something to be rid of, character defenses are often regarded as acceptable and valuable to the person who uses them.

Freud not only originated the concept of character defenses but suggested, in *Character and Anal Erotism*, that such character defenses are a consequence of child-rearing practices. Too-strict toilet training, for example, can lead to characterological defenses against anal eroticism and produce such personality traits as parsimony, punctiliousness, and pedantry.

Reich accepted that conception of character formation, but he went much further with it than Freud did. Reich was among the first to suggest that society, through its values and mores, can impose patterns of child rearing and, hence, affect character formation. Commonality of character in a given society thus reflects commonality of child-rearing practices. Such thinking gave a whole new impetus and direction to cultural anthropology.

Reich went beyond Freud in other respects as well. He asked why, if Marx was correct, members of the working class allowed themselves to be oppressed? Why did the world revolution predicted by the Communists not occur? And why did the socialist revolution that did occur in Russia fail in many of its aims? To answer those questions, Reich suggested that the bourgeoisie set the standards for child rearing. In a paternalistic society the seeds are sown for producing persons with an authoritarian character structure who are subservient to those in a higher station than themselves but callous toward those of lesser position. Workers do not revolt because their character structure renders them submissive to authority. Marx assumed that people are by nature opposed to oppression and exploitation and will change any society wherein they occur. Reich argued, in contrast, that society conditions people to accept oppression and exploitation and that resistance to those social injustices is not innate but, rather, comes from a different mode of child rearing. Reich believed that children reared in freedom and openness would, indeed, resist exploitation and oppression.

Reich's (1946) major work on that topic, *The Mass Psychology of Fascism*, which was first published in 1933, won him wide acclaim among the young intellectuals of Europe but made him unacceptable to the Nazis and to the Communists. In stating the relationships between child rearing and culture, Reich made clear that child-rearing practices can be every bit as important as economics in determining the nature of a society's ethical and moral condition. The full force of that argument has only begun to be recognized in America. But in Russia and in Israel, the relation between child rearing and the nature of society is taken seriously.

Character Types

In Freud's discussion of character formation and character types, he stressed the psychosexual dynamics and the predominant behavior traits of each type. Reich generally accepted Freud's interpretation of the dynamics of character formation,

with the exception of the masochistic character, but added to those descriptions revealing details of interpersonal behavior and motoric qualities peculiar to each character type. Reich regarded those aspects of characterological behavior as part of the person's character armor, with which he defends himself against both internal and external dangers. Those behaviors are important, Reich held, because they have to be dealt with in treatment before the analysis of infantile experiences can proceed.

The examples of character types Reich met in psychoanalytic practice were the starting point for his discussion of therapeutic practice. In contrast to Freud, who was rather vague when it came to the specifics of psychotherapeutic practice, Reich was explicit about technical problems. His technical seminar was well attended and one of the few places where therapeutic errors, as well as successes, were used to define and refine therapeutic practice.

HYSTERICAL CHARACTER

Reich (1949) said that the hysterical character shows the least character armoring and the most lability of function. One type of behavior most typical of the hysterical character is sexual or seductive behavior. In general, the body movements of the hysterical person tend to be soft and rolling. The total impression is one of easy excitability. There is, however, a characteristic fearfulness and skittishness, together with high suggestibility and a tendency to disappointment reactions. Hysterical persons give the impression of superficiality and flightiness.

According to Reich, the character armor in the hysterical person has an important defensive function. Basically, the hysterical person is frightened of his or her genital impulses, which are easily aroused by external stimuli that become a threat and a danger. The hysterical person's seductive behavior is, in reality, an attempt to flush out the danger stimuli, which can then be avoided. If, for example, a man responds positively to a female hysteric's seductive postures and remarks, she immediately retreats and becomes hostile. Such persons are seldom aware of their provocative behavior and vehemently deny it when it is brought to their attention. Rather, they project their sexual desires and acuse those who respond to their overtures of having initiated them.

Persons with a hysterical character structure do not sublimate very well and are not motivated toward intellectual achievement or toward sustained endeavors in any domain. Such people are generally so apprehensive that most of their time and energy are taken up with avoiding dangerous situations and people.

COMPULSIVE CHARACTER

Persons of this character type most often show an inordinate concern for orderliness in all aspects of their lives. The concern with thoroughness and detail makes this character structure highly adaptive in such occupations as accounting and bookkeeping. Another common trait is circumstantial, ruminative thinking. Compulsive characters have trouble keeping still at meetings and, once they have the floor, ramble on in a tangential fashion. Thriftiness is still another trait associated with the compulsive character.

Other traits commonly found in persons with compulsive character formations are indecision, doubt, distrust, restraint, and control. More important, in the emotional domain there is a more or less complete affect block. Indeed, many of the compulsive character's behaviors, such as his ruminative thinking and indecision, derive from that affect block. Affective cues allow people to assign priorities to their actions, to make decisions, and to sense when they are becoming bores. The compulsive character lacks access to those cues, and that lack can occasionally lead him into moral lapses by not allowing him to make appropriate judgments about right and wrong.

In contrast to the hysterical character, who gives the impression of physical lability and movement, the compulsive gives the impression of tension and restraint. According to Reich, both facial and bodily muscles are in a constant state of hypertension. The compulsive character often sits, walks, and stands almost ramrod straight. Such persons are likely to be meticulous about their clothing and grooming and to plan all their activities, both minor and major, well in advance.

The basic dynamic in the compulsive character is anxiety about loss of control over instinctual impulses. All the compulsive person's behaviors are designed to eliminate the unexpected, the unforeseen, and, hence, the uncontrolled. Given a situation in which, for one reason or another, the planning did not succeed, the compulsive character panics and may retreat to a child-like state of helplessness and dependency. Even a minor break in routine or pattern is enough to cause the compulsive character considerable concern. The impulses that the compulsive character is desperately trying to control are powerful, sadistic, and angry impulses, and he fears the punishment and guilt that their expression would entail.

PHALLIC-NARCISSISTIC CHARACTER

Reich claimed to have been the first to describe this character type. In his depiction of persons who fall into this category, Reich (1949) said they are "self confident, arrogant, elastic, vigorous and often impressive." Outwardly, phallic-narcissistic people frequently appear cold, reserved, and defensively aggressive. Reich suggested the term "bristly" as appropriate to describe their characteristic demeanor. In general, such persons come across as outspoken and provocative. They are often high achievers and usually hold positions of power and authority in society.

From a psychodynamic point of view, Reich argued that phallic-narcissistic persons have a more or less total identification with the phallus (in women, with the fantasy of having a penis). Men of this type think of the phallus as a symbol of power and aggression. Reich argued that such men have strong erective potency but are unable to experience orgasm. In Reich's clinical experience, such men are frustrated at the genital exhibitionistic level of development, with a consequent negative hostile attitude toward women. Many men of this character type become homosexual as a consequence of their negative attitudes toward the mother in particular and women in general. Women who as children were frustrated in their exhibitionistic activities in relation to the father develop negative attitudes toward men and a propensity toward lesbianism.

MASOCHISTIC CHARACTER

Ironically, Reich's most original contribution to psychoanalytic theory is the one that most alienated him from Freud. In trying to account for the masochistic or self-punishing character, Freud posited a death instinct (Thanatos), which operates against a life instinct (Eros). In so doing, he abandoned the pleasure principle, which he formerly regarded as the major motivational principle of psychic functioning. In his classic paper on masochism, Reich (1949) demonstrated convincingly that the pleasure principle is sufficient to account for masochism and that the postulation of a death instinct is unnecessary. Although that position is generally accepted today, his stance against Freud's death instinct appears to be one of the reasons Reich was ousted from the psychoanalytic organization.

Despite the disagreement about dynamics, there was no disagreement about the behavior and demeanor of the masochistic character. It is generally accepted that persons of a masochistic bent report a subjective sense of chronic suffering and have a chronic tendency to complain and to manifest self-damaging and self-deprecating words and actions. Such persons often tend to provoke and torture others and may assume a stance of stupidity and ignorance about matters in the real world and regarding their own behavior.

In the traditional analytic interpretation, the masochistic person is supposed to experience unpleasure (pain) as pleasure. That accounts for the many behaviors engaged in by the masochist that are clearly designed to bring negative reactions down about his head. Reich, however, argued that the reverse is true and that, in fact, the masochistic person experiences pleasure as painful. In that formulation, the masochist avoids the build-up of pleasure in anticipation of the pain it causes. The masochist would rather have someone beat him than love him because the beating is less painful than love. Indeed, Reich argued that the masochistic character has an inordinate craving for love but a low tolerance for accepting love. In proving himself unlovable, the masochist avoids the pain of being loved but is frustrated in his need for love. The masochist is in the impossible position of being hurt the most by that which he wants and needs the most—namely, love.

Character Analyses

Perhaps Reich's major contribution to therapeutic practice was his insistence on the analysis of the character resistance before the initiation of psychoanalysis proper. Reich (1949) pointed out that, before a patient can follow the basic rule of free association to say everything that comes to mind, interpersonal issues between the patient and the therapist have to be resolved. Reich's discussion of character analysis was a detailed, clinically exampled exposition of how to cope with the character resistances manifested by patients in their attempts to prevent treatment from getting underway.

Although much of what Reich had to say about the pacing, level, and formulation of interpretations is regarded as standard therapeutic lore today, it was a novelty when Reich wrote about it. He was among the first analysts to take such matters seriously and to highlight the importance of the interpersonal dynamics of the patient and the therapist outside of and before the analysis proper. In many ways Reich's work foreshadowed that of later neo-Freudians, such as Horney and Sullivan, who made the interpersonal dynamics of therapy the core of the process.

Reich argued that the character armor of the patient appears not so much in what the patient says and does but rather in how the words are said and the actions done. The words "I hate you" can be said aggressively and intrusively or quietly and passively. What the person says has to be interpreted in relation to the way in which it is said. In Reich's view, the character armor is an interpersonal defense of the ego that can be used against the analyst and against treatment. Such defenses are more amenable to interpretation than are those against id impulses and, hence, have to be made the starting point of treatment. Reich suggested that a kind of face-to-face therapy is an important prerequisite to the faceless therapy in which the patient lies on the couch and free associates. Reich thus anticipated many of the modern active and transactional modes of treatment.

Mass Psychology

Reich's work on mass psychology gives a good illustration of how his valuable clinical insights became embedded in his paranoid ideation. In his book *The Mass Psychology of Fascism*, Reich (1946) skillfully attacked not only Hitler's fascism but also Marxist revolutionaries. He also gave evidence of their persecution of him: The Gestapo were ordered to confiscate his books, and Marxist envoys were sent to heckle him during his speeches. But he also argued for his strange concepts of sex economy and work democracy, which he posited as being superior to any extant form of government and as most truly reflecting basic human nature.

Reich's (1946) main thesis was that the structure of any given society reflects one of three possible layers of the human personality

On the surface layer of his personality the average man is reserved, polite, compassionate, responsible, conscientious.... The surface layer of social cooperation is not in contact with the deep biologic core of one's selfhood; it is borne by a second, an intermediate character layer which consists exclusively of cruel sadistic lascivious, rapacious and envious impulses.... It represents the sum of the so-called secondary drives.... If one penetrates through this second layer of perversion, deeper into the biological substratum of the human animal, one always discovers the third deepest layer which we call the biologic core. In this core, under favorable social conditions, man is essentially honest, industrious, cooperative, loving and, if motivated, rationally hating animal.

In Reich's view, the positive social traits of the deep biological core must pass through the second layer; as a consequence, they become distorted (Reich, 1946).

This distortion transforms the original social nature of the natural impulses and makes it perverse, thus inhibiting every genuine expression of life.

That secondary layer of the personality is open to social influence, and that is why society can distort human nature. But Reich (1946) saw it as a reciprocal process, rather than as a one-way process:

After social conditions and changes have transformed man's biologic demands and made them part of his character structure, the latter reproduces the social structure of society in the form of ideologies.

When the uppermost layer of the personality is reflected in social organizations, the results are liberal ideologies, which are often superficial, since they hide the vicious secondary core on which they are based. Democratic, socialistic, and communistic societies all fall within that category. Although they espouse liberal humanistic doctrines, the secondary core often erupts, and such societies are filled with aggression, perversion, and moral corruption.

Totalitarian regimes, such as fascism, are a direct projection of the secondary core, and they manifest the cruelty and sadism of that core. What Reich (1946) said—and where his insight was profound—was that the capacity to go along with the fascist ideology is present in everyone. Because the secondary layer of the personality is, in part, social in origin, it is the mass layer. Appeals to that layer of the personality by charismatic figures and national symbols enable individuals to submerge

themselves in a mass movement. But, for Reich, fascism does not bring out the worst in people; rather, the worst in people is reflected in fascism. Fascism could never appear on the social scene were it not for the secondary core of the personality.

No contemporary society, in Reich's view, gave adequate expression to the biological core, the truly social and cooperative self. Societies, of whatever stamp, armor people against that core and plate that armor with a thin veneer of social accommodation. Modern men and women are inhibited and repressed because no society provides adequate opportunities for true human nature to be expressed.

Reich's concept of a work democracy was meant to rectify that situation. It was Reich's contention that Marx had ignored the animal nature in humans, whereas Freud had merely paid lip service to the social nature of humans. Marx erred because he attributed different character structures to different classes. But, as Reich (1946) said, "There are no class distinctions when it comes to character." Freud, on the other hand, erred in assuming that character was the result of developmental fixations. Marx attributed too much to society; Freud attributed too much to biology. The details of Reich's work democracy were never clearly worked out, but what he did describe suggests something like the communal society of Walden II, with a little bit of sexual license thrown in.

As in much of his writing, Reich's discussions of the mass psychology of fascism and of work democracy are filled with contradictions and with logical errors. Despite those obvious flaws, his social psychological insights are still worth reflecting on, particularly in today's rapidly changing world.

Vegetotherapy

After Reich's rejection by the psychoanalytic association, he moved away from traditional psychoanalysis in his theoretical work and in his therapeutic practice. To Reich, who believed that he was supporting Freudian theory in his emphasis on the role of sexuality in neurosis and his advocacy of the pleasure principle, rejection by the psychoanalysts was a bitter experience. Not surprisingly, he decided to go his own way and not to be bound any longer by the canons of psychoanalysis.

Reich's therapeutic innovations were a direct outgrowth of his theories of character armor as reflecting muscular tension. In his new approach to the treatment of the character armor, Reich attempted to deal directly with that muscular tension and sought to relax the patient by interpreting the patient's muscular patterns and by actual massage. Reich (1942) called that type of therapy "vegetotherapy."

Vegetotherapy occasionally had dramatic, positive effects on some patients, but the results were not always salutary. Moreover, Reich rationalized his therapy on the basis of what can, at best, be called a bizarre theory of the autonomic nervous system. Here again, Reich hit on a partial truth for the wrong reasons. The need to relax the patient as part of the therapeutic process has been elaborated by others into relaxation therapy. And the use of actual physical encounters with patients was the forerunner of the many contemporary action therapies, such as rolfing and primal-scream procedures. Reich was, in his advocacy of vegetotherapy, much ahead of his time. But his extremism, his lack of caution, and his unbridled advocacy of his techniques obscured the merit of some of the things he was doing.

Orgonomy

At the same time that Reich was devising his vegetotherapy, he was doing research and theorizing about the dammed-up energy that was causing individuals and society so much trouble. Reich, who was influenced by Newtonian physics and Bergsonian notions of *élan vital*, wanted to find a form of energy that was at once biological and physical. By means of a series of rather strange experiments and shaky theorizing, he arrived at the sought-for energy in the pulsating radiation he produced from inert coal dust. That energy, which Reich held to be both physical and biological, exists all about and can be harnessed. He called it orgone.

The discovery of orgone energy led Reich in two different directions, toward a new therapy and toward a new theology. As far as the therapy was concerned, Reich devised an orgone accumulator, a box covered with alternating layers of rock wool and steel wool, that supposedly trapped orgone energy from the atmosphere. Reich believed that people with various diseases could be cured by being placed in the orgone box. Among the diseases most amenable to such treatment, according to Reich, was cancer. Reich built and distributed a number of those orgone accumulators about the country.

Reich's discovery of orgone energy also led him to reconsider the nature of humans and their place in the universe. Before the discovery of orgone energy, humans could be classified as mechanists or mystics. Mechanists have so armored themselves against their life forces that they deny the existence of those forces and argue that all energy is physical. Mystics, on the other hand, are aware of their own life energy but attribute it to a source outside themselves. Reich, however, believed that orgone energy resolves the difficulty, inasmuch as it is both biological and physical.

Reich thought that he had found a solution to the age-old contradiction between the naturalistic, poetic view and the mechanistic view of the universe. It is not an either-or situation but, rather, a higher order synthesis that ushers in new forms of thinking, feeling, and experiencing that Reich called "functional." In arriving at that insight, Reich (1969) compared himself to Christ and to Giordano Bruno, both of whom were martyred for heretical beliefs. Reich thought that he was being persecuted, and there was some basis for his belief. The Food and Drug Administration was observing him because of his alleged cancer cure.

In the end, Reich believed that he had found the answer to human salvation. Orgone energy was most exemplified in fully experienced orgasms. If people could be freed of their mechanistic and mystical character armors, they would be free to truly enjoy life and to realize their full potential. But Reich felt that elite groups in society feed on the armored persons and are opposed to freeing people from their armoring. And the little person, because of his armoring, was frightened by the very person (Reich) who promised him the hope of freedom. In that way Reich accounted for the abhorrence of the man on the street toward his sexual and orgone theories. In several countries, including the United States, Reich was viciously attacked in the popular press. The little men were persecuting the very man who might relieve them of their suffering. Reich, too, could say, "Father, forgive them; for they know not what they do."

Suggested Cross References

Freud's theories are discussed at length in Chapter 8. Karen Horney and Harry Stack Sullivan are discussed in Sections 9.2 and 9.3, respectively. Transactional analysis is discussed in Section 9.6. Personality disorders are discussed in Chapter 22. Psychoanalytic techniques are described in Section 30.1. New psychotherapy techniques are described in Section 30.8.

REFERENCES

Higgins, M. B., editor. *Wilhelm Reich: Selected Writings.* Farrar, Straus & Cudahy, New York, 1960.
* Reich, W. *The Function of the Orgasm.* Noonday Press, New York, 1942.
Reich, W. *The Mass Psychology of Fascism.* Farrar, Straus, New York, 1946.
* Reich, W. *Character Analysis.* Farrar, Straus & Young, New York, 1949.
* Reich, W. *The Sexual Revolution.* Farrar, Straus & Giroux, New York, 1969.
* Reich, W. and Ollendorf, I. *Wilhelm Reich: A Personal Biography.* St. Martin's Press, New York, 1969.
Ritter, P., editor. *Wilhelm Reich.* Ritter Press, Nottingham, England, 1958.
* Rycroft, C. *Wilhelm Reich.* Viking Press, New York, 1969.

10.7   Existential Psychotherapy

WILLIAM V. OFMAN, Ph.D.

Premises

Existentialism has its roots, as does phenomenology, in a movement of revolt against a view of man that has held fast in Western thought since the Middle Ages and that has directed much psychiatric and psychological thinking—Cartesian thought and its offspring, scientific materialism. The Cartesian conceptual paradigm imposes a framework for the manner in which phenomena are to be selected and ordered, and it provides those physical arrangements and apparatuses in which those selected phenomena may be studied—but studied in the manner that the paradigm prescribes (Yankelovich and Barrett, 1970). The nature of the revolt has been and is essentially that humans stand in paradoxical relation to the world of nature. They are at once, *of* that world—intrinsically intertwined with it—and, through their unique consciousness, free *in* it, free in relation to it. No idealistic, materialistic, or mechanomorphic notion will do.

In this sense current humanistic—that is, nontheistic—existentialism rejects the blind application of technological-based, physics-based methods of science as the only way to study and to treat humans. It offers, instead, a possibility of a new objectivity that is adequate in that it includes human subjectivity (Sartre, 1948; Laing and Cooper, 1971; Chein, 1972; Esterson, 1972; Poole, 1972) in its study of humans. As May et al. (1958) wrote:

Existentialism, in short, is the endeavor to understand man by cutting below the cleavage between subject and object which has bedevilled Western thought and science since shortly after the Renaissance.

Existentialism provides the philosophical base for what may be called humanistic psychology and its approach to persons—an approach that is person centered, homeoergic, one that underscores the symmetrical relationship between subject and subject and between subject and object, rather than any essentialistic view that supposes certain a priori conditions of human nature governing human behavior.

In current existentialist thought, particularly in humanistic existentialist thought, the revolt still obtains against any system that sees humans as secondary to any theory, paradigm of science, system, method, or treatment. The thrust of existentialism in dealing with persons directs that scientific attention be directed toward the primacy of experience and thus toward the subjective (Bugental, 1967). Man must not be traded in on a theory of man.

EXISTENTIALISM AND ESSENTIALISM

It was Tillich's (1961) terse comment—that existentialism, to be understood, must be paired with its opposite, essentialism—that helped clarify the basic meaning of existentialism. When one thinks of any concept or thing—whether it is Sartre's paper cutter, a steady-state universe, instinct, eros, or schizophrenia—one is considering that concept in essentialistic terms. Those attributes without which an object or event would be known as something different constitute its essence.

In the mind of the sculptor, for instance, the idea of a form must precede the molding of the clay. In humanistic existentialist thought, this essentialistic doctrine holds true in the language and grammar of things but not for humans. Humans develop in a way that is radically different from other objects in the universe. For humans alone, existence precedes essence. By dint of human reflexive consciousness, by the consequent ability to use propositional speech, and by the ability to introduce a psychic distance between himself and the objects of his thought, a human has no essence. His being has been not predecided or determined by any structure other than himself. Tillich (1961) wrote:

There are ... only rare moments ... in which an almost pure existentialism has been reached. An example is Sartre's doctrine of man. I refer to the sentence in which the whole problem of essentialism and existentialism comes into the open, his famous statement that man's essence is his existence. The meaning of this sentence is that man is a being of whom no essence can be affirmed, for such an essence would introduce a permanent element, contradictory to man's power of transforming himself indefinitely.

BASIC PRINCIPLE

The canon of existentialism and of existential psychology is that humans exist first. No theory of man, no theory of therapy, no theory of psychopathic genesis precedes humans. Nor must that person who is there before one in hospital, clinic, or consulting room take second place to a theory or preconception of man.

Humans exist; what they are or will be does not predate their reality, as a schematic diagram or blueprint does. To the contrary, the question of what that person there is can only be settled in the course of his life, in the course of his actions, as a function of his choices—basically, as a function of his intentions.

A person's unique choices, then, define him. But they do so in an ephemeral and flexible way, for a person is always free to choose anew and, thus, to redefine himself radically. A human has no identity that is given him by a predetermined epigenetic process or one that unfolds when the conditions are right to actualize his potential. For the humanistic existentialist, a human, by his every choice, forms and defines his selfhood and his essence.

If a human's existence precedes his essence, then a definition of a human is impossible, for his nature absolutely precludes his being cast into any permanent mold. A human appears embedded in human possibility and then conceives himself thus. Perhaps the most radical and important contribution of humanistic existentialism to a different view of human nature is the concept that, paradoxically, there is no human nature.

There is only the nature by which each human chooses, through his choices, to define himself.

In this manner, the humanistic existentialist stands in radical revolt to much of contemporary, formal, academic psychology and psychiatry, as exemplified in Wilson's (1975) essentialistic view of humans. It needs only to be added that the essentialistic view is part of the paradigm of current normal science (Kuhn, 1970) and the influence therein of scientific materialism on the human sciences. Psychology and psychiatry are heir to that paradigm but in a strange way. The physical sciences have been able to move away from a strict Cartesianism or a dated scientific materialism (Oppenheimer, 1954, 1956; Chein, 1972; Wheeler, 1975), but the psychological sciences are less open to such movement.

For example, in considering the basic philosophical question of what is really real, the strict adherent of a scientific materialism answers by bracketing reality with the property of simple location. In psychological terms, instinctual energies, rooted in bodily processes, are really real. The psychoanalytic conception of the psychic apparatus, thus, mirrors the Cartesian paradigm, inasmuch as it is strictly analogous to physical objects and processes.

In actual practice, how one answers the question makes a great difference. If a therapist is committed to the notions of a scientific materialism, he tends to think about his patients' productions in atomistic-unit terms—a unit of energy, a drive, an impulse, a need, an instinct, a stimulus-response link—or in transformation-of-energy terms. The therapist seeks to place his data on what the paradigm deems to be indisputable data, data having the reality of simple location, and he naturally looks behind experience to find the correct explanation of it (Lazerowitz, 1959).

Yankelovich and Barrett (1970) conclude that it is very difficult for most behavioral scientists to proceed in any other way than the scientific materialistic one if they have been trained within current university structures. They note:

No other way appeals to what has become, after centuries, a heritage of common sense. The human sciences have let themselves be boxed in.

It is to the credit of the physical sciences that they are open to more adequately objective views. Note the break with Cartesian materialism in Wheeler's (1975) conception, which has great relevance for the therapist:

The quantum principle has demolished the view we once had that the universe sits safely "out there," that we can observe what goes on in it from behind a foot-thick slab of plate glass without ourselves being involved in what goes on. . . . [To the degree that we measure it,] to the degree the future of the universe is changed. We change it. We have to cross out the old word "observer" and replace it by the new word "participator." In some strange sense the quantum principle tells us that we are dealing with a participatory universe.

The existential psychotherapist could translate that position almost directly to his dealings with patients. In this translation there is no subject-object split but a mutual process. Analogously, the existential principle demolishes the view that human nature or human essence—biologically determined, socially determined—the definition of a human, sits safely out there or that one can devise experiments that create such a situation of objectivity (Zimbardo, 1969 a, b). By every choice a person makes, his future becomes his. By every intervention, experimental or therapeutic, he participates with others in the invention of a new future. Instead of the normal science paradigm's view that such participation must be limited in experiments by controls or in therapy by maintained objectivity or by planned manipulations of interventions, the humanistic existentialist holds that the proper study of humans is just that participatory principle that mutually co-determines the future (Polyani, 1964). As Sartre (1967) wrote:

> Man is nothing else but what he makes of himself. Such is the first principle of existentialism.

The notion that a person is totally responsible for a constant process of self-definition and that this process constitutes his reality has profound implications for the helping process and the therapist's view of what patterns of behavior a diagnostician terms sick or healthy. Ultimately, it affects whether a diagnostician believes a person needs hospitalization, therapy, or help of any kind at all (Singer, 1970).

In opposing the various essentialistic doctrines that predominate in the field of psychiatry and psychotherapy and in denying the existence of a fixed human nature, the existentialist asserts the emptiness of historicity (Popper, 1960) and biological determinism (Wilson, 1975). For the existentialist there is nothing at all to determine a person; each person is free to define his own life, even to end it if he so chooses.

The therapist's image of the nature of humans is crucial in that divergent images—essentialistic or existential—lead to widely varying and distinctly different response options in therapeutic interventions (Wheelis, 1973). This notion is based on the inescapable conclusion that the definition of psychopathology depends mainly on the therapist's position regarding what he considers to be the essential nature of humans and how the person before him fits or does not fit that view or that belief system (Singer, 1970).

THROWN CONDITION

A corollary to the basic principle of existentialism is the key concept of the human's thrown condition. The implications of such a thrown condition have been explored by Heidegger (1962) as *gevorfenheit*, Bugental (1967), Wild (1955, 1963), and Ofman (1976). The major implication of this view is that a person has no blueprint that has predefined his life, and thus there are no external, superpersonal answers to the questions that life raises. There is nothing at all, then, to fall back on to explain the nature of life, nothing to guide a person—not biology, not history, nothing other than his definition of himself for which he and he alone is totally responsible. And for the humanistic existentialist—as opposed to the theistic or Heideggerian existentialist—there is no possibility for a voice from beyond, no God beyond God, no lure of Nirvana, no basic principle or energy or cause or beingness on which to hope and to rely, to mitigate what the existentialist calls the leap—the risk to action without any guarantees. For the existentialist, the future is in principle unknown and unknowable. A person, therefore, has no alternative but to act, and for that act—as for every other—he is totally responsible. The importance of one's actions, further, is that a person acts not only for himself but for all others when he acts. By his actions, he creates and invents value in the world, and so his actions are followed by anguish. A person's actions and choices are definitive; they cannot be undone, and their significance is given by the fact that his life will end. There is nothing that can be redone, as is hoped for by revenge. Authentic guilt, then, is the partner of this conception that acts are definitive and of the conception

that the ambiguity of interpersonal existence includes the periodic, intermittent reality of objectifying the other.

How a person leads his life, how he acts, depends on his willingness or his unwillingness to see his situation clearly and on the manner in which he sees his relationship to the world and to others. At bottom, existentialism—humanistic existentialism, specifically—speaks to the possibility of adequate relationships between the person, others, and the world. The adequacy of the relationships, of course, hinges on the clarity with which one sees that the person is free and intentional and that his acts are participatory.

When the humanistic existentialist speaks of the human's forlorn or thrown condition or no-hope position, he does not speak of pessimism but of clarity. Sartre (1967) stated that what the humanistic existentialist is accused of is not pessimism but an optimistic toughness—an unwillingness to fog oneself into unclarity, into a position of waiting, a fond hope and quietism, and a willingness to see that, because a person's destiny is wholly within himself, the only thing that enables him to live is responsible action. Responsible is not synonymous with obligatory. Responsibility refers to the embracing of action as one's free choice. Obligation refers to acting in terms of others, living in the serious world (Sartre, 1956; Barnes, 1959). The humanistic existentialist believes that a person is able to live without illusions, that his embracing of humanity and his situation does not mean that he will dampen his freedom and succumb to the repetition of a mythic past, to the following of an essentialistic, determined view of himself but, rather, that he will embrace his freedom. In the embracing of freedom is the creation of a tomorrow, and the acceptance of a tomorrow means the determining of one's future.

CONSCIOUSNESS, INTENTIONALITY, AND FREEDOM

The humanistic existentialist conceives of reality as bipartite, as (1) being-in-itself, which includes all of nonconscious reality, together with nonverbal animals (Washburn, 1978) and (2) being-for-itself, which is the being of sentient humans. The being of humans is distinguished by a person's ability to be self-aware. Consciousness or conscious self-awareness connotes a break, a withdrawal from the world. Consciousness is a uniquely human event that, by its self-awareness, assumes a distance between itself and the object of its perusal; thus, it is an attitude toward events and objects. There is a gulf of nothingness between itself and its object of purview. Consciousness is not a thing, not a process, but, because of this gulf, it is a free intending. It is always a free engagement with the world. It cannot exist alone; it is at once dependent on and free of (due to the rupture) the world of things. It is, then, the unique nature of human consciousness that leads the existential therapist to concentrate on experience, specifically on the experience of the person there before one (not to categorize him) and to construct a language that befits humans, one that is far different from the language of things (as is espoused by the behavioral science approach) that is in the Cartesian paradigm (Keen, 1970).

Subsumed to the concept of consciousness is the concept of intentionality. Consciousness itself has no interiority; it is always a consciousness of something; as such, it is an attitude. That attitude has an intention, a way of relating to the object of purview according to the deepest project, cosmology, or personal myth. This basic project or personal myth suffuses all of a person's actions. It is evident everywhere. In effect, the person defines himself by his freely chosen personal ideology.

It is the organizing principle of his life, freely chosen by the person as a commitment. Thus, a person may change himself—radically alter his life—if he finds that the negative consequences of that way of organizing existence become onerous. But note a basic principle here: Any commitment to action contains both negative and positive aspects. In therapy it is often found that the negative aspects of a choice are negated; instead, one attributes some malfunction in the self. Withdrawal from reality in such a retroflexive fashion is one of the basic modes by which persons deny reality. ("Nothing of consequence really exists out there; it is all within me.") The recurrent existential theme of placing humans in correct relationship to the world is expressed by the concept of intentionality. Knowing, for instance, is not consciousness passively observing the impact of the world through one's senses. Instead, experience (consciousness) of the object (or person or event) is interwoven with the object. This binding together of the act of perception is intentionality. A person acts or perceives as a whole person, freely, according to his deepest motives. He intends. In fact, consciousness is not something that intends an object; it is the intention. And this is so because existential psychology stands against the paradigm of natural science, which fostered the subject-object split. Instead, existential psychology links humans inextricably but freely to the world through intentionality (Husserl, 1962; Yankelovich and Barrett, 1970; Poole, 1972).

Based on the conception of a nothingness between consciousness and its object is the assertion of human freedom. It could be said that existentialism is a psychology of freedom and of its antithesis, self-deception (*mauvais-foi*)—the deception that one is determined, unfree, a victim of forces of human nature, biology, instinct, history, or others.

The existential psychologist rejects the behavioristic and the Freudian determinism, in which the person (ego) functions in partial awareness, the person is driven by libidinal drives or instincts, and the person's life is epigenetic, an evolutionary, mechanistic unfolding of a determined, ordered process. The humanistic existentialist also rejects the subject-excluded notion of the behavioral science therapist in which the person is wholly determined by stimuli impinging on him.

What is this human freedom? It is the existential position that the argument hinges on an adequate conception of a human act. Since human consciousness is intentional, every human act has a goal, and it has a cause. All behavior is caused. But, although the determinist locates the cause outside the person, the existentialist holds that each act is caused or motivated by the person in light of those things he has freely chosen to value. "My behavior is undoubtedly caused, but it is I who have freely determined the cause, the motive for my act."

But human freedom is not synonymous with unbridled power. Human freedom is a freedom to choose, and this freedom implies limited, finite alternatives. Each choice limits another, and a person is limited by the facticity of his body and the things around him. Thus, the resistance of others and the situation of the material world is the matrix from which human freedom grows. The basic meaning of psychological determinism is the establishment within the person of an absolute, unbroken continuity of existence in itself and attempts, in the Cartesian mold, to make causes, motives, and intentions into things with properties of location. But, for the existentialist, freedom is not a thing, not a being; instead, it is the being of humans.

Because self-awareness is human consciousness, there is or can be awareness of the causes that lead to action. With such awareness of cause, the cause is already transcended as a determining cause. By seeing the motive through reflexive consciousness, the person is free to follow the motive or not. Humans seem condemned to exist beyond their essence, beyond the cause, beyond the reasons and motives of their acts. It is in this manner that humans, as Sartre (1956) said, are "condemned to be free."

THE UNCONSCIOUS AND BAD FAITH

Existential psychotherapy stands against the psychoanalytic conception of the unconscious as outlined by Freud and his current followers (MacIntyre, 1958; Rappaport, 1959; Loewenstein et al., 1966; Greenson, 1967; Marmor, 1968; Trilling, 1971). The psychoanalytic doctrine of the unconscious is that portion of the psychic apparatus that is the storehouse of repressed personal and racial memories (primal repression and repression proper) and desires that are not directly accessible to consciousness. Repression occurs automatically and without awareness (Healy et al., 1930; Hall, 1954), and, even though material is repressed, it influences conscious life at all times (Healy et al., 1930); repression must occur, and mental health and civilization are a function of adequate repression and sublimation (Freud, 1961; Roheim, 1971).

The existentialist challenges the conception of the unconscious on three grounds: on the evidence of a unity in psychological functioning, on the assertion that there cannot be censorship without a knowing censor, and on the ground that consciousness cannot be blind to itself because consciousness, by its very nature, is a consciousness of itself.

Because consciousness is intentional, that very concept—intentionality—stands in opposition to the psychoanalytic conception of the unconscious. Inasmuch as consciousness is consciousness *of* something (itself, others, or events), what reveals itself to consciousness must be all of consciousness. There is, thus, no possibility of any act or of any intention *in* the unconscious or beneath consciousness. There is no opacity. If the humanistic existentialist (Merleau-Ponty, 1962, 1963; Van Den Berg, 1972) is correct in his perception of the meaning of human consciousness, then to posit unconscious acts and an unconscious that is obscure to the self is to regress to what Needleman (1967, 1968) called an unacceptable level of reduction.

Psychoanalysis, heir to the Cartesian paradigm and following the science of the period, divested from it the very essence of consciousness—intentionality. In direct contradistinction to this conception, existential psychotherapy holds that the phenomena with which it concerns itself and with which it deals in the consulting room constitute the person's intentionality—his way of constituting his reality, his way of constituting his past, his future, his day, his hour, and the way that he is now, this moment, speaking to his therapist.

BAD FAITH AND SELF-DECEPTION

Instead of resorting to the concept of the unconscious in explaining the ubiquitous "I don't know" in personality, the existential therapist resorts to the concept of bad faith (Sartre, 1956) or self-deception (Kaufmann, 1956; Ofman, 1976). Self-deception is the hiding of the truth from oneself. Note that there is no duality here, no division between the lie and the liar. Self-deception is based on the unity and transparency of consciousness. There is no black box of an unconscious that seems to have a reservoir (primal repression) and life (press) of its own.

Self-deception is not a state. It is a choice, a commitment to a way of being that denies what one knows and sees. One denies by choosing not to look. It is in this context that the humanistic existentialist therapist thinks of the common phrase "I don't know" in therapy; the therapist says, "By saying, 'I don't know,' you really mean, 'I don't want to look.' " Instead of looking, one chooses to believe that one is unfree, a being-in-itself. Self-deception is the opposite of authenticity. It implies that one is a victim of essentialistic strivings ("I can't help it!"), socially accepted norms ("It's just not done!"), living for others ("I must protect her or him from the truth."), the denial of one's own vision, and a mistrust of what one feels and experiences.

Any denial of the truth of one's vision on the basis of any other structure—social, historical, or biological—is a lapse of authenticity and a fall into self-deception.

Because, for the existentialist, consciousness can hold no secrets from itself, when a person chooses self-deception, he is or can quickly be aware of his bad faith. This is in direct contradistinction to the psychoanalytic concept of repression, of unconscious impulses or instincts, automatic censorship by repression, resulting in symptoms that are compromises between the unknown, unknowable unconscious impulse and the demands of reality. This process implies the idea of censorship without an aware censor, of automatic psychological functioning with functionaries.

Clearly, if there is censorship, there must be knowledge of what needs to be censored. And in encountering the idea of an unconscious impulse disguising itself in parapraxes, one encounters similar difficulties. How can the repressed impulse or drive disguise itself if it is not aware of being repressed?

In psychoanalytic terms, the humanistic existentialist avers, there is no way in which resistance, symbolization, censorship, or repression can be coherently or logically understood. There cannot be censorship without a censor, and there is no way that any person cannot know (1) what needs to be repressed, (2) that what needs to be repressed has been repressed, and (3) what the content of the repression was. Experiences cannot be hidden or denied if one does not know what needs to be hidden. But if the psychoanalytic formulation is bought, as many lay persons have been sold it (Laing, 1971); only one recourse is left—the concept of the person—being possessed or inhabited by forces that lie beyond his awareness. As Conkling (1968) pointed out:

it would be hard to conceive of a meaningful foundation of repression which was not inordinately mechanistic and relied on viewing man as a peculiar kind of robot.

And this would be a robot who has no choice about becoming sick, inasmuch as he is completely unconscious of his impulses and at the mercy of an implacable superego (Trilling, 1971), but who, nevertheless, is given the choice by the analyst of cooperating or not cooperating with the treatment and the choice of accepting or not accepting the analyst's interpretations. If he does not accept the interpretations, (1) they are too early, (2) they are too deep, or (3) the patient is resisting—and unaware of the resistance. These interpretations are based on the analyst's theory and on his world view (Sullivan, 1941), and in the final analysis the therapist teaches the patient what life is all about, what man is all about, what his cosmology should be. When the patient accepts the cosmology with all its subordinate corollaries, he is pronounced cured (Storr, 1968; Ofman, 1976).

How then, does the humanistic existentialist deal with the fact that there are things about a person that he does not know, of which he is unaware? Clearly, the existentialist must account for different modes of consciousness, and he does this by distinguishing between two: reflective modes and prereflective modes. The difference between prereflective (passive) and reflective (active) modes is that in the reflective mode the person chooses (intends) to pay close attention to his responses and to the situation in which he finds himself. In the prereflective mode such close awareness is not exercised—but it can be. In the reflective mode the person observes himself, pays attention to his inner process. He knows what is going on. This is, in truth, what the therapist intends while practicing psychotherapy. The therapist participates in the person's choice to look closely at himself, to pay keen attention to his personal and interpersonal process. In the prereflective mode the person is aware of others, of objects, and of events, but the choice is not to attend closely to the person's own awareness of them.

In the existential view of consciousness, the person himself, by the way in which he has chosen to live his life, decides what things he will permit himself to be aware of and what things he will choose to ignore and, by denying them close attention, insist that they are outside of his awareness (not known) and, therefore, phenomena for which he cannot be responsible.

Self-deception, then, is a way of organizing reality in order to avoid responsibility. The essential condition of bad faith is the grasping of a person's essential freedom and his possibilities. Self-deception is a person's attempt to avoid the anguish when confronted with this freedom and its twin, responsibility.

Humanistic existentialism posits that to the degree a person is conscious, he intends his environment and organizes it as a situation. Within this situation he freely chooses his actions. In psychosis, for instance, in which the person appears to live a different existence, that person has choosen, in a long progression of choices born of violation, to withdraw from a painful world—a confusing, unclear, maddening one—and to construct one of his own. The choice is to live his life according to a mythical system of his own, a lone construction in which the world outside does not exist. In this world, everything is totally within his own control, in his own head. Confronted with a violating environment over which he had no power or control, the person chose to break the engagement with the world and with others and to change himself instead. He has retroflexively withdrawn into himself and seems willing to pay a great price for that way of being. Such is the strong commitment of some (Barnes, 1959).

In sum, self-deception is the motivated refusal to attend explicitly to responses in the situation that one has organized and in which one has chosen to live. The person chooses to believe, instead, that he is determined. It is a way of making oneself ignorant of what the self is that he has constructed; thus, he does not wish to acknowledge and embrace what is, in fact, true for him at this moment in his existence. If he believed what he felt or saw, he might have to confront the situation directly and be in danger of receiving an unpredictable response from the important others in his life. So the person denies, based on the belief or hope that there must be something other than what he sees and experiences. Usually, the person opts for an essentialistic, serious-attitude system that runs counter to the truth of his own vision, a system based on the hope that—if he believes the system, rather than himself—he will somehow be cured of the negative aspects of his life.

VIOLATION: BASIS FOR PSYCHOPATHOLOGY

If self-deception is the major motive force of psychopathology and if the person is unwilling to attend closely to his priorities, commitments, and what he sees in the world and in himself in an explicitly aware fashion, if he is unwilling to spell out the way he operates in the world, the way others around him operate in his day-to-day living, and to lay out his personal myth clearly by focused, explicit attending, then there must be a good reason for his withdrawal and retroflexion into an intrapsychic, mythical world of his own construction.

The humanistic existentialist has found that, if a person does not deny but is authentic, he may be faced with a world he cannot control or manipulate according to his wishes. He may have to face the truth about how he deals with the violations and violence that have been perpetrated by the important others in his life—that is, he would have to demystify his situation—how he has responded to the existential crises in his life, and how he may have sold out by not declaring himself fully as he has been and as he now is.

The person who looks may recognize how he has responded to the violation of his own experience as others questioned its validity. He may have to accept that he himself began to question his own vision, his own experience, thus weakening his self-confidence and growing alienated from himself. This response initiates the retroflexive withdrawal process and the construction of an insular intrapsychic reality. It is this broken encounter with others and with reality to which the existential therapist basically addresses himself in his work.

These modes of transforming or changing oneself in the face of an uncontrollable, violating, and maddening reality are called alchemical operations that seemingly change the nature of the outside world or, more commonly, change the nature of the self. "They are right, my own perceptions cannot be correct." Because the person denies the independent existence of others ("because they hurt me terribly, and I cannot face that they are as they are"), the other seems to remain under some measure of control by the person. The person who, as a young child, is dependent on others for his very survival participates in the violation process in the following retroflexive manner:

My mother cannot dislike me for her own reasons—reasons that are independent of me. It must somehow be my fault. I was bad! I was not good enough. Therefore, if it is my fault alone, there is something I can do. I will change myself in order to change her. Then she will love me. Her loving me—now, in later life, anybody's loving me—is entirely in my own hands. Thus, I retain my illusion of omnipotence. She (eventually, "they") is not independent. I will not look at the facts as I see them. I will pay attention, instead, to another manipulative structure that is in service of a reduction of painful, violating reality and of a controlling omnipotence that further breaks the reciprocal dyadic circuit.

The consequences of such self-deception born of violation are far-reaching. In denying an independent existence to others, the person must also not attend to his own personal autonomy, to his own freedom (French, 1977). To be aware that the person is doing what he is doing as a consequence of his free commitment, for the best of all possible reasons, would grant that same autonomy to others, and this would endanger the integrity of his illusory system of retroflexive omnipotence and control. In other words, the person would have to place himself in a different—more adequate, more authentic—relationship with others and with the world—a participatory one. Such a relationship would eschew the use of deception and power but would engage about those very issues in an equal manner.

By following the road to a very different existence, a lonely existence (Van Den Berg, 1972), by choosing not to declare himself as he is, the person accelerates the process of self-obliviousness (Singer, 1970), with the consequent loosening of self-confidence and of the natural causal connections in the world. The person becomes more and more unaware and lives more and more in a changed world, a world of uncertainty and anxious confusion in which there seems to be no connection among feelings, acts, and events (Kaiser, 1965; Van Den Berg, 1972).

In many instances this changed world cannot be tolerated and is ordered by means of a purely intrapsychic system in which things gain supernatural or magical significance. In such a system the appropriate relationship—again, the basic theme—with the world is denied, and everything becomes internal. Watzlawick et al. (1967) call this event the double-bind; Laing (1971) calls it invalidation. The humanistic existentialist extends the model and terms it violation (Ofman, 1974, 1976). Blount, in an unpublished dissertation, has found that this concept of violation is central to the thinking about psychopathology in the work of Harry Stack Sullivan, Carl R. Rogers, and Rollo May.

Another way in which violation and self-deception lead to disordered behavior is by ignoring or distracting oneself from the situation by attending to things peripheral. Attention is paid to such structures as the past, the future, a preoccupying thought or movement, omens of the body—pains, tensions, and so on—a self-created world of perpetual crisis, the salvation that may exist in a move to Arizona, another profession, or another spouse. Each response to the violating situation other than one in clarity ("The person does not want to hear me, to see me as I am, and to deal with me on that basis") leads to a break in the engaged encounter with the other and with the world.

AUTHENTICITY AND EXPLICIT AWARENESS

The humanistic existentialist view espouses violation as the nidus of psychopathology. Its motive force is self-deception. A violating situation is any situation in which the person's vision is disconfirmed, in which the person's integrity is placed in jeopardy or not accepted, in which his interiority is ruptured or his subjectivity violated, and in which he is forced to submit to another's perspective. The submission to the other usually results from the other's not declaring his true intention, as when another refuses to declare his objection ("I don't like it!") but, instead, tries to change the person ("You are wrong; you can't mean what you're saying. You must change!") by criticizing him or by intimidating him (Ofman, 1976). Blount analyzed the violating act and concluded that it must consist of three ingredients: a relationship of power or influence; a disconfirmation of experience by denial, intimidation, or silence; and a denial of that disconfirmation.

For good interpersonal reasons—in contrast to the psychoanalytic model, which is essentially intrapsychic (Laing, 1971)—a person initially chooses not to be aware and then continues an unaware, unspelled-out life style. In choosing an authentic life, one needs the courage to make explicit, to utter clearly and in fully articulated ways what one wants (who one is) specifically and generally in life and in any particular situation. The essence of reality is just that kind of specificity.

There seems general agreement here, because this making explicit is, after all, central to most nonbehavioristic psychotherapy. The person is invited to talk and to explore himself deeply. This exploring (Truax and Carkhuff, 1967; Carkhuff and Berenson, 1967; Carkhuff, 1969) implies a conscious effort to spell out those specific features that have heretofore been ignored or denied. Such a process of explicit awareness establishes the crucial connection between one's wants, actions, and outcomes (Boileau, 1958; Murphy, 1975). The spelling-out process provides an opportunity for a person to see deeply the good reasons for the things that he does and feels and how his basic personal myth casts him. The authentic spelling-out, the good reasons, and the embracing of the positive and negative aspects of any choice are the glue that holds the personality together (Corey, 1966). As French (1977) wrote:

> A good life is one in which no part of the self is stifled, denied, or permitted to oppress another part of the self, in which the whole being has room to grow. But room costs something, everything costs something, and no matter what we choose, we are never happy about paying for it.

For the existentialist the fundamental principle of being is authenticity—the belief that the only way for a person to fulfill his full humanity is to recognize that his being is his individual freedom cleaved to its twin, responsibility. One is fully responsible for all one's acts and is determined by nothing. Second, authenticity implies a full recognition of the other's freedom, as well as one's own. Just as it is in bad faith to make an object of oneself, one must seek not to make an object of the other but, rather, to embrace the oscillating nature of relationships and to deal with the inevitable violations by attending to them and by not raising a pragmatic occurrence to a virtue. This kind of attention to potentially violating situations is especially important in psychotherapy, in which the social system has strongly defined the role of the doctor vis-à-vis the patient. In psychotherapy both the follower of the behavior modification school and the follower of the so-called humanistic psychology movement evade the problem of power and manipulation in therapy by grasping a different horn of this fundamental dilemma in human relationships. The behavior controller says, in effect:

> There is no way out of manipulation; that's all there is anyway. Let us, then, frankly manipulate, use our power, and do it well.

The humanist says, in effect:

> We must overcome, somehow, this issue in human relationships by circumventing it and focusing, instead, on love, creativity, emotionalized expression, and an enhancement of self-actualization.

Although the behavior modifier is clearly in bad faith, the humanist acts in hope.

The way out of the dilemma of power, influence, violation, and objectification is to see that there is no permanent way out. It is a constant engaged dealing or encounter with that recurrent central human paradox, the issue of manipulation, control, freedom, and determinism. In humanistic existential terms the issue of transference and projection is dealt with in just those terms—that the person himself (and perhaps even the therapist) alternately wants to deny the full reality of the other and either succumb to power and objectification or dispose of power by assuming it. Rollo May, in *Love and Will*

(1969), conceives of the objectification of persons as the major problem of this time, as an endemic disease. That disease is modern man's tendency to view himself as passive and as the product of powerful psychological drives over which he has no control.

Authenticity also implies the honest dealing with the inevitability of power—its assumption and abrogation—in a therapeutic relationship, together with a quest toward the discovery and building of symmetry in the therapeutic relationship, as in all other relationships into which the person enters. The danger is that the therapist will be blind to the issue, partly because the person who is his patient does not wish him to see it. The therapist who loves his expertness and denies it imposes his system even more strongly, inasmuch as the patient wants just that imposition, on a patient who already suffers from a self-deceiving system of unattended-to power relationships. Thus, there is an overteaching of irresponsibility, a denial of symmetry, and a fostering of inauthenticity (Frankel, 1970; Wheelis, 1973; Ofman, 1976).

Feelings and Emotion

It is appropriate after the discussion of authenticity to give a brief explication of the existentialist view of feelings and emotions. This is especially important, because great weight and attention are given to feelings ("How do you feel? How do you feel about it? What was the feeling?") as important events in a person's life story and in his way of relating to others. Often, the discussion is closed after a person asserts, "Well, that's the way I really feel about it!" as if the feeling or the emotion is the bedrock court of last resort that serves as the explanatory efficient cause of behavior. In effect, such an explanation constitutes an explaining away.

The basic principles of affect are these: Feelings are the ever-present mood, tone, or energized expression that accompanies and underscores a particular way or mode of being in the world—such as sadness, fearfulness, or joy. The feeling of affection for someone accompanies, strengthens, and informs the person that he has chosen to value the attributes that are seen in the loved one (Solomon, 1976). Feelings are an accompaniment of intentionality, and they inform the bipersonal field of that intentionality. If one's value, for instance, is to remain alive at all costs, one feels fear when one's life is threatened. However, if one's commitment is that this world is unimportant and that another is everlasting and filled with peace, the oncoming truck may even be perceived as welcomed. Feeling, then, accompanies and informs one of one's relationship with the world.

Emotion, on the other hand, is seen as an instrument of intentionality. When a person wishes to accomplish ends by means that he has learned have a high probability of success and the world or the world of others exhibits its coefficient of adversity (Sartre, 1948, 1956) that tends to frustrate his motives and his acts to fulfill them, then, if his relations with the world are disrupted, he cannot bear such difficulties, and he resorts to a prereflexive transformation of the world. Emotion is a magical attempt to transform a world that does not conform to one's image of the world. Emotion breaks the normal causal connections between events and intends the instrumentality of magic to change both the self and the world.

But in order not to be a mere charade, the magical transformation, which is emotion, must be accompanied by seriousness and by the body's being incarnated. The body undergoes the emotion because it incarnates and makes real the magical process. The bodily changes, the perceptual changes that occur in emotion, are the attributes of the true belief and of the seriousness of emotional consciousness.

The reason for the humanistic existentialist therapist's attention to a person's feelings and his emotional life is connected with this principle: Feeling and emotions illuminate the basic intentions of the person. As such, they are no more and no less important than any other aspect with which the person deals in his quest for authentic being.

In such a quest the person may say and feel that he wants to spell out his commitments and to look at his life, but he is, in fact, unwilling to do so, and he denies his unwillingness. The humanistic existentialist therapist readily admits that the person has very good reasons for that denial, for maintaining his commitments and his personal myth intact, that there is no a priori, ideal reason for the examination of life in explicit fashion. It is wholly up to the person.

Applications

THERAPEUTIC RELATIONSHIP

Clearly, therapy occurs between persons. The major goal of existential therapy is, if the person so chooses, to help the person come into clarity and authenticity and into what the existentialist sees as a more real relationship with himself and others, the world, and his conception of who he is as a person and what it means to be a person (Kaufmann, 1973; Bugental, 1976).

Authentic behavior does not simply mean frankness—telling people what one thinks of them and walking away. What is usually the motive in simple frankness is a kind of morally superior position without consequences. Nor does authenticity mean simple sincerity. Persons seem able to state sentences that are uninspected regarding their ramifications, and they believe, for the moment, what they are saying; persons proclaim false-hoods with sincerity, believing what they are saying while they are saying it, but earlier they know it to be untrue, and, if questioned a few hours later, they deny that it is true (Kaufmann, 1973).

If authenticity is a central theme, it most certainly is the core for the therapist's behavior. For in the final analysis it is the therapist's own work on himself toward the attainment of clarity, awareness, and authenticity that is the substance of the therapist's merchandise (Kempler, 1969). This implies that the existential therapist engages the person in such a way that each is co-responsible for the therapy and for a constant, mutual vigilance about each seeing the other as a unique other, not as a patient or as a doctor according to the medical model (Jourard, 1969; Truax and Mitchell, 1971; Wheelis, 1971; Colm, 1973) or as belonging to a category, or as in any way unequal (Glad, 1959; Lomas, 1973).

Violation, in existential therapy, is the essential ensickening act. Any maneuver on the part of the therapist that implies an unequal position is a violation. Unfortunately, what is often called psychotherapy is, in reality, getting the person to once again abandon his subjectivity, his own experience, for the therapist's view of the person's situation, for society's view, or for some objective reality. But the person's experiential perspective is his appropriate invention that enabled him to survive his situation (Sartre, 1964). Attempting to move or to change the person is a reactivating, albeit in much more subtle form ("It is for your own good, after all; and you said you wanted help, didn't you?"), of the basic violating paradigm from which the person suffers in the first place.

The quality of the therapeutic relationship, either reciprocally dyadic and mutual or hierarchical, teaches the person about the possibilities in relationships and what it means to be a person-in-relation. The existential therapists seem to agree that psychotherapy is much less a science or a technique than it is a way that one person is (a way of being) with another (Steinzor, 1967; Stein, 1973). A review of the research literature on therapist variables in effective psychotherapy strongly supports this position (Truax and Mitchell, 1971).

The existentialist maintains that, with every act he performs, the therapist asserts that way of acting as a value in the world. A hierarchical, superior relationship with a doctorly expert is deleterious to the main task of psychotherapy, as any superiority in human relationships is degrading to both parties to the relationship (Agel, 1971, 1973; Corey and Maas, 1976).

THERAPEUTIC TASK

To the existential therapist, the therapeutic task is not the discovery of connections between family cathexes and current relationships, nor is it the discovery of connections between the past and the present, because the past has a task in the present and is seen as a function of both the present and the future (Van Den Berg, 1972). The therapeutic task is, rather, the fostering of explicit awareness, of what John Fowles (1977) called whole sight. The goals are for the person to utter and clarify his projects, his basic personal myth; to assume ownership, validity, and responsibility for his projects; to embrace both the positive and the negative aspects of his relationships with others and with the world, so that the divided, unattended-to parts of his personality become integrated (Bugental, 1976). It seems also to lead to much greater autonomy and an attendant symmetry in relationships. Progress toward these goals is sought by means of affirmation and authentic relating.

ACCEPTANCE AND CHANGE

One of the basic suppositions in most psychotherapeutic approaches is that acceptance is an absolute necessity for personality growth. The common assertion is that one must accept the person as he is and where he is. But authentic acceptance, like love, cannot be willed. It can, however, be dissembled. But the existentialist, for whom authenticity is a prime virtue, cannot tolerate such dissembling, whatever its purpose. On what basis, then, can a therapist really accept a person as he is without being condescending? The accepting attitude can occur as a function of the vision that a person has freely chosen to do and to be what he is and that he has chosen this way for the best of all possible reasons. The person who comes to the therapist needs to see that he has chosen his way for the best of all possible reasons. He needs to see his situation in abject clarity and to note that, in terms of his perspectival position, he has chosen to be the way he is for just those good reasons. He further needs to see how his reasons are intimately connected with his overarching way of being, how his choices—each and every one—are emblematic of what Solomon (1976) terms his personal ideology, and how he denies the negative aspects of those choices on the basis of his mythical system. ("Things cannot be the way they are. It must be that there is something wrong with me.") In T. S. Eliot's (1950) *The Cocktail Party*, Celia has a dialogue with her psychiatrist and states that she would rather be sick than see the world as it is.

For the humanistic existentialist therapist, it is contradictory to, on one hand, accept a person as he is and, on the other hand, work for his change. By working for movement, change, actualization, growth, genital primacy, mental health, or adjustment, however defined, the therapist is in danger of reinforcing the person's self-deception. Those goals imply that the therapist, too, believes covertly or overtly that the person is somehow inhabited, bedeviled, or possessed—that he is somehow trapped by internal or external forces and is in a position that he should not be in, does not want to be in, but cannot help being in.

The basic position of the existential therapist is that a person is in precisely the state he should be in; if he truly believed he would be better off in some other state, he would be there. And the person is where he is for the best of all possible reasons. His suffering is a result of his priorities or more specifically, because he denies the negative consequences of those priorities. The psychological pain that persons experience is because they would rather turn on themselves—call themselves deficient, inadequate, depressed, or sick—and thus still maintain the lonely, encapsulated control over basic ontological realities. The world's coefficients of adversity are painful, but they are of a different order of pain than the pain that is caused by the psychic, retroflexive withdrawal in which the person chooses to hurt as a way of denying his being-in-the-world where "it" and "they" exist autonomously of his will.

It is the existential therapist's task not to point out alternatives—that is arrogant—but merely to help the person become aware and attend to the situation in which he lives—to his life as he has structured it and to those structures in his life that are independent of him. The therapist's goal is to help the person see the meaning and integrity of his life, that he is doing what he wants but elects to break an appropriate encounter with the world by denying the negative aspects of his wants. The person's denial is through his removal from the world into an uninvolved, self-involved, omnipotent, decoupled position. The denial, in therapy, is that, instead of seeing things clearly, the person wants to change himself ("There is something wrong with me"). In this project of self-change, there is overt passivity but secret or covert transcendent subjectivity and control. ("If I become different—cured—they and it will do what I want them to.")

The person's fear of being authentic was born of violating situations and has resulted in a plethora of inauthentic and self-deceptive ways of dealing; a minimum of self-awareness is the result. It is in this way that a person's behavior seems to have only a distant relation to his appropriate but unstated wants. Further, the person denies the significance of the reality that his feelings show him by tearing his feelings away from their objects. The person prefers to see his feelings as wholly intrapsychic events. The existential position is that feelings are a way in which the person apprehends the world; thus, they are between the person and the world and, by their intentionality, illuminate the truth of the situation. An example of this is when a woman says:

I know I must love him; I live with him, have children with him. We are supposed to be a married couple. He *is* mean. But there is something wrong with my vagina. It does not respond to his stimulation. Now, doctor, if you could fix that. . . . "

The intention of the therapist's communication is to affirm the reality of the person as he is ("Your body does not lie"), to help him come into reality by helping him utter, in explicit detail, and affirm the validity of his position as he sees and experiences it now and as his feelings inform him of it. Always, it is a mutual search for the truth and correctness of the person's vision, rather than a pointing out of distortions, projections, or displacements (Colm, 1973).

Affirmation helps the person reclaim what he but has lost through denial of awareness—his inner sense. The therapist in the existential mode points out that the negative aspects of the person's choice are real; they exist in the world. And he points out the positive and negative aspects of the person's choice of withdrawal and retroflexion. He has no advice to offer him as to which choice to make. It is wholly up to the person.

Affirmation of the person's needs and wants, not of his behavior, is a crucial element in existential psychotherapy. This element and a therapist who is himself struggling toward authenticity and is willing to be real, utterly human, with the person—one who is willing to see that in the final analysis both are in the same human boat—are the major pillars on which existential therapy rests.

The therapist's affirmation, leading to the person's continuing self-affirmation, of his ability to declare authentically, "This is me, and this is you; this is what I want, and I am willing to pay the price for it," bonded to the most provocative and seminal question of all, "How may we be equally together?" is change enough.

Suggested Cross References

The Freudian theories are discussed in Chapter 8. Psychoanalysis and psychoanalytic psychotherapy are discussed in Section 30.1. Behavior therapy is discussed in Section 30.2. Harry Stack Sullivan's theories are discussed in Section 9.3, and Carl R. Rogers discusses his own theories in Section 30.3.

REFERENCES

Adler, M. *The Difference of Man and the Difference It Makes.* Henry Holt, New York, 1967.
Agel, J. *The Radical Therapist.* Ballantine Books, New York, 1971.
Agel, J. *Rough Times.* Ballantine Books, New York, 1973.
* Barnes, H. *Humanistic Existentialism.* University of Nebraska Press, Lincoln, 1959.
Barnes, H. *An Existentialist Ethics.* Alfred A. Knopf, New York, 1967.
Binswanger, L. Existential analysis and psychotherapy. In *Progress in Psychotherapy,* F. Fromm-Reichmann and J. Moreno, editors, p. 144. Grune & Stratton, New York, 1956.
Blount, H. The existential psychotherapy of phobias. Psychother. Theory, Res. Prac., *3:* 79, 1979.
Boileau, V. New techniques in brief psychotherapy. Psychol. Rep., *4:* 627, 1958.
Brown, N. *Life Against Death.* Vintage, New York, 1959.
* Bugental, J. *The Search for Authenticity.* Holt, Rinehart, and Winston, New York, 1965.
Bugental, J., editor. *Challenges of Humanistic Psychology.* McGraw-Hill, New York, 1967.
Bugental, J. Psychotherapy as a source of the therapist's own authenticity and inauthenticity. In *The Analytic Situation,* H. Ruitenbeek, editor, p. 200. Aldine Publishing Co., Chicago, 1973.
Bugental, J. *The Search for Existential Identity.* Jossey-Bass, San Francisco, 1976.
Carkhuff, R. *Helping and Human Relations.* Holt, Rinehart and Winston, New York, 1969.
Carkhuff, R., and Berenson, B. *Beyond Counseling and Therapy.* Holt, Rinehart, and Winston, New York, 1967.
Chein, I. *The Science of Behavior and the Image of Man.* Basic Books, New York, 1972.
Colm, H. The therapeutic encounter. In *The Analytic Situation,* H. Ruitenbeek, editor, p. 151. Aldine Publishing Co., Chicago, 1973.
Conkling, M. Sartre's refutation of the Freudian unconscious. Rev. Exist. Psychol. Psychiatry, *8:* 86, 1968.
Cooper, D. *Psychiatry and Anti-psychiatry.* Ballantine, New York, 1967.
Corey, D. The use of a reverse format in now psychotherapy. Psychoanal. Rev. *53:* 107, 1966.
Corey, D., and Maas, J. *The Existential Bible.* Na Pali, Honolulu, 1976.
Corlis, R., and Rabe, P. *Psychotherapy from the Center.* International Textbook Co., Scranton, Pa., 1969.
Delbruck, M. Mind from matter? Am. Scholar. 339 Summer, 1978.
Eliot, T. S. *The Cocktail Party.* Harcourt, Brace, and World, New York, 1950.
Esterson, A. *The Leaves of Spring.* Penguin Books, Baltimore, 1972.
Foucault, M. *Mental Illness and Psychology.* Harper Colophon, New York, 1976.
Fowles, J. *Daniel Martin.* Little, Brown, and Co., Boston, 1977.
Foy, J. The existential school. In *American Handbook of Psychiatry,* S. Arieti, editor, p. 926. Basic Books, New York, 1977.
Frankel, M. Morality in psychotherapy. In *Readings in Clinical Psychology Today,* B. Henker, editor, p. 81. Psychology Today, Del Mar, Calif., 1970.
French, M. *The Women's Room.* Simon & Schuster, New York, 1977.

Freud, S. *An Outline of Psychoanalysis.* W. W. Norton, New York, 1949.

Freud, S. The unconscious. In *Standard Edition of the Complete Psychological Works of Sigmund Freud,* p. 98. Hogarth Press, London, 1953.

Freud, S. *Beyond the Pleasure Principle.* W. W. Norton, New York, 1961.

Gendlin, E. *Experiencing and the Creation of Meaning.* Free Press of Glencoe, New York, 1962.

Gendlin, E. Existentialism and experiental psychotherapy. In *New Directions in Client-Centered Therapy,* J. Hart and T. Tomlinson, editors, p. 70. Houghton Mifflin, Boston, 1970.

Glad, D. *Operational Values in Psychotherapy.* Oxford University Press, New York, 1959.

Greene, M. *Introduction to Existentialism.* Phoenix, Chicago, 1959.

Greenson, R. *The Technique and Practice of Psychoanalysis.* International Universities Press, New York, 1967.

Hall, C. *A Primer of Freudian Psychology.* World Book Company, New York, 1954.

Havens, L. Clinical methods in psychiatry. Int. J. Psychiatry, *10:* 7, 1972a.

Havens, L. The development of existential psychiatry. J. Nerv. Ment. Dis., *151:* 309, 1972b.

Havens, L. The existential use of the self. Am. J. Psychiatry, *131:* 1, 1974.

Healy, W., Bronner, A., and Bowers, A. *The Structure and Meaning of Psychoanalysis.* Alfred A. Knopf, New York, 1930.

Heidegger, M. *Being and Time.* Harper & Row, New York, 1962.

Hook, S., editor. *Determinism and Freedom.* New York University Press, New York, 1958.

Hook, S. editor. *Psychoanalysis: Scientific Method and Philosophy.* Grove Press, New York, 1959

Hora, T. The process of existential psychotherapy. Psychiatr. Q., *34:* 495, 1960.

Husserl, E. *Ideas.* Collier Books, New York, 1962.

Jourard, S. The therapist as Guru. Voices, 49, Summer-Fall, 1969.

Jourard, S. *The Transparent Self.* D. Van Nostrand, New York, 1971.

Kaiser, H. *Effective Psychotherapy.* Free Press of Glencoe, New York, 1965.

Kaufmann, W. *Existentialism from Dostoevsky to Sartre.* Meridian, Cleveland, 1956.

Kaufmann, W. *Without Guilt and Justice.* Dell, New York, 1973.

* Keen, E. *Three Faces of Being.* Meredith, New York, 1970.

Kempler, W. The therapist's merchandise. Voices, 49, Winter-Spring, 1969.

Koch, S. Psychology and emerging conceptions of knowledge as unitary. In *Behaviorism and Phenomenology,* T. Wann, editor, p. 1. University of Chicago Press, Chicago, 1964.

Kuhn, T. *The Structure of Scientific Revolutions.* University of Chicago Press, Chicago, 1970.

Laing, R. *The Politics of the Family and Other Essays.* Pantheon Books, New York, 1971.

Laing, R., and Cooper, D. *Reason and Violence.* Vintage, New York, 1971.

Lamont, C. *Freedom of Choice Affirmed.* Horizon, New York, 1967.

Laszlo, E. *Introduction to Systems Philosophy.* Harper & Row, New York, 1972.

Lazerowitz, M. The relevance of psychoanalysis to philosophy. In *Psychoanalysis: Scientific Method and Philosophy,* S. Hook, editor, p. 133. Grove Press, New York, 1959.

Loewenstein, R., Newman, L., Shur, M., and Solnit, A., editors. *Psychoanalysis: A General Psychology.* International Universities Press, New York, 1966.

Lomas, P. *True and False Experience.* Taplinger, New York, 1973.

London, P. *The Modes and Morals of Psychotherapy.* Holt, Rinehart and Winston, New York, 1964.

MacIntyre, A. *The Unconscious.* Routledge and Kegan Paul, London, 1958.

Marmor, J., editor. *Modern Psychoanalysis.* Basic Books, New York, 1968.

May, R. Contributions of existential psychotherapy. In *Existence,* R. May, E. Angel, and H. Ellenberger, editors, p. 37. Basic Books, New York, 1959.

May, R. *Love and Will.* W. W. Norton, New York, 1969.

May, R., Angel, E., and Ellenberger, H., editors. *Existence.* Basic Books, New York, 1958.

May, R., and Van Kaam, A. Existential theory and therapy. In *Current Psychiatric Therapies,* J. Masserman, editor, vol. 3, p. 74. Grune & Stratton, New York, 1963.

Merleau-Ponty, M. *Phenomenology of Perception.* Routledge and Kegan Paul, London, 1962.

Merleau-Ponty, M. *The Structure of Behavior.* Beacon Press, Boston, 1963.

Misiak, H., and Sexton, V. *Phenomenological, Existential, and Humanistic Psychologies: A Historical Survey.* Grune & Stratton, New York, 1973.

Murphy, G. *Outgrowing Self-deception.* Basic Books, New York, 1975.

Needleman, J. Existential psychoanalysis. In *The Encyclopedia of Philosophy,* P. Edwards, editor, p. 154. Collier and The Free Press of Glencoe, New York, 1967.

Needleman, J. *Being-in-the-World.* Harper Torchbooks, New York, 1968.

Ofman, W. *A Primer of Humanistic Existentialist Counseling and Therapy.* Psychological Affiliates Press, Los Angeles, 1974.

* Ofman, W. *Affirmation and Reality,* Western Psychological Services, Los Angeles, 1976.

Oppenheimer, R. *Science and the Common Understanding.* Simon & Schuster, New York, 1954.

Oppenheimer, R. Analogy in science. Am. Psychol., *11:* 127, 1956.

Polyani, M. *Personal Knowledge.* Harper & Row, New York, 1964.

Poole, R. *Towards Deep Subjectivity.* Harper & Row, New York, 1972.

Popper, K. *The Poverty of Historicism.* Basic Books, New York, 1960.

Rappaport, D. The structure of psychoanalytic theory. In *Psychology: A Study of a Science,* S. Koch, editor, vol. 3, p. 55. McGraw-Hill, New York, 1959.

Rogers, C. *On Personal Power.* Delacorte, New York, 1977.

Roheim, G. *The Origin and Function of Culture.* Doubleday, Garden City, N. Y., 1971.

Rychlak, J. *A Philosophy of Science for Personality Theory.* Houghton Mifflin, Boston, 1968.

Rychlak, J. *The Psychology of Rigorous Humanism.* John Wiley & Sons, New York, 1977.

Sanborn, P. *Existentialism.* Pegasus, New York, 1968.

Sartre, J.-P. *The Emotions.* Philosophical Library, New York, 1948.

* Sartre, J.-P. *Being and Nothingness.* Philosophical Library, New York, 1956.

Sartre, J.-P. Foreword. In *Reason and Violence,* R. Laing and D. Cooper, editor, p. 6. Vintage, New York, 1964.

Sartre, J.-P. *Essays in Existentialism.* Citadel Press, New York, 1967.

Schipp, P., editor. *The Philosophy of Karl Jaspers.* Tudor, New York, 1957.

Singer, E. *Key Concepts in Psychotherapy.* Basic Books, New York, 1970.

Solomon, R. *The Passions.* Anchor Press, New York, 1976.

Sonnemann, U. *Existence and Therapy.* Grune & Stratton, New York, 1954.

Spielberg, H. *The Phenomenological Movement.* Martinus Nijhoff, The Hague, 1971.

Spielberg, H. *Phenomenology in Psychology and Psychiatry: A Historical Introduction.* Northwestern University Press, Evanston, 1972.

Stein, R. *Incest and Human Love.* The Third Press, New York, 1973.

Steinzor, B. *The Healing Partnership.* Harper & Row, New York, 1967.

Storr, A. The concept of cure. In *Psychoanalysis Observed,* C. Rycroft, editor, p. 50. Penguin Books, Baltimore, 1968.

Sullivan H. *Conceptions of Modern Psychiatry.* W. W. Norton, New York, 1941.

Tillich, P. Existentialism and psychotherapy. Rev. Exist. Psychol. Psychiatry, *1:* 8, 1961.

Trilling, L. Authenticity and the modern unconscious. Commentary, *52:* 39, 1971.

Truax, C., and Carkhuff, R. *Towards Effective Counseling and Psychotherapy.* Aldine Publishing Co., Chicago, 1967.

Truax, C., and Mitchell, K. Research on certain therapist interpersonal skills in relation to process and outcome. In *Handbook of Psychotherapy and Behavior Change,* A. Bergin and S. Garfield, editors, p. 20. John Wiley & Sons, New York, 1971.

Unamuno, M. *Tragic Sense of Life.* Dover, New York, 1954.

Van Den Berg, J. *The Phenomenological Approach to Psychiatry.* Charles C Thomas, Springfield, Ill., 1955.

Van Den Berg, J. *A Different Existence.* Duquesne University Press, Pittsburgh, 1972.

Van Dusen, W. The theory and practice of existential analysis. In *Psychoanalysis and Existential Philosophy,* H. Ruitenbeek, editor, p. 24. E. P. Dutton, New York, 1962.

Wahl, J. *A Short History of Existentialism.* Philosophical Library, New York, 1949.

Washburn, S. Human behavior and the behavior of other animals. Am. Psychol., *33:* 405, 1978.

Watzlawick, P., Beavin, J., and Jackson, D. *Pragmatics of Human Communication.* W. W. Norton, New York, 1967.

Wheeler, J. The universe as a home for man. In *The Nature of Scientific Discovery,* O. Gingerich, editor, p. 261. Smithsonian Institution Press, Washington, D.C., 1975.

Wheelis, A. *The End of the Modern Age.* Basic Books, New York, 1971.

Wheelis, A. *How People Change.* Harper & Row, New York, 1973.

Wild, J. *The Challenge of Existentialism.* Indiana University Press, Bloomington, 1955.

Wild, J. *Existence and the World of Freedom.* Prentice-Hall, Englewood Cliffs, N. J., 1963.

Wilson, O. *Sociobiology.* Harvard University Press, Cambridge, Mass., 1975.

* Yankelovich, D., and Barrett, W. *Ego and Instinct.* Random House, New York, 1970.

Zimbardo, P. *The Cognitive Control of Motivation.* Scott, Foresman, Chicago, 1969a.

Zimbardo, P. The human choice. In *Nebraska Symposium on Motivation,* W. Arnold and D. Levine, editors, p. 237. University of Nebraska Press, Lincoln, 1969b.

chapter

11

Theories of Personality and Psychopathology: Schools Derived from Psychology and Philosophy

11.1 Personality Theory Derived from Quantitative Experiment

RAYMOND BERNARD CATTELL, Ph.D., D.Sc.

Introduction

EXPERIMENT AND MEASUREMENT IN SCIENTIFIC THEORY

The birth of modern science is frequently placed around the year 1600, when Galileo began to apply quantitative methods to mechanical observation. It is recognized that chemistry separated itself from alchemy and entered a new phase of vigorous development when Dalton, Lavoisier, and others began to apply quantitative methods to establish laws in chemistry. Indeed, it is generally accepted today, as Mach has said, that "the aim of science is to find the formulae which express the relations among observed phenomena." By these touchstones, what is the status, as a science, of psychiatry today?

That it lacks the stability of concepts, the maturity, and the practical effectiveness that are characteristic of a developed science based on quantitative laws and experiment is surely evidenced by the considerable divergencies of theoretical viewpoints represented in this book. However, this lack is even more apparent in the excessive swings of emphasis in approved practice—for example, the recent change from psychoanalytic therapy to behavior therapy and from the predominance of psychoanalytic treatment in private practice to chemotherapy in mental hospitals. Young and uncertain sciences characteristically seek to create the illusion of progress by concentration on rapid movement. As to progress, Eysenck (1960), in an expectedly unpopular—but nevertheless sound—survey has pointed out that psychotherapy has failed to demonstrate that it can bring about recovery at a more rapid rate than would occur spontaneously, without treatment. At this moment there is actually little evidence—except for limited studies by Rickels and Cattell (1965) and Hunt et al. (1959)—of objectively measured gain from psychotherapy. However, to argue this point would serve little purpose. Even more optimistic psychiatrists, as realistic practitioners, readily admit that present methods of diagnosis, control of treatment, and insights into the necessary tactical steps fall far short of the standards required of a developed science.

The present section takes the position that psychiatry is an applied science. As such, it has elements of artistic skill; but in its essentials it must be based on what the sciences of psychology, physiology, and sociology offer. Among the most recent developments in psychology, those that are most relevant concern the concepts, laws, and predictive powers arising out of the experimental and, especially, the sophisticated quantitative studies conducted in the past 30 years. Psychology, like psychiatry, has never lacked theories; indeed, it has assembled an orchestra of resounding scholarship that enjoys a considerable scientific reputation.

The correlation between the development of a technology and the development of pure theory in science cannot be perfect; but it is also true that impressive technological development cannot occur unless the basic scientific theory possesses real potency. If one uses an acid test, as proposed here, the technological capacity to eliminate mental disorder or reeducate delinquent personalities does not provide convincing evidence that more than elementary advances in the basic science of psychology have been made.

UNIFICATION OF THEORY AND MEASUREMENT

The twin pillars that psychology offers in its support of the development of psychiatry are personality theory and learning theory. Until 50 years ago, personality theory developed mainly as a result of clinical observation—as exemplified by the formulations of Kraepelin, Freud, Jung, and Janet—or was based on what might be called literary and general human observation—as exemplified by the work of William James, McDougall, Allport, Klages, and Spranger. The subsequent, quantitative and experimental phase initially framed its questions in terms of the theories inherited from the earlier clinical and literary phase. More recently, however, the quantitative phase has built on a theoretical structure of its own. To date, it has failed to produce scientific laws that can aspire to the scope and elaborateness of the scientific speculations derived from the earlier phase. On the other hand, there is every indication that it has constructed a sound foundation. It is the kind of foundation that will produce definite results, expressed as basic laws and having predictive powers. One can expect these laws and powers to develop in applied science with increasing rapidity in the next decade.

Multivariate Personality Theory

PRELIMINARY ISSUES

One reason why the message from the quantitative, experimental approach has not yet come through as clearly as it might is that the dust of conflict hangs over the area, sustained by a battle between the bivariate and the multivariate schools of experimental design. The bivariate school follows the classical plan of experiments in physical science; typically, it deals with one independent and one dependent variable. For example, it manipulates a stimulus and measures a response, trying and often claiming to hold all else constant while doing so. Wundt, Pavlov, and Skinner are among the advocates of this method, which has been inherited in its entirety by the reflexological school of learning.

The second school of experimental design, favoring the multivariate method, springs from Galton, Spearman, and Thurstone, and it is more concerned with correlational methods and the simultaneous study of measurement of many variables

ADVANTAGES OF THE MULTIVARIATE METHOD

The Galton tradition, enriched by the contributions of many mathematical statisticians in the multivariate field, has recently given scientists remarkably enhanced access, by the electronic computer, to problems that were previously unapproachable. Thus, the multivariate method has two major claims to superiority over the classical bivariate experimental design. First, the multivariate experimental can grasp wholes—that is, complex pattern entities, such as the clinician deals with—whereas the classical experimentalist usually deals with a single atomistic variable, which is often of minor importance and incapable of representing a complex concept. Second, the multivariate method can claim to uncover complex causal relationships without the actual manipulation of people and circumstances that has always been considered essential to classical experiment.

Manipulation in the life sciences has two serious drawbacks. First, it is apt to upset the phenomena it wishes to study. For example, a dog whose adrenal glands have been dissected out is suffering from something more than the removal of adrenalin from his blood stream. Second, manipulation in the life of human beings of those cardinal emotional attachments that are typically involved in clinical generalizations is practically and ethically impossible. It is primarily for this reason that the experimentalist who understands only bivariate designs has turned increasingly to animal experiments. But, even under the most ideal circumstances, the application of conclusions drawn from animal experiments, which do not include cultural concepts or concepts of self, to happenings in the minds of men propels the scientist toward speculative reasoning to a degree that is grotesquely out of keeping with the precision that characterized his animal experimentation.

THREE-CORNERED ARGUMENT

The familiar cleavage between the clinical observer, on the one hand, and the laboratory experimentalist, on the other hand, is not the most important dichotomy in research methodology. Actually, there is

a three-cornered argument in progress. Or rather, although it might serve a purpose if it were an argument, it is actually in danger of becoming a mere regression into three camps that are isolated from each other—clinician, brass-instrument experimentalist, and multivariate experimentalist. In some respects, there is a stronger bond between the clinician and the multivariate experimentalist than there is between the multivariate and the bivariate experimentalists. Both the clinician and the multivariate experimentalist are concerned with seeking generalizations, while keeping the totality of behavior in view, through the formulation of hypotheses that cannot be caught or operationally represented by a single variable. For example, both can handle the concepts of drives and of such multifaceted personality structures as the psychoanalytic concepts of ego and superego. But, in another respect, the multivariate experimentalist has more in common with the bivariate experimentalist than the clinician in that both the multivariate and the bivariate experimentalists demand that concepts be referable to measurable operations and reproducible experiments, whereas the clinician makes no such claim and is, very often, prepared to proceed without the kind of recorded and statistically treated results that the experimentalist regards as indispensible.

Then the third side of the triangle becomes shorter once again when one realizes that the relatively sophisticated mathematical models and statistical analytical procedures used by the multivariate experimentalist are stronger and more remote from the clinician's training than are the experimental and control groups used in the typical bivariate experiment, despite the fact that the multivariate experimentalist's methods are comparatively simple. One of the unfortunate results of the development of mathematics in the multivariate approach has been that, although the clinician and the multivariate researcher are close in principle and in their formal modes of reasoning, the clinician, when he attempts to carry out an experiment, all too frequently reverts to the simple designs of the bivariate methodologist. Because, except for a few brilliant examples, psychiatrists cannot also be mathematicians, the effective interdisciplinary organization of research today requires the multivariate experimentalist to convey to the clinician the emerging structural concepts but not their detailed mathematical support. His task, then, is to equip the clinician with measuring instruments that correspond to these concepts. The clinical researcher can use these in all manner of criterion experiments, using a purely logical comprehension of the dimensions measured rather than a mathematical one. After all, the psychiatrist's unique skills involve the application of these measuring instruments in conjunction with his ability to communicate with the patient. It is as unreasonable to expect him to exhibit equal competence in every area of the field of mathematical, quantitative behavioral research as it would be to expect the multivariate experimentalist to be able to conduct a psychiatric interview competently.

To be realistic, it will certainly be a long time before the mathematical prediction of behavior reaches such a level of comparative completeness that it reduces appreciably the need for considerable supplemental data from the human intuitive arts. However, there is every reason to believe that the results and implements of multivariate experimental research can ultimately be made available for intelligent use by those not engaged in the research of their production and that they will add accuracy to psychiatric procedures. Thus, one can hope that future training in psychiatry will integrate these new concepts. This integration is certainly a possibility, but it is equally certain that little has been done as yet to bring it about. Indeed, too many teachers in the field of personality theory are still not facing in the direction from which the advances in integration of diagnostic measurement and theory are most likely to come.

Structural Measurement versus Psychological Testing

Although theory and measurement need to be closely united, the quantitiative approach to psychological theory involves much more than psychological testing. Psychologists have constructed projective and nonprojective scales for thousands of variables, and laboratory workers have measured myriads of described variables. Nor is this surprising, for the number of aspects of behavior susceptible to being measured by a scale and labeled is infinite, and there is small chance that even two or three of the finite number of psychologists will choose to think the same variable important. Nevertheless, few of these scales have uncovered anything of theoretical importance, and most lie forgotten in professional journals.

Wherein lies the escape from this triviality of measurement? Certainly, as in any science, important concepts must be established, essential in the sense that they wield more predictive power and basic in the sense that they can be correlated with more psychological laws than concepts less happily chosen. Even when they are found, they may not correspond operationally with some single variable. For example, an anxiety score does not correspond with counted beads of prespiration on the brow but may correspond to the average measure of a whole pattern of manifestations. But how are these more vital concepts to be discovered and the choice of variables most suitable for their measurement determined?

APPLICATIONS OF FACTOR ANALYSIS

There are essentially two ways in which a science can move toward the development of its truly efficacious concepts. One is by the process of conceptual trial and error, in which investigator after investigator pits his brain against the obscurities of nature and tries out concept after concept until one is found that fits the facts better than any other and provides more accurate predictions. The second is to develop a representative experimental design in which one samples variables according to some sampling technique and then uses a mathematical method, such as factor analysis, to isolate the comparatively small number of underlying influences responsible for the observed relationships of co-variation among the individually measured variables.

In such sciences as physics and chemistry, the trial-and-error approach has been quite successful and not unduly arduous or wasteful. The concepts of mass, time, temperature, radiation by wave transmission, and valency were, in general, the survivors of no more than half a dozen alternative hypotheses. But, unfortunately, it is a fact of history that psychology has not achieved a comparable degree of success, and students of behavior should realize that they are confronted by a quite different kind of problem, requiring a different method. The number of influences to take into account in deciding whether the home team will win a basketball game or whether Mrs. Jones will decide to speak to Mrs. Smith at a cocktail party or whether patient X will try to commit suicide is of greater magnitude than the number of influences that affect the orbit of Neptune or the rate of the emission of electrons from a heated filament. Something more drastic must be done if one is to cut his way through the thickets of primal phenomena in order to reach the significant variables or concepts, concepts that, at the same time, will not be too numerous to make prediction possible.

The reader must understand the philosophy and the impact of multivariate experimental methods if he is to grasp its revolutionary implications for behavioral research. The evaluator of theory must realize that methods now exist, particularly in factor analysis, that, when they are used flexibly with rotation to simple structure, are capable of reducing the multitudes of variables to a limited set of underlying functional unities capable of predicting those variables. However, correlational methods and factor analysis must be used with the added restrictions of a scientific method, rather than the bare postulates of a purely mathematical method. Only then are they capable of isolating underlying structures and influences in complex phenomena. Even its critics have agreed that factor analysis is capable of predicting—that is, of accounting for the variances in large numbers of variables by identifying the variance in a comparatively limited number of intervening or underlying variables.

A simple demonstration of the method was provided by Dickman and Cattell, who made 32 physical and kinetic measurement observations on the behavior of 100 balls; the factor analysis of these 32 variables yielded four factors—weight, diameter of the ball, elasticity coefficient, and the length of the string on which the ball was swung. These are the concepts that the physicist would use in formulas to explain the 32 measurements. The clinician may not be able to spare the time to follow the mathematical argument in detail. Yet he can be reassured at the common-sense level by demonstrations of this kind that, through behavioral measurements, the method is capable of elucidating the same root influences he perceives clinically as accounting for individual differences in behavior.

Surface and Source Traits

For 100 years psychiatry has struggled with the opposing views that taxonomic schemes are its main stock in trade and that understanding the individual patient through insight makes diagnostic categories unnecessary and even misleading. Finding that pigeonholing patients in types of syndrome grouping did not immediately provide such insight or reliable criteria with regard to therapeutic indications, many psychiatrists suggested the elimination of diagnostic procedures altogether. Instead, they advocated deeper, direct understanding of the dynamics of each case.

To get the full value from diagnostic approaches, such as those developed by Kraepelin and Bleuler, the real need was to press beyond the concept of gross syndromes to a more sophisticated taxonomic system, rather than to retreat. The statistical, quantitative methodology of multivariate experimentation provides a means of doing this with the mathematical model concepts that are briefly designated by the terms "surface trait," "source trait," "type," and "process."

DEFINITIONS

A surface trait is simply a set of behaviors that are observed to go together, to appear together, and to disappear together; as such, it has the form of a simple correlation cluster. A syndrome is one form of surface trait. Computer programs such as Taxonome are capable of rapidly finding such clusters among the observations fed into a computer. In contrast, the source trait is defined as a simple structure factor—that is, one of the underlying influences that may be located by factor analysis. Examples of the source traits found by factor analysis generally include intelligence, the primary mental abilities described by Thurstone, personality source traits such as anxiety, surgency, ego strength, and superego strength, and a number of drive patterns, technically called "ergs." Essentially, the surface traits are heapings up of behavior that derive from interactions of underlying source traits.

It may be useful to review the developments in personality theory that have already occurred through the application of the concept of surface and source traits. Typically, the multivariate experimentalist measures about 300 people with regard to 80 different manifestations in behavior. He then produces a correlation matrix among these 80 variables and by factor analysis finds the factors—that is, the source traits—underlying the variables. When he finds, say, a dozen source traits, he is reasonably sure that he is finding patterns with a high likelihood of replication, as patterns, by others and with psychological predictive value.

This empirically derived emergence of structure provides the dependable concepts for the construction of testing devices. Indeed, it provides a statistical psychometric basis for hitting the bull's eye of such conceptual targets. Herein lies the vast difference between ordinary psychological testing and what may be called functional psychological testing. In psychological testing, one simply constructs scales for a priori notions or for quite specific bits of behavior; in functional psychological testing, one discovers the structures to be measured first. That is, one unearths the inherent dynamic, temperamental, or ability structures—the source traits—in the human personality and then sets out to devise functional factor tests that permit the precise measurement of these structures and nothing else.

Factor dimensions. Forty years of psychometric research in the personality field, using all three possible media of human observation—namely, behavior rating in situ; introspective evidence, as in the questionnaire or the consulting room; and objective test evidence by laboratory or performance measurements—have yielded a steadily increasing harvest of new concepts in personality theory with which the psychiatrist needs to become acquainted.

Analyses of rating and self-rating (introspective) data yield much the same concepts, around 20 in number. These source traits were indexed initially as factors A, B, C, D, etc., in much the same way the vitamin researchers first indexed their vitamin influences. A period of time must elapse between the simple identification of a behavior pattern as behavior and its thorough interpretation and understanding.

Descriptions of source traits. It is reassuring for clinicians to find that the first broad factor found by multivariate experimental psychologists had been observed clinically by Kraepelin, Bleuler, Kretschmer, and others. Kretschmer called it the "cyclothyme versus schizothyme dimension." Every factor must have a convention as to positive direction of score, although mathematically it is a toss up. Thus, at the positive pole one finds easy expression of affect, good contact with people, and a tendency toward mood swings. At the opposite pole, one finds aloofness and rigidity, together with some dissociation of affect from cognition.

For the most part, factor analytical work is based on observations on normal subjects. Consequently, there is no reason to suppose that either the cyclothyme or the schizothyme temperament intrinsically connotes abnormality. Historically, they were first seen in their pathological dress, and it is possible that what was seen was in each case a specific disease process superimposed on an essentially normal deviation. Certainly, the expressions of the A factor pattern within the normal range are sufficiently different from schizophrenic and manic-depressive phenomena to justify a more conservative terminology. Consequently, in normal subjects, the A factor dimension has been called "affectothymia versus sizothymia." The term sizothymia is derived from a Latin root meaning flatness, which is characteristic of the schizothyme temperament apart from any abnormality. After this first major A factor, a second source trait, B, which connotes intelligence, was found to have the greatest influence quantitatively on a random set of behavior variables measured in regard to individual differences. Then, in the third place, comes the ego strength factor, indexed as C, which has most of the properties assigned to it by the psychoanalyst. Factor D is a general excitability dimension. Source trait E is clearly recognizable as a dimension of dominance versus submissiveness that has also been studied in mammals and primates and has been correlated with hormone concentration. The F factor is called surgency-desurgency. At the surgent pole, it seems to be related to creative capacity, which is associated with comparatively little general inhibition; at the desurgent pole, one sees a pattern with many features of what is clinically recognized as depression.

The personality theorist who wants to get a real grasp of this field should study the exact nature—that is, the magnitudes of factor loadings in various behaviors—of from 15 to 20 source traits until he recognizes them easily and understands their mode of expression fairly thoroughly. Some of the most important source traits are set out in bipolar form in Table I. For example, he might be particularly interested in the G factor of superego strength, which has all the ineluctable categorical imperativeness of the Freudian superego and has a special relationship to anxiety. As he studies this factor, he encounters a number of interesting refinements, such as the correlations among factors and the existence of second-order factors. For instance, some patterns show themselves more obviously in overt behavior (L data),

whereas others emerge clearly only in the questionnaire and consulting room (Q data) responses. A "Q" prefix is used for the latter, and prominent among them, in the Sixteen Personality Factor Test (16 PF Test) is Q_3, self-sentiment strength. The score on this factor measures the development of the sentiment about the self, which seems to indicate the extent to which the person's behavior is determined by attitudes that evolve from a consciously precise self-concept.

The Q_4 factor, called ergic tension, seems to represent the general persisting level of drive frustration in the total drive endowment of the person. As far as one can judge from its correlations and manifestations, this factor does not merely indicate undischarged libido level in the Freudian sense but represents the amount of undischarged drive from sex, pugnacity, and any other ergs that may be encountering some of the frustration inevitable in this culture in one's personal life.

Assessment of source traits. Granted that these structures and concepts give precision and potential measurability to some of the older, important parameters that are the basis for understanding any person, how is the practitioner to assess them? In part, he will want to do so directly by clinical interview. Normal persons, such as officer candidates for the Air Force, have often been evaluated by careful rating procedures. In administering tests, one can use either questionnaires or objective, miniature situation performances (the Objective-Analytic Battery, or O-A). The latter is ideal but cumbersome, so that the most convenient way to assess source trait levels is by a questionnaire, provided that the questionnaire can be constructed with sufficient ingenuity to avoid excessive motivational distortion by faking. The Sixteen Personality Factor Test has been used widely in both clinical and occupational situations to evaluate the level of the person on 16 of the 20 factors that have proved most relevant and most reliable. The test yields 16 scores, each on a 10-point scale. However, the psychologist or social worker who has not received sufficient training in this area should be warned that, in assessing personality source traits either by this method or by the Objective-Analytic Battery, he is not dealing with a profile of immutable levels, which he is likely to associate with I.Q. tests or ability measures, but with personality traits that can develop and be modified by life circumstances, psychotherapy, and other factors. Nevertheless, repeat measurements with these scales at intervals of 1 or more years have shown that, when life circumstances remain fairly stable, most of these traits demonstrate considerable stability, from the age of 10 on.

The original factor analyses that showed these patterns in normal adult subjects have been applied in the past 15 years to groups of abnormal persons and pathological subjects and at different ages—specifically, at 12 and 13 years of age, at 11, at 7, and at 4 and 5 years of age. The evidence produced in the questionnaire type of response clearly indicates that most of these factors have a continuity of form that is, of loading pattern—over the whole age range and in groups representing different cultures. Thus, high and low surgency is a recognizable pattern at all age levels that have been investigated to date, as are the affectothyme versus sizothyme temperament dimension, ego strength, and the various other factors. Furthermore, studies performed in Italy, Germany, Japan, India, and Australia have shown that the essential form of these patterns survives cultural translation. Therefore, the evidence accumulated to date supports the view that these functional unities are relatively fundamental dimensions of human personality, which may undergo some modification in expression with age and cultural changes, but which retain a real continuity. This has been an important consideration in recent years for the planning of developmental studies.

The 16 primary trait dimensions are normal in the sense that they are found equally in factoring normal and clinical patient groups, although more deviant score magnitudes may appear in the patient groups. But the advances in factorial research in the past decade have not only added seven more normal factors but have shown that patients are distinguishable by more than deviancy on the now 23 normal primaries. Comprehensive factoring of the abnormal realm of behavior (ratings by Lorr; questionnaire items by Cattell, Delhees, and Sells, including the Minnesota Multiphasic Personality Inventory content)

TABLE I
Brief Descriptions of Some Primary Source Traits Found by Factor Analysis*

| Low-score Description | Technical Labels | | Standard Symbol | High-score Description |
	Low Pole	High Pole		
Reserved, detached, critical, cool	Sizothymia	Affectothymia	A	Outgoing, warm hearted, easy going, participating
Less intelligent, concrete thinking	Low general mental capacity	Intelligence	B	More intelligent, abstract thinking, bright
Affected by feelings, emotionally less stable, easily upset	Lower ego strength	Higher ego strength	C	Emotionally stable, faces reality, calm
Phlegmatic, relaxed	Low excitability	High excitability	D	Excitable, strident, attention seeking
Humble, mild, obedient, conforming	Submissiveness	Dominance	E	Assertive, independent, aggressive, stubborn
Sober, prudent, serious, taciturn	Desurgency	Surgency	F	Happy-go-lucky, heedless, gay, enthusiastic
Expedient, a law to himself, bypasses obligations	Low superego strength	Superego strength	G	Conscientious, preservering, staid, rule bound
Shy, restrained, diffident, timid	Threctia	Parmia	H	Venturesome, socially bold, uninhibited, spontaneous
Tough minded, self-reliant, realistic, no nonsense	Harria	Premsia	I	Tender minded, dependent, overprotected, sensitive
Trusting, adaptable, free of jealousy, easy to get on with	Alaxia	Protension	L	Suspicious, self-opinionated, hard to fool
Practical, careful, conventional, regulated by external realities, proper	Praxernia	Autia	M	Imaginative, preoccupied with inner urgencies, careless of practical matters, Bohemian
Forthright, natural, artless, sentimental	Artlessness	Shrewdness	N	Shrewd, calculating, worldly, penetrating
Placid, self-assured, confident, serene	Untroubled adequacy	Guilt proneness	O	Apprehensive, worried, depressive, troubled
Conservative, respecting established ideas, tolerant of traditional difficulties	Conservatism	Radicalism	Q_1	Experimental, critical, liberal, analytical, free thinking
Group dependent, a joiner and sound follower	Group adherence	Self-sufficiency	Q_2	Self-sufficient, prefers to make decisions, resourceful
Casual, careless of protocol, untidy, follows own urges	Weak self-sentiment	Strong self-sentiment	Q_3	Controlled, socially precise, self-disciplined, compulsive
Relaxed, tranquil, torpid, unfrustrated	Low ergic tension	High ergic tension	Q_4	Tense, driven, overwrought, fretful

* In ratings and questionnaires and now embodied in the 16 Personality Factor Test.

has shown some 12 disease dimensions that can be picked up only in pathology items such as the six depression factors, schizoid tendency, hypochondria, and psychopathic tendencies. These 12 scales have recently been represented along with the 16 normal dimensions in the Clinical Analysis Questionnaire (CAQ), now standardized by Cattell, Krug, and Sells on large clinical groups. It has been shown by May, using the weightings of these scales given by discriminant functions, that the main clinical syndrome groups of the American Psychiatric Association classification can be well separated by the CAQ.

Essentially parallel findings appear when personality source traits are measured through the objective—performance or laboratory—type of test. There are some interesting modifications, however, due to the difference in the power of the eyepiece, so to speak. Some magnification

occurs in questionnaires, so that second-order factors in the questionnaire realm—broad factors that take the form of groupings of primaries—emerge only as first-order factors, narrower in the total field, in the objective test realm. For example, the single general anxiety factor that appears in objective laboratory test measures fractionates into an interrelated set of subfactors in the questionnaire—for example, the factors of ego weakness, guilt proneness, and tension.

The weakness of the questionnaire—that it is vulnerable to faking—can nowadays be partly overcome by correction for social desirability, which is only rough, or, better, by the trait-view correction. But if clinical researchers would afford the time and skill necessary to use the objective (behavioral test) devices, as in the IPAT Objective-Analytic Batteries, they would escape all this. The factors in the O-A Battery that most distinguish most varieties of psychopathology from normal behavior are indexed UI (Universal Index) 16 (ego strength: low), UI 19 (independence: low), UI 21 (exuberance: low), UI 23 (regression: high), UI 24 (anxiety: high; neurotics only); UI 25 (realism: low; Eysenck's psychoticism), UI 30 (somindence: high). Most of these differences are significant at the 0.05 to 0.001 level on single factors (Cattell and Schmidt, 1972), but in combination, as specific patterns, the scores come close to a complete separation of diagnostic categories—for example, schizophrenics, involutional depressives, neurotics, manics (Cattell and Scheier, 1961; Tatro, 1966; Cattell and Tatro, 1966; Cattell and Schmidt, 1972; May, 1972; Cattell and Schuerger, 1978). The extraordinary delay in bringing the O-A Battery and its associated theory of personality factors into diagnostic use, inasmuch as diagnostic power far exceeds such current and ad hoc tests as the Rorschach, belongs with the same mysteries as the 50-year delay in combatting scurvy with vitamin C or replacing Ptolemy by Copernicus in astronomy textbooks. Probably the hitch is partly at a practical level—that the O-A Battery requires 3 times as long to administer as a questionnaire and requires more skill in administration and scoring. However, if diagnosticians became seriously convinced of the power of the O-A Battery and of the theoretical concepts connected with it, doubtless the ensuing due increment of technological attention will find ways to shorten and simplify the procedure, as in other applications of science.

Construction of the Theoretical Model

Elaborate personality theories that do not offer, as a basic prerequisite, the ability to measure recognizable trait structures involved in the theory will not get very far. On the other hand, a system that has nothing to offer but a set of traits cannot be considered potentially significant, no matter how these traits describe the natural history of the observed species. It follows, then, that psychology must experiment with models that will account for trait interaction and development and for the role of situations and that will permit accurate prediction of the outcome of trait combinations and conflicts.

Moreover, this model must have diagnostic validity, and it must be applicable to pathological phenomena, despite the fact that at least half the data on which it is based are derived from observations of normal subjects. Obviously, there may be special disease processes described in clinical material that are never manifested in any aspect of normal behavior. But a description of the main model is the first concern. This is called the factorial systems (intersection) model, for it treats any behavioral event as something that can be accounted for only in terms of concepts of personality, of situation, and of ongoing process. Each of these variables is clearly represented by a specific formula.

THE FACTORIAL SYSTEMS (INTERSECTION) MODEL

Any act is thought, as far as personality is concerned, to involve the total personality—that is, the whole profile of source trait scores. The simplest mathematical way of handling this totality is to assign various appropriate and experimentally obtained weights to the action of specific traits in each given situation and then simply to add these contributions together to get the total strength of the final response. However, if one suspects that the relation obtaining in nature is more complicated than a linear one, the formula may be modified by introducing, for example, products or exponentials among the trait scores. But, so far, this modification has not been necessary, and the basic equation in this intersectional factor analysis model remains what is sometimes called the linear specification equation. It can be represented for k traits as follows:

$$a_j = b_j T_1 + b_{j2} T_2 + \cdots + b_{jk} T_k \qquad (1)$$

where $T_1, T_2 \ldots T_k$ are a person's scores on the traits; a is the act to be predicted, and $b_{j1}, b_{j2} \ldots b_{jk}$ are behavioral indices or weights for these traits when they are manifested in the context of the situation f.

Concept of the linear specification equation. This is a simple linear equation. It states that the magnitude of any particular behavior manifestation (a), such as a symptom, is determined by a whole set of source traits or factors, here indicated by the letters A, B, C, etc., from Table I. So far, this is in accordance with good psychiatric principles, which postulate that most behavior is multiply determined and is not due to the independent action of any single trait or dynamic need. The weights or behavioral indices, that express the extent to which each of the standard common factors is involved in performance, are determined by an experiment, using a factor analysis, and can be assigned any values, ranging from +1 to −1. The application of this specification equation can be illustrated by two examples. The first of these is an equation discovered by Pierson and Kelly (1963) for the probability of recovery from delinquency in adolescent children. The second is also an empirically derived equation and expresses the success of psychiatric technicians, evaluated in their own institutions, as a function of their personality factor scores on the 16 PF Test. These may be stated (see Table I for trait identification) as follows:

Response to treatment = .1B—.5C + .3D—.1F + .6G
$$\qquad —.2H + .2I + .2J + 2Q—.3Q_2 + .2Q_4 \qquad (2)$$

Psychiatric success = .2A + .5C—.2E + .3G + .3H
$$\qquad —.3M—.2O—.3Q_1 + .3Q_3—.2Q_4 \qquad (3)$$

In any actual calculation the values for the source trait scores—which, typically, represent the values on a 10-point scale, based on the stens in the test score—always represent the individual scores on these common traits. ("Sten" is an abbreviation of "standard ten," meaning a standard score in which sigma equals 2 and the total range is 1 to 10.) The I.Q. (B), the affectothyme (A), and the ego strength (C) factor measures are familiar instances of such source trait scores. The T's in equation 1 are replaced with letters to denote particular source traits in equations 2 and 3. The meaning of these letters is given in Table I. Whereas the T values that express the unique qualities of the person constitute the profile of his trait scores, the values that define the situation in which he stands are represented by the b values or behavioral indices. These indices are unique to the particular situation, not to the person. They can be identified only by factoring data that include that situation. These behavioral indices describe the extent to which the given situation evokes certain personality traits. It becomes more evident at this point that the general approach is called the intersection theory because it considers the acts as the intersection of a multidimensional personality with a multidimensional situation. "Intersection" is no figure of speech but refers to an equation for actual computations that can be applied to any related problem. The validity of these modes of representation of the person and the situation can be tested in other ways as well.

Predictive validity. The theory has a practical, testable application. Thus, the practitioner can take the particular scores of a patient on a test, such as the 16 PF Test or the High School Personality Questionnaire (HSPQ) or the O-A Battery. After entering these figures in a familiar equation, obtained by previous researches, for some important situation, he can make a rough prediction of the patient's response. For example, the psychiatrist may be interested in the way a particular person will respond to a certain therapeutic treatment; provided general research has been used earlier to establish the behavioral indices for this situation, he will be able to make an estimate that is probably much better than one that could be made from intuition alone. The accuracy of the estimate can be calculated by finding the magnitude of the multiple correlation obtainable from the given weights.

Some psychometrists have been content to use personality source trait measurements and ability factor measurements in just this way, restricting themselves to purely actuarial statistical methods. But such restrictive practice does not use the resources of the intersectional theory of behavior to their full capacity. Surely, the characteristic that distinguishes a good psychiatrist or psychologist from an accountant or a computer is his desire to use psychological laws as well as actuarial and statistical laws. Here, once again, one encounters a substantial advantage of functional psychological testing over mere psychological testing. If these source traits are the natural structures of personality or if they correspond to functional states—such as anxiety, stress, and elation-depression—one can project the prediction beyond what is possible actuarially. One can reason and predict to future dates and different occasions by adding to the formal calculation or to an estimate that is made in one's head what he knows about the way in which these source traits will change with time and situation and as a result of other influences.

Modifications in source traits. With this potential capability, it becomes important for personality theory to develop, as soon as possible, its repertoire of laws and resources of information about these source traits. One of the obvious and immediate directions of possible research is to find the way in which each source trait changes and develops characteristically with age. When it became known, for example, that the general intelligence factor, as defined by Spearman, grew rapidly in childhood and reached a definite plateau at about 15 to 16 years of age rather than at a much later age, as was generally assumed, predictions about learning rate and future achievement began to be made with much greater reliability and insight. In the past 10 years, as information has accumulated about the life course of several well-known personality factors, many psychologists who had been sitting on the fence too long and looked askance at factors as mere mathematical abstractions became convinced of their reality. For one sees that each factor shows a highly characteristic age course, quite different from that which would arise from a mere averaging of any mathematical but unpsychological set of subtest scores. For example, when the anxiety factor is scored on the eight subtests found to load it most consistently, one discovers that anxiety is high in adolescence, then drops steadily until the age of about 35, after which it stays low until old age, when, apparently, it rises again. The ego strength factor also follows an unstable course in adolescence; thereafter, it continues to rise very slowly and steadily with life experience. The provision of such norms should also help to enhance the psychiatrist's understanding of how far individual cases may be deviating from the normal development.

In the next decade, however, research on intersection theory has many other important things to explore in regard to source traits. Central among these things is the relative importance of constitution and environmental learning in determining individual differences. Preliminary research shows great differences among them in this respect. Personality theory could also be pushing ahead to manipulative, bivariate experiments carried out on factor measurements, such as anxiety, ego strength, surgency, and superego strength. Inasmuch as measures are now available, no factor analysis would be necessary; the aim of such research would simply be to determine, for example, which physiological influences and family learning situations determine levels of these primary structures.

Diagnosis and prognosis by the intersection model. In regard to the establishment of the patterns of functional unities in personality that are called traits, the contention of the factor analyst is that he really needs no check from clinical, nonmetric types of observation, although he welcomes the enrichment of meaning given thereby to the bare bones of his framework. For he has rested his case on the most fundamental principle for establishing functional connections in science—namely, what John Stuart Mill called "the principle of joint variation." Thereby causal and other connections can be proved, and thereby it can be shown that certain elements of behavior do, in fact, go together when examined by more precise methods than are available to the clinician's eye and memory. Consequently, it is not surprising that the factor analytical experimental methods first elucidated some of the major patterns that have been observed clinically, for the clinician is using the same principles but without benefit of a computer. Correlational investigations have confirmed the validity of such con-

cepts as ego strength, a general factor of anxiety, superego strength, schizothyme tendency, and ergic tension.

Although the basis of the newer concept is different, more precise, and more verifiable, these new factors have been given the labels by which the vaguer shapes that preceded them have been clinically recognized. For example, there can no longer be any justification for several different views of the exact pattern of ego strength expression or for conflicting views about whether ego structure is a single pattern or several. These issues can be quickly decided by experiment, and in Cattell's *Personality and Mood by Questionnaire* (1973), precise loadings are given for the various expressions of ego strength, schizothyme tendency, anxiety, and so on. Table II shows, for example, how various introspected and observed anxiety manifestations load the anxiety factor.

Universal Index series. The factor analyst usually uses indices for traits to avoid possibly false connotations in popular labels. For example, in the Universal Index series, UI 24 corresponds to the general anxiety factor. After this pattern is tied down, the psychometrist must also show how UI 24 measures behave in clinical situations. In this case, the factor behaves exactly as the popular conception of anxiety has always behaved. That is, measurements on the UI 24 show that the measurements for neurotics are decidedly higher than they are for normal subjects. They show that under psychotherapy and chemotherapy the score on UI 24 is reduced. They show that UI 24 measures increase in persons subjected to anxiety-provoking situations. The exact identification of a measurable behavioral pattern for anxiety, UI 24, permits these associations to be demonstrated and, incidentally, also permits more precise research to uncover those physiological variables that are related to anxiety. Understanding of physiological associations has been enhanced since factor analytical separation of the response patterns has shown that a stress reaction pattern exists, now called effort stress. This resembles and was frequently confused with anxiety before the advent of correlational factor analytical evidence, but it behaves differently in several ways. For example cholesterol in the blood stream seems to be related positively to effort stress measurements but not to anxiety measurements.

Diagnostic criteria. The difference between the theories developed from multivariate quantitative research and those based on clinical observation does not stop at some variations in emphasis in descriptive patterns, at some greater clarity in the separation of distinct concepts, and at the possibility of resolving otherwise unending verbal disputes by reference to quantitative experimental results. It may alter the whole theoretical picture, as has happened through findings on the number and nature of the factors involved in a specific process, such as neurosis. It appears that clinical observation has succeeded in locating only the more grossly obvious of these functional unities and that a much larger number must be considered. Whereas Freud believed that "anxiety is the central problem in the neuroses," and many psychoanalysts continue to treat neurosis as if the main problem were to reduce the deviant degree of anxiety, the factor analytical approach, by the intersection model, has identified at least seven primary factors that distinguish diagnosed neurotics from normal subjects beyond the P < 0.01 level of significance. According to current tentative labels, these include C− (ego weakness), E− (submissiveness), F− (desurgency), H− (threctia), I+ (premsia), O+ (guilt proneness), Q_3 (inadequate self-sentiment development), and Q_4+ (high undischarged ergic tension level), as presented in Table I.

In the Objective-Analytic Battery, seven factors have also been found that distinguish the neurotics from the normal subjects with the same statistical potency (P < 0.01), although they cover a broader area than was measured in the questionnaire. The degree of separation of neurotics and normal subjects that can, in fact, be obtained just by the use of the O-A battery is shown in Figure 1.

If one examines these factors in terms of their clinical association, one recognizes that classical psychoanalysis has designated ego weakness, guilt proneness, and ergic tension as factors in the neurotic breakdown, but it has said nothing about H− factor (threctia), I+ factor (premsia), or Q_3 (deficient self-sentiment). The evidence pro-

TABLE II

Psychiatric Symptoms Expressive of Anxiety
A. Self-Rating*

Item No.	Correlations with Pure Anxiety Factor			Symptom
	Average of 1 and 2	Research 1 (Sample of 90)	Research 2 (Sample of 150)	
1	+.40	+.32	+48	Jumpy, nervous
2	+.39	+.32	+.45	Feel lonely
3	+.38	+.36	+.39	Want to get away from it all
4	+.36	+.29	+.43	Worry
5	+.36	+.32	+.40	Do foolish or clumsy things, say the wrong thing
6	+.36	+.27	+.45	Nervous movements (finger tapping)
7	+.36	+.31	+.41	Feel depressed or despondent
8	+.34	+.36	+.31	Excitable
9	+.34	+.32	+.35	Have silly, groundless fears
10	+.33	+.30	+.36	Have a fatalistic attitude
11	+.31	+.36	+.26	Lack of self-confidence
12	+.31	+.32	+.29	Irritable
13	+.31	+.22	+.39	Heart pounds when excited
14	+.31	+.29	+.32	Easily distracted
15	+.30	+.28	+.32	Daydream
16	+.30	+.21	+.39	Get confused for certain lengths of time
17	+.30	+.26	+.33	Tense
18	+.29	+.33	+.24	Cry
19	+.28	+.30	+.25	Pulse rapid
20	+.27	+.21	+.32	Easily embarrassed
21	+.26	+.23	+.29	Get cold shivers
22	+.26	+.46	+.05	Moody
23	+.25	+.33	+.17	Have rapid emotional changes (hate to liking)
24	+.25	+.28	+.22	Cannot concentrate
25	+.25	+.24	+.26	Get tired easily

* From Cattell, R. B., and Scheier, I. H. *The Meaning and Measurement of Neuroticism and Anxiety.* Ronald Press, New York, 1961.

B. Psychiatrist's Ratings

Symptom	Correlations with Pure Anxiety Factor
Irritability	+.42
Anxiety	+.33
Depression	+.32
Phobic behavior	+.22
Sleep disturbances	+.13

duced by studies of twins is that H factor is appreciably hereditary and represents a general autonomic sensitivity to threat in the low-score direction—hence the name "threctia." Presumably, this finding of low H in neurotics merely indicates that the person who is highly susceptible to external threats also reacts excessively to threats from internal forces or impulses. It may be that Freud considered this temperamental component too obvious to state, but, in any actual calculation of individual differences in neurosis, it cannot be overlooked.

The concept of premsia versus harria (I factor), on the other hand, adds an entirely new dimension to the theory of neurosis. This factor is largely environmentally determined, although some association has

been shown with blood groups. It seems to represent the extent to which the person has been brought up in an overindulgent and unrealistic environment, as opposed to a disciplined, more self-restrictive atmosphere. The term "premsia" is an acronym from "protected emotional sensitivity," and the ratings given to children and adults high on this factor stress sensitivity, plaintiveness, dependence, preference for art and drama over science and mathematics, and a tendency toward fussiness in personal relations. In school, these children are rated as attentive to and dependent on the teacher, demanding of attention, sensitive to criticism, and unpopular with their peers. An unusually high I factor is found in neurotics, drug addicts, alcoholics, and a number of other pathological categories. The question of how this predisposition leads into neurosis must be considered still open to experimental check. But, presumably, the attitudes and patterns of behavior generated by this overprotective and indulgent early environment produce the neurotic hesitation—that is, the inability to make a firm decision either to give up some satisfaction or to accept its consequences fully—which has often been noted as one of the origins of the neurotic's unrealistic perceptions.

It is not difficult to identify the mechanisms whereby subnormal self-sentiment development (Q_3) becomes associated with neuroticism. Low Q_3 indicates insufficient shaping of and attention to a clear-cut self-sentiment, which helps to direct decisions and actions. It has been shown that persons low on Q_3 develop more anxiety, presumably because they get into more unstructured and conflicting situations by reason of lack of guidance from the more decided self-concept present in the high Q_3 person. Lack of integration follows because behavior is not referred as readily to a defined self-concept.

Similarly, operational explanations have been put forward for the action of various new source traits identified through this experimental approach. The hypotheses they have given rise to have already been put to experimental check in some cases. Certain statistically significant source trait score differences have been found among various pathological groups that have resulted in certain diagnostic potencies for the scales concerned. In addition, rich theoretical developments have occurred with respect to these concepts that require further validation from measurement and experimental findings.

Some clinicians may justifiably feel that, in terms of stimulating clinical research, the approach of the psychometrists has been unduly cautious. Specifically, most experimentalists have been very conservative in speculating about the nature of these entities. Although there is

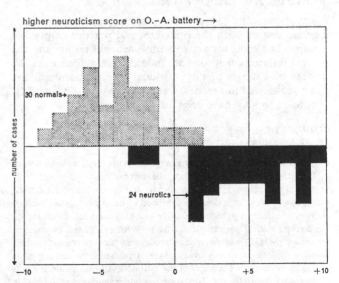

FIGURE 1. Frequency histogram of the linear discriminant function, showing degree of diagnostic separation obtainable for 30 normal and 24 neurotic subjects on objective test personality factors. (From Cattell, R. B. *The Scientific Analysis of Personality*, p. 331. Penguin Books, Baltimore, 1965.)

no question that these functional entities are real, one hesitates to name and theorize about them until additional criterion evidence has appeared. And this evidence has not appeared nearly as rapidly as it should because of the communication gap between the clinicians—who have been inclined, when they take to testing, to use some clinically derived test, regardless of its factorial base in research—and the statisticians. The statisticians, whose skills and realm of action have not included the trial of these tests in clinical situations or the testing of them against psychiatric diagnoses, have in the main constructed factor-pure tests—and then simply left them in the clinician's lap. However, now that these factored scales and batteries have been made available in formal publications in such instruments as the 16 PF, the HSPQ, the IPAT Anxiety scale, the various factor depression scales, the Objective-Analytic Battery, and the Motivational Analysis Test (MAT), one can anticipate a more rapid accumulation of checks against standard psychiatric diagnostic judgments and evaluations of therapeutic gain. From the theoretical point of view, these checks will result in a much greater understanding of each functionally unitary source trait, which lacks definitive interpretation with respect to its relationship to age, family background, neurological associates, and the degree to which it may be modified by therapeutic procedures.

As far as questionnaires are concerned, it has been recognized for some time that, although the 16 PF factors—either scored as primaries or combined in such secondaries as anxiety, exvia, and independence—function well in diagnosing the various forms of neurosis, behavior disorders, homosexuality, and drug addiction (Cattell et al., 1970), they are not sufficient to give full separation of the psychoses. For this purpose the Clinical Analysis Questionnaire (CAQ) or the Minnesota Multiphasic Personality Inventory is necessary, although the CAQ is preferable because, along with its 12-scale scores of a psychotic (definitely pathological) nature, such as schizophrenic and psychopathic scales, it retains the measurement of normal personality dimensions, as in the 16 PF. This finding that the 16 PF is adequate for neuroses, incidentally, fits the now generally accepted theory that neurosis is explicable by normal functions in disequilibrium, but psychosis is a disease process of a distinct and more fundamental kind. The CAQ is able, in its 16 factors corresponding to the 16 PT, to tell about the prepsychotic or apsychotic personality—for example, it shows that the schizophrenic is unusually introverted. But at the same time it tells in the remaining scales the extent of abnormality on specific psychotic disease processes.

Therapeutic Guidelines

Any personality theory worthy of the name should have intimate contact with the principles and practice of psychotherapy. The traits connected with functional testing and the general intersection theory do, indeed, give guidance on the strategy and tactics of the individual therapeutic procedure. But discussion of this relationship also reveals a gap—namely, in relation to what have been called unique traits.

COMBINATION OF SOURCE AND SURFACE TRAIT MEASUREMENTS

Attention must be focused for a moment on the relationship between surface and source traits. Before the advent of basic research in personality structure as implemented by the factor analytical experiment, most psychological scales consisted of measurements of surface traits or of attempts to relate behavior to a particular test by a kind of blind empiricism. For example, the Minnesota Multiphasic Personality Inventory (MMPI) was directed to syndromes (surface traits) that had been recognized previously by the psychiatrist. Thus, the test served as an aid in assessing the severity of the symptoms of that syndrome in a given case. Essentially, the Rorschach has had a similar aim: to provide independent evidence as to the severity of a particular syndrome and thereby help to classify the patient's disorder. Ultimately, a host of clinical psychologists discovered many blind empirical relationships between pathological syndromes and response to inkblots.

This approach to diagnosis, through special-purpose tests, is the exact opposite of the goal and orientation of the general-purpose structural test. In the latter, meaningful structures are found first, and tests are then directed to the elucidation of these concepts. However a surface trait, such as an MMPI scale may offer, can be as much a natural structure as a source trait outlined in the 16 PF test, for example. Therefore, some reference must now be made to the possible advantages of insightfully combining surface and source trait measurements in diagnosis. It is denied by psychologists, such as Wiggins, who have examined the MMPI by correlations that its scales have the homogeneity required by the surface trait definition. But in a clinical sense they may have the homogeneity of correlations with actual psychiatric case syndromes. A certain correlation cluster or surface trait such as the severity of a conversion hysteria syndrome, may be created by several fairly different patterns of source traits. This can be illustrated by the two following specification equations, each of which describes a group of anxiety reaction symptoms of the same severity. The first makes the general statement that, typically, anxiety (a in the equation) is due $-.4$ to ego strength ($+.4$ to ego weakness), $+.5$ to guilt proneness, and $+.5$ to ergic tension (frustrated drive level). Other factors are omitted for simplicity of illustration.

$$a = -.4C + .50 + .5Q_4$$

One can now take two persons, J and K, with the following scores on the 16 PF test:

	C	O	Q_4
J:	.5	.2	.8
K:	.5	.8	.2

When these values are substituted for C, O, and Q_4 in the specification equation, one gets the following result:

$$a_j = (-.4 \text{x} .5) + (.5 \text{x} .2) + (.5 \text{x} .8) = .3$$
$$a_k = (-.4 \text{x} .5) + (.5 \text{x} .8) + (.5 \text{x} .2) = .3$$

In one case this high anxiety reaction score of 3 (0 is average) can be ascribed to a higher guilt proneness, and in the other case it can be ascribed to a greater ergic tension. In general, this shows that the same surface trait score (overt symptom level) can be understood in terms of different source trait profile scores. The latter provides the understanding essential for effective therapeutic intervention, and the whole movement of recent years to discount the docketing of cases by surface trait scores rests on this fact. On the other hand, experimental examination of the personality factor profiles of psychiatric patients assigned to a given syndrome group does reveal a certain similarity of profiles. For example, neurotics tend to be low in ego strength and surgency, high in ergic tension (Q_4), high in guilt proneness (O factor), and high in premsia (I factor). This still leaves enough room for individual differences. In one patient the level of overt severity of symptoms—that is, the surface traits—may be accounted for by a marked ego weakness and a relatively minor guilt reaction; in another patient, the test results may show that, although the patient's ego strength is not deficient to any conspicuous degree, his reaction is much more severe.

Scores expressed simultaneously in surface and source trait structures should be of great value to the therapist in planning his campaign of therapy for the individual patient. Table III provides the weights necessary to estimate the typical MMPI surface trait scores from the 16 PF source traits. Thus, the former can be analyzed in terms of the latter. To date, this computational approach has had relatively little impact on psychiatric practice. However, several articles have appeared in the literature in which a different prognostic outcome has been established experimentally on the basis of one person's source trait profile as compared with another's when the actual syndrome measurement by a surface trait scale, such as the MMPI, has been equally severe in both cases and indistinguishable. This does not mean that surface trait measurement, such as the MMPI, has been equally severe in both cases and indistinguishable. This does not mean that surface trait measurement, such as the MMPI, should be dropped. The purpose of this discussion is to point up the value of a good two-handed use of

TABLE III

Predictions (Average Makeup) of MMPI Surface Trait Scales in Terms of 16 PF Source Trait Scale Scores with Various Attenuation Corrections

For any row in the figures on 16 PF trait measures, the weights (rounded to one decimal) are given to apply to the 16 PF source trait scores to get the best estimate of the MMPI surface trait scale. The values in the last four columns are the multiple correlations, showing how far the 16 PF can be expected to estimate the surface syndromes. For example, psychasthenia and anxiety are fairly well estimated, but hysteria and masculinity-femininity are not. These values are based on studies of a normal group of three cases and should be taken as tentative until checked against the findings derived from investigation of a mixed group of normal and clinical subjects. $N = 300$.

MMPI Surface Trait Estimates	Weights on 16 PF Source Trait Measures																Theoretical Value with Reliability Corrections			
	A	B	C	E	F	G	H	I	L	M	N	O	Q_1	Q_2	Q_3	Q_4	Corrected for MMPI Scale Unreliabilities Only	Corrected for 16 PF Scale Unreliabilities Only	Corrected to Ideal Scales for Both	Uncorrected
Anxiety	0	0	−1	−2	0	0	−1	0	0	0	0	2	0	0	−1	3	49	64	68	58
Lie L scale	0	0	2	−2	0	0	0	−2	0	1	1	−1	0	0	0	1	27	35	40	32
Validity F	0	−1	0	1	−2	−2	1	0	0	0	−2	0	1	0	−1	1	46	58	73	51
Correction K	0	0	1	−1	0	0	0	−1	−1	0	1	−2	0	0	1	0	37	49	55	43
Hypochrondriasis	1	−1	0	0	0	−1	1	−1	−1	1	−1	2	−1	1	−1	1	42	55	62	49
Depression	0	0	−1	−2	−1	−1	0	0	0	0	0	1	−1	0	0	2	32	36	47	32
Hysteria	0	0	1	−2	0	−1	0	−1	0	2	0	−1	0	0	0	1	28	29	43	26
Psychopathic	0	0	1	1	0	−2	1	−1	0	1	1	0	0	0	−1	2	32	32	48	29
Masculinity-femininity	1	0	0	−2	0	0	−1	1	−1	1	0	1	0	0	0	1	25	33	38	29
Paranoia	−1	0	0	−1	−1	−1	1	−2	0	1	0	−1	0	0	1	1	30	36	48	32
Psychasthenia	0	−1	−1	−1	−1	0	−1	1	0	0	0	1	−1	0	−2	3	55	70	78	63
Schizophrenia	0	−1	−1	0	−1	0	0	0	0	0	−1	0	−1	1	0	2	48	66	75	58
Hypomania	0	−1	2	−1	2	−1	0	0	1	1	1	−1	1	0	0	2	33	35	48	32
Social introversion	−1	0	1	−3	1	0	−2	−1	0	0	1	0	1	0	2	1	47	52	64	47

surface trait (MMPI) and source trait (16 PF) measurements in what has been called psychometric depth analysis. One needs to ascertain as accurately as possible both the severity of the actual symptoms and what combination of source traits is most involved in their production. The typical relationships for general surface-source traits have already been established for the average patient, as indicated in Table III.

Knowing the causal nexus in a particular patient at the level of source trait structure is of obvious value from both a theoretical and practical standpoint. It can be illustrated from actual measurements by the work of Pierson and Kelly (1963) on young delinquents. This study showed that in a group of delinquents whose antisocial behavior (surface trait) was equally severe, those with greater ego strength were less likely to modify their behavior in the foreseeable future. On the other hand, subjects who scored high on D factor (excitability) were more likely to return to normal behavior. The obvious conclusion to be drawn here is that high D factor may result in antisocial, impulsive, behavior, although there is really no serious dynamic (antisocial tendency) distortion in character structure. On the other hand, if the person has settled down to socially maladjusted behavior and achieved high ego strength, the reconstruction of his modes of reaction is going to be more difficult because he has a well-formed ego and is experiencing comparatively little anxiety. The theories concerning the treatment of delinquency arising from this quantitative experimental approach, as stated by Pierson and Kelly, have turned out to be quite antithetical to those developed on previous purely clinical grounds. Theories based on clinical observation have treated the delinquent as a neurotic who is acting out. As such, he was considered a candidate for the same therapeutic approach, including the reduction of anxiety. The experimental results that showed that delinquents were actually deficient in anxiety led Pierson to argue, instead, that the first task in therapy is to increase the anxiety level of the delinquent, and his results seem to justify this approach.

Precise practical applications of the intersection model theories require far more survey research than has yet been accomplished, research that focuses on discovering specification equations for a wide variety of pathological behaviors. That is, one needs to know which personality source traits are involved and to what quantitative extent

in response to a wide variety of standard life situations, such as occupation, clinical settings, marriage, and the family. This is a considerable undertaking and can only be accomplished if psychiatrists provide more extensive encouragement in getting systematic measurements than they have to date. Specific theories about the role of particular source traits in certain disorders already exist, but the cautious therapist is not going to feel that he can depend on them until the necessary measurement relations have been cross-validated by larger samples.

OBSERVATION OF INDIVIDUAL CONFLICTS AND MEASUREMENT OF COMMON SOURCE TRAITS

There is a theoretical difficulty in reconciling observations of conflicts and fixations that are specific and idiosyncratic to the patient with measures of source traits that are by definition common forms. Is patient X's symptom formation to be related to a sexual trauma at age 3 or to a low score on the ego strength factor (C), and what bearing does the answer to the question have on therapeutic techniques?

When the factor analyst studies individual differences and correlates behavior measures, he is, essentially developing concepts of common *traits*. That is to say, the intelligence or the anxiety he is measuring is thought to have the same typical pattern for all people, as a measure of mass does for all objects; therefore, he ignores certain variations in form in the individual person. He does not ignore them completely, however, for to a great extent the peculiarity of expression visible in one source trait is due to the fact that it is combined in particular measures with some other source trait. For example, in the expression of dominance of a person rated high on the common dominance trait who is also high on the common measure of anxiety, there is some measure of anxiety, some qualities of rigidity, and so on that are not present in the person who scores at the same level on the dominance trait but at a far lower level on the anxiety trait. In short, a great deal of what is recognized as the uniqueness of the person can be adequately represented by his unique combination of scores on absolutely common traits.

On the other hand, one must also recognize unique traits, particularly in the dynamic field and in regard to the patient's interests. For example, the interest of a person in the house in which he was born and in the sexual life of his grandmother are continua on which other people cannot be given any real score. At best, one can say that the rest of humanity has a zero score on this scale, and a scale that is useful to only one person is not very useful. One of the most common causes of misunderstanding between the psychometrician and the psychiatrist is that the psychometrician is rarely concerned with unique traits, and the psychiatrist has not grasped the conceptual distinction between a common trait and a unique trait. A good deal of clinical work is concerned with the immediate observation of unique traits, and this concern is apt to obscure the fact that in the long run the psychiatrist may have to give more attention to common traits. For example, initially, the clinician may be interested in the specific dynamic conflicts and personal history fixations indicated above, but his ultimate objective is to raise the level of the common trait of ego strength and to reduce, say, the level of the common trait of anxiety. Obviously, he must attend to the idiosyncratic and cultural attachments in which a common trait, such as the sex drive or the superego, has become entangled; but his final concern is with a general economics of energy that produces changes that can be recognized by measurements of the massive common traits.

Parenthetically, there exist potent but costly ways of objectively exploring and measuring individual unique trait structure, dynamic or otherwise—notably, through what has been called "P technique." P technique repeats a battery of measures on the patient for, say, 100 days; his scores are then correlated over time, revealing the functionally unitary factors. When ways can be found to simplify these research approaches for routine application, one hopes that there will be a more extensive use of measurement in psychiatry in regard to the structure and strength of the unique traits. Meanwhile, psychiatry can go a long way in terms of common traits alone, provided the psychiatrist recognizes that both unique and common patterns exist and that the direct manipulation of the unique trait may frequently contribute to change in the common trait measurement.

SPECIFICITY OF INDIVIDUAL CONFLICTS

In principle, the specificity of conflicts and fixations in the individual patient is no different from the specificity of form of a house. A unique dwelling does not prevent the builder or carpenter from using his knowledge of common materials to construct or manipulate the structure of the house. Similarly, one can account for much of a unique psychological structure in terms of different quantitative combinations of common traits. But in the last resort one finds attachments that are unique to the individual person and his history.

Application of Dynamic Calculus to Conflict Measurement

If the universal applicability of mathematical-statistical methods to the discovery of structure is valid, then the dynamic, interest-motivation aspects of personality should also admit of an analysis at least equal in precision to that based on clinical

methods. Developments from such research, under the name of "dynamic calculus," have fully justified these expectations.

The two main devices for dynamic analysis that were developed primarily in the clinical field—namely, free association and hypnotism—have been based mainly on the verbal report of the patient. This is true of the early contributions of the psychometrists as well. Tests of interest, such as the Strong and the Kuder, and approaches to conflict evaluation through such devices as the ordinary questionnaire have also depended on the patient's verbal self-evaluation. It is true that, in principle, the evaluation in free association is at a more sophisticated level than are the self-statements about occupational interests in the Strong Interest Test, for example; but, ultimately, both depend on verbal and self-directed evaluation.

In projective tests the psychologist has offered the psychiatrist an avenue to dynamic trait measurement that is somewhat more sophisticated. Unfortunately, it has also proved very unreliable, as numerous studies of the Thematic Apperception Test (TAT) and other projective tests have shown. A fundamentally different approach from all of these began when some 90 different objective devices for measuring motivational strength—ranging from measures of perceptual distortion to ego defense mechanisms, through information and physiological responses; such as blood pressure and galvanic skin reflex—were subjected to factor analysis in order to identify their components. One cannot assume that all motivational manifestations have a single underlying factor. The results show seven types of motivation components that appear regularly, no matter how diverse the content of interest may be. This finding has permitted the measurement of motivational factors by tests that can themselves be construct validated against the factors. From such objective measures the generalizations that are commonly called the dynamic calculus have emerged.

At present, the nature of the seven distinct primary motivational components is not fully understood. One theory believes them to be the contributions to any interest emanating from the id, the ego, the superego, physiological (autonomic) response, complexes, and certain other sources—that is, the sum total of interest in any response or course of action. For example, wanting to succeed in one's profession is analyzed, by such a battery of tests as the MAT, into relative strengths in these components. However, more recent investigations have shown that for both adults and children the seven components fall into two groups; to be precise, they are organized by two second-order factors. From their nature these second-order factors have been called, respectively, the integrated and the unintegrated components in interest. Thus, a U and an I score can be assigned by the battery to the strength of any interest in any given course of action. Such subtests as autism, perceptual distortion, and galvanic skin response are found to contribute to the unintegrated component, and such responses as word association, information, and penetrating perception of jumbled sentences contribute to the integrated component.

Current theory in this area favors the view that the unintegrated component, although not wholly unconscious, corresponds to many manifestations that have been clinically described as emanating from the unconscious and has to do with the component of interest that has never found any reality testing. On the other hand, the integrated component in the battery corresponds to interest that has been tested out, invested in adjusted performances, educated, and integrated with the self-concept. These two components show relatively little correlation in any person, but Sweney's work (Sweney and Cattell, 1964) suggests that, in general, a high magnitude of the unintegrated relative to the integrated component score occurs whenever there is conflict in that particular drive or need area. The validities of these batteries are not yet raised to the same level as those familiar in ability batteries, and their reliabilities are lower, but experiment is broad enough to show that these factor structures exist, and promising beginnings have been made toward their theoretical interpretation.

Being able to measure interest strength by objective tests is, however, only a beginning. The next step is to apply such a battery over a wide array of the typical person's life interests to attempt to correlate the grouping and structuring of action-interests.

DYNAMIC STRUCTURE FACTORS

Suppose a battery of half a dozen objective subtests (to give a single intensity of interest score), applied to about 300 normal subjects, is made for each of about 50 attitudes and interest areas. The 50 widely sampled attitudes each measured by a score on the total battery, are then correlated. Through factor analysis one then has the basis for discovering empirically the way in which interests are commonly interrelated in the culture. The factor analysis of such matrices has yielded about 20 distinct factors, which are called "dynamic structure factors" to differentiate them from the motivational component factors just described. The motivational component factors are groupings within measurement devices, which hold over all areas of interest, whereas the dynamic structure factors are statements about the way in which interests fall into some functional unities.

The main result of the dynamic calculus research, as applied to dynamic structure factors, has been the finding that interest factors are essentially biological drives, on the one hand, and sentiments or aggregates of interests, acquired by education, about certain objects and institutions, on the other hand. These two distinct kinds of dynamic structure factors must be taken into account in almost any area in which one works. One consequence of this work has been that the theorizing about the nature of drives in man is no longer on a speculative basis; it is now based on experimental verification by suitable calculation. This work seems to have verified the psychoanalytic, rather than the biological, position that there are two distinct sexual needs, which Freud described. One, which is directed toward object love, is mainly heterosexual in character; the other is narcissistic in character.

On the other hand, this research has not supported the list of drives hypothesized by Murray (1938). In fact, among the schemas adopted in various historically important writings, McDougall's (1926) analysis is closest to the experimentally based structures. In particular, it disagrees with the Freudian reduction of all drives to merely two or three instincts. It may be that libido, Thanatos, and so on will yet appear as patterns at a high order of factor analysis, but initially one certainly gets no less than 9 or 10 drives, including the two sex drives, fear, gregariousness, curiosity, parental protective behavior, self-assertiveness, pugnacity—a picture that is more closely akin to what the ethologists have observed in the primates. To avoid confusion with instincts, these new, empirical patterns have been called "ergs," and the measures have subsequently been set up for them in terms of the objective motivational devices have been called measures of ergic tension level.

In terms of the mathematical model, these findings can be brought into exactly the same framework as the general personality source traits. Thus, a particular attitude-interest—that is, a strength of interest as evidenced by responding with a particular course of action in a particular situation, such as "I want so much to go out with X"—can be translated into the specification form as before, namely:

$$I_j = b_{j1}E_1 + \ldots + b_{jk} + b_{jm1}M_1 + \ldots + b_{jmp}M_p$$

where I is strength of interest in course of action j; E_1 to E_k are strengths on k ergs; M_1 to M_p are scores on p sentiments; and the b's are the usual appropriate behavioral indices, found by correlation, which express the involvement of the drive in the action and so on.

The factoring of objective dynamic measures to reveal these b values amounts to a quantitative psychoanalysis. By this method one is able to say how much, although still in terms of common traits of all people, a given interest derives from certain ergic roots. Some interesting findings have resulted in this field, and several of them confirm psychoanalytic positions. For example, interest in smoking is found to be loaded in sex interest, fitting the oral erotic explanation. Some new insights into the nature of drives (ergs) have also emerged, in that a fair number of aggressive attitudes are found to be more loaded by the fear drive than by a pugnacity or sadistic erg as such.

Clinical research with these instruments, such as the factored MAT, and theory construction have only just begun. Ergs and sentiments, including self-sentiment, can be measured, and equations can be stated in two distinct forms—by the integrated component strength and the unintegrated component strength—and there are many indications that differences in these forms have special significance for understanding the dynamic makeup of the person, notably in regard to conflict.

CONFLICT

One of the most important propositions arising from the above theorems is that conflict over a given course of action should be recognizable by the coexistence of positive and negative signs in the specification equation. For example, in equation 4, the negative behavioral indices for E_2 and E_4 show that, to follow the interest I, one must lose satisfactions on E_2 and E_4, while gaining on E_1 and E_3.

$$I_j = .4E_1 \quad .3E_2 + .5E_3 - .4E_4 \tag{4}$$

$$I_k = .4E_1 + .2E_2 + .3E_3 - .1E_4 \tag{5}$$

Furthermore, the model supposes that the severity of conflict is measurable, in theory, by the magnitude of the amount of canceled (negative) behavioral index variance, relative to the total magnitude loading. Thus, in equation 4, there would be decidedly more conflict than in equation 5, indicating that the interest in equation 4 is an interest that, for most people, involves conflict, whereas the other has presumably developed in a less conflictful atmosphere and situation. The second equation offers .9(+) to .1(−), whereas the first equation offers only .9(+) to .7(−), a balance of satisfaction of +.8 versus +.2.

It also follows from this theory that—if one took a broad, representative array of the typical persons' total life interest, determined the amount of conflict in each interest, and then added the scores for the whole field of self-expression—a person who showed a high conflict score would be expected to be in a more frustrated and conflictful psychiatric state. In practice, to check this by experimentally determining the values for such a calculation is costly, because the behavioral indices must be determined by a separate experiment on each person. It requires the use of the factor analytical method called P technique. That is, it is necessary to do a factor analysis of the person, by scoring him on a wide array of interests each day for perhaps 100 days and then correlating the changes in these interests over time and identifying the factors that define the influences behind the day-to-day variation of symptoms. In principle, the multivariate experimentalist is doing something similar to what the clinician does. The two main differences between them are that the experimenter actually measures the changing strength of the symptoms from day to day and calculates co-variation to see what is connected with what, instead of forming his judgments about connections on the basis of chance observation and mere intuition. Yet the multivariate experimentalist has the same goal as the clinician who tries to establish interconnections by observing the co-variation of symptoms with the impact of daily events and the clinical interaction of psychiatrist and patient.

Some years ago, Williams (1959) undertook the monumental task of doing factor analyses on as many as a dozen subjects, each measured daily over months. Six of the subjects were patients in a mental hospital; the remaining six were normal control subjects. The results of this research clearly supported the theory—that is, the behavioral indices derived from the specification equations for the psychotics indicated a much higher level of internal conflict, disagreement of algebraic sign, than did those for the normals. Promising as this theoretical advance is, it may be several years more before the methods on which it is based can be applied to everyday clinical practice.

Fortunately, the demand for extensive calculation has now been overcome by the computer, so that it is now possible for a psychiatrist to hand his measurements to a technician, who then translates the dynamic structure of an individual patient into quantitative form within the hour. The difficulty lies in collecting the data; it has not proved possible statistically to get clear results after fewer than 100 days of repeated measurements. This is a lot of time to devote to one patient, but perhaps before long a short cut will be found. The advantage of P technique and its associated diagnostic methods lies not only in the objectivity of the findings and in the fact that it provides an index of total conflict but also in its ability to locate conflict by measures of severity of conflict in particular areas. Certain valid objections can be anticipated at this point. It is not enough for the psychiatrist—on the basis of classical psychoanalysis, but not behavior therapy—to identify clearly the areas of conflict. The patient must also achieve insight and awareness of his conflicts and their origins. But if the therapist can from an early stage in treatment, see more exactly where the tensions lie, this insight will be a great aid to him in bringing the patient to the point of achieving such awareness by the best-chosen routes.

To summarize briefly the potential advantages of the dynamic calculus theory and measurement: First, they equip the psychiatrist with a set of objective measurements in a field where the psychologist and the psychometrist previously had little but loose, projective devices to offer. Second, and more importantly, they offer a theoretical foundation for calculations based on these measurements to guide diagnostic and therapeutic decisions. In general, the dynamic calculus concepts do not differ radically from those that have been presented in a variety of psychiatric theories. That is, they describe a series of drives (redefined with the special properties of ergs), a series of acquired dynamic structures (such as sentiment with regard to parents, to occupation, and, above all, to self), notions of conflict, and integrated attitudes. What is new in dynamic calculus is the possibility it provides for measurement of the properties and the existence of formulas for calculation and prediction in conformity with these concepts. A difference from the traditional psychoanalytic conceptualization appears at certain points, notably in the discovery of two structures regulating morals and manners—the superego and self-sentiment—instead of just the superego. This inference is supported by the fact that the self-sentiment structure is elicited both through the medium of the questionnaire (Q_3) and through the medium of objective measures of motivation in the MAT. Similarly, these independent instrumentalities agree on the superego factor (G in the 16 PF Test).

Third, the findings derived from application of the dynamic calculus theory leave less doubt about the number and nature of ergs (constitutional drives). At present, the dynamic specification equations also take into account about eight or nine sentiment structures, but they give predominant weight to self-sentiment and to the superego among these learned structures. Measurement of ergic tension levels over time enables the psychiatrist to evaluate the patient's progress in terms of whether there is a building up or a reduction of tension levels and drives, and the same instruments throw light on development in dynamic structures. At present, the MAT measures 10 factors—five ergs and five sentiments. It confines itself to these factors because it is unlikely that clinicians will initially be prepared to handle a more complex predictive system than 10 variables. While the clinical usefulness of these factors is being explored, research should continue to focus on the remaining ergs and drives to improve the validity of their measurement.

In brief, the dynamic calculus theory involves the concept of a dynamic lattice, which is a map of the way in which interests within the person become subordinate to ultimate ergic goals through intermediate subgoals. Factor analysis is only one way of unraveling the structure of this lattice; however it is done, one cannot lose sight of the fact that the clinician seeks to understand this lattice as he attempts to bring about the patient's readjustment in terms of those interests and goals that permit greater satisfaction. Using the model of a lattice enables the psychometrist to avail himself of some of the mathematical treatments applied by electricians to understanding complex electrical circuits, as well as certain propositions in information theory. Another important adjunct of the dynamic calculus is the concept of a series of dynamic crossroads at which decisions are made in a necessary, typical sequence.

DYNAMIC DIAGNOSIS BY P TECHNIQUE

A dynamic lattice, as shown in Figure 2, has been considered so far as derived by factor analysis of objective motivation strength measures, as in the MAT, carried out from correlations in the general population, i.e., it is the common structure of sentiments and ergic goal subsidiations in our culture.

Useful though objective evidence on the main features of this dynamic map may be—e.g., in confirming the general hypothesis that smoking is partly sexual in satisfaction—the immense variety of human experience and attachments requires that a way be found to map the dynamic lattice structure of a single individual. The clinician at present uses free association, dreams, and some crude projective devices like the TAT to track these connections; but, as already mentioned, the theory of the dynamic calculus developed a technique called, among correlational methods, "P technique" (factoring the single *person*), for objectively deciphering dynamic connections. It requires about 100 successive days of observation on the client (its routine practicality can be considered later), and rests on the simple principle that if, say, the level of ergic tension on sex, and the client's interest, in, say, alcohol, are found to go up and down together, some real causal connection exists between them. Factor analysis is the necessary, more refined tool—applied to longitudinal correlations of measures of, say, 30 distinct dynamic interests over, say, 100 days—for teasing out the significance and nature of the subsidiations in the dynamic lattice and opening them to the dynamic calculus of conflict.

Birkett and Cattell (1978) applied P technique to the case of an outstanding man in his profession who was dismissed for severe episodic alcoholism. The objective measures were on the 10 main factors in the MAT (sex, fear, narcism, pugnacity, sentiment to wife, to career, etc.) plus a measure of interest in alcohol measured by the same objective devices (projection, galvanic skin response, reaction time in word association, autistic distortion of perception, etc.) as the MAT dynamic

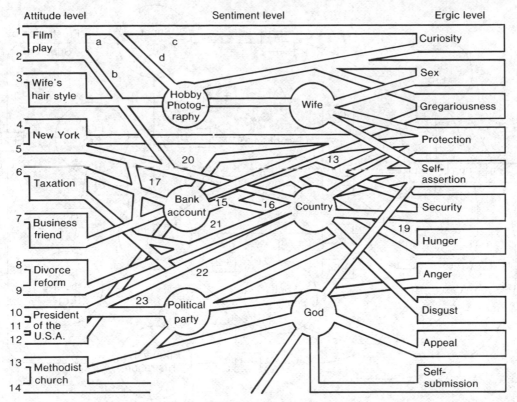

FIGURE 2. The form of a dynamic lattice.

traits. The upshot is shown in Figure 3, which is essentially a dynamic lattice and in which the numbers represent the magnitudes and signs of the actual correlations (convertible to path coefficients by hypotheses). The main conclusion here was that the frustration of narcissism and the self-sentiment were factors in releasing the sex erg, which (for historical reasons appearing in subsequent discussion) was incapable of satisfaction through his wife. The symptom, a yearning for alcohol, was thus indicated to be multiply determined by rising sex tension, situational deprivation of narcissistic and self-sentiment satisfactions, and (to the extent of .22 only) superego pressure.

Therapy—resting on the patient's gaining insight into these connections and reaching substitute satisfactions—proved successful where treatment by five previous psychiatrists, with virtually as many different theories, had always failed. The failure of clinical psychology to develop this research-proved, theoretical basis into a practicable procedure is probably due to the apparent statistical requirement for a sample of 100 days. However Birkett and Cattell (1978) have demonstrated that P technique can be cut down to at least 50 sessions without loss of the diagnostic result. In fact if P technique were taken in hand by developmental research, as, say, the steam engine was by Watt and Stephenson, leading in this case to automatic computer recordings and calculations, there is every reason to believe that this positive, objective method of revealing dynamic connections would far exceed the reliability of existing diagnostic procedures.

Measurement of Temporary States and Role Effects

The theoretical developments that have resulted from the use of correlational methods to locate functional unities in behavior have succeeded to the degree that experiments have continued to replicate about 20 factors in the general area of

personality and some 10 to 15 in the motivational area. The ultimate aim of research is to clarify the individual nature of these factors by relating them to specific criteria, by plots of the typical life course, by nature-nurture investigations, and by exploration of physiological relationships. However, some 30 years of basic research and much debate and refinement of methods with existing resources have been necessary before the point was reached at which instruments could be given to the clinician. Consequently, this last phase—in which hypotheses are developed about the nature of the factors according to various clinical criteria—has been belated. Even while some armchair theorists continue to manufacture alleged unitary traits or concepts and describe their predictive importance before they have even been confirmed as patterns, a dozen or more well-confirmed and measured factor patterns are waiting to be used and enriched in explanation.

ORIGINS OF FACTOR PATTERNS

Since it has become increasingly evident that the desire to interpret these confirmed, constantly reappearing unitary factor patterns is gathering momentum, one should inquire first about the general types of influence that can be expected to produce them. It is clear from the earlier description of schizothyme temperament, ego strength, ergs, and sentiments that some appreciable fraction can be considered to correspond to genetic endowments, probably with associated physiological variables, and that the pattern of behavior emanates from a gene or genes. For example, it seems from genetic research that the H factor (parmia—a toughness associated with predominance of the parasympathetic over the sympathetic reactivity) in the 16 PF Test can be so classified, and possibly the A factor (the schizothyme temperament) as well. In both instances this interpretation is supported by physiological associations and by the fact that they have high nature-nurture ratios examined in studies of twins. Thus, one might look to a temperamental mechanism—such as autonomic, sympathetic high responsiveness as apparently shown in the threctic (H-) pole of the H factor—for several such factors.

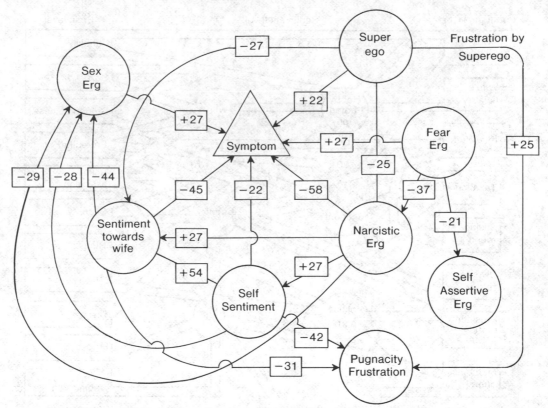

FIGURE 3. The dynamic lattice for a clinical case: Correlations and hypothesized causal path coefficients.

On the other hand, it is equally clear from the same initial nature-nurture studies that environmental influences must be largely responsible for other source trait patterns. Consequently, in these patterns the theorist looks to the family atmosphere, to traumatic experiences, and to associations with particular social institutions, such as school and church, as sources. Here one is presumably dealing with a set of habits, laid down by systematic learning experience, that appear in the same mold for everyone because of some standard social institution but to different degrees of intensity.

Like some ribonucleic acid template, the institution fashions the trait to much the same form in the human molecules exposed to it. To appear as a factor, however, it is necessary that people be exposed to the same experiences and yet adopt the pattern to different degrees. Thus, although the factor pattern one is dealing with in these cases may not correspond to some presently active force but to a deposit of learned habit skills representing a force once active, the pattern is still worth scoring as a unitary entity, for it remains descriptively and predictively useful to score all people on the degrees to which they possess it. A well-known example is what is called the crystallized general ability factor, G, which represents the extent to which intelligence has been channeled into scholastic work and skills and which enables psychometricians to define and measure the person's cognitive apparatus by the traditional intelligence test in terms of the typical pattern of verbal and numerical skills that the bright child picks up in the school system.

MEASUREMENT OF STATES

So far, it has been assumed that factor patterns represent relatively permanent traits, but at this point one needs to ask whether a particular pattern represents some transient state, such as a state of excitement or of depression, or an adrenergic response. At the onset, the formal mathematical-statistical models included process. The question is now being asked, how would a process, a changing state, appear in mathematical analysis. When one measures individual differences by testing 300 people at a given hour, one normally catches everyone in a transient mood. It is as if one took a snapshot that captured the deviations of that instant. Consequently, some factors thought to be traits when subjected to individual factor analysis may actually be frozen states.

The usual factor analytical search for structure—across, say, 300 people—is called R technique. Earlier, a different factoring (P technique) was described, in which one measures one person across, say, 300 occasions. There is also a differential R technique (dR) in which the 300 people are measured once today and once next week, and their change scores on all the variables are then correlated. From such P and dR technique experiments, one is able to discover how many dimensions of change are necessary to account for the complex changes in emotional state that human beings experience. When this analysis is done, some nine dimensions have been reasonably confirmed that represent state dimensions, such as anxiety, effort stress response, elation-depression, and general fatigue. Just as bateries can be set up for measuring traits, so collections of performance subtests, identified as highly loading such factors, can be built up into batteries for measuring the level at which a person stands on a particular state at a given moment.

Thus, a complete description of a person at a certain time requires not only scores on a set of coordinates corresponding to the common traits but also a position in the hyperspace defined by the coordinates for these nine states and others yet to be discovered. The measurement of relatively pure states that, when combined, describe the complex state of a person at a given moment has considerable importance for both psychiatric therapy and pharmacology. Previously in ataractic drug research, the precision on the side of the chemist has been matched by a rather vague evaluation on the part of psychologists with regard to the nature and measurements of the states induced by drugs. Within this new framework, it becomes possible to assign to any drug administered in standard dose an exact vector describing in terms of states the unique combination of changes it may produce. It also becomes possible for the therapist to use a state measurement—for example, on anxiety—in much the same way the internist uses a clinical thermometer to study the patient's changing adaptations in response to various therapeutic measures.

Despite the fact that they are still in a psychometrically rudimentary form, some theories have already begun to emerge in regard to these measures of states. For example, the newly acquired ability to differentiate the effort stress state dimension from the anxiety dimension offers a different interpretation of serum cholesterol changes. Scheier's (1962) simultaneous mesurement of distinct effort stress and anxiety factors has also had some interesting results. For example, the anxiety level of students in relation to examinations was found to be higher 2 or 3 weeks before the examination, and the anxiety level seems to fall during the examination itself, but the effort stress reaction rises as anxiety falls. Studies by Pawlik and others (1965) have related these behavioral state measurements to electroencephalogram records. And other investigations have revealed that serum cholinesterase rises in an anxiety state. Work has also begun on motivational states in terms of particular ergic tensions, as measured by the MAT. This work is only in its infancy, but it has considerable potential importance for clinical work.

Role modulation. From the standpoint of an adequate personality theory, a consideration of trait factors alone is not enough. One must consider the transforming effect of the situation, as well as the inherent nature of the person's traits. In the general class of transient states presently under consideration, it is particularly important to include those special transients called roles. How is one to know when a given piece of behavior is due to the essential personality and when it reflects an adopted role? The theoretical model handles this dilemma by conceiving of role as a dynamic structure in the person that is provoked only by a particular set of stimuli, which are usually related to social situations. In all probability, such dynamic factors are organized as facets of the self-sentiment, but just how this organization comes about has not been properly investigated experimentally. The theoretical possibility also exists that the role behaviors not only arise from this single factor but also evolve from some modulation it produces in certain personality factors. To illustrate, a policeman out of uniform may respond to a traffic violation according to his personality factor profile. But in uniform, under the same circumstances, a whole set of new habits appears, causing a response to an over-all situation, rather than the original focal situation, that may lead to an expression of personality that differs from the ordinary specification equation.

Whether one adopts the theory that a simple new role factor intrudes or moves to this slightly more complex theory, which has been called the *theory of personality modulators,* one adopts a model that accounts for both temporary role action and the reaction of the states. Role modulator action is likely to appear as a second-order factor among personality factors, one that appears only in the analysis of certain types of situations.

It is still too early to judge the extent to which this temporary modulation device in personality theory will prove of practical importance to the psychiatrist. However, the factoring of psychiatrist and patient interaction by Rickels points to the existence of a substantial role reaction factor that simultaneously affects both the patient and the psychiatrist in the interview situation. According to this evidence, certain patients adopt the patient role more completely than do others, and their dependent, demanding behavior evokes a more concerned reaction from the therapist. This reaction affects the therapist's rating of the severity of the patient's symptoms, to the extent that about as much statistical variance in the ratings of anxiety arises from the intensity of this role factor as from the actual patient differences in anxiety and symptom level as revealed by objective tests. It seems, therefore, that a personality theory without any model and mode of measurement of temporary states and situation-provoked role effects— that is, one based only on traits—is unnecessarily crude. These additional techniques for locating and measuring state components have their most obvious application in giving precision to the understanding of the psychological effects of pharmacological agents.

Structured Learning Theory and Psychotherapy

Structured learning theory, as developed by Cattell (1978), is an integral part of personality theory. It adds new features

and laws to classical, reflexological learning theory by the following: (1) It requires that the theory shall account not only for specific conditioned responses, as at present, but also for the rise of those well-defined structures which personality theory, as set out above, has long discovered and found useful. (2) It requires that the total personality be included in any attempt to predict learning, because the evidence is that over and above the particular conditioning influence the whole personality structure enters into the prediction of the learning gain. The last specification equation above (with *E*'s and *M*'s) and the earlier one with ability and temperament terms, can thus be transferred from describing a response to describing a gain in response—provided a reward term is added. (3) Appreciable confusion has haunted classical learning theory through the ambiguous use of the term "reinforcement" simultaneously for the amount of a *learning gain* and for the *reward.* Structured learning theory disentangles this and proceeds to an altogether richer treatment of the concept of reward. Because the dynamic calculus (discussed above) renders possible the recognition and measurement in structured learning of distinct ergic tensions, and reward is defined as drive tension reduction, the reward of any operant response can be defined as a vector of particular ergic satisfactions. Classical reinforcement theory begs the question of whether learning and forgetting under one drive may have different parameters from each other. However, a more important gain of structured learning theory is that it permits, by this ergic tension reduction analysis, a tracing of the subsidiation paths of the satisfaction of a given means-end learning experience (operant conditioning) to ergic goals and the satisfactions of intermediate sentiment structures.

For more precise support of structured learning theory in relation to personality theory, starting from the dynamic calculus from which it draws its more novel concepts, the reader must be referred to Cattell and Child (1975) and Cattell's (1978) latest formulation, *Personality and Learning Theory.* The upshot is that a learning gain, n_j, as engramming, is explained in this theory as a function of the strength of existing traits, including the arousal level of dynamic traits (all of which is represented summed to P—total personality—in the following) plus a function of drive reduction, E_r, of the distance of the response from its reward, $w(t_2 - t_1)$, and the cognitive strength of the S-R bond, n_{sr} at the time, $E_t n_{sr}$, thus

$$n_j = P + [E_t n_{sr} - w(t_2 - t_1)] E_r$$

This equation for the learning of a response potential (engram) to a particular stimulus-response situation *j* (at which reflexology would stop as a "conditioned response," but lacking the *E* (ergic) terms) is carried farther by structured learning theory into three laws of unity-producing action to explain the rise of the unitary dynamic trait structures known to exist from factor analysis.

In the application of theory to psychotherapy the situation today is essentially that reflexology ("behavior therapy") and psychoanalysis are at loggerheads. Structured learning theory, accepting certain truths in both, offers a release from the log-jam. On one hand it respects the experimental methods and findings of reflexology, and on the other it recognizes the reality of the dynamic structures, such as ego and superego, and the dynamic reward complexities of psychoanalytic theory. However, it continues exploration of the latter to structures and, by methods Freud never knew, quantifies those structures by objective measurement in the process. At the same time it builds on the former—reflexology—a second story of patterning laws.

The prospect opened by these steps, while illuminating and integrating, is one of almost appalling complexity. It considers personality change by learning as a multidimensional change produced by a multidimensional situation. First steps have nevertheless been taken to handle this complexity by the best first-approximating mathematical model, which uses the tool of matrix algebra, convenient to the computer.

ADJUSTMENT PATH ANALYSIS

The aim of adjustment path analysis and analytical adjustment theory is to set up a standard paradigm to analyze the possible outcomes from a basic, universal psychological situation. This elementary situation is one that begins with the stimulation of a particular drive in a particular situation. Cattell and Scheier (1961) have described this process in some detail in connection with neurosis; however, such adjustment path analysis theory could apply to any kind of dynamic learning. The paradigm is one of a series of choice points, at each of which two or more standard possibilities exist. These series of dynamic crossroads include such outcomes as whether or not the drive is frustrated, whether or not the barrier is attacked, and whether or not the barrier is overcome. A decision at one point leads to other possible choice points. In the event that the barrier is not overcome, the alternative is suppression or repression—or continual nonadjustive behavior. From these possible adjustment paths only a certain combination of choices will eventually terminate in the neurotic end path.

Granted that this adjustment path theory assigns certain consequences to certain experimental adjustments, one can proceed to an adjustment analysis theory, in which assumptions are made regarding the effects of particular choices on the dynamic and general personality structure. Indeed, the whole aim of the analytical adjustment theory, which includes these and other concepts, is to provide a framework within which personality learning—particularly the personality learning that has to do with the acquisition of a neurosis and its resolution by relearning—can be brought to experimental study through quantification.

This adjustment theory provides a framework of analysis and matrix calculations that is intended to furnish guidance in research designs and to permit statistical analysis of life record data that can serve as the basis for the formulation of laws about personality factor change in learning. It does not merely assume that exposure to a frustrating, traumatic, repressive, anxiety-provoking, or similar unfavorable experience influences personality, but it maintains that personality may exert a reciprocal influence over the choice of such experiences at the various chiasms or dynamic crossroads that the person encounters in the adjustment process. Admittedly, analytical adjustment theory is only a model that expresses in final form the mass of clinical and other evidence accumulated as to the general manner in which personality and situation interact. But if it should prove an effective model in the gathering and reduction of quantitative data, it will further enhance development of personality theories based on functionally unitary traits.

According to the model described above, analytical adjustment theory arises from the conceptual analysis of personality into functionally unitary traits and assumes that they interact with the environment. Unlike the reflexological approach, it assumes that any experience produces a multiple change in personality, potentially affecting any and all scores in the personality profile. This brings one to a consideration of the aspect of analytical adjustment theory called path transformation theory and introduces, by means of matrix algebra, the concept that the effect of any path in the adjustment path diagram provides a certain total pattern of changes in the personality factor profile.

The contributions to such volumes as the *Kentucky Symposium on Learning Theory, Personality Theory and Clinical Research* clearly illustrate that attempts by psychologists over the past 30 years to unify learning theory and personality theory have been far from successful, especially from the standpoint of the clinician. The central but perhaps insufficiently appreciated reason for this lack of success is that most learning theorists have conceived of learning purely in terms of a reflexological and atomistic model. By this is meant reflexology in the classical, Pavlovian sense, not in the sense of punishment and reward

for various drive expressions. Some of the latter behavior, by a feat of semantic acrobatics, has been subsumed by some reflexologists under reflexology.

The technical potency of the multivariate method is revealed, in that it can hope to elicit from actual life behavior, without manipulation, evidence of the causal sequences through which personality is affected by environmental learning. To date, this goal has produced only the statement of a theoretical position—namely, that new and different learning principles remain to be unearthed—for, as yet, virtually no concrete experimental evidence has emerged from this proposal.

Meanwhile, an attempt has been under way for some time to apply the more obvious reflexological principles to relearning in the clinical situation, under the name of behavior therapy. The work of such leaders as Wolpe, Rachman, and Costello has resulted in an impressive array of evidence of removal of symptoms by reflexological extinction methods. As yet, there is no clear indication of what this therapy does to the measurements of functionally unitary traits as such. Provided this approach uses a broader concept of learning theory than that stated above, it may either proceed to greater successes or provide clear evidence as to the areas in which it is not succeeding. Definite evidence of that kind would be an advance over any therapeutic technique currently available. It will almost certainly be open to criticism, however, if it is used merely—as it is now being used, for the most part—to remove some specific symptom, such as a phobia to a particular object.

Most clinicians are thoroughly familiar with the phenomenon of one symptom disappearing and another appearing when there has not been a fundamental change in personality structure. The implication of the theoretical position on personality that runs through this section is that whole source traits must be modified if therapy is to be considered successful. This position does not rule out the possibility that the amelioration of a weak ego structure (C factor), for example, or the reduction of the general ergic tension level (Q factor) may be affected by the cumulative effect of a number of highly specific readjustments. But, any general personality learning theory must operate on the basis of the measurement of source traits as a whole.

MATRICES FOR MULTIDIMENSIONAL LEARNING IN PATH LEARNING ANALYSIS

The reasons that classical bivariate experiment has spent 50 years—for the most part fruitlessly—in personality research are mainly: (1) Ethical and practical considerations forbid any major manipulations of human lives. The gap from man to rat is so large in personality that experiment on the latter is no substitute. Multivariate analysis, as in factor analysis, can work without manipulation. (2) Real life influences on personality are complex and multiple, requiring appropriate concepts and measurement, and multivariate analysis.

The present personality theory has grown from response to these realities, beginning with (1) handling the multiplicity by matrix algebra and by the use of vector quantities which express the given situation and the given person each as a vector (of trait scores in the person and feature scores in the situation); (2) introducing the concept of "life paths"—studying for a degree, getting married, working at an uncongenial job—which can be quantified as vectors in an assembly of the total life situation. The combination of (1) and (2) has resulted in analytical procedures, applicable to the individual cases, known as path learning analysis, adjustment process analysis, and determiner path analysis. These are at present relatively crude in that they omit calculation of intervening steps of gain by the first kind of equation above and give simply the expected learning change in a given personality trait from a given amount of experience of a particular path—marriage, going to war, succeeding in a profession. But they offer a tangible experimental link between personality theory and measurement observations.

Adjustment process analysis and path learning analyses. Space forbids more than a lead here to adjustment process analysis (Cattell and Scheier, 1961; Cattell and Child, 1975; Cattell and Dreger, 1978), and after a brief description the discussion will proceed to path learning analysis. This sets out to bring together personality and situation, each in its multiple dimensionality. On the one hand, one has the natural complexity of life experiences over an interval of time, analyzed according to an adjustment process diagram. On the other hand, one has the equally complex and composite personality change over the period of interaction with the situation, expressed and measured as change in profile on the measured source traits. From these two matrices (see Figure 4), the possibility exists of arriving by statistical analysis at an understanding of the specific effects that particular situations have on particular source traits.

Suppose that there exists, as shown in Figure 4, a matrix that relates the fate of a particular choice to the change in a particular personality factor. In addition, there is a record of the person's historical associations with such choices. The causal direction is presumed to be both from personality to choice and from choice to personality. But the two together can, if necessary, be considered simply as an empirical association. The second matrix in Figure 4, which is called a path frequency matrix, aims to express by numbers in the cells the frequency with which particular subjects—p^1, p^2, and so on—involved in the research have followed and repeated certain paths of attempted adjustment.

From these two matrices one can, by multiplication, produce a third, as shown, which indicates the extent to which a certain personality profile is likely to be associated with particular persons in view of this history.

CHIEF MATRIX CALCULATIONS IN ANALYTICAL ADJUSTMENT THEORY

1. *Calculation of Expected Personality Profiles from Record of Path Frequencies (Experience)*

Formula (i) C = AB, which can be set out in detail as follows:

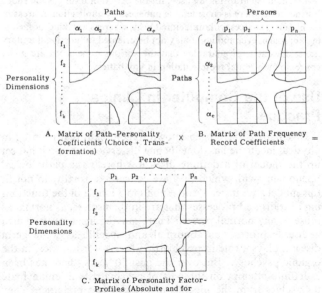

2. *Calculation of Path Frequency Experience from Personality Profile*

Formula (ii) $B = A^{-1}D^{-1}C$, where $D = AA^1$

3. *Calculation of General Path-Personality Coefficients from Experimental Data*

Formula (iii) $A = CB^1D^{-1}$, where $D = BB^1$

FIGURE 4. Chief matrix calculations in analytical adjustment theory. (From Cattell, R. B., and Scheier, I. H. *The Meaning and Measurement of Neuroticism and Anxiety*, p. 341. Ronald Press, New York, 1961.)

On the whole, this mathematical expression of analytical adjustment theory is nothing more than a means of recognizing that the experience of a particular path of adjustment simultaneously affects several personality dimensions in characteristic ways and that different persons characteristically attempt certain paths of adjustment with characteristic frequency. This calculation could be used primarily as a means of calculating what the associations of persons with different personality paths will eventually produce in terms of personality change. However, the calculations and inferences could be made in either direction. If one prefers to make certain assumptions, this calculation can be applied to the solution of unknowns in original personality to facilitate a desirable set of therapeutic experiences. Thus, the therapist should eventually be able to consider therapy or various alternatives in therapy as possible adjustment paths and to work out the effects these alternative therapies would be likely to have on the average personality or a given personality. For example, there is some indication that, quite apart from any other effect it may have, group therapy increases the extroversion of the patient, whereas some other mode of therapy may not do this, and chemotherapy, for example, may reduce anxiety and raise ego strength.

Whereas, in relation to the over-all structural theory outlined here, objective personality measurement and its clinical applications constitute an immediately available practical aid today, applications from the analysis of personality learning are entirely a matter for the future. No experimental use of the design yet exists; consequently, certain technical problems remain to be solved. But it is a development that is consistent with the theoretical position and one that would give new power to therapeutic procedure and planning if implemented.

Functional Testing in Clinical Diagnosis and Therapy

There is a widespread illusion on the part of both psychiatrist and psychometrist that the increasingly liberal use of psychological testing by psychiatrists in this generation implies a real use of true quantitatively based theory. Useful though psychological testing practices have been, their application has often had a nonorganic and even patchwork quality. This quality has been due to the fact that psychiatric theory itself originates from quite different sources from that of test theory. Consequently, tests have tended to be extraneous gadgets—for example, special-purpose tests, like the Rorschach—subordinated as diagnostic instruments to concepts that originated within a different frame of reference.

One can now hope that this relatively ineffective, scientifically unsatisfactory compromise is likely to change radically in the near future, as psychologists trained in functional testing—related to personality theory from experimental origins—become more active in clinical practice and theory. Although much of the new, quantitative theory has turned out to be consistent with earlier clinical impressions, which have thereby been extended and made more precise, it has also produced radically new theories and created a demand that theory and measurement now enter into a truly fruitful relationship.

To get the most out of these possibilities, perhaps the average psychiatrist needs to get over the inferiority complex—or, at least, the diffidence—with which he has often approached the technical aspects of psychological testing. In fact, he has no need to apply advanced statistics, such as factor analysis; he must only apply a logical principle that is close to his own—that is, the concept of a unitary trait. He needs only the simple algebraic formula that sees traits as acting in additive fashion and linearly in the specification equation. Similarly, although he uses his knowledge of chemistry to get a general idea of the composition of pharmacological products he prescribes, he would be quite unprepared to understand the steps of synthesis or the abstruse issues of stereochemistry.

Effective use of the proposed measures of anxiety, ego strength, surgency, intelligence, and schizothymia does, however, require that the psychiatrist comprehend the logical properties of the source trait concepts with which he is dealing and the theoretical setting in which they are embedded. That is, he needs to understand that these source traits derive from factors obtained by correlational methods; that they have a demonstrated functional independence; that they can be considered to interact additively—at least, at first approximation—according to weightings decided by the situation in which the action takes place. It would help, too, if he had some idea of second-order factors as influences that modify first-order factors and if he would undertake to become as thoroughly familiar with the nature of 20 or so factors and their typical nature-nurture origins and life history as he is with anatomy and the action of the principal organs in the body.

It has been asserted for some years, partly on the basis of Meehl's work, (1954) that six independent bits of information constitute about as much as the human mind can effectively handle in forming a composite judgment. This assertion is supported in the clinical field by the fact that there is no appreciable increase in predictive power when more than six bits are added to the clinician's basic information. However, in connection with the possible harnessing of computers to clinical work, this conclusion that information on more than six factors is lost must depend on the way in which clinical work is conducted. In terms of how many trait descriptions can be absorbed in psychiatric education, no one is going to make the absurd claim that instruction has to be restricted to half a dozen concepts. Still less will convenience and acceptability be allowed to dictate that nature be simplified to the trinity id, ego, and superego, which is for some the main attraction of Freudian theory. In factor analysis, too, there have been oversimplifications of the real personality factor position described here. If biochemists can keep 21 amino acids in mind and if chemists can remember more than 100 elements, it is surely no harsh dictum that the psychiatrist should be well aware of the properties of some 20 general personality factors and perhaps an equal number of factors in the motivational structure field. He may not be able to keep the scores on all of them in mind in making a particular diagnosis, but his psychological theory should include them all. And his quantitative and diagnostic use of them can be augmented and assisted by computational aids, beginning with the choice of tests themselves.

The choice of psychological tests is difficult for the psychologist and perhaps even more difficult for the psychiatrist, but their bewildering array is brought into some order by the standard Buros' (1966) *Mental Measurements Yearbook*, which, like a pharmacopoeia, condenses evaluative research evidence. Actually, the number of tests based on replicated oblique simple structure factor analyses is perhaps 5 per cent of the published total, and, if this is one's criterion, the choice is much simplified. However, in making a measurement of a factor, one has a choice of several media. For example, the superego strength factor (G in the 16 PF Test) can be measured by questionnaire, by objective motivation measure (in the MAT), or by objective tests (including projective, stylistic, and many other varieties of performance) in the O-A. The psychiatrist can also take his choice as to whether he will operate at the primary factor level, as in the factors in the 16 PF Tests and the HSPQ, or at the second-order factor level, using such concepts as anxiety, extroversion, and cortertia. Secondaries can be derived from primary scores by suitable weighting. The second orders enable one to use fewer scores but give rougher results, and for most purposes, especially with clerical or computer aid, primaries are better.

In using factors that psychologists have currently been able to incorporate in their tests, the psychiatrist may well ask whether the methods of investigation have been such as to guarantee an inclusion of most dimensions of theoretical and practical importance. The basing of the first sweep on the personality sphere concept has done much to ensure this guarantee, but undoubtedly some factors are not yet included in available tests. Research in this area of personality theory is almost certain to add a few new testable dimensions. For example, preliminary work suggests that there are no fewer than eight factors in the area of depression, and a pathology supplement of several new scales for psychiatric deviations is being added to the 16 PF test to expand its clinical coverage. There is also some value in measuring certain surface traits (symptom strengths) directly—for example, by the MMPI—while getting at the general personality source traits by such tests as those just discussed through psychometric depth analysis. There is, of course, room for improvement in all these tests, but the techniques for progressively moving to more valid factor measurements are being mastered to an increasing extent.

Granted a certain adequacy in source trait measurements themselves, the practice of clinical measurement will also require procedural revisions. The psychiatrist must expect that the time allotted to testing will have to increase. At the present stage of psychometric research, it is not possible to cover 20 or 30 personality factor measurements in an hour or two. Even so, the efficiency will be much higher; for testing, as it is traditionally carried out in mental hospitals and clinics today, is wasteful in terms of the number of demonstrably independent pieces of information it yields in an hour. Typically, the psychologist spends as much as an hour in getting just one factor, intelligence, and then spends only 5 minutes on some two or three other personality factors, each of greater clinical importance than intelligence. Whereas with tests of the prefactor era he gets two dimensions in, say, 80 minutes, the 16 PF test, which takes about 40 minutes, gives a score on no fewer than 16 dimensions, including intelligence. Of course, one could not recommend such an extreme condensation as measuring a factor in 2½ minutes by about 12 items. Indeed, it is strongly recommended that no fewer than 5 and preferably no fewer than 10 minutes be given to one factor. The compromise presented by the former results in the practice of using the 80 minutes to give both A and B forms of the 16 PF test; the latter makes possible the use of the full quota of forms (A, B, C, and D), thus giving about 8 to 10 minutes to each of 16 factors, including intelligence. No adequate reliabilities can be expected unless several equivalent forms are used, for the period of testing is too short. Furthermore, there is considerable unnecessary duplication of areas in traditional practices with unfactored tests, whereas any kind of factoring approach, even though it may not be oriented to functional unitary traits, does at least guarantee that the various dimensions are given approximately equal representation in any battery.

Use of the Computer in Clinical Practice

Psychiatrists have been known to complain that training in physical medicine has done them a disservice because it has set up the model of a definite disease, whereas the pathological phenomena with which they are concerned usually do not fit this model and, instead, correspond to a tangle in the functioning of traits and processes that are in themselves, as normal as those in any normal person. There may be instances in which a disease process, as abnormal and specific as some germ disease, plays a role in psychiatric illness—for instance, in the organic psychoses. But over the past 30 years, there has been a definite attempt on the part of psychiatrists to emancipate themselves from the incubus of the sickness prejudice. They have become disposed to question sharp-line disease categories drawn between normality and pathology and even to regard the behaviors of the psychotic as essentially normal processes that are merely exaggerated and out of control and context. The whole of the intersection model and the dynamic calculus theory that forms part of it are in accord with this view of psychopathology as a problem of disequilibrium and loss of adjustment, rather than one of the appearance of specifically malignant disease processes.

The factor analytical studies of mental hospital populations, as carried out by Dubin with Cattell some 30 years ago and by Tatro more recently (see Cattell and Schuerger, 1978), showed quite early that essentially the same personality dimensions can be found in psychotic as in control groups, even though they stand at significantly different absolute levels of score. Theoretically, pathology is either an extreme deviation in particular source traits on a normal continuum or, probably with greater frequency, an extreme combination of malfunctioning source traits that are not so deviate individually. Empirical evidence that could give a decision on the latter point has not been accumulated in sufficient quantity. However, one constantly sees suggested indications. For example, in the paranoiac it is not acute anxiety alone or rigidity alone but a particular combination of acute anxiety with acute addiction to the reduction of tension by the projective mechanism that seems to characterize this profile. Also, although the source traits of anxiety (UI 24) and regression (UI 23) are uncorrelated in the general population, they show specific correlation in neurotics. That is, there is not only the repeated evidence, notably from the work of Eysenck and the Maudsley group, but also from Rickels (1965) at Philadelphia and from Cattell's laboratory (1978) that neurotics are highly deviant on each of these factors; there is also evidence that anxiety and regression become highly correlated. The most promising indication for these findings is that some spiral of interaction between them is setting in. Still another empirical indication that this is a functional type of disorder, rather than the appearance of a disease due to some foreign agent, lies in the evidence, as yet sparse but significant, that under therapy the deviant measurements retreat toward normal values. If the process is reversible in this way and if grades of deviation can be found in the population, this is something best described as maladaptive or having to do with the economics of energy, rather than with some qualitatively distinct disease entity.

If a theory properly consists of a model plus a set of laws about its operation, the intersection theory and the dynamic calculus concepts represent only the beginnings of a theory. It is true that the model is clear and that it fits the facts closely enough to permit a great deal of effective research to be done. For example, it has sufficed to produce experiments that reveal the nature of several source traits, and it has been demonstrated that their interactions are close to the additive model. But all this has occurred too recently for the measurement devices to have been widely circulated among psychiatrists, so that only a brief early harvest from the use of the concepts and the measurements that arise from them is available as yet. Consequently, the body of laws about the way in which these factors behave is quite fragmentary. Compared with many other theories discussed in this book, the present structure inevitably lacks several necessary floors. To see the theory in its proper perspective, however, one may claim that its foundation is such as to admit in the long run a far higher and more effective architectonic growth than is possible from the nonexperimental and unquantitative theories. The later theories are still preeminent in the field of psychiatry in terms of a sheer count of adherents, but it is to be hoped that a progressive minority can appreciate what the radical difference of method here means in long-term promise. The architectonic growth believed possible will occur most readily if the communication barriers between the psychological model theorist and statistician working with the computer in the backroom and the psychiatrist working with the patient in the clinic are dissolved. The writings of such psychiatrists as Werry and Rickels (1965) and such psychologists as Cohen (1966) and Lorr do much to convey a sense of the gains possible from such communication. What the theoretical development most needs at the present moment are a clear grasp of the particular source trait concepts (temperamental and dynamic) by psychiatrists and an application of these concepts in relation to the rich clinical criteria to which they alone have ready access and in relation to which new intuitive leads for confirmatory research are needed.

Two important matters have found little or no space in this condensed section: the blending of a scientific theory with psychiatric art, on the one hand, and the specific aids that a quantitative theory can gain from the electronic computer, on the other hand. If little has been said about the art of psychiatry and if little space is given to illustration by individual cases here, it is because the primary purpose had to be to provide a highly condensed statement of a still tentative theoretical structure, with wide ramifications to be followed up. In the application of any theory, however precise and complete, there must ultimately be art and intuition. However, the theories described here are as different from the most common species of clinical theory in their scientific structure as they are in their suggestions for the art of application. Essentially, these developments imply that the psychiatrist may advantageously be using his art and intuition at a very different level from that of direct observation and interaction with the patient. Effective interaction at the human level with the patient is, of course, absolutely necessary. But the more developed model presented here means that the psychiatrist can be presented with an array of quantitative evidence of a hitherto unprecedented richness and precision and that he will need to develop his artistic judgment especially in inferring from this evidence what steps are to be taken in his immediate relation with the patient. He is being asked to stand off for a moment from immediate impressions about the patient and to view the patient's makeup and his environmental problem in the perspective of a complex quantitative model.

This approach will be seen by some as a threat and by others as a remarkable opportunity. The opportunity is inherent in the fact that, if the theories are truly quantitative theories, they should admit of all kinds of actual computations helpful in the diagnostic and therapeutic action with individual patients. This fortunate conjunction of the scientific advent of quantitative theories with the social advent of electronic computers needs to be recognized and seized. Here one has an opportunity to inaugurate a sensitive use of theoretically required computations without involving the time and brain power of the psychiatrist in the more routine phases of it.

People have been accustomed to an engineer's needing mathematics and to a physician's getting along without any at all. But as physical medicine and psychological medicine assume more and more the status of advanced sciences, they will necessarily require quantitative methods to be applied to the individual case for their most outstanding feats. Already this fact is becoming evident in the use of technicians' estimates on hormone concentrations and on basal metabolic rates and in calculations in physical medicine, in which the doctor either has some calculation carried out for him or makes a rough estimate as he proceeds. Because a human being has a more complicated organization than a bridge or an automobile engine, the psychiatrist of the future is likely to need to have more subtle calculations carried out for him than those carried out in engineering.

At a simple level, this impact of this theoretical position can be seen in the use of the specification equation given earlier. It should be possible to store in a computer the weights reached by research for a considerable array of behavioral predictions and prognoses. Profiles can also be stored for an array of patterns needed in diagosis. However, the psychiatrist may be in need of something more than a service in which the data are sent to the computer and come back in tomorrow's mail. The psychiatrist is surely almost as much in need as the surgeon is of information and analyses fed back swiftly. Practical decisions have been made in therapy in the light of information appearing at the same session or test results made an hour or two before. Fortunately, the physicists have given their answer to this type of need in the Telstar satellite, which is capable of instantly feeding back answers from a considerable bank of information to any location.

Probably, the practical use of such an information bank in computer calculations of diagnoses and dynamic probabilities is still one or two decades away. In recognizing this radical new direction as an important and likely one, one must also recognize that, as an organic outgrowth from quantitative personality theory, its effective development must depend on the shaping of theories and effectively predictive laws. What has been described here is only a clearing of the foundations, a statement of principles, and some fragmentary beginnings of the super-structure yet to be built. The computer technological development will follow easily enough. The more difficult task is to call psychiatrists and psychologists from their verbal theorizing to the quantitative methods that can build this superstructure of behavioral science.

Suggested Cross References

Freud's theories are discussed in Chapter 8. Learning theory is discussed in Section 4.3. Behavior therapy is discussed in Section 30.2. Psychiatric treatment is evaluated in Chapter 33. Psychological tests are discussed in Sections 12.5, 12.6, and 12.7. Computers and clinical psychiatry are discussed in Section 6.2

REFERENCES

Berg, I. A., and Pennington, L. A., editors. *An Introduction to Clinical Psychology,* ed. 3. Ronald Press, New York, 1966.
Birkett, H., and Cattell, R. B. Diagnosis of the dynamic roots of a clinical symptom by P-technique. Multi. Clin. Exp. Res., *3:* 240, 1978.
Buros, O. K., editor. *The Sixth Mental Measurements Yearbook.* Gryphon Press, Highland Park, N. J., 1966.
Cattell, R. B. P-technique: A new method for analyzing the structure of personal motivation. Trans. N. Y. Acad. Sci. Ser. II, *14:* 29, 1951.
Cattell, R. B. *Personality and Motivation Structure and Measurement.* Harcourt, Brace and World, New York, 1957.
Cattell, R. B. *The Scientific Analysis of Personality.* Penguin Books, Baltimore, 1965.
Cattell, R. B. *Personality and Mood by Questionnaire: A Handbook of Question-naire Theory and Use.* Jossey-Bass, San Francisco, 1973.
Cattell, R. B. *The Clinical Analysis Questionnaire.* Institute for Personality and Ability Testing, Champaign, Ill., 1973.
Cattell, R. B. *The Scientific Use of Factor Analysis.* Plenum Publishing Corp., 1978.
Cattell, R. B. *Personality and Learning Theory.* Springer, New York, 1979.
Cattell, R. B., and Child, D. *Motivation and Dynamic Structure.* John Wiley & Sons, New York, 1975.
Cattell, R. B., and Delhees, K. H. Seven missing normal personality factors in the questionnaire primaries. Mult. Behav. Res., *8:* 173, 1973.
Cattell, R. B., and Dreger, R. M. *Handbook of Modern Personality Theory.* Halsted Press, New York, 1977.
*Cattell, R. B., Eber, H. J., and Tatsuokas, M. *The Sixteen Personality Factor Questionnaire,* ed. 3. Institute for Personality and Ability Testing, Champaign, Ill., 1970.
*Cattell, R. B., and Scheier, I. H. *The Meaning and Measurement of Neuroticism and Anxiety.* Ronald Press, New York, 1961.
Cattell, R. B., and Schmidt, L. R. Clinical diagnosis by the objective-analytic personality batteries. J. Clin. Psychol., monogr. suppl. 34, 1972.
Cattell, R. B., and Schuerger, J. *The O-A (Objective-Analytic) Personality Factor Battery,* ed. 2. Institute for Personality and Ability Testing, Champaign, Ill., 1978.
Cattell, R. B., Stice, G. F., and Kristy, N. F. A first approximation to nature-nurture ratios for eleven primary personality factors in objective tests. J. Abnorm. Soc. Psychol., *54:* 143, 1957.
Cattell, R. B., and Tatro, D. F. The personality factors, objectively measured, which distinguish psychotics from normals. Behav. Res. Ther., *4:* 39, 1966.
Cohen, J. The impact of multivariate research in clinical psychology. In *Handbook of Multivariate Experimental Psychology,* R. B. Cattell, editor. Rand McNally, Chicago, 1966.
*Eysenck, H. J. *The Dynamics of Anxiety and Hysteria.* Routledge and Kegan Paul, London, 1957.
Eysenck, H. J. A rational system of diagnosis and therapy in mental illness. In *Progress in Clinical Psychology,* vol. 4. Grune & Stratton, New York, 1960.
Freud, S. A. *General Introduction to Psychoanalysis.* Doubleday, New York, 1917.
Horn, J. L., Cattell, R. B., and Sweney, A. B. *The Motivational Analysis Test (MAT).* Institute of Personality and Ability Testing, Champaign, Ill., 1964.
Hundleby, J. D., Pawlik, K., and Cattell, R. B. *Personality Factors in Objective Test Devices.* R. R. Knapp, San Diego, 1965.
Kentucky Symposium on Learning Theory, Personality Theory and Clinical Re-search. John Wiley & Sons, New York, 1954.
Kretschmer, E. *Physique and Character,* ed. 2. Routledge and Kegan Paul, London, 1936.
Lindzey, G. *Assessment of Human Motives,* Rinehart, New York, 1958.
Lorr, M., Rubenstein, E., and Jenkins, R. L. A factor analysis of personality ratings of outpatients in psychotherapy. J. Abnorm. Soc. Psychol., *48:* 511, 1953.
May, D. The separation of clinical diagnostic syndrome groups by the clinical analysis questionnaire. Ph.D. thesis, University of Illinois, 1970.

McDougall, W. *An Outline of Abnormal Psychology.* Methuen, London, 1926.
Meehl, P. E. *Clinical versus Statistical Prediction.* University of Minnesota Press, Minneapolis, 1954.
Murray, H. A. *Explorations in Personality.* Oxford University Press, New York, 1938.
Pawlik, K., and Cattell, R. B. The relationship between certain personality factors and measures of cortical arousal. Neuropsychologia, *3:* 129, 1965.
Pierson, G. R., and Kelly, R. F. Anxiety, extraversion, and personality idiosyn-crasy in delinquency. J. Psychol., *56:* 441, 1963.
*Rickels, K., and Cattell, R. B. The clinical factor validity and trueness of the IPAT verbal and objective batteries for anxiety and regression. J. Clin. Psychol., *21:* 257, 1965.
Scheier, I. H. *The 8-parallel Form Battery.* Institute of Personality and Ability Testing, Champaign, Ill., 1962.
Sweney, A. B., and Cattell, R. B. Components measurable in manifestations of mental conflicts. J. Abnorm. Soc. Psychol., *68:* 749, 1964.
Werry, J. S. *Automation and Medicine: The Views from a 19th Century Window.* University of Illinois Press, Urbana, 1965.
Williams, J. R. A test of the validity of the P-technique in the measurement of internal conflict. J. Pers., *27:* 418, 1959.

11.2 Other Psychological Personality Theories

WILLIAM N. THETFORD, Ph.D.

HELEN SCHUCMAN, Ph.D.

**ROGER WALSH, M.B., Ph.D.
MRANZCP**

Introduction

Erich Fromm, Gordon W. Allport, Henry A. Murray, Kurt Goldstein, Abraham Maslow, Gardner Murphy, Kurt Lewin, Frederick S. Perls, Herbert Marcuse, and Norman O. Brown are a highly diversified group of theorists, but they have certain broad areas of general agreement. Most notably, their orienta-tions are essentially consistent with the humanistic point of view. Three of them—Goldstein, Maslow, and Murray—were among the founding sponsors of the Association for Humanistic Psychology, along with Carl Rogers and other eminent figures. The humanistic movement in psychology aims at extending psychological theory and practice into many areas beyond the boundaries of behaviorism and traditional psychoanalytic the-ory. The movement is, therefore, often referred to as the third force in psychology, a term introduced by Maslow.

Goldstein was the first leading exponent and perhaps the most consistent advocate of the organismic approach, an exten-sion of Gestalt psychology that the humanistic orientation favors because of its emphasis on the individual person as an integrated, holistic unit. Perhaps a technical exception to that generalization is Lewin, who emphasizes the psychological or phenomenological field but is not concerned with the biological aspects of the organism. Some of the theorists, especially Murray and Murphy, stress the importance of developmental history, but many others focus on contemporary experience and conscious awareness in the present. In fact, the group in some ways resembles the ego psychologists in emphasizing the more conscious areas of personality structure and function. Most prominent in that respect are Allport, Goldstein, and Lewin. The uniqueness of the individual person, the key con-cept in the thinking of Allport in particular, is also central to the theories of Fromm, Murphy, Murray, and Lewin.

The writers as a group share another basic humanistic con-cept. They believe that the betterment of the human condition is at least theoretically possible. Marcuse and Brown, in particular, emphasize societal transformation. Most of the theorists hold a fundamentally optimistic view of human potentialities, maintaining that the limited and fragmented view of the human being that characterizes traditional scientific approaches obscures the actual range of his or her capabilities. Many of the theorists agree that the human being is being excluded from areas of awareness that are vital aspects of humanness and is living a constricted, unsatisfying, and unfulfilled life. In their attempts to reach a more inclusive view of the potential ranges of human experience, some members of the group are interested in Eastern philosophy and in higher states of consciousness, as reflected in the thought of both East and West, past and present. Areas such as self-actualization, creativity, love, joy, and levels of transpersonal experience become for them legitimate areas of psychological investigation, as well as major goals of psychotherapy, education, and day-to-day living.

Despite such areas of fairly general agreement, however, each of the theorists considered here has contributed significant concepts of his own to the study of personality, as well as a particular frame of reference from which to approach it.

Erich Fromm

Erich Fromm was born in Germany in 1900 and studied sociology, psychology, and philosophy at the University of Heidelberg, where he earned his Ph.D. degree at the age of 22. After completing his training at the Berlin Psychoanalytic Institute, he and Frieda Fromm-Reichmann were among the founders of the Psychoanalytic Institute in Frankfurt. In 1933 he came to the United States at the invitation of the Chicago Psychoanalytic Institute and later became one of the founders and trustees of the William Alanson White Institute in New York City. Fromm has been in private practice in New York for many years and has also been a faculty member of a number of colleges and universities, including Bennington, Yale, Michigan State, Columbia, and New York University. In 1949 he became a professor at the National Autonomous University of Mexico, where he instituted the department of psychoanalysis in the graduate department of the university's medical school. He was also founder and director of the Mexican Psychoanalytic Institute. Since his retirement in 1965 as an honorary professor at the university, Fromm has continued to commute to New York for his various teaching activities and other professional commitments. A volume of essays published in his honor (Landis and Tauber, 1971) paid tribute to his "lifelong efforts to aid us in putting aside the veils of illusion."

Erich Fromm—social philosopher, psychoanalyst, and personality theorist—has been labeled neo-Freudian and a humanistic psychoanalyst. He prefers to regard himself as a dialectic humanist. He has retained a strong interest in the role of social factors in determining personality development, and his early writings in particular show a definite Marxist influence. An essentially dialectic approach is still evident in much of his work. His later publications place increasing emphasis on Eastern and Western philosophy and religion. In a book of essays (Fromm, 1970), he anticipated publishing a fuller exposition of his still-developing ideas in a work tentatively entitled, *Humanist Psychoanalysis.*

BEGINNINGS OF INDIVIDUATION

According to Fromm (1956), the human being has been confronted with one basic problem throughout all ages and in all cultures:

how to overcome separateness, how to achieve union, how to transcend one's individual life and find at-onement.

The terrible sense of isolation that no one can escape as he begins to experience himself as a separate being gives rise to intense anxiety and a deep need to reunite with himself, his fellow humans, and the world. The whole process of his development depends on how he reacts to this fundamental problem.

Fromm finds a parallel between the developmental progress of the individual and of the whole human race. Both are seen as beginning in a state of deep peace and belongingness that comes from feeling completely at one with the surrounding environment. That primitive experience of unity is possible only within the shelter of what Fromm calls "primary ties," the protective bonds in which life begins. For the individual person, such ties lie in his close initial bond to his mother, on whom he is completely dependent and who cares for him without any demand for reciprocity. He does not doubt his safety, and he experiences no anxiety. The race felt similar peace and protection as long as it regarded itself as part of nature and of all that nature comprises. As the child is dependent and sheltered for some time, so Western humans during the medieval period remained under the wing of the Church, accepting unquestioningly its answers to questions about themselves, and their universe. The primary ties were not yet seriously disrupted. Fromm sees further parallels. As the individual person cannot remain a child forever, so Western humans at the time of the Reformation began the painful and frightening process of separating from their primitive unity and going toward independence. Once the process of individuation has begun, there is no hope of return to the primary peace for either the individual or the race. The primary ties are permanently shattered. At best, humans can only follow, however grimly, the way to true selfhood. They have become those most uncomfortable of beings: reasoning persons. They must, therefore, accept the fact of their separation, refuse to let anxiety force them to turn back, and continue on to full independence.

Once the human being has emerged from the primary ties, his one task becomes, as Fromm (1941) said:

To orient and root himself in the world and find security in other ways than those which were characteristic of his preindividualistic existence.

The proper goal of therapy, as of life, is to help him do just that.

THE HUMAN SITUATION

A man is in the unique situation of being partly animal and partly human, aspects of his being that Fromm maintains must be recognized and unified. As a separate person, the human being must accept many bitter facts of which animals are not aware. If he looks honestly at himself and the world about him, he is confronted with two major areas of challenge. The first area Fromm calls historical dichotomies—the many social and cultural tragedies that, being made by humans, can at least theoretically be overcome by them. Existential dichotomies, on the other hand, are immutable. Humans are subject to disease, loss, and death. The span of life is too short to allow them to reach their full potential stature, and, however far a person may advance, he knows what the end must be. Yet, Fromm (1947) wrote:

there is nothing for us to do but accept the fact of death; hence, as far as our life is concerned, defeat.

Although a person cannot change the essential paradox inherent in the human situation, he can deal with it in many different ways. He may, for example, choose to halt the process of individuation, attempting to regress to a parody of the primary ties by throwing away his frightening freedom and putting himself into a new kind of bondage. He will, however, only defeat himself. The primary ties are no longer available to him, and escape will merely destroy his realistic hope of using his freedom for his own well-being and for that of society. The only constructive synthesis for him is to emerge willingly from his prehuman existence, regaining his shattered sense of unity on a new and higher level. He can do so, said Fromm, only by accepting his separateness, going through the attendant anxiety, and becoming "fully born" (Fromm, 1960) as a productive being, finding a fair share of happiness and contributing what he can to his society and culture.

He may, however, be too terrified to accept the pain in which true individuation is born, adopting various regressive strategies in frantic attempts to escape from freedom. In so doing, he may find an illusion of safety but at the cost of frustrating his genuine potentialities, his creativity, and, in fact, his real self. A pseudoself, with pseudothoughts and pseudointerests, will seem to be his own reality. His genuine human needs will remain unfulfilled, for they can be met only in the freedom that he has thrown away.

BASIC HUMAN NEEDS

Fromm identified five intrinsic human needs that, he believes, must be met if a person is to continue to grow. He needs relatedness, a deep feeling of unity with himself and others. He needs transcendence, a sense of rising above the animal in him and becoming genuinely creative. He needs rootedness and identity, through which he feels he belongs and can accept his personal uniqueness accordingly. And, finally, he needs a frame of orientation, a reference point for establishing and maintaining a meaningful and stable perception of himself and his world. Those needs, to Fromm, are inherent in humanness, and no one can continue along the difficult path toward individuation unless they are fulfilled. However, a person must have a kind early environment and a beneficent society in which his progress continues. As society treats a person, so will he come to treat himself and society, for the health or illness of both are inextricably interwoven. The child needs external guidance based on what Fromm called "rational authority," which is democratic, modifiable, and willingly withdrawn when the need for it ceases. Such guidance prepares the growing child to accept independence, fostering a rational conscience that will direct him to what is human and good. Irrational authority, on the other hand, demands submission, rather than cooperation, and tends to induce an irrational conscience. Such a conscience becomes demanding and punitive, promoting guilt and anxiety and frightening the person into submissiveness. Lacking a true inner guide, he is poorly prepared to meet the challenge of individuation and is likely to turn aside into perilous detours.

All human beings are religious in one way or another, as Fromm (1950) used the term, a man's religion being defined as

any system of thought and action which . . . gives the individual the frame of orientation and object of devotion which he needs.

Religion, like conscience, can be either repressive or constructive. In its more authoritarian and immature forms (Fromm, 1960), religion is nothing more than an attempt to regress to

prehuman, preconscious existence. To do away with reason . . . and thus to become one with nature again.

The more productive forms of religion, on the other hand, help a person develop his specifically human capacity to reason, to love, and to work productively, reaching a new level of harmony with himself and others. Fromm sees the ultimate validation of a person's religion in the extent to which it helps him achieve a truly productive orientation. Fromm himself does not advocate any particular form of religion, nor does he insist that the term necessarily have theistic connotations. In fact, his studies of the world's great religions have been sufficiently open minded to lead to his statement (Fromm and Xirau, 1968) that the human experience potentially includes

what has been called "salvation" by the Christian, "liberation" and "enlightenment" by the Buddhist, and love and union by the nontheistic humanists.

Although Fromm's later writings have shown increasing interest in transcendence and mystical experience, he offers no specific guideposts. Everyone must find his own religion, for every human being must believe in something. To Fromm, each person's religion is the particular answer he gives to the basic question of the meaning of existence.

UNPRODUCTIVE ORIENTATIONS

Unless a person is willing and able to win through to freedom, his fear of separation and aloneness may be so intense that he resorts to what Fromm (1941) called "mechanisms of escape." Fromm conceives of many such escapes, including withdrawal from the world and engaging in grandiose fantasies at the expense of reality. Although such mechanisms may be of great importance in understanding a particular person, they are not of major significance from the social point of view. Fromm, therefore, lays greater emphasis on three major escape routes that he sees as prominent factors in the context of society: (1) The person may seek an authoritarian solution, in which he hopes to live through someone or something external to himself. The most obvious form of such a symbiotic life style is the sadomasochistic relationship, in which a person depends on someone else for his sense of personal adequacy and does not conceive of himself as a person in his own right. (2) Destructiveness, as a generalized attitude toward life, is an attempt to eliminate the source of perceived stress. In this potentially dangerous orientation, the person strives indiscriminately to remove all standards against which he may be unfavorably compared. (3) In automation conformity, the person tries to escape from being himself by becoming as like those around him as possible. Laying aside his own ability to think, act, and feel, he becomes painfully eager to live up to the expectations and wishes of others. That escape route Fromm regards as perhaps the least likely to be recognized and also as the commonest in modern society.

Once a person has turned away from freedom, he is headed toward an unproductive adjustment to life, the nature of which depends on the dominant mechanism of escape he has chosen. Fromm identifies four unproductive orientations on this basis: (1) The receptive character is the passive receiver who seeks a magic helper to solve his problems for him. He may seem to be friendly, optimistic, and even helpful, but his prime concern is actually to win favor and approval. (2) The exploitative character is also concerned with getting things from outside, but he tries to take them away from others. He is more aggressive, demanding, and envious, and he uses guile, cunning, and sometimes outright theft to get what he wants. (3) The hoarding character saves, stores, and puts away. He is distant and even remote toward others, values thrift, and may regard miserliness as a virtue. (4) The marketing character is the conformer who, feeling empty and anxious, tries to compensate for his uncertainty by gaining material success. His personality, being regarded as a commodity to be bought or sold, changes as the situation demands. Fromm regards all such unproductive adjustments as evil, because they lead to the loss of the person's good and ultimately to a corrupt and vicious society. Although he does not regard evil as instinctual, he does not deny the extent of the destructiveness of which humans and society are capable. His views on the sources of human aggression are elaborated in one of his latest books (Fromm, 1973). He has also restated in later writings his views on good and evil by identifying two opposing forces that he sees in humans: the necrophilous orientation, the syndrome of decay that propels a person toward death, and the biophilous orientation, the syndrome of life, which points in the opposite direction. Neither is thought to operate exclusively. Fromm (1964) maintained that

> each man goes forward in the direction he has chosen; that of life or that of death; that of good or that of evil.

PRODUCTIVE ORIENTATION

As Fromm believes there is only one basic human problem—namely, the overcoming of separateness and the transcendence of one's individual life—so he sees only one constructive resolution to that problem—namely, the productive orientation. Although he finds the potentialities for that resolution inherent in humanness itself, it is achieved only by the productive character. Fromm regards reaching this orientation as a truly gigantic achievement, and he sees many temptations to regress along the way. Nevertheless, those who do not yield to them have the hope of arriving at a true sense of belongingness and developing the peculiarly human genius for productive living, working, and loving. Productive love (Fromm, 1968) is the higher synthesis—the level at which the person rises above

> the narrow prison of his ego, his greed, his selfishness, his separation from his fellow man, and, hence, his basic loneliness.

At this level he becomes mature, courageous, and fulfilled. Fromm believes that productive love, being an art in itself, requires considerable practice. Once it is achieved, however, it becomes the actual expression of being alive. By it, the productive character's intellect and affect are unified, helping him to work for his own further growth and for that of society. Fromm sees a fairly consistent pattern in the development of the ability to love as the person proceeds from the narcissism of the infant to a sense of unity that is universal in its potential application. He also speaks of different kinds or levels of love that are possible in human relationships.

Brotherly love is perhaps the most fundamental form, inasmuch as it entails a deep sense of caring, respect, responsibility, and knowledge of someone else and is at least potentially reciprocal. Motherly love, on the other hand, is necessarily unequal, because the child needs and the mother gives. Motherly love is not, however, entirely exclusive, because it can be made available to more than one child. Fromm regards erotic love as perhaps the most deceptive form, being based by definition on exclusion, rather than on universality. It is the attempt of two people to fuse into each other and reach an illusory sense of uniting. Self-love can be either destructive or constructive, depending on whether it is false or genuine. If it is selfish, Fromm sees it as actually self-hatred, for it is merely uncaring and self-centered vanity. In the truer sense, self-love

and love of others become one, because each is really impossible without the other. The love of God is the highest form that Fromm recognizes. This love need not be theistic, because the term is used in the context of each person's particular religion. It is, therefore, an individual matter and is as diversified as is the love of humans. At the highest level, love of God and love of humans become unified, just as love for others and love for the self become indistinguishable.

The attainment of that all-inclusive love is seen as the final answer to the human dilemma, giving a new dimension to the human situation and raising a person to his full creative height. Fromm sees cause for profound pessimism in what the human being has become, without losing faith in what he may yet be. Despite the devastation that society has produced, he still believes that humans are capable of transcending their destructiveness and becoming genuinely at peace with themselves, with others, and with the world (Fromm, 1955, 1973, 1978). He makes no pretense that it will occur effortlessly, but he clearly feels it is possible through an evolutionary synthesis of rationality and spirit, and in 1976 Fromm concluded

> a new synthesis is the only alternative to chaos: the synthesis between the spiritual core of the Late Medieval world and the development of rational thought and science since the Renaissance.

Gordon W. Allport

Gordon W. Allport (1897–1967) was born in Indiana and did his undergraduate and graduate work at Harvard University, spending a year teaching at Robert College in Istanbul in between. He returned to Harvard to receive his Ph.D. degree in 1922 and was awarded a 2-year fellowship for foreign study. He attended the universities of Berlin, Hamburg, and Cambridge. He particularly referred to "the powerful impact of my German teachers" on his thinking (Allport, 1967). After a brief period as an instructor at Harvard, where he taught the first course in the psychology of personality to be offered in an American college, Allport moved to Dartmouth, where he spent the next 4 years. Returning again to Harvard, he remained there for the rest of his life. He became a major figure in founding the department of social relations, which provided an integrated program of psychological, sociological, and anthropological study and which Allport chaired for 18 years. He served as president of the American Psychological Association in 1939, of the Eastern Psychological Association in 1943, and of the Society for the Psychological Study of Social Issues in 1947. He was presented with the Gold Medal Award of the American Psychological Foundation in 1963 and the Distinguished Scientific Award of the American Psychological Association in 1964. During the last year of his life, he was appointed the first Richard Clarke Cabot Professor of Social Ethics at Harvard. In an evaluation survey of clinical psychologists conducted some years before his death, the impact of Allport's thinking in terms of influence on psychological practice was rated second only to that of Freud.

Allport was essentially an academician; his theories were based primarily on academic psychology, rather than on clinical experience. Some of his concepts opposed the prevailing scientific and academic thinking of his time, although many of them received increasing endorsement from his former critics. Allport made every effort to judge both criticism and praise with equal fairness. He was always willing to revise his theories whenever and wherever he thought it appropriate to do so. He was precise and scholarly in formulating his concepts and never lost his unusual degree of scientific open mindedness. His writings reflect considerable changes in his viewpoint over the years, and the wide range of his contributions attests to the breadth of interest that characterized his work. A complete bibliography of his many publications (Ghougassian, 1972) is impressive not only for its imposing length but also for the many areas included.

Allport's views have been described as humanistic and personalistic, and he himself agreed with both descriptions up to a point. He preferred, however, to consider his personality theory as an eclecticism that conceives of personality as "a unique and open system." An open system was defined (Allport, 1968b) as

one in which constant intake and output of energy occur . . . with two additional criteria: progressive internal organization over time and creative transaction with the environment.

NECESSITY FOR ECLECTICISM

Allport held that, above all, psychology should study a real person and not be satisfied with constructing an artificial person. No area of possible contribution to understanding human behavior should be discouraged or neglected. His own broad interests included work in such diverse areas as values, motivation, morale, prejudice, communication, expressive movement, handwriting, and practical questions in guidance, teaching, and mental health. All those areas, as he stated in the preface to his last book (Allport, 1968a), represent no more than a partial list of the many aspects of personhood in psychology with which he was concerned.

From Allport's wide horizon and inclusive emphasis, a psychology that would exclude religion hardly deserves to be called a psychology at all. Although he believed that formalized or extrinsic religion often "seems merely symptomatic of fear and frustration" (Allport, 1960a), a mature religious sentiment he regarded as a cardinal feature of many healthy personalities. Allport called such beliefs "intrinsic," a term he applied to those who serve their religion, rather than demanding that it serve them. Nor was Allport's interest in religious experience restricted to Western forms. He deplored the narrow perspective that fails to consider the many highly evolved thought forms of the East, noting (Allport, 1965) that

such ignorance of our Eastern cousin's mind is as dangerous as it is inexcusable.

Uniqueness is the essence of Allport's theoretical approach to personality, but he recognized the anomalous position of science in relation to the individual person. Science as presently constituted is able to investigate primarily groups, common areas, broad generalizations, and common laws. That methodological weakness restricts scientific study largely to nomothetic procedures that, at best, can construct an artificial man and must, therefore, violate personality as it really is. Science is unable as yet to deal adequately with the essential aspect of personality. Allport did not deny the importance of nomothetic investigations, and he acknowledged that his own research was largely of that nature, despite his conceptual emphasis on individuality. Allport's plea, therefore, was for the development of more suitable methods for studying the individual person by morphogenic or idiographic techniques, which would be capable of approaching the uniqueness that, for him, was the core of personality (Allport, 1968b). Despite numerous attempts to decide it one way or another, the debate over the appropriateness for psychology of nomothetic versus the idiographic models and techniques remains today and is one of the areas most frequently associated with Allport's name (Marceil, 1977). Allport frequently used this issue to support one of his major life aims—namely, to make psychologists aware of the effects that models of human behavior have on the type of scientific data subsequently gathered.

PERSONALITY AND MOTIVATION

For Allport, then, a science of personality must be based on the recognition that individuality is the chief characteristic of human nature. What he called "patterned individuality" is, therefore, a proper datum for a scientific study of personality. Everyone has his own unique growth potential, which will never be understood by merely adding up the various ways in which he differs from a purely hypothetical average. Instead, Allport (1961) saw personality as

the dynamic organization within the individual of those psychological systems that determine his characteristic behavior and thought.

Personality is what the person really is, the special way in which he works out his own survival. The personal formula is never static or complete; it remains a becoming throughout his whole life.

Allport regarded the self as a central point of focus in the psychology of personality, for sense of self is a person's only real guarantee of his own personal existence. Selfhood, in Allport's view, develops in a series of stages. The process begins with the early self of the infant, which proceeds through the awareness of a body to self-identity and then to ego enhancement. A sense of self-extension and a self-image is reached in early childhood, followed by a feeling of the self as a rational, coping being. From adolescence into adulthood, the person becomes capable of striving toward long-range goals with a stability and persistence of which a child is incapable. Allport regarded those stages of becoming as constituting the "me" that a person recognizes and accepts as himself. For that self-as-known, Allport used the term "proprium," a major concept in his theory of personality structure. Propriate strivings are thought to unify personality and enable the person to maintain his integrity of functioning. The development of the proprium, in Allport's (1955) view:

distinguishes the human being from the animal, the adult from the child, and in many cases the healthy personality from the sick.

Traits, in Allport's system, are not only the chief unit of personality structure but also the major dynamic source of human motivation. Allport (1961) defined a trait as

a neuropsychic structure having the capability to render many stimuli functionally equivalent, and to initiate and guide equivalent . . . forms of adaptive and expressive behavior.

He made several assumptions regarding traits and ascribed certain specific characteristics to them. To summarize these special features as Allport described them: A trait has actual existence. It is more generalized than a habit and is dynamic or, at least, determinative in behavior. It is neither independent of other traits nor synonymous with moral or social judgments. It can be seen within a person or distributed in a population. And, finally, it cannot be disproved by acts or habits that are inconsistent with it. Allport drew up this list early in his career and did not substantially change it. As his theories developed, however, the term "traits" was reserved for what he later called "common traits," those that characterize people in the same culture. "Personal dispositions," on the other hand, came to be the term used for individual characteristics. Allport distinguished three major levels of such dispositions. Cardinal dispositions are master sentiments or ruling passions, which are outstanding, dominant, and quite rare. More characteristic of most people are the relatively few but easily recognized central dispositions, which tend to govern their lives. Secondary dispositions are less clear cut, more diffuse in expression, and less often manifested. According to Allport, such personal dispositions are the essence of personality, because they represent "unique patterned individuality."

Functional autonomy, through which dispositions are maintained, is probably Allport's most original, best-known, and most controversial theoretical construct. Allport (1961) defined it as

any acquired system of motivation in which the tensions involved are not of the same kind as the antecedent tensions from which the acquired system developed.

That concept brings motivation out of the past and into the framework of the present. For Allport, whatever makes a person act must be operating now. Therefore, the adult cannot be said to act as he did when he was a child. Functional autonomy includes all his present motives that seek new goals—continuous, perhaps, with the past but not dependent on or explained by it. Contemporary motivation looks ahead rather than back, and represents the essential core of purposive behavior. In Allport's own statement, the concept of functional autonomy allows for the concrete uniqueness of personal motives on which he insisted. At the same time, it also permits the emergence of the varied and self-sustaining motivational systems that characterize adult human behavior. When the concept of functional autonomy was advanced in the 1930's, it met with considerable adverse criticism, because its emphasis on contemporary motivation was antithetical to the views of more orthodox psychoanalytic thinkers. However, the same concept was also the precursor of some of the theoretical formulations of the psychoanalytic ego psychologists, whose views permeate contemporary thought.

In addition to the major importance of traits, Allport also recognized a wide range of motives, including interests, abilities, intentions, plans, habits, and attitudes. He further accepted certain lower order self-sustaining systems, such as addictions, routines, and various other types of essentially repetitive behavior patterns. Although behaviors of that kind may be necessary for efficient living, Allport hardly regarded them as sufficient to account for the actual nature of humans. For that he emphasized the role of propriate functional autonomy, the higher order motives that contribute to the organization of the total posture of a human being. Motives of that kind are thought to predominate in the mature and healthy adult. Allport did not, however, regard the mentally ill as necessarily without functional autonomy. He made an interesting distinction in that connection. He maintained that a maladaptive state of adjustment may sometimes become so tightly structured and firmly entrenched that it actually represents the person's style of life. In that event, Allport regarded the illness as an acquired and functionally autonomous motivational system with contemporary meaning to the person in its own right. Such a system, in Allport's view, is probably not amenable to so-called depth analysis. On the other hand, he also believed that in other cases the illness may yield to conventional psychoanalytic procedures. When change occurs on that basis, he did not think that the person's maladaptive life style had achieved the functionally autonomous state in the first place and could, therefore, be altered in the course of a review of the past.

MATURE PERSONALITY

Allport recognized that it is difficult if not impossible to arrive at a satisfactory definition of a mature or healthy or even normal personality. He did, however, identify several specific criteria that he felt—in American culture, at least—can be said to characterize maturity. For example, the mature person in Allport's view has a greatly extended sense of self and can relate warmly to others in both intimate and casual relationships. He is emotionally secure, accepting of others, and aware of outer reality in his thinking, perceiving, and acting. He has zest, enthusiasm, insight, and humor and has achieved a sufficiently unified philosophy of life to use it in directing his living harmoniously. Allport stressed the vital importance of directing human development along those lines from infancy through old age, for the uniqueness of the person remains throughout life. He also regarded all those criteria as essential goals for psychotherapy, maintaining that, at present, stress is usually laid on only a few of the criteria.

Allport saw no inherent reason in basic behavior patterns for the loss of the mutuality and cooperativeness that represent the natural human state. The social smile of the infant suggests his contentment with himself and the world, and the child approaches, rather than avoids or attacks, unless negative emotions of anger and fear have led him to reverse the pattern. Allport saw no reason for that contented, approaching state not to continue under favorable circumstances. In fact, Allport (1960b) regarded the affiliative basis of human behavior as so apparent that

one must perform contortions in order to give equal footing to the alleged aggressive instincts.

It is, therefore, the proper function of psychology, psychotherapy, and education to work toward their common goal of fostering the kind of human progress that enables people to work cooperatively, rather than competitively, with each other.

THE UNIQUE AND OPEN SYSTEM

Allport has been described (Hall and Lindzey, 1970) as one of the few personality theorists who

provides an effective bridge between academic psychology and its traditions on the one hand, and the rapidly developing field of clinical and personality psychology on the other hand.

Perhaps the chief reasons for that bridge were his consistent open mindedness to different points of view and his insistence that no closed system of psychology can possibly enable people to understand the complexities of human behavior. As personality itself is constantly changing, so Allport urged that the psychology of personality must remain an open system as well. A particular theorist or investigator has the right to pursue his own particular interests, but Allport (1968a) insisted

he has no right to forget what he has decided to neglect.

Above all, Allport constantly said that it is psychology's duty to be concerned with the individual person, because personality actually exists only in specific and unique patterns. The person transcends all his aspects and has striven for his own personal integrity and fulfillment in every known society and under all existing conditions because he is the true center of life itself.

Henry A. Murray

Henry A. Murray was born in New York City in 1893. He majored in history as a Harvard undergraduate and then received an M.D. degree in 1919 from the College of Physicians and Surgeons of Columbia University. After earning an M.A. in biology the next year, he taught physiology at Harvard for a short time, later completing a surgical internship at the Presbyterian Hospital in New York. After 2 years of research in embryology at the Rockefeller Institute, he went to England and in 1927 was awarded a Ph.D. in biochemistry from Cambridge University. Becoming increasingly convinced of the importance of psychology, he returned to the United States as an instructor at the newly founded Harvard Psychological Clinic and later became its director. Murray practiced as a psychoanalyst and became one of the founders of the Boston Psychoanalytic Society. He joined the Army Medical Corps in World War II, instituting a comprehensive assessment program for the Office of Strategic Services (Murray, 1948), for which he was awarded the Legion of Merit in 1946. After the war he joined the department of social relations at Harvard, where he set up the psychological clinic annex for personality study. He received the Distinguished Scientific Award and the Gold Medal Award of the American Psychological Foundation. He retired as professor emeritus in 1962 and is continuing to clarify his conceptual framework and to refine some of his personality constructs.

Murray (1938) proposed the term "personology" for the study of personality, defining it as

the branch of psychology which principally concerns itself with the study of human lives and the factors that influence their course.

Inasmuch as personology is the science of humans, Murray considers it the most inclusive area of psychology, other branches being essentially special areas within it. The ultimate aim of the personologist is regarded as 3-fold: to construct a theory of personality, to devise suitable techniques for studying its more important attributes, and to discover its basic facts through careful and extensive investigations of actual human lives. Although Murray has made significant contributions to those aims, he does not regard his theoretical formulations as complete and continues to develop certain aspects of his thinking, which he discussed in some detail in his autobiography (Murray, 1967).

SCOPE OF PERSONOLOGY

Murray has always been an advocate of interdisciplinary personality studies and accepts a wide range of approaches as useful in personology. He himself prefers to emphasize new areas, because he sees no need to concentrate on those already crowded with competent investigators. However, he is quite willing to use existing constructs in his theoretical formulations, although typically adding some ideas of his own before adopting them. Murray was among the first personality theorists to bring psychoanalytic concepts into academic psychology. Although it was the impact of Jung that first turned Murray's interest to psychology, Freud's influence on his thinking is more apparent. Murray includes several classical Freudian concepts in his own developmental theory, along with some additional categories. A strong Freudian emphasis is also notable in his stress on the importance of the past in understanding the present, although he does not neglect the present or fail to consider the role of future-oriented processes. Intention has, in fact, become of increasing importance in his thinking, and

he has noted (Murray, 1971) that

of all the single terms, or concepts, that we have in psychology to refer to one or another variable . . . involved in determining the course of behavior, none is more powerful than the concept of *intention*.

Biological, historical, cultural, social, and evolutionary concepts, as well as those in virtually all areas of psychology, are important to personality, as Murray sees it.

Murray himself stresses the physiological substrate of personality in his own thinking but never approaches psychological phenomena through reduction. Interpersonal, intrapersonal, and impersonal forces are all of concern to him. He recognizes the value of the case history approach and chose to write his own autobiographical statement (Murray, 1967) as a case study of himself, because he found that method most suited to his personal preference and professional experience. Subjective material is of great concern to him, but he does not neglect objective observation. He has constructed and developed a number of special evaluation techniques designed to study both unconscious and conscious psychological processes. Without forgetting the importance of the individual person, he recognizes the need for investigating the common areas of human behavior. He is interested in health, as well as sickness, and one of his stated aims is to furnish a health-oriented continuation or extension of "the illness-oriented Freudian system" (Murray, 1968). Organismic, Gestalt, and field theories are given full recognition. Although Murray recognizes personality as a whole functioning unit, he also sees a need for studying its parts. Among his better-known contributions are his careful lists of the more important determiners of personality functioning as he sees it.

Over-all, Murray's work is a combination of the boldly adventurous and the extremely cautious and precise. He objects to what he regards as premature scientific rigor and does not hesitate to enter into fresh territory and to break new ground. His interests include such diverse areas as dyadic interaction, creativity, imagination, the abolition of warfare, and the possibility of a world state. He edited a book on mythology (Murray, 1960a) and undertook an extensive study of Melville's *Moby Dick* (Murray, 1965). Along with other eminent scientists, Murray (1960b) became a founder of the Institute of Religion in an Age of Science, envisioning a religion

that is compatible with science and understands its aim and destiny.

The development of religion suitable for today remains one of his abiding interests. He is willing to investigate a wide range of areas on a tentative basis, but he is also continually engaged in careful and frequent revisions, reconsiderations, and reevaluations of his more detailed concepts, never regarding them as in final form. He noted (Murray, 1959) that his training emphasized the need to pursue limited goals but admitted to having succumbed

to the dream of an all-embracing scheme, a unified science, not, of course, to be achieved in my own lifetime, but in the distant future.

DEFINITION OF PERSONALITY

Murray (Murray and Kluckhohn, 1953) defined personality as

the hypothetical structure of the mind, the consistent establishments and processes of which are manifested over and over again . . . in the internal and external proceedings which constitute a person's life.

Personality is hypothetical because it can perhaps be inferred from the facts of a person's life but still transcends them all. It is manifested repeatedly because, although it is constantly changing, it also has recognizable features that persist over time. The term "proceedings" that the definition includes refers to the units of time during which a person attends to either the internal or the external circumstances of his life. When he engages in internal proceedings, he is focusing on inner-oriented mental processes, such as feelings, fantasies, judgments, anticipations, and intentions. When his attention turns to external proceedings, he is occupied in coping with the environment. Serials are series of proceedings, related to each other but separate in time, that permit the pursuit of long-range goals. Murray sees the person as continually planning and arranging schedules for achieving those goals and setting up serial programs, sequences of subgoals, which serve as steps along the way. Proceedings, serials, schedules, and serial programs constantly arise, shift, and give way to others as circumstances change, and personality inevitably changes with them.

Murray also sees the person as constantly pressured by conflicting internal and external demands, so that throughout his life he must give up, as well as take for himself. From that point of view, Murray regards personality as a compromise formation resulting from the inevitable conflict between the person's own desires and impulses and those of others. Personality is made up of integrated and interdependent processes, functionally inseparable and always operating as a whole. That unity, Murray maintains, is possible only because the processes of personality refer to organizations in the brain, without which personality could not exist at all. In Murray's terms, the brain is regnant, and regnant processes, whether conscious or unconscious, underlie all psychological functions. Although Murray has altered his theoretical position to some extent in the course of time, he has never ceased to emphasize the centrality of the brain-personality relationship in his thinking. Certain aspects of human experience may soar above physiological considerations, but Murray insists that personality can never be meaningfully separated from its biological roots.

DEVELOPMENT OF PERSONALITY

Murray holds an essentially Freudian picture of personality development, conceiving of certain specific mental structures thought to arise sequentially. The three childhood stages that he identified are Freudian in both name and general conception, although with several notable alterations. The id remains the source of energy and the reservoir of unacceptable impulses, as it was for Freud. In Murray's view, however, the id also contains some acceptable and constructive impulses. Not only is the ego a repressor and an inhibitor, but it also has energy of its own and helps some of the id drives find suitable expression. The superego, although still the internal regulator of behavior derived from early experiences, can be significantly changed later by peer group and other influences, including those associated with literary, historical, and mythological characters with whom the person identifies. Murray's ego ideal, which is associated with the superego, consists of all the various self-images that represent the person at his very best. Those ideals help the person maintain goal-directed living and, if they are reasonably in accord with the requirements of his society and culture, enable him to cope with the environment without relinquishing too many desires of his own. In a healthy development Murray sees those three structures changing in relative dominance as the personality unfolds, the id losing its original preeminence first to the superego and later to the ego.

Murray also identified certain relatively specific temporal sequences in childhood that in many ways resemble the Freudian view of psychosexual development. Oral, anal, and phallic states closely resemble their Freudian counterparts, although Murray's are somewhat more broadly interpreted. He also introduced two further stages, the claustral and the urethral. The claustral is the tranquil state of prenatal existence, and the urethral, which falls between the oral and the anal stages developmentally, involves the pleasurable sensations associated with urethral erotism. If a child is too deprived at any particular stage or lacks sufficient impetus to go ahead, Murray sees the possibility of a fixation in much the Freudian sense. Although some amount of fixation is considered normal and even inevitable, overly strong fixations may lead to complexes, later inducing the adult to strive for enjoyments more suited to earlier periods of his life. Murray evolved a character typology based on the predominant developmental influence in the person's life, again following Freud. He did, however, include two further character types which are associated with the additional stages he introduced. The claustral complex tends to produce a passive, dependent personality development, with prominent withdrawal tendencies. The urethral complex, on the other hand, results in an overly ambitious, strongly narcissistic adult, with a prominent concern for achieving immortality. The urethral complex is also called the Icarus complex because the legend of Icarus symbolizes many of the hypothesized urethral characteristics. The extremely detailed individual history that Murray called "An American Icarus" is probably his best-known case study (Murray, 1955).

THEORY OF MOTIVATION

A primary concept in Murray's theory of motivation is the need (Murray and Kluckhohn, 1953), which he regards as

perhaps the nearest thing to an all-embracing principle which avoids reference to final causes.

The need, to Murray, represents a force in the brain that can be aroused by either internal or external stimulation. Once aroused, it produces continued activity until it is reduced or satisfied. Murray does not, however, believe that need-tension reduction is the chief purpose of living except, perhaps, in the case of the excessively conflict ridden or overly anxious. Rather, he feels that, under normal circumstances, it is the process of tension reduction that is the most satisfying condition. A major goal of personality functioning is, therefore, to reach states in which reducing tension is possible. The person may actually seek out arousal in order to experience this tension reduction. The more obvious aspect of this situation is the tension, but, according to Murray (1938), the need itself remains an inference or a useful fiction that has heuristic existence, rather than demonstrable existence. It is a construct to be inferred from behavior:

an organic potentiality or readiness to respond in a certain way under given conditions.

Murray has experimented with various lists of needs in his continuing efforts at greater precision. In one such system, he distinguished between activity and effect needs, activity needs being directed toward activity for its own sake and effect needs toward the goal to be achieved. He has also worked out a classification involving mental, viscerogenic, and sociorelational needs, the mental arising from the character of the human mind, the viscerogenic from properties of physiological tissues, and the sociorelational from the human being's inherent social nature. Murray also added creative needs, which promote novel and productive activities, as opposed to negative needs, which induce avoidance of the unpleasant or undesirable. A further distinction was made between proactive needs, those arising within the person, and reactive needs, those induced by environmental factors. The emphasis on humans as proactive beings removes them from being merely acted on and gives them a substantial role in their own destiny. Murray never abandoned his stress on the importance of needs but, dissatisfied with his early efforts in this respect, later attempted to retain the essentials of his need concept through the use of a value-vector schema. The purpose of that approach was to portray simultaneously what a person sees as important in a situation and what he does to achieve it. The vectors are used to show the direction of his behavior, and the values represent what he holds in esteem.

Needs must be triggered, and Murray finds the source of need arousal in his concept of press. A press is seen as a force in the environment that, whether real or perceived, has the capacity to arouse need tension in the person. Murray has drawn up lists of press intended for use in specific contexts. Perhaps his most important distinction, however, is between α-press, those aspects of an object or situation that reflect what it really is, and β-press, which is the force of the object or situation as the person interprets it. The need-press combination becomes a thema, simple themas combining into serial themas and more deeply entrenched themas becoming need integrates. Of particular importance in Murray's view of personality is the unity thema, in which dominant needs and press are linked in early childhood through repeated associations that may be either satisfying or traumatic. Murray believes that much of the adult's behavior can be traced to such unity themas, which, in his opinion tend to retain considerable motivational power.

The thema, to Murray, is the proper molar unit for psychological study. A method he developed for uncovering dominant themas in the life of a person is the Thematic Apperception Test (TAT), a projective technique widely used in clinical practice. The data can be analyzed to permit inferences about the dominant needs and press affecting the person's thought and behavior. That is done through the intermediary device of heroes or central figures in the TAT pictures, about which the person is asked to make up stories. It is assumed that his responses indicate his own mental processes and problem areas, unconscious and conscious. The ways in which he handles the issues he projects into the pictures are thought to indicate his characteristic problem-solving approaches, and the endings he gives his stories are assumed to reflect the outcomes he envisions for his own conflicts. Repeated or prevalent themas are considered of special importance. Formal study of the test data is designed to provide clues to a person's temperament, intellectual abilities, imagination, reality awareness, emotional states, perceptual and cognitive styles, and many other personality characteristics. Murray emphasizes that the data cannot yield more than hypotheses, conjectures and indications of areas for further study. And that, indeed, is Murray's over-all evaluation of his whole extensive and varied contribution to the field of personality study. Nevertheless, although he continues to insist that he has never made more than a beginning, his work has been described in a book of essays published in his honor as "a unique and inexhaustible house of treasures" (White, 1963).

Kurt Goldstein

Kurt Goldstein (1878–1965) was born in Germany and received his M.D. degree from the University of Breslau in 1903. After serving several years in the psychiatric clinic at the University of Konigsberg, he became director of the Neurological Institute and professor of neurology at the University of Frankfurt. There during World War I, Goldstein conducted a number of the intensive long-term studies of brain-injured soldiers on which many of his theoretical personality concepts are based. He also spent 3 years as director of the Neurological Hospital and professor of neurology at the University of Berlin. He came to New York City in 1935 as clinical professor of neurology at the College of Physicians and Surgeons of Columbia University and later accepted an appointment as professor of neurology at Tufts Medical School, where he remained until he retired in 1945. Goldstein then continued his private practice in New York City, also teaching at Columbia University, the College of the City of New York, and the New School for Social Research. In his late seventies he began a new teaching career, commuting weekly to Brandeis University. His many honors extended over a long and productive life. He delivered the William James lectures at Harvard University in 1939, published the next year as *Human Nature in the Light of Psychopathology*. On the occasion of his eightieth birthday in 1958, he was awarded an honorary doctorate by the University of Frankfurt. Along with other distinguished figures, he was one of the founding sponsors of the Association for Humanistic Psychology.

Goldstein's early involvement with Gestalt psychology, phenomenology, and existentialism reflected a pervasive interest in philosophical issues that he retained throughout his career. On the basis of extensive studies with thousands of patients, he concluded that the philosophical point of view is necessary for understanding what the organism actually is and how it really functions. Goldstein was a leader of the holistic or organismic theorists, and two of his major constructs were the organismic viewpoint and self-actualization, around which his personality theory is built. His contributions in connection with the organismic viewpoint are unique in that (Murphy, 1968a)

among the proponents of holistic thinking . . . he went all the way.

Self-actualization became an integral part of the conceptual framework of many later personality theorists. A memorial volume of essays (Simmel, 1968) provided an overview by a number of Goldstein's closest colleagues of his life and major contributions.

ORGANISMIC APPROACH

Largely on the basis of his extensive work with brain-injured patients and those with language disorders in particular, Goldstein became increasingly certain that an atomistic approach is fundamentally inadequate to any real understanding of the organism (Goldstein, 1939, 1948). He, therefore, came to believe with increasing conviction that all aspects of living—be they symptoms, disease states, or any of the various forms of behavior a person may manifest—can be appreciated only in terms of the total organism. To him, the organism is always a unit, and anything occurring on either the physiological or the psychological level gains in meaning from the context of this totality. The organism comprises differentiated but interrelated parts that, under normal conditions, are never isolated. What happens in one part must affect every other part as well.

In Goldstein's organismic framework, a person's interrelations with his society, the similarities and differences that exist between him and other members of that society, and even his broader relationships to his culture and to other cultures must all be taken into consideration. The organism in sickness and in health was brought by Goldstein into this comprehensive holistic framework. Symptoms become meaningful only in terms of their functional significance for the whole organism. They do not merely affect a damaged part but involve attempts of the total organism to handle environmental demands for which his former problem-solving techniques are now inadequate or inapplicable. Because of the vast amount of information that Goldstein considered necessary to understand the person from a truly organismic point of view, he strongly favored intensive, long-term studies of single persons in preference to more superficial investigations of groups.

SELF-ACTUALIZATION

Goldstein did not hesitate to assume that a living organism has genuinely creative power. This power is inherent in his concept of self-actualization, the single need that he believed to underlie all human behavior. What may appear to be many different needs are merely different expressions of this one imperative source of motivation. As Goldstein (1966) stated:

The organism has definite potentialities, and because it has them it has the need to actualize and realize them.

Although he regarded the need to actualize the self as universal, its outlets and expressions vary from one person to another and from society to society. The specific potentialities of a person, Goldstein maintained, can be inferred from two factors: what the person himself prefers to do and what he does best. His likes and his skills, therefore, point to his actual possibilities. Goldstein's view of the organism as a totality did not waiver, but he did identify certain fundamental behaviors, attitudes, and performances that tend to facilitate self-actualization in health and hinder it in pathology. The major concepts are coming to terms, figure and ground, and abstract and concrete behavior.

To function reasonably well, the organism must somehow manage to come to terms with the environment in fairly comfortable interaction, because the environment encroaches on the organism, disturbing its equilibrium but also acting as its source of supply. Coming to terms with the environment is, therefore, a double problem that demands resolution. As the person's coping methods become more effective, his chances of self-actualization increase. The undisturbed organism, according to Goldstein, remains in a more or less equal state of tension distribution and normally strives to regain that state when it is upset. That process of equalization was thought to permit the smooth, ordered behavior that adaptive living requires. The organism is thereby aided in coming to satisfactory terms with the environment, which he regarded as a prerequisite for self-actualization.

In Goldstein's view of the person's organismic strivings toward self-actualization, there are constant shifts between a central figure and the background from which it emerges. In any particular activity the organism undertakes, Goldstein (1952) noted:

The capacity that is particularly important for the task is the foreground; the others are in the background.

That selecting-out process enables the organism to actualize itself in any given situation. In perceptual terms, the figure is whatever stands out and occupies the center of attention at any time. As attention shifts, part of what was background before is raised to centrality, and what was formerly the figure recedes into the background. The ability to keep this process smooth and plastic is seen as essential for adequate coping with the environment, because it facilitates appropriate problem solving. Perception, Goldstein maintained, is organized around that process, as is living itself. He also distinguished between the conscious and the unconscious in much the same way. The unconscious becomes the background reservoir for previously conscious aids to self-actualization that can become central again, should they be required. Impairments in the ability to shift figure and ground rapidly and appropriately represent a serious handicap to functioning efficiently at virtually all levels. Goldstein saw that handicap as a major source of difficulty for the brain injured.

The ability to react abstractly or concretely as the situation demands was seen as another cardinal requirement for self-actualization, and Goldstein stated (1967):

the two behavioral attitudes ... abstract and concrete behavior belong together and represent a unit in which each plays a particular role.

Action was thought of as in the realm of the concrete. The abstract attitude may lead to action but does not in itself include it. In the concrete situation, the response aroused is triggered directly by the actual stimulus. In the abstract attitude, the person prepares himself to act by such processes as considering, evaluating, and deciding. Goldstein regarded the abstract attitude as the human organism's highest and essential ability, but he also insisted that concrete behavior is imperative at times. Smooth functioning actually depends on the person's skill in shifting appropriately from concrete responses to abstract responses as the situation requires. Disturbances in that ability represent a serious problem area for the brain-injured organism, imposing severe limitations on the capacity for effective self-actualization.

ORGANISMIC GOALS IN SICKNESS AND HEALTH

Goldstein saw self-actualization as involving somewhat different goals in sickness and in health. The organism in a pathological state may, for example, be forced to limit his expressions of self-actualization to maintenance of the status quo, discharging tension as best he can and perhaps concentrating merely on survival. He may be compelled to abandon the adventurous and creative spirit in order to defend what little remains to him. Goldstein regarded pathology as always associated with isolation to some degree, so that the organism's whole integrity is threatened. Faced with that threat, the sick person may respond rigidly and compulsively, fall back to more primitive levels of behavior, constrict his interests and activity, or withdraw into routines. He may become perseverative, repeating previously successful responses in later situations to which they are no longer appropriate. He may manifest fatigue and retreat from challenge or merely refuse to undertake any task in which he envisions the possibility of failure. Goldstein regarded all such behaviors as catastrophic reactions, responses of the damaged person to what he interprets as devastating conditions with which he cannot cope. However, even that was thought of as an attempt at self-actualization, within the limits available to the modified organism with a curtailed response repertory.

Goldstein's concept of self-actualization had considerable influence on his interpretation of the psychotherapeutic process, which he referred to as "organismic psychotherapy." He believed that patient and therapist enter into a relationship that he referred to as a "communion," a union that enhances the self-realization of both patient and therapist. He regarded this communion as a prerequisite for successful treatment (Goldstein, 1959), because the patient's problems

arise basically from the disruption of the mutual relationship between him and others, the basis of all human existence.

In contrast to the limited expressions of self-actualization that may remain available to the impaired organism—whether the impairment is neurotic, schizophrenic, or organic—Goldstein saw the healthy person's drive to actualize himself as inducing spontaneity, creativeness, and genuine self-expression. The self-actualizing drive in health can enable the person to accept some amount of risk without retreating into fear because he has retained the spirit of adventure and confidence that Goldstein found inherent in the self-actualization principle. The healthy person is, therefore, able to reach what Goldstein referred to as the "sphere of immediacy," the level at which the human being becomes truly dynamic and finds the source of genuine wholeness and creativity. Goldstein recognized that language tends to become more poetic than precise in speaking of experiences at that level. Nevertheless, he regarded experiences of that kind as essential aspects of the whole organismic picture of the human being. He also insisted that those areas are ultimately capable of being investigated with the same scientific exactness as is used in studies of the physical sciences. In the sphere of immediacy, he saw the possibility of humanizing science and of making humanity open to science, for it is here that artificial distinctions disappear and a truly holistic approach becomes possible. The sphere of immediacy and its dynamic character become the vital aspect of human living. As Goldstein (1965) wrote, it is the truly central factor

in friendship, in love, in the instigation of creative production, in the religious attitude: it is not even missing as an instigating part of our scientific work.

Abraham Maslow

Abraham Maslow (1908–1970) was born in Brooklyn, New York, and completed both his undergraduate and his graduate work at the University of Wisconsin, where he received his Ph.D. degree in 1934. Maslow's predoctoral studies placed heavy emphasis on Watsonian behaviorism, and his early postdoctoral research was in the area of animal behavior. However, as the range of his own interests broadened, he came to recognize that many of the more orthodox concepts of scientific psychology were insufficient as a basis for a meaningful approach to human behavior and experience. He was a Carnegie fellow at Columbia University in 1935, after which he joined the faculty of Brooklyn College, where he remained until 1951. At Brandeis University, where he served as professor and chairman of the department of psychology until 1969, he wrote voluminously, lectured extensively, and received many honors. He was president of the division of personality and social psychology and also the division of esthetics, serving as president of the American Psychological Association in 1967. As a leading spokesman for the third-force movement in psychology, Maslow spent the last year of his life as resident fellow at the W. P. Laughlin Foundation in Menlo Park, California. In addition to a memorial volume published posthumously and edited by his wife (B. Maslow, 1972), publications dealing with his life, work, and continuing influence have appeared since his death (Goble, 1970; Wilson, 1972; Roberts, 1978).

Maslow felt strongly that the rigid application of the scientific model of the physical sciences to psychology merely allowed for a partial picture of the human being, in which he is seen in pieces, rather than as a whole. A pervasive influence on Maslow's thinking was the organismic self-actualization theory of Kurt Goldstein. Believing in the need to understand the totality in order to understand at all, Maslow appealed for considerable broadening of psychology both in content and in method. Such a psychology should be firmly based on the humanistic approach and willing to accept and understand the human being as he is. Maslow did not attempt to overthrow the more conventional methods of studying human behavior, for he saw his version of humanistic psychology as complementary, rather than as an alternative to them. The additions he proposed would, he believed, restore to scientific study the many important aspects of human functioning and levels of awareness that are customarily omitted in the restricted scope of traditional investigation. Those omissions, Maslow suggested, have cut the person down to a size that can be handled by already available instruments but have done so at the cost of losing sight of the reality of the human being. Change, expansion, and growth may be painful, said Maslow, but they are absolutely necessary. Oversimplification has obscured the very realities that science seeks. Scientific study must, therefore, be expanded sufficiently to restore its own legitimate goals. That shift he described as the transition from a means-oriented to a problem-oriented science.

Maslow invested with scientific respectability such vital human areas as individuality, consciousness, purpose, ethics, morality, goodness, beauty, authenticity, identity, and the whole range of potentialities that he saw as inherent in humanness. Maslow (1966) included

the person-transcending values and realities, i.e. of a higher level of humanness and self-actualization . . . in which the person becomes part of the world rather than its center.

The truly scientific investigator must try to devise new methods for studying all areas of human behavior and experience. He must learn to be open minded, adventurous, and willing to make mistakes, and he should not neglect his own hunches, inspirations, and subjective reactions. Maslow was well aware that the initial attempts to penetrate into new areas are apt to lack precision and to be poorly conceived. They are, nevertheless, important beginnings. Maslow emphasized that, without such first times, science cannot progress beyond its present constricted boundaries. He himself devoted much of his professional life to such first times, opening up a number of areas of psychological experience hitherto considered as scientifically out of bounds.

Maslow regarded the overconcern of many personality theorists with psychopathology as a further limit on understanding human behavior. That emphasis, said Maslow, has fostered a one-sided picture of the human being and an unnecessarily pessimistic view of human potentialities. Some of Maslow's major contributions are his studies of healthy people, those who have largely overcome areas of deficiency and have realized levels of self-fulfillment and creativity. Maslow maintained that essentially different psychologies arise from studying the sick and the healthy, and he insisted that both are part of a more complete picture of humanness. Human strengths, as well as weaknesses, must make their legitimate contributions to such a comprehensive view. Maslow looked to the healthy for strengths, because they can teach people about the higher levels of human awareness and how to approach them. He emphasized the value of such features as spontaneity, self-acceptance, impulsive-awareness, naturalness, and release as important counteracting agents, acting against the destructive tendencies that come from thwarting a person's higher nature. The sick indicate what happens if human needs, values, and wants are not fulfilled, but the healthy person shows what is needed for self-fulfillment.

HIERARCHY OF NEEDS

One of Maslow's major contributions was his recognition of the hierarchical organization of needs according to their potency and primacy. He identified a broad range of needs that he regarded as intrinsic and present in everyone and hence labeled them as basic or instinctual. The most powerful and prepotent are fundamental survival-oriented needs with a clear physiological basis aimed at removing a deficit, such as hunger or thirst. As those needs are fulfilled, other less powerful needs—such as the needs for shelter, sex, affection, and self-esteem—can become effective motivators in their turn. Only after those prepotent deficiency or D-needs are filled can more subtle growth-oriented being, B-needs or metaneeds, play a primary motivational role. To this second group Maslow assigned such uniquely human desires as impulses to freedom, beauty, goodness, unity, and justice. Initially, he saw self-actualization as the highest need, but in his later years he considered the desire for self-transcendence to be higher still (Roberts, 1978). Those higher needs are initially weak, subtle, and easily disturbed by adverse environments, attitudes, and habits. For most people, they require considerable nurturing if they are to flourish, but flourish they must if the person is to find full expression for his or her basic humanity and avoid what Maslow termed the "metapathologies," such as boredom, cynicism, and lack of inspiration. The rank ordering of the hierarchy may actually reverse once the person discovers the existence and attraction of the metaneeds. For example, the person committed to self-actualization or transcendence may willingly undergo almost all other forms of deprivation to obtain the desired goal.

CONFLICT OF NEEDS

Maslow saw D-needs and B-needs as generating a fundamental and inherent conflict. D-needs induce behavior aimed at supplying deficiencies, and the person must depend on other people and external things. The resulting dependency tends to make him fearful, because the source of supply may fail. The pressure of D-needs is, therefore, apt to induce regressive behavior and lead to defensiveness, clinging to the past, and fear of growth and independence. B-needs, on the other hand, are essentially growth-oriented. They minimize the sense of threat, reduce hostility, and allow the person to become more self-directed, self-sufficient, and self-contained. D-needs and B-needs, then, pressure the person in opposite directions, and the whole process of developing becomes what Maslow (1968) described as

a never ending series of free choice situations, the choice being between safety and growth, dependence and independence, regression and progression, immaturity and maturity.

Conflict is regarded as more or less inevitable, although its intensity varies considerably, and genuine growth can do much to minimize it. In addition, Maslow recognized another kind of conflict that he believed the healthy can escape. The thwarting of basic needs leads to the development of neurotic needs that, being actually impossible to satisfy, result in wasted human potentiality and the depletion of human energy. Mas-

low saw that as the fundamental tragedy of mental illness. Basic needs, on the other hand, can at least be gratified to a reasonable extent, because they entail comparatively free choices and foster a growth process that "makes people healthy and better" (Maslow, 1970a).

From Maslow's theoretical framework, all forms of human behavior can be thought of in terms of the joint operation of D-needs and B-needs. The particular form of the behavior depends on the ratio of regressive to progressive motivation involved. Maslow used the need to know as an example of how the same need can operate under different conditions and with different outcomes. On the one hand, the need to know can serve primarily as a stimulus to lessen the anxiety of an observer faced with something unknown. In that case, the resulting behavior aims at threat reduction, detoxification of the frightening object. The same need to know can, however, also lead beyond the limited goal of reducing anxiety and offer the person higher satisfactions as well. Shifting the balance from D-needs to B-needs becomes the real purpose of education, therapy, and life itself. Whole cultures and thought systems can be studied in those terms, for their essential character depends on which set of needs predominates within them. In fact, Maslow suggested that the unwillingness of the traditional scientist to extend the areas of his investigation may be the result of too little B-motivation and too much investment in D-satisfactions, with the characteristic fear of change, expansion, and taking chances that such a ratio produces.

SELF-ACTUALIZATION AND PEAK EXPERIENCES

Maslow's chief way of approaching health was through studies of its best examples—those persons who are the most fully developed and creative. They are characterized by what Maslow called "self-actualizing creativeness," which he considered a generalized orientation that leads toward health and growth. Special talents may or may not be involved, inasmuch as the truly creative actualize themselves in everything they do. Self-actualization, a central concept in his thinking, was defined (Maslow 1971) as

experiencing fully, vividly, selflessly, with full concentration and total absorption . . . the person is wholly and fully human.

Inner human nature contains all the potentialities for such experiencing, but it is the process of self-actualization that leads to its accomplishment. Using his studies of self-actualizers past and present, Maslow drew up a list of what he saw as their shared characteristics. He found them all, for example, to be realistically oriented, problem centered, and generally accepting of themselves and others. They were also spontaneous, independent, and creative; they identified with mankind and were able to transcend their environments. Their values were democratic and their sense of humor genuine, and most of them reported having had mystical or ego-transcending experiences at some level. Maslow's increasing interest in ego-transcending experiences led him to specific studies of what he referred to as "peak experiences."

The peak experience was described as an episodic, brief occurrence in which the person suddenly experiences a powerful transcendental state of consciousness. In this state the person experiences a sense of heightened noematic clarity and understanding; intense euphoria; appreciation of the holistic, unitive, and integrated nature of the universe and one's unity with it; an altered perception of space and time; and ineffability, in that the experience is so powerful and different from ordinary experience as to give the sense of defying description. Such experiences have been recognized in different cultures and periods and have been called by many names, including mystical, transcendental, cosmic consciousness, and satori. They tend to occur most often in the psychologically healthy and may produce long-lasting beneficial effects, because, as Maslow (1972) noted, the experience

is so profound and shaking . . . that it can change the person's character . . . forever after.

Paradoxically, although those exalted states can arouse fear, they also offer freedom from fear, for in them the person manages to turn away from aggression and self-destructiveness and come close to his Self, his Being, and even to his God, however he may elect to define the term. Maslow had good reason for capitalizing terms like "Being" and "Self" as he used them, for, in the highest levels of peak experiences, the person becomes truly god-like, recognizing and identifying with a wholly unified world. Initially, he believed that such high reaches were available only to the chosen few, but he later came to believe that they are available to most if not all— nonpeakers being merely those who are too fearful to accept and acknowledge them. Subsequent research has borne out many of those assumptions (Walsh and Vaughan, 1979).

Maslow maintained that studies of peak experiences should and must include investigations of mysticism, religious phenomena of all sorts, and all the ways in which human limitations have been reportedly transcended. He believed that all such approaches may be only different avenues to the great transpersonal values that are part of the universal human heritage. It was his hope that such studies would ultimately help to bridge the gap between the relative and the absolute and establish a truly scientific basis for experiences of unity and eternity, which, from Maslow's point of view, are legitimate aspects of the realm of B-values. As such, they are merely a natural part of being human. He believed that it is possible for the human being to live fairly consistently at this higher level of awareness and experience. Although Maslow saw the peak experience itself as essentially transitory, he also maintained that it is possible for the person to achieve a sustained and lofty sense of plateau living, in which, said Maslow (1971), he can

live casually in heaven and be on easy terms with the eternal and the infinite.

In the creative, positive, and healthy characteristics of self-actualizing people, Maslow found justification for the positive view of inherent human nature, which is a prominent emphasis in the whole third-force movement in psychology.

Gardner Murphy

Gardner Murphy, born in Ohio in 1895, did his undergraduate work at Yale. He began graduate training at Harvard, where he received an M.A. degree, and continued at Columbia for his Ph.D., which was awarded in 1923. After postdoctoral study at Harvard as a Hodgson fellow, he joined the psychology department of the City College of New York. At the invitation of the Indian government, he served briefly as a consultant to the United Nations Educational, Scientific, and Cultural Organization in New Delhi. In 1952 he accepted the Dr. Henry March Pfeiffer Research-Training Chair in Psychiatry and also became director of research at the Menninger Foundation. He remained there for 15 years, after which he took his present position as professor of psychology at George Washington University. Murphy

has received many honors, including the Butler Medal of Columbia University in 1932 and the Gold Medal Award of the American Psychological Foundation in 1972. He served as president of the Society for the Psychological Study of Social Issues in 1938, and of the American Psychological Association in 1944. He has also been president of both the American Society for Psychical Research and the Society for Psychical Research in London. The wide range of his honors and professional affiliations reflects the breadth of his interests and the wide horizons of his perspective on human potentialities.

All the theorists discussed here are eclectic to some extent, but Murphy is perhaps the most thoroughgoing in this respect. He consistently argues for increasing interaction of all relevant approaches to the investigation of humans and for the inclusion of as many vantage points as possible from which to study them. Murphy is deeply interested in the many specialized areas of psychology and in numerous related disciplines as well. The range of his own investigations extends well beyond the conventional academic and clinical bounds into the areas of parapsychology and the largely unexplored limits of human potentialities. The psychologies of East and West, old and new, are all of concern to him.

ECLECTICISM WITH A DIFFERENCE

Murphy selects ideas from virtually all the major concepts, principles, and methods of the various branches of psychology. In doing so, he does not merely pick out an idea here or a principle there without considering the whole context in which it is embedded. His own aim is comprehensive indeed. Murphy (1966) intends to approach personality

in such a way as to help clarify the little that we know and to show its possible relations to the vast and confused domain that we do not yet understand.

Murphy has done much to achieve that aim. He is determined in his open mindedness, regarding his passion for inclusiveness as one of his outstanding characteristics. He was among the first to publish a comprehensive history of psychology, which, in its current revision, remains a classic in its field (Murphy and Kovach, 1972). He has made major contributions to social, general, and educational psychology. His firm belief in the lifelong capacity of personality to change and grow has led him to envision almost unlimited human potentialities (Murphy and Leeds, 1975). Nor does he remain comfortably within the scientifically safe areas of investigation in considering what those potentialities may be.

Murphy has long been interested in psychic or paranormal phenomena, considering them part of the total reality of human beings. Although he approaches those areas with caution and considerable rigor, he accepts telepathic and clairvoyant data as part of real human experience, noting that, throughout his pursuit of the more usual approaches to psychology, he was actually leading a double life. He speculates that the scattered and unsystematized parapsychological fragments thus far identified may actually be clues to a still larger universe of which people know virtually nothing as yet. Unusual or altered states of consciousness—such as those accompanying experiences of ecstasy, revelation, and expanded awareness—may have important implications for understanding the potentialities of the human being. Murphy (1967) warned that

he proceeds at his peril who takes a cavalier attitude toward anything in heaven or earth.

BIOSOCIAL THEORY OF PERSONALITY

Murphy accepts no real distinction between the biological and the social aspects of personality. Biological being is seen as the bedrock of personality, but personality is by no means regarded as limited to what is inside the skin. Murphy (1966) conceived of a person as

an inner-outer structure which is the product of a particular organism-culture interaction ... [and] part of a still larger context, as an aspect not only of a community but of a cosmos.

A separate person, to Murphy, is largely a fiction, for personality is seen as a structured organism-environment field that is part of a still larger field, the two aspects being engaged in constant reciprocal interaction. Murphy considers many definitions of personality, recognizing that every investigator sees in it what he is trained to see. Nevertheless, Murphy advocates not fewer lines of study but more. He believes that personality is as complex as human beings and as little understood, and anything that can contribute to the present meager knowledge is made welcome within the broad framework of Murphy's biosocial theory.

PERSONALITY DEVELOPMENT AND STRUCTURE

Murphy describes three essential stages in personality development. The person begins in the stage of undifferentiated wholeness, progresses to differentiation of function, and then proceeds on to the stage of integration. Regression, as well as progression, is possible along the way, and the process is frequently quite uneven. Each developmental stage is thought to involve functions peculiar to itself, so that adult personality is by no means merely an extension of earlier characteristics. Increasing complexity introduces real changes into the developmental process, and the range of individual differences broadens steadily as development continues. The whole complex pattern of the adult's preferences, interests, and values, according to Murphy, derives from the ways in which the person's sensory and motor needs, in particular, have found gratification. However, because such needs and their behavioral expressions are virtually limitless, the potential for human versatility is considered equally unlimited.

The most basic structural units in Murphy's schema are psychological dispositions or organic traits. Those tissue tensions are gradually reconstituted into symbolic traits in the course of development. Personality characteristics derive from organic traits that have been either channeled into specific forms of behavior or redirected by conditioning as the person develops. Learning thus plays a major role in the process, but, characteristically, Murphy sees learning itself as a series of organism-environment interactions in which the biological given is guided and modified by external factors, a process that has recently been more widely recognized by biologists and named "probabilistic epigenesis." Murphy identifies four broad categories of inborn human needs: visceral, motor, sensory, and emergency related. Those needs are thought to become increasingly specific in time, as they are molded by the person's experiences in various social and environmental contexts. A major factor in bringing those changes about is canalization, the process by which a connection is established between a need and a specific way of satisfying it. Canalization, then, permits discharging the energy concentration of the need in the form of behavior, and, as Murphy and Spohn (1968) wrote:

the structure of the environment, both its temporal and spatial structure, is built within the person.

Early canalizations are particularly important in Murphy's view of personality development, for those are the bases for later canalizations, and they also retain the power to induce regressive behavior under stress in the adult. Early body-oriented canalizations represent the origin of the self, which, after going through a series of developmental phases, emerges as the dominant organization of the whole personality. The self is regarded as the unifying aspect that integrates the many disunities and discontinuities with which the person must cope. Murphy also gives conditioning a heavy responsibility in the process of acquired change. Unlike canalizations, which produce actual changes in tension levels, conditioning is seen as a preparatory process that readies the organism for tension reduction but does not affect the tension changes themselves. Also unlike canalization, conditioned responses can be readily generalized and easily shifted, extinguished, and replaced.

In Murphy's schema, canalization and conditioning together account for perceptual learning, as well as behavioral learning. Perception follows much the same progression as personality development. Beginning with the global blur of the infant, perception proceeds through the stage of differentiation and finally reaches integration. The process is greatly influenced by a person's internal needs, for to a large extent a person sees what he wants to see, and Murphy refers to such internally directed perception as autistic. Because of the importance ascribed to autistic percepts, needs become major determiners of individual differences in perception, as well as in behavior and in cognitive styles. However, the role of external reality is not disregarded. Perception, therefore, becomes a double organization, involving outer determiners and internal tissue tensions. In ambiguous situations, autistic perception tends to predominate, but under more clearly defined conditions, Murphy believes, perception usually remains in reasonable accord with external reality.

Murphy has incorporated many concepts from general psychology into his personality framework. In fact, he himself maintains (Murphy, 1968b) that only three major aspects of personality study really exceed the sphere of general psychology, and

these ... are the problem of self, the problem of uniqueness of the stimulating situation, and the problem of the uniqueness of the integrated response.

Murphy contributes substantially to the theoretical understanding of those salient issues, but his own interests include other areas that are not part of general psychology, at least as it is usually now constituted. Those areas, which are discussed below, represent the other side of Murphy's double life.

PARAPSYCHOLOGY

Murphy's contributions to parapsychology are both theoretical and experimental. He suggests that, inasmuch as parapsychological or paranormal experiences may reflect essential aspects of personality, to disregard them may, indeed, be to impose arbitrary restrictions on actual human potentialities (Murphy, 1975). Murphy (1963) urges applying a genuinely experimental method to the area in order to arouse serious interest and to encourage

the expansion of psychology into a vast realm in which it has been taboo.

His approach to parapsychology has been scientific in method and cautious in interpretation, and he advocates austere ground rules for those interested in the subject. He hypothesizes that phenomena such as clairvoyance and mental telepathy may be more normal than paranormal, being found comparatively rarely because most people prefer to uphold their psychological insulation from each other. Murphy notes that some states—such as sleep, drowsiness, certain drug and toxic conditions, hypnosis, and delirium—are apt to be favorable to paranormal experiences. Relaxation, the will to believe, and the ability to escape temporarily from the usual sensory dominance are also regarded as favorable circumstances. Impediments to paranormal awareness, on the other hand, include various intrapsychic barriers, conditions in the general social environment, and a heavy investment in the ordinary types of sensory experience. Recently, he has developed a schema relating the occurrence of specific types of paranormal phenomena to the presence of those facilitating and inhibitory factors and to autonomic nervous system function (Leeds and Murphy, 1979). Murphy advances a possible explanation for paranormal phenomena in strict accord with his general interactional emphasis. He suggests that such abilities may not be associated with a single person but may involve a relationship between, say, a subject and an investigator, each representing an aspect of one organic whole. Such theoretical hypotheses led to a number of careful studies conducted by Murphy and his students. The results tend to support the possibility that paranormal processes are within the range of ordinary human capabilities.

Murphy envisions a truly scientific discipline within parapsychology, one that will build on and extend the pioneering insights of William James (Murphy and Ballou, 1960). Among his own efforts in that direction is an extensive survey of documented examples of parapsychological experiences, in which he discusses telepathic dreams, experimental clairvoyance, precognition, and other events apparently beyond ordinary sensory awareness (Murphy, 1970). He is well aware of the lack of precision often found in areas of that kind, but he insists that unfortunate fact should not be taken as scientific grounds for discontinuing investigations or disregarding legitimate findings. Prejudices associated with parapsychology can become barriers to knowledge, rather than honest scientific caution. Murphy himself is, in fact, willing to go still further beyond ordinary sensory experience in his search for the true range of human potentialities. His deep interest in transpersonal and unitive phenomena has led him to serious speculations regarding the higher states of consciousness, which he believes to be a legitimate part of the whole human experience.

REMOTE ENVIRONMENT

Murphy finds as much place in his thinking for the immediate and remote environments as he does for the inner and outer realities, and here again he recognizes no clear-cut dichotomy. The self remains the core of personality in his theoretical framework, but he does not accept a narrow view of selfhood. On the contrary, he believes that the expanded potential of human experience may well be in opening up the usual constricted borders of the self, thus enabling the person to enter into states of higher awareness. Alterations in levels of awareness, including so-called mystical experiences, have been reported in all cultures and throughout all times. Despite differences associated with time and place, Murphy finds areas of commonality that, he believes, should not be ignored and argues that such experiences are not as different as may be thought. A person can, for example, be lost in an intense aesthetic reaction, in a sudden transporting fantasy, or in a strong sense of religious union with God and the universe. In the more extreme forms, such experiences may be felt as loss of self or as self-expansion, as merging with the outer world or

entering more fully into inner awareness. Either way, the experience itself is real to the person.

Murphy suggests several possibilities for the feeling of cosmic consciousness that such states often entail. He prefers, however, one that fits best with his own biosocial viewpoint. Because the experiences are usually extremely joyful, they may, said Murphy and Spohn (1968), indicate

that tissues are doing what they came into existence to do,

giving rise to a state of extreme well-being. The pleasure centers of the brain, Murphy further suggests, are likely to be strongly activated when truly adaptive orientations are reached. That experience may then be psychologically felt as a sense of true integration in which the person temporarily escapes from the general frustrations and fragmentations that characterize ordinary human living. Murphy's overview of human potentialities includes a wide range of phenomena that seem, at least, to transcend the usual limitations of reality as customarily defined. Studies of biofeedback are of great interest to him, and he sees them as representing a particularly hopeful line of future investigation. Murphy (1973) also considers various approaches to

altered states of consciousness, mystical depersonalization, and the abrogation of personal awareness through hypnosis, drugs, or meditation.

His interests have broadened over the years, and his productivity has, if anything, increased with time. The full range of human potentialities remains as a challenge to him. At one stage, he and his wife, Lois, worked on an intended multivolume summation of the psychologies of the world that sought to include the contributions of sociocultural, experimental, genetic, comparative, and physiological psychology and to interrelate them in a meaningful synthesis with concepts of philosophy. Two volumes have been published (Murphy and Murphy, 1968, 1969). Murphy has suggested the title of *The World of the Mind* for this series, which is hardly an exaggeration in view of its proposed scope. Nor is it out of line with the scientific imperative to investigate all kinds of people, methods, and ideas—as Murphy (1967) says:

none arbitrarily rejected and none arbitrarily accepted, but all brought humbly yet systematically before the reviewing stand of determined reality seeking.

Kurt Lewin

Kurt Lewin (1890–1947) was born in the Prussian village of Mongilno, now a part of Poland. He attended the universities of Freiberg and Munich briefly before matriculating at the University of Berlin, where he received his Ph.D. degree in 1914. After spending 4 years in military service, he returned to the Psychological Institute of the University of Berlin, where he rose to professorial rank in 1927. There he was closely associated with the founders of Gestalt psychology. During those years Lewin's fame became international. His presentation at the International Congress of Psychology at Yale University in 1929 resulted in an invitation to spend 6 months as a visiting professor at Stanford University. When Hitler came to power, Lewin made a hasty return to Germany to arrange his affairs before moving permanently to the United States with his family. He spent the next 2 years as a professor of child psychology at Cornell University, and in 1935 he accepted an appointment as professor of psychology in the child welfare station at the University of Iowa, remaining there for 9 years. He spent the last 2 years of his life at the Massachusetts Institute of Technology as professor and director of the Research Center for Group Dynamics.

Lewin is credited with the well-known remark, "There is nothing so practical as a good theory," and the major biographical account of his life and work is appropriately called *The Practical Theorist* (Marrow, 1969). Lewin shifted his major areas of focus several times during his career, but he never abandoned his emphasis on a sound theory as a cardinal prerequisite for practical applications of psychological concepts. His professional career began with studies of learning and perception, from which he turned his attention to the dynamics of conflict, frustration, and the problems of individual motivation, becoming increasingly concerned in his later years with social issues and group processes. Unfortunately, he did not live to draw up an organized overview of his personality theories.

Two of his chief theoretical contributions are the field approach and group dynamics. He borrowed the field approach from physics and adapted it to psychology. That methodological and conceptual framework stimulated considerable research during and after Lewin's lifetime. Although his particular diagrammatic symbol system is no longer widely used, there is little doubt that field theory remains a strong influence on current personality theory. Group dynamics has also had an impact on later developments in psychology. In this connection Lewin's influence is highly contemporary.

FIELD THEORY

Lewin regarded the person and the environment as parts or regions of the same psychological field. Lewin (1963) defined a field as

the totality of coexisting facts which are conceived of as mutually interdependent.

Behavior thus becomes a function of the person and the environment or, in Lewin's well-known formula, $B = F(P,E)$. Beginning with this first single division of the field into the two regions of person and environment, Lewin attempted to work out a framework suitable for the scientific study of human behavior in general and the prediction of its specific expressions. He preferred to use mathematics, the traditional language of science, rather than verbal descriptions, in representing the person-environment field and the influences acting on it at a given time. He considered two general influences in this connection, which he called topological or structural and dynamic.

Topological concepts. Lewin used topology, a nonmetric branch of mathematics, both to present his structural field concepts in mathematical terms and to depict them in diagrammatic form. Through that approach he attempted to clarify the interconnections of the different regions of the field at a particular moment and to show the nature of the boundaries separating them from each other. Person and environment together make up what Lewin called the "life space." Within that area, which represents a field in constant flux, Lewin placed everything that influences behavior at a given time. In his topological diagrams, person and environment are depicted as two separated areas that together constitute the life space and that are enclosed within it. The whole area is bounded off from the nonpsychological environment or foreign hull, much as the person and the environment are separated from each other by a boundary within it. The environment, as Lewin regarded it, does not necessarily correspond to external reality. The term refers, rather, to the psychological environment, the environment as the person interprets it. The person and his environment are the basic structural elements in Lewin's concept of topological space. Group and individual behavior are thought of in terms of the interactions of regions within the life space, along with those interactions between the life space and adjacent areas of the nonpsychological environment that lie outside.

Within the life space, the person and the environment are both regarded as further subdivided into areas or cells by additional boundaries, the subdivisions being represented by increasingly complex topological diagrams. Different kinds of cells are identified in the person region and are so represented in diagrammatic form. Cells that are closest to the boundary that separates the person from the environment make up what Lewin calls a perceptual-motor region. The more central inner-person area has no direct access to the environment, being bounded off by the ring of perceptual-motor cells. The inner-person region is further subdivided into peripheral and central cells; the peripheral cells are closer to the perceptual-motor boundary, and the central cells are still deeper within the region of the person. In topological diagrams, then, the person is represented as a differentiated area of the life space, which is made up of cells of different kinds and with different functions. Those cells interact with a similarly differentiated environment, although in that case the subdivisions are considered essentially alike in structure. To predict behavior, one must identify all the environmental regions influencing the field, as well as all those operating at the time within the person and in impinging segments of the foreign hull, and one must recognize and understand the quality of their interactions.

The interactions of different regions in the life space are possible in Lewinian theory because the boundaries that set off the various areas from each other are more or less permeable. That basic property of the boundaries of the topological space permits interregional influences to operate. Accessibility, the openness of one region in the field to the effect of another region, depends on a number of theoretical considerations. For example, the degree of remoteness is involved; other things being equal, regions that are close together are regarded as more accessible to each other's influence than are those farther apart. However, the factor of resistance is also relevant, inasmuch as highly resistant boundaries can render even adjacent areas of the field inaccessible to each other's influence. The quality of the surfaces of the regions, too, may be a determining factor. For example, the greater the fluidity of the medium, the easier it is for regions to interconnect. Groups, as well as individuals, are thought to differ in those same respects. They can, for example, be more or less accessible to each other, more or less remote, more or less resistant to change, and more or less rigid in interaction. In the extreme, they can become virtually isolated from the external world by what seem to be impenetrable barriers.

According to Lewin, when regions of the field have become accessible to each other, the result is a locomotion, a penetration by the person into the environment. That penetration need not be real in the sense that actual activity occurs; locomotions may also involve psychological processes, such as planning, anticipation, and fantasizing. By definition, however, locomotions involve the interaction of the person and the environment at some level, real or imaginary. Lewin conceived of a process of communication, rather than locomotion as the means by which regions within the person reach each other. Through communication, the perceptual-motor cells are said to connect with those in the outer region of the inner-personal sphere, which, in turn, exerts a more inner-directed influence. In the same way, the central cells in the person communicate in an outward direction. Both locomotions and communications are seen as directed by certain specific principles, a major principle being what Lewin called "related." This principle states that a single area of the field cannot induce behavior by itself. At least two regions must be involved. Another influencing principle is concreteness, which implies that only facts already present in the field can promote behavior. A related principle is that of contemporaneity, which emphasizes Lewin's strong belief that only present facts are relevant. Those that are past or yet to come can and do have a psychological effect in terms of attitudes and anticipations, but they are literally not present in the field as it is constituted at the time.

Dynamic concepts. Lewin (1936) used the term "dynamic" to refer to conditions of change, especially to forces. Those concepts were depicted somewhat differently from the structural aspects of his field theory, and some distinctions in terminology were also made. For example, at the dynamic level, a region in the person was referred to as a system, and a locomotion became a path. Those aspects of the field were represented mathematically by what Lewin called "hodology," the science of paths. A primary dynamic concept in the person system is the need, which was Lewin's chief motivational construct. A need arouses tension, which is then reduced or equalized as the need is met through either action or ideation. Regardless of the method used to restore the person's equilibrium, Lewin identified three stages through which needs typically proceed: hunger, satiation, and oversatiation. Those states are associated with another dynamic concept, that of valency. A valence was defined as the value with which a person invests a particular environmental region in terms of its potential for need satisfaction. A positive valence is associated with the hunger stage of need arousal, a neutral valence with satiation, and a negative valence with oversatiation. For example, a hungry person is likely to be strongly attracted to a restaurant, the investment lessening as his hunger is satisfied. Should he eat too much, he is apt to react to the restaurant with actual aversion.

In Lewinian terms, then, an unsatisfied need arouses tension, tension induces disequilibrium, and the person reacts to restore his equilibrium through either realistic or unrealistic means. The actual motive power for making the restoration is reserved in Lewin's system for the concept of force, a dynamic construct diagrammatically represented by a vector. The need arises in the person, but the force exists in the environment. A force of sufficient strength pressures the person toward tension reduction, and he selects a path into the environment by which to accomplish the reduction. He may also respond by restructuring the environment or simply by changing his perception of the situation, so that it no longer arouses tension in him. His reactions are largely influenced by what Lewin called his level of aspiration, the degree of difficulty presented by the goal toward which he is striving. His level of aspiration establishes the goal he invests with the highest positive valence or perceived reward, and that goal, in turn, is influenced by a number of subjectively determined factors, as well as social pressures and group evaluations.

The concept of level of aspiration has probably promoted more research than any other single Lewinian construct, and its implications are of continuing importance. Much of the current work in achievement motivation, for example, is based on Lewin's finding (Lewin et al., 1944) that difficult goals carry greater positive valence than do easier goals. Further, the current emphasis on cognitive theories of personality derives from Lewin's (1963) view of goal striving in terms of

the relation between cognitive structure (learning, insight, roundabout route) and the direction and strength of the psychological forces.

Lewin maintained that his topological and dynamic theories have much in common with psychoanalysis (Lewin, 1937). He noted, for example, that both are concerned with emotional problems and the development of personality. Both also place major emphasis on the psychological meaning that people, situations, and things have for the person, rather than on an external reality apart from his perception of it. Further, both are involved with such concepts as need, will, and personality. And both are unwilling to remain at the superficial level of description; they attempt to discover deeper meanings by uncovering causal interrelationships.

GROUP DYNAMICS

Lewin's emphasis on psychological facts as major influences on behavior led naturally to his insistence (Lewin, 1963) that the social scientist deals with problems that are

no less real than physical facts and which can be studied no less objectively.

Lewin also consistently maintained that field theory is as applicable to groups as it is to individuals, although with some structural differences. Seen as a dynamic whole, the group must be studied through the interrelationships of its parts. The individual cannot be neglected as a part of the larger field, but social scientists must also take into consideration the structure of the group as a whole—its cultural values, its ideologies, and the economic factors operating within it. To Lewin, group life was a functioning unit, to be studied through careful searching out of all the interrelationships involved and all the relevant aspects of the larger field of which the group is a part.

The now popular term "group dynamics" was introduced by Lewin, and it is probably in this area that his influence is still most strongly felt. Many contemporary techniques originated here, including action-research programs for altering undesirable social conditions and T-groups for facilitating insight into group processes as a means for reeducation. Lewin's social studies involved such diversified areas as leadership, child rearing, prejudice, civic planning, city housing, and education. He became increasingly involved with social issues toward the end of his career. Theory remained of primary interest to him in that connection, largely because he was convinced that a sound theoretical framework provides the only dependable basis for a feasible program of social improvement. Changing group standards were of major concern to Lewin, largely because he believed that persons resist change unless or until group values change. Above all, as Marrow (1969) wrote, Lewin wanted

to seek deeper explanations of why people behave as they do and to discover how they learn to behave better.

With that inclusive goal in mind, he established the Research Center for Group Dynamics at the Massachusetts Institute of Technology and helped to found the Commission on Community Interrelations in New York City at the request of the American Jewish Congress.

The essence of a group, for Lewin, was the interdependence of its parts, and much of the research at the center was directed toward identifying some of the special qualities of interaction that groups achieve. Lewin's students contributed their own research interests to the program, notably in the areas of group cohesiveness and group communication. The laboratory settings that Lewin approved for studying group dynamics were by no means limited to the usual narrow sense of the term. He believed, for example, that a factory can serve as a laboratory in its own right, as can any other situation in which a total group culture can be studied. As the program at M.I.T. developed, broad avenues of investigation were mapped out for intensive study. Those avenues included group productivity, group roles, intergroup conflict, group communication, individual and group adjustment, and the identification of methods for improving group functioning. After Lewin's death, the program was moved to the University of Michigan, where it continues to function under the powerful impetus he provided.

SENSITIVITY TRAINING AND T-GROUPS

A major Lewinian contribution resulted from a request by the Connecticut State Inter-Racial Commission for help in leadership training and in improving racial and religious tensions. With three of his colleagues serving as trainers, Lewin undertook the preliminary work that led to sensitivity training. The initial change experiment was conducted at a workshop in 1946, with the aim of training the participants to handle people more effectively and to gather data on the changes that took place in the process. That training group, the first of the now famous T-groups, consisted of more than 40 trainees, about half of them blacks or Jews and most of them educators or social workers. They participated in an intensive 2-week training program that focused on attitudinal and behavioral change during the group interaction. Lewin himself broke the process of group change down into three phases, which he called unfreezing, restructuring, and refreezing. Rigid attitudes and beliefs must first be unfrozen, raised to critical consideration and evaluation. A restructuring of perspective, a change in viewpoint, then becomes possible. Thereafter, shifts in attitude and behavior can occur, to be refrozen at more constructive levels.

The success of Lewin's initial training workshop and the later evaluation of its long-range effects introduced a novel approach to reeducation, leading to the establishment of the National Training Laboratory for Group Development. Although Lewin died before the institute was officially opened, it has grown into a major center for the application of behavioral science to social practice, particularly through the use of T-group techniques. Lewin, in fact, provided the theoretical and experimental basis for many later extensions in sensitivity training and encounter groups. The procedures he initiated have been adapted to a widening range of problems in interpersonal relationships and have gained international recognition. Sensitivity training stemming from Lewin's original work has been called, "the most significant social invention of this century" (Rogers, 1968). The approach has shown increasing implications for education and industry and has exerted a profound impact on a variety of related theoretical concepts and psychotherapeutic activities.

Gestalt Therapy

The influence of Einstein's field theory on psychological thought led to the development of Gestalt psychology in Germany in the early part of the century. Its chief exponents were Max Wertheimer, Wolfgang Kohler, and Kurt Koffka, three eminent German psychologists of the period. Frederick S. Perls (1893–1970) extended some of the principles of Gestalt psychology into the special form of psychotherapy that bears its name.

Perls was born in Berlin and received his M.D. degree from the University of Berlin. After serving in the German army, he worked briefly with Paul Schilder in Vienna and then spent a year at the Frankfurt Neurological Institute, assisting Kurt Goldstein. He attended the Vienna and Berlin institutes of psychoanalysis, left Germany for South Africa in the early 1940's with the help of Ernest Jones, and founded the South African Institute for Psychoanalysis in Johannesburg. During that period he wrote his first book, in which he outlined some of the procedures later incorporated into the practice of Gestalt therapy. Perls came to the United States in 1946. He engaged in private practice in New York City and later established the New York Institute for Gestalt Therapy. In 1966 he accepted an appointment as associate psychiatrist at the Esalen Institute in California, where he remained for several years. Shortly before his death, he moved to Vancouver, British Columbia, and founded the Institute for Gestalt Therapy there.

GESTALT PSYCHOLOGY AND GESTALT THERAPY

Although Gestalt psychology provides the underlying themes, it is by no means the only contributor to Gestalt therapy, which is heavily indebted to Freudian theory, to the concepts of Wilhelm Reich and Otto Rank, and to existential thought as well. It is considered one of three types of existential therapy (Perls, 1969b), along with Frankl's logotherapy and Binswanger's *Daseins Analyse*. Gestalt therapy leans prominently toward the third force in psychology, accepting its humanistic, holistic, and essentially positive view of human beings and their potentialities. It is concerned with such areas of experience as self-enhancement, creativity, and transcendence. It regards the mere absence of misery and pain as an insufficient goal for living, looking at the person as at least potentially capable of achieving real joy.

A Gestalt, a whole, was defined by Asch (1968) as

an extended event, whether an experience or an action, that cannot be adequately described as a sum of smaller, independent events.

It is chiefly that distinctive emphasis on looking to the whole for the meaning of the parts that unites a group of theorists into what is called the Gestalt school of psychology. According to the Gestalt point of view, any atomistic approach omits essential characteristics of actual experience, such as value, meaning, and form. A number of additional Gestalt principles elaborate that concept further. Gestalts are thought of as unified wholes that reflect a balanced distribution of the forces underlying their organization. When that balance is disturbed, the organism exerts efforts to restore it. The field in which the organism does so involves an internal unity between the organism and its environment. A Gestalt may be considered "a unit segregated from its surroundings" (Kohler, 1947), but the whole relevant field is included in the Gestalt itself. It is emphasized that Gestalten need not correspond to external properties, because the person putting the Gestalt together selects the perception out of a larger field and thus puts something of himself into it. It is also held that the strength of a particular Gestalt depends on "the degree of interdependence of the parts" (Koffka, 1935). Much of the early Gestalt experimental work focused on perception, particularly visual and auditory, but Gestalt concepts have been applied to a wider range of areas, including memory, learning, cognition, activity, and emotional responsiveness. Gestalt principles thus constitute a basic approach potentially applicable to virtually all areas of human behavior and in many ways overlap with recent developments in general systems theory.

Gestalt therapists, in general, consider those principles as similarly basic. In fact, beginning with Perls, the attempt has been to bring the whole area of motivation into line with Gestalt concepts, thus providing a holistic approach to human experience. The phenomenal world is seen as organized around needs, and those needs both integrate and energize behavior.

Needs are hierarchical and shifting, the central figure in the field being the most dominant or pressing need that the person is experiencing at that moment. As that need is met, it recedes into the background, making room for the next most pressing need to assume the dominant position. That process allows need gratification to proceed in appropriate and orderly sequences, the most relevant need organizing the whole person-environment field at any particular time. The environment is an essential part of the field because the person must look to it for need satisfaction.

The Gestalt therapist also accepts other concepts from Gestalt psychology. The marked emphasis on the here and now, perhaps the most outstanding characteristic of Gestalt therapy, is in accord with the importance that Gestalt psychology places on data from immediate experience. Gestalt thinking also stresses the relations between processes in the perceiver and what is perceived in the Gestalten. The perceiver himself contributes significantly to the construction of the Gestalten that direct his behavior, and his internal needs are highly relevant in determining what those Gestalten shall be. However, the plasticity of figure and ground relationships must be retained, or the person becomes severely hampered in his adjustment potential. Adjustment, like perception, is thought of as an organismic process that requires the continual destruction of obsolete Gestalten and the organization of new ones. That destruction and reorganization process is considered essential to all phases of living, even to the most basic requirement of simple survival.

For the process of shifting to function smoothly and efficiently, the person must be able to make sharp differentiations between figure and ground. In terms of motivation, he must recognize what he needs most at a given time, see it clearly as the central figure in the field, and thus put himself in a position in which need satisfaction is possible. Well-organized motor responsiveness and goal-directed behavior result. As one need is met, the next must arise with equal clarity, to be met with similar effectiveness. In a healthy person that shifting is a smooth, continuous process. In the neurotic, the process suffers from considerable impairment. Lacking the ability to make sharp distinctions between figure and ground, the neurotic has a cluttered field, and his differentiations are uncertain. He becomes confused and does not know what he really wants. He cannot distinguish between the important and the unimportant, between the relevant and the irrelevant. Being without consistent motivation, he tends to be disinterested in what he is doing and to find even simple activities hard to pursue. His reactions become stereotypic and repetitive, rather than spontaneous and problem centered. Unable to actualize himself, he attempts to actualize a self-image. Unaware of his real needs, he directs his efforts at manipulating himself, controlling his environment, and maintaining the status quo.

AIMS OF GESTALT THERAPY

Perls saw the person as engaged in a constant struggle for balance, because his equilibrium is continually being disturbed by the pressures of internal needs or by environmental demands. The result is increased tension, which is reduced as balance is restored. That process, which is called organismic self-regulation, is considered basic to all motivation. In the neurotic, the fundamental problem, as Wallen (1970) put it, is that

the whole self-regulation of the environment-organism relationship is destroyed.

To the extent to which pathology disturbs the person's equilibrium:

the object of every treatment, psychotherapeutic or otherwise, is to facilitate organismic balance, to reestablish optimal functions.

Disturbances in organismic balance are thought to engender fear and avoidance of actual awareness, so that the genuine reactivity and excitement that characterize healthy experience are not available. The crucial factor in restoring balance is thought to be awareness, which "by and of itself can be curative" (Perls, 1969b), and, when awareness has returned:

the organism can work on the healthy Gestalt principle that the most important unfinished situation will always emerge and can be dealt with.

Unfinished situations kept out of awareness remain unsettled and highly unsettling, making balance impossible. As a result, the person's spontaneity, freedom, competence, creativity, emotional feelings, and expressions all become impoverished. His inability to form clear and complete Gestalten fosters lack of energy, dullness, and confusion. He avoids his essential organismic needs and looks for environmental support, rather than for internal strengths, in his attempt to resolve his conflicts.

In the Gestalt view, the neurotic and, still more, the psychotic cannot deal constructively with the many polarizations or splits that characterize living in general. The polarizations include the dichotomies of body and mind, self and nonself, biological and cultural, unconscious and conscious, and love and aggression. Language, thinking, perceptions, and all phases of living are generally dealt with through opposites and contrasts. Such dichotomies pose threats to integration that everyone must meet and overcome. In neurotic splitting, however, the attempted resolutions are faulty and damaging to the wholeness of the personality. One part of the split may be held out of awareness, separated from overt concern, or isolated from the other part. Unity is lost, and organismic functioning becomes impossible. Therapy must attempt to restore the personality to wholeness, to its true Gestalt. The patient must be helped to achieve a flexible figure-ground relationship and an increased tolerance for frustration and stress.

And that must be done here and now, as avoidances and distortions are encountered in the actual therapeutic situation. The therapist works with the patient to help him make a genuinely creative adjustment to a present situation, completing Gestalten that would otherwise remain unfinished and would, therefore, become disruptive. Integration is facilitated by the strengthening and supporting of the patient's real needs, interests, and wishes. As Perls (1966) put it:

when the individual attempts to live according to preconceived ideas of what the world "should" be like, he brackets off his own feelings and needs. The result . . . is the blocking off of his potential and the distortion of his perspective.

Integration requires the fusion of splits that, if left as dichotomies, produce conflict and, in the extreme, incapacitation. The integration of conflicting tendencies, on the other hand, leads to the development of constructive traits. For example, a fusing of impulses toward love and aggression may result in healthy self-assertion and genuinely reciprocal relationships. Such integrations enable the person to give up outworn response patterns, unrealistic aspirations, and attempts at overcontrol. Figure and ground can then be more sharply differentiated, and appropriate and real need satisfaction becomes possible. Being aware of what is really happening to him, the patient recognizes that he is in charge of himself. He relinquishes reliance on the therapist and begins to take responsibility for his treatment, just as he gives up his overdependence on environmental support and starts to take charge of his own life.

The immediate goal of Gestalt therapy, then, is restoration of full awareness to the patient. From a long-range point of view, the purpose is to restore to him all his previously crippled personality functions so that he can release his inherent potentialities. Healthy contact with himself and with the environment must be established, replacing the unhealthy processes that substitute for growth and impede integration. The neurotic is unable to be himself, cannot interact comfortably with the environment, and is reduced to manipulation through playing roles. A crucial aspect of Gestalt therapy is, therefore, opening up the field to all that the unhealthy mechanisms have excluded. Other aspects of personality development that may have been crippled along the way must also be restored. For example, frustration tolerance must be increased, for frustration fosters growth, rather than impedes it. Increased frustration tolerance becomes essential for proper ego functioning. The ego is considered an organismic function with major integrative responsibility whose basic purpose is "to structure the environment . . . in terms of the organism's need" (Patterson, 1973). If the structuring can take place easily and consistently, the person is free to continue smooth psychological growth. Such growth requires the ability for contact, sensing, excitement, and Gestalt formation; those processes, in turn, depend on proper fulfillment of the ego's function. From that viewpoint, Gestalt therapy aims at restoring the integrative role of the ego that healthy personality demands. To a large extent, the various subgoals to be met during treatment can be subsumed under the concept of achieving total awareness. In a sense, that is regarded as both a means and an end. The truly aware person has no need for neurotic mechanisms because he is free to actualize himself as he really is. The full awareness at which Gestalt therapy finally aims is thought to lead to a state of completeness and joy in which, wrote Naranjo (1968), the person opens himself

> to the bliss of the eternal Here and Now . . . being one with life, surrendering to the push of it and being "it" at the same time, relinquishing any individual will other than the will of life through us, our true self.

TECHNIQUES OF GESTALT THERAPY

Because the basic purpose of Gestalt therapy is to restore the patient to full awareness, the techniques used are largely directed toward opening up direct, immediate experience—what he is feeling, doing, and thinking right now. That is the only reality in the therapeutic situation. In that experience the patient can recognize just how he operates, how he defeats and deceives himself and frustrates his own best interests. He sees a sample of his life style right in front of him. He is trained to observe himself by bringing his ongoing experience into awareness and keeping it there. Interpretation, intellectual activity in general, and all forms of merely "thinking about" are discouraged. Efforts are directed toward finding out what he experiences, not why he experiences what he does. The focus is on his behavior at as many levels as possible—all that he is expressing verbally and nonverbally, all indications of avoidance, and, particularly, all discrepancies in different forms of expression as they occur. He may, for example, speak of

someone with love but in a hostile tone of voice. He may state that he enjoys his work, although his face expresses dissatisfaction. Discrepancies of that kind indicate to the therapist that the patient is avoiding part of his actual experience and is not responding as a whole person. The therapist is alert to signs of feelings that are being denied awareness, whether in facial expression, vocal tone, posture, or body movements. The therapist's chief function is to bring the patient's attention back to his immediate experience whenever it wanders, helping him to use the continuum of awareness as a means to return to health.

In Gestalt therapy, then, the patient encounters himself. Perls extended the term "encounter," which is becoming increasingly popular in other therapeutic contexts, to include both intrapersonal and interpersonal communication. Conflicts of either kind must entail at least two sides, and the patient must experience and accept both sides if the conflict is to be resolved. He must take back into his awareness everything that he has excluded, and he cannot let anxiety hold him back. The process is often unpleasant and sometimes quite upsetting. The patient's retroflections, projections, and introjections must be brought into his own awareness as he actually watches himself using them. Only as he recognizes them can he begin to take responsibility for them. And only as he takes responsibility for them can he decide to let them go. As he attempts to use various defensive maneuvers to avoid looking at his unacceptable feelings, the therapist consistently redirects his attention to them. However painful it may be, the patient must look at what he has tried to avoid and must accept responsibility for it. The process is facilitated by certain techniques, referred to as rules and games, which were described by Levitsky and Perls (1970). The purpose of the rules is to help establish a therapeutic situation in which the attention of the patient is kept in the context of his present experience. For example, it may be suggested that he use the present tense in verbalizing, that he use "I" instead of "it" in referring to his body and what it does, or that he address other people directly, rather than talking about them. The games are more explicit techniques for bringing the patient into increasing contact with himself.

In the game of taking sides, the patient is encouraged to bring both sides of a particular conflict into conscious experience. It is often done through dialogue, a kind of encounter technique in which the patient carries on an overt discussion between both parts of the split in his personality. Probably the primary encounter in Gestalt therapy is that between top dog and underdog, the passive-aggressive split in the personality. Top dog is the bullying, demanding, authoritarian, and self-righteous side of the split. Underdog, on the other hand, is dependent and overtly compliant but passively manipulative. The dialogue aims at bringing both sides together, enabling them to declare a truce long enough to listen to each other and become reconciled. Other conflicts can be resolved in the same way. The patient may also be urged to take responsibility. That represents an attempt to impress on him that he must not avoid accepting his feelings as his own. He is, therefore, asked to express what he feels openly and without reserve, concluding his statements by adding, "and I take responsibility for it."

The therapist, as well as the patient, plays an extremely active role in the therapeutic process. The patient attempts to avoid his problems and to defend himself against pain. The therapist serves to counteract such attempts. He draws the patient's attention to his avoidance mechanisms, to signs of phobic behavior, and to other defensive and unproductive attitudes and feelings. The Gestalt viewpoint emphasizes the value of frustration in fostering growth. The therapist may, therefore, deliberately frustrate the patient to help him increase his frustration tolerance and break through his impasse by finding his own way out. Above all, the patient must come to place his confidence in himself, and to do so, he must recognize the fantasy nature of the impasse he experiences. He must come to grips with all that he is resisting in himself. Although he approaches that task with great anxiety, it nevertheless represents his one way out. The role of dreams is considered particularly important in the process. The dream was regarded by Perls (1970) as

an existential message ... a message of yourself to yourself ... possibly the most spontaneous expression of the human being.

The therapist does not approach the dream through interpretation. Instead, he urges the patient to relive it in the immediate situation. He acts it out like a drama, playing the roles of the people and even the objects that the dream contains. A game that may be used for that purpose is the empty chair, a technique in which the patient is instructed to change his seat as he takes the role of different figures in his dream. In recent years a variety of Gestalt techniques have been broadly incorporated into a range of other therapies, and other therapies—such as dance, body work, and Reichian techniques—have, in turn, been combined with Gestalt (Marcus, 1978).

The handling of the dreamwork in Gestalt therapy may be considered a miniature form of the whole therapeutic process. The dream is a story woven around different parts of the self in its various conflicting aspects. If the different levels of the dream can be brought into the patient's full awareness and accepted there, he is put into a position in which integration can replace conflict. That restoration of wholeness is the goal of all the techniques of Gestalt therapy because it is regarded as the goal of life. Gestalt therapy implies a prescription for the good life that is quite similar to its therapeutic procedures. The elements of the prescription, as suggested by Naranjo (1970), include the following: Live now. Live here. Stop imagining and needless thinking. Express, rather than manipulate, justify, and judge. Do not restrict awareness. Accept only your own "shoulds." Take responsibility for your own feelings, thoughts, and actions. And, finally, surrender to being what you are.

Herbert Marcuse

Herbert Marcuse is a political philosopher whose critical philosophical and psychological analyses of mid-20th century society have aroused intense controversy among social theorists of all persuasions.

Born in Berlin in 1898, he attended the University of Berlin and then the University of Freiburg, where he studied with Heidegger and received his Ph.D. degree in philosophy magna cum laude in 1922. Three factors were especially powerful in shaping his world views: first, the nascent discipline of sociology; second, the failure of democracy in Germany and the unchecked rise to power of the Nazis; third, the work of Wilhelm Riech, whose Marxist brand of psychoanalysis gave Marcuse a perspective from which to understand the irrational and inhuman facts of life in Nazi Germany and provided him with the seeds of his theory relating sexual repression to political and social repression.

Marcuse was a co-founder of the Frankfurt School of Social Research, which subsequently became the object of intense denunciation and threat by the Nazis. When Hitler assumed power in 1933, the school closed, and Marcuse fled to Geneva before coming to the United States in 1934 to lecture at Columbia University.

During World War II Marcuse functioned as a European intelligence analyst with the Office of Strategic Services and after the war turned

his analysis toward the Soviet Union, quickly establishing himself as an expert on the Russian language and Soviet affairs. He returned to teaching in 1951 at Columbia, Harvard, and Brandeis. In 1967 he became professor of philosophy at the University of California at San Diego and has continued to teach there well past the usual age of retirement.

His magnus opus, *Eros and Civilization* (1955), is his most complete and profound presentation of his ideas on the neurotic nature of social and political repression. The theories of *Eros and Civilization* were applied specifically to contemporary American society in *One Dimensional Man* (1964) which remains his most popular book. Marcuse has written prolifically (Marcuse, 1970, 1972, 1973, 1976, 1978), but, although his major theses are widely known, relatively few of his books are read outside academic circles.

Marcuse has met with a mixture of powerful reactions. His trenchant criticisms of the societal status quo have been enthusiastically accepted as providing a theoretical foundation for a variety of radical causes. He has been especially popular among student rebels, and his name became associated with the 1968 university rebellions in Rome, Berlin, Paris, and the United States. On the other hand, he has not hesitated to criticize Marxism (Marcuse, 1978), and he has been excoriated by hard-line Communists as a pernicious influence on world youth. To all that, Marcuse responded:

If somebody really believes that my opinions seriously endanger society, then he and society must be very badly off indeed.

PSYCHOSOCIAL PERSPECTIVE

Marcuse's perspective involves elements of Marxism, Freudianism, and libertarianism. The fundamental neurosis in today's affluent society he sees as stemming from an unresolved conflict between human life instincts and the oppressive, irrational, consciousness-reducing forces of anachronistic, self-perpetuating social structures. For Marcuse the belief that freedom and satisfaction are provided by today's affluent society is illusory. People believe they have freedom and satisfaction not because they exist in any fundamental sense but, rather, because the populace is narcotized. People are taught to "produce and consume the unnecessary" (Marcuse, 1969). The result, according to Marcuse, is maintenance of the social and psychodynamic status quo, in which a person learns to desire what the system can produce. That fosters the survival of a scarcity mentality and economy to make sure that production and consumption are continuously increased. The system reinforces repression and sublimation, rather than allowing the search for personal pleasure, despite the fact that free persons in an affluent society can afford such gratification.

The idea that artificial consumer needs must be created and maintained by the society and its media is central to Marcuse's philosophy. The spawning of those consumer needs necessarily involves tinkering with the psychic process of the populace and, in particular, stimulating sexual fantasies. However, because those artificially created needs are never completely satisfied, a chronic sense of frustration is developed. That frustration may be directed internally against the self or outwardly against any suitable targets, such as potential enemies and scapegoats. Another consequence of those processes is that society effectively acts to repress transcendence. On that point Marcuse finds himself in close agreement with Norman O. Brown and Ronald Laing. Behind the widespread destructiveness, Marcuse sees Freud's Thanatos, the death instinct, manifesting and magnifying itself through modern technology.

PSYCHOANALYTIC CONCEPTS

Marcuse makes use of several other psychoanalytic concepts but does not hesitate to modify and adapt them to accommodate changing societal patterns and forces. He lays great emphasis on the role of environmental factors in the determination of what Freud took to be inherent components of human nature. For Freud, repression was the sine qua non for civilization. Repression and sublimation, he held, freed sexual energy for the general good of society, because he saw civilization as being founded on two fundamental dichotomies: (1) freedom versus happiness and (2) sexuality versus civilization. Only where the ego-based reality principle governs the id-based pleasure principle can civilization succeed. For Marcuse (1969), on the other hand, no such dichotomies are necessary, and he sees

happiness as the fulfillment of all potentialities of the individual . . . at root, it is freedom.

Similarly, Marcuse sees nothing impossible in a social order in which sexual energy and gratification form the basis of all human relationships. He believes that social order is possible once society has reached a stage at which material scarcities have been removed and basic repressions, which were necessary in times of scarcity, are no longer essential. Marcuse expands on Freud's constructs by introducing the notion of surplus repression, which he distinguishes from the basic repression necessary for the establishment of a successful civilization. Marcuse maintains that, although repressions could be removed in affluent societies to allow people freer access to their instinctual lives, unnecessary controls are maintained, and basic repression becomes surplus repression. Marcuse holds that affluence has essentially removed the struggle for abundance. What was for Freud a reality principle, demanding repression as essential for survival, has become, so Marcuse argues, a performance principle, which sets inappropriate demands for productivity.

SOCIAL REVOLUTION AS RESOLUTION

For Marcuse, then, the only hope for a transcendence of the mass neurosis of modern people lies in a thoroughgoing revolution and the creation of a new social order (Marcuse, 1976). But, in contradistinction to traditional Marxist thinking, he sees the working class as too anesthetized to be effective. The major hope that Marcuse (1969) sees lies with the intelligentsia and the ghetto populations, who alone may be motivated to undergo the necessary

radical change in consciousness . . . the first step in changing social existence.

Norman O. Brown

Norman O. Brown has become widely known for his unique and iconoclastic blending of psychoanalysis, philology, philosophy, classical studies, and social criticism.

Born in Mexico in 1913, he attended the universities of Oxford, Chicago, and Wisconsin, where he received his Ph.D. He began teaching at Nebraska Wesleyan University, moved to the University of Rochester, and is presently located at the University of California at Santa Cruz. In 1936 and 1958 he was awarded Commonwealth Fund and Guggenheim Fellowships.

Like Marcuse, Brown holds that modern society fosters harmful repression and inhibits freedom and transcendence. Both theorists also believe that such societal restrictions are responsible for an unrecognized proportion of human suffering. In *Life against Death* Brown (1959) explicitly addressed the book

to all who are ready to call into question old assumptions and to entertain new possibilities.

Brown's unique style as a symbolist poet and mystic frequently makes assessment and criticism difficult. He takes themes out of world literature and translates them through analogy and metaphor into a mystical vision of the universe whose essence is sexuality. Believing that organized thought and traditional logic are the source of much distress, Brown pleads for a willing suspension of common sense, a suspension he himself uses frequently, much to the occasional distress of critics. But then for Brown (1966):

Wisdom is in wit, in fooling, most excellent fooling; in play, and not in heavy puritanical seriousness

and (Brown, 1973):

poetic truth is metaphysical truth, and physical truth which is not in conformity with it should be considered false.

Many of Brown's most provocative ideas come from applying Freud's principles to areas untouched by Freud himself (Brown, 1959):

The hard thing is to follow Freud into that dark underworld which he explored, and stay there; and also to have the courage to let go his hand when it becomes apparent that his pioneering map needs to be redrawn.

For Brown (1959):

mankind is unconscious of its real desires, and therefore unable to obtain satisfaction, is hostile to life, and ready to destroy itself.

The major factor in that dilemma he sees as repression, and the way out involves two components: first, a realignment of societal reality with the pleasure principle; second, a process of unification extending across many levels of being to heal the illusory fragmentation and divisions imposed by ego and society.

Brown defined man as the animal which represses himself. Thus, repression forms the basis of the universal human neurosis and

because man has preferred death to life, repression rather than liberation, the society he has created for himself is one of insatiable discontent.

The fundamental nature of the repressed forces are Eros and Thanatos, which are the energies molding human culture. To recognize the nature of those forces, one must reinterpret culture as an expression of the human body, which is the source of those energies. For Freud, Eros and Thanatos were inherent in human nature and necessarily linked. Because Brown identifies Eros with good and Thanatos with evil, he suggests that people discard Thanatos entirely or, at least, come to see it as a friend.

Traditionally, sublimation has been viewed as a healthy mode of adaptation to the reality principle, but for Brown it is more problematic and paradoxical. Brown (1959) sees sublimation as

essentially an attempt to relate the organic and superorganic levels, as part of the general effort of psychoanalysis to rediscover the animal in man and to heal the war between body and soul.

Brown emphasizes, however, that the attempt to integrate across different levels—such as cultural ideals and bodily desires, adult rationality and infantile irrationality—is fraught with paradox and the potential for misuse. Thus (Brown, 1959):

Man has convinced himself that sublimation has been a conquest of lower instincts whereas in reality, progressively greater sublimation has meant that the death instinct has gained.

For Brown then, culture and instinct are necessarily diametrically opposed, as are the pleasure and reality principles.

Freud's work demonstrates that the allegiance of the human psyche to the pleasure principle is indestructable and that the path of instinctual renunciation is the path of sickness and self-destruction.

For Brown the resolution of the conflict is to change social reality toward increasing concordance with the pleasure principle.

He believes that usual sexuality represents but a fragment of a larger picture. The fulfillment of human sexual potential involves an expansion of the range of libidinal expression from the genital to the polymorphous perverse. That expansion will occur when people relinquish their current limited psychosexual identity and move to a higher level of being involving polymorphous ecstasy. Thus, the present social order is to be replaced with one in which instinctual drives are affirmed.

DICHOTOMIES OF THE EGO

For Brown, the ego operates by perceiving differences and divisions, a perceptual mode manifested at the societal level as the division and fragmentation of humanity into separate classes, nations, and other groups. In recognizing the role of the ego in creating a pervasive and divisive picture of reality and true human nature, Brown echoes the millenia-old insights of the great mystics. He also goes beyond traditional egoic definitions of health in suggesting that selfhood and a strong sense of separate identity are not desirable goals. Rather, they represent divisive and limited identifications with individual components of the larger body of humanity.

Real human nature, Brown claims, is unified and transcendent to such dichotomies as man-woman, life-death, me-you. In fact, a basic human drive is toward unity, a unity that transcends the ego-imposed fragmentation of reality and of the corporate body of humanity (Brown, 1966):

The rents, the tears, splits and divisions, are mind made: they are not based on the truth but on what the Buddhists call illusion.

For Brown, that fragmented atomistic picture of the world and people is a function only of superficial egoic functioning. Deep within the unconscious lies (Brown, 1966) the "principle of communion buried beneath the surface separations." By seeking and following the deeper psychic system and the reality it reveals, one releases a drive toward unity and wholeness that can encompass dichotomies and negate conflicts (Brown, 1966):

embracing all mankind, without distinction . . . in one mystical or symbolic body.

New Developments in Personality Theory

A number of the personality theorists considered in this section have emphasized approaches to an expanded view of human potentialities. Throughout history and in all cultures, there have been numerous reports of alterations in awareness, including such phenomena as states of consciousness, which may be experienced as an expanded sense of self or even a loss of selfhood. Any overview of human potentialities must, then, include a broad spectrum of phenomena that seemingly transcend the customary definitions of the limits of reality.

Abraham Maslow, Gardner Murphy, and Gordon Allport have been among the most influential theorists in recognizing and stressing the importance of exploring the extremes of human potential and psychological well-being. Unable to find more than passing reference to those areas in Western literature, they turned toward Eastern psychologies, which have long focused on such questions. There they found a wealth of information that careful examination led them to believe had been significantly underestimated in the past and that pointed toward a radically different picture of human psychology. Their inquiries led them to investigate such subjects as altered states of consciousness, self-transcendence, meditation, yoga, and a range of related experiences and phenomena that had not previously been subject to Western psychological examination. At the same time, a body of empirical and theoretical data was emerging from studies of such phenomena as biofeedback, peak experiences, psychedelic therapy, and the personal experiences of related phenomena and practices reported by initially skeptical Western behavioral scientists.

That growing body of information proved significant enough for Maslow (1968) to conclude:

I consider Humanistic, Third Force Psychology to be transitional, a preparation for a still "higher" Fourth Psychology, transpersonal, transhuman, centered in the cosmos rather than in human needs and interest, going beyond humanness, identity, self-actualization, and the like.

To provide a forum for such interests, Maslow joined several eminent pioneers of humanistic psychology—including Anthony Sutich, Jim Fadiman, and Miles Vich—in founding the *Journal of Transpersonal Psychology* and the Association for Transpersonal Psychology. Thus, the field of transpersonal psychology, the so-called fourth force of Western psychology, emerged, drawing on the contributions of both Eastern wisdom and Western science.

The term "transpersonal" was selected after considerable deliberation in an effort to reflect the extension of psychological inquiry into areas going beyond, *trans,* the individual and his or her *persona* or personality. In many of the experiences under investigation, the subjects experienced an extension of identity beyond both individuality and personality. One of the primary concerns of transpersonal psychology is the study of optimum psychological health and well-being, with a focus on a wide spectrum of states of consciousness. The goal of transpersonal psychotherapy is to facilitate growth and awareness beyond traditionally recognized levels of health.

TRANSPERSONAL MODELS

The transpersonal model of the human being differs in several aspects from traditional models and can be conceptualized under four major dimensions: consciousness, conditioning, personality, and identification (Walsh and Vaughan (1979, 1980).

Consciousness. The transpersonal model holds consciousness to be a central dimension that constitutes the essence, context, or matrix of the human experience. Traditional Western psychologies have held differing positions with regard to consciousness, ranging from behaviorism, which ignores it, to psychodynamic and humanistic approaches, which acknowledge it but, in general, pay more attention to its contents that to consciousness itself. The transpersonal perspective holds that a spectrum of states of consciousness exists, that some of those states are potentially useful, and that some of them represent true higher states. Literature from a variety of cultures and ages, as well as from more recent empirical studies of such areas as meditation and state-dependent learning, attest to the attainability of those states (Buddhagosa, 1923; Grof, 1975; Tart, 1975 a, b; Goleman, 1977; Shapiro and Walsh, 1980). On the other hand, the traditional view holds that only a limited range of states exist—for example, waking, dreaming, intoxication, and psychosis. The usual waking state is considered optimal, and nearly all other states are seen as secondary, unimportant, or detrimental.

However, the transpersonal model views the usual state of consciousness as less than optimal. Meticulous and prolonged self-observation, such as in meditation, reveals that the usual state is filled to a remarkable and unrecognized extent with a continuous and largely uncontrollable flow of thoughts, emotions, and fantasies. They are continuously, automatically, and unconsciously blended with sensory inputs, according to the person's needs and defenses, to exert an extraordinarily powerful but usually unrecognized distorting influence on perception, cognition, and behavior. That part of the model is in agreement with the claims of a variety of Eastern psychologies and consciousness disciplines, which state that, whether they know it or not, untrained persons are prisoners of their own minds. As such, they are totally and unwittingly trapped in a continuous perception-distorting fantasy that creates an all-consuming illusion called "maya" or "samsara." That statement has often been misunderstood to mean that the world is an illusion and does not really exist. Rather, what it suggests is that human perception of the world is colored to an unrecognized degree by mental productions.

Full awareness, in place of that conditioned distortion of the mind, is one of the aims of transpersonal therapy. A variety of approaches may be used, including traditional psychotherapeutic techniques, but, to date, advanced work on that problem has necessitated the use of techniques that are at least partially derived from non-Western psychologies, such as meditation and yoga. They all involve training in controlling one or more aspects of perceptual sensitivity, concentration, affect, and cognition. The intensity and the duration of the training usually needed to attain mastery are quite extraordinary by traditional Western standards. Ultimately, such approaches point the way to the possibility of an enduring state of consciousness—known by a variety of names, such as enlightenment, samadhi, moksha, and Nirvana—that is free of the usual limitations and distortions. A person who has reached that condition is said to be able to look back at his former self and at humanity in general and to recognize those previously unnoticed perceptual errors. In the words of Satprem (1968):

> Having started from a small mental construction wherein he believed himself quite at ease and very enlightened, the seeker looks behind him and asks himself how he has managed to live in such a prison.

Technically, that process of reevaluation of a lower state from a higher state is known as subrationing (Deutsch, 1969).

Conditioning. The transpersonal perspective emphasizes two phenomena related to conditioning that go beyond traditional psychological approaches. The first involves the possibility of freedom from conditioning, at least phenomenologically. Such a possibility is hard to conceive from the perspective of the traditional models, but it follows logically from the process of the disidentification of awareness from mental content. The second phenomenon is a form of conditioning that Eastern psychologies have examined in detail but that has been largely ignored in the West—namely, the specific consequences of attachment. Attachment is closely associated with desire and signifies that the nonfulfillment of the desire will result in psychological pain. Attachment is, therefore, held to play a central role in the causation of suffering, and letting go of attachment is held to be central to the cessation of suffering. Those principles were perhaps most clearly enunciated in the Buddha's four noble truths (Buddhagosa, 1923; Byrom, 1976) but have also been described by some Western practitioners, such as Jung (1973), who stated:

> whenever we are still attached, we are still possessed; and when one is possessed it means the existence of something stronger than oneself.

Personality. In earlier Western psychologies, personality has been accorded a central place, and, indeed, most theories hold that a person *is* his personality. Transpersonal theory, however, places less importance on personality, which is seen as only one aspect of being, an aspect with which the person may identify but does not have to. Psychotherapists have usually viewed the attainment of health as involving some modification of personality. However, from the transpersonal perspective, health is seen as primarily involving a shift from an exclusive identification with personality to a broader identity and sense of being, extending beyond traditional egoic limits and encompassing pure consciousness. Such a shift is accompanied by a sense of relative freedom from the habitual dictates of personality, even in those cases in which the personality itself remains relatively unmodified.

Identification. Identification is seen as a crucial transpersonal concept and is conceptually extended beyond customary Western limits. Traditional psychologies have recognized identification with external phenomena and have defined the process as an unconscious one in which the person becomes like or feels the same as an external object or person.

Transpersonal psychology on the other hand, recognizes external identification but states that identification with intrapsychic phenomena is of even greater significance. Thoughts and feelings may be observed with detachment and exert little or no influence on the person. However, if the person identifies with them, they come to determine his sense of identity and reality. For example, if the thought "I'm scared" arises and is seen to be what it is—that is, just another thought—it exerts little influence. However, if the thought is identified with, then the person's reality at that moment is that he is frightened. Through identification a self-fulfilling prophetic process ensues in which one believes himself to be what he thinks.

THE EGO AS ILLUSION

This process extends into the most fundamental aspects of identity. Even the sense that a relatively stable and permanent ego exists within one may be illusory. Identification of awareness with the thoughts and feelings that continuously flow through the mind in rapid succession results in the illusion that a continuous observer exists, just as a rapid succession of still pictures results in the illusion of continuous motion (Byrom, 1976; Wilber, 1977). However, awareness of sufficient sensitivity and precision, such as occurs in advanced meditation, may cut through those perceptual distortions and result in the recognition that no ego, self, or I is buried deep within the psyche but only a ceaseless, impersonal flux of thoughts and emotions and the awareness that observes them (Goleman, 1977; Kornfield, 1977). That recognition is said to be an extremely salutary one, freeing the person from significant amounts of egocentric concern. However, a full understanding and appreciation of the phenomena and their implications is held to be best obtained by and, at least partially dependent on, direct experiences of them, rather than by intellectual discussion alone.

From that model follow possibilities for psychological growth and well-being that extend beyond the possibilities of traditional Western psychology and psychotherapy. Western psychotherapy usually has as its final goal a strong ego capable of living with and adapting to the existentially inevitable realities, such as continuous ego-superego conflict. For transpersonal theorists, however, more is possible. They agree with the premise that a strong ego is better than a weak, ineffective one in meeting the demands of everyday life, but they suggest that the relinquishing of identification with ego may be essential to higher development.

The conflicts and suffering associated with ego and the existential givens of life may, indeed, be unresolvable. However, from the transpersonal perspective, they are transcendable through the expansion of awareness and identity beyond the exclusive identification with ego and personality (Fadiman and Frager, 1976; Wilber, 1977; Fadiman, 1979). In the words of Needleman (1976):

> The self that psychology talks about is too small, too egotistical and too introverted.

LIBERATION FROM THE EGO

A variety of non-Western psychologies report a state in which the individual sense of identity shifts beyond traditional egoic confines to awareness itself. They view that state as the discovery of one's own true nature or identity, which is experienced as liberation or enlightenment. That pinnacle of psychological development and well-being has been described across cultures and centuries. It is characterized by such features as sensitive clear perception, a sense of the perfection of the universe and one's place in it, love and compassion for others, and an absence of greed, anger, and hatred (Johannson, 1969; Goleman, 1977; Walsh and Shapiro, 1980).

Even transient experiences of that nature may have significant therapeutic effects. As Carl Jung (1973), perhaps the first Western psychotherapist to affirm their importance, wrote:

> The fact is that the approach to the numinous is the real therapy and inasmuch as you attain the numinous experience you are released from the curse of pathology.

Such a recognition is of both theoretical and practical importance, because there has been a tendency for some psychiatrists to make a priori assumptions that such transcendental experiences must represent pathological ego regressions akin to schizophrenic processes (Alexander and Selesnick, 1966; Group for the Advancement of Psychiatry, 1976). Such an interpretation may be understandable from the traditional perspective, which does not recognize the existence of a spectrum of altered states, but it is at variance with recent theoretical and empirical findings (Greeley, 1975; Grof, 1975; Hood, 1976; Walsh and Vaughan, 1979).

CONCEPTUAL CONVERGENCE

Those studies and the transpersonal multistate model also hold significant implications for a new understanding of religion and religious experience. They point to the recognition that certain aspects of the great religions can be considered as state-specific technologies whose practices are designed to alter the practitioner's state of consciousness and induce in him or her a transcendental state (Grof, 1975; Tart, 1975 a, b; Wilber, 1977). Thus, the potential for achieving deeply significant and noematic states—which may be interpreted either theistically or nontheistically, as one chooses—may be inherent in everyone.

Transpersonal psychology provides a framework for intensive investigation of the range of human potential. The need for more refined instruments to measure nonordinary states of consciousness is apparent, as well as the need for greater clarity and precision in delineating the parameters of such phenomena.

Suggested Cross References

Other theories bear on this section, including the theories of Freud (Chapter 8), Berne (Section 9.6), Erikson (Section 10.1), Jung (Section 10.3), Rank (Section 10.4), Reich (Section 10.6), and learning theory (Section 4.3). General living systems theory is discussed in Section 1.2. Perception and cognition are discussed in Section 4.1. Parapsychology is discussed in Section 56.15. Psychoanalysis and psychoanalytic psychotherapy are discussed in Section 30.1, behavior therapy in Section 30.2, group psychotherapy and psychodrama in Section 30.5, and recent methods of psychotherapy in Section 30.8. Biofeedback is discussed in Section 4.9. Hyponosis is discussed in Section 30.4.

REFERENCES

Alexander, F. G., and Selesick, S. T. *The History of Psychiatry.* New American Library, New York, 1966.

Allport, G. W. *Becoming: Basic Considerations for a Psychology of Personality.* Yale University Press, New Haven, Conn., 1955.

Allport, G. W. *The Individual and His Religion.* Macmillan, New York, 1960a.

Allport, G. W. *Personality and Social Encounter.* Beacon Press, Boston, 1960b.

Allport, G. W. *Pattern and Growth in Personality.* Holt, Rinehart and Winston, New York, 1961.

Allport, G. W. Introduction. In *Hindu Psychology,* by S. Akhilananda, p. ix. Routledge and Kegan Paul, London, 1965.

Allport, G. W. Autobiography. In *A History of Psychology in Autobiography,* E. G. Boring and G. Lindzey, editors, vol. 5, p. 10. Appleton-Century-Crofts, New York, 1967.

Allport, G. W. *The Person in Psychology: Selected Essays.* Beacon Press, Boston, 1968a.

Allport, G. W. A unique and open system. In *International Encyclopedia of the Social Sciences,* D. L. Sills, editor, vol. 12, p. 1. Macmillan, New York, 1968b.

Asch, S. E. Gestalt theory. In *International Encyclopedia of the Social Sciences,* D. L. Sills, editor, vol. 6, p. 158. Macmillan, New York, 1968.

*Bischof, L. J. *Interpreting Personality Theories,* ed. 2. Harper & Row, New York, 1970.

*Boring, E. G., and Lindzey, G., editors. *A History of Psychology in Autobiography,* vol. 5. Appleton-Century-Crofts, New York, 1967.

Brown, N. O. *Life against Death: The Psychoanalytic Meaning of History.* Wesleyan University Press, Middletown, Conn., 1959.

Brown, N. O. *Love's Body.* Random House, New York, 1966.

Brown, N. O. *Closing Time.* Random House, New York, 1973.

Buddhagosa. *The Path of Purity.* Pali Text Society, Kandy, Ceylon, 1923.

Byrom, T. *The Dhammapada: The Sayings of the Buddha.* Random House, New York, 1976.

Deutsch, E. *Advaita Vedanta: A Philosophical Reconstruction.* East-West Center Press, Honolulu, 1969.

Fadiman, J. The transpersonal stance. In *Cognition and Clinical Science,* M. Mahoney, editor, p. 102. Pergamon Press, New York, 1979.

Fadiman, J., and Frager, L. *Personality and Personal Growth.* Harper & Row, New York, 1976.

Fromm, E. *Escape from Freedom.* Holt, Rinehart and Winston, New York, 1941.

Fromm, E. *Man for Himself.* Holt, Rinehart and Winston, New York, 1947.

Fromm, E. *Psychoanalysis and Religion.* Yale University Press, New Haven, Conn., 1950.

Fromm, E. *The Sane Society.* Holt, Rinehart and Winston, New York, 1955.

Fromm, E. *The Art of Loving.* Harper & Row, New York, 1956.

Fromm, E. Psychoanalysis and Zen Buddhism. In *Zen Buddhism and Psychoanalysis,* E. Fromm, D. Suzuki, and R. DeMartino, editors, p. 93. Harper & Row, New York, 1960.

Fromm, E. *The Heart of Man.* Harper & Row, New York, 1964.

Fromm, E. *The Revolution of Hope.* Harper & Row, New York, 1968.

Fromm, E. *The Crisis of Psychoanalysis.* Holt, Rinehart and Winston, New York, 1970.

Fromm, E. *The Anatomy of Human Destructiveness.* Holt, Rinehart and Winston, New York, 1973.

Fromm, E. *To Have or to Be.* Harper & Row, New York, 1976.

Fromm, E. *Wellbeing of Man and Society.* Seabury, New York, 1978.

Fromm, E., and Xirau, R. *The Nature of Man.* Macmillan, New York, 1968.

Ghougassian, J. P. *Gordon W. Allport's Ontopsychology of the Person.* Philosophical Library, New York, 1972.

Goble, F. *The Third Force: The Psychology of Abraham Maslow.* Grossman, New York, 1970.

Goldstein, K. *The Organism.* American Book Company, New York, 1939.

Goldstein, K. *Language and Language Disturbances.* Grune & Stratton, New York, 1948.

Goldstein, K. The effect of brain damage on the personality. Psychiatry, *15:* 246, 1952.

Goldstein, K. The organismic approach. In *American Handbook of Psychiatry,* S. Arieti, editor, vol. 2, p. 1345. Basic Books, New York, 1959.

Goldstein, K. Stress and the concept of self-realization. In *The Quest for Self-control,* S. Z. Klausner, editor, p. 351. Free Press of Glencoe (Macmillan), New York, 1965.

Goldstein, K. *Human Nature in the Light of Psychopathology.* Schocken Books, New York, 1966.

Goldstein, K. Autobiography. In *A History of Psychology in Autobiography,* E. G. Boring and G. Lindzey, editors, vol. 5, p. 160. Appleton-Century-Crofts, New York, 1967.

Goleman, D. *The Varieties of the Meditative Experience.* E. P. Dutton, New York, 1977.

Greeley, A. M. *The Sociology of the Paranormal.* Sage, Beverly Hills, Calif., 1975.

Grof, S. *Realms of the Human Unconscious.* Viking Press, New York, 1975.

Group for the Advancement of Psychiatry. *Mysticism: Spritual Quest or Psychic Disorder.* Group for the Advancement of Psychiatry, New York, 1976.

*Hall, C., and Lindzey, G. *Theories of Personality,* ed. 2. John Wiley & Sons, New York, 1970.

Hood, R. W. Conceptual criticisms of regressive explanations of mysticism. Rev. Religious Res., *17:* 179, 1976.

Johannson, R. *The Psychology of Nirvana.* George Allen and Unwin, London, 1969.

Jung, C. G. *Letters.* Princeton University Press, Princeton, 1973.

Koffka, K. *Principles of Gestalt Psychology.* Harcourt, Brace and World, New York, 1935.

Kohler, W. *Gestalt Psychology.* Liveright, New York, 1947.

Kornfield, J. *Living Buddhist Masters.* Unity Press, Santa Cruz, Calif., 1977.

Landis, B., and Tauber, E. *In the Name of Life: Essays in Honor of Erich Fromm.* Holt, Rinehart and Winston, New York, 1971.

Leeds, M., and Murphy, G. *The Paranormal and the Normal.* Paul Elek, London, 1979.

Levitsky, A., and Perls, F. S. The rules and games of Gestalt therapy. In *Gestalt Therapy Now,* J. Fagan and I. L. Shepherd, editors, p. 140. Science and Behavior Books, Palo Alto, Calif., 1970.

Lewin, K. *A Dynamic Theory of Personality,* McGraw-Hill, New York, 1935.

Lewin, K. *Principles of Topological Psychology,* McGraw-Hill, New York, 1936.

Lewin, K. Psychoanalysis and topological psychology. Bull. Menninger Clin., *1:* 202, 1937.

Lewin, K. *Resolving Social Conflicts: Selected Papers on Group Dynamics.* Harper & Row, New York, 1948.

Lewin, K. *Field Theory in Social Sciences: Selected Theoretical Papers.* Tavistock Publications, London, 1963.

Lewin, K., Dembo, T., Festinger, L., and Sears, P. Level of aspiration. In *Personality and the Behavior Disorders,* J. McV. Hunt, editor, vol. 1, p. 333. Ronald Press, New York, 1944.

*Maddi, S. R. *Personality Theories: A Comparative Analysis.* Dorsey Press, Homewood, Ill., 1968.

Marceil, J. C. Implicit dimensions of idiography and nomothesis: A reformulation. Am. Psychol., *32:* 1046, 1977.

Marcus, E. *Gestalt Therapy and Beyond.* Meta Press, Palo Alto, Calif., 1978.

Marcuse, H. *Eros and Civilization: A Philosophical Inquiry into Freud.* Beacon Press, Boston, 1955.

Marcuse, H. *One Dimensional Man.* Beacon Press, Boston, 1964.

Marcuse, H. *An Essay on Liberation.* Beacon Press, Boston, 1969.

Marcuse, H. *Five Lectures: Psychoanalysis, Politics, and Utopia.* Beacon Press, Boston, 1970.

Marcuse, H. *Counterrevolution and Revolt.* Beacon Press, Boston, 1972.

Marcuse, H. *Studies in Critical Philosophy.* Beacon Press, Boston, 1973.

Marcuse, H. *Revaluation of Progress.* New University Press, New York, 1976.

Marcuse, H. *Aesthetic Dimensions: Towards a Critique of Marxist Aesthetics.* Beacon Press, Boston, 1978.

Marrow, A. J. *The Practical Theorist: The Life and Work of Kurt Lewin.* Basic Books, New York, 1969.

Maslow, A. H. *The Psychology of Science: A Reconnaissance.* Harper & Row, New York, 1966.

Maslow, A. H. *Toward a Psychology of Being,* ed. 2. D. Van Nostrand, Princeton, 1968.

Maslow, A. H. *Motivation and Personality,* ed. 2. Harper & Row, New York, 1970a.

Maslow, A. H. *Religions, Values, and Peak-Experiences.* Viking Press, New York, 1970b.

Maslow, A. H. *The Farther Reaches of Human Nature.* Viking Press, New York, 1971.

Maslow, B. G. *Abraham H. Maslow: A Memorial Volume.* Brooks-Cole, Belmont, Calif., 1972.

Murphy, G. Parapsychology. In *Taboo Topics,* N. L. Fareberow, editor, p. 61. Atherton, New York, 1963.

Murphy, G. *Personality: A Biosocial Approach to Origins and Structure.* Basic Books, New York, 1966.

Murphy, G. Autobiography. In *A History of Psychology in Autobiography,* E. G. Boring and G. Lindzey, editors, vol. 5, p. 280. Appleton-Century-Crofts, New York, 1967.

Murphy, G. Personal impressions of Kurt Goldstein. In *The Reach of Mind: Essays in Memory of Kurt Goldstein,* M. Simmel, editor, p. 32. Springer, New York, 1968a.

Murphy, G. Psychological views of personality and contributions to its study. In *The Study of Personality,* E. Norbeck, D. Price-Williams, and W. McCord, editors, p. 30. Holt, Rinehart and Winston, New York, 1968b.

Murphy, G. *Challenge of Psychical Research.* Harper & Row, New York, 1970.

Murphy, G. A Caringtonian approach to reincarnation cases. J. Am. Soc. Psychol., Res., *67:* 126, 1973.

Murphy, G. *Human Potentialities.* Penguin Press, Baltimore, 1975.

Murphy, G., and Ballou, R. O. *William James on Psychical Research.* Viking Press, New York, 1960.

Murphy, G., and Kovach, J. K. *Historical Introduction to Modern Psychology.* Harcourt, Brace, Jovanovich, New York, 1972.

Murphy, G., and Leeds, M. *Outgrowing Self-deception.* Basic Books, New York, 1975.

Murphy, G., and Murphy, L. *Asian Psychology.* Basic Books, New York, 1968.

Murphy, G., and Murphy, L. *Western Psychology.* Basic Books, New York, 1969.

Murphy, G., and Spohn, E. *Encounter with Reality.* Houghton Mifflin, Boston, 1968.

Murray, H. A. *Explorations in Personality.* Oxford University Press, New York, 1938.

Murray, H. A. *Assessment of Men.* Holt, Rinehart and Winston, New York, 1948.

Murray, H. A. An American Icarus. In *Clinical Studies in Personality,* A. Burton and R. E. Harris, editors, vol. 2, p. 615. Harper & Row, New York, 1955.

Murray, H. A. Preparations for the scaffold of a comprehensive system. In *Psychology: A Study of a Science,* S. Koch, editor, vol. 3, p. 47. McGraw-Hill, New York, 1959.

Murray, H. A. The possible nature of a "mythology" to come. In *Myth and Mythmaking,* H. A. Murray, editor. Braziller, New York, 1960a.

Murray, H. A. Two versions of man. In *Science Ponders Religion,* H. Shapley, editor, p. 147. Appleton-Century-Crofts, New York, 1960b.

Murray, H. A. In nomine diaboli. In *Theories of Personality: Primary Sources and Research,* G. Lindzey and C. Hall, editors, p. 153. John Wiley & Sons, New York, 1965.

Murray, H. A. Autobiography. In a *History of Psychology in Autobiography,* E. G. Boring and G. Lindzey, editors, vol. 5, p. 283. Appleton-Century-Crofts, New York, 1967.

Murray, H. A. Components of an evolving personological system. In *International Encyclopedia of the Social Sciences,* D. L. Sills, editor, vol. 12, p. 6. Macmillan, New York, 1968.

Murray, H. A. Foreword. In *Perception of Other People,* by F. From, p. xxii. Columbia University Press, New York, 1971.

Murray, H. A., and Kluckhohn, C. Outline of a conception of personality. In *Personality in Nature, Society, and Culture,* C. Kluckhohn, H. A. Murray, and D. Schneider, editors, ed. 2, p. 30. Alfred A. Knopf, New York, 1953.

Naranjo, C. Contributions of Gestalt therapy. In *Ways of Growth,* H. Otto and J. Mann, editors, p. 134. Grossman, New York, 1968.

Naranjo, C. Present-centeredness: Technique, prescription, and ideal. In *Gestalt Therapy Now,* J. Fagan and I. L. Shepherd, editors, p. 49. Science and Behavior Books, Palo Alto, Calif., 1970.

Naranjo, C. *The Techniques of Gestalt Therapy.* SAT Press, Berkeley, Calif., 1973.

Needleman, J. *A Sense of the Cosmos.* E. P. Dutton, New York, 1976.

Overton, D. A. Discriminative control of behavior by drug states. In *Stimulus Properties of Drugs,* T. Thompson and R. Pickens, editors, p. 112. Appleton-Century-Croft, New York, 1971.

Patterson, C. H. *Theories of Counseling and Psychotherapy,* ed. 2. Harper & Row, New York, 1973.

Perls, F. S. Gestalt therapy and human potentialities. In *Explorations in Human Potentialities,* H. A. Otto, editor, p. 543. Charles C Thomas, Springfield, Ill., 1966.

Perls, F. S. *Ego, Hunger, and Aggression.* Random House, New York, 1969a.

Perls, F. S. *Gestalt Therapy Verbatim.* Real People Press, Moab, Utah, 1969b.

Perls, F. S. *In and Out of the Garbage Pail.* Real People Press. Moab, Utah, 1969c.

Perls, F. S. Four lectures. In *Gestalt Therapy Now,* J. Fagan and I. L. Shepherd, editors, p. 27. Science and Behavior Books, Palo Alto, Calif., 1970.

Perls, F. S., Hefferline, R. F., and Goodman, P. *Gestalt Therapy.* Dell, New York, 1965.

Roberts, T. Beyond Self-actualization. Re-Vision, *1*: 42, 1978.

Rogers, C. Interpersonal relationships USA. J. Appl. Behav. Sci., *3*: 4, 1968.

*Sahakian, W. S. *Psychology of Personality: Readings in Theory.* Rand McNally, Chicago, 1965.

Satprem. *Sri Aurobindo or the Adventure of Consciousness.* Harper & Row, New York, 1968.

Shapiro, D. H., and Walsh, R. N., editors. *The Art and Science of Meditation: Research, Theory, and Experience.* Aldine Publishing Co., Chicago, 1980.

Simmel, M., editor. *The Reach of the Mind: Essays in Memory of Kurt Goldstein.* Springer, New York, 1968.

Tart, C. *States of Conciousness.* E. P. Dutton, New York, 1975a.

Tart, C., editor. *Transpersonal Psychologies.* Harper & Row, New York, 1975b.

Wallen, R. Gestalt therapy and Gestalt psychology. In *Gestalt Therapy Now,* J, Fagan and I. L. Shepherd, editors, p. 10. Science and Behavior Books, Palo Alto, Calif., 1970.

Walsh, R. N., and Shapiro, D. H., editors, *Beyond Health and Normality: An Exploration of Extreme Psychological Wellbeing.* Van Nostrand Reinhold, New York, 1980.

Walsh, R. N., and Vaughan, F. Transpersonal models of the person and psychotherapy. In *Beyond Health and Normality: An Exploration of Extreme Psychological Wellbeing,* R. Walsh and D. H. Shapiro, editors. Van Nostrand Reinhold, New York, 1980.

Walsh, R. N., and Vaughan, F. V., editors. *Beyond Ego: Transpersonal Dimensions in Psychology.* J. P. Tarcher, Los Angeles, 1979.

*Wepman, J. M., and Heine, R. *Concepts of Personality.* Aldine Publishing Co., Chicago, 1963.

White, R. *The Study of Lives.* Atherton, New York, 1963.

Wilber, K. *The Spectrum of Consciousness.* Theosophical Publishing House, Wheatstone, Ill., 1977.

Wilson, C. *New Pathways in Psychology: Maslow and the Post-Freudian Revolution.* Taplinger, New York, 1972.

chapter

12

Diagnosis and Psychiatry: Examination of the Psychiatric Patient

12.1 Psychiatric Interview

ROGER A. MacKINNON, M.D.

Introduction

The modern psychiatric interview is based on a clear understanding of psychopathology and psychodynamics. It is not a random or arbitrary meeting between doctor and patient.

In the psychiatric interview, like all medical interviews, one person is suffering and desires relief; the other person is expected to provide that relief. It is the patient's hope of obtaining relief from his suffering that motivates him to expose himself and to tell all (MacKinnon and Michels, 1971).

That process is facilitated by the confidentiality of the doctor-patient relationship. As long as the patient views the doctor as a potential source of help, he communicates more or less freely any information that he feels may be pertinent to his difficulty. Therefore, it is frequently possible to obtain a considerable amount of information about the patient and his suffering merely by listening. That viewpoint is supported by the non-directive approach of Rogers.

The psychiatric interview is characterized by the fact that the psychiatrist is an expert in the field of interpersonal relations and, accordingly offers the patient more than a sympathetic ear. Indeed, the psychiatric patient or his family expects and deserves expert handling in the interview. The psychiatrist demonstrates his expertise by the questions he both asks and does not ask and by certain other activities discussed later in this section.

The interview is further complicated by the fact that not all psychiatric patients have voluntarily sought the physician's help, and their willingness or ability to cooperate may be impaired. The psychiatrist, like his colleagues in other branches of medicine, is interested in the patient's symptoms, their dates of onset, and significant factors in the patient's life that may explain them. However, psychiatric diagnosis and treatment are based as much on the total life history of the patient as on the present illness. That life history includes the patient's life style, self-appraisal, and traditional coping mechanisms. Psy-

chiatric symptoms, unlike medical symptoms, involve the defensive functions of the ego and represent unconscious psychological conflicts. To the extent that the patient defends himself from awareness of those conflicts, he also conceals them from the interviewer. Therefore, although the psychiatric patient is motivated to reveal himself in order to gain relief from his suffering, he is also motivated to conceal his innermost feelings and the fundamental causes of his psychological disturbance.

Another factor contributing to the patient's concealment during the interview is his concern with the impression he makes on others. The doctor, as a figure of authority, often symbolically represents the patient's parents; consequently, his reactions are particularly important to the patient. If the patient suspects that some of the less admirable aspects of his personality are involved in his illness, he may be unwilling to disclose such material until he is certain that he will not lose the doctor's respect as he exposes himself. For that reason the psychiatrist's relationship with the patient strongly influences what the patient tells him or does not tell him.

In other branches of medicine, the physician finds that there is less chance of omitting important details of the patient's illness if he follows a routine. The experienced psychiatrist avoids stereotyped approaches, and he cannot expect to always learn things in the same order or even always cover the same material in the initial interviews.

Factors Influencing the Interview

Many factors influence both the content and the process of the interview:

The nature of the patient's symptoms and character style significantly influence the transference and the way in which the interview unfolds.

Special clinical situations—such as the patient seen on a general hospital ward, the patient with psychosomatic symptoms, the psychologically unsophisticated patient, and the emergency patient—introduce specific dimensions that shape the interveiw.

Technical factors affect the interview, such as telephone interruptions, the use of an interpreter, note taking, and the physical space and comfort of the room.

The timing of the interview in the patient's illness influences the content and the process of the interview.

The interviewer's style, orientation, and experience have a significant influence on the interview. Even the timing of interjections such as "uh-huh" influence the patient's production as he unconsciously seeks to follow the subtle leads provided by the interviewer.

Purpose of the Interview

Psychiatric interviewers often distinguish between a diagnostic orientation and a therapeutic orientation for an initial interview. However, the interview that is oriented largely toward establishing a diagnosis gives the patient the feeling that he is a specimen of pathology being examined and, therefore, actually inhibits him from revealing certain problems. If there is any single mark of a successful interview, it is the degree to which the patient and the doctor develop a shared feeling of understanding. The beginner frequently misinterprets that statement as advice to provide reassurance or approval. For example, statements that begin "Don't worry" or "That's perfectly normal" are reassuring but do not indicate understanding. Remarks such as "I can see how you felt . . . " and those that pinpoint the circumstances in which the patient became upset do indicate understanding. Even if the interviewer sees a patient only once, a truly therapeutic interaction is possible. It requires great sensitivity, tact, and skill to help the patient maintain his sense of human dignity while exposing his most embarrassing or humiliating experiences. The psychiatrist who adopts a therapeutic attitude toward the patient usually elicits better diagnostic material than if he does not adopt that attitude. In addition, he is better able to assess the patient's attitude toward psychotherapy.

The subject of questionnaires is sometimes raised in connection with supplementing the history obtained during the interview. It is the author's opinion that the chief value of questionnaires or standardized history forms is for research purposes. Although given in the interest of objectivity or completeness, they deprive the interviewer of the opportunity to observe the patient's inner responses to the questions, and they do not facilitate the beginning of a trusting relationship between the patient and the doctor that will lead to the development of the therapeutic alliance.

Initial and Later Interviews

At first glance, the definition of an initial interview seems rather simple: It is the first time that a particular psychiatrist speaks to a particular patient. However, the situation is somewhat more complicated. The patient may never have discussed his personal feelings with anyone, or he may have discussed them with a relative, a friend, a clergyman, a family physician, or another psychiatrist. In fact, the patient may have had a substantial amount of prior psychiatric contact or may have studied psychology, so that he has arrived at a point of self-understanding that may require months of treatment for another patient to reach. There is also the question of time: How long is the initial interview? One hour, 2 hours, 6 hours? Certainly, some issues differentiate the initial interview from later interviews; however, they often prevail for more than one session. Topics that may be discussed with one patient in the first or second interview may not be discussed with another patient until the second year of treatment.

It is sometimes possible to conduct an adequate evaluation of a patient in one interview, but most practitioners prefer to see the patient at least twice before rendering their recommendations. That practice gives the interviewer an opportunity to assess the patient's reactions to their first meeting and thus adds depth to his perspective of the patient. Obviously, the patient should be advised if the consultant plans more than one meeting.

Role of the Interviewer

The most important role of the interviewer is to listen and understand the patient. That understanding is then used to establish rapport and to develop a treatment plan based on sound clinical judgment and acceptable to the patient. The interviewer uses his own empathic responses to facilitate the development of rapport. For example, it is more effective when the patient describes a terrible experience to reply, "How awful" than to say, "You must have felt awful." In general, the interviewer is nonjudgmental, interested, concerned, and kind.

The interviewer frequently asks questions, which may seem to obtain information or to clarify his own or the patient's understanding. Questions can be a subtle form of suggestion; or, by the tone of voice in which they are asked, they may give the patient permission to do something. For example, the interviewer may ask, "Did you ever tell your husband how you feel about that?"

The interviewer makes suggestions to the patient either implicitly or explicitly. He may suggest that the patient discuss major decisions with him before acting on them or that it would or would not be a good idea to discuss certain feelings with important persons in his life. He may, at times, give the patient some advice or practical suggestions about his life. Many of the interviewer's activities serve to gratify the patient's emotional need to feel protected or loved. However, on many occasions the interviewer frustrates the patient's emotional needs, since he cannot realistically make the patient's problems disappear by magic or find him a better job or a better spouse.

The interviewer may offer the patient reassurance concerning specific fears or offer general reassurance, such as, "Please continue; you're doing fine."

The interviewer may, in some situations, have to set limits with a patient who has trouble controlling his impulses, or he may attempt to strengthen drives with another patient who is severely repressed.

The interviewer also helps to build the patient's self-esteem when he focuses on the patient's successful achievements and talents, and he can reduce the patient's guilt through interventions aimed to mollify the patient's harsh superego.

The interviewer offers interpretations that aim at undoing the process of repression, allowing unconscious thoughts and feelings to become conscious, thereby enabling the patient to develop new methods of coping with his conflicts without the formation of symptoms. The two preliminary steps of an interpretation are confrontation, pointing out that the patient is avoiding something, and clarification, formulating the area to be explored.

A complete interpretation delineates a pattern of behavior in the patient's current life, showing the basic conflict between wish and fear, the defenses that are involved, and any resulting symptom formation. That pattern is traced to its origin in his early life, its manifestation in the transference is pointed out, and the secondary gain is formulated. It is never possible to encompass all of those aspects at one time. It requires substantial skill and experience to successfully make interpretations in the first few sessions. The earliest interpretations are aimed at the area in which conscious anxiety is greatest, which is usually the patient's presenting symptoms, his resistance or negative transference. Unconscious material is not interpreted until it has become preconscious. A premature interpretation is threatening; it increases the patient's anxiety and intensifies his resistance. Interpretations are first directed at manifestations of the patient's resistance—but in an empathic and understanding tone that does not make the patient defensive. For example, the interviewer may comment, "If I understand you correctly, you feel it is really your wife who should be seeing a psychiatrist, rather than you" or "You're so worried about your symptoms that it's difficult for you to tell me very much about the other aspects of your life."

Practical Issues

TIME FACTORS

Psychiatric interviews last for varying lengths of time. The average consultation or therapeutic interview is 45 or 50 minutes long. Interviews with psychotic or medically ill patients are often brief, since the patient may find the interview stressful after 20 or 30 minutes. However in the emergency room interviews longer than 50 minutes may be required. In most situations the patient should know in advance approximately how long the interview will last.

The patient's management of time reveals an important facet of his personality. In most cases the patient arrives a few minutes early for his appointment. An anxious patient may arrive as much as a half hour early. If the patient arrives very early and does not seem anxious, that fact probably deserves some exploration during the early part of the interview. The patient who arrives significantly late creates a problem for the interviewer. The first time it occurs the interviewer might listen to the explanation if one is offered and even respond sympathetically if the lateness was clearly due to circumstances beyond the patient's control but should avoid making such comments as, "That's quite all right." If the patient indicates a blatant resistance—such as, "I forgot all about the appointment"—the interviewer might ask, "Did you feel some reluctance about coming?" If the answer is "Yes," he can explore the matter further. But if the reply is "No," then it is better to drop the matter for the time being. It is sometimes appropriate to comment, "Well, we'll cover as much as we can in the time remaining."

The psychiatrist's handling of time is also an important factor in the interview. Chronic carelessness regarding time indicates a lack of concern for the patient. If the physician is unavoidably detained for a first interview, it is quite appropriate for him to express his regret that the patient was kept waiting.

SPACE CONSIDERATIONS

Most patients do not speak freely unless they have privacy and are sure that their conversations cannot be overheard. Quiet surroundings offer fewer distractions for both parties than does a noisy atmosphere, and interruptions are undesirable except for an occasional brief telephone call, preferably not more than one during an interview.

Proper seating arrangements also facilitate the interview. Both chairs should be of approximately equal heights, so that neither person looks down on the other, and it is desirable to place the chairs so that no furniture is between the doctor and the patient. If the room contains several chairs, the doctor indicates his own chair and then allows the patient to choose the chair in which he will feel most comfortable. Overly dependent patients, for example, prefer the chair that is closest

to the doctor; oppositional or competitive patients choose a farther chair, often the one that is directly across from the doctor.

NOTE TAKING

Many opinions exist among experienced psychiatrists concerning the quantity and the method of note taking. The psychiatrist in training often takes written notes during the session in order to present the material to a supervisor. That process may disturb either the patient or the interviewer, particularly if the supervisor requested verbatim notes.

As there is a legal and moral responsibility to maintain an adequate record of each patient's diagnosis and treatment, the need for keeping written records about patients is clear. The patient's record also serves to aid the psychiatrist's memory concerning his patient. Therefore, each interviewer must decide what type of information he has the most difficulty remembering and use that knowledge as a guideline for his own system of record keeping.

The most common practice is to make fairly complete notes during the first few sessions, while eliciting historical data. After that, most psychiatrists record only new historical information, important events in the patient's life, medications prescribed and their effects, transference or countertransference trends, dreams, and general comments about the patient's progress.

Some patients express resentment if the psychiatrist recorded no notes during the interview; they feel that what they said must not have been sufficiently important to record or that the doctor was uninterested. Other patients cannot tolerate note taking and in such cases it should be discontinued. There are times during the interview when the doctor may want to establish a heightened sense of intimacy by putting his pen and paper aside. That practice is customary when the patient reticently discusses such matters as his sex life and his negative feelings about a previous doctor and when he makes transference comments.

Since it is easier to write while listening than it is to write while talking, there is a tendency for notes concerning the remarks made by the patient to be more complete and accurate than are those made by the interviewer.

Data of the Interview

SYSTEMS OF CLASSIFICATION

There are a number of ways to classify or organize the data of the interview. One system is content and process. The content of the interview refers both to the factual information provided by the patient and to the specific verbal interventions of the interviewer. The process of the interview refers to the developing relationship between the doctor and the patient. It is particularly concerned with the implicit meanings of the communications. The patient's awareness of the process varies but is usually limited to his sense of trust or confidence in the doctor or perhaps in his fantasies about him. The interviewer strives for a continuing awareness of the process, which reveals the unfolding of the early transference and countertransference.

Process includes both the manner in which the patient relates to the interviewer and many of the issues in his mental status. With increasing experience the interviewer learns to become aware of his own emotional responses to the patient. If he examines those responses in the light of what the patient has just said or done, he may broaden his understanding of the interview. For example, if he feels bored, he may realize that the patient is avoiding emotional contact and has become preoccupied with his symptoms. If he feels titillated by the sexual details provided by a patient of the opposite sex, he may realize that the patient is using sex to distract him from other issues.

The data of the interview may also be classified as introspective or inspective. Introspective data refer to the patient's subjective report of his feelings and experiences; such data focus on his inner life. Inspective data refer to the nonverbal behavior of the patient and the interviewer. The interviewer is particularly interested in that aspect of the interview with regard to its relationship to the verbal content. For example, the patient who nervously takes his wedding ring on and off is communicating more than general anxiety.

Still another classification of data concerns the affect and thought content of the interview. Both the patient and the doctor experience anxiety in the initial interview, as in any other meeting between strangers. Most people find the idea of having to consult a psychiatrist rather upsetting. The patient is anxious about his illness, the doctor's reaction to him, and the practical problems of psychiatric treatment.

Any display of emotion by the patient during the interview takes priority over other matters, because such a display provides the interviewer with an opportunity to express empathy. It is often useful for the physician to name the emotion the patient is displaying. If the patient denies having the emotion named by the interviewer but suggests a synonym, the physician accepts the correction and asks what evoked that feeling, rather than arguing with the patient.

THE PATIENT

The interview reveals data about the patient's psychopathology, psychodynamics, personality strengths, motivation, transference, and resistance.

Frequently, a patient comes to a psychiatrist expecting the doctor to be interested only in his symptoms and possible deficiencies of character. It can be reassuring for such a patient when the psychiatrist shows some interest in his assets, talents, and other personality strengths. Some patients volunteer such information, but others must be asked, "Can you tell me some of the things you like about yourself." Sensitivity and proper timing are required in the asking of such questions. There is little likelihood that the patient will demonstrate his capacity for joy and pride if, just after revealing painful material, he is asked, "Tell me, what do you do for fun?" It is preferable to lead the patient gently away from upsetting topics, allowing him the opportunity of a transition period before exploring his capacities for warmth and tenderness.

The interviewer should always look at anything the patient has brought to show him. Through those exchanges, some positive aspect of the patient's life is often revealed. When a patient spontaneously says something like, "Would you like to see a picture of my children?" interviewer neutrality at such a moment is experienced by the patient as a rebuff or indifference. Likewise, if the interviewer looks at the picture and returns it without comment, there is little likelihood that the patient will reveal his capacity for warmth. Rapport is facilitated by the interviewer's interest and appropriate questions or observations about whatever the patient shows him.

Transference. Transference is a process in which the patient unconsciously and inappropriately displaces onto persons in his current life those patterns of behavior and emotional reac-

tions that originated with significant figures from his childhood. The relative anonymity of the psychiatrist and his role as a parent surrogate facilitates that displacement to him. The patient's realistic and appropriate reactions to his doctor are not transference.

Furthermore, positive transference is to be distinguished from the therapeutic alliance, which is the relationship between the doctor's analyzing ego and the healthy, observing, rational component of the patient's ego. The therapeutic alliance also has its origin during infancy and is based on the bond of real trust between the child and his mother. Positive transference, therefore, is limited to those responses that are truly displaced from childhood figures and are now inappropriate. The omnipotent power that the patient delegates to the physician is an example. The same principles apply in defining negative transference which stems from the child's fear, anger, or mistrust of his parents.

Realistic factors concerning the doctor can be starting points for the initial transference. Age, sex, personal manner, and social and ethnic background—all influence the rapidity and the direction of the patient's responses. The patient's desire for affection, respect, and gratification of dependent needs is the most widespread form of transference. Requests for special time, financial considerations, pills, matches, cigarettes, tissues, or a glass of water can be concrete examples of such needs or feelings. The inexperienced interviewer has great difficulty in differentiating legitimate demands from irrational demands; consequently, many errors are made in the management of such matters. The problem can be simplified if it is assumed that all requests have an unconscious transference component. The question then becomes when to gratify and when to interpret. The decision is based on the timing of the request, its content, the type of patient, and the reality of the situation. For example, at the first meeting a new patient might greet the interviewer by saying, "Do you have a tissue, Doctor?" Such a patient begins the relationship by making a demand. The physician simply gratifies that request, since immediate refusals or interpretations would be premature and would quickly alienate the patient.

Omnipotent transference feelings are revealed by such remarks as, "I know you can help me" and "Why do I keep getting into these situations?" and "You must know the answer" and "What does my dream mean?" Try to avoid the worn-out Hollywood cliché, "What do you think?" A more effective comment would be, "Do you feel I'm not being helpful enough?" It is even better to tell the patient, "I need to know more about you, and then perhaps I can answer that question."

Questions about the interviewer's personal life may involve several different types of transference. However, they most often reveal concern about his status or his ability to understand or help the patient. Such questions are usually about his age, marital status, ethnic background, and place of residence or training. The experienced interviewer recognizes the true nature of the patient's interest and intuitively recognizes the situations in which it is preferable to give the patient a direct answer. With or without a direct reply, the doctor can inquire, "What led to that question?" or, after answering the question, he can ask the patient, "Now, tell me what you learned from that information that was important to you." It may then be appropriate to interpret the meaning of the patient's question by stating, "Your question about my having children sounds as though you really want to know if I'm able to understand what it feels like to be a parent." On other occasions those personal questions signify the patient's desire to become a social friend, since he either feels he cannot be helped as a patient or he considers the role of patient to be degrading. The latter situation is seen most often in patients who develop competitive transferences and tend to experience the role of the one down position.

Resistance. As MacKinnon and Michels (1971) wrote:

Resistance is any attitude on the part of the patient that opposes the objectives of the treatment.

Any psychological exploration of the patient's symptoms and behavior patterns can elicit anxiety; as a defense against that anxiety, the patient seeks to maintain repression and denial, and he resists insight. Even the most highly motivated patient cannot tell the doctor what he does not know about himself.

Resistances can be classified in many ways. Resistance may be expressed by the patterns of communication during the interview. Silence, garrulousness, censoring or editing thoughts, intellectualization, generalization, and preoccupation with one phase of his life—such as symptoms, current events, or past history—are common examples of resistance.

The patient who resists by talking excessively in order to control the interview can be interrupted by the psychiatrist with a comment such as, "I find it difficult to say anything without interrupting you." That type of intervention may expose the patient's underlying fear.

Affective display can, at times, serve as a resistance to meaningful communication. The hysterical patient often uses one emotion to ward off deeper painful affects; for example, constant anger may be used to defend against injured pride.

Arriving late, forgetting the appointment, using a minor physical illness to avoid the session, seductive behavior, and competitive behavior are other common examples of resistance.

Silence is one of the most common forms of resistance. Prolonged or uncomfortable silences are rarely useful in an initial interview. The interviewer can address himself to the silence, if it develops, with comments such as, "You seem to feel at a loss for words" or "What are you thinking about right now?" or "Perhaps there's something that's difficult for you to discuss." Sometimes interviewers unwittingly provoke silences by assuming a disproportionate responsibility for keeping the interview going. Asking questions that can be answered "Yes" or "No" or providing the patient with multiple-choice answers to a question discourages his sense of responsibility for the interview. Such questions limit the patient's spontaneity and constrict his flow of ideas. The patient retreats to passivity, and the interviewer struggles for the right question that will open the patient up.

Not all silences are a function of resistance. Some patients tolerate silences rather well and, in fact, often use them to gather their thoughts before speaking; if the patient is engrossed in his story, he may not even notice the silences. When the patient uses silence to edit his thoughts, he becomes uncomfortable, thereby providing a clue to the interviewer about the meaning of the silence.

THE INTERVIEWER

The principal tool of the psychiatric interview is the psychiatrist himself. Each psychiatrist brings a different personal and professional background to the interview. His character structure, values, and sensitivity to the feelings of others influence his attitude toward fellow human beings, patients and nonpatients alike. Differences in the social, educational, and intellectual backgrounds of the patient and the interviewer may inter-

fere with the development of rapport. It is an obvious advantage for the psychiatrist to acquire as much understanding and familiarity as possible with the patient's subculture. In any case, the psychiatrist must know what effect his own personality has on a wide variety of people in order to better recognize the patient responses he has stimulated.

In some respects the inexperienced interviewer is similar to the histology student who first peers into the microscope and sees only myriad pretty colors. As his experience increases, he becomes aware of structures and relationships that had previously escaped his attention and recognizes an ever-increasing number of subtleties. Another common problem the novice interviewer faces is when to interrupt the patient in order to cover all his questions; the experienced interviewer uses the clues provided by the patient to provide a sense of structure, rather than a preset outline for psychiatric examination.

Countertransference. Psychiatrists have two classes of emotional responses to a patient. First, there are reactions to the patient as he actually is. The doctor may like or dislike the patient or even be antagonized by him without countertransference implications, provided those are reactions that the patient would elicit in most people. Second, countertransference responses are specific for an individual psychiatrist; although inappropriate, those responses can become a useful source of information if the interviewer allows himself to be aware of them.

Countertransference may be defined as the doctor's responses to the patient as if he were an important figure from the doctor's past. A narrower definition is the interviewer's unconscious response to the patient's transference. The more the patient actually resembles figures from the doctor's past, the greater is the likelihood of such reactions. Examples include becoming dependent on the patient's praise or approval, intolerance and frustration when the patient is angry, being exhibitionistic to court the patient's favor, inability to see inconsistencies in certain interpretations, insisting on one's own infallibility, being critical of prior psychiatrists the patient saw, overidentification with the patient, experiencing vicarious pleasure from the patient's sexual or aggressive behavior, power struggles, arguing with the patient, and wishing to be the patient's child. Boredom or inability to concentrate on what the patient is saying often reflects unconscious anger or anxiety on the part of the interviewer.

Another common countertransference problem stems from the therapist's failing to see occasions when the patient's observing ego is actually a transference masquerade. The result is an overly intellectualized interview devoid of emotion.

The direct expression of emotion in the transference frequently provides an opportunity for countertransference responses. For example, the doctor tells the patient, "It isn't really me you're angry at; it's your father." Telling a patient his feelings are displaced implies that they are not real and is disrespectful and belittling. Similarly, responding to the patient's anger with a comment such as, "It's good that you're able to get angry at me," is contemptuous and is aimed to keep the psychiatrist one up on the patient. The patient's emotions must be taken seriously and dealt with in a forthright and open manner.

Preinterview Considerations

PATIENT'S EXPECTATIONS

The patient's prior knowledge and expectations of the doctor play a role in the unfolding of the interview. Even though the patient at a hospital or clinic does not select the doctor personally, the institutional transference is of considerable importance, and the doctor can explore the patient's reasons for selecting a particular hospital or clinic. A preinterview transference may be disclosed if the patient seems surprised by the doctor's appearance or remarks, "You don't look like a psychiatrist." The doctor can ask, "What did you expect a psychiatrist to be like?" If the patient replies, "Well, someone much older." The doctor may answer, "Perhaps you feel an older doctor would be more experienced and could help you more quickly." Another patient may express relief by indicating that he had expected the psychiatrist to be a more frightening figure.

In private practice a patient is usually referred to a specific doctor. The interviewer is interested to learn what the patient was told about him at the time of the referral. Was he given one name or a list of names? If he was given a list of names, how did he decide which doctor to call first, and was the interviewer the first one he contacted? One patient may indicate that he was influenced by the location of the doctor's office; another may have selected the doctor whose name suggested a particular ethnic background.

DOCTOR'S EXPECTATIONS

The interviewer usually has some knowledge of the patient before the start of the first meeting. That knowledge may have been provided by the referring physician or by a nurse if the patient is seen in a hospital setting. Some clues about the patient may have been obtained directly by the physician during the initial telephone call that led to the appointment.

Experienced psychiatrists have personal preferences concerning the amount of information they want from the referring source. Some prefer to learn as much as possible; others desire only the bare minimum, on the ground that it allows them to interview with a fully open mind.

Anytime the interviewer experiences a feeling of surprise when he meets his new patient, he must question himself. Was he misled about the patient by the person who referred the patient, or was his surprise due to some unrealistic anticipation of his own?

The positive attraction that the psychiatrist and the patient often experience initially is chiefly derived from their unconscious fantasied expectations of each other. As their relationship evolves, the initial somewhat formal behavior is replaced by more intimate behavior that reveals more about the real person of the patient and of the doctor. It is at that point, when their magical expectations are threatened by reality, that the expertise of the psychiatrist is crucial.

Opening Phase

MEETING THE PATIENT

The doctor obtains much information when he first meets a new patient. He can observe who, if anyone, has accompanied the patient and how the patient was passing the time while waiting for the interview to begin. The physician can greet the patient by name and then introduce himself. Such social pleasantries as, "It's nice to meet you" are inappropriate. If the patient is unduly anxious, the doctor may introduce a brief social comment, perhaps inquiring if he had any difficulty in finding the office. A natural and pleasant manner on the part of the psychiatrist is useful to make the patient feel more at ease.

DEVELOPMENT OF RAPPORT

Initial greeting. The experienced interviewer learns so much about the patient during the initial greeting that he may appropriately vary the opening minutes of the interview according to the patient's needs. A suitable beginning is to ask the patient to be seated and then inquire, "What problem brings you here?" or "Could you tell me about your difficulty?" A less directive approach is to ask the patient, "Where shall we start?" or "Where would you prefer to begin?"

Sullivan (1954) discussed the value of a summary statement about the referring person's communications concerning the patient or a restatement of what the physician learned during the initial telephone conversation. It is comforting for the patient who is not self-referred to feel that the physician already knows something about his problem. A presentation of all the details is likely to be harmful, as they rarely seem completely accurate to the patient, and the interview gets underway with the patient defending himself from misunderstanding. General statements are preferable. For example, the interviewer may say, "Dr. Jones has told me that you and your wife have had some difficulties" or "I understand that you've been quite depressed." Usually, the patient continues the story, but occasionally the patient asks, "Didn't he give you all the details?" The interviewer can reply, "He did go into more details than that, but I'd like to hear more about it from you."

Understanding the patient. To establish rapport, the interviewer must communicate a feeling of understanding the patient. That communication is accomplished by both the doctor's attitude and the expertise of his remarks. He does not wish to create the impression that he can read the patient's mind, but he does want the patient to realize that he has treated other people with similar problems and that he understands those problems—not only neurotic and psychotic symptoms but ordinary problems in living. For example, if a young housewife reveals that she has four young children and no household help, the interviewer can ask, "How do you manage?" A question such as, "Do they ever get on your nerves?" shows a lack of understanding.

Doctor's interest. The doctor's interest helps the patient to talk. However, the more the doctor speaks, the more the patient is concerned with what the doctor wants to hear, instead of what is on his own mind. On the other hand, if the doctor is unresponsive, the patient is inhibited from revealing his feelings. Guiding the patient gently with comments such as, "Then what happened?" or "Please continue" may suffice except when a more empathic response is required. For example, the interviewer may remark, "A child is bound to be upset by his parents' divorce" or "It sounds as though your mother was able to control you by making you feel guilty." Such comments really do not constitute premature interpretations, as they do not deal with unconscious wishes and defenses. However, they do encourage the patient to reveal more by creating an atmosphere of safety with the psychiatrist.

Sometimes patients are reluctant to speak freely because they fear the doctor will betray their confidence. The patient may say, "I don't want you to tell this to my husband" or "I hope you don't tell everything to my internist." The interviewer should assure the patient that his privacy will be maintained.

Patient's shame. At times the patient may seem to bog down or behave evasively. That impasse usually stems from feelings of shame or the patient's concern that the interviewer will judge him. Shame causes the patient to attempt to hide; guilt feelings make him want to confess. The sensitive physician perceives that distinction and responds with an empathic comment, such as, "It's hard to discuss embarrassing topics with a stranger" or "Is there something that makes you feel too ashamed to continue?" It is often a mistake to coerce the patient to go further with the use of implied threats, such as, "If you don't tell me everything, I won't be able to help you." It is preferable during the opening phase to either let the matter drop or tell the patient, "Perhaps you can tell me later when you feel more at ease with me." A patient who persists in keeping conscious secrets from the doctor is unable to cooperate in his own best interest, and the doctor may have to tell such a patient that his ability to help depends on and is limited by the patient's capacity to confide in him.

If the patient describes a situation in which he was able to assert himself and the psychiatrist offers the supportive comment, "That must have made you feel better" and the patient replies, "No," it is necessary to develop the subject further in order to sharpen the shared feeling of understanding. It is a mistake for the interviewer to feel that he made an error and try to let the issue slide past. When the psychiatrist is unclear how the experience being described affected the patient, he should ask, rather than conclude that the patient experienced no emotion because he is able to discuss the subject without revealing his feelings.

Uncovering feelings. A helpful technique to get the patient better in touch with his emotions is to ask for specific examples when the patient makes general statements about his life, such as, "My husband doesn't understand me" or "My mother was too overprotective" or "I wasn't as popular as my brother." When the psychiatrist replies, "Can you give me an example?" or "What do you remember about that?" he is obliging the patient to focus on those events and, in part, to relive them. Further questions should emphasize the patient's role in the experience under discussion, such as, "What did you do then?" or "How did you react to that?" That sort of guidance gives the patient an idea of the material that is significant to the interviewer, and the patient responds accordingly. He experiences some relief from the emotional catharsis, which also encourages him to continue.

Frequently, a patient struggles to maintain control over his emotions as the reliving of upsetting experiences reawakens their accompanying affects. If the interviewer observes that the patient stops speaking and has a tear in his eye, he may comment, "It makes you sad to speak of that" or "You're trying not to cry." Anger is another emotion that may be difficult to acknowledge. When the patient manifests no response, the doctor may indicate that a certain experience would make most people angry. The depressed patient, for example, is particularly unable to tolerate his angry feelings and may reply, "No, I only felt hurt." The interviewer accepts that formulation for the time being, rather than argue with the patient.

Middle Phase

ABRUPT TRANSITION

An abrupt transition is sometimes required after the patient has discussed his present illness. For example, the physician can say, "I have a picture of the problems that brought you here; now I'd like to learn more about you as a person" or "Can you tell me something about yourself in addition to the problems that brought you here?" Usually, the interviewer then devotes his attention to the patient's history. Just where to start depends on what aspects of the patient's life have been revealed while discussing the present illness. In most cases the patient

talks about his current life before revealing his past. If the patient has not already mentioned his age, his marital status, the length of his marriage, the age and the name of his spouse, the ages and names of his children and parents, his occupational history, a description of his current living circumstances, and so forth, the interviewer can ask for those details. It is preferable to obtain as much of that information as possible during the description of the present illness. A question such as, "How have your symptoms interfered with your life?" may allow the patient the opportunity to provide data concerning all or any of the topics mentioned above.

If the patient seems preoccupied with his symptoms, past illnesses, or any other subject, it may be necessary for the interviewer to firmly but gently deflect him. That deflection can be done with a comment such as, "You seem to have trouble getting away from that topic; is there something about it that you feel I don't understand?" or "We have a lot of things that we haven't discussed yet, and, if we don't move on, we may not get to them" or "Our time is limited today, and we haven't talked about your marriage."

The number of possibilities in the middle portion of the interview is infinite; consequently, it is impossible to provide precise instructions about which choices to make. Most leads provided by the patient should be followed up at the time of presentation. Doing so gives smooth continuity to the interview, even though there may be numerous topical digressions.

PATIENT'S PERSONALITY

When the interviewer has some ideas concerning the present illness and the patient's current life situation, he may turn his attention to what sort of person the patient is. A question such as, "What sort of person are you?" comes as a surprise to most people, since they are not accustomed to thinking of themselves in that fashion. Some patients respond easily; others become uncomfortable and reply with concrete details that reiterate the facts of their current life situation, such as, "Well, I'm a lawyer" or "I'm just a housewife." Nevertheless, such answers provide both phenomenological and dynamic information. The first reply was made by an obsessive-compulsive man who was preoccupied with rules and regulations, not merely in his job but in his human relationships as well. What he was telling the interviewer was, "I am first and foremost a lawyer, and, in fact, I can never cease being a lawyer." The second reply was offered by a phobic woman who had secret ambitions for a career. She was letting the psychiatrist know that she had a depreciatory view of women, particularly women who are housewives. Like the first patient, she was never able to forget about herself.

Some of the questions that pertain to the patient's view of himself were suggested earlier in this section under the topic of exploring the patient's assets. Questions such as, "What things bring you the most pleasure?" and "What things about yourself give you the most pride?" are additional examples. The interviewer can ask the patient to describe himself both as he appears to others and as he appears to himself in the major areas of his life, including his family, work, social situations, sex, and situations of stress. It is often revealing to ask a patient to describe a typical 24-hour day. The patient may even experience some increase in his self-awareness while reflecting on that question.

EXPLORING THE PAST

Depending on the amount of time available and whether there will be more than one interview, the psychiatrist plans his inquiry into the patient's past. The question of which past issues are most significant varies with the patient's problems and the nature of the consultation.

NEEDS FOR REASSURANCE

At various times during the interview, the patient may become uncomfortable with the material he is discussing. That feeling of discomfort is due to his wish to be accepted by the interviewer and, what is often more important, because of his fear concerning partial insight into himself. For example, he may pause and remark, "I know lots of people who do the same thing" or "Isn't that normal, Doctor?" or "Do you think I'm a bad mother?" Certain patients require a reassuring reply in order to become engaged in the interview; others profit by the doctor's asking, "What did you have in mind?" or "Just what is it that you're concerned about?"

STIMULATING CURIOSITY

Stimulating the patient's curiosity is a fundamental technique in all interviews aimed at uncovering deep feelings. Basically, the doctor uses his own genuine curiosity to awaken the patient's interest in himself. The doctor's curiosity is best directed not toward the most deeply repressed or the most highly defended issues but, rather, at the more superficial layer of the patient's conflict. The doctor's expressed curiosity about the motives of the patient and his loved ones is seldom therapeutic in the first few interviews, as it is threatening to the patient's defenses. For example, if the physician were to say, "I wonder why your husband spends more time at the office than is necessary?" the patient might construe that remark as a hostile accusation or innuendo.

Likewise, confronting the patient with inconsistencies in his story must be done tactfully, so that the patient does not feel accused of lying or being confused. In that situation, the doctor's tone of voice is all important. He may say in a gentle, nonconfronting tone, "I'm a bit confused; I thought I understood you to say the situation was thus and so" or "Earlier in the session you described your husband as generous, but now you tell me that he keeps you on a very tight budget; do you have conflicted feelings about him?" Those interventions focus on the inconsistency without embarrassing the patient and thus serve to protect the patient's sense of dignity and self-respect.

USING THE PATIENT'S WORDS

Using the patient's own words not only facilitates the development of rapport but actually helps avoid the resistance of the patient who argues over terms and different shades of meaning. That technique is particularly important when the psychiatrist wishes to return to a statement the patient made earlier in the interview. Such occasions occur when the interviewer wanted to allow the patient to continue with a point he was developing, rather than to deflect him by pursuing another issue that the patient raised while telling his story. For example, a patient was describing how his impulsiveness had gotten him into trouble with his supervisors at work when he mentioned, as an aside, "My wife gets pretty upset about it, too." After the patient had finished the story of his problems at work, the psychiatrist commented, "You said your wife gets pretty upset about it, too?" thereby exploring another manifestation of the problem while maintaining a smooth sense of continuity in the interview. It is sometimes possible to conduct an entire and thorough interview without the doctor's having to introduce a new topic merely by developing the patient's own references.

OPEN-ENDED QUESTIONS

In most situations questions that can be answered "Yes" or "No" tend to place an undue burden on the interviewer and allow the patient to assume too little responsibility for keeping the interview moving. That does not mean that it may not be necessary to ask an evasive patient for a yes or no answer on certain occasions. Even when the interviewer wants to explore a particular topic, he can phrase his question in such a way as to give the patient the greatest possible leeway in answering. For example, a patient may indicate that her husband seems distant and overly involved with his work. The interviewer can ask, "What things do you do together for fun?" or "Has he always been that way?" or "What things do you argue about?" Those questions may uncover important information, but the interviewer might have learned even more by asking the patient, "Please go on" or "Tell me more about your marriage."

SENSITIVE TOPICS

Tact is required at all times during the interview but particularly when exploring sensitive topics. What makes a given topic particularly sensitive is determined by a complex set of factors, including the patient's predominant character type and the timing of certain events in the patient's life. For example, an obsessive patient may find questions about his financial affairs more difficult to discuss than questions about his sex life. The more recently a traumatic event has taken place, the more likely it is that the patient finds it difficult to discuss.

The interviewer can lead into the sensitive areas gently by saving such questions until the patient has led the discussion to a related topic. An obsessive patient commented that he had received a significant raise when he moved to his new job. The interviewer was then able to ask, "What is your salary now?"

The same principle can be followed when exploring the topic of sex. A young man was describing his awakening interest in girls during his early adolescence. In that context it was easy for the psychiatrist to ask, "What sexual experiences have you had?"

STRESSING THE PATIENT

The psychiatrist occasionally finds it necessary to use stress during an interview to help clarify the patient's diagnosis. For example, a patient with a suspected memory deficit was skillful at covering up his problem. The interviewer confronted the patient in the memory area to establish the shared awareness of the patient's incapacity. For example, early in the interview an elderly patient indicated that she had been in the hospital for a week. Later in the interview she referred to having eaten dinner at her sister's home the day before. The psychiatrist replied, "Are you sure that was yesterday?" The patient hesitated, and the interviewer continued, "You told me earlier that you have been in the hospital for a week; are you having trouble with your memory?" Another example: A borderline patient may or may not have been psychotic. The clear establishment of a delusion would have clarified the diagnosis. The psychiatrist's firm but kindly confrontation of the patient's idiosyncratic ideas revealed the extent of the patient's thought disorder.

When the interviewer has made some stressful confrontation, he should always cause the patient as little pain as possible and should offer the patient some reassurance that is specifically designed to neutralize the effects of the confrontation.

The use of stress in an interview does not imply that the patient can be treated in a callous or insensitive manner. In the example above, asking an elderly patient who seems to be confused about the date, "Are you sure?" is stressful.

Providing too little structure during the interview is a stress for the disorganized patient. Once the technique has demonstrated the patient's disorganization, there is no point in stressing the patient further. The psychiatrist should then provide a structure to help the patient reorganize.

MANAGING THE PATIENT'S ANXIETY

There is an optimum level of anxiety that drives the patient to seek help but does not incapacitate him to such an extent that he is unable to tell his story or answer the interviewer's questions. Clinical experience is required to accurately assess the amount of anxiety that is optimum for each patient. If the interviewer has the feeling that the patient may abruptly leave the office or if he feels that the patient may not return for a second interview, the patient has been allowed to become too anxious. On the other hand, if the patient seems quite composed and manages the interview as though it were a social meeting, the interviewer can become more confronting of the patient's evasion of problem areas.

Closing Phase

PATIENT'S QUESTIONS

Five or 10 minutes should always be set aside near the end of the initial interview to deal with certain issues. The patient who has been crying needs some time to regain his composure before he leaves the office. And a patient who has come with a written or mental list of questions he wanted to ask the psychiatrist needs time to ask them.

The patient has consulted with an expert, and he is entitled to professional opinion concerning his situation, including an appropriate formulation of his problem and recommendations concerning treatment or some other helpful advice (MacKinnon and Michels, 1971).

As the end of the session nears, the psychiatrist can say, "We have about 10 minutes remaining. Perhaps there are some questions you would like to ask." The patient may then reveal material that has been of concern to him throughout the interview; obsessive patients are noted for that behavior. Most often, the patient raises questions pertaining to his illness or his need for treatment.

In today's world of an informed public, patients often ask questions concerning specific modalities of treatment, such as psychotherapy, psychoanalysis, behavior modification, hypnosis, pharmacotherapy, group therapy, and marital therapy. Although the patient is entitled to direct answers to his questions at the completion of his evaluation, the psychiatrist can correctly assume that such questions reveal a great deal concerning the patient's motivation for treatment in general and for, say, intensive psychotherapy in particular. They also reveal an important attitude concerning the role the patient expects to play in the treatment process and the speed with which he expects relief of his symptoms. Significant resistances uncovered at that time may require the psychiatrist to alter his treatment plan. It is a well-known phenomenon that people do not always accept their physician's advice, and many patients have passively accepted prescriptions they never fill, both literally and metaphorically.

TREATMENT PLAN

It is often necessary to recommend a second or even a third interview to complete a thorough evaluation of a complex problem. The patient may have come unprepared for that fact, and, if his expectations are not adequately dealt with in the final 10 minutes of the first interview, he may not return for the second appointment. When the patient accepts the need for additional sessions, the interviewer can advise him that adequate time will be reserved at the completion of the consultation to discuss all the various issues of concern to the patient. Although the more thorough presentation of the psychiatrist's ideas has been deferred, it is still necessary to give the patient some brief summary of the doctor's findings thus far. By presenting the treatment plan in stepwise fashion, the interviewer can discover the areas in which the patient has questions, confusion, or disagreement. That cannot happen when the doctor hands down his opinion like a royal decree.

Formal diagnostic labels have little value to the patient and may even be harmful, since the physician is unaware of the conscious or unconscious significance they hold for the patient or his family. The best clues for the proper terminology are often provided by the patient. The patient may say, "I realize it's all in my mind" or "I know it's some psychological hang-up" or "I know I have to do something about my relationship with my mother."

Although the patient's statement may have been made earlier in the session, the doctor can use it as a foundation for his own formulation, provided the patient really believed what he said. For example, a patient with psychosomatic headaches said, "I know it's all in my mind, Doctor." But that patient did not really accept the psychological causation of his headaches and was merely appeasing the psychiatrist.

The interviewer may start his formulation by repeating the patient's own remark: "As you said before, you do have a psychological problem." The doctor may then refer to what he considers the patient's predominant symptoms and indicate that they are all interrelated and part of the same condition. It is a good plan to separate the patient's acute problems from those that are chronic. The problems of recent origin are generally the ones that respond most quickly to treatment. By confining the formulation to the major area of disturbance, the psychiatrist avoids the danger of overwhelming the patient with a comprehensive statement covering all his psychopathology.

When the psychiatrist and the patient have mutually identified the major problem areas, the doctor can then move on to the subject of treatment. If several forms of therapy are available, the doctor can acknowledge that fact, but the patient still expects the psychiatrist to advise him concerning the treatment that would be best suited for him. "Best suited" is a complex notion that includes not only the subtleties of diagnosis but the patient's emotional, financial, and life situational resources as well. On occasion, the patient may reveal his alarm over the treatment plan by a comment such as, "You don't really think it's that serious do you?" or "Well, is there any hope for me?" or "How long do you think the treatment will take?" It is difficult at the outset to predict exactly how long treatment will take, and it is rarely useful to tell a patient that he will require many years of therapy. Instead, the psychiatrist can point out that the acute symptoms will respond first, and then the patient can reassess his desire for help with the lifelong problems, which require longer periods of treatment. In that way the doctor provides the patient and himself time to explore the interrelation between acute and chronic symptoms, as well as more time to assess the patient's motivation and capacity to work with deep personality problems. The patient's concern with the duration of treatment is not merely a desire for a magical cure or some other resistance. Therapy is costly in terms of both expense and time involved, and it interferes with other aspects of the patient's life. If there is a time limit on the duration of therapy or if the doctor will not be available as long as the patient expects treatment to last, the patient should be told at once. Also, the patient deserves to know from the outset if the consultant will not be the treating physician. If the patien 's financial resources seem to play a limiting role in determining the treatment plan, it is the consultant's responsibility to advise the patient where and how to get the most for his money.

PROGNOSIS

The patient may reveal a great deal of concern over his prognosis with comments such as, "Well, I'm a real basket case, aren't I?" or "Have you ever seen someone like me get better?" The patient is helped by the doctor's empathetic recognition of his feeling of hopelessness. However, prognosis is often difficult early on, and the doctor may harm the patient and himself by being overly reassuring and by guaranteeing cures. In the case of the depressed patient, some positive statement concerning the doctor's belief that the patient will recover is part of the therapy.

Subsequent Interviews

A single meeting with a patient permits only a cross-sectional study. Therefore, it is a good plan to allow a few days to intervene between the first and the second interviews. That time provides both the patient and the physician an opportunity to reflect on and react to the first interview. The added perspective provides supplementary information concerning how the patient may react to further treatment. The subsequent interview also provides an opportunity for the patient to correct any misinformation that he provided in the first meeting. It is often helpful to begin the second interview by asking the patient if he has thought about the first interview and asking for his reactions to the experience. Another variation of that technique is for the doctor to say, "Frequently, people think of additional things they wanted to discuss after they have left. What thoughts did you have?" The patient may begin to speak at that point, or he may indicate that he had no afterthoughts. In that case, the doctor may raise his eyebrows in surprise and wait a few moments. If the patient is floundering, the doctor can go back to a topic the patient had previously discussed productively.

The patient's reactions to the initial interview carry some prognostic implications for psychoanalytically oriented psychotherapy. On the positive side is the patient who reflected further on a topic from the last meeting and arrived at some increased understanding. The patient may bring in some additional history or clarify a point that was previously discussed. The patient may have tried to obtain more historical detail by consulting with a relative, or he may report a dream that occurred after the first meeting.

The author routinely inquires about dreams that have occurred between the first and second meetings, since they reveal the patient's unconscious reactions to the physician and show key emotional problems and dominant transference attitudes. Interviewers who are interested in psychoanalytic psychotherapy subtly or overtly encourage such activities, as they facilitate the treatment process and are more important than whether the patient felt better or worse after the session.

Another group of responses have more negative implications. The patient may have thought about what he reported the first time concerning some criticism of an important figure in his life and later decided that he was wrong. Or a patient may say that he cannot understand why the doctor asked about thus and such (often an obvious point) or that he feels the doctor did not understand him. Such responses typically occur when the patient feels he has been too critical of some important person in his life, and he becomes guilty and withdraws, often feeling angry with the doctor for encouraging him to criticize a loved one. A patient may feel humiliated for having demonstrated a strong emotional response in the presence of the doctor. The doctor must identify the process that led to such negative responses and, he must respond with empathetic understanding, or the therapeutic alliance will not develop.

The psychiatrist often learns something of value when he asks the patient if he discussed the interview with anyone else. If the patient has done so, it is enlightening to learn the details of that conversation and with whom the patient spoke.

There is no set of rules concerning which topics are best put off for the second interview, but, in general, as the patient's comfort and familiarity with the physician increases, he is more able to reveal the most intimate details of his life.

Interviews with Relatives

In recent years psychiatrists have developed flexible attitudes about speaking with the patient's closest family members. Few psychoanalysts now flatly refuse to speak with a patient's spouse or parents. At the other extreme, few psychiatrists obtain a patient's history only from other informants on the grounds that the patient is incapable of giving an accurate history. Virtually every modern residency training program provides some experience in family and couples therapy and crisis intervention with many family members. Those experiences have made it easier for psychiatrists to meet with important family members.

BASIC GROUND RULES

There are three important guidelines in speaking with the relatives of adult patients. One is to always see the patient first. Another is to obtain the patient's permission before speaking with a family member; comatose or severely confused patients are the only exceptions to that principle. The third cardinal rule is not to directly or indirectly violate the patient's confidence. If any information provided by the patient needs to be discussed with a family member, the psychiatrist should obtain the patient's permission first.

The only exceptions to the third rule arise when the life of the patient or someone else is in danger. If the psychiatrist cannot obtain the patient's permission to reveal a plan for suicide or homicide and the patient refuses hospitalization, the doctor has an obligation to advise the family and to recommend commitment. If the doctor cannot obtain the patient's permission to disclose such data, he can at least give the patient the courtesy of telling him that he plans to disclose that information and why. Some part of the patient may be relieved, even though he consciously objects. The patient's relatives may provide valuable information concerning the patient that helps the physician arrive at a treatment plan more quickly.

The opportunity to directly observe the patient's spouse or parents—or children, in the case of elderly patients—provides the psychiatrist with an objective view of those people, who are vitally important in the patient's life. With the aid of such data, the psychiatrist may be more alert to conflicting data in the views provided by his patient, thereby allowing him to more quickly help the patient expand his awareness of certain distortions and conflicting feelings concerning his loved ones.

REASSURANCE AND QUESTIONS

It is normal for relatives to feel concern about the illness of their loved one and to have questions concerning the diagnosis and treatment plan, including duration and prognosis. The same general principles apply as when the psychiatrist discusses such matters with the patient. By first exploring the extent of the relatives' knowledge and understanding of the patient's problems, the psychiatrist can often indicate that they have grasped the essentials of the patient's illness without disclosing any confidential information. The psychiatrist can follow the same guidelines in discussing treatment recommendations and prognosis. The relatives may express some overt or covert feeling of guilt or responsibility for the patient's illness. It is important that the psychiatrist not gang up with the patient against his relatives. Doing so would support only one side of the patient's ambivalent feelings, and it alienates the relatives, who then become more antagonistic to the patient and his psychiatrist. The doctor is not a judge, but occasionally he may have some constructive recommendation for the relative who asks, "Is there anything I can do to help?"

SEEING THE RELATIVE ALONE

Some psychiatrists flatly refuse to speak with a relative except in the presence of the patient; others are willing to meet with relatives alone. The second group is further subdivided into those who do and those who do not feel it is essential to report to the patient everything that was said by the relative. For many years the author has not reported everything to the patients concerned, and he has seen no untoward incidents. However, there are risks in that position, and it requires training, sensitivity, and judgment regarding what to disclose and what not to disclose in the way of information provided by a relative. One current school of thought holds that families have no secrets but only conspiracies not to discuss certain topics. Although that viewpoint applies in many situations, there are still secrets that are best left alone.

For example, a woman revealed to a psychiatrist that there was some cause for doubt in her mind concerning the paternity of the patient, her 35-year-old son. She had a casual affair with another man 35 years earlier and had never seen him since. She had worked out the conflict with her husband that had precipitated the affair and had maintained a monogamous relationship thereafter. That was a clear case of unresolved guilt feeling in the patient's mother, and there was nothing to be gained by disclosing that information to the patient, who had no suspicions. If it turned out later on that the patient did unconsciously know about that event and was ready to face it, he could always broach the subject to his mother himself if there was something to be gained.

Interviewing relatives alone is not an innocuous procedure. It requires skill.

Conclusion

The psychiatric interview encompasses all the basic psychological sciences and requires the integration and clinical application of all the psychiatrist's training. Although each psychiatrist develops his own stylistic variations, studies show that, as interviewers become more experienced, it is more and more difficult for an observing third party to correctly identify their theoretical persuasion.

No one ever conducts an interview that is totally free of mistakes. That human frailty provides the psychiatrist with an ever-continuing opportunity for professional growth.

Suggested Cross References

The remaining sections in this chapter consider other aspects of the examination of the psychiatric patient—the psychiatric history and the mental status examination (Section 12.2), the psychiatric report (Section 12.3), typical signs and symptoms of psychiatric illness (Section 12.4), psychological testing of intelligence and personality (Sections 12.5 and 12.6, respectively), psychological testing for brain damage (Section 12.7), psychiatric social service information (Section 12.8), and medical assessment in psychiatric practice (Section 12.9). The clinical manifestations of psychiatric disorders are described in Chapter 13. Various psychotherapies are discussed in Chapter 30. Confidentiality is discussed in Section 56.14.

REFERENCES

Bird, B. *Talking with Patients*, J. B. Lippincott, Philadelphia, 1973.
Bleneer-Finesinger, J. Psychiatric interviewing: Some principles and procedure in insight therapy. Am. J. Psychiatry, *105*: 187, 1948.
Fromm-Reichmann, F. *Principles of Intensive Psychotherapy*. University of Chicago Press, Chicago, 1950.
* Garrett, A. M. *Interviewing: Its Principles and Methods*. Family Welfare Association of America, New York, 1942.
* Gill, M., Newman, R., and Redlich, F. C. *The Initial Interview in Psychiatric Practice*. International Universities Press, New York, 1954.
Greenson, R. R., and Wexler, M. The Non-transference relationship in the psychoanalytic situation. Int. J. Psychoanal., *51*: 143, 1970.
Group for the Advancement of Psychiatry. *Initial Interviews*. Group for the Advancement of Psychiatry, New York, 1961.
Hendrickson, W. J., Coffer, R. H., and Cross, T. N. The initial interview. Arch. Neurol. Psychiatry, *71*: 24, 1954.
London University Institute of Psychiatry. *Notes on Eliciting and Recording Clinical Information*. Oxford University Press, London, 1973.
* MacKinnon, R. A., and Michels, R. *The Psychiatric Interview in Clinical Practice*. W. B. Saunders, Philadelphia, 1971.
Menninger, K. *A Manual for Psychiatric Case Study*. Grune & Stratton, New York, 1952.
* Powdermaker, F. The techniques of the initial interview and methods of teaching them. Am. J. Psychiatry, *104*: 642, 1948.
Rogers, C. R. *Client-centered Therapy*. Houghton Mifflin, Boston, 1951.
Roth, M. The clinical interview and psychiatric diagnosis: Have they a future in psychiatric practice? Compr. Psychiatry, *8*: 427, 1967.
Saul, L. J. The psychoanalytic diagnostic interview. Psychoanal. Q., *26*: 76, 1957.
Schafer, R. Talking to patients in psychotherapy. Bull. Menninger Clin., *12*: 503, 1974.
Spitzer, R. L., and Endicott, J. DIAGNO II: Further developments in a computer program for psychiatric diagnosis. Am. J. Psychiatry, *125*: 12, 1969.
Stevenson, I. *Medical History Taking*. Hoeber Medical Division, Harper & Row, New York, 1960.
* Sullivan, H. S. *The Psychiatric Interview*. W. W. Norton, New York, 1954.
Tarachow, S. *An Introduction to Psychotherapy*. International Universities Press, New York, 1963.
Tumulty, P. A. What is a clinician and what does he do? N. Engl. J. Med., *283*: 20, 1970.
Weed, L. L. Medical records that guide and teach. N. Engl. J. Med., *278*: 593, 1968.
Whitehorn, J. C. Guide to interviewing and clinical personality study. Arch. Neurol. Psychiatry, *52*: 197, 1944.

12.2 Psychiatric History and Mental Status Examination

ROGER A. MacKINNON, M.D.

Introduction

The technique of obtaining a psychiatric history and performing a mental status examination is a special component of the psychiatric interview. Although the written record must include specific data and adhere to a traditional organized format, the clinician must be ever aware that he is engaging in a therapeutic process with his patient while eliciting information.

As in every therapeutic situation, the patient's recollections and responses are accompanied by specific feelings, of which the interviewer must be aware and to which he must be sensitive. The patient's feelings, associations, and movements and his reactions to the interviewer provide crucial data that enable the psychiatrist to evaluate both content and process while gaining insight into the continuity between the patient's past and his present problems in living. The most common error made while obtaining a psychiatric history is the physician's interference with the patient's natural unfolding of his history by overstructuring the interview with excessive questions in order to follow a particular interview schedule.

The organization of the psychiatric history outlined in this section is for the patient's written record; it is not a script to follow during the interview. That is especially true for the mental status examination, which the skilled interviewer blends and weaves into the process of eliciting the patient's history.

The customary division of the record into the patient's history and his mental status is based on the traditional medical model. In theory, the history contains the patient's experience of his illness and is, therefore, subjective; the mental status examination, like the physical examination, is concerned with objective data that can be observed or verified by the physician. In actual clinical practice, the situation is more complex, since many aspects of the patient's mental status cannot be observed directly, as in a physical examination, and the interviewer is dependent on subjective data provided by the patient.

Psychiatric History

PURPOSE

Psychiatrists, like other specialists in medicine, rely on a careful history as the foundation for the diagnosis and treatment of every illness. Each branch of medicine has its own method for gathering and organizing an accurate comprehensive story of the patient's illness. The usual technique is to secure, in the patient's own words, the onset, duration, and severity of his presenting complaints; to review his past medical problems; and to question the patient regarding the present functioning of his organs and anatomical systems. The emphasis is chiefly on the internal economy of the body and how any malfunctions affect the patient's physical or social life patterns.

The psychiatric history strives to convey the more elusive picture of the patient's individual personality characteristics, including both his strengths and his weaknesses. It provides insight into the nature of his relationships with those closest to him and includes all the important people in his past and present life. A complete story of the patient's life would be impossible to obtain, as it would require another lifetime to tell; however, a reasonably comprehensive picture of the patient's development from his earliest formative years until the present can usually be elicited.

Like other professionals, the novice psychiatrist must progress through certain steps in the mastery of his profession. Whether it be school figures for the skater, finger exercises for the pianist, or the classical third-year medical student history for the future physician, those techniques are time-proved steps to be mastered in the pursuit of professionalism. The third-year medical student history, which may require 3 hours, evolves into a medical or surgical resident's history, which is condensed into 20 minutes. Similarly, in psychiatry, time and experience are required in order to respond quickly to the initial cues provided by the patient that tell the clinician how to proceed with the history. Many clinical situations and diagnostic categories require particular modification with regard to history taking. For example, in a situation of crisis, whether the patient is neurotic or psychotic, it is not appropriate to elicit a complete story of the patient's past life unless the patient is a child (MacKinnon and Michels, 1971).

TECHNIQUES

The most important technique in obtaining the psychiatric history is to allow the patient to tell the story in his own words in the order that he feels is most important to him. The skillful interviewer recognizes those points, as the patient relates his story, at which he can introduce relevant questions concerning the various important areas described in the outline of the psychiatric history and the mental status examination.

Some psychiatrists obtain the history by providing the patient with a questionnaire to fill out before their first meeting. Although that technique saves the psychiatrist time and may be useful in clinics or other places where professional resources are severely limited, that efficiency is obtained at a severe price: It deprives the psychiatrist and the patient of the opportunity to explore the patient's feelings that are elicited while filling out his answers to the questions. It also suggests that, when he finally meets the psychiatrist, he will encounter yet another bureaucratic functionary who is more interested in pieces of paper than in him. A good psychiatrist can overcome that undesirable mental set, but it is an unnecessary bit of pseudoefficiency to create it in the first place.

PROBLEMS

The greatest strengths of most psychiatric histories are in the area of delineating and diagnosing structured neurotic or psychotic illnesses. However, in the realm of personality diagnosis, many psychiatric histories are of relatively little use. That is particularly true of those histories filled out by the patient.

Another major deficiency in the average psychiatric history is its representation as a collection of dates and events that are organized together in a calendar fashion, with relatively little about the impact of those experiences on the patient or understanding of the role he may have played in bringing about those events. The history is often filled with data indicating that the patient went to a certain school, held a certain number of jobs, married at a certain age, and had a certain number of children. Often, none of that material provides any distinctive characteristics about the person that help to distinguish him from another human being with similar vital statistics.

In most training programs there is relatively little formal psychiatric teaching in the techniques involved in eliciting historical data. The beginning psychiatrist is given an outline and is somehow expected to magically learn how to acquire the information requested. It is unusual for his written records to be corrected by his teachers and still more unusual for him to be required to rewrite the report to incorporate any suggested corrections. In his supervised psychotherapy training, the resident usually begins with a presentation of the history as it has been organized for the written record, rather than as it flowed from the patient, and usually the supervisor is not aware of the timing of the questions. Supervisors are usually more interested in the manifestations of early transference and resistance than in teaching the technique of eliciting a smooth, flowing history.

ORGANIZATION OF DATA

Once again, the author wishes to emphasize that the organization for this section is only for the purpose of preparing the written record.

Preliminary Identification

The psychiatrist should begin the written history by stating the patient's name, age, marital status, sex, occupation, language if other than English, race, nationality, religion, and a brief statement about the patient's place of residence and circumstances of living. Comments such as, "The patient lives alone in a furnished room" or "The patient lives with her husband and three children in a three-bedroom apartment," provide adequate detail for this part. If the patient is hospitalized, a statement can be included as to the number of previous admissions for similar conditions. In most written psychiatric records one or more of the above-mentioned items has been omitted. In some instances an omission is the result of a lack of thoroughness by the interviewer, but it is frequently a reflection of some countertransference problem or blind spot in the interviewer.

Chief Complaint

The chief complaint is the presenting problem for which the patient seeks professional help. The chief complaint should be stated in the patient's own words; if the information is not supplied by the patient, the record should contain a description of the person who supplied it and his relationship to the patient. Although at first glance, this part seems to be the briefest and simplest of the various subdivisions of the psychiatric history, in actuality it is often one of the most complex. In many cases the patient does not begin his story with a chief complaint. One or more sessions may be required for the physician to learn what it is that the patient finds most disturbing or why he seeks treatment at this particular time. In other situations the chief complaint is provided by someone other than the patient. For example, an acutely confused and disoriented patient may be brought in by someone else, who provides the chief complaint concerning the patient's confusion. Occasionally, a patient who has multiple symptoms of long duration has great difficulty in explaining precisely why he seeks treatment at this time. Ideally, the chief complaint should give the explanation for why the patient seeks treatment now. That concept must not be confused with the precipitating stress that results in the collapse of the patient's defenses at a particular time. The precipitating stress may be equally difficult to determine. There is usually a direct correlation between the ease of determining the chief complaint and the ease of determining the precipitating stress. At times, the physician uncovers the chief complaint in the course of looking for a precipitating stress or in considering the patient's unconscious expectations.

For example, a woman arrived at a psychiatrist's office feeling distraught after her husband confronted her with the fact that he had been unhappy with their relationship for the past 10 years and that he wanted a separation. She felt depressed and upset and was convinced that her husband was going through some midlife crisis phase. She was certain that he did not know what he was feeling and that they had, in actuality, been happily married during all their years together. Although she consulted the psychiatrist voluntarily, she had no chief complaint and suffered from no psychiatric illness. Her reaction to the confrontation with her husband was quite normal. She wanted the psychiatrist to interview her husband and convince him that he was going through some phase for which he might need treatment and that he should remain with his wife. She did not see herself as a patient, although she had some striking personality pathology that at the time was ego-syntonic and was not directly involved in her reason for seeking psychiatric help. She seemed unaware of her inability to look critically at her own behavior and its effects on others and was unaware of her tendency to project her own tension state onto her husband. Those traits were cental aspects of her neurotic character.

Personal Identification

Although a detailed description of the patient appears at the beginning of the mental status part of the record, it is useful to have a brief, nontechnical description of the patient's appearance and behavior as it might be written by a novelist. What is needed here is not a stereotyped medical description of a "well-developed, well-nourished white male" but, rather, a description that would enable someone who had never met the patient to identify him when he was sitting in a waiting room with many other people. The following description is a good illustration of what is desired:

Mrs. B is a 5'8" tall, formidable, large-framed, dark-skinned woman with a big Afro and medium-height heels. Behind tinted, gold-rimmed glasses, her eyes are alert, penetrating, and wary. Her meticulously clean and neat pants outfit is somber in hue. Her bearing is erect and proud and often arrogant, but she is easily embarrassed into an incongruous sheepishness. She does not fidget, despite obvious anxiety, usually sitting with her knees pressed together. She keeps her coat on and her handbag in her lap. Her speech is clear and precise and pleasant in tone except when she feels misunderstood or criticized; then she lapses into a resentful whine.

Significant omissions in the description of the patient may result from a lack of careful observation, or they may reflect countertransference problems on the part of the examiner.

History of Present Illness

Onset. The psychiatrist must allow an adequate amount of time during the initial interview to explore the details of the patient's presenting symptoms. Those symptoms are usually the prime reason the patient decided to consult a psychiatrist. Beginning psychiatrists, particularly those with an interest in psychodynamic psychiatry, often have difficulty in determining precisely when a present illness begins. They frequently feel that the present illness must have begun sometime in the patient's early life, perhaps even during the first 2 years. Although such developmental concepts are useful in understanding the patient's psychodynamic development, they are of relatively little value in determining when the patient's current failure in adaptation began. For that reason, it is essential to determine the patient's highest level of functioning, even though that adaptation may not be considered healthy by normative standards. The patient's best level of adaptation must be considered the baseline from which his current loss of functioning is measured and new patterns of maladaptation appeared. Most often, a relatively unstructured question, such as, "How did it all begin?" leads to an adequate unfolding of the present illness. A well-organized patient is able to present a reasonably chronological account of his difficulties.

Major modifications may be necessary in interviewing a disorganized patient. For the patient who suffers from a psychotic process or from a severe personality disorder, it is necessary for the physician to provide more structure in order to elicit a coherent, chronological, organized story of the patient's present illness. The patient's lack of an organizing ego requires the interviewer to provide that modification. The purpose of providing such structure is not merely to enable the interviewer to write a more organized psychiatric report but to serve a therapeutic value: The patient uses the physician's organizing ego in an effort to compensate for his own confusion and lack of structure. In that fashion the therapeutic alliance is formed at the same time that the requisite historical data are secured.

Precipitating factors. As the patient recounts the background and the development of the symptoms and behavioral changes that culminated in his seeking assistance, the psychiatrist should attempt to learn the details of the patient's life circumstances at the time of their onset. In many cases the patient is unable to give correlations between the beginning of his illness and the stresses that occurred in his life when he is asked to make such connections directly. A technique referred to as the "parallel history" is particularly useful with the patient who is suffering from a psychosomatic disorder. Such a patient denies any connection between emotional stress and his physical symptoms; therefore, the skilled psychiatrist elicits the parallel history without the patient's becoming aware that he is making connections as he studies the internal and external stresses that the patient experienced just before or coincident with the onset of his psychosomatic disorder. If the patient is in an open and exploratory frame of mind, he himself may notice some striking temporal connection between a certain stress and the appearance of his symptoms. That connection may impress the patient and arouse his curiosity about the role of emotional factors in his illness. But the psychiatrist may undermine that process and intensify the patient's resistance by prematurely offering psychological interpretations concerning the interrelationship of the stress and the symptom.

Secondary gain. The ways in which the patient's illness has affected his life activities and personal relationships highlight the secondary gain of the patient's illness. In attempting to understand the secondary gain, the interviewer must explore that area in a sympathetic and empathic fashion, careful to share the pain of the patient's illness and the loss of the many things he is unable to do as a result of his symptoms. Any implication to the patient that he may unconsciously be attempting to get out of something would immediately destroy any rapport the psychiatrist has established.

For example, a married woman with three children complained of severe backaches with no organic cause. After listening to the description of her pain, the psychiatrist asked in a sympathetic voice, "How do you manage to take care of the housework?" "Oh," replied the patient, "my husband has been very kind, and he does it after he comes home from work." The obvious secondary gain was not interpreted; instead, it provided a clue that the husband may not have been very helpful or understanding of his wife's feelings concerning her role before the onset of her backaches. Later, the psychiatrist explored that area with the patient, who, after her resentment unfolded, was herself aware of the secondary gain.

Overlap with the mental status. There is often an artificial separation between the mental status and the present illness section of the history. For example, changes in personality, interests, mood, attitudes toward others, dress, habits, levels of tenseness, activity, attention, concentration, memory, speech, and psychophysiological symptoms may all be part of the present illness, depending on the nature of the condition from which the patient is suffering. On the other hand, that information could just as well be included in the mental status section of the report.

For example, a patient's phobic symptoms can be described under disorders of thought processes (content of thought in the mental status examination). However, if the patient's present illness involves phobic symptoms, that material is elicited during the discussion of the present illness and is described under present illness in the history. The material need not be repeated in the mental status part of the written record but may be cross-referenced to the present illness, stating the page of the reference. On the other hand, if a patient seeks help because of a marital problem and the psychiatrist uncovers phobic symptoms, it is not appropriate to explore those symptoms during the discussion of the present illness, as the patient does not consider them part of her problem. Indeed, the psychiatrist may choose to postpone that exploration to a later interview to avoid alienating the patient, who does not consider the problem central to her reason for seeking psychiatric help. When the psychiatrist prepares the written record of the patient, he may place the discussion of the phobic symptoms under mental status and cross-reference them in the history of the patient's present illness.

Previous Illnesses

This section is a transition between the story of the present illness and the past personal history. Here prior episodes of emotional and mental disturbances are described. The extent of incapacity, the type of treatment received, the names of hospitals, the length of each illness, and the effects of prior treatments should all be explored and recorded chronologically.

Past Personal History

In the usual medical history the presenting illness gives the physician important information that enables him to focus his questions in his review of systems. As it is impossible to obtain a complete history of a person's life, the psychiatrist uses the patient's present illness to disclose significant clues for further exploration of his past personal history. When the interviewer has acquired a general impression as to the most likely diagnosis, he can then direct his attention to the areas that are pertinent to the patient's major complaints and to defining the underlying personality structure. Each interview is modified according to the underlying condition from which the patient suffers and according to important situational factors that relate to the setting and the circumstances of the interview. In order to modify the form of the interview, the psychiatrist must be familiar with the theories of psychological development and with the phases and conflicts that are of the greatest importance for each condition. In that way, he may concentrate his questions on the areas that will be most significant in explaining the patient's psychological development.

For example, a patient with obsessive-compulsive symptoms should have a thorough study of obedience-defiance behavior in his early relationships to authority figures and how power struggles were dealt with in his home. The psychiatrist should also inquire about the patient's development of rigidity and tyranny of conscience and any early history of rituals. He can expect to find conflicts over the emergence of the patient's aggressive and sexual impulses.

In another type of case, the recognition that the patient was sociopathic led the interviewer to focus his exploration on a different aspect of the lifelong story of the patient's relationships with figures of authority. He began with the patient's parents and his interactions with teachers and then continued into the area of conflicts with the law. For that patient, the emphasis was more on his success in getting away with things and his failure to develop appropriate conscience mechanisms for self-control. Questions designed to elicit the unconscious collaboration on the part of one or both parents were appropriate, as were questions about overt sociopathic behavior on the part of the parents. Questions about lying, cheating, and stealing were gently worked into the interview by the clinician's indicating an understanding of the patient's lifelong struggle against impulses that other people have more easily been able to control. Similar questions pertaining to the developmental history of a patient with a diagnosis of obsessive personality would be experienced as confusing, inappropriate, and offensive.

In addition to studying the patient's present illness and current life situation, the psychiatrist needs an equally thorough understanding of the patient's past life and its relationship to his presenting emotional problem. A thorough psychodynamic explanation of the patient's illness and personality structure requires an understanding of the intricate relationship between the ways in which the patient reacts to the external stresses of his environment and also requires the recognition that he has, in some way, been largely responsible for the creation of that environment. Through a careful understanding of that interrelationship between external stress and the patient's capacity to seek out situations that frustrate him, the psychiatrist develops a concept of intrapsychic conflict.

The past history is perhaps the most deficient section of the typical psychiatric record. It is usually divided into the major developmental periods of prenatal, infancy, early childhood, middle childhood or latency, puberty, adolescence, and adulthood. The past history usually begins with some statement as to whether the patient was breast-fed or bottle-fed and is followed by statements of questionable veracity concerning the patient's toilet training and early developmental landmarks, such as sitting, walking, and talking. That entire area may be condensed into a statement such as, "Developmental landmarks were normal." Just what of value one learns from the fact that the patient was breast-fed or bottle-fed and weaned at the age of 6 months has always mystified the author. The psychiatrist might replace those routine and often meaningless inquiries by an attempt to use significant new areas of knowledge concerning child development.

Prenatal history. The psychiatrist considers the nature of the home situation into which the patient was born and whether the patient was planned and wanted. Were there any problems with the mother's pregnancy and delivery? Was there any evidence of defect or injury at birth?

Early childhood. This period considers the first 3 years of the patient's life. The quality of the mother-child interaction during feeding is certainly more important than whether the child was breast-fed or bottle-fed. Although an accurate account of that experience is difficult to obtain, it is frequently possible to learn whether the child presented problems in feeding and whether the baby was colicky or required special formulas. Early disturbances in sleep patterns and signs of unmet needs, such as head banging and body rocking, provide clues about possible maternal deprivation. In addition, it is important to obtain a history of human constancy during the first 3 years. Were there auxiliary maternal objects? The psychiatrist should attempt to complete an accurate list of who was living in the patient's home during that period and should try to determine the role that each person played in the patient's upbringing. Did the patient exhibit problems at any early period, with stranger anxiety or separation anxiety?

It is helpful to know if the loving mother and the disciplining mother were one and the same person. In one case, a child received most of her love from a grandmother but was trained and disciplined by a maid. In her adult life she rejected housework, which she associated with the cold and punitive authority of the maid, but pursued a career in music, which made her feel close to her loving grandmother. Her actual mother did not enjoy child rearing, and that reaction caused further problems in maternal identification. It is not surprising that the patient did not have a cohesive sense of self and of women and had great difficulty in attempting to integrate her career with being a wife and mother.

The patient's toilet-training history is another area that is usually relatively useless. The problem is that useful and accurate information concerning that important interaction between mother and child is usually impossible to obtain. It is one of the areas in which the will of the mother and the will of the child are pitted against each other. Whether the child experienced toilet training chiefly as a defeat in the power struggle with his mother or whether he experienced it more as enhancing his own mastery is of critical importance for characterological development.

Unmet emotional needs, as well as excessive power struggles, give rise to various problems of behavior, including thumb sucking, temper tantrums, tics, nightmares, fears, eating disorders, masturbation, bed wetting, and nail biting.

The patient's siblings and the details of his relationship to them are other important areas that are often unemphasized in the psychiatric history. That deficiency is often reflected in the psychodynamic formulations as well. The case is too often conceptualized only in terms of oedipal or preoedipal conflicts. Intense sibling rivalries and positive sibling relationships may significantly influence the patient's social adaptation, and care must be taken to include that area. The death of a sibling before the patient's birth or during his early years is an event that had a profound effect on his developmental experience. The parents, and particularly the mother, may have responded to the death of the sibling with significant depression, fear, or anger, which may have resulted in her being incapable of providing adequate emotional nourishment to her other children. Siblings may also play a critical role in supporting one another emotionally by providing the child with the opportunity to develop multiple alliances. They may provide significant support at times when the patient experiences feelings of rejection or isolation from the parents.

A young woman revealed that she shared a room with her grandmother and sister until she was 9 years old, when her grandmother died. The patient stated:

She was blind and diabetic. I was very close to her [tears]. She used to make my lunch. I would set her hair. I remember having lots of nightmares. I realized that she was blind when I would wake her up in the middle of the night and she would say, "is it time to go to school?"

The patient then revealed that she continued to write valentines to her dead grandmother for several years after her death. In spite of her supportive efforts, the grandmother was unable to comfort the patient during those nightmares, and the patient experienced a sense of abandonment by her mother, who had left her under her grandmother's supervision.

The emerging personality of the child is a topic of crucial importance. Was the child shy, restless, overactive, withdrawn, studious, outgoing, timid, athletic, friendly? Play is a useful area to explore in studying the development of the child's personality. This includes the earliest activities of the infant, who plays with bodily parts, and continues on through the complex play of adolescents. This portion of the history not only reveals the child's growing capacity for social relationships but also provides information concerning his developing ego structure. The clinician should seek data concerning the child's increasing ability to concentrate, to tolerate frustration, to postpone gratification, and, as he became older, to cooperate with peers, to be fair, to understand and comply with rules, and to develop mature conscience mechanisms. The child's preference for active or passive roles in physical play should also be noted. The development of intellectual play becomes crucial as the child becomes older. His capacity to entertain himself—playing alone, in contrast to his need for companionship—reveals important information concerning his developing personality. The fairy tales and stories of childhood contain all the conflicts, wishes, and fears of the various developmental phases, so it is useful to learn which stories were the patient's favorites. They may provide clues concerning the patient's most significant problem areas during those particular years.

The psychiatrist should also ask the patient for his earliest memory and for any recurrent dreams or fantasies that occurred during the first 3 years of his life.

Middle childhood (ages 3 to 11). In this section the psychiatrist can address such important subjects as gender identification, punishments used in the home, and who provided the discipline and influenced early conscience formation. The psychiatrist must inquire about the patient's early school experiences, especially how the patient first tolerated being separated from his mother. Data about the patient's earliest friendships and peer relations are valuable. The psychiatrist should identify and define the number and the closeness of the patient's friends, describe whether or not the patient took the role of leader or follower, and describe his social popularity and participation in group or gang activities. Early patterns of assertion, impulsiveness, aggression, passivity, anxiety, or antisocial behavior emerge in the context of school relationships. A history of the patient's learning to read and the development of other intellectual and motor skills is important. A history of minimal cerebral dysfunction or of learning disabilities, their management, and their impact on the child is of particular significance. The presence of nightmares, phobias, bed wetting, fire setting, cruelty to animals, and masturbation should also be explored.

Late childhood (prepuberty through adolescence). During this period of development, the final unfolding and consolidation of the adult personality occurs. The psychiatrist should continue to trace the evolution of social relationships as they achieve increasing importance. During that time and through relationships with peers and in group activities, a person begins to develop independence from his parents. The psychiatrist should attempt to define the values of the patient's social groups and determine who were the patient's idealized figures. That information provides useful clues concerning the patient's emerging idealized self-image.

Further exploration is indicated of the patient's school history, his relationships with teachers, and his favorite studies and interests both in school and in the extracurricular area. The psychiatrist should ask about his participation in sports and hobbies and inquire about any emotional or physical problems that may have made their first appearance during this phase. Common examples include feelings of inferiority, weight problems, smoking, running away from home, and any drug or alcohol use or abuse.

Psychosexual history. Inasmuch as the sexual history is often the most personal and embarrassing area for the patient, it can be useful to elicit this material all at one time. Such a concentration of attention on the patient's sexual history provides a therapeutic structure that is supportive of the sensitive patient and that makes sure the therapist will not fail, as a result of countertransference, to obtain relevant sexual data.

Much of the history of infantile sexuality is not recoverable, although many patients are able to recollect curiosities and sexual games played during the ages of 3 to 6. The interviewer should ask how the patient learned about sex and what attitudes he felt his parents had about his sexual development. The interviewer can also inquire about sexual transgressions imposed on the patient during childhood. Those important incidents are conflict laden and are seldom voluntarily recollected by the patient. The patient often experiences relief when a sensitively phrased question allows him to reveal some particularly difficult material that he might otherwise not reveal for months or even years.

No history is complete without a discussion of the onset of puberty and the patient's feelings about that important milestone. Female patients should be questioned about preparation for the onset of their menses and about the circumstances and their feelings concerning the development of secondary sexual characteristics. Children whose secondary sexual characteristics developed unusually early or unusually late typically suffer from embarrassment and often take elaborate measures to attempt to conceal the fact that they differ from the norm of their peer group. Any exception to that general principle is well worth describing. The adolescent masturbatory history, including the nature of the patient's fantasies and his feelings about them is of significance. The interviewer should routinely inquire about dating, petting, crushes, parties, and sex games. Attitudes toward the opposite sex should be described in detail. Was the patient shy, timid, or aggressive, or did he need to impress others and boast of his sexual conquests? Did the patient experience anxiety in the sexual setting? Was there promiscuity? Did the patient participate in homosexual, group masturbatory, incestuous, aggressive, or perverse sexual behavior?

Religious background. The psychiatrist should describe the religious background of both parents and the details of the patient's religious instruction. Was the family attitude toward religion strict or permissive, and were there any conflicts between the two parents over the religious education of the child? The psychiatrist should trace the evolution of the patient's adolescent religious practices to his present beliefs and activities.

Adulthood

Occupational and advanced educational history. The psychiatrist should describe the patient's choice of occupation, the requisite training and preparation, and his long-term ambitions and goals. The interviewer should also explore his relationships at work with authorities, peers, and if applicable, subordinates and describe the number of jobs the patient has had and their duration, the reasons for changes in jobs, and any changes in job status. What is the patient's current job, and what are his feelings about it?

Social activity. The psychiatrist should describe the patient's social life and the nature of his friendships, with emphasis on the depth, duration, and quality of his human relations. What type of social, intellectual, and physical interests does he share with his friends?

Adult sexuality. Although the written record has organized adult sexuality and marriage into separate categories, in the conduct of the clinical interview it is usually easiest to elicit that material together. The premarital sexual history should include any sexual symptoms—such as frigidity, vaginismus, impotence, premature or retarded ejaculation, and sexual perversion.

Military history. With the cessation of the draft, young psychiatrists will probably overlook the patient's military history. However, for those persons who have been in the military, it has usually been a significant experience. The psychiatrist should inquire about the patient's general adjustment to the military, whether or not he saw combat or sustained an injury, and the nature of his discharge. Was he ever referred for psychiatric consultation, and did he suffer any disciplinary action during his period of service?

Marital history. In this section the interviewer describes each marriage, legal or common law, that the patient has had. Also to be included are significant relationships with members of the opposite sex with whom the patient has lived for a protracted period of time. The story of the marriage should include a description of the courtship and the role played by each partner. The evolution of the relationship should be explored and should describe the areas of agreement and disagreement, including the management of money, the roles of the in-laws, attitudes toward raising children, and their sexual adjustment. The topic of their sexual adjustment should include a description of how their sexual activity is usually initiated, the frequency of their sexual relations, and their sexual preferences, variations, and techniques. It is usually appropriate to inquire if either party has engaged in extramarital relationships and, if so, under what circumstances and whether the spouse learned of the affair. If the spouse did learn of the affair, it is important to describe what happened. The reasons underlying an extramarital affair are just as important as an understanding of its effect on the marriage. Attitudes toward contraception and family planning are important, and the names, ages, descriptions, and relationships to the patient of all the children involved should be obtained. It is important to obtain some assessment of the patient's capacity to function adequately in the parental role.

Current Social Situation

The psychiatrist should inquire about where the patient lives in sufficient detail to describe the neighborhood, as well as the patient's residence. He should include the number of rooms, the number of family members living in the home, and the sleeping arrangements, and he should inquire as to how issues of privacy are handled, with particular emphasis on parental and sibling nudity and bathroom arrangements. The interviewer should ask about the sources of family income and any financial hardships. If applicable, he might inquire about public assistance and the patient's feeling about it. If the patient has been hospitalized, have provisions been made so that he will not lose his job or apartment? The psychiatrist should ask who is caring for the children at home and who visits the patient in the hospital and how frequently.

Dreams, Fantasies, and Value Systems

Freud stated that the dream is the royal road to the unconscious. There is no more direct way to learn about the patient's unconscious fears, wishes, and conflicts than through an understanding of his dreams. Repetitive dreams are of particular value. If the patient has nightmares, what are their repetitive themes? Some of the most common themes of dreams are food (either the patient is being gratified or the patient is being denied while others eat), aggression (the patient is involved in adventures, battles, and chases or, most often, is in the defensive position), examinations (the patient feels unprepared or is late for the examination or cannot find the proper room), helplessness or impotence (the patient is shooting at someone with a gun that has rubber bullets, or the patient is fighting, and his blows seem to have no effect on his opponent; often, the patient is being chased and is unable to run or to cry out for help), and sex dreams of all varieties, both with and without orgasm. The manifest dream may be viewed according to the figures, the activity or motion, the plot or problem, affects, color, the role of the dreamer (active or observer), dream style, and defenses contained within the dream.

It is useful to ask the patient for a recent dream. If the patient cannot produce one, the interviewer may say, "Perhaps you'll have one between now and our next appointment; if you do, try to make a note of it." The patient frequently produces a dream in the second interview that reveals his unconscious feelings about the physician, treatment, his illness, or all three.

Fantasies or daydreams are another valuable source of unconscious material. As with dreams, the psychiatrist can explore and record all manifest details and attendant feelings.

Finally, he may inquire about the patient's system of values—both social and moral values, including values that concern work, play, children, parents, friends, and community and cultural concerns or interests.

Family History

Recent contributions from the field of genetics demonstrate the importance of hereditary factors in a variety of emotional disorders. A brief statement about any psychiatric illnesses, hospitalization, and treatments of the patient's parents, grandparents, siblings, children, and other immediate family members should be placed in this part of the report. In addition, the family history should provide a description of the personalities of the various people living in the patient's home from childhood to the present. The psychiatrist should also define the role each person has played in the patient's upbringing and their current relationships with the patient. Informants other than the patient may be available to contribute to the family history, and the source should be cited in the written record.

Frequently, data concerning the background and the upbringing of the patient's parents suggest probable behaviors that they exhibited toward the patient, despite wishes to do the contrary. Finally, the psychiatrist should determine the family's attitude toward and insight into the patient's illness. Does the patient feel that they are customarily supportive, indifferent, or destructive?

CONCLUSIONS

In summary, the author would like to emphasize the following points: (1) The dynamic treatment process is not postponed or interrupted for the purpose of data collection. (2) There is no one kind of history-taking technique for all patients or all clinical situations. (3) Initially, it is necessary to devote much attention to learning whether or not the patient is willing or able to cooperate with treatment. (4) The history is never complete or fully accurate. (5) The description of the patient, the psychopathology, and the developmental history should all fit together; the best data are those that reveal those interrelationships. (6) The patient's inner mental life should be linked with his symptoms and behaviors. (7) The sciences of psychodynamics and developmental psychology explain the important connections between past and present; without that foundation, psychotherapy is not based on personality theory but on vague concepts about communication, and the psychiatrist can use only mechanistic therapy of interpersonal relationships. (8) The psychiatrist cannot answer every question raised in this section for any patient he treats.

Mental Status Examination

The outlines for mental status examinations in use today have changed relatively little in the past 40 years. In consulting the leading textbooks of psychiatry, one readily sees that each book has a similar but somewhat different organization. Likewise, the various state departments of mental hygiene and the many university departments of psychiatry all have individual variations of the mental status examination.

Ideally, the mental status examination should classify and describe all the areas and components of mental functioning that are involved in modern diagnostic classification. It should serve a role for the psychiatrist similar to the one that the physical examination serves for the internist. However, much of the physical examination can be done without any subjective participation by the patient. The boundary between the history and the mental status is less well defined in that many areas of the mental status require subjective information from the patient or other informants. An adequate mental status examination must relate to personality disorders, neuroses, and psychoses. Current developments in the understanding of personality disorders and the complexities of ego functioning make it abundantly clear that present-day mental status examinations are of little value in those areas. The typical mental status examination is most useful in describing the psychopathology of the psychoses and the neuroses. Personality or character diagnosis is based largely on the patient's history or the nature of the patients interaction with the psychiatrist and requires a careful understanding of the various complex aspects of ego functioning.

Several groups have attempted to develop systematic rating scales of ego functioning in order to quantify the measurement of ego strength. Prelinger and Zimet (1964), the Menninger Foundation Psychotherapy Research Group (Wallerstein and Robbins, 1956), Karush et al. (1964), Grunher et al. (1973),

Greenspan and Cullander (1973)—all have developed related but differing methods toward that end. None of those efforts has produced a system for the assessment of ego function that has been incorporated into any outline for the mental status part of the report. In some cases a number of areas of ego functioning are not included in the mental status examination. Other areas of ego functioning, although included in the mental status examinations, are not described in a way that is useful for the diagnosis of personality disorders. For example, disorders of impulse control are nowhere to be found in the typical mental status outline. Nor is there any category where one can evaluate the sublimatory capacity of the ego or the capacity for object relations. However, inferential data about the capacity for object relations can be gathered from the psychiatric history. That is a typical example of the inescapable blurring of boundaries between the history and the mental status parts of the report. The reality-testing functions of the ego can be evaluated and described under disorders of thought process if the patient has delusions or under perceptual disturbances if the patient has hallucinations. Reality testing is also described under disorders of orientation in considering the patient's ability to identify those persons who are in his immediate environment and to accurately appreciate their roles. The kinds of impairment of reality testing found in personality disorders are usually described under insight and judgment.

The stimulus barrier function of the ego can be assessed under distractibility, provided the examiner understands and agrees not only that distractibility refers to the ego's capacity to attend a particular theme or task, rejecting interfering stimuli from the environment, but that the ego also must maintain the ability to reject interfering visceral or affective stimuli from inside as well. That aspect of the stimulus barrier function of the ego is undoubtedly related to the ego's capacity to repress conflicted thoughts or affects, which is described under the defense formation function of the ego. The distracting awareness of visceral sensations that intrude into a patient's consciousness while engrossed in conversation is a common example of the ego's loss of capacity to reject unwanted internal stimuli. The patient who is overloaded by environmental stimulation and cannot attend to adaptive coping tasks has an impairment in stimulus rejection.

The ego's capacities for adaptive regression—which is required for creativity, for falling in love, and for the enjoyment of sex, music and art—are not assessed in the mental status examination. However, information can be gathered about those important functions from a good psychiatric history. The ego's defensive functions are not directly included in the mental status examination, but conclusions can be made from data found under the description of structured neurotic symptoms. The problem is further complicated by the fact that not all psychiatrists accept the idea that symptoms serve a defensive function or that their mechanism of formation is derived from the ego's attempt to resolve intrapsychic conflict.

The synthetic integrative functions of the ego are not addressed directly in the mental status examination. But inferential conclusions can be drawn from the fact that a patient appears disorganized and unable to integrate and process data, either internal or external.

Many outlines for the mental status contain items that, although of questionable value, are, nonetheless, passed on from one generation of psychiatrists to another. An example is the cowboy story. In *Outlines for Psychiatric Examinations* by N. D. C. Lewis, (1943) that story is listed as a test for memory function, particularly for immediate retention and recall. The story is scored on the basis of 32 components. The story is about a cowboy and his dog, who does not recognize the cowboy in his new clothes but does recognize him when he returns in his old familiar clothes. The patient is asked to repeat the story. The instructions regarding the scoring of the patient's response pertain only to memory, although the interviewer is advised to determine whether or not the patient seems to comprehend the meaning of the story. How does one score the response if the patient says, "Dogs recognize their masters by smell, more than sight, and the writer of that story must never have owned a dog" or if the patient has never owned a dog and fails to spot the illogicality in the story? Another patient may merely find the story boring and irrelevant to his concerns and dismiss the examiner with a comment such as, "I don't know what it means." Or the patient may merely remain silent. Nevertheless, the story has been passed on from one generation of psychiatrists to another without any critical examination of its usefulness.

Table I summarizes the ego's functions. Some of the ego functions may be assessed from the patient's current mental status; others must be assessed from the psychiatric history. The table of ego functions does not lend itself to easy integration into the mental status examination proposed in this section.

TABLE I
Organization of Ego Functions

Defense formation	Conflict resolution: Defenses successfully mediate between id and superego demands, providing gratification Defenses fail to mediate, leading to inhibition and restricted functions Defenses mediate unsuccessfully, with symptoms or pathological character traits resulting Types of defense: Mature defenses, including repression, rationalization, displacement, identification, symbolization, reaction formation, and undoing; must function in service of sublimation Primitive defenses, including denial, projection, introjection, splitting, dissociation, isolation, regression, conversion, and avoidance; can have less primitive manifestations Stability and flexibility of defenses
Regulation and control of drives, affects, and impulses	Postponement of gratification, with ability to tolerate tension and frustration Appropriate control of direct discharge, maintaining adequate fulfillment of pleasures (sublimatory capacity)
Relationship to others	Capacity for subordination of narcissistic or symbiotic choices, fusion of good and bad images; others experienced as separate and whole Capacity to mourn losses and establish new relationships Depth of relationships; empathic capacity Stability and duration of relationships
Self-representation	Actual competence regarding active mastery of environment as seen by others and contrasted with person's self-perception of competence Relationship of self-image to idealized self-image or ego ideal Capacity to fuse good and bad self-images

TABLE I—*continued*

Synthetic integrative functioning	Thinking, memory, language, visual and motor functions, concentration, and attention Anticipation and learning, including cognitive or planning aspect of fantasy Judgment: Requires analytic and synthetic use of the above components Capacity to integrate new experiences, with reconciliation of inconsistencies Executive interaction with environment; requires use of all the above components, with resulting ability to select, control, and integrate systems of mental activity designed to gratify needs and assure security while adapting to outer world
Stimulus regulation	Passive threshold for regulation of excessive external or internal stimuli (a neurophysiological substrate of the ego) Active management of excess stimulation (includes selective attention) Maintenance of adequate stimulus nutrient (tonic homeostasis)
Adaptive regression in service of ego	Capacity to regressively relax perceptual and cognitive acuity; necessary for emotional enjoyment of sex, music, art, food, literature, theater, sleep, creative imagery, and falling in love Openness to new experiences in those areas
Reality testing and sense of reality	Perception of whether stimulus originates inside or outside the organism Accuracy of perception; prevalence of objectivity over wishful perception Selective attention as an organizing process Inner reality testing; reflective awareness, knowing one's self, openness of self Sense of reality; depends on clarity of boundaries between self and world. Depersonalization or derealization

Therefore, it seems logical to introduce the table before discussing the more traditional aspects of the mental status examination. The concept of ego functioning is useful for the assessment of ego strength. With all the controversy about the diagnosis of personality disorders, it is clear both that certain disorders imply a more serious prognosis than do others and that within any given diagnostic category there are patients with varying degrees of psychopathology. The psychiatrist uses his knowledge of ego strength to assess the severity of the patient's disorder.

EGO FUNCTIONS

Definition

The ego is the executive apparatus of the mind; it mediates between the internal demands of biologically determined motives (the id), the socially determined values and behaviors, (the superego), and the external demands of reality. All ego functions serve the basic task of the organism's adaptation to the environment to ensure survival while allowing for the gratification of needs. The biological substrate of the ego lies within the basic physiological processes of perception, concentration, motor behavior, memory, cognition, learning, language, and stimulus control and the integration and syntheses of all those functions. The infant's biologically developing ego processes blend and interact with the psychological processes mediated by the infant's experience with an attentive and responsive mother and significant other humans.

It is difficult to organize ego functions into a hierarchical table because of their intricacies, subtleties, and overlapping of function and because many of the ego functions currently listed are of different levels of abstraction or transect the same structures through different planes. For example, perception and memory are relatively simple functions that are understandable in both physiological and psychological terms. However, the more complex functions—such as the synthetic-integrative function, reality testing, and the defensive functions—do not easily lend themselves to study by the neurochemist and are difficult to measure directly either clinically or in the psychology laboratory.

Ego Strength

No single function of the ego can provide an accurate measurement of ego strength. It is the balance of all ego functions and their effectiveness in promoting the adaptation of the organism to the environment that creates the broad picture of ego strength or weakness. Glover (1958) stated that ego strength depends on the quality and the stability of the emotional ties to others, on the elastic adaptation to instinctual demands, and on optimum freedom from the reactive effects of anxiety and guilt.

Hartmann (1958) added to the understanding of ego functioning with his emphasis on the autonomy of certain operations of the ego. Hartmann (1958) referred to the ego's apparatuses of primary autonomy as

perception, intention, object comprehension, thinking, language, recall-phenomena, productivity . . . motor development . . . and . . . the maturation and learning processes implicit in all of these.

Those functions evolve outside of the sphere of conflict formation and are not dependent on the drives. They are called the ego's primary autonomy from the id. Hartmann (1958) further postulated a secondary autonomy:

an attitude which arose originally in the service of defense against an instinctual drive may, in the course of time, become an independent structure, in which case the instinctual drive merely triggers this response but does not determine the details of its action.

He went on to indicate that the pattern of behavior or symptom may then serve other functions, such as adaptation and synthesis, and thus become a goal in its own right. Rapaport, in a 1955 seminar, extended those concepts to the autonomy of the ego from external reality. By that he meant that a person can "likewise modify and postpone his reaction to external stimulation." He indicated, further, that it was a "relative freedom at best."

Later developments in ego psychology formulate autonomous functioning as a process concept and not a unitary function. The term "autonomous functioning" is best understood when it is used to describe the property of other ego functions.

In the clinical assessment of a patient, the psychiatrist finds ego strength when the functions of primary autonomy—language, motor function, conceptualization, memory, concentration, attention—show no impairment and have remained relatively free from the influence of psychological conflict. A further indication of ego strength is the freedom from psychological impairment of more complex autonomous patterns, such as work routines, hobbies, interests, learned complex skills, and adaptive patterns. Impairment in any of those areas is indicative of ego weakness.

Ego functions must be viewed in terms of the interrelationship between the defensive functions and the synthetic or organizing functions. The early view that the ego mediates between the demands of the id and the demands of the superego is vastly oversimplified and incomplete. Hartmann (1958) stated the appraisal of ego strength must focus on the

nature and maturational stage of the ego apparatuses which underlie intelligence, will and action and not merely on the intensity of instinctual drives and the tolerance for tension which usually are assumed to determine ego strength.

Ego function is best understood in terms of adaptation, a concept that is broader than defense formation and includes all the coping mechanisms necessary for health and survival.

Ego Functions Table

The ego functions table (see Table I) represents a compromise in its method of organization. It reflects a partial attempt at a hierarchical classification of functions and component aspects. One alternative system would be to organize ego functions according to the ego's relationships with other mental structures and to the external environment. Such a system could classify functions according to ego's (1) relationship to the id or drives, (2) relationship to the superego and the ego ideal, (3) relationship to outer reality, and (4) relationship to inner reality and the representational world. Numerous other systems are possible, each with its individual advantages and disadvantages. The emphasis in this section is not on psychoanalytic theory but on its practical application in the clinical evaluation of the patient.

Defense formation. Defense formation includes the effectiveness of the patient's defenses, the general style and maturational level of his defenses, and the stability and flexibility of his defense mechanisms. The assessment should specifically consider each of the following items:

Conflict resolution. Successful defenses resolve intrapsychic conflict between the instinctual wishes of the id and the demands of the superego; they permit some measure of instinctual gratification with freedom from the dysphoric affects of fear, guilt, anger, anxiety, and depression while protecting other ego functions. Unsuccessful defenses lead to inhibition or restrictions of function, specific symptoms, or pathological character traits.

Types of defense. Mature defenses include repression, rationalization, displacement, identification, symbolization, reaction formation, and undoing. For a defense to be considered mature, it must serve a sublimatory function. Primitive defenses include denial, projection, introjection, splitting, dissociation, isolation, regression, conversion, and avoidance. Those defenses can occur in mild or attenuated forms in mature persons.

It is impossible to create a complete list of defense mechanisms, since the ego can use practically anything in the service of defense, including the defensive use of humor and the substitution of one affect for another.

Stability and flexibility of defenses. The stability and flexibility of defenses is revealed by the patient's resilience under stress and his ability not to regress to more immature levels of defense organization.

Defenses must be distinguished from the relatively autonomous character traits that may have originated in defense but that, through the process of formation of psychic structures, operate outside of the defense organization. Examples include conscientiousness and kindliness that evolved through reaction formation. However, reaction formation does not account for all instances of conscientiousness and kindliness, since those traits can also occur through the process of identification.

Regulation and control of drives, affects, and impulses. Ego strength is present when the person is capable of postponing gratification of drives while tolerating the resulting sense of frustration and tension. Ego weakness is indicated by low frustration tolerance and the need for immediate gratification. The appropriate control of the direct discharge of drives, affects, and impulses while maintaining adequate supplies of pleasure is a sign of ego strength. It is facilitated by the ego's capacity to maintain gratification through the mechanism of sublimation. Patients with ego weakness show poor impulse control, and their aggressive and sexual drives are expressed directly and often inappropriately. Neurotic acting out of instinctual wishes is a sign of moderate ego weakness, depending on the degree of displacement or sublimation involved.

In a healthy ego, many primitive impulses must be repressed, and repression is the area of overlap between the first two functions. A mature person has both effective defense mechanisms and effective delay mechanisms. The dysphoric affects of frustration and rage indicate impairment of that function when it is correlated with poor impulse control and inability to postpone the gratification of needs.

Relationship to others. This function has received increasing attention with the current interest in narcissistic and borderline character structures. Ego weakness is indicated by the patient's placing his own needs before those of others, his selection of persons with whom he can form symbiotic attachments, or an inability to relate to others except in a primitive and infantile manner, using others for the enhancement of the need to feel unique and superior. Sadomasochistic relationships with the accompanying primitive aggression are another example of ego weakness. Ego strength is indicated by the patient's capacity to fuse the good and bad mental images of the important people in his past and present life and to experience others as whole people and as separate from himself.

The capacity for deep relationships with others manifested by mutual loving, sharing, and empathy is another sign of ego strength. The ability to maintain stable relationships over sustained periods of time is an indication of maturity, particularly when that ability is coupled with the ability to tolerate the frustrations and anger evoked by the relationship and the frustrations caused by separation from that person. Finally, the capacity to mourn the loss of a loved one and the ability to form new and lasting relations are examples of ego strength.

Self-representation. Ego strength is indicated by the over-all competence of the patient's performance in his interaction with the external world. That competence includes not only the successful mastery of the environment as perceived by others but the patient's subjective sense of competence or self-confidence. The person is self-confident when he perceives himself as able to obtain gratification of his needs and to ensure survival.

In addition to his self-representation or mental image of

what he is actually like, each person has an image of what he would like to be or what he thinks he ought to be—his ego ideal. The closeness of the approximation of his ego ideal and his actual self-image reflects his sense of self-esteem. Both high self-confidence and high self-esteem are an indication of a strong ego. This, of course, must be differentiated from narcissistic grandiosity. Finally, the self-representation must fuse the patient's good and bad self-images into a cohesive unit. Ego weakness is evidenced by fluctuations in the patient's sense of self-worth or alternations between experiencing himself as all good and experiencing himself as all bad.

Synthetic integrative functioning. The synthetic integrative function is probably the most complex of the ego functions. A number of more primary ego functions must be intact in order for synthesis to take place. Those functions include thinking, memory, language, visual and motor functions, attention, and concentration. In progressing upward in the development of the ego, one encounters the more complex functions of anticipation and learning, including the cognitive or planning aspect of fantasy. Next in complexity is judgment, which requires the analytic and synthetic use of all the above components, coordinated with reality testing and a capacity for self-reflection.

Stress tolerance is one measurement of the synthetic integrative function. The patient who can integrate new experiences and use that new knowledge appropriately shows ego strength. The capacity to reconcile inconsistent or contradictory values, affects, attitudes, and behavior in one's self and in others is another measure of the strength of the synthetic function.

Finally, the ego's executive interaction with the environment uses all the above-described functions. Through that function the organism knows which mental system to select at any given time to assure security and to provide for need gratification while adapting to both inner and outer worlds.

Stimulus regulation. The stimulus barrier function is initially a passive, neurophysiological mechanism that protects the infant from excessive stimulation. The mother plays a vital role for the developing child in protecting him from excessive stimulation. At about the age of 4 to 8 weeks, the infant is capable of using active measures to ward off excessive stimulation.

The patient's capacity to read and concentrate in noisy surroundings is an example of the use of selective attention as an organizing ego function to adapt to a disorganizing environment. The person who reads or employs fantasy in an unpleasant environment is using the process of active accommodation to disturbing stimuli.

A patient with the symptoms of eating binges, stealing food from grocery stores, and anxiety attacks stated:

> I'm afraid to go out of the apartment. All those people, the overstimulation—too damn many people. I feel swept along in a current, overwhelmed. I feel like I haven't got much structure, like my body's a wisp in the ocean, like nothing, like I'm struggling to assert myself, struggling through the crowd—a few blocks is a million miles; seems like you'll never get there—all the distraction—too many stores—too many possibilities.

She described similar situations in school when the "flood of information" caused her to panic. In addition to the failure of the stimulus regulation function, she illustrated a weakness of the synthetic integrative function, the drive regulation function, the defense formation function, and judgment, plus other impairments implied but not described in the vignette.

The healthy ego must not block out too many sensory stimuli; the person must receive adequate stimulus nutriment. Sensory deprivation experiments demonstrate the need for stimulus nutriment. Adequate sensory stimulation requires intact functioning of the perceptual and motor apparatuses. The integrative function allows the patient to shift back and forth from external to internal supplies of stimulation as his needs dictate, maintaining what Holt (1965) referred to as "tonic support."

Adaptive regression in service of ego. Adaptive regression in the service of the ego requires the capacity to relax perceptual and cognitive acuity and other ego controls in order to allow the ego to experience preconscious and unconscious material. This function is necessary to fall in love, for the creative process, and for the full emotional enjoyment of sex, music, art, literature, theater, and falling asleep. Ego strength is indicated by the degree of capacity for pleasurable functioning that the patient shows in those areas. Flexibility of ego structure implies a capacity to allow new experiences in those areas that add to the over-all adaptive pleasure balance. There is some controversy as to whether or not this phenomenon actually involves the process of regression or more a type of relaxation of other ego functions.

Reality testing and sense of reality. The reality-testing function of the ego depends on the perceptual apparatus as well as the ability to discriminate whether a given stimulus originates inside or outside the organism. Perception is not merely the passive registration of data, as with a tape recorder. Perception and selective attention to a particular stimulus or experience also serve an organizing function for the ego. The strength of the patient's ego is also reflected in the accuracy of his perceptions. Patients with delusions or hallucinations reveal gross impairments of reality testing. An example of a more subtle impairment of reality testing is the man who erroneously believes that his wife's lack of orderliness is for the deliberate purpose of provoking him.

Reflective awareness refers to the awareness of being aware and the ability to differentiate varieties of conscious experiences and to distinguish dreams, fantasy, memory, and percepts. In other words, reflective awareness is the person's realization that he is the thinker of a thought (Schafer, 1968). When a patient loses his ability to distinguish between a thought and the concrete reality to which the thought refers, he suffers from an impairment of reality testing and exhibits ego weakness.

Reality testing can be impaired through mechanisms that relate primarily to the id, other ego mechanisms, or the superego. An example of the first is a perception distorted by an unconscious wish or fear; the second is exemplified by a defensive denial that an event occurred; the third is illustrated by a situation misperceived as the result of excessive guilt, with anticipation of blame or punishment. Inner reality testing refers to the patient's perception of himself and of how he is viewed by others. Inner reality testing is similar to the concepts contained in the term "insight," coupled with an accurate appraisal of his inner mental state.

The sense of reality refers to the patient's ability to experience external events as real and to sense routine events as familiar. Experiences of derealization reveal an ego defect of this function. The patient's sense of familiarity with his own body and its parts and with his own behavior as belonging to himself is impaired when he experiences feelings of depersonalization. Such a patient might say, "my body does not feel like it belongs to me. My hands don't look familiar and I feel

numb." The patient with derealization would report, "Nothing seems real or familiar; everything looks new, strange, or unnatural." Finally, the sense of reality requires that the patient be able to accurately differentiate between self and others (intact ego boundaries). This function overlaps somewhat with relationship to others and self-representation. A subtle example of impairment of ego boundaries is the patient who feels that he need not report details of his personal experiences to his doctor "because the doctor knows me so well he can tell what is on my mind." A more obvious example is the patient who states, "I feel like I'm my mother."

ORGANIZATION OF DATA

General description

Appearance. Almost every written mental status report begins with a description of the patient's appearance and the over-all physical and emotional impression he conveys to the interviewer, as reflected by his posture, bearing, clothing, grooming, and dominant attitude toward the interviewer. Other aspects of the patient that contribute to his over-all appearance include his degree of poise, the amount of anxiety he manifests, and the manner in which it is expressed. Those aspects, together with his appearance in relationship to his stated age and his attractiveness, should all be covered in a narrative paragraph that would allow someone who does not know the patient to easily recognize him in a room full of other people. Avoid vague and editorial words such as "unkempt," "inappropriate," or "attractive." What is attractive to one clinician may be unkempt to another. Instead describe the patient's appearance precisely, such as "He wore a dirty T-shirt on which he had written in red nail polish 'born to raise hell!'"

Behavior and psychomotor activity. This category refers to both the quantitative and the qualitative aspects of the patient's motor behavior. The psychiatrist should describe any mannerisms, tics, gestures, twitches, stereotyped behavior, echopraxia, hyperactivity, agitation, combativeness, flexibility, or rigidity, as well as the patient's gait and agility.

Attitude toward examiner. The patient's attitude toward the examiner may be described as cooperative, friendly, attentive, interested, frank, seductive, defensive, hostile, playful, ingratiating, evasive, or guarded; any number of other adjectives may be used. It is necessary for the psychiatrist to know the kinds of responses he typically elicits from various personality types so that he may estimate what aspects of the patient's attitude are a personal response to him and how much of it is a true reflection of the patient's mental status at the time of the examination. It must be realized that the patient's attitudes are not constant and that the patient's appearance may depend on the circumstance and the time the mental status examination is performed. The same patient examined by a different psychiatrist may be found to have a different mental status, and the same physician may find a different mental status on a different day of the week.

Speech. Speech is somewhat artificially separated from thought, although it is chiefly through speech that thought is revealed. Traditionally, this part of the report is used to describe the physical characteristics of speech. Disordered thought processes are reflected in certain language impairments, such as word salad, clang associations, and neologisms; they are typically included under thought process disorders. In the traditional outline, speech may be described in terms of its over-all quantity, its rate of production, and its quality. The patient may be described as talkative, garrulous, voluble, taciturn, unspontaneous, or normally responsive to cues from the interviewer. Speech may be rapid or slow, pressured, hesitant, emotional, monotonous, loud, whispered, slurred, or mumbled. Impairments of speech, such as stuttering and echolalia are included in this section.

Mood, feelings, and affect

Mood. Mood may be defined as a pervasive and sustained emotion that colors the patient's perception of the world. The psychiatrist is interested in whether the patient remarks voluntarily about his feeling state or whether it is necessary for him to ask the patient how he feels. Statements about the patient's mood should include depth, intensity, duration, and fluctuations. Some of the more common moods include depressed, expansive, euphoric, calm, neutral, irritable, anxious, terrified, angry, guilty, empty, awed, and self-contemptuous.

Affective expression. To accurately express the patient's full affective capacity or range of emotionality, the interviewer must cover a diversity of topics in a flexible way. The dominant emotion of the interview is related to the patient's mood. Therefore, the psychiatrist must be certain that the interview includes varied subject matter to assure a true test of whether or not the patient shows a constriction or limitation of affect. The interviewer may fail to tap the patient's full affective range, in which case the patient cannot be fairly labeled as constricted. In assessing constriction of affect, the psychiatrist must also be aware of the marked cultural differences in outward affective expression. One can use the same criteria in assessing the affective capacity of an Englishman and an Italian, but it is necessary to use the patient's subjective awareness of his own emotions. The two persons in question may both experience their emotions to an equal degree, but the outward manifestations are, for cultural reasons, more restrained in the English patient. Other patients have learned to simulate emotions but do not really experience their feelings very deeply. When asking the patient about his subjective experience of emotion, the psychiatrist must include the range of feelings that he recognizes in order to make an adequate evaluation of this aspect of the mental status examination.

Some patients experience difficulty in initiating, sustaining, or terminating an emotional response. Any example of this problem should be quoted in the written record. The examiner should comment on the patient's affect as broad or restricted, on its depth and range, and on its quantity.

In the normal expression of affect, there is a variation in facial expression, tone of voice, the use of hands, and body movements. When affect is restricted, there is a clear reduction in the expressive range and intensity of affect. In blunted affect there is severe reduction in the intensity of affective expression. To diagnose flat affect, one should find virtually no signs of affective expressions, the patient's voice should be monotonous and his face should be immobile. It may be difficult to differentiate flat affect from a stuporous depression. The interviewer can note any lability of emotion and then characterize the dominant affect of the interview, if there is one. Blunted, flat, and shallow refer to the depth of emotion; depressed, proud, angry, fearful, anxious, guilty, euphoric, and expansive refer to particular affects.

Appropriateness. The appropriateness of the patient's emotional responses can be considered only in the context of the subject matter the patient is discussing. The paranoid patient who is describing a delusion of persecution should be angry about the experiences he believes are happening to him. Anger in that context is not inappropriate affect; a lack of anger or concern would be inappropriate affect. Some psychiatrists have

reserved the term "inappropriateness of affect" for a quality of response found in the schizophrenic patient.

One patient smiled while discussing the death of her brother. The inappropriate response occurred because some thought entered the patient's mind that amused her but that was topically irrelevant to her feelings about her brother's death. It was an example of the kind of splitting between affect and ideation that was originally described by Bleuler. In another patient the smile while discussing the death of her brother might be because she actually hated him and did not feel sorry or saddened by his loss.

The psychiatrist needs to understand what elicited any emotion the patient displays during the interview. However, when the cause-and-effect relationship is apparent, the psychiatrist need not inquire what elicited the feeling. The interviewer's failure to inquire about emotional responses he does not understand deprives him of opportunities to facilitate rapport. In some situations the patient may not understand his own emotional response. That condition provides an important opportunity for the physician and the patient to collaborate to increase the patient's understanding of his own feelings.

Perception. In some of the old outlines for the mental status part of the report, perceptual disturbances were considered under the category of thought disorders, with hallucinations, illusions, and delusions all lumped together. The author agrees with those psychiatrists who think that hallucinations and illusions deserve a separate category in the outline. The sensory system involved should be described, as well as the content of the hallucinatory experiences. The circumstances of the occurrence of any hallucinatory experience are important, as hypnogogic and hypnopompic hallucinations are of much less serious significance than other types of hallucinations. Feelings of depersonalization and derealization are also examples of perceptual disturbance. Unlike hallucinations and delusions, they are not pathognomonic for psychosis and may be found in a wide variety of neurotic and personality disturbances. The extreme feelings of detachment from oneself or from the environment may have a more serious significance.

Thought process (form of thinking). The term "thought disorder" is an extremely controversial one in the field of psychiatry, as it is used in varied ways by different clinicians. For some, the term "formal thought disorder" has become a euphemistic expression for schizophrenic thought. Many others do not accept that narrow usage of the term and consider thought disorder to include all disorders of thinking that affect language, communication, or thought content. This is the area of the mental status examination with the greatest amount of controversy and variation from one outline to another.

Stream of thought. The stream or flow of thought may be divided into three components. The first comprises the over-all amount of thought and its rate of production. The patient may have an overabundance of ideas or a paucity of ideas. There may be rapid thinking, which, if carried to the extreme, is called a flight of ideas. Another patient may exhibit slow or hesitant thinking.

The second component of the stream of thought involves the continuity of ideas. Do the patient's replies really answer the questions he was asked, and does the patient have the capacity for goal-directed thinking? Is there a clear cause-and-effect relationship in the patient's explanations? Does he have loose associations? Other disturbances of the continuity of thought involve statements that are tangential, circumstantial, rambling, evasive, or perseverative. Blocking is an interruption of the train of speech before a thought or idea has been completed; the period of silence may last seconds or minutes, and the patient indicates that he cannot recall what he was saying or intended to say. Circumstantiality indicates the loss of capacity for goal-directed thinking; in the process of explaining an idea, the patient brings in many irrelevant details and parenthetical comments; the interviewer may need to interrupt the patient in order to help him get on to his point. Distractibility is a disturbance of thought process in which the patient loses the thread of the conversation and pursues tangential thoughts stimulated by various external or internal irrelevant stimuli.

The third area of disturbance in the stream of thought involves severe language impairments that reflect highly disordered mentation. Examples include incoherent or incomprehensible speech (word salad), clang associations, and neologisms. Some psychiatrists consider this area the only true manifestation of a thought disorder.

Content of thought. Disturbances in content of thought are subdivided into two major categories. The first is preoccupations, which may involve the patient's illness, environmental problems, obsessions, compulsions, phobias, suicide, homicidal ideas, hypochondriacal symptoms, or specific antisocial urges. Since those abnormal thoughts appear in a wide variety of neurotic and psychotic illnesses, psychiatrists disagree as to whether or not those symptoms should be considered disorders of thought.

The second category of disturbances of thought content involves delusions. The content of any delusional system should be described, and the psychiatrist should attempt to evaluate its organization and the patient's conviction as to its validity. The manner in which it affects his life is appropriately described in the history of the present illness. Somatic delusions should be included here. Are the delusions isolated, or are they associated with a pervasive suspiciousness in relationship to the environment? Ideas of reference and ideas of influence should also be described, as well as how such ideas began, their content, and the meaning the patient attributes to them.

Abstract thinking. Abstract thought is the last and most advanced level of thought to evolve in the development of the child. The way in which the patient conceptualizes or handles his ideas reveals his capacity for concept formation. The ability to abstract can be tested through similarities, differences, absurdities, and the capacity to use and understand metaphors and to understand the meaning of simple proverbs. A skilled clinician does not need to ask the patient to explain proverbs in order to make an accurate evaluation of his capacity to think abstractly. It is difficult to assess the reply of a patient who finds the proverb boring and irrelevant to his problems. His concrete answer may be only a reflection of his attitude toward the interviewer's question. The patient's thinking may also be overly concrete or overly abstract.

Information and intelligence. While taking the patient's history, the psychiatrist has learned about the patient's formal education and self-education. It is, therefore, unnecessary for the experienced psychiatrist to say to the patient, "Now I'm going to ask you some silly questions." The psychiatrist who apologizes to the patient for asking silly questions creates the impression that it is he who is silly. It is insulting to the patient to ask him questions that are too easy for him. If the psychiatrist is uncertain about the patient's ability to function at his level of basic endowment, he should ask questions that are relevant to the patient's educational and cultural background. If the patient shows some organic mental impairment, that will be

revealed during the history taking as the psychiatrist attempts to explore the ways in which the patient experiences his deficit in the problems of daily living. For example, if the physician has detected a possible organic mental impairment, he can inquire whether the patient has trouble with mental tasks, such as counting the change from $10.00 after a purchase of $6.37. If that task is too difficult, easier problems may be substituted. The skilled and sensitive clinician does not humiliate the patient by repeatedly asking questions that are too difficult or too easy.

Concentration and cognition. Subtracting serial 7's from 100 is a traditional part of every formal mental status examination. That simple task requires both concentration and cognitive capacities to be intact. It may not always be clear to the examiner whether the patient's difficulty in performing the task is due to anxiety, a disturbance of mood, some alteration of consciousness, or, at times, a combination of all three. In any event, the psychiatrist should attempt to estimate which of the above functions seems to be responsible for the patient's difficulty. If the patient cannot perform serial 7's, he can be asked to attempt easier multiplications or divisions. This test can be omitted when there is no suspected impairment.

Consciousness. Disturbances of consciousness usually indicate organic brain impairment. An exception is seen in the altered level of consciousness found in fugue or dream states. The term "clouding of consciousness" describes a dual impairment of the mind. One impairment is reduced wakefulness; the other is an impairment of the capacity to sustain attention to environmental stimuli or to sustain goal-directed thinking or behavior. Clouding or obtunding of consciousness is frequently not a fixed mental state. The typical patient manifests fluctuations in his level of awareness of the surrounding environment. Drowsiness or somnolence is often found in acute delirium. Minor impairments of consciousness may be expressed by decreasing ability to perform mental tasks, heightened effort, perseveration, frequent hesitation, starting, or irritability. The patient who has an altered state of consciousness often shows some impairment of orientation as well, although the reverse is not true. The patient with a stuporous depression and the catatonic patient may be totally unresponsive, but there is no alteration in those patients' states of consciousness.

Orientation. True disturbances in orientation are usually found only in organic mental disorders. It is common for a patient who has been hospitalized for several months to miss the date by a day or two. That mistake is not a sign of disorientation but is the result of sensory deprivation and a loss of interest or contact with the environment. A normal person may mistake the date by as much as 2 days in the middle of a month-long vacation and may temporarily mistake the day of the week by 1 day without showing signs of organic impairment. A good history usually reveals when the patient is fully oriented, and the psychiatrist should not insult the patient or make himself appear foolish by unnecessarily asking the patient if he is oriented. When the history has provided clues that the patient has some organic problem, the manner in which he performs the task of answering the interviewer's questions about orientation may provide useful clues. If for example, the patient is asked to name the season and he looks out the window and comments "Well, the leaves are turning, so it must be autumn," the interviewer has found a deficit. The sensitive clinician corrects the patient's errors in a respectful manner in a therapeutic effort to improve the patient's contact with his environment.

Disorders of orientation are traditionally separated according to time, place, and person. Any impairment usually appears in that order; as the patient improves, the impairment clears in the reverse order. It is necessary to determine whether the patient can give the approximate date. In addition, if he is in a hospital, does he know how long he has been there? And does the patient behave as though he is oriented to the present? In questions about the patient's orientation for place, it is not sufficient that the patient be able to correctly state the name and the location of the hospital; he should also behave as though he knows where he is. If more subtle signs of disorientation to place are suspected, the interviewer may ask the patient the routes and the means by which he would travel from the hospital to his home. In assessing orientation for person, the interviewer asks the patient whether he knows the names of the persons who are around him and whether he understands their roles in relationship to him. It is only in the most severe instances that the patient does not know who he is; in those cases the psychiatrist must be careful to differentiate a disorientation for person from a delusion in which, for example, the patient believes that he is Jesus Christ. When impairments for orientation are suspected, it is useful for the examiner to consult the patient's chart or the nurses' notes or speak with the patient's relatives or ward personnel. Disorders of orientation are often inconstant; for example, the patient may show no impairment at the time of the examination although he may be up wandering about the ward in a state of confusion at night.

Memory. Memory functions have been traditionally divided into four areas: remote memory, recent past memory, recent memory, and immediate retention and recall. Although the traditional view is that remote memory is better preserved than recent memory, there is some difference of opinion concerning the matter. Some psychiatrists and psychologists think that the patient's apparent capacity to recall remote events is actually due to constant repetition and reinforcement of the same material and that detailed testing of remote memory shows that it is just as impaired as recent memory.

The experienced clinician does not find it necessary to ask the patient structured questions about his memory, since he has learned about that function during the course of his interview. If the history does reveal memory problems, he then asks the patient questions that do not seem silly but are relevant to the difficulties from which the patient is suffering.

Recent memory may be checked by asking the patient about his appetite and then inquiring what he had for breakfast or for dinner the previous evening. He may be asked at that point if he recalls the interviewer's name. Asking the patient to repeat six digits forward and then backward is a traditional test for immediate retention. However, the results are often difficult to evaluate. Adults with minimal brain dysfunction may show particular difficulty in repeating the digits backward or may even reverse numbers in repeating them forward. Patients who routinely respond to test questions with anxiety may have difficulty with the digit span. Impaired concentration may also interfere with the patient's ability to repeat digits.

If the examiner has any questions concerning the functions that may be impaired, detailed psychological testing should be performed. Finally, no assessment of memory function is complete without determining the effects of the deficit on the patient and making note of what compensatory mechanisms the patient has developed to cope with his loss of capacity.

Impulse control. This important ego function is not tradi-

tionally part of the mental status examination. It may be disturbed in a variety of emotional disorders, both psychotic and neurotic. Is the patient able to control his aggressive, hostile, and sexual impulses?

A female patient showed no such lack of control during the course of the interview with a resident psychiatrist, but at the end of the session she walked over, pinched his cheek, and said, "You're so cute; are you married?"

The patient who is restless and cannot remain in his chair during the interview is suffering from agitation; however, if he walks over and reads the notes the interviewer is making, he also suffers from a disorder of impulse control.

Judgment. During the course of the history taking, the examiner should be able to assess many aspects of the patient's capacity for social judgment. Does the patient understand the likely outcome of his behavior, and is he influenced by that understanding? The psychiatrist should give examples of the patient's impairment if it is evident. If the patient shows some impairment of judgment, he may be asked hypothetical questions, such as, "What would you do if you found a stamped addressed letter in the street?"

Insight. Insight refers to the patient's degree of awareness and understanding that he is ill. The patient may exhibit a complete denial of his illness; he may show some awareness that he is ill but blame that fact on others, on external factors, or even on organic factors. He may acknowledge that he has an illness but ascribe it to something unknown or mysterious in himself.

Intellectual insight is present when the patient can admit that he is ill and acknowledge his symptoms or failures in adaptation with a realization that they are, in part, due to his own irrational feelings. However, the major limitation to intellectual insight is that the patient is unable to apply his knowledge in order to alter his future experiences. True emotional insight is present when the patient's awareness of his own motives and deep feelings leads to a change in his personality or behavior patterns. He is open to new ideas about himself and the important people in his life.

Reliability. The mental status part of the report concludes with the examiner's impression of the patient's reliability and capacity to report his situation accurately.

Suggested Cross References

The psychiatric interview is discussed in Section 12.1 and the psychiatric report in Section 12.3. Psychological testing is discussed in Sections 12.5, 12.6, and 12.7. Psychiatric classification is discussed in Chapter 14. Genetics is discussed in Section 2.1, sleep in Section 2.3, perception, cognition, and attention in Section 4.1, and sensory deprivation in Section 6.5. Classical psychoanalysis is described in Chapter 8. Schizophrenic disorders are discussed in Chapter 15 and personality disorders in Chapter 22. Disorders of impulse control are discussed in Section 25.2.

REFERENCES

Altman, H., Evenson, R., and Cho, D. New discriminant functions for computer diagnosis. Multivariate Behav. Res., *11:* 367, 1976.
Fenichel, O. Ego strength and ego weakness. In *Collected Papers,* series 2, p. 70. W. W. Norton, New York, 1954.
Freud, A. *The Ego and the Mechanisms of Defence.* International Universities Press, New York, 1946.
Garland, L., II. The problem of observer error. Bull. N. Y. Acad. Med., *36:* 570, 1960.
Gediman, H. K. The concept of the stimulus barrier: Its review and reformulation as an adaptive ego function. Int. J. Psychoanal., *52:* 243, 1971.
Glover, E. Ego distortion. Int. J. Psychoanal., *39:* 260, 1958.

Glueck, B., and Stroebel, C. The computer and the clinical decision process. II. Am. J. Psychiatry, *125* (Suppl.): 2, 1969.

Greenspan, S., and Cullander, C. C. A systematic metapsychological assessment of the personality. J. Am. Psychoanal. Assoc., *21:* 303, 1973.

Hartmann, H. Psychoanalytic theory of the ego. Psychoanal. Study Child, *5:* 93, 1950.

Hartmann, H. *Ego Psychology and the Problem of Adaptation.* International Universities Press, New York, 1958.

Hartmann, H. Technical implications of ego psychology. In *Essays on Ego Psychology,* p. 142. Hogarth Press, London, 1964.

Hartmann, H., Kris, E., and Loewenstein, R. Comments on the formation of psychic structure. Psychoanal. Study Child, *2:* 11, 1946.

Herron, W. G. The assessment of ego strength. J. Psychol. Stud., *13:* 173, 1962.

Hollingshead, A. B., and Redlich, F. C. *Social Class and Mental Illness.* John Wiley & Sons, New York, 1958.

Holt, R. H. Ego autonomy revisited. Int. J. Psychoanal., *46:* 151, 1965.

Hurvich, M. On the concept of reality testing. Int. J. Psychoanal., *51:* 299, 1970.

Hurvich, M., and Bellak, L. Ego function patterns in schizophrenics. Psychol. Rep., *22:* 299, 1968.

Karush, A. Ego strength: An unsolved problem in ego psychology. In *Science and Psychoanalysis,* J. H. Masserman, editor, vol. 11, p. 103. Grune & Stratton, New York, 1967.

Karush, A., Easser, B., Cooper, A., and Swerdloff, B. The evaluation of ego strength. I. A profile of adaptive balance. J. Nerv. Ment. Dis., *139:* 332, 1964.

Kernberg, O. Borderline personality organization. J. Am. Psychoanal. Assoc., *15:* 641, 1967.

Kernberg, O. A psychoanalytic classification of character pathology. J. Am. Psychoanal. Assoc., *18:* 800, 1970.

Kramer, M., Ornstein, P. H., Whitman, R. M., and Baldridge, B. J. The contribution of early memories and dreams to the diagnostic process. Compr. Psychiatry, *8:* 344, 1967.

Langs, R. J. Earliest memories and personality. Arch. Gen. Psychiatry, *12:* 379, 1965.

* Lewis, N. D. C. *Outlines for Psychiatric Examinations,* ed. 3. New York State Department of Mental Hygiene, Albany, 1943.

Lieberman, M. G. Childhood memories as a projective technique. J. Proj. Tech. *21:* 32, 1957.

Lyerly, S. B., and Abbott, P. S. *Handbook of Psychiatric Rating Scales (1950–1964).* National Institute of Mental Health, Bethesda, 1966.

* MacKinnon, R. A., and Michels, R. *The Psychiatric Interview in Clinical Practice.* W. B. Saunders, Philadelphia, 1971.

Mayman, M. Early memories and character structure. J. Proj. Tech. Pers. Assess., *32:* 303, 1968.

Menninger, K. Regulatory devices of the ego under major stress. Int. J. Psychoanal., *35:* 412, 1954.

Menninger, K. A., Mayman, M., and Pruyser, P. W., editors. The psychological examination. In *A Manual for Psychiatric Case Study,* ed. 2, p. 61. Grune & Stratton, New York, 1962.

Mosak, H. H. Early recollections as a projective technique. J. Proj. Tech., *22:* 302, 1958.

Nunberg, H. Ego strength and ego weakness. Am. Imago, *111:* 19, 1942.

Prelinger, E., and Zimet, C. *An Ego Psychological Approach to Character Assessment.* Free Press of Glencoe (Macmillan), New York, 1964.

Rapaport, D., Gill, M., and Schafer, R. *Diagnostic Psychological Testing,* vols. 1 and 2. Year Book, Chicago, 1946.

Roessler, R., Greenfield, M., and Alexander, A. Ego strength and response stereotype. Psychophysiology, *1:* 142, 1961.

* Ryback, R. *The Problem-oriented Record in Psychiatry and Mental Health Care.* Grune & Stratton, New York, 1974.

Schafer, R. *Aspects of Internalization.* International Universities Press, New York, 1968.

Schafer, R. An overview of Hartmann's contributions. Int. J. Psychoanal., *51:* 425, 1970.

Spitzer, R. L. Immediately available record of mental status exam: The mental status schedule inventory. Arch. Gen. Psychiatry, *13:* 76, 1965.

Spitzer, R., and Endicott, J. DIAGNO: A computer program for psychiatric diagnosis utilizing the differential diagnostic procedures. Arch. Gen. Psychiatry, *18:* 746, 1968.

Spitzer, R., and Endicott, J. DIAGNO II: Further developments in a computer program for psychiatric diagnosis. Am. J. Psychiatry, *125* (Suppl): 12, 1969.

Spitzer, R., and Endicott, J. Can the computer assist clinicians in psychiatric diagnosis? Am. J. Psychiatry, *131:* 523, 1974.

Spitzer, R., Endicott, J., and Cohen, J. Constraints on the validity of computer diagnosis. Arch. Gen. Psychiatry, *31:* 197, 1974.

Spitzer, R. L., Fleiss, J. L., Burdock, E. I., and Hardesty, A. S. The mental status schedule: Rationale, reliability, and validity. Compr. Psychiatry, *5:* 384, 1964.

Spitzer, R. L., Fleiss, J. L., Endicott, J., and Cohen, J. Mental status schedule: Properties of factor-analytically derived scales. Arch. Gen. Psychiatry, *16:* 479, 1967.

Spitzer, R. L., Fleiss, J. L., Kernohan, W., Lee, J. C., and Baldwin, I. T. Mental status schedule: Comparing Kentucky and New York schizophrenics. Arch Gen. Psychiatry, *12:* 448, 1965.

Stevenson, I. *The Psychiatric Examination.* Little, Brown, and Co., Boston, 1969.

Ulett, G. Automation in a state mental health system. Hosp. Community Psychiatry, *25:* 77, 1974.

Wallerstein, R. S., and Robbins, C. L. The psychotherapy research project of the Menninger Foundation. IV. Concepts. Bull. Menninger Clin., *20:* 244, 1956.

Weiner, H. Some thoughts on the concept of primary autonomous ego functions. In *Psychoanalysis: A General Psychology: Essays in Honor of Heinz Hartmann,* R. Loewenstein, L. Neuman, M. Schur, and A. Solnit, editors, p. 583. International Universities Press, New York, 1966.

12.3 Psychiatric Report

HAROLD I. KAPLAN, M.D.

BENJAMIN J. SADOCK, M.D.

I. Psychiatric history

A. *Preliminary identification:* name; age; marital status; sex; occupation; language if other than English; race, nationality, and religion insofar as they are pertinent; previous admissions to a hospital for the same or a different condition; with whom the patient lives

B. *Chief complaint:* exactly why the patient came to the psychiatrist, preferably in the patient's own words; if that information does not come from the patient, note who supplied it

C. *Personal identification:* brief, nontechnical description of the patient's appearance and behavior as a novelist might write it

D. *History of present illness:* chronological background and development of the symptoms or behavioral changes that culminated in the patient's seeking assistance; patient's life circumstances at the time of onset; personality when well; how illlness has affected life activities and personal relations—changes in personality, interests, mood, attitudes toward others, dress, habits, level of tenseness, irritability, activity, attention, concentration, memory, speech; psychophysiological symptoms—nature and details of dysfunction, location, intensity, fluctuation; whether anxieties are generalized and nonspecific (free floating) or specifically related to particular situations, activities, or objects; how anxieties are handled—avoidance, repetition of feared situation, use of drugs or other activities for distraction

E. *Previous illnesses:* emotional or mental disturbances—extent of incapacity, type of treatment, names of hospitals, length of illness, effect of treatment

F. *Past personal history:* history (anamnesis) of the patient's life from infancy to the present to the extent it can be recalled, including age of onset, duration, and impact of significant medical illnesses on patient; gaps in history as spontaneously related by the patient; emotions associated with those life periods—painful, stressful, conflictual

  1. Prenatal history: nature of mother's pregnancy and delivery: length of pregnancy, spontaneity and normality of delivery, birth trauma, whether patient was planned and wanted, birth defects

  2. Early childhood (through age 3)

    a. Feeding habits: breast-fed or bottle-fed, eating problems

    b. Maternal deprivation, early development, language development, motor development, signs of unmet needs, sleep pattern, object constancy, stranger anxiety, separation anxiety

    c. Toilet training: age, attitude of parents, feelings about it

    d. Symptoms of behavior problems: thumb sucking, temper tantrums, tics, head bumping, rocking, night-terrors, fears, bed wetting or bed soiling, nail biting, masturbation

    e. Personality as a child: shy, restless, overactive, withdrawn, studious, outgoing, timid, athletic, friendly, patterns of play, reactions to siblings

    f. Early or recurrent dreams or fantasies

  3. Middle childhood (ages 3 to 11): early school history—feelings about going to school, early adjustment, gender identification, conscience development, punishment

  4. Later childhood (from prepuberty through adolescence)

    a. Social relationships: attitudes toward siblings and playmates, number and closeness of friends, leader or follower, social popularity, participation in group or gang activities, idealized figures; patterns of aggression, passivity, anxiety, antisocial behavior

    b. School history: how far the patient went, adjustment to school, relationships with teachers—teacher's pet or rebellious—favorite studies or interests, particular abilities or assets, extracurricular activities, sports, hobbies, relationships of problems or symptoms to any school period

    c. Cognitive and motor development: learning to read and other intellectual and motor skills, minimal cerebral dysfunction, learning disabilities—their management and effects on the child

    d. Particular adolescent emotional or physical problems: nightmares, phobias, masturbation, bed wetting, running away, delinquency, smoking, drug or alcohol use, weight problems, feeling of inferiority

    e. Psychosexual history

      i. Early curiosity, infantile masturbation, sex play

      ii. Acquiring of sexual knowledge, attitude of parents toward sex

      iii. Onset of puberty, feelings about it, kind of preparation, feelings about menstruation, development of secondary sexual characteristics

      iv. Adolescent sexual activity: crushes, parties, dating, petting, masturbation, wet dreams and attitudes toward them

      v. Attitudes toward opposite sex: timid, shy, aggressive, need to impress, seductive, sexual conquests, anxiety

      vi. Sexual practices: sexual problems, homosexual experiences, paraphilias, promiscuity

    f. Religious background: strict, liberal, mixed (possible conflicts), relationship of background to current religious practices

  5. Adulthood

    a. Occupational history: choice of occupation, training, ambitions, conflicts; relations with authority, peers, and subordinates; number of jobs and duration; changes in job status; current job and feelings about it

    b. Social activity: does patient have friends; is he or she withdrawn or socializing well; kind of social, intellectual, and physical interests; relationships with same sex and opposite sex; depth, duration, and quality of human relations

    c. Adult sexuality

      i. Premarital sexual relationships

      ii. Marital history: common-law marriages, legal marriages, description of courtship and role played by each partner, age at marriage, family planning and contraception, names and ages of children, attitudes toward the raising of children, problems of any family members, housing difficulties if important to the marriage, sexual adjustment, areas of agreement and disagreement, management of money, role of in-laws

      iii. Sexual symptoms: anorgasmia, impotence

      iv. Attitudes toward pregnancy and having children; contraceptive practices and feelings about them

      v. Sexual practices: paraphilias

    d. Military history: general adjustment, combat, injuries, referral to psychiatrists, veteran status

G. *Family history:* elicited from patient and from someone else, since quite different descriptions may be given of the same people and events; ethnic, national, and religious traditions; other people in the home, descriptions of them—personality and intelligence—and what has become of them since patient's childhood; descriptions of different households lived in; present relationships between patient and those who were in family; role of illness in the family; history of mental illness

H. *Current social situation:* where does patient live—neighborhood and particular residence of the patient; is home crowded; privacy of family members from each other and from other families; sources of family income and difficulties in obtaining it; public assistance, if any, and attitude about it; will patient lose job or apartment by remaining in the hospital; who is caring for children

I. *Dreams, fantasies, and value systems*

  1. Dreams: prominent ones, if patient will tell them; nightmares

  2. Fantasies: recurrent, favorite, or unshakable daydreams; hypnogogic phenomena

3. Value systems: whether children are seen as a burden or a joy; whether work is seen as a necessary evil, an avoidable chore, or an opportunity

II. **Mental status:** sum total of the examiner's observations and impressions derived from the initial interviews

   A. General description

      1. Appearance: posture, bearing, clothes, grooming, hair, nails; healthy, sickly, angry, frightened, apathetic, perplexed, contemptuous, ill at ease, poised, old looking, young looking, effeminate, masculine; signs of anxiety—moist hands, perspiring forehead, restlessness, tense posture, strained voice, wide eyes; shifts in level of anxiety during interview or abrupt changes of topic

      2. Behavior and psychomotor activity: gait, mannerisms, tics, gestures, twitches, stereotypes, picking, touching examiner, echopraxia, clumsy, agile, limp, rigid, retarded, hyperactive, agitated, combative, waxy

      3. Speech: rapid, slow, pressured, hesitant, emotional, monotonous, loud, whispered, slurred, mumbled, stuttering, echolalia; intensity, pitch, ease, spontaneity, productivity, manner, reaction time, vocabulary

      4. Attitude toward examiner: cooperative, attentive, interested, frank, seductive, defensive, hostile, playful, ingratiating, evasive, guarded

   B. Mood, feelings, and affect

      1. Mood (a pervasive and sustained emotion that colors the person's perception of the world): how does patient say he feels; depth, intensity, duration, and fluctuations of mood—depressed, despairing, irritable, anxious, terrified, angry, expansive, euphoric, empty, guilty, awed, futile, self-contemptuous

      2. Affective expression: how examiner evaluates patient's affects—broad, restricted, depressed, blunted or flat, shallow, anhedonic, labile, proud, angry, fearful, anxious, guilty; amount and range of expression; difficulty in initiating, sustaining, or terminating an emotional response

      3. Appropriateness: is the emotional expression appropriate to the thought content, the culture, and the setting of the examination; examples if emotional expression is not appropriate

   C. Perceptual disturbances

      1. Hallucinations and illusions: does patient hear voices or see visions; content, sensory system involved, circumstances of the occurrence; hypnogogic or hypnopompic hallucinations

      2. Depersonalization and derealization: extreme feelings of detachment from one's self or the environment

   D. Thought process

      1. Stream of thought: quotations from patient

         a. Productivity: overabundance of ideas, paucity of ideas, flight of ideas, rapid thinking, slow thinking, hesitant thinking; does patient speak spontaneously or only when questions are asked

         b. Continuity of thought: do patient's replies really answer questions; are they goal directed and relevant or irrelevant; are there loose associations; is there a lack of cause-and-effect relationships in patient's explanations; are statements illogical, tangential, circumstantial, rambling, evasive, perseverative; is there blocking or distractibility

         c. Language impairments: impairments that reflect disordered mentation, such as incoherent or incomprehensible speech (word salad), clang associations, neologisms

      2. Content of thought

         a. Preoccupations: about the illness, environmental problems; obsessions, compulsions, phobias; obsessions about suicide, homicide, hypochondriacal symptoms, specific antisocial urges

         b. Thought disturbances

            1. Delusions: content of any delusional system, its organization, the patient's convictions as to its validity, how it affects his life; somatic delusions—isolated or associated with pervasive suspiciousness

            2. Ideas of reference and ideas of influence: how ideas began, their content, and the meaning the patient attributes to them

      3. Abstract thinking: disturbances in concept formation; manner in which the patient conceptualizes or handles his ideas; similarities, differences, absurdities; meanings of simple proverbs, such as, "A rolling stone gathers no moss"; answers may be concrete (giving specific examples to illustrate the meaning) or overly abstract (giving generalized explanation); appropriateness of answers

      4. Information and intelligence: patient's level of formal education and self-education; estimate of the patient's intellectual capability and whether he is capable of functioning at the level of his basic endowment; counting, calculation, general knowledge; questions that have some relevance to the patient's educational and cultural background

      5. Concentration: subtract 7 from 100 and keep subtracting 7's; if patient cannot subtract 7's, can he do easier tasks—4 times 9, 5 times 4; whether anxiety or some disturbance of mood or consciousness seems to be responsible for difficulty

   E. Orientation

      1. Time: does patient identify the date correctly; can he approximate date, time of day; if he is in a hospital, does he know how along he has been there; does patient behave as if he is oriented to the present

      2. Place: does patient know where he is

      3. Person: does patient know who the examiner is; does he know the roles or names of the persons with whom he is in contact

   F. Memory: impairment, efforts made to cope with impairment—denial, confabulation, catastrophic reaction, circumstantiality used to conceal deficit; whether the process of registration, retention, or recollection of material is involved

      1. Remote memory: childhood data, important events known to have occurred when the patient was younger or free of illness, personal matters, neutral material

      2. Recent past memory: the past few months

      3. Recent memory: the past few days; what did patient do yesterday, the day before; what did he have for breakfast, lunch, dinner

   4. Immediate retention and recall: ability to repeat six figures after examiner dictates them—first forward, then backward, then after a few minutes' interruption; other test questions; did same questions, if repeated, call forth different answers at different times; digit-span measures; other mental functions, such as anxiety level and concentration

   5. Effect of defect on patient: mechanisms patient has developed to cope with his defect

  G. *Impulse control:* is patient able to control hostile, aggressive, sexual, and amorous impulses

  H. *Judgment*

   1. Social judgment: subtle manifestations of behavior that is harmful to the patient and contrary to acceptable behavior in the culture; does he understand the likely outcome of his behavior and is he influenced by this understanding; examples of impairment

   2. Test judgment: patient's prediction of what he would do in imaginary situations—what he would do if he found a stamped, addressed letter in the street

  I. *Insight:* degree of awareness and understanding the patient has that he is ill

   1. Complete denial of illness

   2. Slight awareness of being sick and needing help but denying it at the same time

   3. Awareness of being sick but blaming it on others, on external factors, on organic factors

   4. Awareness that illness is due to something unknown in himself

   5. Intellectual insight: admission that he is ill and that his symptoms or failures in social adjustment are due to his own particular irrational feelings of disturbances, without applying that knowledge to future experience

   6. True emotional insight: emotional awareness of the motives and feelings within himself of the underlying meaning of symptoms; does the awareness lead to changes in personality and future behavior; openness to new ideas about himself and the important people in his life

  J. *Reliability:* estimate of examiner's impression of patient's veracity or ability to report his situation accurately

III. Further diagnostic studies

  A. *Physical examination*

  B. *Additional psychiatric diagnostic interviews*

  C. *Interviews with family members, friends, or neighbors by social worker*

  D. *Psychological tests by psychologist: type and purpose*

  E. *Specialized tests as indicated:* electroencephalogram, computerized tomography scan, laboratory tests, tests of other medical conditions, reading comprehension and handwriting tests, tests for aphasia

IV. Summary of positive findings: mental symptoms, laboratory findings, psychological test results, if available; drugs patient has been taking, including dosage and duration of intake

V. Diagnosis: diagnostic classification according to the American Psychiatric Association's *Diagnostic and Statistical Manual of Mental Disorders*—nomenclature, classification number, severity, chronicity; supplemental diagnosis; diagnoses to be ruled out

VI. Prognosis: opinion as to the probable future course, extent, and outcome of the illness; specific goals of therapy

VII. Psychodynamic formulation: causes of the patient's psychodynamic breakdown—influences in the patient's life that contributed to his present illness; environmental, genetic, and personality factors relevant in determining patient's symptoms; primary and secondary gains

VIII. Treatment plan: modalities of treatment recommended, role of medication, inpatient or outpatient treatment, frequency of sessions, probable duration of therapy; individual, group, or family therapy; type of psychotherapy; symptoms or problems to be treated

The authors wish to thank Roger A. MacKinnon, M.D., for his help in integrating this section with Sections 12.1 and 12.2.

12.4 Typical Signs and Symptoms of Psychiatric Illness

HAROLD I. KAPLAN, M.D.
BENJAMIN J. SADOCK, M.D.

I. Consciousness: state of awareness

Apperception: perception modified by one's own emotions and thoughts

Sensorium: state of functioning of the special senses

  A. *Disturbances of consciousness*

   1. Confusion: disturbance of orientation as to time, place, or person

2. Clouding of consciousness: incomplete clear-mindedness with disturbance in perception and attitudes
3. Stupor: lack of reaction to and unawareness of surroundings
4. Delirium: bewildered, restless, confused, disoriented reaction associated with fear and hallucinations
5. Coma: profound degree of unconsciousness
6. Coma vigil: coma in which eyes remain open
7. Dreamy state (twilight): disturbed consciousness with hallucinations

B. *Disturbances of attention:* the amount of effort exerted in focusing on certain portions of an experience
  1. Distractibility: inability to concentrate attention
  2. Selective inattention: blocking out of things that generate anxiety

C. *Disturbances in suggestibility:* compliant and uncritical response to an idea or influence
  1. *Folie á deux* (or *folie á trois*): communicated emotional illness between two (or three) persons
  2. Hypnosis: artificially induced modification of consciousness

II. **Affect:** emotional feeling tone

A. *Disturbances in affect*
  1. Inappropriate affect: disharmony of affect and ideation
  2. Pleasurable affects
    a. Euphoria: heightened feeling of psychological well-being inappropriate to apparent events
    b. Elation: air of confidence and enjoyment associated with increased motor activity
    c. Exaltation: intense elation with feelings of grandeur
    d. Ecstasy: feeling of intense rapture
  3. Unpleasurable affects
    a. Depression: psychopathological feeling of sadness
    b. Grief or mourning: sadness appropriate to a real loss
  4. Other affects
    a. Anxiety: feeling of apprehension due to unconscious conflicts
    b. Fear: anxiety due to consciously recognized and realistic danger
    c. Agitation: anxiety associated with severe motor restlessness
    d. Tension with increased motor and psychological activity that is unpleasant
    e. Panic: acute intense attack of anxiety associated with personality disorganization
    f. Free-floating anxiety: pervasive fear not attached to any idea
    g. Apathy: dulled emotional tone associated with detachment or indifference
    h. Ambivalence: coexistence of two opposing impulses toward the same thing in the same person at the same time
    i. Depersonalization: feeling of unreality concerning oneself or one's environment
    j. Derealization: distortion of spatial relationships so that the environment becomes unfamiliar
    k. Aggression: forceful goal-directed action that may be verbal or physical and that is the motor counterpart of the affect of rage, anger, or hostility
    l. Mood swings: oscillations between periods of euphoria and depression or anxiety

III. **Motor behavior (conation):** the capacity to initiate action or motor discharge that concerns the basic strivings of a person as expressed through his behavior

A. *Disturbances of conation*
  1. Echolalia: psychopathological repeating of words of one person by another
  2. Echopraxia: pathological imitation of movements of one person by another
  3. *Cerea flexibilitas* (waxy flexibility): state in which patient maintains body position into which he is placed
  4. Catalepsy: state of unconsciousness in which immobile position is constantly maintained
  5. Command automatism: automatic following of suggestions
  6. Automatism: automatic performance of acts representative of unconscious symbolic activity
  7. Cataplexy: temporary loss of muscle tone and weakness precipitated by a variety of emotional states
  8. Stereotypy: continuous repetition of speech or physical activities
  9. Negativism: frequent opposition to suggestions
  10. Mannerisms: stereotyped involuntary movements
  11. Verbigeration: meaningless repetitions of speech
  12. Overactivity
    a. Hyperactivity (hyperkinesis): restless, aggressive, destructive activity
    b. Tic: spasmodic repetitive motor movements
    c. Sleepwalking (somnambulism): motor activity during sleep
    d. Compulsion: uncontrollable impulse to perform an act repetitively
      (1) Dipsomania: compulsion to drink alcohol
      (2) Egomania: pathological self-preoccupation
      (3) Erotomania: pathological preoccupation with sex
      (4) Kleptomania: compulsion to steal
      (5) Megalomania: pathological sense of power
      (6) Monomania: preoccupation with a single subject
      (7) Nymphomania: excessive need for coitus in female
      (8) Satyriasis: excessive need for coitus in male
      (9) Trichotilomania: compulsion to pull out one's hair

(10) Ritual: automatic activity compulsive in nature, emotional in origin
13. Hypoactivity: decreased activity or retardation, as in psychomotor retardation; slowing of psychological and physical functioning
14. Mimicry: simple, imitative motion activity of childhood

IV. **Thinking:** goal-directed flow of ideas, symbols, and associations, initiated by a problem or task and leading toward a reality-oriented conclusion; when a logical sequence occurs, thinking is normal
   A. *Disturbances in form of thinking*
      1. Dereism: mental activity not concordant with logic or experience
      2. Autistic thinking: thinking that gratifies unfulfilled desires but has no regard for reality; term used somewhat synonymously with dereism
   B. *Disturbances in structure of associations*
      1. Neologism: new words created by the patient for psychological reasons
      2. Word salad: incoherent mixture of words and phrases
      3. Circumstantiality: digression of inappropriate thoughts into ideational processes, but patient eventually gets from desired point to desired goal
      4. Tangentiality: inability to have goal-directed associations of thought; patient never gets from desired point to desired goal
      5. Incoherence: running together of thoughts with no logical connection, resulting in disorganization
      6. Perseveration: psychopathological repetition of the same word or idea in response to different questions
      7. Condensation: fusion of various concepts into one
      8. Irrelevant answer: answer that is not in harmony with question asked
   C. *Disturbances in speed of associations*
      1. Flight of ideas: rapid verbalizations so that there is a shifting from one idea to another
      2. Clang associations: words similar in sound but not in meaning call up new thoughts
      3. Blocking: interruption in train of thinking, unconscious in origin
      4. Pressure of speech: voluble speech difficult to interrupt
      5. Volubility (logorrhea): copious, coherent, logical speech
   D. *Disturbances in type of associations*
      1. Motor aphasia: disturbance of speech due to organic brain disorder in which understanding remains but ability to speak is lost
      2. Sensory aphasia: loss of ability to comprehend the meaning of words or the use of objects
      3. Nominal aphasia: difficulty in finding right name for an object
      4. Syntactical aphasia: inability to arrange words in proper sequence
   E. *Disturbances in content of thought*
      1. Delusion: false belief, not consistent with patient's intelligence and cultural background, that cannot be corrected by reasoning
         a. Delusion of grandeur: exaggerated conception of one's importance
         b. Delusion of persecution: false belief that one is being persecuted; often found in litigious patients
         c. Delusion of reference: false belief that the behavior of others refers to oneself; derived from ideas of reference in which patient falsely feels he is being talked about by others
         d. Delusion of self-accusation: false feeling of remorse
         e. Delusion of control: false feeling that one is being controlled by others
         f. Delusion of infidelity: false belief derived from pathological jealousy that one's lover is unfaithful
         g. Paranoid delusions: oversuspiciousness leading to persecutory delusions
      2. Trend or preoccupation of thought: centering of thought content around a particular idea, associated with a strong affective tone
      3. Hypochondria: exaggerated concern over one's health that is not based on real organic pathology
      4. Obsession: pathological persistence of an irresistible thought, feeling, or impulse that cannot be eliminated from consciousness by logical effort
      5. Phobia: exaggerated and invariably pathological dread of some specific type of stimulus or situation
         a. Acrophobia: dread of high places
         b. Agoraphobia: dread of open places
         c. Algophobia: dread of pain
         d. Claustrophobia: dread of closed places
         e. Xenophobia: dread of strangers
         f. Zoophobia: dread of animals

V. **Perception:** awareness of objects and relations that follows stimulation of peripheral sense organs
   A. *Disturbances associated with organic brain disease* such as agnosia—that is, an inability to recognize and interpret the significance of sensory impressions
   B. *Disturbances associated with hysteria:* illnesses characterized by emotional conflict, the use of the defense mechanism of conversion, and the development of physical symptoms involving the voluntary muscles or special sense organs
      1. Hysterical anesthesia: loss of sensory modalities resulting from emotional conflicts
      2. Macropsia: state in which objects seem larger than they are
      3. Micropsia: state in which objects seem smaller than they are
   C. *Hallucinations:* false sensory perceptions not associated with real external stimuli

    1. Hypnagogic hallucination: false sensory perception occurring midway between falling asleep and being awake
    2. Auditory hallucination: false auditory perception
    3. Visual hallucination: false visual perception
    4. Olfactory hallucination: false perception of smell
    5. Gustatory hallucination: false perception of taste, such as unpleasant taste due to an uncinate fit
    6. Tactile (haptic) hallucination: false perception of touch, such as the feeling of worms under the skin
    7. Kinesthetic hallucination: false perception of movement or sensation, as from an amputated limb (phantom limb)
    8. Lilliputian hallucination: perception of objects as reduced in size
  D. *Illusions:* false sensory perceptions of real external sensory stimuli
VI. **Memory:** function by which information stored in the brain is later recalled to consciousness
  A. *Disturbances of memory*
    1. Amnesia: partial or total inability to recall past experiences
    2. Paramnesia: falsification of memory by distortion of recall
      a. *Fausse reconnaissance:* false recognition
      b. Retrospective falsification: recollection of a true memory to which the patient adds false details
      c. Confabulation: unconscious filling of gaps in memory by imagined or untrue experiences that patient believes but that have no basis in fact
      d. *Déjà vu:* illusion of visual recognition in which a new situation is incorrectly regarded as a repetition of a previous memory
      e. *Déjà entendu:* illusion of auditory recognition
      f. *Jamais vu:* false feeling of unfamiliarity with a real situation one has experienced
    3. Hypermnesia: exaggerated degree of retention and recall
VII. **Intelligence:** the ability to understand, recall, mobilize, and integrate constructively previous learning in meeting new situations
  A. *Mental retardation:* lack of intelligence to a degree in which there is interference with social and vocational performance: mild (I.Q. of 52 to 67), moderate (I.Q. of 36 to 51), severe (I.Q. of 20 to 35), or profound (I.Q. below 20); obsolescent terms are idiot (mental age less than 3 years), imbecile (mental age of 3 to 7 years), and moron (mental age of 8 or more)
  B. *Dementia:* organic loss of mental function

12.5 Psychological Assessment of Intelligence

JOSEPH D. MATARAZZO, Ph.D.

Introduction

Although frequently and erroneously used interchangeably, psychological testing and psychological assessment are vastly different, even though assessment includes testing. Personnel technicians, grammar school teachers, and graduate counselors monitoring a group administration of the College Board's Scholastic Achievement Tests are each involved in the relatively limited professional activity called psychological testing, an activity with little or no continuing relationship or responsibility between examinee and examiner. Psychological assessment, on the other hand, is engaged in by a clinician in a one-to-one relationship with clearly defined or implied professional responsibilities. The distinction between psychological testing and psychological assessment is similar to the distinction between the physical examination carried out by a technician and the assessment of the same patient's medical status by an internist or other highly trained and experienced clinician. Although each examiner may obtain the same basic preliminary information—physical and vital signs and results of blood, urine, and other laboratory tests—the technician merely records it, whereas the clinician both records and interprets it—

that is, gives the findings some meaning within a context of relevant aspects from the examinee's total life situation. Similarly, a senior neurologist in a medical center or general hospital rarely sees a patient for a neurological examination. Rather, in common with colleagues from other specialties, he or she is called in consultation as part of the further understanding of a patient from whom much other information has already been collected. Likewise, a psychologist who is a psychodiagnostic-clinician-consultant in a medical center or hospital is not asked by a colleague to do a psychometric or psychological testing on a patient in the abstract. In common with the internist, orthopaedist, neurologist, and other specialists, the clinical psychologist is requested to carry out a psychological examination, one that is geared specifically to the needs of this particular patient as these needs are determined from a careful reading of the patient's hospital chart or, in the case of an outpatient, from a telephone call or letter of referral.

ASSESS POTENTIAL NOT DEFICIT

Clinical psychologists who specialize in the assessment of individual intelligence did not suffer attacks during the 1960's and 1970's from parents, civil rights leaders, the courts, and Congress, as did educational and personnel specialists involved in the mass testing of intelligence in the schools and in the use of intelligence and personality tests in industry, largely because of this distinction between testing and assessment. As an activity carried on outside a clinical setting, the testing of intelligence, with few exceptions, was and all too often continues to be carried out to benefit someone else—colleges, employers—who, because of an oversupply of applicants, often are searching for deficits and frailty among the mass of individual

·examinees that will help weed out those believed to be unqualified. On the other hand, for the practicing clinical psychologist whose focus of interest is the individual examinee, the challenge in the assessment of intelligence is to assess human potential, not deficit, in each person. In the practice of clinical psychology, each patient or client, with the exception of some court-mandated referrals, is seen as a professional challenge within a framework of diagnosis, with rehabilitation or an improvement in the human condition as the end.

Psychological assessment techniques, in common with most tools, can be used for a diversity of purposes, some destructive and some constructive, and their use cannot be separated from the training, competence, and ethical values of the psychologist. In the hands of a good clinician, the results of an I.Q. examination, when correlated with other information from the person's history or present status, are as useful as comparable laboratory data in the hands of a good surgeon, internist, accountant, or plumber. Such I.Q.-related data in the hands of a fool—whether a psychologist, physician, physicist, grammar school teacher, college admissions officer, surgeon, or plumber—are tools of potential harm. It is important in this day of continuing attacks on intelligence testing to remember that trite as the statement may appear, a scalpel is neither a good tool nor a bad tool. In the hands of a skilled surgeon, it is an exquisite extension of his fingers. In the hands of a fool, it is a lethal weapon for evil. So with a modern test of individual intelligence; by itself, it is a rather bland, innocuous instrument, neither good nor bad, merely a tool to be used by persons of competence or incompetence. This last point cannot be overemphasized. In the hands of a competent clinical psychologist, a test of measured intelligence frequently yields information that, when correlated with other assessment information and a clinical history, proves highly useful both to the patient or client and to those whose professional help such a person has sought. When used in isolation by a technician with little other knowledge of the examinee or by a professional with little experience in its use and interpretation, more harm than good is frequently the outcome.

History

Before the revolutionary contribution of Binet and Simon in 1905, the word "intelligence" had not yet appeared in psychology textbooks because a means for its assessment was not yet available. For example, in William James' 1890 two-volume classic, *The Principles of Psychology,* the word "intelligence" appears only twice and then only in its philosophical sense, with no hint in this first major textbook produced by the young science of psychology that there were quantifiable individual differences among humans along a dimension that would soon be recognized as differing levels of intelligence. Possibly just as surprising, as much as a decade later the word "intelligence" did not appear in Baldwin's 1901 *Dictionary of Philosophy and Psychology.*

BINET

In 1896, in his new position as director of the laboratory of physiological psychology at the Sorbonne and after dabbling for a decade with the problem of objectively measuring differences in intelligence, Alfred Binet published a paper with V. Henri in which they described a multifaceted approach in a projected 10-year program of research. They intended to use systematically a variety of then available tests—memory, attention, imagination, motor skill, and others—in a quest for an objective measure by which to quantify individual differences in mental abilities (intelligence). However, in a paper read in Rome in 1904, Binet and Henri admitted that after 8 years, and in common with the failure of others of the world's then few psychologists, their own research designed to produce such an intelligence test had failed.

However, Binet was involved concurrently in other interests, and it was from one of these, his association with a group called the Society for the Psychological Study of Children, that the keys to his breakthrough emerged (Wolf, 1969, 1973; Matarazzo, 1972). This society was organized in 1899 from a loose association of teachers, school administrators, lawyers, and many other interested persons and had as its purpose the study of children. From its inception Binet dominated the monthly meetings, and his counsel was sought regularly by the various committees or commissions, as they were called, of the society, including commissions on graphology, on memory, on arithmetic, and on mental retardation.

It was the isolated discoveries of these commissions, plus his own ongoing research with his student, Simon, that Binet, after almost a decade of frustrating failure, would weld together into the 1905 Binet-Simon Scale. Specifically, one of the teachers (Parison) working on the society's commission on memory was commended by Binet for the former's report in 1904 of the discovery that a child's score on several objective tests of memory that the teacher had administered was correlated with intelligence (aptitude or brightness) as subjectively rated by all the child's previous teachers. Binet's observation was that this finding suggested that one could ignore these less reliable teachers' subjective judgments and use this objective measure of memory to compare children quantitatively, one relative to another of the same age, who were in the different grades taught by these various teachers. Binet asked other members on that same commission to repeat the study and soon found reproducible evidence that youngsters of the same age—say, 12—but in two different grades—say, the fifth versus the seventh—performed vastly differently on these tests of memory. Thus, for example, the mean memory score on the objective memory tests of 12-year-olds who were in the seventh grade was twice the mean memory score of 12-year-olds who had fallen behind their age-mates and were still in the fifth grade.

Soon thereafter, as an isolated but fortuitous event, a member of another of the society's commissions, a school principal named Vaney, reported in January 1905 that he had developed an *age-related achievement test for arithmetic* by which it was possible for the first time to describe and quantify objectively a child's academic retardation in arithmetic—for example, to say that, relative to his or her age peers, a child was retarded in arithmetic by one, two, or three school grades. More important for Binet was the fact that, as part of its development, this achievement test included norms for each grade and, thus, each age level up through the seventh grade. In the development and standardization of this arithmetic achievement test, Vaney discovered, for example, that the typical 7-year-old first-grader could read and write from dictation the numbers 1 to 20 and add and subtract them orally. At age 8, in the second grade, he could do the same up to 100 and multiply any number from 1 to 10 by 2, 3, 4, and 5 and divide numbers from 1 to 10 by the same. Although standardized arithmetic and other tests of this type were developed by Horace Mann in the United States as early as 1845, his tests contained a hodgepodge, mixed assortment of arithmetic problems, and by the end of the 1800's no one had yet tied them into age-related benchmarks that could serve as an objective measure of individual differences in mental abilities among children of different ages, as well as of the same age.

From these two isolated events Binet discerned that the pegging of performance on Parison's memory tests and on Vaney's arithmetic tests to the chronological age of each child, in contrast to his or her grammar school grade, was the ingredient that the recent contemporary French developers of a crude intelligence test, the Blin-Damaye, had overlooked. These latter two investigators had recently put together a 20-item, grab-bag scale for quantifying the degree of mental retardation in patients in a home for the feebleminded. The Blin-Damaye Scale included items such as, "What is your name?" "What color is this pencil?" and "Is Brittany in France?"—items typical of those that would later appear in every intelligence test; unfortunately, the scale yielded only a total score—an important datum but, as yet, an insufficient benchmark to take into account the rapid growth that takes place in the intellectual skills of children through the adolescent years.

The Binet-Simon Scale—which Binet and his student, Theodore

Simon, published a mere 6 months after Vaney provided Binet with the critical ingredient—was designed, in common with the Blin-Damaye Scale, to provide a quantitative index of the degree of retardation. However, unlike the earlier Blin-Damaye Scale, the 1905 Binet-Simon Scale placed the items in an ascending order of difficulty, from the very easiest to the very hardest item (Binet and Simon, 1905). Data for this arrangement were obtained by Binet and Simon on standardization groups both in an institution for the retarded, where Simon worked as a physician, with an unspecified number of patients, and on 100 youngsters, aged 3 to 12 years, in the public schools of Paris, where Binet had access as a member of a group, newly appointed by the City of Paris' Minister of Public Instruction, for the study of retarded children. This crude 1905 Binet-Simon Scale consisted of only 30 items. The first and easiest of these items required the child to follow a moving object. Items later in the scale ranged from requiring the repetition of three digits to telling how two common objects are alike (similar items) to the thirtieth and most difficult item, defining abstract terms, such as the difference between such complex concepts as esteem and friendship.

This 1905 Scale of Intelligence, as they called it, contained an excellent description of how to score each response objectively. However, although this first scale contained items loosely graduated by age, it contained no precise quantitative method for arriving at a total score or other index of each child's relative ability once the items had been administered and scored. Not until the publication of their second and restandardized 58-item 1908 scale did Binet and Simon (1908) formally introduce the concept of *mental age*. They did so by listing the several items that could be *passed by a majority of children at each age level* from age 3 to age 13. With this 1908 introduction of precisely standardized and designated mental age levels for items differing progressively in level of difficulty, mankind had its first tool for ordering the mental ability of children and retarded adults relative to each other. With the introduction of the 1911 scale, Binet (1911) extended the potential use of the 1908 scale to normal adults and suggested its use someday in industrial psychology, but the norms for adults that were included in the 1911 revision were meager indeed. The 1911 Binet-Simon Scale, like its two predecessors, was still primarily a scale for quantifying the mental abilities of school children.

From the outset, Binet the clinician cautioned in print that the quantitative score (mental age) obtained from his scale was not to be used in isolation as the sole index of one's intelligence; that is, that measured intelligence is not synonymous with over-all intelligence. The father of intelligence assessment made this last point very clearly when in 1905 and 1908 he asserted, almost in the language used today by the American Association on Mental Deficiency and similar groups, that a responsible assessment of the intelligence of an individual child must of necessity involve the integration by a compassionate clinician of information obtained about the child from three totally independent sources. These three sources were (1) the results (mental age) from the objective psychological examination, (2) indices of performance in the classroom, and (3) relevant medical or related items of physiological function (Binet and Simon, 1908, 1916). The means for obtaining the second and third of these three were already available at the close of the 19th century. It was because Binet, with the help of Theodore Simon, in 1905 unlocked the riddle to the first by developing an objective method of measuring relative intelligence that his name has become so well known (Matarazzo, 1972; Wolf, 1973).

STERN

Although Binet died in 1911 at 54 years of age after publication of the revised 1911 Binet-Simon Scale, one can guess today that he would have resisted the developments that began with William Stern's 1912 conversion of Binet's mental age (M.A.) into an intelligence quotient (I.Q.). Stern recommended that a precise quantitative index of relative ability be computed by dividing the child's earned score on the Binet-Simon Scale—the child's earned mental age (M.A.) in years and months—by that child's actual or chronological age (C.A.) and, to remove the decimal, by multiplying that resulting value by 100. The

formula I.Q. equals M.A. divided by C.A., with the sum multiplied by 100, is merely a device for quantitatively relating each child's test age to his or her own actual age, thereby indicating whether the child scores better or worse than his own chronological development dictated. As an example, an 8-year-old child who could successfully answer the same number of items that are typically answered by an 8-year-old would earn an I.Q. of 100. If he could answer more items— say, those answered by the 10-year-old—he would earn an I.Q. of 125 (10 divided by 8 and multiplied by 100). Conversely, if this 8-year-old child were slower, answering only as many items as the typical 6-year-old, his I.Q. would be 6 divided by 8 and multiplied by 100 for a score of 75, a relative score considerably below the average of his peers.

GODDARD

Within a year of Binet's death, the 1911 scale—which Binet had extended to the 15-year-old child and, in an ungraded section, adults— was being translated into many languages. Almost immediately, an American, Goddard, introduced it for use in helping to identify and better serve mentally retarded persons in the Vineland, New Jersey Training School for Feebleminded Boys and Girls. However, Goddard's research on the inheritance of mental retardation in the Kallikak family and his other mentally retarded patients led him to reach a conclusion that would have startled Binet: Mental retardation—which Goddard, forgetting Binet's two other ingredients, defined solely in terms of I.Q.—was inherited and followed the Mendelian laws of heredity from one generation to another. As Cronbach (1975) has chronicled, Goddard soon became an influential spokesman both for a national eugenics policy (enacted into law by a majority of states) involving the sterilization of the retarded and for an administration of America's immigration policies, which in 1917 effectively began to deny admission into this country of 80 to 90 per cent of all Russian, Jewish, Hungarian, and Italian potential immigrants who were waiting at Ellis Island and who, by their at that time not surprisingly low scores on Goddard's English form of Binet's test, Goddard believed were feebleminded.

It was 1959 before the American Association on Mental Deficiency (AAMD) reversed this trend in the United States of relying on I.Q. scores alone. In 1959 the AAMD, following Binet, declared that a diagnosis of mental retardation could be made only when both a person's measured intelligence, as ascertained by an individually administered I.Q. test, and a person's adaptive intelligence, as ascertained by an evaluation of day-to-day performance in the classroom for a child or in the home or work situation for an adult, were defective relative to his or her age peers. Had this second assessment index been used with the earlier immigrants at Ellis Island, only a small number would have been found to be mentally retarded. But before this 1959 AAMD development came about, much more happened in the field of intelligence *testing* of groups and in intelligence *assessment* of individuals in clinics and special education classrooms.

TERMAN

One of the most significant of these developments was Lewis Terman's construction and restandardization at Stanford University of his American revision of the Binet-Simon Scale on a cross-section of American children. This 1916 scale, called by Terman the Stanford Revision of the Binet Intelligence Scale (Terman, 1916, 1937), was adopted in the United States almost overnight for use both for placing slow children in public schools and training schools and for assessing the intelligence of individual children then being treated in increasing numbers in child guidance clinics around the country. It was imperative in the treatment of behavioral dysfunctions in these new child guidance clinics that an attempt be made to sort out the relative contributions of personality-related psychopathology from psychopathology that was a function of low intelligence. It is an unfortunate historical note that, within a short time of his introduction of the revised 1916 scale, Terman added the weight of his university base and professional reputation to Goddard's thesis that the capacity underlying score on an I.Q. test was inherited. It was another 50 years before university-based psychologists of stature equal to that of Terman and Goddard presented impressive evidence that the score on an I.Q. test, although obviously showing a strong hereditary component, equally clearly was very malleable and could potentially be influenced by a rich or stultifying human and educational environment. Among these later psychologists who presented convincing evidence supporting the role of environment on I.Q. scores were Hunt (1961, 1975), Heber and Garber (1975), and Scarr and Weinberg (1976, 1977). Although Jensen (1969) is equally as forceful a proponent of the role of heredity as he lately has become of environment (Jensen, 1977) and, therefore, is the best modern proponent of Terman's views, the research of the other psychologists has shown that a massively enriched environment can profoundly increase a child's I.Q. score, whether the child is black or white and no matter how dull his own biological parents. Matarazzo (1978a) provided an overview of some of the most robust evidence relating to the influence of heredity and environment on I.Q. scores.

To return, however, to Terman, one should note that, within a year of the publication of his 1916 revised Stanford-Binet Scale, the United States entered World War I, and Terman carried a paper-and-pencil offshoot of his 1916 scale—which was developed by his student, Otis, for *mass testing*—to Washington, D.C. There, Terman, Yerkes, Boring, and others used the Otis Test as the prototype for their rapid development of the Army Alpha as well as the Army Beta Batteries for illiterate and non-English-speaking recruits. Almost 2 million American draftees were examined before the cessation of hostilities in 1918. Data from these American draftees were published (Yerkes, 1921) and, with hundreds of other tabular presentations, they suggested that blacks and new immigrants were inferior in either Alpha or Beta I.Q. scores to native and nonnative Americans of other ancestry. That level of education, language difficulties, or prior experience with tests could influence such an I.Q. score, ideas that quite likely would have occurred to Binet, were not considered by Yerkes, Terman, and the other university-based American psychologists.

Relative Intelligence

DISTRIBUTION OF I.Q. SCORES

Both the newly standardized revised Stanford-Binet (Terman, 1916) and the Army Alpha Battery, which was used in mass testing in World War I (Yerkes, 1921), examined larger numbers of persons than had heretofore been examined with one test anywhere in the world. Just as Galton (1869, 1883) had reported from his analysis of the distributions of the equally objective entrance examination achievement scores used by the University of Cambridge, when plotted as a frequency distribution, the I.Q. values of these large numbers of persons examined by Terman or by Yerkes and his colleagues yielded a strikingly clear bell-shaped curve similar to the modern one presented in Figure 1. This figure incorporates the categories later introduced in 1939 by Wechsler for the middle and upper ranges of measured intelligence and the various gradations of mental retardation adopted by the AAMD in its 1959 publication.

ASCERTAINING RELATIVE MEASURED INTELLIGENCE

Although the I.Q. values shown in Figure 1 are those for the Wechsler Adult Intelligence Scale, nothing in either the shape or the categories outlined there is a fixed characteristic of a particular I.Q. test or scale. The I.Q. values shown in Figure 1 are strictly arbitrary and can be derived in this or any other manner for any test or measure of ability. One need only take one of today's measures of ability (say, an 80-item vocabulary test with the items ordered from easiest to hardest level of difficulty) and administer it to a large sample of persons (say, 1,000 persons between 25 and 35 years of age). If the average score on this 80-item vocabulary test for this sample of persons is 43 items correct, one may at his or her discretion arbitrarily convert this same mean score of 43 into an I.Q. of 100 or into a scaled score of 500, as is done on the verbal section of the Scholastic Achievement Test of the College Entrance Examination Board and on the Medical College Admissions Test. Once this raw score of 43 is assigned an I.Q. value of 100 or a SAT or MCAT value of 500, the assigned conversion score for each raw vocabulary score below 43 and each score above 43 is easily obtainable from knowledge of that mean score of 43, the standard deviation for this total sample of examinees, and knowledge of the probability tables.

Terman arbitrarily defined the normal range of measured intelligence on his scale one way, Wechsler slightly differently. For example, Wechsler arbitrarily asserted that the range for the measured intelligence of normal persons falls between an I.Q. of 90 and an I.Q. of 110, thereby statistically encompassing 50 per cent of the total sample (25 per cent below and 25 per cent above the statistical mean of 100). Wechsler could just as easily have defined normal measured intelligence arbitrarily as those scores falling between an I.Q. of 88 and an I.Q. of 112 or between 95 and 105.

Use of the combined empirical sampling and statistical approach just described for converting a raw score into an I.Q. yields a distribution of persons at each I.Q. level for each test.

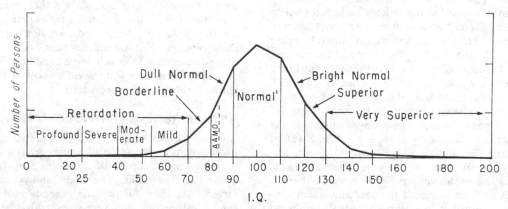

FIGURE 1. The distribution of Wechsler Adult Intelligence Scale I.Q. categories. These categories of measured intelligence serve as only one of several indices of intelligence. A second, equally critical index is an estimate of the same person's adaptive intelligence in school, in the home, at work, and in the community. (From Matarazzo, J. D. *Wechsler's Measurement and Appraisal of Adult Intelligence*, ed. 5, p. 124. Oxford University Press, New York, 1972. Reprinted by permission of Oxford University Press, New York, copyright holder.)

An example of such a distribution—presented in percentile values rather than visually as in Figure 1—is provided in Table I for the Wechsler-Bellevue I (W-B I) and Wechsler Adult Intelligence Scale (WAIS). There it can be seen that with the fixed point of an I.Q. of 100 as the 50th percentile (with 50 per cent of all persons arbitrarily assigned above and 50 per cent below this value), a person who earns an I.Q. of 135 on the WAIS or an I.Q. of 130 on the earlier W-B I scores on this I.Q. index of measured intelligence in the top 1 percent (99th percentile) of all persons that age. Likewise, a WAIS I.Q. of 119 falls at the 90th percentile, 110 at the 75th, 100 at the 50th (by definition), 96 at the 40th, 90 at the 25th, 81 at the 10th, and 65 at the lowest 1 percentile.

Thus, according to Figure 1—in which, by the AAMD criteria of measured intelligence, mental retardation begins at a WAIS I.Q. of 70, the lowest 2.2 per cent of the population on the WAIS—the four levels of retardation shown (mild, moderate, severe, and profound) fortunately encompass only about 2 of every 100 persons.

PERCENTILE RANK

When describing their findings for a particular patient or client to workers in other disciplines, clinical psychologists and other practicing clinicians often find it useful to translate the obtained I.Q. score into the more useful relative index shown in Table I. For example:

Mary Smith's measured intelligence of 113 on the WAIS is a score higher than that earned by 80 out of every 100 men and women her age and thus places her in the upper 20 per cent of the adult population when judged solely on this index of measured intelligence of I.Q.

Or:

John Smith's measured intelligence on the WAIS earned him an I.Q. of 80, a score that exceeds only 9 of every 100 adults in his own age group on this scale.

Data from other indices of adaptive intelligence—from work, the home, and so on—are, typically, then described by the psychologist-practitioner.

I.Q. SCORE IS NOT IMMUTABLE

It was responsible uses of this last type that Binet envisioned for his 1905, 1908, and 1911 scales, both for persons scoring below average in measured ability, whom he hoped to help reach their potential, and for those who were above average relative to their peers. However, as reviewed at length elsewhere (Matarazzo, 1972; Cronbach, 1975), Goddard and Terman and other university-based psychologists soon became sidetracked as they used this new tool to marshall evidence that I.Q. followed the same Mendelian laws of heredity as did eye color and other human characteristics. Between 1910 and 1920 none of the handful of then-practicing clinical psychologists in the United States dared to disagree with these giants of Stanford University or of the Vineland Training School. As a result, I.Q. scores alone played a role in the eugenics movement and in the immigration practices of this country. However, soon thereafter, although not publicized outside the academy, much acrimony could be discerned in the learned journals published from 1920 to 1940 as a few practitioners and other university-based psychologists dared question the assertions of these giants of psychology by suggesting, albeit timidly, that I.Q. was

TABLE I

Equivalent Percentile Ranks for Wechsler-Bellevue I (W-B I) and Wechsler Adult Intelligence Scale (WAIS) Full-Scale I.Q. Scores

Percentile Rank	W-B I*	WAIS†
99	130	135
97	125	128
95	123	125
90	118	119
85	114	115
80	112	113
75	110	110
70	108	108
65	106	105
60	105	104
50	101	100
45	99	98
40	98	96
35	96	95
30	94	92
25	91	90
20	89	87
15	86	85
10	81	81
5	73	75
3	68	72
1	59	65

* Ages 10 to 60.
† Ages 16 to 64

not fixed and immutable and that, for some, admittedly relatively few retarded individuals, repeated examination sometimes yielded fluctuations in I.Q. of as much as 40 or more points in such a supposedly *permanently* retarded person. These critics were few, and soon their dissent disappeared. The thesis that I.Q., although relatively stable in adults, was not fixed at birth did not surface again in the textbooks or journals until Hunt (1961) challenged the whole establishment by marshaling considerable evidence that the I.Q. is amenable to environmental influences, especially in developing children. Although Hunt's book later became influential, initially it stirred little response outside of academic psychology. However, Arthur Jensen (1969) published what he and later impartial reviewers considered in 1969, on balance, a rather tepid restatement of the earlier Goddard and Terman thesis that the I.Q. is mostly inherited. The dam burst, and soon not only academic psychology but much of American society was drawn into a debate as to whether or not I.Q. is inherited and into the related debate regarding the meaning of the differences in the mean I.Q. of blacks versus whites on most tests.

Assessment of Individual Intelligence

It is a curious historical fact that the American university psychologists and their British counterparts who helped spawn the impersonal group intelligence testing movement—Terman, Spearman, Thorndike, Thurstone, and so on—concurrently served as teachers for the first generation of practitioners of clinical psychology who were spawned by the introduction of the 1905 Binet-Simon Scale and, later, such psychological assessment devices as the Rorschach Test, Thematic Apperception Test, and Strong Vocational Interest Blank. Long before

World War II provided the impetus for the revitalization of the training received by today's psychiatrists and clinical psychologists who practice the modern brands of psychology and psychiatry, Thorndike, Cattell, and Woodworth at Columbia were turning out such fledgling Ph.D. graduates as David Wechsler (in 1925) and his counterparts.

WECHSLER

Wechsler was initiated into the field of assessment even before he began the graudate studies leading to his doctorate. For example, before receiving his doctorate but after completing his undergraduate studies, Wechsler was inducted in 1917 into the Army, where, under the direction of E. G. Boring, he was assigned the job of administering the Army Alpha Battery to hundreds of new recruits at an Army camp on Long Island. Army service in France came next, after which Wechsler spent an extra year in England, where he met Charles Spearman and Karl Pearson, and in France, where he met Theodore Simon. Although his 1925 doctoral dissertation, completed under the direction of Woodworth, was not on intelligence but on the use of the galvanic response as a measure of emotion, Wechsler's earlier work with the Army Alpha and Beta Batteries persuaded him that paper-and-pencil tests for mass administration had little place in the new field of clinical psychology in which he began to work shortly before being awarded his doctorate. The route to full-time clinical work was a bit circuitous for him and involved a stint as a clinical psychologist in the newly created New York City Bureau of Child Guidance (1922–1924); a summer's internship at Boston Psychopathic Hospital, during which he also attended conferences in Boston led by Healy and Bronner; and a small private practice combined with odd jobs in New York City (1925–1932).

It was his new position of chief psychologist at the teeming Bellevue Hospital of New York University, which he assumed in 1932 and held until 1967, that helped usher in the second major development in the history of the assessment of intelligence, a development that ranked with the 1905 Binet-Simon Scale. Binet, with his concept of a mental age, had provided the clinician with a highly useful benchmark for determining measured intelligence. When Wechsler joined the staff at Bellevue, Terman's 1916 revision was still an assessment technique that was useful primarily with children, although it did provide a few norms for adults. Wechsler found it clumsy to use the Stanford-Binet's upper limit of age 15 as the chronological age for all examinees older than 15 years, including those in their fifties and sixties. Using the statistical training he had received at Columbia University and under Spearman and Pearson at the University of London, Wechsler decided in one bold sweep that one could completely do away with the use of the mental age by merely, at each age, comparing the performance of an examinee against the performance of his or her own age-mates on the same test items. That is, a 12-year-old examinee's raw score on an I.Q. test would be evaluated only against the distribution of such scores earlier produced by a large, representative sample of all 12-year-olds on exactly the same test, a 25-year-old examinee's score would be compared with that of only 25-year-olds on the same test, and a 60-year-old's performance would be compared with that of only the 60-year-olds given that test in the standardization sample. Wechsler had discerned that with few exceptions any sample of persons whom he or others could select and examine with an intelligence test would yield a frequency distribution of *raw scores* on that test similar in shape to the bell shape in Figure 1. Thorndike, his Columbia University mentor, and others, following Galton, had no doubt repeatedly shown this to be the case for any single age group of grammar or high school or college students. It was Wechsler's insight to assign an I.Q. of 100 to the *different mean raw scores* obtained on the same test by different age groups and, using the standard score statistic as described above, determine the I.Q. equivalent for that age sample of each remaining raw score above and below that age group's own mean raw score.

This statistical innovation, the substitution of a deviation I.Q. at each age level for Binet's universal non-age-specific mental age, was

only the first of Wechsler's three major contributions to this field. The second was his belief that the total or global personality, not just intellectual capacities in isolation, is expressed in an I.Q. score. That is, the total I.Q. score reflects, in addition to intellect, the equally important by-products of motivation, drive, emotional state, and, especially, the psychopathologies that he and his colleagues daily diagnosed in the patients brought to them in the emergency room of Bellevue Hospital. Therefore, a clinically useful device for assessing intelligence must of necessity provide standardized stimuli to reflect the effect of this pathology on intellectual processes, if at all possible. Binet, who worked primarily with children in the public schools and in homes for the mentally retarded, had also believed this, but Wechsler's position at Bellevue Hospital led him to emphasize the role in intelligence of these nonintellective factors, as Wechsler referred to them.

Wechsler's third contribution to the field arose from his earlier examinations of nonliterate draftees with the Army Beta Battery and his need for a nonverbal test with which to examine those segments of New York City's large immigrant population who daily came to Bellevue Hospital for observation and examination but who could not speak or understand English.

The result of Wechsler's three contributions was the 1939 Bellevue-Wechsler Scale for the individual examination of adult intelligence. Soon referred to as the Wechsler-Bellevue I (or W-B I), it contained 10 subtests—five verbal (plus one alternate subtest), and five performance subtests—and it yielded a Full-Scale I.Q., a separate Verbal I.Q., and a Performance I.Q. By his own trial-and-error use of many of the individual tests tried out during World War I by Yerkes (1921) and his colleagues, as well as other tests later published for individual use in training schools, state hospitals, and clinics, Wechsler settled on this battery of 10 subtests as a single omnibus instrument for assessing intelligence because it fulfilled the following important requirements: First, the 10 subtests represented enough of the probable domains of global intelligence that they were both good measures of I.Q. and reflections of personality and psychopathological features that could conceivably suppress the full expression of an examinee's measurable intelligence. Second, they provided a nonverbal, as well as verbal, means of assessing intelligence. And, third, the same instrument—all 10 subtests—could be given to a person of any age from 10 through 60 to provide a yardstick (I.Q.) for that person that was meaningfully related to his or her same-aged peers.

The 1939 W-B I helped to revolutionize and vitalize the practice of clinical psychology. In common with the 1905 Binet-Simon and the 1916 and 1937 revised Stanford-Binet Scales, the W-B I could be administered only individually, typically by a clinician who was presumably examining a patient whom he and his colleagues were trying to assess to help him or her toward a better personal, educational, occupational, or psychiatric rehabilitation. This was Binet's professional orientation, and it was also one that was emulated by the practicing clinical psychologists who followed in Binet's footsteps during the next 75 years. Probably, it was this professional orientation of using the I.Q. test merely as a clinical tool to help each examinee better understand and thereby realize his or her full potential that spared these practitioners of individual clinical psychology—those in private practice, in the schools, and in the hospitals and clinics—the vitriolic abuse that was heaped on the intelligence-testing industry in the 1960's. The results of such an individual, clinically based psychological assessment were typically discussed privately with the patient himself, his family, his physician, or his school principal. Thus, the results were used constructively, in contrast to the impersonal group tests that were used for placement in classrooms and for admission or nonadmission to college or the job of one's choice.

WECHSLER SCALES

Wechsler's first test, the 1939 Bellevue-Wechsler Scale, was an instant success, despite what Wechsler privately acknowledged later was its lack of psychometric and methodological rigor in development and standardization relative to what had been done by Terman with the 1916 and 1937 revisions of the Stanford-Binet. Nevertheless, the 10 quite distinct subtests that made up the W-B I were soon found to be very useful clinically both by psychodiagnosticians and by psychotherapists trying to help their individual patients better understand themselves. The five subtests making up the Bellevue-Wechsler Verbal Scale were: (1) Information, (2) Comprehension, (3) Arithmetic, (4) Similarities, and (5) Digit Span or, as an alternate subtest, Vocabulary. The five subtests making up the Performance Scale were: (1) Block Design, (2) Picture Completion, (3) Picture Arrangement, (4) Object Assembly, and (5) Digit Symbol.

Two years after Wechsler published the W-B I, the United States found itself in World War II and the U.S. Army turned to him for a modern substitute for the Army Beta Battery for use in the individual assessment of those soldiers who needed more in-depth evaluation than could be provided by the group-administered, exclusively verbal Army General Classification Test. Wechsler had already begun intermittent work on an alternate form of the W-B I, which he called the W-B II. Renaming it the Army Wechsler, he quickly pressed it into the service of his country, and it figured prominently in the newly emerging psychodynamic assessment approaches that characterized the World War II era.

In a few years this W-B II was used by Wechsler as the core around which he developed still another Wechsler scale, one designed for use with children. With the help of the professional personnel who were on the staff of his publisher, The Psychological Corporation, this new children's test, the Wechsler Intelligence Scale for Children (WISC), was carefully and meticulously standardized on a representative sample of American children (ages 6 through 16) and was published in 1949. Now there were two Wechsler scales for the clinical psychologist, the W-B I and the WISC.

Acknowledging the fact shortly thereafter that the W-B I was by then an assessment instrument for adults that was used by almost every clinical, school, and industrial assessment psychologist in the land, Wechsler and The Psychological Corporation began a revision and restandardization of the W-B I. In 1955 they brought out its successor, the Wechsler Adult Intelligence Scale (WAIS) for use with all age groups, beginning where the WISC left off, at age 16, and continuing through age 64, with supplementary norms through age 75 added later (Wechsler, 1958). The success of the WAIS was immediate and continues to the present day.

Because the WISC began only at age 6, Wechsler and The Psychological Corporation next extended the range downward with their introduction in 1967 of the Wechsler Preschool and Primary Scale of Intelligence (WPPSI), a scale that was developed to be used for preschoolers and other children in the age range 4 to 6½ years.

Thus, by 1967 Wechsler scales were available to assess children and adults, from ages 4 to 75 years. The scales overlapped in the younger years and had almost the same age range as the 1960 and 1972 revisions of the Stanford-Binet (ages 2 to 18 years). In the 1960 revision of the Stanford-Binet, Terman and Merrill (1960)—later aided by R. L. Thorndike (1973), who provided 1972 norms for their Stanford-Binet—dropped the now psychometrically cumbersome mental age and adopted, instead, a form of deviation I.Q. with clinical advantages comparable to the deviation I.Q. introduced by Wechsler in his 1939 W-B I.

In 1974 Wechsler published an up-to-date, restandardized revision of the WISC, which he named the WISC-R. He next authorized work to begin on a revision of the WAIS to be called the WAIS-R when published around 1980. Throughout the development of each of his scales, Wechsler has retained the same format, the use of an omnibus battery made up of 10 subtests. Sometimes he included a supplementary or an alternate subtest that could serve as a substitute for one or more of the others. The names of these various subtests are shown in Table II. Although the names of the subtests are similar from one age group to another, the content of each is clearly different and is designed to appeal to that specific age group. Thus, to the common question "Tell me the way in which a —— and

TABLE II

Composition of the Verbal and Performance Scales of Four Wechsler Scales

WPPSI*	WISC-R†	WAIS‡	WAIS-R§
Preschool-Primary (4–6½ years)	Children (6–16½ years)	Adults (16–75 years)	Adults
		Verbal Subtests	
Information	Information	Information	Information
Comprehension	Comprehension	Comprehension	Comprehension
Arithmetic	Arithmetic	Arithmetic	Arithmetic
Similarities	Similarities	Similarities	Similarities
Vocabulary	Vocabulary	Vocabulary	Vocabulary
(Sentences)**	(Digit Span)	Digit Span	Digit Span
		Performance Subtests	
Block Design	Block Design	Block Design	Block Design
Picture Completion	Picture Completion	Picture Completion	Picture Completion
	Picture Arrangement	Picture Arrangement	Picture Arrangement
	Object Assembly	Object Assembly	Object Assembly
	Coding	Digit Symbol	Digit Symbol
Animal House	(Mazes)		Level of Aspiration
Mazes			
Geometric Design			

* Wechsler Preschool and Primary Scale of Intelligence.

† Wechsler Intelligence Scale for Children-Revised.

‡ Wechsler Adult Intelligence Scale.

§ Wechsler Adult Intelligence Scale-Revised; this column is tentative, since the WAIS-R is currently being standardized.

** Parentheses indicate subtests that may be used as alternates or as supplementary tests.

a —— are alike," comparable items from the similarities subtests of the WPPSI, the WISC-R, and the WAIS are: WPPSI ("plum and a peach"), WISC-R ("apple and a banana"), and WAIS ("orange and a banana"). Inasmuch as items on each of Wechsler's subtests are arranged from the easiest to the most difficult items, the "plum and peach" item in the WPPSI is one of the hardest (thirteenth out of the 16 items) in that subtest, but its two counterparts are the fifth of 17 items in the WISC-R and the first of 13 in the WAIS.

RELIABILITY OF MEASURED INTELLIGENCE

From the introduction of the 1905 Binet-Simon Scale to the 1974 WISC-R, these and their counterpart clinical scales and all but a few of their hundreds of group-administered paper-and-pencil offshoots have been found to be highly reliable when the same test or an alternate form of the same test is readministered to a given person. These test-retest reliability coefficients of correlation frequently reach .80, .90, and even higher. For persons above 18 years of age, the retest I.Q. is rarely found to change even several years later. When the I.Q. test is administered by an experienced clinical psychologist, even to youngsters 2 to 3 years of age, and readministered weeks or several months later, the I.Q.'s obtained even months apart rarely differ significantly from test to retest. Thus, this same high level of reliability (stability) is typically found. It is only when a youngster is examined at, for example, ages 2 to 8 and is reexamined, even by an experienced clinical psychologist, as many as 2 to 5 years later that the I.Q. obtained the second time may be substantially different from that obtained during the first administration. If the test-retest interval is many years, considerably lower reliability is obtained.

In adults the picture is fortunately better. For example, the 5-year test-retest correlation for the W-B I Full-Scale I.Q. is .82 (Matarazzo, 1972), and the 20-week retest reliability of the WAIS is .91 (R. Matarazzo et al., 1973). The WAIS maintains this same high level (.91) of reliability even over a retest interval of some 2 years (Dodrill and Troupin, 1975). However, Kangas and Bradway (1971) reported that use of the Stanford-Binet in 1956 on the first examination with a sample of then adults and the WAIS in 1969 on these same adults yielded a 13-year retest correlation of only .58, despite the fact that the test-retest correlation yielded a considerably higher value of .83 between the Stanford-Binet and the WAIS administered concurrently in 1956 for these same 48 adults.

The lesson for the clinician is clear; the I.Q. as the sole and quantitative index of measured intelligence is quite reliable and clinically useful for any of a variety of current uses and careful follow-up, such as placement in special educational classes, college planning, and competency hearings. However, a datum such as single I.Q. score may be considerably less reliable or less stable when the examination was conducted years earlier and one attempts to use that earlier finding as a basis for a new diagnosis or decision many years later. Many practicing clinicians can recount instances of adult patients who have been discovered in homes for the mentally retarded after, for example, having been placed there at age 5 and who now, at age 40, earn a WAIS I.Q. of 120. Although the majority of persons tested with an I.Q. measure after they have reached the ages of 15 to 18 rarely show more than a plus or minus 5- to 10-point discrepancy when retested, even many years later, the occasional dramatic finding of a 30- or 40-point difference, even if rare, must be considered a possibility by clinicians whose work can profoundly affect administrative, quasi-judicial, judicial, or personal decisions involving their patients.

VALIDITY OF MEASURED INTELLIGENCE

More than half of the author's 572-page textbook on intelligence (Matarazzo, 1972) was devoted to a review and discussion of the now massive amount of evidence gathered in clinical and school settings for the validity of the Wechsler, Stanford-Binet, and similar scales of measured intelligence. Clearly, such a review is not possible here, and so only highlights of this issue are presented.

Probably the signal and most convincing evidence of the validity of these scales for assessing measured intelligence came from the field of mental retardation. Within only a year or two of Binet's introduction of the 1905 scale, the objective index it produced was substituted throughout the developed nations of the Western world for the more fallible and all too subjective clinical estimate based on each clinician's own understanding and clinical examination. The substitution was so thorough that after the introduction of the 1916 revised Stanford-Binet in the United States, state after state unfortunately passed legislation that made the I.Q. score so obtained the necessary and sole criterion of mental retardation. Although many clinicians, following Binet's clearly stated recommendation, continued to use other indices of social-behavioral adaptive retardation besides the I.Q., the potential for misuse and overreliance on the I.Q. alone became manifest. This potential for abuse was ultimately removed in each state through corrective legislation that required that adaptive-behavioral retardation coexist with measured intellectual retardation for a diagnosis of mental retardation to be valid.

Obviously, these examples of misuse through sole reliance on an I.Q. score were the fault of the individual clinicians and others who had failed to heed Binet's instructions for the use of his test and were not the fault of the test product, the I.Q., itself. In the hands of a compassionate clinician who integrates it with the patient's clinical history, the use of the I.Q. score improves the diagnosis of mental retardation to a level of validity more accurate than that of any other diagnosis in the field of psychopathology, a level of validity that during the two decades since the 1959 AAMD pronouncements has made the diagnosis of mental retardation a trusted one in medicine, clinical psychology, pediatrics, and child psychiatry. (The reader interested in the way group tests of intelligence administered in the schools can lead to abuses in the diagnosis of mental retardation even today can find the story in Mercer, 1973.)

Today's practitioner who specializes in mental retardation never uses the score from an intelligence assessment instrument in isolation. To the resulting I.Q. score obtained by such an instrument, he or she invariably adds either a clinically still not fully quantifiable score for social maturity or another index of socioadaptive behavior, such as the Vineland Social Maturity Scale or the more modern AAMD Adaptive Behavior Scales, and integrates both of those indices with information from the clinical history. The result in the field of mental retardation is the use of the I.Q. as a tool that is patient centered and directed toward using available community and family resources, as well as each patient's own many assets, for better self-fulfillment.

Table III, adapted from Heber (1961), presents the measured intelligence (I.Q.) ranges for each level of mental retardation that clinicians today use to satisfy the first of the three indices suggested by Binet for the diagnosis of mental retardation. That clinical judgment is still required in the diagnosis of mental retardation is clear from the fact that in its 1973 revision of the levels of measured intelligence (Grossman, 1973), the AAMD deleted the "borderline" category of mental retardation from the 1959 definitions shown here in Table III. Clearly, no value in Table III or in its 1973 revision should be used as a substitute for clinical judgment.

Use of I.Q. for Initial Identification of Children at Risk

Binet sought a method whereby he could objectively identify in the earliest grades those children who were slower than their age peers and who needed special help, lest they be unrecognized and passed from grade to grade, learning little until one day they were too old to profit further from public schooling. The experiences with thousands of children who were subsequently diagnosed as truly mentally retarded with the help of an I.Q. measure is too well known to repeat here. However, the results of a study by Dillon (1949) provide excellent additional evidence of the test's validity, including its validity for primary prevention of school dropout in children scoring above the range of mental retardation.

What was needed to provide validational support for Binet's humanistic hope for his index of measured intelligence was a longitudinal study of the same child examined and then followed up as he or she progressed through the years of formal schooling. Dillon's study, although focusing its interest on school dropouts, contained the necessary ingredients for such a study.

As can be seen in Table IV, Dillon began with the individual I.Q. data obtained for 2,600 youngsters in the seventh grade. These 2,600 children were distributed along the I.Q. measure as follows: 400 of them had earned an I.Q. below 85; 575 an I.Q. between 85 and 94; 650 between 95 and 104; 575 between 105 and 114; and 400 an I.Q. of 115 or above. As one reads down each of these columns, one can see, for example, that, of

the 400 seventh graders whose I.Q.'s measured below 85, a total of 93 had dropped out of school by the ninth grade, leaving only 307. The attrition in grades 9 and 10 was 241 additional youngsters, leaving only 66 who entered grade 11. A total of 52 of these 66 dropped out during grades 11 and 12, leaving only 14 of the original 400 who graduated. As is shown in the bottom row of Table IV, this number, 14, constitutes only 4 per cent of the original group of 400 seventh graders. In retrospect, one can see that 96 per cent of the youngsters in this lowest I.Q. group were at risk as potential dropouts and, by this I.Q. index alone, were potentially identifiable as early as the seventh grade, when they, their parents, and their teachers might have been encouraged to take whatever actions, especially motivational and educational actions, were appropriate and desired in each instance to reduce this risk of becoming a school dropout. That the I.Q. measure is an excellent, although not perfectly valid, index of school adaptability is clear as one examines the increasingly lower rate of attrition for the original group of 2,600 seventh graders as one moves progressively up through each higher I.Q. group in Table IV. Thus, as one moves through each group from the lowest group with I.Q.'s of 85 and below and finally reaches the group of youngsters with I.Q.'s of 115 and above, the proportion of those dropping out before graduation is seen to be 96 (that is, 100 minus the 4 per cent shown in the first column of the bottom row), 46, 37, 24, and 14 per cent, respectively. Data from more recent studies that support those in Table IV are reviewed elsewhere (Matarazzo, 1972).

The results of each of these studies and the thousands of others that show that academic grades in school correlate .50 with the I.Q. score are convincing evidence that the I.Q. as an index of measured intelligence is, even alone, a respectably valid predictor of educational-social-personal success in the

TABLE III
*American Association on Mental Deficiency (AAMD) Levels of Measured Intelligence**

Word Description of Retardation in Measured Intelligence	Level of Deviation in Measured Intelligence	Range in Standard Deviation Units	Corresponding I.Q. Range	
			Stanford-Binet S.D.-16	Wechsler S.D.-15
Borderline	−1	−1.01 to −2.00	68–83	70–84
Mild	−2	−2.01 to −3.00	52–67	55–69
Moderate	−3	−3.01 to −4.00	36–51	40–54
Severe	−4	−4.01 to −5.00	20–35	25–39
Profound	−5	below −5.00	below 20	below 25

* Adapted from Heber, R. A manual on terminology and classification in mental retardation. Am. J. Ment. Defic., *64* (Suppl.): 59, 1959; and Modifications in the manual on terminology and classification in mental retardation. Am. J. Ment. Defic., *65:* 500, 1961; and Grossman, H. J., editor. *Manual on Terminology and Classification in Mental Retardation.* American Association on Mental Deficiency, Washington, D.C., 1973, 1977. The borderline category shown here was deleted in the 1973 and 1977 revisions.

TABLE IV
*I.Q. and School Attrition as a Measure of Adaptive Behavior for 2600 Seventh Graders**

	Intelligence Quotient				
	<85	85–94	95–104	105–114	115+
All students in grade 7	400	575	650	575	400
Remainder entering grade 9	307	545	636	570	398
Remainder entering grade 11	66	374	493	492	369
Remainder continuing to graduation	14	309	412	437	344
% grade 7	4%	54%	63%	76%	86%

* Adapted from Dillon, H. J. *Early School Leavers: A Major Educational Problem.* National Child Labor Committee, New York, 1949; and Cronbach, L. J. *Essentials of Psychological Testing*, ed. 3, p. 219. Harper & Row, New York, 1970.

academic setting. And when such an I.Q. score is used in conjunction with indices of educational, medical, and socio-behavioral adaptation—such as grades in high school, annual income, level of responsibility assumed in occupational setting, and neurological findings—the validity of the I.Q. score is even more impressive.

Additional Correlates and Exemplars of I.Q.

Tables V and VI summarize the results of many other studies on the validity of the I.Q. index. For physicians and other practitioners, the data in Table V can serve as a useful rule of thumb in everyday practice. One item in Table VI is especially noteworthy—the fact that the many studies of the relationship between the I.Q. of adults and their success on the job reveal that this correlation is only .20. Although Binet predicted the future widespread use of scales such as his in industry, he was fully aware that employment opportunity, motivation, personality, drive, and a host of other noncognitive variables are as important as measured intelligence in the success of any employee. In spite of such variables as these, the fact that the correlation reaches the statistically significant value of .20 is impressive.

A host of federal and state laws were enacted in the United States during the 1960's and 1970's requiring that before any psychological test or intelligence test is used in employee selection, the employer must first carry out research to show that such a test is a valid predictor of the on-the-job performance of employees. To date, few tests have met this standard. Because of the considerable published validity data comparable to those shown in Table IV, no such laws have been enacted relative to the still considerable use of tests of measured intelligence—such as Scholastic Achievement Tests, Medical College Admission Test, and Graduate Record Examination—as supplementary aids in college and professional school admissions.

Differential Diagnosis

Neurosis and psychosis. Binet was the first to suggest that his scale could provide more than a cognitive index when he wrote that psychotic or alcoholic patients *scatter* their passes and failures on the Binet-Simon Scale over a larger number of year levels of mental age than do mentally retarded patients. However, comprehensive reviews of the literature in the 1930's of the subsequent research published over the next three decades concluded that this observation that psychopathology leads to more than normal unevenness of functioning in sub-

TABLE V
Measured Intelligence and Education*

WAIS I.Q.†	Educational Equivalent
125	Mean of persons receiving Ph.D. and M.D. degrees
115	Mean of college graduates
105	Mean of high school graduates
100	Average for total population
75	About 50–50 chance of reaching ninth grade

* From Matarazzo, J. D. *Wechsler's Measurement and Appraisal of Adult Intelligence,* ed. 5. Oxford University Press, New York, 1972. Reprinted by permission of Oxford University Press, New York, copyright holder.

† These I.Q. values are averages only. Many individual exceptions can be found. For example, some college graduates earn I.Q.'s of 100 or less, and many persons with I.Q.'s above 125 fail to complete high school.

TABLE VI
Exemplars or Validity Coefficients of I.Q.*

Exemplars	Correlation
I.Q. with adaptive behavior measure	
I.Q. × mental retardation	.90
I.Q. × educational attainment (in years)	.70
I.Q. × academic success (grade point)	.50
I.Q. × occupational attainment	.50
I.Q. × socioeconomic status	.40
I.Q. × success on the job	.20
Related variables	
I.Q. × independently judged prestige of one's occupation	.95
I.Q. × parents' educational attainment	.50

* From Matarazzo, J. D. *Wechsler's Measurement and Appraisal of Adult Intelligence,* ed. 5, p. 296. Oxford University Press, New York, 1972. Reprinted by permission of Oxford University Press, New York, copyright holder.

parts of the Stanford-Binet Scale was not supported, either for adults or for children. These literature reviews notwithstanding, beginning with his first book and the test manual that accompanied the 1939 W-B I, Wechsler clearly believed in and devoted large sections of this and his subsequent books to the ways in which the patterning or scatter of the profile of individual subtest scores may be useful in the differential diagnosis of such conditions as schizophrenia, anxiety neurosis, psychopathic personality, brain damage, and senile psychosis. But hundreds of studies on the use of profile, pattern, and scatter analysis published between 1940 and 1972 failed to produce evidence that such a search was fruitful (Matarazzo, 1972).

As is more easily acknowledged today, the problem was that the criterion (the specific clinical diagnosis) was unreliable. Specifically, the clinician-to-clinician reliabilities, even for such major diagnostic categories as psychotic and neurotic as the criterion rarely reached levels that were clinically acceptable. Consequently, no profile or test pattern, no matter how objective it was, could be used in the differential diagnosis of a clinical criterion as fickle as psychotic until the diagnosis was given more precise definition. Fortunately, the objective definitions of these clinical diagnostic categories have improved considerably during the past decade, and published clinician-to-clinician reliabilities of .80 and .90 for a number of the most common psychiatric diagnostic categories are today common (Matarazzo, 1978b). It is now more appropriate than ever before to carry out research on pattern analyses of Wechsler subtest profiles and their usefulness in differential diagnosis. However, for the present and until better studies are carried out, the still widespread tendency among many older practicing clinical psychologists and psychiatrists to base their clinical personality and differential diagnostic interpretations on Wechsler Scale profiles that were derived from research published between 1939 and 1980 is not justified. This recommendation is no doubt unnecessary for those clinicians who have had the unfortunate experience of undergoing severe cross-examination in the courtroom from an attorney who insisted that the witness provide published references to bear out the clinical belief that a Wechsler profile is a valid basis for the just offered differential diagnosis of a condition such as schizophrenia.

To conclude, however, that both Binet and Wechsler were completely incorrect in their hope that their scales could offer information about an examinee's personality functioning would also be incorrect. Actually, as reviewed in detail elsewhere (Matarazzo, 1972), there is considerable published evidence that the Wechsler subtests are heuristically sensitive mirrors of (1) state (momentary) anxiety (but not of chronic or trait anxiety), (2) concern with bodily intactness, (3) negativism, (4) introversion, and (5) other single dimensions of personality. Furthermore, the results of several longitudinal studies that have been going on for some four decades have revealed such additional findings as robust correlations between type and strength of emotional bond between the toddler child and his or her mother and between the mother and the father at that time, on one side, and the scaled scores on specific Wechsler subtests earned by the child at age 18 and even at age 36, on the other side. These early findings point up the types of findings that can be obtained when one uses a very robust outcome (an I.Q. or subtest score) and a demonstrably equally

reliable description or clinical rating of a personality measure. The likelihood is high that considerable research of this type will be forthcoming after the publication of the WAIS-R, the third edition of the *Diagnostic and Statistical Manual of Mental Disorders*, and other equally useful assessment tools.

In addition to sensing that Wechsler subtest profile analysis *may* be clinically useful, clinicians have long been aware that verbal content, whether in an interview or during a standardized psychological examination, often provides a clue to the presence of psychopathology. The Wechsler and other scales serve as excellent vehicles for revealing such clinically rich material. Table VII presents the mean ratings on a scale from 1.00 (normal) to 7.00 (very schizophrenic) given by 16 expert clinical psychologists to the verbatim answers provided by different persons to items from two Wechsler subtests. Beginning students of psychopathology may find it especially instructive to study the differing cues as these clinicians' ratings of the

TABLE VII

Hunt-Arnhoff Standardized Scale for Disorganization in Schizophrenic Thinking*

Vocabulary Scale				Comprehension Scale			
Scale Point†	Response	Mean	S.D.	Scale Point†	Response	Mean	S.D.
1	Gamble—To take a chance, a risk	1.00	0.00	1	Envelope—Deposit it in the mail box	1.06	0.25
	Seclude—To go away and be alone, to seclude oneself	1.50	0.63		Taxes—Taxes are necessary to support the government	1.06	0.25
	Donkey—A type of four-legged animal	1.50	0.52	2	Land in the city—Because they got more accommodations in the city than in the country	2.00	0.96
2	Gown—Garment you wear for lounging	1.75	0.93		Envelope—Best thing is to bring it to post office	2.00	0.73
	Shrewd—Careful in a sneaky, clever way	2.19	0.75	3	Envelope—Pass it by or mail it	2.87	0.81
	Nail—A bit of metal used to pound on	2.37	0.81		Theater—Turn in an alarm so that everyone wouldn't get burned up	3.00	0.82
3	Plural—Means plus another	2.94	0.93	4	Marriage—Proof and identification so you wouldn't get someone else's wife	4.50	1.03
	Join—Has to do with organization	2.62	0.96		Shoes—Probably just tradition, Dutch use wood	3.69	1.25
	Peculiarity—Action one doesn't usually engage in	3.00	1.15	5	Laws—It is reasonable for a group of people to come to some agreement and acceptance of a common good and to aid what has proven to be the best for the many; that is they are made to prevent illegal activities	4.87	0.96
4	Milksop—A sympathetic listener, but lacking in understanding	4.19	1.17
	Espionage—Crooked, not truthful	4.12	1.09
	Seclude—To put somewhere in the dark	3.81	1.11
5	Armory—Combined form of some sort of organization	4.94	0.77
	Juggler—Acts in front of a person, respects himself as a juggler	5.00	0.82		Shoes—Because leather has undoubtedly proved to be the most durable of all that which has been utilized for the preservation of the feet and to continue the comfort of those, that is the people who have chosen to wear shoes	5.06	1.12
	Espionage—A type of sinful devilment	5.44	0.89
6	Nail—Metal I guess, let's say a metal which is made scientifically for purpose of good and bad use	5.75	0.93
	Armory—Part of army subject to call without banner	5.94	0.85	6	Marriage—For ownership you might say and to take care of each other according to health	5.87	0.96
	Diamond—A piece of glass made from roses	6.44	0.63		Marriage—Some people get married in church and some people get married outside of church	5.69	1.09
7	Cushion—To sleep on a pillow of God's sheep	6.75	0.45	7	Forest—I'm not good at telling directions. Just walk uphill and when you get to the top it is easier going down	6.31	0.71
	Fable—Trade good sheep to hide in the beginning	6.81	0.40		Marriage—For scientific purposes and for the identification of siblings, siblings of the association of the parents	6.31	1.01
	Guillotine—Part of law subject only to those without call to stay on earth	6.62	0.62

* Adapted from Hunt, W. A., and Arnhoff, F. N. Some standardized scales for disorganization in schizophrenic thinking. J. Consult. Psychol., *19:* 173, 1955. Copyright 1955 by the American Psychological Association. Reprinted by permission.

† Level of bizarreness or schizophrenicity from none (1) to maximum (7) as judged by 16 experienced clinicians.

content of the responses deteriorates progressively from no pathology (ratings of 1) to pathology in its most extreme forms (ratings of 5, 6, and 7).

Neuropsychology. In the publication of his 1939 W-B I, Wechsler included the clinical suggestion that some (which he labeled don't-hold-up subtests) of the 10 subtests were vulnerable to brain damage, whereas other subtests were less vulnerable (they would hold up), even in brain damage, injury, or disease. He proposed as an aid in differential diagnosis a deterioration index, computed as the ratio of the don't-hold-up to the hold-up subtests. Unfortunately, the clinical diagnosis by neurologists and neurosurgeons of brain damage during the first decades after the introduction of the Wechsler scales was so unreliable that despite the published efforts of a number of investigators, little clinical validity could be demonstrated for the use of the Wechsler subtests in the diagnosis of brain damage.

These early failures notwithstanding, in the early 1940's Ward Halstead at Chicago and later his student, Ralph Reitan, who during the 1950's and 1960's was a member of the neurosurgery faculty of the Indiana University Medical Center, began the painstaking work of improving the reliability for research purposes of this hodgepodge criterion diagnosis loosely labeled brain damage. In time, Reitan was able to gather assessment data on neurologically and neurosurgically carefully composed clinically homogeneous groups of patients with left hemisphere injury or lesion and other equally carefully diagnosed and compiled groups with right hemisphere and generalized involvement (diffused across both hemispheres). Reitan included patients in each of his samples only after extensive evaluation of each one had been carried out by his colleagues in neurology, neurosurgery, and, for those coming to autopsy, pathology. As his predictor variables, Reitan used many assessment techniques, including a clinically promising one that is today called the Halstead-Reitan Battery of Neuropsychological Tests (Matarazzo, 1972; Reitan and Davison, 1974; Matarazzo et al., 1976). We will confine ourselves in the present section to a discussion of the ways in which measured intelligence, per se, is mirrored in the Wechsler scales in patients with demonstrable brain disorders. That practicing clinicians never use these findings from an intelligence test in isolation but, rather, attempt to integrate such Wechsler scale findings with those of the Halstead-Reitan Battery *and* the clinical history and other findings before offering a differential diagnosis in the individual case needs no further discussion or elaboration here.

In his first publication on the validity of the W-B I in the diagnosis of brain-behavior relationships, Reitan in 1955 reported a finding that was later confirmed many times: His group of patients with clinically verifiable lesions in the left hemisphere scored significantly poorer on the Wechsler Verbal Scale subtests than on the Performance Scale subtests. In all, 13 of his 14 individual patients in this first left-hemisphere-dysfunction group showed this finding. Conversely, his homogeneous group of patients with right hemisphere lesions did significantly poorer on the Performance Scale subtests than they did on the Verbal Scale subtests. Fifteen of the 17 individual patients in this right-hemisphere group showed a pattern similar to this total group pattern. Patients with diffuse damage across both hemispheres performed on the W-B I subtests like the group of patients in the right-hemisphere group—that is, they earned a significantly lower Performance I.Q. However, only 17 out of the 31 patients in the diffuse group showed this lower Performance subtest pattern; 12 reversed the pattern, and two had equal Verbal and Performance I.Q.'s.

A review of the literature that followed this initial publication by Reitan (Matarazzo, 1972) showed that a total of eight studies of this type had been published after 1955, and all eight confirmed the basic finding by Reitan in 1955. These first eight studies are shown in the top two-thirds of Table VIII. Since this 1972 literature review three additional studies have been published, and these studies have also been included in Table VIII. The study by Becker (1975) confirmed the finding that the mean scores of patients with diffuse head injury show a lower Performance Scale I.Q. The study by Black (1976) of young American soldiers with missile wounds in the Vietnam War disconfirmed this finding for right-hemisphere patients. However, like all the previous studies summarized in Table VIII, Black's left-hemisphere soldiers did show the predicted lower Verbal I.Q. Black (1974) did publish an earlier study of such soldiers that was consistent with the other findings shown in Table VIII, but no reference is made to it in his 1976 study. The study by Todd et al. (1977) confirmed two of Reitan's 1955 findings—namely, a lower Performance I.Q. than Verbal I.Q. in patients with right-hemisphere involvement and in patients with diffuse involvement—but, unlike the other studies, Todd and his colleagues also found a higher Verbal I.Q. in the group of left-hemisphere patients.

Thus, confirmation of Reitan's initial 1955 findings in these 11 post-1955 studies occurred in 9 out of 10 studies for the left-hemisphere patients, in 9 out of 10 studies for the right-hemisphere patients, and in 9 out of 9 studies for the patients with diffuse involvement. These confirmations are impressive, but the recent failure of cross-validation reported by Black and by Todd and his colleagues with right- and left-hemisphere patients should be taken very seriously by other investigators and especially by the practicing clinician dealing with the individual case. There had been cogent criticisms by Aaron Smith (1966a, 1966b), at the Neuropsychological Laboratory of the University of Michigan Medical Center, of the type of research findings summarized in Table VIII. These criticisms—for example, that the samples of patients with left-hemisphere lesions may include some aphasic patients whose very low verbal scores disproportionally distort the mean verbal scores of left-hemisphere samples—need to be addressed by any serious clinician practicing neuropsychology. However, this caution—plus the necessary reminder that the data in Table VIII are group means and, therefore, do not represent the individual patient in each of the patient samples represented there—should not obscure the increasing confidence among clinicians that when used in context with other pertinent findings on a given patient, the verbal versus performance discrepancies demonstrated in Table VIII may provide another clinically meaningful datum on the patient.

Two case histories demonstrate this point, although the first case is unusual in that the Wechsler scale data were strikingly helpful in and of themselves. This is a mere fortuitous happening. The second case reveals a considerable discrepancy between the diagnostic findings on the WAIS and the more robust findings from other assessment indices.

Brain tumor. The following case represents a dramatic example of the clinical usefulness of the Wechsler scales in an occasional individual clinical case.

The patient was a 21-year-old woman admitted on November 6, 1957 to the neurosurgery service of the University of Oregon Health Sciences Center with symptoms of amnesia, weight loss, anorexic somnolence, and memory loss. As is shown in Table IX, the author and his colleagues examined her preoperatively with the WAIS 5 days after her admission (11-11-57) and reexamined and followed her over

TABLE VIII

Wechsler Verbal and Performance I.Q. for Subgroups of Adult Patients with Lesions in Different Hemispheres of the Brain*

	Left	Right	Diffuse	Control	Investigator(s)
W-B I					
VIQ	79.7†	91.1	80.7		Kløve and Reitan (1958)
PIQ	90.3	80.1	78.2		
VIQ	88.4	99.7	93.4	100.7	Kløve (1959)
PIQ	98.4	87.8	93.1	102.6	
VIQ	88.0	101.0	95.0	114.0	Doehring et al. (1961)
PIQ	97.0	84.0	93.0	117.0	
WAIS					
VIQ	94.9	107.2	90.2	100.0	Satz (1966)
PIQ	105.1	99.7	87.0	97.0	
VIQ	92.3	106.6	98.3	104.2	Satz et al. (1967)
PIQ	104.9	96.1	95.3	99.3	
VIQ	90.3	98.8	92.0		Zimmerman et al. (1970)
PIQ	91.3	93.4	81.5		
VIQ	75.8	89.1			Parsons et al. (1969)
PIQ	83.7	78.7			
VIQ	79.8	91.5	83.2		Simpson and Vega (1971)
PIQ	83.4	78.7	79.5		
VIQ			93.7	106.0	Becker (1975)
PIQ			80.3		
VIQ	99.2	99.0			Black (1976)
PIQ	102.5	100.1‡			
VIQ	96.6‡	102.6	95.9	102.0	Todd et al. (1977)
PIQ	90.6	94.9	88.3	97.5	

* The practicing psychologist should study the many qualifications that must be considered when attempting to apply the findings in this table to the *individual* patient. The research psychologist should also adhere to the requirements outlined by Reitan for classifying groups of patients.

† In this table, each patient subgroup is compared *with itself* on Verbal I.Q. versus Performance I.Q.—that is, 79.7 versus 90.3; 91.1 versus 80.1; and 80.7 versus 78.2, respectively, for the three Kløve and Reitan (1958) subgroups.

‡ A disconfirmation of previous findings.

the next 5 years. The results in Table IX of the first WAIS examination are striking and show a Verbal I.Q. of 98, which was 28 points higher than her Performance I.Q. of 70. Even before the publication of the research findings on brain-behavior relationships shown in Table VIII, it was noticed by many clinicians and confirmed in an analysis of the WAIS standardization data and subsequent reviews of the literature (Matarazzo, 1972, p. 389; pp. 428–449) that large performance-versus-verbal discrepancies are rare and that no other form of psychopathology regularly produces such a pathognomonically marked discrepancy of 28 points between Verbal and Performance functioning within the normal range of the WAIS I.Q. Consequently, in the context of this patient's history and other findings, these WAIS results were interpreted by the psychologist and the neurosurgeon as strongly suggestive of a brain tumor in the right hemisphere. As shown in Table IX, the patient was operated on, a brain tumor was removed from the right hemisphere, and she was retested 2 days after surgery (11-19-57). After two additional retests over the next 3 months, the patient's scatter or discrepancy in Verbal versus Performance I.Q. had totally disappeared—on 2-14-58 she had a Verbal I.Q. of 104 and a Performance I.Q. of 104—thereby validating the original diagnostic impression that this young woman had both a premorbid Verbal I.Q. and Performance I.Q. of about 98 and that her Performance I.Q. had been reduced some 28 points by the presence of the brain tumor. Table IX shows confirmation of this post hoc clinical hypothesis when the patient returned

a year later (1-6-59) with a 23-point Verbal-to-Performance discrepancy; she had a Verbal I.Q. of 108 and Performance I.Q. of 85. The resulting additional surgery, her recovery in intellectual function, and her later history are summarized in Table IX. The improvement, decline, and improvement of her concurrent Wechsler Memory Quotient during these reexaminations are also shown in Table IX.

Brain injury. The following case also illustrates use of the Wechsler Scales.

A 54-year-old woman had experienced a spontaneous subarachnoid hemorrhage 7 years earlier and did not appear to have recovered fully. Her initial psychological examination lasted 10 hours and included the WAIS, Wechsler Memory Scale, Halstead-Reitan Battery, Trail Making Test, MMPI, Cornell Medical Index, Jastak Wide Range Reading Test, Wepman Sensory-Perceptual Examination, and an extensive clinical interview.

The history and, especially, the results of the Halstead-Reitan Battery—namely, a Halstead Impairment Index of .71, a value well above the cut-off of .51 that separates an abnormal index from a normal one, according to Reitan's norms (Matarazzo et al., 1976)—all suggested residual brain injury. But the results of the WAIS showed only a modest scatter of eight points—a Verbal I.Q. of 118 and a Performance

TABLE IX

Wechsler Scale Findings in Successive Reexamination of a 21-Year-Old Woman with a Tumor in the Right Cerebral Hemisphere*

	11-11-57 Preop 1	11-19-57 Postop 1a	12-1-57 Postop 1b	2-14-58 Postop 1c	1-6-59 Preop 2	2-10-59 Postop 2a	6-20-59 Postop 2b
Verbal I.Q.	98	97	102	104	108	110	105
Performance I.Q.	70	52	74	104	85	91	99
Memory Quotient	80	76	108	106	92	116	110

11-6-57	First admission. Her husband reported a 2-month history of amnesia, weight loss, anorexia, somnolence, and memory loss.
11-17-57	Right frontal craniotomy with removal of approximately 90 per cent of cystic craniopharyngioma in the retrochiasmal position. Postoperatively developed diabetes insipidus. Discharged 12-7-57.
2-12-58	Readmitted for evaluation of endocrine function. Considerable clinical improvement.
12-31-58	Third admission. Recurrence of weight loss, somnolence, anorexia, and memory loss. Differential diagnosis of possible further growth of craniopharyngioma.
1-16-59	Right frontal craniotomy with removal of entire cyst and nodule. Consequent loss of useful vision in right eye.
5-6-60	Fourth admission. Right frontal craniotomy and excision of 80 to 90 per cent of recurrent craniopharyngioma. Discharged 7-12-60. Fifth admission on 1-25-62 for recurrence of symptoms. Sixth admission on 11-15-62; patient discharged in care of own family physician. Death associated with craniopharyngioma recorded on 3-30-63.

* From Matarazzo, J. D. *Wechsler's Measurement and Appraisal of Adult Intelligence*, ed. 5, p. 415. Oxford University Press, New York, 1972. Reprinted by permission of Oxford University Press, New York, copyright holder.

I.Q. of 110—and a Full-Scale I.Q. of 115. A 10-point discrepancy between Verbal I.Q. and Performance I.Q. occurs in 30 of every 100 examinations of normal persons (Matarazzo, 1972, p. 389) so this eight-point difference was *clinically unremarkable*.

Negative findings such as in this case remind the practicing clinician that despite the considerable clinical validity for indices of measured intelligence, findings from the Wechsler scales and other tests of measured intelligence can rarely stand alone. This fact is as true in the diagnosis of mental retardation as it is in all other clinical psychological and psychiatric conditions. The modern successors to Binet's 1905 scale, such as the Wechsler and the revised Stanford-Binet scales, have come a long way as aids and tools for clinical practice. However, they are still not substitutes for clinical judgment.

Suggested Cross References

Concepts of perception and cognition, fundamental in the intelligence tests, are discussed in Section 4.1. Psychological testing of personality is presented in Section 12.6 and of children is presented in Section 35.3.

REFERENCES

Becker, B. Intellectual changes after closed head injury. J. Clin. Psychol., *31:* 307, 1975.

Binet, A. Nouvelles recherches sur la mesure du niveau intellectuel cher les enfants d'ecole. L'Ann. Psychol., *17:* 145, 1911.

* Binet, A., and Simon, T. Sur la necessite d'etablir un diagnostic scientifique des etats inferieurs de l'intelligence. L'Ann. Psychol., *11:* 162, 1905.

Binet, A., and Simon, T. Le developpement de l'intelligence chez les enfants. L'Ann. Psychol., *14:* 1, 1908.

Binet, A., and Simon, T. *The Development of Intelligence in Children.* Williams & Wilkins, Baltimore, 1916.

Black, F. W. Cognitive effects of unilateral brain lesions secondary to penetrating missile wounds. Percept. Mot. Skills, *38:* 387, 1974.

Black, F. W. Cognitive deficits in patients with unilateral war-related frontal lobe lesions. J. Clin. Psychol., *32:* 366, 1976.

Cronbach, L. J. *Essentials of Psychological Testing*, ed. 3. Harper & Row, New York, 1970.

* Cronbach, L. J. Five decades of public controversy over mental testing. Am. Psychol., *30:* 1, 1975.

Dillon, H. J. *Early School Leavers: A Major Educational Problem.* National Child Labor Committee, New York, 1949.

Dodrill, C. B., and Troupin, A. S. Effects of repeated administrations of a comprehensive neuropsychological battery among chronic epileptics. J. Nerv. Ment. Dis., *161:* 185, 1975.

Doehring, D. G., Reitan, R. M., and Kløve, H. Changes in patterns of intelligence test performance associated with homonymous visual field defects. J. Nerv. Ment. Dis., *132:* 227, 1961.

Galton, F. *Hereditary Genius: An Inquiry into Its Laws and Consequences.* Macmillan, London, 1869.

Galton, F. *Inquiries into Human Faculty and Its Development.* Macmillan, London, 1883.

Grossman, H. J., editor. *Manual on Terminology and Classification in Mental Retardation*, rev. ed. American Association on Mental Deficiency, Washington D.C., 1973, 1977.

Heber, R. A manual on terminology and classification in mental retardation. Am. J. Ment. Defic., *64* (Suppl.): 59, 1959.

Heber, R. Modification in the manual on terminology and classification in mental retardation. Am. J. Ment. Defic. *65:* 500, 1961.

Heber, R., and Garber, H. The Milwaukee project: A study of the use of family intervention to prevent cultural-familial mental retardation. In *Exceptional Infant*, B. Z. Friedlander, G. M. Sterritt, and G. E. Kirk, editors, vol. 3. Brunner/Mazel, New York, 1975.

Hunt, J. McV. *Intelligence and Experience.* Ronald Press, New York, 1961.

Hunt, J. McV., Paraskevopoulos, J., Schickendancc, D., and Usgiriz, I. C. Variations in the mean ages of achieving object permanence under diverse conditions of rearing. In *Exceptional Infant*, B. Z. Friedlander, G. M. Sterritt and G. E. Kirk, editors. vol. 3. Brunner/Mazel, New York, 1975.

Hunt, W. A., and Arnhoff, F. N. Some standardized scales for disorganization in schizophrenic thinking. J. Consult. Psychol. *19:* 171, 1955.

* Jensen, A. R. How much can we boost I.Q. and scholastic achievement? Harvard Educ. Rev., *39:* 1, 1969.

* Jensen, A. R. Cumulative deficit in I.Q. of blacks in the rural South. Dev. Psychol., *13:* 184, 1977.

Kangas, J., and Bradway, K. Intelligence at middle age: A 38-year follow-up. Dev. Psychol., *5:* 333, 1971.

Kløve, H. Relationship of differential electroencephalographic patterns to distribution of Wechsler-Bellevue scores. Neurology, *9:* 871, 1959.

Kløve, H., and Reitan, R. M. Effect of dysphasia and distortion on Wechsler-Bellevue results. Arch. Neurol. Psychiatry, *80:* 708, 1958.

* Matarazzo, J. D. *Wechsler's Measurement and Appraisal of Adult Intelligence*, ed. 5. Oxford University Press, New York, 1972.

Matarazzo, J. D. Heredity and environmental correlates of I.Q. J. Contin. Educ. Psychiatry, *39:* 35, 1978a.

Matarazzo, J. D. The interview: Its reliability and validity in psychiatric diagnosis. In *Clinical Diagnosis of Mental Disorders: A Handbook*, B. B. Wolman, editor, p. 47. Plenum Publishing Corp., New York, 1978b.

Matarazzo, J. D., Matarazzo, R. G., Wiens, A. N., Gallo, A. E., Jr., and Klonoff, H. Retest reliability of the Halstead Impairment Index in a normal, a schizophrenic, and two samples of organic patients. J. Clin. Psychol., *32:* 338, 1976.

Matarazzo, R. G., Wiens, A. N., Matarazzo, J. D., and Manaugh, T. S. Testretest reliability of the WAIS in a normal population. J. Clin. Psychol. *29:* 194, 1973.

* Mercer, J. R. *Labeling the Mentally Retarded.* University of California Press, Los Angeles, 1973.

Parsons, O. A., Vega, A., Jr., and Burn, J. Different psychological effects of lateralized brain damage. J. Consult. Clin. Psychol., *33:* 551, 1969.

Reitan, R. M., and Davison, L. A., editors. *Clinical Neuropsychology: Current Status and Applications.* Winston & Sons, Washington D.C., 1974.

Satz, P. Specific and nonspecific effects of brain lesions in man. J. Abnorm. Psychol., *71:* 65, 1966.

Satz, P., Richard, W., and Daniels, A. The alteration of intellectual performance after lateralized brain-injury in man. Psychonom. Sci., *7:* 369, 1967.

* Scarr, S., and Weinberg, R. A. I.Q. test performance of black children adopted by white families. Am. Psychol. *31:* 726, 1976.

Scarr, S., and Weinberg, R. A. Intellectual similarities within families of both adopted and biological children. Intelligence, *1:* 170, 1977.

Simpson, C. D., and Vega, A. Unilateral brain damage and patterns of age-corrected WAIS subtest scores. J. Clin. Psychol. *27:* 204, 1971.

Smith, A. Certain hypothesized hemispheric differences in language and visual functions in human adults. Cortex, *2:* 109, 1966a.

Smith, A. Speech and other functions after left (dominant) hemispherectomy. J. Neurol. Neurosurg. Psychiatry, *29:* 467, 1966b.

Terman, L. M. *The Measurement of Intelligence.* Houghton-Mifflin, Boston, 1916.

Terman, L. M., and Merrill, M. A. *Measuring Intelligence.*, Houghton-Mifflin, Boston, 1937.

* Terman, L. M., and Merrill, M. A. *Stanford-Binet Intelligence Scale.* Houghton-Mifflin, Boston, 1960.

Thorndike, R. E. *Stanford-Binet Intelligence Scale, Form L-M, 1972 Norms Edition.* Houghton-Mifflin, Boston, 1973.

Todd, J., Coolidge, F., and Satz, P. The Wechsler Adult Intelligence Scale Discrepancy Index: A neuropsychological evaluation. J. Consult. Clin. Psychol. *3:* 450, 1977.

* Wechsler, D. *The Measurement and Appraisal of Adult Intelligence,* ed. 4. Williams & Wilkins, Baltimore, 1958.

Wolf, T. H. The emergence of Binet's conception and measurement of intelligence: A case history of the creative process. J. Hist. Behav. Sci., *5:* 113, 207, 1969.

Wolf, T. H. *Alfred Binet.* University of Chicago Press, Chicago, 1973.

Yerkes, R. M. editor. Psychological examining in the U.S. Army. Mem. Natl. Acad. Sci. *15:* 1921.

Zimmerman, S. F., Whitmyre, J. W., and Fields, F. R. J. Factor analytic structure of the Wechsler Adult Intelligence Scale in patients with diffuse and lateralized cerebral dysfunction. J. Clin. Psychol., *26:* 462, 1970.

12.6 Psychological Testing of Personality

ARTHUR C. CARR, Ph.D.

Introduction

When properly administered and interpreted by an experienced clinician, psychological tests make a significant contribution to an understanding of the patient and clarify issues related to his psychiatric classification, his psychodynamics, and his management. Although it is debatable whether psychological tests should ever be the sole basis for determining such decisions, they are an important part of the diagnostic armamentarium available for evaluating the functioning of a patient.

Psychological tests vary in form and purpose; they include some tests concerned primarily with what the patient does and others concerned primarily with why he does it. In spite of their differences, psychological tests have important common features that contribute to their effectiveness and reflect their advantage over informal interview procedures or unstandardized examinations.

1. *Standard psychological tests provide a fairly objective means for comparing a relatively controlled sample of the patient's behavior with available normative data representative of a larger reference group.*

Adequate standardization of tests has probably been achieved most extensively in the area of intelligence testing. For example, determining the patient's relative intellectual strengths and weaknesses, as well as his intelligence quotient (I.Q.), is made possible on the Wechsler Adult Intelligence Scale (WAIS) through the use of normative data gathered for various age ranges from a carefully selected sample presumably representative of the general population of the United States. Although the degree of sophistication represented by this sampling procedure does not characterize the more limited standardization in the area of personality testing, there does exist a substantial body of research and clinical data on the major personality-assessment techniques that can serve as a basis for evaluating a patient's response patterns. For example, the bibliography on the Rorschach Test now comprises thousands of references that cover the major diagnostic groups and clinical entities.

Related to the standardization of any test are the available data that presumably demonstrate whether the test is both valid and reliable. Although often stated as simple and separate questions (Does the test measure what it purports to measure? Does the test yield consistent results over time with different examiners?), these issues are extremely complicated, particularly in the area of personality testing when the goal is that of a global measure of what is referred to as the whole personality. As used with psychiatric patients, the typical test battery elicits a wide variety of behavior that serves as the basis for making clinical inferences that usually do not depend on single scores or test signs. A survey of clinical psychologists (Wade and Baker, 1977) indicates that clinicians view clinical experience with a test as more important in their test-use decisions than those psychometric considerations reflected in reliability and validity studies. In a real sense, tests merely elicit behavior, but clinical insights are arrived at through inference. The experience and knowledge of the particular examiner are highly relevant variables, particularly in the use of projective techniques that assume all responses are in some way expressive of the patient's personality. Some authorities are able to make a comprehensive personality evaluation solely on the basis of a single test, but most psychologists require a test battery. Consistencies and inconsistencies between tests are helpful in establishing the level of confidence that can be held about any specific inference and in relating surface behavioral characteristics to their motivational origins.

2. *In the test battery a broad range of stimuli on the continuum of structure-ambiguity is available for eliciting a patient's response samples.*

In contrast to specific or highly structured questions such as those on an intelligence test or a standard psychiatric interview, the projective techniques presumably have no right or wrong answers—"No two people see exactly the same thing; just be sure to tell me *all* that you see." Unlike the typical test or examination, the essential characteristic of a projective technique is that it is unstructured; cues for appropriate action are not clearly specified, and the person being tested must give meaning to (interpret) the stimulus in accordance with his or her own inner needs, drives, abilities, defenses, impulses—in short, according to the dictates of his or her own personality. Whether the stimuli are inkblots (the Rorschach Test) or ambiguous pictures (the TAT), the patient's task is to impose or project his own structure and meaning onto materials that have relatively little meaning or structure and that, in a purely objective sense, are only inkblots or ambiguous pictures. The rationale for choosing tests of varying ambiguity stems from a recognition that social situations vary along this same dimension. A basic assumption is that persons who show a certain kind of disturbance in a test situation of a given degree of ambiguity will in all probability show a similar reaction in a social situation of equal ambiguity. Many persons can function without readily apparent defect when they are in situations that offer cues for what would be an appropriate response. It is only when they are placed in relatively ambiguous or unstructured situations that their basic disturbances become discernible.

The discussion that follows deals with the test battery most widely used in clinical practice for evaluation of psychiatric patients. In addition to an individual intelligence test, it generally includes an association technique (most frequently the Rorschach Test), a storytelling test (most frequently the Thematic Apperception Test, TAT), completion methods (most frequently the Sentence Completion Test, SCT), and graphomotor tests (most frequently the Bender-Gestalt Test and the Draw-a-Person Test). As a personality test widely used in research, the Minnesota Multiphasic Personality Inventory, MMPI, is also discussed. (Table V describes other commonly used personality tests.)

Because the most valid evaluation of the patient's functioning can be obtained only through the use of a battery of carefully chosen tests, administered in a face-to-face relationship between examiner and patient (see Figure 1), a psychological evaluation is usually a time-consuming and expensive procedure. In a typical test battery, 3 to 4 hours are necessary for administration, with at least an equal amount of time spent by the examiner on scoring and interpreting test results. Consequently, psychological evaluations usually are not done routinely, except for simple screening procedures, and in most clinics and hospitals they are done only on specific referral. Therefore, referring sources, who are usually psychotherapists, should have some understanding of what tests can and cannot do, what constitutes a legitimate referral problem for psychological examination, and, in general, how best to use limited diagnostic services.

Proper referral usually requires that the therapist have prior knowledge of the patient, recognizing what areas of his functioning need clarification or evaluation. It is generally well to consider whether the question being asked is actually relevant to the treatment or disposition of the given patient. If the crucial decisions about the patient have already been made, it may be a waste of time and money to submit him and the examiner to the lengthy process of an evaluation at that particular time. In addition, referral should be made at a time the patient seems able to give an adequate sample of his functioning ability—that is, when he is testable. For example, a patient in a profound depression, in a catatonic stupor or excitement, under heavy drug effects, or experiencing the effects of electroconvulsive therapy is not a suitable candidate for testing. Test

results offer maximum usefulness when the patient views the purpose of testing as one designed for his best interests within essentially a therapeutic milieu, unlike what may exist when tests are used with job applicants or prison inmates, who have a compelling reason for deliberately concealing or dissimulating.

Referral Purposes

INTELLECTUAL EVALUATION

Intellectual evaluation can best be accomplished by an individual intelligence test, such as the WAIS. The WAIS comprises 11 different subtests that tap 11 somewhat different abilities. Since the I.Q. represents, in a sense, a score that averages together quite different abilities, the I.Q., as a number, can be grossly misleading. Unless the psychologist delineates the patterning of strengths and weaknesses represented by the variability between verbal I.Q. and performance I.Q. and within and between subtests, he is not adequately presenting the potential contribution of an intellectual evaluation. An intellectual evaluation is usually also part of any personality evaluation, since a good intelligence test elicits evidences of such personality features as obsessive thinking, repressive defenses, awareness of social conventions, and idiosyncratic thought processes.

DIFFERENTIAL DIAGNOSIS

Problems of differential diagnosis can best be answered by recourse to a full test battery in which relationships between tests may offer significant insight into the patient's total pattern of functioning. Although the reference to test signs or test scores may obscure the fact, the psychologist is attending basically to similar criteria for diagnosis, as is the person evaluating interview data. For example, reality-testing ability is a crucial variable in the distinction between neurosis and psychosis, regardless of what data source is used. This fact may not be obvious when reference is made to relevant Rorschach symbols, such as "low P," "low F+%," and "M-." Similarly, the deficits summarized in such symbols as "Impot," "low R," "persev," and "perplex" are suggestive of cerebral malfunctioning, whether expressed on formal tests or revealed through clinical interviews.

ORGANIC IMPAIRMENT

Deficiencies that accompany organic brain malfunctioning are frequently highlighted by means of psychological tests. On occasion, they are most apparent in areas ordinarily conceptualized as intellectual—for example, in memory ability, in arithmetical skills, and in the analysis and synthesis of visual designs. In other instances, they are most apparent in graphomotor productions, such as the Draw-a-Person Test and the Bender-Gestalt Test, in which such distortions as rotations of the designs, difficulties in angulation, fragmentation or oversimplification of the figures, and perseverative phenomena may occur. Brain malfunctioning may often be apparent in responses to the projective techniques in which, for example, the patient's limitations become apparent because he cannot rely on earlier learned skills to conceal his deficit. As there is no way to anticipate where the patient's disturbance is most likely to be apparent, a battery of tests is required. Because of the limitations of the standard test battery when used for this purpose, some psychologists have devised special tests and procedures solely for the purpose of detecting brain damage, such as the Halstead-Reitan Neuropsychological Battery (Reitan, 1973). In any event, psychological tests should be only one part of the total diagnostic battery to be used when the existence of brain damage is suspected. When its presence is confirmed, psychological tests may help document the extent of the resulting incapacities.

PERSONALITY DYNAMICS

Elucidation of personality dynamics usually requires recourse to techniques that vary in the degree to which their stimulus value is obvious and clear, making possible a statement that is dynamically oriented in the sense of its relating consciously expressed attitudes to feelings less available to awareness or to assumed early genetic determinants. In general, the level of inference from the SCT to the TAT to the Rorschach varies directly with the assumed level of awareness that is presumably being tapped. A thorough knowledge of the individual tests and of personality theory is required to be able to relate the overt (conscious, surface, or behavioral) aspects of functioning to the covert (motivational, unconscious) components.

IMPLICATIONS FOR TREATMENT

The patient's relative strengths and weaknesses can be interpreted from the standpoint of their implications for his treatment or management. Important areas for consideration include the patient's thought processes, disturbances in affect, disturbances in ego boundaries, and difficulties in interpersonal relationships. Where weak reality-testing abilities are revealed, supportive treatment is generally considered more advisable than intensive, psychoanalytic treatments that may precipitate further decompensation of already weakened defenses. Motivation for personality change, ability to tolerate frustration, degree of insight, and flexibility of defenses are among the relevant issues.

SPECIALIZED REFERRAL PROBLEMS

Psychological tests may be helpful in answering specific questions related to a particular patient, such as whether there is evidence of suicidal ideation or whether the patient is likely to be dangerous or homicidal. And, although not invariably used by clinical psychologists, many specialized tests are designed to evaluate such issues as educational fitness, occupational interest, and vocational aptitudes that may contribute to the planning for a particular patient. The Buros *Mental Measurements Yearbooks* are an excellent source of information on available tests.

Classification of Tests

Tests have traditionally been divided into various types, depending on their purpose, their content, or the manner in which they are administered. In practice, some of these distinctions become obscured, since how the examiner chooses or is able to use the test is often the determinant of what use the test has. Typical traditional classifications follow.

INTELLIGENCE VERSUS PERSONALITY TESTS

Usual distinctions involve whether the test was devised to evaluate intellectual and cognitive abilities or whether it was designed to measure those other nonintellectual modes of responding assumed to be related to personality. Typical ex-

amples of the former include the WAIS and the Stanford-Binet Intelligence Scale; the latter are represented by the Rorschach Test, the MMPI, and the TAT. A recent innovation in the field, however, involves the conceptualization that intellectual functioning is much more intimately interrelated with the psychodynamics of personality functioning than the dichotomy implies. Many experienced clinicians are able to infer important personality features from the patterning of intellectual strengths and weaknesses represented by the WAIS profile. Similarly, the Rorschach is used by some clinicians to infer the patient's effective intellectual resources. With usage, a test's original purpose may even change. For example, the Draw-a-Person Test was originally used primarily as a measure of intelligence; today the test is used primarily as a projective personality technique.

INDIVIDUAL VERSUS GROUP TESTS

Another traditional distinction involves whether the test is individually administered or whether it can be given simultaneously to a group. Individual testing has the advantage of providing an opportunity for the examiner to evaluate rapport and motivational factors and to observe and record the patient's behavior during testing. Careful timing of responses is also possible. Group tests, on the other hand, are usually more easily administered. They have generally been devised for easier scoring and more objective interpretation. But this distinction is not as clear-cut as may be thought; some tests can be administered in either individual or group forms, with the resulting advantages or disadvantages depending on the test and the examiner. The MMPI was originally devised as an individual test, but today a group form of the test is used predominantly. The advantages of easy scoring and interpretation (now frequently both done by computer) have been retained with each form of the test.

OBJECTIVE VERSUS PROJECTIVE TESTS

Objective personality tests are typically pencil-and-paper tests based on items and questions having obvious meaning and having the advantage of yielding numerical scores and profiles easily subjected to mathematical or statistical analysis. Since response categories in such tests are usually limited (often "true" or "false"), manuals for interpretation may require little experience or sophistication on the part of the user. Projective tests, on the other hand, are so classified on the basis of their presenting stimuli whose meaning is not immediately obvious—that is, where some degree of ambiguity forces the subject to project his own needs into or onto an amorphous, somewhat unstructured situation. In some instances this effect is compounded by the test instructions that also reinforce the element of ambiguity. Interpretation of the elicited free-association data usually requires more experience and greater knowledge of personality theory on the part of the examiner. However, it also provides an opportunity for a richer, more complete understanding of personality functioning than is usually possible with objective tests that traditionally are concerned primarily with what the subject does or with how he feels, rather than with motivational aspects of his behavior.

Although the distinction between objective and projective tests implies a dichotomy, it is really a continuum of ambiguity that is provided within and between tests so that, in many instances, examiners may attend to different aspects of the test results. A readily understood example is handwriting, an expressive technique that conveys only its literal message until it is interpreted otherwise. How far even the untrained layman may read between the lines or infer on the basis of the writing that the writer is sloppy or meticulous or scholarly varies greatly from person to person and from occasion to occasion. With respect to more formal techniques, both the Draw-a-Person Test and the Bender-Gestalt Test, although originally devised for other purposes, are today frequently exploited for their projections of personality features. Similarly, increasing attention is currently being given to the projective interpretation possibilities of the WAIS, the prototype of the objective, nonprojective test. Hence, the philosophy and the interpretative approach of the examiner are important in determining whether the given tool is serving as an objective test, as a projective technique, or as something perhaps alternating between the two. Again, such flexibility in the examiner's interpretative skill is achieved only through extensive training and experience.

Personality Testing

The tests in the psychological test battery used in most psychiatric settings are usually chosen in terms of how well they serve the purpose of a psychodynamic formulation of personality functioning. Basic to this selection is the assumption that behavior is often motivated by forces that vary as to their degree of accessibility to awareness or behavioral expression, with behaviorally dissimilar responses possibly being motivationally identical. The need for a battery of tests arises not because of the possible invalidity of any single test but because different tests detect different areas and levels of functioning and because the relationships between tests reflect the person's multilevel system of functioning.

RORSCHACH TEST

Surveys over the years suggest that the Rorschach Test is the most frequently used individual test, with the possible exception of the WAIS, in clinical settings throughout the United States. In a real sense, the technique does not conform to the usual expectations of a test and quite properly should be referred to as the Rorschach method or the Rorschach technique. Nevertheless, the shorter reference is most frequently used; in fact, the most common designation is probably simply, "the Rorschach."

The Rorschach was devised by Hermann Rorschach (see Figure 2), a Swiss psychiatrist, who began around 1910 to experiment with ambiguous inkblots (see Figure 3). Others before him, including Leonardo da Vinci and Alfred Binet, had used indeterminate forms to stimulate the creative imagination. Shakespeare may have been showing intuitive understanding of the importance of one's associations to ambiguous forms when Hamlet, feigning madness, associates to a cloud formation with images that reflect important aspects of his real personality. Rorschach's accomplishment was the conceptualization of a system for eliciting and scoring responses in terms of their formal qualities to reveal important personality features. A selection of 10 inkblots (limited to this number by the dictates of his publisher) reached publication in the now famous monograph *Psychodiagnostik* (1921).

The Rorschach is a standard set of 10 inkblots that serve as the stimuli for associations. In the standard series the blots, administered in order, are reproduced on cards 7 by 9½ inches and are numbered from I to X. Five of the blots (I, IV, V, VI, and VII) are in black and white; the remainder include other colors as well. The instructions used by most authorities are something as follows:

I am going to be showing you these cards, one at a time. I'd like you

FIGURE 2. Hermann Rorschach. (Courtesy of New York Academy of Medicine).

FIGURE 3 (*left*). Plate I of the Rorschach Test. (Reprinted by permission. Hans Huber Medical Publisher, Berne.)
FIGURE 4 (*right*). Holtzman Inkblot. (Reproduced from the Holtzman Inkblot Technique by permission. Copyright © 1958, 1961 by The Psychological Corporation, New York. All rights reserved.)

to look at each card carefully and tell me anything it looks like or anything that it reminds you of. You can take as long as you like. There are no right or wrong answers. No two people see exactly the same thing. Just be sure to tell me *all* that you see.

A verbatim record is kept of the patient's responses, along with initial reaction times and total time spent on each card. After completion of what is called the free association, an inquiry is then conducted by the examiner to determine important aspects of each response that will be crucial to its scoring (see Table I).

Present scoring systems rest heavily on Rorschach's original formulations. Numerous authorities, however, have made modifications or refinements in Rorschach's scoring system, as well as important contributions to test methodology and interpretation. These authorities include Bruno Klopfer (1942), Samuel J. Beck (1944), Molly Harrower (1946), Roy Schafer (1954), Zygmunt Piotrowski (1957), E. G. Schactel (1966), Marguerite Hertz (1970), and Louise Bates Ames (1971). Toomey and Rickers-Ovsiankina (1977) have presented a tabular compari-

TABLE I
*Responses to Rorschach Card I by Five Male Patients**

Free Association	Inquiry
Patient A: A bug with two witches attached to it.	This whole thing in the middle, just the way it looks. [Points] Just the wings here. Looks like a witch.
Also a halloween mask. About all I can see.	That—the whole thing. The eyes, the mouth. [White space] [?] Nothing else about it.
Patient B: A bat, a bug.	Bat. [Whole] The blackness and the wings. Bug—that was just a pure reference to the color. I just see it as unpleasant.
One of the furies. A headless woman with black wings, grasping hands, claws, whatever. Bottom part of her torso is compressed, held in, like she's reaching forward.	Furies. [Whole] The central portion could represent legs pressed together. She represents a figure of death launching forward, and the head gets lost. Sort of snake-like, and the outer parts are reaching forth at the shadow of the earth.
Patient C: It looks like a monster bat. It has pincers.	The whole thing. It has wings. It's kind of ragged, that's all.
And an ass over here.	[Top center] Arches. Just shaped that way. Feel uptight, knowing I'm taking a test[?] Shape, two mounds.
And a butterfly.	Whole object. The wings, the shape. I just feel I want to get out of here.
Patient D: Must be some kind of bird or butterfly or insect.	[Whole] Wings, center line the body. [Most like?] An insect because of this section. Head looking section with two little feelers.
It could be some sort of oriental building.	[Whole, upside-down] Stands of two outer legs with profile of building sloping forward.
Within the collage may be many profile, hidden pictures of people, the dark spots being the eyes.	[Outer edge] Outlines of two men.
Patient E: Looks like a bat? That's all I can make of it.	Whole blot—the middle makes it look like a body. And it looks like he has a tail and two short feet.

* Table I gives the Rorschach responses, both free associations and inquiries, given to card I by five male patients whose responses to other tests will be given in similar order. These extracted test responses are reported primarily to illustrate the range given by different patients to the same stimulus. As such, these responses may not themselves always delineate the varying psychiatric conditions or medical diagnoses represented.

Patient A: 26 years old, multiple psychiatric hospitalizations within past 4 years. Unable to care for himself, believing himself controlled by a force that makes him act inappropriately. Suffers from chronic delusions, obsessional thinking, and social withdrawal.

Paient B: 23 years old, long history of social isolation, repetitive self-destructive behavior, depression, and inability to function academically. Has shown depersonalization and derealization phenomena but no admitted delusions or hallucinations.

Patient C: 28 years old, complaints of chronic and overwhelming anxiety, feelings of loneliness, and ambivalence about homosexual identification. History of excessive use of psychotropic medication. Borderline personality organization.

Patient D: 22 years old, denies psychological difficulties other than being high strung. Recurring headaches diagnosed as being without organic cause.

Patient E: 33 years old, hospitalized on neurology service for organic mental disorder assumed to be related to occupational hazard: Mercury poisoning. Prior history of behavior difficulties.

son of the major scoring systems, and Exner (1974, 1978) has integrated the varying systems into a comprehensive approach to Rorschach scoring and interpretation. Although the presentation that follows does not attempt to identify individual contributions, it should be realized that present Rorschachiana reflect the achievements of many outstanding psychologists and psychiatrists, some of whom have devoted the major efforts of their lives to the study of this one technique.

Scoring of responses converts the important aspects of each response into a symbol system related to the following variables.

Location areas. The location is scored in terms of what portion of the blot was used as the basis for the response. Grossest differentiations involve whether it was the whole blot (W), a common detail of the blot (D), an unusual detail of the blot (Dd), or a white space area (S).

The relative emphasis on location areas reflects intellectual manner of approach. High W% with accurate form perception may reflect good organizational ability and high intelligence. D% represents interest in the practical aspects of life, and a certain percentage of D responses offers some assurance that the patient has interest in practical affairs. Dd% reflects ability to attend to minor detail and is sometimes overly prominent in the obsessive or the paranoid person. The prominent use of white space may reflect stubborn, oppositional, resistive tendencies that, when in overabundance, imply paranoid features.

Determinants. The determinants of each response reflect what there was about the blot that made it look the way the patient thought it looked. Determinants include form (F), shading (K, k, or c), color (C or C'), movement, either of humans or of animals (M or FM), inanimate movement (m), and various combinations of these determinants with varying emphases. Thus, an FC response is determined primarily by form or shape and secondarily by color; a CF response is determined primarily by color and secondarily by shape.

Human movement (M) responses reflect accessibility to fantasy activities. If in a context of good reality testing, they may indicate high level of integration and ability to use imaginal processes to enrich perception of the world. They can also reflect unrealistic, autistic fantasy, as indicated primarily by poor form accuracy. Animal movement (FM) responses reflect availability to awareness of impulses to immediate gratification; spontaneity; in excess, also related to immaturity; they relate to more primitive, instinctual layers than do M responses. Inanimate movement (m) responses reflect tension and conflict stemming from awareness of forces outside one's control. Form (F) responses reflect responses stripped of the emotional affectional nuances implied by color and shading. Overemphasis on form alone suggests rigidity, impoverishment, and constriction. Insufficient form may mean inadequate control. Form accuracy (F+%) reflects the percentage of form responses in which the form is accurately perceived. As a measure of reality-testing ability, it is an important aspect of ego strength. It may be high in depressions and the very intelligent but low in manic excitement, schizophrenia, and mental retardation. Shading to give a diffuse, unstructured, but three-dimensional effect (KF and K) reflects anxiety of a diffuse and free-floating nature, reflecting a frustration of affectional needs. Shading to give a structured but three-dimensional effect (FK) reflects attempts to handle affectional anxiety by introspective efforts, objectifying the problem by gaining perspective on it. Used excessively, it may reflect strong inferiority feelings. Shading to give the impression of a three-dimensional expanse projected on a two-dimensional plane (k, kF, Fk) reflects affectional anxiety behind a good front of outward control, covering up with an intellectual cloak. Texture responses (c, cF, Fc) relate to the degree of awareness of and differentiation of one's needs for affection and dependency. Achromatic color responses (C', C'F, FC') relate to the artistically impressionable; when excessive, they reflect dysphoria and depression. Color responses (C, CF, FC) relate to the overt emotional reactions of the person to the impact of social environment, affective contact, and control of affect. Experience balance (relative amount of M to total C) reflects the degree to which the person is introversive or extratensive (Rorschach's terms for Jung's familiar dichotomy).

Content areas. Responses are also scored in terms of the content reflected in the responses: human, animal, anatomy, sex, food, nature, and so forth.

In general, content areas reflect breadth and range of interests. Human responses imply interest in and awareness of others but not necessarily involvement with them. In excess, animal responses reflect stereopathy or immaturity in thought, lack of cultural breadth. Anatomy responses reflect fears of bodily harm and preoccupation with bodily functioning, and guarding against the expression of hostile, destructive impulses. Food responses imply a passive, regressive need for nurturance. Traditionally scored content categories often obscure a similarity in underlying themes. For example, such Rorschach responses as "ice cream," "mother bird feeding a chick," "a person kneeling," and "Santa Claus" are scored differently, but all reflect themes pertaining to an oral-receptive orientation. Similarly, "vulture," "teeth," "scarecrow," and "Dracula" all reflect an oral-agressive one. A contribution by Aronow and Reznikoff (1976) summarizes various systems for organizing Rorschach content along meaningful specified dimensions, such as affect categories (Elizur, 1949; DeVos, 1952), primary process manifestations (Holt, 1977), and repressive style (Levine and Spivack, 1964).

The number of popular (P) responses is related to the ability to think along usual, conventional lines.

Sequence analysis. Although traditional Rorschach interpretation placed heavy reliance on the formal aspects of responses reflected in the summary of test scores, the more psychodynamic approach relies on an analysis of qualitative aspects of the associations that are not easily summarized numerically. With awareness of the nature of each stimulus and experience with the kinds of responses usually elicited by blot areas, the skilled clinician draws inferences from the sequence of responses, noting the defenses and defensive failures that are being called into operation (see Table II).

Research use. The Rorschach does not easily lend itself for research purposes, despite the extensive studies that have been conducted. It is difficult to convert the significance of a total profile to numerical figures or signs or to make records comparable, since the number of responses is not controlled for in the administration of the test. Unfortunately, the frequency of many response categories does not increase proportionally to the total number of responses. Hence, the Rorschach lacks many of the psychometric qualities that would make it a good research tool. In spite of the sometimes unsatisfactory research findings (Goldfried et al., 1971), the Rorschach continues to play an important part in the test battery.

Differential diagnosis. The Rorschach is particularly useful as a diagnostic tool. Although a certain mystique has developed around Rorschach interpretation, it is worth reiterating that the test, like any other test, merely serves, under standard conditions, to elicit behavior that can then be evaluated in terms of standard diagnostic or other criteria. The thinking and associational patterns of the patient are highlighted or brought more clearly into focus largely because the ambiguity of the stimulus provides relatively few cues to what may be conventional or standard responses.

With a knowledge of the nature of the task imposed on the patient and with awareness of what the various clinical entities are, one can often correctly infer what patients of the various diagnostic groups will do on the Rorschach or any other projective technique. Recognizing the behavioral differences between hysterical and obsessive-compulsive patients, for example, one could correctly infer that the former have fewer and vaguer responses, are less systematic in approach, and use fewer unusual detail responses than do the latter. The presumed emotional lability of the hysteric should also dictate that he will probably more freely show uncontrolled color responses

---

TABLE II
Psychologist's Interpretation of Patient's Responses to Rorschach Card I

1. A bat (Inquiry: It's the whole. Its wings and these are its claws. This is the place where he goes to the bathroom—anus. Rest of body is here: The whole blot.)	Although the popular percept (bat) is given, the elaboration is highly unusual. Introduction of "anus" is idiosyncratic, forewarning of a theme that reaches greater intensity on subsequent cards. Anal responses or the tendency to see figures from the rear are often found in the records of paranoid patients.
2. A lobster (Inquiry: The whole blot. These wings could be claws, too. [?] Just its head is beaked, sort of like a lobster. It's hard and stony-like. [?] Shading of the color.)	With its central detail frequently seen as a female, card I is sometimes assumed to elicit responses reflecting early attitudes toward the mother figure. Note the incorporative characteristics attributed to aspects of this card, as well as "beaked . . . hard and stony-like."
3. Ugh! A monster of some kind. Whatever it is, I don't like it at all. That's just disgusting—horrible. Frightens me somewhat. (Inquiry: Whole. It looks as if they are reaching for something, trying to engulf and eat it up. It looks like a big hand or something trying to engulf all around it. Just an ugly thing. They are all ugly. These are trying to close in on something.)	The theme of incorporation implied in the lobster responses breaks through in blatant form in the last response. Loss of distance occurs ("Frightens me somewhat"). Such attributes as "disgusting," "horrible," and "frightens me" connote significant projection, found in phobic if not paranoid patients. The departure from convention ("anus") and the disturbance in ego boundaries suggest as early as card I that the patient is schizophrenic. In this context the tendency throughout the test to give responses primarily to the whole blot is consistent with grandiose features.

(CF and C) on the Rorschach than does the obsessive-compulsive. Similar test correlates exist for many of the other distinguishing personality features found in the various disorders.

Schizophrenia is sometimes difficult to detect through structured interview only, but it may be expressed on the Rorschach as indicated below.

Poor contact with reality. The best single Rorschach indicator of reality-testing ability is the accuracy of form perception (F+%), reflecting the degree to which the person perceives with adequate critical capacity. In the schizophrenic, the poor form response is not caused by any visual-perceptual difficulty but is attributable to associational processes that are no longer subject to logical or critical control. Extremely poor responses in terms of form accuracy may alternate with accurately perceived responses.

Overgeneralization. Disturbances in thinking are sometimes reflected in the patient's tendency to overgeneralize or to make interpretations or come to conclusions based on inadequate or inaccurate inferences. The difficulty may be reflected in instances in which a tiny detail of the blot is used for making an inaccurate generalization pertaining to the whole blot—for example, card VI: "It [the whole blot] looks like a cat because here are its whiskers" (tiny detail of the blot). In other instances, the spatial relationship between discrete areas of the blot is assumed to indicate an actual relationship, albeit highly unusual in terms of reality standards. For example, card X, center bottom detail: "This is a rabbit's head, and these must be snakes coming out of the rabbit's eyes." Such combinations found in adults are most frequently schizophrenic, as are those involving the fusing of two separate responses to the same area into a single percept. For example, card I: "A butterfly woman with wings." In positional responses, the association is derived solely from the fact that the area of the blot is located where it is. For example, card III, center detail: "These must be kidneys because they are in the middle." In all such instances, the ordinary rules of logic are ignored; generalizations and conclusions are the products of illogical thought processes.

Unconventionality of thinking. Alienation and estrangement from conventional thought, with inability to think along usual, conventional lines, may be reflected in a paucity of popular responses—those commonly given by normal groups. In a record of average length, at least five or six P responses are necessary to indicate that the patient is sufficiently in contact with how other people perceive and think. While giving many unusual, even creative responses, the schizophrenic may fail to see what others feel is definite and obvious.

Idiosyncrasy of thought. The schizophrenic's thought processes are often highly personalized and idiosyncratic. For example, both schizophrenic patients and patients with organic disorders may perseverate the same response from one card to another, but the perseveration of the schizophrenic tends to be related to more bizarre, personalized material, often dealing with sex, unusual anatomy, or other personal preoccupations. In some instances the meaning given to the cards is so personalized and private as to suggest that the schizophrenic feels the blots were made as they are for him personally.

Peculiarities of language. Language peculiarities may include obvious clang associations, neologisms, and word salad. They may be extremely subtle. On the Rorschach they may be reflected in the tendency to resort to symbolic responses that have little relation to the blot itself. For example, "This looks like the history of the struggle of good and evil" (card VIII). Contaminated responses may give rise to bizarre verbalizations. For example, card IV: "The back of a tree-bear"; card V: "A bat-rabbit, no . . . I meant a rabbit-bat."

In relation to differential diagnosis, recent conceptualizations of borderline personality organization (Kernberg, 1975) have separated in terms of structural criteria a group of patients who are neither clearly neurotic nor psychotic but who previously may have been classified as borderline or pseudoneurotic schizophrenics. Singer (1977) has reported that these patients may show thinking disturbances on the Rorschach similar to those of schizophrenic patients but that unlike schizophrenics, they function adequately on the WAIS. Singer's findings support the contention that a full test battery, including both structured and projective tests, is important in evaluating a patient's functioning.

Suicide indicators. As an example of one of many kinds of predictions based on Rorschach records, suicide is an important one. It readily demonstrates the methodological difficulties in predicting an act that itself is sometimes difficult to define, that can occur only once in a single lifetime, that is sufficiently infrequent as to have low base rates in the general population, and that can be studied only in retrospect or as a future prediction without knowledge of variables other than that of personality organization that may contribute to a suicidal resolution. Nevertheless, it is clinically observed that depressed and potentially suicidal patients tend to use dark shading and black as frequent determinants in their Rorschach responses. Morbidity in thinking is frequently reflected directly in content categories with responses that suggest decay, damage, and death. The presence of rebirth fantasies is believed to enhance the likelihood of suicide. One single Rorschach sign has often been found in the records of suicidal patients. This is the color-shading response that involves the presence of shading as a determinant in a colored blot area; for example, "a red piece of velvet material, shiny like velvet." Appelbaum and Holzman (1962) suggested this response as a diagnostic indicator of suicidal potential, its significance in this regard believed to be the heightened sensitivity to affect that is thought to be characteristic of suicide. As with many other predictive signs, however, one difficulty has been with the number of false positives occurring—that is, persons who have this sign but who are not suicidal. Exner and Wylie (1977) have more recently presented a well-controlled study on effected suiciders, pretested attempters, and posttested attempters. They offer 11 signs, the color-shading response included, and report that a combination of any eight were found to have greatest probability of identifying suicidal records, while yielding a minimum number of false positives.

Body image and ego boundary difficulties. How the person views inkblots may reflect how he views or evaluates his own body, just as minutely and just as judgmentally. Hence, Rorschach responses that emphasize things or bodies being broken, damaged, with parts missing, deformed, and so forth, can often be taken as a projection of attitudes about the body and its parts.

Disturbances in ego boundaries may be reflected through the adequacy with which the patient perceives movement in the blots, particularly human movement (M). An absence of human movement responses may indicate defective empathic ability, but an overabundance of such responses may indicate withdrawal into fantasy and, in the context of poor form level, may suggest the presence of autistic features.

Disturbances in ego boundaries may also be indicated in the manner by which the patient gives his responses and his attitude toward them. In some instances, the blots may be reacted to as if they were real—for example, "A vampire and it's coming right out after me"— reflecting a loss of distance, basic to which is an inability to distinguish reality from fantasy. In other instances, the blots may be perceived as literally changing in front of the observer's eyes ("It's a larvae . . . now it's becoming a moth"). It is as though the observer were a passive participant in an event over which he has no control. Such response changes suggest alternating states of consciousness. In other instances, feelings of inner disintegration are projected onto the world—that is, the inkblots—in such a way that things are seen as falling apart, exploding, rotting away, or decomposing. World-destruction fantasies may be implied, particularly if accuracy of form perception is poor. Restitutive efforts in the form of world-reconstruction fantasies are suggested by themes of religiosity, power, strength, and so forth. The presence of numerous anatomy responses, particularly of the soft organ variety, often of poor form quality (F−), are reflections of concern related to bodily integrity, fear of bodily damage, and preoccupation with bodily functioning.

Directly related to the concept of body image is evidence presented by Fisher and Cleveland (1958) suggesting that Rorschach content in terms of the degree to which definite structure is assigned to the periphery of the inkblot image may reflect how the person perceives his body boundaries. Percepts in which the boundary is highlighted—for example, "turtle with shell," "man in armor"— are labeled barrier responses; percepts emphasizing weakness and permeability—for example, "a broken body," "a torn rug"—are labeled penetration responses. Originally, the barrier dimension was seen as being the opposite of the penetration dimension. Research findings, however, have been more supportive of the barrier index, which has been correlated with psychosomatic disturbances having an external bodily site. High barrier subjects have greater reactivity on exterior bodily indices, and low barrier subjects have greater reactivity on interior bodily indices. Perhaps most important, high barrier scores appear to be correlated with various personality characteristics that have in common what has been called self-steering behavior and include better ability to respond to a stressful situation, including surgery.

Difficulties in interpersonal relationships. One of the best single indicators of the person's basic interest in and relation to other people is contained in the Rorschach human responses, particularly when combined with movement that is appropriate to the form of the blot area and is in the context of an activity appropriate to reality as experienced by others. Cards that typically elicit human movement responses are II, III, and VII. "Withdrawal from interpersonal relationships," "lack of empathic ability," "inability to identify with others," "confused identification," and "overly critical in approach to other people" are examples of inferences made on the basis of human percepts seen or rejected by the patient. Distancing from others is suggested by responses of human beings from other cultures or worlds—for example, "18th-century dames," "Chinese ladies," "men from Mars." In contrast to records with few or no human responses, an overabundance of these responses may reflect an extreme anxiety and overconcern the patient may have about other people.

In the schizophrenic, human movement responses often occur in the context of poor form level or are inappropriately attributed to tiny details of the blot or to unusual parts of the human body. The characteristics or the activity attributed to perceived humans is often hostile in nature. Chaotic sexuality may be suggested by numerous sexual responses, often given in a bland, matter-of-fact way. Although the form qualities of certain blot areas elicit sexual responses even in normal subjects, schizophrenics tend to see sexual responses in atypical areas or delineate them with autistic elaborations.

Problems in sexual identification are often reflected in the patient's ambivalence over the sex of figures seen in ambiguous blot areas. It is normally expected that such ambiguous figures will be interpreted as of the same sex as the viewer, with a contrary identification suggesting the possibility of an opposite sex role identification. Using changing norms over recent years related to interpretation of the sex of ambiguous figures on card III, Brown (1971) concluded that there has been an increasing shift in gender blurring and confusion of sex roles in our culture. Such Rorschach signs, however, are not necessarily related to overt homosexuality, which may be difficult to infer from any sign approach to the Rorschach (Carr et al., 1960). Recent emphasis in psychoanalytic theory on structural derivatives of object relationships (Kohut, 1970; Kernberg, 1975) has led to renewed interest in the intensified analyses of Rorschach human responses given by borderline and narcissistic patients—for example, see Blatt et al. (1976) and Urist (1977). "Splitting," a characteristic defense of borderline patients, may be suggested by contrasting images, such as "a king" (implying idealization) and "a silly clown" (implying devaluation of other humans).

Prognosis. The Rorschach Test is frequently used as a basis for inferring a patient's treatment potential. Piotrowski (1961) presented long-term prognostic criteria for schizophrenics, and Klopfer (1954) developed a widely used prognostic rating scale based on Rorschach scores that has been shown to be correlated with improvement in both treated and untreated groups of patients (Endicott and Endicott, 1964). In general, prognostic indicators have not been shown to be related to specificity of treatment choice. Good prognostic indicators on the Rorschach are well-perceived and active human movement responses (related to ability to identify and empathize with other humans), well-perceived and active animal movement responses (related to impulse expression), adequate use of good form as a basis for responses (related to control and good reality-testing ability), sufficiently adequate shading and color responses (related to sensitivity, need for affection, and emotional responsivity to the environment) in a record of sufficient productivity and diversity (suggestive of personality potentialities). A recent report on the use of the Rorschach and other tests for evaluating the effects of psychotherapy (Appelbaum, 1977) suggests that the better endowed patients do better in psychotherapy than do those less endowed—essentially a manifestation of the rich-get-richer phenomenon.

OTHER INKBLOT SERIES

In an effort to overcome the psychometric limitations of the Rorschach, in which only 10 cards are used and in which there is no control on the number of responses (see Fig. 4), Holtzman (1961) constructed two parallel forms containing 45 inkblots each. The Holtzman Inkblot Technique (HIT) presumably offers richer and more varied stimuli while holding the number of responses constant by encouraging the subject to give only one response per card. The HIT offers substantially greater objectivity and precision in analysis, although it has yet to be shown to offer the clinical sensitivity of the Rorschach blots. In spite of its original promises of ultimately replacing the Rorschach, the HIT seemingly has not rivaled the Rorschach in clinical usage.

Harrower (1946) offered an inkblot test that can be both self-administered and group administered. Expendable inkblots permit the subject to mark his responses, which is time saving and effective. The test was devised as an alternate to the Rorschach, thus being particularly useful for test-retest purposes.

THEMATIC APPERCEPTION TEST

The Thematic Apperception Test (TAT) was designed by Henry Murray (see Figure 5) and Christiana Morgan as part of a case study exploration of the normal personality conducted

FIGURE 5. Henry A. Murray.

at the Harvard Psychological Clinic in 1943. It consists of a series of 30 pictures (see Figure 6) and one blank card. Only 20 of the cards were originally expected to be used with an individual subject, with the choice of some pictures depending on the subject's sex and age. It was also developed so that the test would be divided throughout two occasions, with differing instructions for each.

Today, fewer pictures are usually used, with the selection depending on the examiner's card preference and on what conflict areas he wishes to clarify with a particular patient. Frequently used pictures are the following:

1. A young boy contemplating a violin.
2. A country scene of a young woman with books in her hand, a man working in the fields, and an older woman looking on.
3BM. A huddled form of a boy with his head bowed.
3GF. A young woman standing with downcast head, her face covered with her right hand.
4. A woman clutching the shoulders of a man who looks angry.
6BM. An elderly woman with her back turned to a tall young man, who looks perplexed.
6GF. A young woman on the edge of a sofa, looking over her shoulder at an older man, who may have surprised her.
7BM. A gray-haired man looking at a younger man, who could be his son.
7GF. An older woman sitting on a sofa close beside a girl, who holds a doll in her lap.
12M. A young man on a couch and an elderly man leaning over him.
13MF. A young man standing with downcast head beside a partially clad woman lying in bed.
16. A blank card.

In the single administration, instructions are usually somewhat as follows:

I shall be showing you some pictures one at a time. I'd like you to make up a story about each picture. In your story I'd like you to tell

FIGURE 6. Card 12F of the Thematic Apperception Test. (Reprinted by permission of the publishers from *Thematic Apperception Test* by Henry A. Murray, Cambridge, Mass.: Harvard University Press, Copyright © 1943 by the President and Fellows of Harvard College; 1971 by Henry A. Murray.)

me what is happening now, what led up to this scene, and what the outcome will be. In other words, don't describe the picture to me, but make up a story about it.

Although most of the pictures obviously depict people, thus making the test stimuli more structured than the inkblots of the Rorschach Test, there is ambiguity in all the pictures. Often, one cannot be certain what the feeling state of the people is, whether they are sleeping, dead, or resting; and in some instances even the sex of the character is ambiguous. Unlike the Rorschach blots, to which the patient is asked to associate, the TAT requires that he construct or create a story (see Table III).

Approaches to the interpretation of TAT stories vary greatly. As the test was originally conceived, an important aspect of each story was the figure (the hero) with whom the storyteller seemed to identify and to whom he was presumably attributing his own wishes, strivings, and conflicts. Murray's scoring approach was directly related to his own theory of personality. Stories were viewed from the standpoint of what feelings, trends, and impulses (needs) were attributed to each hero, what forces existed in the hero's environment (press), and what resolution (outcome) resulted from the reaction between needs and press. In this approach the characteristics of people other than the hero are most easily considered as representing the subject's view of other people in his environment.

Piotrowski (1950) offered principles of TAT interpretation that assumed all the figures in a TAT story are equally representative of the subject, with more acceptable and conscious traits and motives being attributed to figures closest to the subject in age, sex, and appearance and the more unacceptable and unconscious traits and motives attributed to figures most unlike the subject. Thus, what is being projected into any TAT story presumably is related more to the multilevel facets of the

TABLE III
Stories in Response to Thematic Apperception Test Card 1 by Five Male Patients

Patient A: The boy has just flunked a test and he seems downcast, and now he's looking over work again to see what he may have missed. [Outcome?] He feels very bad. That's the outcome. Cause he failed the test.

Patient B: I just feel like I'll come up with clichés. A young boy is being forced to study the violin by his father. Reminds me of my father forcing me to do things. He could be the poor little rich kid who has everything and nothing simultaneously. More appropriately, the poor little middle-class kid. The last remark makes me think of someone I used to know. He's the opposite of this kid cause he's the happy little middle-class kid. I wish his happiness would have rubbed off on me. Sometimes I think my sadness rubs off on everyone else. The ironic thing is that the father is forcing him to do things to make him happy, but it makes him unhappy.

Patient C: This little boy is looking at his violin, wondering whether he should play. He's been practicing very hard. He practices on his own. He will want to play the violin. That's all.

Patient D: This young boy has been reading for a long time and is becoming very tired and bored. Oh, I take that back. I wasn't even looking at the picture carefully. Was reading music and playing his violin and became tired and bored and put his violin down. One earlier comment—he had been told to practice the violin by his mother, and he put it down and will fall asleep.

Patient E: Boy and music. The boy is studying parts of violin. Has music sheet underneath. Concentrating on becoming a good violinist. He's thinking that, to be good, he has to know the instrument itself as well as the music.

subject's personality than simply to his view of other people, although those two approaches to interpretation are not mutually exclusive. Other authorities (Tomkins, 1947; Aron, 1949; Shneidman et al., 1951; Bellak, 1954; Fine, 1955; Henry, 1956) offer other approaches to TAT interpretation.

The TAT offers material that can be used for many different purposes. It can be used for inferring aspects of functioning that are more easily inferred from other tests—for example, the patient's intellectual potential or his reality-testing ability. It can also be related to highly specific variables of behavior, such as has been demonstrated in its use in the extensive research on achievement motivation (McClelland et al., 1953). Perhaps the greatest contribution of the TAT lies in its potential for revealing psychodynamics as reflected in the patient's conceptions and patterns of interaction with other significant figures.

Basic to any interpretation of TAT stories is a knowledge of how the pictures are most often interpreted. Normative data are offered by Eron (1950) and Murstein (1972). Stories must be considered from the standpoint of unusualness of theme or plot. Whether the patient is dealing with a common or an uncommon theme, however, his story still reflects his own idiosyncratic approach to organization, sequence, vocabulary, style, preconceptions, assumptions, and outcome.

TAT cards have different stimulus values and can be assumed to elicit data pertaining to different areas of functioning. Thus, the interpreter brings with him certain assumptions about what is tapped by each card. For example, card 1 (boy-violin scene) implicitly deals with achievement motivation and with attitudes toward authority. Quite frequently, the boy is viewed as being made to practice. It is relevant to note who is exerting this pressure on him and what his reaction is. Does the story suggest that the boy identifies with the wishes of the authority? Is his reaction compliance or resistance? Some clinicians are willing to assume that expressed attitudes about the violin and the task posed by it may reflect underlying attitudes concerning sex role identification and body image, obviously dealing with issues other than attitudes toward music lessons.

Card 2 is usually viewed as a family scene, eliciting stories about a schoolgirl, her mother, and her father. The interests, ambitions, and goals of the girl are often at odds with the parent farmers, and resolutions of this difference are varied. Other plots may be developed. Frequently, the women are viewed as competitors for the love and attention of the man, leading to interpretations related to the oedipal complex. On other occasions, no interaction between the characters occurs, suggesting a similar absence of communication in the patient's family.

Generally, the TAT is most useful as a technique for inferring motivational aspects of behavior, expression of which may be influenced by environmental and other factors not directly related to the strength of the drive or impulse. TAT stories cannot be accepted as a direct report of the patient's overt behavior. As with dream reports, interpretation is necessary. In spite of attempts to formulate principles for inferring overt behavior from projective techniques (Carr et al., 1960), such inferences are often difficult to make. In some instances TAT themes directly mirror overt behavior. In the author's experience, for example, TAT references to aberrant sexual practices or to drug addiction have been given primarily by those persons who have engaged in such experiences. Nevertheless, the correlation is not an invariable one, and the absence of such references in no way precludes the presence of these events in the patient's life.

Similar tell-a-story tests include the Shneidman Make-a-

Picture Story (MAPS) Test (see Figure 7), in which figures and backgrounds may be chosen by either the examiner or the patient to create unlimited kinds of scenes, and the Symonds Picture Story Test, designed specifically for adolescents and composed of pictures of more youthful figures than those in the TAT.

SENTENCE COMPLETION TEST

Sentence Completion Test (SCT) responses are often most helpful in establishing level of confidence regarding predictions of overt behavior. The SCT is designed to tap the patient's conscious associations to areas of functioning in which the psychologist may be interested. It is composed of series of sentence stems (usually 75 to 100)—such as, "I like . . . " "Sex is . . . " "Sometimes I wish . . . "—which the patient is asked to complete in his own words. Since such tests are easily constructed, many psychologists have devised their own form of this test, although copyrighted forms are available. Test instructions often vary. Most frequently, some time pressure is applied, with the patient told:

Complete these sentences by writing down the first thing that comes to your mind. Don't think long about it—just try to express your real feelings.

In other instances the patient is encouraged to take all the time he needs, thus allowing him to consider thoroughly how he wishes to present himself. The test may also be administered verbally by the examiner, similar to the word-association technique, in which the patient is told he should reply with the very first thing that comes to his mind. In interpreting results, the examiner should be aware of what instructions were given, since they may influence the nature of the results obtained in terms of the degree to which the patient is given an opportunity to control and censor his responses. Sentence stems vary in their ambiguity, hence some items serve more as a projective test stimulus ("Sometimes I . . . "). Others more closely resemble direct-response questionnaires ("My greatest fear is . . . ") (see Table IV).

Numerous scoring methods have been devised for the SCT and are particularly useful when the test is being used for research purposes in which responses of different groups are to be compared. With the individual protocol, however, most psychologists simply use an inspection technique, noting particularly those responses that are expressive of strong affects, that tend to be given repetitively, or that are unusual or particularly informative in any way. Areas in which denial operates are often revealed through omissions, bland expressions, or factual reports—for example, My mother "is a woman." Humor may also reflect an attempt to deny anxiety

FIGURE 7. Shneidman MAPS. (Courtesy of The Psychological Corporation, New York.)

TABLE IV

*Examples of Sentence Completion Test Responses to the Same Stimulus by Five Male Patients**

I feel happiest when
  A. I eat.
  B. I am alone or with people I like and who like me.
  C. I'm alone.
  D. I'm enjoying being with a girl and she's enjoying being with me.
  E. Thing are right [sic].

I am afraid of
  A. life.
  B. the inevitability of life.
  C. the dark.
  D. loneliness.
  E. geting a beating [sic].

As a child, my greatest fear was
  A. of being picked on.
  B. of snakes.
  C. the truth.
  D. darkness.
  E. of bats.

I feel guilty about
  A. my life.
  B. most things.
  C. love.
  D. very few things.
  E. not done a good job [sic].

When they talked about sex, I
  A. left the room.
  B. always blushed.
  C. crawled into a ball.
  D. was relaxed and conversed freely.
  E. I said nothen [sic].

I dislike to
  A. take orders.
  B. feel weak.
  C. cheat.
  D. go places, or do things, just to be able to say I went somewhere or did something.
  E. talked about marriage [sic].

* Forer Structured Sentence Completion Test items reproduced by permission of the publisher. Copyright © 1957 by Bertram R. Forer, reprinted by permission of Western Psychological Services.

about a particular issue, person, or event. Important historical material is sometimes revealed directly—for example, I feel guilty about "the way my sister was drowned."

With a cooperative patient, sentence completions can usually be taken at face value. Relatively speaking, more conscious data are directly reported in the SCT than in other projective techniques. Since the SCT usually elicits information that the patient is quite willing to give, the level of inference is usually less than in the Rorschach Test or TAT interpretations. However, the SCT is a test on which it is also easy for the patient to deny, conceal, and defend, since the intent of most items is obvious. At times, judicious questioning of the patient clarifies the intent of ambiguous completions.

Less experience and special training are probably required to make meaningful inferences from sentence completions than from responses to most other tests. For example, compare two patients who respond as follows:

Patient A:
I like "to swim."
At night "I sleep."
My mother "is home."
My ambition is "to be the best."

I need "a rest."
Sexual relations "are habit-forming."
I consider myself to be "too fat."

Patient B:
I like "to create objects of art."
At night "I very often think of problems I dealt with during the day."
My mother "seems always to cook meals for me alone which would suffice for two or three."
My ambition is "to become a good university professor."
I need "a good set of watercolor brushes."
Sexual relations "are a fine pastime, in the right place, at the right time."
I consider myself to be "a relatively average man."

No great professional skill or knowledge is necessary to infer that important differences exist between these two patients in terms of interest patterns, drive, activity level, vocabulary, abstracting ability, self-concept, and ideal self-concept. Direct quotations from such SCT data, when included in the psychologist's report, can illustrate the patient's idiosyncratic characteristics and his major preoccupations, fears, and ambitions in a more meaningful way than can any abstraction or generalization about them made by the psychologist.

Greater difficulty is posed in the task of relating SCT data to inferences from other tests and formulating interpretations that relate overt (behavioral or conscious) aspects of functioning to the more covert (unconscious). Only through inferences from other tests and a knowledge of personality theory, for example, could it be recognized that the passivity characterizing patient A is a reaction against underlying rage over early feelings of oral deprivation. Similarly, although patient B is revealed to be a more intelligent person than A, his adjustment, as reflected in other data, is essentially schizoid; obsessive interests—art, professional career—isolate him from others, in relation to whom he has deep inferiority feelings and marked castration anxieties. SCT data help directly isolate the way unconscious motivations and impulses actually reach behavioral expression, something that is sometimes difficult to do with only fantasy (Rorschach Test and TAT) data.

The Forer Structured Sentence Completion Test (FSSCT) is a copyrighted sentence completion test designed by Bertram Forer (1957) that is ideally suited for eliciting data that can be easily integrated with and that complement other tests in the battery. The FSSCT is structured in the sense that a well-planned organization is readily revealed through the use of a check sheet, which can be used to score completions in terms of their expressed characteristics or affect. In the 100 stems, for example, six pertain to each of the important interpersonal figures: mother, father, females, males, people, and authority figures. Items are expressed variously in the first person singular ("I wish that my father . . . "), the third person singular ("Whenever he was with his father, he felt . . . "), and the third person plural ("Most fathers . . . "). Other items are designed to tap the patient's dominant wishes and drives, as reflected in responses to such items as, "He often wished he could . . . " and "Most of all I want . . . ". Particularly meaningful are specified items that tap the causes of the person's aggression ("I could hate a person who . . . "), anxiety and fear ("He felt very tense when . . . "), depression ("I was most depressed when . . . "), failure and frustration ("He felt his lack of success was due to . . . "), and guilt ("He felt to blame when . . . "). Other items tap the patient's reported reactions to such external states as aggression, rejection, failure, responsibility, sexual stimuli, and love. Alternate forms of the test are used for men, women, adolescent boys, and adolescent girls.

Other relevant sentence completion tests have been designed by J. B. Rotter, A. R. Rodhe, J. M. Sacks and S. Levy, J. G. Holsopple and F. R. Miale, and M. Stein. For reference to and a review of these and other SCT methods in personality assessment, see Goldberg (1965).

WORD-ASSOCIATION TECHNIQUE

Although one of the first projective techniques, the word-association method has been less frequently used in recent years with the advent of newer procedures, particularly the sentence completion test, which offers much more precise data. Nevertheless, the word-association test can still be of considerable value in eliciting areas of complexes and conflicts, particularly when the patient is not willing or able to discuss them openly or directly.

The technique consists of presenting stimulus words to the patient and having him respond with the first word that comes to his mind. Frequently used lists have been presented by Jung (1918) and Kent and Rosanoff (1910). Other words can be chosen to tap associations to ideas that may have emotional significance for the particular patient. Rapaport et al. (see Holt, 1968) used a list particularly suitable for psychiatric patients; it included such stimulus words as "hospital," "gun," "suicide," and "doctor," as well as words with oral, anal, and sexual connotations. Recent normative data for schizophrenic patients and normal college students have been provided by Holt. Specially designed lists have also been used for such special purposes as the detection of guilt.

Complex indicators include long reaction times, blocking difficulties in making responses, unusual responses, repetition of the stimulus word, apparent misunderstanding of the word, clang associations, perseveration of earlier responses or ideas, or unusual mannerisms or movements accompanying the response. After the initial administration of the list, some clinicians repeat the list, asking the patient to respond with the same words that he used previously; discrepancies between the two administrations may reveal associational difficulties. Judicious inquiry in the area of any suggested difficulty may clarify the nature of the problem. Because it is easily quantified, the test has continued to be used as a research instrument, although its popularity has diminished greatly over the years.

BENDER (VISUAL-MOTOR) GESTALT TEST

The Bender-Gestalt Test is a test of visual-motor coordination, useful for both children and adults. It was designed by Lauretta Bender (1938) (see Figure 8), who used it to evaluate maturational levels in children. Developmentally, a child below the age of 3 is generally unable to reproduce any of the designs meaningfully. Around 4 he may be able to copy several designs—but poorly. At about 6 he should give some recognizable representation of all the designs, though still unevenly. By 10 and certainly by 12 his copies should be reasonably accurate and well organized (see Figure 9). Bender also presented studies of adults with organic brain defects, mental retardation, aphasias, psychoses, neuroses, and malingering.

The test material consists of nine separate designs, adapted from those used by Wertheimer in his studies in Gestalt psychology. Each design is printed against a white background on a separate card. The introductory figure is a circle joined to a diagonally placed square on the horizontal plane (see Figure 10). Thereafter, figures 1 through 8 follow in sequence. Presented with unlined paper, the patient is asked to copy each one, with the card in front of him. Usually, instructions include

FIGURE 8. Lauretta Bender.

the information, "There will be nine of them in all," so that planning ability can be evaluated in terms of actual placement of designs on the page. There is no time limit. This phase of the test is quite highly structured and does not investigate memory function, since the cards remain in front of the patient while he copies them (see Figure 11, A–E). Many clinicians include a subsequent recall phase, in which, after an interval of 45 to 60 seconds, the patient is asked to reproduce as many of the designs as he can from memory. This phase not only investigates visual memory but also presents a less structured situation, since the patient must now rely essentially on his own resources. It is often particularly helpful to compare the patient's functioning under the two conditions.

Probably the most frequent clinical use for the test with adults is as a screening device for detecting signs of organically based interference, especially in gross forms. Evaluation of the protocol depends both on the form of the reproduced figures and on their relationship to each other and to the whole spatial background. Among the indicators for which the clinician looks are rotations of the designs, difficulties in angulation, faulty awareness of part-whole relationships, fragmentation or oversimplification of the figures, variability in line pressure, closure problems, distortions, omission of essential segments or additions of extraneous ones, progressive or isolated increase or decrease in size, and perseverative phenomena. The last indicator may occur either in the form of carrying over parts of previously copied figures into later ones or as the continuation of a design beyond the actual stimulus limits. Scoring

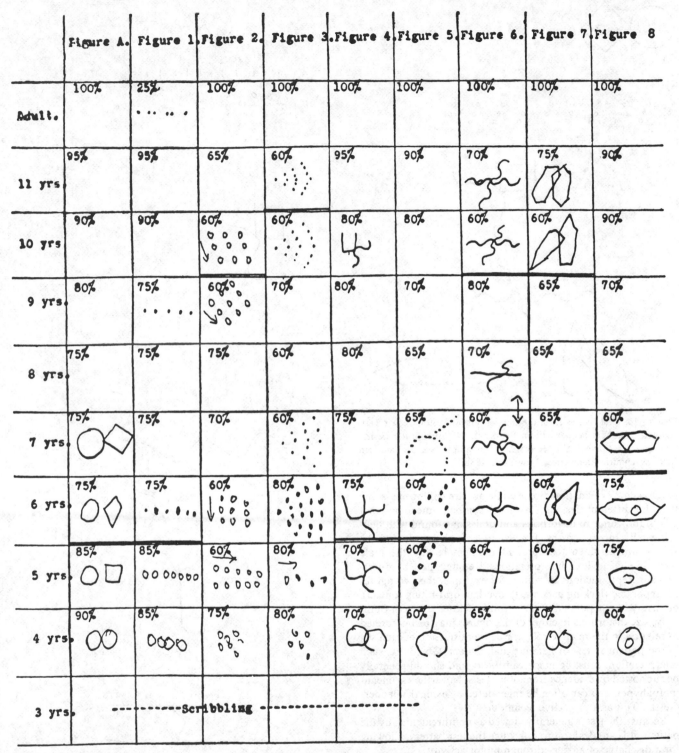

	Figure A	Figure 1	Figure 2	Figure 3	Figure 4	Figure 5	Figure 6	Figure 7	Figure 8
Adult	100%	25%	100%	100%	100%	100%	100%	100%	100%
11 yrs	95%	95%	65%	60%	95%	90%	70%	75%	90%
10 yrs	90%	90%	60%	60%	80%	80%	60%	60%	90%
9 yrs	80%	75%	60%	70%	80%	70%	80%	65%	70%
8 yrs	75%	75%	75%	60%	80%	65%	70%	65%	65%
7 yrs	75%	75%	70%	60%	75%	65%	60%	65%	60%
6 yrs	75%	75%	60%	80%	75%	60%	60%	60%	75%
5 yrs	85%	85%	60%	80%	70%	60%	60%	60%	75%
4 yrs	90%	85%	75%	80%	70%	60%	65%	60%	60%
3 yrs	----------Scribbling----------------------								

FIGURE 9. Summary of Bender-Gestalt responses for each year of age in developing children. (From Bender, L. *A Visual-Motor Gestalt Test and Its Clinical Use*, Research Monograph No. 3. American Orthopsychiatric Association, New York, 1938.)

systems have been designed for reflecting accuracy of drawings (Pascal and Suttell, 1951); although useful for research purposes, they have not gained widespread use for the analysis of an individual patient's productions.

Although the test is chiefly an instrument for studying perceptual-motor acuity, a number of other skills and attributes are tapped. For example, all the designs can be reproduced on one page and, in fact, can be cramped into one section of one page. It is also possible to use a whole page for each of the designs if the patient so chooses. Further, the designs can be reproduced meticulously or carelessly, quickly or slowly, precisely located or casually placed. Such features reflect individual personality traits, rather than visual-motor coordination as such.

If distortions in reproduction cannot be accounted for in terms of some organically based deficit, they may call for a

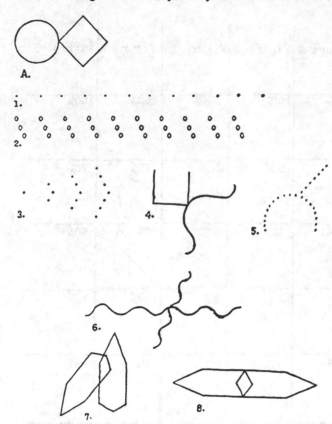

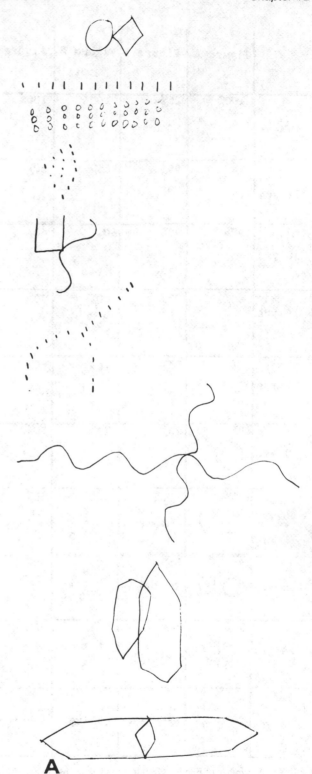

FIGURE 10. Test figures from the Bender Visual-Motor Gestalt Test, adapted from Wertheimer. (From Bender, L. *A Visual-Motor Gestalt Test and Its Clinical Use*, Research Monograph No. 3. American Orthopsychiatric Association, New York, 1938.)

psychogenic explanation. Some clinicians are willing to assume that the different designs may have symbolic meanings that give significance to distortions and omissions found with neurologically intact persons. For example, if the circle and the square are assumed to represent the female and the male respectively, obvious interpretations are suggested by differences in reproductions in which, for example, the two figures are separated (lacking in contact), overlap (oral-biting contact), or fuse without pointed contact (oral-sucking contact). Similarly, size distortions in either of the figures may be interpreted in relation to the relative role or role identification of each sex in the patient's view of heterosexual contact. Obviously, such interpretations must be made cautiously and should generally be supported by evidence from other tests. Nevertheless, meaningful hypotheses can often be engendered by using the Bender-Gestalt Test as a projective technique.

Because the test is generally viewed as nonthreatening by the patient, it is an ideal test to introduce the test battery, allowing for a discharge of anxiety through motor activity.

DRAW-A-PERSON TEST

Another graphomotor test which is frequently used as part of the test battery is the Draw-a-Person Test (DAP), first used as a measure of intelligence with children (Goodenough, 1926). Important contributions to its use as a projective technique have been made by Buck (1948), Machover (1949), and Hammer (1958). The test is easily administered, usually with the instructions, "I'd like you to draw a picture of a person; draw the best person you can" (see Figure 12, A–E). After the

FIGURE 11A. Bender-Gestalt drawings of patient A.

completion of the first drawing, the patient is asked to draw a picture of a person of the opposite sex to that of his first drawing. Some clinicians use an interrogation procedure in which the patient is questioned about his drawings—for example, "What is he doing?" "What are his best qualities?". Modifications include asking also for a drawing of a house and a tree (House-Tree-Person Test) as devised by Buck (1948), of one's family, and of an animal.

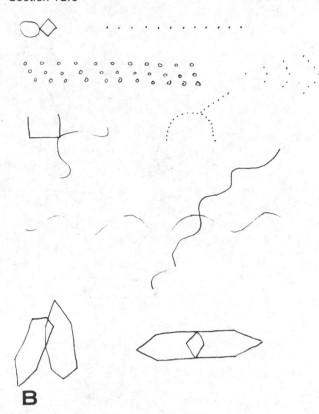

FIGURE 11B. Bender-Gestalt drawings of patient B.

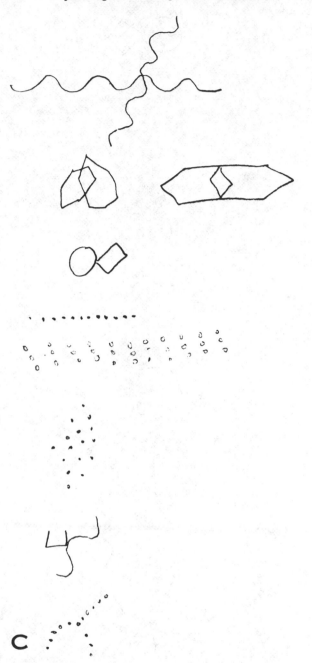

FIGURE 11C. Bender-Gestalt drawings of patient C.

A general assumption is that the drawing of a person represents the expression of the self or of the body in the environment, thus representing the self-image or body image of the drawer. Interpretative principles rest largely on the assumed functional significance of each body part. For example, since the head is the seat of the intellect and fantasy, distortions of it may lead to interpretations related to these factors. Some authorities use figure drawings for comprehensive evaluations of the personality, but most clinicians use drawings primarily as a screening technique, particularly for the detection of organic brain damage. Brain-damaged patients often have great difficulty projecting their image of the body into a figure drawing. Most clinicians do not rely on interpretation of parts or features of the drawing, since drawing ability, like handwriting, is generally subject to many influences other than personality factors. Nevertheless, experience with the drawing technique, using a gestalt approach to interpretation, allows for recognition of differences in the drawings of brain-damaged and schizophrenic patients.

MINNESOTA MULTIPHASIC PERSONALITY INVENTORY

Although usually used independently from the standard test battery, the Minnesota Multiphasic Personality Inventory (MMPI) has become an important test in research and clinical practice. The test was developed by Starke Hathaway, a psychologist, and J. Charnley McKinley, a psychiatrist, and was first published in 1943. Basic references to the MMPI include Hathaway and Meehl (1951), Welsh and Dahlstrom (1956), and Dahlstrom and Welsh (1960).

The test consists of 550 statements covering many areas of functioning, including the physical and the psychological. The patient is asked to indicate whether each statement, as applied to himself, is True or False. A "Cannot say" option is also provided for those items that are considered unanswerable or inapplicable.

Three formats for the test are available: The original (an individual card form in which each individual statement is placed in a "True," "False," or "Cannot say" pile); a group form (statements are contained in a booklet, and answers are placed on an IBM answer sheet); and Form R (a more recently modified group form with rearranged items so that basic scores can be obtained from the first 399 items, thus providing a shorter version of the test, although sacrificing items used in special scales or for research purposes). Raw scores for each scale are converted to T-scores by means of profile forms differentiated for males and females.

T-scores are obtained for nine clinical scales that carry the name for the abnormal conditions on which they were constructed (see Figure 13). An important aspect of these scales is

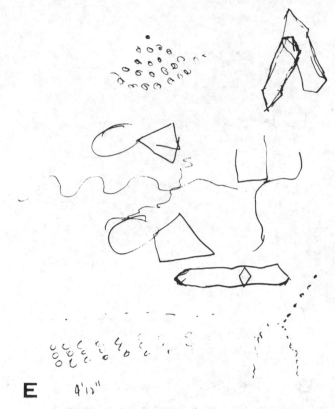

FIGURE 11E. Bender-Gestalt drawings of patient E.

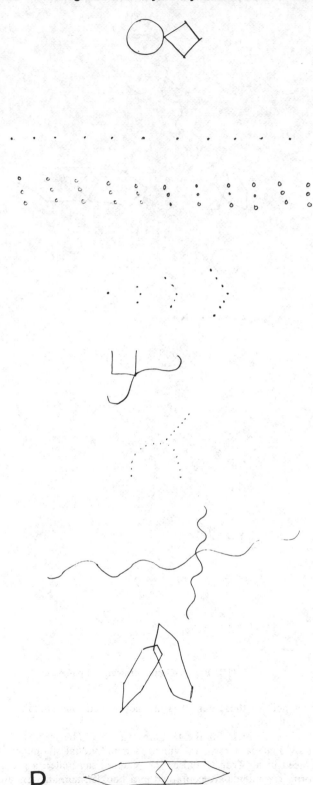

D

FIGURE 11D. Bender-Gestalt drawings of patient D.

that they were derived empirically—that is, in terms of what each of the diagnostic groups in the chosen sample actually reported about themselves that differed from what the normative population reported. Consequently, it is sometimes difficult to predict on which scale many of the items appear, since common sense or clinical intuition may be misleading.

For example, the behavior of crossing the street to avoid meeting someone may be thought to be suggestive of paranoia or schizophrenia but was more frequently claimed or admitted to by normals than by schizophrenics. Thus, even when knowing on which scale a particular item appears, one may find it difficult to predict in what direction (True or False) the item is to be scored. This empirical derivation of the scales gives the MMPI special strengths that do not characterize many other personality inventories.

The nine clinical scales are:

Hypochondriasis (Hs) Scale: 33 items of a fairly obvious nature having to do with bodily function and malfunction. The scale is assumed to reflect abnormal concern over bodily health. Although the scale rises slightly with actual physical disease, it is mainly a character scale. Physically ill patients generally score higher on the depression scale.

Depression (D) Scale: 60 items relating to such things as worry, discouragement, and self-esteem. Depression is frequently the highest scale in the profiles of psychiatric patients. As a mood scale, it may fluctuate widely over time and often reflects changes in outlook that occur with improvement in psychotherapy.

Hysteria (Hy) Scale: 60 items referring either to specific somatic complaints or to a happy acceptance of things in general (denial). As suggested by its name, the scale is reflective of massive repression. High scorers on this scale are frequently naïve and insightless people.

Psychopathic Deviate (Pd) Scale: 50 items that reflect maladjustment and absence of pleasant experiences or strong interpersonal ties. High scores are generally characterized by angry disidentification with recognized conventions. Elevation on this scale is a fairly stable feature in character disorders and the psychoses, reflecting moodiness and brooding resentment.

Masculinity-Femininity (Mf) Scale: 60 items having to do with aesthetic and vocational interests, as well as a passivity-activity dimension. Although originally intended to measure masculinity-femininity, it is

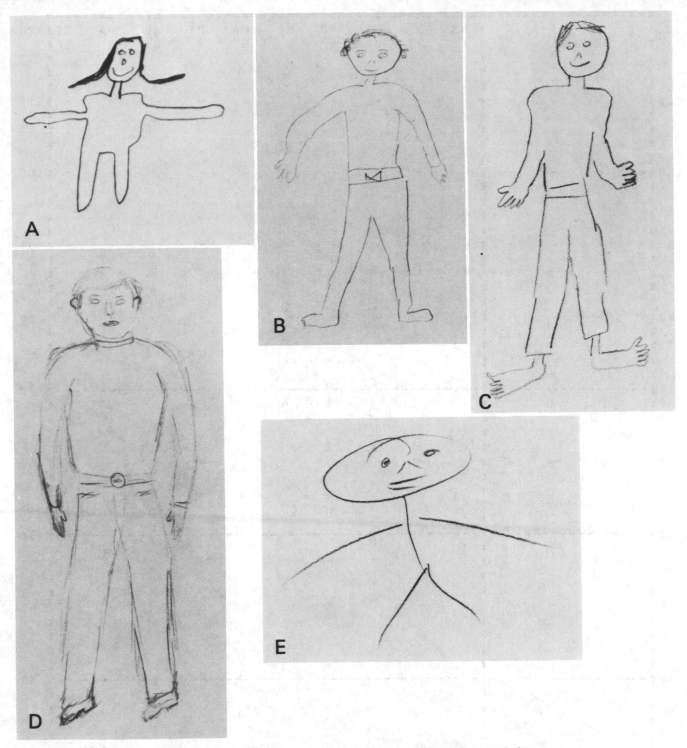

FIGURE 12. A through E. "Draw-a-Person" of patients A through E, respectively.

definitely correlated with such other factors as education and intelligence. Hence, high scores on this scale should not be taken as an indication of homosexuality, although they may reflect lack of identification with the culturally prescribed masculine and feminine roles.

Paranoia (Pa) Scale: 40 items having to do with sensitivity and being easily hurt, excessive moral virtue and claimed rationality, and complaints of persecution and suspiciousness. This scale is generally recognized as the weakest of the clinical scales, since paranoiacs may avoid detection—sometimes scoring low, rather than high. Combined with a high score on the schizophrenia scale, however, an elevation on this scale is often found with paranoid schizophrenia.

Psychasthenia (Pt) Scale: 40 items relating to narcissism, magical thinking, masochistic-sadistic tendencies, and feelings of being forced. The scale is a general measure of anxiety, self-concern, and self-doubt. Marked elevations on this scale correlate highly with an obsessive-compulsive defense system, although obsessive-compulsive persons rigidly defended against anxiety or self-doubt may actually score low on this scale.

Schizophrenia (Sc) Scale: 78 items covering social and family alienation, bizarre emotions, delusions, somatic symptoms, influence of external agents, peculiar bodily dysfunction, dissatisfaction, and depression. High scorers have fundamental questions about their own

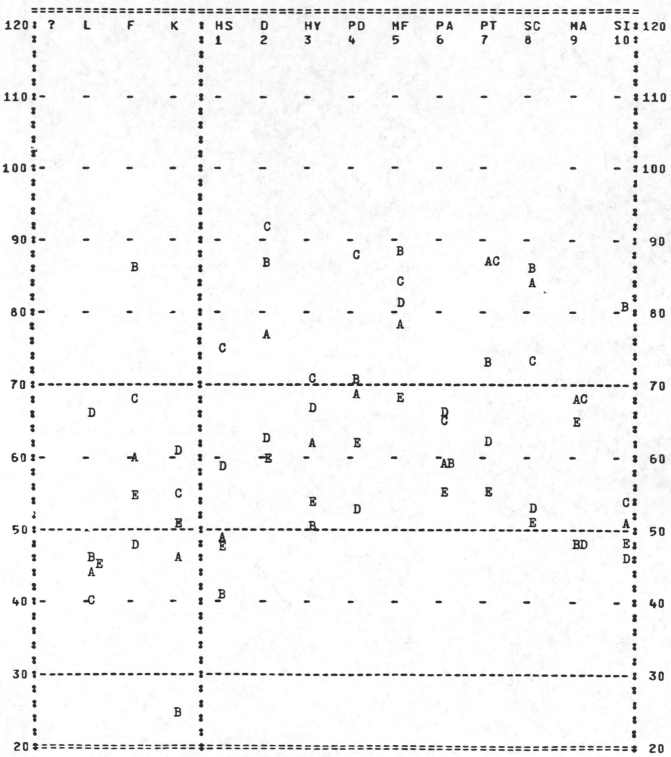

FIGURE 13. MMPI profiles of five male patients (A through E).

identity and may be confused about their lives. Difficulties in thinking and communication are also found in high scorers on this scale.

Hypomania (Ma) Scale: 46 items having generally to do with expansiveness, egotism, and irritability. Moderate ranged scorers may be enthusiastic, outgoing, and pleasant; increasingly higher scores reflect a likelihood of maladaptive hyperactivity and flightiness.

In addition to a social distance (Si) Scale that deals with items that relate to social participation, four scales reflect test-taking attitudes:

Question (?) Score: Properly speaking, one cannot call this a scale; it is simply the number of items to which the person has not answered "True" or "False." The average is considered 0 to 30 items.

L Scale: 15 items chosen to identify persons who attempt to present an overly perfectionistic view of themselves.

F Scale: 64 items that were answered almost always in the same direction by the normal standardized group. Discrepantly high F scores suggest that the profile may be invalid, either because of scoring errors or because the person failed to understand the instructions. Otherwise, it may be assumed that the person is characterized by unusual or markedly unconventional thinking or that he wishes to put himself in a bad light, since he is admitting to relatively deviant items.

K Scale: 30 items selected as a measure of guardedness or defensiveness in test-taking attitude. High scorers are people who cannot tolerate suggestions that they are insecure, having difficulty in social relations, or do not have their lives well ordered.

F-K Index: The ratio of F to K has been used with some success as an indication of faking good or bad. When F minus K taken as raw scores is positive and greater than 11, it suggests a conscious attempt to look bad. When the index is negative and greater than 12, it suggests an effort to look good and to deny emotional problems.

Although the MMPI was designed and is labeled as an objective personality test, the characterization "objective" may be misleading. It must be stressed that individual scales cannot be taken at face value. For example, a high Sc score does not indicate that the patient is necessarily schizophrenic, nor does a high Mf score necessarily indicate either latent or overt homosexuality. It is necessary to relate each scale to all the other scales for an accurate profile interpretation, which requires great experience with the test and some understanding of the social, educational, and class background from which the patient comes. Recent evidence suggests that religion and race are both potential variables in MMPI responses (Costello, 1977; Groesch and Davis, 1977).

Apart from profile interpretation, however, it is often helpful to examine MMPI responses on an inspection basis, using the test simply as a form of interview. Checking responses to critical items may reveal important facts about what or how the patient chooses to report himself in relation to questions that may not otherwise have been asked. For example, it may not be known that the patient admits to being fascinated by fire or having used alcohol excessively only because the patient has not been asked about these matters; the MMPI asks these and other diverse questions and provides an organization of the responses to them in a systematic way.

Commercial computer services are available that offer fairly sophisticated interpretations of the MMPI, although these interpretations should always be evaluated against the total clinical evidence. Two widely used services are Roche Psychiatric Service Institute in Nutley, New Jersey, and The Psychological Corporation in New York.

INTEGRATION OF TEST FINDINGS

The integration of test findings into a comprehensive, meaningful report is probably the most difficult aspect of psychological evaluations. Inferences from different tests must be related to each other in terms of the confidence the psychologist holds about them and of the presumed level of the patient's awareness or consciousness of being tapped.

Most psychologists follow some general outline in preparing a psychological report. The following discussion indicates aspects of functioning that are often included and reveals what tests are most likely to contribute to the formulation of each section of the report. In some instances, important references are noted.

TEST BEHAVIOR

This section is best confined to strict behavioral data; deep-level inferences or high-level abstractions are to be avoided—for example, "autistic," "delusional," "manic." It is better to report, "The patient hung her head and cried" than to say, "Depression was evidenced." Reports often include much extraneous material in this section. In most settings there is no need to report, "The patient has blue eyes" or even that she "has pretty blue eyes." Basically, the major purpose of

this section is to convey whether the test results can be assumed to be valid and, if not, what reservations should be placed on them.

INTELLECTUAL FUNCTIONING

Presentation of the findings regarding intellectual functioning is easily accomplished and is most directly represented by WAIS interpretations. In addition to I.Q.'s, the scaled subtest scores should be reported and interpreted in terms of the patient's revealed relative strengths and weaknesses in the intellectual sphere. If possible, the patient's potential should be inferred.

PERSONALITY FUNCTIONING

Reality-testing ability. Judgment about reality-testing ability can generally be made most directly from the WAIS and the Rorschach, although other tests may also contribute to the judgment. The distinction between reality testing in structured and unstructured situations is called for. For structured situations, the Comprehension and Picture Completion WAIS Subtests are probably most relevant. For unstructured situations, the Rorschach form level and number of popular responses must be considered specifically, along with the general adequacy of the Rorschach protocol. In evaluating the Rorschach from this standpoint, the psychologist must keep in mind that even the Rorschach blots differ in their unstructuredness or ambiguity, just as do all the projective tests in the battery.

Impulse control. Judgments about impulse control obviously cannot be made independently of those pertaining to reality-testing ability. Other factors to be evaluated include availability of recourse to fantasy gratification and the presence of anxiety, depression, or guilt, which may serve to inhibit impulse expression. Use of the Rorschach is directly relevant, particularly as reflected in the FC/CF,C, and the Fc/cF,c relationships. The SCT includes statements eliciting causes of aggression, anxiety, fear, depression, failure, responsibility, sex, and love. The psychologist must keep in mind that SCT data are more subject to the conscious control of the patient in terms of the image he is choosing to present. Hence, even the rapport with the examiner and motivation at the time of testing may be variables relevant to an analysis of the relationships between tests.

Manifest depression and guilt. Manifest depression and guilt are often most directly revealed through TAT themes and SCT completions. As a measure of psychomotor speed, the Digit Symbol Subtest of the WAIS is particularly vulnerable to the effects of depression, as may be all the timed performance tests. One must be alert to the presence of compensatory mechanisms that obscure an underlying depression, probably best inferred from the Rorschach. A discrepantly high Digit Symbol score on the WAIS is sometimes found to reflect such reactive strategies.

Manifestations of major dysfunction. Judgments regarding manifestations of major dysfunction include such issues as general variability in function, difficulties in thought processes, affective disturbances, interpersonal difficulties, and ego boundaries. Recourse to the full test battery must usually be taken in order to make such judgments. The Rorschach is relevant for clarifying some of these issues.

Major defenses. No proper evaluation of major defenses should be undertaken without thorough knowledge of Schafer's *Psychoanalytic Interpretation in Rorschach Testing* (1954). Some defenses are often highlighted dramatically on tests other than the Rorschach. For example, a discrepantly high Information Subtest score on the WAIS reflects attempts at intellectualization; the avoidance of depressive themes on the TAT, in spite of the stimulus value of the cards, reflects a manifestation of denial; and the negation of cause for anger on the SCT reflects reaction formation.

Overt symptoms. The present symptoms may be detected from the patient's direct report on the SCT (I wish "I were dead"), or they may be inferred from other test data. It should be recognized that the prediction of overt behavior solely through the use of projective techniques may be very difficult to do with certain disorders. Some helpful principles are presented in *The Prediction of Overt Behavior through the Use of Projective Techniques* (Carr et al., 1960).

Interpersonal conflicts. Examination of the total test results usually allows the psychologist to make a statement about the patient's relationship with each of the interpersonal figures or representatives indicated. Ideally, it is a dynamic statement in the sense of its relating consciously expressed attitudes to feelings less available to the patient's awareness or to assumed early genetic determinants. The basis for such a statement typically involves data from more than one test. The FSSCT includes sentence stems that specifically elicit conscious attitudes to each of the important interpersonal figures, such as the mother. The TAT includes particular cards that presumably tap similar attitudes to these figures, such as the mother-son and the mother-daughter cards. The Rorschach elicits responses that, because of their content significance (such as oral content) or because of the assumed stimulus value of what elicited the response, are also relevant to such interpersonal figures as the mother. Research has shown that responses to such stimuli can be scored reliably in terms of such affective content areas as dependency, hostility, anxiety, and positive feelings. In general, the level of inference from SCT to TAT to the Rorschach varies directly with the assumed level of awareness that is presumably being tapped. Attention should be directed to all such relevant test data before the final inference is formulated about the mother or any other interpersonal figure. If meaningful inferences cannot invariably be formulated about each of these figures, it is often most helpful to quote the evidence that may be potentially meaningful in light of the full clinical history.

Self-concept. Evaluation of the self-concept involves reference to the full test battery. Figure drawings may be especially revealing. On the SCT, dominant drives (wishes) should be inspected. Interpretation of Rorschach content and TAT themes may be most helpful for inferring unconscious self-perceptions.

Affects. The FSSCT was especially designed to elicit both causes of and reactions to the major affects: aggression, anxiety, depression, guilt, and dependency. The ideal formulation, however, must take recourse to other evidence as well, particularly TAT and Rorschach data, which presumably tap deeper levels of awareness. Defenses often become highlighted through direct reference to test responses or data, even without interpretation or high-level inference.

INFERRED DIAGNOSIS

Tests merely elicit samples of behavior that can be recorded. Clinical insights are arrived at on the basis of inference. The inferential process regarding clinical diagnosis leaves much to be desired. A relevant caution is that the suggested diagnosis should be consistent with the reported findings. To maintain such consistency, the clinician must have a knowledge of psychodynamic theory. For example, if repression is the only defense listed, a diagnosis of paranoid schizophrenia is hardly appropriate. If the psychologist achieves adequate understanding of the patient, the diagnostic label generally follows logically. Hence, diagnosis should be more than simply a labeling of the patient, since, when properly used, it reflects his total hierarchical functioning.

DEGREE OF PRESENT OVERT DISTURBANCE

Regardless of diagnosis offered, it is often helpful to indicate the degree of present overt disturbance, including the patient's ability to handle practical details of everyday life and some judgment as to his degree of incapacitation. In making this inference, the psychologist should base his statements on the patient's present condition, without reference to potential or likelihood of change.

PROGNOSIS FOR SOCIAL RECOVERY

Particularly when the degree of present incapacitation is marked, it is helpful to evaluate the prognosis for social recovery. In this regard, it is relevant to indicate the correlation between good social recovery and the presence of strong affective features, regardless of type of treatment or even in the absence of any treatment. The use of color

and shading on the Rorschach and an evaluation of all assets should be indicated.

MOTIVATION FOR PERSONALITY CHANGE

Related to the issue of motivation for personality change is the judgment of what, if anything, the patient may want changed about himself. Many patients really desire the change to occur in others or in reality. Some seek mere symptom removal. The psychologist's judgment should be made in relation to all the available evidence.

PRIMARY ASSETS AND WEAKNESSES

These sections of the report should include a discussion of the patient's strengths and weaknesses, as reflected in intellectual functioning and personality functioning.

RECOMMENDATIONS

This section is used to elicit whatever recommendations stem from the previously reported inferences. It may involve suggestions ranging from occupation or vocational guidance, suicidal cautions, and recommended type of treatment. Whatever the recommendation, it should follow logically from the previously reported data.

SUMMARY

This section should include a succinct summary of the patient's personality functioning. However fragmented the previous conclusions may have been, this section should be integrated into a coherent summary.

Psychological Report

The following presents an example of a routine psychological report for patient D:

Name: Patient D
Date of birth: January 4, 1956
Age: 22   Sex: Male
          Date of testing: April 7, 1978
Tests Administered:
WAIS
Rorschach
TAT, SCT, MMPI
Bender-Gestalt Test
Draw-a-Person Test

The patient is a mild, pleasant-appearing young man of 22 who reports having headaches for the past 2 or 3 years. He has recently graduated from college and is looking forward to beginning law school in the fall. He readily cooperated with the test instructions but seemed most comfortable when given structure by the examiner.

The patient is functioning at the superior level of intelligence, with a Full-Scale I.Q. of 127. His Verbal I.Q. is at the very superior level (132), and his Performance I.Q. is at the bright normal level (116). Variability in functioning ranges from the average to the very superior levels, with subtest scores as indicated below:

Information	16
Comprehension	16
Arithmetic	17
Similarities	14
Digit Span	14
Vocabulary	—
Digit Symbol	12
Picture Completion	14
Block Design	13
Picture Arrangement	15
Object Assembly	9

Within a structured situation as typified by the WAIS, the patient functions with ease and efficiency. All subtest scores are average or above, with relative strengths in arithmetic (computational) skills, accumulated factual knowledge, and awareness of social convention. He did poorest on a motor task dealing with part-whole relationships, particularly when working toward an unknown goal. There is no evidence to suggest any cerebral malfunctioning. In fact, the evidence appears to contraindicate this possibility: His graphomotor productions are well executed; he has a perfect score in arithmetic computations; immediate, recent, and remote recall are intact. His intellectual potential is clearly in the superior to very superior range.

Personality functioning appears to be consistent with an outwardly controlled, perfectionistic, status-oriented, tense person whose ability to think along usual conventional lines appears assured and whose reality-testing ability is adequate. Although he has a very good intellect, he harbors underlying fears that he is not adequate, with his anxiety about relating to others probably greater than his presently felt depression.

Related to his tension is the threat of loss of control over hostile impulses about which he has little insight. Pressure of these impulses is inferred from "explosion" and "atom bomb" percepts on the Rorschach Test. Hostility may be projected onto others, with a threat or fear of retaliation from others in the form of bodily harm as punishment for his projected anger. On the SCT, he states: *I could hate a person* "who enjoyed killing others." Nevertheless, his TAT productions involve a great deal of fantasied aggression, typical of which is his story to the picture of an older man bending over a young boy: "Two men had a business disagreement and the older man is in the process of killing by smothering his business associate. The older gentleman will be caught and sent to prison." Punishment is invariably viewed as the outcome of any expression of anger or rage.

While able to maintain a façade of being involved and capable (*People seem to think that I* "can do whatever I want"), he is much less sure of himself and less at ease than he appears (*In a group of people I generally feel* "lost in the crowd"; *More than anything else he needed* "security"; *I am afraid of* "loneliness"). Consistent with such insecurity is the report that, as a child, he had a fear of the dark. He generally reacts against his underlying passive-dependency needs, without being aware of his motivations.

Although he stresses his heterosexual satisfactions, it may be that the patient is not as confident about his sexual functioning as he would like, since his interest patterns, as revealed on the MMPI, are somewhat feminine for a youth from his culture. Guilt over and fear of self-damage from masturbation are suggested. His earliest memory is from the age of 5 (oedipal stage) and concerns falling through a window while searching for a ball and cutting his nose. The father has been viewed as generally unavailable, presumably because he spends so much time on his business. The patient is not totally comfortable in the presence of the mother, undoubtedly partially because of unresolved oedipal conflicts. To the story of an operation scene on the TAT, the patient told this story: "A young boy has shot an older man when he saw the man with his mother. The injured man is being operated on. The bullet is being removed from his stomach. The young man feels partial remorse but only partial guilt. He felt it necessary to protect his mother."

Another story also suggests that the patient feels in some way he must be protective of the mother, who is viewed as being too concerned with material things. Although she is reportedly more available for communication than the father, secrets within the family are an issue (the patient reports being upset at the age of 17 when he learned, a couple of years after the fact, that the sister had had an abortion, and on the SCT he indicates: *I was most annoyed when* "my oldest sister repeated things that I told her in confidence"). The patient may tend to harbor grudges about such perceived misdemeanors and be suspicious, particularly toward women. In its mildest form, this feeling comes out in his admitted view that women act as though they can manipulate men. In general, he may alternate between devaluating and idealizing others (human-like responses on the Rorschach range from

"clowns" to "supernatural beings" and "the emblem of Jesus Christ Superstar, the play").

Admitting that he is not absolutely certain of his present choice of law for graduate work, the patient feels some pull toward the father's business, which the father would prefer the son's entering. His felt responsibilities to others leave him feeling somewhat pressured and harried. Although law school may be a way of avoiding the father's business in an acceptable way, the patient has strong exhibitionist impulses that are thereby not being satisfied (*He often wished he could* "become a movie star"). In the latter respect, the patient loves to play the guitar and sing for himself and others, but his level of achievement motivation toward parental goals is probably more closely reflected in his TAT story to the boy-violin scene. "This young boy has been reading for a long time and is becoming very tired and bored. Oh, I take that back, I wasn't even looking at the picture carefully. Was reading music and playing his violin and became tired and bored and put his violin down. One earlier comment—He had been told to practice the violin by his mother and he will put it down and will fall asleep." Strong passive-aggressive components may be expected in his behavior.

Over-all evidence seems most consistent with a neurotic personality organization, although some borderline features are present. With strong needs to be accepted and defensive about admitting any psychological weakness (other than being tense and harried), he is somewhat naïve about psychological motivations, particularly in regard to his own competition and aggression. Seeking symptomatic relief of his headaches, he would probably be resistive to and resent any psychological interpretations, so that getting him established in psychotherapy may be a difficult task. He has many assets, however, including a relatively intact and high-level intellectual functioning, so that psychotherapy should be given a trial period. Resolution of career goals may be helpful in alleviating his physical symptom.

In summary, the patient is functioning at the superior level of intelligence with a Full-Scale I.Q. of 127. His reality-testing ability seems adequate, although insight into his own motivations is poor. He is tense and defensive about admitting psychological weakness and shows denial and mild projection as defenses. A somatic resolution is quite likely in the present setting. In any event, there is no evidence of any cerebral malfunctioning in the test results to account for his headaches.

Supplementary Data

Opinions differ among both psychiatrists and psychologists as to whether test results should be interpreted blindly—that is, without knowledge of other clinical data about the patient—or with knowledge of all relevant clinical information. At times, referring sources may prefer that psychological evaluations be done only on the basis of test findings, totally independent of any knowledge about the patient other than his age and sex. Most psychologists have no difficulty in functioning in this manner, although it cannot be denied that the richest interpretation of test data can be made in the light of certain clinical and historical information about the patient. For example, the religion of the patient is usually not relevant to the interpretation of test results; nevertheless, if the patient reports the Rorschach response, "Christ on the cross," it may be helpful to know something of his religious beliefs. Similarly, "embryo" responses on the Rorschach may be interpreted differently if it is known that the patient recently had an abortion. If the psychologist is viewed as an expert diagnostic consultant, there should be no concern that he will be biased or intimidated by a knowledge of background information on the patient. Ideally, it should be the psychologist's function to determine what information he would like and to seek it from appropriate sources.

The present author has found it especially valuable to elicit certain reports from the patient through the use of a self-report questionnaire that elicits material of psychodynamic and genetic relevance, material usually not elicited directly by the psychological test battery. Although designed specifically to be used in conjunction with this battery, it has also been found helpful when used in the absence of any formal test data, either independently or as a complement to a standard case history or psychiatric interview.

In its present form the questionnaire comprises three pages, usually requiring 15 to 25 minutes for completion. As such, it elicits a more complete sample of handwriting and expressive ability than does the standard test battery as usually administered. The clarity of expression and detail varies strikingly between patients, as does the obvious conscientiousness with which the task has been approached. A discussion of the items follows:

Describe the kind of person your mother is and your relationship to her. Describe the kind of person your father is and your relationship to him.

Experience has demonstrated the value of eliciting directly from the patient his perceptions of and his relationship to each parental figure. The importance of the patient's relationship to each parent not only as a parent but as a representation of sexual role hardly needs justification.

The test battery provides stimuli to elicit attitudes to parental figures ranging from the presumed conscious (on the SCT) through other levels, as provided by the TAT and the Rorschach. The SCT presumably taps conscious attitudes toward the referrent; however, it does not invariably do so. Asking patients to check their completions for those that express their own feelings reveals wide differences in the proportion of responses that are accepted as self-descriptions. Even first person singular items (*When my father came home, I. . .; I wish that my mother. . . .*) have been shown to alternate between that of projective stimulus and that of a direct-response questionnaire. SCT completions may themselves be ambiguous—*Most mothers are great* may carry the meaning that *Most mothers are great,* " particularly my own" or *Most mothers are great,* "but mine isn't." Undoubtedly, the nature of the response elicited by the SCT is influenced somewhat by test instructions, particularly the application of time pressures, although even here patients have been found to be very inconsistent in their manner of response. For these and other reasons, it is worthwhile to pinpoint exactly how the patient does choose to present each parent when there is no disguise as to the intent of the stimulus and little ambiguity regarding the response itself.

These data must be carefully evaluated in terms of their source and the level of inference involved, with the psychologist being particularly alert to any apparent inconsistency of inferred affect. For example, the figure toward whom the greater threat appears to be projected on the Rorschach is frequently the figure decribed most lovingly in conscious descriptions. The impression gained is similar to the finding of Harris (1948) that a large number of persons who report dreams presumably reflecting a fear of loss of love and support (a threat in our culture generally emanating from the mother figure) more frequently report conscious hostility to the father. Likewise, those who report dreams presumably reflecting fear of castration and bodily harm (a threat generally emanating from the father figure) more commonly report conscious hostility to the mother. It is as if hostility were expressed to the safer figure, rather than to the more threatening one. Denials, reaction formations, projections, and so forth, can most easily be recognized when the examiner has a clear idea of what the patient is willing and able to report directly.

List by age and sex your brothers and sisters, indicating whether they are living or dead.

Although a vast literature on the correlation between birth order and personality characteristics has been developed, the original and continuing intent of eliciting the above data is not for any routine attribution of invariable personality qualities to the patient in terms of his birth order. In the context of other test and clinical data, however, the information pertaining to the age and the sex of siblings often helps to establish critical experiences in the life of the patient, facilitating an understanding of the setting in which the patient was reared. Assumed to be particularly important in this effort are the periods at which the

patient's relationship with parental figures may have been substantially changed. Obviously, the mother's pregnancy and the arrival of a new competitor would have had quite different meanings and consequences to a child still in the oral stage of development as opposed to a child in the phallic stage or in adolescence when the sibling arrived. The death of a sibling, either before or after the patient's own birth, would have had other consequences, possibly establishing inordinate expectations or feelings in both parent and child and serving as a basis for feelings in the child that range from his being something very special because he escaped the sibling's fate to the assumption that in some way he was responsible for it. Consistent with the assumption underlying the rationale for the total questionnaire is reliance on the important temporal relationships that may reveal anniversary reactions, a phenomenon that exists with much greater frequency than is usually recognized and that is difficult to detect with only the usual test battery.

List any childhood difficulties, such as bed wetting, temper tantrums, and fears.

Although the data elicited herewith have not always been found to enrich the interpretation of test data in any direct way, the report of childhood symptoms provides a fuller understanding of the atmosphere in which the patient was raised and offers an indication of whether childhood hurdles were taken in a progressive way without the development of serious symptoms. It may be particularly helpful in determining whether the patient's present symptoms are simply a continuation of a pattern established in childhood or whether they represent a shift or change from earlier functioning. For example, psychogenic headaches in adult patients referred to the author for evaluation have been found to vary in date of onset from the age of 7 to that of quite recent origin. Similarly, phobic adult patients have shown wide variation as to whether their present phobia is a continuation of a fear held since childhood, when it may have been appropriate, or whether it emerged in adulthood. Consistent with interpretation of other sections of the questionnaire, approximate times of events are important in evaluating their significance within a life history.

Indicate time and nature of any experiences that were especially upsetting to you.

A report from the patient's view of what experiences were upsetting is helpful in gauging the kinds of threat that have been perceived by the patient as traumatic. The variety of such experiences is wide, although frequently focusing on such events as those that involve separation and loss or threat to bodily integrity. The kinds of experiences upsetting in adulthood can be assumed to represent repetitions of experiences in early childhood. Denial may operate, of course; hence, the total evidence must be examined to determine how the patient's self-report is to be interpreted.

Describe in detail the earliest experience you remember, regardless of whether or not it seems important. Indicate age at which experience occurred.

The practice of eliciting the patient's first memory often uncovers important data that can be usefully exploited within the context of the full test battery. Both Freud (1953, 1960) and Adler (1937) illustrated relevant aspects of the earliest memory, although from different viewpoints, since Freud was more concerned with the concealing or screen function of memories at a time when interest was essentially in id psychology. Adler's view that the earliest memory reflects the person's life style appears closer to present conceptions of psychoanalytic ego psychology. Important contributions to the classification and interpretation of earliest memories have been made by Lieberman (1957), Mosak (1958), and Mayman (1968). An important predictive study with a useful classificatory system has been offered by Langs (1965); Kramer et al. (1971) compared a survey of dream content with early memories, following up an earlier suggestion (Kramer et al., 1967) that early memories reflect more long-standing, characterological problems, while the dream may be more related to current stresses.

Indicate any recurring dream(s) you may have had any time in your life.
Indicate any recent dream(s) you recall.

The rationale for eliciting dreams, whether recent or those of a recurring nature, hardly needs explication to the dynamically oriented reader. Two specially relevant notes, however, may be highlighted.

1. The contribution of Piotrowski (1971) illustrates the application of rules of interpretation originally developed for the TAT. Earlier studies have shown consistencies between inferred affective components of dream imagery and Rorschach responses (Bolgar, 1954), but Piotrowski has formulated a specific theory and explicit rules of interpretation that bring dreams directly into the area of projective test theory. Using the concept of remoteness—a reference to the degree to which various dream figures resemble the dreamer, in turn reflecting the degree to which the dream figure's characteristics are acceptable to the dream—Piotrowski offers what may ultimately be classified as a breakthrough in the difficult task of predicting overt behavior, removing dream interpretation from the field of art to that of science.

2. Dreams occurring just before scheduled testing should always be considered from the standpoint of possibly reflecting potential transference attitudes toward the evaluation procedure. How the patient is essentially viewing the process (benevolently or malevolently) and what may be the defenses erected against the perceived threat are often apparent in the dream occurring at this time.

Describe your present sleep habits, indicating any difficulties in going to sleep, waking up, nightmares, etc. Indicate whether there has been any recent change in your sleep patterns.

The patient's sleep patterns are often a good index to whether depression and anxiety are kept in bounds and whether there are periods when the patient can relax sufficiently to surrender easily to sleep. Some authorities accept the view that people who have difficulty going to sleep are more anxious, whereas those who go to sleep easily but awaken early are more depressed. Onset of sleep difficulties often serves as an index to time of precipitating events of the disorder. The patient's response to sleeping disturbances is also of interest. Risk of suicide is enhanced if patient reports being unable to sleep.

List your present physical difficulties and complaints.
List your previous illnesses and operations.

The richest interpretation of thematic content can be made if the examiner has some awareness of any real or imagined physical illnesses or limitations. Even what may be assumed to be obvious physical attributes are often not readily observable. The prediction of the specificity of symptom choice in the area of the psychosomatic disorders can present dramatic evidence of the soothsaying abilities of the clinician, but it is usually much easier and efficient simply to ask a cooperative patient whether he had any illnesses, operations, or physical symptoms other than the usual childhood disorders. The time of the reported event (accident, surgery, or onset of illness) may be important in elucidating character or symptom formation.

What do you like best about yourself?
What do you like least about yourself?

The patient's self-report on what he likes best and least about himself is often of great help in evaluating the general strengths and weaknesses reflected throughout the other data. Particularly relevant is the fact that the patient often reports aspects of his functioning that add or diminish his self-esteem in terms of characteristics not evaluated in the usual psychological or psychiatric evaluation ("courage," "sense of humor," "responsibility"). Although such assets may be considered as rather superficial aspects of functioning in a report presumably dealing with psychodynamics, these characteristics play an important role in determining how the patient is accepted or responded to by others in critical areas of living. It is relevant to note how enduring the qualities are that are chosen as best and least liked, whether or not they pertain to important values in society, and whether they pertain to physical, intellectual, or personality issues—in short, where the areas of self-pride and self-criticism reside.

What would you change about your personality, if possible?
What would you change about your body, if possible?

These questions direct specific attention to two different aspects of the self that the patient may desire to change. Often the answers reflect what it is the patient really is seeking to change in psychotherapy and may point up wishes that cannot reasonably be fulfilled—for example, the patient who really wants only to be young again. The answers offer an opportunity for the clinician to evaluate the insight of the patient in the degree that he holds realistic appraisals of his own personality and his body. It is interesting to note patients who, with what are obvious bodily defects or personality liabilities, select other seemingly minor or undiscernible things that they wish were changed. Patients may report the desire to change things that the examiner feels are the very strengths and assets of the patient.

Indicate nature and duration of your present psychological problems. (Try to be as explicit as you can be.)

The patient's report of his own psychological problems is often of inestimable value in gauging how he perceives himself and his relationship to the outside world. It is surprising how many patients referred presumably because of psychiatric reasons, report that they feel they have no problems other than some physiological complaint, such as headaches. There is often a major discrepancy between what the referring source reports as the patient's difficulty and what the patient reports. In some instances, patients appear to be giving emphasis to minor issues while ignoring seemingly more important ones. On the other hand, patients often report in a most meaningful way what their difficulties are when viewed from the internal frame of reference, recorded without recourse to abstract generalizations or professional jargon.

What do you feel has been the cause of your present difficulties?

Again, patients vary tremendously as to what they perceive will help them. It is believed that professional assistance will have its best chances of succeeding if it is somewhat consistent with what the patient views himself as needing. Patients' responses often highlight the inappropriateness of a clinician's recommendations based only on what the clinician deems the patient really needs.

Conclusion

Psychological tests may make an important contribution to the understanding of how the patient acts (behavior) and why he acts that way (motivation). Their usefulness is sometimes enhanced if the examiner has access to some supplementary (nontest) data. Nevertheless, the interpretation of psychological tests requires training and experience on the part of the examiner if competent evaluations are to be made.

Suggested Cross References

For further information about psychological tests used to find evidence of brain damage, see Section 12.7. Section 35.3 discusses psychological testing of children. Concepts of perception and cognition, fundamental in the projective and intelligence tests, are covered in Sections 4.1 and 12.5.

TABLE V

Personality Tests Commonly Used by Clinical Psychologists

The table below provides a brief reference to the major personality tests used by clinical psychologists. More detailed references to these and other techniques may be found in the Buros *Mental Measurements Yearbooks.*

Name	General Classification	Description	Special Features
Rorschach Technique	Projective technique	Ten inkblots used as basis for eliciting associations	Especially revealing of personality structure. Most widely used projective technique.
Holtzman Inkblot Technique	Projective technique	Two parallel forms containing 45 inkblots each	Unlike Rorschach, the number of responses is held constant.
Harrower Inkblot Technique	Projective technique	Ten inkblots similar to Rorschach	Devised as alternate form of Rorschach. May be self-administered or group administered.
Thematic Apperception Test (TAT)	Projective technique	Ambiguous pictures used as stimuli for making up a story	Especially useful for revealing personality dynamics. Some pictures are designed specifically for women, men, adolescent girls, and adolescent boys.
Shneidman Make-a-Picture Story (MAPS) Test	Projective technique	Pictures created with cut-outs and background settings	Great flexibility, since combinations are unlimited.
Symonds Picture Story Test	Projective technique	Pictures of adolescents	Designed specifically for adolescents.
Bellak Children's Apperception Test	Projective technique	Drawings of animals for children	Designed specifically for children.
Van Lennep Four-Picture Test	Projective technique	Four very ambiguous pictures	Order of pictures is determined by storyteller in creating a single story.
Kahn Test of Symbol Arrangement	Projective technique	Sixteen symbolic objects that subject arranges on cloth strip	Identifies subject's cultural-symbolic thinking pattern. Allows for free projection. Test may also be objectively scored.
Lowenfeld Mosaic Test	Projective technique	Plastic pieces in varied colors and shapes	Subject is instructed, "Make anything you like out of the pieces."
Rosenzweig Picture Frustration Test	Projective technique	Cartoon situations, dialogue to be completed by subject	Designed specifically to assess patterns of reaction to typical stress situations. Child, adolescent, and adult forms.
Word-Association Technique	Projective technique	Stimulus words to which patient responds with first association that comes to mind	Flexible; may be used to tap associations to different conflict areas. Generally not as revealing as SCT responses.
Sentence Completion Test	Varies from direct-response questionnaire to projective technique	Incomplete sentence stems that vary as to their ambiguity	Highly flexible; may be used to tap specific conflict areas. Reveals generally more conscious, overt attitudes and feelings.
Blacky Test	Projective technique	Cartoons about a dog and his or her family used to elicit stories with subsequent interrogation about each	Systematized approach to different stages of psychosexual development. Designed for both children and adults, it is used more widely with children.

TABLE V—*Continued*

Name	General Classification	Description	Special Features
Draw-a-Person Test	Graphomotor projective technique	Patient asked to draw a person and then one of the sex opposite to the first drawing	Projects body image, how the body is conceived and perceived. Sometimes useful for detecting brain damage. Modifications include: Draw an animal; draw a house, a tree, and a person (H-T-P); draw your family; draw the most unpleasant concept you can think of.
Bender (Visual-Motor) Gestalt Test	Graphomotor technique; may be used as projective technique	Geometric designs that the patient is asked to draw or copy, with design in view	Useful for detecting psychomotor difficulties correlated with brain damage.
Minnesota Multiphasic Personality Inventory (MMPI) (Forms: Individual, Group, and Shortened R)	Objective personality test	Questionnaire yielding scores for 9 clinical scales in addition to other scales	Includes scales related to test-taking attitudes. Empirically constructed on basis of clinical criteria. Computer interpretation services available.
Cattell 16 Personality Factor Questionnaire (16 PF)	Objective personality test	Questionnaire covering 16 personality factors derived from factor-analytic studies	Bipolar variables allow for interpretation of scores varying either above or below the norm, such as reserved versus outgoing; trusting versus suspicious; timid versus venturesome.
California Personality Inventory	Objective personality test	Seventeen scales developed presumably for normal populations for use in guidance and selection	Less emphasis on mental illness than MMPI scales, such as, dominance, responsibility, socialization.
Edwards Personal Preference Schedule	Objective personality test	Forced-choice inventory to show relative importance of 15 key needs or motives, such as nurturance, achievement, order, autonomy	Related to Murray's needs theory. Format presumably reduces effects of social desirability.

REFERENCES

Adler, A. The significance of early recollections. Int. J. Indiv. Psychol., *3:* 283, 1937.

Ames, L. B., Métraux, R. W., and Walker, R. N. *Adolescent Rorschach Responses,* rev. ed. Brunner/Mazel, New York, 1971.

Appelbaum, S. A. *The Anatomy of Change: A Menninger Foundation Report on Testing the Effects of Psychotherapy.* Plenum Publishing Corp., New York, 1977.

Appelbaum, S. A., and Holzman, P. S. The color-shading response and suicide. J. Proj. Tech., *26:* 155, 1962.

Aron, B. *A Manual for Analysis of the Thematic Apperception Test: A Method and Technique for Personality Research.* Willis E. Berg, Berkeley, Calif., 1949.

Aronow, E., and Reznikoff, M. *Rorschach Content Interpretation.* Grune & Stratton, New York, 1976.

* Beck, S. J. *Rorschach's Test,* vols. 1, 2, and 3. Grune & Stratton, New York, 1944–1952.

Bellak, L. *The Thematic Apperception Test and the Children's Apperception Test in Clinical Use.* Grune & Stratton, New York, 1954.

* Bender, L. *A Visual Motor Gestalt Test and Its Clinical Use.* American Orthopsychiatric Association, New York, 1938.

Blatt, S. J., Brenners, C. B., Schimck, J. G., and Glick, M. Normal development and psychological impairment of the concept of the object on the Rorschach. J. Abnorm. Psychol., *85:* 364, 1976.

Bolgar, H. Consistency of affect and symbolic expression: A comparison between dreams and Rorschach responses. Am. J. Orthopsychiatry, *24:* 538, 1954.

Brown, F. Changes in sexual identification and role over a decade and their implications. J. Psychol., *77:* 229, 1971.

Buck, J. M. The H-T-P Technique, a qualitative and quantitative scoring method. J. Clin. Psychol., *4:* 317, 1948.

Buros, O. K. *Mental Measurements Yearbooks.* Gryphon, Highland Park, N. J., 1938–1978.

Carr, A. C., Forer, B. R., Henry, W. E., Hooker, E., Hutt, M. L., and Piotrowski, Z. A. *The Prediction of Overt Behavior Through the Use of Projective Techniques.* Charles C Thomas, Springfield, Ill., 1960.

Costello, R. M. Construction and cross-validation of an MMPI black-white scale. J. Pers. Assess., *41:* 514, 1977.

Dahlstrom, W. G., and Welsh, G. S. *An MMPI Handbook: A Guide to Use in Clinical Practice and Research.* University of Minnesota Press, Minneapolis, 1960.

DeVos, G. A quantitative approach to affective symbolism in Rorschach responses. J. Proj. Tech., *16:* 133, 1952.

Elizur, A. Content analysis of the Rorschach with regard to anxiety and hostility. Rors. Res. Exch. J. Pers. Tech., *13:* 247, 1949.

Endicott, N. A., and Endicott, J. Prediction of improvement in treated and untreated patients using the Rorschach prognostic rating scale. J. Consult. Psychol., *28:* 342, 1964.

Eron, L. A normative study of the Thematic Apperception Test. Psychol. Monogr., *64:* 1, 1950.

* Exner, J. E. *The Rorschach: A Comprehensive System,* vols. 1 and 2. John Wiley & Sons, New York, 1978.

Exner, J. E., and Wylie, J. Some Rorschach data concerning suicide. J. Pers. Assess., *41:* 339, 1977.

Fine, R. A scoring scheme for the TAT and other verbal projective techniques. J. Proj. Tech., *19:* 306, 1955.

Fisher, S., and Cleveland, S. E. *Body Image and Personality.* D. Van Nostrand, New York, 1958.

Forer, B. R. *The Forer Structured Sentence Completion Test Manual.* Western Psychological Services, Beverly Hills, 1957.

Freud, S. Leonardo da Vinci and a memory of his childhood. In *Standard Edition of the Complete Psychological Works of Sigmund Freud*, vol. 11, p. 59. Hogarth Press, London, 1953.

Freud, S. Childhood memories and screen memories. In *Standard Edition of the Complete Psychological Works of Sigmund Freud*, vol. 6, p. 43. Hogarth Press, London, 1960.

* Goldberg, P. A. A review of sentence completion methods in personality assessment. J. Proj. Tech. Pers. Assess., *29:* 12, 1965.

Goldfried, M. R., Stricker, G., and Weiner, I. B. *Rorschach Handbook of Clinical and Research Applications.* Prentice-Hall, Englewood Cliffs, N. J., 1971.

Goodenough, F. L. *Measurement of Intelligence by Drawings.* World Book Company, New York, 1926.

Groesch, S. J., and Davis, W. E. Psychiatric patients' religion and MMPI responses. J. Clin. Psychol., *33:* 168, 1977.

Hammer, E. F., editor. *The Clinical Application of Projective Drawings.* Charles C Thomas, Springfield, Ill., 1958.

Harris, I. Observations concerning typical anxiety dreams. Psychiatry, *11:* 301, 1948.

Harrower, M. *Manual for Psychodiagnostic Ink Blots and Parallel Series of Ink Blots.* Grune & Stratton, New York, 1946.

Hathaway, S. R., and Meehl, P. E. *An Atlas for the Clinical Use of the MMPI.* University of Minnesota Press, Minneapolis, 1951.

Henry, W. E. *The Analysis of Fantasy: The Thematic Apperception Technique in the Study of Personality.* John Wiley & Sons, New York, 1956.

Hertz, M. R. *Frequency Tables for Scoring Rorschach Responses,* ed. 5. Press of Western Reserve University, Cleveland, 1970.

* Holt, R. R., editor. *Diagnostic Psychological Testing,* by D. Rapaport, M. M. Gill, and R. Schafer, rev. ed. International Universities Press, New York, 1968.

Holt, R. R. A method for assessing primary process manifestations and their control in the Rorschach. In *Rorschach Psychology*, M. A. Rickers-Ovsiankina, editor, ed. 2, p. 375. Krieger, Huntington, N.Y., 1977.

Holt, R. R. *Methods in Clinical Psychology,* vols. I and II. Plenum Publishing Corp., New York, 1978.

Holtzman, W. H. *Holtzman Inkblot Technique.* Psychological Corporation, New York, 1961.

Jung, C. G. *Studies in Word Association.* Dodd, Mead & Co., New York, 1918.

Kent, G. H., and Rosanoff, A. A study of (word) association in insanity. Am. J. Insanity, *67:* 37 and 317, 1910.

Kernberg, O. *Borderline Conditions and Pathological Narcissism.* Jason Aronson, New York, 1975.

Klopfer, B. *Developments in the Rorschach Technique,* 2 vols. World Book Company, New York, 1954–1956.

Klopfer, B., and Kelley, D. M. *The Rorschach Technique.* World Book Company, New York, 1942.

Kohut, H. *Analysis of the Self.* International Universities Press, New York, 1970.

Kramer, M., Ornstein, P. H., Whitman, R. M., and Baldridge, B. J. The contribution of early memories and dreams to the diagnostic process. Compr. Psychiatry, *8:* 344, 1967.

Kramer, M., Winget, C., and Whitman, R. M. A city dreams: A survey approach to normative dream content. Am. J. Psychiatry, *127:* 1350, 1971.

Langs, R. J. Earliest memories and personality. Arch. Gen. Psychiatry, *12:* 379, 1965.

Levine, M., and Spivack, G. *The Rorschach Index of Repressive Style.* Charles C Thomas, Springfield, Ill., 1964.

Lieberman, M. G. Childhood memories as a projective technique. J. Proj. Tech., *21:* 32, 1957.

* Machover, K. *Personality Projection in the Drawing of the Human Figure.* Charles C Thomas, Springfield, Ill., 1949.

Mayman, M. Early memories and character structure. J. Proj. Tech. Pers. Assess., *32:* 303, 1968.

McClelland, D. C., Atkinson, J. W., Clark, R. A., and Lowell, E. I. *The Achievement Motive.* Appleton-Century-Crofts, New York, 1953.

Mosak, H. H. Early recollections as a projective technique. J. Proj. Tech., *22:* 302, 1958.

* Murray, H. A. *Thematic Apperception Test Manual.* Harvard University Press, Cambridge, 1943.

Murstein, B. I. Normative written TAT responses for a college sample. J. Pers. Assess., *36:* 109, 1972.

Pascal, C. R., and Suttell, B. J. *The Bender-Gestalt Test.* Grune & Stratton, New York, 1951.

Piotrowski, Z. A. A new evaluation of the Thematic Apperception Test. Psychoanal. Rev., *37:* 101, 1950.

Piotrowski, Z. A. *Perceptanalysis: A Fundamentally Reworked, Expanded, and Systemized Rorschach Method.* Macmillan, New York, 1957.

Piotrowski, Z. A. A rational explanation of the irrational: Freud's and Jung's own dreams reinterpreted. J. Pers. Assess., *35:* 503, 1971.

Piotrowski, Z. A., and Bricklin, B. A second validation of a long-term Rorschach diagnostic index for schizophrenic patients. J. Consult. Psychol., *25:* 135, 1961.

Reitan, R. M. Psychological testing of neurological diagnosis. In *Neurosurgery: A Comprehensive Reference Guide to the Diagnosis and Management of Neurosurgical Problems.* J. R. Youmans, editor, p. 423. W. B. Saunders, Philadelphia, 1973.

Rorschach, H. *Psychodiagnostik.* Bircher, Bern, 1921.

Schachtel, E. G. *Experiential Foundations of Rorschach's Test.* Basic Books, New York, 1966.

* Schafer, R. *Psychoanalytic Interpretation in Rorschach Testing.* Grune & Stratton, New York, 1954.

Shneidman, E. S., Joel, W., and Little, K. B., editors. *Thematic Test Analysis.* Grune & Stratton, New York, 1951.

Singer, M. T. The borderline diagnosis and psychological tests: Review and research. In *Borderline Personality Disorders*, B. Hartocollis, editor, p. 193. International Universities Press, New York, 1977.

Tomkins, S. S. *The Thematic Apperception Test: The Theory and Technique of Interpretation.* Grune & Stratton, New York, 1947.

Toomey, L. C., and Rickers-Ovsiankina, M. A. Tabular comparisons of scoring systems. In *Rorschach Psychology*, M. A. Rickers-Ovsiankina, editor, ed. 2, p. 609. Krieger, Huntington, N.Y., 1977.

Urist, J. The Rorschach test and the assessment of object relations. J. Pers. Assess., *41:* 3, 1977.

Wade, T. C., and Baker, T. B. Opinions and use of psychological tests. Am. Psychol., *32:* 874, 1977.

Welsh, G. S., and Dahlstrom, W. G., editors. *Basic Readings on the MMPI in Psychology and Medicine.* University of Minnesota Press, Minneapolis, 1956.

12.7 Psychological Testing for Brain Damage

ARTHUR L. BENTON, Ph.D., D.Sc.

Introduction

As the primary integrative mechanism of the human organism, the central nervous system (CNS) mediates mental processes and complex behavioral reactions, as well as somatic and vegetative responses. Consequently, disease or injury at the higher levels of the CNS is likely to be reflected in disturbances in mentation, feeling, and conduct. This basic fact makes behavioral assessment an integral part of clinical neurological evaluation, particularly when the question of disease involving the cerebral hemispheres has been raised. Such behavioral assessment can be accomplished in various ways: by direct observation of the patient's behavior in a natural setting, from the description of informants of the patient's present and past conduct, by questioning and observation during the interview, and by the use of neuropsychological tests. All these approaches have proved to be useful in aiding diagnostic inference.

The method of tests differs from the other approaches in a number of respects. A test is essentially an attempt to elicit a specific type of behavior under relatively controlled stimulus conditions. This control is achieved by presenting a defined task or stimulus-complex in a standardized manner to every patient. Moreover, the task or stimulus-complex is of such a nature as to evoke behavior that is relatively easily described in objective and quantitative terms.

Because of their relatively objective and quantitative nature, psychological test methods are often designated as laboratory procedures, comparable to serology, electroencephalography, and radiology with respect to the role that they play in neuropsychiatric diagnosis. The designation is accurate in one sense and inaccurate in another. It emphasizes the distinctive contribution that these methods can make, as contrasted with the more global forms of behavioral evaluation, in providing findings characterized by a degree of precision and objectivity that cannot be obtained through the use of the other methods.

Moreover, it assigns neuropsychological test methods their proper role as an aid to or component of the total clinicodiagnostic process. However, there is also a fundamental difference between such procedures as serology or electroencephalography and neuropsychological test methods. The former deal with infrabehavioral events, the latter with behavioral events. Classes of phenomena not otherwise open to analysis are disclosed through the use of the infrabehavioral techniques. In contrast, neuropsychological test methods deal with overt behavior, a class of phenomena already available, actually or potentially, to global clinical evaluation. As a matter of fact, many neuropsychological tests were developed to objectify and quantify impressions already gained from general clinical observations.

To a considerable degree, the aspects of behavior sampled by clinical observation and by neuropsychological tests are the same—for example, speed of response, level of comprehension, and use of language—but the test procedures assess these aspects of behavior with greater reliability and precision. The tests go on to sample other aspects of behavior, such as visual memory and psychomotor skill, that are not readily elicitable in the general examination. Thus, the use of neuropsychological tests serves both to validate the impressionistic findings of the general clinical examination and to provide additional information about other aspects of intellect and personality (see Table I).

It is a truism that behavior has multiple determinants and that the same behavioral deviation may be produced by factors of a diverse nature. Hence, when behavioral deficits that raise the question of cerebral dysfunction are observed in a patient, one must consider other possible determinants of defective performance before making the inference of cerebral disease. Among these possible determinants are: (1) lack of adequate cooperation and effort on the part of apathetic, hostile, asocial, or paranoid patients; (2) lack of mental energy in patients who are depressed or seriously depleted by systemic extracerebral disease; (3) inattention and concentration difficulty associated with preoccupation or intense anxiety; (4) simulation or exaggeration of mental incompetence, particularly when there are questions of a pension or compensation for injuries received; (5) poor understanding and task adjustment on the part of culturally handicapped patients.

General Intelligence and Dementia

The clinical observation that patients with cerebral disease may show an over-all behavioral inefficiency and be unable to meet the diverse intellectual demands associated with the responsibilities of daily life dates back many centuries. The observation is expressed in the global concepts of dementia or deterioration. The normal counterpart of these pathological concepts is the concept of general intelligence, which is equally global in nature. The application of this concept in clinical practice assumes that there is a sufficient degree of positive intercorrelation among various intellectual abilities to warrant the conclusion that a single general ability is a significant component in performance on diverse intellectual tasks—verbal skills, perceptual capacities, abstract reasoning, and the like. Granted this reasonable assumption, one can derive a single score from a battery of mental tests and use this score as an index of general intelligence. This is what is done when a mental test battery such as the Wechsler Adult Intelligence Scale (WAIS) (Wechsler, 1958; Matarazzo, 1972), the Halstead-Reitan battery (Halstead, 1947; Reitan, 1955a; Chapman and

Wolff, 1959), or any other reasonably comprehensive set of tests is given to a patient and his scores on the various subtests are combined into a total score yielding an I.Q. or an equivalent measure.

Dementia implies an over-all impairment in mental capacity, with consequent decline in social and economic competence. The concept has always been the target of criticism. In 1911, Bleuler (1950) characterized dementia as "an unclear concept ... almost as broad as mental disease itself." More recent authors, such as Stengel (1964) and Zangwill (1964), have condemned the concept as being too vague to be useful and as discouraging identification of the specific cognitive defects that a patient may show. These strictures are justified. There are, in fact, clinically distinguishable types of dementia—for example, an aphasic type, an amnesic type, a type showing prominent visuoperceptual and somatoperceptual defects, and a relatively pure type manifesting impairment in abstract reasoning and problem solving within a setting of fairly intact linguistic and perceptual capacity. It is also true that all too often the diagnosis of dementia has been applied inappropriately to patients with specific aphasic and amnesic disorders, as well as to those who are confused or psychotic.

Nevertheless, despite its limitations, the global concept of dementia has demonstrable neurological significance, as well as pragmatic value. Chapman and Wolff (1959) found that both the Wechsler-Bellevue Performance Scale I.Q. and the Impairment Index derived from the Halstead battery correlated to a significant degree with the estimated amount of cerebral tissue loss in patients with excised neoplasms. Even stronger evidence that a measure of dementia is useful for inferring both the presence and the extent of cerebral disease comes from the study by Blessed et al. (1968) in which senile patients were given a mental test battery, the results of which were correlated with postmortem findings. A highly significant and fairly close association ($r = .59$) was found between the total score on the mental test battery and the mean number of senile plaques counted in samples of cortex from different areas of the brain. Similarly, Willanger (1970) was able to demonstrate a significant correlation between general intellectual impairment and the degree of cortical atrophy as estimated from pneumoencephalography.

As noted, a number of more or less distinctive subtypes of dementia can be identified on clinical grounds. For example, although some degree of memory defect is characteristic of all cases of dementia, a subgroup of patients show pronounced impairment comparable in severity to that seen in Korsakoff's syndrome or in the amnesic syndrome associated with bilateral temporal lobe disease. It was on the basis of the clinicopathological correlations in a demented patient with particularly severe memory defects that Glees and Griffith (1952) first suggested the importance of bilateral hippocampal destruction in the genesis of memory disorders. Other demented patients show striking agnosic defects, pointing to significant focal brain involvement within the context of diffuse disease (Horenstein, 1971). Aphasic dementia, indicating particularly severe involvement of the zone of language in the left hemisphere, is another recognized subtype. A subcortical dementia—the major features of which are slowness in thinking, poor calculating and abstracting ability, and emotional alterations, with relatively intact verbal and perceptuomotor capacities—has also been identified (Albert et al., 1974). Finally, of tremendous importance because of the possibility of effective therapeutic intervention are the potentially reversible dementias associated with hyperlipidemia and normal pressure hydrocephalus (Adams et al., 1965; Adams, 1966; Benson et al., 1970; Heilman

TABLE I

Tests for Assessing Brain Damage

Category	Subcategories	Remarks
General scales	Wechsler scales (WAIS, WISC, WPSSI) Stanford-Binet Halstead-Reitan battery	Given the availability of adequate normative standards in relation to the patient's educational and cultural background, a performance significantly below expectations should raise the question of cerebral damage. This generalization applies to both adults and children.
Reasoning and problem solving	Shipley Abstractions Raven Progressive Matrices Gorham Proverbs Elithorn Perceptual Mazes Porteus Mazes Goldstein-Scheerer Sorting Tests Wisconsin Card-Sorting Test	Performance level is closely related to educational background and premorbid intellectual level. In general, the clinical application of these tests is more useful in the case of educated patients. If specific language and perceptual defect can be ruled out as determinants of defective performance, failure suggests frontal lobe involvement or diffuse cerebral disease.
Memory and orientation	Repetition and reversal of digits Visual memory for designs Auditory memory for words or stories Visual memory for words or pictures Temporal orientation Serial digit learning	For complete assessment, a number of memory tasks (auditory versus visual, verbal versus nonverbal, immediate versus recent) should be given. Defects in temporal orientation suggestive of impairment in recent memory may be elicited.
Visuoperceptive and visuoconstructive	Identification of hidden figures Discrimination of complex patterns Facial recognition Inkblot interpretation Block design construction Stick arranging Copying designs Three-dimensional block construction Visuospatial judgment	These tasks are useful indicators of the presence of cerebral disease. Analysis of qualitative features of performance and comparison of performance level with the status of language and reasoning abilities often provide indications with regard to the locus of the lesion.
Somatoperceptual	Finger recognition Right-left orientation Responsiveness to double tactile stimulation	These are useful indicators of the presence and the locus of cerebral disease.
Language	Token Test Controlled Word Association Illinois Test of Psycholinguistic Abilities Diagnostic reading tests	Test performance depends on educational background, and clinical interpretation must allow for this and other possibly significant factors. In adult patients, defective performance (particularly in relation to other abilities) suggests dysfunction of the cerebral hemisphere that is dominant for language. In children, defective performance does not have this localizing significance but does raise the question of the presence of cerebral damage. Performance on verbal reasoning tests, such as Shipley Abstractions and Gorham Proverbs may also disclose specific impairment in language function.
Attention, concentration, motor abilities, information processing	Simple and choice reaction time Visual vigilance Imitation of movements Paced Serial Addition	There are useful behavioral indicators of the presence and sometimes the locus of cerebral disease that deserve more extensive clinical application.

and Fisher, 1974; Messert and Wannamaker, 1974; Mathew et al., 1975).

OBTAINED I.Q. VERSUS EXPECTED I.Q.

In this country, the WAIS is by far the most widely used test battery to assess general intelligence in adults. In its clinical application a number of procedures have been used to evaluate the possibility of a decline in general intelligence that may be ascribable to the presence of cerebral disease. The most direct approach is to compare a patient's obtained age-corrected I.Q. score with the age-corrected I.Q. score that may be expected in view of his educational background, cultural level, and occu-

pational history. A negative discrepancy—an obtained I.Q. below the expected I.Q.—that is beyond empirically established normal limits may be interpreted as raising the question of the presence of cerebral disease. This procedure has been shown to have some clinical usefulness (Fogel, 1964). However, many patients with unquestionable cerebral disease do not show an over-all decline in general intelligence of sufficient severity to be reflected in a significant lowering of their WAIS I.Q. score. Consequently, this procedure yields a fair proportion of false negative results. This is perhaps to be expected when an instrument is used for a purpose for which it was not originally designed.

A variant of this procedure is to compare obtained and

expected I.Q. scores on the WAIS Performance Scale, which consists, for the most part, of nonverbal and relatively novel tasks. This comparison has proved to be practically as useful as the comparison of Full-Scale I.Q. scores (Fogel, 1964).

SENSITIVE VERSUS INSENSITIVE TASKS

Since it has been found, at least in nonaphasic patients, that certain types of performance tend to be more seriously affected by cerebral damage than are others, a second approach has been to compare performance level on presumably less sensitive tasks with that on more sensitive tasks. Thus, Verbal Scale I.Q. is compared to Performance Scale I.Q. or performance on a set of insensitive tests, such as Information or Picture Completion, is compared with performance on a set of sensitive tests, such as Arithmetic or Block Designs. Although widely used by clinical psychologists, procedures that rely on a discrepancy score or a deterioration ratio within the test battery itself have been found to possess only relatively modest clinical usefulness (Fogel, 1964; Violon and Rustin, 1971).

IMPAIRED PERFORMANCES

A third approach has been to focus attention on those subtest performances—Block Designs, Arithmetic, Digit Symbol— that clinical experience indicates are most frequently and severely impaired in patients with cerebral disease. This is a rational procedure, but full exploitation of its clinical value depends on the availability of valid and precise normative standards of performance in relation to age, educational background, and sex. In a given clinical setting the establishment of such standards may require the development of local norms, since test performance patterns may vary in different parts of the country and among different cultural groups.

Reasoning and Problem Solving

Impairment of the capacity for abstract reasoning and reduction in behavioral flexibility when confronted with an unfamiliar situation are well-known behavioral characteristics of the brain-damaged patient. Both types of deficit are important components of Goldstein's (1948) concept that the fundamental behavioral change resulting from cerebral disease is a "loss of the abstract attitude."

A relatively large number of special tests designed to measure each of these capacities have been devised. Among those that have shown clinical usefulness are the Shipley Abstractions (Shipley and Burlingame, 1941), the Progressive Matrices of Raven (1958; Irving et al., 1970), the Proverbs Test of Gorham (1956; Fogel, 1965), the Mazes of Porteus (1959; Sterne, 1969), the Elithorn Perceptual Mazes (Benton et al., 1963), the Sorting Tests of Goldstein and Scheerer (1941), and the Wisconsin Card-sorting Test (Berg, 1948; Milner, 1963).

Defective performance by brain-damaged patients is frequent enough, but one must determine the basis for a given patient's failure. Language skills play an important role in performance on some tests; other tests make demands on visuoperceptive capacity. Hence, one must rule out language and perceptual handicaps as determinants of a defective performance before making the inference that the performance indicates impaired reasoning or impaired problem-solving ability.

These tests have proved to be particularly valuable for disclosing behavioral deficit in the neurologically negative patient with frontal lobe or beginning diffuse cerebral disease who shows no specific sensory, perceptual, language, or motor impairments and who, on initial encounter, may appear to have a functional psychiatric disorder. Conversely, these tests are less useful for the specific purpose of inferring brain disease when applied to unintelligent or uneducated subjects or those suffering from psychosis.

The following case report illustrates the usefulness of both general intelligence tests and abstract reasoning tests in arriving at a diagnosis of a neurologically negative patient whose behavior raised the question of cerebral disease.

A 49-year-old married woman was referred for neurological evaluation because of a recent personality change and her own complaint of inability to carry on a conversation. Her educational background was 3 years of college. The family noted lapses of memory and a loss of interest in household affairs over the preceding several months. In addition, she had had frequent crying spells. She had lost some weight but was not anorectic. Her medical history consisted essentially of a variety of somatic complaints, including nervous stomach and irregular menses with long periods of amenorrhea, for which she had been hospitalized and surgically explored, always with negative results. A recent check-up at a local hospital had also failed to disclose an organic basis for her distress.

The findings on neurological examination were uniformly negative. Cranial nerve function was completely intact, and sensory and motor status was normal. She showed satisfactory orientation for time, place, and person, showed normal expression and comprehension of speech, repeated seven digits and reversed four digits, and performed serial sevens adequately. The electroencephalogram (EEG), which showed some mixed slightly slow activity, was interpreted as nonspecifically abnormal. The neurologist's impression at this stage of the work-up was that there was no definite evidence of CNS disease and that a functional psychiatric disorder was a possibility. Nevertheless, features of the clinical picture had an organic flavor, and a neuropsychological examination was requested to secure details about cognitive functioning.

When seen for neuropsychological examination, the patient was friendly and cooperative but showed a rather bland affect. Attention and concentration were good. She seemed fatigued after 40 minutes of testing but made no complaints; on being asked, she acknowledged that she was tired, and the examination was terminated. Performance on a large segment of the examination was on a normal level. Aphasia testing disclosed no disturbances in object recognition, object naming, oral language comprehension, reading, or writing. She repeated seven digits and reversed four. Immediate visual memory (Benton Visual Retention Test) was within normal limits. Tactile formboard performance (modified Halstead-Reitan procedure), constructional praxis, temporal orientation, right-left discrimination, and finger recognition were also normal.

However, in contrast to these adequate performances, she showed significant impairment on tasks requiring abstract reasoning or capacity for deliberation. Her performance on the Gorham Proverbs Test was grossly defective, with many responses indicative of a concrete level of thinking. The same concreteness in thinking was shown in her handling of the items of the WAIS Similarities and Comprehension Subtests, both of which were almost completely failed (scaled scores of 4 and 2, respectively). Her performance on the Elithorn Perceptual Mazes was characterized by failure to deliberate before responding and by a grossly defective over-all performance level. Her WAIS Full-Scale I.Q. was 80, Verbal Scale I.Q. was 72, and Performance Scale I.Q. was 92.

The obtained WAIS Full-Scale I.Q., which was at least 25 points below expectation, was considered presumptive evidence of the presence of cerebral disease, since she was alert and cooperative and, at the same time, neither depressed nor preoccupied. It may be noted that the use of deterioration ratios (Verbal Scale I.Q. versus Performance Scale I.Q., sensitive versus insensitive subtests) would not have led to the inference of cerebral disease, since her Performance Scale I.Q. was actually higher than her Verbal Scale I.Q., and her performance on such sensitive subtests as Arithmetic Reasoning and Digit Span was higher than on such relatively insensitive subtests as Comprehension.

The distinctive performance pattern, with its positive and negative features—adequate performance on linguistic, visuoperceptive, visuoconstructive, and somatoperceptual tasks versus gross defect in abstract reasoning and problem solving—led the examiner to infer cerebral disease with bilateral frontal lobe involvement. Pneumoencephalography subsequently disclosed cortical atrophy apparently limited to the frontal areas, and a diagnosis of early presenile dementia was made. Her progressive deterioration over the course of the next year substantiated the diagnosis.

Memory

Impairment of various types of memory, most notably short-term and recent memory, is a prominent behavioral deficit in brain-damaged patients, and it is often the first sign of beginning cerebral disease and of aging. For this reason, procedures for the assessment of memory functions have always found a prominent place in the mental status examination and in psychological test batteries.

Memory is a comprehensive term that covers the retention of all types of material over different periods of time and involving diverse forms of response. Empirical study has shown that a person's performance on retention tasks may vary significantly as a function of a number of factors, such as the sensory modality involved (auditory versus visual), the type of material to be remembered (verbal versus nonverbal), and the form of response required (recognition versus reproduction, vocal versus manual). Consequently, the neuropsychological examiner is more inclined to give specific memory tests and evaluate them separately than to use an omnibus battery that provides for a brief assessment of a large variety of performances and yields a single score in the form of a memory quotient. The Wechsler (1945) Memory Scale, for example, consists of seven brief tests—Personal and Current Information, Orientation for Time and Place, Counting, Paragraph Memory, Digit Span, Immediate Visual Memory, and Paired Associated Verbal Learning—the scores of which are added together to obtain a total score. However, this type of instrument has some usefulness as a screening device, despite the fact that it does not adequately measure some memory functions, such as visual retention, and also despite the fact that combining the separate scores into a single total score is a procedure of dubious validity. Age-corrected standard scores that may be helpful in clinical interpretation are provided by Osborne and Davis (1978) for four subtests of the Wechsler Memory Scale.

A differentiation among immediate memory, short-term memory, recent memory, and remote memory is often made. Immediate memory is assumed to involve only registration of information, and the other forms of memory are assumed to involve the storage of information over some period of time. This differentiation is meaningful from a clinical standpoint. For example, patients with Korsakoff's syndrome who show a pervasive and severe impairment in short-term or recent memory may be able to perform well on tasks involving the immediate repetition of digits or sentences. Conversely, anxious or depressed patients may fail immediate memory tasks because of disturbances in attention and concentration but show intact recent memory.

IMMEDIATE MEMORY

Immediate memory may be defined as the reproduction, recognition, or recall of perceived material directly after presentation. It is most often assessed by digit repetition and reversal (auditory) and memory-for-designs (visual) tests (Graham and Kendall, 1960; Benton, 1974). Both types of task discriminate significantly between brain-damaged and control subjects, but the visual task has been found to be the more sensitive indicator (Heilbrun, 1958; Sterne, 1969). The precise reason for this difference in discriminating power is not known; the relatively novel and more demanding nature of the task of drawing designs from memory may be an important factor here, or the difference in sensory modality may be the crucial factor. A comparative study of the discriminative efficiency of auditory and visual digit span tasks would be of interest in this regard and might provide information of clinical interest.

In any case, both an auditory-verbal task, such as digit span or memory for words or sentences, and a nonverbal visual task, such as memory for designs or for objects or faces, should be given to assess the patient's immediate memory. Despite the fact that group studies show a significant positive correlation between performances on the two types of task, dissociation—that is, adequate performance on the one and defective performance on the other—is not rare and may be of clinical significance. Patients with lesions of the right hemisphere are likely to show more severe defect on visual nonverbal tasks than on auditory-verbal tasks. Conversely, patients with left hemisphere disease, including those who are not aphasic, are likely to show more severe deficit on the auditory-verbal tests with variable performance on the visual nonverbal tasks.

SHORT-TERM AND RECENT MEMORY

These terms refer to the recognition, recall, or reproduction of information some time after the initial presentation. Short-term memory is typically assessed either by measuring the patient's retention of information a brief time (ranging from 10 seconds to 10 minutes) after the presentation or acquisition of the information or by assessing his learning of the material over repeated trials, the improvement in performance presumably being dependent on intact short-term retention. A useful test of short-term retention is serial digit learning—that is, the memorization of a series of digits longer than the patient's immediate memory span for digits over successive trials. This supraspan test has been used to evaluate short-term memory deficit in patients with temporal lobe abnormalities (Drachman and Hughes, 1971), and it has been demonstrated to be superior to the conventional digit span test in detecting the presence of brain disease (Zangwill, 1943; Schinka, 1975).

Recent memory refers to the retention of information over hours, days, weeks, or months. Defects in recent memory are often reflected in impaired temporal orientation. In a hospital setting, defective recent memory is disclosed by inaccurate reporting of current events, failure to remember visits by relatives or friends, and inability to recall earlier instructions by the physician or the nurse.

REMOTE MEMORY

It is commonly believed that remote memory is well preserved in patients who show pronounced defects in recent memory. The impression is probably based on the circumstance that the capacity to recall the events of early life is not as critically assessed as is immediate or recent memory. In fact, the remote memory of senile and amnesic patients is usually significantly inferior to that of normal persons of comparable age and education (Williams and Pennybacker, 1954; Shapiro et al., 1956; Talland, 1965; Brunschwig et al., 1971). Even patients who appear to be able to recount their past fairly accurately will, on close examination, show gaps and inconsistency in their recital. Although events in the remote past are recalled, their placement within a temporal framework is likely to be imprecise, and uncertainty about such items as the dates of presidential terms or wars or even the birth dates of their children is more the rule than the exception.

In recent years clinical investigators have developed and used standardized objective tests for the assessment of remote memory. Typically, these tests require the patient to identify the photographs of public figures who were prominent in past decades and to recall public events that occurred many years before the onset of his illness (Sanders and Warrington, 1971; Seltzer and Benson, 1974; Squire, 1974; Marslen-Wilson and Teuber, 1975). The tenor of the results has been that patients with brain disease do show impairment in remote memory and, further, that their deficiency in recall and recognition is as severe for the oldest and most remote events as it is for less remote material. Squire and Slater (1975) devised a technique of assessment that requires the patient to identify the names of television shows of earlier years. Adopting this procedure, Levin et al. (1977) found that brain-diseased patients showed a significant defect in remote memory, as reflected in their poor identification of television programs broadcast 3 to 10 years before the examination. There was no evidence of better memory for earlier programs shown 9 to 10 years before than for programs shown 3 to 4 years before examination.

Orientation

Orientation for person or place is rarely disturbed in the brain-damaged patient who is not psychotic or severely demented, but defects in temporal orientation, which can be considered to reflect the integrity of recent memory, are not at all uncommon. These defects are often missed by the clinical examiner because of his tendency to regard a slight inaccuracy in giving the day of the week or of the month as being inconsequential. However, objective assessment, using a fixed schedule of questions and based on empirically derived normative standards, discloses that about 25 per cent of nonpsychotic patients with hemispheric cerebral disease are likely to show significant inferiority with respect to precision of temporal orientation (Benton et al., 1964; Levin and Benton, 1975).

A schedule of this type is shown in Table II. Using the same questions that are asked in the conventional Mental Status Examination, it provides a basis for evaluating a patient's performance in terms of the responses given by an unselected sample of control patients. Table III shows the distributions of scores on this inventory in groups of control and brain-damaged patients. As shown, 14 patients (23 per cent of the total number) with cerebral disease proved to have defective orientation, as defined by a performance level below that of 97 per cent of the control patients. It is noteworthy that only five patients with relatively severe impairment had been noted on clinical neurological examination as having defects in temporal orientation, the others having been designated as normal in this regard. In short, use of the inventory identified nine additional patients (15 per cent of the total group) as being significantly inaccurate in temporal orientation. Further analysis indicated that the reason for the discrepancy between the clinical judgments and the test results was that the neurologists' standards of normality tended to be too liberal. A number of them believed that at least a few normal subjects could be expected to misidentify the year or the month when, in fact, no control patient showed such gross inaccuracy. Thus, the value of a brief schedule such as this is not in the specific questions asked, which are essentially the same as those posed in the clinical examination, but in the use of empirically derived norms as a basis for interpreting performance.

TABLE II
Temporal Orientation Schedule

Administration

What is today's date? (The patient is required to give month, day, and year.)

What day of the week is it?

What time is it now? (Examiner makes sure that the patient cannot look at a watch or clock.)

Scoring

Day of week: 1 point off for each day removed from the correct day to a maximum of 3 points.

Day of month: 1 point off for each day removed from the correct day to a maximum of 15 points.

Month: 5 points off for each month removed from the correct month with the qualification that, if the stated date is within 15 days of the correct date, no points are taken off for the incorrect month (for example, May 29 for June 2 = 4 points off).

Year: 10 points off for each year removed from the correct year to a maximum of 60 points with the qualification that, if the stated date is within 15 days of the correct date, no points are taken off for the incorrect year (for example, December 26, 1982 for January 2, 1983 = 7 points off).

Time of day: 1 point off for each 30 minutes removed from the correct time to a maximum of 5 points.

The total number of points off for errors is subtracted from 100, and the remainder is considered as the patient's obtained score.

TABLE III
Distribution of Temporal Orientation Scores in Control and Brain-damaged Patients

Score	Controls (N = 110)	Brain-damaged (N = 60)
100	67	27
99	33	6
98	4	12
97	3	1
96	2	3
95	1	3
94		
93		1
92		
91		1
90		
89		1
88		1
0–87		4

Perceptual and Perceptuomotor Performances

Many patients with brain disease, when examined by means of special techniques, show defective capacity to analyze complex stimulus constellations or inability to translate their perceptions into appropriate motor action. Unless the impairment is of a gross nature, as in visual object agnosia or dressing apraxia, or interferes with a specific occupational skill, these deficits are not likely to be the subject of spontaneous complaint. However, appropriate testing discloses a remarkably high incidence of impaired performance on visuoanalytic, visuospatial, and visuoconstructive tasks in brain-damaged patients, particularly in those with disease involving the right hemisphere (Benton, 1969; Warrington, 1969; Hécaen and Albert, 1978). This type of impairment also extends to tactile and auditory perceptual task performances (Milner, 1962; Carmon and Bechtoldt, 1969; Fontenot and Benton, 1971).

Many tests have been devised to measure these capacities; only a few of them can be mentioned here. Higher level visuoperceptive capacity may be assessed by means of tests involving the recognition of hidden figures and fragmented figures (Teuber and Weinstein, 1956; Russo and Vignolo, 1967), the discrimination of similar visual patterns differing only slightly in structure (Meier and French, 1965), and the identification of faces (Benton and Van Allen, 1968). Visuo-constructive capacity may be assessed by tests calling for block design construction (Critchley, 1953), stick arranging (Critchley, 1953), copying designs (Bender, 1938, 1962), and three-dimensional block model construction (Benton, 1969, 1973). Defective capacity for visual analysis and synthesis is also brought out in the Rorschach Test by such performance characteristics as poor percepts (F−), failure to see movement (low M), and paucity of response (Reitan, 1955b).

Performance on the Elithorn Perceptual Mazes often discloses the same type of impairment (Benton et al., 1963). Patients with apparently intact stereognostic capacity, as evidenced by their accurate recognition of palpated objects in the neurological examination, often show defects in tactile recognition when subjected to more demanding test procedures (Critchley, 1953). Defects in auditory discrimination and memory may also be manifested (Milner, 1962). Somatoperceptual defects, such as impairment in finger recognition or in the identification of the right and left sides of one's body, may be brought to light by appropriate testing (Critchley, 1953; Benton, 1959). Defective capacity for perceptual integration within the visual and tactile modalities may be disclosed by application of the method of double simultaneous sensory stimulation (Bender, 1952; Critchley, 1953).

The application of these perceptual and perceptuomotor tests to detect the presence of cerebral disease has proved to be quite rewarding and to possess certain advantages. Although not culture free (no behavioral performances are), they are generally less dependent on educational level and cultural background than are many of the more intellectual types of task. Many of the perceptual and perceptuomotor tests are relatively sensitive indicators of the presence of cerebral disease. In addition, they often provide suggestions with regard to the probable locus of the cerebral lesion and thus may help to offer a focus for further neurological exploration.

An example of this type of procedure is provided by tests of constructional praxis. These tests require the patient to assemble or articulate elements to form a more complex unity, such as a block pattern or a design. Design copying and three-dimensional block construction are perhaps the most useful of these tests from the standpoint of clinical application. The tests devised to assess these capacities generally present easy tasks that most normal adults perform on a perfect or nearly perfect level. In contrast, a significant proportion of patients with brain disease, particularly those with lesions of the right hemisphere who do not show obvious impairment in language behavior, perform defectively. Figure 1 shows the stimulus figures of the Bender-Gestalt Test. Figure 2 shows the models used in a standardized test of three-dimensional constructional praxis and presents examples of strikingly defective performances made by patients with disease of the right hemisphere. Similarly, Figure 3 shows some of the designs in a standardized copying test and the reproductions of a patient with disease of the right hemisphere.

Another test procedure that is useful in eliciting evidence of right hemisphere disease in right-handed patients requires discrimination of the slope of visually presented lines (Benton et al., 1978). As shown in Figure 4, pairs of lines in different

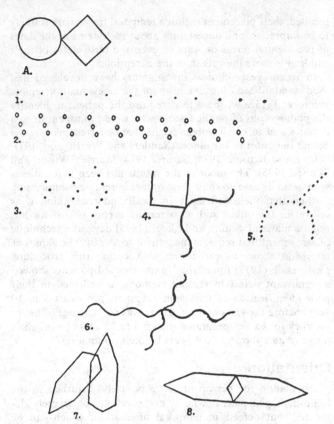

FIGURE 1. Test figures from the Bender (Visual-Motor) Gestalt Test, adapted from Wertheimer. (From Bender, L. *A Visual-Motor Gestalt Test and Its Clinical Use.* Research Monograph No. 3. American Orthopsychiatric Association, New York, 1938.)

directions, together with a multiple-choice display consisting of an array of numbered lines, are presented to the patient who indicates by naming or pointing the two lines in the multiple-choice display that correspond to the presented pair of lines. Analysis of the performances of patients with focal lesions indicates that defective performance is characteristic of those with right posterior parietal disease. Patients with left hemisphere disease, including aphasics, and those with anterior right hemisphere lesions generally perform on a normal level.

Language Functions

Gross impairment in language functions in the form of frank aphasia can scarcely be overlooked by the psychiatrist, although the less experienced examiner may sometimes misinterpret paraphasic or jargon speech as a sign of dementia or psychosis. On the other hand, it is quite likely that less severe disturbances of language expression and comprehension go unrecognized for the simple reason that the interview or the application of a few simple tests for aphasia fails to bring them out.

Yet relatively minor defects in the use of the instrument of language may be valid indicators of the presence of brain disease, particularly if it involves the dominant hemisphere. These defects are often the first signs of a developing aphasic disorder or the early stage of cerebral degeneration. Higher level language tests have been successfully used to probe for the presence of such a latent, minimal, or subclinical aphasia. A number of instruments can be used for this purpose. The Token Test of De Renzi and Vignolo (1962; Boller and Vig-

FIGURE 2. Three-dimensional constructional praxis: Performances of patients with right hemisphere disease. *Upper half* shows failure to construct left half of model, indicative of unilateral spatial neglect; *lower half* illustrates closing-in phenomenon (use of part of model in making the construction).

nolo, 1966) brings subtle and gross disturbances in the comprehension of oral language into sharp relief. The Shipley Abstractions make demands on verbal reasoning that the patient with latent aphasia is unable to meet. Understanding of the meaning of proverbs is often poor (Fogel, 1965). Verbal-ideational impoverishment is shown by defective performance on word fluency tests.

An example of a standardized verbal fluency task with established clinical usefulness is the controlled word-association test in which the patient is asked to give all the words he can think of beginning with a given letter of the alphabet. Aphasic patients, of course, fail this task. But a substantial proportion of nonaphasic patients, particularly those with left hemisphere disease, also perform defectively (Borkowski et al., 1967; Benton, 1968; Ramier and Hécaen, 1970). Analyzing the performances of patients with unilateral frontal lobe disease, Ramier and Hécaen concluded that two components underlay performance on the controlled word-association test—a linguistic component specifically associated with left hemisphere function and an ideational component associated with frontal lobe function.

Performance on all these language tests depends on educational background, and allowance must be made for this variable, as well as for other possibly significant factors, such as age and sex, in clinical interpretation. When these corrections are made, the tests provide valuable information that can aid in diagnosis. The sensitivity of performance level to the presence of brain disease, particularly when it involves the dominant hemisphere, negates the assumption that verbal abilities remain intact in nonaphasic patients with cerebral damage while nonverbal skills decline. It is a question of what tests are used to assess verbal abilities.

Speed and Flexibility of Response

Some brain-damaged patients are quite slow in responding to diverse stimuli and have notable difficulty in modifying their behavior to meet the changing demands of a shifting situation. Objective quantitative methods of assessment not only confirm these clinical observations in such patients but also disclose the same response retardation and behavioral rigidity in many others who may appear on clinical grounds to be unremarkable in these respects.

Reaction time studies have shown that both simple and choice reactions are significantly retarded in 40 to 45 per cent of nonpsychotic brain-damaged patients (Blackburn and Benton, 1955; Dee and Van Allen, 1973). Moreover, patients with unilateral brain disease show clear retardation, even when the ipsilateral hand (the hand on the unaffected side of the body) is used to effect the response (Benton and Joynt, 1959). There is suggestive evidence that complex reaction time may be a more sensitive indicator of brain function than simple reaction time (Gronwall and Sampson, 1974). These results demonstrate that reaction time is a sensitive indicator of over-all cerebral integrity and that retardation in reaction time reflects the presence of a cerebral lesion, regardless of its locus. Comparison of the reaction times of the right and left hands often provides an indication of the hemisphere locus of the lesion in a patient with unilateral cerebral disease. The method deserves more extensive application as a diagnostic procedure, particularly when the question of differentiation between neurosis and cerebral disease is raised.

A variant of the simple reaction time experiment—in which the patient is required to react to successive presentations of different stimuli instead of to successive presentations of the same stimulus, as in the conventional procedure—provides an opportunity to measure behavioral flexibility on a basic sensorimotor level. Excessive slowness in response to a stimulus that has been preceded by a stimulus in another sense modality (cross-modal retardation effect) is shown both by schizophrenic and by nonpsychotic brain-damaged patients (Benton et al., 1962). Neurotic patients do not show this marked susceptibility to the cross-modal retardation effect.

A useful technique for assessing speed of information processing in patients with suspected cerebral dysfunction is the Paced Serial Addition Task of Gronwall (1977). The procedure involves the presentation of digits at a constant rate to the subject who is required to add the first two digits and announce the sum, then add the third digit to the second digit and announce the sum, and so on. The digits are presented at four different rates 2.4, 2.0, 1.6, and 1.2 a second. Studying patients with closed-head injuries, Gronwall has found that even mildly concussed patients who are hospitalized for fewer than 3 days show defects in performance under these fixed pacing conditions, but their performances under unpaced conditions are usually without error.

Other measures of behavioral flexibility are provided by tasks in which the patient must modify his approach to a problem in accordance with changing requirements—color-form-sorting tests, object-sorting tests, and concept formation tests. The concept formation test, when considered in relation to other test performances, has been found to be particularly

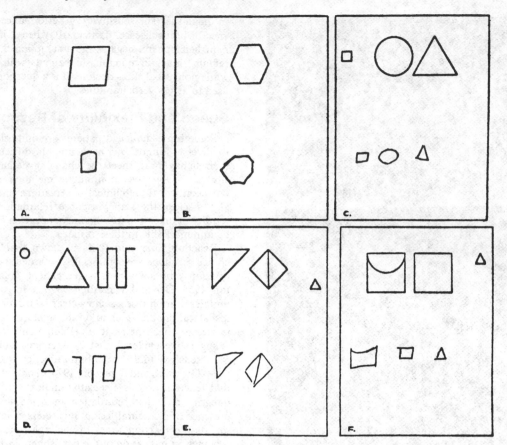

FIGURE 3. Copying of designs by a patient with right hemisphere disease. *A.* Distortion. *B.* Distortion. *C.* Size error in reproduction of left peripheral figure. *D.* Omission of left peripheral figure, size error in reproduction of left major figure, distortion of right major figure. *E.* Omission of right peripheral figure. *F.* Distortion of left major figure, size error in reproduction of right major figure.

valuable in identifying patients with frontal lobe disease, who are likely to show strong perseverative tendencies (Milner, 1963, 1964).

Attention and Concentration

The capacity to sustain a maximal level of attention over a period of time is sometimes impaired in brain-damaged patients, and this impairment is reflected in oscillation in performance level on a continuous or repeated activity. There is some evidence that this instability in performance is related to electroencephalographic (EEG) abnormality and that the occurrence of inexplicable declines in performance is related temporally to the appearance of certain types of abnormal electrical activity. For example, Prechtl et al. (1961) showed that episodes of response retardation in a continuous performance task in epileptic patients coincided with the occurrence of diffuse flattening of the EEG.

Various tests have been devised to assess vigilance and capacity for sustained attention. Simple reaction time provides a convenient measure of variability and speed of simple responses and possibly is as discriminative and informative as assessments of performance on more complex and lengthy tasks. The patient's median reaction time can be used as an index of speed, and the standard deviation of his reaction times provides an index of variability that can be conceptualized as reflecting limitations in capacity for sustaining maximal attention. Intraindividual variability in both simple and choice reaction time is significantly higher in brain-damaged patients than in matched controls (Blackburn and Benton, 1955). Among the tests that have been developed to measure attention

and concentration is the continuous performance test of Rosvold and associates (1965), which has been shown to discriminate reasonably well between brain-damaged patients (both adults and children) and controls. Another test is a vigilance task, involving the detection of visual signals, developed by McDonald and Burns (1964), which also discriminates significantly between brain-damaged patients and controls.

The clinical usefulness of these tests of attention and vigilance has not been precisely determined, and whether they deserve a place in the armamentarium of the clinical examiner is still an open question. Study along these lines has to take into account the possible effects of drugs and of deviations in mood. These tests seem to warrant further exploration, particularly since they furnish a type of task that includes the possibility of establishing a temporal correlation between performance and specified neural events.

Suggested Cross References

Basic concepts of intelligence are discussed in Section 4.1. Learning is discussed in Section 4.3. Neurophysiology of behavior is discussed in Section 2.5. Psychological assessment of intelligence and psychological testing of personality are discussed in Sections 12.5 and 12.6, respectively. Psychological use of language and psycholinguistics is covered in Section 4.8. The clinical disorders to which the psychological tests mentioned in this section are applicable are discussed in detail in Chapter 20 on organic mental disorders. Attention deficit disorders are covered in Chapter 38. For a discussion of the assessment of brain damage by means of the psychiatric examination, see Section 12.2.

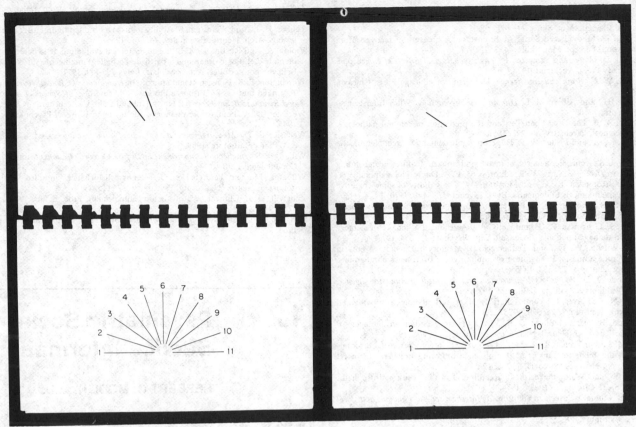

FIGURE 4. Two items of a test of visuospatial judgment. A pair of lines and the multiple-choice display are presented simultaneously to the patient. He is instructed to identify the presented pair of lines by pointing to them or calling out their numbers on the multiple-choice display. (From Benton, A. L., Varney, N. R., and Hamsher, K. Visuospatial judgment: A clinical test. Arch. Neurol., *18:* 364, 1978.)

REFERENCES

Adams, R. D. Further observations on normal pressure hydrocephalus. Proc. R. Soc. Med., *59:* 1135, 1966.

Adams, R. D., Fisher, C. M., and Hakin S. Symptomatic occult hydrocephalus with "normal" cerebrospinal fluid pressure. N. Engl. J. Med., *273:* 117, 1965.

Albert, M. L., Feldman, R. G., and Willis, A. L. The "subcortical dementia" of progressive nuclear palsy. J. Neurol. Neurosurg. Psychiatry 37: 121, 1974.

Bender, L. *A Visual-Motor Gestalt Test and Its Clinical Use.* Research Monograph No. 3. American Orthopsychiatric Association, New York, 1938.

Bender, M. B. *Disorders in Perception.* Charles C Thomas, Springfield, Ill., 1952.

Benson, D. F., LeMay, M., Patten, D. H., and Rubens, A. B. Diagnosis of normal-pressure hydrocephalus. N. Engl. J. Med., *283:* 609, 1970.

Benton, A. L. *Right-Left Discrimination and Finger Localization: Development and Pathology.* Harper & Row, New York, 1959.

Benton, A. L. The visual retention test as a constructional praxis task. Confin. Neurol., *22:* 141, 1962.

Benton, A. L. Differential behavioral effects in frontal lobe disease. Neuropsychologia, *6:* 53, 1968.

* Benton, A. L. Disorders of spatial orientation. In *Handbook of Clinical Neurology,* P. J. Vinken and G. W. Bruyn, editors, vol. 3, *Disorders of Higher Nervous Activity,* p. 212. North Holland Publ. Co., Amsterdam, 1969.

Benton, A. L. Visuoconstructive disability in patients with cerebral disease: Its relationship to side of lesion and aphasic disorder. Doc. Ophthalmol., *34:* 67, 1973.

Benton, A. L. *The Visual Retention Test: Clinical and Experimental Applications,* ed. 4. Psychological Corporation, New York, 1974.

Benton, A. L., Elithorn, A., Fogel, M. L., and Kerr, M. A perceptual maze test sensitive to brain damage. J. Neurol. Neurosurg. Psychiatry, *26:* 540, 1963.

Benton, A. L., and Joynt, R. J. Reaction time in unilateral cerebral disease. Confin. Neurol., *19:* 247, 1959.

Benton, A. L., Sutton, S., Kennedy, J. A., and Brokaw, J. R. The cross-modal retardation in reaction times of patients with cerebral disease. J. Nerv. Ment. Dis., *135:* 413, 1962.

* Benton, A. L., and Van Allen, M. W. Impairment in facial recognition in patients with cerebral disease. Cortex, *4:* 344, 1968.

Benton, A. L., Van Allen, M. W., and Fogel, M. L. Temporal orientation in cerebral disease. J. Nerv. Ment. Dis., *139:* 110, 1964.

* Benton, A. L., Varney, N. R., and Hamsher, K. Visuospatial judgment: A clinical test. Arch. Neurol., *18:* 364, 1978.

Berg, E. A. A simple objective technique for measuring flexibility in thinking. J. Gen. Psychol., *39:* 15, 1948.

Blackburn, H. L., and Benton, A. L. Simple and choice reaction time in cerebral disease. Confin. Neurol., *15:* 327, 1955.

Blessed, G., Tomlinson, B. E., and Roth, M. The association between quantitative measures of dementia and of senile change in the cerebral grey matter of elderly subjects. Br. J. Psychiatry, *114:* 797, 1968.

Bleuler, E. *Dementia Praecox or the Group of Schizophrenias.* International Universities Press, New York, 1950.

Boller, F., and Vignolo, L. A. Latent sensory aphasia in hemisphere-damaged patients: An experimental study with the Token Test. Brain, *89:* 815, 1966.

Borkowski, J. G., Benton, A. L., and Spreen, O. Word fluency and brain damage. Neuropsychologia, *5:* 135, 1967.

Brunschwig, L., Strain, J. J., and Bidder, T. G. Issues in the assessment of post-ECT memory changes. Br. J. Psychiatry, *119:* 73, 1971.

Carmon, A., and Bechtoldt, H. P. Dominance of the right cerebral hemisphere for stereopsis. Neuropsychologia, *7:* 29, 1969.

Chapman, L. F., and Wolff, H. G. The cerebral hemispheres and the highest integrative functions of man. Arch. Neurol., *1:* 357, 1959.

Critchley, M. *The Parietal Lobes.* Edward Arnold, London, 1953.

Dee, H. L., and Van Allen, M. W. Speed of decision-making processes in patients with unilateral cerebral disease. Arch. Neurol., *28:* 163, 1973.

De Renzi, E., and Vignolo, L. A. The Token Test: A sensitive test to detect receptive disturbances in aphasics. Brain, *85:* 665, 1962.

Drachman, D., and Hughes, J. R. Memory and the hippocampal complexes: III. Aging and temporal lobe abnormalities. Neurology (Minneap.), *21:* 1, 1971.

Fogel, M. L. The intelligence quotient as an index of brain damage. Am. J. Orthopsychiatry, *34:* 555, 1964.

Fogel, M. L. The Gorham Proverbs Test in the appraisal of cerebral disease. J. Gen. Psychol., *72:* 269, 1965.

Fontenot, D. J., and Benton, A. L. Tactile perception of direction in relation to hemispheric locus of lesion. Neuropsychologia, *9:* 83, 1971.

Glees, P., and Griffith, H. B. Bilateral destruction of the hippocampus (cornu ammonis) in a case of dementia. Monatsscher. Psychiat. Neurol., *129:* 193, 1952.

Goldstein, K. *Language and Language Disturbances.* Grune & Stratton, New York, 1948.

Goldstein, K., and Scheerer, M. Abstract and concrete behavior: An experimental study with special tests. Psychol. Monogr., *53:* No. 2, 1941.

Gorham, D. R. A proverbs test for clinical and experimental use. Psychol. Rep.,

(Suppl.) No. 1, 1956.

Graham, F. K., and Kendall, B. Memory-for-Designs Test: Revised general manual. Percept. Mot. Skills, *11:* 147, 1960.

Gronwall, D. M. A. Paced Serial Addition task: A measure of recovery from concussion. Percept. Mot. Skills, *44:* 367, 1977.

Gronwall, D. M. A., and Sampson, H. *The Psychological Effects of Concussion.* University Press, Auckland, 1974.

Halstead, W. C. *Brain and Intelligence.* University of Chicago Press, Chicago, 1947.

* Hécaen, H., and Albert, M. L. *Human Neuropsychology.* Wiley-Interscience, New York, 1978.

Heilbrun, A. B. The Digit Span Test and the prediction of cerebral pathology. Arch. Neurol. Psychiatry, *80:* 228, 1958.

Heilman, K. M., and Fisher, W. R. Hyperlipidemic dementia. Arch. Neurol., *31:* 67, 1974.

Horenstein, S. Amnestic, agnosic, apractic, and aphasic features in dementing illness. In *Dementia,* C. E. Wells, editor, p. 61. F. A. Davis, Philadelphia, 1971.

Irving, G., Robinson, R. A., and McAdam, W. The validity of some cognitive tests in the diagnosis of dementia. Br. J. Psychol. *117:* 149, 1970.

* Levin, H. S., and Benton, A. L. Temporal orientation in patients with brain disease. Appl. Neurophysiol. *38:* 56, 1975.

Levin, H. S., Grossman, R. G., and Kelly, P. J. Assessment of long-term memory in brain-damaged patients. J. Consult. Clin. Psychol., *45:* 684, 1977.

Marslen-Wilson, W. D., and Teuber, H. L. Memory for remote events in anterograde amnesia: Recognition of public figures from news photographs. Neuropsychologia, *13:* 353, 1975.

* Matarazzo, J. D. *Wechsler's Measurement and Appraisal of Adult Intelligence,* ed. 5. Williams & Wilkins, Baltimore, 1972.

Mathew, N. T., Meyer, J. S., and Achari, A. N. Hyperlipidemic neuropathy and dementia. Neurology, *25:* 373, 1975.

McDonald, R. D., and Burns, S. B. Visual vigilance and brain damage: An empirical study. J. Neurol. Neurosurg. Psychiatry, *27:* 206, 1964.

Meier, M. J., and French, L. A. Lateralized deficits in complex visual discrimination and bilateral transfer of reminiscence following unilateral temporal lobectomy. Neuropsychologia, *3:* 261, 1965.

Messert, B., and Wannamaker, B. B. Reappraisal of the occult hydrocephalus syndrome. Neurology, *24:* 224, 1974.

Milner, B. Laterality effects in audition. In *Interhemispheric Relations and Cerebral Dominance,* V. B. Mountcastle, editor, p. 177. Johns Hopkins University Press, Baltimore, 1962.

Milner, B. Effects of different brain lesions on card sorting. Arch. Neurol., *9:* 90, 1963.

Milner, B. Some effects of prefrontal lobectomy in man. In *The Frontal Granular Cortex and Behavior,* J. M. Warren and K. Akert, editors, p. 313. McGraw-Hill, New York, 1964.

Osborne, D., and Davis, L. J. Standard scores for Wechsler Memory Scale subtests. J. Clin. Psychol., *34:* 115, 1978.

Porteus, S. D. *The Maze Test and Clinical Psychology.* Pacific Books, Palo Alto, Calif., 1959.

Prechtl, H. F. R., Bocke, P. E., and Schut, T. The electroencephalogram and performance in epileptic patients. Neurology (Minneap)., *11:* 296, 1961.

Ramier, A.-M., and Hécaen, H. Rôle respectif des atteintes frontales et de la latéralisation lésionnelle dans des déficits de la "fluence verbale." Rev. Neurol. (Paris), *123:* 17, 1970.

Raven, J. C. *Guide to Using the Mill Hill Vocabulary Scale with the Progressive Matrices Scales.* H. K. Lewis, London, 1958.

Reitan, R. M. Investigation of the validity of Halstead's measure of biological intelligence. Arch. Neurol. Psychiatry, *73:* 28, 1955a.

Reitan, R. M. Validity of Rorschach Test as a measure of psychological effects of brain damage. Arch. Neurol. Psychiatry, *73:* 445, 1955b.

Rosvold, H. E., Mirsky, A. F., Sarason, I., Bransome, E. D., and Beck, L. H. A continuous performance test for brain damage. J. Consult. Psychol., *20:* 243, 1965.

Russo, M., and Vignolo, L. A. Visual figure-ground discrimination in patients with unilateral cerebral disease. Cortex, *3:* 113, 1967.

Sanders, H. I., and Warrington, E. K. Memory for remote events in amnesic patients. Brain, *94:* 661, 1971.

Schinka, J. A. Performance of brain-damaged subjects on tests of short-term and long-term memory. Dissertation Abstracts Int. B. The Sciences and Engineering, *35:* 6112, 1975.

Seltzer, B., and Benson, D. F. The temporal pattern of retrograde amnesia in Korsakoff's disease. Neurology, *24:* 527, 1974.

Shapiro, M. B., Pote, F., Lofring, B., and Inglis, J. "Memory function" in psychiatric patients over sixty. J. Ment. Sci., *102:* 233, 1956.

Shipley, W. C., and Burlingame, C. C. A convenient self-administering scale for measuring intellectual impairment in psychotics. Am. J. Psychiatry, *97:* 1313, 1941.

Squire, L. R. Remote memory as affected by aging. Neuropsychologia, *12:* 429, 1974.

Squire, L. R., and Slater, P. C. Forgetting in very long-term memory as assessed by an improved questionnaire technique. J. Exp. Psychol. Hum. Learning Memory, *1:* 50, 1975.

Stengel, E. The psychopathology of dementia. Proc. R. Soc. Med., *57:* 911, 1964.

Sterne, D. M. The Benton, Porteus, and WAIS Digit Span Tests with normal and brain-damaged subjects. J. Clin. Psychol., *25:* 173, 1969.

Talland, G. A. *Deranged Memory: A Psychonomic Study of the Amnesic Syndrome.* Academic Press, New York, 1965.

Teuber, H.-L., and Weinstein, S. Ability to discover hidden figures after cerebral lesions. Arch. Neurol. Psychiatry, *76:* 369, 1956.

Violon, A., and Rustin, R. M. Etude des critères d'évaluation de la détérioration mentale d'étiologie organique à partir de l'échelle d'intelligence de Wechsler-Bellevue pour adultes. Acta Psychiatr. Belg., *71:* 449, 1971.

Warrington, E. K. Constructional apraxia. In *Handbook of Clinical Neurology,* P. J. Vinken and G. W. Bruyn, editors, vol. 4, *Disorders of Speech, Perception, and Symbolic Behavior,* p. 67. North Holland Publ. Co., Amsterdam, 1969.

Wechsler, D. A standardized memory scale for clinical use. J. Psychol., *19:* 87, 1945.

Wechsler, D. *The Measurement and Appraisal of Adult Intelligence,* ed. 4. Williams & Wilkins, Baltimore, 1958.

Willanger, R. *Intellectual Impairment in Diffuse Cerebral Lesions.* Munksgaard, Copenhagen, 1970.

Williams, M., and Pennybacker, J. Memory disturbances in third ventricle tumors. J. Neurol. Neurosurg. Psychiatry, *17:* 115, 1954.

Zangwill, O. L. Clinical tests of memory impairment. Proc. R. Soc. Med., *36:* 576, 1943.

Zangwill, O. L. The psychopathology of dementia. Proc. R. Soc. Med., *57:* 914, 1964.

12.8   Psychiatric Social Service Information

HERBERT C. MODLIN, M.D.

Introduction

The profession of social work evolved from a confluence of sources in the early 20th century. One tributary, which originated in England, was a strong 19th-century trend among many compassionate ladies and gentlemen to give charitable goods and services to the unfortunate. Those well-meaning volunteers were concerned with the moral behavior and the physical well-being of their beneficiaries; donations of clothing and grocery baskets and preachments were interdigitated.

With the rapid and massive shift of population to urban living in the United States at the turn of the century and concurrently arriving waves of European immigrants, ghettos and slums appeared, and the settlement house movement was born. Unlike the visiting, volunteer gentry, settlement house workers found it important, if they were to render service of real value, that they work day and night and live in the ghetto. Clothing, food, education, and medical care were parceled out according to evaluated need. Their emphasis was more on the Americanization of immigrants than on moral uplift.

As charitable endeavors expanded, organizations were formed. Salaried full-time staff members eventually became self-taught professionals. The publication of Mary E. Richmond's (1917) *Social Diagnosis* is frequently credited as a cornerstone in the structure of the social work profession. She emphasized the importance of case evaluation—the collection of data by thoroughly studying a client and his immediate environment on the proposition that, given sufficient information, the case worker can determine what action is needed. Consequently, *Social Diagnosis* is concerned almost entirely with the framework for and manner of collecting and evaluating data about cases, the process Richmond called "social study and social diagnosis" (Briar, 1971).

Subsequently, the social work discipline discovered dynamic psychiatry (Freud and Rank), and the psychological phase in the development of social case work overshadowed the earlier diagnostic phase. Social work progress in the past 30 years has been therapeutic, rather than diagnostic, in nature. Case work, counseling, psychotherapy, group work, family therapy, community organization, social action, and crisis intervention are now represented in the curriculums of most social work training schools.

In the 1960's, diagnosis as a social work skill was further denigrated as members of the profession became involved in welfare reform, civil rights, social planning, community action, and client advocacy. These interests generated a nearly anti-diagnostic stance, marked by much protest against the restrictive limits of the medical model. However, the pendulum swings inexorably. As Turner (1976) observed, the whole existence of clinical practice was under attack. Labeling, classification, and treatment based on diagnosis were targets of severe criticism. But, because the conflict now

appears to be waning, once again we can turn to further efforts in making our work more precise and effective.

In other words, a modern, sophisticated version of Richmond's social diagnosis survives as one of the basic skills that social workers are taught and practice.

The Psychiatric Team

The proliferation of child guidance clinics in the 1920's and 1930's brought the social case worker firmly into the psychiatric fold and fostered a subspecialty, psychiatric social work. Through the demonstrated usefulness of skilled diagnostic and therapeutic work with parents of disturbed children and the adoption of the signal contributions of psychometric and projective testing, the formation of the classical tripartite team of psychiatrist, clinical psychologist, and psychiatric social worker eventuated. The application of this team concept in a variety of settings—mental hospital, mental retardation institution, adult outpatient clinic, college student health service, military service, mental health center—encouraged flexibility; and many other professionals—nurse, occupational therapist, vocational rehabilitation specialist, neurologist, chaplain, neighborhood worker—became established team members.

The diagnostic process, as defined in this context, is applied most often to people who have just acquired the tentative label "psychiatric patient" and who have been newly admitted to an outpatient clinic, a psychiatric unit in a general hospital, or the admissions ward of a psychiatric hospital. The three-member team of mental health professionals approaches a relatively unknown situation; their objective is to evaluate the quality and the quantity of illness and the assets and strengths in the patient and his immediate environment, formulate a treatment plan, and present their findings and recommendations to interested and involved persons.

The team concept implies that a comprehensive evaluation requires more data than the psychiatrist obtained from a patient, more than clarification concerning the patient's psychopathological status. A thorough understanding of assets, limitations, and noxious elements in the environment and of assets, limitations, and noxious elements in the patient must be gained. Thus, the team members can better judge what they have to work with and what they have to work against.

Because members of a patient's family are a valuable source of such data, the psychiatrist interviews the patient, and the social worker traditionally interviews his family. An advantage of this arrangement is that it provides the relatives with one particular professional person to relate to, one who they can feel cares about their needs and the affliction the patient's illness brings them. Another advantage is that the psychiatrist does not need to communicate directly with the relatives, and thus he is able to avoid the appearance and risk of revealing his patient's confidences to anyone.

Diagnostic Social Work

PERSPECTIVES OF THE PATIENT'S ILLNESS

Relatives' observations of changes from preillness functioning in the patient's thinking, mood, verbalizations, and behavior provide valuable information to compare with what the psychiatrist obtains from the patient and to check for concordances, differences, omissions, and distortions from either source. It may become apparent that the patient is minimizing his illness, that the mother is denying the seriousness of her child's difficulties, that his wife is exaggerating the patient's misbehavior, or that both the patient and his relatives are engaged in an entrenched practice of reciprocal blaming and recrimination.

EARLY DEVELOPMENT

Parents and older siblings can give clues to the understanding of significant early interpersonal relationships, lags, or distortions in growth, early traumata, and factors establishing basic character traits. The psychiatrist may be concerned about a patient's suspiciousness. Learning from his intimates through the social worker that from childhood he has always been reserved and wary helps the psychiatrist to understand the patient's projective maneuvers.

GENERAL LIFE CIRCUMSTANCES

The social and cultural mores, taboos, rules, and directives peculiar to the environment within which the patient and his family interact must be investigated. Class, culture, value systems, religion, family economics, child care practices, and attitudes toward mental illness and psychiatry are among the pertinent realities to be considered. Is the woman's passivity and dependence on her husband's decision making a manifestation of masochism or a disguised depression, or is it simply characteristic of her particular role in her particular class and culture?

The social worker is a team's procurator and interpreter of information from a wide variety of sources. He or she can be instrumental in obtaining school, military, court, medical, and work records; in discovering the patient's and the family's previous experiences with community agencies; in providing a preliminary evaluation of community resources available and acceptable to the family and possibly to be enlisted in the eventual treatment plan.

Sixteen-year-old Nan was referred for diagnostic evaluation by her attorney before the court trial of a civil suit that had been pending for 3 years. In the automobile accident that killed her mother, Nan, then 13, sustained multiple fractures and deep cuts. Her face, chest, breasts, arms, and hands were mutilated and burned; the many plastic surgery procedures that were necessary accomplished disappointingly meager cosmetic improvement. At the time of the accident, the mother had been living with her third husband, who flatly refused responsibility for his three orphaned stepchildren and who consigned them to their aging and inhospitable grandparents. Sensing her grandparents' ambivalent acceptance of child-rearing burdens, Nan became negativistic, ran away, engaged in indiscriminate sexual relations, was adjudicated a neglected and abandoned child, and was made a ward of the state welfare department, which placed her in a girls' school. The school's age-limit rules required her discharge after her sixteenth birthday.

The psychiatrist of a diagnostic team interviewed resistive, uncommunicative Nan for 6 hours. The psychologist spent 5 hours with her in testing. The social worker spent days interviewing the grandmother, a responsible state welfare worker, and a school social worker and in unearthing preaccident and postaccident school records, medical records from three hospitals, and depositions, held by the attorney, from Nan and witnesses to the accident.

From material thus garnered it was possible to reconstruct a reasonably clear picture of Nan's preaccident relationships with her mother, two stepfathers, and siblings; her classroom behavior and achievements; her relationships with peers; her postaccident adaptation to the loss of her mother, the many surgical procedures, her disfigurement, her grandparents' attitude, and her experiencing of the school. The social worker apprised the team concerning each involved person's (lawyer, grandmother, welfare worker, school social worker) individual expectation that answers to his questions would be forthcoming from the diagnostic team, and his impression of what those questions were likely to be.

PREILLNESS FUNCTIONING

It is useful to establish a baseline of the patient's preillness functioning for measuring in a rough way the degree of deviance manifested in his present symptoms and for determining a potential therapeutic goal that will signify, when reached, the patient's return to his particular normalcy. Comparison of the social worker's data and the psychiatrist's data should be routine. The patient may submit reasonable-sounding explanations of his erratic work history; his wife may more objectively describe his lifelong, mostly futile search for occupational success.

SOURCES OF STRESS

Psychiatrists generally assume clearly definable mental illness to be effected by the impact of a precipitating set of environmental stresses on a predisposed innately or developmentally defective personality. An oversimplified statement regarding a diagnostician's task is 3-fold: He needs to determine (1) how a patient is reacting, (2) what psychological resources he possesses to react with, and (3) what he is reacting to.

With information from relatives and other pertinent sources, the social worker can present for the team's consideration an objective evaluation of environmental stresses that may serve to clear up unresolved questions in the mind of one or another team member. How precarious is the patient's position with his firm; is his foreboding of imminent discharge part of his illness? How adamant is his wife's decision to sue the patient for divorce; is her ultimatum partly intended to incite change in his behavior? Has the patient actually no practicable defense in a pending court action against him; has the feasibility of restitution, compromise, or modification of the charges been exhaustively explored? How nearly irreversible was the patient's scholastic failure; were there other precipitating stresses relevant to his dropping out of school?

USES AND MISUSES OF THE PATIENT'S ILLNESS

Relatives can usually describe much more graphically than the patient the factors of secondary gain that serve to sustain the patient's symptoms. Through his illness the patient is unconsciously trying to cope with real or imagined stresses; but, even though he is paying a heavy price, he may be realizing secondary compensations. He may be avoiding work and social responsibilities, tyrannizing his family, punishing his spouse, evading his wife's sexual invitations, or denying his waning powers in aging.

Conversely, astute observations of the relatives' productions can reveal the family's uses of the patient's illness for secondary advantages. Focus on the sick patient alone may divert attention from a sick family constellation. A spouse's vindictiveness may be expressed in collusion with the patient to resist treatment or in "forgetting" to remove barbiturates from the medicine cabinet. Merely the appearance together of patient and relative for evaluation does not establish that either is unambivalently committed to the patient's regaining health.

Work with Children

In diagnostic evaluations of children, the social worker's contributions to the total team effort are more crucial than when the patient is an adult. Many adult patients are relatively competent reporters concerning their current difficulties, past history, life style, interpersonal relationships, and the milieu in which they live. Not so with children, particularly children under the age of 6. Their limitations as reporters are attributable not only to their state of being ill but also to their incompleteness of cognitive, verbal, mnemonic, and experiential development (Group for the Advancement of Psychiatry, 1957).

The child is more firmly and exclusively embedded in the nuclear family matrix than is the average adult, who has acquired some direct contact with his social class, culture, and community. The child has few options for independent behavior; his family's intercommunication, mores, style, values, and standards constitute nearly the whole of his social life. Also, those close to him, chiefly his parents, exercise functions in his behalf that he will assume for himself when older. Parents are his auxiliary or supplemental ego and superego. Diagnostic study of the whole young person must encompass scrutiny of environmental structures and functions in a manner qualitatively and quantitatively different from the procedure in evaluating a relatively self-sufficient adult.

In child psychiatry practice the basic team is frequently augmented by a pediatrician, a neurologist, and a speech therapist. As the evaluation proceeds, the social worker must be prepared to organize, sort, and relay information from the accumulating data relevant to the tasks of each team member. This information may concern not only developmental history, family relationships, onset of symptoms, and present functioning but also such factors as inadequate housing, nutritional deficiencies, and lead ingestion; family history of hereditary disorders, including allergies; deviation from growth norms suggesting a degree of mental retardation; learning disabilities; hearing, sight, and speech defects; life crises and traumata, possibly including child abuse.

Ordinarily, a child is not presented for diagnostic study until his parents are sufficiently distressed; they provide the motivation. Emotional illness in a child is a mysterious and frightening thing in that the child usually cannot point to a particular place where his body hurts. He cannot define or specify the nature of his distress; he can only express it through symptoms that often seem irrational and without cause. His dilemma, however, does not invoke psychiatric help unless its impact is felt by his parents and it involves them. When they are drawn into the child's distress, when they sense his pain as, in part, indistinguishable from their own and are bewildered and angry that their own attempts to give help fail, they may seek assistance (Menninger Clinic Children's Division, 1969).

Several years ago the husband of Mrs. C., 40, committed suicide. He had been despondent for many years, and she had rescued him from many business failures and lawsuits. Their only child, Sally, had seemed shadowy and insubstantial to her father and also to Mrs. C., who had perforce given so much attention to her husband. The quiet, withdrawn, and lonely child made fairly good grades in elementary school. Now 15 and in high school, her academic work began to decline. As she observed that her mother was increasingly depressed and drinking, she began to stay away from home and, finally, with another girl ran away to a distant city, where the police found her living in a motel. Interpreting her daughter's behavior as expressing a cry of distress for both herself and her mother, Mrs. C. felt constrained to apply for help (Menninger Clinic Children's Division, 1969).

Social case work with the parents of a child in diagnostic study must of necessity have a certain therapeutic dimension; they, too, always need help. Particularly may this be so at the end of evaluation, when recommendations for treatment are presented.

To a degree not required of adult patients' relatives, a disturbed child's parents are often expected to play a large role in the implementation of a treatment program. In fact, one or both parents may need to accept a direct therapeutic assignment. One team recommendation for a preschool child may be enrollment in a remedial or therapeutic nursery school that requires the mother's active participation up to the point of enrollment in a mother-training program.

Two of the most trying experiences for parents occur when recommendations for helping the child include (1) separating him from their home and (2) suggesting needed alterations in the parents' attitudes, behavior, and marital interaction. A total team effort must be mobilized, including, for example, the psychiatrist's exercise of empathic medical authority and the clinical psychologist's firm delineation of irrefutable findings. The social worker carries the chief burden, however, for he or she must work through the implications of the needed changes with the parents and, if indicated, maintain an ongoing professional relationship with them during the implementation of the prescribed therapeutic program.

Team Functioning

The diagnostic goals of the psychiatric team involve more than gathering information and labeling the patient's psychopathology. The informants—the patients and their relatives—must become engaged with the team's members in a diagnostic process. The informants' attitudes and feelings must be discovered, assayed, and understood in the context of their life circumstances. Their resistance, defense, evasion, reticence, and denial must be invalidated sufficiently for the actual state of affairs to emerge and be viewed.

In the psychiatrist's office many patients and relatives adopt the social role of medical patient. They expect the doctor and his assistants in the medical hierarchy to question, examine, synthesize, diagnose, and then institute appropriate measures to alleviate the distress. In psychiatric work, these stereotypes of doctor and patient roles must be relinquished rapidly. Optimally, the informants become the team's co-workers in the diagnostic process. As Modlin et al. (1958) wrote:

They must participate actively in the solution of the clinical problem which they brought.

The presenting symptoms, complaints, or problem frequently mask the real difficulty, and the patient and his relatives must be guided toward a comprehension of the conflicts underlying the patient's symptoms.

A 40-year-old attorney, accompanied by his wife, came for evaluation and medical assistance in solving his excessive drinking problem. A year of psychological counseling and membership in Alcoholics Anonymous had not helped; they intimated that admission to a sanitarium for alcoholics was the recommendation they expected. It became apparent during the course of evaluation that the patient's successful father had dominated his life in a way that seriously injured and scarred his self-esteem. It was also observable that the patient's wife had learned to use her father-in-law's techniques to disparage and demoralize her husband, even as she complained about his inefficacy. With a social worker's help, she soon came to understand the father's destructive influence inasmuch as her view as a daughter-in-law was more objective than the patient's view as a son. The social worker helped her also to a limited insight of the damage her own behavior had contributed to her husband's psychological difficulties. The four participants—husband, wife, psychiatrist, and social worker—were then able to focus on the complex interaction of patient, wife, and father. Only then was the crucial effect of the patient's older brother brought to light. A chip off the old block, he was the patient's immediate supervisor in the family's business enterprise.

The skillfully directed diagnostic process is time oriented; it has a beginning, a middle phase, and an end point, related generally to defining the problem, working it through, and presenting recommendations. Many teams schedule three conferences timed to these three phases: a preevaluation planning conference, a midpoint strategy conference, and a final conference, usually on the day before termination.

To function smoothly, economically, and flexibly, the team needs to become more than a group of competent mental health professionals cooperating with one another. It becomes an integrated team through a process of group growth over time. It is not enough that each member accomplishes his specific discipline-oriented work well; he needs to contribute to the work of each of the other team members. The psychologist can apprise the psychiatrist of a psychometrically exposed depressive component underlying a patient's optimistic facade. The psychiatrist can inform the social worker that a patient's wife rejects marital sexuality. The social worker can alert the psychologist to a young patient's sadistic abuse of animals.

Before a team can function with maximal effectiveness, it must reach a stage of group maturity in which style of leadership has become established, redefinition of professional roles has been accomplished, and easy communication has become routine. The significance of integration is that each member identifies himself with the group as a whole; in his professional participation he acts as an agent of the team in accomplishing a team purpose. As Modlin and Faris (1956) wrote:

In a well-integrated team, the patient, the relatives and their several problems "belong" to the team,

not separately to the psychiatrist or the social worker.

In such a flexible team, the patient and his relatives are easily admitted as temporary members to contribute to and participate in the team's tasks with as much responsibility as the team considers reasonable to expect. Thus the diagnostic process advances.

In one sense the diagnostic process includes a therapeutic process as well (Meyers, 1956). By "process" is meant a series of actions continuous in time directed to a specific end; process denotes change. By a "therapeutic process" is meant a series of experiences tending to promote better understanding, better reality adaptation, and better motivation for constructive action (Modlin et al., 1958). A therapeutic process is realized by the patient through his relationship with the psychiatrist and possibly the clinical psychologist, by the relatives through their relationship with the social worker, and by the family group through their shifting intrafamilial interactions during the evaluation. Also, as the patient and his relatives become ad hoc team members, a kind of over-all process involves the total membership, including the professionals.

A 27-year-old single man came for evaluation with his 50-year-old parents, who were dissatisfied with their son's current psychotherapy and his disorganized way of life. His precarious, schizoid adjustment was well documented in material from the attending psychotherapist. At the beginning of evaluation, each person of the family trio was preoccupied with his personal wants. The patient came not unwillingly because his therapist had recommended it, but he was wary of the clinical team because he wanted to retain his therapist and move from his parents' home to an apartment. His mother wanted a change in treatment and therapist for her son, and she wanted also to talk lengthily of her own symptoms and her frustrating husband. His father wanted a concrete, foolproof, painless plan that would stiffen his son's spine, subdue his wife, and relieve his own mind's concern.

Near the end of the evaluation, each of the three family members and the several team members revealed, in one way or another, improved skill in focusing on the major problem, the maladjusted patient. Although his mother became willing to consider psychotherapy for herself, she could not recognize that her repeated interference in her son's therapy and living arrangements had not been helpful. Her husband, viewing the neurotic maternal maneuvers more realistically, began to envision himself in a more positive and less egocentric role—controlling his wife's impulsive interference and supporting his son's self-growth. The patient expressed new awareness of ways in which he provoked his mother to interfere with his psychotherapy, of ways in which his fear and anger toward his father contaminated their relationship, and of ways in which he could start finding for himself a more satisfying and independent life (Modlin et al., 1958).

This case vignette illustrates the flexible, shifting interplay among team members, the patient, and his relatives, leading to a satisfactory outcome of the diagnostic process. It also illustrates the central role of the social worker in assessing and altering parental attitudes, without which the team's final recommendations would have had little chance to succeed.

The joint conference of the patient, his relatives, the psychiatrist, and the social worker is a useful team technique in varied circumstances, notably at the beginning and end of the evaluation period (Hall and Wheeler, 1957). An initial meeting of the patient and his relatives with the team members should facilitate introducing them to the team concept, to the diagnostic process, and to each other. Such a meeting allows the patient and his relatives to become acquainted with each other's professional associate and thus largely avoids the distracting speculation and fantasy about team members that commonly occurs if they remain strangers. When the patient is a child, the joint conference allows his parents to look over the child psychiatrist, who, from that time on, is closeted exclusively with the child and supposedly is ferreting out family secrets. It also affords the child his first contact with the psychiatrist while feeling the comforting security of his parents' supportive presence. It gives the patient an opportunity to obtain at least a visual impression of the social worker, whom the relatives will probably be mentioning or quoting as the evaluation proceeds.

At termination, the complex task of presenting recommendations for treatment can be facilitated in a joint conference. If the patient and his relatives have been successfully drawn into the evolving treatment plan during the diagnostic process, the final team recommendations hold few surprises for them; otherwise, the recommendations may come as a shock.

The joint conference offers an opportunity for the team, the patient, and his relatives to examine the implications of the recommendations and to gain a shared understanding of what is being proposed, including the fixing of responsibility for implementing various parts of the proposals. If the recommendations are presented to the patient and his relatives separately, each may hear what he is pretuned to expect, and each may receive a different message. In that event the successful execution of the treatment plan will be seriously jeopardized. The social worker may suggest that he meet again with the relatives to help them digest and assimilate the recommendations. If some aspects of the remedial program need to be communicated to a court, probation office, school, employer, or welfare department, the social worker may be assigned as the team representative to explain the program, enlist the agency's cooperation, and maintain contact until assured that the desired program is actually in operation.

Social Worker Diagnostician

The social worker may exercise diagnostic skills in a variety of roles and settings besides in his essential contributive part of the classical psychiatric team's diagnostic work.

INTAKE

In many psychiatric clinics, hospitals, mental health centers, and service agencies, one of the psychiatric social worker's responsibilities is to interview prospective patients or clients and to determine their suitability for admission to the agency or institution. In systems language, the social worker has a boundary function in determining who is to be admitted to the subsystem and who is to be excluded. This function requires the social worker to make at least three determinations: (1) the type and severity of the prospective client's problem, (2) the functions and limitations of his agency in handling such problems, and (3) other community resources possibly better qualified to meet the client's needs.

In every instance someone—patient, relative, minister, physician—or some community agency—probate court, probation office, public welfare department, police department, public health department—has made a primary diagnosis: "This person needs to see a psychiatrist." The intake social worker's task is to check the referring diagnosis and agree or disagree with it or modify it. A social worker needs considerable knowledge, skill, clinical experience, and professional poise to feel comfortable and competent in performing this important decision-making duty.

DISCHARGE

When a person is deemed ready for termination of treatment or a move from one facility to another—hospital to halfway house, prison to probation, orphanage to foster home—the social worker must evaluate the readiness or reluctance of a family, the community at large, or specific helping agencies to accept him. Discharge planning implicitly includes a large diagnostic or evaluative component with respect not only to the dischargee but also to the milieu into which he will move.

As in formulation of a treatment plan by the original diagnostic team, a discharge plan must be made optimally suitable, which may necessitate its being modified for adaptability to reality factors in the new environment as the social worker assesses them.

COMMUNITY MENTAL HEALTH CENTER

In these centers the psychiatric social worker fills many roles: administrator, supervisor, teacher, researcher, clinician. Because many centers serve mostly the economically, racially, and socially disadvantaged, the center's staff must learn a kind of psychosocial practice, a coordination of intrapsychic, interpersonal, intrafamilial, and person-environment perspectives. The psychiatrist, the clinical psychologist, and the psychiatric social worker assimilate some of each other's skills and perspectives and interchangeably work to carry out much of the center's program. Storefront operations, satellite clinics, and remote rural centers are commonly staffed by social workers, clinical psychologists, and paraprofessional mental health workers. A consulting psychiatrist may visit weekly or simply be on call. In these facilities the social worker functions as an all-purpose clinician, and his or her diagnostic-evaluative skills are fully used.

CRISIS INTERVENTION

In clinical practice, crisis is a stress-producing discrepancy between an environmental stressor impinging on a client and the resources he has available to manage and resolve it. The stressor is usually an unanticipated environmental change of some magnitude, not readily amenable to the stress-reducing maneuvers on which the client normally relies. A resultant sense of stress, distress, immobilizes the client and blocks possible action. The clinician-social worker, through his or her understanding of client-environment interactions and his or her experience in suitable environmental manipulation, can promptly assist the client to cope temporarily with his seemingly overwhelming problem while initiating measures to correct it. He or she can sort through the client's fears and complaints, focus on the real problem, insist that there is a solution, suggest helping resources available, and shift the client from a position of helplessness into active participation in a problem-solving effort (Edwards, 1977).

The proper initial goal of the clinician is anxiety reduction. When the crisis has been successfully resolved, attention may then be directed to a search for explanations concerning the client's collapse in the situation. The client may accept a recommendation to become a patient and enter short-term psychotherapy, family therapy, or a formal psychiatric diagnostic evaluation.

Psychiatric Education

Classical psychiatric diagnostic teams function in varying degrees of cooperation, coordination, and integration achieved by their members. Still, traditional distinctions of specialty disciplines obtain in the division of labor: The psychiatrist sees the patient, and the social worker sees the relatives. In many practice settings this distinction has been or is being discarded. Today's psychiatrist interviews, evaluates, and treats families and groups; today's social worker interviews, evaluates, and treats individual patients.

Team practice is common to psychiatric residency training centers, which usually have a plentiful supply of professional personnel and the goal of teaching thorough, detailed diagnosis and treatment. Staffs of these centers are aware that their graduates will practice in a variety of situations—solo practice, mental hospital, community clinic, social agency—in which traditional team practice will not always be possible or appropriate. During training, the resident should be afforded ample opportunity to work with families and negotiate with community agencies in his patients' behalf. This training applies most importantly to child psychiatry trainees. In some centers two child psychiatry residents are assigned to a new case. One, supervised by a child psychiatrist, works with the family. The social worker's possible contributions to the education of today's multifunctioning psychiatrist are, therefore, considerable.

Suggested Cross References

The family in relation to psychiatry is discussed in Section 5.3. Family therapy is discussed in Section 30.6. Community psychiatry is discussed in Chapter 45. For a further discussion of social workers in psychiatric settings see Chapter 51.

REFERENCES

* Briar, S. Social casework and social group work: Historical and social science foundations. In *Encyclopedia of Social Work*, R. Morris, editor, p. 1237. National Association of Social Workers, New York, 1971.
Edwards, R. *Crisis Intervention and How It Works*. Charles C Thomas, Springfield, Ill., 1977.
* Group for the Advancement of Psychiatry. *The Diagnostic Process in Child Psychiatry*. Group for the Advancement of Psychiatry, New York, 1957.
* Hall, B., and Wheeler, W. The patient and his relatives: Initial joint interview. Soc. Work, 2: 75, 1957.
* Menninger Clinic Children's Division. *Disturbed Children: Examination and Assessment through Team Process*. Jossey-Bass, San Francisco, 1969.
* Meyers, H. L. The therapeutic functions of the evaluation process. Bull. Menninger Clin., 20: 9, 1956.
Modlin, H. C., and Faris, M. T. Group adaptation and integration in psychiatric team practice. Psychiatry, 19: 97, 1956.
* Modlin, H. C., Gardner, R. W., and Faris, M. T. Implications of a therapeutic process in evaluations by psychiatric teams. Am. J. Orthopsychiatry, 28: 647, 1958.
Richmond, M. E. *Social Diagnosis*. Russell Sage Foundation, New York, 1917.
Turner, F. J. *Differential Diagnosis and Treatment in Social Work*. Free Press of Glencoe, New York, 1976.

12.9 Medical Assessment in Psychiatric Practice

MARC H. HOLLENDER, M.D.

CHARLES E. WELLS, M.D.

Introduction

The place of medical assessment in the care of psychiatric patients remains controversial. Some psychiatrists contend that a complete medical work-up is essential for every patient; others maintain that for many patients it is unnecessary and that for a few it is even contraindicated. It is clear, however, that the medical status of every psychiatric patient should be considered at the outset and that usually it is the psychiatrist who decides if a medical evaluation is needed and, if so, what it should include.

Selection of Patients for Medical Assessment

In the selection of those patients who should undergo a complete medical examination and those who need not, the nature of the complaints is the critical criterion. Complaints can be divided into three groups: those involving (1) the body, (2) the mind, and (3) social interactions.

If symptoms involve the body—as with headache, impotence, and palpitations—a medical examination is required to determine, insofar as possible, the part that somatic processes play in causing the distress. The same approach is indicated for symptoms involving the mind—such as depression, anxiety, hallucinations, and paranoid delusions—because they can be expressions of somatic processes. The situation is different if the patient complains only of being upset because of long-standing difficulties in interactions with teachers, employers, parents, or spouse. When the problem is clearly limited to the social sphere, there is no special indication for a medical examination.

A periodic medical check-up may be desirable for everyone, but it is not appropriate, except under special circumstances, for the psychiatrist to require a complete medical examination for a person without physical or mental complaints. To rule that all patients consulting a psychiatrist must undergo such an examination seems unwarranted.

Performance of the Medical Assessment

Psychoanalysts do not perform physical examinations on their analysands, nor should they. Unfortunately, this rule, like that of not conferring with family members, has spilled over into situations for which it was never intended. Misapplication of this injunction, especially on the part of the neophyte, has resulted sometimes in an inappropriate hands-off policy, even in a hospital setting.

Role blurring, characteristic of the community mental health movement, has also interfered with obtaining adequate medical diagnostic studies. Here the shift of focus to social issues has resulted in neglect of the biological dimension by nonmedical personnel taking primary responsibility for patients they refer to as clients.

For practical reasons, most psychiatric patients who require a medical assessment should have it performed by an internist or a family practitioner, rather than by a psychiatrist. Few psychiatrists see enough patients requiring complete medical evaluations to maintain their skills in performing physical examinations. Moreover, the demands on psychiatrists' time are such that it is impractical for them to do what other physicians regard as their primary responsibility.

Although practical and technical reasons can be adduced to excuse psychiatrists from performing complete physical examinations routinely, they should still be expected to elicit a complete medical history and to use their visual, auditory, and olfactory powers fully. Whereas loss of skill in palpation, percussion, and auscultation can be justified, loss of skill in observation cannot. If the detection of nonverbal psychological cues is a cardinal part of the psychiatrists' function, the detection of indications of somatic illness, subtle as well as striking, should also be part of their function.

The Psychiatrist's Role in Medical Assessment

The objectives of the medical evaluation of a psychiatric patient are (1) the detection of underlying and perhaps unsuspected organic pathology that may be primarily responsible for psychiatric symptoms, (2) an understanding of demonstrated disease as a factor in over-all psychiatric debility, and (3) an appreciation of somatic symptoms that reflect primarily psychological, rather than organic, disease.

When the psychiatrist does not conduct the medical examination, he or she should make certain that it has been carried out properly and should become fully conversant with the results and their implications.

Patients reach psychiatrists for evaluation and treatment by various routes, and planning for proper medical examinations must take this diversity into account.

THE REFERRED PATIENT

The situation is probably simplest when the patient is referred by a primary physician. Here the psychiatrist turns to the referring physician for information about the patient's general health and the extent of physical pathology, if any. This information usually provides a reliable baseline.

Occasionally, however, the patient's psychological status suggests the possibility of a specific disease not identified during a recent medical examination. It may then be necessary to ask the primary physician if this possibility has been explored adequately; if not, the patient should be sent back for additional studies.

The patient aware of physical changes but who is told that there is no evidence of disease and that any indisposition is imaginary or emotional is likely to become depressed, precipitating a referral to the psychiatrist. In the early stages of myasthenia gravis or multiple sclerosis, for example, this phenomenon is not unusual. The physician must remember that diagnostic studies, however thorough, seldom exclude pathology with certainty. Therefore, if new signs or symptoms develop or if it seems that old ones were ignored, it is advisable to request another physical examination or perhaps additional laboratory studies.

A similar situation is presented by the patient with unexplained or unusual somatic symptoms who is referred for psychiatric treatment on the assumption that the complaints must, therefore, be psychological in origin. If the psychiatrist cannot adduce definite evidence of psychological problems, the patient should be returned to the referring physician for additional medical studies and continuing surveillance.

THE EMERGENCY ROOM PATIENT

In most instances the patient in the emergency room is seen first by a primary physician, who elicits a history, performs a physical examination, and orders pertinent laboratory tests and X-ray studies. Only if the findings are essentially negative and there is a suspicion of an emotional or mental disorder is the psychiatrist called.

In some instances, when the triaging person, perhaps a nurse, immediately labels the patient as psychiatric, the psychiatrist may be the first physician called. In these cases it is especially important that clues be sought that point to medical, as well as psychiatric, disorders and that all appropriate studies be performed.

Acutely psychotic patients, especially if they are obstreperous or assaultive, may be precipitously labeled psychiatric by the primary physician who is eager to dispose of disruptive and unwelcome problems. The psychiatrist—mindful of how often delirium, encephalitis, and seizure disorders present in this manner—should perform a thorough examination.

THE SELF-REFERRED PATIENT

If the patient's complaints are clearly the result of faulty interactions or problems in living—especially if the problems are long-standing—a medical examination is not required. If, on the other hand, features of the history presented by the self-identified psychiatric patient suggest a physical disorder, the lead should be carefully pursued. For example, when a patient who has rarely experienced emotional upsets complains of depression, anxiety, and irritability that cannot readily be explained on a psychodynamic basis, an underlying disease that has triggered these symptoms should be suspected. In women whose symptoms come on 4 or 5 days before each period, the possibility of water retention, a phenomenon that also produces premenstrual weight gain, can be suspected.

THE PATIENT IN PSYCHIATRIC TREATMENT

Because intercurrent illnesses may arise while patients are being treated for their psychological problems, it is essential for the psychiatrist to be alert to factors calling for additional diagnostic studies. Seidenberg (1963) noted that patients in psychoanalysis may be "all too willing or desirous of attributing their illness to psychological problems." Attention should be paid to the possible use of denial, especially if the complaints do not seem to be related to the conflicts currently in focus.

At a time of increased stress, a long-term psychotherapy patient developed urinary frequency, which she attributed to the pressure she was under. Only after much urging did she agree to a medical evaluation, which revealed severe cystitis.

Not only do patients attribute somatic disorders to psychological problems, but therapists sometimes do so, too. There is the danger of providing psychodynamic explanations for physical symptoms. For example, it was observed that a disturbed young woman in a psychiatric unit would curl up in a clothes basket and remain for long periods in this position, described as fetal and ascribed to regression. Later, when the diagnosis of meningoencephalitis was established, it seemed that a better explanation for her behavior was the need to relieve pressure on nerve roots.

The appearance of symptoms such as dizziness and drowsiness or signs such as skin eruption and gait disturbance, which are common side effects of psychotropic medications, calls for a medical reevaluation if the patient fails to respond in a reasonable period of time to changes in the kind or the dosage of the medications administered.

Early in an illness, paucity or an absence of significant physical or laboratory findings is common. In such an instance and especially if there is glaring evidence of psychic trauma or emotional conflict, all symptoms are likely to be attributed to a psychiatric disorder and new symptoms seen in this light. Indicators for repeating the medical work-up may be missed unless the physician is alert to clues suggesting that some symptoms do not fit the original diagnosis and point, instead, to a medical illness. Occasionally, a patient with an acute illness, like encephalitis, is hospitalized with the diagnosis of schizophrenia, or a patient with a subacute illness, like carcinoma of the pancreas, is treated in a private office or clinic with the diagnosis of depression. Although it may not be possible to make the correct diagnosis at the time of the initial psychiatric evaluation, continued surveillance and attention to clinical details usually provide clues leading to the recognition of the underlying disease.

The likelihood of intercurrent illnesses is greater with some psychiatric disorders than with others. An example is drug abuse, in which there is lowered resistance to infection and a heightened likelihood of trauma, dietary deficiencies, and skin diseases—such as scabies, impetigo, and pediculosis—commonly associated with poor hygiene.

When somatic and psychological dysfunctions are known to coexist, the psychiatrist should be fully conversant with the patient's medical status. In the presence of cardiac decompensation, peripheral neuropathy, or other physical disorders, it is essential to assess the nature and degree of impairment attributable to the physical disorder and to establish a realistic baseline for physical endeavors. Does the patient exploit a disability, or is it ignored with resultant overexertion? If activity and complaints seem out of keeping with the physical disability, a psychiatric consultation is likely to be sought. To render a meaningful opinion, the psychiatrist should carefully review the medical findings and also take a detailed psychiatric history. One pitfall for medical practitioners, including psychiatrists, is to assume that a diagnostic label defines the extent of the disability. The situation is compounded if the physician imparts this viewpoint to the patient. It is essential for the psychiatrist to assess functional capabilities and limitations, rather than to make a sweeping judgment based on a diagnostic label.

With certain patients under care for psychophysiological disorders, it is necessary to be especially vigilant about their medical conditions. Such is the case with patients with ulcerative colitis who are bleeding profusely and patients with anorexia nervosa who are losing appreciable weight. In these circumstances there is the possibility that the patients' lives are endangered.

The Medical Assessment

The medical assessment consists of more than the physical examination; it includes all the procedures conducted for patient evaluation. With each patient the psychiatrist depends on history taking and observation to gauge general health. In selected instances the information derived serves as a guide in conducting the physical examination and performing laboratory procedures.

HISTORY

When patients are seen for psychiatric evaluation, two aspects of the medical history should be developed (1) facts about known physical disease and dysfunction, (2) information about specific physical complaints.

The first objective can usually be achieved by the routine inquiry about disease or dysfunction involving the cardiovascular, pulmonary, gastrointestinal, endocrine, genitourinary, hepatic, musculoskeletal, and nervous systems. As a rule, it is not necessary to carry out a minutely detailed review of the bodily systems. However, detailed information should be gathered when appropriate. An inquiry should be made into the present and past use of coffee, tea, tobacco, alcohol, other drugs, and medications. Such information is essential not only for a full understanding of the patient's problems but also for planning appropriate treatment. One should hesitate, for example, before using a medication such as chlorpromazine, with its potential for causing hypotension, in a patient with known cerebrovascular insufficiency or imipramine or amitriptyline, with their cardiotoxic effects, in a patient with a history of myocardial irritability. These three medications may also be contraindicated in a patient whose hypertension is being controlled by guanethidine, because their actions are antagonistic to this particular antihypertensive agent.

Information about previous illnesses may provide valuable clues. For example, if the present disorder is paranoid in nature and there is a history of several similar episodes, each of which responded promptly to diverse forms of treatment and left no residuals, the possibility of amphetamine psychosis is strongly suggested. A drug screen should be ordered to pursue this lead.

An occupational history may provide essential information. Exposure to inorganic mercury may result in complaints suggesting a neurosis or functional psychosis, and exposure to lead, as in smelting, may produce an organic mental disorder. The latter clinical picture may also result from imbibing moonshine with a high lead content.

More difficult and more variable is the second aspect of history taking—eliciting information concerning specific complaints presented by the patient. Here the complementary nature of the physician's medical and psychological knowledge comes into full play. For example, the physician must be able to obtain from the patient complaining of headache sufficient information to predict with considerable certainty whether the pain is or is not the result of cranial pathology. At the same time the examiner should be alert enough to recognize that the pain in the right shoulder of a hypochondriacal patient with abdominal discomfort may be the classical referred pain of gallbladder disease.

The medical history should always include information concerning medications currently being taken by the patient. Many medications, such as reserpine and isoniazid, may produce side effects of a psychiatric nature. A prescribed medication taken in therapeutic dosage may for various reasons occasionally reach high blood levels. Digitalis intoxication, for example, may occur under such circumstances and result in an impairment of mental functioning.

Differential diagnosis. It is essential that the psychiatrist listen to the recital of symptoms not only in terms of diagnosing psychiatric disorders and understanding psychodynamic connections but also in terms of diagnosing medical diseases.

Consider the patient who is dyspneic or breathless. Is the disorder due to pulmonary disease or depression? In pulmonary or obstructive airway disease, the onset of the symptom is usually insidious, whereas in depression it is sudden. In depression, breathlessness is experienced at rest, shows little change with exertion, and may fluctuate even within a matter of minutes. The onset of the respiratory distress coincides with the onset of the affective disturbance and is often accompanied by attacks of dizziness, sweating, palpitations, and paresthesias. Only patients with the most advanced respiratory incapacity experience breathlessness at rest. Most striking and of the greatest assistance in making a differential diagnosis is the emphasis placed on difficulty experienced on inspiration by patients with depression and difficulty on expiration by patients with pulmonary disease (Burns, 1971).

A young woman was evaluated on a psychiatric unit for anxiety attacks of 2 years' duration. The attacks began suddenly, were accompanied by a rapid pulse, and lasted from several minutes to half an hour. Symptoms during the attack included palpitations, rapid breathing, anxiety, perioral and hand paresthesia, anterior neck discomfort, trembling, lightheadedness, a feeling of unreality, and fear of dying. Episodes occurred as often as two or three times a day but occasionally disappeared for as long as 3 weeks. They were more common when the patient felt under pressure, but she could identify no specific precipitating factor. She described herself as very anxious between attacks and as clinging to her husband for security. The patient fulfilled the criteria for panic disorder and anxiety neurosis. Yet the diagnosis of mitral valve prolapse syndrome needed to be considered in the differential diagnosis.

The cardiology consultant made the diagnosis of mitral valve prolapse syndrome on the basis of auscultatory, stress electrocardiographic (ECG), and echocardiographic findings. Typical auscultatory findings included a midsystolic click and a blowing musical apical late systolic murmur that varied with position change. The stress ECG revealed tachycardia (190 beats a minute), sinus arrythmia, and wandering atrial pacemaker. The echocardiogram demonstrated abnormal mitral valve movement, considered to be diagnostic of mitral valve prolapse syndrome (Pariser et al., 1978).

Awareness of how symptoms cluster into patterns typical of particular disorders is as important for the psychiatrist as it is for other physicians. For example, fleeting, periodic stabbing pains in the left side of the neck may suggest angina pectoris, coronary artery disease, or hyperventilation syndrome. Hyperventilation syndrome is most likely if other symptoms include a few or all the following: onset at rest, sighing respirations, apprehension, anxiety, depersonalization, palpitations, feelings of an inability to swallow, numbness of the feet and hands, and carpal pedal spasm.

Diagnostic aids. Symptoms that are atypical for functional psychiatric disorders should also be alerters. For example, if a patient with hallucinations and delusions complains of a severe or excruciating headache at the onset of the psychosis and during its early phase, the symptom should not be written off as being of little consequence or as part of a schizophrenic process. Such a symptom suggests the possibility of brain pathology and calls for careful and repeated neurological examinations. Similarly, if a psychotic patient remains incontinent after treatment for several days with psychotropic medication, some cause other than schizophrenia should be suspected.

Organic brain dysfunction. This topic has been singled out because of its special importance for the psychiatrist. Few patients seen for diagnostic evaluation by the psychiatrist present textbook symptoms and signs of organic brain disease. When they do, the recognition of organicity is easy, but detecting its cause may be a formidable task. More often, patients with organic brain disease are seen early in the course of the illness, when the evidence of organicity is relatively slight. Liston (1977) has emphasized, for example, the frequency with which depression is the initial symptom in presenile dementia and the frequency with which the correct diagnosis is obscured by the affective symptoms. The diagnosis should be seriously entertained in three particular circumstances: (1) when patients present numerous somatic complaints that conform to no recognizable pattern of disease, especially if these complaints are not consonant with their long-standing life style; (2) when patients present numerous psychiatric symptoms that conform to no definite diagnostic category, especially if similar complaints have been uncommon in the past; and (3) when patients' histories remain vague and unclear, even after lengthy and precise questioning.

The possibility of organic brain dysfunction should routinely be considered, but, when specific features suggest that this diagnosis is likely, the course of the examination is more firmly fixed. In history taking particular information is sought. Has memory loss been noted? Have there been difficulties with concentration, dealing with complex materials, or keeping information and routines in order? What is the course of the illness—abrupt or gradual in onset; stuttering, stable, or slowly progressive? Is there a history of head injury? Have there been headaches, changes in the level of consciousness, loss of consciousness, or epileptiform seizures? Have sedatives, tranquilizers, antidepressants, analgesics, alcohol, or other drugs been used? Are there symptoms that suggest discrete focal brain lesions—aphasia, apraxia, agnosia, or focal motor or sensory changes? Are there symptoms of a generalized systemic disease that commonly impairs brain function, such as hypertension, systemic lupus erythematosus, or pernicious anemia? Often, accurate answers to these questions can be obtained only from family members or associates of the patient.

The suspicion of organic brain disease also modifies the form of the psychiatric examination. Although the evaluation for brain pathology is an integral part of every psychiatric evaluation, the intactness of the cerebral structures is frequently gathered from the general demeanor of the patient and the tenor of the interview, rather than demonstrated directly. When organic brain dysfunction is specifically suggested, however, the examiner is more likely to use those parts of the mental status examination especially affected by cerebral pathology. Orientation, taken for granted in most interviews, should be ascertained by direct questions. Specific memory components—immediate recall, recent memory, and remote memory—are evaluated. The level of intellectual function is ascertained by questions measuring general information, by tasks requiring calculations, and by problems involving discrimination and judgment, the questions being chosen for their appropriateness to the patient's general cultural and educational level.

Occasionally, symptoms usually associated with a psychiatric disorder, if pursued in detail, alert the examiner to the possibility of a medical disorder. Examples are auditory hallucinations in which voices are heard only toward one side and visual hallucinations in which a person or an object is seen only in one part of the visual field. Although phenomena like these may be encountered in schizophrenia, they should first suggest the possibility of a cerebral lesion, and neurological studies should be conducted with special care.

OBSERVATION

When psychiatrists-in-training are exhorted to develop their powers of observation, it usually means that they should learn to recognize unconsciously determined nonverbal clues. To the same extent they should also develop their powers of observation in assessing general health and in recognizing manifestations of physical illness.

Visual evaluation. The scrutiny of the patient begins at the first encounter. In moving from the waiting room to the interview room, the gait is observed for telltale signs of dysfunction. Is there unsteadiness? Ataxia suggests diffuse brain disease, alcohol or other drug intoxication, chorea, spinocerebellar degeneration or weakness based on general physical disease, or on an esoteric underlying disorder, such as myotonic dystrophy. Does the patient walk without the usual associated arm movements and turn in a rigid fashion, like a toy soldier, as is seen in early Parkinson's disease? Is there an asymmetry of gait, such as turning one foot outward, dragging a leg, or absent swing of one arm, suggesting a focal brain lesion?

As soon as the patient is seated, the examiner's attention should be directed to grooming. Is the patient's hair combed, and are nails clean and teeth brushed? Has clothing been chosen with care, and is it appropriate? Although inattention to dress and hygiene is common in emotional disorders, it is also a hallmark of organic brain disease, and particular lapses—such as the mismatching of socks, stockings, or shoes—should strongly suggest an organic brain disease.

The patient's posture and automatic movements or the lack of them should be noted. A stooped, flexed posture with a paucity of automatic movements should bring to mind the possibility of Parkinson's disease, diffuse hemispheric disease, or the side effects of psychotropic medications. An unusual tilt of the head may be adopted to avoid eye contact, but it can also result from diplopia, visual field defect, or focal cerebellar dysfunction. Frequent quick, purposeless movements are characteristic of anxiety, but they are equally characteristic of chorea or hyperthyroidism. Tremors, although commonly seen with anxiety, may point to Parkinson's disease or essential tremor. Patients with essential tremor sometimes seek psychiatric treatment because they believe their tremor must be due to unrecognized fear and anxiety, as they have often been told by their associates. Finally, unilateral paucity or excess of movement suggests focal brain disease.

Next, the appearance of the patient is scrutinized to assess general health. Does the patient appear robust, or is there a certain indefinable sense of ill health? Does looseness of clothing indicate recent weight loss? Is there shortness of breath or coughing? Does the general physiognomy suggest a specific disease? Persons with Klinefelter's syndrome, who may be seen for emotional troubles and intellectual impairment, show a feminine fat distribution and lack of development of secondary sexual characteristics. The person with acromegaly is usually immediately recognizable.

What is the status of the patient's nutrition? Recent weight loss, although often encountered in depression and schizophrenia, may be due to gastrointestinal disease, diffuse carcinomatosis, Addison's disease, hyperthyroidism, and many other somatic disorders. Obesity may result from either emotional distress or organic disease. The moon facies, truncal obesity, and buffalo hump are striking findings in Cushing's syndrome, as are symptoms of emotional distress. The puffy, bloated appearance of hypothyroidism and the massive obesity and periodic respiration of the Pickwickian syndrome are also easily recognized in those patients who may present psychiatric symptoms.

The skin frequently provides valuable information. The yellow coloration of hepatic dysfunction and the pallor of anemia are reasonably distinctive. Intense reddening may be due to carbon monoxide poisoning or photosensitivity resulting from porphyria or phenothiazines. Eruptions may be manifestations of disorders such as systemic lupus erythematosus, tuberous sclerosis with adenoma sebaceum, and sensitivity to drugs. A dusky purplish cast of the face plus telangiectasia are almost pathognomonic of alcoholism.

The psychiatrist may be involved in situations in which it is suspected that the patient is creating his or her own disease,

FIGURE 1. Patient prior to developing Cushing's syndrome.

FIGURE 2. Patient with Cushing's syndrome.

whether it is a dermatitis, bleeding disorder, or hyperinsulinism. Careful observation may result in pursuing clues that lead to the correct diagnosis. For example, the location and the shape of the skin lesions and the time of their appearance may suggest the likelihood of dermatitis factitia (Hollender and Abram, 1973).

The examiner should scan the face and head for evidence of disease. Premature whitening of the hair occurs in pernicious anemia and thinning and coarseness of the hair in myxedema. Pupillary changes are produced by various drugs—constriction by opiates and dilatation by anticholinergic agents and hallucinogens. The combination of dilated and fixed pupils and a dry skin and mucous membranes should immediately suggest the likelihood of atropine or atropine-like toxicity. Suffusion of the conjunctivae suggests alcoholism, the use of marijuana, or obstruction of the superior vena cava. Flattening of the nasolabial fold on one side may be the result of focal dysfunction of the contralateral cerebral hemisphere, as may weakness of one side of the face, as manifested in speaking, smiling, and grimacing.

The patient's state of alertness and responsiveness is carefully evaluated. Drowsiness and inattentiveness may be due to a psychological problem, but they are more likely to result from organic brain dysfunction, whether secondary to intrinsic brain disease or to an exogenous factor, such as drug intoxication.

Auditory evaluation. Examiners should listen as intently as they look for evidence of physical disease. Slowed speech is characteristic not only of depression but of diffuse brain dysfunction; unusually rapid speech is characteristic not only of mania and anxiety but also of hyperthyroidism. A weak voice with monotony of tone is heard in Parkinson's disease, and psychiatrists frequently see patients in an early stage of this disease who complain mainly of depression. A slow, low pitched, hoarse voice should suggest to the attentive listener the possibility of hypothyroidism. Asher (1949) described the voice quality as like that of

a bad gramophone record of a drowsy, slightly intoxicated person with a bad cold and a plum in the mouth.

Difficulty in initiating speech may be due to anxiety or stuttering, or it may be the hallmark of Parkinson's disease. Easy fatigability of speech, which may be a manifestation of an emotional problem, is also characteristic of myasthenia gravis, and these patients are sometimes seen by psychiatrists before the correct diagnosis has been made because their symptoms suggest a psychological, rather than an organic, disorder. Slurring of speech may result from alcohol, other drugs, or structural brain changes.

Word production, as well as the quality of the speech, is important. Even occasional mispronunciations or choice of an incorrect word suggest aphasia and, thus, the possibility of a lesion of the dominant hemisphere. The same possibility exists when the patient perseverates, has trouble finding a name or a word, or describes an object or an event in an indirect fashion (paraphasia). Coarseness, profanity, or inappropriate disclosures when not consonant with the patient's socioeconomic status or educational level may indicate loss of inhibition due to dementia. Even so ill defined a quality as vagueness of speech suggests the possibility of organic brain dysfunction, as well as various psychological disorders.

Olfactory evaluation. Although the human sense of smell is neither so well developed nor so eminently useful as the senses of sight and hearing, it sometimes provides information of value. The unpleasant odor of a patient who fails to bathe makes one suspicious not only of depression but also of organic brain dysfunction. The odor of alcohol or of substances used to hide it is revealing in a patient who attempts to conceal a drinking problem. Similarly, recognizing the burnt-rope odor of marihuana smoke may be informative. Occasionally, a uriniferous odor calls attention to bladder dysfunction secondary to nervous system disease. Characteristic odors are also noted in patients with diabetic acidosis and uremia or in hepatic coma.

PHYSICAL EXAMINATION

Psychological considerations. The effect on the patient of even a routine physical examination should be borne in mind. Instruments and procedures may be frightening. A simple running account of what is being done can prevent much needless anxiety. Moreover, if the patient is consistently forewarned of what will be done, there is not the dread of being suddenly and painfully surprised. Comments such as, "There's nothing to this" or, "You don't have to be afraid because this won't hurt" leave the patient in the dark and are much less reassuring than a few words about what actually will be done (Hollender, 1958).

Although the physical examination is most likely to stimulate or intensify a reaction of fear and anxiety, it can also stir up sexual feelings. Weiss and English (1957) warned that a suspicious, hysterical woman with fantasies of being seduced may misinterpret an ordinary movement in the physical examination as an amorous advance. Similarly, a paranoid man with homosexual fears may perceive a rectal examination as a sexual attack.

In considering the implications of a procedure, the physician should remember that if he or she lingers over the examination of a particular organ because of scientific interest in an unusual but normal variation, the patient is likely to assume that a serious pathological process has been discovered. Such a reaction is most likely to be profound in an anxious or hypochondriacal patient.

The physical examination occasionally serves a psychotherapeutic function. An anxious patient may be relieved to learn that in spite of troublesome symptoms, there is no evidence of the serious illness that is feared. The young man or woman who complains of chest pain and is certain that this pain heralds a heart attack can usually be reassured by the report of a normal physical examination and electrocardiogram. The reassurance, however, relieves only the acute episode. Unless psychiatric treatment succeeds in dealing with the determinants of the reaction, recurrent episodes are likely.

Sending a patient who has a deeply ingrained fear of malignancy for still another study intended to be reassuring usually proves unrewarding. Lederer (1953) reported this case:

> In spite of repeated examinations, a patient (a physician) was certain he had carcinoma of the pharynx. Finally, a colleague, in an effort to produce proof positive, biopsied the area of complaint. When the patient was shown a section of normal tissue, he immediately declared that this section had been substituted for one showing malignant cells.

During the performance of the physical examination, an observant physician may note indications of emotional distress. Indeed, this observation may be the starting point for a train of events leading to a psychiatric referral. Tunnadine (1973), in writing about the vaginal examination, stated that if the physician observes the patient's behavior, much may be learned about her sexual attitude and problems. On the basis of observation, the physician may ask a few questions that encourage the patient to describe her distress and to express her desire for help.

Deferring the physical examination. Occasionally, circumstances make it necessary or desirable to defer a complete medical assessment. An example is the paranoid or manic patient who is combative and resistive. In this instance a medical history should be elicited from a family member if possible; unless there is a pressing reason, the physical examination should be deferred until the patient is more amenable to being examined.

The medical assessment should also be deferred in some office evaluations in which for psychological reasons it is ill advised or unwise to recommend it. For example, with today's increased sensitivity and openness about sexual matters and a greater proneness to turn quickly for psychiatric help, male patients may complain about the failure at an initial attempt to consummate a sexual relationship. After taking a detailed history, the psychiatrist may conclude that the failure has prematurely been defined as a problem requiring attention. If this is the case, it is advisable to recommend neither a physical examination nor a course of psychotherapy, because doing so would reinforce the notion of pathology.

The neurological examination. If psychiatrists suspect the existence of an underlying somatic disorder, such as diabetes mellitus or Cushing's syndrome, they almost always refer the patient to another physician for examination and treatment. If, however, organic brain dysfunction is suspected, psychiatrists may wish to assume this responsibility themselves. The task of detecting signs and making the diagnosis is especially difficult when the brain disease is in an early stage.

A careful neurological examination is mandatory for each patient suspected of having organic brain dysfunction. During the history taking process, the level of awareness, attentiveness to details of the examination, understanding, facial expression, speech, posture, and gait are noted. The neurological examination should then be performed with two objectives in mind: (1) to elicit signs pointing to focal, circumscribed cerebral dysfunction and (2) to elicit signs pointing to diffuse, bilateral cerebral disease. The first objective is met by the routine neurological examination, which primarily reveals asymmetries in the motor, perceptual, and reflex functions of the two sides of the body due to focal hemispheric disease. The second objective is met by performing specific maneuvers designed to elicit signs of diffuse brain dysfunction, as described in detail by Paulson (1977). These signs include the corneomandibular, sucking, snout, palmomental, grasp, and toe grasp reflexes and

the persistence of the glabella tap response. Such signs strongly suggest diffuse brain dysfunction.

Incidental findings. Psychiatrists should be able to evaluate the significance of findings uncovered by consultants. For example, the patient who complains of a lump in the throat (globus hystericus) may be found on examination of the pharynx to have hypertrophied lymphoid tissue. It is then tempting to think of a cause-and-effect relationship, and, indeed, some textbooks of otolaryngology (Lederer, 1952) have ascribed the sensation of the lump in the throat to the hypertrophied tissue. But how can one be sure that this finding is not incidental? Has the patient been observed to have hypertrophied lymphoid tissue at a time when no complaint is registered? And are there many persons who usually have hypertrophied tissue but never experience the sensation of a lump in the throat?

Another example is the patient with multiple sclerosis who complains of an inability to walk but on neurological examination has only mild spasticity and unilateral Babinski's sign. Again, it is tempting to ascribe the symptom to the neurological disorder, but in this instance the findings are totally out of keeping with the manifest dysfunction.

Often, some lesion may be found that may account for a symptom, but the psychiatrist should make every effort to separate a causative lesion from an incidental one, to separate a lesion that produces the symptom from one that is merely found in the area of the symptom.

DIAGNOSTIC STUDIES

Even in this era of defensive medicine, diagnostic studies should never be performed merely for the sake of completeness. To do so would subject patients to unwarranted discomfort and expense. Procedures recently performed and reported as negative should not be repeated unless new signs or symptoms appear or indications for follow-up are present. Diagnostic procedures that involve a significant expense, that are likely to produce much discomfort, or that entail appreciable risk should be ordered only if there is reasonable likelihood that the findings may alter the plan of treatment and thereby favorably influence the outcome.

If a procedure is pressingly indicated for medical reasons, it should be done regardless of the patient's emotional or mental state. Every effort, of course, should be made to assuage anxiety, reduce pain, and make the timing as favorable as possible.

Selecting diagnostic procedures. In patient care the medical evaluation and the psychological evaluation should be addressed as separate processes, each having its own rules, procedures, and limitations. Thus, to evaluate somatic illness, the physician selects diagnostic tests to measure physical functions. Data obtained from the physical examination and from laboratory procedures do not serve as evidence for or against the existence of a psychological disorder. Conversely, data obtained from the psychological investigation do not serve as evidence for or against the existence of a somatic disorder. In practice, both aspects of the investigation should and usually do proceed concurrently but independently (Hollender and Robbins, 1958).

Possible organic brain disease. Not infrequently, even after a thorough history and a neurological examination, the psychiatrist is still in doubt as to the presence or absence of organic brain dysfunction and may have to turn for help to ancillary testing procedures. Psychological assessment (Wells and Buchanan, 1977) is often the most useful of the available procedures. The clinical psychologist has tests capable of revealing small defects in function resulting from focal or diffuse brain disease, but the psychologist must be apprised of the problems so that he or she can make appropriate choices among the many tests available. The psychiatrist should also be familiar with the psychological tests used. The expectation then is not for the psychologist to make the diagnosis but, rather, to provide a set of observations helpful in reaching a definitive diagnosis. Regrettably, when the presence or absence of organicity is unclear on the basis of clinical observations, the uncertainty is often borne out, rather than resolved, by psychological testing. In such cases, repeat psychological evaluation, after an interval of several months, often helps to resolve the problem.

The growing availability of computerized cranial tomography (CT-scan) has greatly expanded the psychiatrist's capacity to explore the intracranial cavity for possible brain lesions. Although a relatively costly procedure, computerized cranial tomography is safe and painless and is capable of demonstrating even small lesions, whether vascular, neoplastic, or atrophic in character. The routine use of CT-scans in psychiatric patients is impractical, but it is often the first ancillary diagnostic procedure chosen when organicity is recognized or seriously suspected. Woods (1976) suggested the following indications for CT-scans in psychiatric patients: (1) a focal abnormality on neurological examination, (2) dementia, (3) a persistent or unexplained confusional state, (4) seizures, (5) a focal or generalized electroencephalographic abnormality, (6) a history of rage attacks or impulsive aggressive behavior, (7) psychological test findings that suggest organicity, and (8) an unusual headache history.

Increased use of the CT-scan has led to decreased reliance on skull X-rays and electroencephalography. Nevertheless, both remain useful procedures. The diagnostic yield from routine skull radiography is low, but, since it is a relatively harmless procedure that occasionally reveals significant abnormalities, its use should be continued, especially for those patients in whom the indications of organicity are insufficient to warrant the expense of a CT-scan. The electroencephalogram (EEG), another safe and painless procedure, is capable of revealing clear evidence of organic brain dysfunction that is sometimes undemonstrable by other means. For example, the EEG may reveal evidence of delirium or epilepsy, disorders often producing no abnormalities on the CT-scan. For the psychiatrist the EEG has its greatest usefulness in cases in which the distinction between delirium and functional psychosis is unclear, and in episodic disorders.

Definite evidence of organic dysfunction demonstrated by any of the diagnostic steps—interview, neurological examination, psychological testing, computerized cranial tomography, skull X-rays, and electroencephalography—may point to the need for additional procedures—spinal fluid examination, radioactive brain scan, radioiodinated serum albumin scan, arteriography. These studies should be reserved, however, for those patients in whom simpler studies have demonstrated unequivocal organic involvement, and even then they should be ordered only when there is a clear likelihood that they will yield information of specific diagnostic or therapeutic value. These additional procedures are painful or expensive or both, and their diagnostic yield when organic damage is only suspected is extremely low.

IMPORTANCE OF MEDICAL ILLNESS IN PSYCHIATRIC PATIENTS

Numerous articles call attention to the need for thorough medical screening of patients seen in psychiatric hospital units and clinics. To assess the magnitude of the problem, Penick and Carrier (1967) reviewed the records of 4,032 patients admitted to a private psychiatric hospital during a 30-month period. They found that 106 patients (2.4 per cent) had been transferred to a general hospital for the treatment of medical or surgical illnesses. In many of the patients in whom medical or surgical illnesses coexisted with psychiatric disorders, treatment of the physical illnesses took precedence over treatment of the psychiatric disorders. In 38 patients (about 1 per cent of all admissions), medical illnesses presented primarily with psychiatric symptoms. Twenty-three of these patients had brain tumors, three thyrotoxicosis, two each herpes simplex encephalitis, lupus erythematosus, and myxedema, and one each Addison's disease, Cushing's syndrome, carcinomatosis, hyperparathyroidism, porphyria, and regional enteritis.

FIGURE 3. Patient with myxedema on admission to hospital. (From Haughton, C. S. Psychosis with myxoedema. Med. J. Aust., 2: 766, 1959.)

FIGURE 4. Hospitalized patient with myxedema following treatment (2 months later). (From Haughton, C. S. Psychosis with myxoedema. Med. J. Aust., 2: 766, 1959.)

In another report, physical illness was diagnosed in 67 of 200 consecutive patients admitted to the psychiatric unit of a general hospital. In almost half these patients, the medical disorder had not been diagnosed before admission. Cardiovascular disorders (16) and orthopaedic disorders (15) were most common, but the list also included cases of cerebellar hemangioblastoma, subarachnoid hemorrhage, thyrotoxicosis, myxedema, and bromism. Physical illness was found significantly more often in patients with organic mental disorders, and, as expected, the physical morbidity for all patients increased with age (Maguire and Granville-Grossman, 1968).

The medical literature also abounds with descriptions of patients whose disorders were initially considered functional but ultimately proved to be organic, especially neurological. The most encouraging aspect of such reports is that a careful reading of the histories and clinical manifestations reveals features pointing toward organicity in almost every instance (Williams et al., 1974; Wells, 1978). Diagnostic errors arose not because there were no features to suggest organicity but because such features were accorded too little weight.

Special Considerations

MEDICAL CONSIDERATIONS FOR PSYCHIATRIC TREATMENT

Specific medical considerations arise immediately if psychotropic medications and electroconvulsive therapy are considered in planning psychiatric treatment.

Medication. The dangers of a particular medication must be weighed against its possible benefits. As Klein and Davis (1969) stated, the psychiatrist is often in

the unenviable position of having to balance the hazards concomitant with the use of psychotropic agents with the hazards of continued psychiatric illness.

Contraindications to the use of specific medications can be ascertained readily from drug house package inserts or from *Physicians' Desk Reference* (PDR). The chief contraindications are cardiovascular, renal, and hepatic diseases, but diseases of other organs must also be considered. In deciding whether a given medication can be or should be prescribed for a patient with a somatic illness, the physician may find that statistical guidelines are of only limited value. In the final analysis, the clinician's experience and judgment may prove to be the best basis for decision making.

If medications with potential dangers are prescribed, precautions should be taken when possible. For example, if phenothiazines or other medications with anticholinergic action are given to patients with glaucoma, tonometry should be performed regularly to monitor the effect of the medications on the eyes and a local miotic agent should be used as needed (Klein and Davis, 1969).

Electroconvulsive therapy. Relatively few special medical considerations arise when electroconvulsive therapy is being considered. The regular use of a muscle relaxant, such as succinylcholine, to modify the convulsive manifestations has greatly reduced both its dangers and its complications. A chest X-ray and an electrocardiogram are required before instituting treatment, but the necessity for routine spinal X-rays has been eliminated by the use of succinylcholine modification. The physician should use electroconvulsive therapy cautiously in patients with myocardial disease, thrombophlebitis, hyperten-

sion, pulmonary disease, and bone disease, although Detre and Jerecki (1971) considered increased intracranial pressure the only absolute contraindication.

THE MEDICALLY AND PSYCHIATRICALLY ILL PATIENT

Occasionally, the psychiatrist treats a patient in need of hospital care who is suffering concurrently from a psychiatric disorder and a medical illness. It is then necessary to choose where the patient is to be treated. Although local circumstances vary, if the psychiatric disorder is such that it will not interfere with medical care, the patient should generally be hospitalized first on a medical unit and then transferred to a psychiatric unit when medical needs become less pressing. However, if the patient's psychiatric status threatens to interfere seriously with the administration of medical care, hospitalization on a psychiatric unit may be necessary first.

Suggested Cross References

For additional material on psychiatric evaluation and diagnosis see the other sections in this chapter, in particular, Sections 12.5, 12.6, and 12.7, on assessment of intelligence, and tests of personality and brain damage, respectively; Section 12.6 includes information on instruments used by psychologists. Chapter 13 provides a detailed discussion of some of the clinical manifestations mentioned here. See also Chapter 20, on organic mental disorders, Chapter 26, on psychological factors affecting physical conditions, and Section 28.1, on psychiatry and medicine. Organic therapies, including tranquilizers and convulsive therapies, are described in Chapter 31.

REFERENCES

Asher, R. Myxoedematous madness. Br. Med. J., *2:* 555, 1949.
Burns, B. H. Breathlessness in depression. Br. J. Psychiatry, *119:* 39, 1971.
Detre, T. P., and Jerecki, H. G. *Modern Psychiatric Treatment.* J. B. Lippincott, Philadelphia, 1971.
* Hollender, M. H. *The Psychology of Medical Practice.* W. B. Saunders, Philadelphia, 1958.
Hollender, M. H., and Abram, H. S. Dermatitis factitia. South. Med. J., *66:* 1279, 1973.
Hollender, M. H., and Robbins, F. P. The psychosomatic approach to medicine. In *Tice's Practice of Medicine,* J. C. Harvey, editor-in-chief, vol. 10, p. 859. W. F. Prior, Hagerstown, Md., 1958.
* Klein, D. F., and Davis, J. M. *Diagnosis and Drug Treatment of Psychiatric Disorders.* Williams & Wilkins, Baltimore, 1969.
Lederer, F. L. *Diseases of the Ear, Nose, and Throat,* ed. 6. F. A. Davis, Philadelphia, 1952.
Lederer, F. L. Prevention of iatrogenic trauma in otolaryngology. J. Int. College Surg., *19:* 43, 1953.
Liston, E. H. Occult presenile dementia. J. Nerv. Ment. Dis., *164:* 263, 1977.
* Maguire, G. P., and Granville-Grossman, K. L. Physical illness in psychiatric patients. Br. J. Psychiatry, *114:* 1365, 1968.
Pariser, S. F., Pinta, E. R., and Jones, B. A. Mitral valve prolapse syndrome and anxiety neurosis/panic disorder. Am. J. Psychiatry, *135:* 246, 1978.
* Paulson, G. W. The neurological examination in dementia. In *Dementia,* C. E. Wells, editor, ed. 2, p. 169. F. A. Davis, Philadelphia, 1977.
* Penick, S. B., and Carrier, R. N. Serious medical illness in an acute psychiatric hospital. J. Med. Soc. N. J., *64:* 651, 1967.
Seidenberg, R. Omnipotence, denial, and psychosomatic medicine. Psychosom. Med., *25:* 31, 1963.
Tunnadine, P. Psychologic aspects of the vaginal examination. Med. Asp. Hum. Sex., *7:* 116, 1973.
Weiss, E., and English, O. S. *Psychosomatic Medicine,* ed. 3, p. 5. W. B. Saunders, Philadelphia, 1957.
Wells, C. E. Dementia, pseudodementia, and dementia praecox. In *Phenomenology and Treatment of Schizophrenia,* W. E. Fann, I. Karacan, A. D. Pokorny, and R. L. Williams, editors, p. 39. Spectrum Publications, New York, 1978.
Wells, C. E., and Buchanan, D. C. The clinical use of psychological testing in evaluation for dementia. In *Dementia,* C. E. Wells, editor, ed. 2, p. 189. F. A. Davis, Philadelphia, 1977.
Williams, S. E., Bell, D. S., and Gye, R. S. Neurosurgical disease encountered in a psychiatric service. J. Neurol. Neurosurg. Psychiatry, *37:* 112, 1974.
* Woods, B. T. C-T scanning in an adult psychiatric population. McLean Hosp. J., *1:* 150, 1976.

chapter

13

Clinical Manifestations of Psychiatric Disorders

LOUIS LINN, M.D.

Introduction

General medicine tends to deal with separate organs and their functions in health and disease. By contrast, the object of psychiatry is the entire person—the totality of one's thoughts, feelings, and actions. Whereas general medicine concerns itself essentially with adaptational breakdowns in relation to the nonhuman environment, the adaptational interactions with other human beings provide the primary focus of psychiatry. Indeed, for Freud, the most reliable single measure of mental health was to be found precisely here, in the quality of human relationships.

Much of the confusion, for example, concerning the nature of schizophrenia is a consequence of the failure to comprehend its most outstanding characteristic—namely, the specific antihuman bias of the schizophrenic. When permitted to operate in isolation, the schizophrenic may be capable of prodigies of abstract thinking and creative work, and yet all that capacity characteristically disappears when the schizophrenic is trapped in human relationships to which he cannot adapt.

Furthermore, the less challenging the environment from a human interactional point of view, the less the need for medication, the poorer the social milieu, the greater the need (Wing, 1978). Criminal recidivism often represents a need for the simplicities of a sheltered inpatient, albeit prison, environment.

For example, on November 3, 1966, a New York City grand jury indicted a 31-year-old man for the first-degree strangulation murder of a young woman. He never stood trial. Because he pleaded guilty, he was sentenced on a less serious charge, first-degree manslaughter. He became a model prisoner, seemingly a star example of a rehabilitation program working at its best, so much so that he was released after 5 years. Fourteen months later he was again imprisoned for a crime almost identical to the first homicide. The prison director's comment was:

> He became a model inmate who seemed to learn his lesson. But I guess underneath it all he was a con-man. He certainly fooled me.

That case illustrates how bewildering recidivist criminal behavior can be unless considered from an adaptational point of view.

Obsessive-compulsive symptoms may subside entirely in an inpatient setting, only to return with redoubled fury in a setting of family stress (Stern and Cobb, 1978). Epidemics of elopement and suicide have often been reported in inpatient settings torn by staff conflict; the epidemics subside when rational staff interactions have been restored.

Because the quality of human interaction is the primary concern of psychiatry, one must obtain accurate information about the patient's relationships within his family, at work, at play, and in the community. In the Munchausen syndrome, the patient consciously falsifies and simulates symptoms in order to obtain hospitalization and drugs. In other cases, data are distorted unconsciously because of the nature of the presenting mental disorder. Obviously, a complete and reliable case history cannot always be obtained in a simple one-to-one interview, particularly if the interview is conducted in the sheltered setting of an inpatient unit. Whenever possible, psychiatric evaluation should include data concerning outpatient behavior as described by observers other than the patient—namely, his family, friends, and physicians.

More than a cross-sectional view of a person is needed for diagnosis. That is the rationale for including in the third edition of the American Psychiatric Association's (1980) *Diagnostic and Statistical Manual of Mental Disorders* (DSM-III) a statement on Axis IV that permits the clinician to indicate (1) the specific psychosocial stressors that contribute significantly to the development or the exacerbation of the current disorder and (2) a rating of the over-all severity of the stress when compared with the reactions of the average person of that socioeconomic and cultural background. In evaluating the stressors, the psychiatrist must note, in particular, pressures relating to family, work, play, and the community. An evaluation on Axis IV is necessary not only for diagnosis but for treatment. In some instances certain outpatient treatments are not possible unless the patient is surrounded by a supportive social network.

If the stress is connected with physical illness, that fact is listed on Axis III, which permits the clinician to indicate any current physical disorder, outside of the mental disorder section of the ninth edition of the International Classification of Diseases, that is potentially relevant to the understanding or management of the case. In addition, DSM-III provides Axis V, which permits the clinican to indicate the highest level of adaptive functioning during the previous year. Here, too, the clinician must scrutinize human relationships within the family, at work, at play, and in the community on a six-point scale ranging from number 1 (superior) to number 6 (grossly impaired). Axis V allows the clinician to scrutinize the functional, historical, and predictive aspects of the present illness (Weiner, 1978).

The psychiatrist depends on objective data collected with precision. He concerns himself with pathological issues involving anatomy, physiology, chemistry, toxins, metabolism, endocrinology, and genetics. Significant sociocultural factors can also be measured quantitatively.

The most outstanding example is socioeconomic status, which is an index based on educational level, occupation, income, and rent and which correlates significantly with the incidence, prevalence, nature, and severity of the mental disorder. In the psychological sphere, the intelligence quotient, which is an index comparing a person's performance on specific intelligence tests with the performances of others of the same age group, is an important piece of quantitative information included in the psychiatric examination. The presence or absence of specific disturbances in thoughts, feelings, or actions can be objectively checked in a carefully conducted anamnesis and mental status.

However, the psychiatrist also depends on another category of data. Just as the general physician compares the patient's pulse and temperature, for example, with average expected norms collected under specific conditions, so does the psychiatrist constantly compare his patient's thoughts, feelings, and actions with average expected reactions under more or less average conditions. To do so, he often has to depend on data derived from empathic observation—that is, on data based on his own memories, thoughts, and feelings as they are evoked by the patient. It is not surprising, therefore, that the qualities that best measure a good psychiatric resident include the ability to relate flexibly and sensitively to patients, their relatives, and other staff members. Conversely, personality problems that would not necessarily affect the ability to gather objective data could disqualify a psychiatric trainee because they may cause countertransference, a neurotic disturbance that impairs the capacity for empathic observation.

The life process in health and disease consists of an ongoing series of adaptations. Depending on their effectiveness, a person may be healthy and functioning with unimpaired efficiency, or he may be mortally affected by stress, or he may display a number of intermediate reactive patterns representing disease states that are, in effect, the continuation of life in the face of handicaps. Thus, a symptom or even a complex disease process in its entirety may be viewed as a reaction pattern having adaptational significance.

The clinical manifestations of all illness, nonpsychiatric as well as psychiatric, are the outcome of three complex interacting sets of forces—biological, sociocultural, and psychological. Although that point of view is often touted as a new clinical approach, it is at least a quarter-century old (see Figure 1).

The biological factor represents the organic—that is, the anatomical, chemical, and physiological component. It is a consequence of hereditary, congenital, and postnatal environmental influences. In addition to those physical influences, the person is also what he has learned to be. Those learned elements and adaptational resources that derive largely from family experiences during the early formative years make up the psychological factor. And those learned elements and adaptational resources that are derived from extrafamilial experiences and that begin essentially with schooling are what is meant by the sociocultural factor.

That psychiatric abnormalities are the outgrowth of several factors acting in concert has been expressed in the past by such terms as a psychosocial or a psychobiological point of view. To express the thesis embodied in Figure 1, one has to say that the clinical manifestations of psychiatric disorder are in all instances biopsychosocial. The weight of the biological, psychological, and social factors differs from case to case and from

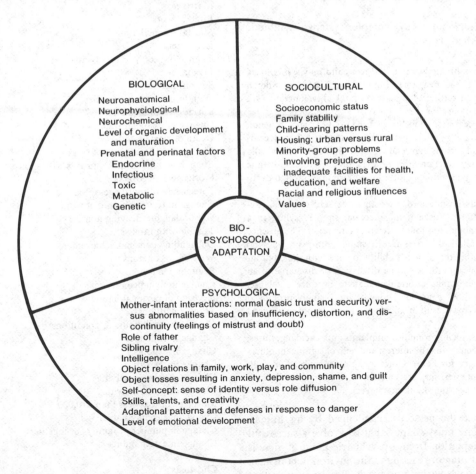

FIGURE 1. Biological, sociocultural, and psychological forces. All the forces interact and affect the psychiatric health of the person. (Modified after Richmond, J. B., and Lustman, S. L. Total health: A conceptual visual aid. J. Med. Educ., 29: 23, 1954).

day to day in a given case. They vary, too, according to the stage of the illness, whether one is dealing with the preclinical, acute, chronic, or convalescent phase.

In a study of patients chronically incapacitated after accidental head injuries sustained at work, it was found that many such workers gave a history of personality change during the weeks or months preceding the accident. That preclinical phase was characterized by depression, irritability, argumentativeness, alcoholism, and a variety of somatic complaints expressed at frequent sick calls. If one searched for it, one could often elicit a history of some stressful life change, like the birth of a baby or the loss of a wife. Against that background, a person with a previously unblemished work record may start having industrial accidents due to carelessness. On occasion, the carelessness may result in a crippling injury or death. In other instances, a mild and transient cerebral concussion can become for that worker a face-saving device for escaping from an intolerable life situation. Thus, what started out as an acute neurological disorder related to head injury—concussion—may merge almost imperceptibly into a chronic incapacitating psychiatric disorder characterized by severe somatic complaints without adequate physical basis and by paranoid and litigious trends.

Once started, such symptom complexes resist all therapeutic efforts until a lump-sum financial settlement and a suitable work reassignment have been made. A consideration of the life stress and the chronic depression that initiated the process is often neglected in the over-all management of the case.

The foregoing sequence of events occurs largely among poorly paid, unskilled workers involved in work that is hazardous, monotonous, or physically exhausting. Thus, there is also a crucial social component that should not be overlooked. In short, the whole process is understandable only from a biopsychosocial point of view.

The individual patient lives in a complex system of symbiotic states involving other people.

To a certain schizophrenic woman, her own child may symbolize a hated sibling whom she is incapable of mothering. That same woman living in the sheltered setting of a state hospital may function as a perfectly competent nanny for the children of staff members.

In the armed forces, precariously balanced soldiers may function competently for years in relation to a specific leader and then decompensate psychiatrically when that leader is lost. Similarly, chronically depressed persons may function more or less unnoticed for a long time and then commit suicide suddenly after losing a spouse through death or desertion.

For many patients hospitalized after an acute schizophrenic psychosis, a suicide attempt, or a panic reaction, simple asylum in a sheltered setting is enough to produce symptomatic relief. The absence of symptoms in a relatively stress-free hospital setting provides no reliable clue concerning the patient's ability to cope with the environment in which he became ill. A simple discussion of discharge to an unchanged life circumstance is often enough to produce a relapse. Actual discharge without a graded series of increasingly prolonged preliminary test visits may result in suicide or a more deeply entrenched psychotic regression.

Certain symptoms, such as somatic complaints and suicidal gestures, serve the function of engaging the interest and help of significant others (the symptom as a cry for help). Other symptoms, such as uncouth dress and bizarre mannerisms, are calculated to keep other human beings at a safe distance (the skunk maneuver).

In every instance the person is challenged by his human environment, and he must adapt—that is, evolve a successful response to it. Adaptation from a psychiatric point of view is a process of conforming or reacting to the environment in such a way as to fulfill one's wishes and needs. Breakdowns in that process are expressed psychiatrically as abnormalities of thoughts, feelings, and actions. Currently, work with the phys-

ically handicapped emphasizes the relativity of the handicapped state. Providing a patient with prosthetic devices, for example, makes him less handicapped. Provision for greater wheelchair mobility reduces the degree of physical handicap. A similar relativistic point of view must be developed in relation to patients who are psychiatrically handicapped.

Efforts at self-change through insight constitute the autoplastic pattern of adaptation. Efforts at environmental change constitute the alloplastic pattern of adaptation. A rational treatment plan takes both patterns into consideration.

A stressful or a traumatic life situation is one that generates challenges to which the organism cannot competently respond. Holmes and Rahe (1967) devised a social readjustment rating scale that lists 43 life events associated with varying amounts of disruption in the average person's life (see Table I). The

TABLE I
The Stress of Adjusting to Change*

Events	Scale of Impact
Death of spouse	100
Divorce	73
Marital separation	65
Jail term	63
Death of close family member	63
Personal injury or illness	53
Marriage	50
Fired at work	47
Marital reconciliation	45
Retirement	45
Change in health of family member	44
Pregnancy	40
Sex difficulties	39
Gain of new family member	39
Business readjustment	39
Change in financial state	38
Death of close friend	37
Change to different line of work	36
Change in number of arguments with spouse	35
Mortgage over $10,000	31
Foreclosure of mortgage or loan	30
Change in responsibilities at work	29
Son or daughter leaving home	29
Trouble with in-laws	29
Outstanding personal achievement	28
Wife begins or stops work	26
Begin or end school	26
Change in living conditions	25
Revision of personal habits	24
Trouble with boss	23
Change in work hours or conditions	20
Change in residence	20
Change in schools	20
Change in recreation	19
Change in church activities	19
Change in social activities	18
Mortgage or loan less than $10,000	17
Change in sleeping habits	16
Change in number of family get-togethers	15
Change in eating habits	15
Vacation	13
Christmas	12
Minor violations of the law	11

* From Dr. Thomas J. Holmes. *The New York Times*, June 10, 1973.

scale was constructed by having hundreds of persons of different ages, cultures, and walks of life rank the relative amount of adjustment necessitated by those life events. Holmes and Rahe named those stress values "life-change units." They found that an accumulation of 200 or more life-change units in a single year was followed by a significantly increased incidence of such diseases as myocardial infarction, peptic ulcer, infection, and a variety of psychiatric disorders. An estimate of the life-change unit score may provide a basis for recommending caution before proceeding with further change.

The death of a spouse, which received the highest rating on the Holmes and Rahe scale, is often followed by a change in financial state, revisions in personal habits and social activities, and so on. If in that same year the bereaved spouse undertakes changes in residence and work that can be postponed, an unnecessarily high accumulation of life-change units occurs, frequently with disastrous medical and psychiatric consequences. The corollary is to postpone all elective life changes for a year or more after bereavement.

Psychiatric symptoms may be variously classified. For example, Bleuler (1972) divided the symptoms of schizophrenia into two groups, the primary and the secondary symptoms. Bleuler believed that the primary symptoms (also referred to as the fundamental or basic symptoms) were pathognomonic of the disorder and included disturbances in association, disturbances of affect, ambivalence, autism, attention defects, disturbances of the will, changes in the personality, disturbances of activity and behavior, and dementia. Bleuler's secondary (or accessory) symptoms included delusions, hallucinations, ideas of reference, and certain types of memory disturbances.

A purely empirical symptom classification is Schneider's list of first-rank or supposedly pathognomonic signs and symptoms of schizophrenia and includes delusions, hearing one's thoughts spoken aloud, auditory hallucinations concerning one's behavior (giving orders, pejoratively describing or mocking the described behavior), somatic hallucinations, feeling that one's thoughts are controlled, feeling that one's thoughts spread to other people and affect their behavior, and feeling that one's actions are controlled or influenced from the outside. Although those symptoms are often used in research projects to define the population under study, the fact is that many schizophrenic patients do not display those symptoms.

From another point of view, there are two primary symptoms of schizophrenia. The first is an irrational fear of intimate human relationships. That symptom results in a generalized pattern of social withdrawal. The second primary symptom is an intolerable feeling of loneliness consequent to the social withdrawal. The schizophrenic patient is thus trapped between his need for human contact because of loneliness and his fear of human contact. Together, those primary symptoms constitute the need-fear dilemma, which is at the root of the schizophrenic reaction. All other manifestations of schizophrenia may be appropriately regarded as secondary symptoms. Freud in 1911 regarded the secondary symptoms of schizophrenia as attempts to solve the problem of schizophrenic loneliness and referred to them accordingly as restitutive symptoms. The ambivalence and the almost limitless variety of abnormalities of thought, perception, feelings, speech, and actions represent attempts to resolve that dilemma. Thus, the patient may elaborate a series of rationalizations about the surrounding world that form the basis for his delusions and hallucinations. As a result of such secondary or restitutive symptoms, the patient becomes less lonely. He becomes capable even of survival in his privately elaborated delusional world.

The foregoing classification of schizophrenic symptoms points up the fallacy of the search for hallucinogenic metabolic abnormalities as the exclusive or even major cause of schizophrenia. Delusions and hallucinations are secondary symptoms and represent an attempt to cope with loneliness. Before the loneliness there is a dysphoric state that is responsible for the schizophrenic's antihuman bias. The availability of hallucinogens, endogenous or exogenous, may lead to one specific type of resolution of the schizophrenic need-fear dilemma, to one specific group of secondary symptoms. However, that resolution does not by itself explain the basis of the primary schizophrenic disorder.

The need-fear dilemma concept is actually broadly applicable not only to cases of schizophrenia but to human behavior in general. The psychological defense mechanisms represent a static point of view, referring as they do to only one pole of the need-fear dilemma—namely, the need to avoid unendurable intimacy. Left out of consideration is a problem of equal importance, that of loneliness. The life conduct of each patient—indeed, of each person in health and disease—may be viewed as a process of active searching for that precise distance between intimacy and loneliness that is most comfortable. Thus, one may speak more accurately of the interpersonal distance-regulating mechanisms when describing recurrent behavior patterns clinically.

By the same token, one may recognize secondary or restitutive symptoms in nonschizophrenic categories. For example, depressed patients in the early stages of their illness are particularly prone to combat primary feelings of emptiness by secondary symptoms, such as acting out sexually, developing addictions, reckless behavior, shoplifting, and self-inflicted injuries.

There is a theory in sociology that, if a person has been labeled mentally ill, his ability to function in normal social roles is seriously compromised because of the reactions of others, which tend to keep him channeled in a deviant role (labeling theory).

That theory states further that social groups create deviance by making arbitrary rules whose infractions constitute deviance and by applying those rules to particular persons and labeling them as outsiders. For example, there are reports that certain totalitarian states are applying psychiatric labels to political dissidents and are using involuntary confinement in psychiatric institutions for punitive purposes. In American society, too, certain patterns of behavior deviate from prevailing norms but cause no outsider to suffer, such as certain addictive states, homosexuality and some other sexual practices, social isolation and eccentricity, and parentally disapproved adolescent religious involvements. If those persons cause no community disruption and do not ask for help, labeling theorists ask, should one search for them with militant outreach programs, put clinical labels on them, and force treatments on them that they do not want?

The further point is made by labeling theorists that a synthetic and arbitrarily created state of primary deviance may be followed by a loss of social skills—as a result, for example, of unnecessary hospitalization or prison incarceration—that in time gives rise to patterns of secondary deviance. Although there is much validity to that point of view, some extremists have carried it to a perhaps caricatured extreme and have ended up concluding that mental illness does not exist at all.

In accordance with Hughlings Jackson's (1932) theoretical formulations, one may speak of deficit symptoms and release symptoms. For example, a focal cortical brain injury may result in a circumscribed language disorder, aphasia, which is a deficit symptom. However, if the cortical injury is widespread, there may be generalized personality changes associated with inappropriate social behavior, which may be interpreted as release symptoms that, Jackson theorized, result from the dissolution of higher controlling levels of brain functioning.

In the pages that follow, symptoms are considered from an adaptational point of view and are traced from their roots in essentially normal behavior through a variety of abnormal behavior patterns. How the patient thinks, feels, and acts; the degree to which he is alert and oriented; how well he observes and remembers; his personal eccentricities and the ways in which he relates to other persons in his family, at work, at play, and in the community—all are explored.

Disturbances in Thinking

NORMAL THOUGHT

Normal thought or cognition refers to ideational or informational experience, as contrasted to affects or feelings. It refers to a broad range of psychic phenomena, including abstract and concrete thinking, judgment, orientation, memory, perception, and imagery. In dreams the prevailing mode of thought representation is visual, whereas in waking thinking the verbal or lexical mode predominates. Convincing evidence indicates that verbal thinking or cognition is a left brain function, whereas nonverbal modes of cognition are right brain functions.

Normal rational thinking consists of a goal-directed flow of ideas, symbols, and associations initiated by a problem and leading to reality-oriented conclusions. Normally, the attentive listener is able to follow logically the verbal and ideational sequences of speech. In actuality, a perfectly logical associative flow is rarely observed. Much more often, speech sequences are interrupted by the forgetting of a familiar name or fact, a slip of the tongue, a period of relative incoherence during which the thread of thought is momentarily lost, or a digression that is irrelevant to the main topic.

Those lapses from logic (parapraxes), which are part of normal thinking, were described by Freud in *The Psychopathology of Everyday Life* as follows:

> Slips of the tongue are the best examples of conflicts between strivings for discharge and opposing forces. Some tendency that has been warded off either definitely by regression or by a wish not to express it here and now finds a distorted expression counter to the opposing conscious will.

The essence of the parapraxis, then, is that it constitutes a compromise or the solution to a problem arising from conflicting psychological drives.

Cognitive controls are the psychological mechanisms governing selective attention and inattention; in response to stress, they may lead to delays or detours in the thought process. In potentially traumatic situations, thoughts may be blocked entirely or distorted in characteristic ways that make up, in part, the defense mechanisms.

The flow of thought becomes available for clinical scrutiny when it is verbalized in speech or writing. In addition to thought content, evaluation of speech includes attention to volume, pitch, voice quality, rate, phrasing, fluency, emphasis, intonation, inflection, and articulation.

Dysprosody is a loss of normal speech melody. Inflection and rhythm are disturbed, resulting in speech that is monotonous, halting, and occasionally suggesting a foreign accent. It can be the result of organic brain disease, as in parkinsonism, for example. It can also be a psychological defensive device seen most markedly in schizophrenia and serving the function of maintaining a safe distance in social encounters.

At every point the expressed flow of ideas is part of a dialogue in which the personal significance of the other member is crucial.

Some mothers of schizophrenic children characteristically tend to be unclear in communicating with their children. The children, in turn, respond to that verbal ambiguity by puzzlement, disinterest, and social withdrawal. Conversely, the verbal communications of a skillful therapist may elicit meaningful responses from a previously inaccessible patient. By the same token, a powerful authority figure or a sexually threatening figure modifies the dialogue accordingly.

Dreaming represents another normal setting in which lapses from logical thought and expression occur. Although dreams often seem bizarre, meaningless, and illogical, Freud demonstrated that a characteristic organization or pattern of thinking can be identified within the dream. He used the term "primary process" to signify that that pattern of thinking is primary in the chronological sense that it occurs first in the developmental process. In primary-process thinking, there is a tendency toward concrete thinking, condensation of separate psychological items into one item, displacement of feelings from one item to another, and a disregard for time sequence, so that past and present may be treated as simultaneities. There is also a considerable use of metaphor and symbolism. According to psychoanalytic theory, all those departures from logical thinking avoid painful feelings and fulfill forbidden pleasures. It has been suggested that essentially nonverbal primary-process thinking is a right brain function that undergoes continuing development through the years paralleling verbal, left brain, secondary-process thinking.

Free association may be cited as an example of an artificially induced disturbance in association. In psychoanalytic psychotherapy, the patient is encouraged to express spontaneously every thought, without selection. In effect, he is encouraged to suspend the demands of logic and reality, at least on a purely verbal level, for the duration of the psychotherapeutic session. By that device the normal associative stream is deliberately disrupted, and the flow of associations assumes qualities of unpredictability, strangeness, and disconnection with reality. Poets and stream-of-consciousness writers may also suspend the normal associative stream, either inspirationally or deliberately, as a creative literary device.

In the loosening of the associations, the flow of thought may seem haphazard, purposeless, illogical, confused, incorrect, abrupt, and bizarre. For Bleuler (1950) that disturbance in association constituted one of the fundamental symptoms of schizophrenia. That seemingly illogical and confusing progression of thought results when the observer is not in tune with the patient's private frame of reference. When he cracks the code, he discerns that there is a communicative and self-defensive method in the patient's madness.

DISTURBANCES IN FORM AND STREAM OF THOUGHT

Dereism or dereistic thinking emphasizes the disconnections from reality. Autism emphasizes the preoccupation with inner thoughts, daydreams, fantasies, delusions, and hallucinations that occur after disconnection from reality. In common usage the two terms are interchangeable. Autistic trends may occur as a character trait, referring to persons who are bashful, shy, retiring, shut in, inaccessible, or introverted. In its extreme form, autism constitutes one of Bleuler's primary symptoms of schizophrenia. As a consequence of the preoccupation with inner fantasies, autistic thinking is not readily subject to correction by reality and is not likely to be followed by action.

Early infantile autism is related to autism in general by its prevailing quality of extreme withdrawal and absorption with inner thoughts. Specifically, it refers to a form of childhood schizophrenia that is characterized by profound withdrawal and lack of contact from the first years of life, an obsessive demand for sameness in the environment, a personalized use of language that is ineffective for communication, and a preference for relationships with inanimate objects. Kanner (1948), who introduced the term, regarded it as a form of behavior resulting from the mother's inability to create a climate of emotional warmth. Infantile autism is associated with varying degrees of organic brain disease. It occurs more often after measles, encephalitis, and rubeola during pregnancy.

In schizophrenia, the entire speech mechanism is drafted in the service of the need-fear dilemma. The schizophrenic repels intimacy by an almost endless variety of abnormalities of voice and speech. The manner of speech may be rendered conspicuously stilted by unusual choices of words or phrases, inaudibility or inappropriate shouting, extreme intellectualization, and so on.

For example, when asked the function of the heart, a schizophrenic patient answered, "It invigorates the blood by putting red and white corpuscles in the blood stream." When asked how yeast causes dough to rise, another schizophrenic patient answered: "Something takes place in the bacteriologic context. When heat is applied, molecules become active and cause it to rise."

Although those verbal mannerisms often have a clearly repelling effect, they also retain some communicative value. By regulating the balance of those opposite effects, the schizophrenic can carefully determine the emotional distance between himself and others, becoming maximally unintelligible when he is most threatened and even entirely normal with others—for example, with a skilled therapist or some other person whom the patient trusts.

Neologism is the coinage of new words, usually by condensing several other words that have special meaning for the patient. In extreme forms of neologism, a word salad ensues that is characterized most of all by its unintelligibility. In certain religious sects, babbling nonsense syllables in a nonlanguage is a form of prayer. The phenomenon is called "speaking in tongues" or glossolalia. For the believer, that type of speech is thought to come from God as a special gift and represents a particularly intimate form of communication with Him. Occasionally, certain forms of aphasia may be misdiagnosed as a schizophrenic speech disorder.

Magical thinking refers to the belief that specific thoughts, verbalizations, associations, gestures, or postures can in some mystical manner lead to the fulfillment of certain wishes or the warding off of certain evils. That type of thinking may occur normally in superstitious or religious beliefs that are appropriate in specific sociocultural settings. Young children are prone to that form of thinking as a consequence of their limited understanding of causality. It is a prominent aspect of obsessive-compulsive thinking. It achieves its most extreme expression in schizophrenia.

In his attempt to mollify a threatening world, the schizophrenic may use certain words or gestures to control evil forces. A schizophrenic patient may believe he is engaged in the most significant work in the universe while standing rigidly in a catatonic stupor. The catatonic schizophrenic is often trapped in a double bind—that is, a set of contradictory parental messages generate unbearable guilt, regardless of the action chosen. In such a case, statue-like immobility may become the patient's only solution. Added to that solution may be the magical belief that any movement on his part will cause the destruction of himself or others.

Intellectualization is a flight into intellectual concepts and words that are emotionally neutral in order to avoid objectionable feelings or impulses of a sexual or aggressive nature. It may take the form of brooding or anxious pondering about abstract, theoretical, or philosophical issues. It often occurs in normal adolescence. It is also seen in obsessive-compulsive neurotics, as a cognitive style in certain character types, and as a mechanism of defense in some schizophrenics.

A patient may torment himself with questions like, "What existed before the creation of the world?" "Why is God a man?" "How is immaculate conception possible?" Such questions, couched in religious terms, often contain a thinly disguised sexual preoccupation.

When a teenaged member of a religious Jewish sect first heard of parthenogenesis, he thought "If parthenogenesis is possible, then immaculate conception and virgin birth are possible, and perhaps my mother did not have to submit sexually to my father. In that case, I myself am the product of an immaculate conception and represent the second coming of Christ." That group of ideas made up the central content of a delusional system that went on for many months.

Circumstantiality is a disorder of association in which too many associated ideas come into consciousness because of too little selective suppression. The circumstantial patient eventually reaches his goal in spite of many digressions. Circumstantiality may thus be distinguished from tangential thinking, in which the goal is never clearly defined or ever reached. In circumstantiality, excessive detail is used to describe simple events, at times to an absurd or bizarre degree. Like intellectualization, circumstantiality often represents a way of avoiding objectionable impulses and feelings.

For the psychiatrist whose task it is to collect much information in little time, the circumstantial patient presents a special problem. A direct verbal assault on that mechanism of defense is apt to be frustrating and futile. It is more fruitful to recognize the underlying anxiety and to relieve it with appropriate psychotherapeutic measures.

For example, a cardiologist complained that many patients exhausted him with trivial details about minor complaints whenever he queried them about their heart conditions. He found that behavior particularly exasperating, since he was unable to influence it by cajolery or stern remonstration. It was explained to him that those patients were fearful and were seeking to postpone as long as possible confronting what they feared most—namely, the possibility of cardiac invalidism or death. By prefacing his crisp inquiry about the patient's cardiac symptoms with a few words of reassurance, he found that such patients very quickly became more cooperative.

Tangential thinking involves verbal interjections that derail the dialogue. By moving at a tangent to the main orbit of the discussion, the patient avoids intimate interactions. A similar effect can result from punning, which is a form of tangential thinking.

Clang associations represent a thought disturbance in which the mere sound of the word, rather than its meaning, touches off a new train of thought. It is thus related to tangential thinking. It occurs most often in manic states with flight or ideas and may result in a series of punning and rhyming nonsensical associations.

Stereotypy is the constant repetition of a speech or action from force of habit or limitations of choice, based on irrational fear or chronic mental disorder. When stereotypy expresses itself as the reiteration of a specific word or phrase, it is called verbigeration. It may occur in either spoken or written form. It is most often seen in schizophrenia.

Perseveration is the persisting response to a prior stimulus after a new stimulus has been presented. It is most often associated with organic brain disease.

A patient with left hemiplegia after a stroke named a key correctly but then called every other object presented to her during that examination "a key." Another hemiplegic patient was able to demonstrate the proper use of a comb but then subsequently attempted to comb her hair with a fountain pen.

Abstract thinking, as described by Kurt Goldstein (1939), includes the ability to assume a mental set voluntarily, to shift voluntarily from one aspect of a situation to another, to keep in mind simultaneously various aspects of a situation, to grasp the essentials of a whole and to break a whole into its parts, to abstract common properties, to plan ahead, to assume make-believe attitudes, to use symbolism in one's thoughts and actions, and to interpret proverbs. By means of a series of specialized tests, Goldstein was able to demonstrate that the capacity for abstract thinking is impaired in many patients with organic brain disease.

It has been erroneously assumed that in schizophrenia, too, the capacity for abstract thinking is impaired. That incapacity is purportedly demonstrated in the schizophrenic's impaired capacity to interpret proverbs. As a matter of fact, schizophrenics are often capable of a high order of abstract thinking in the context of mathematics and other scientific work. Their difficulties with the interpretation of proverbs are the result of a tendency to bizarre idiosyncratic thinking, particularly in relation to a strange examiner in a test situation, rather than a primary defect in the capacity to think abstractly.

From a developmental point of view, concrete thinking—which involves specific objects, creatures, things, and phenomena, as contrasted with qualities that can be ascribed only to classes of objects and so on—appears first in early childhood. The capacity for abstract thinking, characterized by symbols that cannot be directly perceived through the senses, develops later but probably not as late as was once believed. Considerable verbal skill is needed to communicate abstract ideas; therefore, in overt expression, at least, abstract thinking does not appear definitely until adolescence.

The ease with which one produces thoughts is an important clinical variable.

After a fumbling and relatively inarticulate social evening, one may experience a flood of bright thoughts and witticisms on the way home, too late for social display (*l'esprit d'escalier, treppen gedanken*). Similarly, patients who are inarticulate during a psychotherapy session may report a rich flow of "important" thoughts as soon as they leave the therapist's office, only to forget them by the time they return for the next session. The psychiatrist, too, may appreciate the significance of a communication from a patient only after the patient leaves his office. Those familiar examples emphasize the primary significance of the role of the partner in a dialogue; inhibitory influences mediated by the partner, for whatever reason, may be lifted as soon as separation takes place. Communication inhibitions based on neurotic misconceptions concerning the psychotherapist are classified psychoanalytically as transference phenomena. The therapist's neurotic failure to understand the patient represents countertransference.

Foreign-language patients who are depressed or frightened fall back on their mother tongues and seem incapable of speaking English. As such patients improve, they often surprise their physicians with the amount they do understand and the degree to which they can make themselves understood.

It is not enough simply to know a foreign patient's language to establish contact with him. It is also necessary to help him overcome his distrust of the foreign examiner. As that distrust is overcome psychotherapeutically, the patient often prefers to communicate in the prevailing language of the community.

Blocking consists of sudden suppressions in the flow of thought or speech in the middle of a sentence. Commonly, the patient is unable to explain the reason for the interruption, which is usually the result of an unconscious mental intrusion. When, with conscious effort, the patient endeavors to continue the thought, new thoughts may crop up that neither the patient nor the observer can bring into connection with the previous stream of thought. The complete blanking out of the flow of thought, the effort to renew it, and the inability to account for the interruption create an unpleasant feeling state within the patient. Blocking is also known as thought deprivation. Although the phenomenon occurs intermittently in normal persons and in a variety of diagnostic categories, it occurs most strikingly in schizophrenia.

The rate at which thoughts are produced is an important clinical variable.

In depressed states, the flow of associations is slowed up—not intermittently in response to hallucinatory or delusional intrusions, as in blocking, but as an ongoing consequence of sadness. The patient thinks and speaks slowly. He is essentially unresponsive to his environment. The range of his thoughts is limited to a perseverative repetition of his pessimism and despair. Such a patient commonly complains that thinking requires considerable conscious effort, that his concentration is poor and his memory impaired. In extreme states of slowing due to depression, the clinical picture may resemble the mutism of a catatonic schizophrenic.

Withdrawal from human relationships is the first step in the schizophrenic process. Associated with the retreat is usually a reduction in the amount of spontaneous speech. Thus, the flow of speech in schizophrenia may be slowed up and show blocking. That blocking may progress to total mutism. In his loneliness and in his drive to recontact the world on less frightening terms, the schizophrenic may elaborate a "successful" psychotic system, on the basis of which his suffering is temporarily relieved. At that point, the patient may speak rapidly and animatedly, giving full expression to his delusional beliefs and responding actively to his hallucinations.

As depression lifts, the rate of thought and speech also accelerates. If the condition swings over to a manic state, pressure of speech occurs; that is, voluble speech difficult for the listener to interrupt. Pressure of speech may progress to flight of ideas, a nearly continuous high-speed flow of speech. The patient leaps rapidly from one topic to another, each topic being more or less meaningfully related to the preceding topic or to adventitious environmental stimuli, but his progression of thought is illogical, and the goal is never reached. The speed and cleverness with which the manic patient leaps from one idea to another can be dazzling. From a qualitative point of view, the manic patient's associations are not strange or absurd. In fact, the connections and identifiable events in the environment are usually understandable, amusing, and even convincing. Puns and witticisms are common.

The flight of ideas of a manic patient must be differentiated from the disturbance of association displayed in the rapid speech of schizophrenic catatonic excitement. The shifts in schizophrenic talk are confusing because of the indiscriminate overinclusion of material belonging to both shared social contexts and private fantasy contexts. It is the fact that the schizophrenic patient draws largely on an autistic reservoir for his ideas and verbal symbols that makes his productions strange, as contrasted to those of the manic patient.

In spite of those qualitative differences between the associative stream of the manic patient and that of the catatonic-excited schizophrenic patient, both show a pattern of flight from the pain of some intolerable external reality, even though one draws on an inner and essentially inaccessible repertoire and the other on an outer and socially evident repertoire for the specific words and ideas that make up the associative flow.

For all the appearance of joy and inner freedom that the manic patient displays, the careful observer can usually detect the sham. With firm reality-testing interventions, he can break through the mask, even if only for a moment, and reduce the manic patient to sobriety and even to tears.

Often the differentiation between the inner and the outer defensive resources in psychosis is not a sharp one. A differential diagnosis is not possible, and the term "schizoaffective" is used to emphasize that fact.

Pressure of speech may occur more or less within the limits of normal conversation, and one then speaks of volubility. In certain neurotic disorders, talkativeness may acquire a compulsive quality that is called logorrhea. That talkativeness may be associated with peculiarities of speech rhythm in which the patient pauses for breath unexpectedly in the middle of a sentence and rushes on without pause to the next sentence, thereby cutting off the listener from the give and take of a normal dialogue. Logorrhea occasionally occurs episodically as a manifestation of temporal lobe epilepsy.

Organic brain disease is a major cause of disturbances in the flow of speech. Aphasia is a disturbance of language output, resulting almost always from damage to the left side of the brain. However distorted a patient's speech may sound, if his productions read as correct English sentences when transcribed, he is suffering not from aphasia but from some form of articulatory speech disability.

Traditionally, it is said that an aphasic patient with trouble in speaking has an expressive or motor aphasia and that it is due to a lesion in Broca's area (anterior temporal and adjoining frontal regions), whereas, if he cannot comprehend language, he has a receptive aphasia due to a lesion in Wernicke's area (temperoparietal region).

That classification can mislead and should probably be abandoned. Geschwind (1971) observed that the most important distinction in disorders of language output is that between fluent aphasia and nonfluent aphasia. Patients with nonfluent aphasia produce little speech, and what is produced is uttered slowly, with great effort and poor articulation. Characteristically, the speech of such patients lacks the small grammatical words and endings, so that it may take on the quality of a telegram. Asked about the weather, such a patient may say, "Sunny." If urged to produce a full sentence, he may say, "Weather—sunny."

By contrast, patients with fluent aphasia effortlessly produce well-articulated long phrases or sentences with a normal grammatical skeleton, having normal rhythm and melody. Such patients often speak more rapidly than normal. Despite the many words produced, however, their speech is often remarkably devoid of content. Thus, a knob may become "what you use to open a door" or a "thing." A knife may become a "fork," a spoon a "spoot," a thumb an "Argentinian rifle."

In some cases, the words produced are totally neologistic. One patient, for example, responded to all questions with animated but perseverative responses consisting of two nonsense words, "itsi potsi," repeated with various intonations and inflections (jargon aphasia).

Nonfluent aphasias result from lesions in Broca's area. Those lesions generally involve the adjacent motor cortex and cause an associated hemiplegia, which is usually greater in the arm than in other areas; facial weakness is less prominent because the lower face has substantial bilateral innervation. By contrast, fluent aphasias result from lesions in Wernicke's area and typically have no associated hemiplegia.

There are several forms of fluent aphasia, distinguished on the basis of the patient's ability to comprehend and repeat spoken language. In Wernicke's aphasia (lesion in the posterior superior temporal region) the patient cannot comprehend or repeat the examiner's words. In conduction aphasia (lesion deep in the parietal lobe above the Sylvian fissure) the patient shows normal comprehension of spoken language but repeats the examiner's words incorrectly. Paradoxically, the use of short words is most difficult for the patient. "No ifs, ands, or buts" is the hardest of all phrases for such patients to repeat.

Anomic or amnestic aphasia is manifested by a difficulty in finding the right name for an object or person, even though the patient retains full comprehension concerning the test object involved and is able to repeat test phrases easily. It is closely related to the familiar experience, within normal limits, of not being able to recall the name of an object or a person. In its mildest form it is seen in fatigue, anxiety, acute alcoholic intoxication, diffuse brain disease, and a variety of toxic-metabolic states. When the aphasia occurs acutely as a result of vascular occlusion, the lesion most often lies in the region of the angular gyrus.

Isolation-of-the-speech-area aphasia is a rare form of fluent aphasia in which the patient has a severe loss of comprehension but repeats test phrases with ease.

Global aphasia is the result of a massive lesion affecting both Broca's area and Wernicke's area. A patient with global aphasia almost always has a severe hemiplegia and suffers from a grossly nonfluent aphasia, combined with a severe loss of comprehension and repetition.

Every patient who is aphasic in speech is also aphasic in writing, although there are rare patients who are aphasic in writing but not in speech. Therefore, if a patient is able to produce full normal language in a written form but does not speak, one must conclude that he is suffering not from aphasia but from some form of mutism. Mutism may occur in catatonic schizophrenia, severe depression, hysterical aphonia, and a variety of organic disorders involving the speech apparatus, as contrasted to the language areas of the left cerebral cortex. Patients with organic disorders of the speech apparatus may, on recovery, show dysarthria—that is, difficulty in articulation but not in word finding or in grammar.

Fluent aphasia is frequently misdiagnosed, since many physicians are unaware of the frequency of aphasia without hemiplegia. The patient may be called psychotic or confused, particularly when there is a rapid outpouring of abnormal speech.

Although aphasia has been discussed here in purely biological terms, the severity of the disorder may wax and wane within certain limits in response to changing object relationships. When brain-injured patients are pushed to perform tasks they can no longer do, they may respond with agitation, panic, and intensification of the neurological deficit, a response termed by Kurt Goldstein (1939) the catastrophic reaction.

Perseveration is a device for warding off catastrophic reactions by clinging to a specific response with which the patient feels comfortable. Aphasic patients often use clichés as evidence of their verbal impoverishment and their reliance on easy devices to make themselves understood.

DISTURBANCES IN THOUGHT CONTENT

Certain types of thought content are essentially nonverbal. They are probably manifestations of right brain functioning. The most outstanding example is the mystical experience. That phenomenon can occur fleetingly in normal persons during the induction phase of general anesthesia. It may be chemically induced in addicts. It can occur transiently in schizophrenia and in the experiences of religious mystics.

The mystical experience, whatever the circumstance that elicits it, has certain distinguishing qualities:

1. Ineffability. The person insists that his experience is inexpressible and indescribable, that it is impossible to convey what it is like to one who has never experienced it.

2. Noesis. The person feels that the mystery of the universe has been plumbed, that an immense illumination or revelation has occurred. Along with that feeling may go a curious sense of authority, the conviction that one is privileged to lead and to command. As for the revelation itself, it seems to consist of layer upon layer of truth that, as it unfolds, may find expression in some familiar or even commonplace thought that suddenly seems pregnant with new meaning. On occasion, the expressions of the truth may take the form of a document of poetic beauty and great moral significance, such as the writings of the biblical prophets. On the other hand, the revelation may be expressed in unintelligible words or nonsense syllables (glossolalia, speaking in tongues).

3. Transiency. The actual mystical state may last only a moment or go on for an hour or two; but, when the experience ceases, the particular quality of feeling it aroused is only imperfectly reproducible in memory. Yet it is unforgettable and highly treasured and may color all subsequent activity.

4. Passivity. In the mystical state there is an abeyance of will, as if the person were in the grip of a superior power to whose direction he is highly responsive.

5. Unio mystica. There is a sense of mystic unity with an infinite power, an oceanic feeling in which opposites are reconciled, in which there are "darknesses that dazzle" and "voices of silence." There is a quality of timelessness, in which minutes and centuries are one and in which past and present are one.

The mystical experience seems to represent a specific state of consciousness, since it tends to occur in settings of exhaustion and toxicity in which full alert consciousness is impaired. It also seems to represent psychological regression at its most extreme. It has been hypothesized that it is a retreat to the beginnings of conscious psychological life, and in that sense it may represent an ultimate counsel of despair. As the person travels back in memory in search of a time when life was endurable, finding no one on earth to whom he can turn for help, he comes at last to a time of contentment that preceded language and preceded conscious awareness of other human beings. It is a retreat to a time when infant and mother were indistinguishably fused in the infant mind. In recapturing that mood, the person may find in the mystical experience a way out in the form of psychosis or a compelling religious experience that may be lifesaving in its impact.

A fantasy is a mental representation of a scene or occurrence that is recognized as unreal but is either expected or hoped for. There are two types of fantasy: creative fantasy, which prepares for some later action, and daydreaming fantasy, which is the refuge for wishes that cannot be fulfilled. Creative fantasy may start in inspirational moments that are rooted deep in the unconscious. However, it is then elaborated systematically and is translated into a realistic program of action. The daydream

as a refuge for wishes that cannot be fulfilled is self-explanatory. It tends to diminish with psychological and biological maturation. Increasingly, daydreaming is replaced by direct sexual satisfaction with appropriate love objects and by sublimations at work and at play. Sublimation is the replacement of forbidden behavior with related activities that are personally satisfying and socially approved—for example, the choice of a medical career to replace death wishes toward an ailing parent or sibling. To some extent, daydreaming persists within normal limits throughout life. However, in autistic characters and in borderline psychotic states, daydreaming may preempt so much time and energy that it seriously impairs the person's capacity for normal relationships and responsibilities.

Pseudologia fantastica or pathological lying differs from normal daydreaming in that the person believes in the reality of his fantasies intermittently and for long enough intervals of time to act on them.

Such a patient tends to outrage the moral sensibilities of his victims and commonly provokes punishment. When confronted with damning evidence, the patient usually acknowledges his falsehoods readily. However, he has a compulsive need to act out his fantasies repeatedly. It is often difficult to ascertain whether the untruths are expressed with conscious or unconscious intent to deceive or as part of an actual delusional distortion of reality.

The imposter is a type of pathological liar who seeks to gain some advantage by imposing on others various lies about his attainments, social position, or worldly possessions.

The imposter is obviously suffering from a severe identity problem. He is attempting to foist a false identity, but perhaps of greater significance is his need to reject his own real identity. Such persons are often quite gifted and capable of authentic success in the real world, but an unconscious fear of success causes them to misspend their talents. They tend to be self-defeating in their dramatizations and usually end up with humiliation and punishment.

A phobia is an exaggerated and invariably pathological dread of some specific type of stimulus or situation. Table II presents a small list of common phobias. Many others have been described, and phobias are probably limitless in number.

TABLE II
*Phobias**

Phobia	Dread of	Phobia	Dread of
Acro-	High places	Nycto-	Darkness, night
Agora-	Open places	Patho- (noso-)	Disease, suffering
Algo-	Pain	Peccato-	Sinning
Astra- (astrapo-)	Thunder and lightning	Phono-	Speaking aloud
Claustro-	Closed (confined) places	Photo-	Strong light
Copro-	Excreta	Sito-	Eating
Hemato-	Sight of blood	Tapho-	Being buried alive
Hydro-	Water	Thanato-	Death
Lalo- (glosso-)	Speaking	Toxo-	Being poisoned
Myso-	Dirt, contamination	Xeno-	Strangers
Necro-	Dead bodies	Zoo-	Animals

* Modified from Warren, H. C. *Dictionary of Psychology.* Houghton Mifflin, New York, 1934.

Whereas a setting that elicits pleasure evokes approach behavior, one that elicits fear evokes avoidance. There are probably biological differences in the readiness to respond with fear. Certainly, one can breed animals for more or less timidity. A few fear responses in humans seem to be innate. Around the eighth month of development, for example, a child usually becomes capable of distinguishing the familiar face of his mother. At that time, the infant reacts with anxiety to the face of a stranger (eighth-month anxiety, stranger anxiety). A crawling infant reacts with fear to perceived heights. Loud noises and sudden rough movements can elicit startle reactions at any age.

Fears become attached to specific situations as the outcome of a learning process. For example, a patient may develop a fear of sea or air travel as a result of specific traumatic experiences. A child may develop a school phobia because his fearful mother inculcates her own fear of separation. Punitive parents may inculcate childhood fears that emerge in adult life as a variety of sexual, eating, and excretory fears. Psychoanalytic theory emphasizes the role of symbolism in phobia formation.

A 3-year-old child developed an acute fear of appendages of all kinds—door knobs, hanging light fixtures, and so on—after viewing in the nude for the first time her father, who had just come home after several years of overseas military duty.

In psychotherapy it was brought out that the sight of her father's penis had evoked in her fears concerning her own genitalia, fears that her genitals had been mutilated as a punishment for hateful thoughts toward that intruding stranger, and fears of further mutilation based on her necessarily distorted childish fantasies concerning sexual intercourse.

That specific fear of appendages rapidly generalized to include a fear of physical imperfections of all kinds—for example, a fear of cracks in the wall, of broken cookies, of imperfections in her clothing, and of bald men. One day she was carrying a toy pinwheel. When a gust of wind suddenly tore it from the stick, she developed a fear of the wind. When she saw leaves in a tree shaking in response to a breeze, she developed a fear of leaves. Thus, what started as a specific phobia connected with a fear of genital mutilation rapidly generalized and became an almost panphobic state. She was relieved of her symptoms by means of psychoanalytically oriented therapy that focused on her ambivalent attitudes toward her parents, her guilt concerning sexual and angry feelings, and her fear of punitive genital mutilation.

Sometimes the associative connections in phobias seem rather direct. A forbidden wish to suck, bite, or devour, for example, may result in a fear of eating specific foods or a fear of eating in specific places. A fear of loss of control of violent impulses may lead to a fear of all scenes of violence. A fear of sexual penetration may lead to a fear of being cut or stabbed, and that fear may lead to a fear of contact with all sharp instruments.

In other instances the associative connections are more obscure. A fear of walking on the street (agoraphobia), for example, may be based on unconscious prostitution fantasies. The sexual excitement and fear of punishment connected with those fantasies may result in palpitation and breathlessness, which then presents clinically as a cardiac neurosis. Most often, the phobia for which the patient seeks treatment is like the manifest content of a dream. Behind the expressed fear is a chain of other fears. However, entwined in the fears that are supposed to guard against forbidden impulses are thoughts, feelings, and actions that secretly fulfill those drives. The incorporation of a wish fulfillment in the symptom that is supposed to ward off that wish is called the return of the repressed.

A pretty young married woman, the mother of a 5-year-old daughter, became pregnant. She was aborted illegally at her husband's behest. When the abortionist let her see the bottle containing the curetted fetal tissue, she experienced a sharp pain in her eyes. Thereafter, she was afraid to go out into the street because of a fear that a foreign body would fly into her eyes. Psychoanalysis showed that her fear was a displacement from below upward—that is, her eye fear concealed a fear that she would be impregnated as a result of prostitution fantasies. Those fantasies were the result of rage against her husband, whom she identified with her punitive mother, for not permitting her to have a baby. When she did venture out into the street, and she did so very often, she would experience a foreign-body sensation in her eye, which would send her flying in a panic to her family doctor, who lived nearby. The doctor's search for the foreign body was regularly associated with much fluttering of eyelashes, fearful breathing, and struggling—all of which resulted in her seducing her doctor into sexual play, consisting mostly of kissing and caressing. Since she unconsciously identified her family doctor with her father, that sex play represented a revival of her childhood attachment to her overly demonstrative father. As a result, it aroused much guilt and anxiety.

The phobic reactions of childhood usually have a good prognosis. On the other hand, they sometimes persist and may be forerunners of later schizophrenic reactions. Phobic reactions that start in adult life are more resistant to treatment or to spontaneous remission.

Many phobic patients who are otherwise immobilized by their fears can function if accompanied by some trusted person who is called a "phobic companion."

Because of the tendency of any single phobia to generalize, widespread life impairments can occur, affecting relationships within the family, at work, and in society at large and impairing self-esteem to a crushing degree. Relief of a secondary or peripheral phobia by the simple techniques of behavior therapy can often interrupt that vicious cycle and initiate a spreading upward spiral of rehabilitation (the ripple effect).

The foregoing discussion has emphasized those phobic reactions that have been learned and that are connected psychologically with specific objects (for example, animals, insects, knives, dirt, and vomitus), specific places (high places, closed places, hospitals), and social situations (public performances, such as eating, speaking, and signing one's name). Those specific and circumscribed phobic reactions respond best to psychotherapy—analytic, supportive, or behavior modifying—and require enforced exposure to the frightening situation as part of the treatment plan. The phobias tend to arise early in life and may become incapacitating in early adult years. In addition, some phobic reactions associated with panic attacks occur unpredictably in a variety of settings that generate in the patient a fear of leaving home because he dreads having a panic attack away from home. That is classified as agoraphobia with panic attacks, and it often begins during the adult years. A purely psychological treatment approach is often unsuccessful. On the other hand, preliminary therapy with a tricyclic antidepressant usually brings the panic attacks under control, after which psychological treatment becomes more effective. Occasionally, the monoamine oxidase inhibitors are successful in controlling the panic attacks.

An obsession is the pathological presence of a persistent and irresistible thought, feeling, or impulse that cannot be eliminated from consciousness by any logical effort. Typically, the patient feels compelled to carry out specific ritualized or stereotyped acts, known as compulsions, in order to minimize their distressing effects—hence, obsessive-compulsive neurosis. Obsessive fears and doubts may overlap the phobias.

Whereas the phobic or hysterical patient dramatizes fantasies in the form of relatively simple fears and bodily sensations, the fantasies of the obsessional neurotic are converted into intellectually complex word games. Patients with the disorder invest words and thoughts with unrealistic power. They imagine that an inadvertent thought or comment or some innocent act may cause great harm to a loved one or punishment to one's self. Conversely, a given verbal formula may ward off danger to self or to others. Thus, much time and energy are spent by the obsessional patient in undoing with one set of thoughts or actions the harm he feels he has already accomplished with another set. Since words are powerful, it becomes necessary to choose one's words carefully. And, for the obsessional neurotic, no matter how carefully he chooses his words, he is never sure that he chose carefully enough, and so he repeats himself with verbal formulas of ever-increasing complexity. Those formulas may take the form of prayers. Behind that preoccupation with seemingly magical but actually trivial words is concealed an intrapsychic struggle involving erotic and aggressive impulses in every conceivable combination of activity and passivity, of masculinity and femininity, of piety and blasphemy, of obedience and rebellion. Such verbal gymnastics demand a great mastery of language, which requires considerable intelligence. Conversely, whenever verbal skills are limited because of limitations of intelligence or education, obsessional defenses usually do not appear.

Scrupulosity is characterized by a pathological sense of guilt and a preoccupation with repetitious religious ritual and a caricatured concern for detail. Recognition of that disorder by clergy leads to psychiatric referral, rather than futile attempts at religious reassurance.

An obsessional patient was constantly concerned lest he inadvertently harm someone and be legally punished for the accidental wrongdoing. He feared that germs on his hands would infect others. As a result, he washed his hands endlessly and used all kinds of stratagems to avoid handshaking. In a restaurant, he would inspect and clean his glass and his silverware with his napkin. Having done so, he would feel that he offended the waiter and that the waiter would now spoil his food or give him poor service in retaliation. In his home he would remove flower pots or any loose object lying on or close to a windowsill, lest they roll out and injure someone in the street below. If he drove up to a traffic light, he would apply his brakes forcefully during the red-light interval so as not to drive through accidentally. When the light turned green, he would proceed cautiously. Moments later, he would be seized with the fear that he had driven through the red light and had injured a pedestrian. He had to return to the scene of the "crime" and assure himself that no accident had actually occurred. At the end of a day's work in his office in a skyscraper building, he would remember, on reaching the street, that he had dropped the wrapper of a pack of cigarettes on the office floor. He would develop the fear that that piece of paper would somehow ignite and burn the building down and that the conflagration would be traced to him through the cigarette wrapper. He would have to return to his office and retrieve the paper, even if it meant searching out cleaning women who had already swept the floor. Before falling asleep at night, he had to visualize a cross resting precisley in the middle of his forehead. He had to keep working in his imagination to place the cross just right. When he achieved that, he had to recite a series of prayers to protect the health of various friends and relatives. If blasphemous thoughts intruded in the midst of his prayer, he had to start all over again. The bedtime ritual was often prolonged and at times could seriously interfere with his sleep.

Just as phobic patients can function if accompanied by a phobic companion, obsessive-compulsive patients can function if some trusted person, such as a parent, spouse, or doctor—

that is, an obsessional companion—provides reassurance. Often, a reassuring message recorded on a cassette during a psychotherapy session substitutes effectively as an obsessional companion. The use of an inanimate substitute for the living companion is reminiscent of the transitional object phenomenon (Winnicott, 1953). Dependency in early childhood on a security blanket or a favorite toy as a source of comfort during periods of enforced separation from the mother is a familiar example of the phenomenon.

A paradoxical concern with cleanliness is common in obsessional patients. For example, extreme meticulousness in outer garments may conceal slovenliness in the undergarments and a neglect of bathing. Freud felt that the cleanliness preoccupation was a consequence of excessively harsh toilet-training experiences and was associated commonly with a constellation of anal character traits—stubbornness, orderliness, stinginess, and punctuality.

When thought content centers on a particular idea and is associated with a strong affective tone, the patient is said to be dominated by a trend or preoccupation—for example, a paranoid trend or a suicidal preoccupation.

When a patient ascribes personal significance to neutral remarks or comments, he is said to show referential thinking or to display ideas of reference. For example, those ideas arise when the patient attributes to others thoughts and feelings that he himself has imagined, a process called projection. The associated pattern of oversuspiciousness is called paranoid thinking. When a shy but essentially normal person enters a social situation, he may experience a series of self-observing, self-criticizing thoughts, which he succeeds in brushing aside in favor of the social encounter. Such thoughts, if intensified to the point of paralyzing shyness but recognized as unreasonable, are designated as neurotic hypersensitivity.

A tendency to referential thinking is regularly encountered in patients undergoing psychoanalysis. By a studied attitude of neutrality and inconspicuousness, the analyst deliberately encourages the patient to fill the gaps in his knowledge concerning the analyst with his imagination. In this way, the analyst can ascertain aspects of the patient's personality development not otherwise available. The patient's uncritical belief in those projections is called transference. The resulting set of thoughts and feelings about the analyst is called the transference neurosis and typically re-creates certain traumatic aspects of the patient's childhood. The systematic correction of those distortions of reality by the analyst is called the process of interpretation. The method depends on the psychoanalyst's emotional stability and maturity. If maturity is not present, he may accept the patient's projections literally and act out with the patient in a *folie à deux*, with projections of his own. Such a pathological response on the part of the psychoanalyst is called countertransference.

Between ages 3 and 6, a child often devises an imaginary companion. That companion typically appears after a traumatic event, like the birth of a sibling or the death of a grandparent. The imaginary companion may be a simple double who helps assuage loneliness or a scapegoat who is the recipient of endless scoldings and punishments for misbehavior. With emotional maturation, the need for the companion subsides, and he is gradually forgotten. The imaginary companion can be likened to a transitional object. Persistent attachment to the transitional object into adolescence is evidence of a maturational lag.

In settings of extreme social deprivation, adults may conjure up imaginary companions. That tendency has been documented by men circumnavigating the globe alone in sailboats. One man would engage himself in loud, active conversations whenever he made navigational measurements, checking and praising himself for accuracy and skill. Another sailor who was temporarily incapacitated by a fever fixed his course, lay on his bed, and engaged in high-spirited conversations with a vividly hallucinated pirate—a large, jovial, parent figure who stood at the helm and cared for his boat until his fever subsided.

A delusion is a false belief that arises without appropriate external stimulation and that is maintained unshakably in the face of reason. Furthermore, the belief held is not one ordinarily shared by other members of the patient's sociocultural and educational group; for example, it is not a commonly believed superstition or a religious or political conviction. Delusions are pathognomonic of the psychoses. They occur most frequently in schizophrenia, but they can be observed in all psychotic states, including those of organic origin.

An 85-year-old widow living alone in a city apartment complained to a visiting nurse that a man living above her was making forays into her apartment in her absence, rearranging her furniture, and doing all kinds of minor mischief to annoy her. She often beat on her ceiling with a broomstick and hurled imprecations at him for tormenting her. When the nurse tried to point out the delusional nature of her beliefs, the woman became furious and ordered her out of the house. The nurse was advised not to attack the delusional thinking directly but, instead, to tell the woman that she must feel lonely living by herself and to offer to visit her more often. She did so, and the woman quieted down.

In that case the "persecutor" was an imaginary companion the patient needed to combat feelings of loneliness. Her need to endow him with objectionable qualities necessitating endless quarreling related to a lifelong inability to tolerate intimacy, even on an imaginary basis.

A patient had the delusion that her husband's girlfriends were taunting her with insulting phone calls. At her husband's insistence, an unlisted telephone was installed. As a result, the few friends she had no longer knew how to call her. She became lonely and depressed. It became clear in retrospect that those callers were imaginary companions whose company she needed, for all her persecutory complaints to the contrary.

In the well-known Schreber case, Freud hypothesized that homosexual impulses, which were repugnant and consciously unacceptable to Schreber, underwent a series of transformations in which Schreber declared, first, that he did not really love his imagined homosexual companion but hated him. In a still further development of his thought disturbance, Schreber declared that he did not hate his companion but, rather, that his companion hated him. In that way, the unconsciously loved homosexual imaginary companion emerged into consciousness as Schreber's persecutor.

In some delusional states, persecutory feelings become attached to body feelings, such as intestinal movements or the sensation of stool in the rectum. Somatic delusions are characterized by their bizarre quality. For example, a patient may believe that his intestinal tract has become occluded with solid paraffin or that his internal organs are rotting and worm infested. Those delusions are to be differentiated from the localized or circumscribed somatic symptoms of hysterics and the generalized physical complaints of hypochondriacs.

Although delusions of almost unlimited variety occur clinically, certain syndromes are more common than others. For example, there is the delusion of the influencing machine. In that condition, certain feelings are attributed to a distantly located influencing machine operated by a persecutor. The

patient may claim that the imagined machine compels him to see pictures, forces certain thoughts and feelings on him, or abruptly drains off all thoughts and feelings. He may attribute to the machine erections, cutaneous eruptions, and so on. The description of the influencing machine necessarily draws on the patient's cultural and technological background. In some instances one can connect the influencing machine associatively to the patient's own genitals and his sexual excitement, which he is attempting to deny. The persecutor operating the machine is connected with an imagined sexual partner, whom the patient cannot acknowledge consciously, out of a sense of guilt.

In Capgras' syndrome, the patient develops the delusion that certain important persons—spouse, offspring, parent, siblings, nurse—have been replaced by a bad look-alike imposter. (Capgras' delusion, incidentally, provides the basic theme for the popular science-fiction film *Invasion of the Body Snatchers*.) The delusion can occur as a transient belief during childhood after a period of separation from a parent. It occurs most often as a schizophrenic delusion. For some reason it is less common in men than in women. Although the onset of the delusion is experienced as a sudden insight (Aha! phenomenon), it develops against a background of considerable ambivalence. The psychotic state resolves the ambivalence by splitting the world into good objects and bad objects. That mechanism is facilitated in states of diffuse organic brain disease, including tumors, postoperative neurosurgical states, and arteriosclerotic brain disease. In organic brain disease the phenomenon may express itself in relation to the hospital. For example, the patient may say:

There are two Mount Sinai Hospitals. I am in the bad one. The good Mount Sinai Hospital is several blocks away.

The patient may acknowledge the presence of a paralyzed left arm, for example, but insist that he has an additional left arm that is not paralyzed. That is called the phenomenon of reduplication.

In erotomania or de Clérambault syndrome, the patient, always female, maintains a fixed delusional belief that a man, usually considerably older and of higher social status, is much in love with her. The psychotic patient growing up with the belief that she is unloved or unlovable solves that narcissistic wound by the grandiose fantasy. The delusional system may overflow into complicating and socially embarrassing situations. It is particularly resistant to treatment.

Pathological jealousy may occur in marital settings in which a spouse has unconscious extramarital sexual impulses, either heterosexual or homosexual, which are then projected onto the marital partner and may emerge clinically as delusions of infidelity.

The difference between normal and pathological jealousy is similar to that between normal grief and pathological mourning. Every child suffers jealousy when a third person—whether father or sibling—intrudes between himself and his mother. The occurrence of pathological jealousy in adult life is related to unresolved early childhood attachments. At times, a pathological lack of jealousy can occur.

A patient was referred for psychiatric treatment by her family physician because of alleged sexual acting out on her part that had scandalized the small community in which they lived. The patient described a sexual pattern within the marriage in which her husband would ask her to dress for bed like a whore. He would revile her for a variety of sordid make-believe sexual infidelities, tear her nightclothes off, and rape her as her punishment. That dramatization became a necessary precursor for his sexual excitement—a game, incidentally, that the patient engaged in willingly because of her own psychopathology.

In time, the sexual excitement generated by the game wore off, and the husband involved her in actual flirtations with friends, which had the effect of reviving his flagging sexual drive. Those flirtations gave rise to transient sexual liaisons and, finally, to a loving relationship with a man who courted her actively. When the patient tried to break off that relationship in a desperate attempt to save her marriage, her husband remained pointedly unaware of the conspicuous evidences of infidelity that she left about in a vain cry for help. It was then that she consulted her family physician, who referred her for psychiatric treatment.

Early in treatment, the husband was interviewed. His striking lack of jealousy was a consequence of an almost delusional refusal to accept the evidence of his wife's extramarital involvements. He refused to discuss his peculiar sexual habits and indignantly rejected the suggestion that he, too, needed treatment if the marriage was to be saved. The wife's treatment culminated in her divorce and then by her marriage to her suitor.

Litigiousness is a pathological tendency to take legal action because of imagined mistreatment or persecution. Delusions of persecution may involve a surgeon because of delusional fantasies concerning the surgical procedure. Hostile relatives may project their negative impulses onto the hospital staff. In compensation neurosis or accident neurosis, somatic complaints initiated by an industrial accident or other situation involving compensation may resist all therapeutic interventions and lead to endless litigations until a lump-sum settlement is made.

The thought content encountered clinically is determined by, among other things, the patient's mood. Ecstatic states may be associated with delusions of grandeur or megalomania, a delusionally exaggerated idea of one's importance. A male patient may express the idea that he is the Savior or a latter-day saint; a female patient may believe that she is the Virgin Mary and is about to give birth to the Baby Jesus. Delusions of grandeur may result in identifications with political or military figures of great power. The salvation of the world is the basic delusional goal. Often, that grandiose goal is to compensate for feelings of inadequacy. In manic states, inappropriate delusions of great wealth may result in crippling financial expenditures.

The wish to save the world is commonly a projection onto the outer world of a wish to overcome the feeling that one's inner world is crumbling. If one asks adolescents what they wish for most of all, a large percentage wish for world peace. That is perhaps not a surprising response in an idealistic youth. However, one commonly encounters the same response on questioning schizophrenics in whom contact with the outer world has, for all practical purposes, ceased. In their artwork such schizophrenic patients often depict a world at war. In their responses to the Rorschach Test, they often see the symmetrical halves of an inkblot as contending forces.

Patients with postoperative delirious states often have the delusion that some type of violent activity is going on in the streets—fires, riots, wars (the delusion of violence in the streets). Here, too, the patient is projecting his own sense of inner turmoil onto the outer world.

A shift of mood from elation to depression may result in the self-accusatory delusion of having committed an unpardonable sin. That delusion is associated with intense guilt and remorse. In place of the delusions of saving the world, there may appear the end-of-the-world fantasy, the delusional belief that the world is about to come to an end. The patient may be convinced

that the salvation of the world depends on his own death; as a consequence, he may destroy or seriously mutilate himself. In less bizarre terms the depressed patient may feel that the world would be better off without him and may have suicidal impulses or ideation on an altruistic basis. In contrast to the delusion of great wealth, there may be, in the depressed state, a delusion of poverty. The complaint, "I am poor," is characteristic of depression, almost independently of the patient's true economic state. In addition to feelings of guilt, worthlessness, and impoverishment, the patient may express a loss of interest in all previously satisfying spheres of activity. He may lose his appetite for food, family, sex, work, and play. Loss of appetite for food may be the result of delusions of poisoning.

Paradoxically, some patients invest the process of not eating and weight loss with such intense emotional satisfaction that they lapse into anorexia nervosa, which, on occasion, may lead to death by starvation, in spite of an apparent continued interest in other aspects of life. That condition is associated with a delusional denial of the cachectic state.

In addition to the content of the patient's productions, one must also take into account the intent.

As a result primarily of depression and anxiety, many clinging patients have a desperate need for the company and attention of the therapist. In return for his attention, those patients are motivated to say almost anything calculated to engage his interest. Is the therapist interested in dreams? Then the patient dwells on dreams. Is he interested in infantile sexuality, in orality, in the castration complex? Does he use a Kleinian or a Jungian frame of reference? In each instance, the patient tunes in on the therapist's special interest. He responds to subtle cues almost telepathically. Such patients seem to prove almost any theory that the therapist cherishes, a phenomenon known as doctrinal compliance. For the beginner in psychotherapy, the flood of associations provided by such patients can be an endless source of interest and yet prove, in the long run, to be of questionable psychotherapeutic value. It often takes great clinical skill to differentiate between productions offered with the intent of seducing or clinging and content that can be used to foster authentic self-understanding and positive clinical change.

Thus, the therapy calculated to foster autonomy, separation, and individuation may inadvertently reinforce the opposite—that is, a state of continuing passive dependence. Because actions speak louder than words, the patient in therapy must perform those acts that he dreads doing, as in the treatment of phobias, or refrain from doing those acts he feels compelled to do, as in the treatment of compulsions. In brief, behavioral change must precede insight. Repetition of morbid behavior interferes with the acquisition of insight. That is what Freud meant when he said that psychoanalytic therapy can proceed successfully only in a setting of abstinence.

Just as the content of one patient's productions may be rendered interesting in a spirit of doctrinal compliance, so can another patient offer productions that are boring or irritating as a device for keeping the therapist at a safe distance. Whether the intent is to draw the therapist closer or to repel him, the actual content of the verbal production in such instances is of secondary importance.

To understand the disturbances in mental functioning seen in patients with widespread, as contrasted with focal, organic brain disease, one may find certain theoretical considerations helpful.

In most cases a hospitalized patient suffering from a serious physical impairment of any kind is preoccupied with a wish to be well and a wish to go home. In general, he accepts the realities of the illness and the necessity for hospitalization and makes an adaptation based on his premorbid personality.

A patient with widespread brain injury presents a different picture. In many ways he acts like a person in a waking dream. Is there a wish to be out of the hospital? Then the patient speaks and acts as if he were not in a hospital. Is there a wish to be well? Then wishing makes it so, and he displays the syndrome of anosognosia, the denial that physical illness is present. A blind person insists that he can see, and a paralyzed patient says that he can walk. In some cases the patient denies the major illness and ascribes the need for hospitalization to a trivial illness or to a previous illness from which he has long since recovered. A patient who has just had a craniotomy, for example, may insist that all he had was a tonsillectomy or an appendectomy. On occasion, a patient admits that he cannot move a paralyzed leg but rationalizes that inability as a result of fatigue or laziness. A patient with a paralyzed limb may disown the incapacitated extremity by saying that it belongs to someone else or that a paralyzed arm is lying on a bedside table like a set of false teeth. When questioned about his own illness, an anosognosic patient may respond by discussing the illness of some other family member or may agree that he had a hemiplegia in the past but is fully recovered at this time. A blind patient may give detailed descriptions of objects he is looking at; another patient may alter the name of the hospital so as to deny its medical function or to move it closer to home or business. The patient fills in memory gaps with extensive confabulations, the common denominator of which is the absence of physical disability.

The anosognosic patient may be mute and unresponsive when questioned by a physician and yet speak freely to a relative.

Anosognosic patients may show a language disorder called paraphasia, the use of word substitutes, a form of fluent aphasia.

The paraphasic abnormality occurs frequently in relation to hospital- or disease- connected words. When a word is produced, it is usually a neologism or an inappropriate word that tends to deny illness. For example, a clinical thermometer is called a "gradient" and a wheelchair is a "chaise." At times, anosognosic patients speak of themselves in the third person. In response to a query about surgery already performed, a patient answered, "He did not have an operation." A paralyzed limb may be referred to as "he," "she," or "it," as if to disclaim possession of the sick part.

Other language patterns seen in anosognosic patients include intellectualization and the liberal use of clichés as facile platitudes available to the patient with the expenditure of little thought or energy. Characteristic of anosognosic patients is the fact that they do not alter their basic errors, in spite of repeated corrections by the examiner.

If the patient is corrected as to the year, he repeats the wrong year if questioned just a few moments later. However, he does not give just any wrong year. He carefully and persistently repeats the identically same wrong year, such as 1962. Thus, it is not that his memory is simply bad but, rather, that he persists in accurately "remembering" the wrong date. The patient's history usually discloses that the date selected by the brain-injured patient is one that precedes the onset of his illness and is part of the carefully structured anosognosic state.

In purely quantitative terms, the success with which the brain-damaged patient succeeds in denying his illness is determined to some degree by the extent of the brain disease. In acute reversible brain disease, the period of maximal brain damage is associated with equanimity or euphoria. In the euphoric stage the patient's speech may resemble that of a mild hypomanic reaction. However, the humor (*Witzelsucht*) is characteristically shallow, and the range of ideas is sharply circum-scribed. It is a type of facetiousness, with a tendency to punning. In intermediate stages of brain damage, the flow of associations tends to show a paranoid trend, although again with a relatively limited ideational content. With further improvement in brain function, the entire capacity for denial of illness may dissolve. At that point a depressive reaction, not entirely inappropriate to the clinical realities, may emerge. The slowed-up flow of associations then reflects the affective state. The emergence of a depressive reaction in a patient with reversible brain disease is evidence of improvement in brain functioning—that is, it takes brain power to be depressed.

When a barbiturate, such as amobarbital sodium (Amytal) is injected intravenously into a depressed and no longer anosognosic brain-injured patient so that he shows nystagmus and slurring of speech, all the previously noted denial-of-illness patterns can be temporarily reestablished. That fact forms the basis for a presumptive test of organic brain disease.

The manic and paranoid states seen in brain-injured patients have a certain stability that resists correction. However, during the transitions from one level of somatopsychic organization to another level, there are intervening stages during which hallucinatory phenomena and terror predominate and the flow of associations is maximally disorganized. In many ways, that stage is comparable to the abstinence syndrome or withdrawal reaction, which is seen whenever a patient who has maintained some form of psychosocial adaptation with the help of a drug is suddenly called on to readapt to his environment without the help of the drug. It is possible to see in a single patient all the clinical manifestations that at one time or another have been associated with organic brain disease. The basic and fixed element in the clinical picture is the patient's premorbid personality. The variables derive from the location, extent, and severity of the brain lesion.

Since the fact of brain damage impairs the availability of language and ideas, anosognosic patients tend to lack verbal and ideational complexity. Nevertheless, the delusional fulfillment of the wish to be well draws into its train wish fulfillments from other layers in the emotional development, exactly as takes place in a dream. For example, an unhappily married woman may "forget" that she is married and persistently give her maiden name.

DISTURBANCES IN JUDGMENT

Judgment, from a psychiatric point of view, is the mental act of comparing or evaluating alternatives within the framework of a given set of values for the purpose of deciding on a course of action. The comparison may be in terms of magnitude, rightness, goodness, beauty, or economic worth. If the course of action decided on is consonant with reality as measured by mature adult standards, judgment is said to be good, intact, or normal. If, on the other hand, wish-fulfilling impulses predominate and lead to impulsive decisions based on the need for immediate infantile gratification, whether directly or as part of a psychotic delusional system, then judgment is said to be poor, impaired, or abnormal.

The capacity to decide whether or not to take action depends on the capacity to think—that is, to anticipate the future in the imagination. That capacity depends on the capacity to bring before the mind once again something that has been previously perceived, to reproduce an object in the imagination without requiring the actual presence of the object. The imagined or internalized representation of an object is not always a faithful one. It may be modified by omissions or changed as a result of merging elements. Reality testing determines how far such distortions have gone.

The thought process involved in reality testing takes time. Freud described thinking as "experimental action." It begins with a tentative sampling of data from the outer world; those data are then compared with data from the reservoir of stored memories. That process culminates in a decision, which puts an end to the postponement of action. Thus, the controlled postponement of action is the essence of judgment. The person with good judgment looks before he leaps. But judgment leads from thought to action. Reality testing makes it possible to try out actively and in small doses an experience that may be traumatic if permitted to happen passively and in unknown doses.

The ability to recognize reality begins long before speech is learned. The infant becomes aware of reality as represented by the human face at about 3 months of age. The infant reacts reflexly to the sight of the human face with a smile. At about 8 months of age, the infant begins to compare and evaluate human faces. He learns to differentiate the face of his mother from all other faces. The infant reacts with love to her face and with fear and anger to others. Psychoanalytically, it is hypothesized that the infant takes in her face with his eyes as he eagerly swallows her food. He turns away from others and expels the food offered by those strangers as bad objects. Those simple nonverbal relationships provide the model for the process of judgment—paying attention (as well as selective inattention), comparing, evaluating, decision making, and acting. They also provide the basis for learning how to learn. The learned capacity for selective exclusion of irrelevant stimuli constitutes an important element in the barrier against stimuli (*Reizschutz*), without which ordinary social encounters may have a traumatic impact and learning in a classroom situation becomes difficult or impossible.

One of the developmental hurdles is to be able to accept the fact that a person—one's mother, for example—who is judged to be good today is the same person judged to be bad tomorrow. Object constancy, the ability to maintain a positive loving relationship in spite of periods of frustration and separation, is a hallmark of the maturing mind. Some persons fail to achieve that fusion. They see others only in terms that are purely good or purely bad. Such persons, characterized clinically as suffering from borderline disorders, are constantly suffering from episodes of rage and depression because those on whom they depend are not unfailingly supportive.

Speech initiates a decisive step in the development of reality testing and judgment. Words permit more precise communication and more precise anticipations of trial actions.

The function of judgment, then, depends on maturation of the mental apparatus. Intelligence and education are required for the inculcation of values.

For good judgment to prevail, the sensory apparatus must be capable of accurate perception and discrimination. Memory must provide a reservoir of data as a basis for comparison. The motor apparatus must have the skills to carry out decisions and the inhibitory mechanisms for postponing action. Thus, a developmental process is automatically implied in the concept of judgment. Although rudimentary manifestations of judgment can be found in infancy and early childhood, judgment develops steadily with biopsychosocial maturation. It is maximal in the fully alert, emotionally mature adult. It is impaired in all circumstances associated with regression.

If judgment is a mental function calculated to ensure reality-oriented action, then mental states that avoid painful reality are inevitably associated with impairment of judgment. Those states may occur transitorily in relation to parapraxes. A suspension of logical judgment is characteristic of dreams. Impaired judgment is a regular accompaniment of all psychotic states.

Adolescents display impaired judgment for many reasons. Through lack of education and experience, they may fail to recognize which situations or ideas merit attention. Adolescence, with its characteristic intensification of intrapsychic conflict, may be associated one moment with excellent reality testing based on adult goals and aspirations and a moment later with impaired reality testing based on persistent, unmastered infantile longings. Undeveloped values and self-discipline may precipitate ill-advised actions. Thus, judgment in the adolescent is notoriously uneven and unpredictable.

Estimates of judgment may be based on responses to test questions or standard hypothetical situations. For example, a mentally defective patient with a long history of deliquency and fire setting was asked:

What would you do if you found a stamped, addressed and sealed envelope in the street?

He answered:

I would put it in the mailbox if it didn't have anything in it for me.

Wechsler (1971) observed that a significantly higher score in the performance scale than in the verbal scale in the Wechsler Adult Intelligence Scale suggests a character disorder associated with impairment of judgment and impulsivity.

DISTURBANCES IN INTELLIGENCE

Intelligence may be defined as the capacity to meet a novel situation by improvising a novel adaptive response. That capacity is composed of three factors: abstract intelligence, which is the capacity to understand and manage abstract ideas and symbols; mechanical intelligence, which is the capacity to understand, invent, and manage mechanisms; and social intelligence, which is the capacity to act reasonably and wisely in human relations and social affairs.

Efforts to quantify intelligence have been made by means of various tests that consist of questions or tasks the subject is required to answer or perform. Depending on the difficulty of the items used, the accuracy and speed with which they are completed, and the frequency with which they are passed, numerical values are assigned to the responses; those values are added up to give a total score. Scores so obtained are then used as a basis for defining different levels of intelligence.

The most frequently used score for measuring intelligence is the intelligence quotient (I.Q.). The I.Q. is a numerical ratio derived from a comparison of the score that a person makes on a given test of intelligence with the average score that subjects of his own age have attained on the same or a similar test. The result is an index of relative brightness. It is a measure not of absolute ability but only of relative ability. It purports to tell how bright or dull a person is compared with persons of his own age or, if a comparison is made between two groups, how the brightness of the average person in the first group compares with the brightness of the average person of the same age in the second group.

The abilities measured by those tests do not in themselves constitute intelligence or even represent the only ways in which it may express itself. The rationale of the I.Q. is that those scores do, indeed, correlate with widely accepted criteria of intelligent behavior. Wechsler (1971) emphasized that, in addition to the cognitive or intellective factors measured by those tests, other nonintellective factors, not so readily quantifiable, are crucial for intelligent behavior. Those factors include energy or drive, persistence, motivation, and goal awareness.

Concerning the I.Q., Wechsler (1971) said:

One must obviously be careful as to how one interprets as well as how one arrives at an I.Q. It is not, however, a fault of the I.Q. that incompetent or mischievous people misuse it. Nor does the observation that educationally, economically, and otherwise deprived subjects generally score lower on I.Q. tests invalidate the I.Q. as an index. Of course, the factors that affect the I.Q. are important, but it is the social conditions that produce the factors and not the I.Q. that is the culprit. No one, for example, would suggest the elimination of tests for tuberculosis in the public schools because it was found that children from deprived areas showed up more often with positive signs than children from "good" neighborhoods. Similarly, if the I.Q. test scores of children coming from deprived and depressed areas are significantly lower than those of children from better neighborhoods, the reason can no more be ascribed to the inadequacy of the I.Q. test than the greater incidence of tuberculosis to the possible limitations of the tuberculin test. The cause is elsewhere, and the remedy not in denigrating or banishing the I.Q. but in attacking and removing the several causes that impair it.

Mental retardation is a lack of intelligence to a degree in which there is interference with social and vocational performance. Mild degrees of impairment (I.Q. of 50 to 70) are associated with trainability and the capacity to function in sheltered settings. Moderate impairment (I.Q. of 35 to 49), severe impairment (I.Q. of 20 to 34), and profound impairment (I.Q. below 20) are usually the result of gross organic brain disease and require ongoing supervision, usually in a specialized institution.

The I.Q. correlates with prognosis in schizophrenia. In a family predisposed to schizophrenia, the child with the lowest I.Q. is the most vulnerable to clinical disease. In a retrospective study of the childhood I.Q.'s of hospitalized adult schizophrenics, Offord and Cross (1971) found that patients with childhood I.Q.'s below 80 were more than 4 years younger on first admission for mental disorder than those with I.Q's between 80 and 90 and almost 10 years younger than patients with I.Q's of 100 or more. In addition, at ages 20, 30, and 40, patients with lower I.Q.'s accumulated more institutional time than did patients with average or superior I.Q.'s. Thus, an adequate or superior I.Q. can, in some way, protect a person predisposed to schizophrenia from becoming overtly psychotic early on and spending considerable time in an institution. The failure to detect a low I.Q. in psychiatric assessment may lead to gross errors in diagnosis and treatment planning.

Reading ability is crucial to formal education. Dyslexia—a syndrome characterized by a specific difficulty in learning to read, spell, and write—can masquerade as an impairment of intelligence. Frequently, secondary emotional and behavioral disorders confuse the clinical picture even further. The ratio of boys to girls with dyslexia is about five to one.

Thompson (1973) emphasized that dyslexia is a consequence of an inherent maturational lag, rather than minimal brain dysfunction. With early recognition and adequate remedial reading instruction, the great majority of dyslexic children can attain reading competence, but their typical spelling errors—reversal of symbols and confused directionality—persist, so that, for example, a "b" becomes a "d," and "m" becomes a "w," "was" becomes "saw," and "girl" may become "grill."

Children and adolescents suffering from depression may surface clinically as academic underachievers and must be differentiated from those with other causes of learning disability.

Disorders of Consciousness

Consciousness has been defined as the distinguishing feature of mental life. It is synonymous with the quality of being aware and of having knowledge. Thus, it is a faculty of perception that draws on information from the outer world directly through the sense organs and indirectly through stored memory traces. The term "sensorium" is sometimes used as a synonym for consciousness. When a person is clearly aware of the nature of his surroundings, his sensorium is said to be clear or intact. For example, correct orientation is a manifestation of a clear sensorium. Conversely, a person whose contact with reality is impaired as a consequence of organic brain disease is said to have a cloudy or an impaired sensorium. Implicit in the concept of full consciousness is the capacity to understand information and to use it effectively to influence the relationship of the self to the environment. Consciousness may be said to have a sensory component or a degree of receptive awareness, which is measured as cognitive intensity or level of cognition, and a motor component or a degree of kinesthetic readiness to initiate and execute a voluntary act, which is conative intensity or level of conation.

LEVELS OF CONSCIOUSNESS

One can discuss levels of consciousness from biological, psychological, and social points of view.

Biological considerations

The reticular activating system (RAS) acts as an arousing mechanism that increases alertness when stimulated. It may be likened to the volume dial on an audio system. In response to specific stimuli, it turns on (Linn, 1953).

Sensory stimuli serve a 2-fold function from the point of view of consciousness. First, they bring information from the environment to the cerebral cortex, thus fulfilling a cognitive function. Second, through collateral pathways to the RAS, they arouse and alert the organism, thus playing a consciousness-raising role.

Corticofugal pathways also send collaterals to the RAS, thereby placing that system under cortical control. Incoming information undergoes cortical elaboration, and then impulses are sent to the RAS, producing either further alerting or a reduction in the level of consciousness, depending on the significance of the information.

Consciousness may be said to exist on a continuum, with maximum alertness at one extreme and absolute unconsciousness or coma at the other extreme, with varying degrees of alertness in between. There is, indeed, a continuum, but striking discontinuities can also be recognized. One may consider alcohol as a paradigm.

An ounce or two of whiskey can reduce sensory and memory input enough to transform a tense, anxious, and mildly depressed person into a *bon vivant*. The whiskey accomplishes the transformation by facilitating repression and denial and by reducing self-criticizing tendencies. Increased fluency, a quickening of the wit, heightened sociability, and even flashes of brilliance may occur. At that point perhaps only a spouse can detect the personality transformation and the changes in appearance, and perhaps only sensitive tests can detect changes in motor coordination. In any event, an apparent heightening of mental functioning has taken place by minimally reducing the effect of neurotic inhibition.

More alcohol further reduces brain functioning to the stage of manifest drunkenness. Slurring of speech and unsteadiness of gait become apparent. At that point, emotional and behavioral controls are greatly reduced. An extraordinarily high percentage of suicides, murders, and fatal automobile accidents take place during that stage of reduced consciousness. That is the basis for the old saying that the superego or conscience is an alcohol-soluble substance.

With still greater alcohol intake, stupor sets in, a state of relative nonresponsiveness to the environment that differs from the total insensibility of coma in purely quantitative terms. In the deepest stages of coma, reflex responses to painful stimuli and even to breathing obstructions are abolished. Function is reduced to the mere vegetative persistence of circulation and respiration. For the maintenance of respiration, tracheotomy and mechanically assisted breathing may be necessary.

The chronic alcoholic may maintain his adaptation to his surroundings in a chronically reduced state of consciousness by means of an intake of 16 to 32 ounces of alcohol a day. If his alcohol supply is suddenly stopped, he undergoes a characteristic withdrawal or abstinence syndrome. By the end of 24 hours, he has developed a coarse tremor, hypersensitivity to all stimuli, and frequent startle reactions. That condition of central nervous system hyperirritability gradually increases, and, at the end of 48 hours of abstinence, grand mal seizures may occur (rum fits). During that period, responsiveness to stimuli is so heightened that illusions—that is, brief frightening misinterpretations of real stimuli—may occur. By the end of 72 hours of abstinence, that stage merges into the stage of alcoholic hallucinosis, during which auditory hallucinations predominate. Those hallucinations are frightening to the patient, but he has insight as to their unreality, and they occur characteristically and paradoxically in what seems to be a state of clear consciousness. By the end of 96 hours of abstinence, delirium tremens occurs. An indescribably terrifying psychotic state erupts. Visual and tactile hallucinations predominate. The tactile hallucinations are often experienced as small animals crawling over the skin. Death occurs in about 3 or 4 per cent of the patients. Most persons recover in 3 to 6 days, with an amnesia for the episode and a resumption of heavy drinking.

About 15 per cent of all cases of delirium tremens go on to Korsakoff's psychosis (chronic alcoholic psychosis), characterized by memory impairment, disorientation, and, particularly, confabulation. There is also the phenomenon of pathological intoxication, in which a small alcohol intake can release a brief psychotic reaction characterized by acts of extreme violence and followed by a total amnesia for the psychotic episode. It is often seen in soldiers in rest areas after prolonged exposure to combat.

Although alcohol was cited to illustrate the variety of states of consciousness that can be elicited by brain poisons, various other pharmacological agents could have served as well.

The varieties of states of consciousness seen in hospitalized patients recovering from acute reversible brain disease—for example, on recovery from subarachnoid hemorrhage or encephalitis—was alluded to earlier. Characteristically, patients display a euphoric reaction during the earliest stages of recovery, a paranoid reaction during the intermediate state, and a depressive reaction in the final stage of recovery.

Akinetic mutism or coma vigil is a syndrome usually associated with tumors of the third ventricle. Characteristically, the patient lies inertly in bed. He is able to swallow, but he has to be fed. Although essentially unresponsive to stimuli, the patient does follow the human face. Tracking movements of the eyes can be elicited by means of a two-dimensional pictorial representation of the face, as well as by the face itself. Sucking and grasping reflexes are also usually present. The phenomenon seems to represent a regression to an early developmental stage, when the infant tracks the mother's face and relates to her primarily with respect to feeding.

It has been hypothesized that the major tranquilizers selectively diminish the activity within the multisynaptic short circuits of the reticular activating system, reducing the affective component of consciousness; by leaving the cerebral cortex relatively unaffected, they do not reduce the cognitive component of consciousness. That effect is in contrast to the barbiturates and other sedative medications, which diminish central nervous system activity diffusely, including the cerebral cortex and the long pathways, thus reducing both affective and cognitive aspects of consciousness simultaneously. Because of neurochemical differences in the locus of action and the varying effects on level of consciousness with or without affecting cerebral cortical functioning, different pharmacological agents have different clinical effects.

Psychological factors

Attention. Attention is an aspect of consciousness that relates to the amount of effort exerted in focusing on certain portions of an experience so that they become relatively more vivid. One may speak of primary attention—which is passive, involuntary, automatic, instinctive, or reflexive—and secondary attention, which is active or voluntary.

Attention may fluctuate in intensity from moment to moment in acute brain disorders and toxic metabolic states. Attention may remain alert and vigilant and shift flexibly from topic to topic. In distractibility a person's attention is too easily drawn away from a given focus by extraneous stimuli. In its most extreme form it occurs in manic states. However, in milder forms it characterizes neurotic reactions of anxiety and depression and, in relation to depression, may play an important role in learning disabilities. Distractions may also be a result of the intrusion of fantasies, and those occur most intensely in schizophrenia. Attention span may be defined as the reciprocal of distractibility. In selective inattention or denial the person blocks out those environmental details that generate unpleasant feelings. An extreme form is seen in childhood schizophrenia as pain anosognosia, in which the child is not only unresponsive to pain but may inflict mutilating wounds on himself.

Self-consciousness. Self-consciousness is typically associated with lowered self-esteem and the expectation of rejection by others. Although it may occur fleetingly in anyone, it occurs in neurotic states of anxiety and depression, as well as in schizophrenia and the depressive psychoses. In the psychotic states the consciousness of self may become so extreme that one's own thoughts acquire the vividness of auditory hallucinations. In psychoanalytic terminology, self-consciousness is an expression of the superego or conscience.

In manic or exalted schizophrenic states, the patient no longer feels he is the victim of a rejecting loved one. On the contrary, he feels he has joined triumphantly in a blissful union with a loving, all-accepting parent. Under those circumstances, self-consciousness disappears completely.

Suggestibility. Suggestibility exists when a person responds compliantly and with unusual readiness. It can occur acutely when the person is overwhelmed by feelings of helplessness and passivity, as in the relationship of a frightened child to a parent or any adult in a psychologically traumatic situation.

Freud hypothesized that acutely frightening situations were associated with an alteration of consciousness that he called the hypnoid state, characterized by heightened suggestibility, feelings of depersonalization, and a special vulnerability to hysterical symptom formations.

Suggestibility can occur as an ongoing character trait in certain emotionally immature persons, and it expresses itself as gullibility. Extreme forms of suggestibility occur in catatonic stupor in the form of automatic obedience as echolalia, echopraxia, and waxy flexibility (cerea flexibilitas).

In catatonic stupor the patient is motionless, mute, and more or less nonresponsive to painful stimuli. The patient is aware of his environment with a clarity and intensity that is belied by his superficially stuporous appearance. After the stupor has subsided, the patient is able to give detailed retrospective accounts of the happenings during the catatonic episode. Thus, it is necessary to be circumspect in one's conversations in the presence of a catatonic patient.

The catatonic stupor may be regarded as one type of solution to the schizophrenic need-fear dilemma. Having convinced himself that any movement or remark will elicit a pain-producing response from the environment, the patient ceases entirely to move or to speak. If he relates at all, it is only in terms of the characteristic and, for him, safe catatonic automatism. Most of all, he keeps himself safely locked up in his world of private fantasy.

Suggestibility also plays an important role in communicated insanity (*folie à deux*), a psychotic reaction in which two or more closely related and associated persons simultaneously show the same symptoms and in which one member seems to have influenced or suggested the clinical picture to the other. Cultism is a variant of *folie à deux* in which one person, the leader, inculcates a group with his private ideology and then creates living conditions which prevent reality-testing social contacts.

In hypnosis the subject enters into a hyperattentive relationship with the hypnotist during which a trance state occurs, characterized by heightened suggestibility. As a result, a variety of hysteria-like sensory and motor abnormalities may be induced, as well as dissociative states and hypermnesia. Although the trance state may be superficially made to simulate sleep as a result of specific suggestions by the hypnotist, it is physiologically distinct from sleep.

According to Spiegel and Spiegel (1978), hypnotizability is a specific character trait that they quantify on a five-point scale. Types zero and one are essentially not hypnotizable. Types four and five are so hypnotizable that they are constantly lapsing into dissociative states as a result of chance suggestions from the environment. Most persons are two or three on the Spiegel scale.

Dissociative states. Dissociation means a loss of the usual consistency and relatedness between various groups of mental processes, with resultant apparent independent functioning of one of them. Although dissociation and splitting are used more or less synonymously, "dissociation" usually refers to hysterical or hypnosis-induced dissociative states, whereas "splitting" is used with reference to schizophrenia.

Although dissociation underlies every symptom of hysteria, there are occasions when the splitting is so profound as to alter the whole personality and behavior of the patient. Double and multiple personalities are the terms applied when a person at different times appears to be in possession of entirely different mental contents, dispositions, and characters and when one of the different phases seems to show complete ignorance of the other phase or phases. In trance states, which may occur spontaneously in hysteria or in response to hypnotic suggestion, the apparently sleeping subject may express the dissociative state in the form of automatic writing—that is, the subject may express in written form ideas and feelings that he will not recognize as his own when the trance state is ended. The performance of automatic writing and other actions during a trance state in response to a command or a suggestion is called command automatism. A command automatism may manifest itself after the trance state is presumably over as a posthypnotic suggestion.

In naïve cultural settings the dissociative phenomenon may give rise to a belief that the victim has been possessed by an alien spirit. For example, in Jewish folklore, the alien spirit, called a dybbuk, is believed to be the soul of a dead person wandering the earth to correct an injustice or to seek revenge. The mystical ceremony elaborated to drive out the alien spirit is called exorcism. Such rather widespread superstitious beliefs and practices form the basis for specific delusions in schizophrenia.

Perhaps the most familiar example of a dissociative state is that experienced during a nightmare. At a particularly terrifying moment in the dream, the dreamer may suddenly reassure himself:

This is only a dream. You are not in real danger. You can wake up any time you want.

And when he wakes up, he experiences the transition from a mental state that felt absolutely real just a moment ago to a new mental state to which the feeling of reality is now attached.

A teenage boy with a schizoid personality often daydreamed that his current unhappy life situation was a scene in a play. Momentarily, he expected a director from somewhere on high to say, "The scene is over; you can now take a rest from playing this painful role."

A hospitalized schizophrenic patient was convinced that every other patient on the ward was really a staff member and that all together were engaging her in an elaborate psychodrama, the basic theme of which she had not yet fathomed.

A teenage girl was hospitalized for a hysterical paraplegia. Under hypnosis she was asked, "Where are you?" In response, she acted out in dramatic detail a sexual incident involving a male high school classmate. When the episode came to an end, she was asked again, "Where are you?" She acted out a second drama, from an earlier period in her life, dealing with her grief about the death of her grandmother. Each repetition of the question, "Where are you?" resulted, spontaneously, in a regression to an earlier age, during which she acted out an incident involving erotic or aggressive impulses that generated guilt.

Schreiber (1973) described a patient who would go into a dissociative state whenever she was in a traumatic situation. In that state she would create a new personality, who would suffer the abuse and punishment in her place. By the time she was a grown woman, she had elaborated 16 separate personalities, each with a distinctive name, a particular manner of speaking, and distinctive personality traits.

Patients displaying dramatic dissociative states like the foregoing give the clinical impression of psychosis. The last patient mentioned did, indeed, have psychotic episodes with depression and suicidal behavior and required hospitalization and shock therapy. However, such patients usually retain a hold on reality through the basic personality and can be worked with psychotherapeutically.

An automatism is an activity performed without conscious knowledge on the part of the subject and usually followed by complete amnesia. It occurs most often after a grand mal seizure, head trauma, or pathological alcoholic intoxication. It may also occur as a posthypnotic suggestion.

Social factors. Some teenagers display one moral code while at home or in school and a completely dissociated (delinquent) code while with the gang. The ease with which they slip from one moral position to another suggests the term cassette-type superego, analogous to the ease with which one slips a new cassette into a tape recorder.

Students of mob psychology have studied the elation, impulsivity, general emotional regression, and personality dissociation that can occur in a seemingly normal adult when he becomes part of a mob (Freud).

Marxists speak of class consciousness and class ideology as key elements in a person's interpretation of reality. Those in the women's liberation movement speak of the consciousness-raising impact of their newfound self-respect as human beings, in contrast to the self-demeaning attitudes they had previously accepted as the reality of their female lot.

Sociologists refer to cognitive dissonance as the state of mind that occurs when there is an incongruity between one's daily life experiences and one's expectations based on prevailing social beliefs. It is hypothesized that an optimal level of cognitive dissonance is required to maintain an active creative relationship to the environment. When the level is too high, the person tends to withdraw. When it is too low, boredom results, and the person tends to seek change. Normally, a feeling of cognitive dissonance is a prod to reexamine and correct one's comprehension of reality. However, cultists—that is, members of religious or political sects who share a particular ideology that has become a vital personal source of hope—tend to respond to incongruities between cherished beliefs and observable facts not with the correction or rejection of one's basic premises but, rather, with new rationalizations that reintensify their basic fanatical zeal. The need to believe and the capacity to maintain belief in the face of maximum cognitive dissonance is the Festinger phenomenon.

The mass suicide in 1978 by the followers of cultist leader Jim Jones awakened a horrified world to the possible consequences of human suggestibility. Socially alienated persons by the thousands joined his church in a quest for personal security and significance. They turned over to him their worldly possessions, addressed him as "Dad," and accepted extremes of physical hardship and self-degradation at his command, including the ultimate command to end their lives. That phenomenon is by no means new or rare. Throughout recorded history, lonely, frightened masses have followed false messiahs in pursuit of the millennium, attributing to their leader qualities of omnipotence and omniscience normally seen in little children in relation to their parents and accepting living conditions which prevent reality-testing social contacts.

SLEEP

Sleep is a complex state of altered consciousness consisting of separate stages that have been variously labeled and classified. For example, as the subject falls asleep, his waking electroencelphalogram (EEG), characterized by α or 8 to 12 waves a second, is gradually replaced by low-voltage desynchronized activity. From an EEG point of view, that is stage 1 sleep. After some minutes that EEG pattern is replaced by a sequence of spindle-shape tracings made up of 13 to 15 waves a second. Those are called sleep spindles. In addition, occasional high-voltage spikes called K-complexes occur. Together they make up stage 2. After a few minutes slow waves appear, 0.5 to 2.5 a second. Those are called δ-waves, and their appearance marks the onset of stage 3 sleep. δ-waves gradually increase, when they make up most of the record, the subject is in stage 4 sleep. In the foregoing sequence, stage 1 is considered the lightest stage of sleep and stage 4 the deepest.

Sleep is cyclical, with four or five periods, occurring approximately every 90 minutes, of emerging consciousness from stages 4, 3, and 2 to a stage whose EEG resembles stage 1 but is fundamentally different. First, there occur rapid conjugate eye movements (REM), as a result of which the stage is commonly called the REM stage. In addition, there is a generalized loss of tone in most of the striated musculature, great increases and irregularities in pulse rate, respiratory rate, and blood pressure; penile erections, and nonresponsiveness to external stimuli. In addition to those phenomena, there are characteristic neurological, physiological, and chemical con-

comitants. If a subject is awakened during REM sleep, he reports having been in the midst of a dream in 60 to 90 per cent of all awakenings. REM sleep has also been called D sleep, for desynchronized or dreaming. It has also been called paradoxical sleep and active sleep. The remainder of sleep has been called S (synchronized) or NREM (non-REM) sleep, orthodox sleep, and quiet sleep.

The first D period occurs about 90 minutes after the onset of sleep. It may be longer in some normal persons particularly fatigued subjects, but it is significantly shorter in persons with affective disorders. D sleep constitutes 20 to 25 per cent of total sleep. The first D period is the shortest, about 5 minutes. Subsequent D periods are successively longer, and the final, awakening period lasts up to 40 minutes.

The percentage of REM sleep is much higher in the newborn and in young children than in older persons. It can go as high as 70 per cent in a premature infant. It drops somewhat below 20 per cent in old age. REM sleep shows a rebound increase after experimental suppression.

Monoamine oxidase inhibitors, which are effective antidepressant medications, bring about prolonged and total suppression of REM sleep. On the theory that the effect may be a factor in the therapeutic activity of the drug, the prevention of REM sleep by appropriate wakenings during the night has been used to treat depression, apparently with some success.

Reserpine, which reduces brain amine activity is one of the few drugs that increases D sleep; coincidentally, it often produces a clinical state of depression when used to treat essential hypertension.

Narcolepsy is characterized by a sudden overpowering desire to sleep. The patient goes to sleep anywhere, anytime—at work, while eating, while conversing or playing, and even while standing or walking. The sleep may last from a few seconds to several minutes; only rarely does it last a few hours. The patient can generally be aroused easily, and, when he wakes, he is perfectly fresh and able to go on with his work. He may have several attacks in a day. Associated with narcolepsy is cataplexy, which consists of attacks of sudden weakness, limpness of the arms or legs, or falling of the head to one side. During the cataplectic attack, the patient cannot speak. The attacks are often brought on by strong emotion, such as a sudden burst of laughter, anger, surprise, or pleasure.

In addition to the foregoing symptoms, a narcoleptic patient also displays sleep paralysis, which occurs just as the patient is falling asleep or waking up. Although mentally alert, the patient is totally unable to move. Hypnagogic and hypnopompic hallucinations also occur frequently. Pathognomonic of narcolepsy is an EEG pattern that shows REM at the very onset of sleep instead of the customary 90 to 100 minutes delay after the onset of sleep.

It has been found that narcolepsy or paroxymal daytime attacks of uncontrollable sleep consist of daytime seizures of REM sleep. The condition can be successfully treated by means of a monoamine oxidase inhibitor (Wyatt et al., 1971).

The other most clearly distinguishable form of sleep is stage 4 sleep, also known as NREM (non-REM) sleep or slow-wave sleep.

Stage 4 sleep probably plays a role in physiological restitution, and it has been shown to increase in response to fatigue, muscular activity, and sleep deprivation. It shows a rebound increase after experimental suppression. Peak secretion of growth hormone, which is supposed to increase protein synthesis, occurs in the early part of the night during stage 4 sleep.

Dreams are infrequently reported by subjects awakened during NREM sleep. However, a variety of motor phenomena—such as enuresis, somnambulism, and talking in one's sleep—do occur at that time.

Perhaps the most curious phenomenon that occurs in stage 4 sleep is the attack of night-terror, also known as *pavor nocturnus*. Most often, those attacks occur during the first non-REM sleep period, some as early as 15 to 30 minutes after sleep onset. In its most severe form, the stage 4 night-terror is a combination of extreme panic, a fight-flight reaction in the form of motility and somnambulism, and sleep utterances in the form of gasps, moans, groans, curses, and blood-curdling, piercing screams. Although the attack starts in stage 4, the episode itself is part of an arousal response characterized by a waking α-EEG. The person may be hallucinating and delusional while he acts out the night-terror. Heart rates attain levels of 160 to 170 a minute in 15 to 30 seconds, an acceleration rate greater than in any other human response. The respiratory rate is increased, but the most striking change is a tremendous increase in respiratory amplitude. The entire episode lasts 1 to 2 minutes, and the person returns to sleep rapidly. The content of the episode usually consists of a single brief, frightening image or thought, such as the idea of an intruder in the room, and it contrasts strikingly with the REM nightmare, which is more complex in content and far less severe in its somatic concomitants.

Because night-terrors have their origin in stage 4 sleep, Fisher and co-workers (1973) administered diazepam, a mild tranquilizer, which has a strong suppressional effect on stage 4 sleep. They found that, in general, when stage 4 sleep disappeared, the night-terrors disappeared.

Sleep apnea, can occur both during REM and NREM sleep. It is a cessation of airflow for more than 10 seconds at a time that occurs more than 30 times a night and is followed by periods of loud snoring. It is the most dangerous of all the sleep disorders. In obese patients it has been called the Pickwickian syndrome. It has also been called Ondine's curse. Despite the absence of evidence of cardiorespiratory disease, such patients may show polycythemia, hypoxemia, and hypercapnia. The disorder is also associated with cardiac arrhythmias during sleep, sudden death in adults, and sudden infant death syndrome (SIDS). Daytime drowsiness is also a common accompaniment of sleep apnea. There is a strong genetic influence, and it is associated with a high familial incidence. In cases of sleep apnea, one should avoid the use of sedatives. Many patients who are ill advisedly taking sedatives and hypnotics because of insomnia due to sleep apnea report that the medication aggravates the insomnia. Overweight patients should be placed on weight-reducing diets. When the associated cardiorespiratory complications become alarming, it may be necessary to perform a tracheostomy and to install a diaphragmatic pacemaker as lifesaving measures. In addition, electronic monitoring devices may be used to alert family members to awaken the apneic patient.

Nocturnal myoclonus consists of leg twitchings that occur once or twice a minute throughout the night. The condition is rarely a serious cause of insomnia. The use of an appropriate hypnotic at bedtime may have the effect of reducing the intensity of the muscle twitchings and the number of awakenings.

Some type of monitoring of the external world takes place during sleep, so that, for example, a mother may sleep soundly, unmindful of loud noises all about her, and yet awaken at the first soft cry of her baby. Another expression of consciousness in sleep is the commonly experienced ability to wake up at a specific time in the morning.

Sleep occupies most of the 24 hours of the day at birth and is interrupted only briefly because of hunger or physical discomfort. The period of sleep gradually shortens until it occupies 7 to 8 hours in the normal adult and becomes still shorter with advancing age. Normal sleep requirements vary widely from 4 hours a night to 10 hours or more.

Insomnia is a pathological inability to sleep. In catatonic or manic excitement the patient may remain uninterruptedly sleepless for 24 to 48 hours at a time. Those reactions of extreme excitement may go on to hyperthermia and death due to exhaustion.

Depressed patients usually complain of frequent awakenings during the night but most of all of early-morning insomnia—that is, the patient wakes up too early and is often bathed in anguished perspiration. That sleep pattern is commonly associated with anorexia, weight loss, feelings of sadness, and suicidal ideation.

Inability to fall asleep is a form of insomnia characteristic of the neuroses. The patient often fears sleep because of nightmares. That phenomenon is particularly common in the traumatic neuroses induced by battlefield experiences. Sleep disturbances may result from circadian rhythm disturbances; most commonly due to jet travel, they may be of unknown causes. Treatment may require alterations in the patient's life style—that is, accepting the necessity for periodic reversals in night-day wakefulness patterns or deliberately inducing nights of sleep deprivation. It is believed that some reactions of depression are connected with such circadian rhythm disturbances.

Recent studies have shown that depressed patients have significantly longer sleep latency—that is, the time it takes to fall asleep. Such patients also spend less time asleep than do other persons. They spend significantly more time in stage 1 sleep and often show considerable diminution in δ-sleep. REM latency is also significantly less—that is, the first REM period tends to start about 55 minutes after sleep onset, compared with about 90 minutes in normal persons. In addition, the percentage of time spent in REM sleep is significantly less than normal—less than 20 per cent in depressed patients compared with a normal of about 25 per cent.

The detection of penile tumescence during REM sleep has been used to differentiate potency disturbances of functional origin from cases of organic impotence.

Somnambulism can be precipitated in adult patients taking large bedtime doses of the major tranquillizers, antidepressants, and antihistamines. There is often a premonitory period, during which the patient complains of too much dreaming.

EEG-monitored transcendental meditation (TM) shows that much of TM time is spent in sleep stages 2, 3, and 4. Thus, much of the refreshment reported after a TM seance may be the result of a much-needed nap.

The fact that dreaming sleep is triggered cyclically by a neurobiological clock and is associated with a period of nonresponsiveness to external waking stimuli requires a reconsideration of Freud's theory, particularly the implications of his proposition that dreams occur in response to waking stimuli and function primarily as guardians of sleep.

Hypersomnia or excessive sleeping is often seen in depressive reactions occurring in neurosis. It is commonly associated with other depressive equivalents, such as overeating, and a variety of other addictive states, as well as sexual and aggressive acting out and academic underachievement. It may also occur in the early stages of a psychotic depressive illness, before more advanced stages of decompensation have occurred.

Reversal of sleep habit is a common accompaniment of hypersomnia. The patient tends to sleep soundly through the early morning hours, wake up gradually in the early afternoon, and achieve full wakefulness at a time when most people are going to bed. That pattern is most likely a psychologically caused interpersonal distance-regulating device for a person whose pattern is one of avoidance and retreat.

Drowsiness is a state of consciousness that intervenes normally between sleep and waking. It is characterized by a tendency to concrete thinking and transient hallucinatory phenomena, auditory and visual, which can occur normally just before sleep (hypnagogic hallucinations) and just before waking up (hypnopompic hallucinations).

Somnolence is abnormal drowsiness. It occurs in a variety of toxic, metabolic, and inflammatory diseases of the brain and with brain tumors that press on the floor of the third ventricle.

EPILEPTIC AND CONVULSIVE DISORDERS

The essence of epilepsy from the standpoint of diagnosis is the periodic recurrence of transient disturbances of consciousness.

Petit mal and grand mal seizures are characteristically associated with the full loss of consciousness in the midst of the attack. In petit mal, consciousness blinks on and off for intervals lasting between 1 and 40 seconds each. Those individual attacks are not associated with a preattack warning and are not followed by characteristic subjective or objective sequelae. EEG records in the midst of such attacks invariably reveal a spike-and-wave pattern having a frequency of about three of those complexes a second. The attacks may occur as often as 100 times in a single day or as occasional, isolated attacks days or weeks apart.

The disturbances of consciousness associated with grand mal epilepsy are more complicated. The actual muscular movements are typically preceded by an aura, which in itself may consist of a variety of clouded states of general awareness, including feelings of unreality and depersonalization. Commonly, those feeling states are not only vividly experienced but remembered by the patient. Such preconvulsive alterations of consciousness may last for hours or even days before the actual seizure and may give the patient an opportunity to get to a place of safety. During the actual convulsion, loss of consciousness is complete, and amnesia for the events during the actual seizure is also complete. After the grand mal seizure, the patient displays a clouded state of consciousness, which varies in duration from a few minutes to a period of hours. During that time, the EEG may show diffuse, symmetrical slow-wave activity. Amnesia for the postseizure period may be complete or interspersed with fragmentary islands of recall. That period has been called the postictal twilight state.

Twilight states, dream-like states of consciousness, can occur as independent seizure phenomena apart from grand mal seizures and are called psychomotor epilepsy. If the associated EEG abnormality is confined to the temporal lobe, one may speak of temporal lobe epilepsy; if the twilight states are associated with unpleasant olfactory and gustatory hallucinations with tasting tongue and lip movements, one may speak of uncinate fits. They are also characterized by circumscribed periods of intellectual dulling, disturbance in consciousness, confusion, and disorientation. Brief auditory and visual hallucinatory symptoms and schizophrenic-like psychotic reactions have been described. Generally, there is an amnesia for actions during that period. Characteristically, all those seizure patterns are associated with electroencephalographic abnormalities, which coincide in duration with the duration of the abnormality in the state of consciousness.

Because the seizure disorders represent precipitous interruptions in the patient's customary life style, they are commonly confused with other episodic behavior disorders—for example, the syndrome of pathological alcoholic intoxication; acute episodes of violence after other addicting substances, such as the barbiturates, lysergic acid diethylamide (LSD), cocaine, and the amphetamines; and toxic delirium after major surgery or various metabolic disorders. Severe breath-holding spells in children between the ages of 2 and 6 may go on to cyanosis, loss of consciousness, and opisthotonus-like seizures. The normal EEG and a history of a disturbed home environment help to clarify the differential diagnosis. In catatonic schizophrenia there may be a sudden eruption of extreme violence, leading to suicide, self-mutilation, or mutilating acts of homicide. Such an attack is sometimes called raptus.

A 21-year-old male schizophrenic severely abraded his cornea in a sudden attempt at self-enucleation. A 38-year-female schizophrenic suddenly seized a kitchen knife and stabbed herself to death with about two dozen self-inflicted wounds.

Impulsive characters may be goaded in a family quarrel to tantrum-like outbursts, with suicidal or homicidal results. Hysterical characters may undergo dissociative states, with a sudden complete change in personality. Sexual exhibitionism or homosexual acting out may occur episodically in response to a sudden loss of self-esteem.

Needless to say, none of the foregoing instances of episodic behavior disorder is connected with epilepsy.

Patients with episodes of unexplained paroxysms of abdominal pain that are associated with transient confusional reactions, syncope, or headache may show seizure patterns on the EEG. Those are instances of abdominal epilepsy and may be relieved by appropriate antiseizure medication.

Because seizures may be precipitated by flickering lights, some patients are unable to tolerate television.

In monitoring delirium reactions with EEG, one occasionally uncovers instances in which the mental disorder is the consequence of a petit mal status, with its characteristic sequence of spike-and-dome waves on the EEG. Those reactions can be controlled with appropriate antiseizure medication.

Episodes of syncope can occur in a physically debilitated male while urinating in an upright position. Careful nursing attention is necessary to prevent physical injury.

It is sometimes said that seizure disorders are associated with a higher incidence of sociopathy—that is, with convictions for crime. Most likely, epilepsy itself is not the cause of sociopathy; rather, the social ostracism that is often the fate of the epileptic may lead to adaptational problems, including sociopathy.

Disturbances of Orientation

Orientation may be defined as the ability to recognize one's surroundings and their temporal and spatial relationships to one's self or to appreciate one's relations to the social environment. The capacity for orientation involves the following categories: (1) Time: knowledge of the hour, day of the week, date, month, season, year. (2) Place: name of present location and home address, reason for being in this place at this time; inquiries in this area may reveal pathological denial of physical illness and the existence of other types of delusional systems. (3) Person: identity of self and others in the immediate environment, including not only a knowledge of names but also an appreciation of the role of each person in that setting.

The capacity for orientation depends, in the main, on three factors: the availability of perceptual data from the outer world, the availability of the stored data of recent memory, and to the demands of reality, which is part of the emotional equipment of the mature adult.

One may speak of a specific drive to seek out and maintain accurate orientation as a psychological quality characterizing the mature adult. Normally, the inability to establish one's bearings generates anxiety and appropriate orientation-seeking behavior. A normal person, for example, on awakening in strange surroundings from a deep sleep, may have a brief period of bewilderment, during which he scans his environment for clues, draws on his stored memory for recent events, and, finally, with a sense of relief, orients himself correctly. If he awakens from a particularly vivid dream characterized by a deep sense of the reality of the events in the dream, he may have a similar brief struggle to reestablish his orientation. If a patient wakes up from a coma, he may not be able to marshal sufficient data to orient himself. He may suffer from anxiety and bewilderment and respond to specific inquiries concerning orientation with panic and requests for information or by admitting that he does not know the answers to the questions.

In a variety of settings, persons abdicate their firm commitment to reality. Adults in normal recreational settings, for example, deliberately cultivate flight from reality as part of the recreational process. In the theater, surrender to the make-believe of the play may be so complete that it takes a period of active struggle to reestablish contact with the real world when the performance is over. Alcohol and other common central nervous system inhibitory substances encourage and temporarily make possible flights from reality and facilitate rapprochement with the world of make-believe.

A vivid feeling of reality is not necessarily associated with actual contact with reality. The delusional patient, for example, reorganizes his entire comprehension of the surrounding world to conform to his psychotic system, a process called rationalization, the purpose of which is to reduce the feeling of cognitive dissonance.

Disorientations in different spheres tend to parallel and to support—that is, to rationalize—each other. Through secondary elaboration, an inner consistency is achieved, like that often characterizing a dream. If the time precedes the onset of the patient's illness, the place is apt to be consistent with that time. People are similarly misidentified, and the reason for everyone's being together at that time and in that place is rationalized by a complex delusional system. When the disorientations in the delusional system are logically organized so that they have a rational inner consistency, the delusional system has been systematized.

When systematized delusions occur in schizophrenia, they are generally expressive of chronicity. They are resistant to psychotherapeutic intervention and carry a serious prognosis.

For many years the incorrect orientation answers of brain-injured patients were too briefly dismissed with, "The patient is confused" or "The patient shows memory impairment." On close observation, orderly patterns can be discerned within the over-all picture of disorientation.

DISORIENTATION FOR TIME

Hospitalized patients without organic brain disease commonly lose track of the date, the day of the week, and even the month. Thus, correct answers may be expressive of an alert and intact sensorium, but errors in those categories are not diagnostic of organic brain disease. An error in the year, on the other hand, is of diagnostic significance. It is in relation to the year that one commonly encounters a persistent pattern of misremembering.

A patient may give the year as 1958, and, even though he is corrected repeatedly, on each subsequent questioning he persists in stating that the year is 1958. Thus, he remembers quite dependably the wrong year. To characterize that misremembering as a simple lapse of memory is to miss the point that the patient is remembering what he wishes to remember—that is, he is responding to a wish or to a feeling that he is living in a year that was, perhaps, the last time he was in good health. The incorrect response, "The year is 1958," expresses a wish to be well, rather than a simple failure of memory.

Errors for the time of day are not significant as evidence of organic brain disease unless the error crosses a mealtime. Brain-injured patients commonly show errors for time of day if awakened from a nap—thinking, for example, that lunch or supper is actually breakfast.

A patient cited by Weinstein and Kahn (1955) always gave the time of day as 7 P.M. "because that is when my daughter comes to visit me." That patient deliberately avoided contact with a clearly visible wall clock in the process of denying the correct time.

In giving his personal history, a patient often condenses incidents in time that should actually be separated.

A patient giving a psychiatric history may report the birth of a younger sibling and the occurrence of an operation, such as a tonsillectomy, as taking place in the same year, when, in fact, the younger sibling was born when the patient was age 3 and the operation took place at age 6. In some such instances, it is possible to demonstrate that guilt over sibling rivalry on the one hand and the childish misinterpretation of an operative procedure as a punitive act on the other, although temporally separated, are condensed as a retrospective temporal falsification, so that crime and punishment become fused in memory as a single event.

Neurotic problems involving rebellious attitudes or a need to avoid painful reality may result in patterns of persistent tardiness. The affective state also plays a role in temporal orientation. During moods of elation, time seems to move quickly, whereas depressive moods are associated with a feeling that time is dragging.

Some anxious patients are unable to tolerate free time and have a need to fill all the temporal nooks and crannies of the day with prearranged activities. Such patients often suffer from a fear of loss of impulse control and defend themselves against acting out by overscheduling themselves. On the other hand, some patients, with a fear of their own passivity, complain that they are too tightly scheduled. The outer controlling elements are experienced as potentially dangerous forces capable of overwhelming the victim. Such patients are incapable of tolerating authority and may present particular problems in relation to school and military service, where punctuality is a sine qua non for successful performance.

DISORIENTATION FOR PLACE

The brain-injured patient in a general hospital may express the wish to be well by insisting that he is not in a hospital but in his home.

When one such patient was asked to explain the presence of the doctors and nurses who were all around her, she answered, "These people have taken over my home and have made it over to look like a hospital, but it is really my home." Other patients give the name of the institution correctly but characterize it as a hotel, a restaurant, or a convalescent home—that is, in various ways they deny the gravity of the illness by denying that they are in a hospital. On occasion, the patient gives the name of the hospital correctly but places the hospital close to home, saying, "I live a block away" or "I live across the street," when, in fact, home may be miles away. At times the patient locates himself in another hospital in which he was treated many years ago for a relatively minor illness from which he recovered. In that spatial dislocation he is expressing a *déjà vu*. He says, in effect, "I've been here before, and I went home to good health." Temporal disorientation commonly accompanies the pattern of spatial disorientation.

Those meaningful alterations, which are clear in the case of the patient with diffuse brain disease, provide the clue for the disorientations in place encountered without organic brain disease. Schizophrenic patients may be disoriented for place in less predictable ways than are patients with organic brain disease but always meaningfully in terms of their delusions.

DISORIENTATION FOR PERSON

A married female patient displaying disorientation for person may give her maiden name and insist that she is not married. Such denials often express elements of marital disharmony from which the patient wishes to take flight. They may also be associated with temporal disorientation, representing regression to a time preceding the onset of illness.

Anosognosic patients tend to misidentify in a manner to confirm the denial of illness. The hospital doctor in a white coat may be identified as a fish peddler and the place of their encounter as the Fulton Fish Market. Some physical or characterological trait in a doctor or a nurse may be the basis for a persistent misidentification of that person as a friend from the past who has no connection with illness. The doctor may be identified under such circumstances as a former teacher or an insurance salesman.

The tendency to divide the world into good and bad elements and then to create delusional systems that, in effect, embody that split resulted in a delusion expressed by a woman with one son named William. She claimed she had two sons, one named Bill, who was a good son, and one named Willie, who was bad.

Duplication may involve not only the entire person but part of a person. For instance, a hemiplegic patient may insist that he has two left arms, one good left arm and one bad left arm.

In patients without organic brain disease, the concept of self may be so chaotic that the vulnerable patient tends to be highly suggestible and to identify with any dominant person he is with. He may incorporate specific mannerisms of speech and dress and self-destructive patterns of behavior, such as narcotic addiction. That instability of self-concept is particularly conspicuous in teenaged girls. For that reason, they are vulnerable to mass hysterical behavior, as television audiences know from watching their responses to popular public performers. The chaotic concept of self most characteristic of adolescents is what Erikson (1963) referred to as the identity crisis. Confronted with an essentially insoluble dilemma concerning one's role in life, some teenagers go beyond experimental introjections and identifications and take flight into psychosis.

A teenaged girl could not decide whether to be a successful writer and civic-spirited citizen like her father or a beautiful, narcissistic woman like her mother. The patient had a prominent nose that caused her to resemble her father. A plastic surgeon modified her nose, achieved an excellent cosmetic result, and succeeded in emphasizing delicate feminine features resembling those of her mother. Postoperatively, she went into an acute schizophrenic state, characterized by delusions that she was a sought-after beauty who had a great mission to save the world as a second Florence Nightingale.

Disturbances of Memory

Memory is based on three essential processes: (1) registration, the ability to establish a record of an experience in the central nervous system; (2) retention, the persistence or permanence of a registered experience; and (3) recall, the ability to arouse and report in consciousness a previously registered experience.

A good memory involves the capacity to register data swiftly and accurately, the capacity to retain those data for long periods of time, and the capacity to recall them promptly in relation to reality-oriented goals.

During the process of registration, there must be a physiologically intact alert central nervous system. There must also be a sufficient number of repetitions of exposure to the data to stabilize the memory trace. An actor who needs many repetitions to memorize a script is called a slow study. At the other extreme are gifted persons who in a single exposure can master a dramatic script, a musical score, or a school lesson.

Emotions associated with the learning process play a crucial role in determining the permanence of memories. In infancy and early childhood, the entire learning process is tied up with satisfactions based on the relief of biological needs by loving parents. Thus, in early childhood the brain is maximally receptive to learning in purely biological terms, attentive adults are prepared to provide the repetitions necessary for learning, and there is a pattern of reward based on the loving responses of the parents as teachers. For all those reasons, it is no accident that the first language learned is called the mother tongue and that the mother tongue is normally the first language that returns on recovery from brain injury in patients who knew more than one language before the injury.

Although a good memory is one of the factors in the complex of mental capacities that make up intelligence, phenomenal feats of memory are occasionally encountered in settings of apparent mental retardation. Those feats of memory usually involve rote memory, the capacity to retain and reproduce data verbatim, without reference to meaning. In logical memory, on the other hand, problem solving in relation to a reality-oriented goal is paramount.

Mentally retarded memory prodigies are rare. They are encountered occasionally in institutions and are called idiot savants. It is likely that they are not really retarded persons but are schizophrenics who are protecting themselves from human contact with a facade of pseudo-idiocy.

In addition to quantitative, there are also qualitative differences in memory. Some persons are particularly well endowed with visual memory and can recall images with virtual hallucinatory intensity. They are called eidetic persons, and the reproduced memories are called eidetic images. That eidetic capacity tends to occur in childhood and subside with age, so that it is rare after adolescence. Eidetic mental retardates tend to retain that quality longer than do normal persons.

Memory for music, mathematics, muscular movements such as those involved in the performing arts, spatial relationships, and emotional feelings may be cited as examples of nonverbal memory which seems to reside in the right brain. Verbal memory depends on the development of verbal skills and resides in the left brain.

DISTURBANCES IN REGISTRATION

Registration depends on the level of consciousness. Anything that diminishes consciousness, such as alcoholism or concussion, interferes with registration. A prizefighter may go on for several rounds to win a fight after a dazing blow to the head and yet have no recoverable memory for the events after the blow. A circumscribed memory loss of that kind occurring during the time after an acute brain injury is called anterograde amnesia. An alcoholic may behave in a socially acceptable manner for an entire evening and yet have no recoverable memory of the events of that evening (alcoholic blackout). Disturbed states of consciousness lasting for weeks and months associated with encephalitis, subarachnoid hemorrhage, and severe brain trauma may be followed by a permanent inability to recall the events experienced during that period. In all those instances, the subsequent defect in recall starts with primary defects involving registration and retention.

Electroshock therapy (ECT) may be followed by both anterograde amnesia and retrograde amnesia, memory loss for events preceding shock therapy. With cessation of ECT, memory functioning rapidly improves. The term "retrograde amnesia" is used to refer not only to memory losses in relation to events preceding a specific incident of brain trauma but also to a memory pattern found in chronic organic brain disease, such as senile dementia, in which the capacity to recall recent events is primarily impaired, whereas memory for remote events remains relatively intact. Depending on the number of ECT treatments, memory returns more or less to normal within weeks after the last treatment. However, islands of amnesia may persist and resist all psychotherapeutic efforts at recall.

There are conditions in which registration seems to be impaired because the patient appears to be totally nonreactive. That impairment occurs in catatonic schizophrenia and in severe panic states. However, when the brain is intact from an organic point of view but perceived experiences are repressed or denied for purely emotional reasons, registration is normal. In those instances, seemingly nonobserved events can be recalled later, either directly or with the use of specific techniques for eliciting forgotten or repressed memories, such as hypnosis, narcoanalysis, and psychoanalysis.

DISTURBANCES IN RETENTION

In the establishment of lasting memories, there is a preliminary learning stage during which the memory trace is unstable. The memory curve or the curve of forgetting is a graphic representation of the relative amounts of memorized material that can be recalled after various intervals of time. For persons with good memories, memory traces are quickly established, and the curve of forgetting is prolonged and may extend over the entire lifetime of the person. In some instances of organic brain disease, the curve of forgetting is accelerated. In Korsakoff's psychosis, memory for recently acquired facts may decay in a matter of seconds, without any residual capacity for recall.

Information storage takes place in at least three separate stages. A preliminary processing takes place on a sensory level. An intermediate processing leads to short-term storage. A definitive processing leads to long-term storage. Short-term storage is what is used when, for example, a telephone number is remembered for a few seconds. It is a highly fragile memory trace and is easily disturbed by interference or distraction. With repetition and sufficient motivation, the memory trace may be transformed into a long-term storage item.

Retention is a property of nerve tissues in general. Nerve cells and their processes may be compared to tape recorders that retain a record of the impulses that have passed along them. There is an enormous capacity for units of information and for specificity of records of that kind in the brain.

It has been hypothesized that synaptic conductance is altered as a result of learning, in the direction of making the postsynaptic membrane increasingly sensitive to acetylcholine with time after learning, up to a certain point. After that point is passed, sensitivity declines, leading to the phenomenon of forgetting. According to that theory, increased learning leads to an increase in conductance in each set of synapses without an increase in their number.

There is evidence that stage 4 sleep may facilitate long-term storage.

It has been hypothesized that the registration stage of memory depends on the formation of ribonucleic acid (RNA) within the nerve cells and their processes and that specific memories derive their individuality from specific modifications in the RNA molecule. According to that hypothesis, each such RNA molecule is the storage device for the memory system and, at the same time, a template or stencil that can run off duplicates of the molecule as part of the mechanism of recall.

It has also been hypothesized that in the aging brain the basic supply of RNA is diminished and that the diminished supply is the specific organic deficit underlying the weakness of memory in the aged.

Certain antibiotics that are inhibitors of protein synthesis have a demonstrated ability to interfere with long-term memory storage in experimental animals.

DISTURBANCES IN RECALL

Amnesia is the partial or total inability to recall past experiences. Any process that interferes with the formation of a short-term memory or its fixation into long-term memory results in complete or permanent amnesia. That type of amnesia may also be called registration amnesia. Chronic brain disease impairs both registration and recall. That is seen in Korsakoff's syndrome, vascular disease, senile dementia, and brain tumor. When memories are presumed to have been formed and stored permanently but access to them is somehow prevented, the result is an amnesia that in many cases is temporary and treatable. That is referred to as recall amnesia.

According to psychoanalytic theory, an important basis for an adult's amnesia for the events in his childhood is the need to control and repress various infantile wishes that are forbidden by parents. As infantile fears of parental punishment are relieved during psychoanalysis, many of the events of childhood amnesia become increasingly accessible to voluntary recall. In that way psychoanalytic treatment may lead to a recovery of much of the essentially normal childhood amnesia.

The sharp distinction between amnesia of organic origin and amnesia of emotional origin is made for purposes of description and clarification. Most amnesias seen in relation to organic brain disease are, in fact, mixed amnesias in which organic deficits and emotional interference with recall both play a role.

Hysterical amnesia is a loss of memory for a particular period of past life or for certain situations associated with great fear, rage, or shameful humiliation. That form of amnesia is highly selective and systematized to fulfill the patient's specific emotional needs.

The rule of Pitrés states that, in a person who knew more than one language before a brain insult, the first language that returns is the mother tongue.

A case of polyglot aphasia illustrates the negative role which emotion can play during the period of recovery. A brain-injured young man grew up in a Spanish-speaking country, but his mother tongue was English. In that case the mother-child relationship was a highly disturbed one, and the patient grew up with the image of his mother as a menacing figure. As memory for language returned to the brain-injured man, he clearly preferred Spanish. A reduction in his comprehension of English was especially noticeable during his mother's visits.

In another case, on recovery from a severe head injury, a Hebrew-speaking man whose mother tongue was English followed the rule of Pitrés and used English first. However, on return from the hospital to his Hebrew-speaking wife and children, he went into a severe depression when he found he could not communicate with them. During the next days his fluency in Hebrew returned more rapidly than did his fluency in English.

The brain-injured patient who is highly motivated may succeed in overcoming organically determined impairments of recall by a variety of mnemonic devices. For example, in response to a request to name an abstract word or concept, he may start with a concrete visual image that is charged with highly personal significance. In his search for the correct word, he may then go on to make writing movements with his head. Finally, after much effort exerted over that tortuous path, he arrives at the abstract word for which he is searching. Thus, in order to discover subtle memory defects in brain-injured patients, one must inquire into the mechanism of recall, as well as the actual content of what is remembered.

In contrast to the aphasic impairments of recall, which are highly circumscribed and involve specific words or actions, is the impairment of recall associated with the hysterical fugue state, a form of dissociative reaction that sets in after a severe emotional trauma.

A terrifying experience on the battlefront or a momentary loss of impulse control that nearly leads to the murder of a loved one may be followed by a complete loss of memory concerning all personal identifying data. After the precipitating psychological trauma, the patient enters into a period of actual physical flight, which takes place in a state of panic. When the victim comes to, he finds himself far removed from his accustomed habitat and unable to identify his surroundings, his reason for being there, or anything about his past. That form of amnesia is associated with a flattening of affect characteristic of hysteria. Usually, the lost memory is readily recoverable with hypnosis, narcoanalysis, or strong suggestion, particularly when offered in a setting that promises extended relief or actual physical separation from the traumatic life situation.

The dramatic extreme embodied in a hysterical fugue state provides a model for more circumscribed examples of functional forgetting. What is referred to as repression in relation to early childhood traumas is indistinguishable from simple forgetting or recall amnesia, in which long-term registration is intact. Such circumscribed amnesias may be the basis for a chronic state of psychological stress. According to psychoanalytic theory, those forgotten traumas constantly threaten to erupt into consciousness. Symptom formation, to some degree, has its origin in the ongoing need to keep those memories out of consciousness or to distort and disguise them if they do return. In a sense, the neurotic patient can be said to suffer from memories that he is forgetting with only partial success; in that way the psychopathology of memory is related to the psychopathology of the emotions. By the same token, the treatment of recall amnesia is most effectively accomplished by a systematic desensitization of the patient to the traumatic aspects of the forgotten events.

Paramnesia is a distortion of recall resulting from the inclusion of false details, meanings, or emotions or wrong temporal relationships. It is also known as *fausse reconnaisance* and retrospective falsification.

Distortions in recall are encountered in normal persons. Witness's errors in the courtroom are examples. There is in everyone a readiness to distortion whenever accurate recall elicits painful affects. The presence of diffuse organic brain disease has the effect of facilitating and fixating that universally present tendency toward paramnesia.

Confabulation is the unconscious filling in of memory gaps by imagined experiences. It is characteristic of diffuse organic brain disease. Those recollections change from moment to moment and are easily induced by suggestion.

A simple test for confabulation is to ask the hospitalized patient, "Where were you last night?" That question is usually enough to elicit the phenomenon if it is present.

Déjà vu is an illusion of recognition in which a new situation is incorrectly regarded as a repetition of a previous memory. It

can occur in normal persons, particularly in settings generating anxiety. It is more common in neurotic states and occurs occasionally in the aura of grand mal epilepsy. In *jamais vu* there is a feeling of unfamiliarity with a situation that one has actually experienced.

Related to *déjà vu* are *déjà entendu*, in which a comment never heard before is incorrectly regarded as a repetition of a previous conversation, and *déjà pensé*, in which a thought never entertained before is incorrectly regarded as a repetition of a previous thought.

Although the causes of those related phenomena are not known, psychoanalytic evidence suggests that they share with screen memories and daydreaming the function of psychological defense. Implicit in the feeling "I have experienced this before" is the reassuring further thought "and I have survived in spite of my fears." In short, *déjà vu* is a device to control the intensity of anticipatory anxiety.

The familiar type of nightmare known as the examination dream seems to serve the same function as *déjà vu*. Such dreams occur typically before a school examination or some other life trial. In the dream the sleeper is asked to answer examination questions concerning a subject he never studied. In spite of the manifest anxiety in such dreams, the content typically deals with a test that in actuality was successfully passed some time ago. As such, it serves to reassure the dreamer that he will pass this test as well.

A tennis player, at a taut moment in a doubles match, expressed to his partner the following reassuring words: "Don't worry, we've been here before."

Hypermnesia is the capacity for an exaggerated degree of recall. It can be elicited episodically in a hypnotic trance, particularly when regression in time is specifically suggested to the subject. It is seen as an ongoing state in certain prodigies, obsessive-compulsive neurosis, paranoia, and mania.

A screen memory consists of fragments of childhood recollection that break through the barrier of childhood amnesia. The screen memory is often striking for the minutiae recalled. There are often associated recollections of bright light. Characteristic also of the screen memory is its tendency to return to consciousness repeatedly in an obsessive fashion. Paradoxically, the qualities of exaggerated accuracy and feelings of certainty that accompany those hypermnesias are deceptive. Temporal and spatial alterations and an emphasis on trivia combine to ward off from conscious recall specific traumatic memories of childhood. Thus, those memories may be more accurately classified among the paramnesias, and in some ways they can be said to resemble the structure of a dream.

In settings of depression without organic brain disease, patients often complain of severe memory impairment, even though objective memory testing does not confirm such an impairment. On the other hand, brain-injured patients with objectively demonstrative memory impairment commonly fail to complain of it.

Disturbances in Perception

Perception is the awareness of objects, qualities, or relations that follows the stimulation of peripheral sense organs, as distinct from the awareness that results from memory. Thus, perception is the necessary precursor of memory and is connected with memory through the process of memory registration.

There are as many categories of perceived data as there are types of end organs, including visual, auditory, olfactory, gustatory, tactile, and kinesthetic. Accurate perception depends, first of all, on an intact perceptual apparatus at every level of organization, and impairments in perception set the stage for delusions, hallucinations, and a variety of misinterpretations of reality.

A neuroma in an amputation stump, for example, may set the stage for a phantom-limb delusion. Deaf persons may fill in the gaps of hearing with paranoid projections. A lesion in Wernicke's area gives rise to agnosia, an inability to recognize and interpret the significance of sensory impressions. That inability sets the stage for anosognosia, the delusional denial of physical illness. Clouding of consciousness due to diffuse brain disease gives rise to a variety of perceptual disturbances. Many central nervous system toxins are hallucinogens with differing effects on specific sensory modalities.

One theory of schizophrenia postulates a metabolic abnormality that generates hallucinogens. Such disturbances may, indeed, occur in some schizophrenics and provide a specific hallucinatory component to the clinical picture. It has been claimed, for example, that schizophrenics with delusions of poisoning are particularly prone to hallucinations in the olfactory and gustatory spheres and less prone to auditory hallucinations.

Perception does not consist of simple somatic responses. It depends on a complex maturational process with psychological and social components. The *Reizschutz*, a complex barrier against traumatic stimuli, is developed gradually in the mother-child interactions of infancy. Schizophrenic children do not develop that perceptual shield, and for them ordinary stimuli exert a traumatic effect and give rise to a chronic posture of negativism and retreat.

Perception begins with a tuning-in process, an act of paying attention. What one pays attention to and with what intensity are determined by personal values. At every step of the perceptual process, the somatic mechanism interacts in a complex dialogue with the percept. The mood plays a role. Depressed patients see less than others do because of lack of interest. Schizophrenics are inclined to see less than others do because they fear what they see. Manic patients may seem to take in everything, but their perceptual pattern is primarily in the service of avoiding key issues—that is, the seemingly hyperalert attention of the manic is really a form of selective inattention.

Fish and Haggin (1973) observed a visuomotor disorder in infants at risk for schizophrenia. In those infants visual exploration seemed to go on normally. However, visual exploration was not associated with normal amounts of reaching, grasping, and manipulating. As a result, visual impressions were not associated with the usual tactile and proprioceptive impressions. Fish and Haggin thought that the disconnection between visual perception and motor response was primary and etiological in childhood schizophrenia. It seems more likely that what is seen here are manifestations of anhedonia—that is, dysphoric or unpleasurable feelings on contacting the world—and that the lack of motor response is an early manifestation of the core schizophrenic pattern, one of avoidance and retreat.

The well-defended schizophrenic is one who preserves his nonpsychotic state by astute avoidance of traumatic perceptions, particularly those involving human interactions. The schizophrenic state is associated with a significantly reduced amount of incoming stimuli. The greater the reduction, the greater the tendency to autistic and idiosyncratic thinking and to unusual perceptual experiences, such as hallucinations.

Apperception is conscious awareness of the significance of a percept. It is based on the complex psychological components that determine its total impact.

Perception may be the result of relatively simple, affectively neutral stimuli, presented one at a time or two at a time (double simultaneous stimulation). Stimuli may be complex, involving both visual and kinesthetic factors in making a discriminatory judgment, as in binocular vision; or stimuli may be a combination of visual, olfactory, and gustatory in an essentially gustatory perception.

A disturbance of perception associated with organic brain disease forms the basis for the face-hand test (Bender, 1952). If a normal alert adult with eyes closed is touched on his face and hand simultaneously, he recognizes both touches accurately and promptly. In settings of diffuse organic brain disease, including cerebral arteriosclerosis, the patient reports the face touch accurately but does not report the hand touch at all or displaces it up toward the face and locates it inaccurately. Persistent errors on double simultaneous stimulation are a positive result and provide presumptive evidence of organic brain disease. The test is normally positive in children up to the age of 4 or 5. It then becomes negative until age 60, after which it tends to become positive again. In the intervening age groups, the test provides a useful presumptive sign. In elderly patients who are depressed and who give a positive response, the test tends to become negative as the depression lifts. In all instances of a positive response, further neurological studies are required to demonstrate absolutely that organic brain disease is present.

Between the presentation of a stimulus and its recognition by the observer, there is a time lapse called the perception time. That lapse involves time for the transmission of the nerve impulse from the sensory receptor to the appropriate brain centers. More significant is the time involved to overcome an emotionally determined barrier to perception, a barrier that exists to protect the person against traumatic stimuli.

Traumatic stimuli of all categories are modified adaptively by the barrier against stimuli. Functional alterations in the level of consciousness may be cited, with complete loss of consciousness (fainting) as an extreme example of the way in which the barrier against stimuli operates.

Whereas emotionally induced fainting eliminates all perception, circumscribed eliminations of perception may occur as a device for coping with traumatic stimuli. In negative hallucination, a person with a physiologically intact nervous system fails to perceive a stimulus. It can be induced through hypnosis. When the nonperceived stimulus is excluded from conscious awareness because it is traumatic, it is usually part of the syndrome of hysteria.

Any modality of perception may be disordered in hysteria. Total anesthesia can occur, but diminution in sensation is more common. Those perceptual disturbances do not follow recognizable neuroanatomical distributions but involve, rather, a part of a limb (glove-and-stocking distribution), half the body, and the mucous membranes (vagina, rectum, nose, mouth, and pharynx). Peculiar to the hysterical anesthesias is the simultaneous involvement of all forms of sensation, superficial and deep, without the sensory dissociation that frequently characterizes organic sensory disturbances. If the sensory loss is limited to half the body, it is found to stop exactly at the midline, a condition contrary to the normal cutaneous innervative overlapping. Similarly, psychogenic loss of sensation is attested to by the hysteric's perception of the tuning fork on only one side of the sternum or on only one side of the head, an obvious impossibility in view of the normal bone conduction of vibrations.

Repeated testing of visual fields in hysteria may result in a spiral contraction of the visual field. Hysterical blindness may occur.

Macropsia is a condition characteristic of hysteria in which objects appear larger than they really are. They may assume terrifying proportions.

Micropsia is a condition in which objects appear smaller than they really are. The condition may alternate with macropsia in hysteria, but it has also been described as an aura in some cases of epilepsy.

Hysterical patterns of perceptual disturbance do not by any means rule out organic disease. The perceptual disturbances often seem to emerge in response to repeated sensory testing. That is not at all the result of a conscious intent to deceive the examiner but more likely the outcome of a naïve appeal for help.

Brain-injured patients with left hemiplegia, hemianesthesia, and hemianopsia often steadfastly neglect the entire left side of the visual field. For example, they eat all the food on the right side of the hospital tray up to the midline; they write only on the right half of the page; they read the right half of a word. In drawing the human figure, they draw only the mirrored representation of the right half of the body, neglecting entirely to draw the other half. In all those instances, there seems to be a selective inattention to the sick side, an inattention that manifests itself as an essentially hysterical disturbance in vision. The relationship of the hysterical disturbance to denial of illness seems quite clear: "The sick side does not exist."

It has been suggested that the term "hysteria" be replaced entirely by the term "psychogenic sensory and motor disorders" and that those disorders be described along with the associated disease entity or personality disorder. In that way one could avoid the confusion that arises when one attaches the term "hysteria" to all sorts of conditions, including psychosis, neurosis, and organic brain disease.

Patients with organic hearing impairments have selectively more difficulty than do others in hearing emotionally disturbing auditory stimuli. In a sense, those patients with mixed (organic and functional) hearing disturbances are expressing in a selective and more circumscribed fashion the same phenomenon that is encountered in complete hysterical deafness without organic hearing impairment—namely, a blocking out of potentially traumatic auditory percepts.

Hysterical anesthesia has been described as a kind of localized fainting. Frigidity, including all degrees of anesthesia of the vagina and external genitalia, is a common hysterical defense against sexual excitement. In each circumstance there is a withdrawal of attention from potentially traumatic external events. Hysterical anesthesia of the nasopharynx leads to absent gag reflex, commonly observed in hysteria.

Just as withdrawal of attention from a body part can reduce perception to the point of complete anesthesia, so can a sensory end organ be overinvested with attention because of anxiety. In the latter instance, there may be areas of hyperalgesia to touch and to headaches and other body pains. In spite of verbal expressions of great suffering, the hysterical patient may show a characteristic attitude of unconcern (*la belle indifférence*). Complaints of pain may be associated with rigidity of muscles and occasionally bizarre flexion deformities of the extremities and spine.

Although the physical complaints typically do not conform to recognizable clinical syndromes, actual physical disease, past or present, may set the stage for use of a specific body part in symptom formation that is without organic basis. The return to a previous symptom or the perpetuation and intensification of a present organic symptom in the formation of a hysterical symptom is termed somatic compliance. The preoccupation with headache after a head injury in an industrial accident involving compensation is an example of somatic compliance.

In all the perceptual disturbances of hysteria, it is not enough to demonstrate that the pattern of sensory abnormality is impossible from the point of view of known neuroanatomical facts. One must also search out the emotional meaning of the perceptual disturbance in adaptational terms, recalling that anesthesia, hyperesthesia, and paralysis commonly serve to defend the patient against sexual or violent impulses that he fears may get out of control or serve as a cry for help in patients whose verbal skills are limited.

HYPOCHONDRIASIS

A generalized withdrawal of attention from external objects is almost always followed by an increase in the attention focused on the self as an object. If the retreat from the world of real objects is complete enough, a pathological awareness of body feelings emerges, and that awareness is the basis for hypochondriasis. One normally encounters a transiently increased awareness of somatic sensations on drifting off to sleep—an awareness of the heart beat, endoptic visual phenomena, and so on.

Hypochondriasis is the unshakable belief that widespread physical disease is present, in the face of all evidence to the contrary. As a symptom, it occurs in many forms of mental illness. It is most common in the depressions, particularly those of the involutional period. It may take bizarre forms in schizophrenia, in which case one may speak more appropriately of somatic delusions. It may occur in a chronic, low-grade form over a period of years as part of a neurotic reaction.

Abnormal body feelings associated with hysteria tend to be localized and serve to protect the person against the still longed for but potentially traumatic encounters with circumscribed portions of the outer world. Abnormal body feelings associated with hypochondriasis, on the other hand, tend to be generalized, in the sense that the entire body is involved, and result from a relatively complete withdrawal from external objects. Thus, an important difference between the hysteric and the hypochondriac is the degree to which contacts with real objects in the external world have been retained or surrendered.

A fear of sexual intercourse can occur as part of a neurosis and may be associated with specific hysterical perceptual impairments involving the genitalia. Other aspects of human interaction may be preserved relatively intact. In a psychotic reaction there is a generalized fear of human interaction and a relative breaking off of all real relationships. With that withdrawal goes a generalized somatic preoccupation, as in hypochondriasis.

Neurotic fears tend to center on a specific body part, with expectation of injury to the "offending" organ. In psychoanalytic terminology that fear is referred to as the castration complex. Psychotic fears tend to center on a fear of extinction or total annihilation (aphinisis).

When severe identity confusion exists, as in certain instances of homosexual panic, there is fear of annihilation, which may express itself as hypochondriasis. Hypochondriacal preoccupations are commonly seen for the same reason in institutionalized disturbed children.

DSM-III places those various complaints under the general heading of somatoform disorders. The essential features are symptoms suggesting physical illness for which there is no organic basis. In addition, there is evidence that the symptom is linked to psychological factors or conflicts. Unlike the symptoms of factitious illness and malingering, the symptoms of somatoform disorders are not under the patient's voluntary control. They occur more often in women than in men. DSM-III suggests four subgroups. The first is somatization disorder or Briquet's syndrome. It consists of recurrent multiple somatic complaints starting in adolescence and is associated with a characteristically vague and overdramatic history. Along with marked anxiety, depression, and sociopathy, there are various physical complaints, many of which are clearly psychogenic—that is, hysterical. The second subgroup is conversion disorder. It usually involves a single disturbance during a given episode but may vary in site and in kind if there are subsequent episodes. It commonly has an onset in the later years of life. The third subgroup is psychogenic pain disorder in which intractable pain without organic basis is the main feature. The fourth subgroup is atypical somatoform disorder which consists of a preoccupation with bodily function and a fear of disease without organic basis. Many patients with that disorder were previously labeled "hypochondriacs."

ILLUSIONS

In an illusion there is perceptual misinterpretation of a real external sensory experience.

In a state of anxiety and loneliness, a traveler is apt to mistake a tree trunk for a menacing adversary or a mist for a terrifying apparition. That tendency does not necessarily imply psychopathology. However, a schizophrenic patient may hear an insulting remark in the chime of a clock or feel the sinister hand of death in a casual handshake. That kind of misinterpretation is also known as an illusion.

Illusions may occur in certain toxic states. For example, in the stage of alcohol withdrawal syndrome just preceding hallucinosis, the sound of a match striking can elicit a startled leap into the air, with fear and trembling. Such frightened reactions to ambiguous or neutral stimuli indicate that the patient is projecting and is on the threshold of ideas of reference.

HALLUCINATIONS

A hallucination is the apparent perception of an external object when no corresponding real object exists—that is, an internal psychological event is mistakenly attributed to an external source. A dream is a simple example of a hallucination in normal experience.

Any modality of perception may be involved. Within the framework of normal hallucinatory experience, hypnagogic and hypnopompic hallucinations should be mentioned. Hypnagogic hallucinations occur in the drowsy state preceding deep sleep. They may contain both auditory and visual elements with great clarity and intensity. At times, they are associated with paresthesias in the mouth and hand, the sound of murmured voices, and vague visual images of large objects approaching and receding. Those hypnagogic hallucinations have been called the Isakower phenomenon and seem to represent a reawakening of the memory of early nursing experiences.

Although it is said that hypnagogic hallucinations occur most often in persons suffering from hysteria, they can also occur in normal persons, particularly during childhood and early adolescence. What has been said of hypnagogic hallucinations is also true of hypnopompic hallucinations, except that hypnopompic hallucinations occur during the drowsy state after deep sleep and before awakening. They also occur as part of the syndrome of narcolepsy.

When the schizophrenic patient is wide awake by all neurophysiological criteria, he may experience hallucinations as vivid as those experienced by normal people during dreams. He often acts on those inner perceptions, as though they were more compelling than the external realities that compete for his attention. He may incorporate illusions into his hallucinations, so that the hallucinations occur alongside external perceptions and even intermingle with them.

Hallucinosis is a psychotic state in which the patient seems to be alert and well oriented, in spite of the fact that he is hallucinating. Such patients may slip in and out of the hallucinatory state, with intervals of insight and lucidity—hence, Hughlings Jackson's term "mental diplopia."

A group of hallucinogenic psychotomimetic drugs characteristically elicit hallucinosis—that is, hallucinations in a setting of relatively clear consciousness. Mescaline and lysergic acid diethylamide (LSD) are well-known representatives of that group of drugs. The person's relative alertness makes it possible for him to communicate his hallucinations in considerable detail in an experimental situation.

Under mescaline, visual hallucinations, combined with visual illusions, are most frequently reported. Those visual phenomena are vivid and change rapidly. Auditory hallucinations also occur but less frequently than do visual illusions. In LSD toxicity a patient may experience a colorful hallucination after hearing a loud voice, or he may have an auditory hallucination in response to a bright light (synesthesia). There is also the LSD phenomenon known as trailing, a perceptual abnormality in which moving objects are seen as a series of discrete and discontinuous images, reminiscent of a stroboscopic photograph with multiple exposures.

After repeated ingestions of LSD, one may precipitate a disorder, called flashbacks, that may last for months after the last usage. The disorder is characterized by spontaneous recurrences of illusions and visual hallucinations similar to those experienced during the acute toxic state. There may be bursts of color and visions of formed objects. Depersonalization, perceptual distortions, hallucinations, and episodes of catatonia may occur. The trailing phenomenon, too, may make its reappearance.

In the convulsive disorders, relatively unformed percepts may occur during the aura. Olfactory and gustatory hallucinations occur in temporal lobe lesions in uncinate fits. Characteristically, the patient is unable to describe those sensations clearly, except to say that they are unpleasant. Other patients may experience nausea or flashes of light as part of the aura. Less often, the aura in uncinate fits is associated with complex hallucinatory experiences involving visual and auditory components and possessing an affective quality of reminiscence—for example, déjà vu. The nature of the preseizure sensory disturbance often provides important clues for the localization of seizure foci amenable to surgical extirpation.

Generalized organic brain disease of almost any cause can be associated with hallucinatory states that are at times indistinguishable from schizophrenia. Those reactions may be expressive of drug sensitivities. Atropine and its derivatives may cause characteristic Lilliputian hallucinations in drug-sensitive adults receiving relatively small quantities in the form of eyedrops or in children being treated for enuresis with atropine derivatives. In Lilliputian hallucinations the hallucinated objects, usually people, appear greatly reduced in size. Although they occur most characteristically in psychotic reactions to a variety of drugs and toxic-metabolic states, they can, on occasion, occur in psychotic reactions without organic brain disease. They are to be differentiated from micropsia, a hysterical phenomenon in which real objects in the environment appear reduced in size.

Similarly, relatively small doses of alcohol or marihuana can produce hallucinations in sensitive subjects. Even the major tranquilizers, which are administered to decrease psychotic manifestations, may intensify hallucinations or elicit new ones in patients hypersensitive to anticholinergic substances.

Patients who are chronically habituated to any sedative substance—such as alcohol, barbiturates, meprobamate, or diazepoxide—often experience hallucinations when those drugs are withdrawn (abstinence syndrome or withdrawal reaction). Those hallucinatory states are commonly associated with great terror.

Brain tumors, subarachnoid hemorrhage, uremia, strokes, a broad range of endocrine abnormalities, and a variety of drugs may all play a role in initiating hallucinatory states. Different chemical agents may have the same hallucinatory effect on a given person, and, conversely, a given chemical may produce widely varying responses in different persons.

In addition, the effect of a given chemical agent varies with the mood, the social setting, and the physical condition of the patient.

In describing a hallucinatory state, one should consider the following elements:

Projection to the outer world. At times, hallucinations are perceived with great intensity; at other times, they are perceived as barely audible whispers or barely visible shadows. At times, the hallucination is clearly placed in the outer world; at other times, it is experienced within the body—a picture or a voice located in the head, the chest, or some other part of the body. The images and words may be distinct or blurred.

They shade off from unmistakable sensory experiences at one extreme, through vivid imaginations and inspired thoughts, to ordinary thoughts and ideas at the other extreme. Thus, hallucinations and delusions occur on a continuum and are measured by the degree of the patient's conviction of the objective reality of a bizarre experience.

Sensory modality. A haptic hallucination is one associated with the sensation of touch. Although it may occur in schizophrenia, it is more common in delirium tremens, in which those cutaneous hallucinations are commonly associated with visual hallucinations of tiny, crawling animals. Creeping sensations under the skin are known as formication. Among cocaine users, the phenomenon is known as the cocaine bug. Olfactory and gustatory hallucinations of bad tastes and odors may be encountered as part of the aura of temporal lobe epilepsy (uncinate fit). They may also occur in schizophrenia, with complex delusional elaborations of being poisoned. The auditory sphere is probably the most frequently involved sensory modality in the hallucinations of schizophrenia. Reflex hallucinations may occur in one sensory sphere as the result of irritation in another; for example, a toothache may stimulate an auditory hallucination. Kinesthetic hallucinations may occur in amputees, as part of the phantom-limb experience.

Circumstances that have elicited the hallucinations. A careful history and physical and laboratory examinations identify some organic hallucinatory states otherwise indistinguishable from schizophrenia. Toxic delirium is apt to occur at night. Acute hallucinatory states may be precipitated in certain schizoid persons by the enforced physical intimacy of army barracks life.

Insight. Insight is most likely to be present in the early stages of any psychosis and during the period of recovery. In either case, its presence tends to be associated with a good prognosis, and patients showing insight are usually cooperative for treatment.

Emotional and ideational content of the hallucinations. The acute reactions of withdrawal from drugs and the toxic deliriums are typically associated with great terror. Reactions of flight are common, and the patient, if unattended, may leap out of a hospital window.

During psychotic states of ecstasy and elation, hallucinatory experiences may involve sexual excitement and feelings of being infused with impregnating rays. In paranoid states, voices may be threatening. Rays may "cause" diseases, poisonings, or strange feelings. Voices may order the patient to commit acts of violence to save himself or the world from unspeakable sin. In depressive states, voices may be derisive and humiliating. They may accuse the patient of sexual perversion and order him to commit some expiatory act of self-mutilation or self-destruction.

As in dreams, memory traces constitute the building blocks of hallucinations. Indeed, it has been theorized that hallucinations may be the result of abnormalities in the memory retrieval system. The past history of each patient provides the clue for understanding hallucinatory content. The content reflects the effort to master anxiety and to fulfill various wishes and needs. Whereas patients with organic brain disease tend to express simple ideas related to the wish to be well and to be home, patients with functional psychoses express more complex ideas based on interactions with imagined partners and concern themselves primarily with sexual and aggressive drives that the patient has been unable to master in real life.

Disturbances in Affect

Affect is the feeling tone, pleasurable or unpleasurable, that accompanies an idea. Affect and emotion are used interchangeably and include such feelings as rage, grief, and joy. Affect determines the general attitude, whether of rejection, acceptance, flight, fight, or indifference. Thus, the affects provide the motivational drive or psychodynamic component in relation to every life situation and play a determining role in the thoughts and actions of a person in health and disease. When an affective state is sustained for a considerable period, one speaks of a mood. Affect may be described as shallow or inadequate (emotional flatness), inappropriate (when the emotion does not correspond to the stimulus), or labile (changeable).

Attitude refers to the affective state with which a person habitually confronts his environment. Attitude is determined in early childhood by what Erikson (1963) called basic trust.

In the normal developmental sequence, a person acquires a capacity to relate to parents and to later parent figures in school and at work with a positive attitude of love and basic trust. In settings of family disorganization and in the absence of dependable sources of love and safety, the person grows up with an attitude of basic distrust, in which case he tends to be rigidly hostile, suspicious, cynical, and pessimistic toward everyone, even when others attempt to relate to him in a positive way, as in a classroom. Thus, preschool experiences within the family may weigh more heavily in the long run in the future educational record of the child than does the quality of the schooling itself.

Disposition refers to the affective state with which a person habitually confronts himself. Whenever what Erikson (1963) called basic security has evolved, there is also a clear sense of personal identity. Associated with that sense is a sustaining sense of well-being and optimism. Basic security is part of self-esteem or normal narcissism.

Conscious human behavior is the result, primarily, of certain felt needs and can be divided simply into two main categories, those associated with pleasure, which result in movements toward a goal, and those associated with pain, which result in movements away.

Pleasurable activity begins with a series of goal-directed orienting or appetitive acts, which are associated with anticipatory pleasure, and culminates in a final act in which there is a surge of consummatory pleasure, which is followed by satiety.

The tie to the person who promises consummatory fulfillment is, essentially, the bond of love. That bond is associated with attachment behavior—clinging, smiling, following, searching, calling—and maintenance behavior, which consists of acts of tenderness and consideration. Freud referred to maintenance behavior, expressed as tenderness, as aim-inhibited love, which can exist between parent and child, between friends, and in a variety of other nonsexual situations.

Attachment and maintenance call for behavior that is appetitive and consummatory to the loved partner, a fact that defines the essential bond of love—namely, that it is mutually appetitive and consummatory.

Lack of mutuality occurs in pseudolove relationships in which one person exploits the partner in a neurotic bond. For example, a phobic patient may enter into a sexual relationship or even marriage in a neurotic search for a phobic companion.

A marital partner may represent a parent surrogate in various ways. In those instances there is not a mature love bond characterized by mutuality and complementarity but a transference attachment. The unrealistic and essentially unfulfillable expectations of the transference attachment generate much of the disturbed or neurotic interaction in an unhappy marriage. The successful treatment of that type of marital conflict depends on the resolution of transference expectations, on fostering emotional growth, and on the development of reality-based attachments.

Patients suffering from borderline or overtly schizophrenic disorders often develop an overly intense attachment to the therapist, with unfulfillable expectations that result in frustration, depression, rage, and much ambivalence. Successful therapy depends on the patient's ability to accept the therapist as an entity separate from the patient, with needs and rights of his own.

Before a person can establish an authentic loving bond with anyone else, he must possess a sufficiency of self-love—self-esteem or normal narcissism. Throughout life, whatever threatens self-esteem threatens his ability to relate to others.

Hence, he defends his self-esteem as fiercely as he defends his life. The small child loses self-esteem when he loses love and attains self-esteem when he regains love. That is what makes children educable. They need supplies of affection so badly that they are ready to renounce all other satisfactions if rewards of affection are promised or if withdrawal of affection is threatened. That model characterizes all relationships throughout life, including those that are artificially induced in the course of behavior modification therapy and those that are excessively present in adult attachments to a cultist leader.

With maturation, the person develops an increasing range of substitutive outlets and sources of self-esteem. As a result, he increases his capacity to tolerate frustrations and to postpone immediate gratification. With that increased capacity there is a tendency for mood stabilization.

Normal recreation may be cited as an example of a substitutive outlet. Recreation is characterized by a quality of irresponsibility, spontaneity, enthusiasm, hilarity, euphoria, elation, and other relatively uncontrolled expressions of positive emotion. During play, the emotionally mature adult is permitted to become a child again. Not only is that regression socially approved, but the capacity to act childishly in a controlled setting is a distinct asset. In play, it is possible to vent aggressive feelings against one's opponent. Mounting excitation culminating in a victorious climax may represent sublimation of sexual drives. Repetitive motor discharge through the playing of games is a device for successfully achieving motor mastery in childhood and for recalling and reliving the joy of that success as an adult. Although there are regressive elements in normal play, they are always within limits strictly set by the rules of the game. The capacity to regress while maintaining disciplined contact with reality is not only part of recreation but part of the esthetic experience in general and was referred to by Kris (1952) as regression in the service of the ego.

Euphoria refers to the first, moderate level in the scale of pleasurable affects. It has been defined as a positive feeling of emotional and physical well-being. When it occurs in a manifestly inappropriate setting, it is indicative of mental disorder. Although it is usually psychogenic, it may be observed in organic brain disease.

Elation may be thought of as a second level in the scale of pleasurable affects. It is characterized by a definite affect of gladness in which there is an air of enjoyment and self-confidence, and motor activity is increased. That affect belongs within the limits of normal life experience, yet it may be indicative of mental disorders when it occurs in a manifestly inappropriate setting.

Various pharmacological agents may induce euphoria or elation. Alcohol, narcotics, and the amphetamines may be cited as examples. Underlying most cases of addiction is an anxious-depressive state that drives the patient to use agents that relieve the painful affective state. Those substances enable the person to repress or deny the existence of painful affects. Brain lesions may have a similar impact on painful affects.

Exaltation may be defined as extreme elation; it is usually associated with delusions of grandeur. It merges into ecstasy, which represents a peak state of rapture. Those affects in inappropriate circumstances are found almost exclusively in relation to psychosis, as in schizophrenia. They are also encountered in religious emotional transports, which may occur in certain persons as private mystical experiences, or they may be mass induced in revivalist ceremonies.

It was once thought that lesions of the frontal lobe specifically elicited a mood of euphoria. It is now known that any brain impairment—anywhere and from any cause—that lowers the level of consciousness can have that effect. A small lesion involving the floor of the third ventricle may have a greater mood-elevating effect than does a much larger lesion occurring elsewhere. Affability encountered in patients with senile dementia is an example of mood elevation associated with diffuse organic brain disease.

Research has identified normally occurring brain substances—enkephalins and β-endorphins—that mimic the effects of opiates and that may have the effect of relieving physical and mental pain during traumatic emergencies and that may also contribute to states of mental well-being. It has also been hypothesized that opiate dependency states result from a deficiency in the supply of normally available endorphins.

So far, the role of drugs and toxic and organic factors as affect-elevating agents has been emphasized. Some patients are able to eliminate painful affects from consciousness without the aid of chemical consciousness-impairing agents. By using the psychological defense mechanism of denial or selective inattention, they avoid confrontations with traumatic percepts, and, by means of repression, they avoid confrontations with painful memories. If those mechanisms are sufficiently successful, a psychotic state supervenes. The manic patient does not feel deprived; he feels elated. In place of pessimism and despair, he has feelings of unwarranted optimism and self-confidence, and he is physically overactive and high spirited. He feels that he has unlimited resources and, as a result, squanders money with reckless abandon. That pattern is called the manic reaction or mania. When less intense, the behavior is described as a hypomanic reaction.

Often, the manic reaction thinly disguises an underlying depression, by which it may be abruptly replaced. Manic reactions tend to be relatively short lived and are typically followed by depression. In some instances, a hypomanic reaction may be indefinitely prolonged and may be regarded as a hypomanic character disorder.

Manic psychosis occurs in self-limited episodes. Individual attacks may be separated by months or years. If recurring episodes are exclusively of the manic type, it is called a manic psychosis of the unipolar type. If the manic episodes alternate with episodes of depression, it is the more typical manic-depressive psychosis of the bipolar type. In DSM-III, manic attacks are classified among the affective disorders as manic disorder, single episode, and manic disorder, recurrent.

DEPRESSION

Depression is one of the most common illnesses to which humans are subject. Paradoxically, it is probably the most frequently overlooked symptom, and, even when recognized, it is probably the single most incorrectly treated symptom in clinical practice. Not only are the signs and symptoms of depression multiple and complex at any given stage of the disorder, but there are many stages and different problems in different age groups. Its symptoms at onset, for example, differ considerably from those that develop later on and from those that appear penultimately in the depressed patient who commits suicide. There is also the age factor. The manifestations in the teenager differ considerably from those seen in late life.

From a purely descriptive point of view, the phenomena associated with depression are often indistinguishable from those seen in bereavement—that is, in the normal reaction of grief and mourning.

In bereavement, the intensity of the grief is a function of the intensity of the attachment. Somatic complaints are common, and there is evidence of considerable anxiety. There may be loud crying. Thoughts are preoccupied with the loss. A child in a hospital, for example, looks eagerly for any sight or sound that may prove to be the missing mother. People and objects that are reminders of the loss are treasured. An attitude of active searching results in dreams, misidentifications, illnesses, and even hallucinations. Conversely, there is a disappearance of interest in anything not connected with the loss. There may be a suicidal drive to heal the loss by joining the loved one in death.

There is a tendency to a compulsive review of events leading up to the loss—that is, a process of painful, repetitious recall. That is part of a need to make sense of the loss. It is also a kind of immunizing process to master the trauma of the loss and is part of what Freud called the work of mourning.

Mitigating behavior also occurs in bereavement. There is irritability and quarreling that may alienate bewildered friends at a time when their presence is much needed. To a smaller degree there is anger at the one who died.

Guilt is also present. There are obsessional questions: What could I have done to prevent it? Why did this happen to me? The presence of guilt in the bereavement process was particularly striking in survivors who lost relatives in concentration camps during World War II (survivor guilt, concentration camp syndrome).

A love object is an important source of self-esteem, and so with bereavement commonly goes a feeling of lost self-esteem.

The bereaved person may cope with the loss at first by trying to become the lost person—that is, by adopting specific symptoms, interests, and mannerisms (introjection). In time, however, it is necessary to move on from introjection to the establishment of a new identity and a new contact with the world that may necessitate, for example, courtship and marriage.

The bereavement process has been likened to a physical injury that has to heal. Complications may delay healing. Further injuries may open the wound, and healing may occur with disfigurment. The injury may be fatal. Or, as in the case of a broken bone, healing may result in even greater strength than before the injury.

In his study of bereavement, Parkes (1972) described the highest risk case as follows: a young widow with children, living at home without relatives, who is timid and clinging and intolerant of separation, with a history of previous depressive episodes, a history of intense but hostile dependency on her husband, an inability to express grief, and postbereavement stress, such as loss of income, loss of home, and difficulty with the children.

In the ordinary course of bereavement, the loss is followed by a characteristic psychological digestive process, the work of mourning, which ultimately does come to an end, and after a period of time the bereaved person resumes his regular activities. In certain cases, however, a chronic state of mental illness supervenes. If the patient has been rendered vulnerable by psychological traumas in early childhood, he tends to relate to the love object lost in adult life in symbolic terms, transferring unresolved infantile longings onto present-day objects and life experiences. He displays considerable ambivalence concerning the loss. It is precisely that mixture of hatred persisting in substantial quantity from early childhood, operating largely unconsciously, that gives rise to anger, guilt, and self-reproach, as well as to self-perpetuating psychological mechanisms that prevent the mourning process from coming to a normal conclusion. A chronic depression sets in, or one recurs periodically, often in relation to anniversaries, when the original mourning process is reawakened (pathological mourning, anniversary reaction).

Failure to complete the work of mourning means the failure to accept the reality and the finality of a loss. That nucleus of impaired reality testing can exert a negative ripple effect of impaired reality testing in other associated life areas. The working through of the problem in psychotherapy is necessarily associated with a revival of the mourning process, with overt symptoms of depression and anxiety.

In addition to depressogenic factors of psychological and social origin, biological inputs must not be overlooked. Certain medications can precipitate a severe depression in a previously functioning person. Reserpine and corticosteroids in high doses and phenothiazines are familiar examples. Retroperitoneal neoplasms, such as lymphoma and carcinoma of the pancreas, can precipitate depression. Depressive illness may set in after certain viral infections, such as hepatitis, infectious mononucleosis, and influenza. In addition, there is evidence for a biologically based hereditary factor in vulnerability to depression, particularly in the recurrent depressions of manic-depressive illness.

Premenstrually, many women are subject to mood swings. Depression and anger are common, as well as suicidal behavior and sociopathy. There may be a breakthrough of compulsive cleaning. The phenomenon undoubtedly has both psychological and endocrinological causative components.

Depression equivalents, masked depression, depressive practices, defenses against depression. Certain depressive symptoms are best understood as cries for help. When depressogenic factors first appear, the victim often displays a reaction of protest. A grade-school child, for instance, may show hyperkinetic behavior, fire setting, accident proneness, and enuresis. The adolescent may indulge in conspicuous displays of antisocial behavior that compel the adult world to pay attention. All too often, those cries for help are misinterpreted and dealt with punitively, with resultant intensification of the depressogenic mechanism. An older person often seeks out his physician with physical complaints because he does not known how else to express his cry for help.

Deviations in sexual behavior may occur episodically and acutely in response to situations that impair self-esteem. For example, homosexual cruising, the compulsive search for a promiscuous partner, may occur in a bisexual man after a marital quarrel. Perverse exhibitionistic behavior may occur when the birth of a new child gives rise, in the father, to feelings of being rejected. One patient had transvestite episodes as an anniversary mourning reaction to the childhood loss of his mother. By dressing like her, he could make believe that she was still alive.

The somatic complaints commonly seen in depression are of several varieties. They may have symbolic connections with a loved one from whom separation is dreaded or has already occurred. In those instances one is dealing primarily with conversion hysteria. In other instances the patient may complain of an existing relatively mild physical disorder, such as an inguinal hernia, in the hope that hospitalization will provide an escape from an unbearable conflict or compel attention that is not otherwise obtainable. Access to medical echelons of help may be achieved through injuries "accidentally" incurred at work.

The patient may develop a reaction of detachment associated with feelings of depersonalization, derealization, and long-lasting personality impairments. The entire spectrum of addictive states can be understood as attempts to ward off depression. Those states include overeating, alcoholism, the various drug dependency states, addiction to television, people addiction (including "telephonitis"), delinquent gang formation, and logorrhea. The patient may seek to overcome feelings of emptiness by various forms of acting out—reckless driving, antisocial behavior, compulsive gambling, and sexual disturbances, including nymphomania, Don Juanism, recurrent out-of-wedlock pregnancy, and perverse sexual acting out. The addictive state may express itself as a compulsive preoccupation with work or as religious or political activism. The patient may inflict on himself a variety of minor injuries in which self-stimulation is the primary goal, such as wrist slitting, hair pulling (trichotillomania), and scratching. The patient may retreat into patterns of excessive sleep.

While those defenses against depression continue to operate, the person may seem to be cheerful, on occasion even functioning competently and successfully. Yet closer inspection reveals a joylessness in those activities. The patient lives rigidly and compulsively. His life has a quality of desperation based on the threat of depressogenic breakthrough.

Clinically overt depression. When the breakthrough occurs—as it inevitably must—what emerges are the commonly recognized symptoms of depression. The very appearance of the victim changes: He looks old and sad. His face is lined. His posture is stooped and bent. Indeed, the gait and facial expression may bear a superficial resemblance to the signs of parkinsonism. In so-called simple depression, psychological and motor spontaneity are lost. The patient tends to be slowed-up and mute. His voice is low; his replies to questions are brief and monosyllabic. All previous interests are lost. There is anorexia, with weight loss. There is loss of sexual desire and a loss of interest in recreation, work, family, and friends. The patient complains of an indescribable misery that he sometimes locates in his chest or abdomen. He is filled with self-reproach and is convinced that he is a failure, that his money is gone, that he is old, and that he has become stupid. He expresses feelings of pessimism, poverty, hopelessness, and futility. He is filled with guilt and shame. He expects punishment. He has suicidal thoughts and impulses. In addition, he displays characteristic somatic concomitants: dryness of the mouth with *fetor oris*, sighing respiration, and constipation. In place of a prior tendency to hypersomnia, insomnia sets in and is most commonly associated with frequent waking spells during the night and early-morning agitation, with sweating and feelings of anguish. As interest in the outer world is withdrawn, there comes an intensified awareness of the body, with hypochondriasis and somatic delusions. Many patients describe a deeply felt need to weep but complain of an inability to do so and say, "I believe I'd feel better if I could only cry." On the other hand, there may be periods of uncontrollable sobbing. In contrast to the foregoing picture of the psychological and motor-slowing characteristic of simple depression, some patients display a state of agitated depression characterized by much pacing, wringing of the hands, weeping, and loud vocalizations of despair.

Some patients show schizophrenic symptoms mixed with depression. Too often, the schizophrenia is recognized, and the depressive component is ignored, to the detriment of the patient. Patients with mixed symptoms often have a history of episodic illness, with intervals of relatively normal functioning, and are classified as having a schizoaffective disorder.

The diagnostic issues are more complicated when one turns to the diverse manifestations of the struggle to ward off depression. Many of those manifestations are given diagnostic labels of their own, such as sexual deviations, alcoholism, drug dependency, psychophysiological disorders, antisocial personality disorder, and obsessive-compulsive personality disorder. Although those rubrics are essential in the diagnostic description of the patient, one must not lose sight of the essential role of those conditions in the patient's struggle against depression. Proper therapy for those conditions depends on the treatment of the underlying depression.

Anaclitic depression refers to the syndrome shown by infants during the first years of life if they are deprived of the attentions of a suitable mothering figure. Anaclitic means "leaning on" and is a psychoanalytic term denoting an infant's dependency on his mother for his sense of well-being. On separation from the mother, the infant goes through a characteristic sequence of changes. There is an initial phase of protest, characterized by intense crying and struggling. If the state of deprivation continues, the infant lapses into the phase of despair. At that point, his behavior suggests hopelessness. Struggling decreases,

and his crying is monotonous and softer than before. In children's hospitals that quieter state is commonly misinterpreted as a state of diminished distress. Actually, it is a state of mourning. Some of those infants fail to thrive. They may stop eating and then waste away and die, a state called marasmus. Most survive but lapse into a phase of detachment in which the infant withdraws from human relationships and becomes preoccupied with inanimate objects or his own body parts, engaging in masturbation, fecal smearing, head banging, or rocking.

It is often said that depression is the most common psychiatric disorder of old age. One can go further and say that a tendency to depression is the universal fate of humans if they live long enough. Depression is the clinical syndrome that reflects a patient's response to loss and his attempts to cope with loss. In the aged, the loss of love objects presents a universal psychological problem. The loss of an accustomed work role presents a number of social problems. And the loss of general physical health and brain power represents a major loss on a biological level.

Most important about the depressive reactions of late life is the fact that it takes brain power to become depressed. The extensively damaged brain provides a setting that somehow facilitates wishful thinking and regression. Such a brain-injured patient may become silly, elated, apathetic, or paranoid as part of the previously alluded-to delusional system called denial of illness. As the patient's brain damage subsides, however, his capacity for denial also subsides. As the grim reality of his life situation becomes inescapable, the previously cheerful patient becomes depressed. Thus, the emergence of a severe depression is a paradoxical sign that signals clinical improvement. By the same token, depression that is the most common psychiatric symptom in old age is also the most hopeful sign. Depression is never caused by brain damage except in a reactive psychological sense. It is a feeling that can be generated only if a substantial part of the brain is still intact. It is a realistic cry for help and an attempt to reestablish a remembered state of previous intact functioning. For that reason, late-life depressions deserve the most serious and even heroic therapeutic efforts, regardless of the age or general physical condition of the patient.

Geriatric patients often show a mixture of organic brain defect, usually aphasia and apraxia, combined with depression. The effect of the depression may be to intensify the manifestations of organicity. The combined picture is the pseudodementia often seen in late-life depression. Unwarranted pessimism may lead to therapeutic nihilism, whereas adequate antidepression treatment may result in striking improvement in the depression and, indeed, in some reversal of the organic deficits. Heart-damaged geriatric patients tolerate electroconvulsive therapy better than they do the antidepression medications.

The appearance of depressive symptoms may also signal the onset of recovery from an acute schizophrenic episode, as if the delusional state represented a respite from life's problems; as a consequence, recovery is associated with a sense of loss. Some schizoaffective patients retreat into manic grandiose psychotic states as a lifesaving escape from an intolerably depressing situation. Such patients are understandably reluctant to keep taking the major tranquilizers that, in effect, deprive them of that escape route and have been known to commit suicide when injected with long-acting depot tranquilizers.

Depression can appear pradoxically as the aftermath of some great success in those who are destroyed by success. Many instances may be cited in current literary history in which the production of a successful novel or play was followed by severe depression and suicide. The depression appears when success is unconsciously symbolized as a destruction and displacement of the father. To avoid that kind of depression, patients are characteristically self-defeating, or they may assume an imposter role that makes it possible to deny the actuality of one's achievements.

A change in the mood not only changes one's whole life outlook but may change the content of delusions and alter the entire symptom complex. A schizophrenic who believed he was saving the world when he was in an exalted mood felt he was responsible for the end of the world when he became depressed. A male patient who would derive sexual excitement from fantasies of being whipped on the buttocks during depressed moods would excite himself sexually with fantasies of receiving an enema from a loving mother in more elated moods. A superstitious patient, who saw all kinds of evil omens in a depressed mood, felt himself surrounded by lucky signs and omens when elated.

Suicide is an important consideration in the problems of depression. It is the primary issue in deciding whether to treat a given patient as an outpatient or in an inpatient setting. The physician must ask the depressed patient if he has suicidal thoughts or impulses. Some physicians hesitate to do so for fear that they will plant the thought in the patient's mind de novo; the contrary is true. Patients appreciate the inquiry as an expression of concern, particularly if the examining physician explains that the prognosis in depression is good and that he does not want harm to befall the patient before improvement can be effected.

It often happens that a patient who threatens suicide while he is an outpatient is more comfortable in an inpatient setting. He then presses for discharge and evinces no interest in further psychiatric care. One may draw a superficial impression of clinical improvement and sanction discharge to an unchanged and essentially intolerable life situation. The result is an unusually high suicide rate in that patient group. Active clinical contact should be maintained for at least 6 months, the period of maximum suicidal danger.

One often hears the cliché, "The period of improvement from depression is the time of the greatest suicidal danger." There is a small grain of truth in the sense that some depressed patients are so immobilized by lack of energy and drive that those depressive symptoms do exert some lifesaving function. However, more often the improvement referred to is pseudoimprovement, which occurs in the sheltered hospital setting, and death is the result of inadequate posthospital treatment planning.

It is erroneous to regard clinical depression as the only or even the major cause of suicide. In a general hospital the delirious patient who is either postoperative or suffering from some toxic metabolic disorder presents the greatest suicidal risk of all, particularly at night. Schizophrenic patients may commit suicide or some act of self-mutilation in the delusional belief that they are saving others in so doing.

Hysterical patients who are prone to suicidal gestures may die accidentally. Patients with perverse sexual practices involving playing at tying themselves and hanging themselves (bonding) may die accidentally.

Suicidal patients sometimes plan well in advance of the act, setting their affairs in order and writing a suicidal note. On occasion, the note becomes a full-fledged novel. A work of art sometimes fulfills needs that may have the effect of averting the suicidal act.

ANXIETY

Anxiety may be defined as a disagreeable emotional state in which there are feelings of impending danger, characterized by uneasiness, tension, or apprehension. The cause is usually unconscious or unrecognized intrapsychic conflict. Anxiety is associated with a characteristic pattern of autonomic nervous system discharge involving altered respiration rate, increased heart rate, pallor, dryness of the mouth, increased sweating, and musculoskeletal disturbances, involving trembling and feelings of weakness. Every organ system in the body, including the orgasm mechanism, may participate in the expression of anxiety.

Anxiety is to be differentiated from fear, in which the foregoing combination of feelings and nervous discharges occurs as a reaction to a real, conscious, and external danger that is present or that threatens to materialize.

Panic is a state of extreme, acute, intense anxiety accompanied by disorganization of personality and function.

In infancy, anxiety is hypothesized to be a diffuse, objectless feeling of dread stemming from the discomforts of unsatisfied needs. As the infant comes to identify the people in the environment who satisfy his needs, anxiety appears as a response to separation from them. With biological development, he is able to make complex behavioral responses calculated to prevent separation or to take action to bring separation to an end. As part of the child's anxiety reaction, he develops physical maneuvers to protect his body, to fight off the attentions of unwelcome persons, or to take flight. Anxiety at that point involves not only a feeling of dread and the concept of danger but also a positive relationship to a specific person, usually his mother, capable of relieving the danger. As a consequence of that relationship, the anxiety reaction becomes mingled with a feeling of hope.

As the child develops, he learns to anticipate the danger of separation and to initiate maneuvers to avoid it before it starts. As that avoidance is accomplished with increasing success, the gross reaction of discomfort subsides, and in time anxiety is reduced to a mere signal of danger, which sets off appropriate responses so swiftly and silently that there may be no conscious awareness of danger in the entire process.

When confronted with an unprecedented danger or when the previous solutions are no longer available, the silent signal of danger again becomes a conscious clamor, and once again there are psychologically meaningful actions representing calls for help and preparations for fight or flight. If a solution is still not forthcoming, anxiety increases progressively. At one point, expressions of helplessness and hopelessness ensue, with panic and various pathological forms of withdrawal from the traumatic environment. When it reaches paralyzing levels, anxiety no longer functions as a signal of danger but becomes a source of danger in its own right and is then designated traumatic anxiety.

Traumatic anxiety in its extreme forms can provoke neurovegetative responses, involving both the flight-fight and the conservation-withdrawal systems, conducive to lethal cardiac events, particularly in persons with preexisting cardiovascular diseases.

As the infant develops strength and understanding, he becomes increasingly capable of accepting periods of separation from his mother and increasingly capable of accepting suitable substitutes for her during periods of enforced separation.

Realistic dangers continue throughout life. Such stressful situations still call forth the feeling of dread, the impulse to fight or to take flight, and all the associated physiological concomitants. Commonly, the stressor is readily identifiable—for example, an impending operation. At other times the source of anxiety is more difficult to identify. In the early stages of organic disease, a reaction of anxiety to the vaguely sensed organic impairment may be the earliest clinical symptom preceding the appearance of any other localizing somatic symptoms.

Whenever the psychological adaptational mechanisms threaten to decompensate, anxiety appears. It may appear in a chronic, low-grade form as a constant accompaniment to life. That occurs when a more or less compensated mental disorder exists. Sudden changes in one's life situation may evoke an increase of anxiety or precipitate an episode of panic as a warning that more disastrous emotional decompensation is in the offing. Thus, the presence of generalized anxiety or the occurrence of anxiety attacks is not indicative of any one clinical entity but is, rather, a psychophysiological signal of danger that can occur in any diagnostic category of physical or emotional disease.

Free-floating anxiety is the nucleus and key symptom of neurosis. It consists of a feeling of dread that the patient cannot logically assign to a specific cause. In the quest for causality, patients suffering from free-floating anxiety are always ready to attach it to some suitable ideational content.

Generalized anxiety disorder is a neurotic state based primarily on free-floating anxiety. It is characterized by irritability, anxious expectation, pangs of conscience, and episodes of panic. There is a hypersensitivity to ordinary sights and sounds, as a result of which startle reactions occur frequently and with minimal sensory provocation. Cardiac palpitation, breathlessness, giddiness, nausea, dryness of mouth, diarrhea, compulsive eating, urinary frequency, seminal emissions, blurring of vision, general physical weakness, and other physical manifestations may occur chronically as part of anxiety neurosis. In an effort to reduce the unpleasant feelings associated with anxiety, the person evolves a variety of defensive devices that in their entirety constitute many of the clinical manifestations of psychiatric disorder.

Conversion hysteria, for example, is a well-known pathological device for reducing or eliminating free-floating anxiety. It is a neurosis characterized by sensory and motor deficits without a corresponding structural organic lesion. The effect of a hysterical paraplegia, for example, may be to prevent access to a situation feared by the patient because of unconsciously desired and rejected erotic or aggressive impulses. Often, the physical symptom is so effective in alleviating the anxiety that the patient displays an attitude of calm (*la belle indifférence*) that contrasts strangely with the extent of the physical disability. Because overt anxiety is not necessarily a clinical manifestation of conversion, the condition is classified in DSM-III with the somatoform disorders.

Social phobia and simple phobia occur when the patient develops fears or phobias in relation to specific situations that may stimulate erotic or aggressive impulses unconsciously desired and rejected by the patient. A similar anxiety-relieving role can be made out for many of the symptoms of obsessive-compulsive neurosis and schizophrenia.

In all instances the clinical picture is best understood in adaptation terms in which a "dangerous" impulse is permitted some modicum of indirect or disguised discharge, and the need for restraint and punishment is also permitted some degree of disguised gratification. Those conflicting strivings are synthesized and harmonized in a way to reduce the amount of suffering caused by anxiety, and together they form the clinical symptom or neurosis.

A young woman was brought into the emergency room of a general hospital by her sister and brother-in-law with an adductor spasm of both legs and an inability to walk. The motor abnormality was without accompanying organic disease. The emergency room physician gave her a small quantity of amobarbital sodium (Amytal) intravenously, with the strong suggestion that her leg muscles would relax and return to normal when he finished counting to 10. At the appropriate signal, the patient relaxed, got off the table, and walked out of the emergency room, apparently elated. Four hours later, she was returned to the emergency room in a catatonic stupor, for which she had to be hospitalized. At that point, information was elicited for the first time that the patient had recently moved into her sister's household and had suffered from guilt and anxiety as a result of illicit sexual play with her brother-in-law. Thus, removal of the hysterical defense (adductor spasm) caused her to regress to a psychotic defense (catatonia).

In classifying the anxiety disorders, DSM-III emphasizes in particular those cases in which panic attacks occur in an essentially unpredictable way with respect to time, place, or social circumstances. That is particularly characteristic of agoraphobia with panic attacks. It is also true of panic disorder. Most phobic states with panic are mixtures—that is, they are associated with panic in specific phobia-generating situations, as well as with the seemingly nonspecific episodes of panic. From the point of view of clinical management, differential diagnosis is important, since the nonspecific panic reactions respond rather specifically to the tricyclic and monoamine oxidase inhibitor antidepressants.

AGGRESSION

Aggression is defined as a constellation of specific thoughts, feelings, and actions that are mobilized by an obstruction to a wish or need and whose goal is to remove the obstruction in order to permit drive discharge.

Not all the specific thoughts, feelings, and actions characteristic of aggression are manifest. For example, one may feel rage and have no conscious thoughts that rationally explain it. One may kill in cold blood without feelings of anger. One may consciously harbor angry thoughts and feelings and commit no overt act. Or one may repress the entire process so completely that its only overt expression is a psychosomatic disorder whose psychological component can be made manifest only through psychoanalytic uncovering.

Aggression is inseparable from the complex of wishes and needs that together make up the life drive or the wish to live. Indeed, the greater the amount of love energy impelling a specific wish or need, the greater is the amount of aggressive energy mobilized to remove the obstacles in its path.

Infants brought up in a setting of sensory and emotional deprivation develop a hunger for inputs. In the absence of a suitable mothering person, the developing infant evolves his own inputs. His intensified search leads to a precocious discovery of his genitalia and masturbation or to a precocious discovery of his feces and fecal play. With developing motor skills, the affect-deprived infant may add scratching, body rocking, head banging, and hair pulling to his repertoire of autonomously available sensory inputs. The aggressive drive makes it possible for the infant literally to tear from his own bodily substance objects with which to interact pleasurably and which he desperately needs for normal growth and development.

The role of aggression in masked depression or in the defense against depression has already been alluded to in hyperkinetic behavior, fire setting, accident proneness, and general destructiveness manifest at a grade-school level, as well as in reckless driving, sociopathy, wrist slitting, and hair pulling in the adolescent struggle with depression.

For the developing infant, the key issue of his life becomes one of maintaining contact with his mother. As desperately as he needs her, so desperately does he hate all who obstruct his path to her, hence sibling rivalry and the Oedipus complex. Intrafamilial aggression must be channeled in such a way as to prevent dissolution of the family. A parentally inculcated sense of right and wrong is what is referred to psychoanalytically as superego formation. One family may proscribe all external expressions of aggression; another may permit scapegoating of a single family member, which may give rise to child battering; and another may sanction only extrafamilial expressions of aggression.

The quantity of aggression that wells up from within the developing person is an escapable part of his drive to survive and to fulfill himself and is probably rooted in biological factors. However, the target of his aggression and the specific way he expresses his aggression—whether by words or by deeds, whether with unrestrained violence or with self-discipline—these are learned patterns determined first by family structure and later by a variety of parent substitutes in extrafamilial educational and social experiences.

Just as the family can survive only by channeling intrafamilial aggression, so can animal species in general and human society in particular survive only by techniques for channeling aggression. When two adult animals of the same species who are strangers to each other are brought together for the first time, one invariably attempts to dominate the other. In the ordinary course of events, dominance is achieved, whether by bluff or by battle, in a few minutes. In that process the surrender ritual is the key issue, the primary function of which is to prevent killing in the process of establishing dominance. The surrender ritual is a formal pattern of behavior, the display of which by the losing animal has the effect of inhibiting further attack by the winner. Thus, in those fights for dominance, killing of the lower ranks is not at all the goal.

It is often claimed that man is unique among beasts in his supposed lack of a surrender ritual. The fact is that man has surrender rituals and, in general, in unarmed fighting he respects them in his opponent. However, in man's brain resides a potentially fatal flaw. Man the tool maker has devised weapons, tools for killing. The more lethal the weapon, the more readily available, the easier to use, the swifter and more deadly the effect, the more does that tool rob fighting man of the opportunity to express surrender rituals himself or to respond to those of a weaker opponent. Thus, killing tools have disconnected man from the delicately evolved surrender mechanism by which species are protected from self-destruction. But man knows of that disconnection and is constantly devising rules of conduct in an attempt to overcome that recently acquired behavioral defect.

Another even more deadly flaw issues from man's brain. Man the symbol maker has devised ideologies that relegate vast categories of fellow humans to subhuman status (dehumanization). By simply declaring, on any basis, that a given human category really consists of vermin, a person can clean out a pocket of resistance in a "virtuous" act that wins parental or parent surrogate approval. It is the dehumanization process most of all that neutralizes the surrender ritual reflexes and that most endangers mankind.

In pathological mother-child relationships, a spectrum of rage reactions may be discerned, with postpartum depression and suicide at one end of the scale and child battering and infanticide at the other. Schizophrenic mothers may have infanticidal impulses (Medea syndrome) because the newborn child symbolizes a hated sibling or other family member. Those same women may be capable of normal mothering behavior in relation to someone else's child.

Child battering. A battered child is any child who receives nonaccidental injuries as a result of acts or omissions on the part of the parents.

It is estimated that only 10 per cent of child batterers are overtly psychotic. One parent is usually the active batterer, and the other parent is an accomplice through passivity and silence. Battering parents commonly give a history of exposure to parental violence in their own childhoods. They are usually emotionally immature and tend to reverse the parent-child role in the sense that they have unrealistic needs for emotional gratification from the child. One child, in particular, tends to be selected for battering. In some instances the scapegoated child is battered not only by the parents but also by his siblings. Battering tends to occur episodically. Many times a mother who fears loss of self-control presents herself with a minimally injured child in the hospital emergency service. Admitting that child for a day or two may prevent more serious injury to him. Battering parents need the opportunity for separation from the child during periods of emotional crisis.

They also need supportive psychotherapy to give them the love they never had in their own childhoods, as well as instruction in the normal techniques of mothering. Kempe and Helfer (1972), who pioneered in this field, promulgated an attitude of compassion toward battering parents. Professionals involved in the management of a battered child should know the local laws determining which children must be reported, by whom, and to what agencies. They must also know the resources for emergency remanding of an endangered child for safety. The forms of child abuse are varied and, at times, strain credulity. There are whiplash injuries producing intramuscular and intracranial hemorrhage, scalding in hot water, burning in a direct flame, sexual abuse, administration of poisonous substances to a child who is then presented at the hospital as a medical or surgical emergency. Children with a history of previous battering are particularly prone to suicide and self-mutilating behavior.

Kempe and Helfer (1972) suggested a series of warning signs in relation to families with a potential for child abuse. During the prenatal period, there may be an overconcern about the sex of the child or a total denial of the pregnancy itself in terms of making plans for the future. There may be a prevailing mood of hopelessness concerning the responsibilities associated with an additional child. In addition, the potential batterers tend to be socially isolated couples who often have unlisted telephones. During the postpartum period, the parents may be persistently disappointed in the sex of the child, display indecision in choosing a name for the child, and show impatience and hostility toward the baby, particularly in relation to his crankiness or feeding. An important warning sign consists of frequent "emergency" calls to the physician about minor matters. Kempe and Helfer (1972) urged that, if such calls occur more than twice in a single day, they should be interpreted as signals of an impending loss of parental self-control and the need for hospitalization of the child.

Wife abuse. It has been estimated that 90 per cent of familial homicides are preceded by at least one major domestic disturbance. That statistic makes it imperative to be alert to the phenomenon of wife abuse and render appropriate counseling when indicated. Many battered wives give a history of taking antidepressants or tranquilizers. The phenomenon seems to be distributed equally among all socioeconomic strata. The physician should invoke community resources and legislation in efforts to help those victims of violence.

Parent battering. Culturally, this society seems to be in a transitional stage during which traditional family hierarchies are breaking down and the readiness by children to accept parental authority has been eroded. As a result, episodes of parent batterings and other manifestations of community violence require study and a therapeutic response from a psychosocial point of view.

Family quarrels and social situations that threaten self-esteem commonly precipitate acts of violence. For some persons the statement, "I am wrong; I apologize," is associated with an unendurable blow to self-esteem. Such persons cannot apologize, even on pain of death. Murders have occurred in family quarrels in just such circumstances.

Other expressions of aggression. Episodes of violence may occur as manifestations of a seizure disorder. To make the diagnosis, one has to demonstrate temporally related electroencephalographic abnormalities.

Schizophrenics may become violent when confronted with unwanted intimacies from which they feel that they cannot escape. Violence may erupt when a naïve therapist does not understand or respect the schizophrenic patient's need to maintain a safe interpersonal distance—that is, a need to avoid intimacy.

Violence associated with criminal acts of breaking and entering may be connected with perverse sexual impulses. Sadistic and masochistic fantasies may inadvertently lead to violence, as in the accidental suicides of patients with bonding fantasies.

Irritability is a chronic diffuse state of anger that occurs as an interpersonal distance-regulating device. It may occur in paranoid personality disorder. It is commonly encountered in adolescents who are warding off sexually charged encounters with parents or siblings.

Vandalism is an act of indiscriminate violence that has many qualities in common with a child's temper tantrum. It represents a displacement from the true target of the rage and is associated with a personal feeling of impotent fury. It may occur in privacy as the act of one person. More often, it occurs semipublicly in socioeconomically deprived areas. It is directed at community property in general and is associated with a prevailing cultural attitude of approval of the behavior. It may also occur episodically in settings of mob violence and may be associated with looting and a general mood of festivity.

Ambivalence refers to the coexistence of antithetical emotions, attitudes, ideas, or wishes toward a given object or situation. Usually, only one attitude emerges into consciousness, the other remaining unconscious. Ambivalence is encountered in all instances of affective instability. Thus, it plays a role in the mood swings that occur within normal limits. However, it is fundamental in many pathological mental states. There is the familiar doing and undoing characteristic of obsessive-compulsive neurosis and the pathologically prolonged mourning that takes place when there is ambivalence toward the lost object. However, the most dramatic aspects of ambivalence are seen in schizophrenia, and for Bleuler (1950) ambivalence was one of the primary symptoms of that disease.

Underlying the ambivalence of the schizophrenic is the need-fear dilemma and the unending search for a suitable human relationship. The schizophrenic's interpersonal needs are so highly specialized that a suitable person is not easily come by; if one is found, the schizophrenic clings with abnormal intensity. Such relationships are filled with ambivalence and instability. Any suggestion of intimacy immediately moves the patient to dread and the need to retreat. His usual distance-regulating mechanism is hostility, which causes the partner also to retreat. The partner's retreat terrifies the patient and leads to intensified clinging. That is the nightmare fate of the schizophrenic—to swing eternally between two poles, unendurable loneliness and an unendurable dread of intimacy. Almost all the symptoms of schizophrenia can be traced to that ambivalent dilemma.

Alcohol intoxication remains the most important contributor to many episodes of destructive dyscontrol. The amphetamines, cocaine, a variety of hallucinogens, the barbiturates, the tricyclic antidepressants, and the prolonged use of benzodiazepines have all been implicated in episodes of violent dyscontrol. With or without the involvement of substance abuse, suicide remains the third leading cause of death among 15- to 24-year-olds in the United States. Accidents and homicides account for even more deaths in that age group.

The act of rape is essentially an expression of rage and the wish to dominate the victim. In rape, male sexuality is always in the service of other nonsexual needs.

Extreme forms of self-mutilation are sometimes seen in adult schizophrenics who enucleate their eyeballs, castrate themselves, inflict burns, eviscerate surgical incisions, and stab themselves to death with frightful wounds. Smaller degrees of self-inflicted wounds—notably wrist slitting, as contrasted to wrist cutting with serious suicidal intent, and trichotillomania (compulsive hair pulling)—occur more often in women than in men. Severe self-inflicted injuries are seen in childhood schizophrenia and in the Lesch-Nyhan syndrome, an X-linked recessive defect in purine metabolism associated with severe mental retardation.

Children may display tantrum-like attacks of rage on reunion with their parents after enforced periods of physical separation. Adolescents may react with tantrum-like violence against inappropriately intimate physical approaches by parents, particularly in settings of marital disturbance.

Perhaps the most impressive clinical fact about violent behavior is its unpredictability. Many patients show a potential for violence on psychological testing and may even threaten it verbally over a period of years and yet do not erupt overtly as long as the patient's supportive social network remains intact. Sudden loss or rejection by a loved one or some other event that sharply reduces self-esteem may provoke violent behavior. Many patients who have been protected from violent outbursts in the sheltered inpatient setting of a mental hospital are often embroiled in antisocial acts involving violence and police action as a result of unsupervised deinstitutionalization.

COMPOUND EMOTIONS

In addition to the primary emotional states already described, there are many compound emotional states. The list of emotions in Table III is by no means exhaustive.

For example, smugness is compounded of self-satisfaction, self-absorption, and a reduced awareness of the environment. With it, there is also greediness and grasping, without associated guilt. There is a characteristic pleased look about the mouth of the smug person. A negative reaction to smugness, based on envy and rivalry, is present to some degree in everyone. Enviousness designates a behavior pattern that elicits envy in others. It occurs characteristically in people with strong narcissistic needs who provoke others into attitudes of grudging admiration in an unending quest for new inputs to bolster their fragile self-esteem. Bitterness is a feeling of resentment over what appears to be a justified grievance. It is associated with demands for redress. Confusion occurs when one cannot resolve the normally present ambivalence that creates a split attitude of love and hate, good and bad, toward most objects. Boredom is a state of dissatisfaction and disinclination to act. Time drags, as it does in depression, but the feeling in boredom is one of emptiness or apathy. Some instances of seemingly unmotivated violence in adolescents may represent an attempt to overcome boredom. Pathological jealousy has been compared to normal jealousy, as pathological mourning is compared to normal mourning. Pathological jealousy is compounded of grief, hatred, loss of self-esteem, and ambivalence. It may have its roots in unconscious homosexual attachments

TABLE III
Catalogue of the Emotions

Anger	Envy	Petulance
Anxiety	Faith	Poise
Arrogance	Fear	Querulence
Bitterness	Gloating	Rage
Boredom	Gratitude	Sadism
Cheating	Grief	Sarcasm
Confusion	Guilt	Shame
Curiosity	Gullibility	Shyness
Cynicism	Hate	Smugness
Depression	Homesickness	Teasing
Derision	Hope	Trust
Disillusionment	Jealousy	Uncanny feelings
Elation	Masochism	Vengefulness
Enthusiasm	Nostalgia	

and merge into paranoid delusional thinking. Vengefulness is a striving toward an object, as in love, but for the purpose of ensuring its destruction. It is associated with a desire to get even and is calculated to assuage guilt and to relieve feelings of fear and hatred. Curiosity is a feeling state that gives rise to exploratory behavior. It is a drive to generate and increase anticipatory pleasure. In a creative person it can prevail over hunger, fear, pain, or pleasure. It is a craving for increasing tension that is as urgent as the quest for tension relief or satiety that follows consummatory pleasure.

MECHANISMS FOR MAINTAINING MOOD CONTROL

Mood is a sustained and prevailing emotional set. Since emotional set determines the direction and the intensity of behavioral response, a large part of mental functioning is related specifically to mood control.

Psychogenic fainting or loss of consciousness in response to an emotionally traumatic event is a model for the mechanisms of defense in the sense that it is a way of breaking off contact with an excessively painful reality. Similarly, a child may cover his eyes or ears to exclude unpleasant impressions. The defense mechanisms that evolve with emotional maturation provide a repertoire of techniques for controlling the emotional impact of events. Those techniques include repression, denial, projection, sublimation, intellectualization, rationalization, regression, suppression, reaction formation, undoing, introjection, identification, isolation, displacement, depersonalization, and derealization.

Depersonalization is a mental phenomenon characterized by a feeling of unreality and strangeness about one's self. The patient says, in effect, "This experience does not hurt me because I am not me." The term "depersonalization" includes feelings of unreality, estrangement, amnesia, multiple personality states, and distortions in the body image. Depersonalization may be partial or complete, transient or long lasting. It may be encountered in hysteria or as part of the aura of epilepsy, but in schizophrenic states it tends to be more complete and lasting than in other disorders.

Derealization is a mental phenomenon characterized by the loss of the sense of reality concerning one's surroundings. The patient says, in effect, "This environment is not dangerous to me because this environment does not really exist." Derealization includes distortions of spatial and temporal relationships so that an essentially neutral environment seems strangely familiar (*déjà vu*) or strangely unfamiliar (*jamais vu*) or otherwise strange and distorted. Like depersonalization, to which it is closely related, derealization can be partial or complete, transient or long lasting. Similarly, it may occur in hysteria or as part of the aura of epilepsy, but derealization, too, tends to be most complete and persistent in schizophrenic states.

Although depersonalization and derealization occur as adaptational mechanisms to reduce unpleasant affects, they may in their own right create a feeling of impending catastrophe. Depersonalization and derealization are sometimes seen in atypical depressive reactions. A tendency to misconstrue them as schizophrenic phenomena may lead to the inappropriate use of major tranquilizers, with intensification of the symptoms. An antidepressant, on the other hand, may provide symptomatic relief.

A feeling that could be shattering if experienced in a single episode becomes tolerable if digested piecemeal over an extended time.

The traumatic neuroses of wartime may be cited as an example. An experience capable of generating overwhelming terror may be dealt with at the moment of occurrence by depersonalization and dereali-

zation. When the catastrophe is over and the person is no longer in danger, delayed reactions of anxiety may appear. Sleep may be disturbed by recurrent battle dreams. There may be an intolerance for sudden loud noises and for displays of aggression. After memories of the traumatic incident have been revisited repeatedly and the anxiety slowly mastered in small doses, the traumatic neurosis subsides, a mechanism that has been compared to the process of immunization or allergic desensitization.

The concept of an interpersonal distance-regulating mechanism seems closer to the clinical facts than is the more static concept of defense.

A father was teaching his young daughter to ride a bicycle. They had reached a stage in their lesson in which all she needed, literally, to maintain her balance was her father's finger, lightly touching the seat. She did not need or, indeed, want more support, and yet any less was unmanageable.

After childbirth there is a mother-child symbiosis in which independent existence for the child is impossible. Subsequent development occurs in a series of steps that make it possible for the child to tolerate increasing separations from the mother until he is capable of functioning with true autonomy. Mahler (1968) called that the separation-individuation process. Failure to complete the process results in a broad range of psychopathological states in which true separation from the mother or various mother substitutes cannot be tolerated.

Conversely, the need to maintain distance can be the dominant theme. Among prisoners, for example, it has been found that inmates differ in the size of the body-buffer zone they need for peace of mind. Outbursts of seemingly irrational physical violence are often motivated by a need to drive away intruders from the body-buffer zone. The size of a person's body-buffer zone varies with the significance for that person of a given intruder.

So important is the body-buffer zone in normal life that it is protected by laws expressing the concept that every person has a right to his zone of privacy.

Just as certain inputs can be traumatic, a total absence of input can be traumatic. For certain depressed patients a major complaint is an absence of feelings. Old-fashioned physiotherapy techniques like massage and hydrotherapy may be reassuring in those instances. The patient says, in effect, "I feel; therefore, I am." Every person experiences a need for a certain level of background tension or feeling. If that level drops too low, he is moved to stimulate himself in order to maintain an optimal level. The repertoire of autostimulatory phenomena is probably limitless. From a psychoanalytic point of view, masturbation is the paradigm, and all other autostimulatory phenomena are regarded as displacements from that basic mechanism. Some familiar examples of autostimulatory phenomena are deliberate self-injury, addictions of all kinds, scratching, nail biting, cuticle picking, hair pulling (trichotillomania), skin slicing, smoking, eating, grimacing, leg shaking, tics, physical overactivity, compulsive sexual behavior of all kinds (including promiscuity), compulsive watching of television and movies, and compulsive listening to hi-fi music.

A patient who was a severe nail biter from early childhood sustained a median nerve injury in an automobile accident. He stopped biting the nails of the anesthetized fingertips, even though he continued to bite with unabated fury the nails of the normally innervated fingers. That case suggests that the satisfaction derived from nail biting resides in the pain inflicted on the fingers primarily, rather than on hypothetical oral satisfactions residing in the mouth.

Defense or distance-regulating mechanisms may be established during a developmental period, when they fulfill a more or less useful adaptational function. With further maturation, those mechanisms may outlive that function and become counterproductive. A childhood fear of dogs, for example, may become an institutionalized part of an ongoing life style that impairs freedom of action and reduces self-esteem. The removal of such a symptom with behavior therapy is easily accomplished. However, some mechanisms fulfill an important distance-regulating function, even in adult life. The removal of such mechanisms can result in depression or substitute symptom formation or may necessitate alterations in basic relationships.

A patient had a symptom of premature ejaculation, which was a chronic source of lowered self-esteem. Years of psychotherapy focusing on his passivity, his symbolizing intercourse as a physically destructive act, and his fear of vengeful retaliation accomplished little change. Removal of his symptoms was easily accomplished with hypnosis. In response to his improved sexual performance, his wife developed an acute cancerophobia. She feared that his physically vigorous attentions might injure her breast or her cervix and produce a malignancy. In response to her panic, he, in effect, unhypnotized himself back to his previous state of premature ejaculation, with which his wife, for her own neurotic reasons, was apparently more comfortable.

The foregoing case may also be cited as an instance of alternating reciprocal *folie à deux* in the sense that one partner's well-being seems to depend on a state of overt symptom formation in the other and vice versa.

A married woman developed a postpartum depression after the birth of her son, an only child. During the ensuing years the depression remained severe. It became associated with alcoholism. When the alcoholism was controlled by membership in Alcoholics Anonymous, she developed a barbiturate dependency. Her little son suffered accidental injuries when she tried to care for him during states of intoxication. During that time her husband, a successful businessman, was always ready to expound on his martyrdom to all who would listen.

When her son was 19 years old, the woman developed submucous uterine fibroids, with heavy bleeding. A hysterectomy was performed, after which there was not only considerable physical improvement but an extraordinary psychiatric transformation. Liberated from a chronic unceasing fear of pregnancy, which she had never disclosed to previous therapists, she was now content and self-confident. She became a successful businesswoman in her own right. Coincident with those improvements, her husband went into a decline. He became chronically depressed. He began psychiatric treatment, in spite of which his depression deepened, and he became suicidal. Two years after his wife's hysterectomy, he committed suicide. His wife continued to function satisfactorily.

Disturbances in Motor Aspects of Behavior

Conation or the conative aspect of mental functioning refers to the capacity to initiate action or motor discharge and concerns the basic strivings of a person as expressed through his behavior. The affective component of an idea determines the force and the direction of the action that follows that idea. Thus, conation can not be considered apart from affects, and, conversely, all affects represent potential energy through their conative components.

The simple schizophrenic has difficulty initiating goal-directed activity. He may in some instances be capable of useful work if it is initiated for him and carried out under supervision, as in a sheltered workshop or state hospital or any other setting where self-support and independent functioning are not expected of him. Indeed, the lack of a self-starting mechanism—that is, the inability of a schizophrenic to initiate and carry out goal-directed behavior in any sphere, whether it be vocational, recreational or familial—is a hallmark of schizophrenia and is associated with a poor outcome in any activities program unless

hospital staff leaders are constantly and actively on the scene to keep the activity in progress.

Lacking the capacity to initiate their own actions, some schizophrenics respond to suggestions automatically and uncritically (command automatism) or by echolalia, which is the pathological repetition by imitation of the speech of another person; by echopraxia, the pathological repetition by imitation of the movements of another person; or by waxy flexibility (cerea flexibilitas), the maintenance by a patient of imposed postures with increased muscle tone, as when a limb remains passively in the position in which it is placed, however long or uncomfortable. Waxy flexibility is most characteristic of catatonic schizophrenia. Catalepsy is often used as a synonym for waxy flexibility; it is also used in a wider sense to include the intense muscular rigidities that can be induced by hypnotic suggestion.

Learned sphincter control may be lost during periods of emotional stress. Thus, a precociously toilet-trained youngster may become enuretic, with episodes of lost urethral sphincter control, or encopretic, with episodes of lost anal sphincter control, during periods of enforced separation from his mother or on returning to a disturbed home after a successful adjustment with foster parents. The undoubted psychological role in the enuretic syndrome notwithstanding, the fact remains that enuresis has a clear-cut biological substrate—occurring as it does during arousal from NREM (usually stage 4) sleep—is not typically associated with dreaming, and is associated with an increase in the number and the intensity of spontaneous and evoked bladder muscle contractions during NREM sleep. In almost all instances, there seems to be maturational lag. Most cases of enuresis yield in time to a patient, nonpunitive, nonshaming approach. The use of a tricyclic antidepressant and a bed buzzer may spare the enuretic child much suffering because of a one-sided psychoanalytic or behavior-modification treatment approach. In adult patients, encopresis is usually a result of organic disease. In its absence, encopresis is usually associated with schizophrenia.

A mannerism is a gesture or other form of motor expression peculiar to a given person. It is used interchangeably with stereotypy and posturing, the assuming of specific physical attitudes.

Some persons display a mannerism of staring upward to the right or the left while lost in thought. That same posture may occur in a schizophrenic listening to an auditory hallucination. An inappropriately fixed smile may occur as a mannerism in schizophrenia.

The startle reaction is a reflex response to an unexpected stimulus of great intensity. It is associated with a sudden increase in the level of consciousness and a diffuse motor response involving flexion movements of the trunk and extremities, hence, in German, *Zusammenschrecken* reflex. It occurs in normal people, but it may be elicited more readily and with a greater motor excursion in acute anxiety neurosis, as occurs after a traumatic battlefield experience during wartime.

Cyclic changes in motor activity are commonly observed in women. Premenstrually, women often go through periods of compulsive cleaning, a pattern that has been compared to nest building.

OVERACTIVITY

Some persons are endowed biologically with a tendency to increased motor output, which can be demonstrated in fetal movements studied in utero (Fries, 1953).

The hyperkinetic child is characterized by overactivity, distractibility, impulsiveness, and excitability. The condition occurs predominantly in boys. It is associated with difficulties in peer relationships, with disciplinary problems, and with severe learning impairments. Although the hyperkinetic state tends to subside with age, residual learning problems and academic underachieving may continue into adult life. In the patient's middle twenties, he may continue to show evidences of emotional immaturity and inability to maintain goal-directed behavior. His long history of social impairment is commonly associated in adult life with a state of chronic depression, with feelings of hopelessness, and with lack of self-esteem. Occasionally, an acute schizophrenic psychosis may erupt. Treatment must be instituted early and depends on the use of appropriate medication and schooling in a setting with a high staff-to-student ratio. Although organic brain disease is often suspected in hyperkinetic children, it can rarely be convincingly demonstrated. Nevertheless, the condition is often referred to clinically as minimal brain damage.

Children and adolescents suffering from depression often show hyperactivity. Depressed adolescents may be reckless, antisocial, and sexually promiscuous.

Agitation refers to a state of pacing, hand wringing, and verbalized complaints of suffering, which occurs in agitated depression.

The phenothiazines and other antipsychotic drugs can cause a variety of motor abnormalities that are regarded as extrapyramidal side effects.

Parkinsonism is the most common side effect. In acute dystonic reactions, occurring in some patients sensitive to the major tranquilizers, the muscles of the head and the neck are predominantly involved. Spasm of the tongue and mouth muscles may cause difficulty in speaking and swallowing. There may be opisthotonos, torticollis, and oculogyric crisis. The reaction occurs most often in young patients, somewhat more in males than in females; it starts on the first day or two of treatment and is sometimes misdiagnosed as hysteria. The symptoms are rapidly reversed by antiparkinsonism medications.

Akathisia is a subjective desire to be in constant motion. A manifestation of drug sensitivity, it may be confused with psychotic agitation and incorrectly treated by increasing the dose of the offending medication. The symptom subsides promptly when the offending medication is discontinued and replaced by another one better tolerated by the patient.

Perhaps the most unpleasant of all the motor side effects of the major tranquilizers is tardive dyskinesia. It is characterized by rhythmical, involuntary movements of the tongue, face, mouth, and jaw—for example, protrusion of the tongue, puffing of the cheeks, puckering of the mouth, and chewing movements. Sometimes those movements are accompanied by involuntary movements of the extremities and trunk. Tardive dyskinesia was once thought to affect mostly elderly female patients on high and prolonged doses of antipsychotic medication and most likely to appear when the medication was discontinued. It is now known to affect youngsters and young adults and to appear as a breakthrough phenomenon—that is, while the patient is still receiving the antipsychotic medication. Although often regarded as an irreversible disorder, many patients, fortunately, do improve after a period of months when the medication is gradually withdrawn after the appearance of the symptom. Although drug holidays, the periodic discontinuation of the medication, are widely recommended as a device to reduce the likelihood of tardive dyskinesia, evidence suggests that the more frequent the drug holidays, the higher the incidence of persistent tardive dyskinesia. That the involuntary movements associated with tardive dyskinesia can be a source of social and functional impairment is quite clear. However, in addition to the typical orofacial and trunkal dyskinesis, life-threatening muscular disturbances may

involve respiration and peristalsis, giving the physician no choice but to reinstitute neuroleptic medications in sufficient quantities to control the dyskinesia. Indeed, evidence suggests that tardive dyskinesia patients in general tend to have a reduced life expectancy. One must conclude from those facts that the major tranquilizers should not be used unless urgently indicated and then should be withdrawn when the patient goes into remission or shows the first signs of tardive dyskinesia.

Patients with systemic lupus erythematosus or under treatment with prednisone are particularly prone to the extrapyramidal side effects of antipsychotic medications.

Hysterical convulsions usually consist of pantomimic expressions of sexual and aggressive fantasies. Occasionally, a hysterical patient mimics a grand mal seizure with extraordinary fidelity. The differential diagnosis depends on the absence of electroencephalographic abnormalities during the seizure and the absence of abnormal reflexes immediately thereafter.

Sleepwalking, somnambulism, is primarily a motor disturbance of childhood. It is often associated with sleeptalking and enuresis. On a motivational level, it seems related to nocturnal fears and loneliness and a wish to enter the parental bed. It is also associated with night-terrors, pavor nocturnus. When electroencephalographically monitored, the foregoing phenomena all take place in stage 4 (slow-wave) sleep.

Neurotic reactions of the obsessive-compulsive type are characterized by obsessive thoughts and by complex compulsive rituals. Most common are compulsive hand washing, counting, and repetitive ceremonial rituals, including the recitation of prayers and the repeated checking of door locks, water faucets, gas jets, and windows. In each instance, the compulsive act simultaneously carries out a forbidden wish and then undoes it. The endlessly repeated cycle of anxiety by carrying out the compulsive act, and the need to undo the act characterizes the compulsive symptoms.

Other types of compulsive acts are not usually connected with obsessive-compulsive neurosis—for example, alcoholism (dipsomania), compulsive stealing (kleptomania), compulsive fire setting (pyromania), and compulsive sexual acting out in a woman (nymphomania). Included in that category too, is compulsive gambling, for which a program like Alcoholics Anonymous is available.

Compulsive drinking of great quantities of water in a relatively short span of time is occasionally seen in schizophrenia in response to specific delusions or hallucinations. For example, the Virgin Mary "commanded" a psychotic patient to drink holy water. Another patient momentarily expected to be sucked into the sun and had to drink much water in preparation for that dehydrating ordeal. Severe electrolyte disturbances with grand mal seizures can occur in those instances. The electrolyte imbalance can itself be a cause of a toxic-metabolic psychotic reaction that complicates the basic schizophrenic disorder and can on occasion result in a fatal outcome.

The compulsive eating of scaling wall paint in children is called pica. It has been hypothesized that an underlying nutritional deficiency is the cause. For example, it is often contended that an iron deficiency is regularly found in those cases. On the other hand, in a study of families in an inner-city walk-up apartment house complex, pica occurred most often in children living above the third floor, who seemed to have less opportunity for out-of-doors play than did children living on lower floors.

A tic is an intermittent spasmodic twitching of the face or other body part that is repeated at frequent intervals and without external stimulus.

Gilles de la Tourette's disease, *maladie des tics*, is a disorder characterized by a facial tic, which may spread to involve the head, neck, and upper and lower extremities. The tic is associated with stereotyped gestures, echolalia, coprolalia (compulsive use of obscene spoken words), and compulsive thoughts. It usually begins between the ages of 7 and 15. The muscular movements begin in the face and extend to the rest of the body. The patient opens his mouth, spits, jerks his head, claps his hands, scratches, jumps, and dances. Articulation and phonation are affected, and barking noises are often made. The patient repeats certain words or phrases, frequently expressing compulsive ideas. Although causative organic changes are often postulated, the nature of the pathology is unknown. Early diagnosis is important, since haloperidol can effectively reduce the symptoms. The tricyclic antidepressants may make them worse. There is a familial incidence of the disorder and a high male-to-female ratio. Onset during childhood carries a better prognosis than does onset in later years.

Most patients with anorexia nervosa tend to be hyperactive before, during, and after hospitalization. The threat of enforced physical restriction often stimulates a cachectic anorectic patient to start eating, and enlargement of the sphere of activity may be used as the reward to encourage further eating and weight gain. Curiously, many anorectic patients retain the pattern of physical hyperactivity in posthospital settings, and the weight gain is successfully maintained. Such patients may give a clinical impression of depression. In any case, a trial of therapeutic doses of a tricyclic antidepressant is indicated.

Bulimia (compulsive overeating) is commonly associated with anorexia nervosa and occurs with self-induced vomiting for purposes of weight control.

Institutionalized patients who are retarded and psychotic may indulge in self-injurious behavior—for example, head slapping and head banging. Behavior modification has been tried in such instances. Reward for non-self-injury seems to result in relatively little improvement. On the other hand, a program of overcorrection—that is, encouraging even more severe self-attack—may have a rapidly positive effect in some instances. Once improvement by the latter technique has occurred, verbal reprimands may suffice to prevent further self-injury.

Manic patients may talk, sing, dance, and joke with apparently inexhaustible energy and good spirit. In agitated depression, there may be crying, pacing, and wringing of hands. In catatonic excitement, the pattern of overactivity is extreme from a quantitative point of view and bewildering from the point of view of content. Talking, which may be loud and voluble, is in response to delusions and hallucinations. The talk may consist of endless repetitions of sentences or phrases, the meaning of which is obscure. The severe ambivalence characterizing the schizophrenic process may result in great mood swings, ranging from abject terror to exaltation. There may be sudden eruptions of terror and rage, in response to which the patient may become homicidal. There may be moments of deep guilt and an urge to self-sacrifice, which may result in acts of self-mutilation. The excited catatonic patient may execute various gestures that have the intent of influencing the world by means of magic. Catatonic excitement, because of extreme intensity and prolongation, may result in severe exhaustion states, with dehydration, hyperthermia, and sudden death. The use of physical restraint tends to increase terror, intensify excitement, and increase the dangers of exhaustion and death. In addition, the major tranquilizers commonly used in treating catatonic excitement affect temperature control through hypothalamic suppression, further increasing the danger of hyperthermal death.

An outburst of homicidal rage can follow a severe blow to one's self-esteem. If the patient is a young adult, separated from home, frustrated, and exposed to constant danger, as in a combat zone, a small intake of alcohol may precipitate a homicidal episode (pathological intoxication). In Southeast Asia an episode like the foregoing that results in an act of homicide against a group of people who are usually strangers to the killer is called amok.

For persons lacking in self-esteem or suffering from identity uncertainty, an automobile or a motorcycle can act as an ego prosthesis. A preoccupation with motorcycles, in particular, can occur in adolescent males with accident-prone histories since childhood, persistent fears of bodily injury, extreme passivity, identification with the mother, inability to compete, poor impulse control, potency problems, homosexual fears, and counterphobic involvements with aggressive girls. The motorcycle imparts a sense of strength and virility. Mingled with those positive feelings, however, is a continual awareness of the risk of serious injury.

The following vignette, observed in a park zoo, illustrates somewhat humorously a complex behavioral pattern by which a schizophrenic maintains a safe distance from other human beings and yet enters into limited interactions that combat loneliness.

A somewhat obese, eccentrically dressed woman was at the elephant enclosure. As the elephant approached, she spoke tenderly, "Come here, darling. Have a peanut. That's a sweet elephant!" If any human being approached, particularly if he accidentally touched her, she would snarl, "Get out of my way, you dirty bastard!" To a little child wandering over to her side, she said, "Stay out of my way, you little bastard, or I'll knock the shit out of you." To another approaching child she said, "I'll break your jaw if you don't stay away from here!" The effect of those vituperations was to keep everyone effectively at a distance. Thus isolated, she could resume her loving ministrations with her bag of peanuts.

UNDERACTIVITY (PSYCHOMOTOR RETARDATION)

Just as there are persons constitutionally predisposed to hyperkinesis, so there are others who react to stress with motor inhibition. In childhood and early adolescence, generalized patterns of inhibition and retreat tend to have a graver clinical significance than they do in later years, and they suggest a potential for a schizophrenic reaction.

Simple depression, in contrast to agitated depression, is characterized by the absence of anxiety and by decreased motor activity. There is a feeling of pronounced fatigue and great difficulty in initiating any activity, including speech. Responses to stimuli are slowed up on an ideational, verbal, and motor level. The patient's posture is expressive of the underlying affect of hopelessness and futility.

Hysterical motor disturbances can affect any of the voluntary muscle groups in patterns calculated to ward off forbidden sexual and aggressive discharges or to avoid situations of physical danger. They may present clinically as paralysis or muscular weakness (asthenia); abnormal posture, such as torticollis, camptocormia, pseudocontractures, and stiffness; gait disturbances ranging from hysterical paraplegia to astasia-abasia. The speech apparatus may be affected with aphonia, hoarseness, and stammering. Blepharospasm may occur in relation to forbidden scoptophilic wishes. The muscular abnormalities of hysteria are usually associated with an increase in muscular tonus. If sustained, they may produce painful orthopaedic and gynecological disorders. For example, hysterical spasm of the muscles of the pelvic floor may cause vaginismus.

Concerning the physical findings in hysterical paralysis, Freud wrote:

> The hysteric acts in his paralyses and other manifestations as if anatomy were nonexistent or as if he had no knowledge of it.

Although hysterical paralyses are usually associated with increased muscle tone and rigidity, on some occasions a total flaccidity, except for the retention of normal reflexes, is encountered. On occasion, an attitude of ambivalence expresses itself in variations in muscle tone.

In childhood schizophrenia, in particular, there are wide and unpredictable changes in muscle tone, so that a child being carried holds himself with inappropriate stiffness at one moment and goes totally limp at another.

Cataplexy, commonly associated with narcolepsy, is characterized by sudden loss of motor tone, with profound weakness of the arms, legs, neck, and speech apparatus. Those attacks are brought on by unexpected strong emotional reactions involving laughter, anger, surprise, or pleasure.

According to behavior therapists, anxiety is necessarily associated with an increase in muscle tone, and, conversely, an induced state of physical relaxation must have an anxiety-relieving effect. That is the theoretical basis for the behavioral technique known as reciprocal inhibition, in which systematic desensitization to phobic situations takes place while the patient simultaneously cultivates a state of generalized physical relaxation.

In schizophrenic catatonic stupor, the patient is immobile. His face may be mask-like. He is unresponsive to questions and commands, except occasionally when he manifests echolalia or echopraxia. When an attempt is made to bend his arm at the elbow, he may vigorously extend it. He may close his eyes tightly when asked to open them. Those qualities, which may be regarded as contrariness or countersuggestibility, are manifestations of a generalized oppositional attitude called negativism. Ambivalence may modify the muscle tonus of the patient with catatonic stupor to the extent that he permits bending of his arm but against a resistance, so that a characteristic tonus quality emerges known as waxy flexibility.

The extreme degree of motor retardation in catatonic stupor may be regarded as a way of splinting or restraining the total self. Beneath the facade of immobility is a seething volcano of potential violence. That volcano can erupt at any moment as catatonic excitement, bringing in its wake homicide, suicide, self-mutilation, and generalized destructiveness.

Speech disturbances may express themselves as motoric inhibitions—for example, hysterical hoarseness and mutism.

Stammering is a disorder characterized by spasmodic, halting, or hesitating speech. Stuttering is a more severe degree of stammering. It tends to have an explosive quality, based on violent expulsive respiratory movements associated with the production of speech. It usually appears between the ages of 2 and 6 years. It occurs much more frequently in males than in females and is said to be more frequent in those who are left-handed than in the right-handed.

When a person encounters an affect-laden idea while speaking, he may hesitate and stammer. Such an interruption in the flow of words is analogous to a slip of the tongue and represents a momentary speech impediment based on an encounter with a circumscribed, personalized conflict. However, when the function of speech itself has acquired an objectionable emotional overlay, there is an ongoing disturbance in the capacity to speak more or less independently of the ideas themselves. Such is the situation in stuttering.

The hyperventilation syndrome is associated with massive overbreathing, paresthesia, tetany, and precordial pain. Although the episode may be precipitated by an identifiable attack of anxiety, that is not always so. Diagnosis rests on reproducing the symptoms by controlled voluntary hyperventilation. Treatment consists of teaching the patient to become aware of his disordered breathing habits and to change to a slow diaphragmatic pattern of breathing.

Globus hystericus usually presents clinically as the sensation of a lump in the throat. X-ray studies often show accompanying spasms of the cricopharyngeal muscle, esophagitis, and gastroesophageal reflux. Although significant psychosocial factors contribute to the symptom and should be treated, associated local somatic disorders also require correction.

In male sexual functioning, motor inhibition may be expressed as impotence, premature ejaculation, and retarded ejaculation. In certain sexual perversions a male patient deliberately cultivates physical immobilization by tying himself up as a way of increasing sexual excitement (bonding).

Heroin addicts have a high incidence of sexual inhibition. Such patients characteristically describe normal sexual functioning before heroin addiction and a rapid return to normal functioning after heroin withdrawal. Patients receiving methadone treatment seem to have a more satisfactory sexual performance than do those using heroin.

In childhood, exhibitionism occurs as a normal technique for riveting the attention of a loving parent. Persistent strong needs for such attention provide the basis for exhibitionism in the adult. The adult exhibitionist exposes himself before a child in a symbolic act in which he identifies both with the child and with the adult whose attention is desired.

Adult exhibitionists tend to display their symptoms episodically, in relation to specific settings of stress, such as intolerable emotional deprivation associated with the birth of a new child in the family or physical illness of the wife.

Disturbances of Personality

Personality refers to the sum total of the thoughts, feelings, and actions that a person habitually uses in his ongoing adaptations to life. Personality is essentially synonymous with character. Deeply ingrained behavior patterns are clearly recognizable by adolescence and occasionally earlier. The element of continuity is perhaps the most distinguishing element of personality, as contrasted with the episodic or discontinuous nature of most other diagnostic categories.

Although personality development entails a certain loss of freedom of thought and action, it also protects against trauma and overt symptom formation. That protective function of personality has given rise to the term "character armor."

The structural rigidities of personality may conceal deep-seated psychopathology. For example, a patient with a schizoid personality may function satisfactorily in civilian life as long as he is permitted to work on the night shift in the post office and to lead a hermit-like existence by day. If drafted into the armed forces, with its group living and inescapable physical intimacy, an acute schizophrenic episode may erupt. Or a woman with a passive-dependent personality disorder may live for decades in a satisfactory symbiosis with a strong, controlling father figure of a husband and then collapse with a depressive psychosis when her husband dies.

Thomas et al. (1963) delineated the following categories of temperament that are identifiable in early childhood and that influence personality development: activity level (the proportions of active and inactive periods during the day); rhythmicity (the predictability of such functions as hunger, feeding pattern, elimination, and the sleep-wake cycle); approach or withdrawal (speed and ease with which behavior is modified in response to altered environment); intensity of reaction (energy level); threshold of responsiveness (to sensory stimuli, the environment, and human relationships); quality of mood (pleasant and sociable versus unpleasant and unsociable); distractibility; and attention span and persistence.

The American Psychiatric Association's (1980) DSM-III lists a number of identifiable personality disorders: paranoid, introverted, schizotypal, histrionic, narcissistic, antisocial, borderline, avoidant, dependent, compulsive, and passive-aggressive.

Although the enduring nature of personality traits has been emphasized thus far, at each stage of life the person tends to select an environment that reinforces his basic pattern (repetition compulsion). Thus, the enduring quality of early learned behavior is probably more the result of continuous reinforcement by specific environments than the result of any special durability of the early learned system. The seemingly superficial approaches of behavior therapy and environmental manipulation may produce unsuspectedly profound personality changes, and psychoanalytically oriented insight therapy may depend ultimately on environmental change in order to complete the crucial working-through process.

In addition to the official rubrics, there are other suggested personality classifications.

From a psychosomatic point of view, type A and type B personalities have been identified. Type A people show excessive ambition, a tendency to be overscheduled, overwhelming aggression, and impatience. They are particularly prone to myocardial infarction and probably many other somatic disorders. In contrast is the more easy-going, relaxed type B personality.

The Rip van Winkle personality defect occurs in one who has been out of touch with his environment for many years because of illness, family peculiarities, or social circumstance. When the patient comes to, he discovers that he is a stranger in a strange land, with a broken family, no social ties, and lost occupational skills. In certain family settings, the defect may present as an inhibition in the development of specific skills—social, athletic, mechanical, musical. Those developmental omissions may contribute to lowered self-esteem. Successful treatment may call for a catching-up process by means of direct education.

Existential neurosis is associated with the conviction that life is meaningless or with the chronic inability to believe in the importance or usefulness of anything one does. It is a state of nihilism and is associated with the feeling that one is deliberately and self-consciously playing out a series of essentially empty roles to fulfill social obligations and body needs.

The psychoanalytic literature describes personality types in terms of levels of emotional development. Thus, the oral character or personality is a passive-dependent person who tries to re-create in his relationships the pattern of being fed by a loving mother. There is some evidence to suggest that such persons are particularly prone to depressive illness. In the anal character the outstanding qualities are excessive orderliness, frugality, and obstinacy—qualities presumably developed in the interactions with his mother during bowel training. The "genital character" is a term used to designate the emotionally mature ideal, with maximally effective adaptability.

Masculine and feminine character traits are associated with assigned social roles, the details of which are culturally determined. Certain symptom complexes are associated more with one sex or another. For example, somatization and nailbiting are more frequent among females, and the addictions and sociopathy are more frequent among males.

Disturbances in Appearance

Excessive fastidiousness may suggest an obsessive-compulsive disorder. Deterioration from a previous normal level of neatness may be an early sign of depression or schizophrenia. When a female patient seeks to arouse sexual desire by her seductive dress and manner, a hysterical character disorder may be suspected. Male homosexuals may be distinguished by their exhibitionistic attire. A sexually fearful woman may deliberately choose neutral or drab clothing to discourage the interest of potential sexual partners. Regressive clinging to childhood may be expressed in childish patterns of dress.

Rejection of normal sexual identity may be implied in adolescent girls who affect boys' haircuts and blue jeans and in adolescent boys who affect female or childhood hair styles. Repulsive body odor due to lack of bathing is designated the skunk maneuver, which is calculated to keep a frightening world at a safe distance. Paranoid patients may wear dark glasses so that they can spy on others without themselves being spied on. Eccentric patterns of dress, including unkempt beards, may become a badge of rebellion or conformity for membership in teenage groups.

Transvestites are sometimes acting out complex fantasies involving a wish to recapture a lost parent figure. Schizophrenic patients may first reveal the delusion of body change by complaining that a hat or a pair of eyeglasses no longer fits properly. Powerful automobiles and other possessions may be ego prostheses and serve to compensate for feelings of inferiority.

Patterns of Human Relationships

After enumerating in detail the clinical manifestations of psychiatric disorders, one is left with a fundamental fact—that the mental health or illness of a given person is measured not by his symptoms but by the quality of his human relationships. To evaluate those relationships, one must systematically explore four separate areas—family, work, play, and community—with careful notations included on each of those items in the psychiatric history.

FAMILY

A stable family mediates in behalf of its members vis-à-vis the nonfamily environment, providing nourishment, protection, and an unfailing source of self-esteem. The family is the transmitter of culture, instructing each child concerning his social role. Thus, a culture stands or falls on the quality and the stability of family life. For that reason, family-centered holiday seasons are often traumatic for the social isolate and for the person whose family has been broken by death or divorce. It explains, too, why the anniversary of a loss can precipitate a breakdown and the importance of searching specifically for that possibility in the psychiatric history.

To ensure family survival, society has evolved a number of protective devices. Most important are the learned taboos against intrafamilial sex and violence that, as unconsciously operating psychological mechanisms, constitute the superego. The effect of the superego is to direct those drives toward extrafamilial targets; when the superego fails in its function, pathology erupts.

The schizophrenic family member constitutes a major threat to the family stability. Because of his fear of the outer world, he is forced to invest his drives within the family. In response, the family has the choice of extruding this offending member (the schismatic-family solution) or of twisting itself into some pathological pattern of accommodation that makes his continued presence possible (the skewed-family solution).

In relation to aggression, a specific family member may be scapegoated. As a consequence, that person may become a battered child and later in life grow up to be a battering parent and to display other forms of psychopathology.

Within a family group, one can identify the following roles: spouse (husband, wife), parent (father, mother, grandparents), and child (son, daughter, sibling). Each of those roles involves a complex of capacities and responsibilities. The husband must be not only the wage earner but also the sexual partner and companion for his wife. The capacity for satisfactory sexual performance is implicit in his role. Potency disturbances can have a severe undermining effect on family happiness. Just as satisfactory sexual performance reinforces the husband's concept of himself as a man, the satisfaction he gives to his wife reinforces her identity as a woman and promotes acceptance of her female role.

In their studies of human sexuality, Masters and Johnson (1966) emphasized that most sexual malfunctioning in marriage is the result of a communication breakdown. Their focus was not on an impotent husband or a frigid wife but on the marital unit, on the human transactions in their totality that take place within that unit. The focus on the marital unit applies not only to the treatment of sexual dysfunction but to a broad range of psychiatric disorders and to psychosomatic medicine. The onset, the course, and the outcome of a myocardial infarction, for example, may be determined more by the functioning of the marital unit than by any other detail in the treatment plan. The ideal marital goal is a noncompetitive state, with room for autonomous functioning and a dovetailing of skills and interests that makes for complementarity. Most of all, the ideal marriage is a relationship based on reality, not on a variety of communication distortions based on projective identification and the need to complete the unfinished business of a childhood neurosis. Much effective marital counseling deals specifically with that issue, and much psychotherapy has found its richest application in the form of family therapy, in which the family, as the biological unit, is really the patient.

Perhaps the most important aspect of the parental role is the capacity to accept an attitude of passive dependence in others. Periods of helplessness and dependency fall within the range of normal, and a sine qua non for normal functioning as a spouse or parent is the mastery of one's own infantile dependency needs. A person who has achieved that mastery is capable of providing maximal opportunity for normal emotional development in others. On the other hand, a reversal of roles is often seen in disturbed households in which an emotionally immature parent makes unrealistic demands on a young child. For example, a schizophrenic or depressed mother may take to her bed and expect her little daughter to mother her.

The ideal parental attitude is one of unconditional positive regard, which communicates to the child the message, "Whether I approve of your actions or not, my love for you remains intact." One may contrast that message with the schizophrenogenic parental attitude of unconditional negative regard, which says, "Whatever you do is wrong and makes me love you less," to which the response is often one of generalized social withdrawal.

The responses of a mother to her newborn child depend on his specific symbolic significance to her. For example, if he reminds her of the trauma she experienced decades before, when she was displaced by a younger sibling, the infant arouses feelings of hatred and rejection, which may eventuate in severe postpartum mental illness.

Fathers who refuse to relinquish their primary hold on the mother's attention and who compete actively for her love may seriously impair the emotional development of their children.

A woman who is childless often retains a greater capacity for tenderness toward her husband than does a woman with children. Conversely, a woman who has a child, particularly a much-wanted son, may lose sexual interest in her husband entirely, and a previously satisfactory marital relationship may then deteriorate.

Loss of a spouse is a major life stress and may play a causative role in a wide range of mental and physical disorders. The relative loss of a wife when she has given birth to a child may precipitate various postpartum disorders in the husband, including depression, accident proneness and injury at work, and episodes of sexual deviation.

Grandparents play an important role in family life, with variations that are determined largely by cultural factors. Perhaps the most striking aspect of the grandparent relationship is its relative freedom from ambivalence. Because of that attitude of unconditional positive regard, grandparents contribute much to the self-esteem of the growing child. By the same token, the loss of a grandparent may in certain instances be traumatic.

That the mother plays a role of special importance in the emotional development of the child is self-evident. However, the importance of the father in the developmental process is equally great. Not only does he consolidate the self-esteem of the mother, but he also provides an identification for the son and, in his relation to the mother, an identification model for the daughter. Families without fathers are particularly prone to psychopathology, and that is true more or less independently of the cause of his absence—that is, whether due to death, occupation, or divorce.

Children develop basic security and basic trust in their relationships with their parents. When the opportunity for that trust does not exist, attitudes of cynicism and distrust emerge and seriously impair the social, intellectual, and emotional development process.

One result of effective parental participation in family life is the setting of limits on the outward expression of sibling rivalry. The birth of a sibling is universally experienced as a trauma, resulting as it does in a displacement of the older child from the bosom of the mother. The displaced youngster has feelings of rage, with which he needs help from his parents. If that help is not forthcoming, the youngster does not internalize his aggression or learn to sublimate it. Instead, he expresses it outwardly. That is why the likelihood of homicide and other forms of violence is greatly increased in communities characterized by family disorganization and absent parents.

WORK

If successfully managed, the work role makes personal autonomy possible in the extrafamilial community. It is probably the single most important prerequisite for entering into marriage and for raising a family.

Work is a major source of self-esteem. It fulfills a need to be needed. Loss of work for any reason can be a crushing narcissistic blow, with major mental and physical repercussions. The work role is also important in relation to one's identity or concept of self. For those reasons, Freud observed that man is bound most closely to reality through his work.

A minimum level of mental health is necessary to be able to work at all or to work with maximal effectiveness. A remarkable measure of the significance of work vis-à-vis health is the fact that job satisfaction is the strongest predictor of longevity. Conversely, heart attacks, addictions of all kinds, depression, and suicide correlate highly with job dissatisfaction. In addition, extraoccupational life changes may alter work attitudes so that a previously steady worker becomes accident prone and liable to crippling injury or accident neurosis.

If a specific job threatens to disrupt a state of dependency on parents or involves separation from the parental home, it is unacceptable to a person who has not achieved the stage of separation-individuation in his emotional growth. The schizophrenic's attitude toward work can be baffling. In general, people enjoy having a work role. Schizophrenics are anhedonic—that is, they get little pleasure out of anything, including work. Most people have a need to be needed. The schizophrenic's main need is to be left alone. Thus, programs to motivate the unemployed schizophrenic are often wrecked by those basic schizophrenic qualities. Nevertheless, many schizophrenics, particularly borderline patients, are capable of performing outstandingly at jobs of great professional responsibility as long as the work does not demand intimate contact with fellow workers.

At each stage of life, there is a work role. For the school-age youngster, his role involves his capacity to function as a student. The wage earner must be able to work with reasonable effectiveness and personal satisfaction. The same is true for a housewife in relation to her household chores.

Because of prevailing attitudes of denigration, women have been getting less pay than men for identical work. In addition, they have been arbitrarily excluded from a number of professions. That bigoted point of view has deprived women of self-esteem. By correcting that situation, society at large will benefit.

Many women have successfully embarked on a profession as a second career after their children have been launched into the school system. Some women are unable to be homemakers because of a fundamental inability to accept the nurturing role. Ideally, that inability should be corrected with treatment. From a mental health point of view, it may be necessary to accept that limitation in specific cases and to arrange for work outside the home. However, the emotional development of the children may be compromised as a consequence, particularly if the mother's outside work occurs during the children's preschool years of life.

Many people work far below their potential because of psychopathological work inhibitions. Some are self-defeating out of a sense of guilt. Others are self-defeating because of a fear of success. Some fall behind because they must rebel in their quest for identity. On a school level, that rebellion expresses itself as an impaired capacity for learning and in the school dropout problem.

Retirement from work may have a severe disruptive impact on the adaptational patterns in a family and may touch off a vicious cycle of psychopathology. Some people can be termed work addicts. They are guilt-ridden people who work compulsively. For them, in particular, loss of a job or retirement upsets a delicately balanced adaptational state.

Specific types of employment are associated with special problems. For example, doctors and nurses are particularly prone to narcotic addiction because of the pressures of their work and their relatively easy access to opiates. The father who commutes a long distance to work may create a family void as traumatic as an absent father. Unskilled jobs associated with danger, monotony, and poor pay are particularly associated

with accident neurosis and litigiousness. The higher the socioeconomic status of the family of origin, the greater is the likelihood of normal growth and development in the offspring, and the greater is the likelihood of good medical care and education.

PLAY

Normal emotional development calls for a capacity to enjoy one's leisure. That capacity involves not only a range of skills and interests but also freedom from guilt and anxiety. The capacity for spontaneity, enthusiasm, and elation has been mentioned in the description of normal recreation. Some people in recreational situations are like work addicts. They play compulsively, angrily, and anxiously. They are so demanding of themselves that they suffer severely if they make errors; if they lose a game, they become depressed. In those instances, the superego remains too much in control, and there is no opportunity for genuine sublimation. In any event, inquiry into the play area is a necessary element in a good psychiatric history.

COMMUNITY

A concern for the welfare of others should extend beyond the confines of the family. The emotionally mature adult has a sense of duty toward his community and ideally involves himself in charitable, educational, or political groups to provide service to others without financial reward. Community work involves a capacity for idealism and self-sacrifice and the ability to get along with others. However, many people become involved in the area for pathological reasons, such as guilt, exhibitionism, and a need for self-aggrandizement. In such instances the formal goal of the group may clash with the person's pathological informal goals. If such persons have positions of leadership, they may exert a highly destructive influence on the group, necessitating their removal if formal group goals are to be achieved.

Suggested Cross References

Chapter 12 discusses the examination and assessment of the psychiatric patient. Chapter 14 discusses classification in psychiatry. The various mental disorders mentioned in this chapter are discussed at length in Chapters 15 through 27. Child psychiatric disorders are discussed in Chapters 37 through 41. Sleep is discussed in Section 2.3. Aggression is discussed in Sections 4.5 and 56.6. Suicide is discussed in Section 29.1.

REFERENCES

American Psychiatric Association. *Diagnostic and Statistical Manual of Mental Disorders*, ed. 3. American Psychiatric Association, Washington, D. C., 1980.
* Bender, M. B. *Disorders of Perception*. Charles C Thomas, Springfield, 1952.
Bleuler, E. *Dementia Praecox: The Group of Schizophrenias*. International Universities Press, New York, 1950.
Bleuler, M. *Die Schizophrenen Geistesstoerungen in Lichte Langjahriger Kranken und Familiengeschichten*. Thieme, Stuttgart, 1972.
* Burnham, D. L., Gladstone, S. I., and Gibson, R. W. *Schizophrenia and the Need-Fear Dilemma*. International Universities Press, New York, 1969.
Cohn, N. *The Pursuit of the Millennium*. Oxford University Press, New York, 1970.
Crosby, W. H. Pica. J. A. M. A., *235*: 2765, 1976.
Dicks, H. V. *Marital Tensions*. Basic Books, New York, 1967.
Erikson, E. H. *Childhood and Society*. W. W. Norton, New York, 1963.
* Fenichel, O. *Psychoanalytic Theory of the Neuroses*. W. W. Norton, New York, 1945.
Fish, B., and Haggin, R. Visual-motor disorders in infants at risk for schizophrenia. Arch. Gen. Psychiatry, *28*: 900, 1973.
Fisher, C., Kahn, E., Edwards, A., and Davis, D. M. A psychophysiological study of nightmares and night terrors. Arch. Gen. Psychiatry, *28*: 252, 1973.
Freud, S. *Standard Edition of the Complete Psychological Works of Sigmund*

Freud. Hogarth Press, London, 1953–1966.

Fries, M. E., and Wolf, P. J. Some hypotheses on the role of congenital activity types in personality development. Psychoanal. Study Child, *8:* 48, 1953.

* Geschwind, N. Aphasia. N. Engl. J. Med., *284:* 654, 1971.

Gift, T. E., Strauss, J. S., and Ritzler, B. A. The failure to detect low I.Q. in psychiatric assessment. Am. J. Psychiatry, *135:* 345, 1978.

Goldstein, K. *The Organism.* American Book Company, New York, 1939.

Gove, W. R. Societal reaction as an explanation of mental illness: An evaluation. Am. Soc. Rev., *35:* 873, 1970.

Gunderson, J. G., and Singer, M. T. Defining borderline patients: An overview. Am. J. Psychiatry, *132:* 1, 1975.

Hartmann, E. *The Function of Sleep.* Yale University Press, New Haven, Conn., 1973.

Hollender, M. H., and Callahan, A. S., III. Erotomania or de Clérambault syndrome. Arch. Gen. Psychiatry, *32:* 1574, 1975.

* Holmes, T. H., and Rahe, R. H. The social readjustment rating scale. J. Psychosom. Res., *11:* 213, 1967.

Jackson, H. *Selected Writings,* J. Taylor, editor. Hodder & Stroughton, London, 1932.

Kalinowsky, L. B., and Hippius, M. *Pharmacologic, Convulsive, and Other Somatic Treatments in Psychiatry.* Grune & Stratton, New York, 1969.

Kanner, L. Early infantile autism. Am. J. Orthopsychiatry, *19:* 416, 1948.

Kaplus, D., and Reich, R. The murdered child and his killers. Am. J. Psychiatry, *133:* 809, 1976.

Kempe, C. H., and Helfer, R. E. *Helping the Battered Child and His Family.* J. B. Lippincott, Philadelphia, 1972.

Kovacs, M., and Beck, A. T. Maladaptive cognitive structures in depression. Am. J. Psychiatry, *135:* 525, 1978.

Kris, E. *Psychoanalytic Explorations in Art.* International Universities Press, New York, 1952.

Kupfer, D. J., Foster, F. G., Coble, P., McPartland, R. J., and Ulrich, R. F. The application of EEG sleep for the differential diagnosis of affective disorders. Am. J. Psychiatry, *135:* 69, 1978.

Linn, L. Psychological implications of the reticular activating system. Am. J. Psychiatry, *110:* 61, 1953.

Mahler, M. S. *Infantile Psychosis.* International Universities Press, New York, 1968.

Masters, W. H., and Johnson, V. E. *Human Sexual Response.* Little, Brown & Co., Boston, 1966.

McLaughlin, J. T. Primary and secondary process in the context of cerebral hemispheric specialization. Psychoanal. Q., *47:* 237, 1978.

Mehta, D., Mallya, A., and Volavka, J. Mortality of patients with tardive dyskinesia. Am. J. Psychiatry, *135:* 371, 1978.

Offord, D. R., and Cross, L. A. Adult schizophrenia with scholastic failure or low I.Q. in childhood. Arch. Gen. Psychiatry, *24:* 431, 1971.

Ostow, M. *The Psychology of Melancholy.* Harper & Row, New York, 1970.

* Parkes, C. M. *Bereavement: Studies of Grief in Adult Life.* International Universities Press, New York, 1972.

Pembrook, L. Child abuse: Heavy hands, heavy hearts: An interview with C. Henry Kempe, M.D. Mod. Med., *2:* 52, 1975.

Peppercorn, M. A., Herzog, A. G., Dichter, M. A., and Mayman, C. I. Abdominal epilepsy: A cause of abdominal pain in adults. J. A. M. A., *240:* 2450, 1978.

Rendell, M., McGrane, D., and Cuesta, M. Fatal compulsive water drinking. J. A. M. A., *240:* 2557, 1978.

Schreiber, F. R. *Sybil.* Henry Regency, Chicago, 1973.

Snyder, S. H. The opiate receptor and morphine-like peptides in the brain. Am. J. Psychiatry, *135:* 645, 1978.

Spiegel, H., and Spiegel, D. *Trance and Treatment: The Clinical Uses of Hypnosis.* Basic Books, New York, 1978.

Stern, R. S., and Cobb, J. P. Phenomenology of obsessive-compulsive neurosis. Br. J. Psychiatry, *132:* 233, 1978.

Strub, R. L., and Black, F. W. *The Mental Status Examination in Neurology.* F. A. Davis, Philadelphia, 1977.

Sugar, O. In search of Ondine's curse. J. A. M. A., *240:* 236, 1978.

Thomas, A., Chess, S., Birch, H. G., and Korn, K. *Behavioral Individuality in Early Childhood.* New York University Press, New York, 1963.

Thompson, L. J. Learning disabilities: An overview. Am. J. Psychiatry, *130:* 393, 1973.

Turino, G. M., and Goldring, R. M. Sleeping and breathing. N. Engl. J. Med. *299:* 1009, 1978.

Van Allen, M. W. Epilepsy among persons convicted of crimes. J. A. M. A., *239:* 2694, 1978.

Wechsler, D. Intelligence: Definition, theory, and I.Q. In *Intelligence: Influence of Heredity and Environment,* R. Cancro, editor, p. 50. Grune & Stratton, New York, 1971.

Weiner, H. The illusion of simplicity: The medical model revisited. Am. J. Psychiatry, *135* (Suppl.): 27, 1978.

Weinstein, E. A., and Kahn, R. L. *Denial of Illness.* Charles C Thomas, Springfield, Ill., 1955.

Wing, J. K. The social context of schizophrenia. Am. J. Psychiatry, *135:* 1333, 1978.

Winncott, D. W. Transitional objects and transitional phenomena. Int. J. Psychoanal. *34:* 89, 1953.

Wyatt, R. J., Fram, D. H., Buchbinder, R., and Snyder, F. Treatment of intractable narcolepsy with a monoamine oxidase inhibitor. N. Engl. J. Med., *285:* 987, 1971.

chapter

14

Classification in Psychiatry

14.1 Classification of Mental Disorders and DSM-III

ROBERT L. SPITZER, M.D.
JANET B. W. WILLIAMS, M.S.W.

Introduction

Classification is the process by which the complexity of phenomena is reduced by arranging them into categories according to some established criteria for one or more purposes. A classification of mental disorders consists of a list of categories of specific mental disorders grouped into various classes on the basis of some shared characteristics.

Purposes of a Classification of Mental Disorders

The purposes of classifications differ according to what is being classified. The purposes of a classification of mental disorders always involve, in the broadest sense, communication, control, and comprehension.

COMMUNICATION

A classification enables users to communicate with each other about the disorders with which they deal. This involves using names of categories as standard shorthand ways of summarizing certain agreed-on important features of categories that would otherwise require the use of a larger number of terms. For example, when a clinician refers to a particular personality disorder, he is attempting to communicate a cluster of clinical features about a person without having to list all the features that together constitute the disorder. For communication to be effective, there must be a high level of agreement among clinicians when those categories are actually applied to people.

CONTROL

The control of mental disorders ideally involves the ability either to prevent their occurrence or to modify their courses with treatment. For that reason, control is the most important purpose of a classification of mental disorders. If no forms of

prevention or treatment are known, only a limited degree of control is possible by knowledge of the natural course of the condition and commonly associated features which are often important in management.

COMPREHENSION

Comprehension implies understanding the causes of mental disorders and the processes involved in their development and maintenance. Frequently, a mental disorder can be treated effectively without understanding either its cause or its pathological process. Comprehension is not an end in itself but is desired because it usually leads to better control of the disorder.

Assumptions

ASSUMPTIONS NECESSARY FOR A CLASSIFICATION OF MENTAL DISORDERS

It is useful to examine what assumptions are necessary for a classification of mental disorders. Frequently, in the extensive and controversial literature dealing with the appropriateness of various models for conceptualizing psychopathology, such as the medical model, assertions are made about assumptions implicit in a classification of mental disorders. On examination, many of those assumptions are not at all necessary and only provide fuel for interprofessional rivalry.

The following assumptions seem to represent all the assumptions that are necessarily implicit in a classification of mental disorders:

1. There are individuals with relatively distinct and clinically significant behavioral or psychological syndromes or patterns of signs or symptoms. That means that the behavioral manifestations of interest do not occur randomly but cluster meaningfully into syndromes or patterns. The phrase "clinically significant" acknowledges that a classification of mental disorders generally does not include conditions that are so mild or so self-limited that they rarely require professional intervention—for example, caffeine withdrawal.

A syndrome is a grouping of symptoms or signs that recurrently appear temporally together in many persons. An example is the depressive syndrome in which depressed mood or loss of interest or pleasure is accompanied by such symptoms as insomnia, loss of appetite, poor concentration, decreased self-esteem, and psychomotor disturbance. Almost all conditions termed mental disorders consist of behavioral syndromes. However, a few mental disorders are characterized by only a single essential symptom or sign in the absence of other symptoms or signs. For example, the psychosexual dysfunction of functional dyspareunia is characterized by painful sexual intercourse and the absence of any other symptoms or signs indicating an organic

1035

basis for the disturbance. An adjustment disorder with depressed mood is characterized by depressed mood following a psychosocial stressor in the absence of a full depressive syndrome. Strictly speaking in such cases a pattern of behavioral features, rather than a syndrome, characterizes the disorder.

2. The behavioral syndromes or patterns are undesirable, since they are typically associated with either a painful symptom (distress) or impairment in one or more important areas of functioning (disability). Because of that, there should be methods for preventing or treating those conditions. That assumption does not speak to the issue of who—the patient, society, a mental health professional—is to decide that the condition is undesirable or under what circumstances treatment should be given.

3. There is an inference that there is a behavioral, psychological, or biological dysfunction in the person, and that the disturbance is not only in the relationship between the person and society. Put in simple language, the concept of mental disorder assumes that something is wrong with the person. Whether the nature of what is wrong is conceptualized as behavioral, psychological, or biological, one cannot avoid the inference that some function in the person is disturbed. As a corollary, when the disturbance is limited to a conflict between a person and society, it may represent social deviance, which may or may not be commendable but is not by itself a mental disorder.

4. Behavioral syndromes or patterns are differentially related to variables not included in the definition of the syndrome, such as associated features, course, treatment response, familial pattern, and etiology. That means that knowledge that a person has the characteristics of a behavioral syndrome or pattern implies useful information beyond that necessary to make the diagnosis. For example, if it is known that a person has a persistent and full depressive syndrome, the clinician knows that there is a likelihood of such associated features as hypochondriasis and anxiety and is in a position to predict the likely outcome, select an effective treatment, and hypothesize about possible causal factors. Implicit is the notion that the additional information results from identifying a particular behavioral syndrome, as opposed to merely noting each of its component clinical features.

5. The extent of the relationship of a behavioral syndrome or pattern to various external correlates is increased with the inclusion of features other than the cross-sectional picture into the definition of the category. Such features include duration, historical behavioral features, and causes. For example, bipolar disorder is distinguished from major depression by the historical presence of both manic and depressive episodes in the bipolar disorder. The psychotic syndrome associated with use of amphetamine is defined as a different mental disorder than similarly appearing psychotic syndromes occurring in the absence of substance use. Adding such features to the definition of a disorder provides more useful information about external correlates than the definition would have if it were limited to a cross-sectional behavioral syndrome.

When the cause is known or presumed, it is usually incorporated into the definition and the name of a disorder because a knowledge of etiology can be an important aid to prevention and treatment (control). For example, amphetamine delusional disorder indicates the etiological role of amphetamine.

Since only some of the categories in a classification of mental disorders have etiology included in their definitions, it has become customary to use the generic term "disorder," which does not imply that the cause is necessarily known. Although the manifestations of those conditions are primarily psychological and behavioral, by tradition they are referred to as "*mental* disorders."

6. Mental disorders vary in their symptomatic inclusiveness. For that reason it is possible to organize some of the diagnostic classes into a hierarchy such that a category in a class high in the hierarchy may have features found in disorders in classes that are lower in the hierarchy, but the reverse is not true. For example, the organic brain syndrome of dementia hierarchically comes before schizophrenia because all the manifestations of schizophrenia, such as delusions and hallucinations, can occur in persons with organic mental disorders,

although the reverse is not true. Similarly, affective disorders hierarchically come before anxiety disorders because all the manifestations of anxiety disorders can occur in persons with affective disorders, although the reverse is not true.

ASSUMPTIONS OFTEN MADE BUT NOT NECESSARY

When a classification of mental disorders is conceptualized as within the medical model, the following assumptions are often thought to be necessary, but in fact they are not.

1. A biological abnormality or dysfunction within the organism fully accounts for the condition. However, a biological abnormality cannot be demonstrated for most of the conditions that are, by tradition, listed as mental disorders. Historically, when a specific treatable biological abnormality is demonstrated, the condition is often removed from a classification of mental disorders and is conceptualized as a physical disorder—for example, general paresis. The notion that every mental disorder can be fully explained by a biological dysfunction within the organism is certainly not a necessary assumption, since there are other models for accounting for the disordered behavior of many conditions that have, by tradition, been included in classifications of mental disorders, as in the use of reinforcement theory to explain phobias.

That there may be a biological abnormality for some of the major mental disorders is certainly an assumption that underlies much of the current research into such conditions as schizophrenia and bipolar disorder. However, for many other disorders, such as some gender identity disorders—for example, transsexualism—research efforts to understand their development have involved primarily psychological constructs, rather than biological constructs. (Green and Money, 1969; Green, 1975).

Most users of a classification of mental disorders assume that the etiology of most, if not all, mental disorders is not limited to a single factor but is multifactorial. The assumption of multifactorial causation certainly applies to most physical illnesses—that is, they are the result of a combination of causal factors which include host resistance, environmental influences, and severity of exposure to causative agents.

2. Each mental disorder exists as a discrete entity with discontinuity between it and other categories, as well as discontinuity between it and normality. The usefulness of categorization does not require that there be discontinuity in the subject matter being classified. For example, even if in the real world a particular personality pattern is distributed on a continuum of severity so that mild forms are more common than either its absence or its severe forms, it may be useful to define a category for that portion of the distribution of the personality pattern that is associated with social or occupational impairment. The assumption of discrete entities is not even met for all physical disorders, such as essential hypertension and some endocrine disorders.

3. There is complete homogeneity of psychopathology within each diagnostic category. That assumption implies that all persons with a specific diagnosis have the same psychopathology and do not differ in any significant respects. The assumption is incorrect because classification into any category only assumes that the members of that category share certain characteristics used as defining features of that category. Americans, Lithuanians, trees, and cats differ among themselves, yet within each group they share those features that qualify them for membership in those groups. So too, persons with schizophrenia, major depression, and narcissistic personality disorder vary in many important respects within each diagnostic category but share certain features used to define membership in each diagnostic category.

The most unfortunate result of that incorrect assumption is the equation of a person with the mental disorder with which he or she is afflicted. For example, reference is made to "Mr. Jones, the schizophrenic," rather than to "Mr. Jones, who has schizophrenia." That practice extends to references to physical disorders, particularly chronic disorders, as in referring to "Mrs. Smith, the diabetic."

Validity

The validity of a classification of mental disorders is the extent to which the entire classification and each of its specific diagnostic categories achieve the purposes of communication, control, and comprehension. How well those purposes are fulfilled is related to the establishment of several different types of validity.

The literature dealing with the validity of mental disorders rarely distinguishes among the different types of validity. When certain types of validity are discussed, such as concurrent validity, the terminology is borrowed from the psychometric literature and applied in an inconsistent manner and without an appreciation of the differences in the subject matter to which it is applied. In psychometrics one is generally interested in how valid a particular procedure, such as an intelligence test, is for measuring a particular dimension of behavior, such as intelligence. That is clearly different from the problem of assessing the validity of a classification of mental disorders in which it is necessary to distinguish between the validity of the procedure for making a diagnosis, such as the clinical diagnostic evaluation, and the validity of each of the categories themselves, such as schizophrenia and affective disorder.

TYPES OF VALIDITY

The following types of validity should be distinguished when assessing the validity of a classification of mental disorders and its component categories. Table I summarizes the types of validity and the different kinds of evidence required for their demonstration.

Face validity. Face validity is the extent to which the description of a particular category seems, on the face of it, to describe accurately the characteristic features of persons with a particular disorder. Face validity is the first step in the identification of a category; it is the result of clinicians' agreeing on the identification of a particular syndrome or pattern of clinical features as a mental disorder. Once a category is identified, with some agreement as to its characteristic features, to some extent the purpose of communication has been achieved. The rationale for including, in the initial development of a classification system, a category for which only face validity has been demonstrated is the assumption that other kinds of valid-

TABLE I

Purposes of Classification and Evidence Required to Demonstrate Different Types of Validity for a Specific Mental Disorder

Purpose of Classification	Type of Validity	Evidence Required
Communication	Face	Expert consensus regarding description
	Descriptive	Characteristic features unique
Control	Predictive	Follow-up studies indicating homogeneous course and complications specific to that mental disorder
		Differential treatment response
Comprehension	Construct	Familial pattern
		Genetic relationship to other disorders
		Biological abnormality
		Relationship to environmental or demographic variables

ity exist, even if not yet demonstrated. (The extent of face validity can be said to be directly proportional to the number of approving faces and the wisdom of the people behind those faces.)

In psychometrics, face validity is the extent to which a procedure seems to be obviously related to the dimension of behavior being assessed—for example, a spelling test and spelling ability. Because other more powerful kinds of validity can be demonstrated without great difficulty, face validity in psychometrics is by itself never accepted as a justification for recommending the general use of a particular procedure. However, because of the far greater difficulty of demonstrating the more powerful types of validity for diagnostic categories, it is necessary to recommend for general use some categories of mental disorder for which, admittedly, only face validity can be demonstrated. Clinicians need to be able to communicate with each other about the different types of disorders they recognize in their professional work; they cannot wait for a fully validated classification system (Rosenhan, 1973; Spitzer, 1976). Obviously, the profession still has a responsibility to assess the existence of other types of validity for those categories. If other types of validity cannot be demonstrated after a thorough investigation, there is no justification for the continued inclusion of those categories in a classification of mental disorders for general use.

Descriptive validity. Descriptive validity is the extent to which the characteristic features of a particular mental disorder are unique to that category, relative to other mental disorders and conditions. Furthermore, the joint occurrence of the characteristic features in a heterogeneous group of persons is more common than would be expected by chance alone. Characteristic features are either single features that are always present—for example, loss of memory in dementia—or components of syndromes when the syndromes are always present in a disorder—for example, loss of pleasure as part of the depressive syndrome that is always present in major depression. Whereas the frequency of the joint occurrence of characteristic depressive symptoms that would be expected by chance alone is very low, calculated by the serial multiplication of the base rate of each symptom, the actual frequency of the syndrome in a heterogeneous sample is relatively high.

The presence of descriptive validity justifies the assumption that a category represents a relatively distinct behavioral syndrome or pattern, rather than a random collection of clinical features. Historically, disorders such as mania and dementia were among the first mental disorders to be identified (face validity) because they have considerable descriptive validity. The characteristic symptoms of each of those disorders—for example, sustained euphoric mood and decreased need for sleep in mania; memory loss and deterioration in intellectual functions in dementia—are rarely seen in persons with other mental disorders.

A category with little descriptive validity is one in which the characteristic features are commonly seen in persons with other mental disorders or with no mental disorder. In the second edition of the American Psychiatric Association's (1968) *Diagnostic and Statistical Manual of Mental Disorders* (DSM-II), the category of inadequate personality, whose characteristic features were

ineffectual responses to emotional, social, intellectual and physical demands . . . inadaptability, ineptness, poor judgment, social instability, and lack of physical and emotional stamina,

had little, if any, descriptive validity. Most of those features are often seen in a variety of other mental disorders.

Descriptive validity serves the purpose of communication in that, the more nearly unique a category is, the more likely it is that clinicians will be able to agree with each other in its identification. Furthermore, a category with considerable descriptive validity almost certainly has more powerful types of validity, such as predictive and construct validity. Categories whose over-all validity is most in doubt tend to be categories with little descriptive validity.

Descriptive validity can be examined by comparing the relative frequency of each of the characteristic features of a disorder in persons with the disorder and in persons without the disorder. The characteristic features of a disorder are, by definition, always more common in persons with the disorder than in those without the disorder. What is important is the *relative* frequency with which the features are seen in persons without the disorder. The relative frequency of the features in each group is a function of how the features are defined. For example, if one used merely sadness as a characteristic feature of a depressive disorder, that feature would contribute little to the descriptive validity of the category because sadness is common in persons without a depressive disorder. However, if one used, instead, persistent and pervasive depressed mood as a characteristic feature of a depressive disorder, it would contribute significantly to the descriptive validity of the category because it is not commonly seen in persons without a depressive disorder. Descriptive validity can also be examined by calculating the actual rate of joint occurrence of characteristic features of a disorder and comparing it with the expected rate of joint occurrence, in a heterogeneous sample, calculated by the serial multiplication of the frequency of each symptom.

A category may have considerable descriptive validity with respect to one or more categories but limited descriptive validity with respect to other categories. Thus, although dementia, when compared with a heterogeneous group of disorders, has considerable descriptive validity, it has much less descriptive validity when compared with delirium because both disorders share features of global cognitive impairment.

As an example of how the descriptive validity of categories can be assessed, Figure 1 presents data from the International Pilot Study of Schizophrenia (World Health Organization, 1973) for the diagnostic categories of psychotic depression, schizophrenia, and schizoaffective schizophrenia. The items on the left side of the abscissa are common in both schizoaffective schizophrenia and schizophrenia but are rarely seen in psychotic depression. In contrast, the items on the right side are more common in psychotic depression than in the other two categories. These data provide evidence for the descriptive validity of each of the three categories.

Predictive validity. Predictive validity is the extent to which knowledge that a person has a particular mental disorder is useful in predicting some aspects of the future for that person, such as subsequent course of the illness, complications, and response to treatment. Clearly, that kind of validity is most directly related to the major practical purposes of a classification of mental disorders, management and treatment.

Historically, it was largely on the basis of predictive validity that Kraepelin distinguished manic-depressive psychosis from dementia precox according to their differences in course. A more recent example is the demonstration of the relative specificity with which persons with bipolar disorder respond to treatment with lithium carbonate, providing predictive validity for the unipolar-bipolar distinction in the classification of affective disorders. The fact that suicide is so much more common as a complication of major depression than of most

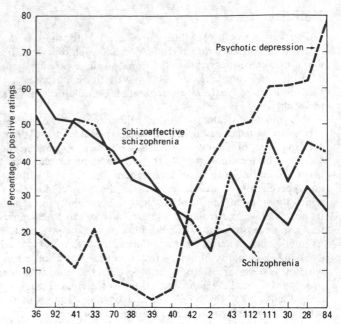

FIGURE 1. Percentage of positive ratings on selected units of analysis for all schizophrenia, psychotic depression, and schizoaffective schizophrenia. In this figure, "percentage" refers to the number of patients on whom the units were positive in relation to the total number of patients in the group. (From World Health Organization. *Report of the International Pilot Study of Schizophrenia*, vol. 1, p. 220. World Health Organization, Geneva, 1973.)

other mental disorders provides predictive validity for the category of major depression.

Follow-up studies of persons with a particular mental disorder are used to determine whether the course is typically self-limiting, episodic, or chronic. If a sizable proportion of persons with a presumed diagnosis recover and a sizable proportion show a deteriorating course, these two distinctly different outcomes suggest that the original group may actually have been composed of persons with different disorders. Similarly, if a sizable proportion of persons at follow-up appear to suffer from disorders other than the originally diagnosed disorder, that also suggests that the original group was diagnostically heterogeneous (Akiskal et al., 1978). There is no logical reason why the course of a disorder should be exactly the same in all persons with that disorder, but—in the absence of knowledge of the etiology or pathophysiological process involved in a disorder, as is the case for most of the mental disorders—it is reasonable to question whether a disorder represents a single condition if its course is extremely variable in different persons.

Treatment studies can provide evidence for the predictive validity of a category either by showing that a particular treatment is more effective for one diagnostic category than for another—for example, that lithium carbonate is more effective in the treatment of manic episodes than in the treatment of schizophrenia—or by showing that persons with a particular mental disorder respond differentially to two treatments—for example, persons with psychosexual dysfunctions respond better to behaviorally oriented therapy than to somatic therapy.

Follow-up studies of persons with different disorders can reveal the extent to which specific disorders are associated with specific complications. For example, studies indicating that incarceration in a penal institution is far more common in persons with antisocial personality disorder than in persons with other disorders provides predictive validity for that category.

Construct validity. Construct validity is the extent to which evidence supports a theory that is helpful in explaining the etiology of a disorder or the nature of the pathophysiological process. Construct validity fulfills the purpose of comprehension. Current research efforts to understand the relationship of genetic, environmental, social, and biological factors to the development of mental disorders are attempts to provide construct validity for the different mental disorders. Although the etiology of most mental disorders is unknown, some construct validity is available for many of the major categories. For example, evidence that certain mental disorders are more common among family members than in the general population suggests a genetic mechanism in the transmission of those disorders. The finding that certain mental disorders occur with high frequency among family members of persons with another disorder suggests that all those disorders may be related by a biological spectrum (Rosenthal and Kety, 1968; Winokur, 1972). The finding that the effectiveness of antipsychotic drugs is highly correlated with their antidopaminergic effect supports the dopamine theory of schizophrenia and provides construct validity for the category of schizophrenia. Similarly, the finding that persons with depression report more stressful life events than do persons without depression suggests a causal role of stress in the development of depression (Paykel et al., 1969).

MODIFYING A CLASSIFICATION ON THE BASIS OF VALIDITY EVIDENCE

As Robins, Winokur, Guze, and their colleagues (Feighner et al., 1972) noted, the usual process of validating a diagnostic category begins with a description of a distinctive clinical picture (face and descriptive validity) and proceeds with the collection of further evidence supporting the hypothesis that the original group is homogeneous. Such evidence results from follow-up studies and studies of treatment response (predictive validity) or the demonstration of a familial pattern to the disorder (construct validity).

In some instances, however, knowledge gained from studies demonstrating construct or predictive validity is used to refine or subclassify the original diagnostic category. For example, mental retardation was originally thought of as a single diagnostic entity, idiocy. With the demonstration that some cases of mental retardation had distinct biological abnormalities, the diagnostic category was subdivided into a number of specific subtypes, each defined by its association with a specific biological etiology. Further, some of those subtypes have distinctive features, such as association with particular I.Q. ranges or certain behavioral abnormalities. Therefore, a knowledge of etiology (construct validity) resulted in a refinement of the classification into specific subtypes, each with more descriptive and predictive validity than the original heterogeneous group.

Klein and Davis (1969) used the term "pharmacological dissection" to describe a similar process in which the results of differential response to pharmacological treatment (predictive validity) are used to subdivide a heterogeneous diagnostic category. For example, response to tricyclic antidepressants was useful in distinguishing persons with recurrent panic attacks from persons with other patterns of anxiety (Klein et al., 1978). Genetic studies (construct validity) can also be used in that way to refine a classification of mental disorders.

Shields and Gottesman (1972) showed how the validity of various sets of diagnostic criteria for a single psychiatric disorder can be tested by examining the relative heritability found in persons classified by those different sets of criteria. They used that approach in a large study of twins with schizophrenia. The highest heritability (ratio of identical to fraternal twin concordance rates) was found for a concept of schizophrenia that would have been regarded as too narrow in the United States and too broad in the United Kingdom. That finding suggests that both a too narrow concept and a too broad concept of schizophrenia have less validity than a less extreme concept. Genetic studies can also be used to examine whether a single phenotype (distinctive clinical picture) is the expression of more than one genotype (Gottesman and Shields, 1976). In such a case the phenotype would be subclassified according to the different genotypes.

PROCEDURAL VALIDITY: VALIDITY OF THE DIAGNOSTIC PROCESS

In much of the literature on the validity of mental disorders, there is confusion between the validity of a category of mental disorder and the validity of the evaluation procedure that a clinician uses to arrive at a diagnosis. Thus, Rosenhan (1973), in a discussion of his famous study of "pseudopatients," noted the absence of laboratory procedures, such as X-ray examination to validate a diagnosis of a fracture, that can be applied to mental disorders. Rosenhan (1973) concluded that:

> unlike most medical diagnoses, which can be validated in numerous ways, psychiatric diagnoses are maintained by consensus alone.

Whereas Rosenhan was largely correct in observing the lack of laboratory procedures to validate the evelution procedure used in arriving at a diagnosis of a mental disorder, it is not true that the diagnostic categories themselves are maintained by consensus alone (face validity). There are objective methods for demonstrating other types of validity, as described above. (The reader is likely to enjoy and benefit from a critical analysis made by Spitzer (1976) of this important study.)

One often judges the adequacy of a new diagnostic procedure by using some existing procedure as the criterion. For example, if a structured interview has been developed to permit persons with little clinical experience to make diagnoses of mental disorders, one is interested in knowing the extent to which diagnoses made in that manner agree with diagnoses made by experienced clinicians doing routine diagnostic evaluations. If one uses the experienced clinicians' judgments as the criterion and if the agreement between the two diagnostic procedures is high, the structured interview, as a new procedure, has been demonstrated to be valid as a diagnostic procedure. Similarly, if one wanted to develop specified criteria for a diagnostic category that clinicians cannot diagnose reliably because of lack of agreement on the defining features, one would want to demonstrate some agreement between diagnoses arrived at by using the proposed specified criteria for the category and diagnoses arrived at by clinical judgments not based on specified criteria (the procedure that is used as the criterion). Agreement would indicate that use of the specified criteria is valid as a procedure for making the diagnosis.

The term "procedural validity" can be used in such cases—that is, whenever the question being asked concerns the extent to which the new diagnostic procedure yields results similar to the results of an established diagnostic procedure that is used as a criterion. Procedural validity, as already noted, speaks only to the issue of the validity of the evaluation procedure and not to the validity of the diagnostic categories themselves.

It is important to demonstrate procedural validity for a new procedure, whether or not the ultimate purpose of the new procedure is to replace an existing procedure. For example, the purpose of a structured interview for use by persons with little clinical training is to establish an adequate alternative diagnostic procedure for use only in situations in which the use of experienced clinicians is not feasible, as in large-scale community surveys. On the other hand, the purpose of developing specified criteria for a diagnostic category is to modify actual clinical diagnostic practice by having clinicians use the same criteria for diagnosis and thus increase diagnostic reliability. In the example of specified criteria, one is interested in replacing the usual clinical procedure—that is, clinical judgments not based on specified criteria—with another procedure that is expected to be superior in some way to the criterion measure, with the use of specified criteria resulting in increased reliability. In that case one would be satisfied with a minimum of procedural validity—that is, low levels of agreement between the two procedures. In the example of the structured interview, however, one is interested in simulating the usual clinical procedure and would, therefore, require high levels of agreement (procedural validity).

Not all instances in which one is interested in the relationship between the results of a clinical diagnostic procedure and the results of some other test or procedure are related to the concept of procedural validity. Several examples illustrate the point: a study of the relationship between a clinical diagnosis of endogenous depression and the results of a procedure to measure urinary 3-methoxy-4-hydroxyphenylglycol (MHPG) excretion, a study of the diagnosis of borderline personality disorder and the results of the Rorschach psychological test, a study of the relationship between galvanic skin response (GSR) and a diagnosis of an anxiety disorder. In none of those cases is one asking the question, "What is the extent to which one diagnostic procedure yields results similar to another diagnostic procedure?" Rather, in all those examples the goal is to better understand the nature of the pathological process or the etiology. A finding of a relationship between MHPG excretion and endogenous depression would support a theory about the role of certain neurotransmitters in the causation of a certain kind of depressive disorder. A finding of certain characteristic responses on the Rorschach Test of persons with borderline personality disorder might clarify the nature of the psychological disturbances in that disorder. A finding of a relationship between GSR and a diagnosis of an anxiety disorder would provide clues to the nature of the pathophysiological process. In each case, positive findings provide construct validity for the diagnostic categories. Procedural validity is not involved, since in none of the cases does the alternative procedure have the immediate purpose of simulating or replacing the clinical diagnostic procedure. Of course, one of those alternative procedures may eventually be found to be powerful enough to be used as a diagnostic procedure, in which case the concept of procedural validity would become relevant.

CONCURRENT VALIDITY AND THE VALIDITY OF MENTAL DISORDERS

In psychometrics the term "concurrent validity" has been used to refer to the relationship between the results of two procedures that measure related dimensions of behavior and that are applied at the same time. Thus, in developing a self-rating scale of depressed mood, one would be interested in knowing the relationship of the severity of depressed mood to clinical judgments.

As applied to the problems of validating either diagnostic categories or diagnostic procedures, the concept of concurrent validity is confusing because it does not indicate what is being validated, either the procedure or the categories. It seems that there is little need to use the concept of concurrent validity if one makes use of the concepts of descriptive validity, construct validity, and procedural validity.

VALIDITY OF AN ENTIRE CLASSIFICATION

The validity of an entire classification of mental disorders is largely a function of the extent to which each of the individual categories in the classification has the different kinds of validity already discussed. However, two other factors contribute to the validity of an entire classification.

Coverage. Coverage is the extent to which a classification of mental disorders has specific categories for all the persons who have a mental disorder. A classification that includes only well-validated categories will not have categories for a sizable group of persons who, nevertheless, seem to have some form of mental disorder. The coverage of a classification can be indexed by the proportion of persons that cannot be adequately classified into any of the specific categories included in the classification.

The coverage of a classification of mental disorders is likely to vary according to the setting in which the classification is used. Coverage is likely to be lower in settings with large numbers of persons who are only mildly ill. That is because mild disturbances are not easily classifiable into recognized syndromes or patterns of behavior. Largely for that reason, clinicians in outpatient settings have always been more dissatisfied with standard classifications than have their colleagues practicing in inpatient settings.

Feasibility. Feasibility is the extent to which a classification of mental disorders can be successfully used by the professionals for whom it is designed. A classification that has demonstrated validity in a restricted setting, such as a research ward with diagnostically focused professionals, may be too complicated to be feasible in general outpatient clinical settings. The feasibility of the classification in such settings would need to be demonstrated by determining the extent to which practitioners in those settings are actually able to use it and judge it to be useful (face validity of entire classification).

Reliability

The reliability of a classification of mental disorders or of a specific diagnostic category is the extent to which users can agree on diagnoses applied to a series of cases. Strictly speaking, reliability is the extent to which subjects can be discriminated from each other. For that reason, a series of cases is required. If one examines the extent to which clinicians classify a single case in the same way, only agreement is determined.

Although a classification can be used reliably but may not be valid, the validity of a classification is limited by the extent to which it can be used reliably. If reliability is totally lacking, the system can have no validity. If reliability is present but only fair, there can be some validity, but that validity is limited. For that reason, it is not logical to require that reliability be good before a category is included in a classification of mental disorders for general use, as long as the category seems to have some type of validity. For example, even if a diagnosis of schizophrenia could be judged with only fair reliability, its inclusion in a classification is justified by the important treatment considerations implicit in making the diagnosis.

THE DIAGNOSTIC PROCESS AND SOURCES OF UNRELIABILITY

Typically, a diagnosis of a mental disorder is made by a clinician after interviewing a person. In addition to information collected during the interview, the clinician may have other sources of information, such as referral notes, a previous case record, or another informant. During the interview, the clinician asks a series of questions to which the person responds. The questions are, in part, guided by what areas of functioning the clinician deems most relevant, the clinician's observations, and the interpretation that the clinician makes of the person's responses and other behavior during the course of the interview. Finally, the clinician summarizes his or her clinical judgments into a diagnosis.

The reliability of diagnosis is determined by having two or more clinicians examine a series of cases and independently make diagnostic judgments. It is useful to identify different sources of unreliability in order to improve diagnostic reliability. Technically, these are referred to as sources of error variance.

Information variance. This source of unreliability is present when clinicians have different sources of information. For example, one clinician may speak with a family member who indicates that the patient has problems with alcohol; another clinician may not be told of those problems, and during the interview the patient may deny having them. Or a patient may give different responses because of different interviewing techniques and different questions being asked, as when one clinician elicits delusional material after intensive questioning about psychotic symptoms, whereas another clinician in a separate interview does not elicit such material because he or she made only a perfunctory inquiry into the presence of psychotic symptoms.

Observation and interpretation variance. This source of unreliability is present when clinicians presented with the same stimuli differ in what they notice and remember. For example, one clinician may notice that a person showed signs of psychomotor retardation, whereas another clinician may not notice the signs. This type of variance also includes differences in the significance that clinicians attach to what they observe and differences in the threshold for attaching clinical significance to certain observations. For example, two clinicians may hear the same account of how a patient believes he is being harassed by neighbors. One clinician may conclude that the context of the belief makes it uncertain whether or not a delusion is present; the other clinician may conclude that it is certainly a delusion.

Criterion variance. This source of unreliability is present when there are differences in the criteria that clinicians use to summarize data into diagnoses. When clinicians use a classification system that does not provide explicit criteria, they are forced to use their own idiosyncratic criteria for the disorders, basing these on their own personal concepts. For example, there may be disagreements as to whether or not some degree of chronicity is necessary for a diagnosis of schizophrenia.

Criterion variance also includes differences in the definitions of technical terms that clinicians use. For example, one clinician may include tangentiality as an example of "formal thought disorder," whereas another clinician may insist on disorganization of speech that renders it difficult to follow.

Subject variance and occasion variance. Subject variance refers to the true differences that exist among subjects and is not a source of error in the sense of unreliability, since it is actually the variable being measured. Occasion variance is present when a person's condition is actually different at different times. Since occasion variance reflects true facts, it is not a source of error in that it represents not disagreement but a true change.

Relative contributions. Few studies of diagnostic reliability have examined the diagnostic process in order to determine the relative contribution of each of those different sources of diagnostic disagreement to diagnostic unreliability. A notable exception is a study by Ward et al. (1962) involving independent diagnostic evaluations of 40 patients by a pair of psychiatrists who subsequently discussed the reasons for any diagnostic disagreements. Although the study used the classification in the first edition of the American Psychiatric Association's (1952) *Diagnostic and Statistical Manual, Mental Disorders* (DSM-I), it is likely that the results are generalizable to DSM-II as well, since both manuals presented similar descriptions of the diagnostic categories and neither had specified criteria. Nearly a third of the diagnostic disagreements involved either different interviewing techniques that led to differences in the material elicited (information variance) or differential weighting of the significance of symptoms and how patient material was conceptualized in terms of psychopathological symptoms (observation and interpretation variance). Almost all the remaining diagnostic disagreements, nearly two-thirds, were apparently the result of ambiguities in the definitions of the categories and in the rules for differential diagnosis (criterion variance).

METHODS FOR IMPROVING DIAGNOSTIC RELIABILITY

For each type of variance discussed above, certain procedures may be useful to minimize its effect in causing diagnostic unreliability.

Information variance can be minimized by making sure that the clinicians consider the same body of information. That can be done by making sure that the clinicians review the same sources of information, such as case records, and that the clinicians observe the same interview. Information variance can also be minimized by the use of structured interviews, so that clinicians doing separate evaluations ask the same questions.

Observation and interpretation variance is best minimized by adequate training in the skills of observation and the interpretation of behavior. Differences in interpreting the significance of certain behaviors can be minimized by the use of guidelines for determining thresholds for significance. One example is a guideline that specifies that a symptom is not considered significant unless it either interferes with functioning or leads the person to seek professional help.

Criterion variance can be minimized by clinicians' using the same specified inclusion and exclusion criteria for diagnosis. In addition, this type of variance is reduced by clinicians' using the same definitions of the technical terms that are relevant to diagnosis.

METHODS FOR ASSESSING DIAGNOSTIC RELIABILITY

There are three common methods for determining diagnostic reliability, each with its own advantages and limitations.

Joint assessment method. The most widely used method for determining diagnostic reliability is to have two or more clinicians jointly observe the same interviews, live or recorded, of a series of cases. Usually, one of the clinicians conducts the interview, and the others observe, perhaps asking occasional additional questions. The purest form of this way of determining reliability is to limit the clinicians to the use of information gathered during the interview.

The advantage of this procedure is that the subject is evaluated only once, avoiding the need for a repeat assessment that the subject may not welcome. Because information variance is minimized with this procedure, it is most helpful when the purpose of the reliability study is to focus on the adequacy of criteria for summarizing clinical information into a diagnosis. However, a disadvantage of this procedure is that it provides an inflated value for diagnostic reliability if one is interested in generalizing to the real world, in which different interviewers do ask different questions. Furthermore, with this procedure there is a likelihood that the diagnostic judgment of the interviewer, as it affects the questions asked, will inadvertently become known to the other clinicians present, so that their diagnosis may not be totally independent.

Test-retest method. Less widely used than joint assessment is a procedure in which one clinician evaluates a person at one time and another evaluates the same person at a later time. That is done for a series of cases. The two assessments must be as close together in time as possible, usually within a day or two, so as to minimize the possibility that the subject's condition changes.

The advantage of this procedure is that it helps answer the question of what is the reliability of diagnostic judgments made by clinicians, each performing his or her own evaluation. As expected, reliability obtained by this method is generally lower than that obtained by joint assessment, since information variance is minimized in the joint assessment method.

The disadvantages of the test-retest method are that it taxes the subjects with extra interviews and it is often difficult to arrange logistically. (Yet another disadvantage of this method is that the lower reliability values obtained often have a negative effect on the self-esteem of the participating clinicians and the investigators responsible for the study!)

Case record method. Less often used is the case record method, in which clinical records of a series of cases are read and evaluated independently by two or more clinicians. Usually, the clinical records have been prepared according to some standard format.

The major advantage of the case record method is that it is possible to preselect cases. For example, one may wish to include rare diagnostic cases that are unlikely to be seen in a small series of cases selected for live interviews. One may also wish to stratify the cases to make sure that the series is representative of some defined population. Since all information variance is eliminated with this method, it is particularly suited to assessing the clarity of the rules for categorization.

An important disadvantage of the case record method is that it is difficult to get case records with sufficient detail to enable a clinician to make a differential diagnosis with any degree of certainty. Another disadvantage is that it is difficult to generalize to the live situation, since the writer of the case record has already processed the raw data—that is, made judgments about the significance of various behaviors that determine what is either included or not included in the case record.

Generally, the reliability of diagnoses obtained by using case records is lower than the reliability of diagnoses based on live interviews, either joint or test-retest assessments. That is contrary to what one might expect, since information variance has been eliminated in the case record method. The explanation may be that live interviews provide important diagnostic information that is left out of case records or, conversely, that case records frequently provide ambiguous information that interferes with making a differential diagnosis.

INDEXING RELIABILITY

It is possible to index the reliability of a diagnostic class—for example, agreement on whether or not an affective disorder is present—or a specific diagnosis, such as Major Depression. Less useful and more difficult to interpret is the over-all reliability of the diagnostic classes—that is, the extent to which there is agreement on class membership across classes—and over-all reliability of the specific diagnoses—that is, the extent to which there is agreement on membership in each specific diagnostic category across all categories.

One of the problems that occurs in comparing the results of different studies of diagnostic reliability is an inconsistency and incompleteness in the manner of reporting results. Moreover, there are statistical problems in choosing an appropriate index of agreement for nominal categories, such as diagnostic categories, as opposed to ordinal categories, such as severity of psychopathology.

A suitable statistic was proposed by Cohen (1960) and was later generalized to the problems of diagnosis of mental disorders. The index, kappa, contrasts the observed rate of agreement with the rate expected by chance. Kappa varies from negative values for less than chance agreement through zero for chance agreement to +1.0 for perfect agreement. Kappa has an advantage over the usual methods of reporting agreement, such as simple percentage agreement, in that it takes into account the base rates of the diagnoses, so that only agreement not accounted for by chance alone is indexed.

All reliability studies of diagnosis should report their results in terms of kappa for a single rater, even if more than two raters are involved. Whenever the study includes diagnostic categories that are rarely diagnosed—for example, fewer than 5 per cent of all the persons in the study—it is also helpful to note the proportion of persons given each diagnosis by at least one of the raters. In that way, the reader can assess the stability of the results (Bartko and Carpenter, 1976).

History of Classifications of Mental Disorders

Menninger et al. (1963) presented a compendium of classifications of mental disorders from ancient times to the modern era. According to Menninger et al., the first specific description of a mental illness appeared about 3000 B.C. in a depiction of senile deterioration ascribed to Prince Ptah-hotep. The syndromes of melancholia and hysteria appeared in the Sumerian and Egyptian literature as far back as 2600 B.C. In the Ebers Papyrus (about 1500 B.C.) both senile deterioration and alcoholism were described.

Hippocrates (about 460–370 B.C.) is usually regarded as the one who introduced the concept of psychiatric illness into medicine. His writings described acute mental disturbances with fever (perhaps delirium), acute mental disturbances without fever (probably analogous to functional psychoses but called mania), chronic disturbances without fever (called melancholia), hysteria (broader than its later use), and Scythian disease (similar to transvestism).

Caelius Aurelianus, a 5th-century physician living in the Roman Empire, described homosexuality as an affliction of a diseased mind found in both men and women. Mental deficiency and dementia were noted by Swiss Renaissance physician Felix Platter (1536–1614).

Before the time of the English physician Thomas Sydenham (1624–1689), all illness, despite the differences in appearance between the different syndromes, was attributed to a single pathogenic process, either a disturbance of the humoral balance or a disturbance in the tensions of the solid tissues. Sydenham, on the other hand, believed that each illness had a specific cause. He called for the study of morbid processes and likened the investigation of the specificity of diseases to the botanist's search for species of plants.

Philippe Pinel (1745–1826), a French physician, simplified the complex diagnostic systems that preceded him by recognizing four fundamental clinical types: mania (conditions with acute excitement or fury), melancholia (depressive disorders and delusions with limited topics), dementia (lack of cohesion in ideas), and idiotism (idiocy and organic dementia). Pinel thus reacted against the specific disease entity tradition of Sydenham and went back to a noncomplex Hippocratic system of classification. All mental illnesses were in a category of physical illnesses called neuroses, which were defined as functional diseases of the nervous system—that is, illnesses that were not accompanied by fever, inflammation, hemorrhage, or anatomical lesion.

By the 19th century, mental disorder began to be regarded consistently as the manifestation of physical pathology, and scientists searched for specific lesions, parallel to the investigation of bodily diseases. Benedict-Augustin Morel (1809–1873) was the first to use the course of an illness as a basis for classification. His *démence précoce* was not a disease entity but a particular form of the course of mental disease.

Karl Ludwig Kahlbaum (1828–1899), a German descriptive psychiatrist who foreshadowed Kraepelin, introduced the concepts of (1) temporary symptom complex, as opposed to the underlying disease, (2) the distinction between organic and nonorganic mental disorder, and (3) considering the patient's age at the time of onset and the characteristic development of the disorder as bases for classification.

The finding made by Antoine Bayle in 1822 that progressive paresis was a specific organic disease of the brain and the discovery of Paul Broca (1824–1880) in 1861 that some forms of aphasia were related to definite lesions of the cortex increased attempts to base all classifications of mental disorders on demonstrated brain lesions or disturbances in vascular and nutritional physiology. Those findings led Wilhelm Griesinger (1818–1868) to coin the slogan "mental diseases are brain diseases." Because the knowledge of brain pathology was limited, he recognized the need for a provisional functional category for mental illnesses with as-yet unknown somatic pathology.

In the last 2 decades of the 19th century, Emil Kraepelin (1856–1926) synthesized three approaches: the clinical-descriptive, the somatic, and the consideration of the course of the disorder. He viewed mental illnesses as organic disease entities that could be classified on the basis of knowledge about their causes, courses, and outcomes. He brought the manic and depressive disturbances together into one illness, manic-depressive psychosis, and distinguished it, on the basis of its periods of remission, from the chronic deteriorating illness called dementia precox, which Bleuler later renamed schizophrenia. Kraepelin also recognized paranoia as distinct from dementia precox, distinguished delirium from dementia, and, for the first time in a classification system of mental disorders, included the concepts of psychogenic neuroses and psychopathic personalities (the "born criminal," the "unstable," "pathological liars and swindlers," and "litigious paranoiacs").

The basic approach of Kraepelin toward classification was to search for that combination of clinical features that would best predict outcome. In contrast, Eugen Bleuler (1857–1939) based his classification system on an inferred psychopathological process, such as a disturbance in the associative process in schizophrenia.

The personality disorders were first noted in the psychiatric literature by J. C. Prichard in 1835 with his introduction of the concepts of moral insanity and moral imbecility. In 1891 August Koch coined the phrases "psychopathic personality" and "psychopathic constitutional inferiority."

Sigmund Freud (1856–1939), after studying hysteria, the prototypical neurosis, went on to divide the neuroses into the actual neuroses, the result of dammed-up sexual excitation, and the psychoneuroses, the result of unconscious conflict and compromise symptom formation (Freud, 1963). As interest in the actual neuroses diminished, the term "neurosis" came to be synonymous with "psychoneurosis." Freud recognized only the following subtypes of neurosis: anxiety neurosis, anxiety hysteria (phobia), obsessive-compulsive neurosis, and hysteria. It was not until much later, in the American Medical Association's (1935) *Standard Classified Nomenclature of Disease*, that reactive depression was added as an additional subtype of the neuroses, later to find its way, with other neurotic subtypes, into DSM-I and DSM-II. Freud's dynamic concepts and interest in the psychopathology of everyday life led to an expansion of the boundaries of what was considered mental illness to include mild forms of personality deviation.

As Akiskal and McKinney (1973) noted, despite the advances in the understanding of mental disorders in the past 50 years, the major categories of mental disorders in the standard classification systems are based primarily on the concepts of Kraepelin and Bleuler—organic mental disorders, affective disorders, and schizophrenia—and Freud—neuroses and personality disorders.

ALTERNATIVES TO THE CLASSIFICATION OF MENTAL DISORDERS

In the 1960's several schools of thought challenged the need for a classification of mental disorders or even for the concept of mental disorder. The most radical critique came from Thomas S. Szasz (1961), who summarized his position in the title of one of his books, *The Myth of Mental Illness*. His arguments rest on four assumptions, all based on equating the concept of mental disorder with mental disease: (1) Only symptoms with demonstrable physical lesions qualify as manifestations of disease. (2) Mental symptoms are subjective in nature and depend on sociocultural norms, whereas physical symptoms are objective and independent of cultural and ethical norms. (3) Mental symptoms are expressions of problems of living. (4) Mental problems are not illnesses but, rather, conflicts over ways of achieving social values that are disguised by the psychiatric profession through the use of medical terminology.

However, the concept of mental disorder does not necessarily imply acceptance of the medical model and the equation of mental disorder with disease. The other assumptions made by Szasz were found wanting in critical commentaries by Akiskal and McKinney (1973), Ausubel (1961), Reiss (1972), and Pies (1979). Szasz never offered evidence that conceptualizing the kinds of problems that are ordinarily classified as mental disorders as mere interpersonal conflicts, as he advocated, is useful in solving or managing those problems.

Menninger et al. (1963) set forth the notion that there is only one mental illness; therefore, there is no need for a classification of mental disorders. Menninger et al. argued that all the so-called mental disorders are merely manifestations of five stages of dyscontrol in the unitary process of mental illness. The first stage of dyscontrol is nervousness, a slight but definite impairment of adaptive control, organization, and coping. The second stage is increased disorganization and includes the traditional neurotic syndromes. The third stage is undisguised aggression. The fourth stage is extreme disorganization, regression, and reality repudiation, which includes the traditional psychoses. The fifth stage is malignant anxiety and depression eventuating in death. Menninger et al. apparently recognized the traditional diagnostic categories but believed that distinctions between them are trivial compared with the level of disorganization that they represent.

Social learning theorists—such as Bandura (1969), Kanfer and Saslow (1969), and Paul (1974)—presented comprehensive criticisms of classifications of mental disorders. They pointed to the low reliability of existing classifications and the generally poor relationship between diagnosis and treatment. They even questioned the value of diagnosis as a shorthand method for communicating an accurate clinical picture. They argued that the importance of environmental variables in initiating and maintaining pathological behavior is ignored when attention is focused on the classification of mental *disorders*. They asserted that all behavior is subject to the principles of learning and that what distinguishes normal from pathological behavior are the value judgments made by an observer, rather than an intrinsic property of the behavior.

The alternative to classifying mental disorders that Kanfer and Saslow (1969) proposed was a behavioral diagnosis, in which the person's problems are described in seven areas: (1) the behavioral excesses or deficits that constitute the person's complaint and the behavioral assets available for use in therapy; (2) the factors that maintain the problem behaviors; (3) a motivational analysis to determine the dominant positive and negative reinforcement contingencies; (4) an analysis of the relevant biological, sociological, and behavioral events in the person's history; (5) the person's capacity for participation in the treatment as measured by his self-control; (6) social resources in the person's environment that affect his current behavior or may affect the treatment; and (7) an analysis of the limits placed on therapeutic goals by the person's social and physical environment.

Although the notion of behavioral diagnosis was originally presented as an alternative to traditional diagnosis, it can be viewed as a valuable system that can be used in conjunction with a standard diagnostic formulation and treatment plan.

HISTORY OF OFFICIAL CLASSIFICATIONS

The first official system for tabulating mental disorder in the United States was initially used for the decennial census of 1840. It contained only one category and lumped together the idiotic and the insane. Forty years later, great progress was made when, in the census of 1880, the mentally ill were subdivided into seven separate categories. It is sobering to realize that the conceptual issues that modern classifiers wrestle with today were well recognized by the authors of that system. In the introductory remarks to the census office report, the authors lamented about the difficulties of creating a classification system for the mentally ill (Kramer, 1973):

> Much effort has been put forth to secure uniformity in the classification of the insane in every country of the world; but it seems impossible for those best qualified to form an opinion to agree upon any scheme which can be devised. Some classifications are based upon symptoms and some upon physical causes; others are a mixture of the two; and still others take into account the complications of insanity. For the purposes of the census, it seemed to us advisable to disregard all minute subdivisions and to adopt a simple analysis on the broadest possible outlines.

In 1889 the International Congress of Mental Science in Paris adopted a classification proposed by a commission headed by Morel that included 11 categories (Tuke, 1890):

> including all those "upon which the majority [of the commission's members] was unanimous" and omitting those "upon which opinion was divided."

Those early classifications are presented in Table II.

In 1923, in order to conduct a special census of patients in hospitals for mental disease, the Bureau of the Census used a classification system developed in collaboration with the American Psychiatric Association (then the American Medico-Psychological Association) and

TABLE II
Early Classifications of Mental Disorders

1840 U. S. Census	1880 U. S. Census	1889 International Congress of Mental Science
Idiocy (insanity)	Mania	Mania
	Melancholia	Melancholia
	Monomania	Periodical insanity
	Paresis	Progressive systematic insanity
	Dementia	Dementia
	Dipsomania	Organic and senile dementia
	Epilepsy	General paralysis
		Insane neuroses
		Toxic insanity
		Moral and impulsive insanity
		Idiocy, etc.

the National Committee for Mental Health. That system had been adopted by the American Psychiatric Association in 1917 and was used until 1935, when it was revised for incorporation into the first edition of the American Medical Association's (1935) *Standard Classified Nomenclature of Disease.*

That 1935 classification was designed primarily for chronic inpatients and, therefore, proved inadequate for use with World War II psychiatric casualties, who required classifications for acute disturbances, psychosomatic disorders, and personality disorders, which were not represented in the 1935 classification. In addition, the system was considered anachronistic by the increasing number of psychodynamically oriented psychiatrists who were emerging from training programs and whose interests lay more in the treatment of private outpatients. For those reasons, shortly after World War II the Veterans Administration and the military services developed their own systems.

In 1948 the World Health Organization (WHO) assumed the responsibility for revising what had previously been called the International List of Causes of Death and that had been revised every 10 or 20 years since its inception in 1900. The sixth revision (World Health Organization, 1948) was renamed the *Manual of the International Classification of Diseases, Injuries, and Causes of Death* (ICD-6) and contained for the first time a classification of mental disorders, entitled "mental, psychoneurotic, and personality disorders." It contained 10 categories of psychosis, nine categories of psychoneurosis, and seven categories of disorders of character, behavior, and intelligence.

In spite of the fact that American psychiatrists had participated in the development of the mental disorders section of ICD-6, the absence of such important categories as the dementias, many personality disorders, and adjustment disorders rendered it unsatisfactory for use in the United States. Other countries apparently also found the mental disorders section unsatisfactory, since only Finland, New Zealand, Peru, Thailand, and the United Kingdom made official use of it.

The lack of widespread international acceptance of that section of ICD-6 led the World Health Organization to ask Erwin Stengel, a British psychiatrist, to investigate the situation. Stengel (1959) concluded that the lack of general acceptance of the international classification of mental disorders was due to the fact that the diagnostic terms frequently had etiological implications that were at odds with various theoretical schools of psychiatry. His suggestion was to develop a classification in which all diagnoses should be described operationally and without etiological implications in a companion glossary. (As the furor over the elimination of neuroses in DSM-III has indicated, this is not so easily done!)

DSM-I. In 1951 the United States Public Health Service commissioned a working party, with representation from the American Psychiatric Association, to develop an alternative to the mental disorders section of ICD-6 for use in this country. That document, prepared largely by George Raines and based heavily on the Veterans Administration classification system developed by William Menninger, was published in 1952 by the American Psychiatric Association as *Diagnostic and Statistical Manual, Mental Disorders* (DSM-I).

The significance of DSM-I was that it replaced the outdated mental disorders section of the AMA's *Standard Classified Nomenclature of Disease* and the systems devised by the military and the Veterans Administration, and for the first time it provided a glossary of definitions of categories.

In the definitions of the diagnostic categories, the frequent use of the term "reaction," as in "schizophrenic reaction" and "psychoneurotic reaction," expressed the strong environmental orientation of Adolf Meyer; and the frequent reference to defense mechanisms, particularly as an explanation of the neuroses and personality disorders, reflected the wide acceptance of psychoanalytic concepts. Despite its widespread influence and impact on American psychiatric literature, DSM-I was not universally accepted as the official nomenclature throughout the country. The New York State Department of Mental Hygiene, for example, retained the old *Standard Classified Nomenclature of Disease* until 1968.

Because most of the other countries that used ICD also found the mental disorders section of the sixth revision unsatisfactory, the World

Health Organization sponsored an international effort to develop a classification system for mental disorders that would improve on ICD-6 and be acceptable to all member nations. That task was coordinated in this country by the United States Public Health Service, which sent American representatives to the international committees preparing revisions of the mental disorders section. ICD-8 was approved by the World Health Organization in 1966 and became effective in 1968. (The mental disorders section of ICD-7, which appeared in 1955, was identical to the mental disorders section of ICD-6.)

DSM-II. In 1965 the American Psychiatric Association, which had maintained close ties with the international committees preparing ICD-8, assigned its Committee on Nomenclature and Statistics, under the chairmanship of Ernest M. Gruenberg, the task of preparing for the American Psychiatric Association a new diagnostic manual of mental disorders based on the ICD-8 classification but defining each disorder for use in the United States. Such definitions were necessary because, when ICD-8 was first published, it did not have an accompanying glossary. It was only much later, in 1972, 4 years after DSM-II was adopted, that a glossary was published.

A draft of the second edition of the American Psychiatric Association's *Diagnostic and Statistical Manual of Mental Disorders* (DSM-II) was circulated in 1967 to 120 psychiatrists known to have a special interest in the area of diagnosis, and it was revised on the basis of their criticisms and suggestions. After further study the draft was adopted by the American Psychiatric Association in 1967 and published and officially accepted throughout the country in 1968. At about the same time, the General Register Office in Great Britain published its own glossary, largely written by Sir Aubrey Lewis, which interpreted the ICD-8 classification (General Register Office, 1968).

The DSM-II classification consisted of 10 major categories:

I. Mental retardation. This category had been called "mental deficiency" in DSM-I and had been limited to idiopathic or familial varieties of the disorder. In DSM-II it was subdivided according to both severity and etiology.

II. Organic brain syndromes. The DSM-I distinction of acute (reversible) versus chronic (irreversible) was dropped and replaced by the subdivision into psychoses associated with organic brain syndromes and nonpsychotic organic brain syndromes.

III. Psychoses not attributed to physical conditions listed previously. This section included the functional psychoses: schizophrenia, major affective disorders, paranoid states, and other psychoses (psychotic depressive reaction). The DSM-II category of schizophrenia included latent type, not included in DSM-I. The DSM-I category of involutional psychotic reaction was subdivided into involutional melancholia and involutional paranoid state in DSM-II.

IV. Neuroses. This category included disorders in which the chief characteristic was anxiety, whether "felt and expressed directly" or "controlled unconsciously and automatically by conversion, displacement and various other psychological mechanisms." The DSM-I subtypes were retained, with the addition in DSM-II of neurasthenic neurosis, depersonalization neurosis, and hypochondriacal neurosis.

V. Personality disorders and certain other nonpsychotic mental disorders. This category included personality disorders, sexual deviation, alcoholism, and drug dependence. In DSM-I all those categories were subsumed under the rubric of "personality disorders." In the personality disorders section itself, DSM-II added hysterical personality and eliminated the somewhat related DSM-I category of emotionally unstable personality.

VI. Psychophysiological disorders. This group of disorders was characterized by physical symptoms caused by emotional factors and involving a single organ system, usually under autonomic nervous system innervation. The disorders were subdivided by the organ system involved.

VII. Special symptoms. This category was for a small list of symptoms occurring in the absence of any other mental disorder and most likely seen in children. DSM-II added several symptoms to the DSM-I list.

VIII. Transient situational disturbances. This category was reserved for more or less transient disorders of any severity, including those of psychotic proportions, that occurred as acute reactions to overwhelming environmental stress in persons without any apparent underlying mental disorders. Transient situational personality disorders in DSM-I did not specifically include acute reactions to stress that reached psychotic proportions, as did the category of transient situational disturbances in DSM-II.

IX. Behavior disorders of childhood and adolescence. This category included six specific diagnoses. DSM-I had not provided a separate category for disorders of childhood and adolescence.

X. Conditions without manifest psychiatric disorder and nonspecific conditions. This category, not present in DSM-I, performed the function of encompassing the "conditions of individuals who are psychiatrically normal but who nevertheless have severe enough problems to warrant examination by a psychiatrist." These conditions are, therefore, not mental disorders. This category was subdivided into three groups: social maladjustment without manifest psychiatric disorder, nonspecific conditions, and no mental disorder.

Unlike DSM-I, which discouraged multiple diagnoses, DSM-II explicitly encouraged clinicians to diagnose every disorder that was present, even if one was causally related to another—for example, alcoholism secondary to a depression.

The reaction to the publication of DSM-II in 1968 was mixed. Those who were most critical of DSM-II regarded it, as one commentator stated, as a

> giant leap into the 19th century and a return to a Kraepelinian view of mental disorders as fixed disease entities.

That despite the fact that the word "disease" was limited to certain categories in the mental retardation and organic brain syndromes sections and even though the word "illness" appeared only in the manic-depressive conditions, where it was adopted to avoid the ICD term manic-depressive psychosis. Karl Menninger (1969) summarized the view when he said:

> This year the American Psychiatric Association took a great step backward when it abandoned the principle used in the simple useful nosology [DSM-I] which Dr. Will [William Menninger] worked so hard to get installed. . . . In the interest of uniformity, in the interest of having some kind of international code of designations for different kinds of human troubles, in the interest of statistics and computers, the American medical scientists were asked to repudiate some of the advances they had made in conceptualization and in designation of mental illness.

Although child psychiatrists were pleased that DSM-II, unlike DSM-I, had a special category for children and adolescents, many were disappointed that the Group for the Advancement of Psychiatry's (1966) *Psychopathological Disorders in Childhood: Theoretical Considerations and a Proposed Classification*, which had been available for several years, was not used by the committee that developed DSM-II.

Many applauded the elimination of the term "reaction," which had been appended to most of the DSM-I terms, as an honest retreat from the position that, by adding the term "reaction" to diagnostic labels, one thereby somehow communicates some important knowledge about the etiology of the mental disorders. As Gruenberg (1969) explained:

> The routinizing of the word "reaction" in our standard nomenclature [DSM-I] has accomplished little that is positive—it has given many psychiatrists the false notion that mental disorders are reactions of the organism to circumstances but that tuberculosis and diabetes and nephritis and measles and mumps are "things" independent of the patient's nature. For all medical diseases are also reactions of the organism to certain life circumstances and do not exist independently of the people who are sick.

TABLE III
ICD-9 Classification of Mental Disorders*

ORGANIC PSYCHOTIC CONDITIONS
Senile and pre-senile organic psychotic conditions
290.0 Senile dementia, simple type
290.1 Pre-senile dementia
290.2 Senile dementia, depressed or paranoid type
290.3 Senile dementia with acute confusional state
290.4 Arteriosclerotic dementia
290.8 Other
290.9 Unspecified

Alcoholic psychoses
291.0 Delirium tremens
291.1 Korsakov's psychosis, alcoholic
291.2 Other alcoholic dementia
291.3 Other alcoholic hallucinosis
291.4 Pathological drunkenness
291.5 Alcoholic jealousy
291.8 Other
291.9 Unspecified

Drug psychoses
292.0 Drug withdrawal syndrome
292.1 Paranoid and/or hallucinatory states induced by drugs
292.2 Pathological drug intoxication
292.8 Other
292.9 Unspecified

Transient organic psychotic conditions
293.0 Acute confusional state
293.1 Subacute confusional state
293.8 Other
293.9 Unspecified

Other organic psychotic conditions (chronic)
294.0 Korsakov's psychosis (non-alcoholic)
294.1 Dementia in conditions classified elsewhere
294.8 Other
294.9 Unspecified

OTHER PSYCHOSES
Schizophrenic psychoses
295.0 Simple type
295.1 Hebephrenic type
295.2 Catatonic type
295.3 Paranoid type
295.4 Acute schizophrenic episode
295.5 Latent schizophrenia
295.6 Residual schizophrenia
295.7 Schizo-affective type
295.8 Other
295.9 Unspecified

Affective psychoses
296.0 Manic-depressive psychosis, manic type
296.1 Manic depressive psychosis, depressed type
296.2 Manic-depressive psychosis, circular type but currently manic
296.3 Manic-depressive psychosis, circular type but currently depressed

296.4 Manic-depressive psychosis, circular type, mixed
296.5 Manic-depressive psychosis, circular type, current condition not specified
296.6 Manic-depressive psychosis, other and unspecified
296.8 Other
296.9 Unspecified

Paranoid states
297.0 Paranoid state, simple
297.1 Paranoia
297.2 Paraphrenia
297.3 Induced psychosis
297.8 Other
297.9 Unspecified

Other nonorganic psychoses
298.0 Depressive type
298.1 Excitative type
298.2 Reactive confusion
298.3 Acute paranoid reaction
298.4 Psychogenic paranoid psychosis
298.8 Other and unspecified reactive psychosis
298.9 Unspecified psychosis

Psychoses with origin specific to childhood
299.0 Infantile autism
299.1 Disintegrative psychosis
299.8 Other
299.9 Unspecified

NEUROTIC DISORDERS, PERSONALITY DISORDERS, AND OTHER NONPSYCHOTIC MENTAL DISORDERS
Neurotic disorders
300.0 Anxiety states
300.1 Hysteria
300.2 Phobic state
300.3 Obsessive-compulsive disorder
300.4 Neurotic depression
300.5 Neurasthenia
300.6 Depersonalization syndrome
300.7 Hypochondriasis
300.8 Other
300.9 Unspecified

Personality disorders
301.0 Paranoid
301.1 Affective
301.2 Schizoid
301.3 Explosive
301.4 Anankastic
301.5 Hysterical
301.6 Asthenic
301.7 With predominantly sociopathic or asocial manifestations
301.8 Other
301.9 Unspecified

Sexual deviations and disorders
302.0 Homosexuality
302.1 Bestiality
302.2 Paedophilia

302.3 Transvestism
302.4 Exhibitionism
302.5 Transsexualism
302.6 Disorders of psychosexual identity
302.7 Frigidity and impotence
302.8 Other
302.9 Unspecified

303. Alcohol dependence

Drug dependence
304.0 Morphine type
304.1 Barbiturate type
304.2 Cocaine
304.3 Cannabis
304.4 Amphetamine type and other psycho-stimulants
304.5 Hallucinogens
304.6 Other
304.7 Combinations of morphine type drug with any other
304.8 Combinations excluding morphine type drug
304.9 Unspecified

Nondependent abuse of drugs
305.0 Alcohol
305.1 Tobacco
305.2 Cannabis
305.3 Hallucinogens
305.4 Barbiturates and tranquilizers
305.5 Morphine type
305.6 Cocaine type
305.7 Amphetamine type
305.8 Antidepressants
305.9 Other, mixed or unspecified

Physical conditions arising from mental factors
306.0 Musculoskeletal
306.1 Respiratory
306.2 Cardiovascular
306.3 Skin
306.4 Gastro-intestinal
306.5 Genito-urinary
306.6 Endocrine
306.7 Organs of special sense
306.8 Other
306.9 Unspecified

Special symptoms or syndromes not elsewhere classified
307.0 Stammering and stuttering
307.1 Anorexia nervosa
307.2 Tics
307.3 Stereotyped repetitive movements
307.4 Specific disorders of sleep
307.5 Other disorders of eating
307.6 Enuresis
307.7 Encopresis
307.8 Psychalgia
307.9 Other and unspecified

Acute reaction to stress
308.0 Predominant disturbance of emotions
308.1 Predominant disturbance of

TABLE III—*Continued*

		consciousness
308.2	Predominant psychomotor disturbance	
308.3	Other	
308.4	Mixed	
308.9	Unspecified	

Adjustment reaction
309.0　Brief depressive reaction
309.1　Prolonged depressive reaction
309.2　With predominant disturbance of other emotions
309.3　With predominant disturbance of conduct
309.4　With mixed disturbance of emotions and conduct
309.8　Other
309.9　Unspecified

Specific nonpsychotic mental disorders following organic brain damage
310.0　Frontal lobe syndrome
310.1　Cognitive or personality change of other type
310.2　Postconcussional syndrome
310.8　Other
310.9　Unspecified

311.　Depressive disorder, not elsewhere classified
Disturbance of conduct not elsewhere classified
312.0　Unsocialized disturbance of conduct
312.1　Socialized disturbance of conduct
312.2　Compulsive conduct disorder
312.3　Mixed disturbance of conduct and emotions
312.8　Other
312.9　Unspecified

Disturbance of emotions specific to childhood and adolescence
313.0　With anxiety and fearfulness
313.1　With misery and unhappiness
313.2　With sensitivity, shyness and social withdrawal
313.3　Relationship problems
313.8　Other or mixed
313.9　Unspecified

Hyperkinetic syndrome of childhood
314.0　Simple disturbance of activity and attention

314.1　Hyperkinesis with developmental delay
314.2　Hyperkinetic conduct disorder
314.8　Other
314.9　Unspecified

Specific delays in development
315.0　Specific reading retardation
315.1　Specific arithmetical retardation
315.2　Other specific learning difficulties
315.3　Developmental speech or language disorder
315.4　Specific motor retardation
315.5　Mixed development disorder
315.8　Other
315.9　Unspecified

316.　Psychic factors associated with diseases classified elsewhere

317.　Mild mental retardation

Other specified mental retardation
318.0　Moderate mental retardation
318.1　Severe mental retardation
318.2　Profound mental retardation

319.　Unspecified mental retardation

* From World Health Organization. *Manual of the International Classification of Diseases, Injuries, and Causes of Death*, rev. 9. World Health Organization, Geneva, 1978.

Those who were most enthusiastic pointed to the potential benefits that might accrue to international research and to communication between psychiatrists of different nations because this country had adopted a system based on the *International Classification of Diseases.*

In 1975 the ninth revision of the ICD classification of mental disorders was published, together with a glossary, to go into effect in 1978. Although many minor changes in the ICD-8 classification and glossary were made, there were no radical changes. As with ICD-8, psychiatrists from the United States provided some limited input into the final document.

An examination of the ICD-9 classification (see Table III) reveals a major difficulty in developing a classification that is acceptable internationally. It is far easier to allow each country to introduce terms that will be used only by that country than it is to insist that different countries use a single agreed-on terminology. Thus, as Kendell (1975) noted, the ICD-9 classification actually includes several "alternative and quite incompatible" ways of classifying depression. For example, definitions of the categories of manic-depressive psychosis, depressed type, and depressive type of nonorganic psychosis are not mutually exclusive.

Recent Methodological Developments

In the past 2 decades there have been several significant methodological developments in the study of the diagnostic process, in procedures for making diagnoses, and in ways to classify and define the diagnostic categories.

CROSS-NATIONAL STUDIES

Two major cross-national studies have investigated the diagnostic process in several countries. The United States-United Kingdom Diagnostic Project (Cooper et al., 1972) was begun in the early 1960's to investigate the wide discrepancy with which affective disorders and schizophrenia were diagnosed in the United States and England. A large number of patients

were studied in each country by a group of project psychiatrists who used the Present State Examination (PSE) to evaluate the patients in order to determine whether the differences in diagnostic practices in the two countries were due to differences in the patients or to differences in the diagnostic concepts used in the two countries. The findings indicated that there were only insignificant differences in the patients in the two countries and that differences in the rates of diagnoses were due to a very broad concept of schizophrenia in use in the United States as compared with a quite narrow concept in England.

By showing groups of American and British psychiatrists videotapes of interviews, the project also demonstrated important cross-national differences in the threshold for recognizing certain symptoms (observation and interpretation variance) and in the definitions of certain technical terms (criterion variance). American psychiatrists tended to rate higher levels of psychopathology in all areas, particularly those suggesting schizophrenia, and had a much broader concept of thought disorder than did British psychiatrists. Those findings suggest that international standardization of diagnostic terminology requires reducing not only criterion variance (a difficult task in itself) but also observation and interpretation variance (an even more difficult task).

The International Pilot Study of Schizophrenia, sponsored by the World Health Organization (1973), set out to determine whether the use of standardized instruments and procedures by teams of clinicians working in both developed and undeveloped countries would result in reliable judgments of psychopathology. The project also sought to determine whether similar groups of persons with schizophrenia could be identified in each of the participating countries and whether follow-up studies would reveal cross-national differences in outcome. The major assessment instrument was the Present State Examination, which was translated into seven languages so that it could be used with patients in all the participating field research centers—Aarhus in Denmark, Agra in India, Ibadan in Nigeria, London, Moscow, Prague, Taipei, and Washington, D.C.

The results indicated that high reliability among interviewers was achieved in all the various countries in the study. Furthermore, in all the centers except Moscow and Washington, the same concept of schizophrenia was held by virtually all the local psychiatrists; in Moscow and Washington there was a much broader conception of schizophrenia. Despite those differences, with the use of a computer program (CATEGO, discussed below) for summarizing the data into diagnoses, it was possible to identify, in each center, a group of persons with a distinct clinical picture of schizophrenia that was consistent across all centers.

Follow-up studies indicated a complicated interaction between duration of illness prior to evaluation, level of development of the country, and outcome (Sartorius et al., 1978) that has implications for defining schizophrenia in a way that maximizes its predictive validity.

COMPUTER PROGRAMS

Because of the large contribution of criterion variance to the unreliability of diagnosis, it was logical to turn to computers in the hope that a standardized computer program would replace the clinician's task of summarizing data into a diagnosis. All the clinician needs to do is make accurate observations that are then fed into a computer program. The computer program, using some kind of algorithm, processes the data and yields a diagnosis. The problem of reliability is resolved in the sense that, given the same data, the computer program always yields the same diagnosis.

Computer programs for diagnosis have used either a statistical approach or a logical decision-tree model. In the statistical approach (Birnbaum and Maxwell, 1960; Melrose et al., 1970; Sletten et al., 1971) data are first collected on a sample of persons, for each of whom the diagnosis is known and for each of whom a series of measures is available. This is called the developmental sample, and it is used to derive the empirical classification scheme. Using each person's observed series of scores, the computerized classification scheme quantifies how close the person is to each diagnostic group, and the person is assigned the diagnosis to which he or she is closest. Whatever statistical method is used, it must be validated on new samples because of chance features in the developmental sample that contributed to the effectiveness of the algorithm.

In the logical decision-tree model the computer program consists of a sequence of statements, each of which is evaluated as either true or false. The truth or falsity of each statement rules out one or more diagnoses and determines which statement is to be examined next. Some statements may specify the presence of a single sign or symptom, others specify that a numeric score is in a certain range, and still others specify a complex pattern of both signs and scores. That approach is similar to the differential diagnostic method used by clinicians in making a diagnosis. It has an obvious advantage over the statistical model, in that it does not require a data base and does not depend on the specific characteristics of a developmental sample.

The logical decision-tree model was first used by Spitzer and Endicott (1968, 1969, 1974) in a series of computer programs—DIAGNO I, DIAGNO II, and DIAGNO III. DIAGNO I and DIAGNO II used information collected on structured interview schedules; DIAGNO III used information collected during routine clinical diagnostic interviews and recorded on forms used in an automated record-keeping system. DIAGNO III was the most complicated of the programs; it used information about both current and past psychopathology as input data to yield an output that included 46 standard DSM-II diagnoses. All the DIAGNO programs attempted to simulate established clinical practice. Therefore, no attempt was made to improve the validity of the diagnoses themselves by using decision rules that deviated from routine clinical practice.

Wing et al. (1974) have used the same logical decision-tree model to develop a computer program, CATEGO, that uses data collected on their structured interview schedule, the Present State Examination (Wing et al., 1967). In the DIAGNO approach, diagnoses or groups of diagnoses are ruled out sequentially, as in the differential diagnostic process. In the CATEGO program, all the data are reduced to a number of syndromes that are then condensed to six descriptive categories. The final output for each case includes all the syndromes and descriptive categories present and provisional diagnostic class or diagnosis.

The CATEGO program focuses on the major categories of schizophrenia and affective disorders, with a heavy reliance on the use of Schneiderian first-rank symptoms in identifying schizophrenia. Unlike the DIAGNO programs, whose major contribution was limited to the demonstration that computer programs could simulate clinical diagnostic practice, the CATEGO program has been successfully used to derive standard diagnoses in the International Pilot Study of Schizophrenia and in many other major diagnostic studies. The greater usefulness of the CATEGO program is largely due to the fact that the algorithms are based on a carefully thought-out conceptual scheme, rather than designed merely to simulate established clinical practice.

MATHEMATICALLY DERIVED DIAGNOSTIC TYPES

With the advent of computers, it became possible to explore the possibility of deriving diagnostic categories by applying various statistical methods to clinical ratings. It has been hoped that new diagnostic categories or syndromes would emerge that had not been detected by clinical practice. The simplest model, factor analysis, is based on correlating a large number of traits, usually symptoms of the person's current episode of illness. The result is a series of factors that describe dimensions of symptoms on which people vary (Lorr, 1966). A factor represents a dimension of behavior composed of a group of items that co-vary; however, many clinically useful diagnostic categories are composed of several dimensions of behavior. Another method, pattern analysis, involves comparing profiles of patients so that similarity on all traits taken together is examined (Overall and Hollister, 1964). The major difficulty with that procedure is ignorance as to what should constitute the item set of traits and the arbitrariness of the various measures of similarity. Another procedure, cluster analysis, involves an attempt to derive clusters of items that identify homogeneous sets of persons. A similar problem of the arbitrariness of indexing similarity exists with that procedure.

Unfortunately, mathematical techniques have not fulfilled their promise. Even when a mathematical procedure is able to identify a new diagnostic type and cross-validate the result in another sample, it is a far cry from demonstrating that the new category has predictive validity and, therefore, clinical usefulness. Only a few attempts to test that kind of validity have been made for a mathematically derived category (Paykel, 1972). In fact, no category has ever been added to a classification of mental disorders for clinical use that was first identified by a mathematical procedure designed to generate diagnostic categories.

DIAGNOSTIC CRITERIA

Although the inclusion in standard glossaries, such as DSM-I and DSM-II, of brief descriptions of the most important features of each mental disorder has been of some value in reducing criterion variance in diagnostic practice, serious problems have remained. The clinician is usually still forced to rely heavily on his or her own concepts of the diagnostic categories because no formal definitions are offered for most of them; features that are invariably present in the disorder are often not clearly distinguished from features that are often but not invariably present. In addition, there is often no clear indication of which features distinguish a particular condition from similar conditions. There are usually few if any guidelines to specify which diagnoses are mutually exclusive or which should be joint diagnoses to help the clinician faced with a patient with clinical features suggesting two different conditions. Sometimes the classification forces the clinician to choose between competing classificatory principles without a rule as to which takes precedence. And, even when concepts are clearly presented, there are no specified rules that the clinician can apply to a given case to determine whether or not the criteria of a particular diagnostic category have been met.

The inadequacies of the standard glossaries have been most apparent to research investigators because of their need to identify relatively homogeneous groups for study. Therefore, researchers began to develop their own explicit criteria and classification schemes that often had little resemblance to the standard nomenclature.

The group associated with the department of psychiatry at Washington University School of Medicine in St. Louis, Missouri, is responsible for having first developed, for research use, specific criteria for a large number of diagnostic categories (Feighner et al., 1972). The criteria include certain features that are required (inclusion criteria) and, in some instances, certain features whose presence rules out the diagnosis (exclusion criteria). Those criteria are sometimes referred to as operational criteria, although technically they are not operational, in that they do not specify the operations that a clinician has to perform—for example, specific questions to be asked—to make clinical judgments. Hence, it is more accurate to refer to them as diagnostic criteria. In research settings, clinicians were expected to use the criteria regardless of their own personal concepts of the disorders. Studies indicated high reliability for those criteria (Helzer et al., 1977 a, b).

As part of a collaborative project on the psychobiology of the depressive disorders, sponsored by the Clinical Research Branch of the National Institute of Mental Health, the Feighner et al. (1972) criteria were modified, and criteria for other diagnoses were added, resulting in the Research Diagnostic Criteria (RDC) (Spitzer et al., 1978b). The RDC has criteria for 23 diagnostic categories. In addition, many different non-mutually exclusive ways of subcategorizing some of the more important groups, such as major depression, are included.

A special form of the RDC, the Family History-RDC, has been developed to provide diagnostic criteria for use in determining the diagnosis of a family member when the family member himself is not available for direct evaluation and the information must be obtained from another source, such as a close relative (Andreasen et al., 1977). In such instances, when only limited information may be available from the informant, the criteria cannot be as stringent as when a diagnosis is being made on the basis of a direct interview. Studies indicate high reliability for both the RDC (Spitzer et al., 1978b) and the Family History-RDC (Andreasen et al., 1977).

The criteria in the RDC provided a preliminary basis for those RDC categories that were included in the third edition of the American Psychiatric Association's (1980) *Diagnostic and Statistical Manual of Mental Disorders* (DSM-III). For some disorders—such as panic disorder, manic episode of bipolar disorder, and obsessive-compulsive disorder—the criteria are virtually the same in both the RDC and DSM-III. For other categories—such as schizophrenia, schizoaffective disorder, and major depression—there are significant differences resulting from experience with the RDC and the interpretation of recent research findings.

So that the reader can appreciate the greater clarity in the boundaries of a disorder that is possible with the use of diagnostic criteria, Table IV presents the DSM-II description of schizophrenia contrasted with the DSM-III diagnostic criteria. DSM-III also provides a narrative description of the disorder.

It is apparent that the DSM-II description of schizophrenia has many of the inadequacies mentioned above. For example, are disturbances in thinking required, or, as specified in the DSM-III criteria, are other psychotic symptoms sufficient? The DSM-II definition suggests that corollary mood changes are always present; the DSM-III criteria make no such requirement and, in fact, explicitly exclude cases in which a full affective syndrome precedes the development of the psychotic symptoms. The DSM-II reference to the mental status as "attributable primarily to a *thought* disorder" perpetuates a widely held assumption about the nature of the underlying disturbance in schizophrenia but offers no guidelines for making such a determination. In contrast, the DSM-III diagnostic criteria make no reference to the nature of the underlying disturbance but concentrate on the descriptive features that distinguish the disorder from other disorders. And the DSM-II description offers no guidelines as to whether or not any degree of chronicity is required for the diagnosis; the DSM-III criteria explicitly refer to a certain degree of chronicity.

In developing diagnostic criteria, one ordinarily starts with a clinical concept for which there is some degree of face validity. Initial criteria are developed by asking clinicians to describe what they consider to be the most characteristic features of the disorder.

In constructing individual items, one tries to increase descriptive validity by defining each item in such a way that it helps discriminate persons with the disorder from those without the disorder. It is useful to attempt to identify features that are expected to be present always in every person with the disorder. For example, when the DSM-III criteria for schizophrenia were developed, a decision was made to include the criterion that, at some time during the course of the illness, some kind of psychotic feature was present. Frequently, it is helpful to construct an index of symptoms, a certain number of which are needed in order to establish the presence of a syndrome. For example, in constructing diagnostic criteria for a depressive episode, one wants to list the characteristic features of the depressive syndrome and then determine how many are needed for the diagnosis.

Once the criteria have been drafted, they need to be field tested. What may seem to be unambiguous wording to the authors of the criteria may seem to be gobbledygook to clinicians trying to use them. Repeated use by clinicians may lead to several revisions. Formal reliability trials should then be conducted and efforts made to establish predictive validity for

DSM-II Description of Schizophrenia*	DSM-III Diagnostic Criteria for Schizophrenia†
This large category includes a group of disorders manifested by characteristic disturbances of thinking, mood and behavior. Disturbances in thinking are marked by alterations of concept formation which may lead to misinterpretation of reality and sometimes to delusions and hallucinations, which frequently appear psychologically self-protective. Corollary mood changes include ambivalent, constricted and inappropriate emotional responsiveness and loss of empathy with others. Behavior may be withdrawn, regressive and bizarre. The schizophrenias, in which the mental status is attributable primarily to a *thought* disorder, are to be distinguished from the *Major affective illnesses* (q.v.) which are dominated by a *mood* disorder. The *Paranoid states* (q.v.) are distinguished from schizophrenia by the narrowness of their distortions of reality and by the absence of other psychotic symptoms.	A. At least one of the following during a phase of the illness: (1) Bizarre delusions (content is patently absurd and has *no* possible basis in fact), such as delusions of being controlled, thought broadcasting, thought insertion, or thought withdrawal. (2) Somatic, grandiose, religious, nihilistic or other delusions without persecutory or jealous content. (3) Delusions with persecutory or jealous content, if accompanied by hallucinations of any type. (4) Auditory hallucinations in which either a voice keeps up a running commentary on the individual's behavior or thoughts, or two or more voices converse with each other. (5) Auditory hallucinations on several occasions with content of more than one or two words having no apparent relation to depression or elation. (6) Incoherence, marked loosening of associations, markedly illogical thinking or marked poverty of content of speech, if associated with at least one of the following: (a) blunted, flat or inappropriate affect (b) delusions or hallucinations (c) catatonic or other grossly disorganized behavior B. Deterioration from a previous level of functioning in such areas as work, social relations, and self-care. C. *Duration:* Continuous signs of the illness for at least six months at some time during the person's life with some signs of the illness at present. The six-month period must include an active phase during which there were symptoms from A, with or without a prodromal or residual phase, as defined below: *Prodromal phase:* A clear deterioration in functioning before the active phase of the illness not due to a disturbance in mood or to a Substance Use Disorder, and involving at least *two* of the symptoms noted below. *Residual phase:* Persistence following the active phase of the illness, of at least *two* of the symptoms noted below, not due to a disturbance in mood or to a Substance Use Disorder. *Prodromal or Residual Symptoms* (a) social isolation or withdrawal (b) marked impairment in role functioning as wage-earner, student, or homemaker (c) markedly peculiar behavior (e.g., collecting garbage, talking to self in public, hoarding food) (d) marked impairment in personal hygiene and grooming (e) blunted, flat, or inappropriate affect (f) digressive, vague, overelaborate, circumstantial, or metaphorical speech (g) odd or bizarre ideation, or magical thinking, e.g., superstitiousness, clairvoyance, telepathy, "sixth sense," "others can feel my feelings," overvalued ideas, ideas of reference (h) unusual perceptual experiences, e.g., recurrent illusions, sensing the presence of a force or person not actually present *Examples:* Six months of prodromal symptoms with 1 week of symptoms from A; no prodromal symptoms with six months of symptoms from A; no prodromal symptoms with two weeks of symptoms from A and six months of residual symptoms; six months of symptoms from A, apparently followed by several years of complete remission, with 1 week of symptoms in A in current episode. D. The full depressive or manic syndrome (criteria A and B of major depressive or manic episode), if present, developed after any psychotic symptoms, or was brief in duration relative to the duration of the psychotic symptoms in A. E. Onset of prodomal or active phase of the illness before age 45. F. Not due to any Organic Mental Disorder or Mental Retardation.

* Adapted from American Psychiatric Association. *Diagnostic and Statistical Manual of Mental Disorders*, ed. 2. American Psychiatric Association, Washington, D.C., 1968.

† Adapted from American Psychiatric Association. *Diagnostic and Statistical Manual of Mental Disorders*, ed. 3. American Psychiatric Association, Washington, D.C., 1980.

the category itself. If there are alternate sets of criteria for the same category, comparative validity studies are necessary.

An important consequence of having specified criteria is that some persons with obvious disturbances do not meet the criteria for any of the specific categories. Thus, there is a need for residual categories. In the Feighner et al. (1972) criteria that problem was handled by having a single category called undiagnosed psychiatric disorder. In DSM-III, the problem is handled by having, for almost all classes of disorder, an atypical category—for example, atypical depression for persons with a depressive disorder that does not meet the criteria for any of the specified depressive disorders. That solution is in marked contrast to the usual approach that was taken in both DSM-I and DSM-II, in which the diagnostician was encouraged to select the diagnostic category that the person most resembled. That approach increased false positives; that is, some persons were incorrectly identified as fitting specific categories when they actually should have been diagnosed in a manner that acknowledged a lack of diagnostic certainty.

The potential costs or consequences associated with a false-positive diagnosis are generally greater than those associated with a false-negative diagnosis. A false-positive diagnosis may lead to a wrong course of treatment that is expensive or potentially toxic. On the other hand, a false-negative diagnosis usually results only in a delay of indicated treatment. Since most mental disorders are not lethal, that cost is usually minor.

With the development of specified criteria for diagnosis, many questions emerge. If different sets of criteria are proposed for the same category—as they have been, for example, for schizophrenia—how does one choose the most appropriate set (Strauss and Gift, 1977; Endicott et al., 1978)? To date, only a few studies have compared different sets of diagnostic criteria for a single category by using an external validating criterion, such as outcome (Brockington et al., 1978, Kendell et al., 1979). It has been suggested that computerized forms can facilitate the comparison of alternative sets (Overall and Hollister, 1979), but that approach is problematic unless efforts are made to ensure that the clinicians use each set as actually intended (Spitzer et al., 1979a).

Another question is: Will the use of diagnostic criteria result in a mechanized checklist attitude toward evaluation? Certainly diagnostic criteria do not eliminate the need for clinical judgment. It may well be that different degrees of flexibility are appropriate, depending on whether the purpose is to identify as homogeneous a group as possible for research study or to make a diagnosis for strictly clinical purposes.

And one wonders to what extent diagnostic criteria are adhered to in actual practice and to what extent the clinician forms a clinical judgment based on his or her own concepts and then bends the clinical data to fit the criteria. It seems that diagnostic criteria are here to stay; the only issues are what particular criteria to use and how they should be used.

STRUCTURED INTERVIEWS

As noted earlier, an important source of information variance contributing to the unreliability of diagnosis of mental disorders is variability in the way clinicians conduct diagnostic interviews. That variability can be minimized by the use of structured interview schedules (Spitzer et al., 1964). In that way, each person is asked the same questions in the same order, so that differences between persons are likely to be real, rather than due to differences in the interviews given by different clinicians.

Three major instruments designed for diagnostic use that include rating scales with structured or semistructured interview schedules have been developed. The Present State Examination (PSE) (Wing et al., 1967) consists of a structured interview schedule that focuses on symptoms that have occurred during the past month. Diagnoses are made by the application of a computer program, CATEGO. The Schedule for Affective Disorders and Schizophrenia (SADS) (Endicott and Spitzer, 1978) contains two sections, one dealing with the present episode of illness and the other dealing with past history. The diagnostic decisions are made by the interviewer after the assessment by the use of the Research Diagnostic Criteria (RDC). The National Institute of Mental Health Diagnostic Interview Schedule (DIS) (Robins et al., 1979) was developed for use in situations in which it is not feasible to require that the interviewers have professional training in psychopathology as both the PSE and the SADS require. As with the PSE, the diagnostic decisions are made by a computer program that uses algorithms to make certain diagnoses according to the Feighner et al. (1972) criteria, the Research Diagnostic Criteria, and DSM-III.

EPIDEMIOLOGICAL COMMUNITY SURVEYS

Efforts to assess the prevalence of both treated and untreated specific mental disorders have been hampered by the lack of suitable assessment procedures that could be used in community surveys; obviously, the cost of using diagnostically trained professional interviewers in large-scale studies is prohibitive. For that reason, up until recently, surveys have used indirect methods, such as self-report scales that tapped over-all severity of illness but provided little information about specific types of disorders.

With the advent of structured interviews and specified criteria for diagnosis, it has become possible to train personnel with limited or no professional experience to conduct diagnostic interviews. A special version of the Schedule for Affective Disorders and Schizophrenia (SADS) was designed to assess persons who may not be in a current episode of illness but who may have had a previous episode of illness. That instrument was used successfully in a large-scale community survey by Weissman and Myers (1978) with raters whose education was below the doctorate level.

To facilitate similar studies conducted by persons without any graduate-level education, the Office of Biometry and Epidemiology of the National Institute of Mental Health sponsored the development of the NIMH Diagnostic Interview Schedule (DIS), referred to above. That instrument can be used by lay interviewers who undergo an intensive training program. The task of the DIS interviewer is limited to rating a person's response to highly structured questions. As noted above, the diagnostic decisions are all made by a computer program. The DIS will be used in several epidemiological catchment areas in the United States to determine the prevalence of certain treated and untreated mental disorders and their relationship to various risk factors and the use of health facilities. The Present State Examination (PSE) has also been used in community surveys (Wing et al., 1978).

MULTIAXIAL CLASSIFICATION

In 1947 the Swedish psychiatrists Essen-Möller and Wohlfahrt proposed that a classification of mental disorders include separate axes for symptomatology and etiology. They believed that the axes would not only make it possible to identify cases with the same etiology, such as infection, but make it possible to identify cases that have common symptomatology but different etiology, such as deliriums. Such a system would also reduce unreliability caused by different etiological conceptions of the disorder. And it was hoped that, if clinicians were asked to classify possible etiological factors for each patient, knowledge would be gained about the etiology of mental disorders.

Since that time several other investigators have proposed multiaxial models that have contained various axes variously defined (Mezzich, 1979). Ottosson and Perris (1973) proposed a four-axis system. Axis I is for symptomatology and is itself divided into a number of different symptoms, of which several are further subdivided, and more than one symptom may be noted; also included are a number of personality disturbances. Axis II codes severity, divided into neurosis and psychosis on the basis of reality testing. Axis III is for course, and each symptom noted on Axis I may have its course coded separately. Axis IV, etiology, is divided into four categories: somatogenic, psychogenic, multifactorial, and cryptogenic.

Rutter et al. (1975a) proposed a five-axis system for children as part of a World Health Organization effort to explore the feasibility of a multiaxial approach to classification. Axis I, called the clinical psychiatric syndrome, contained all the mental disorders from the mental disorders section of ICD-9 with the exception of specific delays in development, which were noted on Axis II, and mental retardation, which was coded on Axis III. Axis III also had a code for normal intellectual functioning. Axis IV provided for the coding of all current nonpsychiatric medical conditions, whether or not they were thought to have caused the mental disorders coded on the first three axes. Axis V provided a classification of current abnormal psychosocial situations, regardless of whether or not they were thought to have a causal relationship to the current mental disorders.

Strauss (1975) proposed a different five-axis system. Axis I comprised symptoms, which could be described with DSM-II categories devoid of any implications regarding etiology or course. Axis II coded duration and course of symptoms. Axis III was for circumstances associated with symptoms and included possible environmental stresses, physical illness, drug or alcohol abuse, and other associated factors. Axis IV rated the quality of personal relationships on a five-point scale. Axis V coded work function, also on a five-point scale.

Other multiaxial systems have been proposed with yet other axes including such concepts as certainty with which the diagnosis is being made (Helmchen, 1975). The DSM-III multiaxial system is discussed in detail below but is included in Table V so that the reader can compare the various axes of the major multiaxial systems that have been proposed.

In the most radical systems, such as those proposed by Essen-Möller and Wohlfahrt (1947) and Ottosson and Perris (1973),

traditional diagnostic categories are replaced by symptoms or symptom pictures; in the other systems, traditional diagnoses are coded on one or more axes, which are then supplemented with other nondiagnostic information. For example, the clinical pictures of what in DSM-III are called amphetamine delusional disorder and paranoid schizophrenia would, in the Ottosson and Perris system, receive the same coding on the axis for symptomatology since the two disorders usually present with an indistinguishable psychotic symptom picture. However, on the axis for etiology, the disorders would be differentiated by coding the amphetamine delusional disorder as somatogenic and coding paranoid schizophrenia as cryptogenic.

In other systems, such as that of Rutter et al. (1975a) and DSM-III, various sections of the traditional classification of mental disorders are distributed on two (DSM-III) or three (Rutter et al., 1975a) axes in order to make sure that attention is given to those parts of the classification that are likely to be overlooked when attention is directed to the usually more florid Axis I condition. Some of the multiaxial systems proposed include ordinal scales for some of the axes—for example, Strauss's (1975) scales for Axes IV and V and the DSM-III scales for Axes IV and V. In some cases an axis provides an extensive classification itself, as with Rutter et al.'s (1975a) Axis V classification of abnormal psychosocial situations.

Clearly, with any multiaxial classification there is a conflict between comprehensiveness and feasibility. One can always think of additional useful information that could be the basis for another axis. The trick is to choose a small number of axes that are of maximal clinical usefulness in a variety of clinical situations. Before the development of DSM-III, none of the systems that have been proposed has had more than limited clinical use, and it remains to be seen to what extent the full DSM-III multiaxial system will be used.

On the basis of experience gained with the major multiaxial systems, it seems that the reliability of diagnostic judgments is increased if certain portions of the classification system are coded separately on different axes. However, the initial hope of Essen-Möller and Wohlfahrt that such systems would lead to increased knowledge about etiology does not seem to have been realized, and it is unlikely that such knowledge can be expected from the collection of routine clinical data. What is needed is a promising etiological hypothesis that is then put to the test in a well-designed study.

DSM-III

As the mental disorders chapter of the ninth revision of the *International Classification of Diseases* (ICD-9) was being de-

TABLE V
Multiaxial Approaches to Classification

	Essen-Möller and Wohlfahrt (1947)	Ottosson and Perris (1973)	Rutter et al. (1975a)	Strauss (1975)	DSM-III (1980)
Axis I	Syndrome	Symptomatology	Clinical psychiatric syndrome	Symptoms	Clinical syndromes and other conditions
Axis II	Etiology	Severity	Specific delays in development	Duration and course of symptoms	Personality disorders and specific developmental disorders
Axis III		Course	Intellectual level	Associated etiological factors	Physical disorders and conditions
Axis IV		Etiology	Physical conditions	Quality of personal relationships	Severity of psychosocial stressors
Axis V			Abnormal psychosocial situations	Work function	Highest level of adaptive functioning past year

veloped, the American Psychiatric Association's Committee on Nomenclature and Statistics reviewed it to assess its adequacy for use in the United States. Although the ICD-9 classification and glossary incorporated many improvements over the ICD-8 classification and glossary, there was some concern that it had not made sufficient use of recent methodological developments, such as specified diagnostic criteria and multiaxial diagnosis, and that, in many specific areas of the classification, there was insufficient subtyping for clinical and research use. For example, the ICD-9 classification contains only one category for frigidity and impotence, despite the well-known work in the area of psychosexual dysfunctions that has identified several specific types with different clinical pictures and treatment implications. For those reasons, the American Psychiatric Association in June 1974 appointed Robert L. Spitzer to chair a Task Force on Nomenclature and Statistics to develop a new diagnostic manual, the third edition of the American Psychiatric Association's (1980) *Diagnostic and Statistical Manual of Mental Disorders* (DSM-III).

The mandate given to the task force was to develop a classification system that would, as much as possible, reflect the current state of knowledge regarding mental disorders and maximize its usefulness for both clinical practice and research studies. Secondarily, the classification was to be, as much as possible, compatible with ICD-9.

PROCESS

Selection of the task force. Each member or consultant of the task force was selected by the chairperson because of his or her interest in or contribution to the classification of mental disorders. As the work progressed, additional members were added to ensure representation of different perspectives and areas of expertise. In particular, because it had become evident that not enough members of the task force had a primarily psychodynamic orientation, persons who held that perspective were added.

Shared goals. The task force functioned as a steering committee overseeing the ongoing work. All members of the task force shared a commitment to the maximal attainment in DSM-III of the following goals: clinical usefulness (validity) for making treatment and management decisions in varied clinical settings; reliability of the diagnostic categories; acceptability to clinicians and research investigators of varying theoretical orientations; usefulness for educating health professionals; maintaining compatibility with ICD-9, except when departures were unavoidable; avoiding the introduction of new terminology and concepts that broke with tradition, except when clearly needed; reaching a consensus as to the meaning of necessary diagnostic terms that have been used inconsistently and avoiding the use of terms that have outlived their usefulness; consistency with data from research studies bearing on the validity of diagnostic categories; suitability for describing subjects in research studies; and being responsive during the development of DSM-III to critiques made by mental health professionals.

Functions of the task force. The major job of the task force was to determine the most effective strategies for making sure that the final document attained each goal to as great an extent as possible without sacrificing the other goals. In addition, the task force had the job of evaluating all proposals for changes in DSM-III that might affect the attainment of those goals. Those proposals came from individual task force members and the chair, liaison committees with professional groups, and participants in the DSM-III field trials. In a few instances the task force had to resolve an important issue for which a consensus could not be reached by an advisory committee. And the task force was responsible for reviewing drafts of the text and criteria.

In addition to annual or semiannual meetings of the entire task force, memoranda were constantly circulated, and individual members were frequently in touch by phone. Most issues were resolved by consensus without a formal vote, although in many instances a formal vote had to be taken after prolonged discussions or exchanges of memoranda. In some of those cases, even though data were available from relevant research studies, the members of the task force differed in their interpretation of the findings.

Advisory committees and other consultants. Advisory committees to the task force were selected for each of 12 major areas of the classification, the multiaxial system, and the glossary of technical terms. Each advisory committee was composed of persons with expertise in that area. Most of the members of the committees were psychiatrists, but psychologists, social workers, and other mental health professionals were also included. In all, the advisory committees included more than 100 people.

In beginning its work, each advisory committee usually held a few meetings in order to reach a tentative agreement on the categories to be included in its area and how the categories were to be defined. Next, drafts of each category were prepared either by individual members or by small groups of members of each advisory committee. Those drafts were then reviewed by the entire committee and revised, usually many times. After undergoing a number of revisions, drafts were circulated to the task force, to a group of other consultants, and to some outside experts. Frequently, when an outside expert made a significant contribution to the revision of a draft, he or she was asked to join the advisory committee.

BASIC FEATURES

Descriptive approach. DSM-III is generally atheoretical with regard to etiology with the exception of those few disorders in which the etiology or pathophysiological processes are known, such as the organic mental disorders. Thus, DSM-III attempts to describe comprehensively what the manifestations of the mental disorders are and only rarely attempts to account for how the disturbances come about, unless the mechanism is included in the definition of the disorder. That general approach can be said to be descriptive in that the definitions of the disorders by and large consist of descriptions of the clinical features of the disorders.

Diagnostic criteria. Specified diagnostic criteria are provided for each specific mental disorder. The only exception is the category of schizoaffective disorder.

Multiaxial evaluation. DSM-III is a multiaxial system for evaluation that includes the following five axes: Axis I, clinical syndromes, conditions not attributable to a mental disorder that are a focus of attention or treatment and additional codes; Axis II, personality disorders and specific developmental disorders; Axis III, physical disorders or conditions; Axis IV, severity of psychosocial stressors; and Axis V, highest level of adaptive functioning past year.

Axes I and II comprise the mental disorders and conditions not attributable to a mental disorder that are a focus of attention or treatment. Axis III permits the clinician to indicate any current physical disorder or condition outside of the mental disorders section of the ICD-9-CM that is potentially relevant to the understanding or management of the person.

Axis IV provides a seven-point rating scale for coding the over-all severity of stress that is judged to have been a significant contributor to the development or exacerbation of the current disorder. Each scale level is anchored with examples for adults and for children and adolescents. The person's prognosis may be better when a disorder develops as a consequence of marked stress than when it develops after minimal or no stress.

The rating of severity of stress should be based on the clinician's assessment of the stress that an average person with similar sociocultural values and circumstances would experience from the psychosocial stressors. That judgment involves a consideration of the amount of change in the person's life due to the stressor, the degree to which the event is desired and under the person's control, and the number of stressors. In addition, in certain settings it may be useful to note the specific psychosocial stressors. That information may be important in formulating a treatment plan that includes attempts to remove the psychosocial stressors or to help the person cope with them.

Axis V permits the clinician to indicate his or her judgment of the person's highest level of adaptive functioning, for at least a few months, during the past year. A seven-point rating scale is provided, and it is anchored with examples for adults and for children and adolescents. Adaptive functioning is conceptualized as a composite of three major areas: social relations, occupational functioning, and the use of leisure time.

An example of the results of a DSM-III multiaxial evaluation follows:

Axis I: 303.92 Alcohol dependence, episodic
Axis II: 301.60 Dependent personality disorder
Axis III: Alcoholic cirrhosis of liver
Axis IV: Psychosocial stressors: anticipated retirement and change in residence with loss of contact with friends. Severity: 4 moderate
Axis V: Highest level of adaptive functioning past year: 3 good

Levels of diagnostic certainty. Most diagnostic systems, such as DSM-II and ICD-9, provide only limited opportunities for expressing diagnostic uncertainty. In contrast, DSM-III provides a number of ways that can be done. Table VI presents the DSM-III terms for different clinical situations in which a diagnosis of a specific mental disorder is not possible or appropriate.

Systematic description. The text of DSM-III systematically describes each disorder in terms of current knowledge in the following areas: essential features, associated features, age at onset, course, impairment, complications, predisposing factors, prevalence, sex ratio, familial pattern, and differential diagnosis.

Appendices. DSM-III contains the following appendices: decision trees for differential diagnosis, a glossary of technical terms, an annotated comparative listing of DSM-II and DSM-III with explanations for the major changes made and new categories added and with references from the scientific liter-ature (see Table VIII), a historical review of the development of the ICD-9 glossary and classification and the ICD-9-CM classification (a clinical modification for use in the United States), a classification of sleep and arousal disorders, and a description of the DSM-III field trials and interrater reliability.

CONTROVERSIAL ISSUES

During the development of DSM-III, the task force had to resolve a variety of controversial issues. What follows is a brief discussion of several of those issues.

Should DSM-III contain a definition of mental disorder? Initially, the task force believed that it would be useful, since no definition is present in DSM-I, DSM-II, ICD-8, or ICD-9 and since a frequent charge made by critics of nosology is that there has never been an accepted definition of mental disorder. After reviewing two complicated proposals (Klein, 1978; Spitzer and Endicott, 1978), the task force decided that no definition would be satisfactory and that the attempt to formulate one was doomed to failure. However, in the final months of the development of DSM-III, the authors, with assistance from task force members, drafted the following definition, which is included in the introduction to DSM-III and which incorporates many of the necessary assumptions in a classification of mental disorders that were previously discussed:

> In DSM-III each of the mental disorders is conceptualized as a clinically significant behavioral or psychological syndrome or pattern that occurs in an individual and that is typically associated with either a painful symptom (distress) or impairment in one or more important areas of functioning (disability). In addition, there is an inference that there is a behavioral, psychological, or biological dysfunction, and that the disturbance is not only in the relationship between the individual and society. (When the disturbance is *limited* to a conflict between an individual and society, this may represent social deviance, which may or may not be commendable, but is not by itself a mental disorder.)

Should DSM-III contain a statement that mental disorders are a subset of medical disorders? The initial definitions of mental disorder considered by the task force explicitly conceptualized mental disorders as medical disorders. When the task force initially decided not to include any definition of mental disorder, there was still a plan to

TABLE VI
Provisions in DSM-III for Expressing Different Levels of Diagnostic Certainty

Frequently, there is insufficient information after a diagnostic evaluation to make a specific diagnosis. The following table indicates the various ways in which a clinician may indicate diagnostic uncertainty.

DSM-III Term	Clinical Situation
V Codes (for conditions not attributable to a mental disorder that are a focus of attention or treatment)	Insufficient information to know whether or not a presenting problem is attributable to a mental disorder—for example, academic problem or adult antisocial behavior.
799.90 Diagnosis or condition deferred on Axis I	Information too inadequate to make any diagnostic judgment about an Axis I diagnosis or condition.
799.90 Diagnosis deferred on Axis II	Information too inadequate to make any diagnostic judgment about an Axis II diagnosis.
300.90 Unspecified mental disorder (nonpsychotic)	Enough information available to rule out a psychotic disorder, but further specification is not possible.
298.90 Atypical psychosis	Enough information available to determine the presence of a psychotic disorder, but further specification is not possible.
Atypical (class of disorder)	Enough information available to indicate the class of disorder that is present, but further specification is not possible because either there is not sufficient information to make a more specific diagnosis, or the clinical features of the disorder do not meet the criteria for any of the other categories—for example, atypical affective disorder.
Specific diagnosis (provisional)	Enough information available to make a working diagnosis, but the clinician wishes to indicate a significant degree of diagnostic uncertainty—for example, schizophreniform disorder (provisional).

include a statement that the DSM-III mental disorders were a subset of medical disorders, noting that the statement did not necessarily imply that only physicians could treat those conditions. The rationale for that plan was that, in fact, the DSM-III categories are included in the ICD-9-CM, a medical classification, and making that fact explicit would be useful in emphasizing that psychiatry is a branch of medicine and, furthermore, that differential diagnosis of mental disorders requires medical training.

The reaction of psychologists to that plan, as might be expected, was less than enthusiastic (Schacht and Nathan, 1977; Zubin, 1978). It became clear that the inclusion of such a statement would only fan the fires of professional rivalry and might be a real obstacle to the use of DSM-III by nonmedical health professionals who had used DSM-I and DSM-II in their clinical and research work. After an agonizing reappraisal, the task force concluded that the purpose of DSM-III was to describe and classify mental disorders, not to clarify the relationship of psychiatry to medicine. Therefore, DSM-III contains no explicit reference to mental disorders' being a subset of medical disorders, although it is noted that the DSM-III categories are all included in ICD-9-CM.

Should the text for each disorder be largely limited to descriptive material, or should it include various theories about the etiology or mechanism for each disorder? From the beginning, the task force assumed that the text and the criteria for the categories in DSM-III would be limited to descriptive material. DSM-I and DSM-II, with only a few exceptions—several sentences in the section on neuroses—were also largely descriptive. However, the liaison committee of the American Psychoanalytic Association took strong exception to that approach and urged that psychodynamic material be included in the text and the criteria for many of the disorders. The task force, after reviewing specific proposals made by the liaison committee for the inclusion of such material, determined that the inclusion of the material would cause several problems: The material was not necessary to enable the clinician to make a diagnosis, and its inclusion would be an obstacle to the use of the manual by clinicians of other theoretical orientations, since it would not be feasible to present all reasonable theories about etiology or the underlying mechanisms involved in each disorder.

Should there be a diagnostic class of neuroses in DSM-III, as in DSM-II? Throughout the development of DSM-III, the task force on nomenclature and statistics believed that there should not be a diagnostic class of neuroses. When Freud first used the term "psychoneurosis," he was referring to only four subtypes: anxiety neurosis, anxiety hysteria (phobia), obsessive-compulsive neurosis, and hysteria. Freud used the term descriptively to indicate a painful symptom in a person with intact reality testing and to describe the etiological process—unconscious conflict arouses anxiety and leads to the maladaptive use of defensive mechanisms that result in symptom formation.

The term "neuroses" in DSM-II had both descriptive and etiological meanings. The task force believed that the inclusion of the etiological implications of the term would be inconsistent with the generally descriptive approach taken in DSM-III. Thus, drafts of the DSM-III classification prepared before April 1979 contained no reference to the terms "neuroses" and "neurotic disorders" and the DSM-II neuroses subtypes were dispersed among several DSM-III classes.

Although there had been widespread dissatisfaction with the omission of neuroses as a diagnostic class, it was only in February 1979, with the approval of the manual imminent, that organized opposition to that approach developed. Several local societies of the American Psychiatric Association and the American Psychoanalytic Association went on record as being opposed to the adoption of DSM-III unless the neuroses were reinstated.

In an attempt to satisfy the demands of those groups while preserving the descriptive approach taken in DSM-III, a series of compromises evolved. The following final solution was generally accepted, and it avoided the possibility of an organized effort to prevent the formal adoption of DSM-III by the American Psychiatric Association.

At the present time, there is no consensus as to how to define "neurosis." Some clinicians limit the term to its descriptive meaning;

others include the concept of a specific etiological process. The term "neurotic disorder" is used in DSM-III when only a descriptive meaning is intended. It refers to a mental disorder in which the predominant disturbance is a symptom or a group of symptoms that is distressing to the person and is recognized by him or her as unacceptable and alien (ego-dystonic); reality testing is grossly intact; behavior does not actively violate gross social norms, although functioning may be markedly impaired; the disturbance is relatively enduring or recurrent without treatment and is not limited to a mild transitory reaction to stress; and there is no demonstrable organic cause or factor.

The term "neurotic process" is recommended for use when the clinician wishes to indicate the concept of a specific etiological process involving the following sequence: (1) unconscious conflicts between opposing wishes or between wishes and prohibitions that cause (2) an unconscious perception of anticipated danger or dysphoria, which leads to (3) the use of defense mechanisms that result in (4) either symptoms or personality disturbance or both.

In DSM-III the neurotic disorders are included in affective, anxiety, somatoform, dissociative, and psychosexual disorders. Those diagnostic classes are listed together in the DSM-III classification to facilitate the location of neurotic disorders. Preceding the listing of the class of affective disorders is a statement that indicates that neurotic disorders are included in those five DSM-III classes.

The ICD-9 category of neurotic disorders, also defined descriptively, includes only those categories that historically have been included as neuroses in previous standard classifications. Those previous classifications did not have some DSM-III categories, such as psychosexual disorders, that unquestionably include some disorders falling within the concept of neurotic disorders.

Alternative approaches to the issue of the relationship of neurotic disorders to the DSM-III classification were considered. If the DSM-III classification had included a category of neurotic disorders that was limited to those disorders that are included in the ICD-9 category, the potential value of the term "neurotic disorders" would have been limited by a lack of adherence to its descriptive meaning. On the other hand, to have grouped together all the specific DSM-III categories that are almost always considered to be neurotic disorders would have required separating some affective disorders from the other affective disorders, some psychosexual disorders from the other psychosexual disorders, and some dissociative disorders from the other dissociative disorders. The possible advantages of that approach seemed to be far outweighed by the disadvantage of fragmenting several diagnostic classes. Similarly, it was judged unwise to group all psychotic disorders together, as does ICD-9.

To facilitate the identification of the categories that in DSM-II were grouped together in the class of neuroses, the task force agreed to add the DSM-II terms in parentheses after the corresponding categories.

Should the diagnostic criteria be presented as requirements for making each diagnosis? The task force agreed that the diagnostic criteria should be recommended as guidelines. That decision was based partly on the recognition that in actual practice, regardless of what instructions are given to clinicians, most clinicians use them only as guides for diagnosis, not as requirements. In addition, many argued for the elimination of diagnostic criteria from DSM-III because of their potential for misuse. Those persons accepted the inclusion of diagnostic criteria only when it was stated that they would be presented as guidelines only.

Should Axes IV and V be optional and only for use in special clinical and research settings? The American Psychiatric Association's Committee on Confidentiality was concerned that information on Axes IV and V might be misused and was not necessary for purposes of third-party review. They therefore suggested that those two axes not be considered part of the official DSM-III diagnosis. With appreciation of the concern about confidentiality, the task force accepted that suggestion.

Should there be a classification of psychosocial stressors for Axis IV? When work started on the multiaxial system, Axis IV provided a 30-category classification of psychosocial stressors that was a modification and expansion of the fifth axis, associated abnormal psychosocial situations, in the World Health Organization-sponsored multiaxial classification scheme developed by Rutter et al. (1975a). Since trial use indicated that the 30-category scheme was inadequate in coverage and definition, that scheme was simplified into a classification of 10 major areas of stressors, each with subdivisions. Trial use indicated that scheme also was unsatisfactory. Furthermore, it became apparent that categorization of the psychosocial stressor, such as by family problem, was not as clinically useful as describing the specific situation—for example, mother at home with terminal cancer. Therefore, further attempts at categorization of psychosocial stressors were abandoned. Instead, Axis IV uses a scale of severity of stressors and allows the clinician to note the specific psychosocial stressor.

Should the multiaxial system include a sixth axis, for prominent defense mechanisms or coping styles? The impetus for that idea came from the controversy regarding the inclusion of psychodynamic material in DSM-III. An ad hoc committee was created to explore the possibility. It concluded that, at the present time, a classification of defense mechanisms or coping styles that was generally acceptable could not be developed. At best, DSM-III might provide a list of coping styles to which the reader could refer, and the clinician could note appropriate coping styles in addition to the formal diagnosis. For example, the clinician might wish to note that a diagnosis of alcohol dependence was accompanied by marked denial.

The task force reviewed a list of coping styles proposed by the ad hoc committee and decided that, at the present time, no list of coping styles would find general acceptance and use.

Should there be a sixth axis, for etiology? In view of the fact that many multiaxial systems include an axis for etiology or associated factors, a proposal was made for an axis that would allow the clinician to express his judgment about the relative importance of various etiological factors. The clinician could choose from among a list of causal factors and then rank order the categories in terms of their relative importance. The factors could include, for example, psychosocial stress, environmental reinforcement, intrapsychic conflict, constitutional factors, and genetic factors. The task force concluded that such an axis would actually reflect more about the clinician's orientation than about the patient being evaluated. Furthermore, it would put the clinician in the position of being expected to speculate about the etiology of mental disorders whose etiology was unknown.

Should DSM-III include a classification of disturbed family units? As already noted above, mental disorders are conditions that occur in persons. Some have argued for a classification in which the focus of attention is the disturbed relationship between persons, as in a family. Early in the development of DSM-III, requests were made for the inclusion of a classification of disordered family units. A proposed classification was circulated to a group of experts in the area of family therapy for their review. Most of them had serious reservations about the proposed classification, and several questioned the feasibility of developing such a classification, given the current state of knowledge in the area. The task force, which had initially been receptive to the idea of including such a classification in an appendix, concluded that, for DSM-III, it would not be possible to develop a classification of family units that would be generally acceptable.

Since DSM-III contains no material on statistical reporting, as did DSM-I and DSM-II, should the name of the manual be changed to Diagnostic Manual (DM-1)? Despite the compelling logic of the proposed name change, there was widespread agreement that, in this case, there was something to be said for historical continuity.

CLASSIFICATION OF MENTAL DISORDERS

Table VII presents the DSM-III classification of mental disorders (Axes I and II). There are 16 major diagnostic classes and a total of 187 specific diagnostic categories. Although one of the criticisms of DSM-III has been the proliferation of diagnostic categories, DSM-III had 146 specific categories. Thus, the difference between DSM-II and DSM-III is rather small, far smaller than the average increase in the number of

specific diagnostic categories for other sections of ICD-8 and ICD-9-CM.

Disorders usually first evident in infancy, childhood, or adolescence. The disorders in this section are those that usually arise and first manifest themselves in infancy, childhood, or adolescence. This class appears first in the classification to encourage clinicians to first consider these disorders when diagnosing adults. And disorders from the other sections of the classification are often appropriate for children or adolescents.

There are more than 4 times as many categories in this section as there were for children in DSM-II, reflecting a great increase in research in this area.

The minor classes of disorders in this section can be grouped into the following five major groups, based on the predominant area of disturbance: (1) intellectual (mental retardation); (2) behavioral (overt) (attention deficit disorder, conduct disorder); (3) emotional (anxiety disorders of childhood or adolescence; other disorders of infancy, childhood, or adolescence); (4) physical (eating disorders, stereotyped movement disorders, other disorders with physical manifestations); and (5) developmental (pervasive developmental disorders, specific developmental disorders).

Organic mental disorders. The essential feature of all these disorders is a psychological or behavioral disturbance that is due to transient or permanent dysfunction of the brain. DSM-III recognizes the following organic brain syndromes: (1) delirium and dementia, with relatively global cognitive impairment; (2) amnestic syndrome and organic hallucinosis, with relatively selective areas of cognitive impairment; (3) organic delusional syndrome and organic affective syndrome, with features resembling schizophrenic or affective disorders; (4) organic personality syndrome, with features affecting the personality; (5) intoxication and withdrawal, associated with drug ingestion or cessation and not meeting the criteria for any of the previous syndromes; strictly speaking, these two categories are etiologically rather than syndromally, defined; and (6) other organic brain syndrome, a residual category for any other organic brain syndrome not classifiable as any of the previous syndromes.

The organic mental disorders contain two sections. Section 1 includes those disorders in which the etiology or the pathophysiological process involves either aging (senile and presenile dementias, such as multiinfarct dementia) or the ingestion of a substance (substance-induced organic brain syndromes, such as opioid intoxication). Section 2 includes organic brain syndromes whose etiology or pathophysiological process is either noted as an additional diagnosis from outside the mental disorders section of ICD-9-CM—for example, delirium due to pneumonia—or is unknown.

Substance use disorders. This section of the classification includes disorders in which behavioral changes are caused by taking substances that affect the central nervous system and that in almost all subcultures are viewed as extremely undesirable. The categories of substance abuse are defined by a minimal duration of use (1 month), social complications of use (such as impairment in social or occupational functioning), and a pathological pattern of use (such as the inability to cut down or stop use, remaining intoxicated throughout the day). Substance dependence is generally defined by the presence of either tolerance or withdrawal.

There are categories of abuse and dependence for the following substances: alcohol, barbiturates or similarly acting sedatives or hypnotics, opioids, amphetamines or similarly acting sympathomimetics, and cannabis. Substances for which there is abuse but no demonstrated dependence include cocaine, phencyclidine (PCP) or similarly acting arylcyclohexylamines

TABLE VII
DSM-III Classification: Axes I and II Categories and Codes*

All official DSM-III codes and terms are included in ICD-9-CM. However, in order to differentiate those DSM-III categories that use the same ICD-9-CM codes, unofficial non-ICD-9-CM codes are provided in parentheses for use when greater specificity is necessary. The long dashes indicate the need for a fifth-digit subtype or other qualifying term.

DISORDERS USUALLY FIRST EVIDENT IN INFANCY, CHILDHOOD OR ADOLESCENCE

Mental retardation
(Code in fifth digit: 1 = with other behavioral symptoms [requiring attention or treatment and that are not part of another disorder], 0 = without other behavioral symptoms.)
317.0(x)   Mild mental retardation, _____
318.0(x)   Moderate mental retardation, _____
318.1(x)   Severe mental retardation, _____
318.2(x)   Profound mental retardation, _____
319.0(x)   Unspecified mental retardation, _____

Attention deficit disorder
314.01   with hyperactivity
314.00   without hyperactivity
314.80   residual type

Conduct disorder
312.00   undersocialized aggressive
312.10   undersocialized, nonaggressive
312.23   socialized, aggressive
312.21   socialized, nonaggressive
312.90   atypical

Anxiety disorders of childhood or adolescence
309.21   Separation anxiety disorder
313.21   Avoidant disorder of childhood or adolescence
313.00   Overanxious disorder

Other disorders of infancy, childhood or adolescence
313.89   Reactive attachment disorder of infancy
313.22   Schizoid disorder of childhood or adolescence
313.23   Elective mutism
313.81   Oppositional disorder
313.82   Identity disorder

Eating disorders
307.10   Anorexia nervosa
307.51   Bulimia
307.52   Pica
307.53   Rumination disorder of infancy
307.50   Atypical eating disorder

Stereotyped movement disorders
307.21   Transient tic disorder
307.22   Chronic motor tic disorder
307.23   Tourette's disorder
307.20   Atypical tic disorder
307.30   Atypical stereotyped movement disorder

Other disorders with physical manifestations
307.00   Stuttering
307.60   Functional enuresis
307.70   Functional encopresis
307.46   Sleepwalking disorder
307.46   Sleep terror disorder (307.49)

Pervasive developmental disorders
Code in fifth digit: 0 = full syndrome present, 1 = residual state.
299.0x   Infantile autism, _____

299.9x   Childhood onset pervasive developmental disorder, _____

299.8x   Atypical, _____

Specific developmental disorders
Note: These are coded on Axis II.
315.00   Developmental reading disorder
315.10   Developmental arithmetic disorder
315.31   Developmental language disorder
315.39   Developmental articulation disorder
315.50   Mixed specific developmental disorder
315.90   Atypical specific developmental disorder

ORGANIC MENTAL DISORDERS
Section 1. Organic mental disorders whose etiology or pathophysiological process is listed below (taken from the mental disorders section of ICD-9-CM).
Dementias arising in the senium and presenium
           Primary degenerative dementia, senile onset,
290.30   with delirium
290.20   with delusions
290.21   with depression
290.00   uncomplicated
Code in fifth digit: 1 = with delirium, 2 = with delusions, 3 = with depression, 0 = uncomplicated.
290.1x   Primary degenerative dementia, presenile onset, _____

290.4x   Multi-infarct dementia, _____

Substance-induced
           Alcohol
303.00   intoxication
291.40   idiosyncratic intoxication
291.80   withdrawal
291.00   withdrawal delirium
291.30   hallucinosis
291.10   amnestic disorder
Code severity of dementia in fifth digit: 1 = mild, 2 = moderate, 3 = severe, 0 = unspecified.
291.2x   Dementia associated with alcoholism, _____
           Barbiturate or similarly acting sedative or hypnotic
305.40   intoxication (327.00)
292.00   withdrawal (327.01)
292.00   withdrawal delirium (327.02)
292.83   amnestic disorder (327.04)
           Opioid
305.50   intoxication (327.10)
292.00   withdrawal (327.11)
           Cocaine
305.60   intoxication (327.20)
           Amphetamine or similarly acting sympathomimetic
305.70   intoxication (327.30)
292.81   delirium (327.32)
292.11   delusional disorder (327.35)
292.00   withdrawal (327.31)
           Phencyclidine (PCP) or similarly acting arylcyclohexylamine
305.90   intoxication (327.40)
292.81   delirium (327.42)
292.90   mixed organic mental disorder (327.49)
           Hallucinogen
305.30   hallucinosis (327.56)
292.11   delusional disorder (327.55)

TABLE VII—*Continued*

292.84	affective disorder (327.57)
	Cannabis
305.20	intoxication (327.60)
292.11	delusional disorder (327.65)
	Tobacco
292.00	withdrawal (327.71)
	Caffeine
305.90	intoxication (327.80)
	Other or unspecified substance
305.90	intoxication (327.90)
292.00	withdrawal (327.91)
292.81	delirium (327.92)
292.82	dementia (327.93)
292.83	amnestic disorder (327.94)
292.11	delusional disorder (327.95)
292.12	hallucinosis (327.96)
292.84	affective disorder (327.97)
292.89	personality disorder (327.98)
292.90	atypical or mixed organic mental disorder (327.99)

Section 2. Organic brain syndromes whose etiology or pathophysiological process is either noted as an additional diagnosis from outside the mental disorders section of ICD-9-CM or is unknown.

293.00	Delirium
294.10	Dementia
294.00	Amnestic syndrome
293.81	Organic delusional syndrome
293.82	Organic hallucinosis
293.83	Organic affective syndrome
310.10	Organic personality syndrome
294.80	Atypical or mixed organic brain syndrome

SUBSTANCE USE DISORDERS

Code in fifth digit: 1 = continuous, 2 = episodic, 3 = in remission, 0 = unspecified.

305.0x	Alcohol abuse, _____
303.9x	Alcohol dependence (Alcoholism), _____
305.4x	Barbiturate or similarly acting sedative or hypnotic abuse, _____
304.1x	Barbiturate or similarly acting sedative or hypnotic dependence, _____
305.5x	Opioid abuse, _____
304.0x	Opioid dependence, _____
305.6x	Cocaine abuse, _____
305.7x	Amphetamine or similarly acting sympathomimetic abuse, _____
304.4x	Amphetamine or similarly acting sympathomimetic dependence, _____
305.9x	Phencyclidine (PCP) or similarly acting arylcyclohexylamine abuse, _____ (328.4x)
305.3x	Hallucinogen abuse, _____
305.2x	Cannabis abuse, _____
304.3x	Cannabis dependence, _____
305.1x	Tobacco dependence, _____
305.9x	Other, mixed or unspecified substance abuse, _____
304.6x	Other specified substance dependence, _____
304.9x	Unspecified substance dependence, _____
304.7x	Dependence on combination of opioid and other non-alcoholic substance, _____
304.8x	Dependence on combination of substances, excluding opioids and alcohol, _____

SCHIZOPHRENIC DISORDERS

Code in fifth digit: 1 = subchronic, 2 = chronic, 3 = subchronic with acute exacerbation, 4 = chronic with acute exacerbation, 5 = in remission, 0 = unspecified.

Schizophrenia,

295.1x	disorganized, _____
295.2x	catatonic, _____
295.3x	paranoid, _____
295.9x	undifferentiated, _____
295.6x	residual, _____

PARANOID DISORDERS

297.10	Paranoia
297.30	Shared paranoid disorder
298.30	Acute paranoid disorder
297.90	Atypical paranoid disorder

PSYCHOTIC DISORDERS NOT ELSEWHERE CLASSIFIED

295.40	Schizophreniform disorder
298.80	Brief reactive psychosis
295.70	Schizoaffective disorder
298.90	Atypical psychosis

NEUROTIC DISORDERS: These are included in Affective, Anxiety, Somatoform, Dissociative and Psychosexual Disorders. In order to facilitate the identification of the categories that in DSM-II were grouped together in the class of Neuroses, the DSM-II terms are included separately in parentheses after the corresponding categories. These DSM-II terms are included in ICD-9-CM and therefore are acceptable as alternatives to the recommended DSM-III terms that precede them.

AFFECTIVE DISORDERS
Major affective disorders

Code major depressive episode in fifth digit: 6 = in remission, 4 = psychotic features (the unofficial non-ICD-9-CM fifth digit 7 may be used instead to indicate that the psychotic features are mood-incongruent), 3 = with melancholia, 2 = without melancholia, 0 = unspecified.

Code manic episode in fifth digit: 6 = in remission, 4 = with psychotic features (the unofficial non-ICD-9-CM fifth digit 7 may be used instead to indicate that the psychotic features are mood-incongruent), 2 = without psychotic features, 0 = unspecified.

	Bipolar disorder,
296.6x	mixed, _____
296.4x	manic, _____
296.5x	depressed, _____
	Major depression,
296.2x	single episode, _____
296.3x	recurrent, _____

Other specific affective disorders

301.13	Cyclothymic disorder
300.40	Dysthymic disorder (or Depressive neurosis)

Atypical affective disorders

296.70	Atypical bipolar disorder
296.82	Atypical depression

ANXIETY DISORDERS

	Phobic disorders (or Phobic neuroses)
300.21	Agoraphobia with panic attacks
300.22	Agoraphobia without panic attacks
300.23	Social phobia
300.29	Simple phobia
	Anxiety states (or Anxiety neuroses)
300.01	Panic disorder
300.02	Generalized anxiety disorder
300.30	Obsessive compulsive disorder (or Obsessive compulsive neurosis)

TABLE VII—*Continued*

	Post-traumatic stress disorder
308.30	acute
309.81	chronic or delayed
300.00	Atypical anxiety disorder

SOMATOFORM DISORDERS

300.81	Somatization disorder
300.11	Conversion disorder (or Hysterical neurosis, conversion type)
307.80	Psychogenic pain disorder
300.70	Hypochondriasis (or Hypochondriacal neurosis)
300.70	Atypical somatoform disorder (300.71)

DISSOCIATIVE DISORDERS (OR HYSTERICAL NEUROSES, DISSOCIATIVE TYPE)

300.12	Psychogenic amnesia
300.13	Psychogenic fugue
300.14	Multiple personality
300.60	Depersonalization disorder (or Depersonalization neurosis)
300.15	Atypical dissociative disorder

PSYCHOSEXUAL DISORDERS

Gender identity disorders

Indicate sexual history in the fifth digit of Transsexualism code: 1 = asexual, 2 = homosexual, 3 = heterosexual, 0 = unspecified.

302.5x	Transsexualism,_____
302.60	Gender identity disorder of childhood
302.85	Atypical gender identity disorder

Paraphilias

302.81	Fetishism
302.30	Transvestism
302.10	Zoophilia
302.20	Pedophilia
302.40	Exhibitionism
302.82	Voyeurism
302.83	Sexual masochism
302.84	Sexual sadism
302.90	Atypical paraphilia

Psychosexual dysfunctions

302.71	Inhibited sexual desire
302.72	Inhibited sexual excitement
302.73	Inhibited female orgasm
302.74	Inhibited male orgasm
302.75	Premature ejaculation
302.76	Functional dyspareunia
306.51	Functional vaginismus
302.70	Atypical psychosexual dysfunction

Other psychosexual disorders

| 302.00 | Ego-dystonic homosexuality |
| 302.89 | Psychosexual disorder not elsewhere classified |

FACTITIOUS DISORDERS

300.16	Factitious disorder with psychological symptoms
301.51	Chronic factitious disorder with physical symptoms
300.19	Atypical factitious disorder with physical symptoms

DISORDERS OF IMPULSE CONTROL NOT ELSEWHERE CLASSIFIED

| 312.31 | Pathological gambling |
| 312.32 | Kleptomania |

312.33	Pyromania
312.34	Intermittent explosive disorder
312.35	Isolated explosive disorder
312.39	Atypical impulse control disorder

ADJUSTMENT DISORDER

309.00	with depressed mood
309.24	with anxious mood
309.28	with mixed emotional features
309.30	with disturbance of conduct
309.40	with mixed disturbance of emotions and conduct
309.23	with work (or academic) inhibition
309.83	with withdrawal
309.90	with atypical features

PSYCHOLOGICAL FACTORS AFFECTING PHYSICAL CONDITION

Specify physical condition on Axis III.

| 316.00 | Psychological factors affecting physical condition |

PERSONALITY DISORDERS

Note: These are coded on Axis II.

301.00	Paranoid
301.20	Schizoid
301.22	Schizotypal
301.50	Histrionic
301.81	Narcissistic
301.70	Antisocial
301.83	Borderline
301.82	Avoidant
301.60	Dependent
301.40	Compulsive
301.84	Passive-Aggressive
301.89	Atypical, mixed or other personality disorder

V CODES FOR CONDITIONS NOT ATTRIBUTABLE TO A MENTAL DISORDER THAT ARE A FOCUS OF ATTENTION OR TREATMENT

V65.20	Malingering
V62.89	Borderline intellectual functioning (V62.88)
V71.01	Adult antisocial behavior
V71.02	Childhood or adolescent antisocial behavior
V62.30	Academic problem
V62.20	Occupational problem
V62.82	Uncomplicated bereavement
V15.81	Noncompliance with medical treatment
V62.89	Phase of life problem or other life circumstance problem
V61.10	Marital problem
V61.20	Parent-child problem
V61.80	Other specified family circumstances
V62.81	Other interpersonal problem

ADDITIONAL CODES

300.90	Unspecified mental disorder (non-psychotic)
V71.09	No diagnosis or condition on Axis I
799.90	Diagnosis or condition deferred on Axis I

| V71.09 | No diagnosis on Axis II |
| 799.90 | Diagnosis deferred on Axis II |

* From American Psychiatric Association. *Diagnostic and Statistical Manual of Mental Disorders*, ed. 3, American Psychiatric Association, Washington, D.C., 1980.

and hallucinogens. And there is a category for tobacco dependence but not tobacco abuse.

The pattern of use is coded in the fifth digit as continuous, episodic, or in remission.

Schizophrenic disorders. As defined in DSM-III, at some time during the illness a schizophrenic disorder always involves at least one of the following: delusions, hallucinations, or certain characteristic disturbances in the form of thought. No single clinical feature is unique to schizophrenia or evident in every case or at every phase of the illness, except that, by definition, the diagnosis is not made unless the period of illness, including the prodromal and residual phases, has persisted for at least 6 months.

The following phenomenological subtypes are recognized: disorganized, catatonic, paranoid, undifferentiated, and residual. In addition, the course of the illness is coded as subchronic, chronic, subchronic with acute exacerbation, chronic with acute exacerbation, and in remission.

Paranoid disorders. The essential feature is a clinical picture in which the predominant symptoms are persistent persecutory delusions or delusions of jealousy that are not explainable by some other psychotic disorder. There are three specific paranoid disorders: paranoia, shared paranoid disorder, and acute paranoid disorder.

Psychotic disorders not elsewhere classified. This is a residual class for psychotic disorders that are not classified as an organic mental disorder, a schizophrenic disorder, a paranoid disorder, or an affective disorder. It contains three specific categories: schizophreniform disorder, brief reactive psychosis, and schizoaffective disorder.

Affective disorders. The essential feature of this group of disorders is a disturbance of mood accompanied by related symptoms. This major class contains two specific minor classes. The first, major affective disorders, includes bipolar disorder and major depression. Bipolar disorder is subdivided according to the current episode as mixed, manic, or depressed. Major depression is subdivided according to whether the disturbance is a single episode or recurrent. There is also provision for further characterizing the current episode as in remission, with psychotic features, with or without melancholia (for a major depressive episode), and without psychotic features (for manic episodes). The second minor class, other specific affective disorders, includes cyclothymic disorder and dysthymic disorder (chronic mild depression).

Anxiety disorders. In this group of disorders, some form of anxiety is the most predominant disturbance or is experienced if the person tries to resist giving in to his or her symptoms.

Phobic disorders are characterized by persistent avoidance behavior secondary to irrational fears of a specific object, activity, or situation. In anxiety states the predominant disturbance is the experience of anxiety itself, which may be episodic, as in panic disorder, or chronic and persistent, as in generalized anxiety disorder. In obsessive-compulsive disorder there are recurrent obsessions or compulsions or both. In posttraumatic stress disorder the essential feature is the development of characteristic symptoms after experiencing a psychologically traumatic event or events that are outside the range of human experience usually considered to be normal.

Somatoform disorders. In this class, all the disorders involve physical symptoms suggesting physical disorder for which no demonstrable organic findings are adequate to explain the symptoms and for which positive evidence or a strong presumption indicates that the symptoms are linked to psychological factors or conflicts. The first disorder in this category is somatization disorder, a chronic polysymptomatic disorder that begins early in life. The second disorder is conversion disorder,

in which the predominant disturbance is conversion symptoms that are not symptomatic of another disorder. Psychogenic pain disorder is for psychologically induced pain not attributable to any other mental or physical disorder. Hypochondriasis involves an unrealistic and persistent interpretation of physical symptoms or sensations as abnormal, leading to the preoccupation with the fear or belief of having a serious disease.

Dissociative disorders. The essential feature of these disorders is a sudden, temporary alteration in the normally integrated functions of consciousness, identity, or motor behavior. This class includes psychogenic amnesia, psychogenic fugue, multiple personality, and depersonalization disorder.

Psychosexual disorders. There are four minor classes: gender identity disorders, characterized by the person's feelings of discomfort and inappropriateness about his or her anatomical sex and by persistent behaviors generally associated with the other sex; paraphilias, characterized by arousal in response to sexual objects or situations that are not part of normative arousal-activity patterns; psychosexual dysfunctions, characterized by inhibitions in sexual desire or the psychophysiological changes that characterize the sexual response cycle; and other psychosexual disorders, which include ego-dystonic homosexuality.

Factitious disorders. These disorders are characterized by physical or psychological symptoms that are produced by the person and are under his or her voluntary control. The judgment that a particular piece of behavior is under voluntary control is made by the exclusion of all other possible causes for the behavior. Factitious disorders are distinguished from acts of malingering, in which the "patient" is also in voluntary control of the symptom production but for a goal that is obviously recognizable with a knowledge of the environmental circumstances, rather than of his or her psychology.

Disorders of impulse control not elsewhere classified. This is a residual category for disorders of impulse control that are not classified elsewhere as, for example, substance use disorders or paraphilias. A disorder of impulse control is characterized by a failure to resist an impulse to perform some action that is harmful to the person or to others; there is an increasing sense of tension before performing the act; and, at the time of performing the act, there is an experience of pleasure, gratification, or release. This class includes pathological gambling, kleptomania, pyromania, intermittent explosive disorder, and isolated explosive disorder.

Adjustment disorder. This category is for maladaptive reactions to identifiable life events or circumstances that do not meet the criteria for and are not merely exacerbations of one of the other mental disorders and that are expected to remit when the stressor ceases or when a new level of adaptation is reached. Predominant symptoms, such as depressed mood, can be coded.

Psychological factors affecting physical condition. This category documents the certainty with which a clinician judges psychological factors to be contributory to the initiation or the exacerbation of a physical condition. The physical condition is noted on Axis III. The judgment that psychological factors are affecting the physical condition requires evidence of a temporal relationship between the environmental stimulus and the meaning given to it, on the one hand, and the initiation or exacerbation of the physical condition, on the other.

Personality disorders. The essential features are deeply ingrained, inflexible, maladaptive patterns of relating to, perceiving, and thinking about the environment and oneself that are of sufficient severity to cause either a significant impairment in adaptive functioning or subjective distress. The personality disorders have been grouped into three clusters. The first cluster includes paranoid, schizoid, and schizotypal personality disorders. Persons with those disorders often seem odd or eccentric. The second cluster includes histrionic, narcissistic, antisocial, and borderline personality disorders. Persons with those disorders often seem dramatic, emotional, or erratic. The third cluster includes avoidant, dependent, compulsive, and passive-aggressive personality disorders. Persons with those disorders often seem anxious or fearful. A residual category for atypical, mixed, or other personality disorders can be used for other specific personality disorders or for cases with mixed features that do not qualify for any of the specific personality disorders described in DSM-III.

V Codes. This category includes codes for conditions that are a focus of attention or treatment but are not attributable to any of the mental disorders noted previously. In some instances, one of those conditions is noted because, after a thorough evaluation, no mental disorder is found to be present. In other instances, the scope of the diagnostic evaluation was not such as to adequately determine the presence or absence of a mental disorder, but there is a need to note the reason for contact with the mental health care system. Or a person may have a mental disorder, but the focus of attention or treatment is a condition that is not due to the mental disorder. For example, a person with bipolar disorder may have marital problems that are not directly related to the manifestations of the affective disorder but are the principal focus of treatment. The 13 DSM-III V codes have been taken from a much larger list of V codes that appear in ICD-9-CM.

FIELD TRIALS

An important step in the development of DSM-III has been a series of field trials using draft versions of the manual. These have been valuable in assessing the clinical usefulness of DSM-III in a variety of clinical settings and in identifying problems in the descriptions of the categories, the diagnostic criteria, and the classification itself so that improvements could be made in subsequent revisions. In addition, the field trials made it possible to determine the interrater reliability of the diagnostic categories.

Over 700 clinicians participated in several phases of the field trials using successive drafts of the manual. The last phase involved more than 500 clinicians participating in a formal field trial sponsored by the National Institute of Mental Health. The clinical acceptability of DSM-III was demonstrated by the fact that approximately three-quarters of the participants judged DSM-III to be "more helpful in making treatment and management decisions than DSM-II." Over 80 per cent judged the multiaxial system to be "a useful addition to traditional psychiatric diagnosis." Despite the concerns with the potential misuse of diagnostic criteria, more than 80 per cent believed that "the diagnostic criteria represent one of DSM-III's major contributions." Seventy-five per cent agreed with the generally atheoretical approach taken in the descriptions of the diagnostic categories.

Interrater reliability was determined by both the test-retest and joint assessment methods using pairs of clinicians working at the same facilities (Spitzer et al., 1979a). For most of the diagnostic classes, the reliability for both interview situations was quite good and, in general, higher than that previously achieved using DSM-I and DSM-II. The over-all kappa coefficient of agreement for Axis I diagnoses of 281 adult patients was .78 for joint interviews and .66 for diagnoses made after separate interviews. For Axis II, the coefficients of agreement on the presence of a personality disorder were .61 (joint assessment) and .54 (test-retest). The high interrater reliability of DSM-III may be due to improvements in the classification itself (e.g., grouping all the affective disorders together), the separation of Axis I and Axis II disorders, the systematic description of the various disorders, and the inclusion of diagnostic criteria.

The reliability of Axes IV and V was also determined (Spitzer and Forman, 1979). The kappa coefficient of agreement for Axis IV was .62 for joint interviews and .58 for separate interviews, which is at least fair. Reliability for Axis V was quite good—.80 for joint interviews and .69 for separate interviews.

Suggested Cross References

DSM-III is reflected in all the clinical chapters of this textbook—particularly Chapters 13, 15 through 27, and 36 through 41. The application of statistics to psychiatry is discussed in Chapter 7, and computers are discussed in Section 6.2.

TABLE VIII

Annotated Comparative Listing of DSM-II and DSM-III*

This table lists all the specific categories included in the second edition of the *Diagnostic and Statistical Manual of Mental Disorders* (DSM-II), and the specific DSM-III categories that are equivalent to or subsumed by them. Because of the greater precision with which the DSM-III categories are described and because the diagnostic concepts have often been modified, the degree of equivalence varies. (For example, in DSM-III the category of Schizophrenia is more restrictive than the DSM-II category.) Whenever a category in one manual corresponds to several categories in the other, those categories are enclosed by one brace. In some instances, several categories from one manual are equivalent to several categories from the other manual. In such cases, a double brace is used. This text should not be used as a conversion between DSM-II and ICD-9-CM. In a number of instances, the conceptual reclassification of disorders is unique to DSM-III and does not conform to the classification of these disorders in ICD-9-CM. Where these departures occur, the DSM-III titles have been asterisked.

When a DSM-II category is listed without a corresponding DSM-III category, it indicates that the DSM-II category was not included in DSM-III. Likewise, when a DSM-III category is listed with no corresponding DSM-II category, it indicates that the DSM-III diagnostic concept was not included in DSM-II.

Included in the table are comments that attempt to explain the reasons for major changes in the DSM-II classification, terminology, or definitions of the categories. References are cited when the reason for a change is based on evidence cited in the literature or when the article referred to provides a fuller discussion of the rationale for the change.

The DSM-II classification follows, in order to assist the reader in locating specific categories, since the diagnostic categories are listed in the order in which they appear in DSM-II.

DSM-II	DSM-III
I. Mental Retardation	**Mental Retardation**

Since the large majority of persons with borderline intellectual functioning (I.Q.=71-84) do not have significant impairment in adaptive behavior, this range of intellectual functioning is no longer included within Mental Retardation (Gross, 1977). DSM-III includes Borderline Intellectual Functioning as a V code for Conditions Not Attributable to a Mental Disorder because of the frequent need to attend to that condition when planning treatment (Gift et al., 1978).

TABLE VIII—*Continued*

DSM-II	DSM-III
310.x Borderline mental retardation	V62.89 Borderline intellectual functioning (included as a condition not attributable to a mental disorder)
311.x Mild mental retardation	317.0 Mild mental retardation
312.x Moderate mental retardation	318.0 Moderate mental retardation
313.x Severe mental retardation	318.1 Severe mental retardation
314.x Profound mental retardation	318.2 Profound mental retardation
315.x Unspecified mental retardation	319.0 Unspecified mental retardation

In DSM-II the fourth digit was used to note associated physical conditions. In DSM-III, the multiaxial system permits a more specific designation of associated physical conditions, noted on Axis III. In DSM-III the fifth digit is used to indicate other psychiatric symptoms requiring attention or treatment that are not part of another disorder. Frequently, such symptoms as aggressiveness and self-mutilation are the primary focus of attention.

II. Organic Brain Syndromes   **Organic Mental Disorders**

The introduction to the organic brain syndromes section of DSM-II implied the concept of a *single* organic brain syndrome with a limited number of manifestations. They were divided into the Psychoses and the Nonpsychotic Organic Brain Syndromes. Because psychosis was defined in terms of "severity of functional impairment" and the "capacity to meet the ordinary demands of life," the psychotic-nonpsychotic distinction was difficult to make. Within the Psychotic Organic Brain Syndromes, DSM-II retained the DSM-I distinction of acute versus chronic brain syndrome. That distinction was based on the potential reversibility of the syndrome and not on the course of the illness, as the terms "acute" and "chronic" are ordinarily used. This approach had many limitations (Lipowski, 1978; Seltzer and Sherwin, 1978; Wells, 1978); for example, it discouraged recognition of the possible reversibility of seemingly "chronic" brain syndromes, such as "reversible dementia."

The DSM-III approach recognizes nine different organic brain syndromes: intoxication, withdrawal, delirium, dementia, amnestic syndrome, delusional syndrome, hallucinosis, affective syndrome, and personality syndrome. When the etiological factor is either associated with aging or is substance-induced, the etiological factor, together with the specific organic brain syndrome, constitutes the DSM-III Organic Mental Disorder. When there is some other etiology (e.g. pneumonia) or the etiology or pathophysiological process is unknown, the organic brain syndrome from section 2 of the Organic Mental Disorders section of DSM-III is noted on Axis I, and the specific physical disorder, if known, is noted on Axis III. In DSM-II the category of "Drug Intoxication (other than alcohol)" did not allow for identifying the class of drug or the more specific brain syndrome.

The DSM-II categories that have equivalent specific DSM-III categories are presented below.

The large number of specific DSM-III Organic Mental Disorders that have no direct DSM-II equivalents are not listed in this table.

DSM-II	DSM-III
290 Senile and presenile dementia	290.xx Dementias arising in the senium and presenium
290.0 Senile dementia	290.xx Primary degenerative dementia, senile onset
290.1 Presenile dementia	290.1x Primary degenerative dementia, presenile onset

Fourth and fifth digits in DSM-III are used to code complications of delirium, delusional features, and depressive features.

DSM-II	DSM-III
291 Alcoholic psychosis	
291.0 Delirium tremens	291.00 Alcohol withdrawal delirium
291.1 Korsakov's psychosis, alcoholic	291.10 Alcohol amnestic disorder
291.2 Other alcoholic hallucinosis	291.30 Alcohol hallucinosis
291.3 Alcohol paranoid state	303.9x Alcohol Dependence* and 297.90 Atypical paranoid disorder*

Because there is no compelling evidence that a paranoid state due to chronic alcohol use is a distinct entity, DSM-III does not include a category for alcohol paranoid state.

DSM-II	DSM-III
291.4 Acute alcohol intoxication	303.00 Alcohol intoxication*
291.5 Alcoholic deterioration	291.2x Dementia associated with alcoholism

There is no compelling evidence that alcohol itself is the causative factor in Dementia in individuals with chronic Alcohol Dependence. For this reason, the ICD-9 term "Alcoholic Dementia" is avoided, since it implies that alcohol is known to be the causative factor (Goodwin and Hill, 1975).

291.6 Pathological intoxication	291.40 Alcohol idiosyncratic intoxication

The DSM-III term is more precise than the DSM-II term.

293.0 Psychosis with cerebral arteriosclerosis	290.4x Multi-infarct dementia

There is evidence that the dementia is related to the presence of multiple infarcts, rather than the degree of cerebral arteriosclerosis (Fisher, 1968; Hachinski et al., 1974).

294.4 Psychosis with childbirth	298.90 Atypical psychosis*

As with DSM-II, the DSM-III category is to be used only when no other psychotic disorder can be diagnosed. There is no compelling evidence that post-partum psychosis is a distinct entity.

II-B. Nonpsychotic Organic Brain Syndromes

DSM-II	DSM-III
309.13 Nonpsychotic organic brain syndrome with alcohol (simple drunkenness)	303.00 Alcohol intoxication*
309.30 Nonpsychotic organic brain syndrome with circulatory disturbance	290.4x Multi-infarct dementia*
309.60 Nonpsychotic organic brain syndrome with senile or presenile brain disease	290.xx Primary degenerative dementia, senile onset
	290.1x Primary degenerative dementia, presenile onset

TABLE VIII—*Continued*

DSM-II	DSM-III

III. Psychoses Not Attributed to Physical Conditions Listed Previously

DSM-III does not use "psychotic" as a fundamental basis for classifying the nonorganic mental disorders in order to avoid classifying the Major Affective Disorders as psychotic, since such disorders usually do not have psychotic features.

Schizophrenia   Schizophrenic disorders

The DSM-III concept is more restrictive in order to identify a group that is more homogeneous with regard to differential response to somatic therapy, presence of a familial pattern, a tendency toward onset in early adult life, and recurrence and severe functional impairment (Spitzer et al., 1978a).

In DSM-II, two of the subtypes were defined by course, and the remaining subtypes were defined only by symptomatology. In DSM-III, the fourth digit is used to characterize symptomatology of the current episode, and the fifth digit is used to code the course of the illness as subchronic, chronic, subchronic with acute exacerbation, chronic with acute exacerbation, or in remission.

295.0   Schizophrenia, simple type   301.22   Schizotypal personality disorder*

The DSM-III concept of Schizophrenia requires the presence of psychotic features at some time during the illness. Furthermore, the validity of the category of Simple Schizophrenia has been questioned (Stone et al., 1968; Munoz et al., 1972). The closest approximation is Schizotypal Personality Disorder.

295.1   Schizophrenia, hebephrenic type   295.1x   Schizophrenia, disorganized type

The term "hebephrenic" in this country has included only cases with regressive and silly behavior, whereas the more common meaning has emphasized the disorganized aspect of the behavior (Tsuang and Winokur, 1974).

295.2   Schizophrenia, catatonic type
295.23   Schizophrenia, catatonic type, excited   } { 295.2x   Schizophrenia, catatonic type
295.24   Schizophrenia, catatonic type, withdrawn   { 296.4x   Bipolar disorder, manic*

Because of changes in the concepts of Schizophrenia and Affective Disorders, some cases of the DSM-II category of catatonic type will be diagnosed as having an Affective Disorder in DSM-III (Abrams and Taylor, 1977).

295.3   Schizophrenia, paranoid type   295.3x   Schizophrenia, paranoid type
                                                         { 295.40   Schizophreniform disorder
295.4   Acute schizophrenic episode   { 298.80   Brief reactive psychosis*
                                                         { 295.70   Schizoaffective disorder*

The DSM-III category of Schizophrenia requires a duration of 6 months (including prodromal and residual phases) as this criterion defined a group that is more homogeneous with regard to familial pattern and course (Astrup and Noreik, 1966; Tsuang et al., 1976; Sartorius et al., 1978).

295.5   Schizophrenia, latent type   { 301.22   Schizotypal personality disorder
                                                          { 301.83   Borderline Personality Disorder

The criteria for Schizotypal Personality Disorder were developed to identify a group of individuals clinically diagnosed as having Borderline Schizophrenia, a term included with the DSM-II category (Spitzer et al., 1979b). However, this category is not included with the DSM-III category of Schizophrenia, since the category requires psychotic features at some time during the illness. Some individuals diagnosed as having Schizophrenia, latent type, in DSM-II may meet the criteria for Borderline Personality Disorder in DSM-III, instead of, or in addition to, Schizotypal Personality Disorder (Spitzer et al., 1979b).

295.6   Schizophrenia, residual type   { 295.6x   Schizophrenia, residual type
295.7   Schizophrenia, schizoaffective type   { 296.4x   Major affective disorder (depressed or manic) with psychotic
295.73   Schizophrenia, schizoaffective type, excited   }   features*
295.74   Schizophrenia, schizoaffective type, depressed   { 295.40   Schizophreniform disorder
                                                          { 298.80   Brief reactive psychosis*
                                                          { 295.xx   Schizophrenia* with superimposed Atypical affective disor-
                                                          {   der*
                                                          { 295.70   Schizoaffective disorder

DSM-III acknowledges that certain bizarre psychotic symptoms are not incompatible with otherwise fully validated Affective Disorder (Pope and Lipinski, 1978). The other DSM-III categories are included here because of the hetereogeneous nature of individuals previously classified as having Schizoaffective Schizophrenia (Procci, 1976; Brockington and Leff, 1979). In DSM-III Schizoaffective Disorder is a residual category, not included in Schizophrenia, and is to be used when there is uncertainty about the differential diagnosis between an Affective Disorder and either Schizophrenia or Schizophreniform Disorder.

295.8   Schizophrenia, childhood type   { 299.0x   Infantile autism
                                                          { 299.9x   Childhood-onset pervasive developmental disorder

When children or adolescents have an illness that meets the criteria for Schizophrenia in DSM-III, that diagnosis is given. There is evidence that the syndrome of Infantile Autism has little relationship to the psychotic disorders of adult life, particularly adult onset Schizophrenia (Rutter and Schopler, 1978). The relationship between the DSM-III category of Childhood Onset Pervasive Developmental Disorder and the psychotic disorders of adult life is unclear (Kolvin et al., 1960; Brown, 1963; Rutter, 1974). The criteria for this disorder describe children who have been described by some clinicians as Childhood Schizophrenia, Childhood Psychosis, Atypical Children, and Symbiotic Psychosis. It is likely that some children with this disorder will, indeed, develop Schizophrenia as adults. However, there is currently no way of predicting which children will develop Schizophrenia as adults.

295.9   Schizophrenia, chronic undifferentiated type   295.9x   Schizophrenia, undifferentiated type

Major affective disorders   Affective disorders

In DSM-II Major Affective Disorders were included within the Nonorganic Psychoses, Affective Disorders that seemed to be "related directly to a precipitating life experience" were excluded. In contrast, the DSM-III category of Affective Disorders groups all the Affective Disorders together, regardless of the presence or absence of psychotic features or association with precipitating life experiences. The DSM-III classification recognizes the heterogeneous nature of a major depressive episode (Nelson and Channey, unpublished) and uses the term melancholia to designate the subtype that tends to be more severe, associated with a constellation of characteristic symptoms, and is apparently particularly responsive to somatic therapy (Bielski and Friedel, 1976).

TABLE VIII—*Continued*

DSM-II	DSM-III

296.0   Involutional melancholia .... 296.23   Major depression, single episode, with melancholia

There is no compelling evidence that depression occurring in the involutional period is distinct from depression occurring in other stages of life (Weissman, 1979).

296.1   Manic-depressive illness, manic type   296.4x   Bipolar disorder, manic*

Since virtually all individuals with manic episodes eventually develop depressive episodes, most investigators now conceptualize manic episodes as being subsumed under Bipolar Disorder (Nurnberger et al., 1979). Therefore, in DSM-III the diagnosis of Bipolar Disorder is made when there is a manic episode, whether or not there has been a depressive episode.

296.2   Manic-depressive illness, depressed type   Major depression
                                                                                 296.2x   single episode
                                                                                 296.3x   recurrent

296.3   Manic-depressive illness, circular type ....   Bipolar disorder
296.33   manic ....   296.4x   manic
296.34   depressed ....   296.5x   depressed
                                                                                 296.6x   mixed

The DSM-II classification implied the unity of manic-depressive illness. DSM-III accepts the evidence pointing to the importance of the distinction between unipolar and bipolar forms of Affective Disorder (Perris, 1966; Winokur et al., 1969).

Paranoid states ....   Paranoid disorders

297.0   Paranoia ....   297.10   Paranoia

297.1   Involutional paranoid state ....   { 297.10   Paranoia*
                                                                    { 297.90   Atypical paranoid disorder*

There is no compelling evidence that a paranoid disorder occurring in the involutional period is distinct from paranoid disorders occurring in other periods of life (Retterstol, 1966).

                                                                                 297.30   Shared paranoid disorder

This category is the traditional category of Folie à deux. The justification for its inclusion in DSM-III, despite its rarity, rests on the distinct clinical picture and the treatment implications (Gralnick, 1942; McNeil et al., 1972).

                                                                                 298.30   Acute paranoid disorder

This category permits the identification of the most common form of Paranoid Disorder, which is of acute onset and of brief duration (Retterstol, 1966).

298.0   Psychotic depressive reaction ....   296.24   Major depression, single episode, with psychotic features,*
                                                                             with coding of severity of psychosocial stressor on Axis IV

There is no compelling evidence that, once a Major Depression has developed, its course and response to treatment are affected by whether or not its onset was associated with a stressor.

IV. Neuroses

In DSM-II, disorders in which the "chief characteristic" was anxiety, whether "felt and expressed directly" or "controlled unconsciously and automatically by conversion, displacement and various other psychological mechanisms" were grouped together as Neuroses. In contrast, in DSM-III the disorders in which anxiety is experienced directly are grouped together in the class of Anxiety Disorders. The other DSM-II neuroses are distributed among other classes, each defined by shared symptoms or other descriptive characteristics. So that one can identify the categories that in DSM-II were grouped together in the class of Neuroses, the DSM-II terms are included separately in parentheses after the corresponding DSM-III categories.

300.0   Anxiety neurosis ....   { 300.01   Panic disorder
                                                                    { 300.02   Generalized anxiety disorder

There is compelling evidence that Panic Disorder, as a distinct entity, has differential treatment response, as compared with other disorders in which anxiety is prominent (Klein et al., 1978; Zitrin et al., 1978).

300.13   Hysterical neurosis

In DSM-III, the concept and the term "hysteria" have been avoided. Instead, the multiple meanings of the term have been included within new categories, such as Somatoform Disorders and Dissociative Disorders (Hyler and Spitzer, 1978).

300.1   Hysterical neurosis, conversion type ....   { 300.11   Conversion disorder
                                                                    { 307.80   Psychogenic pain disorder*

This latter DSM-III category permits the identification of individuals whose predominant complaint is pain, apparently of psychogenic origin (Sternbach, 1968).

                                                                    { 300.12   Psychogenic amnesia
                                                                    { 300.13   Psychogenic fugue
300.14   Hysterical neurosis, dissociative type .... { 300.14   Multiple personality
                                                                    { 307.46   Sleepwalking disorder
                                                                    {   (in the childhood section)

In DSM-III, the four disorders included in the DSM-II description are defined as separate disorders because of differing clinical pictures, predisposing factors, and courses (Ludwig et al., 1972; Nemiah, 1975). The first three disorders are included within the Dissociative Disorders. Sleepwalking disorder is listed in the section Disorders Usually First Evident in Infancy, Childhood, or Adolescence and is defined as a disturbance of a particular state of sleep (Jacobson et al., 1965, 1969).

                                                                    Phobic disorders
                                                                    { 300.21   Agoraphobia with panic attacks
                                                                    { 300.22   Agoraphobia without panic attacks
300.2   Phobic neurosis ....   { 300.23   Social phobia
                                                                    { 300.29   Simple phobia
                                                                    { 309.21   Separation anxiety disorder* (in the childhood section)

TABLE VIII—*Continued*

DSM-II	DSM-III

DSM-III subdivides phobias into separate categories because of differing clinical pictures, age at onset, and differential treatment responses (Marles, 1969). Even though Separation Anxiety Disorder is a form of Phobia, because it characteristically begins in infancy or childhood and rarely persists into adulthood, it is classified in the section Disorders Usually First Evident in Infancy, Childhood, or Adolescence (Bowlby, 1960; Gittelman-Klein and Klein, 1973).

300.3 Obsessive compulsive neurosis	300.30 Obsessive compulsive disorder
	300.40 Dysthmic disorder
	Major depression
300.4 Depressive neurosis	296.22 single episode, without melancholia
	296.32 recurrent, without melancholia
	309.00 Adjustment disorder with depressed mood*

The DSM-II category was defined merely as "an excessive reaction of depression due to an internal conflict or to an identifiable event. . . ." For this reason, it was applied to a heterogeneous group of conditions (Klerman et al., 1979). The three major conditions to which it was applied have each been defined descriptively without reference to etiology. When an "identifiable event" is judged to have contributed to the development of the illness, this factor can be noted on Axis IV.

300.5   Neurasthenic neurosis

This DSM-II category was rarely used.

300.6 Depersonalization neurosis	300.60 Depersonalization disorder

The DSM-III category is included within the class of Dissociative Disorders even though it is controversial, because the feeling of one's own reality, a component of identity, is lost (Lehmann, 1974).

300.7 Hypochondriacal neurosis	300.70 Hypochondriasis

Hypochondriasis is included within the class of Somatoform Disorders because of the presentation of symptoms suggestive of physical disorder.

	300.81 Somatization disorder

This disorder has been described in the literature as either "Hysteria" or "Briquet's syndrome," and validity data have been gathered in a series of studies (Guze, 1975).

	Post-traumatic stress disorder
	308.30 acute
	309.81 chronic or delayed

This DSM-III category used to be referred to as Traumatic Neurosis (Keiser, 1968). Its subdivision into acute and chronic forms is justified by longitudinal studies showing differential outcomes for the two forms (Adler, 1943, 1945; Kamman, 1951).

V. Personality Disorders	**Personality Disorders**

Personality Disorders in DSM-III are coded on Axis II to insure that they are not overlooked when attention is directed to the usually more florid Axis I disorder.

DSM-III recognizes the distinction between personality traits and personality disorders. For that reason, the term "disorder" appears in the diagnostic term. Although prominent personality traits may be noted on Axis II, they are not given code numbers, since they do not represent mental disorders.

301.0 Paranoid personality	301.00 Paranoid personality disorder
301.1 Cyclothymic personality	301.13 Cyclothymic disorder

Cyclothymic disorder is included in DSM-III within the Affective Disorders, rather than the Personality Disorders, because of evidence that it is related to Bipolar Disorder (Akiskal et al., 1977).

	301.22 Schizotypal personality disorder
301.2 Schizoid personality	301.21 Schizoid personality disorder
	301.82 Avoidant personality disorder*

The DSM-II category included "shyness, over-sensitivity, seclusiveness, avoidance of close or competitive relationships, and often eccentricity." In DSM-III Schizotypal Personality Disorder describes individuals with the eccentric features referred to in the DSM-II description.

The criteria for Schizotypal Personality Disorder were developed to identify individuals who had been described as having Borderline Schizophrenia (Spitzer et al., 1979b). There is evidence that Chronic Schizophrenia is more common among family members of individuals who were described as having Borderline Schizophrenia than in the general population (Rosenthal and Kety, 1968). The distinction between the DSM-III categories of Schizoid and Avoidant Personality Disorders is based on whether or not there is a defect in the motivation and capacity for emotional involvement (Millon, 1969). It is expected that this descriptive distinction will have therapeutic and prognostic implications.

301.3 Explosive personality	312.34 Intermittent explosive disorder*

Because the explosive behavior is, by definition, in contrast to the individual's usual behavior, the disorder in DSM-III is not classified among the personality disorders.

301.4 Obsessive compulsive personality	301.40 Compulsive personality disorder

The DSM-III label omits the term "obsessive" in order to avoid confusion with Obsessive Compulsive disorder.

301.5 Hysterical personality	301.50 Histrionic personality disorder

The term "hysterical" has many irrelevant historical connotations and suggests a relationship to conversion symptoms (Chadoff and Lyons, 1958; Chadoff, 1974). The essential feature of this disorder, as described in both DSM-II and DSM-III, is the histrionic pattern of behavior.

301.6   Asthenic personality

This DSM-II category was rarely used.

301.7 Antisocial personality	301.70 Antisocial personality disorder

The DSM-III description and criteria are based on longitudinal studies of children whose antisocial behavior persisted into adult life (Robins, 1974).

301.81 Passive-aggressive personality	301.84 Passive-aggressive personality disorder
301.82 Inadequate personality	

This DSM-II category was defined primarily in terms of functional impairment, rather than by a distinctive behavior pattern.

	301.81 Narcissistic personality disorder

TABLE VIII—*Continued*

DSM-II	DSM-III

In recent years, considerable attention has been given in the psychoanalytic literature to narcissistic disturbances in personality (Kohut, 1971; Kernberg, 1975).

301.83   Borderline personality disorder

This category identifies a constellation of relatively enduring personality features of instability and vulnerability believed to have important treatment and outcome implications (Gunderson and Singer, 1975). The criteria for this category are supported by the results of a factor analytic study of symptom data from patients clinically designated as having a borderline condition and are consistent with the literature describing borderline conditions (Spitzer et al., 1979b). Some of these individuals were diagnosed as having Schizophrenia, latent type, in DSM-II.

301.60   Dependent personality disorder

This category is roughly equivalent to the DSM-I category of Passive-aggressive personality, dependent type.

Sexual deviations   Paraphilias

The term "paraphilias" is preferable to "sexual deviations" in that it correctly emphasizes that the deviation (para) is in that to which the individual is attracted (philia).

302.0   Homosexuality (replaced in 1973 with Sexual orientation disturbance)   302.00   Ego-dystonic homosexuality (included in Other Psychosexual Disorders)

Whether or not homosexuality per se should be classified as a mental disorder has been the focus of considerable controversy (Stoller et al., 1973). In December 1973, the Board of Trustees of the American Psychiatric Association voted to eliminate homosexuality per se as a mental disorder and to substitute a new category, Sexual Orientation Disturbance, reserved for those homosexuals who are "disturbed by, in conflict with, or wish to change their sexual orientation." That change appeared in the seventh and subsequent printings of DSM-II.

The removal of homosexuality per se from DSM-II was supported by the following rationale: the crucial issue in determining whether or not homosexuality per se should be regarded as a mental disorder is not the etiology of the condition but its consequences and the definition of mental disorder (Spitzer and Endicott, 1978). A significant proportion of homosexuals are apparently satisfied with their sexual orientation, show no significant signs of manifest psychopathology (unless homosexuality, by itself, is considered psychopathology), and are able to function socially and occupationally with no impairment (Hooker, 1963; Siegelman, 1972 a, b; Bell and Weinberg, 1978). If one uses the criteria of *distress* or *disability*, homosexuality per se is not a mental disorder. If one uses the criterion of *inherent disadvantage*, it is not at all clear that homosexuality is a disadvantage in all cultures or subcultures (Ford and Beach, 1951; Davenport, 1965).

In DSM-III, the category of Ego-dystonic Homosexuality is a modification of the DSM-II category of Sexual Orientation Disturbance. The change in terminology was made to make it clear that the category is limited to individuals with a homosexual arousal pattern. Changes in the definition of the category emphasize the impairment in heterosexual functioning. Ego-dystonic Homosexuality is not included as a Paraphilia in DSM-III, in contrast to the inclusion of both Homosexuality and Sexual Orientation Disturbance in DSM-II as Sexual Deviations, because in DSM-III the Paraphilias are limited to conditions that are associated with (1) preference for the use of a nonhuman object for sexual arousal, (2) repetitive sexual activity with humans involving real or simulated suffering or humiliation, or (3) repetitive sexual activity with nonconsenting or inappropriate partners. In contrast, the DSM-II category of Sexual Deviations also included those "individuals whose sexual interests are directed primarily toward objects other than people of the opposite sex."

302.1	Fetishism	302.81	Fetishism
302.2	Pedophilia	302.20	Pedophilia
302.3	Transvestism	302.30	Transvestism
302.4	Exhibitionism	302.40	Exhibitionism
302.5	Voyeurism	302.82	Voyeurism
302.6	Sadism	302.84	Sexual sadism
302.7	Masochism	302.83	Sexual masochism

The DSM-III terms for the above two categories avoid any confusion with nonsexual meanings of these terms.

302.10   Zoophilia (Shenken, 1964)

Gender identity disorders

302.5x   Transsexualism (Benjamin, 1966; Green and Money, 1969)

302.60   Gender identity disorder of childhood (Green, 1975)

Psychosexual dysfunctions

302.71   Inhibited sexual desire

302.72   Inhibited sexual excitement

302.73   Inhibited female orgasm

302.74   Inhibited male orgasm

302.75   Premature ejaculation

302.76   Functional dyspareunia

306.51   Functional vaginismus

DSM-II listed, as examples of Psychophysiological Genitourinary Disorder, both Dyspareunia and Impotence, whose DSM-III equivalents are Functional Dyspareunia and Inhibited Sexual Excitement (in a male). The justification for including the other specific Psychosexual Dysfunctions rests on their clinical importance and differential treatments (Masters and Johnson, 1970; Kaplan, 1974).

Alcoholism   Alcohol Abuse and Dependence (included within Substance Use Disorders)

In DSM-III, the equivalent categories are included within the Substance Use Disorders to emphasize the fact that the effects of the maladaptive use of alcohol are similar to the effects of the maladaptive use of other substances of potential abuse and dependence.

303.0	Episodic excessive drinking	305.02	Alcohol abuse, episodic*
303.1	Habitual excessive drinking	305.01	Alcohol abuse, continuous*
303.2	Alcohol addiction	303.9x	Alcohol dependence

In DSM-III, for each Substance Use Disorder, the course of the illness may be noted in the fifth digit as continuous, episodic, or in remission.

TABLE VIII—*Continued*

DSM-II	DSM-III

Drug Dependence .... Substance Use Disorders

The DSM-II Drug Dependence category included what in DSM-III is referred to as Substance Abuse and Substance Dependence. In DSM-II, the term "dependence" included both psychological dependence and physiological dependence. In DSM-III, dependence is used only in the physiological sense and generally requires evidence of either tolerance or withdrawal. The DSM-II Drug Dependence category specifically excluded alcohol (coded separately) and tobacco, whereas these substances are both included within the DSM-III Substance Use Disorders.

304.0	Drug dependence, opium, opium alkaloids and their derivatives		305.5x	Opioid abuse
304.1	Drug dependence, synthetic analgesics with morphine-like effects		304.0x	Opioid dependence
304.2	Drug dependence, barbiturates		305.4x	Barbiturate or similarly acting sedative or hypnotic abuse
304.3	Drug dependence, other hypnotics and sedatives or "tranquilizers"		304.1x	Barbiturate or similarly acting sedative or hypnotic dependence
304.4	Drug dependence, cocaine		305.6x	Cocaine abuse
304.5	Drug dependence, *Cannabis sativa* (hashish, marihuana)		305.2x	Cannabis abuse
			304.3x	Cannabis dependence

The existence and significance of tolerance or withdrawal with regular heavy use of cannabis (Cannabis dependence) is controversial (Jones et al., 1976; Petersen, 1977).

304.6	Drug dependence, other psychostimulants (amphetamines, etc.)		305.7x	Amphetamine or similarly acting sympathomimetic abuse
			304.4x	Amphetamine or similarly acting sympathomimetic dependence
304.7	Drug dependence, hallucinogens		305.3x	Hallucinogen abuse

No withdrawal syndrome from hallucinogens has ever been described.

305.9x   Phencyclidine (PCP) or similarly acting arylcyclohexylamine abuse

This relatively new substance of abuse is distinguished from hallucinogens, despite some similarities in their effects (Petersen and Stillman, 1978).

305.1x   Tobacco dependence

The justification for the inclusion of Tobacco Dependence in DSM-III (as it is in the ninth revision of the International Classification of Diseases) rests on the serious medical complications of long-term use (Larson and Silvetle, 1975; Jaffe and Jarvik, 1978; Office of the Surgeon General, 1979). It could be argued that the absence of both an intoxication state and the kinds of social complications associated with other substances of dependence speak for classifying Tobacco Dependence as a physical disorder, not a mental disorder. However, the behavioral manifestations of the dependence (inability to control use) and the withdrawal syndrome are by no means inconsequential. Furthermore, by tradition, substance dependence is classified as a mental disorder.

304.7x   Dependence on combination of an opioid and other nonalcoholic substance

304.8x   Dependence on combination of substances, excluding opioids and alcohol

These two categories are necessary to indicate poly-substance use when it is not possible to identify all the specific substances involved.

VI. Psychophysiological Disorders (305) ....   **316.00   Psychological Factors Affecting Physical Condition**

The DSM-II approach to the classification of so-called "psychophysiological" or "psychosomatic" disorders had several practical and theoretical shortcomings. The categories of psychophysiological disorders were rarely used. The choice between a psychophysiological diagnosis and an "organic" diagnosis tends to be made idiosyncratically. The DSM-II approach did not encourage collaboration between psychiatrists and other medical specialists. The theoretical basis for the category perpetuated a simplistic, unicausational concept about disease etiology. The DSM-III approach attempts to overcome those shortcomings by the use of the multiaxial system. When the clinician judges that a psychological factor is associated with either the initiation or the exacerbation of a physical condition or disorder, the category of Psychological Factors Affecting Physical Condition is noted on Axis I. The physical condition or disorder is noted on Axis III. The limitations of the DSM-II approach and the potential advantages of this approach are discussed more fully elsewhere (Looney et al., 1978; Latimer, 1979).

VII. Special Symptoms (306)

This section of DSM-II was intended for "discrete, specific symptoms" as distinguished from mental disorders. The names of the symptoms were listed with no descriptions. In DSM-III most of the "symptoms" are included as mental disorders because of their syndromal nature (e.g. Anorexia Nervosa), or because they represent a distinct clinical pattern (e.g. Functional Enuresis).

306.0   Speech disturbance ....   307.00   Stuttering

The only speech disturbance included in DSM-III is Stuttering. Other speech disturbances are unlikely to come to the attention of a mental health professional.

Specific Developmental Disorders

	315.00	Developmental reading disorder
	315.10	Developmental arithmetic disorder
306.1 Specific learning disturbance	315.31	Developmental language disorder
	315.39	Developmental articulation disorder
	315.50	Mixed specific developmental disorder

The DSM-III term Specific Developmental Disorders indicates that these disorders are characterized by specific delays in development. Because of differential treatment implications, they are divided according to the predominant area of functioning that is impaired (Rutter and Yule, 1973). They are coded on Axis II in order to insure that they are considered when the person has a more florid Axis I disorder.

Stereotyped movement disorders

	307.21	Transient tic disorder
306.2 Tic	307.22	Chronic motor tic disorder
	307.23	Tourette's disorder

TABLE VIII—*Continued*

DSM-II	DSM-III

The three major forms of Tic Disorders are described separately because of differing clinical pictures, courses, and treatment implications (Shapiro et al., 1978).

306.4   Disorders of sleep ....

{ 307.46*   Sleepwalking disorder
{ 307.46*   Sleep terror disorder

Of the many disorders of sleep, DSM-III includes only these two because of their marked behavioral manifestations, because of frequency with which they come to the attention of mental health professionals, and because, by tradition, they are thought of as mental disorders (Jacobson et al., 1969; Fisher et al., 1973, 1974).

Eating disorders
{ 307.10   Anorexia nervosa
{ 307.51   Bulimia
306.5   Feeding disturbance ....   { 307.52   Pica
{ 307.53   Rumination disorder of infancy

The Eating Disorders are described separately because of differing clinical pictures, courses, and treatment implications.

306.6   Enuresis ....   307.60   Functional enuresis
306.7   Encopresis ....   307.70   Functional encopresis

The DSM-III terms emphasize the exclusion of known physical etiology.

306.80   Cephalalgia

It is not clear what was included within this DSM-II category.

VIII. Transient Situational Disturbances (307) ....   **Adjustment Disorder**

The DSM-II category was "reserved for more or less transient disorders of any severity (including those of psychotic proportions) that occur in individuals without any apparent underlying mental disorders. . . ."

The DSM-III category of Adjustment Disorder excludes reactions of psychotic proportions, since they are adequately classified elsewhere. Adjustment Disorder can be given as an additional diagnosis to an individual with an underlying disorder, e.g., a Personality Disorder, since there is evidence that individuals with Personality Disorders are particularly vulnerable to stress (Looney and Gunderson, 1978).

The DSM-II classification of Transient Situational Disturbances by developmental stage, infancy to late life, offered no information about the manifestations of the disturbance that would be of importance in planning treatment. For that reason, in DSM-III Adjustment Disorder is subtyped by predominant symptomatology.

	{ 309.00 with depressed mood
307.0 Adjustment reaction of infancy	309.24 with anxious mood
307.1 Adjustment reaction of childhood	309.28 with mixed emotional features
307.2 Adjustment reaction of adolescence	{ 309.30 with disturbance of conduct
307.3 Adjustment reaction of adult life	309.40 with mixed disturbance of emotions and conduct
307.4 Adjustment reaction of late life	309.23 with work (or academic) inhibition
	{ 309.83 with withdrawal

IX. Behavior Disorders of Childhood and Adolescence   **Disorders Usually First Evident in Infancy, Childhood, or Adolescence**

The DSM-II category was limited to a small number of categories appropriate only for children or adolescents. They were conceptualized as midway between Transient Situational Disturbances, on the one hand, and Psychoses, Neuroses, and Personality Disorders, on the other hand, in terms of stability and resistance to treatment. In contrast, the DSM-III section includes a large number of diagnoses of varying degrees of severity and stability. Furthermore, when appropriate, some of the diagnoses may be given to adults.

308.0   Hyperkinetic reaction of childhood (or adolescence) ....   314.01   Attention deficit disorder, with hyperactivity

The DSM-III term is used to reflect the observation that attentional difficulties are prominent and virtually always present in hyperkinetic children. Alternative terms for this disorder, such as Minimal Brain Dysfunction, are based on unproved assumptions (Cantwell, 1975 a, b).

308.1   Withdrawing reaction of childhood (or adolescence) ....   { 313.21   Avoidant disorder of childhood or adolescence
{ 313.22   Schizoid disorder of childhood or adolescence

The distinction between Avoidant and Schizoid Disorders of Childhood or Adolescence is based on whether or not there is a defect in the motivation and capacity for emotional involvement. It is expected that this descriptive distinction will have therapeutic and prognostic implications.

308.2   Overanxious reaction of childhood (or adolescence) ....   313.00   Overanxious disorder
308.3   Runaway reaction of childhood (or adolescence) ....   312.10   Conduct disorder, undersocialized, nonaggressive
308.4   Unsocialized aggressive reaction of childhood (or adolescence)   312.00   Conduct disorder, undersocialized, aggressive
308.5   Group delinquent reaction of childhood (or adolescence) ....   { 312.23   Conduct disorder, socialized, aggressive
{ 312.21   Conduct disorder, socialized, nonaggressive

In DSM-III the category of Conduct Disorder includes cases in which there is a repetitive and persistent pattern of aggressive or nonaggressive conduct in which either the rights of others or major age-appropriate societal norms or rules are violated. The subdivision of Conduct Disorders is controversial. There is evidence that the frequency and the variety of childhood antisocial behaviors are predictive of adult antisocial behavior (Kirkegaard-Sorensen and Mednick, 1977; Cloninger et al., 1978; Robins, 1978). At the same time, there is evidence that the presence or the absence of adequate social attachments (socialization) in children with antisocial behavior has prognostic significance (Lewis, 1954; Jenkins, 1973). The DSM-III approach divides Conduct Disorder into four subtypes. The justification for the aggressive-nonaggressive distinction rests on an obvious difference in clinical picture, with management considerations. The socialized-undersocialized dichotomy is likely to have treatment implications, even if the prognostic implications are still unclear.

314.00   Attention deficit disorder, without hyperactivity

It is clinically recognized that some children with attentional difficulties have never had concomitant hyperactivity (Wender, 1971).

314.80   Attention deficit disorder, residual type

There is evidence that some individuals who, as children, had Attention Deficit Disorder, with Hyperactivity, in adolescence or adulthood no longer have hyperactivity, although they continue to have attentional difficulties (Weiss et al., 1971; Wood et al., 1976).

313.89   Reactive attachment disorder of infancy

TABLE VIII—Continued

DSM-II	DSM-III

This category has been described in the literature under a variety of names, including "failure to thrive without organic basis" (Lozoff et al., 1977; Fischhoff, 1979).

    313.23   Elective mutism

This is a well-recognized syndrome (Browne et al., 1963; Elson et al., 1965).

    313.81   Oppositional disorder

This category was included as a Personality Disorder in a classification of disorders in childhood proposed by the Group for the Advancement of Psychiatry (1966). It is included in DSM-III in modified form and is to be distinguished from Passive-Aggressive Personality Disorder and from Conduct Disorder, Socialized, Nonaggressive.

    313.82   Identity disorder

There is a large literature on identity problems in adolescence (Erikson, 1968; Lichtenstein, 1977). This category is to be distinguished from the DSM-III category of Borderline Personality Disorder.

Factitious Disorders
    300.16   Factitious disorder with psychological symptoms
    301.51   Chronic factitious disorder with physical symptoms (Munchausen syndrome)

The prototype of Factitious Disorders, Munchausen Syndrome, has been recognized in the literature as have other factitious illnesses with physical symptoms, such as Factitious Dermatitis (Asher, 1951; Kingsley, 1967). Despite the rarity of the disorders, it seems useful to distinguish them as a class of disorders (Hyler and Spitzer, 1978).

Disorders of Impulse Control Not Elsewhere Classified
    312.31   Pathological gambling
    312.32   Kleptomania
    312.33   Pyromania
    312.35   Isolated explosive disorder

These disorders have been recognized in the literature as having distinct clinical pictures with differing treatment implications and with obvious relevance to forensic issues (Wihels, 1942; Lewis and Yarnell, 1951; Bolen and Boyd, 1968; Bach-y-Rita et al., 1971; Lesieur, 1979). In DSM-III, this class also includes Intermittent Explosive Disorder, which is roughly equivalent to the DSM-II category of Explosive Personality Disorder, as noted above.

X. Conditions Without Manifest Psychiatric Disorder and Nonspecific Conditions

316   Social Maladjustments Without Manifest Psychiatric Disorder   V   Codes for Conditions Not Attributable to a Mental Disorder That Are a Focus of Attention or Treatment

The DSM-II category was limited to "individuals who are psychiatrically normal but who nevertheless have severe enough problems to warrant examination by a psychiatrist." No definition of normality was provided. As the DSM-III name implies, these categories may be given to an individual who has a mental disorder, as long as the condition itself is not attributable to a mental disorder.

316.0 Marital maladjustment	V61.10	Marital problem
316.1 Social maladjustment	V62.89	Phase-of-life problem or other life circumstance problem*
316.2 Occupational maladjustment	V62.20	Occupational problem
	{ V71.01	Adult antisocial behavior
316.3 Dyssocial behavior	{ V71.02	Childhood or adolescent antisocial behavior
	V65.20	Malingering

Malingering (Weiss and David, 1974) has been included because of its obvious relevance to forensic psychiatry.

    V62.30   Academic problem
    V62.82   Uncomplicated bereavement
    V15.81   Noncompliance with medical treatment
    V61.20   Parent-child problem
    V61.80   Other specified family circumstances
    V62.81   Other interpersonal problem

It seems useful to be able to distinguish these problems from mental disorders. The study of bereavement has made it possible to distinguish it from Major Depressive Disorder (Clayton et al., 1971, 1974).

317 Nonspecific conditions	{ 300.90	Unspecified mental disorder (nonpsychotic)
	{ 298.90	Atypical psychosis*
318 No mental disorder	{ V71.09	No diagnosis or condition on Axis I
	{ V71.09	No diagnosis on Axis II
319.0 Diagnosis deferred	{ 799.90	Diagnosis or condition deferred on Axis I
	{ 799.90	Diagnosis deferred on Axis II

* Prepared by Robert L. Spitzer, M.D., Steven E. Hyler, M.D., and Janet B. W. Williams, M.S.W. From American Psychiatric Association. *Diagnostic and Statistical Manual of Mental Disorders*, ed. 3, American Psychiatric Association, Washington, D.C., 1980.

The authors gratefully acknowledge the assistance of Doctors Jean Endicott, Steven Hyler, and Andrew Skodol in the preparation of this manuscript. In describing various aspects of DSM-III, some material was taken directly from the manual, with the permission of the American Psychiatric Association.

REFERENCES

Abrams, R., and Taylor, M. A. Catatonia: Prediction of response to somatic treatments. Am. J. Psychiatry, *134:* 78, 1977.
Adler, A. Neuropsychiatric complications in victims of Boston's Cocoanut Grove Disaster. J. A. M. A., *123:* 1098, 1943.

Adler, A. Mental symptoms following head injury: A statistical analysis of 200 cases. Arch Neurol. Psychiatry, *53:* 34, 1945.

Akiskal, H. S., Bitar, A. H., Puzantian, V. R., Rosenthal, T. L., and Walker, P. W. The nosological status of neurotic depression. Arch. Gen. Psychiatry, *35:* 756, 1978.

Akiskal, H. S., Djenderedjian, A. H., Rosenthal, R. H., and Khani, M. K. Cyclothymic disorder: Validating criteria for inclusion in the bipolar affective group. Am. J. Psychiatry, *134:* 1227, 1977.

Akiskal, H. S., and McKinney, W. T., Jr. Psychiatry and pseudopsychiatry. Arch. Gen. Psychiatry, *28:* 367, 1973.

American Medical Association. *Standard Classified Nomenclature of Disease.* American Medical Association, Chicago, 1935.

American Psychiatric Association. *Diagnostic and Statistical Manual, Mental Disorders,* ed. 1. American Psychiatric Association, Washington, D.C., 1952.

American Psychiatric Association. *Diagnostic and Statistical Manual of Mental Disorders,* ed. 2. American Psychiatric Association, Washington, D.C., 1968.

* American Psychiatric Association. *Diagnostic and Statistical Manual of Mental Disorders,* ed. 3. American Psychiatric Association, Washington, D.C., 1980.

Andreasen, N. C., Endicott, J., Spitzer, R. L., and Winokur, G. The family history method using diagnostic criteria: Reliability and validity. Arch. Gen. Psychiatry, *34:* 1220, 1977.

Asher, R. The Munchausen syndrome. Lancet, *1:* 339, 1951.

Astrup, C., and Noreik, K. *Functional Psychoses: Diagnostic and Prognostic Models.* Charles C Thomas, Springfield, Ill., 1966.

Ausubel, D. P. Personality disorder *is* disease. Am. Psychol., *16:* 69, 1961.

Bach-y-Rita, G., Lion, J. R., Climent, C. S., and Ervin, F. R. Episodic dyscontrol: A study of 130 violent patients. Am. J. Psychiatry, *127:* 1473, 1971.

Bandura, A. *Principles of Behavior Modification.* Holt, Rinehart and Winston, New York, 1969.

Bartko, J. J., and Carpenter, W. T. On the methods and theory of reliability. J. Nerv. Ment. Dis., *163:* 307, 1976.

Bell, A. P., and Weinberg, M. S. *Homosexualities: A Study of Diversity among Men and Women.* Simon & Schuster, New York, 1978.

Benjamin, H. *The Transsexual Phenomenon.* Julian Press, New York, 1966.

Bielski, R. J., and Friedel, R. O. Prediction of tricyclic antidepressant response: A critical review. Arch. Gen. Psychiatry, *33:* 1479, 1976.

Birnbaum, A., and Maxwell, A. Classification procedures based on Bayes' formula. Appl. Stat., *9:* 152, 1960.

Bolen, D. W., and Boyd, W. H. Gambling and the gambler. Arch. Gen. Psychiatry, *18:* 617, 1968.

Bowlby, J. Separation anxiety: A critical review of the literature. J. Child Psychol. Psychiatry, *1:* 251, 1960.

Brockington, I. F., Kendell, R. E., and Leff, J. P. Definitions of schizophrenia: Concordance and prediction of outcome. Psychol. Med., *8:* 387, 1978.

Brockington, I. F., and Leff, J. P. Schizo-affective psychosis: Definitions and incidence. Psychol. Med., *9:* 91, 1979.

Brown, J. Follow-up of children with atypical development (infantile psychosis). Am. J. Orthopsychiatry, *33:* 855, 1963.

Browne, E., Wilson, V., and Layborne, P. C. Diagnosis and treatment of elective mutism in children. J. Am. Acad. Child Psychiatry, *2:* 605, 1963.

Cantwell, D. *The Hyperactive Child: Diagnosis and Management and Current Research.* Spectrum, New York, 1975a.

Cantwell, D. Scientific myth of minimal brain damage. Frontiers Psychiatry, 5, June 1, 1975b.

Chodoff, P. The diagnosis of hysteria: An overview. Am. J. Psychiatry, *131:* 1073, 1974.

Chodoff, P., and Lyons, H. Hysteria, the hysterical personality, and hysterical conversion. Am. J. Psychiatry, *114:* 734, 1958.

Clayton, P. J., Halikas, J. A., and Maurice, W. L. The bereavement of the widowed. Dis. Nerv. Syst., *32:* 597, 1971.

Clayton, P. J., Herjanic, M., Murphy G. E., and Woodruff, R. Mourning and depression: Their similarities and differences. Can. Psychiatr. Assoc. J., *19:* 309, 1974.

Cloninger, C. R., Christiansen, K. O., Reich, T., and Gottesman, I. I. Implications of sex differences in the prevalence of antisocial personality, alcoholism, and criminality for familial transmission. Arch. Gen. Psychiatry, *35:* 941, 1978.

Cohen, J. A coefficient of agreement for nominal scales. Educ. Psychol. Measurement, *20:* 37, 1960.

Cooper, J. E., Kendell, R. E., Gurland, B. J., Sharpe, L., Copeland, J. R. M., and Simon, R. *Psychiatric Diagnosis in New York and London.* Oxford University Press, London, 1972.

Davenport, W. Sexual patterns and their regulation in a society of the Southwest Pacific. In *Sex and Behavior,* F. A. Beach, editor, p. 164. John Wiley & Sons, New York, 1965.

Elson, A., Pearson, C., Jones, C. D., and Schumacher, E. Follow-up study of childhood elective mutism. Arch. Gen. Psychiatry, *13:* 182, 1965.

Endicott, J., Forman, J. B. W., and Spitzer, R. L. Research approaches to diagnostic classification in schizophrenia. In *Neurochemical and Immunological Components in Schizophrenia,* D. Bergsma and A. L. Goldstein, editors, p. 41. Allan R. Liss, New York, 1978.

Endicott, J., and Spitzer, R. L. A diagnostic interview: The schedule for affective disorders and schizophrenia. Arch. Gen. Psychiatry, *35:* 837, 1978.

Erikson, E. *Identity, Youth, and Crisis.* W. W. Norton, New York, 1968.

Essen-Möller, E., and Wohlfahrt, S. Suggestions for the amendment of the official Swedish classification of mental disorders. Acta Psychiat. Scand., *47* (Suppl.): 551, 1947.

* Feighner, J. P., Robins, E., Guze, S. B., Woodruff, R. A., Winokur, G., and Muñoz, R. Diagnostic criteria for use in psychiatric research. Arch. Gen. Psychiatry, *26:* 57, 1972.

Fisher, C. Dementia and cerebral vascular disease. In *Cerebral Vascular Diseases: Sixth Conference,* J. F. Toole, R. G. Siekert, and J. P. Whisnant, editors, p. 232. Grune & Stratton, New York, 1968.

Fisher, C., Kahn, E., Edwards, A., and Davis, D. M. A psychophysiological study of nightmares and night terrors. I. Physiological aspects of stage 4 night terrors. J. Nerv. Ment. Dis., *157:* 75, 1973.

Fisher, C., Kahn, E., Edwards, A., Davis, D. M., and Fine, J. A psychophysiological study of nightmares and night terrors. III. Mental content and recall of stage 4 night terrors. J. Nerv. Ment. Dis., *158:* 174, 1974.

Fischhoff, J. Failure to thrive. In *Handbook of Child Psychiatry,* J. Noshpitz, editor. Basic Books, New York, 1979.

Ford, C. S., and Beach, F. A. *Pattern of Sexual Behavior.* Harper & Row, New York, 1951.

Freud, S. *Introductory Lectures on Psycho-analysis.* Hogarth Press, London, 1963.

General Register Office. *A Glossary of Mental Disorders.* Her Majesty's Stationery Office, London, 1968.

Gift, J. E., Strauss, J. S., Ritzler, B. A. Failure to detect low I. Q. in psychiatric assessment. Am. J. Psychiatry, *135:* 345, 1978.

Gittelman-Klein, R., and Klein, D. F. School phobia diagnostic considerations in the light of imipramine effects. J. Nerv. Ment. Dis., *156:* 199, 1973.

Goodwin, D. W., and Hill, S. Y. Chronic effects of alcohol and other psychoactive drugs on intellect, learning and memory. In *Alcohol, Drugs, and Brain Damage,* J. G. Rankin, editor, p. 55, Addiction Research Foundation, Toronto, 1975.

Gottesman, I. I., and Shields, J. A critical review of recent adoption, twin, and family studies of schizophrenia: Behavioral genetics perspectives. Schizophr. Bull., *2:* 360, 1976.

Gralnick, A. Folie a deux, the psychoses of association. Parts I and II. Psychiatr. Q., *16:* 230, 491, 1942.

Green, R. *Sexual Identity Conflict in Children and Adults.* Penguin Books, New York, 1975.

Green, R., and Money, J. *Transsexualism and Sex Reassignment.* Johns Hopkins University Press, Baltimore, 1969.

Gross, H. J. *Manual on Terminology and Classification in Mental Retardation.* Garamond/Pridemark Press, Baltimore, 1977.

Group for the Advancement of Psychiatry. *Psychopathological Disorders in Childhood: Theoretical Considerations and a Proposed Classification.* Group for the Advancement of Psychiatry, New York, 1966.

Gruenberg, E. M. How can the new diagnostic manual help? Int. J. Psychiatry, *7:* 368, 1969.

Gunderson, J. G., and Singer, M. T. Defining borderline patients: An overview. Am. J. Psychiatry, *132:* 1, 1975.

Guze, S. The validity and significance of the clinical diagnosis of hysteria (Briquet's syndrome). Am. J. Psychiatry, *132:* 138, 1975.

Hachinski, V. C., Lassen, N. A., and Marshall, J. Multi-infarct dementia: A cause of mental deterioration in the elderly. Lancet, *2:* 207, 1974.

Helmchen, H. Schizophrenia: Diagnositc concepts in the ICD-8. Br. J. Psychiatry, *10:* 10, 1975.

Helzer, J. E., Clayton, P. H., Pambakian, R., Reich, T., Woodruff, R. A., and Reverley, M. A. Reliability of psychiatric diagnosis. II. The test/retest reliability of diagnostic classification. Arch. Gen. Psychiatry, *34:* 136, 1977a.

Helzer, J. E., Robins, L. N., Taibleson, M., Woodruff, R. A., Reich, T., and Wish, E. D. Reliability of psychiatric diagnosis. I. A methodological review. Arch. Gen. Psychiatry, *34:* 129, 1977b.

Hooker, E. The adjustment of the male overt homosexual. In *The Problem of Homosexuality in Modern Society,* H. M. Ruitenbeck, editor, p. 141. E. P. Dutton, New York, 1963.

Hyler, S. E., and Spitzer, R. L. Hysteria split asunder. Am. J. Psychiatry, *135:* 1500, 1978.

Jacobson, A., Kales, J. D., and Kales, A. Clinical and electrophysiological correlates of sleep disorders in children. In *Sleep, Physiology, and Pathology,* A. Kales, editor, p. 109. J. B. Lippincott, Philadelphia, 1969.

Jacobson, A., Kales, A., Lehmann, D., and Zweizig, J. R. Somnambulism: All-night electroencephalographic studies. Science, *148:* 975, 1965.

Jaffe, J. H., and Jarvik, M. E. Tobacco use and tobacco use disorder. In *Psychopharmacology: A Generation of Progress,* M. A. Lipton, A. DiMascio, and K. F. Killam, editors, p. 1665. Raven Press, New York, 1978.

Jenkins, R. L. *Behavior Disorders of Childhood and Adolescence.* Charles C Thomas, Springfield, Ill., 1973.

Jones, R. T., Benowitz, N., and Bachman, J. Clinical studies of cannabis tolerance and dependance. Ann. N. Y. Acad. Sci., *282:* 221, 1976.

Kamman, G. R. Traumatic neurosis, compensation neurosis, or attitudinal pathosis. Arch. Neurol. Psychiatry, *65:* 593, 1951.

Kanfer, F. H., and Saslow, G. Behavioral diagnosis. In *Behavior Therapy: Appraisal and Status,* C. M. Franks, editor, p. 417. McGraw-Hill, New York, 1969.

Kaplan, H. S. *The New Sex Therapy.* Brunner/Mazel, New York, 1974.

Keiser, L. *The Traumatic Neurosis.* J. B. Lippincott, Philadelphia, 1968.

* Kendell, R. E. *The Role of Diagnosis in Psychiatry.* Blackwell, Oxford, 1975.

Kendell, R. E., Brockington, I. F., and Leff, J. P. Prognostic implications of six alternative definitions of schizophrenia. Arch. Gen. Psychiatry, *36:* 25, 1979.

Kernberg, O. *Borderline Conditions and Pathological Narcissism.* Jason Aronson, New York, 1975.

Kingsley, H. J. Peculiarities in dermatology: A case of dermatitis artefacta. Cent.

Afr. J. Med., *13:* 264, 1967.

Kirkegaard-Sorensen, L., and Mednick, S. A. A prospective study of predictors of criminality: School behavior. In *Biosocial Bases of Criminal Behavior,* S. Mednick and K. O. Christiansen, editors, p. 255. Gardner Press, New York, 1977.

Klein, D. F. Delineation of two drug-responsive anxiety syndromes. Psychopharmacologia, *5:* 397, 1964.

Klein, D. F. A proposed definition of mental illness. In *Critical Issues in Psychiatric Diangosis,* R. L. Spitzer and D. F. Klein, editors, p. 41. Raven Press, New York, 1978.

Klein, D. F., and Davis, J. *Diagnosis and Drug Treatment of Psychiatric Disorders.* Williams & Wilkins, Baltimore, 1969.

Klein, D. F., Zitrin, C. M., and Woerner, M. G. Antidepressants, anxiety, panic, and phobia. in *Psychopharmacology: A Generation of Progress,* M. A. Lipton, A. DiMascio, K. F. Killam, editors, p. 1401. Raven Press, New York, 1978.

Klerman, G. L., Endicott, J., Spitzer, R. L., and Hirschfeld, R. M. A. Neurotic depressions: A systematic analysis of multiple criteria and multiple meanings. Am. J. Psychiatry, *136:* 57, 1979.

Kohut, H. *Analysis of the Self: A Systematic Approach to the Psychoanalytic Treatment of Narcissistic Personality Disorders.* International Universities Press, New York, 1971.

Kolvin, I. Studies in the childhood psychoses. I. Diagnostic criteria and classification. Br. J. Psychiatry, *118:* 381, 1971.

Kolvin, I., Garside, R. F., and Kidd, J. S. H. IV. Parental personality and attitude and childhood psychoses. Br. J. Psychiatry, *118:* 403, 1971.

Kolvin, I., Humphrey, M., and McNay, A. Cognitive factors in childhood psychoses. Br. J. Psychiatry, *118:* 415, 1971.

Kolvin, I., Ounsted, C., Humphrey, M., and McNay, A. II. The phenomenology of childhood psychoses. Br. J. Psychiatry, *118:* 385, 1971.

Kolvin, I., Ounsted, C., Richardson, L. M., and Garside, R. F. III. The family and social background in childhood psychoses. Br. J. Psychiatry, *118:* 396, 1971.

Kolvin, I., Ounsted, C., and Roth, M. V. Cerebral dysfunction and childhood psychoses. Br. J. Psychiatry, *118:* 407, 1971.

Kramer, M. The history of the efforts to agree on an international classification of mental disorders. In *Diagnostic and Statistical Manual of Mental Disorders,* ed. 2. p. 135. American Psychiatric Association, Washington, D.C., 1973.

Larson, P. S., and Silvetle, H. *Tobacco: Experimental and Clinical Studies.* Williams & Wilkins, Baltimore, 1975.

Latimer, P. Psychophysiologic disorders: A critical appraisal of concept and theory illustrated with reference to the irritable bowel syndrome (IBS). Psychol. Med., *9:* 71, 1979.

Lehmann, L. Depersonalization. Am. J. Psychiatry, *131:* 1221, 1974.

Lesieur, H. R. The compulsive gambler's spiral of options and involvement. Psychiatry, *42:* 79, 1979.

Lewis, H. *Deprived Children.* Oxford University Press, New York, 1954.

Lewis, N. D. C., and Yarnell, H. *Pathological Firesetting.* Nervous and Mental Diseases, New York, 1951.

Lichtenstein, H. *The Dilemma of Human Identity.* Jason Aronson, New York, 1977.

Lipowski, Z. B. Organic brain syndromes: A reformulation. Compr. Psychiatry, *19:* 309, 1978.

Looney, J. G., and Gunderson, E. K. E. Transient situational disturbances: Course and outcome. Am. J. Psychiatry, *135:* 660, 1978.

Looney, J. G., Lipp, M. R., and Spitzer, R. L. A new method of classification for psychophysiologic disorders. Am. J. Psychiatry, *135:* 304, 1978.

Lorr, M., editor. *Explanations in Typing Psychotics.* Pergamon Press, Oxford, 1966.

Lozoff, B., Brittenham, G. M., Trause, M. A., Kennell, J. H., and Klaus, M. H. The mother-newborn relationship: Limits of adaptability. J. Pediatr., *91:* 1, 1977.

Ludwig, A. M., Brandsma, J. M., Wilbur, C. B., Bendfeldt, F., and Jameson, D. H. The objective study of a multiple personality. Arch. Gen. Psychiatry, *26:* 298, 1972.

Marks, I. *Fears and Phobias.* Academic Press, New York, 1969.

Masters, W. H., and Johnson, V. E. *Human Sexual Inadequacy.* Little, Brown, and Co., Boston, 1970.

McNeil, J. N., Verwaerdt, A., and Peak, D. Folie a deux in the aged: Review and case report of role reversal. *Am. Geriatr. Soc.,* 20: 316, 1972.

Melrose, J. P., Stroebel, C., and Glueck, B. Diagnosis of psychopathology using stepwise multiple discriminant analysis. Compr. Psychiatry, *11:* 43, 1970.

Menninger, K. Sheer verbal mickey mouse. Int. J. Psychiatry, *7:* 415, 1969.

Menninger, K., Mayman, M., and Pruyser, P. *The Vital Balance: The Life Process in Mental Health and Illness.* Viking Press, New York, 1963.

Mezzich, J. E. Patterns and issues in multiaxial psychiatric diagnosis. Psychol. Med., *9:* 125, 1979.

Millon, T. *Modern Psychopathology.* W. B. Saunders, Philadelphia, 1969.

MMPI Research Laboratory. *Comprehensive MMPI Code Book for Males.* MMPI Research Laboratory, Veterans Administration, Minneapolis, 1970.

Muñoz, R. A., Kulak, G., Marten, S., and Tvason, V. B. Simple and hebephrenic schizophrenia: A Follow-up study in life history research. In *Psychopathology,* M. Roff, L. Robins, and M. Pollack, editors, vol. 2, p. 228. University of Minnesota Press, Minneapolis, 1972.

Nemiah, J. C. Hysterical neurosis, dissociative type. In *Comprehensive Textbook of Psychiatry,* A. M. Freedman, H. I. Kaplan, B. J. Sadock, editors, ed. 2, p. 1220. Williams & Wilkins, Baltimore, 1975.

Nurnberger, J., Roose, S., Dunner D., and Fieve, R. R. Unipolar mania: A distinct clinical entity? Am. J. Psychiatry, *136:* 1420, 1979.

Office of the Surgeon General. *Report on Smoking and Health.* United States Department of Health, Education, and Welfare, Rockville, Md., 1979.

Ottosson, J. O., and Perris, C. Multidimensional classification of mental disorders. Psychol. Med., *3:* 238, 1973.

Overall, J. E., and Hollister, L. E. Computer procedures for psychiatric classification. J. A. M. A., *187:* 583, 1964.

Overall, J. E., and Hollister, L. E. Comparative evaluation of research diagnostic criteria for schizophrenia. Arch. Gen. Psychiatry, *36:* 1198, 1979.

Paul, G. L. Experimental-behavioral approaches to "schizophrenia." In *Strategic Intervention in Schizophrenia,* R. Cancro, N. Fox, and L. Shapiro, editors, p. 187. Behavioral Publications, New York, 1974.

Paykel, E. S. Depressive typologies and response to amitriptyline. Br. J. Psychiatry, *120:* 147, 1972.

Paykel, E., Myers, J. K., Dienelt, M. N., Klerman, G. L., Lindenthal, J. J., and Pepper, M. P. Life events and depression: A controlled study. Arch. Gen. Psychiatry, *21:* 753, 1969.

Perris, C. A study of bipolar (manic depressive) and unipolar recurrent depressive psychosis. Acta Psychiatr. Scand., *42* (Suppl): 9, 1966.

Petersen, R. C. *Marihuana Research Findings.* United States Department of Health, Education, and Welfare, Rockville, Md., 1977.

Petersen, R. C., and Stillman, R. C. *Phencyclidine (PCP) Abuse: An Appraisal.* United States Department of Health, Education, and Welfare, Rockville, Md., 1978.

Pies, R. On myths and countermyths: More on Szaszian fallacies. Arch. Gen. Psychiatry, *36:* 139, 1979.

Pope, H. G., Jr., and Lipinski, J. Diagnosis in schizophrenia and manic-depressive illness: A reassessment of the specificity of "schizophrenic" symptoms in the light of current research. Arch. Gen. Psychiatry, *35:* 811, 1978.

Procci, W. R. Schizo-affective psychosis: Fact or fiction. Arch. Gen. Psychiatry, *33:* 1167, 1976.

Reiss, S. A critique of Thomas Szasz's *Myth of Mental Illness.* Am. J. Psychiatry, *128:* 71, 1972.

Retterstol, N. *Paranoid and Paranoiac Psychosis.* Charles C Thomas, Springfield, Ill., 1966.

Robins, L. *Deviant Children Grown Up.* Kreiger, Huntington, N. Y., 1974.

Robins, L. Sturdy childhood predictors of adult outcomes: Replications from longitudinal studies. Psychol. Med., *8:* 611, 1978.

Robins, L., Helzer, J., and Croughan, J. L. *NIMH-Diagnostic Interview.* National Institute of Mental Health, Bethesda, 1979.

Rosenhan, D. L. On being sane in insane places. Science, *179:* 250, 1973.

Rosenthal, D., and Kety, S. S., editors, *The Transmission of Schizophrenia.* Pergamon Press, London, 1968.

Rutter, M. The development of infantile autism. Psychol. Med., *4:* 147, 1974.

Rutter, M., and Schopler, E. *Autism: A Re-appraisal of Concepts and Treatments.* Plenum Publishing Corp., New York, 1978.

Rutter, M., Shaffer, D., and Sheperd, M. *A Multiaxial Classification of Child Psychiatric Disorders* World Health Organization, Geneva, 1975a.

Rutter, M., Shaffer, D., and Sturge, C. *A Guide to a Multiaxial Classification Scheme for Psychiatric Disorders in Childhood and Adolescence.* Institute of Psychiatry, London, 1975b.

Rutter, M., and Yule, W. The concept of specific reading retardation. J. Child Psychol. Psychiatry, *16:* 181, 1975.

Sartorius, N., Jablensky, A., and Shapiro, R. Cross-cultural differences in the short-term prognosis of schizophrenic psychoses. Schizophr. Bull., *4:* 102, 1978.

Schact, T., and Nathan, P. E. But is it good for the psychologists? Appraisal and status of DSM-III. Am. Psychol., *32:* 1017, 1977.

Seltzer, B., and Sherwin, I. "Organic brain syndromes": An empirical study and critical review. Am. J. Psychiatry, *135:* 13, 1978.

Shapiro, A. K., Shapiro, E. S., Bruun, R. D., and Sweet, R. D. *Gilles de la Tourette Syndrome.* Raven Press, New York, 1978.

Shenken, L. I. Some clinical and psychopathological aspects of bestiality. J. Nerv. Ment. Dis., *139:* 137, 1964.

Shields, J., and Gottesman, I. I. Cross-national diagnosis of schizophrenia in twins. Arch. Gen. Psychiatry, *27:* 725, 1972.

Siegelman, M. Adjustment of homosexual and heterosexual women. Br. J. Psychiatry, *120:* 477, 1972a.

Siegelman, M. Adjustment of male homosexuals and heterosexuals. Arch. Sex. Behav., *2:* 9, 1972b.

Sletten, I., Altman, H., and Ulett, G. Routine diagnosis by computer. Am. J. Psychiatry, *127:* 1147, 1971.

Spitzer, R. L. More on pseudoscience in science and the case for psychiatric diagnosis: A critique of D. L. Rosenhan's "On Being Sane in Insane Places" and "The Contextual Nature of Psychiatric Diagnosis." Arch. Gen. Psychiatry, *33:* 459, 1976.

Spitzer, R. L., Andreasen, N., and Endicott, J. Schizophrenia and other psychotic disorders in DSM-III. Schizophr. Bull., *4:* 489, 1978a.

Spitzer, R. L., and Endicott, J. DIAGNO: A computer program for psychiatric diagnosis utilizing the differential diagnostic procedure. Arch. Gen. Psychiatry, *18:* 746, 1968.

Spitzer, R. L., and Endicott, J. DIAGNO II: Further developments in a computer program for psychiatric diagnosis. Am. J. Psychiatry, *125* (Suppl.): 12, 1969.

Spitzer, R. L., and Endicott, J. Computer diagnosis in an automated record keeping system: A study in clinical acceptability. In *Progress in Psychiatric Information Systems: Computer Application,* J. D. Crawford, D. W. Morgan, and D. T. Giantinco, editors, p. 73. Ballinger Press, Cambridge, Mass., 1974.

Spitzer, R. L., and Endicott, J. Medical and mental disorder: Proposed definition and criteria. In *Critical Issues in Psychiatric Diagnosis.* R. L. Spitzer and D. F. Klein, editors, p. 15. Raven Press, New York, 1978.

Spitzer, R. L., Endicott, J., and Williams, J. B. W. Letter to the editor: Research diagnostic criteria. Arch. Gen. Psychiatry, *36:* 1381, 1979a.

Spitzer, R. L., Endicott, J., and Gibbon, M. Crossing the border into borderline personality and borderline schizophrenia: The development of criteria. Arch. Gen. Psychiatry, *36:* 17, 1979b.

Spitzer, R. L., Endicott, J., and Robins, E. Research diagnostic criteria: Rationale and reliability. Arch. Gen. Psychiatry, *35:* 773, 1978b.

Spitzer, R. L., Fleiss, J. L., Burdock, E. I., and Hardesty, A. S. The mental status schedule: Rationale, reliability, and validity. Compr. Psychiatry, *5:* 384, 1964.

Stengel, E. Classification of mental disorders. Bull. WHO, *21:* 601, 1959.

Sternbach, R. A. *Pain: A Psychophysiological Analysis.* Academic Press, New York, 1968.

Stoller, R. J., Marmor, J., Bieber, I., Gold, R., Socarides, C. W., Green, R., and Spitzer, R. L. A symposium: Should homosexuality be in the APA nomenclature? Am. J. Psychiatry, *130:* 1207, 1973.

Stone, A. A., Hopkins, R., Mahnke, M. W., Shapiro, D. W., and Silverglate, H. A. Simple schizophrenia: Syndrome or shibboleth. Am. J. Psychiatry, *125:* 305, 1968.

Strauss, J. S. A comprehensive approach to psychiatric diagnosis. Am. J. Psychiatry, *132:* 1193, 1975.

Strauss, J. S., and Gift, T. E. Choosing an approach for diagnosing schizophrenia. Arch. Gen. Psychiatry, *34:* 1248, 1977.

Szasz, T. *The Myth of Mental Illness.* Harper & Row, New York, 1961.

Tsuang, M., Dempsey, M., and Rauscher, F. A study of atypical schizophrenia: Comparison with schizophrenia and affective disorder by sex, age of admission, precipitant, outcome, and family history. Arch. Gen. Psychiatry, *33:* 1157, 1976.

Tsuang, M., and Winokur, G. Criteria for subtyping schizophrenia: Clinical differentiation of hebephrenic and paranoid schizophrenia. Arch. Gen. Psychiatry, *31:* 43, 1974.

Tuke, H. French retrospective. J. Ment. Sci., *36:* 117, 1890.

Ward, C. H., Beck, A. T., Mendelson, M., Mock, J. E., and Erbaugh, J. K. The psychiatric nomenclature: Reasons for diagnostic disagreement. Arch. Gen. Psychiatry, *7:* 198, 1962.

Weiss, G., Minde, K., Werry, J. S., Douglas, V., and Nemeth, E. Studies on the hyperactive child. VIII. Five-year follow-up. Arch. Gen. Psychiatry, *24:* 409, 1971.

Weiss, J. M. A., and David, D. Malingering and associated syndromes. In *American Handbook of Psychiatry,* S. Arieti and E. Brody, editors, ed. 2, vol. 2, p. 270. Basic Books, New York, 1974.

Weissman, M. The myth of involutional melancholia. J. A. M. A., *242:* 742, 1979.

Weissman, M. M., and Myers, J. K. Affective disorders in a U. S. urban community: The use of research diagnostic criteria in an epidemiological survey. Arch. Gen. Psychiatry, *35:* 1304, 1978.

Wells, C. E. Chronic brain diseases: An overview. Am. J. Psychiatry, *135:* 22, 1978.

Wender, P. *Minimal Brain Dysfunction in Children.* John Wiley & Sons, New York, 1971.

Wihels, F. Kleptomania and other psychopathic crimes. J. Crim. Psychopathol., *4:* 205, 1942.

Wing, J. K., Birley, J. L. T., Cooper, J. E., Reliability of a procedure for measuring and classifying "present psychiatric state." Br. J. Psychiatry, *113:* 449, 1967.

Wing, J. K., Cooper, J. E., and Sartorius, N. *Measurement and Classification of Psychiatric Symptoms: An Instruction Manual for the PSE and Catego Program.* Cambridge University Press, London, 1974.

Wing, J. K., Mann, S. A., Leff, J. P., and Nixon, J. M. The concept of a "case" in psychiatric population surveys. Psychol. Med., *8:* 203, 1978.

Winokur, G. Family studies. VIII. Secondary depression is alive and well and . . . Dis. Nerv. Syst., *33:* 94, 1972.

Winokur, G., Clayton, P., and Reich, T. *Manic Depressive Illness.* C. V. Mosby, St. Louis, 1969.

Wood, D. R., Reimherr, F. W., Wender, P. H., and Johnson, G. E. Diagnosis and treatment of minimal brain dysfunction in adults. Arch. Gen. Psychiatry, *33:* 1453, 1976.

World Health Organization. *Manual of the International Classification of Diseases, Injuries, and Causes of Death,* rev. 6, vol. 1. World Health Organization, Geneva, 1948.

* World Health Organization. *The International Pilot Study of Schizophrenia,* vol. 1. World Health Organization, Geneva, 1973.

Zitrin, C. M., Klein, D. F., and Woerner, M. G. Behavior therapy, supportive psychotherapy, imipramine, and phobias. Arch. Gen. Psychiatry, *35:* 307, 1978.

Zubin, J. But is it good for science? Clin. Psychol., *31:* 1, 1978.

14.2 Multiaxial Diagnostic Systems in Psychiatry

JUAN E. MEZZICH, M.D., Ph.D.

Introduction

Although the word "diagnosis" can refer to the act of identifying the nature of a disease in medicine and the precise description of the characteristics of an organism for taxonomic classification in biology, it is useful to focus attention on its etymological meaning. Diagnosis is a New Latin word coming from the Greek *diagignōskein,* meaning "to know thoroughly." It is that more thorough, comprehensive, or complete knowledge, in this instance about the patient and his condition, that the multiaxial model intends to reflect.

The multiaxial diagnostic model essentially consists in the systematic formulation of the patient's condition and its causative and associated factors in terms of several variables, aspects, or axes that are thought to have high clinical information value and are conceptualized and rated as quasi-independent from each other. It has attracted considerable attention on the basis of its potential both to describe and to handle more effectively the complexity of the clinical condition and to articulate a multitheoretical approach to psychiatry and medicine in general. Interest in the model is reflected in the use of a transitional multiaxial framework in the third edition of the American Psychiatric Association's (1980) *Diagnostic and Statistical Manual of Mental Disorders* (DSM-III) and the serious consideration of a multiaxial system for the tenth revision of the *International Classification of Diseases.*

To understand better the possibilities and problems encompassed by the multiaxial model, one must review its historical roots, specific multiaxial systems proposed in the literature, and the trends and issues involved in the conceptualization, organization, and scaling of diagnostic axes.

History and Overview of Multiaxial Diagnostic Systems

ORIGINS

Although the impact of multiaxial diagnosis is relatively recent, its origins are not. The contrast between the multiaxial and the conventional uniaxial diagnostic system may be traced perhaps to the old nosological controversy reviewed by Kendell (1975) between, on the one hand, the idealized and abstract platonic disease entity and, on the other hand, the Hippocratic approach, which was closer to the patient and, therefore, more clinical.

That contrast was revived early in this century by the argument between Kraepelin (1902), who thoroughly endorsed the disease-entity model, and Hoche (1912), who did not believe in it and proposed the separation of syndrome and cause in the diagnostic formulation. Kraepelin's position prevailed, and nothing much was heard about the issue until 1947, when Essen-Möller and Wohlfahrt suggested an amendment of the official Swedish classification of mental disorders, separating syndrome and cause.

Increased interest in multiaxial models for psychiatric diagnosis was then prompted by various symposiums on the classification of mental disorders sponsored by the World Health Organization and by the American Psychopathological Association. Those symposiums reviewed a number of fundamental methodological issues in diagnosis and also some germinal multiaxial ideas (Stengel, 1959; Zubin, 1961; Rutter et al., 1969). More recently, building on the diagnostic separation of syndrome and etiology put forward by Essen-Möller and Wohlfahrt (1947) and Essen-Möller (1961, 1971), a number of multiaxial models have been proposed in various parts of the world.

OVERVIEW OF PROPOSED MULTIAXIAL SYSTEMS

The international psychiatric literature shows nine representative psychiatric diagnostic systems developed in the following countries: England (Wing, 1970; Rutter et al., 1975b), Germany (Helmchen, 1975; von Cranach, 1977), Japan (Kato, 1977), Sweden (Ottosson and Perris, 1973), and the United States (Strauss, 1975; American Psychiatric Association, 1980). Those systems are outlined in Table I to highlight their conceptual and structural trends and issues. The axes and subaxes included in those systems are listed with the actual order numbers and wordings used by the respective authors. The years appearing after the authors' names indicate the representative publications or reports containing the various versions of the proposed system. In each case, the system outlined corresponds to the most recent publication.

Perhaps because of the particular complexity of child psychiatry, workers in that field have long been important contributors in the development of multiaxial diagnostic systems. Rutter et al. (1969), as participants in the Third World Health Organization Seminar on psychiatric diagnosis, proposed a triaxial classification of childhood mental disorders that included clinical psychiatric syndrome, intellectual level, and associated or etiological factors. The third axis was split into biological factors and abnormal psychosocial influences at the Fifth World Health Organization Seminar, which focused on the diagnosis of mental retardation (Tarjan et al., 1972). The most recent version of that classification has five axes, obtained by splitting the first axis into "psychiatric syndrome" and "specific delays of development" (Rutter et al., 1975b).

There were some relatively early American suggestions for multiaxial conceptualization of psychiatric nosology. Gardner (1965) suggested the consideration of type of disorder, level and course of disability, and personality structure in the classification of psychiatric outpatients. The same year, Ziskind (1965) made a plea for a psychiatric classification by symptom and etiology. More recently, Bahn (1971) proposed a multidisciplinary scheme for the classification of psychosocial functioning, and Spitzer (1971) suggested the use of statements on impairment level, stage of illness, prognosis, precipitating stresses, and environmental deficits as a complement to the standard diagnostic formulation. In 1973, Strauss challenged the single-label diagnostic model on scientific grounds, and in 1975 he proposed the first systematic and comprehensive multiaxial model generated in the United States. It includes axes dealing with symptoms, duration and course of symptoms, associated factors, personal relationships, and work functioning. The last two axes, which cover the area of social functioning, represent a distinct innovation in the history of multiaxial systems.

The task force on nomenclature and statistics of the American Psychiatric Association (1980) prepared during the past few years a third edition of the *Diagnostic and Statistical Manual of Mental Disorders* (DSM-III). Major characteristics of DSM-III are the use of operational or explicit criteria for assigning patients to diagnostic categories and the implementation of a multiaxial framework. It includes the following five axes: clinical psychiatric syndrome (which is not a purely symptomatological axis, as it has some categories rated according to severity, periodicity, or chronicity); personality disorders for adults and specific developmental disorders for children and adolescents; nonmental medical or physical disorders; severity of psychosocial stressors; and highest level of adaptive functioning in the past year. The first three axes are typological, and the last two are dimensional—that is, measured on seven-point scales. Shortly before the adoption of DSM-III, the use of the psychosocial-stressors and the adaptive-functioning axes became optional.

An atypical system is that proposed by Kato (1977), from the Japanese National Institute of Mental Health, which includes only two axes, illness (medically evaluated) and caseness (culturally evaluated). In addition, Kato endorsed the appropriateness of considering axes on symptoms, cause, intelligence level, and personality, but he did not elaborate on them. The usefulness of differentiating between a taxonomy based on biomedical concepts and another based on alternative sociocultural concepts was well explained by Fabrega (1976).

Trends and Issues in Axial Content, Organization, and Scaling

CONCEPTUALIZATION OF AXIAL CONTENT

The axes considered in the various diagnostic systems presented in Table I can be grouped, according to their content, into the following major types or themes: (1) phenomenology, including symptoms, personality disorders, developmental delays, and intellectual functioning; (2) etiological or associated factors, including axes on biological and psychosocial factors conceptualized and organized in various ways; causation may include predisposing, precipitating, and maintaining factors; (3) time frame, including axes dealing with onset, duration, and course of psychopathology; (4) social functioning, including axes dealing with work performance, interpersonal relations, and other aspects of adaptive functioning; and (5) other, including psychopathological severity, certainty, and the illness versus caseness contrast; some axes, such as certainty, have a moderator meaning, rather than being conceptually independent axes.

Almost universal consensus is found on the inclusion of symptoms or syndrome and causative or associated factors, which always included both biological and psychosocial factors (as separate axes in Rutter et al., 1975b and DSM-III).

Social or adaptive functioning is considered only in the two American proposals. It is implemented as a single axis in DSM-III and as two axes (personal relationships and work functioning) in Strauss's (1975) system.

The innovation in the structure of psychiatric diagnosis represented by the multiaxial model has opened the door to the proposal of new axes as additions to or modifications of those formulated above. Examples of such other axes are family relationships (Strauss, 1975) and interaction with other individuals and groups, which, together with work functioning and

TABLE I

*A Synopsis of Multiaxial Psychiatric Diagnostic Systems**

Type of axes	Essen-Möller and Wohlfahrt (1947) Essen-Möller (1961, 1971)	Wing (1970)	Ottosson & Perris (1973) von Knorring et al. (1977)	Helmchen (1975)	Rutter et al. (1975b)

Phenomenology	I. Syndrome
	  A. Specific syndrome
	  B. Gross syndrome
	    1. Psychosis
	    2. Neurosis
	    3. Habitual abnormality (personality disorder, mental retardation)
		II. Psychiatric condition
		
		III. Mental subnormality (I.Q. also coded)
			I. Symptomatology	I. Symptomatology	I. Psychiatric syndrome
					
					II. Specific delays in development
					III. Intellectual level

Etiological or associated factors	II. Etiology
	  A. Classic somatic diseases
	  B. Additional items
	    1. Hereditary taint
	    2. Situational stress
	    3. Postpsychotic
	    4. Cryptogenic
		I. Cause (organic or psychological)
		IV. Additional physical illness or handicap
			IV. Etiopathogenesis
			  Somatogenic
			  Histogenic
			  Chemogenic
			  Hereditary
			  Psychogenic
			  Sociogenic
			  Characterological
			  Multifactorial
			  Cryptogenic
			     or
				II. Etiology
				  1. Disposition
				  2. Precipitation
				  3. Fixation
					IV. Medical conditions
					
					V. Abnormal psychosocial situations

Time frame			III. Course
			  Episodic
			  Periodic, same disorder
			  Periodic, different disorder
			  Chronic stable
			  Chronic progressive
				III. Time
				  Onset age
				  Onset speed
				  Duration
				  Course	

Social functioning					

Other			II. Severity
			  Healthy
			  Nonpsychotic
			  Psychotic
			  Occasionally psychotic
				IV. Intensity (of Axes I and II)
				
				V. Certainty (of Axes I, II, and III)	

Types of axes	Strauss (1975)	DSM-III, APA (1980)	Kato (1977)	von Cranach (1977)
Phenomenology	I. Symptoms	I. Clinical psychiatric syndrome (some categories subclassified according to duration, course, and severity) II. Personality disorder (adults) or specific developmental disorder (child)		I. Symptomatology V. Personality disorder
Etiological or associated factors	III. Associated factors B. Physical illness C. Drug-alcohol abuse A. Environment stresses	III. Physical disorder IV. Psychosocial stressors severity (seven-point scale)		IV. Etiology A. Biological B. Psychosocial
Time frame	II. Duration and course of symptoms A. Duration Long term Moderate duration Recent onset B. Course Remittent Fluctuating Continuous			II. Acuity of episodes III. Course of illness Episodic Intermittent First episode Chronic
Social functioning	IV. Personal relations (5-point scale) V. Work functioning (5-point scale)	V. Highest level of adaptive functioning in past year (7-point scale)		
Other			I. Illness (medically evaluated) II. Caseness (culturally evaluated)	

* Modified from Mezzich, J.E. Patterns and issues in multiaxial psychiatric diagnosis. Psychol. Med., 9: 125, 1979.

functioning in family, attempt to cover the social functioning area (Mezzich et al., 1978).

The fulfillment of the potential of the multiaxial approach to improve data organization, reliability, and validity may be facilitated if new axes are formulated in a way that is clear and explicit, as well as conceptually distinct from others.

NUMBER AND ORGANIZATION OF AXES

Decisions about the number of axes in a system entail a consideration of the relative importance given to two conflicting objectives in diagnostic development. One objective is greater comprehensiveness and informational richness of the diagnostic formulation, which tends to increase the number of axes. The other objective is parsimony, addressed to limiting the number of axes in order to prevent overloading the clinician when he tries to conceptualize the patient's problems and make management decisions. As can be seen in Table I, the number of axes in most systems was four or five, with five being the most frequent number.

Some multiaxial systems include subaxes that, in fact, increase their number of effective axes in that they involve separate statements for conceptually different clinical aspects. For example, Strauss's (1975) approach proposes separate statements for duration and course of symptoms (Axis II).

DIMENSIONAL VERSUS TYPOLOGICAL SCALING

In regard to their scaling, axes can be either typological or dimensional. A typological axis consists of categories that are qualitatively different from each other and can be represented by patient clusters or groups. A common example of a typological axis is syndrome description, involving a set of states such as generalized anxiety and paranoid schizophrenia. In contrast, a dimensional axis represents continuous, ordered, quantitative variation. The mathematical scale underlying it may be either of the rank type, in which only ordinal information is considered, or of the interval type, in which information about the size of the differences between objects or points is also considered. Persons diagnosed according to a dimensional axis are done so by defining the point on the scale which most closely corresponds to their condition. Examples of dimensional axes are chronicity and level of social functioning.

If one compares their diagnostic merits, a typological axis has the advantage of its traditional and generalized use in standard diagnostic systems, such as the current edition of the *International Classification of Diseases*. The predilection for the use of categorical labels may extend beyond the clinical area and respond to deep psychological needs for simplified description, as suggested by Raven et al. (1971). On the other hand, a dimensional axis or scale, when suitable to the data (e.g., I.Q.), involves a fuller use of the available information than does a typological scale. Besides the above considerations, the choice between a typological or a dimensional scale to assess a particular clinical aspect may depend on the scientific nature or basis of that problem and the type of information about it which is available, as determined by clinical judgment and data-based research.

Multiaxial diagnostic models can be classified, according to the scaling of their component axes, into purely typological, purely dimensional, and mixed. A review of Table I shows that most multiaxial systems are of the mixed type. That predominance is probably warranted by the comprehensiveness and

the flexibility provided by the inclusion of both typological and dimensional axes to handle the complexity and the varied informational structures of important clinical aspects.

Roles of Multiaxial Diagnosis

The functions of multiaxial diagnosis in general psychiatry include etiological and theoretical elucidation, optimization of clinical service, promotion of public health, and facilitation of clinical training. The application of multiaxial systems to circumscribed or special areas may also be useful.

ETIOLOGICAL ELUCIDATION AND THEORY DEVELOPMENT

One of the purposes that Essen-Möller and Wohlfahrt (1947) had in mind when they proposed the separation of syndrome and etiology was the discovery of atypical constellations—that is, new syndrome-cause connections. The fact that some multiaxial systems also include axes such as social functioning enhances the possibilities of finding innovative and useful nosological patterns.

Another potential theoretical role of the multiaxial model is related to the holistic and ecological movement in medicine and psychiatry, which proposes an integrative view of the biological and the psychosocial, the organismic and the environmental. Such propositions have recently attained new heights of conceptual rigor and clinical persuasiveness through the writings of Fabrega (1974, 1975)—who critically examined the relationship of disease, social behavior, and human adaptation, and argued for the development of an ethnomedical science—and the work of Engel (1976), who proposed a new biopsychosocial medical model. The multiaxial model offers the possibility of embracing multiple theories of psychopathology and of articulating empirically a holistic and ecological approach to psychiatry and medicine.

OPTIMIZATION OF CLINICAL SERVICE

The generic purposes of diagnosis in patient care involve organization of clinical information, communication among clinicians, and prediction of course and outcome. Multiaxial systems may be helpful in each of those regards.

Organization of clinical information. Multiaxial diagnosis may be useful here by promoting comprehensiveness in the description of the clinical condition. It involves ensuring that in the diagnostic formulation systematic consideration is given to such aspects as level of social functioning and concomitant physical disorders, in addition to the obviously important psychopathological syndromes.

Communication among clinicians. Communication may be improved by the above-mentioned comprehensiveness of the diagnostic formulation and by the teasing out or conceptual delineation of various aspects of the clinical condition and their separate ratings. It can contribute to a clear and precise communication among clinicians.

Treatment planning and prediction of outcome. The comprehensiveness of the multiaxial diagnostic formulation should facilitate the rational selection of the components of a comprehensive treatment plan. The multiaxial delineation of various clinical aspects may also optimize the prediction of important outcome measures. For example, it has been suggested that, at least among schizophrenics, the best predictors of future work adjustment and social functioning are past work adjustment and social functioning, respectively (Strauss and Carpenter, 1974).

PROMOTION OF PUBLIC HEALTH

The improvement of public health statistics afforded by the multiaxial model is illustrated by the case described by Rutter et al. (1975a) of a child with mental retardation, epilepsy, and emotional disturbance. The use of a multiaxial system that includes axes dealing with I.Q., physical disorders, and psychiatric syndromes facilitates the formulation of each of those three conditions and, therefore, promotes more accurate and complete incidence and prevalence statistics. An axis on social functioning also gives an opportunity to obtain systematic information on the disability associated with mental disorders. The development of such improved epidemiological statistics should, in turn, lead to a more rational planning and monitoring of prevention and treatment programs.

FACILITATION OF CLINICAL TRAINING

Authors of multiaxial systems who have implemented them in academic settings have explicitly reported the value of those systems for teaching psychiatric assessment (Helmchen, 1977; von Cranach, 1977; von Knorring et al., 1977). The use of a multiaxial diagnostic system seems to be helpful to organize the interview process, to ensure the consideration and careful assessment of important clinical aspects, and to facilitate the monitoring of the learning process.

MULTIAXIAL SYSTEMS FOR SPECIAL AREAS

Multiaxial systems, in addition to being useful for the classification of general psychiatric patients, may be productively applied to special areas.

One special area in which there is considerable experience with multiaxial systems is child psychiatry. In fact, some child psychiatrists, such as Rutter and his associates, have been pioneers in the development of multiaxial thinking.

Another special area may be defined by type of disorder. Illustrative of multiaxial systems in such an area is the work of Tarjan et al. (1972) on the classification of mental retardation.

In other cases, the multiaxial model may be applied not to a person but to alternative levels of organization, such as the family. An example is the triaxial system for the diagnosis of family dysfunction developed by Tseng and McDermott (1979).

Evaluation of Multiaxial Systems

The development of a diagnostic system can be seen, from a scientific method viewpoint, as a hypothesis-generating process. It is to be followed by a hypothesis-testing process, which, in the case of a diagnostic system, is represented by the evaluation of the various forms of its validity or usefulness and its reliability. The need for evaluation is especially great in the case of multiaxial diagnostic systems because of the number of potentially useful axes and the various alternative ways of organizing and scaling them. The rationale for the development of multiaxial diagnostic systems includes its presumed potential for raising the levels of reliability (by separately coding various clinical aspects) and validity—in general, by making the diagnostic formulation more comprehensive and reflective of the complexity of the clinical condition and, more specifically, by

explicitly considering variables, such as social functioning, with presumed value for predicting corresponding outcome aspects. The degree in which the potential is being fulfilled needs to be evaluated.

Frequently considered aspects of the validity of a diagnostic system include descriptive validity, predictive validity, and consensual validity.

Descriptive validity refers to the power of the diagnostic system to organize clinical information. It is usually estimated by the fit of the diagnostic system to real patient data—for example, actual homogeneity of diagnostic groups and degree of coverage of the psychiatric population under consideration.

Predictive validity refers to the power of a diagnostic system to predict clinically relevant future events, such as course of the disorder and treatment response. This criterion has high scientific value for hypothesis testing, although its assessment is not without potential pitfalls.

Consensual validity refers to the degree of acceptability—perceived appropriateness and usefulness—of a given diagnostic system among experienced clinicians. Although not always recognized as such, this validity criterion seems to be the major one underlying the adoption of most standard diagnostic systems.

Another interesting validity aspect is construct validity (Cronbach and Mehl, 1955). In the case of psychiatric diagnosis (Zubin, 1978), it is more readily applicable to a specific diagnostic category, rather than to a whole axis, and refers to the extent to which the diagnosis satisfies a given theoretical model.

Reliability or replicability of a diagnostic system is a necessary, although not sufficient, requirement for its validity or usefulness. It is usually assessed in terms of agreement among clinicians formulating diagnoses on the same patient.

In the mid-1970's pioneer comparative evaluations of multiaxial diagnostic systems versus conventional uniaxial systems, dealing mainly with reliability and more limitedly with validity, were conducted by Rutter et al. (1975a), Cantwell (1977), and von Knorring et al. (1977). Some methodological problems were noted in those studies, including the use of a reliability index (percentage of raters using the most common diagnosis) not corrected for chance agreement and the assessment of the reliability of a dimensional axis under a reduced typological frame, which involves loss of information. Recently, procedures have been described for assessing agreement on dimensional scales using intraclass correlation coefficients (Shrout and Fleiss, 1979) and procedures for assessing chance-corrected agreement among multiple raters formulating multiple typological diagnoses and for assessing the statistical significance of reliability differences between axes and between diagnostic systems (Mezzich et al., 1979). Using those newly developed procedures, Mezzich and Mezzich (1979) comparatively evaluated the reliability and some validity aspects of the multiaxial DSM-III versus the uniaxial DSM-II in child psychiatry cases. Their results were quite similar to those of the above-mentioned studies in that the reliabilities of Axes I and II of DSM-III, encompassing all mental disorders, were above chance level and similar to the reliability of DSM-II. Adaptive functioning seemed to be the only axis with reliability significantly higher than other DSM-III axes and DSM-II. Using the criterion of consensual validity, it was found that DSM-III was preferred to DSM-II because of its greater suitability, conceptual correctness, and clarity of diagnostic criteria and because of its systematic consideration of developmental disorders, psychosocial stress, and adaptive functioning.

The preliminary reports of the validity of the multiaxial

systems are encouraging, but additional studies are required to assess their consensual, descriptive, and, especially, predictive validities in general psychiatric populations.

Development of Improved Multiaxial Diagnostic Systems

The development of a multiaxial system involves first the identification of axes and then the determination of the content and the structure of the identified axes. Most of the current multiaxial systems and all standard uniaxial systems have been based almost exclusively on clinical intuition and judgment. However, the coordinated and synergetic use of clinical judgment and empirical (data-based) procedures is likely to be helpful. These procedures involve the evaluation of the validity and the reliability of potential diagnostic axes, as discussed in the preceding section, as well as the investigation of patterns in appropriate patient data bases. Such investigation may include the use of general exploratory procedures and the specific exploration of patient clusters or types, dimensions, and longitudinal patterns.

General exploratory procedures may include graphical analysis and ordinal multidimensional scaling (Shepard, 1962; Kruskal, 1964) for a maximally candid, visual appraisal of what is in the data. Graphical approaches allow a bidimensional or a tridimensional plotting of patients as multivariate data points. Special procedures such as Chernoff's (1973) faces and Fourier series (Mezzich and Worthington, 1978) permit the graphical representation of higher dimensionality. Interactive computer graphics provide the additional benefit of rotation and tilting of the spatial display and the ability to use flexibly alternative sets of elementary or composite variables to frame the representation.

The exploration of patient clusters or types can be conducted by using cluster analytic techniques after such general exploratory procedures. Besides the exploration of the existence of clusters, the visual analysis can suggest the form of the clusters, if any, which can then suggest the type of cluster analysis to use—for example, complete linkage for spheroid clusters and single linkage for elongated clusters. Comparative evaluations of taxonomic methods on psychopathological data (Strauss et al., 1973; Mezzich, 1977, 1978) suggest that the complete linkage agglomerative hierarchical method (Johnson, 1967) and the k-means-partition method (MacQueen, 1967) may be the most helpful techniques in many cases.

The exploration of dimensions—for example, investigation of hypothetical constructs underlying social functioning—may be helped by factor analysis. A discussion of that general method, including procedures for factor extraction and rotation and its options and pitfalls, can be found in Harman (1967).

The exploration of longitudinal patterns is usually addressed to the elucidation of groups of patients who move together in time when measured on a given set of variables. A variety of graphic approaches to the appraisal of temporal variation can be used (Siegel et al., 1971; Mezzich and Worthington, 1978).

A step complementary to the development of a multiaxial system consists in the formulation of diagnostic rules. That refers to the determination of rules for assigning new patients to the established diagnostic categories in the case of typological axes and for patient description, using rank or interval scales, in the case of dimensional axes. Clinical judgment and statistical procedures, such as discriminant function analysis, can again be used interactively in the process.

Central to the current conceptualizations of the multiaxial model is the separate rating of various clinical aspects, which are thus considered as quasi-independent of each other. However, in reality, the variables represented by the axes may have, at least for some psychopathological areas, a significant relationship to each other, in the sense that knowledge of the standing of a person on one axis may provide information on his standing on another axis. Knowledge of interaxis relations may even lead to the integration or lumping of some of the axes into higher order patterns, which would represent a second-generation development in multiaxial diagnostic modeling.

Conclusion

The multiaxial diagnostic model consists in the systematic formulation of a patient's condition and its associated factors according to separate variables or aspects. The model has old roots and an international trajectory. It seems to be useful for promoting the various purposes of psychiatric diagnosis, including the organization of clinical information, communication, prediction of course and outcome, etiological and theoretical elucidation, promotion of public health, and facilitation of clinical education and training.

By questioning the traditional nosological paradigm in psychiatry and promoting the empirical development and testing of innovative approaches, the multiaxial model is inaugurating a new and more active epoch in the investigation of diagnostic systems, not only in regard to assessment and formulation but also in the conceptualization of psychiatric disorders.

Suggested Cross References

The multiaxial system used in DSM-III is discussed in Section 14.1. The application of statistics to psychiatry is discussed in Chapter 7.

The author gratefully acknowledges the suggestions provided by Doctors Anthony J. Costello, Horacio Fabrega, Jr., Jonathan M. Himmelhoch, David J. Kupfer, and Ada C. Mezzich.

REFERENCES

American Psychiatric Association. *Diagnostic and Statistical Manual of Mental Disorders*, ed. 3. American Psychiatric Association, Washington, D.C., 1980.

Bahn, A. K. A multi-disciplinary psychosocial classification scheme. Am. J. Orthopsychiatry, *41*: 830, 1971.

Cantwell, D. A DSM-III field trial and reliability study. Paper presented at the 130th annual meeting of the American Psychiatric Association, Toronto, 1977.

Chernoff, H. The use of faces to represent points in k-dimensional space graphically. J. Am. Statistical Assoc., *68*: 361, 1973.

Cronbach, L. J., and Mehl, P. E. Construct validity in psychological tests. Psychol. Bull., *52*: 281, 1955.

Engel, G. L. The need for a new medical model: A challenge for biomedicine. Science, *196*: 129, 1976.

Essen-Möller, E. On classification of mental disorders. Acta Psychiatr. Scand., *37*: 119, 1961.

Essen-Möller, E. Suggestions for further improvement on the international classification of mental disorders. Psychol. Med., *1*: 308, 1971.

Essen-Möller, E., and Wohlfahrt, S. Suggestions for the amendment of the official Swedish classification of mental disorders. Acta Psychiatr. Scand., *47* (Suppl.): 551, 1947.

Fabrega, H. *Disease and Social Behavior: An Interdisciplinary Perspective*. MIT Press, Cambridge, Mass., 1974.

Fabrega, H. The need for an ethnomedical science. Science, *189*: 969, 1975.

Fabrega, H. The biological significance of taxonomies of disease. J. Theor. Biol., *63*: 191, 1976.

Gardner, E. G. The role of the classification system in outpatient psychiatry. In *The Role and Methodology of Classification in Psychiatry and Psychopathology*, M. M. Katz, J. O. Cole, and W. E. Barton, editors. United States Public Health Service, Bethesda, 1965.

Harman, H. H. *Modern Factor Analysis*, ed. 2. University of Chicago Press, Chicago, 1967.

Helmchen, H. Schizophrenia: Diagnostic concepts in the ICD-8. In *Studies in*

Schizophrenia, M. H. Lader, editor, p. 10. British Journal of Psychiatry, Special Publication No. 10, 1975.

Helmchen, H. Multiaxial systems of classification. Paper presented at the VI World Congress of Psychiatry, Honolulu, 1977.

Hoche, A. Die Bedeutung der Symptomenkomplexe in der Psychiatrie. Z. Gesamte Neurol. Psychiatrie, 12: 540, 1912.

Johnson, S. C. Hierarchical clustering schemes. Psychometrika, 32: 241, 1967.

Kato, M. Multiaxial diagnosis in adult psychiatry. Paper presented at the VI World Congress of Psychiatry, Honolulu, 1977.

Kendell, R. E. The Role of Diagnosis in Psychiatry. Blackwell, Oxford, 1975.

Kraepelin, E. Clinical Psychiatry. Macmillan, New York, 1902.

Kruskal, J. B. Multidimensional scaling by optimizing goodness of fit to a nonmetric hypothesis. Psychometrika, 29: 1, 1964.

MacQueen, J. B. Some methods for classification and analysis of multivariate observations. Proc. Fifth Berkeley Symp. Math. Stat. Prob., 1: 281, 1967.

Mezzich, A. C., and Mezzich, J. E. Reliability of DSM-III vs. DSM-II in child psychiatry. Paper presented at the 132nd meeting of the American Psychiatric Association, Chicago, 1979.

Mezzich, J. E. A comprehensive comparison of cluster analytic methods. Paper presented at the National Science Foundation Workshop on Classifying Social and Cultural Data, Charleston, S. C., 1977.

Mezzich, J. E. Evaluating clustering methods for psychiatric diagnosis. Biol. Psychiatry, 13: 265, 1978.

Mezzich, J. E. Patterns and issues in multiaxial psychiatric diagnosis. Psychol. Med., 9: 125, 1979.

Mezzich, J. E., Keener, M. A., Kraemer, H. C., and Worthington, D. R. L. Comparative Reliability of Three Psychiatric Diagnostic Systems: Technical Report. Department of Psychiatry and Behavioral Sciences, Stanford University, Palo Alto, Calif., 1978.

Mezzich, J. E., Kraemer, H. C., and Worthington, D. R. L. Reliability assessment of multiaxial diagnostic systems. Paper presented at the tenth annual meeting of The Classification Society, Gainesville, Fla., 1979.

Mezzich, J. E., and Worthington, D. R. L. A comparison of graphical representations of multidimensional psychiatric diagnostic data. In Graphical Representation of Multivariate Data, P. Wang, editor, p. 123. Academic Press, New York, 1978.

Ottosson, J. O., and Perris, C. Multidimensional classification of mental disorders. Psychol. Med., 3: 238, 1973.

Raven, P. H., Berlin, B., and Breedlove, D. E. The origins of taxonomy. Science, 174: 1210, 1971.

Rutter, M., Lebovici, S., Eisenberg, L., Sneznevskij, A. V., Sadoun, R., Brooke, E., and Lin, T. Y. A tri-axial classification of mental disorders in childhood. J. Child Psychol. Psychiatry, 10: 41, 1969.

Rutter, M., Shaffer, D., and Shepherd, M. A Multiaxial Classification of Child Psychiatric Disorders. World Health Organization, Geneva, 1975a.

Rutter, M., Shaffer, D., and Sturge, C. A Guide to a Multiaxial Classification Scheme for Psychiatric Disorders in Childhood and Adolescence. Institute of Psychiatry, London, 1975b.

Shepard, R. N. The analysis of proximities: Multidimensional scaling with an unknown distance function. Psychometrika, 27: 125, 1962.

Shrout, P. E., and Fleiss, J. L. Intraclass correlations: Uses in assessing rater reliability. Psychol. Bull., 2: 420, 1979.

Siegel, H. J., Goldwyn, R. M., and Friedman, H. P. Pattern and process in the evolution of human shock. Surgery, 70: 232, 1971.

Spitzer, R. L. A response to the threat of a classification scheme for the psychosocial disorders: Some specific suggestions. Am. J. Orthopsychiatry, 41: 838, 1971.

Stengel, E. Classification of mental disorders. Bull. W. H. O., 21: 601, 1959.

Strauss, J. S. Diagnostic models and the nature of psychiatric disorder. Arch. Gen. Psychiatry, 29: 445, 1973.

Strauss, J. S. A comprehensive approach to psychiatric diagnosis. Am. J. Psychiatry, 132: 1193, 1975.

Strauss, J. S., Bartko, J. J., and Carpenter, W. T. The use of clustering techniques for the classification of psychiatric patients. Br. J. Psychiatry, 122: 531, 1973.

Strauss, J. S., and Carpenter, W. T. The prediction of outcome in schizophrenia. II. Relationships between predictors and outcome variables: A report from the International Pilot Study of Schizophrenia. Arch. Gen. Psychiatry, 31: 37, 1974.

Tarjan, G., Tizard, J., and Rutter, M. Classification and mental retardation: Issues arising in the Fifth WHO Seminar on Psychiatric Diagnosis, Classification and Statistics. Am. J. Psychiatry, 128 (Suppl.): 34, 1972.

Tseng, W. S., and McDermott, J., Jr. Triaxial family classification. J. Am. Acad. Child Psychiatry, 18: 22, 1979.

von Cranach, M. Categorical vs. multiaxial classification. Paper presented at the VI World Congress of Psychiatry, Honolulu, 1977.

von Knorring, L., Perris, C., and Jacobsson, L. A multiaxial classification of mental disorders: Experiences from clinical routine work and preliminary studies of inter-rater reliability. Paper presented at the VI World Congress of Psychiatry, Honolulu, 1977.

Wing, L. Observations on the psychiatric section of the International Classification of Diseases and the British Glossary of Mental Disorders. Psychol. Med., 1: 79, 1970.

Ziskind, E. Some nosologic concepts related to mental diseases. Acta Psychiatr. Scand., 41: 303, 1965.

Zubin, J. Field Studies in the Mental Disorders: Proceedings of the American Psychopathological Association. Grune & Stratton, New York, 1961.

Zubin, J. Research in clinical diagnosis. In Clinical Diagnosis of Mental Disorders, B. B. Wolman, editor, p. 3. Plenum Publishing Corp., New York, 1978.

14.3 Neurosis, Psychosis, and the Borderline States

OTTO F. KERNBERG, M.D.

Classification Problems

Early approaches to psychiatric diagnosis conceived of three broad groups of disorders: the psychoneuroses and character pathologies, the organic mental disorders, and the functional psychoses, which included schizophrenia, the affective disorders (manic-depressive illness and related conditions), and the paranoid states. The term "functional" as applied to those disorders was helpful in signaling a contrast to the gross organic disturbances associated with the organic mental disorders, but it was a misnomer because genetic, constitutional, and biochemical alterations are also present in the functional psychoses. Although that classification system did not include all specific psychiatric disorders and although certain syndromes, such as depression, cut across those major groups, it had one definite advantage: The relatively few and rather easily detectable key symptoms that differentiated clinical syndromes did belong to one of those three broad groups, thus facilitating differential diagnoses.

The neuroses and character pathologies could be discerned by a quantitative decrease in the capacity for adaptation to the external and intrapsychic world without gross alteration or loss of the capacity to relate to the environment and the maintenance of reality testing; and the extent to which the symptoms were ego-alien or ego-syntonic differentiated symptomatic neuroses from character pathology within that group. For the chronic organic mental disorders, loss of memory and of intelligence, particularly of abstracting ability, represented the key symptoms, symptoms usually obscured in the acute organic mental disorders by the alterations in the sensorium—attention, orientation, consciousness, apperception, and judgment. The psychoses were characterized by a severe loss of the capacity to adapt to external and intrapsychic reality, a shift from quantitative to qualitative alterations in the psychosocial interaction, a loss of reality testing, and gross alterations in behavior, affect, and thought—both thought content and formal organization of thought processes. The productive psychotic symptoms, true hallucinations and delusions, permitted an additional differentiation of the psychoses, both functional and those superimposed on organic mental disorders, from the neuroses and character pathologies.

Thus, the evaluation in a mental status examination of the

key symptoms of (1) subjective complaints or neurotic symptoms; (2) pathological character traits; (3) reality testing; (4) behavior; (5) affect; (6) thought content and organization, including delusion formation; (7) pathological perceptions, particularly hallucinations; (8) attention; (9) orientation; (10) consciousness; (11) apperception; (12) judgment; (13) memory; and (14) intelligence jointly permitted the classification of a psychiatric patient into one of those three groups.

But certain developments have led to increasing dissatisfaction with the traditional method of classifying psychiatric illnesses. First, sophisticated genetic studies of schizophrenia and the affective disorders have indicated the possibility of a schizophrenic spectrum and an affective spectrum of disorders that may overlap with the neuroses and character pathologies. Second, in a reaction to the relative neglect of descriptive syndromes that stemmed from both oversimplified psychodynamic approaches and community psychiatry models, current research efforts are focusing on discrete, descriptive, or phenomenological symptom constellations, rather than on broader groupings. Third, the exploration of the vast field of character pathologies, which has undergone bewildering and confusing changes in labeling throughout the various editions of the American Psychiatric Association's *Diagnostic and Statistical Manual of Mental Disorders,* has brought about an interest in the complex intermediate area between severe character pathology and the major (functional) psychoses—that is, the borderline states. Fourth, new treatment methods evolving from a psychoanalytically oriented therapeutic viewpoint of those borderline conditions, new psychopharmacological approaches to them, and genetic studies of the major psychoses— all indicate the need to reexamine the border area between character pathologies and the psychoses, as well as the grouping or classification of character pathologies themselves.

In the third edition of the American Psychiatric Association's (1980) *Diagnostic and Statistical Manual of Mental Disorders* (DSM-III), the organic mental disorders still constitute one group, but the old functional grouping of certain psychoses has been abandoned and replaced by the specific groupings of schizophrenic disorders, paranoid disorders, affective disorders, and psychotic disorders not elsewhere classified. The entire area of neuroses and character pathology has been replaced by the headings of anxiety disorders, factitious disorders, somatoform disorders, dissociative disorders, personality disorders, psychosexual disorders, disorders of impulse control not elsewhere classified, and adjustment disorders. Most character pathologies are incorporated in the personality disorders, which are coded on Axis II, but certain personality constellations are grouped within other disorders, such as the multiple personality syndrome, which is placed within the dissociative disorders, and the Munchausen syndrome, which is placed within the factitious disorders. A majority of the predominant constellations of character or personality disorders are preserved as such under the heading of "personality disorders," and the subheading "atypical, mixed, or other personality disorders" provides helpful flexibility for classifying other constellations of pathological character traits.

The major disadvantage of the new classification of psychiatric disorders is that it may deemphasize or obscure the potential relationship of a certain clinical syndrome to other underlying disorders, thus missing a dimension to a psychopathological depth that may be relevant to differential diagnosis, prognosis, and treatment.

In an effort to establish diagnostic validity as a guideline, Guze (1975) suggested five criteria for the recognition and definition of a valid psychiatric syndrome: clinical description, laboratory studies, delimitation from other disorders, follow-up studies, and family studies. In theory, those are straightforward criteria; in practice, however, they do not sufficiently consider the complex relationships between a clinical syndrome and the underlying disease or illness in the sense of psychopathological or causative entity. The definition of depression as a clinical syndrome, for example, is different from the diagnosis of major depressive disorder and of a bipolar affective disorder or manic-depressive illness as an underlying clinical entity. Depression may, indeed, reflect an episodic affective disorder; it may also develop periodically in a depressive character structure as a chronic minor depressive disorder and, in later stages of life, in a narcissistic personality. In still other cases, depression as a clinical syndrome may reflect an abnormal grief reaction, probably best classified under adjustment disorder with depressed mood or even an uncomplicated bereavement. In short, depression may evolve as part of a genetically or biochemically determined disorder, as a direct reaction to psychosocial stress, as a neurotic symptom, or as a secondary development in various types of character pathology.

The present classification of clinical psychiatric disorders is enhanced by an additional dimension, the relationship between underlying psychobiological, psychodynamic, characterological, and psychosocial dispositions and a specific clinical disorder. Although how genetic, biochemical, psychodynamic, characterological, and environmentally determined psychological disturbances are interrelated is still a matter of some controversy, a flexible analysis of clinical data in terms of both clinical syndromes and underlying structured predispositions, such as altered personality structure and altered psychophysiological matrix of affective response patterns, should give depth and sophistication to what otherwise might become mechanistic groupings and regroupings of symptoms.

A structural approach to diagnosis is useful as a complement to psychiatric classification. The structural model refers to an over-all intrapsychic organization that has stability, continuity, and sameness throughout time. The model should permit the maintenance or reintroduction of valuable aspects of the traditional classification of nonorganic psychiatric disorders into a neurotic, psychotic, and an intermediary or borderline field, while refining the diagnosis of specific clinical disorders.

The concept of mental structure has had a complex development in psychological and psychoanalytic theory. It has been a valuable hypothesis in developmental theory (Inhelder and Piaget, 1958). In the topographic theory of the mind, Freud (1958) described three systems: unconscious, preconscious, and conscious. Later, Freud (1961) organized mental processes and functions into three structures: id, ego, and superego. Maintaining Freud's structural theory, Hartmann et al. (1946) and Rapaport and Gill (1959) proposed viewing the ego as (1) a combination of slowly changing structures or configurations that determine the channeling of mental processes; (2) the mental processes or functions themselves; and (3) thresholds for the activation of those functions. More recently, the term "structural analysis" has been used to describe the development and vicissitudes of the structural derivatives of internalized object relations and the various levels of organization of mental functioning in terms of hierarchy of motivational systems that are closely linked to internalized object relations (Kernberg, 1976a).

Three types of structural organizations correspond to normal and neurotic, borderline, and psychotic levels of personality organization (Kernberg, 1977). Those structures are laid down on the basis of the developmental interactions of genetic, constitutional, biochemical, familial, and psychosocial factors with the individual history of unconscious intrapsychic conflicts. Psychological functioning stabilizes in terms of that structure, which then becomes the underlying matrix from which behavioral symptoms develop. Those three structural types—neurotic, borderline, and psychotic—are reflected in the patient's structural characteristics, three of which—the degree of identity integration, the level of defensive operations, and the capacity for reality testing—have particular relevance for clinical diagnosis. The neurotic personality structure presents an integrated identity, whereas borderline and psychotic structures present identity diffusion or lack of integration of identity. The neurotic personality structure presents a defensive organization centering on repression and other advanced or high-level defensive operations. In contrast, borderline and psychotic structures show a predominance of primitive defensive operations centering on the mechanism of splitting. Reality testing is maintained in neurotic and borderline personality organizations but is severely impaired in psychotic organization.

That classification of neurotic, borderline, and psychotic personality structures cuts across the classification used in DSM-III. For practical purposes, however, it should be possible to classify most patients presenting borderline personality organization within the personality disorders and the disorders of impulse control not elsewhere classified. The proposed diagnosis based on the three structural organizations is intended not to replace but to supplement and enrich the diagnosis of clinical disorders, particularly those falling within the borderline field. A patient's placement into any of those three proposed categories is definitely not sufficient for the classification of mental disorders. For cases in which the diagnosis of borderline personality organization is an appropriate qualification of a symptomatic or characterological constellation that may also be grouped elsewhere, using the two conjointly may be helpful in terms of diagnosis, prognosis, and therapy. In addition to providing a discriminating dimension of the character pathologies, which permits their classification as neurotic and borderline structures, the proposed structural approach should also contribute significantly to the differential diagnosis of schizophrenic reactions from their respective spectrum of personality disorders, with schizoid, paranoid, and hypomanic features. Similarly, the approach may permit the differentiation of depressions with psychotic structure from those with borderline and neurotic structures, thus contributing to a clarification of the affective disorders spectrum.

Borderline Personality Organization

Many distinguished clinicians have attempted to define and differentiate a group of borderline patients. Adolph Stern (1938) was the first to refer to borderline conditions. In the early literature various terms were used—"borderline states" (Knight, 1954 a, b), "preschizophrenic" personality structure (Rapaport et al., 1945–1946), "psychotic characters" (Frosch, 1964), "borderline personality" (Rangell, 1955; Robbins, 1956). Some authors did not make it clear whether the term "ambulatory schizophrenia" referred to borderline personality disorder or to more regressed, psychotic patients whose symptoms resemble the borderline conditions. Psychoanalytic investigations of "as-if" personalities (Deutsch, 1942), schizoid personality structure (Fairbairn, 1952), and patients with severe ego distortions (Gitelson, 1958) appeared to deal with patients who were also related to the borderline group.

The early literature also contained clinical descriptions of many patients who might now be considered borderline—for example, descriptions by Zilboorg (1941, 1957) and Hoch and Polatin (1949). Hoch

and Cattell (1959) elaborated on the diagnosis of "pseudoneurotic schizophrenic." Other aspects of the symptoms of some borderline patients were studied by Bychowski (1953), who also described such important structural characteristics as the persistence of dissociated primitive ego states and the cleavage of parental images into good and bad objects.

Until recently, much confusion was caused by the fact that the term "borderline" was used to refer both to patients who showed acute transitory signs that they were rapidly regressing from neurotic symptoms to an overt psychotic reaction and to patients who were functioning chronically in a stable way at a level considered to be on a borderline between neurosis and psychosis (Rangell, 1955; Robbins, 1956; Waelder, 1958). Frosch (1964) contributed to the differential diagnosis of borderline personality organization from psychosis. He stressed that, although borderline patients have alterations in their relationships with reality and in their subjective experiences of reality, their capacity to test reality—in contrast to patients with psychotic reactions—is preserved. Knight (1954 a, b) synthesized the general descriptive features of borderline patients with suggestions for the treatment of their ego deficits. He called attention to the severe regression in the transference and to the need to modify the psychotherapeutic approach to borderline patients.

The most important contribution to the understanding of borderline personality organization and to its treatment came from the analysis of the pathology of internalized object relations. Helen Deutsch's (1942) article on "as-if" personalities was the first and fundamental contribution. The independent conclusions of Melanie Klein (1946) and Fairbairn (1952) followed. Additional contributions to the analysis of the pathology in internalized object relations have come from ego psychology—Jacobson (1964), Greenson (1954, 1958), and Erikson (1956), whose ideas point toward phenomena similar to those described in different terms by the British school of psychoanalysis influenced by Fairbairn and Klein. Khan (1960), for example, stressed the structural elements in regard to both specific defensive operations and the specific pathology of the object relations of borderline patients.

Rapaport's (1957) analysis of the level of cognitive structures focused on the degree to which primary-process thinking predominates over secondary-process thinking in borderline patients. That difference is still considered a distinctive clinical manifestation of borderline personality organization. Much of the thinking of Rapaport et al. (1945–1946) with regard to structural differentiation was linked to their analysis of levels of cognitive structures; they used a battery of psychological tests to evaluate the degree to which secondary-process thinking or primary-process thinking predominated.

Grinker et al.'s (1968) *The Borderline Syndrome* made a major contribution to the diagnosis of the borderline syndrome. They described as characteristic of the borderline syndrome

anger as the main or only affect, defect in affectional relationships, absence of indication of self-identity, and depressive loneliness.

They defined four subgroups within that clinical constellation: (1) the psychotic border, characterized by inappropriate and negativistic behavior and affects toward other patients and hospital staff; (2) the borderline syndrome, characterized by negativistic and chaotic feelings and behavior, contradictory behavior, and a strong potential for acting out; (3) the adaptive, affectless, defended "as-if" person, characterized by superficially adaptive but affectively deficient interactions; and (4) the border with the neuroses, which presents child-like clinging depression. They concluded that the borderline syndrome, in contrast to schizophrenia, does not present disturbances in intellectual associational processes, autistic or regressive thinking, a characteristic family structure with pseudomutuality or skewing, delusions or hallucinations, or any deficit in the connotative aspects of language. In comparing the borderline syndrome with the neuroses, they stated that, although depression as an affect is found in several of the borderline categories, it does not correspond with that seen in the depressive syndrome.

More recently, Collum (1972), combining the viewpoints of Grinker and Kernberg, focused on the central nature of identity diffusion. Cary (1972) developed further the structural-dynamic analysis of borderline conditions, stressing the following characteristics: depression accompanied by a sense of futility and pervasive feelings of loneliness and isolation—a feeling of isolation and angry demandingness—rather than by feelings of guilt and self-derogation, which are characteristic of neurotic and psychotic depression. He also stressed schizoid detachment as a major defense of borderline patients.

Bergeret (1970, 1972), examining the structural and dynamic characteristics of borderline states from a psychoanalytic viewpoint, concluded that the states are characterized by a predominance of pregenital conflicts and primitive structural and defensive characteristics of the ego and the superego. He saw the ego's immaturity of object relations as constituting a psychopathological category different from both neurotic structures and psychotic structures. Duvocelle, in an unpublished 1971 thesis, integrated Bergeret's and Kernberg's ideas into a clinical and theoretical overview of borderline personality organization.

Mahler (1971) proposed that children who do not resolve the rapprochement crisis normally may, during the rapprochement subphase of the separation-individuation process, develop a bad introject, which becomes infiltrated with the derivatives of aggressive drive and may evolve into a more or less permanent split of the object world into good objects and bad objects.

> These mechanisms, coercion and splitting of the object world, are characteristic in most cases of borderline transference.

That pathological development is in contrast to the consequences of the normal resolution of the rapprochement subphase in the form of normal identity formation in the third year of life.

Other recent studies presenting an overview of the borderline syndrome and a discussion of its descriptive and structural diagnostic criteria included those of Wolberg (1973), Gunderson and Singer (1975), and Kernberg (1975a). A recent review of some of the important current controversial issues regarding the diagnosis and treatment of borderline conditions may be found in Mack's (1975) book.

Gunderson and Singer (1975) reviewed the literature critically and proposed some basic paradigms for the diagnosis of borderline conditions. They suggested that most writers have characterized borderline patients as presenting intense affect, usually of a strongly hostile or depressed nature; a history of impulsive behavior, including such episodic acts as self-mutilation and overdoses of drugs, and more chronic behavior patterns, such as drug dependency and promiscuity; superficial social adaptiveness, which may reflect a disturbed identity masked by mimicry; brief psychotic episodes, which may become evident during drug use or unstructured situations and relationships; performance on psychological tests wherein disturbed functioning is revealed on unstructured tests, as contrasted to relatively intact performance on structured tests; and characteristic interpersonal relationships that oscillate between those that are transiently superficial and those that are intensely dependent and marred by devaluation, manipulation, and demandingness. They said that those six features provide a rational basis for diagnosis and can be assessed readily on initial evaluation.

In comparing borderline and schizophrenic patients, Gunderson et al. (1975) found that borderline patients, although presenting more confusing diagnostic pictures, could be differentiated from schizophrenic patients by the absence of a definite or prolonged psychotic episode, by the relative severity of their dissociated experiences, by more severe anger, and by less anxiety. Despite discrepant symptom pictures in the two patient groups, a systematic review of prehospitalization functioning and a 2-year posthospitalization course did not reveal significant differences between them. A 5-year follow-up study (Carpenter et al., 1977) revealed that the schizophrenic group showed some deterioration in the quality of their social relating over time, while the borderline group remained constant. In addition, the borderline patients were readily distinguished from other hospitalized groups,

with the exception of neurotic depressive patients. In a later study, Gunderson and Kolb (1978) found that borderline patients can be discriminated with high accuracy from matched comparison groups of schizophrenic patients and patients with neurotic depression. They concluded that the best discriminating symptoms in a variety of differential diagnostic problems were low achievement, impulsivity, manipulative suicide, heightened affectivity, mild psychotic experiences, high socialization, and disturbed close relationships.

Perry and Klerman (1978)—comparing the approaches of Knight, Kernberg, Grinker, and Gunderson and Singer for borderline patients—were concerned by the impression conveyed that the whole range of psychopathology of personality is represented, thereby presenting a large amount of overlap with other personality disorder diagnoses. The question of overlap resulting from the numerous definitions of the term "borderline" led them to recommend the definition of and a search for subtypes within the group of borderline patients.

Research is currently under way comparing Gunderson's approach to the diagnosis of borderline conditions with that of Kernberg. Preliminary findings indicate that the structural diagnosis of patients on the basis of an initial structural interview (Kernberg, 1977) without previous information about the patient, except name and age, correlates highly with the diagnosis of borderline personality arrived at independently by means of Gunderson's diagnostic interview for borderlines, on the one hand, and psychological testing, on the other hand. Although Gunderson's borderline syndrome may be more restrictive than Kernberg's and probably corresponds to the subgroups of infantile and narcissistic personalities within Kernberg's borderline character pathology, the approaches complement each other. In addition, Kernberg's structural diagnosis may permit the differentiation of schizophrenic from pseudoschizophrenic, schizoid, and schizotypal personality structures, thus refining the mapping of the boundaries of the borderline syndrome.

In that connection, Spitzer et al.'s (1979) differentiation of two subtypes of borderline conditions, their schizotypal and unstable borderline cases, also pointed to the importance of differentiating subgroups within the borderline syndrome and the relative ease with which that appears to be feasible. Clinically, their schizotypal subgroup probably corresponds to the schizoid personality and the unstable subgroup to the infantile personality. Such subgroups may be relevant for research on treatment response and may also help in evaluating the causative effect of genetic predispositions to borderline conditions in terms of the influence of schizophrenic and manic-depressive predisposition to character structure.

The major questions are: Do common characteristics exist that span the spectrum of the entire borderline syndrome, that have discriminating value for both inpatients and outpatients, and that can at the same time permit a delimitation of the borderline syndrome from schizophrenia, nonborderline character pathology, and the affective disorders? And if such characteristics do exist, will they say something about the specific response of patients to a certain type of treatment and about their prognoses?

A major incentive for the study of borderline conditions came from the need to study the schizophrenia spectrum from a genetic viewpoint; another incentive came from the need to differentiate schizophrenic patients from pseudoschizophrenic patients; a third focus of interest derived from the treatment complications and failures in patients with character pathologies treated with psychoanalysis and psychoanalytic psychotherapy on an outpatient basis. That last point probably represents the most frequent and clinically the most challenging aspect of the borderline syndrome. The lack of sufficient emphasis on outpatient populations has seriously limited research in the area. The definition and clarification of a common borderline structure cutting across various subgroups and constituting an underlying personality structure that determines, fixates, or modifies the specific character constellations of all those patients may have practical relevance for the treatment and prognosis of the vast, confusing range of characterological illnesses that extend beyond the neuroses without being part of the major psychoses.

DIAGNOSIS

The proposed classification of borderline personality organization (Kernberg, 1975a, 1977) explains the clinical features of borderline patients on the basis of certain underlying structural characteristics that differentiate them from patients with neurotic and psychotic levels of personality structure. Those three structural characteristics have to do with the degree of identity integration, the level of defensive operations, and the capacity for reality testing.

Table I summarizes the structural criteria for each proposed diagnostic group. The chart schematically represents the differential diagnosis of neurotic, borderline, and psychotic conditions.

Degree of identity integration. Neurotic personality organization presents a well-integrated ego identity. In contrast, borderline personality organization and psychotic organization present identity diffusion. However, severely regressed psychotic patients may present a psychotic, delusional identity. Clinically, identity diffusion is represented by a poorly integrated concept of the self and of significant others. The patient with identity diffusion has a chronic feeling of emptiness, contradictory perceptions of the self, contradictory behavior that he cannot integrate in an emotionally meaningful way, and an impoverished perception of others. Identity diffusion manifests itself in the patient's inability to convey significant interactions with others to an interviewer, who, as a consequence, experiences difficulty in empathizing with the patient's conception of himself and others. Thus, the degree of identity integration or diffusion may be inferred from interview behavior if the interview is geared to elicit the data pertinent to evaluating that characteristic.

The following is assumed to underlie that lack of integration: (1) In borderline personality organization, internal differentiation of self-representation from object representations is sufficient to permit a sharp differentiation between the self and others; in psychotic structures, on the other hand, they are poorly distinguished. (2) In borderline personality organization, contradictory aspects of the self and of others have not been integrated into comprehensive conceptions; from that stem the clinical manifestations of identity diffusion. (3) The failure to integrate contradictory images of the self and of others is presumed to result from the predominance of severe early aggression activated in the patient and the related predominance of primitive defenses.

Level of defensive operations. In neurotic personality organization there is a defensive organization centering on repression and other advanced or high-level defensive operations—reaction formation, isolation, undoing, intellectualization, rationalization—that protect the conscious ego from intrapsychic conflict by rejecting drive derivatives or their ideational representations. In contrast, borderline and psychotic structures are reflected in the predominance of primitive defensive operations centering on splitting and other mechanisms related to it—primitive idealization, projective identification, denial, omnipotence, and devaluation—that protect the ego from conflict by means of dissociating contradictory experiences of the self and of significant others.

Splitting is the division of the self and external objects into "all good" and "all bad," with a concomitant possibility of sudden and complete reversals of all feelings and conceptualizations about one's self or about a particular person.

Primitive idealization enhances the tendency to see external objects as either totally good or totally bad. The goodness or badness in others is pathologically exaggerated, so that primitive idealization creates unrealistic, all-good or all-bad images that are endowed with extraordinary powers.

Projective identification—in contrast to higher levels of projection, which are characterized by attributing to the other person an impulse the patient has repressed in himself—may be defined as attributing a dissociated impulse to another person and at the same time continuing to experience the impulse, as if in reaction to the other person's expressing it, which causes the patient to fear the other person, experienced as under the control of that impulse, and, hence, to feel the need to control him.

Denial in the borderline patient is the inability to bring together two emotionally contradictory areas of consciousness. The patient is aware of the contradictory perceptions and feelings he has about himself and others at different times, but his cognitive awareness has no emotional relevance for him and, therefore, no influence on his feelings. Denial may be manifest as a complete lack of concern, anxiety, or emotional reaction about an immediate, serious, pressing need, conflict,

TABLE I
Differentiation of Personality Structures

	Neurotic	Borderline	Psychotic
Identity integration	Self-representations and object representations are sharply delimited.		Self-representations and object representations are poorly delimited, or else there is delusional identity.
	Integrated identity: contradictory images of self and others are integrated into comprehensive conceptions.	Identity diffusion: contradictory aspects of self and others are poorly integrated and kept apart.	
Defensive operations	Repression and high-level defenses: reaction formation, isolation, undoing, rationalization, intellectualization.	Mainly splitting and low-level defenses: primitive idealization, projective identification, denial, omnipotence, and devaluation.	
	Defenses protect patient from intrapsychic conflict. Interpretation improves functioning.		Defenses protect patients from disintegration and self-object merging. Interpretation leads to regression.
Reality testing	Capacity to test reality is preserved—differentiation of self from nonself, intrapsychic from external origins of perceptions and stimuli.		Capacity to test reality is lost.
	Capacity to evaluate self and others realistically and in depth.	Alterations in relationship with reality and in their feelings of reality.	

or danger in the patient's life; the patient calmly conveys his cognitive awareness of the situation while denying its emotional implications.

Omnipotence and devaluation both derive from splitting operations and are represented by the activation of ego states containing representations of a highly inflated, grandiose, omnipotent self in relation to depreciated and devalued representations of others.

The above defenses protect borderline patients from intrapsychic conflict but at the cost of weakening their ego functioning. Those same primitive defensive operations can be found in psychotic organization, in which they serve the purpose of protecting the patient from further disintegration and self-object merging. That the same defensive mechanisms operate in borderline patients and psychotic patients and yet serve different functions can be observed in clinical interviews. When a psychiatrist interprets splitting and other primitive mechanisms to a patient with borderline personality organization, the patient's functioning immediately improves, if only transitorily, as a result of improved ego integration, as can be seen in an increase in social adaptation and in reality testing. Interpretation of those defenses to a psychotic patient, however, brings about further transitory regression in the patient's functioning. Thus, whether the patient immediately improves or deteriorates under the effect of such interpretation contributes in a crucial way to the diagnostic differentiation of borderline organization from psychotic organization. Similarly, because neurotic personality organization reflects a level of defensive operations centering on repression and borderline personality organization centers on splitting, determining the predominant level of defensive operation in the diagnostic interviews permits the differentiation of those two structural types. As a matter of fact, advanced, high-level, or neurotic defensive operations centering on repression are only manifest in subtle and unobtrusive ways in the initial interviews. In contrast, the predominance of primitive defensive operations rapidly infiltrates the interpersonal field of the diagnostic interviews, thus facilitating their diagnosis and, potentially, their interpretation.

Capacity for reality testing. Reality testing is defined by the capacity to differentiate self from nonself and intrapsychic from external origins of perceptions and stimuli and the capacity to evaluate realistically one's own affect, behavior, and thought content in terms of ordinary social norms. Both neurotic personality organization and borderline personality organization present maintenance of reality testing, in contrast to the psychotic level of personality organization, so that reality testing permits the differentiation of borderline personality organization from the major psychotic syndromes. Clinically, reality testing is reflected in the patient's capacity—when confronted with discrepancies between social norms and his own behavior, affect, or thought contents in the immediate social interaction with the therapist—to empathize with the therapist's observations of such discrepancies and to reduce them by self-reflection. Reality testing, thus defined, needs to be differentiated from alterations in the subjective experience of reality that may exist at the same time in any patient with psychological distress and from the alteration of the relationship with reality that is present in all character pathologies and in more regressive, psychotic conditions and is of diagnostic value by itself only in extreme forms. The capacity for reality testing may be observed in clinical interviews on the basis of how the patient responds, verbally and nonverbally, to the interviewer's probing.

Whether the patient's reality testing is intact can be discerned in the diagnostic interviews in several ways: The psychiatrist can assume that reality testing is preserved if the patient's information indicates that he has not suffered from hallucinations or delusions in the past or manifests them in the present or that, if he has had hallucinations or delusions in the past, he has the capacity to evaluate them fully and totally and can express appropriate concern or puzzlement over such phenomena.

In patients who have not had hallucinations or delusions, reality testing can be further evaluated by the interviewer's focusing sharply on whatever inappropriate affect, thought content, or behavior can be observed. Reality testing is reflected in the patient's capacity to empathize with the interviewer's perception of those characteristics and, in a more subtle way, in the patient's capacity to empathize with the interviewer's perception of his interaction with the patient in general. The structural interview, therefore, constitutes an ideal testing ground for reality testing and, thus, for the differentiation of borderline organization from psychotic organization.

Reality testing may also be evaluated by interpreting primitive defensive operations in the patient-interviewer interaction. An improvement in the patient's immediate functioning as a consequence of such interpretation reflects a maintenance of reality testing; an immediate deterioration of the patient's functioning as a consequence of such intervention indicates a loss of reality testing.

Kernberg (1975a) described additional structural criteria of borderline personality organization that are less essential in the differential diagnosis. They include aspects of ego weakness, such as lack of anxiety tolerance, lack of impulse control, and lack of developed channels for sublimation. In addition, borderline patients usually suffer from severe pathology of object relations and a certain lack of integration of superego functioning.

Although some borderline patients present remarkably few symptoms, most of them present the polysymptomatic neuroses described in the literature, including chronic, diffuse anxiety; multiple phobias; obsessive-compulsive symptoms; multiple, elaborate, or bizarre conversion symptoms; dissociative reactions; hypochondriasis; paranoid trends; polymorphous perverse sexual trends; and the classical prepsychotic personality structures—namely, paranoid personality, schizoid personality, and hypomanic personality structures. That confusing variety of symptoms and severe character pathologies leads to the questions raised in the literature about the extent to which the borderline syndrome overlaps with character pathologies at large. Therefore, it is highly desirable to make the diagnosis on the basis of the structural characteristics of the patient while preserving the label of his predominant character pathology.

What follows is a summary of the descriptive—in contrast to structural—characteristics most frequently found in borderline personality organization; the neurotic symptoms and pathological character traits function as presumptive evidence. (1) Anxiety; borderline patients tend to present chronic, diffuse, free-floating anxiety. (2) Polysymptomatic neurosis; many patients present several neurotic symptoms, but one may consider only those presenting two or more of the following neurotic symptoms: multiple phobias, especially those imposing severe restrictions on the patient's daily life; obsessive-compulsive symptoms that have acquired secondary ego-syntonicity and, therefore, a quality of overvalued thoughts and actions; multiple, elaborate, or bizarre conversion symptoms, especially if they are chronic; dissociative reactions, especially hysterical twilight states and fugues, and amnesia accompanied by disturbances of consciousness; hypochondriasis; and paranoid and hypochondriacal trends with any other symptomatic neurosis; that is a typical combination, indicating a presumptive diagnosis of borderline personality organization. (3) Polymorphous perverse sexual trends, as seen in patients who present a manifest sexual deviation within which several perverse trends coexist. The more chaotic and multiple the perverse fantasies and actions and the more unstable the object relations connected with those interactions, the more strongly should the presence of borderline personality organization be considered. Bizarre forms of perversion, especially those involving manifestations of primitive aggression or primitive replacement of genital aims by eliminatory ones (urination, defecation), are also indicative of an underlying borderline personality organization. (4) Classical prepsychotic personality structures, including the paranoid personality (paranoid trends of such intensity that they themselves determine the main descriptive diagnosis), the schizoid personality, the hypomanic personality, and the cyclothymic personality organization with strong hypomanic trends. (5) Impulse neurosis and addictions, as seen in those forms of severe character pathology in which chronic, repetitive eruptions of an impulse gratify instinctual needs in a way that is ego-dystonic outside of the impulse-ridden episodes but is ego-syntonic and actually highly pleasurable during the episode itself. Alcoholism, drug addiction, certain forms of psychogenic obesity, and kleptomania are all typical examples. (6) Lower level character disorders, as seen in severe character pathologies typically represented by the chaotic and impulse-ridden character, in contrast to the classical reaction-formation types of character structures and the milder avoidance-trait characters. From a clinical standpoint, most typical hysterical personalities are not borderline structures; the same holds true for most obsessive-compulsive personalities and for the depressive personality (Laughlin, 1956) structures and better-integrated masochistic personalities. In contrast, many infantile personalities, the as-if personalities, and most typical narcissistic personalities present underlying borderline organization. All clear-cut antisocial personality structures the author has examined have presented a typical borderline personality organization.

ORIGIN

The internalization of object relations is a crucial organizing factor for both ego and superego development. Introjections, identifications, and ego identity formation constitute a progressive sequence in the process of internalization of object relations (Erikson, 1956.) The essential components of internalized object relations are self-representations, object representations, and specific affect states or dispositions linking each self-representation with a corresponding object representation. Two essential tasks that the early ego has to accomplish in rapid succession are to differentiate the self-representation from object representations and to integrate self-representations and object representations built up under the influence of libidinal drive derivatives and their related affects with their corresponding self-representations and object representations built up under the influence of aggressive drive derivatives and their related affects (Kernberg, 1976a).

The first task is accomplished in part under the influence of the development of the apparatuses of primary autonomy; perception and memory traces help to sort out the origin of stimuli and gradually differentiate self-representations and ob-

ject representations. That first task fails to a major extent in the psychoses; a pathological fusion between self-representations and object representations results in a failure in the differentiation of ego boundaries and, therefore, in the differentiation of self from nonself. In borderline personality organization, differentiation of self-representations from object representations is sufficient to permit the establishment of firm ego boundaries and a concomitant differentiation of the self from others.

The second task, the integration of libidinally associated and aggressively associated self-representations and object representations, fails to a great extent in borderline patients, mainly because of the pathological predominance of pregenital aggression. The resulting lack of synthesis of contradictory self-representations and object representations interferes with the integration of the self-concept and with the integration of object representations—the establishment of total object relations and object constancy. The need to preserve the good self-representations and the good object representations and good external objects in the presence of dangerous all-bad self-representations and object representations leads to a defensive division of the ego. What was at first a simple defect in integration is used actively to keep good and bad self-representations and object representations apart. That is, in essence, the mechanism of splitting. It is reinforced by subsidiary defensive operations, especially projective mechanisms, and thus results in an ego organization different from that in which repression and related mechanism are used.

All-good and all-bad self-representations and object representations seriously interfere with superego integration because they create fantastic ideals of power, greatness, and perfection, rather than the more realistic demands and goals of an ego ideal constructed under the influence of more integrated, toned-down, ideal self-representations and object representations. Projection of bad self-representations and object representations results, through reintrojection of distorted experiences of the frustrating and punishing aspects of the parents, in a pathological predominance of sadistic superego forerunners and a subsequent incapacity to integrate the idealized superego components with the sadistically threatening ones. All that leads to a lack of superego integration and a concomitant tendency to reproject superego nuclei. Thus, dissociative or splitting processes in the ego are reinforced by the absence of the normal integrative contribution of the superego, so that contradictory internalized demands, together with the insufficiency of the ego's repressive mechanisms, contribute to the establishment of contradictory, instinctually infiltrated, pathological character traits. That development is characteristic of borderline personality organization.

In contrast, when good and bad internalized object relations are so integrated that an integrated self-concept and a related integrated representational world of object representations develops, a stable ego identity is achieved. At that point, a central ego core is protected from unacceptable drive derivatives by a stable repressive barrier, and the defensive character traits that develop have the characteristics of reaction formations or inhibitory traits. The development of that level of integration within the ego also creates the preconditions for the integration of the sadistically determined superego forerunners with the ego ideal, and the subsequent capacity to internalize the realistic, demanding, and prohibitive aspects of the parents. All that fosters further superego integration and, eventually, depersonification and abstraction within the superego. The superego may then act as a higher level organizer of the ego, providing further pressures for a harmonious integration of any remaining contradictory trends within the ego. The toning down of such an integrated, more realistically determined superego permits a more flexible management of instinctual drive derivatives on the ego's part, with the appearance of sublimatory character traits.

At the neurotic—in contrast to borderline—level of organization of character pathology, the integration of the superego is still very much under the influence of sadistic forerunners, to the extent that the superego, although well integrated, remains harsh and overdemanding. Repressive and sublimatory handling of pregenital drive derivatives, especially of pregenital aggression, is effective to the extent that there is less infiltration of genital drive derivatives by pregenital, especially aggressive, trends; and the oedipal-genital level of development clearly predominates. At that neurotic level of organization of character pathology, the excessive severity of the superego centers on excessive prohibition or conflicts around infantile sexuality. Object constancy, a capacity for stable and deep object relations, and a stable ego identity have all been reached at that level.

Normality represents a further and final progression along the continuum, with a well-integrated, less severe and punitive superego, realistic superego demands, an ego ideal and ego goals that permit an over-all harmony in dealing with the external world and with instinctual needs. The predominance of sublimatory character traits reflects such an optimal expression of instinctual needs, of adaptive and sublimatory integration of pregenital trends under the primacy of genitality, in the context of mature, adult object relations. A firm repressive barrier against a residuum of unacceptable, infantile instinctual needs is complemented by a large sector of a conflict-free, flexibly functioning ego and the capacity to suppress some realistically ungratifiable needs without excessive stress.

TREATMENT

The early references in the literature to the therapeutic problems with borderline patients were predominantly on the side of recommending modified psychotherapy of a supportive type, in contrast to classical psychoanalysis. Stern (1938, 1945) recommended an expressive, interpretive approach, with the constant focus on the transference, rather than on historical material, and with constant efforts to reduce the clinging, child-like dependency of the patient on the analyst. He felt that borderline patients need a new and realistic relationship, in contrast to the traumatic ones of their childhoods; he believed that such patients can only gradually develop a capacity to establish a transference neurosis similar to that of the usual analytic patient. Schmideberg (1947) recommended an approach probably best designated as psychoanalytic psychotherapy.

Knight's (1954 a, b) contributions to the psychotherapeutic strategy with borderline patients leaned definitely in the direction of a purely supportive approach. He stressed the importance of strengthening the ego of the patient and of respecting his neurotic defenses; Knight considered deep interpretations dangerous because of the regressive pull that such interpretations have and because the patient's weak ego makes it hard enough for him to keep functioning on a secondary-process level. Knight stressed the importance of structure, both within the psychotherapeutic setting and in the utilization of the hospital and day hospital, as part of the total treatment program for borderline patients.

In contrast to that emphasis on a supportive approach, a number of analysts, influenced to varying degrees by the British school of psychoanalysis, believe that classical psychoanalytic treatment can, indeed, be attempted with many, if not all, borderline patients. Some of their contributions have been of crucial importance to the better understanding of the defensive organization and the particular resistances char-

acteristic of patients with borderline personality organization. Despite the author's disagreement with their assumptions about the possibility of treating most borderline patients with psychoanalysis and with many of their theoretical assumptions in general, the author believes that the findings of those analysts permit modifications of psychoanalytic psychotherapies specifically adapted to the transference complications of borderline patients. (Little, 1957, 1960, 1966; Winnicott, 1958, 1965; Segal, 1964; Rosenfeld, 1964, 1971, 1975; Bion, 1965, 1967, 1970; Khan, 1974).

In the United States Boyer and Giovacchini (1967) also recommended a nonmodified psychoanalytic approach to schizophrenic and characterological disorders. Although Giovacchini (1975), in writing about character disorders, did not refer specifically to borderline conditions, as against severe character pathology in general, his observations focused on the technical problems posed by what most authors would consider patients with borderline conditions.

In a somewhat intermediate position between supportive and nonmodified analytic approaches are the techniques recommended by Stone (1954) and Eissler (1953). Stone thought that borderline patients may need preparatory psychotherapy but that at least some of them may be treated with classical psychoanalysis either from the beginning of treatment or after a working relationship with the therapist has been established. Stone also agreed with Eissler that switching from therapy to analysis is possible only if psychotherapy has not created transference distortions of such magnitude that they cannot be resolved through interpretation. In following Eissler's and Stone's approaches, various authors in this country have recommended a modified psychoanalytic procedure or expressive psychotherapeutic approach for borderline patients that has influenced and is related to Kernberg's treatment recommendations, outlined below.

Frosch (1970, 1971) spelled out the clinical approach to borderline patients within a modified psychoanalytic procedure. Greenson (1954, 1958) proposed a similar approach, illustrating his modified psychoanalytic technique with clinical cases. Both Frosch and Greenson stressed the importance of clarifying the patient's perceptions and his attitudes toward the therapist's interventions. Their approach, with which the author basically agrees, implies that the therapist should adopt a technically neutral position and deviate as little as possible from such a position.

In contrast, other psychoanalytically derived psychotherapeutic approaches to borderline conditions involve more modifications of technique. Masterson (1972, 1976, 1978), for example, designed a psychotherapy specifically geared to the resolution of the abandonment depression and to the correction and repair of the ego defects that accompany the narcissistic oral fixation of borderline patients by encouraging growth through the stages of separation-individuation to autonomy. He proposed that psychotherapy with borderline patients start out as supportive and that intensive reconstructive, psychoanalytically oriented psychotherapy be an expansion and outgrowth of supportive psychotherapy. He stressed the importance of the analysis of primitive transferences and expanded on the description of two mutually split-off part-object-relations units—the rewarding or libidinal part-object-relations unit and the withdrawing or aggressive part-object-relations unit—thus combining an object relations viewpoint with a developmental model based on the work of Margaret Mahler (Mahler and Furer, 1968).

Rinsley (1977) and Furer (1977) are others among a growing group of psychoanalytically oriented therapists who are combining an ego psychological object relations theory with a developmental model stemming from Mahler's work (Mahler and Furer, 1968; Mahler, 1971, 1972; Mahler et al., 1975; Mahler and Kaplan, 1977). Giovacchini (1975), Bergeret (1970), Green (1977), Searles (1977), and Volkan (1975) have also been applying models derived from object relations theory. Searles, particularly, has focused on the understanding of the characteristics of transference and countertransference developments in the treatment of borderline and psychotic patients. Comprehensive overviews of some of those approaches can be found in Hartocollis (1977) and Masterson (1978).

Although American authors base their approach on an essentially ego psychological model that incorporates recent developmental findings and ego psychological object relations theories, the British school of psychoanalysis, which was originally identified with certain object relations theories, has continued to influence the technical approaches to borderline patients. Little (1957, 1960, 1966) focused largely on technique. Although she assumed that the patients she described had mostly borderline conditions, her implication that her patients presented a lack of differentiation between self and object and her technical proposals for helping them develop a sense of uniqueness and separateness seemed to focus on the pathology of the early differentiation subphase of separation-individuation. Her views are somewhat similar to those of Winnicott (1965), but her patients seem to be more regressed than those he described.

Winnicott (1965) stressed the need to permit the patient to develop his true self by avoiding an impingement on him at certain stages of therapeutic regression. The therapist acts as a holding object, a function akin to basic mothering, for patients who, for whatever reason, lacked normal mothering. At such times, the analyst's intuitive, empathically understanding presence may be more therapeutic than the disturbing, intrusively experienced effects of verbal interpretation.

That concept is related to Bion's (1965, 1967, 1970) theory that a mother's intuitive daydreaming or "reverie," in Bion's terms, permits her to incorporate the projected, dispersed, fragmented, primitive experiences of the baby at points of frustration and to integrate them by means of her intuitive understanding of the baby's total predicament at that point. The mother's intuition, Bion said, thus acts as a container that organizes the projected content. Similarly, Bion went on, the dispersed, distorted, pathological elements of the regressed patient's experience are projected onto the analyst in order to use him as a container—an organizer, one might say, of what the patient cannot tolerate experiencing in himself.

In short, both Winnicott and Bion stressed that it is important for the therapist working with borderline patients to be able to integrate both cognitive and emotional aspects in his understanding of the therapeutic situation. Although Bion focused on the cognitive (containing) and Winnicott emphasized the emotional (holding), the two ideas seem closely related.

In recent years, there has been a gradual shift away from the recommendation that borderline patients be treated with supportive psychotherapy; Zetzel (1971) and Grinker (1975) seem to be the last proponents of the purely supportive approach that was predominant 20 years ago. Zetzel recommended regular but limited contact—seldom more than once a week—with borderline patients, to decrease the intensity of the transference and countertransference manifestations, and a stress on reality issues and structuralization of treatment hours—all of which jointly constituted an essentially supportive approach. Zetzel acknowledged that the supportive approach requires that the therapist remain at least potentially available over an indefinitely extended period. The problem is that the supportive approach, although effective in permitting the patient to adjust better to reality, may contribute to an interminable psychotherapeutic relationship. Zetzel and Grinker shared the fear, expressed in earlier literature, regarding the presumed frailty of the defensive system, personality organization, and transferences of borderline patients. Implicitly, that fear is also reflected in various psychoanalytically based but operationally manipulative approaches, such as those of Marie Nelson (1967) and Arlene Wolberg (1973).

In summary, a majority of clinicians who have worked intensively with borderline patients have been shifting in recent years from a supportive approach, inspired by Knight's early work, to modified psychoanalytic techniques or psychoanalytic psychotherapy for most patients but still consider the possibility that some patients should be treated by nonmodified psychoanalysis from the beginning of treatment and others with a modified psychoanalytic procedure that may gradually evolve into a standard psychoanalytic situation at advanced stages of the treatment (Stone, 1954; Frosch, 1971; Jacobson, 1971; Kernberg, 1975a, 1976 a, b, 1978).

Although some borderline patients may respond to a nonmodified psychoanalytic approach, the vast majority respond best to a modified psychoanalytic procedure or psychoanalytic psychotherapy. For some borderline patients a psychoanalytic approach—standard or modified—is contraindicated, and those patients do require supportive psychotherapy—that is, an approach based on a psychoanalytic model for psychotherapy relying mostly on the supportive techniques outlined by Bibring (1954), Gill (1954), and Zetzel (1971). Psychoanalysis and psychotherapy should be most carefully differentiated (Gill, 1954).

In addition, much of what appears as ego weakness, in the sense of a defect in borderline patients, turns out, under a psychoanalytically based exploration, to be based on conflict. Obviously, that conviction underlies the author's stress on the value of an interpretive, in contrast to a supportive, approach with borderline patients. A major source for that conviction stems from a psychotherapy research project of the Menninger Foundation (Kernberg et al., 1972) that revealed, contrary to initial expectations, that borderline patients did much better with an interpretive or expressive approach than with a purely supportive one.

Psychoanalytic psychotherapy. If psychoanalysis is defined by a position of technical neutrality, the predominant use of interpretation as a major psychotherapeutic tool, and the systematic analysis of the transference (Gill, 1951, 1954), psychoanalytic psychotherapies may be defined in terms of modification in all or any of those three technical paradigms. In fact, a definition of a spectrum of psychoanalytic psychotherapies—ranging from psychoanalysis, on the one extreme, to supportive psychotherapies, on the other—is possible in terms of those three basic paradigms.

Within an ego psychological approach, psychoanalytic psychotherapy may be defined as a psychoanalytically based or oriented treatment that does not aim for a systematic resolution of unconscious conflicts and, therefore, of all impulse-defense configurations and the respective resistances. Rather, it attempts a partial resolution of some resistances and a reinforcement of other resistances, with a subsequent, partial integration of previously repressed impulses into the adult ego. As a result, a partial increase of ego strength and flexibility may take place, thereby permitting a more effective repression of residual, dynamically unconscious impulses and a modified impulse-defense configuration that increases the adaptive—in contrast to the maladaptive—aspects of character formation. That definition differentiates psychoanalysis from psychoanalytic psychotherapy both in the goals and in the underlying theory of change implicit in those different goals.

In regard to the techniques used in psychoanalytic psychotherapy geared to the achievement of those goals, the ego psychological approach defines two major modalities of treatment based on the psychoanalytic framework: (1) exploratory, uncovering, or, simply, expressive psychoanalytic psychotherapy and (2) suppressive or supportive psychotherapy.

Expressive psychotherapy is characterized by the use of clarification and interpretation as major tools. Partial aspects of the transference are interpreted, and the therapist actively selects such transferences to be interpreted in the light of the particular goals of treatment, the predominant transference resistances, and the patient's external reality. Technical neutrality is usually maintained, but a systematic analysis of all transference manifestations or a systematic resolution of the transference neurosis by interpretation alone is definitely not attempted.

Supportive psychotherapy is characterized by the partial use of clarification and the predominance of the use of suggestion and manipulation. Bibring (1954) defined those techniques and illustrated their technical use. Insofar as supportive psychotherapy still implies an acute awareness and monitoring of the transference on the part of the psychotherapist and a careful consideration of transference resistances as part of his technique in dealing with characterological problems and their connections to the patient's life difficulties, it is still a psychoanalytic psychotherapy in a broad sense. By definition, however, transference is not interpreted in purely supportive psychotherapy, and the use of technical tools such as suggestion and manipulation eliminates technical neutrality.

The major problem with that psychoanalytic theory and technique of psychoanalytic psychotherapy has been the contradiction between the theoretical model from which it stems and the structural intrapsychic organization of many patients with whom it has been used. The theoretical model underlying the approach holds remarkably well for patients with good ego strength, but applying it to patients with severe psychopathologies, particularly the borderline conditions has led to puzzling and contradictory findings.

First, those patients present a constellation of primitive defensive mechanisms centering on dissociation of contradictory ego states, rather than on repression. Second, their transferences have peculiarities that are very different from the more usual transference developments in better-functioning patients. Third and most important, their primitive impulses are not unconscious but mutually dissociated in consciousness. Hence, the evaluation of defense-impulse constellations often does not permit a clarification of what agency within the tripartite structure—ego, superego, id—is motivating and activating a defense against what impulse within what other agency. In other words, the transference seems to reflect contradictory ego states that incorporate contradictory, primitive internalized object relations within an over-all psychic matrix that does not present a clear differentiation of ego, superego, and id.

Those findings led to an additional, special psychoanalytic approach—namely, psychoanalytic object relations theory, which attempts to deal with the phenomena just described.

According to object relations theory, unconscious intrapsychic conflicts are never simply conflicts between impulse and defense but are conceptualized as being between self-representations and object representations under the impact of a determined drive derivative—clinically, a certain affect disposition—and other, contradictory or opposing, units of self-representations and object representations under the impact of their respective affect dispositions. That is, the drive derivative finds expression through a certain primitive object relation—a certain unit of self-representation and object representation—and the defense also finds expression through a certain internalized object relation. The conflict is between those intrapsychic structures. For example, in obsessive, characterological submissiveness, a chronically submissive self-image in relation to a powerful and protective parental image may defend the patient against the repressed, violently rebellious self relating to a sadistic and controlling parental image. Thus, clinically, both repressed impulses and defenses against them involve mutually opposed internal object relations.

From the viewpoint of object relations theory, the consolidation of the over-all intrapsychic structures—ego, superego, and id—results in an integration of internalized object relations that obscures the self-representation-object representation-affect units within each of the structures (Kernberg, 1976a). The psychopathology of the symptomatic neuroses and less severe character neuroses is produced by *inter*systemic conflicts between such integrated ego, superego, and id systems. In contrast, in the psychopathology of borderline personality organization, such an integration of the major intrapsychic agencies is not achieved, and conflicts are, therefore, largely or mostly *intra*systemic—within an undifferentiated ego-id matrix. In severe psychopathologies—particularly the borderline condi-

tions—early, primitive units of internalized object relations are directly manifest in the transference, in the context of mutually conflictual drive derivatives reflected in contradictory ego states.

In those cases the predominance of a constellation of early defense mechanisms centering on primitive dissociation or splitting immediately activates, in the transference, mutually contradictory, primitive, but conscious intrapsychic conflicts (Kernberg, 1975a). What appear on the surface as inappropriate, primitive, chaotic character traits and interpersonal interactions, impulsive behavior, and affect storms actually reflect the fantastic, early object relations-derived structures that are the building blocks of the later tripartite system. Those object relations determine the characteristics of primitive transferences—that is, of highly fantastic, unreal derivatives of early object relations. They do not reflect directly the actual external object relations of infancy and childhood but do reflect internalized object relations and have to be interpreted integratively until, by reconstitution of total—in contrast to partial or split—object relations, more actual aspects of the developmental history emerge (Kernberg, 1975b). In treatment, structural integration through interpretation precedes genetic reconstructions.

Because primitive transferences are immediately available, predominate as resistances, and, in fact, determine the severity of intrapsychic and interpersonal disturbances, they can be and need to be focused on immediately, starting out from their interpretation only in the here and now and leading into genetic reconstructions only in the late stages of treatment, when primitive transferences determined by part-object relations have been transformed into advanced transferences or total-object relations, thus approaching the more realistic experiences of childhood that lend themselves to genetic reconstruction. Interpretation of the transference requires the therapist to maintain a position of technical neutrality, because there can be no interpretation of primitive transferences without a firm, consistent, stable maintenance of reality boundaries in the therapeutic situation and without the therapist's active caution not to be sucked into the reactivation of pathological primitive object relations by the patient. Insofar as both transference interpretation and a position of technical neutrality require the use of clarification and interpretation and contraindicate the use of suggestive and manipulative techniques, clarification and interpretation are maintained as principal techniques.

However, in contrast to psychoanalysis proper, transference interpretation is not systematic. Because there is a need to focus on the severity of acting out and on the disturbances in the patient's external reality, which may threaten the continuity of the treatment and the patient's psychosocial survival, and also because, as part of the acting out of primitive transferences, the treatment easily comes to replace life, transference interpretation has to be co-determined by (1) the predominant nature of the transference, (2) the prevailing conflicts in immediate reality, and (3) the specific goals of treatment.

In addition, technical neutrality is limited by the need to establish parameters of technique, including, in certain cases, the structuring of the patient's external life and the establishment of a teamwork approach with patients who cannot function autonomously during long stretches of their psychotherapy. Technical neutrality, therefore, is a theoretical baseline from which deviations occur again and again, to be reduced—again and again—by interpretation. One crucial aspect of psychoanalytic psychotherapy with patients presenting severe psychopathology is the systematic interpretation of defenses.

In contrast to expressive psychotherapies in better-functioning patients in which certain defenses are selectively interpreted while others are not touched, the systematic interpretation of defenses in severe psychopathology is crucial to improve ego functioning and to permit the transformation and resolution of primitive transferences.

Therefore, the similarity between expressive psychoanalytic psychotherapy and psychoanalysis is greater in the case of severe psychopathology than in the case of patients with milder psychological illness. One might say that, in psychoanalytic psychotherapy of borderline conditions, the tactical approach to each session may be almost indistinguishable from psychoanalysis proper and that only from a long-term, strategic viewpoint do the differences between the two techniques emerge. By the same token, the cleavage between expressive and supportive psychotherapy is sharp and definitive in the case of patients with borderline conditions but blurred in patients with less severe illnesses. In other words, it is not possible to bring about significant personality modifications by means of psychoanalytic psychotherapy in patients with severe psychopathologies without the exploration and resolution of primitive transferences, and that requires a purely expressive, meticulously analytic approach, although not psychoanalysis proper.

Manipulative or suggestive techniques destroy technical neutrality and interfere with the possibility of analyzing primitive transferences and resistances—the most important ego-strengthening aspect of the psychoanalytic psychotherapy of borderline patients. Technical neutrality means equidistance from the forces co-determining the patient's intrapsychic conflicts and not lack of warmth or empathy with him. One still hears comments implying that borderline patients need, first of all, empathic understanding, rather than a precise theory and cognitively sharpened interpretations based on such a theory. All psychotherapy requires as a baseline the therapist's capacity for authentic human warmth and empathy; those qualities are preconditions for any appropriate psychotherapeutic work but, by themselves, are not enough.

Empathy, however, is not only the therapist's intuitive, emotional awareness of the patient's central emotional experience at a certain point but must also include the therapist's capacity to empathize with what the patient cannot tolerate within himself; therapeutic empathy, therefore, transcends the empathy of ordinary human interactions and includes the therapist's cognitive and emotional understanding of what is actively dissociated or split in borderline patients.

In addition, when serious distortions in the patient's reality testing in the psychotherapeutic hours evolve as part of the activation of primitive transferences and primitive defensive operations, particularly that of projective identification, it may be crucial for the therapist to begin his interpretive efforts by clarifying the reality of the therapeutic situation. Such initial interventions often require a great deal of active work on the part of the therapist, a direct dealing with what is real in the sessions or in the patient's external life. The patient may misunderstand those interventions as technically supportive, suggestive, or manipulative.

Transference interpretation. The predominantly negative transference of borderline patients should be systematically elaborated only in the here and now, without attempting to achieve full genetic reconstructions. The reason is that lack of differentiation of the self-concept and lack of differentiation and individualization of objects interfere with the ability of borderline patients to differentiate present and past object relationships, resulting in their confusing transference and

reality and failing to differentiate the analyst from the transference object. Full genetic reconstructions, therefore, have to await advanced stages of the treatment.

The typical defensive constellations should be interpreted as they enter the transference; the implication is that the interpretation of the predominant, primitive defensive operations characteristic of borderline personality organization strengthens the patient's ego and brings about structural intrapsychic changes that contribute to resolving that organization.

Limits should be set to block acting out of the transference, with as much structuring of the patient's life outside the hours as is necessary to protect the therapist's neutrality. The implications are that, although interventions in the patient's external life may sometimes be needed, the therapist's technical neutrality is essential for the treatment. Moreover, it is important to avoid allowing the therapeutic relationship, with its gratifying and sheltered nature, to replace ordinary life, lest primitive pathological needs be gratified in the acting out of the transference during and outside treatment hours.

The less primitively determined, modulated aspects of the positive transference should not be interpreted. That fosters the gradual development of the therapeutic alliance; however, the primitive idealizations that reflect the splitting of all-good from all-bad object relations need to be interpreted systematically as part of the effort to work through those primitive defenses.

Interpretations should be formulated so that the patient's distortions of the therapist's interventions and of present reality, especially of the patient's perceptions in the treatment hour, can be systematically clarified. The patient's magical use of the therapist's interpretations needs to be interpreted.

The highly distorted transferences—at times, of an almost psychotic nature—reflecting fantastic internal object relations related to early ego disturbances should be worked through first, in order to later reach the transferences related to actual childhood experiences. All transferences, of course, recapitulate childhood fantasies, actual experiences, and defensive formations against them, and it is often difficult to sort out fantasies from reality. However, the extreme nature of the fantasied relationships reflecting early object relations gives the transference of borderline patients special characteristics.

Transformation of primitive into advanced or neurotic transferences. The over-all strategical aim in working through the transference developments of borderline patients is to resolve those primitive dissociations of the self and of internalized objects, thus transforming primitive transferences—the primitive level of internalized object relations activated in the transference—into the transference reactions of the integrated, more realistic type related to real childhood experiences. Obviously, that resolution requires intensive, long-term treatment (Kernberg, 1975a), usually not less than three sessions a week over years of treatment. The strategy of interpretation of the transference occurs in three consecutive stages.

The first step consists in the therapist's efforts to reconstruct—on the basis of his gradual understanding of what is emotionally predominant in the chaotic, meaningless, empty, distorted, or suppressed material—the nature of the primitive or part-object relation that has become activated in the transference. He needs to evaluate what in the contradictory bits of verbal and behavioral communication and in the patient's confused and confusing thoughts and feelings and expressions is of predominant emotional relevance in the patient's present relation with him and how that can be understood in the context of the patient's total communications. In other words, the therapist transforms what literally amounts to a dehumanization of the therapeutic relationship into an emotionally significant, although highly distorted, fantastic transference relationship.

As a second step, the therapist must evaluate that crystallizing predominant object relation in the transference in terms of the self-representation and the object representation involved and clarify the affect of the corresponding interaction of self and object. The therapist may represent one aspect of the patient's dissociated self-representation or one aspect of the primitive object representation or both; and patient and therapist may interchange their enactment of, respectively, self-representation or object representation. Those aspects of the self-representation and of object representations need to be interpreted, and the respective internal object relation needs to be clarified in the transference.

As a third step, the particular part-object relation activated in the transference has to be integrated with other part-object relations reflecting other, related and opposite, defensively dissociated part-object relations until the patient's self-concept and his internal conception of objects can be integrated and consolidated.

Integration of the self-concept and of the representations of objects and thus of the entire world of internalized object relations is a major strategic aim in the treatment of patients with borderline personality organization. Integration of affects with their related, fantasied or real, human relation involving the patient and the significant objects is another aspect of the work. The patient's affect dispositions reflect the libidinal or aggressive investment of certain internalized object relations, and the integration of split-off, fragmented affect states is a corollary of the integration of split-off, fragmented internalized object relations. When such a resolution of primitive transferences has occurred, the integrated affect dispositions that now emerge reflect more coherent and differentiated drive derivatives. The integrated object images now reflect more realistic parental images, as perceived in early childhood.

Arrangements and difficulties. A major question in the early stages of treatment is to what extent an external structure is necessary to protect the patient and the treatment situation from premature, violent acting out that may threaten the patient's life or other people's lives or the continuation of the treatment. When the treatment starts out right after a recent or still active psychotic episode, which borderline patients may experience under excessive emotional turmoil—under the effect of drugs, alcohol, or in the course of a transference psychosis—hospital treatment for a few days or even a few weeks may be indicated. A well-structured hospital milieu provides clarification of the immediate reality and a combination of understanding and limit setting.

A generally chaotic life situation, particularly when it is complicated by the patient's difficulty in providing meaningful information about his life to the psychotherapist, may present another indication for short-term hospitalization. Severe suicidal threats or attempts, a deteriorating social situation, or severe acting out involving the law are all typical examples of situations that threaten the patient's life or the continuation of treatment.

The most important objective regarding the degree of structuring required is to set up treatment arrangements that permit the psychotherapist to remain in a position of technical neutrality—that is, equidistant from external reality, the patient's superego, instinctual needs, and acting, in contrast to observing, ego (A. Freud, 1946). That objective can sometimes be achieved by using part-hospitalization arrangements, foster-home placement, or the intervention of a social worker within the patient's environment.

Borderline patients who do not have a sufficient degree of observing ego for intensive, outpatient psychoanalytic psychotherapy—for example, they may have extremely low motivation for treatment, severe lack of anxiety tolerance and of impulse control, and very poor object relationships—may require a long-term environmental structuring of their lives in order to make an expressive psychotherapeutic approach possible. Severe and chronic acting-out, suicidal or generally self-destructive trends that the patient cannot control, and some types of negative therapeutic reactions may require such a long-term environmental structuring by means of long hospitalization, part-time hospital structures, or extramural social services.

However, many borderline patients, without external structuring of their lives, are able to participate actively in setting limits to certain types of acting out that threaten their treatment or their safety. Sometimes, the psychotherapist has to spell out certain conditions the patient must meet for outpatient psychoanalytic psychotherapy to proceed. Setting up such conditions for treatment constitutes, of course, an abandonment of technical neutrality and the setting up of parameters of technique. Such parameters should be kept to a minimum.

Psychopharmacological treatment. Sarwer-Foner (1977) suggested that pharmacotherapy be used as part of the therapeutic approach to borderline conditions to control target symptoms such as hyperactivity, impulsivity with poor control, poorly controlled aggression, inability to sleep, psychomotor agitation, and psychomotor retardation. He suggested using antidepressant drugs for patients with severe psychomotor retardation and questioned the use of long-term pharmacotherapy for borderline patients. Although he felt that pharmacotherapy is helpful in dealing with the emergency or emergent aspects of certain disruptive symptoms or acute psychotic states, it is not in itself the ideal approach to the treatment of borderline patients. Donald Klein (1975, 1976, 1977) suggested that borderline conditions are an extremely heterogeneous group and that responses to medication may be useful in isolating homogeneous subgroups. Such treatment responses led him to describe the phobic anxious patient, the emotionally unstable character disorder, and the hysteroid dysphoric. He thought thioridazine, in doses of about 300 mg. at bed time, and lithium carbonate might be helpful to borderline patients who present predominant emotional lability and that cases of rejection-sensitive dysphoria—which he also designated as "hysteroid dysphoria"—might respond to monoamine oxidase inhibitors. For chronic anxiety-tension states, Klein recommended minor tranquilizers. He felt that histrionic states, the hysterical and possibly infantile personalities, would not respond well to medication and that the same would be true for hysteroschizophrenic patients.

Klein's differentiation of hysteroid dysphoria from histrionic states on the basis of their respective response or nonresponse to medication does not seem to be sufficiently clarified clinically at this time. His use of the term "histrionic states" as equivalent to or overlapping "hysteroschizophrenia" complicates matters further. It is not clear what made Klein include the phobic anxious patients with the borderline conditions. Further, Liebowitz (1979) pointed out that the several patient types described by Klein showed differences in degree of homogeneity of drug response and in the amount of data available on their diagnostic overlap with the borderline syndrome. Klein's interest in exploring subgroups of borderline conditions as potentially belonging to the affective-disorders spectrum seems of definite interest. It may well turn out that a subgroup of borderline patients presents a genetic or biochemical disposition to schizophrenia or affective disorders and that such predisposition influences the patients' responses or lack of response to pharmacotherapy.

In the author's experience, antidepressant medication may be helpful in acute severe depressive reactions in borderline conditions, and he agrees with the questions raised by Sarwer-Foner (1977) regarding the long-term use of pharmacotherapy in borderline patients undergoing psychotherapeutic treatment. Pharmacotherapy may have a place in those cases in which a supportive approach has been decided on, but intensive psychoanalytic psychotherapy along the lines defined above, geared to bringing about significant personality reorganization of the patient, can be best carried out without the use of any medication at all.

In conclusion, although there is clinical and research evidence (Kernberg et al., 1972) to support the view that borderline patients may require and benefit optimally from an expressive or psychoanalytically oriented psychotherapeutic approach and, in selected cases, from concomitant external structuring of their lives, those findings need to be examined further, alongside other studies suggesting the usefulness of psychopharmacological and other treatment approaches to certain subgroups of borderline patients.

Suggested Cross References

DSM-III is discussed in Section 14.1. The psychiatric interview is discussed in Section 12.1, and the psychiatric history and the mental status examination are discussed in Section 12.2. Clinical manifestations of psychiatric disorders are described in Chapter 13. The schizophrenic disorders are discussed at length in Chapter 15, paranoid disorders in Chapter 16, schizoaffective disorders in Chapter 17, and affective disorders in Chapters 18 and 19. Neurotic disorders are discussed in Chapter 21. Personality disorders are discussed in Chapter 22. Adjustment and impulse control disorders are discussed in Chapter 25. Psychotherapies are discussed in Chapter 30, organic therapies in Chapter 31, and hospitalization and milieu therapy in Chapter 32.

REFERENCES

American Psychiatric Association. *Diagnostic and Statistical Manual of Mental Disorders*, ed. 3. American Psychiatric Association, Washington, D. C., 1980.
Bergeret, J. Les etats limites. Rev. Fr. Psychanal., *34*: 605, 1970.
Bergeret, J. *Abrege de Psychologie Pathologique*. Masson, Paris, 1972.
Bibring, E. Psychoanalysis and the dynamic psychotherapies. J. Am. Psychoanal. Assoc., *2*: 745, 1954.
Bion, W. R. *Transformations*. Heinemann, London, 1965.
Bion, W. R. *Second Thoughts: Selected Papers on Psychoanalysis*. Heinemann, London, 1967.
Bion, W. R. *Attention and Interpretation*. Heinemann, London, 1970.
Boyer, L. B., and Giovacchini, P. *Psychoanalytic Treatment of Characterological and Schizophrenic Disorders*. Jason Aronson, New York, 1967.
Bychowski, G. The problem of latent psychosis. J. Am. Psychoanal. Assoc., *1*: 484, 1953.
Carpenter, W., Gunderson, J., and Strauss, J. Considerations of the borderline syndrome: A longitudinal comparative study of borderline and schizophrenic patients. In *Borderline Personality Disorders*, P. Hartocollis, editor, p. 231. International Universities Press, New York, 1977.
Cary, G. L. The borderline condition: A structural-dynamic viewpoint. Psychoanal. Rev., *59*: 33, 1972.
Collum, J. Identity diffusion and the borderline maneuver. Compr. Psychiatry, *13*: 179, 1972.
Deutsch, H. Some forms of emotional disturbance and their relationship to schizophrenia. Psychoanal. Q., *11*: 301, 1942.
Eissler, K. R. The effects of the structure of the ego on psychoanalytic technique. J. Am. Psychoanal. Assoc., *1*: 104, 1953.
Erikson, E. H. The problem of ego identity. J. Am. Psychoanal. Assoc., *4*: 56, 1956.
Fairbairn, W. R. D. *An Object-Relations Theory of the Personality*. Basic Books, New York, 1952.
Freud, A. *The Ego and the Mechanisms of Defense: The Writings of Anna Freud*. International Universities Press, New York, 1946.

Freud, S. The interpretation of dreams. In *Standard Edition of the Complete Psychological Works of Sigmund Freud*, vols. 4 and 5. Hogarth Press, London, 1958.
Freud, S. The ego and the id. In *Standard Edition of the Complete Psychological Works of Sigmund Freud*, vol. 19, p. 12. Hogarth Press, London, 1961.
Frosch, J. The psychotic character: Clinical psychiatric considerations. Psychiatr. Q., *38*: 81, 1964.
Frosch, J. Psychoanalytic consideration of the psychotic character. J. Am. Psychoanal. Assoc., *18*: 24, 1970.
Frosch, J. Technique in regard to some specific ego defects in the treatment of borderline patients. Psychiatr. Q., *45*: 216, 1971.
Furer, M. Personality organization during the recovery of a severely disturbed young child. In *Borderline Personality Disorders*, P. Hartocollis, editor, p. 457. International Universities Press, New York, 1977.
Gill, M. Ego psychology and psychotherapy. Psychoanal. Q., *20*: 62, 1951.
Gill, M. Psychoanalysis and exploratory psychotherapy. J. Am. Psychoanal. Assoc., *2*: 771, 1954.
Giovacchini, P. *Psychoanalysis of Character Disorders*. Jason Aronson, New York, 1975.
Gitelson, M. Ego distortion. Int. J. Psychoanal., *39*: 245, 1958.
Green, A. The borderline concept. In *Borderline Personality Disorder*, P. Hartocollis, editor, p. 15. International Universities Press, New York, 1977.
Greenson, R. R. The struggle against identification. J. Am. Psychoanal. Assoc., *2*: 200, 1954.
Greenson, R. R. On screen defenses, screen hunger, and screen identity. J. Am. Psychoanal. Assoc., *6*: 242, 1958.
Grinker, R. R. Neurosis, psychosis, and the borderline states. In *Comprehensive Textbook of Psychiatry*, A. M. Freedman, H. I. Kaplan, and B. J. Sadock, editors, ed. 2, p. 845. Williams & Wilkins, Baltimore, 1975.
Grinker, R. R. The borderline syndrome: A phenomenological view. In *Borderline Personality Disorders*, P. Hartocollis, editor, p. 159. International Universities Press, New York, 1977.
* Grinker, R. R., Sr., Werble, B., and Drye, R. C. *The Borderline Syndrome*. Basic Books, New York, 1968.
Gunderson, J. G. Characteristics of borderlines. In *Borderline Personality Disorders*, P. Hartocollis, editor, p. 173. International Universities Press, New York, 1977.
Gunderson, J. G., Carpenter, W., and Strauss, J. Borderline and schizophrenic patients: A comparative study. Am. J. Psychiatry, *132*: 1257, 1975.
Gunderson, J. G., and Kolb, J. E. Discriminating features of borderline patients. Am. J. Psychiatry, *135*: 792, 1978.
Gunderson, J., and Singer, M. Defining borderline patients: An overview. Am. J. Psychiatry, *132*: 1, 1975.
Guze, S. B. Differential diagnosis of the borderline personality syndrome. In *Borderline States in Psychiatry*, J. Mack, editor, p. 69. Grune & Stratton, New York, 1975.
Hartmann, H., Kris, E., and Loewenstein, R. M. Comments on the formation of psychic structure. Psychoanal. Study Child, *2*: 11, 1946.
* Hartocollis, P., editor. *Borderline Personality Disorders*. International Universities Press, New York, 1977.
Hoch, P., and Cattell, J. P. The diagnosis of pseudoneurotic schizophrenia. Psychiatr. Q., *33*: 17, 1959.
Hoch, P., and Polatin, R. Pseudoneurotic forms of schizophrenia. Psychiatr. Q., *23*: 248, 1949.
Inhelder, B., and Piaget, J. *The Growth of Logical Thinking from Childhood to Adolescence: An Essay on the Construction of Formal Operational Structures*. Basic Books, New York, 1958.
Jacobson, E. *The Self and the Object World*. International Universities Press, New York, 1964.
Jacobson, E. *Depression*. International Universities Press, New York, 1971.
Kernberg, O. Early ego integration and object relations. Ann. N. Y. Acad. Sci., *193*: 233, 1972.
* Kernberg, O. *Borderline Conditions and Pathological Narcissism*. Jason Aronson, New York, 1975a.
Kernberg, O. Transference and countertransference in the treatment of borderline patients. J. Natl. Assoc. Priv. Psychiatr. Hosp., *7*: 14, 1975b.
Kernberg, O. *Object Relations Theory and Clinical Psychoanalysis*. Jason Aronson, New York, 1976a.
Kernberg, O. Technical considerations in the treatment of borderline personality organization. J. Am. Psychoanal. Assoc., *24*: 795, 1976b.
Kernberg, O. Structural diagnosis of borderline personality organization. In *Borderline Personality Disorders*, P. Hartocollis, editor, p. 87. International Universities Press, New York, 1977.
Kernberg, O. Contrasting approaches to the psychotherapy of borderline conditions. In *New Perspectives of Psychotherapy of the Borderline Adult*, J. Masterson, editor, chap. 3, p. 77. Brunner/Mazel, New York, 1978.
Kernberg, O., Burnstein, E., Coyne, L., Appelbaum, A., Horwitz, L., and Voth, H. Psychotherapy and psychoanalysis: Final report of the Menninger Foundations' psychotherapy research project. Bull. Menninger Clin., *36*: 1, 1972.
Khan, M. Clinical aspects of the schizoid personality: Affects and technique. Int. J. Psychoanal., *41*: 430, 1960.
Khan, M. *The Privacy of the Self: Papers on Psychoanalytic Theory and Technique*. International Universities Press, New York, 1974.
Klein, M. Notes on some schizoid mechanisms. Int. J. Psychoanal., *27*: 99, 1946.
Klein, D. Psychopharmacology and the borderline patient. In *Borderline States*

in Psychiatry, J. E. Mack, editor, p. 75. Grune & Stratton, New York, 1975.

Klein, D. The borderline state: Psychopharmacologic treatment approaches to the undiagnosed case. In *Manual of Psychiatric Therapeutics*, R. Shader, editor, p. 281. Little, Brown, and Co., Boston, 1976.

Klein, D. Pharmacological treatment and delineation of borderline disorders. In *Borderline Personality Disorders*, P. Hartocollis, editor, p. 365. International Universities Press, New York, 1977.

Knight, R. P. Borderline states. In *Psychoanalytic Psychiatry and Psychology*, R. P. Knight and C. R. Friedman, editors, vol. 1, p. 97. International Universities Press, New York, 1954a.

Knight, R. P. Management and psychotherapy of the borderline schizophrenic patient. In *Psychoanalytic Psychiatry and Psychology*, R. P. Knight and R. R. Friedman, editors, p. 110. International Universities Press, New York, 1954b.

Laughlin, H. P. *The Neuroses in Clinical Practice*. W. B. Saunders, Philadelphia, 1956.

Liebowitz, M. Is borderline a distinct entity? Schizophr. Bull., *5*: 23, 1979.

Little, M. "R": The analyst's total response to his patient's needs. Int. J. Psychoanal., *38*: 240, 1957.

Little, M. On basic unity. Int. J. Psychoanal., *41*: 377, 1960.

Little, M. Transference in borderline states. Int. J. Psychoanal., *47*: 476, 1966.

* Mack, J. *Borderline States in Psychiatry*. Grune & Stratton, New York, 1975.

Mahler, M. S. A study of the separation-individuation process and its possible application to borderline phenomena in the psychoanalytic situation. Psychoanal. Study Child, *26*: 403, 1971.

Mahler, M. S. Rapprochement subphase of the separation-individuation process. Psychoanal. Q., *41*: 487, 1972.

Mahler, M. S., and Furer, M. *On Human Symbiosis and the Vicissitudes of Individuation*. International Universities Press, New York, 1968.

Mahler, M. S., and Kaplan, L. Developmental aspects in the assessment of narcissistic and so-called borderline personalities. In *Borderline Personality Disorders*, P. Hartocollis, editor, p. 71. International Universities Press, New York, 1977.

Mahler, M. S., Pine, F., and Bergman, A. *The Psychological Birth of the Human Infant*. Basic Books, New York, 1975.

Masterson, J. *Treatment of the Borderline Adolescent: A Developmental Approach*. Wiley-Interscience, New York, 1972.

Masterson, J. *Psychotherapy of the Borderline Adult: A Developmental Approach*. Brunner/Mazel, New York, 1976.

* Masterson, J. *New Perspective on Psychotherapy of the Borderline Adult*. Brunner/Mazel, New York, 1978.

Nelson, M. Effect of paradigmatic techniques on the psychic economy of the borderline patients. In *Active Psychotherapy*, H. Greenwald, editor, p. 63. Atherton, New York, 1967.

Perry, J. C., and Klerman, G. L. The borderline patient: A comparative analysis of four sets of diagnostic criteria. Arch. Gen. Psychiatry, *35*: 141, 1978.

Rangell, L. Panel report: The borderline case. J. Am. Psychoanal. Assoc., *3*: 285, 1955.

Rapaport, D. Cognitive structures. In *Contemporary Approaches to Cognition*, J. S. Bruner, editor, p. 157. Harvard University Press, Cambridge, Mass., 1957.

Rapaport, D., and Gill, M. M. The points of view of assumptions of metapsychology. Int. J. Psychoanal., *40*: 153, 1959.

Rapaport, D., Gill, M. M., and Schafer, R. Diagnostic Psychological Testing. Year Book Medical Publishers, Chicago, 1945-1946.

Rinsley, D. An object-relation view of borderline personality. In *Borderline Personality Disorders*, P. Hartocollis, editor, p. 47. International Universities Press, New York, 1977.

Robbins, L. Panel report: The borderline case. J. Am. Psychoanal. Assoc., *4*: 550, 1956.

Rosenfeld, H. Notes on psychopathology and psychoanalytic treatment of schizophrenia. In *Psychotherapy of Schizophrenia and Manic-Depressive States*, H. Azima and B. C. Glueck, Jr., editors, p. 61. American Psychiatric Association, Washington, D. C., 1963.

Rosenfeld, H. On the psychopathology of narcissism: A clinical approach. Int. J. Psychoanal., *45*: 332, 1964.

Rosenfeld, H. A clinical approach to the psychoanalytic theory of the life and death instincts: An investigation into the aggressive aspects of narcissism. Int. J. Psychoanal., *52*: 169, 1971.

Rosenfeld, H. Negative therapeutic reaction. In *Tactics and Techniques in Psychoanalytic Therapy*, P. L. Giovacchini, editor, vol. 2, p. 217. Jason Aronson, New York, 1975.

Sarwer-Foner, G. L. An approach to the global treatment of the borderline patient: Psychoanalytic, psychotherapeutic, and psychopharmacological considerations. In *Borderline Personality Disorders*, P. Hartocollis, editor, p. 345. International Universities Press, New York, 1977.

Schmideberg, M. The treatment of psychopaths and borderline patients. Am. J. Psychother., *1*: 45, 1947.

Searles, H. Dual- and multi-identity processes in borderline ego functioning. In *Borderline Personality Disorders*, P. Hartocollis, editor, p. 441. International Universities Press, New York, 1977.

Segal, H. *Introduction to the Work of Melanie Klein*. Basic Books, New York, 1964.

Spitzer, R. L., Endicott, J., and Gibbon, M. Crossing the border into borderline personality and borderline schizophrenia: The development of criteria. Arch. Gen. Psychiatry, *36*: 17, 1979.

Stern, A. Psychoanalytic investigation of and therapy in the borderline group of neuroses. Psychoanal. Q., *7*: 467, 1938.

Stern, A. Psychoanalytic therapy in the borderline neuroses. Psychoanal. Q., *14*: 190, 1945.

Stone, L. The widening scope of indications for psychoanalysis. J. Am. Psychoanal. Assoc., *2*: 567, 1954.

Volkan, V. *Clinical Correlates of Primitive Internalized Object Relations*. International Universities Press, New York, 1975.

Waelder, R. Ego distortion. Int. J. Psychoanal., *39*: 243, 1958.

Winnicott, D. W. *Collected Papers: Through Paediatrics to Psychoanalysis*. Basic Books, New York, 1958.

Winnicott, D. W. *The Maturational Process and the Facilitating Environment*. International Universities Press, New York, 1965.

Wolberg, A. R. *The Borderline Patient*. Intercontinental Medical Books, New York, 1973.

Zetzel, E. R. A developmental approach to the borderline patient. Am. J. Psychoanal., *127*: 867, 1971.

Zilboorg, G. Ambulatory schizophrenia. Psychiatry, *4*: 149, 1941.

Zilboorg, G. Further observations on ambulatory schizophrenia. Am. J. Orthopsychiatry, *27*: 677, 1957.

Index

VOLUME 1–pages 1–1092; VOLUME 2–pages 1093–2256; VOLUME 3–pages 2257–3365.

xxvii

medication for, 1524
prognosis, 1523
psychoanalytic theories, 1520
psychotherapy for, 1524
rehabilitation, 1524
treatment, 1524–1525
Posttraumatic syndrome, 1427
Posture, in neurological examination, 255
Post-Vietnam syndrome (see also Prisoner of war syndrome), 2893–2894
Posturing, 3348
clinical features, 1837
course, 1837–1838
definition, 1836–1837
epidemiology, 1837
history, 1836–1837
prognosis, 1837–1838
treatment, 1838
Potash, H., 1990
Potassium
deficiency, 182
disorders, 308
Potency, 3348
Potentials, evoked, 264
Pottenger, M., 1334
Potter, H. W., 2527
Pound, Ezra, 3128
Pouraghabagher, A. R., 349
Poussaint, Alvin F., 3155–3160
Poussin, 58
Poverty
children in, 523–525
learning problems and, 2702–2703
mental retardation and, 2505
psychiatric implications, 3177–3179
suicide and, 2087
Powell, D. H., 1602
Power
in middle age, 3017
struggles, in family, 2222
violence and, 3150
Power, H., 232
Powers, M. H., 2567
Poznanski, E., 2683, 2801
Practical Aspects of Psychoanalysis, 86
Practice effect, 3348
Practical Theorist, The, 883
Prader-Willi syndrome 2502
Pragmatism, 5
Praise of Folly, The, 39
Prange, A. J., 179, 208, 1347
Pratt, Joseph H., 2179, 3348
Pratt, R. T. C., 1414
Praxis Medica, 48
Prazepam (Verstran)
dose, 2323
efficacy, 2317–2318
Prechtl, H. F. R., 2588, 2792
Precision, statistical, 614–615
Precognition, 3241
Preconscious, 657, 681, 2115, 3348
Precox feeling, 1180–1181
Prediction of Overt Behavior through the Use of Projective Techniques, The, 960
Prednisone, dose, 1446
Pregenital stages, 3348
Pregnancy
benzodiazepines during, 2328–2329
complications, 2502–2503
central nervous system and, 2428
ECT in, 2338
father illness during, 2763
hypoxia during, 2792
in heroin addict, 1598, 1600
maternal infections during, 2502
meprobamate during, 2328–2329
of adopted women, 2757
premarital, 1711
sex and, 1714–1715
sex hormones in, 2518

sexual intercourse in, 1663–1664
syphilis during, 2502
unwanted, 1712
Prehistoric era, mind-body problem, 1844
Prejudice (see also Racism), 3348–3349
cultural values, 3158–3159
professional, 3158
racial
history, 3155–3156
nature of, 3156–3157
Preliminary Communication, 641, 647
Prelinger, E., 912
Preliterate cultures
psychiatry in, 11–15
psychological aspects, 10
Prell, D. B., 151
Preludin (see Phenmetrazine)
Premenstrual tension syndrome
causes, 1925
mental manifestations, 1925
mental retardation and, 2503
physical signs and symptoms, 1925
treatment, 1925
Premorbid, 3349
Prenatal influences, mental illness and, 495
Prentice, N. B., 2797
Preodor, E., 1322
Preoperational stage of child development, 376
Prepsychotic personality, 1179–1180
Presamine (see Imipramine)
Pre-Sate (see Chlorophentermine)
Preschool years, 121–123
Presenile dementia, 3020, 3349
Present State Examination (PSE), 554, 1047, 1051, 2407
President's Commission on Mental Health, 2360
Presley, A. S., 1575
Press, 876
environmental, 784
Preston, D., 437
Preston, J. H., 3115
Prevalence, 3349
statistical, 628
Prevention, 546–547
in clinic, 2992
miscarried, 778
schools and, 2697
Preventive psychiatry, 3349
biotechnical interventions, 2863–2865
developmental strategies, 2862
early intervention effects, 2867
epidemiological strategies, 2861–2862
financing programs, 2871
primary, 2859–2867
strategies, 2860–2862
techniques, 2863–2867
psychosocial techniques, 2865–2867
public health approach, 2859
public health disease model, 2860–2861
secondary, 2867–2868
target groups, 2866
tertiary, 2868–2871
Priapism, 1740
Pribram, Karl H., 401, 446, 553, 816
Price, A. L., 2205
Price, G. R., 230, 3236–3237
Price, J. S., 1336
Price, R. H., 345, 1283
Prichard, Cowles, 67
Prichard, James, 64
Prichard, J. C., 1043, 1361, 1374, 1563, 2817
Prien, R. F., 1187, 2266–2267, 2350–2351
Prigogine, 6
Prilipko, L. L., 1968
Primal images, 791–792
Primal pool, 2236

Primal scene, 1707, 2236, 3349
Primal therapy, 2235–2236, 3257, 3349
Primary care, 2077–2078
Primary care physician
psychiatry and, 2077–2084
psychiatric education of, 2079–2080
Primary process, 3349
Primary-process intervention, 1199–1200
Primary ties, 869
Primate Ethology, 425
Prime of life, 3016
Primidone (Mysoline), 1443, 1461, 1480
dosage, 312
EEG and, 264
Primitive Cultures, 486
Prince, G. R., 3239
Prince, J., 1821
Prince, Morton, 1497–1498, 1553–1554, 3341, 3349
Prince, V., 1702, 2778
Principle of joint variation, 854
Principles of Intensive Psychotherapy, The, 88
Principles of Medical Ethics, 3217
Principles of Medical Psychology, The, 6, 66
Principles of Psychology, The, 927, 1544
Principles of Sociology, 486
Principles of Topological Psychology, 89
Pringle, M. L. K., 2728, 2755–2756
Prioleau, W. H., 605
Prison
neurosis, 3316
psychiatry (see Correctional psychiatry)
psychosis, 1294–1295, 3349
sensory deprivation, 604
staff, 3087
Prisoner of war syndrome (see also Post-Vietnam syndrome), 1838
causes, 1838–1839
clinical features, 1839–1840
Prisoners (see Inmate population, prison)
Prisoners of war, 2891–2893, 2912
Privilege, 3349
Pro, J. D., 1372
Probability, statistical, 619
Pro-Banthine (see Propantheline)
Probetazine (see Carphenazine)
Problem Child, The, 733
Problem of Ego Identity, The, 3014
Problem-oriented medical record, 554, 559, 2409–2416
computerized, 2414
problems, 2415
Problem-Oriented Medical Informational System (PROMIS), 2414
Problem solving, tests for, 969–970
Problems, of Aristotle, 26, 33
Problems of Neurosis, 733, 736
Procainamide, 306
Procaine (Novocain), 1446
Process, as concept in general living systems theory, 100
Processing (see Information processing)
Prochazka, J., 1714
Prochlorperazine (Compazine), 1741, 2280, 2335, 2337
available preparation, 2276
cost, 2263–2264
-dextroamphetamine combination (Eskatrol), 2327
dose, 2274–2275
efficacy, 2258, 2262
for children, 2679
structure, 2274
Proctor, W. C., 2897
Procyclidine (Kemadrin)
available preparations, 2282
dose, 2282–2283
structure, 2282

Prodrome, 3349
Producer, as subsystem in general living systems theory, 102–103
Profession (see Helping professions)
Professional Standards Review Organization (PSRO), 2985, 3231–3232, 3284, 3286–3287, 3289
Profile of Mood States (POMS), 2405
Progesterone, 1343, 1345
Prognosis, 788
Rorschach Test to assess, 947
Progoff, I., 819
Program for Special Training and Qualifications (PSTQ), 2964
Programing (see also Reinforcement), 385–388
Progressive supranuclear palsy, 1418
Project for a Scientific Psychology, 587, 637–640, 646, 654–655, 663, 675, 680, 1530, 2114
Project Head Start, 2434–2435, 2506
Project Re-Ed, 2703
Projection (see also Identification, projective), 691, 695, 821, 1000, 3349
aging and, 3027
future, in psychodrama, 2215
in dream formation, 652
in group psychotherapy, 2185
in middle age, 3019
in paranoid disorders, 691, 712, 1290, 1574
in personality disorders, 1570
Projective tests (see Tests)
Proketazine (see Carphenazine)
Prolactin, 180
Prolactin release-inhibiting factor (PIF), 1918
Prolactin-releasing factor (PRF), 1918
Prolixin decanoate or enanthate (see Fluphenazine)
Promazine (Sparine), 1440, 1741
available preparation, 2276
dose, 2274
efficacy, 2258, 2262
Promethazine (Phenergan), 161, 320, 1415
addictive level, 2321
available preparations, 2321
dose, 2320
structure, 2320
Promiscuity, 1665, 1729, 1796–1797
Promotion depression, 131
Propantheline (Pro-Banthine), 1444
Prophecy, 22
Propoxyphene (Darvon), 1637
Propranolol (Inderal), 1622, 1858, 2318, 2323–2324, 2356–2357
Proprioceptive impairment, 316
Proprium, 872
Prosen, H., 1794
Proskauer, S., 2663
Prosopagnosia, 3349
Prospects and Proposals: Lifetime Learning for Psychiatrists, 2975
Prosser, W., 3062–3063, 3073
Prostaglandins
brain, 181
for abortion, 1758
Prostheses, behavioral, 2150–2151
Prostigmin (see Neostigmine)
Protagonist, in psychodrama, 2212
Protagoras, 24
Protean man, 3110
Protein (see also S-100)
brain, 179–181
in cerebrospinal fluid, 268
liquid protein diet, 1879
memory and, 209
nervous system-specific, 179, 181
Protestant ethic, 63
Protofemininity, 1696
Protoperverse, 1773–1774
Prototaxic, 3349

School period of child development, 2434-2438
School phobia (see also Separation anxiety), 999, 2109-2110, 3355
  causes, 2701-2702
  prevalence, 2701
  prognosis, 2702
  treatment, 2702
Schoop, T., 1200
Schopenhauer, 76, 3016
Schorer, C. E., 1114
Schorr, J., 788
Schou, M., 1313, 2348, 2350-2351
Schrag, P., 1226
Schramel, D. J., 2891
Schreber case, 671, 711-712, 1001, 1288, 1290, 3020, 3201-3202, 3355
Schreiber, F. R., 1007
Schreiber, R. F., 1545
Schroder, H. M., 603
Schubert, D. S. P., 2828
Schucker, B., 1858
Schuckit, M. A., 1638, 2821, 2899
Schucman, Helen, 868-894
Schuell, H., 2579
Schuerger, J., 853, 867
Schuettler, R., 1176
Schulman, R. E., 2096-2097
Schulsinger, F., 150, 1137, 1140, 1180, 1565-1566, 1580, 2819
Schulte, W., 2356
Schultz, D. P., 603
Schultz, J. H., 1938
Schulz, B., 1098, 1125
Schur, M., 3117
Schuri, U., 478
Schuster, C. R., 1601
Schwab, J. J., 543, 1984
Schwab, M. E., 543
Schwab, P. J., 1289, 1295
  studies of hospitalized paranoid patients, 1289
Schwann, Theodor, 70
Schwannoma, 279-280
Schwarcz, R., 162
Schwartz, A. D., 1253
Schwartz, Arthur H., 1953-1956
Schwartz, B., 3108
Schwartz, E. M., 2756-2757
Schwartz, G. E., 222, 478, 1979
Schwartz, H., 1822
Schwartz, I. L., 197
Schwartz, M., 1229, 2190, 2195, 2200
Schwartz, M. S., 491, 1147, 1194, 2359, 2366, 2369, 3093
Schwartz, R. S., 1967
Schwartzbaum, J. S., 398
Schwartzberg, N. S., 415
Schwarz, B. E., 3241
Schweber, S. S., 3117
Schweid, D. E., 1144, 2888, 2900
Schweitzer, Albert, 22
Schwing, G., 1199
Schwirian, P. M., 1624
Schwitzgebel, R., 2638
Schyve, D. M., 2286
Sciarra, D., 1465
Scibetta, R. C., 2899
Science of Living, The, 733
Sclare, A. B., 1911-1912
Sclerosis, amyotrophic lateral, 1421
Scodel, A., 1820
Scopolamine, 1368, 2107
Scot, Michael, 34
Scot, Reginald, 41, 45
Scotch, N. A., 1119, 1139
Scotoma, 3355
Scotophilia, 664
Scotophobin, 180
Scott, J. P., 230, 1230, 2437
Scott, M. B., 3276
Scott, P., 2529
Scott, W. C. M., 2655

Scoville, W. B., 1620, 2343
Screening, 3355
Scripts, 795
  in TA, 2237
Scull, A., 1
Scurvy, 291
Seager, C. P., 2308
Seaman, B., 2954
Search Within, The, 83
Searle, J. R., 462
Searles, H., 1086, 1199-1200
Sears, R., 2728
Seashore, M. J., 2761
Seashore Tonal Memory Test, 3254
Seay, B. M., 435, 437, 580
Sebeok, T. A., 107
Sechehaye, M., 334, 353, 1200
Sechenov, Ivan, 70
Secobarbital (Seconal), 1438, 1622, 1637, 2465
  dose, 2326
Secobarbital-amobarbital combination (Tuinal), 2327
Seconal (see Secobarbital)
Second Sex, The, 3163
Second Thoughts: Selected Papers on Psycho-Analysis, 829
Secondary process, 3355
Secondary-process intervention, 1200
Secret of the Golden Flower, The, 20
Secret of the Totem, 486
Security (see Basic security)
Security operations, 761, 770-771
Sedation
  in alcoholism, 1643
  threshold, 267, 1565-1566
Sedatives, 1438-1441, 2324-2328, 3335
  hypoglycemia as, 2353-2355
  overdose, 2106
  side effects, 2320-2321
  withdrawal from, 2106
Seduction hypothesis, 647-649, 680
Seductive patient, 1527
Seefeldt, C., 2745
Seeley, J. R., 2926
Seeman, J., 2163
Seeman, P., 162
Seeman, W., 1185
Seeress of Prevost, The, 65
Sefrovná, M., 2218
Segal, B. M., 1340
Segal, Hanna, 823, 826-827, 1086, 3132
Segal, J., 1359, 1838, 2912, 3303
Segal, S. P., 512
Segantini, 3130
Seglow, J., 2755, 2757
Segraves, R. T., 1788
Séguin, Edward, 68, 2484-2485, 2521, 2695
Seidel, U. P., 2435
Seiden, Anne M., 2950-2959
Seidenberg, R., 983, 1345
Seidensticker, J. F., 1882, 1886
Seigler, M., 1201
Seitz, M. R., 461
Seitz, P. F. D., 1936, 2116, 2119, 2128
Seizures (see also Epileptic seizures; Hysterical seizures)
  akinetic, 1472
  atonic, 1472
  clonic, 1472
  febrile, 310
  focal, 1472-1474
  generalized, 1469
  grand mal, 1471
  myoclonic, 1472
    of infancy, mental retardation and, 2504
  petit mal, 1469
  primary, 1477
  secondary, 1478
  tonic, 1472
  uncinate, 204

unilateral, 1474
  withdrawal, 310
  with psychic phenomena, 310
Selesnick, S. T., 892
Self, 81, 750-751, 777-778, 815
  concept of, in client-centered psychotherapy, 2161
  fragmentation of, 1595
  perceptions of, in depersonalization disorder, 1558-1559
  personification of, 755, 773
  sense of, 3356
  supervisory patterns, 762
  theories
    of Horney, 742
    of Jung, 81, 815
    of Rado, 777-778
  therapeutic use of, 2383, 2664
Self-actualization, 876
  theories
    of Goldstein, 877
    of Maslow, 879-880
Self-analysis, 3355
Self-Analysis, 742
Self-as-known, 872
Self-centeredness, in alcoholics, 1639
Self-concept, sexuality and, 1708
Self-consciousness, 1006
Self-deception, bad faith and, 841-842
Self-discovery, 3355
Self-esteem
  loss of, in bereavement, 1020
  mental retardation and, 2508
  negative, of adopted child, 2756
  violence and, 3151
  work as source of, 1032-1033
Self-expression, development, 455
Self-hatred, 745
Self-help groups (see also specific groups), 2840, 2884
Self-hypnosis, 2168
Self-idealization, 828
Self-image, 3355
  aging and, 3025-3026
Self-indulgence, 3199
Self-mutilation, 1025, 1176
Self-observation, capacity, in children, 2654
Self-realization, 3355
Self-reference, 3356
Self-report questionnaire, 2395
Self-representation, 915
Self-stimulation, intracranial, 400
Self-system, 755, 3356
Self-therapy (see also Biofeedback)
  for stuttering, 2582
Selfe, L., 3118
Selfishness, 234
Selfridge, J. A., 463
Seligman, M. E. P., 230, 474, 566-567, 571-572, 582, 1333, 2088
Sellers, E. M., 1636, 2331
Selltiz, C., 3299, 3301
Seltzer, B., 971
Selvillano, M., 595
Selye, H., 110, 221, 1345, 1517, 1850-1851, 1859
Selzer, Melvin L., 1629-1644
Semans, J. H., 1712, 1788, 1801
Semantic component, 460
Semantic differential, 459, 489
Semantogenic theory of stuttering, 2580
Semélaigne, 26
Semon, R. G., 75, 1257
Semrad, E. V., 715, 1200, 2253
Seneca, 27
Senescence, 3026
Senescu, Robert A., 774-781
Senile chorea, 289-290
Senile dementia (see also Alzheimer's disease), 1374-1375, 3356
  age-specific prevalence rate, 538
  in aging persons, 3037

Senility, 133
Senn, M. J. E., 2419
Senn, Milton, 88
Sensation, 3356
Sensitivity groups, 2203
Sensitivity, in schizophrenia, 1154
Sensitivity training, 885
Sensitivity training group, 3356
Sensorimotor period of child development, 375-376
Sensorium, 3356
Sensory awakening, 2202
Sensory deprivation, 110-111, 600-607, 2731, 3356
  after surgery, 605
  cardiac psychosis and, 604
  cognitive theory, 603-604
  delirium and, 1370
  expectation and, 603
  experimentation, 601-602
  geriatrics and, 605
  history, 600-601
  in factory workers, 604
  in hospitalization, 604
  in military, 604
  in prison, 604
  in public health, 604
  in respirator, 606
  in trucking, 604
  instincts and, 603
  mental retardation and, 2506
  neurology and, 605-606
  ophthalmology and, 605
  orthopaedics and, 605
  personality and, 603
  physiological theories, 603
  psychological theory, 603
  psychology and, 606
Sensory disturbances
  hysterical, 1534-1535
  in psychiatric patients, 345-350
Sensory examination, in neurological evaluation, 251
Sensory extinction, 3356
Sensory habituation, 200
Sensory restriction, 577-578
Sensory stimuli, nocturnal, effect on dream content, 650
Sentence Completion Test (SCT), 941, 950-952, 959, 964
Senturia, A., 2756
Separation (see also Maternal separation)
  childhood depression and, 2801
  from father, 2729
  in military service, 2894
  in schizophrenia, 1238
  mastery of, 521, 527
  meaning of, to child, 2729
  responses to, in institutionalized children, 2729
  temporary, infant monkey reaction to, 580
  tolerance of, 721-722
Separation anxiety (see also School phobia), 120, 686, 1487, 3356
  characteristics, 2623
  clinical features, 2624-2625
  complications, 2625
  course, 2625
  diagnosis, 2626, 2630
  drugs for, 2684
  epidemiology, 2623-2624
  pathology, 2624
  predisposing factors, 2625-2626
  prognosis, 2625
  treatment, 2626
Separation-individuation (see also Child development), 119, 128, 1026, 1033, 1774, 2453, 2589, 2755, 2764
  borderline personality and, 1583
  depression and, 701, 704-705